The Holy Bible

King James Version

Theme Rheme Edition

Arete Publishing, LLC
www.AretePublishing.com

The Holy Bible, King James Version
Theme Rheme Edition

Copyright © 2025 by Arete Publishing, LLC

Published by Arete Publishing, LLC
Marshall, MI
www.AretePublishing.com
All rights reserved.

ISBN 978-1-964118-05-5 Paperback
ISBN 978-1-964118-01-7 Hardcover

No part of this book may be reproduced in any form, or by any means electronic or mechanical, including photocopying, recording, or by any information storage or retrieval system, without written permission of Arete Publishing, LLC, except in the case of brief quotations in articles and reviews, or as provided by USA copyright law.

Table of Contents

Preface

The Theme Rheme Bible (TRB) you're holding is different than any other Bible you've read. The idea of a TRB came to me shortly after I retired from a tenure-track teaching position at a large university. After over fifty years in the workforce, it didn't take me long to realize that I didn't like retirement. Of course, I love spending more time with my grandchildren and children, but they can't fill the sixteen hours of awake time I face daily. Eventually, my longing to do something more, especially related to my faith and trust in Jesus Christ, led me back to my first love: the arts. This was not just a hobby but a deep-seated passion that I couldn't ignore.

So with an educational background and decades of experience in Advertising and Journalism (B.S.), English Composition (M.A.), and English with an emphasis on linguistics, semiotics, and psychology (Ph.D.), I opened one of my favorite graduate school books on linguistics, hoping to find something meaningful that I could work on during my retirement. And there it was: Theme and Rheme. It didn't take long to realize that I could work with these two linguistic elements and help make the Bible easier to read and understand. An Introduction to Theme and Rheme appears after this Preface, and I strongly encourage you to read it. But you don't need to know how Theme and Rheme work to use this Bible. That's the beauty of it. It's designed to be user-friendly and accessible to all.

Most of us are familiar with various forms of a Theme concept. For example, an essay can have a thesis statement that informs readers about the entire text. The thesis statement is a type of Theme. We're also familiar with the idea of a topic sentence for a paragraph, another kind of Theme. For our purposes, we won't work with essays and paragraphs. Instead, we'll focus on the clause, which is one step below a sentence. The concept of a Theme Rheme Bible involves breaking down every Bible passage into a series of clauses and reading the Bible one clause at a time. Research has shown that reading shorter chunks of information (e.g., clauses) can enhance our ability to understand the meaning of what we're reading. And that's the whole concept behind a Theme Rheme Bible. This new approach can revolutionize the way we read and understand the Bible, making it more accessible and meaningful.

The following Theme-Rheme rendition of Ezekiel 1:21-22 shows how reading a complex Bible passage one clause at a time is easier to understand. Here's the traditional passage:

"When those went, these went; and when those stood, these stood; and when those were lifted up from the earth, the wheels were lifted up over against them: for the spirit of the living creature was in the wheels. And the likeness of the firmament upon the heads of the living creature was as the colour of the terrible crystal, stretched forth over their heads above" (Ezekiel 1:21-22).

Here's a Theme Rheme rendition:

When those went,
these went;
and when those stood,
these stood;
and when those were lifted up from the earth,
the wheels were lifted up over against them;
for the spirit of the living creature was in the wheels.

And the likeness of the firmament upon the heads of the living creatures was as the colour of the terrible crystal,
stretched forth over their heads above.

The Theme-Rheme rendition is easier to follow and understand. Here's why:

1. Organizing the Bible passage one clause at a time helps readers to focus on the meaning of each clause rather than the entire sentence or paragraph.

2. A clause-by-clause format forces a reader to slow down, thus improving comprehension.

3. The bold-highlighted Themes <u>signal</u> the reader's brain about the context in which the clause takes place, which also helps improve comprehension.

This last point deserves further explanation. A brief lesson in semiotics or *sign systems* is warranted . . . and it's easier than you may think. When we go outside and see dark clouds rolling in, we automatically know to grab an umbrella because it's going to rain. Notice how we intuitively know this without the use of language. The sky doesn't flash the following words: "It's going to rain! Grab your umbrella!" Instead, the dark clouds are a *sign* that it's going to rain. We even use that phrase commonly, that something is a *sign* of something else (e.g., his droopy eyes are a sign that he didn't sleep well last night).

In the same way, a written text includes *signs* as well. For example, a period <u>*signals*</u> us that the end of a sentence has occurred. We know a thought has been completed, so we pause before the next sentence. Similarly, a comma <u>*signals*</u> that we should briefly pause before continuing. Punctuation marks divide a large text into smaller chunks of information. Just as a punctuation mark helps aid one's reading process, so does a clause-by-clause organization of a written text. It does so by separating one chunk of information (i.e., one clause) from other chunks of information (i.e., other clauses). However, a Theme Rheme format involves more than just providing us with smaller chunks of information to focus on. It goes one step further, and here's where a sign system comes into play.

Just like we interpret the sign of rain in the sky or a sign of sleepiness in a person with droopy eyes, we also interpret signs in a written text. Or more accurately, our brains interpret signs in a written text without consciously thinking about it. One such sign is the *Theme* of a clause, the part that is highlighted in a bold typeface. It functions as a *sign* for our brains that the Theme forms the context for the remainder of the clause.

Let's look at an example from the Ezekiel passage, specifically the following clause:

the wheels were lifted up over against them;

In this clause, everything in the Rheme (were lifted up over against them) makes sense only within the context of the Theme (the wheels). Your brain automatically knows this.

While this example sounds simple enough and all too obvious, a written text such as a chapter or book in the Bible can involve hundreds of clauses, all of which contain a continuous series of Theme-Rheme structures that our brains process intuitively in order for us to understand what we've just read. A Theme-Rheme organization of the Bible takes advantage of this thinking process: It helps slow down our often-hurried reading process, enabling us to focus consciously on one clause at a time, all while trusting (for a good reason) that our brains are putting everything together to make sense of it all. Therefore, the bold-highlighted Themes should <u>not</u> be the focus of our attention. In fact, unless you plan on conducting a linguistic analysis of the Bible, you don't need to pay attention to the bold type at all. Just read each clause as you normally would, and your brain will handle the rest automatically. The bold type is there to help visually separate the Theme from the Rheme to make the text more readable.

Now let's move on to other details about the Theme Rheme Bible. You may wonder why I chose the King James Version (KJV) as the world's first TRB. Here are two reasons. First, the KJV is in the public domain, so copyright permissions and restrictions don't exist. Second and perhaps more importantly, the KJV has not been substantially updated (other than the New King James Version) in several hundred years, so it has become more challenging to understand because of its archaic language and style. In fact, publishers of the KJV have seen the market share of this translation decline in recent years. However, the KJV remains the translation of choice for millions of people. Organizing the KJV in a Theme-Rheme format does not change the fact that word meanings have changed since Elizabethan times. But it does help address its more complex sentence structures. Reading the KJV one clause at a time is easier to understand.

Four points remain. First, you may notice a Christian Ichthys symbol (🐟) before the first verse of some chapters. These symbols are part of a *Read Through the Bible in One Year* feature that enables you to start reading through the Bible on any day, not just at the beginning of the year. The symbol indicates the start of each day's reading passage. Second, the TRB can be used by the general public and as a research tool for scholarly purposes. However, what constitutes a Theme and a Rheme is not set in stone. Differences do exist among linguists. Third, the various nuances of the English language sometimes make identifying what constitutes a clause complicated and somewhat arbitrary, especially when words or phrases that represent understood or implied information are left out of a text. The *inferred you* in a command is just one example. Fourth, readers should know that a Theme-Rheme format does not change the Biblical text. The wording, verse numbers, chapters, and books are identical to those in a traditionally-formatted Bible.

My final point concerns the introductory summaries at the beginning of each book. They are intended to provide a general overview of each book and, therefore, are not the focus of this publication. God's Word is. These summaries were written with the assistance of Artificial Intelligence (AI) during my fact-gathering stage. Many people don't realize that AI is the search engine of tomorrow. Instead of returning *sources* of information, it returns the information itself. The book information that I gleaned from AI and other sources was verified using on-line publications, print publications, and the Bible. From there, I composed the summaries. These summaries, therefore, are not pure AI creations. Human hands (typing) and a human brain (thinking, organizing, composing, and editing) are responsible for them.

Putting together this Theme Rheme Bible has been a three-year project that I wouldn't trade for any other. Not only did it familiarize me with all sixty-six books of the Bible in a more meaningful way, but it also helped me to see the world and its history from God's perspective. After all, it is God's story. I hope and pray that reading the Bible in this Theme Rheme format will open up new avenues of discovery for you as it did for me.

With Many Blessings,

Editor,
Theme Rheme Bible

Introduction

This Theme-Rheme edition of the Bible is not just a new way to read and study the King James Version; it's a more accessible way. It leads to a more careful reading and a better and fuller understanding of God's Word. Theme and Rheme, part of a language theory called Functional Grammar, are not just for scholars. Their practical application to Biblical texts allows everyone to read the Bible from the inspired perspectives of each book's author.

Most of us are used to reading a Bible organized into verses, sentences, paragraphs, sections, and chapters, none of which are part of the original Greek and Hebrew texts. Without these classical grammatical structures, a straightforward reading of the Bible would remain inaccessible to the general public. However, these structures are not the only way to organize the Bible. Some publishers offer a verse-by-verse format without paragraphs, others use paragraphs with or without section headings, and others use no verses or a range of verses. As one can see, while God inspires the Bible itself, each publisher determines its format. The Theme-Rheme edition of the Bible offers a new way to interpret the text, empowering readers to engage with God's written Word in a more personal and meaningful way.

Functional Grammar

Most readers are familiar with traditional grammatical terms—nouns, verbs, adjectives, subjects, predicates, clauses, and others—all of which focus on the *structure* of a language and how various elements are organized to make meaning apart from their contextual use. Functional Grammar, however, focuses on how the elements of language, such as Theme and Rheme, communicate meaning within the context of language use. More generally, traditional grammar focuses on *form without context*, while Functional Grammar focuses on *function within context*.[1] This theory is the foundation of a Theme-Rheme edition of the Bible. It helps readers understand the underlying concerns of each passage in their specific context.

Neither one of these linguistic approaches to language is more important or better than the other. Most, if not all, publications of the Bible, however, are presented exclusively using traditional grammatical structures. But different ways can exist as well. A Theme-Rheme edition of the Bible does not replace traditional grammar but rather complements it, offering a new perspective that provides deeper insights into the text.

Furthermore, a Theme-Rheme Bible is not a reinterpretation of the text. It changes nothing about a translation's wording, verse numbers, chapters, and books. It differs by presenting Biblical texts one clause at a time. The result is a reader-friendly Bible that enables everyone to focus more easily on the meaning of a text based on the inspired writer's intent. You can trust that this King James Version of the Bible is a faithful representation of the original text, designed to enhance your understanding and appreciation of God's Word.

What is a Theme?

In Functional Grammar, a Theme "is the element that serves as the point of departure of the message; it is that which locates and orients the clause within its context "[2] and thus identifies what a clause is concerned about. People familiar with traditional grammar's Subject and Predicate might assume that Theme is equivalent to Subject, and Rheme is equivalent to Predicate. Let's investigate this assumption further.

Theme = Subject

Some sentences are constructed in a way that makes their Themes the same as their Subjects, such as the following one-clause sentence:

The Bible is God's inspired Word.

In this example, The Bible is both Subject and Theme:

Subject = *The Bible*
Theme = *The Bible*

Here's why. In traditional grammar, the Subject of a sentence is the person, place, or thing that is (a) doing the action or (b) what the sentence is about. In the sentence above, *The Bible* is what the sentence is about.

In Functional Grammar, the Theme places the clause within a particular context, and it must meet the following three criteria: (a) it is always located at the beginning of the clause, and (b) it extends from the beginning up to and including the first experiential element of the clause, which is (c) in the form of a participant (noun, pronoun, or noun phrase), process (verb or verb phrase), or circumstance (adverb, adverb phrase, or prepositional phrase). In the sentence above, *The Bible* is the first experiential element of the clause, in this case, in the form of a participant (i.e., a noun).

Theme ≠ Subject

Not every clause has a Theme = Subject structure, such as the following one-clause sentence:

And immediately the spirit driveth him into the wilderness. (Mark 1:12)

This example has a Theme that is different from the Subject:

Subject = *the spirit*
Theme = *And immediately*

We can explore why they are different using the same definitions as before. In the verse above, *the spirit* is the Person doing the action, hence *the spirit* is the Subject. The Theme, however, provides the context through which everything else in the clause is filtered. The Theme extends from the beginning of the clause up to and including the first experiential element. In this case, *immediately* is the first experiential element, a circumstance in the form of an adverb; hence, *And immediately* is the Theme.[3]

The author chose to construct the sentence in this manner, revealing his underlying concern to place the entire clause within the context of when the spirit drove Jesus into the wilderness. Otherwise, if his underlying concern was a focus on the spirit, the sentence would have been written as follows:

The spirit driveth him immediately into the wilderness.

Writers make choices when expressing their thoughts in written form. Identifying each clause's Theme helps readers better understand the writer's inspired intent.

What is a Rheme?

In Functional Grammar, the Rheme develops the Theme by providing information about it. All information in a Rheme must relate to or be connected to the Theme. Every major clause (both independent and dependent) contains a Theme + Rheme construction.

In the Mark 1:12 example, the Theme (identified as *And immediately*) is followed by the Rheme:

Theme = *And immediately*
Rheme = *the spirit driveth him into the wilderness*

The Bible as a Theme + Rheme Structure

As Michael Alexander Kirkwood (M.A.K.) Halliday stated in his seminal book on Functional Grammar, "[By] analysing the thematic structure of a text clause by clause, we can gain an insight into its texture and understand how the writer made clear to us the nature of his underlying concerns."[4] In this case, readers can gain insight into the underlying concerns of all God-inspired passages in the Bible. For instance, in the Mark 1:12 example, the Theme *And immediately* sets the context, while the Rheme *the spirit driveth him into the wilderness* provides the action. This analysis can help us understand the urgency and immediacy of the spirit's action in driving Jesus into the wilderness.

The Theme and Rheme were identified on two lines in the previously mentioned examples. All 66 books of the Bible could be organized in this way, but doing so would lead to a visually busy format that is difficult and ponderous to read.

Instead, all 66 books will identify the Theme and the Rheme of each clause in a way that makes reading more enjoyable and productive. For example, John 3:16 contains four clauses:

#1 = For God so loved the world
#2 = that he gave his only begotten Son,
#3 = that whosoever believeth in him should not perish,
#4 = but have everlasting life.

Note how the following format identifies both the Theme and Rheme in each clause:

For God so loved the world,
that he gave his only begotten Son,
that whosoever believeth in him should not perish,
but have everlasting life.

In this Theme-Rheme edition of the Bible, every sentence will be organized as a list of one or more clauses, with each Theme highlighted in bold type and each Rheme in regular type. The only variation on this format would involve the embedding of one clause within another clause. For example, Matthew 6:6 has a clause (in italics) embedded in another clause:

But thou, *when thou prayest,* enter into thy closet,
and when thou has shut thy door,
pray to thy Father which is in secret;
and thy Father which seeth in secret shall reward thee openly.

In such passages, curly brackets will surround an embedded clause, and the Theme will be underlined, as shown below:

But thou, {<u>when thou</u> prayest}, enter into thy closet,
and when thou has shut thy door,
pray to thy Father which is in secret;
and thy Father which seeth in secret shall reward thee openly.

Some passages in the Bible show an embedded clause surrounded by traditional parentheses. In such cases, the Theme will be underlined. Other passages in the Bible show a clause between two traditional parentheses but without any embedded clauses; in such cases, the Theme will be highlighted in bold type. In summary, Themes in embedded clauses will be underlined, and Themes in non-embedded clauses will be highlighted in bold type.

Using a Theme-Rheme Bible

While this Theme-Rheme format of the Bible can be useful for scholarly work, it is intended to be used by the general public to better understand God's Word—one clause at a time. Therefore, reading it like any other Bible is the best way to start.

The semantic organization of each sentence as a list of one or more clauses essentially involves dividing larger units of information into smaller *chunks* of information that are easier to comprehend. The result is a more productive and more enjoyable reading process—all without altering the beauty and divine message of the King James Version.

Footnotes

[1] Theme and Rheme are a small part of Functional Grammar, and the general discussion about Functional Grammar in this Introduction is not meant to be all-inclusive. A more comprehensive analysis of the Bible using all the tools presented in Functional Grammar is possible, but it would (a) be a lifetime of work in progress, and (b) result in an incredibly complex document, rendering it inaccessible to the general public and thus useful only as a scholarly study. For our purposes, a Theme-and-Rheme organization of the Bible provides the general public with a practical application for reading Biblical texts in a new, simple, and easily accessible way, one that highlights the inspired writer's underlying concerns about each passage.

[2] Halliday, M. A. K. *Halliday's Introduction to Functional Grammar, 4th Edition*. Revised by Christian M. I. M. Matthiessen (London and New York: Routledge, Taylor & Francis Group, 2014), 89.

[3] Some translated sentences in the Bible are expressed as imperative clauses, which have an inferred *You* at the beginning. For example, Psalm 6:8 states the following: *Depart from me, all ye workers of iniquity; for the LORD hath heard the voice of my weeping.* This verse has two Theme-Rheme structures: (a) *Depart from me, all ye workers of iniquity;* and (b) *for the LORD hath heard the voice of my weeping.* The first clause has an inferred *You* as traditional grammar's Subject: *[You] Depart from me, all ye workers of iniquity*. In Functional Grammar, the Theme of an imperative clause can be either (a) the inferred You or (b) the verb. Both are correct. However, to avoid adding any words to this King James Bible translation, the verb will be considered the Theme.

[4] Halliday, M. A. K. *Halliday's Introduction to Functional Grammar, 4th Edition*. Revised by Christian M. I. M. Matthiessen (London and New York: Routledge, Taylor & Francis Group, 2014), 133.

The Old Testament

King James Version

Theme Rheme Edition

Genesis

Moses, a significant figure in Biblical history, provides a historical and theological foundation for understanding God and His relationship with the future nation of Israel. He recounts how God created the universe, the earth, and all living things, including Adam and Eve, and their eventual fall from grace. Genesis then tells the well-known story of how God floods the earth as a punishment for human wickedness and how he saves Noah and his family on the Ark.

The narrative about the Tower of Babel recalls a time when the people in ancient Mesopotamia began building a tower to reach heaven and to serve as a monument to their glory. In response, God scatters them across the earth, each with their unique language and culture. Finally, Moses provides historical information about Abraham, Isaac, and Jacob, all considered the founders of the Israelite nation.

These stories establish the background in which God makes a covenant with His chosen people. They also construct the moral and religious framework for the Israelites. This pivotal moment sets the stage for the rest of the Bible, providing guidance and direction as the Israelites navigate their relationship with God.

1 **In the beginning** God created the heaven and the earth.

2 **And the earth** was without form, and void;
and darkness was upon the face of the deep.
And the Spirit of God moved upon the face of the waters.

3 **And God** said,
Let there be light:
and there was light.

4 **And God** saw the light,
that it was good:
and God divided the light from the darkness.

5 **And God** called the light Day,
and the darkness he called Night.
And the evening and the morning were the first day.

6 **And God** said,
Let there be a firmament in the midst of the waters,
and let it divide the waters from the waters.

7 **And God** made the firmament,
and divided the waters which were under the firmament from the waters which were above the firmament:
and it was so.

8 **And God** called the firmament Heaven.
And the evening and the morning were the second day.

9 **And God** said,
Let the waters under the heaven be gathered together unto one place,
and let the dry land appear:
and it was so.

10 **And God** called the dry land Earth;
and the gathering together of the waters called he Seas:
and God saw that it was good.

11 **And God** said,
Let the earth bring forth grass,
the herb yielding seed,
and the fruit tree yielding fruit after his kind,
whose seed is in itself, upon the earth:
and it was so.

12 **And the earth** brought forth grass,
and herb yielding seed after his kind,
and the tree yielding fruit,
whose seed was in itself, after his kind:
and God saw that it was good.

13 **And the evening and the morning** were the third day.

14 **And God** said,
Let there be lights in the firmament of the heaven
to divide the day from the night;
and let them be for signs, and for seasons, and for days, and years:

15 **And let them** be for lights in the firmament of the heaven
to give light upon the earth:
and it was so.

16 **And God** made two great lights; the greater light to rule the day, and the lesser light to rule the night:
he made the stars also.

17 **And God** set them in the firmament of the heaven
to give light upon the earth,

18 **And** to rule over the day and over the night,
and to divide the light from the darkness:
and God saw that it was good.

19 **And the evening and the morning** were the fourth day.

20 **And God** said,
Let the waters bring forth abundantly the moving creature that hath life, and fowl that may fly above the earth in the open firmament of heaven.

21 **And God** created great whales, and every living creature that moveth,
which the waters brought forth abundantly, after their kind, and every winged fowl after his kind:
and God saw that it was good.

22 **And God** blessed them,
saying,
Be fruitful,
and multiply,
and fill the waters in the seas,
and let fowl multiply in the earth.

23 **And the evening and the morning** were the fifth day.

24 **And God** said,
Let the earth bring forth the living creature after his kind, cattle, and creeping thing, and beast of the earth after his kind:
and it was so.

25 **And God** made the beast of the earth after his kind, and cattle after their kind, and every thing

that creepeth upon the earth after his kind:
and God saw that it was good.

26 **And God** said,
Let us make man in our image, after our likeness:
and let them have dominion over the fish of the sea, and over the fowl of the air, and over the cattle, and over all the earth, and over every creeping thing that creepeth upon the earth.

27 **So God** created man in his own image,
in the image of God created he him;
male and female created he them.

28 **And God** blessed them,
and God said unto them,
Be fruitful, and multiply,
and replenish the earth,
and subdue it:
and have dominion over the fish of the sea, and over the fowl of the air, and over every living thing that moveth upon the earth.

29 **And God** said,
Behold,
I have given you every herb bearing seed,
which is upon the face of all the earth, and every tree,
in the which is the fruit of a tree yielding seed;
to you it shall be for meat.

30 **And to every beast of the earth, and to every fowl of the air, and to every thing that creepeth upon the earth, {wherein} there is life},** I have given every green herb for meat:
and it was so.

31 **And God** saw every thing that he had made,
and, {behold}, it was very good.
And the evening and the morning were the sixth day.

2

Thus the heavens and the earth were finished, and all the host of them.

2 **And on the seventh day** God ended his work which he had made;
and he rested on the seventh day from all his work which he had made.

3 **And God** blessed the seventh day,
and sanctified it:
because that in it he had rested from all his work which God created and made.

4 **These** are the generations of the heavens and of the earth when they were created, in the day that the LORD God made the earth and the heavens,
5 And every plant of the field before it was in the earth, and every herb of the field before it grew:
for the LORD God had not caused it to rain upon the earth,
and there was not a man to till the ground.

6 **But there** went up a mist from the earth,
and watered the whole face of the ground.

7 **And the LORD God** formed man of the dust of the ground,
and breathed into his nostrils the breath of life;
and man became a living soul.

8 **And the LORD God** planted a garden eastward in Eden;
and there he put the man whom he had formed.

9 **And out of the ground** made the LORD God to grow every tree that is pleasant to the sight, and good for food; the tree of life also in the midst of the garden, and the tree of knowledge of good and evil.

10 **And a river** went out of Eden
to water the garden;
and from thence it was parted,
and became into four heads.

11 **The name of the first** is Pison:
that is it which compasseth the whole land of Havilah,
where there is gold;
12 **And the gold of that land** is good:
there is bdellium and the onyx stone.

13 **And the name of the second river** is Gihon:
the same is it that compasseth the whole land of Ethiopia.

14 **And the name of the third river** is Hiddekel:
that is it which goeth toward the east of Assyria.

And the fourth river is Euphrates.

15 **And the LORD God** took the man,
and put him into the garden of Eden
to dress it
and to keep it.

16 **And the LORD God** commanded the man,
saying,
Of every tree of the garden thou mayest freely eat:
17 **But of the tree of the knowledge of good and evil,** thou shalt not eat of it:
for in the day that thou eatest thereof thou shalt surely die.

18 **And the LORD God** said,
It is not good that the man should be alone;
I will make him an help meet for him.

19 **And out of the ground** the LORD God formed every beast of the field, and every fowl of the air;
and brought them unto Adam
to see what he would call them:
and whatsoever Adam called every living creature,
that was the name thereof.

20 **And** Adam gave names to all cattle, and to the fowl of the air, and to every beast of the field;
but for Adam there was not found an help meet for him.

21 **And the LORD God** caused a deep sleep to fall upon Adam,
and he slept:
and he took one of his ribs,
and closed up the flesh instead thereof;
22 **And the rib**, {which the LORD God had taken from man}, made he a woman,
and brought her unto the man.

23 **And Adam** said,
This is now bone of my bones, and flesh of my flesh:
she shall be called Woman,
because she was taken out of Man.

24 **Therefore** shall a man leave his father and his mother,
and shall cleave unto his wife:
and they shall be one flesh.

25 **And they** were both naked, the man and his wife,
and were not ashamed.

3

Now the serpent was more subtil than any beast of the field which the LORD God had made.

And he said unto the woman,
Yea, hath God said,
Ye shall not eat of every tree of the garden?

2 **And the woman** said unto the
serpent,
We may eat of the fruit of the trees
of the garden:
3 **But of the fruit of the tree which
is in the midst of the garden,**
God hath said,
Ye shall not eat of it,
neither shall ye touch it,
lest ye die.
4 **And the serpent** said unto the
woman,
Ye shall not surely die:
5 **For God** doth know
that in the day ye eat thereof,
then your eyes shall be opened,
and ye shall be as gods,
knowing good and evil.
6 **And when the woman** saw that
the tree was good for food,
and that it was pleasant to the
eyes,
and a tree to be desired
to make one wise,
she took of the fruit thereof,
and did eat,
and gave also unto her husband
with her;
and he did eat.
7 **And the eyes of them both** were
opened,
and they knew
that they were naked;
and they sewed fig leaves together,
and made themselves aprons.
8 **And they** heard the voice of the
LORD God walking in the garden
in the cool of the day:
and Adam and his wife hid
themselves from the presence of
the LORD God amongst the trees
of the garden.
9 **And the LORD God** called unto
Adam,
and said unto him,
Where art thou?
10 **And he** said,
I heard thy voice in the garden,
and I was afraid,
because I was naked;
and I hid myself.
11 **And he** said,
Who told thee
that thou wast naked?
Hast thou eaten of the tree,
whereof I commanded thee
that thou shouldest not eat?
12 **And the man** said,
**The woman whom thou gavest to
be with me,** she gave me of the
tree,
and I did eat.
13 **And the LORD God** said unto the
woman,
What is this that thou hast done?
And the woman said,
The serpent beguiled me,
and I did eat.
14 **And the LORD God** said unto the
serpent,
Because thou hast done this,
thou art cursed above all cattle, and
above every beast of the field;
upon thy belly shalt thou go,
and dust shalt thou eat all the days
of thy life:
15 **And I** will put enmity between
thee and the woman, and
between thy seed and her seed;
it shall bruise thy head,
and thou shalt bruise his heel.
16 **Unto the woman** he said,
I will greatly multiply thy sorrow
and thy conception;
in sorrow thou shalt bring forth
children;
and thy desire shall be to thy
husband,
and he shall rule over thee.
17 **And unto Adam** he said,
Because thou hast hearkened unto
the voice of thy wife,
and hast eaten of the tree,
of which I commanded thee,
saying,
Thou shalt not eat of it:
cursed is the ground for thy sake;
in sorrow shalt thou eat of it all the
days of thy life;
18 **Thorns also and thistles** shall it
bring forth to thee;
and thou shalt eat the herb of the
field;
19 **In the sweat of thy face** shalt
thou eat bread,
till thou return unto the ground;
for out of it wast thou taken:
for dust thou art,
and unto dust shalt thou return.
20 **And Adam** called his wife's name
Eve;
because she was the mother of all
living.
21 **Unto Adam also and to his wife**
did the LORD God make coats of
skins,
and clothed them.
22 **And the LORD God** said,
Behold,
the man is become as one of us,
to know good and evil:
and now, lest he put forth his hand,
and take also of the tree of life,
and eat,
and live for ever:
23 **Therefore the LORD God** sent
him forth from the garden of
Eden,
to till the ground from whence he
was taken.
24 **So he** drove out the man;
and he placed at the east of the
garden of Eden Cherubims, and a
flaming sword which turned
every way,
to keep the way of the tree of life.

4 ∞ **And Adam** knew Eve his
wife;
and she conceived,
and bare Cain,
and said,
I have gotten a man from the LORD.
2 **And she** again bare his brother
Abel.
And Abel was a keeper of sheep,
but Cain was a tiller of the ground.
3 **And in process of time** it came to
pass,
that Cain brought of the fruit of the
ground an offering unto the
LORD.
4 **And Abel**, he also brought of the
firstlings of his flock and of the fat
thereof.
And the LORD had respect unto
Abel and to his offering:
5 **But unto Cain and to his offering**
he had not respect.
And Cain was very wroth,
and his countenance fell.
6 **And the LORD** said unto Cain,
Why art thou wroth?
and why is thy countenance fallen?
7 **If thou** doest well,
shalt thou not be accepted?
and if thou doest not well,
sin lieth at the door.
And unto thee shall be his desire,
and thou shalt rule over him.
8 **And Cain** talked with Abel his
brother:
and it came to pass,
when they were in the field,
that Cain rose up against Abel his
brother,
and slew him.

9 **And the LORD** said unto Cain,
Where is Abel thy brother?
And he said,
I know not:
Am I my brother's keeper?
10 **And he** said,
What hast thou done?
the voice of thy brother's blood crieth unto me from the ground.
11 **And now** art thou cursed from the earth,
which hath opened her mouth to receive thy brother's blood from thy hand;
12 **When thou** tillest the ground,
it shall not henceforth yield unto thee her strength;
a fugitive and a vagabond shalt thou be in the earth.
13 **And Cain** said unto the LORD,
My punishment is greater than I can bear.
14 **Behold,**
thou hast driven me out this day from the face of the earth;
and from thy face shall I be hid;
and I shall be a fugitive and a vagabond in the earth;
and it shall come to pass,
that every one that findeth me shall slay me.
15 **And the LORD** said unto him,
Therefore whosoever slayeth Cain,
vengeance shall be taken on him sevenfold.
And the LORD set a mark upon Cain,
lest any finding him should kill him.
16 **And Cain** went out from the presence of the LORD,
and dwelt in the land of Nod, on the east of Eden.
17 **And Cain** knew his wife;
and she conceived,
and bare Enoch:
and he builded a city,
and called the name of the city, after the name of his son, Enoch.
18 **And unto Enoch** was born Irad:
and Irad begat Mehujael:
and Mehujael begat Methusael:
and Methusael begat Lamech.
19 **And Lamech** took unto him two wives:
the name of the one was Adah,
and the name of the other Zillah.
20 **And Adah** bare Jabal:
he was the father of such as dwell in tents, and of such as have cattle.
21 **And his brother's name** was Jubal:
he was the father of all such as handle the harp and organ.
22 **And Zillah,** she also bare Tubalcain, an instructer of every artificer in brass and iron:
and the sister of Tubalcain was Naamah.
23 **And Lamech** said unto his wives, Adah and Zillah,
Hear my voice; ye wives of Lamech,
hearken unto my speech:
for I have slain a man to my wounding, and a young man to my hurt.
24 **If Cain** shall be avenged sevenfold, truly Lamech seventy and sevenfold.
25 **And Adam** knew his wife again;
and she bare a son,
and called his name Seth:
For God, {said she}, hath appointed me another seed instead of Abel,
whom Cain slew.
26 **And to Seth,** to him also there was born a son;
and he called his name Enos:
then began men to call upon the name of the LORD.

5 **This** is the book of the generations of Adam.
In the day that God created man,
in the likeness of God made he him;
2 **Male and female** created he them;
and blessed them,
and called their name Adam,
in the day when they were created.
3 **And Adam** lived an hundred and thirty years,
and begat a son in his own likeness, and after his image;
and called his name Seth:
4 **And the days of Adam after he had begotten Seth** were eight hundred years:
and he begat sons and daughters:
5 **And all the days that Adam lived** were nine hundred and thirty years:
and he died.
6 **And Seth** lived an hundred and five years,
and begat Enos:
7 **And Seth** lived after he begat Enos eight hundred and seven years,
and begat sons and daughters:
8 **And all the days of Seth** were nine hundred and twelve years:
and he died.
9 **And Enos** lived ninety years,
and begat Cainan:
10 **And Enos** lived after he begat Cainan eight hundred and fifteen years,
and begat sons and daughters:
11 **And all the days of Enos** were nine hundred and five years:
and he died.
12 **And Cainan** lived seventy years
and begat Mahalaleel:
13 **And Cainan** lived after he begat Mahalaleel eight hundred and forty years,
and begat sons and daughters:
14 **And all the days of Cainan** were nine hundred and ten years:
and he died.
15 **And Mahalaleel** lived sixty and five years,
and begat Jared:
16 **And Mahalaleel** lived after he begat Jared eight hundred and thirty years,
and begat sons and daughters:
17 **And all the days of Mahalaleel** were eight hundred ninety and five years:
and he died.
18 **And Jared** lived an hundred sixty and two years,
and he begat Enoch:
19 **And Jared** lived after he begat Enoch eight hundred years,
and begat sons and daughters:
20 **And all the days of Jared** were nine hundred sixty and two years:
and he died.
21 **And Enoch** lived sixty and five years,
and begat Methuselah:
22 **And Enoch** walked with God after he begat Methuselah three hundred years,
and begat sons and daughters:
23 **And all the days of Enoch** were three hundred sixty and five years:
24 **And Enoch** walked with God:
and he was not;
for God took him.
25 **And Methuselah** lived an hundred eighty and seven years,
and begat Lamech.

26 **And Methuselah** lived after he begat Lamech seven hundred eighty and two years,
and begat sons and daughters:
27 **And all the days of Methuselah** were nine hundred sixty and nine years:
and he died.

28 **And Lamech** lived an hundred eighty and two years,
and begat a son:
29 **And he** called his name Noah, saying,
This same shall comfort us concerning our work and toil of our hands, because of the ground which the LORD hath cursed.

30 **And Lamech** lived after he begat Noah five hundred ninety and five years,
and begat sons and daughters:
31 **And all the days of Lamech** were seven hundred seventy and seven years:
and he died.

32 **And Noah** was five hundred years old:
and Noah begat Shem, Ham, and Japheth.

6

And it came to pass,
when men began to multiply on the face of the earth,
and daughters were born unto them,
2 **That the sons of God** saw the daughters of men that they were fair;
and they took them wives of all which they chose.

3 **And the LORD** said,
My spirit shall not always strive with man,
for that he also is flesh:
yet his days shall be an hundred and twenty years.

4 **There** were giants in the earth in those days;
and also after that, {when the sons of God came in unto the daughters of men}, {and they bare children to them}, the same became mighty men which were of old, men of renown.

5 **And God** saw that the wickedness of man was great in the earth, and that every imagination of the thoughts of his heart was only evil continually.

6 **And it repented the LORD** that he had made man on the earth,
and it grieved him at his heart.

7 **And the LORD** said,
I will destroy man whom I have created from the face of the earth; both man, and beast, and the creeping thing, and the fowls of the air;
for it repenteth me that I have made them.

8 **But Noah** found grace in the eyes of the LORD.

9 **These** are the generations of Noah:
Noah was a just man and perfect in his generations,
and Noah walked with God.

10 **And Noah** begat three sons, Shem, Ham, and Japheth.

11 **The earth** also was corrupt before God,
and the earth was filled with violence.

12 **And God** looked upon the earth,
and, {behold}, it was corrupt;
for all flesh had corrupted his way upon the earth.

13 **And God** said unto Noah,
The end of all flesh is come before me;
for the earth is filled with violence through them;
and, {behold}, I will destroy them with the earth.

14 **Make thee** an ark of gopher wood;
rooms shalt thou make in the ark,
and shalt pitch it within and without with pitch.

15 **And this** is the fashion which thou shalt make it of:
The length of the ark shall be three hundred cubits, the breadth of it fifty cubits, and the height of it thirty cubits.

16 **A window** shalt thou make to the ark,
and in a cubit shalt thou finish it above;
and the door of the ark shalt thou set in the side thereof;
with lower, second, and third stories shalt thou make it.

17 **And, {behold}, I, even I,** do bring a flood of waters upon the earth,
to destroy all flesh,
wherein is the breath of life, from under heaven;
and every thing that is in the earth shall die.

18 **But with thee** will I establish my covenant;
and thou shalt come into the ark, thou, and thy sons, and thy wife, and thy sons' wives with thee.

19 **And of every living thing of all flesh,** two of every sort shalt thou bring into the ark,
to keep them alive with thee;
they shall be male and female.

20 **Of fowls after their kind, and of cattle after their kind, of every creeping thing of the earth after his kind,** two of every sort shall come unto thee,
to keep them alive.

21 **And take thou** unto thee of all food that is eaten,
and thou shalt gather it to thee;
and it shall be for food for thee, and for them.

22 **Thus** did Noah; according to all that God commanded him,
so did he.

7

And the LORD said unto Noah,
Come thou and all thy house into the ark;
for thee have I seen righteous before me in this generation.

2 **Of every clean beast** thou shalt take to thee by sevens, the male and his female: and of beasts that are not clean by two, the male and his female.

3 **Of fowls also of the air** by sevens, the male and the female;
to keep seed alive upon the face of all the earth.

4 **For yet seven days,** and I will cause it to rain upon the earth forty days and forty nights;
and every living substance that I have made will I destroy from off the face of the earth.

5 **And Noah** did according unto all that the LORD commanded him.

6 **And Noah** was six hundred years old
when the flood of waters was upon the earth.

7 **And Noah** went in, and his sons, and his wife, and his sons' wives with him, into the ark, because of the waters of the flood.

8 **Of clean beasts, and of beasts
that are not clean, and of fowls,
and of every thing that creepeth
upon the earth,**
9 There went in two and two unto
Noah into the ark, the male and
the female,
as God had commanded Noah.
10 **And it** came to pass after seven
days,
that the waters of the flood were
upon the earth.
11 **In the six hundredth year of
Noah's life, in the second
month, the seventeenth day of
the month,** the same day were all
the fountains of the great deep
broken up,
and the windows of heaven were
opened.
12 **And the rain** was upon the earth
forty days and forty nights.
13 **In the selfsame day** entered
Noah, and Shem, and Ham, and
Japheth, the sons of Noah, and
Noah's wife, and the three wives
of his sons with them, into the
ark;
14 They, and every beast after his
kind, and all the cattle after their
kind, and every creeping thing
that creepeth upon the earth after
his kind, and every fowl after his
kind, every bird of every sort.
15 **And they** went in unto Noah into
the ark, two and two of all flesh,
wherein is the breath of life.
16 **And they that went in,** went in
male and female of all flesh,
as God had commanded him:
and the LORD shut him in.
17 **And the flood** was forty days
upon the earth;
and the waters increased,
and bare up the ark,
and it was lift up above the earth.
18 **And the waters** prevailed,
and were increased greatly upon
the earth;
and the ark went upon the face of
the waters.
19 **And the waters** prevailed
exceedingly upon the earth;
and all the high hills, {that were
under the whole heaven}, were
covered.
20 **Fifteen cubits upward** did the
waters prevail;
and the mountains were covered.
21 **And all flesh** died that moved
upon the earth, both of fowl, and
of cattle, and of beast, and of
every creeping thing that
creepeth upon the earth, and
every man:
22 **All in whose nostrils was the
breath of life, of all that was in
the dry land,** died.
23 **And every living substance** was
destroyed which was upon the
face of the ground, both man, and
cattle, and the creeping things,
and the fowl of the heaven;
and they were destroyed from the
earth:
and Noah only remained alive, and
they that were with him in the
ark.
24 **And the waters** prevailed upon
the earth an hundred and fifty
days.

8

∞ **And God** remembered
Noah, and every living thing,
and all the cattle that was with
him in the ark:
and God made a wind to pass over
the earth,
and the waters assuaged;
2 **The fountains also of the deep
and the windows of heaven**
were stopped,
and the rain from heaven was
restrained;
3 **And the waters** returned from off
the earth continually:
**and after the end of the hundred
and fifty days** the waters were
abated.
4 **And the ark** rested in the seventh
month, on the seventeenth day of
the month, upon the mountains
of Ararat.
5 **And the waters** decreased
continually until the tenth
month:
**in the tenth month, on the first
day of the month,** were the tops
of the mountains seen.
6 **And it** came to pass at the end of
forty days,
that Noah opened the window of
the ark which he had made:
7 **And he** sent forth a raven,
which went forth to and fro,
until the waters were dried up
from off the earth.
8 **Also he** sent forth a dove from
him,
to see if the waters were abated
from off the face of the ground;
9 **But the dove** found no rest for the
sole of her foot,
and she returned unto him into the
ark,
for the waters were on the face of
the whole earth:
then he put forth his hand,
and took her,
and pulled her in unto him into the
ark.
10 **And he** stayed yet other seven
days;
and again he sent forth the dove
out of the ark;
11 **And the dove** came in to him in
the evening;
and, {lo}, in her mouth was an
olive leaf pluckt off:
so Noah knew
that the waters were abated from
off the earth.
12 **And he** stayed yet other seven
days;
and sent forth the dove;
which returned not again unto him
any more.
13 **And it** came to pass in the six
hundredth and first year, in the
first month, the first day of the
month,
the waters were dried up from off
the earth:
and Noah removed the covering of
the ark,
and looked,
**and, {behold}, the face of the
ground** was dry.
14 **And in the second month, on
the seven and twentieth day of
the month,** was the earth dried.
15 **And God** spake unto Noah,
saying,
16 **Go forth** of the ark, thou, and thy
wife, and thy sons, and thy sons'
wives with thee.
17 **Bring forth** with thee every living
thing that is with thee, of all flesh,
both of fowl, and of cattle, and of
every creeping thing that
creepeth upon the earth;
that they may breed abundantly in
the earth,
and be fruitful,
and multiply upon the earth.
18 **And Noah** went forth, and his
sons, and his wife, and his sons'
wives with him:

19 **Every beast, every creeping thing, and every fowl, and whatsoever creepeth upon the earth, after their kinds,** went forth out of the ark.

20 **And Noah** builded an altar unto the LORD;
and took of every clean beast, and of every clean fowl,
and offered burnt offerings on the altar.

21 **And the LORD** smelled a sweet savour;
and the LORD said in his heart,
I will not again curse the ground any more for man's sake;
for the imagination of man's heart is evil from his youth;
neither will I again smite any more every thing living,
as I have done.

22 **While the earth** remaineth,
seedtime and harvest, and cold and heat, and summer and winter, and day and night shall not cease.

9 **And God** blessed Noah and his sons,
and said unto them,
Be fruitful,
and multiply,
and replenish the earth.

2 **And the fear of you and the dread of you** shall be upon every beast of the earth, and upon every fowl of the air, upon all that moveth upon the earth, and upon all the fishes of the sea;
into your hand are they delivered.

3 **Every moving thing that liveth** shall be meat for you;
even as the green herb have I given you all things.

4 **But flesh with the life thereof,** {which is the blood thereof}, shall ye not eat.

5 **And surely your blood of your lives** will I require;
at the hand of every beast will I require it,
and at the hand of man; at the hand of every man's brother will I require the life of man.

6 **Whoso** sheddeth man's blood,
by man shall his blood be shed:
for in the image of God made he man.

7 **And you,** be ye fruitful,
and multiply;
bring forth abundantly in the earth,
and multiply therein.

8 **And God** spake unto Noah, and to his sons with him,
saying,

9 **And I, {behold}, I** establish my covenant with you, and with your seed after you;

10 And with every living creature that is with you, of the fowl, of the cattle, and of every beast of the earth with you; from all that go out of the ark, to every beast of the earth.

11 **And I** will establish my covenant with you,
neither shall all flesh be cut off any more by the waters of a flood;
neither shall there any more be a flood to destroy the earth.

12 **And God** said,
This is the token of the covenant which I make between me and you and every living creature that is with you, for perpetual generations:

13 **I** do set my bow in the cloud,
and it shall be for a token of a covenant between me and the earth.

14 **And it** shall come to pass,
when I bring a cloud over the earth,
that the bow shall be seen in the cloud:

15 **And I** will remember my covenant,
which is between me and you and every living creature of all flesh;
and the waters shall no more become a flood to destroy all flesh.

16 **And the bow** shall be in the cloud;
and I will look upon it,
that I may remember the everlasting covenant between God and every living creature of all flesh that is upon the earth.

17 **And God** said unto Noah,
This is the token of the covenant,
which I have established between me and all flesh that is upon the earth.

18 **And the sons of Noah**, {that went forth of the ark}, were Shem, and Ham, and Japheth:
and Ham is the father of Canaan.

19 **These** are the three sons of Noah:
and of them was the whole earth overspread.

20 **And Noah** began to be an husbandman,
and he planted a vineyard:
21 **And he** drank of the wine,
and was drunken;
and he was uncovered within his tent.

22 **And Ham, the father of Canaan,** saw the nakedness of his father,
and told his two brethren without.

23 **And Shem and Japheth** took a garment,
and laid it upon both their shoulders,
and went backward,
and covered the nakedness of their father;
and their faces were backward,
and they saw not their father's nakedness.

24 **And Noah** awoke from his wine,
and knew
what his younger son had done unto him.

25 **And he** said,
Cursed be Canaan;
a servant of servants shall he be unto his brethren.

26 **And he** said,
Blessed be the LORD God of Shem;
and Canaan shall be his servant.

27 **God** shall enlarge Japheth,
and he shall dwell in the tents of Shem;
and Canaan shall be his servant.

28 **And Noah** lived after the flood three hundred and fifty years.

29 **And all the days of Noah** were nine hundred and fifty years:
and he died.

10 **Now these** are the generations of the sons of Noah, Shem, Ham, and Japheth:
and unto them were sons born after the flood.

2 **The sons of Japheth;** Gomer, and Magog, and Madai, and Javan, and Tubal, and Meshech, and Tiras.

3 **And the sons of Gomer;** Ashkenaz, and Riphath, and Togarmah.

4 **And the sons of Javan;** Elishah, and Tarshish, Kittim, and Dodanim.

5 **By these** were the isles of the
Gentiles divided in their lands;
every one after his tongue, after
their families, in their nations.
6 **And the sons of Ham;** Cush, and
Mizraim, and Phut, and Canaan.
7 **And the sons of Cush;** Seba, and
Havilah, and Sabtah, and
Raamah, and Sabtechah: and the
sons of Raamah; Sheba, and
Dedan.
8 **And Cush** begat Nimrod:
he began to be a mighty one in the
earth.
9 **He** was a mighty hunter before the
LORD:
wherefore it is said,
Even as Nimrod the mighty hunter
before the LORD.
10 **And the beginning of his
kingdom** was Babel, and Erech,
and Accad, and Calneh, in the
land of Shinar.
11 **Out of that land** went forth
Asshur,
and builded Nineveh, and the city
Rehoboth, and Calah,
12 And Resen between Nineveh and
Calah:
the same is a great city.
13 **And Mizraim** begat Ludim, and
Anamim, and Lehabim, and
Naphtuhim,
14 And Pathrusim, and Casluhim,
(out of whom came Philistim,)
and Caphtorim.
15 **And Canaan** begat Sidon his first
born, and Heth,
16 And the Jebusite, and the Amorite,
and the Girgasite,
17 And the Hivite, and the Arkite, and
the Sinite,
18 And the Arvadite, and the
Zemarite, and the Hamathite:
and afterward were the families of
the Canaanites spread abroad.
19 **And the border of the
Canaanites** was from Sidon,
as thou comest to Gerar, unto Gaza;
as thou goest, unto Sodom, and
Gomorrah, and Admah, and
Zeboim, even unto Lasha.
20 **These** are the sons of Ham, after
their families, after their tongues,
in their countries, and in their
nations.
21 **Unto Shem** also, the father of all
the children of Eber, the brother
of Japheth the elder,
even to him were children born.
22 **The children of Shem;** Elam, and
Asshur, and Arphaxad, and Lud,
and Aram.
23 **And the children of Aram;** Uz,
and Hul, and Gether, and Mash.
24 **And Arphaxad** begat Salah;
and Salah begat Eber.
25 **And unto Eber** were born two
sons:
the name of one was Peleg;
for in his days was the earth
divided;
and his brother's name was
Joktan.
26 **And Joktan** begat Almodad, and
Sheleph, and Hazarmaveth, and
Jerah,
27 And Hadoram, and Uzal, and
Diklah,
28 And Obal, and Abimael, and
Sheba,
29 And Ophir, and Havilah, and
Jobab:
all these were the sons of Joktan.
30 **And their dwelling** was from
Mesha,
as thou goest unto Sephar a mount
of the east.
31 **These** are the sons of Shem, after
their families, after their tongues,
in their lands, after their nations.
32 **These** are the families of the sons
of Noah, after their generations,
in their nations:
and by these were the nations
divided in the earth after the
flood.

11

And the whole earth was of
one language, and of one
speech.
2 **And it** came to pass,
as they journeyed from the east,
that they found a plain in the land
of Shinar;
and they dwelt there.
3 **And they** said one to another,
Go to,
let us make brick,
and burn them thoroughly.
And they had brick for stone,
and slime had they for morter.
4 **And they** said,
Go to,
let us build us a city and a tower,
whose top may reach unto heaven;
and let us make us a name,
lest we be scattered abroad upon
the face of the whole earth.
5 **And the LORD** came down to see
the city and the tower,
which the children of men
builded.
6 **And the LORD** said,
Behold,
the people is one,
and they have all one language;
and this they begin to do:
and now nothing will be restrained
from them,
which they have imagined to do.
7 **Go to,**
let us go down,
and there confound their language,
that they may not understand one
another's speech.
8 **So the LORD** scattered them
abroad from thence upon the face
of all the earth:
and they left off to build the city.
9 **Therefore** is the name of it called
Babel;
because the LORD did there
confound the language of all the
earth:
and from thence did the LORD
scatter them abroad upon the face
of all the earth.
10 **These** are the generations of
Shem:
Shem was an hundred years old,
and begat Arphaxad two years after
the flood:
11 **And Shem** lived after he begat
Arphaxad five hundred years,
and begat sons and daughters.
12 **And Arphaxad** lived five and
thirty years,
and begat Salah:
13 **And Arphaxad** lived after he
begat Salah four hundred and
three years,
and begat sons and daughters.
14 **And Salah** lived thirty years,
and begat Eber:
15 **And Salah** lived after he begat
Eber four hundred and three
years,
and begat sons and daughters.
16 **And Eber** lived four and thirty
years,
and begat Peleg:
17 **And Eber** lived after he begat
Peleg four hundred and thirty
years,
and begat sons and daughters.

[18] **And Peleg** lived thirty years,
and begat Reu:
[19] **And Peleg** lived after he begat Reu two hundred and nine years,
and begat sons and daughters.

[20] **And Reu** lived two and thirty years,
and begat Serug:
[21] **And Reu** lived after he begat Serug two hundred and seven years,
and begat sons and daughters.

[22] **And Serug** lived thirty years,
and begat Nahor:
[23] **And Serug** lived after he begat Nahor two hundred years,
and begat sons and daughters.

[24] **And Nahor** lived nine and twenty years,
and begat Terah:
[25] **And Nahor** lived after he begat Terah an hundred and nineteen years,
and begat sons and daughters.

[26] **And Terah** lived seventy years,
and begat Abram, Nahor, and Haran.

[27] **Now these** are the generations of Terah:
Terah begat Abram, Nahor, and Haran;
and Haran begat Lot.

[28] **And Haran** died before his father Terah in the land of his nativity, in Ur of the Chaldees.

[29] **And Abram and Nahor** took them wives:
the name of Abram's wife was Sarai;
and the name of Nahor's wife, Milcah, the daughter of Haran, the father of Milcah, and the father of Iscah.

[30] **But Sarai** was barren;
she had no child.

[31] **And Terah** took Abram his son, and Lot the son of Haran his son's son, and Sarai his daughter in law, his son Abram's wife;
and they went forth with them from Ur of the Chaldees,
to go into the land of Canaan;
and they came unto Haran,
and dwelt there.

[32] **And the days of Terah** were two hundred and five years:
and Terah died in Haran.

12

Now the LORD had said unto Abram,
Get thee out of thy country, and from thy kindred, and from thy father's house, unto a land that I will shew thee:
[2] **And I** will make of thee a great nation,
and I will bless thee,
and make thy name great;
and thou shalt be a blessing:
[3] **And I** will bless them that bless thee, and curse him that curseth thee:
and in thee shall all families of the earth be blessed.

[4] **So Abram** departed,
as the LORD had spoken unto him;
and Lot went with him:
and Abram was seventy and five years old
when he departed out of Haran.

[5] **And Abram** took Sarai his wife, and Lot his brother's son, and all their substance that they had gathered, and the souls that they had gotten in Haran;
and they went forth to go into the land of Canaan;
and into the land of Canaan they came.

[6] **And Abram** passed through the land unto the place of Sichem, unto the plain of Moreh.
And the Canaanite was then in the land.

[7] **And the LORD** appeared unto Abram,
and said,
Unto thy seed will I give this land:
and there builded he an altar unto the LORD,
who appeared unto him.

[8] **And he** removed from thence unto a mountain on the east of Bethel,
and pitched his tent,
having Bethel on the west, and Hai on the east:
and there he builded an altar unto the LORD,
and called upon the name of the LORD.

[9] **And Abram** journeyed,
going on still toward the south.

[10] **And there** was a famine in the land:
and Abram went down into Egypt to sojourn there;
for the famine was grievous in the land.

[11] **And it** came to pass,
when he was come near to enter into Egypt,
that he said unto Sarai his wife,
Behold now,
I know
that thou art a fair woman to look upon:
[12] **Therefore it** shall come to pass,
when the Egyptians shall see thee,
that they shall say,
This is his wife:
and they will kill me,
but they will save thee alive.

[13] **Say,**
I pray thee,
thou art my sister:
that it may be well with me for thy sake;
and my soul shall live because of thee.

[14] **And it** came to pass,
that, {when Abram was come into Egypt}, the Egyptians beheld the woman that she was very fair.

[15] **The princes also of Pharaoh** saw her,
and commended her before Pharaoh:
and the woman was taken into Pharaoh's house.

[16] **And he** entreated Abram well for her sake:
and he had sheep, and oxen, and he asses, and menservants, and maidservants, and she asses, and camels.

[17] **And the LORD** plagued Pharaoh and his house with great plagues because of Sarai Abram's wife.

[18] **And Pharaoh** called Abram and said,
What is this that thou hast done unto me?
why didst thou not tell me
that she was thy wife?
[19] **Why** saidst thou,
She is my sister?
so I might have taken her to me to wife:
now therefore behold thy wife,
take her,
and go thy way.

[20] **And Pharaoh** commanded his men concerning him:
and they sent him away, and his wife, and all that he had.

13

And Abram went up out of Egypt, he, and his wife, and

all that he had, and Lot with him, into the south.

2 **And Abram** was very rich in cattle, in silver, and in gold.

3 **And he** went on his journeys from the south even to Bethel, unto the place where his tent had been at the beginning, between Bethel and Hai;

4 Unto the place of the altar,
which he had make there at the first:
and there Abram called on the name of the LORD.

5 **And Lot** also, {which went with Abram}, had flocks, and herds, and tents.

6 **And the land** was not able to bear them,
that they might dwell together:
for their substance was great,
so that they could not dwell together.

7 **And there** was a strife between the herdmen of Abram's cattle and the herdmen of Lot's cattle:
and the Canaanite and the Perizzite dwelled then in the land.

8 **And Abram** said unto Lot,
Let there be no strife, {I pray thee}, between me and thee, and between my herdmen and thy herdmen;
for we be brethren.

9 **Is not the whole land** before thee?
separate thyself, {I pray thee}, from me:
if thou wilt take the left hand,
then I will go to the right;
or if thou depart to the right hand,
then I will go to the left.

10 **And Lot** lifted up his eyes,
and beheld all the plain of Jordan,
that it was well watered every where,
before the LORD destroyed Sodom and Gomorrah, even as the garden of the LORD, like the land of Egypt, as thou comest unto Zoar.

11 **Then Lot** chose him all the plain of Jordan;
and Lot journeyed east:
and they separated themselves the one from the other.

12 **Abram** dwelled in the land of Canaan,
and Lot dwelled in the cities of the plain,
and pitched his tent toward Sodom.

13 **But the men of Sodom** were wicked and sinners before the LORD exceedingly.

14 **And the LORD** said unto Abram,
after that Lot was separated from him,
Lift up now thine eyes,
and look from the place where thou art northward, and southward, and eastward, and westward:

15 **For all the land which thou seest,** to thee will I give it, and to thy seed for ever.

16 **And I** will make thy seed as the dust of the earth:
so that if a man can number the dust of the earth,
then shall thy seed also be numbered.

17 **Arise,**
walk through the land in the length of it and in the breadth of it;
for I will give it unto thee.

18 **Then Abram** removed his tent,
and came and dwelt in the plain of Mamre,
which is in Hebron,
and built there an altar unto the LORD.

14 **And it** came to pass in the days of Amraphel king of Shinar, Arioch king of Ellasar, Chedorlaomer king of Elam, and Tidal king of nations;

2 **That these** made war with Bera king of Sodom, and with Birsha king of Gomorrah, Shinab king of Admah, and Shemeber king of Zeboiim, and the king of Bela,
which is Zoar.

3 **All these** were joined together in the vale of Siddim,
which is the salt sea.

4 **Twelve years** they served Chedorlaomer,
and in the thirteenth year they rebelled.

5 **And in the fourteenth year** came Chedorlaomer, and the kings that were with him,
and smote the Rephaims in Ashteroth Karnaim, and the Zuzims in Ham, and the Emins in Shaveh Kiriathaim,

6 And the Horites in their mount Seir, unto Elparan,
which is by the wilderness.

7 **And they** returned,
and came to Enmishpat,
which is Kadesh,
and smote all the country of the Amalekites, and also the Amorites,
that dwelt in Hazezontamar.

8 **And there** went out the king of Sodom, and the king of Gomorrah, and the king of Admah, and the king of Zeboiim, and the king of Bela (the same is Zoar;)
and they joined battle with them in the vale of Siddim;

9 With Chedorlaomer the king of Elam, and with Tidal king of nations, and Amraphel king of Shinar, and Arioch king of Ellasar; four kings with five.

10 **And the vale of Siddim** was full of slimepits;
and the kings of Sodom and Gomorrah fled,
and fell there;
and they that remained fled to the mountain.

11 **And they** took all the goods of Sodom and Gomorrah, and all their victuals,
and went their way.

12 **And they** took Lot, Abram's brother's son, {who dwelt in Sodom}, and his goods,
and departed.

13 **And there** came one that had escaped,
and told Abram the Hebrew;
for he dwelt in the plain of Mamre the Amorite, brother of Eshcol, and brother of Aner:
and these were confederate with Abram.

14 **And when Abram** heard that his brother was taken captive,
he armed his trained servants, born in his own house, three hundred and eighteen,
and pursued them unto Dan.

15 **And he** divided himself against them, he and his servants, by night,
and smote them,
and pursued them unto Hobah,
which is on the left hand of Damascus.

16 **And he** brought back all the goods,

and also brought again his brother Lot, and his goods, and the women also, and the people.

17 **And the king of Sodom** went out to meet him after his return from the slaughter of Chedorlaomer, and of the kings that were with him, at the valley of Shaveh,
which is the king's dale.

18 **And Melchizedek king of Salem** brought forth bread and wine:
and he was the priest of the most high God.

19 **And he** blessed him,
and said,
Blessed be Abram of the most high God, possessor of heaven and earth:

20 **And blessed** be the most high God,
which hath delivered thine enemies into thy hand.
And he gave him tithes of all.

21 **And the king of Sodom** said unto Abram,
Give me the persons,
and take the goods to thyself.

22 **And Abram** said to the king of Sodom,
I have lift up mine hand unto the LORD, the most high God, the possessor of heaven and earth,

23 **That I** will not take from a thread even to a shoelatchet,
and that I will not take any thing that is thine,
lest thou shouldest say,
I have made Abram rich:

24 Save only that which the young men have eaten, and the portion of the men which went with me, Aner, Eshcol, and Mamre;
let them take their portion.

15 **After these things** the word of the LORD came unto Abram in a vision,
saying,
Fear not, Abram:
I am thy shield, and thy exceeding great reward.

2 **And Abram** said,
LORD God, what wilt thou give me,
seeing I go childless,
and the steward of my house is this Eliezer of Damascus?

3 **And Abram** said,
Behold,
to me thou hast given no seed:
and, {lo}, one born in my house is mine heir.

4 **And, {behold}, the word of the LORD** came unto him,
saying,
This shall not be thine heir;
but he that shall come forth out of thine own bowels shall be thine heir.

5 **And he** brought him forth abroad,
and said,
Look now toward heaven,
and tell the stars,
if thou be able to number them:
and he said unto him,
So shall thy seed be.

6 **And he** believed in the LORD;
and he counted it to him for righteousness.

7 **And he** said unto him,
I am the LORD that brought thee out of Ur of the Chaldees,
to give thee this land to inherit it.

8 **And he** said,
Lord GOD, whereby shall I know
that I shall inherit it?

9 **And he** said unto him,
Take me an heifer of three years old, and a she goat of three years old, and a ram of three years old, and a turtledove, and a young pigeon.

10 **And he** took unto him all these,
and divided them in the midst,
and laid each piece one against another:
but the birds divided he not.

11 **And when the fowls** came down upon the carcases,
Abram drove them away.

12 **And when the sun** was going down,
a deep sleep fell upon Abram;
and, {lo}, an horror of great darkness fell upon him.

13 **And he** said unto Abram,
Know of a surety
that thy seed shall be a stranger in a land that is not theirs,
and shall serve them;
and they shall afflict them four hundred years;

14 **And also that nation**, {whom they shall serve}, will I judge:
and afterward shall they come out with great substance.

15 **And thou** shalt go to thy fathers in peace;
thou shalt be buried in a good old age.

16 **But in the fourth generation** they shall come hither again:
for the iniquity of the Amorites is not yet full.

17 **And it** came to pass,
that, {when the sun went down}, {and it was dark}, behold a smoking furnace, and a burning lamp that passed between those pieces.

18 **In the same day** the LORD made a covenant with Abram,
saying,
Unto thy seed have I given this land, from the river of Egypt unto the great river, the river Euphrates:

19 The Kenites, and the Kenizzites, and the Kadmonites,

20 And the Hittites, and the Perizzites, and the Rephaims,

21 And the Amorites, and the Canaanites, and the Girgashites, and the Jebusites.

16 **Now Sarai Abram's wife** bare him no children:
and she had an handmaid, an Egyptian,
whose name was Hagar.

2 **And Sarai** said unto Abram,
Behold now,
the LORD hath restrained me from bearing:
I pray thee,
go in unto my maid;
it may be that I may obtain children by her.
And Abram hearkened to the voice of Sarai.

3 **And Sarai Abram's wife** took Hagar her maid the Egyptian,
after Abram had dwelt ten years in the land of Canaan,
and gave her to her husband Abram to be his wife.

4 **And he** went in unto Hagar,
and she conceived:
and when she saw that she had conceived,
her mistress was despised in her eyes.

5 **And Sarai** said unto Abram,
My wrong be upon thee:
I have given my maid into thy bosom;
and when she saw that she had conceived,

I was despised in her eyes:
the LORD judge between me and thee.
6 **But Abram** said unto Sarai,
Behold,
thy maid is in thine hand;
do to her as it pleaseth thee.
And when Sarai dealt hardly with her,
she fled from her face.
7 **And the angel of the LORD** found her by a fountain of water in the wilderness, by the fountain in the way to Shur.
8 **And he** said,
Hagar, Sarai's maid, whence camest thou?
and whither wilt thou go?
And she said,
I flee from the face of my mistress Sarai.
9 **And the angel of the LORD** said unto her,
Return to thy mistress,
and submit thyself under her hands.
10 **And the angel of the LORD** said unto her,
I will multiply thy seed exceedingly,
that it shall not be numbered for multitude.
11 **And the angel of the LORD** said unto her,
Behold,
thou art with child
and shalt bear a son,
and shalt call his name Ishmael;
because the LORD hath heard thy affliction.
12 **And he** will be a wild man;
his hand will be against every man, and every man's hand against him;
and he shall dwell in the presence of all his brethren.
13 **And she** called the name of the LORD that spake unto her,
Thou God seest me:
for she said,
Have I also here looked after him that seeth me?
14 **Wherefore the well** was called Beerlahairoi;
behold,
it is between Kadesh and Bered.
15 **And Hagar** bare Abram a son:
and Abram called his son's name, {which Hagar bare}, Ishmael.
16 **And Abram** was fourscore and six years old,
when Hagar bare Ishmael to Abram.

17

And when Abram was ninety years old and nine,
the LORD appeared to Abram,
and said unto him,
I am the Almighty God;
walk before me,
and be thou perfect.
2 **And I** will make my covenant between me and thee,
and will multiply thee exceedingly.
3 **And Abram** fell on his face:
and God talked with him,
saying,
4 **As for me**, {behold}, my covenant is with thee,
and thou shalt be a father of many nations.
5 **Neither** shall thy name any more be called Abram,
but thy name shall be Abraham;
for a father of many nations have I made thee.
6 **And I** will make thee exceeding fruitful,
and I will make nations of thee,
and kings shall come out of thee.
7 **And I** will establish my covenant between me and thee and thy seed after thee in their generations for an everlasting covenant,
to be a God unto thee, and to thy seed after thee.
8 **And I** will give unto thee, and to thy seed after thee, the land wherein thou art a stranger, all the land of Canaan, for an everlasting possession;
and I will be their God.
9 **And God** said unto Abraham,
Thou shalt keep my covenant therefore, thou, and thy seed after thee in their generations.
10 **This** is my covenant,
which ye shall keep, between me and you and thy seed after thee;
Every man child among you shall be circumcised.
11 **And ye** shall circumcise the flesh of your foreskin;
and it shall be a token of the covenant betwixt me and you.
12 **And he that is eight days old** shall be circumcised among you, every man child in your generations, he that is born in the house, or bought with money of any stranger,
which is not of thy seed.
13 **He that is born in thy house, and he that is bought with thy money,** must needs be circumcised:
and my covenant shall be in your flesh for an everlasting covenant.
14 **And the uncircumcised man child whose flesh of his foreskin is not circumcised,** that soul shall be cut off from his people;
he hath broken my covenant.
15 **And God** said unto Abraham,
As for Sarai thy wife, thou shalt not call her name Sarai,
but Sarah shall her name be.
16 **And I** will bless her,
and give thee a son also of her:
yea, I will bless her,
and she shall be a mother of nations;
kings of people shall be of her.
17 **Then Abraham** fell upon his face,
and laughed,
and said in his heart,
Shall a child be born unto him that is an hundred years old?
and shall Sarah, {that is ninety years old}, bear?
18 **And Abraham** said unto God,
O that Ishmael might live before thee!
19 **And God** said,
Sarah thy wife shall bear thee a son indeed;
and thou shalt call his name Isaac:
and I will establish my covenant with him for an everlasting covenant, and with his seed after him.
20 **And as for Ishmael,** I have heard thee:
Behold,
I have blessed him,
and will make him fruitful,
and will multiply him exceedingly;
twelve princes shall he beget,
and I will make him a great nation.
21 **But my covenant** will I establish with Isaac,
which Sarah shall bear unto thee at this set time in the next year.
22 **And he** left off talking with him,
and God went up from Abraham.
23 **And Abraham** took Ishmael his son, and all that were born in his

house, and all that were bought with his money, every male among the men of Abraham's house;
and circumcised the flesh of their foreskin in the selfsame day,
as God had said unto him.

24 **And Abraham** was ninety years old and nine,
when he was circumcised in the flesh of his foreskin.

25 **And Ishmael his son** was thirteen years old,
when he was circumcised in the flesh of his foreskin.

26 **In the selfsame day** was Abraham circumcised, and Ishmael his son.

27 **And all the men of his house**, born in the house, and bought with money of the stranger, were circumcised with him.

18 **And the LORD** appeared unto him in the plains of Mamre:
and he sat in the tent door in the heat of the day;
2 **And he** lift up his eyes and looked,
and, {lo}, three men stood by him:
and when he saw them,
he ran to meet them from the tent door,
and bowed himself toward the ground,
3 **And** said,
My Lord, if now I have found favour in thy sight,
pass not away, {I pray thee}, from thy servant:
4 **Let a little water**, {I pray you}, be fetched,
and wash your feet,
and rest yourselves under the tree:
5 **And I** will fetch a morsel of bread,
and comfort ye your hearts;
after that ye shall pass on:
for therefore are ye come to your servant.

And they said,
So do,
as thou hast said.

6 **And Abraham** hastened into the tent unto Sarah,
and said,
Make ready quickly three measures of fine meal,
knead it,
and make cakes upon the hearth.

7 **And Abraham** ran unto the herd,
and fetcht a calf tender and good,
and gave it unto a young man;
and he hasted to dress it.

8 **And he** took butter, and milk, and the calf which he had dressed,
and set it before them;
and he stood by them under the tree,
and they did eat.

9 **And they** said unto him,
Where is Sarah thy wife?

And he said,
Behold, in the tent.

10 **And he** said,
I will certainly return unto thee according to the time of life;
and, {lo}, Sarah thy wife shall have a son.

And Sarah heard it in the tent door,
which was behind him.

11 **Now Abraham and Sarah** were old and well stricken in age;
and it ceased to be with Sarah after the manner of women.

12 **Therefore Sarah** laughed within herself,
saying,
After I am waxed old
shall I have pleasure,
my lord being old also?

13 **And the LORD** said unto Abraham,
Wherefore did Sarah laugh,
saying,
Shall I of a surety bear a child,
which am old?

14 **Is any thing** too hard for the LORD?

At the time appointed I will return unto thee, according to the time of life,
and Sarah shall have a son.

15 **Then Sarah** denied,
saying,
I laughed not;
for she was afraid.

And he said,
Nay;
but thou didst laugh.

16 **And the men** rose up from thence,
and looked toward Sodom:
and Abraham went with them
to bring them on the way.

17 **And the LORD** said,
Shall I hide from Abraham that thing which I do;
18 **Seeing that Abraham** shall surely become a great and mighty nation,
and all the nations of the earth shall be blessed in him?

19 **For I** know him,
that he will command his children and his household after him,
and they shall keep the way of the LORD,
to do justice and judgment;
that the LORD may bring upon Abraham that which he hath spoken of him.

20 **And the LORD** said,
Because the cry of Sodom and Gomorrah is great,
and because their sin is very grievous;
21 **I** will go down now,
and see whether they have done altogether according to the cry of it,
which is come unto me;
and if not, I will know.

22 **And the men** turned their faces from thence,
and went toward Sodom:
but Abraham stood yet before the LORD.

23 **And Abraham** drew near,
and said,
Wilt thou also destroy the righteous with the wicked?

24 **Peradventure there** be fifty righteous within the city:
wilt thou also destroy and not spare the place for the fifty righteous that are therein?

25 **That** be far from thee to do after this manner,
to slay the righteous with the wicked:
and that the righteous should be as the wicked,
that be far from thee:
Shall not the Judge of all the earth do right?

26 **And the LORD** said,
If I find in Sodom fifty righteous within the city,
then I will spare all the place for their sakes.

27 **And Abraham** answered and said,
Behold now,
I have taken upon me to speak unto the Lord,
which am but dust and ashes:
28 **Peradventure there** shall lack five of the fifty righteous:
wilt thou destroy all the city for lack of five?

And he said,

If I find there forty and five,
I will not destroy it.
29 **And he** spake unto him yet again,
and said,
Peradventure there shall be forty found there.
And he said,
I will not do it for forty's sake.
30 **And he** said unto him,
Oh let not the Lord be angry,
and I will speak:
Peradventure there shall thirty be found there.
And he said,
I will not do it,
if I find thirty there.
31 **And he** said,
Behold now,
I have taken upon me to speak unto the Lord:
Peradventure there shall be twenty found there.
And he said,
I will not destroy it for twenty's sake.
32 **And he** said,
Oh let not the Lord be angry,
and I will speak yet but this once:
Peradventure ten shall be found there.
And he said,
I will not destroy it for ten's sake.
33 **And the LORD** went his way,
as soon as he had left communing with Abraham:
and Abraham returned unto his place.

19 ∞ **And there** came two angels to Sodom at even;
and Lot sat in the gate of Sodom:
and Lot seeing them rose up
to meet them;
and he bowed himself with his face toward the ground;
2 **And he** said,
Behold now, my lords,
turn in, {I pray you}, into your servant's house,
and tarry all night,
and wash your feet,
and ye shall rise up early,
and go on your ways.
And they said,
Nay;
but we will abide in the street all night.
3 **And he** pressed upon them greatly;
and they turned in unto him,
and entered into his house;
and he made them a feast,
and did bake unleavened bread,
and they did eat.
4 **But before they** lay down,
the men of the city, even the men of Sodom, compassed the house round, both old and young, all the people from every quarter:
5 **And they** called unto Lot,
and said unto him,
Where are the men which came in to thee this night?
bring them out unto us,
that we may know them.
6 **And Lot** went out at the door unto them,
and shut the door after him,
7 **And** said,
I pray you, brethren,
do not so wickedly.
8 **Behold** now,
I have two daughters which have not known man;
let me, {I pray you}, bring them out unto you,
and do ye to them as is good in your eyes:
only unto these men do nothing;
for therefore came they under the shadow of my roof.
9 **And they** said,
Stand back.
And they said again,
This one fellow came in to sojourn,
and he will needs be a judge:
now will we deal worse with thee, than with them.
And they pressed sore upon the man, even Lot,
and came near to break the door.
10 **But the men** put forth their hand,
and pulled Lot into the house to them,
and shut to the door.
11 **And they** smote the men that were at the door of the house with blindness, both small and great:
so that they wearied themselves to find the door.
12 **And the men** said unto Lot,
Hast thou here any besides?
son in law, and thy sons, and thy daughters, and whatsoever thou hast in the city, bring them out of this place:
13 **For we** will destroy this place,
because the cry of them is waxen great before the face of the LORD;
and the LORD hath sent us
to destroy it.
14 **And Lot** went out,
and spake unto his sons in law,
which married his daughters,
and said,
Up,
get you out of this place;
for the LORD will destroy this city.
But he seemed as one that mocked unto his sons in law.
15 **And when the morning** arose,
then the angels hastened Lot,
saying,
Arise,
take thy wife, and thy two daughters,
which are here;
lest thou be consumed in the iniquity of the city.
16 **And while he** lingered,
the men laid hold upon his hand, and upon the hand of his wife, and upon the hand of his two daughters;
the LORD being merciful unto him:
and they brought him forth,
and set him without the city.
17 **And it** came to pass,
when they had brought them forth abroad,
that he said,
Escape for thy life;
look not behind thee,
neither stay thou in all the plain;
escape to the mountain,
lest thou be consumed.
18 **And Lot** said unto them,
Oh, not so, my Lord:
19 **Behold** now,
thy servant hath found grace in thy sight,
and thou hast magnified thy mercy,
which thou hast shewed unto me in saving my life;
and I cannot escape to the mountain,
lest some evil take me,
and I die:
20 **Behold** now,
this city is near to flee unto,
and it is a little one:
Oh, let me escape thither,
(is it not a little one?)
and my soul shall live.
21 **And he** said unto him,
See,
I have accepted thee concerning this thing also,
that I will not overthrow this city,
for the which thou hast spoken.
22 **Haste thee,**

escape thither;
for I cannot do anything
till thou be come thither.

Therefore the name of the city was called Zoar.

23 **The sun** was risen upon the earth
when Lot entered into Zoar.

24 **Then the LORD** rained upon Sodom and upon Gomorrah brimstone and fire from the LORD out of heaven;

25 **And he** overthrew those cities, and all the plain, and all the inhabitants of the cities, and that which grew upon the ground.

26 **But his wife** looked back from behind him,
and she became a pillar of salt.

27 **And Abraham** gat up early in the morning to the place where he stood before the LORD:

28 **And he** looked toward Sodom and Gomorrah, and toward all the land of the plain,
and beheld,
and, {lo}, the smoke of the country went up as the smoke of a furnace.

29 **And it** came to pass,
when God destroyed the cities of the plain,
that God remembered Abraham,
and sent Lot out of the midst of the overthrow,
when he overthrew the cities in the which Lot dwelt.

30 **And Lot** went up out of Zoar,
and dwelt in the mountain, and his two daughters with him;
for he feared to dwell in Zoar:
and he dwelt in a cave, he and his two daughters.

31 **And the firstborn** said unto the younger,
Our father is old,
and there is not a man in the earth to come in unto us after the manner of all the earth:

32 **Come,**
let us make our father drink wine,
and we will lie with him,
that we may preserve seed of our father.

33 **And they** made their father drink wine that night:
and the firstborn went in,
and lay with her father;
and he perceived not when she lay down, nor when she arose.

34 **And it** came to pass on the morrow,
that the firstborn said unto the younger,
Behold,
I lay yesternight with my father:
let us make him drink wine this night also;
and go thou in,
and lie with him,
that we may preserve seed of our father.

35 **And they** made their father drink wine that night also:
and the younger arose,
and lay with him;
and he perceived not when she lay down, nor when she arose.

36 **Thus** were both the daughters of Lot with child by their father.

37 **And the first born** bare a son,
and called his name Moab:
the same is the father of the Moabites unto this day.

38 **And the younger,** she also bare a son,
and called his name Benammi:
the same is the father of the children of Ammon unto this day.

20

And Abraham journeyed from thence toward the south country,
and dwelled between Kadesh and Shur,
and sojourned in Gerar.

2 **And Abraham** said of Sarah his wife,
She is my sister:
and Abimelech king of Gerar sent,
and took Sarah.

3 **But God** came to Abimelech in a dream by night,
and said to him,
Behold,
thou art but a dead man, for the woman which thou hast taken;
for she is a man's wife.

4 **But Abimelech** had not come near her:
and he said,
Lord, wilt thou slay also a righteous nation?

5 **Said he not** unto me,
She is my sister?
and she, even she herself said,
He is my brother:
in the integrity of my heart and innocency of my hands have I done this.

6 **And God** said unto him in a dream,
Yea, I know
that thou didst this in the integrity of thy heart;
for I also withheld thee from sinning against me:
therefore suffered I thee not to touch her.

7 **Now therefore restore** the man his wife;
for he is a prophet,
and he shall pray for thee,
and thou shalt live:
and if thou restore her not,
know thou
that thou shalt surely die, thou, and all that are thine.

8 **Therefore Abimelech** rose early in the morning,
and called all his servants,
and told all these things in their ears:
and the men were sore afraid.

9 **Then Abimelech** called Abraham,
and said unto him,
What hast thou done unto us?
and what have I offended thee,
that thou hast brought on me and on my kingdom a great sin?
thou hast done deeds unto me that ought not to be done.

10 **And Abimelech** said unto Abraham,
What sawest thou,
that thou hast done this thing?

11 **And Abraham** said,
Because I thought,
Surely the fear of God is not in this place;
and they will slay me for my wife's sake.

12 **And yet indeed she** is my sister;
she is the daughter of my father, but not the daughter of my mother;
and she became my wife.

13 **And it** came to pass,
when God caused me to wander from my father's house,
that I said unto her,
This is thy kindness which thou shalt shew unto me;
at every place whither we shall come, say of me,
He is my brother.

14 **And Abimelech** took sheep, and oxen, and menservants, and womenservants,
and gave them unto Abraham,
and restored him Sarah his wife.

15 **And Abimelech** said,
Behold,
my land is before thee:
dwell where it pleaseth thee.
16 **And unto Sarah** he said,
Behold,
I have given thy brother a thousand pieces of silver:
behold,
he is to thee a covering of the eyes, unto all that are with thee, and with all other:
thus she was reproved.
17 **So Abraham** prayed unto God:
and God healed Abimelech, and his wife, and his maidservants;
and they bare children.
18 **For the LORD** had fast closed up all the wombs of the house of Abimelech, because of Sarah Abraham's wife.

21 **And the LORD** visited Sarah as he had said,
and the LORD did unto Sarah as he had spoken.
2 **For Sarah** conceived,
and bare Abraham a son in his old age, at the set time of which God had spoken to him.
3 **And Abraham** called the name of his son that was born unto him, {whom Sarah bare to him}, Isaac.
4 **And Abraham** circumcised his son Isaac being eight days old,
as God had commanded him.
5 **And Abraham** was an hundred years old,
when his son Isaac was born unto him.
6 **And Sarah** said,
God hath made me to laugh,
so that all that hear will laugh with me.
7 **And she** said,
Who would have said unto Abraham,
that Sarah should have given children suck?
for I have born him a son in his old age.
8 **And the child** grew,
and was weaned:
and Abraham made a great feast the same day that Isaac was weaned.
9 **And Sarah** saw the son of Hagar the Egyptian, {which she had born unto Abraham}, mocking.
10 **Wherefore she** said unto Abraham,
Cast out this bondwoman and her son:
for the son of this bondwoman shall not be heir with my son, even with Isaac.
11 **And the thing** was very grievous in Abraham's sight because of his son.
12 **And God** said unto Abraham,
Let it not be grievous in thy sight because of the lad, and because of thy bondwoman;
in all that Sarah hath said unto thee, hearken unto her voice;
for in Isaac shall thy seed be called.
13 **And also of the son of the bondwoman** will I make a nation,
because he is thy seed.
14 **And Abraham** rose up early in the morning,
and took bread, and a bottle of water,
and gave it unto Hagar,
putting it on her shoulder, and the child,
and sent her away:
and she departed,
and wandered in the wilderness of Beersheba.
15 **And the water** was spent in the bottle,
and she cast the child under one of the shrubs.
16 **And she** went,
and sat her down over against him a good way off, as it were a bow shot:
for she said,
Let me not see the death of the child.
And she sat over against him,
and lift up her voice,
and wept.
17 **And God** heard the voice of the lad;
and the angel of God called to Hagar out of heaven,
and said unto her,
What aileth thee, Hagar?
fear not;
for God hath heard the voice of the lad where he is.
18 **Arise,**
lift up the lad,
and hold him in thine hand;
for I will make him a great nation.
19 **And God** opened her eyes,
and she saw a well of water;
and she went,
and filled the bottle with water,
and gave the lad drink.
20 **And God** was with the lad;
and he grew,
and dwelt in the wilderness,
and became an archer.
21 **And he** dwelt in the wilderness of Paran:
and his mother took him a wife out of the land of Egypt.
22 **And it** came to pass at that time,
that Abimelech and Phichol the chief captain of his host spake unto Abraham,
saying,
God is with thee in all that thou doest:
23 **Now therefore swear** unto me here by God
that thou wilt not deal falsely with me, nor with my son, nor with my son's son:
but according to the kindness that I have done unto thee, thou shalt do unto me, and to the land wherein thou hast sojourned.
24 **And Abraham** said,
I will swear.
25 **And Abraham** reproved Abimelech because of a well of water,
which Abimelech's servants had violently taken away.
26 **And Abimelech** said,
I wot not
who hath done this thing;
neither didst thou tell me,
neither yet heard I of it, but to day.
27 **And Abraham** took sheep and oxen,
and gave them unto Abimelech;
and both of them made a covenant.
28 **And Abraham** set seven ewe lambs of the flock by themselves.
29 **And Abimelech** said unto Abraham,
What mean these seven ewe lambs which thou hast set by themselves?
30 **And he** said,
For these seven ewe lambs shalt thou take of my hand,
that they may be a witness unto me,
that I have digged this well.

31 **Wherefore he** called that place Beersheba;
because there they sware both of them.
32 **Thus they** made a covenant at Beersheba:
then Abimelech rose up, and Phichol the chief captain of his host,
and they returned into the land of the Philistines.
33 **And Abraham** planted a grove in Beersheba,
and called there on the name of the LORD, the everlasting God.
34 **And Abraham** sojourned in the Philistines' land many days.

22 **And it** came to pass after these things,
that God did tempt Abraham,
and said unto him,
Abraham:
and he said,
Behold,
here I am.
2 **And he** said,
Take now thy son, thine only son Isaac,
whom thou lovest,
and get thee into the land of Moriah;
and offer him there for a burnt offering upon one of the mountains which I will tell thee of.
3 **And Abraham** rose up early in the morning,
and saddled his ass,
and took two of his young men with him, and Isaac his son,
and clave the wood for the burnt offering,
and rose up,
and went unto the place of which God had told him.
4 **Then on the third day** Abraham lifted up his eyes,
and saw the place afar off.
5 **And Abraham** said unto his young men,
Abide ye here with the ass;
and I and the lad will go yonder and worship,
and come again to you.
6 **And Abraham** took the wood of the burnt offering,
and laid it upon Isaac his son;
and he took the fire in his hand, and a knife;
and they went both of them together.
7 **And Isaac** spake unto Abraham his father,
and said,
My father:
and he said,
Here am I, my son.
And he said,
Behold the fire and the wood:
but where is the lamb for a burnt offering?
8 **And Abraham** said,
My son, God will provide himself a lamb for a burnt offering:
so they went both of them together.
9 **And they** came to the place which God had told him of;
and Abraham built an altar there,
and laid the wood in order,
and bound Isaac his son,
and laid him on the altar upon the wood.
10 **And Abraham** stretched forth his hand,
and took the knife
to slay his son.
11 **And the angel of the LORD** called unto him out of heaven,
and said,
Abraham, Abraham:
and he said,
Here am I.
12 **And he** said,
Lay not thine hand upon the lad,
neither do thou any thing unto him:
for now I know
that thou fearest God,
seeing thou hast not withheld thy son, thine only son from me.
13 **And Abraham** lifted up his eyes,
and looked,
and behold
behind him a ram caught in a thicket by his horns:
and Abraham went and took the ram,
and offered him up for a burnt offering in the stead of his son.
14 **And Abraham** called the name of that place Jehovahjireh:
as it is said to this day, In the mount of the LORD it shall be seen.
15 **And the angel of the LORD** called unto Abraham out of heaven the second time,
16 **And** said,
By myself have I sworn,
saith the LORD, for because thou hast done this thing,
and hast not withheld thy son, thine only son:
17 **That in blessing** I will bless thee,
and in multiplying I will multiply thy seed as the stars of the heaven, and as the sand which is upon the sea shore;
and thy seed shall possess the gate of his enemies;
18 **And in thy seed** shall all the nations of the earth be blessed;
because thou hast obeyed my voice.
19 **So Abraham** returned unto his young men,
and they rose up and went together to Beersheba;
and Abraham dwelt at Beersheba.
20 **And it** came to pass after these things,
that it was told Abraham,
saying,
Behold,
Milcah, she hath also born children unto thy brother Nahor;
21 Huz his firstborn, and Buz his brother, and Kemuel the father of Aram,
22 And Chesed, and Hazo, and Pildash, and Jidlaph, and Bethuel.
23 And Bethuel begat Rebekah:
these eight Milcah did bear to Nahor, Abraham's brother.
24 **And his concubine,** {whose name was Reumah}, she bare also Tebah, and Gaham, and Thahash, and Maachah.

23 **And Sarah** was an hundred and seven and twenty years old:
these were the years of the life of Sarah.
2 **And Sarah** died in Kirjatharba;
the same is Hebron in the land of Canaan:
and Abraham came to mourn for Sarah,
and to weep for her.
3 **And Abraham** stood up from before his dead, **and** spake unto the sons of Heth,
saying,
4 **I** am a stranger and a sojourner with you:
give me a possession of a buryingplace with you,

that I may bury my dead out of my sight.
5 **And the children of Heth** answered Abraham,
saying unto him,
6 **Hear** us, my lord:
thou art a mighty prince among us:
in the choice of our sepulchres bury thy dead;
none of us shall withhold from thee his sepulchre,
but that thou mayest bury thy dead.
7 **And Abraham** stood up,
and bowed himself to the people of the land, even to the children of Heth.
8 **And he** communed with them,
saying,
If it be your mind that I should bury my dead out of my sight;
hear me,
and intreat for me to Ephron the son of Zohar,
9 **That he** may give me the cave of Machpelah,
which he hath,
which is in the end of his field;
for as much money as it is worth he shall give it me for a possession of a buryingplace amongst you.
10 **And Ephron** dwelt among the children of Heth:
and Ephron the Hittite answered Abraham in the audience of the children of Heth, even of all that went in at the gate of his city,
saying,
11 **Nay, my lord, hear** me:
the field give I thee,
and the cave that is therein, I give it thee;
in the presence of the sons of my people give I it thee: bury thy dead.
12 **And Abraham** bowed down himself before the people of the land.
13 **And he** spake unto Ephron in the audience of the people of the land,
saying,
But if thou wilt give it,
I pray thee,
hear me:
I will give thee money for the field;
take it of me,
and I will bury my dead there.
14 **And Ephron** answered Abraham,
saying unto him,
15 **My lord, hearken** unto me:
the land is worth four hundred shekels of silver;
what is that betwixt me and thee?
bury therefore thy dead.
16 **And Abraham** hearkened unto Ephron;
and Abraham weighed to Ephron the silver,
which he had named in the audience of the sons of Heth, four hundred shekels of silver, current money with the merchant.
17 **And the field of Ephron which was in Machpelah, which was before Mamre, the field, and the cave which was therein, and all the trees that were in the field, that were in all the borders round about,** were made sure
18 Unto Abraham for a possession in the presence of the children of Heth, before all that went in at the gate of his city.
19 **And after this,** Abraham buried Sarah his wife in the cave of the field of Machpelah before Mamre:
the same is Hebron in the land of Canaan.
20 **And the field, and the cave that is therein,** were made sure unto Abraham for a possession of a buryingplace by the sons of Heth.

24

And Abraham was old,
and well stricken in age:
and the LORD had blessed Abraham in all things.
2 **And Abraham** said unto his eldest servant of his house,
that ruled over all that he had,
Put, {I pray thee}, thy hand under my thigh:
3 **And I** will make thee swear by the LORD, the God of heaven, and the God of the earth,
that thou shalt not take a wife unto my son of the daughters of the Canaanites,
among whom I dwell:
4 **But thou** shalt go unto my country, and to my kindred,
and take a wife unto my son Isaac.
5 **And the servant** said unto him,
Peradventure the woman will not be willing to follow me unto this land:
must I needs bring thy son again unto the land from whence thou camest?
6 **And Abraham** said unto him,
Beware thou that thou bring not my son thither again.
7 **The LORD God of heaven**, {which took me from my father's house, and from the land of my kindred}, {and which spake unto me}, {and that sware unto me}, {saying}, {Unto thy seed will I give this land}; he shall send his angel before thee,
and thou shalt take a wife unto my son from thence.
8 **And if the woman** will not be willing to follow thee,
then thou shalt be clear from this my oath:
only bring not my son thither again.
9 **And the servant** put his hand under the thigh of Abraham his master,
and sware to him concerning that matter.
10 **And the servant** took ten camels of the camels of his master,
and departed;
for all the goods of his master were in his hand:
and he arose,
and went to Mesopotamia, unto the city of Nahor.
11 **And he** made his camels to kneel down without the city by a well of water at the time of the evening, even the time that women go out to draw water.
12 **And he** said
O LORD God of my master Abraham, {I pray thee}, send me good speed this day,
and shew kindness unto my master Abraham.
13 **Behold,**
I stand here by the well of water;
and the daughters of the men of the city come out
to draw water:
14 **And let it** come to pass,
that the damsel to whom I shall say, {Let down thy pitcher}, {I pray thee}, {that I may drink}; {and she shall say}, {Drink}, {and I will give thy camels drink also}: let the same be she that thou hast appointed for thy servant Isaac;
and thereby shall I know
that thou hast shewed kindness unto my master.

15 **And it** came to pass,
before he had done speaking,
that, {behold}, Rebekah came out,
who was born to Bethuel, son of Milcah, the wife of Nahor, Abraham's brother, with her pitcher upon her shoulder.
16 **And the damsel** was very fair to look upon, a virgin,
neither had any man known her:
and she went down to the well,
and filled her pitcher,
and came up.
17 **And the servant** ran to meet her,
and said,
Let me, {I pray thee}, drink a little water of thy pitcher.
18 **And she** said,
Drink, my lord:
and she hasted,
and let down her pitcher upon her hand,
and gave him drink.
19 **And when she** had done giving him drink,
she said,
I will draw water for thy camels also,
until they have done drinking.
20 **And she** hasted,
and emptied her pitcher into the trough,
and ran again unto the well
to draw water,
and drew for all his camels.
21 **And the man wondering at her** held his peace,
to wit
whether the LORD had made his journey prosperous or not.
22 **And it** came to pass,
as the camels had done drinking,
that the man took a golden earring of half a shekel weight, and two bracelets for her hands of ten shekels weight of gold;
23 **And** said,
Whose daughter art thou?
tell me,
I pray thee:
is there room in thy father's house for us to lodge in?
24 **And she** said unto him,
I am the daughter of Bethuel the son of Milcah,
which she bare unto Nahor.
25 **She** said moreover unto him,
We have both straw and provender enough, and room to lodge in.
26 **And the man** bowed down his head,
and worshipped the LORD.
27 **And he** said,
Blessed be the LORD God of my master Abraham,
who hath not left destitute my master of his mercy and his truth:
I being in the way,
the LORD led me to the house of my master's brethren.
28 **And the damsel** ran,
and told them of her mother's house these things.
29 **And Rebekah** had a brother,
and his name was Laban:
and Laban ran out unto the man, unto the well.
30 **And it** came to pass,
when he saw the earring and bracelets upon his sister's hands,
and when he heard the words of Rebekah his sister,
saying,
Thus spake the man unto me;
that he came unto the man;
and, {behold}, he stood by the camels at the well.
31 **And he** said,
Come in, thou blessed of the LORD;
wherefore standest thou without?
for I have prepared the house, and room for the camels.
32 **And the man** came into the house:
and he ungirded his camels,
and gave straw and provender for the camels, and water to wash his feet, and the men's feet that were with him.
33 **And there** was set meat before him to eat:
but he said,
I will not eat,
until I have told mine errand.
And he said,
Speak on.
34 **And he** said,
I am Abraham's servant.
35 **And the LORD** hath blessed my master greatly;
and he is become great:
and he hath given him flocks, and herds, and silver, and gold, and menservants, and maidservants, and camels, and asses.
36 **And Sarah my master's wife** bare a son to my master
when she was old:
and unto him hath he given all that he hath.
37 **And my master** made me swear,
saying,
Thou shalt not take a wife to my son of the daughters of the Canaanites,
in whose land I dwell:
38 **But thou** shalt go unto my father's house, and to my kindred,
and take a wife unto my son.
39 **And I** said unto my master,
Peradventure the woman will not follow me.
40 **And he** said unto me,
The LORD, {before whom I walk}, will send his angel with thee,
and prosper thy way;
and thou shalt take a wife for my son of my kindred, and of my father's house:
41 **Then** shalt thou be clear from this my oath,
when thou comest to my kindred;
and if they give not thee one,
thou shalt be clear from my oath.
42 **And I** came this day unto the well,
and said,
O LORD God of my master Abraham, if now thou do prosper my way which I go:
43 **Behold,**
I stand by the well of water;
and it shall come to pass,
that when the virgin cometh forth
to draw water,
and I say to her,
Give me, {I pray thee}, a little water of thy pitcher to drink;
44 **And she** say to me,
Both drink thou,
and I will also draw for thy camels:
let the same be the woman whom the LORD hath appointed out for my master's son.
45 **And before I** had done speaking in mine heart,
behold,
Rebekah came forth with her pitcher on her shoulder;
and she went down unto the well,
and drew water:
and I said unto her,
Let me drink,
I pray thee.
46 **And she** made haste,
and let down her pitcher from her shoulder,
and said,
Drink,

and I will give thy camels drink also:
so I drank,
and she made the camels drink also.
47 **And I** asked her,
and said,
Whose daughter art thou?
And she said,
the daughter of Bethuel, Nahor's son,
whom Milcah bare unto him:
and I put the earring upon her face, and the bracelets upon her hands.
48 **And I** bowed down my head,
and worshipped the LORD,
and blessed the LORD God of my master Abraham,
which had led me in the right way to take my master's brother's daughter unto his son.
49 **And now if ye** will deal kindly and truly with my master,
tell me:
and if not, tell me;
that I may turn to the right hand, or to the left.
50 **Then Laban and Bethuel** answered and said,
The thing proceedeth from the LORD:
we cannot speak unto thee bad or good.
51 **Behold, Rebekah** is before thee,
take her,
and go,
and let her be thy master's son's wife,
as the LORD hath spoken.
52 **And it** came to pass,
that, {when Abraham's servant heard their words}, he worshipped the LORD,
bowing himself to the earth.
53 **And the servant** brought forth jewels of silver, and jewels of gold, and raiment,
and gave them to Rebekah:
he gave also to her brother and to her mother precious things.
54 **And they** did eat and drink, he and the men that were with him,
and tarried all night;
and they rose up in the morning,
and he said,
Send me away unto my master.
55 **And her brother and her mother** said,
Let the damsel abide with us a few days, at the least ten;
after that she shall go.
56 **And he** said unto them,
Hinder me not,
seeing the LORD hath prospered my way;
send me away
that I may go to my master.
57 **And they** said,
We will call the damsel,
and enquire at her mouth.
58 **And they** called Rebekah,
and said unto her,
Wilt thou go with this man?
And she said,
I will go.
59 **And they** sent away Rebekah their sister, and her nurse, and Abraham's servant, and his men.
60 **And they** blessed Rebekah,
and said unto her,
Thou art our sister,
be thou the mother of thousands of millions,
and let thy seed possess the gate of those which hate them.
61 **And Rebekah** arose, and her damsels,
and they rode upon the camels,
and followed the man:
and the servant took Rebekah,
and went his way.
62 **And Isaac** came from the way of the well Lahairoi;
for he dwelt in the south country.
63 **And Isaac** went out to meditate in the field at the eventide:
and he lifted up his eyes,
and saw, {and, behold}, the camels were coming.
64 **And Rebekah** lifted up her eyes,
and when she saw Isaac,
she lighted off the camel.
65 **For she** had said unto the servant,
What man is this that walketh in the field to meet us?
And the servant had said,
It is my master:
therefore she took a vail,
and covered herself.
66 **And the servant** told Isaac all things that he had done.
67 **And Isaac** brought her into his mother Sarah's tent,
and took Rebekah,
and she became his wife;
and he loved her:
and Isaac was comforted after his mother's death.

25 **Then again Abraham** took a wife,
and her name was Keturah.
2 **And she** bare him Zimran, and Jokshan, and Medan, and Midian, and Ishbak, and Shuah.
3 **And Jokshan** begat Sheba, and Dedan.
And the sons of Dedan were Asshurim, and Letushim, and Leummim.
4 **And the sons of Midian;** Ephah, and Epher, and Hanoch, and Abidah, and Eldaah.
All these were the children of Keturah.
5 **And Abraham** gave all that he had unto Isaac.
6 **But unto the sons of the concubines**, {which Abraham had}, Abraham gave gifts,
and sent them away from Isaac his son, {while he yet lived}, eastward, unto the east country.
7 **And these** are the days of the years of Abraham's life which he lived, an hundred threescore and fifteen years.
8 **Then Abraham** gave up the ghost,
and died in a good old age, an old man, and full of years;
and was gathered to his people.
9 **And his sons Isaac and Ishmael** buried him in the cave of Machpelah, in the field of Ephron the son of Zohar the Hittite,
which is before Mamre;
10 The field which Abraham purchased of the sons of Heth:
there was Abraham buried, and Sarah his wife.
11 **And it** came to pass after the death of Abraham,
that God blessed his son Isaac;
and Isaac dwelt by the well Lahairoi.
12 **Now these** are the generations of Ishmael, Abraham's son,
whom Hagar the Egyptian, Sarah's handmaid, bare unto Abraham:
13 **And these** are the names of the sons of Ishmael, by their names, according to their generations: the firstborn of Ishmael, Nebajoth; and Kedar, and Adbeel, and Mibsam,

14 And Mishma, and Dumah, and Massa,
15 Hadar, and Tema, Jetur, Naphish, and Kedemah:
16 **These** are the sons of Ishmael,
and these are their names, by their towns, and by their castles; twelve princes according to their nations.
17 **And these** are the years of the life of Ishmael, an hundred and thirty and seven years:
and he gave up the ghost and died;
and was gathered unto his people.
18 **And they** dwelt from Havilah unto Shur, that is before Egypt,
as thou goest toward Assyria:
and he died in the presence of all his brethren.
19 **And these** are the generations of Isaac, Abraham's son:
Abraham begat Isaac:
20 **And Isaac** was forty years old
when he took Rebekah to wife, the daughter of Bethuel the Syrian of Padanaram, the sister to Laban the Syrian.
21 **And Isaac** intreated the LORD for his wife,
because she was barren:
and the LORD was intreated of him,
and Rebekah his wife conceived.
22 **And the children** struggled together within her;
and she said,
If it be so,
why am I thus?
And she went to enquire of the LORD.
23 **And the LORD** said unto her,
Two nations are in thy womb,
and two manner of people shall be separated from thy bowels;
and the one people shall be stronger than the other people;
and the elder shall serve the younger.
24 **And when her days to be delivered** were fulfilled,
behold,
there were twins in her womb.
25 **And the first** came out red, all over like an hairy garment;
and they called his name Esau.
26 **And after that** came his brother out,
and his hand took hold on Esau's heel;
and his name was called Jacob:
and Isaac was threescore years old
when she bare them.
27 **And the boys** grew:
and Esau was a cunning hunter, a man of the field;
and Jacob was a plain man, dwelling in tents.
28 **And Isaac** loved Esau,
because he did eat of his venison:
but Rebekah loved Jacob.
29 **And Jacob** sod pottage:
and Esau came from the field,
and he was faint:
30 **And Esau** said to Jacob,
Feed me, {I pray thee}, with that same red pottage;
for I am faint:
therefore was his name called Edom.
31 **And Jacob** said,
Sell me this day thy birthright.
32 **And Esau** said,
Behold,
I am at the point to die:
and what profit shall this birthright do to me?
33 **And Jacob** said,
Swear to me this day;
and he sware unto him:
and he sold his birthright unto Jacob.
34 **Then Jacob** gave Esau bread and pottage of lentiles;
and he did eat and drink,
and rose up,
and went his way:
thus Esau despised his birthright.

26

And there was a famine in the land, beside the first famine that was in the days of Abraham.
And Isaac went unto Abimelech king of the Philistines unto Gerar.
2 **And the LORD** appeared unto him,
and said,
Go not down into Egypt;
dwell in the land which I shall tell thee of:
3 **Sojourn** in this land,
and I will be with thee,
and will bless thee;
for unto thee, and unto thy seed, I will give all these countries,
and I will perform the oath which I sware unto Abraham thy father;
4 **And I** will make thy seed to multiply as the stars of heaven,
and will give unto thy seed all these countries;
and in thy seed shall all the nations of the earth be blessed;
5 **Because that Abraham** obeyed my voice,
and kept my charge, my commandments, my statutes, and my laws.
6 **And Isaac** dwelt in Gerar:
7 **And the men of the place** asked him of his wife;
and he said,
She is my sister:
for he feared to say,
She is my wife;
lest, {said he}, the men of the place should kill me for Rebekah;
because she was fair to look upon.
8 **And it** came to pass,
when he had been there a long time,
that Abimelech king of the Philistines looked out at a window,
and saw,
and, {behold}, Isaac was sporting with Rebekah his wife.
9 **And Abimelech** called Isaac,
and said,
Behold,
of a surety she is thy wife;
and how saidst thou,
She is my sister?
And Isaac said unto him,
Because I said,
Lest I die for her.
10 **And Abimelech** said,
What is this thou hast done unto us?
one of the people might lightly have lien with thy wife,
and thou shouldest have brought guiltiness upon us.
11 **And Abimelech** charged all his people,
saying,
He that toucheth this man or his wife shall surely be put to death.
12 **Then Isaac** sowed in that land,
and received in the same year an hundredfold:
and the LORD blessed him.
13 **And the man** waxed great,
and went forward,
and grew until he became very great:
14 **For he** had possession of flocks, and possession of herds, and great store of servants:

and the Philistines envied him.
15 **For all the wells which his father's servants** had digged in the days of Abraham his father,
the Philistines had stopped them,
and filled them with earth.
16 **And Abimelech** said unto Isaac,
Go from us;
for thou art much mightier than we.
17 **And Isaac** departed thence,
and pitched his tent in the valley of Gerar,
and dwelt there.
18 **And Isaac** digged again the wells of water,
which they had digged in the days of Abraham his father;
for the Philistines had stopped them after the death of Abraham:
and he called their names after the names by which his father had called them.
19 **And Isaac's servants** digged in the valley,
and found there a well of springing water.
20 **And the herdmen of Gerar** did strive with Isaac's herdmen,
saying,
The water is ours:
and he called the name of the well Esek;
because they strove with him.
21 **And they** digged another well,
and strove for that also:
and he called the name of it Sitnah.
22 **And he** removed from thence,
and digged another well;
and for that they strove not:
and he called the name of it Rehoboth;
and he said,
For now the LORD hath made room for us,
and we shall be fruitful in the land.
23 **And he** went up from thence to Beersheba.
24 **And the LORD** appeared unto him the same night,
and said,
I am the God of Abraham thy father:
fear not,
for I am with thee,
and will bless thee,
and multiply thy seed for my servant Abraham's sake.
25 **And he** builded an altar there,
and called upon the name of the LORD,
and pitched his tent there:
and there Isaac's servants digged a well.
26 **Then Abimelech** went to him from Gerar, and Ahuzzath one of his friends, and Phichol the chief captain of his army.
27 **And Isaac** said unto them,
Wherefore come ye to me,
seeing ye hate me,
and have sent me away from you?
28 **And they** said,
We saw certainly that the LORD was with thee:
and we said,
Let there be now an oath betwixt us, even betwixt us and thee,
and let us make a covenant with thee;
29 **That thou** wilt do us no hurt,
as we have not touched thee,
and as we have done unto thee nothing but good,
and have sent thee away in peace:
thou art now the blessed of the LORD.
30 **And he** made them a feast,
and they did eat and drink.
31 **And they** rose up betimes in the morning,
and sware one to another:
and Isaac sent them away,
and they departed from him in peace.
32 **And it** came to pass the same day,
that Isaac's servants came,
and told him concerning the well which they had digged,
and said unto him,
We have found water.
33 **And he** called it Shebah:
therefore the name of the city is Beersheba unto this day.
34 **And Esau** was forty years old
when he took to wife Judith the daughter of Beeri the Hittite, and Bashemath the daughter of Elon the Hittite:
35 **Which** were a grief of mind unto Isaac and to Rebekah.

27

And it came to pass,
that when Isaac was old,
and his eyes were dim,
so that he could not see,
he called Esau his eldest son,
and said unto him, My son:
and he said unto him,
Behold,
here am I.
2 **And he** said,
Behold now,
I am old,
I know not the day of my death:
3 **Now therefore take**, {I pray thee}, thy weapons, thy quiver and thy bow,
and go out to the field,
and take me some venison;
4 **And make** me savoury meat,
such as I love,
and bring it to me,
that I may eat;
that my soul may bless thee
before I die.
5 **And Rebekah** heard when Isaac spake to Esau his son.
And Esau went to the field to hunt for venison,
and to bring it.
6 **And Rebekah** spake unto Jacob her son,
saying,
Behold,
I heard thy father speak unto Esau thy brother,
saying,
7 **Bring** me venison,
and make me savoury meat,
that I may eat,
and bless thee before the LORD before my death.
8 **Now therefore, my son, obey** my voice according to that which I command thee.
9 **Go** now to the flock,
and fetch me from thence two good kids of the goats;
and I will make them savoury meat for thy father,
such as he loveth:
10 **And thou** shalt bring it to thy father,
that he may eat,
and that he may bless thee before his death.
11 **And Jacob** said to Rebekah his mother,
Behold,
Esau my brother is a hairy man,
and I am a smooth man:
12 **My father** peradventure will feel me,
and I shall seem to him as a deceiver;
and I shall bring a curse upon me, and not a blessing.
13 **And his mother** said unto him,

Upon me be thy curse, my son:
only obey my voice,
and go fetch me them.
14 **And he** went,
and fetched,
and brought them to his mother:
and his mother made savoury meat,
such as his father loved.
15 **And Rebekah** took goodly raiment of her eldest son Esau,
which were with her in the house,
and put them upon Jacob her younger son:
16 **And she** put the skins of the kids of the goats upon his hands, and upon the smooth of his neck:
17 **And she** gave the savoury meat and the bread,
which she had prepared, into the hand of her son Jacob.
18 **And he** came unto his father,
and said,
My father:
and he said,
Here am I;
who art thou, my son?
19 **And Jacob** said unto his father,
I am Esau thy first born;
I have done according as thou badest me:
arise,
I pray thee,
sit and eat of my venison,
that thy soul may bless me.
20 **And Isaac** said unto his son,
How is it that thou hast found it so quickly, my son?
And he said,
Because the LORD thy God brought it to me.
21 **And Isaac** said unto Jacob,
Come near,
I pray thee,
that I may feel thee, my son,
whether thou be my very son Esau or not.
22 **And Jacob** went near unto Isaac his father;
and he felt him,
and said,
The voice is Jacob's voice,
but the hands are the hands of Esau.
23 **And he** discerned him not,
because his hands were hairy, as his brother Esau's hands:
so he blessed him.
24 **And he** said,
Art thou my very son Esau?
And he said,
I am.
25 **And he** said,
Bring it near to me,
and I will eat of my son's venison,
that my soul may bless thee.
And he brought it near to him,
and he did eat:
and he brought him wine
and he drank.
26 **And his father Isaac** said unto him,
Come near now,
and kiss me, my son.
27 **And he** came near,
and kissed him:
and he smelled the smell of his raiment,
and blessed him,
and said,
See,
the smell of my son is as the smell of a field which the LORD hath blessed:
28 **Therefore God** give thee of the dew of heaven, and the fatness of the earth, and plenty of corn and wine:
29 **Let people** serve thee,
and nations bow down to thee:
be lord over thy brethren,
and let thy mother's sons bow down to thee:
cursed be every one that curseth thee,
and blessed be he that blesseth thee.
30 **And it** came to pass,
as soon as Isaac had made an end of blessing Jacob,
and Jacob was yet scarce gone out from the presence of Isaac his father,
that Esau his brother came in from his hunting.
31 **And he** also had made savoury meat,
and brought it unto his father,
and said unto his father,
Let my father arise,
and eat of his son's venison,
that thy soul may bless me.
32 **And Isaac his father** said unto him,
Who art thou?
And he said,
I am thy son, thy firstborn Esau.
33 **And Isaac** trembled very exceedingly,
and said,
Who?
where is he that hath taken venison,
and brought it me,
and I have eaten of all before thou camest,
and have blessed him?
yea, and he shall be blessed.
34 **And when Esau** heard the words of his father,
he cried with a great and exceeding bitter cry,
and said unto his father,
Bless me, even me also, O my father.
35 **And he** said,
Thy brother came with subtilty,
and hath taken away thy blessing.
36 **And he** said,
Is not he rightly named Jacob?
for he hath supplanted me these two times:
he took away my birthright;
and, {behold}, now he hath taken away my blessing.
And he said,
Hast thou not reserved a blessing for me?
37 **And Isaac** answered and said unto Esau,
Behold,
I have made him thy lord,
and all his brethren have I given to him for servants;
and with corn and wine have I sustained him:
and what shall I do now unto thee, my son?
38 **And Esau** said unto his father,
Hast thou but one blessing, my father?
bless me, even me also, O my father.
And Esau lifted up his voice,
and wept.
39 **And Isaac his father** answered and said unto him,
Behold, thy dwelling shall be the fatness of the earth, and of the dew of heaven from above;
40 **And by thy sword** shalt thou live,
and shalt serve thy brother;
and it shall come to pass
when thou shalt have the dominion,
that thou shalt break his yoke from off thy neck.

41 **And Esau** hated Jacob because of the blessing wherewith his father blessed him:
and Esau said in his heart,
The days of mourning for my father are at hand;
then will I slay my brother Jacob.

42 **And these words of Esau her elder son** were told to Rebekah:
and she sent and called Jacob her younger son,
and said unto him,
Behold,
thy brother Esau, as touching thee, doth comfort himself,
purposing to kill thee.

43 **Now therefore, my son, obey** my voice;
arise,
flee thou to Laban my brother to Haran;
44 **And** tarry with him a few days,
until thy brother's fury turn away;
45 **Until thy brother's anger** turn away from thee,
and he forget that which thou hast done to him:
then I will send,
and fetch thee from thence:
why should I be deprived also of you both in one day?

46 **And Rebekah** said to Isaac,
I am weary of my life because of the daughters of Heth:
if Jacob take a wife of the daughters of Heth, such as these which are of the daughters of the land,
what good shall my life do me?

28 **And Isaac** called Jacob,
and blessed him,
and charged him,
and said unto him,
Thou shalt not take a wife of the daughters of Canaan.

2 **Arise,**
go to Padanaram, to the house of Bethuel thy mother's father;
and take thee a wife from thence of the daughers of Laban thy mother's brother.

3 **And God Almighty** bless thee,
and make thee fruitful,
and multiply thee,
that thou mayest be a multitude of people;
4 **And** give thee the blessing of Abraham, to thee, and to thy seed with thee;
that thou mayest inherit the land wherein thou art a stranger,
which God gave unto Abraham.

5 **And Isaac** sent away Jacob:
and he went to Padanaram unto Laban, son of Bethuel the Syrian, the brother of Rebekah, Jacob's and Esau's mother.

6 **When Esau** saw that Isaac had blessed Jacob, and sent him away to Padanaram, to take him a wife from thence; and that as he blessed him he gave him a charge, saying, Thou shalt not take a wife of the daughters of Canaan;
7 And that Jacob obeyed his father and his mother, and was gone to Padanaram;
8 **And Esau** seeing that the daughters of Canaan pleased not Isaac his father;
9 **Then** went Esau unto Ishmael,
and took unto the wives which he had Mahalath the daughter of Ishmael Abraham's son, the sister of Nebajoth, to be his wife.

10 **And Jacob** went out from Beersheba,
and went toward Haran.

11 **And he** lighted upon a certain place,
and tarried there all night,
because the sun was set;
and he took of the stones of that place,
and put them for his pillows,
and lay down in that place
to sleep.

12 **And he** dreamed,
and {behold} a ladder set up on the earth,
and the top of it reached to heaven:
and {behold} the angels of God ascending and descending on it.

13 **And, {behold}, the LORD** stood above it,
and said,
I am the LORD God of Abraham thy father, and the God of Isaac:
the land whereon thou liest, to thee will I give it, and to thy seed;
14 **And thy seed** shall be as the dust of the earth,
and thou shalt spread abroad to the west, and to the east, and to the north, and to the south:
and in thee and in thy seed shall all the families of the earth be blessed.

15 **And, {behold}, I** am with thee,
and will keep thee in all places whither thou goest,
and will bring thee again into this land;
for I will not leave thee,
until I have done that which I have spoken to thee of.

16 **And Jacob** awaked out of his sleep,
and he said,
Surely the LORD is in this place;
and I knew it not.

17 **And he** was afraid,
and said,
How dreadful is this place!
this is none other but the house of God,
and this is the gate of heaven.

18 **And Jacob** rose up early in the morning,
and took the stone that he had put for his pillows,
and set it up for a pillar,
and poured oil upon the top of it.
19 **And he** called the name of that place Bethel:
but the name of that city was called Luz at the first.

20 **And Jacob** vowed a vow,
saying,
If God will be with me,
and will keep me in this way that I go,
and will give me bread to eat, and raiment to put on,
21 **So that I** come again to my father's house in peace;
then shall the LORD be my God:
22 **And this stone,** {which I have set for a pillar}, shall be God's house:
and of all that thou shalt give me I will surely give the tenth unto thee.

29 **Then Jacob** went on his journey,
and came into the land of the people of the east.

2 **And he** looked,
and behold a well in the field,
and, {lo}, there were three flocks of sheep lying by it;
for out of that well they watered the flocks:
and a great stone was upon the well's mouth.

3 **And thither** were all the flocks gathered:
and they rolled the stone from the well's mouth,
and watered the sheep,
and put the stone again upon the well's mouth in his place.

4 **And Jacob** said unto them,
My brethren, whence be ye?
And they said,
Of Haran are we.
5 **And he** said unto them,
Know ye Laban the son of Nahor?
And they said,
We know him.
6 **And he** said unto them,
Is he well?
And they said,
He is well:
and, {behold}, Rachel his daughter cometh with the sheep.
7 **And he** said,
Lo,
it is yet high day,
neither is it time that the cattle should be gathered together:
water ye the sheep,
and go and feed them.
8 **And they** said,
We cannot,
until all the flocks be gathered together,
and till they roll the stone from the well's mouth;
then we water the sheep.
9 **And while he** yet spake with them,
Rachel came with her father's sheep;
for she kept them.
10 **And it** came to pass,
when Jacob saw Rachel the daughter of Laban his mother's brother, and the sheep of Laban his mother's brother,
that Jacob went near,
and rolled the stone from the well's mouth,
and watered the flock of Laban his mother's brother.
11 **And Jacob** kissed Rachel,
and lifted up his voice,
and wept.
12 **And Jacob** told Rachel
that he was her father's brother,
and that he was Rebekah's son:
and she ran and told her father.
13 **And it** came to pass,
when Laban heard the tidings of Jacob his sister's son,
that he ran to meet him,
and embraced him,
and kissed him,
and brought him to his house.
And he told Laban all these things.
14 **And Laban** said to him,
Surely thou art my bone and my flesh.
And he abode with him the space of a month.
15 **And Laban** said unto Jacob,
Because thou art my brother,
shouldest thou therefore serve me for nought?
tell me,
what shall thy wages be?
16 **And Laban** had two daughters:
the name of the elder was Leah,
and the name of the younger was Rachel.
17 **Leah** was tender eyed;
but Rachel was beautiful and well favoured.
18 **And Jacob** loved Rachel;
and said,
I will serve thee seven years for Rachel thy younger daughter.
19 **And Laban** said,
It is better that I give her to thee,
than that I should give her to another man:
abide with me.
20 **And Jacob** served seven years for Rachel;
and they seemed unto him but a few days, for the love he had to her.
21 **And Jacob** said unto Laban,
Give me my wife,
for my days are fulfilled,
that I may go in unto her.
22 **And Laban** gathered together all the men of the place,
and made a feast.
23 **And it** came to pass in the evening,
that he took Leah his daughter,
and brought her to him;
and he went in unto her.
24 **And Laban** gave unto his daughter Leah Zilpah his maid for an handmaid.
25 **And it** came to pass,
that in the morning, {behold}, it was Leah:
and he said to Laban,
What is this thou hast done unto me?
did not I serve with thee for Rachel?
wherefore then hast thou beguiled me?
26 **And Laban** said,
It must not be so done in our country,
to give the younger before the firstborn.
27 **Fulfil** her week,
and we will give thee this also for the service which thou shalt serve with me yet seven other years.
28 **And Jacob** did so,
and fulfilled her week:
and he gave him Rachel his daughter to wife also.
29 **And Laban** gave to Rachel his daughter Bilhah his handmaid to be her maid.
30 **And he** went in also unto Rachel,
and he loved also Rachel more than Leah,
and served with him yet seven other years.
31 **And when the LORD** saw that Leah was hated,
he opened her womb:
but Rachel was barren.
32 **And Leah** conceived,
and bare a son,
and she called his name Reuben:
for she said,
Surely the LORD hath looked upon my affliction;
now therefore my husband will love me.
33 **And she** conceived again,
and bare a son;
and said,
Because the LORD hath heard I was hated,
he hath therefore given me this son also:
and she called his name Simeon.
34 **And she** conceived again,
and bare a son;
and said,
Now this time will my husband be joined unto me,
because I have born him three sons:
therefore was his name called Levi.
35 **And she** conceived again,
and bare a son:
and she said,
Now will I praise the LORD:
therefore she called his name Judah;
and left bearing.

30 **And when Rachel** saw that she bare Jacob no children,
Rachel envied her sister;
and said unto Jacob,
Give me children,
or else I die.

2 **And Jacob's anger** was kindled against Rachel:
and he said,
Am I in God's stead,
who hath withheld from thee the fruit of the womb?
3 **And she** said,
Behold my maid Bilhah,
go in unto her;
and she shall bear upon my knees,
that I may also have children by her.
4 **And she** gave him Bilhah her handmaid to wife:
and Jacob went in unto her.
5 **And Bilhah** conceived,
and bare Jacob a son.
6 **And Rachel** said,
God hath judged me,
and hath also heard my voice,
and hath given me a son:
therefore called she his name Dan.
7 **And Bilhah Rachel's maid** conceived again,
and bare Jacob a second son.
8 **And Rachel** said,
With great wrestlings have I wrestled with my sister,
and I have prevailed:
and she called his name Naphtali.
9 **When Leah** saw that she had left bearing,
she took Zilpah her maid,
and gave her Jacob to wife.
10 **And Zilpah Leah's maid** bare Jacob a son.
11 **And Leah** said,
A troop cometh:
and she called his name Gad.
12 **And Zilpah Leah's maid** bare Jacob a second son.
13 **And Leah** said,
Happy am I,
for the daughters will call me blessed:
and she called his name Asher.
14 **And Reuben** went in the days of wheat harvest,
and found mandrakes in the field,
and brought them unto his mother Leah.
Then Rachel said to Leah,
Give me, {I pray thee}, of thy son's mandrakes.
15 **And she** said unto her,
Is it a small matter that thou hast taken my husband?
and wouldest thou take away my son's mandrakes also?
And Rachel said, **Therefore he** shall lie with thee to night for thy son's mandrakes.
16 **And Jacob** came out of the field in the evening,
and Leah went out to meet him,
and said,
Thou must come in unto me;
for surely I have hired thee with my son's mandrakes.
And he lay with her that night.
17 **And God** hearkened unto Leah,
and she conceived,
and bare Jacob the fifth son.
18 **And Leah** said,
God hath given me my hire,
because I have given my maiden to my husband:
and she called his name Issachar.
19 **And Leah** conceived again,
and bare Jacob the sixth son.
20 **And Leah** said,
God hath endued me with a good dowry;
now will my husband dwell with me,
because I have born him six sons:
and she called his name Zebulun.
21 **And afterwards** she bare a daughter,
and called her name Dinah.
22 **And God** remembered Rachel,
and God hearkened to her,
and opened her womb.
23 **And she** conceived,
and bare a son;
and said,
God hath taken away my reproach:
24 **And she** called his name Joseph;
and said,
The LORD shall add to me another son.
25 **And it** came to pass,
when Rachel had born Joseph,
that Jacob said unto Laban,
Send me away,
that I may go unto mine own place, and to my country.
26 **Give** me my wives and my children,
for whom I have served thee,
and let me go:
for thou knowest my service which I have done thee.
27 **And Laban** said unto him,
I pray thee,
if I have found favour in thine eyes,
tarry:
for I have learned by experience that the LORD hath blessed me for thy sake.
28 **And he** said,
Appoint me thy wages,
and I will give it.
29 **And he** said unto him,
Thou knowest
how I have served thee,
and how thy cattle was with me.
30 **For it** was little which thou hadst before I came,
and it is now increased unto a multitude;
and the LORD hath blessed thee since my coming:
and now when shall I provide for mine own house also?
31 **And he** said,
What shall I give thee?
And Jacob said,
Thou shalt not give me any thing:
if thou wilt do this thing for me,
I will again feed and keep thy flock.
32 **I** will pass through all thy flock to day,
removing from thence all the speckled and spotted cattle, and all the brown cattle among the sheep, and the spotted and speckled among the goats:
and of such shall be my hire.
33 **So** shall my righteousness answer for me in time to come,
when it shall come for my hire before thy face:
every one that is not speckled and spotted among the goats, and brown among the sheep, that shall be counted stolen with me.
34 **And Laban** said,
Behold,
I would it might be according to thy word.
35 **And he** removed that day the he goats that were ringstraked and spotted, and all the she goats that were speckled and spotted, and every one that had some white in it, and all the brown among the sheep,
and gave them into the hand of his sons.
36 **And he** set three days' journey betwixt himself and Jacob:
and Jacob fed the rest of Laban's flocks.

37 **And Jacob** took him rods of green poplar, and of the hazel and chesnut tree;
and pilled white strakes in them,
and made the white appear which was in the rods.
38 **And he** set the rods which he had pilled before the flocks in the gutters in the watering troughs
when the flocks came to drink,
that they should conceive when they came to drink.
39 **And the flocks** conceived before the rods,
and brought forth cattle ringstraked, speckled, and spotted.
40 **And Jacob** did separate the lambs,
and set the faces of the flocks toward the ringstraked, and all the brown in the flock of Laban;
and he put his own flocks by themselves,
and put them not unto Laban's cattle.
41 **And it** came to pass,
whensoever the stronger cattle did conceive,
that Jacob laid the rods before the eyes of the cattle in the gutters,
that they might conceive among the rods.
42 **But when the cattle** were feeble,
he put them not in:
so the feebler were Laban's, and the stronger Jacob's.
43 **And the man** increased exceedingly,
and had much cattle, and maidservants, and menservants, and camels, and asses.

31

And he heard the words of Laban's sons,
saying,
Jacob hath taken away all that was our father's;
and of that which was our father's hath he gotten all this glory.
2 **And Jacob** beheld the countenance of Laban,
and, {behold}, it was not toward him as before.
3 **And the LORD** said unto Jacob,
Return unto the land of thy fathers, and to thy kindred;
and I will be with thee.
4 **And Jacob** sent and called Rachel and Leah to the field unto his flock,
5 **And** said unto them,
I see your father's countenance,
that it is not toward me as before;
but the God of my father hath been with me.
6 **And ye** know
that with all my power I have served your father.
7 **And your father** hath deceived me,
and changed my wages ten times;
but God suffered him not to hurt me.
8 **If he** said thus,
The speckled shall be thy wages;
then all the cattle bare speckled:
and if he said thus,
The ringstraked shall be thy hire;
then bare all the cattle ringstraked.
9 **Thus God** hath taken away the cattle of your father,
and given them to me.
10 **And it** came to pass at the time that the cattle conceived,
that I lifted up mine eyes,
and saw in a dream,
and, {behold}, the rams which leaped upon the cattle were ringstraked, speckled, and grisled.
11 **And the angel of God** spake unto me in a dream,
saying,
Jacob:
And I said,
Here am I.
12 **And he** said,
Lift up now thine eyes,
and see,
all the rams which leap upon the cattle are ringstraked, speckled, and grisled:
for I have seen all that Laban doeth unto thee.
13 **I** am the God of Bethel,
where thou anointedst the pillar,
and where thou vowedst a vow unto me:
now arise,
get thee out from this land,
and return unto the land of thy kindred.
14 **And Rachel and Leah** answered and said unto him,
Is there yet any portion or inheritance for us in our father's house?
15 **Are we not** counted of him strangers?
for he hath sold us,
and hath quite devoured also our money.
16 **For all the riches which God hath taken from our father,** that is ours, and our children's:
now then, whatsoever God hath said unto thee, do.
17 **Then Jacob** rose up,
and set his sons and his wives upon camels;
18 **And he** carried away all his cattle, and all his goods which he had gotten, the cattle of his getting,
which he had gotten in Padanaram,
for to go to Isaac his father in the land of Canaan.
19 **And Laban** went to shear his sheep:
and Rachel had stolen the images that were her father's.
20 **And Jacob** stole away unawares to Laban the Syrian,
in that he told him not
that he fled.
21 **So he** fled with all that he had;
and he rose up,
and passed over the river,
and set his face toward the mount Gilead.
22 **And it was told Laban on the third day** that Jacob was fled.
23 **And he** took his brethren with him,
and pursued after him seven days' journey;
and they overtook him in the mount Gilead.
24 **And God** came to Laban the Syrian in a dream by night,
and said unto him,
Take heed that thou speak not to Jacob either good or bad.
25 **Then Laban** overtook Jacob.
Now Jacob had pitched his tent in the mount:
and Laban with his brethren pitched in the mount of Gilead.
26 **And Laban** said to Jacob,
What hast thou done,
that thou hast stolen away unawares to me,
and carried away my daughters, as captives taken with the sword?
27 **Wherefore** didst thou flee away secretly,
and steal away from me;

and didst not tell me,
that I might have sent thee away with mirth, and with songs, with tabret, and with harp?

28 **And** hast not suffered me to kiss my sons and my daughters?
thou hast now done foolishly in so doing.

29 **It is in the power of my hand** to do you hurt:
but the God of your father spake unto me yesternight,
saying,
Take thou heed that thou speak not to Jacob either good or bad.

30 **And now, though thou** wouldest needs be gone,
because thou sore longedst after thy father's house,
yet wherefore hast thou stolen my gods?

31 **And Jacob** answered and said to Laban,
Because I was afraid:
for I said,
Peradventure thou wouldest take by force thy daughters from me.

32 **With whomsoever** thou findest thy gods,
let him not live:
before our brethren discern thou what is thine with me,
and take it to thee.

For Jacob knew not
that Rachel had stolen them.

33 **And Laban** went into Jacob's tent, and into Leah's tent, and into the two maidservants' tents;
but he found them not.

Then went he out of Leah's tent,
and entered into Rachel's tent.

34 **Now Rachel** had taken the images,
and put them in the camel's furniture,
and sat upon them.

And Laban searched all the tent,
but found them not.

35 **And she** said to her father,
Let it not displease my lord that I cannot rise up before thee;
for the custom of women is upon me.

And he searched but found not the images.

36 **And Jacob** was wroth,
and chode with Laban:
and Jacob answered and said to Laban,
What is my trespass?
what is my sin,
that thou hast so hotly pursued after me?

37 **Whereas thou** hast searched all my stuff,
what hast thou found of all thy household stuff?
set it here before my brethren and thy brethren,
that they may judge betwixt us both.

38 **This twenty years** have I been with thee;
thy ewes and thy she goats have not cast their young,
and the rams of thy flock have I not eaten.

39 **That which was torn of beasts** I brought not unto thee;
I bare the loss of it;
of my hand didst thou require it, whether stolen by day, or stolen by night.

40 **Thus I** was;
in the day the drought consumed me, and the frost by night;
and my sleep departed from mine eyes.

41 **Thus** have I been twenty years in thy house;
I served thee fourteen years for thy two daughters, and six years for thy cattle:
and thou hast changed my wages ten times.

42 **Except the God of my father, the God of Abraham, and the fear of Isaac,** had been with me,
surely thou hadst sent me away now empty.

God hath seen mine affliction and the labour of my hands,
and rebuked thee yesternight.

43 **And Laban** answered and said unto Jacob,
These daughters are my daughters,
and these children are my children,
and these cattle are my cattle,
and all that thou seest is mine:
and what can I do this day unto these my daughters, or unto their children which they have born?

44 **Now therefore come thou,**
let us make a covenant, I and thou;
and let it be for a witness between me and thee.

45 **And Jacob** took a stone,
and set it up for a pillar.

46 **And Jacob** said unto his brethren,
Gather stones;
and they took stones,
and made an heap:
and they did eat there upon the heap.

47 **And Laban** called it Jegarsahadutha:
but Jacob called it Galeed.

48 **And Laban** said,
This heap is a witness between me and thee this day.

Therefore was the name of it called Galeed;
49 And Mizpah;
for he said,
The LORD watch between me and thee,
when we are absent one from another.

50 **If thou** shalt afflict my daughters,
or if thou shalt take other wives beside my daughters,
no man is with us;
see,
God is witness betwixt me and thee.

51 **And Laban** said to Jacob,
Behold this heap,
and behold this pillar,
which I have cast betwixt me and thee:
52 **This heap** be witness,
and this pillar be witness,
that I will not pass over this heap to thee,
and that thou shalt not pass over this heap and this pillar unto me, for harm.

53 **The God of Abraham, and the God of Nahor, the God of their father,** judge betwixt us.

And Jacob sware by the fear of his father Isaac.

54 **Then Jacob** offered sacrifice upon the mount,
and called his brethren to eat bread:
and they did eat bread,
and tarried all night in the mount.

55 **And early in the morning** Laban rose up,
and kissed his sons and his daughters,
and blessed them:
and Laban departed,
and returned unto his place.

32 ∞ **And Jacob** went on his way,
and the angels of God met him.

[2] **And when Jacob** saw them,
he said,
This is God's host:
and he called the name of that place Mahanaim.
[3] **And Jacob** sent messengers before him to Esau his brother unto the land of Seir, the country of Edom.
[4] **And he** commanded them,
saying,
Thus shall ye speak unto my lord Esau;
Thy servant Jacob saith thus,
I have sojourned with Laban,
and stayed there until now:
[5] **And I** have oxen, and asses, flocks, and menservants, and womenservants:
and I have sent to tell my lord,
that I may find grace in thy sight.
[6] **And the messengers** returned to Jacob,
saying,
We came to thy brother Esau,
and also he cometh to meet thee, and four hundred men with him.
[7] **Then Jacob** was greatly afraid and distressed:
and he divided the people that was with him, and the flocks, and herds, and the camels, into two bands;
[8] **And** said,
If Esau come to the one company,
and smite it,
then the other company which is left shall escape.
[9] **And Jacob** said,
O God of my father Abraham, and God of my father Isaac, the LORD which saidst unto me, {Return unto thy country, and to thy kindred}, {and I will deal well with thee}:
[10] **I** am not worthy of the least of all the mercies, and of all the truth,
which thou hast shewed unto thy servant;
for with my staff I passed over this Jordan;
and now I am become two bands.
[11] **Deliver** me, {I pray thee}, from the hand of my brother, from the hand of Esau:
for I fear him,
lest he will come and smite me, and the mother with the children.
[12] **And thou** saidst,
I will surely do thee good,
and make thy seed as the sand of the sea,
which cannot be numbered for multitude.
[13] **And he** lodged there that same night;
and took of that which came to his hand a present for Esau his brother;
[14] Two hundred she goats, and twenty he goats, two hundred ewes, and twenty rams,
[15] Thirty milch camels with their colts, forty kine, and ten bulls, twenty she asses, and ten foals.
[16] **And he** delivered them into the hand of his servants, every drove by themselves;
and said unto his servants,
Pass over before me,
and put a space betwixt drove and drove.
[17] **And he** commanded the foremost,
saying,
When Esau my brother meeteth thee,
and asketh thee,
saying,
Whose art thou?
and whither goest thou?
and whose are these before thee?
[18] **Then thou** shalt say,
They be thy servant Jacob's;
it is a present sent unto my lord Esau:
and, {behold}, also he is behind us.
[19] **And so** commanded he the second, and the third, and all that followed the droves,
saying,
On this manner shall ye speak unto Esau,
when ye find him.
[20] **And say ye** moreover,
Behold,
thy servant Jacob is behind us.
For he said,
I will appease him with the present that goeth before me,
and afterward I will see his face;
peradventure he will accept of me.
[21] **So** went the present over before him:
and himself lodged that night in the company.
[22] **And he** rose up that night,
and took his two wives, and his two womenservants, and his eleven sons,
and passed over the ford Jabbok.
[23] **And he** took them,
and sent them over the brook,
and sent over that he had.
[24] **And Jacob** was left alone;
and there wrestled a man with him until the breaking of the day.
[25] **And when he** saw that he prevailed not against him,
he touched the hollow of his thigh;
and the hollow of Jacob's thigh was out of joint,
as he wrestled with him.
[26] **And he** said,
Let me go,
for the day breaketh.
And he said,
I will not let thee go,
except thou bless me.
[27] **And he** said unto him,
What is thy name?
And he said,
Jacob.
[28] **And he** said,
Thy name shall be called no more Jacob, but Israel:
for as a prince hast thou power with God and with men,
and hast prevailed.
[29] **And Jacob** asked him,
and said,
Tell me, {I pray thee}, thy name.
And he said,
Wherefore is it that thou dost ask after my name?
And he blessed him there.
[30] **And Jacob** called the name of the place Peniel:
for I have seen God face to face,
and my life is preserved.
[31] **And as he** passed over Penuel
the sun rose upon him,
and he halted upon his thigh.
[32] **Therefore the children of Israel** eat not of the sinew which shrank,
which is upon the hollow of the thigh, unto this day:
because he touched the hollow of Jacob's thigh in the sinew that shrank.

33

And Jacob lifted up his eyes,
and looked,
and, {behold}, Esau came, and with him four hundred men.
And he divided the children unto Leah, and unto Rachel, and unto the two handmaids.

2 **And he** put the handmaids and their children foremost, and Leah and her children after, and Rachel and Joseph hindermost.

3 **And he** passed over before them,
and bowed himself to the ground seven times,
until he came near to his brother.

4 **And Esau** ran to meet him,
and embraced him,
and fell on his neck,
and kissed him:
and they wept.

5 **And he** lifted up his eyes,
and saw the women and the children;
and said,
Who are those with thee?

And he said,
The children which God hath graciously given thy servant.

6 **Then the handmaidens** came near, they and their children,
and they bowed themselves.

7 **And Leah also with her children** came near,
and bowed themselves:
and after came Joseph near and Rachel,
and they bowed themselves.

8 **And he** said,
What meanest thou by all this drove which I met?

And he said,
These are to find grace in the sight of my lord.

9 **And Esau** said,
I have enough, my brother;
keep that thou hast unto thyself.

10 **And Jacob** said,
Nay, {I pray thee}, if now I have found grace in thy sight,
then receive my present at my hand:
for therefore I have seen thy face,
as though I had seen the face of God,
and thou wast pleased with me.

11 **Take**, {I pray thee}, my blessing that is brought to thee;
because God hath dealt graciously with me,
and because I have enough.

And he urged him,
and he took it.

12 **And he** said,
Let us take our journey,
and let us go,
and I will go before thee.

13 **And he** said unto him,
My lord knoweth
that the children are tender,
and the flocks and herds with young are with me:
and if men should overdrive them one day,
all the flock will die.

14 **Let my lord**, {I pray thee}, pass over before his servant:
and I will lead on softly, according as the cattle that goeth before me and the children be able to endure,
until I come unto my lord unto Seir.

15 **And Esau** said,
Let me now leave with thee some of the folk that are with me.

And he said,
What needeth it?
let me find grace in the sight of my lord.

16 **So Esau** returned that day on his way unto Seir.

17 **And Jacob** journeyed to Succoth,
and built him an house,
and made booths for his cattle:
therefore the name of the place is called Succoth.

18 **And Jacob** came to Shalem, a city of Shechem,
which is in the land of Canaan,
when he came from Padanaram;
and pitched his tent before the city.

19 **And he** bought a parcel of a field,
where he had spread his tent, at the hand of the children of Hamor, Shechem's father, for an hundred pieces of money.

20 **And he** erected there an altar,
and called it EleloheIsrael.

34 **And Dinah the daughter of Leah**, {which she bare unto Jacob}, went out to see the daughters of the land.

2 **And when Shechem the son of Hamor the Hivite**, prince of the country, saw her,
he took her,
and lay with her,
and defiled her.

3 **And his soul** clave unto Dinah the daughter of Jacob,
and he loved the damsel,
and spake kindly unto the damsel.

4 **And Shechem** spake unto his father Hamor,
saying,
Get me this damsel to wife.

5 **And Jacob** heard that he had defiled Dinah his daughter:
now his sons were with his cattle in the field:
and Jacob held his peace
until they were come.

6 **And Hamor the father of Shechem** went out unto Jacob
to commune with him.

7 **And the sons of Jacob** came out of the field
when they heard it:
and the men were grieved,
and they were very wroth,
because he had wrought folly in Israel in lying with Jacob's daughter:
which thing ought not to be done.

8 **And Hamor** communed with them,
saying,
The soul of my son Shechem longeth for your daughter:
I pray you give her him to wife.

9 **And make ye** marriages with us,
and give your daughters unto us,
and take our daughters unto you.

10 **And ye** shall dwell with us:
and the land shall be before you;
dwell and trade ye therein,
and get you possessions therein.

11 **And Shechem** said unto her father and unto her brethren,
Let me find grace in your eyes,
and what ye shall say unto me
I will give.

12 **Ask** me never so much dowry and gift,
and I will give according as ye shall say unto me:
but give me the damsel to wife.

13 **And the sons of Jacob** answered Shechem and Hamor his father deceitfully,
and said,
because he had defiled Dinah their sister:

14 **And they** said unto them,
We cannot do this thing,
to give our sister to one that is uncircumcised;
for that were a reproach unto us:

15 **But in this** will we consent unto you:
If ye will be as we be,
that every male of you be circumcised;

16 **Then** will we give our daughters unto you,

and we will take your daughters to us,
and we will dwell with you,
and we will become one people.
17 **But if ye** will not hearken unto us,
to be circumcised;
then will we take our daughter,
and we will be gone.
18 **And their words** pleased Hamor, and Shechem Hamor's son.
19 **And the young man** deferred not to do the thing,
because he had delight in Jacob's daughter:
and he was more honourable than all the house of his father.
20 **And Hamor and Shechem his son** came unto the gate of their city,
and communed with the men of their city,
saying,
21 **These men** are peaceable with us;
therefore let them dwell in the land,
and trade therein;
for the land, {behold}, it is large enough for them;
let us take their daughters to us for wives,
and let us give them our daughters.
22 **Only herein** will the men consent unto us for to dwell with us,
to be one people,
if every male among us be circumcised,
as they are circumcised.
23 **Shall not their cattle and their substance and every beast of their's** be our's?
only let us consent unto them,
and they will dwell with us.
24 **And unto Hamor and unto Shechem his son** hearkened all that went out of the gate of his city;
and every male was circumcised, all that went out of the gate of his city.
25 **And it** came to pass on the third day,
when they were sore,
that two of the sons of Jacob, Simeon and Levi, Dinah's brethren, took each man his sword,
and came upon the city boldly,
and slew all the males.
26 **And they** slew Hamor and Shechem his son with the edge of the sword,
and took Dinah out of Shechem's house,
and went out.
27 **The sons of Jacob** came upon the slain,
and spoiled the city,
because they had defiled their sister.
28 **They** took their sheep, and their oxen, and their asses, and that which was in the city, and that which was in the field,
29 And all their wealth, and all their little ones,
and their wives took they captive,
and spoiled even all that was in the house.
30 **And Jacob** said to Simeon and Levi,
Ye have troubled me to make me to stink among the inhabitants of the land, among the Canaanites and the Perizzites:
and I being few in number,
they shall gather themselves together against me,
and slay me;
and I shall be destroyed, I and my house.
31 **And they** said,
Should he deal with our sister as with an harlot?

35

And God said unto Jacob,
Arise,
go up to Bethel,
and dwell there:
and make there an altar unto God,
that appeared unto thee
when thou fleddest from the face of Esau thy brother.
2 **Then Jacob** said unto his household, and to all that were with him,
Put away the strange gods that are among you,
and be clean,
and change your garments:
3 **And let us** arise,
and go up to Bethel;
and I will make there an altar unto God,
who answered me in the day of my distress,
and was with me in the way which I went.
4 **And they** gave unto Jacob all the strange gods which were in their hand, and all their earrings which were in their ears;
and Jacob hid them under the oak which was by Shechem.
5 **And they** journeyed:
and the terror of God was upon the cities that were round about them,
and they did not pursue after the sons of Jacob.
6 **So Jacob** came to Luz,
which is in the land of Canaan, that is, Bethel, he and all the people that were with him.
7 **And he** built there an altar,
and called the place Elbethel:
because there God appeared unto him,
when he fled from the face of his brother.
8 **But Deborah, Rebekah's nurse** died,
and she was buried beneath Bethel under an oak:
and the name of it was called Allonbachuth.
9 **And God** appeared unto Jacob again,
when he came out of Padanaram,
and blessed him.
10 **And God** said unto him,
Thy name is Jacob:
thy name shall not be called any more Jacob,
but Israel shall be thy name:
and he called his name Israel.
11 **And God** said unto him,
I am God Almighty:
be fruitful
and multiply;
a nation and a company of nations shall be of thee,
and kings shall come out of thy loins;
12 **And the land which I gave Abraham and Isaac,** to thee I will give it,
and to thy seed after thee will I give the land.
13 **And God** went up from him in the place where he talked with him.
14 **And Jacob** set up a pillar in the place where he talked with him, even a pillar of stone:
and he poured a drink offering thereon,
and he poured oil thereon.

[15] **And Jacob** called the name of the place where God spake with him, Bethel.

[16] **And they** journeyed from Bethel;
and there was but a little way to come to Ephrath:
and Rachel travailed,
and she had hard labour.

[17] **And it** came to pass,
when she was in hard labour,
that the midwife said unto her,
Fear not;
thou shalt have this son also.

[18] **And it** came to pass,
as her soul was in departing,
(for she died)
that she called his name Benoni:
but his father called him Benjamin.

[19] **And Rachel** died,
and was buried in the way to Ephrath,
which is Bethlehem.

[20] **And Jacob** set a pillar upon her grave:
that is the pillar of Rachel's grave unto this day.

[21] **And Israel** journeyed,
and spread his tent beyond the tower of Edar.

[22] **And it** came to pass,
when Israel dwelt in that land,
that Reuben went and lay with Bilhah his father's concubine:
and Israel heard it.

Now the sons of Jacob were twelve:

[23] **The sons of Leah;** Reuben, Jacob's firstborn, and Simeon, and Levi, and Judah, and Issachar, and Zebulun:

[24] **The sons of Rachel;** Joseph, and Benjamin:

[25] **And the sons of Bilhah, Rachel's handmaid;** Dan, and Naphtali:

[26] **And the sons of Zilpah, Leah's handmaid:** Gad, and Asher:
these are the sons of Jacob,
which were born to him in Padanaram.

[27] **And Jacob** came unto Isaac his father unto Mamre, unto the city of Arbah,
which is Hebron,
where Abraham and Isaac sojourned.

[28] **And the days of Isaac** were an hundred and fourscore years.

[29] **And Isaac** gave up the ghost,
and died,
and was gathered unto his people, being old and full of days:
and his sons Esau and Jacob buried him.

36

Now these are the generations of Esau,
who is Edom.

[2] **Esau** took his wives of the daughters of Canaan; Adah the daughter of Elon the Hittite, and Aholibamah the daughter of Anah the daughter of Zibeon the Hivite;

[3] And Bashemath Ishmael's daughter, sister of Nebajoth.

[4] **And Adah** bare to Esau Eliphaz;
and Bashemath bare Reuel;

[5] **And Aholibamah** bare Jeush, and Jaalam, and Korah:
these are the sons of Esau,
which were born unto him in the land of Canaan.

[6] **And Esau** took his wives, and his sons, and his daughters, and all the persons of his house, and his cattle, and all his beasts, and all his substance,
which he had got in the land of Canaan;
and went into the country from the face of his brother Jacob.

[7] **For their riches** were more than that they might dwell together;
and the land wherein they were strangers could not bear them because of their cattle.

[8] **Thus** dwelt Esau in mount Seir:
Esau is Edom.

[9] **And these** are the generations of Esau the father of the Edomites in mount Seir:

[10] **These** are the names of Esau's sons; Eliphaz the son of Adah the wife of Esau, Reuel the son of Bashemath the wife of Esau.

[11] **And the sons of Eliphaz** were Teman, Omar, Zepho, and Gatam, and Kenaz.

[12] **And Timna** was concubine to Eliphaz Esau's son;
and she bare to Eliphaz Amalek:
these were the sons of Adah Esau's wife.

[13] **And these** are the sons of Reuel; Nahath, and Zerah, Shammah, and Mizzah:
these were the sons of Bashemath Esau's wife.

[14] **And these** were the sons of Aholibamah, the daughter of Anah the daughter of Zibeon, Esau's wife:
and she bare to Esau Jeush, and Jaalam, and Korah.

[15] **These** were dukes of the sons of Esau: the sons of Eliphaz the firstborn son of Esau; duke Teman, duke Omar, duke Zepho, duke Kenaz,

[16] Duke Korah, duke Gatam, and duke Amalek:
these are the dukes that came of Eliphaz in the land of Edom;
these were the sons of Adah.

[17] **And these** are the sons of Reuel Esau's son; duke Nahath, duke Zerah, duke Shammah, duke Mizzah:
these are the dukes that came of Reuel in the land of Edom;
these are the sons of Bashemath Esau's wife.

[18] **And these** are the sons of Aholibamah Esau's wife; duke Jeush, duke Jaalam, duke Korah:
these were the dukes that came of Aholibamah the daughter of Anah, Esau's wife.

[19] **These** are the sons of Esau,
who is Edom,
and these are their dukes.

[20] **These** are the sons of Seir the Horite,
who inhabited the land; Lotan, and Shobal, and Zibeon, and Anah,

[21] And Dishon, and Ezer, and Dishan:
these are the dukes of the Horites, the children of Seir in the land of Edom.

[22] **And the children of Lotan** were Hori and Hemam;
and Lotan's sister was Timna.

[23] **And the children of Shobal** were these; Alvan, and Manahath, and Ebal, Shepho, and Onam.

[24] **And these** are the children of Zibeon; both Ajah, and Anah:
this was that Anah that found the mules in the wilderness,
as he fed the asses of Zibeon his father.

[25] **And the children of Anah** were these; Dishon, and Aholibamah the daughter of Anah.

[26] **And these** are the children of Dishon; Hemdan, and Eshban, and Ithran, and Cheran.

27 **The children of Ezer** are these; Bilhan, and Zaavan, and Akan.

28 **The children of Dishan** are these; Uz, and Aran.

29 **These** are the dukes that came of the Horites; duke Lotan, duke Shobal, duke Zibeon, duke Anah,
30 Duke Dishon, duke Ezer, duke Dishan:
these are the dukes that came of Hori, among their dukes in the land of Seir.

31 **And these** are the kings that reigned in the land of Edom,
before there reigned any king over the children of Israel.

32 **And Bela the son of Beor** reigned in Edom:
and the name of his city was Dinhabah.

33 **And Bela** died,
and Jobab the son of Zerah of Bozrah reigned in his stead.

34 **And Jobab** died,
and Husham of the land of Temani reigned in his stead.

35 **And Husham** died,
and Hadad the son of Bedad, {who smote Midian in the field of Moab}, reigned in his stead:
and the name of his city was Avith.

36 **And Hadad** died,
and Samlah of Masrekah reigned in his stead.

37 **And Samlah** died,
and Saul of Rehoboth by the river reigned in his stead.

38 **And Saul** died,
and Baalhanan the son of Achbor reigned in his stead.

39 **And Baalhanan the son of Achbor** died,
and Hadar reigned in his stead:
and the name of his city was Pau;
and his wife's name was Mehetabel, the daughter of Matred, the daughter of Mezahab.

40 **And these** are the names of the dukes that came of Esau, according to their families, after their places, by their names; duke Timnah, duke Alvah, duke Jetheth,
41 Duke Aholibamah, duke Elah, duke Pinon,
42 Duke Kenaz, duke Teman, duke Mibzar,
43 Duke Magdiel, duke Iram:
these be the dukes of Edom, according to their habitations in the land of their possession:
he is Esau the father of the Edomites.

37 **And Jacob** dwelt in the land wherein his father was a stranger, in the land of Canaan.

2 **These** are the generations of Jacob.
Joseph, {being seventeen years old}, was feeding the flock with his brethren;
and the lad was with the sons of Bilhah, and with the sons of Zilpah, his father's wives:
and Joseph brought unto his father their evil report.

3 **Now Israel** loved Joseph more than all his children,
because he was the son of his old age:
and he made him a coat of many colours.

4 **And when his brethren** saw that their father loved him more than all his brethren,
they hated him,
and could not speak peaceably unto him.

5 **And Joseph** dreamed a dream,
and he told it his brethren:
and they hated him yet the more.

6 **And he** said unto them,
Hear, {I pray you}, this dream which I have dreamed:
7 **For, {behold}, we** were binding sheaves in the field,
and, {lo}, my sheaf arose,
and also stood upright;
and, {behold}, your sheaves stood round about,
and made obeisance to my sheaf.

8 **And his brethren** said to him,
Shalt thou indeed reign over us?
or shalt thou indeed have dominion over us?
And they hated him yet the more for his dreams, and for his words.

9 **And he** dreamed yet another dream,
and told it his brethren,
and said,
Behold,
I have dreamed a dream more;
and, {behold}, the sun and the moon and the eleven stars made obeisance to me.

10 **And he** told it to his father, and to his brethren:
and his father rebuked him,
and said unto him,
What is this dream that thou hast dreamed?
Shall I and thy mother and thy brethren indeed come to bow down ourselves to thee to the earth?

11 **And his brethren** envied him;
but his father observed the saying.

12 **And his brethren** went to feed their father's flock in Shechem.

13 **And Israel** said unto Joseph,
Do not thy brethren feed the flock in Shechem?
come,
and I will send thee unto them.
And he said to him,
Here am I.

14 **And he** said to him,
Go,
I pray thee,
see whether it be well with thy brethren, and well with the flocks;
and bring me word again.
So he sent him out of the vale of Hebron,
and he came to Shechem.

15 **And a certain man** found him,
and, {behold}, he was wandering in the field:
and the man asked him,
saying,
What seekest thou?

16 **And he** said,
I seek my brethren:
tell me,
I pray thee,
where they feed their flocks.

17 **And the man** said,
They are departed hence;
for I heard them say,
Let us go to Dothan.
And Joseph went after his brethren,
and found them in Dothan.

18 **And when they** saw him afar off,
even before he came near unto them,
they conspired against him to slay him.

19 **And they** said one to another,
Behold,
this dreamer cometh.

20 **Come** now therefore,
and let us slay him,
and cast him into some pit,
and we will say,

Some evil beast hath devoured him:
and we shall see what will become of his dreams.
21 **And Reuben** heard it,
and he delivered him out of their hands;
and said,
Let us not kill him.
22 **And Reuben** said unto them,
Shed no blood,
but cast him into this pit that is in the wilderness,
and lay no hand upon him;
that he might rid him out of their hands,
to deliver him to his father again.
23 **And it** came to pass,
when Joseph was come unto his brethren,
that they stript Joseph out of his coat, his coat of many colours that was on him;
24 **And they** took him,
and cast him into a pit:
and the pit was empty,
there was no water in it.
25 **And they** sat down to eat bread:
and they lifted up their eyes and looked,
and, {behold}, a company of Ishmeelites came from Gilead with their camels bearing spicery and balm and myrrh,
going to carry it down to Egypt.
26 **And Judah** said unto his brethren,
What profit is it
if we slay our brother,
and conceal his blood?
27 **Come,**
and let us sell him to the Ishmeelites,
and let not our hand be upon him;
for he is our brother and our flesh.
And his brethren were content.
28 **Then there** passed by Midianites merchantmen;
and they drew and lifted up Joseph out of the pit,
and sold Joseph to the Ishmeelites for twenty pieces of silver:
and they brought Joseph into Egypt.
29 **And Reuben** returned unto the pit;
and, {behold}, Joseph was not in the pit;
and he rent his clothes.
30 **And he** returned unto his brethren,
and said,
The child is not;
and I, whither shall I go?
31 **And they** took Joseph's coat,
and killed a kid of the goats,
and dipped the coat in the blood;
32 **And they** sent the coat of many colours,
and they brought it to their father;
and said,
This have we found:
know now
whether it be thy son's coat or no.
33 **And he** knew it,
and said,
It is my son's coat;
an evil beast hath devoured him;
Joseph is without doubt rent in pieces.
34 **And Jacob** rent his clothes,
and put sackcloth upon his loins,
and mourned for his son many days.
35 **And all his sons and all his daughters** rose up
to comfort him;
but he refused to be comforted;
and he said,
For I will go down into the grave unto my son mourning.
Thus his father wept for him.
36 **And the Midianites** sold him into Egypt unto Potiphar, an officer of Pharaoh's, and captain of the guard.

38

And it came to pass at that time,
that Judah went down from his brethren,
and turned in to a certain Adullamite,
whose name was Hirah.
2 **And Judah** saw there a daughter of a certain Canaanite,
whose name was Shuah;
and he took her,
and went in unto her.
3 **And she** conceived,
and bare a son;
and he called his name Er.
4 **And she** conceived again,
and bare a son;
and she called his name Onan.
5 **And she** yet again conceived,
and bare a son;
and called his name Shelah:
and he was at Chezib,
when she bare him.
6 **And Judah** took a wife for Er his firstborn,
whose name was Tamar.
7 **And Er,** Judah's firstborn, was wicked in the sight of the LORD;
and the LORD slew him.
8 **And Judah** said unto Onan,
Go in unto thy brother's wife,
and marry her,
and raise up seed to thy brother.
9 **And Onan** knew
that the seed should not be his;
and it came to pass,
when he went in unto his brother's wife,
that he spilled it on the ground,
lest that he should give seed to his brother.
10 **And the thing which he did** displeased the LORD:
wherefore he slew him also.
11 **Then** said Judah to Tamar his daughter in law,
Remain a widow at thy father's house,
till Shelah my son be grown:
for he said,
Lest peradventure he die also,
as his brethren did.
And Tamar went and dwelt in her father's house.
12 **And in process of time** the daughter of Shuah Judah's wife died;
and Judah was comforted,
and went up unto his sheepshearers to Timnath, he and his friend Hirah the Adullamite.
13 **And it** was told Tamar,
saying,
Behold
thy father in law goeth up to Timnath
to shear his sheep.
14 **And she** put her widow's garments off from her,
and covered her with a vail,
and wrapped herself,
and sat in an open place,
which is by the way to Timnath;
for she saw that Shelah was grown,
and she was not given unto him to wife.
15 **When Judah** saw her,
he thought her to be an harlot;
because she had covered her face.
16 **And he** turned unto her by the way,

and said,
Go to,
I pray thee,
let me come in unto thee;
(for he knew not
that she was his daughter in law.)
And she said,
What wilt thou give me,
that thou mayest come in unto me?

17 **And he** said,
I will send thee a kid from the flock.

And she said,
Wilt thou give me a pledge,
till thou send it?

18 **And he** said,
What pledge shall I give thee?

And she said,
Thy signet, and thy bracelets, and thy staff that is in thine hand.

And he gave it her,
and came in unto her,
and she conceived by him.

19 **And she** arose,
and went away,
and laid by her vail from her,
and put on the garments of her widowhood.

20 **And Judah** sent the kid by the hand of his friend the Adullamite,
to receive his pledge from the woman's hand:
but he found her not.

21 **Then he** asked the men of that place,
saying,
Where is the harlot,
that was openly by the way side?

And they said,
There was no harlot in this place.

22 **And he** returned to Judah,
and said,
I cannot find her;
and also the men of the place said,
that there was no harlot in this place.

23 **And Judah** said,
Let her take it to her,
lest we be shamed:
behold,
I sent this kid,
and thou hast not found her.

24 **And it** came to pass about three months after,
that it was told Judah,
saying,
Tamar thy daughter in law hath played the harlot;
and also, {behold}, she is with child by whoredom.

And Judah said,
Bring her forth,
and let her be burnt.

25 **When she** was brought forth,
she sent to her father in law,
saying,
By the man, {whose these are}, am I with child:
and she said,
Discern,
I pray thee,
whose are these, the signet, and bracelets, and staff.

26 **And Judah** acknowledged them,
and said,
She hath been more righteous than I;
because that I gave her not to Shelah my son.

And he knew her again no more.

27 **And it** came to pass in the time of her travail,
that, {behold}, twins were in her womb.

28 **And it** came to pass,
when she travailed, that the one put out his hand:
and the midwife took and bound upon his hand a scarlet thread,
saying,
This came out first.

29 **And it** came to pass,
as he drew back his hand,
that, {behold}, his brother came out:
and she said,
How hast thou broken forth?
this breach be upon thee:
therefore his name was called Pharez.

30 **And afterward** came out his brother,
that had the scarlet thread upon his hand:
and his name was called Zarah.

39

And Joseph was brought down to Egypt;
and Potiphar, an officer of Pharaoh, captain of the guard, an Egyptian, bought him of the hands of the Ishmeelites,
which had brought him down thither.

2 **And the LORD** was with Joseph,
and he was a prosperous man;
and he was in the house of his master the Egyptian.

3 **And his master** saw that the LORD was with him, and that the LORD made all that he did to prosper in his hand.

4 **And Joseph** found grace in his sight,
and he served him:
and he made him overseer over his house, and all that he had he put into his hand.

5 **And it** came to pass from the time that he had made him overseer in his house, and over all that he had,
that the LORD blessed the Egyptian's house for Joseph's sake;
and the blessing of the LORD was upon all that he had in the house, and in the field.

6 **And he** left all that he had in Joseph's hand;
and he knew not ought he had, save the bread which he did eat.

And Joseph was a goodly person, and well favoured.

7 **And it** came to pass after these things,
that his master's wife cast her eyes upon Joseph;
and she said,
Lie with me.

8 **But he** refused,
and said unto his master's wife,
Behold,
my master wotteth not
what is with me in the house,
and he hath committed all that he hath to my hand;

9 **There** is none greater in this house than I;
neither hath he kept back any thing from me but thee,
because thou art his wife:
how then can I do this great wickedness,
and sin against God?

10 **And it** came to pass,
as she spake to Joseph day by day,
that he hearkened not unto her,
to lie by her,
or to be with her.

11 **And it** came to pass about this time,
that Joseph went into the house
to do his business;
and there was none of the men of the house there within.

12 **And she** caught him by his garment,
saying,
Lie with me:

and he left his garment in her hand,
and fled,
and got him out.

13 **And it** came to pass,
when she saw that he had left his garment in her hand, and was fled forth,
14 **That she** called unto the men of her house,
and spake unto them,
saying,
See,
he hath brought in an Hebrew unto us
to mock us;
he came in unto me
to lie with me,
and I cried with a loud voice:
15 **And it** came to pass,
when he heard that I lifted up my voice and cried,
that he left his garment with me,
and fled,
and got him out.

16 **And she** laid up his garment by her,
until his lord came home.

17 **And she** spake unto him according to these words,
saying,
The Hebrew servant, {which thou hast brought unto us}, came in unto me
to mock me:
18 **And it** came to pass,
as I lifted up my voice and cried,
that he left his garment with me,
and fled out.

19 **And it** came to pass,
when his master heard the words of his wife,
which she spake unto him,
saying,
After this manner did thy servant to me;
that his wrath was kindled.

20 **And Joseph's master** took him,
and put him into the prison, a place where the king's prisoners were bound:
and he was there in the prison.

21 **But the LORD** was with Joseph,
and shewed him mercy,
and gave him favour in the sight of the keeper of the prison.

22 **And the keeper of the prison** committed to Joseph's hand all the prisoners that were in the prison;
and whatsoever they did there,
he was the doer of it.

23 **The keeper of the prison** looked not to any thing that was under his hand;
because the LORD was with him,
and that which he did, the LORD made it to prosper.

40

And it came to pass after these things,
that the butler of the king of Egypt and his baker had offended their lord the king of Egypt.

2 **And Pharaoh** was wroth against two of his officers, against the chief of the butlers, and against the chief of the bakers.

3 **And he** put them in ward in the house of the captain of the guard, into the prison,
the place where Joseph was bound.

4 **And the captain of the guard** charged Joseph with them,
and he served them:
and they continued a season in ward.

5 **And they** dreamed a dream both of them, each man his dream in one night, each man according to the interpretation of his dream, the butler and the baker of the king of Egypt,
which were bound in the prison.

6 **And Joseph** came in unto them in the morning,
and looked upon them,
and, {behold}, they were sad.

7 **And he** asked Pharaoh's officers that were with him in the ward of his lord's house,
saying,
Wherefore look ye so sadly to day?

8 **And they** said unto him,
We have dreamed a dream,
and there is no interpreter of it.

And Joseph said unto them,
Do not interpretations belong to God?
tell me them,
I pray you.

9 **And the chief butler** told his dream to Joseph,
and said to him,
In my dream, {behold}, a vine was before me;
10 **And in the vine** were three branches:
and it was as though it budded,
and her blossoms shot forth;
and the clusters thereof brought forth ripe grapes:
11 **And Pharaoh's cup** was in my hand:
and I took the grapes,
and pressed them into Pharaoh's cup,
and I gave the cup into Pharaoh's hand.

12 **And Joseph** said unto him,
This is the interpretation of it:
The three branches are three days:
13 **Yet within three days** shall Pharaoh lift up thine head,
and restore thee unto thy place:
and thou shalt deliver Pharaoh's cup into his hand, after the former manner when thou wast his butler.

14 **But think** on me
when it shall be well with thee,
and shew kindness, {I pray thee}, unto me,
and make mention of me unto Pharaoh,
and bring me out of this house:
15 **For indeed I** was stolen away out of the land of the Hebrews:
and here also have I done nothing that they should put me into the dungeon.

16 **When the chief baker** saw that the interpretation was good,
he said unto Joseph,
I also was in my dream,
and, {behold}, I had three white baskets on my head:
17 **And in the uppermost basket** there was of all manner of bakemeats for Pharaoh;
and the birds did eat them out of the basket upon my head.

18 **And Joseph** answered and said,
This is the interpretation thereof:
The three baskets are three days:
19 **Yet within three days** shall Pharaoh lift up thy head from off thee,
and shall hang thee on a tree;
and the birds shall eat thy flesh from off thee.

20 **And it** came to pass the third day,
which was Pharaoh's birthday,
that he made a feast unto all his servants:
and he lifted up the head of the chief butler and of the chief baker among his servants.

21 **And he** restored the chief butler unto his butlership again;
and he gave the cup into Pharaoh's hand:
22 **But he** hanged the chief baker:
as Joseph had interpreted to them.
23 **Yet** did not the chief butler remember Joseph,
but forgat him.

41 **And it** came to pass at the end of two full years,
that Pharaoh dreamed:
and, {behold}, he stood by the river.
2 **And, {behold}, there** came up out of the river seven well favoured kine and fatfleshed;
and they fed in a meadow.
3 **And, {behold}, seven other kine** came up after them out of the river, ill favoured and leanfleshed;
and stood by the other kine upon the brink of the river.
4 **And the ill favoured and leanfleshed kine** did eat up the seven well favoured and fat kine.
So Pharaoh awoke.
5 **And he** slept and dreamed the second time:
and, {behold}, seven ears of corn came up upon one stalk, rank and good.
6 **And, {behold}, seven thin ears and blasted with the east wind** sprung up after them.
7 **And the seven thin ears** devoured the seven rank and full ears.
And Pharaoh awoke,
and, {behold}, it was a dream.
8 **And it** came to pass in the morning
that his spirit was troubled;
and he sent and called for all the magicians of Egypt, and all the wise men thereof:
and Pharaoh told them his dream;
but there was none that could interpret them unto Pharaoh.
9 **Then** spake the chief butler unto Pharaoh,
saying,
I do remember my faults this day:
10 **Pharaoh** was wroth with his servants,
and put me in ward in the captain of the guard's house, both me and the chief baker:
11 **And we** dreamed a dream in one night, I and he;
we dreamed each man according to the interpretation of his dream.
12 **And there** was there with us a young man, an Hebrew, servant to the captain of the guard;
and we told him,
and he interpreted to us our dreams;
to each man according to his dream he did interpret.
13 **And it** came to pass,
as he interpreted to us,
so it was;
me he restored unto mine office,
and him he hanged.
14 **Then Pharaoh** sent and called Joseph,
and they brought him hastily out of the dungeon:
and he shaved himself,
and changed his raiment,
and came in unto Pharaoh.
15 **And Pharaoh** said unto Joseph,
I have dreamed a dream,
and there is none that can interpret it:
and I have heard say of thee,
that thou canst understand a dream to interpret it.
16 **And Joseph** answered Pharaoh,
saying,
It is not in me:
God shall give Pharaoh an answer of peace.
17 **And Pharaoh** said unto Joseph,
In my dream, {behold}, I stood upon the bank of the river:
18 **And, {behold}, there** came up out of the river seven kine, fatfleshed and well favoured;
and they fed in a meadow:
19 **And, {behold}, seven other kine** came up after them, poor and very ill favoured and leanfleshed,
such as I never saw in all the land of Egypt for badness:
20 **And the lean and the ill favoured kine** did eat up the first seven fat kine:
21 **And when they** had eaten them up,
it could not be known that they had eaten them;
but they were still ill favoured, as at the beginning.
So I awoke.
22 **And I** saw in my dream,
and, {behold}, seven ears came up in one stalk, full and good:
23 **And, {behold}, seven ears, withered, thin, and blasted with the east wind,** sprung up after them:
24 **And the thin ears** devoured the seven good ears:
and I told this unto the magicians;
but there was none that could declare it to me.
25 **And Joseph** said unto Pharaoh,
The dream of Pharaoh is one:
God hath shewed Pharaoh what he is about to do.
26 **The seven good kine** are seven years;
and the seven good ears are seven years:
the dream is one.
27 **And the seven thin and ill favoured kine that came up after them** are seven years;
and the seven empty ears blasted with the east wind shall be seven years of famine.
28 **This** is the thing which I have spoken unto Pharaoh:
What God is about to do
he sheweth unto Pharaoh.
29 **Behold,**
there come seven years of great plenty throughout all the land of Egypt:
30 **And there** shall arise after them seven years of famine;
and all the plenty shall be forgotten in the land of Egypt;
and the famine shall consume the land;
31 **And the plenty** shall not be known in the land by reason of that famine following;
for it shall be very grievous.
32 **And for that the dream** was doubled unto Pharaoh twice;
it is
because the thing is established by God,
and God will shortly bring it to pass.
33 **Now therefore let Pharaoh** look out a man discreet and wise,
and set him over the land of Egypt.
34 **Let Pharaoh** do this,
and let him appoint officers over the land,
and take up the fifth part of the land of Egypt in the seven plenteous years.

35 **And let them** gather all the food of those good years that come,
and lay up corn under the hand of Pharaoh,
and let them keep food in the cities.
36 **And that food** shall be for store to the land against the seven years of famine,
which shall be in the land of Egypt;
that the land perish not through the famine.
37 **And the thing** was good in the eyes of Pharaoh, and in the eyes of all his servants.
38 **And Pharaoh** said unto his servants,
Can we find such a one as this is,
a man in whom the Spirit of God is?
39 **And Pharaoh** said unto Joseph,
Forasmuch as God hath shewed thee all this,
there is none so discreet and wise as thou art:
40 **Thou** shalt be over my house,
and according unto thy word shall all my people be ruled:
only in the throne will I be greater than thou.
41 **And Pharaoh** said unto Joseph,
See,
I have set thee over all the land of Egypt.
42 **And Pharaoh** took off his ring from his hand,
and put it upon Joseph's hand,
and arrayed him in vestures of fine linen,
and put a gold chain about his neck;
43 **And he** made him to ride in the second chariot which he had;
and they cried before him,
Bow the knee:
and he made him ruler over all the land of Egypt.
44 **And Pharaoh** said unto Joseph,
I am Pharaoh,
and without thee shall no man lift up his hand or foot in all the land of Egypt.
45 **And Pharaoh** called Joseph's name Zaphnathpaaneah;
and he gave him to wife Asenath the daughter of Potipherah priest of On.
And Joseph went out over all the land of Egypt.
46 **And Joseph** was thirty years old
when he stood before Pharaoh king of Egypt.
And Joseph went out from the presence of Pharaoh,
and went throughout all the land of Egypt.
47 **And in the seven plenteous years** the earth brought forth by handfuls.
48 **And he** gathered up all the food of the seven years,
which were in the land of Egypt,
and laid up the food in the cities:
the food of the field, {which was round about every city}, laid he up in the same.
49 **And Joseph** gathered corn as the sand of the sea, very much,
until he left numbering;
for it was without number.
50 **And unto Joseph** were born two sons
before the years of famine came,
which Asenath the daughter of Potipherah priest of On bare unto him.
51 **And Joseph** called the name of the firstborn Manasseh:
For God, {said he}, hath made me forget all my toil, and all my father's house.
52 **And the name of the second** called he Ephraim:
For God hath caused me to be fruitful in the land of my affliction.
53 **And the seven years of plenteousness**, {that was in the land of Egypt}, were ended.
54 **And the seven years of dearth** began to come,
according as Joseph had said:
and the dearth was in all lands;
but in all the land of Egypt there was bread.
55 **And when all the land of Egypt** was famished,
the people cried to Pharaoh for bread:
and Pharaoh said unto all the Egyptians,
Go unto Joseph;
what he saith to you,
do.
56 **And the famine** was over all the face of the earth:
and Joseph opened all the storehouses,
and sold unto the Egyptians;
and the famine waxed sore in the land of Egypt.
57 **And all countries** came into Egypt to Joseph
for to buy corn;
because that the famine was so sore in all lands.

42 **Now when Jacob** saw that there was corn in Egypt,
Jacob said unto his sons,
Why do ye look one upon another?
2 **And he** said,
Behold,
I have heard that there is corn in Egypt:
get you down thither,
and buy for us from thence;
that we may live,
and not die.
3 **And Joseph's ten brethren** went down to buy corn in Egypt.
4 **But Benjamin, Joseph's brother,** Jacob sent not with his brethren;
for he said,
Lest peradventure mischief befall him.
5 **And the sons of Israel** came to buy corn among those that came:
for the famine was in the land of Canaan.
6 **And Joseph** was the governor over the land,
and he it was that sold to all the people of the land:
and Joseph's brethren came,
and bowed down themselves before him with their faces to the earth.
7 **And Joseph** saw his brethren,
and he knew them,
but made himself strange unto them,
and spake roughly unto them;
and he said unto them,
Whence come ye?
And they said,
From the land of Canaan
to buy food.
8 **And Joseph** knew his brethren,
but they knew not him.
9 **And Joseph** remembered the dreams which he dreamed of them,
and said unto them,
Ye are spies;
to see the nakedness of the land ye are come.
10 **And they** said unto him,

Nay, my lord, but to buy food are thy servants come.
11 **We** are all one man's sons;
we are true men,
thy servants are no spies.
12 **And he** said unto them,
Nay, but to see the nakedness of the land
ye are come.
13 **And they** said,
Thy servants are twelve brethren, the sons of one man in the land of Canaan;
and, {behold}, the youngest is this day with our father,
and one is not.
14 **And Joseph** said unto them,
That is it that I spake unto you,
saying,
Ye are spies:
15 **Hereby** ye shall be proved:
By the life of Pharaoh ye shall not go forth hence,
except your youngest brother come hither.
16 **Send** one of you,
and let him fetch your brother,
and ye shall be kept in prison,
that your words may be proved,
whether there be any truth in you:
or else by the life of Pharaoh surely ye are spies.
17 **And he** put them all together into ward three days.
18 **And Joseph** said unto them the third day,
This do,
and live;
for I fear God:
19 **If ye** be true men,
let one of your brethren be bound in the house of your prison:
go ye,
carry corn for the famine of your houses:
20 **But bring** your youngest brother unto me;
so shall your words be verified,
and ye shall not die.
And they did so.
21 **And they** said one to another,
We are verily guilty concerning our brother,
in that we saw the anguish of his soul,
when he besought us,
and we would not hear;
therefore is this distress come upon us.
22 **And Reuben** answered them,
saying,
Spake I not unto you,
saying,
Do not sin against the child;
and ye would not hear?
therefore, {behold}, also his blood is required.
23 **And they** knew not
that Joseph understood them;
for he spake unto them by an interpreter.
24 **And he** turned himself about from them,
and wept;
and returned to them again,
and communed with them,
and took from them Simeon,
and bound him before their eyes.
25 **Then Joseph** commanded
to fill their sacks with corn,
and to restore every man's money into his sack,
and to give them provision for the way:
and thus did he unto them.
26 **And they** laded their asses with the corn,
and departed thence.
27 **And as one of them** opened his sack
to give his ass provender in the inn,
he espied his money;
for, {behold}, it was in his sack's mouth.
28 **And he** said unto his brethren,
My money is restored;
and, {lo}, it is even in my sack:
and their heart failed them,
and they were afraid,
saying one to another,
What is this that God hath done unto us?
29 **And they** came unto Jacob their father unto the land of Canaan,
and told him all that befell unto them;
saying,
30 **The man**, {who is the lord of the land}, spake roughly to us,
and took us for spies of the country.
31 **And we** said unto him,
We are true men;
we are no spies:
32 **We** be twelve brethren, sons of our father;
one is not,
and the youngest is this day with our father in the land of Canaan.
33 **And the man, the lord of the country,** said unto us,
Hereby shall I know
that ye are true men;
leave one of your brethren here with me,
and take food for the famine of your households,
and be gone:
34 **And bring** your youngest brother unto me:
then shall I know
that ye are no spies,
but that ye are true men:
so will I deliver you your brother,
and ye shall traffick in the land.
35 **And it** came to pass
as they emptied their sacks,
that, {behold}, every man's bundle of money was in his sack:
and when both they and their father saw the bundles of money,
they were afraid.
36 **And Jacob their father** said unto them,
Me have ye bereaved of my children:
Joseph is not,
and Simeon is not,
and ye will take Benjamin away:
all these things are against me.
37 **And Reuben** spake unto his father,
saying,
Slay my two sons,
if I bring him not to thee:
deliver him into my hand,
and I will bring him to thee again.
38 **And he** said,
My son shall not go down with you;
for his brother is dead,
and he is left alone:
if mischief befall him by the way in the which ye go,
then shall ye bring down my gray hairs with sorrow to the grave.

43

And the famine was sore in the land.
2 **And it** came to pass,
when they had eaten up the corn which they had brought out of Egypt,
their father said unto them,
Go again,
buy us a little food.
3 **And Judah** spake unto him,
saying,
The man did solemnly protest unto us,
saying,

Ye shall not see my face,
except your brother be with you.
[4] **If thou** wilt send our brother with us,
we will go down and buy thee food:
[5] **But if thou** wilt not send him,
we will not go down:
for the man said unto us,
Ye shall not see my face,
except your brother be with you.
[6] **And Israel** said,
Wherefore dealt ye so ill with me,
as to tell the man
whether ye had yet a brother?
[7] **And they** said,
The man asked us straitly of our state, and of our kindred,
saying,
Is your father yet alive?
have ye another brother?
and we told him according to the tenor of these words:
could we certainly know
that he would say,
Bring your brother down?
[8] **And Judah** said unto Israel his father,
Send the lad with me,
and we will arise and go;
that we may live,
and not die, both we, and thou, and also our little ones.
[9] **I** will be surety for him;
of my hand shalt thou require him:
if I bring him not unto thee,
and set him before thee,
then let me bear the blame for ever:
[10] **For except we** had lingered,
surely now we had returned this second time.
[11] **And their father Israel** said unto them,
If it must be so now,
do this;
take of the best fruits in the land in your vessels,
and carry down the man a present, a little balm, and a little honey, spices, and myrrh, nuts, and almonds:
[12] **And take** double money in your hand;
and the money that was brought again in the mouth of your sacks, carry it again in your hand;
peradventure it was an oversight:
[13] **Take** also your brother,
and arise,
go again unto the man:
[14] **And God Almighty** give you mercy before the man,
that he may send away your other brother, and Benjamin.
If I be bereaved of my children,
I am bereaved.
[15] **And the men** took that present,
and they took double money in their hand and Benjamin;
and rose up,
and went down to Egypt,
and stood before Joseph.
[16] **And when Joseph** saw Benjamin with them,
he said to the ruler of his house,
Bring these men home,
and slay,
and make ready;
for these men shall dine with me at noon.
[17] **And the man** did as Joseph bade;
and the man brought the men into Joseph's house.
[18] **And the men** were afraid,
because they were brought into Joseph's house;
and they said,
Because of the money that was returned in our sacks at the first time are we brought in;
that he may seek occasion against us,
and fall upon us,
and take us for bondmen, and our asses.
[19] **And they** came near to the steward of Joseph's house,
and they communed with him at the door of the house,
[20] **And** said,
O sir, we came indeed down at the first time
to buy food:
[21] **And it** came to pass,
when we came to the inn,
that we opened our sacks,
and, {behold}, every man's money was in the mouth of his sack, our money in full weight:
and we have brought it again in our hand.
[22] **And other money** have we brought down in our hands
to buy food:
we cannot tell
who put our money in our sacks.
[23] **And he** said,
Peace be to you,
fear not:
your God, and the God of your father, hath given you treasure in your sacks:
I had your money.
And he brought Simeon out unto them.
[24] **And the man** brought the men into Joseph's house,
and gave them water,
and they washed their feet;
and he gave their asses provender.
[25] **And they** made ready the present against Joseph came at noon:
for they heard that they should eat bread there.
[26] **And when Joseph** came home,
they brought him the present which was in their hand into the house,
and bowed themselves to him to the earth.
[27] **And he** asked them of their welfare,
and said,
Is your father well, the old man of whom ye spake?
Is he yet alive?
[28] **And they** answered,
Thy servant our father is in good health,
he is yet alive.
And they bowed down their heads,
and made obeisance.
[29] **And he** lifted up his eyes,
and saw his brother Benjamin, his mother's son,
and said,
Is this your younger brother,
of whom ye spake unto me?
And he said,
God be gracious unto thee, my son.
[30] **And Joseph** made haste;
for his bowels did yearn upon his brother:
and he sought where to weep;
and he entered into his chamber,
and wept there.
[31] **And he** washed his face,
and went out,
and refrained himself,
and said,
Set on bread.
[32] **And they** set on for him by himself, and for them by themselves, and for the Egyptians,
which did eat with him, by themselves:

because the Egyptians might not eat bread with the Hebrews;
for that is an abomination unto the Egyptians.

33 **And they** sat before him, the firstborn according to his birthright, and the youngest according to his youth:
and the men marvelled one at another.

34 **And he** took and sent messes unto them from before him:
but Benjamin's mess was five times so much as any of their's.

And they drank,
and were merry with him.

44

And he commanded the steward of his house, saying,
Fill the men's sacks with food,
as much as they can carry,
and put every man's money in his sack's mouth.

2 **And put** my cup, the silver cup, in the sack's mouth of the youngest, and his corn money.

And he did according to the word that Joseph had spoken.

3 **As soon as the morning** was light,
the men were sent away, they and their asses.

4 **And when they** were gone out of the city, and not yet far off,
Joseph said unto his steward,
Up,
follow after the men;
and when thou dost overtake them,
say unto them,
Wherefore have ye rewarded evil for good?

5 **Is not this** it in which my lord drinketh,
and whereby indeed he divineth?
ye have done evil in so doing.

6 **And he** overtook them,
and he spake unto them these same words.

7 **And they** said unto him,
Wherefore saith my lord these words?

God forbid that thy servants should do according to this thing:

8 **Behold,**
the money, {which we found in our sacks' mouths}, we brought again unto thee out of the land of Canaan:
how then should we steal out of thy lord's house silver or gold?

9 **With whomsoever of thy servants** it be found,
both let him die,
and we also will be my lord's bondmen.

10 **And he** said,
Now also let it be according unto your words:
he with whom it is found shall be my servant;
and ye shall be blameless.

11 **Then they** speedily took down every man his sack to the ground,
and opened every man his sack.

12 **And he** searched,
and began at the eldest,
and left at the youngest:
and the cup was found in Benjamin's sack.

13 **Then they** rent their clothes,
and laded every man his ass,
and returned to the city.

14 **And Judah and his brethren** came to Joseph's house;
for he was yet there:
and they fell before him on the ground.

15 **And Joseph** said unto them,
What deed is this that ye have done?
wot ye not
that such a man as I can certainly divine?

16 **And Judah** said,
What shall we say unto my lord?
what shall we speak?
or how shall we clear ourselves?

God hath found out the iniquity of thy servants:
behold,
we are my lord's servants, both we, and he also with whom the cup is found.

17 **And he** said,
God forbid that I should do so:
but the man in whose hand the cup is found, he shall be my servant;
and as for you, get you up in peace unto your father.

18 **Then Judah** came near unto him,
and said,
Oh my lord, let thy servant, {I pray thee}, speak a word in my lord's ears,
and let not thine anger burn against thy servant:
for thou art even as Pharaoh.

19 **My lord** asked his servants, saying,
Have ye a father, or a brother?

20 **And we** said unto my lord,
We have a father, an old man, and a child of his old age, a little one;
and his brother is dead,
and he alone is left of his mother,
and his father loveth him.

21 **And thou** saidst unto thy servants,
Bring him down unto me,
that I may set mine eyes upon him.
22 **And we** said unto my lord,
The lad cannot leave his father:
for if he should leave his father,
his father would die.

23 **And thou** saidst unto thy servants,
Except your youngest brother come down with you,
ye shall see my face no more.

24 **And it** came to pass
when we came up unto thy servant my father,
we told him the words of my lord.

25 **And our father** said,
Go again,
and buy us a little food.

26 **And we** said,
We cannot go down:
if our youngest brother be with us,
then will we go down:
for we may not see the man's face,
except our youngest brother be with us.

27 **And thy servant my father** said unto us,
Ye know
that my wife bare me two sons:
28 **And the one** went out from me,
and I said,
Surely he is torn in pieces;
and I saw him not since:
29 **And if ye** take this also from me,
and mischief befall him,
ye shall bring down my gray hairs with sorrow to the grave.

30 **Now therefore when I** come to thy servant my father,
and the lad be not with us;
seeing that his life is bound up in the lad's life;
31 **It** shall come to pass,
when he seeth that the lad is not with us,
that he will die:

and thy servants shall bring down
the gray hairs of thy servant our
father with sorrow to the grave.
32 **For thy servant** became surety
for the lad unto my father,
saying,
If I bring him not unto thee,
then I shall bear the blame to my
father for ever.
33 **Now therefore, {I pray thee}, let
thy servant** abide instead of the
lad a bondman to my lord;
and let the lad go up with his
brethren.
34 **For how** shall I go up to my
father,
and the lad be not with me?
lest peradventure I see the evil that
shall come on my father.

45 **Then Joseph** could not
refrain himself before all
them that stood by him;
and he cried,
Cause every man to go out from me.
And there stood no man with him,
while Joseph made himself known
unto his brethren.
2 **And he** wept aloud:
**and the Egyptians and the house
of Pharaoh** heard.
3 **And Joseph** said unto his brethren,
I am Joseph;
doth my father yet live?
And his brethren could not answer
him;
for they were troubled at his
presence.
4 **And Joseph** said unto his brethren,
Come near to me,
I pray you.
And they came near.
And he said,
I am Joseph your brother,
whom ye sold into Egypt.
5 **Now therefore be not** grieved, nor
angry with yourselves,
that ye sold me hither:
for God did send me before you
to preserve life.
6 **For these two years** hath the
famine been in the land:
and yet there are five years,
in the which there shall neither be
earing nor harvest.
7 **And God** sent me before you
to preserve you a posterity in the
earth,
and to save your lives by a great
deliverance.
8 **So now it** was not you that sent
me hither, but God:
and he hath made me a father to
Pharaoh, and lord of all his house,
and a ruler throughout all the
land of Egypt.
9 **Haste ye,**
and go up to my father,
and say unto him,
Thus saith thy son Joseph,
God hath made me lord of all Egypt:
come down unto me,
tarry not:
10 **And thou** shalt dwell in the land
of Goshen,
and thou shalt be near unto me,
thou, and thy children, and thy
children's children, and thy
flocks, and thy herds, and all that
thou hast:
11 **And there** will I nourish thee;
for yet there are five years of
famine;
**lest thou, and thy household, and
all that thou hast,** come to
poverty.
12 **And, {behold}, your eyes** see, and
the eyes of my brother Benjamin,
that it is my mouth that speaketh
unto you.
13 **And ye** shall tell my father of all
my glory in Egypt, and of all that
ye have seen;
and ye shall haste and bring down
my father hither.
14 **And he** fell upon his brother
Benjamin's neck,
and wept;
and Benjamin wept upon his neck.
15 **Moreover he** kissed all his
brethren,
and wept upon them:
and after that his brethren talked
with him.
16 **And the fame thereof** was heard
in Pharaoh's house,
saying,
Joseph's brethren are come:
and it pleased Pharaoh well, and
his servants.
17 **And Pharaoh** said unto Joseph,
Say unto thy brethren,
This do ye;
lade your beasts,
and go,
get you unto the land of Canaan;
18 **And take** your father and your
households,
and come unto me:
and I will give you the good of the
land of Egypt,
and ye shall eat the fat of the land.
19 **Now thou** art commanded,
this do ye;
take you wagons out of the land of
Egypt for your little ones, and for
your wives,
and bring your father,
and come.
20 **Also regard not** your stuff;
**for the good of all the land of
Egypt** is your's.
21 **And the children of Israel** did so:
and Joseph gave them wagons,
according to the commandment
of Pharaoh,
and gave them provision for the
way.
22 **To all of them** he gave each man
changes of raiment;
but to Benjamin he gave three
hundred pieces of silver, and five
changes of raiment.
23 **And to his father** he sent after
this manner; ten asses laden with
the good things of Egypt, and ten
she asses laden with corn and
bread and meat for his father by
the way.
24 **So he** sent his brethren away,
and they departed:
and he said unto them,
See that ye fall not out by the way.
25 **And they** went up out of Egypt,
and came into the land of Canaan
unto Jacob their father,
26 **And** told him,
saying,
Joseph is yet alive,
and he is governor over all the land
of Egypt.
And Jacob's heart fainted,
for he believed them not.
27 **And they** told him all the words
of Joseph,
which he had said unto them:
and when he saw the wagons
which Joseph had sent to carry
him,
the spirit of Jacob their father
revived:
28 **And Israel** said,
It is enough;
Joseph my son is yet alive:
I will go and see him
before I die.

46

And Israel took his journey with all that he had,
and came to Beersheba,
and offered sacrifices unto the God of his father Isaac.
2 **And God** spake unto Israel in the visions of the night,
and said,
Jacob, Jacob.
And he said,
Here am I.
3 **And he** said,
I am God, the God of thy father:
fear not to go down into Egypt;
for I will there make of thee a great nation:
4 **I** will go down with thee into Egypt;
and I will also surely bring thee up again:
and Joseph shall put his hand upon thine eyes.
5 **And Jacob** rose up from Beersheba:
and the sons of Israel carried Jacob their father, and their little ones, and their wives, in the wagons which Pharaoh had sent to carry him.
6 **And they** took their cattle, and their goods,
which they had gotten in the land of Canaan,
and came into Egypt, Jacob, and all his seed with him:
7 **His sons, and his sons' sons with him, his daughters, and his sons' daughters, and all his seed** brought he with him into Egypt.
8 **And these** are the names of the children of Israel,
which came into Egypt, Jacob and his sons: Reuben, Jacob's firstborn.
9 **And the sons of Reuben;** Hanoch, and Phallu, and Hezron, and Carmi.
10 **And the sons of Simeon;** Jemuel, and Jamin, and Ohad, and Jachin, and Zohar, and Shaul the son of a Canaanitish woman.
11 **And the sons of Levi;** Gershon, Kohath, and Merari.
12 **And the sons of Judah;** Er, and Onan, and Shelah, and Pharez, and Zarah:
but Er and Onan died in the land of Canaan.
And the sons of Pharez were Hezron and Hamul.
13 **And the sons of Issachar;** Tola, and Phuvah, and Job, and Shimron.
14 **And the sons of Zebulun;** Sered, and Elon, and Jahleel.
15 **These** be the sons of Leah,
which she bare unto Jacob in Padanaram, with his daughter Dinah:
all the souls of his sons and his daughters were thirty and three.
16 **And the sons of Gad;** Ziphion, and Haggi, Shuni, and Ezbon, Eri, and Arodi, and Areli.
17 **And the sons of Asher;** Jimnah, and Ishuah, and Isui, and Beriah, and Serah their sister:
and the sons of Beriah; Heber, and Malchiel.
18 **These** are the sons of Zilpah,
whom Laban gave to Leah his daughter,
and these she bare unto Jacob, even sixteen souls.
19 **The sons of Rachel Jacob's wife;** Joseph, and Benjamin.
20 **And unto Joseph in the land of Egypt** were born Manasseh and Ephraim,
which Asenath the daughter of Potipherah priest of On bare unto him.
21 **And the sons of Benjamin** were Belah, and Becher, and Ashbel, Gera, and Naaman, Ehi, and Rosh, Muppim, and Huppim, and Ard.
22 **These** are the sons of Rachel,
which were born to Jacob:
all the souls were fourteen.
23 **And the sons of Dan;** Hushim.
24 **And the sons of Naphtali;** Jahzeel, and Guni, and Jezer, and Shillem.
25 **These** are the sons of Bilhah,
which Laban gave unto Rachel his daughter,
and she bare these unto Jacob:
all the souls were seven.
26 **All the souls that came with Jacob into Egypt**, {which came out of his loins, besides Jacob's sons' wives}, all the souls were threescore and six;
27 **And the sons of Joseph**, {which were born him in Egypt}, were two souls:
all the souls of the house of Jacob, {which came into Egypt}, were threescore and ten.
28 **And he** sent Judah before him unto Joseph,
to direct his face unto Goshen;
and they came into the land of Goshen.
29 **And Joseph** made ready his chariot,
and went up to meet Israel his father, to Goshen,
and presented himself unto him;
and he fell on his neck,
and wept on his neck a good while.
30 **And Israel** said unto Joseph,
Now let me die,
since I have seen thy face,
because thou art yet alive.
31 **And Joseph** said unto his brethren, and unto his father's house,
I will go up,
and shew Pharaoh,
and say unto him,
My brethren, and my father's house, {which were in the land of Canaan}, are come unto me;
32 **And the men** are shepherds,
for their trade hath been to feed cattle;
and they have brought their flocks, and their herds, and all that they have.
33 **And it** shall come to pass,
when Pharaoh shall call you,
and shall say,
What is your occupation?
34 **That ye** shall say,
Thy servants' trade hath been about cattle from our youth even until now, both we, and also our fathers:
that ye may dwell in the land of Goshen;
for every shepherd is an abomination unto the Egyptians.

47

Then Joseph came and told Pharaoh,
and said,
My father and my brethren, and their flocks, and their herds, and all that they have, are come out of the land of Canaan;
and, {behold}, they are in the land of Goshen.
2 **And he** took some of his brethren, even five men,
and presented them unto Pharaoh.

3 **And Pharaoh** said unto his brethren,
What is your occupation?
And they said unto Pharaoh,
Thy servants are shepherds, both we, and also our fathers.
4 **They** said morever unto Pharaoh,
For to sojourn in the land are we come;
for thy servants have no pasture for their flocks;
for the famine is sore in the land of Canaan:
now therefore, {we pray thee}, let thy servants dwell in the land of Goshen.
5 **And Pharaoh** spake unto Joseph, saying,
Thy father and thy brethren are come unto thee:
6 **The land of Egypt** is before thee;
in the best of the land make thy father and brethren to dwell;
in the land of Goshen let them dwell:
and if thou knowest any men of activity among them,
then make them rulers over my cattle.
7 **And Joseph** brought in Jacob his father,
and set him before Pharaoh:
and Jacob blessed Pharaoh.
8 **And Pharaoh** said unto Jacob,
How old art thou?
9 **And Jacob** said unto Pharaoh,
The days of the years of my pilgrimage are an hundred and thirty years:
few and evil have the days of the years of my life been,
and have not attained unto the days of the years of the life of my fathers in the days of their pilgrimage.
10 **And Jacob** blessed Pharaoh,
and went out from before Pharaoh.
11 **And Joseph** placed his father and his brethren,
and gave them a possession in the land of Egypt, in the best of the land, in the land of Rameses,
as Pharaoh had commanded.
12 **And Joseph** nourished his father, and his brethren, and all his father's household, with bread, according to their families.
13 **And there** was no bread in all the land;
for the famine was very sore,
so that the land of Egypt and all the land of Canaan fainted by reason of the famine.
14 **And Joseph** gathered up all the money that was found in the land of Egypt, and in the land of Canaan, for the corn which they bought:
and Joseph brought the money into Pharaoh's house.
15 **And when money** failed in the land of Egypt, and in the land of Canaan,
all the Egyptians came unto Joseph,
and said,
Give us bread:
for why should we die in thy presence?
for the money faileth.
16 **And Joseph** said,
Give your cattle;
and I will give you for your cattle,
if money fail.
17 **And they** brought their cattle unto Joseph:
and Joseph gave them bread in exchange for horses, and for the flocks, and for the cattle of the herds, and for the asses:
and he fed them with bread for all their cattle for that year.
18 **When that year** was ended,
they came unto him the second year,
and said unto him,
We will not hide it from my lord,
how that our money is spent;
my lord also hath our herds of cattle;
there is not ought left in the sight of my lord, but our bodies, and our lands:
19 **Wherefore** shall we die before thine eyes, both we and our land?
buy us and our land for bread,
and we and our land will be servants unto Pharaoh:
and give us seed,
that we may live,
and not die,
that the land be not desolate.
20 **And Joseph** bought all the land of Egypt for Pharaoh;
for the Egyptians sold every man his field,
because the famine prevailed over them:
so the land became Pharaoh's.
21 **And as for the people,** he removed them to cities from one end of the borders of Egypt even to the other end thereof.
22 **Only the land of the priests** bought he not;
for the priests had a portion assigned them of Pharaoh,
and did eat their portion which Pharaoh gave them:
wherefore they sold not their lands.
23 **Then Joseph** said unto the people,
Behold,
I have bought you this day and your land for Pharaoh:
lo,
here is seed for you,
and ye shall sow the land.
24 **And it** shall come to pass in the increase,
that ye shall give the fifth part unto Pharaoh,
and four parts shall be your own, for seed of the field, and for your food, and for them of your households, and for food for your little ones.
25 **And they** said,
Thou hast saved our lives:
let us find grace in the sight of my lord,
and we will be Pharaoh's servants.
26 **And Joseph** made it a law over the land of Egypt unto this day,
that Pharaoh should have the fifth part, except the land of the priests only,
which became not Pharaoh's.
27 **And Israel** dwelt in the land of Egypt, in the country of Goshen;
and they had possessions therein,
and grew,
and multiplied exceedingly.
28 **And Jacob** lived in the land of Egypt seventeen years:
so the whole age of Jacob was an hundred forty and seven years.
29 **And the time** drew nigh that Israel must die:
and he called his son Joseph,
and said unto him,
If now I have found grace in thy sight,
put, {I pray thee}, thy hand under my thigh,
and deal kindly and truly with me;
bury me not, {I pray thee}, in Egypt:

30 **But I** will lie with my fathers,
and thou shalt carry me out of Egypt,
and bury me in their buryingplace.
And he said,
I will do as thou hast said.
31 **And he** said,
Swear unto me.
And he sware unto him.
And Israel bowed himself upon the bed's head.

48

And it came to pass after these things,
that one told Joseph,
Behold,
thy father is sick:
and he took with him his two sons, Manasseh and Ephraim.
2 **And one** told Jacob,
and said,
Behold,
thy son Joseph cometh unto thee:
and Israel strengthened himself,
and sat upon the bed.
3 **And Jacob** said unto Joseph,
God Almighty appeared unto me at Luz in the land of Canaan,
and blessed me,
4 **And** said unto me,
Behold,
I will make thee fruitful,
and multiply thee,
and I will make of thee a multitude of people;
and will give this land to thy seed after thee for an everlasting possession.
5 **And now thy two sons, Ephraim and Manasseh,** {which were born unto thee in the land of Egypt} {before I came unto thee into Egypt}, are mine;
as Reuben and Simeon, they shall be mine.
6 **And thy issue,** {which thou begettest after them}, shall be thine,
and shall be called after the name of their brethren in their inheritance.
7 **And as for me,** {when I came from Padan}, Rachel died by me in the land of Canaan in the way,
when yet there was but a little way to come unto Ephrath:
and I buried her there in the way of Ephrath;
the same is Bethlehem.
8 **And Israel** beheld Joseph's sons,
and said,
Who are these?
9 **And Joseph** said unto his father,
They are my sons,
whom God hath given me in this place.
And he said,
Bring them, {I pray thee}, unto me,
and I will bless them.
10 **Now the eyes of Israel** were dim for age,
so that he could not see.
And he brought them near unto him;
and he kissed them,
and embraced them.
11 **And Israel** said unto Joseph,
I had not thought to see thy face:
and, {lo}, God hath shewed me also thy seed.
12 **And Joseph** brought them out from between his knees,
and he bowed himself with his face to the earth.
13 **And Joseph** took them both, Ephraim in his right hand toward Israel's left hand, and Manasseh in his left hand toward Israel's right hand,
and brought them near unto him.
14 **And Israel** stretched out his right hand,
and laid it upon Ephraim's head,
who was the younger, and his left hand upon Manasseh's head,
guiding his hands wittingly;
for Manasseh was the firstborn.
15 **And he** blessed Joseph,
and said,
God, {before whom my fathers Abraham and Isaac did walk}, the God which fed me all my life long unto this day,
16 The Angel which redeemed me from all evil, bless the lads;
and let my name be named on them, and the name of my fathers Abraham and Isaac;
and let them grow into a multitude in the midst of the earth.
17 **And when Joseph** saw that his father laid his right hand upon the head of Ephraim,
it displeased him:
and he held up his father's hand,
to remove it from Ephraim's head unto Manasseh's head.
18 **And Joseph** said unto his father,
Not so, my father:
for this is the firstborn;
put thy right hand upon his head.
19 **And his father** refused,
and said,
I know it, my son,
I know it:
he also shall become a people,
and he also shall be great:
but truly his younger brother shall be greater than he,
and his seed shall become a multitude of nations.
20 **And he** blessed them that day,
saying,
In thee shall Israel bless,
saying,
God make thee as Ephraim and as Manasseh:
and he set Ephraim before Manasseh.
21 **And Israel** said unto Joseph,
Behold,
I die:
but God shall be with you,
and bring you again unto the land of your fathers.
22 **Moreover I** have given to thee one portion above thy brethren,
which I took out of the hand of the Amorite with my sword and with my bow.

49

And Jacob called unto his sons,
and said,
Gather yourselves together,
that I may tell you that which shall befall you in the last days.
2 **Gather** yourselves together,
and hear, ye sons of Jacob;
and hearken unto Israel your father.
3 **Reuben, thou** art my firstborn, my might, and the beginning of my strength, the excellency of dignity, and the excellency of power:
4 **Unstable as water,** thou shalt not excel;
because thou wentest up to thy father's bed;
then defiledst thou it:
he went up to my couch.
5 **Simeon and Levi** are brethren;
instruments of cruelty are in their habitations.
6 **O my soul, come not thou** into their secret;
unto their assembly, mine honour, be not thou united:

for in their anger they slew a man,
and in their selfwill they digged down a wall.

7 **Cursed** be their anger, {for it was fierce}; and their wrath, {for it was cruel}:
I will divide them in Jacob,
and scatter them in Israel.

8 **Judah, thou** art he whom thy brethren shall praise:
thy hand shall be in the neck of thine enemies;
thy father's children shall bow down before thee.

9 **Judah** is a lion's whelp:
from the prey, my son, thou art gone up:
he stooped down,
he couched as a lion, and as an old lion;
who shall rouse him up?

10 **The sceptre** shall not depart from Judah, nor a lawgiver from between his feet,
until Shiloh come;
and unto him shall the gathering of the people be.

11 **Binding his foal unto the vine, and his ass's colt unto the choice vine;** he washed his garments in wine, and his clothes in the blood of grapes:

12 **His eyes** shall be red with wine, and his teeth white with milk.

13 **Zebulun** shall dwell at the haven of the sea;
and he shall be for an haven of ships;
and his border shall be unto Zidon.

14 **Issachar** is a strong ass couching down between two burdens:

15 **And he** saw that rest was good, and the land that it was pleasant;
and bowed his shoulder
to bear,
and became a servant unto tribute.

16 **Dan** shall judge his people, as one of the tribes of Israel.

17 **Dan** shall be a serpent by the way, an adder in the path,
that biteth the horse heels,
so that his rider shall fall backward.

18 I have waited for thy salvation, O LORD.

19 **Gad,** a troop shall overcome him:
but he shall overcome at the last.

20 **Out of Asher** his bread shall be fat,
and he shall yield royal dainties.

21 **Naphtali** is a hind let loose:
he giveth goodly words.

22 **Joseph** is a fruitful bough, even a fruitful bough by a well;
whose branches run over the wall:

23 **The archers** have sorely grieved him,
and shot at him,
and hated him:

24 **But his bow** abode in strength,
and the arms of his hands were made strong by the hands of the mighty God of Jacob; (from thence is the shepherd, the stone of Israel:)

25 Even by the God of thy father, {who shall help thee}; and by the Almighty, {who shall bless thee with blessings of heaven above}, blessings of the deep that lieth under, blessings of the breasts, and of the womb:

26 **The blessings of thy father** have prevailed above the blessings of my progenitors unto the utmost bound of the everlasting hills:
they shall be on the head of Joseph, and on the crown of the head of him that was separate from his brethren.

27 **Benjamin** shall ravin as a wolf:
in the morning he shall devour the prey,
and at night he shall divide the spoil.

28 **All these** are the twelve tribes of Israel:
and this is it that their father spake unto them, and blessed them;
every one according to his blessing he blessed them.

29 **And he** charged them,
and said unto them,
I am to be gathered unto my people:
bury me with my fathers in the cave that is in the field of Ephron the Hittite,

30 In the cave that is in the field of Machpelah, {which is before Mamre, in the land of Canaan}, {which Abraham bought with the field of Ephron the Hittite for a possession of a buryingplace}.

31 **There** they buried Abraham and Sarah his wife;
there they buried Isaac and Rebekah his wife;
and there I buried Leah.

32 **The purchase of the field and of the cave that is therein** was from the children of Heth.

33 **And when Jacob** had made an end of commanding his sons,
he gathered up his feet into the bed,
and yielded up the ghost,
and was gathered unto his people.

50

And Joseph fell upon his father's face,
and wept upon him,
and kissed him.

2 **And Joseph** commanded his servants the physicians to embalm his father:
and the physicians embalmed Israel.

3 **And forty days** were fulfilled for him;
for so are fulfilled the days of those which are embalmed:
and the Egyptians mourned for him threescore and ten days.

4 **And when the days of his mourning** were past,
Joseph spake unto the house of Pharaoh,
saying,
If now I have found grace in your eyes,
speak, {I pray you}, in the ears of Pharaoh,
saying,

5 **My father** made me swear,
saying,
Lo,
I die:
in my grave which I have digged for me in the land of Canaan, there shalt thou bury me.
Now therefore let me go up, {I pray thee}, and bury my father,
and I will come again.

6 **And Pharaoh** said,
Go up,
and bury thy father,
according as he made thee swear.

7 **And Joseph** went up to bury his father:
and with him went up all the servants of Pharaoh, the elders of his house, and all the elders of the land of Egypt,

8 And all the house of Joseph, and his brethren, and his father's house:
only their little ones, and their flocks, and their herds, they left in the land of Goshen.

9 **And there** went up with him both
chariots and horsemen:
and it was a very great company.
10 **And they** came to the
threshingfloor of Atad,
which is beyond Jordan,
and there they mourned with a
great and very sore lamentation:
and he made a mourning for his
father seven days.
11 **And when the inhabitants of the**
land, the Canaanites, saw the
mourning in the floor of Atad,
they said,
This is a grievous mourning to the
Egyptians:
wherefore the name of it was
called Abelmizraim,
which is beyond Jordan.
12 **And his sons** did unto him
according as he commanded them:
13 **For his sons** carried him into the
land of Canaan,
and buried him in the cave of the
field of Machpelah,
which Abraham bought with the
field for a possession of a
buryingplace of Ephron the
Hittite, before Mamre.
14 **And Joseph** returned into Egypt,
he, and his brethren, and all that
went up with him
to bury his father,
after he had buried his father.

15 **And when Joseph's brethren** saw
that their father was dead,
they said,
Joseph will peradventure hate us,
and will certainly requite us all the
evil which we did unto him.
16 **And they** sent a messenger unto
Joseph,
saying,
Thy father did command before he
died,
saying,
17 **So** shall ye say unto Joseph,
Forgive, {I pray thee now}, the
trespass of thy brethren, and their
sin;
for they did unto thee evil:
and now, {we pray thee}, forgive
the trespass of the servants of the
God of thy father.
And Joseph wept
when they spake unto him.
18 **And his brethren** also went and
fell down before his face;
and they said,
Behold,
we be thy servants.
19 **And Joseph** said unto them,
Fear not:
for am I in the place of God?
20 **But as for you,** ye thought evil
against me;
but God meant it unto good,

to bring to pass, {as it is this day}, to
save much people alive.
21 **Now therefore fear ye not:**
I will nourish you, and your little
ones.
And he comforted them,
and spake kindly unto them.
22 And Joseph dwelt in Egypt, he,
and his father's house:
and Joseph lived an hundred and
ten years.
23 **And Joseph** saw Ephraim's
children of the third generation:
the children also of Machir the
son of Manasseh were brought
up upon Joseph's knees.
24 **And Joseph** said unto his
brethren,
I die:
and God will surely visit you,
and bring you out of this land unto
the land which he sware to
Abraham, to Isaac, and to Jacob.
25 **And Joseph** took an oath of the
children of Israel,
saying,
God will surely visit you,
and ye shall carry up my bones
from hence.
26 **So Joseph** died,
being an hundred and ten years old:
and they embalmed him,
and he was put in a coffin in Egypt.

Exodus

The Book of Exodus covers many of the Old Testament's most oft-repeated stories as Moses describes the Israelites' rescue from slavery in Egypt and their journey to the Promised Land. It shares how God reveals himself to Moses in the form of a burning bush and how He calls him to lead the Israelites out of slavery in Egypt.

It also tells the story of how God delivered a series of plagues upon Egypt to convince Pharaoh to release the Israelites, culminating in the death of the firstborn son in every household except for the Israeli households. Here, the narrative provides a historical account of the first Passover, when God, through Moses, directed every Israelite household to sacrifice an unblemished lamb and apply its blood to their doorposts. This act would cause the Angel of Death to bypass their dwellings, thereby protecting their firstborn from its fatal touch.

Moses then details the Israelites' hasty departure from Egypt and their crossing of the Red Sea. Soon afterward, the book describes how God revealed the Ten Commandments to Moses on Mount Sinai, which form the foundation of Jewish and Christian law. Finally, Moses details the construction of the Tabernacle, which serves as a portable temple for the Israelites during their wanderings in the wilderness. Exodus is an integral part of the Biblical narrative, as it continues the foundational story of God's deliverance and guidance of His chosen people.

1 **Now these** are the names of the children of Israel,
which came into Egypt;
every man and his household came with Jacob.
2 Reuben, Simeon, Levi, and Judah,
3 Issachar, Zebulun, and Benjamin,
4 Dan, and Naphtali, Gad, and Asher.
5 **And all the souls that came out of the loins of Jacob** were seventy souls:
for Joseph was in Egypt already.
6 **And Joseph** died, and all his brethren, and all that generation.
7 **And the children of Israel** were fruitful,
and increased abundantly,
and multiplied,
and waxed exceeding mighty;
and the land was filled with them.
8 **Now there** arose up a new king over Egypt,
which knew not Joseph.
9 **And he** said unto his people,
Behold,
the people of the children of Israel are more and mightier than we:
10 **Come on,**
let us deal wisely with them;
lest they multiply,
and it come to pass,
that, {when there falleth out any war}, they join also unto our enemies,
and fight against us,
and so get them up out of the land.
11 **Therefore they** did set over them taskmasters
to afflict them with their burdens.
And they built for Pharaoh treasure cities, Pithom and Raamses.
12 **But the more they** afflicted them,
the more they multiplied and grew.
And they were grieved because of the children of Israel.
13 **And the Egyptians** made the children of Israel to serve with rigour:
14 **And they** made their lives bitter with hard bondage, in morter, and in brick, and in all manner of service in the field:
all their service, {wherein they made them serve}, was with rigour.
15 **And the king of Egypt** spake to the Hebrew midwives,
of which the name of the one was Shiphrah, and the name of the other Puah:
16 **And he** said,
When ye do the office of a midwife to the Hebrew women,
and see them upon the stools;
if it be a son,
then ye shall kill him:
but if it be a daughter,
then she shall live.
17 **But the midwives** feared God,
and did not as the king of Egypt commanded them,
but saved the men children alive.
18 **And the king of Egypt** called for the midwives,
and said unto them,
Why have ye done this thing,
and have saved the men children alive?
19 **And the midwives** said unto Pharaoh,
Because the Hebrew women are not as the Egyptian women;
for they are lively,
and are delivered
ere the midwives come in unto them.
20 **Therefore God** dealt well with the midwives:
and the people multiplied,
and waxed very mighty.
21 **And it** came to pass,
because the midwives feared God,
that he made them houses.
22 **And Pharaoh** charged all his people,
saying,
Every son that is born ye shall cast into the river,
and every daughter ye shall save alive.

2 **And there** went a man of the house of Levi,
and took to wife a daughter of Levi.
2 **And the woman** conceived,
and bare a son:
and when she saw him that he was a goodly child,
she hid him three months.

3 **And when she** could not longer hide him,
she took for him an ark of bulrushes,
and daubed it with slime and with pitch,
and put the child therein;
and she laid it in the flags by the river's brink.

4 **And his sister** stood afar off,
to wit
what would be done to him.

5 **And the daughter of Pharaoh** came down to wash herself at the river;
and her maidens walked along by the river's side;
and when she saw the ark among the flags,
she sent her maid to fetch it.

6 **And when she** had opened it,
she saw the child:
and, {behold}, the babe wept.

And she had compassion on him,
and said,
This is one of the Hebrews' children.

7 **Then** said his sister to Pharaoh's daughter,
Shall I go and call to thee a nurse of the Hebrew women,
that she may nurse the child for thee?

8 **And Pharaoh's daughter** said to her,
Go.

And the maid went and called the child's mother.

9 **And Pharaoh's daughter** said unto her,
Take this child away,
and nurse it for me,
and I will give thee thy wages.

And the women took the child,
and nursed it.

10 **And the child** grew,
and she brought him unto Pharaoh's daughter,
and he became her son.

And she called his name Moses:
and she said,
Because I drew him out of the water.

11 **And it** came to pass in those days,
when Moses was grown,
that he went out unto his brethren,
and looked on their burdens:
and he spied an Egyptian smiting an Hebrew, one of his brethren.

12 **And he** looked this way and that way,
and when he saw that there was no man,
he slew the Egyptian,
and hid him in the sand.

13 **And when he** went out the second day,
behold,
two men of the Hebrews strove together:
and he said to him that did the wrong,
Wherefore smitest thou thy fellow?

14 **And he** said,
Who made thee a prince and a judge over us?
intendest thou to kill me,
as thou killedst the Egyptian?

And Moses feared,
and said,
Surely this thing is known.

15 **Now when Pharaoh** heard this thing,
he sought to slay Moses.

But Moses fled from the face of Pharaoh,
and dwelt in the land of Midian:
and he sat down by a well.

16 **Now the priest of Midian** had seven daughters:
and they came and drew water,
and filled the troughs
to water their father's flock.

17 **And the shepherds** came and drove them away:
but Moses stood up and helped them,
and watered their flock.

18 **And when they** came to Reuel their father,
he said,
How is it that ye are come so soon to day?

19 **And they** said,
An Egyptian delivered us out of the hand of the shepherds,
and also drew water enough for us,
and watered the flock.

20 **And he** said unto his daughters,
And where is he?
why is it that ye have left the man?
call him,
that he may eat bread.

21 **And Moses** was content to dwell with the man:
and he gave Moses Zipporah his daughter.

22 **And she** bare him a son,
and he called his name Gershom:
for he said,
I have been a stranger in a strange land.

23 **And it** came to pass in process of time,
that the king of Egypt died:
and the children of Israel sighed by reason of the bondage,
and they cried,
and their cry came up unto God by reason of the bondage.

24 **And God** heard their groaning,
and God remembered his covenant with Abraham, with Isaac, and with Jacob.

25 **And God** looked upon the children of Israel,
and God had respect unto them.

3 **Now Moses** kept the flock of Jethro his father in law, the priest of Midian:
and he led the flock to the backside of the desert,
and came to the mountain of God, even to Horeb.

2 **And the angel of the LORD** appeared unto him in a flame of fire out of the midst of a bush:
and he looked,
and, {behold}, the bush burned with fire,
and the bush was not consumed.

3 **And Moses** said, **I** will now turn aside,
and see this great sight,
why the bush is not burnt.

4 **And when the LORD** saw that he turned aside to see,
God called unto him out of the midst of the bush,
and said,
Moses, Moses.

And he said,
Here am I.

5 **And he** said,
Draw not nigh hither:
put off thy shoes from off thy feet,
for the place whereon thou standest is holy ground.

6 **Moreover he** said,
I am the God of thy father, the God of Abraham, the God of Isaac, and the God of Jacob.

And Moses hid his face;
for he was afraid to look upon God.

7 **And the LORD** said,

I have surely seen the affliction of my people which are in Egypt,
and have heard their cry by reason of their taskmasters;
for I know their sorrows;
8 **And I** am come down
to deliver them out of the hand of the Egyptians,
and to bring them up out of that land unto a good land and a large, unto a land flowing with milk and honey; unto the place of the Canaanites, and the Hittites, and the Amorites, and the Perizzites, and the Hivites, and the Jebusites.

9 **Now therefore, {behold}, the cry of the children of Israel** is come unto me:
and I have also seen the oppression wherewith the Egyptians oppress them.

10 **Come** now therefore,
and I will send thee unto Pharaoh,
that thou mayest bring forth my people the children of Israel out of Egypt.

11 **And Moses** said unto God,
Who am I,
that I should go unto Pharaoh,
and that I should bring forth the children of Israel out of Egypt?

12 **And he** said,
Certainly I will be with thee;
and this shall be a token unto thee,
that I have sent thee:
When thou hast brought forth the people out of Egypt,
ye shall serve God upon this mountain.

13 **And Moses** said unto God,
Behold,
when I come unto the children of Israel,
and shall say unto them,
The God of your fathers hath sent me unto you;
and they shall say to me,
What is his name?
what shall I say unto them?

14 **And God** said unto Moses,
I Am That I Am:
and he said,
Thus shalt thou say unto the children of Israel,
I Am hath sent me unto you.

15 **And God** said moreover unto Moses,
Thus shalt thou say unto the children of Israel,
the LORD God of your fathers, the God of Abraham, the God of Isaac, and the God of Jacob, hath sent me unto you:
this is my name for ever,
and this is my memorial unto all generations.

16 **Go,**
and gather the elders of Israel together,
and say unto them,
The LORD God of your fathers, the God of Abraham, of Isaac, and of Jacob, appeared unto me, saying,
I have surely visited you,
and seen that which is done to you in Egypt:

17 **And I** have said,
I will bring you up out of the affliction of Egypt unto the land of the Canaanites, and the Hittites, and the Amorites, and the Perizzites, and the Hivites, and the Jebusites, unto a land flowing with milk and honey.

18 **And they** shall hearken to thy voice:
and thou shalt come, thou and the elders of Israel, unto the king of Egypt,
and ye shall say unto him,
The LORD God of the Hebrews hath met with us:
and now let us go, {we beseech thee}, three days' journey into the wilderness,
that we may sacrifice to the LORD our God.

19 **And I** am sure that the king of Egypt will not let you go, no, not by a mighty hand.

20 **And I** will stretch out my hand,
and smite Egypt with all my wonders which I will do in the midst thereof:
and after that he will let you go.

21 **And I** will give this people favour in the sight of the Egyptians:
and it shall come to pass,
that, {when ye go}, ye shall not go empty.

22 **But every woman** shall borrow of her neighbour, and of her that sojourneth in her house, jewels of silver, and jewels of gold, and raiment:
and ye shall put them upon your sons, and upon your daughters;
and ye shall spoil the Egyptians.

4

And Moses answered and said,
But, {behold}, they will not believe me,
nor hearken unto my voice:
for they will say,
The LORD hath not appeared unto thee.

2 **And the LORD** said unto him,
What is that in thine hand?
And he said,
A rod.

3 **And he** said,
Cast it on the ground.
And he cast it on the ground,
and it became a serpent;
and Moses fled from before it.

4 **And the LORD** said unto Moses,
Put forth thine hand,
and take it by the tail.
And he put forth his hand,
and caught it,
and it became a rod in his hand:
5 **That they** may believe
that the LORD God of their fathers, the God of Abraham, the God of Isaac, and the God of Jacob, hath appeared unto thee.

6 **And the LORD** said furthermore unto him,
Put now thine hand into thy bosom.
And he put his hand into his bosom:
and when he took it out,
behold,
his hand was leprous as snow.

7 **And he** said,
Put thine hand into thy bosom again.
And he put his hand into his bosom again;
and plucked it out of his bosom,
and, {behold}, it was turned again as his other flesh.

8 **And it** shall come to pass,
if they will not believe thee,
neither hearken to the voice of the first sign,
that they will believe the voice of the latter sign.

9 **And it** shall come to pass,
if they will not believe also these two signs,
neither hearken unto thy voice,
that thou shalt take of the water of the river,
and pour it upon the dry land:

and the water which thou takest out of the river shall become blood upon the dry land.

10 **And Moses** said unto the LORD,
O my Lord, I am not eloquent, neither heretofore,
nor since thou hast spoken unto thy servant:
but I am slow of speech, and of a slow tongue.

11 **And the LORD** said unto him,
Who hath made man's mouth?
or who maketh the dumb, or deaf, or the seeing, or the blind?
have not I the LORD?

12 **Now therefore go,**
and I will be with thy mouth,
and teach thee what thou shalt say.

13 **And he** said,
O my Lord, send, {I pray thee}, by the hand of him whom thou wilt send.

14 **And the anger of the LORD** was kindled against Moses,
and he said,
Is not Aaron the Levite thy brother?
I know
that he can speak well.
And also, {behold}, he cometh forth
to meet thee:
and when he seeth thee,
he will be glad in his heart.

15 **And thou** shalt speak unto him,
and put words in his mouth:
and I will be with thy mouth, and with his mouth,
and will teach you what ye shall do.

16 **And he** shall be thy spokesman unto the people:
and he shall be,
even he shall be to thee instead of a mouth,
and thou shalt be to him instead of God.

17 **And thou** shalt take this rod in thine hand,
wherewith thou shalt do signs.

18 **And Moses** went and returned to Jethro his father in law,
and said unto him,
Let me go, {I pray thee}, and return unto my brethren which are in Egypt,
and see whether they be yet alive.
And Jethro said to Moses,
Go in peace.

19 **And the LORD** said unto Moses in Midian,
Go,
return into Egypt:
for all the men are dead which sought thy life.

20 **And Moses** took his wife and his sons,
and set them upon an ass,
and he returned to the land of Egypt:
and Moses took the rod of God in his hand.

21 **And the LORD** said unto Moses,
When thou goest to return into Egypt,
see that thou do all those wonders before Pharaoh,
which I have put in thine hand:
but I will harden his heart,
that he shall not let the people go.

22 **And thou** shalt say unto Pharaoh,
Thus saith the LORD,
Israel is my son, even my firstborn:
23 **And I** say unto thee,
Let my son go,
that he may serve me:
and if thou refuse to let him go,
behold,
I will slay thy son, even thy firstborn.

24 **And it** came to pass by the way in the inn,
that the LORD met him,
and sought to kill him.

25 **Then Zipporah** took a sharp stone,
and cut off the foreskin of her son,
and cast it at his feet,
and said,
Surely a bloody husband art thou to me.

26 **So he** let him go:
then she said,
A bloody husband thou art, because of the circumcision.

27 **And the LORD** said to Aaron,
Go into the wilderness
to meet Moses.
And he went,
and met him in the mount of God,
and kissed him.

28 **And Moses** told Aaron all the words of the LORD who had sent him, and all the signs which he had commanded him.

29 **And Moses and Aaron** went and gathered together all the elders of the children of Israel:

30 **And Aaron** spake all the words which the LORD had spoken unto Moses,
and did the signs in the sight of the people.

31 **And the people** believed:
and when they heard that the LORD had visited the children of Israel, and that he had looked upon their affliction,
then they bowed their heads and worshipped.

5

And afterward Moses and Aaron went in,
and told Pharaoh,
Thus saith the LORD God of Israel,
Let my people go,
that they may hold a feast unto me in the wilderness.

2 **And Pharaoh** said,
Who is the LORD,
that I should obey his voice to let Israel go?
I know not the LORD,
neither will I let Israel go.

3 **And they** said,
The God of the Hebrews hath met with us:
let us go, {we pray thee}, three days' journey into the desert,
and sacrifice unto the LORD our God;
lest he fall upon us with pestilence, or with the sword.

4 **And the king of Egypt** said unto them,
Wherefore do ye, Moses and Aaron, let the people from their works?
get you unto your burdens.

5 **And Pharaoh** said,
Behold,
the people of the land now are many,
and ye make them rest from their burdens.

6 **And Pharaoh** commanded the same day the taskmasters of the people, and their officers,
saying,
7 **Ye** shall no more give the people straw
to make brick, as heretofore:
let them go and gather straw for themselves.

8 **And the tale of the bricks,** {which they did make heretofore}, ye shall lay upon them;
ye shall not diminish ought thereof:
for they be idle;

therefore they cry,
saying,
Let us go and sacrifice to our God.
9 **Let there** more work be laid upon the men,
that they may labour therein;
and let them not regard vain words.
10 **And the taskmasters of the people** went out, and their officers,
and they spake to the people,
saying,
Thus saith Pharaoh,
I will not give you straw.
11 **Go ye,**
get you straw
where ye can find it:
yet not ought of your work shall be diminished.
12 **So the people** were scattered abroad throughout all the land of Egypt
to gather stubble instead of straw.
13 **And the taskmasters** hasted them,
saying,
Fulfil your works, your daily tasks,
as when there was straw.
14 **And the officers of the children of Israel**, {which Pharaoh's taskmasters had set over them}, were beaten,
and demanded,
Wherefore have ye not fulfilled your task in making brick both yesterday and to day, as heretofore?
15 **Then the officers of the children of Israel** came and cried unto Pharaoh,
saying,
Wherefore dealest thou thus with thy servants?
16 **There** is no straw given unto thy servants,
and they say to us,
Make brick:
and, {behold}, thy servants are beaten;
but the fault is in thine own people.
17 **But he** said,
Ye are idle,
ye are idle:
therefore ye say,
Let us go and do sacrifice to the LORD.
18 **Go** therefore now,
and work;
for there shall no straw be given you,
yet shall ye deliver the tale of bricks.
19 **And the officers of the children of Israel** did see that they were in evil case,
after it was said,
Ye shall not minish ought from your bricks of your daily task.
20 **And they** met Moses and Aaron,
who stood in the way,
as they came forth from Pharaoh:
21 **And they** said unto them,
The LORD look upon you,
and judge;
because ye have made our savour to be abhorred in the eyes of Pharaoh, and in the eyes of his servants,
to put a sword in their hand to slay us.
22 **And Moses** returned unto the LORD,
and said,
Lord, wherefore hast thou so evil entreated this people?
why is it that thou hast sent me?
23 **For since I** came to Pharaoh
to speak in thy name,
he hath done evil to this people;
neither hast thou delivered thy people at all.

6 **Then the LORD** said unto Moses,
Now shalt thou see what I will do to Pharaoh:
for with a strong hand shall he let them go,
and with a strong hand shall he drive them out of his land.
2 **And God** spake unto Moses,
and said unto him,
I am the LORD:
3 **And I** appeared unto Abraham, unto Isaac, and unto Jacob, by the name of God Almighty,
but by my name Jehovah was I not known to them.
4 **And I** have also established my covenant with them,
to give them the land of Canaan, the land of their pilgrimage,
wherein they were strangers.
5 **And I** have also heard the groaning of the children of Israel,
whom the Egyptians keep in bondage;
and I have remembered my covenant.
6 **Wherefore** say unto the children of Israel,
I am the LORD,
and I will bring you out from under the burdens of the Egyptians,
and I will rid you out of their bondage,
and I will redeem you with a stretched out arm, and with great judgments:
7 **And I** will take you to me for a people,
and I will be to you a God:
and ye shall know
that I am the LORD your God,
which bringeth you out from under the burdens of the Egyptians.
8 **And I** will bring you in unto the land,
concerning the which I did swear to give it to Abraham, to Isaac, and to Jacob;
and I will give it you for an heritage:
I am the LORD.
9 **And Moses** spake so unto the children of Israel:
but they hearkened not unto Moses for anguish of spirit, and for cruel bondage.
10 **And the LORD** spake unto Moses,
saying,
11 **Go** in,
speak unto Pharaoh king of Egypt,
that he let the children of Israel go out of his land.
12 **And Moses** spake before the LORD,
saying,
Behold,
the children of Israel have not hearkened unto me;
how then shall Pharaoh hear me,
who am of uncircumcised lips?
13 **And the LORD** spake unto Moses and unto Aaron,
and gave them a charge unto the children of Israel, and unto Pharaoh king of Egypt,
to bring the children of Israel out of the land of Egypt.
14 **These** be the heads of their fathers' houses:
The sons of Reuben the firstborn of Israel; Hanoch, and Pallu, Hezron, and Carmi:
these be the families of Reuben.
15 **And the sons of Simeon;** Jemuel, and Jamin, and Ohad, and Jachin,

and Zohar, and Shaul the son of a Canaanitish woman:
these are the families of Simeon.

16 **And these** are the names of the sons of Levi according to their generations; Gershon, and Kohath, and Merari:
and the years of the life of Levi were an hundred thirty and seven years.

17 **The sons of Gershon;** Libni, and Shimi, according to their families.

18 **And the sons of Kohath;** Amram, and Izhar, and Hebron, and Uzziel:
and the years of the life of Kohath were an hundred thirty and three years.

19 **And the sons of Merari;** Mahali and Mushi:
these are the families of Levi according to their generations.

20 **And Amram** took him Jochebed his father's sister to wife;
and she bare him Aaron and Moses:
and the years of the life of Amram were an hundred and thirty and seven years.

21 **And the sons of Izhar;** Korah, and Nepheg, and Zichri.

22 **And the sons of Uzziel;** Mishael, and Elzaphan, and Zithri.

23 **And Aaron** took him Elisheba, daughter of Amminadab, sister of Naashon, to wife;
and she bare him Nadab, and Abihu, Eleazar, and Ithamar.

24 **And the sons of Korah;** Assir, and Elkanah, and Abiasaph:
these are the families of the Korhites.

25 **And Eleazar Aaron's son** took him one of the daughters of Putiel to wife;
and she bare him Phinehas:
these are the heads of the fathers of the Levites according to their families.

26 **These** are that Aaron and Moses,
to whom the LORD said,
Bring out the children of Israel from the land of Egypt according to their armies.

27 **These** are they which spake to Pharaoh king of Egypt,
to bring out the children of Israel from Egypt:
these are that Moses and Aaron.

28 **And it** came to pass on the day
when the LORD spake unto Moses in the land of Egypt,

29 **That the LORD** spake unto Moses,
saying,
I am the LORD:
speak thou unto Pharaoh king of Egypt all that I say unto thee.

30 **And Moses** said before the LORD,
Behold,
I am of uncircumcised lips,
and how shall Pharaoh hearken unto me?

7 ⤫ **And the LORD** said unto Moses,
See,
I have made thee a god to Pharaoh:
and Aaron thy brother shall be thy prophet.

2 **Thou** shalt speak all that I command thee:
and Aaron thy brother shall speak unto Pharaoh,
that he send the children of Israel out of his land.

3 **And I** will harden Pharaoh's heart,
and multiply my signs and my wonders in the land of Egypt.

4 **But Pharaoh** shall not hearken unto you,
that I may lay my hand upon Egypt,
and bring forth mine armies, and my people the children of Israel, out of the land of Egypt by great judgments.

5 **And the Egyptians** shall know
that I am the LORD,
when I stretch forth mine hand upon Egypt,
and bring out the children of Israel from among them.

6 **And Moses and Aaron** did as the LORD commanded them,
so did they.

7 **And Moses** was fourscore years old, and Aaron fourscore and three years old,
when they spake unto Pharaoh.

8 **And the LORD** spake unto Moses and unto Aaron,
saying,

9 **When Pharaoh** shall speak unto you,
saying,
Shew a miracle for you:
then thou shalt say unto Aaron,
Take thy rod,
and cast it before Pharaoh,
and it shall become a serpent.

10 **And Moses and Aaron** went in unto Pharaoh,
and they did so as the LORD had commanded:
and Aaron cast down his rod before Pharaoh, and before his servants,
and it became a serpent.

11 **Then Pharaoh** also called the wise men and the sorcerers:
now the magicians of Egypt, they also did in like manner with their enchantments.

12 **For they** cast down every man his rod,
and they became serpents:
but Aaron's rod swallowed up their rods.

13 **And he** hardened Pharaoh's heart,
that he hearkened not unto them;
as the LORD had said.

14 **And the LORD** said unto Moses,
Pharaoh's heart is hardened,
he refuseth to let the people go.

15 **Get thee** unto Pharaoh in the morning;
lo,
he goeth out unto the water;
and thou shalt stand by the river's brink
against he come;
and the rod which was turned to a serpent shalt thou take in thine hand.

16 **And thou** shalt say unto him,
The LORD God of the Hebrews hath sent me unto thee,
saying,
Let my people go,
that they may serve me in the wilderness:
and, {behold}, hitherto thou wouldest not hear.

17 **Thus** saith the LORD,
In this thou shalt know
that I am the LORD:
behold,
I will smite with the rod that is in mine hand upon the waters which are in the river,
and they shall be turned to blood.

18 **And the fish that is in the river** shall die,
and the river shall stink;
and the Egyptians shall lothe to drink of the water of the river.

19 **And the LORD** spake unto Moses,
Say unto Aaron,
Take thy rod,
and stretch out thine hand upon the waters of Egypt, upon their

streams, upon their rivers, and upon their ponds, and upon all their pools of water,
that they may become blood;
and that there may be blood throughout all the land of Egypt, both in vessels of wood, and in vessels of stone.

20 **And Moses and Aaron** did so,
as the LORD commanded;
and he lifted up the rod,
and smote the waters that were in the river, in the sight of Pharaoh, and in the sight of his servants;
and all the waters that were in the river were turned to blood.

21 **And the fish that was in the river** died;
and the river stank,
and the Egyptians could not drink of the water of the river;
and there was blood throughout all the land of Egypt.

22 **And the magicians of Egypt** did so with their enchantments:
and Pharaoh's heart was hardened,
neither did he hearken unto them;
as the LORD had said.

23 **And Pharaoh** turned and went into his house,
neither did he set his heart to this also.

24 **And all the Egyptians** digged round about the river for water to drink;
for they could not drink of the water of the river.

25 **And seven days** were fulfilled,
after that the LORD had smitten the river.

8 **And the LORD** spake unto Moses,
Go unto Pharaoh,
and say unto him,
Thus saith the LORD,
Let my people go,
that they may serve me.

2 **And if thou** refuse to let them go,
behold,
I will smite all thy borders with frogs:

3 **And the river** shall bring forth frogs abundantly,
which shall go up and come into thine house, and into thy bedchamber, and upon thy bed, and into the house of thy servants, and upon thy people, and into thine ovens, and into thy kneadingtroughs:

4 **And the frogs** shall come up both on thee, and upon thy people, and upon all thy servants.

5 **And the LORD** spake unto Moses,
Say unto Aaron,
Stretch forth thine hand with thy rod over the streams, over the rivers, and over the ponds,
and cause frogs to come up upon the land of Egypt.

6 **And Aaron** stretched out his hand over the waters of Egypt;
and the frogs came up,
and covered the land of Egypt.

7 **And the magicians** did so with their enchantments,
and brought up frogs upon the land of Egypt.

8 **Then Pharaoh** called for Moses and Aaron,
and said,
Intreat the LORD,
that he may take away the frogs from me, and from my people;
and I will let the people go,
that they may do sacrifice unto the LORD.

9 **And Moses** said unto Pharaoh,
Glory over me:
when shall I intreat for thee, and for thy servants, and for thy people,
to destroy the frogs from thee and thy houses,
that they may remain in the river only?

10 **And he** said,
To morrow.
And he said,
Be it according to thy word:
that thou mayest know
that there is none like unto the LORD our God.

11 **And the frogs** shall depart from thee, and from thy houses, and from thy servants, and from thy people;
they shall remain in the river only.

12 **And Moses and Aaron** went out from Pharaoh:
and Moses cried unto the LORD because of the frogs which he had brought against Pharaoh.

13 **And the LORD** did according to the word of Moses;
and the frogs died out of the houses, out of the villages, and out of the fields.

14 **And they** gathered them together upon heaps:
and the land stank.

15 **But when Pharaoh** saw that there was respite,
he hardened his heart,
and hearkened not unto them;
as the LORD had said.

16 **And the LORD** said unto Moses,
Say unto Aaron,
Stretch out thy rod,
and smite the dust of the land,
that it may become lice throughout all the land of Egypt.

17 **And they** did so;
for Aaron stretched out his hand with his rod,
and smote the dust of the earth,
and it became lice in man, and in beast;
all the dust of the land became lice throughout all the land of Egypt.

18 **And the magicians** did so with their enchantments
to bring forth lice,
but they could not:
so there were lice upon man, and upon beast.

19 **Then the magicians** said unto Pharaoh,
This is the finger of God:
and Pharaoh's heart was hardened,
and he hearkened not unto them;
as the LORD had said.

20 **And the LORD** said unto Moses,
Rise up early in the morning,
and stand before Pharaoh;
lo,
he cometh forth to the water;
and say unto him,
Thus saith the LORD,
Let my people go,
that they may serve me.

21 **Else, if thou** wilt not let my people go,
behold,
I will send swarms of flies upon thee, and upon thy servants, and upon thy people, and into thy houses:
and the houses of the Egyptians shall be full of swarms of flies, and also the ground whereon they are.

22 **And I** will sever in that day the land of Goshen,

in which my people dwell,
that no swarms of flies shall be there;
to the end thou mayest know
that I am the LORD in the midst of the earth.
23 **And I** will put a division between my people and thy people:
to morrow shall this sign be.
24 **And the LORD** did so;
and there came a grievous swarm of flies into the house of Pharaoh, and into his servants' houses, and into all the land of Egypt:
the land was corrupted by reason of the swarm of flies.
25 **And Pharaoh** called for Moses and for Aaron,
and said,
Go ye,
sacrifice to your God in the land.
26 **And Moses** said,
It is not meet so to do;
for we shall sacrifice the abomination of the Egyptians to the LORD our God:
lo,
shall we sacrifice the abomination of the Egyptians before their eyes,
and will they not stone us?
27 **We** will go three days' journey into the wilderness,
and sacrifice to the LORD our God,
as he shall command us.
28 **And Pharaoh** said,
I will let you go,
that ye may sacrifice to the LORD your God in the wilderness;
only ye shall not go very far away:
intreat for me.
29 **And Moses** said,
Behold,
I go out from thee,
and I will intreat the LORD
that the swarms of flies may depart from Pharaoh, from his servants, and from his people, to morrow:
but let not Pharaoh deal deceitfully any more in not letting the people go
to sacrifice to the LORD.
30 **And Moses** went out from Pharaoh,
and intreated the LORD.
31 **And the LORD** did according to the word of Moses;
and he removed the swarms of flies from Pharaoh, from his servants, and from his people;
there remained not one.
32 **And Pharaoh** hardened his heart at this time also,
neither would he let the people go.

9 **Then the LORD** said unto Moses,
Go in unto Pharaoh,
and tell him,
Thus saith the LORD God of the Hebrews,
Let my people go,
that they may serve me.
2 **For if thou** refuse to let them go,
and wilt hold them still,
3 **Behold,**
the hand of the LORD is upon thy cattle which is in the field, upon the horses, upon the asses, upon the camels, upon the oxen, and upon the sheep:
there shall be a very grievous murrain.
4 **And the LORD** shall sever between the cattle of Israel and the cattle of Egypt:
and there shall nothing die of all that is the children's of Israel.
5 **And the LORD** appointed a set time,
saying,
To morrow the LORD shall do this thing in the land.
6 **And the LORD** did that thing on the morrow,
and all the cattle of Egypt died:
but of the cattle of the children of Israel died not one.
7 **And Pharaoh** sent,
and, {behold}, there was not one of the cattle of the Israelites dead.
And the heart of Pharaoh was hardened,
and he did not let the people go.
8 **And the LORD** said unto Moses and unto Aaron,
Take to you handfuls of ashes of the furnace,
and let Moses sprinkle it toward the heaven in the sight of Pharaoh.
9 **And it** shall become small dust in all the land of Egypt,
and shall be a boil breaking forth with blains upon man, and upon beast, throughout all the land of Egypt.
10 **And they** took ashes of the furnace,
and stood before Pharaoh;
and Moses sprinkled it up toward heaven;
and it became a boil breaking forth with blains upon man, and upon beast.
11 **And the magicians** could not stand before Moses because of the boils;
for the boil was upon the magicians, and upon all the Egyptians.
12 **And the LORD** hardened the heart of Pharaoh,
and he hearkened not unto them;
as the LORD had spoken unto Moses.
13 **And the LORD** said unto Moses,
Rise up early in the morning,
and stand before Pharaoh,
and say unto him,
Thus saith the LORD God of the Hebrews,
Let my people go,
that they may serve me.
14 **For I** will at this time send all my plagues upon thine heart, and upon thy servants, and upon thy people;
that thou mayest know
that there is none like me in all the earth.
15 **For now I** will stretch out my hand,
that I may smite thee and thy people with pestilence;
and thou shalt be cut off from the earth.
16 **And in very deed for this cause** have I raised thee up,
for to shew in thee my power;
and that my name may be declared throughout all the earth.
17 **As yet exaltest thou thyself** against my people,
that thou wilt not let them go?
18 **Behold,**
to morrow about this time I will cause it to rain a very grievous hail,
such as hath not been in Egypt since the foundation thereof even until now.
19 **Send** therefore now,
and gather thy cattle, and all that thou hast in the field;
for upon every man and beast which shall be found in the field, and shall not be brought home, the hail shall come down upon them,

and they shall die.

20 **He that feared the word of the LORD among the servants of Pharaoh** made his servants and his cattle flee into the houses:

21 **And he that regarded not the word of the LORD** left his servants and his cattle in the field.

22 **And the LORD** said unto Moses,
Stretch forth thine hand toward heaven,
that there may be hail in all the land of Egypt, upon man, and upon beast, and upon every herb of the field, throughout the land of Egypt.

23 **And Moses** stretched forth his rod toward heaven:
and the LORD sent thunder and hail,
and the fire ran along upon the ground;
and the LORD rained hail upon the land of Egypt.

24 **So there** was hail, and fire mingled with the hail, very grievous,
such as there was none like it in all the land of Egypt
since it became a nation.

25 **And the hail** smote throughout all the land of Egypt all that was in the field, both man and beast;
and the hail smote every herb of the field,
and brake every tree of the field.

26 **Only in the land of Goshen,** {where the children of Israel were}, was there no hail.

27 **And Pharaoh** sent,
and called for Moses and Aaron,
and said unto them,
I have sinned this time:
the LORD is righteous,
and I and my people are wicked.

28 **Intreat** the LORD (for it is enough)
that there be no more mighty thunderings and hail;
and I will let you go,
and ye shall stay no longer.

29 **And Moses** said unto him,
As soon as I am gone out of the city,
I will spread abroad my hands unto the LORD;
and the thunder shall cease,
neither shall there be any more hail;
that thou mayest know
how that the earth is the LORD's.

30 **But as for thee and thy servants,** I know
that ye will not yet fear the LORD God.

31 **And the flax and the barley** was smitten:
for the barley was in the ear,
and the flax was bolled.

32 **But the wheat and the rie** were not smitten:
for they were not grown up.

33 **And Moses** went out of the city from Pharaoh,
and spread abroad his hands unto the LORD:
and the thunders and hail ceased,
and the rain was not poured upon the earth.

34 **And when Pharaoh** saw that the rain and the hail and the thunders were ceased,
he sinned yet more,
and hardened his heart, he and his servants.

35 **And the heart of Pharaoh** was hardened,
neither would he let the children of Israel go;
as the LORD had spoken by Moses.

10

And the LORD said unto Moses,
Go in unto Pharaoh:
for I have hardened his heart, and the heart of his servants,
that I might shew these my signs before him:

2 **And that thou** mayest tell in the ears of thy son, and of thy son's son,
what things I have wrought in Egypt, and my signs which I have done among them;
that ye may know
how that I am the LORD.

3 **And Moses and Aaron** came in unto Pharaoh,
and said unto him,
Thus saith the LORD God of the Hebrews,
How long wilt thou refuse to humble thyself before me?
let my people go,
that they may serve me.

4 **Else, if thou** refuse to let my people go,
behold,
to morrow will I bring the locusts into thy coast:

5 **And they** shall cover the face of the earth,
that one cannot be able to see the earth:
and they shall eat the residue of that which is escaped,
which remaineth unto you from the hail,
and shall eat every tree which groweth for you out of the field:

6 **And they** shall fill thy houses, and the houses of all thy servants, and the houses of all the Egyptians;
which neither thy fathers, nor thy fathers' fathers have seen, since the day that they were upon the earth unto this day.
And he turned himself,
and went out from Pharaoh.

7 **And Pharaoh's servants** said unto him,
How long shall this man be a snare unto us?
let the men go,
hat they may serve the LORD their God:
knowest thou not yet
that Egypt is destroyed?

8 **And Moses and Aaron** were brought again unto Pharaoh:
and he said unto them,
Go,
serve the LORD your God:
but who are they that shall go?

9 **And Moses** said,
We will go with our young and with our old,
with our sons and with our daughters, with our flocks and with our herds will we go;
for we must hold a feast unto the LORD.

10 **And he** said unto them,
Let the LORD be so with you,
as I will let you go, and your little ones:
look to it;
for evil is before you.

11 Not so:
go now ye that are men,
and serve the LORD;
for that ye did desire.
And they were driven out from Pharaoh's presence.

12 **And the LORD** said unto Moses,
Stretch out thine hand over the land of Egypt for the locusts,
that they may come up upon the land of Egypt,

and eat every herb of the land, even all that the hail hath left.

13 **And Moses** stretched forth his rod over the land of Egypt,
and the LORD brought an east wind upon the land all that day, and all that night;
and when it was morning,
the east wind brought the locusts.

14 **And the locust** went up over all the land of Egypt,
and rested in all the coasts of Egypt:
very grievous were they;
before them there were no such locusts as they,
neither after them shall be such.

15 **For they** covered the face of the whole earth,
so that the land was darkened;
and they did eat every herb of the land, and all the fruit of the trees which the hail had left:
and there remained not any green thing in the trees, or in the herbs of the field, through all the land of Egypt.

16 **Then Pharaoh** called for Moses and Aaron in haste;
and he said,
I have sinned against the LORD your God, and against you.

17 **Now therefore forgive**, {I pray thee}, my sin only this once,
and intreat the LORD your God,
that he may take away from me this death only.

18 **And he** went out from Pharaoh,
and intreated the LORD.

19 **And the LORD** turned a mighty strong west wind,
which took away the locusts,
and cast them into the Red sea;
there remained not one locust in all the coasts of Egypt.

20 **But the LORD** hardened Pharaoh's heart,
so that he would not let the children of Israel go.

21 **And the LORD** said unto Moses,
Stretch out thine hand toward heaven,
that there may be darkness over the land of Egypt, even darkness which may be felt.

22 **And Moses** stretched forth his hand toward heaven;
and there was a thick darkness in all the land of Egypt three days:

23 **They** saw not one another,
neither rose any from his place for three days:
but all the children of Israel had light in their dwellings.

24 **And Pharaoh** called unto Moses,
and said,
Go ye,
serve the LORD;
only let your flocks and your herds be stayed:
let your little ones also go with you.

25 **And Moses** said,
Thou must give us also sacrifices and burnt offerings,
that we may sacrifice unto the LORD our God.

26 **Our cattle** also shall go with us;
there shall not an hoof be left behind;
for thereof must we take
to serve the LORD our God;
and we know not
with what we must serve the LORD,
until we come thither.

27 **But the LORD** hardened Pharaoh's heart,
and he would not let them go.

28 **And Pharaoh** said unto him,
Get thee from me,
take heed to thyself,
see my face no more;
for in that day thou seest my face thou shalt die.

29 **And Moses** said,
Thou hast spoken well,
I will see thy face again no more.

11 **And the LORD** said unto Moses,
Yet will I bring one plague more upon Pharaoh, and upon Egypt;
afterwards he will let you go hence:
when he shall let you go,
he shall surely thrust you out hence altogether.

2 **Speak** now in the ears of the people,
and let every man borrow of his neighbour, and every woman of her neighbour, jewels of silver and jewels of gold.

3 **And the LORD** gave the people favour in the sight of the Egyptians.
Moreover the man Moses was very great in the land of Egypt, in the sight of Pharaoh's servants, and in the sight of the people.

4 **And Moses** said,
Thus saith the LORD,
About midnight will I go out into the midst of Egypt:

5 **And all the firstborn in the land of Egypt** shall die, from the first born of Pharaoh that sitteth upon his throne, even unto the firstborn of the maidservant that is behind the mill; and all the firstborn of beasts.

6 **And there** shall be a great cry throughout all the land of Egypt,
such as there was none like it,
nor shall be like it any more.

7 **But against any of the children of Israel** shall not a dog move his tongue, against man or beast:
that ye may know
how that the LORD doth put a difference between the Egyptians and Israel.

8 **And all these thy servants** shall come down unto me,
and bow down themselves unto me,
saying,
Get thee out, and all the people that follow thee:
and after that I will go out.
And he went out from Pharaoh in a great anger.

9 **And the LORD** said unto Moses,
Pharaoh shall not hearken unto you;
that my wonders may be multiplied in the land of Egypt.

10 **And Moses and Aaron** did all these wonders before Pharaoh:
and the LORD hardened Pharaoh's heart,
so that he would not let the children of Israel go out of his land.

12 **And the LORD** spake unto Moses and Aaron in the land of Egypt
saying,

2 **This month** shall be unto you the beginning of months:
it shall be the first month of the year to you.

3 **Speak ye** unto all the congregation of Israel,
saying,
In the tenth day of this month they shall take to them every man

a lamb, according to the house of their fathers, a lamb for an house:

4 **And if the household** be too little for the lamb,
let him and his neighbour next unto his house take it according to the number of the souls;
every man according to his eating shall make your count for the lamb.

5 **Your lamb** shall be without blemish, a male of the first year:
ye shall take it out from the sheep, or from the goats:

6 **And ye** shall keep it up until the fourteenth day of the same month:
and the whole assembly of the congregation of Israel shall kill it in the evening.

7 **And they** shall take of the blood,
and strike it on the two side posts and on the upper door post of the houses,
wherein they shall eat it.

8 **And they** shall eat the flesh in that night, roast with fire, and unleavened bread;
and with bitter herbs they shall eat it.

9 **Eat not** of it raw, nor sodden at all with water, but roast with fire; his head with his legs, and with the purtenance thereof.

10 **And ye** shall let nothing of it remain until the morning;
and that which remaineth of it until the morning ye shall burn with fire.

11 **And thus** shall ye eat it;
with your loins girded, your shoes on your feet, and your staff in your hand;
and ye shall eat it in haste:
it is the LORD's passover.

12 **For I** will pass through the land of Egypt this night,
and will smite all the firstborn in the land of Egypt, both man and beast;
and against all the gods of Egypt I will execute judgment:
I am the LORD.

13 **And the blood** shall be to you for a token upon the houses where ye are:
and when I see the blood,
I will pass over you,
and the plague shall not be upon you to destroy you,
when I smite the land of Egypt.

14 **And this day** shall be unto you for a memorial;
and ye shall keep it a feast to the LORD throughout your generations;
ye shall keep it a feast by an ordinance for ever.

15 **Seven days** shall ye eat unleavened bread;
even the first day ye shall put away leaven out of your houses:
for whosoever eateth leavened bread from the first day until the seventh day,
that soul shall be cut off from Israel.

16 **And in the first day** there shall be an holy convocation,
and in the seventh day there shall be an holy convocation to you;
no manner of work shall be done in them, save that which every man must eat,
that only may be done of you.

17 **And ye** shall observe the feast of unleavened bread;
for in this selfsame day have I brought your armies out of the land of Egypt:
therefore shall ye observe this day in your generations by an ordinance for ever.

18 **In the first month, on the fourteenth day of the month at even,** ye shall eat unleavened bread, until the one and twentieth day of the month at even.

19 **Seven days** shall there be no leaven found in your houses:
for whosoever eateth that which is leavened,
even that soul shall be cut off from the congregation of Israel,
whether he be a stranger,
or born in the land.

20 **Ye** shall eat nothing leavened;
in all your habitations shall ye eat unleavened bread.

21 **Then Moses** called for all the elders of Israel,
and said unto them,
Draw out and take you a lamb according to your families,
and kill the passover.

22 **And ye** shall take a bunch of hyssop,
and dip it in the blood that is in the bason,
and strike the lintel and the two side posts with the blood that is in the bason;
and none of you shall go out at the door of his house until the morning.

23 **For the LORD** will pass through to smite the Egyptians;
and when he seeth the blood upon the lintel, and on the two side posts,
the LORD will pass over the door,
and will not suffer the destroyer to come in unto your houses
to smite you.

24 **And ye** shall observe this thing for an ordinance to thee and to thy sons for ever.

25 **And it** shall come to pass,
when ye be come to the land which the LORD will give you,
according as he hath promised,
that ye shall keep this service.

26 **And it** shall come to pass,
when your children shall say unto you,
What mean ye by this service?

27 **That ye** shall say,
It is the sacrifice of the LORD's passover,
who passed over the houses of the children of Israel in Egypt,
when he smote the Egyptians,
and delivered our houses.

And the people bowed the head and worshipped.

28 **And the children of Israel** went away,
and did as the LORD had commanded Moses and Aaron,
so did they.

29 **And it** came to pass,
that at midnight the LORD smote all the firstborn in the land of Egypt, from the firstborn of Pharaoh that sat on his throne unto the firstborn of the captive that was in the dungeon; and all the firstborn of cattle.

30 **And Pharaoh** rose up in the night, he, and all his servants, and all the Egyptians;
and there was a great cry in Egypt;
for there was not a house where there was not one dead.

31 **And he** called for Moses and Aaron by night,
and said,
Rise up,

and get you forth from among my people, both ye and the children of Israel;
and go,
serve the LORD,
as ye have said.
32 **Also take** your flocks and your herds,
as ye have said,
and be gone;
and bless me also.
33 **And the Egyptians** were urgent upon the people,
that they might send them out of the land in haste;
for they said,
We be all dead men.
34 **And the people** took their dough
before it was leavened,
their kneadingtroughs being bound up in their clothes upon their shoulders.
35 **And the children of Israel** did according to the word of Moses;
and they borrowed of the Egyptians jewels of silver, and jewels of gold, and raiment:
36 **And the LORD** gave the people favour in the sight of the Egyptians,
so that they lent unto them such things as they required.
And they spoiled the Egyptians.
37 **And the children of Israel** journeyed from Rameses to Succoth, about six hundred thousand on foot that were men, beside children.
38 **And a mixed multitude** went up also with them; and flocks, and herds, even very much cattle.
39 **And they** baked unleavened cakes of the dough which they brought forth out of Egypt,
for it was not leavened;
because they were thrust out of Egypt,
and could not tarry,
neither had they prepared for themselves any victual.
40 **Now the sojourning of the children of Israel**, {who dwelt in Egypt}, was four hundred and thirty years.
41 **And it** came to pass at the end of the four hundred and thirty years, even the selfsame day it came to pass,
that all the hosts of the LORD went out from the land of Egypt.
42 **It is a night** to be much observed unto the LORD
for bringing them out from the land of Egypt:
this is that night of the LORD to be observed of all the children of Israel in their generations.
43 **And the LORD** said unto Moses and Aaron,
This is the ordinance of the passover:
There shall no stranger eat thereof:
44 **But every man's servant that is bought for money**, {when thou hast circumcised him}, then shall he eat thereof.
45 **A foreigner and an hired servant** shall not eat thereof.
46 **In one house** shall it be eaten;
thou shalt not carry forth ought of the flesh abroad out of the house;
neither shall ye break a bone thereof.
47 **All the congregation of Israel** shall keep it.
48 **And when a stranger** shall sojourn with thee,
and will keep the passover to the LORD,
let all his males be circumcised,
and then let him come near and keep it;
and he shall be as one that is born in the land:
for no uncircumcised person shall eat thereof.
49 **One law** shall be to him that is homeborn, and unto the stranger that sojourneth among you.
50 **Thus** did all the children of Israel;
as the LORD commanded Moses and Aaron,
so did they.
51 **And it** came to pass the selfsame day,
that the LORD did bring the children of Israel out of the land of Egypt by their armies.

13

And the LORD spake unto Moses,
saying,
2 **Sanctify** unto me all the firstborn,
whatsoever openeth the womb among the children of Israel, both of man and of beast:
it is mine.
3 **And Moses** said unto the people,
Remember this day,
in which ye came out from Egypt, out of the house of bondage;
for by strength of hand the LORD brought you out from this place:
there shall no leavened bread be eaten.
4 **This day** came ye out in the month Abib.
5 **And it** shall be
when the LORD shall bring thee into the land of the Canaanites, and the Hittites, and the Amorites, and the Hivites, and the Jebusites,
which he sware unto thy fathers to give thee, a land flowing with milk and honey,
that thou shalt keep this service in this month.
6 **Seven days** thou shalt eat unleavened bread,
and in the seventh day shall be a feast to the LORD.
7 **Unleavened bread** shall be eaten seven days;
and there shall no leavened bread be seen with thee,
either shall there be leaven seen with thee in all thy quarters.
8 **And thou** shalt shew thy son in that day,
saying,
This is done because of that which the LORD did unto me
when I came forth out of Egypt.
9 **And it** shall be for a sign unto thee upon thine hand, and for a memorial between thine eyes,
that the LORD's law may be in thy mouth:
for with a strong hand hath the LORD brought thee out of Egypt.
10 **Thou** shalt therefore keep this ordinance in his season from year to year.
11 **And it** shall be
when the LORD shall bring thee into the land of the Canaanites,
as he sware unto thee and to thy fathers,
and shall give it thee,
12 **That thou** shalt set apart unto the LORD all that openeth the matrix, and every firstling that cometh of a beast which thou hast;
the males shall be the LORD's.
13 **And every firstling of an ass** thou shalt redeem with a lamb;
and if thou wilt not redeem it,

then thou shalt break his neck:
and all the firstborn of man among thy children shalt thou redeem.

14 **And it** shall be
when thy son asketh thee in time to come,
saying,
What is this?
that thou shalt say unto him,
By strength of hand the LORD brought us out from Egypt, from the house of bondage:

15 **And it** came to pass,
when Pharaoh would hardly let us go,
that the LORD slew all the firstborn in the land of Egypt, both the firstborn of man, and the firstborn of beast:
therefore I sacrifice to the LORD all that openeth the matrix,
being males;
but all the firstborn of my children I redeem.

16 **And it** shall be for a token upon thine hand, and for frontlets between thine eyes:
for by strength of hand the LORD brought us forth out of Egypt.

17 **And it** came to pass,
when Pharaoh had let the people go,
that God led them not through the way of the land of the Philistines,
although that was near;
for God said,
Lest peradventure the people repent when they see war,
and they return to Egypt:

18 **But God** led the people about, through the way of the wilderness of the Red sea:
and the children of Israel went up harnessed out of the land of Egypt.

19 **And Moses** took the bones of Joseph with him:
for he had straitly sworn the children of Israel,
saying,
God will surely visit you;
and ye shall carry up my bones away hence with you.

20 **And they** took their journey from Succoth,
and encamped in Etham, in the edge of the wilderness.

21 **And the LORD** went before them by day in a pillar of a cloud, {to lead them the way}; and by night in a pillar of fire, {to give them light};
to go by day and night:

22 **He** took not away the pillar of the cloud by day, nor the pillar of fire by night, from before the people.

14

And the LORD spake unto Moses,
saying,

2 **Speak** unto the children of Israel,
that they turn and encamp before Pihahiroth, between Migdol and the sea, over against Baalzephon:
before it shall ye encamp by the sea.

3 **For Pharaoh** will say of the children of Israel,
They are entangled in the land,
the wilderness hath shut them in.

4 **And I** will harden Pharaoh's heart,
that he shall follow after them;
and I will be honoured upon Pharaoh, and upon all his host;
that the Egyptians may know
that I am the LORD.
And they did so.

5 **And it was told the king of Egypt** that the people fled:
and the heart of Pharaoh and of his servants was turned against the people,
and they said,
Why have we done this,
that we have let Israel go from serving us?

6 **And he** made ready his chariot,
and took his people with him:

7 **And he** took six hundred chosen chariots, and all the chariots of Egypt, and captains over every one of them.

8 **And the LORD** hardened the heart of Pharaoh king of Egypt,
and he pursued after the children of Israel:
and the children of Israel went out with an high hand.

9 **But the Egyptians** pursued after them, all the horses and chariots of Pharaoh, and his horsemen, and his army,
and overtook them encamping by the sea, beside Pihahiroth, before Baalzephon.

10 **And when Pharaoh** drew nigh,
the children of Israel lifted up their eyes,
and, {behold}, the Egyptians marched after them;
and they were sore afraid:
and the children of Israel cried out unto the LORD.

11 **And they** said unto Moses,
Because there were no graves in Egypt,
hast thou taken us away
to die in the wilderness?
wherefore hast thou dealt thus with us,
to carry us forth out of Egypt?

12 **Is not this** the word that we did tell thee in Egypt,
saying,
Let us alone,
that we may serve the Egyptians?
For it had been better for us to serve the Egyptians,
than that we should die in the wilderness.

13 **And Moses** said unto the people,
Fear ye not,
stand still,
and see the salvation of the LORD,
which he will shew to you to day:
for the Egyptians whom ye have seen to day, ye shall see them again no more for ever.

14 **The LORD** shall fight for you,
and ye shall hold your peace.

15 **And the LORD** said unto Moses,
Wherefore criest thou unto me?
speak unto the children of Israel,
that they go forward:

16 **But lift thou** up thy rod
and stretch out thine hand over the sea,
and divide it:
and the children of Israel shall go on dry ground through the midst of the sea.

17 **And I, {behold}, I** will harden the hearts of the Egyptians,
and they shall follow them:
and I will get me honour upon Pharaoh, and upon all his host, upon his chariots, and upon his horsemen.

18 **And the Egyptians** shall know
that I am the LORD,
when I have gotten me honour upon Pharaoh, upon his chariots, and upon his horsemen.

19 **And the angel of God**, {which went before the camp of Israel}, removed and went behind them;
and the pillar of the cloud went from before their face,

and stood behind them:

20 **And it** came between the camp of the Egyptians and the camp of Israel;
and it was a cloud and darkness to them,
but it gave light by night to these:
so that the one came not near the other all the night.

21 **And Moses** stretched out his hand over the sea;
and the LORD caused the sea to go back by a strong east wind all that night,
and made the sea dry land,
and the waters were divided.

22 **And the children of Israel** went into the midst of the sea upon the dry ground:
and the waters were a wall unto them on their right hand, and on their left.

23 **And the Egyptians** pursued,
and went in after them to the midst of the sea, even all Pharaoh's horses, his chariots, and his horsemen.

24 **And it** came to pass,
that in the morning watch the LORD looked unto the host of the Egyptians through the pillar of fire and of the cloud,
and troubled the host of the Egyptians,

25 **And** took off their chariot wheels,
that they drave them heavily:
so that the Egyptians said,
Let us flee from the face of Israel;
for the LORD fighteth for them against the Egyptians.

26 **And the LORD** said unto Moses,
Stretch out thine hand over the sea,
that the waters may come again upon the Egyptians, upon their chariots, and upon their horsemen.

27 **And Moses** stretched forth his hand over the sea,
and the sea returned to his strength
when the morning appeared;
and the Egyptians fled against it;
and the LORD overthrew the Egyptians in the midst of the sea.

28 **And the waters** returned,
and covered the chariots, and the horsemen, and all the host of Pharaoh that came into the sea after them;
there remained not so much as one of them.

29 **But the children of Israel** walked upon dry land in the midst of the sea;
and the waters were a wall unto them on their right hand, and on their left.

30 **Thus the LORD** saved Israel that day out of the hand of the Egyptians;
and Israel saw the Egyptians dead upon the sea shore.

31 **And Israel** saw that great work which the LORD did upon the Egyptians:
and the people feared the LORD,
and believed the LORD, and his servant Moses.

15 **Then** sang Moses and the children of Israel this song unto the LORD,
and spake,
saying,
I will sing unto the LORD,
for he hath triumphed gloriously:
the horse and his rider hath he thrown into the sea.

2 **The LORD** is my strength and song,
and he is become my salvation:
he is my God, {and I will prepare him an habitation}; my father's God, {and I will exalt him}.

3 **The LORD** is a man of war:
the LORD is his name.

4 **Pharaoh's chariots and his host** hath he cast into the sea:
his chosen captains also are drowned in the Red sea.

5 **The depths** have covered them:
they sank into the bottom as a stone.

6 **Thy right hand,** O LORD, is become glorious in power:
thy right hand, O LORD, hath dashed in pieces the enemy.

7 **And in the greatness of thine excellency** thou hast overthrown them that rose up against thee:
thou sentest forth thy wrath,
which consumed them as stubble.

8 **And with the blast of thy nostrils** the waters were gathered together,
the floods stood upright as an heap,
and the depths were congealed in the heart of the sea.

9 **The enemy** said,
I will pursue,
I will overtake,
I will divide the spoil;
my lust shall be satisfied upon them;
I will draw my sword,
my hand shall destroy them.

10 **Thou** didst blow with thy wind,
the sea covered them:
they sank as lead in the mighty waters.

11 **Who** is like unto thee, O LORD, among the gods?
who is like thee, glorious in holiness, fearful in praises,
doing wonders?

12 **Thou** stretchedst out thy right hand,
the earth swallowed them.

13 **Thou in thy mercy** hast led forth the people which thou hast redeemed:
thou hast guided them in thy strength unto thy holy habitation.

14 **The people** shall hear,
and be afraid:
sorrow shall take hold on the inhabitants of Palestina.

15 **Then the dukes of Edom** shall be amazed;
the mighty men of Moab, {trembling} shall take hold upon them;
all the inhabitants of Canaan shall melt away.

16 **Fear and dread** shall fall upon them;
by the greatness of thine arm they shall be as still as a stone;
till thy people pass over, O LORD,
till the people pass over,
which thou hast purchased.

17 **Thou** shalt bring them in,
and plant them in the mountain of thine inheritance, in the place, O LORD, which thou hast made for thee to dwell in, in the Sanctuary, O Lord, which thy hands have established.

18 **The LORD** shall reign for ever and ever.

19 **For the horse of Pharaoh** went in with his chariots and with his horsemen into the sea,
and the LORD brought again the waters of the sea upon them;
but the children of Israel went on dry land in the midst of the sea.

20 **And Miriam the prophetess, the sister of Aaron,** took a timbrel in her hand;
and all the women went out after her with timbrels and with dances.

21 **And Miriam** answered them,
Sing ye to the LORD,
for he hath triumphed gloriously;
the horse and his rider hath he thrown into the sea.

22 **So Moses** brought Israel from the Red sea,
and they went out into the wilderness of Shur;
and they went three days in the wilderness,
and found no water.

23 **And when they** came to Marah,
they could not drink of the waters of Marah,
for they were bitter:
therefore the name of it was called Marah.

24 **And the people** murmured against Moses,
saying,
What shall we drink?

25 **And he** cried unto the LORD;
nd the LORD shewed him a tree,
which when he had cast into the waters,
the waters were made sweet:
there he made for them a statute and an ordinance,
and there he proved them,
26 **And** said,
If thou wilt diligently hearken to the voice of the LORD thy God,
and wilt do that which is right in his sight,
and wilt give ear to his commandments,
and keep all his statutes,
I will put none of these diseases upon thee,
which I have brought upon the Egyptians:
for I am the LORD that healeth thee.

27 **And they** came to Elim,
where were twelve wells of water, and threescore and ten palm trees:
and they encamped there by the waters.

16

And they took their journey from Elim,
and all the congregation of the children of Israel came unto the wilderness of Sin, {which is between Elim and Sinai}, on the fifteenth day of the second month after their departing out of the land of Egypt.

2 **And the whole congregation of the children of Israel** murmured against Moses and Aaron in the wilderness:

3 **And the children of Israel** said unto them,
Would to God we had died by the hand of the LORD in the land of Egypt,
when we sat by the flesh pots,
and when we did eat bread to the full;
for ye have brought us forth into this wilderness,
to kill this whole assembly with hunger.

4 **Then** said the LORD unto Moses,
Behold,
I will rain bread from heaven for you;
and the people shall go out and gather a certain rate every day,
that I may prove them,
whether they will walk in my law, or no.

5 **And it** shall come to pass,
that on the sixth day they shall prepare that which they bring in;
and it shall be twice as much as they gather daily.

6 **And Moses and Aaron** said unto all the children of Israel,
At even, then ye shall know
at the LORD hath brought you out from the land of Egypt:
7 **And in the morning,** then ye shall see the glory of the LORD;
for that he heareth your murmurings against the LORD:
and what are we,
that ye murmur against us?

8 **And Moses** said,
This shall be,
when the LORD shall give you in the evening flesh to eat, and in the morning bread to the full;
for that the LORD heareth your murmurings which ye murmur against him:
and what are we?
your murmurings are not against us, but against the LORD.

9 **And Moses** spake unto Aaron,
Say unto all the congregation of the children of Israel,
Come near before the LORD:
for he hath heard your murmurings.

10 **And it** came to pass,
as Aaron spake unto the whole congregation of the children of Israel,
that they looked toward the wilderness,
and, {behold}, the glory of the LORD appeared in the cloud.

11 **And the LORD** spake unto Moses, saying,

12 **I** have heard the murmurings of the children of Israel:
speak unto them,
saying,
At even ye shall eat flesh,
and in the morning ye shall be filled with bread;
and ye shall know
that I am the LORD your God.

13 **And it** came to pass
that at even the quails came up,
and covered the camp:
and in the morning the dew lay round about the host.

14 **And when the dew that lay** was gone up,
behold,
upon the face of the wilderness there lay a small round thing, as small as the hoar frost on the ground.

15 **And when the children of Israel** saw it,
they said one to another,
It is manna:
for they wist not
what it was.

And Moses said unto them,
This is the bread which the LORD hath given you to eat.

16 **This** is the thing which the LORD hath commanded,
Gather of it every man according to his eating, an omer for every man, according to the number of your persons;
take ye every man for them which are in his tents.

17 **And the children of Israel** did so,
and gathered, some more, some less.

18 **And when they** did mete it with an omer,
he that gathered much had nothing over,
and he that gathered little had no lack;

they gathered every man according to his eating.
19 **And Moses** said,
Let no man leave of it till the morning.
20 **Notwithstanding they** hearkened not unto Moses;
but some of them left of it until the morning,
and it bred worms,
and stank:
and Moses was wroth with them.
21 **And they** gathered it every morning, every man according to his eating:
and when the sun waxed hot,
it melted.
22 **And it** came to pass,
that on the sixth day they gathered twice as much bread, two omers for one man:
and all the rulers of the congregation came and told Moses.
23 **And he** said unto them,
This is that which the LORD hath said,
To morrow is the rest of the holy sabbath unto the LORD:
bake that which ye will bake to day,
and seethe that ye will seethe;
and that which remaineth over lay up for you to be kept until the morning.
24 **And they** laid it up till the morning,
as Moses bade:
and it did not stink,
neither was there any worm therein.
25 **And Moses** said,
Eat that to day;
for to day is a sabbath unto the LORD:
to day ye shall not find it in the field.
26 **Six days** ye shall gather it;
but on the seventh day, {which is the sabbath}, in it there shall be none.
27 **And it** came to pass,
that there went out some of the people on the seventh day
for to gather,
and they found none.
28 **And the LORD** said unto Moses,
How long refuse ye to keep my commandments and my laws?
29 **See,**
for that the LORD hath given you the sabbath,
therefore he giveth you on the sixth day the bread of two days;
abide ye every man in his place,
let no man go out of his place on the seventh day.
30 **So the people** rested on the seventh day.
31 **And the house of Israel** called the name thereof Manna:
and it was like coriander seed, white;
and the taste of it was like wafers made with honey.
32 **And Moses** said,
This is the thing which the LORD commandeth,
Fill an omer of it to be kept for your generations;
that they may see the bread wherewith I have fed you in the wilderness,
when I brought you forth from the land of Egypt.
33 **And Moses** said unto Aaron,
Take a pot,
and put an omer full of manna therein,
and lay it up before the LORD,
to be kept for your generations.
34 **As the LORD** commanded Moses,
so Aaron laid it up before the Testimony,
to be kept.
35 **And the children of Israel** did eat manna forty years,
until they came to a land inhabited;
they did eat manna,
until they came unto the borders of the land of Canaan.
36 **Now an omer** is the tenth part of an ephah.

17 **And all the congregation of the children of Israel** journeyed from the wilderness of Sin, after their journeys, according to the commandment of the LORD,
and pitched in Rephidim:
and there was no water for the people to drink.
2 **Wherefore the people** did chide with Moses,
and said,
Give us water
that we may drink.
And Moses said unto them,
Why chide ye with me?
wherefore do ye tempt the LORD?
3 **And the people** thirsted there for water;
and the people murmured against Moses,
and said,
Wherefore is this that thou hast brought us up out of Egypt,
to kill us and our children and our cattle with thirst?
4 **And Moses** cried unto the LORD,
saying,
What shall I do unto this people?
they be almost ready to stone me.
5 **And the LORD** said unto Moses,
Go on before the people,
and take with thee of the elders of Israel; and thy rod,
wherewith thou smotest the river,
take in thine hand,
and go.
6 **Behold,**
I will stand before thee there upon the rock in Horeb;
and thou shalt smite the rock,
and there shall come water out of it,
that the people may drink.
And Moses did so in the sight of the elders of Israel.
7 **And he** called the name of the place Massah, and Meribah, because of the chiding of the children of Israel,
and because they tempted the LORD,
saying,
Is the LORD among us, or not?
8 **Then** came Amalek,
and fought with Israel in Rephidim.
9 **And Moses** said unto Joshua,
Choose us out men,
and go out,
fight with Amalek:
to morrow I will stand on the top of the hill with the rod of God in mine hand.
10 **So Joshua** did as Moses had said to him,
and fought with Amalek:
and Moses, Aaron, and Hur went up to the top of the hill.
11 **And it** came to pass,
when Moses held up his hand,
that Israel prevailed:
and when he let down his hand,
Amalek prevailed.
12 **But Moses hands** were heavy;
and they took a stone,

and put it under him,
and he sat thereon;
and Aaron and Hur stayed up his hands, the one on the one side, and the other on the other side;
and his hands were steady
until the going down of the sun.
13 **And Joshua** discomfited Amalek and his people with the edge of the sword.
14 **And the LORD** said unto Moses,
Write this for a memorial in a book,
and rehearse it in the ears of Joshua:
for I will utterly put out the remembrance of Amalek from under heaven.
15 **And Moses** built an altar,
and called the name of it Jehovahnissi:
16 **For he** said,
Because the LORD hath sworn
that the LORD will have war with Amalek from generation to generation.

18 **When Jethro, the priest of Midian, Moses' father in law,** heard of all that God had done for Moses, and for Israel his people, and that the LORD had brought Israel out of Egypt;
2 **Then Jethro, Moses' father in law,** took Zipporah, Moses' wife,
after he had sent her back,
3 And her two sons;
of which the name of the one was Gershom;
for he said,
I have been an alien in a strange land:
4 **And the name of the other** was Eliezer;
for the God of my father, {said he}, was mine help,
and delivered me from the sword of Pharaoh:
5 **And Jethro, Moses' father in law,** came with his sons and his wife unto Moses into the wilderness,
where he encamped at the mount of God:
6 **And he** said unto Moses,
I thy father in law Jethro am come unto thee, and thy wife, and her two sons with her.
7 **And Moses** went out
to meet his father in law,
and did obeisance,
and kissed him;
and they asked each other of their welfare;
and they came into the tent.
8 **And Moses** told his father in law all that the LORD had done unto Pharaoh and to the Egyptians for Israel's sake, and all the travail that had come upon them by the way,
and how the LORD delivered them.
9 **And Jethro** rejoiced for all the goodness which the LORD had done to Israel,
whom he had delivered out of the hand of the Egyptians.
10 **And Jethro** said,
Blessed be the LORD,
who hath delivered you out of the hand of the Egyptians, and out of the hand of Pharaoh,
who hath delivered the people from under the hand of the Egyptians.
11 **Now I** know
that the LORD is greater than all gods:
for in the thing wherein they dealt proudly he was above them.
12 **And Jethro, Moses' father in law,** took a burnt offering and sacrifices for God:
and Aaron came, and all the elders of Israel,
to eat bread with Moses' father in law before God.
13 **And it** came to pass on the morrow,
that Moses sat to judge the people:
and the people stood by Moses from the morning unto the evening.
14 **And when Moses' father in law** saw all that he did to the people,
he said,
What is this thing that thou doest to the people?
why sittest thou thyself alone,
and all the people stand by thee from morning unto even?
15 **And Moses** said unto his father in law,
Because the people come unto me to enquire of God:
16 **When they** have a matter,
they come unto me;
and I judge between one and another,
and I do make them know the statutes of God, and his laws.
17 **And Moses' father in law** said unto him,
The thing that thou doest is not good.
18 **Thou** wilt surely wear away, both thou, and this people that is with thee:
for this thing is too heavy for thee;
thou art not able to perform it thyself alone.
19 **Hearken** now unto my voice,
I will give thee counsel,
and God shall be with thee:
Be thou for the people to God-ward,
that thou mayest bring the causes unto God:
20 **And thou** shalt teach them ordinances and laws,
and shalt shew them the way wherein they must walk, and the work that they must do.
21 **Moreover thou** shalt provide out of all the people able men,
such as fear God, men of truth, hating covetousness;
and place such over them,
to be rulers of thousands, and rulers of hundreds, rulers of fifties, and rulers of tens:
22 **And let them** judge the people at all seasons:
and it shall be,
that every great matter they shall bring unto thee,
but every small matter they shall judge:
so shall it be easier for thyself,
and they shall bear the burden with thee.
23 **If thou** shalt do this thing,
and God command thee so,
then thou shalt be able to endure,
and all this people shall also go to their place in peace.
24 **So Moses** hearkened to the voice of his father in law,
and did all that he had said.
25 **And Moses** chose able men out of all Israel,
and made them heads over the people, rulers of thousands, rulers of hundreds, rulers of fifties, and rulers of tens.
26 **And they** judged the people at all seasons:
the hard causes they brought unto Moses,
but every small matter they judged themselves.

27 **And Moses** let his father in law
depart;
and he went his way into his own
land.

19

In the third month,
{when the children of Israel
were gone forth out of the land of
Egypt}, the same day came they
into the wilderness of Sinai.
2 **For they** were departed from
Rephidim,
and were come to the desert of
Sinai,
and had pitched in the wilderness;
and there Israel camped before the
mount.
3 **And Moses** went up unto God,
and the LORD called unto him out
of the mountain,
saying,
hus shalt thou say to the house of
Jacob,
and tell the children of Israel;
4 **Ye** have seen what I did unto the
Egyptians,
and how I bare you on eagles'
wings,
and brought you unto myself.
5 **Now therefore, if ye** will obey my
voice indeed,
and keep my covenant,
then ye shall be a peculiar treasure
unto me above all people:
for all the earth is mine:
6 **And ye** shall be unto me a
kingdom of priests, and an holy
nation.
These are the words which thou
shalt speak unto the children of
Israel.
7 **And Moses** came and called for
the elders of the people,
and laid before their faces all these
words which the LORD
commanded him.
8 **And all the people** answered
together,
and said,
All that the LORD hath spoken we
will do.
And Moses returned the words of
the people unto the LORD.
9 **And the LORD** said unto Moses,
Lo,
I come unto thee in a thick cloud,
that the people may hear when I
speak with thee,
and believe thee for ever.
And Moses told the words of the
people unto the LORD.
10 **And the LORD** said unto Moses,
Go unto the people,
and sanctify them to day and to
morrow,
and let them wash their clothes,
11 **And be** ready against the third
day:
for the third day the LORD will
come down in the sight of all the
people upon mount Sinai.
12 **And thou** shalt set bounds unto
the people round about,
saying,
Take heed to yourselves,
that ye go not up into the mount,
or touch the border of it:
whosoever toucheth the mount
shall be surely put to death:
13 **There** shall not an hand touch it,
but he shall surely be stoned,
or shot through;
whether it be beast or man,
it shall not live:
hen the trumpet soundeth long,
they shall come up to the mount.
14 **And Moses** went down from the
mount unto the people,
and sanctified the people;
and they washed their clothes.
15 **And he** said unto the people,
Be ready against the third day:
come not at your wives.
16 **And it** came to pass on the third
day in the morning,
that there were thunders and
lightnings, and a thick cloud upon
the mount, and the voice of the
trumpet exceeding loud;
**so that all the people that was in
the camp** trembled.
17 **And Moses** brought forth the
people out of the camp
to meet with God;
and they stood at the nether part of
the mount.
18 **And mount Sinai** was altogether
on a smoke,
because the LORD descended upon
it in fire:
and the smoke thereof ascended
as the smoke of a furnace,
and the whole mount quaked
greatly.
19 **And when the voice of the
trumpet** sounded long,
and waxed louder and louder,
Moses spake,
and God answered him by a voice.
20 **And the LORD** came down upon
mount Sinai, on the top of the
mount:
and the LORD called Moses up to
the top of the mount;
and Moses went up.
21 **And the LORD** said unto Moses,
Go down,
charge the people,
lest they break through unto the
LORD to gaze,
and many of them perish.
22 **And let the priests** also, {which
come near to the LORD}, sanctify
themselves,
lest the LORD break forth upon
them.
23 **And Moses** said unto the LORD,
The people cannot come up to
mount Sinai:
for thou chargedst us, saying,
Set bounds about the mount,
and sanctify it.
24 **And the LORD** said unto him,
Away,
get thee down,
and thou shalt come up, thou, and
Aaron with thee:
**but let not the priests and the
people** break through to come up
unto the LORD,
lest he break forth upon them.
25 **So Moses** went down unto the
people,
and spake unto them.

20

And God spake all these
words,
saying,
2 **I** am the LORD thy God,
which have brought thee out of the
land of Egypt, out of the house of
bondage.
3 **Thou** shalt have no other gods
before me.
4 **Thou** shalt not make unto thee
any graven image, or any likeness
of any thing that is in heaven
above, or that is in the earth
beneath, or that is in the water
under the earth.
5 **Thou** shalt not bow down thyself
to them,
nor serve them:
for I the LORD thy God am a jealous
God,
visiting the iniquity of the fathers
upon the children unto the third
and fourth generation of them
that hate me;

6 **And** shewing mercy unto thousands of them that love me,
and keep my commandments.

7 **Thou** shalt not take the name of the LORD thy God in vain;
for the LORD will not hold him guiltless that taketh his name in vain.

8 **Remember** the sabbath day,
to keep it holy.

9 **Six days** shalt thou labour,
and do all thy work:
10 **But the seventh day** is the sabbath of the LORD thy God:
in it thou shalt not do any work, thou, nor thy son, nor thy daughter, thy manservant, nor thy maidservant, nor thy cattle, nor thy stranger that is within thy gates:
11 **For in six days** the LORD made heaven and earth, the sea, and all that in them is,
and rested the seventh day:
wherefore the LORD blessed the sabbath day,
and hallowed it.

12 **Honour** thy father and thy mother:
that thy days may be long upon the land which the LORD thy God giveth thee.

13 **Thou** shalt not kill.

14 **Thou** shalt not commit adultery.

15 **Thou** shalt not steal.

16 **Thou** shalt not bear false witness against thy neighbour.

17 **Thou** shalt not covet thy neighbour's house,
thou shalt not covet thy neighbour's wife, nor his manservant, nor his maidservant, nor his ox, nor his ass, nor any thing that is thy neighbour's.

18 **And all the people** saw the thunderings, and the lightnings, and the noise of the trumpet, and the mountain smoking:
and when the people saw it,
they removed,
and stood afar off.

19 **And they** said unto Moses,
Speak thou with us,
and we will hear:
but let not God speak with us,
lest we die.

20 **And Moses** said unto the people,
Fear not:
for God is come to prove you,
and that his fear may be before your faces,
that ye sin not.

21 **And the people** stood afar off,
and Moses drew near unto the thick darkness where God was.

22 **And the LORD** said unto Moses,
Thus thou shalt say unto the children of Israel,
Ye have seen that I have talked with you from heaven.

23 **Ye** shall not make with me gods of silver,
neither shall ye make unto you gods of gold.

24 **An altar of earth** thou shalt make unto me,
and shalt sacrifice thereon thy burnt offerings, and thy peace offerings, thy sheep, and thine oxen:
in all places where I record my name I will come unto thee,
and I will bless thee.

25 **And if thou** wilt make me an altar of stone,
thou shalt not build it of hewn stone:
for if thou lift up thy tool upon it,
thou hast polluted it.

26 **Neither** shalt thou go up by steps unto mine altar,
that thy nakedness be not discovered thereon.

21

Now these are the judgments which thou shalt set before them.

2 **If thou** buy an Hebrew servant,
six years he shall serve:
and in the seventh he shall go out free for nothing.

3 **If he** came in by himself,
he shall go out by himself:
if he were married,
then his wife shall go out with him.

4 **If his master** have given him a wife,
and she have born him sons or daughters;
the wife and her children shall be her master's,
and he shall go out by himself.

5 **And if the servant** shall plainly say,
I love my master, my wife, and my children;
I will not go out free:
6 **Then his master** shall bring him unto the judges;
he shall also bring him to the door, or unto the door post;
and his master shall bore his ear through with an aul;
and he shall serve him for ever.

7 **And if a man** sell his daughter to be a maidservant,
she shall not go out as the menservants do.

8 **If she** please not her master,
who hath betrothed her to himself,
then shall he let her be redeemed:
to sell her unto a strange nation
he shall have no power,
9 **And if he** have betrothed her unto his son,
he shall deal with her after the manner of daughters.

10 **If he** take him another wife;
her food, her raiment, and her duty of marriage, shall he not diminish.

11 **And if he** do not these three unto her,
then shall she go out free without money.

12 **He that smiteth a man, so that he die,** shall be surely put to death.

13 **And if a man** lie not in wait,
but God deliver him into his hand;
then I will appoint thee a place whither he shall flee.

14 **But if a man** come presumptuously upon his neighbour,
to slay him with guile;
thou shalt take him from mine altar,
that he may die.

15 **And he that smiteth his father, or his mother,** shall be surely put to death.

16 **And he that stealeth a man, and selleth him, or if he be found in his hand,** he shall surely be put to death.

17 **And he that curseth his father, or his mother,** shall surely be put to death.

18 **And if men** strive together,
and one smite another with a stone, or with his fist,
and he die not,
but keepeth his bed:
19 **If he** rise again,
and walk abroad upon his staff,
then shall he that smote him be quit:

only he shall pay for the loss of his time,
and shall cause him to be thoroughly healed.

20 **And if a man** smite his servant, or his maid, with a rod,
and he die under his hand;
he shall be surely punished.

21 **Notwithstanding, if he** continue a day or two,
he shall not be punished:
for he is his money.

22 **If men** strive,
and hurt a woman with child,
so that her fruit depart from her,
and yet no mischief follow:
he shall be surely punished,
according as the woman's husband will lay upon him;
and he shall pay as the judges determine.

23 **And if any mischief** follow,
then thou shalt give life for life,
24 Eye for eye, tooth for tooth, hand for hand, foot for foot,
25 Burning for burning, wound for wound, stripe for stripe.

26 **And if a man** smite the eye of his servant, or the eye of his maid,
that it perish;
he shall let him go free for his eye's sake.

27 **And if he** smite out his manservant's tooth, or his maidservant's tooth;
he shall let him go free for his tooth's sake.

28 **If an ox** gore a man or a woman,
that they die:
then the ox shall be surely stoned,
and his flesh shall not be eaten;
but the owner of the ox shall be quit.

29 **But if the ox** were wont to push with his horn in time past,
and it hath been testified to his owner,
and he hath not kept him in,
but that he hath killed a man or a woman;
the ox shall be stoned,
and his owner also shall be put to death.

30 **If there** be laid on him a sum of money,
then he shall give for the ransom of his life whatsoever is laid upon him.

31 **Whether he** have gored a son,
or have gored a daughter,
according to this judgment shall it be done unto him.

32 **If the ox** shall push a manservant or a maidservant;
he shall give unto their master thirty shekels of silver,
and the ox shall be stoned.

33 **And if a man** shall open a pit,
or if a man shall dig a pit,
and not cover it,
and an ox or an ass fall therein;
34 **The owner of the pit** shall make it good,
and give money unto the owner of them;
and the dead beast shall be his.

35 **And if one man's ox** hurt another's,
that he die;
en they shall sell the live ox,
and divide the money of it;
and the dead ox also they shall divide.

36 **Or if it be known** that the ox hath used to push in time past, and his owner hath not kept him in;
he shall surely pay ox for ox;
and the dead shall be his own.

22

If a man shall steal an ox, or a sheep,
and kill it,
or sell it;
he shall restore five oxen for an ox, and four sheep for a sheep.

2 **If a thief** be found breaking up,
and be smitten
that he die,
there shall no blood be shed for him.

3 **If the sun** be risen upon him,
there shall be blood shed for him;
for he should make full restitution;
if he have nothing,
then he shall be sold for his theft.

4 **If the theft** be certainly found in his hand alive,
whether it be ox, or ass, or sheep;
he shall restore double.

5 **If a man** shall cause a field or vineyard to be eaten,
and shall put in his beast,
and shall feed in another man's field;
of the best of his own field, and of the best of his own vineyard, shall he make restitution.

6 **If fire** break out,
and catch in thorns,
so that the stacks of corn, or the standing corn, or the field, be consumed therewith;
he that kindled the fire shall surely make restitution.

7 **If a man** shall deliver unto his neighbour money or stuff to keep,
and it be stolen out of the man's house;
if the thief be found,
let him pay double.

8 **If the thief** be not found,
then the master of the house shall be brought unto the judges,
to see whether he have put his hand unto his neighbour's goods.

9 **For all manner of trespass,** {whether it be for ox, for ass, for sheep, for raiment, or for any manner of lost thing which another challengeth to be his}, the cause of both parties shall come before the judges;
and whom the judges shall condemn,
he shall pay double unto his neighbour.

10 **If a man** deliver unto his neighbour an ass, or an ox, or a sheep, or any beast,
to keep;
and it die,
or be hurt,
or driven away,
no man seeing it:
11 **Then** shall an oath of the LORD be between them both,
that he hath not put his hand unto his neighbour's goods;
and the owner of it shall accept thereof,
and he shall not make it good.

12 **And if it** be stolen from him,
he shall make restitution unto the owner thereof.

13 **If it** be torn in pieces,
then let him bring it for witness,
and he shall not make good that which was torn.

14 **And if a man** borrow ought of his neighbour,
and it be hurt,
or die,
the owner thereof being not with it,
he shall surely make it good.

15 **But if the owner thereof** be with it,
he shall not make it good:

if it be an hired thing,
it came for his hire.

16 **And if a man** entice a maid that is not betrothed,
and lie with her,
he shall surely endow her to be his wife.

17 **If her father** utterly refuse to give her unto him,
he shall pay money according to the dowry of virgins.

18 **Thou** shalt not suffer a witch to live.

19 **Whosoever lieth with a beast** shall surely be put to death.

20 **He that sacrificeth unto any god, save unto the LORD only,** he shall be utterly destroyed.

21 **Thou** shalt neither vex a stranger,
nor oppress him:
for ye were strangers in the land of Egypt.

22 **Ye** shall not afflict any widow, or fatherless child.

23 **If thou** afflict them in any wise,
and they cry at all unto me,
I will surely hear their cry;
24 **And my wrath** shall wax hot,
and I will kill you with the sword;
and your wives shall be widows, and your children fatherless.

25 **If thou** lend money to any of my people that is poor by thee,
thou shalt not be to him as an usurer,
neither shalt thou lay upon him usury.

26 **If thou** at all take thy neighbour's raiment to pledge,
thou shalt deliver it unto him
by that the sun goeth down:
27 **For that** is his covering only,
it is his raiment for his skin:
wherein shall he sleep?
and it shall come to pass,
when he crieth unto me,
that I will hear;
for I am gracious.

28 **Thou** shalt not revile the gods,
nor curse the ruler of thy people.

29 **Thou** shalt not delay to offer the first of thy ripe fruits, and of thy liquors:
the firstborn of thy sons shalt thou give unto me.

30 **Likewise** shalt thou do with thine oxen, and with thy sheep:
seven days it shall be with his dam;
on the eighth day thou shalt give it me.

31 **And ye** shall be holy men unto me:
neither shall ye eat any flesh that is torn of beasts in the field;
ye shall cast it to the dogs.

23 **Thou** shalt not raise a false report:
put not thine hand with the wicked to be an unrighteous witness.

2 **Thou** shalt not follow a multitude to do evil;
neither shalt thou speak in a cause to decline after many
to wrest judgment:
3 **Neither** shalt thou countenance a poor man in his cause.

4 **If thou** meet thine enemy's ox or his ass going astray,
thou shalt surely bring it back to him again.

5 **If thou** see the ass of him that hateth thee lying under his burden,
and wouldest forbear to help him,
thou shalt surely help with him.

6 **Thou** shalt not wrest the judgment of thy poor in his cause.

7 **Keep thee** far from a false matter;
and the innocent and righteous slay thou not:
for I will not justify the wicked.

8 **And thou** shalt take no gift:
for the gift blindeth the wise,
and perverteth the words of the righteous.

9 **Also thou** shalt not oppress a stranger:
for ye know the heart of a stranger,
seeing ye were strangers in the land of Egypt.

10 **And six years** thou shalt sow thy land,
and shalt gather in the fruits thereof:
11 **But the seventh year** thou shalt let it rest and lie still
that the poor of thy people may eat:
and what they leave
the beasts of the field shall eat.
In like manner thou shalt deal with thy vineyard, and with thy oliveyard.

12 **Six days** thou shalt do thy work,
and on the seventh day thou shalt rest:
that thine ox and thine ass may rest,
and the son of thy handmaid, and the stranger, may be refreshed.

13 **And in all things that I have said unto you** be circumspect:
and make no mention of the name of other gods,
neither let it be heard out of thy mouth.

14 **Three times** thou shalt keep a feast unto me in the year.

15 **Thou** shalt keep the feast of unleavened bread: ({thou shalt eat unleavened bread seven days}, {as I commanded thee, in the time appointed of the month Abib}; {for in it thou camest out from Egypt}: {and none shall appear before me empty}:)
16 And the feast of harvest, the firstfruits of thy labours, {which thou hast sown in the field}: and the feast of ingathering, {which is in the end of the year}, {when thou hast gathered in thy labours out of the field}.

17 **Three times in the year** all thy males shall appear before the Lord GOD.

18 **Thou** shalt not offer the blood of my sacrifice with leavened bread;
neither shall the fat of my sacrifice remain until the morning.

19 **The first of the firstfruits of thy land** thou shalt bring into the house of the LORD thy God.
Thou shalt not seethe a kid in his mother's milk.

20 **Behold,**
I send an Angel before thee,
to keep thee in the way,
and to bring thee into the place which I have prepared.

21 **Beware** of him,
and obey his voice,
provoke him not;
for he will not pardon your transgressions:
for my name is in him.

22 **But if thou** shalt indeed obey his voice,
and do all that I speak;
then I will be an enemy unto thine enemies, and an adversary unto thine adversaries.

23 **For mine Angel** shall go before thee,
and bring thee in unto the Amorites, and the Hittites, and the Perizzites, and the

Canaanites, the Hivites, and the Jebusites:
and I will cut them off.
24 **Thou** shalt not bow down to their gods,
nor serve them,
nor do after their works:
but thou shalt utterly overthrow them,
and quite break down their images.
25 **And ye** shall serve the LORD your God,
and he shall bless thy bread, and thy water;
and I will take sickness away from the midst of thee.
26 **There** shall nothing cast their young,
nor be barren, in thy land:
the number of thy days I will fulfil.
27 **I** will send my fear before thee,
and will destroy all the people to whom thou shalt come,
and I will make all thine enemies turn their backs unto thee.
28 **And I** will send hornets before thee,
which shall drive out the Hivite, the Canaanite, and the Hittite, from before thee.
29 **I** will not drive them out from before thee in one year;
lest the land become desolate,
and the beast of the field multiply against thee.
30 **By little and little** I will drive them out from before thee,
until thou be increased,
and inherit the land.
31 **And I** will set thy bounds from the Red sea even unto the sea of the Philistines, and from the desert unto the river:
for I will deliver the inhabitants of the land into your hand;
and thou shalt drive them out before thee.
32 **Thou** shalt make no covenant with them, nor with their gods.
33 **They** shall not dwell in thy land,
lest they make thee sin against me:
for if thou serve their gods,
it will surely be a snare unto thee.

24

And he said unto Moses,
Come up unto the LORD, thou, and Aaron, Nadab, and Abihu, and seventy of the elders of Israel;
and worship ye afar off.
2 **And Moses alone** shall come near the LORD:
but they shall not come nigh;
neither shall the people go up with him.
3 **And Moses** came and told the people all the words of the LORD, and all the judgments:
and all the people answered with one voice,
and said,
All the words which the LORD hath said will we do.
4 **And Moses** wrote all the words of the LORD,
and rose up early in the morning,
and builded an altar under the hill, and twelve pillars, according to the twelve tribes of Israel.
5 **And he** sent young men of the children of Israel,
which offered burnt offerings,
and sacrificed peace offerings of oxen unto the LORD.
6 **And Moses** took half of the blood,
and put it in basons;
and half of the blood he sprinkled on the altar.
7 **And he** took the book of the covenant,
and read in the audience of the people:
and they said,
All that the LORD hath said will we do,
and be obedient.
8 **And Moses** took the blood,
and sprinkled it on the people,
and said,
Behold the blood of the covenant,
which the LORD hath made with you concerning all these words.
9 **Then** went up Moses, and Aaron, Nadab, and Abihu, and seventy of the elders of Israel:
10 **And they** saw the God of Israel:
and there was under his feet as it were a paved work of a sapphire stone, and as it were the body of heaven in his clearness.
11 **And upon the nobles of the children of Israel** he laid not his hand:
also they saw God,
and did eat and drink.
12 **And the LORD** said unto Moses,
Come up to me into the mount,
and be there:
and I will give thee tables of stone, and a law, and commandments which I have written;
that thou mayest teach them.
13 **And Moses** rose up, and his minister Joshua:
and Moses went up into the mount of God.
14 **And he** said unto the elders,
Tarry ye here for us,
until we come again unto you:
and, {behold}, Aaron and Hur are with you:
if any man have any matters to do,
let him come unto them.
15 **And Moses** went up into the mount,
and a cloud covered the mount.
16 **And the glory of the LORD** abode upon mount Sinai,
and the cloud covered it six days:
and the seventh day he called unto Moses out of the midst of the cloud.
17 **And the sight of the glory of the LORD** was like devouring fire on the top of the mount in the eyes of the children of Israel.
18 **And Moses** went into the midst of the cloud,
and gat him up into the mount:
and Moses was in the mount forty days and forty nights.

25

And the LORD spake unto Moses,
saying,
2 **Speak** unto the children of Israel,
that they bring me an offering:
of every man that giveth it willingly with his heart ye shall take my offering.
3 **And this** is the offering which ye shall take of them; gold, and silver, and brass,
4 And blue, and purple, and scarlet, and fine linen, and goats' hair,
5 And rams' skins dyed red, and badgers' skins, and shittim wood,
6 Oil for the light, spices for anointing oil, and for sweet incense,
7 Onyx stones, and stones to be set in the ephod, and in the breastplate.
8 **And let them** make me a sanctuary;
that I may dwell among them.
9 **According to all that I shew thee, after the pattern of the**

tabernacle, and the pattern of all the instruments thereof, even so shall ye make it.

10 **And they** shall make an ark of shittim wood:
two cubits and a half shall be the length thereof, and a cubit and a half the breadth thereof, and a cubit and a half the height thereof.

11 **And thou** shalt overlay it with pure gold,
within and without shalt thou overlay it,
and shalt make upon it a crown of gold round about.

12 **And thou** shalt cast four rings of gold for it,
and put them in the four corners thereof;
and two rings shall be in the one side of it, and two rings in the other side of it.

13 **And thou** shalt make staves of shittim wood,
and overlay them with gold.

14 **And thou** shalt put the staves into the rings by the sides of the ark,
that the ark may be borne with them.

15 **The staves** shall be in the rings of the ark:
they shall not be taken from it.

16 **And thou** shalt put into the ark the testimony which I shall give thee.

17 **And thou** shalt make a mercy seat of pure gold:

18 **And thou** shalt make two cherubims of gold,
of beaten work shalt thou make them, in the two ends of the mercy seat.

19 **And make** one cherub on the one end, and the other cherub on the other end:
even of the mercy seat shall ye make the cherubims on the two ends thereof.

20 **And the cherubims** shall stretch forth their wings on high,
covering the mercy seat with their wings,
and their faces shall look one to another;
toward the mercy seat shall the faces of the cherubims be.

21 **And thou** shalt put the mercy seat above upon the ark;
and in the ark thou shalt put the testimony that I shall give thee.

22 **And there** I will meet with thee,
and I will commune with thee from above the mercy seat, from between the two cherubims which are upon the ark of the testimony, of all things which I will give thee in commandment unto the children of Israel.

23 **Thou** shalt also make a table of shittim wood:
two cubits shall be the length thereof, and a cubit the breadth thereof, and a cubit and a half the height thereof.

24 **And thou** shalt overlay it with pure gold,
and make thereto a crown of gold round about.

25 **And thou** shalt make unto it a border of an hand breadth round about,
and thou shalt make a golden crown to the border thereof round about.

26 **And thou** shalt make for it four rings of gold,
and put the rings in the four corners that are on the four feet thereof.

27 **Over against the border** shall the rings be for places of the staves to bear the table.

28 **And thou** shalt make the staves of shittim wood,
and overlay them with gold,
that the table may be borne with them.

29 **And thou** shalt make the dishes thereof, and spoons thereof, and covers thereof, and bowls thereof,
to cover withal:
of pure gold shalt thou make them.

30 **And thou** shalt set upon the table shewbread before me alway.

31 **And thou** shalt make a candlestick of pure gold:
of beaten work shall the candlestick be made:
his shaft, and his branches, his bowls, his knops, and his flowers, shall be of the same.

32 **And six branches** shall come out of the sides of it; three branches of the candlestick out of the one side, and three branches of the candlestick out of the other side:

33 Three bowls made like unto almonds, with a knop and a flower in one branch; and three bowls made like almonds in the other branch, with a knop and a flower: so in the six branches that come out of the candlestick.

34 **And in the candlesticks** shall be four bowls made like unto almonds, with their knops and their flowers.

35 **And there** shall be a knop under two branches of the same, and a knop under two branches of the same, and a knop under two branches of the same, according to the six branches that proceed out of the candlestick.

36 **Their knops and their branches** shall be of the same:
all it shall be one beaten work of pure gold.

37 **And thou** shalt make the seven lamps thereof:
and they shall light the lamps thereof,
that they may give light over against it.

38 **And the tongs thereof, and the snuffdishes thereof,** shall be of pure gold.

39 **Of a talent of pure gold** shall he make it, with all these vessels.

40 **And look** that thou make them after their pattern,
which was shewed thee in the mount.

26

Moreover thou shalt make the tabernacle with ten curtains of fine twined linen, and blue, and purple, and scarlet:
with cherubims of cunning work shalt thou make them.

2 **The length of one curtain** shall be eight and twenty cubits, and the breadth of one curtain four cubits:
and every one of the curtains shall have one measure.

3 **The five curtains** shall be coupled together one to another;
and other five curtains shall be coupled one to another.

4 **And thou** shalt make loops of blue upon the edge of the one curtain from the selvedge in the coupling;
and likewise shalt thou make in the uttermost edge of another curtain, in the coupling of the second.

5 **Fifty loops** shalt thou make in the one curtain,

and fifty loops shalt thou make in the edge of the curtain that is in the coupling of the second;
that the loops may take hold one of another.

6 **And thou** shalt make fifty taches of gold,
and couple the curtains together with the taches:
and it shall be one tabernacle.

7 **And thou** shalt make curtains of goats' hair to be a covering upon the tabernacle:
eleven curtains shalt thou make.

8 **The length of one curtain** shall be thirty cubits, and the breadth of one curtain four cubits:
and the eleven curtains shall be all of one measure.

9 **And thou** shalt couple five curtains by themselves, and six curtains by themselves,
and shalt double the sixth curtain in the forefront of the tabernacle.

10 **And thou** shalt make fifty loops on the edge of the one curtain that is outmost in the coupling, and fifty loops in the edge of the curtain which coupleth the second.

11 **And thou** shalt make fifty taches of brass,
and put the taches into the loops,
and couple the tent together,
that it may be one.

12 **And the remnant that remaineth of the curtains of the tent, the half curtain that remaineth,** shall hang over the backside of the tabernacle.

13 **And a cubit on the one side, and a cubit on the other side of that which remaineth in the length of the curtains of the tent,** it shall hang over the sides of the tabernacle on this side and on that side,
to cover it.

14 **And thou** shalt make a covering for the tent of rams' skins dyed red, and a covering above of badgers' skins.

15 **And thou** shalt make boards for the tabernacle of shittim wood standing up.

16 **Ten cubits** shall be the length of a board,
and a cubit and a half shall be the breadth of one board.

17 **Two tenons** shall there be in one board,
set in order one against another:
thus shalt thou make for all the boards of the tabernacle.

18 **And thou** shalt make the boards for the tabernacle, twenty boards on the south side southward.

19 **And thou** shalt make forty sockets of silver under the twenty boards; two sockets under one board for his two tenons, and two sockets under another board for his two tenons.

20 **And for the second side of the tabernacle on the north side** there shall be twenty boards:
21 And their forty sockets of silver; two sockets under one board, and two sockets under another board.

22 **And for the sides of the tabernacle westward** thou shalt make six boards.

23 **And two boards** shalt thou make for the corners of the tabernacle in the two sides.

24 **And they** shall be coupled together beneath,
and they shall be coupled together above the head of it unto one ring:
thus shall it be for them both;
they shall be for the two corners.

25 **And they** shall be eight boards, and their sockets of silver, sixteen sockets; two sockets under one board, and two sockets under another board.

26 **And thou** shalt make bars of shittim wood; five for the boards of the one side of the tabernacle,
27 And five bars for the boards of the other side of the tabernacle, and five bars for the boards of the side of the tabernacle, for the two sides westward.

28 **And the middle bar in the midst of the boards** shall reach from end to end.

29 **And thou** shalt overlay the boards with gold,
and make their rings of gold for places for the bars:
and thou shalt overlay the bars with gold.

30 **And thou** shalt rear up the tabernacle according to the fashion thereof which was shewed thee in the mount.

31 **And thou** shalt make a vail of blue, and purple, and scarlet, and fine twined linen of cunning work:
with cherubims shall it be made:

32 **And thou** shalt hang it upon four pillars of shittim wood overlaid with gold:
their hooks shall be of gold, upon the four sockets of silver.

33 **And thou** shalt hang up the vail under the taches,
that thou mayest bring in thither within the vail the ark of the testimony:
and the vail shall divide unto you between the holy place and the most holy.

34 **And thou** shalt put the mercy seat upon the ark of the testimony in the most holy place.

35 **And thou** shalt set the table without the vail, and the candlestick over against the table on the side of the tabernacle toward the south:
and thou shalt put the table on the north side.

36 **And thou** shalt make an hanging for the door of the tent, of blue, and purple, and scarlet, and fine twined linen,
wrought with needlework.

37 **And thou** shalt make for the hanging five pillars of shittim wood,
and overlay them with gold,
and their hooks shall be of gold:
and thou shalt cast five sockets of brass for them.

27

And thou shalt make an altar of shittim wood, five cubits long, and five cubits broad;
the altar shall be foursquare:
and the height thereof shall be three cubits.

2 **And thou** shalt make the horns of it upon the four corners thereof:
his horns shall be of the same:
and thou shalt overlay it with brass.

3 **And thou** shalt make his pans to receive his ashes, and his shovels, and his basons, and his fleshhooks, and his firepans:
all the vessels thereof thou shalt make of brass.

4 **And thou** shalt make for it a grate of network of brass;

and upon the net shalt thou make four brasen rings in the four corners thereof.

5 **And thou** shalt put it under the compass of the altar beneath,
that the net may be even to the midst of the altar.

6 **And thou** shalt make staves for the altar, staves of shittim wood,
and overlay them with brass.

7 **And the staves** shall be put into the rings,
and the staves shall be upon the two sides of the altar,
to bear it.

8 **Hollow with boards** shalt thou make it:
as it was shewed thee in the mount,
so shall they make it.

9 **And thou** shalt make the court of the tabernacle:
for the south side southward there shall be hangings for the court of fine twined linen of an hundred cubits long for one side:

10 **And the twenty pillars thereof and their twenty sockets** shall be of brass;
the hooks of the pillars and their fillets shall be of silver.

11 **And likewise for the north side in length** there shall be hangings of an hundred cubits long, and his twenty pillars and their twenty sockets of brass; the hooks of the pillars and their fillets of silver.

12 **And for the breadth of the court on the west side** shall be hangings of fifty cubits: their pillars ten, and their sockets ten.

13 **And the breadth of the court on the east side eastward** shall be fifty cubits.

14 **The hangings of one side of the gate** shall be fifteen cubits: their pillars three, and their sockets three.

15 **And on the other side** shall be hangings fifteen cubits: their pillars three, and their sockets three.

16 **And for the gate of the court** shall be an hanging of twenty cubits, of blue, and purple, and scarlet, and fine twined linen,
wrought with needlework:
and their pillars shall be four, and their sockets four.

17 **All the pillars round about the court** shall be filleted with silver;
their hooks shall be of silver, and their sockets of brass.

18 **The length of the court** shall be an hundred cubits, and the breadth fifty every where, and the height five cubits of fine twined linen, and their sockets of brass.

19 **All the vessels of the tabernacle in all the service thereof, and all the pins thereof, and all the pins of the court,** shall be of brass.

20 **And thou** shalt command the children of Israel,
that they bring thee pure oil olive beaten for the light,
to cause the lamp to burn always.

21 **In the tabernacle of the congregation without the vail**, {which is before the testimony}, Aaron and his sons shall order it from evening to morning before the LORD:
it shall be a statute for ever unto their generations on the behalf of the children of Israel.

28

And take thou unto thee Aaron thy brother, and his sons with him, from among the children of Israel,
that he may minister unto me in the priest's office, even Aaron, Nadab and Abihu, Eleazar and Ithamar, Aaron's sons.

2 **And thou** shalt make holy garments for Aaron thy brother for glory and for beauty.

3 **And thou** shalt speak unto all that are wise hearted,
whom I have filled with the spirit of wisdom,
that they may make Aaron's garments
to consecrate him,
that he may minister unto me in the priest's office.

4 **And these** are the garments which they shall make; a breastplate, and an ephod, and a robe, and a broidered coat, a mitre, and a girdle:
and they shall make holy garments for Aaron thy brother, and his sons,
that he may minister unto me in the priest's office.

5 **And they** shall take gold, and blue, and purple, and scarlet, and fine linen.

6 **And they** shall make the ephod of gold, of blue, and of purple, of scarlet, and fine twined linen, with cunning work.

7 **It** shall have the two shoulderpieces thereof joined at the two edges thereof;
and so it shall be joined together.

8 **And the curious girdle of the ephod**, {which is upon it}, shall be of the same, according to the work thereof; even of gold, of blue, and purple, and scarlet, and fine twined linen.

9 **And thou** shalt take two onyx stones,
and grave on them the names of the children of Israel:

10 Six of their names on one stone, and the other six names of the rest on the other stone, according to their birth.

11 **With the work of an engraver in stone, like the engravings of a signet,** shalt thou engrave the two stones with the names of the children of Israel:
thou shalt make them to be set in ouches of gold.

12 **And thou** shalt put the two stones upon the shoulders of the ephod for stones of memorial unto the children of Israel:
and Aaron shall bear their names before the LORD upon his two shoulders for a memorial.

13 **And thou** shalt make ouches of gold;

14 And two chains of pure gold at the ends;
of wreathen work shalt thou make them,
and fasten the wreathen chains to the ouches.

15 **And thou** shalt make the breastplate of judgment with cunning work;
after the work of the ephod thou shalt make it;
of gold, of blue, and of purple, and of scarlet, and of fine twined linen, shalt thou make it.

16 **Foursquare** it shall be
being doubled;
a span shall be the length thereof,
and a span shall be the breadth thereof.

17 **And thou** shalt set in it settings of stones, even four rows of stones:
the first row shall be a sardius, a topaz, and a carbuncle:
this shall be the first row.
18 **And the second row** shall be an emerald, a sapphire, and a diamond.
19 **And the third row** a ligure, an agate, and an amethyst.
20 **And the fourth row** a beryl, and an onyx, and a jasper:
they shall be set in gold in their inclosings.
21 **And the stones** shall be with the names of the children of Israel, twelve, according to their names, like the engravings of a signet;
every one with his name shall they be according to the twelve tribes.
22 **And thou** shalt make upon the breastplate chains at the ends of wreathen work of pure gold.
23 **And thou** shalt make upon the breastplate two rings of gold,
and shalt put the two rings on the two ends of the breastplate.
24 **And thou** shalt put the two wreathen chains of gold in the two rings which are on the ends of the breastplate.
25 **And the other two ends of the two wreathen chains** thou shalt fasten in the two ouches,
and put them on the shoulderpieces of the ephod before it.
26 **And thou** shalt make two rings of gold,
and thou shalt put them upon the two ends of the breastplate in the border thereof,
which is in the side of the ephod inward.
27 **And two other rings of gold** thou shalt make,
and shalt put them on the two sides of the ephod underneath, toward the forepart thereof, over against the other coupling thereof, above the curious girdle of the ephod.
28 **And they** shall bind the breastplate by the rings thereof unto the rings of the ephod with a lace of blue,
that it may be above the curious girdle of the ephod
and that the breastplate be not loosed from the ephod.
29 **And Aaron** shall bear the names of the children of Israel in the breastplate of judgment upon his heart,
when he goeth in unto the holy place, for a memorial before the LORD continually.
30 **And thou** shalt put in the breastplate of judgment the Urim and the Thummim;
and they shall be upon Aaron's heart,
when he goeth in before the LORD:
and Aaron shall bear the judgment of the children of Israel upon his heart before the LORD continually.
31 **And thou** shalt make the robe of the ephod all of blue.
32 **And there** shall be an hole in the top of it, in the midst thereof:
it shall have a binding of woven work round about the hole of it,
as it were the hole of an habergeon,
that it be not rent.
33 **And beneath upon the hem of it** thou shalt make pomegranates of blue, and of purple, and of scarlet, round about the hem thereof; and bells of gold between them round about:
34 A golden bell and a pomegranate, a golden bell and a pomegranate, upon the hem of the robe round about.
35 **And it** shall be upon Aaron to minister:
and his sound shall be heard when he goeth in unto the holy place before the LORD, and when he cometh out,
that he die not.
36 **And thou** shalt make a plate of pure gold,
and grave upon it, like the engravings of a signet, Holiness To The LORD.
37 **And thou** shalt put it on a blue lace,
that it may be upon the mitre;
upon the forefront of the mitre it shall be.
38 **And it** shall be upon Aaron's forehead,
that Aaron may bear the iniquity of the holy things,
which the children of Israel shall hallow in all their holy gifts;
and it shall be always upon his forehead,
that they may be accepted before the LORD.
39 **And thou** shalt embroider the coat of fine linen, and thou shalt make the mitre of fine linen, and thou shalt make the girdle of needlework.
40 And for Aaron's sons thou shalt make coats,
and thou shalt make for them girdles,
and bonnets shalt thou make for them, for glory and for beauty.
41 **And thou** shalt put them upon Aaron thy brother, and his sons with him;
and shalt anoint them,
and consecrate them,
and sanctify them,
that they may minister unto me in the priest's office.
42 **And thou** shalt make them linen breeches
to cover their nakedness;
from the loins even unto the thighs they shall reach:
43 **And they** shall be upon Aaron, and upon his sons,
when they come in unto the tabernacle of the congregation,
or when they come near unto the altar
to minister in the holy place;
that they bear not iniquity,
and die:
it shall be a statute for ever unto him and his seed after him.

29 **And this** is the thing that thou shalt do unto them to hallow them,
to minister unto me in the priest's office:
Take one young bullock, and two rams without blemish,
2 And unleavened bread, and cakes unleavened tempered with oil, and wafers unleavened anointed with oil:
of wheaten flour shalt thou make them.
3 **And thou** shalt put them into one basket,
and bring them in the basket, with the bullock and the two rams.
4 **And Aaron and his sons** thou shalt bring unto the door of the tabernacle of the congregation,
and shalt wash them with water.
5 **And thou** shalt take the garments,

and put upon Aaron the coat, and the robe of the ephod, and the ephod, and the breastplate,
and gird him with the curious girdle of the ephod:

6 **And thou** shalt put the mitre upon his head,
and put the holy crown upon the mitre.

7 **Then** shalt thou take the anointing oil,
and pour it upon his head,
and anoint him.

8 **And thou** shalt bring his sons,
and put coats upon them.

9 **And thou** shalt gird them with girdles, Aaron and his sons,
and put the bonnets on them:
and the priest's office shall be theirs for a perpetual statute:
and thou shalt consecrate Aaron and his sons.

10 **And thou** shalt cause a bullock to be brought before the tabernacle of the congregation:
and Aaron and his sons shall put their hands upon the head of the bullock.

11 **And thou** shalt kill the bullock before the LORD, by the door of the tabernacle of the congregation.

12 **And thou** shalt take of the blood of the bullock,
and put it upon the horns of the altar with thy finger,
and pour all the blood beside the bottom of the altar.

13 **And thou** shalt take all the fat that covereth the inwards, and the caul that is above the liver, and the two kidneys, and the fat that is upon them,
and burn them upon the altar.

14 **But the flesh of the bullock, and his skin, and his dung,** shalt thou burn with fire without the camp:
it is a sin offering.

15 **Thou** shalt also take one ram;
and Aaron and his sons shall put their hands upon the head of the ram.

16 **And thou** shalt slay the ram,
and thou shalt take his blood,
and sprinkle it round about upon the altar.

17 **And thou** shalt cut the ram in pieces,
and wash the inwards of him, and his legs,
and put them unto his pieces, and unto his head.

18 **And thou** shalt burn the whole ram upon the altar:
it is a burnt offering unto the LORD:
it is a sweet savour, an offering made by fire unto the LORD.

19 **And thou** shalt take the other ram;
and Aaron and his sons shall put their hands upon the head of the ram.

20 **Then** shalt thou kill the ram,
and take of his blood,
and put it upon the tip of the right ear of Aaron, and upon the tip of the right ear of his sons, and upon the thumb of their right hand, and upon the great toe of their right foot,
and sprinkle the blood upon the altar round about.

21 **And thou** shalt take of the blood that is upon the altar, and of the anointing oil,
and sprinkle it upon Aaron, and upon his garments, and upon his sons, and upon the garments of his sons with him:
and he shall be hallowed, and his garments, and his sons, and his sons' garments with him.

22 **Also thou** shalt take of the ram the fat and the rump, and the fat that covereth the inwards, and the caul above the liver, and the two kidneys, and the fat that is upon them, and the right shoulder;
for it is a ram of consecration:

23 And one loaf of bread, and one cake of oiled bread, and one wafer out of the basket of the unleavened bread that is before the LORD:

24 **And thou** shalt put all in the hands of Aaron, and in the hands of his sons;
and shalt wave them for a wave offering before the LORD.

25 **And thou** shalt receive them of their hands,
and burn them upon the altar for a burnt offering, for a sweet savour before the LORD:
it is an offering made by fire unto the LORD.

26 **And thou** shalt take the breast of the ram of Aaron's consecration,
and wave it for a wave offering before the LORD:
and it shall be thy part.

27 **And thou** shalt sanctify the breast of the wave offering, and the shoulder of the heave offering,
which is waved,
and which is heaved up, of the ram of the consecration, even of that which is for Aaron, and of that which is for his sons:

28 **And it** shall be Aaron's and his sons' by a statute for ever from the children of Israel:
for it is an heave offering:
and it shall be an heave offering from the children of Israel of the sacrifice of their peace offerings, even their heave offering unto the LORD.

29 **And the holy garments of Aaron** shall be his sons' after him,
to be anointed therein,
and to be consecrated in them.

30 **And that son that is priest in his stead** shall put them on seven days,
when he cometh into the tabernacle of the congregation
to minister in the holy place.

31 **And thou** shalt take the ram of the consecration,
and seethe his flesh in the holy place.

32 **And Aaron and his sons** shall eat the flesh of the ram, and the bread that is in the basket by the door of the tabernacle of the congregation.

33 **And they** shall eat those things wherewith the atonement was made,
to consecrate and to sanctify them:
but a stranger shall not eat thereof,
because they are holy.

34 **And if ought of the flesh of the consecrations, or of the bread,** remain unto the morning,
then thou shalt burn the remainder with fire:
it shall not be eaten,
because it is holy.

35 **And thus** shalt thou do unto Aaron, and to his sons, according to all things which I have commanded thee:
seven days shalt thou consecrate them.

36 **And thou** shalt offer every day a bullock for a sin offering for atonement:
and thou shalt cleanse the altar,
when thou hast made an atonement for it,
and thou shalt anoint it,
to sanctify it.
37 **Seven days** thou shalt make an atonement for the altar,
and sanctify it;
and it shall be an altar most holy:
whatsoever toucheth the altar shall be holy.
38 **Now this** is that which thou shalt offer upon the altar; two lambs of the first year day by day continually.
39 **The one lamb** thou shalt offer in the morning;
and the other lamb thou shalt offer at even:
40 **And with the one lamb** a tenth deal of flour mingled with the fourth part of an hin of beaten oil; and the fourth part of an hin of wine for a drink offering.
41 **And the other lamb** thou shalt offer at even,
and shalt do thereto according to the meat offering of the morning, and according to the drink offering thereof, for a sweet savour, an offering made by fire unto the LORD.
42 **This** shall be a continual burnt offering throughout your generations at the door of the tabernacle of the congregation before the LORD:
where I will meet you,
to speak there unto thee.
43 **And there** I will meet with the children of Israel,
and the tabernacle shall be sanctified by my glory.
44 **And I** will sanctify the tabernacle of the congregation, and the altar:
I will sanctify also both Aaron and his sons,
to minister to me in the priest's office.
45 **And I** will dwell among the children of Israel,
and will be their God.
46 **And they** shall know
that I am the LORD their God,
that brought them forth out of the land of Egypt,
that I may dwell among them:
I am the LORD their God.

30 ∞ **And thou** shalt make an altar to burn incense upon:
of shittim wood shalt thou make it.
2 **A cubit** shall be the length thereof, and a cubit the breadth thereof;
foursquare shall it be:
and two cubits shall be the height thereof:
the horns thereof shall be of the same.
3 **And thou** shalt overlay it with pure gold, the top thereof, and the sides thereof round about, and the horns thereof;
and thou shalt make unto it a crown of gold round about.
4 **And two golden rings** shalt thou make to it under the crown of it, by the two corners thereof,
upon the two sides of it shalt thou make it;
and they shall be for places for the staves
to bear it withal.
5 **And thou** shalt make the staves of shittim wood,
and overlay them with gold.
6 **And thou** shalt put it before the vail that is by the ark of the testimony, before the mercy seat that is over the testimony,
where I will meet with thee.
7 **And Aaron** shall burn thereon sweet incense every morning:
when he dresseth the lamps,
he shall burn incense upon it.
8 **And when Aaron** lighteth the lamps at even,
he shall burn incense upon it, a perpetual incense before the LORD throughout your generations.
9 **Ye** shall offer no strange incense thereon, nor burnt sacrifice, nor meat offering;
neither shall ye pour drink offering thereon.
10 **And Aaron** shall make an atonement upon the horns of it once in a year with the blood of the sin offering of atonements:
once in the year shall he make atonement upon it throughout your generations:
it is most holy unto the LORD.
11 **And the LORD** spake unto Moses, saying,
12 **When thou** takest the sum of the children of Israel after their number,
then shall they give every man a ransom for his soul unto the LORD,
when thou numberest them;
that there be no plague among them,
when thou numberest them.
13 **This** they shall give, every one that passeth among them that are numbered, half a shekel after the shekel of the sanctuary:
(a shekel is twenty gerahs:)
an half shekel shall be the offering of the LORD.
14 **Every one that passeth among them that are numbered, from twenty years old and above,** shall give an offering unto the LORD.
15 **The rich** shall not give more,
and the poor shall not give less than half a shekel,
when they give an offering unto the LORD,
to make an atonement for your souls.
16 **And thou** shalt take the atonement money of the children of Israel,
and shalt appoint it for the service of the tabernacle of the congregation;
that it may be a memorial unto the children of Israel before the LORD,
to make an atonement for your souls.
17 **And the LORD** spake unto Moses, saying,
18 **Thou** shalt also make a laver of brass, and his foot also of brass,
to wash withal:
and thou shalt put it between the tabernacle of the congregation and the altar,
and thou shalt put water therein.
19 **For Aaron and his sons** shall wash their hands and their feet thereat:
20 **When they** go into the tabernacle of the congregation,
they shall wash with water,
that they die not;
or when they come near to the altar
to minister,

to burn offering made by fire unto the LORD:
21 **So they** shall wash their hands and their feet,
that they die not:
and it shall be a statute for ever to them, even to him and to his seed throughout their generations.

22 **Moreover the LORD** spake unto Moses,
saying,
23 **Take thou** also unto thee principal spices, of pure myrrh five hundred shekels, and of sweet cinnamon half so much, even two hundred and fifty shekels, and of sweet calamus two hundred and fifty shekels,
24 And of cassia five hundred shekels, after the shekel of the sanctuary, and of oil olive an hin:
25 **And thou** shalt make it an oil of holy ointment, an ointment compound after the art of the apothecary:
it shall be an holy anointing oil.

26 **And thou** shalt anoint the tabernacle of the congregation therewith, and the ark of the testimony,
27 And the table and all his vessels, and the candlestick and his vessels, and the altar of incense,
28 And the altar of burnt offering with all his vessels, and the laver and his foot.

29 **And thou** shalt sanctify them,
that they may be most holy:
whatsoever toucheth them shall be holy.

30 **And thou** shalt anoint Aaron and his sons,
and consecrate them,
that they may minister unto me in the priest's office.

31 **And thou** shalt speak unto the children of Israel,
saying,
This shall be an holy anointing oil unto me throughout your generations.

32 **Upon man's flesh** shall it not be poured,
neither shall ye make any other like it, after the composition of it:
it is holy,
and it shall be holy unto you.

33 **Whosoever compoundeth any like it, or whosoever putteth any of it upon a stranger,** shall even be cut off from his people.

34 **And the LORD** said unto Moses,
Take unto thee sweet spices, stacte, and onycha, and galbanum; these sweet spices with pure frankincense:
of each shall there be a like weight:
35 **And thou** shalt make it a perfume, a confection after the art of the apothecary,
tempered together, pure and holy:
36 **And thou** shalt beat some of it very small,
and put of it before the testimony in the tabernacle of the congregation,
where I will meet with thee:
it shall be unto you most holy.

37 **And as for the perfume which thou shalt make,** ye shall not make to yourselves according to the composition thereof:
it shall be unto thee holy for the LORD.

38 **Whosoever shall make like unto that**, {to smell thereto}, shall even be cut off from his people.

31 **And the LORD** spake unto Moses,
saying,
2 **See,**
I have called by name Bezaleel the son of Uri, the son of Hur, of the tribe of Judah:
3 **And I** have filled him with the spirit of God, in wisdom, and in understanding, and in knowledge, and in all manner of workmanship,
4 To devise cunning works,
to work in gold, and in silver, and in brass,
5 And in cutting of stones, {to set them}, and in carving of timber, {to work in all manner of workmanship}.

6 **And I, {behold}, I** have given with him Aholiab, the son of Ahisamach, of the tribe of Dan:
and in the hearts of all that are wise hearted I have put wisdom,
that they may make all that I have commanded thee;
7 The tabernacle of the congregation, and the ark of the testimony, and the mercy seat that is thereupon, and all the furniture of the tabernacle,
8 And the table and his furniture, and the pure candlestick with all his furniture, and the altar of incense,
9 And the altar of burnt offering with all his furniture, and the laver and his foot,
10 And the cloths of service, and the holy garments for Aaron the priest, and the garments of his sons,
to minister in the priest's office,
11 And the anointing oil, and sweet incense for the holy place:
according to all that I have commanded thee shall they do.

12 **And the LORD** spake unto Moses,
saying,
13 **Speak thou** also unto the children of Israel,
saying,
Verily my sabbaths ye shall keep:
for it is a sign between me and you throughout your generations;
that ye may know
that I am the LORD that doth sanctify you.

14 **Ye** shall keep the sabbath therefore;
for it is holy unto you:
every one that defileth it shall surely be put to death:
for whosoever doeth any work therein,
that soul shall be cut off from among his people.

15 **Six days** may work be done;
but in the seventh is the sabbath of rest, holy to the LORD:
whosoever doeth any work in the sabbath day,
he shall surely be put to death.

16 **Wherefore the children of Israel** shall keep the sabbath, {to observe the sabbath throughout their generations}, for a perpetual covenant.

17 **It** is a sign between me and the children of Israel for ever:
for in six days the LORD made heaven and earth,
and on the seventh day he rested,
and was refreshed.

18 **And he** gave unto Moses, {when he had made an end of communing with him upon mount Sinai}, two tables of testimony, tables of stone, written with the finger of God.

32 **And when the people** saw that Moses delayed to come down out of the mount,

the people gathered themselves together unto Aaron,
and said unto him,
Up,
make us gods,
which shall go before us;
for as for this Moses, the man that brought us up out of the land of Egypt, we wot not
what is become of him.
2 **And Aaron** said unto them,
Break off the golden earrings,
which are in the ears of your wives, of your sons, and of your daughters,
and bring them unto me.
3 **And all the people** brake off the golden earrings which were in their ears,
and brought them unto Aaron.
4 **And he** received them at their hand,
and fashioned it with a graving tool,
after he had made it a molten calf:
and they said,
These be thy gods, O Israel,
which brought thee up out of the land of Egypt.
5 **And when Aaron** saw it,
he built an altar before it;
and Aaron made proclamation,
and said,
To morrow is a feast to the LORD.
6 **And they** rose up early on the morrow,
and offered burnt offerings,
and brought peace offerings;
and the people sat down
to eat and to drink,
and rose up
to play.
7 **And the LORD** said unto Moses,
Go,
get thee down;
for thy people, {which thou broughtest out of the land of Egypt}, have corrupted themselves:
8 **They** have turned aside quickly out of the way which I commanded them:
they have made them a molten calf,
and have worshipped it,
and have sacrificed thereunto,
and said,
These be thy gods, O Israel,
which have brought thee up out of the land of Egypt.
9 **And the LORD** said unto Moses,
I have seen this people,
and, {behold}, it is a stiffnecked people:
10 **Now therefore let me** alone,
that my wrath may wax hot against them,
and that I may consume them:
and I will make of thee a great nation.
11 **And Moses** besought the LORD his God,
and said,
LORD, why doth thy wrath wax hot against thy people,
which thou hast brought forth out of the land of Egypt with great power, and with a mighty hand?
12 **Wherefore** should the Egyptians speak,
and say,
For mischief did he bring them out,
to slay them in the mountains,
and to consume them from the face of the earth?
Turn from thy fierce wrath,
and repent of this evil against thy people.
13 **Remember** Abraham, Isaac, and Israel, thy servants,
to whom thou swarest by thine own self,
and saidst unto them,
I will multiply your seed as the stars of heaven,
and all this land that I have spoken of will I give unto your seed,
and they shall inherit it for ever.
14 **And the LORD** repented of the evil which he thought to do unto his people.
15 **And Moses** turned,
and went down from the mount,
and the two tables of the testimony were in his hand:
the tables were written on both their sides;
on the one side and on the other were they written.
16 **And the tables** were the work of God,
and the writing was the writing of God,
graven upon the tables.
17 **And when Joshua** heard the noise of the people as they shouted,
he said unto Moses,
There is a noise of war in the camp.
18 **And he** said,
It is not the voice of them that shout for mastery,
neither is it the voice of them that cry for being overcome:
but the noise of them that sing do I hear.
19 **And it** came to pass,
as soon as he came nigh unto the camp,
that he saw the calf, and the dancing:
and Moses' anger waxed hot,
and he cast the tables out of his hands,
and brake them beneath the mount.
20 **And he** took the calf which they had made,
and burnt it in the fire,
and ground it to powder,
and strawed it upon the water,
and made the children of Israel drink of it.
21 **And Moses** said unto Aaron,
What did this people unto thee,
that thou hast brought so great a sin upon them?
22 **And Aaron** said,
Let not the anger of my lord wax hot:
thou knowest the people,
that they are set on mischief.
23 **For they** said unto me,
Make us gods,
which shall go before us:
for as for this Moses, the man that brought us up out of the land of Egypt, we wot not
what is become of him.
24 **And I** said unto them,
Whosoever hath any gold,
let them break it off.
So they gave it me:
then I cast it into the fire,
and there came out this calf.
25 **And when Moses** saw that the people were naked;
(for Aaron had made them naked unto their shame among their enemies:)
26 **Then Moses** stood in the gate of the camp,
and said,
Who is on the LORD's side?
let him come unto me.
And all the sons of Levi gathered themselves together unto him.
27 **And he** said unto them,
Thus saith the LORD God of Israel,
Put every man his sword by his side,

and go in and out from gate to gate throughout the camp,
and slay every man his brother, and every man his companion, and every man his neighbour.

28 **And the children of Levi** did according to the word of Moses:
and there fell of the people that day about three thousand men.

29 **For Moses** had said,
Consecrate yourselves today to the LORD, even every man upon his son, and upon his brother;
that he may bestow upon you a blessing this day.

30 **And it** came to pass on the morrow,
that Moses said unto the people,
Ye have sinned a great sin:
and now I will go up unto the LORD;
peradventure I shall make an atonement for your sin.

31 **And Moses** returned unto the LORD,
and said,
Oh, this people have sinned a great sin,
and have made them gods of gold.

32 **Yet now, {if thou wilt}** forgive their sin—;
and if not, blot me, {I pray thee}, out of thy book which thou hast written.

33 **And the LORD** said unto Moses,
Whosoever hath sinned against me,
him will I blot out of my book.

34 **Therefore now go,**
lead the people unto the place of which I have spoken unto thee:
behold,
mine Angel shall go before thee:
nevertheless in the day when I visit I will visit their sin upon them.

35 **And the LORD** plagued the people,
because they made the calf,
which Aaron made.

33

And the LORD said unto Moses,
Depart,
and go up hence, thou and the people which thou hast brought up out of the land of Egypt, unto the land which I sware unto Abraham, to Isaac, and to Jacob,
saying,
Unto thy seed will I give it:

2 **And I** will send an angel before thee;
and I will drive out the Canaanite, the Amorite, and the Hittite, and the Perizzite, the Hivite, and the Jebusite:

3 Unto a land flowing with milk and honey:
for I will not go up in the midst of thee;
for thou art a stiffnecked people:
lest I consume thee in the way.

4 **And when the people** heard these evil tidings,
they mourned:
and no man did put on him his ornaments.

5 **For the LORD** had said unto Moses,
Say unto the children of Israel,
Ye are a stiffnecked people:
I will come up into the midst of thee in a moment,
and consume thee:
therefore now put off thy ornaments from thee,
that I may know
what to do unto thee.

6 **And the children of Israel** stripped themselves of their ornaments by the mount Horeb.

7 **And Moses** took the tabernacle,
and pitched it without the camp, afar off from the camp,
and called it the Tabernacle of the congregation.
And it came to pass,
that every one which sought the LORD went out unto the tabernacle of the congregation,
which was without the camp.

8 **And it** came to pass,
when Moses went out unto the tabernacle,
that all the people rose up,
and stood every man at his tent door,
and looked after Moses,
until he was gone into the tabernacle.

9 **And it** came to pass,
as Moses entered into the tabernacle,
the cloudy pillar descended,
and stood at the door of the tabernacle,
and the LORD talked with Moses.

10 **And all the people** saw the cloudy pillar stand at the tabernacle door:
and all the people rose up and worshipped, every man in his tent door.

11 **And the LORD** spake unto Moses face to face,
as a man speaketh unto his friend.
And he turned again into the camp:
but his servant Joshua, the son of Nun, a young man, departed not out of the tabernacle.

12 **And Moses** said unto the LORD,
See,
thou sayest unto me,
Bring up this people:
and thou hast not let me know
whom thou wilt send with me.
Yet thou hast said,
I know thee by name,
and thou hast also found grace in my sight.

13 **Now therefore, {I pray thee}, if I** have found grace in thy sight,
shew me now thy way,
that I may know thee,
that I may find grace in thy sight:
and consider that this nation is thy people.

14 **And he** said,
My presence shall go with thee,
and I will give thee rest.

15 **And he** said unto him,
If thy presence go not with me,
carry us not up hence.

16 **For wherein** shall it be known here
that I and thy people have found grace in thy sight?
is it not in that thou goest with us?
so shall we be separated, I and thy people, from all the people that are upon the face of the earth.

17 **And the LORD** said unto Moses,
I will do this thing also that thou hast spoken:
for thou hast found grace in my sight,
and I know thee by name.

18 **And he** said,
I beseech thee,
shew me thy glory.

19 **And he** said,
I will make all my goodness pass before thee,
and I will proclaim the name of the LORD before thee;
and will be gracious to whom I will be gracious,
and will shew mercy on whom I

will shew mercy.
20 **And he** said,
Thou canst not see my face:
for there shall no man see me,
and live.
21 **And the LORD** said,
Behold,
there is a place by me,
and thou shalt stand upon a rock:
22 **And it** shall come to pass,
while my glory passeth by,
that I will put thee in a clift of the rock,
and will cover thee with my hand
while I pass by:
23 **And I** will take away mine hand,
and thou shalt see my back parts:
but my face shall not be seen.

34 **And the LORD** said unto Moses,
Hew thee two tables of stone like unto the first:
and I will write upon these tables the words that were in the first tables,
which thou brakest.
2 **And be** ready in the morning,
and come up in the morning unto mount Sinai,
and present thyself there to me in the top of the mount.
3 **And no man** shall come up with thee,
neither let any man be seen throughout all the mount;
neither let the flocks nor herds feed before that mount.
4 **And he** hewed two tables of stone like unto the first;
and Moses rose up early in the morning,
and went up unto mount Sinai,
as the LORD had commanded him,
and took in his hand the two tables of stone.
5 **And the LORD** descended in the cloud,
and stood with him there
and proclaimed the name of the LORD.
6 **And the LORD** passed by before him,
and proclaimed,
The LORD, The LORD God, merciful and gracious, longsuffering, and abundant in goodness and truth,
7 Keeping mercy for thousands,
forgiving iniquity and transgression and sin,
and that will by no means clear the guilty;
visiting the iniquity of the fathers upon the children, and upon the children's children, unto the third and to the fourth generation.
8 **And Moses** made haste,
and bowed his head toward the earth,
and worshipped.
9 **And he** said,
If now I have found grace in thy sight, O Lord,
let my Lord, {I pray thee}, go among us;
for it is a stiffnecked people;
and pardon our iniquity and our sin,
and take us for thine inheritance.
10 **And he** said,
Behold,
I make a covenant:
before all thy people I will do marvels,
such as have not been done in all the earth, nor in any nation:
and all the people among which thou art shall see the work of the LORD:
for it is a terrible thing that I will do with thee.
11 **Observe thou** that which I command thee this day:
behold,
I drive out before thee the Amorite, and the Canaanite, and the Hittite, and the Perizzite, and the Hivite, and the Jebusite.
12 **Take heed** to thyself,
lest thou make a covenant with the inhabitants of the land whither thou goest,
lest it be for a snare in the midst of thee:
13 **But ye** shall destroy their altars,
break their images,
and cut down their groves:
14 **For thou** shalt worship no other god:
for the LORD, {whose name is Jealous}, is a jealous God:
15 **Lest thou** make a covenant with the inhabitants of the land,
and they go a whoring after their gods,
and do sacrifice unto their gods,
and one call thee,
and thou eat of his sacrifice;
16 **And thou** take of their daughters unto thy sons,
and their daughters go a whoring after their gods,
and make thy sons go a whoring after their gods.
17 **Thou** shalt make thee no molten gods.
18 **The feast of unleavened bread** shalt thou keep.
Seven days thou shalt eat unleavened bread,
as I commanded thee, in the time of the month Abib:
for in the month Abib thou camest out from Egypt.
19 **All that openeth the matrix** is mine; and every firstling among thy cattle, whether ox or sheep, that is male.
20 **But the firstling of an ass** thou shalt redeem with a lamb:
and if thou redeem him not,
then shalt thou break his neck.
All the firstborn of thy sons thou shalt redeem.
And none shall appear before me empty.
21 **Six days** thou shalt work,
but on the seventh day thou shalt rest:
in earing time and in harvest thou shalt rest.
22 **And thou** shalt observe the feast of weeks, of the firstfruits of wheat harvest, and the feast of ingathering at the year's end.
23 **Thrice in the year** shall all your menchildren appear before the Lord GOD, the God of Israel.
24 **For I** will cast out the nations before thee,
and enlarge thy borders:
neither shall any man desire thy land,
when thou shalt go up to appear before the LORD thy God thrice in the year.
25 **Thou** shalt not offer the blood of my sacrifice with leaven;
neither shall the sacrifice of the feast of the passover be left unto the morning.
26 **The first of the firstfruits of thy land** thou shalt bring unto the house of the LORD thy God.
Thou shalt not seethe a kid in his mother's milk.
27 **And the LORD** said unto Moses,

Write thou these words:
for after the tenor of these words I have made a covenant with thee and with Israel.
28 **And he** was there with the LORD forty days and forty nights;
he did neither eat bread,
nor drink water.
And he wrote upon the tables the words of the covenant, the ten commandments.
29 **And it** came to pass,
when Moses came down from mount Sinai with the two tables of testimony in Moses' hand,
when he came down from the mount,
that Moses wist not
that the skin of his face shone
while he talked with him.
30 **And when Aaron and all the children of Israel** saw Moses,
behold,
the skin of his face shone; and they were afraid to come nigh him.
31 **And Moses** called unto them;
and Aaron and all the rulers of the congregation returned unto him:
and Moses talked with them.
32 **And afterward** all the children of Israel came nigh:
and he gave them in commandment all that the LORD had spoken with him in mount Sinai.
33 **And till Moses** had done speaking with them,
he put a vail on his face.
34 **But when Moses** went in before the LORD
to speak with him,
he took the vail off,
until he came out.
And he came out,
and spake unto the children of Israel that which he was commanded.
35 **And the children of Israel** saw the face of Moses,
that the skin of Moses' face shone:
and Moses put the vail upon his face again,
until he went in
to speak with him.

35 **And Moses** gathered all the congregation of the children of Israel together,
and said unto them,
These are the words which the LORD hath commanded,
that ye should do them.
2 **Six days** shall work be done,
but on the seventh day there shall be to you an holy day, a sabbath of rest to the LORD:
whosoever doeth work therein shall be put to death.
3 **Ye** shall kindle no fire throughout your habitations upon the sabbath day.
4 **And Moses** spake unto all the congregation of the children of Israel,
saying,
This is the thing which the LORD commanded,
saying,
5 **Take ye** from among you an offering unto the LORD:
whosoever is of a willing heart,
let him bring it, an offering of the LORD; gold, and silver, and brass,
6 And blue, and purple, and scarlet, and fine linen, and goats' hair,
7 And rams' skins dyed red, and badgers' skins, and shittim wood,
8 And oil for the light, and spices for anointing oil, and for the sweet incense,
9 And onyx stones, and stones to be set for the ephod, and for the breastplate.
10 **And every wise hearted among you** shall come,
and make all that the LORD hath commanded;
11 The tabernacle, his tent, and his covering, his taches, and his boards, his bars, his pillars, and his sockets,
12 The ark, and the staves thereof, with the mercy seat, and the vail of the covering,
13 The table, and his staves, and all his vessels, and the shewbread,
14 The candlestick also for the light, and his furniture, and his lamps, with the oil for the light,
15 And the incense altar, and his staves, and the anointing oil, and the sweet incense, and the hanging for the door at the entering in of the tabernacle,
16 The altar of burnt offering, with his brasen grate, his staves, and all his vessels, the laver and his foot,
17 The hangings of the court, his pillars, and their sockets, and the hanging for the door of the court,
18 The pins of the tabernacle, and the pins of the court, and their cords,
19 The cloths of service, {to do service in the holy place}, the holy garments for Aaron the priest, and the garments of his sons, {to minister in the priest's office}.
20 **And all the congregation of the children of Israel** departed from the presence of Moses.
21 **And they** came, every one whose heart stirred him up, and every one whom his spirit made willing,
and they brought the LORD's offering to the work of the tabernacle of the congregation, and for all his service, and for the holy garments.
22 **And they** came, both men and women,
as many as were willing hearted,
and brought bracelets, and earrings, and rings, and tablets, all jewels of gold:
and every man that offered offered an offering of gold unto the LORD.
23 **And every man**, {with whom was found blue, and purple, and scarlet, and fine linen, and goats' hair, and red skins of rams, and badgers' skins}, brought them.
24 **Every one that did offer an offering of silver and brass** brought the LORD's offering:
and every man, {with whom was found shittim wood for any work of the service}, brought it.
25 **And all the women that were wise hearted** did spin with their hands,
and brought that which they had spun, both of blue, and of purple, and of scarlet, and of fine linen.
26 **And all the women whose heart stirred them up in wisdom** spun goats' hair.
27 **And the rulers** brought onyx stones,
and stones to be set, for the ephod, and for the breastplate;
28 And spice, and oil for the light, and for the anointing oil, and for the sweet incense.
29 **The children of Israel** brought a willing offering unto the LORD, every man and woman,

whose heart made them willing to bring for all manner of work,
which the LORD had commanded to be made by the hand of Moses.

30 **And Moses** said unto the children of Israel,
See,
the LORD hath called by name Bezaleel the son of Uri, the son of Hur, of the tribe of Judah;
31 **And he** hath filled him with the spirit of God, in wisdom, in understanding, and in knowledge, and in all manner of workmanship;
32 **And** to devise curious works,
to work in gold, and in silver, and in brass,
33 And in the cutting of stones, {to set them}, and in carving of wood, {to make any manner of cunning work}.

34 **And he** hath put in his heart that he may teach, both he, and Aholiab, the son of Ahisamach, of the tribe of Dan.

35 **Them** hath he filled with wisdom of heart,
to work all manner of work, of the engraver, and of the cunning workman, and of the embroiderer, in blue, and in purple, in scarlet, and in fine linen, and of the weaver, even of them that do any work, and of those that devise cunning work.

36

Then wrought Bezaleel and Aholiab, and every wise hearted man,
in whom the LORD put wisdom and understanding to know how to work all manner of work for the service of the sanctuary, according to all that the LORD had commanded.

2 **And Moses** called Bezaleel and Aholiab, and every wise hearted man,
in whose heart the LORD had put wisdom, even every one whose heart stirred him up to come unto the work to do it:
3 **And they** received of Moses all the offering,
which the children of Israel had brought for the work of the service of the sanctuary,
to make it withal.
And they brought yet unto him free offerings every morning.

4 **And all the wise men,** {that wrought all the work of the sanctuary}, came every man from his work which they made;
5 **And they** spake unto Moses,
saying,
The people bring much more than enough for the service of the work,
which the LORD commanded to make.

6 **And Moses** gave commandment,
and they caused it to be proclaimed throughout the camp,
saying,
Let neither man nor woman make any more work for the offering of the sanctuary.

So the people were restrained from bringing.

7 **For the stuff they had** was sufficient for all the work to make it, and too much.

8 **And every wise hearted man among them that wrought the work of the tabernacle** made ten curtains of fine twined linen, and blue, and purple, and scarlet:
with cherubims of cunning work made he them.

9 **The length of one curtain** was twenty and eight cubits, and the breadth of one curtain four cubits:
the curtains were all of one size.

10 **And he** coupled the five curtains one unto another:
and the other five curtains he coupled one unto another.

11 **And he** made loops of blue on the edge of one curtain from the selvedge in the coupling:
likewise he made in the uttermost side of another curtain, in the coupling of the second.

12 **Fifty loops** made he in one curtain,
and fifty loops made he in the edge of the curtain which was in the coupling of the second:
the loops held one curtain to another.

13 **And he** made fifty taches of gold,
and coupled the curtains one unto another with the taches:
so it became one tabernacle.

14 **And he** made curtains of goats' hair for the tent over the tabernacle:
eleven curtains he made them.

15 **The length of one curtain** was thirty cubits,
and four cubits was the breadth of one curtain:
the eleven curtains were of one size.

16 **And he** coupled five curtains by themselves, and six curtains by themselves.

17 **And he** made fifty loops upon the uttermost edge of the curtain in the coupling,
and fifty loops made he upon the edge of the curtain which coupleth the second.

18 **And he** made fifty taches of brass
to couple the tent together,
that it might be one.

19 **And he** made a covering for the tent of rams' skins dyed red, and a covering of badgers' skins above that.

20 **And he** made boards for the tabernacle of shittim wood,
standing up.

21 **The length of a board** was ten cubits, and the breadth of a board one cubit and a half.

22 **One board** had two tenons, equally distant one from another:
thus did he make for all the boards of the tabernacle.

23 **And he** made boards for the tabernacle; twenty boards for the south side southward:
24 **And forty sockets of silver** he made under the twenty boards; two sockets under one board for his two tenons, and two sockets under another board for his two tenons.

25 **And for the other side of the tabernacle,** {which is toward the north corner}, he made twenty boards,
26 And their forty sockets of silver; two sockets under one board, and two sockets under another board.

27 **And for the sides of the tabernacle westward** he made six boards.

28 **And two boards** made he for the corners of the tabernacle in the two sides.

29 **And they** were coupled beneath,
and coupled together at the head thereof, to one ring:
thus he did to both of them in both the corners.

30 **And there** were eight boards;
and their sockets were sixteen
sockets of silver, under every
board two sockets.
31 **And he** made bars of shittim
wood; five for the boards of the
one side of the tabernacle,
32 And five bars for the boards of the
other side of the tabernacle, and
five bars for the boards of the
tabernacle for the sides westward.
33 **And he** made the middle bar to
shoot through the boards from
the one end to the other.
34 **And he** overlaid the boards with
gold,
and made their rings of gold to be
places for the bars,
and overlaid the bars with gold.
35 **And he** made a vail of blue, and
purple, and scarlet, and fine
twined linen:
with cherubims made he it of
cunning work.
36 **And he** made thereunto four
pillars of shittim wood,
and overlaid them with gold:
their hooks were of gold;
and he cast for them four sockets of
silver.
37 **And he** made an hanging for the
tabernacle door of blue, and
purple, and scarlet, and fine
twined linen, of needlework;
38 And the five pillars of it with their
hooks:
and he overlaid their chapiters and
their fillets with gold:
but their five sockets were of
brass.

37 **And Bezaleel** made the ark
of shittim wood:
two cubits and a half was the
length of it, and a cubit and a half
the breadth of it, and a cubit and a
half the height of it:
2 **And he** overlaid it with pure gold
within and without,
and made a crown of gold to it
round about.
3 **And he** cast for it four rings of
gold,
to be set by the four corners of it;
even two rings upon the one side
of it, and two rings upon the other
side of it.
4 **And he** made staves of shittim
wood,
and overlaid them with gold.
5 **And he** put the staves into the
rings by the sides of the ark,
to bear the ark.
6 **And he** made the mercy seat of
pure gold:
two cubits and a half was the
length thereof, and one cubit and
a half the breadth thereof.
7 **And he** made two cherubims of
gold, {beaten out of one piece
made he them}, on the two ends
of the mercy seat;
8 One cherub on the end on this
side, and another cherub on the
other end on that side:
out of the mercy seat made he the
cherubims on the two ends
thereof.
9 **And the cherubims** spread out
their wings on high,
and covered with their wings over
the mercy seat, with their faces
one to another;
even to the mercy seatward were
the faces of the cherubims.
10 **And he** made the table of shittim
wood:
two cubits was the length thereof,
and a cubit the breadth thereof,
and a cubit and a half the height
thereof:
11 **And he** overlaid it with pure gold,
and made thereunto a crown of
gold round about.
12 **Also he** made thereunto a border
of an handbreadth round about;
and made a crown of gold for the
border thereof round about.
13 **And he** cast for it four rings of
gold,
and put the rings upon the four
corners that were in the four feet
thereof.
14 **Over against the border** were the
rings,
the places for the staves to bear
the table.
15 **And he** made the staves of shittim
wood,
and overlaid them with gold,
to bear the table.
16 **And he** made the vessels which
were upon the table, his dishes,
and his spoons, and his bowls,
and his covers to cover withal, of
pure gold.
17 **And he** made the candlestick of
pure gold:
of beaten work made he the
candlestick;
**his shaft, and his branch, his
bowls, his knops, and his
flowers**, were of the same:
18 And six branches going out of the
sides thereof; three branches of
the candlestick out of the one side
thereof, and three branches of the
candlestick out of the other side
thereof:
19 Three bowls made after the
fashion of almonds in one branch,
a knop and a flower; and three
bowls made like almonds in
another branch, a knop and a
flower: so throughout the six
branches going out of the
candlestick.
20 **And in the candlestick** were four
bowls made like almonds, his
knops, and his flowers:
21 And a knop under two branches of
the same, and a knop under two
branches of the same, and a knop
under two branches of the same,
according to the six branches
going out of it.
22 **Their knops and their branches**
were of the same:
all of it was one beaten work of
pure gold.
23 **And he** made his seven lamps,
and his snuffers, and his
snuffdishes, of pure gold.
24 **Of a talent of pure gold** made he
it, and all the vessels thereof.
25 **And he** made the incense altar of
shittim wood:
the length of it was a cubit, and the
breadth of it a cubit;
it was foursquare;
and two cubits was the height of it;
the horns thereof were of the
same.
26 **And he** overlaid it with pure gold,
both the top of it, and the sides
thereof round about, and the
horns of it:
also he made unto it a crown of
gold round about.
27 **And he** made two rings of gold for
it under the crown thereof, by the
two corners of it, upon the two
sides thereof, to be places for the
staves to bear it withal.
28 **And he** made the staves of shittim
wood,
and overlaid them with gold.
29 **And he** made the holy anointing
oil, and the pure incense of sweet

spices, according to the work of
the apothecary.

38 **And he** made the altar of
burnt offering of shittim
wood:
five cubits was the length thereof,
and five cubits the breadth
thereof;
it was foursquare; and three cubits
the height thereof.
2 **And he** made the horns thereof on
the four corners of it;
the horns thereof were of the
same:
and he overlaid it with brass.
3 **And he** made all the vessels of the
altar, the pots, and the shovels,
and the basons, and the
fleshhooks, and the firepans:
all the vessels thereof made he of
brass.
4 **And he** made for the altar a brasen
grate of network under the
compass thereof beneath unto the
midst of it.
5 **And he** cast four rings for the four
ends of the grate of brass,
to be places for the staves.
6 **And he** made the staves of shittim
wood,
and overlaid them with brass.
7 **And he** put the staves into the
rings on the sides of the altar,
to bear it withal;
he made the altar hollow with
boards.
8 **And he** made the laver of brass,
and the foot of it of brass, of the
lookingglasses of the women
assembling,
which assembled at the door of the
tabernacle of the congregation.
9 **And he** made the court:
on the south side southward the
hangings of the court were of fine
twined linen, an hundred cubits:
10 **Their pillars** were twenty, and
their brasen sockets twenty;
**the hooks of the pillars and their
fillets** were of silver.
11 **And for the north side the
hangings** were an hundred
cubits,
their pillars were twenty, and their
sockets of brass twenty; the hooks
of the pillars and their fillets of
silver.
12 **And for the west side** were
hangings of fifty cubits, their
pillars ten, and their sockets ten;
the hooks of the pillars and their
fillets of silver.
13 **And for the east side eastward**
fifty cubits.
14 **The hangings of the one side of
the gate** were fifteen cubits; their
pillars three, and their sockets
three.
15 **And for the other side of the
court gate, on this hand and
that hand,** were hangings of
fifteen cubits; their pillars three,
and their sockets three.
16 **All the hangings of the court
round about** were of fine twined
linen.
17 **And the sockets for the pillars**
were of brass; the hooks of the
pillars and their fillets of silver;
and the overlaying of their
chapiters of silver;
and all the pillars of the court
were filleted with silver.
18 **And the hanging for the gate of
the court** was needlework, of
blue, and purple, and scarlet, and
fine twined linen:
and twenty cubits was the length,
and the height in the breadth was
five cubits,
answerable to the hangings of the
court.
19 **And their pillars** were four, and
their sockets of brass four; their
hooks of silver, and the overlaying
of their chapiters and their fillets
of silver.
20 **And all the pins of the
tabernacle, and of the court
round about,** were of brass.
21 **This** is the sum of the tabernacle,
even of the tabernacle of
testimony,
as it was counted, according to the
commandment of Moses, for the
service of the Levites, by the hand
of Ithamar, son to Aaron the
priest.
22 **And Bezaleel the son Uri, the
son of Hur, of the tribe of Judah,**
made all that the LORD
commanded Moses.
23 **And with him** was Aholiab, son
of Ahisamach, of the tribe of Dan,
an engraver, and a cunning
workman, and an embroiderer in
blue, and in purple, and in scarlet,
and fine linen.
24 **All the gold that was occupied
for the work in all the work of
the holy place, even the gold of
the offering,** was twenty and
nine talents, and seven hundred
and thirty shekels, after the
shekel of the sanctuary.
25 **And the silver of them that were
numbered of the congregation**
was an hundred talents, and a
thousand seven hundred and
threescore and fifteen shekels,
after the shekel of the sanctuary:
26 A bekah for every man, that is,
half a shekel, after the shekel of
the sanctuary, for every one that
went to be numbered, from
twenty years old and upward, for
six hundred thousand and three
thousand and five hundred and
fifty men.
27 **And of the hundred talents of
silver** were cast the sockets of the
sanctuary, and the sockets of the
vail; an hundred sockets of the
hundred talents, a talent for a
socket.
28 **And of the thousand seven
hundred seventy and five
shekels** he made hooks for the
pillars,
and overlaid their chapiters,
and filleted them.
29 **And the brass of the offering**
was seventy talents, and two
thousand and four hundred
shekels.
30 **And therewith** he made the
sockets to the door of the
tabernacle of the congregation,
and the brasen altar, and the
brasen grate for it, and all the
vessels of the altar,
31 And the sockets of the court round
about, and the sockets of the
court gate, and all the pins of the
tabernacle, and all the pins of the
court round about.

39 ✂ **And of the blue, and
purple, and scarlet,** they
made cloths of service,
to do service in the holy place,
and made the holy garments for
Aaron;
as the LORD commanded Moses.
2 **And he** made the ephod of gold,
blue, and purple, and scarlet, and
fine twined linen.
3 **And they** did beat the gold into

thin plates,
and cut it into wires,
to work it in the blue, and in the purple, and in the scarlet, and in the fine linen, with cunning work.

4 **They** made shoulderpieces for it,
to couple it together:
by the two edges was it coupled together.

5 **And the curious girdle of his ephod,** {that was upon it}, was of the same, according to the work thereof; of gold, blue, and purple, and scarlet, and fine twined linen;
as the LORD commanded Moses.

6 **And they** wrought onyx stones inclosed in ouches of gold, graven, {as signets are graven}, with the names of the children of Israel.

7 **And he** put them on the shoulders of the ephod,
that they should be stones for a memorial to the children of Israel;
as the LORD commanded Moses.

8 **And he** made the breastplate of cunning work, like the work of the ephod; of gold, blue, and purple, and scarlet, and fine twined linen.

9 **It** was foursquare;
they made the breastplate double:
a span was the length thereof, and a span the breadth thereof,
being doubled.

10 **And they** set in it four rows of stones:
the first row was a sardius, a topaz, and a carbuncle:
this was the first row.

11 **And the second row,** an emerald, a sapphire, and a diamond.

12 **And the third row,** a ligure, an agate, and an amethyst.

13 **And the fourth row,** a beryl, an onyx, and a jasper:
they were inclosed in ouches of gold in their inclosings.

14 **And the stones** were according to the names of the children of Israel, twelve, according to their names, like the engravings of a signet, every one with his name, according to the twelve tribes.

15 **And they** made upon the breastplate chains at the ends, of wreathen work of pure gold.

16 **And they** made two ouches of gold, and two gold rings;
and put the two rings in the two ends of the breastplate.

17 **And they** put the two wreathen chains of gold in the two rings on the ends of the breastplate.

18 **And the two ends of the two wreathen chains** they fastened in the two ouches,
and put them on the shoulderpieces of the ephod, before it.

19 **And they** made two rings of gold,
and put them on the two ends of the breastplate, upon the border of it,
which was on the side of the ephod inward.

20 **And they** made two other golden rings,
and put them on the two sides of the ephod underneath, toward the forepart of it, over against the other coupling thereof, above the curious girdle of the ephod.

21 **And they** did bind the breastplate by his rings unto the rings of the ephod with a lace of blue,
that it might be above the curious girdle of the ephod,
and that the breastplate might not be loosed from the ephod;
as the LORD commanded Moses.

22 **And he** made the robe of the ephod of woven work, all of blue.

23 **And there** was an hole in the midst of the robe, as the hole of an habergeon, with a band round about the hole,
that it should not rend.

24 **And they** made upon the hems of the robe pomegranates of blue, and purple, and scarlet, and twined linen.

25 **And they** made bells of pure gold,
and put the bells between the pomegranates upon the hem of the robe, round about between the pomegranates;

26 A bell and a pomegranate, a bell and a pomegranate, round about the hem of the robe to minister in;
as the LORD commanded Moses.

27 **And they** made coats of fine linen of woven work for Aaron, and for his sons,

28 And a mitre of fine linen, and goodly bonnets of fine linen, and linen breeches of fine twined linen,

29 And a girdle of fine twined linen, and blue, and purple, and scarlet, of needlework;
as the LORD commanded Moses.

30 **And they** made the plate of the holy crown of pure gold,
and wrote upon it a writing, like to the engravings of a signet, Holiness To The LORD.

31 **And they** tied unto it a lace of blue,
to fasten it on high upon the mitre;
as the LORD commanded Moses.

32 **Thus** was all the work of the tabernacle of the tent of the congregation finished:
and the children of Israel did according to all that the LORD commanded Moses,
so did they.

33 **And they** brought the tabernacle unto Moses, the tent, and all his furniture, his taches, his boards, his bars, and his pillars, and his sockets,

34 And the covering of rams' skins dyed red, and the covering of badgers' skins, and the vail of the covering,

35 The ark of the testimony, and the staves thereof, and the mercy seat,

36 The table, and all the vessels thereof, and the shewbread,

37 The pure candlestick, with the lamps thereof, even with the lamps to be set in order, and all the vessels thereof, and the oil for light,

38 And the golden altar, and the anointing oil, and the sweet incense, and the hanging for the tabernacle door,

39 The brasen altar, and his grate of brass, his staves, and all his vessels, the laver and his foot,

40 The hangings of the court, his pillars, and his sockets, and the hanging for the court gate, his cords, and his pins, and all the vessels of the service of the tabernacle, for the tent of the congregation,

41 The cloths of service {to do service in the holy place}, and the holy garments for Aaron the priest, and his sons' garments, {to minister in the priest's office}.

42 **According to all that the LORD commanded Moses,** so the children of Israel made all the work.

43 **And Moses** did look upon all the work,
and, {behold}, they had done it
as the LORD had commanded,
even so had they done it:
and Moses blessed them.

40 **And the LORD** spake unto Moses,
saying,
2 **On the first day of the first month** shalt thou set up the tabernacle of the tent of the congregation.
3 **And thou** shalt put therein the ark of the testimony,
and cover the ark with the vail.
4 **And thou** shalt bring in the table,
and set in order the things that are to be set in order upon it;
and thou shalt bring in the candlestick,
and light the lamps thereof.
5 **And thou** shalt set the altar of gold for the incense before the ark of the testimony,
and put the hanging of the door to the tabernacle.
6 **And thou** shalt set the altar of the burnt offering before the door of the tabernacle of the tent of the congregation.
7 **And thou** shalt set the laver between the tent of the congregation and the altar,
and shalt put water therein.
8 **And thou** shalt set up the court round about,
and hang up the hanging at the court gate.
9 **And thou** shalt take the anointing oil,
and anoint the tabernacle, and all that is therein,
and shalt hallow it, and all the vessels thereof:
and it shall be holy.
10 **And thou** shalt anoint the altar of the burnt offering, and all his vessels,
and sanctify the altar:
and it shall be an altar most holy.
11 **And thou** shalt anoint the laver and his foot,
and sanctify it.
12 **And thou** shalt bring Aaron and his sons unto the door of the tabernacle of the congregation,
and wash them with water.
13 **And thou** shalt put upon Aaron the holy garments,
and anoint him,
and sanctify him;
that he may minister unto me in the priest's office.
14 **And thou** shalt bring his sons,
and clothe them with coats:
15 **And thou** shalt anoint them,
as thou didst anoint their father,
that they may minister unto me in the priest's office:
for their anointing shall surely be an everlasting priesthood throughout their generations.
16 **Thus** did Moses:
according to all that the LORD commanded him, so did he.
17 **And it** came to pass in the first month in the second year, on the first day of the month,
that the tabernacle was reared up.
18 **And Moses** reared up the tabernacle,
and fastened his sockets,
and set up the boards thereof,
and put in the bars thereof,
and reared up his pillars.
19 **And he** spread abroad the tent over the tabernacle,
and put the covering of the tent above upon it;
as the LORD commanded Moses.
20 **And he** took and put the testimony into the ark,
and set the staves on the ark,
and put the mercy seat above upon the ark:
21 **And he** brought the ark into the tabernacle,
and set up the vail of the covering,
and covered the ark of the testimony;
as the LORD commanded Moses.
22 **And he** put the table in the tent of the congregation, upon the side of the tabernacle northward, without the vail.
23 **And he** set the bread in order upon it before the LORD;
as the LORD had commanded Moses.
24 **And he** put the candlestick in the tent of the congregation, over against the table, on the side of the tabernacle southward.
25 **And he** lighted the lamps before the LORD;
as the LORD commanded Moses.
26 **And he** put the golden altar in the tent of the congregation before the vail:
27 **And he** burnt sweet incense thereon;
as the LORD commanded Moses.
28 **And he** set up the hanging at the door of the tabernacle.
29 **And he** put the altar of burnt offering by the door of the tabernacle of the tent of the congregation,
and offered upon it the burnt offering and the meat offering;
as the LORD commanded Moses.
30 **And he** set the laver between the tent of the congregation and the altar,
and put water there,
to wash withal.
31 **And Moses and Aaron and his sons** washed their hands and their feet thereat:
32 **When they** went into the tent of the congregation,
and when they came near unto the altar,
they washed;
as the LORD commanded Moses.
33 **And he** reared up the court round about the tabernacle and the altar,
and set up the hanging of the court gate.
So Moses finished the work.
34 **Then a cloud** covered the tent of the congregation,
and the glory of the LORD filled the tabernacle.
35 **And Moses** was not able to enter into the tent of the congregation,
because the cloud abode thereon,
and the glory of the LORD filled the tabernacle.
36 **And when the cloud** was taken up from over the tabernacle,
the children of Israel went onward in all their journeys:
37 **But if the cloud** were not taken up,
then they journeyed not till the day that it was taken up.
38 **For the cloud of the LORD** was upon the tabernacle by day,
and fire was on it by night, in the sight of all the house of Israel, throughout all their journeys.

Leviticus

The Book of Leviticus provides the Israelites with a comprehensive set of instructions for worship, purity, and conduct. These instructions are not just for their benefit but to establish a righteous and holy people who would be a light to the nations. It outlines the required sacrifices and offerings and establishes a priest's role and duties, as well as the requirements for becoming a priest.

The book also explains the procedures for offering sacrifices and performing other religious rituals. It outlines the various festivals and holy days that are to be observed by the people, each with its unique significance in the religious calendar. Moses emphasizes the importance of holiness and purity in the lives of the Israelites, and he provides detailed instructions on how to maintain them, including rules for cleanliness, dietary restrictions, and sexual conduct. In addition, Leviticus contains a wide range of moral and civil laws related to personal conduct, property rights, and justice, all guiding the Israelites in living a life pleasing to God and establishing a just and harmonious society.

Moses closes the book with a series of blessings and curses that God will bestow upon the Israelites according to their adherence to His laws. These blessings are a testament to the profound benefits of following His commands. The laws and rituals that Moses covers in Leviticus are designed to create a sense of order and structure in the lives of the Israelites. They establish a system of worship, devotion, and personal conduct that guides them in their relationship with God and one another.

1 **And the LORD** called unto Moses,
and spake unto him out of the tabernacle of the congregation, saying,
2 **Speak** unto the children of Israel,
and say unto them,
If any man of you bring an offering unto the LORD,
ye shall bring your offering of the cattle, even of the herd, and of the flock.

3 **If his offering** be a burnt sacrifice of the herd,
let him offer a male without blemish:
he shall offer it of his own voluntary will at the door of the tabernacle of the congregation before the LORD.

4 **And he** shall put his hand upon the head of the burnt offering;
and it shall be accepted for him to make atonement for him.

5 **And he** shall kill the bullock before the LORD:
and the priests, Aaron's sons, shall bring the blood,
and sprinkle the blood round about upon the altar that is by the door of the tabernacle of the congregation.

6 **And he** shall flay the burnt offering,
and cut it into his pieces

7 **And the sons of Aaron the priest** shall put fire upon the altar,
and lay the wood in order upon the fire:
8 **And the priests, Aaron's sons,** shall lay the parts, the head, and the fat, in order upon the wood that is on the fire which is upon the altar:
9 **But his inwards and his legs** shall he wash in water:
and the priest shall burn all on the altar,
to be a burnt sacrifice, an offering made by fire, of a sweet savour unto the LORD.

10 **And if his offering** be of the flocks, namely, of the sheep, or of the goats, for a burnt sacrifice;
he shall bring it a male without blemish.

11 **And he** shall kill it on the side of the altar northward before the LORD:
and the priests, Aaron's sons, shall sprinkle his blood round about upon the altar.

12 **And he** shall cut it into his pieces, with his head and his fat:
and the priest shall lay them in order on the wood that is on the fire which is upon the altar:
13 **But he** shall wash the inwards and the legs with water:
and the priest shall bring it all,
and burn it upon the altar:
it is a burnt sacrifice, an offering made by fire, of a sweet savour unto the LORD.

14 **And if the burnt sacrifice for his offering to the LORD** be of fowls,
then he shall bring his offering of turtledoves, or of young pigeons.

15 **And the priest** shall bring it unto the altar,
and wring off his head,
and burn it on the altar;
and the blood thereof shall be wrung out at the side of the altar:
16 **And he** shall pluck away his crop with his feathers,
and cast it beside the altar on the east part, by the place of the ashes:
17 **And he** shall cleave it with the wings thereof,
but shall not divide it asunder:
and the priest shall burn it upon the altar, upon the wood that is upon the fire:
it is a burnt sacrifice, an offering made by fire, of a sweet savour unto the LORD.

2 **And when any** will offer a meat offering unto the LORD,
his offering shall be of fine flour;
and he shall pour oil upon it,
and put frankincense thereon:
2 **And he** shall bring it to Aaron's sons the priests:
and he shall take thereout his handful of the flour thereof, and of the oil thereof, with all the frankincense thereof;
and the priest shall burn the memorial of it upon the altar,

to be an offering made by fire, of a sweet savour unto the LORD:
[3] **And the remnant of the meat offering** shall be Aaron's and his sons':
it is a thing most holy of the offerings of the LORD made by fire.
[4] **And if thou** bring an oblation of a meat offering baken in the oven,
it shall be unleavened cakes of fine flour mingled with oil, or unleavened wafers anointed with oil.
[5] **And if thy oblation** be a meat offering baken in a pan,
it shall be of fine flour unleavened, mingled with oil.
[6] **Thou** shalt part it in pieces,
and pour oil thereon:
it is a meat offering.
[7] **And if thy oblation** be a meat offering baken in the fryingpan,
it shall be made of fine flour with oil.
[8] **And thou** shalt bring the meat offering that is made of these things unto the LORD:
and when it is presented unto the priest,
he shall bring it unto the altar.
[9] **And the priest** shall take from the meat offering a memorial thereof,
and shall burn it upon the altar:
it is an offering made by fire, of a sweet savour unto the LORD.
[10] **And that which is left of the meat offering** shall be Aaron's and his sons':
it is a thing most holy of the offerings of the LORD made by fire.
[11] **No meat offering**, {which ye shall bring unto the LORD}, shall be made with leaven:
for ye shall burn no leaven, nor any honey, in any offering of the LORD made by fire.
[12] **As for the oblation of the firstfruits,** ye shall offer them unto the LORD:
but they shall not be burnt on the altar for a sweet savour.
[13] **And every oblation of thy meat offering** shalt thou season with salt;
neither shalt thou suffer the salt of the covenant of thy God to be lacking from thy meat offering:
with all thine offerings thou shalt offer salt.
[14] **And if thou** offer a meat offering of thy firstfruits unto the LORD,
thou shalt offer for the meat offering of thy firstfruits green ears of corn dried by the fire, even corn beaten out of full ears.
[15] **And thou** shalt put oil upon it,
and lay frankincense thereon:
it is a meat offering.
[16] **And the priest** shall burn the memorial of it, part of the beaten corn thereof, and part of the oil thereof, with all the frankincense thereof:
it is an offering made by fire unto the LORD.

3 **And if his oblation** be a sacrifice of peace offering,
if he offer it of the herd;
whether it be a male or female,
he shall offer it without blemish before the LORD.
[2] **And he** shall lay his hand upon the head of his offering,
and kill it at the door of the tabernacle of the congregation:
and Aaron's sons the priests shall sprinkle the blood upon the altar round about.
[3] **And he** shall offer of the sacrifice of the peace offering an offering made by fire unto the LORD;
the fat that covereth the inwards, and all the fat that is upon the inwards,
[4] **And the two kidneys, and the fat that is on them, {which is by the flanks}, and the caul above the liver, with the kidneys,** it shall he take away.
[5] **And Aaron's sons** shall burn it on the altar upon the burnt sacrifice,
which is upon the wood that is on the fire:
it is an offering made by fire, of a sweet savour unto the LORD.
[6] **And if his offering for a sacrifice of peace offering unto the LORD** be of the flock; male or female,
he shall offer it without blemish.
[7] **If he** offer a lamb for his offering,
then shall he offer it before the LORD.
[8] **And he** shall lay his hand upon the head of his offering,
and kill it before the tabernacle of the congregation:
and Aaron's sons shall sprinkle the blood thereof round about upon the altar.
[9] **And he** shall offer of the sacrifice of the peace offering an offering made by fire unto the LORD;
the fat thereof, and the whole rump, {it shall he take off hard by the backbone}; and the fat that covereth the inwards, and all the fat that is upon the inwards,
[10] **And the two kidneys, and the fat that is upon them, {which is by the flanks}, and the caul above the liver, with the kidneys,** it shall he take away.
[11] **And the priest** shall burn it upon the altar:
it is the food of the offering made by fire unto the LORD.
[12] **And if his offering** be a goat,
then he shall offer it before the LORD.
[13] **And he** shall lay his hand upon the head of it,
and kill it before the tabernacle of the congregation:
and the sons of Aaron shall sprinkle the blood thereof upon the altar round about.
[14] **And he** shall offer thereof his offering, even an offering made by fire unto the LORD;
the fat that covereth the inwards, and all the fat that is upon the inwards,
[15] **And the two kidneys, and the fat that is upon them, {which is by the flanks}, and the caul above the liver, with the kidneys,** it shall he take away.
[16] **And the priest** shall burn them upon the altar:
it is the food of the offering made by fire for a sweet savour:
all the fat is the LORD's.
[17] **It shall be a perpetual statute for your generations throughout all your dwellings,** that ye eat neither fat nor blood.

4 **And the LORD** spake unto Moses,
saying,
[2] **Speak** unto the children of Israel,
saying,
If a soul shall sin through ignorance against any of the commandments of the LORD

concerning things which ought not to be done,
and shall do against any of them:
3 **If the priest that is anointed** do sin according to the sin of the people;
then let him bring for his sin,
which he hath sinned, a young bullock without blemish unto the LORD for a sin offering.

4 **And he** shall bring the bullock unto the door of the tabernacle of the congregation before the LORD;
and shall lay his hand upon the bullock's head,
and kill the bullock before the LORD.

5 **And the priest that is anointed** shall take of the bullock's blood,
and bring it to the tabernacle of the congregation:
6 **And the priest** shall dip his finger in the blood,
and sprinkle of the blood seven times before the LORD, before the vail of the sanctuary.

7 **And the priest** shall put some of the blood upon the horns of the altar of sweet incense before the LORD, **which** is in the tabernacle of the congregation;
and shall pour all the blood of the bullock at the bottom of the altar of the burnt offering,
which is at the door of the tabernacle of the congregation.

8 **And he** shall take off from it all the fat of the bullock for the sin offering;
the fat that covereth the inwards, and all the fat that is upon the inwards,
9 **And the two kidneys, and the fat that is upon them, which is by the flanks, and the caul above the liver, with the kidneys,** it shall he take away,
10 **As it** was taken off from the bullock of the sacrifice of peace offerings:
and the priest shall burn them upon the altar of the burnt offering.

11 **And the skin of the bullock, and all his flesh, with his head, and with his legs, and his inwards, and his dung,**
12 **Even the whole bullock** shall he carry forth without the camp unto a clean place,
where the ashes are poured out,
and burn him on the wood with fire:
where the ashes are poured out shall he be burnt.

13 **And if the whole congregation of Israel** sin through ignorance,
and the thing be hid from the eyes of the assembly,
and they have done somewhat against any of the commandments of the LORD concerning things which should not be done,
and are guilty;
14 **When the sin**, {which they have sinned against it}, is known,
then the congregation shall offer a young bullock for the sin,
and bring him before the tabernacle of the congregation.

15 **And the elders of the congregation** shall lay their hands upon the head of the bullock before the LORD:
and the bullock shall be killed before the LORD.

16 **And the priest that is anointed** shall bring of the bullock's blood to the tabernacle of the congregation:
17 **And the priest** shall dip his finger in some of the blood,
and sprinkle it seven times before the LORD, even before the vail.

18 **And he** shall put some of the blood upon the horns of the altar which is before the LORD,
that is in the tabernacle of the congregation,
and shall pour out all the blood at the bottom of the altar of the burnt offering,
which is at the door of the tabernacle of the congregation.

19 **And he** shall take all his fat from him,
and burn it upon the altar.

20 **And he** shall do with the bullock as he did with the bullock for a sin offering,
so shall he do with this:
and the priest shall make an atonement for them,
and it shall be forgiven them.

21 **And he** shall carry forth the bullock without the camp,
and burn him as he burned the first bullock:
it is a sin offering for the congregation.

22 **When a ruler** hath sinned,
and done somewhat through ignorance against any of the commandments of the LORD his God concerning things which should not be done,
and is guilty;
23 **Or if his sin**, {wherein he hath sinned}, come to his knowledge;
he shall bring his offering, a kid of the goats, a male without blemish:
24 **And he** shall lay his hand upon the head of the goat,
and kill it in the place where they kill the burnt offering before the LORD:
it is a sin offering.

25 **And the priest** shall take of the blood of the sin offering with his finger,
and put it upon the horns of the altar of burnt offering,
and shall pour out his blood at the bottom of the altar of burnt offering.

26 **And he** shall burn all his fat upon the altar, as the fat of the sacrifice of peace offerings:
and the priest shall make an atonement for him as concerning his sin,
and it shall be forgiven him.

27 **And if any one of the common people** sin through ignorance,
while he doeth somewhat against any of the commandments of the LORD concerning things which ought not to be done,
and be guilty;
28 **Or if his sin**, {which he hath sinned}, come to his knowledge:
then he shall bring his offering, a kid of the goats, a female without blemish, for his sin which he hath sinned.

29 **And he** shall lay his hand upon the head of the sin offering,
and slay the sin offering in the place of the burnt offering.

30 **And the priest** shall take of the blood thereof with his finger,
and put it upon the horns of the altar of burnt offering,
and shall pour out all the blood thereof at the bottom of the altar.

31 **And he** shall take away all the fat thereof,
as the fat is taken away from off the sacrifice of peace offerings;
and the priest shall burn it upon the altar for a sweet savour unto the LORD;
and the priest shall make an atonement for him,
and it shall be forgiven him.
32 **And if he** bring a lamb for a sin offering,
he shall bring it a female without blemish.
33 **And he** shall lay his hand upon the head of the sin offering,
and slay it for a sin offering in the place where they kill the burnt offering.
34 **And the priest** shall take of the blood of the sin offering with his finger,
and put it upon the horns of the altar of burnt offering,
and shall pour out all the blood thereof at the bottom of the altar:
35 **And he** shall take away all the fat thereof,
as the fat of the lamb is taken away from the sacrifice of the peace offerings;
and the priest shall burn them upon the altar, according to the offerings made by fire unto the LORD:
and the priest shall make an atonement for his sin that he hath committed,
and it shall be forgiven him.

5 **And if a soul** sin,
and hear the voice of swearing,
and is a witness,
whether he hath seen or known of it;
if he do not utter it,
then he shall bear his iniquity.
2 **Or if a soul** touch any unclean thing,
whether it be a carcase of an unclean beast, or a carcase of unclean cattle, or the carcase of unclean creeping things,
and if it be hidden from him;
he also shall be unclean, and guilty.
3 **Or if he** touch the uncleanness of man,
whatsoever uncleanness it be that a man shall be defiled withal,
and it be hid from him;
when he knoweth of it,
then he shall be guilty.
4 **Or if a soul** swear,
pronouncing with his lips to do evil,
or to do good,
whatsoever it be that a man shall pronounce with an oath,
and it be hid from him;
when he knoweth of it,
then he shall be guilty in one of these.
5 **And it** shall be,
when he shall be guilty in one of these things,
that he shall confess
that he hath sinned in that thing:
6 **And he** shall bring his trespass offering unto the LORD for his sin which he hath sinned, a female from the flock, a lamb or a kid of the goats, for a sin offering;
and the priest shall make an atonement for him concerning his sin.
7 **And if he** be not able to bring a lamb,
then he shall bring for his trespass,
which he hath committed, two turtledoves, or two young pigeons, unto the LORD; one for a sin offering, and the other for a burnt offering.
8 **And he** shall bring them unto the priest,
who shall offer that which is for the sin offering first,
and wring off his head from his neck,
but shall not divide it asunder:
9 **And he** shall sprinkle of the blood of the sin offering upon the side of the altar;
and the rest of the blood shall be wrung out at the bottom of the altar:
it is a sin offering.
10 **And he** shall offer the second for a burnt offering, according to the manner:
and the priest shall make an atonement for him for his sin which he hath sinned,
and it shall be forgiven him.
11 **But if he** be not able to bring two turtledoves, or two young pigeons,
then he that sinned shall bring for his offering the tenth part of an ephah of fine flour for a sin offering;
he shall put no oil upon it,
neither shall he put any frankincense thereon:
for it is a sin offering.
12 **Then** shall he bring it to the priest,
and the priest shall take his handful of it, even a memorial thereof,
and burn it on the altar, according to the offerings made by fire unto the LORD:
it is a sin offering.
13 **And the priest** shall make an atonement for him as touching his sin that he hath sinned in one of these,
and it shall be forgiven him:
and the remnant shall be the priest's, as a meat offering.
14 **And the LORD** spake unto Moses, saying,
15 **If a soul** commit a trespass,
and sin through ignorance, in the holy things of the LORD;
then he shall bring for his trespass unto the LORD a ram without blemish out of the flocks, with thy estimation by shekels of silver, after the shekel of the sanctuary, for a trespass offering.
16 **And he** shall make amends for the harm that he hath done in the holy thing,
and shall add the fifth part thereto,
and give it unto the priest:
and the priest shall make an atonement for him with the ram of the trespass offering,
and it shall be forgiven him.
17 **And if a soul** sin,
and commit any of these things which are forbidden to be done by the commandments of the LORD;
though he wist it not,
yet is he guilty,
and shall bear his iniquity.
18 **And he** shall bring a ram without blemish out of the flock, with thy estimation, for a trespass offering, unto the priest:
and the priest shall make an atonement for him concerning his ignorance wherein he erred and wist it not,
and it shall be forgiven him.
19 **It** is a trespass offering:
he hath certainly trespassed against the LORD.

6

And the LORD spake unto Moses,
saying,
2 **If a soul** sin,
and commit a trespass against the LORD,
and lie unto his neighbour in that which was delivered him to keep, or in fellowship, or in a thing taken away by violence,
or hath deceived his neighbour;
3 **Or** have found that which was lost,
and lieth concerning it,
and sweareth falsely; in any of all these that a man doeth,
sinning therein:
4 **Then it** shall be,
because he hath sinned,
and is guilty,
that he shall restore that which he took violently away, or the thing which he hath deceitfully gotten, or that which was delivered him to keep, or the lost thing which he found,
5 Or all that about which he hath sworn falsely;
he shall even restore it in the principal,
and shall add the fifth part more thereto,
and give it unto him to whom it appertaineth, in the day of his trespass offering.
6 **And he** shall bring his trespass offering unto the LORD, a ram without blemish out of the flock, with thy estimation, for a trespass offering, unto the priest:
7 **And the priest** shall make an atonement for him before the LORD:
and it shall be forgiven him for any thing of all that he hath done in trespassing therein.
8 **And the LORD** spake unto Moses,
saying,
9 **Command** Aaron and his sons,
saying,
This is the law of the burnt offering:
It is the burnt offering, because of the burning upon the altar all night unto the morning,
and the fire of the altar shall be burning in it.
10 **And the priest** shall put on his linen garment,
and his linen breeches shall he put upon his flesh,
and take up the ashes which the fire hath consumed with the burnt offering on the altar,
and he shall put them beside the altar.
11 **And he** shall put off his garments,
and put on other garments,
and carry forth the ashes without the camp unto a clean place.
12 **And the fire upon the altar** shall be burning in it;
it shall not be put out:
and the priest shall burn wood on it every morning,
and lay the burnt offering in order upon it;
and he shall burn thereon the fat of the peace offerings.
13 **The fire** shall ever be burning upon the altar;
it shall never go out.
14 **And this** is the law of the meat offering:
the sons of Aaron shall offer it before the LORD, before the altar.
15 **And he** shall take of it his handful, of the flour of the meat offering, and of the oil thereof, and all the frankincense which is upon the meat offering,
and shall burn it upon the altar for a sweet savour, even the memorial of it, unto the LORD.
16 **And the remainder thereof** shall Aaron and his sons eat:
with unleavened bread shall it be eaten in the holy place;
in the court of the tabernacle of the congregation they shall eat it.
17 **It** shall not be baken with leaven.
I have given it unto them for their portion of my offerings made by fire;
it is most holy, as is the sin offering, and as the trespass offering.
18 **All the males among the children of Aaron** shall eat of it.
It shall be a statute for ever in your generations concerning the offerings of the LORD made by fire:
every one that toucheth them shall be holy.
19 **And the LORD** spake unto Moses,
saying,
20 **This** is the offering of Aaron and of his sons,
which they shall offer unto the LORD in the day when he is anointed; the tenth part of an ephah of fine flour for a meat offering perpetual, half of it in the morning, and half thereof at night.
21 **In a pan** it shall be made with oil;
and when it is baken,
thou shalt bring it in:
and the baken pieces of the meat offering shalt thou offer for a sweet savour unto the LORD.
22 **And the priest of his sons that is anointed in his stead** shall offer it:
it is a statute for ever unto the LORD;
it shall be wholly burnt.
23 **For every meat offering for the priest** shall be wholly burnt:
it shall not be eaten.
24 **And the LORD** spake unto Moses,
saying,
25 **Speak** unto Aaron and to his sons,
saying,
This is the law of the sin offering:
In the place where the burnt offering is killed shall the sin offering be killed before the LORD:
it is most holy.
26 **The priest that offereth it for sin** shall eat it:
in the holy place shall it be eaten, in the court of the tabernacle of the congregation.
27 **Whatsoever shall touch the flesh thereof** shall be holy:
and when there is sprinkled of the blood thereof upon any garment,
thou shalt wash that whereon it was sprinkled in the holy place.
28 **But the earthen vessel wherein it is sodden** shall be broken:
and if it be sodden in a brasen pot,
it shall be both scoured,
and rinsed in water.
29 **All the males among the priests** shall eat thereof:
it is most holy.
30 **And no sin offering**, {whereof any of the blood is brought into the tabernacle of the congregation} {to reconcile withal in the holy place}, shall be eaten:
it shall be burnt in the fire.

7 **Likewise this** is the law of the trespass offering:
it is most holy.

2 **In the place where they kill the burnt offering** shall they kill the trespass offering:
and the blood thereof shall he sprinkle round about upon the altar.

3 **And he** shall offer of it all the fat thereof;
the rump, and the fat that covereth the inwards,

4 **And the two kidneys, and the fat that is on them, {which is by the flanks}, and the caul that is above the liver, with the kidneys,** it shall he take away:

5 **And the priest** shall burn them upon the altar for an offering made by fire unto the LORD:
it is a trespass offering.

6 **Every male among the priests** shall eat thereof:
it shall be eaten in the holy place:
it is most holy.

7 **As the sin offering** is,
so is the trespass offering:
there is one law for them:
the priest that maketh atonement therewith shall have it.

8 **And the priest that offereth any man's burnt offering**, even the priest shall have to himself the skin of the burnt offering which he hath offered.

9 **And all the meat offering that is baken in the oven, and all that is dressed in the fryingpan, and in the pan,** shall be the priest's that offereth it.

10 **And every meat offering, {mingled with oil, and dry},** shall all the sons of Aaron have, one as much as another.

11 **And this** is the law of the sacrifice of peace offerings,
which he shall offer unto the LORD.

12 **If he** offer it for a thanksgiving,
then he shall offer with the sacrifice of thanksgiving unleavened cakes mingled with oil, and unleavened wafers anointed with oil, and cakes mingled with oil, of fine flour, fried.

13 **Besides the cakes,** he shall offer for his offering leavened bread with the sacrifice of thanksgiving of his peace offerings.

14 **And of it** he shall offer one out of the whole oblation for an heave offering unto the LORD,
and it shall be the priest's that sprinkleth the blood of the peace offerings.

15 **And the flesh of the sacrifice of his peace offerings for thanksgiving** shall be eaten the same day that it is offered;
he shall not leave any of it until the morning.

16 **But if the sacrifice of his offering** be a vow, or a voluntary offering,
it shall be eaten the same day that he offereth his sacrifice:
and on the morrow also the remainder of it shall be eaten:

17 **But the remainder of the flesh of the sacrifice on the third day** shall be burnt with fire.

18 **And if any of the flesh of the sacrifice of his peace offerings** be eaten at all on the third day,
it shall not be accepted,
neither shall it be imputed unto him that offereth it:
it shall be an abomination,
and the soul that eateth of it shall bear his iniquity.

19 **And the flesh that toucheth any unclean thing** shall not be eaten;
it shall be burnt with fire:
and as for the flesh, all that be clean shall eat thereof.

20 **But the soul that eateth of the flesh of the sacrifice of peace offerings**, {that pertain unto the LORD}, {having his uncleanness upon him}, even that soul shall be cut off from his people.

21 **Moreover the soul that shall touch any unclean thing, as the uncleanness of man, or any unclean beast, or any abominable unclean thing, and eat of the flesh of the sacrifice of peace offerings, {which pertain unto the LORD},** even that soul shall be cut off from his people.

22 **And the LORD** spake unto Moses, saying,

23 **Speak** unto the children of Israel, saying,
Ye shall eat no manner of fat, of ox, or of sheep, or of goat.

24 **And the fat of the beast that dieth of itself, and the fat of that which is torn with beasts,** may be used in any other use:
but ye shall in no wise eat of it.

25 **For whosoever** eateth the fat of the beast,
of which men offer an offering made by fire unto the LORD,
even the soul that eateth it shall be cut off from his people.

26 **Moreover ye** shall eat no manner of blood, {whether it be of fowl or of beast}, in any of your dwellings.

27 **Whatsoever soul it be that eateth any manner of blood,** even that soul shall be cut off from his people.

28 **And the LORD** spake unto Moses, saying,

29 **Speak** unto the children of Israel, saying,
He that offereth the sacrifice of his peace offerings unto the LORD shall bring his oblation unto the LORD of the sacrifice of his peace offerings.

30 **His own hands** shall bring the offerings of the LORD made by fire, the fat with the breast,
it shall he bring,
that the breast may be waved for a wave offering before the LORD.

31 **And the priest** shall burn the fat upon the altar:
but the breast shall be Aaron's and his sons'.

32 **And the right shoulder** shall ye give unto the priest for an heave offering of the sacrifices of your peace offerings.

33 **He among the sons of Aaron**, {that offereth the blood of the peace offerings, and the fat}, shall have the right shoulder for his part.

34 **For the wave breast and the heave shoulder** have I taken of the children of Israel from off the sacrifices of their peace offerings,
and have given them unto Aaron the priest and unto his sons by a statute for ever from among the children of Israel.

35 **This** is the portion of the anointing of Aaron, and of the anointing of his sons, out of the offerings of the LORD made by

fire, in the day when he presented them to minister unto the LORD in the priest's office;
36 {Which the LORD commanded to be given them of the children of Israel}, in the day that he anointed them, by a statute for ever throughout their generations.
37 **This** is the law of the burnt offering, of the meat offering, and of the sin offering, and of the trespass offering, and of the consecrations, and of the sacrifice of the peace offerings;
38 {Which the LORD commanded Moses in mount Sinai}, in the day that he commanded the children of Israel to offer their oblations unto the LORD, in the wilderness of Sinai.

8 ⤫ **And the LORD** spake unto Moses,
saying,
2 **Take** Aaron and his sons with him, and the garments, and the anointing oil, and a bullock for the sin offering, and two rams, and a basket of unleavened bread;
3 **And gather thou** all the congregation together unto the door of the tabernacle of the congregation.
4 **And Moses** did as the LORD commanded him;
and the assembly was gathered together unto the door of the tabernacle of the congregation.
5 **And Moses** said unto the congregation,
This is the thing which the LORD commanded to be done.
6 **And Moses** brought Aaron and his sons,
and washed them with water.
7 **And he** put upon him the coat,
and girded him with the girdle,
and clothed him with the robe,
and put the ephod upon him,
and he girded him with the curious girdle of the ephod,
and bound it unto him therewith.
8 **And he** put the breastplate upon him:
also he put in the breastplate the Urim and the Thummim.
9 **And he** put the mitre upon his head;
also upon the mitre, even upon his forefront, did he put the golden plate, the holy crown;
as the LORD commanded Moses.
10 **And Moses** took the anointing oil,
and anointed the tabernacle and all that was therein,
and sanctified them.
11 **And he** sprinkled thereof upon the altar seven times,
and anointed the altar and all his vessels, both the laver and his foot,
to sanctify them.
12 **And he** poured of the anointing oil upon Aaron's head,
and anointed him,
to sanctify him.
13 **And Moses** brought Aaron's sons,
and put coats upon them,
and girded them with girdles,
and put bonnets upon them;
as the LORD commanded Moses.
14 **And he** brought the bullock for the sin offering:
and Aaron and his sons laid their hands upon the head of the bullock for the sin offering.
15 **And he** slew it;
and Moses took the blood,
and put it upon the horns of the altar round about with his finger,
and purified the altar,
and poured the blood at the bottom of the altar,
and sanctified it,
to make reconciliation upon it.
16 **And he** took all the fat that was upon the inwards, and the caul above the liver, and the two kidneys, and their fat,
and Moses burned it upon the altar.
17 **But the bullock, and his hide, his flesh, and his dung,** he burnt with fire without the camp;
as the LORD commanded Moses.
18 **And he** brought the ram for the burnt offering:
and Aaron and his sons laid their hands upon the head of the ram.
19 **And he** killed it;
and Moses sprinkled the blood upon the altar round about.
20 **And he** cut the ram into pieces;
and Moses burnt the head, and the pieces, and the fat.
21 **And he** washed the inwards and the legs in water;
and Moses burnt the whole ram upon the altar:
it was a burnt sacrifice for a sweet savour, and an offering made by fire unto the LORD;
as the LORD commanded Moses.
22 **And he** brought the other ram, the ram of consecration:
and Aaron and his sons laid their hands upon the head of the ram.
23 **And he** slew it;
and Moses took of the blood of it,
and put it upon the tip of Aaron's right ear, and upon the thumb of his right hand, and upon the great toe of his right foot.
24 **And he** brought Aaron's sons,
and Moses put of the blood upon the tip of their right ear, and upon the thumbs of their right hands, and upon the great toes of their right feet:
and Moses sprinkled the blood upon the altar round about.
25 **And he** took the fat, and the rump, and all the fat that was upon the inwards, and the caul above the liver, and the two kidneys, and their fat, and the right shoulder:
26 **And out of the basket of unleavened bread**, {that was before the LORD}, he took one unleavened cake, and a cake of oiled bread, and one wafer,
and put them on the fat, and upon the right shoulder:
27 **And he** put all upon Aaron's hands, and upon his sons' hands,
and waved them for a wave offering before the LORD.
28 **And Moses** took them from off their hands,
and burnt them on the altar upon the burnt offering:
they were consecrations for a sweet savour:
it is an offering made by fire unto the LORD.
29 **And Moses** took the breast,
and waved it for a wave offering before the LORD:
for of the ram of consecration it was Moses' part;
as the LORD commanded Moses.
30 **And Moses** took of the anointing oil, and of the blood which was upon the altar,
and sprinkled it upon Aaron, and upon his garments, and upon his

sons, and upon his sons' garments with him;
and sanctified Aaron, and his garments, and his sons, and his sons' garments with him.
31 **And Moses** said unto Aaron and to his sons,
Boil the flesh at the door of the tabernacle of the congregation:
and there eat it with the bread that is in the basket of consecrations,
as I commanded,
saying,
Aaron and his sons shall eat it.
32 **And that which remaineth of the flesh and of the bread** shall ye burn with fire.
33 **And ye** shall not go out of the door of the tabernacle of the congregation in seven days,
until the days of your consecration be at an end:
for seven days shall he consecrate you.
34 **As he** hath done this day,
so the LORD hath commanded to do,
to make an atonement for you.
35 **Therefore** shall ye abide at the door of the tabernacle of the congregation day and night seven days,
and keep the charge of the LORD,
that ye die not:
for so I am commanded.
36 **So Aaron and his sons** did all things which the LORD commanded by the hand of Moses.

9 **And it** came to pass on the eighth day,
that Moses called Aaron and his sons, and the elders of Israel;
2 **And he** said unto Aaron,
Take thee a young calf for a sin offering, and a ram for a burnt offering, without blemish,
and offer them before the LORD.
3 **And unto the children of Israel** thou shalt speak,
saying,
Take ye a kid of the goats for a sin offering; and a calf and a lamb, both of the first year, without blemish, for a burnt offering;
4 Also a bullock and a ram for peace offerings, {to sacrifice before the LORD}; and a meat offering mingled with oil:
for to day the LORD will appear unto you.
5 **And they** brought that which Moses commanded before the tabernacle of the congregation:
and all the congregation drew near and stood before the LORD.
6 **And Moses** said,
This is the thing which the LORD commanded that ye should do:
and the glory of the LORD shall appear unto you.
7 **And Moses** said unto Aaron,
Go unto the altar,
and offer thy sin offering, and thy burnt offering,
and make an atonement for thyself, and for the people:
and offer the offering of the people,
and make an atonement for them;
as the LORD commanded.
8 **Aaron** therefore went unto the altar,
and slew the calf of the sin offering,
which was for himself.
9 **And the sons of Aaron** brought the blood unto him:
and he dipped his finger in the blood,
and put it upon the horns of the altar,
and poured out the blood at the bottom of the altar:
10 **But the fat, and the kidneys, and the caul above the liver of the sin offering,** he burnt upon the altar;
as the LORD commanded Moses.
11 **And the flesh and the hide** he burnt with fire without the camp.
12 **And he** slew the burnt offering;
and Aaron's sons presented unto him the blood,
which he sprinkled round about upon the altar.
13 **And they** presented the burnt offering unto him, with the pieces thereof, and the head:
and he burnt them upon the altar.
14 **And he** did wash the inwards and the legs,
and burnt them upon the burnt offering on the altar.
15 **And he** brought the people's offering,
and took the goat,
which was the sin offering for the people,
and slew it,
and offered it for sin, as the first.
16 **And he** brought the burnt offering,
and offered it according to the manner.
17 **And he** brought the meat offering,
and took an handful thereof,
and burnt it upon the altar, beside the burnt sacrifice of the morning.
18 **He** slew also the bullock and the ram for a sacrifice of peace offerings,
which was for the people:
and Aaron's sons presented unto him the blood, {which he sprinkled upon the altar round about},
19 And the fat of the bullock and of the ram, the rump, and that which covereth the inwards, and the kidneys, and the caul above the liver:
20 **And they** put the fat upon the breasts,
and he burnt the fat upon the altar:
21 **And the breasts and the right shoulder** Aaron waved for a wave offering before the LORD;
as Moses commanded.
22 **And Aaron** lifted up his hand toward the people,
and blessed them,
and came down from offering of the sin offering, and the burnt offering, and peace offerings.
23 **And Moses and Aaron** went into the tabernacle of the congregation,
and came out,
and blessed the people:
and the glory of the LORD appeared unto all the people.
24 **And there** came a fire out from before the LORD,
and consumed upon the altar the burnt offering and the fat:
which when all the people saw,
they shouted,
and fell on their faces.

10 **And Nadab and Abihu, the sons of Aaron,** took either of them his censer,
and put fire therein,
and put incense thereon,
and offered strange fire before the LORD,
which he commanded them not.
2 **And there** went out fire from the LORD,

and devoured them,
and they died before the LORD.

3 **Then Moses** said unto Aaron,
This is it that the LORD spake, saying,
I will be sanctified in them that come nigh me,
and before all the people I will be glorified.

And Aaron held his peace.

4 **And Moses** called Mishael and Elzaphan, the sons of Uzziel the uncle of Aaron,
and said unto them,
Come near,
carry your brethren from before the sanctuary out of the camp.

5 **So they** went near,
and carried them in their coats out of the camp;
as Moses had said.

6 **And Moses** said unto Aaron, and unto Eleazar and unto Ithamar, his sons,
Uncover not your heads,
neither rend your clothes;
lest ye die,
and lest wrath come upon all the people:
but let your brethren, the whole house of Israel, bewail the burning which the LORD hath kindled.

7 **And ye** shall not go out from the door of the tabernacle of the congregation,
lest ye die:
for the anointing oil of the LORD is upon you.

And they did according to the word of Moses.

8 **And the LORD** spake unto Aaron, saying,
9 **Do not** drink wine nor strong drink, thou, nor thy sons with thee,
when ye go into the tabernacle of the congregation,
lest ye die:
it shall be a statute for ever throughout your generations:
10 **And that ye** may put difference between holy and unholy, and between unclean and clean;
11 **And that ye** may teach the children of Israel all the statutes which the LORD hath spoken unto them by the hand of Moses.

12 **And Moses** spake unto Aaron, and unto Eleazar and unto Ithamar, his sons that were left,
Take the meat offering that remaineth of the offerings of the LORD made by fire,
and eat it without leaven beside the altar:
for it is most holy:
13 **And ye** shall eat it in the holy place,
because it is thy due, and thy sons' due, of the sacrifices of the LORD made by fire:
for so I am commanded.

14 **And the wave breast and heave shoulder** shall ye eat in a clean place; thou, and thy sons, and thy daughters with thee:
for they be thy due, and thy sons' due,
which are given out of the sacrifices of peace offerings of the children of Israel.

15 **The heave shoulder and the wave breast** shall they bring with the offerings made by fire of the fat,
to wave it for a wave offering before the LORD;
and it shall be thine, and thy sons' with thee, by a statute for ever;
as the LORD hath commanded.

16 **And Moses** diligently sought the goat of the sin offering,
and, {behold}, it was burnt:
and he was angry with Eleazar and Ithamar, the sons of Aaron which were left alive,
saying,
17 **Wherefore** have ye not eaten the sin offering in the holy place,
seeing it is most holy,
and God hath given it you to bear the iniquity of the congregation,
to make atonement for them before the LORD?

18 **Behold,**
the blood of it was not brought in within the holy place:
ye should indeed have eaten it in the holy place,
as I commanded.

19 **And Aaron** said unto Moses,
Behold,
this day have they offered their sin offering and their burnt offering before the LORD;
and such things have befallen me:
and if I had eaten the sin offering to day,
should it have been accepted in the sight of the LORD?

20 **And when Moses** heard that,
he was content.

11

And the LORD spake unto Moses and to Aaron, saying unto them,
2 **Speak** unto the children of Israel, saying,
These are the beasts which ye shall eat among all the beasts that are on the earth.

3 **Whatsoever** parteth the hoof,
and is clovenfooted,
and cheweth the cud, among the beasts,
that shall ye eat.

4 **Nevertheless these** shall ye not eat of them that chew the cud, or of them that divide the hoof:
as the camel, {because he cheweth the cud}, {but divideth not the hoof}; he is unclean unto you.

5 **And the coney**, {because he cheweth the cud}, {but divideth not the hoof}; he is unclean unto you.

6 **And the hare**, {because he cheweth the cud}, {but divideth not the hoof}; he is unclean unto you.

7 **And the swine**, {though he divide the hoof}, {and be clovenfooted}, {yet he cheweth not the cud}; he is unclean to you.

8 **Of their flesh** shall ye not eat,
and their carcase shall ye not touch;
they are unclean to you.

9 **These** shall ye eat of all that are in the waters:
whatsoever hath fins and scales in the waters, in the seas, and in the rivers,
them shall ye eat.

10 **And all that have not fins and scales in the seas, and in the rivers, of all that move in the waters, and of any living thing which is in the waters**, they shall be an abomination unto you:
11 **They** shall be even an abomination unto you;
ye shall not eat of their flesh,
but ye shall have their carcases in abomination.

12 **Whatsoever** hath no fins nor scales in the waters,
that shall be an abomination unto you.
13 **And these** are they which ye shall have in abomination among the fowls;
they shall not be eaten,
they are an abomination: the eagle, and the ossifrage, and the ospray,
14 And the vulture, and the kite after his kind;
15 Every raven after his kind;
16 And the owl, and the night hawk, and the cuckow, and the hawk after his kind,
17 And the little owl, and the cormorant, and the great owl,
18 And the swan, and the pelican, and the gier eagle,
19 And the stork, the heron after her kind, and the lapwing, and the bat.
20 **All fowls that creep**, {going upon all four}, shall be an abomination unto you.
21 **Yet these** may ye eat of every flying creeping thing that goeth upon all four,
which have legs above their feet,
to leap withal upon the earth;
22 **Even these of them** ye may eat; the locust after his kind, and the bald locust after his kind, and the beetle after his kind, and the grasshopper after his kind.
23 **But all other flying creeping things**, {which have four feet}, shall be an abomination unto you.
24 **And for these** ye shall be unclean:
whosoever toucheth the carcase of them shall be unclean until the even.
25 **And whosoever beareth ought of the carcase of them** shall wash his clothes,
and be unclean until the even.
26 **The carcases of every beast which divideth the hoof, and is not clovenfooted, nor cheweth the cud,** are unclean unto you:
every one that toucheth them shall be unclean.
27 **And whatsoever goeth upon his paws, among all manner of beasts that go on all four,** those are unclean unto you:
whoso toucheth their carcase shall be unclean until the even.
28 **And he that beareth the carcase of them** shall wash his clothes,
and be unclean until the even:
they are unclean unto you.
29 **These** also shall be unclean unto you among the creeping things that creep upon the earth; the weasel, and the mouse, and the tortoise after his kind,
30 And the ferret, and the chameleon, and the lizard, and the snail, and the mole.
31 **These** are unclean to you among all that creep:
whosoever doth touch them, {when they be dead}, shall be unclean until the even.
32 **And upon whatsoever any of them**, {when they are dead}, doth fall,
it shall be unclean;
whether it be any vessel of wood, or raiment, or skin, or sack,
whatsoever vessel it be,
wherein any work is done,
it must be put into water,
and it shall be unclean until the even;
so it shall be cleansed.
33 **And every earthen vessel**, {whereinto any of them falleth}, {whatsoever is in it} shall be unclean;
and ye shall break it.
34 **Of all meat which may be eaten,** that on which such water cometh shall be unclean:
and all drink that may be drunk in every such vessel shall be unclean.
35 **And every thing whereupon any part of their carcase falleth** shall be unclean;
whether it be oven, or ranges for pots,
they shall be broken down:
for they are unclean
and shall be unclean unto you.
36 **Nevertheless a fountain or pit**, {wherein there is plenty of water}, shall be clean:
but that which toucheth their carcase shall be unclean.
37 **And if any part of their carcase** fall upon any sowing seed which is to be sown,
it shall be clean.
38 **But if any water** be put upon the seed,
and any part of their carcase fall thereon,
it shall be unclean unto you.
39 **And if any beast**, {of which ye may eat}, die;
he that toucheth the carcase thereof shall be unclean until the even.
40 **And he that eateth of the carcase of it** shall wash his clothes,
and be unclean until the even:
he also that beareth the carcase of it shall wash his clothes,
and be unclean until the even.
41 **And every creeping thing that creepeth upon the earth** shall be an abomination;
it shall not be eaten.
42 **Whatsoever** goeth upon the belly,
and whatsoever goeth upon all four,
or whatsoever hath more feet among all creeping things that creep upon the earth,
them ye shall not eat;
for they are an abomination.
43 **Ye** shall not make yourselves abominable with any creeping thing that creepeth,
neither shall ye make yourselves unclean with them,
that ye should be defiled thereby.
44 **For I** am the LORD your God:
ye shall therefore sanctify yourselves,
and ye shall be holy;
for I am holy:
neither shall ye defile yourselves with any manner of creeping thing that creepeth upon the earth.
45 **For I** am the LORD that bringeth you up out of the land of Egypt,
to be your God:
ye shall therefore be holy,
for I am holy.
46 **This** is the law of the beasts, and of the fowl, and of every living creature that moveth in the waters, and of every creature that creepeth upon the earth:
47 To make a difference between the unclean and the clean, and between the beast that may be eaten and the beast that may not be eaten.

12 **And the LORD** spake unto Moses,
saying,
2 **Speak** unto the children of Israel, saying,
If a woman have conceived seed,
and born a man child:
then she shall be unclean seven days;
according to the days of the separation for her infirmity shall she be unclean.

3 **And in the eighth day** the flesh of his foreskin shall be circumcised.

4 **And she** shall then continue in the blood of her purifying three and thirty days;
she shall touch no hallowed thing,
nor come into the sanctuary,
until the days of her purifying be fulfilled.

5 **But if she** bear a maid child,
then she shall be unclean two weeks, as in her separation:
and she shall continue in the blood of her purifying threescore and six days.

6 **And when the days of her purifying** are fulfilled, for a son, or for a daughter,
she shall bring a lamb of the first year for a burnt offering, and a young pigeon, or a turtledove, for a sin offering, unto the door of the tabernacle of the congregation, unto the priest:
7 **Who** shall offer it before the LORD,
and make an atonement for her;
and she shall be cleansed from the issue of her blood.

This is the law for her that hath born a male or a female.

8 **And if she** be not able to bring a lamb,
then she shall bring two turtles, or two young pigeons; the one for the burnt offering, and the other for a sin offering:
and the priest shall make an atonement for her,
and she shall be clean.

13 **And the LORD** spake unto Moses and Aaron,
saying,
2 **When a man** shall have in the skin of his flesh a rising, a scab, or bright spot,
and it be in the skin of his flesh like the plague of leprosy;
then he shall be brought unto Aaron the priest, or unto one of his sons the priests:
3 **And the priest** shall look on the plague in the skin of the flesh:
and when the hair in the plague is turned white,
and the plague in sight be deeper than the skin of his flesh,
it is a plague of leprosy:
and the priest shall look on him,
and pronounce him unclean.

4 **If the bright spot** be white in the skin of his flesh,
and in sight be not deeper than the skin,
and the hair thereof be not turned white;
then the priest shall shut up him that hath the plague seven days:
5 **And the priest** shall look on him the seventh day:
and, {behold}, if the plague in his sight be at a stay,
and the plague spread not in the skin;
then the priest shall shut him up seven days more:
6 **And the priest** shall look on him again the seventh day:
and, {behold}, if the plague be somewhat dark,
and the plague spread not in the skin,
the priest shall pronounce him clean:
it is but a scab:
and he shall wash his clothes,
and be clean.

7 **But if the scab** spread much abroad in the skin,
after that he hath been seen of the priest for his cleansing,
he shall be seen of the priest again.

8 **And if the priest** see that,
behold,
the scab spreadeth in the skin,
then the priest shall pronounce him unclean:
it is a leprosy.

9 **When the plague of leprosy** is in a man,
then he shall be brought unto the priest;
10 **And the priest** shall see him:
and, {behold}, if the rising be white in the skin,
and it have turned the hair white,
and there be quick raw flesh in the rising;
11 **It** is an old leprosy in the skin of his flesh,
and the priest shall pronounce him unclean,
and shall not shut him up:
for he is unclean.

12 **And if a leprosy** break out abroad in the skin,
and the leprosy cover all the skin of him that hath the plague from his head even to his foot,
wheresoever the priest looketh;
13 **Then the priest** shall consider:
and, {behold}, if the leprosy have covered all his flesh,
he shall pronounce him clean that hath the plague:
it is all turned white:
he is clean.

14 **But when raw flesh** appeareth in him,
he shall be unclean.

15 **And the priest** shall see the raw flesh,
and pronounce him to be unclean:
for the raw flesh is unclean:
it is a leprosy.

16 **Or if the raw flesh** turn again,
and be changed unto white,
he shall come unto the priest;
17 **And the priest** shall see him:
and, {behold}, if the plague be turned into white;
then the priest shall pronounce him clean that hath the plague:
he is clean.

18 **The flesh also, in which, even in the skin thereof,** was a boil,
and is healed,
19 **And in the place of the boil** there be a white rising, or a bright spot, white, and somewhat reddish,
and it be shewed to the priest;
20 **And if**, {when the priest seeth it},
behold,
it be in sight lower than the skin,
and the hair thereof be turned white;
the priest shall pronounce him unclean:
it is a plague of leprosy broken out of the boil.

21 **But if the priest** look on it,
and, {behold}, there be no white hairs therein,
and if it be not lower than the skin,
but be somewhat dark;
then the priest shall shut him up seven days:

22 **And if it** spread much abroad in the skin,
then the priest shall pronounce him unclean:
it is a plague.

23 **But if the bright spot** stay in his place,
and spread not,
it is a burning boil;
and the priest shall pronounce him clean.

24 **Or if there** be any flesh, in the skin whereof there is a hot burning,
and the quick flesh that burneth have a white bright spot, somewhat reddish, or white;

25 **Then the priest** shall look upon it:
and, {behold}, if the hair in the bright spot be turned white,
and it be in sight deeper than the skin;
it is a leprosy broken out of the burning:
wherefore the priest shall pronounce him unclean:
it is the plague of leprosy.

26 **But if the priest** look on it,
and, {behold}, there be no white hair in the bright spot,
and it be no lower than the other skin,
but be somewhat dark;
then the priest shall shut him up seven days:

27 **And the priest** shall look upon him the seventh day:
and if it be spread much abroad in the skin,
then the priest shall pronounce him unclean:
it is the plague of leprosy.

28 **And if the bright spot** stay in his place,
and spread not in the skin,
but it be somewhat dark;
it is a rising of the burning,
and the priest shall pronounce him clean:
for it is an inflammation of the burning.

29 **If a man or woman** have a plague upon the head or the beard;

30 **Then the priest** shall see the plague:
and, {behold}, if it be in sight deeper than the skin;
and there be in it a yellow thin hair;
then the priest shall pronounce him unclean:
it is a dry scall, even a leprosy upon the head or beard.

31 **And if the priest** look on the plague of the scall,
and, {behold}, it be not in sight deeper than the skin,
and that there is no black hair in it;
then the priest shall shut up him that hath the plague of the scall seven days:

32 **And in the seventh day** the priest shall look on the plague:
and, {behold}, if the scall spread not,
and there be in it no yellow hair,
and the scall be not in sight deeper than the skin;

33 **He** shall be shaven,
but the scall shall he not shave;
and the priest shall shut up him that hath the scall seven days more:

34 **And in the seventh day** the priest shall look on the scall:
and, {behold}, if the scall be not spread in the skin,
nor be in sight deeper than the skin;
then the priest shall pronounce him clean:
and he shall wash his clothes,
and be clean.

35 **But if the scall** spread much in the skin after his cleansing;

36 **Then the priest** shall look on him:
and, {behold}, if the scall be spread in the skin,
the priest shall not seek for yellow hair;
he is unclean.

37 **But if the scall** be in his sight at a stay,
and that there is black hair grown up therein;
the scall is healed,
he is clean:
and the priest shall pronounce him clean.

38 **If a man also or a woman** have in the skin of their flesh bright spots, even white bright spots;

39 **Then the priest** shall look:
and, {behold}, if the bright spots in the skin of their flesh be darkish white;
it is a freckled spot that groweth in the skin;
he is clean.

40 **And the man whose hair is fallen off his head,** he is bald;
yet is he clean.

41 **And he that hath his hair fallen off from the part of his head toward his face,** he is forehead bald:
yet is he clean.

42 **And if there** be in the bald head, or bald forehead, a white reddish sore;
it is a leprosy sprung up in his bald head, or his bald forehead.

43 **Then the priest** shall look upon it:
and, {behold}, if the rising of the sore be white reddish in his bald head, or in his bald forehead,
as the leprosy appeareth in the skin of the flesh;

44 **He** is a leprous man,
he is unclean:
the priest shall pronounce him utterly unclean;
his plague is in his head.

45 **And the leper in whom the plague is,** his clothes shall be rent,
and his head bare,
and he shall put a covering upon his upper lip,
and shall cry,
Unclean, unclean.

46 **All the days wherein the plague shall be in him** he shall be defiled;
he is unclean:
he shall dwell alone;
without the camp shall his habitation be.

47 **The garment also that the plague of leprosy is in,** {whether it be a woollen garment, or a linen garment};

48 {Whether it be in the warp, or woof; of linen, or of woollen; whether in a skin, or in any thing made of skin};

49 {And if the plague be greenish or reddish in the garment, or in the skin, either in the warp, or in the woof, or in any thing of skin;
it is a plague of leprosy,
and shall be shewed unto the priest:

50 **And the priest** shall look upon the plague,
and shut up it that hath the plague seven days:

51 **And he** shall look on the plague on the seventh day:

if the plague be spread in the garment, either in the warp, or in the woof, or in a skin, or in any work that is made of skin;
the plague is a fretting leprosy;
it is unclean.

52 **He** shall therefore burn that garment, whether warp or woof, in woollen or in linen, or any thing of skin,
wherein the plague is:
for it is a fretting leprosy;
it shall be burnt in the fire.

53 **And if the priest** shall look,
and, {behold}, the plague be not spread in the garment, either in the warp, or in the woof, or in any thing of skin;
54 **Then the priest** shall command
that they wash the thing wherein the plague is,
and he shall shut it up seven days more:
55 **And the priest** shall look on the plague,
after that it is washed:
and, {behold}, if the plague have not changed his colour,
and the plague be not spread;
it is unclean;
thou shalt burn it in the fire;
it is fret inward,
whether it be bare within or without.

56 **And if the priest** look,
and, {behold}, the plague be somewhat dark after the washing of it;
then he shall rend it out of the garment, or out of the skin, or out of the warp, or out of the woof:
57 **And if it** appear still in the garment, either in the warp, or in the woof, or in any thing of skin;
it is a spreading plague:
thou shalt burn that wherein the plague is with fire.

58 **And the garment, either warp, or woof, or whatsoever thing of skin it be**, which thou shalt wash,
if the plague be departed from them,
then it shall be washed the second time,
and shall be clean.

59 **This** is the law of the plague of leprosy in a garment of woollen or linen, either in the warp, or woof, or any thing of skins,
to pronounce it clean,
or to pronounce it unclean.

14 ✕ **And the LORD** spake unto Moses,
saying,
2 **This** shall be the law of the leper in the day of his cleansing:
He shall be brought unto the priest:
3 **And the priest** shall go forth out of the camp;
and the priest shall look,
and, behold, if the plague of leprosy be healed in the leper;
4 **Then** shall the priest command
to take for him that is to be cleansed two birds alive and clean, and cedar wood, and scarlet, and hyssop:
5 **And the priest** shall command
that one of the birds be killed in an earthen vessel over running water:
6 **As for the living bird,** he shall take it, and the cedar wood, and the scarlet, and the hyssop,
and shall dip them and the living bird in the blood of the bird that was killed over the running water:
7 **And he** shall sprinkle upon him that is to be cleansed from the leprosy seven times,
and shall pronounce him clean,
and shall let the living bird loose into the open field.

8 **And he that is to be cleansed** shall wash his clothes,
and shave off all his hair,
and wash himself in water,
that he may be clean:
and after that he shall come into the camp,
and shall tarry abroad out of his tent seven days.

9 **But it** shall be on the seventh day,
that he shall shave all his hair off his head and his beard and his eyebrows,
even all his hair he shall shave off:
and he shall wash his clothes,
also he shall wash his flesh in water,
and he shall be clean.

10 **And on the eighth day** he shall take two he lambs without blemish, and one ewe lamb of the first year without blemish, and three tenth deals of fine flour for a meat offering, {mingled with oil}, and one log of oil.

11 **And the priest that maketh him clean** shall present the man that is to be made clean, and those things, before the LORD, at the door of the tabernacle of the congregation:
12 **And the priest** shall take one he lamb,
and offer him for a trespass offering, and the log of oil,
and wave them for a wave offering before the LORD:
13 **And he** shall slay the lamb in the place where he shall kill the sin offering and the burnt offering, in the holy place:
for as the sin offering is the priest's,
so is the trespass offering:
it is most holy:
14 **And the priest** shall take some of the blood of the trespass offering,
and the priest shall put it upon the tip of the right ear of him that is to be cleansed, and upon the thumb of his right hand, and upon the great toe of his right foot:
15 **And the priest** shall take some of the log of oil,
and pour it into the palm of his own left hand:
16 **And the priest** shall dip his right finger in the oil that is in his left hand,
and shall sprinkle of the oil with his finger seven times before the LORD:
17 **And of the rest of the oil that is in his hand** shall the priest put upon the tip of the right ear of him that is to be cleansed, and upon the thumb of his right hand, and upon the great toe of his right foot, upon the blood of the trespass offering:
18 **And the remnant of the oil that is in the priest's hand** he shall pour upon the head of him that is to be cleansed:
and the priest shall make an atonement for him before the LORD.

19 **And the priest** shall offer the sin offering,
and make an atonement for him that is to be cleansed from his uncleanness;
and afterward he shall kill the burnt offering:
20 **And the priest** shall offer the burnt offering and the meat offering upon the altar:

and the priest shall make an atonement for him,
and he shall be clean.

21 **And if he** be poor,
and cannot get so much;
then he shall take one lamb for a trespass offering to be waved,
to make an atonement for him, and one tenth deal of fine flour mingled with oil for a meat offering, and a log of oil;
22 And two turtledoves, or two young pigeons,
such as he is able to get;
and the one shall be a sin offering, and the other a burnt offering.

23 **And he** shall bring them on the eighth day for his cleansing unto the priest, unto the door of the tabernacle of the congregation, before the LORD.

24 **And the priest** shall take the lamb of the trespass offering, and the log of oil,
and the priest shall wave them for a wave offering before the LORD:
25 **And he** shall kill the lamb of the trespass offering,
and the priest shall take some of the blood of the trespass offering,
and put it upon the tip of the right ear of him that is to be cleansed, and upon the thumb of his right hand, and upon the great toe of his right foot:
26 **And the priest** shall pour of the oil into the palm of his own left hand:
27 **And the priest** shall sprinkle with his right finger some of the oil that is in his left hand seven times before the LORD:
28 **And the priest** shall put of the oil that is in his hand upon the tip of the right ear of him that is to be cleansed, and upon the thumb of his right hand, and upon the great toe of his right foot, upon the place of the blood of the trespass offering:
29 **And the rest of the oil that is in the priest's hand** he shall put upon the head of him that is to be cleansed,
to make an atonement for him before the LORD.

30 **And he** shall offer the one of the turtledoves, or of the young pigeons,
such as he can get;
31 **Even such as he** is able to get, the one for a sin offering, and the other for a burnt offering, with the meat offering:
and the priest shall make an atonement for him that is to be cleansed before the LORD.

32 **This** is the law of him in whom is the plague of leprosy,
whose hand is not able to get that which pertaineth to his cleansing.

33 **And the LORD** spake unto Moses and unto Aaron,
saying,
34 **When ye** be come into the land of Canaan,
which I give to you for a possession,
and I put the plague of leprosy in a house of the land of your possession;
35 **And he that owneth the house** shall come and tell the priest,
saying,
It seemeth to me there is as it were a plague in the house:
36 **Then the priest** shall command
that they empty the house,
before the priest go into it
to see the plague,
that all that is in the house be not made unclean:
and afterward the priest shall go in to see the house:
37 **And he** shall look on the plague,
and, {<u>behold</u>}, if the plague be in the walls of the house with hollow strakes, greenish or reddish,
which in sight are lower than the wall;
38 **Then the priest** shall go out of the house to the door of the house,
and shut up the house seven days:
39 **And the priest** shall come again the seventh day,
and shall look:
and, {<u>behold</u>}, if the plague be spread in the walls of the house;
40 **Then the priest** shall command
that they take away the stones in which the plague is,
and they shall cast them into an unclean place without the city:
41 **And he** shall cause the house to be scraped within round about,
and they shall pour out the dust that they scrape off without the city into an unclean place:
42 **And they** shall take other stones,
and put them in the place of those stones;
and he shall take other morter,
and shall plaister the house.

43 **And if the plague** come again,
and break out in the house,
after that he hath taken away the stones,
and after he hath scraped the house,
and after it is plaistered;
44 **Then the priest** shall come and look,
and, {<u>behold</u>}, if the plague be spread in the house,
it is a fretting leprosy in the house;
it is unclean.

45 **And he** shall break down the house, the stones of it, and the timber thereof, and all the morter of the house;
and he shall carry them forth out of the city into an unclean place.

46 **Moreover he that goeth into the house all the while that it is shut up** shall be unclean until the even.

47 **And he that lieth in the house** shall wash his clothes;
and he that eateth in the house shall wash his clothes.

48 **And if the priest** shall come in,
and look upon it,
and, {<u>behold</u>}, the plague hath not spread in the house,
after the house was plaistered:
then the priest shall pronounce the house clean,
because the plague is healed.

49 **And he** shall take to cleanse the house two birds, and cedar wood, and scarlet, and hyssop:
50 **And he** shall kill the one of the birds in an earthen vessel over running water:
51 **And he** shall take the cedar wood, and the hyssop, and the scarlet, and the living bird,
and dip them in the blood of the slain bird, and in the running water,
and sprinkle the house seven times:
52 **And he** shall cleanse the house with the blood of the bird, and with the running water, and with the living bird, and with the cedar wood, and with the hyssop, and with the scarlet:
53 **But he** shall let go the living bird out of the city into the open fields,

and make an atonement for the house:
and it shall be clean.
54 **This** is the law for all manner of plague of leprosy, and scall,
55 And for the leprosy of a garment, and of a house,
56 And for a rising, and for a scab, and for a bright spot:
57 To teach
when it is unclean,
and when it is clean:
this is the law of leprosy.

15 **And the LORD** spake unto Moses and to Aaron,
saying,
2 **Speak** unto the children of Israel,
and say unto them,
When any man hath a running issue out of his flesh,
because of his issue he is unclean.
3 **And this** shall be his uncleanness in his issue:
whether his flesh run with his issue,
or his flesh be stopped from his issue,
it is his uncleanness.
4 **Every bed**, {whereon he lieth that hath the issue}, is unclean:
and every thing, {whereon he sitteth], shall be unclean.
5 **And whosoever toucheth his bed** shall wash his clothes,
and bathe himself in water,
and be unclean until the even.
6 **And he that sitteth on any thing whereon he sat that hath the issue** shall wash his clothes,
and bathe himself in water,
and be unclean until the even.
7 **And he that toucheth the flesh of him that hath the issue** shall wash his clothes,
and bathe himself in water,
and be unclean until the even.
8 **And if he that hath the issue** spit upon him that is clean;
then he shall wash his clothes,
and bathe himself in water,
and be unclean until the even.
9 **And what saddle soever he rideth upon that hath the issue** shall be unclean.
10 **And whosoever toucheth any thing that was under him** shall be unclean until the even:
and he that beareth any of those things shall wash his clothes,
and bathe himself in water,
and be unclean until the even.
11 **And whomsoever he toucheth that hath the issue, and hath not rinsed his hands in water,** he shall wash his clothes,
and bathe himself in water,
and be unclean until the even.
12 **And the vessel of earth, that he toucheth which hath the issue,** shall be broken:
and every vessel of wood shall be rinsed in water.
13 **And when he that hath an issue** is cleansed of his issue;
then he shall number to himself seven days for his cleansing,
and wash his clothes,
and bathe his flesh in running water,
and shall be clean.
14 **And on the eighth day** he shall take to him two turtledoves, or two young pigeons,
and come before the LORD unto the door of the tabernacle of the congregation,
and give them unto the priest:
15 **And the priest** shall offer them, the one for a sin offering, and the other for a burnt offering;
and the priest shall make an atonement for him before the LORD for his issue.
16 **And if any man's seed of copulation** go out from him,
then he shall wash all his flesh in water,
and be unclean until the even.
17 **And every garment, and every skin**, {whereon is the seed of copulation}, shall be washed with water,
and be unclean until the even.
18 **The woman also with whom man shall lie with seed of copulation,** they shall both bathe themselves in water,
and be unclean until the even.
19 **And if a woman** have an issue,
and her issue in her flesh be blood,
she shall be put apart seven days:
and whosoever toucheth her shall be unclean until the even.
20 **And every thing that she lieth upon in her separation** shall be unclean:
every thing also that she sitteth upon shall be unclean.
21 **And whosoever toucheth her bed** shall wash his clothes,
and bathe himself in water,
and be unclean until the even.
22 **And whosoever toucheth any thing that she sat upon** shall wash his clothes,
and bathe himself in water,
and be unclean until the even.
23 **And if it** be on her bed, or on any thing whereon she sitteth,
when he toucheth it,
he shall be unclean until the even.
24 **And if any man** lie with her at all,
and her flowers be upon him,
he shall be unclean seven days;
and all the bed whereon he lieth shall be unclean.
25 **And if a woman** have an issue of her blood many days out of the time of her separation,
or if it run beyond the time of her separation;
all the days of the issue of her uncleanness shall be as the days of her separation:
she shall be unclean.
26 **Every bed whereon she lieth all the days of her issue** shall be unto her as the bed of her separation:
and whatsoever she sitteth upon shall be unclean, as the uncleanness of her separation.
27 **And whosoever toucheth those things** shall be unclean,
and shall wash his clothes,
and bathe himself in water,
and be unclean until the even.
28 **But if she** be cleansed of her issue,
then she shall number to herself seven days,
and after that she shall be clean.
29 **And on the eighth day** she shall take unto her two turtles, or two young pigeons,
and bring them unto the priest, to the door of the tabernacle of the congregation.
30 **And the priest** shall offer the one for a sin offering, and the other for a burnt offering;
and the priest shall make an atonement for her before the LORD for the issue of her uncleanness.

31 **Thus** shall ye separate the children of Israel from their uncleanness;
that they die not in their uncleanness,
when they defile my tabernacle that is among them.

32 **This** is the law of him that hath an issue, and of him whose seed goeth from him,
and is defiled therewith;

33 And of her that is sick of her flowers, and of him that hath an issue, of the man, and of the woman, and of him that lieth with her that is unclean.

16 **And the LORD** spake unto Moses after the death of the two sons of Aaron,
when they offered before the LORD,
and died;

2 **And the LORD** said unto Moses,
Speak unto Aaron thy brother,
that he come not at all times into the holy place within the vail before the mercy seat,
which is upon the ark;
that he die not:
for I will appear in the cloud upon the mercy seat.

3 **Thus** shall Aaron come into the holy place: with a young bullock for a sin offering, and a ram for a burnt offering.

4 **He** shall put on the holy linen coat,
and he shall have the linen breeches upon his flesh,
and shall be girded with a linen girdle,
and with the linen mitre shall he be attired:
these are holy garments;
therefore shall he wash his flesh in water,
and so put them on.

5 **And he** shall take of the congregation of the children of Israel two kids of the goats for a sin offering, and one ram for a burnt offering.

6 **And Aaron** shall offer his bullock of the sin offering,
which is for himself,
and make an atonement for himself, and for his house.

7 **And he** shall take the two goats,
and present them before the LORD at the door of the tabernacle of the congregation.

8 **And Aaron** shall cast lots upon the two goats; one lot for the LORD, and the other lot for the scapegoat.

9 **And Aaron** shall bring the goat upon which the LORD's lot fell,
and offer him for a sin offering.

10 **But the goat**, {on which the lot fell to be the scapegoat}, shall be presented alive before the LORD,
to make an atonement with him,
and to let him go for a scapegoat into the wilderness.

11 **And Aaron** shall bring the bullock of the sin offering,
which is for himself,
and shall make an atonement for himself, and for his house,
and shall kill the bullock of the sin offering which is for himself:

12 **And he** shall take a censer full of burning coals of fire from off the altar before the LORD, and his hands full of sweet incense beaten small,
and bring it within the vail:

13 **And he** shall put the incense upon the fire before the LORD,
that the cloud of the incense may cover the mercy seat that is upon the testimony,
that he die not:

14 **And he** shall take of the blood of the bullock,
and sprinkle it with his finger upon the mercy seat eastward;
and before the mercy seat shall he sprinkle of the blood with his finger seven times.

15 **Then** shall he kill the goat of the sin offering,
that is for the people,
and bring his blood within the vail,
and do with that blood as he did with the blood of the bullock,
and sprinkle it upon the mercy seat, and before the mercy seat:

16 **And he** shall make an atonement for the holy place, because of the uncleanness of the children of Israel, and because of their transgressions in all their sins:
and so shall he do for the tabernacle of the congregation,
that remaineth among them in the midst of their uncleanness.

17 **And there** shall be no man in the tabernacle of the congregation
when he goeth in to make an atonement in the holy place,
until he come out,
and have made an atonement for himself, and for his household, and for all the congregation of Israel.

18 **And he** shall go out unto the altar that is before the LORD,
and make an atonement for it;
and shall take of the blood of the bullock, and of the blood of the goat,
and put it upon the horns of the altar round about.

19 **And he** shall sprinkle of the blood upon it with his finger seven times,
and cleanse it,
and hallow it from the uncleanness of the children of Israel.

20 **And when he** hath made an end of reconciling the holy place, and the tabernacle of the congregation, and the altar,
he shall bring the live goat:

21 **And Aaron** shall lay both his hands upon the head of the live goat,
and confess over him all the iniquities of the children of Israel, and all their transgressions in all their sins,
putting them upon the head of the goat,
and shall send him away by the hand of a fit man into the wilderness:

22 **And the goat** shall bear upon him all their iniquities unto a land not inhabited:
and he shall let go the goat in the wilderness.

23 **And Aaron** shall come into the tabernacle of the congregation,
and shall put off the linen garments,
which he put on
when he went into the holy place,
and shall leave them there:

24 **And he** shall wash his flesh with water in the holy place,
and put on his garments,
and come forth,
and offer his burnt offering, and the burnt offering of the people,
and make an atonement for himself, and for the people.

25 **And the fat of the sin offering** shall he burn upon the altar.

26 **And he that let go the goat for the scapegoat** shall wash his clothes,
and bathe his flesh in water,
and afterward come into the camp.

27 **And the bullock for the sin offering, and the goat for the sin offering**, {whose blood was brought in to make atonement in the holy place}, shall one carry forth without the camp;
and they shall burn in the fire their skins, and their flesh, and their dung.

28 **And he that burneth them** shall wash his clothes,
and bathe his flesh in water,
and afterward he shall come into the camp.

29 **And this** shall be a statute for ever unto you:
that in the seventh month, on the tenth day of the month, ye shall afflict your souls,
and do no work at all,
whether it be one of your own country, or a stranger that sojourneth among you:

30 **For on that day** shall the priest make an atonement for you,
to cleanse you,
that ye may be clean from all your sins before the LORD.

31 **It** shall be a sabbath of rest unto you,
and ye shall afflict your souls, by a statute for ever.

32 **And the priest**, {whom he shall anoint}, {and whom he shall consecrate to minister in the priest's office in his father's stead}, shall make the atonement,
and shall put on the linen clothes, even the holy garments:

33 **And he** shall make an atonement for the holy sanctuary,
and he shall make an atonement for the tabernacle of the congregation, and for the altar,
and he shall make an atonement for the priests, and for all the people of the congregation.

34 **And this** shall be an everlasting statute unto you,
to make an atonement for the children of Israel for all their sins once a year.
And he did as the LORD commanded Moses.

17 **And the LORD** spake unto Moses,
saying,

2 **Speak** unto Aaron, and unto his sons, and unto all the children of Israel,
and say unto them;
This is the thing which the LORD hath commanded,
saying,

3 **What man soever there** be of the house of Israel,
that killeth an ox, or lamb, or goat, in the camp,
or that killeth it out of the camp,

4 **And** bringeth it not unto the door of the tabernacle of the congregation,
to offer an offering unto the LORD before the tabernacle of the LORD;
blood shall be imputed unto that man;
he hath shed blood;
and that man shall be cut off from among his people:

5 **To the end that the children of Israel** may bring their sacrifices,
which they offer in the open field,
even that they may bring them unto the LORD, unto the door of the tabernacle of the congregation, unto the priest,
and offer them for peace offerings unto the LORD.

6 **And the priest** shall sprinkle the blood upon the altar of the LORD at the door of the tabernacle of the congregation,
and burn the fat for a sweet savour unto the LORD.

7 **And they** shall no more offer their sacrifices unto devils,
after whom they have gone a whoring.
This shall be a statute for ever unto them throughout their generations.

8 **And thou** shalt say unto them,
Whatsoever man there be of the house of Israel, or of the strangers which sojourn among you,
that offereth a burnt offering or sacrifice,

9 **And** bringeth it not unto the door of the tabernacle of the congregation,
to offer it unto the LORD;
even that man shall be cut off from among his people.

10 **And whatsoever man there** be of the house of Israel, or of the strangers that sojourn among you,
that eateth any manner of blood;
I will even set my face against that soul that eateth blood,
and will cut him off from among his people.

11 **For the life of the flesh** is in the blood:
and I have given it to you upon the altar
to make an atonement for your souls:
for it is the blood that maketh an atonement for the soul.

12 **Therefore I** said unto the children of Israel,
No soul of you shall eat blood,
neither shall any stranger that sojourneth among you eat blood.

13 **And whatsoever man there** be of the children of Israel, or of the strangers that sojourn among you,
which hunteth and catcheth any beast or fowl that may be eaten;
he shall even pour out the blood thereof,
and cover it with dust.

14 **For it** is the life of all flesh;
the blood of it is for the life thereof:
therefore I said unto the children of Israel,
Ye shall eat the blood of no manner of flesh:
for the life of all flesh is the blood thereof:
whosoever eateth it shall be cut off.

15 **And every soul that eateth that which died of itself, or that which was torn with beasts**, {whether it be one of your own country, or a stranger}, he shall both wash his clothes,
and bathe himself in water,
and be unclean until the even:
then shall he be clean.

16 **But if he** wash them not,
nor bathe his flesh;
then he shall bear his iniquity.

18 **And the LORD** spake unto Moses,
saying,

2 **Speak** unto the children of Israel,
and say unto them,
I am the LORD your God.

3 **After the doings of the land of Egypt**, {wherein ye dwelt}, shall ye not do:
and after the doings of the land of Canaan, {whither I bring you}, shall ye not do:
neither shall ye walk in their ordinances.
4 **Ye** shall do my judgments,
and keep mine ordinances,
to walk therein:
I am the LORD your God.
5 **Ye** shall therefore keep my statutes, and my judgments:
which if a man do,
he shall live in them:
I am the LORD.
6 **None of you** shall approach to any that is near of kin to him,
to uncover their nakedness:
I am the LORD.
7 **The nakedness of thy father, or the nakedness of thy mother,** shalt thou not uncover:
she is thy mother;
thou shalt not uncover her nakedness.
8 **The nakedness of thy father's wife** shalt thou not uncover:
it is thy father's nakedness.
9 **The nakedness of thy sister, the daughter of thy father, or daughter of thy mother,** {whether she be born at home, or born abroad}, even their nakedness thou shalt not uncover.
10 **The nakedness of thy son's daughter, or of thy daughter's daughter**, even their nakedness thou shalt not uncover:
for theirs is thine own nakedness.
11 **The nakedness of thy father's wife's daughter**, {begotten of thy father}, {she is thy sister}, thou shalt not uncover her nakedness.
12 **Thou** shalt not uncover the nakedness of thy father's sister:
she is thy father's near kinswoman.
13 **Thou** shalt not uncover the nakedness of thy mother's sister:
for she is thy mother's near kinswoman.
14 **Thou** shalt not uncover the nakedness of thy father's brother,
thou shalt not approach to his wife:
she is thine aunt.
15 **Thou** shalt not uncover the nakedness of thy daughter in law:
she is thy son's wife;
thou shalt not uncover her nakedness.
16 **Thou** shalt not uncover the nakedness of thy brother's wife:
it is thy brother's nakedness.
17 **Thou** shalt not uncover the nakedness of a woman and her daughter,
neither shalt thou take her son's daughter, or her daughter's daughter,
to uncover her nakedness;
for they are her near kinswomen:
it is wickedness.
18 **Neither** shalt thou take a wife to her sister, {to vex her}, {to uncover her nakedness}, beside the other in her life time.
19 **Also thou** shalt not approach unto a woman
to uncover her nakedness,
as long as she is put apart for her uncleanness.
20 **Moreover thou** shalt not lie carnally with thy neighbour's wife,
to defile thyself with her.
21 **And thou** shalt not let any of thy seed pass through the fire to Molech,
neither shalt thou profane the name of thy God:
I am the LORD.
22 **Thou** shalt not lie with mankind, as with womankind:
it is abomination.
23 **Neither** shalt thou lie with any beast
to defile thyself therewith:
neither shall any woman stand before a beast
to lie down thereto:
it is confusion.
24 **Defile not ye** yourselves in any of these things:
for in all these the nations are defiled which I cast out before you:
25 **And the land** is defiled:
therefore I do visit the iniquity thereof upon it,
and the land itself vomiteth out her inhabitants.
26 **Ye** shall therefore keep my statutes and my judgments,
and shall not commit any of these abominations; neither any of your own nation, nor any stranger that sojourneth among you:
27 (For all these abominations have the men of the land done,
which were before you,
and the land is defiled;)
28 **That the land** spue not you out also,
when ye defile it,
as it spued out the nations that were before you.
29 **For whosoever shall commit any of these abominations,** even the souls that commit them shall be cut off from among their people.
30 **Therefore** shall ye keep mine ordinance,
that ye commit not any one of these abominable customs,
which were committed before you,
and that ye defile not yourselves therein:
I am the LORD your God.

19

And the LORD spake unto Moses,
saying,
2 **Speak** unto all the congregation of the children of Israel,
and say unto them,
Ye shall be holy:
for I the LORD your God am holy.
3 **Ye** shall fear every man his mother, and his father,
and keep my sabbaths:
I am the LORD your God.
4 **Turn ye not** unto idols,
nor make to yourselves molten gods:
I am the LORD your God.
5 **And if ye** offer a sacrifice of peace offerings unto the LORD,
ye shall offer it at your own will.
6 **It** shall be eaten the same day ye offer it, and on the morrow:
and if ought remain until the third day,
it shall be burnt in the fire.
7 **And if it** be eaten at all on the third day,
it is abominable;
it shall not be accepted.
8 **Therefore every one that eateth it** shall bear his iniquity,
because he hath profaned the hallowed thing of the LORD:
and that soul shall be cut off from among his people.

9 **And when ye** reap the harvest of your land,
thou shalt not wholly reap the corners of thy field,
neither shalt thou gather the gleanings of thy harvest.

10 **And thou** shalt not glean thy vineyard,
neither shalt thou gather every grape of thy vineyard;
thou shalt leave them for the poor and stranger:
I am the LORD your God.

11 **Ye** shall not steal,
neither deal falsely,
neither lie one to another.

12 **And ye** shall not swear by my name falsely,
neither shalt thou profane the name of thy God:
I am the LORD.

13 **Thou** shalt not defraud thy neighbour,
neither rob him:
the wages of him that is hired shall not abide with thee all night until the morning.

14 **Thou** shalt not curse the deaf,
nor put a stumblingblock before the blind,
but shalt fear thy God:
I am the LORD.

15 **Ye** shall do no unrighteousness in judgment:
thou shalt not respect the person of the poor,
nor honor the person of the mighty:
but in righteousness shalt thou judge thy neighbour.

16 **Thou** shalt not go up and down as a talebearer among thy people:
neither shalt thou stand against the blood of thy neighbour;
I am the LORD.

17 **Thou** shalt not hate thy brother in thine heart:
thou shalt in any wise rebuke thy neighbour,
and not suffer sin upon him.

18 **Thou** shalt not avenge,
nor bear any grudge against the children of thy people,
but thou shalt love thy neighbour as thyself:
I am the LORD.

19 **Ye** shall keep my statutes.
Thou shalt not let thy cattle gender with a diverse kind:
thou shalt not sow thy field with mingled seed:
neither shall a garment mingled of linen and woollen come upon thee.

20 **And whosoever lieth carnally with a woman**, {that is a bondmaid}, {betrothed to an husband}, {and not at all redeemed}, {nor freedom given her}; she shall be scourged;
they shall not be put to death,
because she was not free.

21 **And he** shall bring his trespass offering unto the LORD, unto the door of the tabernacle of the congregation, even a ram for a trespass offering.

22 **And the priest** shall make an atonement for him with the ram of the trespass offering before the LORD for his sin which he hath done:
and the sin which he hath done shall be forgiven him.

23 **And when ye** shall come into the land,
and shall have planted all manner of trees for food,
then ye shall count the fruit thereof as uncircumcised:
three years shall it be as uncircumcised unto you:
it shall not be eaten of.

24 **But in the fourth year** all the fruit thereof shall be holy to praise the LORD withal.

25 **And in the fifth year** shall ye eat of the fruit thereof,
that it may yield unto you the increase thereof:
I am the LORD your God.

26 **Ye** shall not eat any thing with the blood:
neither shall ye use enchantment,
nor observe times.

27 **Ye** shall not round the corners of your heads,
neither shalt thou mar the corners of thy beard.

28 **Ye** shall not make any cuttings in your flesh for the dead,
nor print any marks upon you:
I am the LORD.

29 **Do not** prostitute thy daughter,
to cause her to be a whore;
lest the land fall to whoredom,
and the land become full of wickedness.

30 **Ye** shall keep my sabbaths,
and reverence my sanctuary:
I am the LORD.

31 **Regard not** them that have familiar spirits,
neither seek after wizards,
to be defiled by them:
I am the LORD your God.

32 **Thou** shalt rise up before the hoary head,
and honour the face of the old man,
and fear thy God:
I am the LORD.

33 **And if a stranger** sojourn with thee in your land,
ye shall not vex him.

34 **But the stranger that dwelleth with you** shall be unto you as one born among you,
and thou shalt love him as thyself;
for ye were strangers in the land of Egypt:
I am the LORD your God.

35 **Ye** shall do no unrighteousness in judgment, in meteyard, in weight, or in measure.

36 **Just balances, just weights, a just ephah, and a just hin,** shall ye have:
I am the LORD your God,
which brought you out of the land of Egypt.

37 **Therefore** shall ye observe all my statutes, and all my judgments,
and do them:
I am the LORD.

20

And the LORD spake unto Moses,
saying,

2 **Again, thou** shalt say to the children of Israel,
Whosoever he be of the children of Israel, or of the strangers that sojourn in Israel,
that giveth any of his seed unto Molech;
he shall surely be put to death:
the people of the land shall stone him with stones.

3 **And I** will set my face against that man,
and will cut him off from among his people;
because he hath given of his seed unto Molech,
to defile my sanctuary,
and to profane my holy name.

4 **And if the people of the land** do any ways hide their eyes from the man,
when he giveth of his seed unto Molech,
and kill him not:

5 **Then I** will set my face against that man, and against his family,
and will cut him off, and all that go a whoring after him, {to commit whoredom with Molech}, from among their people.

6 **And the soul that turneth after such as have familiar spirits, and after wizards,** {to go a whoring after them}, I will even set my face against that soul,
and will cut him off from among his people.

7 **Sanctify** yourselves therefore,
and be ye holy:
for I am the LORD your God.

8 **And ye** shall keep my statutes,
and do them:
I am the LORD which sanctify you.

9 **For every one that curseth his father or his mother** shall be surely put to death:
he hath cursed his father or his mother;
his blood shall be upon him.

10 **And the man that committeth adultery with another man's wife, even he that committeth adultery with his neighbour's wife,** the adulterer and the adulteress shall surely be put to death.

11 **And the man that lieth with his father's wife** hath uncovered his father's nakedness:
both of them shall surely be put to death;
their blood shall be upon them.

12 **And if a man** lie with his daughter in law,
both of them shall surely be put to death:
they have wrought confusion;
their blood shall be upon them.

13 **If a man** also lie with mankind,
as he lieth with a woman,
both of them have committed an abomination:
they shall surely be put to death;
their blood shall be upon them.

14 **And if a man** take a wife and her mother,
it is wickedness:
they shall be burnt with fire, both he and they;
that there be no wickedness among you.

15 **And if a man** lie with a beast,
he shall surely be put to death:
and ye shall slay the beast.

16 **And if a woman** approach unto any beast,
and lie down thereto,
thou shalt kill the woman, and the beast:
they shall surely be put to death;
their blood shall be upon them.

17 **And if a man** shall take his sister, his father's daughter, or his mother's daughter,
and see her nakedness,
and she see his nakedness;
it is a wicked thing;
and they shall be cut off in the sight of their people:
he hath uncovered his sister's nakedness;
he shall bear his iniquity.

18 **And if a man** shall lie with a woman having her sickness,
and shall uncover her nakedness;
he hath discovered her fountain,
and she hath uncovered the fountain of her blood:
and both of them shall be cut off from among their people.

19 **And thou** shalt not uncover the nakedness of thy mother's sister, nor of thy father's sister:
for he uncovereth his near kin:
they shall bear their iniquity.

20 **And if a man** shall lie with his uncle's wife,
he hath uncovered his uncle's nakedness:
they shall bear their sin;
they shall die childless.

21 **And if a man** shall take his brother's wife,
it is an unclean thing:
he hath uncovered his brother's nakedness;
they shall be childless.

22 **Ye** shall therefore keep all my statutes, and all my judgments,
and do them:
that the land, {whither I bring you to dwell therein}, spue you not out.

23 **And ye** shall not walk in the manners of the nation,
which I cast out before you:
for they committed all these things,
and therefore I abhorred them.

24 **But I** have said unto you,
Ye shall inherit their land,
and I will give it unto you to possess it, a land that floweth with milk and honey:
I am the LORD your God,
which have separated you from other people.

25 **Ye** shall therefore put difference between clean beasts and unclean, and between unclean fowls and clean:
and ye shall not make your souls abominable by beast, or by fowl, or by any manner of living thing that creepeth on the ground,
which I have separated from you as unclean.

26 **And ye** shall be holy unto me:
for I the LORD am holy,
and have severed you from other people,
that ye should be mine.

27 **A man also or woman that hath a familiar spirit, or that is a wizard,** shall surely be put to death:
they shall stone them with stones:
their blood shall be upon them.

21 **And the LORD** said unto Moses,
Speak unto the priests the sons of Aaron,
and say unto them,
There shall none be defiled for the dead among his people:

2 **But for his kin, {that is near unto him}, that is, for his mother, and for his father, and for his son, and for his daughter, and for his brother,**

3 **And for his sister a virgin, {that is nigh unto him}, {which hath had no husband};** for her may he be defiled.

4 **But he** shall not defile himself,
being a chief man among his people,
to profane himself.

5 **They** shall not make baldness upon their head,
neither shall they shave off the corner of their beard,
nor make any cuttings in their flesh.

6 **They** shall be holy unto their God,
and not profane the name of their God:

for the offerings of the LORD made by fire, and the bread of their God, they do offer:
therefore they shall be holy.

7 **They** shall not take a wife that is a whore, or profane;
neither shall they take a woman put away from her husband:
for he is holy unto his God.

8 **Thou** shalt sanctify him therefore;
for he offereth the bread of thy God:
he shall be holy unto thee:
for I the LORD, {which sanctify you}, am holy.

9 **And the daughter of any priest**, {if she profane herself by playing the whore}, she profaneth her father:
she shall be burnt with fire.

10 **And he that is the high priest among his brethren, upon whose head the anointing oil was poured, and that is consecrated to put on the garments,** shall not uncover his head,
nor rend his clothes;
11 **Neither** shall he go in to any dead body,
nor defile himself for his father, or for his mother;
12 **Neither** shall he go out of the sanctuary,
nor profane the sanctuary of his God;
for the crown of the anointing oil of his God is upon him:
I am the LORD.

13 **And he** shall take a wife in her virginity.

14 **A widow, or a divorced woman, or profane, or an harlot,** these shall he not take:
but he shall take a virgin of his own people to wife.

15 **Neither** shall he profane his seed among his people:
for I the LORD do sanctify him.

16 **And the LORD** spake unto Moses,
saying,
17 **Speak** unto Aaron,
saying,
Whosoever he be of thy seed in their generations that hath any blemish, let him not approach to offer the bread of his God.

18 **For whatsoever man he be that hath a blemish,** he shall not approach: a blind man, or a lame, or he that hath a flat nose, or any thing superfluous,
19 Or a man that is brokenfooted, or brokenhanded,
20 Or crookbackt, or a dwarf, or that hath a blemish in his eye, or be scurvy, or scabbed, or hath his stones broken;
21 **No man that hath a blemish of the seed of Aaron the priest** shall come nigh to offer the offerings of the LORD made by fire:
he hath a blemish;
he shall not come nigh to offer the bread of his God.

22 **He** shall eat the bread of his God, both of the most holy, and of the holy.

23 **Only he** shall not go in unto the vail,
nor come nigh unto the altar,
because he hath a blemish;
that he profane not my sanctuaries:
for I the LORD do sanctify them.

24 **And Moses** told it unto Aaron, and to his sons, and unto all the children of Israel.

22

And the LORD spake unto Moses,
saying,
2 **Speak** unto Aaron and to his sons,
that they separate themselves from the holy things of the children of Israel,
and that they profane not my holy name in those things which they hallow unto me:
I am the LORD.

3 **Say** unto them,
Whosoever he be of all your seed among your generations, {that goeth unto the holy things}, {which the children of Israel hallow unto the LORD}, {having his uncleanness upon him}, that soul shall be cut off from my presence:
I am the LORD.

4 **What man soever of the seed of Aaron** is a leper,
or hath a running issue;
he shall not eat of the holy things,
until he be clean.

And whoso toucheth any thing that is unclean by the dead, or a man whose seed goeth from him;
5 **Or whosoever toucheth any creeping thing, {whereby he may be made unclean}, or a man of whom he may take uncleanness, {whatsoever uncleanness he hath};**
6 The soul which hath touched any such shall be unclean until even,
and shall not eat of the holy things,
unless he wash his flesh with water.

7 **And when the sun** is down,
he shall be clean,
and shall afterward eat of the holy things;
because it is his food.

8 **That which dieth of itself, or is torn with beasts,** he shall not eat to defile himself therewith;
I am the LORD.

9 **They** shall therefore keep mine ordinance,
lest they bear sin for it,
and die therefore,
if they profane it:
I the LORD do sanctify them.

10 **There** shall no stranger eat of the holy thing:
a sojourner of the priest, or an hired servant, shall not eat of the holy thing.

11 **But if the priest** buy any soul with his money,
he shall eat of it,
and he that is born in his house: they shall eat of his meat.

12 **If the priest's daughter** also be married unto a stranger,
she may not eat of an offering of the holy things.

13 **But if the priest's daughter** be a widow,
or divorced,
and have no child,
and is returned unto her father's house, as in her youth,
she shall eat of her father's meat:
but there shall be no stranger eat thereof.

14 **And if a man** eat of the holy thing unwittingly,
then he shall put the fifth part thereof unto it,
and shall give it unto the priest with the holy thing.

15 **And they** shall not profane the holy things of the children of Israel,
which they offer unto the LORD;
16 **Or** suffer them to bear the iniquity of trespass,
when they eat their holy things:

for I the LORD do sanctify them.

17 **And the LORD** spake unto Moses,
saying,

18 **Speak** unto Aaron, and to his sons, and unto all the children of Israel,
and say unto them,
Whatsoever he be of the house of Israel, or of the strangers in Israel, {that will offer his oblation for all his vows, and for all his freewill offerings}, {which they will offer unto the LORD for a burnt offering};

19 Ye shall offer at your own will a male without blemish, of the beeves, of the sheep, or of the goats.

20 **But whatsoever** hath a blemish,
that shall ye not offer:
for it shall not be acceptable for you.

21 **And whosoever offereth a sacrifice of peace offerings unto the LORD {to accomplish his vow}, or a freewill offering in beeves or sheep,** it shall be perfect to be accepted;
there shall be no blemish therein.

22 **Blind, or broken, or maimed, {or having a wen, or scurvy, or scabbed},** ye shall not offer these unto the LORD,
nor make an offering by fire of them upon the altar unto the LORD.

23 **Either a bullock or a lamb that hath any thing superfluous or lacking in his parts,** that mayest thou offer for a freewill offering;
but for a vow it shall not be accepted.

24 **Ye** shall not offer unto the LORD that which is bruised, or crushed, or broken, or cut;
neither shall ye make any offering thereof in your land.

25 **Neither from a stranger's hand** shall ye offer the bread of your God of any of these;
because their corruption is in them,
and blemishes be in them:
they shall not be accepted for you.

26 **And the LORD** spake unto Moses,
saying,

27 **When a bullock, or a sheep, or a goat,** is brought forth,
then it shall be seven days under the dam;
and from the eighth day and thenceforth it shall be accepted for an offering made by fire unto the LORD.

28 **And whether it** be cow, or ewe,
ye shall not kill it and her young both in one day.

29 **And when ye** will offer a sacrifice of thanksgiving unto the LORD,
offer it at your own will.

30 **On the same day** it shall be eaten up;
ye shall leave none of it until the morrow:
I am the LORD.

31 **Therefore** shall ye keep my commandments,
and do them:
I am the LORD.

32 **Neither** shall ye profane my holy name;
but I will be hallowed among the children of Israel:
I am the LORD which hallow you,

33 **That** brought you out of the land of Egypt,
to be your God:
I am the LORD.

23

And the LORD spake unto Moses,
saying,

2 **Speak** unto the children of Israel,
and say unto them,
Concerning the feasts of the LORD, {which ye shall proclaim to be holy convocations}, even these are my feasts.

3 **Six days** shall work be done:
but the seventh day is the sabbath of rest, an holy convocation;
ye shall do no work therein:
it is the sabbath of the LORD in all your dwellings.

4 **These** are the feasts of the LORD, even holy convocations,
which ye shall proclaim in their seasons.

5 **In the fourteenth day of the first month at even** is the LORD's passover.

6 **And on the fifteenth day of the same month** is the feast of unleavened bread unto the LORD:
seven days ye must eat unleavened bread.

7 **In the first day** ye shall have an holy convocation:
ye shall do no servile work therein.

8 **But ye** shall offer an offering made by fire unto the LORD seven days:
in the seventh day is an holy convocation:
ye shall do no servile work therein.

9 **And the LORD** spake unto Moses,
saying,

10 **Speak** unto the children of Israel,
and say unto them,
When ye be come into the land which I give unto you,
and shall reap the harvest thereof,
then ye shall bring a sheaf of the firstfruits of your harvest unto the priest:

11 **And he** shall wave the sheaf before the LORD,
to be accepted for you:
on the morrow after the sabbath the priest shall wave it.

12 **And ye** shall offer that day when ye wave the sheaf an he lamb without blemish of the first year for a burnt offering unto the LORD.

13 **And the meat offering thereof** shall be two tenth deals of fine flour mingled with oil, an offering made by fire unto the LORD for a sweet savour:
and the drink offering thereof shall be of wine, the fourth part of an hin.

14 **And ye** shall eat neither bread, nor parched corn, nor green ears, until the selfsame day that ye have brought an offering unto your God:
it shall be a statute for ever throughout your generations in all your dwellings.

15 **And ye** shall count unto you from the morrow after the sabbath, from the day that ye brought the sheaf of the wave offering;
seven sabbaths shall be complete:

16 **Even unto the morrow after the seventh sabbath** shall ye number fifty days;
and ye shall offer a new meat offering unto the LORD.

17 **Ye** shall bring out of your habitations two wave loaves of two tenth deals;
they shall be of fine flour;
they shall be baken with leaven;
they are the firstfruits unto the LORD.

18 **And ye** shall offer with the bread seven lambs without blemish of

the first year, and one young bullock, and two rams:
they shall be for a burnt offering unto the LORD, with their meat offering, and their drink offerings, even an offering made by fire, of sweet savour unto the LORD.
19 **Then ye** shall sacrifice one kid of the goats for a sin offering, and two lambs of the first year for a sacrifice of peace offerings.
20 **And the priest** shall wave them with the bread of the firstfruits for a wave offering before the LORD, with the two lambs:
they shall be holy to the LORD for the priest.
21 **And ye** shall proclaim on the selfsame day,
that it may be an holy convocation unto you:
ye shall do no servile work therein:
it shall be a statute for ever in all your dwellings throughout your generations.
22 **And when ye** reap the harvest of your land,
thou shalt not make clean riddance of the corners of thy field when thou reapest,
neither shalt thou gather any gleaning of thy harvest:
thou shalt leave them unto the poor, and to the stranger:
I am the LORD your God.
23 **And the LORD** spake unto Moses, saying,
24 **Speak** unto the children of Israel, saying,
In the seventh month, in the first day of the month, shall ye have a sabbath, a memorial of blowing of trumpets, an holy convocation.
25 **Ye** shall do no servile work therein:
but ye shall offer an offering made by fire unto the LORD.
26 **And the LORD** spake unto Moses, saying,
27 **Also on the tenth day of this seventh month** there shall be a day of atonement:
it shall be an holy convocation unto you;
and ye shall afflict your souls,
and offer an offering made by fire unto the LORD.
28 **And ye** shall do no work in that same day:
for it is a day of atonement, to make an atonement for you before the LORD your God.
29 **For whatsoever soul it be that shall not be afflicted in that same day,** he shall be cut off from among his people.
30 **And whatsoever soul it be that doeth any work in that same day,** the same soul will I destroy from among his people.
31 **Ye** shall do no manner of work:
it shall be a statute for ever throughout your generations in all your dwellings.
32 **It** shall be unto you a sabbath of rest,
and ye shall afflict your souls:
in the ninth day of the month at even, from even unto even, shall ye celebrate your sabbath.
33 **And the LORD** spake unto Moses, saying,
34 **Speak** unto the children of Israel, saying,
The fifteenth day of this seventh month shall be the feast of tabernacles for seven days unto the LORD.
35 **On the first day** shall be an holy convocation:
ye shall do no servile work therein.
36 **Seven days** ye shall offer an offering made by fire unto the LORD:
on the eighth day shall be an holy convocation unto you;
and ye shall offer an offering made by fire unto the LORD:
it is a solemn assembly;
and ye shall do no servile work therein.
37 **These** are the feasts of the LORD,
which ye shall proclaim to be holy convocations,
to offer an offering made by fire unto the LORD, a burnt offering, and a meat offering, a sacrifice, and drink offerings, every thing upon his day:
38 Beside the sabbaths of the LORD, and beside your gifts, and beside all your vows, and beside all your freewill offerings,
which ye give unto the LORD.
39 **Also in the fifteenth day of the seventh month**, {when ye have gathered in the fruit of the land}, ye shall keep a feast unto the LORD seven days:
on the first day shall be a sabbath,
and on the eighth day shall be a sabbath.
40 **And ye** shall take you on the first day the boughs of goodly trees, branches of palm trees, and the boughs of thick trees, and willows of the brook;
and ye shall rejoice before the LORD your God seven days.
41 **And ye** shall keep it a feast unto the LORD seven days in the year.
It shall be a statute for ever in your generations:
ye shall celebrate it in the seventh month.
42 **Ye** shall dwell in booths seven days;
all that are Israelites born shall dwell in booths:
43 **That your generations** may know
that I made the children of Israel to dwell in booths,
when I brought them out of the land of Egypt:
I am the LORD your God.
44 **And Moses** declared unto the children of Israel the feasts of the LORD.

24

And the LORD spake unto Moses, saying,
2 **Command** the children of Israel,
that they bring unto thee pure oil olive beaten for the light,
to cause the lamps to burn continually.
3 **Without the vail of the testimony, in the tabernacle of the congregation,** shall Aaron order it from the evening unto the morning before the LORD continually:
it shall be a statute for ever in your generations.
4 **He** shall order the lamps upon the pure candlestick before the LORD continually.
5 **And thou** shalt take fine flour,
and bake twelve cakes thereof:
two tenth deals shall be in one cake.
6 **And thou** shalt set them in two rows, six on a row, upon the pure table before the LORD.
7 **And thou** shalt put pure frankincense upon each row,

that it may be on the bread for a memorial, even an offering made by fire unto the LORD.

8 **Every sabbath** he shall set it in order before the LORD continually,
being taken from the children of Israel by an everlasting covenant.

9 **And it** shall be Aaron's and his sons';
and they shall eat it in the holy place:
for it is most holy unto him of the offerings of the LORD made by fire by a perpetual statute.

10 **And the son of an Israelitish woman**, {whose father was an Egyptian}, went out among the children of Israel:
and this son of the Israelitish woman and a man of Israel strove together in the camp;
11 **And the Israelitish woman's son** blasphemed the name of the LORD,
and cursed.

And they brought him unto Moses:
(and his mother's name was Shelomith, the daughter of Dibri, of the tribe of Dan:)
12 **And they** put him in ward,
that the mind of the LORD might be shewed them.

13 **And the LORD** spake unto Moses,
saying,
14 **Bring forth** him that hath cursed without the camp;
and let all that heard him lay their hands upon his head,
and let all the congregation stone him.

15 **And thou** shalt speak unto the children of Israel,
saying,
Whosoever curseth his God shall bear his sin.

16 **And he that blasphemeth the name of the LORD,** he shall surely be put to death,
and all the congregation shall certainly stone him:
as well the stranger, as he that is born in the land, {when he blasphemeth the name of the LORD}, shall be put to death.

17 **And he that killeth any man** shall surely be put to death.

18 **And he that killeth a beast** shall make it good; beast for beast.

19 **And if a man** cause a blemish in his neighbour;
as he hath done,
so shall it be done to him;
20 Breach for breach, eye for eye, tooth for tooth:
as he hath caused a blemish in a man,
so shall it be done to him again.

21 **And he that killeth a beast,** he shall restore it:
and he that killeth a man, he shall be put to death.

22 **Ye** shall have one manner of law, as well for the stranger, as for one of your own country:
for I am the LORD your God.

23 **And Moses** spake to the children of Israel,
that they should bring forth him that had cursed out of the camp,
and stone him with stones.

And the children of Israel did as the LORD commanded Moses.

25

And the LORD spake unto Moses in mount Sinai,
saying,
2 **Speak** unto the children of Israel,
and say unto them,
When ye come into the land which I give you,
then shall the land keep a sabbath unto the LORD.

3 **Six years** thou shalt sow thy field,
and six years thou shalt prune thy vineyard,
and gather in the fruit thereof;
4 **But in the seventh year** shall be a sabbath of rest unto the land, a sabbath for the LORD:
thou shalt neither sow thy field,
nor prune thy vineyard.

5 **That which groweth of its own accord of thy harvest** thou shalt not reap,
neither gather the grapes of thy vine undressed:
for it is a year of rest unto the land.

6 **And the sabbath of the land** shall be meat for you; for thee, and for thy servant, and for thy maid, and for thy hired servant, and for thy stranger that sojourneth with thee.

7 **And for thy cattle, and for the beast that are in thy land,** shall all the increase thereof be meat.

8 **And thou** shalt number seven sabbaths of years unto thee, seven times seven years;
and the space of the seven sabbaths of years shall be unto thee forty and nine years.

9 **Then** shalt thou cause the trumpet of the jubile to sound on the tenth day of the seventh month,
in the day of atonement shall ye make the trumpet sound throughout all your land.

10 **And ye** shall hallow the fiftieth year,
and proclaim liberty throughout all the land unto all the inhabitants thereof:
it shall be a jubile unto you;
and ye shall return every man unto his possession,
and ye shall return every man unto his family.

11 **A jubile** shall that fiftieth year be unto you:
ye shall not sow,
neither reap that which groweth of itself in it,
nor gather the grapes in it of thy vine undressed.

12 **For it** is the jubile;
it shall be holy unto you:
ye shall eat the increase thereof out of the field.

13 **In the year of this jubile** ye shall return every man unto his possession.

14 **And if thou** sell ought unto thy neighbour,
or buyest ought of thy neighbour's hand,
ye shall not oppress one another:
15 **According to the number of years after the jubile** thou shalt buy of thy neighbour,
and according unto the number of years of the fruits he shall sell unto thee:

16 **According to the multitude of years** thou shalt increase the price thereof,
and according to the fewness of years thou shalt diminish the price of it:
for according to the number of the years of the fruits doth he sell unto thee.

17 **Ye** shall not therefore oppress one another;
but thou shalt fear thy God:
for I am the LORD your God.

18 **Wherefore ye** shall do my statutes,

and keep my judgments,
and do them;
and ye shall dwell in the land in safety.

19 **And the land** shall yield her fruit,
and ye shall eat your fill,
and dwell therein in safety.

20 **And if ye** shall say,
What shall we eat the seventh year?
behold,
we shall not sow,
nor gather in our increase:
21 **Then I** will command my blessing upon you in the sixth year,
and it shall bring forth fruit for three years.

22 **And ye** shall sow the eighth year,
and eat yet of old fruit until the ninth year;
until her fruits come in
ye shall eat of the old store.

23 **The land** shall not be sold for ever:
for the land is mine,
for ye are strangers and sojourners with me.

24 **And in all the land of your possession** ye shall grant a redemption for the land.

25 **If thy brother** be waxen poor,
and hath sold away some of his possession,
and if any of his kin come to redeem it,
then shall he redeem that which his brother sold.

26 **And if the man** have none to redeem it,
and himself be able to redeem it;
27 **Then let him** count the years of the sale thereof,
and restore the overplus unto the man to whom he sold it;
that he may return unto his possession.

28 **But if he** be not able to restore it to him,
then that which is sold shall remain in the hand of him that hath bought it until the year of jubile:
and in the jubile it shall go out,
and he shall return unto his possession.

29 **And if a man** sell a dwelling house in a walled city,
then he may redeem it within a whole year after it is sold;
within a full year may he redeem it.

30 **And if it** be not redeemed within the space of a full year,
then the house that is in the walled city shall be established for ever to him that bought it throughout his generations:
it shall not go out in the jubile.

31 **But the houses of the villages which have no wall round about them** shall be counted as the fields of the country:
they may be redeemed,
and they shall go out in the jubile.

32 **Notwithstanding the cities of the Levites, and the houses of the cities of their possession,** may the Levites redeem at any time.

33 **And if a man** purchase of the Levites,
then the house that was sold, and the city of his possession, shall go out in the year of jubile:
for the houses of the cities of the Levites are their possession among the children of Israel.

34 **But the field of the suburbs of their cities** may not be sold;
for it is their perpetual possession.

35 **And if thy brother** be waxen poor,
and fallen in decay with thee;
then thou shalt relieve him:
yea, though he be a stranger, or a sojourner;
that he may live with thee.

36 **Take thou** no usury of him, or increase:
but fear thy God;
that thy brother may live with thee.

37 **Thou** shalt not give him thy money upon usury,
nor lend him thy victuals for increase.

38 **I** am the LORD your God,
which brought you forth out of the land of Egypt,
to give you the land of Canaan,
and to be your God.

39 **And if thy brother that dwelleth by thee** be waxen poor,
and be sold unto thee;
thou shalt not compel him to serve as a bondservant:
40 **But as an hired servant, and as a sojourner,** he shall be with thee,
and shall serve thee unto the year of jubile.

41 **And then** shall he depart from thee, both he and his children with him,
and shall return unto his own family,
and unto the possession of his fathers shall he return.

42 **For they** are my servants,
which I brought forth out of the land of Egypt:
they shall not be sold as bondmen.

43 **Thou** shalt not rule over him with rigour;
but shalt fear thy God.

44 **Both thy bondmen, and thy bondmaids,** {which thou shalt have}, shall be of the heathen that are round about you;
of them shall ye buy bondmen and bondmaids.

45 **Moreover of the children of the strangers that do sojourn among you,** of them shall ye buy, and of their families that are with you,
which they begat in your land:
and they shall be your possession.

46 **And ye** shall take them as an inheritance for your children after you,
to inherit them for a possession;
they shall be your bondmen for ever:
but over your brethren the children of Israel, ye shall not rule one over another with rigour.

47 **And if a sojourner or stranger** wax rich by thee,
and thy brother that dwelleth by him wax poor,
and sell himself unto the stranger or sojourner by thee, or to the stock of the stranger's family:
48 **After that he** is sold
he may be redeemed again;
one of his brethren may redeem him:
49 **Either his uncle, or his uncle's son,** may redeem him,
or any that is nigh of kin unto him of his family may redeem him;
or if he be able,
he may redeem himself.

50 **And he** shall reckon with him that bought him from the year that he was sold to him unto the year of jubile:
and the price of his sale shall be according unto the number of years,

according to the time of an hired servant shall it be with him.

51 **If there** be yet many years behind,
according unto them he shall give again the price of his redemption out of the money that he was bought for.

52 **And if there** remain but few years unto the year of jubile,
then he shall count with him,
and according unto his years shall he give him again the price of his redemption.

53 **And as a yearly hired servant** shall he be with him:
and the other shall not rule with rigour over him in thy sight.

54 **And if he** be not redeemed in these years,
then he shall go out in the year of jubile, both he, and his children with him.

55 **For unto me** the children of Israel are servants;
they are my servants whom I brought forth out of the land of Egypt:
I am the LORD your God.

26

Ye shall make you no idols nor graven image,
neither rear you up a standing image,
neither shall ye set up any image of stone in your land,
to bow down unto it:
for I am the LORD your God.

2 **Ye** shall keep my sabbaths,
and reverence my sanctuary:
I am the LORD.

3 **If ye** walk in my statutes,
and keep my commandments,
and do them;

4 **Then I** will give you rain in due season,
and the land shall yield her increase,
and the trees of the field shall yield their fruit.

5 **And your threshing** shall reach unto the vintage,
and the vintage shall reach unto the sowing time:
and ye shall eat your bread to the full,
and dwell in your land safely.

6 **And I** will give peace in the land,
and ye shall lie down,
and none shall make you afraid:
and I will rid evil beasts out of the land,
neither shall the sword go through your land.

7 **And ye** shall chase your enemies,
and they shall fall before you by the sword.

8 **And five of you** shall chase an hundred,
and an hundred of you shall put ten thousand to flight:
and your enemies shall fall before you by the sword.

9 **For I** will have respect unto you,
and make you fruitful,
and multiply you,
and establish my covenant with you.

10 **And ye** shall eat old store,
and bring forth the old because of the new.

11 **And I** set my tabernacle among you:
and my soul shall not abhor you.

12 **And I** will walk among you,
and will be your God,
and ye shall be my people.

13 **I** am the LORD your God,
which brought you forth out of the land of Egypt,
that ye should not be their bondmen;
and I have broken the bands of your yoke,
and made you go upright.

14 **But if ye** will not hearken unto me,
and will not do all these commandments;

15 **And if ye** shall despise my statutes,
or if your soul abhor my judgments,
so that ye will not do all my commandments,
but that ye break my covenant:

16 **I** also will do this unto you;
I will even appoint over you terror, consumption, and the burning ague,
that shall consume the eyes,
and cause sorrow of heart:
and ye shall sow your seed in vain,
for your enemies shall eat it.

17 **And I** will set my face against you,
and ye shall be slain before your enemies:
they that hate you shall reign over you;
and ye shall flee **when none** pursueth you.

18 **And if ye** will not yet for all this hearken unto me,
then I will punish you seven times more for your sins.

19 **And I** will break the pride of your power;
and I will make your heaven as iron, and your earth as brass:

20 **And your strength** shall be spent in vain:
for your land shall not yield her increase,
neither shall the trees of the land yield their fruits.

21 **And if ye** walk contrary unto me,
and will not hearken unto me;
I will bring seven times more plagues upon you according to your sins.

22 **I** will also send wild beasts among you,
which shall rob you of your children,
and destroy your cattle,
and make you few in number;
and your high ways shall be desolate.

23 **And if ye** will not be reformed by me by these things,
but will walk contrary unto me;

24 **Then** will I also walk contrary unto you,
and will punish you yet seven times for your sins.

25 **And I** will bring a sword upon you,
that shall avenge the quarrel of my covenant:
and when ye are gathered together within your cities,
I will send the pestilence among you;
and ye shall be delivered into the hand of the enemy.

26 **And when I** have broken the staff of your bread,
ten women shall bake your bread in one oven,
and they shall deliver you your bread again by weight:
and ye shall eat,
and not be satisfied.

27 **And if ye** will not for all this hearken unto me,
but walk contrary unto me;

28 **Then I** will walk contrary unto you also in fury;
and I, even I, will chastise you seven times for your sins.

29 **And ye** shall eat the flesh of your sons,
and the flesh of your daughters shall ye eat.
30 **And I** will destroy your high places,
and cut down your images,
and cast your carcases upon the carcases of your idols,
and my soul shall abhor you.
31 **And I** will make your cities waste,
and bring your sanctuaries unto desolation,
and I will not smell the savour of your sweet odours.
32 **And I** will bring the land into desolation:
and your enemies which dwell therein shall be astonished at it.
33 **And I** will scatter you among the heathen,
and will draw out a sword after you:
and your land shall be desolate, and your cities waste.
34 **Then** shall the land enjoy her sabbaths,
as long as it lieth desolate,
and ye be in your enemies' land;
even then shall the land rest,
and enjoy her sabbaths.
35 **As long as it** lieth desolate
it shall rest;
because it did not rest in your sabbaths,
when ye dwelt upon it.
36 **And upon them that are left alive of you** I will send a faintness into their hearts in the lands of their enemies;
and the sound of a shaken leaf shall chase them;
and they shall flee,
as fleeing from a sword;
and they shall fall when none pursueth.
37 **And they** shall fall one upon another,
as it were before a sword,
when none pursueth:
and ye shall have no power to stand before your enemies.
38 **And ye** shall perish among the heathen,
and the land of your enemies shall eat you up.
39 **And they that are left of you** shall pine away in their iniquity in your enemies' lands;
and also in the iniquities of their fathers shall they pine away with them.
40 **If they** shall confess their iniquity, and the iniquity of their fathers, with their trespass which they trespassed against me,
and that also they have walked contrary unto me;
41 **And that I** also have walked contrary unto them,
and have brought them into the land of their enemies;
if then their uncircumcised hearts be humbled,
and they then accept of the punishment of their iniquity:
42 **Then** will I remember my covenant with Jacob,
and also my covenant with Isaac, and also my covenant with Abraham will I remember;
and I will remember the land.
43 **The land** also shall be left of them,
and shall enjoy her sabbaths,
while she lieth desolate without them:
and they shall accept of the punishment of their iniquity:
because, even because they despised my judgments,
and because their soul abhorred my statutes.
44 **And yet for all that,** {<u>when they</u> be in the land of their enemies}, I will not cast them away,
neither will I abhor them,
to destroy them utterly,
and to break my covenant with them:
for I am the LORD their God.
45 **But I** will for their sakes remember the covenant of their ancestors,
whom I brought forth out of the land of Egypt in the sight of the heathen,
that I might be their God:
I am the LORD.
46 **These** are the statutes and judgments and laws,
which the LORD made between him and the children of Israel in mount Sinai by the hand of Moses.

27 **And the LORD** spake unto Moses,
saying,
2 **Speak** unto the children of Israel,
and say unto them,
When a man shall make a singular vow,
the persons shall be for the LORD by thy estimation.
3 **And thy estimation** shall be of the male from twenty years old even unto sixty years old,
even thy estimation shall be fifty shekels of silver, after the shekel of the sanctuary.
4 **And if it** be a female,
then thy estimation shall be thirty shekels.
5 **And if it** be from five years old even unto twenty years old,
then thy estimation shall be of the male twenty shekels, and for the female ten shekels.
6 **And if it** be from a month old even unto five years old,
then thy estimation shall be of the male five shekels of silver,
and for the female thy estimation shall be three shekels of silver.
7 **And if it** be from sixty years old and above;
if it be a male,
then thy estimation shall be fifteen shekels, and for the female ten shekels.
8 **But if he** be poorer than thy estimation,
then he shall present himself before the priest,
and the priest shall value him;
according to his ability that vowed shall the priest value him.
9 **And if it** be a beast,
whereof men bring an offering unto the LORD,
all that any man giveth of such unto the LORD shall be holy.
10 **He** shall not alter it,
nor change it, a good for a bad, or a bad for a good:
and if he shall at all change beast for beast,
then it and the exchange thereof shall be holy.
11 **And if it** be any unclean beast,
of which they do not offer a sacrifice unto the LORD,
then he shall present the beast before the priest:
12 **And the priest** shall value it,
whether it be good or bad:
as thou valuest it,
who art the priest,
so shall it be.

13 **But if he** will at all redeem it,
then he shall add a fifth part
thereof unto thy estimation.

14 **And when a man** shall sanctify
his house to be holy unto the
LORD,
then the priest shall estimate it,
whether it be good or bad:
as the priest shall estimate it,
so shall it stand.

15 **And if he that sanctified it** will
redeem his house,
then he shall add the fifth part of
the money of thy estimation unto
it,
and it shall be his.

16 **And if a man** shall sanctify unto
the LORD some part of a field of
his possession,
then thy estimation shall be
according to the seed thereof:
an homer of barley seed shall be
valued at fifty shekels of silver.

17 **If he** sanctify his field from the
year of jubile,
according to thy estimation it
shall stand.

18 **But if he** sanctify his field after
the jubile,
then the priest shall reckon unto
him the money according to the
years that remain, even unto the
year of the jubile,
and it shall be abated from thy
estimation.

19 **And if he that sanctified the
field** will in any wise redeem it,
then he shall add the fifth part of
the money of thy estimation unto
it,
and it shall be assured to him.

20 **And if he** will not redeem the
field,
or if he have sold the field to
another man,
it shall not be redeemed any more.

21 **But the field**, {when it goeth out
in the jubile}, shall be holy unto
the LORD, as a field devoted;
the possession thereof shall be the
priest's.

22 **And if a man** sanctify unto the
LORD a field which he hath
bought,
which is not of the fields of his
possession;

23 **Then the priest** shall reckon unto
him the worth of thy estimation,
even unto the year of the jubile:
and he shall give thine estimation
in that day, as a holy thing unto
the LORD.

24 **In the year of the jubile** the field
shall return unto him of whom it
was bought, even to him to whom
the possession of the land did
belong.

25 **And all thy estimations** shall be
according to the shekel of the
sanctuary:
twenty gerahs shall be the shekel.

26 **Only the firstling of the beasts**,
{which should be the LORD's
firstling}, no man shall sanctify it;
whether it be ox, or sheep:
it is the LORD's.

27 **And if it** be of an unclean beast,
then he shall redeem it according to
thine estimation,
and shall add a fifth part of it
thereto:
or if it be not redeemed,
then it shall be sold according to
thy estimation.

28 **Notwithstanding no devoted
thing**, {that a man shall devote
unto the LORD of all that he hath,
both of man and beast, and of the
field of his possession}, shall be
sold or redeemed:
every devoted thing is most holy
unto the LORD.

29 **None devoted**, {which shall be
devoted of men}, shall be
redeemed;
but shall surely be put to death.

30 **And all the tithe of the land,
whether of the seed of the land,
or of the fruit of the tree,** is the
LORD's:
it is holy unto the LORD.

31 **And if a man** will at all redeem
ought of his tithes,
he shall add thereto the fifth part
thereof.

32 **And concerning the tithe of the
herd, or of the flock, even of
whatsoever passeth under the
rod,** the tenth shall be holy unto
the LORD.

33 **He** shall not search whether it be
good or bad,
neither shall he change it:
and if he change it at all,
**then both it and the change
thereof** shall be holy;
it shall not be redeemed.

34 **These** are the commandments,
which the LORD commanded
Moses for the children of Israel in
mount Sinai.

Numbers

The Book of Numbers, authored by Moses, narrates the long and arduous journey through the wilderness after the Israelite nation's exodus from Egypt. The Hebrew title of the book, Bamidbar, means in the wilderness, which reflects the book's focus on the people's passage through this challenging and inhospitable environment. Additionally, Numbers contains numerous lists, counts, and other numerical data, such as the organization of the tribes into camps, the allocation of resources, and the distribution of land and property. These numerical aspects, meticulously planned by God, provide a sense of order and structure to the story and demonstrate His careful attention to detail in guiding and providing for His people.

Numbers begins with a census of the tribes of Israel, revealing the number of men capable of bearing arms. The tribes are organized into four camps, each with its own flag and designated place. Moses then proceeds to recount the wilderness journey, marked by encounters with various hardships and hurdles, such as the scarcity of food and water and the uprisings and grievances of the people against Moses and Aaron. Throughout the book, God imparts to Moses a diverse array of laws and ordinances that the Israelites must adhere to, including the laws of purity, sacrifice, and warfare. These laws, far from mere regulations, represent a divine roadmap for the Israelites, guiding them in their relationship with God and each other and invoking a profound sense of reverence and obedience.

In one of the book's most pivotal narratives, Moses dispatches twelve spies, one from each tribe, to survey the land of Canaan, which was promised to the Israelites as their inheritance. On their return, ten of the spies declare that the land is insurmountable, leading the people to lose faith in God and revolt against Moses and Aaron. As a consequence of their disbelief and defiance against God, the Israelites are struck with a plague and are compelled to wander in the wilderness for forty years. The book culminates with the anointing of Joshua as Moses' successor, who will lead the Israelites into the land of Canaan and establish them as a nation. The Book of Numbers serves as a stark reminder of the consequences of disobedience, invoking a sense of caution and respect for God's authority.

1 **And the LORD** spake unto Moses in the wilderness of Sinai, in the tabernacle of the congregation, on the first day of the second month, in the second year after they were come out of the land of Egypt,
saying,

2 **Take ye** the sum of all the congregation of the children of Israel, after their families, by the house of their fathers, with the number of their names, every male by their polls;

3 From twenty years old and upward, all that are able to go forth to war in Israel:
thou and Aaron shall number them by their armies.

4 **And with you** there shall be a man of every tribe; every one head of the house of his fathers.

5 **And these** are the names of the men that shall stand with you:
of the tribe of Reuben; Elizur the son of Shedeur.

6 **Of Simeon;** Shelumiel the son of Zurishaddai.

7 **Of Judah;** Nahshon the son of Amminadab.

8 **Of Issachar;** Nethaneel the son of Zuar.

9 **Of Zebulun;** Eliab the son of Helon.

10 **Of the children of Joseph:** of Ephraim; Elishama the son of Ammihud: of Manasseh; Gamaliel the son of Pedahzur.

11 **Of Benjamin;** Abidan the son of Gideoni.

12 **Of Dan;** Ahiezer the son of Ammishaddai.

13 **Of Asher;** Pagiel the son of Ocran.

14 **Of Gad;** Eliasaph the son of Deuel.

15 **Of Naphtali;** Ahira the son of Enan.

16 **These** were the renowned of the congregation, princes of the tribes of their fathers, heads of thousands in Israel.

17 **And Moses and Aaron** took these men which are expressed by their names:

18 **And they** assembled all the congregation together on the first day of the second month,
and they declared their pedigrees after their families, by the house of their fathers, according to the number of the names, from twenty years old and upward, by their polls.

19 **As the LORD** commanded Moses,
so he numbered them in the wilderness of Sinai.

20 **And the children of Reuben, Israel's eldest son,** by their generations, after their families, by the house of their fathers, according to the number of the names, by their polls, every male from twenty years old and upward, all that were able to go forth to war;

21 **Those that were numbered of them, even of the tribe of Reuben,** were forty and six thousand and five hundred.

22 **Of the children of Simeon,** by their generations, after their families, by the house of their fathers, those that were

numbered of them, according to the number of the names, by their polls, every male from twenty years old and upward, all that were able to go forth to war;
23 **Those that were numbered of them, even of the tribe of Simeon,** were fifty and nine thousand and three hundred.
24 **Of the children of Gad,** by their generations, after their families, by the house of their fathers, according to the number of the names, from twenty years old and upward, all that were able to go forth to war;
25 **Those that were numbered of them, even of the tribe of Gad,** were forty and five thousand six hundred and fifty.
26 **Of the children of Judah,** by their generations, after their families, by the house of their fathers, according to the number of the names, from twenty years old and upward, all that were able to go forth to war;
27 **Those that were numbered of them, even of the tribe of Judah,** were threescore and fourteen thousand and six hundred.
28 **Of the children of Issachar,** by their generations, after their families, by the house of their fathers, according to the number of the names, from twenty years old and upward, all that were able to go forth to war;
29 **Those that were numbered of them, even of the tribe of Issachar,** were fifty and four thousand and four hundred.
30 **Of the children of Zebulun,** by their generations, after their families, by the house of their fathers, according to the number of the names, from twenty years old and upward, all that were able to go forth to war;
31 **Those that were numbered of them, even of the tribe of Zebulun,** were fifty and seven thousand and four hundred.
32 **Of the children of Joseph, namely, of the children of Ephraim,** by their generations, after their families, by the house of their fathers, according to the number of the names, from twenty years old and upward, all that were able to go forth to war;
33 **Those that were numbered of them, even of the tribe of Ephraim,** were forty thousand and five hundred.
34 **Of the children of Manasseh,** by their generations, after their families, by the house of their fathers, according to the number of the names, from twenty years old and upward, all that were able to go forth to war;
35 **Those that were numbered of them, even of the tribe of Manasseh,** were thirty and two thousand and two hundred.
36 **Of the children of Benjamin,** by their generations, after their families, by the house of their fathers, according to the number of the names, from twenty years old and upward, all that were able to go forth to war;
37 **Those that were numbered of them, even of the tribe of Benjamin,** were thirty and five thousand and four hundred.
38 **Of the children of Dan,** by their generations, after their families, by the house of their fathers, according to the number of the names, from twenty years old and upward, all that were able to go forth to war;
39 **Those that were numbered of them, even of the tribe of Dan,** were threescore and two thousand and seven hundred.
40 **Of the children of Asher,** by their generations, after their families, by the house of their fathers, according to the number of the names, from twenty years old and upward, all that were able to go forth to war;
41 **Those that were numbered of them, even of the tribe of Asher,** were forty and one thousand and five hundred.
42 **Of the children of Naphtali,** throughout their generations, after their families, by the house of their fathers, according to the number of the names, from twenty years old and upward, all that were able to go forth to war;
43 **Those that were numbered of them, even of the tribe of Naphtali,** were fifty and three thousand and four hundred.
44 **These** are those that were numbered,
which Moses and Aaron numbered, and the princes of Israel,
being twelve men:
each one was for the house of his fathers.
45 **So** were all those that were numbered of the children of Israel, by the house of their fathers, from twenty years old and upward, all that were able to go forth to war in Israel;
46 **Even all they that were numbered** were six hundred thousand and three thousand and five hundred and fifty.
47 **But the Levites after the tribe of their fathers** were not numbered among them.
48 **For the LORD** had spoken unto Moses,
saying,
49 **Only thou** shalt not number the tribe of Levi,
neither take the sum of them among the children of Israel:
50 **But thou** shalt appoint the Levites over the tabernacle of testimony, and over all the vessels thereof, and over all things that belong to it:
they shall bear the tabernacle, and all the vessels thereof;
and they shall minister unto it,
and shall encamp round about the tabernacle.
51 **And when the tabernacle** setteth forward,
the Levites shall take it down:
and when the tabernacle is to be pitched,
the Levites shall set it up:
and the stranger that cometh nigh shall be put to death.
52 **And the children of Israel** shall pitch their tents, every man by his own camp, and every man by his own standard, throughout their hosts.
53 **But the Levites** shall pitch round about the tabernacle of testimony,
that there be no wrath upon the congregation of the children of Israel:

and the Levites shall keep the charge of the tabernacle of testimony.

54 **And the children of Israel** did according to all that the LORD commanded Moses,
so did they.

2 **And the LORD** spake unto Moses and unto Aaron, saying,

2 **Every man of the children of Israel** shall pitch by his own standard, with the ensign of their father's house:
far off about the tabernacle of the congregation shall they pitch.

3 **And on the east side toward the rising of the sun** shall they of the standard of the camp of Judah pitch throughout their armies:
and Nahshon the son of Amminadab shall be captain of the children of Judah.

4 **And his host, and those that were numbered of them,** were threescore and fourteen thousand and six hundred.

5 **And those that do pitch next unto him** shall be the tribe of Issachar:
and Nethaneel the son of Zuar shall be captain of the children of Issachar.

6 **And his host, and those that were numbered thereof,** were fifty and four thousand and four hundred.

7 **Then** the tribe of Zebulun:
and Eliab the son of Helon shall be captain of the children of Zebulun.

8 **And his host, and those that were numbered thereof,** were fifty and seven thousand and four hundred.

9 **All that were numbered in the camp of Judah** were an hundred thousand and fourscore thousand and six thousand and four hundred, throughout their armies.
These shall first set forth.

10 **On the south side** shall be the standard of the camp of Reuben according to their armies:
and the captain of the children of Reuben shall be Elizur the son of Shedeur.

11 **And his host, and those that were numbered thereof,** were forty and six thousand and five hundred.

12 **And those which pitch by him** shall be the tribe of Simeon:
and the captain of the children of Simeon shall be Shelumiel the son of Zurishaddai.

13 **And his host, and those that were numbered of them,** were fifty and nine thousand and three hundred.

14 **Then** the tribe of Gad:
and the captain of the sons of Gad shall be Eliasaph the son of Reuel.

15 **And his host, and those that were numbered of them,** were forty and five thousand and six hundred and fifty.

16 **All that were numbered in the camp of Reuben** were an hundred thousand and fifty and one thousand and four hundred and fifty, throughout their armies.
And they shall set forth in the second rank.

17 **Then the tabernacle of the congregation** shall set forward with the camp of the Levites in the midst of the camp:
as they encamp, so shall they set forward, every man in his place by their standards.

18 **On the west side** shall be the standard of the camp of Ephraim according to their armies:
and the captain of the sons of Ephraim shall be Elishama the son of Ammihud.

19 **And his host, and those that were numbered of them,** were forty thousand and five hundred.

20 **And by him** shall be the tribe of Manasseh:
and the captain of the children of Manasseh shall be Gamaliel the son of Pedahzur.

21 **And his host, and those that were numbered of them,** were thirty and two thousand and two hundred.

22 **Then** the tribe of Benjamin:
and the captain of the sons of Benjamin shall be Abidan the son of Gideoni.

23 **And his host, and those that were numbered of them,** were thirty and five thousand and four hundred.

24 **All that were numbered of the camp of Ephraim** were an hundred thousand and eight thousand and an hundred, throughout their armies.
And they shall go forward in the third rank.

25 **The standard of the camp of Dan** shall be on the north side by their armies:
and the captain of the children of Dan shall be Ahiezer the son of Ammishaddai.

26 **And his host, and those that were numbered of them,** were threescore and two thousand and seven hundred.

27 **And those that encamp by him** shall be the tribe of Asher:
and the captain of the children of Asher shall be Pagiel the son of Ocran.

28 **And his host, and those that were numbered of them,** were forty and one thousand and five hundred.

29 **Then** the tribe of Naphtali:
and the captain of the children of Naphtali shall be Ahira the son of Enan.

30 **And his host, and those that were numbered of them,** were fifty and three thousand and four hundred.

31 **All they that were numbered in the camp of Dan** were an hundred thousand and fifty and seven thousand and six hundred.
They shall go hindmost with their standards.

32 **These** are those which were numbered of the children of Israel by the house of their fathers:
all those that were numbered of the camps throughout their hosts were six hundred thousand and three thousand and five hundred and fifty.

33 **But the Levites** were not numbered among the children of Israel;
as the LORD commanded Moses.

34 **And the children of Israel** did according to all that the LORD commanded Moses:
so they pitched by their standards,

and so they set forward, every one after their families, according to the house of their fathers.

3

These also are the generations of Aaron and Moses in the day that the LORD spake with Moses in mount Sinai.

2 **And these** are the names of the sons of Aaron; Nadab the firstborn, and Abihu, Eleazar, and Ithamar.

3 **These** are the names of the sons of Aaron, the priests which were anointed,
whom he consecrated to minister in the priest's office.

4 **And Nadab and Abihu** died before the LORD,
when they offered strange fire before the LORD, in the wilderness of Sinai,
and they had no children:
and Eleazar and Ithamar ministered in the priest's office in the sight of Aaron their father.

5 **And the LORD** spake unto Moses,
saying,

6 **Bring** the tribe of Levi near,
and present them before Aaron the priest,
that they may minister unto him.

7 **And they** shall keep his charge, and the charge of the whole congregation before the tabernacle of the congregation,
to do the service of the tabernacle.

8 **And they** shall keep all the instruments of the tabernacle of the congregation, and the charge of the children of Israel,
to do the service of the tabernacle.

9 **And thou** shalt give the Levites unto Aaron and to his sons:
they are wholly given unto him out of the children of Israel.

10 **And thou** shalt appoint Aaron and his sons,
and they shall wait on their priest's office:
and the stranger that cometh nigh shall be put to death.

11 **And the LORD** spake unto Moses,
saying,

12 **And I, {behold}, I** have taken the Levites from among the children of Israel instead of all the firstborn that openeth the matrix among the children of Israel:
therefore the Levites shall be mine;

13 **Because all the firstborn** are mine;
for on the day that I smote all the firstborn in the land of Egypt I hallowed unto me all the firstborn in Israel, both man and beast:
mine shall they be:
I am the LORD.

14 **And the LORD** spake unto Moses in the wilderness of Sinai,
saying,

15 **Number** the children of Levi after the house of their fathers, by their families:
every male from a month old and upward shalt thou number them.

16 **And Moses** numbered them according to the word of the LORD,
as he was commanded.

17 **And these** were the sons of Levi by their names; Gershon, and Kohath, and Merari.

18 **And these** are the names of the sons of Gershon by their families; Libni, and Shimei.

19 **And the sons of Kohath by their families;** Amram, and Izehar, Hebron, and Uzziel.

20 **And the sons of Merari by their families;** Mahli, and Mushi.
These are the families of the Levites according to the house of their fathers.

21 **Of Gershon** was the family of the Libnites, and the family of the Shimites:
these are the families of the Gershonites.

22 **Those that were numbered of them, according to the number of all the males, from a month old and upward, even those that were numbered of them** were seven thousand and five hundred.

23 **The families of the Gershonites** shall pitch behind the tabernacle westward.

24 **And the chief of the house of the father of the Gershonites** shall be Eliasaph the son of Lael.

25 **And the charge of the sons of Gershon in the tabernacle of the congregation** shall be the tabernacle, and the tent, the covering thereof, and the hanging for the door of the tabernacle of the congregation,

26 And the hangings of the court, and the curtain for the door of the court, {which is by the tabernacle}, and by the altar round about, and the cords of it for all the service thereof.

27 **And of Kohath** was the family of the Amramites, and the family of the Izeharites, and the family of the Hebronites, and the family of the Uzzielites:
these are the families of the Kohathites.

28 **In the number of all the males, from a month old and upward,** were eight thousand and six hundred, keeping the charge of the sanctuary.

29 **The families of the sons of Kohath** shall pitch on the side of the tabernacle southward.

30 **And the chief of the house of the father of the families of the Kohathites** shall be Elizaphan the son of Uzziel.

31 **And their charge** shall be the ark, and the table, and the candlestick, and the altars, and the vessels of the sanctuary wherewith they minister, and the hanging, and all the service thereof.

32 **And Eleazar the son of Aaron the priest** shall be chief over the chief of the Levites,
and have the oversight of them that keep the charge of the sanctuary.

33 **Of Merari** was the family of the Mahlites, and the family of the Mushites:
these are the families of Merari.

34 **And those that were numbered of them, according to the number of all the males, from a month old and upward,** were six thousand and two hundred.

35 **And the chief of the house of the father of the families of Merari** was Zuriel the son of Abihail:
these shall pitch on the side of the tabernacle northward.

36 **And under the custody and charge of the sons of Merari** shall be the boards of the tabernacle, and the bars thereof, and the pillars thereof, and the sockets thereof, and all the vessels

thereof, and all that serveth thereto,
37 And the pillars of the court round about, and their sockets, and their pins, and their cords.

38 **But those that encamp before the tabernacle toward the east, even before the tabernacle of the congregation eastward,** shall be Moses, and Aaron and his sons,
keeping the charge of the sanctuary for the charge of the children of Israel;
and the stranger that cometh nigh shall be put to death.

39 **All that were numbered of the Levites, {which Moses and Aaron numbered at the commandment of the LORD}, throughout their families, all the males from a month old and upward,** were twenty and two thousand.

40 **And the LORD** said unto Moses,
Number all the firstborn of the males of the children of Israel from a month old and upward,
and take the number of their names.

41 **And thou** shalt take the Levites for me (I am the LORD) instead of all the firstborn among the children of Israel; and the cattle of the Levites instead of all the firstlings among the cattle of the children of Israel.

42 **And Moses** numbered, {as the LORD commanded him}, all the firstborn among the children of Israel.

43 **And all the firstborn males by the number of names, from a month old and upward, of those that were numbered of them,** were twenty and two thousand two hundred and threescore and thirteen.

44 **And the LORD** spake unto Moses, saying,
45 **Take** the Levites instead of all the firstborn among the children of Israel, and the cattle of the Levites instead of their cattle;
and the Levites shall be mine:
I am the LORD.

46 **And for those that are to be redeemed of the two hundred and threescore and thirteen of the firstborn of the children of Israel,** {which are more than the Levites};
47 Thou shalt even take five shekels apiece by the poll,
after the shekel of the sanctuary shalt thou take them: (the shekel is twenty gerahs:)
48 **And thou** shalt give the money, {wherewith the odd number of them is to be redeemed}, unto Aaron and to his sons.

49 **And Moses** took the redemption money of them that were over and above them that were redeemed by the Levites:
50 **Of the firstborn of the children of Israel** took he the money; a thousand three hundred and threescore and five shekels, after the shekel of the sanctuary:
51 **And Moses** gave the money of them that were redeemed unto Aaron and to his sons, according to the word of the LORD,
as the LORD commanded Moses.

4 **And the LORD** spake unto Moses and unto Aaron, saying,
2 **Take** the sum of the sons of Kohath from among the sons of Levi, after their families, by the house of their fathers,
3 From thirty years old and upward even until fifty years old, all that enter into the host,
to do the work in the tabernacle of the congregation.

4 **This** shall be the service of the sons of Kohath in the tabernacle of the congregation, about the most holy things:
5 **And when the camp** setteth forward,
Aaron shall come, and his sons,
and they shall take down the covering vail,
and cover the ark of testimony with it:
6 **And** shall put thereon the covering of badgers' skins,
and shall spread over it a cloth wholly of blue,
and shall put in the staves thereof.

7 **And upon the table of shewbread** they shall spread a cloth of blue,
and put thereon the dishes, and the spoons, and the bowls, and covers to cover withal:
and the continual bread shall be thereon:
8 **And they** shall spread upon them a cloth of scarlet,
and cover the same with a covering of badgers' skins,
and shall put in the staves thereof.

9 **And they** shall take a cloth of blue,
and cover the candlestick of the light, and his lamps, and his tongs, and his snuffdishes, and all the oil vessels thereof,
wherewith they minister unto it:
10 **And they** shall put it and all the vessels thereof within a covering of badgers' skins,
and shall put it upon a bar.

11 **And upon the golden altar** they shall spread a cloth of blue,
and cover it with a covering of badgers' skins,
and shall put to the staves thereof:
12 **And they** shall take all the instruments of ministry,
wherewith they minister in the sanctuary,
and put them in a cloth of blue,
and cover them with a covering of badgers' skins,
and shall put them on a bar:
13 **And they** shall take away the ashes from the altar,
and spread a purple cloth thereon:
14 **And they** shall put upon it all the vessels thereof,
wherewith they minister about it, even the censers, the fleshhooks, and the shovels, and the basons, all the vessels of the altar;
and they shall spread upon it a covering of badgers' skins,
and put to the staves of it.

15 **And when Aaron and his sons** have made an end of covering the sanctuary, and all the vessels of the sanctuary,
as the camp is to set forward;
after that, the sons of Kohath shall come to bear it:
but they shall not touch any holy thing,
lest they die.

These things are the burden of the sons of Kohath in the tabernacle of the congregation.

16 **And to the office of Eleazar the son of Aaron the priest** pertaineth the oil for the light, and the sweet incense, and the daily meat offering, and the anointing oil, and the oversight of all the tabernacle, and of all that

therein is, in the sanctuary, and in the vessels thereof.

17 **And the LORD** spake unto Moses and unto Aaron
saying,

18 **Cut ye not off** the tribe of the families of the Kohathites from among the Levites:

19 **But thus do** unto them,
that they may live,
and not die,
when they approach unto the most holy things:
Aaron and his sons shall go in,
and appoint them every one to his service and to his burden:

20 **But they** shall not go in to see when the holy things are covered,
lest they die.

21 **And the LORD** spake unto Moses,
saying,

22 **Take** also the sum of the sons of Gershon, throughout the houses of their fathers, by their families;

23 **From thirty years old and upward until fifty years old** shalt thou number them; all that enter in to perform the service,
to do the work in the tabernacle of the congregation.

24 **This** is the service of the families of the Gershonites,
to serve, and for burdens:

25 **And they** shall bear the curtains of the tabernacle, and the tabernacle of the congregation, his covering, and the covering of the badgers' skins that is above upon it, and the hanging for the door of the tabernacle of the congregation,

26 And the hangings of the court, and the hanging for the door of the gate of the court,
which is by the tabernacle and by the altar round about, and their cords, and all the instruments of their service, and all that is made for them:
so shall they serve.

27 **At the appointment of Aaron and his sons** shall be all the service of the sons of the Gershonites, in all their burdens, and in all their service:
and ye shall appoint unto them in charge all their burdens.

28 **This** is the service of the families of the sons of Gershon in the tabernacle of the congregation:
and their charge shall be under the hand of Ithamar the son of Aaron the priest.

29 **As for the sons of Merari,** thou shalt number them after their families, by the house of their fathers;

30 **From thirty years old and upward even unto fifty years old** shalt thou number them, every one that entereth into the service,
to do the work of the tabernacle of the congregation.

31 **And this** is the charge of their burden, according to all their service in the tabernacle of the congregation; the boards of the tabernacle, and the bars thereof, and the pillars thereof, and sockets thereof,

32 And the pillars of the court round about, and their sockets, and their pins, and their cords, with all their instruments, and with all their service:
and by name ye shall reckon the instruments of the charge of their burden.

33 **This** is the service of the families of the sons of Merari, according to all their service, in the tabernacle of the congregation, under the hand of Ithamar the son of Aaron the priest.

34 **And Moses and Aaron and the chief of the congregation** numbered the sons of the Kohathites after their families, and after the house of their fathers,

35 From thirty years old and upward even unto fifty years old, every one that entereth into the service, for the work in the tabernacle of the congregation:

36 **And those that were numbered of them by their families** were two thousand seven hundred and fifty.

37 **These** were they that were numbered of the families of the Kohathites, all that might do service in the tabernacle of the congregation,
which Moses and Aaron did number according to the commandment of the LORD by the hand of Moses.

38 **And those that were numbered of the sons of Gershon, throughout their families, and by the house of their fathers,**

39 **From thirty years old and upward even unto fifty years old, every one that entereth into the service, for the work in the tabernacle of the congregation,**

40 **Even those that were numbered of them, throughout their families, by the house of their fathers,** were two thousand and six hundred and thirty.

41 **These** are they that were numbered of the families of the sons of Gershon, of all that might do service in the tabernacle of the congregation,
whom Moses and Aaron did number according to the commandment of the LORD.

42 **And those that were numbered of the families of the sons of Merari, throughout their families, by the house of their fathers,**

43 **From thirty years old and upward even unto fifty years old, every one that entereth into the service, for the work in the tabernacle of the congregation,**

44 **Even those that were numbered of them after their families,** were three thousand and two hundred.

45 **These** be those that were numbered of the families of the sons of Merari,
whom Moses and Aaron numbered according to the word of the LORD by the hand of Moses.

46 **All those that were numbered of the Levites, {whom Moses and Aaron and the chief of Israel numbered}, after their families, and after the house of their fathers,**

47 **From thirty years old and upward even unto fifty years old, every one that came to do the service of the ministry, and the service of the burden in the tabernacle of the congregation,**

48 **Even those that were numbered of them,** were eight thousand and five hundred and fourscore,

49 **According to the commandment of the LORD** they were numbered by the hand of Moses, every one according to

his service, and according to his burden:
thus were they numbered of him,
as the LORD commanded Moses.

5

And the LORD spake unto Moses,
saying,
[2] **Command** the children of Israel,
that they put out of the camp every leper, and every one that hath an issue, and whosoever is defiled by the dead:
[3] **Both male and female** shall ye put out,
without the camp shall ye put them;
that they defile not their camps,
in the midst whereof I dwell.
[4] **And the children of Israel** did so,
and put them out without the camp:
as the LORD spake unto Moses,
so did the children of Israel.
[5] **And the LORD** spake unto Moses,
saying,
[6] **Speak** unto the children of Israel,
When a man or woman shall commit any sin that men commit,
to do a trespass against the LORD,
and that person be guilty;
[7] **Then they** shall confess their sin which they have done:
and he shall recompense his trespass with the principal thereof,
and add unto it the fifth part thereof,
and give it unto him against whom he hath trespassed.
[8] **But if the man** have no kinsman to recompense the trespass unto,
let the trespass be recompensed unto the LORD, even to the priest; beside the ram of the atonement,
whereby an atonement shall be made for him.
[9] **And every offering of all the holy things of the children of Israel,** {which they bring unto the priest}, shall be his.
[10] **And every man's hallowed things** shall be his:
whatsoever any man giveth the priest, it shall be his.
[11] **And the LORD** spake unto Moses,
saying,
[12] **Speak** unto the children of Israel,
and say unto them,
If any man's wife go aside,
and commit a trespass against him,
[13] **And a man** lie with her carnally,
and it be hid from the eyes of her husband,
and be kept close,
and she be defiled,
and there be no witness against her,
neither she be taken with the manner;
[14] **And the spirit of jealousy** come upon him,
and he be jealous of his wife,
and she be defiled:
or if the spirit of jealousy come upon him,
and he be jealous of his wife,
and she be not defiled:
[15] **Then** shall the man bring his wife unto the priest,
and he shall bring her offering for her, the tenth part of an ephah of barley meal;
he shall pour no oil upon it,
nor put frankincense thereon;
for it is an offering of jealousy, an offering of memorial,
bringing iniquity to remembrance.
[16] **And the priest** shall bring her near,
and set her before the LORD:
[17] **And the priest** shall take holy water in an earthen vessel;
and of the dust that is in the floor of the tabernacle the priest shall take,
and put it into the water:
[18] **And the priest** shall set the woman before the LORD,
and uncover the woman's head,
and put the offering of memorial in her hands,
which is the jealousy offering:
and the priest shall have in his hand the bitter water that causeth the curse:
[19] **And the priest** shall charge her by an oath,
and say unto the woman,
If no man have lain with thee,
and if thou hast not gone aside to uncleanness with another instead of thy husband,
be thou free from this bitter water that causeth the curse:
[20] **But if thou** hast gone aside to another instead of thy husband,
and if thou be defiled,
and some man have lain with thee beside thine husband:
[21] **Then the priest** shall charge the woman with an oath of cursing,
and the priest shall say unto the woman,
The LORD make thee a curse and an oath among thy people,
when the LORD doth make thy thigh to rot,
and thy belly to swell;
[22] **And this water that causeth the curse** shall go into thy bowels,
to make thy belly to swell,
and thy thigh to rot:
And the woman shall say,
Amen, amen.
[23] **And the priest** shall write these curses in a book,
and he shall blot them out with the bitter water:
[24] **And he** shall cause the woman to drink the bitter water that causeth the curse:
and the water that causeth the curse shall enter into her,
and become bitter.
[25] **Then the priest** shall take the jealousy offering out of the woman's hand,
and shall wave the offering before the LORD,
and offer it upon the altar:
[26] **And the priest** shall take an handful of the offering, even the memorial thereof,
and burn it upon the altar,
and afterward shall cause the woman to drink the water.
[27] **And when he** hath made her to drink the water,
then it shall come to pass,
that, {if she be defiled}, {and have done trespass against her husband}, that the water that causeth the curse shall enter into her,
and become bitter,
and her belly shall swell,
and her thigh shall rot:
and the woman shall be a curse among her people.
[28] **And if the woman** be not defiled,
but be clean;
then she shall be free,
and shall conceive seed.
[29] **This** is the law of jealousies,
when a wife goeth aside to another instead of her husband,
and is defiled;
[30] **Or when the spirit of jealousy** cometh upon him,
and he be jealous over his wife,

and shall set the woman before the LORD,
and the priest shall execute upon her all this law.
31 **Then** shall the man be guiltless from iniquity,
and this woman shall bear her iniquity.

6 **And the LORD** spake unto Moses,
saying,
2 **Speak** unto the children of Israel,
and say unto them,
When either man or woman shall separate themselves to vow a vow of a Nazarite,
to separate themselves unto the LORD:
3 **He** shall separate himself from wine and strong drink,
and shall drink no vinegar of wine, or vinegar of strong drink,
neither shall he drink any liquor of grapes,
nor eat moist grapes, or dried.
4 **All the days of his separation** shall he eat nothing that is made of the vine tree, from the kernels even to the husk.
5 **All the days of the vow of his separation** there shall no razor come upon his head:
until the days be fulfilled,
in the which he separateth himself unto the LORD,
he shall be holy,
and shall let the locks of the hair of his head grow.
6 **All the days that he separateth himself unto the LORD** he shall come at no dead body.
7 **He** shall not make himself unclean for his father, or for his mother, for his brother, or for his sister,
when they die:
because the consecration of his God is upon his head.
8 **All the days of his separation** he is holy unto the LORD.
9 **And if any man** die very suddenly by him,
and he hath defiled the head of his consecration;
then he shall shave his head in the day of his cleansing,
on the seventh day shall he shave it.
10 **And on the eighth day** he shall bring two turtles, or two young pigeons, to the priest, to the door of the tabernacle of the congregation:
11 **And the priest** shall offer the one for a sin offering, and the other for a burnt offering,
and make an atonement for him,
for that he sinned by the dead,
and shall hallow his head that same day.
12 **And he** shall consecrate unto the LORD the days of his separation,
and shall bring a lamb of the first year for a trespass offering:
but the days that were before shall be lost,
because his separation was defiled.
13 **And this** is the law of the Nazarite,
when the days of his separation are fulfilled:
he shall be brought unto the door of the tabernacle of the congregation:
14 **And he** shall offer his offering unto the LORD, one he lamb of the first year without blemish for a burnt offering, and one ewe lamb of the first year without blemish for a sin offering, and one ram without blemish for peace offerings,
15 And a basket of unleavened bread, cakes of fine flour mingled with oil, and wafers of unleavened bread anointed with oil, and their meat offering, and their drink offerings.
16 **And the priest** shall bring them before the LORD,
and shall offer his sin offering, and his burnt offering:
17 **And he** shall offer the ram for a sacrifice of peace offerings unto the LORD, with the basket of unleavened bread:
the priest shall offer also his meat offering, and his drink offering.
18 **And the Nazarite** shall shave the head of his separation at the door of the tabernacle of the congregation,
and shall take the hair of the head of his separation,
and put it in the fire which is under the sacrifice of the peace offerings.
19 **And the priest** shall take the sodden shoulder of the ram, and one unleavened cake out of the basket, and one unleavened wafer,
and shall put them upon the hands of the Nazarite,
after the hair of his separation is shaven:
20 **And the priest** shall wave them for a wave offering before the LORD:
this is holy for the priest, with the wave breast and heave shoulder:
and after that the Nazarite may drink wine.
21 **This** is the law of the Nazarite who hath vowed, and of his offering unto the LORD for his separation, beside that that his hand shall get:
according to the vow which he vowed, so he must do after the law of his separation.
22 **And the LORD** spake unto Moses,
saying,
23 **Speak** unto Aaron and unto his sons,
saying,
On this wise ye shall bless the children of Israel,
saying unto them,
24 **The LORD** bless thee,
and keep thee:
25 **The LORD** make his face shine upon thee,
and be gracious unto thee:
26 **The LORD** lift up his countenance upon thee,
and give thee peace.
27 **And they** shall put my name upon the children of Israel,
and I will bless them.

7 **And it** came to pass on the day that Moses had fully set up the tabernacle,
and had anointed it,
and sanctified it, and all the instruments thereof, both the altar and all the vessels thereof,
and had anointed them,
and sanctified them;
2 **That the princes of Israel, heads of the house of their fathers**, {who were the princes of the tribes}, {and were over them that were numbered}, offered:
3 **And they** brought their offering before the LORD, six covered wagons, and twelve oxen; a wagon for two of the princes, and for each one an ox:

and they brought them before the tabernacle.

4 **And the LORD** spake unto Moses, saying,
5 **Take** it of them,
that they may be to do the service of the tabernacle of the congregation;
and thou shalt give them unto the Levites, to every man according to his service.

6 **And Moses** took the wagons and the oxen,
and gave them unto the Levites.

7 **Two wagons and four oxen** he gave unto the sons of Gershon, according to their service:
8 **And four wagons and eight oxen** he gave unto the sons of Merari, according unto their service, under the hand of Ithamar the son of Aaron the priest.

9 **But unto the sons of Kohath** he gave none:
because the service of the sanctuary belonging unto them was that they should bear upon their shoulders.

10 **And the princes** offered for dedicating of the altar in the day that it was anointed,
even the princes offered their offering before the altar.

11 **And the LORD** said unto Moses,
They shall offer their offering, each prince on his day, for the dedicating of the altar.

12 **And he that offered his offering the first day** was Nahshon the son of Amminadab, of the tribe of Judah:
13 **And his offering** was one silver charger, {the weight thereof was an hundred and thirty shekels}, one silver bowl of seventy shekels, after the shekel of the sanctuary;
both of them were full of fine flour mingled with oil for a meat offering:
14 One spoon of ten shekels of gold, full of incense:
15 One young bullock, one ram, one lamb of the first year, for a burnt offering:
16 One kid of the goats for a sin offering:
17 And for a sacrifice of peace offerings, two oxen, five rams, five he goats, five lambs of the first year:
this was the offering of Nahshon the son of Amminadab.

18 **On the second day** Nethaneel the son of Zuar, prince of Issachar, did offer:
19 **He** offered for his offering one silver charger, {the weight whereof was an hundred and thirty shekels}, one silver bowl of seventy shekels, after the shekel of the sanctuary; both of them full of fine flour mingled with oil for a meat offering:
20 One spoon of gold of ten shekels, full of incense:
21 One young bullock, one ram, one lamb of the first year, for a burnt offering:
22 One kid of the goats for a sin offering:
23 And for a sacrifice of peace offerings, two oxen, five rams, five he goats, five lambs of the first year:
this was the offering of Nethaneel the son of Zuar.

24 **On the third day** Eliab the son of Helon, prince of the children of Zebulun, did offer:
25 **His offering** was one silver charger, {the weight whereof was an hundred and thirty shekels}, one silver bowl of seventy shekels, after the shekel of the sanctuary; both of them full of fine flour mingled with oil for a meat offering:
26 One golden spoon of ten shekels, full of incense:
27 One young bullock, one ram, one lamb of the first year, for a burnt offering:
28 One kid of the goats for a sin offering:
29 And for a sacrifice of peace offerings, two oxen, five rams, five he goats, five lambs of the first year:
this was the offering of Eliab the son of Helon.

30 **On the fourth day** Elizur the son of Shedeur, prince of the children of Reuben, did offer:
31 **His offering** was one silver charger of the weight of an hundred and thirty shekels, one silver bowl of seventy shekels, after the shekel of the sanctuary; both of them full of fine flour mingled with oil for a meat offering:
32 One golden spoon of ten shekels, full of incense:
33 One young bullock, one ram, one lamb of the first year, for a burnt offering:
34 One kid of the goats for a sin offering:
35 And for a sacrifice of peace offerings, two oxen, five rams, five he goats, five lambs of the first year:
this was the offering of Elizur the son of Shedeur.

36 **On the fifth day** Shelumiel the son of Zurishaddai, prince of the children of Simeon, did offer:
37 **His offering** was one silver charger, {the weight whereof was an hundred and thirty shekels}, one silver bowl of seventy shekels, after the shekel of the sanctuary; both of them full of fine flour mingled with oil for a meat offering:
38 One golden spoon of ten shekels, full of incense:
39 One young bullock, one ram, one lamb of the first year, for a burnt offering:
40 One kid of the goats for a sin offering:
41 And for a sacrifice of peace offerings, two oxen, five rams, five he goats, five lambs of the first year:
this was the offering of Shelumiel the son of Zurishaddai.

42 **On the sixth day** Eliasaph the son of Deuel, prince of the children of Gad, offered:
43 **His offering** was one silver charger of the weight of an hundred and thirty shekels, a silver bowl of seventy shekels, after the shekel of the sanctuary; both of them full of fine flour mingled with oil for a meat offering:
44 One golden spoon of ten shekels, full of incense:
45 One young bullock, one ram, one lamb of the first year, for a burnt offering:
46 One kid of the goats for a sin offering:
47 And for a sacrifice of peace offerings, two oxen, five rams, five he goats, five lambs of the first year:
this was the offering of Eliasaph the son of Deuel.

48 **On the seventh day** Elishama the son of Ammihud, prince of the children of Ephraim, offered:
49 **His offering** was one silver charger, {the weight whereof was an hundred and thirty shekels}, one silver bowl of seventy shekels, after the shekel of the sanctuary; both of them full of fine flour mingled with oil for a meat offering:
50 One golden spoon of ten shekels, full of incense:
51 One young bullock, one ram, one lamb of the first year, for a burnt offering:
52 One kid of the goats for a sin offering:
53 And for a sacrifice of peace offerings, two oxen, five rams, five he goats, five lambs of the first year:
this was the offering of Elishama the son of Ammihud.

54 **On the eighth day** offered Gamaliel the son of Pedahzur, prince of the children of Manasseh:
55 **His offering** was one silver charger of the weight of an hundred and thirty shekels, one silver bowl of seventy shekels, after the shekel of the sanctuary; both of them full of fine flour mingled with oil for a meat offering:
56 One golden spoon of ten shekels, full of incense:
57 One young bullock, one ram, one lamb of the first year, for a burnt offering:
58 One kid of the goats for a sin offering:
59 And for a sacrifice of peace offerings, two oxen, five rams, five he goats, five lambs of the first year:
this was the offering of Gamaliel the son of Pedahzur.

60 **On the ninth day** Abidan the son of Gideoni, prince of the children of Benjamin, offered:
61 **His offering** was one silver charger, {the weight whereof was an hundred and thirty shekels}, one silver bowl of seventy shekels, after the shekel of the sanctuary; both of them full of fine flour mingled with oil for a meat offering:
62 One golden spoon of ten shekels, full of incense:
63 One young bullock, one ram, one lamb of the first year, for a burnt offering:
64 One kid of the goats for a sin offering:
65 And for a sacrifice of peace offerings, two oxen, five rams, five he goats, five lambs of the first year:
this was the offering of Abidan the son of Gideoni.

66 **On the tenth day** Ahiezer the son of Ammishaddai, prince of the children of Dan, offered:
67 **His offering** was one silver charger, {the weight whereof was an hundred and thirty shekels}, one silver bowl of seventy shekels, after the shekel of the sanctuary; both of them full of fine flour mingled with oil for a meat offering:
68 One golden spoon of ten shekels, full of incense:
69 One young bullock, one ram, one lamb of the first year, for a burnt offering:
70 One kid of the goats for a sin offering:
71 And for a sacrifice of peace offerings, two oxen, five rams, five he goats, five lambs of the first year:
this was the offering of Ahiezer the son of Ammishaddai.

72 **On the eleventh day** Pagiel the son of Ocran, prince of the children of Asher, offered:
73 **His offering** was one silver charger, {the weight whereof was an hundred and thirty shekels}, one silver bowl of seventy shekels, after the shekel of the sanctuary; both of them full of fine flour mingled with oil for a meat offering:
74 One golden spoon of ten shekels, full of incense:
75 One young bullock, one ram, one lamb of the first year, for a burnt offering:
76 One kid of the goats for a sin offering:
77 And for a sacrifice of peace offerings, two oxen, five rams, five he goats, five lambs of the first year:
this was the offering of Pagiel the son of Ocran.

78 **On the twelfth day** Ahira the son of Enan, prince of the children of Naphtali, offered:
79 **His offering** was one silver charger, {the weight whereof was an hundred and thirty shekels}, one silver bowl of seventy shekels, after the shekel of the sanctuary; both of them full of fine flour mingled with oil for a meat offering:
80 One golden spoon of ten shekels, full of incense:
81 One young bullock, one ram, one lamb of the first year, for a burnt offering:
82 One kid of the goats for a sin offering:
83 And for a sacrifice of peace offerings, two oxen, five rams, five he goats, five lambs of the first year:
this was the offering of Ahira the son of Enan.

84 **This** was the dedication of the altar, in the day when it was anointed, by the princes of Israel: twelve chargers of silver, twelve silver bowls, twelve spoons of gold:
85 **Each charger of silver** weighing an hundred and thirty shekels, each bowl seventy:
all the silver vessels weighed two thousand and four hundred shekels, after the shekel of the sanctuary:
86 **The golden spoons** were twelve, full of incense,
weighing ten shekels apiece, after the shekel of the sanctuary:
all the gold of the spoons was an hundred and twenty shekels.

87 **All the oxen for the burnt offering** were twelve bullocks, the rams twelve, the lambs of the first year twelve, with their meat offering: and the kids of the goats for sin offering twelve.

88 **And all the oxen for the sacrifice of the peace offerings** were twenty and four bullocks, the rams sixty, the he goats sixty, the lambs of the first year sixty.

This was the dedication of the altar, **after that it** was anointed.

89 **And when Moses** was gone into the tabernacle of the congregation to speak with him,

then he heard the voice of one speaking unto him from off the mercy seat that was upon the ark of testimony, from between the two cherubims:
and he spake unto him.

8 **And the LORD** spake unto Moses,
saying,
2 **Speak** unto Aaron
and say unto him,
When thou lightest the lamps,
the seven lamps shall give light over against the candlestick.

3 **And Aaron** did so;
he lighted the lamps thereof over against the candlestick,
as the LORD commanded Moses.

4 **And this work of the candlestick** was of beaten gold,
unto the shaft thereof, unto the flowers thereof, was beaten work:
according unto the pattern which the LORD had shewed Moses, so he made the candlestick.

5 **And the LORD** spake unto Moses,
saying,
6 **Take** the Levites from among the children of Israel,
and cleanse them.

7 **And thus** shalt thou do unto them,
to cleanse them:
Sprinkle water of purifying upon them,
and let them shave all their flesh,
and let them wash their clothes,
and so make themselves clean.

8 **Then let them** take a young bullock with his meat offering, even fine flour mingled with oil,
and another young bullock shalt thou take for a sin offering.

9 **And thou** shalt bring the Levites before the tabernacle of the congregation:
and thou shalt gather the whole assembly of the children of Israel together:
10 **And thou** shalt bring the Levites before the LORD:
and the children of Israel shall put their hands upon the Levites:
11 **And Aaron** shall offer the Levites before the LORD for an offering of the children of Israel,
that they may execute the service of the LORD.

12 **And the Levites** shall lay their hands upon the heads of the bullocks:
and thou shalt offer the one for a sin offering, and the other for a burnt offering, unto the LORD,
to make an atonement for the Levites.

13 **And thou** shalt set the Levites before Aaron, and before his sons,
and offer them for an offering unto the LORD.

14 **Thus** shalt thou separate the Levites from among the children of Israel:
and the Levites shall be mine.

15 **And after that** shall the Levites go in to do the service of the tabernacle of the congregation:
and thou shalt cleanse them,
and offer them for an offering.

16 **For they** are wholly given unto me from among the children of Israel;
instead of such as open every womb, even instead of the firstborn of all the children of Israel, have I taken them unto me.

17 **For all the firstborn of the children of Israel** are mine, both man and beast:
on the day that I smote every firstborn in the land of Egypt I sanctified them for myself.

18 **And I** have taken the Levites for all the firstborn of the children of Israel.

19 **And I** have given the Levites as a gift to Aaron and to his sons from among the children of Israel,
to do the service of the children of Israel in the tabernacle of the congregation,
and to make an atonement for the children of Israel:
that there be no plague among the children of Israel,
when the children of Israel come nigh unto the sanctuary.

20 **And Moses, and Aaron, and all the congregation of the children of Israel,** did to the Levites according unto all that the LORD commanded Moses concerning the Levites,
so did the children of Israel unto them.

21 **And the Levites** were purified,
and they washed their clothes;
and Aaron offered them as an offering before the LORD;
and Aaron made an atonement for them
to cleanse them.

22 **And after that** went the Levites in to do their service in the tabernacle of the congregation before Aaron, and before his sons:
as the LORD had commanded Moses concerning the Levites,
so did they unto them.

23 **And the LORD** spake unto Moses,
saying,
24 **This** is it that belongeth unto the Levites:
from twenty and five years old and upward they shall go in to wait upon the service of the tabernacle of the congregation:
25 **And from the age of fifty years** they shall cease waiting upon the service thereof,
and shall serve no more:
26 **But** shall minister with their brethren in the tabernacle of the congregation,
to keep the charge,
and shall do no service.

Thus shalt thou do unto the Levites touching their charge.

9 **And the LORD** spake unto Moses in the wilderness of Sinai, in the first month of the second year after they were come out of the land of Egypt,
saying,
2 **Let the children of Israel** also keep the passover at his appointed season.

3 **In the fourteenth day of this month, at even,** ye shall keep it in his appointed season:
according to all the rites of it, and according to all the ceremonies thereof, shall ye keep it.

4 **And Moses** spake unto the children of Israel,
that they should keep the passover.

5 **And they** kept the passover on the fourteenth day of the first month at even in the wilderness of Sinai:
according to all that the LORD commanded Moses, so did the children of Israel.

6 **And there** were certain men,
who were defiled by the dead body of a man,

that they could not keep the passover on that day:
and they came before Moses and before Aaron on that day:

7 **And those men** said unto him,
We are defiled by the dead body of a man:
wherefore are we kept back,
that we may not offer an offering of the LORD in his appointed season among the children of Israel?

8 **And Moses** said unto them,
Stand still,
and I will hear what the LORD will command concerning you.

9 **And the LORD** spake unto Moses, saying,
10 **Speak** unto the children of Israel, saying,
If any man of you or of your posterity shall be unclean by reason of a dead body,
or be in a journey afar off,
yet he shall keep the passover unto the LORD.

11 **The fourteenth day of the second month at even** they shall keep it,
and eat it with unleavened bread and bitter herbs.

12 **They** shall leave none of it unto the morning,
nor break any bone of it:
according to all the ordinances of the passover they shall keep it.

13 **But the man that is clean, and is not in a journey, and forbeareth to keep the passover,** even the same soul shall be cut off from among his people:
because he brought not the offering of the LORD in his appointed season,
that man shall bear his sin.

14 **And if a stranger** shall sojourn among you,
and will keep the passover unto the LORD;
according to the ordinance of the passover, and according to the manner thereof, so shall he do:
ye shall have one ordinance, both for the stranger, and for him that was born in the land.

15 **And on the day that the tabernacle was reared up** the cloud covered the tabernacle, namely, the tent of the testimony:
and at even there was upon the tabernacle as it were the appearance of fire, until the morning.

16 **So it** was alway:
the cloud covered it by day, and the appearance of fire by night.

17 **And when the cloud** was taken up from the tabernacle,
then after that the children of Israel journeyed:
and in the place where the cloud abode, there the children of Israel pitched their tents.

18 **At the commandment of the LORD** the children of Israel journeyed,
and at the commandment of the LORD they pitched:
as long as the cloud abode upon the tabernacle
they rested in their tents.

19 **And when the cloud** tarried long upon the tabernacle many days,
then the children of Israel kept the charge of the LORD,
and journeyed not.

20 **And so** it was,
when the cloud was a few days upon the tabernacle;
according to the commandment of the LORD they abode in their tents,
and according to the commandment of the LORD they journeyed.

21 **And so** it was,
when the cloud abode from even unto the morning,
and that the cloud was taken up in the morning,
then they journeyed:
whether it was by day or by night that the cloud was taken up,
they journeyed.

22 **Or whether it were two days, or a month, or a year,** that the cloud tarried upon the tabernacle, remaining thereon,
the children of Israel abode in their tents,
and journeyed not:
but when it was taken up,
they journeyed.

23 **At the commandment of the LORD** they rested in the tents,
and at the commandment of the LORD they journeyed:
they kept the charge of the LORD, at the commandment of the LORD by the hand of Moses.

10

And the LORD spake unto Moses, saying,

2 **Make thee** two trumpets of silver;
of a whole piece shalt thou make them:
that thou mayest use them for the calling of the assembly, and for the journeying of the camps.

3 **And when they** shall blow with them,
all the assembly shall assemble themselves to thee at the door of the tabernacle of the congregation.

4 **And if they** blow but with one trumpet,
then the princes, {which are heads of the thousands of Israel}, shall gather themselves unto thee.

5 **When ye** blow an alarm,
then the camps that lie on the east parts shall go forward.

6 **When ye** blow an alarm the second time,
then the camps that lie on the south side shall take their journey:
they shall blow an alarm for their journeys.

7 **But when the congregation** is to be gathered together,
ye shall blow,
but ye shall not sound an alarm.

8 **And the sons of Aaron, the priests,** shall blow with the trumpets;
and they shall be to you for an ordinance for ever throughout your generations.

9 **And if ye** go to war in your land against the enemy that oppresseth you,
then ye shall blow an alarm with the trumpets;
and ye shall be remembered before the LORD your God,
and ye shall be saved from your enemies.

10 **Also in the day of your gladness, and in your solemn days, and in the beginnings of your months,** ye shall blow with the trumpets over your burnt offerings, and over the sacrifices of your peace offerings;
that they may be to you for a memorial before your God:
I am the LORD your God.

11 **And it** came to pass on the twentieth day of the second month, in the second year,
that the cloud was taken up from off the tabernacle of the testimony.

12 **And the children of Israel** took their journeys out of the wilderness of Sinai;
and the cloud rested in the wilderness of Paran.

13 **And they first** took their journey according to the commandment of the LORD by the hand of Moses.

14 **In the first place** went the standard of the camp of the children of Judah according to their armies:
and over his host was Nahshon the son of Amminadab.

15 **And over the host of the tribe of the children of Issachar** was Nethaneel the son of Zuar.

16 **And over the host of the tribe of the children of Zebulun** was Eliab the son of Helon.

17 **And the tabernacle** was taken down;
and the sons of Gershon and the sons of Merari set forward,
bearing the tabernacle.

18 **And the standard of the camp of Reuben** set forward according to their armies:
and over his host was Elizur the son of Shedeur.

19 **And over the host of the tribe of the children of Simeon** was Shelumiel the son of Zurishaddai.

20 **And over the host of the tribe of the children of Gad** was Eliasaph the son of Deuel.

21 **And the Kohathites** set forward,
bearing the sanctuary:
and the other did set up the tabernacle
against they came.

22 **And the standard of the camp of the children of Ephraim** set forward according to their armies:
and over his host was Elishama the son of Ammihud.

23 **And over the host of the tribe of the children of Manasseh** was Gamaliel the son of Pedahzur.

24 **And over the host of the tribe of the children of Benjamin** was Abidan the son of Gideoni.

25 **And the standard of the camp of the children of Dan** set forward,
which was the rereward of all the camps throughout their hosts:
and over his host was Ahiezer the son of Ammishaddai.

26 **And over the host of the tribe of the children of Asher** was Pagiel the son of Ocran.

27 **And over the host of the tribe of the children of Naphtali** was Ahira the son of Enan.

28 **Thus** were the journeyings of the children of Israel according to their armies,
when they set forward.

29 **And Moses** said unto Hobab, the son of Raguel the Midianite, Moses' father in law,
We are journeying unto the place of which the LORD said,
I will give it you:
come thou with us,
and we will do thee good:
for the LORD hath spoken good concerning Israel.

30 **And he** said unto him,
I will not go;
but I will depart to mine own land, and to my kindred.

31 **And he** said,
Leave us not,
I pray thee;
forasmuch as thou knowest
how we are to encamp in the wilderness,
and thou mayest be to us instead of eyes.

32 **And it** shall be,
if thou go with us,
yea, it shall be,
that what goodness the LORD shall do unto us,
the same will we do unto thee.

33 **And they** departed from the mount of the LORD three days' journey:
and the ark of the covenant of the LORD went before them in the three days' journey,
to search out a resting place for them.

34 **And the cloud of the LORD** was upon them by day,
when they went out of the camp.

35 **And it** came to pass,
when the ark set forward,
that Moses said, **Rise up,** LORD,
and let thine enemies be scattered;
and let them that hate thee flee before thee.

36 **And when** it rested,
he said,
Return, O LORD, unto the many thousands of Israel.

11 **And when the people** complained,
it displeased the LORD:
and the LORD heard it;
and his anger was kindled;
and the fire of the LORD burnt among them,
and consumed them that were in the uttermost parts of the camp.

2 **And the people** cried unto Moses;
and when Moses prayed unto the LORD,
the fire was quenched.

3 **And he** called the name of the place Taberah:
because the fire of the LORD burnt among them.

4 **And the mixt multitude that was among them** fell a lusting:
and the children of Israel also wept again,
and said,
Who shall give us flesh to eat?

5 **We** remember the fish,
which we did eat in Egypt freely;
the cucumbers, and the melons, and the leeks, and the onions, and the garlick:

6 **But now our soul** is dried away:
there is nothing at all, beside this manna, before our eyes.

7 **And the manna** was as coriander seed, and the colour thereof as the colour of bdellium.

8 **And the people** went about,
and gathered it,
and ground it in mills,
or beat it in a mortar,
and baked it in pans,
and made cakes of it:
and the taste of it was as the taste of fresh oil.

9 **And when the dew** fell upon the camp in the night,
the manna fell upon it.

10 **Then Moses** heard the people weep throughout their families, every man in the door of his tent:
and the anger of the LORD was kindled greatly;
Moses also was displeased.

11 **And Moses** said unto the LORD,

Wherefore hast thou afflicted thy servant?
and wherefore have I not found favour in thy sight,
that thou layest the burden of all this people upon me?

12 **Have I** conceived all this people?
have I begotten them,
that thou shouldest say unto me,
Carry them in thy bosom,
as a nursing father beareth the sucking child, unto the land which thou swarest unto their fathers?

13 **Whence** should I have flesh to give unto all this people?
for they weep unto me,
saying,
Give us flesh,
that we may eat.

14 **I** am not able to bear all this people alone,
because it is too heavy for me.

15 **And if thou** deal thus with me,
kill me, {I pray thee}, out of hand,
if I have found favour in thy sight;
and let me not see my wretchedness.

16 **And the LORD** said unto Moses,
Gather unto me seventy men of the elders of Israel,
whom thou knowest to be the elders of the people, and officers over them;
and bring them unto the tabernacle of the congregation,
that they may stand there with thee.

17 **And I** will come down and talk with thee there:
and I will take of the spirit which is upon thee,
and will put it upon them;
and they shall bear the burden of the people with thee,
that thou bear it not thyself alone.

18 **And say thou** unto the people,
Sanctify yourselves against to morrow,
and ye shall eat flesh:
for ye have wept in the ears of the LORD,
saying,
Who shall give us flesh to eat?
for it was well with us in Egypt:
therefore the LORD will give you flesh,
and ye shall eat.

19 **Ye** shall not eat one day, nor two days, nor five days, neither ten days, nor twenty days;

20 But even a whole month,
until it come out at your nostrils,
and it be loathsome unto you:
because that ye have despised the LORD which is among you,
and have wept before him,
saying,
Why came we forth out of Egypt?

21 **And Moses** said,
The people, {among whom I am}, are six hundred thousand footmen;
and thou hast said,
I will give them flesh,
that they may eat a whole month.

22 **Shall the flocks and the herds** be slain for them,
to suffice them?
or shall all the fish of the sea be gathered together for them,
to suffice them?

23 **And the LORD** said unto Moses,
Is the LORD's hand waxed short?
thou shalt see now whether my word shall come to pass unto thee or not.

24 **And Moses** went out,
and told the people the words of the LORD,
and gathered the seventy men of the elders of the people,
and set them round about the tabernacle.

25 **And the LORD** came down in a cloud,
and spake unto him,
and took of the spirit that was upon him,
and gave it unto the seventy elders:
and it came to pass,
that, {when the spirit rested upon them}, they prophesied,
and did not cease.

26 **But there** remained two of the men in the camp,
the name of the one was Eldad, and the name of the other Medad:
and the spirit rested upon them;
and they were of them that were written,
but went not out unto the tabernacle:
and they prophesied in the camp.

27 **And there** ran a young man,
and told Moses,
and said,
Eldad and Medad do prophesy in the camp.

28 **And Joshua the son of Nun, the servant of Moses, one of his young men,** answered and said,
My lord Moses, forbid them.

29 **And Moses** said unto him,
Enviest thou for my sake?
would God that all the LORD's people were prophets,
and that the LORD would put his spirit upon them!

30 **And Moses** gat him into the camp, he and the elders of Israel.

31 **And there** went forth a wind from the LORD,
and brought quails from the sea,
and let them fall by the camp, as it were a day's journey on this side, and as it were a day's journey on the other side, round about the camp, and as it were two cubits high upon the face of the earth.

32 **And the people** stood up all that day, and all that night, and all the next day,
and they gathered the quails:
he that gathered least gathered ten homers:
and they spread them all abroad for themselves round about the camp.

33 **And while the flesh** was yet between their teeth,
ere it was chewed,
the wrath of the LORD was kindled against the people,
and the LORD smote the people with a very great plague.

34 **And he** called the name of that place Kibrothhattaavah:
because there they buried the people that lusted.

35 **And the people** journeyed from Kibrothhattaavah unto Hazeroth;
and abode at Hazeroth.

12

And Miriam and Aaron spake against Moses because of the Ethiopian woman whom he had married:
for he had married an Ethiopian woman.

2 **And they** said,
Hath the LORD indeed spoken only by Moses?
hath he not spoken also by us?
And the LORD heard it.

3 (**Now the man Moses** was very meek, above all the men which were upon the face of the earth.)

4 **And the LORD** spake suddenly unto Moses, and unto Aaron, and unto Miriam,
Come out ye three unto the tabernacle of the congregation.

And they three came out.

5 **And the LORD** came down in the pillar of the cloud,
and stood in the door of the tabernacle,
and called Aaron and Miriam:
and they both came forth.

6 **And he** said,
Hear now my words:
If there be a prophet among you,
I the LORD will make myself known unto him in a vision,
and will speak unto him in a dream.

7 **My servant Moses** is not so,
who is faithful in all mine house.

8 **With him** will I speak mouth to mouth, even apparently, and not in dark speeches;
and the similitude of the LORD shall he behold:
wherefore then were ye not afraid to speak against my servant Moses?

9 **And the anger of the LORD** was kindled against them;
and he departed.

10 **And the cloud** departed from off the tabernacle;
and, {behold}, Miriam became leprous, white as snow:
and Aaron looked upon Miriam,
and, {behold}, she was leprous.

11 **And Aaron** said unto Moses,
Alas, my lord, I beseech thee,
lay not the sin upon us,
wherein we have done foolishly,
and wherein we have sinned.

12 **Let her not** be as one dead,
of whom the flesh is half consumed
when he cometh out of his mother's womb.

13 **And Moses** cried unto the LORD,
saying,
Heal her now, O God,
I beseech thee.

14 **And the LORD** said unto Moses,
If her father had but spit in her face,
should she not be ashamed seven days?
let her be shut out from the camp seven days,
and after that let her be received in again.

15 **And Miriam** was shut out from the camp seven days:
and the people journeyed not
till Miriam was brought in again.

16 **And afterward** the people removed from Hazeroth,
and pitched in the wilderness of Paran.

13

And the LORD spake unto Moses,
saying,

2 **Send thou** men,
that they may search the land of Canaan,
which I give unto the children of Israel:
of every tribe of their fathers shall ye send a man, every one a ruler among them.

3 **And Moses by the commandment of the LORD** sent them from the wilderness of Paran:
all those men were heads of the children of Israel.

4 **And these** were their names:
of the tribe of Reuben, Shammua the son of Zaccur.

5 **Of the tribe of Simeon,** Shaphat the son of Hori.

6 **Of the tribe of Judah,** Caleb the son of Jephunneh.

7 **Of the tribe of Issachar,** Igal the son of Joseph.

8 **Of the tribe of Ephraim,** Oshea the son of Nun.

9 **Of the tribe of Benjamin,** Palti the son of Raphu.

10 **Of the tribe of Zebulun,** Gaddiel the son of Sodi.

11 **Of the tribe of Joseph, namely, of the tribe of Manasseh,** Gaddi the son of Susi.

12 **Of the tribe of Dan,** Ammiel the son of Gemalli.

13 **Of the tribe of Asher,** Sethur the son of Michael.

14 **Of the tribe of Naphtali,** Nahbi the son of Vophsi.

15 **Of the tribe of Gad,** Geuel the son of Machi.

16 **These** are the names of the men which Moses sent to spy out the land.
And Moses called Oshea the son of Nun Jehoshua.

17 **And Moses** sent them to spy out the land of Canaan,
and said unto them,
Get you up this way southward,
and go up into the mountain:

18 **And see** the land,
what it is, and the people that dwelleth therein,
whether they be strong or weak, few or many;

19 **And what** the land is that they dwell in,
whether it be good or bad;
and what cities they be that they dwell in, whether in tents, or in strong holds;

20 **And what** the land is,
whether it be fat or lean,
whether there be wood therein, or not.

And be ye of good courage,
and bring of the fruit of the land.

Now the time was the time of the firstripe grapes.

21 **So they** went up,
and searched the land from the wilderness of Zin unto Rehob,
as men come to Hamath.

22 **And they** ascended by the south,
and came unto Hebron;
where Ahiman, Sheshai, and Talmai, the children of Anak, were.

(**Now Hebron** was built seven years before Zoan in Egypt.)

23 **And they** came unto the brook of Eshcol,
and cut down from thence a branch with one cluster of grapes,
and they bare it between two upon a staff;
and they brought of the pomegranates, and of the figs.

24 **The place** was called the brook Eshcol, because of the cluster of grapes which the children of Israel cut down from thence.

25 **And they** returned from searching of the land after forty days.

26 **And they** went and came to Moses, and to Aaron, and to all the congregation of the children of Israel, unto the wilderness of Paran, to Kadesh;
and brought back word unto them, and unto all the congregation,

and shewed them the fruit of the land.

27 **And they** told him,
and said,
We came unto the land whither thou sentest us,
and surely it floweth with milk and honey;
and this is the fruit of it.

28 **Nevertheless the people** be strong that dwell in the land,
and the cities are walled, and very great:
and moreover we saw the children of Anak there.

29 **The Amalekites** dwell in the land of the south:
and the Hittites, and the Jebusites, and the Amorites, dwell in the mountains:
and the Canaanites dwell by the sea, and by the coast of Jordan.

30 **And Caleb** stilled the people before Moses,
and said,
Let us go up at once,
and possess it;
for we are well able to overcome it.

31 **But the men that went up with him** said,
We be not able to go up against the people;
for they are stronger than we.

32 **And they** brought up an evil report of the land which they had searched unto the children of Israel,
saying,
The land, {through which we have gone to search it}, is a land that eateth up the inhabitants thereof;
and all the people that we saw in it are men of a great stature.

33 **And there** we saw the giants, the sons of Anak,
which come of the giants:
and we were in our own sight as grasshoppers,
and so we were in their sight.

14

And all the congregation lifted up their voice,
and cried;
and the people wept that night.

2 **And all the children of Israel** murmured against Moses and against Aaron:
and the whole congregation said unto them,
Would God that we had died in the land of Egypt!
or would God we had died in this wilderness!

3 **And wherefore** hath the LORD brought us unto this land,
to fall by the sword,
that our wives and our children should be a prey?
were it not better for us to return into Egypt?

4 **And they** said one to another,
Let us make a captain,
and let us return into Egypt.

5 **Then Moses and Aaron** fell on their faces before all the assembly of the congregation of the children of Israel.

6 **And Joshua the son of Nun, and Caleb the son of Jephunneh,** {which were of them that searched the land}, rent their clothes:

7 **And they** spake unto all the company of the children of Israel,
saying,
The land, {which we passed through to search it}, is an exceeding good land.

8 **If the LORD** delight in us,
then he will bring us into this land,
and give it us; a land which floweth with milk and honey.

9 **Only rebel not ye** against the LORD,
neither fear ye the people of the land;
for they are bread for us:
their defence is departed from them,
and the LORD is with us:
fear them not.

10 **But all the congregation** bade stone them with stones.

And the glory of the LORD appeared in the tabernacle of the congregation before all the children of Israel.

11 **And the LORD** said unto Moses,
How long will this people provoke me?
and how long will it be ere they believe me, for all the signs which I have shewed among them?

12 **I** will smite them with the pestilence,
and disinherit them,
and will make of thee a greater nation and mightier than they.

13 **And Moses** said unto the LORD,
Then the Egyptians shall hear it,
(for thou broughtest up this people in thy might from among them;)

14 **And they** will tell it to the inhabitants of this land:
for they have heard that thou LORD art among this people, that thou LORD art seen face to face, and that thy cloud standeth over them, and that thou goest before them, by day time in a pillar of a cloud, and in a pillar of fire by night.

15 **Now if thou** shalt kill all this people as one man,
then the nations which have heard the fame of thee will speak,
saying,

16 **Because the LORD** was not able to bring this people into the land which he sware unto them,
therefore he hath slain them in the wilderness.

17 **And now, {I beseech thee}, let the power of my Lord** be great,
according as thou hast spoken,
saying,

18 **The LORD** is longsuffering, and of great mercy,
forgiving iniquity and transgression,
and by no means clearing the guilty,
visiting the iniquity of the fathers upon the children unto the third and fourth generation.

19 **Pardon**, {I beseech thee}, the iniquity of this people according unto the greatness of thy mercy,
and as thou hast forgiven this people, from Egypt even until now.

20 **And the LORD** said,
I have pardoned according to thy word:

21 **But as truly as I** live,
all the earth shall be filled with the glory of the LORD.

22 **Because all those men which have seen my glory, and my miracles,** {which I did in Egypt and in the wilderness}, and have tempted me now these ten times,
and have not hearkened to my voice;

23 **Surely they** shall not see the land which I sware unto their fathers,

neither shall any of them that provoked me see it:
24 **But my servant Caleb,** {because he had another spirit with him}, {and hath followed me fully}, him will I bring into the land whereinto he went;
and his seed shall possess it.
25 (**Now the Amalekites and the Canaanites** dwelt in the valley.)
Tomorrow turn you,
and get you into the wilderness by the way of the Red sea.
26 **And the LORD** spake unto Moses and unto Aaron,
saying,
27 **How long** shall I bear with this evil congregation,
which murmur against me?
I have heard the murmurings of the children of Israel,
which they murmur against me.
28 **Say** unto them,
As truly as I live,
saith the LORD,
as ye have spoken in mine ears,
so will I do to you:
29 **Your carcases** shall fall in this wilderness; and all that were numbered of you, according to your whole number, from twenty years old and upward which have murmured against me.
30 **Doubtless ye** shall not come into the land,
concerning which I sware to make you dwell therein, save Caleb the son of Jephunneh, and Joshua the son of Nun.
31 **But your little ones,** {which ye said should be a prey}, them will I bring in,
and they shall know the land which ye have despised.
32 **But as for you,** your carcases, they shall fall in this wilderness.
33 **And your children** shall wander in the wilderness forty years,
and bear your whoredoms,
until your carcases be wasted in the wilderness.
34 **After the number of the days in which ye searched the land, even forty days, each day for a year,** shall ye bear your iniquities, even forty years,
and ye shall know my breach of promise.
35 **I the LORD** have said,
I will surely do it unto all this evil congregation,
that are gathered together against me:
in this wilderness they shall be consumed,
and there they shall die.
36 **And the men,** {which Moses sent to search the land}, {who returned}, {and made all the congregation to murmur against him}, {by bringing up a slander upon the land},
37 Even those men that did bring up the evil report upon the land, died by the plague before the LORD.
38 **But Joshua the son of Nun, and Caleb the son of Jephunneh,** {which were of the men that went to search the land}, lived still.
39 **And Moses** told these sayings unto all the children of Israel:
and the people mourned greatly.
40 **And they** rose up early in the morning,
and gat them up into the top of the mountain,
saying,
Lo,
we be here,
and will go up unto the place which the LORD hath promised:
for we have sinned.
41 **And Moses** said,
Wherefore now do ye transgress the commandment of the LORD?
but it shall not prosper.
42 **Go not up,**
for the LORD is not among you;
that ye be not smitten before your enemies.
43 **For the Amalekites and the Canaanites** are there before you,
and ye shall fall by the sword:
because ye are turned away from the LORD,
therefore the LORD will not be with you.
44 **But they** presumed to go up unto the hill top:
nevertheless the ark of the covenant of the LORD, and Moses, departed not out of the camp.
45 **Then the Amalekites** came down, and the Canaanites which dwelt in that hill,
and smote them,
and discomfited them, even unto Hormah.

15 **And the LORD** spake unto Moses,
saying,
2 **Speak** unto the children of Israel,
and say unto them,
When ye be come into the land of your habitations,
which I give unto you,
3 **And** will make an offering by fire unto the LORD, a burnt offering,
or a sacrifice in performing a vow, or in a freewill offering, or in your solemn feasts,
to make a sweet savour unto the LORD, of the herd or of the flock:
4 **Then** shall he that offereth his offering unto the LORD bring a meat offering of a tenth deal of flour mingled with the fourth part of an hin of oil.
5 **And the fourth part of an hin of wine for a drink offering** shalt thou prepare with the burnt offering or sacrifice, for one lamb.
6 **Or for a ram,** thou shalt prepare for a meat offering two tenth deals of flour mingled with the third part of an hin of oil.
7 **And for a drink offering** thou shalt offer the third part of an hin of wine, for a sweet savour unto the LORD.
8 **And when thou** preparest a bullock for a burnt offering,
or for a sacrifice in performing a vow, or peace offerings unto the LORD:
9 **Then** shall he bring with a bullock a meat offering of three tenth deals of flour mingled with half an hin of oil.
10 **And thou** shalt bring for a drink offering half an hin of wine, for an offering made by fire, of a sweet savour unto the LORD.
11 **Thus** shall it be done for one bullock, or for one ram, or for a lamb, or a kid.
12 **According to the number that ye shall prepare,** so shall ye do to every one according to their number.
13 **All that are born of the country** shall do these things after this manner,
in offering an offering made by fire, of a sweet savour unto the LORD.
14 **And if a stranger** sojourn with you,

or whosoever be among you in your generations,
and will offer an offering made by fire, of a sweet savour unto the LORD;
as ye do,
so he shall do.

15 **One ordinance** shall be both for you of the congregation, and also for the stranger that sojourneth with you, an ordinance for ever in your generations:
as ye are,
so shall the stranger be before the LORD.

16 **One law and one manner** shall be for you, and for the stranger that sojourneth with you.

17 **And the LORD** spake unto Moses, saying,
18 **Speak** unto the children of Israel,
and say unto them,
When ye come into the land whither I bring you,
19 **Then it** shall be,
that, {when ye eat of the bread of the land}, ye shall offer up an heave offering unto the LORD.

20 **Ye** shall offer up a cake of the first of your dough for an heave offering:
as ye do the heave offering of the threshingfloor,
so shall ye heave it.

21 **Of the first of your dough** ye shall give unto the LORD an heave offering in your generations.

22 **And if ye** have erred,
and not observed all these commandments,
which the LORD hath spoken unto Moses,
23 Even all that the LORD hath commanded you by the hand of Moses, from the day that the LORD commanded Moses, and henceforward among your generations;
24 **Then it** shall be,
if ought be committed by ignorance without the knowledge of the congregation,
that all the congregation shall offer one young bullock for a burnt offering, for a sweet savour unto the LORD, with his meat offering, and his drink offering, according to the manner, and one kid of the goats for a sin offering.

25 **And the priest** shall make an atonement for all the congregation of the children of Israel,
and it shall be forgiven them;
for it is ignorance:
and they shall bring their offering, a sacrifice made by fire unto the LORD, and their sin offering before the LORD, for their ignorance:
26 **And it** shall be forgiven all the congregation of the children of Israel, and the stranger that sojourneth among them;
seeing all the people were in ignorance.

27 **And if any soul** sin through ignorance,
then he shall bring a she goat of the first year for a sin offering.

28 **And the priest** shall make an atonement for the soul that sinneth ignorantly,
when he sinneth by ignorance before the LORD,
to make an atonement for him;
and it shall be forgiven him.

29 **Ye** shall have one law for him that sinneth through ignorance, both for him that is born among the children of Israel, and for the stranger that sojourneth among them.

30 **But the soul that doeth ought presumptuously**, {whether he be born in the land, or a stranger}, the same reproacheth the LORD;
and that soul shall be cut off from among his people.

31 **Because he** hath despised the word of the LORD,
and hath broken his commandment,
that soul shall utterly be cut off;
his iniquity shall be upon him.

32 **And while the children of Israel** were in the wilderness,
they found a man that gathered sticks upon the sabbath day.

33 **And they that found him gathering sticks** brought him unto Moses and Aaron, and unto all the congregation.

34 **And they** put him in ward,
because it was not declared what should be done to him.

35 **And the LORD** said unto Moses,
The man shall be surely put to death:
all the congregation shall stone him with stones without the camp.

36 **And all the congregation** brought him without the camp,
and stoned him with stones,
and he died;
as the LORD commanded Moses.

37 **And the LORD** spake unto Moses, saying,
38 **Speak** unto the children of Israel,
and bid them
that they make them fringes in the borders of their garments throughout their generations,
and that they put upon the fringe of the borders a ribband of blue:
39 **And it** shall be unto you for a fringe,
that ye may look upon it,
and remember all the commandments of the LORD,
and do them;
and that ye seek not after your own heart and your own eyes,
after which ye use to go a whoring:
40 **That ye** may remember,
and do all my commandments,
and be holy unto your God.

41 **I** am the LORD your God,
which brought you out of the land of Egypt,
to be your God:
I am the LORD your God.

16 **Now Korah, the son of Izhar, the son of Kohath, the son of Levi, and Dathan and Abiram, the sons of Eliab, and On, the son of Peleth, sons of Reuben,** took men:
2 **And they** rose up before Moses, with certain of the children of Israel, two hundred and fifty princes of the assembly, famous in the congregation, men of renown:
3 **And they** gathered themselves together against Moses and against Aaron,
and said unto them,
Ye take too much upon you,
seeing all the congregation are holy, every one of them,
and the LORD is among them:
wherefore then lift ye up yourselves above the congregation of the LORD?
4 **And when Moses** heard it,
he fell upon his face:

5 **And he** spake unto Korah and unto all his company,
saying,
Even to morrow the LORD will shew
who are his,
and who is holy;
and will cause him to come near unto him:
even him whom he hath chosen will he cause to come near unto him.

6 **This do;**
Take you censers, Korah, and all his company;
7 **And put** fire therein,
and put incense in them before the LORD to morrow:
and it shall be that the man whom the LORD doth choose,
he shall be holy:
ye take too much upon you, ye sons of Levi.

8 **And Moses** said unto Korah,
Hear, {I pray you}, ye sons of Levi:
9 **Seemeth it but a small thing unto you,** that the God of Israel hath separated you from the congregation of Israel,
to bring you near to himself
to do the service of the tabernacle of the LORD,
and to stand before the congregation
to minister unto them?

10 **And he** hath brought thee near to him, and all thy brethren the sons of Levi with thee:
and seek ye the priesthood also?

11 **For which cause** both thou and all thy company are gathered together against the LORD:
and what is Aaron,
that ye murmur against him?

12 **And Moses** sent to call Dathan and Abiram, the sons of Eliab:
which said,
We will not come up:
13 **Is it a small thing** that thou hast brought us up out of a land that floweth with milk and honey,
to kill us in the wilderness,
except thou make thyself altogether a prince over us?

14 **Moreover thou** hast not brought us into a land that floweth with milk and honey,
or given us inheritance of fields and vineyards:
wilt thou put out the eyes of these men?
we will not come up.

15 **And Moses** was very wroth,
and said unto the LORD,
Respect not thou their offering:
I have not taken one ass from them,
neither have I hurt one of them.

16 **And Moses** said unto Korah,
Be thou and all thy company before the LORD, thou, and they, and Aaron, to morrow:
17 **And take** every man his censer,
and put incense in them,
and bring ye before the LORD every man his censer, two hundred and fifty censers; thou also, and Aaron, each of you his censer.

18 **And they** took every man his censer,
and put fire in them,
and laid incense thereon,
and stood in the door of the tabernacle of the congregation with Moses and Aaron.

19 **And Korah** gathered all the congregation against them unto the door of the tabernacle of the congregation:
and the glory of the LORD appeared unto all the congregation.

20 **And the LORD** spake unto Moses and unto Aaron,
saying,
21 **Separate** yourselves from among this congregation,
that I may consume them in a moment.

22 **And they** fell upon their faces,
and said,
O God, the God of the spirits of all flesh, shall one man sin,
and wilt thou be wroth with all the congregation?

23 **And the LORD** spake unto Moses,
saying,
24 **Speak** unto the congregation,
saying,
Get you up from about the tabernacle of Korah, Dathan, and Abiram.

25 **And Moses** rose up and went unto Dathan and Abiram;
and the elders of Israel followed him.

26 **And he** spake unto the congregation,
saying,
Depart, {I pray you}, from the tents of these wicked men,
and touch nothing of their's,
lest ye be consumed in all their sins.

27 **So they** gat up from the tabernacle of Korah, Dathan, and Abiram, on every side:
and Dathan and Abiram came out,
and stood in the door of their tents, and their wives, and their sons, and their little children.

28 **And Moses** said,
Hereby ye shall know
that the LORD hath sent me to do all these works;
for I have not done them of mine own mind.

29 **If these men** die the common death of all men,
or if they be visited after the visitation of all men;
then the LORD hath not sent me.

30 **But if the LORD** make a new thing,
and the earth open her mouth,
and swallow them up, with all that appertain unto them,
and they go down quick into the pit;
then ye shall understand
that these men have provoked the LORD.

31 **And it** came to pass,
as he had made an end of speaking all these words,
that the ground clave asunder that was under them:
32 **And the earth** opened her mouth,
and swallowed them up, and their houses, and all the men that appertained unto Korah, and all their goods.

33 **They, and all that appertained to them,** went down alive into the pit,
and the earth closed upon them:
and they perished from among the congregation.

34 **And all Israel that were round about them** fled at the cry of them:
for they said,
Lest the earth swallow us up also.

35 **And there** came out a fire from the LORD,
and consumed the two hundred and fifty men that offered incense.

36 **And the LORD** spake unto Moses,
saying,

37 **Speak** unto Eleazar the son of Aaron the priest,
that he take up the censers out of the burning,
and scatter thou the fire yonder;
for they are hallowed.

38 **The censers of these sinners against their own souls,** let them make them broad plates for a covering of the altar:
for they offered them before the LORD,
therefore they are hallowed:
and they shall be a sign unto the children of Israel.

39 **And Eleazar the priest** took the brasen censers,
wherewith they that were burnt had offered;
and they were made broad plates for a covering of the altar:
40 To be a memorial unto the children of Israel,
that no stranger, {which is not of the seed of Aaron}, come near to offer incense before the LORD;
that he be not as Korah, and as his company:
as the LORD said to him by the hand of Moses.

41 **But on the morrow** all the congregation of the children of Israel murmured against Moses and against Aaron,
saying,
Ye have killed the people of the LORD.

42 **And it** came to pass,
when the congregation was gathered against Moses and against Aaron,
that they looked toward the tabernacle of the congregation:
and, {behold}, the cloud covered it,
and the glory of the LORD appeared.

43 **And Moses and Aaron** came before the tabernacle of the congregation.

44 **And the LORD** spake unto Moses,
saying,
45 **Get you up** from among this congregation,
that I may consume them as in a moment.
And they fell upon their faces.

46 **And Moses** said unto Aaron,
Take a censer,
and put fire therein from off the altar,
and put on incense,
and go quickly unto the congregation,
and make an atonement for them:
for there is wrath gone out from the LORD;
the plague is begun.

47 **And Aaron** took as Moses commanded,
and ran into the midst of the congregation;
and, {behold}, the plague was begun among the people:
and he put on incense,
and made an atonement for the people.

48 **And he** stood between the dead and the living;
and the plague was stayed.

49 **Now they that died in the plague** were fourteen thousand and seven hundred, beside them that died about the matter of Korah.

50 **And Aaron** returned unto Moses unto the door of the tabernacle of the congregation:
and the plague was stayed.

17

And the LORD spake unto Moses,
saying,
2 **Speak** unto the children of Israel,
and take of every one of them a rod according to the house of their fathers, of all their princes according to the house of their fathers twelve rods:
write thou every man's name upon his rod.

3 **And thou** shalt write Aaron's name upon the rod of Levi:
for one rod shall be for the head of the house of their fathers.

4 **And thou** shalt lay them up in the tabernacle of the congregation before the testimony,
where I will meet with you.

5 **And it** shall come to pass,
that the man's rod, {whom I shall choose}, shall blossom:
and I will make to cease from me the murmurings of the children of Israel,
whereby they murmur against you.

6 **And Moses** spake unto the children of Israel,
and every one of their princes gave him a rod apiece, for each prince one, according to their fathers' houses, even twelve rods:
and the rod of Aaron was among their rods.

7 **And Moses** laid up the rods before the LORD in the tabernacle of witness.

8 **And it** came to pass,
that on the morrow Moses went into the tabernacle of witness;
and, {behold}, the rod of Aaron for the house of Levi was budded,
and brought forth buds,
and bloomed blossoms,
and yielded almonds.

9 **And Moses** brought out all the rods from before the LORD unto all the children of Israel:
and they looked,
and took every man his rod.

10 **And the LORD** said unto Moses,
Bring Aaron's rod again before the testimony,
to be kept for a token against the rebels;
and thou shalt quite take away their murmurings from me,
that they die not.

11 **And Moses** did so:
as the LORD commanded him,
so did he.

12 **And the children of Israel** spake unto Moses,
saying,
Behold,
we die,
we perish,
we all perish.

13 **Whosoever cometh any thing near unto the tabernacle of the LORD** shall die:
shall we be consumed with dying?

18

And the LORD said unto Aaron,
Thou and thy sons and thy father's house with thee shall bear the iniquity of the sanctuary:
and thou and thy sons with thee shall bear the iniquity of your priesthood.

2 **And thy brethren also of the tribe of Levi, the tribe of thy father,** bring thou with thee,
that they may be joined unto thee,
and minister unto thee:

but thou and thy sons with thee shall minister before the tabernacle of witness.

3 **And they** shall keep thy charge, and the charge of all the tabernacle:
only they shall not come nigh the vessels of the sanctuary and the altar,
that neither they, nor ye also, die.

4 **And they** shall be joined unto thee,
and keep the charge of the tabernacle of the congregation, for all the service of the tabernacle:
and a stranger shall not come nigh unto you.

5 **And ye** shall keep the charge of the sanctuary, and the charge of the altar:
that there be no wrath any more upon the children of Israel.

6 **And I, {behold}, I** have taken your brethren the Levites from among the children of Israel:
to you they are given as a gift for the LORD,
to do the service of the tabernacle of the congregation.

7 **Therefore thou and thy sons with thee** shall keep your priest's office for everything of the altar, and within the vail;
and ye shall serve:
I have given your priest's office unto you as a service of gift:
and the stranger that cometh nigh shall be put to death.

8 **And the LORD** spake unto Aaron,
Behold,
I also have given thee the charge of mine heave offerings of all the hallowed things of the children of Israel;
unto thee have I given them by reason of the anointing, and to thy sons, by an ordinance for ever.

9 **This** shall be thine of the most holy things,
reserved from the fire:
every oblation of their's, every meat offering of their's, and every sin offering of their's, and every trespass offering of their's which they shall render unto me, shall be most holy for thee and for thy sons.

10 **In the most holy place** shalt thou eat it;
every male shall eat it:
it shall be holy unto thee.

11 **And this** is thine; the heave offering of their gift, with all the wave offerings of the children of Israel:
I have given them unto thee, and to thy sons and to thy daughters with thee, by a statute for ever:
every one that is clean in thy house shall eat of it.

12 **All the best of the oil, and all the best of the wine, and of the wheat, the firstfruits of them which they shall offer unto the LORD,** them have I given thee.

13 **And whatsoever is first ripe in the land**, {which they shall bring unto the LORD}, shall be thine;
every one that is clean in thine house shall eat of it.

14 **Every thing devoted in Israel** shall be thine.

15 **Every thing that openeth the matrix in all flesh**, {which they bring unto the LORD}, {whether it be of men or beasts}, shall be thine:
nevertheless the firstborn of man shalt thou surely redeem,
and the firstling of unclean beasts shalt thou redeem.

16 **And those that are to be redeemed from a month old** shalt thou redeem, according to thine estimation, for the money of five shekels, after the shekel of the sanctuary,
which is twenty gerahs.

17 **But the firstling of a cow, or the firstling of a sheep, or the firstling of a goat,** thou shalt not redeem;
they are holy:
thou shalt sprinkle their blood upon the altar,
and shalt burn their fat for an offering made by fire, for a sweet savour unto the LORD.

18 **And the flesh of them** shall be thine,
as the wave breast and as the right shoulder are thine.

19 **All the heave offerings of the holy things**, {which the children of Israel offer unto the LORD}, have I given thee, and thy sons and thy daughters with thee, by a statute for ever:
it is a covenant of salt for ever before the LORD unto thee and to thy seed with thee.

20 **And the LORD** spake unto Aaron,
Thou shalt have no inheritance in their land,
neither shalt thou have any part among them:
I am thy part and thine inheritance among the children of Israel.

21 **And, {behold}, I** have given the children of Levi all the tenth in Israel for an inheritance, for their service which they serve, even the service of the tabernacle of the congregation.

22 **Neither** must the children of Israel henceforth come nigh the tabernacle of the congregation,
lest they bear sin,
and die.

23 **But the Levites** shall do the service of the tabernacle of the congregation,
and they shall bear their iniquity:
it shall be a statute for ever throughout your generations,
that among the children of Israel they have no inheritance.

24 **But the tithes of the children of Israel**, {which they offer as an heave offering unto the LORD}, I have given to the Levites to inherit:
therefore I have said unto them,
Among the children of Israel they shall have no inheritance.

25 **And the LORD** spake unto Moses, saying,
26 **Thus** speak unto the Levites,
and say unto them,
When ye take of the children of Israel the tithes which I have given you from them for your inheritance,
then ye shall offer up an heave offering of it for the LORD, even a tenth part of the tithe.

27 **And this your heave offering** shall be reckoned unto you,
as though it were the corn of the threshingfloor, and as the fulness of the winepress.

28 **Thus ye** also shall offer an heave offering unto the LORD of all your tithes,
which ye receive of the children of Israel;

and ye shall give thereof the LORD's heave offering to Aaron the priest.

29 **Out of all your gifts** ye shall offer every heave offering of the LORD, of all the best thereof, even the hallowed part thereof out of it.

30 **Therefore thou** shalt say unto them,
When ye have heaved the best thereof from it,
then it shall be counted unto the Levites as the increase of the threshingfloor, and as the increase of the winepress.

31 **And ye** shall eat it in every place, ye and your households:
for it is your reward for your service in the tabernacle of the congregation.

32 **And ye** shall bear no sin by reason of it,
when ye have heaved from it the best of it:
neither shall ye pollute the holy things of the children of Israel,
lest ye die.

19 **And the LORD** spake unto Moses and unto Aaron, saying,
2 **This** is the ordinance of the law which the LORD hath commanded,
saying,
Speak unto the children of Israel,
that they bring thee a red heifer without spot,
wherein is no blemish,
and upon which never came yoke:
3 **And ye** shall give her unto Eleazar the priest,
that he may bring her forth without the camp,
and one shall slay her before his face:
4 **And Eleazar the priest** shall take of her blood with his finger,
and sprinkle of her blood directly before the tabernacle of the congregation seven times:
5 **And one** shall burn the heifer in his sight;
her skin, and her flesh, and her blood, with her dung, shall he burn:
6 **And the priest** shall take cedar wood, and hyssop, and scarlet,
and cast it into the midst of the burning of the heifer.

7 **Then the priest** shall wash his clothes,
and he shall bathe his flesh in water,
and afterward he shall come into the camp,
and the priest shall be unclean until the even.

8 **And he that burneth her** shall wash his clothes in water,
and bathe his flesh in water,
and shall be unclean until the even.

9 **And a man that is clean** shall gather up the ashes of the heifer,
and lay them up without the camp in a clean place,
and it shall be kept for the congregation of the children of Israel for a water of separation:
it is a purification for sin.

10 **And he that gathereth the ashes of the heifer** shall wash his clothes,
and be unclean until the even:
and it shall be unto the children of Israel, and unto the stranger that sojourneth among them, for a statute for ever.

11 **He that toucheth the dead body of any man** shall be unclean seven days.

12 **He** shall purify himself with it on the third day,
and on the seventh day he shall be clean:
but if he purify not himself the third day,
then the seventh day he shall not be clean.

13 **Whosoever toucheth the dead body of any man that is dead, {and purifieth not himself},** defileth the tabernacle of the LORD;
and that soul shall be cut off from Israel:
because the water of separation was not sprinkled upon him,
he shall be unclean;
his uncleanness is yet upon him.

14 **This** is the law,
when a man dieth in a tent:
all that come into the tent, and all that is in the tent, shall be unclean seven days.

15 **And every open vessel**, {which hath no covering bound upon it}, is unclean.

16 **And whosoever toucheth one that is slain with a sword in the open fields, or a dead body, or a bone of a man, or a grave,** shall be unclean seven days.

17 **And for an unclean person** they shall take of the ashes of the burnt heifer of purification for sin,
and running water shall be put thereto in a vessel:

18 **And a clean person** shall take hyssop,
and dip it in the water,
and sprinkle it upon the tent, and upon all the vessels, and upon the persons that were there, and upon him that touched a bone, or one slain, or one dead, or a grave:

19 **And the clean person** shall sprinkle upon the unclean on the third day, and on the seventh day:
and on the seventh day he shall purify himself,
and wash his clothes,
and bathe himself in water,
and shall be clean at even.

20 **But the man that shall be unclean, and shall not purify himself,** that soul shall be cut off from among the congregation,
because he hath defiled the sanctuary of the LORD:
the water of separation hath not been sprinkled upon him;
he is unclean.

21 **And it** shall be a perpetual statute unto them,
that he that sprinkleth the water of separation shall wash his clothes;
and he that toucheth the water of separation shall be unclean until even.

22 **And whatsoever the unclean person toucheth** shall be unclean;
and the soul that toucheth it shall be unclean until even.

20 **Then** came the children of Israel, even the whole congregation, into the desert of Zin in the first month:
and the people abode in Kadesh;
and Miriam died there,
and was buried there.

2 **And there** was no water for the congregation:
and they gathered themselves together against Moses and against Aaron.

3 **And the people** chode with Moses,
and spake,

saying,
Would God that we had died
when our brethren died before the LORD!
4 **And why** have ye brought up the congregation of the LORD into this wilderness,
that we and our cattle should die there?
5 **And wherefore** have ye made us to come up out of Egypt,
to bring us in unto this evil place?
it is no place of seed, or of figs, or of vines, or of pomegranates;
neither is there any water to drink.
6 **And Moses and Aaron** went from the presence of the assembly unto the door of the tabernacle of the congregation,
and they fell upon their faces:
and the glory of the LORD appeared unto them.
7 **And the LORD** spake unto Moses,
saying,
8 **Take** the rod,
and gather thou the assembly together, thou, and Aaron thy brother,
and speak ye unto the rock before their eyes;
and it shall give forth his water,
and thou shalt bring forth to them water out of the rock:
so thou shalt give the congregation and their beasts drink.
9 **And Moses** took the rod from before the LORD,
as he commanded him.
10 **And Moses and Aaron** gathered the congregation together before the rock,
and he said unto them,
Hear now, ye rebels;
must we fetch you water out of this rock?
11 **And Moses** lifted up his hand,
and with his rod he smote the rock twice:
and the water came out abundantly,
and the congregation drank, and their beasts also.
12 **And the LORD** spake unto Moses and Aaron,
Because ye believed me not,
to sanctify me in the eyes of the children of Israel,
therefore ye shall not bring this congregation into the land which I have given them.
13 **This** is the water of Meribah;
because the children of Israel strove with the LORD,
and he was sanctified in them.
14 **And Moses** sent messengers from Kadesh unto the king of Edom,
Thus saith thy brother Israel,
Thou knowest all the travail that hath befallen us:
15 **How** our fathers went down into Egypt,
and we have dwelt in Egypt a long time;
and the Egyptians vexed us, and our fathers:
16 **And when we** cried unto the LORD,
he heard our voice,
and sent an angel,
and hath brought us forth out of Egypt:
and, {behold}, we are in Kadesh, a city in the uttermost of thy border:
17 **Let us** pass, {I pray thee{, through thy country:
we will not pass through the fields, or through the vineyards,
neither will we drink of the water of the wells:
we will go by the king's high way,
we will not turn to the right hand nor to the left,
until we have passed thy borders.
18 **And Edom** said unto him,
Thou shalt not pass by me,
lest I come out against thee with the sword.
19 **And the children of Israel** said unto him,
We will go by the high way:
and if I and my cattle drink of thy water,
then I will pay for it:
I will only, {without doing anything else}, go through on my feet.
20 **And he** said,
Thou shalt not go through.
And Edom came out against him with much people, and with a strong hand.
21 **Thus Edom** refused to give Israel passage through his border:
wherefore Israel turned away from him.
22 **And the children of Israel, even the whole congregation,** journeyed from Kadesh,
and came unto mount Hor.
23 **And the LORD** spake unto Moses and Aaron in mount Hor, by the coast of the land of Edom,
saying,
24 **Aaron** shall be gathered unto his people:
for he shall not enter into the land which I have given unto the children of Israel,
because ye rebelled against my word at the water of Meribah.
25 **Take** Aaron and Eleazar his son,
and bring them up unto mount Hor:
26 **And strip** Aaron of his garments,
and put them upon Eleazar his son:
and Aaron shall be gathered unto his people,
and shall die there.
27 **And Moses** did as the LORD commanded:
and they went up into mount Hor in the sight of all the congregation.
28 **And Moses** stripped Aaron of his garments,
and put them upon Eleazar his son;
and Aaron died there in the top of the mount:
and Moses and Eleazar came down from the mount.
29 **And when all the congregation** saw that Aaron was dead,
they mourned for Aaron thirty days, even all the house of Israel.

21 ∞ **And when king Arad the Canaanite,** {which dwelt in the south}, heard tell that Israel came by the way of the spies;
then he fought against Israel,
and took some of them prisoners.
2 **And Israel** vowed a vow unto the LORD,
and said,
If thou wilt indeed deliver this people into my hand,
then I will utterly destroy their cities.
3 **And the LORD** hearkened to the voice of Israel,
and delivered up the Canaanites;
and they utterly destroyed them and their cities:
and he called the name of the place Hormah.
4 **And they** journeyed from mount Hor by the way of the Red sea,
to compass the land of Edom:

and the soul of the people was much discouraged because of the way.

5 **And the people** spake against God, and against Moses,
Wherefore have ye brought us up out of Egypt to die in the wilderness?
for there is no bread,
neither is there any water;
and our soul loatheth this light bread.

6 **And the LORD** sent fiery serpents among the people,
and they bit the people;
and much people of Israel died.

7 **Therefore the people** came to Moses,
and said,
We have sinned,
for we have spoken against the LORD, and against thee;
pray unto the LORD,
that he take away the serpents from us.

And Moses prayed for the people.

8 **And the LORD** said unto Moses,
Make thee a fiery serpent,
and set it upon a pole:
and it shall come to pass,
that every one that is bitten, {when he looketh upon it}, shall live.

9 **And Moses** made a serpent of brass,
and put it upon a pole,
and it came to pass,
that if a serpent had bitten any man,
when he beheld the serpent of brass,
he lived.

10 **And the children of Israel** set forward,
and pitched in Oboth.

11 **And they** journeyed from Oboth,
and pitched at Ijeabarim, in the wilderness which is before Moab, toward the sunrising.

12 **From thence** they removed,
and pitched in the valley of Zared.
13 **From thence** they removed,
and pitched on the other side of Arnon,
which is in the wilderness that cometh out of the coasts of the Amorites:
for Arnon is the border of Moab, between Moab and the Amorites.

14 **Wherefore it** is said in the book of the wars of the LORD,
What he did in the Red sea, and in the brooks of Arnon,
15 And at the stream of the brooks that goeth down to the dwelling of Ar, and lieth upon the border of Moab,
16 **And from thence** they went to Beer:
that is the well whereof the LORD spake unto Moses,
Gather the people together,
and I will give them water.

17 **Then Israel** sang this song,
Spring up, O well;
sing ye unto it:
18 **The princes** digged the well,
the nobles of the people digged it, by the direction of the lawgiver, with their staves.

And from the wilderness they went to Mattanah:
19 And from Mattanah to Nahaliel:
and from Nahaliel to Bamoth:
20 And from Bamoth in the valley, {that is in the country of Moab}, to the top of Pisgah, {which looketh toward Jeshimon}.

21 **And Israel** sent messengers unto Sihon king of the Amorites,
saying,
22 **Let me** pass through thy land:
we will not turn into the fields, or into the vineyards;
we will not drink of the waters of the well:
but we will go along by the king's high way,
until we be past thy borders.

23 **And Sihon** would not suffer Israel to pass through his border:
but Sihon gathered all his people together,
and went out against Israel into the wilderness:
and he came to Jahaz,
and fought against Israel.

24 **And Israel** smote him with the edge of the sword,
and possessed his land from Arnon unto Jabbok, even unto the children of Ammon:
for the border of the children of Ammon was strong.

25 **And Israel** took all these cities:
and Israel dwelt in all the cities of the Amorites, in Heshbon, and in all the villages thereof.

26 **For Heshbon** was the city of Sihon the king of the Amorites,
who had fought against the former king of Moab,
and taken all his land out of his hand, even unto Arnon.

27 **Wherefore they that speak in proverbs** say,
Come into Heshbon,
let the city of Sihon be built and prepared:
28 **For there** is a fire gone out of Heshbon, a flame from the city of Sihon:
it hath consumed Ar of Moab, and the lords of the high places of Arnon.

29 **Woe** to thee, Moab!
thou art undone, O people of Chemosh:
he hath given his sons that escaped, and his daughters, into captivity unto Sihon king of the Amorites.

30 **We** have shot at them;
Heshbon is perished even unto Dibon,
and we have laid them waste even unto Nophah,
which reacheth unto Medeba.

31 **Thus Israel** dwelt in the land of the Amorites.

32 **And Moses** sent to spy out Jaazer,
and they took the villages thereof,
and drove out the Amorites that were there.

33 **And they** turned and went up by the way of Bashan:
and Og the king of Bashan went out against them, he, and all his people, to the battle at edrei.

34 **And the LORD** said unto Moses,
Fear him not:
for I have delivered him into thy hand, and all his people, and his land;
and thou shalt do to him
as thou didst unto Sihon king of the Amorites,
which dwelt at Heshbon.

35 **So they** smote him, and his sons, and all his people,
until there was none left him alive:
and they possessed his land.

22 **And the children of Israel** set forward,
and pitched in the plains of Moab on this side Jordan by Jericho.

2 **And Balak the son of Zippor** saw all that Israel had done to the Amorites.

3 **And Moab** was sore afraid of the people,
because they were many:
and Moab was distressed because of the children of Israel.

4 **And Moab** said unto the elders of Midian,
Now shall this company lick up all that are round about us,
as the ox licketh up the grass of the field.

And Balak the son of Zippor was king of the Moabites at that time.

5 **He** sent messengers therefore unto Balaam the son of Beor to Pethor,
which is by the river of the land of the children of his people,
to call him,
saying,
Behold,
there is a people come out from Egypt:
behold,
they cover the face of the earth,
and they abide over against me:

6 **Come** now therefore,
I pray thee,
curse me this people;
for they are too mighty for me:
peradventure I shall prevail,
that we may smite them,
and that I may drive them out of the land:
for I wot
that he whom thou blessest is blessed,
and he whom thou cursest is cursed.

7 **And the elders of Moab and the elders of Midian** departed with the rewards of divination in their hand;
and they came unto Balaam,
and spake unto him the words of Balak.

8 **And he** said unto them,
Lodge here this night,
and I will bring you word again,
as the LORD shall speak unto me:
and the princes of Moab abode with Balaam.

9 **And God** came unto Balaam,
and said,
What men are these with thee?

10 **And Balaam** said unto God,
Balak the son of Zippor, king of Moab, hath sent unto me,
saying,

11 **Behold,**
there is a people come out of Egypt,
which covereth the face of the earth:
come now,
curse me them;
peradventure I shall be able to overcome them,
and drive them out.

12 **And God** said unto Balaam,
Thou shalt not go with them;
thou shalt not curse the people:
for they are blessed.

13 **And Balaam** rose up in the morning,
and said unto the princes of Balak,
Get you into your land:
for the LORD refuseth to give me leave to go with you.

14 **And the princes of Moab** rose up,
and they went unto Balak,
and said,
Balaam refuseth to come with us.

15 **And Balak** sent yet again princes, more, and more honourable than they.

16 **And they** came to Balaam,
and said to him,
Thus saith Balak the son of Zippor,
Let nothing, {I pray thee}, hinder thee from coming unto me:

17 **For I** will promote thee unto very great honour,
and I will do whatsoever thou sayest unto me:
come therefore,
I pray thee,
curse me this people.

18 **And Balaam** answered and said unto the servants of Balak,
If Balak would give me his house full of silver and gold,
I cannot go beyond the word of the LORD my God,
to do less or more.

19 **Now therefore, {I pray you}, tarry ye** also here this night,
that I may know
what the LORD will say unto me more.

20 **And God** came unto Balaam at night,
and said unto him,
If the men come to call thee,
rise up,
and go with them;
but yet the word which I shall say unto thee, that shalt thou do.

21 **And Balaam** rose up in the morning,
and saddled his ass,
and went with the princes of Moab.

22 **And God's anger** was kindled
because he went:
and the angel of the LORD stood in the way for an adversary against him.

Now he was riding upon his ass,
and his two servants were with him.

23 **And the ass** saw the angel of the LORD standing in the way, and his sword drawn in his hand:
and the ass turned aside out of the way,
and went into the field:
and Balaam smote the ass,
to turn her into the way.

24 **But the angel of the LORD** stood in a path of the vineyards,
a wall being on this side, and a wall on that side.

25 **And when the ass** saw the angel of the LORD,
she thrust herself unto the wall,
and crushed Balaam's foot against the wall:
and he smote her again.

26 **And the angel of the LORD** went further,
and stood in a narrow place,
where was no way to turn either to the right hand or to the left.

27 **And when the ass** saw the angel of the LORD,
she fell down under Balaam:
and Balaam's anger was kindled,
and he smote the ass with a staff.

28 **And the LORD** opened the mouth of the ass,
and she said unto Balaam,
What have I done unto thee,
that thou hast smitten me these three times?

29 **And Balaam** said unto the ass,
Because thou hast mocked me:
I would there were a sword in mine hand,
for now would I kill thee.

30 **And the ass** said unto Balaam,
Am not I thine ass,
upon which thou hast ridden
ever since I was thine unto this day?
was I ever wont to do so unto thee?
and he said,
Nay.

31 **Then the LORD** opened the eyes of Balaam,
and he saw the angel of the LORD standing in the way, and his sword drawn in his hand:
and he bowed down his head,
and fell flat on his face.

32 **And the angel of the LORD** said unto him,
Wherefore hast thou smitten thine ass these three times?
behold,
I went out to withstand thee,
because thy way is perverse before me:

33 **And the ass** saw me,
and turned from me these three times:
unless she had turned from me,
surely now also I had slain thee,
and saved her alive.

34 **And Balaam** said unto the angel of the LORD,
I have sinned;
for I knew not
that thou stoodest in the way against me:
now therefore, {if it displease thee}, I will get me back again.

35 **And the angel of the LORD** said unto Balaam,
Go with the men: but only the word that I shall speak unto thee,
that thou shalt speak.

So Balaam went with the princes of Balak.

36 **And when Balak** heard that Balaam was come,
he went out to meet him unto a city of Moab,
which is in the border of Arnon,
which is in the utmost coast.

37 **And Balak** said unto Balaam,
Did I not earnestly send unto thee to call thee?
wherefore camest thou not unto me?
am I not able indeed to promote thee to honour?

38 **And Balaam** said unto Balak,
Lo,
I am come unto thee:
have I now any power at all to say any thing?
the word that God putteth in my mouth, that shall I speak.

39 **And Balaam** went with Balak,
and they came unto Kirjathhuzoth.

40 **And Balak** offered oxen and sheep,
and sent to Balaam, and to the princes that were with him.

41 **And it** came to pass on the morrow,
that Balak took Balaam,
and brought him up into the high places of Baal,
that thence he might see the utmost part of the people.

23

And Balaam said unto Balak,
Build me here seven altars,
and prepare me here seven oxen and seven rams.

2 **And Balak** did as Balaam had spoken;
and Balak and Balaam offered on every altar a bullock and a ram.

3 **And Balaam** said unto Balak,
Stand by thy burnt offering,
and I will go:
peradventure the LORD will come to meet me:
and whatsoever he sheweth me
I will tell thee.

And he went to an high place.

4 **And God** met Balaam:
and he said unto him,
I have prepared seven altars,
and I have offered upon every altar a bullock and a ram.

5 **And the LORD** put a word in Balaam's mouth,
and said,
Return unto Balak,
and thus thou shalt speak.

6 **And he** returned unto him,
and, {lo}, he stood by his burnt sacrifice, he, and all the princes of Moab.

7 **And he** took up his parable,
and said,
Balak the king of Moab hath brought me from Aram, out of the mountains of the east,
saying,
Come,
curse me Jacob,
and come,
defy Israel.

8 **How** shall I curse,
whom God hath not cursed?
or how shall I defy,
whom the LORD hath not defied?

9 **For from the top of the rocks** I see him,
and from the hills I behold him:
lo,
the people shall dwell alone,
and shall not be reckoned among the nations.

10 **Who** can count the dust of Jacob,
and the number of the fourth part of Israel?

Let me die the death of the righteous,
and let my last end be like his!

11 **And Balak** said unto Balaam,
What hast thou done unto me?

I took thee to curse mine enemies,
and, {behold}, thou hast blessed them altogether.

12 **And he** answered and said,
Must I not take heed to speak that which the LORD hath put in my mouth?

13 **And Balak** said unto him,
Come, {I pray thee}, with me unto another place,
from whence thou mayest see them:
thou shalt see but the utmost part of them,
and shalt not see them all:
and curse me them from thence.

14 **And he** brought him into the field of Zophim, to the top of Pisgah,
and built seven altars,
and offered a bullock and a ram on every altar.

15 **And he** said unto Balak,
Stand here by thy burnt offering,
while I meet the LORD yonder.

16 **And the LORD** met Balaam,
and put a word in his mouth,
and said,
Go again unto Balak,
and say thus.

17 **And when he** came to him,
behold,
he stood by his burnt offering, and the princes of Moab with him.

And Balak said unto him,
What hath the LORD spoken?

18 **And he** took up his parable,
and said,
Rise up, Balak,
and hear;
hearken unto me, thou son of Zippor:

19 **God** is not a man, {that he should lie}; neither the son of man, {that he should repent}:
hath he said,
and shall he not do it?
or hath he spoken,
and shall he not make it good?

20 **Behold,**

I have received commandment to bless:
and he hath blessed;
and I cannot reverse it.

21 **He** hath not beheld iniquity in Jacob,
neither hath he seen perverseness in Israel:
the LORD his God is with him,
and the shout of a king is among them.

22 **God** brought them out of Egypt;
he hath as it were the strength of an unicorn.

23 **Surely there** is no enchantment against Jacob,
neither is there any divination against Israel:
according to this time it shall be said of Jacob and of Israel,
What hath God wrought!

24 **Behold,**
the people shall rise up as a great lion,
and lift up himself as a young lion:
he shall not lie down
until he eat of the prey,
and drink the blood of the slain.

25 **And Balak** said unto Balaam,
Neither curse them at all,
nor bless them at all.

26 **But Balaam** answered and said unto Balak,
Told not I thee,
saying,
All that the LORD speaketh, that I must do?

27 **And Balak** said unto Balaam,
Come,
I pray thee,
I will bring thee unto another place;
peradventure it will please God that thou mayest curse me them from thence.

28 **And Balak** brought Balaam unto the top of Peor,
that looketh toward Jeshimon.

29 **And Balaam** said unto Balak,
Build me here seven altars,
and prepare me here seven bullocks and seven rams.

30 **And Balak** did as Balaam had said,
and offered a bullock and a ram on every altar.

24 **And when Balaam** saw that it pleased the LORD to bless Israel,
he went not, as at other times, to seek for enchantments,
but he set his face toward the wilderness.

2 **And Balaam** lifted up his eyes,
and he saw Israel abiding in his tents according to their tribes;
and the spirit of God came upon him.

3 **And he** took up his parable,
and said,
Balaam the son of Beor hath said,
and the man whose eyes are open hath said:

4 **He** hath said,
which heard the words of God,
which saw the vision of the Almighty,
falling into a trance,
but having his eyes open:

5 **How goodly** are thy tents, O Jacob, and thy tabernacles, O Israel!

6 **As the valleys** are they spread forth, as gardens by the river's side, as the trees of lign aloes which the LORD hath planted, and as cedar trees beside the waters.

7 **He** shall pour the water out of his buckets,
and his seed shall be in many waters,
and his king shall be higher than Agag,
and his kingdom shall be exalted.

8 **God** brought him forth out of Egypt;
he hath as it were the strength of an unicorn:
he shall eat up the nations his enemies,
and shall break their bones,
and pierce them through with his arrows.

9 **He** couched,
he lay down as a lion, and as a great lion:
who shall stir him up?
Blessed is he that blesseth thee,
and cursed is he that curseth thee.

10 **And Balak's anger** was kindled against Balaam,
and he smote his hands together:
and Balak said unto Balaam,
I called thee to curse mine enemies,
and, {behold}, thou hast altogether blessed them these three times.

11 **Therefore now flee thou** to thy place:
I thought
to promote thee unto great honour;
but, lo, the LORD hath kept thee back from honour.

12 **And Balaam** said unto Balak,
Spake I not also to thy messengers which thou sentest unto me,
saying,

13 **If Balak** would give me his house full of silver and gold,
I cannot go beyond the commandment of the LORD,
to do either good or bad of mine own mind;
but what the LORD saith,
that will I speak?

14 **And now, {behold}, I** go unto my people:
come therefore,
and I will advertise thee
what this people shall do to thy people in the latter days.

15 **And he** took up his parable,
and said,
Balaam the son of Beor hath said,
and the man whose eyes are open hath said:

16 **He** hath said,
which heard the words of God,
and knew the knowledge of the most High,
which saw the vision of the Almighty,
falling into a trance,
but having his eyes open:

17 **I** shall see him, but not now:
I shall behold him, but not nigh:
there shall come a Star out of Jacob,
and a Sceptre shall rise out of Israel,
and shall smite the corners of Moab,
and destroy all the children of Sheth.

18 **And Edom** shall be a possession,
Seir also shall be a possession for his enemies;
and Israel shall do valiantly.

19 **Out of Jacob** shall come he that shall have dominion,
and shall destroy him that remaineth of the city.

20 **And when he** looked on Amalek,
he took up his parable,
and said,
Amalek was the first of the nations;
but his latter end shall be that he perish for ever.

21 **And he** looked on the Kenites,
and took up his parable,

and said,
Strong is thy dwellingplace,
and thou puttest thy nest in a rock.
22 **Nevertheless the Kenite** shall be wasted,
until Asshur shall carry thee away captive.
23 **And he** took up his parable,
and said,
Alas, who shall live
when God doeth this!
24 **And ships** shall come from the coast of Chittim,
and shall afflict Asshur,
and shall afflict Eber,
and he also shall perish for ever.
25 **And Balaam** rose up,
and went and returned to his place:
and Balak also went his way.

25 **And Israel** abode in Shittim,
and the people began to commit whoredom with the daughters of Moab.
2 **And they** called the people unto the sacrifices of their gods:
and the people did eat,
and bowed down to their gods.
3 **And Israel** joined himself unto Baalpeor:
and the anger of the LORD was kindled against Israel.
4 **And the LORD** said unto Moses,
Take all the heads of the people,
and hang them up before the LORD against the sun,
that the fierce anger of the LORD may be turned away from Israel.
5 **And Moses** said unto the judges of Israel,
Slay ye every one his men that were joined unto Baalpeor.
6 **And, {behold}, one of the children of Israel** came and brought unto his brethren a Midianitish woman in the sight of Moses, and in the sight of all the congregation of the children of Israel,
who were weeping before the door of the tabernacle of the congregation.
7 **And when Phinehas, the son of Eleazar, the son of Aaron the priest,** saw it,
he rose up from among the congregation,
and took a javelin in his hand;
8 **And he** went after the man of Israel into the tent,
and thrust both of them through, the man of Israel, and the woman through her belly.
So the plague was stayed from the children of Israel.
9 **And those that died in the plague** were twenty and four thousand.
10 **And the LORD** spake unto Moses,
saying,
11 **Phinehas, the son of Eleazar, the son of Aaron the priest,** hath turned my wrath away from the children of Israel,
while he was zealous for my sake among them,
that I consumed not the children of Israel in my jealousy.
12 **Wherefore say,**
Behold,
I give unto him my covenant of peace:
13 **And he** shall have it, and his seed after him, even the covenant of an everlasting priesthood;
because he was zealous for his God,
and made an atonement for the children of Israel.
14 **Now the name of the Israelite that was slain, even that was slain with the Midianitish woman,** was Zimri, the son of Salu, a prince of a chief house among the Simeonites.
15 **And the name of the Midianitish woman that was slain** was Cozbi, the daughter of Zur;
he was head over a people, and of a chief house in Midian.
16 **And the LORD** spake unto Moses,
saying,
17 **Vex** the Midianites,
and smite them:
18 **For they** vex you with their wiles,
wherewith they have beguiled you in the matter of Peor, and in the matter of Cozbi, the daughter of a prince of Midian, their sister,
which was slain in the day of the plague for Peor's sake.

26 ⤳ **And it** came to pass after the plague,
that the LORD spake unto Moses and unto Eleazar the son of Aaron the priest,
saying,
2 **Take** the sum of all the congregation of the children of Israel, from twenty years old and upward, throughout their fathers' house, all that are able to go to war in Israel.
3 **And Moses and Eleazar the priest** spake with them in the plains of Moab by Jordan near Jericho,
saying,
4 **Take** the sum of the people, from twenty years old and upward;
as the LORD commanded Moses and the children of Israel,
which went forth out of the land of Egypt.
5 **Reuben,** the eldest son of Israel:
the children of Reuben; Hanoch, {of whom cometh the family of the Hanochites}: of Pallu, the family of the Palluites:
6 Of Hezron, the family of the Hezronites: of Carmi, the family of the Carmites.
7 **These** are the families of the Reubenites:
and they that were numbered of them were forty and three thousand and seven hundred and thirty.
8 **And the sons of Pallu;** Eliab.
9 **And the sons of Eliab;** Nemuel, and Dathan, and Abiram.
This is that Dathan and Abiram,
which were famous in the congregation,
who strove against Moses and against Aaron in the company of Korah,
when they strove against the LORD:
10 **And the earth** opened her mouth,
and swallowed them up together with Korah,
when that company died,
what time the fire devoured two hundred and fifty men:
and they became a sign.
11 **Notwithstanding the children of Korah** died not.
12 **The sons of Simeon after their families:** of Nemuel, the family of the Nemuelites: of Jamin, the family of the Jaminites: of Jachin, the family of the Jachinites:
13 Of Zerah, the family of the Zarhites: of Shaul, the family of the Shaulites.

[14] **These** are the families of the Simeonites, twenty and two thousand and two hundred.

[15] **The children of Gad after their families:** of Zephon, the family of the Zephonites: of Haggi, the family of the Haggites: of Shuni, the family of the Shunites:
[16] Of Ozni, the family of the Oznites: of Eri, the family of the Erites:
[17] Of Arod, the family of the Arodites: of Areli, the family of the Arelites.

[18] **These** are the families of the children of Gad according to those that were numbered of them, forty thousand and five hundred.

[19] **The sons of Judah** were Er and Onan:
and Er and Onan died in the land of Canaan.

[20] **And the sons of Judah after their families** were; of Shelah, the family of the Shelanites: of Pharez, the family of the Pharzites: of Zerah, the family of the Zarhites.

[21] **And the sons of Pharez** were; of Hezron, the family of the Hezronites: of Hamul, the family of the Hamulites.

[22] **These** are the families of Judah according to those that were numbered of them, threescore and sixteen thousand and five hundred.

[23] **Of the sons of Issachar after their families:** of Tola, the family of the Tolaites: of Pua, the family of the Punites:
[24] Of Jashub, the family of the Jashubites: of Shimron, the family of the Shimronites.

[25] **These** are the families of Issachar according to those that were numbered of them, threescore and four thousand and three hundred.

[26] **Of the sons of Zebulun after their families:** of Sered, the family of the Sardites: of Elon, the family of the Elonites: of Jahleel, the family of the Jahleelites.

[27] **These** are the families of the Zebulunites according to those that were numbered of them, threescore thousand and five hundred.

[28] **The sons of Joseph after their families** were Manasseh and Ephraim.

[29] **Of the sons of Manasseh:** of Machir, the family of the Machirites:
and Machir begat Gilead:
of Gilead come the family of the Gileadites.
[30] **These** are the sons of Gilead: of Jeezer, the family of the Jeezerites: of Helek, the family of the Helekites:
[31] And of Asriel, the family of the Asrielites: and of Shechem, the family of the Shechemites:
[32] And of Shemida, the family of the Shemidaites: and of Hepher, the family of the Hepherites.

[33] **And Zelophehad the son of Hepher** had no sons, but daughters:
and the names of the daughters of Zelophehad were Mahlah, and Noah, Hoglah, Milcah, and Tirzah.

[34] **These** are the families of Manasseh, and those that were numbered of them, fifty and two thousand and seven hundred.

[35] **These** are the sons of Ephraim after their families: of Shuthelah, the family of the Shuthalhites: of Becher, the family of the Bachrites: of Tahan, the family of the Tahanites.

[36] **And these** are the sons of Shuthelah: of Eran, the family of the Eranites.

[37] **These** are the families of the sons of Ephraim according to those that were numbered of them, thirty and two thousand and five hundred.
These are the sons of Joseph after their families.

[38] **The sons of Benjamin after their families:** of Bela, the family of the Belaites: of Ashbel, the family of the Ashbelites: of Ahiram, the family of the Ahiramites:
[39] Of Shupham, the family of the Shuphamites: of Hupham, the family of the Huphamites.

[40] **And the sons of Bela** were Ard and Naaman: of Ard, the family of the Ardites: and of Naaman, the family of the Naamites.

[41] **These** are the sons of Benjamin after their families:
and they that were numbered of them were forty and five thousand and six hundred.

[42] **These** are the sons of Dan after their families: of Shuham, the family of the Shuhamites.
These are the families of Dan after their families.

[43] **All the families of the Shuhamites, according to those that were numbered of them,** were threescore and four thousand and four hundred.

[44] **Of the children of Asher after their families:** of Jimna, the family of the Jimnites: of Jesui, the family of the Jesuites: of Beriah, the family of the Beriites.

[45] **Of the sons of Beriah:** of Heber, the family of the Heberites: of Malchiel, the family of the Malchielites.

[46] **And the name of the daughter of Asher** was Sarah.

[47] **These** are the families of the sons of Asher according to those that were numbered of them;
who were fifty and three thousand and four hundred.

[48] **Of the sons of Naphtali after their families:** of Jahzeel, the family of the Jahzeelites: of Guni, the family of the Gunites:
[49] Of Jezer, the family of the Jezerites: of Shillem, the family of the Shillemites.

[50] **These** are the families of Naphtali according to their families:
and they that were numbered of them were forty and five thousand and four hundred.

[51] **These** were the numbered of the children of Israel, six hundred thousand and a thousand seven hundred and thirty.

[52] **And the LORD** spake unto Moses, saying,
[53] **Unto these** the land shall be divided for an inheritance according to the number of names.

[54] **To many** thou shalt give the more inheritance,
and to few thou shalt give the less inheritance:
to every one shall his inheritance be given according to those that were numbered of him.

55 **Notwithstanding the land** shall be divided by lot:
according to the names of the tribes of their fathers they shall inherit.

56 **According to the lot** shall the possession thereof be divided between many and few.

57 **And these** are they that were numbered of the Levites after their families: of Gershon, the family of the Gershonites: of Kohath, the family of the Kohathites: of Merari, the family of the Merarites.

58 **These** are the families of the Levites: the family of the Libnites, the family of the Hebronites, the family of the Mahlites, the family of the Mushites, the family of the Korathites.
And Kohath begat Amram.

59 **And the name of Amram's wife** was Jochebed, the daughter of Levi,
whom her mother bare to Levi in Egypt:
and she bare unto Amram Aaron and Moses, and Miriam their sister.

60 **And unto Aaron** was born Nadab, and Abihu, Eleazar, and Ithamar.

61 **And Nadab and Abihu** died,
when they offered strange fire before the LORD.

62 **And those that were numbered of them** were twenty and three thousand, all males from a month old and upward:
for they were not numbered among the children of Israel,
because there was no inheritance given them among the children of Israel.

63 **These** are they that were numbered by Moses and Eleazar the priest,
who numbered the children of Israel in the plains of Moab by Jordan near Jericho.

64 **But among these** there was not a man of them whom Moses and Aaron the priest numbered,
when they numbered the children of Israel in the wilderness of Sinai.

65 **For the LORD** had said of them,
They shall surely die in the wilderness.
And there was not left a man of them, save Caleb the son of Jephunneh, and Joshua the son of Nun.

27

Then came the daughters of Zelophehad, the son of Hepher, the son of Gilead, the son of Machir, the son of Manasseh, of the families of Manasseh the son of Joseph:
and these are the names of his daughters; Mahlah, Noah, and Hoglah, and Milcah, and Tirzah.

2 **And they** stood before Moses, and before Eleazar the priest, and before the princes and all the congregation, by the door of the tabernacle of the congregation,
saying,
3 **Our father** died in the wilderness,
and he was not in the company of them that gathered themselves together against the LORD in the company of Korah;
but died in his own sin,
and had no sons.

4 **Why** should the name of our father be done away from among his family,
because he hath no son?
Give unto us therefore a possession among the brethren of our father.

5 **And Moses** brought their cause before the LORD.

6 **And the LORD** spake unto Moses,
saying,
7 **The daughters of Zelophehad** speak right:
thou shalt surely give them a possession of an inheritance among their father's brethren;
and thou shalt cause the inheritance of their father to pass unto them.

8 **And thou** shalt speak unto the children of Israel,
saying,
If a man die,
and have no son,
then ye shall cause his inheritance to pass unto his daughter.

9 **And if he** have no daughter,
then ye shall give his inheritance unto his brethren.

10 **And if he** have no brethren,
then ye shall give his inheritance unto his father's brethren.

11 **And if his father** have no brethren,
then ye shall give his inheritance unto his kinsman that is next to him of his family,
and he shall possess it:
and it shall be unto the children of Israel a statute of judgment,
as the LORD commanded Moses.

12 **And the LORD** said unto Moses,
Get thee up into this mount Abarim,
and see the land which I have given unto the children of Israel.

13 **And when thou** hast seen it,
thou also shalt be gathered unto thy people,
as Aaron thy brother was gathered.

14 **For ye** rebelled against my commandment in the desert of Zin, in the strife of the congregation,
to sanctify me at the water before their eyes: that is the water of Meribah in Kadesh in the wilderness of Zin.

15 **And Moses** spake unto the LORD,
saying,
16 **Let the LORD, the God of the spirits of all flesh,** set a man over the congregation,
17 **Which** may go out before them,
and which may go in before them,
and which may lead them out,
and which may bring them in;
that the congregation of the LORD be not as sheep which have no shepherd.

18 **And the LORD** said unto Moses,
Take thee Joshua the son of Nun, a man in whom is the spirit,
and lay thine hand upon him;
19 **And set** him before Eleazar the priest, and before all the congregation;
and give him a charge in their sight.

20 **And thou** shalt put some of thine honour upon him,
that all the congregation of the children of Israel may be obedient.

21 **And he** shall stand before Eleazar the priest,
who shall ask counsel for him after the judgment of Urim before the LORD:
at his word shall they go out,
and at his word they shall come in,
both he, and all the children of Israel with him, even all the congregation.

22 **And Moses** did as the LORD
commanded him:
and he took Joshua,
and set him before Eleazar the
priest, and before all the
congregation:
23 **And he** laid his hands upon him,
and gave him a charge,
as the LORD commanded by the
hand of Moses.

28

And the LORD spake
unto Moses,
saying,
2 **Command** the children of Israel,
and say unto them,
**My offering, and my bread for my
sacrifices made by fire, for a
sweet savour unto me,** shall ye
observe to offer unto me in their
due season.

3 **And thou** shalt say unto them,
This is the offering made by fire
which ye shall offer unto the
LORD; two lambs of the first year
without spot day by day, for a
continual burnt offering.

4 **The one lamb** shalt thou offer in
the morning,
and the other lamb shalt thou offer
at even;
5 And a tenth part of an ephah of
flour for a meat offering,
mingled with the fourth part of an
hin of beaten oil.

6 **It** is a continual burnt offering,
which was ordained in mount Sinai
for a sweet savour, a sacrifice
made by fire unto the LORD.

7 **And the drink offering thereof**
shall be the fourth part of an hin
for the one lamb:
in the holy place shalt thou cause
the strong wine to be poured unto
the LORD for a drink offering.

8 **And the other lamb** shalt thou
offer at even:
**as the meat offering of the
morning, and as the drink
offering thereof,** thou shalt offer
it, a sacrifice made by fire, of a
sweet savour unto the LORD.

9 **And on the sabbath day two
lambs of the first year without
spot, and two tenth deals of
flour for a meat offering,
{mingled with oil}, and the
drink offering thereof:**
10 This is the burnt offering of every
sabbath, beside the continual
burnt offering, and his drink
offering.

11 **And in the beginnings of your
months** ye shall offer a burnt
offering unto the LORD; two
young bullocks, and one ram,
seven lambs of the first year
without spot;
12 And three tenth deals of flour for a
meat offering, {mingled with oil},
for one bullock; and two tenth
deals of flour for a meat offering,
{mingled with oil}, for one ram;
13 And a several tenth deal of flour
mingled with oil for a meat
offering unto one lamb; for a
burnt offering of a sweet savour, a
sacrifice made by fire unto the
LORD.

14 **And their drink offerings** shall
be half an hin of wine unto a
bullock, and the third part of an
hin unto a ram, and a fourth part
of an hin unto a lamb:
this is the burnt offering of every
month throughout the months of
the year.

15 **And one kid of the goats for a sin
offering unto the LORD** shall be
offered, beside the continual
burnt offering, and his drink
offering.

16 **And in the fourteenth day of the
first month** is the passover of the
LORD.

17 **And in the fifteenth day of this
month** is the feast:
seven days shall unleavened bread
be eaten.

18 **In the first day** shall be an holy
convocation;
ye shall do no manner of servile
work therein:
19 **But ye** shall offer a sacrifice made
by fire for a burnt offering unto
the LORD; two young bullocks,
and one ram, and seven lambs of
the first year:
they shall be unto you without
blemish:
20 **And their meat offering** shall be
of flour mingled with oil:
three tenth deals shall ye offer for a
bullock, and two tenth deals for a
ram;
21 **A several tenth deal** shalt thou
offer for every lamb, throughout
the seven lambs:
22 And one goat for a sin offering,
to make an atonement for you.

23 **Ye** shall offer these beside the
burnt offering in the morning,
which is for a continual burnt
offering.

24 **After this manner** ye shall offer
daily, throughout the seven days,
the meat of the sacrifice made by
fire, of a sweet savour unto the
LORD:
it shall be offered beside the
continual burnt offering, and his
drink offering.

25 **And on the seventh day** ye shall
have an holy convocation;
ye shall do no servile work.

26 **Also in the day of the firstfruits,**
{when ye bring a new meat
offering unto the LORD}, {after
your weeks be out}, ye shall have
an holy convocation;
ye shall do no servile work:
27 **But ye** shall offer the burnt
offering for a sweet savour unto
the LORD; two young bullocks,
one ram, seven lambs of the first
year;
28 And their meat offering of flour
mingled with oil, three tenth
deals unto one bullock, two tenth
deals unto one ram,
29 A several tenth deal unto one
lamb, throughout the seven
lambs;
30 And one kid of the goats,
to make an atonement for you.

31 **Ye** shall offer them beside the
continual burnt offering, and his
meat offering, (they shall be unto
you without blemish) and their
drink offerings.

29

**And in the seventh
month, on the first day
of the month,** ye shall have an
holy convocation;
ye shall do no servile work:
it is a day of blowing the trumpets
unto you.

2 **And ye** shall offer a burnt offering
for a sweet savour unto the LORD;
one young bullock, one ram, and
seven lambs of the first year
without blemish:
3 **And their meat offering** shall be
of flour mingled with oil, three
tenth deals for a bullock, and two
tenth deals for a ram,
4 And one tenth deal for one lamb,
throughout the seven lambs:
5 And one kid of the goats for a sin
offering,

to make an atonement for you:
6 Beside the burnt offering of the month, and his meat offering, and the daily burnt offering, and his meat offering, and their drink offerings, according unto their manner, for a sweet savour, a sacrifice made by fire unto the LORD.

7 **And ye** shall have on the tenth day of this seventh month an holy convocation;
and ye shall afflict your souls:
ye shall not do any work therein:
8 **But ye** shall offer a burnt offering unto the LORD for a sweet savour; one young bullock, one ram, and seven lambs of the first year;
they shall be unto you without blemish:
9 **And their meat offering** shall be of flour mingled with oil, three tenth deals to a bullock, and two tenth deals to one ram,
10 A several tenth deal for one lamb, throughout the seven lambs:
11 One kid of the goats for a sin offering; beside the sin offering of atonement, and the continual burnt offering, and the meat offering of it, and their drink offerings.

12 **And on the fifteenth day of the seventh month** ye shall have an holy convocation;
ye shall do no servile work,
and ye shall keep a feast unto the LORD seven days:
13 **And ye** shall offer a burnt offering, a sacrifice made by fire, of a sweet savour unto the LORD; thirteen young bullocks, two rams, and fourteen lambs of the first year;
they shall be without blemish:
14 **And their meat offering** shall be of flour mingled with oil, three tenth deals unto every bullock of the thirteen bullocks, two tenth deals to each ram of the two rams,
15 And a several tenth deal to each lamb of the fourteen lambs:
16 And one kid of the goats for a sin offering; beside the continual burnt offering, his meat offering, and his drink offering.

17 **And on the second day** ye shall offer twelve young bullocks, two rams, fourteen lambs of the first year without spot:
18 **And their meat offering and their drink offerings for the bullocks, for the rams, and for the lambs,** shall be according to their number, after the manner:
19 And one kid of the goats for a sin offering; beside the continual burnt offering, and the meat offering thereof, and their drink offerings.

20 **And on the third day** eleven bullocks, two rams, fourteen lambs of the first year without blemish;
21 **And their meat offering and their drink offerings for the bullocks, for the rams, and for the lambs,** shall be according to their number, after the manner:
22 And one goat for a sin offering; beside the continual burnt offering, and his meat offering, and his drink offering.

23 **And on the fourth day** ten bullocks, two rams, and fourteen lambs of the first year without blemish:
24 **Their meat offering and their drink offerings for the bullocks, for the rams, and for the lambs,** shall be according to their number, after the manner:
25 And one kid of the goats for a sin offering; beside the continual burnt offering, his meat offering, and his drink offering.

26 **And on the fifth day** nine bullocks, two rams, and fourteen lambs of the first year without spot:
27 **And their meat offering and their drink offerings for the bullocks, for the rams, and for the lambs,** shall be according to their number, after the manner:
28 And one goat for a sin offering; beside the continual burnt offering, and his meat offering, and his drink offering.

29 **And on the sixth day** eight bullocks, two rams, and fourteen lambs of the first year without blemish:
30 **And their meat offering and their drink offerings for the bullocks, for the rams, and for the lambs,** shall be according to their number, after the manner:
31 And one goat for a sin offering; beside the continual burnt offering, his meat offering, and his drink offering.

32 **And on the seventh day** seven bullocks, two rams, and fourteen lambs of the first year without blemish:
33 **And their meat offering and their drink offerings for the bullocks, for the rams, and for the lambs,** shall be according to their number, after the manner:
34 And one goat for a sin offering; beside the continual burnt offering, his meat offering, and his drink offering.

35 **On the eighth day** ye shall have a solemn assembly:
ye shall do no servile work therein:
36 **But ye** shall offer a burnt offering, a sacrifice made by fire, of a sweet savour unto the LORD: one bullock, one ram, seven lambs of the first year without blemish:
37 **Their meat offering and their drink offerings for the bullock, for the ram, and for the lambs,** shall be according to their number, after the manner:
38 And one goat for a sin offering; beside the continual burnt offering, and his meat offering, and his drink offering.

39 **These things** ye shall do unto the LORD in your set feasts, beside your vows, and your freewill offerings, for your burnt offerings, and for your meat offerings, and for your drink offerings, and for your peace offerings.

40 **And Moses** told the children of Israel according to all that the LORD commanded Moses.

30 **And Moses** spake unto the heads of the tribes concerning the children of Israel, saying,
This is the thing which the LORD hath commanded.

2 **If a man** vow a vow unto the LORD,
or swear an oath to bind his soul with a bond;
he shall not break his word,
he shall do according to all that proceedeth out of his mouth.

3 **If a woman** also vow a vow unto the LORD,
and bind herself by a bond,
being in her father's house in her youth;

4 **And her father** hear her vow, and her bond wherewith she hath bound her soul,
and her father shall hold his peace at her;
then all her vows shall stand,
and every bond wherewith she hath bound her soul shall stand.
5 **But if her father** disallow her in the day that he heareth;
not any of her vows, or of her bonds wherewith she hath bound her soul, shall stand:
and the LORD shall forgive her,
because her father disallowed her.
6 **And if she** had at all an husband,
when she vowed,
or uttered ought out of her lips,
wherewith she bound her soul;
7 **And her husband** heard it,
and held his peace at her in the day that he heard it:
then her vows shall stand,
and her bonds wherewith she bound her soul shall stand.
8 **But if her husband** disallowed her on the day that he heard it;
then he shall make her vow which she vowed, and that which she uttered with her lips, wherewith she bound her soul, of none effect:
and the LORD shall forgive her.
9 **But every vow of a widow, and of her that is divorced,** {wherewith they have bound their souls}, shall stand against her.
10 **And if she** vowed in her husband's house,
or bound her soul by a bond with an oath;
11 **And her husband** heard it,
and held his peace at her,
and disallowed her not:
then all her vows shall stand,
and every bond wherewith she bound her soul shall stand.
12 **But if her husband** hath utterly made them void on the day he heard them;
then whatsoever proceeded out of her lips concerning her vows, or concerning the bond of her soul, shall not stand:
her husband hath made them void;
and the LORD shall forgive her.
13 **Every vow, and every binding oath to afflict the soul,** her husband may establish it,
or her husband may make it void.
14 **But if her husband** altogether hold his peace at her from day to day;
then he establisheth all her vows, or all her bonds,
which are upon her:
he confirmeth them,
because he held his peace at her in the day that he heard them.
15 **But if he** shall any ways make them void
after that he hath heard them;
then he shall bear her iniquity.
16 **These** are the statutes,
which the LORD commanded Moses, between a man and his wife, between the father and his daughter,
being yet in her youth in her father's house.

31

And the LORD spake unto Moses,
saying,
2 **Avenge** the children of Israel of the Midianites:
afterward shalt thou be gathered unto thy people.
3 **And Moses** spake unto the people,
saying,
Arm some of yourselves unto the war,
and let them go against the Midianites,
and avenge the LORD of Midian.
4 **Of every tribe a thousand, throughout all the tribes of Israel,** shall ye send to the war.
5 **So there** were delivered out of the thousands of Israel, a thousand of every tribe, twelve thousand armed for war.
6 **And Moses** sent them to the war, a thousand of every tribe, them and Phinehas the son of Eleazar the priest, to the war, with the holy instruments, and the trumpets to blow in his hand.
7 **And they** warred against the Midianites,
as the LORD commanded Moses;
and they slew all the males.
8 **And they** slew the kings of Midian, beside the rest of them that were slain; namely, Evi, and Rekem, and Zur, and Hur, and Reba, five kings of Midian:
Balaam also the son of Beor they slew with the sword.
9 **And the children of Israel** took all the women of Midian captives, and their little ones,
and took the spoil of all their cattle, and all their flocks, and all their goods.
10 **And they** burnt all their cities wherein they dwelt, and all their goodly castles, with fire.
11 **And they** took all the spoil, and all the prey, both of men and of beasts.
12 **And they** brought the captives, and the prey, and the spoil, unto Moses, and Eleazar the priest, and unto the congregation of the children of Israel, unto the camp at the plains of Moab,
which are by Jordan near Jericho.
13 **And Moses, and Eleazar the priest, and all the princes of the congregation,** went forth to meet them without the camp.
14 **And Moses** was wroth with the officers of the host, with the captains over thousands, and captains over hundreds,
which came from the battle.
15 **And Moses** said unto them,
Have ye saved all the women alive?
16 **Behold, these** caused the children of Israel, through the counsel of Balaam, to commit trespass against the LORD in the matter of Peor,
and there was a plague among the congregation of the LORD.
17 **Now therefore kill** every male among the little ones,
and kill every woman that hath known man by lying with him.
18 **But all the women children,** [that have not known a man by lying with him], keep alive for yourselves.
19 **And do ye** abide without the camp seven days:
whosoever hath killed any person, and whosoever hath touched any slain, purify both yourselves and your captives on the third day, and on the seventh day.
20 **And purify** all your raiment, and all that is made of skins, and all work of goats' hair, and all things made of wood.

21 **And Eleazar the priest** said unto the men of war which went to the battle,
This is the ordinance of the law which the LORD commanded Moses;
22 **Only the gold, and the silver, the brass, the iron, the tin, and the lead,**
23 **Every thing that may abide the fire,** ye shall make it go through the fire,
and it shall be clean:
nevertheless it shall be purified with the water of separation:
and all that abideth not the fire ye shall make go through the water.
24 **And ye** shall wash your clothes on the seventh day,
and ye shall be clean,
and afterward ye shall come into the camp.
25 **And the LORD** spake unto Moses,
saying,
26 **Take** the sum of the prey that was taken, both of man and of beast, thou, and Eleazar the priest, and the chief fathers of the congregation:
27 **And divide** the prey into two parts; between them that took the war upon them, {who went out to battle}, and between all the congregation:
28 **And levy** a tribute unto the LORD of the men of war which went out to battle: one soul of five hundred, both of the persons, and of the beeves, and of the asses, and of the sheep:
29 **Take** it of their half,
and give it unto Eleazar the priest, for an heave offering of the LORD.
30 **And of the children of Israel's half,** thou shalt take one portion of fifty, of the persons, of the beeves, of the asses, and of the flocks, of all manner of beasts,
and give them unto the Levites,
which keep the charge of the tabernacle of the LORD.
31 **And Moses and Eleazar the priest** did as the LORD commanded Moses.
32 **And the booty**, {being the rest of the prey which the men of war had caught}, was six hundred thousand and seventy thousand and five thousand sheep,
33 And threescore and twelve thousand beeves,
34 And threescore and one thousand asses,
35 And thirty and two thousand persons in all, of women that had not known man by lying with him.
36 **And the half**, {which was the portion of them that went out to war}, was in number three hundred thousand and seven and thirty thousand and five hundred sheep:
37 **And the LORD's tribute of the sheep** was six hundred and threescore and fifteen.
38 **And the beeves** were thirty and six thousand;
of which the LORD's tribute was threescore and twelve.
39 **And the asses** were thirty thousand and five hundred;
of which the LORD's tribute was threescore and one.
40 **And the persons** were sixteen thousand;
of which the LORD's tribute was thirty and two persons.
41 **And Moses** gave the tribute, {which was the LORD's heave offering}, unto Eleazar the priest,
as the LORD commanded Moses.
42 **And of the children of Israel's half**, {which Moses divided from the men that warred},
43 (Now the half that pertained unto the congregation was three hundred thousand and thirty thousand and seven thousand and five hundred sheep,
44 And thirty and six thousand beeves,
45 And thirty thousand asses and five hundred,
46 And sixteen thousand persons;)
47 **Even of the children of Israel's half, Moses** took one portion of fifty, both of man and of beast,
and gave them unto the Levites,
which kept the charge of the tabernacle of the LORD;
as the LORD commanded Moses.
48 **And the officers which were over thousands of the host, the captains of thousands, and captains of hundreds,** came near unto Moses:
49 **And they** said unto Moses,
Thy servants have taken the sum of the men of war which are under our charge,
and there lacketh not one man of us.
50 **We** have therefore brought an oblation for the LORD,
what every man hath gotten, of jewels of gold, chains, and bracelets, rings, earrings, and tablets,
to make an atonement for our souls before the LORD.
51 **And Moses and Eleazar the priest** took the gold of them, even all wrought jewels.
52 **And all the gold of the offering that they offered up to the LORD, of the captains of thousands, and of the captains of hundreds,** was sixteen thousand seven hundred and fifty shekels.
53 (**For the men of war** had taken spoil, every man for himself.)
54 **And Moses and Eleazar the priest** took the gold of the captains of thousands and of hundreds,
and brought it into the tabernacle of the congregation, for a memorial for the children of Israel before the LORD.

32 **Now the children of Reuben and the children of Gad** had a very great multitude of cattle:
and when they saw the land of Jazer, and the land of Gilead,
that, {behold}, the place was a place for cattle;
2 **The children of Gad and the children of Reuben** came and spake unto Moses, and to Eleazar the priest, and unto the princes of the congregation,
saying,
3 **Ataroth, and Dibon, and Jazer, and Nimrah, and Heshbon, and Elealeh, and Shebam, and Nebo, and Beon,**
4 **Even the country which the LORD smote before the congregation of Israel,** is a land for cattle,
and thy servants have cattle:
5 **Wherefore, {said they}, if we** have found grace in thy sight,
let this land be given unto thy servants for a possession,

and bring us not over Jordan.
6 **And Moses** said unto the children of Gad and to the children of Reuben,
Shall your brethren go to war,
and shall ye sit here?
7 **And wherefore** discourage ye the heart of the children of Israel from going over into the land which the LORD hath given them?
8 **Thus** did your fathers,
when I sent them from Kadeshbarnea to see the land.
9 **For when they** went up unto the valley of Eshcol,
and saw the land,
they discouraged the heart of the children of Israel,
that they should not go into the land which the LORD had given them.
10 **And the LORD's anger** was kindled the same time,
and he sware,
saying,
11 **Surely none of the men that came up out of Egypt, from twenty years old and upward,** shall see the land which I sware unto Abraham, unto Isaac, and unto Jacob;
because they have not wholly followed me:
12 Save Caleb the son of Jephunneh the Kenezite, and Joshua the son of Nun:
for they have wholly followed the LORD.
13 **And the LORD's anger** was kindled against Israel,
and he made them wander in the wilderness forty years,
until all the generation, {that had done evil in the sight of the LORD}, was consumed.
14 **And, {behold}, ye** are risen up in your fathers' stead, an increase of sinful men,
to augment yet the fierce anger of the LORD toward Israel.
15 **For if ye** turn away from after him,
he will yet again leave them in the wilderness;
and ye shall destroy all this people.
16 **And they** came near unto him,
and said,
We will build sheepfolds here for our cattle, and cities for our little ones:
17 **But we ourselves** will go ready armed before the children of Israel,
until we have brought them unto their place:
and our little ones shall dwell in the fenced cities because of the inhabitants of the land.
18 **We** will not return unto our houses,
until the children of Israel have inherited every man his inheritance.
19 **For we** will not inherit with them on yonder side Jordan, or forward;
because our inheritance is fallen to us on this side Jordan eastward.
20 **And Moses** said unto them,
If ye will do this thing,
if ye will go armed before the LORD to war,
21 **And** will go all of you armed over Jordan before the LORD,
until he hath driven out his enemies from before him,
22 **And the land** be subdued before the LORD:
then afterward ye shall return,
and be guiltless before the LORD, and before Israel;
and this land shall be your possession before the LORD.
23 **But if ye** will not do so,
behold,
ye have sinned against the LORD:
and be sure
your sin will find you out.
24 **Build** you cities for your little ones, and folds for your sheep;
and do that which hath proceeded out of your mouth.
25 **And the children of Gad and the children of Reuben** spake unto Moses,
saying,
Thy servants will do as my lord commandeth.
26 **Our little ones, our wives, our flocks, and all our cattle,** shall be there in the cities of Gilead:
27 **But thy servants** will pass over, every man armed for war, before the LORD to battle,
as my lord saith.
28 **So concerning them** Moses commanded Eleazar the priest, and Joshua the son of Nun, and the chief fathers of the tribes of the children of Israel:
29 **And Moses** said unto them,
If the children of Gad and the children of Reuben will pass with you over Jordan, every man armed to battle, before the LORD,
and the land shall be subdued before you;
then ye shall give them the land of Gilead for a possession:
30 **But if they** will not pass over with you armed,
they shall have possessions among you in the land of Canaan.
31 **And the children of Gad and the children of Reuben** answered,
saying,
As the LORD hath said unto thy servants,
so will we do.
32 **We** will pass over armed before the LORD into the land of Canaan,
that the possession of our inheritance on this side Jordan may be our's.
33 **And Moses** gave unto them, even to the children of Gad, and to the children of Reuben, and unto half the tribe of Manasseh the son of Joseph, the kingdom of Sihon king of the Amorites, and the kingdom of Og king of Bashan, the land, with the cities thereof in the coasts, even the cities of the country round about.
34 **And the children of Gad** built Dibon, and Ataroth, and Aroer,
35 And Atroth, Shophan, and Jaazer, and Jogbehah,
36 And Bethnimrah, and Bethharan, fenced cities: and folds for sheep.
37 **And the children of Reuben** built Heshbon, and Elealeh, and Kirjathaim,
38 And Nebo, and Baalmeon, (their names being changed,) and Shibmah:
and gave other names unto the cities which they builded.
39 **And the children of Machir the son of Manasseh** went to Gilead,
and took it,
and dispossessed the Amorite which was in it.
40 **And Moses** gave Gilead unto Machir the son of Manasseh;
and he dwelt therein.
41 **And Jair the son of Manasseh** went and took the small towns thereof,
and called them Havothjair.

42 **And Nobah** went and took Kenath, and the villages thereof,
and called it Nobah, after his own name.

33 ⚮ **These** are the journeys of the children of Israel,
which went forth out of the land of Egypt with their armies under the hand of Moses and Aaron.

2 **And Moses** wrote their goings out according to their journeys by the commandment of the LORD:
and these are their journeys according to their goings out.

3 **And they** departed from Rameses in the first month, on the fifteenth day of the first month;
on the morrow after the passover the children of Israel went out with an high hand in the sight of all the Egyptians.

4 **For the Egyptians** buried all their firstborn,
which the LORD had smitten among them:
upon their gods also the LORD executed judgments.

5 **And the children of Israel** removed from Rameses,
and pitched in Succoth.

6 **And they** departed from Succoth,
and pitched in Etham,
which is in the edge of the wilderness.

7 **And they** removed from Etham,
and turned again unto Pihahiroth,
which is before Baalzephon:
and they pitched before Migdol.

8 **And they** departed from before Pihahiroth,
and passed through the midst of the sea into the wilderness,
and went three days'journey in the wilderness of Etham,
and pitched in Marah.

9 **And they** removed from Marah,
and came unto Elim:
and in Elim were twelve fountains of water, and threescore and ten palm trees;
and they pitched there.

10 **And they** removed from Elim,
and encamped by the Red sea.

11 **And they** removed from the Red sea,
and encamped in the wilderness of Sin.

12 **And they** took their journey out of the wilderness of Sin,
and encamped in Dophkah.

13 **And they** departed from Dophkah,
and encamped in Alush.

14 **And they** removed from Alush,
and encamped at Rephidim,
where was no water for the people to drink.

15 **And they** departed from Rephidim,
and pitched in the wilderness of Sinai.

16 **And they** removed from the desert of Sinai,
and pitched at Kibrothhattaavah.

17 **And they** departed from Kibrothhattaavah,
and encamped at Hazeroth.

18 **And they** departed from Hazeroth,
and pitched in Rithmah.

19 **And they** departed from Rithmah,
and pitched at Rimmonparez.

20 **And they** departed from Rimmonparez,
and pitched in Libnah.

21 **And they** removed from Libnah,
and pitched at Rissah.

22 **And they** journeyed from Rissah,
and pitched in Kehelathah.

23 **And they** went from Kehelathah,
and pitched in mount Shapher.

24 **And they** removed from mount Shapher,
and encamped in Haradah.

25 **And they** removed from Haradah,
and pitched in Makheloth.

26 **And they** removed from Makheloth,
and encamped at Tahath.

27 **And they** departed from Tahath,
and pitched at Tarah.

28 **And they** removed from Tarah,
and pitched in Mithcah.

29 **And they** went from Mithcah,
and pitched in Hashmonah.

30 **And they** departed from Hashmonah,
and encamped at Moseroth.

31 **And they** departed from Moseroth,
and pitched in Benejaakan.

32 **And they** removed from Benejaakan,
and encamped at Horhagidgad.

33 **And they** went from Horhagidgad,
and pitched in Jotbathah.

34 **And they** removed from Jotbathah,
and encamped at Ebronah.

35 **And they** departed from Ebronah,
and encamped at Eziongaber.

36 **And they** removed from Eziongaber,
and pitched in the wilderness of Zin,
which is Kadesh.

37 **And they** removed from Kadesh,
and pitched in mount Hor, in the edge of the land of Edom.

38 **And Aaron the priest** went up into mount Hor at the commandment of the LORD,
and died there,
in the fortieth year after the children of Israel were come out of the land of Egypt, in the first day of the fifth month.

39 **And Aaron** was an hundred and twenty and three years old
when he died in mount Hor.

40 **And king Arad the Canaanite**, {<u>which</u> dwelt in the south in the land of Canaan}, heard of the coming of the children of Israel.

41 **And they** departed from mount Hor,
and pitched in Zalmonah.

42 **And they** departed from Zalmonah,
and pitched in Punon.

43 **And they** departed from Punon,
and pitched in Oboth.

44 **And they** departed from Oboth,
and pitched in Ijeabarim, in the border of Moab.

45 **And they** departed from Iim,
and pitched in Dibongad.

46 **And they** removed from Dibongad,
and encamped in Almondiblathaim.

47 **And they** removed from Almondiblathaim,
and pitched in the mountains of Abarim, before Nebo.

48 **And they** departed from the mountains of Abarim,
and pitched in the plains of Moab by Jordan near Jericho.

49 **And they** pitched by Jordan, from Bethjesimoth even unto Abelshittim in the plains of Moab.

50 **And the LORD** spake unto Moses
in the plains of Moab by Jordan
near Jericho,
saying,
51 **Speak** unto the children of Israel,
and say unto them,
When ye are passed over Jordan
into the land of Canaan;
52 **Then ye** shall drive out all the
inhabitants of the land from
before you,
and destroy all their pictures,
and destroy all their molten images,
and quite pluck down all their high
places:
53 **And ye** shall dispossess the
inhabitants of the land,
and dwell therein:
for I have given you the land to
possess it.
54 **And ye** shall divide the land by lot
for an inheritance among your
families:
and to the more ye shall give the
more inheritance,
and to the fewer ye shall give the
less inheritance:
every man's inheritance shall be
in the place where his lot falleth;
**according to the tribes of your
fathers** ye shall inherit.
55 **But if ye** will not drive out the
inhabitants of the land from
before you
then it shall come to pass,
**that those which ye let remain of
them** shall be pricks in your eyes,
and thorns in your sides,
and shall vex you in the land
wherein ye dwell.
56 **Moreover it** shall come to pass,
that I shall do unto you,
as I thought to do unto them.

34 **And the LORD** spake unto
Moses,
saying,
2 **Command** the children of Israel,
and say unto them,
When ye come into the land of
Canaan;
(this is the land that shall fall unto
you for an inheritance, even the
land of Canaan with the coasts
thereof:)
3 **Then your south quarter** shall be
from the wilderness of Zin along
by the coast of Edom,
and your south border shall be the
outmost coast of the salt sea
eastward:
4 **And your border** shall turn from
the south to the ascent of
Akrabbim,
and pass on to Zin:
and the going forth thereof shall
be from the south to
Kadeshbarnea,
and shall go on to Hazaraddar,
and pass on to Azmon:
5 **And the border** shall fetch a
compass from Azmon unto the
river of Egypt,
and the goings out of it shall be at
the sea.
6 **And as for the western border,** ye
shall even have the great sea for a
border:
this shall be your west border.
7 **And this** shall be your north
border:
from the great sea ye shall point
out for you mount Hor:
8 **From mount Hor** ye shall point
out your border unto the entrance
of Hamath;
and the goings forth of the border
shall be to Zedad:
9 **And the border** shall go on to
Ziphron,
and the goings out of it shall be at
Hazarenan:
this shall be your north border.
10 **And ye** shall point out your east
border from Hazarenan to
Shepham:
11 **And the coast** shall go down from
Shepham to Riblah, on the east
side of Ain;
and the border shall descend,
and shall reach unto the side of the
sea of Chinnereth eastward:
12 **And the border** shall go down to
Jordan,
and the goings out of it shall be at
the salt sea:
this shall be your land with the
coasts thereof round about.
13 **And Moses** commanded the
children of Israel,
saying,
This is the land which ye shall
inherit by lot,
which the LORD commanded to
give unto the nine tribes, and to
the half tribe:
14 **For the tribe of the children of
Reuben according to the house
of their fathers, and the tribe of
the children of Gad according to
the house of their fathers,** have
received their inheritance;
and half the tribe of Manasseh
have received their inheritance:
15 **The two tribes and the half tribe**
have received their inheritance on
this side Jordan near Jericho
eastward, toward the sunrising.
16 **And the LORD** spake unto Moses,
saying,
17 **These** are the names of the men
which shall divide the land unto
you: Eleazar the priest, and
Joshua the son of Nun.
18 **And ye** shall take one prince of
every tribe,
to divide the land by inheritance.
19 **And the names of the men** are
these:
Of the tribe of Judah, Caleb the
son of Jephunneh.
20 **And of the tribe of the children
of Simeon,** Shemuel the son of
Ammihud.
21 **Of the tribe of Benjamin,** Elidad
the son of Chislon.
22 **And the prince of the tribe of
the children of Dan,** Bukki the
son of Jogli.
23 **The prince of the children of
Joseph, for the tribe of the
children of Manasseh,** Hanniel
the son of Ephod.
24 **And the prince of the tribe of
the children of Ephraim,** Kemuel
the son of Shiphtan.
25 **And the prince of the tribe of
the children of Zebulun,**
Elizaphan the son of Parnach.
26 **And the prince of the tribe of
the children of Issachar,** Paltiel
the son of Azzan.
27 **And the prince of the tribe of
the children of Asher,** Ahihud
the son of Shelomi.
28 **And the prince of the tribe of
the children of Naphtali,**
Pedahel the son of Ammihud.
29 **These** are they whom the LORD
commanded to divide the
inheritance unto the children of
Israel in the land of Canaan.

35 **And the LORD** spake
unto Moses in the plains of
Moab by Jordan near Jericho,
saying,
2 **Command** the children of Israel,

that they give unto the Levites of the inheritance of their possession cities to dwell in;
and ye shall give also unto the Levites suburbs for the cities round about them.
[3] **And the cities** shall they have to dwell in;
and the suburbs of them shall be for their cattle, and for their goods, and for all their beasts.
[4] **And the suburbs of the cities**, {which ye shall give unto the Levites}, shall reach from the wall of the city and outward a thousand cubits round about.
[5] **And ye** shall measure from without the city on the east side two thousand cubits, and on the south side two thousand cubits, and on the west side two thousand cubits, and on the north side two thousand cubits;
and the city shall be in the midst:
this shall be to them the suburbs of the cities.
[6] **And among the cities which ye shall give unto the Levites** there shall be six cities for refuge,
which ye shall appoint for the manslayer,
that he may flee thither:
and to them ye shall add forty and two cities.
[7] **So all the cities which ye shall give to the Levites** shall be forty and eight cities:
them shall ye give with their suburbs.
[8] **And the cities which ye shall give** shall be of the possession of the children of Israel:
from them that have many ye shall give many;
but from them that have few ye shall give few:
every one shall give of his cities unto the Levites according to his inheritance which he inheriteth.
[9] **And the LORD** spake unto Moses, saying,
[10] **Speak** unto the children of Israel,
and say unto them,
When ye be come over Jordan into the land of Canaan;
[11] **Then ye** shall appoint you cities to be cities of refuge for you;
that the slayer may flee thither,
which killeth any person at unawares.
[12] **And they** shall be unto you cities for refuge from the avenger;
that the manslayer die not,
until he stand before the congregation in judgment.
[13] **And of these cities which ye shall give** six cities shall ye have for refuge.
[14] **Ye** shall give three cities on this side Jordan,
and three cities shall ye give in the land of Canaan,
which shall be cities of refuge.
[15] **These six cities** shall be a refuge, both for the children of Israel, and for the stranger, and for the sojourner among them:
that every one that killeth any person unawares may flee thither.
[16] **And if he** smite him with an instrument of iron,
so that he die,
he is a murderer:
the murderer shall surely be put to death.
[17] **And if he** smite him with throwing a stone,
wherewith he may die,
and he die,
he is a murderer:
the murderer shall surely be put to death.
[18] **Or if he** smite him with an hand weapon of wood,
wherewith he may die,
and he die,
he is a murderer:
the murderer shall surely be put to death.
[19] **The revenger of blood himself** shall slay the murderer:
when he meeteth him,
he shall slay him.
[20] **But if he** thrust him of hatred,
or hurl at him
by laying of wait,
that he die;
[21] **Or in enmity** smite him with his hand,
that he die:
he that smote him shall surely be put to death;
for he is a murderer:
the revenger of blood shall slay the murderer,
when he meeteth him.
[22] **But if he** thrust him suddenly without enmity,
or have cast upon him any thing
without laying of wait,
[23] Or with any stone,
wherewith a man may die,
seeing him not,
and cast it upon him,
that he die,
and was not his enemy,
neither sought his harm:
[24] **Then the congregation** shall judge between the slayer and the revenger of blood according to these judgments:
[25] **And the congregation** shall deliver the slayer out of the hand of the revenger of blood,
and the congregation shall restore him to the city of his refuge,
whither he was fled:
and he shall abide in it unto the death of the high priest,
which was anointed with the holy oil.
[26] **But if the slayer** shall at any time come without the border of the city of his refuge,
whither he was fled;
[27] **And the revenger of blood** find him without the borders of the city of his refuge,
and the revenger of blood kill the slayer;
he shall not be guilty of blood:
[28] **Because he** should have remained in the city of his refuge until the death of the high priest:
but after the death of the high priest the slayer shall return into the land of his possession.
[29] **So these things** shall be for a statute of judgment unto you throughout your generations in all your dwellings.
[30] **Whoso** killeth any person,
the murderer shall be put to death by the mouth of witnesses:
but one witness shall not testify against any person to cause him to die.
[31] **Moreover ye** shall take no satisfaction for the life of a murderer,
which is guilty of death:
but he shall be surely put to death.
[32] **And ye** shall take no satisfaction for him that is fled to the city of his refuge,
that he should come again {to dwell in the land}, until the death of the priest.

33 **So ye** shall not pollute the land
wherein ye are:
for blood it defileth the land:
and the land cannot be cleansed of
the blood that is shed therein, but
by the blood of him that shed it.
34 **Defile not** therefore the land
which ye shall inhabit,
wherein I dwell:
for I the LORD dwell among the
children of Israel.

36 **And the chief fathers of
the families of the
children of Gilead, the son of
Machir, the son of Manasseh, of
the families of the sons of
Joseph,** came near,
and spake before Moses, and before
the princes, the chief fathers of
the children of Israel:
2 **And they** said,
The LORD commanded my lord to
give the land for an inheritance by
lot to the children of Israel:
and my lord was commanded by
the LORD to give the inheritance
of Zelophehad our brother unto
his daughters.
3 **And if they** be married to any of
the sons of the other tribes of the
children of Israel,
then shall their inheritance be
taken from the inheritance of our
fathers,
and shall be put to the inheritance
of the tribe whereunto they are
received:
so shall it be taken from the lot of
our inheritance.
4 **And when the jubile of the
children of Israel** shall be,
then shall their inheritance be put
unto the inheritance of the tribe
whereunto they are received:
so shall their inheritance be taken
away from the inheritance of the
tribe of our fathers.
5 **And Moses** commanded the
children of Israel according to the
word of the LORD,
saying,
The tribe of the sons of Joseph
hath said well.
6 **This** is the thing which the LORD
doth command concerning the
daughters of Zelophehad,
saying,
Let them marry to whom they
think best;
**only to the family of the tribe of
their father** shall they marry.
7 **So** shall not the inheritance of the
children of Israel remove from
tribe to tribe:
**for every one of the children of
Israel** shall keep himself to the
inheritance of the tribe of his
fathers.
8 **And every daughter**, {that
possesseth an inheritance in any
tribe of the children of Israel},
shall be wife unto one of the
family of the tribe of her father,
that the children of Israel may
enjoy every man the inheritance
of his fathers.
9 **Neither** shall the inheritance
remove from one tribe to another
tribe;
**but every one of the tribes of the
children of Israel** shall keep
himself to his own inheritance.
10 **Even as the LORD** commanded
Moses,
so did the daughters of Zelophehad:
11 **For Mahlah, Tirzah, and Hoglah,
and Milcah, and Noah, the
daughters of Zelophehad,** were
married unto their fathers
brothers' sons:
12 **And they** were married into the
families of the sons of Manasseh
the son of Joseph,
and their inheritance remained in
the tribe of the family of their
father.
13 **These** are the commandments
and the judgments,
which the LORD commanded by
the hand of Moses unto the
children of Israel in the plains of
Moab by Jordan near Jericho.

Deuteronomy

The Book of Deuteronomy, authored by Moses, is a historical and theological record of the covenant relationship between God and the Israelites. The word *deuteronomy*, which comes from the Greek Word *deuteronomion*, is often translated as *second law*. However, it does not imply a new set of laws but rather a restatement and reinforcement of the laws first given in Exodus. The book, therefore, derives its namesake in two ways. First, it contains a retelling of the Ten Commandments and other Mosaic laws. Second, it reflects the idea that Moses, as a trusted leader, is reiterating and emphasizing the importance of these laws to the Israelites before they enter the Promised Land.

The Book of Deuteronomy highlights several key elements, including the Ten Commandments, which form the bedrock of God's covenant with the Israelites. These commandments span a range of moral and religious principles, from the prohibition of idolatry to the importance of observing the Sabbath and honoring one's parents. The book also features the Shema, a declaration of faith in one God, considered one of the most significant prayers in Judaism. In addition, Deuteronomy outlines a series of laws and commandments that the Israelites must follow to uphold their covenant with God. These laws, such as kashrut (dietary restrictions) and the laws of justice, provide a framework for daily living and maintaining a righteous relationship with God. Finally, the narrative concludes with the death of Moses, which marks the end of an era for the people of Israel.

The Book of Deuteronomy underscores the gravity of disobeying God's laws. It vividly describes the people's past offenses and warns of the severe consequences of future violations, including exile and punishment. However, this book is not a mere cautionary tale but a stark reminder of the importance of following God's laws and maintaining the covenant. In this final installment of the five Mosaic books known as the Pentateuch, Deuteronomy provides a comprehensive understanding of God's expectations for His chosen people.

1 **These** be the words which Moses spake unto all Israel on this side Jordan in the wilderness, in the plain over against the Red sea, between Paran, and Tophel, and Laban, and Hazeroth, and Dizahab.

2 (**There** are eleven days' journey from Horeb by the way of mount Seir unto Kadeshbarnea.)

3 **And it** came to pass in the fortieth year, in the eleventh month, on the first day of the month,
that Moses spake unto the children of Israel, according unto all that the LORD had given him in commandment unto them;

4 **After he** had slain Sihon the king of the Amorites,
which dwelt in Heshbon, and Og the king of Bashan,
which dwelt at Astaroth in Edrei:

5 **On this side Jordan, in the land of Moab,** began Moses to declare this law,
saying,

6 **The LORD our God** spake unto us in Horeb,
saying,
Ye have dwelt long enough in this mount:

7 **Turn you,**
and take your journey,
and go to the mount of the Amorites, and unto all the places nigh thereunto, in the plain, in the hills, and in the vale, and in the south, and by the sea side, to the land of the Canaanites, and unto Lebanon, unto the great river, the river Euphrates.

8 **Behold,**
I have set the land before you:
go in and possess the land which the LORD sware unto your fathers, Abraham, Isaac, and Jacob,
to give unto them and to their seed after them.

9 **And I** spake unto you at that time,
saying,
I am not able to bear you myself alone:

10 **The LORD your God** hath multiplied you,
and, {behold}, ye are this day as the stars of heaven for multitude.

11 (**The LORD God of your fathers** make you a thousand times so many more as ye are,
and bless you,
as he hath promised you!)

12 **How** can I myself alone bear your cumbrance, and your burden, and your strife?

13 **Take you** wise men, and understanding, and known among your tribes,
and I will make them rulers over you.

14 **And ye** answered me,
and said,
The thing which thou hast spoken is good for us to do.

15 **So I** took the chief of your tribes, wise men, and known,
and made them heads over you, captains over thousands, and captains over hundreds, and captains over fifties, and captains over tens, and officers among your tribes.

16 **And I** charged your judges at that time,
saying,
Hear the causes between your brethren,
and judge righteously between every man and his brother, and the stranger that is with him.

17 **Ye** shall not respect persons in judgment;

but ye shall hear the small as well as the great;
ye shall not be afraid of the face of man;
for the judgment is God's:
and the cause that is too hard for you, bring it unto me,
and I will hear it.

18 **And I** commanded you at that time all the things which ye should do.

19 **And when we** departed from Horeb,
we went through all that great and terrible wilderness,
which ye saw by the way of the mountain of the Amorites,
as the LORD our God commanded us;
and we came to Kadeshbarnea.

20 **And I** said unto you,
Ye are come unto the mountain of the Amorites,
which the LORD our God doth give unto us.

21 **Behold,**
the LORD thy God hath set the land before thee:
go up and possess it,
as the LORD God of thy fathers hath said unto thee;
fear not,
neither be discouraged.

22 **And ye** came near unto me every one of you,
and said,
We will send men before us,
and they shall search us out the land,
and bring us word again by what way we must go up, and into what cities we shall come.

23 **And the saying** pleased me well:
and I took twelve men of you, one of a tribe:

24 **And they** turned and went up into the mountain,
and came unto the valley of Eshcol,
and searched it out.

25 **And they** took of the fruit of the land in their hands,
and brought it down unto us,
and brought us word again,
and said,
It is a good land which the LORD our God doth give us.

26 **Notwithstanding ye** would not go up,
but rebelled against the commandment of the LORD your God:

27 **And ye** murmured in your tents,
and said,
Because the LORD hated us,
he hath brought us forth out of the land of Egypt,
to deliver us into the hand of the Amorites,
to destroy us.

28 **Whither** shall we go up?
our brethren have discouraged our heart,
saying,
The people is greater and taller than we;
the cities are great and walled up to heaven;
and moreover we have seen the sons of the Anakims there.

29 **Then I** said unto you,
Dread not,
neither be afraid of them.

30 **The LORD your God which goeth before you,** he shall fight for you, according to all that he did for you in Egypt before your eyes;

31 And in the wilderness,
where thou hast seen how that the LORD thy God bare thee, {as a man doth bear his son}, in all the way that ye went,
until ye came into this place.

32 **Yet in this thing** ye did not believe the LORD your God,

33 **Who** went in the way before you,
to search you out a place to pitch your tents in, in fire by night,
to shew you by what way ye should go, and in a cloud by day.

34 **And the LORD** heard the voice of your words,
and was wroth,
and sware,
saying,

35 **Surely there** shall not one of these men of this evil generation see that good land,
which I sware to give unto your fathers.

36 **Save Caleb the son of Jephunneh;** he shall see it,
and to him will I give the land that he hath trodden upon, and to his children,
because he hath wholly followed the LORD.

37 **Also the LORD** was angry with me for your sakes,
saying,
Thou also shalt not go in thither.

38 **But Joshua the son of Nun,** {which standeth before thee}, he shall go in thither:
encourage him:
for he shall cause Israel to inherit it.

39 **Moreover your little ones, {which ye said should be a prey, and your children, {which in that day had no knowledge between good and evil},** they shall go in thither,
and unto them will I give it,
and they shall possess it.

40 **But as for you,** turn you,
and take your journey into the wilderness by the way of the Red sea.

41 **Then ye** answered and said unto me,
We have sinned against the LORD,
we will go up and fight, according to all that the LORD our God commanded us.
And when ye had girded on every man his weapons of war,
ye were ready to go up into the hill.

42 **And the LORD** said unto me,
Say unto them,
Go not up,
neither fight;
for I am not among you;
lest ye be smitten before your enemies.

43 **So I** spake unto you;
and ye would not hear,
but rebelled against the commandment of the LORD,
and went presumptuously up into the hill.

44 **And the Amorites,** {which dwelt in that mountain}, came out against you,
and chased you, as bees do,
and destroyed you in Seir, even unto Hormah.

45 **And ye** returned and wept before the LORD;
but the LORD would not hearken to your voice,
nor give ear unto you.

46 **So ye** abode in Kadesh many days, according unto the days that ye abode there.

2 **Then we** turned,
and took our journey into the

wilderness by the way of the Red sea,
as the LORD spake unto me:
and we compassed mount Seir many days.

2 **And the LORD** spake unto me,
saying,
3 **Ye** have compassed this mountain long enough:
turn you northward.

4 **And command thou** the people,
saying,
Ye are to pass through the coast of your brethren the children of Esau,
which dwell in Seir;
and they shall be afraid of you:
take ye good heed unto yourselves therefore:
5 **Meddle not** with them;
for I will not give you of their land, no, not so much as a foot breadth;
because I have given mount Seir unto Esau for a possession.

6 **Ye** shall buy meat of them for money,
that ye may eat;
and ye shall also buy water of them for money,
that ye may drink.

7 **For the LORD thy God** hath blessed thee in all the works of thy hand:
he knoweth thy walking through this great wilderness:
these forty years the LORD thy God hath been with thee;
thou hast lacked nothing.

8 **And when we** passed by from our brethren the children of Esau,
which dwelt in Seir, through the way of the plain from Elath, and from Eziongaber,
we turned and passed by the way of the wilderness of Moab.

9 **And the LORD** said unto me,
Distress not the Moabites,
neither contend with them in battle:
for I will not give thee of their land for a possession;
because I have given Ar unto the children of Lot for a possession.

10 **The Emims** dwelt therein in times past, a people great, and many, and tall, as the Anakims;
11 **Which** also were accounted giants, as the Anakims;
but the Moabites called them Emims.

12 **The Horims** also dwelt in Seir beforetime;
but the children of Esau succeeded them,
when they had destroyed them from before them,
and dwelt in their stead;
as Israel did unto the land of his possession,
which the LORD gave unto them.

13 **Now rise up,**
said I,
and get you over the brook Zered.
And we went over the brook Zered.

14 **And the space in which we came from Kadeshbarnea,** {until we were come over the brook Zered}, was thirty and eight years;
until all the generation of the men of war were wasted out from among the host,
as the LORD sware unto them.

15 **For indeed the hand of the LORD** was against them,
to destroy them from among the host,
until they were consumed.

16 **So it** came to pass,
when all the men of war were consumed and dead from among the people,
17 **That the LORD** spake unto me,
saying,
18 **Thou** art to pass over through Ar, the coast of Moab, this day:
19 **And when thou** comest nigh over against the children of Ammon,
distress them not,
nor meddle with them:
for I will not give thee of the land of the children of Ammon any possession;
because I have given it unto the children of Lot for a possession.

20 (**That** also was accounted a land of giants:
giants dwelt therein in old time;
and the Ammonites call them Zamzummims;
21 A people great, and many, and tall, as the Anakims;
but the LORD destroyed them before them;
and they succeeded them,
and dwelt in their stead:
22 **As he** did to the children of Esau,
which dwelt in Seir,
when he destroyed the Horims from before them;
and they succeeded them,
and dwelt in their stead even unto this day:
23 **And the Avims which dwelt in Hazerim, even unto Azzah, the Caphtorims, {which came forth out of Caphtor},** destroyed them,
and dwelt in their stead.)

24 **Rise ye up,**
take your journey,
and pass over the river Arnon:
behold,
I have given into thine hand Sihon the Amorite, king of Heshbon, and his land:
begin to possess it,
and contend with him in battle.

25 **This day** will I begin to put the dread of thee and the fear of thee upon the nations that are under the whole heaven,
who shall hear report of thee,
and shall tremble,
and be in anguish because of thee.

26 **And I** sent messengers out of the wilderness of Kedemoth unto Sihon king of Heshbon with words of peace,
saying,
27 **Let me** pass through thy land:
I will go along by the high way,
I will neither turn unto the right hand nor to the left.

28 **Thou** shalt sell me meat for money,
that I may eat;
and give me water for money,
that I may drink:
only I will pass through on my feet;
29 (As the children of Esau which dwell in Seir, and the Moabites which dwell in Ar, did unto me;)
until I shall pass over Jordan into the land which the LORD our God giveth us.

30 **But Sihon king of Heshbon** would not let us pass by him:
for the LORD thy God hardened his spirit,
and made his heart obstinate,
that he might deliver him into thy hand,
as appeareth this day.

31 **And the LORD** said unto me,
behold,
I have begun to give Sihon and his land before thee:
begin to possess,
that thou mayest inherit his land.

32 **Then Sihon** came out against us,
he and all his people,

to fight at Jahaz.

33 **And the LORD our God** delivered him before us;
and we smote him, and his sons, and all his people.

34 **And we** took all his cities at that time,
and utterly destroyed the men, and the women, and the little ones, of every city,
we left none to remain:

35 **Only the cattle** we took for a prey unto ourselves, and the spoil of the cities which we took.

36 **From Aroer, {which is by the brink of the river of Arnon}, and from the city that is by the river, even unto Gilead,** there was not one city too strong for us:
the LORD our God delivered all unto us:

37 **Only unto the land of the children of Ammon** thou camest not, nor unto any place of the river Jabbok, nor unto the cities in the mountains, nor unto whatsoever the LORD our God forbad us.

3 **Then we** turned,
and went up the way to Bashan:
and Og the king of Bashan came out against us, he and all his people,
to battle at Edrei.

2 **And the LORD** said unto me,
Fear him not:
for I will deliver him, and all his people, and his land, into thy hand;
and thou shalt do unto him as thou didst unto Sihon king of the Amorites,
which dwelt at Heshbon.

3 **So the LORD our God** delivered into our hands Og also, the king of Bashan, and all his people:
and we smote him
until none was left to him remaining.

4 **And we** took all his cities at that time,
there was not a city which we took not from them, threescore cities, all the region of Argob, the kingdom of Og in Bashan.

5 **All these cities** were fenced with high walls, gates, and bars; beside unwalled towns a great many.

6 **And we** utterly destroyed them,
as we did unto Sihon king of Heshbon,
utterly destroying the men, women, and children, of every city.

7 **But all the cattle, and the spoil of the cities,** we took for a prey to ourselves.

8 **And we** took at that time out of the hand of the two kings of the Amorites the land that was on this side Jordan, from the river of Arnon unto mount Hermon;

9 (Which Hermon the Sidonians call Sirion; and the Amorites call it Shenir;)

10 All the cities of the plain, and all Gilead, and all Bashan, unto Salchah and Edrei, cities of the kingdom of Og in Bashan.

11 **For only Og king of Bashan** remained of the remnant of giants;
behold
his bedstead was a bedstead of iron;
is it not in Rabbath of the children of Ammon?
nine cubits was the length thereof, and four cubits the breadth of it, after the cubit of a man.

12 **And this land, {which we possessed at that time}, from Aroer, {which is by the river Arnon}, and half mount Gilead, and the cities thereof,** gave I unto the Reubenites and to the Gadites.

13 **And the rest of Gilead, and all Bashan,** {being the kingdom of Og}, gave I unto the half tribe of Manasseh; all the region of Argob, with all Bashan,
which was called the land of giants.

14 **Jair the son of Manasseh** took all the country of Argob unto the coasts of Geshuri and Maachathi;
and called them after his own name, Bashanhavothjair, unto this day.

15 **And I** gave Gilead unto Machir.

16 **And unto the Reubenites and unto the Gadites** I gave from Gilead even unto the river Arnon half the valley, and the border even unto the river Jabbok,
which is the border of the children of Ammon;

17 The plain also, and Jordan, and the coast thereof, from Chinnereth even unto the sea of the plain, even the salt sea, under Ashdothpisgah eastward.

18 **And I** commanded you at that time,
saying,
The LORD your God hath given you this land to possess it:
ye shall pass over armed before your brethren the children of Israel, all that are meet for the war.

19 **But your wives, and your little ones, and your cattle,** (for I know} {that ye have much cattle,) shall abide in your cities which I have given you;

20 **Until the LORD** have given rest unto your brethren, as well as unto you,
and until they also possess the land which the LORD your God hath given them beyond Jordan:
and then shall ye return every man unto his possession,
which I have given you.

21 **And I** commanded Joshua at that time,
saying,
Thine eyes have seen all that the LORD your God hath done unto these two kings:
so shall the LORD do unto all the kingdoms whither thou passest.

22 **Ye** shall not fear them:
for the LORD your God he shall fight for you.

23 **And I** besought the LORD at that time,
saying,

24 **O Lord GOD, thou** hast begun to shew thy servant thy greatness, and thy mighty hand:
for what God is there in heaven or in earth,
that can do according to thy works, and according to thy might?

25 **I** pray thee,
let me go over,
and see the good land that is beyond Jordan, that goodly mountain, and Lebanon.

26 **But the LORD** was wroth with me for your sakes,
and would not hear me:
and the LORD said unto me,
Let it suffice thee;
speak no more unto me of this matter.

27 **Get thee** up into the top of Pisgah,

and lift up thine eyes westward,
and northward, and southward,
and eastward,
and behold it with thine eyes:
for thou shalt not go over this
Jordan.

28 **But charge** Joshua,
and encourage him,
and strengthen him:
for he shall go over before this
people,
and he shall cause them to inherit
the land which thou shalt see.

29 **So we** abode in the valley over
against Bethpeor.

4 **Now therefore hearken,** O
Israel, unto the statutes and
unto the judgments,
which I teach you,
for to do them,
that ye may live,
and go in and possess the land
which the LORD God of your
fathers giveth you.

2 **Ye** shall not add unto the word
which I command you,
neither shall ye diminish ought
from it,
that ye may keep the
commandments of the LORD
your God which I command you.

3 **Your eyes** have seen what the
LORD did because of Baalpeor:
**for all the men that followed
Baalpeor,** the LORD thy God hath
destroyed them from among you.

4 **But ye that did cleave unto the
LORD your God** are alive every
one of you this day.

5 **Behold,**
I have taught you statutes and
judgments,
even as the LORD my God
commanded me,
that ye should do so in the land
whither ye go to possess it.

6 **Keep** therefore
and do them;
for this is your wisdom and your
understanding in the sight of the
nations,
which shall hear all these statutes,
and say,
Surely this great nation is a wise
and understanding people.

7 **For what nation** is there so great,
who hath God so nigh unto them,
as the LORD our God is in all
things that we call upon him for?

8 **And what nation** is there so great,
that hath statutes and judgments
so righteous as all this law,
which I set before you this day?

9 **Only take heed** to thyself,
and keep thy soul diligently,
lest thou forget the things which
thine eyes have seen,
and lest they depart from thy heart
all the days of thy life:
but teach them thy sons, and thy
sons' sons;

10 Specially the day that thou
stoodest before the LORD thy God
in Horeb,
when the LORD said unto me,
Gather me the people together,
and I will make them hear my
words,
that they may learn to fear me all
the days that they shall live upon
the earth,
and that they may teach their
children.

11 **And ye** came near and stood
under the mountain;
and the mountain burned with fire
unto the midst of heaven, with
darkness, clouds, and thick
darkness.

12 **And the LORD** spake unto you
out of the midst of the fire:
ye heard the voice of the words,
but saw no similitude;
only ye heard a voice.

13 **And he** declared unto you his
covenant,
which he commanded you to
perform, even ten
commandments;
and he wrote them upon two tables
of stone.

14 **And the LORD** commanded me at
that time
to teach you statutes and
judgments,
that ye might do them in the land
whither ye go over to possess it.

15 **Take ye** therefore good heed unto
yourselves;
for ye saw no manner of similitude
on the day that the LORD spake
unto you in Horeb out of the
midst of the fire:

16 **Lest ye** corrupt yourselves,
and make you a graven image, the
similitude of any figure, the
likeness of male or female,

17 The likeness of any beast that is
on the earth, the likeness of any
winged fowl that flieth in the air,

18 The likeness of any thing that
creepeth on the ground, the
likeness of any fish that is in the
waters beneath the earth:

19 **And lest thou** lift up thine eyes
unto heaven,
and when thou seest the sun, and
the moon, and the stars, even all
the host of heaven,
shouldest be driven to worship
them,
and serve them,
which the LORD thy God hath
divided unto all nations under the
whole heaven.

20 **But the LORD** hath taken you,
and brought you forth out of the
iron furnace, even out of Egypt,
to be unto him a people of
inheritance,
as ye are this day.

21 **Furthermore the LORD** was
angry with me for your sakes,
and sware
that I should not go over Jordan,
and that I should not go in unto
that good land,
which the LORD thy God giveth
thee for an inheritance:

22 **But I** must die in this land,
I must not go over Jordan:
but ye shall go over,
and possess that good land.

23 **Take heed** unto yourselves,
lest ye forget the covenant of the
LORD your God,
which he made with you,
and make you a graven image, or
the likeness of any thing,
which the LORD thy God hath
forbidden thee.

24 **For the LORD thy God** is a
consuming fire, even a jealous
God.

25 **When thou** shalt beget children,
and children's children,
and ye shall have remained long in
the land,
and shall corrupt yourselves,
and make a graven image, or the
likeness of any thing,
and shall do evil in the sight of the
LORD thy God,
to provoke him to anger:

26 **I** call heaven and earth to witness
against you this day,

that ye shall soon utterly perish from off the land whereunto ye go over Jordan to possess it;
ye shall not prolong your days upon it,
but shall utterly be destroyed.

27 **And the LORD** shall scatter you among the nations,
and ye shall be left few in number among the heathen,
whither the LORD shall lead you.

28 **And there** ye shall serve gods, the work of men's hands, wood and stone,
which neither see,
nor hear,
nor eat,
nor smell.

29 **But if from thence** thou shalt seek the LORD thy God,
thou shalt find him,
if thou seek him with all thy heart and with all thy soul.

30 **When thou** art in tribulation,
and all these things are come upon thee, even in the latter days,
if thou turn to the LORD thy God,
and shalt be obedient unto his voice;

31 (For the LORD thy God is a merciful God;)
he will not forsake thee,
neither destroy thee,
nor forget the covenant of thy fathers which he sware unto them.

32 **For ask** now of the days that are past,
which were before thee, since the day that God created man upon the earth,
and ask from the one side of heaven unto the other,
whether there hath been any such thing as this great thing is,
or hath been heard like it?

33 **Did ever people** hear the voice of God
speaking out of the midst of the fire,
as thou hast heard,
and live?

34 **Or hath God** assayed to go and take him a nation from the midst of another nation, by temptations, by signs, and by wonders, and by war, and by a mighty hand, and by a stretched out arm, and by great terrors, according to all that the LORD your God did for you in Egypt before your eyes?

35 **Unto thee** it was shewed,
that thou mightest know
that the LORD he is God;
there is none else beside him.

36 **Out of heaven** he made thee to hear his voice,
that he might instruct thee:
and upon earth he shewed thee his great fire;
and thou heardest his words out of the midst of the fire.

37 **And because he** loved thy fathers,
therefore he chose their seed after them,
and brought thee out in his sight with his mighty power out of Egypt;

38 To drive out nations from before thee greater and mightier than thou art,
to bring thee in,
to give thee their land for an inheritance,
as it is this day.

39 **Know** therefore this day,
and consider it in thine heart,
that the LORD he is God in heaven above, and upon the earth beneath:
there is none else.

40 **Thou** shalt keep therefore his statutes, and his commandments,
which I command thee this day,
that it may go well with thee, and with thy children after thee,
and that thou mayest prolong thy days upon the earth,
which the LORD thy God giveth thee, for ever.

41 **Then Moses** severed three cities on this side Jordan toward the sunrising;

42 **That the slayer** might flee thither,
which should kill his neighbour unawares,
and hated him not in times past;
and that fleeing unto one of these cities he might live:

43 Namely, Bezer in the wilderness, in the plain country, of the Reubenites; and Ramoth in Gilead, of the Gadites; and Golan in Bashan, of the Manassites.

44 **And this** is the law which Moses set before the children of Israel:

45 **These** are the testimonies, and the statutes, and the judgments,
which Moses spake unto the children of Israel,
after they came forth out of Egypt,

46 On this side Jordan, in the valley over against Bethpeor, in the land of Sihon king of the Amorites,
who dwelt at Heshbon,
whom Moses and the children of Israel smote,
after they were come forth out of Egypt:

47 **And they** possessed his land, and the land of Og king of Bashan, two kings of the Amorites,
which were on this side Jordan toward the sunrising;

48 From Aroer,
which is by the bank of the river Arnon, even unto mount Sion,
which is Hermon,

49 And all the plain on this side Jordan eastward, even unto the sea of the plain, under the springs of Pisgah.

5 **And Moses** called all Israel, **and** said unto them,
Hear, O Israel, the statutes and judgments which I speak in your ears this day,
that ye may learn them,
and keep,
and do them.

2 **The LORD our God** made a covenant with us in Horeb.

3 **The LORD** made not this covenant with our fathers, but with us, even us,
who are all of us here alive this day.

4 **The LORD** talked with you face to face in the mount out of the midst of the fire,

5 (I stood between the LORD and you at that time,
to shew you the word of the LORD:
for ye were afraid by reason of the fire,
and went not up into the mount;)
saying,

6 **I** am the LORD thy God,
which brought thee out of the land of Egypt, from the house of bondage.

7 **Thou** shalt have none other gods before me.

8 **Thou** shalt not make thee any graven image, or any likeness of any thing that is in heaven above, or that is in the earth beneath, or that is in the waters beneath the earth:

9 **Thou** shalt not bow down thyself unto them,
nor serve them:
for I the LORD thy God am a jealous God,
visiting the iniquity of the fathers upon the children unto the third and fourth generation of them that hate me,
10 **And** shewing mercy unto thousands of them that love me and keep my commandments.
11 **Thou** shalt not take the name of the LORD thy God in vain:
for the LORD will not hold him guiltless that taketh his name in vain.
12 **Keep** the sabbath day
to sanctify it,
as the LORD thy God hath commanded thee.
13 **Six days** thou shalt labour,
and do all thy work:
14 **But the seventh day** is the sabbath of the LORD thy God:
in it thou shalt not do any work, thou, nor thy son, nor thy daughter, nor thy manservant, nor thy maidservant, nor thine ox, nor thine ass, nor any of thy cattle, nor thy stranger that is within thy gates;
that thy manservant and thy maidservant may rest as well as thou.
15 **And remember**
that thou wast a servant in the land of Egypt,
and that the LORD thy God brought thee out thence through a mighty hand and by a stretched out arm:
therefore the LORD thy God commanded thee
to keep the sabbath day.
16 **Honour** thy father and thy mother,
as the LORD thy God hath commanded thee;
that thy days may be prolonged,
and that it may go well with thee, in the land which the LORD thy God giveth thee.
17 **Thou** shalt not kill.
18 **Neither** shalt thou commit adultery.
19 **Neither** shalt thou steal.
20 **Neither** shalt thou bear false witness against thy neighbour.
21 **Neither** shalt thou desire thy neighbour's wife,
neither shalt thou covet thy neighbour's house, his field, or his manservant, or his maidservant, his ox, or his ass, or any thing that is thy neighbour's.
22 **These words** the LORD spake unto all your assembly in the mount out of the midst of the fire, of the cloud, and of the thick darkness, with a great voice:
and he added no more.
And he wrote them in two tables of stone,
and delivered them unto me.
23 **And it** came to pass,
when ye heard the voice out of the midst of the darkness,
(for the mountain did burn with fire,)
that ye came near unto me, even all the heads of your tribes, and your elders;
24 **And ye** said,
Behold,
the LORD our God hath shewed us his glory and his greatness,
and we have heard his voice out of the midst of the fire:
we have seen this day that God doth talk with man,
and he liveth.
25 **Now therefore why** should we die?
for this great fire will consume us:
if we hear the voice of the LORD our God any more,
then we shall die.
26 **For who** is there of all flesh,
that hath heard the voice of the living God speaking out of the midst of the fire,
as we have,
and lived?
27 **Go thou** near,
and hear all that the LORD our God shall say:
and speak thou unto us all that the LORD our God shall speak unto thee;
and we will hear it,
and do it.
28 **And the LORD** heard the voice of your words,
when ye spake unto me;
and the LORD said unto me,
I have heard the voice of the words of this people,
which they have spoken unto thee:
they have well said all that they have spoken.
29 **O that there** were such an heart in them,
that they would fear me,
and keep all my commandments always,
that it might be well with them, and with their children for ever!
30 **Go say** to them,
Get you into your tents again.
31 **But as for thee,** stand thou here by me,
and I will speak unto thee all the commandments, and the statutes, and the judgments,
which thou shalt teach them,
that they may do them in the land which I give them to possess it.
32 **Ye** shall observe to do therefore as the LORD your God hath commanded you:
ye shall not turn aside to the right hand or to the left.
33 **Ye** shall walk in all the ways which the LORD your God hath commanded you,
that ye may live,
and that it may be well with you,
and that ye may prolong your days in the land which ye shall possess.

6 **Now these** are the commandments, the statutes, and the judgments,
which the LORD your God commanded to teach you,
that ye might do them in the land whither ye go to possess it:
2 **That thou** mightest fear the LORD thy God,
to keep all his statutes and his commandments,
which I command thee, thou, and thy son, and thy son's son, all the days of thy life;
and that thy days may be prolonged.
3 **Hear** therefore, O Israel,
and observe to do it;
that it may be well with thee,
and that ye may increase mightily,
as the LORD God of thy fathers hath promised thee, in the land that floweth with milk and honey.
4 **Hear,** O Israel:
The LORD our God is one LORD:
5 **And thou** shall love the LORD thy God with all thine heart, and with

all thy soul, and with all thy might.

6 **And these words**, {which I command thee this day}, shall be in thine heart:

7 **And thou** shalt teach them diligently unto thy children,
and shalt talk of them
when thou sittest in thine house,
and when thou walkest by the way,
and when thou liest down,
and when thou risest up.

8 **And thou** shalt bind them for a sign upon thine hand,
and they shall be as frontlets between thine eyes.

9 **And thou** shalt write them upon the posts of thy house, and on thy gates.

10 And it shall be,
when the LORD thy God shall have brought thee into the land which he sware unto thy fathers, to Abraham, to Isaac, and to Jacob,
to give thee great and goodly cities, {which thou buildedst not},
11 And houses full of all good things, {which thou filledst not}, and wells digged, {which thou diggedst not}, vineyards and olive trees, {which thou plantedst not};
when thou shalt have eaten and be full;
12 **Then beware**
lest thou forget the LORD,
which brought thee forth out of the land of Egypt, from the house of bondage.

13 **Thou** shalt fear the LORD thy God,
and serve him,
and shalt swear by his name.

14 **Ye** shall not go after other gods, of the gods of the people which are round about you;
15 (For the LORD thy God is a jealous God among you)
lest the anger of the LORD thy God be kindled against thee,
and destroy thee from off the face of the earth.

16 **Ye** shall not tempt the LORD your God,
as ye tempted him in Massah.

17 **Ye** shall diligently keep the commandments of the LORD your God, and his testimonies, and his statutes,
which he hath commanded thee.

18 **And thou** shalt do that which is right and good in the sight of the LORD:
that it may be well with thee,
and that thou mayest go in and possess the good land which the LORD sware unto thy fathers.

19 To cast out all thine enemies from before thee,
as the LORD hath spoken.

20 **And when thy son** asketh thee in time to come,
saying,
What mean the testimonies, and the statutes, and the judgments,
which the LORD our God hath commanded you?
21 **Then thou** shalt say unto thy son,
We were Pharaoh's bondmen in Egypt;
and the LORD brought us out of Egypt with a mighty hand:
22 **And the LORD** shewed signs and wonders, great and sore, upon Egypt, upon Pharaoh, and upon all his household, before our eyes:
23 **And he** brought us out from thence,
that he might bring us in,
to give us the land which he sware unto our fathers.

24 **And the LORD** commanded us to do all these statutes,
to fear the LORD our God, for our good always,
that he might preserve us alive,
as it is at this day.

25 **And it** shall be our righteousness,
if we observe to do all these commandments before the LORD our God,
as he hath commanded us.

7 **When the LORD thy God** shall bring thee into the land whither thou goest to possess it,
and hath cast out many nations before thee, the Hittites, and the Girgashites, and the Amorites, and the Canaanites, and the Perizzites, and the Hivites, and the Jebusites, seven nations greater and mightier than thou;
2 **And when the LORD thy God** shall deliver them before thee;
thou shalt smite them,
and utterly destroy them;
thou shalt make no covenant with them,
nor shew mercy unto them:

3 **Neither** shalt thou make marriages with them;
thy daughter thou shalt not give unto his son,
nor his daughter shalt thou take unto thy son.

4 **For they** will turn away thy son from following me,
that they may serve other gods:
so will the anger of the LORD be kindled against you,
and destroy thee suddenly.

5 **But thus** shall ye deal with them;
ye shall destroy their altars,
and break down their images,
and cut down their groves,
and burn their graven images with fire.

6 **For thou** art an holy people unto the LORD thy God:
the LORD thy God hath chosen thee to be a special people unto himself, above all people that are upon the face of the earth.

7 **The LORD** did not set his love upon you,
nor choose you,
because ye were more in number than any people;
for ye were the fewest of all people:
8 **But because the LORD** loved you,
and because he would keep the oath which he had sworn unto your fathers,
hath the LORD brought you out with a mighty hand,
and redeemed you out of the house of bondmen, from the hand of Pharaoh king of Egypt.

9 **Know** therefore **that the LORD thy God**, he is God, the faithful God,
which keepeth covenant and mercy with them that love him and keep his commandments to a thousand generations;
10 **And** repayeth them that hate him to their face,
to destroy them:
he will not be slack to him that hateth him,
he will repay him to his face.

11 **Thou** shalt therefore keep the commandments, and the statutes, and the judgments,
which I command thee this day,
to do them.

12 **Wherefore it** shall come to pass,
if ye hearken to these judgments,
and keep,

and do them,
that the LORD thy God shall keep unto thee the covenant and the mercy which he sware unto thy fathers:
13 **And he** will love thee,
and bless thee,
and multiply thee:
he will also bless the fruit of thy womb, and the fruit of thy land, thy corn, and thy wine, and thine oil, the increase of thy kine, and the flocks of thy sheep, in the land which he sware unto thy fathers to give thee.
14 **Thou** shalt be blessed above all people:
there shall not be male or female barren among you, or among your cattle.
15 **And the LORD** will take away from thee all sickness,
and will put none of the evil diseases of Egypt, {which thou knowest}, upon thee;
but will lay them upon all them that hate thee.
16 **And thou** shalt consume all the people which the LORD thy God shall deliver thee;
thine eye shall have no pity upon them:
neither shalt thou serve their gods;
for that will be a snare unto thee.
17 **If thou** shalt say in thine heart,
These nations are more than I;
how can I dispossess them?
18 **Thou** shalt not be afraid of them:
but shalt well remember
what the LORD thy God did unto Pharaoh, and unto all Egypt;
19 **The great temptations which thine eyes saw, and the signs, and the wonders, and the mighty hand, and the stretched out arm, {whereby the LORD thy God brought thee out}:** so shall the LORD thy God do unto all the people of whom thou art afraid.
20 **Moreover the LORD thy God** will send the hornet among them,
until they that are left, and hide themselves from thee, be destroyed.
21 **Thou** shalt not be affrighted at them:
for the LORD thy God is among you, a mighty God and terrible.
22 **And the LORD thy God** will put out those nations before thee by little and little:
thou mayest not consume them at once,
lest the beasts of the field increase upon thee.
23 **But the LORD thy God** shall deliver them unto thee,
and shall destroy them with a mighty destruction,
until they be destroyed.
24 **And he** shall deliver their kings into thine hand,
and thou shalt destroy their name from under heaven:
there shall no man be able to stand before thee,
until thou have destroyed them.
25 **The graven images of their gods** shall ye burn with fire:
thou shalt not desire the silver or gold that is on them,
nor take it unto thee,
lest thou be snared therin:
for it is an abomination to the LORD thy God.
26 **Neither** shalt thou bring an abomination into thine house,
lest thou be a cursed thing like it:
but thou shalt utterly detest it,
and thou shalt utterly abhor it;
for it is a cursed thing.

8 **All the commandments which I command thee this day** shall ye observe to do,
that ye may live,
and multiply,
and go in and possess the land which the LORD sware unto your fathers.
2 **And thou** shalt remember all the way which the LORD thy God led thee these forty years in the wilderness,
to humble thee,
and to prove thee,
to know
what was in thine heart,
whether thou wouldest keep his commandments, or no.
3 **And he** humbled thee,
and suffered thee to hunger,
and fed thee with manna,
which thou knewest not,
neither did thy fathers know;
that he might make thee know
that man doth not live by bread only,
but by every word that proceedeth out of the mouth of the LORD doth man live.
4 **Thy raiment** waxed not old upon thee, {neither did thy foot swell}, these forty years.
5 **Thou** shalt also consider in thine heart,
that, {as a man chasteneth his son}, so the LORD thy God chasteneth thee.
6 **Therefore thou** shalt keep the commandments of the LORD thy God,
to walk in his ways,
and to fear him.
7 **For the LORD thy God** bringeth thee into a good land, a land of brooks of water, of fountains and depths that spring out of valleys and hills;
8 A land of wheat, and barley, and vines, and fig trees, and pomegranates; a land of oil olive, and honey;
9 A land wherein thou shalt eat bread without scarceness, {thou shalt not lack any thing in it}; a land whose stones are iron, and out of whose hills thou mayest dig brass.
10 **When thou** hast eaten and art full,
then thou shalt bless the LORD thy God for the good land which he hath given thee.
11 **Beware**
that thou forget not the LORD thy God,
in not keeping his commandments, and his judgments, and his statutes,
which I command thee this day:
12 **Lest when thou** hast eaten and art full,
and hast built goodly houses,
and dwelt therein;
13 **And when thy herds and thy flocks** multiply,
and thy silver and thy gold is multiplied,
and all that thou hast is multiplied;
14 **Then thine heart** be lifted up,
and thou forget the LORD thy God,
which brought thee forth out of the land of Egypt, from the house of bondage;
15 **Who** led thee through that great and terrible wilderness,

wherein were fiery serpents, and scorpions, and drought,
where there was no water;
who brought thee forth water out of the rock of flint;
16 **Who** fed thee in the wilderness with manna,
which thy fathers knew not,
that he might humble thee,
and that he might prove thee,
to do thee good at thy latter end;
17 **And thou** say in thine heart,
My power and the might of mine hand hath gotten me this wealth.
18 **But thou** shalt remember the LORD thy God:
for it is he that giveth thee power to get wealth,
that he may establish his covenant which he sware unto thy fathers,
as it is this day.
19 **And it** shall be,
if thou do at all forget the LORD thy God,
and walk after other gods,
and serve them,
and worship them,
I testify against you this day
that ye shall surely perish.
20 **As the nations which the LORD destroyeth before your face,** so shall ye perish;
because ye would not be obedient unto the voice of the LORD your God.

9 **Hear,** O Israel:
Thou art to pass over Jordan this day,
to go in to possess nations greater and mightier than thyself, cities great and fenced up to heaven,
2 A people great and tall, the children of the Anakims,
whom thou knowest,
and of whom thou hast heard say,
Who can stand before the children of Anak!
3 **Understand** therefore this day,
that the LORD thy God is he which goeth over before thee;
as a consuming fire he shall destroy them,
and he shall bring them down before thy face:
so shalt thou drive them out,
and destroy them quickly,
as the LORD hath said unto thee.
4 **Speak not thou** in thine heart,
after that the LORD thy God hath cast them out from before thee,
saying,
For my righteousness the LORD hath brought me in to possess this land:
but for the wickedness of these nations the LORD doth drive them out from before thee.
5 **Not for thy righteousness, or for the uprightness of thine heart,** dost thou go to possess their land:
but for the wickedness of these nations the LORD thy God doth drive them out from before thee,
and that he may perform the word which the LORD sware unto thy fathers, Abraham, Isaac, and Jacob.
6 **Understand** therefore,
that the LORD thy God giveth thee not this good land to possess it for thy righteousness;
for thou art a stiffnecked people.
7 **Remember,**
and forget not,
how thou provokedst the LORD thy God to wrath in the wilderness:
from the day that thou didst depart out of the land of Egypt, {until ye came unto this place}, ye have been rebellious against the LORD.
8 **Also in Horeb** ye provoked the LORD to wrath,
so that the LORD was angry with you
to have destroyed you.
9 **When I** was gone up into the mount
to receive the tables of stone, even the tables of the covenant which the LORD made with you,
then I abode in the mount forty days and forty nights,
I neither did eat bread
nor drink water:
10 **And the LORD** delivered unto me two tables of stone written with the finger of God;
and on them was written according to all the words,
which the LORD spake with you in the mount out of the midst of the fire in the day of the assembly.
11 **And it** came to pass at the end of forty days and forty nights,
that the LORD gave me the two tables of stone, even the tables of the covenant.
12 **And the LORD** said unto me,
Arise,
get thee down quickly from hence;
for thy people which thou hast brought forth out of Egypt have corrupted themselves;
they are quickly turned aside out of the way which I commanded them;
they have made them a molten image.
13 **Furthermore the LORD** spake unto me,
saying,
I have seen this people,
and, {behold}, it is a stiffnecked people:
14 **Let me** alone,
that I may destroy them,
and blot out their name from under heaven:
and I will make of thee a nation mightier and greater than they.
15 **So I** turned and came down from the mount,
and the mount burned with fire:
and the two tables of the covenant were in my two hands.
16 **And I** looked,
and, {behold}, ye had sinned against the LORD your God,
and had made you a molten calf:
ye had turned aside quickly out of the way which the LORD had commanded you.
17 **And I** took the two tables,
and cast them out of my two hands,
and brake them before your eyes.
18 **And I** fell down before the LORD, as at the first, forty days and forty nights:
I did neither eat bread,
nor drink water, because of all your sins which ye sinned,
in doing wickedly in the sight of the LORD,
to provoke him to anger.
19 **For I** was afraid of the anger and hot displeasure,
wherewith the LORD was wroth against you
to destroy you.
But the LORD hearkened unto me at that time also.
20 **And the LORD** was very angry with Aaron
to have destroyed him:
and I prayed for Aaron also the same time.
21 **And I** took your sin, the calf which ye had made,
and burnt it with fire,

and stamped it,
and ground it very small,
even until it was as small as dust:
and I cast the dust thereof into the brook that descended out of the mount.
22 **And at Taberah, and at Massah, and at Kibrothhattaavah,** ye provoked the LORD to wrath.
23 **Likewise when the LORD** sent you from Kadeshbarnea,
saying,
Go up and possess the land which I have given you;
then ye rebelled against the commandment of the LORD your God,
and ye believed him not,
nor hearkened to his voice.
24 **Ye** have been rebellious against the LORD from the day that I knew you.
25 **Thus I** fell down before the LORD forty days and forty nights,
as I fell down at the first;
because the LORD had said
he would destroy you.
26 **I** prayed therefore unto the LORD,
and said,
O Lord GOD, destroy not thy people and thine inheritance,
which thou hast redeemed through thy greatness,
which thou hast brought forth out of Egypt with a mighty hand.
27 **Remember** thy servants, Abraham, Isaac, and Jacob;
look not unto the stubbornness of this people, nor to their wickedness, nor to their sin:
28 **Lest the land whence thou broughtest us out** say,
Because the LORD was not able to bring them into the land which he promised them,
and because he hated them,
he hath brought them out
to slay them in the wilderness.
29 **Yet they** are thy people and thine inheritance,
which thou broughtest out by thy mighty power and by thy stretched out arm.

10

At that time the LORD said unto me,
Hew thee two tables of stone like unto the first,
and come up unto me into the mount,
and make thee an ark of wood.
2 **And I** will write on the tables the words that were in the first tables which thou brakest,
and thou shalt put them in the ark.
3 **And I** made an ark of shittim wood,
and hewed two tables of stone like unto the first,
and went up into the mount,
having the two tables in mine hand.
4 **And he** wrote on the tables, according to the first writing, the ten commandments,
which the LORD spake unto you in the mount out of the midst of the fire in the day of the assembly:
and the LORD gave them unto me.
5 **And I** turned myself and came down from the mount,
and put the tables in the ark which I had made;
and there they be,
as the LORD commanded me.
6 **And the children of Israel** took their journey from Beeroth of the children of Jaakan to Mosera:
there Aaron died,
and there he was buried;
and Eleazar his son ministered in the priest's office in his stead.
7 **From thence** they journeyed unto Gudgodah; and from Gudgodah to Jotbath, a land of rivers of waters.
8 **At that time** the LORD separated the tribe of Levi,
to bear the ark of the covenant of the LORD,
to stand before the LORD
to minister unto him, {and to bless in his name}, unto this day.
9 **Wherefore Levi** hath no part nor inheritance with his brethren;
the LORD is his inheritance,
according as the LORD thy God promised him.
10 **And I** stayed in the mount, according to the first time, forty days and forty nights;
and the LORD hearkened unto me at that time also,
and the LORD would not destroy thee.
11 **And the LORD** said unto me,
Arise,
take thy journey before the people,
that they may go in and possess the land,
which I sware unto their fathers to give unto them.
12 **And now, Israel, what** doth the LORD thy God require of thee,
but to fear the LORD thy God,
to walk in all his ways,
and to love him,
and to serve the LORD thy God with all thy heart and with all thy soul,
13 To keep the commandments of the LORD, and his statutes,
which I command thee this day for thy good?
14 **Behold,**
the heaven and the heaven of heavens is the LORD's thy God, the earth also, with all that therein is.
15 **Only the LORD** had a delight in thy fathers
to love them,
and he chose their seed after them, even you above all people,
as it is this day.
16 **Circumcise** therefore the foreskin of your heart,
and be no more stiffnecked.
17 **For the LORD your God** is God of gods, and Lord of lords, a great God, a mighty, and a terrible,
which regardeth not persons,
nor taketh reward:
18 **He** doth execute the judgment of the fatherless and widow,
and loveth the stranger,
in giving him food and raiment.
19 **Love ye** therefore the stranger:
for ye were strangers in the land of Egypt.
20 **Thou** shalt fear the LORD thy God;
him shalt thou serve,
and to him shalt thou cleave,
and swear by his name.

21 **He** is thy praise,
and he is thy God,
that hath done for thee these great and terrible things,
which thine eyes have seen.
22 **Thy fathers** went down into Egypt with threescore and ten persons;
and now the LORD thy God hath made thee as the stars of heaven for multitude.

11

Therefore thou shalt love the LORD thy God,

and keep his charge, and his statutes, and his judgments, and his commandments, alway.

2 **And know ye** this day:
for I speak not with your children which have not known, and which have not seen the chastisement of the LORD your God, his greatness, his mighty hand, and his stretched out arm,
3 And his miracles, and his acts, {which he did in the midst of Egypt unto Pharaoh the king of Egypt}, and unto all his land;
4 {And what he did unto the army of Egypt, unto their horses, and to their chariots};
{how he made the water of the Red sea to overflow them}
{as they pursued after you},
{and how the LORD hath destroyed them unto this day};
5 {And what he did unto you in the wilderness},
{until ye came into this place};
6 {And what he did unto Dathan and Abiram, the sons of Eliab, the son of Reuben}:
{how the earth opened her mouth},
{and swallowed them up, and their households, and their tents, and all the substance that was in their possession, in the midst of all Israel}:
7 **But your eyes** have seen all the great acts of the LORD which he did.

8 **Therefore** shall ye keep all the commandments which I command you this day,
that ye may be strong,
and go in and possess the land,
whither ye go to possess it;
9 **And that ye** may prolong your days in the land,
which the LORD sware unto your fathers
to give unto them and to their seed, a land that floweth with milk and honey.

10 **For the land**, {whither thou goest in to possess it}, is not as the land of Egypt,
from whence ye came out,
where thou sowedst thy seed,
and wateredst it with thy foot, as a garden of herbs:
11 **But the land**, {whither ye go to possess it}, is a land of hills and valleys,
and drinketh water of the rain of heaven:
12 A land which the LORD thy God careth for:
the eyes of the LORD thy God are always upon it, from the beginning of the year even unto the end of the year.

13 **And it** shall come to pass,
if ye shall hearken diligently unto my commandments which I command you this day,
to love the LORD your God,
and to serve him with all your heart and with all your soul,
14 **That I** will give you the rain of your land in his due season, the first rain and the latter rain,
that thou mayest gather in thy corn, and thy wine, and thine oil.

15 **And I** will send grass in thy fields for thy cattle,
that thou mayest eat and be full.

16 **Take heed** to yourselves,
that your heart be not deceived,
and ye turn aside,
and serve other gods,
and worship them;
17 **And then the LORD's wrath** be kindled against you,
and he shut up the heaven,
that there be no rain,
and that the land yield not her fruit;
and lest ye perish quickly from off the good land which the LORD giveth you.

18 **Therefore** shall ye lay up these my words in your heart and in your soul,
and bind them for a sign upon your hand,
that they may be as frontlets between your eyes.

19 **And ye** shall teach them your children,
speaking of them
when thou sittest in thine house,
and when thou walkest by the way,
when thou liest down,
and when thou risest up.

20 **And thou** shalt write them upon the door posts of thine house, and upon thy gates:
21 **That your days** may be multiplied, and the days of your children, in the land which the LORD sware unto your fathers to give them, as the days of heaven upon the earth.

22 **For if ye** shall diligently keep all these commandments which I command you,
to do them,
to love the LORD your God,
to walk in all his ways,
and to cleave unto him;
23 **Then** will the LORD drive out all these nations from before you,
and ye shall possess greater nations and mightier than yourselves.

24 **Every place whereon the soles of your feet shall tread** shall be yours:
from the wilderness and Lebanon, from the river, the river Euphrates, even unto the uttermost sea shall your coast be.

25 **There** shall no man be able to stand before you:
for the LORD your God shall lay the fear of you and the dread of you upon all the land that ye shall tread upon,
as he hath said unto you.

26 **Behold,**
I set before you this day a blessing and a curse;
27 A blessing, {if ye obey the commandments of the LORD your God}, {which I command you this day}:
28 And a curse, {if ye will not obey the commandments of the LORD your God}, {but turn aside out of the way which I command you this day}, {to go after other gods}, {which ye have not known}.

29 **And it** shall come to pass,
when the LORD thy God hath brought thee in unto the land whither thou goest to possess it,
that thou shalt put the blessing upon mount Gerizim, and the curse upon mount Ebal.

30 **Are they not** on the other side Jordan, by the way where the sun goeth down, in the land of the Canaanites,
which dwell in the champaign over against Gilgal, beside the plains of Moreh?

31 **For ye** shall pass over Jordan
to go in to possess the land which the LORD your God giveth you,
and ye shall possess it,
and dwell therein.

32 **And ye** shall observe to do all the statutes and judgments which I set before you this day.

12 **These** are the statutes and judgments,
which ye shall observe to do in the land,
which the LORD God of thy fathers giveth thee to possess it, all the days that ye live upon the earth.
2 **Ye** shall utterly destroy all the places,
wherein the nations which ye shall possess served their gods, upon the high mountains, and upon the hills, and under every green tree:
3 **And ye** shall overthrow their altars,
and break their pillars,
and burn their groves with fire;
and ye shall hew down the graven images of their gods,
and destroy the names of them out of that place.
4 **Ye** shall not do so unto the LORD your God.
5 **But unto the place which the LORD your God shall choose out of all your tribes to put his name there,** even unto his habitation shall ye seek,
and thither thou shalt come:
6 **And thither** ye shall bring your burnt offerings, and your sacrifices, and your tithes, and heave offerings of your hand, and your vows, and your freewill offerings, and the firstlings of your herds and of your flocks:
7 **And there** ye shall eat before the LORD your God,
and ye shall rejoice in all that ye put your hand unto, ye and your households,
wherein the LORD thy God hath blessed thee.
8 **Ye** shall not do after all the things that we do here this day,
every man whatsoever is right in his own eyes.
9 **For ye** are not as yet come to the rest and to the inheritance,
which the LORD your God giveth you.
10 **But when ye** go over Jordan,
and dwell in the land which the LORD your God giveth you to inherit,
and when he giveth you rest from all your enemies round about,
so that ye dwell in safety;
11 **Then there** shall be a place which the LORD your God shall choose to cause his name to dwell there;
thither shall ye bring all that I command you; your burnt offerings, and your sacrifices, your tithes, and the heave offering of your hand, and all your choice vows which ye vow unto the LORD:
12 **And ye** shall rejoice before the LORD your God, ye, and your sons, and your daughters, and your menservants, and your maidservants, and the Levite that is within your gates;
forasmuch as he hath no part nor inheritance with you.
13 **Take heed** to thyself
that thou offer not thy burnt offerings in every place that thou seest:
14 **But in the place which the LORD shall choose in one of thy tribes,** there thou shalt offer thy burnt offerings,
and there thou shalt do all that I command thee.
15 **Notwithstanding thou** mayest kill and eat flesh in all thy gates,
whatsoever thy soul lusteth after, according to the blessing of the LORD thy God which he hath given thee:
the unclean and the clean may eat thereof, as of the roebuck, and as of the hart.
16 **Only ye** shall not eat the blood;
ye shall pour it upon the earth as water.
17 **Thou** mayest not eat within thy gates the tithe of thy corn, or of thy wine, or of thy oil, or the firstlings of thy herds or of thy flock, nor any of thy vows which thou vowest, nor thy freewill offerings, or heave offering of thine hand:
18 **But thou** must eat them before the LORD thy God in the place which the LORD thy God shall choose, thou, and thy son, and thy daughter, and thy manservant, and thy maidservant, and the Levite that is within thy gates:
and thou shalt rejoice before the LORD thy God in all that thou puttest thine hands unto.
19 **Take heed** to thyself
that thou forsake not the Levite as long as thou livest upon the earth.
20 **When the LORD thy God** shall enlarge thy border,
as he hath promised thee,
and thou shalt say,
I will eat flesh,
because thy soul longeth to eat flesh;
thou mayest eat flesh,
whatsoever thy soul lusteth after.
21 **If the place which the LORD thy God hath chosen to put his name there** be too far from thee,
then thou shalt kill of thy herd and of thy flock,
which the LORD hath given thee,
as I have commanded thee,
and thou shalt eat in thy gates
whatsoever thy soul lusteth after.
22 **Even as the roebuck and the hart** is eaten,
so thou shalt eat them:
the unclean and the clean shall eat of them alike.
23 **Only be sure** that thou eat not the blood:
for the blood is the life;
and thou mayest not eat the life with the flesh.
24 **Thou** shalt not eat it;
thou shalt pour it upon the earth as water.
25 **Thou** shalt not eat it;
that it may go well with thee, and with thy children after thee,
when thou shalt do that which is right in the sight of the LORD.
26 **Only thy holy things which thou hast, and thy vows,** thou shalt take,
and go unto the place which the LORD shall choose:
27 **And thou** shalt offer thy burnt offerings, the flesh and the blood, upon the altar of the LORD thy God:
and the blood of thy sacrifices shall be poured out upon the altar of the LORD thy God,
and thou shalt eat the flesh.
28 **Observe and hear** all these words which I command thee,
that it may go well with thee, and with thy children after thee for ever,

when thou doest that which is good and right in the sight of the LORD thy God.
29 **When the LORD thy God** shall cut off the nations from before thee,
whither thou goest to possess them,
and thou succeedest them,
and dwellest in their land;
30 **Take heed** to thyself
that thou be not snared by following them,
after that they be destroyed from before thee;
and that thou enquire not after their gods,
saying,
How did these nations serve their gods?
even so will I do likewise.
31 **Thou** shalt not do so unto the LORD thy God:
for every abomination to the LORD, {which he hateth}, have they done unto their gods;
for even their sons and their daughters they have burnt in the fire to their gods.
32 **What thing soever** I command you,
observe to do it:
thou shalt not add thereto,
nor diminish from it.

13 **If there** arise among you a prophet, or a dreamer of dreams,
and giveth thee a sign or a wonder,
2 **And the sign or the wonder** come to pass,
whereof he spake unto thee,
saying,
Let us go after other gods,
which thou hast not known,
and let us serve them;
3 **Thou** shalt not hearken unto the words of that prophet, or that dreamer of dreams:
for the LORD your God proveth you,
to know whether ye love the LORD your God with all your heart and with all your soul.
4 **Ye** shall walk after the LORD your God,
and fear him,
and keep his commandments,
and obey his voice,
and ye shall serve him,
and cleave unto him.
5 **And that prophet, or that dreamer of dreams,** shall be put to death;
because he hath spoken
to turn you away from the LORD your God,
which brought you out of the land of Egypt,
and redeemed you out of the house of bondage,
to thrust thee out of the way which the LORD thy God commanded thee to walk in.
So shalt thou put the evil away from the midst of thee.
6 **If thy brother, the son of thy mother, or thy son, or thy daughter, or the wife of thy bosom, or thy friend,** {which is as thine own soul}, entice thee secretly,
saying,
Let us go and serve other gods,
which thou hast not known, thou, nor thy fathers;
7 Namely, of the gods of the people which are round about you, nigh unto thee, or far off from thee, from the one end of the earth even unto the other end of the earth;
8 **Thou** shalt not consent unto him,
nor hearken unto him;
neither shall thine eye pity him,
neither shalt thou spare,
neither shalt thou conceal him:
9 **But thou** shalt surely kill him;
thine hand shall be first upon him to put him to death, and afterwards the hand of all the people.
10 **And thou** shalt stone him with stones,
that he die;
because he hath sought to thrust thee away from the LORD thy God,
which brought thee out of the land of Egypt, from the house of bondage.
11 **And all Israel** shall hear,
and fear,
and shall do no more any such wickedness as this is among you.
12 **If thou** shalt hear say in one of thy cities,
which the LORD thy God hath given thee to dwell there,
saying,
13 **Certain men, the children of Belial,** are gone out from among you,
and have withdrawn the inhabitants of their city,
saying,
Let us go and serve other gods,
which ye have not known;
14 **Then** shalt thou enquire,
and make search,
and ask diligently;
and, {behold}, if it be truth, and the thing certain,
that such abomination is wrought among you;
15 **Thou** shalt surely smite the inhabitants of that city with the edge of the sword,
destroying it utterly, and all that is therein, and the cattle thereof, with the edge of the sword.
16 **And thou** shalt gather all the spoil of it into the midst of the street thereof,
and shalt burn with fire the city, and all the spoil thereof every whit, for the LORD thy God:
and it shall be an heap for ever;
it shall not be built again.
17 **And there** shall cleave nought of the cursed thing to thine hand:
that the LORD may turn from the fierceness of his anger,
and shew thee mercy,
and have compassion upon thee,
and multiply thee,
as he hath sworn unto thy fathers;
18 **When thou** shalt hearken to the voice of the LORD thy God,
to keep all his commandments which I command thee this day,
to do that which is right in the eyes of the LORD thy God.

14 **Ye** are the children of the LORD your God:
ye shall not cut yourselves,
nor make any baldness between your eyes for the dead.
2 **For thou** art an holy people unto the LORD thy God,
and the LORD hath chosen thee to be a peculiar people unto himself, above all the nations that are upon the earth.
3 **Thou** shalt not eat any abominable thing.
4 **These** are the beasts which ye shall eat: the ox, the sheep, and the goat,

5 The hart, and the roebuck, and the fallow deer, and the wild goat, and the pygarg, and the wild ox, and the chamois.

6 **And every beast that parteth the hoof, and cleaveth the cleft into two claws, and cheweth the cud among the beasts,** that ye shall eat.

7 **Nevertheless these** ye shall not eat of them that chew the cud, or of them that divide the cloven hoof; as the camel, and the hare, and the coney:
for they chew the cud,
but divide not the hoof;
therefore they are unclean unto you.

8 **And the swine,** {because it divideth the hoof}, {yet cheweth not the cud}, it is unclean unto you:
ye shall not eat of their flesh,
nor touch their dead carcase.

9 **These** ye shall eat of all that are in the waters:
all that have fins and scales shall ye eat:
10 **And whatsoever hath not fins and scales** ye may not eat;
it is unclean unto you.

11 **Of all clean birds** ye shall eat.

12 **But these** are they of which ye shall not eat: the eagle, and the ossifrage, and the ospray,
13 And the glede, and the kite, and the vulture after his kind,
14 And every raven after his kind,
15 And the owl, and the night hawk, and the cuckow, and the hawk after his kind,
16 The little owl, and the great owl, and the swan,
17 And the pelican, and the gier eagle, and the cormorant,
18 And the stork, and the heron after her kind, and the lapwing, and the bat.

19 **And every creeping thing that flieth** is unclean unto you:
they shall not be eaten.

20 **But of all clean fowls** ye may eat.

21 **Ye** shall not eat of anything that dieth of itself:
thou shall give it unto the stranger that is in thy gates,
that he may eat it;
or thou mayest sell it unto an alien:
for thou art an holy people unto the LORD thy God.
Thou shalt not seethe a kid in his mother's milk.

22 **Thou** shalt truly tithe all the increase of thy seed,
that the field bringeth forth year by year.

23 **And thou** shalt eat before the LORD thy God, in the place which he shall choose to place his name there, the tithe of thy corn, of thy wine, and of thine oil, and the firstlings of thy herds and of thy flocks;
that thou mayest learn to fear the LORD thy God always.

24 **And if the way** be too long for thee,
so that thou art not able to carry it;
or if the place be too far from thee,
which the LORD thy God shall choose to set his name there,
when the LORD thy God hath blessed thee:
25 **Then** shalt thou turn it into money,
and bind up the money in thine hand,
and shalt go unto the place which the LORD thy God shall choose:
26 **And thou** shalt bestow that money for whatsoever thy soul lusteth after, for oxen, or for sheep, or for wine, or for strong drink, or for whatsoever thy soul desireth:
and thou shalt eat there before the LORD thy God,
and thou shalt rejoice, thou, and thine household,
27 **And the Levite that is within thy gates;** thou shalt not forsake him;
for he hath no part nor inheritance with thee.

28 **At the end of three years** thou shalt bring forth all the tithe of thine increase the same year,
and shalt lay it up within thy gates:
29 **And the Levite, (because he hath no part nor inheritance with thee,) and the stranger, and the fatherless, and the widow, {which are within thy gates},** shall come,
and shall eat and be satisfied;
that the LORD thy God may bless thee in all the work of thine hand which thou doest.

15

At the end of every seven years thou shalt make a release.

2 **And this** is the manner of the release:
Every creditor that lendeth ought unto his neighbour shall release it;
he shall not exact it of his neighbour, or of his brother;
because it is called the LORD's release.

3 **Of a foreigner** thou mayest exact it again:
but that which is thine with thy brother thine hand shall release;
4 **Save when there** shall be no poor among you;
for the LORD shall greatly bless thee in the land which the LORD thy God giveth thee for an inheritance to possess it:
5 **Only if thou** carefully hearken unto the voice of the LORD thy God,
to observe to do all these commandments which I command thee this day.

6 **For the LORD thy God** blesseth thee,
as he promised thee:
and thou shalt lend unto many nations,
but thou shalt not borrow;
and thou shalt reign over many nations,
but they shall not reign over thee.

7 **If there** be among you a poor man of one of thy brethren within any of thy gates in thy land which the LORD thy God giveth thee,
thou shalt not harden thine heart,
nor shut thine hand from thy poor brother:
8 **But thou** shalt open thine hand wide unto him,
and shalt surely lend him sufficient for his need, in that which he wanteth.

9 **Beware**
that there be not a thought in thy wicked heart,
saying,
The seventh year, the year of release, is at hand;
and thine eye be evil against thy poor brother,
and thou givest him nought;
and he cry unto the LORD against thee,
and it be sin unto thee.

10 **Thou** shalt surely give him,

and thine heart shall not be grieved
when thou givest unto him:
because that for this thing the LORD thy God shall bless thee in all thy works, and in all that thou puttest thine hand unto.

11 **For the poor** shall never cease out of the land:
therefore I command thee,
saying,
Thou shalt open thine hand wide unto thy brother, to thy poor, and to thy needy, in thy land.

12 **And if thy brother, an Hebrew man, or an Hebrew woman,** be sold unto thee,
and serve thee six years;
then in the seventh year thou shalt let him go free from thee.

13 **And when thou** sendest him out free from thee,
thou shalt not let him go away empty:

14 **Thou** shalt furnish him liberally out of thy flock, and out of thy floor, and out of thy winepress:
of that wherewith the LORD thy God hath blessed thee thou shalt give unto him.

15 **And thou** shalt remember
that thou wast a bondman in the land of Egypt,
and the LORD thy God redeemed thee:
therefore I command thee this thing to day.

16 **And it** shall be,
if he say unto thee,
I will not go away from thee;
because he loveth thee and thine house,
because he is well with thee;

17 **Then thou** shalt take an aul,
and thrust it through his ear unto the door,
and he shall be thy servant for ever.
And also unto thy maidservant thou shalt do likewise.

18 **It** shall not seem hard unto thee,
when thou sendest him away free from thee;
for he hath been worth a double hired servant to thee,
in serving thee six years:
and the LORD thy God shall bless thee in all that thou doest.

19 **All the firstling males that come of thy herd and of thy flock** thou shalt sanctify unto the LORD thy God:
thou shalt do no work with the firstling of thy bullock,
nor shear the firstling of thy sheep.

20 **Thou** shalt eat it before the LORD thy God year by year in the place which the LORD shall choose, thou and thy household.

21 **And if there** be any blemish therein,
as if it be lame, or blind,
or have any ill blemish,
thou shalt not sacrifice it unto the LORD thy God.

22 **Thou** shalt eat it within thy gates:
the unclean and the clean person shall eat it alike, as the roebuck, and as the hart.

23 **Only thou** shalt not eat the blood thereof;
thou shalt pour it upon the ground as water.

16

Observe the month of Abib, **and keep** the passover unto the LORD thy God:
for in the month of Abib the LORD thy God brought thee forth out of Egypt by night.

2 **Thou** shalt therefore sacrifice the passover unto the LORD thy God, of the flock and the herd, in the place which the LORD shall choose to place his name there.

3 **Thou** shalt eat no leavened bread with it;
seven days shalt thou eat unleavened bread therewith, even the bread of affliction;
for thou camest forth out of the land of Egypt in haste:
that thou mayest remember the day when thou camest forth out of the land of Egypt all the days of thy life.

4 **And there** shall be no leavened bread seen with thee in all thy coast seven days;
neither shall there any thing of the flesh, {which thou sacrificedst the first day at even}, remain all night until the morning.

5 **Thou** mayest not sacrifice the passover within any of thy gates,
which the LORD thy God giveth thee:

6 **But at the place which the LORD thy God shall choose to place his name in,** there thou shalt sacrifice the passover at even, at the going down of the sun, at the season that thou camest forth out of Egypt.

7 **And thou** shalt roast and eat it in the place which the LORD thy God shall choose:
and thou shalt turn in the morning,
and go unto thy tents.

8 **Six days** thou shalt eat unleavened bread:
and on the seventh day shall be a solemn assembly to the LORD thy God:
thou shalt do no work therein.

9 **Seven weeks** shalt thou number unto thee:
begin to number the seven weeks from such time as thou beginnest to put the sickle to the corn.

10 **And thou** shalt keep the feast of weeks unto the LORD thy God with a tribute of a freewill offering of thine hand,
which thou shalt give unto the LORD thy God,
according as the LORD thy God hath blessed thee:

11 **And thou** shalt rejoice before the LORD thy God, thou, and thy son, and thy daughter, and thy manservant, and thy maidservant, and the Levite that is within thy gates, and the stranger, and the fatherless, and the widow, {that are among you}, in the place which the LORD thy God hath chosen to place his name there.

12 **And thou** shalt remember
that thou wast a bondman in Egypt:
and thou shalt observe and do these statutes.

13 **Thou** shalt observe the feast of tabernacles seven days,
after that thou hast gathered in thy corn and thy wine:

14 **And thou** shalt rejoice in thy feast, thou, and thy son, and thy daughter, and thy manservant, and thy maidservant, and the Levite, the stranger, and the fatherless, and the widow,
that are within thy gates.

15 **Seven days** shalt thou keep a solemn feast unto the LORD thy God in the place which the LORD shall choose:

because the LORD thy God shall bless thee in all thine increase, and in all the works of thine hands,
therefore thou shalt surely rejoice.

16 **Three times in a year** shall all thy males appear before the LORD thy God in the place which he shall choose; in the feast of unleavened bread, and in the feast of weeks, and in the feast of tabernacles:
and they shall not appear before the LORD empty:

17 **Every man** shall give as he is able, according to the blessing of the LORD thy God which he hath given thee.

18 **Judges and officers** shalt thou make thee in all thy gates,
which the LORD thy God giveth thee, throughout thy tribes:
and they shall judge the people with just judgment.

19 **Thou** shalt not wrest judgment;
thou shalt not respect persons,
neither take a gift:
for a gift doth blind the eyes of the wise,
and pervert the words of the righteous.

20 **That which is altogether just** shalt thou follow,
that thou mayest live,
and inherit the land which the LORD thy God giveth thee.

21 **Thou** shalt not plant thee a grove of any trees near unto the altar of the LORD thy God,
which thou shalt make thee.

22 **Neither** shalt thou set thee up any image;
which the LORD thy God hateth.

17

Thou shalt not sacrifice unto the LORD thy God any bullock, or sheep, wherein is blemish, or any evilfavouredness:
for that is an abomination unto the LORD thy God.

2 **If there** be found among you, within any of thy gates which the LORD thy God giveth thee, man or woman,
that hath wrought wickedness in the sight of the LORD thy God,
in transgressing his covenant,

3 **And** hath gone and served other gods,
and worshipped them, either the sun, or moon, or any of the host of heaven,
which I have not commanded;

4 **And it** be told thee,
and thou hast heard of it,
and enquired diligently,
and, {behold}, it be true, and the thing certain,
that such abomination is wrought in Israel:

5 **Then** shalt thou bring forth that man or that woman, {which have committed that wicked thing}, unto thy gates, even that man or that woman,
and shalt stone them with stones,
till they die.

6 **At the mouth of two witnesses, or three witnesses,** shall he that is worthy of death be put to death;
but at the mouth of one witness he shall not be put to death.

7 **The hands of the witnesses** shall be first upon him to put him to death, and afterward the hands of all the people.
So thou shalt put the evil away from among you.

8 **If there** arise a matter too hard for thee in judgment, between blood and blood, between plea and plea, and between stroke and stroke,
being matters of controversy within thy gates:
then shalt thou arise,
and get thee up into the place which the LORD thy God shall choose;

9 **And thou** shalt come unto the priests the Levites, and unto the judge that shall be in those days,
and enquire;
and they shall shew thee the sentence of judgment:

10 **And thou** shalt do according to the sentence,
which they of that place which the LORD shall choose shall shew thee;
and thou shalt observe to do according to all that they inform thee:

11 **According to the sentence of the law which they shall teach thee, and according to the judgment which they shall tell thee,** thou shalt do:
thou shalt not decline from the sentence which they shall shew thee, to the right hand, nor to the left.

12 **And the man that will do presumptuously, and will not hearken unto the priest that standeth to minister there before the LORD thy God, or unto the judge,** even that man shall die:
and thou shalt put away the evil from Israel.

13 **And all the people** shall hear,
and fear,
and do no more presumptuously.

14 **When thou** art come unto the land which the LORD thy God giveth thee,
and shalt possess it,
and shalt dwell therein,
and shalt say,
I will set a king over me, like as all the nations that are about me;

15 **Thou** shalt in any wise set him king over thee,
whom the LORD thy God shall choose:
one from among thy brethren shalt thou set king over thee:
thou mayest not set a stranger over thee,
which is not thy brother.

16 **But he** shall not multiply horses to himself,
nor cause the people to return to Egypt,
to the end that he should multiply horses:
forasmuch as the LORD hath said unto you,
Ye shall henceforth return no more that way.

17 **Neither** shall he multiply wives to himself,
that his heart turn not away:
neither shall he greatly multiply to himself silver and gold.

18 **And it** shall be,
when he sitteth upon the throne of his kingdom,
that he shall write him a copy of this law in a book out of that which is before the priests the Levites:

19 **And it** shall be with him,
and he shall read therein all the days of his life:
that he may learn to fear the LORD his God,
to keep all the words of this law and these statutes,

to do them:
20 **That his heart** be not lifted up
above his brethren,
and that he turn not aside from the
commandment, to the right hand,
or to the left:
to the end that he may prolong his
days in his kingdom, he, and his
children, in the midst of Israel.

18

The priests the Levites,
and all the tribe of Levi,
shall have no part nor inheritance
with Israel:
they shall eat the offerings of the
LORD made by fire, and his
inheritance.
2 **Therefore** shall they have no
inheritance among their brethren:
the LORD is their inheritance,
as he hath said unto them.
3 **And this** shall be the priest's due
from the people, from them that
offer a sacrifice,
whether it be ox or sheep;
and they shall give unto the priest
the shoulder, and the two cheeks,
and the maw.
4 **The firstfruit also of thy corn, of**
thy wine, and of thine oil, and
the first of the fleece of thy
sheep, shalt thou give him.
5 **For the LORD thy God** hath
chosen him out of all thy tribes,
to stand to minister in the name of
the LORD, him and his sons for
ever.
6 **And if a Levite** come from any of
thy gates out of all Israel,
where he sojourned,
and come with all the desire of his
mind unto the place which the
LORD shall choose;
7 **Then he** shall minister in the
name of the LORD his God,
as all his brethren the Levites do,
which stand there before the LORD.
8 **They** shall have like portions to
eat, beside that which cometh of
the sale of his patrimony.
9 **When thou** art come into the land
which the LORD thy God giveth
thee,
thou shalt not learn to do after the
abominations of those nations.
10 **There** shall not be found among
you any one that maketh his son
or his daughter to pass through
the fire, or that useth divination,
or an observer of times, or an
enchanter, or a witch,
11 Or a charmer, or a consulter with
familiar spirits, or a wizard, or a
necromancer.
12 **For all that do these things** are
an abomination unto the LORD:
and because of these
abominations the LORD thy God
doth drive them out from before
thee.
13 **Thou** shalt be perfect with the
LORD thy God.
14 **For these nations,** {which thou
shalt possess}, hearkened unto
observers of times, and unto
diviners:
but as for thee, the LORD thy God
hath not suffered thee so to do.
15 **The LORD thy God** will raise up
unto thee a Prophet from the
midst of thee, of thy brethren, like
unto me;
unto him ye shall hearken;
16 According to all that thou
desiredst of the LORD thy God in
Horeb in the day of the assembly,
saying,
Let me not hear again the voice of
the LORD my God,
neither let me see this great fire
any more,
that I die not.
17 **And the LORD** said unto me,
They have well spoken that which
they have spoken.
18 **I** will raise them up a Prophet
from among their brethren, like
unto thee,
and will put my words in his
mouth;
and he shall speak unto them all
that I shall command him.
19 **And it** shall come to pass,
that whosoever will not hearken
unto my words which he shall
speak in my name,
I will require it of him.
20 **But the prophet,** {which shall
presume to speak a word in my
name}, {which I have not
commanded him to speak}, {or
that shall speak in the name of
other gods}, even that prophet
shall die.
21 **And if thou** say in thine heart,
How shall we know the word which
the LORD hath not spoken?
22 **When a prophet** speaketh in the
name of the LORD,
if the thing follow not,
nor come to pass,
that is the thing which the LORD
hath not spoken,
but the prophet hath spoken it
presumptuously:
thou shalt not be afraid of him.

19

When the LORD thy God
hath cut off the nations,
whose land the LORD thy God
giveth thee,
and thou succeedest them,
and dwellest in their cities, and in
their houses;
2 **Thou** shalt separate three cities for
thee in the midst of thy land,
which the LORD thy God giveth
thee to possess it.
3 **Thou** shalt prepare thee a way,
and divide the coasts of thy land,
which the LORD thy God giveth
thee to inherit, into three parts,
that every slayer may flee thither.
4 **And this** is the case of the slayer,
which shall flee thither,
that he may live:
Whoso killeth his neighbour
ignorantly,
whom he hated not in time past;
5 **As when a man** goeth into the
wood with his neighbour
to hew wood,
and his hand fetcheth a stroke with
the axe
to cut down the tree,
and the head slippeth from the
helve,
and lighteth upon his neighbour,
that he die;
he shall flee unto one of those cities,
and live:
6 **Lest the avenger of the blood**
pursue the slayer,
while his heart is hot,
and overtake him,
because the way is long,
and slay him;
whereas he was not worthy of
death,
inasmuch as he hated him not in
time past.
7 **Wherefore I** command thee,
saying,
Thou shalt separate three cities for
thee.
8 **And if the LORD thy God** enlarge
thy coast,
as he hath sworn unto thy fathers,
and give thee all the land which he
promised to give unto thy fathers;

9 **If thou** shalt keep all these commandments to do them,
which I command thee this day,
to love the LORD thy God,
and to walk ever in his ways;
then shalt thou add three cities more for thee, beside these three:
10 **That innocent blood** be not shed in thy land,
which the LORD thy God giveth thee for an inheritance,
and so blood be upon thee.
11 **But if any man** hate his neighbour,
and lie in wait for him,
and rise up against him,
and smite him mortally
that he die,
and fleeth into one of these cities:
12 **Then the elders of his city** shall send and fetch him thence,
and deliver him into the hand of the avenger of blood,
that he may die.
13 **Thine eye** shall not pity him,
but thou shalt put away the guilt of innocent blood from Israel,
that it may go well with thee.
14 **Thou** shalt not remove thy neighbour's landmark,
which they of old time have set in thine inheritance,
which thou shalt inherit in the land that the LORD thy God giveth thee to possess it.
15 **One witness** shall not rise up against a man for any iniquity, or for any sin, in any sin that he sinneth:
at the mouth of two witnesses, or at the mouth of three witnesses, shall the matter be established.
16 **If a false witness** rise up against any man
to testify against him that which is wrong;
17 **Then both the men**, {between whom the controversy is}, shall stand before the LORD, before the priests and the judges,
which shall be in those days;
18 **And the judges** shall make diligent inquisition:
and, {behold}, if the witness be a false witness,
and hath testified falsely against his brother;
19 **Then** shall ye do unto him,
as he had thought to have done unto his brother:
so shalt thou put the evil away from among you.
20 **And those which remain** shall hear,
and fear,
and shall henceforth commit no more any such evil among you.
21 **And thine eye** shall not pity;
but life shall go for life, eye for eye, tooth for tooth, hand for hand, foot for foot.

20

When thou goest out to battle against thine enemies,
and seest horses, and chariots, and a people more than thou,
be not afraid of them:
for the LORD thy God is with thee,
which brought thee up out of the land of Egypt.
2 **And it** shall be,
when ye are come nigh unto the battle,
that the priest shall approach and speak unto the people,
3 **And** shall say unto them,
Hear, O Israel,
ye approach this day unto battle against your enemies:
let not your hearts faint,
fear not,
and do not tremble,
neither be ye terrified because of them;
4 **For the LORD your God** is he that goeth with you,
to fight for you against your enemies,
to save you.
5 **And the officers** shall speak unto the people,
saying,
What man is there that hath built a new house,
and hath not dedicated it?
let him go and return to his house,
lest he die in the battle,
and another man dedicate it.
6 **And what man** is he that hath planted a vineyard,
and hath not yet eaten of it?
let him also go and return unto his house,
lest he die in the battle,
and another man eat of it.
7 **And what man** is there that hath betrothed a wife,
and hath not taken her?
let him go and return unto his house,
lest he die in the battle,
and another man take her.
8 **And the officers** shall speak further unto the people,
and they shall say,
What man is there that is fearful and fainthearted?
let him go and return unto his house,
lest his brethren's heart faint as well as his heart.
9 **And it** shall be,
when the officers have made an end of speaking unto the people
that they shall make captains of the armies to lead the people.
10 **When thou** comest nigh unto a city to fight against it,
then proclaim peace unto it.
11 **And it** shall be,
if it make thee answer of peace,
and open unto thee,
then it shall be,
that all the people that is found therein shall be tributaries unto thee,
and they shall serve thee.
12 **And if it** will make no peace with thee,
but will make war against thee,
then thou shalt besiege it:
13 **And when the LORD thy God** hath delivered it into thine hands,
thou shalt smite every male thereof with the edge of the sword:
14 **But the women, and the little ones, and the cattle, and all that is in the city, even all the spoil thereof,** shalt thou take unto thyself;
and thou shalt eat the spoil of thine enemies,
which the LORD thy God hath given thee.
15 **Thus** shalt thou do unto all the cities which are very far off from thee,
which are not of the cities of these nations.
16 **But of the cities of these people**, {which the LORD thy God doth give thee for an inheritance}, thou shalt save alive nothing that breatheth:
17 **But thou** shalt utterly destroy them; namely, the Hittites, and the Amorites, the Canaanites, and

the Perizzites, the Hivites, and the Jebusites;
as the LORD thy God hath commanded thee:
18 **That they** teach you not to do after all their abominations,
which they have done unto their gods;
so should ye sin against the LORD your God.

19 **When thou** shalt besiege a city a long time,
in making war against it
to take it,
thou shalt not destroy the trees thereof
by forcing an axe against them:
for thou mayest eat of them,
and thou shalt not cut them down
(for the tree of the field is man's life)
to employ them in the siege:
20 **Only the trees which thou knowest that they be not trees for meat,** thou shalt destroy and cut them down;
and thou shalt build bulwarks against the city that maketh war with thee,
until it be subdued.

21

If one be found slain in the land which the LORD thy God giveth thee to possess it,
lying in the field,
and it be not known
who hath slain him:
2 **Then thy elders and thy judges** shall come forth,
and they shall measure unto the cities which are round about him that is slain:
3 **And it** shall be,
that the city which is next unto the slain man, even the elders of that city shall take an heifer,
which hath not been wrought with,
and which hath not drawn in the yoke;
4 **And the elders of that city** shall bring down the heifer unto a rough valley,
which is neither eared
nor sown,
and shall strike off the heifer's neck there in the valley:
5 **And the priests the sons of Levi** shall come near;
for them the LORD thy God hath chosen to minister unto him,
and to bless in the name of the LORD;
and by their word shall every controversy and every stroke be tried:
6 **And all the elders of that city,** {that are next unto the slain man}, shall wash their hands over the heifer that is beheaded in the valley:
7 **And they** shall answer and say,
Our hands have not shed this blood,
neither have our eyes seen it.
8 **Be** merciful, O LORD, unto thy people Israel,
whom thou hast redeemed,
and lay not innocent blood unto thy people of Israel's charge.
And the blood shall be forgiven them.
9 **So** shalt thou put away the guilt of innocent blood from among you,
when thou shalt do that which is right in the sight of the LORD.
10 **When thou** goest forth to war against thine enemies,
and the LORD thy God hath delivered them into thine hands,
and thou hast taken them captive,
11 **And** seest among the captives a beautiful woman,
and hast a desire unto her,
that thou wouldest have her to thy wife;
12 **Then thou** shalt bring her home to thine house,
and she shall shave her head,
and pare her nails;
13 **And she** shall put the raiment of her captivity from off her,
and shall remain in thine house,
and bewail her father and her mother a full month:
and after that thou shalt go in unto her,
and be her husband,
and she shall be thy wife.
14 **And it** shall be,
if thou have no delight in her,
then thou shalt let her go whither she will;
but thou shalt not sell her at all for money,
thou shalt not make merchandise of her,
because thou hast humbled her.
15 **If a man** have two wives, one beloved, and another hated,
and they have born him children, both the beloved and the hated;
and if the firstborn son be hers that was hated:
16 **Then it** shall be,
when he maketh his sons to inherit that which he hath,
that he may not make the son of the beloved firstborn before the son of the hated,
which is indeed the firstborn:
17 **But he** shall acknowledge the son of the hated for the firstborn,
by giving him a double portion of all that he hath:
for he is the beginning of his strength;
the right of the firstborn is his.
18 **If a man** have a stubborn and rebellious son,
which will not obey the voice of his father, or the voice of his mother,
and that, {when they have chastened him}, will not hearken unto them:
19 **Then** shall his father and his mother lay hold on him,
and bring him out unto the elders of his city, and unto the gate of his place;
20 **And they** shall say unto the elders of his city,
This our son is stubborn and rebellious,
he will not obey our voice;
he is a glutton, and a drunkard.
21 **And all the men of his city** shall stone him with stones,
that he die:
so shalt thou put evil away from among you;
and all Israel shall hear,
and fear.
22 **And if a man** have committed a sin worthy of death,
and he be to be put to death,
and thou hang him on a tree:
23 **His body** shall not remain all night upon the tree,
but thou shalt in any wise bury him that day;
(for he that is hanged is accursed of God;)
that thy land be not defiled,
which the LORD thy God giveth thee for an inheritance.

22

Thou shalt not see thy brother's ox or his sheep go astray,
and hide thyself from them:
thou shalt in any case bring them again unto thy brother.

2 **And if thy brother** be not nigh unto thee,
or if thou know him not,
then thou shalt bring it unto thine own house,
and it shall be with thee
until thy brother seek after it,
and thou shalt restore it to him again.

3 **In like manner** shalt thou do with his ass;
and so shalt thou do with his raiment;
and with all lost thing of thy brother's, {which he hath lost}, {and thou hast found}, shalt thou do likewise:
thou mayest not hide thyself.

4 **Thou** shalt not see thy brother's ass or his ox fall down by the way,
and hide thyself from them:
thou shalt surely help him to lift them up again.

5 **The woman** shall not wear that which pertaineth unto a man,
neither shall a man put on a woman's garment:
for all that do so are abomination unto the LORD thy God.

6 **If a bird's nest** chance to be before thee in the way in any tree, or on the ground,
whether they be young ones, or eggs,
and the dam sitting upon the young, or upon the eggs,
thou shalt not take the dam with the young:

7 **But thou** shalt in any wise let the dam go,
and take the young to thee;
that it may be well with thee,
and that thou mayest prolong thy days.

8 **When thou** buildest a new house,
then thou shalt make a battlement for thy roof,
that thou bring not blood upon thine house,
if any man fall from thence.

9 **Thou** shalt not sow thy vineyard with divers seeds:
lest the fruit of thy seed which thou hast sown, and the fruit of thy vineyard, be defiled.

10 **Thou** shalt not plow with an ox and an ass together.

11 **Thou** shalt not wear a garment of divers sorts, as of woollen and linen together.

12 **Thou** shalt make thee fringes upon the four quarters of thy vesture,
wherewith thou coverest thyself.

13 **If any man** take a wife,
and go in unto her,
and hate her,
14 **And** give occasions of speech against her,
and bring up an evil name upon her,
and say,
I took this woman,
and when I came to her,
I found her not a maid:
15 **Then** shall the father of the damsel, and her mother, take and bring forth the tokens of the damsel's virginity unto the elders of the city in the gate:
16 **And the damsel's father** shall say unto the elders,
I gave my daughter unto this man to wife,
and he hateth her;
17 **And, {lo}, he** hath given occasions of speech against her,
saying,
I found not thy daughter a maid;
and yet these are the tokens of my daughter's virginity.

And they shall spread the cloth before the elders of the city.

18 **And the elders of that city** shall take that man and chastise him;
19 **And they** shall amerce him in an hundred shekels of silver,
and give them unto the father of the damsel,
because he hath brought up an evil name upon a virgin of Israel:
and she shall be his wife;
he may not put her away all his days.

20 **But if this thing** be true,
and the tokens of virginity be not found for the damsel:
21 **Then they** shall bring out the damsel to the door of her father's house,
and the men of her city shall stone her with stones
that she die:
because she hath wrought folly in Israel,
to play the whore in her father's house:
so shalt thou put evil away from among you.

22 **If a man** be found lying with a woman married to an husband,
then they shall both of them die, both the man that lay with the woman, and the woman:
so shalt thou put away evil from Israel.

23 **If a damsel that is a virgin** be betrothed unto an husband,
and a man find her in the city,
and lie with her;
24 **Then ye** shall bring them both out unto the gate of that city,
and ye shall stone them with stones
that they die;
the damsel, because she cried not, being in the city;
and the man, because he hath humbled his neighbour's wife:
so thou shalt put away evil from among you.

25 **But if a man** find a betrothed damsel in the field,
and the man force her,
and lie with her:
then the man only that lay with her shall die.

26 **But unto the damsel** thou shalt do nothing;
there is in the damsel no sin worthy of death:
for as when a man riseth against his neighbour,
and slayeth him,
even so is this matter:
27 **For he** found her in the field,
and the betrothed damsel cried,
and there was none to save her.

28 **If a man** find a damsel that is a virgin,
which is not betrothed,
and lay hold on her,
and lie with her,
and they be found;
29 **Then the man that lay with her** shall give unto the damsel's father fifty shekels of silver,
and she shall be his wife;
because he hath humbled her,
he may not put her away all his days.

30 **A man** shall not take his father's wife,
nor discover his father's skirt.

23 **He that is wounded in the stones, or hath his privy member cut off,** shall not enter into the congregation of the LORD.

2 **A bastard** shall not enter into the congregation of the LORD;
even to his tenth generation shall he not enter into the congregation of the LORD.
3 **An Ammonite or Moabite** shall not enter into the congregation of the LORD;
even to their tenth generation shall they not enter into the congregation of the LORD for ever:
4 **Because they** met you not with bread and with water in the way,
when ye came forth out of Egypt;
and because they hired against thee Balaam the son of Beor of Pethor of Mesopotamia,
to curse thee.
5 **Nevertheless the LORD thy God** would not hearken unto Balaam;
but the LORD thy God turned the curse into a blessing unto thee,
because the LORD thy God loved thee.
6 **Thou** shalt not seek their peace nor their prosperity all thy days for ever.
7 **Thou** shalt not abhor an Edomite;
for he is thy brother:
thou shalt not abhor an Egyptian;
because thou wast a stranger in his land.
8 **The children that are begotten of them** shall enter into the congregation of the LORD in their third generation.
9 **When the host** goeth forth against thine enemies,
then keep thee from every wicked thing.
10 **If there** be among you any man,
that is not clean by reason of uncleanness that chanceth him by night,
then shall he go abroad out of the camp,
he shall not come within the camp:
11 **But it** shall be,
when evening cometh on,
he shall wash himself with water:
and when the sun is down,
he shall come into the camp again.
12 **Thou** shalt have a place also without the camp,
whither thou shalt go forth abroad:
13 **And thou** shalt have a paddle upon thy weapon;
and it shall be,
when thou wilt ease thyself abroad,
thou shalt dig therewith,
and shalt turn back and cover that which cometh from thee:
14 **For the LORD thy God** walketh in the midst of thy camp,
to deliver thee,
and to give up thine enemies before thee;
therefore shall thy camp be holy:
that he see no unclean thing in thee,
and turn away from thee.
15 **Thou** shalt not deliver unto his master the servant which is escaped from his master unto thee:
16 **He** shall dwell with thee, even among you, in that place which he shall choose in one of thy gates,
where it liketh him best:
thou shalt not oppress him.
17 **There** shall be no whore of the daughters of Israel, nor a sodomite of the sons of Israel.
18 **Thou** shalt not bring the hire of a whore, or the price of a dog, into the house of the LORD thy God for any vow:
for even both these are abomination unto the LORD thy God.
19 **Thou** shalt not lend upon usury to thy brother; usury of money, usury of victuals, usury of any thing that is lent upon usury:
20 **Unto a stranger** thou mayest lend upon usury;
but unto thy brother thou shalt not lend upon usury:
that the LORD thy God may bless thee in all that thou settest thine hand to in the land whither thou goest to possess it.
21 **When thou** shalt vow a vow unto the LORD thy God,
thou shalt not slack to pay it:
for the LORD thy God will surely require it of thee;
and it would be sin in thee.
22 **But if thou** shalt forbear to vow,
it shall be no sin in thee.
23 **That which is gone out of thy lips** thou shalt keep and perform; even a freewill offering,
according as thou hast vowed unto the LORD thy God,
which thou hast promised with thy mouth.
24 **When thou** comest into thy neighbour's vineyard,
then thou mayest eat grapes thy fill at thine own pleasure;
but thou shalt not put any in thy vessel.
25 **When thou** comest into the standing corn of thy neighbour,
then thou mayest pluck the ears with thine hand;
but thou shalt not move a sickle unto thy neighbour's standing corn.

24 ∞ **When a man** hath taken a wife,
and married her,
and it come to pass
that she find no favour in his eyes,
because he hath found some uncleanness in her:
then let him write her a bill of divorcement,
and give it in her hand,
and send her out of his house.
2 **And when she** is departed out of his house,
she may go and be another man's wife.
3 **And if the latter husband** hate her,
and write her a bill of divorcement,
and giveth it in her hand,
and sendeth her out of his house;
or if the latter husband die,
which took her to be his wife;
4 **Her former husband**, {which sent her away}, may not take her again to be his wife,
after that she is defiled;
for that is abomination before the LORD:
and thou shalt not cause the land to sin,
which the LORD thy God giveth thee for an inheritance.
5 **When a man** hath taken a new wife,
he shall not go out to war,
neither shall he be charged with any business:
but he shall be free at home one year,
and shall cheer up his wife which he hath taken.
6 **No man** shall take the nether or the upper millstone to pledge:
for he taketh a man's life to pledge.

7 **If a man** be found stealing any of his brethren of the children of Israel,
and maketh merchandise of him,
or selleth him;
then that thief shall die;
and thou shalt put evil away from among you.

8 **Take heed** in the plague of leprosy,
that thou observe diligently,
and do according to all that the priests the Levites shall teach you:
as I commanded them,
so ye shall observe to do.

9 **Remember**
what the LORD thy God did unto Miriam by the way,
after that ye were come forth out of Egypt.

10 **When thou** dost lend thy brother any thing,
thou shalt not go into his house
to fetch his pledge.

11 **Thou** shalt stand abroad,
and the man to whom thou dost lend shall bring out the pledge abroad unto thee.

12 **And if the man** be poor,
thou shalt not sleep with his pledge:

13 **In any case thou** shalt deliver him the pledge again
when the sun goeth down,
that he may sleep in his own raiment,
and bless thee:
and it shall be righteousness unto thee before the LORD thy God.

14 **Thou** shalt not oppress an hired servant that is poor and needy,
whether he be of thy brethren, or of thy strangers that are in thy land within thy gates:

15 **At his day** thou shalt give him his hire,
neither shall the sun go down upon it;
for he is poor,
and setteth his heart upon it:
lest he cry against thee unto the LORD,
and it be sin unto thee.

16 **The fathers** shall not be put to death for the children,
neither shall the children be put to death for the fathers:
every man shall be put to death for his own sin.

17 **Thou** shalt not pervert the judgment of the stranger, nor of the fatherless;
nor take a widow's raiment to pledge:

18 **But thou** shalt remember
that thou wast a bondman in Egypt,
and the LORD thy God redeemed thee thence:
therefore I command thee
to do this thing.

19 **When thou** cuttest down thine harvest in thy field,
and hast forgot a sheaf in the field,
thou shalt not go again to fetch it:
it shall be for the stranger, for the fatherless, and for the widow:
that the LORD thy God may bless thee in all the work of thine hands.

20 **When thou** beatest thine olive tree,
thou shalt not go over the boughs again:
it shall be for the stranger, for the fatherless, and for the widow.

21 **When thou** gatherest the grapes of thy vineyard,
thou shalt not glean it afterward:
it shall be for the stranger, for the fatherless, and for the widow.

22 **And thou** shalt remember
that thou wast a bondman in the land of Egypt:
therefore I command thee
to do this thing.

25

If there be a controversy between men,
and they come unto judgment,
that the judges may judge them;
then they shall justify the righteous,
and condemn the wicked.

2 **And it** shall be,
if the wicked man be worthy to be beaten,
that the judge shall cause him to lie down,
and to be beaten before his face, according to his fault, by a certain number.

3 **Forty stripes** he may give him, and not exceed:
lest, {if he should exceed}, {and beat him above these with many stripes}, then thy brother should seem vile unto thee.

4 **Thou** shalt not muzzle the ox
when he treadeth out the corn.

5 **If brethren** dwell together,
and one of them die,
and have no child,
the wife of the dead shall not marry without unto a stranger:
her husband's brother shall go in unto her,
and take her to him to wife,
and perform the duty of an husband's brother unto her.

6 **And it** shall be,
that the firstborn which she beareth shall succeed in the name of his brother which is dead,
that his name be not put out of Israel.

7 **And if the man** like not to take his brother's wife,
then let his brother's wife go up to the gate unto the elders,
and say,
My husband's brother refuseth to raise up unto his brother a name in Israel,
he will not perform the duty of my husband's brother.

8 **Then the elders of his city** shall call him,
and speak unto him:
and if he stand to it,
and say,
I like not to take her;

9 **Then** shall his brother's wife come unto him in the presence of the elders,
and loose his shoe from off his foot,
and spit in his face,
and shall answer and say,
So shall it be done unto that man that will not build up his brother's house.

10 **And his** name shall be called in Israel,
The house of him that hath his shoe loosed.

11 **When men** strive together one with another,
and the wife of the one draweth near
for to deliver her husband out of the hand of him that smiteth him,
and putteth forth her hand,
and taketh him by the secrets:

12 **Then thou** shalt cut off her hand,
thine eye shall not pity her.

13 **Thou** shalt not have in thy bag divers weights, a great and a small.

14 **Thou** shalt not have in thine house divers measures, a great and a small.

15 **But thou** shalt have a perfect and just weight,
a perfect and just measure shalt thou have:
that thy days may be lengthened in the land which the LORD thy God giveth thee.

16 **For all that do such things, and all that do unrighteously,** are an abomination unto the LORD thy God.

17 **Remember**
what Amalek did unto thee by the way,
when ye were come forth out of Egypt;
18 **How** he met thee by the way,
and smote the hindmost of thee, even all that were feeble behind thee,
when thou wast faint and weary;
and he feared not God.

19 **Therefore it** shall be,
when the LORD thy God hath given thee rest from all thine enemies round about, in the land which the LORD thy God giveth thee for an inheritance to possess it,
that thou shalt blot out the remembrance of Amalek from under heaven;
thou shalt not forget it.

26

And it shall be,
when thou art come in unto the land which the LORD thy God giveth thee for an inheritance,
and possessest it,
and dwellest therein;
2 **That thou** shalt take of the first of all the fruit of the earth,
which thou shalt bring of thy land that the LORD thy God giveth thee,
and shalt put it in a basket,
and shalt go unto the place which the LORD thy God shall choose to place his name there.

3 **And thou** shalt go unto the priest that shall be in those days,
and say unto him,
I profess this day unto the LORD thy God,
that I am come unto the country which the LORD sware unto our fathers for to give us.

4 **And the priest** shall take the basket out of thine hand,
and set it down before the altar of the LORD thy God.

5 **And thou** shalt speak and say before the LORD thy God,
A Syrian ready to perish was my father,
and he went down into Egypt,
and sojourned there with a few,
and became there a nation, great, mighty, and populous:
6 **And the Egyptians** evil entreated us,
and afflicted us,
and laid upon us hard bondage:
7 **And when we** cried unto the LORD God of our fathers,
the LORD heard our voice,
and looked on our affliction, and our labour, and our oppression:
8 **And the LORD** brought us forth out of Egypt with a mighty hand, and with an outstretched arm, and with great terribleness, and with signs, and with wonders:
9 **And he** hath brought us into this place,
and hath given us this land, even a land that floweth with milk and honey.

10 **And now, <u>{behold}</u>, I** have brought the firstfruits of the land,
which thou, O LORD, hast given me.

And thou shalt set it before the LORD thy God,
and worship before the LORD thy God:
11 **And thou** shalt rejoice in every good thing which the LORD thy God hath given unto thee, and unto thine house, thou, and the Levite, and the stranger that is among you.

12 **When thou** hast made an end of tithing all the tithes of thine increase the third year,
which is the year of tithing,
and hast given it unto the Levite, the stranger, the fatherless, and the widow,
that they may eat within thy gates,
and be filled;
13 **Then thou** shalt say before the LORD thy God,
I have brought away the hallowed things out of mine house,
and also have given them unto the Levite, and unto the stranger, to the fatherless, and to the widow, according to all thy commandments which thou hast commanded me:
I have not transgressed thy commandments,
neither have I forgotten them.

14 **I** have not eaten thereof in my mourning,
neither have I taken away ought thereof for any unclean use,
nor given ought thereof for the dead:
but I have hearkened to the voice of the LORD my God,
and have done according to all that thou hast commanded me.

15 **Look down** from thy holy habitation, from heaven,
and bless thy people Israel, and the land which thou hast given us,
as thou swarest unto our fathers, a land that floweth with milk and honey.

16 **This day** the LORD thy God hath commanded thee
to do these statutes and judgments:
thou shalt therefore keep and do them with all thine heart, and with all thy soul.

17 **Thou** hast avouched the LORD this day to be thy God,
and to walk in his ways,
and to keep his statutes, and his commandments, and his judgments,
and to hearken unto his voice:
18 **And the LORD** hath avouched thee this day to be his peculiar people,
as he hath promised thee,
and that thou shouldest keep all his commandments;
19 **And** to make thee high above all nations which he hath made, in praise, and in name, and in honour;
and that thou mayest be an holy people unto the LORD thy God,
as he hath spoken.

27

And Moses with the elders of Israel
commanded the people,
saying,
Keep all the commandments which I command you this day.

2 **And it** shall be on the day when ye shall pass over Jordan unto the land which the LORD thy God giveth thee,

that thou shalt set thee up great stones,
and plaister them with plaister:
3 **And thou** shalt write upon them all the words of this law,
when thou art passed over,
that thou mayest go in unto the land which the LORD thy God giveth thee, a land that floweth with milk and honey;
as the LORD God of thy fathers hath promised thee.
4 **Therefore it** shall be when ye be gone over Jordan,
that ye shall set up these stones,
which I command you this day, in mount Ebal,
and thou shalt plaister them with plaister.
5 **And there** shalt thou build an altar unto the LORD thy God, an altar of stones:
thou shalt not lift up any iron tool upon them.
6 **Thou** shalt build the altar of the LORD thy God of whole stones:
and thou shalt offer burnt offerings thereon unto the LORD thy God:
7 **And thou** shalt offer peace offerings,
and shalt eat there,
and rejoice before the LORD thy God.
8 **And thou** shalt write upon the stones all the words of this law very plainly.
9 **And Moses and the priests the Levites** spake unto all Israel,
saying,
Take heed,
and hearken, O Israel;
this day thou art become the people of the LORD thy God.
10 **Thou** shalt therefore obey the voice of the LORD thy God,
and do his commandments and his statutes,
which I command thee this day.
11 **And Moses** charged the people the same day,
saying,
12 **These** shall stand upon mount Gerizim to bless the people,
when ye are come over Jordan;
Simeon, and Levi, and Judah, and Issachar, and Joseph, and Benjamin:
13 **And these** shall stand upon mount Ebal to curse;
Reuben, Gad, and Asher, and Zebulun, Dan, and Naphtali.
14 **And the Levites** shall speak,
and say unto all the men of Israel with a loud voice,
15 **Cursed** be the man that maketh any graven or molten image, an abomination unto the LORD, the work of the hands of the craftsman,
and putteth it in a secret place.
And all the people shall answer and say,
Amen.
16 **Cursed** be he that setteth light by his father or his mother.
And all the people shall say,
Amen.
17 **Cursed** be he that removeth his neighbour's landmark.
And all the people shall say,
Amen.
18 **Cursed** be he that maketh the blind to wander out of the way.
And all the people shall say,
Amen.
19 **Cursed** be he that perverteth the judgment of the stranger, fatherless, and widow.
And all the people shall say,
Amen.
20 **Cursed** be he that lieth with his father's wife;
because he uncovereth his father's skirt.
And all the people shall say,
Amen.
21 **Cursed** be he that lieth with any manner of beast.
And all the people shall say,
Amen.
22 **Cursed** be he that lieth with his sister, the daughter of his father, or the daughter of his mother.
And all the people shall say,
Amen.
23 **Cursed** be he that lieth with his mother in law.
And all the people shall say,
Amen.
24 **Cursed** be he that smiteth his neighbour secretly.
And all the people shall say,
Amen.
25 **Cursed** be he that taketh reward to slay an innocent person.
And all the people shall say,
Amen.
26 **Cursed** be he that confirmeth not all the words of this law
to do them.
And all the people shall say,
Amen.

28

And it shall come to pass,
if thou shalt hearken diligently unto the voice of the LORD thy God,
to observe and to do all his commandments which I command thee this day,
that the LORD thy God will set thee on high above all nations of the earth:
2 **And all these blessings** shall come on thee,
and overtake thee,
if thou shalt hearken unto the voice of the LORD thy God.
3 **Blessed** shalt thou be in the city,
and blessed shalt thou be in the field.
4 **Blessed** shall be the fruit of thy body, and the fruit of thy ground, and the fruit of thy cattle, the increase of thy kine, and the flocks of thy sheep.
5 **Blessed** shall be thy basket and thy store.
6 **Blessed** shalt thou be
when thou comest in,
and blessed shalt thou be
when thou goest out.
7 **The LORD** shall cause thine enemies that rise up against thee to be smitten before thy face:
they shall come out against thee one way,
and flee before thee seven ways.
8 **The LORD** shall command the blessing upon thee in thy storehouses, and in all that thou settest thine hand unto;
and he shall bless thee in the land which the LORD thy God giveth thee.
9 **The LORD** shall establish thee an holy people unto himself,
as he hath sworn unto thee,
if thou shalt keep the commandments of the LORD thy God,
and walk in his ways.
10 **And all people of the earth** shall see that thou art called by the name of the LORD;

and they shall be afraid of thee.

11 **And the LORD** shall make thee plenteous in goods, in the fruit of thy body, and in the fruit of thy cattle, and in the fruit of thy ground, in the land which the LORD sware unto thy fathers to give thee.

12 **The LORD** shall open unto thee his good treasure,
the heaven to give the rain unto thy land in his season,
and to bless all the work of thine hand:
and thou shalt lend unto many nations,
and thou shalt not borrow.

13 **And the LORD** shall make thee the head, and not the tail;
and thou shalt be above only,
and thou shalt not be beneath;
if that thou hearken unto the commandments of the LORD thy God,
which I command thee this day,
to observe and to do them:

14 **And thou** shalt not go aside from any of the words which I command thee this day, to the right hand, or to the left,
to go after other gods
to serve them.

15 **But it** shall come to pass,
if thou wilt not hearken unto the voice of the LORD thy God,
to observe to do all his commandments and his statutes which I command thee this day;
that all these curses shall come upon thee,
and overtake thee:

16 **Cursed** shalt thou be in the city,
and cursed shalt thou be in the field.

17 **Cursed** shall be thy basket and thy store.

18 **Cursed** shall be the fruit of thy body, and the fruit of thy land, the increase of thy kine, and the flocks of thy sheep.

19 **Cursed** shalt thou be
when thou comest in,
and cursed shalt thou be
when thou goest out.

20 **The LORD** shall send upon thee cursing, vexation, and rebuke, in all that thou settest thine hand unto for to do,
until thou be destroyed,
and until thou perish quickly;
because of the wickedness of thy doings,
whereby thou hast forsaken me.

21 **The LORD** shall make the pestilence cleave unto thee,
until he have consumed thee from off the land,
whither thou goest to possess it.

22 **The LORD** shall smite thee with a consumption, and with a fever, and with an inflammation, and with an extreme burning, and with the sword, and with blasting, and with mildew;
and they shall pursue thee
until thou perish.

23 **And thy heaven that is over thy head** shall be brass,
and the earth that is under thee shall be iron.

24 **The LORD** shall make the rain of thy land powder and dust:
from heaven shall it come down upon thee,
until thou be destroyed.

25 **The LORD** shall cause thee to be smitten before thine enemies:
thou shalt go out one way against them,
and flee seven ways before them:
and shalt be removed into all the kingdoms of the earth.

26 **And thy carcase** shall be meat unto all fowls of the air, and unto the beasts of the earth,
and no man shall fray them away.

27 **The LORD** will smite thee with the botch of Egypt, and with the emerods, and with the scab, and with the itch,
whereof thou canst not be healed.

28 **The LORD** shall smite thee with madness, and blindness, and astonishment of heart:

29 **And thou** shalt grope at noonday,
as the blind gropeth in darkness,
and thou shalt not prosper in thy ways:
and thou shalt be only oppressed and spoiled evermore,
and no man shall save thee.

30 **Thou** shalt betroth a wife,
and another man shall lie with her:
thou shalt build an house,
and thou shalt not dwell therein:
thou shalt plant a vineyard,
and shalt not gather the grapes thereof.

31 **Thine ox** shall be slain before thine eyes,
and thou shalt not eat thereof:
thine ass shall be violently taken away from before thy face,
and shall not be restored to thee:
thy sheep shall be given unto thine enemies,
and thou shalt have none to rescue them.

32 **Thy sons and thy daughters** shall be given unto another people,
and thine eyes shall look,
and fail with longing for them all the day long;
and there shall be no might in thine hand.

33 **The fruit of thy land, and all thy labours,** shall a nation which thou knowest not eat up;
and thou shalt be only oppressed and crushed alway:

34 **So that thou** shalt be mad for the sight of thine eyes which thou shalt see.

35 **The LORD** shall smite thee in the knees, and in the legs, with a sore botch that cannot be healed, from the sole of thy foot unto the top of thy head.

36 **The LORD** shall bring thee, and thy king which thou shalt set over thee, unto a nation which neither thou nor thy fathers have known;
and there shalt thou serve other gods, wood and stone.

37 **And thou** shalt become an astonishment, a proverb, and a byword, among all nations whither the LORD shall lead thee.

38 **Thou** shalt carry much seed out into the field,
and shalt gather but little in;
for the locust shall consume it.

39 **Thou** shalt plant vineyards,
and dress them,
but shalt neither drink of the wine,
nor gather the grapes;
for the worms shall eat them.

40 **Thou** shalt have olive trees throughout all thy coasts,
but thou shalt not anoint thyself with the oil;
for thine olive shall cast his fruit.

41 **Thou** shalt beget sons and daughters,
but thou shalt not enjoy them;
for they shall go into captivity.

42 **All thy trees and fruit of thy land** shall the locust consume.

43 **The stranger that is within thee** shall get up above thee very high;
and thou shalt come down very low.

44 **He** shall lend to thee,
and thou shalt not lend to him:
he shall be the head,
and thou shalt be the tail.

45 **Moreover all these curses** shall come upon thee,
and shall pursue thee,
and overtake thee,
till thou be destroyed;
because thou hearkenedst not unto the voice of the LORD thy God,
to keep his commandments and his statutes which he commanded thee:
46 **And they** shall be upon thee for a sign and for a wonder, and upon thy seed for ever.

47 **Because thou** servedst not the LORD thy God with joyfulness, and with gladness of heart, for the abundance of all things;
48 **Therefore** shalt thou serve thine enemies which the LORD shall send against thee, in hunger, and in thirst, and in nakedness, and in want of all things:
and he shall put a yoke of iron upon thy neck,
until he have destroyed thee.

49 **The LORD** shall bring a nation against thee from far, from the end of the earth,
as swift as the eagle flieth; a nation whose tongue thou shalt not understand;
50 A nation of fierce countenance,
which shall not regard the person of the old,
nor shew favour to the young:
51 **And he** shall eat the fruit of thy cattle, and the fruit of thy land,
until thou be destroyed:
which also shall not leave thee either corn, wine, or oil, or the increase of thy kine, or flocks of thy sheep,
until he have destroyed thee.

52 **And he** shall besiege thee in all thy gates,
until thy high and fenced walls come down,
wherein thou trustedst, throughout all thy land:
and he shall besiege thee in all thy gates throughout all thy land,
which the LORD thy God hath given thee.

53 **And thou** shalt eat the fruit of thine own body, the flesh of thy sons and of thy daughters,
which the LORD thy God hath given thee, in the siege, and in the straitness,
wherewith thine enemies shall distress thee:
54 **So that the man that is tender among you, and very delicate,** his eye shall be evil toward his brother, and toward the wife of his bosom, and toward the remnant of his children which he shall leave:
55 **So that he** will not give to any of them of the flesh of his children whom he shall eat:
because he hath nothing left him in the siege, and in the straitness,
wherewith thine enemies shall distress thee in all thy gates.

56 **The tender and delicate woman among you**, {which would not adventure to set the sole of her foot upon the ground for delicateness and tenderness}, her eye shall be evil toward the husband of her bosom, and toward her son, and toward her daughter,
57 And toward her young one that cometh out from between her feet, and toward her children which she shall bear:
for she shall eat them for want of all things secretly in the siege and straitness,
wherewith thine enemy shall distress thee in thy gates.

58 **If thou** wilt not observe to do all the words of this law that are written in this book,
that thou mayest fear this glorious and fearful name,
The LORD Thy God;
59 **Then the LORD** will make thy plagues wonderful, and the plagues of thy seed, even great plagues, and of long continuance, and sore sicknesses, and of long continuance.

60 **Moreover he** will bring upon thee all the diseases of Egypt,
which thou wast afraid of;
and they shall cleave unto thee.

61 **Also every sickness, and every plague**, {which is not written in the book of this law}, them will the LORD bring upon thee,
until thou be destroyed.

62 **And ye** shall be left few in number,
whereas ye were as the stars of heaven for multitude;
because thou wouldest not obey the voice of the LORD thy God.

63 **And it** shall come to pass,
that as the LORD rejoiced over you to do you good,
and to multiply you;
so the LORD will rejoice over you to destroy you,
and to bring you to nought;
and ye shall be plucked from off the land whither thou goest to possess it.

64 **And the LORD** shall scatter thee among all people, from the one end of the earth even unto the other;
and there thou shalt serve other gods,
which neither thou nor thy fathers have known, even wood and stone.

65 **And among these nations** shalt thou find no ease,
neither shall the sole of thy foot have rest:
but the LORD shall give thee there a trembling heart, and failing of eyes, and sorrow of mind:
66 **And thy life** shall hang in doubt before thee;
and thou shalt fear day and night,
and shalt have none assurance of thy life:
67 **In the morning** thou shalt say, {Would God it were even!}
and at even thou shalt say, {Would God it were morning!} for the fear of thine heart wherewith thou shalt fear, and for the sight of thine eyes which thou shalt see.

68 **And the LORD** shall bring thee into Egypt again with ships, by the way whereof I spake unto thee,
Thou shalt see it no more again:
and there ye shall be sold unto your enemies for bondmen and bondwomen,
and no man shall buy you.

29

These are the words of the covenant,
which the LORD commanded Moses to make with the children of Israel in the land of Moab, beside the covenant which he made with them in Horeb.
2 **And Moses** called unto all Israel,
and said unto them,
Ye have seen all that the LORD did before your eyes in the land of Egypt unto Pharaoh, and unto all his servants, and unto all his land;
3 The great temptations which thine eyes have seen, the signs, and those great miracles:
4 **Yet the LORD** hath not given you {an heart to perceive}, {and eyes to see}, {and ears to hear}, unto this day.
5 **And I** have led you forty years in the wilderness:
your clothes are not waxen old upon you,
and thy shoe is not waxen old upon thy foot.
6 **Ye** have not eaten bread,
neither have ye drunk wine or strong drink:
that ye might know
that I am the LORD your God.
7 **And when ye** came unto this place,
Sihon the king of Heshbon, and Og the king of Bashan, came out against us unto battle,
and we smote them:
8 **And we** took their land,
and gave it for an inheritance unto the Reubenites, and to the Gadites, and to the half tribe of Manasseh.
9 **Keep** therefore the words of this covenant,
and do them,
that ye may prosper in all that ye do.
10 **Ye** stand this day all of you before the LORD your God; your captains of your tribes, your elders, and your officers, with all the men of Israel,
11 Your little ones, your wives, and thy stranger that is in thy camp, from the hewer of thy wood unto the drawer of thy water:
12 **That thou** shouldest enter into covenant with the LORD thy God, and into his oath,
which the LORD thy God maketh with thee this day:
13 **That he** may establish thee to day for a people unto himself,
and that he may be unto thee a God,
as he hath said unto thee,
and as he hath sworn unto thy fathers, to Abraham, to Isaac, and to Jacob.
14 **Neither with you only** do I make this covenant and this oath;
15 But with him that standeth here with us this day before the LORD our God, and also with him that is not here with us this day:
16 (For ye know
how we have dwelt in the land of Egypt;
and how we came through the nations which ye passed by;
17 And ye have seen their abominations, and their idols, wood and stone, silver and gold,
which were among them:)
18 **Lest there** should be among you man, or woman, or family, or tribe,
whose heart turneth away this day from the LORD our God,
to go and serve the gods of these nations;
lest there should be among you a root that beareth gall and wormwood;
19 **And it** come to pass,
when he heareth the words of this curse,
that he bless himself in his heart,
saying,
I shall have peace,
though I walk in the imagination of mine heart,
to add drunkenness to thirst:
20 **The LORD** will not spare him,
but then the anger of the LORD and his jealousy shall smoke against that man,
and all the curses that are written in this book shall lie upon him,
and the LORD shall blot out his name from under heaven.
21 **And the LORD** shall separate him unto evil out of all the tribes of Israel, according to all the curses of the covenant that are written in this book of the law:
22 **So that the generation to come of your children that shall rise up after you, and the stranger that shall come from a far land,** shall say,
when they see the plagues of that land, and the sicknesses which the LORD hath laid upon it;
23 **And that the whole land thereof** is brimstone, and salt,
and burning,
that it is not sown,
nor beareth,
nor any grass groweth therein, like the overthrow of Sodom, and Gomorrah, Admah, and Zeboim,
which the LORD overthrew in his anger, and in his wrath:
24 **Even all nations** shall say,
Wherefore hath the LORD done thus unto this land?
what meaneth the heat of this great anger?
25 **Then men** shall say,
Because they have forsaken the covenant of the LORD God of their fathers,
which he made with them
when he brought them forth out of the land of Egypt:
26 **For they** went and served other gods,
and worshipped them, gods whom they knew not, and whom he had not given unto them:
27 **And the anger of the LORD** was kindled against this land,
to bring upon it all the curses that are written in this book:
28 **And the LORD** rooted them out of their land in anger, and in wrath, and in great indignation,
and cast them into another land,
as it is this day.
29 **The secret things** belong unto the LORD our God:
but those things which are revealed belong unto us and to our children for ever,
that we may do all the words of this law.

30

∞ **And it** shall come to pass,
when all these things are come upon thee, the blessing and the curse,
which I have set before thee,
and thou shalt call them to mind among all the nations,
whither the LORD thy God hath driven thee,
2 **And** shalt return unto the LORD thy God,

and shalt obey his voice according to all that I command thee this day, thou and thy children, with all thine heart, and with all thy soul;
3 **That then the LORD thy God** will turn thy captivity,
and have compassion upon thee,
and will return and gather thee from all the nations,
whither the LORD thy God hath scattered thee.
4 **If any of thine** be driven out unto the outmost parts of heaven,
from thence will the LORD thy God gather thee,
and from thence will he fetch thee:
5 **And the LORD thy God** will bring thee into the land which thy fathers possessed,
and thou shalt possess it;
and he will do thee good,
and multiply thee above thy fathers.
6 **And the LORD thy God** will circumcise thine heart, and the heart of thy seed,
to love the LORD thy God with all thine heart, and with all thy soul,
that thou mayest live.
7 **And the LORD thy God** will put all these curses upon thine enemies, and on them that hate thee, which persecuted thee.
8 **And thou** shalt return and obey the voice of the LORD,
and do all his commandments which I command thee this day.
9 **And the LORD thy God** will make thee plenteous in every work of thine hand, in the fruit of thy body, and in the fruit of thy cattle, and in the fruit of thy land, for good:
for the LORD will again rejoice over thee for good,
as he rejoiced over thy fathers:
10 **If thou** shalt hearken unto the voice of the LORD thy God,
to keep his commandments and his statutes which are written in this book of the law,
and if thou turn unto the LORD thy God with all thine heart, and with all thy soul.
11 **For this commandment which I command thee this day,** it is not hidden from thee,
neither is it far off.
12 **It** is not in heaven,
that thou shouldest say,
Who shall go up for us to heaven,
and bring it unto us,
that we may hear it,
and do it?
13 **Neither** is it beyond the sea,
that thou shouldest say,
Who shall go over the sea for us,
and bring it unto us,
that we may hear it,
and do it?
14 **But the word** is very nigh unto thee, in thy mouth, and in thy heart,
that thou mayest do it.
15 **See,**
I have set before thee this day life and good, and death and evil;
16 **In that I** command thee this day
to love the LORD thy God,
to walk in his ways,
and to keep his commandments and his statutes and his judgments,
that thou mayest live and multiply:
and the LORD thy God shall bless thee in the land whither thou goest to possess it.
17 **But if thine heart** turn away,
so that thou wilt not hear,
but shalt be drawn away,
and worship other gods,
and serve them;
18 **I** denounce unto you this day,
that ye shall surely perish,
and that ye shall not prolong your days upon the land,
whither thou passest over Jordan
to go to possess it.
19 **I** call heaven and earth to record this day against you,
that I have set before you life and death, blessing and cursing:
therefore choose life,
that both thou and thy seed may live:
20 **That thou** mayest love the LORD thy God,
and that thou mayest obey his voice,
and that thou mayest cleave unto him:
for he is thy life, and the length of thy days:
that thou mayest dwell in the land which the LORD sware unto thy fathers, to Abraham, to Isaac, and to Jacob,
to give them.

31

And Moses went and spake these words unto all Israel.
2 **And he** said unto them,
I am an hundred and twenty years old this day;
I can no more go out and come in:
also the LORD hath said unto me,
Thou shalt not go over this Jordan.
3 **The LORD thy God**, he will go over before thee,
and he will destroy these nations from before thee,
and thou shalt possess them:
and Joshua, he shall go over before thee,
as the LORD hath said.
4 **And the LORD** shall do unto them as he did to Sihon and to Og, kings of the Amorites, and unto the land of them,
whom he destroyed.
5 **And the LORD** shall give them up before your face,
that ye may do unto them according unto all the commandments which I have commanded you.
6 **Be** strong and of a good courage,
fear not,
nor be afraid of them:
for the LORD thy God, he it is that doth go with thee;
he will not fail thee,
nor forsake thee.
7 **And Moses** called unto Joshua,
and said unto him in the sight of all Israel,
Be strong and of a good courage:
for thou must go with this people unto the land which the LORD hath sworn unto their fathers to give them;
and thou shalt cause them to inherit it.
8 **And the LORD,** he it is that doth go before thee;
he will be with thee,
he will not fail thee,
neither forsake thee:
fear not,
neither be dismayed.
9 **And Moses** wrote this law,
and delivered it unto the priests the sons of Levi,
which bare the ark of the covenant of the LORD, and unto all the elders of Israel.
10 **And Moses** commanded them, saying,

At the end of every seven years, in the solemnity of the year of release, in the feast of tabernacles,
11 {When all Israel is come to appear before the LORD thy God in the place which he shall choose}, thou shalt read this law before all Israel in their hearing.
12 **Gather** the people together, men and women, and children, and thy stranger that is within thy gates,
that they may hear,
and that they may learn,
and fear the LORD your God,
and observe to do all the words of this law:
13 **And that their children**, {which have not known any thing}, may hear,
and learn to fear the LORD your God,
as long as ye live in the land whither ye go over Jordan to possess it.
14 **And the LORD** said unto Moses,
Behold,
thy days approach that thou must die:
call Joshua,
and present yourselves in the tabernacle of the congregation,
that I may give him a charge.
And Moses and Joshua went,
and presented themselves in the tabernacle of the congregation.
15 **And the LORD** appeared in the tabernacle in a pillar of a cloud:
and the pillar of the cloud stood over the door of the tabernacle.
16 **And the LORD** said unto Moses,
Behold,
thou shalt sleep with thy fathers;
and this people will rise up,
and go a whoring after the gods of the strangers of the land,
whither they go to be among them,
and will forsake me,
and break my covenant which I have made with them.
17 **Then my anger** shall be kindled against them in that day,
and I will forsake them,
and I will hide my face from them,
and they shall be devoured,
and many evils and troubles shall befall them;
so that they will say in that day,
Are not these evils come upon us,
because our God is not among us?
18 **And I** will surely hide my face in that day for all the evils which they shall have wrought,
in that they are turned unto other gods.
19 **Now therefore write ye** this song for you,
and teach it the children of Israel:
put it in their mouths,
that this song may be a witness for me against the children of Israel.
20 **For when I** shall have brought them into the land which I sware unto their fathers,
that floweth with milk and honey;
and they shall have eaten and filled themselves,
and waxen fat;
then will they turn unto other gods,
and serve them,
and provoke me,
and break my covenant.
21 **And it** shall come to pass,
when many evils and troubles are befallen them,
that this song shall testify against them as a witness;
for it shall not be forgotten out of the mouths of their seed:
for I know their imagination which they go about,
even now, before I have brought them into the land which I sware.
22 **Moses** therefore wrote this song the same day,
and taught it the children of Israel.
23 **And he** gave Joshua the son of Nun a charge,
and said,
Be strong and of a good courage:
for thou shalt bring the children of Israel into the land which I sware unto them:
and I will be with thee.
24 **And it** came to pass,
when Moses had made an end of writing the words of this law in a book,
until they were finished,
25 **That Moses** commanded the Levites,
which bare the ark of the covenant of the LORD,
saying,
26 **Take** this book of the law,
and put it in the side of the ark of the covenant of the LORD your God,
that it may be there for a witness against thee.
27 **For I** know thy rebellion, and thy stiff neck:
behold,
while I am yet alive with you this day,
ye have been rebellious against the LORD; and how much more after my death?
28 **Gather** unto me all the elders of your tribes, and your officers,
that I may speak these words in their ears,
and call heaven and earth to record against them.
29 **For I** know
that after my death ye will utterly corrupt yourselves,
and turn aside from the way which I have commanded you;
and evil will befall you in the latter days;
because ye will do evil in the sight of the LORD,
to provoke him to anger through the work of your hands.
30 **And Moses** spake in the ears of all the congregation of Israel the words of this song,
until they were ended.

32 **Give ear,** O ye heavens,
and I will speak;
and hear, O earth, the words of my mouth.
2 **My doctrine** shall drop as the rain,
my speech shall distil as the dew,
as the small rain upon the tender herb, and as the showers upon the grass:
3 **Because I** will publish the name of the LORD:
ascribe ye greatness unto our God.
4 **He** is the Rock,
his work is perfect:
for all his ways are judgment: a God of truth and without iniquity,
just and right is he.
5 **They** have corrupted themselves,
their spot is not the spot of his children:
they are a perverse and crooked generation.
6 **Do ye** thus requite the LORD, O foolish people and unwise?
is not he thy father that hath bought thee?
hath he not made thee,
and established thee?

7 **Remember** the days of old,
consider the years of many generations:
ask thy father, {and he will shew thee}; thy elders, {and they will tell thee}.

8 **When the Most High** divided to the nations their inheritance,
when he separated the sons of Adam,
he set the bounds of the people according to the number of the children of Israel.

9 **For the LORD's portion** is his people
Jacob is the lot of his inheritance.

10 **He** found him in a desert land, and in the waste howling wilderness;
he led him about,
he instructed him,
he kept him as the apple of his eye.

11 **As an eagle** stirreth up her nest,
fluttereth over her young,
spreadeth abroad her wings,
taketh them,
beareth them on her wings:
12 **So the LORD alone** did lead him,
and there was no strange god with him.

13 **He** made him ride on the high places of the earth,
that he might eat the increase of the fields;
and he made him to suck honey out of the rock, and oil out of the flinty rock;
14 Butter of kine, and milk of sheep, with fat of lambs, and rams of the breed of Bashan, and goats, with the fat of kidneys of wheat;
and thou didst drink the pure blood of the grape.

15 **But Jeshurun** waxed fat,
and kicked:
thou art waxen fat,
thou art grown thick,
thou art covered with fatness;
then he forsook God which made him,
and lightly esteemed the Rock of his salvation.

16 **They** provoked him to jealousy with strange gods,
with abominations provoked they him to anger.

17 **They** sacrificed unto devils, not to God; to gods whom they knew not, to new gods that came newly up,
whom your fathers feared not.

18 **Of the Rock that begat thee** thou art unmindful,
and hast forgotten God that formed thee.

19 **And when the LORD** saw it,
he abhorred them, because of the provoking of his sons, and of his daughters.

20 **And he** said,
I will hide my face from them,
I will see what their end shall be:
for they are a very froward generation, children in whom is no faith.

21 **They** have moved me to jealousy with that which is not God;
they have provoked me to anger with their vanities:
and I will move them to jealousy with those which are not a people;
I will provoke them to anger with a foolish nation.

22 **For a fire** is kindled in mine anger,
and shall burn unto the lowest hell,
and shall consume the earth with her increase,
and set on fire the foundations of the mountains.

23 I will heap mischiefs upon them;
I will spend mine arrows upon them.

24 **They** shall be burnt with hunger,
and devoured with burning heat, and with bitter destruction:
I will also send the teeth of beasts upon them, with the poison of serpents of the dust.

25 **The sword without, and terror within,** shall destroy both the young man and the virgin, the suckling also with the man of gray hairs.

26 I said,
I would scatter them into corners,
I would make the remembrance of them to cease from among men:
27 **Were it not that I** feared the wrath of the enemy,
lest their adversaries should behave themselves strangely,
and lest they should say,
Our hand is high,
and the LORD hath not done all this.

28 **For they** are a nation void of counsel,
neither is there any understanding in them.

29 **O that they** were wise,
that they understood this,
that they would consider their latter end!

30 **How** should one chase a thousand,
and two put ten thousand to flight,
except their Rock had sold them,
and the LORD had shut them up?

31 **For their rock** is not as our Rock,
even our enemies themselves being judges.

32 **For their vine** is of the vine of Sodom, and of the fields of Gomorrah:
their grapes are grapes of gall,
their clusters are bitter:
33 **Their wine** is the poison of dragons, and the cruel venom of asps.

34 **Is not this** laid up in store with me,
and sealed up among my treasures?

35 **To me** belongeth vengeance and recompence;
their foot shall slide in due time:
for the day of their calamity is at hand,
and the things that shall come upon them make haste.

36 **For the LORD** shall judge his people,
and repent himself for his servants,
when he seeth that their power is gone, and there is none shut up, or left.

37 **And he** shall say,
Where are their gods, their rock in whom they trusted,
38 **Which** did eat the fat of their sacrifices,
and drank the wine of their drink offerings?
let them rise up and help you,
and be your protection.

39 **See** now that I, even I, am he,
and there is no god with me:
I kill,
and I make alive;
I wound,
and I heal:
neither is there any that can deliver out of my hand.

40 **For I** lift up my hand to heaven,
and say,
I live for ever.

41 **If I** whet my glittering sword,

and mine hand take hold on
judgment;
I will render vengeance to mine
enemies,
and will reward them that hate me.
42 **I** will make mine arrows drunk
with blood,
and my sword shall devour flesh;
and that with the blood of the
slain and of the captives, from the
beginning of revenges upon the
enemy.
43 **Rejoice,** O ye nations, with his
people:
for he will avenge the blood of his
servants,
and will render vengeance to his
adversaries,
and will be merciful unto his land,
and to his people.
44 **And Moses** came and spake all
the words of this song in the ears
of the people, he, and Hoshea the
son of Nun.
45 **And Moses** made an end of
speaking all these words to all
Israel:
46 **And he** said unto them,
Set your hearts unto all the words
which I testify among you this
day,
which ye shall command your
children to observe to do, all the
words of this law.
47 **For it** is not a vain thing for you;
because it is your life:
and through this thing ye shall
prolong your days in the land,
whither ye go over Jordan to
possess it.
48 **And the LORD** spake unto Moses
that selfsame day,
saying,
49 **Get thee up** into this mountain
Abarim, unto mount Nebo,
which is in the land of Moab,
that is over against Jericho;
and behold the land of Canaan,
which I give unto the children of
Israel for a possession:
50 **And die** in the mount whither
thou goest up,
and be gathered unto thy people;
as Aaron thy brother died in
mount Hor,
and was gathered unto his people:
51 **Because ye** trespassed against me
among the children of Israel at
the waters of MeribahKadesh, in
the wilderness of Zin;
because ye sanctified me not in the
midst of the children of Israel.
52 **Yet thou** shalt see the land before
thee;
but thou shalt not go thither unto
the land which I give the children
of Israel.

33 **And this** is the blessing,
wherewith Moses the man
of God blessed the children of
Israel before his death.
2 **And he** said,
The LORD came from Sinai,
and rose up from Seir unto them;
he shined forth from mount Paran,
and he came with ten thousands of
saints:
from his right hand went a fiery
law for them.
3 **Yea, he** loved the people;
all his saints are in thy hand:
and they sat down at thy feet;
every one shall receive of thy
words.
4 **Moses** commanded us a law, even
the inheritance of the
congregation of Jacob.
5 **And he** was king in Jeshurun,
**when the heads of the people and
the tribes of Israel** were gathered
together.
6 **Let Reuben** live,
and not die;
and let not his men be few.
7 **And this** is the blessing of Judah:
and he said,
Hear, LORD, the voice of Judah,
and bring him unto his people:
let his hands be sufficient for him;
and be thou an help to him from
his enemies.
8 **And of Levi** he said,
Let thy Thummim and thy Urim
be with thy holy one,
whom thou didst prove at Massah,
and with whom thou didst strive
at the waters of Meribah;
9 **Who** said unto his father and to
his mother,
I have not seen him;
neither did he acknowledge his
brethren,
nor knew his own children:
for they have observed thy word,
and kept thy covenant.
10 **They** shall teach Jacob thy
judgments, and Israel thy law:
they shall put incense before thee,
and whole burnt sacrifice upon
thine altar.
11 **Bless,** LORD, his substance,
and accept the work of his hands;
smite through the loins of them
that rise against him, and of them
that hate him,
that they rise not again.
12 **And of Benjamin** he said,
The beloved of the LORD shall
dwell in safety by him;
and the LORD shall cover him all
the day long,
and he shall dwell between his
shoulders.
13 **And of Joseph** he said,
Blessed of the LORD be his land,
for the precious things of heaven,
for the dew, and for the deep that
coucheth beneath,
14 And for the precious fruits
brought forth by the sun, and for
the precious things put forth by
the moon,
15 And for the chief things of the
ancient mountains, and for the
precious things of the lasting
hills,
16 And for the precious things of the
earth and fulness thereof, and for
the good will of him that dwelt in
the bush:
let the blessing come upon the
head of Joseph, and upon the top
of the head of him that was
separated from his brethren.
17 **His glory** is like the firstling of his
bullock,
and his horns are like the horns of
unicorns:
with them he shall push the people
together to the ends of the earth:
and they are the ten thousands of
Ephraim,
and they are the thousands of
Manasseh.
18 **And of Zebulun** he said,
Rejoice, Zebulun, in thy going out;
and, Issachar, in thy tents.
19 **They** shall call the people unto
the mountain;
there they shall offer sacrifices of
righteousness:
for they shall suck of the
abundance of the seas, and of
treasures hid in the sand.
20 **And of Gad** he said,
Blessed be he that enlargeth Gad:
he dwelleth as a lion,
and teareth the arm with the crown
of the head.

21 **And he** provided the first part for himself,
because there, in a portion of the lawgiver, was he seated;
and he came with the heads of the people,
he executed the justice of the LORD, and his judgments with Israel.

22 **And of Dan** he said,
Dan is a lion's whelp:
he shall leap from Bashan.

23 **And of Naphtali** he said,
O Naphtali, satisfied with favour, and full with the blessing of the LORD: possess thou the west and the south.

24 **And of Asher** he said,
Let Asher be blessed with children;
let him be acceptable to his brethren,
and let him dip his foot in oil.

25 **Thy shoes** shall be iron and brass;
and as thy days, so shall thy strength be.

26 **There** is none like unto the God of Jeshurun,
who rideth upon the heaven in thy help, and in his excellency on the sky.

27 **The eternal God** is thy refuge,
and underneath are the everlasting arms:
and he shall thrust out the enemy from before thee;
and shall say,
Destroy them.

28 **Israel** then shall dwell in safety alone:
the fountain of Jacob shall be upon a land of corn and wine;
also his heavens shall drop down dew.

29 **Happy** art thou, O Israel:
who is like unto thee, O people saved by the LORD, the shield of thy help,
and who is the sword of thy excellency!
and thine enemies shall be found liars unto thee;
and thou shalt tread upon their high places.

34

And Moses went up from the plains of Moab unto the mountain of Nebo, to the top of Pisgah, that is over against Jericho.
And the LORD shewed him all the land of Gilead, unto Dan,
2 And all Naphtali, and the land of Ephraim, and Manasseh, and all the land of Judah, unto the utmost sea,
3 And the south, and the plain of the valley of Jericho, the city of palm trees, unto Zoar.

4 **And the LORD** said unto him,
This is the land which I sware unto Abraham, unto Isaac, and unto Jacob,
saying,
I will give it unto thy seed:
I have caused thee to see it with thine eyes,
but thou shalt not go over thither.

5 **So Moses the servant of the LORD** died there in the land of Moab, according to the word of the LORD.

6 **And he** buried him in a valley in the land of Moab, over against Bethpeor:
but no man knoweth of his sepulchre unto this day.

7 **And Moses** was an hundred and twenty years old when he died:
his eye was not dim,
nor his natural force abated.

8 **And the children of Israel** wept for Moses in the plains of Moab thirty days:
so the days of weeping and mourning for Moses were ended.

9 **And Joshua the son of Nun** was full of the spirit of wisdom;
for Moses had laid his hands upon him:
and the children of Israel hearkened unto him,
and did as the LORD commanded Moses.

10 **And there** arose not a prophet since in Israel like unto Moses,
whom the LORD knew face to face,
11 In all the signs and the wonders,
which the LORD sent him to do in the land of Egypt to Pharaoh, and to all his servants, and to all his land,
12 And in all that mighty hand, and in all the great terror which Moses shewed in the sight of all Israel.

Joshua

God, in His divine wisdom, anoints Joshua to guide the people into the Promised Land. The book unfolds with the Israelites crossing a flooded Jordan River on dry ground, a miraculous event reminiscent of the crossing of the Red Sea. Under Joshua's leadership, the Israelites then conquer the city of Jericho. They march around it for seven days, blowing trumpets and shouting, and witness the city walls collapse in another miraculous event.

Joshua then records the conquest of Canaan, highlighting the battles, alliances, and leadership decisions that culminate in victory and settlement in the land. These historical accounts are a powerful testament to God's unwavering faithfulness. They also attest to the reliability of His promises, as the battles are marked by divine intervention, with God actively aiding the Israelites in their conquests.

After the triumphant conquest of Canaan, Joshua divides the territories among the twelve tribes of Israel, assigning each tribe a portion of the land based on its population and needs. Israel's leader then gathers the people and solemnly renews the covenant between them and God. The Book of Joshua is a powerful reminder of God's unwavering faithfulness. It also emphasizes the Israelites' sacred obligations to follow His law, maintain their faith and obedience, and serve Him alone.

1 **Now after the death of Moses the servant of the LORD** it came to pass,
that the LORD spake unto Joshua the son of Nun, Moses' minister,
saying,
2 **Moses my servant** is dead;
now therefore arise,
go over this Jordan, thou, and all this people, unto the land which I do give to them, even to the children of Israel.
3 **Every place that the sole of your foot shall tread upon,** that have I given unto you,
as I said unto Moses.
4 **From the wilderness and this Lebanon even unto the great river, the river Euphrates, all the land of the Hittites, and unto the great sea toward the going down of the sun,** shall be your coast.
5 **There** shall not any man be able to stand before thee all the days of thy life:
as I was with Moses,
so I will be with thee:
I will not fail thee,
nor forsake thee.
6 **Be** strong and of a good courage:
for unto this people shalt thou divide for an inheritance the land,
which I sware unto their fathers to give them.
7 **Only be thou** strong and very courageous,
that thou mayest observe to do according to all the law,
which Moses my servant commanded thee:
turn not from it to the right hand or to the left,
that thou mayest prosper
withersoever thou goest.
8 **This book of the law** shall not depart out of thy mouth;
but thou shalt meditate therein day and night,
that thou mayest observe to do according to all that is written therein:
for then thou shalt make thy way prosperous,
and then thou shalt have good success.
9 **Have not I** commanded thee?
Be strong and of a good courage;
be not afraid,
neither be thou dismayed:
for the LORD thy God is with thee
whithersoever thou goest.
10 **Then Joshua** commanded the officers of the people,
saying,
11 **Pass through** the host,
and command the people,
saying,
Prepare you victuals;
for within three days ye shall pass over this Jordan,
to go in to possess the land,
which the LORD your God giveth you to possess it.
12 **And to the Reubenites, and to the Gadites, and to half the tribe of Manasseh,** spake Joshua,
saying,
13 **Remember** the word which Moses the servant of the LORD commanded you,
saying,
The LORD your God hath given you rest,
and hath given you this land.
14 **Your wives, your little ones, and your cattle,** shall remain in the land which Moses gave you on this side Jordan;
but ye shall pass before your brethren armed, all the mighty men of valour,
and help them;
15 **Until the LORD** have given your brethren rest,
as he hath given you,
and they also have possessed the land which the LORD your God giveth them:
then ye shall return unto the land of your possession,
and enjoy it,
which Moses the LORD's servant gave you on this side Jordan toward the sunrising.
16 **And they** answered Joshua,
saying,
All that thou commandest us we will do,
and whithersoever thou sendest us,
we will go.

17 **According as we** hearkened unto Moses in all things,
so will we hearken unto thee:
only the LORD thy God be with thee,
as he was with Moses.

18 **Whosoever he** be that doth rebel against thy commandment,
and will not hearken unto thy words in all that thou commandest him,
he shall be put to death:
only be strong and of a good courage.

2

And Joshua the son of Nun sent out of Shittim two men to spy secretly,
saying,
Go view the land, even Jericho.

And they went,
and came into an harlot's house, named Rahab,
and lodged there.

2 **And it** was told the king of Jericho,
saying,
Behold,
there came men in hither to night of the children of Israel
to search out the country.

3 **And the king of Jericho** sent unto Rahab,
saying,
Bring forth the men that are come to thee,
which are entered into thine house:
for they be come to search out all the country.

4 **And the woman** took the two men,
and hid them,
and said thus,
There came men unto me,
but I wist not
whence they were:

5 **And it** came to pass about the time of shutting of the gate,
when it was dark,
that the men went out:
whither the men went
I wot not:
pursue after them quickly;
for ye shall overtake them.

6 **But she** had brought them up to the roof of the house,
and hid them with the stalks of flax,
which she had laid in order upon the roof.

7 **And the men** pursued after them the way to Jordan unto the fords:
and as soon as they which pursued after them were gone out,
they shut the gate.

8 **And before they** were laid down,
she came up unto them upon the roof;

9 **And she** said unto the men,
I know
that the LORD hath given you the land,
and that your terror is fallen upon us,
and that all the inhabitants of the land faint because of you.

10 **For we** have heard how the LORD dried up the water of the Red sea for you,
when ye came out of Egypt;
and what ye did unto the two kings of the Amorites,
that were on the other side Jordan, Sihon and Og,
whom ye utterly destroyed.

11 **And as soon as we** had heard these things,
our hearts did melt,
neither did there remain any more courage in any man, because of you:
for the LORD your God, he is God in heaven above, and in earth beneath.

12 **Now therefore, {I pray you}, swear** unto me by the LORD,
since I have shewed you kindness,
that ye will also shew kindness unto my father's house,
and give me a true token:

13 **And that ye** will save alive my father, and my mother, and my brethren, and my sisters, and all that they have,
and deliver our lives from death.

14 **And the men** answered her,
Our life for yours,
if ye utter not this our business.

And it shall be,
when the LORD hath given us the land,
that we will deal kindly and truly with thee.

15 **Then she** let them down by a cord through the window:
for her house was upon the town wall,
and she dwelt upon the wall.

16 **And she** said unto them,
Get you to the mountain,
lest the pursuers meet you;
and hide yourselves there three days,
until the pursuers be returned:
and afterward may ye go your way.

17 **And the men** said unto her,
We will be blameless of this thine oath which thou hast made us swear.

18 **Behold,**
when we come into the land,
thou shalt bind this line of scarlet thread in the window which thou didst let us down by:
and thou shalt bring thy father, and thy mother, and thy brethren, and all thy father's household, home unto thee.

19 **And it** shall be,
that whosoever shall go out of the doors of thy house into the street,
his blood shall be upon his head,
and we will be guiltless:
and whosoever shall be with thee in the house,
his blood shall be on our head,
if any hand be upon him.

20 **And if thou** utter this our business,
then we will be quit of thine oath which thou hast made us to swear.

21 **And she** said,
According unto your words, so be it.

And she sent them away,
and they departed:
and she bound the scarlet line in the window.

22 **And they** went,
and came unto the mountain,
and abode there three days,
until the pursuers were returned:
and the pursuers sought them throughout all the way,
but found them not.

23 **So the two men** returned,
and descended from the mountain,
and passed over,
and came to Joshua the son of Nun,
and told him all things that befell them:

24 **And they** said unto Joshua,
Truly the LORD hath delivered into our hands all the land;
for even all the inhabitants of the country do faint because of us.

3

And Joshua rose early in the morning;
and they removed from Shittim,

and came to Jordan, he and all the children of Israel,
and lodged there
before they passed over.
2 **And it** came to pass after three days,
that the officers went through the host;
3 **And they** commanded the people, saying,
When ye see the ark of the covenant of the LORD your God,
and the priests the Levites bearing it,
then ye shall remove from your place,
and go after it.
4 **Yet there** shall be a space between you and it, about two thousand cubits by measure:
come not near unto it,
that ye may know the way by which ye must go:
for ye have not passed this way heretofore.
5 **And Joshua** said unto the people,
Sanctify yourselves:
for to morrow the LORD will do wonders among you.
6 **And Joshua** spake unto the priests, saying,
Take up the ark of the covenant,
and pass over before the people.
And they took up the ark of the covenant,
and went before the people.
7 **And the LORD** said unto Joshua,
This day will I begin to magnify thee in the sight of all Israel,
that they may know
that, {as I was with Moses}, so I will be with thee.
8 **And thou** shalt command the priests that bear the ark of the covenant,
saying,
When ye are come to the brink of the water of Jordan,
ye shall stand still in Jordan.
9 **And Joshua** said unto the children of Israel,
Come hither,
and hear the words of the LORD your God.
10 **And Joshua** said,
Hereby ye shall know
that the living God is among you,
and that he will without fail drive out from before you the Canaanites, and the Hittites, and the Hivites, and the Perizzites, and the Girgashites, and the Amorites, and the Jebusites.
11 **Behold,**
the ark of the covenant of the Lord of all the earth passeth over before you into Jordan.
12 **Now therefore take you** twelve men out of the tribes of Israel, out of every tribe a man.
13 **And it** shall come to pass,
as soon as the soles of the feet of the priests that bear the ark of the LORD, the Lord of all the earth, shall rest in the waters of Jordan,
that the waters of Jordan shall be cut off from the waters that come down from above;
and they shall stand upon an heap.
14 **And it** came to pass,
when the people removed from their tents,
to pass over Jordan, and the priests bearing the ark of the covenant before the people;
15 **And as they that bare the ark** were come unto Jordan,
and the feet of the priests that bare the ark were dipped in the brim of the water, (for Jordan overfloweth all his banks all the time of harvest,)
16 **That the waters which came down from above** stood and rose up upon an heap very far from the city Adam, that is beside Zaretan:
and those that came down toward the sea of the plain, even the salt sea, failed,
and were cut off:
and the people passed over right against Jericho.
17 **And the priests that bare the ark of the covenant of the LORD** stood firm on dry ground in the midst of Jordan,
and all the Israelites passed over on dry ground,
until all the people were passed clean over Jordan.

4 **And it** came to pass,
when all the people were clean passed over Jordan,
that the LORD spake unto Joshua, saying,
2 **Take you** twelve men out of the people, out of every tribe a man,
3 **And command ye** them,
saying,
Take you hence out of the midst of Jordan, out of the place where the priests' feet stood firm, twelve stones,
and ye shall carry them over with you,
and leave them in the lodging place,
where ye shall lodge this night.
4 **Then Joshua** called the twelve men,
whom he had prepared of the children of Israel, out of every tribe a man:
5 **And Joshua** said unto them,
Pass over before the ark of the LORD your God into the midst of Jordan,
and take you up every man of you a stone upon his shoulder, according unto the number of the tribes of the children of Israel:
6 **That this** may be a sign among you,
that when your children ask their fathers in time to come,
saying,
What mean ye by these stones?
7 **Then ye** shall answer them,
That the waters of Jordan were cut off before the ark of the covenant of the LORD;
when it passed over Jordan,
the waters of Jordan were cut off:
and these stones shall be for a memorial unto the children of Israel for ever.
8 **And the children of Israel** did so as Joshua commanded,
and took up twelve stones out of the midst of Jordan,
as the LORD spake unto Joshua, according to the number of the tribes of the children of Israel,
and carried them over with them unto the place where they lodged,
and laid them down there.
9 **And Joshua** set up twelve stones in the midst of Jordan, in the place where the feet of the priests which bare the ark of the covenant stood:
and they are there unto this day.
10 **For the priests which bare the ark** stood in the midst of Jordan,
until everything was finished that the LORD commanded Joshua to speak unto the people, according to all that Moses commanded Joshua:

and the people hasted and passed over.

11 **And it** came to pass,
when all the people were clean passed over,
that the ark of the LORD passed over, and the priests, in the presence of the people.

12 **And the children of Reuben, and the children of Gad, and half the tribe of Manasseh,** passed over armed before the children of Israel,
as Moses spake unto them:

13 **About forty thousand prepared for war** passed over before the LORD unto battle, to the plains of Jericho.

14 **On that day** the LORD magnified Joshua in the sight of all Israel;
and they feared him,
as they feared Moses, all the days of his life.

15 **And the LORD** spake unto Joshua,
saying,
16 **Command** the priests that bear the ark of the testimony,
that they come up out of Jordan.

17 **Joshua** therefore commanded the priests,
saying,
Come ye up out of Jordan.

18 **And it** came to pass,
when the priests that bare the ark of the covenant of the LORD were come up out of the midst of Jordan,
and the soles of the priests' feet were lifted up unto the dry land,
that the waters of Jordan returned unto their place,
and flowed over all his banks,
as they did before.

19 **And the people** came up out of Jordan on the tenth day of the first month,
and encamped in Gilgal, in the east border of Jericho.

20 **And those twelve stones**, {which they took out of Jordan}, did Joshua pitch in Gilgal.

21 **And he** spake unto the children of Israel,
saying,
When your children shall ask their fathers in time to come,
saying,
What mean these stones?

22 **Then ye** shall let your children know,
saying,
Israel came over this Jordan on dry land.

23 **For the LORD your God** dried up the waters of Jordan from before you,
until ye were passed over,
as the LORD your God did to the Red sea,
which he dried up from before us,
until we were gone over:
24 **That all the people of the earth** might know the hand of the LORD,
that it is mighty:
that ye might fear the LORD your God for ever.

5 **And it** came to pass,
when all the kings of the Amorites, {which were on the side of Jordan westward}, and all the kings of the Canaanites, {which were by the sea}, heard that the LORD had dried up the waters of Jordan from before the children of Israel,
until we were passed over,
that their heart melted,
neither was there spirit in them any more, because of the children of Israel.

2 **At that time** the LORD said unto Joshua,
Make thee sharp knives,
and circumcise again the children of Israel the second time.

3 **And Joshua** made him sharp knives,
and circumcised the children of Israel at the hill of the foreskins.

4 **And this** is the cause why Joshua did circumcise:
All the people that came out of Egypt, that were males, even all the men of war, died in the wilderness by the way,
after they came out of Egypt.

5 **Now all the people that came out** were circumcised:
but all the people that were born in the wilderness by the way as they came forth out of Egypt, them they had not circumcised.

6 **For the children of Israel** walked forty years in the wilderness,
till all the people that were men of war, {which came out of Egypt}, were consumed,
because they obeyed not the voice of the LORD:
unto whom the LORD sware
that he would not shew them the land,
which the LORD sware unto their fathers
that he would give us, a land that floweth with milk and honey.

7 **And their children**, {whom he raised up in their stead}, them Joshua circumcised:
for they were uncircumcised,
because they had not circumcised them by the way.

8 **And it** came to pass,
when they had done circumcising all the people,
that they abode in their places in the camp,
till they were whole.

9 **And the LORD** said unto Joshua,
This day have I rolled away the reproach of Egypt from off you.
Wherefore the name of the place is called Gilgal unto this day.

10 **And the children of Israel** encamped in Gilgal,
and kept the passover on the fourteenth day of the month at even in the plains of Jericho.

11 **And they** did eat of the old corn of the land on the morrow after the passover, unleavened cakes, and parched corn in the selfsame day.

12 **And the manna** ceased on the morrow after they had eaten of the old corn of the land;
neither had the children of Israel manna any more;
but they did eat of the fruit of the land of Canaan that year.

13 **And it** came to pass,
when Joshua was by Jericho,
that he lifted up his eyes and looked,
and, {behold}, there stood a man over against him with his sword drawn in his hand:
and Joshua went unto him,
and said unto him,
Art thou for us, or for our adversaries?

14 **And he** said,
Nay;
but as captain of the host of the LORD am I now come.
And Joshua fell on his face to the earth,

and did worship,
and said unto him,
What saith my LORD unto his servant?

15 **And the captain of the LORD's host** said unto Joshua,
Loose thy shoe from off thy foot;
for the place whereon thou standest is holy.

And Joshua did so.

6 **Now Jericho** was straitly shut up because of the children of Israel:
none went out,
and none came in.

2 **And the LORD** said unto Joshua,
See,
I have given into thine hand Jericho, and the king thereof, and the mighty men of valour.

3 **And ye** shall compass the city, all ye men of war,
and go round about the city once.

Thus shalt thou do six days.

4 **And seven priests** shall bear before the ark seven trumpets of rams' horns:
and the seventh day ye shall compass the city seven times,
and the priests shall blow with the trumpets.

5 **And it** shall come to pass,
that when they make a long blast with the ram's horn,
and when ye hear the sound of the trumpet,
all the people shall shout with a great shout;
and the wall of the city shall fall down flat,
and the people shall ascend up every man straight before him.

6 **And Joshua the son of Nun** called the priests,
and said unto them,
Take up the ark of the covenant,
and let seven priests bear seven trumpets of rams' horns before the ark of the LORD.

7 **And he** said unto the people,
Pass on,
and compass the city,
and let him that is armed pass on before the ark of the LORD.

8 **And it** came to pass,
when Joshua had spoken unto the people,
that the seven priests bearing the seven trumpets of rams' horns passed on before the LORD,
and blew with the trumpets:
and the ark of the covenant of the LORD followed them.

9 **And the armed men** went before the priests that blew with the trumpets,
and the rereward came after the ark,
the priests going on,
and blowing with the trumpets.

10 **And Joshua** had commanded the people,
saying,
Ye shall not shout,
nor make any noise with your voice,
neither shall any word proceed out of your mouth,
until the day I bid you shout;
then shall ye shout.

11 **So the ark of the LORD** compassed the city,
going about it once:
and they came into the camp,
and lodged in the camp.

12 **And Joshua** rose early in the morning,
and the priests took up the ark of the LORD.

13 **And seven priests bearing seven trumpets of rams' horns before the ark of the LORD** went on continually,
and blew with the trumpets:
and the armed men went before them;
but the rereward came after the ark of the LORD,
the priests going on,
and blowing with the trumpets.

14 **And the second day** they compassed the city once,
and returned into the camp:
so they did six days.

15 **And it** came to pass on the seventh day,
that they rose early about the dawning of the day,
and compassed the city after the same manner seven times:
only on that day they compassed the city seven times.

16 **And it** came to pass at the seventh time,
when the priests blew with the trumpets,
Joshua said unto the people,
Shout;
for the LORD hath given you the city.

17 **And the city** shall be accursed, even it, and all that are therein, to the LORD:
only Rahab the harlot shall live, she and all that are with her in the house,
because she hid the messengers that we sent.

18 **And ye, in any wise** keep yourselves from the accursed thing,
lest ye make yourselves accursed,
when ye take of the accursed thing,
and make the camp of Israel a curse,
and trouble it.

19 **But all the silver, and gold, and vessels of brass and iron,** are consecrated unto the LORD:
they shall come into the treasury of the LORD.

20 **So the people** shouted
when the priests blew with the trumpets:
and it came to pass,
when the people heard the sound of the trumpet,
and the people shouted with a great shout,
that the wall fell down flat,
so that the people went up into the city, every man straight before him,
and they took the city.

21 **And they** utterly destroyed all that was in the city, both man and woman, young and old, and ox, and sheep, and ass, with the edge of the sword.

22 **But Joshua** had said unto the two men that had spied out the country,
Go into the harlot's house,
and bring out thence the woman, and all that she hath,
as ye sware unto her.

23 **And the young men that were spies** went in,
and brought out Rahab, and her father, and her mother, and her brethren, and all that she had;
and they brought out all her kindred,
and left them without the camp of Israel.

24 **And they** burnt the city with fire, and all that was therein:
only the silver, and the gold, and the vessels of brass and of iron,

they put into the treasury of the house of the LORD.

25 **And Joshua** saved Rahab the harlot alive, and her father's household, and all that she had;
and she dwelleth in Israel even unto this day;
because she hid the messengers,
which Joshua sent to spy out Jericho.

26 **And Joshua** adjured them at that time,
saying,
Cursed be the man before the LORD,
that riseth up and buildeth this city Jericho:
he shall lay the foundation thereof in his firstborn,
and in his youngest son shall he set up the gates of it.

27 **So the LORD** was with Joshua;
and his fame was noised throughout all the country.

7 **But the children of Israel** committed a trespass in the accursed thing:
for Achan, the son of Carmi, the son of Zabdi, the son of Zerah, of the tribe of Judah, took of the accursed thing:
and the anger of the LORD was kindled against the children of Israel.

2 **And Joshua** sent men from Jericho to Ai,
which is beside Bethaven, on the east of Bethel,
and spake unto them,
saying,
Go up and view the country.
And the men went up and viewed Ai.

3 **And they** returned to Joshua,
and said unto him,
Let not all the people go up;
but let about two or three thousand men go up and smite Ai;
and make not all the people to labour thither;
for they are but few.

4 **So there** went up thither of the people about three thousand men:
and they fled before the men of Ai.

5 **And the men of Ai** smote of them about thirty and six men:
for they chased them from before the gate even unto Shebarim,
and smote them in the going down:
wherefore the hearts of the people melted,
and became as water.

6 **And Joshua** rent his clothes,
and fell to the earth upon his face before the ark of the LORD until the eventide, he and the elders of Israel,
and put dust upon their heads.

7 **And Joshua** said,
Alas, O Lord GOD, wherefore hast thou at all brought this people over Jordan,
to deliver us into the hand of the Amorites,
to destroy us?
would to God we had been content,
and dwelt on the other side Jordan!

8 **O Lord, what** shall I say,
when Israel turneth their backs before their enemies!

9 **For the Canaanites and all the inhabitants of the land** shall hear of it,
and shall environ us round,
and cut off our name from the earth:
and what wilt thou do unto thy great name?

10 **And the LORD** said unto Joshua,
Get thee up;
wherefore liest thou thus upon thy face?

11 **Israel** hath sinned,
and they have also transgressed my covenant which I commanded them:
for they have even taken of the accursed thing,
and have also stolen,
and dissembled also,
and they have put it even among their own stuff.

12 **Therefore the children of Israel** could not stand before their enemies,
but turned their backs before their enemies,
because they were accursed:
neither will I be with you any more,
except ye destroy the accursed from among you.

13 **Up,**
sanctify the people,
and say,
Sanctify yourselves against to morrow:
for thus saith the LORD God of Israel,
There is an accursed thing in the midst of thee, O Israel:
thou canst not stand before thine enemies,
until ye take away the accursed thing from among you.

14 **In the morning** therefore ye shall be brought according to your tribes:
and it shall be,
that the tribe which the LORD taketh shall come according to the families thereof;
and the family which the LORD shall take shall come by households;
and the household which the LORD shall take shall come man by man.

15 **And it** shall be, that he that is taken with the accursed thing shall be burnt with fire, he and all that he hath:
because he hath transgressed the covenant of the LORD,
and because he hath wrought folly in Israel.

16 **So Joshua** rose up early in the morning,
and brought Israel by their tribes;
and the tribe of Judah was taken:
17 **And he** brought the family of Judah;
and he took the family of the Zarhites:
and he brought the family of the Zarhites man by man;
and Zabdi was taken:
18 **And he** brought his household man by man;
and Achan, the son of Carmi, the son of Zabdi, the son of Zerah, of the tribe of Judah, was taken.

19 **And Joshua** said unto Achan,
My son, give, {I pray thee}, glory to the LORD God of Israel,
and make confession unto him;
and tell me now
what thou hast done;
hide it not from me.

20 **And Achan** answered Joshua,
and said,
Indeed I have sinned against the LORD God of Israel,
and thus and thus have I done:

21 **When I** saw among the spoils a goodly Babylonish garment, and two hundred shekels of silver, and a wedge of gold of fifty shekels weight,
then I coveted them,
and took them;
and, {behold}, they are hid in the earth in the midst of my tent, and the silver under it.

22 **So Joshua** sent messengers
and they ran unto the tent;
and, {behold}, it was hid in his tent, and the silver under it.

23 **And they** took them out of the midst of the tent,
and brought them unto Joshua, and unto all the children of Israel,
and laid them out before the LORD.

24 **And Joshua, and all Israel with him,** took Achan the son of Zerah, and the silver, and the garment, and the wedge of gold, and his sons, and his daughters, and his oxen, and his asses, and his sheep, and his tent, and all that he had:
and they brought them unto the valley of Achor.

25 **And Joshua** said,
Why hast thou troubled us?
the LORD shall trouble thee this day.

And all Israel stoned him with stones,
and burned them with fire,
after they had stoned them with stones.

26 **And they** raised over him a great heap of stones unto this day.

So the LORD turned from the fierceness of his anger.

Wherefore the name of that place was called, The valley of Achor, unto this day.

8 **And the LORD** said unto Joshua,
Fear not,
neither be thou dismayed:
take all the people of war with thee,
and arise,
go up to Ai:
see,
I have given into thy hand the king of Ai, and his people, and his city, and his land:

2 **And thou** shalt do to Ai and her king as thou didst unto Jericho and her king:
only the spoil thereof, and the cattle thereof, shall ye take for a prey unto yourselves:
lay thee an ambush for the city behind it.

3 **So Joshua** arose, and all the people of war,
to go up against Ai:
and Joshua chose out thirty thousand mighty men of valour,
and sent them away by night.

4 **And he** commanded them, saying,
Behold,
ye shall lie in wait against the city, even behind the city:
go not very far from the city,
but be ye all ready:

5 **And I, and all the people that are with me,** will approach unto the city:
and it shall come to pass,
when they come out against us, as at the first,
that we will flee before them,

6 (For they will come out after us)
till we have drawn them from the city;
for they will say,
They flee before us, as at the first:
therefore we will flee before them.

7 **Then ye** shall rise up from the ambush,
and seize upon the city:
for the LORD your God will deliver it into your hand.

8 **And it** shall be,
when ye have taken the city,
that ye shall set the city on fire:
according to the commandment of the LORD shall ye do.

See,
I have commanded you.

9 **Joshua** therefore sent them forth:
and they went to lie in ambush,
and abode between Bethel and Ai, on the west side of Ai:
but Joshua lodged that night among the people.

10 **And Joshua** rose up early in the morning,
and numbered the people,
and went up, he and the elders of Israel, before the people to Ai.

11 **And all the people, even the people of war that were with him,** went up,
and drew nigh,
and came before the city,
and pitched on the north side of Ai:
now there was a valley between them and Ai.

12 **And he** took about five thousand men,
and set them to lie in ambush between Bethel and Ai, on the west side of the city.

13 **And when they** had set the people, even all the host that was on the north of the city, and their liers in wait on the west of the city,
Joshua went that night into the midst of the valley.

14 **And it** came to pass,
when the king of Ai saw it,
that they hasted and rose up early,
and the men of the city went out against Israel to battle, he and all his people, at a time appointed, before the plain;
but he wist not
that there were liers in ambush against him behind the city.

15 **And Joshua and all Israel** made as if they were beaten before them,
and fled by the way of the wilderness.

16 **And all the people that were in Ai** were called together to pursue after them:
and they pursued after Joshua,
and were drawn away from the city.

17 **And there** was not a man left in Ai or Bethel,
that went not out after Israel:
and they left the city open,
and pursued after Israel.

18 **And the LORD** said unto Joshua,
Stretch out the spear that is in thy hand toward Ai;
for I will give it into thine hand.

And Joshua stretched out the spear that he had in his hand toward the city.

19 **And the ambush** arose quickly out of their place,
and they ran as soon as he had stretched out his hand:
and they entered into the city,
and took it,
and hasted and set the city on fire.

20 **And when the men of Ai** looked behind them,
they saw,
and, {behold}, the smoke of the city ascended up to heaven,

and they had no power to flee this way or that way:
and the people that fled to the wilderness turned back upon the pursuers.

21 **And when Joshua and all Israel** saw that the ambush had taken the city,
and that the smoke of the city ascended
then they turned again,
and slew the men of Ai.

22 **And the other** issued out of the city against them;
so they were in the midst of Israel, some on this side, and some on that side:
and they smote them,
so that they let none of them remain or escape.

23 **And the king of Ai** they took alive,
and brought him to Joshua.

24 **And it** came to pass,
when Israel had made an end of slaying all the inhabitants of Ai in the field, in the wilderness wherein they chased them,
and when they were all fallen on the edge of the sword,
until they were consumed,
that all the Israelites returned unto Ai,
and smote it with the edge of the sword.

25 **And so it** was,
that all that fell that day, both of men and women, were twelve thousand, even all the men of Ai.

26 **For Joshua** drew not his hand back,
wherewith he stretched out the spear,
until he had utterly destroyed all the inhabitants of Ai.

27 **Only the cattle and the spoil of that city** Israel took for a prey unto themselves, according unto the word of the LORD which he commanded Joshua.

28 **And Joshua** burnt Ai,
and made it an heap for ever, even a desolation unto this day.

29 **And the king of Ai** he hanged on a tree until eventide:
and as soon as the sun was down,
Joshua commanded
that they should take his carcase down from the tree,
and cast it at the entering of the gate of the city,
and raise thereon a great heap of stones, that remaineth unto this day.

30 **Then Joshua** built an altar unto the LORD God of Israel in mount Ebal,

31 **As Moses the servant of the LORD** commanded the children of Israel,
as it is written in the book of the law of Moses, an altar of whole stones,
over which no man hath lift up any iron
and they offered thereon burnt offerings unto the LORD,
and sacrificed peace offerings.

32 **And he** wrote there upon the stones a copy of the law of Moses,
which he wrote in the presence of the children of Israel.

33 **And all Israel, and their elders, and officers, and their judges,** stood on this side the ark and on that side before the priests the Levites,
which bare the ark of the covenant of the LORD, as well the stranger, as he that was born among them; half of them over against mount Gerizim, and half of them over against mount Ebal;
as Moses the servant of the LORD had commanded before,
that they should bless the people of Israel.

34 **And afterward** he read all the words of the law, the blessings and cursings, according to all that is written in the book of the law.

35 **There** was not a word of all that Moses commanded,
which Joshua read not before all the congregation of Israel, with the women, and the little ones, and the strangers that were conversant among them.

9

And it came to pass,
when all the kings which were on this side Jordan, in the hills, and in the valleys, and in all the coasts of the great sea over against Lebanon, the Hittite, and the Amorite, the Canaanite, the Perizzite, the Hivite, and the Jebusite, heard thereof;

2 **That they** gathered themselves together,
to fight with Joshua and with Israel, with one accord.

3 **And when the inhabitants of Gibeon** heard what Joshua had done unto Jericho and to Ai,
4 **They** did work wilily,
and went and made as if they had been ambassadors,
and took old sacks upon their asses, and wine bottles, old, and rent, and bound up;
5 And old shoes and clouted upon their feet, and old garments upon them;
and all the bread of their provision was dry and mouldy.

6 **And they** went to Joshua unto the camp at Gilgal,
and said unto him, and to the men of Israel,
We be come from a far country:
now therefore make ye a league with us.

7 **And the men of Israel** said unto the Hivites,
Peradventure ye dwell among us;
and how shall we make a league with you?

8 **And they** said unto Joshua,
We are thy servants.

And Joshua said unto them,
Who are ye?
and from whence come ye?

9 **And they** said unto him,
From a very far country thy servants are come because of the name of the LORD thy God:
for we have heard the fame of him, and all that he did in Egypt,
10 And all that he did to the two kings of the Amorites, {that were beyond Jordan}, to Sihon king of Heshbon, and to Og king of Bashan, {which was at Ashtaroth}.

11 **Wherefore our elders and all the inhabitants of our country** spake to us,
saying,
Take victuals with you for the journey,
and go to meet them,
and say unto them,
We are your servants:
therefore now make ye a league with us.

12 **This our bread** we took hot for our provision out of our houses

on the day we came forth to go unto you;
but now, {behold}, it is dry,
and it is mouldy:
13 **And these bottles of wine,** {which we filled}, were new;
and, {behold}, they be rent:
and these our garments and our shoes are become old by reason of the very long journey.

14 **And the men** took of their victuals,
and asked not counsel at the mouth of the LORD.

15 **And Joshua** made peace with them,
and made a league with them,
to let them live:
and the princes of the congregation sware unto them.

16 **And it** came to pass at the end of three days after they had made a league with them,
that they heard that they were their neighbours, and that they dwelt among them.

17 **And the children of Israel** journeyed,
and came unto their cities on the third day.
Now their cities were Gibeon, and Chephirah, and Beeroth, and Kirjathjearim.

18 **And the children of Israel** smote them not,
because the princes of the congregation had sworn unto them by the LORD God of Israel.
And all the congregation murmured against the princes.

19 **But all the princes** said unto all the congregation,
We have sworn unto them by the LORD God of Israel:
now therefore we may not touch them.

20 **This** we will do to them;
we will even let them live,
lest wrath be upon us, because of the oath which we sware unto them.

21 **And the princes** said unto them,
Let them live;
but let them be hewers of wood and drawers of water unto all the congregation;
as the princes had promised them.

22 **And Joshua** called for them,
and he spake unto them,
saying,
Wherefore have ye beguiled us,
saying,
We are very far from you;
when ye dwell among us?

23 **Now therefore ye** are cursed,
and there shall none of you be freed from being bondmen, and hewers of wood and drawers of water for the house of my God.

24 **And they** answered Joshua,
and said,
Because it was certainly told thy servants,
how that the LORD thy God commanded his servant Moses
to give you all the land,
and to destroy all the inhabitants of the land from before you,
therefore we were sore afraid of our lives because of you,
and have done this thing.

25 **And now, {behold}, we** are in thine hand:
as it seemeth good and right unto thee to do unto us,
do.

26 **And so** did he unto them,
and delivered them out of the hand of the children of Israel,
that they slew them not.

27 **And Joshua** made them that day hewers of wood and drawers of water for the congregation, and for the altar of the LORD, even unto this day, in the place which he should choose.

10

Now it came to pass,
when Adonizedec king of Jerusalem had heard how Joshua had taken Ai,
and had utterly destroyed it;
as he had done to Jericho and her king,
so he had done to Ai and her king;
and how the inhabitants of Gibeon had made peace with Israel,
and were among them;
2 **That they** feared greatly,
because Gibeon was a great city, as one of the royal cities,
and because it was greater than Ai,
and all the men thereof were mighty.

3 **Wherefore Adonizedec king of Jerusalem,** sent unto Hoham king of Hebron, and unto Piram king of Jarmuth, and unto Japhia king of Lachish, and unto Debir king of Eglon,
saying,
4 **Come up** unto me,
and help me,
that we may smite Gibeon:
for it hath made peace with Joshua and with the children of Israel.

5 **Therefore the five kings of the Amorites, the king of Jerusalem, the king of Hebron, the king of Jarmuth, the king of Lachish, the king of Eglon,** gathered themselves together,
and went up, they and all their hosts,
and encamped before Gibeon,
and made war against it.

6 **And the men of Gibeon** sent unto Joshua to the camp to Gilgal,
saying,
Slack not thy hand from thy servants;
come up to us quickly,
and save us,
and help us:
for all the kings of the Amorites that dwell in the mountains are gathered together against us.

7 **So Joshua** ascended from Gilgal, he, and all the people of war with him, and all the mighty men of valour.

8 **And the LORD** said unto Joshua,
Fear them not:
for I have delivered them into thine hand;
there shall not a man of them stand before thee.

9 **Joshua** therefore came unto them suddenly,
and went up from Gilgal all night.

10 **And the LORD** discomfited them before Israel,
and slew them with a great slaughter at Gibeon,
and chased them along the way that goeth up to Bethhoron,
and smote them to Azekah, and unto Makkedah.

11 **And it** came to pass,
as they fled from before Israel,
and were in the going down to Bethhoron,
that the LORD cast down great stones from heaven upon them unto Azekah,
and they died:
they were more which died with hailstones than they whom the

children of Israel slew with the sword.
12 **Then** spake Joshua to the LORD in the day when the LORD delivered up the Amorites before the children of Israel,
and he said in the sight of Israel,
Sun, stand thou still upon Gibeon; and thou, Moon, in the valley of Ajalon.
13 **And the sun** stood still,
and the moon stayed,
until the people had avenged themselves upon their enemies.
Is not this written in the book of Jasher?
So the sun stood still in the midst of heaven,
and hasted not to go down about a whole day.
14 **And there** was no day like that before it or after it,
that the LORD hearkened unto the voice of a man:
for the LORD fought for Israel.
15 **And Joshua** returned, and all Israel with him, unto the camp to Gilgal.
16 **But these five kings** fled,
and hid themselves in a cave at Makkedah.
17 **And it** was told Joshua,
saying,
The five kings are found hid in a cave at Makkedah.
18 **And Joshua** said,
Roll great stones upon the mouth of the cave,
and set men by it
for to keep them:
19 **And stay ye not,**
but pursue after your enemies,
and smite the hindmost of them;
suffer them not to enter into their cities:
for the LORD your God hath delivered them into your hand.
20 **And it** came to pass,
when Joshua and the children of Israel had made an end of slaying them with a very great slaughter,
till they were consumed,
that the rest which remained of them entered into fenced cities.
21 **And all the people** returned to the camp to Joshua at Makkedah in peace:
none moved his tongue against any of the children of Israel.
22 **Then** said Joshua,
Open the mouth of the cave,
and bring out those five kings unto me out of the cave.
23 **And they** did so,
and brought forth those five kings unto him out of the cave, the king of Jerusalem, the king of Hebron, the king of Jarmuth, the king of Lachish, and the king of Eglon.
24 **And it** came to pass,
when they brought out those kings unto Joshua,
that Joshua called for all the men of Israel,
and said unto the captains of the men of war which went with him,
Come near,
put your feet upon the necks of these kings.
And they came near,
and put their feet upon the necks of them.
25 **And Joshua** said unto them,
Fear not,
nor be dismayed,
be strong and of good courage:
for thus shall the LORD do to all your enemies against whom ye fight.
26 **And afterward** Joshua smote them,
and slew them,
and hanged them on five trees:
and they were hanging upon the trees until the evening.
27 **And it** came to pass at the time of the going down of the sun,
that Joshua commanded,
and they took them down off the trees,
and cast them into the cave wherein they had been hid,
and laid great stones in the cave's mouth,
which remain until this very day.
28 **And that day** Joshua took Makkedah,
and smote it with the edge of the sword,
and the king thereof he utterly destroyed, them, and all the souls that were therein;
he let none remain:
and he did to the king of Makkedah as he did unto the king of Jericho.
29 **Then Joshua** passed from Makkedah, and all Israel with him, unto Libnah,
and fought against Libnah:
30 **And the LORD** delivered it also, and the king thereof, into the hand of Israel;
and he smote it with the edge of the sword, and all the souls that were therein;
he let none remain in it;
but did unto the king thereof as he did unto the king of Jericho.
31 **And Joshua** passed from Libnah, and all Israel with him, unto Lachish,
and encamped against it,
and fought against it:
32 **And the LORD** delivered Lachish into the hand of Israel,
which took it on the second day,
and smote it with the edge of the sword, and all the souls that were therein, according to all that he had done to Libnah.
33 **Then Horam king of Gezer** came up to help Lachish;
and Joshua smote him and his people,
until he had left him none remaining.
34 **And from Lachish** Joshua passed unto Eglon, and all Israel with him;
and they encamped against it,
and fought against it:
35 **And they** took it on that day,
and smote it with the edge of the sword,
and all the souls that were therein he utterly destroyed that day, according to all that he had done to Lachish.
36 **And Joshua** went up from Eglon, and all Israel with him, unto Hebron;
and they fought against it:
37 **And they** took it,
and smote it with the edge of the sword, and the king thereof, and all the cities thereof, and all the souls that were therein;
he left none remaining, according to all that he had done to Eglon;
but destroyed it utterly, and all the souls that were therein.
38 **And Joshua** returned, and all Israel with him, to Debir;
and fought against it:
39 **And he** took it, and the king thereof, and all the cities thereof;
and they smote them with the edge of the sword,

and utterly destroyed all the souls that were therein;
he left none remaining:
as he had done to Hebron,
so he did to Debir, and to the king thereof;
as he had done also to Libnah, and to her king.
40 **So Joshua** smote all the country of the hills, and of the south, and of the vale, and of the springs, and all their kings:
he left none remaining,
but utterly destroyed all that breathed,
as the LORD God of Israel commanded.
41 **And Joshua** smote them from Kadeshbarnea even unto Gaza, and all the country of Goshen, even unto Gibeon.
42 **And all these kings and their land** did Joshua take at one time,
because the LORD God of Israel fought for Israel.
43 **And Joshua** returned, and all Israel with him, unto the camp to Gilgal.

11 **And it** came to pass,
when Jabin king of Hazor had heard those things,
that he sent to Jobab king of Madon, and to the king of Shimron, and to the king of Achshaph,
2 And to the kings that were on the north of the mountains, and of the plains south of Chinneroth, and in the valley, and in the borders of Dor on the west,
3 And to the Canaanite on the east and on the west, and to the Amorite, and the Hittite, and the Perizzite, and the Jebusite in the mountains, and to the Hivite under Hermon in the land of Mizpeh.
4 **And they** went out, they and all their hosts with them, much people, even as the sand that is upon the sea shore in multitude, with horses and chariots very many.
5 **And when all these kings** were met together,
they came and pitched together at the waters of Merom,
to fight against Israel.
6 **And the LORD** said unto Joshua,
Be not afraid because of them:
for to morrow about this time will I deliver them up all slain before Israel:
thou shalt hough their horses,
and burn their chariots with fire.
7 **So Joshua** came, and all the people of war with him, against them by the waters of Merom suddenly;
and they fell upon them.
8 **And the LORD** delivered them into the hand of Israel,
who smote them,
and chased them unto great Zidon, and unto Misrephothmaim, and unto the valley of Mizpeh eastward;
and they smote them,
until they left them none remaining.
9 **And Joshua** did unto them
as the LORD bade him:
he houghed their horses,
and burnt their chariots with fire.
10 **And Joshua at that time** turned back,
and took Hazor,
and smote the king thereof with the sword:
for Hazor beforetime was the head of all those kingdoms.
11 **And they** smote all the souls that were therein with the edge of the sword,
utterly destroying them:
there was not any left to breathe:
and he burnt Hazor with fire.
12 **And all the cities of those kings, and all the kings of them,** did Joshua take,
and smote them with the edge of the sword,
and he utterly destroyed them,
as Moses the servant of the LORD commanded.
13 **But as for the cities that stood still in their strength,** Israel burned none of them, save Hazor only;
that did Joshua burn.
14 **And all the spoil of these cities, and the cattle,** the children of Israel took for a prey unto themselves;
but every man they smote with the edge of the sword,
until they had destroyed them,
neither left they any to breathe.
15 **As the LORD** commanded Moses his servant,
so did Moses command Joshua,
and so did Joshua;
he left nothing undone of all that the LORD commanded Moses.
16 **So Joshua** took all that land, the hills, and all the south country, and all the land of Goshen, and the valley, and the plain, and the mountain of Israel, and the valley of the same;
17 Even from the mount Halak, {that goeth up to Seir}, even unto Baalgad in the valley of Lebanon under mount Hermon:
and all their kings he took,
and smote them,
and slew them.
18 **Joshua** made war a long time with all those kings.
19 **There** was not a city that made peace with the children of Israel, save the Hivites the inhabitants of Gibeon:
all other they took in battle.
20 **For it was of the LORD** to harden their hearts,
that they should come against Israel in battle,
that he might destroy them utterly,
and that they might have no favour,
but that he might destroy them,
as the LORD commanded Moses.
21 **And at that time** came Joshua,
and cut off the Anakims from the mountains, from Hebron, from Debir, from Anab, and from all the mountains of Judah, and from all the mountains of Israel:
Joshua destroyed them utterly with their cities.
22 **There** was none of the Anakims left in the land of the children of Israel:
only in Gaza, in Gath, and in Ashdod, there remained.
23 **So Joshua** took the whole land, according to all that the LORD said unto Moses;
and Joshua gave it for an inheritance unto Israel according to their divisions by their tribes.
And the land rested from war.

12 **Now these** are the kings of the land,
which the children of Israel smote,
and possessed their land on the other side Jordan toward the

rising of the sun, from the river Arnon unto mount Hermon, and all the plain on the east:
2 Sihon king of the Amorites, {who dwelt in Heshbon}, {and ruled from Aroer}, {which is upon the bank of the river Arnon, and from the middle of the river, and from half Gilead, even unto the river Jabbok}, {which is the border of the children of Ammon};
3 And from the plain to the sea of Chinneroth on the east, and unto the sea of the plain, even the salt sea on the east, the way to Bethjeshimoth; and from the south, under Ashdothpisgah:
4 And the coast of Og king of Bashan, {which was of the remnant of the giants}, {that dwelt at Ashtaroth and at Edrei},
5 {And reigned in mount Hermon, and in Salcah, and in all Bashan}, unto the border of the Geshurites and the Maachathites, and half Gilead, the border of Sihon king of Heshbon.
6 **Them** did Moses the servant of the LORD and the children of Israel smite:
and Moses the servant of the LORD gave it for a possession unto the Reubenites, and the Gadites, and the half tribe of Manasseh.
7 **And these** are the kings of the country which Joshua and the children of Israel smote on this side Jordan on the west, from Baalgad in the valley of Lebanon even unto the mount Halak, {that goeth up to Seir}; {which Joshua gave unto the tribes of Israel for a possession according to their divisions};
8 In the mountains, and in the valleys, and in the plains, and in the springs, and in the wilderness, and in the south country; the Hittites, the Amorites, and the Canaanites, the Perizzites, the Hivites, and the Jebusites:
9 **The king of Jericho,** one;
the king of Ai, {which is beside Bethel}, one;
10 **The king of Jerusalem,** one;
the king of Hebron, one;
11 **The king of Jarmuth,** one;
the king of Lachish, one;
12 **The king of Eglon,** one;
the king of Gezer, one;
13 **The king of Debir,** one;
the king of Geder, one;
14 **The king of Hormah,** one;
the king of Arad, one;
15 **The king of Libnah,** one;
the king of Adullam, one;
16 **The king of Makkedah,** one;
the king of Bethel, one;
17 **The king of Tappuah,** one;
the king of Hepher, one;
18 **The king of Aphek,** one;
the king of Lasharon, one;
19 **The king of Madon,** one;
the king of Hazor, one;
20 **The king of Shimronmeron,** one;
the king of Achshaph, one;
21 **The king of Taanach,** one;
the king of Megiddo, one;
22 **The king of Kedesh,** one;
the king of Jokneam of Carmel, one;
23 **The king of Dor in the coast of Dor,** one;
the king of the nations of Gilgal, one;
24 **The king of Tirzah,** one:
all the kings thirty and one.

13

Now Joshua was old and stricken in years;
and the LORD said unto him,
Thou art old and stricken in years,
and there remaineth yet very much land to be possessed.
2 **This** is the land that yet remaineth: all the borders of the Philistines, and all Geshuri,
3 From Sihor, {which is before Egypt}, even unto the borders of Ekron northward, {which is counted to the Canaanite}: five lords of the Philistines; the Gazathites, and the Ashdothites, the Eshkalonites, the Gittites, and the Ekronites; also the Avites:
4 From the south, all the land of the Canaanites, and Mearah that is beside the Sidonians unto Aphek, to the borders of the Amorites:
5 And the land of the Giblites, and all Lebanon, toward the sunrising, from Baalgad under mount Hermon unto the entering into Hamath.
6 **All the inhabitants of the hill country from Lebanon unto Misrephothmaim, and all the Sidonians,** them will I drive out from before the children of Israel:
only divide thou it by lot unto the Israelites for an inheritance,
as I have commanded thee.
7 **Now therefore divide** this land for an inheritance unto the nine tribes, and the half tribe of Manasseh,
8 **With whom** the Reubenites and the Gadites have received their inheritance,
which Moses gave them, beyond Jordan eastward,
even as Moses the servant of the LORD gave them;
9 From Aroer, {that is upon the bank of the river Arnon, and the city that is in the midst of the river, and all the plain of Medeba unto Dibon};
10 And all the cities of Sihon king of the Amorites, {which reigned in Heshbon}, unto the border of the children of Ammon;
11 And Gilead, and the border of the Geshurites and Maachathites, and all mount Hermon, and all Bashan unto Salcah;
12 All the kingdom of Og in Bashan, {which reigned in Ashtaroth and in Edrei}, {who remained of the remnant of the giants}:
for these did Moses smite,
and cast them out.
13 **Nevertheless the children of Israel** expelled not the Geshurites, nor the Maachathites:
but the Geshurites and the Maachathites dwell among the Israelites until this day.
14 **Only unto the tribes of Levi** he gave none inheritance;
the sacrifices of the LORD God of Israel made by fire are their inheritance,
as he said unto them.
15 **And Moses** gave unto the tribe of the children of Reuben inheritance according to their families.
16 **And their coast** was from Aroer, {that is on the bank of the river Arnon, and the city that is in the midst of the river, and all the plain by Medeba};
17 Heshbon, and all her cities that are in the plain; Dibon, and Bamothbaal, and Bethbaalmeon,
18 And Jahaza, and Kedemoth, and Mephaath,

19 And Kirjathaim, and Sibmah, and Zarethshahar in the mount of the valley,
20 And Bethpeor, and Ashdothpisgah, and Bethjeshimoth,
21 And all the cities of the plain, and all the kingdom of Sihon king of the Amorites, {which reigned in Heshbon},
whom Moses smote with the princes of Midian, Evi, and Rekem, and Zur, and Hur, and Reba,
which were dukes of Sihon, dwelling in the country.
22 **Balaam also the son of Beor, the soothsayer,** did the children of Israel slay with the sword among them that were slain by them.
23 **And the border of the children of Reuben** was Jordan, and the border thereof.
This was the inheritance of the children of Reuben after their families, the cities and the villages thereof.
24 **And Moses** gave inheritance unto the tribe of Gad, even unto the children of Gad according to their families.
25 **And their coast** was Jazer, and all the cities of Gilead, and half the land of the children of Ammon, unto Aroer that is before Rabbah;
26 And from Heshbon unto Ramathmizpeh, and Betonim; and from Mahanaim unto the border of Debir;
27 And in the valley, Betharam, and Bethnimrah, and Succoth, and Zaphon, the rest of the kingdom of Sihon king of Heshbon, Jordan and his border, even unto the edge of the sea of Chinnereth on the other side Jordan eastward.
28 **This** is the inheritance of the children of Gad after their families, the cities, and their villages.
29 **And Moses** gave inheritance unto the half tribe of Manasseh:
and this was the possession of the half tribe of the children of Manasseh by their families.
30 **And their coast** was from Mahanaim, all Bashan, all the kingdom of Og king of Bashan, and all the towns of Jair, {which are in Bashan}, threescore cities:
31 **And half Gilead, and Ashtaroth, and Edrei, cities of the kingdom of Og in Bashan,** were pertaining unto the children of Machir the son of Manasseh, even to the one half of the children of Machir by their families.
32 **These** are the countries which Moses did distribute for inheritance in the plains of Moab, on the other side Jordan, by Jericho, eastward.
33 **But unto the tribe of Levi** Moses gave not any inheritance:
the LORD God of Israel was their inheritance,
as he said unto them.

14 **And these** are the countries which the children of Israel inherited in the land of Canaan,
which Eleazar the priest, and Joshua the son of Nun, and the heads of the fathers of the tribes of the children of Israel, distributed for inheritance to them.
2 **By lot** was their inheritance, {as the LORD commanded by the hand of Moses}, for the nine tribes, and for the half tribe.
3 **For Moses** had given the inheritance of two tribes and an half tribe on the other side Jordan:
but unto the Levites he gave none inheritance among them.
4 **For the children of Joseph** were two tribes, Manasseh and Ephraim:
therefore they gave no part unto the Levites in the land,
save cities to dwell in, with their suburbs for their cattle and for their substance.
5 **As the LORD** commanded Moses,
so the children of Israel did,
and they divided the land.
6 **Then the children of Judah** came unto Joshua in Gilgal:
and Caleb the son of Jephunneh the Kenezite said unto him,
Thou knowest the thing that the LORD said unto Moses the man of God concerning me and thee in Kadeshbarnea.
7 **Forty years old** was I
when Moses the servant of the LORD sent me from Kadeshbarnea
to espy out the land;
and I brought him word again as it was in mine heart.
8 **Nevertheless my brethren that went up with me** made the heart of the people melt:
but I wholly followed the LORD my God.
9 **And Moses** sware on that day, saying,
Surely the land whereon thy feet have trodden shall be thine inheritance, and thy children's for ever,
because thou hast wholly followed the LORD my God.
10 **And now, {behold}, the LORD** hath kept me alive, {as he said}, these forty and five years,
even since the LORD spake this word unto Moses,
while the children of Israel wandered in the wilderness:
and now, {lo}, I am this day fourscore and five years old.
11 **As yet I** am as strong this day as I was in the day that Moses sent me:
as my strength was then,
even so is my strength now, for war,
both to go out,
and to come in.
12 **Now therefore give** me this mountain,
whereof the LORD spake in that day;
for thou heardest in that day how the Anakims were there,
and that the cities were great and fenced:
if so be the LORD will be with me,
then I shall be able to drive them out,
as the LORD said.
13 **And Joshua** blessed him,
and gave unto Caleb the son of Jephunneh Hebron for an inheritance.
14 **Hebron** therefore became the inheritance of Caleb the son of Jephunneh the Kenezite unto this day,
because that he wholly followed the LORD God of Israel.
15 **And the name of Hebron before** was Kirjatharba;
which Arba was a great man among the Anakims.
And the land had rest from war.

15 **This** then was the lot of the tribe of the children of Judah by their families;
even to the border of Edom the wilderness of Zin southward was the uttermost part of the south coast.
2 **And their south border** was from the shore of the salt sea, from the bay that looketh southward:
3 **And it** went out to the south side to Maalehacrabbim,
and passed along to Zin,
and ascended up on the south side unto Kadeshbarnea,
and passed along to Hezron,
and went up to Adar,
and fetched a compass to Karkaa:
4 **From thence** it passed toward Azmon,
and went out unto the river of Egypt;
and the goings out of that coast were at the sea:
this shall be your south coast.
5 **And the east border** was the salt sea, even unto the end of Jordan.
And their border in the north quarter was from the bay of the sea at the uttermost part of Jordan:
6 **And the border** went up to Bethhogla,
and passed along by the north of Betharabah;
and the border went up to the stone of Bohan the son of Reuben:
7 **And the border** went up toward Debir from the valley of Achor, and so northward,
looking toward Gilgal,
that is before the going up to Adummim,
which is on the south side of the river:
and the border passed toward the waters of Enshemesh,
and the goings out thereof were at Enrogel:
8 **And the border** went up by the valley of the son of Hinnom unto the south side of the Jebusite;
the same is Jerusalem:
and the border went up to the top of the mountain that lieth before the valley of Hinnom westward,
which is at the end of the valley of the giants northward:
9 **And the border** was drawn from the top of the hill unto the fountain of the water of Nephtoah,
and went out to the cities of mount Ephron;
and the border was drawn to Baalah,
which is Kirjathjearim:
10 **And the border** compassed from Baalah westward unto mount Seir,
and passed along unto the side of mount Jearim,
which is Chesalon, on the north side,
and went down to Bethshemesh,
and passed on to Timnah:
11 **And the border** went out unto the side of Ekron northward:
and the border was drawn to Shicron,
and passed along to mount Baalah,
and went out unto Jabneel;
and the goings out of the border were at the sea.
12 **And the west border** was to the great sea, and the coast thereof.
This is the coast of the children of Judah round about according to their families.
13 **And unto Caleb the son of Jephunneh** he gave a part among the children of Judah, according to the commandment of the LORD to Joshua, even the city of Arba the father of Anak,
which city is Hebron.
14 **And Caleb** drove thence the three sons of Anak, Sheshai, and Ahiman, and Talmai, the children of Anak.
15 **And he** went up thence to the inhabitants of Debir:
and the name of Debir before was Kirjathsepher.
16 **And Caleb** said,
He that smiteth Kirjathsepher, and taketh it, to him will I give Achsah my daughter to wife.
17 **And Othniel the son of Kenaz, the brother of Caleb,** took it:
and he gave him Achsah his daughter to wife.
18 **And it** came to pass,
as she came unto him,
that she moved him to ask of her father a field:
and she lighted off her ass;
and Caleb said unto her,
What wouldest thou?
19 **Who** answered,
Give me a blessing;
for thou hast given me a south land;
give me also springs of water.
And he gave her the upper springs, and the nether springs.
20 **This** is the inheritance of the tribe of the children of Judah according to their families.
21 **And the uttermost cities of the tribe of the children of Judah toward the coast of Edom southward** were Kabzeel, and Eder, and Jagur,
22 And Kinah, and Dimonah, and Adadah,
23 And Kedesh, and Hazor, and Ithnan,
24 Ziph, and Telem, and Bealoth,
25 And Hazor, Hadattah, and Kerioth, and Hezron, {which is Hazor},
26 Amam, and Shema, and Moladah,
27 And Hazargaddah, and Heshmon, and Bethpalet,
28 And Hazarshual, and Beersheba, and Bizjothjah,
29 Baalah, and Iim, and Azem,
30 And Eltolad, and Chesil, and Hormah,
31 And Ziklag, and Madmannah, and Sansannah,
32 And Lebaoth, and Shilhim, and Ain, and Rimmon:
all the cities are twenty and nine, with their villages:
33 And in the valley, Eshtaol, and Zoreah, and Ashnah,
34 And Zanoah, and Engannim, Tappuah, and Enam,
35 Jarmuth, and Adullam, Socoh, and Azekah,
36 And Sharaim, and Adithaim, and Gederah, and Gederothaim;
fourteen cities with their villages:
37 Zenan, and Hadashah, and Migdalgad,
38 And Dilean, and Mizpeh, and Joktheel,
39 Lachish, and Bozkath, and Eglon,
40 And Cabbon, and Lahmam, and Kithlish,
41 And Gederoth, Bethdagon, and Naamah, and Makkedah;
sixteen cities with their villages:
42 Libnah, and Ether, and Ashan,
43 And Jiphtah, and Ashnah, and Nezib,
44 And Keilah, and Achzib, and Mareshah;
nine cities with their villages:

45 Ekron, with her towns and her villages:
46 From Ekron even unto the sea,
all that lay near Ashdod, with their villages:
47 Ashdod with her towns and her villages,
Gaza with her towns and her villages, unto the river of Egypt, and the great sea, and the border thereof:
48 And in the mountains, Shamir, and Jattir, and Socoh,
49 And Dannah, and Kirjathsannah, {which is Debir},
50 And Anab, and Eshtemoh, and Anim,
51 And Goshen, and Holon, and Giloh;
eleven cities with their villages:
52 Arab, and Dumah, and Eshean,
53 And Janum, and Bethtappuah, and Aphekah,
54 And Humtah, and Kirjatharba, {which is Hebron}, and Zior;
nine cities with their villages:
55 Maon, Carmel, and Ziph, and Juttah,
56 And Jezreel, and Jokdeam, and Zanoah,
57 Cain, Gibeah, and Timnah;
ten cities with their villages:
58 Halhul, Bethzur, and Gedor,
59 And Maarath, and Bethanoth, and Eltekon;
six cities with their villages:
60 Kirjathbaal, which is Kirjathjearim, and Rabbah;
two cities with their villages:
61 In the wilderness, Betharabah, Middin, and Secacah,
62 And Nibshan, and the city of Salt, and Engedi;
six cities with their villages.

63 **As for the Jebusites the inhabitants of Jerusalem,** the children of Judah could not drive them out;
but the Jebusites dwell with the children of Judah at Jerusalem unto this day.

16

And the lot of the children of Joseph fell from Jordan by Jericho, unto the water of Jericho on the east, to the wilderness that goeth up from Jericho throughout mount Bethel,
2 **And** goeth out from Bethel to Luz,
and passeth along unto the borders of Archi to Ataroth,
3 **And** goeth down westward to the coast of Japhleti, unto the coast of Bethhoron the nether, and to Gezer;
and the goings out thereof are at the sea.

4 **So the children of Joseph, Manasseh and Ephraim,** took their inheritance.

5 **And the border of the children of Ephraim according to their families** was thus:
even the border of their inheritance on the east side was Atarothaddar, unto Bethhoron the upper;
6 **And the border** went out toward the sea to Michmethah on the north side;
and the border went about eastward unto Taanathshiloh,
and passed by it on the east to Janohah;
7 **And it** went down from Janohah to Ataroth, and to Naarath,
and came to Jericho,
and went out at Jordan.

8 **The border** went out from Tappuah westward unto the river Kanah;
and the goings out thereof were at the sea.
This is the inheritance of the tribe of the children of Ephraim by their families.

9 **And the separate cities for the children of Ephraim** were among the inheritance of the children of Manasseh, all the cities with their villages.

10 **And they** drave not out the Canaanites that dwelt in Gezer:
but the Canaanites dwell among the Ephraimites unto this day,
and serve under tribute.

17

There was also a lot for the tribe of Manasseh;
for he was the firstborn of Joseph; to wit, for Machir the firstborn of Manasseh, the father of Gilead:
because he was a man of war,
therefore he had Gilead and Bashan.

2 **There** was also a lot for the rest of the children of Manasseh by their families; for the children of Abiezer, and for the children of Helek, and for the children of Asriel, and for the children of Shechem, and for the children of Hepher, and for the children of Shemida:
these were the male children of Manasseh the son of Joseph by their families.

3 **But Zelophehad, the son of Hepher, the son of Gilead, the son of Machir, the son of Manasseh,** had no sons, but daughters:
and these are the names of his daughters, Mahlah, and Noah, Hoglah, Milcah, and Tirzah.
4 **And they** came near before Eleazar the priest, and before Joshua the son of Nun, and before the princes,
saying,
The LORD commanded Moses
to give us an inheritance among our brethren.
Therefore according to the commandment of the LORD he gave them an inheritance among the brethren of their father.

5 **And there** fell ten portions to Manasseh, beside the land of Gilead and Bashan,
which were on the other side Jordan;
6 **Because the daughters of Manasseh** had an inheritance among his sons:
and the rest of Manasseh's sons had the land of Gilead.

7 **And the coast of Manasseh** was from Asher to Michmethah,
that lieth before Shechem;
and the border went along on the right hand unto the inhabitants of Entappuah.
8 **Now Manasseh** had the land of Tappuah:
but Tappuah on the border of Manasseh belonged to the children of Ephraim;
9 **And the coast** descended unto the river Kanah, southward of the river:
these cities of Ephraim are among the cities of Manasseh:
the coast of Manasseh also was on the north side of the river,
and the outgoings of it were at the sea:
10 **Southward** it was Ephraim's,
and northward it was Manasseh's,
and the sea is his border;

and they met together in Asher on the north, and in Issachar on the east.
11 **And Manasseh** had in Issachar and in Asher Bethshean and her towns, and Ibleam and her towns, and the inhabitants of Dor and her towns, and the inhabitants of Endor and her towns, and the inhabitants of Taanach and her towns, and the inhabitants of Megiddo and her towns, even three countries.
12 **Yet the children of Manasseh** could not drive out the inhabitants of those cities;
but the Canaanites would dwell in that land.
13 **Yet it** came to pass,
when the children of Israel were waxen strong,
that they put the Canaanites to tribute,
but did not utterly drive them out.
14 **And the children of Joseph** spake unto Joshua,
saying,
Why hast thou given me but one lot and one portion to inherit,
seeing I am a great people,
forasmuch as the LORD hath blessed me hitherto?
15 **And Joshua** answered them,
If thou be a great people,
then get thee up to the wood country,
and cut down for thyself there in the land of the Perizzites and of the giants,
if mount Ephraim be too narrow for thee.
16 **And the children of Joseph** said,
The hill is not enough for us:
and all the Canaanites that dwell in the land of the valley have chariots of iron, both they who are of Bethshean and her towns, and they who are of the valley of Jezreel.
17 **And Joshua** spake unto the house of Joseph, even to Ephraim and to Manasseh,
saying,
Thou art a great people,
and hast great power:
thou shalt not have one lot only:
18 **But the mountain** shall be thine;
for it is a wood,
and thou shalt cut it down:
and the outgoings of it shall be thine:
for thou shalt drive out the Canaanites,
though they have iron chariots,
and though they be strong.

18 **And the whole congregation of the children of Israel** assembled together at Shiloh,
and set up the tabernacle of the congregation there.
And the land was subdued before them.
2 **And there** remained among the children of Israel seven tribes,
which had not yet received their inheritance.
3 **And Joshua** said unto the children of Israel,
How long are ye slack to go to possess the land,
which the LORD God of your fathers hath given you?
4 **Give out** from among you three men for each tribe:
and I will send them,
and they shall rise,
and go through the land,
and describe it according to the inheritance of them;
and they shall come again to me.
5 **And they** shall divide it into seven parts:
Judah shall abide in their coast on the south,
and the house of Joseph shall abide in their coasts on the north.
6 **Ye** shall therefore describe the land into seven parts,
and bring the description hither to me,
that I may cast lots for you here before the LORD our God.
7 **But the Levites** have no part among you;
for the priesthood of the LORD is their inheritance:
and Gad, and Reuben, and half the tribe of Manasseh, have received their inheritance beyond Jordan on the east,
which Moses the servant of the LORD gave them.
8 **And the men** arose,
and went away:
and Joshua charged them that went to describe the land,
saying,
Go and walk through the land,
and describe it,
and come again to me,
that I may here cast lots for you before the LORD in Shiloh.
9 **And the men** went and passed through the land,
and described it by cities into seven parts in a book,
and came again to Joshua to the host at Shiloh.
10 **And Joshua** cast lots for them in Shiloh before the LORD:
and there Joshua divided the land unto the children of Israel according to their divisions.
11 **And the lot of the tribe of the children of Benjamin** came up according to their families:
and the coast of their lot came forth between the children of Judah and the children of Joseph.
12 **And their border on the north side** was from Jordan;
and the border went up to the side of Jericho on the north side,
and went up through the mountains westward;
and the goings out thereof were at the wilderness of Bethaven.
13 **And the border** went over from thence toward Luz, to the side of Luz,
which is Bethel, southward;
and the border descended to Atarothadar, near the hill that lieth on the south side of the nether Bethhoron.
14 **And the border** was drawn thence,
and compassed the corner of the sea southward, from the hill that lieth before Bethhoron southward;
and the goings out thereof were at Kirjathbaal,
which is Kirjathjearim, a city of the children of Judah:
this was the west quarter.
15 **And the south quarter** was from the end of Kirjathjearim,
and the border went out on the west,
and went out to the well of waters of Nephtoah:
16 **And the border** came down to the end of the mountain that lieth before the valley of the son of Hinnom,

and which is in the valley of the giants on the north,
and descended to the valley of Hinnom, to the side of Jebusi on the south,
and descended to Enrogel,
17 **And** was drawn from the north,
and went forth to Enshemesh,
and went forth toward Geliloth,
which is over against the going up of Adummim,
and descended to the stone of Bohan the son of Reuben,
18 **And** passed along toward the side over against Arabah northward,
and went down unto Arabah:
19 **And the border** passed along to the side of Bethhoglah northward:
and the outgoings of the border were at the north bay of the salt sea at the south end of Jordan:
this was the south coast.

20 **And Jordan** was the border of it on the east side.

This was the inheritance of the children of Benjamin, by the coasts thereof round about, according to their families.

21 **Now the cities of the tribe of the children of Benjamin according to their families** were Jericho, and Bethhoglah, and the valley of Keziz,
22 And Betharabah, and Zemaraim, and Bethel,
23 And Avim, and Pharah, and Ophrah,
24 And Chepharhaammonai, and Ophni, and Gaba;
twelve cities with their villages:
25 Gibeon, and Ramah, and Beeroth,
26 And Mizpeh, and Chephirah, and Mozah,
27 And Rekem, and Irpeel, and Taralah,
28 And Zelah, Eleph, and Jebusi, {which is Jerusalem}, Gibeath, and Kirjath;
fourteen cities with their villages.

This is the inheritance of the children of Benjamin according to their families.

19 ⥈ **And the second lot** came forth to Simeon, even for the tribe of the children of Simeon according to their families:
and their inheritance was within the inheritance of the children of Judah.
2 **And they** had in their inheritance Beersheba, and Sheba, and Moladah,
3 And Hazarshual, and Balah, and Azem,
4 And Eltolad, and Bethul, and Hormah,
5 And Ziklag, and Bethmarcaboth, and Hazarsusah,
6 And Bethlebaoth, and Sharuhen; thirteen cities and their villages:
7 Ain, Remmon, and Ether, and Ashan;
four cities and their villages:
8 And all the villages that were round about these cities to Baalathbeer, Ramath of the south.

This is the inheritance of the tribe of the children of Simeon according to their families.

9 **Out of the portion of the children of Judah** was the inheritance of the children of Simeon:
for the part of the children of Judah was too much for them:
therefore the children of Simeon had their inheritance within the inheritance of them.

10 **And the third lot** came up for the children of Zebulun according to their families:
and the border of their inheritance was unto Sarid:
11 **And their border** went up toward the sea, and Maralah,
and reached to Dabbasheth,
and reached to the river that is before Jokneam;
12 **And** turned from Sarid eastward toward the sunrising unto the border of Chislothtabor,
and then goeth out to Daberath,
and goeth up to Japhia,
13 **And from thence** passeth on along on the east to Gittahhepher, to Ittahkazin,
and goeth out to Remmonmethoar to Neah;
14 **And the border** compasseth it on the north side to Hannathon:
and the outgoings thereof are in the valley of Jiphthahel:
15 And Kattath, and Nahallal, and Shimron, and Idalah, and Bethlehem:
twelve cities with their villages.

16 **This** is the inheritance of the children of Zebulun according to their families, these cities with their villages.

17 **And the fourth lot** came out to Issachar, for the children of Issachar according to their families.

18 **And their border** was toward Jezreel, and Chesulloth, and Shunem,
19 And Haphraim, and Shihon, and Anaharath,
20 And Rabbith, and Kishion, and Abez,
21 And Remeth, and Engannim, and Enhaddah, and Bethpazzez;
22 And the coast reacheth to Tabor, and Shahazimah, and Bethshemesh;
and the outgoings of their border were at Jordan:
sixteen cities with their villages.

23 **This** is the inheritance of the tribe of the children of Issachar according to their families, the cities and their villages.

24 **And the fifth lot** came out for the tribe of the children of Asher according to their families.

25 **And their border** was Helkath, and Hali, and Beten, and Achshaph,
26 And Alammelech, and Amad, and Misheal;
and reacheth to Carmel westward, and to Shihorlibnath;
27 **And** turneth toward the sunrising to Bethdagon,
and reacheth to Zebulun, and to the valley of Jiphthahel toward the north side of Bethemek, and Neiel,
and goeth out to Cabul on the left hand,
28 And Hebron, and Rehob, and Hammon, and Kanah, even unto great Zidon;
29 **And then the coast** turneth to Ramah, and to the strong city Tyre;
and the coast turneth to Hosah;
and the outgoings thereof are at the sea from the coast to Achzib:
30 Ummah also, and Aphek, and Rehob:
twenty and two cities with their villages.

31 **This** is the inheritance of the tribe of the children of Asher according to their families, these cities with their villages.

32 **The sixth lot** came out to the children of Naphtali, even for the children of Naphtali according to their families.

33 **And their coast** was from Heleph, from Allon to Zaanannim, and Adami, Nekeb, and Jabneel, unto Lakum;
and the outgoings thereof were at Jordan:

34 **And then the coast** turneth westward to Aznothtabor,
and goeth out from thence to Hukkok,
and reacheth to Zebulun on the south side,
and reacheth to Asher on the west side, and to Judah upon Jordan toward the sunrising.

35 **And the fenced cities** are Ziddim, Zer, and Hammath, Rakkath, and Chinnereth,
36 And Adamah, and Ramah, and Hazor,
37 And Kedesh, and Edrei, and Enhazor,
38 And Iron, and Migdalel, Horem, and Bethanath, and Bethshemesh;
nineteen cities with their villages.

39 **This** is the inheritance of the tribe of the children of Naphtali according to their families, the cities and their villages.

40 **And the seventh lot** came out for the tribe of the children of Dan according to their families.

41 **And the coast of their inheritance** was Zorah, and Eshtaol, and Irshemesh,
42 And Shaalabbin, and Ajalon, and Jethlah,
43 And Elon, and Thimnathah, and Ekron,
44 And Eltekeh, and Gibbethon, and Baalath,
45 And Jehud, and Beneberak, and Gathrimmon,
46 And Mejarkon, and Rakkon, with the border before Japho.

47 **And the coast of the children of Dan** went out too little for them:
therefore the children of Dan went up to fight against Leshem,
and took it,
and smote it with the edge of the sword,
and possessed it,
and dwelt therein,
and called Leshem, Dan, after the name of Dan their father.

48 **This** is the inheritance of the tribe of the children of Dan according to their families, these cities with their villages.

49 **When they** had made an end of dividing the land for inheritance by their coasts,
the children of Israel gave an inheritance to Joshua the son of Nun among them:

50 **According to the word of the LORD** they gave him the city which he asked, even Timnathserah in mount Ephraim:
and he built the city,
and dwelt therein.

51 **These** are the inheritances,
which Eleazar the priest, and Joshua the son of Nun, and the heads of the fathers of the tribes of the children of Israel, divided for an inheritance by lot in Shiloh before the LORD, at the door of the tabernacle of the congregation.
So they made an end of dividing the country.

20 **The LORD** also spake unto Joshua,
saying,
2 **Speak** to the children of Israel,
saying,
Appoint out for you cities of refuge,
whereof I spake unto you by the hand of Moses:

3 **That the slayer that killeth any person unawares and unwittingly** may flee thither:
and they shall be your refuge from the avenger of blood.

4 **And when he that doth flee unto one of those cities** shall stand at the entering of the gate of the city,
and shall declare his cause in the ears of the elders of that city,
they shall take him into the city unto them,
and give him a place,
that he may dwell among them.

5 **And if the avenger of blood** pursue after him,
then they shall not deliver the slayer up into his hand;
because he smote his neighbour unwittingly,
and hated him not beforetime.

6 **And he** shall dwell in that city,
until he stand before the congregation for judgment, and until the death of the high priest that shall be in those days:
then shall the slayer return,
and come unto his own city, and unto his own house, unto the city from whence he fled.

7 **And they** appointed Kedesh in Galilee in mount Naphtali, and Shechem in mount Ephraim, and Kirjatharba, {which is Hebron}, in the mountain of Judah.

8 **And on the other side Jordan by Jericho eastward,** they assigned Bezer in the wilderness upon the plain out of the tribe of Reuben, and Ramoth in Gilead out of the tribe of Gad, and Golan in Bashan out of the tribe of Manasseh.

9 **These** were the cities appointed for all the children of Israel, and for the stranger that sojourneth among them,
that whosoever killeth any person at unawares might flee thither,
and not die by the hand of the avenger of blood,
until he stood before the congregation.

21 **Then** came near the heads of the fathers of the Levites unto Eleazar the priest, and unto Joshua the son of Nun, and unto the heads of the fathers of the tribes of the children of Israel;

2 **And they** spake unto them at Shiloh in the land of Canaan,
saying,
The LORD commanded by the hand of Moses
to give us cities to dwell in, with the suburbs thereof for our cattle.

3 **And the children of Israel** gave unto the Levites out of their inheritance, at the commandment of the LORD, these cities and their suburbs.

4 **And the lot** came out for the families of the Kohathites:
and the children of Aaron the priest, {which were of the Levites}, had by lot out of the tribe of Judah, and out of the tribe of Simeon, and out of the tribe of Benjamin, thirteen cities.

5 **And the rest of the children of Kohath** had by lot out of the families of the tribe of Ephraim,

and out of the tribe of Dan, and out of the half tribe of Manasseh, ten cities.

6 **And the children of Gershon** had by lot out of the families of the tribe of Issachar, and out of the tribe of Asher, and out of the tribe of Naphtali, and out of the half tribe of Manasseh in Bashan, thirteen cities.

7 **The children of Merari by their families** had out of the tribe of Reuben, and out of the tribe of Gad, and out of the tribe of Zebulun, twelve cities.

8 **And the children of Israel** gave by lot unto the Levites these cities with their suburbs,
as the LORD commanded by the hand of Moses.

9 **And they** gave out of the tribe of the children of Judah, and out of the tribe of the children of Simeon, these cities which are here mentioned by name.

10 **Which the children of Aaron**, {being of the families of the Kohathites}, {who were of the children of Levi}, had:
for theirs was the first lot.

11 **And they** gave them the city of Arba the father of Anak,
which city is Hebron, in the hill country of Judah, with the suburbs thereof round about it.

12 **But the fields of the city, and the villages thereof,** gave they to Caleb the son of Jephunneh for his possession.

13 **Thus they** gave to the children of Aaron the priest Hebron with her suburbs, {to be a city of refuge for the slayer}; and Libnah with her suburbs,

14 And Jattir with her suburbs, and Eshtemoa with her suburbs,

15 And Holon with her suburbs, and Debir with her suburbs,

16 And Ain with her suburbs, and Juttah with her suburbs, and Bethshemesh with her suburbs;
nine cities out of those two tribes.

17 **And out of the tribe of Benjamin,** Gibeon with her suburbs, Geba with her suburbs,

18 Anathoth with her suburbs, and Almon with her suburbs;
four cities.

19 **All the cities of the children of Aaron, the priests,** were thirteen cities with their suburbs.

20 **And the families of the children of Kohath, the Levites which remained of the children of Kohath,** even they had the cities of their lot out of the tribe of Ephraim.

21 **For they** gave them Shechem with her suburbs in mount Ephraim, {to be a city of refuge for the slayer}; and Gezer with her suburbs,

22 And Kibzaim with her suburbs, and Bethhoron with her suburbs;
four cities.

23 **And out of the tribe of Dan,** Eltekeh with her suburbs, Gibbethon with her suburbs,

24 Aijalon with her suburbs, Gathrimmon with her suburbs;
four cities.

25 **And out of the half tribe of Manasseh,** Tanach with her suburbs, and Gathrimmon with her suburbs;
two cities.

26 **All the cities** were ten with their suburbs for the families of the children of Kohath that remained.

27 **And unto the children of Gershon, of the families of the Levites, out of the other half tribe of Manasseh** they gave Golan in Bashan with her suburbs, {to be a city of refuge for the slayer}; and Beeshterah with her suburbs;
two cities.

28 **And out of the tribe of Issachar,** Kishon with her suburbs, Dabareh with her suburbs,

29 Jarmuth with her suburbs, Engannim with her suburbs;
four cities.

30 **And out of the tribe of Asher,** Mishal with her suburbs, Abdon with her suburbs,

31 Helkath with her suburbs, and Rehob with her suburbs;
four cities.

32 **And out of the tribe of Naphtali,** Kedesh in Galilee with her suburbs, {to be a city of refuge for the slayer}; and Hammothdor with her suburbs, and Kartan with her suburbs;
three cities.

33 **All the cities of the Gershonites according to their families** were thirteen cities with their suburbs.

34 **And unto the families of the children of Merari,** the rest of the Levites, out of the tribe of Zebulun, Jokneam with her suburbs, and Kartah with her suburbs,

35 Dimnah with her suburbs, Nahalal with her suburbs;
four cities.

36 **And out of the tribe of Reuben,** Bezer with her suburbs, and Jahazah with her suburbs,

37 Kedemoth with her suburbs, and Mephaath with her suburbs;
four cities.

38 **And out of the tribe of Gad,** Ramoth in Gilead with her suburbs, {to be a city of refuge for the slayer}; and Mahanaim with her suburbs,

39 Heshbon with her suburbs, Jazer with her suburbs;
four cities in all.

40 **So all the cities for the children of Merari by their families,** {which were remaining of the families of the Levites}, were by their lot twelve cities.

41 **All the cities of the Levites within the possession of the children of Israel** were forty and eight cities with their suburbs.

42 **These cities** were every one with their suburbs round about them:
thus were all these cities.

43 **And the LORD** gave unto Israel all the land which he sware to give unto their fathers;
and they possessed it,
and dwelt therein.

44 **And the LORD** gave them rest round about, according to all that he sware unto their fathers:
and there stood not a man of all their enemies before them;
the LORD delivered all their enemies into their hand.

45 **There** failed not ought of any good thing which the LORD had spoken unto the house of Israel;
all came to pass.

22 **Then Joshua** called the Reubenites, and the Gadites, and the half tribe of Manasseh,

2 **And** said unto them,

Ye have kept all that Moses the servant of the LORD commanded you,
and have obeyed my voice in all that I commanded you:
3 **Ye** have not left your brethren these many days unto this day,
but have kept the charge of the commandment of the LORD your God.

4 **And now the LORD your God** hath given rest unto your brethren,
as he promised them:
therefore now return ye,
and get you unto your tents, and unto the land of your possession,
which Moses the servant of the LORD gave you on the other side Jordan.

5 **But take diligent heed** to do the commandment and the law,
which Moses the servant of the LORD charged you,
to love the LORD your God,
and to walk in all his ways,
and to keep his commandments, and to cleave unto him,
and to serve him with all your heart and with all your soul.

6 **So Joshua** blessed them,
and sent them away:
and they went unto their tents.

7 **Now to the one half of the tribe of Manasseh** Moses had given possession in Bashan:
but unto the other half thereof gave Joshua among their brethren on this side Jordan westward.

And when Joshua sent them away also unto their tents,
then he blessed them,
8 **And he** spake unto them,
saying,
Return with much riches unto your tents, and with very much cattle, with silver, and with gold, and with brass, and with iron, and with very much raiment:
divide the spoil of your enemies with your brethren.

9 **And the children of Reuben and the children of Gad and the half tribe of Manasseh** returned,
and departed from the children of Israel out of Shiloh,
which is in the land of Canaan,
to go unto the country of Gilead, to the land of their possession,
whereof they were possessed, according to the word of the LORD by the hand of Moses.

10 **And when they** came unto the borders of Jordan,
that are in the land of Canaan,
the children of Reuben and the children of Gad and the half tribe of Manasseh built there an altar by Jordan,
a great altar to see to.

11 **And the children of Israel** heard say,
Behold,
the children of Reuben and the children of Gad and the half tribe of Manasseh have built an altar over against the land of Canaan, in the borders of Jordan, at the passage of the children of Israel.

12 **And when the children of Israel** heard of it,
the whole congregation of the children of Israel gathered themselves together at Shiloh,
to go up to war against them.

13 **And the children of Israel** sent unto the children of Reuben, and to the children of Gad, and to the half tribe of Manasseh, into the land of Gilead, Phinehas the son of Eleazar the priest,
14 And with him ten princes, of each chief house a prince throughout all the tribes of Israel;
and each one was an head of the house of their fathers among the thousands of Israel.

15 **And they** came unto the children of Reuben, and to the children of Gad, and to the half tribe of Manasseh, unto the land of Gilead,
and they spake with them,
saying,
16 **Thus** saith the whole congregation of the LORD,
What trespass is this that ye have committed against the God of Israel,
to turn away this day from following the LORD,
in that ye have builded you an altar,
that ye might rebel this day against the LORD?

17 **Is the iniquity of Peor** too little for us,
from which we are not cleansed until this day,
although there was a plague in the congregation of the LORD,
18 **But that ye** must turn away this day from following the LORD?
and it will be,
seeing ye rebel to day against the LORD,
that to morrow he will be wroth with the whole congregation of Israel.

19 **Notwithstanding, if the land of your possession** be unclean,
then pass ye over unto the land of the possession of the LORD,
wherein the LORD's tabernacle dwelleth,
and take possession among us:
but rebel not against the LORD,
nor rebel against us,
in building you an altar beside the altar of the LORD our God.

20 **Did not Achan the son of Zerah** commit a trespass in the accursed thing,
and wrath fell on all the congregation of Israel?
and that man perished not alone in his iniquity.

21 **Then the children of Reuben and the children of Gad and the half tribe of Manasseh** answered,
and said unto the heads of the thousands of Israel,
22 **The LORD God of gods, the LORD God of gods,** he knoweth,
and Israel he shall know;
if it be in rebellion, or if in transgression against the LORD,
(save us not this day,)
23 **That we** have built us an altar to turn from following the LORD,
or if to offer thereon burnt offering or meat offering,
or if to offer peace offerings thereon,
let the LORD himself require it;
24 **And if we** have not rather done it for fear of this thing,
saying,
In time to come your children might speak unto our children,
saying,
What have ye to do with the LORD God of Israel?

25 **For the LORD** hath made Jordan a border between us and you, ye children of Reuben and children of Gad;

ye have no part in the LORD:
so shall your children make our children cease from fearing the LORD.

26 **Therefore we** said,
Let us now prepare to build us an altar, not for burnt offering, nor for sacrifice:
27 **But that it** may be a witness between us, and you, and our generations after us,
that we might do the service of the LORD before him with our burnt offerings, and with our sacrifices, and with our peace offerings;
that your children may not say to our children in time to come,
Ye have no part in the LORD.

28 **Therefore** said we,
that it shall be,
when they should so say to us or to our generations in time to come,
that we may say again,
Behold the pattern of the altar of the LORD,
which our fathers made, not for burnt offerings, nor for sacrifices;
but it is a witness between us and you.

29 **God** forbid
that we should rebel against the LORD,
and turn this day from following the LORD,
to build an altar for burnt offerings, for meat offerings, or for sacrifices, beside the altar of the LORD our God that is before his tabernacle.

30 **And when Phinehas the priest, and the princes of the congregation and heads of the thousands of Israel which were with him,** heard the words that the children of Reuben and the children of Gad and the children of Manasseh spake,
it pleased them.

31 **And Phinehas the son of Eleazar the priest** said unto the children of Reuben, and to the children of Gad, and to the children of Manasseh,
This day we perceive that the LORD is among us,
because ye have not committed this trespass against the LORD:
now ye have delivered the children of Israel out of the hand of the LORD.

32 **And Phinehas the son of Eleazar the priest, and the princes,** returned from the children of Reuben, and from the children of Gad, out of the land of Gilead, unto the land of Canaan, to the children of Israel,
and brought them word again.

33 **And the thing** pleased the children of Israel;
and the children of Israel blessed God,
and did not intend to go up against them in battle,
to destroy the land wherein the children of Reuben and Gad dwelt.

34 **And the children of Reuben and the children of Gad** called the altar Ed:
for it shall be a witness between us
that the LORD is God.

23 **And it** came to pass **a long time after that the LORD** had given rest unto Israel from all their enemies round about,
that Joshua waxed old and stricken in age.

2 **And Joshua** called for all Israel, and for their elders, and for their heads, and for their judges, and for their officers,
and said unto them,
I am old and stricken in age:
3 **And ye** have seen all that the LORD your God hath done unto all these nations because of you;
for the LORD your God is he that hath fought for you.

4 **Behold,**
I have divided unto you by lot these nations that remain,
to be an inheritance for your tribes, from Jordan, with all the nations that I have cut off, even unto the great sea westward.

5 **And the LORD your God,** he shall expel them from before you,
and drive them from out of your sight;
and ye shall possess their land,
as the LORD your God hath promised unto you.

6 **Be ye** therefore very courageous
to keep and to do all that is written in the book of the law of Moses,
that ye turn not aside therefrom to the right hand or to the left;
7 **That ye** come not among these nations, these that remain among you;
neither make mention of the name of their gods,
nor cause to swear by them,
neither serve them,
nor bow yourselves unto them:
8 **But cleave** unto the LORD your God,
as ye have done unto this day.

9 **For the LORD** hath driven out from before you great nations and strong:
but as for you, no man hath been able to stand before you unto this day.

10 **One man of you** shall chase a thousand:
for the LORD your God, he it is that fighteth for you,
as he hath promised you.

11 **Take** good heed therefore unto yourselves,
that ye love the LORD your God.

12 **Else if ye** do in any wise go back,
and cleave unto the remnant of these nations, even these that remain among you,
and shall make marriages with them,
and go in unto them,
and they to you:
13 **Know** for a certainty
that the LORD your God will no more drive out any of these nations from before you;
but they shall be snares and traps unto you, and scourges in your sides, and thorns in your eyes,
until ye perish from off this good land which the LORD your God hath given you.

14 **And, {behold}, this day** I am going the way of all the earth:
and ye know in all your hearts and in all your souls,
that not one thing hath failed of all the good things which the LORD your God spake concerning you;
all are come to pass unto you,
and not one thing hath failed thereof.

15 **Therefore it** shall come to pass,
that as all good things are come upon you,
which the LORD your God promised you;
so shall the LORD bring upon you all evil things,

until he have destroyed you from off this good land which the LORD your God hath given you.

16 **When ye** have transgressed the covenant of the LORD your God,
which he commanded you,
and have gone and served other gods,
and bowed yourselves to them;
then shall the anger of the LORD be kindled against you,
and ye shall perish quickly from off the good land which he hath given unto you.

24

And Joshua gathered all the tribes of Israel to Shechem,
and called for the elders of Israel, and for their heads, and for their judges, and for their officers;
and they presented themselves before God.

2 **And Joshua** said unto all the people,
Thus saith the LORD God of Israel,
Your fathers dwelt on the other side of the flood in old time, even Terah, the father of Abraham, and the father of Nachor:
and they served other gods.

3 **And I** took your father Abraham from the other side of the flood,
and led him throughout all the land of Canaan,
and multiplied his seed,
and gave him Isaac.

4 **And I** gave unto Isaac Jacob and Esau:
and I gave unto Esau mount Seir,
to possess it;
but Jacob and his children went down into Egypt.

5 **I** sent Moses also and Aaron,
and I plagued Egypt, according to that which I did among them:
and afterward I brought you out.

6 **And I** brought your fathers out of Egypt:
and ye came unto the sea;
and the Egyptians pursued after your fathers with chariots and horsemen unto the Red sea.

7 **And when they** cried unto the LORD,
he put darkness between you and the Egyptians,
and brought the sea upon them,
and covered them;
and your eyes have seen what I have done in Egypt:
and ye dwelt in the wilderness a long season.

8 **And I** brought you into the land of the Amorites,
which dwelt on the other side Jordan;
and they fought with you:
and I gave them into your hand,
that ye might possess their land;
and I destroyed them from before you.

9 **Then Balak the son of Zippor, king of Moab,** arose and warred against Israel,
and sent and called Balaam the son of Beor to curse you:

10 **But I** would not hearken unto Balaam;
therefore he blessed you still:
so I delivered you out of his hand.

11 **And you** went over Jordan,
and came unto Jericho:
and the men of Jericho fought against you, the Amorites, and the Perizzites, and the Canaanites, and the Hittites, and the Girgashites, the Hivites, and the Jebusites;
and I delivered them into your hand.

12 **And I** sent the hornet before you,
which drave them out from before you, even the two kings of the Amorites; but not with thy sword, nor with thy bow.

13 **And I** have given you a land for which ye did not labour, and cities which ye built not,
and ye dwell in them;
of the vineyards and oliveyards which ye planted not do ye eat.

14 **Now therefore fear** the LORD,
and serve him in sincerity and in truth:
and put away the gods which your fathers served on the other side of the flood, and in Egypt;
and serve ye the LORD.

15 **And if it seem evil unto you** to serve the LORD,
choose you this day
whom ye will serve; whether the gods which your fathers served that were on the other side of the flood, or the gods of the Amorites,
in whose land ye dwell:
but as for me and my house, we will serve the LORD.

16 **And the people** answered and said,
God forbid
that we should forsake the LORD,
to serve other gods;

17 **For the LORD our God,** he it is that brought us up and our fathers out of the land of Egypt, from the house of bondage,
and which did those great signs in our sight,
and preserved us in all the way wherein we went, and among all the people through whom we passed:

18 **And the LORD** drave out from before us all the people, even the Amorites which dwelt in the land:
therefore will we also serve the LORD;
for he is our God.

19 **And Joshua** said unto the people,
Ye cannot serve the LORD:
for he is an holy God;
he is a jealous God;
he will not forgive your transgressions nor your sins.

20 **If ye** forsake the LORD,
and serve strange gods,
then he will turn and do you hurt,
and consume you,
after that he hath done you good.

21 **And the people** said unto Joshua,
Nay;
but we will serve the LORD.

22 **And Joshua** said unto the people,
Ye are witnesses against yourselves
that ye have chosen you the LORD,
to serve him.
And they said,
We are witnesses.

23 **Now therefore put away**, {said he}, the strange gods which are among you,
and incline your heart unto the LORD God of Israel.

24 **And the people** said unto Joshua,
The LORD our God will we serve,
and his voice will we obey.

25 **So Joshua** made a covenant with the people that day,
and set them a statute and an ordinance in Shechem.

26 **And Joshua** wrote these words in the book of the law of God,
and took a great stone,
and set it up there under an oak,
that was by the sanctuary of the LORD.

27 **And Joshua** said unto all the people,
Behold,
this stone shall be a witness unto us;
for it hath heard all the words of the LORD which he spake unto us:
it shall be therefore a witness unto you,
lest ye deny your God.

28 **So Joshua** let the people depart, every man unto his inheritance.

29 **And it** came to pass after these things,
that Joshua the son of Nun, the servant of the LORD, died,
being an hundred and ten years old.

30 **And they** buried him in the border of his inheritance in Timnathserah,
which is in mount Ephraim, on the north side of the hill of Gaash.

31 **And Israel** served the LORD all the days of Joshua, and all the days of the elders that overlived Joshua, and which had known all the works of the LORD, that he had done for Israel.

32 **And the bones of Joseph**, {which the children of Israel brought up out of Egypt}, buried they in Shechem, in a parcel of ground which Jacob bought of the sons of Hamor the father of Shechem for an hundred pieces of silver:
and it became the inheritance of the children of Joseph.

33 **And Eleazar the son of Aaron** died;
and they buried him in a hill that pertained to Phinehas his son,
which was given him in mount Ephraim.

Judges

The Book of Judges (author unknown but possibly the prophet Samuel) tells the story of the Israelites from the time of Joshua's death until the birth of Samuel. It provides an account of the Israelites' struggles and triumphs as they seek to establish a nation in the land of Canaan. The book describes the period of the judges, a time of political and religious turmoil in Israel when judges ruled the nation before the establishment of its monarchy. These judges are leaders, chosen by God, who help the Israelites maintain their faith and resist the temptations of the surrounding cultures.

Judges contains some of the Bible's most famous passages that scholars and theologians have studied and analyzed for centuries. Deborah, a prophetess and judge, leads the Israelites in a battle against the Canaanites. Gideon, called by God to lead the Israelites against the Midianites, tests God's promise by asking for a sign involving a fleece. When God proves Himself faithful, Gideon gathers an army and defeats the Midianites. Samson, a judge given supernatural strength by God, is betrayed by a Philistine woman he falls in love with, Delilah, who cuts his hair to weaken him. The Philistines then capture him and gouge out his eyes. Still, he regains his strength and destroys their temple, killing himself and many others.

The Book of Judges reminds readers of the challenges faced by the Israelites during this period and the importance of remaining faithful to God in the face of adversity. It also highlights the cyclical nature of Israel's history. This pattern involves a period of disobedience and turning away from God, followed by divine judgment or punishment, leading to repentance and a return to God's favor.

1 **Now after the death of Joshua** it came to pass,
that the children of Israel asked the LORD,
saying,
Who shall go up for us against the Canaanites first,
to fight against them?

2 **And the LORD** said,
Judah shall go up:
behold,
I have delivered the land into his hand.

3 **And Judah** said unto Simeon his brother,
Come up with me into my lot,
that we may fight against the Canaanites;
and I likewise will go with thee into thy lot.
So Simeon went with him.

4 **And Judah** went up;
and the LORD delivered the Canaanites and the Perizzites into their hand:
and they slew of them in Bezek ten thousand men.

5 **And they** found Adonibezek in Bezek:
and they fought against him,
and they slew the Canaanites and the Perizzites.

6 **But Adonibezek** fled;
and they pursued after him,
and caught him,
and cut off his thumbs and his great toes.

7 **And Adonibezek** said,
Threescore and ten kings, {having their thumbs and their great toes cut off}, gathered their meat under my table:
as I have done,
so God hath requited me.
And they brought him to Jerusalem,
and there he died.

8 **Now the children of Judah** had fought against Jerusalem,
and had taken it,
and smitten it with the edge of the sword,
and set the city on fire.

9 **And afterward** the children of Judah went down to fight against the Canaanites,
that dwelt in the mountain, and in the south, and in the valley.

10 **And Judah** went against the Canaanites that dwelt in Hebron:
(now the name of Hebron before was Kirjatharba:)
and they slew Sheshai, and Ahiman, and Talmai.

11 **And from thence** he went against the inhabitants of Debir:
and the name of Debir before was Kirjathsepher:

12 **And Caleb** said,
He that smiteth Kirjathsepher, and taketh it, to him will I give Achsah my daughter to wife.

13 **And Othniel the son of Kenaz, Caleb's younger brother**, took it:
and he gave him Achsah his daughter to wife.

14 **And it** came to pass,
when she came to him,
that she moved him to ask of her father a field:
and she lighted from off her ass;
and Caleb said unto her,
What wilt thou?

15 **And she** said unto him,
Give me a blessing:
for thou hast given me a south land;
give me also springs of water.
And Caleb gave her the upper springs and the nether springs.

16 **And the children of the Kenite, Moses' father in law,** went up out of the city of palm trees with the children of Judah into the wilderness of Judah,
which lieth in the south of Arad;
and they went and dwelt among the people.

17 **And Judah** went with Simeon his brother,
and they slew the Canaanites that inhabited Zephath,
and utterly destroyed it.

And the name of the city was called Hormah.

18 **Also Judah** took Gaza with the coast thereof, and Askelon with the coast thereof, and Ekron with the coast thereof.

19 **And the LORD** was with Judah;
and he drave out the inhabitants of the mountain;
but could not drive out the inhabitants of the valley,
because they had chariots of iron.

20 **And they** gave Hebron unto Caleb,
as Moses said:
and he expelled thence the three sons of Anak.

21 **And the children of Benjamin** did not drive out the Jebusites that inhabited Jerusalem;
but the Jebusites dwell with the children of Benjamin in Jerusalem unto this day.

22 **And the house of Joseph,** they also went up against Bethel:
and the LORD was with them.

23 **And the house of Joseph** sent to descry Bethel.
(**Now the name of the city before** was Luz.)

24 **And the spies** saw a man come forth out of the city,
and they said unto him,
Shew us, {we pray thee}, the entrance into the city,
and we will shew thee mercy.

25 **And when he** shewed them the entrance into the city,
they smote the city with the edge of the sword;
but they let go the man and all his family.

26 **And the man** went into the land of the Hittites,
and built a city,
and called the name thereof Luz:
which is the name thereof unto this day.

27 **Neither** did Manasseh drive out the inhabitants of Bethshean and her towns, nor Taanach and her towns, nor the inhabitants of Dor and her towns, nor the inhabitants of Ibleam and her towns, nor the inhabitants of Megiddo and her towns:
but the Canaanites would dwell in that land.

28 **And it** came to pass,
when Israel was strong,
that they put the Canaanites to tribute,
and did not utterly drive them out.

29 **Neither** did Ephraim drive out the Canaanites that dwelt in Gezer;
but the Canaanites dwelt in Gezer among them.

30 **Neither** did Zebulun drive out the inhabitants of Kitron, nor the inhabitants of Nahalol;
but the Canaanites dwelt among them,
and became tributaries.

31 **Neither** did Asher drive out the inhabitants of Accho, nor the inhabitants of Zidon, nor of Ahlab, nor of Achzib, nor of Helbah, nor of Aphik, nor of Rehob:

32 **But the Asherites** dwelt among the Canaanites, the inhabitants of the land:
for they did not drive them out.

33 **Neither** did Naphtali drive out the inhabitants of Bethshemesh, nor the inhabitants of Bethanath;
but he dwelt among the Canaanites, the inhabitants of the land:
nevertheless the inhabitants of Bethshemesh and of Bethanath became tributaries unto them.

34 **And the Amorites** forced the children of Dan into the mountain:
for they would not suffer them to come down to the valley:

35 **But the Amorites** would dwell in mount Heres in Aijalon, and in Shaalbim:
yet the hand of the house of Joseph prevailed,
so that they became tributaries.

36 **And the coast of the Amorites** was from the going up to Akrabbim, from the rock, and upward.

2 **And an angel of the LORD** came up from Gilgal to Bochim,
and said,
I made you to go up out of Egypt,
and have brought you unto the land which I sware unto your fathers;
and I said,
I will never break my covenant with you.

2 **And ye** shall make no league with the inhabitants of this land;
ye shall throw down their altars:
but ye have not obeyed my voice:
why have ye done this?

3 **Wherefore I** also said,
I will not drive them out from before you;
but they shall be as thorns in your sides,
and their gods shall be a snare unto you.

4 **And it** came to pass,
when the angel of the LORD spake these words unto all the children of Israel,
that the people lifted up their voice,
and wept.

5 **And they** called the name of that place Bochim:
and they sacrificed there unto the LORD.

6 **And when Joshua** had let the people go,
the children of Israel went every man unto his inheritance
to possess the land.

7 **And the people** served the LORD all the days of Joshua, and all the days of the elders that outlived Joshua,
who had seen all the great works of the LORD,
that he did for Israel.

8 **And Joshua the son of Nun, the servant of the LORD,** died,
being an hundred and ten years old.

9 **And they** buried him in the border of his inheritance in Timnathheres, in the mount of Ephraim, on the north side of the hill Gaash.

10 **And also all that generation** were gathered unto their fathers:
and there arose another generation after them,
which knew not the LORD, nor yet the works which he had done for Israel.

11 **And the children of Israel** did evil in the sight of the LORD,
and served Baalim:

12 **And they** forsook the LORD God of their fathers,
which brought them out of the land of Egypt,
and followed other gods, of the gods of the people that were round about them,

and bowed themselves unto them,
and provoked the LORD to anger.
13 **And they** forsook the LORD,
and served Baal and Ashtaroth.14 **And the anger of the LORD** was hot against Israel,
and he delivered them into the hands of spoilers that spoiled them,
and he sold them into the hands of their enemies round about,
so that they could not any longer stand before their enemies.
15 **Whithersoever they** went out,
the hand of the LORD was against them for evil,
as the LORD had said,
and as the LORD had sworn unto them:
and they were greatly distressed.
16 **Nevertheless the LORD** raised up judges,
which delivered them out of the hand of those that spoiled them.
17 **And yet they** would not hearken unto their judges,
but they went a whoring after other gods,
and bowed themselves unto them:
they turned quickly out of the way which their fathers walked in,
obeying the commandments of the LORD;
but they did not so.
18 **And when the LORD** raised them up judges,
then the LORD was with the judge,
and delivered them out of the hand of their enemies all the days of the judge:
for it repented the LORD because of their groanings by reason of them that oppressed them and vexed them.
19 **And it** came to pass,
when the judge was dead,
that they returned,
and corrupted themselves more than their fathers,
in following other gods to serve them,
and to bow down unto them;
they ceased not from their own doings, nor from their stubborn way.
20 **And the anger of the LORD** was hot against Israel;
and he said,
Because that this people hath transgressed my covenant which I commanded their fathers,
and have not hearkened unto my voice;
21 **I** also will not henceforth drive out any from before them of the nations which Joshua left when he died:
22 **That through them** I may prove Israel,
whether they will keep the way of the LORD to walk therein,
as their fathers did keep it, or not.
23 **Therefore the LORD** left those nations,
without driving them out hastily;
neither delivered he them into the hand of Joshua.

3 **Now these** are the nations which the LORD left,
to prove Israel by them, even as many of Israel as had not known all the wars of Canaan;
2 **Only that the generations of the children of Israel** might know,
to teach them war, at the least such as before knew nothing thereof;
3 Namely, five lords of the Philistines, and all the Canaanites, and the Sidonians, and the Hivites that dwelt in mount Lebanon, from mount Baalhermon unto the entering in of Hamath.
4 **And they** were to prove Israel by them,
to know
whether they would hearken unto the commandments of the LORD,
which he commanded their fathers by the hand of Moses.
5 **And the children of Israel** dwelt among the Canaanites, Hittites, and Amorites, and Perizzites, and Hivites, and Jebusites:
6 **And they** took their daughters to be their wives,
and gave their daughters to their sons,
and served their gods.
7 **And the children of Israel** did evil in the sight of the LORD,
and forgat the LORD their God,
and served Baalim and the groves.
8 **Therefore the anger of the LORD** was hot against Israel,
and he sold them into the hand of Chushanrishathaim king of Mesopotamia:
and the children of Israel served Chushanrishathaim eight years.
9 **And when the children of Israel** cried unto the LORD,
the LORD raised up a deliverer to the children of Israel,
who delivered them, even Othniel the son of Kenaz, Caleb's younger brother.
10 **And the Spirit of the LORD** came upon him,
and he judged Israel,
and went out to war:
and the LORD delivered Chushanrishathaim king of Mesopotamia into his hand;
and his hand prevailed against Chushanrishathaim.
11 **And the land** had rest forty years.
And Othniel the son of Kenaz died.
12 **And the children of Israel** did evil again in the sight of the LORD:
and the LORD strengthened Eglon the king of Moab against Israel,
because they had done evil in the sight of the LORD.
13 **And he** gathered unto him the children of Ammon and Amalek,
and went and smote Israel,
and possessed the city of palm trees.
14 **So the children of Israel** served Eglon the king of Moab eighteen years.
15 **But when the children of Israel** cried unto the LORD,
the LORD raised them up a deliverer, Ehud the son of Gera, a Benjamite, a man lefthanded:
and by him the children of Israel sent a present unto Eglon the king of Moab.
16 **But Ehud** made him a dagger which had two edges, of a cubit length;
and he did gird it under his raiment upon his right thigh.
17 **And he** brought the present unto Eglon king of Moab:
and Eglon was a very fat man.
18 **And when he** had made an end to offer the present,
he sent away the people that bare the present.
19 **But he himself** turned again from the quarries that were by Gilgal,
and said,

I have a secret errand unto thee, O king:
who said,
Keep silence.

And all that stood by him went out from him.

20 **And Ehud** came unto him;
and he was sitting in a summer parlour,
which he had for himself alone.

And Ehud said,
I have a message from God unto thee.

And he arose out of his seat.

21 **And Ehud** put forth his left hand,
and took the dagger from his right thigh,
and thrust it into his belly:
22 **And the haft** also went in after the blade;
and the fat closed upon the blade,
so that he could not draw the dagger out of his belly;
and the dirt came out.

23 **Then Ehud** went forth through the porch,
and shut the doors of the parlour upon him,
and locked them.

24 **When he** was gone out,
his servants came;
and when they saw that, {behold}, the doors of the parlour were locked,
they said,
Surely he covereth his feet in his summer chamber.

25 **And they** tarried
till they were ashamed:
and, {behold}, he opened not the doors of the parlour;
therefore they took a key,
and opened them:
and, {behold}, their lord was fallen down dead on the earth.

26 **And Ehud** escaped
while they tarried,
and passed beyond the quarries,
and escaped unto Seirath.

27 **And it** came to pass,
when he was come,
that he blew a trumpet in the mountain of Ephraim,
and the children of Israel went down with him from the mount, and he before them.

28 **And he** said unto them,
Follow after me:
for the LORD hath delivered your enemies the Moabites into your hand.

And they went down after him,
and took the fords of Jordan toward Moab,
and suffered not a man to pass over.

29 **And they** slew of Moab at that time about ten thousand men, all lusty, and all men of valour;
and there escaped not a man.

30 **So Moab** was subdued that day under the hand of Israel.

And the land had rest fourscore years.

31 **And after him** was Shamgar the son of Anath,
which slew of the Philistines six hundred men with an ox goad:
and he also delivered Israel.

4

And the children of Israel again did evil in the sight of the LORD,
when Ehud was dead.

2 **And the LORD** sold them into the hand of Jabin king of Canaan,
that reigned in Hazor;
the captain of whose host was Sisera,
which dwelt in Harosheth of the Gentiles.

3 **And the children of Israel** cried unto the LORD:
for he had nine hundred chariots of iron;
and twenty years he mightily oppressed the children of Israel.

4 **And Deborah, a prophetess, the wife of Lapidoth,** she judged Israel at that time.

5 **And she** dwelt under the palm tree of Deborah between Ramah and Bethel in mount Ephraim:
and the children of Israel came up to her for judgment.

6 **And she** sent and called Barak the son of Abinoam out of Kedeshnaphtali,
and said unto him,
Hath not the LORD God of Israel commanded,
saying,
Go and draw toward mount Tabor,
and take with thee ten thousand men of the children of Naphtali and of the children of Zebulun?

7 **And I** will draw unto thee to the river Kishon Sisera, the captain of Jabin's army, with his chariots and his multitude;
and I will deliver him into thine hand.

8 **And Barak** said unto her,
If thou wilt go with me,
then I will go:
but if thou wilt not go with me,
then I will not go.

9 **And she** said,
I will surely go with thee:
notwithstanding the journey that thou takest shall not be for thine honour;
for the LORD shall sell Sisera into the hand of a woman.

And Deborah arose,
and went with Barak to Kedesh.

10 **And Barak** called Zebulun and Naphtali to Kedesh;
and he went up with ten thousand men at his feet:
and Deborah went up with him.

11 **Now Heber the Kenite,** {which was of the children of Hobab the father in law of Moses}, had severed himself from the Kenites,
and pitched his tent unto the plain of Zaanaim,
which is by Kedesh.

12 **And they** shewed Sisera
that Barak the son of Abinoam was gone up to mount Tabor.

13 **And Sisera** gathered together all his chariots, even nine hundred chariots of iron, and all the people that were with him, from Harosheth of the Gentiles unto the river of Kishon.

14 **And Deborah** said unto Barak,
Up;
for this is the day in which the LORD hath delivered Sisera into thine hand:
is not the LORD gone out before thee?

So Barak went down from mount Tabor, and ten thousand men after him.

15 **And the LORD** discomfited Sisera, and all his chariots, and all his host, with the edge of the sword before Barak;
so that Sisera lighted down off his chariot,
and fled away on his feet.

16 **But Barak** pursued after the chariots, and after the host, unto Harosheth of the Gentiles:

and all the host of Sisera fell upon the edge of the sword;
and there was not a man left.

17 **Howbeit Sisera** fled away on his feet to the tent of Jael the wife of Heber the Kenite:
for there was peace between Jabin the king of Hazor and the house of Heber the Kenite.

18 **And Jael** went out to meet Sisera,
and said unto him,
Turn in, my lord,
turn in to me;
fear not.

And when he had turned in unto her into the tent,
she covered him with a mantle.

19 **And he** said unto her,
Give me, {I pray thee}, a little water to drink;
for I am thirsty.

And she opened a bottle of milk,
and gave him drink,
and covered him.

20 **Again he** said unto her,
Stand in the door of the tent,
and it shall be,
when any man doth come and enquire of thee,
and say,
Is there any man here?
that thou shalt say,
No.

21 **Then Jael Heber's wife** took a nail of the tent,
and took an hammer in her hand,
and went softly unto him,
and smote the nail into his temples,
and fastened it into the ground:
for he was fast asleep and weary.

So he died.

22 **And, {behold}, as Barak** pursued Sisera,
Jael came out
to meet him,
and said unto him,
Come,
and I will shew thee the man whom thou seekest.

And when he came into her tent,
behold,
Sisera lay dead,
and the nail was in his temples.

23 **So God** subdued on that day Jabin the king of Canaan before the children of Israel.

24 **And the hand of the children of Israel** prospered,
and prevailed against Jabin the king of Canaan,
until they had destroyed Jabin king of Canaan.

5 **Then** sang Deborah and Barak the son of Abinoam on that day,
saying,

2 **Praise ye** the LORD for the avenging of Israel,
when the people willingly offered themselves.

3 **Hear,** O ye kings;
give ear, O ye princes;
I, even I, will sing unto the LORD;
I will sing praise to the LORD God of Israel.

4 **LORD, when thou** wentest out of Seir,
when thou marchedst out of the field of Edom,
the earth trembled,
and the heavens dropped,
the clouds also dropped water.

5 **The mountains** melted from before the LORD, even that Sinai from before the LORD God of Israel.

6 **In the days of Shamgar the son of Anath, in the days of Jael,** the highways were unoccupied,
and the travellers walked through byways.

7 **The inhabitants of the villages** ceased,
they ceased in Israel,
until that I Deborah arose,
that I arose a mother in Israel.

8 **They** chose new gods;
then was war in the gates:
was there a shield or spear seen among forty thousand in Israel?

9 **My heart** is toward the governors of Israel,
that offered themselves willingly among the people.

Bless ye the LORD.

10 **Speak,** ye that ride on white asses, ye that sit in judgment,
and walk by the way.

11 **They that are delivered from the noise of archers in the places of drawing water,** there shall they rehearse the righteous acts of the LORD, even the righteous acts toward the inhabitants of his villages in Israel:
then shall the people of the LORD go down to the gates.

12 **Awake,**
awake, Deborah:
awake,
awake,
utter a song:
arise, Barak,
and lead thy captivity captive, thou son of Abinoam.

13 **Then he** made him that remaineth have dominion over the nobles among the people:
the LORD made me have dominion over the mighty.

14 **Out of Ephraim** was there a root of them against Amalek; after thee, Benjamin, among thy people;
out of Machir came down governors, and out of Zebulun they that handle the pen of the writer.

15 **And the princes of Issachar** were with Deborah; even Issachar, and also Barak:
he was sent on foot into the valley.

For the divisions of Reuben there were great thoughts of heart.

16 **Why** abodest thou among the sheepfolds,
to hear the bleatings of the flocks?

For the divisions of Reuben there were great searchings of heart.

17 **Gilead** abode beyond Jordan:
and why did Dan remain in ships?

Asher continued on the sea shore,
and abode in his breaches.

18 **Zebulun and Naphtali** were a people that jeoparded their lives unto the death in the high places of the field.

19 **The kings** came and fought,
then fought the kings of Canaan in Taanach by the waters of Megiddo;
they took no gain of money.

20 **They** fought from heaven;
the stars in their courses fought against Sisera.

21 **The river of Kishon** swept them away, that ancient river, the river Kishon.

O my soul, thou hast trodden down strength.

22 **Then** were the horsehoofs broken by the means of the pransings, the pransings of their mighty ones.

23 **Curse ye Meroz,** said the angel of the LORD,

curse ye bitterly the inhabitants thereof;
because they came not to the help of the LORD,
to the help of the LORD against the mighty.

24 **Blessed above women** shall Jael the wife of Heber the Kenite be,
blessed shall she be above women in the tent.

25 **He** asked water,
and she gave him milk;
she brought forth butter in a lordly dish.

26 **She** put her hand to the nail, and her right hand to the workmen's hammer;
and with the hammer she smote Sisera,
she smote off his head,
when she had pierced and stricken through his temples.

27 **At her feet** he bowed,
he fell,
he lay down:
at her feet he bowed,
he fell:
where he bowed,
there he fell down dead.

28 **The mother of Sisera** looked out at a window,
and cried through the lattice,
Why is his chariot so long in coming?
why tarry the wheels of his chariots?

29 **Her wise ladies** answered her,
yea, she returned answer to herself,
30 **Have they not** sped?
have they not divided the prey; to every man a damsel or two; to Sisera a prey of divers colours, a prey of divers colours of needlework, of divers colours of needlework on both sides, meet for the necks of them that take the spoil?

31 **So let all thine enemies** perish, O LORD:
but let them that love him be as the sun when he goeth forth in his might.
And the land had rest forty years.

6

And the children of Israel did evil in the sight of the LORD:
and the LORD delivered them into the hand of Midian seven years.

2 **And the hand of Midian** prevailed against Israel:
and because of the Midianites the children of Israel made them the dens which are in the mountains, and caves, and strong holds.

3 **And so it was**, {when Israel had sown}, that the Midianites came up, and the Amalekites, and the children of the east,
even they came up against them;
4 **And they** encamped against them,
and destroyed the increase of the earth,
till thou come unto Gaza,
and left no sustenance for Israel, neither sheep, nor ox, nor ass.

5 **For they** came up with their cattle and their tents,
and they came as grasshoppers for multitude;
for both they and their camels were without number:
and they entered into the land
to destroy it.

6 **And Israel** was greatly impoverished because of the Midianites;
and the children of Israel cried unto the LORD.

7 **And it** came to pass,
when the children of Israel cried unto the LORD because of the Midianites,
8 **That the LORD** sent a prophet unto the children of Israel,
which said unto them,
Thus saith the LORD God of Israel,
I brought you up from Egypt,
and brought you forth out of the house of bondage;
9 **And I** delivered you out of the hand of the Egyptians, and out of the hand of all that oppressed you,
and drave them out from before you,
and gave you their land;
10 **And I** said unto you,
I am the LORD your God;
fear not the gods of the Amorites,
in whose land ye dwell:
but ye have not obeyed my voice.

11 **And there** came an angel of the LORD,
and sat under an oak which was in Ophrah,
that pertained unto Joash the Abiezrite:
and his son Gideon threshed wheat by the winepress,
to hide it from the Midianites.

12 **And the angel of the LORD** appeared unto him,
and said unto him,
The LORD is with thee, thou mighty man of valour.

13 **And Gideon** said unto him,
Oh my Lord, if the LORD be with us,
why then is all this befallen us?
and where be all his miracles which our fathers told us of,
saying,
Did not the LORD bring us up from Egypt?
but now the LORD hath forsaken us,
and delivered us into the hands of the Midianites.

14 **And the LORD** looked upon him,
and said,
Go in this thy might,
and thou shalt save Israel from the hand of the Midianites:
have not I sent thee?

15 **And he** said unto him,
Oh my Lord, wherewith shall I save Israel?
behold,
my family is poor in Manasseh,
and I am the least in my father's house.

16 **And the LORD** said unto him,
Surely I will be with thee,
and thou shalt smite the Midianites as one man.

17 **And he** said unto him,
If now I have found grace in thy sight,
then shew me a sign that thou talkest with me.

18 **Depart not** hence,
I pray thee,
until I come unto thee,
and bring forth my present,
and set it before thee.

And he said,
I will tarry
until thou come again.

19 **And Gideon** went in,
and made ready a kid, and unleavened cakes of an ephah of flour:
the flesh he put in a basket,
and he put the broth in a pot,
and brought it out unto him under the oak,
and presented it.

20 **And the angel of God** said unto him,
Take the flesh and the unleavened cakes,
and lay them upon this rock,
and pour out the broth.
And he did so.

21 **Then the angel of the LORD** put forth the end of the staff that was in his hand,
and touched the flesh and the unleavened cakes;
and there rose up fire out of the rock,
and consumed the flesh and the unleavened cakes.
Then the angel of the LORD departed out of his sight.

22 **And when Gideon** perceived that he was an angel of the LORD,
Gideon said,
Alas, O Lord GOD!
for because I have seen an angel of the LORD face to face.

23 **And the LORD** said unto him,
Peace be unto thee;
fear not:
thou shalt not die.

24 **Then Gideon** built an altar there unto the LORD,
and called it Jehovahshalom:
unto this day it is yet in Ophrah of the Abiezrites.

25 **And it** came to pass the same night,
that the LORD said unto him,
Take thy father's young bullock, even the second bullock of seven years old,
and throw down the altar of Baal that thy father hath,
and cut down the grove that is by it:

26 **And build** an altar unto the LORD thy God upon the top of this rock, in the ordered place,
and take the second bullock,
and offer a burnt sacrifice with the wood of the grove which thou shalt cut down.

27 **Then Gideon** took ten men of his servants,
and did as the LORD had said unto him:
and so it was,
because he feared his father's household, and the men of the city,
that he could not do it by day,
that he did it by night.

28 **And when the men of the city** arose early in the morning,
behold,
the altar of Baal was cast down,
and the grove was cut down that was by it,
and the second bullock was offered upon the altar that was built.

29 **And they** said one to another,
Who hath done this thing?
And when they enquired and asked,
they said,
Gideon the son of Joash hath done this thing.

30 **Then the men of the city** said unto Joash,
Bring out thy son,
that he may die:
because he hath cast down the altar of Baal,
and because he hath cut down the grove that was by it.

31 **And Joash** said unto all that stood against him,
Will ye plead for Baal?
will ye save him?
he that will plead for him, let him be put to death whilst it is yet morning:
if he be a god,
let him plead for himself,
because one hath cast down his altar.

32 **Therefore on that day** he called him Jerubbaal,
saying,
Let Baal plead against him,
because he hath thrown down his altar.

33 **Then all the Midianites and the Amalekites and the children of the east** were gathered together,
and went over,
and pitched in the valley of Jezreel.

34 **But the Spirit of the LORD** came upon Gideon,
and he blew a trumpet;
and Abiezer was gathered after him.

35 **And he** sent messengers throughout all Manasseh;
who also was gathered after him:
and he sent messengers unto Asher, and unto Zebulun, and unto Naphtali;
and they came up
to meet them.

36 **And Gideon** said unto God,
If thou wilt save Israel by mine hand,
as thou hast said,

37 **Behold,**
I will put a fleece of wool in the floor;
and if the dew be on the fleece only,
and it be dry upon all the earth beside,
then shall I know
that thou wilt save Israel by mine hand,
as thou hast said.

38 **And it** was so:
for he rose up early on the morrow,
and thrust the fleece together,
and wringed the dew out of the fleece, a bowl full of water.

39 **And Gideon** said unto God,
Let not thine anger be hot against me,
and I will speak but this once:
let me prove, {I pray thee}, but this once with the fleece;
let it now be dry only upon the fleece,
and upon all the ground let there be dew.

40 **And God** did so that night:
for it was dry upon the fleece only,
and there was dew on all the ground.

7 **Then Jerubbaal, {who is Gideon}, and all the people that were with him**, rose up early,
and pitched beside the well of Harod:
so that the host of the Midianites were on the north side of them, by the hill of Moreh, in the valley.

2 **And the LORD** said unto Gideon,
The people that are with thee are too many for me to give the Midianites into their hands,
lest Israel vaunt themselves against me,
saying,
Mine own hand hath saved me.

3 **Now therefore go to,**
proclaim in the ears of the people,
saying,
Whosoever is fearful and afraid,
let him return and depart early from mount Gilead.
And there returned of the people twenty and two thousand;
and there remained ten thousand.

4 **And the LORD** said unto Gideon,
The people are yet too many;
bring them down unto the water,
and I will try them for thee there:
and it shall be,
that of whom I say unto thee,
This shall go with thee,
the same shall go with thee;
and of whomsoever I say unto thee,
This shall not go with thee,
the same shall not go.

5 **So he** brought down the people unto the water:
and the LORD said unto Gideon,
Every one that lappeth of the water with his tongue, as a dog lappeth, him shalt thou set by himself; likewise every one that boweth down upon his knees to drink.

6 **And the number of them that lapped**, {putting their hand to their mouth}, were three hundred men:
but all the rest of the people bowed down upon their knees
to drink water.

7 **And the LORD** said unto Gideon,
By the three hundred men that lapped will I save you,
and deliver the Midianites into thine hand:
and let all the other people go every man unto his place.

8 **So the people** took victuals in their hand, and their trumpets:
and he sent all the rest of Israel every man unto his tent,
and retained those three hundred men:
and the host of Midian was beneath him in the valley.

9 **And it** came to pass the same night,
that the LORD said unto him,
Arise,
get thee down unto the host;
for I have delivered it into thine hand.

10 **But if thou** fear to go down,
go thou with Phurah thy servant down to the host:

11 **And thou** shalt hear what they say;
and afterward shall thine hands be strengthened to go down unto the host.
Then went he down with Phurah his servant unto the outside of the armed men that were in the host.

12 **And the Midianites and the Amalekites and all the children of the east** lay along in the valley like grasshoppers for multitude;
and their camels were without number, as the sand by the sea side for multitude.

13 **And when Gideon** was come,
behold,
there was a man that told a dream unto his fellow,
and said,
Behold,
I dreamed a dream,
and, {lo}, a cake of barley bread tumbled into the host of Midian,
and came unto a tent,
and smote it
that it fell,
and overturned it,
that the tent lay along.

14 **And his fellow** answered and said,
This is nothing else save the sword of Gideon the son of Joash, a man of Israel:
for into his hand hath God delivered Midian, and all the host.

15 **And it** was so,
when Gideon heard the telling of the dream, and the interpretation thereof,
that he worshipped,
and returned into the host of Israel,
and said,
Arise;
for the LORD hath delivered into your hand the host of Midian.

16 **And he** divided the three hundred men into three companies,
and he put a trumpet in every man's hand, with empty pitchers, and lamps within the pitchers.

17 **And he** said unto them,
Look on me,
and do likewise:
and, {behold}, when I come to the outside of the camp,
it shall be
that, {as I do}, so shall ye do.

18 **When I** blow with a trumpet, I and all that are with me,
then blow ye the trumpets also on every side of all the camp,
and say,
The sword of the LORD, and of Gideon.

19 **So Gideon, and the hundred men that were with him,** came unto the outside of the camp in the beginning of the middle watch;
and they had but newly set the watch:
and they blew the trumpets,
and brake the pitchers that were in their hands.

20 **And the three companies** blew the trumpets,
and brake the pitchers,
and held the lamps in their left hands, and the trumpets in their right hands
to blow withal:
and they cried,
The sword of the LORD, and of Gideon.

21 **And they** stood every man in his place round about the camp;
and all the host ran,
and cried,
and fled.

22 **And the three hundred** blew the trumpets,
and the LORD set every man's sword against his fellow, even throughout all the host:
and the host fled to Bethshittah in Zererath, and to the border of Abelmeholah, unto Tabbath.

23 **And the men of Israel** gathered themselves together out of Naphtali, and out of Asher, and out of all Manasseh,
and pursued after the Midianites.

24 **And Gideon** sent messengers throughout all mount Ephraim,
saying,
come down against the Midianites,
and take before them the waters unto Bethbarah and Jordan.
Then all the men of Ephraim gathered themselves together,
and took the waters unto Bethbarah and Jordan.

25 **And they** took two princes of the Midianites, Oreb and Zeeb;
and they slew Oreb upon the rock Oreb,
and Zeeb they slew at the winepress of Zeeb,
and pursued Midian,
and brought the heads of Oreb and Zeeb to Gideon on the other side Jordan.

8 ∞ **And the men of Ephraim** said unto him,
Why hast thou served us thus,
that thou calledst us not,
when thou wentest to fight with the Midianites?
And they did chide with him sharply.
2 **And he** said unto them,
What have I done now in comparison of you?
Is not the gleaning of the grapes of Ephraim better than the vintage of Abiezer?
3 **God** hath delivered into your hands the princes of Midian, Oreb and Zeeb:
and what was I able to do in comparison of you?
Then their anger was abated toward him,
when he had said that.
4 **And Gideon** came to Jordan,
and passed over, he, and the three hundred men that were with him, faint,
yet pursuing them.
5 **And he** said unto the men of Succoth,
Give, {I pray you}, loaves of bread unto the people that follow me;
for they be faint,
and I am pursuing after Zebah and Zalmunna, kings of Midian.
6 **And the princes of Succoth** said,
Are the hands of Zebah and Zalmunna now in thine hand,
that we should give bread unto thine army?
7 **And Gideon** said,
Therefore when the LORD hath delivered Zebah and Zalmunna into mine hand,
then I will tear your flesh with the thorns of the wilderness and with briers.
8 **And he** went up thence to Penuel,
and spake unto them likewise:
and the men of Penuel answered him
as the men of Succoth had answered him.
9 **And he** spake also unto the men of Penuel,
saying,
When I come again in peace,
I will break down this tower.
10 **Now Zebah and Zalmunna** were in Karkor, and their hosts with them, about fifteen thousand men, all that were left of all the hosts of the children of the east:
for there fell an hundred and twenty thousand men that drew sword.
11 **And Gideon** went up by the way of them that dwelt in tents on the east of Nobah and Jogbehah,
and smote the host;
for the host was secure.
12 **And when Zebah and Zalmunna** fled,
he pursued after them,
and took the two kings of Midian, Zebah and Zalmunna,
and discomfited all the host.
13 **And Gideon the son of Joash** returned from battle
before the sun was up,
14 **And** caught a young man of the men of Succoth,
and enquired of him:
and he described unto him the princes of Succoth, and the elders thereof, even threescore and seventeen men.
15 **And he** came unto the men of Succoth,
and said,
Behold Zebah and Zalmunna,
with whom ye did upbraid me,
saying,
Are the hands of Zebah and Zalmunna now in thine hand,
that we should give bread unto thy men that are weary?
16 **And he** took the elders of the city, and thorns of the wilderness and briers,
and with them he taught the men of Succoth.
17 **And he** beat down the tower of Penuel,
and slew the men of the city.
18 **Then** said he unto Zebah and Zalmunna,
What manner of men were they whom ye slew at Tabor?
And they answered,
As thou art,
so were they;
each one resembled the children of a king.
19 **And he** said,
They were my brethren, even the sons of my mother:
as the LORD liveth,
if ye had saved them alive,
I would not slay you.
20 **And he** said unto Jether his firstborn,
Up,
and slay them.
But the youth drew not his sword:
for he feared,
because he was yet a youth.
21 **Then Zebah and Zalmunna** said,
Rise thou,
and fall upon us:
for as the man is,
so is his strength.
And Gideon arose,
and slew Zebah and Zalmunna,
and took away the ornaments that were on their camels' necks.
22 **Then the men of Israel** said unto Gideon,
Rule thou over us, both thou, and thy son, and thy son's son also:
for thou hast delivered us from the hand of Midian.
23 **And Gideon** said unto them,
I will not rule over you,
neither shall my son rule over you:
the LORD shall rule over you.
24 **And Gideon** said unto them,
I would desire a request of you,
that ye would give me every man the earrings of his prey.
(**For they** had golden earrings,
because they were Ishmaelites.)
25 **And they** answered,
We will willingly give them.
And they spread a garment,
and did cast therein every man the earrings of his prey.
26 **And the weight of the golden earrings that he requested** was a thousand and seven hundred shekels of gold; beside ornaments, and collars, and purple raiment that was on the kings of Midian, and beside the chains that were about their camels' necks.
27 **And Gideon** made an ephod thereof,
and put it in his city, even in Ophrah:
and all Israel went thither a whoring after it:
which thing became a snare unto Gideon, and to his house.
28 **Thus** was Midian subdued before the children of Israel,
so that they lifted up their heads no more.

And the country was in quietness forty years in the days of Gideon.

29 **And Jerubbaal the son of Joash** went and dwelt in his own house.

30 **And Gideon** had threescore and ten sons of his body begotten:
for he had many wives.

31 **And his concubine that was in Shechem,** she also bare him a son,
whose name he called Abimelech.

32 **And Gideon the son of Joash** died in a good old age,
and was buried in the sepulchre of Joash his father, in Ophrah of the Abiezrites.

33 **And it** came to pass,
as soon as Gideon was dead,
that the children of Israel turned again,
and went a whoring after Baalim,
and made Baalberith their god.

34 **And the children of Israel** remembered not the LORD their God,
who had delivered them out of the hands of all their enemies on every side:

35 **Neither** shewed they kindness to the house of Jerubbaal, namely, Gideon, according to all the goodness which he had shewed unto Israel.

9 **And Abimelech the son of Jerubbaal** went to Shechem unto his mother's brethren,
and communed with them, and with all the family of the house of his mother's father,
saying,

2 **Speak**, {I pray you}, in the ears of all the men of Shechem,
Whether is better for you,
either that all the sons of Jerubbaal, {which are threescore and ten persons}, reign over you,
or that one reign over you?
remember also
that I am your bone and your flesh.

3 **And his mother's brethren** spake of him in the ears of all the men of Shechem all these words:
and their hearts inclined to follow Abimelech;
for they said,
He is our brother.

4 **And they** gave him threescore and ten pieces of silver out of the house of Baalberith,
wherewith Abimelech hired vain and light persons,
which followed him.

5 **And he** went unto his father's house at Ophrah,
and slew his brethren the sons of Jerubbaal,
being threescore and ten persons, upon one stone:
notwithstanding yet Jotham the youngest son of Jerubbaal was left;
for he hid himself.

6 **And all the men of Shechem** gathered together, and all the house of Millo,
and went,
and made Abimelech king, by the plain of the pillar that was in Shechem.

7 **And when they** told it to Jotham,
he went and stood in the top of mount Gerizim,
and lifted up his voice,
and cried,
and said unto them,
Hearken unto me, ye men of Shechem,
that God may hearken unto you.

8 **The trees** went forth on a time
to anoint a king over them;
and they said unto the olive tree,
Reign thou over us.

9 **But the olive tree** said unto them,
Should I leave my fatness,
wherewith by me they honour God and man,
and go to be promoted over the trees?

10 **And the trees** said to the fig tree,
Come thou,
and reign over us.

11 **But the fig tree** said unto them,
Should I forsake my sweetness, and my good fruit,
and go to be promoted over the trees?

12 **Then** said the trees unto the vine,
Come thou,
and reign over us.

13 **And the vine** said unto them,
Should I leave my wine,
which cheereth God and man,
and go to be promoted over the trees?

14 **Then** said all the trees unto the bramble,
Come thou,
and reign over us.

15 **And the bramble** said unto the trees,
If in truth ye anoint me king over you,
then come and put your trust in my shadow:
and if not, let fire come out of the bramble,
and devour the cedars of Lebanon.

16 **Now therefore, if ye** have done truly and sincerely,
in that ye have made Abimelech king,
and if ye have dealt well with Jerubbaal and his house,
and have done unto him according to the deserving of his hands;

17 (For my father fought for you,
and adventured his life far,
and delivered you out of the hand of Midian:

18 And ye are risen up against my father's house this day,
and have slain his sons, threescore and ten persons, upon one stone,
and have made Abimelech, the son of his maidservant, king over the men of Shechem,
because he is your brother;)

19 **If ye** then have dealt truly and sincerely with Jerubbaal and with his house this day,
then rejoice ye in Abimelech,
and let him also rejoice in you:

20 **But if not, let fire** come out from Abimelech,
and devour the men of Shechem, and the house of Millo;
and let fire come out from the men of Shechem, and from the house of Millo,
and devour Abimelech.

21 **And Jotham** ran away, and fled,
and went to Beer,
and dwelt there, for fear of Abimelech his brother.

22 **When Abimelech** had reigned three years over Israel,

23 **Then God** sent an evil spirit between Abimelech and the men of Shechem;
and the men of Shechem dealt treacherously with Abimelech:

24 **That the cruelty done to the threescore and ten sons of Jerubbaal** might come,
and their blood be laid upon Abimelech their brother,
which slew them; and upon the men of Shechem,

which aided him in the killing of his brethren.

25 **And the men of Shechem** set liers in wait for him in the top of the mountains,
and they robbed all that came along that way by them:
and it was told Abimelech.

26 **And Gaal the son of Ebed** came with his brethren,
and went over to Shechem:
and the men of Shechem put their confidence in him.

27 **And they** went out into the fields,
and gathered their vineyards,
and trode the grapes,
and made merry,
and went into the house of their god,
and did eat and drink,
and cursed Abimelech.

28 **And Gaal the son of Ebed** said,
Who is Abimelech,
and who is Shechem,
that we should serve him?
is not he the son of Jerubbaal? and Zebul his officer?
serve the men of Hamor the father of Shechem:
for why should we serve him?

29 **And would to God this people** were under my hand!
then would I remove Abimelech.

And he said to Abimelech,
Increase thine army,
and come out.

30 **And when Zebul the ruler of the city** heard the words of Gaal the son of Ebed,
his anger was kindled.

31 **And he** sent messengers unto Abimelech privily,
saying,
Behold,
Gaal the son of Ebed and his brethren be come to Shechem;
and, {behold}, they fortify the city against thee.

32 **Now therefore up** by night, thou and the people that is with thee,
and lie in wait in the field:

33 **And it** shall be,
that in the morning, {as soon as the sun is up}, thou shalt rise early,
and set upon the city:
and, {behold}, when he and the people that is with him come out against thee,
then mayest thou do to them
as thou shalt find occasion.

34 **And Abimelech** rose up, and all the people that were with him, by night,
and they laid wait against Shechem in four companies.

35 **And Gaal the son of Ebed** went out,
and stood in the entering of the gate of the city:
and Abimelech rose up, and the people that were with him,
from lying in wait.

36 **And when Gaal** saw the people,
he said to Zebul,
Behold,
there come people down from the top of the mountains.

And Zebul said unto him,
Thou seest the shadow of the mountains
as if they were men.

37 **And Gaal** spake again,
and said,
See
there come people down by the middle of the land,
and another company come along by the plain of Meonenim.

38 **Then** said Zebul unto him,
Where is now thy mouth,
wherewith thou saidst,
Who is Abimelech,
that we should serve him?
is not this the people that thou hast despised?
go out, {I pray now}, and fight with them.

39 **And Gaal** went out before the men of Shechem,
and fought with Abimelech.

40 **And Abimelech** chased him,
and he fled before him,
and many were overthrown and wounded, even unto the entering of the gate.

41 **And Abimelech** dwelt at Arumah:
and Zebul thrust out Gaal and his brethren,
that they should not dwell in Shechem.

42 **And it** came to pass on the morrow,
that the people went out into the field;
and they told Abimelech.

43 **And he** took the people,
and divided them into three companies,
and laid wait in the field,
and looked,
and, {behold}, the people were come forth out of the city;
and he rose up against them,
and smote them.

44 **And Abimelech, and the company that was with him,** rushed forward,
and stood in the entering of the gate of the city:
and the two other companies ran upon all the people that were in the fields,
and slew them.

45 **And Abimelech** fought against the city all that day;
and he took the city,
and slew the people that was therein,
and beat down the city,
and sowed it with salt.

46 **And when all the men of the tower of Shechem** heard that,
they entered into an hold of the house of the god Berith.

47 **And it** was told Abimelech,
that all the men of the tower of Shechem were gathered together.

48 **And Abimelech** gat him up to mount Zalmon, he and all the people that were with him;
and Abimelech took an axe in his hand,
and cut down a bough from the trees,
and took it,
and laid it on his shoulder,
and said unto the people that were with him,
What ye have seen me do,
make haste,
and do as I have done.

49 **And all the people** likewise cut down every man his bough,
and followed Abimelech,
and put them to the hold,
and set the hold on fire upon them;
so that all the men of the tower of Shechem died also, about a thousand men and women.

50 **Then** went Abimelech to Thebez,
and encamped against Thebez,
and took it.

51 **But there** was a strong tower within the city,
and thither fled all the men and women, and all they of the city,
and shut it to them,

and gat them up to the top of the
tower.
52 **And Abimelech** came unto the
tower,
and fought against it,
and went hard unto the door of the
tower
to burn it with fire.
53 **And a certain woman** cast a
piece of a millstone upon
Abimelech's head,
and all to brake his skull.
54 **Then he** called hastily unto the
young man his armourbearer,
and said unto him,
Draw thy sword,
and slay me,
that men say not of me,
A women slew him.
And his young man thrust him
through,
and he died.
55 **And when the men of Israel** saw
that Abimelech was dead,
they departed every man unto his
place.
56 **Thus God** rendered the
wickedness of Abimelech,
which he did unto his father,
in slaying his seventy brethren:
57 **And all the evil of the men of
Shechem** did God render upon
their heads:
and upon them came the curse of
Jotham the son of Jerubbaal.

10 ✡ **And after Abimelech**
there arose to defend Israel
Tola the son of Puah, the son of
Dodo, a man of Issachar;
and he dwelt in Shamir in mount
Ephraim.
2 **And he** judged Israel twenty and
three years,
and died,
and was buried in Shamir.
3 **And after him** arose Jair, a
Gileadite,
and judged Israel twenty and two
years.
4 **And he** had thirty sons that rode
on thirty ass colts,
and they had thirty cities,
which are called Havothjair unto
this day,
which are in the land of Gilead.
5 **And Jair** died,
and was buried in Camon.
6 **And the children of Israel** did evil
again in the sight of the LORD,
and served Baalim, and Ashtaroth,
and the gods of Syria, and the
gods of Zidon, and the gods of
Moab, and the gods of the
children of Ammon, and the gods
of the Philistines,
and forsook the LORD,
and served not him.
7 **And the anger of the LORD** was
hot against Israel,
and he sold them into the hands of
the Philistines, and into the hands
of the children of Ammon.
8 **And that year** they vexed and
oppressed the children of Israel:
eighteen years, all the children of
Israel that were on the other side
Jordan in the land of the
Amorites, which is in Gilead.
9 **Moreover the children of
Ammon** passed over Jordan
to fight also against Judah, and
against Benjamin, and against the
house of Ephraim;
so that Israel was sore distressed.
10 **And the children of Israel** cried
unto the LORD,
saying,
We have sinned against thee,
both because we have forsaken our
God,
and also served Baalim.
11 **And the LORD** said unto the
children of Israel,
Did not I deliver you from the
Egyptians, and from the Amorites,
from the children of Ammon, and
from the Philistines?
12 **The Zidonians also, and the
Amalekites, and the Maonites,**
did oppress you;
and ye cried to me,
13 **Yet ye** have forsaken me,
and served other gods:
wherefore I will deliver you no
more.
14 **Go and cry** unto the gods which
ye have chosen;
let them deliver you in the time of
your tribulation.
15 **And the children of Israel** said
unto the LORD,
We have sinned:
do thou unto us whatsoever
seemeth good unto thee;
deliver us only, {we pray thee}, this
day.
16 **And they** put away the strange
gods from among them,
and served the LORD:
and his soul was grieved for the
misery of Israel.
17 **Then the children of Ammon**
were gathered together,
and encamped in Gilead.
And the children of Israel
assembled themselves together,
and encamped in Mizpeh.
18 **And the people and princes of
Gilead** said one to another,
What man is he that will begin to
fight against the children of
Ammon?
he shall be head over all the
inhabitants of Gilead.

11 **Now Jephthah the
Gileadite** was a mighty man
of valour,
and he was the son of an harlot:
and Gilead begat Jephthah.
2 **And Gilead's wife** bare him sons;
and his wife's sons grew up,
and they thrust out Jephthah,
and said unto him,
Thou shalt not inherit in our
father's house;
for thou art the son of a strange
woman.
3 **Then Jephthah** fled from his
brethren,
and dwelt in the land of Tob:
and there were gathered vain men
to Jephthah,
and went out with him.
4 **And it** came to pass in process of
time,
that the children of Ammon made
war against Israel.
5 **And it** was so,
that when the children of Ammon
made war against Israel,
the elders of Gilead went to fetch
Jephthah out of the land of Tob:
6 **And they** said unto Jephthah,
Come,
and be our captain,
that we may fight with the children
of Ammon.
7 **And Jephthah** said unto the elders
of Gilead,
Did not ye hate me,
and expel me out of my father's
house?
and why are ye come unto me now
when ye are in distress?
8 **And the elders of Gilead** said
unto Jephthah,
Therefore we turn again to thee
now,

that thou mayest go with us,
and fight against the children of Ammon,
and be our head over all the inhabitants of Gilead.

9 **And Jephthah** said unto the elders of Gilead,
If ye bring me home again to fight against the children of Ammon,
and the LORD deliver them before me,
shall I be your head?

10 **And the elders of Gilead** said unto Jephthah,
The LORD be witness between us,
if we do not so according to thy words.

11 **Then Jephthah** went with the elders of Gilead,
and the people made him head and captain over them:
and Jephthah uttered all his words before the LORD in Mizpeh.

12 **And Jephthah** sent messengers unto the king of the children of Ammon,
saying,
What hast thou to do with me,
that thou art come against me
to fight in my land?

13 **And the king of the children of Ammon** answered unto the messengers of Jephthah,
Because Israel took away my land,
when they came up out of Egypt, from Arnon even unto Jabbok, and unto Jordan:
now therefore restore those lands again peaceably.

14 **And Jephthah** sent messengers again unto the king of the children of Ammon:

15 **And** said unto him,
Thus saith Jephthah,
Israel took not away the land of Moab, nor the land of the children of Ammon:

16 **But when Israel** came up from Egypt,
and walked through the wilderness unto the Red sea,
and came to Kadesh;

17 **Then Israel** sent messengers unto the king of Edom,
saying,
Let me, {I pray thee}, pass through thy land:
but the king of Edom would not hearken thereto.
And in like manner they sent unto the king of Moab:
but he would not consent:
and Israel abode in Kadesh.

18 **Then they** went along through the wilderness,
and compassed the land of Edom, and the land of Moab,
and came by the east side of the land of Moab,
and pitched on the other side of Arnon,
but came not within the border of Moab:
for Arnon was the border of Moab.

19 **And Israel** sent messengers unto Sihon king of the Amorites, the king of Heshbon;
and Israel said unto him,
Let us pass, {<u>we</u> pray thee}, through thy land into my place.

20 **But Sihon** trusted not Israel to pass through his coast:
but Sihon gathered all his people together,
and pitched in Jahaz,
and fought against Israel.

21 **And the LORD God of Israel** delivered Sihon and all his people into the hand of Israel,
and they smote them:
so Israel possessed all the land of the Amorites, the inhabitants of that country.

22 **And they** possessed all the coasts of the Amorites, from Arnon even unto Jabbok, and from the wilderness even unto Jordan.

23 **So now the LORD God of Israel** hath dispossessed the Amorites from before his people Israel,
and shouldest thou possess it?

24 **Wilt not thou** possess that which Chemosh thy god giveth thee to possess?
So whomsoever the LORD our God shall drive out from before us,
them will we possess.

25 **And now art thou** any thing better than Balak the son of Zippor, king of Moab?
did he ever strive against Israel,
or did he ever fight against them,

26 **While Israel** dwelt in Heshbon and her towns, and in Aroer and her towns, and in all the cities that be along by the coasts of Arnon, three hundred years?
why therefore did ye not recover them within that time?

27 **Wherefore I** have not sinned against thee,
but thou doest me wrong to war against me:
the LORD the Judge be judge this day between the children of Israel and the children of Ammon.

28 **Howbeit the king of the children of Ammon** hearkened not unto the words of Jephthah which he sent him.

29 **Then the Spirit of the LORD** came upon Jephthah,
and he passed over Gilead, and Manasseh,
and passed over Mizpeh of Gilead,
and from Mizpeh of Gilead he passed over unto the children of Ammon.

30 **And Jephthah** vowed a vow unto the LORD,
and said,
If thou shalt without fail deliver the children of Ammon into mine hands,

31 **Then it** shall be,
that whatsoever cometh forth of the doors of my house to meet me, {<u>when I</u> return in peace from the children of Ammon}, shall surely be the LORD's,
and I will offer it up for a burnt offering.

32 **So Jephthah** passed over unto the children of Ammon
to fight against them;
and the LORD delivered them into his hands.

33 **And he** smote them from Aroer,
even till thou come to Minnith, even twenty cities, and unto the plain of the vineyards, with a very great slaughter.
Thus the children of Ammon were subdued before the children of Israel.

34 **And Jephthah** came to Mizpeh unto his house,
and, {<u>behold</u>}, his daughter came out to meet him with timbrels and with dances:
and she was his only child;
beside her he had neither son nor daughter.

35 **And it** came to pass,
when he saw her,
that he rent his clothes,
and said,
Alas, my daughter!
thou hast brought me very low,

and thou art one of them that trouble me:
for I have opened my mouth unto the LORD,
and I cannot go back.
36 **And she** said unto him,
My father, if thou hast opened thy mouth unto the LORD,
do to me according to that which hath proceeded out of thy mouth;
forasmuch as the LORD hath taken vengeance for thee of thine enemies, even of the children of Ammon.
37 **And she** said unto her father,
Let this thing be done for me:
let me alone two months,
that I may go up and down upon the mountains,
and bewail my virginity, I and my fellows.
38 **And he** said,
Go.
And he sent her away for two months:
and she went with her companions,
and bewailed her virginity upon the mountains.
39 **And it** came to pass at the end of two months,
that she returned unto her father,
who did with her according to his vow which he had vowed:
and she knew no man.
And it was a custom in Israel,
40 That the daughters of Israel went yearly to lament the daughter of Jephthah the Gileadite four days in a year.

12 **And the men of Ephraim** gathered themselves together,
and went northward,
and said unto Jephthah,
Wherefore passedst thou over to fight against the children of Ammon,
and didst not call us to go with thee?
we will burn thine house upon thee with fire.
2 **And Jephthah** said unto them,
I and my people were at great strife with the children of Ammon;
and when I called you,
ye delivered me not out of their hands.
3 **And when I** saw that ye delivered me not,
I put my life in my hands,
and passed over against the children of Ammon,
and the LORD delivered them into my hand:
wherefore then are ye come up unto me this day,
to fight against me?
4 **Then Jephthah** gathered together all the men of Gilead,
and fought with Ephraim:
and the men of Gilead smote Ephraim,
because they said,
Ye Gileadites are fugitives of Ephraim among the Ephraimites, and among the Manassites.
5 **And the Gileadites** took the passages of Jordan before the Ephraimites:
and it was so,
that when those Ephraimites which were escaped said,
Let me go over;
that the men of Gilead said unto him,
Art thou an Ephraimite?
If he said,
Nay;
6 **Then** said they unto him,
Say now Shibboleth:
and he said Sibboleth:
for he could not frame to pronounce it right.
Then they took him,
and slew him at the passages of Jordan:
and there fell at that time of the Ephraimites forty and two thousand.
7 **And Jephthah** judged Israel six years.
Then died Jephthah the Gileadite,
and was buried in one of the cities of Gilead.
8 **And after him Ibzan of Bethlehem** judged Israel.
9 **And he** had thirty sons, and thirty daughters,
whom he sent abroad,
and took in thirty daughters from abroad for his sons.
And he judged Israel seven years.
10 **Then** died Ibzan,
and was buried at Bethlehem.
11 **And after him** Elon, a Zebulonite, judged Israel;
and he judged Israel ten years.
12 **And Elon the Zebulonite** died,
and was buried in Aijalon in the country of Zebulun.
13 **And after him** Abdon the son of Hillel, a Pirathonite, judged Israel.
14 **And he** had forty sons and thirty nephews,
that rode on threescore and ten ass colts:
and he judged Israel eight years.
15 **And Abdon the son of Hillel the Pirathonite** died,
and was buried in Pirathon in the land of Ephraim, in the mount of the Amalekites.

13 ✂ **And the children of Israel** did evil again in the sight of the LORD;
and the LORD delivered them into the hand of the Philistines forty years.
2 **And there** was a certain man of Zorah, of the family of the Danites,
whose name was Manoah;
and his wife was barren,
and bare not.
3 **And the angel of the LORD** appeared unto the woman,
and said unto her,
Behold now,
thou art barren,
and bearest not:
but thou shalt conceive,
and bear a son.
4 **Now therefore beware,**
I pray thee,
and drink not wine nor strong drink,
and eat not any unclean thing:
5 **For, {lo}, thou** shalt conceive,
and bear a son;
and no razor shall come on his head:
for the child shall be a Nazarite unto God from the womb:
and he shall begin to deliver Israel out of the hand of the Philistines.
6 **Then the woman** came and told her husband,
saying,
A man of God came unto me,
and his countenance was like the countenance of an angel of God, very terrible:
but I asked him not
whence he was,
neither told he me his name:
7 **But he** said unto me,
Behold,

thou shalt conceive,
and bear a son;
and now drink no wine nor strong drink,
neither eat any unclean thing:
for the child shall be a Nazarite to God from the womb to the day of his death.

8 **Then Manoah** intreated the LORD,
and said,
O my Lord, let the man of God which thou didst send come again unto us,
and teach us what we shall do unto the child that shall be born.

9 **And God** hearkened to the voice of Manoah;
and the angel of God came again unto the woman
as she sat in the field:
but Manoah her husband was not with her.

10 **And the woman** made haste,
and ran,
and shewed her husband,
and said unto him,
Behold,
the man hath appeared unto me,
that came unto me the other day.

11 **And Manoah** arose,
and went after his wife,
and came to the man,
and said unto him,
Art thou the man that spakest unto the woman?

And he said,
I am.

12 **And Manoah** said,
Now let thy words come to pass.

How shall we order the child,
and how shall we do unto him?

13 **And the angel of the LORD** said unto Manoah,
Of all that I said unto the woman let her beware.

14 **She** may not eat of any thing that cometh of the vine,
neither let her drink wine or strong drink,
nor eat any unclean thing:
all that I commanded her let her observe.

15 **And Manoah** said unto the angel of the LORD,
I pray thee,
let us detain thee,
until we shall have made ready a kid for thee.

16 **And the angel of the LORD** said unto Manoah,
Though thou detain me,
I will not eat of thy bread:
and if thou wilt offer a burnt offering,
thou must offer it unto the LORD.

For Manoah knew not
that he was an angel of the LORD.

17 **And Manoah** said unto the angel of the LORD,
What is thy name,
that when thy sayings come to pass
we may do thee honour?

18 **And the angel of the LORD** said unto him,
Why askest thou thus after my name,
seeing it is secret?

19 **So Manoah** took a kid with a meat offering,
and offered it upon a rock unto the LORD:
and the angel did wonderously;
and Manoah and his wife looked on.

20 **For it** came to pass,
when the flame went up toward heaven from off the altar,
that the angel of the LORD ascended in the flame of the altar.

And Manoah and his wife looked on it,
and fell on their faces to the ground.

21 **But the angel of the LORD** did no more appear to Manoah and to his wife.

Then Manoah knew
that he was an angel of the LORD.

22 **And Manoah** said unto his wife,
We shall surely die,
because we have seen God.

23 **But his wife** said unto him,
If the LORD were pleased to kill us,
he would not have received a burnt offering and a meat offering at our hands,
neither would he have shewed us all these things,
nor would as at this time have told us such things as these.

24 **And the woman** bare a son,
and called his name Samson:
and the child grew,
and the LORD blessed him.

25 **And the Spirit of the LORD** began to move him at times in the camp of Dan between Zorah and Eshtaol.

14 **And Samson** went down to Timnath,
and saw a woman in Timnath of the daughters of the Philistines.

2 **And he** came up,
and told his father and his mother,
and said,
I have seen a woman in Timnath of the daughters of the Philistines:
now therefore get her for me to wife.

3 **Then his father and his mother** said unto him,
Is there never a woman among the daughters of thy brethren, or among all my people,
that thou goest to take a wife of the uncircumcised Philistines?

And Samson said unto his father,
Get her for me;
for she pleaseth me well.

4 **But his father and his mother** knew not
that it was of the LORD,
that he sought an occasion against the Philistines:
for at that time the Philistines had dominion over Israel.

5 **Then** went Samson down, and his father and his mother, to Timnath,
and came to the vineyards of Timnath:
and, {behold}, a young lion roared against him.

6 **And the Spirit of the LORD** came mightily upon him,
and he rent him as he would have rent a kid,
and he had nothing in his hand:
but he told not his father or his mother
what he had done.

7 **And he** went down,
and talked with the woman;
and she pleased Samson well.

8 **And after a time** he returned to take her,
and he turned aside
to see the carcase of the lion:
and, {behold}, there was a swarm of bees and honey in the carcase of the lion.

9 **And he** took thereof in his hands,
and went on eating,
and came to his father and mother,
and he gave them,

and they did eat:
but he told not them
that he had taken the honey out of the carcase of the lion.

10 **So his father** went down unto the woman:
and Samson made there a feast;
for so used the young men to do.

11 **And it** came to pass,
when they saw him,
that they brought thirty companions to be with him.

12 **And Samson** said unto them,
I will now put forth a riddle unto you:
if ye can certainly declare it me within the seven days of the feast,
and find it out,
then I will give you thirty sheets and thirty change of garments:
13 **But if ye** cannot declare it me,
then shall ye give me thirty sheets and thirty change of garments.

And they said unto him,
Put forth thy riddle,
that we may hear it.

14 **And he** said unto them,
Out of the eater came forth meat,
and out of the strong came forth sweetness.

And they could not in three days expound the riddle.

15 **And it** came to pass on the seventh day,
that they said unto Samson's wife,
Entice thy husband,
that he may declare unto us the riddle,
lest we burn thee and thy father's house with fire:
have ye called us to take that we have?
is it not so?

16 **And Samson's wife** wept before him,
and said,
Thou dost but hate me,
and lovest me not:
thou hast put forth a riddle unto the children of my people,
and hast not told it me.

And he said unto her,
Behold,
I have not told it my father nor my mother,
and shall I tell it thee?

17 **And she** wept before him the seven days,
while their feast lasted:
and it came to pass on the seventh day,
that he told her,
because she lay sore upon him:
and she told the riddle to the children of her people.

18 **And the men of the city** said unto him on the seventh day before the sun went down,
What is sweeter than honey?

And what is stronger than a lion?
and he said unto them,
If ye had not plowed with my heifer,
ye had not found out my riddle.

19 **And the Spirit of the LORD** came upon him,
and he went down to Ashkelon,
and slew thirty men of them,
and took their spoil,
and gave change of garments unto them which expounded the riddle.

And his anger was kindled,
and he went up to his father's house.

20 **But Samson's wife** was given to his companion,
whom he had used as his friend.

15

But it came to pass within a while after, in the time of wheat harvest,
that Samson visited his wife with a kid;
and he said,
I will go in to my wife into the chamber.

But her father would not suffer him to go in.

2 **And her father** said,
I verily thought
that thou hadst utterly hated her;
therefore I gave her to thy companion:
is not her younger sister fairer than she?
take her, {I pray thee}, instead of her.

3 **And Samson** said concerning them,
Now shall I be more blameless than the Philistines,
though I do them a displeasure.

4 **And Samson** went and caught three hundred foxes,
and took firebrands,
and turned tail to tail,
and put a firebrand in the midst between two tails.

5 **And when he** had set the brands on fire,
he let them go into the standing corn of the Philistines,
and burnt up both the shocks, and also the standing corn, with the vineyards and olives.

6 **Then the Philistines** said,
Who hath done this?

And they answered, Samson, the son in law of the Timnite,
because he had taken his wife,
and given her to his companion.

And the Philistines came up,
and burnt her and her father with fire.

7 **And Samson** said unto them,
Though ye have done this,
yet will I be avenged of you,
and after that I will cease.

8 **And he** smote them hip and thigh with a great slaughter:
and he went down and dwelt in the top of the rock Etam.

9 **Then the Philistines** went up,
and pitched in Judah,
and spread themselves in Lehi.

10 **And the men of Judah** said,
Why are ye come up against us?

And they answered,
To bind Samson are we come up,
to do to him as he hath done to us.

11 **Then three thousand men of Judah** went to the top of the rock Etam,
and said to Samson,
Knowest thou not
that the Philistines are rulers over us?
what is this that thou hast done unto us?

And he said unto them,
As they did unto me,
so have I done unto them.

12 **And they** said unto him,
We are come down
to bind thee,
that we may deliver thee into the hand of the Philistines.

And Samson said unto them,
Swear unto me,
that ye will not fall upon me yourselves.

13 **And they** spake unto him,
saying,
No;
but we will bind thee fast,
and deliver thee into their hand:
but surely we will not kill thee.

And they bound him with two new cords,
and brought him up from the rock.
14 **And when he** came unto Lehi,
the Philistines shouted against him:
and the Spirit of the LORD came mightily upon him,
and the cords that were upon his arms became as flax that was burnt with fire,
and his bands loosed from off his hands.
15 **And he** found a new jawbone of an ass,
and put forth his hand,
and took it,
and slew a thousand men therewith.
16 **And Samson** said,
With the jawbone of an ass, heaps upon heaps, with the jaw of an ass have I slain a thousand men.
17 **And it** came to pass,
when he had made an end of speaking,
that he cast away the jawbone out of his hand,
and called that place Ramathlehi.
18 **And he** was sore athirst,
and called on the LORD,
and said,
Thou hast given this great deliverance into the hand of thy servant:
and now shall I die for thirst,
and fall into the hand of the uncircumcised?
19 **But God** clave an hollow place that was in the jaw,
and there came water thereout;
and when he had drunk,
his spirit came again,
and he revived:
wherefore he called the name thereof Enhakkore,
which is in Lehi unto this day.
20 **And he** judged Israel in the days of the Philistines twenty years.

16 **Then** went Samson to Gaza,
and saw there an harlot,
and went in unto her.
2 **And it** was told the Gazites,
saying,
Samson is come hither.
And they compassed him in,
and laid wait for him all night in the gate of the city,
and were quiet all the night,
saying,
In the morning, {when it is day},
we shall kill him.
3 **And Samson** lay till midnight,
and arose at midnight,
and took the doors of the gate of the city, and the two posts,
and went away with them, bar and all,
and put them upon his shoulders,
and carried them up to the top of an hill that is before Hebron.
4 **And it** came to pass afterward,
that he loved a woman in the valley of Sorek,
whose name was Delilah.
5 **And the lords of the Philistines** came up unto her,
and said unto her,
Entice him,
and see wherein his great strength lieth,
and by what means we may prevail against him,
that we may bind him
to afflict him;
and we will give thee every one of us eleven hundred pieces of silver.
6 **And Delilah** said to Samson,
Tell me,
I pray thee,
wherein thy great strength lieth,
and wherewith thou mightest be bound to afflict thee.
7 **And Samson** said unto her,
If they bind me with seven green withs that were never dried,
then shall I be weak,
and be as another man.
8 **Then the lords of the Philistines** brought up to her seven green withs which had not been dried, and she bound him with them.
9 **Now there** were men lying in wait, abiding with her in the chamber.
And she said unto him,
The Philistines be upon thee, Samson.
And he brake the withs,
as a thread of tow is broken
when it toucheth the fire.
So his strength was not known.
10 **And Delilah** said unto Samson,
Behold,
thou hast mocked me,
and told me lies:
now tell me,
I pray thee,
wherewith thou mightest be bound.
11 **And he** said unto her,
If they bind me fast with new ropes that never were occupied,
then shall I be weak,
and be as another man.
12 **Delilah** therefore took new ropes,
and bound him therewith,
and said unto him,
The Philistines be upon thee, Samson.
And there were liers in wait abiding in the chamber.
And he brake them from off his arms like a thread.
13 **And Delilah** said unto Samson,
Hitherto thou hast mocked me,
and told me lies:
tell me
wherewith thou mightest be bound.
And he said unto her,
If thou weavest the seven locks of my head with the web.
14 **And she** fastened it with the pin,
and said unto him,
The Philistines be upon thee, Samson.
And he awaked out of his sleep,
and went away with the pin of the beam, and with the web.
15 **And she** said unto him,
How canst thou say,
I love thee,
when thine heart is not with me?
thou hast mocked me these three times,
and hast not told me
wherein thy great strength lieth.
16 **And it** came to pass,
when she pressed him daily with her words,
and urged him,
so that his soul was vexed unto death;
17 **That he** told her all his heart,
and said unto her,
There hath not come a razor upon mine head;
for I have been a Nazarite unto God from my mother's womb:
if I be shaven,
then my strength will go from me,
and I shall become weak,
and be like any other man.
18 **And when Delilah** saw that he had told her all his heart,

she sent and called for the lords of the Philistines,
saying,
Come up this once,
for he hath shewed me all his heart.

Then the lords of the Philistines came up unto her,
and brought money in their hand.

19 **And she** made him sleep upon her knees;
and she called for a man,
and she caused him to shave off the seven locks of his head;
and she began to afflict him,
and his strength went from him.

20 **And she** said,
The Philistines be upon thee, Samson.

And he awoke out of his sleep,
and said,
I will go out as at other times before,
and shake myself.

And he wist not
that the LORD was departed from him.

21 **But the Philistines** took him,
and put out his eyes,
and brought him down to Gaza,
and bound him with fetters of brass;
and he did grind in the prison house.

22 **Howbeit the hair of his head** began to grow again
after he was shaven.

23 **Then the lords of the Philistines** gathered them together
for to offer a great sacrifice unto Dagon their god,
and to rejoice:
for they said,
Our god hath delivered Samson our enemy into our hand.

24 **And when the people** saw him,
they praised their god:
for they said,
Our god hath delivered into our hands our enemy, and the destroyer of our country,
which slew many of us.

25 **And it** came to pass,
when their hearts were merry,
that they said,
Call for Samson,
that he may make us sport.

And they called for Samson out of the prison house;
and he made them sport:
and they set him between the pillars.

26 **And Samson** said unto the lad that held him by the hand,
Suffer me
that I may feel the pillars whereupon the house standeth,
that I may lean upon them.

27 **Now the house** was full of men and women;
and all the lords of the Philistines were there;
and there were upon the roof about three thousand men and women,
that beheld while Samson made sport.

28 **And Samson** called unto the LORD,
and said,
O Lord GOD, remember me, {I pray thee},
and strengthen me, {I pray thee}, only this once, O God,
that I may be at once avenged of the Philistines for my two eyes.

29 **And Samson** took hold of the two middle pillars upon which the house stood, and on which it was borne up, of the one with his right hand, and of the other with his left.

30 **And Samson** said,
Let me die with the Philistines.

And he bowed himself with all his might;
and the house fell upon the lords, and upon all the people that were therein.

So the dead which he slew at his death were more than they which he slew in his life.

31 **Then his brethren and all the house of his father** came down,
and took him,
and brought him up,
and buried him between Zorah and Eshtaol in the buryingplace of Manoah his father.

And he judged Israel twenty years.

17

And there was a man of mount Ephraim,
whose name was Micah.

2 **And he** said unto his mother,
The eleven hundred shekels of silver that were taken from thee, {about which thou cursedst}, {and spakest of also in mine ears}, {behold}, the silver is with me;
I took it.

And his mother said,
Blessed be thou of the LORD, my son.

3 **And when he** had restored the eleven hundred shekels of silver to his mother,
his mother said,
I had wholly dedicated the silver unto the LORD from my hand for my son,
to make a graven image and a molten image:
now therefore I will restore it unto thee.

4 **Yet he** restored the money unto his mother;
and his mother took two hundred shekels of silver,
and gave them to the founder,
who made thereof a graven image and a molten image:
and they were in the house of Micah.

5 **And the man Micah** had an house of gods,
and made an ephod, and teraphim,
and consecrated one of his sons,
who became his priest.

6 **In those days** there was no king in Israel,
but every man did that which was right in his own eyes.

7 **And there** was a young man out of Bethlehemjudah of the family of Judah,
who was a Levite,
and he sojourned there.

8 **And the man** departed out of the city from Bethlehemjudah
to sojourn where he could find a place:
and he came to mount Ephraim to the house of Micah,
as he journeyed.

9 **And Micah** said unto him,
Whence comest thou?

And he said unto him,
I am a Levite of Bethlehemjudah,
and I go to sojourn where I may find a place.

10 **And Micah** said unto him,
Dwell with me,
and be unto me a father and a priest,
and I will give thee ten shekels of silver by the year, and a suit of apparel, and thy victuals.

So the Levite went in.

11 **And the Levite** was content to dwell with the man;
and the young man was unto him as one of his sons.
12 **And Micah** consecrated the Levite;
and the young man became his priest,
and was in the house of Micah.
13 **Then** said Micah,
Now know I
that the LORD will do me good,
seeing I have a Levite to my priest.

18 **In those days** there was no king in Israel:
and in those days the tribe of the Danites sought them an inheritance to dwell in;
for unto that day all their inheritance had not fallen unto them among the tribes of Israel.
2 **And the children of Dan** sent of their family five men from their coasts, men of valour, from Zorah, and from Eshtaol,
to spy out the land,
and to search it;
and they said unto them,
Go,
search the land:
who when they came to mount Ephraim, to the house of Micah,
they lodged there.
3 **When they** were by the house of Micah,
they knew the voice of the young man the Levite:
and they turned in thither,
and said unto him,
Who brought thee hither?
and what makest thou in this place?
and what hast thou here?
4 **And he** said unto them,
Thus and thus dealeth Micah with me,
and hath hired me,
and I am his priest.
5 **And they** said unto him,
Ask counsel, {we pray thee}, of God,
that we may know
whether our way which we go shall be prosperous.
6 **And the priest** said unto them,
Go in peace:
before the LORD is your way wherein ye go.
7 **Then the five men** departed,
and came to Laish,
and saw the people that were therein,
how they dwelt careless, after the manner of the Zidonians, quiet and secure;
and there was no magistrate in the land,
that might put them to shame in any thing;
and they were far from the Zidonians,
and had no business with any man.
8 **And they** came unto their brethren to Zorah and Eshtaol:
and their brethren said unto them,
What say ye?
9 **And they** said,
Arise,
that we may go up against them:
for we have seen the land,
and, {behold}, it is very good:
and are ye still?
be not slothful to go,
and to enter to possess the land.
10 **When ye** go,
ye shall come unto a people secure, and to a large land:
for God hath given it into your hands; a place where there is no want of any thing that is in the earth.
11 **And there** went from thence of the family of the Danites, out of Zorah and out of Eshtaol, six hundred men appointed with weapons of war.
12 **And they** went up,
and pitched in Kirjathjearim, in Judah:
wherefore they called that place Mahanehdan unto this day:
behold,
it is behind Kirjathjearim.
13 **And they** passed thence unto mount Ephraim,
and came unto the house of Micah.
14 **Then** answered the five men that went to spy out the country of Laish,
and said unto their brethren,
Do ye know
that there is in these houses an ephod, and teraphim, and a graven image, and a molten image?
now therefore consider
what ye have to do.
15 **And they** turned thitherward,
and came to the house of the young man the Levite, even unto the house of Micah,
and saluted him.
16 **And the six hundred men appointed with their weapons of war**, {which were of the children of Dan}, stood by the entering of the gate.
17 **And the five men that went to spy out the land** went up,
and came in thither,
and took the graven image, and the ephod, and the teraphim, and the molten image:
and the priest stood in the entering of the gate with the six hundred men that were appointed with weapons of war.
18 **And these** went into Micah's house,
and fetched the carved image, the ephod, and the teraphim, and the molten image.
Then said the priest unto them,
What do ye?
19 **And they** said unto him,
Hold thy peace,
lay thine hand upon thy mouth,
and go with us,
and be to us a father and a priest:
is it better for thee to be a priest unto the house of one man, or that thou be a priest unto a tribe and a family in Israel?
20 **And the priest's heart** was glad,
and he took the ephod, and the teraphim, and the graven image,
and went in the midst of the people.
21 **So they** turned and departed,
and put the little ones and the cattle and the carriage before them.
22 **And when they** were a good way from the house of Micah,
the men that were in the houses near to Micah's house were gathered together,
and overtook the children of Dan.
23 **And they** cried unto the children of Dan.
And they turned their faces,
and said unto Micah,
What aileth thee,
that thou comest with such a company?
24 **And he** said,
Ye have taken away my gods
which I made, and the priest,

and ye are gone away:
and what have I more?
and what is this that ye say unto me,
What aileth thee?
25 **And the children of Dan** said unto him,
Let not thy voice be heard among us,
lest angry fellows run upon thee,
and thou lose thy life, with the lives of thy household.
26 **And the children of Dan** went their way:
and when Micah saw that they were too strong for him,
he turned and went back unto his house.
27 **And they** took the things which Micah had made, and the priest which he had,
and came unto Laish, unto a people that were at quiet and secure:
and they smote them with the edge of the sword,
and burnt the city with fire.
28 **And there** was no deliverer,
because it was far from Zidon,
and they had no business with any man;
and it was in the valley that lieth by Bethrehob.
And they built a city,
and dwelt therein.
29 **And they** called the name of the city Dan, after the name of Dan their father,
who was born unto Israel:
howbeit the name of the city was Laish at the first.
30 **And the children of Dan** set up the graven image:
and Jonathan, the son of Gershom, the son of Manasseh, he and his sons were priests to the tribe of Dan until the day of the captivity of the land.
31 **And they** set them up Micah's graven image, {which he made}, all the time that the house of God was in Shiloh.

19 ∞ **And it** came to pass in those days,
when there was no king in Israel,
that there was a certain Levite sojourning on the side of mount Ephraim,
who took to him a concubine out of Bethlehemjudah.
2 **And his concubine** played the whore against him,
and went away from him unto her father's house to Bethlehemjudah,
and was there four whole months.
3 **And her husband** arose,
and went after her,
to speak friendly unto her,
and to bring her again,
having his servant with him, and a couple of asses:
and she brought him into her father's house:
and when the father of the damsel saw him,
he rejoiced to meet him.
4 **And his father in law, the damsel's father,** retained him;
and he abode with him three days:
so they did eat and drink,
and lodged there.
5 **And it** came to pass on the fourth day,
when they arose early in the morning,
that he rose up to depart:
and the damsel's father said unto his son in law,
Comfort thine heart with a morsel of bread,
and afterward go your way.
6 **And they** sat down,
and did eat and drink both of them together:
for the damsel's father had said unto the man,
Be content,
I pray thee,
and tarry all night,
and let thine heart be merry.
7 **And when the man** rose up to depart,
his father in law urged him:
therefore he lodged there again.
8 **And he** arose early in the morning on the fifth day
to depart;
and the damsel's father said,
Comfort thine heart,
I pray thee.
And they tarried until afternoon,
and they did eat both of them.
9 **And when the man** rose up to depart,
he, and his concubine, and his servant, his father in law, the damsel's father, said unto him,
Behold,
now the day draweth toward evening,
I pray you tarry all night:
behold,
the day groweth to an end,
lodge here,
that thine heart may be merry;
and to morrow get you early on your way,
that thou mayest go home.
10 **But the man** would not tarry that night,
but he rose up and departed,
and came over against Jebus,
which is Jerusalem;
and there were with him two asses saddled,
his concubine also was with him.
11 **And when they** were by Jebus,
the day was far spent;
and the servant said unto his master,
Come,
I pray thee,
and let us turn in into this city of the Jebusites,
and lodge in it.
12 **And his** master said unto him,
We will not turn aside hither into the city of a stranger,
that is not of the children of Israel;
we will pass over to Gibeah.
13 **And he** said unto his servant,
Come,
and let us draw near to one of these places {to lodge all night}, in Gibeah, or in Ramah.
14 **And they** passed on and went their way;
and the sun went down upon them
when they were by Gibeah,
which belongeth to Benjamin.
15 **And they** turned aside thither,
to go in and to lodge in Gibeah:
and when he went in,
he sat him down in a street of the city:
for there was no man that took them into his house to lodging.
16 **And, {behold}, there** came an old man from his work out of the field at even,
which was also of mount Ephraim;
and he sojourned in Gibeah:
but the men of the place were Benjamites.
17 **And when he** had lifted up his eyes,
he saw a wayfaring man in the street of the city:

and the old man said,
Whither goest thou?
and whence comest thou?
18 **And he** said unto him,
We are passing from Bethlehemjudah toward the side of mount Ephraim;
from thence am I:
and I went to Bethlehemjudah,
but I am now going to the house of the LORD;
and there is no man that receiveth me to house.
19 **Yet there** is both straw and provender for our asses;
and there is bread and wine also for me, and for thy handmaid, and for the young man which is with thy servants:
there is no want of any thing.
20 **And the old man** said,
Peace be with thee;
howsoever let all thy wants lie upon me;
only lodge not in the street.
21 **So he** brought him into his house,
and gave provender unto the asses:
and they washed their feet,
and did eat and drink.
22 **Now as they** were making their hearts merry,
behold,
the men of the city, certain sons of Belial, beset the house round about,
and beat at the door,
and spake to the master of the house, the old man,
saying,
Bring forth the man that came into thine house,
that we may know him.
23 **And the man, the master of the house,** went out unto them,
and said unto them,
Nay, my brethren, nay,
I pray you,
do not so wickedly;
seeing that this man is come into mine house,
do not this folly.
24 **Behold,**
here is my daughter a maiden, and his concubine;
them I will bring out now,
and humble ye them,
and do with them what seemeth good unto you:
but unto this man do not so vile a thing.
25 **But the men** would not hearken to him:
so the man took his concubine,
and brought her forth unto them;
and they knew her,
and abused her all the night until the morning:
and when the day began to spring,
they let her go.
26 **Then** came the woman in the dawning of the day,
and fell down at the door of the man's house where her lord was,
till it was light.
27 **And her lord** rose up in the morning,
and opened the doors of the house,
and went out to go his way:
and, {behold}, the woman his concubine was fallen down at the door of the house,
and her hands were upon the threshold.
28 **And he** said unto her,
Up,
and let us be going.
But none answered.
Then the man took her up upon an ass,
and the man rose up,
and gat him unto his place.
29 **And when he** was come into his house,
he took a knife,
and laid hold on his concubine,
and divided her, together with her bones, into twelve pieces,
and sent her into all the coasts of Israel.
30 **And it** was so,
that all that saw it said,
There was no such deed done nor seen from the day that the children of Israel came up out of the land of Egypt unto this day:
consider of it,
take advice,
and speak your minds.

20

Then all the children of Israel went out,
and the congregation was gathered together as one man, from Dan even to Beersheba, with the land of Gilead, unto the LORD in Mizpeh.
2 **And the chief of all the people, even of all the tribes of Israel,** presented themselves in the assembly of the people of God, four hundred thousand footmen that drew sword.
3 **(Now the children of Benjamin** heard that the children of Israel were gone up to Mizpeh.)
Then said the children of Israel,
Tell us,
how was this wickedness?
4 **And the Levite, the husband of the woman that was slain,** answered and said,
I came into Gibeah that belongeth to Benjamin, I and my concubine,
to lodge.
5 **And the men of Gibeah** rose against me,
and beset the house round about upon me by night,
and thought to have slain me:
and my concubine have they forced,
that she is dead.
6 **And I** took my concubine, and cut her in pieces,
and sent her throughout all the country of the inheritance of Israel:
for they have committed lewdness and folly in Israel.
7 **Behold,**
ye are all children of Israel;
give here your advice and counsel.
8 **And all the people** arose as one man,
saying,
We will not any of us go to his tent,
neither will we any of us turn into his house.
9 **But now this** shall be the thing which we will do to Gibeah;
we will go up by lot against it;
10 **And we** will take ten men of an hundred throughout all the tribes of Israel, and an hundred of a thousand, and a thousand out of ten thousand,
to fetch victual for the people,
that they may do, {when they come to Gibeah of Benjamin}, according to all the folly that they have wrought in Israel.
11 **So all the men of Israel** were gathered against the city,
knit together as one man.
12 **And the tribes of Israel** sent men through all the tribe of Benjamin,
saying,
What wickedness is this that is done among you?

13 **Now therefore deliver** us the men, the children of Belial,
which are in Gibeah,
that we may put them to death,
and put away evil from Israel.
But the children of Benjamin would not hearken to the voice of their brethren the children of Israel.

14 **But the children of Benjamin** gathered themselves together out of the cities unto Gibeah,
to go out to battle against the children of Israel.

15 **And the children of Benjamin** were numbered at that time out of the cities twenty and six thousand men that drew sword, beside the inhabitants of Gibeah,
which were numbered seven hundred chosen men.

16 **Among all this people** there were seven hundred chosen men lefthanded;
every one could sling stones at an hair breadth,
and not miss.

17 **And the men of Israel, beside Benjamin,** were numbered four hundred thousand men that drew sword:
all these were men of war.

18 **And the children of Israel** arose,
and went up to the house of God,
and asked counsel of God,
and said,
Which of us shall go up first to the battle against the children of Benjamin?
And the LORD said,
Judah shall go up first.

19 **And the children of Israel** rose up in the morning,
and encamped against Gibeah.

20 **And the men of Israel** went out to battle against Benjamin;
and the men of Israel put themselves in array to fight against them at Gibeah.

21 **And the children of Benjamin** came forth out of Gibeah,
and destroyed down to the ground of the Israelites that day twenty and two thousand men.

22 **And the people the men of Israel** encouraged themselves,
and set their battle again in array in the place where they put themselves in array the first day.

23 (**And the children of Israel** went up and wept before the LORD until even,
and asked counsel of the LORD,
saying,
Shall I go up again to battle against the children of Benjamin my brother?
And the LORD said,
Go up against him.)

24 **And the children of Israel** came near against the children of Benjamin the second day.

25 **And Benjamin** went forth against them out of Gibeah the second day,
and destroyed down to the ground of the children of Israel again eighteen thousand men;
all these drew the sword.

26 **Then all the children of Israel, and all the people,** went up,
and came unto the house of God,
and wept,
and sat there before the LORD,
and fasted that day until even,
and offered burnt offerings and peace offerings before the LORD.

27 **And the children of Israel** enquired of the LORD, (for the ark of the covenant of God was there in those days,

28 And Phinehas, the son of Eleazar, the son of Aaron, stood before it in those days,)
saying,
Shall I yet again go out to battle against the children of Benjamin my brother,
or shall I cease?
And the LORD said,
Go up;
for to morrow I will deliver them into thine hand.

29 **And Israel** set liers in wait round about Gibeah.

30 **And the children of Israel** went up against the children of Benjamin on the third day,
and put themselves in array against Gibeah, as at other times.

31 **And the children of Benjamin** went out against the people,
and were drawn away from the city;
and they began to smite of the people,
and kill, as at other times, in the highways,
of which one goeth up to the house of God, and the other to Gibeah in the field, about thirty men of Israel.

32 **And the children of Benjamin** said,
They are smitten down before us, as at the first.
But the children of Israel said,
Let us flee,
and draw them from the city unto the highways.

33 **And all the men of Israel** rose up out of their place,
and put themselves in array at Baaltamar:
and the liers in wait of Israel came forth out of their places, even out of the meadows of Gibeah.

34 **And there** came against Gibeah ten thousand chosen men out of all Israel,
and the battle was sore:
but they knew not
that evil was near them.

35 **And the LORD** smote Benjamin before Israel:
and the children of Israel destroyed of the Benjamites that day twenty and five thousand and an hundred men:
all these drew the sword.

36 **So the children of Benjamin** saw that they were smitten:
for the men of Israel gave place to the Benjamites,
because they trusted unto the liers in wait which they had set beside Gibeah.

37 **And the liers in wait** hasted,
and rushed upon Gibeah;
and the liers in wait drew themselves along,
and smote all the city with the edge of the sword.

38 **Now there** was an appointed sign between the men of Israel and the liers in wait,
that they should make a great flame with smoke rise up out of the city.

39 **And when the men of Israel** retired in the battle,
Benjamin began to smite and kill of the men of Israel about thirty persons:
for they said,
Surely they are smitten down before us, as in the first battle.

40 **But when the flame** began to arise up out of the city with a pillar of smoke,
the Benjamites looked behind them,
and, {behold}, the flame of the city ascended up to heaven.

41 **And when the men of Israel** turned again,
the men of Benjamin were amazed:
for they saw that evil was come upon them.

42 **Therefore they** turned their backs before the men of Israel unto the way of the wilderness;
but the battle overtook them;
and them which came out of the cities they destroyed in the midst of them.

43 **Thus they** inclosed the Benjamites round about,
and chased them
and trode them down with ease over against Gibeah toward the sunrising.

44 **And there** fell of Benjamin eighteen thousand men;
all these were men of valour.

45 **And they** turned and fled toward the wilderness unto the rock of Rimmon:
and they gleaned of them in the highways five thousand men;
and pursued hard after them unto Gidom,
and slew two thousand men of them.

46 **So that all which fell that day of Benjamin** were twenty and five thousand men that drew the sword;
all these were men of valour.

47 **But six hundred men** turned and fled to the wilderness unto the rock Rimmon,
and abode in the rock Rimmon four months.

48 **And the men of Israel** turned again upon the children of Benjamin,
and smote them with the edge of the sword, as well the men of every city, as the beast, and all that came to hand:
also they set on fire all the cities that they came to.

21 **Now the men of Israel** had sworn in Mizpeh,
saying,
There shall not any of us give his daughter unto Benjamin to wife.

2 **And the people** came to the house of God,
and abode there till even before God,
and lifted up their voices,
and wept sore;

3 **And** said,
O LORD God of Israel, why is this come to pass in Israel,
that there should be to day one tribe lacking in Israel?

4 **And it** came to pass on the morrow,
that the people rose early,
and built there an altar,
and offered burnt offerings and peace offerings.

5 **And the children of Israel** said,
Who is there among all the tribes of Israel that came not up with the congregation unto the LORD?
For they had made a great oath concerning him that came not up to the LORD to Mizpeh,
saying,
He shall surely be put to death.

6 **And the children of Israel** repented them for Benjamin their brother,
and said,
There is one tribe cut off from Israel this day.

7 **How** shall we do for wives for them that remain,
seeing we have sworn by the LORD
that we will not give them of our daughters to wives?

8 **And they** said,
What one is there of the tribes of Israel that came not up to Mizpeh to the LORD?
And, {behold}, there came none to the camp from Jabeshgilead to the assembly.

9 **For the people** were numbered,
and, {behold}, there were none of the inhabitants of Jabeshgilead there.

10 **And the congregation** sent thither twelve thousand men of the valiantest,
and commanded them,
saying,
Go and smite the inhabitants of Jabeshgilead with the edge of the sword, with the women and the children.

11 **And this** is the thing that ye shall do,
Ye shall utterly destroy every male, and every woman that hath lain by man.

12 **And they** found among the inhabitants of Jabeshgilead four hundred young virgins,
that had known no man by lying with any male:
and they brought them unto the camp to Shiloh,
which is in the land of Canaan.

13 **And the whole congregation** sent some to speak to the children of Benjamin that were in the rock Rimmon,
and to call peaceably unto them.

14 **And Benjamin** came again at that time;
and they gave them wives which they had saved alive of the women of Jabeshgilead:
and yet so they sufficed them not.

15 **And the people** repented them for Benjamin,
because that the LORD had made a breach in the tribes of Israel.

16 **Then the elders of the congregation** said,
How shall we do for wives for them that remain,
seeing the women are destroyed out of Benjamin?

17 **And they** said,
There must be an inheritance for them that be escaped of Benjamin,
that a tribe be not destroyed out of Israel.

18 **Howbeit we** may not give them wives of our daughters:
for the children of Israel have sworn,
saying,
Cursed be he that giveth a wife to Benjamin.

19 **Then they** said,
Behold,
there is a feast of the LORD in Shiloh yearly in a place which is on the north side of Bethel, on the east side of the highway that goeth up from Bethel to Shechem, and on the south of Lebonah.

20 **Therefore they** commanded the children of Benjamin,

saying,
Go and lie in wait in the vineyards;
21 **And see,**
and, {behold}, if the daughters of Shiloh come out to dance in dances,
then come ye out of the vineyards,
and catch you every man his wife of the daughters of Shiloh,
and go to the land of Benjamin.
22 **And it** shall be,
when their fathers or their brethren come unto us to complain,
that we will say unto them,
Be favourable unto them for our sakes:
because we reserved not to each man his wife in the war:
for ye did not give unto them at this time,
that ye should be guilty.
23 **And the children of Benjamin** did so,
and took them wives, according to their number, of them that danced,
whom they caught:
and they went and returned unto their inheritance,
and repaired the cities,
and dwelt in them.
24 **And the children of Israel** departed thence at that time, every man to his tribe and to his family,
and they went out from thence every man to his inheritance.
25 **In those days** there was no king in Israel:
every man did that which was right in his own eyes.

Ruth

The Book of Ruth (author unknown but traditionally attributed to the prophet Samuel) provides a narrative about the lineage of King David and, ultimately, Jesus. The story takes place during the time of the Judges, a period of transition between the exodus from Egypt and the establishment of the Kingdom of Israel. It focuses on Ruth, a Moabite woman, and her loyalty to her mother-in-law, Naomi, after the death of their husbands. When Naomi decides to return to her homeland in Israel, Ruth chooses to accompany her.

After arriving in Israel, Ruth works in the fields, gleaning the leftover grain from the harvest. She ends up working in the field of Boaz, a relative of Naomi, who takes notice of her and shows her favor. Boaz, impressed by Ruth's loyalty and hard work, agrees to be the kinsman-redeemer for Naomi and Ruth, and he eventually proposes to the Moabite woman. Ruth and Boaz marry, ensuring her future and the future of her mother-in-law. The Book of Ruth concludes by tracing the genealogy of Ruth and Boaz's son, Obed, who becomes the grandfather of King David.

The genealogy of Ruth and Boaz's son, Obed, highlights Ruth's inclusion in the lineage of the Israelite monarchy and underscores the integration of foreigners into the Israelite community. Ruth's unwavering loyalty to her mother-in-law and her profound trust in God's provision are not just personal traits, but they embody the central values of the Bible: loyalty, faith, and commitment. Her story is a testament to how God's providence works through ordinary people to bring about His plan. It also highlights the importance of following God's will and the blessings that come from doing so.

1 **Now it** came to pass in the days when the judges ruled,
that there was a famine in the land.
And a certain man of Bethlehemjudah went to sojourn in the country of Moab, he, and his wife, and his two sons.
2 **And the name of the man** was Elimelech,
and the name of his wife Naomi,
and the name of his two sons Mahlon and Chilion, Ephrathites of Bethlehemjudah.
And they came into the country of Moab,
and continued there.
3 **And Elimelech Naomi's husband** died;
and she was left, and her two sons.
4 **And they** took them wives of the women of Moab;
the name of the one was Orpah, and the name of the other Ruth:
and they dwelled there about ten years.
5 **And Mahlon and Chilion** died also both of them;
and the woman was left of her two sons and her husband.
6 **Then she** arose with her daughters in law,
that she might return from the country of Moab:
for she had heard in the country of Moab how that the LORD had visited his people
in giving them bread.
7 **Wherefore she** went forth out of the place where she was, and her two daughters in law with her;
and they went on the way to return unto the land of Judah.
8 **And Naomi** said unto her two daughters in law,
Go,
return each to her mother's house:
the LORD deal kindly with you,
as ye have dealt with the dead, and with me.
9 **The LORD** grant you that ye may find rest, each of you in the house of her husband.
Then she kissed them;
and they lifted up their voice,
and wept.
10 **And they** said unto her,
Surely we will return with thee unto thy people.
11 **And Naomi** said,
Turn again, my daughters:
why will ye go with me?
are there yet any more sons in my womb,
that they may be your husbands?
12 **Turn again,** my daughters,
go your way;
for I am too old to have an husband.
If I should say,
I have hope,
if I should have an husband also to night,
and should also bear sons;
13 **Would ye** tarry for them
till they were grown?
would ye stay for them from having husbands?
nay, my daughters;
for it grieveth me much for your sakes that the hand of the LORD is gone out against me.
14 **And they** lifted up their voice,
and wept again:
and Orpah kissed her mother in law;
but Ruth clave unto her.
15 **And she** said,
Behold,
thy sister in law is gone back unto her people, and unto her gods:
return thou after thy sister in law.
16 **And Ruth** said,
Intreat me not to leave thee,
or to return from following after thee:
for whither thou goest,
I will go;
and where thou lodgest,
I will lodge:
thy people shall be my people,
and thy God my God:
17 **Where thou** diest,
will I die,

and there will I be buried:
the LORD do so to me, and more also,
if ought but death part thee and me.

18 **When she** saw that she was stedfastly minded to go with her,
then she left speaking unto her.

19 **So they two** went
until they came to Bethlehem.

And it came to pass,
when they were come to Bethlehem,
that all the city was moved about them,
and they said,
Is this Naomi?

20 **And she** said unto them,
Call me not Naomi,
call me Mara:
for the Almighty hath dealt very bitterly with me.

21 **I** went out full
and the LORD hath brought me home again empty:
why then call ye me Naomi,
seeing the LORD hath testified against me,
and the Almighty hath afflicted me?

22 **So Naomi** returned, and Ruth the Moabitess, her daughter in law, with her,
which returned out of the country of Moab:
and they came to Bethlehem in the beginning of barley harvest.

2

And Naomi had a kinsman of her husband's, a mighty man of wealth, of the family of Elimelech;
and his name was Boaz.

2 **And Ruth the Moabitess** said unto Naomi,
Let me now go to the field,
and glean ears of corn after him in whose sight I shall find grace.

And she said unto her,
Go, my daughter.

3 **And she** went,
and came,
and gleaned in the field after the reapers:
and her hap was to light on a part of the field belonging unto Boaz,
who was of the kindred of Elimelech.

4 **And, {behold}, Boaz** came from Bethlehem,
and said unto the reapers,
The LORD be with you.

And they answered him,
The LORD bless thee.

5 **Then** said Boaz unto his servant that was set over the reapers,
Whose damsel is this?

6 **And the servant that was set over the reapers** answered and said,
It is the Moabitish damsel
that came back with Naomi out of the country of Moab:
7 **And she** said,
I pray you,
let me glean and gather after the reapers among the sheaves:
so she came,
and hath continued even from the morning until now,
that she tarried a little in the house.

8 **Then** said Boaz unto Ruth,
Hearest thou not, my daughter?

Go not to glean in another field,
neither go from hence,
but abide here fast by my maidens:
9 **Let thine eyes** be on the field that they do reap,
and go thou after them:
have I not charged the young men
that they shall not touch thee?
and when thou art athirst,
go unto the vessels,
and drink of that which the young men have drawn.

10 **Then she** fell on her face,
and bowed herself to the ground,
and said unto him,
Why have I found grace in thine eyes,
that thou shouldest take knowledge of me,
seeing I am a stranger?

11 **And Boaz** answered and said unto her,
It hath fully been shewed me, all that thou hast done unto thy mother in law since the death of thine husband:
and how thou hast left thy father and thy mother, and the land of thy nativity,
and art come unto a people which thou knewest not heretofore.

12 **The LORD** recompense thy work,
and a full reward be given thee of the LORD God of Israel,
under whose wings thou art come to trust.

13 **Then she** said,
Let me find favour in thy sight, my lord;
for that thou hast comforted me,
and for that thou hast spoken friendly unto thine handmaid,
though I be not like unto one of thine handmaidens.

14 **And Boaz** said unto her,
At mealtime come thou hither,
and eat of the bread,
and dip thy morsel in the vinegar.

And she sat beside the reapers:
and he reached her parched corn,
and she did eat,
and was sufficed,
and left.

15 **And when she** was risen up to glean,
Boaz commanded his young men, saying,
Let her glean even among the sheaves,
and reproach her not:
16 **And let fall** also some of the handfuls of purpose for her,
and leave them,
that she may glean them,
and rebuke her not.

17 **So she** gleaned in the field until even,
and beat out that she had gleaned:
and it was about an ephah of barley.

18 **And she** took it up,
and went into the city:
and her mother in law saw what she had gleaned:
and she brought forth,
and gave to her that she had reserved after she was sufficed.

19 **And her mother in law** said unto her,
Where hast thou gleaned to day?
and where wroughtest thou?
blessed be he that did take knowledge of thee.

And she shewed her mother in law
with whom she had wrought,
and said,
The man's name with whom I wrought to day is Boaz.

20 **And Naomi** said unto her daughter in law,
Blessed be he of the LORD,
who hath not left off his kindness to the living and to the dead.

And Naomi said unto her,
The man is near of kin unto us, one of our next kinsmen.

21 **And Ruth the Moabitess** said,
He said unto me also,
Thou shalt keep fast by my young men,
until they have ended all my harvest.

22 **And Naomi** said unto Ruth her daughter in law,
It is good, my daughter, that thou go out with his maidens,
that they meet thee not in any other field.

23 **So she** kept fast by the maidens of Boaz
to glean unto the end of barley harvest and of wheat harvest;
and dwelt with her mother in law.

3

Then Naomi her mother in law said unto her,
My daughter, shall I not seek rest for thee,
that it may be well with thee?

2 **And now is not Boaz** of our kindred,
with whose maidens thou wast?
Behold,
he winnoweth barley to night in the threshingfloor.

3 **Wash** thyself therefore,
and anoint thee,
and put thy raiment upon thee,
and get thee down to the floor:
but make not thyself known unto the man,
until he shall have done eating and drinking.

4 **And it** shall be,
when he lieth down,
that thou shalt mark the place where he shall lie,
and thou shalt go in,
and uncover his feet,
and lay thee down;
and he will tell thee
what thou shalt do.

5 **And she** said unto her,
All that thou sayest unto me I will do.

6 **And she** went down unto the floor,
and did according to all that her mother in law bade her.

7 **And when Boaz** had eaten and drunk,
and his heart was merry,
he went to lie down at the end of the heap of corn:
and she came softly,
and uncovered his feet,
and laid her down.

8 **And it** came to pass at midnight,
that the man was afraid,
and turned himself:
and, {behold}, a woman lay at his feet.

9 **And he** said,
Who art thou?
And she answered,
I am Ruth thine handmaid:
spread therefore thy skirt over thine handmaid;
for thou art a near kinsman.

10 **And he** said,
Blessed be thou of the LORD, my daughter:
for thou hast shewed more kindness in the latter end than at the beginning,
inasmuch as thou followedst not young men, whether poor or rich.

11 **And now, my daughter,** fear not;
I will do to thee all that thou requirest:
for all the city of my people doth know
that thou art a virtuous woman.

12 **And now it is true** that I am thy near kinsman:
howbeit there is a kinsman nearer than I.

13 **Tarry** this night,
and it shall be in the morning,
that if he will perform unto thee the part of a kinsman, well;
let him do the kinsman's part:
but if he will not do the part of a kinsman to thee,
then will I do the part of a kinsman to thee,
as the LORD liveth:
lie down until the morning.

14 **And she** lay at his feet until the morning:
and she rose up
before one could know another.
And he said,
Let it not be known
that a woman came into the floor.

15 **Also he** said,
Bring the vail that thou hast upon thee,
and hold it.
And when she held it,
he measured six measures of barley,
and laid it on her:
and she went into the city.

16 **And when she** came to her mother in law,
she said,
Who art thou, my daughter?
And she told her all that the man had done to her.

17 **And she** said,
These six measures of barley gave he me;
for he said to me,
Go not empty unto thy mother in law.

18 **Then** said she,
Sit still, my daughter,
until thou know
how the matter will fall:
for the man will not be in rest,
until he have finished the thing this day.

4

Then went Boaz up to the gate,
and sat him down there:
and, {behold}, the kinsman of whom Boaz spake came by;
unto whom he said,
Ho, such a one!
turn aside,
sit down here.
And he turned aside,
and sat down.

2 **And he** took ten men of the elders of the city,
and said,
Sit ye down here.
And they sat down.

3 **And he** said unto the kinsman,
Naomi, {that is come again out of the country of Moab}, selleth a parcel of land,
which was our brother Elimelech's:
4 **And I** thought to advertise thee,
saying,
Buy it before the inhabitants, and before the elders of my people.
If thou wilt redeem it,
redeem it:
but if thou wilt not redeem it,
then tell me,
that I may know:
for there is none to redeem it beside thee;
and I am after thee.
And he said,
I will redeem it.

5 **Then** said Boaz,
What day thou buyest the field of the hand of Naomi,
thou must buy it also of Ruth the Moabitess, the wife of the dead,
to raise up the name of the dead upon his inheritance.

6 **And the kinsman** said,

I cannot redeem it for myself,
lest I mar mine own inheritance:
redeem thou my right to thyself;
for I cannot redeem it.

7 **Now this** was the manner in former time in Israel concerning redeeming and concerning changing,
for to confirm all things;
a man plucked off his shoe,
and gave it to his neighbour:
and this was a testimony in Israel.

8 **Therefore the kinsman** said unto Boaz,
Buy it for thee.

So he drew off his shoe.

9 **And Boaz** said unto the elders, and unto all the people,
Ye are witnesses this day,
that I have bought all that was Elimelech's, and all that was Chilion's and Mahlon's, of the hand of Naomi.

10 **Moreover Ruth the Moabitess, the wife of Mahlon,** have I purchased to be my wife,
to raise up the name of the dead upon his inheritance,
that the name of the dead be not cut off from among his brethren, and from the gate of his place:
ye are witnesses this day.

11 **And all the people that were in the gate, and the elders,** said,
We are witnesses.

The LORD make the woman that is come into thine house like Rachel and like Leah,
which two did build the house of Israel:
and do thou worthily in Ephratah,
and be famous in Bethlehem:

12 **And let thy house** be like the house of Pharez, {whom Tamar bare unto Judah}, of the seed which the LORD shall give thee of this young woman.

13 **So Boaz** took Ruth,
and she was his wife:
and when he went in unto her,
the LORD gave her conception,
and she bare a son.

14 **And the women** said unto Naomi,
Blessed be the LORD,
which hath not left thee this day without a kinsman,
that his name may be famous in Israel.

15 **And he** shall be unto thee a restorer of thy life, and a nourisher of thine old age:
for thy daughter in law, {which loveth thee}, {which is better to thee than seven sons}, hath born him.

16 **And Naomi** took the child,
and laid it in her bosom,
and became nurse unto it.

17 **And the women her neighbours** gave it a name,
saying,
There is a son born to Naomi;
and they called his name Obed:
he is the father of Jesse, the father of David.

18 **Now these** are the generations of Pharez:
Pharez begat Hezron,
19 **And Hezron** begat Ram,
and Ram begat Amminadab,
20 **And Amminadab** begat Nahshon,
and Nahshon begat Salmon,
21 **And Salmon** begat Boaz,
and Boaz begat Obed,
22 **And Obed** begat Jesse,
and Jesse begat David.

1 Samuel

First Samuel (author unknown) focuses on the transition of Israel from a nation ruled by judges to the establishment of a monarchy, a significant turning point in their history. The book, guided by divine inspiration, highlights the importance of seeking God's guidance in governance and leadership, as evidenced by the lives of Saul and David, Israel's first two kings, whose relationship with God and Samuel influenced their reigns. First Samuel begins with Samuel's birth, a miraculous event. His mother, Hannah, is barren, but she prays fervently for a child. God grants her prayer, and she dedicates her son, Samuel, to God's service.

As a young boy, Samuel hears the voice of God for the first time, and he eventually becomes a prophet and judge in Israel. He also plays a crucial role in anointing Saul as the first king of Israel. Saul, a handsome young man, leads the Israelites to victory in several battles. Still, his insecurities and jealousy eventually lead to his downfall. His reign becomes increasingly troubled, so God sends Samuel to anoint a new king: a young shepherd boy named David, who becomes the hero of the book's most famous story: the battle between David and Goliath.

David's rise to fame is not without its trials. Saul's jealousy and fear of him escalate as his popularity grows, leading to numerous attempts on David's life. These circumstances force David, God's newly-anointed one, to live as an outlaw, constantly on the run. The book's final chapters see Saul's demise in a battle against the Philistines. The Book of First Samuel is a captivating narrative that delves into themes of leadership, faith, and the nature of God's will. It also serves as a crucial backdrop for the establishment of the Israelite monarchy, setting the stage for the reign of Israel's most renowned monarch: King David, a leader chosen by God.

1 **Now there** was a certain man of Ramathaimzophim, of mount Ephraim,
and his name was Elkanah, the son of Jeroham, the son of Elihu, the son of Tohu, the son of Zuph, an Ephrathite:
2 **And he** had two wives;
the name of the one was Hannah, and the name of the other Peninnah:
and Peninnah had children,
but Hannah had no children.
3 **And this man** went up out of his city yearly
to worship and to sacrifice unto the LORD of hosts in Shiloh.
And the two sons of Eli, Hophni and Phinehas, the priests of the LORD, were there.
4 **And when the time** was that Elkanah offered,
he gave to Peninnah his wife, and to all her sons and her daughters, portions:
5 **But unto Hannah** he gave a worthy portion;
for he loved Hannah:
but the LORD had shut up her womb.
6 **And her adversary** also provoked her sore,
for to make her fret,
because the LORD had shut up her womb.
7 **And as he** did so year by year,
when she went up to the house of the LORD,
so she provoked her;
therefore she wept,
and did not eat.
8 **Then** said Elkanah her husband to her,
Hannah, why weepest thou?
and why eatest thou not?
and why is thy heart grieved?
am not I better to thee than ten sons?
9 **So Hannah** rose up
after they had eaten in Shiloh,
and after they had drunk.
Now Eli the priest sat upon a seat by a post of the temple of the LORD.
10 **And she** was in bitterness of soul,
and prayed unto the LORD,
and wept sore.
11 **And she** vowed a vow,
and said,
O LORD of hosts, if thou wilt indeed look on the affliction of thine handmaid,
and remember me,
and not forget thine handmaid,
but wilt give unto thine handmaid a man child,
then I will give him unto the LORD all the days of his life,
and there shall no razor come upon his head.
12 **And it** came to pass,
as she continued praying before the LORD,
that Eli marked her mouth.
13 **Now Hannah,** she spake in her heart;
only her lips moved,
but her voice was not heard:
therefore Eli thought she had been drunken.
14 **And Eli** said unto her,
How long wilt thou be drunken?
put away thy wine from thee.
15 **And Hannah** answered and said,
No, my lord, I am a woman of a sorrowful spirit:
I have drunk neither wine nor strong drink,
but have poured out my soul before the LORD.
16 **Count not** thine handmaid for a daughter of Belial:
for out of the abundance of my complaint and grief have I spoken hitherto.
17 **Then Eli** answered and said,

Go in peace:
and the God of Israel grant thee thy petition that thou hast asked of him.
18 **And she** said,
Let thine handmaid find grace in thy sight.
So the woman went her way,
and did eat,
and her countenance was no more sad.
19 **And they** rose up in the morning early,
and worshipped before the LORD,
and returned,
and came to their house to Ramah:
and Elkanah knew Hannah his wife;
and the LORD remembered her.
20 **Wherefore it** came to pass,
when the time was come about after Hannah had conceived,
that she bare a son,
and called his name Samuel,
saying,
Because I have asked him of the LORD.
21 **And the man Elkanah, and all his house,** went up to offer unto the LORD the yearly sacrifice, and his vow.
22 **But Hannah** went not up;
for she said unto her husband,
I will not go up until the child be weaned,
and then I will bring him,
that he may appear before the LORD,
and there abide for ever.
23 **And Elkanah her husband** said unto her,
Do what seemeth thee good;
tarry
until thou have weaned him;
only the LORD establish his word.
So the woman abode,
and gave her son suck
until she weaned him.
24 **And when she** had weaned him,
she took him up with her, with three bullocks, and one ephah of flour, and a bottle of wine,
and brought him unto the house of the LORD in Shiloh:
and the child was young.
25 **And they** slew a bullock,
and brought the child to Eli.
26 **And she** said,
Oh my lord, as thy soul liveth, my lord,
I am the woman that stood by thee here,
praying unto the LORD.
27 **For this child** I prayed;
and the LORD hath given me my petition which I asked of him:
28 **Therefore also I** have lent him to the LORD;
as long as he liveth
he shall be lent to the LORD.
And he worshipped the LORD there.

2 **And Hannah** prayed,
and said,
My heart rejoiceth in the LORD,
mine horn is exalted in the LORD:
my mouth is enlarged over mine enemies;
because I rejoice in thy salvation.
2 **There** is none holy as the LORD:
for there is none beside thee:
neither is there any rock like our God.
3 **Talk** no more so exceeding proudly;
let not arrogancy come out of your mouth:
for the LORD is a God of knowledge,
and by him actions are weighed.
4 **The bows of the mighty men** are broken,
and they that stumbled are girded with strength.
5 **They that were full** have hired out themselves for bread;
and they that were hungry ceased:
so that the barren hath born seven;
and she that hath many children is waxed feeble.
6 **The LORD** killeth,
and maketh alive:
he bringeth down to the grave,
and bringeth up.
7 **The LORD** maketh poor,
and maketh rich:
he bringeth low,
and lifteth up.
8 **He** raiseth up the poor out of the dust,
and lifteth up the beggar from the dunghill,
to set them among princes,
and to make them inherit the throne of glory:
for the pillars of the earth are the LORD's,
and he hath set the world upon them.
9 **He** will keep the feet of his saints,
and the wicked shall be silent in darkness;
for by strength shall no man prevail.
10 **The adversaries of the LORD** shall be broken to pieces;
out of heaven shall he thunder upon them:
the LORD shall judge the ends of the earth;
and he shall give strength unto his king,
and exalt the horn of his anointed.
11 **And Elkanah** went to Ramah to his house.
And the child did minister unto the LORD before Eli the priest.
12 **Now the sons of Eli** were sons of Belial;
they knew not the LORD.
13 **And the priest's custom with the people** was, that, {when any man offered sacrifice}, the priest's servant came, {while the flesh was in seething}, with a fleshhook of three teeth in his hand;
14 **And he** struck it into the pan, or kettle, or caldron, or pot;
all that the fleshhook brought up the priest took for himself.
So they did in Shiloh unto all the Israelites that came thither.
15 **Also before they** burnt the fat,
the priest's servant came,
and said to the man that sacrificed,
Give flesh to roast for the priest;
for he will not have sodden flesh of thee, but raw.
16 **And if any man** said unto him,
Let them not fail to burn the fat presently,
and then take as much as thy soul desireth;
then he would answer him,
Nay;
but thou shalt give it me now:
and if not, I will take it by force.
17 **Wherefore the sin of the young men** was very great before the LORD:
for men abhorred the offering of the LORD.
18 **But Samuel** ministered before the LORD,
being a child,
girded with a linen ephod.

19 **Moreover his mother** made him a little coat,
and brought it to him from year to year,
when she came up with her husband to offer the yearly sacrifice.
20 **And Eli** blessed Elkanah and his wife,
and said,
The LORD give thee seed of this woman for the loan which is lent to the LORD.
And they went unto their own home.
21 **And the LORD** visited Hannah,
so that she conceived,
and bare three sons and two daughters.
And the child Samuel grew before the LORD.
22 **Now Eli** was very old,
and heard all that his sons did unto all Israel;
and how they lay with the women that assembled at the door of the tabernacle of the congregation.
23 **And he** said unto them,
Why do ye such things?
for I hear of your evil dealings by all this people.
24 Nay, my sons;
for it is no good report that I hear:
ye make the LORD's people to transgress.
25 **If one man** sin against another,
the judge shall judge him:
but if a man sin against the LORD,
who shall intreat for him?
Notwithstanding they hearkened not unto the voice of their father,
because the LORD would slay them.
26 **And the child Samuel** grew on,
and was in favour both with the LORD, and also with men.
27 **And there** came a man of God unto Eli,
and said unto him,
Thus saith the LORD,
Did I plainly appear unto the house of thy father,
when they were in Egypt in Pharaoh's house?
28 **And did I** choose him out of all the tribes of Israel to be my priest,
to offer upon mine altar,
to burn incense,
to wear an ephod before me?
and did I give unto the house of thy father all the offerings made by fire of the children of Israel?
29 **Wherefore kick ye** at my sacrifice and at mine offering,
which I have commanded in my habitation;
and honourest thy sons above me,
to make yourselves fat with the chiefest of all the offerings of Israel my people?
30 **Wherefore the LORD God of Israel** saith,
I said indeed
that thy house, and the house of thy father, should walk before me for ever:
but now the LORD saith,
Be it far from me;
for them that honour me I will honour,
and they that despise me shall be lightly esteemed.
31 **Behold,**
the days come,
that I will cut off thine arm, and the arm of thy father's house,
that there shall not be an old man in thine house.
32 **And thou** shalt see an enemy in my habitation, in all the wealth which God shall give Israel:
and there shall not be an old man in thine house for ever.
33 **And the man of thine**, {whom I shall not cut off from mine altar}, shall be to consume thine eyes,
and to grieve thine heart:
and all the increase of thine house shall die in the flower of their age.
34 **And this** shall be a sign unto thee,
that shall come upon thy two sons, on Hophni and Phinehas;
in one day they shall die both of them.
35 **And I** will raise me up a faithful priest,
that shall do according to that which is in mine heart and in my mind:
and I will build him a sure house;
and he shall walk before mine anointed for ever.
36 **And it** shall come to pass,
that every one that is left in thine house shall come and crouch to him for a piece of silver and a morsel of bread,
and shall say,
Put me, {I pray thee}, into one of the priests' offices,
that I may eat a piece of bread.

3

And the child Samuel ministered unto the LORD before Eli.
And the word of the LORD was precious in those days;
there was no open vision.
2 **And it** came to pass at that time,
when Eli was laid down in his place,
and his eyes began to wax dim,
that he could not see;
3 **And ere the lamp of God** went out in the temple of the LORD,
where the ark of God was,
and Samuel was laid down to sleep;
4 **That the LORD** called Samuel:
and he answered,
Here am I.
5 **And he** ran unto Eli,
and said,
Here am I;
for thou calledst me.
And he said,
I called not;
lie down again.
And he went and lay down.
6 **And the LORD** called yet again, Samuel.
And Samuel arose and went to Eli,
and said,
Here am I;
for thou didst call me.
And he answered,
I called not, my son;
lie down again.
7 **Now Samuel** did not yet know the LORD,
neither was the word of the LORD yet revealed unto him.
8 **And the LORD** called Samuel again the third time.
And he arose and went to Eli,
and said,
Here am I;
for thou didst call me.
And Eli perceived that the LORD had called the child.
9 **Therefore Eli** said unto Samuel,
Go,
lie down:
and it shall be,
if he call thee,
that thou shalt say,
Speak, LORD;
for thy servant heareth.

So Samuel went and lay down in his place.

10 **And the LORD** came,
and stood,
and called as at other times,
Samuel, Samuel.

Then Samuel answered,
Speak;
for thy servant heareth.

11 **And the LORD** said to Samuel,
Behold,
I will do a thing in Israel,
at which both the ears of every one that heareth it shall tingle.

12 **In that day** I will perform against Eli all things which I have spoken concerning his house:
when I begin,
I will also make an end.

13 **For I** have told him
that I will judge his house for ever for the iniquity which he knoweth;
because his sons made themselves vile,
and he restrained them not.

14 **And therefore I** have sworn unto the house of Eli,
that the iniquity of Eli's house shall not be purged with sacrifice nor offering for ever.

15 **And Samuel** lay until the morning,
and opened the doors of the house of the LORD.

And Samuel feared to shew Eli the vision.

16 **Then Eli** called Samuel,
and said,
Samuel, my son.

And he answered,
Here am I.

17 **And he** said,
What is the thing that the LORD hath said unto thee?

I pray thee
hide it not from me:
God do so to thee, and more also,
if thou hide any thing from me of all the things that he said unto thee.

18 **And Samuel** told him every whit,
and hid nothing from him.

And he said,
It is the LORD:
let him do what seemeth him good.

19 **And Samuel** grew,
and the LORD was with him,
and did let none of his words fall to the ground.

20 **And all Israel from Dan even to Beersheba** knew
that Samuel was established to be a prophet of the LORD.

21 **And the LORD** appeared again in Shiloh:
for the LORD revealed himself to Samuel in Shiloh by the word of the LORD.

4

And the word of Samuel came to all Israel.

Now Israel went out against the Philistines to battle,
and pitched beside Ebenezer:
and the Philistines pitched in Aphek.

2 **And the Philistines** put themselves in array against Israel:
and when they joined battle,
Israel was smitten before the Philistines:
and they slew of the army in the field about four thousand men.

3 **And when the people** were come into the camp,
the elders of Israel said,
Wherefore hath the LORD smitten us to day before the Philistines?

Let us fetch the ark of the covenant of the LORD out of Shiloh unto us,
that, {when it cometh among us}, it may save us out of the hand of our enemies.

4 **So the people** sent to Shiloh,
that they might bring from thence the ark of the covenant of the LORD of hosts,
which dwelleth between the cherubims:
and the two sons of Eli, Hophni and Phinehas, were there with the ark of the covenant of God.

5 **And when the ark of the covenant of the LORD** came into the camp,
all Israel shouted with a great shout,
so that the earth rang again.

6 **And when the Philistines** heard the noise of the shout,
they said,
What meaneth the noise of this great shout in the camp of the Hebrews?

And they understood
that the ark of the LORD was come into the camp.

7 **And the Philistines** were afraid,
for they said,
God is come into the camp.

And they said,
Woe unto us!
for there hath not been such a thing heretofore.

8 **Woe** unto us!
who shall deliver us out of the hand of these mighty Gods?
these are the Gods that smote the Egyptians with all the plagues in the wilderness.

9 **Be** strong
and quit yourselves like men, O ye Philistines,
that ye be not servants unto the Hebrews,
as they have been to you:
quit yourselves like men,
and fight.

10 **And the Philistines** fought,
and Israel was smitten,
and they fled every man into his tent:
and there was a very great slaughter;
for there fell of Israel thirty thousand footmen.

11 **And the ark of God** was taken;
and the two sons of Eli, Hophni and Phinehas, were slain.

12 **And there** ran a man of Benjamin out of the army,
and came to Shiloh the same day
with his clothes rent, and with earth upon his head.

13 **And when** he came,
lo,
Eli sat upon a seat by the wayside watching:
for his heart trembled for the ark of God.

And when the man came into the city,
and told it,
all the city cried out.

14 **And when Eli** heard the noise of the crying,
he said,
What meaneth the noise of this tumult?

And the man came in hastily,
and told Eli.

15 **Now Eli** was ninety and eight years old;
and his eyes were dim,
that he could not see.

16 **And the man** said unto Eli,

I am he that came out of the army,
and I fled to day out of the army.
And he said,
What is there done, my son?
17 **And the messenger** answered and said,
Israel is fled before the Philistines,
and there hath been also a great slaughter among the people,
and thy two sons also, Hophni and Phinehas, are dead,
and the ark of God is taken.
18 **And it** came to pass,
when he made mention of the ark of God,
that he fell from off the seat backward by the side of the gate,
and his neck brake,
and he died:
for he was an old man, and heavy.
And he had judged Israel forty years.
19 **And his daughter in law, Phinehas' wife,** was with child,
near to be delivered:
and when she heard the tidings that the ark of God was taken, and that her father in law and her husband were dead,
she bowed herself and travailed;
for her pains came upon her.
20 **And about the time of her death** the women that stood by her said unto her,
Fear not;
for thou hast born a son.
But she answered not,
neither did she regard it.
21 **And she** named the child Ichabod, saying,
The glory is departed from Israel:
because the ark of God was taken, and because of her father in law and her husband.
22 **And she** said,
The glory is departed from Israel:
for the ark of God is taken.

5

And the Philistines took the ark of God,
and brought it from Ebenezer unto Ashdod.
2 **When the Philistines** took the ark of God,
they brought it into the house of Dagon,
and set it by Dagon.
3 **And when they of Ashdod** arose early on the morrow,
behold,
Dagon was fallen upon his face to the earth before the ark of the LORD.
And they took Dagon,
and set him in his place again.
4 **And when they** arose early on the morrow morning,
behold,
Dagon was fallen upon his face to the ground before the ark of the LORD;
and the head of Dagon and both the palms of his hands were cut off upon the threshold;
only the stump of Dagon was left to him.
5 **Therefore neither the priests of Dagon, nor any that come into Dagon's house,** tread on the threshold of Dagon in Ashdod unto this day.
6 **But the hand of the LORD** was heavy upon them of Ashdod,
and he destroyed them,
and smote them with emerods, even Ashdod and the coasts thereof.
7 **And when the men of Ashdod** saw that it was so,
they said,
The ark of the God of Israel shall not abide with us:
for his hand is sore upon us, and upon Dagon our god.
8 **They** sent therefore and gathered all the lords of the Philistines unto them,
and said,
What shall we do with the ark of the God of Israel?
And they answered,
Let the ark of the God of Israel be carried about unto Gath.
And they carried the ark of the God of Israel about thither.
9 **And it** was so,
that, {after they had carried it about}, the hand of the LORD was against the city with a very great destruction:
and he smote the men of the city, both small and great,
and they had emerods in their secret parts.
10 **Therefore they** sent the ark of God to Ekron.
And it came to pass,
as the ark of God came to Ekron,
that the Ekronites cried out, saying,
They have brought about the ark of the God of Israel to us,
to slay us and our people.
11 **So they** sent and gathered together all the lords of the Philistines,
and said,
Send away the ark of the God of Israel,
and let it go again to his own place,
that it slay us not, and our people:
for there was a deadly destruction throughout all the city;
the hand of God was very heavy there.
12 **And the men that died not** were smitten with the emerods:
and the cry of the city went up to heaven.

6

And the ark of the LORD was in the country of the Philistines seven months.
2 **And the Philistines** called for the priests and the diviners,
saying,
What shall we do to the ark of the LORD?
tell us
wherewith we shall send it to his place.
3 **And they** said,
If ye send away the ark of the God of Israel,
send it not empty;
but in any wise return him a trespass offering:
then ye shall be healed,
and it shall be known to you why his hand is not removed from you.
4 **Then** said they,
What shall be the trespass offering which we shall return to him?
They answered, Five golden emerods, and five golden mice, according to the number of the lords of the Philistines:
for one plague was on you all, and on your lords.
5 **Wherefore ye** shall make images of your emerods, and images of your mice that mar the land;
and ye shall give glory unto the God of Israel:
peradventure he will lighten his hand from off you, and from off your gods, and from off your land.
6 **Wherefore** then do ye harden your hearts,

as the Egyptians and Pharaoh hardened their hearts?
when he had wrought wonderfully among them,
did they not let the people go,
and they departed?

7 **Now therefore make** a new cart,
and take two milch kine,
on which there hath come no yoke,
and tie the kine to the cart,
and bring their calves home from them:
8 **And take** the ark of the LORD,
and lay it upon the cart;
and put the jewels of gold, {which ye return him for a trespass offering}, in a coffer by the side thereof;
and send it away,
that it may go.

9 **And see,**
if it goeth up by the way of his own coast to Bethshemesh,
then he hath done us this great evil:
but if not, then we shall know
that it is not his hand that smote us:
it was a chance that happened to us.

10 **And the men** did so;
and took two milch kine,
and tied them to the cart,
and shut up their calves at home:
11 **And they** laid the ark of the LORD upon the cart, and the coffer with the mice of gold and the images of their emerods.

12 **And the kine** took the straight way to the way of Bethshemesh,
and went along the highway,
lowing as they went,
and turned not aside to the right hand or to the left;
and the lords of the Philistines went after them unto the border of Bethshemesh.

13 **And they of Bethshemesh** were reaping their wheat harvest in the valley:
and they lifted up their eyes,
and saw the ark,
and rejoiced to see it.

14 **And the cart** came into the field of Joshua, a Bethshemite,
and stood there,
where there was a great stone:
and they clave the wood of the cart,
and offered the kine a burnt offering unto the LORD.

15 **And the Levites** took down the ark of the LORD, and the coffer that was with it,
wherein the jewels of gold were,
and put them on the great stone:
and the men of Bethshemesh offered burnt offerings and sacrificed sacrifices the same day unto the LORD.

16 **And when the five lords of the Philistines** had seen it,
they returned to Ekron the same day.

17 **And these** are the golden emerods which the Philistines returned for a trespass offering unto the LORD; for Ashdod one, for Gaza one, for Askelon one, for Gath one, for Ekron one;
18 And the golden mice, according to the number of all the cities of the Philistines belonging to the five lords, both of fenced cities, and of country villages, even unto the great stone of Abel, {whereon they set down the ark of the LORD}: {which stone remaineth unto this day in the field of Joshua, the Bethshemite}.

19 **And he** smote the men of Bethshemesh,
because they had looked into the ark of the LORD,
even he smote of the people fifty thousand and threescore and ten men:
and the people lamented,
because the LORD had smitten many of the people with a great slaughter.

20 **And the men of Bethshemesh** said,
Who is able to stand before this holy LORD God?
and to whom shall he go up from us?

21 **And they** sent messengers to the inhabitants of Kirjathjearim,
saying,
The Philistines have brought again the ark of the LORD;
come ye down,
and fetch it up to you.

7 **And the men of Kirjathjearim** came,
and fetched up the ark of the LORD,
and brought it into the house of Abinadab in the hill,
and sanctified Eleazar his son to keep the ark of the LORD.

2 **And it** came to pass,
while the ark abode in Kirjathjearim,
that the time was long;
for it was twenty years:
and all the house of Israel lamented after the LORD.

3 **And Samuel** spake unto all the house of Israel,
saying,
If ye do return unto the LORD with all your hearts,
then put away the strange gods and Ashtaroth from among you,
and prepare your hearts unto the LORD,
and serve him only:
and he will deliver you out of the hand of the Philistines.

4 **Then the children of Israel** did put away Baalim and Ashtaroth,
and served the LORD only.

5 **And Samuel** said,
Gather all Israel to Mizpeh,
and I will pray for you unto the LORD.

6 **And they** gathered together to Mizpeh,
and drew water,
and poured it out before the LORD,
and fasted on that day,
and said there,
We have sinned against the LORD.

And Samuel judged the children of Israel in Mizpeh.

7 **And when the Philistines** heard that the children of Israel were gathered together to Mizpeh,
the lords of the Philistines went up against Israel.

And when the children of Israel heard it,
they were afraid of the Philistines.

8 **And the children of Israel** said to Samuel,
Cease not to cry unto the LORD our God for us,
that he will save us out of the hand of the Philistines.

9 **And Samuel** took a sucking lamb,
and offered it for a burnt offering wholly unto the LORD:
and Samuel cried unto the LORD for Israel;
and the LORD heard him.

10 **And as Samuel** was offering up the burnt offering,
the Philistines drew near to battle against Israel:

but the LORD thundered with a great thunder on that day upon the Philistines,
and discomfited them;
and they were smitten before Israel.
11 **And the men of Israel** went out of Mizpeh,
and pursued the Philistines,
and smote them,
until they came under Bethcar.
12 **Then Samuel** took a stone,
and set it between Mizpeh and Shen,
and called the name of it Ebenezer,
saying,
Hitherto hath the LORD helped us.
13 **So the Philistines** were subdued,
and they came no more into the coast of Israel:
and the hand of the LORD was against the Philistines all the days of Samuel.
14 **And the cities which the Philistines had taken from Israel** were restored to Israel, from Ekron even unto Gath;
and the coasts thereof did Israel deliver out of the hands of the Philistines.
And there was peace between Israel and the Amorites.
15 **And Samuel** judged Israel all the days of his life.
16 **And he** went from year to year in circuit to Bethel, and Gilgal, and Mizpeh,
and judged Israel in all those places.
17 **And his return** was to Ramah;
for there was his house;
and there he judged Israel;
and there he built an altar unto the LORD.

8

And it came to pass,
when Samuel was old,
that he made his sons judges over Israel.
2 **Now the name of his firstborn** was Joel; and the name of his second, Abiah:
they were judges in Beersheba.
3 **And his sons** walked not in his ways,
but turned aside after lucre,
and took bribes,
and perverted judgment.
4 **Then all the elders of Israel** gathered themselves together,
and came to Samuel unto Ramah,
5 **And** said unto him,
Behold,
thou art old,
and thy sons walk not in thy ways:
now make us a king {to judge us} like all the nations.
6 **But the thing** displeased Samuel,
when they said,
Give us a king to judge us.
And Samuel prayed unto the LORD.
7 **And the LORD** said unto Samuel,
Hearken unto the voice of the people in all that they say unto thee:
for they have not rejected thee,
but they have rejected me,
that I should not reign over them.
8 **According to all the works which they have done since the day that I brought them up out of Egypt even unto this day,** {wherewith they have forsaken me}, {and served other gods}, so do they also unto thee.
9 **Now therefore hearken** unto their voice:
howbeit yet protest solemnly unto them,
and shew them the manner of the king that shall reign over them.
10 **And Samuel** told all the words of the LORD unto the people that asked of him a king.
11 **And he** said,
This will be the manner of the king that shall reign over you:
He will take your sons,
and appoint them for himself, for his chariots, and to be his horsemen;
and some shall run before his chariots.
12 **And he** will appoint him captains over thousands, and captains over fifties;
and will set them to ear his ground,
and to reap his harvest,
and to make his instruments of war, and instruments of his chariots.
13 **And he** will take your daughters to be confectionaries, and to be cooks, and to be bakers.
14 **And he** will take your fields, and your vineyards, and your oliveyards, even the best of them,
and give them to his servants.
15 **And he** will take the tenth of your seed, and of your vineyards,
and give to his officers, and to his servants.
16 **And he** will take your menservants, and your maidservants, and your goodliest young men, and your asses,
and put them to his work.
17 **He** will take the tenth of your sheep:
and ye shall be his servants.
18 **And ye** shall cry out in that day because of your king which ye shall have chosen you;
and the LORD will not hear you in that day.
19 **Nevertheless the people** refused to obey the voice of Samuel;
and they said,
Nay;
but we will have a king over us;
20 **That we** also may be like all the nations;
and that our king may judge us,
and go out before us,
and fight our battles.
21 **And Samuel** heard all the words of the people,
and he rehearsed them in the ears of the LORD.
22 **And the LORD** said to Samuel,
Hearken unto their voice,
and make them a king.
And Samuel said unto the men of Israel,
Go ye every man unto his city.

9

Now there was a man of Benjamin,
whose name was Kish, the son of Abiel, the son of Zeror, the son of Bechorath, the son of Aphiah, a Benjamite, a mighty man of power.
2 **And he** had a son, {whose name was Saul}, a choice young man, and a goodly:
and there was not among the children of Israel a goodlier person than he:
from his shoulders and upward he was higher than any of the people.
3 **And the asses of Kish Saul's father** were lost.
And Kish said to Saul his son,
Take now one of the servants with thee,
and arise,
go seek the asses.
4 **And he** passed through mount Ephraim,

and passed through the land of Shalisha,
but they found them not:
then they passed through the land of Shalim,
and there they were not:
and he passed through the land of the Benjamites,
but they found them not.

5 **And when they** were come to the land of Zuph,
Saul said to his servant that was with him,
Come,
and let us return;
lest my father leave caring for the asses,
and take thought for us.

6 **And he** said unto him,
Behold now,
there is in this city a man of God,
and he is an honourable man;
all that he saith cometh surely to pass:
now let us go thither;
peradventure he can shew us our way that we should go.

7 **Then** said Saul to his servant,
But, {behold}, if we go,
what shall we bring the man?
for the bread is spent in our vessels,
and there is not a present to bring to the man of God:
what have we?

8 **And the servant** answered Saul again,
and said,
Behold,
I have here at hand the fourth part of a shekel of silver:
that will I give to the man of God,
to tell us our way.

9 (**Beforetime in Israel**, {when a man went to enquire of God},
thus he spake,
Come,
and let us go to the seer:
for he that is now called a Prophet was beforetime called a Seer.)

10 **Then** said Saul to his servant,
Well said;
come,
let us go.

So they went unto the city where the man of God was.

11 **And as they** went up the hill to the city,
they found young maidens going out to draw water,
and said unto them,
Is the seer here?

12 **And they** answered them,
and said,
He is;
behold,
he is before you:
make haste now,
for he came to day to the city;
for there is a sacrifice of the people to day in the high place:

13 **As soon as ye** be come into the city,
ye shall straightway find him,
before he go up to the high place to eat:
for the people will not eat until he come,
because he doth bless the sacrifice;
and afterwards they eat that be bidden.

Now therefore get you up;
for about this time ye shall find him.

14 **And they** went up into the city:
and when they were come into the city,
behold,
Samuel came out against them,
for to go up to the high place.

15 **Now the LORD** had told Samuel in his ear
a day before Saul came,
saying,

16 **To morrow about this time** I will send thee a man out of the land of Benjamin,
and thou shalt anoint him to be captain over my people Israel,
that he may save my people out of the hand of the Philistines:
for I have looked upon my people,
because their cry is come unto me.

17 **And when Samuel** saw Saul,
the LORD said unto him,
Behold the man whom I spake to thee of!
this same shall reign over my people.

18 **Then Saul** drew near to Samuel in the gate,
and said,
Tell me,
I pray thee,
where the seer's house is.

19 **And Samuel** answered Saul,
and said,
I am the seer:
go up before me unto the high place;
for ye shall eat with me to day,
and to morrow I will let thee go,
and will tell thee all that is in thine heart.

20 **And as for thine asses that were lost three days ago,** set not thy mind on them;
for they are found.

And on whom is all the desire of Israel?

Is it not on thee, and on all thy father's house?

21 **And Saul** answered and said,
Am not I a Benjamite, of the smallest of the tribes of Israel?
and my family the least of all the families of the tribe of Benjamin?
wherefore then speakest thou so to me?

22 **And Samuel** took Saul and his servant,
and brought them into the parlour,
and made them sit in the chiefest place among them that were bidden,
which were about thirty persons.

23 **And Samuel** said unto the cook,
Bring the portion which I gave thee,
of which I said unto thee,
Set it by thee.

24 **And the cook** took up the shoulder, and that which was upon it,
and set it before Saul.

And Samuel said,
Behold that which is left!
set it before thee,
and eat:
for unto this time hath it been kept for thee
since I said,
I have invited the people.

So Saul did eat with Samuel that day.

25 **And when they** were come down from the high place into the city,
Samuel communed with Saul upon the top of the house.

26 **And they** arose early:
and it came to pass about the spring of the day,
that Samuel called Saul to the top of the house,
saying,
Up,
that I may send thee away.
And Saul arose,

and they went out both of them, he and Samuel, abroad.
27 **And as they** were going down to the end of the city,
Samuel said to Saul,
Bid the servant pass on before us,
(and he passed on),
but stand thou still a while,
that I may shew thee the word of God.

10 **Then Samuel** took a vial of oil,
and poured it upon his head,
and kissed him,
and said,
Is it not because the LORD hath anointed thee to be captain over his inheritance?
2 **When thou** art departed from me to day,
then thou shalt find two men by Rachel's sepulchre in the border of Benjamin at Zelzah;
and they will say unto thee,
The asses which thou wentest to seek are found:
and, {lo}, thy father hath left the care of the asses,
and sorroweth for you,
saying,
What shall I do for my son?
3 **Then** shalt thou go on forward from thence,
and thou shalt come to the plain of Tabor,
and there shall meet thee three men going up to God to Bethel, one carrying three kids, and another carrying three loaves of bread, and another carrying a bottle of wine:
4 **And they** will salute thee,
and give thee two loaves of bread;
which thou shalt receive of their hands.
5 **After that thou** shalt come to the hill of God,
where is the garrison of the Philistines:
and it shall come to pass,
when thou art come thither to the city,
that thou shalt meet a company of prophets coming down from the high place with a psaltery, and a tabret, and a pipe, and a harp, before them;
and they shall prophesy:
6 **And the Spirit of the LORD** will come upon thee,
and thou shalt prophesy with them,
and shalt be turned into another man.
7 **And let it be**, {when these signs are come unto thee}, that thou do as occasion serve thee;
for God is with thee.
8 **And thou** shalt go down before me to Gilgal;
and, {behold}, I will come down unto thee,
to offer burnt offerings,
and to sacrifice sacrifices of peace offerings:
seven days shalt thou tarry,
till I come to thee,
and shew thee
what thou shalt do.
9 **And it** was so,
that when he had turned his back to go from Samuel,
God gave him another heart:
and all those signs came to pass that day.
10 **And when they** came thither to the hill,
behold,
a company of prophets met him;
and the Spirit of God came upon him,
and he prophesied among them.
11 **And it** came to pass,
when all that knew him beforetime saw that,
behold,
he prophesied among the prophets,
then the people said one to another,
What is this that is come unto the son of Kish?
Is Saul also among the prophets?
12 **And one of the same place** answered and said,
But who is their father?
Therefore it became a proverb,
Is Saul also among the prophets?
13 **And when he** had made an end of prophesying,
he came to the high place.
14 **And Saul's uncle** said unto him and to his servant,
Whither went ye?
And he said,
To seek the asses:
and when we saw that they were no where,
we came to Samuel.
15 **And Saul's uncle** said,
Tell me,
I pray thee,
what Samuel said unto you.
16 **And Saul** said unto his uncle,
He told us plainly
that the asses were found.
But of the matter of the kingdom, {whereof Samuel spake}, he told him not.
17 **And Samuel** called the people together unto the LORD to Mizpeh;
18 **And** said unto the children of Israel,
Thus saith the LORD God of Israel,
I brought up Israel out of Egypt,
and delivered you out of the hand of the Egyptians, and out of the hand of all kingdoms, and of them that oppressed you:
19 **And ye** have this day rejected your God,
who himself saved you out of all your adversities and your tribulations;
and ye have said unto him,
Nay,
but set a king over us.
Now therefore present yourselves before the LORD by your tribes, and by your thousands.
20 **And when Samuel** had caused all the tribes of Israel to come near,
the tribe of Benjamin was taken.
21 **When he** had caused the tribe of Benjamin to come near by their families,
the family of Matri was taken,
and Saul the son of Kish was taken:
and when they sought him,
he could not be found.
22 **Therefore they** enquired of the LORD further,
if the man should yet come thither.
And the LORD answered,
Behold
he hath hid himself among the stuff.
23 **And they** ran and fetched him thence:
and when he stood among the people,
he was higher than any of the people from his shoulders and upward.
24 **And Samuel** said to all the people,

See ye him whom the LORD hath chosen,
that there is none like him among all the people?

And all the people shouted,
and said,
God save the king.

25 **Then Samuel** told the people the manner of the kingdom,
and wrote it in a book,
and laid it up before the LORD.

And Samuel sent all the people away, every man to his house.

26 **And Saul** also went home to Gibeah;
and there went with him a band of men,
whose hearts God had touched.

27 **But the children of Belial** said,
How shall this man save us?

And they despised him,
and brought no presents.

But he held his peace.

11 **Then Nahash the Ammonite** came up,
and encamped against Jabeshgilead:
and all the men of Jabesh said unto Nahash,
Make a covenant with us,
and we will serve thee.

2 **And Nahash the Ammonite** answered them,
On this condition will I make a covenant with you,
that I may thrust out all your right eyes,
and lay it for a reproach upon all Israel.

3 **And the elders of Jabesh** said unto him,
Give us seven days' respite,
that we may send messengers unto all the coasts of Israel:
and then, {if there be no man to save us}, we will come out to thee.

4 **Then** came the messengers to Gibeah of Saul,
and told the tidings in the ears of the people:
and all the people lifted up their voices,
and wept.

5 **And, behold, Saul** came after the herd out of the field;
and Saul said,
What aileth the people
that they weep?

And they told him the tidings of the men of Jabesh.

6 **And the Spirit of God** came upon Saul
when he heard those tidings,
and his anger was kindled greatly.

7 **And he** took a yoke of oxen,
and hewed them in pieces,
and sent them throughout all the coasts of Israel by the hands of messengers,
saying,
Whosoever cometh not forth after Saul and after Samuel
so shall it be done unto his oxen.

And the fear of the LORD fell on the people,
and they came out with one consent.

8 **And when he** numbered them in Bezek,
the children of Israel were three hundred thousand, and the men of Judah thirty thousand.

9 **And they** said unto the messengers that came,
Thus shall ye say unto the men of Jabeshgilead,
To morrow, by that time the sun be hot, ye shall have help.

And the messengers came and shewed it to the men of Jabesh;
and they were glad.

10 **Therefore the men of Jabesh** said,
To morrow we will come out unto you,
and ye shall do with us all that seemeth good unto you.

11 **And it** was so on the morrow,
that Saul put the people in three companies;
and they came into the midst of the host in the morning watch,
and slew the Ammonites until the heat of the day:
and it came to pass,
that they which remained were scattered,
so that two of them were not left together.

12 **And the people** said unto Samuel,
Who is he that said,
Shall Saul reign over us?
bring the men,
that we may put them to death.

13 **And Saul** said,
There shall not a man be put to death this day:
for to day the LORD hath wrought salvation in Israel.

14 **Then said** Samuel to the people,
Come,
and let us go to Gilgal,
and renew the kingdom there.

15 **And all the people** went to Gilgal;
and there they made Saul king before the LORD in Gilgal;
and there they sacrificed sacrifices of peace offerings before the LORD;
and there Saul and all the men of Israel rejoiced greatly.

12 **And Samuel** said unto all Israel,
Behold,
I have hearkened unto your voice in all that ye said unto me,
and have made a king over you.

2 **And now, {behold}, the king** walketh before you:
and I am old and grayheaded;
and, {behold}, my sons are with you:
and I have walked before you from my childhood unto this day.

3 **Behold, here** I am:
witness against me before the LORD, and before his anointed:
whose ox have I taken?
or whose ass have I taken?
or whom have I defrauded?
whom have I oppressed?
or of whose hand have I received any bribe to blind mine eyes therewith?
and I will restore it you.

4 **And they** said,
Thou hast not defrauded us,
nor oppressed us,
neither hast thou taken ought of any man's hand.

5 **And he** said unto them,
The LORD is witness against you,
and his anointed is witness this day,
that ye have not found ought in my hand.

And they answered,
He is witness.

6 **And Samuel** said unto the people,
It is the LORD that advanced Moses and Aaron, and that brought your fathers up out of the land of Egypt.

7 **Now therefore stand still,**

that I may reason with you before the LORD of all the righteous acts of the LORD,
which he did to you and to your fathers.
8 **When Jacob** was come into Egypt,
and your fathers cried unto the LORD,
then the LORD sent Moses and Aaron,
which brought forth your fathers out of Egypt,
and made them dwell in this place.
9 **And when they** forgat the LORD their God,
he sold them into the hand of Sisera, captain of the host of Hazor, and into the hand of the Philistines, and into the hand of the king of Moab,
and they fought against them.
10 **And they** cried unto the LORD,
and said,
We have sinned,
because we have forsaken the LORD,
and have served Baalim and Ashtaroth:
but now deliver us out of the hand of our enemies,
and we will serve thee.
11 **And the LORD** sent Jerubbaal, and Bedan, and Jephthah, and Samuel,
and delivered you out of the hand of your enemies on every side,
and ye dwelled safe.
12 **And when ye** saw that Nahash the king of the children of Ammon came against you,
ye said unto me,
Nay;
but a king shall reign over us:
when the LORD your God was your king.
13 **Now therefore behold** the king whom ye have chosen, and whom ye have desired!
and, {behold}, the LORD hath set a king over you.
14 **If ye** will fear the LORD,
and serve him,
and obey his voice,
and not rebel against the commandment of the LORD,
then shall both ye and also the king that reigneth over you continue following the LORD your God:
15 **But if ye** will not obey the voice of the LORD,
but rebel against the commandment of the LORD,
then shall the hand of the LORD be against you,
as it was against your fathers.
16 **Now therefore stand and see** this great thing,
which the LORD will do before your eyes.
17 **Is it not** wheat harvest to day?
I will call unto the LORD,
and he shall send thunder and rain;
that ye may perceive and see that your wickedness is great,
which ye have done in the sight of the LORD,
in asking you a king.
18 **So Samuel** called unto the LORD;
and the LORD sent thunder and rain that day:
and all the people greatly feared the LORD and Samuel.
19 **And all the people** said unto Samuel,
Pray for thy servants unto the LORD thy God,
that we die not:
for we have added unto all our sins this evil,
to ask us a king.
20 **And Samuel** said unto the people,
Fear not:
ye have done all this wickedness:
yet turn not aside from following the LORD,
but serve the LORD with all your heart;
21 **And turn ye not aside:**
for then should ye go after vain things,
which cannot profit
nor deliver;
for they are vain.
22 **For the LORD** will not forsake his people for his great name's sake:
because it hath pleased the LORD to make you his people.
23 **Moreover as for me,** God forbid
that I should sin against the LORD
in ceasing to pray for you:
but I will teach you the good and the right way:
24 **Only fear** the LORD,
and serve him in truth with all your heart:
for consider
how great things he hath done for you.
25 **But if ye** shall still do wickedly,
ye shall be consumed, both ye and your king.

13 **Saul** reigned one year;
and when he had reigned two years over Israel,
2 **Saul** chose him three thousand men of Israel;
whereof two thousand were with Saul in Michmash and in mount Bethel,
and a thousand were with Jonathan in Gibeah of Benjamin:
and the rest of the people he sent every man to his tent.
3 **And Jonathan** smote the garrison of the Philistines that was in Geba,
and the Philistines heard of it.
And Saul blew the trumpet throughout all the land,
saying,
Let the Hebrews hear.
4 **And all Israel** heard say
that Saul had smitten a garrison of the Philistines,
and that Israel also was had in abomination with the Philistines.
And the people were called together after Saul to Gilgal.
5 **And the Philistines** gathered themselves together to fight with Israel, thirty thousand chariots, and six thousand horsemen, and people as the sand which is on the sea shore in multitude:
and they came up,
and pitched in Michmash, eastward from Bethaven.
6 **When the men of Israel** saw that they were in a strait,
(for the people were distressed,)
then the people did hide themselves in caves, and in thickets, and in rocks, and in high places, and in pits.
7 **And some of the Hebrews** went over Jordan to the land of Gad and Gilead.
As for Saul, he was yet in Gilgal,
and all the people followed him trembling.
8 **And he** tarried seven days, according to the set time that Samuel had appointed:
but Samuel came not to Gilgal;
and the people were scattered from him.
9 **And Saul** said,

Bring hither a burnt offering to me, and peace offerings.

And he offered the burnt offering.

10 **And it** came to pass,
that as soon as he had made an end of offering the burnt offering,
behold,
Samuel came;
and Saul went out to meet him,
that he might salute him.

11 **And Samuel** said,
What hast thou done?

And Saul said,
Because I saw that the people were scattered from me, and that thou camest not within the days appointed, and that the Philistines gathered themselves together at Michmash;
12 **Therefore** said I,
The Philistines will come down now upon me to Gilgal,
and I have not made supplication unto the LORD:
I forced myself therefore,
and offered a burnt offering.

13 **And Samuel** said to Saul,
Thou hast done foolishly:
thou hast not kept the commandment of the LORD thy God,
which he commanded thee:
for now would the LORD have established thy kingdom upon Israel for ever.

14 **But now thy kingdom** shall not continue:
the LORD hath sought him a man after his own heart,
and the LORD hath commanded him to be captain over his people,
because thou hast not kept that which the LORD commanded thee.

15 **And Samuel** arose,
and gat him up from Gilgal unto Gibeah of Benjamin.

And Saul numbered the people that were present with him, about six hundred men.

16 **And Saul, and Jonathan his son, and the people that were present with them,** abode in Gibeah of Benjamin:
but the Philistines encamped in Michmash.

17 **And the spoilers** came out of the camp of the Philistines in three companies:
one company turned unto the way that leadeth to Ophrah, unto the land of Shual:
18 **And another company** turned the way to Bethhoron:
and another company turned to the way of the border that looketh to the valley of Zeboim toward the wilderness.

19 **Now there** was no smith found throughout all the land of Israel:
for the Philistines said,
Lest the Hebrews make them swords or spears:
20 **But all the Israelites** went down to the Philistines,
to sharpen every man his share, and his coulter, and his axe, and his mattock.
21 **Yet they** had a file for the mattocks, and for the coulters, and for the forks, and for the axes,
and to sharpen the goads.

22 **So it** came to pass in the day of battle,
that there was neither sword nor spear found in the hand of any of the people that were with Saul and Jonathan:
but with Saul and with Jonathan his son was there found.

23 **And the garrison of the Philistines** went out to the passage of Michmash.

14

Now it came to pass upon a day,
that Jonathan the son of Saul said unto the young man that bare his armour,
Come,
and let us go over to the Philistines' garrison,
that is on the other side.

But he told not his father.

2 **And Saul** tarried in the uttermost part of Gibeah under a pomegranate tree which is in Migron:
and the people that were with him were about six hundred men;
3 **And Ahiah, the son of Ahitub, Ichabod's brother, the son of Phinehas, the son of Eli, the LORD's priest in Shiloh,** wearing an ephod.

And the people knew not
that Jonathan was gone.

4 **And between the passages,** {by which Jonathan sought to go over unto the Philistines' garrison},
there was a sharp rock on the one side, and a sharp rock on the other side:
and the name of the one was Bozez, and the name of the other Seneh.

5 **The forefront of the one** was situate northward over against Michmash, and the other southward over against Gibeah.

6 **And Jonathan** said to the young man that bare his armour,
Come,
and let us go over unto the garrison of these uncircumcised:
it may be that the LORD will work for us:
for there is no restraint to the LORD to save by many or by few.

7 **And his armourbearer** said unto him,
Do all that is in thine heart:
turn thee;
behold,
I am with thee according to thy heart.

8 **Then** said Jonathan,
Behold,
we will pass over unto these men,
and we will discover ourselves unto them.

9 **If they** say thus unto us,
Tarry until we come to you;
then we will stand still in our place,
and will not go up unto them.
10 **But if they** say thus,
Come up unto us;
then we will go up:
for the LORD hath delivered them into our hand:
and this shall be a sign unto us.

11 **And both of them** discovered themselves unto the garrison of the Philistines:
and the Philistines said,
Behold,
the Hebrews come forth out of the holes where they had hid themselves.

12 **And the men of the garrison** answered Jonathan and his armourbearer,
and said,
Come up to us,
and we will shew you a thing.

And Jonathan said unto his armourbearer,
Come up after me:

for the LORD hath delivered them into the hand of Israel.

13 **And Jonathan** climbed up upon his hands and upon his feet, and his armourbearer after him:
and they fell before Jonathan;
and his armourbearer slew after him.

14 **And that first slaughter**, {which Jonathan and his armourbearer made}, was about twenty men, within as it were an half acre of land,
which a yoke of oxen might plow.

15 **And there** was trembling in the host, in the field, and among all the people:
the garrison, and the spoilers, they also trembled,
and the earth quaked
so it was a very great trembling.

16 **And the watchmen of Saul in Gibeah of Benjamin** looked;
and, {behold}, the multitude melted away,
and they went on beating down one another.

17 **Then** said Saul unto the people that were with him,
Number now,
and see who is gone from us.

And when they had numbered,
behold,
Jonathan and his armourbearer were not there.

18 **And Saul** said unto Ahiah,
Bring hither the ark of God.

For the ark of God was at that time with the children of Israel.

19 **And it** came to pass,
while Saul talked unto the priest,
that the noise that was in the host of the Philistines went on and increased:
and Saul said unto the priest,
Withdraw thine hand.

20 **And Saul and all the people that were with him** assembled themselves,
and they came to the battle:
and, {behold}, every man's sword was against his fellow,
and there was a very great discomfiture.

21 **Moreover the Hebrews that were with the Philistines before that time**, {which went up with them into the camp from the country round about}, even they also turned to be with the Israelites that were with Saul and Jonathan.

22 **Likewise all the men of Israel which had hid themselves in mount Ephraim**, {when they heard that the Philistines fled}, even they also followed hard after them in the battle.

23 **So the LORD** saved Israel that day:
and the battle passed over unto Bethaven.

24 **And the men of Israel** were distressed that day:
for Saul had adjured the people,
saying,
Cursed be the man that eateth any food until evening,
that I may be avenged on mine enemies.

So none of the people tasted any food.

25 **And all they of the land** came to a wood;
and there was honey upon the ground.

26 **And when the people** were come into the wood,
behold,
the honey dropped;
but no man put his hand to his mouth:
for the people feared the oath.

27 **But Jonathan** heard not when his father charged the people with the oath:
wherefore he put forth the end of the rod that was in his hand,
and dipped it in an honeycomb,
and put his hand to his mouth;
and his eyes were enlightened.

28 **Then** answered one of the people,
and said,
Thy father straitly charged the people with an oath,
saying,
Cursed be the man that eateth any food this day.

And the people were faint.

29 **Then** said Jonathan,
My father hath troubled the land:
see, {I pray you}, how mine eyes have been enlightened,
because I tasted a little of this honey.

30 **How much more**, if haply the people had eaten freely to day of the spoil of their enemies which they found?
for had there not been now a much greater slaughter among the Philistines?

31 **And they** smote the Philistines that day from Michmash to Aijalon:
and the people were very faint.

32 **And the people** flew upon the spoil,
and took sheep, and oxen, and calves,
and slew them on the ground:
and the people did eat them with the blood.

33 **Then they** told Saul,
saying,
Behold,
the people sin against the LORD,
in that they eat with the blood.

And he said,
Ye have transgressed:
roll a great stone unto me this day.

34 **And Saul** said,
Disperse yourselves among the people,
and say unto them,
Bring me hither every man his ox, and every man his sheep,
and slay them here,
and eat;
and sin not against the LORD
in eating with the blood.

And all the people brought every man his ox with him that night,
and slew them there.

35 **And Saul** built an altar unto the LORD:
the same was the first altar that he built unto the LORD.

36 **And Saul** said,
Let us go down after the Philistines by night,
and spoil them until the morning light,
and let us not leave a man of them.

And they said,
Do whatsoever seemeth good unto thee.

Then said the priest,
Let us draw near hither unto God.

37 **And Saul** asked counsel of God,
Shall I go down after the Philistines?
wilt thou deliver them into the hand of Israel?

But he answered him not that day.

38 **And Saul** said,

Draw ye near hither, all the chief of the people:
and know and see
wherein this sin hath been this day.

39 **For, {as the LORD liveth}**, {which saveth Israel}, {though it be in Jonathan my son}, he shall surely die.

But there was not a man among all the people that answered him.

40 **Then** said he unto all Israel,
Be ye on one side,
and I and Jonathan my son will be on the other side.

And the people said unto Saul,
Do what seemeth good unto thee.

41 **Therefore Saul** said unto the LORD God of Israel,
Give a perfect lot.

And Saul and Jonathan were taken:
but the people escaped.

42 **And Saul** said,
Cast lots between me and Jonathan my son.

And Jonathan was taken.

43 **Then Saul** said to Jonathan,
Tell me
what thou hast done.

And Jonathan told him,
and said,
I did but taste a little honey with the end of the rod that was in mine hand,
and, {lo}, I must die.

44 **And Saul** answered,
God do so and more also:
for thou shalt surely die, Jonathan.

45 **And the people** said unto Saul,
Shall Jonathan die,
who hath wrought this great salvation in Israel?

God forbid:
as the LORD liveth,
there shall not one hair of his head fall to the ground;
for he hath wrought with God this day.

So the people rescued Jonathan,
that he died not.

46 **Then Saul** went up from following the Philistines:
and the Philistines went to their own place.

47 **So Saul** took the kingdom over Israel,
and fought against all his enemies on every side, against Moab, and against the children of Ammon, and against Edom, and against the kings of Zobah, and against the Philistines:
and whithersoever he turned himself,
he vexed them.

48 **And he** gathered an host,
and smote the Amalekites,
and delivered Israel out of the hands of them that spoiled them.

49 **Now the sons of Saul** were Jonathan, and Ishui, and Melchishua:
and the names of his two daughters were these; the name of the firstborn Merab, and the name of the younger Michal:

50 **And the name of Saul's wife** was Ahinoam, the daughter of Ahimaaz:
and the name of the captain of his host was Abner, the son of Ner, Saul's uncle.

51 **And Kish** was the father of Saul;
and Ner the father of Abner was the son of Abiel.

52 **And there** was sore war against the Philistines all the days of Saul:
and when Saul saw any strong man, or any valiant man,
he took him unto him.

15 **Samuel** also said unto Saul,
The LORD sent me to anoint thee to be king over his people, over Israel:
now therefore hearken thou unto the voice of the words of the LORD.

2 **Thus** saith the LORD of hosts,
I remember that which Amalek did to Israel,
how he laid wait for him in the way,
when he came up from Egypt.

3 **Now go and smite** Amalek,
and utterly destroy all that they have,
and spare them not;
but slay both man and woman, infant and suckling, ox and sheep, camel and ass.

4 **And Saul** gathered the people together,
and numbered them in Telaim, two hundred thousand footmen, and ten thousand men of Judah.

5 **And Saul** came to a city of Amalek,
and laid wait in the valley.

6 **And Saul** said unto the Kenites,
Go,
depart,
get you down from among the Amalekites,
lest I destroy you with them:
for ye shewed kindness to all the children of Israel,
when they came up out of Egypt.

So the Kenites departed from among the Amalekites.

7 **And Saul** smote the Amalekites from Havilah
until thou comest to Shur,
that is over against Egypt.

8 **And he** took Agag the king of the Amalekites alive,
and utterly destroyed all the people with the edge of the sword.

9 **But Saul and the people** spared Agag, and the best of the sheep, and of the oxen, and of the fatlings, and the lambs, and all that was good,
and would not utterly destroy them:
but every thing that was vile and refuse, that they destroyed utterly.

10 **Then** came the word of the LORD unto Samuel,
saying,

11 **It repenteth me** that I have set up Saul to be king:
for he is turned back from following me,
and hath not performed my commandments.

And it grieved Samuel;
and he cried unto the LORD all night.

12 **And when Samuel** rose early to meet Saul in the morning,
it was told Samuel, {saying}, Saul came to Carmel,
and, {behold}, he set him up a place,
and is gone about,
and passed on,
and gone down to Gilgal.

13 **And Samuel** came to Saul:
and Saul said unto him,
Blessed be thou of the LORD:
I have performed the commandment of the LORD.

14 **And Samuel** said,

What meaneth then this bleating of the sheep in mine ears, and the lowing of the oxen which I hear?
15 **And Saul** said,
They have brought them from the Amalekites:
for the people spared the best of the sheep and of the oxen,
to sacrifice unto the LORD thy God;
and the rest we have utterly destroyed.
16 **Then Samuel** said unto Saul,
Stay,
and I will tell thee
what the LORD hath said to me this night.
And he said unto him,
Say on.
17 **And Samuel** said,
When thou wast little in thine own sight,
wast thou not made the head of the tribes of Israel,
and the LORD anointed thee king over Israel?
18 **And the LORD** sent thee on a journey,
and said,
Go and utterly destroy the sinners the Amalekites,
and fight against them
until they be consumed.
19 **Wherefore** then didst thou not obey the voice of the LORD,
but didst fly upon the spoil,
and didst evil in the sight of the LORD?
20 **And Saul** said unto Samuel,
Yea,
I have obeyed the voice of the LORD,
and have gone the way which the LORD sent me,
and have brought Agag the king of Amalek,
and have utterly destroyed the Amalekites.
21 **But the people** took of the spoil, sheep and oxen, the chief of the things which should have been utterly destroyed,
to sacrifice unto the LORD thy God in Gilgal.
22 **And Samuel** said,
Hath the LORD as great delight in burnt offerings and sacrifices,
as in obeying the voice of the LORD?
Behold, to obey is better than sacrifice,
and to hearken than the fat of rams.
23 **For rebellion** is as the sin of witchcraft,
and stubbornness is as iniquity and idolatry.
Because thou hast rejected the word of the LORD,
he hath also rejected thee from being king.
24 **And Saul** said unto Samuel,
I have sinned:
for I have transgressed the commandment of the LORD, and thy words:
because I feared the people,
and obeyed their voice.
25 **Now therefore, {I pray thee}, pardon** my sin,
and turn again with me,
that I may worship the LORD.
26 **And Samuel** said unto Saul,
I will not return with thee:
for thou hast rejected the word of the LORD,
and the LORD hath rejected thee from being king over Israel.
27 **And as Samuel** turned about to go away,
he laid hold upon the skirt of his mantle,
and it rent.
28 **And Samuel** said unto him,
The LORD hath rent the kingdom of Israel from thee this day,
and hath given it to a neighbour of thine,
that is better than thou.
29 **And also the Strength of Israel** will not lie nor repent:
for he is not a man,
that he should repent.
30 **Then he** said,
I have sinned:
yet honour me now, {I pray thee}, before the elders of my people, and before Israel,
and turn again with me,
that I may worship the LORD thy God.
31 **So Samuel** turned again after Saul;
and Saul worshipped the LORD.
32 **Then** said Samuel,
Bring ye hither to me Agag the king of the Amalekites.
And Agag came unto him delicately.
And Agag said,
Surely the bitterness of death is past.
33 **And Samuel** said,
As thy sword hath made women childless,
so shall thy mother be childless among women.
And Samuel hewed Agag in pieces before the LORD in Gilgal.
34 **Then Samuel** went to Ramah;
and Saul went up to his house to Gibeah of Saul.
35 **And Samuel** came no more to see Saul until the day of his death:
nevertheless Samuel mourned for Saul:
and the LORD repented that he had made Saul king over Israel.

16

And the LORD said unto Samuel,
How long wilt thou mourn for Saul,
seeing I have rejected him from reigning over Israel?
fill thine horn with oil,
and go,
I will send thee to Jesse the Bethlehemite:
for I have provided me a king among his sons.
2 **And Samuel** said,
How can I go?
if Saul hear it,
he will kill me.
And the LORD said,
Take an heifer with thee,
and say,
I am come to sacrifice to the LORD.
3 **And call** Jesse to the sacrifice,
and I will shew thee
what thou shalt do:
and thou shalt anoint unto me him whom I name unto thee.
4 **And Samuel** did that which the LORD spake,
and came to Bethlehem.
And the elders of the town trembled at his coming,
and said,
Comest thou peaceably?
5 **And he** said,
Peaceably:
I am come to sacrifice unto the LORD:
sanctify yourselves,
and come with me to the sacrifice.

And he sanctified Jesse and his sons,
and called them to the sacrifice.
6 **And it** came to pass,
when they were come,
that he looked on Eliab,
and said,
Surely the LORD's anointed is before him.
7 **But the LORD** said unto Samuel,
Look not on his countenance, or on the height of his stature;
because I have refused him:
for the LORD seeth not as man seeth;
for man looketh on the outward appearance,
but the LORD looketh on the heart.
8 **Then Jesse** called Abinadab,
and made him pass before Samuel.
And he said,
Neither hath the LORD chosen this.
9 **Then Jesse** made Shammah to pass by.
And he said,
Neither hath the LORD chosen this.
10 **Again, Jesse** made seven of his sons to pass before Samuel.
And Samuel said unto Jesse,
The LORD hath not chosen these.
11 **And Samuel** said unto Jesse,
Are here all thy children?
And he said,
There remaineth yet the youngest,
and, {behold}, he keepeth the sheep.
And Samuel said unto Jesse,
Send and fetch him:
for we will not sit down
till he come hither.
12 **And he** sent,
and brought him in.
Now he was ruddy, and withal of a beautiful countenance, and goodly to look to.
And the LORD said,
Arise,
anoint him:
for this is he.
13 **Then Samuel** took the horn of oil,
and anointed him in the midst of his brethren:
and the Spirit of the LORD came upon David from that day forward.
So Samuel rose up,
and went to Ramah.
14 **But the Spirit of the LORD** departed from Saul,
and an evil spirit from the LORD troubled him.
15 **And Saul's servants** said unto him,
Behold now,
an evil spirit from God troubleth thee.
16 **Let our lord** now command thy servants,
which are before thee,
to seek out a man,
who is a cunning player on an harp:
and it shall come to pass,
when the evil spirit from God is upon thee,
that he shall play with his hand,
and thou shalt be well.
17 **And Saul** said unto his servants,
Provide me now a man that can play well,
and bring him to me.
18 **Then** answered one of the servants,
and said,
Behold,
I have seen a son of Jesse the Bethlehemite,
that is cunning in playing, and a mighty valiant man, and a man of war, and prudent in matters, and a comely person,
and the LORD is with him.
19 **Wherefore Saul** sent messengers unto Jesse,
and said,
Send me David thy son,
which is with the sheep.
20 **And Jesse** took an ass laden with bread, and a bottle of wine, and a kid,
and sent them by David his son unto Saul.
21 **And David** came to Saul,
and stood before him:
and he loved him greatly;
and he became his armourbearer.
22 **And Saul** sent to Jesse,
saying,
Let David, {I pray thee}, stand before me;
for he hath found favour in my sight.
23 **And it** came to pass,
when the evil spirit from God was upon Saul,
that David took an harp,
and played with his hand:
so Saul was refreshed,
and was well,
and the evil spirit departed from him.

17

Now the Philistines gathered together their armies to battle,
and were gathered together at Shochoh,
which belongeth to Judah,
and pitched between Shochoh and Azekah, in Ephesdammim.
2 **And Saul and the men of Israel** were gathered together,
and pitched by the valley of Elah,
and set the battle in array against the Philistines.
3 **And the Philistines** stood on a mountain on the one side,
and Israel stood on a mountain on the other side:
and there was a valley between them.
4 **And there** went out a champion out of the camp of the Philistines, named Goliath, of Gath,
whose height was six cubits and a span.
5 **And he** had an helmet of brass upon his head,
and he was armed with a coat of mail;
and the weight of the coat was five thousand shekels of brass.
6 **And he** had greaves of brass upon his legs, and a target of brass between his shoulders.
7 **And the staff of his spear** was like a weaver's beam;
and his spear's head weighed six hundred shekels of iron:
and one bearing a shield went before him.
8 **And he** stood and cried unto the armies of Israel,
and said unto them,
Why are ye come out to set your battle in array?
am not I a Philistine,
and ye servants to Saul?
choose you a man for you,
and let him come down to me.
9 **If he** be able to fight with me,
and to kill me,
then will we be your servants:
but if I prevail against him,
and kill him,
then shall ye be our servants,
and serve us.
10 **And the Philistine** said,

I defy the armies of Israel this day;
give me a man,
that we may fight together.

11 **When Saul and all Israel** heard those words of the Philistine,
they were dismayed,
and greatly afraid.

12 **Now David** was the son of that Ephrathite of Bethlehemjudah,
whose name was Jesse;
and he had eight sons:
and the man went among men for an old man in the days of Saul.

13 **And the three eldest sons of Jesse** went and followed Saul to the battle:
and the names of his three sons that went to the battle were Eliab the firstborn, and next unto him Abinadab, and the third Shammah.

14 **And David** was the youngest:
and the three eldest followed Saul.

15 **But David** went and returned from Saul
to feed his father's sheep at Bethlehem.

16 **And the Philistine** drew near morning and evening,
and presented himself forty days.

17 **And Jesse** said unto David his son,
Take now for thy brethren an ephah of this parched corn, and these ten loaves,
and run to the camp of thy brethren;

18 **And carry** these ten cheeses unto the captain of their thousand,
and look how thy brethren fare,
and take their pledge.

19 **Now Saul, and they, and all the men of Israel,** were in the valley of Elah,
fighting with the Philistines.

20 **And David** rose up early in the morning,
and left the sheep with a keeper,
and took,
and went,
as Jesse had commanded him;
and he came to the trench,
as the host was going forth to the fight,
and shouted for the battle.

21 **For Israel and the Philistines** had put the battle in array, army against army.

22 **And David** left his carriage in the hand of the keeper of the carriage,
and ran into the army,
and came and saluted his brethren.

23 **And as he** talked with them,
behold,
there came up the champion, the Philistine of Gath, Goliath by name, out of the armies of the Philistines,
and spake according to the same words:
and David heard them.

24 **And all the men of Israel**, {when they saw the man}, fled from him,
and were sore afraid.

25 **And the men of Israel** said,
Have ye seen this man that is come up?
surely to defy Israel is he come up:
and it shall be,
that the man who killeth him, the king will enrich him with great riches,
and will give him his daughter,
and make his father's house free in Israel.

26 **And David** spake to the men that stood by him,
saying,
What shall be done to the man that killeth this Philistine,
and taketh away the reproach from Israel?
for who is this uncircumcised Philistine,
that he should defy the armies of the living God?

27 **And the people** answered him after this manner,
saying,
So shall it be done to the man that killeth him.

28 **And Eliab his eldest brother** heard when he spake unto the men;
and Eliab's anger was kindled against David,
and he said,
Why camest thou down hither?
and with whom hast thou left those few sheep in the wilderness?
I know thy pride, and the naughtiness of thine heart;
for thou art come down
that thou mightest see the battle.

29 **And David** said,
What have I now done?
Is there not a cause?

30 **And he** turned from him toward another,
and spake after the same manner:
and the people answered him again after the former manner.

31 **And when the words** were heard which David spake,
they rehearsed them before Saul:
and he sent for him.

32 **And David** said to Saul,
Let no man's heart fail because of him;
thy servant will go and fight with this Philistine.

33 **And Saul** said to David,
Thou art not able to go against this Philistine to fight with him:
for thou art but a youth,
and he a man of war from his youth.

34 **And David** said unto Saul,
Thy servant kept his father's sheep,
and there came a lion, and a bear,
and took a lamb out of the flock:
35 **And I** went out after him,
and smote him,
and delivered it out of his mouth:
and when he arose against me,
I caught him by his beard,
and smote him,
and slew him.

36 **Thy servant** slew both the lion and the bear:
and this uncircumcised Philistine shall be as one of them,
seeing he hath defied the armies of the living God.

37 **David** said moreover,
The LORD that delivered me out of the paw of the lion, and out of the paw of the bear, he will deliver me out of the hand of this Philistine.
And Saul said unto David,
Go,
and the LORD be with thee.

38 **And Saul** armed David with his armour,
and he put an helmet of brass upon his head;
also he armed him with a coat of mail.

39 **And David** girded his sword upon his armour,
and he assayed to go;
for he had not proved it.
And David said unto Saul,
I cannot go with these;
for I have not proved them.

And David put them off him.

40 **And he** took his staff in his hand,
and chose him five smooth stones out of the brook,
and put them in a shepherd's bag which he had, even in a scrip;
and his sling was in his hand:
and he drew near to the Philistine.

41 **And the Philistine** came on and drew near unto David;
and the man that bare the shield went before him.

42 **And when the Philistine** looked about,
and saw David,
he disdained him:
for he was but a youth, and ruddy, and of a fair countenance.

43 **And the Philistine** said unto David,
Am I a dog,
that thou comest to me with staves?

And the Philistine cursed David by his gods.

44 **And the Philistine** said to David,
Come to me,
and I will give thy flesh unto the fowls of the air, and to the beasts of the field.

45 **Then** said David to the Philistine,
Thou comest to me with a sword, and with a spear, and with a shield:
but I come to thee in the name of the LORD of hosts, the God of the armies of Israel,
whom thou hast defied.

46 **This day** will the LORD deliver thee into mine hand;
and I will smite thee,
and take thine head from thee;
and I will give the carcases of the host of the Philistines this day unto the fowls of the air, and to the wild beasts of the earth;
that all the earth may know
that there is a God in Israel.

47 **And all this assembly** shall know
that the LORD saveth not with sword and spear:
for the battle is the LORD's,
and he will give you into our hands.

48 **And it** came to pass,
when the Philistine arose,
and came,
and drew nigh to meet David,
that David hastened,
and ran toward the army to meet the Philistine.

49 **And David** put his hand in his bag,
and took thence a stone,
and slang it,
and smote the Philistine in his forehead,
that the stone sunk into his forehead;
and he fell upon his face to the earth.

50 **So David** prevailed over the Philistine with a sling and with a stone,
and smote the Philistine,
and slew him;
but there was no sword in the hand of David.

51 **Therefore David** ran,
and stood upon the Philistine,
and took his sword,
and drew it out of the sheath thereof,
and slew him,
and cut off his head therewith.

And when the Philistines saw their champion was dead,
they fled.

52 **And the men of Israel and of Judah** arose,
and shouted,
and pursued the Philistines,
until thou come to the valley, and to the gates of Ekron.

And the wounded of the Philistines fell down by the way to Shaaraim, even unto Gath, and unto Ekron.

53 **And the children of Israel** returned from chasing after the Philistines,
and they spoiled their tents.

54 **And David** took the head of the Philistine,
and brought it to Jerusalem;
but he put his armour in his tent.

55 **And when Saul** saw David go forth against the Philistine,
he said unto Abner, the captain of the host,
Abner, whose son is this youth?

And Abner said,
As thy soul liveth, O king,
I cannot tell.

56 **And the king** said,
Enquire thou
whose son the stripling is.

57 **And as David** returned from the slaughter of the Philistine,
Abner took him,
and brought him before Saul with the head of the Philistine in his hand.

58 **And Saul** said to him,
Whose son art thou, thou young man?

And David answered,
I am the son of thy servant Jesse the Bethlehemite.

18 ✂ **And it** came to pass,
when he had made an end of speaking unto Saul,
that the soul of Jonathan was knit with the soul of David,
and Jonathan loved him as his own soul.

2 **And Saul** took him that day,
and would let him go no more home to his father's house.

3 **Then Jonathan and David** made a covenant,
because he loved him as his own soul.

4 **And Jonathan** stripped himself of the robe that was upon him,
and gave it to David, and his garments, even to his sword, and to his bow, and to his girdle.

5 **And David** went out whithersoever Saul sent him,
and behaved himself wisely:
and Saul set him over the men of war,
and he was accepted in the sight of all the people, and also in the sight of Saul's servants.

6 **And it** came to pass as they came,
when David was returned from the slaughter of the Philistine,
that the women came out of all cities of Israel,
singing and dancing, {to meet king Saul}, with tabrets, with joy, and with instruments of musick.

7 **And the women** answered one another as they played,
and said,
Saul hath slain his thousands,
and David his ten thousands.

8 **And Saul** was very wroth,
and the saying displeased him;
and he said,
They have ascribed unto David ten thousands,
and to me they have ascribed but thousands:

and what can he have more but the kingdom?

9 **And Saul** eyed David from that day and forward.

10 **And it** came to pass on the morrow,
that the evil spirit from God came upon Saul,
and he prophesied in the midst of the house:
and David played with his hand, as at other times:
and there was a javelin in Saul's hand.

11 **And Saul** cast the javelin;
for he said,
I will smite David even to the wall with it.

And David avoided out of his presence twice.

12 **And Saul** was afraid of David,
because the LORD was with him,
and was departed from Saul.

13 **Therefore Saul** removed him from him,
and made him his captain over a thousand;
and he went out and came in before the people.

14 **And David** behaved himself wisely in all his ways;
and the LORD was with him.

15 **Wherefore when Saul** saw that he behaved himself very wisely,
he was afraid of him.

16 **But all Israel and Judah** loved David,
because he went out and came in before them.

17 **And Saul** said to David,
Behold my elder daughter Merab,
her will I give thee to wife:
only be thou valiant for me,
and fight the LORD's battles.

For Saul said,
Let not mine hand be upon him,
but let the hand of the Philistines be upon him.

18 **And David** said unto Saul,
Who am I?
and what is my life, or my father's family in Israel,
that I should be son in law to the king?

19 **But it** came to pass at the time
when Merab Saul's daughter should have been given to David,
that she was given unto Adriel the Meholathite to wife.

20 **And Michal Saul's daughter** loved David:
and they told Saul,
and the thing pleased him.

21 **And Saul** said,
I will give him her,
that she may be a snare to him,
and that the hand of the Philistines may be against him.
Wherefore Saul said to David,
Thou shalt this day be my son in law in the one of the twain.

22 **And Saul** commanded his servants,
saying,
Commune with David secretly,
and say,
Behold,
the king hath delight in thee,
and all his servants love thee:
now therefore be the king's son in law.

23 **And Saul's servants** spake those words in the ears of David.

And David said,
Seemeth it to you a light thing to be a king's son in law,
seeing that I am a poor man, and lightly esteemed?

24 **And the servants of Saul** told him,
saying,
On this manner spake David.

25 **And Saul** said,
Thus shall ye say to David,
The king desireth not any dowry, but an hundred foreskins of the Philistines,
to be avenged of the king's enemies.

But Saul thought to make David fall by the hand of the Philistines.

26 **And when his servants** told David these words,
it pleased David well to be the king's son in law:
and the days were not expired.

27 **Wherefore David** arose and went, he and his men,
and slew of the Philistines two hundred men;
and David brought their foreskins,
and they gave them in full tale to the king,
that he might be the king's son in law.

And Saul gave him Michal his daughter to wife.

28 **And Saul** saw and knew
that the LORD was with David,
and that Michal Saul's daughter loved him.

29 **And Saul** was yet the more afraid of David;
and Saul became David's enemy continually.

30 **Then the princes of the Philistines** went forth:
and it came to pass,
after they went forth,
that David behaved himself more wisely than all the servants of Saul;
so that his name was much set by.

19 **And Saul** spake to Jonathan his son, and to all his servants,
that they should kill David.

2 **But Jonathan Saul's son** delighted much in David:
and Jonathan told David,
saying,
Saul my father seeketh to kill thee:
now therefore, {I pray thee}, take heed to thyself until the morning,
and abide in a secret place,
and hide thyself:
3 **And I** will go out and stand beside my father in the field where thou art,
and I will commune with my father of thee;
and what I see,
that I will tell thee.

4 **And Jonathan** spake good of David unto Saul his father,
and said unto him,
Let not the king sin against his servant, against David;
because he hath not sinned against thee,
and because his works have been to thee-ward very good:
5 **For he** did put his life in his hand,
and slew the Philistine,
and the LORD wrought a great salvation for all Israel:
thou sawest it,
and didst rejoice:
wherefore then wilt thou sin against innocent blood,
to slay David without a cause?

6 **And Saul** hearkened unto the voice of Jonathan:
and Saul sware,
As the LORD liveth,
he shall not be slain.

7 **And Jonathan** called David,
and Jonathan shewed him all those things.

And Jonathan brought David to Saul,
and he was in his presence, as in times past.
8 **And there** was war again:
and David went out,
and fought with the Philistines,
and slew them with a great slaughter;
and they fled from him.
9 **And the evil spirit from the LORD** was upon Saul,
as he sat in his house with his javelin in his hand:
and David played with his hand.
10 **And Saul** sought to smite David even to the wall with the javelin:
but he slipped away out of Saul's presence,
and he smote the javelin into the wall:
and David fled,
and escaped that night.
11 **Saul** also sent messengers unto David's house,
to watch him,
and to slay him in the morning:
and Michal David's wife told him,
saying,
If thou save not thy life to night,
to morrow thou shalt be slain.
12 **So Michal** let David down through a window:
and he went,
and fled,
and escaped.
13 **And Michal** took an image,
and laid it in the bed,
and put a pillow of goats' hair for his bolster,
and covered it with a cloth.
14 **And when Saul** sent messengers to take David,
she said,
He is sick.
15 **And Saul** sent the messengers again to see David,
saying,
Bring him up to me in the bed,
that I may slay him.
16 **And when the messengers** were come in,
behold,
there was an image in the bed, with a pillow of goats' hair for his bolster.
17 **And Saul** said unto Michal,
Why hast thou deceived me so,
and sent away mine enemy,
that he is escaped?
And Michal answered Saul,
He said unto me,
Let me go;
why should I kill thee?
18 **So David** fled,
and escaped,
and came to Samuel to Ramah,
and told him all that Saul had done to him.
And he and Samuel went and dwelt in Naioth.
19 **And it** was told Saul,
saying,
Behold,
David is at Naioth in Ramah.
20 **And Saul** sent messengers to take David:
and when they saw the company of the prophets prophesying,
and Samuel standing as appointed over them,
the Spirit of God was upon the messengers of Saul,
and they also prophesied.
21 **And when it** was told Saul,
he sent other messengers,
and they prophesied likewise.
And Saul sent messengers again the third time,
and they prophesied also.
22 **Then** went he also to Ramah,
and came to a great well that is in Sechu:
and he asked and said,
Where are Samuel and David?
And one said,
Behold,
they be at Naioth in Ramah.
23 **And he** went thither to Naioth in Ramah:
and the Spirit of God was upon him also,
and he went on,
and prophesied,
until he came to Naioth in Ramah.
24 **And he** stripped off his clothes also,
and prophesied before Samuel in like manner,
and lay down naked all that day and all that night.
Wherefore they say,
Is Saul also among the prophets?

20 **And David** fled from Naioth in Ramah,
and came and said before Jonathan,
What have I done?
what is mine iniquity?
and what is my sin before thy father,
that he seeketh my life?
2 **And he** said unto him,
God forbid;
thou shalt not die:
behold,
my father will do nothing either great or small,
but that he will shew it me:
and why should my father hide this thing from me?
it is not so.
3 **And David** sware moreover,
and said,
Thy father certainly knoweth
that I have found grace in thine eyes;
and he saith,
Let not Jonathan know this,
lest he be grieved:
but truly as the LORD liveth,
and as thy soul liveth,
there is but a step between me and death.
4 **Then** said Jonathan unto David,
Whatsoever thy soul desireth,
I will even do it for thee.
5 **And David** said unto Jonathan,
Behold,
to morrow is the new moon,
and I should not fail to sit with the king at meat:
but let me go,
that I may hide myself in the field unto the third day at even.
6 **If thy father at all** miss me,
then say,
David earnestly asked leave of me
that he might run to Bethlehem his city:
for there is a yearly sacrifice there for all the family.
7 **If he** say thus,
It is well;
thy servant shall have peace:
but if he be very wroth,
then be sure that evil is determined by him.
8 **Therefore thou** shalt deal kindly with thy servant;
for thou hast brought thy servant into a covenant of the LORD with thee:
notwithstanding, {if there be in me iniquity}, slay me thyself;
for why shouldest thou bring me to thy father?
9 **And Jonathan** said,

Far be it from thee:
for if I knew certainly
that evil were determined by my father to come upon thee,
then would not I tell it thee?
10 **Then** said David to Jonathan,
Who shall tell me?
or what if thy father answer thee roughly?
11 **And Jonathan** said unto David,
Come,
and let us go out into the field.

And they went out both of them into the field.
12 **And Jonathan** said unto David,
O LORD God of Israel, when I have sounded my father about to morrow any time, or the third day,
and, {behold}, if there be good toward David,
and I then send not unto thee,
and shew it thee;
13 **The LORD** do so and much more to Jonathan:
but if it please my father to do thee evil,
then I will shew it thee,
and send thee away,
that thou mayest go in peace:
and the LORD be with thee,
as he hath been with my father.
14 **And thou** shalt {not only while yet I live} shew me the kindness of the LORD,
that I die not:
15 **But also thou** shalt not cut off thy kindness from my house for ever:
no, not when the LORD hath cut off the enemies of David every one from the face of the earth.
16 **So Jonathan** made a covenant with the house of David,
saying,
Let the LORD even require it at the hand of David's enemies.
17 **And Jonathan** caused David to swear again,
because he loved him:
for he loved him as he loved his own soul.
18 **Then Jonathan** said to David,
To morrow is the new moon:
and thou shalt be missed,
because thy seat will be empty.
19 **And when thou** hast stayed three days,
then thou shalt go down quickly,
and come to the place where thou didst hide thyself when the business was in hand,
and shalt remain by the stone Ezel.
20 **And I** will shoot three arrows on the side thereof,
as though I shot at a mark.
21 **And, {behold}, I** will send a lad,
saying,
Go,
find out the arrows.
If I expressly say unto the lad,
Behold,
the arrows are on this side of thee,
take them;
then come thou:
for there is peace to thee, and no hurt;
as the LORD liveth.
22 **But if I** say thus unto the young man,
Behold,
the arrows are beyond thee;
go thy way:
for the LORD hath sent thee away.
23 **And as touching the matter which thou and I have spoken of**, {behold}, the LORD be between thee and me for ever.
24 **So David** hid himself in the field:
and when the new moon was come,
the king sat him down to eat meat.
25 **And the king** sat upon his seat, as at other times, even upon a seat by the wall:
and Jonathan arose,
and Abner sat by Saul's side,
and David's place was empty.
26 **Nevertheless Saul** spake not any thing that day:
for he thought,
Something hath befallen him,
he is not clean;
surely he is not clean.
27 **And it** came to pass on the morrow,
which was the second day of the month,
that David's place was empty:
and Saul said unto Jonathan his son,
Wherefore cometh not the son of Jesse to meat, neither yesterday, nor to day?
28 **And Jonathan** answered Saul,
David earnestly asked leave of me to go to Bethlehem:
29 **And he** said,
Let me go,
I pray thee;
for our family hath a sacrifice in the city;
and my brother, he hath commanded me to be there:
and now, {if I have found favour in thine eyes}, let me get away,
I pray thee,
and see my brethren.
Therefore he cometh not unto the king's table.
30 **Then Saul's anger** was kindled against Jonathan,
and he said unto him,
Thou son of the perverse rebellious woman, do not I know
that thou hast chosen the son of Jesse to thine own confusion, and unto the confusion of thy mother's nakedness?
31 **For as long as the son of Jesse** liveth upon the ground,
thou shalt not be established, nor thy kingdom.
Wherefore now send and fetch him unto me,
for he shall surely die.
32 **And Jonathan** answered Saul his father,
and said unto him,
Wherefore shall he be slain?
what hath he done?
33 **And Saul** cast a javelin at him to smite him:
whereby Jonathan knew
that it was determined of his father to slay David.
34 **So Jonathan** arose from the table in fierce anger,
and did eat no meat the second day of the month:
for he was grieved for David,
because his father had done him shame.
35 **And it** came to pass in the morning,
that Jonathan went out into the field at the time appointed with David, and a little lad with him.
36 **And he** said unto his lad,
Run,
find out now the arrows which I shoot.
And as the lad ran,
he shot an arrow beyond him.

37 **And when the lad** was come to the place of the arrow which Jonathan had shot,
Jonathan cried after the lad,
and said,
Is not the arrow beyond thee?

38 **And Jonathan** cried after the lad,
Make speed,
haste,
stay not.

And Jonathan's lad gathered up the arrows,
and came to his master.

39 **But the lad** knew not any thing:
only Jonathan and David knew the matter.

40 **And Jonathan** gave his artillery unto his lad,
and said unto him,
Go,
carry them to the city.

41 **And as soon as the lad** was gone,
David arose out of a place toward the south,
and fell on his face to the ground,
and bowed himself three times:
and they kissed one another,
and wept one with another,
until David exceeded.

42 **And Jonathan** said to David,
Go in peace,
forasmuch as we have sworn both of us in the name of the LORD,
saying,
The LORD be between me and thee, and between my seed and thy seed for ever.

And he arose and departed:
and Jonathan went into the city.

21

Then came David to Nob to Ahimelech the priest:
and Ahimelech was afraid at the meeting of David,
and said unto him,
Why art thou alone, and no man with thee?

2 **And David** said unto Ahimelech the priest,
The king hath commanded me a business,
and hath said unto me,
Let no man know any thing of the business whereabout I send thee, and what I have commanded thee:
and I have appointed my servants to such and such a place.

3 **Now therefore what** is under thine hand?
give me five loaves of bread in mine hand,
or what there is present.

4 **And the priest** answered David,
and said,
There is no common bread under mine hand,
but there is hallowed bread;
if the young men have kept themselves at least from women.

5 **And David** answered the priest,
and said unto him,
Of a truth women have been kept from us about these three days,
since I came out,
and the vessels of the young men are holy,
and the bread is in a manner common,
yea, though it were sanctified this day in the vessel.

6 **So the priest** gave him hallowed bread:
for there was no bread there but the shewbread,
that was taken from before the LORD,
to put hot bread in the day when it was taken away.

7 **Now a certain man of the servants of Saul** was there that day,
detained before the LORD;
and his name was Doeg, an Edomite, the chiefest of the herdmen that belonged to Saul.

8 **And David** said unto Ahimelech,
And is there not here under thine hand spear or sword?
for I have neither brought my sword nor my weapons with me,
because the king's business required haste.

9 **And the priest** said,
The sword of Goliath the Philistine, {whom thou slewest in the valley of Elah},
behold,
it is here wrapped in a cloth behind the ephod:
if thou wilt take that,
take it:
for there is no other save that here.

And David said,
There is none like that;
give it me.

10 **And David** arose and fled that day for fear of Saul,
and went to Achish the king of Gath.

11 **And the servants of Achish** said unto him,
Is not this David the king of the land?
did they not sing one to another of him in dances,
saying,
Saul hath slain his thousands, and David his ten thousands?

12 **And David** laid up these words in his heart,
and was sore afraid of Achish the king of Gath.

13 **And he** changed his behaviour before them,
and feigned himself mad in their hands,
and scrabbled on the doors of the gate,
and let his spittle fall down upon his beard.

14 **Then** said Achish unto his servants,
Lo,
ye see the man is mad:
wherefore then have ye brought him to me?

15 **Have I** need of mad men,
that ye have brought this fellow to play the mad man in my presence?
shall this fellow come into my house?

22

David therefore departed thence,
and escaped to the cave Adullam:
and when his brethren and all his father's house heard it,
they went down thither to him.

2 **And every one that was in distress, and every one that was in debt, and every one that was discontented,** gathered themselves unto him;
and he became a captain over them:
and there were with him about four hundred men.

3 **And David** went thence to Mizpeh of Moab:
and he said unto the king of Moab,
Let my father and my mother, {I pray thee}, come forth,
and be with you,
till I know
what God will do for me.

4 **And he** brought them before the king of Moab:

and they dwelt with him all the while that David was in the hold.

5 **And the prophet Gad** said unto David,
Abide not in the hold;
depart,
and get thee into the land of Judah.

Then David departed,
and came into the forest of Hareth.

6 **When Saul** heard that David was discovered, and the men that were with him,
(now Saul abode in Gibeah under a tree in Ramah,
having his spear in his hand,
and all his servants were standing about him;)
7 **Then Saul** said unto his servants that stood about him,
Hear now, ye Benjamites;
will the son of Jesse give every one of you fields and vineyards,
and make you all captains of thousands, and captains of hundreds;
8 **That all of you** have conspired against me,
and there is none that sheweth me that my son hath made a league with the son of Jesse,
and there is none of you that is sorry for me,
or sheweth unto me that my son hath stirred up my servant against me, {to lie in wait}, as at this day?

9 **Then** answered Doeg the Edomite,
which was set over the servants of Saul,
and said,
I saw the son of Jesse coming to Nob, to Ahimelech the son of Ahitub.

10 **And he** enquired of the LORD for him,
and gave him victuals,
and gave him the sword of Goliath the Philistine.

11 **Then the king** sent to call Ahimelech the priest, the son of Ahitub, and all his father's house, the priests that were in Nob:
and they came all of them to the king.

12 **And Saul** said,
Hear now, thou son of Ahitub.

And he answered,
Here I am, my lord.

13 **And Saul** said unto him,
Why have ye conspired against me, thou and the son of Jesse,
in that thou hast given him bread, and a sword,
and hast enquired of God for him,
that he should rise against me, {to lie in wait}, as at this day?

14 **Then Ahimelech** answered the king,
and said,
And who is so faithful among all thy servants as David,
which is the king's son in law,
and goeth at thy bidding,
and is honourable in thine house?

15 **Did I** then begin to enquire of God for him?
be it far from me:
let not the king impute any thing unto his servant, nor to all the house of my father:
for thy servant knew nothing of all this, less or more.

16 **And the king** said,
Thou shalt surely die, Ahimelech, thou, and all thy father's house.

17 **And the king** said unto the footmen that stood about him,
Turn,
and slay the priests of the LORD:
because their hand also is with David,
and because they knew
when he fled,
and did not shew it to me.

But the servants of the king would not put forth their hand to fall upon the priests of the LORD.

18 **And the king** said to Doeg,
Turn thou,
and fall upon the priests.

And Doeg the Edomite turned,
and he fell upon the priests,
and slew on that day fourscore and five persons that did wear a linen ephod.

19 **And Nob, the city of the priests,** smote he with the edge of the sword, both men and women, children and sucklings, and oxen, and asses, and sheep, with the edge of the sword.

20 **And one of the sons of Ahimelech the son of Ahitub, named Abiathar,** escaped,
and fled after David.

21 **And Abiathar** shewed David
that Saul had slain the LORD's priests.

22 **And David** said unto Abiathar,
I knew it that day,
when Doeg the Edomite was there,
that he would surely tell Saul:
I have occasioned the death of all the persons of thy father's house.

23 **Abide thou** with me,
fear not:
for he that seeketh my life seeketh thy life:
but with me thou shalt be in safeguard.

23

Then they told David, saying,
Behold,
the Philistines fight against Keilah,
and they rob the threshingfloors.

2 **Therefore David** enquired of the LORD,
saying,
Shall I go and smite these Philistines?

And the LORD said unto David,
Go,
and smite the Philistines,
and save Keilah.

3 **And David's men** said unto him,
Behold,
we be afraid here in Judah:
how much more then if we come to Keilah against the armies of the Philistines?

4 **Then David** enquired of the LORD yet again.

And the LORD answered him and said,
Arise,
go down to Keilah;
for I will deliver the Philistines into thine hand.

5 **So David and his men** went to Keilah,
and fought with the Philistines,
and brought away their cattle,
and smote them with a great slaughter.

So David saved the inhabitants of Keilah.

6 **And it** came to pass,
when Abiathar the son of Ahimelech fled to David to Keilah,
that he came down with an ephod in his hand.

7 **And it was told Saul** that David was come to Keilah.

And Saul said,

God hath delivered him into mine hand;
for he is shut in,
by entering into a town that hath gates and bars.

8 **And Saul** called all the people together to war,
to go down to Keilah,
to besiege David and his men.

9 **And David** knew
that Saul secretly practised mischief against him;
and he said to Abiathar the priest,
Bring hither the ephod.

10 **Then** said David,
O LORD God of Israel, thy servant hath certainly heard that Saul seeketh to come to Keilah,
to destroy the city for my sake.

11 **Will the men of Keilah** deliver me up into his hand?
will Saul come down,
as thy servant hath heard?

O LORD God of Israel, {I beseech thee}, tell thy servant.

And the LORD said,
He will come down.

12 **Then** said David,
Will the men of Keilah deliver me and my men into the hand of Saul?

And the LORD said,
They will deliver thee up.

13 **Then David and his men**, {which were about six hundred}, arose and departed out of Keilah,
and went whithersoever they could go.

And it was told Saul that David was escaped from Keilah;
and he forbare to go forth.

14 **And David** abode in the wilderness in strong holds,
and remained in a mountain in the wilderness of Ziph.

And Saul sought him every day,
but God delivered him not into his hand.

15 **And David** saw that Saul was come out to seek his life:
and David was in the wilderness of Ziph in a wood.

16 **And Jonathan Saul's son** arose,
and went to David into the wood,
and strengthened his hand in God.

17 **And he** said unto him,
Fear not:
for the hand of Saul my father shall not find thee;
and thou shalt be king over Israel,
and I shall be next unto thee;
and that also Saul my father knoweth.

18 **And they two** made a covenant before the LORD:
and David abode in the wood,
and Jonathan went to his house.

19 **Then** came up the Ziphites to Saul to Gibeah,
saying,
Doth not David hide himself with us in strong holds in the wood, in the hill of Hachilah,
which is on the south of Jeshimon?

20 **Now therefore, O king, come down** according to all the desire of thy soul to come down;
and our part shall be to deliver him into the king's hand.

21 **And Saul** said,
Blessed be ye of the LORD;
for ye have compassion on me.

22 **Go,**
I pray you,
prepare yet,
and know and see his place where his haunt is,
and who hath seen him there:
for it is told me that he dealeth very subtilly.

23 **See** therefore,
and take knowledge of all the lurking places where he hideth himself,
and come ye again to me with the certainty,
and I will go with you:
and it shall come to pass,
if he be in the land,
that I will search him out throughout all the thousands of Judah.

24 **And they** arose,
and went to Ziph before Saul:
but David and his men were in the wilderness of Maon, in the plain on the south of Jeshimon.

25 **Saul also and his men** went to seek him.

And they told David;
wherefore he came down into a rock,
and abode in the wilderness of Maon.

And when Saul heard that,
he pursued after David in the wilderness of Maon.

26 **And Saul** went on this side of the mountain, and David and his men on that side of the mountain:
and David made haste to get away for fear of Saul;
for Saul and his men compassed David and his men round about
to take them.

27 **But there** came a messenger unto Saul,
saying,
Haste thee,
and come;
for the Philistines have invaded the land.

28 **Wherefore Saul** returned from pursuing after David,
and went against the Philistines:
therefore they called that place Selahammahlekoth.

29 **And David** went up from thence,
and dwelt in strong holds at Engedi.

24 **And it** came to pass,
when Saul was returned from following the Philistines,
that it was told him,
saying,
Behold,
David is in the wilderness of Engedi.

2 **Then Saul** took three thousand chosen men out of all Israel,
and went to seek David and his men upon the rocks of the wild goats.

3 **And he** came to the sheepcotes by the way,
where was a cave;
and Saul went in to cover his feet:
and David and his men remained in the sides of the cave.

4 **And the men of David** said unto him,
Behold the day of which the LORD said unto thee,
Behold,
I will deliver thine enemy into thine hand,
that thou mayest do to him as it shall seem good unto thee.

Then David arose,
and cut off the skirt of Saul's robe privily.

5 **And it** came to pass afterward,
that David's heart smote him,
because he had cut off Saul's skirt.

6 **And he** said unto his men,

The LORD forbid
that I should do this thing unto my master, the LORD's anointed,
to stretch forth mine hand against him,
seeing he is the anointed of the LORD.
7 **So David** stayed his servants with these words,
and suffered them not to rise against Saul.
But Saul rose up out of the cave,
and went on his way.
8 **David** also arose afterward,
and went out of the cave,
and cried after Saul,
saying,
My lord the king.
And when Saul looked behind him,
David stooped with his face to the earth,
and bowed himself.
9 **And David** said to Saul,
Wherefore hearest thou men's words,
saying,
Behold,
David seeketh thy hurt?
10 **Behold,**
this day thine eyes have seen how that the LORD had delivered thee to day into mine hand in the cave:
and some bade me kill thee:
but mine eye spared thee;
and I said,
I will not put forth mine hand against my lord;
for he is the LORD's anointed.
11 **Moreover, my father, see, yea, see** the skirt of thy robe in my hand:
for in that I cut off the skirt of thy robe,
and killed thee not,
know thou and see
that there is neither evil nor transgression in mine hand,
and I have not sinned against thee;
yet thou huntest my soul to take it.
12 **The LORD** judge between me and thee,
and the LORD avenge me of thee:
but mine hand shall not be upon thee.
13 **As** saith the proverb of the ancients,
Wickedness proceedeth from the wicked:
but mine hand shall not be upon thee.
14 **After whom** is the king of Israel come out?
after whom dost thou pursue?
after a dead dog, after a flea.
15 **The LORD** therefore be judge,
and judge between me and thee,
and see,
and plead my cause,
and deliver me out of thine hand.
16 **And it** came to pass,
when David had made an end of speaking these words unto Saul,
that Saul said,
Is this thy voice, my son David?
And Saul lifted up his voice,
and wept.
17 **And he** said to David,
Thou art more righteous than I:
for thou hast rewarded me good,
whereas I have rewarded thee evil.
18 **And thou** hast shewed this day
how that thou hast dealt well with me:
forasmuch as when the LORD had delivered me into thine hand,
thou killedst me not.
19 **For if a man** find his enemy,
will he let him go well away?
wherefore the LORD reward thee good for that thou hast done unto me this day.
20 **And now, {behold}, I** know well
that thou shalt surely be king,
and that the kingdom of Israel shall be established in thine hand.
21 **Swear** now therefore unto me by the LORD,
that thou wilt not cut off my seed after me,
and that thou wilt not destroy my name out of my father's house.
22 **And David** sware unto Saul.
And Saul went home;
but David and his men gat them up unto the hold.

25 **And Samuel** died;
and all the Israelites were gathered together,
and lamented him,
and buried him in his house at Ramah.
And David arose,
and went down to the wilderness of Paran.
2 **And there** was a man in Maon,
whose possessions were in Carmel;
and the man was very great,
and he had three thousand sheep, and a thousand goats:
and he was shearing his sheep in Carmel.
3 **Now the name of the man** was Nabal; and the name of his wife Abigail:
and she was a woman of good understanding, and of a beautiful countenance:
but the man was churlish and evil in his doings;
and he was of the house of Caleb.
4 **And David** heard in the wilderness that Nabal did shear his sheep.
5 **And David** sent out ten young men,
and David said unto the young men,
Get you up to Carmel,
and go to Nabal,
and greet him in my name:
6 **And thus** shall ye say to him that liveth in prosperity,
Peace be both to thee,
and peace be to thine house,
and peace be unto all that thou hast.
7 **And now I** have heard that thou hast shearers:
now thy shepherds which were with us, we hurt them not,
neither was there ought missing unto them,
all the while they were in Carmel.
8 **Ask** thy young men,
and they will shew thee.
Wherefore let the young men find favour in thine eyes:
for we come in a good day:
give, {I pray thee}, whatsoever cometh to thine hand unto thy servants, and to thy son David.
9 **And when David's young men** came,
they spake to Nabal according to all those words in the name of David,
and ceased.
10 **And Nabal** answered David's servants,
and said,
Who is David?
and who is the son of Jesse?
there be many servants now a days that break away every man from his master.
11 **Shall I** then take my bread, and my water, and my flesh that I have killed for my shearers,
and give it unto men,

whom I know not
whence they be?
12 **So David's young men** turned their way,
and went again,
and came and told him all those sayings.
13 **And David** said unto his men,
Gird ye on every man his sword.
And they girded on every man his sword;
and David also girded on his sword:
and there went up after David about four hundred men;
and two hundred abode by the stuff.
14 **But one of the young men** told Abigail, Nabal's wife,
saying,
Behold,
David sent messengers out of the wilderness to salute our master;
and he railed on them.
15 **But the men** were very good unto us,
and we were not hurt,
neither missed we any thing,
as long as we were conversant with them,
when we were in the fields:
16 **They** were a wall unto us both by night and day, all the while we were with them
keeping the sheep.
17 **Now therefore know and consider**
what thou wilt do;
for evil is determined against our master, and against all his household:
for he is such a son of Belial,
that a man cannot speak to him.
18 **Then Abigail** made haste,
and took two hundred loaves, and two bottles of wine, and five sheep ready dressed, and five measures of parched corn, and an hundred clusters of raisins, and two hundred cakes of figs,
and laid them on asses.
19 **And she** said unto her servants,
Go on before me;
behold,
I come after you.
But she told not her husband Nabal.
20 **And it** was so,
as she rode on the ass,
that she came down by the covert on the hill,
and, {behold}, David and his men came down against her;
and she met them.
21 **Now David** had said,
Surely in vain have I kept all that this fellow hath in the wilderness,
so that nothing was missed of all that pertained unto him:
and he hath requited me evil for good.
22 **So and more also** do God unto the enemies of David,
if I leave of all that pertain to him by the morning light any that pisseth against the wall.
23 **And when Abigail** saw David,
she hasted,
and lighted off the ass,
and fell before David on her face,
and bowed herself to the ground,
24 **And** fell at his feet,
and said,
Upon me, my lord, upon me let this iniquity be:
and let thine handmaid, {I pray thee}, speak in thine audience,
and hear the words of thine handmaid.
25 **Let not my lord**, {I pray thee}, regard this man of Belial, even Nabal:
for as his name is,
so is he;
Nabal is his name,
and folly is with him:
but I thine handmaid saw not the young men of my lord,
whom thou didst send.
26 **Now therefore, my lord, as the LORD** liveth,
and as thy soul liveth,
seeing the LORD hath withholden thee from coming to shed blood,
and from avenging thyself with thine own hand,
now let thine enemies, and they that seek evil to my lord, be as Nabal.
27 **And now this blessing which thine handmaid hath brought unto my lord,** let it even be given unto the young men that follow my lord.
28 **I** pray thee,
forgive the trespass of thine handmaid:
for the LORD will certainly make my lord a sure house;
because my lord fighteth the battles of the LORD,
and evil hath not been found in thee all thy days.
29 **Yet a man** is risen to pursue thee,
and to seek thy soul:
but the soul of my lord shall be bound in the bundle of life with the LORD thy God;
and the souls of thine enemies, them shall he sling out, as out of the middle of a sling.
30 **And it** shall come to pass,
when the LORD shall have done to my lord according to all the good that he hath spoken concerning thee,
and shall have appointed thee ruler over Israel;
31 **That this** shall be no grief unto thee, nor offence of heart unto my lord,
either that thou hast shed blood causeless,
or that my lord hath avenged himself:
but when the LORD shall have dealt well with my lord,
then remember thine handmaid.
32 **And David** said to Abigail,
Blessed be the LORD God of Israel,
which sent thee this day to meet me:
33 **And blessed** be thy advice,
and blessed be thou,
which hast kept me this day from coming to shed blood,
and from avenging myself with mine own hand.
34 **For in very deed,** {as the LORD God of Israel liveth}, {which hath kept me back from hurting thee}, {except thou hadst hasted and come to meet me}, surely there had not been left unto Nabal by the morning light any that pisseth against the wall.
35 **So David** received of her hand that which she had brought him,
and said unto her,
Go up in peace to thine house;
see,
I have hearkened to thy voice,
and have accepted thy person.
36 **And Abigail** came to Nabal;
and, {behold}, he held a feast in his house, like the feast of a king;
and Nabal's heart was merry within him,
for he was very drunken:

wherefore she told him nothing, less or more, until the morning light.

37 **But it** came to pass in the morning,
when the wine was gone out of Nabal,
and his wife had told him these things,
that his heart died within him,
and he became as a stone.

38 **And it** came to pass about ten days after,
that the LORD smote Nabal,
that he died.

39 **And when David** heard that Nabal was dead,
he said,
Blessed be the LORD,
that hath pleaded the cause of my reproach from the hand of Nabal,
and hath kept his servant from evil:
for the LORD hath returned the wickedness of Nabal upon his own head.

And David sent and communed with Abigail,
to take her to him to wife.

40 **And when the servants of David** were come to Abigail to Carmel,
they spake unto her,
saying,
David sent us unto thee,
to take thee to him to wife.

41 **And she** arose,
and bowed herself on her face to the earth,
and said,
Behold,
let thine handmaid be a servant to wash the feet of the servants of my lord.

42 **And Abigail** hasted,
and arose and rode upon an ass, with five damsels of hers that went after her;
and she went after the messengers of David,
and became his wife.

43 **David** also took Ahinoam of Jezreel;
and they were also both of them his wives.

44 **But Saul** had given Michal his daughter, David's wife, to Phalti the son of Laish,
which was of Gallim.

26

And the Ziphites came unto Saul to Gibeah,
saying,
Doth not David hide himself in the hill of Hachilah,
which is before Jeshimon?

2 **Then Saul** arose,
and went down to the wilderness of Ziph,
having three thousand chosen men of Israel with him,
to seek David in the wilderness of Ziph.

3 **And Saul** pitched in the hill of Hachilah, {which is before Jeshimon}, by the way.
But David abode in the wilderness,
and he saw that Saul came after him into the wilderness.

4 **David** therefore sent out spies,
and understood
that Saul was come in very deed.

5 **And David** arose,
and came to the place where Saul had pitched:
and David beheld the place where Saul lay, and Abner the son of Ner, the captain of his host:
and Saul lay in the trench,
and the people pitched round about him.

6 **Then** answered David and said to Ahimelech the Hittite, and to Abishai the son of Zeruiah, brother to Joab,
saying,
Who will go down with me to Saul to the camp?
And Abishai said,
I will go down with thee.

7 **So David and Abishai** came to the people by night:
and, {behold}, Saul lay sleeping within the trench,
and his spear stuck in the ground at his bolster:
but Abner and the people lay round about him.

8 **Then** said Abishai to David,
God hath delivered thine enemy into thine hand this day:
now therefore let me smite him, {I pray thee}, with the spear even to the earth at once,
and I will not smite him the second time.

9 **And David** said to Abishai,
Destroy him not:
for who can stretch forth his hand against the LORD's anointed,
and be guiltless?

10 **David** said furthermore,
As the LORD liveth,
the LORD shall smite him;
or his day shall come to die;
or he shall descend into battle,
and perish.

11 **The LORD** forbid
that I should stretch forth mine hand against the LORD's anointed:
but, {I pray thee}, take thou now the spear that is at his bolster, and the cruse of water,
and let us go.

12 **So David** took the spear and the cruse of water from Saul's bolster;
and they gat them away,
and no man saw it,
nor knew it,
neither awaked:
for they were all asleep;
because a deep sleep from the LORD was fallen upon them.

13 **Then David** went over to the other side,
and stood on the top of an hill afar off;
a great space being between them:

14 **And David** cried to the people, and to Abner the son of Ner,
saying,
Answerest thou not, Abner?
Then Abner answered and said,
Who art thou that criest to the king?

15 **And David** said to Abner,
Art not thou a valiant man?
and who is like to thee in Israel?
wherefore then hast thou not kept thy lord the king?
for there came one of the people in to destroy the king thy lord.

16 **This thing** is not good that thou hast done.
As the LORD liveth,
ye are worthy to die,
because ye have not kept your master, the LORD's anointed.
And now see where the king's spear is, and the cruse of water that was at his bolster.

17 **And Saul** knew David's voice,
and said,
Is this thy voice, my son David?
And David said,
It is my voice, my lord, O king.

[18] **And he** said,
Wherefore doth my lord thus pursue after his servant?
for what have I done?
or what evil is in mine hand?

[19] **Now therefore, {I pray thee}, let my lord the king** hear the words of his servant.
If the LORD have stirred thee up against me,
let him accept an offering:
but if they be the children of men,
cursed be they before the LORD;
or they have driven me out this day from abiding in the inheritance of the LORD,
saying,
Go,
serve other gods.

[20] **Now therefore, let not my blood** fall to the earth before the face of the LORD:
for the king of Israel is come out to seek a flea,
as when one doth hunt a partridge in the mountains.

[21] **Then said** Saul,
I have sinned:
return, my son David:
for I will no more do thee harm,
because my soul was precious in thine eyes this day:
behold,
I have played the fool,
and have erred exceedingly.

[22] **And David** answered and said,
Behold the king's spear!
and let one of the young men come over and fetch it.

[23] **The LORD** render to every man his righteousness and his faithfulness;
for the LORD delivered thee into my hand to day,
but I would not stretch forth mine hand against the LORD's anointed.

[24] **And, {behold}, as thy life** was much set by this day in mine eyes,
so let my life be much set by in the eyes of the LORD,
and let him deliver me out of all tribulation.

[25] **Then Saul** said to David,
Blessed be thou, my son David:
thou shalt both do great things,
and also shalt still prevail.
So David went on his way,
and Saul returned to his place.

27

And David said in his heart,
I shall now perish one day by the hand of Saul:
there is nothing better for me than that I should speedily escape into the land of the Philistines;
and Saul shall despair of me,
to seek me any more in any coast of Israel:
so shall I escape out of his hand.

[2] **And David** arose,
and he passed over with the six hundred men that were with him unto Achish, the son of Maoch, king of Gath.

[3] **And David** dwelt with Achish at Gath, he and his men, every man with his household, even David with his two wives, Ahinoam the Jezreelitess, and Abigail the Carmelitess, Nabal's wife.

[4] **And it was told Saul** that David was fled to Gath:
and he sought no more again for him.

[5] **And David** said unto Achish,
If I have now found grace in thine eyes,
let them give me a place in some town in the country,
that I may dwell there:
for why should thy servant dwell in the royal city with thee?

[6] **Then Achish** gave him Ziklag that day:
wherefore Ziklag pertaineth unto the kings of Judah unto this day.

[7] **And the time that David dwelt in the country of the Philistines** was a full year and four months.

[8] **And David and his men** went up,
and invaded the Geshurites, and the Gezrites, and the Amalekites:
for those nations were of old the inhabitants of the land, {as thou goest to Shur}, even unto the land of Egypt.

[9] **And David** smote the land,
and left neither man nor woman alive,
and took away the sheep, and the oxen, and the asses, and the camels, and the apparel,
and returned,
and came to Achish.

[10] **And Achish** said,
Whither have ye made a road to day?
And David said, Against the south of Judah, and against the south of the Jerahmeelites, and against the south of the Kenites.

[11] **And David** saved neither man nor woman alive,
to bring tidings to Gath,
saying,
Lest they should tell on us,
saying,
So did David,
and so will be his manner all the while he dwelleth in the country of the Philistines.

[12] **And Achish** believed David,
saying,
He hath made his people Israel utterly to abhor him;
therefore he shall be my servant for ever.

28

And it came to pass in those days,
that the Philistines gathered their armies together for warfare,
to fight with Israel.
And Achish said unto David,
Know thou assuredly,
that thou shalt go out with me to battle, thou and thy men.

[2] **And David** said to Achish,
Surely thou shalt know
what thy servant can do.
And Achish said to David,
Therefore will I make thee keeper of mine head for ever.

[3] **Now Samuel** was dead,
and all Israel had lamented him,
and buried him in Ramah, even in his own city.
And Saul had put away those that had familiar spirits, and the wizards, out of the land.

[4] **And the Philistines** gathered themselves together,
and came and pitched in Shunem:
and Saul gathered all Israel together,
and they pitched in Gilboa.

[5] **And when Saul** saw the host of the Philistines,
he was afraid,
and his heart greatly trembled.

[6] **And when Saul** enquired of the LORD,
the LORD answered him not, neither by dreams, nor by Urim, nor by prophets.

[7] **Then** said Saul unto his servants,

Seek me a woman that hath a familiar spirit,
that I may go to her,
and enquire of her.
And his servants said to him,
Behold,
there is a woman that hath a familiar spirit at Endor.
8 **And Saul** disguised himself,
and put on other raiment,
and he went, and two men with him,
and they came to the woman by night:
and he said,
I pray thee,
divine unto me by the familiar spirit,
and bring me him up,
whom I shall name unto thee.
9 **And the woman** said unto him,
Behold,
thou knowest
what Saul hath done,
how he hath cut off those that have familiar spirits, and the wizards, out of the land:
wherefore then layest thou a snare for my life,
to cause me to die?
10 **And Saul** sware to her by the LORD,
saying,
As the LORD liveth,
there shall no punishment happen to thee for this thing.
11 **Then** said the woman,
Whom shall I bring up unto thee?
And he said,
Bring me up Samuel.
12 **And when the woman** saw Samuel,
she cried with a loud voice:
and the woman spake to Saul,
saying,
Why hast thou deceived me?
for thou art Saul.
13 **And the king** said unto her,
Be not afraid:
for what sawest thou?
And the woman said unto Saul,
I saw gods ascending out of the earth.
14 **And he** said unto her,
What form is he of?
And she said,
An old man cometh up;
and he is covered with a mantle.
And Saul perceived that it was Samuel,
and he stooped with his face to the ground,
and bowed himself.
15 **And Samuel** said to Saul,
Why hast thou disquieted me,
to bring me up?
And Saul answered,
I am sore distressed;
for the Philistines make war against me,
and God is departed from me,
and answereth me no more, neither by prophets, nor by dreams:
therefore I have called thee,
that thou mayest make known unto me
what I shall do.
16 **Then** said Samuel,
Wherefore then dost thou ask of me,
seeing the LORD is departed from thee,
and is become thine enemy?
17 **And the LORD** hath done to him,
as he spake by me:
for the LORD hath rent the kingdom out of thine hand,
and given it to thy neighbour, even to David:
18 **Because thou** obeyedst not the voice of the LORD,
nor executedst his fierce wrath upon Amalek,
therefore hath the LORD done this thing unto thee this day.
19 **Moreover the LORD** will also deliver Israel with thee into the hand of the Philistines:
and to morrow shalt thou and thy sons be with me:
the LORD also shall deliver the host of Israel into the hand of the Philistines.
20 **Then Saul** fell straightway all along on the earth,
and was sore afraid, because of the words of Samuel:
and there was no strength in him;
for he had eaten no bread all the day, nor all the night.
21 **And the woman** came unto Saul,
and saw that he was sore troubled,
and said unto him,
Behold,
thine handmaid hath obeyed thy voice,
and I have put my life in my hand,
and have hearkened unto thy words which thou spakest unto me.
22 **Now therefore, {I pray thee}, hearken thou** also unto the voice of thine handmaid,
and let me set a morsel of bread before thee;
and eat,
that thou mayest have strength,
when thou goest on thy way.
23 **But he** refused,
and said,
I will not eat.
But his servants, together with the woman, compelled him;
and he hearkened unto their voice.
So he arose from the earth,
and sat upon the bed.
24 **And the woman** had a fat calf in the house;
and she hasted,
and killed it,
and took flour,
and kneaded it,
and did bake unleavened bread thereof:
25 **And she** brought it before Saul, and before his servants;
and they did eat.
Then they rose up,
and went away that night.

29 **Now the Philistines** gathered together all their armies to Aphek:
and the Israelites pitched by a fountain which is in Jezreel.
2 **And the lords of the Philistines** passed on by hundreds, and by thousands:
but David and his men passed on in the rereward with Achish.
3 **Then** said the princes of the Philistines,
What do these Hebrews here?
And Achish said unto the princes of the Philistines,
Is not this David, the servant of Saul the king of Israel,
which hath been with me these days, or these years,
and I have found no fault in him
since he fell unto me unto this day?
4 **And the princes of the Philistines** were wroth with him;
and the princes of the Philistines said unto him,
Make this fellow return,
that he may go again to his place which thou hast appointed him,

and let him not go down with us to battle,
lest in the battle he be an adversary to us:
for wherewith should he reconcile himself unto his master?
should it not be with the heads of these men?

5 **Is not this** David,
of whom they sang one to another in dances,
saying,
Saul slew his thousands, and David his ten thousands?

6 **Then Achish** called David,
and said unto him,
Surely, {as the LORD liveth}, thou hast been upright,
and thy going out and thy coming in with me in the host is good in my sight:
for I have not found evil in thee since the day of thy coming unto me unto this day:
nevertheless the lords favour thee not.

7 **Wherefore now return,**
and go in peace,
that thou displease not the lords of the Philistines.

8 **And David** said unto Achish,
But what have I done?
and what hast thou found in thy servant so long as I have been with thee unto this day,
that I may not go fight against the enemies of my lord the king?

9 **And Achish** answered and said to David,
I know
that thou art good in my sight, as an angel of God:
notwithstanding the princes of the Philistines have said,
He shall not go up with us to the battle.

10 **Wherefore now rise up** early in the morning with thy master's servants that are come with thee:
and as soon as ye be up early in the morning,
and have light,
depart.

11 **So David and his men** rose up early to depart in the morning,
to return into the land of the Philistines.

And the Philistines went up to Jezreel.

30

And it came to pass,
when David and his men were come to Ziklag on the third day,
that the Amalekites had invaded the south, and Ziklag,
and smitten Ziklag,
and burned it with fire;

2 **And** had taken the women captives,
that were therein:
they slew not any, either great or small,
but carried them away,
and went on their way.

3 **So David and his men** came to the city,
and, {behold}, it was burned with fire;
and their wives, and their sons, and their daughters, were taken captives.

4 **Then David and the people that were with him** lifted up their voice and wept,
until they had no more power to weep.

5 **And David's two wives** were taken captives, Ahinoam the Jezreelitess, and Abigail the wife of Nabal the Carmelite.

6 **And David** was greatly distressed;
for the people spake of stoning him,
because the soul of all the people was grieved, every man for his sons and for his daughters:
but David encouraged himself in the LORD his God.

7 **And David** said to Abiathar the priest, Ahimelech's son,
I pray thee,
bring me hither the ephod.

And Abiathar brought thither the ephod to David.

8 **And David** enquired at the LORD,
saying,
Shall I pursue after this troop?
shall I overtake them?

And he answered him,
Pursue:
for thou shalt surely overtake them,
and without fail recover all.

9 **So David** went, he and the six hundred men that were with him,
and came to the brook Besor,
where those that were left behind stayed.

10 **But David** pursued, he and four hundred men:
for two hundred abode behind,
which were so faint that they could not go over the brook Besor.

11 **And they** found an Egyptian in the field,
and brought him to David,
and gave him bread,
and he did eat;
and they made him drink water;

12 **And they** gave him a piece of a cake of figs, and two clusters of raisins:
and when he had eaten,
his spirit came again to him:
for he had eaten no bread, {nor drunk any water}, three days and three nights.

13 **And David** said unto him,
To whom belongest thou?
and whence art thou?

And he said,
I am a young man of Egypt, servant to an Amalekite;
and my master left me,
because three days agone I fell sick.

14 **We** made an invasion upon the south of the Cherethites, and upon the coast which belongeth to Judah, and upon the south of Caleb;
and we burned Ziklag with fire.

15 **And David** said to him,
Canst thou bring me down to this company?

And he said,
Swear unto me by God,
that thou wilt neither kill me,
nor deliver me into the hands of my master,
and I will bring thee down to this company.

16 **And when he** had brought him down,
behold,
they were spread abroad upon all the earth,
eating and drinking,
and dancing, because of all the great spoil that they had taken out of the land of the Philistines, and out of the land of Judah.

17 **And David** smote them from the twilight even unto the evening of the next day:
and there escaped not a man of them, save four hundred young men,

which rode upon camels,
and fled.

18 **And David** recovered all that the Amalekites had carried away:
and David rescued his two wives.

19 **And there** was nothing lacking to them, neither small nor great, neither sons nor daughters, neither spoil, nor any thing that they had taken to them:
David recovered all.

20 **And David** took all the flocks and the herds,
which they drave before those other cattle,
and said,
This is David's spoil.

21 **And David** came to the two hundred men,
which were so faint that they could not follow David,
whom they had made also to abide at the brook Besor:
and they went forth to meet David,
and to meet the people that were with him:
and when David came near to the people,
he saluted them.

22 **Then** answered all the wicked men and men of Belial, of those that went with David,
and said,
Because they went not with us,
we will not give them ought of the spoil that we have recovered, save to every man his wife and his children,
that they may lead them away,
and depart.

23 **Then** said David,
Ye shall not do so, my brethren, with that which the LORD hath given us,
who hath preserved us,
and delivered the company that came against us into our hand.

24 **For who** will hearken unto you in this matter?
but as his part is that goeth down to the battle,
so shall his part be that tarrieth by the stuff:
they shall part alike.

25 **And it** was so from that day forward,
that he made it a statute and an ordinance for Israel unto this day.

26 **And when David** came to Ziklag,
he sent of the spoil unto the elders of Judah, even to his friends,
saying,
Behold a present for you of the spoil of the enemies of the LORD;

27 To them which were in Bethel, and to them which were in south Ramoth, and to them which were in Jattir,

28 And to them which were in Aroer, and to them which were in Siphmoth, and to them which were in Eshtemoa,

29 And to them which were in Rachal, and to them which were in the cities of the Jerahmeelites, and to them which were in the cities of the Kenites,

30 And to them which were in Hormah, and to them which were in Chorashan, and to them which were in Athach,

31 And to them which were in Hebron, and to all the places where David himself and his men were wont to haunt.

31

Now the Philistines fought against Israel:
and the men of Israel fled from before the Philistines,
and fell down slain in mount Gilboa.

2 **And the Philistines** followed hard upon Saul and upon his sons;
and the Philistines slew Jonathan, and Abinadab, and Melchishua, Saul's sons.

3 **And the battle** went sore against Saul,
and the archers hit him;
and he was sore wounded of the archers.

4 **Then** said Saul unto his armourbearer,
Draw thy sword,
and thrust me through therewith;
lest these uncircumcised come and thrust me through,
and abuse me.

But his armourbearer would not;
for he was sore afraid.

Therefore Saul took a sword,
and fell upon it.

5 **And when his armourbearer** saw that Saul was dead,
he fell likewise upon his sword,
and died with him.

6 **So Saul** died, and his three sons, and his armourbearer, and all his men, that same day together.

7 **And when the men of Israel that were on the other side of the valley, and they that were on the other side Jordan,** saw that the men of Israel fled, and that Saul and his sons were dead,
they forsook the cities,
and fled;
and the Philistines came and dwelt in them.

8 **And it** came to pass on the morrow,
when the Philistines came to strip the slain,
that they found Saul and his three sons fallen in mount Gilboa.

9 **And they** cut off his head,
and stripped off his armour,
and sent into the land of the Philistines round about,
to publish it in the house of their idols, and among the people.

10 **And they** put his armour in the house of Ashtaroth:
and they fastened his body to the wall of Bethshan.

11 **And when the inhabitants of Jabeshgilead** heard of that which the Philistines had done to Saul;

12 **All the valiant men** arose,

and went all night,
and took the body of Saul and the bodies of his sons from the wall of Bethshan,
and came to Jabesh,
and burnt them there.
13 **And they** took their bones,
and buried them under a tree at Jabesh,
and fasted seven days.

2 Samuel

The Book of Second Samuel (author unknown) vividly narrates the triumphs and trials of King David's reign. It commences with the captivating tale of David's anointing as the king of Israel, a divine appointment following the demise of King Saul. The narrative then unfolds David's ascent to power, marked by his resounding victories over the Philistines and increasing influence among the people of Israel. The book also chronicles the story of the Ark of the Covenant, a sacred object symbolizing the presence of God among the Israelites.

One of the most well-known passages in Second Samuel is the story of David and Bathsheba. In a moment of human frailty, David succumbs to sin with Bathsheba, another man's wife. This transgression culminates in the tragic murder of her husband, Uriah the Hittite. The entire incident casts a deep shadow of shame upon David. Yet his sincere repentance paves the way for restoring his relationship with God. The book concludes with an account of the succession of David's kingdom, a legacy passed on to his son, Solomon.

The Book of Second Samuel weaves a compelling narrative of King David's reign, offering many instances that illuminate his devotion to God and his battles with sin. In doing so, it stands as a testament to the intricate nature of human existence, the pivotal role of repentance in fostering restoration, and the necessity of seeking divine guidance in all facets of life.

1 **Now it** came to pass after the death of Saul,
when David was returned from the slaughter of the Amalekites,
and David had abode two days in Ziklag;
2 **It** came even to pass on the third day,
that, {behold}, a man came out of the camp from Saul with his clothes rent, and earth upon his head:
and so it was,
when he came to David,
that he fell to the earth,
and did obeisance.
3 **And David** said unto him,
From whence comest thou?
And he said unto him,
Out of the camp of Israel am I escaped.
4 **And David** said unto him,
How went the matter?
I pray thee,
tell me.
And he answered,
That the people are fled from the battle,
and many of the people also are fallen and dead;
and Saul and Jonathan his son are dead also.
5 **And David** said unto the young man that told him,
How knowest thou
that Saul and Jonathan his son be dead?
6 **And the young man that told him** said,
As I happened by chance upon mount Gilboa,
behold,
Saul leaned upon his spear;
and, {lo}, the chariots and horsemen followed hard after him.
7 **And when he** looked behind him,
he saw me,
and called unto me.
And I answered,
Here am I.
8 **And he** said unto me,
Who art thou?
And I answered him,
I am an Amalekite.
9 **He** said unto me again,
Stand, {I pray thee}, upon me,
and slay me:
for anguish is come upon me,
because my life is yet whole in me.
10 **So I** stood upon him,
and slew him,
because I was sure that he could not live after that he was fallen:
and I took the crown that was upon his head, and the bracelet that was on his arm,
and have brought them hither unto my lord.
11 **Then David** took hold on his clothes,
and rent them; and likewise all the men that were with him:
12 **And they** mourned,
and wept,
and fasted until even, for Saul, and for Jonathan his son, and for the people of the LORD, and for the house of Israel;
because they were fallen by the sword.
13 **And David** said unto the young man that told him,
Whence art thou?
And he answered,
I am the son of a stranger, an Amalekite.
14 **And David** said unto him,
How wast thou not afraid to stretch forth thine hand to destroy the LORD's anointed?
15 **And David** called one of the young men,
and said,
Go near,
and fall upon him.
And he smote him that he died.
16 **And David** said unto him,
Thy blood be upon thy head;
for thy mouth hath testified against thee,
saying,
I have slain the LORD's anointed.
17 **And David** lamented with this lamentation over Saul and over Jonathan his son:
18 (Also he bade them teach the children of Judah the use of the bow:
behold,
it is written in the book of Jasher.)

19 **The beauty of Israel** is slain upon thy high places:
how are the mighty fallen!
20 **Tell it not** in Gath,
publish it not in the streets of Askelon;
lest the daughters of the Philistines rejoice,
lest the daughters of the uncircumcised triumph.
21 **Ye mountains of Gilboa, let there** be no dew,
neither let there be rain, upon you, nor fields of offerings:
for there the shield of the mighty is vilely cast away, the shield of Saul,
as though he had not been anointed with oil.
22 **From the blood of the slain, from the fat of the mighty,** the bow of Jonathan turned not back,
and the sword of Saul returned not empty
23 **Saul and Jonathan** were lovely and pleasant in their lives,
and in their death they were not divided:
they were swifter than eagles,
they were stronger than lions.
24 **Ye daughters of Israel, weep** over Saul,
who clothed you in scarlet, with other delights,
who put on ornaments of gold upon your apparel.
25 **How** are the mighty fallen in the midst of the battle!
O Jonathan, thou wast slain in thine high places.
26 **I** am distressed for thee, my brother Jonathan:
very pleasant hast thou been unto me:
thy love to me was wonderful,
passing the love of women.
27 **How** are the mighty fallen,
and the weapons of war perished!

2

And it came to pass after this, **that David** enquired of the LORD,
saying,
Shall I go up into any of the cities of Judah?
And the LORD said unto him,
Go up.
And David said,
Whither shall I go up?
And he said,
Unto Hebron.
2 **So David** went up thither, and his two wives also, Ahinoam the Jezreelitess, and Abigail Nabal's wife the Carmelite.
3 **And his men that were with him** did David bring up, every man with his household:
and they dwelt in the cities of Hebron.
4 **And the men of Judah** came,
and there they anointed David king over the house of Judah.
And they told David,
saying,
That the men of Jabeshgilead were they that buried Saul.
5 **And David** sent messengers unto the men of Jabeshgilead,
and said unto them,
Blessed be ye of the LORD,
that ye have shewed this kindness unto your lord, even unto Saul,
and have buried him.
6 **And now the LORD** shew kindness and truth unto you:
and I also will requite you this kindness,
because ye have done this thing.
7 **Therefore now let your hands** be strengthened,
and be ye valiant:
for your master Saul is dead,
and also the house of Judah have anointed me king over them.
8 **But Abner the son of Ner, captain of Saul's host,** took Ishbosheth the son of Saul,
and brought him over to Mahanaim;
9 **And** made him king over Gilead, and over the Ashurites, and over Jezreel, and over Ephraim, and over Benjamin, and over all Israel.
10 **Ishbosheth Saul's son** was forty years old
when he began to reign over Israel,
and reigned two years.
But the house of Judah followed David.
11 **And the time that David was king in Hebron over the house of Judah** was seven years and six
months.12 **And Abner the son of Ner, and the servants of Ishbosheth the son of Saul,** went out from Mahanaim to Gibeon.
13 **And Joab the son of Zeruiah, and the servants of David,** went out,
and met together by the pool of Gibeon:
and they sat down, the one on the one side of the pool, and the other on the other side of the pool.
14 **And Abner** said to Joab,
Let the young men now arise,
and play before us.
And Joab said,
Let them arise.
15 **Then there** arose and went over by number twelve of Benjamin, {which pertained to Ishbosheth the son of Saul}, and twelve of the servants of David.
16 **And they** caught every one his fellow by the head,
and thrust his sword in his fellow's side;
so they fell down together:
wherefore that place was called Helkathhazzurim,
which is in Gibeon.
17 **And there** was a very sore battle that day;
and Abner was beaten, and the men of Israel, before the servants of David.
18 **And there** were three sons of Zeruiah there, Joab, and Abishai, and Asahel:
and Asahel was as light of foot as a wild roe.
19 **And Asahel** pursued after Abner;
and in going he turned not to the right hand nor to the left from following Abner.
20 **Then Abner** looked behind him,
and said,
Art thou Asahel?
And he answered,
I am.
21 **And Abner** said to him,
Turn thee aside to thy right hand or to thy left,
and lay thee hold on one of the young men,
and take thee his armour.
But Asahel would not turn aside from following of him.
22 **And Abner** said again to Asahel,
Turn thee aside from following me:
wherefore should I smite thee to the ground?
how then should I hold up my face to Joab thy brother?
23 **Howbeit he** refused to turn aside:

wherefore Abner with the hinder end of the spear smote him under the fifth rib,
that the spear came out behind him;
and he fell down there,
and died in the same place:
and it came to pass,
that as many as came to the place where Asahel fell down and died stood still.

24 **Joab also and Abishai** pursued after Abner:
and the sun went down
when they were come to the hill of Ammah,
that lieth before Giah by the way of the wilderness of Gibeon.

25 **And the children of Benjamin** gathered themselves together after Abner,
and became one troop,
and stood on the top of an hill.

26 **Then Abner** called to Joab,
and said,
Shall the sword devour for ever?
knowest thou not
that it will be bitterness in the latter end?
how long shall it be then,
ere thou bid the people return from following their brethren?

27 **And Joab** said,
As God liveth,
unless thou hadst spoken,
surely then in the morning the people had gone up every one from following his brother.

28 **So Joab** blew a trumpet,
and all the people stood still,
and pursued after Israel no more,
neither fought they any more.

29 **And Abner and his men** walked all that night through the plain,
and passed over Jordan,
and went through all Bithron,
and they came to Mahanaim.

30 **And Joab** returned from following Abner:
and when he had gathered all the people together,
there lacked of David's servants nineteen men and Asahel.

31 **But the servants of David** had smitten of Benjamin, and of Abner's men,
so that three hundred and threescore men died.

32 **And they** took up Asahel,
and buried him in the sepulchre of his father,
which was in Bethlehem.

And Joab and his men went all night,
and they came to Hebron at break of day.

3 **Now there** was long war between the house of Saul and the house of David:
but David waxed stronger and stronger,
and the house of Saul waxed weaker and weaker.

2 **And unto David** were sons born in Hebron:
and his firstborn was Amnon, of Ahinoam the Jezreelitess;
3 And his second, Chileab, of Abigail the wife of Nabal the Carmelite; and the third, Absalom the son of Maacah the daughter of Talmai king of Geshur;
4 And the fourth, Adonijah the son of Haggith; and the fifth, Shephatiah the son of Abital;
5 And the sixth, Ithream, by Eglah David's wife.

These were born to David in Hebron.

6 **And it** came to pass,
while there was war between the house of Saul and the house of David,
that Abner made himself strong for the house of Saul.

7 **And Saul** had a concubine,
whose name was Rizpah, the daughter of Aiah:
and Ishbosheth said to Abner,
Wherefore hast thou gone in unto my father's concubine?

8 **Then** was Abner very wroth for the words of Ishbosheth,
and said,
Am I a dog's head,
which against Judah do shew kindness this day unto the house of Saul thy father, to his brethren, and to his friends,
and have not delivered thee into the hand of David,
that thou chargest me to day with a fault concerning this woman?

9 **So** do God to Abner, and more also,
except, {as the LORD hath sworn to David}, even so I do to him;
10 To translate the kingdom from the house of Saul,
and to set up the throne of David over Israel and over Judah, from Dan even to Beersheba.

11 **And he** could not answer Abner a word again,
because he feared him.

12 **And Abner** sent messengers to David on his behalf,
saying,
Whose is the land?
saying also,
Make thy league with me,
and, {behold}, my hand shall be with thee,
to bring about all Israel unto thee.

13 **And he** said,
Well;
I will make a league with thee:
but one thing I require of thee, that is,
Thou shalt not see my face,
except thou first bring Michal Saul's daughter,
when thou comest to see my face.

14 **And David** sent messengers to Ishbosheth Saul's son,
saying,
Deliver me my wife Michal,
which I espoused to me for an hundred foreskins of the Philistines.

15 **And Ishbosheth** sent,
and took her from her husband, even from Phaltiel the son of Laish.

16 **And her husband** went with her
along weeping behind her to Bahurim.

Then said Abner unto him,
Go,
return.
And he returned.

17 **And Abner** had communication with the elders of Israel,
saying,
Ye sought for David in times past to be king over you:
18 **Now then do** it:
for the LORD hath spoken of David,
saying,
By the hand of my servant David I will save my people Israel out of the hand of the Philistines, and out of the hand of all their enemies.

19 **And Abner** also spake in the ears of Benjamin:

and Abner went also to speak in the ears of David in Hebron all that seemed good to Israel, and that seemed good to the whole house of Benjamin.

20 **So Abner** came to David to Hebron, and twenty men with him.

And David made Abner and the men that were with him a feast.

21 **And Abner** said unto David,
I will arise and go,
and will gather all Israel unto my lord the king,
that they may make a league with thee,
and that thou mayest reign over all that thine heart desireth.

And David sent Abner away;
and he went in peace.

22 **And, {behold}, the servants of David and Joab** came from pursuing a troop,
and brought in a great spoil with them:
but Abner was not with David in Hebron;
for he had sent him away,
and he was gone in peace.

23 **When Joab and all the host that was with him** were come,
they told Joab,
saying,
Abner the son of Ner came to the king,
and he hath sent him away,
and he is gone in peace.

24 **Then Joab** came to the king,
and said,
What hast thou done?
behold,
Abner came unto thee;
hy is it that thou hast sent him away,
and he is quite gone?

25 **Thou** knowest Abner the son of Ner,
that he came to deceive thee,
and to know thy going out and thy coming in,
and to know all that thou doest.

26 **And when Joab** was come out from David,
he sent messengers after Abner,
which brought him again from the well of Sirah:
but David knew it not.

27 **And when Abner** was returned to Hebron,
Joab took him aside in the gate to speak with him quietly,
and smote him there under the fifth rib, {that he died}, for the blood of Asahel his brother.

28 **And afterward when David** heard it,
he said,
I and my kingdom are guiltless before the LORD for ever from the blood of Abner the son of Ner:

29 **Let it** rest on the head of Joab, and on all his father's house;
and let there not fail from the house of Joab one that hath an issue, or that is a leper, or that leaneth on a staff, or that falleth on the sword, or that lacketh bread.

30 **So Joab, and Abishai his brother** slew Abner,
because he had slain their brother Asahel at Gibeon in the battle.

31 **And David** said to Joab, and to all the people that were with him,
Rend your clothes,
and gird you with sackcloth,
and mourn before Abner.

And king David himself followed the bier.

32 **And they** buried Abner in Hebron:
and the king lifted up his voice,
and wept at the grave of Abner;
and all the people wept.

33 **And the king** lamented over Abner,
and said,
Died Abner as a fool dieth?

34 **Thy hands** were not bound,
nor thy feet put into fetters:
as a man falleth before wicked men,
so fellest thou.

And all the people wept again over him.

35 **And when all the people** came to cause David to eat meat while it was yet day,
David sware,
saying,
So do God to me, and more also,
if I taste bread, or ought else, till the sun be down.

36 **And all the people** took notice of it,
and it pleased them:
as whatsoever the king did pleased all the people.

37 **For all the people and all Israel** understood that day
that it was not of the king to slay Abner the son of Ner.

38 **And the king** said unto his servants,
Know ye not
that there is a prince and a great man fallen this day in Israel?

39 **And I** am this day weak,
though anointed king;
and these men the sons of Zeruiah be too hard for me:
the LORD shall reward the doer of evil according to his wickedness.

4

And when Saul's son heard that Abner was dead in Hebron,
his hands were feeble,
and all the Israelites were troubled.

2 **And Saul's son** had two men that were captains of bands:
the name of the one was Baanah, and the name of the other Rechab, the sons of Rimmon a Beerothite, of the children of Benjamin:
(for Beeroth also was reckoned to Benjamin.

3 **And the Beerothites** fled to Gittaim,
and were sojourners there until this day.)

4 **And Jonathan, Saul's son,** had a son that was lame of his feet.

He was five years old
when the tidings came of Saul and Jonathan out of Jezreel,
and his nurse took him up,
and fled:
and it came to pass,
as she made haste to flee,
that he fell,
and became lame.

And his name was Mephibosheth.

5 **And the sons of Rimmon the Beerothite, Rechab and Baanah,** went,
and came about the heat of the day to the house of Ishbosheth,
who lay on a bed at noon.

6 **And they** came thither into the midst of the house,
as though they would have fetched wheat;
and they smote him under the fifth rib:
and Rechab and Baanah his brother escaped.

7 **For when they** came into the house,

he lay on his bed in his bedchamber,
and they smote him,
and slew him,
and beheaded him,
and took his head,
and gat them away through the plain all night.

8 **And they** brought the head of Ishbosheth unto David to Hebron,
and said to the king,
Behold the head of Ishbosheth the son of Saul thine enemy,
which sought thy life;
and the LORD hath avenged my lord the king this day of Saul, and of his seed.

9 **And David** answered Rechab and Baanah his brother, the sons of Rimmon the Beerothite,
and said unto them,
As the LORD liveth,
who hath redeemed my soul out of all adversity,
10 **When one** told me,
saying,
Behold,
Saul is dead,
thinking to have brought good tidings,
I took hold of him,
and slew him in Ziklag,
who thought
that I would have given him a reward for his tidings:

11 **How much more, when wicked men** have slain a righteous person in his own house upon his bed?
shall I not therefore now require his blood of your hand,
and take you away from the earth?

12 **And David** commanded his young men,
and they slew them,
and cut off their hands and their feet,
and hanged them up over the pool in Hebron.

But they took the head of Ishbosheth,
and buried it in the sepulchre of Abner in Hebron.

5 **Then** came all the tribes of Israel to David unto Hebron,
and spake,
saying,
Behold,
we are thy bone and thy flesh.

2 **Also in time past,** {when Saul was king over us}, thou wast he that leddest out and broughtest in Israel:
and the LORD said to thee,
Thou shalt feed my people Israel,
and thou shalt be a captain over Israel.

3 **So all the elders of Israel** came to the king to Hebron;
and king David made a league with them in Hebron before the LORD:
and they anointed David king over Israel.

4 **David** was thirty years old
when he began to reign,
and he reigned forty years.

5 **In Hebron** he reigned over Judah seven years and six months:
and in Jerusalem he reigned thirty and three years over all Israel and Judah.

6 **And the king and his men** went to Jerusalem unto the Jebusites, the inhabitants of the land:
which spake unto David,
saying,
Except thou take away the blind and the lame,
thou shalt not come in hither:
thinking,
David cannot come in hither.

7 **Nevertheless David** took the strong hold of Zion:
the same is the city of David.

8 **And David** said on that day,
Whosoever getteth up to the gutter,
and smiteth the Jebusites, and the lame and the blind that are hated of David's soul,
he shall be chief and captain.

Wherefore they said,
The blind and the lame shall not come into the house.

9 **So David** dwelt in the fort,
and called it the city of David.

And David built round about from Millo and inward.

10 **And David** went on,
and grew great,
and the LORD God of hosts was with him.

11 **And Hiram king of Tyre** sent messengers to David, and cedar trees, and carpenters, and masons:
and they built David an house.

12 **And David** perceived that the LORD had established him king over Israel, and that he had exalted his kingdom for his people Israel's sake.

13 **And David** took him more concubines and wives out of Jerusalem,
after he was come from Hebron:
and there were yet sons and daughters born to David.

14 **And these** be the names of those that were born unto him in Jerusalem; Shammuah, and Shobab, and Nathan, and Solomon,
15 Ibhar also, and Elishua, and Nepheg, and Japhia,
16 And Elishama, and Eliada, and Eliphalet.

17 **But when the Philistines** heard that they had anointed David king over Israel,
all the Philistines came up to seek David;
and David heard of it,
and went down to the hold.

18 **The Philistines** also came and spread themselves in the valley of Rephaim.

19 **And David** enquired of the LORD,
saying,
Shall I go up to the Philistines?
wilt thou deliver them into mine hand?

And the LORD said unto David,
Go up:
for I will doubtless deliver the Philistines into thine hand.

20 **And David** came to Baalperazim,
and David smote them there,
and said,
The LORD hath broken forth upon mine enemies before me, as the breach of waters.

Therefore he called the name of that place Baalperazim.

21 **And there** they left their images,
and David and his men burned them.

22 **And the Philistines** came up yet again,
and spread themselves in the valley of Rephaim.

23 **And when David** enquired of the LORD,
he said,
Thou shalt not go up;
but fetch a compass behind them,

and come upon them over against the mulberry trees.

24 **And let it be**, {when thou hearest the sound of a going in the tops of the mulberry trees}, that then thou shalt bestir thyself:
for then shall the LORD go out before thee,
to smite the host of the Philistines.

25 **And David** did so,
as the LORD had commanded him;
and smote the Philistines from Geba until thou come to Gazer.

6 **Again, David** gathered together all the chosen men of Israel, thirty thousand.

2 **And David** arose,
and went with all the people that were with him from Baale of Judah,
to bring up from thence the ark of God,
whose name is called by the name of the LORD of hosts that dwelleth between the cherubims.

3 **And they** set the ark of God upon a new cart,
and brought it out of the house of Abinadab that was in Gibeah:
and Uzzah and Ahio, the sons of Abinadab, drave the new cart.

4 **And they** brought it out of the house of Abinadab which was at Gibeah,
accompanying the ark of God:
and Ahio went before the ark.

5 **And David and all the house of Israel** played before the LORD on all manner of instruments made of fir wood, even on harps, and on psalteries, and on timbrels, and on cornets, and on cymbals.

6 **And when they** came to Nachon's threshingfloor,
Uzzah put forth his hand to the ark of God,
and took hold of it;
for the oxen shook it.

7 **And the anger of the LORD** was kindled against Uzzah;
and God smote him there for his error;
and there he died by the ark of God.

8 **And David** was displeased,
because the LORD had made a breach upon Uzzah:
and he called the name of the place Perezuzzah to this day.

9 **And David** was afraid of the LORD that day,
and said,
How shall the ark of the LORD come to me?

10 **So David** would not remove the ark of the LORD unto him into the city of David:
but David carried it aside into the house of Obededom the Gittite.

11 **And the ark of the LORD** continued in the house of Obededom the Gittite three months:
and the LORD blessed Obededom, and all his household.

12 **And it** was told king David,
saying,
The LORD hath blessed the house of Obededom, and all that pertaineth unto him, because of the ark of God.
So David went and brought up the ark of God from the house of Obededom into the city of David with gladness.

13 **And it** was so,
that when they that bare the ark of the LORD had gone six paces,
he sacrificed oxen and fatlings.

14 **And David** danced before the LORD with all his might;
and David was girded with a linen ephod.

15 **So David and all the house of Israel** brought up the ark of the LORD with shouting, and with the sound of the trumpet.

16 **And as the ark of the LORD** came into the city of David,
Michal Saul's daughter looked through a window,
and saw king David leaping and dancing before the LORD;
and she despised him in her heart.

17 **And they** brought in the ark of the LORD,
and set it in his place, in the midst of the tabernacle that David had pitched for it:
and David offered burnt offerings and peace offerings before the LORD.

18 **And as soon as David** had made an end of offering burnt offerings and peace offerings,
he blessed the people in the name of the LORD of hosts.

19 **And he** dealt among all the people, even among the whole multitude of Israel, as well to the women as men, to every one a cake of bread, and a good piece of flesh, and a flagon of wine.
So all the people departed every one to his house.

20 **Then David** returned to bless his household.
And Michal the daughter of Saul came out to meet David,
and said,
How glorious was the king of Israel to day,
who uncovered himself to day in the eyes of the handmaids of his servants,
as one of the vain fellows shamelessly uncovereth himself!

21 **And David** said unto Michal,
It was before the LORD,
which chose me before thy father, and before all his house,
to appoint me ruler over the people of the LORD, over Israel:
therefore will I play before the LORD.

22 **And I** will yet be more vile than thus,
and will be base in mine own sight:
and of the maidservants which thou hast spoken of, of them shall I be had in honour.

23 **Therefore Michal the daughter of Saul** had no child unto the day of her death.

7 **And it** came to pass,
when the king sat in his house,
and the LORD had given him rest round about from all his enemies;

2 **That the king** said unto Nathan the prophet,
See now,
I dwell in an house of cedar,
but the ark of God dwelleth within curtains.

3 **And Nathan** said to the king,
Go,
do all that is in thine heart;
for the LORD is with thee.

4 **And it** came to pass that night,
that the word of the LORD came unto Nathan,
saying,

5 **Go and tell** my servant David,
Thus saith the LORD,

Shalt thou build me an house for me to dwell in?

6 **Whereas I** have not dwelt in any house since the time that I brought up the children of Israel out of Egypt, even to this day,
but have walked in a tent and in a tabernacle.

7 **In all the places wherein I have walked with all the children of Israel** spake I a word with any of the tribes of Israel,
whom I commanded to feed my people Israel,
saying,
Why build ye not me an house of cedar?

8 **Now therefore so** shalt thou say unto my servant David,
Thus saith the LORD of hosts,
I took thee from the sheepcote, from following the sheep,
to be ruler over my people, over Israel:
9 **And I** was with thee
whithersoever thou wentest,
and have cut off all thine enemies out of thy sight,
and have made thee a great name, like unto the name of the great men that are in the earth.

10 **Moreover I** will appoint a place for my people Israel,
and will plant them,
that they may dwell in a place of their own,
and move no more;
neither shall the children of wickedness afflict them any more, as beforetime,
11 And as since the time that I commanded judges to be over my people Israel,
and have caused thee to rest from all thine enemies.

Also the LORD telleth thee
that he will make thee an house.

12 **And when thy days** be fulfilled,
and thou shalt sleep with thy fathers,
I will set up thy seed after thee,
which shall proceed out of thy bowels,
and I will establish his kingdom.

13 **He** shall build an house for my name,
and I will stablish the throne of his kingdom for ever.

14 **I** will be his father,
and he shall be my son.
If he commit iniquity,
I will chasten him with the rod of men, and with the stripes of the children of men:

15 **But my mercy** shall not depart away from him,
as I took it from Saul,
whom I put away before thee.

16 **And thine house and thy kingdom** shall be established for ever before thee:
thy throne shall be established for ever.

17 **According to all these words, and according to all this vision,** so did Nathan speak unto David.

18 **Then** went king David in,
and sat before the LORD,
and he said,
Who am I, O Lord GOD?
and what is my house,
that thou hast brought me hitherto?

19 **And this** was yet a small thing in thy sight, O Lord GOD;
but thou hast spoken also of thy servant's house for a great while to come.

And is this the manner of man, O Lord GOD?

20 **And what** can David say more unto thee?
for thou, Lord GOD, knowest thy servant.

21 **For thy word's sake, and according to thine own heart,** hast thou done all these great things,
to make thy servant know them.

22 **Wherefore thou** art great, O LORD God:
for there is none like thee,
neither is there any God beside thee, according to all that we have heard with our ears.

23 **And what one nation in the earth** is like thy people, even like Israel,
whom God went to redeem for a people to himself,
and to make him a name,
and to do for you great things and terrible, for thy land, before thy people,
which thou redeemedst to thee from Egypt, from the nations and their gods?

24 **For thou** hast confirmed to thyself thy people Israel to be a people unto thee for ever:
and thou, LORD, art become their God.

25 **And now, O LORD God, the word that thou hast spoken concerning thy servant, and concerning his house,** establish it for ever,
and do as thou hast said.

26 **And let thy name** be magnified for ever,
saying,
The LORD of hosts is the God over Israel:
and let the house of thy servant David be established before thee.

27 **For thou,** O LORD of hosts, God of Israel, hast revealed to thy servant,
saying,
I will build thee an house:
therefore hath thy servant found in his heart to pray this prayer unto thee.

28 **And now,** O Lord GOD, thou art that God,
and thy words be true,
and thou hast promised this goodness unto thy servant:
29 **Therefore now let it** please thee to bless the house of thy servant,
that it may continue for ever before thee:
for thou, O Lord GOD, hast spoken it:
and with thy blessing let the house of thy servant be blessed for ever.

8 ⤜ **And after this** it came to pass
that David smote the Philistines,
and subdued them:
and David took Methegammah out of the hand of the Philistines.

2 **And he** smote Moab,
and measured them with a line,
casting them down to the ground;
even with two lines measured he to put to death, and with one full line to keep alive.

And so the Moabites became David's servants,
and brought gifts.

3 **David** smote also Hadadezer, the son of Rehob, king of Zobah,
as he went to recover his border at the river Euphrates.

4 **And David** took from him a thousand chariots, and seven hundred horsemen, and twenty thousand footmen:
and David houghed all the chariot horses, but reserved of them for an hundred chariots.

5 **And when the Syrians of Damascus** came to succour Hadadezer king of Zobah,
David slew of the Syrians two and twenty thousand men.

6 **Then David** put garrisons in Syria of Damascus:
and the Syrians became servants to David,
and brought gifts.

And the LORD preserved David
whithersoever he went.

7 **And David** took the shields of gold that were on the servants of Hadadezer,
and brought them to Jerusalem.

8 **And from Betah, and from Berothai, cities of Hadadezer,** king David took exceeding much brass.

9 **When Toi king of Hamath** heard that David had smitten all the host of Hadadezer,
10 **Then Toi** sent Joram his son unto king David,
to salute him,
and to bless him,
because he had fought against Hadadezer,
and smitten him:
for Hadadezer had wars with Toi.

And Joram brought with him vessels of silver, and vessels of gold, and vessels of brass:
11 **Which also king David** did dedicate unto the LORD, with the silver and gold that he had dedicated of all nations which he subdued;
12 Of Syria, and of Moab, and of the children of Ammon, and of the Philistines, and of Amalek, and of the spoil of Hadadezer, son of Rehob, king of Zobah.

13 **And David** gat him a name
when he returned from smiting of the Syrians in the valley of salt,
being eighteen thousand men.

14 **And he** put garrisons in Edom;
throughout all Edom put he garrisons,
and all they of Edom became David's servants.

And the LORD preserved David
whithersoever he went.

15 **And David** reigned over all Israel;
and David executed judgment and justice unto all his people.

16 **And Joab the son of Zeruiah** was over the host;
and Jehoshaphat the son of Ahilud was recorder;
17 **And Zadok the son of Ahitub, and Ahimelech the son of Abiathar,** were the priests;
and Seraiah was the scribe;
18 **And Benaiah the son of Jehoiada** was over both the Cherethites and the Pelethites;
and David's sons were chief rulers.

9 **And David** said,
Is there yet any that is left of the house of Saul,
that I may shew him kindness for Jonathan's sake?

2 **And there** was of the house of Saul a servant whose name was Ziba.

And when they had called him unto David,
the king said unto him,
Art thou Ziba?

And he said,
Thy servant is he.

3 **And the king** said,
Is there not yet any of the house of Saul,
that I may shew the kindness of God unto him?

And Ziba said unto the king,
Jonathan hath yet a son,
which is lame on his feet.

4 **And the king** said unto him,
Where is he?

And Ziba said unto the king,
Behold,
he is in the house of Machir, the son of Ammiel, in Lodebar.

5 **Then king David** sent,
and fetched him out of the house of Machir, the son of Ammiel, from Lodebar.

6 **Now when Mephibosheth, the son of Jonathan, the son of Saul,** was come unto David,
he fell on his face,
and did reverence.

And David said,
Mephibosheth.

And he answered,
Behold thy servant!

7 **And David** said unto him,
Fear not:
for I will surely shew thee kindness for Jonathan thy father's sake,
and will restore thee all the land of Saul thy father;
and thou shalt eat bread at my table continually.

8 **And he** bowed himself,
and said,
What is thy servant,
that thou shouldest look upon such a dead dog as I am?

9 **Then the king** called to Ziba, Saul's servant,
and said unto him,
I have given unto thy master's son all that pertained to Saul and to all his house.

10 **Thou therefore, and thy sons, and thy servants,** shall till the land for him,
and thou shalt bring in the fruits,
that thy master's son may have food to eat:
but Mephibosheth thy master's son shall eat bread alway at my table.

Now Ziba had fifteen sons and twenty servants.

11 **Then** said Ziba unto the king,
According to all that my lord the king hath commanded his servant, so shall thy servant do.

As for Mephibosheth, {said the king}, he shall eat at my table, as one of the king's sons.

12 **And Mephibosheth** had a young son,
whose name was Micha.

And all that dwelt in the house of Ziba were servants unto Mephibosheth.

13 **So Mephibosheth** dwelt in Jerusalem:
for he did eat continually at the king's table;
and was lame on both his feet.

10 **And it** came to pass after this,
that the king of the children of Ammon died,
and Hanun his son reigned in his stead.

2 **Then** said David,
I will shew kindness unto Hanun the son of Nahash,
as his father shewed kindness unto me.

And David sent to comfort him by the hand of his servants for his father.
And David's servants came into the land of the children of Ammon.
3 **And the princes of the children of Ammon** said unto Hanun their lord,
Thinkest thou
that David doth honour thy father,
that he hath sent comforters unto thee?
hath not David rather sent his servants unto thee,
to search the city,
and to spy it out,
and to overthrow it?
4 **Wherefore Hanun** took David's servants,
and shaved off the one half of their beards,
and cut off their garments in the middle, even to their buttocks,
and sent them away.
5 **When they** told it unto David,
he sent to meet them,
because the men were greatly ashamed:
and the king said,
Tarry at Jericho
until your beards be grown,
and then return.
6 **And when the children of Ammon** saw that they stank before David,
the children of Ammon sent and hired the Syrians of Bethrehob and the Syrians of Zoba, twenty thousand footmen, and of king Maacah a thousand men, and of Ishtob twelve thousand men.
7 **And when David** heard of it,
he sent Joab, and all the host of the mighty men.
8 **And the children of Ammon** came out,
and put the battle in array at the entering in of the gate:
and the Syrians of Zoba, and of Rehob, and Ishtob, and Maacah, were by themselves in the field.
9 **When Joab** saw that the front of the battle was against him before and behind,
he chose of all the choice men of Israel,
and put them in array against the Syrians:
10 **And the rest of the people** he delivered into the hand of Abishai his brother,
that he might put them in array against the children of Ammon.
11 **And he** said,
If the Syrians be too strong for me,
then thou shalt help me:
but if the children of Ammon be too strong for thee,
then I will come and help thee.
12 **Be** of good courage,
and let us play the men for our people, and for the cities of our God:
and the LORD do that which seemeth him good.
13 **And Joab** drew nigh, and the people that were with him, unto the battle against the Syrians:
and they fled before him.
14 **And when the children of Ammon** saw that the Syrians were fled,
then fled they also before Abishai,
and entered into the city.
So Joab returned from the children of Ammon,
and came to Jerusalem.
15 **And when the Syrians** saw that they were smitten before Israel,
they gathered themselves together.
16 **And Hadarezer** sent,
and brought out the Syrians that were beyond the river:
and they came to Helam;
and Shobach the captain of the host of Hadarezer went before them.
17 **And when it** was told David,
he gathered all Israel together,
and passed over Jordan,
and came to Helam.
And the Syrians set themselves in array against David,
and fought with him.
18 **And the Syrians** fled before Israel;
and David slew the men of seven hundred chariots of the Syrians, and forty thousand horsemen,
and smote Shobach the captain of their host,
who died there.
19 **And when all the kings that were servants to Hadarezer** saw that they were smitten before Israel,
they made peace with Israel,
and served them.
So the Syrians feared to help the children of Ammon any more.

11 **And it** came to pass,
after the year was expired,
at the time when kings go forth to battle,
that David sent Joab, and his servants with him, and all Israel;
and they destroyed the children of Ammon,
and besieged Rabbah.
But David tarried still at Jerusalem.
2 **And it** came to pass in an eveningtide,
that David arose from off his bed,
and walked upon the roof of the king's house:
and from the roof he saw a woman washing herself;
and the woman was very beautiful to look upon.
3 **And David** sent and enquired after the woman.
And one said,
Is not this Bathsheba, the daughter of Eliam, the wife of Uriah the Hittite?
4 **And David** sent messengers,
and took her;
and she came in unto him,
and he lay with her;
for she was purified from her uncleanness:
and she returned unto her house.
5 **And the woman** conceived,
and sent and told David,
and said,
I am with child.
6 **And David** sent to Joab,
saying,
Send me Uriah the Hittite.
And Joab sent Uriah to David.
7 **And when Uriah** was come unto him,
David demanded of him
how Joab did,
and how the people did,
and how the war prospered.
8 **And David** said to Uriah,
Go down to thy house,
and wash thy feet.
And Uriah departed out of the king's house,
and there followed him a mess of meat from the king.
9 **But Uriah** slept at the door of the king's house with all the servants of his lord,

and went not down to his house.
10 **And when they** had told David, saying,
Uriah went not down unto his house,
David said unto Uriah,
Camest thou not from thy journey?
why then didst thou not go down unto thine house?
11 **And Uriah** said unto David,
The ark, and Israel, and Judah, abide in tents;
and my lord Joab, and the servants of my lord, are encamped in the open fields;
shall I then go into mine house,
to eat and to drink,
and to lie with my wife?
as thou livest,
and as thy soul liveth,
I will not do this thing.
12 **And David** said to Uriah,
Tarry here to day also,
and to morrow I will let thee depart.
So Uriah abode in Jerusalem that day, and the morrow.
13 **And when David** had called him,
he did eat and drink before him;
and he made him drunk:
and at even he went out to lie on his bed with the servants of his lord,
but went not down to his house.
14 **And it** came to pass in the morning,
that David wrote a letter to Joab,
and sent it by the hand of Uriah.
15 **And he** wrote in the letter, saying,
Set ye Uriah in the forefront of the hottest battle,
and retire ye from him,
that he may be smitten,
and die.
16 **And it** came to pass,
when Joab observed the city,
that he assigned Uriah unto a place where he knew that valiant men were.
17 **And the men of the city** went out,
and fought with Joab:
and there fell some of the people of the servants of David;
and Uriah the Hittite died also.
18 **Then Joab** sent and told David all the things concerning the war;
19 **And** charged the messenger, saying,
When thou hast made an end of telling the matters of the war unto the king,
20 **And if so be** that the king's wrath arise,
and he say unto thee,
Wherefore approached ye so nigh unto the city
when ye did fight?
knew ye not
that they would shoot from the wall?
21 **Who** smote Abimelech the son of Jerubbesheth?
did not a woman cast a piece of a millstone upon him from the wall,
that he died in Thebez?
why went ye nigh the wall?
then say thou,
Thy servant Uriah the Hittite is dead also.
22 **So the messenger** went,
and came and shewed David all that Joab had sent him for.
23 **And the messenger** said unto David,
Surely the men prevailed against us,
and came out unto us into the field,
and we were upon them even unto the entering of the gate.
24 **And the shooters** shot from off the wall upon thy servants;
and some of the king's servants be dead,
and thy servant Uriah the Hittite is dead also.
25 **Then David** said unto the messenger,
Thus shalt thou say unto Joab,
Let not this thing displease thee,
for the sword devoureth one as well as another:
make thy battle more strong against the city,
and overthrow it:
and encourage thou him.
26 **And when the wife of Uriah** heard that Uriah her husband was dead,
she mourned for her husband.
27 **And when the mourning** was past,
David sent and fetched her to his house,
and she became his wife,
and bare him a son.
But the thing that David had done displeased the LORD.

12

And the LORD sent Nathan unto David.
And he came unto him,
and said unto him,
There were two men in one city; the one rich, and the other poor.
2 **The rich man** had exceeding many flocks and herds:
3 **But the poor man** had nothing, save one little ewe lamb,
which he had bought and nourished up:
and it grew up together with him, and with his children;
it did eat of his own meat,
and drank of his own cup,
and lay in his bosom,
and was unto him as a daughter.
4 **And there** came a traveller unto the rich man,
and he spared to take of his own flock and of his own herd,
to dress for the wayfaring man that was come unto him;
but took the poor man's lamb,
and dressed it for the man that was come to him.
5 **And David's anger** was greatly kindled against the man;
and he said to Nathan,
As the LORD liveth,
the man that hath done this thing shall surely die:
6 **And he** shall restore the lamb fourfold,
because he did this thing,
and because he had no pity.
7 **And Nathan** said to David,
Thou art the man.
Thus saith the LORD God of Israel,
I anointed thee king over Israel,
and I delivered thee out of the hand of Saul;
8 **And I** gave thee thy master's house, and thy master's wives into thy bosom,
and gave thee the house of Israel and of Judah;
and if that had been too little,
I would moreover have given unto thee such and such things.
9 **Wherefore** hast thou despised the commandment of the LORD,
to do evil in his sight?
thou hast killed Uriah the Hittite with the sword,
and hast taken his wife to be thy wife,
and hast slain him with the sword of the children of Ammon.

10 **Now therefore the sword** shall never depart from thine house;
because thou hast despised me,
and hast taken the wife of Uriah the Hittite to be thy wife.

11 **Thus** saith the LORD,
Behold,
I will raise up evil against thee out of thine own house,
and I will take thy wives before thine eyes,
and give them unto thy neighbour,
and he shall lie with thy wives in the sight of this sun.

12 **For thou** didst it secretly:
but I will do this thing before all Israel, and before the sun.

13 **And David** said unto Nathan,
I have sinned against the LORD.

And Nathan said unto David,
The LORD also hath put away thy sin;
thou shalt not die.

14 **Howbeit, because by this deed** thou hast given great occasion to the enemies of the LORD to blaspheme,
the child also that is born unto thee shall surely die.

15 **And Nathan** departed unto his house.

And the LORD struck the child that Uriah's wife bare unto David,
and it was very sick.

16 **David** therefore besought God for the child;
and David fasted,
and went in,
and lay all night upon the earth.

17 **And the elders of his house** arose,
and went to him,
to raise him up from the earth:
but he would not,
neither did he eat bread with them.

18 **And it** came to pass on the seventh day,
that the child died.

And the servants of David feared to tell him
that the child was dead:
for they said,
Behold,
while the child was yet alive,
we spake unto him,
and he would not hearken unto our voice:
how will he then vex himself,
if we tell him
that the child is dead?

19 **But when David** saw that his servants whispered,
David perceived that the child was dead:
therefore David said unto his servants,
Is the child dead?

And they said,
He is dead.

20 **Then David** arose from the earth,
and washed,
and anointed himself,
and changed his apparel,
and came into the house of the LORD,
and worshipped:
then he came to his own house;
and when he required,
they set bread before him,
and he did eat.

21 **Then** said his servants unto him,
What thing is this that thou hast done?
thou didst fast and weep for the child,
while it was alive;
but when the child was dead,
thou didst rise and eat bread.

22 **And he** said,
While the child was yet alive,
I fasted and wept:
for I said,
Who can tell
whether God will be gracious to me
that the child may live?

23 **But now he** is dead,
wherefore should I fast?
can I bring him back again?

I shall go to him,
but he shall not return to me.

24 **And David** comforted Bathsheba his wife,
and went in unto her,
and lay with her:
and she bare a son,
and he called his name Solomon:
and the LORD loved him.

25 **And he** sent by the hand of Nathan the prophet;
and he called his name Jedidiah, because of the LORD.

26 **And Joab** fought against Rabbah of the children of Ammon,
and took the royal city.

27 **And Joab** sent messengers to David,
and said,
I have fought against Rabbah,
and have taken the city of waters.

28 **Now therefore gather** the rest of the people together,
and encamp against the city,
and take it:
lest I take the city,
and it be called after my name.

29 **And David** gathered all the people together,
and went to Rabbah,
and fought against it,
and took it.

30 **And he** took their king's crown from off his head,
the weight whereof was a talent of gold with the precious stones:
and it was set on David's head.

And he brought forth the spoil of the city in great abundance.

31 **And he** brought forth the people that were therein,
and put them under saws, and under harrows of iron, and under axes of iron,
and made them pass through the brick-kiln:
and thus did he unto all the cities of the children of Ammon.

So David and all the people returned unto Jerusalem.

13

And it came to pass after this,
that Absalom the son of David had a fair sister,
whose name was Tamar;
and Amnon the son of David loved her.

2 **And Amnon** was so vexed,
that he fell sick for his sister Tamar;
for she was a virgin;
and Amnon thought it hard for him to do anything to her.

3 **But Amnon** had a friend,
whose name was Jonadab, the son of Shimeah David's brother:
and Jonadab was a very subtil man.

4 **And he** said unto him,
Why art thou, {being the king's son}, lean from day to day?
wilt thou not tell me?

And Amnon said unto him,
I love Tamar, my brother Absalom's sister.

5 **And Jonadab** said unto him,
Lay thee down on thy bed,
and make thyself sick:
and when thy father cometh to see thee,
say unto him,

I pray thee,
let my sister Tamar come,
and give me meat,
and dress the meat in my sight,
that I may see it,
and eat it at her hand.
6 **So Amnon** lay down,
and made himself sick:
and when the king was come to see him,
Amnon said unto the king,
I pray thee,
let Tamar my sister come,
and make me a couple of cakes in my sight,
that I may eat at her hand.
7 **Then David** sent home to Tamar,
saying,
Go now to thy brother Amnon's house,
and dress him meat.
8 **So Tamar** went to her brother Amnon's house;
and he was laid down.
And she took flour,
and kneaded it,
and made cakes in his sight,
and did bake the cakes.
9 **And she** took a pan,
and poured them out before him;
but he refused to eat.
And Amnon said,
Have out all men from me.
And they went out every man from him.
10 **And Amnon** said unto Tamar,
Bring the meat into the chamber,
that I may eat of thine hand.
And Tamar took the cakes which she had made,
and brought them into the chamber to Amnon her brother.
11 **And when she** had brought them unto him to eat,
he took hold of her,
and said unto her,
Come lie with me, my sister.
12 **And she** answered him,
Nay, my brother, do not force me;
for no such thing ought to be done in Israel:
do not thou this folly.
13 **And I,** whither shall I cause my shame to go?
and as for thee, thou shalt be as one of the fools in Israel.
Now therefore, {I pray thee},
speak unto the king;
for he will not withhold me from thee.
14 **Howbeit he** would not hearken unto her voice:
but, {being stronger than she}, forced her,
and lay with her.
15 **Then Amnon** hated her exceedingly;
so that the hatred wherewith he hated her was greater than the love wherewith he had loved her.
And Amnon said unto her,
Arise,
be gone.
16 **And she** said unto him,
There is no cause:
this evil in sending me away is greater than the other that thou didst unto me.
But he would not hearken unto her.
17 **Then he** called his servant that ministered unto him,
and said,
Put now this woman out from me,
and bolt the door after her.
18 **And she** had a garment of divers colours upon her:
for with such robes were the king's daughters that were virgins apparelled.
Then his servant brought her out,
and bolted the door after her.
19 **And Tamar** put ashes on her head,
and rent her garment of divers colours that was on her,
and laid her hand on her head,
and went on crying.
20 **And Absalom her brother** said unto her,
Hath Amnon thy brother been with thee?
but hold now thy peace, my sister:
he is thy brother;
regard not this thing.
So Tamar remained desolate in her brother Absalom's house.
21 **But when king David** heard of all these things,
he was very wroth.
22 **And Absalom** spake unto his brother Amnon neither good nor bad:
for Absalom hated Amnon,
because he had forced his sister Tamar.
23 **And it** came to pass after two full years,
that Absalom had sheepshearers in Baalhazor,
which is beside Ephraim:
and Absalom invited all the king's sons.
24 **And Absalom** came to the king,
and said,
Behold now,
thy servant hath sheepshearers;
let the king, {I beseech thee}, and his servants go with thy servant.
25 **And the king** said to Absalom,
Nay, my son,
let us not all now go,
lest we be chargeable unto thee.
And he pressed him:
howbeit he would not go,
but blessed him.
26 **Then** said Absalom,
If not, {I pray thee}, let my brother Amnon go with us.
And the king said unto him,
Why should he go with thee?
27 **But Absalom** pressed him,
that he let Amnon and all the king's sons go with him.
28 **Now Absalom** had commanded his servants,
saying,
Mark ye now
when Amnon's heart is merry with wine,
and when I say unto you,
Smite Amnon;
then kill him,
fear not:
have not I commanded you?
be courageous,
and be valiant.
29 **And the servants of Absalom** did unto Amnon as Absalom had commanded.
Then all the king's sons arose,
and every man gat him up upon his mule,
and fled.
30 **And it** came to pass,
while they were in the way,
that tidings came to David,
saying,
Absalom hath slain all the king's sons,
and there is not one of them left.
31 **Then the king** arose,
and tare his garments,
and lay on the earth;
and all his servants stood by with their clothes rent.

32 **And Jonadab, the son of Shimeah David's brother,** answered and said,
Let not my lord suppose
that they have slain all the young men the king's sons;
for Amnon only is dead:
for by the appointment of Absalom this hath been determined from the day that he forced his sister Tamar.

33 **Now therefore let not my lord the king** take the thing to his heart,
to think that all the king's sons are dead:
for Amnon only is dead.

34 **But Absalom** fled.

And the young man that kept the watch lifted up his eyes,
and looked,
and, {behold}, there came much people by the way of the hill side behind him.

35 **And Jonadab** said unto the king,
Behold,
the king's sons come:
as thy servant said,
so it is.

36 **And it** came to pass,
as soon as he had made an end of speaking,
that, {behold}, the king's sons came,
and lifted up their voice and wept:
and the king also and all his servants wept very sore.

37 **But Absalom** fled,
and went to Talmai, the son of Ammihud, king of Geshur.

And David mourned for his son every day.

38 **So Absalom** fled,
and went to Geshur,
and was there three years.

39 **And the soul of king David** longed to go forth unto Absalom:
for he was comforted concerning Amnon,
seeing he was dead.

14

Now Joab the son of Zeruiah perceived that the king's heart was toward Absalom.

2 **And Joab** sent to Tekoah,
and fetched thence a wise woman,
and said unto her,
I pray thee,
feign thyself to be a mourner,
and put on now mourning apparel,
and anoint not thyself with oil,
but be as a woman that had a long time mourned for the dead:

3 **And come** to the king,
and speak on this manner unto him.

So Joab put the words in her mouth.

4 **And when the woman of Tekoah** spake to the king,
she fell on her face to the ground,
and did obeisance,
and said,
Help, O king.

5 **And the king** said unto her,
What aileth thee?

And she answered,
I am indeed a widow woman,
and mine husband is dead.

6 **And thy handmaid** had two sons,
and they two strove together in the field,
and there was none to part them,
but the one smote the other,
and slew him.

7 **And, {behold}, the whole family** is risen against thine handmaid,
and they said,
Deliver him that smote his brother,
that we may kill him, for the life of his brother whom he slew;
and we will destroy the heir also:
and so they shall quench my coal which is left,
and shall not leave to my husband neither name nor remainder upon the earth.

8 **And the king** said unto the woman,
Go to thine house,
and I will give charge concerning thee.

9 **And the woman of Tekoah** said unto the king,
My lord, O king, the iniquity be on me, and on my father's house:
and the king and his throne be guiltless.

10 **And the king** said,
Whoever saith ought unto thee,
bring him to me,
and he shall not touch thee any more.

11 **Then** said she,
I pray thee,
let the king remember the LORD thy God,
that thou wouldest not suffer the revengers of blood to destroy any more,
lest they destroy my son.

And he said,
As the LORD liveth,
there shall not one hair of thy son fall to the earth.

12 **Then the woman** said,
Let thine handmaid, {I pray thee}, speak one word unto my lord the king.

And he said,
Say on.

13 **And the woman** said,
Wherefore then hast thou thought such a thing against the people of God?
for the king doth speak this thing as one which is faulty,
in that the king doth not fetch home again his banished.

14 **For we** must needs die,
and are as water spilt on the ground,
which cannot be gathered up again;
neither doth God respect any person:
yet doth he devise means,
that his banished be not expelled from him.

15 **Now therefore that I** am come to speak of this thing unto my lord the king,
it is because the people have made me afraid:
and thy handmaid said,
I will now speak unto the king;
it may be that the king will perform the request of his handmaid.

16 **For the king** will hear,
to deliver his handmaid out of the hand of the man that would destroy me and my son together out of the inheritance of God.

17 **Then thine handmaid** said,
The word of my lord the king shall now be comfortable:
for as an angel of God, so is my lord the king
to discern good and bad:
therefore the LORD thy God will be with thee.

18 **Then the king** answered and said unto the woman,
Hide not from me, {I pray thee}, the thing that I shall ask thee.

And the woman said,

Let my lord the king now speak.
19 **And the king** said,
Is not the hand of Joab with thee in all this?
And the woman answered and said,
As thy soul liveth, my lord the king,
none can turn to the right hand or to the left from ought that my lord the king hath spoken:
for thy servant Joab, he bade me,
and he put all these words in the mouth of thine handmaid:
20 **To fetch about this form of speech** hath thy servant Joab done this thing:
and my lord is wise, according to the wisdom of an angel of God,
to know all things that are in the earth.
21 **And the king** said unto Joab,
Behold now,
I have done this thing:
go therefore,
bring the young man Absalom again.
22 **And Joab** fell to the ground on his face,
and bowed himself,
and thanked the king:
and Joab said,
To day thy servant knoweth
that I have found grace in thy sight, my lord, O king,
in that the king hath fulfilled the request of his servant.
23 **So Joab** arose and went to Geshur,
and brought Absalom to Jerusalem.
24 **And the king** said,
Let him turn to his own house,
and let him not see my face.
So Absalom returned to his own house,
and saw not the king's face.
25 **But in all Israel** there was none to be so much praised as Absalom for his beauty:
from the sole of his foot even to the crown of his head there was no blemish in him.
26 **And when he** polled his head,
(for it was at every year's end that he polled it:
because the hair was heavy on him,
therefore he polled it:)
he weighed the hair of his head at two hundred shekels after the king's weight.
27 **And unto Absalom** there were born three sons, and one daughter,
whose name was Tamar:
she was a woman of a fair countenance.
28 **So Absalom** dwelt two full years in Jerusalem,
and saw not the king's face.
29 **Therefore Absalom** sent for Joab,
to have sent him to the king;
but he would not come to him:
and when he sent again the second time,
he would not come.
30 **Therefore he** said unto his servants,
See,
Joab's field is near mine,
and he hath barley there;
go and set it on fire.
And Absalom's servants set the field on fire.
31 **Then Joab** arose,
and came to Absalom unto his house,
and said unto him,
Wherefore have thy servants set my field on fire?
32 **And Absalom** answered Joab,
Behold,
I sent unto thee,
saying,
Come hither,
that I may send thee to the king,
to say,
Wherefore am I come from Geshur?
it had been good for me to have been there still:
now therefore let me see the king's face;
and if there be any iniquity in me,
let him kill me.
33 **So Joab** came to the king,
and told him:
and when he had called for Absalom,
he came to the king,
and bowed himself on his face to the ground before the king:
and the king kissed Absalom.

15 **And it** came to pass after this,
that Absalom prepared him chariots and horses,
and fifty men to run before him.
2 **And Absalom** rose up early,
and stood beside the way of the gate:
and it was so,
that when any man that had a controversy came to the king for judgment,
then Absalom called unto him,
and said,
Of what city art thou?
And he said,
Thy servant is of one of the tribes of Israel.
3 **And Absalom** said unto him,
See,
thy matters are good and right;
but there is no man deputed of the king to hear thee.
4 **Absalom** said moreover,
Oh that I were made judge in the land,
that every man which hath any suit or cause might come unto me,
and I would do him justice!
5 **And it** was so,
that when any man came nigh to him to do him obeisance,
he put forth his hand,
and took him,
and kissed him.
6 **And on this manner** did Absalom to all Israel that came to the king for judgment:
so Absalom stole the hearts of the men of Israel.
7 **And it** came to pass after forty years,
that Absalom said unto the king,
I pray thee,
let me go and pay my vow, {which I have vowed unto the LORD}, in Hebron.
8 **For thy servant** vowed a vow
while I abode at Geshur in Syria,
saying,
If the LORD shall bring me again indeed to Jerusalem,
then I will serve the LORD.
9 **And the king** said unto him,
Go in peace.
So he arose,
and went to Hebron.
10 **But Absalom** sent spies throughout all the tribes of Israel,
saying,
As soon as ye hear the sound of the trumpet,
then ye shall say,
Absalom reigneth in Hebron.
11 **And with Absalom** went two hundred men out of Jerusalem,

that were called;
and they went in their simplicity,
and they knew not any thing.
12 **And Absalom** sent for Ahithophel the Gilonite, David's counsellor, from his city, even from Giloh,
while he offered sacrifices.
And the conspiracy was strong;
for the people increased continually with Absalom.
13 **And there** came a messenger to David,
saying,
The hearts of the men of Israel are after Absalom.
14 **And David** said unto all his servants that were with him at Jerusalem,
Arise,
and let us flee;
for we shall not else escape from Absalom:
make speed to depart,
lest he overtake us suddenly,
and bring evil upon us,
and smite the city with the edge of the sword.
15 **And the king's servants** said unto the king,
Behold,
thy servants are ready to do whatsoever my lord the king shall appoint.
16 **And the king** went forth, and all his household after him.
And the king left ten women, {which were concubines}, to keep the house.
17 **And the king** went forth, and all the people after him,
and tarried in a place that was far off.
18 **And all his servants** passed on beside him;
and all the Cherethites, and all the Pelethites, and all the Gittites, six hundred men which came after him from Gath, passed on before the king.
19 **Then** said the king to Ittai the Gittite,
Wherefore goest thou also with us?
return to thy place,
and abide with the king:
for thou art a stranger, and also an exile.
20 **Whereas thou** camest but yesterday,
should I this day make thee go up and down with us?
seeing I go whither I may,
return thou,
and take back thy brethren:
mercy and truth be with thee.
21 **And Ittai** answered the king,
and said,
As the LORD liveth,
and as my lord the king liveth,
surely in what place my lord the king shall be, whether in death or life,
even there also will thy servant be.
22 **And David** said to Ittai,
Go and pass over.
And Ittai the Gittite passed over, and all his men, and all the little ones that were with him.
23 **And all the country** wept with a loud voice,
and all the people passed over:
the king also himself passed over the brook Kidron,
and all the people passed over, toward the way of the wilderness.
24 **And {lo} Zadok also, and all the Levites** were with him,
bearing the ark of the covenant of God:
and they set down the ark of God;
and Abiathar went up,
until all the people had done passing out of the city.
25 **And the king** said unto Zadok,
Carry back the ark of God into the city:
if I shall find favour in the eyes of the LORD,
he will bring me again,
and shew me both it, and his habitation:
26 **But if he** thus say,
I have no delight in thee;
behold,
here am I,
let him do to me as seemeth good unto him.
27 **The king** said also unto Zadok the priest,
Art not thou a seer?
return into the city in peace, and your two sons with you, Ahimaaz thy son, and Jonathan the son of Abiathar.
28 **See,**
I will tarry in the plain of the wilderness,
until there come word from you to certify me.
29 **Zadok therefore and Abiathar** carried the ark of God again to Jerusalem:
and they tarried there.
30 **And David** went up by the ascent of mount Olivet,
and wept
as he went up,
and had his head covered,
and he went barefoot:
and all the people that was with him covered every man his head,
and they went up,
weeping
as they went up.
31 **And one** told David,
saying,
Ahithophel is among the conspirators with Absalom.
And David said,
O LORD, {I pray thee}, turn the counsel of Ahithophel into foolishness.
32 **And it** came to pass,
that when David was come to the top of the mount,
where he worshipped God,
behold,
Hushai the Archite came to meet him with his coat rent, and earth upon his head:
33 **Unto whom** David said,
If thou passest on with me,
then thou shalt be a burden unto me:
34 **But if thou** return to the city,
and say unto Absalom,
I will be thy servant, O king;
as I have been thy father's servant hitherto,
so will I now also be thy servant:
then mayest thou for me defeat the counsel of Ahithophel.
35 **And hast thou not** there with thee Zadok and Abiathar the priests?
therefore it shall be,
that what thing soever thou shalt hear out of the king's house,
thou shalt tell it to Zadok and Abiathar the priests.
36 **Behold,**
they have there with them their two sons, Ahimaaz Zadok's son, and Jonathan Abiathar's son;
and by them ye shall send unto me every thing that ye can hear.
37 **So Hushai David's friend** came into the city,
and Absalom came into Jerusalem.

16

And when David was a little past the top of the hill,
behold,
Ziba the servant of Mephibosheth met him, with a couple of asses saddled, and upon them two hundred loaves of bread, and an hundred bunches of raisins, and an hundred of summer fruits, and a bottle of wine.

2 **And the king** said unto Ziba,
What meanest thou by these?

And Ziba said,
The asses be for the king's household to ride on;
and the bread and summer fruit for the young men to eat;
and the wine, that such as be faint in the wilderness may drink.

3 **And the king** said,
And where is thy master's son?

And Ziba said unto the king,
Behold,
he abideth at Jerusalem:
for he said,
To day shall the house of Israel restore me the kingdom of my father.

4 **Then** said the king to Ziba,
Behold,
thine are all that pertained unto Mephibosheth.

And Ziba said,
I humbly beseech thee
that I may find grace in thy sight, my lord, O king.

5 **And when king David** came to Bahurim,
behold,
thence came out a man of the family of the house of Saul,
whose name was Shimei, the son of Gera:
he came forth,
and cursed still as he came.

6 **And he** cast stones at David, and at all the servants of king David:
and all the people and all the mighty men were on his right hand and on his left.

7 **And thus** said Shimei
when he cursed,
Come out,
come out, thou bloody man, and thou man of Belial:
8 **The LORD** hath returned upon thee all the blood of the house of Saul,
in whose stead thou hast reigned;
and the LORD hath delivered the kingdom into the hand of Absalom thy son:
and, {behold}, thou art taken in thy mischief,
because thou art a bloody man.

9 **Then** said Abishai the son of Zeruiah unto the king,
Why should this dead dog curse my lord the king?
let me go over,
I pray thee,
and take off his head.

10 **And the king** said,
What have I to do with you, ye sons of Zeruiah?
so let him curse,
because the LORD hath said unto him,
Curse David.

Who shall then say,
Wherefore hast thou done so?

11 **And David** said to Abishai, and to all his servants,
Behold,
my son, {which came forth of my bowels}, seeketh my life:
how much more now may this Benjamite do it?
let him alone,
and let him curse;
for the LORD hath bidden him.

12 **It may be that the LORD** will look on mine affliction,
and that the LORD will requite me good for his cursing this day.

13 **And as David and his men** went by the way,
Shimei went along on the hill's side over against him,
and cursed as he went,
and threw stones at him,
and cast dust.

14 **And the king, and all the people that were with him,** came weary,
and refreshed themselves there.

15 **And Absalom, and all the people the men of Israel,** came to Jerusalem, and Ahithophel with him.

16 **And it** came to pass,
when Hushai the Archite, David's friend, was come unto Absalom,
that Hushai said unto Absalom,
God save the king,
God save the king.

17 **And Absalom** said to Hushai,
Is this thy kindness to thy friend?
why wentest thou not with thy friend?

18 **And Hushai** said unto Absalom,
Nay;
but whom the LORD, and this people, and all the men of Israel, choose,
his will I be,
and with him will I abide.

19 **And again, whom** should I serve?
should I not serve in the presence of his son?
as I have served in thy father's presence,
so will I be in thy presence.

20 **Then** said Absalom to Ahithophel,
Give counsel among you
what we shall do.

21 **And Ahithophel** said unto Absalom,
Go in unto thy father's concubines,
which he hath left to keep the house;
and all Israel shall hear that thou art abhorred of thy father:
then shall the hands of all that are with thee be strong.

22 **So they** spread Absalom a tent upon the top of the house;
and Absalom went in unto his father's concubines in the sight of all Israel.

23 **And the counsel of Ahithophel,** {which he counselled in those days}, was as if a man had enquired at the oracle of God:
so was all the counsel of Ahithophel both with David and with Absalom.

17

Moreover Ahithophel said unto Absalom,
Let me now choose out twelve thousand men,
and I will arise and pursue after David this night:
2 **And I** will come upon him
while he is weary and weak handed,
and will make him afraid:
and all the people that are with him shall flee;
and I will smite the king only:
3 **And I** will bring back all the people unto thee:
the man whom thou seekest is as if all returned:
so all the people shall be in peace.

4 **And the saying** pleased Absalom
well, and all the elders of Israel.
5 **Then** said Absalom,
Call now Hushai the Archite also,
and let us hear likewise what he
saith.
6 **And when Hushai** was come to
Absalom,
Absalom spake unto him,
saying,
Ahithophel hath spoken after this
manner:
shall we do after his saying?
if not; speak thou.
7 **And Hushai** said unto Absalom,
**The counsel that Ahithophel hath
given** is not good at this time.
8 **For, {said Hushai}, thou** knowest
thy father and his men,
that they be mighty men,
and they be chafed in their minds,
as a bear robbed of her whelps in
the field:
and thy father is a man of war,
and will not lodge with the people.
9 **Behold,**
he is hid now in some pit, or in
some other place:
and it will come to pass,
when some of them be overthrown
at the first,
that whosoever heareth it will say,
There is a slaughter among the
people that follow Absalom.
10 **And he also that is valiant,**
{whose heart is as the heart of a
lion}, shall utterly melt:
for all Israel knoweth
that thy father is a mighty man,
and they which be with him are
valiant men.
11 **Therefore I** counsel
that all Israel be generally gathered
unto thee, from Dan even to
Beersheba, as the sand that is by
the sea for multitude;
and that thou go to battle in thine
own person.
12 **So** shall we come upon him in
some place where he shall be
found,
and we will light upon him as the
dew falleth on the ground:
**and of him and of all the men that
are with him** there shall not be
left so much as one.
13 **Moreover, if he** be gotten into a
city,
then shall all Israel bring ropes to
that city,
and we will draw it into the river,
until there be not one small stone
found there.
14 **And Absalom and all the men of
Israel** said,
The counsel of Hushai the Archite
is better than the counsel of
Ahithophel.
For the LORD had appointed to
defeat the good counsel of
Ahithophel,
to the intent that the LORD might
bring evil upon Absalom.
15 **Then** said Hushai unto Zadok and
to Abiathar the priests,
Thus and thus did Ahithophel
counsel Absalom and the elders of
Israel;
and thus and thus have I
counselled.
16 **Now therefore send** quickly,
and tell David,
saying,
Lodge not this night in the plains of
the wilderness,
but speedily pass over;
lest the king be swallowed up, and
all the people that are with him.
17 **Now Jonathan and Ahimaaz**
stayed by Enrogel;
for they might not be seen to come
into the city:
and a wench went and told them;
and they went and told king David.
18 **Nevertheless a lad** saw them,
and told Absalom:
but they went both of them away
quickly,
and came to a man's house in
Bahurim,
which had a well in his court;
whither they went down.
19 **And the woman** took and spread
a covering over the well's mouth,
and spread ground corn thereon;
and the thing was not known.
20 **And when Absalom's servants**
came to the woman to the house,
they said,
Where is Ahimaaz and Jonathan?
And the woman said unto them,
They be gone over the brook of
water.
And when they had sought and
could not find them,
they returned to Jerusalem.
21 **And it** came to pass,
after they were departed,
that they came up out of the well,
and went and told king David,
and said unto David,
Arise,
and pass quickly over the water:
for thus hath Ahithophel
counselled against you.
22 **Then David** arose, and all the
people that were with him,
and they passed over Jordan:
by the morning light there lacked
not one of them that was not
gone over Jordan.
23 **And when Ahithophel** saw that
his counsel was not followed,
he saddled his ass,
and arose,
and gat him home to his house, to
his city,
and put his household in order,
and hanged himself,
and died,
and was buried in the sepulchre of
his father.
24 **Then David** came to Mahanaim.
And Absalom passed over Jordan,
he and all the men of Israel with
him.
25 **And Absalom** made Amasa
captain of the host instead of
Joab:
which Amasa was a man's son,
whose name was Ithra an Israelite,
that went in to Abigail the daughter
of Nahash, sister to Zeruiah Joab's
mother.
26 **So Israel and Absalom** pitched in
the land of Gilead.
27 **And it** came to pass,
when David was come to
Mahanaim,
**that Shobi the son of Nahash of
Rabbah of the children of
Ammon, and Machir the son of
Ammiel of Lodebar, and
Barzillai the Gileadite of
Rogelim,**
28 Brought beds, and basons, and
earthen vessels, and wheat, and
barley, and flour, and parched
corn, and beans, and lentiles, and
parched pulse,
29 And honey, and butter, and sheep,
and cheese of kine, for David, and
for the people that were with him,
to eat:
for they said,
The people is hungry, and weary,
and thirsty, in the wilderness.

18 **And David** numbered the people that were with him,
and set captains of thousands, and captains of hundreds over them.

2 **And David** sent forth a third part of the people under the hand of Joab, and a third part under the hand of Abishai the son of Zeruiah, Joab's brother, and a third part under the hand of Ittai the Gittite.

And the king said unto the people,
I will surely go forth with you myself also.

3 **But the people** answered,
Thou shalt not go forth:
for if we flee away,
they will not care for us;
neither if half of us die,
will they care for us:
but now thou art worth ten thousand of us:
therefore now it is better that thou succour us out of the city.

4 **And the king** said unto them,
What seemeth you best I will do.

And the king stood by the gate side,
and all the people came out by hundreds and by thousands.

5 **And the king** commanded Joab and Abishai and Ittai,
saying,
Deal gently for my sake with the young man, even with Absalom.

And all the people heard when the king gave all the captains charge concerning Absalom.

6 **So the people** went out into the field against Israel:
and the battle was in the wood of Ephraim;

7 **Where the people of Israel** were slain before the servants of David,
and there was there a great slaughter that day of twenty thousand men.

8 **For the battle** was there scattered over the face of all the country:
and the wood devoured more people that day than the sword devoured.

9 **And Absalom** met the servants of David.

And Absalom rode upon a mule,
and the mule went under the thick boughs of a great oak,
and his head caught hold of the oak,
and he was taken up between the heaven and the earth;
and the mule that was under him went away.

10 **And a certain man** saw it,
and told Joab,
and said,
Behold,
I saw Absalom hanged in an oak.

11 **And Joab** said unto the man that told him,
And, {behold}, thou sawest him,
and why didst thou not smite him there to the ground?
and I would have given thee ten shekels of silver, and a girdle.

12 **And the man** said unto Joab,
Though I should receive a thousand shekels of silver in mine hand,
yet would I not put forth mine hand against the king's son:
for in our hearing the king charged thee and Abishai and Ittai,
saying,
Beware
that none touch the young man Absalom.

13 **Otherwise I** should have wrought falsehood against mine own life:
for there is no matter hid from the king,
and thou thyself wouldest have set thyself against me.

14 **Then** said Joab,
I may not tarry thus with thee.

And he took three darts in his hand,
and thrust them through the heart of Absalom,
while he was yet alive in the midst of the oak.

15 **And ten young men that bare Joab's armour** compassed about and smote Absalom,
and slew him.

16 **And Joab** blew the trumpet,
and the people returned from pursuing after Israel:
for Joab held back the people.

17 **And they** took Absalom,
and cast him into a great pit in the wood,
and laid a very great heap of stones upon him:
and all Israel fled every one to his tent.

18 **Now Absalom in his lifetime** had taken and reared up for himself a pillar,
which is in the king's dale:
for he said,
I have no son to keep my name in remembrance:
and he called the pillar after his own name:
and it is called unto this day,
Absalom's place.

19 **Then** said Ahimaaz the son of Zadok,
Let me now run,
and bear the king tidings,
how that the LORD hath avenged him of his enemies.

20 **And Joab** said unto him,
Thou shalt not bear tidings this day,
but thou shalt bear tidings another day:
but this day thou shalt bear no tidings,
because the king's son is dead.

21 **Then** said Joab to Cushi,
Go tell the king
what thou hast seen.

And Cushi bowed himself unto Joab,
and ran.

22 **Then** said Ahimaaz the son of Zadok yet again to Joab,
But howsoever, let me, {I pray thee}, also run after Cushi.

And Joab said,
Wherefore wilt thou run, my son,
seeing that thou hast no tidings ready?

23 **But howsoever, {said he}, let me** run.

And he said unto him,
Run.

Then Ahimaaz ran by the way of the plain,
and overran Cushi.

24 **And David** sat between the two gates:
and the watchman went up to the roof over the gate unto the wall,
and lifted up his eyes,
and looked,
and {behold} a man running alone.

25 **And the watchman** cried,
and told the king.

And the king said,
If he be alone,
there is tidings in his mouth.

And he came apace,
and drew near.

26 **And the watchman** saw another man running:

and the watchman called unto the porter,
and said,
Behold
another man running alone.
And the king said,
He also bringeth tidings.
27 **And the watchman** said,
Me thinketh
the running of the foremost is like the running of Ahimaaz the son of Zadok.
And the king said,
He is a good man,
and cometh with good tidings.
28 **And Ahimaaz** called,
and said unto the king,
All is well.
And he fell down to the earth upon his face before the king,
and said,
Blessed be the LORD thy God,
which hath delivered up the men that lifted up their hand against my lord the king.
29 **And the king** said,
Is the young man Absalom safe?
And Ahimaaz answered,
When Joab sent the king's servant, and me thy servant,
I saw a great tumult,
but I knew not
what it was.
30 **And the king** said unto him,
Turn aside,
and stand here.
And he turned aside,
and stood still.
31 **And, {behold}, Cushi** came;
and Cushi said,
Tidings, my lord the king:
for the LORD hath avenged thee this day of all them that rose up against thee.
32 **And the king** said unto Cushi,
Is the young man Absalom safe?
And Cushi answered,
The enemies of my lord the king, and all that rise against thee to do thee hurt, be as that young man is.
33 **And the king** was much moved,
and went up to the chamber over the gate,
and wept:
and as he went,
thus he said,
O my son Absalom, my son, my son Absalom!
would God I had died for thee, O Absalom, my son, my son!

19 **And it** was told Joab,
Behold,
the king weepeth and mourneth for Absalom.
2 **And the victory that day** was turned into mourning unto all the people:
for the people heard say that day
how the king was grieved for his son.
3 **And the people** gat them by stealth that day into the city,
as people being ashamed steal away when they flee in battle.
4 **But the king** covered his face,
and the king cried with a loud voice,
O my son Absalom, O Absalom, my son, my son!
5 **And Joab** came into the house to the king,
and said,
Thou hast shamed this day the faces of all thy servants,
which this day have saved thy life, and the lives of thy sons and of thy daughters, and the lives of thy wives, and the lives of thy concubines;
6 **In that thou** lovest thine enemies,
and hatest thy friends.
For thou hast declared this day,
that thou regardest neither princes nor servants:
for this day I perceive,
that if Absalom had lived,
and all we had died this day,
then it had pleased thee well.
7 **Now therefore arise,**
go forth,
and speak comfortably unto thy servants:
for I swear by the LORD,
if thou go not forth,
there will not tarry one with thee this night:
and that will be worse unto thee than all the evil that befell thee from thy youth until now.
8 **Then the king** arose,
and sat in the gate.
And they told unto all the people,
saying,
Behold,
the king doth sit in the gate.
And all the people came before the king:
for Israel had fled every man to his tent.
9 **And all the people** were at strife throughout all the tribes of Israel,
saying,
The king saved us out of the hand of our enemies,
and he delivered us out of the hand of the Philistines;
and now he is fled out of the land for Absalom.
10 **And Absalom**, {whom we anointed over us}, is dead in battle.
Now therefore why speak ye not a word of bringing the king back?
11 **And king David** sent to Zadok and to Abiathar the priests,
saying,
Speak unto the elders of Judah,
saying,
Why are ye the last to bring the king back to his house?
seeing the speech of all Israel is come to the king, even to his house.
12 **Ye are** my brethren,
ye are my bones and my flesh:
wherefore then are ye the last to bring back the king?
13 **And say ye** to Amasa,
Art thou not of my bone, and of my flesh?
God do so to me, and more also,
if thou be not captain of the host before me continually in the room of Joab.
14 **And he** bowed the heart of all the men of Judah, even as the heart of one man;
so that they sent this word unto the king,
Return thou, and all thy servants.
15 **So the king** returned,
and came to Jordan.
And Judah came to Gilgal,
to go to meet the king,
to conduct the king over Jordan.
16 **And Shimei the son of Gera, a Benjamite**, {which was of Bahurim}, hasted and came down with the men of Judah
to meet king David.
17 **And there** were a thousand men of Benjamin with him, and Ziba the servant of the house of Saul, and his fifteen sons and his twenty servants with him;

and they went over Jordan before the king.
18 **And there** went over a ferry boat to carry over the king's household,
and to do what he thought good.
And Shimei the son of Gera fell down before the king,
as he was come over Jordan;
19 **And** said unto the king,
Let not my lord impute iniquity unto me,
neither do thou remember that which thy servant did perversely the day that my lord the king went out of Jerusalem,
that the king should take it to his heart.
20 **For thy servant** doth know
that I have sinned:
therefore, {behold}, I am come the first this day of all the house of Joseph
to go down to meet my lord the king.
21 **But Abishai the son of Zeruiah** answered and said,
Shall not Shimei be put to death for this,
because he cursed the LORD's anointed?
22 **And David** said,
What have I to do with you, ye sons of Zeruiah,
that ye should this day be adversaries unto me?
shall there any man be put to death this day in Israel?
for do not I know
that I am this day king over Israel?
23 **Therefore the king** said unto Shimei,
Thou shalt not die.
And the king sware unto him.
24 **And Mephibosheth the son of Saul** came down to meet the king,
and had neither dressed his feet,
nor trimmed his beard,
nor washed his clothes, from the day the king departed until the day he came again in peace.
25 **And it** came to pass,
when he was come to Jerusalem to meet the king,
that the king said unto him,
Wherefore wentest not thou with me, Mephibosheth?
26 **And he** answered,
My lord, O king, my servant deceived me:
for thy servant said,
I will saddle me an ass,
that I may ride thereon,
and go to the king;
because thy servant is lame.
27 **And he** hath slandered thy servant unto my lord the king;
but my lord the king is as an angel of God:
do therefore what is good in thine eyes.
28 **For all of my father's house** were but dead men before my lord the king:
yet didst thou set thy servant among them that did eat at thine own table.
What right therefore have I
yet to cry any more unto the king?
29 **And the king** said unto him,
Why speakest thou any more of thy matters?
I have said,
Thou and Ziba divide the land.
30 **And Mephibosheth** said unto the king,
Yea, let him take all,
forasmuch as my lord the king is come again in peace unto his own house.
31 **And Barzillai the Gileadite** came down from Rogelim,
and went over Jordan with the king,
to conduct him over Jordan.
32 **Now Barzillai** was a very aged man, even fourscore years old:
and he had provided the king of sustenance
while he lay at Mahanaim;
for he was a very great man.
33 **And the king** said unto Barzillai,
Come thou over with me,
and I will feed thee with me in Jerusalem.
34 **And Barzillai** said unto the king,
How long have I to live,
that I should go up with the king unto Jerusalem?
35 **I** am this day fourscore years old:
and can I discern between good and evil?
can thy servant taste what I eat or what I drink?
can I hear any more the voice of singing men and singing women?
wherefore then should thy servant be yet a burden unto my lord the king?
36 **Thy servant** will go a little way over Jordan with the king:
and why should the king recompense it me with such a reward?
37 **Let thy servant**, {I pray thee}, turn back again,
that I may die in mine own city,
and be buried by the grave of my father and of my mother.
But behold thy servant Chimham;
let him go over with my lord the king;
and do to him what shall seem good unto thee.
38 **And the king** answered,
Chimham shall go over with me,
and I will do to him that which shall seem good unto thee:
and whatsoever thou shalt require of me,
that will I do for thee.
39 **And all the people** went over Jordan.
And when the king was come over,
the king kissed Barzillai,
and blessed him;
and he returned unto his own place.
40 **Then the king** went on to Gilgal,
and Chimham went on with him:
and all the people of Judah conducted the king, and also half the people of Israel.
41 **And, {behold}, all the men of Israel** came to the king,
and said unto the king,
Why have our brethren the men of Judah stolen thee away,
and have brought the king, and his household, and all David's men with him, over Jordan?
42 **And all the men of Judah** answered the men of Israel,
Because the king is near of kin to us:
wherefore then be ye angry for this matter?
have we eaten at all of the king's cost?
or hath he given us any gift?
43 **And the men of Israel** answered the men of Judah,
and said,
We have ten parts in the king,

and we have also more right in David than ye:
why then did ye despise us,
that our advice should not be first had in bringing back our king?

And the words of the men of Judah were fiercer than the words of the men of Israel.

20 **And there** happened to be there a man of Belial,
whose name was Sheba, the son of Bichri, a Benjamite:
and he blew a trumpet,
and said,
We have no part in David,
neither have we inheritance in the son of Jesse:
every man to his tents, O Israel.

2 **So every man of Israel** went up from after David,
and followed Sheba the son of Bichri:
but the men of Judah clave unto their king, from Jordan even to Jerusalem.

3 **And David** came to his house at Jerusalem;
and the king took the ten women his concubines,
whom he had left to keep the house,
and put them in ward,
and fed them,
but went not in unto them.

So they were shut up unto the day of their death,
living in widowhood.

4 **Then** said the king to Amasa,
Assemble me the men of Judah within three days,
and be thou here present.

5 **So Amasa** went to assemble the men of Judah:
but he tarried longer than the set time which he had appointed him.

6 **And David** said to Abishai,
Now shall Sheba the son of Bichri do us more harm than did Absalom:
take thou thy lord's servants,
and pursue after him,
lest he get him fenced cities,
and escape us.

7 **And there** went out after him Joab's men, and the Cherethites, and the Pelethites, and all the mighty men:
and they went out of Jerusalem,
to pursue after Sheba the son of Bichri.

8 **When they** were at the great stone which is in Gibeon,
Amasa went before them.

And Joab's garment that he had put on was girded unto him, and upon it a girdle with a sword fastened upon his loins in the sheath thereof;
and as he went forth **it** fell out.

9 **And Joab** said to Amasa,
Art thou in health, my brother?

And Joab took Amasa by the beard with the right hand to kiss him.

10 **But Amasa** took no heed to the sword that was in Joab's hand:
so he smote him therewith in the fifth rib,
and shed out his bowels to the ground,
and struck him not again;
and he died.

So Joab and Abishai his brother pursued after Sheba the son of Bichri.

11 **And one of Joab's men** stood by him,
and said,
He that favoureth Joab, and he that is for David, let him go after Joab.

12 **And Amasa** wallowed in blood in the midst of the highway.

And when the man saw that all the people stood still,
he removed Amasa out of the highway into the field,
and cast a cloth upon him,
when he saw that every one that came by him stood still.

13 **When he** was removed out of the highway,
all the people went on after Joab,
to pursue after Sheba the son of Bichri.

14 **And he** went through all the tribes of Israel unto Abel, and to Bethmaachah, and all the Berites:
and they were gathered together,
and went also after him.

15 **And they** came and besieged him in Abel of Bethmaachah,
and they cast up a bank against the city,
and it stood in the trench:
and all the people that were with Joab battered the wall,
to throw it down.

16 **Then** cried a wise woman out of the city,
Hear,
hear;
say, {I pray you}, unto Joab,
Come near hither,
that I may speak with thee.

17 **And when he** was come near unto her,
the woman said,
Art thou Joab?

And he answered,
I am he.

Then she said unto him,
Hear the words of thine handmaid.

And he answered,
I do hear.

18 **Then she** spake,
saying,
They were wont to speak in old time,
saying,
They shall surely ask counsel at Abel:
and so they ended the matter.

19 **I** am one of them that are peaceable and faithful in Israel:
thou seekest to destroy a city and a mother in Israel:
why wilt thou swallow up the inheritance of the LORD?

20 **And Joab** answered and said,
Far be it,
far be it from me,
that I should swallow up or destroy.

21 **The matter** is not so:
but a man of mount Ephraim, Sheba the son of Bichri by name, hath lifted up his hand against the king, even against David:
deliver him only,
and I will depart from the city.

And the woman said unto Joab,
Behold,
his head shall be thrown to thee over the wall.

22 **Then the woman** went unto all the people in her wisdom.

And they cut off the head of Sheba the son of Bichri,
and cast it out to Joab.

And he blew a trumpet,
and they retired from the city, every man to his tent.

And Joab returned to Jerusalem unto the king.

23 **Now Joab** was over all the host of Israel:
and Benaiah the son of Jehoiada was over the Cherethites and over the Pelethites:
24 **And Adoram** was over the tribute:
and Jehoshaphat the son of Ahilud was recorder:
25 **And Sheva** was scribe:
and Zadok and Abiathar were the priests:
26 **And Ira also the Jairite** was a chief ruler about David.

21 **Then there** was a famine in the days of David three years, year after year;
and David enquired of the LORD.
And the LORD answered,
It is for Saul, and for his bloody house,
because he slew the Gibeonites.
2 **And the king** called the Gibeonites,
and said unto them;
(now the Gibeonites were not of the children of Israel, but of the remnant of the Amorites;
and the children of Israel had sworn unto them:
and Saul sought to slay them in his zeal to the children of Israel and Judah.)
3 **Wherefore David** said unto the Gibeonites,
What shall I do for you?
and wherewith shall I make the atonement,
that ye may bless the inheritance of the LORD?
4 **And the Gibeonites** said unto him,
We will have no silver nor gold of Saul, nor of his house;
neither for us shalt thou kill any man in Israel.
And he said,
What ye shall say,
that will I do for you.
5 **And they** answered the king,
The man that consumed us, and that devised against us that we should be destroyed from remaining in any of the coasts of Israel,
6 Let seven men of his sons be delivered unto us,
and we will hang them up unto the LORD in Gibeah of Saul,
whom the LORD did choose.
And the king said,
I will give them.
7 **But the king** spared Mephibosheth, the son of Jonathan the son of Saul, because of the LORD's oath that was between them, between David and Jonathan the son of Saul.
8 **But the king** took the two sons of Rizpah the daughter of Aiah, {whom she bare unto Saul, Armoni and Mephibosheth}; and the five sons of Michal the daughter of Saul, {whom she brought up for Adriel the son of Barzillai the Meholathite}:
9 **And he** delivered them into the hands of the Gibeonites,
and they hanged them in the hill before the LORD:
and they fell all seven together,
and were put to death in the days of harvest, in the first days, in the beginning of barley harvest.
10 **And Rizpah the daughter of Aiah** took sackcloth,
and spread it for her upon the rock, from the beginning of harvest until water dropped upon them out of heaven,
and suffered neither the birds of the air to rest on them by day, nor the beasts of the field by night.
11 **And it** was told David
what Rizpah the daughter of Aiah, the concubine of Saul, had done.
12 **And David** went and took the bones of Saul and the bones of Jonathan his son from the men of Jabeshgilead,
which had stolen them from the street of Bethshan,
where the Philistines had hanged them,
when the Philistines had slain Saul in Gilboa:
13 **And he** brought up from thence the bones of Saul and the bones of Jonathan his son;
and they gathered the bones of them that were hanged.
14 **And the bones of Saul and Jonathan his son** buried they in the country of Benjamin in Zelah, in the sepulchre of Kish his father:
and they performed all that the king commanded.
And after that God was intreated for the land.
15 **Moreover the Philistines** had yet war again with Israel;
and David went down, and his servants with him,
and fought against the Philistines:
and David waxed faint.
16 **And Ishbibenob**, {which was of the sons of the giant}, the weight of whose spear weighed three hundred shekels of brass in weight, {he being girded with a new sword},
thought to have slain David.
17 **But Abishai the son of Zeruiah** succoured him,
and smote the Philistine,
and killed him.
Then the men of David sware unto him,
saying,
Thou shalt go no more out with us to battle,
that thou quench not the light of Israel.
18 **And it** came to pass after this,
that there was again a battle with the Philistines at Gob:
then Sibbechai the Hushathite slew Saph,
which was of the sons of the giant.
19 **And there** was again a battle in Gob with the Philistines,
where Elhanan the son of Jaareoregim, a Bethlehemite, slew the brother of Goliath the Gittite, the staff of whose spear was like a weaver's beam.
20 **And there** was yet a battle in Gath,
where was a man of great stature,
that had on every hand six fingers, and on every foot six toes, four and twenty in number;
and he also was born to the giant.
21 **And when he** defied Israel,
Jonathan the son of Shimeah the brother of David slew him.
22 **These four** were born to the giant in Gath,
and fell by the hand of David, and by the hand of his servants.

22 **And David** spake unto the LORD the words of this song in the day that the LORD had delivered him out of the hand of all his enemies, and out of the hand of Saul:
2 **And he** said,

The LORD is my rock, and my fortress, and my deliverer;

3 The God of my rock;
in him will I trust:
he is my shield, and the horn of my salvation, my high tower, and my refuge, my saviour;
thou savest me from violence.

4 **I** will call on the LORD,
who is worthy to be praised:
so shall I be saved from mine enemies.

5 **When the waves of death** compassed me,
the floods of ungodly men made me afraid;

6 **The sorrows of hell** compassed me about;
the snares of death prevented me;

7 **In my distress** I called upon the LORD,
and cried to my God:
and he did hear my voice out of his temple,
and my cry did enter into his ears.

8 **Then the earth** shook and trembled;
the foundations of heaven moved and shook,
because he was wroth.

9 **There** went up a smoke out of his nostrils,
and fire out of his mouth devoured:
coals were kindled by it.

10 **He** bowed the heavens also,
and came down;
and darkness was under his feet.

11 **And he** rode upon a cherub,
and did fly:
and he was seen upon the wings of the wind.

12 **And he** made darkness pavilions round about him, dark waters, and thick clouds of the skies.

13 **Through the brightness before him** were coals of fire kindled.

14 **The LORD** thundered from heaven,
and the most High uttered his voice.

15 **And he** sent out arrows, {and scattered them}; lightning, {and discomfited them}.

16 **And the channels of the sea** appeared,
the foundations of the world were discovered, at the rebuking of the LORD, at the blast of the breath of his nostrils.

17 **He** sent from above,
he took me;
he drew me out of many waters;

18 **He** delivered me from my strong enemy, and from them that hated me:
for they were too strong for me.

19 **They** prevented me in the day of my calamity:
but the LORD was my stay.

20 **He** brought me forth also into a large place:
he delivered me,
because he delighted in me.

21 **The LORD** rewarded me according to my righteousness:
according to the cleanness of my hands hath he recompensed me.

22 **For I** have kept the ways of the LORD,
and have not wickedly departed from my God.

23 **For all his judgments** were before me:
and as for his statutes, I did not depart from them.

24 **I** was also upright before him,
and have kept myself from mine iniquity.

25 **Therefore the LORD** hath recompensed me according to my righteousness; according to my cleanness in his eye sight.

26 **With the merciful** thou wilt shew thyself merciful,
and with the upright man thou wilt shew thyself upright.

27 **With the pure** thou wilt shew thyself pure;
and with the froward thou wilt shew thyself unsavoury.

28 **And the afflicted people** thou wilt save:
but thine eyes are upon the haughty,
that thou mayest bring them down.

29 **For thou** art my lamp, O LORD:
and the LORD will lighten my darkness.

30 **For by thee** I have run through a troop:
by my God have I leaped over a wall.

31 **As for God,** his way is perfect;
the word of the LORD is tried:
he is a buckler to all them that trust in him.

32 **For who** is God, save the LORD?
and who is a rock, save our God?

33 **God** is my strength and power:
and he maketh my way perfect.

34 **He** maketh my feet like hinds' feet:
and setteth me upon my high places.

35 **He** teacheth my hands to war;
so that a bow of steel is broken by mine arms.

36 **Thou** hast also given me the shield of thy salvation:
and thy gentleness hath made me great.

37 **Thou** hast enlarged my steps under me;
so that my feet did not slip.

38 **I** have pursued mine enemies,
and destroyed them;
and turned not again
until I had consumed them.

39 **And I** have consumed them,
and wounded them,
that they could not arise: yea,
they are fallen under my feet.

40 **For thou** hast girded me with strength to battle:
them that rose up against me hast thou subdued under me.

41 **Thou** hast also given me the necks of mine enemies,
that I might destroy them that hate me.

42 **They** looked, {but there was none to save}; even unto the LORD, {but he answered them not}.

43 **Then** did I beat them as small as the dust of the earth,
I did stamp them as the mire of the street,
and did spread them abroad.

44 **Thou** also hast delivered me from the strivings of my people,
thou hast kept me to be head of the heathen:
a people which I knew not shall serve me.

45 **Strangers** shall submit themselves unto me:
as soon as they hear,
they shall be obedient unto me.

46 **Strangers** shall fade away,
and they shall be afraid out of their close places.

47 **The LORD** liveth;

and blessed be my rock;
and exalted be the God of the rock of my salvation.

48 **It is God** that avengeth me, and that bringeth down the people under me.

49 And that bringeth me forth from mine enemies:
thou also hast lifted me up on high above them that rose up against me:
thou hast delivered me from the violent man.

50 **Therefore I** will give thanks unto thee, O LORD, among the heathen,
and I will sing praises unto thy name.

51 **He** is the tower of salvation for his king:
and sheweth mercy to his anointed, unto David, and to his seed for evermore.

23

Now these be the last words of David.
David the son of Jesse said,
and the man who was raised up on high, the anointed of the God of Jacob, and the sweet psalmist of Israel, said,
2 **The Spirit of the LORD** spake by me,
and his word was in my tongue.
3 **The God of Israel** said,
the Rock of Israel spake to me,
He that ruleth over men must be just,
ruling in the fear of God.
4 **And he** shall be as the light of the morning,
when the sun riseth, even a morning without clouds; as the tender grass springing out of the earth by clear shining after rain.
5 **Although my house** be not so with God;
yet he hath made with me an everlasting covenant,
ordered in all things,
and sure:
for this is all my salvation, and all my desire,
although he make it not to grow.
6 **But the sons of Belial** shall be all of them as thorns thrust away,
because they cannot be taken with hands:
7 **But the man that shall touch them** must be fenced with iron and the staff of a spear;
and they shall be utterly burned with fire in the same place.

8 **These** be the names of the mighty men whom David had:
The Tachmonite that sat in the seat, chief among the captains; the same was Adino the Eznite:
he lift up his spear against eight hundred,
whom he slew at one time.

9 **And after him** was Eleazar the son of Dodo the Ahohite, one of the three mighty men with David,
when they defied the Philistines that were there gathered together to battle,
and the men of Israel were gone away:
10 **He** arose,
and smote the Philistines
until his hand was weary,
and his hand clave unto the sword:
and the LORD wrought a great victory that day;
and the people returned after him only to spoil.

11 **And after him** was Shammah the son of Agee the Hararite.
And the Philistines were gathered together into a troop,
where was a piece of ground full of lentiles:
and the people fled from the Philistines.
12 **But he** stood in the midst of the ground,
and defended it,
and slew the Philistines:
and the LORD wrought a great victory.

13 **And three of the thirty chief** went down,
and came to David in the harvest time unto the cave of Adullam:
and the troop of the Philistines pitched in the valley of Rephaim.
14 **And David** was then in an hold,
and the garrison of the Philistines was then in Bethlehem.
15 **And David** longed,
and said,
Oh that one would give me drink of the water of the well of Bethlehem,
which is by the gate!
16 **And the three mighty men** brake through the host of the Philistines,
and drew water out of the well of Bethlehem,
that was by the gate,
and took it,
and brought it to David:
nevertheless he would not drink thereof,
but poured it out unto the LORD.
17 **And he** said,
Be it far from me, O LORD,
that I should do this:
is not this the blood of the men that went in jeopardy of their lives?
therefore he would not drink it.
These things did these three mighty men.

18 **And Abishai, the brother of Joab, the son of Zeruiah,** was chief among three.
And he lifted up his spear against three hundred,
and slew them,
and had the name among three.
19 **Was he not** most honourable of three?
therefore he was their captain:
howbeit he attained not unto the first three.

20 **And Benaiah the son of Jehoiada, the son of a valiant man, of Kabzeel**, {who had done many acts}, he slew two lionlike men of Moab:
he went down also and slew a lion in the midst of a pit in time of snow:
21 **And he** slew an Egyptian, a goodly man:
and the Egyptian had a spear in his hand;
but he went down to him with a staff,
and plucked the spear out of the Egyptian's hand,
and slew him with his own spear.
22 **These things** did Benaiah the son of Jehoiada,
and had the name among three mighty men.
23 **He** was more honourable than the thirty,
but he attained not to the first three.
And David set him over his guard.

24 **Asahel the brother of Joab** was one of the thirty; Elhanan the son of Dodo of Bethlehem,

25 Shammah the Harodite, Elika the Harodite,
26 Helez the Paltite, Ira the son of Ikkesh the Tekoite,
27 Abiezer the Anethothite, Mebunnai the Hushathite,
28 Zalmon the Ahohite, Maharai the Netophathite,
29 Heleb the son of Baanah, a Netophathite, Ittai the son of Ribai out of Gibeah of the children of Benjamin,
30 Benaiah the Pirathonite, Hiddai of the brooks of Gaash,
31 Abialbon the Arbathite, Azmaveth the Barhumite,
32 Eliahba the Shaalbonite, of the sons of Jashen, Jonathan,
33 Shammah the Hararite, Ahiam the son of Sharar the Hararite,
34 Eliphelet the son of Ahasbai, the son of the Maachathite, Eliam the son of Ahithophel the Gilonite,
35 Hezrai the Carmelite, Paarai the Arbite,
36 Igal the son of Nathan of Zobah, Bani the Gadite,
37 Zelek the Ammonite, Nahari the Beerothite, armourbearer to Joab the son of Zeruiah,
38 Ira an Ithrite, Gareb an Ithrite,
39 Uriah the Hittite: thirty and seven in all.

24

And again the anger of the LORD was kindled against Israel,
and he moved David against them to say,
Go,
number Israel and Judah.
2 **For the king** said to Joab the captain of the host,
which was with him,
Go now through all the tribes of Israel, from Dan even to Beersheba,
and number ye the people,
that I may know the number of the people.
3 **And Joab** said unto the king,
Now the LORD thy God add unto the people,
how many soever they be, an hundredfold,
and that the eyes of my lord the king may see it:
but why doth my lord the king delight in this thing?
4 **Notwithstanding the king's word** prevailed against Joab, and against the captains of the host.
And Joab and the captains of the host went out from the presence of the king,
to number the people of Israel.
5 **And they** passed over Jordan,
and pitched in Aroer, on the right side of the city that lieth in the midst of the river of Gad, and toward Jazer:
6 **Then they** came to Gilead, and to the land of Tahtimhodshi;
and they came to Danjaan, and about to Zidon,
7 **And** came to the strong hold of Tyre, and to all the cities of the Hivites, and of the Canaanites:
and they went out to the south of Judah, even to Beersheba.
8 **So when they** had gone through all the land,
they came to Jerusalem at the end of nine months and twenty days.
9 **And Joab** gave up the sum of the number of the people unto the king:
and there were in Israel eight hundred thousand valiant men that drew the sword;
and the men of Judah were five hundred thousand men.
10 **And David's heart** smote him
after that he had numbered the people.
And David said unto the LORD,
I have sinned greatly
in that I have done:
and now, {I beseech thee}, O LORD, take away the iniquity of thy servant;
for I have done very foolishly.
11 **For when David** was up in the morning,
the word of the LORD came unto the prophet Gad, David's seer,
saying,
12 **Go and say** unto David,
Thus saith the LORD,
I offer thee three things;
choose thee one of them,
that I may do it unto thee.
13 **So Gad** came to David,
and told him,
and said unto him,
Shall seven years of famine come unto thee in thy land?
or wilt thou flee three months before thine enemies,
while they pursue thee?
or that there be three days' pestilence in thy land?
now advise,
and see what answer I shall return to him that sent me.
14 **And David** said unto Gad,
I am in a great strait:
let us fall now into the hand of the LORD;
for his mercies are great:
and let me not fall into the hand of man.
15 **So the LORD** sent a pestilence upon Israel from the morning even to the time appointed:
and there died of the people from Dan even to Beersheba seventy thousand men.
16 **And when the angel** stretched out his hand upon Jerusalem to destroy it,
the LORD repented him of the evil,
and said to the angel that destroyed the people,
It is enough:
stay now thine hand.
And the angel of the LORD was by the threshingplace of Araunah the Jebusite.
17 **And David** spake unto the LORD
when he saw the angel that smote the people,
and said,
Lo,
I have sinned,
and I have done wickedly:
but these sheep, what have they done?
let thine hand, {I pray thee}, be against me, and against my father's house.
18 **And Gad** came that day to David,
and said unto him,
Go up,
rear an altar unto the LORD in the threshingfloor of Araunah the Jebusite.
19 **And David**, according to the saying of Gad, went up
as the LORD commanded.
20 **And Araunah** looked,
and saw the king and his servants coming on toward him:
and Araunah went out,
and bowed himself before the king on his face upon the ground.
21 **And Araunah** said,
Wherefore is my lord the king come to his servant?

And David said,
To buy the threshingfloor of thee,
to build an altar unto the LORD,
that the plague may be stayed from the people.

22 **And Araunah** said unto David,
Let my lord the king take and offer up what seemeth good unto him:
behold,
here be oxen for burnt sacrifice, and threshing instruments and other instruments of the oxen for wood.

23 **All these things** did Araunah, as a king, give unto the king.
And Araunah said unto the king,
The LORD thy God accept thee.

24 **And the king** said unto Araunah,
Nay;
but I will surely buy it of thee at a price:
neither will I offer burnt offerings unto the LORD my God of that which doth cost me nothing.
So David bought the threshingfloor and the oxen for fifty shekels of silver.

25 **And David** built there an altar unto the LORD,
and offered burnt offerings and peace offerings.
So the LORD was intreated for the land,
and the plague was stayed from Israel.

1 Kings

The Book of First Kings, a work of profound significance, was penned by an author whose identity remains a mystery, yet it is traditionally attributed to the prophet Jeremiah. This obscure origin adds a layer of intrigue to the text, inviting readers to delve deeper into its historical and theological framework. The book, likely written during the Babylonian Exile, a period of immense upheaval and turmoil for the people of Israel, offers hope and inspiration to those living through this difficult time. Its focus on kingship, prophecy, and the relationship between God and the people of Israel reflects the concerns and struggles of the exiled community, providing important insights into the political, religious, and cultural history of Israel during this tumultuous period.

After the death of King David, Solomon ascends to the throne of Israel and quickly establishes a reputation as a ruler who is both wise and just. His reign, a golden era marked by great prosperity and peace, is not only a testament to his leadership but also to his profound impact on the people of Israel. One of his most significant acts is the construction of the Temple in Jerusalem, a monumental event that symbolizes the covenant between God and the nation, invoking a sense of reverence and awe. After the death of King Solomon, Israel as one nation no longer exists, a result of God's judgment on the people's failure to adhere to His laws and to maintain their devotion to Him. King Jeroboam leads the northern kingdom (Israel), while King Rehoboam leads the southern kingdom (Judah). The book chronicles a succession of kings and details about their reigns. Among them is King Ahab, one of the era's most notorious figures. His marriage to Jezebel, a foreign princess, leads to the introduction of the worship of Baal into Israel, which causes great conflict and unrest.

The book's concluding chapters shine a spotlight on the prophet Elijah, a figure of immense courage and faith. He valiantly opposes King Ahab and the prophets of Baal, striving to steer the people of Israel back to God and to challenge the prevalent false gods and practices of the time. These narratives not only serve as a historical and theological guide to the complexities of ancient Israel's history, but they also underscore the profound impact of God's divine intervention in shaping its destiny.

1 **Now king David** was old and stricken in years;
and they covered him with clothes,
but he gat no heat.

2 **Wherefore his servants** said unto him,
Let there be sought for my lord the king a young virgin:
and let her stand before the king,
and let her cherish him,
and let her lie in thy bosom,
that my lord the king may get heat.

3 **So they** sought for a fair damsel throughout all the coasts of Israel,
and found Abishag a Shunammite,
and brought her to the king.

4 **And the damsel** was very fair,
and cherished the king,
and ministered to him:
but the king knew her not.

5 **Then Adonijah the son of Haggith** exalted himself,
saying,
I will be king:
and he prepared him chariots and horsemen,
and fifty men to run before him.

6 **And his father** had not displeased him at any time in saying,
Why hast thou done so?
and he also was a very goodly man;
and his mother bare him after Absalom.

7 **And he** conferred with Joab the son of Zeruiah, and with Abiathar the priest:
and they following Adonijah helped him.

8 **But Zadok the priest, and Benaiah the son of Jehoiada, and Nathan the prophet, and Shimei, and Rei, and the mighty men which belonged to David,** were not with Adonijah.

9 **And Adonijah** slew sheep and oxen and fat cattle by the stone of Zoheleth,
which is by Enrogel,
and called all his brethren the king's sons, and all the men of Judah the king's servants:

10 **But Nathan the prophet, and Benaiah, and the mighty men, and Solomon his brother,** he called not.

11 **Wherefore Nathan** spake unto Bathsheba the mother of Solomon,
saying,
Hast thou not heard that Adonijah the son of Haggith doth reign,
and David our lord knoweth it not?

12 **Now therefore come,**
let me, {I pray thee}, give thee counsel,
that thou mayest save thine own life, and the life of thy son Solomon.

13 **Go and get thee** in unto king David,
and say unto him,
Didst not thou, my lord, O king, swear unto thine handmaid,
saying,
Assuredly Solomon thy son shall reign after me,
and he shall sit upon my throne?
why then doth Adonijah reign?

14 **Behold,**
while thou yet talkest there with the king,
I also will come in after thee,
and confirm thy words.

15 **And Bathsheba** went in unto the king into the chamber:
and the king was very old;
and Abishag the Shunammite ministered unto the king.

16 **And Bathsheba** bowed,
and did obeisance unto the king.

And the king said,
What wouldest thou?

17 **And she** said unto him,
My lord, thou swarest by the LORD thy God unto thine handmaid,
saying,
Assuredly Solomon thy son shall reign after me,
and he shall sit upon my throne.

18 **And now, {behold}, Adonijah** reigneth;
and now, my lord the king, thou knowest it not:
19 **And he** hath slain oxen and fat cattle and sheep in abundance,
and hath called all the sons of the king, and Abiathar the priest, and Joab the captain of the host:
but Solomon thy servant hath he not called.

20 **And thou, my lord, O king, the eyes of all Israel** are upon thee,
that thou shouldest tell them
who shall sit on the throne of my lord the king after him.

21 **Otherwise it** shall come to pass,
when my lord the king shall sleep with his fathers,
that I and my son Solomon shall be counted offenders.

22 **And, {lo}, while she** yet talked with the king,
Nathan the prophet also came in.

23 **And they** told the king,
saying,
Behold Nathan the prophet.

And when he was come in before the king,
he bowed himself before the king with his face to the ground.

24 **And Nathan** said, My lord, O king, hast thou said,
Adonijah shall reign after me,
and he shall sit upon my throne?
25 **For he** is gone down this day,
and hath slain oxen and fat cattle and sheep in abundance,
and hath called all the king's sons, and the captains of the host, and Abiathar the priest;
and, {behold}, they eat and drink before him,
and say,
God save king Adonijah.

26 **But me, even me thy servant, and Zadok the priest, and Benaiah the son of Jehoiada, and thy servant Solomon,** hath he not called.

27 **Is this thing** done by my lord the king,
and thou hast not shewed it unto thy servant,
who should sit on the throne of my lord the king after him?

28 **Then king David** answered and said,
Call me Bathsheba.

And she came into the king's presence,
and stood before the king.

29 **And the king** sware,
and said,
As the LORD liveth,
that hath redeemed my soul out of all distress,
30 **Even as I** sware unto thee by the LORD God of Israel,
saying,
Assuredly Solomon thy son shall reign after me,
and he shall sit upon my throne in my stead;
even so will I certainly do this day.

31 **Then Bathsheba** bowed with her face to the earth,
and did reverence to the king,
and said,
Let my lord king David live for ever.

32 **And king David** said,
Call me Zadok the priest, and Nathan the prophet, and Benaiah the son of Jehoiada.

And they came before the king.

33 **The king** also said unto them,
Take with you the servants of your lord,
and cause Solomon my son to ride upon mine own mule,
and bring him down to Gihon:
34 **And let Zadok the priest and Nathan the prophet** anoint him there king over Israel:
and blow ye with the trumpet,
and say,
God save king Solomon.

35 **Then ye** shall come up after him,
that he may come and sit upon my throne;
for he shall be king in my stead:
and I have appointed him to be ruler over Israel and over Judah.

36 **And Benaiah the son of Jehoiada** answered the king,
and said,
Amen:
the LORD God of my lord the king say so too.

37 **As the LORD** hath been with my lord the king,
even so be he with Solomon,
and make his throne greater than the throne of my lord king David.

38 **So Zadok the priest, and Nathan the prophet, and Benaiah the son of Jehoiada, and the Cherethites, and the Pelethites,** went down,
and caused Solomon to ride upon king David's mule,
and brought him to Gihon.

39 **And Zadok the priest** took an horn of oil out of the tabernacle,
and anointed Solomon.

And they blew the trumpet;
and all the people said,
God save king Solomon.

40 **And all the people** came up after him,
and the people piped with pipes,
and rejoiced with great joy,
so that the earth rent with the sound of them.

41 **And Adonijah and all the guests that were with him** heard it as they had made an end of eating.

And when Joab heard the sound of the trumpet,
he said,
Wherefore is this noise of the city being in an uproar?

42 **And while he** yet spake,
behold,
Jonathan the son of Abiathar the priest came;
and Adonijah said unto him,
Come in;
for thou art a valiant man,
and bringest good tidings.

43 **And Jonathan** answered and said to Adonijah,
Verily our lord king David hath made Solomon king.

44 **And the king** hath sent with him Zadok the priest, and Nathan the prophet, and Benaiah the son of Jehoiada, and the Cherethites, and the Pelethites,

and they have caused him to ride upon the king's mule:
45 **And Zadok the priest and Nathan the prophet** have anointed him king in Gihon:
and they are come up from thence rejoicing,
so that the city rang again.

This is the noise that ye have heard.

46 **And also Solomon** sitteth on the throne of the kingdom.

47 **And moreover the king's servants** came to bless our lord king David,
saying,
God make the name of Solomon better than thy name,
and make his throne greater than thy throne.

And the king bowed himself upon the bed.

48 **And also thus** said the king,
Blessed be the LORD God of Israel,
which hath given one to sit on my throne this day,
mine eyes even seeing it.

49 **And all the guests that were with Adonijah** were afraid,
and rose up,
and went every man his way.

50 **And Adonijah** feared because of Solomon,
and arose,
and went,
and caught hold on the horns of the altar.

51 **And it** was told Solomon,
saying,
Behold,
Adonijah feareth king Solomon:
for, {lo}, he hath caught hold on the horns of the altar,
saying,
Let king Solomon swear unto me today
that he will not slay his servant with the sword.

52 **And Solomon** said,
If he will shew himself a worthy man,
there shall not an hair of him fall to the earth:
but if wickedness shall be found in him,
he shall die.

53 **So king Solomon** sent,
and they brought him down from the altar.

And he came and bowed himself to king Solomon:
and Solomon said unto him,
Go to thine house.

2 **Now the days of David** drew nigh that he should die;
and he charged Solomon his son,
saying,
2 **I** go the way of all the earth:
be thou strong therefore,
and shew thyself a man;
3 **And keep** the charge of the LORD thy God,
to walk in his ways,
to keep his statutes, and his commandments, and his judgments, and his testimonies,
as it is written in the law of Moses,
that thou mayest prosper in all that thou doest,
and whithersoever thou turnest thyself:
4 **That the LORD** may continue his word which he spake concerning me,
saying,
If thy children take heed to their way,
to walk before me in truth with all their heart and with all their soul,
there shall not fail thee (said he) a man on the throne of Israel.

5 **Moreover thou** knowest also
what Joab the son of Zeruiah did to me,
and what he did to the two captains of the hosts of Israel, unto Abner the son of Ner, and unto Amasa the son of Jether,
whom he slew,
and shed the blood of war in peace,
and put the blood of war upon his girdle that was about his loins, and in his shoes that were on his feet.

6 **Do** therefore according to thy wisdom,
and let not his hoar head go down to the grave in peace.

7 **But shew** kindness unto the sons of Barzillai the Gileadite,
and let them be of those that eat at thy table:
for so they came to me
when I fled because of Absalom thy brother.

8 **And, {behold}, thou** hast with thee Shimei the son of Gera, a Benjamite of Bahurim,
which cursed me with a grievous curse in the day when I went to Mahanaim:
but he came down to meet me at Jordan,
and I sware to him by the LORD,
saying,
I will not put thee to death with the sword.

9 **Now therefore hold** him not guiltless:
for thou art a wise man,
and knowest
what thou oughtest to do unto him;
but his hoar head bring thou down to the grave with blood.

10 **So David** slept with his fathers,
and was buried in the city of David.

11 **And the days that David reigned over Israel** were forty years:
seven years reigned he in Hebron,
and thirty and three years reigned he in Jerusalem.

12 **Then** sat Solomon upon the throne of David his father;
and his kingdom was established greatly.

13 **And Adonijah the son of Haggith** came to Bathsheba the mother of Solomon.

And she said,
Comest thou peaceably?

And he said,
Peaceably.

14 **He** said moreover,
I have somewhat to say unto thee.

And she said,
Say on.

15 **And he** said,
Thou knowest
that the kingdom was mine,
and that all Israel set their faces on me,
that I should reign:
howbeit the kingdom is turned about,
and is become my brother's:
for it was his from the LORD.

16 **And now I** ask one petition of thee,
deny me not.

And she said unto him,
Say on.

17 **And he** said,
Speak, {I pray thee}, unto Solomon the king,
(for he will not say thee nay,)
that he give me Abishag the Shunammite to wife.

18 **And Bathsheba** said,
Well;
I will speak for thee unto the king.

19 **Bathsheba** therefore went unto king Solomon,
to speak unto him for Adonijah.

And the king rose up to meet her,
and bowed himself unto her,
and sat down on his throne,
and caused a seat to be set for the king's mother;
and she sat on his right hand.

20 **Then she** said,
I desire one small petition of thee;
I pray thee,
say me not nay.

And the king said unto her,
Ask on, my mother:
for I will not say thee nay.

21 **And she** said,
Let Abishag the Shunammite be given to Adonijah thy brother to wife.

22 **And king Solomon** answered and said unto his mother,
And why dost thou ask Abishag the Shunammite for Adonijah?
ask for him the kingdom also;
for he is mine elder brother; even for him, and for Abiathar the priest, and for Joab the son of Zeruiah.

23 **Then king Solomon** sware by the LORD,
saying,
God do so to me, and more also,
if Adonijah have not spoken this word against his own life.

24 **Now therefore, {as the LORD liveth}, {which hath established me}, {and set me on the throne of David my father}, {and who hath made me an house}, {as he promised},** Adonijah shall be put to death this day.

25 **And king Solomon** sent by the hand of Benaiah the son of Jehoiada;
and he fell upon him
that he died.

26 **And unto Abiathar the priest** said the king,
Get thee to Anathoth, unto thine own fields;
for thou art worthy of death:
but I will not at this time put thee to death,
because thou barest the ark of the Lord GOD before David my father,
and because thou hast been afflicted in all wherein my father was afflicted.

27 **So Solomon** thrust out Abiathar from being priest unto the LORD;
that he might fulfil the word of the LORD,
which he spake concerning the house of Eli in Shiloh.

28 **Then tidings** came to Joab:
for Joab had turned after Adonijah,
though he turned not after Absalom.

And Joab fled unto the tabernacle of the LORD,
and caught hold on the horns of the altar.

29 **And it was told king Solomon** that Joab was fled unto the tabernacle of the LORD;
and, {behold}, he is by the altar.

Then Solomon sent Benaiah the son of Jehoiada,
saying,
Go,
fall upon him.

30 **And Benaiah** came to the tabernacle of the LORD,
and said unto him,
Thus saith the king,
Come forth.

And he said,
Nay;
but I will die here.

And Benaiah brought the king word again,
saying,
Thus said Joab,
and thus he answered me.

31 **And the king** said unto him,
Do as he hath said,
and fall upon him,
and bury him;
that thou mayest take away the innocent blood,
which Joab shed, from me, and from the house of my father.

32 **And the LORD** shall return his blood upon his own head,
who fell upon two men more righteous and better than he,
and slew them with the sword,
my father David not knowing thereof, to wit, Abner the son of Ner, captain of the host of Israel, and Amasa the son of Jether, captain of the host of Judah.

33 **Their blood** shall therefore return upon the head of Joab, and upon the head of his seed for ever:
but upon David, and upon his seed, and upon his house, and upon his throne, shall there be peace for ever from the LORD.

34 **So Benaiah the son of Jehoiada** went up,
and fell upon him,
and slew him:
and he was buried in his own house in the wilderness.

35 **And the king** put Benaiah the son of Jehoiada in his room over the host:
and Zadok the priest did the king put in the room of Abiathar.

36 **And the king** sent and called for Shimei,
and said unto him,
Build thee an house in Jerusalem,
and dwell there,
and go not forth thence any whither.

37 **For it** shall be,
that on the day thou goest out,
and passest over the brook Kidron,
thou shalt know for certain
that thou shalt surely die:
thy blood shall be upon thine own head.

38 **And Shimei** said unto the king,
The saying is good:
as my lord the king hath said,
so will thy servant do.

And Shimei dwelt in Jerusalem many days.

39 **And it** came to pass at the end of three years,
that two of the servants of Shimei ran away unto Achish son of Maachah king of Gath.

And they told Shimei,
saying,
Behold,
thy servants be in Gath.

40 **And Shimei** arose,
and saddled his ass,
and went to Gath to Achish
to seek his servants:
and Shimei went,
and brought his servants from Gath.

41 **And it was told Solomon** that Shimei had gone from Jerusalem to Gath, and was come again.

42 **And the king** sent and called for Shimei,

and said unto him,
Did I not make thee to swear by the LORD,
and protested unto thee,
saying,
Know for a certain,
on the day thou goest out,
and walkest abroad any whither,
that thou shalt surely die?
and thou saidst unto me,
The word that I have heard is good.
43 **Why** then hast thou not kept the oath of the LORD, and the commandment that I have charged thee with?
44 **The king** said moreover to Shimei,
Thou knowest all the wickedness which thine heart is privy to,
that thou didst to David my father:
therefore the LORD shall return thy wickedness upon thine own head;
45 **And king Solomon** shall be blessed,
and the throne of David shall be established before the LORD for ever.
46 **So the king** commanded Benaiah the son of Jehoiada;
which went out,
and fell upon him,
that he died.
And the kingdom was established in the hand of Solomon.

3 **And Solomon** made affinity with Pharaoh king of Egypt,
and took Pharaoh's daughter,
and brought her into the city of David,
until he had made an end of building his own house, and the house of the LORD, and the wall of Jerusalem round about.
2 **Only the people** sacrificed in high places,
because there was no house built unto the name of the LORD, until those days.
3 **And Solomon** loved the LORD,
walking in the statutes of David his father:
only he sacrificed and burnt incense in high places.
4 **And the king** went to Gibeon
to sacrifice there;
for that was the great high place:
a thousand burnt offerings did Solomon offer upon that altar.
5 **In Gibeon** the LORD appeared to Solomon in a dream by night:
and God said,
Ask
what I shall give thee.
6 **And Solomon** said,
Thou hast shewed unto thy servant David my father great mercy,
according as he walked before thee in truth, and in righteousness, and in uprightness of heart with thee;
and thou hast kept for him this great kindness,
that thou hast given him a son to sit on his throne,
as it is this day.
7 **And now, O LORD my God, thou** hast made thy servant king instead of David my father:
and I am but a little child:
I know not
how to go out or come in.
8 **And thy servant** is in the midst of thy people which thou hast chosen, a great people,
that cannot be numbered
nor counted for multitude.
9 **Give** therefore thy servant an understanding heart
to judge thy people,
that I may discern between good and bad:
for who is able to judge this thy so great a people?
10 **And the speech** pleased the Lord,
that Solomon had asked this thing.
11 **And God** said unto him,
Because thou hast asked this thing,
and hast not asked for thyself long life;
neither hast asked riches for thyself,
nor hast asked the life of thine enemies;
but hast asked for thyself understanding
to discern judgment;
12 **Behold,**
I have done according to thy words:
lo,
I have given thee a wise and an understanding heart;
so that there was none like thee before thee,
neither after thee shall any arise like unto thee.
13 **And I** have also given thee that which thou hast not asked, both riches, and honour:
so that there shall not be any among the kings like unto thee all thy days.
14 **And if thou** wilt walk in my ways,
to keep my statutes and my commandments,
as thy father David did walk,
then I will lengthen thy days.
15 **And Solomon** awoke;
and, {behold}, it was a dream.
And he came to Jerusalem,
and stood before the ark of the covenant of the LORD,
and offered up burnt offerings,
and offered peace offerings,
and made a feast to all his servants.
16 **Then** came there two women,
that were harlots, unto the king,
and stood before him.
17 **And the one woman** said,
O my lord, I and this woman dwell in one house;
and I was delivered of a child with her in the house.
18 **And it** came to pass the third day after that I was delivered,
that this woman was delivered also:
and we were together;
there was no stranger with us in the house, save we two in the house.
19 **And this woman's child** died in the night;
because she overlaid it.
20 **And she** arose at midnight,
and took my son from beside me,
while thine handmaid slept,
and laid it in her bosom,
and laid her dead child in my bosom.
21 **And when I** rose in the morning to give my child suck,
behold,
it was dead:
but when I had considered it in the morning,
behold,
it was not my son,
which I did bear.
22 **And the other woman** said,
Nay;
but the living is my son,
and the dead is thy son.
And this said,
No;
but the dead is thy son,

and the living is my son.
Thus they spake before the king.
23 **Then** said the king,
The one saith,
This is my son that liveth,
and thy son is the dead:
and the other saith,
Nay;
but thy son is the dead,
and my son is the living.
24 **And the king** said,
Bring me a sword.
And they brought a sword before the king.
25 **And the king** said,
Divide the living child in two,
and give half to the one, and half to the other.
26 **Then** spake the woman whose the living child was unto the king,
for her bowels yearned upon her son,
and she said,
O my lord, give her the living child,
and in no wise slay it.
But the other said,
Let it be neither mine nor thine,
but divide it.
27 **Then the king** answered and said,
Give her the living child,
and in no wise slay it:
she is the mother thereof.
28 **And all Israel** heard of the judgment which the king had judged;
and they feared the king:
for they saw that the wisdom of God was in him,
to do judgment.

4 **So king Solomon** was king over all Israel.
2 **And these** were the princes which he had;
Azariah the son of Zadok the priest,
3 **Elihoreph and Ahiah, the sons of Shisha,** scribes;
Jehoshaphat the son of Ahilud, the recorder.
4 **And Benaiah the son of Jehoiada** was over the host:
and Zadok and Abiathar were the priests:
5 **And Azariah the son of Nathan** was over the officers:
and Zabud the son of Nathan was principal officer, and the king's friend:
6 **And Ahishar** was over the household:
and Adoniram the son of Abda was over the tribute.
7 **And Solomon** had twelve officers over all Israel,
which provided victuals for the king and his household:
each man his month in a year made provision.
8 **And these** are their names:
The son of Hur, in mount Ephraim:
9 **The son of Dekar,** in Makaz, and in Shaalbim, and Bethshemesh, and Elonbethhanan:
10 **The son of Hesed,** in Aruboth; {to him pertained Sochoh, and all the land of Hepher}:
11 **The son of Abinadab,** in all the region of Dor; {which had Taphath the daughter of Solomon to wife}:
12 **Baana the son of Ahilud; {to him** pertained Taanach and Megiddo, and all Bethshean}, {which is by Zartanah beneath Jezreel, from Bethshean to Abelmeholah, even unto the place that is beyond Jokneam}:
13 **The son of Geber,** in Ramothgilead; {to him pertained the towns of Jair the son of Manasseh}, {which are in Gilead}; {to him also pertained the region of Argob}, {which is in Bashan, threescore great cities with walls and brasen bars}:
14 **Ahinadab the son of Iddo** had Mahanaim:
15 **Ahimaaz** was in Naphtali;
he also took Basmath the daughter of Solomon to wife:
16 **Baanah the son of Hushai** was in Asher and in Aloth:
17 **Jehoshaphat the son of Paruah,** in Issachar:
18 **Shimei the son of Elah,** in Benjamin:
19 **Geber the son of Uri** was in the country of Gilead, in the country of Sihon king of the Amorites, and of Og king of Bashan;
and he was the only officer which was in the land.
20 **Judah and Israel** were many, as the sand which is by the sea in multitude,
eating and drinking,
and making merry.
21 **And Solomon** reigned over all kingdoms from the river unto the land of the Philistines, and unto the border of Egypt:
they brought presents,
and served Solomon all the days of his life.
22 **And Solomon's provision for one day** was thirty measures of fine flour, and threescore measures of meal,
23 Ten fat oxen, and twenty oxen out of the pastures, and an hundred sheep, beside harts, and roebucks, and fallowdeer, and fatted fowl.
24 **For he** had dominion over all the region on this side the river, from Tiphsah even to Azzah, over all the kings on this side the river:
and he had peace on all sides round about him.
25 **And Judah and Israel** dwelt safely, every man under his vine and under his fig tree, from Dan even to Beersheba, all the days of Solomon.
26 **And Solomon** had forty thousand stalls of horses for his chariots, and twelve thousand horsemen.
27 **And those officers** provided victual for king Solomon, and for all that came unto king Solomon's table, every man in his month:
they lacked nothing.
28 **Barley also and straw for the horses and dromedaries** brought they unto the place where the officers were, every man according to his charge.
29 **And God** gave Solomon wisdom and understanding exceeding much, and largeness of heart, even as the sand that is on the sea shore.
30 **And Solomon's wisdom** excelled the wisdom of all the children of the east country, and all the wisdom of Egypt.
31 **For he** was wiser than all men; than Ethan the Ezrahite, and Heman, and Chalcol, and Darda, the sons of Mahol:
and his fame was in all nations round about.
32 **And he** spake three thousand proverbs:
and his songs were a thousand and five.
33 **And he** spake of trees, from the cedar tree that is in Lebanon even

unto the hyssop that springeth out of the wall:
he spake also of beasts, and of fowl, and of creeping things, and of fishes.

34 **And there** came of all people to hear the wisdom of Solomon, from all kings of the earth,
which had heard of his wisdom.

5 **And Hiram king of Tyre** sent his servants unto Solomon;
for he had heard that they had anointed him king in the room of his father:
for Hiram was ever a lover of David.

2 **And Solomon** sent to Hiram, saying,
3 **Thou** knowest
how that David my father could not build an house unto the name of the LORD his God for the wars which were about him on every side,
until the LORD put them under the soles of his feet.

4 **But now the LORD my God** hath given me rest on every side,
so that there is neither adversary nor evil occurrent.

5 **And, {behold}, I** purpose to build an house unto the name of the LORD my God,
as the LORD spake unto David my father,
saying,
Thy son, {whom I will set upon thy throne in thy room}, he shall build an house unto my name.

6 **Now therefore command thou**
that they hew me cedar trees out of Lebanon;
and my servants shall be with thy servants:
and unto thee will I give hire for thy servants according to all that thou shalt appoint:
for thou knowest
that there is not among us any that can skill to hew timber like unto the Sidonians.

7 **And it** came to pass,
when Hiram heard the words of Solomon,
that he rejoiced greatly,
and said,
Blessed be the LORD this day,
which hath given unto David a wise son over this great people.

8 **And Hiram** sent to Solomon, saying,
I have considered the things which thou sentest to me for:
and I will do all thy desire concerning timber of cedar, and concerning timber of fir.

9 **My servants** shall bring them down from Lebanon unto the sea:
and I will convey them by sea in floats unto the place that thou shalt appoint me,
and will cause them to be discharged there,
and thou shalt receive them:
and thou shalt accomplish my desire,
in giving food for my household.

10 **So Hiram** gave Solomon cedar trees and fir trees according to all his desire.

11 **And Solomon** gave Hiram twenty thousand measures of wheat for food to his household, and twenty measures of pure oil:
thus gave Solomon to Hiram year by year.

12 **And the LORD** gave Solomon wisdom,
as he promised him:
and there was peace between Hiram and Solomon;
and they two made a league together.

13 **And king Solomon** raised a levy out of all Israel;
and the levy was thirty thousand men.

14 **And he** sent them to Lebanon, ten thousand a month by courses:
a month they were in Lebanon, and two months at home:
and Adoniram was over the levy.

15 **And Solomon** had threescore and ten thousand that bare burdens, and fourscore thousand hewers in the mountains;

16 Beside the chief of Solomon's officers which were over the work, three thousand and three hundred,
which ruled over the people that wrought in the work.

17 **And the king** commanded,
and they brought great stones, costly stones, and hewed stones,
to lay the foundation of the house.

18 **And Solomon's builders and Hiram's builders** did hew them, and the stonesquarers:
so they prepared timber and stones to build the house.

6 ✠ **And it** came to pass in the four hundred and eightieth year after the children of Israel were come out of the land of Egypt, in the fourth year of Solomon's reign over Israel, in the month Zif,
which is the second month,
that he began to build the house of the LORD.

2 **And the house which king Solomon built for the LORD,** the length thereof was threescore cubits, and the breadth thereof twenty cubits, and the height thereof thirty cubits.

3 **And the porch before the temple of the house,** twenty cubits was the length thereof, according to the breadth of the house;
and ten cubits was the breadth thereof before the house.

4 **And for the house** he made windows of narrow lights.

5 **And against the wall of the house** he built chambers round about, against the walls of the house round about, both of the temple and of the oracle:
and he made chambers round about:

6 **The nethermost chamber** was five cubits broad,
and the middle was six cubits broad,
and the third was seven cubits broad:
for without in the wall of the house he made narrowed rests round about,
that the beams should not be fastened in the walls of the house.

7 **And the house**, {when it was in building}, was built of stone made ready before it was brought thither:
so that there was neither hammer nor axe nor any tool of iron heard in the house,
while it was in building.

8 **The door for the middle chamber** was in the right side of the house:
and they went up with winding stairs into the middle chamber, and out of the middle into the third.

9 **So he** built the house,

and finished it;
and covered the house with beams and boards of cedar.
10 **And then he** built chambers against all the house, five cubits high:
and they rested on the house with timber of cedar.
11 **And the word of the LORD** came to Solomon,
saying,
12 **Concerning this house which thou art in building,** if thou wilt walk in my statutes,
and execute my judgments,
and keep all my commandments to walk in them;
then will I perform my word with thee,
which I spake unto David thy father:
13 **And I** will dwell among the children of Israel,
and will not forsake my people Israel.
14 **So Solomon** built the house,
and finished it.
15 **And he** built the walls of the house within with boards of cedar, both the floor of the house, and the walls of the ceiling:
and he covered them on the inside with wood,
and covered the floor of the house with planks of fir.
16 **And he** built twenty cubits on the sides of the house, both the floor and the walls with boards of cedar:
he even built them for it within, even for the oracle, even for the most holy place.
17 **And the house, that is, the temple before it,** was forty cubits long.
18 **And the cedar of the house within** was carved with knops and open flowers:
all was cedar;
there was no stone seen.
19 **And the oracle** he prepared in the house within,
to set there the ark of the covenant of the LORD.
20 **And the oracle in the forepart** was twenty cubits in length, and twenty cubits in breadth, and twenty cubits in the height thereof:
and he overlaid it with pure gold;
and so covered the altar which was of cedar.
21 **So Solomon** overlaid the house within with pure gold:
and he made a partition by the chains of gold before the oracle;
and he overlaid it with gold.
22 **And the whole house** he overlaid with gold,
until he had finished all the house:
also the whole altar that was by the oracle he overlaid with gold.
23 **And within the oracle** he made two cherubims of olive tree, each ten cubits high.
24 **And five cubits** was the one wing of the cherub, and five cubits the other wing of the cherub:
from the uttermost part of the one wing unto the uttermost part of the other were ten cubits.
25 **And the other cherub** was ten cubits:
both the cherubims were of one measure and one size.
26 **The height of the one cherub** was ten cubits,
and so was it of the other cherub.
27 **And he** set the cherubims within the inner house:
and they stretched forth the wings of the cherubims,
so that the wing of the one touched the one wall,
and the wing of the other cherub touched the other wall;
and their wings touched one another in the midst of the house.
28 **And he** overlaid the cherubims with gold.
29 **And he** carved all the walls of the house round about with carved figures of cherubims and palm trees and open flowers, within and without.
30 **And the floors of the house** he overlaid with gold, within and without.
31 **And for the entering of the oracle** he made doors of olive tree:
the lintel and side posts were a fifth part of the wall.
32 **The two doors** also were of olive tree;
and he carved upon them carvings of cherubims and palm trees and open flowers,
and overlaid them with gold,
and spread gold upon the cherubims, and upon the palm trees.
33 **So** also made he for the door of the temple posts of olive tree, a fourth part of the wall.
34 **And the two doors** were of fir tree:
the two leaves of the one door were folding,
and the two leaves of the other door were folding.
35 **And he** carved thereon cherubims and palm trees and open flowers:
and covered them with gold fitted upon the carved work.
36 **And he** built the inner court with three rows of hewed stone, and a row of cedar beams.
37 **In the fourth year** was the foundation of the house of the LORD laid, in the month Zif:
38 **And in the eleventh year, in the month Bul**, {which is the eighth month}, was the house finished throughout all the parts thereof, and according to all the fashion of it.
So was he seven years in building it.

7 **But Solomon** was building his own house thirteen years,
and he finished all his house.
2 **He** built also the house of the forest of Lebanon;
the length thereof was an hundred cubits, and the breadth thereof fifty cubits, and the height thereof thirty cubits, upon four rows of cedar pillars, with cedar beams upon the pillars.
3 **And it** was covered with cedar above upon the beams,
that lay on forty five pillars, fifteen in a row.
4 **And there** were windows in three rows,
and light was against light in three ranks.
5 **And all the doors and posts** were square, with the windows:
and light was against light in three ranks.
6 **And he** made a porch of pillars;
the length thereof was fifty cubits, and the breadth thereof thirty cubits:
and the porch was before them:
and the other pillars and the thick beam were before them.

7 **Then he** made a porch for the throne where he might judge, even the porch of judgment:
and it was covered with cedar from one side of the floor to the other.

8 **And his house where he dwelt** had another court within the porch,
which was of the like work.

Solomon made also an house for Pharaoh's daughter,
whom he had taken to wife, like unto this porch.

9 **All these** were of costly stones, according to the measures of hewed stones,
sawed with saws, within and without, even from the foundation unto the coping, and so on the outside toward the great court.

10 **And the foundation** was of costly stones, even great stones, stones of ten cubits, and stones of eight cubits.

11 **And above** were costly stones, after the measures of hewed stones, and cedars.

12 **And the great court round about** was with three rows of hewed stones, and a row of cedar beams, both for the inner court of the house of the LORD, and for the porch of the house.

13 **And king Solomon** sent and fetched Hiram out of Tyre.

14 **He** was a widow's son of the tribe of Naphtali,
and his father was a man of Tyre, a worker in brass:
and he was filled with wisdom, and understanding, and cunning to work all works in brass.

And he came to king Solomon,
and wrought all his work.

15 **For he** cast two pillars of brass, of eighteen cubits high apiece:
and a line of twelve cubits did compass either of them about.

16 **And he** made two chapiters of molten brass,
to set upon the tops of the pillars:
the height of the one chapiter was five cubits,
and the height of the other chapiter was five cubits:

17 And nets of checker work, and wreaths of chain work, for the chapiters which were upon the top of the pillars; seven for the one chapiter, and seven for the other chapiter.

18 **And he** made the pillars, and two rows round about upon the one network,
to cover the chapiters that were upon the top, with pomegranates:
and so did he for the other chapiter.

19 **And the chapiters that were upon the top of the pillars** were of lily work in the porch, four cubits.

20 **And the chapiters upon the two pillars** had pomegranates also above, over against the belly which was by the network:
and the pomegranates were two hundred in rows round about upon the other chapiter.

21 **And he** set up the pillars in the porch of the temple:
and he set up the right pillar,
and called the name thereof Jachin:
and he set up the left pillar,
and called the name thereof Boaz.

22 **And upon the top of the pillars** was lily work:
so was the work of the pillars finished.

23 **And he** made a molten sea, ten cubits from the one brim to the other:
it was round all about,
and his height was five cubits:
and a line of thirty cubits did compass it round about.

24 **And under the brim of it round about** there were knops compassing it, ten in a cubit,
compassing the sea round about:
the knops were cast in two rows,
when it was cast.

25 **It** stood upon twelve oxen,
three looking toward the north,
and three looking toward the west,
and three looking toward the south,
and three looking toward the east:
and the sea was set above upon them,
and all their hinder parts were inward.

26 **And it** was an hand breadth thick,
and the brim thereof was wrought like the brim of a cup, with flowers of lilies:
it contained two thousand baths.

27 **And he** made ten bases of brass;
four cubits was the length of one base, and four cubits the breadth thereof, and three cubits the height of it.

28 **And the work of the bases** was on this manner:
they had borders,
and the borders were between the ledges:

29 **And on the borders that were between the ledges** were lions, oxen, and cherubims:
and upon the ledges there was a base above:
and beneath the lions and oxen were certain additions made of thin work.

30 **And every base** had four brasen wheels, and plates of brass:
and the four corners thereof had undersetters:
under the laver were undersetters molten, at the side of every addition.

31 **And the mouth of it within the chapiter and above** was a cubit:
but the mouth thereof was round after the work of the base, a cubit and an half:
and also upon the mouth of it were gravings with their borders, foursquare, not round.

32 **And under the borders** were four wheels;
and the axletrees of the wheels were joined to the base:
and the height of a wheel was a cubit and half a cubit.

33 **And the work of the wheels** was like the work of a chariot wheel:
their axletrees, and their naves, and their felloes, and their spokes, were all molten.

34 **And there** were four undersetters to the four corners of one base:
and the undersetters were of the very base itself.

35 **And in the top of the base** was there a round compass of half a cubit high:
and on the top of the base the ledges thereof and the borders thereof were of the same.

36 **For on the plates of the ledges thereof, and on the borders thereof,** he graved cherubims, lions, and palm trees, according to the proportion of every one, and additions round about.

37 **After this manner** he made the ten bases:
all of them had one casting, one measure, and one size.

38 **Then** made he ten lavers of brass:
one laver contained forty baths:
and every laver was four cubits: and upon every one of the ten bases one laver.

39 **And he** put five bases on the right side of the house, and five on the left side of the house:
and he set the sea on the right side of the house eastward over against the south.

40 **And Hiram** made the lavers, and the shovels, and the basons.
So Hiram made an end of doing all the work that he made king Solomon for the house of the LORD:

41 The two pillars, and the two bowls of the chapiters that were on the top of the two pillars; and the two networks,
to cover the two bowls of the chapiters which were upon the top of the pillars;

42 And four hundred pomegranates for the two networks, even two rows of pomegranates for one network,
to cover the two bowls of the chapiters that were upon the pillars;

43 And the ten bases, and ten lavers on the bases;

44 And one sea, and twelve oxen under the sea;

45 And the pots, and the shovels, and the basons:
and all these vessels, {which Hiram made to king Solomon for the house of the LORD}, were of bright brass.

46 **In the plain of Jordan** did the king cast them, in the clay ground between Succoth and Zarthan.

47 **And Solomon** left all the vessels unweighed,
because they were exceeding many:
neither was the weight of the brass found out.

48 **And Solomon** made all the vessels that pertained unto the house of the LORD: the altar of gold, and the table of gold, {whereupon the shewbread was},

49 And the candlesticks of pure gold, five on the right side, and five on the left, before the oracle, with the flowers, and the lamps, and the tongs of gold,

50 And the bowls, and the snuffers, and the basons, and the spoons, and the censers of pure gold; and the hinges of gold, both for the doors of the inner house, the most holy place, and for the doors of the house, to wit, of the temple.

51 **So** was ended all the work that king Solomon made for the house of the LORD.
And Solomon brought in the things which David his father had dedicated;
even the silver, and the gold, and the vessels, did he put among the treasures of the house of the LORD.

8 **Then Solomon** assembled the elders of Israel, and all the heads of the tribes, the chief of the fathers of the children of Israel, unto king Solomon in Jerusalem,
that they might bring up the ark of the covenant of the LORD out of the city of David,
which is Zion.

2 **And all the men of Israel** assembled themselves unto king Solomon at the feast in the month Ethanim,
which is the seventh month.

3 **And all the elders of Israel** came,
and the priests took up the ark.

4 **And they** brought up the ark of the LORD, and the tabernacle of the congregation, and all the holy vessels that were in the tabernacle,
even those did the priests and the Levites bring up.

5 **And king Solomon, and all the congregation of Israel**, {that were assembled unto him}, were with him before the ark,
sacrificing sheep and oxen,
that could not be told
nor numbered for multitude.

6 **And the priests** brought in the ark of the covenant of the LORD unto his place, into the oracle of the house, to the most holy place, even under the wings of the cherubims.

7 **For the cherubims** spread forth their two wings over the place of the ark,
and the cherubims covered the ark and the staves thereof above.

8 **And they** drew out the staves,
that the ends of the staves were seen out in the holy place before the oracle,
and they were not seen without:
and there they are unto this day.

9 **There** was nothing in the ark save the two tables of stone,
which Moses put there at Horeb,
when the LORD made a covenant with the children of Israel,
when they came out of the land of Egypt.

10 **And it** came to pass,
when the priests were come out of the holy place,
that the cloud filled the house of the LORD,

11 **So that the priests** could not stand to minister because of the cloud:
for the glory of the LORD had filled the house of the LORD.

12 **Then** spake Solomon,
The LORD said
that he would dwell in the thick darkness.

13 **I** have surely built thee an house to dwell in,
a settled place for thee to abide in for ever.

14 **And the king** turned his face about,
and blessed all the congregation of Israel:
(and all the congregation of Israel stood;)

15 **And he** said,
Blessed be the LORD God of Israel,
which spake with his mouth unto David my father,
and hath with his hand fulfilled it, saying,

16 **Since the day that I brought forth my people Israel out of Egypt,** I chose no city out of all the tribes of Israel to build an house,
that my name might be therein;
but I chose David to be over my people Israel.

17 **And it was in the heart of David my father** to build an house for the name of the LORD God of Israel.

18 **And the LORD** said unto David my father,
Whereas it was in thine heart to build an house unto my name,
thou didst well that it was in thine heart.

19 **Nevertheless thou** shalt not build the house;
but thy son that shall come forth out of thy loins, he shall build the house unto my name.

20 **And the LORD** hath performed his word that he spake,
and I am risen up in the room of David my father,
and sit on the throne of Israel,
as the LORD promised,
and have built an house for the name of the LORD God of Israel.

21 **And I** have set there a place for the ark,
wherein is the covenant of the LORD,
which he made with our fathers,
when he brought them out of the land of Egypt.

22 **And Solomon** stood before the altar of the LORD in the presence of all the congregation of Israel,
and spread forth his hands toward heaven:
23 **And he** said,
LORD God of Israel, there is no God like thee, in heaven above, or on earth beneath,
who keepest covenant and mercy with thy servants that walk before thee with all their heart:
24 **Who** hast kept with thy servant David my father that thou promisedst him:
thou spakest also with thy mouth,
and hast fulfilled it with thine hand,
as it is this day.

25 **Therefore now, LORD God of Israel, keep** with thy servant David my father that thou promisedst him,
saying,
There shall not fail thee a man in my sight to sit on the throne of Israel;
so that thy children take heed to their way,
that they walk before me as thou hast walked before me.

26 **And now, O God of Israel, let thy word**, {I pray thee}, be verified,
which thou spakest unto thy servant David my father.

27 **But** will God indeed dwell on the earth?
behold,
the heaven and heaven of heavens cannot contain thee; how much less this house that I have builded?

28 **Yet have thou** respect unto the prayer of thy servant, and to his supplication, O LORD my God,
to hearken unto the cry and to the prayer,
which thy servant prayeth before thee to day:
29 **That thine eyes** may be open toward this house night and day, even toward the place of which thou hast said,
My name shall be there:
that thou mayest hearken unto the prayer which thy servant shall make toward this place.

30 **And hearken thou** to the supplication of thy servant, and of thy people Israel,
when they shall pray toward this place:
and hear thou in heaven thy dwelling place:
and when thou hearest,
forgive.

31 **If any man** trespass against his neighbour,
and an oath be laid upon him to cause him to swear,
and the oath come before thine altar in this house:
32 **Then hear thou** in heaven,
and do,
and judge thy servants,
condemning the wicked,
to bring his way upon his head;
and justifying the righteous,
to give him according to his righteousness.

33 **When thy people Israel** be smitten down before the enemy,
because they have sinned against thee,
and shall turn again to thee,
and confess thy name,
and pray,
and make supplication unto thee in this house:
34 **Then hear thou** in heaven,
and forgive the sin of thy people Israel,
and bring them again unto the land which thou gavest unto their fathers.

35 **When heaven** is shut up,
and there is no rain,
because they have sinned against thee;
if they pray toward this place,
and confess thy name,
and turn from their sin,
when thou afflictest them:
36 **Then hear thou** in heaven,
and forgive the sin of thy servants, and of thy people Israel,
that thou teach them the good way wherein they should walk,
and give rain upon thy land,
which thou hast given to thy people for an inheritance.

37 **If there** be in the land famine,
if there be pestilence, blasting, mildew, locust,
or if there be caterpiller;
if their enemy besiege them in the land of their cities;
whatsoever plague, whatsoever sickness there be;
38 What prayer and supplication soever be made by any man, or by all thy people Israel,
which shall know every man the plague of his own heart,
and spread forth his hands toward this house:
39 **Then hear thou** in heaven thy dwelling place,
and forgive,
and do,
and give to every man according to his ways,
whose heart thou knowest;
(for thou, even thou only, knowest the hearts of all the children of men;)
40 **That they** may fear thee all the days that they live in the land which thou gavest unto our fathers.

41 **Moreover concerning a stranger**, {that is not of thy people Israel}, {but cometh out of a far country for thy name's sake};
42 (For they shall hear of thy great name, and of thy strong hand, and of thy stretched out arm;)
{when he shall come and pray toward this house};
43 Hear thou in heaven thy dwelling place,
and do according to all that the stranger calleth to thee for:

that all people of the earth may
know thy name,
to fear thee,
as do thy people Israel;
and that they may know
that this house, {which I have
builded}, is called by thy name.
44 **If thy people** go out to battle
against their enemy,
whithersoever thou shalt send
them,
and shall pray unto the LORD
toward the city which thou hast
chosen, and toward the house
that I have built for thy name:
45 **Then hear thou** in heaven their
prayer and their supplication,
and maintain their cause.
46 **If they** sin against thee,
(for there is no man that sinneth
not,)
and thou be angry with them,
and deliver them to the enemy,
so that they carry them away
captives unto the land of the
enemy, far or near;
47 **Yet if they** shall bethink
themselves in the land whither
they were carried captives,
and repent,
and make supplication unto thee in
the land of them that carried
them captives,
saying,
We have sinned,
and have done perversely,
we have committed wickedness;
48 **And so** return unto thee with all
their heart, and with all their
soul, in the land of their enemies,
which led them away captive,
and pray unto thee toward their
land,
which thou gavest unto their
fathers, the city which thou hast
chosen, and the house which I
have built for thy name:
49 **Then hear thou** their prayer and
their supplication in heaven thy
dwelling place,
and maintain their cause,
50 **And forgive** thy people that have
sinned against thee, and all their
transgressions wherein they have
transgressed against thee,
and give them compassion before
them who carried them captive,
that they may have compassion on
them:
51 **For they** be thy people, and thine
inheritance,
which thou broughtest forth out of
Egypt, from the midst of the
furnace of iron:
52 **That thine eyes** may be open
unto the supplication of thy
servant, and unto the
supplication of thy people Israel,
to hearken unto them in all that
they call for unto thee.
53 **For thou** didst separate them
from among all the people of the
earth,
to be thine inheritance,
as thou spakest by the hand of
Moses thy servant,
when thou broughtest our fathers
out of Egypt, O Lord GOD.
54 **And it** was so,
that when Solomon had made an
end of praying all this prayer and
supplication unto the LORD,
he arose from before the altar of the
LORD,
from kneeling on his knees with his
hands spread up to heaven.
55 **And he** stood,
and blessed all the congregation of
Israel with a loud voice,
saying,
56 **Blessed** be the LORD,
that hath given rest unto his people
Israel, according to all that he
promised:
there hath not failed one word of all
his good promise,
which he promised by the hand of
Moses his servant.
57 **The LORD our God** be with us,
as he was with our fathers:
let him not leave us,
nor forsake us:
58 **That he** may incline our hearts
unto him,
to walk in all his ways,
and to keep his commandments,
and his statutes, and his
judgments,
which he commanded our fathers.
59 **And let these my words,**
{wherewith I have made
supplication before the LORD}, be
nigh unto the LORD our God day
and night,
that he maintain the cause of his
servant, and the cause of his
people Israel at all times,
as the matter shall require:
60 **That all the people of the earth**
may know
that the LORD is God,
and that there is none else.
61 **Let your heart** therefore be
perfect with the LORD our God,
to walk in his statutes,
and to keep his commandments, as
at this day.
62 **And the king, and all Israel with
him,** offered sacrifice before the
LORD.
63 **And Solomon** offered a sacrifice
of peace offerings,
which he offered unto the LORD,
two and twenty thousand oxen,
and an hundred and twenty
thousand sheep.
**So the king and all the children of
Israel** dedicated the house of the
LORD.
64 **The same day** did the king
hallow the middle of the court
that was before the house of the
LORD:
for there he offered burnt offerings,
and meat offerings, and the fat of
the peace offerings:
**because the brasen altar that was
before the LORD** was too little to
receive the burnt offerings, and
meat offerings, and the fat of the
peace offerings.
65 **And at that time** Solomon held a
feast, and all Israel with him, a
great congregation, from the
entering in of Hamath unto the
river of Egypt, before the LORD
our God, seven days and seven
days, even fourteen days.
66 **On the eighth day** he sent the
people away:
and they blessed the king,
and went unto their tents joyful
and glad of heart for all the
goodness that the LORD had done
for David his servant, and for
Israel his people.

9 **And it** came to pass,
when Solomon had finished
the building of the house of the
LORD, and the king's house, and
all Solomon's desire which he was
pleased to do,
2 **That the LORD** appeared to
Solomon the second time,
as he had appeared unto him at
Gibeon.
3 **And the LORD** said unto him,
I have heard thy prayer and thy
supplication,
that thou hast made before me:

I have hallowed this house,
which thou hast built,
to put my name there for ever;
and mine eyes and mine heart shall be there perpetually.

4 **And if thou** wilt walk before me,
as David thy father walked, in integrity of heart, and in uprightness,
to do according to all that I have commanded thee,
and wilt keep my statutes and my judgments:

5 **Then I** will establish the throne of thy kingdom upon Israel for ever,
as I promised to David thy father,
saying,
There shall not fail thee a man upon the throne of Israel.

6 **But if ye** shall at all turn from following me, ye or your children,
and will not keep my commandments and my statutes which I have set before you,
but go and serve other gods,
and worship them:
7 **Then** will I cut off Israel out of the land which I have given them;
and this house, {which I have hallowed for my name}, will I cast out of my sight;
and Israel shall be a proverb and a byword among all people:
8 **And at this house**, {which is high}, every one that passeth by it shall be astonished,
and shall hiss;
and they shall say,
Why hath the LORD done thus unto this land, and to this house?

9 **And they** shall answer,
Because they forsook the LORD their God,
who brought forth their fathers out of the land of Egypt,
and have taken hold upon other gods,
and have worshipped them,
and served them:
therefore hath the LORD brought upon them all this evil.

10 **And it** came to pass at the end of twenty years,
when Solomon had built the two houses, the house of the LORD, and the king's house,
11 (Now Hiram the king of Tyre had furnished Solomon with cedar trees and fir trees, and with gold, according to all his desire,)
that then king Solomon gave Hiram twenty cities in the land of Galilee.

12 **And Hiram** came out from Tyre
to see the cities which Solomon had given him;
and they pleased him not.

13 **And he** said,
What cities are these which thou hast given me, my brother?
And he called them the land of Cabul unto this day.

14 **And Hiram** sent to the king sixscore talents of gold.

15 **And this** is the reason of the levy which king Solomon raised;
for to build the house of the LORD, and his own house, and Millo, and the wall of Jerusalem, and Hazor, and Megiddo, and Gezer.

16 **For Pharaoh king of Egypt** had gone up,
and taken Gezer,
and burnt it with fire,
and slain the Canaanites that dwelt in the city,
and given it for a present unto his daughter, Solomon's wife.
17 **And Solomon** built Gezer, and Bethhoron the nether,
18 And Baalath, and Tadmor in the wilderness, in the land,
19 And all the cities of store that Solomon had, and cities for his chariots, and cities for his horsemen, and that which Solomon desired to build in Jerusalem, and in Lebanon, and in all the land of his dominion.

20 **And all the people that were left of the Amorites, Hittites, Perizzites, Hivites, and Jebusites**, {which were not of the children of Israel},
21 Their children that were left after them in the land, {whom the children of Israel also were not able utterly to destroy}, upon those did Solomon levy a tribute of bondservice unto this day.

22 **But of the children of Israel** did Solomon make no bondmen:
but they were men of war, and his servants, and his princes, and his captains, and rulers of his chariots, and his horsemen.

23 **These** were the chief of the officers that were over Solomon's work, five hundred and fifty,
which bare rule over the people that wrought in the work.

24 **But Pharaoh's daughter** came up out of the city of David unto her house which Solomon had built for her:
then did he build Millo.

25 **And three times in a year** did Solomon offer burnt offerings and peace offerings upon the altar which he built unto the LORD,
and he burnt incense upon the altar that was before the LORD.

So he finished the house.

26 **And king Solomon** made a navy of ships in Eziongeber,
which is beside Eloth, on the shore of the Red sea, in the land of Edom.

27 **And Hiram** sent in the navy his servants, shipmen that had knowledge of the sea, with the servants of Solomon.

28 **And they** came to Ophir,
and fetched from thence gold, four hundred and twenty talents,
and brought it to king Solomon.

10 **And when the queen of Sheba** heard of the fame of Solomon concerning the name of the LORD,
she came
to prove him with hard questions.

2 **And she** came to Jerusalem with a very great train, with camels that bare spices, and very much gold, and precious stones:
and when she was come to Solomon,
she communed with him of all that was in her heart.

3 **And Solomon** told her all her questions:
there was not any thing hid from the king,
which he told her not.

4 **And when the queen of Sheba** had seen all Solomon's wisdom, and the house that he had built,
5 And the meat of his table, and the sitting of his servants, and the attendance of his ministers, and their apparel, and his cupbearers, and his ascent by which he went up unto the house of the LORD;
there was no more spirit in her.

6 **And she** said to the king,

It was a true report that I heard in mine own land of thy acts and of thy wisdom.

7 **Howbeit I** believed not the words,
until I came,
and mine eyes had seen it:
and, {behold}, the half was not told me:
thy wisdom and prosperity exceedeth the fame which I heard.

8 **Happy** are thy men,
happy are these thy servants,
which stand continually before thee,
and that hear thy wisdom.

9 **Blessed** be the LORD thy God,
which delighted in thee,
to set thee on the throne of Israel:
because the LORD loved Israel for ever,
therefore made he thee king,
to do judgment and justice.

10 **And she** gave the king an hundred and twenty talents of gold, and of spices very great store, and precious stones:
there came no more such abundance of spices as these which the queen of Sheba gave to king Solomon.

11 **And the navy also of Hiram**, {that brought gold from Ophir}, brought in from Ophir great plenty of almug trees, and precious stones.

12 **And the king** made of the almug trees pillars for the house of the LORD, and for the king's house, harps also and psalteries for singers:
there came no such almug trees,
nor were seen unto this day.

13 **And king Solomon** gave unto the queen of Sheba all her desire,
whatsoever she asked, beside that which Solomon gave her of his royal bounty.
So she turned and went to her own country, she and her servants.

14 **Now the weight of gold that came to Solomon in one year** was six hundred threescore and six talents of gold,
15 Beside that he had of the merchantmen, and of the traffick of the spice merchants, and of all the kings of Arabia, and of the governors of the country.

16 **And king Solomon** made two hundred targets of beaten gold:
six hundred shekels of gold went to one target.

17 **And he** made three hundred shields of beaten gold;
three pound of gold went to one shield:
and the king put them in the house of the forest of Lebanon.

18 **Moreover the king** made a great throne of ivory,
and overlaid it with the best gold.

19 **The throne** had six steps,
and the top of the throne was round behind:
and there were stays on either side on the place of the seat,
and two lions stood beside the stays.

20 **And twelve lions** stood there on the one side and on the other upon the six steps:
there was not the like made in any kingdom.

21 **And all king Solomon's drinking vessels** were of gold,
and all the vessels of the house of the forest of Lebanon were of pure gold;
none were of silver:
it was nothing accounted of in the days of Solomon.

22 **For the king** had at sea a navy of Tharshish with the navy of Hiram:
once in three years came the navy of Tharshish,
bringing gold, and silver, ivory, and apes, and peacocks.

23 **So king Solomon** exceeded all the kings of the earth for riches and for wisdom.

24 **And all the earth** sought to Solomon,
to hear his wisdom,
which God had put in his heart.

25 **And they** brought every man his present, vessels of silver, and vessels of gold, and garments, and armour, and spices, horses, and mules, a rate year by year.

26 **And Solomon** gathered together chariots and horsemen:
and he had a thousand and four hundred chariots, and twelve thousand horsemen,
whom he bestowed in the cities for chariots, and with the king at Jerusalem.

27 **And the king** made silver to be in Jerusalem as stones,
and cedars made he to be as the sycomore trees that are in the vale, for abundance.

28 **And Solomon** had horses brought out of Egypt, and linen yarn:
the king's merchants received the linen yarn at a price.

29 **And a chariot** came up and went out of Egypt for six hundred shekels of silver, and an horse for an hundred and fifty:
and so for all the kings of the Hittites, and for the kings of Syria, did they bring them out by their means.

11

But king Solomon loved many strange women,
together with the daughter of Pharaoh, women of the Moabites, Ammonites, Edomites, Zidonians, and Hittites:

2 **Of the nations concerning which the LORD said unto the children of Israel, {Ye shall not go in to them}, {neither shall they come in unto you}: {for surely they will turn away your heart after their gods}:** Solomon clave unto these in love.

3 **And he** had seven hundred wives, princesses, and three hundred concubines:
and his wives turned away his heart.

4 **For it** came to pass,
when Solomon was old,
that his wives turned away his heart after other gods:
and his heart was not perfect with the LORD his God,
as was the heart of David his father.

5 **For Solomon** went after Ashtoreth the goddess of the Zidonians, and after Milcom the abomination of the Ammonites.

6 **And Solomon** did evil in the sight of the LORD,
and went not fully after the LORD,
as did David his father.

7 **Then** did Solomon build an high place for Chemosh, the abomination of Moab, in the hill that is before Jerusalem, and for Molech, the abomination of the children of Ammon.

8 **And likewise** did he for all his strange wives,
which burnt incense and sacrificed unto their gods.

9 **And the LORD** was angry with Solomon,
because his heart was turned from the LORD God of Israel,
which had appeared unto him twice,

10 **And** had commanded him concerning this thing,
that he should not go after other gods:
but he kept not that which the LORD commanded.

11 **Wherefore the LORD** said unto Solomon,
Forasmuch as this is done of thee,
and thou hast not kept my covenant and my statutes,
which I have commanded thee,
I will surely rend the kingdom from thee,
and will give it to thy servant.

12 **Notwithstanding in thy days** I will not do it for David thy father's sake:
but I will rend it out of the hand of thy son.

13 **Howbeit I** will not rend away all the kingdom;
but will give one tribe to thy son for David my servant's sake, and for Jerusalem's sake which I have chosen.

14 **And the LORD** stirred up an adversary unto Solomon, Hadad the Edomite:
he was of the king's seed in Edom.

15 **For it** came to pass,
when David was in Edom,
and Joab the captain of the host was gone up to bury the slain,
after he had smitten every male in Edom;

16 (For six months did Joab remain there with all Israel, until he had cut off every male in Edom:)

17 **That Hadad** fled, he and certain Edomites of his father's servants with him,
to go into Egypt;
Hadad being yet a little child.

18 **And they** arose out of Midian,
and came to Paran:
and they took men with them out of Paran,
and they came to Egypt, unto Pharaoh king of Egypt;
which gave him an house,
and appointed him victuals,
and gave him land.

19 **And Hadad** found great favour in the sight of Pharaoh,
so that he gave him to wife the sister of his own wife, the sister of Tahpenes the queen.

20 **And the sister of Tahpenes** bare him Genubath his son,
whom Tahpenes weaned in Pharaoh's house:
and Genubath was in Pharaoh's household among the sons of Pharaoh.

21 **And when Hadad** heard in Egypt that David slept with his fathers,
and that Joab the captain of the host was dead,
Hadad said to Pharaoh,
Let me depart,
that I may go to mine own country.

22 **Then Pharaoh** said unto him,
But what hast thou lacked with me,
that, {behold}, thou seekest to go to thine own country?

And he answered,
Nothing:
howbeit let me go in any wise.

23 **And God** stirred him up another adversary, Rezon the son of Eliadah,
which fled from his lord Hadadezer king of Zobah:

24 **And he** gathered men unto him,
and became captain over a band,
when David slew them of Zobah:
and they went to Damascus,
and dwelt therein,
and reigned in Damascus.

25 **And he** was an adversary to Israel all the days of Solomon, beside the mischief that Hadad did:
and he abhorred Israel,
and reigned over Syria.

26 **And Jeroboam the son of Nebat, an Ephrathite of Zereda, Solomon's servant,** {whose mother's name was Zeruah, a widow woman}, even he lifted up his hand against the king.

27 **And this** was the cause that he lifted up his hand against the king:
Solomon built Millo,
and repaired the breaches of the city of David his father.

28 **And the man Jeroboam** was a mighty man of valour:
and Solomon seeing the young man that he was industrious,
he made him ruler over all the charge of the house of Joseph.

29 **And it** came to pass at that time when Jeroboam went out of Jerusalem,
that the prophet Ahijah the Shilonite found him in the way;
and he had clad himself with a new garment;
and they two were alone in the field:

30 **And Ahijah** caught the new garment that was on him,
and rent it in twelve pieces:

31 **And he** said to Jeroboam,
Take thee ten pieces:
for thus saith the LORD, the God of Israel,
Behold,
I will rend the kingdom out of the hand of Solomon,
and will give ten tribes to thee:

32 (But he shall have one tribe for my servant David's sake, and for Jerusalem's sake, the city which I have chosen out of all the tribes of Israel:)

33 **Because that they** have forsaken me,
and have worshipped Ashtoreth the goddess of the Zidonians, Chemosh the god of the Moabites, and Milcom the god of the children of Ammon,
and have not walked in my ways,
to do that which is right in mine eyes,
and to keep my statutes and my judgments,
as did David his father.

34 **Howbeit I** will not take the whole kingdom out of his hand:
but I will make him prince all the days of his life for David my servant's sake,
whom I chose,
because he kept my commandments and my statutes:

35 **But I** will take the kingdom out of his son's hand,
and will give it unto thee, even ten tribes.

36 **And unto his son** will I give one tribe,
that David my servant may have a light alway before me in Jerusalem, the city which I have chosen me to put my name there.

37 **And I** will take thee,

and thou shalt reign according to
all that thy soul desireth,
and shalt be king over Israel.
38 **And it** shall be,
if thou wilt hearken unto all that I
command thee,
and wilt walk in my ways,
and do that is right in my sight,
to keep my statutes and my
commandments,
as David my servant did;
that I will be with thee,
and build thee a sure house,
as I built for David,
and will give Israel unto thee.
39 **And I** will for this afflict the seed
of David, but not for ever.
40 **Solomon** sought therefore to kill
Jeroboam.
And Jeroboam arose,
and fled into Egypt, unto Shishak
king of Egypt,
and was in Egypt until the death of
Solomon.
41 **And the rest of the acts of
Solomon, and all that he did,
and his wisdom,** are they not
written in the book of the acts of
Solomon?
42 **And the time that Solomon
reigned in Jerusalem over all
Israel** was forty years.
43 **And Solomon** slept with his
fathers,
and was buried in the city of David
his father:
and Rehoboam his son reigned in
his stead.

12 **And Rehoboam** went to
Shechem:
for all Israel were come to Shechem
to make him king.
2 **And it** came to pass,
when Jeroboam the son of Nebat,
{who was yet in Egypt}, heard of
it,
({for he was fled from the presence
of king Solomon},
{and Jeroboam dwelt in Egypt};)
3 **That they** sent and called him.
**And Jeroboam and all the
congregation of Israel** came,
and spake unto Rehoboam,
saying,
4 **Thy father** made our yoke
grievous:
now therefore make thou the
grievous service of thy father, and
his heavy yoke which he put upon
us, lighter,
and we will serve thee.
5 **And he** said unto them,
Depart yet for three days,
then come again to me.
And the people departed.
6 **And king Rehoboam** consulted
with the old men,
that stood before Solomon his
father
while he yet lived,
and said,
How do ye advise
that I may answer this people?
7 **And they** spake unto him,
saying,
If thou wilt be a servant unto this
people this day,
and wilt serve them,
and answer them,
and speak good words to them,
then they will be thy servants for
ever.
8 **But he** forsook the counsel of the
old men,
which they had given him,
and consulted with the young men
that were grown up with him, and
which stood before him:
9 **And he** said unto them,
What counsel give ye that we may
answer this people,
who have spoken to me,
saying,
Make the yoke which thy father did
put upon us lighter?
10 **And the young men that were
grown up with him** spake unto
him,
saying,
Thus shalt thou speak unto this
people that spake unto thee,
saying,
Thy father made our yoke heavy,
but make thou it lighter unto us;
thus shalt thou say unto them,
My little finger shall be thicker
than my father's loins.
11 **And now whereas my father** did
lade you with a heavy yoke,
I will add to your yoke:
my father hath chastised you with
whips,
but I will chastise you with
scorpions.
12 **So Jeroboam and all the people**
came to Rehoboam the third day,
as the king had appointed,
saying,
Come to me again the third day.
13 **And the king** answered the
people roughly,
and forsook the old men's counsel
that they gave him;
14 **And** spake to them after the
counsel of the young men,
saying,
My father made your yoke heavy,
and I will add to your yoke:
my father also chastised you with
whips,
but I will chastise you with
scorpions.
15 **Wherefore the king** hearkened
not unto the people;
for the cause was from the LORD,
that he might perform his saying,
which the LORD spake by Ahijah
the Shilonite unto Jeroboam the
son of Nebat.
16 **So when all Israel** saw that the
king hearkened not unto them,
the people answered the king,
saying,
What portion have we in David?
neither have we inheritance in the
son of Jesse:
to your tents, O Israel:
now see to thine own house, David.
So Israel departed unto their tents.
17 **But as for the children of Israel
which dwelt in the cities of
Judah,** Rehoboam reigned over
them.
18 **Then king Rehoboam** sent
Adoram,
who was over the tribute;
and all Israel stoned him with
stones,
that he died.
Therefore king Rehoboam made
speed to get him up to his chariot,
to flee to Jerusalem.
19 **So Israel** rebelled against the
house of David unto this day.
20 **And it** came to pass,
when all Israel heard that
Jeroboam was come again,
that they sent and called him unto
the congregation,
and made him king over all Israel:
there was none that followed the
house of David, but the tribe of
Judah only.
21 **And when Rehoboam** was come
to Jerusalem,
he assembled all the house of
Judah, with the tribe of Benjamin,
an hundred and fourscore
thousand chosen men,

which were warriors,
to fight against the house of Israel,
to bring the kingdom again to Rehoboam the son of Solomon.

22 **But the word of God** came unto Shemaiah the man of God,
saying,
23 **Speak** unto Rehoboam, the son of Solomon, king of Judah, and unto all the house of Judah and Benjamin, and to the remnant of the people,
saying,
24 **Thus** saith the LORD,
Ye shall not go up,
nor fight against your brethren the children of Israel:
return every man to his house;
for this thing is from me.

They hearkened therefore to the word of the LORD,
and returned to depart, according to the word of the LORD.

25 **Then Jeroboam** built Shechem in mount Ephraim,
and dwelt therein;
and went out from thence,
and built Penuel.

26 **And Jeroboam** said in his heart,
Now shall the kingdom return to the house of David:
27 **If this people** go up to do sacrifice in the house of the LORD at Jerusalem,
then shall the heart of this people turn again unto their lord, even unto Rehoboam king of Judah,
and they shall kill me,
and go again to Rehoboam king of Judah.

28 **Whereupon the king** took counsel,
and made two calves of gold,
and said unto them,
It is too much for you to go up to Jerusalem:
behold thy gods, O Israel,
which brought thee up out of the land of Egypt.

29 **And he** set the one in Bethel,
and the other put he in Dan.

30 **And this thing** became a sin:
for the people went to worship before the one, even unto Dan.

31 **And he** made an house of high places,
and made priests of the lowest of the people,
which were not of the sons of Levi.

32 **And Jeroboam** ordained a feast in the eighth month, on the fifteenth day of the month, like unto the feast that is in Judah,
and he offered upon the altar.

So did he in Bethel,
sacrificing unto the calves that he had made:
and he placed in Bethel the priests of the high places which he had made.

33 **So he** offered upon the altar which he had made in Bethel the fifteenth day of the eighth month, even in the month which he had devised of his own heart;
and ordained a feast unto the children of Israel:
and he offered upon the altar,
and burnt incense.

13 **And, {behold}, there** came a man of God out of Judah by the word of the LORD unto Bethel:
and Jeroboam stood by the altar to burn incense.

2 **And he** cried against the altar in the word of the LORD,
and said,
O altar, altar, thus saith the LORD;
Behold,
a child shall be born unto the house of David, Josiah by name;
and upon thee shall he offer the priests of the high places that burn incense upon thee,
and men's bones shall be burnt upon thee.

3 **And he** gave a sign the same day,
saying,
This is the sign which the LORD hath spoken;
Behold,
the altar shall be rent,
and the ashes that are upon it shall be poured out.

4 **And it** came to pass,
when king Jeroboam heard the saying of the man of God,
which had cried against the altar in Bethel,
that he put forth his hand from the altar,
saying,
Lay hold on him.

And his hand, {which he put forth against him}, dried up,
so that he could not pull it in again to him.

5 **The altar** also was rent,
and the ashes poured out from the altar, according to the sign which the man of God had given by the word of the LORD.

6 **And the** king answered and said unto the man of God,
Intreat now the face of the LORD thy God,
and pray for me,
that my hand may be restored me again.

And the man of God besought the LORD,
and the king's hand was restored him again,
and became as it was before.

7 **And the** king said unto the man of God,
Come home with me,
and refresh thyself,
and I will give thee a reward.

8 **And the man of God** said unto the king,
If thou wilt give me half thine house,
I will not go in with thee,
neither will I eat bread
nor drink water in this place:
9 **For so** was it charged me by the word of the LORD,
saying,
Eat no bread,
nor drink water,
nor turn again by the same way that thou camest.

10 **So he** went another way,
and returned not by the way that he came to Bethel.

11 **Now there** dwelt an old prophet in Bethel;
and his sons came and told him all the works that the man of God had done that day in Bethel:
the words which he had spoken unto the king, them they told also to their father.

12 **And their father** said unto them,
What way went he?

For his sons had seen what way the man of God went,
which came from Judah.

13 **And he** said unto his sons,
Saddle me the ass.

So they saddled him the ass:
and he rode thereon,
14 **And** went after the man of God,
and found him sitting under an oak:
and he said unto him,

Art thou the man of God that camest from Judah?
And he said,
I am.
15 **Then he** said unto him,
Come home with me,
and eat bread.
16 **And he** said,
I may not return with thee,
nor go in with thee:
neither will I eat bread
nor drink water with thee in this place:
17 **For it was said to me by the word of the LORD,** Thou shalt eat no bread nor drink water there, nor turn again to go by the way that thou camest.
18 **He** said unto him,
I am a prophet also as thou art;
and an angel spake unto me by the word of the LORD,
saying,
Bring him back with thee into thine house,
that he may eat bread and drink water.
But he lied unto him.
19 **So he** went back with him,
and did eat bread in his house,
and drank water.
20 **And it** came to pass,
as they sat at the table,
that the word of the LORD came unto the prophet that brought him back:
21 **And he** cried unto the man of God that came from Judah,
saying,
Thus saith the LORD,
Forasmuch as thou hast disobeyed the mouth of the LORD,
and hast not kept the commandment which the LORD thy God commanded thee,
22 **But** camest back,
and hast eaten bread
and drunk water in the place,
of the which the LORD did say to thee,
Eat no bread,
and drink no water;
thy carcase shall not come unto the sepulchre of thy fathers.
23 **And it** came to pass,
after he had eaten bread,
and after he had drunk,
that he saddled for him the ass, to wit, for the prophet whom he had brought back.
24 **And when he** was gone,
a lion met him by the way,
and slew him:
and his carcase was cast in the way,
and the ass stood by it,
the lion also stood by the carcase.
25 **And, {behold}, men** passed by,
and saw the carcase cast in the way, and the lion standing by the carcase:
and they came and told it in the city where the old prophet dwelt.
26 **And when the prophet that brought him back from the way** heard thereof,
he said,
It is the man of God,
who was disobedient unto the word of the LORD:
therefore the LORD hath delivered him unto the lion,
which hath torn him,
and slain him, according to the word of the LORD,
which he spake unto him.
27 **And he** spake to his sons,
saying,
Saddle me the ass.
And they saddled him.
28 **And he** went and found his carcase cast in the way, and the ass and the lion standing by the carcase:
the lion had not eaten the carcase,
nor torn the ass.
29 **And the prophet** took up the carcase of the man of God,
and laid it upon the ass,
and brought it back:
and the old prophet came to the city,
to mourn and to bury him.
30 **And he** laid his carcase in his own grave;
and they mourned over him,
saying,
Alas, my brother!
31 **And it** came to pass,
after he had buried him,
that he spake to his sons,
saying,
When I am dead,
then bury me in the sepulchre wherein the man of God is buried;
lay my bones beside his bones:
32 **For the saying which he cried by the word of the LORD against the altar in Bethel, and against all the houses of the high places which are in the cities of Samaria,** shall surely come to pass.
33 **After this thing** Jeroboam returned not from his evil way,
but made again of the lowest of the people priests of the high places:
whosoever would,
he consecrated him,
and he became one of the priests of the high places.
34 **And this thing** became sin unto the house of Jeroboam,
even to cut it off,
and to destroy it from off the face of the earth.

14 **At that time** Abijah the son of Jeroboam fell sick.
2 **And Jeroboam** said to his wife,
Arise,
I pray thee,
and disguise thyself,
that thou be not known to be the wife of Jeroboam;
and get thee to Shiloh:
behold,
there is Ahijah the prophet,
which told me
that I should be king over this people.
3 **And take** with thee ten loaves, and cracknels, and a cruse of honey,
and go to him:
he shall tell thee
what shall become of the child.
4 **And Jeroboam's wife** did so,
and arose,
and went to Shiloh,
and came to the house of Ahijah.
But Ahijah could not see;
for his eyes were set by reason of his age.
5 **And the LORD** said unto
Ahijah, {Behold}, the wife of Jeroboam cometh to ask a thing of thee for her son;
for he is sick:
thus and thus shalt thou say unto her:
for it shall be,
when she cometh in,
that she shall feign herself to be another woman.
6 **And it** was so,
when Ahijah heard the sound of her feet,
as she came in at the door,
that he said,
Come in, thou wife of Jeroboam;

why feignest thou thyself to be another?
for I am sent to thee with heavy tidings.

7 **Go,**
tell Jeroboam,
Thus saith the LORD God of Israel,
Forasmuch as I exalted thee from among the people,
and made thee prince over my people Israel,
8 **And** rent the kingdom away from the house of David,
and gave it thee:
and yet thou hast not been as my servant David,
who kept my commandments,
and who followed me with all his heart,
to do that only which was right in mine eyes;
9 **But** hast done evil above all that were before thee:
for thou hast gone and made thee other gods, and molten images,
to provoke me to anger,
and hast cast me behind thy back:
10 **Therefore, {behold}, I** will bring evil upon the house of Jeroboam,
and will cut off from Jeroboam him that pisseth against the wall, and him that is shut up and left in Israel,
and will take away the remnant of the house of Jeroboam, as a man taketh away dung, till it be all gone.

11 **Him that dieth of Jeroboam in the city** shall the dogs eat;
and him that dieth in the field shall the fowls of the air eat:
for the LORD hath spoken it.

12 **Arise thou** therefore,
get thee to thine own house:
and when thy feet enter into the city,
the child shall die.

13 **And all Israel** shall mourn for him,
and bury him:
for he only of Jeroboam shall come to the grave,
because in him there is found some good thing toward the LORD God of Israel in the house of Jeroboam.

14 **Moreover the LORD** shall raise him up a king over Israel,
who shall cut off the house of Jeroboam that day:
but what? even now.

15 **For the LORD** shall smite Israel, as a reed is shaken in the water,
and he shall root up Israel out of this good land,
which he gave to their fathers,
and shall scatter them beyond the river,
because they have made their groves,
provoking the LORD to anger.

16 **And he** shall give Israel up because of the sins of Jeroboam,
who did sin,
and who made Israel to sin.

17 **And Jeroboam's wife** arose,
and departed,
and came to Tirzah:
and when she came to the threshold of the door,
the child died;
18 **And they** buried him;
and all Israel mourned for him, according to the word of the LORD,
which he spake by the hand of his servant Ahijah the prophet.

19 **And the rest of the acts of Jeroboam**, {how he warred}, {and how he reigned}, {behold}, they are written in the book of the chronicles of the kings of Israel.

20 **And the days which Jeroboam reigned** were two and twenty years:
and he slept with his fathers,
and Nadab his son reigned in his stead.

21 **And Rehoboam the son of Solomon** reigned in Judah.
Rehoboam was forty and one years old when he began to reign,
and he reigned seventeen years in Jerusalem, the city which the LORD did choose out of all the tribes of Israel, to put his name there.

And his mother's name was Naamah an Ammonitess.

22 **And Judah** did evil in the sight of the LORD,
and they provoked him to jealousy with their sins which they had committed, above all that their fathers had done.

23 **For they** also built them high places, and images, and groves, on every high hill, and under every green tree.

24 **And there** were also sodomites in the land:
and they did according to all the abominations of the nations which the LORD cast out before the children of Israel.

25 **And it** came to pass in the fifth year of king Rehoboam,
that Shishak king of Egypt came up against Jerusalem:
26 **And he** took away the treasures of the house of the LORD, and the treasures of the king's house;
he even took away all:
and he took away all the shields of gold which Solomon had made.

27 **And king Rehoboam** made in their stead brasen shields,
and committed them unto the hands of the chief of the guard,
which kept the door of the king's house.

28 **And it** was so,
when the king went into the house of the LORD,
that the guard bare them,
and brought them back into the guard chamber.

29 **Now the rest of the acts of Rehoboam, and all that he did,** are they not written in the book of the chronicles of the kings of Judah?

30 **And there** was war between Rehoboam and Jeroboam all their days.

31 **And Rehoboam** slept with his fathers,
and was buried with his fathers in the city of David.

And his mother's name was Naamah an Ammonitess.

And Abijam his son reigned in his stead.

15 **Now in the eighteenth year of king Jeroboam** the son of Nebat reigned Abijam over Judah.

2 **Three years** reigned he in Jerusalem.

And his mother's name was Maachah, the daughter of Abishalom.

3 **And he** walked in all the sins of his father,
which he had done before him:
and his heart was not perfect with the LORD his God, as the heart of David his father.

[4] **Nevertheless for David's sake** did the LORD his God give him a lamp in Jerusalem,
to set up his son after him,
and to establish Jerusalem:
[5] **Because David** did that which was right in the eyes of the LORD,
and turned not aside from any thing that he commanded him all the days of his life, save only in the matter of Uriah the Hittite.

[6] **And there** was war between Rehoboam and Jeroboam all the days of his life.

[7] **Now the rest of the acts of Abijam, and all that he did,** are they not written in the book of the chronicles of the kings of Judah?

And there was war between Abijam and Jeroboam.

[8] **And Abijam** slept with his fathers;
and they buried him in the city of David:
and Asa his son reigned in his stead.

[9] **And in the twentieth year of Jeroboam king of Israel** reigned Asa over Judah.

[10] **And forty and one years** reigned he in Jerusalem.

And his mother's name was Maachah, the daughter of Abishalom.

[11] **And Asa** did that which was right in the eyes of the LORD,
as did David his father.

[12] **And he** took away the sodomites out of the land,
and removed all the idols that his fathers had made.

[13] **And also Maachah his mother,** even her he removed from being queen,
because she had made an idol in a grove;
and Asa destroyed her idol,
and burnt it by the brook Kidron.

[14] **But the high places** were not removed:
nevertheless Asa's heart was perfect with the LORD all his days.

[15] **And he** brought in the things which his father had dedicated, and the things which himself had dedicated, into the house of the LORD, silver, and gold, and vessels.

[16] **And there** was war between Asa and Baasha king of Israel all their days.

[17] **And Baasha king of Israel** went up against Judah,
and built Ramah,
that he might not suffer any to go out or come in to Asa king of Judah.

[18] **Then Asa** took all the silver and the gold that were left in the treasures of the house of the LORD, and the treasures of the king's house,
and delivered them into the hand of his servants:
and king Asa sent them to Benhadad, the son of Tabrimon, the son of Hezion, king of Syria,
that dwelt at Damascus,
saying,
[19] **There** is a league between me and thee, and between my father and thy father:
behold,
I have sent unto thee a present of silver and gold;
come and break thy league with Baasha king of Israel,
that he may depart from me.

[20] **So Benhadad** hearkened unto king Asa,
and sent the captains of the hosts which he had against the cities of Israel,
and smote Ijon, and Dan, and Abelbethmaachah, and all Cinneroth, with all the land of Naphtali.

[21] **And it** came to pass,
when Baasha heard thereof,
that he left off building of Ramah,
and dwelt in Tirzah.

[22] **Then king Asa** made a proclamation throughout all Judah;
none was exempted:
and they took away the stones of Ramah, and the timber thereof,
wherewith Baasha had builded;
and king Asa built with them Geba of Benjamin, and Mizpah.

[23] **The rest of all the acts of Asa, and all his might, and all that he did, and the cities which he built,** are they not written in the book of the chronicles of the kings of Judah?

Nevertheless in the time of his old age he was diseased in his feet.

[24] **And Asa** slept with his fathers,
and was buried with his fathers in the city of David his father:
and Jehoshaphat his son reigned in his stead.

[25] **And Nadab the son of Jeroboam** began to reign over Israel in the second year of Asa king of Judah,
and reigned over Israel two years.

[26] **And he** did evil in the sight of the LORD,
and walked in the way of his father, and in his sin wherewith he made Israel to sin.

[27] **And Baasha the son of Ahijah, of the house of Issachar,** conspired against him;
and Baasha smote him at Gibbethon,
which belonged to the Philistines;
for Nadab and all Israel laid siege to Gibbethon.

[28] **Even in the third year of Asa king of Judah** did Baasha slay him,
and reigned in his stead.

[29] **And it** came to pass,
when he reigned,
that he smote all the house of Jeroboam;
he left not to Jeroboam any that breathed,
until he had destroyed him,
according unto the saying of the LORD,
which he spake by his servant Ahijah the Shilonite:
[30] Because of the sins of Jeroboam which he sinned, and which he made Israel sin, by his provocation wherewith he provoked the LORD God of Israel to anger.

[31] **Now the rest of the acts of Nadab, and all that he did,** are they not written in the book of the chronicles of the kings of Israel?

[32] **And there** was war between Asa and Baasha king of Israel all their days.

[33] **In the third year of Asa king of Judah** began Baasha the son of Ahijah to reign over all Israel in Tirzah, twenty and four years.

[34] **And he** did evil in the sight of the LORD,
and walked in the way of Jeroboam, and in his sin wherewith he made Israel to sin.

16 **Then the word of the LORD** came to Jehu the son of Hanani against Baasha,
saying,

2 **Forasmuch as I** exalted thee out of the dust,
and made thee prince over my people Israel;
and thou hast walked in the way of Jeroboam,
and hast made my people Israel to sin,
to provoke me to anger with their sins;

3 **Behold,**
I will take away the posterity of Baasha, and the posterity of his house;
and will make thy house like the house of Jeroboam the son of Nebat.

4 **Him that dieth of Baasha in the city** shall the dogs eat;
and him that dieth of his in the fields shall the fowls of the air eat.

5 **Now the rest of the acts of Baasha, and what he did, and his might,** are they not written in the book of the chronicles of the kings of Israel?

6 **So Baasha** slept with his fathers,
and was buried in Tirzah:
and Elah his son reigned in his stead.

7 **And also by the hand of the prophet Jehu the son of Hanani** came the word of the LORD against Baasha, and against his house, even for all the evil that he did in the sight of the LORD,
in provoking him to anger with the work of his hands,
in being like the house of Jeroboam;
and because he killed him.

8 **In the twenty and sixth year of Asa king of Judah** began Elah the son of Baasha to reign over Israel in Tirzah, two years.

9 **And his servant Zimri, captain of half his chariots,** conspired against him,
as he was in Tirzah,
drinking himself drunk in the house of Arza steward of his house in Tirzah.

10 **And Zimri** went in and smote him,
and killed him, in the twenty and seventh year of Asa king of Judah,
and reigned in his stead.

11 **And it** came to pass,
when he began to reign,
as soon as he sat on his throne,
that he slew all the house of Baasha:
he left him not one that pisseth against a wall, neither of his kinsfolks, nor of his friends.

12 **Thus** did Zimri destroy all the house of Baasha, according to the word of the LORD,
which he spake against Baasha by Jehu the prophet.

13 For all the sins of Baasha, and the sins of Elah his son,
by which they sinned,
and by which they made Israel to sin,
in provoking the LORD God of Israel to anger with their vanities.

14 **Now the rest of the acts of Elah, and all that he did,** are they not written in the book of the chronicles of the kings of Israel?

15 **In the twenty and seventh year of Asa king of Judah** did Zimri reign seven days in Tirzah.
And the people were encamped against Gibbethon,
which belonged to the Philistines.

16 **And the people that were encamped** heard say,
Zimri hath conspired,
and hath also slain the king:
wherefore all Israel made Omri, the captain of the host, king over Israel that day in the camp.

17 **And Omri** went up from Gibbethon, and all Israel with him,
and they besieged Tirzah.

18 **And it** came to pass,
when Zimri saw that the city was taken,
that he went into the palace of the king's house,
and burnt the king's house over him with fire,
and died.

19 For his sins which he sinned in doing evil in the sight of the LORD, {in walking in the way of Jeroboam}, and in his sin which he did, {to make Israel to sin}.

20 **Now the rest of the acts of Zimri, and his treason that he wrought,** are they not written in the book of the chronicles of the kings of Israel?

21 **Then** were the people of Israel divided into two parts:
half of the people followed Tibni the son of Ginath,
to make him king;
and half followed Omri.

22 **But the people that followed Omri** prevailed against the people that followed Tibni the son of Ginath:
so Tibni died,
and Omri reigned.

23 **In the thirty and first year of Asa king of Judah** began Omri to reign over Israel, twelve years:
six years reigned he in Tirzah.

24 **And he** bought the hill Samaria of Shemer for two talents of silver,
and built on the hill,
and called the name of the city which he built, after the name of Shemer, owner of the hill, Samaria.

25 **But Omri** wrought evil in the eyes of the LORD,
and did worse than all that were before him.

26 **For he** walked in all the way of Jeroboam the son of Nebat, and in his sin wherewith he made Israel to sin,
to provoke the LORD God of Israel to anger with their vanities.

27 **Now the rest of the acts of Omri which he did, and his might that he shewed,** are they not written in the book of the chronicles of the kings of Israel?

28 **So Omri** slept with his fathers,
and was buried in Samaria:
and Ahab his son reigned in his stead.

29 **And in the thirty and eighth year of Asa king of Judah** began Ahab the son of Omri to reign over Israel:
and Ahab the son of Omri reigned over Israel in Samaria twenty and two years.

30 **And Ahab the son of Omri** did evil in the sight of the LORD above all that were before him.

31 **And it** came to pass,
as if it had been a light thing for him to walk in the sins of Jeroboam the son of Nebat,

that he took to wife Jezebel the
daughter of Ethbaal king of the
Zidonians,
and went and served Baal,
and worshipped him.
32 **And he** reared up an altar for Baal
in the house of Baal,
which he had built in Samaria.
33 **And Ahab** made a grove;
and Ahab did more to provoke the
LORD God of Israel to anger than
all the kings of Israel that were
before him.
34 **In his days** did Hiel the Bethelite
build Jericho:
he laid the foundation thereof in
Abiram his firstborn,
and set up the gates thereof in his
youngest son Segub, according to
the word of the LORD,
which he spake by Joshua the son
of Nun.

17 **And Elijah the Tishbite**,
{who was of the inhabitants
of Gilead}, said unto Ahab,
As the LORD God of Israel liveth,
before whom I stand,
there shall not be dew nor rain
these years, but according to my
word.
2 **And the word of the LORD** came
unto him,
saying,
3 **Get thee** hence,
and turn thee eastward,
and hide thyself by the brook
Cherith,
that is before Jordan.
4 **And it** shall be,
that thou shalt drink of the brook;
and I have commanded the ravens
to feed thee there.
5 **So he** went and did according unto
the word of the LORD:
for he went and dwelt by the brook
Cherith,
that is before Jordan.
6 **And the ravens** brought him
bread and flesh in the morning,
and bread and flesh in the
evening;
and he drank of the brook.
7 **And it** came to pass after a while,
that the brook dried up,
because there had been no rain in
the land.
8 **And the word of the LORD** came
unto him,
saying,
9 **Arise,**
get thee to Zarephath,
which belongeth to Zidon,
and dwell there:
behold,
I have commanded a widow
woman there
to sustain thee.
10 **So he** arose and went to
Zarephath.
And when he came to the gate of
the city,
behold,
the widow woman was there
gathering of sticks:
and he called to her,
and said,
Fetch me, {I pray thee}, a little
water in a vessel,
that I may drink.
11 **And as she** was going to fetch it,
he called to her,
and said,
Bring me, {I pray thee}, a morsel of
bread in thine hand.
12 **And she** said,
As the LORD thy God liveth,
I have not a cake, but an handful of
meal in a barrel, and a little oil in
a cruse:
and, {behold}, I am gathering two
sticks,
that I may go in and dress it for me
and my son,
that we may eat it,
and die.
13 **And Elijah** said unto her,
Fear not;
go and do as thou hast said:
but make me thereof a little cake
first,
and bring it unto me,
and after make for thee and for thy
son.
14 **For thus** saith the LORD God of
Israel,
The barrel of meal shall not waste,
neither shall the cruse of oil fail,
until the day that the LORD
sendeth rain upon the earth.
15 **And she** went and did according
to the saying of Elijah:
and she, and he, and her house,
did eat many days.
16 **And the barrel of meal** wasted
not,
neither did the cruse of oil fail,
according to the word of the
LORD,
which he spake by Elijah.
17 **And it** came to pass after these
things,
**that the son of the woman, the
mistress of the house,** fell sick;
and his sickness was so sore,
that there was no breath left in
him.
18 **And she** said unto Elijah,
What have I to do with thee, O thou
man of God?
art thou come unto me to call my
sin to remembrance,
and to slay my son?
19 **And he** said unto her,
Give me thy son.
And he took him out of her bosom,
and carried him up into a loft,
where he abode,
and laid him upon his own bed.
20 **And he** cried unto the LORD,
and said,
O LORD my God, hast thou also
brought evil upon the widow
with whom I sojourn,
by slaying her son?
21 **And he** stretched himself upon
the child three times,
and cried unto the LORD,
and said,
**O LORD my God, {I pray thee}, let
this child's soul** come into him
again.
22 **And the LORD** heard the voice of
Elijah;
and the soul of the child came into
him again,
and he revived.
23 **And Elijah** took the child,
and brought him down out of the
chamber into the house,
and delivered him unto his mother:
and Elijah said,
See,
thy son liveth.
24 **And the woman** said to Elijah,
Now by this I know
that thou art a man of God,
**and that the word of the LORD in
thy mouth** is truth.

18 **And it** came to pass
after many days,
that the word of the LORD came
to Elijah in the third year,
saying,
Go,
shew thyself unto Ahab;
and I will send rain upon the earth.
2 **And Elijah** went to shew himself
unto Ahab.

And there was a sore famine in Samaria.
3 **And Ahab** called Obadiah,
which was the governor of his house.
(**Now Obadiah** feared the LORD greatly:
4 **For it** was so,
when Jezebel cut off the prophets of the LORD,
that Obadiah took an hundred prophets,
and hid them by fifty in a cave,
and fed them with bread and water.)
5 **And Ahab** said unto Obadiah,
Go into the land, unto all fountains of water, and unto all brooks:
peradventure we may find grass
to save the horses and mules alive,
that we lose not all the beasts.
6 **So they** divided the land between them
to pass throughout it:
Ahab went one way by himself,
and Obadiah went another way by himself.
7 **And as Obadiah** was in the way,
behold,
Elijah met him:
and he knew him,
and fell on his face,
and said,
Art thou that my lord Elijah?
8 **And he** answered him,
I am:
go,
tell thy lord,
Behold,
Elijah is here.
9 **And he** said,
What have I sinned,
that thou wouldest deliver thy servant into the hand of Ahab,
to slay me?
10 **As the LORD thy God** liveth,
there is no nation or kingdom,
whither my lord hath not sent to seek thee:
and when they said,
He is not there;
he took an oath of the kingdom and nation,
that they found thee not.
11 **And now thou** sayest,
Go,
tell thy lord,
Behold,
Elijah is here.
12 **And it** shall come to pass,
as soon as I am gone from thee,
that the Spirit of the LORD shall carry thee
whither I know not;
and so when I come and tell Ahab,
and he cannot find thee,
he shall slay me:
but I thy servant fear the LORD from my youth.
13 **Was it not** told my lord
what I did
when Jezebel slew the prophets of the LORD,
how I hid an hundred men of the LORD's prophets by fifty in a cave,
and fed them with bread and water?
14 **And now thou** sayest,
Go,
tell thy lord,
Behold,
Elijah is here:
and he shall slay me.
15 **And Elijah** said,
As the LORD of hosts liveth,
before whom I stand,
I will surely shew myself unto him to day.
16 **So Obadiah** went to meet Ahab,
and told him:
and Ahab went to meet Elijah.
17 **And it** came to pass,
when Ahab saw Elijah,
that Ahab said unto him,
Art thou he that troubleth Israel?
18 **And he** answered,
I have not troubled Israel; but thou, and thy father's house,
in that ye have forsaken the commandments of the LORD,
and thou hast followed Baalim.
19 **Now therefore send,**
and gather to me all Israel unto mount Carmel, and the prophets of Baal four hundred and fifty, and the prophets of the groves four hundred,
which eat at Jezebel's table.
20 **So Ahab** sent unto all the children of Israel,
and gathered the prophets together unto mount Carmel.
21 **And Elijah** came unto all the people,
and said,
How long halt ye between two opinions?
if the LORD be God,
follow him:
but if Baal,
then follow him.
And the people answered him not a word.
22 **Then** said Elijah unto the people,
I, even I only, remain a prophet of the LORD;
but Baal's prophets are four hundred and fifty men.
23 **Let them** therefore give us two bullocks;
and let them choose one bullock for themselves,
and cut it in pieces,
and lay it on wood,
and put no fire under:
and I will dress the other bullock,
and lay it on wood,
and put no fire under:
24 **And call ye** on the name of your gods,
and I will call on the name of the LORD:
and the God that answereth by fire, let him be God.
And all the people answered and said,
It is well spoken.
25 **And Elijah** said unto the prophets of Baal,
Choose you one bullock for yourselves,
and dress it first;
for ye are many;
and call on the name of your gods,
but put no fire under.
26 **And they** took the bullock which was given them,
and they dressed it,
and called on the name of Baal from morning even until noon,
saying,
O Baal, hear us.
But there was no voice, nor any that answered.
And they leaped upon the altar which was made.
27 **And it** came to pass at noon,
that Elijah mocked them,
and said,
Cry aloud:
for he is a god;
either he is talking,
or he is pursuing,
or he is in a journey,
or peradventure he sleepeth,
and must be awaked.
28 **And they** cried aloud,

and cut themselves after their manner with knives and lancets,
till the blood gushed out upon them.

29 **And it** came to pass,
when midday was past,
and they prophesied until the time of the offering of the evening sacrifice,
that there was neither voice,
nor any to answer,
nor any that regarded.

30 **And Elijah** said unto all the people,
Come near unto me.

And all the people came near unto him.

And he repaired the altar of the LORD that was broken down.

31 **And Elijah** took twelve stones, according to the number of the tribes of the sons of Jacob,
unto whom the word of the LORD came,
saying,
Israel shall be thy name:
32 **And with the stones** he built an altar in the name of the LORD:
and he made a trench about the altar, as great as would contain two measures of seed.

33 **And he** put the wood in order,
and cut the bullock in pieces,
and laid him on the wood,
and said,
Fill four barrels with water,
and pour it on the burnt sacrifice, and on the wood.

34 **And he** said,
Do it the second time.

And they did it the second time.

And he said,
Do it the third time.

And they did it the third time.

35 **And the water** ran round about the altar;
and he filled the trench also with water.

36 **And it** came to pass at the time of the offering of the evening sacrifice,
that Elijah the prophet came near,
and said,
LORD God of Abraham, Isaac, and of Israel, let it be known this day that thou art God in Israel, and that I am thy servant, and that I have done all these things at thy word.

37 **Hear** me, O LORD,
hear me,
that this people may know
that thou art the LORD God,
and that thou hast turned their heart back again.

38 **Then the fire of the LORD** fell,
and consumed the burnt sacrifice, and the wood, and the stones, and the dust,
and licked up the water that was in the trench.

39 **And when all the people** saw it,
they fell on their faces:
and they said,
The LORD, he is the God;
the LORD, he is the God.

40 **And Elijah** said unto them,
Take the prophets of Baal;
let not one of them escape.

And they took them:
and Elijah brought them down to the brook Kishon,
and slew them there.

41 **And Elijah** said unto Ahab,
Get thee up,
eat and drink;
for there is a sound of abundance of rain.

42 **So Ahab** went up to eat and to drink.

And Elijah went up to the top of Carmel;
and he cast himself down upon the earth,
and put his face between his knees,
43 **And** said to his servant,
Go up now,
look toward the sea.

And he went up,
and looked,
and said,
There is nothing.

And he said,
Go again seven times.

44 **And it** came to pass at the seventh time,
that he said,
Behold,
there ariseth a little cloud out of the sea, like a man's hand.

And he said,
Go up,
say unto Ahab,
Prepare thy chariot,
and get thee down
that the rain stop thee not.

45 **And it** came to pass in the mean while,
that the heaven was black with clouds and wind,
and there was a great rain.

And Ahab rode,
and went to Jezreel.

46 **And the hand of the LORD** was on Elijah;
and he girded up his loins,
and ran before Ahab to the entrance of Jezreel.

19

And Ahab told Jezebel all that Elijah had done,
and withal how he had slain all the prophets with the sword.

2 **Then Jezebel** sent a messenger unto Elijah,
saying,
So let the gods do to me, and more also,
if I make not thy life as the life of one of them by to morrow about this time.

3 **And when he** saw that,
he arose,
and went for his life,
and came to Beersheba,
which belongeth to Judah,
and left his servant there.

4 **But he himself** went a day's journey into the wilderness,
and came and sat down under a juniper tree:
and he requested for himself
that he might die;
and said,
It is enough;
now, O LORD, take away my life;
for I am not better than my fathers.

5 **And as he** lay and slept under a juniper tree,
behold,
then an angel touched him,
and said unto him,
Arise and eat.

6 **And he** looked,
and, {behold}, there was a cake baken on the coals, and a cruse of water at his head.

And he did eat and drink,
and laid him down again.

7 **And the angel of the LORD** came again the second time,
and touched him,
and said,
Arise and eat;
because the journey is too great for thee.

8 **And he** arose,
and did eat and drink,

and went in the strength of that meat forty days and forty nights unto Horeb the mount of God.

[9] **And he** came thither unto a cave,
and lodged there;
and, {behold}, the word of the LORD came to him,
and he said unto him,
What doest thou here, Elijah?

[10] **And he** said,
I have been very jealous for the LORD God of hosts:
for the children of Israel have forsaken thy covenant,
thrown down thine altars,
and slain thy prophets with the sword;
and I, even I only, am left;
and they seek my life,
to take it away.

[11] **And he** said,
Go forth,
and stand upon the mount before the LORD.
And, {behold}, the LORD passed by,
and a great and strong wind rent the mountains,
and brake in pieces the rocks before the LORD;
but the LORD was not in the wind:
and after the wind an earthquake;
but the LORD was not in the earthquake:

[12] **And after the earthquake** a fire;
but the LORD was not in the fire:
and after the fire a still small voice.

[13] **And it** was so,
when Elijah heard it,
that he wrapped his face in his mantle,
and went out,
and stood in the entering in of the cave.
And, {behold}, there came a voice unto him,
and said,
What doest thou here, Elijah?

[14] **And he** said,
I have been very jealous for the LORD God of hosts:
because the children of Israel have forsaken thy covenant,
thrown down thine altars,
and slain thy prophets with the sword;
and I, even I only, am left;
and they seek my life,
to take it away.

[15] **And the LORD** said unto him,
Go,
return on thy way to the wilderness of Damascus:
and when thou comest,
anoint Hazael to be king over Syria:

[16] **And Jehu the son of Nimshi** shalt thou anoint to be king over Israel:
and Elisha the son of Shaphat of Abelmeholah shalt thou anoint to be prophet in thy room.

[17] **And it** shall come to pass,
that him that escapeth the sword of Hazael shall Jehu slay:
and him that escapeth from the sword of Jehu shall Elisha slay.

[18] **Yet I** have left me seven thousand in Israel, all the knees which have not bowed unto Baal, and every mouth which hath not kissed him.

[19] **So he** departed thence,
and found Elisha the son of Shaphat,
who was plowing with twelve yoke of oxen before him, and he with the twelfth:
and Elijah passed by him,
and cast his mantle upon him.

[20] **And he** left the oxen,
and ran after Elijah,
and said,
Let me, {I pray thee}, kiss my father and my mother,
and then I will follow thee.
And he said unto him,
Go back again:
for what have I done to thee?

[21] **And he** returned back from him,
and took a yoke of oxen,
and slew them,
and boiled their flesh with the instruments of the oxen,
and gave unto the people,
and they did eat.
Then he arose,
and went after Elijah,
and ministered unto him.

20 **And Benhadad the king of Syria** gathered all his host together:
and there were thirty and two kings with him, and horses, and chariots;
and he went up and besieged Samaria,
and warred against it.

[2] **And he** sent messengers to Ahab king of Israel into the city,
and said unto him,
Thus saith Benhadad,

[3] **Thy silver and thy gold** is mine;
thy wives also and thy children, even the goodliest, are mine.

[4] **And the king of Israel** answered and said,
My lord, O king, according to thy saying, I am thine, and all that I have.

[5] **And the messengers** came again,
and said,
Thus speaketh Benhadad,
saying,
Although I have sent unto thee,
saying,
Thou shalt deliver me thy silver, and thy gold, and thy wives, and thy children;

[6] **Yet I** will send my servants unto thee to morrow about this time,
and they shall search thine house, and the houses of thy servants;
and it shall be,
that whatsoever is pleasant in thine eyes,
they shall put it in their hand,
and take it away.

[7] **Then the king of Israel** called all the elders of the land,
and said,
Mark,
I pray you,
and see how this man seeketh mischief:
for he sent unto me for my wives, and for my children, and for my silver, and for my gold;
and I denied him not.

[8] **And all the elders and all the people** said unto him,
Hearken not unto him,
nor consent.

[9] **Wherefore he** said unto the messengers of Benhadad,
Tell my lord the king,
All that thou didst send for to thy servant at the first I will do:
but this thing I may not do.
And the messengers departed,
and brought him word again.

[10] **And Benhadad** sent unto him,
and said,
The gods do so unto me, and more also,
if the dust of Samaria shall suffice for handfuls for all the people that follow me.

[11] **And the king of Israel** answered and said,
Tell him,

Let not him that girdeth on his harness boast himself as he that putteth it off.

12 **And it** came to pass,
when Ben-hadad heard this message,
as he was drinking, he and the kings in the pavilions,
that he said unto his servants,
Set yourselves in array.

And they set themselves in array against the city.

13 **And, {behold}, there** came a prophet unto Ahab king of Israel,
saying,
Thus saith the LORD,
Hast thou seen all this great multitude?
behold,
I will deliver it into thine hand this day;
and thou shalt know
that I am the LORD.

14 **And Ahab** said,
By whom?

And he said,
Thus saith the LORD,
Even by the young men of the princes of the provinces.

Then he said,
Who shall order the battle?

And he answered,
Thou.

15 **Then he** numbered the young men of the princes of the provinces,
and they were two hundred and thirty two:
and after them he numbered all the people, even all the children of Israel,
being seven thousand.

16 **And they** went out at noon.

But Benhadad was drinking himself drunk in the pavilions, he and the kings, the thirty and two kings that helped him.

17 **And the young men of the princes of the provinces** went out first;
and Benhadad sent out,
and they told him,
saying,
There are men come out of Samaria.

18 **And he** said,
Whether they be come out for peace,
take them alive;
or whether they be come out for war,
take them alive.

19 **So these young men of the princes of the provinces** came out of the city, and the army which followed them.

20 **And they** slew every one his man:
and the Syrians fled;
and Israel pursued them:
and Benhadad the king of Syria escaped on an horse with the horsemen.

21 **And the king of Israel** went out,
and smote the horses and chariots,
and slew the Syrians with a great slaughter.

22 **And the prophet** came to the king of Israel,
and said unto him,
Go,
strengthen thyself,
and mark,
and see what thou doest:
for at the return of the year the king of Syria will come up against thee.

23 **And the servants of the king of Syria** said unto him,
Their gods are gods of the hills;
therefore they were stronger than we;
but let us fight against them in the plain,
and surely we shall be stronger than they.

24 **And do** this thing,
Take the kings away, every man out of his place,
and put captains in their rooms:
25 **And number** thee an army, like the army that thou hast lost, horse for horse, and chariot for chariot:
and we will fight against them in the plain,
and surely we shall be stronger than they.

And he hearkened unto their voice,
and did so.

26 **And it** came to pass at the return of the year,
that Benhadad numbered the Syrians,
and went up to Aphek,
to fight against Israel.

27 **And the children of Israel** were numbered,
and were all present,
and went against them:
and the children of Israel pitched before them like two little flocks of kids;
but the Syrians filled the country.

28 **And there** came a man of God,
and spake unto the king of Israel,
and said,
Thus saith the LORD,
Because the Syrians have said,
The LORD is God of the hills,
but he is not God of the valleys,
therefore will I deliver all this great multitude into thine hand,
and ye shall know
that I am the LORD.

29 **And they** pitched one over against the other seven days.

And so it was,
that in the seventh day the battle was joined:
and the children of Israel slew of the Syrians an hundred thousand footmen in one day.

30 **But the rest** fled to Aphek, into the city;
and there a wall fell upon twenty and seven thousand of the men that were left.

And Benhadad fled,
and came into the city, into an inner chamber.

31 **And his servants** said unto him,
Behold now,
we have heard that the kings of the house of Israel are merciful kings:
let us, {I pray thee}, put sackcloth on our loins, and ropes upon our heads,
and go out to the king of Israel:
peradventure he will save thy life.

32 **So they** girded sackcloth on their loins,
and put ropes on their heads,
and came to the king of Israel,
and said,
Thy servant Benhadad saith,
I pray thee,
let me live.

And he said,
Is he yet alive?
he is my brother.

33 **Now the men** did diligently observe whether any thing would come from him,
and did hastily catch it:
and they said,
Thy brother Benhadad.

Then he said,
Go ye,

bring him.

Then Benhadad came forth to him;
and he caused him to come up into the chariot.

34 **And Ben-hadad** said unto him,
The cities, {which my father took from thy father}, I will restore;
and thou shalt make streets for thee in Damascus,
as my father made in Samaria.

Then said Ahab,
I will send thee away with this covenant.

So he made a covenant with him,
and sent him away.

35 **And a certain man of the sons of the prophets** said unto his neighbour in the word of the LORD,
Smite me,
I pray thee.

And the man refused to smite him.

36 **Then** said he unto him,
Because thou hast not obeyed the voice of the LORD,
behold,
as soon as thou art departed from me,
a lion shall slay thee.

And as soon as he was departed from him,
a lion found him,
and slew him.

37 **Then he** found another man,
and said,
Smite me,
I pray thee.

And the man smote him,
so that in smiting
he wounded him.

38 **So the prophet** departed,
and waited for the king by the way,
and disguised himself with ashes upon his face.

39 **And as the king** passed by,
he cried unto the king:
and he said,
Thy servant went out into the midst of the battle;
and, {behold}, a man turned aside,
and brought a man unto me,
and said,
Keep this man:
if by any means he be missing,
then shall thy life be for his life,
or else thou shalt pay a talent of silver.

40 **And as thy servant** was busy here and there,
he was gone.

And the king of Israel said unto him,
So shall thy judgment be;
thyself hast decided it.

41 **And he** hasted,
and took the ashes away from his face;
and the king of Israel discerned him that he was of the prophets.

42 **And he** said unto him,
Thus saith the LORD,
Because thou hast let go out of thy hand a man whom I appointed to utter destruction,
therefore thy life shall go for his life, and thy people for his people.

43 **And the king of Israel** went to his house heavy and displeased,
and came to Samaria.

21 **And it** came to pass after these things,
that Naboth the Jezreelite had a vineyard,
which was in Jezreel, hard by the palace of Ahab king of Samaria.

2 **And Ahab** spake unto Naboth,
saying,
Give me thy vineyard,
that I may have it for a garden of herbs,
because it is near unto my house:
and I will give thee for it a better vineyard than it;
or, {if it seem good to thee}, I will give thee the worth of it in money.

3 **And Naboth** said to Ahab,
The LORD forbid it me,
that I should give the inheritance of my fathers unto thee.

4 **And Ahab** came into his house heavy and displeased because of the word which Naboth the Jezreelite had spoken to him:
for he had said,
I will not give thee the inheritance of my fathers.

And he laid him down upon his bed,
and turned away his face,
and would eat no bread.

5 **But Jezebel his wife** came to him,
and said unto him,
Why is thy spirit so sad,
that thou eatest no bread?

6 **And he** said unto her,
Because I spake unto Naboth the Jezreelite,
and said unto him,
Give me thy vineyard for money;
or else, {if it please thee}, I will give thee another vineyard for it:
and he answered,
I will not give thee my vineyard.

7 **And Jezebel his wife** said unto him,
Dost thou now govern the kingdom of Israel?
arise,
and eat bread,
and let thine heart be merry:
I will give thee the vineyard of Naboth the Jezreelite.

8 **So she** wrote letters in Ahab's name,
and sealed them with his seal,
and sent the letters unto the elders and to the nobles that were in his city,
dwelling with Naboth.

9 **And she** wrote in the letters,
saying,
Proclaim a fast,
and set Naboth on high among the people:

10 **And set** two men, sons of Belial, before him,
to bear witness against him,
saying,
Thou didst blaspheme God and the king.

And then carry him out,
and stone him,
that he may die.

11 **And the men of his city, even the elders and the nobles who were the inhabitants in his city,** did as Jezebel had sent unto them,
and as it was written in the letters which she had sent unto them.

12 **They** proclaimed a fast,
and set Naboth on high among the people.

13 **And there** came in two men, children of Belial,
and sat before him:
and the men of Belial witnessed against him, even against Naboth, in the presence of the people,
saying,
Naboth did blaspheme God and the king.

Then they carried him forth out of the city,
and stoned him with stones,
that he died.

14 **Then they** sent to Jezebel,
saying,
Naboth is stoned,

and is dead.
15 **And it** came to pass,
when Jezebel heard that Naboth was stoned,
and was dead,
that Jezebel said to Ahab,
Arise,
take possession of the vineyard of Naboth the Jezreelite,
which he refused to give thee for money:
for Naboth is not alive,
but dead.
16 **And it** came to pass,
when Ahab heard that Naboth was dead,
that Ahab rose up to go down to the vineyard of Naboth the Jezreelite,
to take possession of it.
17 **And the word of the LORD** came to Elijah the Tishbite,
saying,
18 **Arise,**
go down to meet Ahab king of Israel,
which is in Samaria:
behold,
he is in the vineyard of Naboth,
whither he is gone down
to possess it.
19 **And thou** shalt speak unto him,
saying,
Thus saith the LORD,
Hast thou killed,
and also taken possession?
And thou shalt speak unto him,
saying,
Thus saith the LORD,
In the place where dogs licked the blood of Naboth shall dogs lick thy blood, even thine.
20 **And Ahab** said to Elijah,
Hast thou found me, O mine enemy?
And he answered,
I have found thee:
because thou hast sold thyself
to work evil in the sight of the LORD.
21 **Behold,**
I will bring evil upon thee,
and will take away thy posterity,
and will cut off from Ahab him that pisseth against the wall, and him that is shut up and left in Israel,
22 **And** will make thine house like the house of Jeroboam the son of Nebat, and like the house of Baasha the son of Ahijah, for the provocation wherewith thou hast provoked me to anger,
and made Israel to sin.
23 **And of Jezebel** also spake the LORD,
saying,
The dogs shall eat Jezebel by the wall of Jezreel.
24 **Him that dieth of Ahab in the city** the dogs shall eat;
and him that dieth in the field shall the fowls of the air eat.
25 **But there** was none like unto Ahab,
which did sell himself
to work wickedness in the sight of the LORD,
whom Jezebel his wife stirred up.
26 **And he** did very abominably in following idols, according to all things as did the Amorites,
whom the LORD cast out before the children of Israel.
27 **And it** came to pass,
when Ahab heard those words,
that he rent his clothes,
and put sackcloth upon his flesh,
and fasted,
and lay in sackcloth,
and went softly.
28 **And the word of the LORD** came to Elijah the Tishbite,
saying,
29 **Seest thou** how Ahab humbleth himself before me?
because he humbleth himself before me,
I will not bring the evil in his days:
but in his son's days will I bring the evil upon his house.

22 **And they** continued three years without war between Syria and Israel.
2 **And it** came to pass in the third year,
that Jehoshaphat the king of Judah came down to the king of Israel.
3 **And the king of Israel** said unto his servants,
Know ye
that Ramoth in Gilead is ours,
and we be still,
and take it not out of the hand of the king of Syria?
4 **And he** said unto Jehoshaphat,
Wilt thou go with me to battle to Ramothgilead?
And Jehoshaphat said to the king of Israel,
I am as thou art, my people as thy people, my horses as thy horses.
5 **And Jehoshaphat** said unto the king of Israel,
Enquire, {I pray thee}, at the word of the LORD to day.
6 **Then the king of Israel** gathered the prophets together, about four hundred men,
and said unto them,
Shall I go against Ramothgilead to battle,
or shall I forbear?
And they said,
Go up;
for the Lord shall deliver it into the hand of the king.
7 **And Jehoshaphat** said,
Is there not here a prophet of the LORD besides,
that we might enquire of him?
8 **And the king of Israel** said unto Jehoshaphat,
There is yet one man, Micaiah the son of Imlah,
by whom we may enquire of the LORD:
but I hate him;
for he doth not prophesy good concerning me, but evil.
And Jehoshaphat said,
Let not the king say so.
9 **Then the king of Israel** called an officer,
and said,
Hasten hither Micaiah the son of Imlah.
10 **And the king of Israel and Jehoshaphat the king of Judah** sat each on his throne,
having put on their robes, in a void place in the entrance of the gate of Samaria;
and all the prophets prophesied before them.
11 **And Zedekiah the son of Chenaanah** made him horns of iron:
and he said,
Thus saith the LORD,
With these shalt thou push the Syrians,
until thou have consumed them.
12 And all the prophets prophesied so,
saying,
Go up to Ramothgilead,

and prosper:
for the LORD shall deliver it into the king's hand.
13 **And the messenger that was gone to call Micaiah** spake unto him,
saying,
Behold now,
the words of the prophets declare good unto the king with one mouth:
let thy word, {I pray thee}, be like the word of one of them,
and speak that which is good.
14 **And Micaiah** said,
As the LORD liveth,
what the LORD saith unto me,
that will I speak.
15 **So he** came to the king.
And the king said unto him,
Micaiah, shall we go against Ramothgilead to battle,
or shall we forbear?
And he answered him,
Go,
and prosper:
for the LORD shall deliver it into the hand of the king.
16 **And the king** said unto him,
How many times shall I adjure thee
that thou tell me nothing but that which is true in the name of the LORD?
17 **And he** said,
I saw all Israel scattered upon the hills, as sheep that have not a shepherd:
and the LORD said,
These have no master:
let them return every man to his house in peace.
18 **And the king of Israel** said unto Jehoshaphat,
Did I not tell thee
that he would prophesy no good concerning me, but evil?
19 **And he** said,
Hear thou therefore the word of the LORD:
I saw the LORD sitting on his throne, and all the host of heaven standing by him on his right hand and on his left.
20 **And the LORD** said,
Who shall persuade Ahab,
that he may go up and fall at Ramothgilead?
And one said on this manner,
and another said on that manner.
21 **And there** came forth a spirit,
and stood before the LORD,
and said,
I will persuade him.
22 **And the LORD** said unto him,
Wherewith?
And he said,
I will go forth,
and I will be a lying spirit in the mouth of all his prophets.
And he said,
Thou shalt persuade him,
and prevail also:
go forth,
and do so.
23 **Now therefore, {behold}, the LORD** hath put a lying spirit in the mouth of all these thy prophets,
and the LORD hath spoken evil concerning thee.
24 **But Zedekiah the son of Chenaanah** went near,
and smote Micaiah on the cheek,
and said,
Which way went the Spirit of the LORD from me to speak unto thee?
25 **And Micaiah** said,
Behold,
thou shalt see in that day,
when thou shalt go into an inner chamber
to hide thyself.
26 **And the king of Israel** said,
Take Micaiah,
and carry him back unto Amon the governor of the city, and to Joash the king's son;
27 **And say,**
Thus saith the king,
Put this fellow in the prison,
and feed him with bread of affliction and with water of affliction,
until I come in peace.
28 **And Micaiah** said,
If thou return at all in peace,
the LORD hath not spoken by me.
And he said,
Hearken, O people, every one of you.
29 **So the king of Israel and Jehoshaphat the king of Judah** went up to Ramothgilead.
30 **And the king of Israel** said unto Jehoshaphat,
I will disguise myself,
and enter into the battle;
but put thou on thy robes.
And the king of Israel disguised himself,
and went into the battle.
31 **But the king of Syria** commanded his thirty and two captains that had rule over his chariots,
saying,
Fight neither with small nor great, save only with the king of Israel.
32 **And it** came to pass,
when the captains of the chariots saw Jehoshaphat,
that they said,
Surely it is the king of Israel.
And they turned aside
to fight against him:
and Jehoshaphat cried out.
33 **And it** came to pass,
when the captains of the chariots perceived that it was not the king of Israel,
that they turned back from pursuing him.
34 **And a certain man** drew a bow at a venture,
and smote the king of Israel between the joints of the harness:
wherefore he said unto the driver of his chariot,
Turn thine hand,
and carry me out of the host;
for I am wounded.
35 **And the battle** increased that day:
and the king was stayed up in his chariot against the Syrians,
and died at even:
and the blood ran out of the wound into the midst of the chariot.
36 **And there** went a proclamation throughout the host about the going down of the sun,
saying,
Every man to his city, and every man to his own country.
37 **So the king** died,
and was brought to Samaria;
and they buried the king in Samaria.
38 **And one** washed the chariot in the pool of Samaria;
and the dogs licked up his blood;
and they washed his armour;
according unto the word of the LORD which he spake.
39 **Now the rest of the acts of Ahab, and all that he did, and the**

ivory house which he made,
and all the cities that he built,
are they not written in the book of the chronicles of the kings of Israel?

40 **So Ahab** slept with his fathers;
and Ahaziah his son reigned in his stead.

41 **And Jehoshaphat the son of Asa** began to reign over Judah in the fourth year of Ahab king of Israel.

42 **Jehoshaphat** was thirty and five years old
when he began to reign;
and he reigned twenty and five years in Jerusalem.

And his mother's name was Azubah the daughter of Shilhi.

43 **And he** walked in all the ways of Asa his father;
he turned not aside from it,
doing that which was right in the eyes of the LORD:
nevertheless the high places were not taken away;
for the people offered and burnt incense yet in the high places.

44 **And Jehoshaphat** made peace with the king of Israel.

45 **Now the rest of the acts of Jehoshaphat, and his might that he shewed, {and how he warred},** are they not written in the book of the chronicles of the kings of Judah?

46 **And the remnant of the sodomites**, {which remained in the days of his father Asa}, he took out of the land.

47 **There** was then no king in Edom:
a deputy was king.

48 **Jehoshaphat** made ships of Tharshish
to go to Ophir for gold:
but they went not;
for the ships were broken at Eziongeber.

49 **Then** said Ahaziah the son of Ahab unto Jehoshaphat,
Let my servants go with thy servants in the ships.

But Jehoshaphat would not.

50 **And Jehoshaphat** slept with his fathers,
and was buried with his fathers in the city of David his father:
and Jehoram his son reigned in his stead.

51 **Ahaziah the son of Ahab** began to reign over Israel in Samaria the seventeenth year of Jehoshaphat king of Judah,
and reigned two years over Israel.

52 **And he** did evil in the sight of the LORD,
and walked in the way of his father, and in the way of his mother, and in the way of Jeroboam the son of Nebat,
who made Israel to sin:
53 **For he** served Baal,
and worshipped him,
and provoked to anger the LORD God of Israel, according to all that his father had done.

2 Kings

The Book of Second Kings, traditionally attributed to the prophet Jeremiah, is a historical account following the kingdom's division, a significant event after King Solomon's death. This division forms two countries: Israel in the north and Judah in the south. The book chronicles the reigns of these two nations' monarchs and their complex relationship with God. It encompasses the rise of the Assyrian Empire, which eventually conquers the northern Kingdom of Israel. It also describes the rise of the Babylonian Empire, which later conquers the southern Kingdom of Judah.

Second Kings emphasizes the role of two influential prophets in the Bible. Elijah is renowned for his miraculous deeds, such as raising the dead and challenging the priests of Baal by calling down fire from heaven. Elisha is celebrated for his healing and prophetic powers. Their prophetic actions help shape the course of Israel's history, as do the wicked actions of King Ahab and Jezebel, the idolatrous rulers of Israel who persecute the prophets of the Lord and worship Baal. The book also chronicles the reign of several righteous leaders. King Jehu of Israel eradicates the worship of Baal and the house of Ahab. King Hezekiah of Judah purges the land of idolatry and restores the worship of the Lord. King Josiah of Judah unearths the Book of the Law and initiates a significant reform in the land.

However, the political, religious, and moral paths of both kingdoms ultimately lead to a heart-wrenching conclusion, underscoring the book's central theme. The prophets tirelessly warn Israel and Judah about the dire consequences of their wicked deeds, including internal conflicts, political instability, and the loss of divine protection. Yet the people and their rulers ignore these warnings, persisting in their disobedience to God's laws and worship of false deities. As a result, both nations are eventually conquered by foreign powers, a direct consequence of forsaking their covenant with God. The Book of Second Kings describes these tragic events, seen as divine retribution, to remind the people about the consequences of disobeying God's commands. It also offers undeniable proof of God's unwavering efforts to guide and safeguard His people through the prophets.

1 **Then Moab** rebelled against Israel after the death of Ahab.
2 **And Ahaziah** fell down through a lattice in his upper chamber that was in Samaria,
and was sick:
and he sent messengers,
and said unto them,
Go,
enquire of Baalzebub the god of Ekron
whether I shall recover of this disease.
3 **But the angel of the LORD** said to Elijah the Tishbite,
Arise,
go up to meet the messengers of the king of Samaria,
and say unto them,
Is it not because there is not a God in Israel,
that ye go to enquire of Baalzebub the god of Ekron?
4 **Now therefore thus** saith the LORD,
Thou shalt not come down from that bed on which thou art gone up,
but shalt surely die.
And Elijah departed.
5 **And when the messengers** turned back unto him,
he said unto them,
Why are ye now turned back?
6 **And they** said unto him,
There came a man up to meet us,
and said unto us,
Go,
turn again unto the king that sent you,
and say unto him,
Thus saith the LORD,
Is it not because there is not a God in Israel,
that thou sendest to enquire of Baalzebub the god of Ekron?
therefore thou shalt not come down from that bed on which thou art gone up,
but shalt surely die.
7 **And he** said unto them,
What manner of man was he which came up to meet you,
and told you these words?
8 **And they** answered him,
He was an hairy man,
and girt with a girdle of leather about his loins.
And he said,
It is Elijah the Tishbite.
9 **Then the king** sent unto him a captain of fifty with his fifty.
And he went up to him:
and, {behold}, he sat on the top of an hill.
And he spake unto him,
Thou man of God, the king hath said,
Come down.
10 **And Elijah** answered and said to the captain of fifty,
If I be a man of God,
then let fire come down from heaven,
and consume thee and thy fifty.
And there came down fire from heaven,
and consumed him and his fifty.
11 **Again also he** sent unto him another captain of fifty with his fifty.
And he answered and said unto him,
O man of God, thus hath the king said,
Come down quickly.
12 **And Elijah** answered and said

unto them,
If I be a man of God,
let fire come down from heaven,
and consume thee and thy fifty.
And the fire of God came down from heaven,
and consumed him and his fifty.
13 **And he** sent again a captain of the third fifty with his fifty.
And the third captain of fifty went up,
and came and fell on his knees before Elijah,
and besought him,
and said unto him,
O man of God, {I pray thee}, let my life, and the life of these fifty thy servants, be precious in thy sight.
14 **Behold,**
there came fire down from heaven,
and burnt up the two captains of the former fifties with their fifties:
therefore let my life now be precious in thy sight.
15 **And the angel of the LORD** said unto Elijah,
Go down with him:
be not afraid of him.
And he arose,
and went down with him unto the king.
16 **And he** said unto him,
Thus saith the LORD,
Forasmuch as thou hast sent messengers to enquire of Baalzebub the god of Ekron,
is it not because there is no God in Israel to enquire of his word?
therefore thou shalt not come down off that bed on which thou art gone up,
but shalt surely die.
17 **So he** died according to the word of the LORD which Elijah had spoken.
And Jehoram reigned in his stead in the second year of Jehoram the son of Jehoshaphat king of Judah;
because he had no son.
18 **Now the rest of the acts of Ahaziah which he did,** are they not written in the book of the chronicles of the kings of Israel?

2 **And it** came to pass,
when the LORD would take up Elijah into heaven by a whirlwind,
that Elijah went with Elisha from Gilgal.
2 **And Elijah** said unto Elisha,
Tarry here,
I pray thee;
for the LORD hath sent me to Bethel.
And Elisha said unto him,
As the LORD liveth,
and as thy soul liveth,
I will not leave thee.
So they went down to Bethel.
3 **And the sons of the prophets that were at Bethel** came forth to Elisha,
and said unto him,
Knowest thou
that the LORD will take away thy master from thy head to day?
And he said,
Yea, I know it;
hold ye your peace.
4 **And Elijah** said unto him,
Elisha, tarry here,
I pray thee;
for the LORD hath sent me to Jericho.
And he said,
As the LORD liveth,
and as thy soul liveth,
I will not leave thee.
So they came to Jericho.
5 **And the sons of the prophets that were at Jericho** came to Elisha,
and said unto him,
Knowest thou
that the LORD will take away thy master from thy head to day?
And he answered,
Yea, I know it;
hold ye your peace.
6 **And Elijah** said unto him,
Tarry, {I pray thee}, here;
for the LORD hath sent me to Jordan.
And he said,
As the LORD liveth,
and as thy soul liveth,
I will not leave thee.
And they two went on.
7 **And fifty men of the sons of the prophets** went,
and stood to view afar off:
and they two stood by Jordan.
8 **And Elijah** took his mantle,
and wrapped it together,
and smote the waters,
and they were divided hither and thither,
so that they two went over on dry ground.
9 **And it** came to pass,
when they were gone over,
that Elijah said unto Elisha,
Ask
what I shall do for thee,
before I be taken away from thee.
And Elisha said,
I pray thee,
let a double portion of thy spirit be upon me.
10 **And he** said,
Thou hast asked a hard thing:
nevertheless, if thou see me when I am taken from thee,
it shall be so unto thee;
but if not, it shall not be so.
11 **And it** came to pass,
as they still went on,
and talked,
that, {behold}, there appeared a chariot of fire, and horses of fire,
and parted them both asunder;
and Elijah went up by a whirlwind into heaven.
12 **And Elisha** saw it,
and he cried,
My father, my father, the chariot of Israel, and the horsemen thereof.
And he saw him no more:
and he took hold of his own clothes,
and rent them in two pieces.
13 **He** took up also the mantle of Elijah that fell from him,
and went back,
and stood by the bank of Jordan;
14 **And he** took the mantle of Elijah that fell from him,
and smote the waters,
and said,
Where is the LORD God of Elijah?
and when he also had smitten the waters,
they parted hither and thither:
and Elisha went over.
15 **And when the sons of the prophets which were to view at Jericho** saw him,
they said,
The spirit of Elijah doth rest on Elisha.
And they came to meet him,
and bowed themselves to the ground before him.
16 **And they** said unto him,
Behold now,

there be with thy servants fifty strong men;
let them go,
we pray thee,
and seek thy master:
lest peradventure the Spirit of the LORD hath taken him up,
and cast him upon some mountain, or into some valley.

And he said,
Ye shall not send.

17 **And when they** urged him till he was ashamed,
he said,
Send.

They sent therefore fifty men;
and they sought three days,
but found him not.

18 **And when they** came again to him,
(for he tarried at Jericho,)
he said unto them,
Did I not say unto you,
Go not?

19 **And the men of the city** said unto Elisha,
Behold,
I pray thee,
the situation of this city is pleasant,
as my lord seeth:
but the water is naught,
and the ground barren.

20 **And he** said,
Bring me a new cruse,
and put salt therein.

And they brought it to him.

21 **And he** went forth unto the spring of the waters,
and cast the salt in there,
and said,
Thus saith the LORD,
I have healed these waters;
there shall not be from thence any more death or barren land.

22 **So the waters** were healed unto this day, according to the saying of Elisha which he spake.

23 **And he** went up from thence unto Bethel:
and as he was going up by the way,
there came forth little children out of the city,
and mocked him,
and said unto him,
Go up, thou bald head;
go up, thou bald head.

24 **And he** turned back,
and looked on them,
and cursed them in the name of the LORD.

And there came forth two she bears out of the wood,
and tare forty and two children of them.

25 **And he** went from thence to mount Carmel,
and from thence he returned to Samaria.

3

Now Jehoram the son of Ahab began to reign over Israel in Samaria the eighteenth year of Jehoshaphat king of Judah,
and reigned twelve years.

2 **And he** wrought evil in the sight of the LORD; but not like his father, and like his mother:
for he put away the image of Baal that his father had made.

3 **Nevertheless he** cleaved unto the sins of Jeroboam the son of Nebat,
which made Israel to sin;
he departed not therefrom.

4 **And Mesha king of Moab** was a sheepmaster,
and rendered unto the king of Israel an hundred thousand lambs, and an hundred thousand rams, with the wool.

5 **But it** came to pass,
when Ahab was dead,
that the king of Moab rebelled against the king of Israel.

6 **And king Jehoram** went out of Samaria the same time,
and numbered all Israel.

7 **And he** went and sent to Jehoshaphat the king of Judah,
saying,
The king of Moab hath rebelled against me:
wilt thou go with me against Moab to battle?

And he said,
I will go up:
I am as thou art, my people as thy people, and my horses as thy horses.

8 **And he** said,
Which way shall we go up?

And he answered,
The way through the wilderness of Edom.

9 **So the king of Israel** went, and the king of Judah, and the king of Edom:
and they fetched a compass of seven days' journey:
and there was no water for the host, and for the cattle that followed them.

10 **And the king of Israel** said,
Alas!
that the LORD hath called these three kings together,
to deliver them into the hand of Moab!

11 **But Jehoshaphat** said,
Is there not here a prophet of the LORD,
that we may enquire of the LORD by him?

And one of the king of Israel's servants answered and said,
Here is Elisha the son of Shaphat,
which poured water on the hands of Elijah.

12 **And Jehoshaphat** said,
The word of the LORD is with him.

So the king of Israel and Jehoshaphat and the king of Edom went down to him.

13 **And Elisha** said unto the king of Israel,
What have I to do with thee?
get thee to the prophets of thy father, and to the prophets of thy mother.

And the king of Israel said unto him,
Nay:
for the LORD hath called these three kings together,
to deliver them into the hand of Moab.

14 **And Elisha** said,
As the LORD of hosts liveth,
before whom I stand,
surely, were it not that I regard the presence of Jehoshaphat the king of Judah,
I would not look toward thee,
nor see thee.

15 **But now bring** me a minstrel.

And it came to pass,
when the minstrel played,
that the hand of the LORD came upon him.

16 **And he** said,
Thus saith the LORD,
Make this valley full of ditches.

17 **For thus** saith the LORD,
Ye shall not see wind,
neither shall ye see rain;
yet that valley shall be filled with water,

that ye may drink, both ye, and your cattle, and your beasts.
18 **And this** is but a light thing in the sight of the LORD:
he will deliver the Moabites also into your hand.
19 **And ye** shall smite every fenced city, and every choice city,
and shall fell every good tree,
and stop all wells of water,
and mar every good piece of land with stones.
20 **And it** came to pass in the morning,
when the meat offering was offered,
that, {behold}, there came water by the way of Edom,
and the country was filled with water.
21 **And when all the Moabites** heard that the kings were come up to fight against them,
they gathered all that were able to put on armour, and upward,
and stood in the border.
22 **And they** rose up early in the morning,
and the sun shone upon the water,
and the Moabites saw the water on the other side as red as blood:
23 **And they** said,
This is blood:
the kings are surely slain,
and they have smitten one another:
now therefore, Moab, to the spoil.
24 **And when they** came to the camp of Israel,
the Israelites rose up and smote the Moabites,
so that they fled before them:
but they went forward
smiting the Moabites, even in their country.
25 **And they** beat down the cities,
and on every good piece of land cast every man his stone,
and filled it;
and they stopped all the wells of water,
and felled all the good trees:
only in Kirharaseth left they the stones thereof;
howbeit the slingers went about it,
and smote it.
26 **And when the king of Moab** saw that the battle was too sore for him,
he took with him seven hundred men that drew swords,
to break through even unto the king of Edom:
but they could not.
27 **Then he** took his eldest son that should have reigned in his stead,
and offered him for a burnt offering upon the wall.
And there was great indignation against Israel:
and they departed from him,
and returned to their own land.

4

Now there cried a certain woman of the wives of the sons of the prophets unto Elisha,
saying,
Thy servant my husband is dead;
and thou knowest
that thy servant did fear the LORD:
and the creditor is come to take unto him my two sons to be bondmen.
2 **And Elisha** said unto her,
What shall I do for thee?
tell me,
what hast thou in the house?
And she said,
Thine handmaid hath not any thing in the house, save a pot of oil.
3 **Then he** said,
Go,
borrow thee vessels abroad of all thy neighbours, even empty vessels;
borrow not a few.
4 **And when thou** art come in,
thou shalt shut the door upon thee and upon thy sons,
and shalt pour out into all those vessels,
and thou shalt set aside that which is full.
5 **So she** went from him,
and shut the door upon her and upon her sons,
who brought the vessels to her;
and she poured out.
6 **And it** came to pass,
when the vessels were full,
that she said unto her son,
Bring me yet a vessel.
And he said unto her,
There is not a vessel more.
And the oil stayed.
7 **Then she** came and told the man of God.
And he said,
Go,
sell the oil,
and pay thy debt,
and live thou and thy children of the rest.
8 **And it** fell on a day,
that Elisha passed to Shunem,
where was a great woman;
and she constrained him to eat bread.
And so it was,
that as oft as he passed by,
he turned in thither
to eat bread.
9 **And she** said unto her husband,
Behold now,
I perceive that this is an holy man of God,
which passeth by us continually.
10 **Let us** make a little chamber, {I pray thee}, on the wall;
and let us set for him there a bed, and a table, and a stool, and a candlestick:
and it shall be,
when he cometh to us,
that he shall turn in thither.
11 **And it** fell on a day,
that he came thither,
and he turned into the chamber,
and lay there.
12 **And he** said to Gehazi his servant,
Call this Shunammite.
And when he had called her,
she stood before him.
13 **And he** said unto him,
Say now unto her,
Behold,
thou hast been careful for us with all this care;
what is to be done for thee?
wouldest thou be spoken for to the king, or to the captain of the host?
And she answered,
I dwell among mine own people.
14 **And he** said,
What then is to be done for her?
And Gehazi answered,
Verily she hath no child,
and her husband is old.
15 **And he** said,
Call her.
And when he had called her,
she stood in the door.
16 **And he** said,
About this season, according to the time of life, thou shalt embrace a son.
And she said,

Nay, my lord,
thou man of God, do not lie unto thine handmaid.

17 **And the woman** conceived,
and bare a son at that season that Elisha had said unto her, according to the time of life.

18 **And when the child** was grown,
it fell on a day,
that he went out to his father to the reapers.

19 **And he** said unto his father,
My head, my head.

And he said to a lad,
Carry him to his mother.

20 **And when he** had taken him,
and brought him to his mother,
he sat on her knees till noon,
and then died.

21 **And she** went up,
and laid him on the bed of the man of God,
and shut the door upon him,
and went out.

22 **And she** called unto her husband,
and said,
Send me, {I pray thee}, one of the young men, and one of the asses,
that I may run to the man of God,
and come again.

23 **And he** said,
Wherefore wilt thou go to him to day?
it is neither new moon, nor sabbath.

And she said,
It shall be well.

24 **Then she** saddled an ass,
and said to her servant,
Drive,
and go forward;
slack not thy riding for me,
except I bid thee.

25 **So she** went and came unto the man of God to mount Carmel.

And it came to pass,
when the man of God saw her afar off,
that he said to Gehazi his servant,
Behold,
yonder is that Shunammite:
26 **Run** now,
I pray thee,
to meet her,
and say unto her,
Is it well with thee?
is it well with thy husband?
is it well with the child?

And she answered,
It is well:

27 **And when she** came to the man of God to the hill,
she caught him by the feet:
but Gehazi came near to thrust her away.

And the man of God said,
Let her alone;
for her soul is vexed within her:
and the LORD hath hid it from me,
and hath not told me.

28 **Then she** said,
Did I desire a son of my lord?
did I not say,
Do not deceive me?

29 **Then he** said to Gehazi,
Gird up thy loins,
and take my staff in thine hand,
and go thy way:
if thou meet any man,
salute him not;
and if any salute thee,
answer him not again:
and lay my staff upon the face of the child.

30 **And the mother of the child** said,
As the LORD liveth,
and as thy soul liveth,
I will not leave thee.

And he arose,
and followed her.

31 **And Gehazi** passed on before them,
and laid the staff upon the face of the child;
but there was neither voice,
nor hearing.

Wherefore he went again to meet him,
and told him,
saying,
The child is not awaked.

32 **And when Elisha** was come into the house,
behold,
the child was dead,
and laid upon his bed.

33 **He** went in therefore,
and shut the door upon them twain,
and prayed unto the LORD.

34 **And he** went up,
and lay upon the child,
and put his mouth upon his mouth, and his eyes upon his eyes, and his hands upon his hands:
and stretched himself upon the child;
and the flesh of the child waxed warm.

35 **Then he** returned,
and walked in the house to and fro;
and went up,
and stretched himself upon him:
and the child sneezed seven times,
and the child opened his eyes.

36 **And he** called Gehazi,
and said,
Call this Shunammite.

So he called her.

And when she was come in unto him,
he said,
Take up thy son.

37 **Then she** went in,
and fell at his feet,
and bowed herself to the ground,
and took up her son,
and went out.

38 **And Elisha** came again to Gilgal:
and there was a dearth in the land;
and the sons of the prophets were sitting before him:
and he said unto his servant,
Set on the great pot,
and seethe pottage for the sons of the prophets.

39 **And one** went out into the field
to gather herbs,
and found a wild vine,
and gathered thereof wild gourds his lap full,
and came and shred them into the pot of pottage:
for they knew them not.

40 **So they** poured out for the men to eat.

And it came to pass,
as they were eating of the pottage,
that they cried out,
and said,
O thou man of God, there is death in the pot.

And they could not eat thereof.

41 **But he** said,
Then bring meal.

And he cast it into the pot;
and he said,
Pour out for the people,
that they may eat.

And there was no harm in the pot.

42 **And there** came a man from Baalshalisha,
and brought the man of God bread of the firstfruits, twenty loaves of barley, and full ears of corn in the

husk thereof.

And he said,
Give unto the people,
that they may eat.

43 **And his servitor** said,
What, should I set this before an hundred men?

He said again,
Give the people,
that they may eat:
for thus saith the LORD,
They shall eat,
and shall leave thereof.

44 **So he** set it before them,
and they did eat,
and left thereof, according to the word of the LORD.

5 **Now Naaman, captain of the host of the king of Syria,** was a great man with his master, and honourable,
because by him the LORD had given deliverance unto Syria:
he was also a mighty man in valour,
but he was a leper.

2 **And the Syrians** had gone out by companies,
and had brought away captive out of the land of Israel a little maid;
and she waited on Naaman's wife.

3 **And she** said unto her mistress,
Would God my lord were with the prophet that is in Samaria!
for he would recover him of his leprosy.

4 **And one** went in,
and told his lord,
saying,
Thus and thus said the maid that is of the land of Israel.

5 **And the king of Syria** said,
Go to,
go,
and I will send a letter unto the king of Israel.

And he departed,
and took with him ten talents of silver, and six thousand pieces of gold, and ten changes of raiment.

6 **And he** brought the letter to the king of Israel,
saying,
Now when this letter is come unto thee,
behold,
I have therewith sent Naaman my servant to thee,
that thou mayest recover him of his leprosy.

7 **And it** came to pass,
when the king of Israel had read the letter,
that he rent his clothes,
and said,
Am I God,
to kill and to make alive,
that this man doth send unto me to recover a man of his leprosy?
wherefore consider, {I pray you},
and see how he seeketh a quarrel against me.

8 **And it** was so,
when Elisha the man of God had heard that the king of Israel had rent his clothes,
that he sent to the king,
saying,
Wherefore hast thou rent thy clothes?
let him come now to me,
and he shall know
that there is a prophet in Israel.

9 **So Naaman** came with his horses and with his chariot,
and stood at the door of the house of Elisha.

10 **And Elisha** sent a messenger unto him,
saying,
Go and wash in Jordan seven times,
and thy flesh shall come again to thee,
and thou shalt be clean.

11 **But Naaman** was wroth,
and went away,
and said,
Behold,
I thought,
He will surely come out to me,
and stand,
and call on the name of the LORD his God,
and strike his hand over the place,
and recover the leper.

12 **Are not Abana and Pharpar,** rivers of Damascus, better than all the waters of Israel?
may I not wash in them,
and be clean?

So he turned and went away in a rage.

13 **And his servants** came near,
and spake unto him,
and said,
My father, if the prophet had bid thee do some great thing,
wouldest thou not have done it?
how much rather then, when he saith to thee,
Wash,
and be clean?

14 **Then** went he down,
and dipped himself seven times in Jordan, according to the saying of the man of God:
and his flesh came again like unto the flesh of a little child,
and he was clean.

15 **And he** returned to the man of God, he and all his company,
and came,
and stood before him:
and he said,
Behold,
now I know
that there is no God in all the earth, but in Israel:
now therefore, {I pray thee}, take a blessing of thy servant.

16 **But he** said,
As the LORD liveth,
before whom I stand,
I will receive none.

And he urged him to take it;
but he refused.

17 **And Naaman** said,
Shall there not then, {I pray thee}, be given to thy servant two mules' burden of earth?
for thy servant will henceforth offer neither burnt offering nor sacrifice unto other gods, but unto the LORD.

18 **In this thing** the LORD pardon thy servant,
that when my master goeth into the house of Rimmon
to worship there,
and he leaneth on my hand,
and I bow myself in the house of Rimmon:
when I bow down myself in the house of Rimmon,
the LORD pardon thy servant in this thing.

19 **And he** said unto him,
Go in peace.

So he departed from him a little way.

20 **But Gehazi, the servant of Elisha the man of God,** said,
Behold,
my master hath spared Naaman this Syrian,
in not receiving at his hands that which he brought:
but, {as the LORD liveth}, I will run after him,

and take somewhat of him.

21 **So Gehazi** followed after Naaman.

And when Naaman saw him running after him,
he lighted down from the chariot
to meet him,
and said,
Is all well?

22 **And he** said,
All is well.

My master hath sent me,
saying,
Behold,
even now there be come to me from mount Ephraim two young men of the sons of the prophets:
give them, {I pray thee}, a talent of silver, and two changes of garments.

23 **And Naaman** said,
Be content,
take two talents.

And he urged him,
and bound two talents of silver in two bags, with two changes of garments,
and laid them upon two of his servants;
and they bare them before him.

24 **And when he** came to the tower,
he took them from their hand,
and bestowed them in the house:
and he let the men go,
and they departed.

25 **But he** went in,
and stood before his master.

And Elisha said unto him,
Whence comest thou, Gehazi?

And he said,
Thy servant went no whither.

26 **And he** said unto him,
Went not mine heart with thee,
when the man turned again from his chariot
to meet thee?

Is it a time to receive money,
and to receive garments, and oliveyards, and vineyards, and sheep, and oxen, and menservants, and maidservants?

27 **The leprosy therefore of Naaman** shall cleave unto thee, and unto thy seed for ever.

And he went out from his presence a leper as white as snow.

6

And the sons of the prophets said unto Elisha,
Behold now,
the place where we dwell with thee is too strait for us.

2 **Let us** go, {we pray thee}, unto Jordan,
and take thence every man a beam,
and let us make us a place there,
where we may dwell.

And he answered,
Go ye.

3 **And one** said,
Be content,
I pray thee,
and go with thy servants.

And he answered,
I will go.

4 **So he** went with them.

And when they came to Jordan,
they cut down wood.

5 **But as one** was felling a beam,
the axe head fell into the water:
and he cried,
and said,
Alas, master!
for it was borrowed.

6 **And the man of God** said,
Where fell it?

And he shewed him the place.

And he cut down a stick,
and cast it in thither;
and the iron did swim.

7 **Therefore** said he,
Take it up to thee.

And he put out his hand,
and took it.

8 **Then the king of Syria** warred against Israel,
and took counsel with his servants,
saying,
In such and such a place shall be my camp.

9 **And the man of God** sent unto the king of Israel,
saying,
Beware that thou pass not such a place;
for thither the Syrians are come down.

10 **And the king of Israel** sent to the place which the man of God told him and warned him of,
and saved himself there, not once nor twice.

11 **Therefore the heart of the king of Syria** was sore troubled for this thing;
and he called his servants,
and said unto them,
Will ye not shew me
which of us is for the king of Israel?

12 **And one of his servants** said,
None, my lord, O king:
but Elisha, the prophet that is in Israel, telleth the king of Israel the words that thou speakest in thy bedchamber.

13 **And he** said,
Go and spy where he is,
that I may send and fetch him.

And it was told him,
saying,
Behold,
he is in Dothan.

14 **Therefore** sent he thither horses, and chariots, and a great host:
and they came by night,
and compassed the city about.

15 **And when the servant of the man of God** was risen early,
and gone forth,
behold,
an host compassed the city both with horses and chariots.

And his servant said unto him,
Alas, my master!
how shall we do?

16 **And he** answered,
Fear not:
for they that be with us are more than they that be with them.

17 **And Elisha** prayed,
and said,
LORD, {I pray thee}, open his eyes,
that he may see.

And the LORD opened the eyes of the young man;
and he saw:
and, {behold}, the mountain was full of horses and chariots of fire round about Elisha.

18 **And when they** came down to him,
Elisha prayed unto the LORD,
and said,
Smite this people, {I pray thee}, with blindness.

And he smote them with blindness according to the word of Elisha.

19 **And Elisha** said unto them,
This is not the way,
neither is this the city:
follow me,
and I will bring you to the man whom ye seek.

But he led them to Samaria.

20 **And it** came to pass,
when they were come into Samaria,

that Elisha said,
LORD, open the eyes of these men,
that they may see.
And the LORD opened their eyes,
and they saw;
and, {behold}, they were in the midst of Samaria.
21 **And the king of Israel** said unto Elisha,
when he saw them,
My father, shall I smite them?
shall I smite them?
22 **And he** answered,
Thou shalt not smite them:
wouldest thou smite those whom thou hast taken captive with thy sword and with thy bow?
set bread and water before them,
that they may eat and drink,
and go to their master.
23 **And he** prepared great provision for them:
and when they had eaten and drunk,
he sent them away,
and they went to their master.
So the bands of Syria came no more into the land of Israel.
24 **And it** came to pass after this,
that Benhadad king of Syria gathered all his host,
and went up,
and besieged Samaria.
25 **And there** was a great famine in Samaria:
and, {behold}, they besieged it,
until an ass's head was sold for fourscore pieces of silver, and the fourth part of a cab of dove's dung for five pieces of silver.
26 **And as the king of Israel** was passing by upon the wall,
there cried a woman unto him,
saying,
Help, my lord, O king.
27 **And he** said,
If the LORD do not help thee,
whence shall I help thee?
out of the barnfloor, or out of the winepress?
28 **And the king** said unto her,
What aileth thee?
And she answered,
This woman said unto me,
Give thy son,
that we may eat him to day,
and we will eat my son to morrow.
29 **So we** boiled my son,
and did eat him:
and I said unto her on the next day,
Give thy son,
that we may eat him:
and she hath hid her son.
30 **And it** came to pass,
when the king heard the words of the woman,
that he rent his clothes;
and he passed by upon the wall,
and the people looked,
and, {behold}, he had sackcloth within upon his flesh.
31 **Then he** said,
God do so and more also to me,
if the head of Elisha the son of Shaphat shall stand on him this day.
32 **But Elisha** sat in his house,
and the elders sat with him;
and the king sent a man from before him:
but ere the messenger came to him,
he said to the elders,
See ye how this son of a murderer hath sent to take away mine head?
look,
when the messenger cometh,
shut the door,
and hold him fast at the door:
is not the sound of his master's feet behind him?
33 **And while he** yet talked with them,
behold,
the messenger came down unto him:
and he said,
Behold,
this evil is of the LORD;
what should I wait for the LORD any longer?

7 **Then Elisha** said,
Hear ye the word of the LORD;
Thus saith the LORD,
To morrow about this time shall a measure of fine flour be sold for a shekel, and two measures of barley for a shekel, in the gate of Samaria.
2 **Then a lord on whose hand the king leaned** answered the man of God,
and said,
Behold,
if the LORD would make windows in heaven,
might this thing be?
And he said,
Behold,
thou shalt see it with thine eyes,
but shalt not eat thereof.
3 **And there** were four leprous men at the entering in of the gate:
and they said one to another,
Why sit we here
until we die?
4 **If we** say,
We will enter into the city,
then the famine is in the city,
and we shall die there:
and if we sit still here,
we die also.
Now therefore come,
and let us fall unto the host of the Syrians:
if they save us alive,
we shall live;
and if they kill us,
we shall but die.
5 **And they** rose up in the twilight,
to go unto the camp of the Syrians:
and when they were come to the uttermost part of the camp of Syria,
behold,
there was no man there.
6 **For the Lord** had made the host of the Syrians to hear a noise of chariots, and a noise of horses, even the noise of a great host:
and they said one to another,
Lo,
the king of Israel hath hired against us the kings of the Hittites, and the kings of the Egyptians,
to come upon us.
7 **Wherefore they** arose and fled in the twilight,
and left their tents, and their horses, and their asses, even the camp as it was,
and fled for their life.
8 **And when these lepers** came to the uttermost part of the camp,
they went into one tent,
and did eat and drink,
and carried thence silver, and gold, and raiment,
and went and hid it;
and came again,
and entered into another tent,
and carried thence also,
and went and hid it.
9 **Then they** said one to another,
We do not well:
this day is a day of good tidings,
and we hold our peace:

if we tarry till the morning light,
some mischief will come upon us:
now therefore come,
that we may go and tell the king's household.
10 **So they** came and called unto the porter of the city:
and they told them,
saying,
We came to the camp of the Syrians,
and, {behold}, there was no man there, neither voice of man, but horses tied, and asses tied, and the tents as they were.
11 **And he** called the porters;
and they told it to the king's house within.
12 **And the king** arose in the night,
and said unto his servants,
I will now shew you
what the Syrians have done to us.
They know
that we be hungry;
therefore are they gone out of the camp
to hide themselves in the field,
saying,
When they come out of the city,
we shall catch them alive,
and get into the city.
13 **And one of his servants** answered and said,
Let some take, {I pray thee}, five of the horses that remain,
which are left in the city,
(behold,
they are as all the multitude of Israel that are left in it:
behold,
I say,
they are even as all the multitude of the Israelites that are consumed:)
and let us send and see.
14 **They** took therefore two chariot horses;
and the king sent after the host of the Syrians,
saying,
Go and see.
15 **And they** went after them unto Jordan:
and, {lo}, all the way was full of garments and vessels,
which the Syrians had cast away in their haste.
And the messengers returned,
and told the king.
16 **And the people** went out,
and spoiled the tents of the Syrians.
So a measure of fine flour was sold for a shekel, and two measures of barley for a shekel, according to the word of the LORD.
17 **And the king** appointed the lord on whose hand he leaned to have the charge of the gate:
and the people trode upon him in the gate,
and he died,
as the man of God had said,
who spake
when the king came down to him.
18 **And it** came to pass
as the man of God had spoken to the king,
saying,
Two measures of barley for a shekel, and a measure of fine flour for a shekel, shall be to morrow about this time in the gate of Samaria:
19 **And that lord** answered the man of God,
and said,
Now, {behold}, if the LORD should make windows in heaven,
might such a thing be?
And he said,
Behold,
thou shalt see it with thine eyes,
but shalt not eat thereof.
20 **And so it** fell out unto him:
for the people trode upon him in the gate,
and he died.

8 **Then** spake Elisha unto the woman,
whose son he had restored to life,
saying,
Arise,
and go thou and thine household,
and sojourn
wheresoever thou canst sojourn:
for the LORD hath called for a famine;
and it shall also come upon the land seven years.
2 **And the woman** arose,
and did after the saying of the man of God:
and she went with her household,
and sojourned in the land of the Philistines seven years.
3 **And it** came to pass at the seven years' end,
that the woman returned out of the land of the Philistines:
and she went forth to cry unto the king for her house and for her land.
4 **And the king** talked with Gehazi the servant of the man of God,
saying,
Tell me, {I pray thee}, all the great things that Elisha hath done.
5 **And it** came to pass,
as he was telling the king
how he had restored a dead body to life,
that, {behold}, the woman, {whose son he had restored to life}, cried to the king for her house and for her land.
And Gehazi said,
My lord, O king, this is the woman,
and this is her son,
whom Elisha restored to life.
6 **And when the king** asked the woman,
she told him.
So the king appointed unto her a certain officer,
saying,
Restore all that was hers, and all the fruits of the field since the day that she left the land, even until now.
7 **And Elisha** came to Damascus;
and Benhadad the king of Syria was sick;
and it was told him,
saying,
The man of God is come hither.
8 **And the king** said unto Hazael,
Take a present in thine hand,
and go,
meet the man of God,
and enquire of the LORD by him,
saying,
Shall I recover of this disease?
9 **So Hazael** went to meet him,
and took a present with him, even of every good thing of Damascus, forty camels' burden,
and came and stood before him,
and said,
Thy son Benhadad king of Syria hath sent me to thee,
saying,
Shall I recover of this disease?
10 **And Elisha** said unto him,
Go,
say unto him,
Thou mayest certainly recover:
howbeit the LORD hath shewed me that he shall surely die.
11 **And he** settled his countenance

stedfastly,
until he was ashamed:
and the man of God wept.

12 **And Hazael** said,
Why weepeth my lord?
And he answered,
Because I know the evil
that thou wilt do unto the children of Israel:
their strong holds wilt thou set on fire,
and their young men wilt thou slay with the sword,
and wilt dash their children,
and rip up their women with child.

13 **And Hazael** said,
But what,
is thy servant a dog,
that he should do this great thing?
And Elisha answered,
The LORD hath shewed me that thou shalt be king over Syria.

14 **So he** departed from Elisha,
and came to his master;
who said to him,
What said Elisha to thee?
And he answered,
He told me
that thou shouldest surely recover.

15 **And it** came to pass on the morrow,
that he took a thick cloth,
and dipped it in water,
and spread it on his face,
so that he died:
and Hazael reigned in his stead.

16 **And in the fifth year of Joram the son of Ahab king of Israel,** {Jehoshaphat being then king of Judah}, Jehoram the son of Jehoshaphat king of Judah began to reign.

17 **Thirty and two years old** was he
when he began to reign;
and he reigned eight years in Jerusalem.

18 **And he** walked in the way of the kings of Israel,
as did the house of Ahab:
for the daughter of Ahab was his wife:
and he did evil in the sight of the LORD.

19 **Yet the LORD** would not destroy Judah for David his servant's sake,
as he promised him to give him alway a light, and to his children.

20 **In his days** Edom revolted from under the hand of Judah,
and made a king over themselves.

21 **So Joram** went over to Zair, and all the chariots with him:
and he rose by night,
and smote the Edomites which compassed him about, and the captains of the chariots:
and the people fled into their tents.

22 **Yet Edom** revolted from under the hand of Judah unto this day.
Then Libnah revolted at the same time.

23 **And the rest of the acts of Joram, and all that he did,** are they not written in the book of the chronicles of the kings of Judah?

24 **And Joram** slept with his fathers,
and was buried with his fathers in the city of David:
and Ahaziah his son reigned in his stead.

25 **In the twelfth year of Joram the son of Ahab king of Israel** did Ahaziah the son of Jehoram king of Judah begin to reign.

26 **Two and twenty years old** was Ahaziah
when he began to reign;
and he reigned one year in Jerusalem.
And his mother's name was Athaliah, the daughter of Omri king of Israel.

27 **And he** walked in the way of the house of Ahab,
and did evil in the sight of the LORD,
as did the house of Ahab:
for he was the son in law of the house of Ahab.

28 **And he** went with Joram the son of Ahab to the war against Hazael king of Syria in Ramothgilead;
and the Syrians wounded Joram.

29 **And king Joram** went back to be healed in Jezreel of the wounds which the Syrians had given him at Ramah,
when he fought against Hazael king of Syria.
And Ahaziah the son of Jehoram king of Judah went down to see Joram the son of Ahab in Jezreel,
because he was sick.

9

And Elisha the prophet called one of the children of the prophets,
and said unto him,
Gird up thy loins,
and take this box of oil in thine hand,
and go to Ramothgilead:

2 **And when thou** comest thither,
look out there Jehu the son of Jehoshaphat the son of Nimshi,
and go in,
and make him arise up from among his brethren,
and carry him to an inner chamber;

3 **Then take** the box of oil,
and pour it on his head,
and say,
Thus saith the LORD,
I have anointed thee king over Israel.
Then open the door,
and flee,
and tarry not.

4 **So the young man, even the young man the prophet,** went to Ramothgilead.

5 **And when he** came,
behold,
the captains of the host were sitting;
and he said,
I have an errand to thee, O captain.
And Jehu said,
Unto which of all us?
And he said,
To thee, O captain.

6 **And he** arose,
and went into the house;
and he poured the oil on his head,
and said unto him,
Thus saith the LORD God of Israel,
I have anointed thee king over the people of the LORD, even over Israel.

7 **And thou** shalt smite the house of Ahab thy master,
that I may avenge the blood of my servants the prophets, and the blood of all the servants of the LORD, at the hand of Jezebel.

8 **For the whole house of Ahab** shall perish:
and I will cut off from Ahab him that pisseth against the wall, and him that is shut up and left in Israel:

9 **And I** will make the house of Ahab like the house of Jeroboam the son of Nebat, and like the house of Baasha the son of Ahijah:

10 **And the dogs** shall eat Jezebel in the portion of Jezreel,

and there shall be none to bury her.

And he opened the door,
and fled.

11 **Then Jehu** came forth to the servants of his lord:
and one said unto him,
Is all well?
wherefore came this mad fellow to thee?

And he said unto them,
Ye know the man, and his communication.

12 **And they** said,
It is false;
tell us now.

And he said,
Thus and thus spake he to me,
saying,
Thus saith the LORD,
I have anointed thee king over Israel.

13 **Then they** hasted,
and took every man his garment,
and put it under him on the top of the stairs,
and blew with trumpets,
saying,
Jehu is king.

14 **So Jehu the son of Jehoshaphat the son of Nimshi** conspired against Joram.

(**Now Joram** had kept Ramothgilead, he and all Israel, because of Hazael king of Syria.

15 **But king Joram** was returned to be healed in Jezreel of the wounds which the Syrians had given him, when he fought with Hazael king of Syria.)

And Jehu said,
If it be your minds,
then let none go forth
nor escape out of the city to go to tell it in Jezreel.

16 **So Jehu** rode in a chariot,
and went to Jezreel;
for Joram lay there.

And Ahaziah king of Judah was come down to see Joram.

17 **And there** stood a watchman on the tower in Jezreel,
and he spied the company of Jehu
as he came,
and said,
I see a company.

And Joram said,
Take an horseman,
and send to meet them,
and let him say,
Is it peace?

18 **So there** went one on horseback to meet him,
and said,
Thus saith the king,
Is it peace?

And Jehu said,
What hast thou to do with peace?
turn thee behind me.

And the watchman told,
saying,
The messenger came to them,
but he cometh not again.

19 **Then he** sent out a second on horseback,
which came to them,
and said,
Thus saith the king,
Is it peace?

And Jehu answered,
What hast thou to do with peace?
turn thee behind me.

20 **And the watchman** told,
saying,
He came even unto them,
and cometh not again:
and the driving is like the driving of Jehu the son of Nimshi;
for he driveth furiously.

21 **And Joram** said,
Make ready.

And his chariot was made ready.

And Joram king of Israel and Ahaziah king of Judah went out, each in his chariot,
and they went out against Jehu,
and met him in the portion of Naboth the Jezreelite.

22 **And it** came to pass,
when Joram saw Jehu,
that he said,
Is it peace, Jehu?

And he answered,
What peace,
so long as the whoredoms of thy mother Jezebel and her witchcrafts are so many?

23 **And Joram** turned his hands,
and fled,
and said to Ahaziah,
There is treachery, O Ahaziah.

24 **And Jehu** drew a bow with his full strength,
and smote Jehoram between his arms,
and the arrow went out at his heart,
and he sunk down in his chariot.

25 **Then** said Jehu to Bidkar his captain,
Take up,
and cast him in the portion of the field of Naboth the Jezreelite:
for remember
how that, {<u>when I</u> and thou rode together after Ahab his father}, the LORD laid this burden upon him;

26 **Surely I** have seen yesterday the blood of Naboth, and the blood of his sons,
saith the LORD;
and I will requite thee in this plat,
saith the LORD.

Now therefore take and cast him into the plat of ground, according to the word of the LORD.

27 **But when Ahaziah the king of Judah** saw this,
he fled by the way of the garden house.

And Jehu followed after him,
and said,
Smite him also in the chariot.

And they did so at the going up to Gur,
which is by Ibleam.

And he fled to Megiddo,
and died there.

28 **And his servants** carried him in a chariot to Jerusalem,
and buried him in his sepulchre with his fathers in the city of David.

29 **And in the eleventh year of Joram the son of Ahab** began Ahaziah to reign over Judah.

30 **And when Jehu** was come to Jezreel,
Jezebel heard of it;
and she painted her face,
and tired her head,
and looked out at a window.

31 **And as Jehu** entered in at the gate,
she said,
Had Zimri peace,
who slew his master?

32 **And he** lifted up his face to the window,
and said,
Who is on my side?
who?

And there looked out to him two or three eunuchs.

33 **And he** said,
Throw her down.

So they threw her down:
and some of her blood was

sprinkled on the wall, and on the horses:
and he trode her under foot.

34 **And when he** was come in,
he did eat and drink,
and said,
Go,
see now this cursed woman,
and bury her:
for she is a king's daughter.

35 **And they** went to bury her:
but they found no more of her than the skull, and the feet, and the palms of her hands.

36 **Wherefore they** came again,
and told him.

And he said,
This is the word of the LORD,
which he spake by his servant Elijah the Tishbite,
saying,
In the portion of Jezreel shall dogs eat the flesh of Jezebel:

37 **And the carcase of Jezebel** shall be as dung upon the face of the field in the portion of Jezreel;
so that they shall not say,
This is Jezebel.

10

And Ahab had seventy sons in Samaria.

And Jehu wrote letters,
and sent to Samaria, unto the rulers of Jezreel, to the elders, and to them that brought up Ahab's children,
saying,

2 **Now as soon as this letter** cometh to you,
seeing your master's sons are with you,
and there are with you chariots and horses, a fenced city also, and armour;

3 **Look even out** the best and meetest of your master's sons,
and set him on his father's throne,
and fight for your master's house.

4 **But they** were exceedingly afraid,
and said,
Behold,
two kings stood not before him:
how then shall we stand?

5 **And he that was over the house, and he that was over the city, the elders also, and the bringers up of the children,** sent to Jehu,
saying,
We are thy servants,
and will do all that thou shalt bid us;
we will not make any king:
do thou that which is good in thine eyes.

6 **Then he** wrote a letter the second time to them,
saying,
If ye be mine,
and if ye will hearken unto my voice,
take ye the heads of the men your master's sons,
and come to me to Jezreel by to morrow this time.

Now the king's sons, {being seventy persons}, were with the great men of the city,
which brought them up.

7 **And it** came to pass,
when the letter came to them,
that they took the king's sons,
and slew seventy persons,
and put their heads in baskets,
and sent him them to Jezreel.

8 **And there** came a messenger,
and told him,
saying,
They have brought the heads of the king's sons.

And he said,
Lay ye them in two heaps at the entering in of the gate until the morning.

9 **And it** came to pass in the morning,
that he went out,
and stood,
and said to all the people,
Ye be righteous:
behold,
I conspired against my master,
and slew him:
but who slew all these?

10 **Know** now
that there shall fall unto the earth nothing of the word of the LORD,
which the LORD spake concerning the house of Ahab:
for the LORD hath done that which he spake by his servant Elijah.

11 **So Jehu** slew all that remained of the house of Ahab in Jezreel, and all his great men, and his kinsfolks, and his priests,
until he left him none remaining.

12 **And he** arose and departed,
and came to Samaria.

And as he was at the shearing house in the way,

13 **Jehu** met with the brethren of Ahaziah king of Judah,
and said,
Who are ye?

And they answered,
We are the brethren of Ahaziah;
and we go down to salute the children of the king and the children of the queen.

14 **And he** said,
Take them alive.

And they took them alive,
and slew them at the pit of the shearing house, even two and forty men;
neither left he any of them.

15 **And when** he was departed thence,
he lighted on Jehonadab the son of Rechab coming to meet him:
and he saluted him,
and said to him,
Is thine heart right,
as my heart is with thy heart?

And Jehonadab answered,
It is.

If it be,
give me thine hand.

And he gave him his hand;
and he took him up to him into the chariot.

16 **And he** said,
Come with me,
and see my zeal for the LORD.

So they made him ride in his chariot.

17 **And when he** came to Samaria,
he slew all that remained unto Ahab in Samaria,
till he had destroyed him, according to the saying of the LORD,
which he spake to Elijah.

18 **And Jehu** gathered all the people together,
and said unto them,
Ahab served Baal a little;
but Jehu shall serve him much.

19 **Now therefore call** unto me all the prophets of Baal, all his servants, and all his priests;
let none be wanting:
for I have a great sacrifice to do to Baal;
whosoever shall be wanting,
he shall not live.

But Jehu did it in subtilty,
to the intent that he might destroy the worshippers of Baal.

20 **And Jehu** said,
Proclaim a solemn assembly for Baal.
And they proclaimed it.
21 **And Jehu** sent through all Israel:
and all the worshippers of Baal came,
so that there was not a man left that came not.
And they came into the house of Baal;
and the house of Baal was full from one end to another.
22 **And he** said unto him that was over the vestry,
Bring forth vestments for all the worshippers of Baal.
And he brought them forth vestments.
23 **And Jehu** went, and Jehonadab the son of Rechab, into the house of Baal,
and said unto the worshippers of Baal,
Search,
and look that there be here with you none of the servants of the LORD, but the worshippers of Baal only.
24 **And when they** went in to offer sacrifices and burnt offerings,
Jehu appointed fourscore men without,
and said,
If any of the men whom I have brought into your hands escape,
he that letteth him go, his life shall be for the life of him.
25 **And it** came to pass,
as soon as he had made an end of offering the burnt offering,
that Jehu said to the guard and to the captains,
Go in,
and slay them;
let none come forth.
And they smote them with the edge of the sword;
and the guard and the captains cast them out,
and went to the city of the house of Baal.
26 **And they** brought forth the images out of the house of Baal,
and burned them.
27 **And they** brake down the image of Baal,
and brake down the house of Baal,
and made it a draught house unto this day.
28 **Thus Jehu** destroyed Baal out of Israel.
29 **Howbeit from the sins of Jeroboam the son of Nebat,** {who made Israel to sin}, Jehu departed not from after them, to wit, the golden calves that were in Bethel, and that were in Dan.
30 **And the LORD** said unto Jehu,
Because thou hast done well in executing that which is right in mine eyes,
and hast done unto the house of Ahab according to all that was in mine heart,
thy children of the fourth generation shall sit on the throne of Israel.
31 **But Jehu** took no heed to walk in the law of the LORD God of Israel with all his heart:
for he departed not from the sins of Jeroboam,
which made Israel to sin.
32 **In those days** the LORD began to cut Israel short:
and Hazael smote them in all the coasts of Israel;
33 From Jordan eastward, all the land of Gilead, the Gadites, and the Reubenites, and the Manassites, from Aroer,
which is by the river Arnon, even Gilead and Bashan.
34 **Now the rest of the acts of Jehu, and all that he did, and all his might,** are they not written in the book of the chronicles of the kings of Israel?
35 **And Jehu** slept with his fathers:
and they buried him in Samaria.
And Jehoahaz his son reigned in his stead.
36 **And the time that Jehu reigned over Israel in Samaria** was twenty and eight years.

11

And when Athaliah the mother of Ahaziah saw that her son was dead,
she arose and destroyed all the seed royal.
2 **But Jehosheba, the daughter of king Joram, sister of Ahaziah,** took Joash the son of Ahaziah,
and stole him from among the king's sons which were slain;
and they hid him, even him and his nurse, in the bedchamber from Athaliah,
so that he was not slain.
3 **And he** was with her hid in the house of the LORD six years.
And Athaliah did reign over the land.
4 **And the seventh year Jehoiada** sent and fetched the rulers over hundreds, with the captains and the guard,
and brought them to him into the house of the LORD,
and made a covenant with them,
and took an oath of them in the house of the LORD,
and shewed them the king's son.
5 **And he** commanded them, saying,
This is the thing that ye shall do;
A third part of you that enter in on the sabbath shall even be keepers of the watch of the king's house;
6 **And a third part** shall be at the gate of Sur; and a third part at the gate behind the guard:
so shall ye keep the watch of the house,
that it be not broken down.
7 **And two parts of all you that go forth on the sabbath,** even they shall keep the watch of the house of the LORD about the king.
8 **And ye** shall compass the king round about, every man with his weapons in his hand:
and he that cometh within the ranges, let him be slain:
and be ye with the king
as he goeth out
and as he cometh in.
9 **And the captains over the hundreds** did according to all things that Jehoiada the priest commanded:
and they took every man his men that were to come in on the sabbath, with them that should go out on the sabbath,
and came to Jehoiada the priest.
10 **And to the captains over hundreds** did the priest give king David's spears and shields,
that were in the temple of the LORD.
11 **And the guard** stood, every man with his weapons in his hand, round about the king, from the right corner of the temple to the left corner of the temple, along by

the altar and the temple.

12 **And he** brought forth the king's son,
and put the crown upon him,
and gave him the testimony;
and they made him king,
and anointed him;
and they clapped their hands,
and said,
God save the king.

13 **And when Athaliah** heard the noise of the guard and of the people,
she came to the people into the temple of the LORD.

14 **And when** she looked,
behold,
the king stood by a pillar, {as the manner was}, and the princes and the trumpeters by the king,
and all the people of the land rejoiced,
and blew with trumpets:
and Athaliah rent her clothes,
and cried,
Treason, Treason.

15 **But Jehoiada the priest** commanded the captains of the hundreds, the officers of the host,
and said unto them,
Have her forth without the ranges:
and him that followeth her kill with the sword.

For the priest had said,
Let her not be slain in the house of the LORD.

16 **And they** laid hands on her;
and she went by the way by the which the horses came into the king's house:
and there was she slain.

17 **And Jehoiada** made a covenant between the LORD and the king and the people,
that they should be the LORD's people; between the king also and the people.

18 **And all the people of the land** went into the house of Baal,
and brake it down;
his altars and his images brake they in pieces thoroughly,
and slew Mattan the priest of Baal before the altars.

And the priest appointed officers over the house of the LORD.

19 **And he** took the rulers over hundreds, and the captains, and the guard, and all the people of the land;
and they brought down the king from the house of the LORD,
and came by the way of the gate of the guard to the king's house.

And he sat on the throne of the kings.

20 **And all the people of the land** rejoiced,
and the city was in quiet:
and they slew Athaliah with the sword beside the king's house.

21 **Seven years old** was Jehoash
when he began to reign.

12 **In the seventh year of Jehu** Jehoash began to reign;
and forty years reigned he in Jerusalem.

And his mother's name was Zibiah of Beersheba.

2 **And Jehoash** did that which was right in the sight of the LORD all his days wherein Jehoiada the priest instructed him.

3 **But the high places** were not taken away:
the people still sacrificed and burnt incense in the high places.

4 **And Jehoash** said to the priests,
All the money of the dedicated things that is brought into the house of the LORD, even the money of every one that passeth the account, the money that every man is set at, and all the money that cometh into any man's heart to bring into the house of the LORD,
5 Let the priests take it to them, every man of his acquaintance:
and let them repair the breaches of the house,
wheresoever any breach shall be found.

6 **But it** was so,
that in the three and twentieth year of king Jehoash the priests had not repaired the breaches of the house.

7 **Then king Jehoash** called for Jehoiada the priest, and the other priests,
and said unto them,
Why repair ye not the breaches of the house?
now therefore receive no more money of your acquaintance,
but deliver it for the breaches of the house.

8 **And the priests** consented to receive no more money of the people,
neither to repair the breaches of the house.

9 **But Jehoiada the priest** took a chest,
and bored a hole in the lid of it,
and set it beside the altar, on the right side as one cometh into the house of the LORD:
and the priests that kept the door put therein all the money that was brought into the house of the LORD.

10 **And it** was so,
when they saw that there was much money in the chest,
that the king's scribe and the high priest came up,
and they put up in bags,
and told the money that was found in the house of the LORD.

11 **And they** gave the money, {being told}, into the hands of them that did the work, that had the oversight of the house of the LORD:
and they laid it out to the carpenters and builders, {that wrought upon the house of the LORD},
12 And to masons, and hewers of stone,
and to buy timber and hewed stone {to repair the breaches of the house of the LORD}, and for all that was laid out for the house {to repair it}.

13 **Howbeit there** were not made for the house of the LORD bowls of silver, snuffers, basons, trumpets, any vessels of gold, or vessels of silver, of the money that was brought into the house of the LORD:
14 **But they** gave that to the workmen,
and repaired therewith the house of the LORD.

15 **Moreover they** reckoned not with the men,
into whose hand they delivered the money to be bestowed on workmen:
for they dealt faithfully.

16 **The trespass money and sin money** was not brought into the house of the LORD:

it was the priests'.

17 **Then Hazael king of Syria** went up,
and fought against Gath,
and took it:
and Hazael set his face to go up to Jerusalem.

18 **And Jehoash king of Judah** took all the hallowed things that Jehoshaphat, and Jehoram, and Ahaziah, his fathers, kings of Judah, had dedicated, and his own hallowed things, and all the gold that was found in the treasures of the house of the LORD, and in the king's house,
and sent it to Hazael king of Syria:
and he went away from Jerusalem.

19 **And the rest of the acts of Joash, and all that he did,** are they not written in the book of the chronicles of the kings of Judah?

20 **And his servants** arose,
and made a conspiracy,
and slew Joash in the house of Millo,
which goeth down to Silla.

21 **For Jozachar the son of Shimeath, and Jehozabad the son of Shomer, his servants,** smote him,
and he died;
and they buried him with his fathers in the city of David:
and Amaziah his son reigned in his stead.

13 **In the three and twentieth year of Joash the son of Ahaziah king of Judah** Jehoahaz the son of Jehu began to reign over Israel in Samaria,
and reigned seventeen years.

2 **And he** did that which was evil in the sight of the LORD,
and followed the sins of Jeroboam the son of Nebat,
which made Israel to sin;
he departed not therefrom.

3 **And the anger of the LORD** was kindled against Israel,
and he delivered them into the hand of Hazael king of Syria, and into the hand of Benhadad the son of Hazael, all their days.

4 **And Jehoahaz** besought the LORD,
and the LORD hearkened unto him:
for he saw the oppression of Israel,
because the king of Syria oppressed them.

5 (**And the LORD** gave Israel a saviour,
so that they went out from under the hand of the Syrians:
and the children of Israel dwelt in their tents, as beforetime.

6 **Nevertheless they** departed not from the sins of the house of Jeroboam,
who made Israel sin,
but walked therein:
and there remained the grove also in Samaria.)

7 **Neither** did he leave of the people to Jehoahaz but fifty horsemen, and ten chariots, and ten thousand footmen;
for the king of Syria had destroyed them,
and had made them like the dust by threshing.

8 **Now the rest of the acts of Jehoahaz, and all that he did, and his might,** are they not written in the book of the chronicles of the kings of Israel?

9 **And Jehoahaz** slept with his fathers;
and they buried him in Samaria:
and Joash his son reigned in his stead.

10 **In the thirty and seventh year of Joash king of Judah** began Jehoash the son of Jehoahaz to reign over Israel in Samaria,
and reigned sixteen years.

11 **And he** did that which was evil in the sight of the LORD;
he departed not from all the sins of Jeroboam the son of Nebat,
who made Israel sin:
but he walked therein.

12 **And the rest of the acts of Joash, and all that he did, and his might wherewith he fought against Amaziah king of Judah,** are they not written in the book of the chronicles of the kings of Israel?

13 **And Joash** slept with his fathers;
and Jeroboam sat upon his throne:
and Joash was buried in Samaria with the kings of Israel.

14 **Now Elisha** was fallen sick of his sickness whereof he died.
And Joash the king of Israel came down unto him,
and wept over his face,
and said,
O my father, my father, the chariot of Israel, and the horsemen thereof.

15 **And Elisha** said unto him,
Take bow and arrows.
And he took unto him bow and arrows.

16 **And he** said to the king of Israel,
Put thine hand upon the bow.
And he put his hand upon it:
and Elisha put his hands upon the king's hands.

17 **And he** said,
Open the window eastward.
And he opened it.
Then Elisha said,
Shoot.
And he shot.
And he said,
The arrow of the LORD's deliverance, and the arrow of deliverance from Syria:
for thou shalt smite the Syrians in Aphek,
till thou have consumed them.

18 **And he** said,
Take the arrows.
And he took them.
And he said unto the king of Israel,
Smite upon the ground.
And he smote thrice,
and stayed.

19 **And the man of God** was wroth with him,
and said,
Thou shouldest have smitten five or six times;
then hadst thou smitten Syria
till thou hadst consumed it:
whereas now thou shalt smite Syria but thrice.

20 **And Elisha** died,
and they buried him.
And the bands of the Moabites invaded the land at the coming in of the year.

21 **And it** came to pass,
as they were burying a man,
that, {behold}, they spied a band of men;
and they cast the man into the sepulchre of Elisha:
and when the man was let down,
and touched the bones of Elisha,
he revived,
and stood up on his feet.

22 **But Hazael king of Syria**

oppressed Israel all the days of Jehoahaz.

23 **And the LORD** was gracious unto them,
and had compassion on them,
and had respect unto them, because of his covenant with Abraham, Isaac, and Jacob,
and would not destroy them,
neither cast he them from his presence as yet.

24 **So Hazael king of Syria** died;
and Benhadad his son reigned in his stead.

25 **And Jehoash the son of Jehoahaz** took again out of the hand of Benhadad the son of Hazael the cities,
which he had taken out of the hand of Jehoahaz his father by war.
Three times did Joash beat him,
and recovered the cities of Israel.

14

In the second year of Joash son of Jehoahaz king of Israel reigned Amaziah the son of Joash king of Judah.

2 **He** was twenty and five years old
when he began to reign,
and reigned twenty and nine years in Jerusalem.
And his mother's name was Jehoaddan of Jerusalem.

3 **And he** did that which was right in the sight of the LORD, yet not like David his father:
he did according to all things as Joash his father did.

4 **Howbeit the high places** were not taken away:
as yet the people did sacrifice and burnt incense on the high places.

5 **And it** came to pass,
as soon as the kingdom was confirmed in his hand,
that he slew his servants which had slain the king his father.

6 **But the children of the murderers** he slew not: according unto that which is written in the book of the law of Moses,
wherein the LORD commanded,
saying,
The fathers shall not be put to death for the children,
nor the children be put to death for the fathers;
but every man shall be put to death for his own sin.

7 **He** slew of Edom in the valley of salt ten thousand,
and took Selah by war,
and called the name of it Joktheel unto this day.

8 **Then Amaziah** sent messengers to Jehoash, the son of Jehoahaz son of Jehu, king of Israel,
saying,
Come,
let us look one another in the face.

9 **And Jehoash the king of Israel** sent to Amaziah king of Judah,
saying, **The thistle that was in Lebanon** sent to the cedar that was in Lebanon,
saying,
Give thy daughter to my son to wife:
and there passed by a wild beast that was in Lebanon,
and trode down the thistle.

10 **Thou** hast indeed smitten Edom,
and thine heart hath lifted thee up:
glory of this,
and tarry at home:
for why shouldest thou meddle to thy hurt,
that thou shouldest fall, even thou, and Judah with thee?

11 **But Amaziah** would not hear.
Therefore Jehoash king of Israel went up;
and he and Amaziah king of Judah looked one another in the face at Bethshemesh,
which belongeth to Judah.

12 **And Judah** was put to the worse before Israel;
and they fled every man to their tents.

13 **And Jehoash king of Israel** took Amaziah king of Judah, the son of Jehoash the son of Ahaziah, at Bethshemesh,
and came to Jerusalem,
and brake down the wall of Jerusalem from the gate of Ephraim unto the corner gate, four hundred cubits.

14 **And he** took all the gold and silver, and all the vessels that were found in the house of the LORD, and in the treasures of the king's house, and hostages,
and returned to Samaria.

15 **Now the rest of the acts of Jehoash which he did, and his might, and how he fought with Amaziah king of Judah,** are they not written in the book of the chronicles of the kings of Israel?

16 **And Jehoash** slept with his fathers,
and was buried in Samaria with the kings of Israel;
and Jeroboam his son reigned in his stead.

17 **And Amaziah the son of Joash king of Judah** lived after the death of Jehoash son of Jehoahaz king of Israel fifteen years.

18 **And the rest of the acts of Amaziah,** are they not written in the book of the chronicles of the kings of Judah?

19 **Now they** made a conspiracy against him in Jerusalem:
and he fled to Lachish;
but they sent after him to Lachish,
and slew him there.

20 **And they** brought him on horses:
and he was buried at Jerusalem with his fathers in the city of David.

21 **And all the people of Judah** took Azariah,
which was sixteen years old,
and made him king instead of his father Amaziah.

22 **He** built Elath,
and restored it to Judah,
after that the king slept with his fathers.

23 **In the fifteenth year of Amaziah the son of Joash king of Judah** Jeroboam the son of Joash king of Israel began to reign in Samaria,
and reigned forty and one years.

24 **And he** did that which was evil in the sight of the LORD:
he departed not from all the sins of Jeroboam the son of Nebat,
who made Israel to sin.

25 **He** restored the coast of Israel from the entering of Hamath unto the sea of the plain, according to the word of the LORD God of Israel,
which he spake by the hand of his servant Jonah, the son of Amittai, the prophet,
which was of Gathhepher.

26 **For the LORD** saw the affliction of Israel,
that it was very bitter:
for there was not any shut up, nor any left, nor any helper for Israel.

27 **And the LORD** said not
that he would blot out the name of

Israel from under heaven:
but he saved them by the hand of Jeroboam the son of Joash.

28 **Now the rest of the acts of Jeroboam, and all that he did, and his might, how he warred, and how he recovered Damascus, and Hamath, which belonged to Judah, for Israel,** are they not written in the book of the chronicles of the kings of Israel?

29 **And Jeroboam** slept with his fathers, even with the kings of Israel;
and Zachariah his son reigned in his stead.

15 **In the twenty and seventh year of Jeroboam king of Israel** began Azariah son of Amaziah king of Judah to reign.

2 **Sixteen years old** was he
when he began to reign,
and he reigned two and fifty years in Jerusalem.
And his mother's name was Jecholiah of Jerusalem.

3 **And he** did that which was right in the sight of the LORD, according to all that his father Amaziah had done;

4 **Save that the high places** were not removed:
the people sacrificed and burnt incense still on the high places.

5 **And the LORD** smote the king,
so that he was a leper unto the day of his death,
and dwelt in a several house.
And Jotham the king's son was over the house,
judging the people of the land.

6 **And the rest of the acts of Azariah, and all that he did,** are they not written in the book of the chronicles of the kings of Judah?

7 **So Azariah** slept with his fathers;
and they buried him with his fathers in the city of David:
and Jotham his son reigned in his stead.

8 **In the thirty and eighth year of Azariah king of Judah** did Zachariah the son of Jeroboam reign over Israel in Samaria six months.

9 **And he** did that which was evil in the sight of the LORD,
as his fathers had done:
he departed not from the sins of Jeroboam the son of Nebat,
who made Israel to sin.

10 **And Shallum the son of Jabesh** conspired against him,
and smote him before the people,
and slew him,
and reigned in his stead.

11 **And the rest of the acts of Zachariah,** {behold}, they are written in the book of the chronicles of the kings of Israel.

12 **This** was the word of the LORD which he spake unto Jehu,
saying,
Thy sons shall sit on the throne of Israel unto the fourth generation.
And so it came to pass.

13 **Shallum the son of Jabesh** began to reign in the nine and thirtieth year of Uzziah king of Judah;
and he reigned a full month in Samaria.

14 **For Menahem the son of Gadi** went up from Tirzah,
and came to Samaria,
and smote Shallum the son of Jabesh in Samaria,
and slew him,
and reigned in his stead.

15 **And the rest of the acts of Shallum, and his conspiracy which he made,** {behold}, they are written in the book of the chronicles of the kings of Israel.

16 **Then Menahem** smote Tiphsah, and all that were therein, and the coasts thereof from Tirzah:
because they opened not to him,
therefore he smote it;
and all the women therein that were with child he ripped up.

17 **In the nine and thirtieth year of Azariah king of Judah** began Menahem the son of Gadi to reign over Israel,
and reigned ten years in Samaria.

18 **And he** did that which was evil in the sight of the LORD:
he departed not all his days from the sins of Jeroboam the son of Nebat,
who made Israel to sin.

19 **And Pul the king of Assyria** came against the land:
and Menahem gave Pul a thousand talents of silver,
that his hand might be with him to confirm the kingdom in his hand.

20 **And Menahem** exacted the money of Israel, even of all the mighty men of wealth, of each man fifty shekels of silver,
to give to the king of Assyria.
So the king of Assyria turned back,
and stayed not there in the land.

21 **And the rest of the acts of Menahem, and all that he did,** are they not written in the book of the chronicles of the kings of Israel?

22 **And Menahem** slept with his fathers;
and Pekahiah his son reigned in his stead.

23 **In the fiftieth year of Azariah king of Judah** Pekahiah the son of Menahem began to reign over Israel in Samaria,
and reigned two years.

24 **And he** did that which was evil in the sight of the LORD:
he departed not from the sins of Jeroboam the son of Nebat,
who made Israel to sin.

25 **But Pekah the son of Remaliah, a captain of his,** conspired against him,
and smote him in Samaria, in the palace of the king's house, with Argob and Arieh, and with him fifty men of the Gileadites:
and he killed him,
and reigned in his room.

26 **And the rest of the acts of Pekahiah, and all that he did,** {behold}, they are written in the book of the chronicles of the kings of Israel.

27 **In the two and fiftieth year of Azariah king of Judah** Pekah the son of Remaliah began to reign over Israel in Samaria,
and reigned twenty years.

28 **And he** did that which was evil in the sight of the LORD:
he departed not from the sins of Jeroboam the son of Nebat,
who made Israel to sin.

29 **In the days of Pekah king of Israel** came Tiglathpileser king of Assyria,
and took Ijon, and Abelbethmaachah, and Janoah, and Kedesh, and Hazor, and Gilead, and Galilee, all the land of Naphtali,

and carried them captive to Assyria.
30 **And Hoshea the son of Elah** made a conspiracy against Pekah the son of Remaliah,
and smote him,
and slew him,
and reigned in his stead, in the twentieth year of Jotham the son of Uzziah.
31 **And the rest of the acts of Pekah, and all that he did,** {behold}, they are written in the book of the chronicles of the kings of Israel.
32 **In the second year of Pekah the son of Remaliah king of Israel** began Jotham the son of Uzziah king of Judah to reign.
33 **Five and twenty years old** was he
when he began to reign,
and he reigned sixteen years in Jerusalem.
And his mother's name was Jerusha, the daughter of Zadok.
34 **And he** did that which was right in the sight of the LORD:
he did according to all that his father Uzziah had done.
35 **Howbeit the high places** were not removed:
the people sacrificed and burned incense still in the high places.
He built the higher gate of the house of the LORD.
36 **Now the rest of the acts of Jotham, and all that he did,** are they not written in the book of the chronicles of the kings of Judah?
37 **In those days** the LORD began to send against Judah Rezin the king of Syria, and Pekah the son of Remaliah.
38 **And Jotham** slept with his fathers,
and was buried with his fathers in the city of David his father:
and Ahaz his son reigned in his stead.

16 **In the seventeenth year of Pekah the son of Remaliah** Ahaz the son of Jotham king of Judah began to reign.
2 **Twenty years old** was Ahaz
when he began to reign,
and reigned sixteen years in Jerusalem,
and did not that which was right in the sight of the LORD his God, like David his father.
3 **But he** walked in the way of the kings of Israel,
yea, and made his son to pass through the fire, according to the abominations of the heathen,
whom the LORD cast out from before the children of Israel.
4 **And he** sacrificed and burnt incense in the high places, and on the hills, and under every green tree.
5 **Then Rezin king of Syria and Pekah son of Remaliah king of Israel** came up to Jerusalem
to war:
and they besieged Ahaz,
but could not overcome him.
6 **At that time** Rezin king of Syria recovered Elath to Syria,
and drave the Jews from Elath:
and the Syrians came to Elath,
and dwelt there unto this day.
7 **So Ahaz** sent messengers to Tiglathpileser king of Assyria,
saying,
I am thy servant and thy son:
come up,
and save me out of the hand of the king of Syria, and out of the hand of the king of Israel,
which rise up against me.
8 **And Ahaz** took the silver and gold that was found in the house of the LORD, and in the treasures of the king's house,
and sent it for a present to the king of Assyria.
9 **And the king of Assyria** hearkened unto him:
for the king of Assyria went up against Damascus,
and took it,
and carried the people of it captive to Kir,
and slew Rezin.
10 **And king Ahaz** went to Damascus
to meet Tiglathpileser king of Assyria,
and saw an altar that was at Damascus:
and king Ahaz sent to Urijah the priest the fashion of the altar, and the pattern of it, according to all the workmanship thereof.
11 **And Urijah the priest** built an altar according to all that king Ahaz had sent from Damascus:
so Urijah the priest made it
against king Ahaz came from Damascus.
12 **And when the king** was come from Damascus,
the king saw the altar:
and the king approached to the altar,
and offered thereon.
13 **And he** burnt his burnt offering and his meat offering, {and poured his drink offering}, {and sprinkled the blood of his peace offerings}, upon the altar.
14 **And he** brought also the brasen altar, {which was before the LORD}, from the forefront of the house, from between the altar and the house of the LORD,
and put it on the north side of the altar.
15 **And king Ahaz** commanded Urijah the priest,
saying,
Upon the great altar burn the morning burnt offering, and the evening meat offering, and the king's burnt sacrifice, and his meat offering, with the burnt offering of all the people of the land, and their meat offering, and their drink offerings;
and sprinkle upon it all the blood of the burnt offering, and all the blood of the sacrifice:
and the brasen altar shall be for me to enquire by.
16 **Thus** did Urijah the priest, according to all that king Ahaz commanded.
17 **And king Ahaz** cut off the borders of the bases,
and removed the laver from off them;
and took down the sea from off the brasen oxen that were under it,
and put it upon the pavement of stones.
18 **And the covert for the sabbath that they had built in the house, and the king's entry without,** turned he from the house of the LORD for the king of Assyria.
19 **Now the rest of the acts of Ahaz which he did,** are they not written in the book of the chronicles of the kings of Judah?
20 **And Ahaz** slept with his fathers,
and was buried with his fathers in the city of David:
and Hezekiah his son reigned in his stead.

17 **In the twelfth year of Ahaz king of Judah** began
Hoshea the son of Elah to reign in
Samaria over Israel nine years.
2 **And he** did that which was evil in
the sight of the LORD, but not as
the kings of Israel that were
before him.
3 **Against him** came up
Shalmaneser king of Assyria;
and Hoshea became his servant,
and gave him presents.
4 **And the king of Assyria** found
conspiracy in Hoshea:
for he had sent messengers to So
king of Egypt,
and brought no present to the king
of Assyria,
as he had done year by year:
therefore the king of Assyria shut
him up,
and bound him in prison.
5 **Then the king of Assyria** came up
throughout all the land,
and went up to Samaria,
and besieged it three years.
6 **In the ninth year of Hoshea** the
king of Assyria took Samaria,
and carried Israel away into
Assyria,
and placed them in Halah and in
Habor by the river of Gozan, and
in the cities of the Medes.
7 **For so** it was,
that the children of Israel had
sinned against the LORD their
God,
which had brought them up out of
the land of Egypt, from under the
hand of Pharaoh king of Egypt,
and had feared other gods,
8 **And** walked in the statutes of the
heathen,
whom the LORD cast out from
before the children of Israel, and
of the kings of Israel,
which they had made.
9 **And the children of Israel** did
secretly those things that were
not right against the LORD their
God,
and they built them high places in
all their cities, from the tower of
the watchmen to the fenced city.
10 **And they** set them up images and
groves in every high hill, and
under every green tree:
11 **And there** they burnt incense in
all the high places,
as did the heathen whom the LORD
carried away before them;
and wrought wicked things to
provoke the LORD to anger:
12 **For they** served idols,
whereof the LORD had said unto
them,
Ye shall not do this thing.
13 **Yet the LORD** testified against
Israel, and against Judah, by all
the prophets, and by all the seers,
saying,
Turn ye from your evil ways,
and keep my commandments and
my statutes, according to all the
law which I commanded your
fathers, and which I sent to you
by my servants the prophets.
14 **Notwithstanding they** would not
hear,
but hardened their necks, like to the
neck of their fathers,
that did not believe in the LORD
their God.
15 **And they** rejected his statutes,
and his covenant that he made
with their fathers, and his
testimonies which he testified
against them;
and they followed vanity,
and became vain,
and went after the heathen that
were round about them,
concerning whom the LORD had
charged them,
that they should not do like them.
16 **And they** left all the
commandments of the LORD
their God,
and made them molten images,
even two calves,
and made a grove,
and worshipped all the host of
heaven,
and served Baal.
17 **And they** caused their sons and
their daughters to pass through
the fire,
and used divination and
enchantments,
and sold themselves to do evil in
the sight of the LORD,
to provoke him to anger.
18 **Therefore the LORD** was very
angry with Israel,
and removed them out of his sight:
there was none left but the tribe of
Judah only.
19 **Also Judah** kept not the
commandments of the LORD
their God,
but walked in the statutes of Israel
which they made.
20 **And the LORD** rejected all the
seed of Israel,
and afflicted them,
and delivered them into the hand of
spoilers,
until he had cast them out of his
sight.
21 **For he** rent Israel from the house
of David;
and they made Jeroboam the son of
Nebat king:
and Jeroboam drave Israel from
following the LORD,
and made them sin a great sin.
22 **For the children of Israel** walked
in all the sins of Jeroboam which
he did;
they departed not from them;
23 **Until the LORD** removed Israel
out of his sight,
as he had said by all his servants
the prophets.
So was Israel carried away out of
their own land to Assyria unto
this day.
24 **And the king of Assyria** brought
men from Babylon, and from
Cuthah, and from Ava, and from
Hamath, and from Sepharvaim,
and placed them in the cities of
Samaria instead of the children of
Israel:
and they possessed Samaria,
and dwelt in the cities thereof.
25 **And so** it was at the beginning of
their dwelling there,
that they feared not the LORD:
therefore the LORD sent lions
among them,
which slew some of them.
26 **Wherefore they** spake to the king
of Assyria,
saying,
**The nations which thou hast
removed, and placed in the
cities of Samaria,** know not the
manner of the God of the land:
therefore he hath sent lions among
them,
and, {behold}, they slay them,
because they know not the manner
of the God of the land.
27 **Then the king of Assyria**
commanded,
saying,
Carry thither one of the priests
whom ye brought from thence;
and let them go and dwell there,

and let him teach them the manner of the God of the land.

28 **Then one of the priests whom they had carried away from Samaria** came and dwelt in Bethel,
and taught them how they should fear the LORD.

29 **Howbeit every nation** made gods of their own,
and put them in the houses of the high places which the Samaritans had made, every nation in their cities wherein they dwelt.

30 **And the men of Babylon** made Succothbenoth,
and the men of Cuth made Nergal,
and the men of Hamath made Ashima,

31 **And the Avites** made Nibhaz and Tartak,
and the Sepharvites burnt their children in fire to Adrammelech and Anammelech, the gods of Sepharvaim.

32 **So they** feared the LORD,
and made unto themselves of the lowest of them priests of the high places,
which sacrificed for them in the houses of the high places.

33 **They** feared the LORD,
and served their own gods, after the manner of the nations whom they carried away from thence.

34 **Unto this day** they do after the former manners:
they fear not the LORD,
neither do they after their statutes, or after their ordinances, or after the law and commandment which the LORD commanded the children of Jacob,
whom he named Israel;

35 **With whom** the LORD had made a covenant,
and charged them,
saying,
Ye shall not fear other gods,
nor bow yourselves to them,
nor serve them,
nor sacrifice to them:

36 **But the LORD**, {who brought you up out of the land of Egypt with great power and a stretched out arm}, him shall ye fear,
and him shall ye worship,
and to him shall ye do sacrifice.

37 **And the statutes, and the ordinances, and the law, and the commandment**, {which he wrote for you}, ye shall observe to do for evermore;
and ye shall not fear other gods.

38 **And the covenant that I have made with you** ye shall not forget;
neither shall ye fear other gods.

39 **But the LORD your God** ye shall fear;
and he shall deliver you out of the hand of all your enemies.

40 **Howbeit they** did not hearken,
but they did after their former manner.

41 **So these nations** feared the LORD,
and served their graven images, both their children, and their children's children:
as did their fathers,
so do they unto this day.

18

Now it came to pass in the third year of Hoshea son of Elah king of Israel,
that Hezekiah the son of Ahaz king of Judah began to reign.

2 **Twenty and five years old** was he when he began to reign;
and he reigned twenty and nine years in Jerusalem.
His mother's name also was Abi, the daughter of Zachariah.

3 **And he** did that which was right in the sight of the LORD, according to all that David his father did.

4 **He** removed the high places,
and brake the images,
and cut down the groves,
and brake in pieces the brasen serpent that Moses had made:
for unto those days the children of Israel did burn incense to it:
and he called it Nehushtan.

5 **He** trusted in the LORD God of Israel;
so that after him was none like him among all the kings of Judah, nor any that were before him.

6 **For he** clave to the LORD,
and departed not from following him,
but kept his commandments,
which the LORD commanded Moses.

7 **And the LORD** was with him;
and he prospered
whithersoever he went forth:
and he rebelled against the king of Assyria,
and served him not.

8 **He** smote the Philistines, even unto Gaza, and the borders thereof, from the tower of the watchmen to the fenced city.

9 **And it** came to pass in the fourth year of king Hezekiah,
which was the seventh year of Hoshea son of Elah king of Israel,
that Shalmaneser king of Assyria came up against Samaria,
and besieged it.

10 **And at the end of three years** they took it:
even in the sixth year of Hezekiah, that is in the ninth year of Hoshea king of Israel, Samaria was taken.

11 **And the king of Assyria** did carry away Israel unto Assyria,
and put them in Halah and in Habor by the river of Gozan, and in the cities of the Medes:

12 **Because they** obeyed not the voice of the LORD their God,
but transgressed his covenant, and all that Moses the servant of the LORD commanded,
and would not hear them,
nor do them.

13 **Now in the fourteenth year of king Hezekiah** did Sennacherib king of Assyria come up against all the fenced cities of Judah,
and took them.

14 **And Hezekiah king of Judah** sent to the king of Assyria to Lachish,
saying,
I have offended;
return from me:
that which thou puttest on me will I bear.
And the king of Assyria appointed unto Hezekiah king of Judah three hundred talents of silver and thirty talents of gold.

15 **And Hezekiah** gave him all the silver that was found in the house of the LORD, and in the treasures of the king's house.

16 **At that time** did Hezekiah cut off the gold from the doors of the temple of the LORD, and from the pillars which Hezekiah king of Judah had overlaid,
and gave it to the king of Assyria.

17 **And the king of Assyria** sent Tartan and Rabsaris and

Rabshakeh from Lachish to king
Hezekiah with a great host
against Jerusalem.
And they went up and came to
Jerusalem.
And when they were come up,
they came and stood by the conduit
of the upper pool,
which is in the highway of the
fuller's field.
18 **And when they** had called to the
king,
there came out to them Eliakim the
son of Hilkiah,
which was over the household, and
Shebna the scribe, and Joah the
son of Asaph the recorder.
19 **And Rabshakeh** said unto them,
Speak ye now to Hezekiah,
Thus saith the great king, the king
of Assyria,
What confidence is this wherein
thou trustest?
20 **Thou** sayest,
(but they are but vain words,)
Now on whom dost thou trust,
that thou rebellest against me?
21 **Now, {behold}, thou** trustest
upon the staff of this bruised reed,
even upon Egypt,
on which if a man lean,
it will go into his hand,
and pierce it:
so is Pharaoh king of Egypt unto all
that trust on him.
22 **But if ye** say unto me,
We trust in the LORD our God:
is not that he,
**whose high places and whose
altars** Hezekiah hath taken away,
and hath said to Judah and
Jerusalem,
Ye shall worship before this altar in
Jerusalem?
23 **Now therefore, {I pray thee},
give** pledges to my lord the king
of Assyria,
and I will deliver thee two
thousand horses,
if thou be able on thy part to set
riders upon them.
24 **How** then wilt thou turn away
the face of one captain of the least
of my master's servants,
and put thy trust on Egypt for
chariots and for horsemen?
25 **Am I** now come up without the
LORD against this place
to destroy it?
The LORD said to me,
Go up against this land,
and destroy it.
26 **Then** said Eliakim the son of
Hilkiah, and Shebna, and Joah,
unto Rabshakeh,
Speak, {I pray thee}, to thy servants
in the Syrian language;
for we understand it:
and talk not with us in the Jews'
language in the ears of the people
that are on the wall.
27 **But Rabshakeh** said unto them,
Hath my master sent me to thy
master, and to thee,
to speak these words?
hath he not sent me to the men
which sit on the wall,
that they may eat their own dung,
and drink their own piss with you?
28 **Then Rabshakeh** stood and cried
with a loud voice in the Jews'
language,
and spake,
saying,
Hear the word of the great king, the
king of Assyria:
29 **Thus** saith the king,
Let not Hezekiah deceive you:
for he shall not be able to deliver
you out of his hand:
30 **Neither let Hezekiah** make you
trust in the LORD,
saying,
The LORD will surely deliver us,
and this city shall not be delivered
into the hand of the king of
Assyria.
31 **Hearken not** to Hezekiah:
for thus saith the king of Assyria,
Make an agreement with me by a
present,
and come out to me,
and then eat ye every man of his
own vine, and every one of his fig
tree,
and drink ye every one the waters
of his cistern:
32 **Until I** come and take you away to
a land like your own land, a land
of corn and wine, a land of bread
and vineyards, a land of oil olive
and of honey,
that ye may live,
and not die:
and hearken not unto Hezekiah,
when he persuadeth you,
saying,
The LORD will deliver us.
33 **Hath any of the gods of the
nations** delivered at all his land
out of the hand of the king of
Assyria?
34 **Where** are the gods of Hamath,
and of Arpad?
where are the gods of Sepharvaim,
Hena, and Ivah?
have they delivered Samaria out of
mine hand?
35 **Who** are they among all the gods
of the countries,
that have delivered their country
out of mine hand,
that the LORD should deliver
Jerusalem out of mine hand?
36 **But the people** held their peace,
and answered him not a word:
for the king's commandment was,
saying,
Answer him not.
37 **Then** came Eliakim the son of
Hilkiah, {which was over the
household}, and Shebna the
scribe, and Joah the son of Asaph
the recorder, to Hezekiah with
their clothes rent,
and told him the words of
Rabshakeh.

19 **And it** came to pass,
when king Hezekiah
heard it,
that he rent his clothes,
and covered himself with sackcloth,
and went into the house of the
LORD.
2 **And he** sent Eliakim, {which was
over the household}, and Shebna
the scribe, and the elders of the
priests, {covered with sackcloth},
to Isaiah the prophet the son of
Amoz.
3 **And they** said unto him,
Thus saith Hezekiah,
This day is a day of trouble, and of
rebuke, and blasphemy;
for the children are come to the
birth,
and there is not strength to bring
forth.
4 **It may be the LORD thy God** will
hear all the words of Rabshakeh,
whom the king of Assyria his
master hath sent to reproach the
living God;
and will reprove the words which
the LORD thy God hath heard:
wherefore lift up thy prayer for the
remnant that are left.
5 **So the servants of king Hezekiah**

came to Isaiah.
6 **And Isaiah** said unto them,
Thus shall ye say to your master,
Thus saith the LORD,
Be not afraid of the words which thou hast heard, with which the servants of the king of Assyria have blasphemed me.
7 **Behold,**
I will send a blast upon him,
and he shall hear a rumour,
and shall return to his own land;
and I will cause him to fall by the sword in his own land.
8 **So Rabshakeh** returned,
and found the king of Assyria warring against Libnah:
for he had heard that he was departed from Lachish.
9 **And when he** heard say of Tirhakah king of Ethiopia,
Behold,
he is come out to fight against thee:
he sent messengers again unto Hezekiah,
saying,
10 **Thus** shall ye speak to Hezekiah king of Judah,
saying,
Let not thy God in whom thou trustest deceive thee,
saying,
Jerusalem shall not be delivered into the hand of the king of Assyria.
11 **Behold,**
thou hast heard what the kings of Assyria have done to all lands,
by destroying them utterly:
and shalt thou be delivered?
12 **Have the gods of the nations** delivered them which my fathers have destroyed; as Gozan, and Haran, and Rezeph, and the children of Eden which were in Thelasar?
13 **Where** is the king of Hamath, and the king of Arpad, and the king of the city of Sepharvaim, of Hena, and Ivah?
14 **And Hezekiah** received the letter of the hand of the messengers,
and read it:
and Hezekiah went up into the house of the LORD,
and spread it before the LORD.
15 **And Hezekiah** prayed before the LORD,
and said,
O LORD God of Israel, {which dwellest between the cherubims}, thou art the God, even thou alone, of all the kingdoms of the earth;
thou hast made heaven and earth.
16 **LORD, bow down** thine ear,
and hear:
open, LORD, thine eyes,
and see:
and hear the words of Sennacherib,
which hath sent him to reproach the living God.
17 **Of a truth, LORD, the kings of Assyria** have destroyed the nations and their lands,
18 **And** have cast their gods into the fire:
for they were no gods, but the work of men's hands, wood and stone:
therefore they have destroyed them.
19 **Now therefore, O LORD our God, I** beseech thee,
save thou us out of his hand,
that all the kingdoms of the earth may know
that thou art the LORD God, even thou only.
20 **Then Isaiah the son of Amoz** sent to Hezekiah,
saying,
Thus saith the LORD God of Israel,
That which thou hast prayed to me against Sennacherib king of Assyria I have heard.
21 **This** is the word that the LORD hath spoken concerning him;
The virgin the daughter of Zion hath despised thee,
and laughed thee to scorn;
the daughter of Jerusalem hath shaken her head at thee.
22 **Whom** hast thou reproached and blasphemed?
and against whom hast thou exalted thy voice,
and lifted up thine eyes on high?
even against the Holy One of Israel.
23 **By thy messengers** thou hast reproached the Lord,
and hast said,
With the multitude of my chariots I am come up to the height of the mountains, to the sides of Lebanon,
and will cut down the tall cedar trees thereof, and the choice fir trees thereof:
and I will enter into the lodgings of his borders, and into the forest of his Carmel.
24 **I** have digged and drunk strange waters,
and with the sole of my feet have I dried up all the rivers of besieged places.
25 **Hast thou not** heard long ago how I have done it, and of ancient times that I have formed it?
now have I brought it to pass,
that thou shouldest be to lay waste fenced cities into ruinous heaps.
26 **Therefore their inhabitants** were of small power,
they were dismayed and confounded;
they were as the grass of the field, and as the green herb, as the grass on the house tops, and as corn blasted before it be grown up.
27 **But I** know thy abode,
and thy going out,
and thy coming in,
and thy rage against me.
28 **Because thy rage against me and thy tumult** is come up into mine ears,
therefore I will put my hook in thy nose, and my bridle in thy lips,
and I will turn thee back by the way by which thou camest.
29 **And this** shall be a sign unto thee,
Ye shall eat this year such things as grow of themselves, and in the second year that which springeth of the same;
and in the third year sow ye,
and reap,
and plant vineyards,
and eat the fruits thereof.
30 **And the remnant that is escaped of the house of Judah** shall yet again take root downward,
and bear fruit upward.
31 **For out of Jerusalem** shall go forth a remnant, and they that escape out of mount Zion:
the zeal of the LORD of hosts shall do this.
32 **Therefore thus** saith the LORD concerning the king of Assyria,
He shall not come into this city,
nor shoot an arrow there,
nor come before it with shield,
nor cast a bank against it.
33 **By the way that he came,** by the same shall he return,
and shall not come into this city,

saith the LORD.

34 **For I** will defend this city, {to save it}, for mine own sake, and for my servant David's sake.

35 **And it** came to pass that night,
that the angel of the LORD went out,
and smote in the camp of the Assyrians an hundred fourscore and five thousand:
and when they arose early in the morning,
behold,
they were all dead corpses.

36 **So Sennacherib king of Assyria** departed,
and went and returned, **and** dwelt at Nineveh.

37 **And it** came to pass,
as he was worshipping in the house of Nisroch his god,
that Adrammelech and Sharezer his sons smote him with the sword:
and they escaped into the land of Armenia.
And Esarhaddon his son reigned in his stead.

20

⤫ **In those days** was Hezekiah sick unto death.
And the prophet Isaiah the son of Amoz came to him,
and said unto him,
Thus saith the LORD,
Set thine house in order;
for thou shalt die,
and not live.

2 **Then he** turned his face to the wall,
and prayed unto the LORD,
saying,
3 **I** beseech thee, O LORD,
remember now
how I have walked before thee in truth and with a perfect heart,
and have done that which is good in thy sight.
And Hezekiah wept sore.

4 **And it** came to pass,
afore Isaiah was gone out into the middle court,
that the word of the LORD came to him,
saying,
5 **Turn again,**
and tell Hezekiah the captain of my people,
Thus saith the LORD, the God of David thy father,
I have heard thy prayer,
I have seen thy tears:
behold,
I will heal thee:
on the third day thou shalt go up unto the house of the LORD.

6 **And I** will add unto thy days fifteen years;
and I will deliver thee and this city out of the hand of the king of Assyria;
and I will defend this city for mine own sake, and for my servant David's sake.

7 **And Isaiah** said,
Take a lump of figs.
And they took and laid it on the boil,
and he recovered.

8 **And Hezekiah** said unto Isaiah,
What shall be the sign that the LORD will heal me,
and that I shall go up into the house of the LORD the third day?

9 **And Isaiah** said,
This sign shalt thou have of the LORD,
that the LORD will do the thing that he hath spoken:
shall the shadow go forward ten degrees,
or go back ten degrees?

10 **And Hezekiah** answered,
It is a light thing for the shadow to go down ten degrees:
nay, but let the shadow return backward ten degrees.

11 **And Isaiah the prophet** cried unto the LORD:
and he brought the shadow ten degrees backward,
by which it had gone down in the dial of Ahaz.

12 **At that time** Berodachbaladan, the son of Baladan, king of Babylon, sent letters and a present unto Hezekiah:
for he had heard that Hezekiah had been sick.

13 **And Hezekiah** hearkened unto them,
and shewed them all the house of his precious things, the silver, and the gold, and the spices, and the precious ointment, and all the house of his armour, and all that was found in his treasures:
there was nothing in his house, nor in all his dominion, that Hezekiah shewed them not.

14 **Then** came Isaiah the prophet unto king Hezekiah,
and said unto him,
What said these men?
and from whence came they unto thee?
And Hezekiah said,
They are come from a far country, even from Babylon.

15 **And he** said,
What have they seen in thine house?
And Hezekiah answered,
All the things that are in mine house have they seen:
there is nothing among my treasures that I have not shewed them.

16 **And Isaiah** said unto Hezekiah,
Hear the word of the LORD.

17 **Behold,**
the days come,
that all that is in thine house, and that which thy fathers have laid up in store unto this day, shall be carried into Babylon:
nothing shall be left,
saith the LORD.

18 **And of thy sons that shall issue from thee,** {which thou shalt beget}, shall they take away;
and they shall be eunuchs in the palace of the king of Babylon.

19 **Then** said Hezekiah unto Isaiah,
Good is the word of the LORD which thou hast spoken.
And he said,
Is it not good,
if peace and truth be in my days?

20 **And the rest of the acts of Hezekiah, and all his might, {and how he made a pool, and a conduit}, {and brought water into the city},** are they not written in the book of the chronicles of the kings of Judah?

21 **And Hezekiah** slept with his fathers:
and Manasseh his son reigned in his stead.

21

Manasseh was twelve years old
when he began to reign,
and reigned fifty and five years in Jerusalem.
And his mother's name was Hephzibah.

2 **And he** did that which was evil in

the sight of the LORD, after the abominations of the heathen,
whom the LORD cast out before the children of Israel.

3 **For he** built up again the high places which Hezekiah his father had destroyed;
and he reared up altars for Baal,
and made a grove,
as did Ahab king of Israel;
and worshipped all the host of heaven,
and served them.

4 **And he** built altars in the house of the LORD,
of which the LORD said,
In Jerusalem will I put my name.

5 **And he** built altars for all the host of heaven in the two courts of the house of the LORD.

6 **And he** made his son pass through the fire,
and observed times,
and used enchantments,
and dealt with familiar spirits and wizards:
he wrought much wickedness in the sight of the LORD,
to provoke him to anger.

7 **And he** set a graven image of the grove that he had made in the house,
of which the LORD said to David, and to Solomon his son,
In this house, and in Jerusalem, {which I have chosen out of all tribes of Israel}, will I put my name for ever:

8 **Neither** will I make the feet of Israel move any more out of the land which I gave their fathers;
only if they will observe to do according to all that I have commanded them, and according to all the law that my servant Moses commanded them.

9 **But they** hearkened not:
and Manasseh seduced them to do more evil than did the nations whom the LORD destroyed before the children of Israel.

10 **And the LORD** spake by his servants the prophets,
saying,

11 **Because Manasseh king of Judah** hath done these abominations,
and hath done wickedly above all that the Amorites did,
which were before him,
and hath made Judah also to sin with his idols:

12 **Therefore thus** saith the LORD God of Israel,
Behold,
I am bringing such evil upon Jerusalem and Judah,
that whosoever heareth of it,
both his ears shall tingle.

13 **And I** will stretch over Jerusalem the line of Samaria, and the plummet of the house of Ahab:
and I will wipe Jerusalem as a man wipeth a dish,
wiping it,
and turning it upside down.

14 **And I** will forsake the remnant of mine inheritance,
and deliver them into the hand of their enemies;
and they shall become a prey and a spoil to all their enemies;

15 **Because they** have done that which was evil in my sight,
and have provoked me to anger,
since the day their fathers came forth out of Egypt, even unto this day.

16 **Moreover Manasseh** shed innocent blood very much,
till he had filled Jerusalem from one end to another; beside his sin wherewith he made Judah to sin,
in doing that which was evil in the sight of the LORD.

17 **Now the rest of the acts of Manasseh, and all that he did, and his sin that he sinned,** are they not written in the book of the chronicles of the kings of Judah?

18 **And Manasseh** slept with his fathers,
and was buried in the garden of his own house, in the garden of Uzza:
and Amon his son reigned in his stead.

19 **Amon** was twenty and two years old
when he began to reign,
and he reigned two years in Jerusalem.
And his mother's name was Meshullemeth, the daughter of Haruz of Jotbah.

20 **And he** did that which was evil in the sight of the LORD,
as his father Manasseh did.

21 **And he** walked in all the way that his father walked in,
and served the idols that his father served,
and worshipped them:

22 **And he** forsook the LORD God of his fathers,
and walked not in the way of the LORD.

23 **And the servants of Amon** conspired against him,
and slew the king in his own house.

24 **And the people of the land** slew all them that had conspired against king Amon;
and the people of the land made Josiah his son king in his stead.

25 **Now the rest of the acts of Amon which he did,** are they not written in the book of the chronicles of the kings of Judah?

26 **And he** was buried in his sepulchre in the garden of Uzza:
and Josiah his son reigned in his stead.

22 **Josiah** was eight years old **when he** began to reign,
and he reigned thirty and one years in Jerusalem.
And his mother's name was Jedidah, the daughter of Adaiah of Boscath.

2 **And he** did that which was right in the sight of the LORD,
and walked in all the way of David his father,
and turned not aside to the right hand or to the left.

3 **And it** came to pass in the eighteenth year of king Josiah,
that the king sent Shaphan the son of Azaliah, the son of Meshullam, the scribe, to the house of the LORD,
saying,

4 **Go up** to Hilkiah the high priest,
that he may sum the silver which is brought into the house of the LORD,
which the keepers of the door have gathered of the people:

5 **And let them** deliver it into the hand of the doers of the work,
that have the oversight of the house of the LORD:
and let them give it to the doers of the work which is in the house of the LORD,
to repair the breaches of the house,

6 Unto carpenters, and builders, and masons,
and to buy timber and hewn stone

to repair the house.

7 **Howbeit there** was no reckoning made with them of the money that was delivered into their hand,
because they dealt faithfully.

8 **And Hilkiah the high priest** said unto Shaphan the scribe,
I have found the book of the law in the house of the LORD.

And Hilkiah gave the book to Shaphan,
and he read it.

9 **And Shaphan the scribe** came to the king,
and brought the king word again,
and said,
Thy servants have gathered the money that was found in the house,
and have delivered it into the hand of them that do the work, that have the oversight of the house of the LORD.

10 **And Shaphan the scribe** shewed the king,
saying,
Hilkiah the priest hath delivered me a book.

And Shaphan read it before the king.

11 **And it** came to pass,
when the king had heard the words of the book of the law,
that he rent his clothes.

12 **And the king** commanded Hilkiah the priest, and Ahikam the son of Shaphan, and Achbor the son of Michaiah, and Shaphan the scribe, and Asahiah a servant of the king's,
saying,
13 **Go ye,**
enquire of the LORD for me, and for the people, and for all Judah, concerning the words of this book that is found:
for great is the wrath of the LORD that is kindled against us,
because our fathers have not hearkened unto the words of this book,
to do according unto all that which is written concerning us.

14 **So Hilkiah the priest, and Ahikam, and Achbor, and Shaphan, and Asahiah,** went unto Huldah the prophetess, the wife of Shallum the son of Tikvah, the son of Harhas, keeper of the wardrobe;
(now she dwelt in Jerusalem in the college;)
and they communed with her.

15 **And she** said unto them,
Thus saith the LORD God of Israel,
Tell the man that sent you to me,
16 **Thus** saith the LORD,
Behold,
I will bring evil upon this place, and upon the inhabitants thereof, even all the words of the book which the king of Judah hath read:
17 **Because they** have forsaken me,
and have burned incense unto other gods,
that they might provoke me to anger with all the works of their hands;
therefore my wrath shall be kindled against this place,
and shall not be quenched.

18 **But to the king of Judah which sent you to enquire of the LORD,** thus shall ye say to him,
Thus saith the LORD God of Israel,
As touching the words which thou hast heard;
19 **Because thine heart** was tender,
and thou hast humbled thyself before the LORD,
when thou heardest what I spake against this place, and against the inhabitants thereof,
that they should become a desolation and a curse,
and hast rent thy clothes,
and wept before me;
I also have heard thee,
saith the LORD.

20 **Behold** therefore,
I will gather thee unto thy fathers,
and thou shalt be gathered into thy grave in peace;
and thine eyes shall not see all the evil which I will bring upon this place.

And they brought the king word again.

23

And the king sent,
and they gathered unto him all the elders of Judah and of Jerusalem.

2 **And the king** went up into the house of the LORD, and all the men of Judah and all the inhabitants of Jerusalem with him, and the priests, and the prophets, and all the people, both small and great:
and he read in their ears all the words of the book of the covenant which was found in the house of the LORD.

3 **And the king** stood by a pillar,
and made a covenant before the LORD,
to walk after the LORD,
and to keep his commandments and his testimonies and his statutes with all their heart and all their soul,
to perform the words of this covenant that were written in this book.

And all the people stood to the covenant.

4 **And the king** commanded Hilkiah the high priest, and the priests of the second order, and the keepers of the door,
to bring forth out of the temple of the LORD all the vessels that were made for Baal, and for the grove, and for all the host of heaven:
and he burned them without Jerusalem in the fields of Kidron,
and carried the ashes of them unto Bethel.

5 **And he** put down the idolatrous priests,
whom the kings of Judah had ordained to burn incense in the high places in the cities of Judah, and in the places round about Jerusalem; them also that burned incense unto Baal, to the sun, and to the moon, and to the planets, and to all the host of heaven.

6 **And he** brought out the grove from the house of the LORD, without Jerusalem, unto the brook Kidron,
and burned it at the brook Kidron,
and stamped it small to powder,
and cast the powder thereof upon the graves of the children of the people.

7 **And he** brake down the houses of the sodomites,
that were by the house of the LORD,
where the women wove hangings for the grove.

8 **And he** brought all the priests out of the cities of Judah,
and defiled the high places where the priests had burned incense, from Geba to Beersheba,
and brake down the high places of the gates that were in the

entering in of the gate of Joshua the governor of the city,
which were on a man's left hand at the gate of the city.

9 **Nevertheless the priests of the high places** came not up to the altar of the LORD in Jerusalem,
but they did eat of the unleavened bread among their brethren.

10 **And he** defiled Topheth,
which is in the valley of the children of Hinnom,
that no man might make his son or his daughter to pass through the fire to Molech.

11 **And he** took away the horses that the kings of Judah had given to the sun, at the entering in of the house of the LORD, by the chamber of Nathanmelech the chamberlain,
which was in the suburbs,
and burned the chariots of the sun with fire.

12 **And the altars that were on the top of the upper chamber of Ahaz, {which the kings of Judah had made}, and the altars which Manasseh had made in the two courts of the house of the LORD,** did the king beat down, and brake them down from thence, and cast the dust of them into the brook Kidron.

13 **And the high places that were before Jerusalem**, {which were on the right hand of the mount of corruption}, {which Solomon the king of Israel had builded for Ashtoreth the abomination of the Zidonians, and for Chemosh the abomination of the Moabites, and for Milcom the abomination of the children of Ammon}, did the king defile.

14 **And he** brake in pieces the images,
and cut down the groves,
and filled their places with the bones of men.

15 **Moreover the altar that was at Bethel, and the high place which Jeroboam the son of Nebat**, {who made Israel to sin}, had made,
both that altar and the high place he brake down,
and burned the high place,
and stamped it small to powder,
and burned the grove.

16 **And as Josiah** turned himself,
he spied the sepulchres that were there in the mount,
and sent,
and took the bones out of the sepulchres,
and burned them upon the altar,
and polluted it, according to the word of the LORD which the man of God proclaimed,
who proclaimed these words.

17 **Then he** said,
What title is that that I see?
And the men of the city told him,
It is the sepulchre of the man of God,
which came from Judah,
and proclaimed these things that thou hast done against the altar of Bethel.

18 **And he** said,
Let him alone;
let no man move his bones.
So they let his bones alone, with the bones of the prophet that came out of Samaria.

19 **And all the houses also of the high places that were in the cities of Samaria**, {which the kings of Israel had made to provoke the LORD to anger}, Josiah took away,
and did to them according to all the acts that he had done in Bethel.

20 **And he** slew all the priests of the high places that were there upon the altars,
and burned men's bones upon them,
and returned to Jerusalem.

21 **And the king** commanded all the people,
saying,
Keep the passover unto the LORD your God,
as it is written in the book of this covenant.

22 **Surely there** was not holden such a passover from the days of the judges that judged Israel, nor in all the days of the kings of Israel, nor of the kings of Judah;

23 **But in the eighteenth year of king Josiah,** wherein this passover was holden to the LORD in Jerusalem.

24 **Moreover the workers with familiar spirits, and the wizards, and the images, and the idols, and all the abominations that were spied in the land of Judah and in Jerusalem,** did Josiah put away,
that he might perform the words of the law which were written in the book that Hilkiah the priest found in the house of the LORD.

25 **And like unto him** was there no king before him,
that turned to the LORD with all his heart, and with all his soul, and with all his might, according to all the law of Moses;
neither after him arose there any like him.

26 **Notwithstanding the LORD** turned not from the fierceness of his great wrath,
wherewith his anger was kindled against Judah, because of all the provocations that Manasseh had provoked him withal.

27 **And the LORD** said,
I will remove Judah also out of my sight,
as I have removed Israel,
and will cast off this city Jerusalem which I have chosen, and the house of which I said,
My name shall be there.

28 **Now the rest of the acts of Josiah, and all that he did,** are they not written in the book of the chronicles of the kings of Judah?

29 **In his days** Pharaohnechoh king of Egypt went up against the king of Assyria to the river Euphrates:
and king Josiah went against him;
and he slew him at Megiddo,
when he had seen him.

30 **And his servants** carried him in a chariot dead from Megiddo,
and brought him to Jerusalem,
and buried him in his own sepulchre.
And the people of the land took Jehoahaz the son of Josiah,
and anointed him,
and made him king in his father's stead.

31 **Jehoahaz** was twenty and three years old
when he began to reign;
and he reigned three months in Jerusalem.
And his mother's name was Hamutal, the daughter of Jeremiah of Libnah.

32 **And he** did that which was evil in the sight of the LORD, according to all that his fathers had done.

33 **And Pharaohnechoh** put him in bands at Riblah in the land of Hamath,
that he might not reign in Jerusalem;
and put the land to a tribute of an hundred talents of silver, and a talent of gold.

34 **And Pharaohnechoh** made Eliakim the son of Josiah king in the room of Josiah his father,
and turned his name to Jehoiakim,
and took Jehoahaz away:
and he came to Egypt,
and died there.

35 **And Jehoiakim** gave the silver and the gold to Pharaoh;
but he taxed the land
to give the money according to the commandment of Pharaoh:
he exacted the silver and the gold of the people of the land, of every one according to his taxation,
to give it unto Pharaohnechoh.

36 **Jehoiakim** was twenty and five years old
when he began to reign;
and he reigned eleven years in Jerusalem.
And his mother's name was Zebudah, the daughter of Pedaiah of Rumah.

37 **And he** did that which was evil in the sight of the LORD, according to all that his fathers had done.

24 **In his days** Nebuchadnezzar king of Babylon came up,
and Jehoiakim became his servant three years:
then he turned and rebelled against him.

2 **And the LORD** sent against him bands of the Chaldees, and bands of the Syrians, and bands of the Moabites, and bands of the children of Ammon,
and sent them against Judah
to destroy it, according to the word of the LORD,
which he spake by his servants the prophets.

3 **Surely at the commandment of the LORD** came this upon Judah,
to remove them out of his sight, for the sins of Manasseh, according to all that he did;

4 And also for the innocent blood that he shed:
for he filled Jerusalem with innocent blood;
which the LORD would not pardon.

5 **Now the rest of the acts of Jehoiakim, and all that he did,** are they not written in the book of the chronicles of the kings of Judah?

6 **So Jehoiakim** slept with his fathers:
and Jehoiachin his son reigned in his stead.

7 **And the king of Egypt** came not again any more out of his land:
for the king of Babylon had taken from the river of Egypt unto the river Euphrates all that pertained to the king of Egypt.

8 **Jehoiachin** was eighteen years old
when he began to reign,
and he reigned in Jerusalem three months.
And his mother's name was Nehushta, the daughter of Elnathan of Jerusalem.

9 **And he** did that which was evil in the sight of the LORD, according to all that his father had done.

10 **At that time** the servants of Nebuchadnezzar king of Babylon came up against Jerusalem,
and the city was besieged.

11 **And Nebuchadnezzar king of Babylon** came against the city,
and his servants did besiege it.

12 **And Jehoiachin the king of Judah** went out to the king of Babylon, he, and his mother, and his servants, and his princes, and his officers:
and the king of Babylon took him in the eighth year of his reign.

13 **And he** carried out thence all the treasures of the house of the LORD, and the treasures of the king's house,
and cut in pieces all the vessels of gold which Solomon king of Israel had made in the temple of the LORD,
as the LORD had said.

14 **And he** carried away all Jerusalem, and all the princes, and all the mighty men of valour, even ten thousand captives, and all the craftsmen and smiths:
none remained, save the poorest sort of the people of the land.

15 **And he** carried away Jehoiachin to Babylon, and the king's mother, and the king's wives, and his officers, and the mighty of the land,
those carried he into captivity from Jerusalem to Babylon.

16 **And all the men of might, even seven thousand, and craftsmen and smiths a thousand, all that were strong and apt for war,** even them the king of Babylon brought captive to Babylon.

17 **And the king of Babylon** made Mattaniah his father's brother king in his stead,
and changed his name to Zedekiah.

18 **Zedekiah** was twenty and one years old
when he began to reign,
and he reigned eleven years in Jerusalem.
And his mother's name was Hamutal, the daughter of Jeremiah of Libnah.

19 **And he** did that which was evil in the sight of the LORD, according to all that Jehoiakim had done.

20 **For through the anger of the LORD** it came to pass in Jerusalem and Judah,
until he had cast them out from his presence,
that Zedekiah rebelled against the king of Babylon.

25 **And it** came to pass in the ninth year of his reign, in the tenth month, in the tenth day of the month,
that Nebuchadnezzar king of Babylon came, he, and all his host, against Jerusalem,
and pitched against it;
and they built forts against it round about.

2 **And the city** was besieged unto the eleventh year of king Zedekiah.

3 **And on the ninth day of the fourth month** the famine prevailed in the city,
and there was no bread for the people of the land.

4 **And the city** was broken up,
and all the men of war fled by night by the way of the gate

between two walls,
which is by the king's garden:
(now the Chaldees were against the
city round about:)
and the king went the way toward
the plain.
5 **And the army of the Chaldees**
pursued after the king,
and overtook him in the plains of
Jericho:
and all his army were scattered
from him.
6 **So they** took the king,
and brought him up to the king of
Babylon to Riblah;
and they gave judgment upon him.
7 **And they** slew the sons of
Zedekiah before his eyes,
and put out the eyes of Zedekiah,
and bound him with fetters of
brass,
and carried him to Babylon.
8 **And in the fifth month, on the
seventh day of the month,**
{which is the nineteenth year of
king Nebuchadnezzar king of
Babylon}, came Nebuzaradan,
captain of the guard, a servant of
the king of Babylon, unto
Jerusalem:
9 **And he** burnt the house of the
LORD, and the king's house, and
all the houses of Jerusalem,
and every great man's house
burnt he with fire.
10 **And all the army of the
Chaldees**, {that were with the
captain of the guard}, brake down
the walls of Jerusalem round
about.
11 **Now the rest of the people that
were left in the city, and the
fugitives that fell away to the
king of Babylon, with the
remnant of the multitude,** did
Nebuzaradan the captain of the
guard carry away.
12 **But the captain of the guard** left
of the poor of the land to be
vinedressers and husbandmen.
13 **And the pillars of brass that
were in the house of the LORD,
and the bases, and the brasen
sea that was in the house of the
LORD,** did the Chaldees break in
pieces,
and carried the brass of them to
Babylon.
14 **And the pots, and the shovels,
and the snuffers, and the
spoons, and all the vessels of
brass wherewith they
ministered,** took they away.
15 **And the firepans, and the bowls,
and such things as were of gold,
in gold, and of silver, in silver,**
the captain of the guard took
away.
16 **The two pillars, one sea, and the
bases which Solomon had made
for the house of the LORD;** the
brass of all these vessels was
without weight.
17 **The height of the one pillar** was
eighteen cubits,
and the chapiter upon it was
brass:
and the height of the chapiter
three cubits;
**and the wreathen work, and
pomegranates upon the
chapiter round about,** all of
brass:
and like unto these had the second
pillar with wreathen work.
18 **And the captain of the guard**
took Seraiah the chief priest, and
Zephaniah the second priest, and
the three keepers of the door:
19 **And out of the city** he took an
officer that was set over the men
of war, and five men of them that
were in the king's presence,
{which were found in the city},
and the principal scribe of the
host, {which mustered the people
of the land}, and threescore men
of the people of the land that were
found in the city:
20 **And Nebuzaradan captain of
the guard** took these,
and brought them to the king of
Babylon to Riblah:
21 **And the king of Babylon** smote
them,
and slew them at Riblah in the land
of Hamath.
So Judah was carried away out of
their land.
22 **And as for the people that
remained in the land of Judah,**
{whom Nebuchadnezzar king of
Babylon had left}, even over them
he made Gedaliah the son of
Ahikam, the son of Shaphan,
ruler.
23 **And when all the captains of the
armies, they and their men,**
heard that the king of Babylon
had made Gedaliah governor,
there came to Gedaliah to Mizpah,
even Ishmael the son of
Nethaniah, and Johanan the son
of Careah, and Seraiah the son of
Tanhumeth the Netophathite,
and Jaazaniah the son of a
Maachathite, they and their men.
24 **And Gedaliah** sware to them, and
to their men,
and said unto them,
Fear not to be the servants of the
Chaldees:
dwell in the land,
and serve the king of Babylon;
and it shall be well with you.
25 **But it** came to pass in the seventh
month,
**that Ishmael the son of
Nethaniah, the son of Elishama,
of the seed royal,** came, and ten
men with him,
and smote Gedaliah,
that he died, and the Jews and the
Chaldees that were with him at
Mizpah.
26 **And all the people, both small
and great, and the captains of
the armies,** arose,
and came to Egypt:
for they were afraid of the
Chaldees.
27 **And it** came to pass in the seven
and thirtieth year of the captivity
of Jehoiachin king of Judah, in the
twelfth month, on the seven and
twentieth day of the month,
**that Evilmerodach king of
Babylon in the year that he
began to reign** did lift up the
head of Jehoiachin king of Judah
out of prison;
28 **And he** spake kindly to him,
and set his throne above the throne
of the kings that were with him in
Babylon;
29 **And** changed his prison
garments:
and he did eat bread continually
before him all the days of his life.
30 **And his allowance** was a
continual allowance given him of
the king, a daily rate for every day,
all the days of his life.

1 Chronicles

First Chronicles, traditionally attributed to the prophet Ezra, provides a historical account of the people of Israel after their return from exile in Babylon. The book is primarily a historical record that focuses on the Israelites' genealogy, the reign of King David, and the preparations for constructing the Temple in Jerusalem. Because of its impact on the development of Jewish and Christian theology, it remains an integral part of the Old Testament canon.

The opening chapters begin with a detailed genealogy of the Israelites, tracing their lineage from the time of Adam to the twelve tribes of Israel, a testament to their shared heritage and collective identity. It also provides a brief account of King Saul's reign, including his selection as king and his battles against the Philistines. But most of the book is devoted to the reign of King David: his rise to power, his conquests, and his deep and intimate relationship with God. It then concludes with King David's death, followed by the accession of his son, King Solomon, who would build the Temple in Jerusalem.

The Book of First Chronicles serves two purposes. It vividly illustrates the potential consequences of deviating from God's path, thus serving as a cautionary tale. Yet it also rekindles the Israeli spirit by recounting the people's storied past and illuminating their potential for a brighter future under the steadfast guidance of God. Intended to resonate deeply within the hearts of God's chosen people, the book provides a message of hope and motivation. And it does so by infusing the Israelites with renewed optimism and faith while urging them to tread God's path with unwavering determination.

1 Adam, Sheth, Enosh,
2 Kenan, Mahalaleel, Jered,
3 Henoch, Methuselah, Lamech,
4 Noah, Shem, Ham, and Japheth.

5 **The sons of Japheth;** Gomer, and Magog, and Madai, and Javan, and Tubal, and Meshech, and Tiras.

6 **And the sons of Gomer;** Ashchenaz, and Riphath, and Togarmah.

7 **And the sons of Javan;** Elishah, and Tarshish, Kittim, and Dodanim.

8 **The sons of Ham;** Cush, and Mizraim, Put, and Canaan.

9 **And the sons of Cush;** Seba, and Havilah, and Sabta, and Raamah, and Sabtecha.

And the sons of Raamah; Sheba, and Dedan.

10 **And Cush** begat Nimrod:
he began to be mighty upon the earth.

11 **And Mizraim** begat Ludim, and Anamim, and Lehabim, and Naphtuhim,
12 And Pathrusim, and Casluhim, (of whom came the Philistines,) and Caphthorim.

13 **And Canaan** begat Zidon his firstborn, and Heth,
14 The Jebusite also, and the Amorite, and the Girgashite,
15 And the Hivite, and the Arkite, and the Sinite,
16 And the Arvadite, and the Zemarite, and the Hamathite.

17 **The sons of Shem;** Elam, and Asshur, and Arphaxad, and Lud, and Aram, and Uz, and Hul, and Gether, and Meshech.

18 **And Arphaxad** begat Shelah,
and Shelah begat Eber.

19 **And unto Eber** were born two sons:
the name of the one was Peleg;
because in his days the earth was divided:
and his brother's name was Joktan.

20 **And Joktan** begat Almodad, and Sheleph, and Hazarmaveth, and Jerah,
21 Hadoram also, and Uzal, and Diklah,
22 And Ebal, and Abimael, and Sheba,
23 And Ophir, and Havilah, and Jobab.

All these were the sons of Joktan.

24 Shem, Arphaxad, Shelah,
25 Eber, Peleg, Reu,
26 Serug, Nahor, Terah,
27 Abram;
the same is Abraham.

28 **The sons of Abraham;** Isaac, and Ishmael.

29 **These** are their generations:
The firstborn of Ishmael,
Nebaioth; then Kedar, and Adbeel, and Mibsam,
30 Mishma, and Dumah, Massa, Hadad, and Tema,
31 Jetur, Naphish, and Kedemah.

These are the sons of Ishmael.

32 **Now the sons of Keturah, Abraham's concubine:**
she bare Zimran, and Jokshan, and Medan, and Midian, and Ishbak, and Shuah.

And the sons of Jokshan; Sheba, and Dedan.

33 **And the sons of Midian;** Ephah, and Epher, and Henoch, and Abida, and Eldaah.

All these are the sons of Keturah.

34 **And Abraham** begat Isaac.

The sons of Isaac; Esau and Israel.

35 **The sons of Esau;** Eliphaz, Reuel, and Jeush, and Jaalam, and Korah.

36 **The sons of Eliphaz;** Teman, and Omar, Zephi, and Gatam, Kenaz, and Timna, and Amalek.

37 **The sons of Reuel;** Nahath, Zerah, Shammah, and Mizzah.

38 **And the sons of Seir;** Lotan, and Shobal, and Zibeon, and Anah, and Dishon, and Ezar, and Dishan.

39 **And the sons of Lotan;** Hori, and Homam: and Timna was Lotan's sister.

40 **The sons of Shobal;** Alian, and Manahath, and Ebal, Shephi, and Onam.
And the sons of Zibeon; Aiah, and Anah.
41 **The sons of Anah;** Dishon.
And the sons of Dishon; Amram, and Eshban, and Ithran, and Cheran.
42 **The sons of Ezer;** Bilhan, and Zavan, and Jakan.
The sons of Dishan; Uz, and Aran.
43 **Now these** are the kings that reigned in the land of Edom
before any king reigned over the children of Israel;
Bela the son of Beor:
and the name of his city was Dinhabah.
44 **And when Bela** was dead,
Jobab the son of Zerah of Bozrah reigned in his stead.
45 **And when Jobab** was dead,
Husham of the land of the Temanites reigned in his stead.
46 **And when Husham** was dead,
Hadad the son of Bedad, {which smote Midian in the field of Moab}, reigned in his stead:
and the name of his city was Avith.
47 **And when Hadad** was dead,
Samlah of Masrekah reigned in his stead.
48 **And when Samlah** was dead,
Shaul of Rehoboth by the river reigned in his stead.
49 **And when Shaul** was dead,
Baalhanan the son of Achbor reigned in his stead.
50 **And when Baalhanan** was dead,
Hadad reigned in his stead:
and the name of his city was Pai;
and his wife's name was Mehetabel, the daughter of Matred, the daughter of Mezahab.
51 **Hadad** died also.
And the dukes of Edom were; duke Timnah, duke Aliah, duke Jetheth,
52 Duke Aholibamah, duke Elah, duke Pinon,
53 Duke Kenaz, duke Teman, duke Mibzar,
54 Duke Magdiel, duke Iram.
These are the dukes of Edom.

2 **These** are the sons of Israel; Reuben, Simeon, Levi, and Judah, Issachar, and Zebulun,
2 Dan, Joseph, and Benjamin, Naphtali, Gad, and Asher.
3 **The sons of Judah;** Er, and Onan, and Shelah:
which three were born unto him of the daughter of Shua the Canaanitess.
And Er, the firstborn of Judah, was evil in the sight of the LORD;
and he slew him.
4 **And Tamar his daughter in law** bore him Pharez and Zerah.
All the sons of Judah were five.
5 **The sons of Pharez;** Hezron, and Hamul.
6 **And the sons of Zerah;** Zimri, and Ethan, and Heman, and Calcol, and Dara: five of them in all.
7 **And the sons of Carmi;** Achar, the troubler of Israel,
who transgressed in the thing accursed.
8 **And the sons of Ethan;** Azariah.
9 **The sons also of Hezron**, {that were born unto him}; Jerahmeel, and Ram, and Chelubai.
10 **And Ram** begat Amminadab;
and Amminadab begat Nahshon, prince of the children of Judah;
11 **And Nahshon** begat Salma,
and Salma begat Boaz,
12 **And Boaz** begat Obed,
and Obed begat Jesse,
13 **And Jesse** begat his firstborn Eliab, and Abinadab the second, and Shimma the third,
14 Nethaneel the fourth, Raddai the fifth,
15 Ozem the sixth, David the seventh:
16 **Whose sisters** were Zeruiah, and Abigail.
And the sons of Zeruiah; Abishai, and Joab, and Asahel, three.
17 **And Abigail** bare Amasa:
and the father of Amasa was Jether the Ishmeelite.
18 **And Caleb the son of Hezron** begat children of Azubah his wife, and of Jerioth:
her sons are these; Jesher, and Shobab, and Ardon.
19 **And when Azubah** was dead,
Caleb took unto him Ephrath,
which bare him Hur.
20 **And Hur** begat Uri,
and Uri begat Bezaleel.
21 **And afterward Hezron** went in to the daughter of Machir the father of Gilead,
whom he married
when he was threescore years old;
and she bare him Segub.
22 **And Segub** begat Jair,
who had three and twenty cities in the land of Gilead.
23 **And he** took Geshur, and Aram, with the towns of Jair, from them, with Kenath, and the towns thereof, even threescore cities.
All these belonged to the sons of Machir the father of Gilead.
24 **And after that Hezron** was dead in Calebephratah,
then Abiah Hezron's wife bare him Ashur the father of Tekoa.
25 **And the sons of Jerahmeel the firstborn of Hezron** were, Ram the firstborn, and Bunah, and Oren, and Ozem, and Ahijah.
26 **Jerahmeel** had also another wife,
whose name was Atarah;
she was the mother of Onam.
27 **And the sons of Ram the firstborn of Jerahmeel** were, Maaz, and Jamin, and Eker.
28 **And the sons of Onam** were, Shammai, and Jada.
And the sons of Shammai; Nadab and Abishur.
29 **And the name of the wife of Abishur** was Abihail,
and she bare him Ahban, and Molid.
30 **And the sons of Nadab;** Seled, and Appaim:
but Seled died without children.
31 **And the sons of Appaim;** Ishi.
And the sons of Ishi; Sheshan.
And the children of Sheshan; Ahlai.
32 **And the sons of Jada the brother of Shammai;** Jether, and Jonathan:
and Jether died without children.
33 **And the sons of Jonathan;** Peleth, and Zaza.
These were the sons of Jerahmeel.
34 **Now Sheshan** had no sons, but daughters.
And Sheshan had a servant, an Egyptian,
whose name was Jarha.

35 **And Sheshan** gave his daughter
to Jarha his servant to wife;
and she bare him Attai.

36 **And Attai** begat Nathan,
and Nathan begat Zabad,
37 **And Zabad** begat Ephlal,
and Ephlal begat Obed,
38 **And Obed** begat Jehu,
and Jehu begat Azariah,
39 **And Azariah** begat Helez,
and Helez begat Eleasah,
40 **And Eleasah** begat Sisamai,
and Sisamai begat Shallum,
41 **And Shallum** begat Jekamiah,
and Jekamiah begat Elishama.

42 **Now the sons of Caleb the
brother of Jerahmeel** were,
Mesha his firstborn,
which was the father of Ziph; and
the sons of Mareshah the father of
Hebron.

43 **And the sons of Hebron;** Korah,
and Tappuah, and Rekem, and
Shema.

44 **And Shema** begat Raham, the
father of Jorkoam:
and Rekem begat Shammai.

45 **And the son of Shammai** was
Maon:
and Maon was the father of
Bethzur.

46 **And Ephah, Caleb's concubine,**
bare Haran, and Moza, and Gazez:
and Haran begat Gazez.

47 **And the sons of Jahdai;** Regem,
and Jotham, and Gesham, and
Pelet, and Ephah, and Shaaph.

48 **Maachah, Caleb's concubine,**
bare Sheber, and Tirhanah.

49 **She** bare also Shaaph the father of
Madmannah, Sheva the father of
Machbenah, and the father of
Gibea:
and the daughter of Caleb was
Achsa.

50 **These** were the sons of Caleb the
son of Hur, the firstborn of
Ephratah; Shobal the father of
Kirjathjearim,
51 Salma the father of Bethlehem,
Hareph the father of Bethgader.

52 **And Shobal the father of
Kirjathjearim** had sons; Haroeh,
and half of the Manahethites.

53 **And the families of
Kirjathjearim;** the Ithrites, and
the Puhites, and the Shumathites,
and the Mishraites;
of them came the Zareathites, and
the Eshtaulites,
54 **The sons of Salma;** Bethlehem,
and the Netophathites, Ataroth,
the house of Joab, and half of the
Manahethites, the Zorites.

55 **And the families of the scribes
which dwelt at Jabez;** the
Tirathites, the Shimeathites, and
Suchathites.
These are the Kenites that came of
Hemath, the father of the house
of Rechab.

3

Now these were the sons
of David,
which were born unto him in
Hebron; the firstborn Amnon, of
Ahinoam the Jezreelitess; the
second Daniel, of Abigail the
Carmelitess:
2 The third, Absalom the son of
Maachah the daughter of Talmai
king of Geshur: the fourth,
Adonijah the son of Haggith:
3 The fifth, Shephatiah of Abital: the
sixth, Ithream by Eglah his wife.

4 **These six** were born unto him in
Hebron;
and there he reigned seven years
and six months:
and in Jerusalem he reigned thirty
and three years.

5 **And these** were born unto him in
Jerusalem; Shimea, and Shobab,
and Nathan, and Solomon, four,
of Bathshua the daughter of
Ammiel:
6 Ibhar also, and Elishama, and
Eliphelet,
7 And Nogah, and Nepheg, and
Japhia,
8 And Elishama, and Eliada, and
Eliphelet, nine.

9 **These** were all the sons of David,
beside the sons of the concubines,
and Tamar their sister.

10 **And Solomon's son** was
Rehoboam, Abia his son, Asa his
son, Jehoshaphat his son,
11 Joram his son, Ahaziah his son,
Joash his son,
12 Amaziah his son, Azariah his son,
Jotham his son,
13 Ahaz his son, Hezekiah his son,
Manasseh his son,
14 Amon his son, Josiah his son.

15 **And the sons of Josiah** were, the
firstborn Johanan, the second
Jehoiakim, the third Zedekiah, the
fourth Shallum.

16 **And the sons of Jehoiakim:**
Jeconiah his son, Zedekiah his
son.

17 **And the sons of Jeconiah;** Assir,
Salathiel his son,
18 Malchiram also, and Pedaiah, and
Shenazar, Jecamiah, Hoshama,
and Nedabiah.

19 **And the sons of Pedaiah** were,
Zerubbabel, and Shimei:
and the sons of Zerubbabel;
Meshullam, and Hananiah, and
Shelomith their sister:
20 And Hashubah, and Ohel, and
Berechiah, and Hasadiah,
Jushabhesed, five.

21 **And the sons of Hananiah;**
Pelatiah, and Jesaiah: the sons of
Rephaiah, the sons of Arnan, the
sons of Obadiah, the sons of
Shechaniah.

22 **And the sons of Shechaniah;**
Shemaiah:
and the sons of Shemaiah;
Hattush, and Igeal, and Bariah,
and Neariah, and Shaphat, six.

23 **And the sons of Neariah;**
Elioenai, and Hezekiah, and
Azrikam, three.

24 **And the sons of Elioenai** were,
Hodaiah, and Eliashib, and
Pelaiah, and Akkub, and Johanan,
and Dalaiah, and Anani, seven.

4

The sons of Judah; Pharez,
Hezron, and Carmi, and Hur,
and Shobal.

2 **And Reaiah the son of Shobal**
begat Jahath;
and Jahath begat Ahumai, and
Lahad.
These are the families of the
Zorathites.

3 **And these** were of the father of
Etam; Jezreel, and Ishma, and
Idbash:
and the name of their sister was
Hazelelponi:
4 And Penuel the father of Gedor,
and Ezer the father of Hushah.
These are the sons of Hur, the
firstborn of Ephratah, the father
of Bethlehem.

5 **And Ashur the father of Tekoa**
had two wives, Helah and Naarah.

6 **And Naarah** bare him Ahuzam,
and Hepher, and Temeni, and
Haahashtari.

These were the sons of Naarah.

7 **And the sons of Helah** were, Zereth, and Jezoar, and Ethnan.

8 **And Coz** begat Anub, and Zobebah, and the families of Aharhel the son of Harum.

9 **And Jabez** was more honourable than his brethren:
and his mother called his name Jabez,
saying,
Because I bare him with sorrow.

10 **And Jabez** called on the God of Israel,
saying,
Oh that thou wouldest bless me indeed,
and enlarge my coast,
and that thine hand might be with me,
and that thou wouldest keep me from evil,
that it may not grieve me!
And God granted him that which he requested.

11 **And Chelub the brother of Shuah** begat Mehir,
which was the father of Eshton.

12 **And Eshton** begat Bethrapha, and Paseah, and Tehinnah the father of Irnahash.
These are the men of Rechah.

13 **And the sons of Kenaz;** Othniel, and Seraiah:
and the sons of Othniel; Hathath.

14 **And Meonothai** begat Ophrah:
and Seraiah begat Joab, the father of the valley of Charashim;
for they were craftsmen.

15 **And the sons of Caleb the son of Jephunneh;** Iru, Elah, and Naam: and the sons of Elah, even Kenaz.

16 **And the sons of Jehaleleel;** Ziph, and Ziphah, Tiria, and Asareel.

17 **And the sons of Ezra** were, Jether, and Mered, and Epher, and Jalon:
and she bare Miriam, and Shammai, and Ishbah the father of Eshtemoa.

18 **And his wife Jehudijah** bare Jered the father of Gedor, and Heber the father of Socho, and Jekuthiel the father of Zanoah.
And these are the sons of Bithiah the daughter of Pharaoh,
which Mered took.

19 **And the sons of his wife Hodiah the sister of Naham,** the father of Keilah the Garmite, and Eshtemoa the Maachathite.

20 **And the sons of Shimon** were, Amnon, and Rinnah, Benhanan, and Tilon.
And the sons of Ishi were, Zoheth, and Benzoheth.

21 **The sons of Shelah the son of Judah** were, Er the father of Lecah, and Laadah the father of Mareshah, and the families of the house of them that wrought fine linen, of the house of Ashbea,

22 And Jokim, and the men of Chozeba, and Joash, and Saraph, {who had the dominion in Moab}, and Jashubilehem.
And these are ancient things.

23 **These** were the potters, and those that dwelt among plants and hedges:
there they dwelt with the king for his work.

24 **The sons of Simeon** were, Nemuel, and Jamin, Jarib, Zerah, and Shaul:

25 Shallum his son, Mibsam his son, Mishma his son.

26 **And the sons of Mishma;** Hamuel his son, Zacchur his son, Shimei his son.

27 **And Shimei** had sixteen sons and six daughters:
but his brethren had not many children,
neither did all their family multiply, like to the children of Judah.

28 **And they** dwelt at Beersheba, and Moladah, and Hazarshual,

29 And at Bilhah, and at Ezem, and at Tolad,

30 And at Bethuel, and at Hormah, and at Ziklag,

31 And at Bethmarcaboth, and Hazarsusim, and at Bethbirei, and at Shaaraim.
These were their cities unto the reign of David.

32 **And their villages** were, Etam, and Ain, Rimmon, and Tochen, and Ashan, five cities:

33 And all their villages that were round about the same cities, unto Baal.
These were their habitations, and their genealogy.

34 And Meshobab, and Jamlech, and Joshah, the son of Amaziah,

35 And Joel, and Jehu the son of Josibiah, the son of Seraiah, the son of Asiel,

36 And Elioenai, and Jaakobah, and Jeshohaiah, and Asaiah, and Adiel, and Jesimiel, and Benaiah,

37 And Ziza the son of Shiphi, the son of Allon, the son of Jedaiah, the son of Shimri, the son of Shemaiah;

38 **These mentioned by their names** were princes in their families:
and the house of their fathers increased greatly.

39 **And they** went to the entrance of Gedor, even unto the east side of the valley,
to seek pasture for their flocks.

40 **And they** found fat pasture and good,
and the land was wide, and quiet, and peaceable;
for they of Ham had dwelt there of old.

41 **And these written by name** came in the days of Hezekiah king of Judah,
and smote their tents, and the habitations that were found there,
and destroyed them utterly unto this day,
and dwelt in their rooms:
because there was pasture there for their flocks.

42 **And some of them, even of the sons of Simeon, five hundred men,** went to mount Seir,
having for their captains Pelatiah, and Neariah, and Rephaiah, and Uzziel, the sons of Ishi.

43 **And they** smote the rest of the Amalekites that were escaped,
and dwelt there unto this day.

5

Now the sons of Reuben the firstborn of Israel,
(for he was the firstborn;
but forasmuch as he defiled his father's bed, his birthright was given unto the sons of Joseph the son of Israel:
and the genealogy is not to be reckoned after the birthright.

2 For Judah prevailed above his brethren,
and of him came the chief ruler;
but the birthright was Joseph's:)

3 **The sons, {I say}, of Reuben the firstborn of Israel** were, Hanoch, and Pallu, Hezron, and Carmi.

4 **The sons of Joel;** Shemaiah his son, Gog his son, Shimei his son,
5 Micah his son, Reaia his son, Baal his son,
6 Beerah his son,
whom Tilgathpilneser king of Assyria carried away captive:
he was prince of the Reubenites.

7 **And his brethren by their families**, {when the genealogy of their generations was reckoned}, were the chief, Jeiel, and Zechariah,
8 And Bela the son of Azaz, the son of Shema, the son of Joel, who dwelt in Aroer, even unto Nebo and Baalmeon:
9 **And eastward** he inhabited unto the entering in of the wilderness from the river Euphrates:
because their cattle were multiplied in the land of Gilead.

10 **And in the days of Saul** they made war with the Hagarites,
who fell by their hand:
and they dwelt in their tents throughout all the east land of Gilead.

11 **And the children of Gad** dwelt over against them, in the land of Bashan unto Salcah:
12 Joel the chief, and Shapham the next, and Jaanai, and Shaphat in Bashan.

13 **And their brethren of the house of their fathers** were, Michael, and Meshullam, and Sheba, and Jorai, and Jachan, and Zia, and Heber, seven.

14 **These** are the children of Abihail the son of Huri, the son of Jaroah, the son of Gilead, the son of Michael, the son of Jeshishai, the son of Jahdo, the son of Buz;
15 Ahi the son of Abdiel, the son of Guni, chief of the house of their fathers.

16 **And they** dwelt in Gilead in Bashan, and in her towns, and in all the suburbs of Sharon, upon their borders.

17 **All these** were reckoned by genealogies in the days of Jotham king of Judah, and in the days of Jeroboam king of Israel.

18 **The sons of Reuben, and the Gadites, and half the tribe of Manasseh, of valiant men, men able to bear buckler and sword, and to shoot with bow, and skilful in war,** were four and forty thousand seven hundred and threescore,
that went out to the war.

19 **And they** made war with the Hagarites, with Jetur, and Nephish, and Nodab.

20 **And they** were helped against them,
and the Hagarites were delivered into their hand, and all that were with them:
for they cried to God in the battle,
and he was intreated of them;
because they put their trust in him.

21 **And they** took away their cattle; of their camels fifty thousand, and of sheep two hundred and fifty thousand, and of asses two thousand, and of men an hundred thousand.

22 **For there** fell down many slain,
because the war was of God.

And they dwelt in their steads until the captivity.

23 **And the children of the half tribe of Manasseh** dwelt in the land:
they increased from Bashan unto Baalhermon and Senir, and unto mount Hermon.

24 **And these** were the heads of the house of their fathers, even Epher, and Ishi, and Eliel, and Azriel, and Jeremiah, and Hodaviah, and Jahdiel, mighty men of valour, famous men, and heads of the house of their fathers.

25 **And they** transgressed against the God of their fathers,
and went a whoring after the gods of the people of the land,
whom God destroyed before them.

26 **And the God of Israel** stirred up the spirit of Pul king of Assyria, and the spirit of Tilgathpilneser king of Assyria,
and he carried them away, even the Reubenites, and the Gadites, and the half tribe of Manasseh,
and brought them unto Halah, and Habor, and Hara, and to the river Gozan, unto this day.

6 **The sons of Levi;** Gershon, Kohath, and Merari.

2 **And the sons of Kohath;** Amram, Izhar, and Hebron, and Uzziel.

3 **And the children of Amram;** Aaron, and Moses, and Miriam.

The sons also of Aaron; Nadab, and Abihu, Eleazar, and Ithamar.

4 **Eleazar** begat Phinehas,
Phinehas begat Abishua,
5 **And Abishua** begat Bukki,
and Bukki begat Uzzi,
6 **And Uzzi** begat Zerahiah,
and Zerahiah begat Meraioth,
7 **Meraioth** begat Amariah,
and Amariah begat Ahitub,
8 **And Ahitub** begat Zadok,
and Zadok begat Ahimaaz,
9 **And Ahimaaz** begat Azariah,
and Azariah begat Johanan,
10 **And Johanan** begat Azariah,
(he it is that executed the priest's office in the temple that Solomon built in Jerusalem:)
11 **And Azariah** begat Amariah,
and Amariah begat Ahitub,
12 **And Ahitub** begat Zadok,
and Zadok begat Shallum,
13 **And Shallum** begat Hilkiah,
and Hilkiah begat Azariah,
14 **And Azariah** begat Seraiah,
and Seraiah begat Jehozadak,
15 **And Jehozadak** went into captivity,
when the LORD carried away Judah and Jerusalem by the hand of Nebuchadnezzar.

16 **The sons of Levi;** Gershom, Kohath, and Merari.

17 **And these** be the names of the sons of Gershom; Libni, and Shimei.

18 **And the sons of Kohath** were, Amram, and Izhar, and Hebron, and Uzziel.

19 **The sons of Merari;** Mahli, and Mushi.

And these are the families of the Levites according to their fathers.

20 **Of Gershom;** Libni his son, Jahath his son, Zimmah his son,
21 Joah his son, Iddo his son, Zerah his son, Jeaterai his son.

22 **The sons of Kohath;** Amminadab his son, Korah his son, Assir his son,
23 Elkanah his son, and Ebiasaph his son, and Assir his son,
24 Tahath his son, Uriel his son, Uzziah his son, and Shaul his son.

25 **And the sons of Elkanah;** Amasai, and Ahimoth.

26 **As for Elkanah:** the sons of Elkanah; Zophai his son, and Nahath his son,
27 Eliab his son, Jeroham his son, Elkanah his son.

28 **And the sons of Samuel;** the firstborn Vashni, and Abiah.

29 **The sons of Merari;** Mahli, Libni his son, Shimei his son, Uzza his son,
30 Shimea his son, Haggiah his son, Asaiah his son.

31 **And these** are they whom David set over the service of song in the house of the LORD,
after that the ark had rest.

32 **And they** ministered before the dwelling place of the tabernacle of the congregation with singing,
until Solomon had built the house of the LORD in Jerusalem:
and then they waited on their office according to their order.

33 **And these** are they that waited with their children.
Of the sons of the Kohathites: Heman a singer, the son of Joel, the son of Shemuel,
34 The son of Elkanah, the son of Jeroham, the son of Eliel, the son of Toah,
35 The son of Zuph, the son of Elkanah, the son of Mahath, the son of Amasai,
36 The son of Elkanah, the son of Joel, the son of Azariah, the son of Zephaniah,
37 The son of Tahath, the son of Assir, the son of Ebiasaph, the son of Korah,
38 The son of Izhar, the son of Kohath, the son of Levi, the son of Israel.

39 **And his brother Asaph**, {who stood on his right hand}, even Asaph the son of Berachiah, the son of Shimea,
40 The son of Michael, the son of Baaseiah, the son of Malchiah,
41 The son of Ethni, the son of Zerah, the son of Adaiah,
42 The son of Ethan, the son of Zimmah, the son of Shimei,
43 The son of Jahath, the son of Gershom, the son of Levi.

44 **And their brethren the sons of Merari** stood on the left hand: Ethan the son of Kishi, the son of Abdi, the son of Malluch,
45 The son of Hashabiah, the son of Amaziah, the son of Hilkiah,
46 The son of Amzi, the son of Bani, the son of Shamer,
47 The son of Mahli, the son of Mushi, the son of Merari, the son of Levi.

48 **Their brethren also the Levites** were appointed unto all manner of service of the tabernacle of the house of God.

49 **But Aaron and his sons** offered upon the altar of the burnt offering, and on the altar of incense,
and were appointed for all the work of the place most holy,
and to make an atonement for Israel, according to all that Moses the servant of God had commanded.

50 **And these** are the sons of Aaron; Eleazar his son, Phinehas his son, Abishua his son,
51 Bukki his son, Uzzi his son, Zerahiah his son,
52 Meraioth his son, Amariah his son, Ahitub his son,
53 Zadok his son, Ahimaaz his son.

54 **Now these** are their dwelling places throughout their castles in their coasts, of the sons of Aaron, of the families of the Kohathites:
for theirs was the lot.

55 **And they** gave them Hebron in the land of Judah, and the suburbs thereof round about it.

56 **But the fields of the city, and the villages thereof,** they gave to Caleb the son of Jephunneh.

57 **And to the sons of Aaron** they gave the cities of Judah, namely, Hebron, the city of refuge, and Libnah with her suburbs, and Jattir, and Eshtemoa, with their suburbs,
58 And Hilen with her suburbs, Debir with her suburbs,
59 And Ashan with her suburbs, and Bethshemesh with her suburbs:
60 And out of the tribe of Benjamin; Geba with her suburbs, and Alemeth with her suburbs, and Anathoth with her suburbs.
All their cities throughout their families were thirteen cities.

61 **And unto the sons of Kohath,** {which were left of the family of that tribe}, were cities given out of the half tribe, namely, out of the half tribe of Manasseh, by lot, ten cities.

62 **And to the sons of Gershom throughout their families out of the tribe of Issachar, and out of the tribe of Asher, and out of the tribe of Naphtali, and out of the tribe of Manasseh in Bashan,** thirteen cities.

63 **Unto the sons of Merari** were given by lot, throughout their families, out of the tribe of Reuben, and out of the tribe of Gad, and out of the tribe of Zebulun, twelve cities.

64 **And the children of Israel** gave to the Levites these cities with their suburbs.

65 **And they** gave by lot out of the tribe of the children of Judah, and out of the tribe of the children of Simeon, and out of the tribe of the children of Benjamin, these cities,
which are called by their names.

66 **And the residue of the families of the sons of Kohath** had cities of their coasts out of the tribe of Ephraim.

67 **And they** gave unto them, of the cities of refuge, Shechem in mount Ephraim with her suburbs;
they gave also Gezer with her suburbs,
68 And Jokmeam with her suburbs, and Bethhoron with her suburbs,
69 And Aijalon with her suburbs, and Gathrimmon with her suburbs:
70 And out of the half tribe of Manasseh; Aner with her suburbs, and Bileam with her suburbs, for the family of the remnant of the sons of Kohath.

71 **Unto the sons of Gershom** were given out of the family of the half tribe of Manasseh, Golan in Bashan with her suburbs, and Ashtaroth with her suburbs:
72 And out of the tribe of Issachar; Kedesh with her suburbs, Daberath with her suburbs,
73 And Ramoth with her suburbs, and Anem with her suburbs:
74 And out of the tribe of Asher; Mashal with her suburbs, and Abdon with her suburbs,
75 And Hukok with her suburbs, and Rehob with her suburbs:

76 And out of the tribe of Naphtali; Kedesh in Galilee with her suburbs, and Hammon with her suburbs, and Kirjathaim with her suburbs.

77 **Unto the rest of the children of Merari** were given out of the tribe of Zebulun, Rimmon with her suburbs, Tabor with her suburbs:

78 **And on the other side Jordan by Jericho, on the east side of Jordan,** were given them out of the tribe of Reuben, Bezer in the wilderness with her suburbs, and Jahzah with her suburbs,

79 Kedemoth also with her suburbs, and Mephaath with her suburbs:

80 And out of the tribe of Gad; Ramoth in Gilead with her suburbs, and Mahanaim with her suburbs,

81 And Heshbon with her suburbs, and Jazer with her suburbs.

7

Now the sons of Issachar were, Tola, and Puah, Jashub, and Shimrom, four.

2 **And the sons of Tola;** Uzzi, and Rephaiah, and Jeriel, and Jahmai, and Jibsam, and Shemuel, heads of their father's house, to wit, of Tola:
they were valiant men of might in their generations;
whose number was in the days of David two and twenty thousand and six hundred.

3 **And the sons of Uzzi;** Izrahiah: and the sons of Izrahiah; Michael, and Obadiah, and Joel, Ishiah, five: all of them chief men.

4 **And with them, by their generations, after the house of their fathers,** were bands of soldiers for war, six and thirty thousand men:
for they had many wives and sons.

5 **And their brethren among all the families of Issachar** were valiant men of might,
reckoned in all by their genealogies fourscore and seven thousand.

6 **The sons of Benjamin;** Bela, and Becher, and Jediael, three.

7 **And the sons of Bela;** Ezbon, and Uzzi, and Uzziel, and Jerimoth, and Iri, five; heads of the house of their fathers, mighty men of valour;
and were reckoned by their genealogies twenty and two thousand and thirty and four.

8 **And the sons of Becher;** Zemira, and Joash, and Eliezer, and Elioenai, and Omri, and Jerimoth, and Abiah, and Anathoth, and Alameth.
All these are the sons of Becher.

9 **And the number of them, after their genealogy by their generations, heads of the house of their fathers, mighty men of valour,** was twenty thousand and two hundred.

10 **The sons also of Jediael;** Bilhan: and the sons of Bilhan; Jeush, and Benjamin, and Ehud, and Chenaanah, and Zethan, and Tharshish, and Ahishahar.

11 **All these the sons of Jediael, by the heads of their fathers, mighty men of valour,** were seventeen thousand and two hundred soldiers,
fit to go out for war and battle.

12 **Shuppim also, and Huppim,** the children of Ir,
and Hushim, the sons of Aher.

13 **The sons of Naphtali;** Jahziel, and Guni, and Jezer, and Shallum, the sons of Bilhah.

14 **The sons of Manasseh;** Ashriel, whom she bare:
(but his concubine the Aramitess bare Machir the father of Gilead:

15 And Machir took to wife the sister of Huppim and Shuppim,
whose sister's name was Maachah;)
and the name of the second was Zelophehad: and Zelophehad had daughters.

16 **And Maachah the wife of Machir** bare a son,
and she called his name Peresh;
and the name of his brother was Sheresh;
and his sons were Ulam and Rakem.

17 **And the sons of Ulam;** Bedan.
These were the sons of Gilead, the son of Machir, the son of Manasseh.

18 **And his sister Hammoleketh** bare Ishod, and Abiezer, and Mahalah.

19 **And the sons of Shemidah** were, Ahian, and Shechem, and Likhi, and Aniam.

20 **And the sons of Ephraim;** Shuthelah, and Bered his son, and Tahath his son, and Eladah his son, and Tahath his son,

21 And Zabad his son, and Shuthelah his son, and Ezer, and Elead,
whom the men of Gath that were born in that land slew,
because they came down to take away their cattle.

22 **And Ephraim their father** mourned many days,
and his brethren came to comfort him.

23 **And when he** went in to his wife,
she conceived,
and bare a son,
and he called his name Beriah,
because it went evil with his house.

24 (**And his daughter** was Sherah,
who built Bethhoron the nether, and the upper, and Uzzensherah.)

25 **And Rephah** was his son, also Resheph, and Telah his son, and Tahan his son,

26 Laadan his son, Ammihud his son, Elishama his son,

27 Non his son, Jehoshuah his son.

28 **And their possessions and habitations** were, Bethel and the towns thereof, and eastward Naaran, and westward Gezer, with the towns thereof; Shechem also and the towns thereof, unto Gaza and the towns thereof:

29 And by the borders of the children of Manasseh, Bethshean and her towns, Taanach and her towns, Megiddo and her towns, Dor and her towns.
In these dwelt the children of Joseph the son of Israel.

30 **The sons of Asher;** Imnah, and Isuah, and Ishuai, and Beriah, and Serah their sister.

31 **And the sons of Beriah;** Heber, and Malchiel, who is the father of Birzavith.

32 **And Heber** begat Japhlet, and Shomer, and Hotham, and Shua their sister.

33 **And the sons of Japhlet;** Pasach, and Bimhal, and Ashvath.
These are the children of Japhlet.

34 **And the sons of Shamer;** Ahi, and Rohgah, Jehubbah, and Aram.

35 **And the sons of his brother Helem;** Zophah, and Imna, and Shelesh, and Amal.

36 **The sons of Zophah;** Suah, and
Harnepher, and Shual, and Beri,
and Imrah,
37 Bezer, and Hod, and Shamma, and
Shilshah, and Ithran, and Beera.
38 **And the sons of Jether;**
Jephunneh, and Pispah, and Ara.
39 **And the sons of Ulla;** Arah, and
Haniel, and Rezia.
40 **All these** were the children of
Asher, heads of their father's
house, choice and mighty men of
valour, chief of the princes.
**And the number throughout the
genealogy of them that were
apt to the war and to battle** was
twenty and six thousand men.

8

Now Benjamin begat Bela his
firstborn, Ashbel the second,
and Aharah the third,
2 Nohah the fourth, and Rapha the
fifth.
3 **And the sons of Bela** were, Addar,
and Gera, and Abihud,
4 And Abishua, and Naaman, and
Ahoah,
5 And Gera, and Shephuphan, and
Huram.
6 **And these** are the sons of Ehud:
these are the heads of the fathers of
the inhabitants of Geba,
and they removed them to
Manahath:
7 And Naaman, and Ahiah, and Gera,
he removed them,
and begat Uzza, and Ahihud.
8 **And Shaharaim** begat children in
the country of Moab,
after he had sent them away;
Hushim and Baara were his wives.
9 **And he** begat of Hodesh his wife,
Jobab, and Zibia, and Mesha, and
Malcham,
10 And Jeuz, and Shachia, and
Mirma.
These were his sons, heads of the
fathers.
11 **And of Hushim** he begat Abitub,
and Elpaal.
12 **The sons of Elpaal;** Eber, and
Misham, and Shamed, {<u>who</u> built
Ono, and Lod, with the towns
thereof}:
13 Beriah also, and Shema, {<u>who</u>
were heads of the fathers of the
inhabitants of Aijalon}, {<u>who</u>
drove away the inhabitants of
Gath}:
14 And Ahio, Shashak, and Jeremoth,
15 And Zebadiah, and Arad, and
Ader,
16 And Michael, and Ispah, and Joha,
the sons of Beriah;
17 And Zebadiah, and Meshullam,
and Hezeki, and Heber,
18 Ishmerai also, and Jezliah, and
Jobab, the sons of Elpaal;
19 And Jakim, and Zichri, and Zabdi,
20 And Elienai, and Zilthai, and Eliel,
21 And Adaiah, and Beraiah, and
Shimrath, the sons of Shimhi;
22 And Ishpan, and Heber, and Eliel,
23 And Abdon, and Zichri, and
Hanan,
24 And Hananiah, and Elam, and
Antothijah,
25 And Iphedeiah, and Penuel, the
sons of Shashak;
26 And Shamsherai, and Shehariah,
and Athaliah,
27 And Jaresiah, and Eliah, and
Zichri, the sons of Jeroham.
28 **These** were heads of the fathers,
by their generations, chief men.
These dwelt in Jerusalem.
29 **And at Gibeon** dwelt the father of
Gibeon;
whose wife's name was Maachah:
30 And his firstborn son Abdon, and
Zur, and Kish, and Baal, and
Nadab,
31 And Gedor, and Ahio, and Zacher.
32 **And Mikloth** begat Shimeah.
And these also dwelt with their
brethren in Jerusalem, over
against them.
33 **And Ner** begat Kish,
and Kish begat Saul,
and Saul begat Jonathan, and
Malchishua, and Abinadab, and
Eshbaal.
34 **And the son of Jonathan** was
Meribbaal;
and Meribbaal begat Micah.
35 **And the sons of Micah** were,
Pithon, and Melech, and Tarea,
and Ahaz.
36 **And Ahaz** begat Jehoadah;
and Jehoadah begat Alemeth, and
Azmaveth, and Zimri;
and Zimri begat Moza,
37 **And Moza** begat Binea:
Rapha was his son, Eleasah his son,
Azel his son:
38 **And Azel** had six sons,
whose names are these, Azrikam,
Bocheru, and Ishmael, and
Sheariah, and Obadiah, and
Hanan.
All these were the sons of Azel.
39 **And the sons of Eshek his
brother** were, Ulam his firstborn,
Jehush the second, and Eliphelet
the third.
40 **And the sons of Ulam** were
mighty men of valour, archers,
and had many sons, and sons' sons,
an hundred and fifty.
All these are of the sons of
Benjamin.

9

So all Israel were reckoned
by genealogies;
and, {<u>behold</u>}, they were written
in the book of the kings of Israel
and Judah,
who were carried away to Babylon
for their transgression.
2 **Now the first inhabitants that
dwelt in their possessions in
their cities** were, the Israelites,
the priests, Levites, and the
Nethinims.
3 **And in Jerusalem** dwelt of the
children of Judah, and of the
children of Benjamin, and of the
children of Ephraim, and
Manasseh;
4 Uthai the son of Ammihud, the son
of Omri, the son of Imri, the son
of Bani, of the children of Pharez
the son of Judah.
5 **And of the Shilonites;** Asaiah the
firstborn, and his sons.
6 **And of the sons of Zerah;** Jeuel,
and their brethren, six hundred
and ninety.
7 **And of the sons of Benjamin;**
Sallu the son of Meshullam, the
son of Hodaviah, the son of
Hasenuah,
8 And Ibneiah the son of Jeroham,
and Elah the son of Uzzi, the son
of Michri, and Meshullam the son
of Shephathiah, the son of Reuel,
the son of Ibnijah;
9 And their brethren, according to
their generations, nine hundred
and fifty and six.
All these men were chief of the
fathers in the house of their
fathers.
10 **And of the priests;** Jedaiah, and
Jehoiarib, and Jachin,
11 And Azariah the son of Hilkiah, the
son of Meshullam, the son of
Zadok, the son of Meraioth, the

son of Ahitub, the ruler of the house of God;

12 And Adaiah the son of Jeroham, the son of Pashur, the son of Malchijah, and Maasiai the son of Adiel, the son of Jahzerah, the son of Meshullam, the son of Meshillemith, the son of Immer;

13 And their brethren, heads of the house of their fathers, a thousand and seven hundred and threescore; very able men for the work of the service of the house of God.

14 **And of the Levites;** Shemaiah the son of Hasshub, the son of Azrikam, the son of Hashabiah, of the sons of Merari;

15 And Bakbakkar, Heresh, and Galal, and Mattaniah the son of Micah, the son of Zichri, the son of Asaph;

16 And Obadiah the son of Shemaiah, the son of Galal, the son of Jeduthun, and Berechiah the son of Asa, the son of Elkanah,
that dwelt in the villages of the Netophathites.

17 **And the porters** were, Shallum, and Akkub, and Talmon, and Ahiman, and their brethren:
Shallum was the chief;

18 **Who** hitherto waited in the king's gate eastward:
they were porters in the companies of the children of Levi.

19 **And Shallum the son of Kore, the son of Ebiasaph, the son of Korah, and his brethren, of the house of his father, the Korahites,** were over the work of the service, keepers of the gates of the tabernacle:
and their fathers, {being over the host of the LORD}, were keepers of the entry.

20 **And Phinehas the son of Eleazar** was the ruler over them in time past,
and the LORD was with him.

21 **And Zechariah the son of Meshelemiah** was porter of the door of the tabernacle of the congregation.

22 **All these which were chosen to be porters in the gates** were two hundred and twelve.
These were reckoned by their genealogy in their villages,
whom David and Samuel the seer did ordain in their set office.

23 **So they and their children** had the oversight of the gates of the house of the LORD, namely, the house of the tabernacle, by wards.

24 **In four quarters** were the porters, toward the east, west, north, and south.

25 **And their brethren**, {which were in their villages}, were to come after seven days from time to time with them.

26 **For these Levites, the four chief porters,** were in their set office,
and were over the chambers and treasuries of the house of God.

27 **And they** lodged round about the house of God,
because the charge was upon them,
and the opening thereof every morning pertained to them.

28 **And certain of them** had the charge of the ministering vessels,
that they should bring them in and out by tale.

29 **Some of them** also were appointed to oversee the vessels, and all the instruments of the sanctuary, and the fine flour, and the wine, and the oil, and the frankincense, and the spices.

30 **And some of the sons of the priests** made the ointment of the spices.

31 **And Mattithiah, one of the Levites**, {who was the firstborn of Shallum the Korahite}, had the set office over the things that were made in the pans.

32 **And other of their brethren, of the sons of the Kohathites,** were over the shewbread,
to prepare it every sabbath.

33 **And these** are the singers, chief of the fathers of the Levites,
who {remaining in the chambers} were free:
for they were employed in that work day and night.

34 **These chief fathers of the Levites** were chief throughout their generations;
these dwelt at Jerusalem.

35 **And in Gibeon** dwelt the father of Gibeon, Jehiel,
whose wife's name was Maachah:

36 And his firstborn son Abdon, then Zur, and Kish, and Baal, and Ner, and Nadab,

37 And Gedor, and Ahio, and Zechariah, and Mikloth.

38 **And Mikloth** begat Shimeam.
And they also dwelt with their brethren at Jerusalem, over against their brethren.

39 **And Ner** begat Kish;
and Kish begat Saul;
and Saul begat Jonathan, and Malchishua, and Abinadab, and Eshbaal.

40 **And the son of Jonathan** was Meribbaal:
and Meribbaal begat Micah.

41 **And the sons of Micah** were, Pithon, and Melech, and Tahrea, and Ahaz.

42 **And Ahaz** begat Jarah;
and Jarah begat Alemeth, and Azmaveth, and Zimri;
and Zimri begat Moza;

43 **And Moza** begat Binea; and Rephaiah his son, Eleasah his son, Azel his son.

44 **And Azel** had six sons,
whose names are these, Azrikam, Bocheru, and Ishmael, and Sheariah, and Obadiah, and Hanan:
these were the sons of Azel.

10

Now the Philistines fought against Israel;
and the men of Israel fled from before the Philistines,
and fell down slain in mount Gilboa.

2 **And the Philistines** followed hard after Saul, and after his sons;
and the Philistines slew Jonathan, and Abinadab, and Malchishua, the sons of Saul.

3 **And the battle** went sore against Saul,
and the archers hit him,
and he was wounded of the archers.

4 **Then** said Saul to his armourbearer,
Draw thy sword,
and thrust me through therewith;
lest these uncircumcised come and abuse me.
But his armourbearer would not;
for he was sore afraid.
So Saul took a sword,
and fell upon it.

5 **And when his armourbearer** saw that Saul was dead,
he fell likewise on the sword,
and died.

6 **So Saul** died, and his three sons,
and all his house died together.

7 **And when all the men of Israel that were in the valley** saw that they fled,
and that Saul and his sons were dead,
then they forsook their cities,
and fled:
and the Philistines came and dwelt in them.

8 **And it** came to pass on the morrow,
when the Philistines came to strip the slain,
that they found Saul and his sons fallen in mount Gilboa.

9 **And when they** had stripped him,
they took his head, and his armour,
and sent into the land of the Philistines round about,
to carry tidings unto their idols, and to the people.

10 **And they** put his armour in the house of their gods,
and fastened his head in the temple of Dagon.

11 **And when all Jabeshgilead** heard all that the Philistines had done to Saul,
12 **They** arose, all the valiant men,
and took away the body of Saul, and the bodies of his sons,
and brought them to Jabesh,
and buried their bones under the oak in Jabesh,
and fasted seven days.

13 **So Saul** died for his transgression which he committed against the LORD, even against the word of the LORD,
which he kept not,
and also for asking counsel of one that had a familiar spirit,
to enquire of it;
14 **And** enquired not of the LORD:
therefore he slew him,
and turned the kingdom unto David the son of Jesse.

11 **Then all Israel** gathered themselves to David unto Hebron,
saying,
Behold,
we are thy bone and thy flesh.

2 **And moreover in time past,** {even when Saul was king}, thou wast he that leddest out and broughtest in Israel:
and the LORD thy God said unto thee,
Thou shalt feed my people Israel,
and thou shalt be ruler over my people Israel.

3 **Therefore** came all the elders of Israel to the king to Hebron;
and David made a covenant with them in Hebron before the LORD;
and they anointed David king over Israel, according to the word of the LORD by Samuel.

4 **And David and all Israel** went to Jerusalem,
which is Jebus;
where the Jebusites were, the inhabitants of the land.

5 **And the inhabitants of Jebus** said to David,
Thou shalt not come hither.

Nevertheless David took the castle of Zion,
which is the city of David.

6 **And David** said,
Whosoever smiteth the Jebusites first shall be chief and captain.

So Joab the son of Zeruiah went first up,
and was chief.

7 **And David** dwelt in the castle;
therefore they called it the city of David.

8 **And he** built the city round about, even from Millo round about:
and Joab repaired the rest of the city.

9 **So David** waxed greater and greater:
for the LORD of hosts was with him.

10 **These** also are the chief of the mighty men whom David had,
who strengthened themselves with him in his kingdom, and with all Israel, {to make him king}, according to the word of the LORD concerning Israel.

11 **And this** is the number of the mighty men whom David had; Jashobeam, an Hachmonite, the chief of the captains:
he lifted up his spear against three hundred slain by him at one time.

12 **And after him** was Eleazar the son of Dodo, the Ahohite,
who was one of the three mighties.

13 **He** was with David at Pasdammim,
and there the Philistines were gathered together to battle,
where was a parcel of ground full of barley;
and the people fled from before the Philistines.

14 **And they** set themselves in the midst of that parcel,
and delivered it,
and slew the Philistines;
and the LORD saved them by a great deliverance.

15 **Now three of the thirty captains** went down to the rock to David, into the cave of Adullam;
and the host of the Philistines encamped in the valley of Rephaim.

16 **And David** was then in the hold,
and the Philistines' garrison was then at Bethlehem.

17 **And David** longed,
and said,
Oh that one would give me drink of the water of the well of Bethlehem,
that is at the gate!

18 **And the three** brake through the host of the Philistines,
and drew water out of the well of Bethlehem,
that was by the gate,
and took it,
and brought it to David:
but David would not drink of it,
but poured it out to the LORD.

19 **And** said,
My God forbid it me,
that I should do this thing:
shall I drink the blood of these men that have put their lives in jeopardy?
for with the jeopardy of their lives they brought it.

Therefore he would not drink it.

These things did these three mightiest.

20 **And Abishai the brother of Joab,** he was chief of the three:
for lifting up his spear against three hundred,
he slew them,
and had a name among the three.

21 **Of the three,** he was more honourable than the two;
for he was their captain:

howbeit he attained not to the first three.
22 **Benaiah the son of Jehoiada, the son of a valiant man of Kabzeel**, {who had done many acts}; he slew two lionlike men of Moab:
also he went down and slew a lion in a pit in a snowy day.
23 **And he** slew an Egyptian, a man of great stature, five cubits high;
and in the Egyptian's hand was a spear like a weaver's beam;
and he went down to him with a staff,
and plucked the spear out of the Egyptian's hand,
and slew him with his own spear.
24 **These things** did Benaiah the son of Jehoiada,
and had the name among the three mighties.
25 **Behold,**
he was honourable among the thirty,
but attained not to the first three:
and David set him over his guard.
26 **Also the valiant men of the armies** were, Asahel the brother of Joab, Elhanan the son of Dodo of Bethlehem,
27 Shammoth the Harorite, Helez the Pelonite,
28 Ira the son of Ikkesh the Tekoite, Abiezer the Antothite,
29 Sibbecai the Hushathite, Ilai the Ahohite,
30 Maharai the Netophathite, Heled the son of Baanah the Netophathite,
31 Ithai the son of Ribai of Gibeah, {that pertained to the children of Benjamin}, Benaiah the Pirathonite,
32 Hurai of the brooks of Gaash, Abiel the Arbathite,
33 Azmaveth the Baharumite, Eliahba the Shaalbonite,
34 The sons of Hashem the Gizonite, Jonathan the son of Shage the Hararite,
35 Ahiam the son of Sacar the Hararite, Eliphal the son of Ur,
36 Hepher the Mecherathite, Ahijah the Pelonite,
37 Hezro the Carmelite, Naarai the son of Ezbai,
38 Joel the brother of Nathan, Mibhar the son of Haggeri,
39 Zelek the Ammonite, Naharai the Berothite, the armourbearer of Joab the son of Zeruiah,
40 Ira the Ithrite, Gareb the Ithrite,
41 Uriah the Hittite, Zabad the son of Ahlai,
42 Adina the son of Shiza the Reubenite, a captain of the Reubenites, and thirty with him,
43 Hanan the son of Maachah, and Joshaphat the Mithnite,
44 Uzzia the Ashterathite, Shama and Jehiel the sons of Hothan the Aroerite,
45 Jediael the son of Shimri, and Joha his brother, the Tizite,
46 Eliel the Mahavite, and Jeribai, and Joshaviah, the sons of Elnaam, and Ithmah the Moabite,
47 Eliel, and Obed, and Jasiel the Mesobaite.

12

Now these are they that came to David to Ziklag,
while he yet kept himself close because of Saul the son of Kish:
and they were among the mighty men, helpers of the war.
2 **They** were armed with bows,
and could use both the right hand and the left {in hurling stones} {and shooting arrows out of a bow}, even of Saul's brethren of Benjamin.
3 **The chief** was Ahiezer, then Joash, the sons of Shemaah the Gibeathite; and Jeziel, and Pelet, the sons of Azmaveth; and Berachah, and Jehu the Antothite,
4 And Ismaiah the Gibeonite, a mighty man among the thirty, and over the thirty; and Jeremiah, and Jahaziel, and Johanan, and Josabad the Gederathite,
5 Eluzai, and Jerimoth, and Bealiah, and Shemariah, and Shephatiah the Haruphite,
6 Elkanah, and Jesiah, and Azareel, and Joezer, and Jashobeam, the Korhites,
7 And Joelah, and Zebadiah, the sons of Jeroham of Gedor.
8 **And of the Gadites** there separated themselves unto David into the hold to the wilderness men of might, and men of war fit for the battle,
that could handle shield and buckler,
whose faces were like the faces of lions,
and were as swift as the roes upon the mountains;
9 Ezer the first, Obadiah the second, Eliab the third,
10 Mishmannah the fourth, Jeremiah the fifth,
11 Attai the sixth, Eliel the seventh,
12 Johanan the eighth, Elzabad the ninth,
13 Jeremiah the tenth, Machbanai the eleventh.
14 **These** were of the sons of Gad, captains of the host:
one of the least was over an hundred,
and the greatest over a thousand.
15 **These** are they that went over Jordan in the first month,
when it had overflown all his banks;
and they put to flight all them of the valleys, both toward the east, and toward the west.
16 **And there** came of the children of Benjamin and Judah to the hold unto David.
17 **And David** went out to meet them,
and answered and said unto them,
If ye be come peaceably unto me to help me,
mine heart shall be knit unto you:
but if ye be come to betray me to mine enemies,
seeing there is no wrong in mine hands,
the God of our fathers look thereon,
and rebuke it.
18 **Then the spirit** came upon Amasai,
who was chief of the captains,
and he said,
Thine are we, David, and on thy side, thou son of Jesse:
peace, peace be unto thee,
and peace be to thine helpers;
for thy God helpeth thee.
Then David received them,
and made them captains of the band.
19 **And there** fell some of Manasseh to David,
when he came with the Philistines against Saul to battle:
but they helped them not:
for the lords of the Philistines upon advisement sent him away,
saying,

He will fall to his master Saul to the jeopardy of our heads.

20 **As he** went to Ziklag,
there fell to him of Manasseh, Adnah, and Jozabad, and Jediael, and Michael, and Jozabad, and Elihu, and Zilthai, captains of the thousands that were of Manasseh.

21 **And they** helped David against the band of the rovers:
for they were all mighty men of valour,
and were captains in the host.

22 **For at that time** day by day there came to David
to help him,
until it was a great host, like the host of God.

23 **And these** are the numbers of the bands that were ready armed to the war,
and came to David to Hebron, {to turn the kingdom of Saul to him}, according to the word of the LORD.

24 **The children of Judah that bare shield and spear** were six thousand and eight hundred,
ready armed to the war.

25 **Of the children of Simeon, mighty men of valour for the war,** seven thousand and one hundred.

26 **Of the children of Levi** four thousand and six hundred.

27 **And Jehoiada** was the leader of the Aaronites,
and with him were three thousand and seven hundred;

28 **And Zadok, a young man mighty of valour, and of his father's house** twenty and two captains.

29 **And of the children of Benjamin, the kindred of Saul,** three thousand:
for hitherto the greatest part of them had kept the ward of the house of Saul.

30 **And of the children of Ephraim** twenty thousand and eight hundred, mighty men of valour, famous throughout the house of their fathers.

31 **And of the half tribe of Manasseh** eighteen thousand,
which were expressed by name,
to come and make David king.

32 **And of the children of Issachar,** {which were men that had understanding of the times}, {to know what Israel ought to do}; the heads of them were two hundred;
and all their brethren were at their commandment.

33 **Of Zebulun, {such as went forth to battle}, expert in war, with all instruments of war,** fifty thousand,
which could keep rank:
they were not of double heart.

34 **And of Naphtali a thousand captains, and with them with shield and spear thirty** and seven thousand.

35 **And of the Danites expert in war** twenty and eight thousand and six hundred.

36 **And of Asher, {such as went forth to battle}, expert in war,** forty thousand.

37 **And on the other side of Jordan, of the Reubenites, and the Gadites, and of the half tribe of Manasseh, with all manner of instruments of war for the battle,** an hundred and twenty thousand.

38 **All these men of war**, {that could keep rank}, came with a perfect heart to Hebron,
to make David king over all Israel:
and all the rest also of Israel were of one heart
to make David king.

39 **And there** they were with David three days,
eating and drinking:
for their brethren had prepared for them.

40 **Moreover they that were nigh them, even unto Issachar and Zebulun and Naphtali,** brought bread on asses, and on camels, and on mules, and on oxen, and meat, meal, cakes of figs, and bunches of raisins, and wine, and oil, and oxen, and sheep abundantly:
for there was joy in Israel.

13 **And David** consulted with the captains of thousands and hundreds, and with every leader.

2 **And David** said unto all the congregation of Israel,
If it seem good unto you,
and that it be of the LORD our God,
let us send abroad unto our brethren every where,
that are left in all the land of Israel, and with them also to the priests and Levites which are in their cities and suburbs,
that they may gather themselves unto us:

3 **And let us** bring again the ark of our God to us:
for we enquired not at it in the days of Saul.

4 **And all the congregation** said
that they would do so:
for the thing was right in the eyes of all the people.

5 **So David** gathered all Israel together, from Shihor of Egypt even unto the entering of Hemath,
to bring the ark of God from Kirjathjearim.

6 **And David** went up, and all Israel, to Baalah, that is, to Kirjathjearim, {which belonged to Judah}, to bring up thence the ark of God the LORD,
that dwelleth between the cherubims,
whose name is called on it.

7 **And they** carried the ark of God in a new cart out of the house of Abinadab:
and Uzza and Ahio drave the cart.

8 **And David and all Israel** played before God with all their might, and with singing, and with harps, and with psalteries, and with timbrels, and with cymbals, and with trumpets.

9 **And when they** came unto the threshingfloor of Chidon,
Uzza put forth his hand to hold the ark;
for the oxen stumbled.

10 **And the anger of the LORD** was kindled against Uzza,
and he smote him,
because he put his hand to the ark:
and there he died before God.

11 **And David** was displeased,
because the LORD had made a breach upon Uzza:
wherefore that place is called Perezuzza to this day.

12 **And David** was afraid of God that day,
saying,

How shall I bring the ark of God home to me?

13 **So David** brought not the ark home to himself to the city of David,
but carried it aside into the house of Obededom the Gittite.

14 **And the ark of God** remained with the family of Obededom in his house three months.
And the LORD blessed the house of Obededom, and all that he had.

14 **Now Hiram king of Tyre** sent messengers to David, and timber of cedars, with masons and carpenters,
to build him an house.

2 **And David** perceived that the LORD had confirmed him king over Israel,
for his kingdom was lifted up on high, because of his people Israel.

3 **And David** took more wives at Jerusalem:
and David begat more sons and daughters.

4 **Now these** are the names of his children which he had in Jerusalem; Shammua, and Shobab, Nathan, and Solomon,
5 And Ibhar, and Elishua, and Elpalet,
6 And Nogah, and Nepheg, and Japhia,
7 And Elishama, and Beeliada, and Eliphalet.

8 **And when the Philistines** heard that David was anointed king over all Israel,
all the Philistines went up to seek David.
And David heard of it,
and went out against them.

9 **And the Philistines** came and spread themselves in the valley of Rephaim.

10 **And David** enquired of God, saying,
Shall I go up against the Philistines?
And wilt thou deliver them into mine hand?
And the LORD said unto him,
Go up;
for I will deliver them into thine hand.

11 **So they** came up to Baalperazim;
and David smote them there.
Then David said,
God hath broken in upon mine enemies by mine hand like the breaking forth of waters:
therefore they called the name of that place Baalperazim.

12 **And when they** had left their gods there,
David gave a commandment,
and they were burned with fire.

13 **And the Philistines** yet again spread themselves abroad in the valley.

14 **Therefore David** enquired again of God;
and God said unto him,
Go not up after them;
turn away from them,
and come upon them over against the mulberry trees.

15 **And it** shall be,
when thou shalt hear a sound of going in the tops of the mulberry trees,
that then thou shalt go out to battle:
for God is gone forth before thee to smite the host of the Philistines.

16 **David** therefore did as God commanded him:
and they smote the host of the Philistines from Gibeon even to Gazer.

17 **And the fame of David** went out into all lands;
and the LORD brought the fear of him upon all nations.

15 ∞ **And David** made him houses in the city of David,
and prepared a place for the ark of God,
and pitched for it a tent.

2 **Then David** said,
None ought to carry the ark of God but the Levites:
for them hath the LORD chosen to carry the ark of God,
and to minister unto him for ever.

3 **And David** gathered all Israel together to Jerusalem,
to bring up the ark of the LORD unto his place,
which he had prepared for it.

4 **And David** assembled the children of Aaron, and the Levites:
5 **Of the sons of Kohath;** Uriel the chief, and his brethren an hundred and twenty:
6 **Of the sons of Merari;** Asaiah the chief, and his brethren two hundred and twenty:
7 **Of the sons of Gershom;** Joel the chief and his brethren an hundred and thirty:
8 **Of the sons of Elizaphan;** Shemaiah the chief, and his brethren two hundred:
9 **Of the sons of Hebron;** Eliel the chief, and his brethren fourscore:
10 **Of the sons of Uzziel;** Amminadab the chief, and his brethren an hundred and twelve.

11 **And David** called for Zadok and Abiathar the priests, and for the Levites, for Uriel, Asaiah, and Joel, Shemaiah, and Eliel, and Amminadab,
12 **And** said unto them,
Ye are the chief of the fathers of the Levites:
sanctify yourselves, both ye and your brethren,
that ye may bring up the ark of the LORD God of Israel unto the place that I have prepared for it.

13 **For because ye** did it not at the first,
the LORD our God made a breach upon us,
for that we sought him not after the due order.

14 **So the priests and the Levites** sanctified themselves
to bring up the ark of the LORD God of Israel.

15 **And the children of the Levites** bare the ark of God upon their shoulders with the staves thereon,
as Moses commanded according to the word of the LORD.

16 **And David** spake to the chief of the Levites to appoint their brethren to be the singers with instruments of musick, psalteries and harps and cymbals, sounding,
by lifting up the voice with joy.

17 **So the Levites** appointed Heman the son of Joel; and of his brethren, Asaph the son of Berechiah; and of the sons of Merari their brethren, Ethan the son of Kushaiah;
18 And with them their brethren of the second degree, Zechariah, Ben, and Jaaziel, and Shemiramoth, and Jehiel, and Unni, Eliab, and Benaiah, and

Maaseiah, and Mattithiah, and
Elipheleh, and Mikneiah, and
Obededom, and Jeiel, the porters.
19 **So the singers, Heman, Asaph, and Ethan,** were appointed to sound with cymbals of brass;
20 **And Zechariah, and Aziel, and Shemiramoth, and Jehiel, and Unni, and Eliab, and Maaseiah, and Benaiah,** with psalteries on Alamoth;
21 **And Mattithiah, and Elipheleh, and Mikneiah, and Obededom, and Jeiel, and Azaziah,** with harps on the Sheminith to excel.
22 **And Chenaniah, chief of the Levites,** was for song:
he instructed about the song,
because he was skilful.
23 **And Berechiah and Elkanah** were doorkeepers for the ark.
24 **And Shebaniah, and Jehoshaphat, and Nethaneel, and Amasai, and Zechariah, and Benaiah, and Eliezer, the priests,** did blow with the trumpets before the ark of God:
and Obededom and Jehiah were doorkeepers for the ark.
25 **So David, and the elders of Israel, and the captains over thousands,** went to bring up the ark of the covenant of the LORD out of the house of Obededom with joy.
26 **And it** came to pass,
when God helped the Levites that bare the ark of the covenant of the LORD,
that they offered seven bullocks and seven rams.
27 **And David** was clothed with a robe of fine linen, and all the Levites that bare the ark, and the singers, and Chenaniah the master of the song with the singers:
David also had upon him an ephod of linen.
28 **Thus all Israel** brought up the ark of the covenant of the LORD with shouting, and with sound of the cornet, and with trumpets, and with cymbals,
making a noise with psalteries and harps.
29 **And it** came to pass,
as the ark of the covenant of the LORD came to the city of David,
that Michal, the daughter of Saul looking out at a window saw king David dancing and playing:
and she despised him in her heart.

16 **So they** brought the ark of God,
and set it in the midst of the tent that David had pitched for it:
and they offered burnt sacrifices and peace offerings before God.
2 **And when David** had made an end of offering the burnt offerings and the peace offerings,
he blessed the people in the name of the LORD.
3 **And he** dealt to every one of Israel, both man and woman, to every one a loaf of bread, and a good piece of flesh, and a flagon of wine.
4 **And he** appointed certain of the Levites to minister before the ark of the LORD,
and to record,
and to thank and praise the LORD God of Israel:
5 Asaph the chief, and next to him Zechariah, Jeiel, and Shemiramoth, and Jehiel, and Mattithiah, and Eliab, and Benaiah, and Obededom: and Jeiel with psalteries and with harps;
but Asaph made a sound with cymbals;
6 **Benaiah also and Jahaziel the priests with trumpets** continually before the ark of the covenant of God.
7 **Then on that day** David delivered first this psalm to thank the LORD into the hand of Asaph and his brethren.
8 **Give** thanks unto the LORD,
call upon his name,
make known his deeds among the people.
9 **Sing** unto him,
sing psalms unto him,
talk ye of all his wondrous works.
10 **Glory ye** in his holy name:
let the heart of them rejoice that seek the LORD.
11 **Seek** the LORD and his strength,
seek his face continually.
12 **Remember** his marvellous works that he hath done, his wonders, and the judgments of his mouth;
13 O ye seed of Israel his servant, ye children of Jacob, his chosen ones.
14 **He** is the LORD our God;
his judgments are in all the earth.
15 **Be ye** mindful always of his covenant; the word which he commanded to a thousand generations;
16 Even of the covenant which he made with Abraham, and of his oath unto Isaac;
17 **And** hath confirmed the same to Jacob for a law, and to Israel for an everlasting covenant,
18 Saying,
Unto thee will I give the land of Canaan, the lot of your inheritance;
19 **When ye** were but few, even a few, and strangers in it.
20 **And when they** went from nation to nation, and from one kingdom to another people;
21 **He** suffered no man to do them wrong:
yea, he reproved kings for their sakes,
22 Saying,
Touch not mine anointed,
and do my prophets no harm.
23 **Sing** unto the LORD, all the earth;
shew forth from day to day his salvation.
24 **Declare** his glory among the heathen; his marvellous works among all nations.
25 **For great** is the LORD,
and greatly to be praised:
he also is to be feared above all gods.
26 **For all the gods of the people** are idols:
but the LORD made the heavens.
27 **Glory and honour** are in his presence;
strength and gladness are in his place.
28 **Give** unto the LORD, ye kindreds of the people,
give unto the LORD glory and strength.
29 **Give** unto the LORD the glory due unto his name:
bring an offering,
and come before him:
worship the LORD in the beauty of holiness.
30 **Fear** before him, all the earth:
the world also shall be stable,

that it be not moved.

31 **Let the heavens** be glad,
and let the earth rejoice:
and let men say among the nations,
The LORD reigneth.

32 **Let the sea** roar, and the fulness thereof:
let the fields rejoice, and all that is therein.

33 **Then** shall the trees of the wood sing out at the presence of the LORD,
because he cometh to judge the earth.

34 **O give** thanks unto the LORD;
for he is good;
for his mercy endureth for ever.

35 **And say ye,**
Save us, O God of our salvation,
and gather us together,
and deliver us from the heathen,
that we may give thanks to thy holy name,
and glory in thy praise.

36 **Blessed** be the LORD God of Israel for ever and ever.

And all the people said, Amen,
and praised the LORD.

37 **So he** left there before the ark of the covenant of the LORD Asaph and his brethren,
to minister before the ark continually,
as every day's work required:
38 And Obededom with their brethren, threescore and eight;
Obededom also the son of Jeduthun and Hosah to be porters:
39 **And** Zadok the priest, and his brethren the priests, before the tabernacle of the LORD in the high place that was at Gibeon,
40 To offer burnt offerings unto the LORD upon the altar of the burnt offering continually morning and evening,
and to do according to all that is written in the law of the LORD,
which he commanded Israel;
41 **And with them** Heman and Jeduthun, and the rest that were chosen, {who were expressed by name}, to give thanks to the LORD,
because his mercy endureth for ever;
42 **And with them** Heman and Jeduthun with trumpets and cymbals for those that should make a sound, and with musical instruments of God.
And the sons of Jeduthun were porters.
43 **And all the people** departed every man to his house:
and David returned to bless his house.

17

Now it came to pass,
as David sat in his house,
that David said to Nathan the prophet,
Lo,
I dwell in an house of cedars,
but the ark of the covenant of the LORD remaineth under curtains.

2 **Then Nathan** said unto David,
Do all that is in thine heart;
for God is with thee.

3 **And it** came to pass the same night,
that the word of God came to Nathan,
saying,
4 **Go and tell** David my servant,
Thus saith the LORD,
Thou shalt not build me an house to dwell in:
5 **For I** have not dwelt in an house since the day that I brought up Israel unto this day;
but have gone from tent to tent, and from one tabernacle to another.

6 **Wheresoever I** have walked with all Israel,
spake I a word to any of the judges of Israel,
whom I commanded to feed my people,
saying,
Why have ye not built me an house of cedars?

7 **Now therefore thus** shalt thou say unto my servant David,
Thus saith the LORD of hosts,
I took thee from the sheepcote, even from following the sheep,
that thou shouldest be ruler over my people Israel:
8 **And I** have been with thee
whithersoever thou hast walked,
and have cut off all thine enemies from before thee,
and have made thee a name like the name of the great men that are in the earth.

9 **Also I** will ordain a place for my people Israel,
and will plant them,
and they shall dwell in their place,
and shall be moved no more;
neither shall the children of wickedness waste them any more, as at the beginning,
10 And since the time that I commanded judges to be over my people Israel.
Moreover I will subdue all thine enemies.
Furthermore I tell thee
that the LORD will build thee an house.

11 **And it** shall come to pass,
when thy days be expired that thou must go to be with thy fathers,
that I will raise up thy seed after thee,
which shall be of thy sons;
and I will establish his kingdom.

12 **He** shall build me an house,
and I will stablish his throne for ever.

13 **I** will be his father,
and he shall be my son:
and I will not take my mercy away from him,
as I took it from him that was before thee:
14 **But I** will settle him in mine house and in my kingdom for ever:
and his throne shall be established for evermore.

15 **According to all these words,**
and according to all this vision,
so did Nathan speak unto David.

16 **And David the king** came and sat before the LORD,
and said,
Who am I, O LORD God,
and what is mine house,
that thou hast brought me hitherto?

17 **And yet this** was a small thing in thine eyes, O God;
for thou hast also spoken of thy servant's house for a great while to come,
and hast regarded me according to the estate of a man of high degree, O LORD God.

18 **What** can David speak more to thee for the honour of thy servant?
for thou knowest thy servant.

19 **O LORD, for thy servant's sake,**
and according to thine own

heart, hast thou done all this greatness,
in making known all these great things.
20 **O LORD, there** is none like thee,
neither is there any God beside thee, according to all that we have heard with our ears.
21 **And what one nation in the earth** is like thy people Israel,
whom God went to redeem to be his own people,
to make thee a name of greatness and terribleness,
by driving out nations from before thy people whom thou hast redeemed out of Egypt?
22 **For thy people Israel** didst thou make thine own people for ever;
and thou, LORD, becamest their God.
23 **Therefore now, LORD, let the thing that thou hast spoken concerning thy servant and concerning his house** be established for ever,
and do as thou hast said.
24 **Let it** even be established,
that thy name may be magnified for ever,
saying,
The LORD of hosts is the God of Israel, even a God to Israel:
and let the house of David thy servant be established before thee.
25 **For thou,** O my God, hast told thy servant
that thou wilt build him an house:
therefore thy servant hath found in his heart to pray before thee.
26 **And now, LORD, thou** art God,
and hast promised this goodness unto thy servant:
27 **Now therefore let it** please thee to bless the house of thy servant,
that it may be before thee for ever:
for thou blessest, O LORD,
and it shall be blessed for ever.

18

Now after this it came to pass,
that David smote the Philistines,
and subdued them,
and took Gath and her towns out of the hand of the Philistines.
2 **And he** smote Moab;
and the Moabites became David's servants,
and brought gifts.
3 **And David** smote Hadarezer king of Zobah unto Hamath,
as he went to stablish his dominion by the river Euphrates.
4 **And David** took from him a thousand chariots, and seven thousand horsemen, and twenty thousand footmen:
David also houghed all the chariot horses,
but reserved of them an hundred chariots.
5 **And when the Syrians of Damascus** came to help Hadarezer king of Zobah,
David slew of the Syrians two and twenty thousand men.
6 **Then David** put garrisons in Syriadamascus;
and the Syrians became David's servants,
and brought gifts.
Thus the LORD preserved David
whithersoever he went.
7 **And David** took the shields of gold that were on the servants of Hadarezer,
and brought them to Jerusalem.
8 **Likewise from Tibhath, and from Chun, cities of Hadarezer,** brought David very much brass,
wherewith Solomon made the brasen sea, and the pillars, and the vessels of brass.
9 **Now when Tou king of Hamath** heard how David had smitten all the host of Hadarezer king of Zobah;
10 **He** sent Hadoram his son to king David,
to enquire of his welfare,
and to congratulate him,
because he had fought against Hadarezer,
and smitten him;
(for Hadarezer had war with Tou;)
and with him all manner of vessels of gold and silver and brass.
11 **Them also king David** dedicated unto the LORD, with the silver and the gold that he brought from all these nations; from Edom, and from Moab, and from the children of Ammon, and from the Philistines, and from Amalek.
12 **Moreover Abishai the son of Zeruiah** slew of the Edomites in the valley of salt eighteen thousand.
13 **And he** put garrisons in Edom;
and all the Edomites became David's servants.
Thus the LORD preserved David
whithersoever he went.
14 **So David** reigned over all Israel,
and executed judgment and justice among all his people.
15 **And Joab the son of Zeruiah** was over the host;
and Jehoshaphat the son of Ahilud, recorder.
16 **And Zadok the son of Ahitub, and Abimelech the son of Abiathar,** were the priests;
and Shavsha was scribe;
17 **And Benaiah the son of Jehoiada** was over the Cherethites and the Pelethites;
and the sons of David were chief about the king.

19

Now it came to pass after this,
that Nahash the king of the children of Ammon died,
and his son reigned in his stead.
2 **And David** said,
I will shew kindness unto Hanun the son of Nahash,
because his father shewed kindness to me.
And David sent messengers to comfort him concerning his father.
So the servants of David came into the land of the children of Ammon to Hanun,
to comfort him.
3 **But the princes of the children of Ammon** said to Hanun,
Thinkest thou
that David doth honour thy father,
that he hath sent comforters unto thee?
are not his servants come unto thee
for to search,
and to overthrow,
and to spy out the land?
4 **Wherefore Hanun** took David's servants,
and shaved them,
and cut off their garments in the midst hard by their buttocks,
and sent them away.
5 **Then there** went certain,
and told David
how the men were served.
And he sent to meet them:
for the men were greatly ashamed.

And the king said,
Tarry at Jericho
until your beards be grown,
and then return.

6 **And when the children of Ammon** saw that they had made themselves odious to David,
Hanun and the children of Ammon sent a thousand talents of silver
to hire them chariots and horsemen out of Mesopotamia, and out of Syriamaachah, and out of Zobah.

7 **So they** hired thirty and two thousand chariots, and the king of Maachah and his people;
who came and pitched before Medeba.

And the children of Ammon gathered themselves together from their cities,
and came to battle.

8 **And when David** heard of it,
he sent Joab, and all the host of the mighty men.

9 **And the children of Ammon** came out,
and put the battle in array before the gate of the city:
and the kings that were come were by themselves in the field.

10 **Now when Joab** saw that the battle was set against him before and behind,
he chose out of all the choice of Israel,
and put them in array against the Syrians.

11 **And the rest of the people** he delivered unto the hand of Abishai his brother,
and they set themselves in array against the children of Ammon.

12 **And he** said,
If the Syrians be too strong for me,
then thou shalt help me:
but if the children of Ammon be too strong for thee,
then I will help thee.

13 **Be** of good courage,
and let us behave ourselves valiantly for our people, and for the cities of our God:
and let the LORD do that which is good in his sight.

14 **So Joab and the people that were with him** drew nigh before the Syrians unto the battle;
and they fled before him.

15 **And when the children of Ammon** saw that the Syrians were fled,
they likewise fled before Abishai his brother,
and entered into the city.

Then Joab came to Jerusalem.

16 **And when the Syrians** saw that they were put to the worse before Israel,
they sent messengers,
and drew forth the Syrians that were beyond the river:
and Shophach the captain of the host of Hadarezer went before them.

17 **And it** was told David;
and he gathered all Israel,
and passed over Jordan,
and came upon them,
and set the battle in array against them.

So when David had put the battle in array against the Syrians,
they fought with him.

18 **But the Syrians** fled before Israel;
and David slew of the Syrians seven thousand men which fought in chariots, and forty thousand footmen,
and killed Shophach the captain of the host.

19 **And when the servants of Hadarezer** saw that they were put to the worse before Israel,
they made peace with David,
and became his servants:
neither would the Syrians help the children of Ammon any more.

20 **And it** came to pass,
that after the year was expired, at the time that kings go out to battle,
Joab led forth the power of the army,
and wasted the country of the children of Ammon,
and came and besieged Rabbah.

But David tarried at Jerusalem.

And Joab smote Rabbah,
and destroyed it.

2 **And David** took the crown of their king from off his head,
and found it to weigh a talent of gold,
and there were precious stones in it;
and it was set upon David's head:
and he brought also exceeding much spoil out of the city.

3 **And he** brought out the people that were in it,
and cut them with saws, and with harrows of iron, and with axes.

Even so dealt David with all the cities of the children of Ammon.

And David and all the people returned to Jerusalem.

4 **And it** came to pass after this,
that there arose war at Gezer with the Philistines;
at which time Sibbechai the Hushathite slew Sippai,
that was of the children of the giant:
and they were subdued.

5 **And there** was war again with the Philistines;
and Elhanan the son of Jair slew Lahmi the brother of Goliath the Gittite,
whose spear staff was like a weaver's beam.

6 **And yet again there** was war at Gath,
where was a man of great stature,
whose fingers and toes were four and twenty, six on each hand, and six on each foot
and he also was the son of the giant.

7 **But when he** defied Israel,
Jonathan the son of Shimea David's brother slew him.

8 **These** were born unto the giant in Gath;
and they fell by the hand of David, and by the hand of his servants.

21 **And Satan** stood up against Israel,
and provoked David to number Israel.

2 **And David** said to Joab and to the rulers of the people,
Go,
number Israel from Beersheba even to Dan;
and bring the number of them to me,
that I may know it.

3 **And Joab** answered,
The LORD make his people an hundred times so many more as they be:
but, my lord the king, are they not all my lord's servants?

why then doth my lord require this thing?
why will he be a cause of trespass to Israel?
4 **Nevertheless the king's word** prevailed against Joab.
Wherefore Joab departed,
and went throughout all Israel,
and came to Jerusalem.
5 **And Joab** gave the sum of the number of the people unto David.
And all they of Israel were a thousand thousand and an hundred thousand men that drew sword:
and Judah was four hundred threescore and ten thousand men that drew sword.
6 **But Levi and Benjamin** counted he not among them:
for the king's word was abominable to Joab.
7 **And God** was displeased with this thing;
therefore he smote Israel.
8 **And David** said unto God,
I have sinned greatly,
because I have done this thing:
but now, {I beseech thee}, do away the iniquity of thy servant;
for I have done very foolishly.
9 **And the LORD** spake unto Gad, David's seer,
saying,
10 **Go and tell** David,
saying,
Thus saith the LORD,
I offer thee three things:
choose thee one of them,
that I may do it unto thee.
11 **So Gad** came to David,
and said unto him,
Thus saith the LORD,
Choose thee
12 **Either** three years' famine;
or three months to be destroyed before thy foes, {while that the sword of thine enemies overtaketh thee};
or else three days the sword of the LORD, even the pestilence, in the land, {and the angel of the LORD destroying throughout all the coasts of Israel}.
Now therefore advise thyself
what word I shall bring again to him that sent me.
13 **And David** said unto Gad,
I am in a great strait:
let me fall now into the hand of the LORD;
for very great are his mercies:
but let me not fall into the hand of man.
14 **So the LORD** sent pestilence upon Israel:
and there fell of Israel seventy thousand men.
15 **And God** sent an angel unto Jerusalem to destroy it:
and as he was destroying,
the LORD beheld,
and he repented him of the evil,
and said to the angel that destroyed,
It is enough,
stay now thine hand.
And the angel of the LORD stood by the threshingfloor of Ornan the Jebusite.
16 **And David** lifted up his eyes,
and saw the angel of the LORD stand between the earth and the heaven,
having a drawn sword in his hand stretched out over Jerusalem.
Then David and the elders of Israel, {who were clothed in sackcloth}, fell upon their faces.
17 **And David** said unto God,
Is it not I that commanded the people to be numbered?
even I it is that have sinned and done evil indeed;
but as for these sheep, what have they done?
let thine hand, {I pray thee}, O LORD my God, be on me, and on my father's house; but not on thy people,
that they should be plagued.
18 **Then the angel of the LORD** commanded Gad to say to David,
that David should go up,
and set up an altar unto the LORD in the threshingfloor of Ornan the Jebusite.
19 **And David** went up at the saying of Gad,
which he spake in the name of the LORD.
20 **And Ornan** turned back,
and saw the angel;
and his four sons with him hid themselves.
Now Ornan was threshing wheat.
21 **And as David** came to Ornan,
Ornan looked and saw David,
and went out of the threshingfloor,
and bowed himself to David with his face to the ground.
22 **Then David** said to Ornan,
Grant me the place of this threshingfloor,
that I may build an altar therein unto the LORD:
thou shalt grant it me for the full price:
that the plague may be stayed from the people.
23 **And Ornan** said unto David,
Take it to thee,
and let my lord the king do that which is good in his eyes:
lo,
I give thee the oxen also for burnt offerings, and the threshing instruments for wood, and the wheat for the meat offering;
I give it all.
24 **And king David** said to Ornan,
Nay;
but I will verily buy it for the full price:
for I will not take that which is thine for the LORD,
nor offer burnt offerings without cost.
25 **So David** gave to Ornan for the place six hundred shekels of gold by weight.
26 **And David** built there an altar unto the LORD,
and offered burnt offerings and peace offerings,
and called upon the LORD;
and he answered him from heaven by fire upon the altar of burnt offering.
27 **And the LORD** commanded the angel;
and he put up his sword again into the sheath thereof.
28 **At that time when David saw that the LORD had answered him in the threshingfloor of Ornan the Jebusite,** then he sacrificed there.
29 **For the tabernacle of the LORD, {which Moses made in the wilderness}, and the altar of the burnt offering,** were at that season in the high place at Gibeon.
30 **But David** could not go before it to enquire of God:
for he was afraid because of the sword of the angel of the LORD.

22 **Then David** said,
This is the house of the LORD God,
and this is the altar of the burnt offering for Israel.
2 **And David** commanded to gather together the strangers that were in the land of Israel;
and he set masons to hew wrought stones to build the house of God.
3 **And David** prepared iron in abundance for the nails for the doors of the gates, and for the joinings; and brass in abundance without weight;
4 Also cedar trees in abundance:
for the Zidonians and they of Tyre brought much cedar wood to David.
5 **And David** said,
Solomon my son is young and tender,
and the house that is to be builded for the LORD must be exceeding magnifical, of fame and of glory throughout all countries:
I will therefore now make preparation for it.
So David prepared abundantly before his death.
6 **Then he** called for Solomon his son,
and charged him to build an house for the LORD God of Israel.
7 **And David** said to Solomon,
My son, as for me, it was in my mind to build an house unto the name of the LORD my God:
8 **But the word of the LORD** came to me,
saying,
Thou hast shed blood abundantly,
and hast made great wars:
thou shalt not build an house unto my name,
because thou hast shed much blood upon the earth in my sight.
9 **Behold,**
a son shall be born to thee,
who shall be a man of rest
and I will give him rest from all his enemies round about:
for his name shall be Solomon,
and I will give peace and quietness unto Israel in his days.
10 **He** shall build an house for my name;
and he shall be my son,
and I will be his father;
and I will establish the throne of his kingdom over Israel for ever.
11 **Now, my son, the LORD** be with thee;
and prosper thou,
and build the house of the LORD thy God,
as he hath said of thee.
12 **Only the LORD** give thee wisdom and understanding,
and give thee charge concerning Israel,
that thou mayest keep the law of the LORD thy God.
13 **Then** shalt thou prosper,
if thou takest heed to fulfil the statutes and judgments which the LORD charged Moses with concerning Israel:
be strong, and of good courage;
dread not,
nor be dismayed.
14 **Now, {behold}, in my trouble** I have prepared for the house of the LORD an hundred thousand talents of gold, and a thousand thousand talents of silver; and of brass and iron without weight;
for it is in abundance:
timber also and stone have I prepared;
and thou mayest add thereto.
15 **Moreover there** are workmen with thee in abundance, hewers and workers of stone and timber, and all manner of cunning men for every manner of work.
16 **Of the gold, the silver, and the brass, and the iron,** there is no number.
Arise therefore,
and be doing,
and the LORD be with thee.
17 **David** also commanded all the princes of Israel to help Solomon his son,
saying,
18 **Is not the LORD your God** with you?
and hath he not given you rest on every side?
for he hath given the inhabitants of the land into mine hand;
and the land is subdued before the LORD, and before his people.
19 **Now set** your heart and your soul to seek the LORD your God;
arise therefore,
and build ye the sanctuary of the LORD God,
to bring the ark of the covenant of the LORD, and the holy vessels of God, into the house that is to be built to the name of the LORD.

23 **So when David** was old and full of days,
he made Solomon his son king over Israel.
2 **And he** gathered together all the princes of Israel, with the priests and the Levites.
3 **Now the Levites** were numbered from the age of thirty years and upward:
and their number by their polls, man by man, was thirty and eight thousand.
4 **Of which, twenty and four thousand** were to set forward the work of the house of the LORD;
and six thousand were officers and judges:
5 **Moreover four thousand** were porters;
and four thousand praised the LORD with the instruments which I made, {said David}, to praise therewith.
6 **And David** divided them into courses among the sons of Levi, namely, Gershon, Kohath, and Merari.
7 **Of the Gershonites** were, Laadan, and Shimei.
8 **The sons of Laadan; the chief** was Jehiel, and Zetham, and Joel, three.
9 **The sons of Shimei;** Shelomith, and Haziel, and Haran, three.
These were the chief of the fathers of Laadan.
10 **And the sons of Shimei** were, Jahath, Zina, and Jeush, and Beriah.
These four were the sons of Shimei.
11 **And Jahath** was the chief, and Zizah the second:
but Jeush and Beriah had not many sons;
therefore they were in one reckoning, according to their father's house.
12 **The sons of Kohath;** Amram, Izhar, Hebron, and Uzziel, four.
13 **The sons of Amram;** Aaron and Moses:

and Aaron was separated,
that he should sanctify the most holy things, he and his sons for ever,
to burn incense before the LORD,
to minister unto him,
and to bless in his name for ever.

14 **Now concerning Moses the man of God,** his sons were named of the tribe of Levi.

15 **The sons of Moses** were, Gershom, and Eliezer.

16 **Of the sons of Gershom,** Shebuel was the chief.

17 **And the sons of Eliezer** were, Rehabiah the chief.

And Eliezer had none other sons;
but the sons of Rehabiah were very many.

18 **Of the sons of Izhar;** Shelomith the chief.

19 **Of the sons of Hebron;** Jeriah the first, Amariah the second, Jahaziel the third, and Jekameam the fourth.

20 **Of the sons of Uzziel;** Micah the first and Jesiah the second.

21 **The sons of Merari;** Mahli, and Mushi.

The sons of Mahli; Eleazar, and Kish.

22 **And Eleazar** died,
and had no sons, but daughters:
and their brethren the sons of Kish took them.

23 **The sons of Mushi;** Mahli, and Eder, and Jeremoth, three.

24 **These** were the sons of Levi after the house of their fathers; even the chief of the fathers,
as they were counted by number of names by their polls, {that did the work for the service of the house of the LORD}, from the age of twenty years and upward.

25 **For David** said,
The LORD God of Israel hath given rest unto his people,
that they may dwell in Jerusalem for ever:

26 **And also unto the Levites;** they shall no more carry the tabernacle, nor any vessels of it for the service thereof.

27 **For by the last words of David** the Levites were numbered from twenty years old and above:

28 **Because their office** was to wait on the sons of Aaron for the service of the house of the LORD, in the courts, and in the chambers, and in the purifying of all holy things, and the work of the service of the house of God;

29 Both for the shewbread, and for the fine flour for meat offering, and for the unleavened cakes, and for that which is baked in the pan, and for that which is fried, and for all manner of measure and size;

30 **And** to stand every morning {to thank and praise the LORD}, and likewise at even:

31 **And** to offer all burnt sacrifices unto the LORD in the sabbaths, in the new moons, and on the set feasts, by number, according to the order commanded unto them, continually before the LORD:

32 **And that they** should keep the charge of the tabernacle of the congregation, and the charge of the holy place, and the charge of the sons of Aaron their brethren, in the service of the house of the LORD.

24

Now these are the divisions of the sons of Aaron.

The sons of Aaron; Nadab, and Abihu, Eleazar, and Ithamar.

2 **But Nadab and Abihu** died before their father,
and had no children:
therefore Eleazar and Ithamar executed the priest's office.

3 **And David** distributed them, both Zadok of the sons of Eleazar, and Ahimelech of the sons of Ithamar, according to their offices in their service.

4 **And there** were more chief men found of the sons of Eleazar than of the sons of Ithamar,
and thus were they divided.
Among the sons of Eleazar there were sixteen chief men of the house of their fathers, and eight among the sons of Ithamar according to the house of their fathers.

5 **Thus** were they divided by lot, one sort with another;
for the governors of the sanctuary, and governors of the house of God, were of the sons of Eleazar, and of the sons of Ithamar.

6 **And Shemaiah the son of Nethaneel the scribe, one of the Levites,** wrote them before the king, and the princes, and Zadok the priest, and Ahimelech the son of Abiathar, and before the chief of the fathers of the priests and Levites:
one principal household being taken for Eleazar,
and one taken for Ithamar.

7 **Now the first lot** came forth to Jehoiarib, the second to Jedaiah,
8 The third to Harim, the fourth to Seorim,
9 The fifth to Malchijah, the sixth to Mijamin,
10 The seventh to Hakkoz, the eighth to Abijah,
11 The ninth to Jeshuah, the tenth to Shecaniah,
12 The eleventh to Eliashib, the twelfth to Jakim,
13 The thirteenth to Huppah, the fourteenth to Jeshebeab,
14 The fifteenth to Bilgah, the sixteenth to Immer,
15 The seventeenth to Hezir, the eighteenth to Aphses,
16 The nineteenth to Pethahiah, the twentieth to Jehezekel,
17 The one and twentieth to Jachin, the two and twentieth to Gamul,
18 The three and twentieth to Delaiah, the four and twentieth to Maaziah.

19 **These** were the orderings of them in their service to come into the house of the LORD, according to their manner, under Aaron their father,
as the LORD God of Israel had commanded him.

20 **And the rest of the sons of Levi** were these:
Of the sons of Amram; Shubael:
of the sons of Shubael; Jehdeiah.

21 Concerning Rehabiah:
of the sons of Rehabiah, the first was Isshiah.

22 **Of the Izharites;** Shelomoth:
of the sons of Shelomoth; Jahath.

23 **And the sons of Hebron;** Jeriah the first, Amariah the second, Jahaziel the third, Jekameam the fourth.

24 **Of the sons of Uzziel;** Michah:
of the sons of Michah; Shamir.

25 **The brother of Michah** was Isshiah:
of the sons of Isshiah; Zechariah.

26 **The sons of Merari** were Mahli and Mushi:
the sons of Jaaziah; Beno.

27 **The sons of Merari by Jaaziah;** Beno, and Shoham, and Zaccur, and Ibri.

28 **Of Mahli** came Eleazar,
who had no sons.

29 Concerning Kish:
the son of Kish was Jerahmeel.

30 **The sons also of Mushi;** Mahli, and Eder, and Jerimoth.

These were the sons of the Levites after the house of their fathers.

31 **These** likewise cast lots over against their brethren the sons of Aaron in the presence of David the king, and Zadok, and Ahimelech, and the chief of the fathers of the priests and Levites, even the principal fathers over against their younger brethren.

25

∞ **Moreover David and the captains of the host** separated to the service of the sons of Asaph, and of Heman, and of Jeduthun,
who should prophesy with harps, with psalteries, and with cymbals:
and the number of the workmen according to their service was:

2 **Of the sons of Asaph;** Zaccur, and Joseph, and Nethaniah, and Asarelah, the sons of Asaph under the hands of Asaph,
which prophesied according to the order of the king.

3 Of Jeduthun:
the sons of Jeduthun; Gedaliah, and Zeri, and Jeshaiah, Hashabiah, and Mattithiah, six, under the hands of their father Jeduthun,
who prophesied with a harp,
to give thanks
and to praise the LORD.

4 Of Heman:
the sons of Heman: Bukkiah, Mattaniah, Uzziel, Shebuel, and Jerimoth, Hananiah, Hanani, Eliathah, Giddalti, and Romamtiezer, Joshbekashah, Mallothi, Hothir, and Mahazioth:

5 **All these** were the sons of Heman the king's seer in the words of God,
to lift up the horn.

And God gave to Heman fourteen sons and three daughters.

6 **All these** were under the hands of their father for song in the house of the LORD, with cymbals, psalteries, and harps, for the service of the house of God, according to the king's order to Asaph, Jeduthun, and Heman.

7 **So the number of them, with their brethren that were instructed in the songs of the LORD, even all that were cunning,** was two hundred fourscore and eight.

8 **And they** cast lots, ward against ward, as well the small as the great, the teacher as the scholar.

9 **Now the first lot** came forth for Asaph to Joseph:
the second to Gedaliah, {who with his brethren and sons were twelve}:

10 **The third to Zaccur, he, his sons, and his brethren,** were twelve:

11 **The fourth to Izri, he, his sons, and his brethren,** were twelve:

12 **The fifth to Nethaniah, he, his sons, and his brethren,** were twelve:

13 **The sixth to Bukkiah, he, his sons, and his brethren,** were twelve:

14 **The seventh to Jesharelah, he, his sons, and his brethren,** were twelve:

15 **The eighth to Jeshaiah, he, his sons, and his brethren,** were twelve:

16 **The ninth to Mattaniah, he, his sons, and his brethren,** were twelve:

17 **The tenth to Shimei, he, his sons, and his brethren,** were twelve:

18 **The eleventh to Azareel, he, his sons, and his brethren,** were twelve:

19 **The twelfth to Hashabiah, he, his sons, and his brethren,** were twelve:

20 **The thirteenth to Shubael, he, his sons, and his brethren,** were twelve:

21 **The fourteenth to Mattithiah, he, his sons, and his brethren,** were twelve:

22 **The fifteenth to Jeremoth, he, his sons, and his brethren,** were twelve:

23 **The sixteenth to Hananiah, he, his sons, and his brethren,** were twelve:

24 **The seventeenth to Joshbekashah, he, his sons, and his brethren,** were twelve:

25 **The eighteenth to Hanani, he, his sons, and his brethren,** were twelve:

26 **The nineteenth to Mallothi, he, his sons, and his brethren,** were twelve:

27 **The twentieth to Eliathah, he, his sons, and his brethren,** were twelve:

28 **The one and twentieth to Hothir, he, his sons, and his brethren,** were twelve:

29 **The two and twentieth to Giddalti, he, his sons, and his brethren,** were twelve:

30 **The three and twentieth to Mahazioth, he, his sons, and his brethren,** were twelve:

31 **The four and twentieth to Romamtiezer, he, his sons, and his brethren,** were twelve.

26

Concerning the divisions of the porters:
Of the Korhites was Meshelemiah the son of Kore, of the sons of Asaph.

2 **And the sons of Meshelemiah** were, Zechariah the firstborn, Jediael the second, Zebadiah the third, Jathniel the fourth,
3 Elam the fifth, Jehohanan the sixth, Elioenai the seventh.

4 **Moreover the sons of Obededom** were, Shemaiah the firstborn, Jehozabad the second, Joah the third, and Sacar the fourth, and Nethaneel the fifth,
5 Ammiel the sixth, Issachar the seventh, Peulthai the eighth:
for God blessed him.

6 **Also unto Shemaiah his son** were sons born,
that ruled throughout the house of their father:
for they were mighty men of valour.

7 **The sons of Shemaiah;** Othni, and Rephael, and Obed, Elzabad,
whose brethren were strong men, Elihu, and Semachiah.

8 All these of the sons of Obededom:

they and their sons and their brethren, able men for strength for the service, were threescore and two of Obededom.

9 **And Meshelemiah** had sons and brethren, strong men, eighteen.

10 **Also Hosah, of the children of Merari,** had sons; Simri the chief,
(for though he was not the firstborn,
yet his father made him the chief;)
11 Hilkiah the second, Tebaliah the third, Zechariah the fourth:
all the sons and brethren of Hosah were thirteen.

12 **Among these** were the divisions of the porters, even among the chief men,
having wards one against another,
to minister in the house of the LORD.

13 **And they** cast lots, as well the small as the great, according to the house of their fathers, for every gate.

14 **And the lot eastward** fell to Shelemiah.
Then for Zechariah his son, a wise counsellor, they cast lots;
and his lot came out northward.
15 **To Obededom** southward;
and to his sons the house of Asuppim.

16 **To Shuppim and Hosah** the lot came forth westward, with the gate Shallecheth, by the causeway of the going up, ward against ward.

17 **Eastward** were six Levites, northward four a day, southward four a day, and toward Asuppim two and two.

18 **At Parbar westward,** four at the causeway, and two at Parbar.

19 **These** are the divisions of the porters among the sons of Kore, and among the sons of Merari.

20 **And of the Levites,** Ahijah was over the treasures of the house of God, and over the treasures of the dedicated things.

21 **As concerning the sons of Laadan; the sons of the Gershonite Laadan, chief fathers, even of Laadan the Gershonite,** were Jehieli.

22 **The sons of Jehieli;** Zetham, and Joel his brother,
which were over the treasures of the house of the LORD.

23 **Of the Amramites, and the Izharites, the Hebronites, and the Uzzielites:**

24 **And Shebuel the son of Gershom, the son of Moses,** was ruler of the treasures.

25 **And his brethren by Eliezer;** Rehabiah his son, and Jeshaiah his son, and Joram his son, and Zichri his son, and Shelomith his son.

26 **Which Shelomith and his brethren** were over all the treasures of the dedicated things,
which David the king, and the chief fathers, the captains over thousands and hundreds, and the captains of the host, had dedicated.

27 **Out of the spoils won in battles** did they dedicate to maintain the house of the LORD.

28 **And all that Samuel the seer, and Saul the son of Kish, and Abner the son of Ner, and Joab the son of Zeruiah,** had dedicated;
and whosoever had dedicated any thing,
it was under the hand of Shelomith, and of his brethren.

29 **Of the Izharites,** Chenaniah and his sons were for the outward business over Israel, for officers and judges.

30 **And of the Hebronites,** Hashabiah and his brethren, men of valour, a thousand and seven hundred, were officers among them of Israel on this side Jordan westward in all the business of the LORD, and in the service of the king.

31 **Among the Hebronites** was Jerijah the chief, even among the Hebronites, according to the generations of his fathers.
In the fortieth year of the reign of David they were sought for,
and there were found among them mighty men of valour at Jazer of Gilead.

32 **And his brethren, men of valour,** were two thousand and seven hundred chief fathers,
whom king David made rulers over the Reubenites, the Gadites, and the half tribe of Manasseh, for every matter pertaining to God, and affairs of the king.

27 **Now the children of Israel after their number, to wit, the chief fathers and captains of thousands and hundreds, and their officers that served the king in any matter of the courses,** {which came in and went out month by month throughout all the months of the year}, of every course were twenty and four thousand.

2 **Over the first course for the first month** was Jashobeam the son of Zabdiel:
and in his course were twenty and four thousand.

3 **Of the children of Perez** was the chief of all the captains of the host for the first month.

4 **And over the course of the second month** was Dodai an Ahohite,
and of his course was Mikloth also the ruler:
in his course likewise were twenty and four thousand.

5 **The third captain of the host for the third month** was Benaiah the son of Jehoiada, a chief priest:
and in his course were twenty and four thousand.

6 **This** is that Benaiah,
who was mighty among the thirty, and above the thirty:
and in his course was Ammizabad his son.

7 **The fourth captain for the fourth month** was Asahel the brother of Joab, and Zebadiah his son after him:
and in his course were twenty and four thousand.

8 **The fifth captain for the fifth month** was Shamhuth the Izrahite:
and in his course were twenty and four thousand.

9 **The sixth captain for the sixth month** was Ira the son of Ikkesh the Tekoite:
and in his course were twenty and four thousand.

10 **The seventh captain for the seventh month** was Helez the Pelonite, of the children of Ephraim:

and in his course were twenty and four thousand.
11 **The eighth captain for the eighth month** was Sibbecai the Hushathite, of the Zarhites:
and in his course were twenty and four thousand.
12 **The ninth captain for the ninth month** was Abiezer the Anetothite, of the Benjamites:
and in his course were twenty and four thousand.
13 **The tenth captain for the tenth month** was Maharai the Netophathite, of the Zarhites:
and in his course were twenty and four thousand.
14 **The eleventh captain for the eleventh month** was Benaiah the Pirathonite, of the children of Ephraim: **and in his course** were twenty and four thousand.
15 **The twelfth captain for the twelfth month** was Heldai the Netophathite, of Othniel:
and in his course were twenty and four thousand.
16 **Furthermore over the tribes of Israel:** the ruler of the Reubenites was Eliezer the son of Zichri:
of the Simeonites, Shephatiah the son of Maachah:
17 **Of the Levites,** Hashabiah the son of Kemuel:
of the Aaronites, Zadok:
18 **Of Judah,** Elihu, one of the brethren of David:
of Issachar, Omri the son of Michael:
19 **Of Zebulun,** Ishmaiah the son of Obadiah:
of Naphtali, Jerimoth the son of Azriel:
20 **Of the children of Ephraim,** Hoshea the son of Azaziah:
of the half tribe of Manasseh, Joel the son of Pedaiah:
21 **Of the half tribe of Manasseh in Gilead,** Iddo the son of Zechariah:
of Benjamin, Jaasiel the son of Abner:
22 **Of Dan,** Azareel the son of Jeroham.
These were the princes of the tribes of Israel.
23 **But David** took not the number of them from twenty years old and under:
because the LORD had said he would increase Israel like to the stars of the heavens.
24 **Joab the son of Zeruiah** began to number,
but he finished not,
because there fell wrath for it against Israel;
neither was the number put in the account of the chronicles of king David.
25 **And over the king's treasures** was Azmaveth the son of Adiel:
and over the storehouses in the fields, in the cities, and in the villages, and in the castles, was Jehonathan the son of Uzziah:
26 **And over them that did the work of the field for tillage of the ground** was Ezri the son of Chelub:
27 **And over the vineyards** was Shimei the Ramathite:
over the increase of the vineyards for the wine cellars was Zabdi the Shiphmite:
28 **And over the olive trees and the sycomore trees that were in the low plains** was Baalhanan the Gederite:
and over the cellars of oil was Joash:
29 **And over the herds that fed in Sharon** was Shitrai the Sharonite:
and over the herds that were in the valleys was Shaphat the son of Adlai:
30 **Over the camels** also was Obil the Ishmaelite:
and over the asses was Jehdeiah the Meronothite:
31 **And over the flocks** was Jaziz the Hagerite.
All these were the rulers of the substance which was king David's.
32 **Also Jonathan David's uncle** was a counsellor, a wise man, and a scribe:
and Jehiel the son of Hachmoni was with the king's sons:
33 **And Ahithophel** was the king's counsellor:
and Hushai the Archite was the king's companion:
34 **And after Ahithophel** was Jehoiada the son of Benaiah, and Abiathar:
and the general of the king's army was Joab.

28

And David assembled all the princes of Israel, the princes of the tribes, and the captains of the companies that ministered to the king by course, and the captains over the thousands, and captains over the hundreds, and the stewards over all the substance and possession of the king, and of his sons, with the officers, and with the mighty men, and with all the valiant men, unto Jerusalem.
2 **Then David the king** stood up upon his feet,
and said,
Hear me, my brethren, and my people:
As for me, I had in mine heart to build an house of rest for the ark of the covenant of the LORD, and for the footstool of our God,
and had made ready for the building:
3 **But God** said unto me,
Thou shalt not build an house for my name,
because thou hast been a man of war,
and hast shed blood.
4 **Howbeit the LORD God of Israel** chose me before all the house of my father to be king over Israel for ever:
for he hath chosen Judah to be the ruler;
and of the house of Judah, the house of my father; and among the sons of my father he liked me to make me king over all Israel:
5 **And of all my sons,** (for the LORD hath given me many sons,) he hath chosen Solomon my son to sit upon the throne of the kingdom of the LORD over Israel.
6 **And he** said unto me,
Solomon thy son, he shall build my house and my courts:
for I have chosen him to be my son,
and I will be his father.
7 **Moreover I** will establish his kingdom for ever, {if he be constant to do my commandments and my judgments}, as at this day.
8 **Now therefore in the sight of all Israel the congregation of the LORD, and in the audience of our God,** keep and seek for all the

commandments of the LORD your God:
that ye may possess this good land,
and leave it for an inheritance for your children after you for ever.

9 **And thou, Solomon my son,** know thou the God of thy father,
and serve him with a perfect heart and with a willing mind:
for the LORD searcheth all hearts,
and understandeth all the imaginations of the thoughts:
if thou seek him,
he will be found of thee;
but if thou forsake him,
he will cast thee off for ever.

10 **Take heed** now;
for the LORD hath chosen thee to build an house for the sanctuary:
be strong,
and do it.

11 **Then David** gave to Solomon his son the pattern of the porch, and of the houses thereof, and of the treasuries thereof, and of the upper chambers thereof, and of the inner parlours thereof, and of the place of the mercy seat,
12 And the pattern of all that he had by the spirit, of the courts of the house of the LORD, and of all the chambers round about, of the treasuries of the house of God, and of the treasuries of the dedicated things:
13 Also for the courses of the priests and the Levites, and for all the work of the service of the house of the LORD, and for all the vessels of service in the house of the LORD.

14 **He** gave of gold by weight for things of gold, for all instruments of all manner of service; silver also for all instruments of silver by weight, for all instruments of every kind of service:
15 Even the weight for the candlesticks of gold, and for their lamps of gold, by weight for every candlestick, and for the lamps thereof: and for the candlesticks of silver by weight, both for the candlestick, and also for the lamps thereof, according to the use of every candlestick.

16 **And by weight** he gave gold for the tables of shewbread, for every table; and likewise silver for the tables of silver:
17 Also pure gold for the fleshhooks, and the bowls, and the cups:
and for the golden basons he gave gold by weight for every bason; and likewise silver by weight for every bason of silver:
18 And for the altar of incense refined gold by weight; and gold for the pattern of the chariot of the cherubims, that spread out their wings, and covered the ark of the covenant of the LORD.

19 **All this**, {said David}, the LORD made me understand in writing by his hand upon me, even all the works of this pattern.

20 **And David** said to Solomon his son,
Be strong and of good courage,
and do it:
fear not,
nor be dismayed:
for the LORD God, even my God, will be with thee;
he will not fail thee,
nor forsake thee,
until thou hast finished all the work for the service of the house of the LORD.

21 **And, {behold}, the courses of the priests and the Levites,** even they shall be with thee for all the service of the house of God:
and there shall be with thee for all manner of workmanship every willing skilful man, for any manner of service:
also the princes and all the people will be wholly at thy commandment.

29 **Furthermore David the king** said unto all the congregation,
Solomon my son, {whom alone God hath chosen}, is yet young and tender,
and the work is great:
for the palace is not for man, but for the LORD God.

2 **Now I** have prepared with all my might for the house of my God the gold for things to be made of gold, and the silver for things of silver, and the brass for things of brass, the iron for things of iron, and wood for things of wood; onyx stones, and stones to be set, glistering stones, and of divers colours, and all manner of precious stones, and marble stones in abundance.

3 **Moreover, because I** have set my affection to the house of my God,
I have of mine own proper good, of gold and silver,
which I have given to the house of my God, over and above all that I have prepared for the holy house,
4 Even three thousand talents of gold, of the gold of Ophir, and seven thousand talents of refined silver,
to overlay the walls of the houses withal:
5 The gold for things of gold, and the silver for things of silver, and for all manner of work to be made by the hands of artificers.
And who then is willing to consecrate his service this day unto the LORD?

6 **Then the chief of the fathers and princes of the tribes of Israel and the captains of thousands and of hundreds, with the rulers of the king's work,** offered willingly,
7 **And** gave for the service of the house of God of gold five thousand talents and ten thousand drams, and of silver ten thousand talents, and of brass eighteen thousand talents, and one hundred thousand talents of iron.

8 **And they with whom precious stones were found** gave them to the treasure of the house of the LORD, by the hand of Jehiel the Gershonite.

9 **Then the people** rejoiced,
for that they offered willingly,
because with perfect heart they offered willingly to the LORD:
and David the king also rejoiced with great joy.

10 **Wherefore David** blessed the LORD before all the congregation:
and David said,
Blessed be thou, LORD God of Israel our father, for ever and ever.

11 **Thine, O LORD** is the greatness, and the power, and the glory, and the victory, and the majesty:
for all that is in the heaven and in the earth is thine;
thine is the kingdom, O LORD,
and thou art exalted as head above all.

12 **Both riches and honour** come of thee,
and thou reignest over all;
and in thine hand is power and might;
and in thine hand it is to make great,
and to give strength unto all.

13 **Now therefore, our God, we** thank thee,
and praise thy glorious name.

14 **But who** am I,
and what is my people,
that we should be able to offer so willingly after this sort?
for all things come of thee,
and of thine own have we given thee.

15 **For we** are strangers before thee, and sojourners,
as were all our fathers:
our days on the earth are as a shadow,
and there is none abiding.

16 **O LORD our God, all this store that we have prepared to build thee an house for thine holy name** cometh of thine hand,
and is all thine own.

17 **I** know also, my God,
that thou triest the heart,
and hast pleasure in uprightness.
As for me, in the uprightness of mine heart I have willingly offered all these things:
and now have I seen with joy thy people,
which are present here,
to offer willingly unto thee.

18 **O LORD God of Abraham, Isaac, and of Israel, our fathers, keep** this for ever in the imagination of the thoughts of the heart of thy people,
and prepare their heart unto thee:

19 **And give** unto Solomon my son a perfect heart,
to keep thy commandments, thy testimonies, and thy statutes,
and to do all these things,
and to build the palace,
for the which I have made provision.

20 **And David** said to all the congregation,
Now bless the LORD your God.
And all the congregation blessed the LORD God of their fathers,
and bowed down their heads,
and worshipped the LORD, and the king.

21 **And they** sacrificed sacrifices unto the LORD,
and offered burnt offerings unto the LORD, on the morrow after that day, even a thousand bullocks, a thousand rams, and a thousand lambs, with their drink offerings, and sacrifices in abundance for all Israel:

22 **And** did eat and drink before the LORD on that day with great gladness.
And they made Solomon the son of David king the second time,
and anointed him unto the LORD to be the chief governor,
and Zadok to be priest.

23 **Then Solomon** sat on the throne of the LORD as king instead of David his father,
and prospered;
and all Israel obeyed him.

24 **And all the princes, and the mighty men, and all the sons likewise of king David,** submitted themselves unto Solomon the king.

25 **And the LORD** magnified Solomon exceedingly in the sight of all Israel,
and bestowed upon him such royal majesty as had not been on any king before him in Israel.

26 **Thus David the son of Jesse** reigned over all Israel.

27 **And the time that he reigned over Israel** was forty years;
seven years reigned he in Hebron,
and thirty and three years reigned he in Jerusalem.

28 **And he** died in a good old age, full of days, riches, and honour:
and Solomon his son reigned in his stead.

29 **Now the acts of David the king, first and last,** {behold}, they are written in the book of Samuel the seer, and in the book of Nathan the prophet, and in the book of Gad the seer,

30 With all his reign and his might, and the times that went over him, and over Israel, and over all the kingdoms of the countries.

2 Chronicles

Traditionally attributed to the prophet Ezra, the Book of Second Chronicles tells the history of the divided kingdoms, especially the southern Kingdom of Judah. It covers the reigns of several kings, including Solomon, and evaluates each one's adherence to God's laws. The final chapters then describe the fall of Jerusalem and the deportation of its citizens to Babylon, the consequence of straying from God's laws.

While Second Chronicles may not feature the well-known Bible stories of other Old Testament books, it remains a valuable document for understanding the two kingdoms: their rulers, religious practices, and cultures. The book highlights many examples of good and bad behavior among the kings and people. These examples provide practical lessons about the benefits of humility, justice, and integrity and the dangers of pride, idolatry, and rebellion.

This connection to the past is not a relic of the past but a vibrant part of the people's national identity. It forms a thread that binds the Israelites to their ancestors' rich heritage and enduring faith. Overall, the Book of Second Chronicles seeks to deepen the people's knowledge of their history, customs, and religion. Furthermore, it underscores the need to repent and restore their covenant with God. The preservation of Jewish culture will depend on it.

1 **And Solomon the son of David** was strengthened in his kingdom,
and the LORD his God was with him,
and magnified him exceedingly.
2 **Then Solomon** spake unto all Israel, to the captains of thousands and of hundreds, and to the judges, and to every governor in all Israel, the chief of the fathers.
3 **So Solomon, and all the congregation with him,** went to the high place that was at Gibeon;
for there was the tabernacle of the congregation of God,
which Moses the servant of the LORD had made in the wilderness.
4 **But the ark of God** had David brought up from Kirjathjearim to the place which David had prepared for it:
for he had pitched a tent for it at Jerusalem.
5 **Moreover the brasen altar**, {that Bezaleel the son of Uri, the son of Hur, had made}, he put before the tabernacle of the LORD:
and Solomon and the congregation sought unto it.
6 **And Solomon** went up thither to the brasen altar before the LORD,
which was at the tabernacle of the congregation,
and offered a thousand burnt offerings upon it.
7 **In that night** did God appear unto Solomon,
and said unto him,
Ask
what I shall give thee.
8 **And Solomon** said unto God,
Thou hast shewed great mercy unto David my father,
and hast made me to reign in his stead.
9 **Now, O LORD God, let thy promise unto David my father** be established:
for thou hast made me king over a people like the dust of the earth in multitude.
10 **Give** me now wisdom and knowledge,
that I may go out and come in before this people:
for who can judge this thy people,
that is so great?
11 **And God** said to Solomon,
Because this was in thine heart,
and thou hast not asked riches, wealth, or honour, nor the life of thine enemies,
neither yet hast asked long life;
but hast asked wisdom and knowledge for thyself,
that thou mayest judge my people,
over whom I have made thee king:
12 **Wisdom and knowledge** is granted unto thee;
and I will give thee riches, and wealth, and honour,
such as none of the kings have had that have been before thee,
neither shall there any after thee have the like.
13 **Then Solomon** came from his journey to the high place that was at Gibeon to Jerusalem, from before the tabernacle of the congregation,
and reigned over Israel.
14 **And Solomon** gathered chariots and horsemen:
and he had a thousand and four hundred chariots, and twelve thousand horsemen,
which he placed in the chariot cities, and with the king at Jerusalem.
15 **And the king** made silver and gold at Jerusalem as plenteous as stones,
and cedar trees made he as the sycomore trees that are in the vale for abundance.
16 **And Solomon** had horses brought out of Egypt, and linen yarn:
the king's merchants received the linen yarn at a price.
17 **And they** fetched up,
and brought forth out of Egypt a chariot for six hundred shekels of silver, and an horse for an hundred and fifty:
and so brought they out horses for all the kings of the Hittites, and for the kings of Syria, by their means.

2 **And Solomon** determined to build an house for the name

of the LORD, and an house for his kingdom.

2 **And Solomon** told out threescore and ten thousand men to bear burdens,
and fourscore thousand to hew in the mountain,
and three thousand and six hundred to oversee them.

3 **And Solomon** sent to Huram the king of Tyre,
saying,
As thou didst deal with David my father,
and didst send him cedars to build him an house to dwell therein,
even so deal with me.

4 **Behold, I** build an house to the name of the LORD my God,
to dedicate it to him,
and to burn before him sweet incense, and for the continual shewbread, and for the burnt offerings morning and evening, on the sabbaths, and on the new moons, and on the solemn feasts of the LORD our God.
This is an ordinance for ever to Israel.

5 **And the house which I build** is great:
for great is our God above all gods.

6 **But who** is able to build him an house,
seeing the heaven and heaven of heavens cannot contain him?
who am I then,
that I should build him an house,
save only to burn sacrifice before him?

7 **Send** me now therefore a man cunning to work in gold, and in silver, and in brass, and in iron, and in purple, and crimson, and blue,
and that can skill to grave with the cunning men that are with me in Judah and in Jerusalem,
whom David my father did provide.

8 **Send** me also cedar trees, fir trees, and algum trees, out of Lebanon:
for I know
that thy servants can skill to cut timber in Lebanon;
and, {behold}, my servants shall be with thy servants,

9 **Even** to prepare me timber in abundance:
for the house which I am about to build shall be wonderful great.

10 **And, {behold}, I** will give to thy servants, the hewers that cut timber, twenty thousand measures of beaten wheat, and twenty thousand measures of barley, and twenty thousand baths of wine, and twenty thousand baths of oil.

11 **Then Huram the king of Tyre** answered in writing,
which he sent to Solomon,
Because the LORD hath loved his people,
he hath made thee king over them.

12 **Huram** said moreover,
Blessed be the LORD God of Israel,
that made heaven and earth,
who hath given to David the king a wise son,
endued with prudence and understanding,
that might build an house for the LORD, and an house for his kingdom.

13 **And now I** have sent a cunning man, {endued with understanding}, of Huram my father's,

14 The son of a woman of the daughters of Dan,
and his father was a man of Tyre,
skilful to work in gold, and in silver, in brass, in iron, in stone, and in timber, in purple, in blue, and in fine linen, and in crimson;
also to grave any manner of graving,
and to find out every device which shall be put to him, with thy cunning men, and with the cunning men of my lord David thy father.

15 **Now therefore the wheat, and the barley, the oil, and the wine,** {which my lord hath spoken of}, let him send unto his servants:

16 **And we** will cut wood out of Lebanon,
as much as thou shalt need:
and we will bring it to thee in floats by sea to Joppa;
and thou shalt carry it up to Jerusalem.

17 **And Solomon** numbered all the strangers that were in the land of Israel, after the numbering wherewith David his father had numbered them;
and they were found an hundred and fifty thousand and three thousand and six hundred.

18 **And he** set threescore and ten thousand of them to be bearers of burdens, and fourscore thousand to be hewers in the mountain, and three thousand and six hundred overseers
to set the people a work.

3 **Then Solomon** began to build the house of the LORD at Jerusalem in mount Moriah,
where the LORD appeared unto David his father, in the place that David had prepared in the threshingfloor of Ornan the Jebusite.

2 **And he** began to build in the second day of the second month, in the fourth year of his reign.

3 **Now these** are the things wherein Solomon was instructed for the building of the house of God.
The length by cubits after the first measure was threescore cubits, and the breadth twenty cubits.

4 **And the porch that was in the front of the house,** the length of it was according to the breadth of the house, twenty cubits,
and the height was an hundred and twenty:
and he overlaid it within with pure gold.

5 **And the greater house** he cieled with fir tree,
which he overlaid with fine gold,
and set thereon palm trees and chains.

6 **And he** garnished the house with precious stones for beauty:
and the gold was gold of Parvaim.

7 **He** overlaid also the house, the beams, the posts, and the walls thereof, and the doors thereof, with gold;
and graved cherubims on the walls.

8 **And he** made the most holy house,
the length whereof was according to the breadth of the house, twenty cubits, and the breadth thereof twenty cubits:
and he overlaid it with fine gold, amounting to six hundred talents.

9 **And the weight of the nails** was fifty shekels of gold.
And he overlaid the upper chambers with gold.

10 **And in the most holy house** he made two cherubims of image work,
and overlaid them with gold.

11 **And the wings of the cherubims** were twenty cubits long:
one wing of the one cherub was five cubits,
reaching to the wall of the house:
and the other wing was likewise five cubits,
reaching to the wing of the other cherub.

12 **And one wing of the other cherub** was five cubits,
reaching to the wall of the house:
and the other wing was five cubits also,
joining to the wing of the other cherub.

13 **The wings of these cherubims** spread themselves forth twenty cubits:
and they stood on their feet,
and their faces were inward.

14 **And he** made the vail of blue, and purple, and crimson, and fine linen,
and wrought cherubims thereon.

15 **Also he** made before the house two pillars of thirty and five cubits high,
and the chapiter that was on the top of each of them was five cubits.

16 **And he** made chains, as in the oracle,
and put them on the heads of the pillars;
and made an hundred pomegranates,
and put them on the chains.

17 **And he** reared up the pillars before the temple, one on the right hand, and the other on the left;
and called the name of that on the right hand Jachin, and the name of that on the left Boaz.

4 **Moreover he** made an altar of brass, twenty cubits the length thereof, and twenty cubits the breadth thereof, and ten cubits the height thereof.

2 **Also he** made a molten sea of ten cubits from brim to brim, round in compass, and five cubits the height thereof;
and a line of thirty cubits did compass it round about.

3 **And under it** was the similitude of oxen,
which did compass it round about: ten in a cubit,
compassing the sea round about.
Two rows of oxen were cast,
when it was cast.

4 **It** stood upon twelve oxen, three looking toward the north, and three looking toward the west, and three looking toward the south, and three looking toward the east:
and the sea was set above upon them,
and all their hinder parts were inward.

5 **And the thickness of it** was an handbreadth, and the brim of it like the work of the brim of a cup, with flowers of lilies;
and it received and held three thousand baths.

6 **He** made also ten lavers,
and put five on the right hand, and five on the left,
to wash in them:
such things as they offered for the burnt offering they washed in them;
but the sea was for the priests to wash in.

7 **And he** made ten candlesticks of gold according to their form,
and set them in the temple, five on the right hand, and five on the left.

8 **He** made also ten tables,
and placed them in the temple, five on the right side, and five on the left.
And he made an hundred basons of gold.

9 **Furthermore he** made the court of the priests, and the great court, and doors for the court,
and overlaid the doors of them with brass.

10 **And he** set the sea on the right side of the east end, over against the south.

11 **And Huram** made the pots, and the shovels, and the basons.
And Huram finished the work that he was to make for king Solomon for the house of God;

12 To wit, the two pillars, and the pommels, and the chapiters which were on the top of the two pillars, {and the two wreaths to cover the two pommels of the chapiters which were on the top of the pillars};

13 And four hundred pomegranates on the two wreaths; two rows of pomegranates on each wreath,
to cover the two pommels of the chapiters which were upon the pillars.

14 **He** made also bases,
and lavers made he upon the bases;

15 One sea, and twelve oxen under it.

16 **The pots also, and the shovels, and the fleshhooks, and all their instruments,** did Huram his father make to king Solomon for the house of the LORD of bright brass.

17 **In the plain of Jordan** did the king cast them, in the clay ground between Succoth and Zeredathah.

18 **Thus Solomon** made all these vessels in great abundance:
for the weight of the brass could not be found out.

19 **And Solomon** made all the vessels that were for the house of God, the golden altar also, and the tables whereon the shewbread was set;

20 **Moreover the candlesticks with their lamps, {that they should burn after the manner before the oracle}, of pure gold;**

21 **And the flowers, and the lamps, and the tongs,** made he of gold, and that perfect gold;

22 And the snuffers, and the basons, and the spoons, and the censers, of pure gold:
and the entry of the house, the inner doors thereof for the most holy place, and the doors of the house of the temple, were of gold.

5 **Thus all the work that Solomon made for the house of the LORD** was finished:
and Solomon brought in all the things that David his father had dedicated;
and the silver, and the gold, and all the instruments, put he among the treasures of the house of God.

2 **Then Solomon** assembled the
elders of Israel, and all the heads
of the tribes, the chief of the
fathers of the children of Israel,
unto Jerusalem,
to bring up the ark of the covenant
of the LORD out of the city of
David,
which is Zion.
3 **Wherefore all the men of Israel**
assembled themselves unto the
king in the feast
which was in the seventh month.
4 **And all the elders of Israel** came;
and the Levites took up the ark.
5 **And they** brought up the ark, and
the tabernacle of the
congregation, and all the holy
vessels that were in the
tabernacle,
these did the priests and the Levites
bring up.
6 **Also king Solomon, and all the
congregation of Israel that were
assembled unto him before the
ark,** sacrificed sheep and oxen,
which could not be told nor
numbered for multitude.
7 **And the priests** brought in the ark
of the covenant of the LORD unto
his place, to the oracle of the
house, into the most holy place,
even under the wings of the
cherubims:
8 **For the cherubims** spread forth
their wings over the place of the
ark,
and the cherubims covered the ark
and the staves thereof above.
9 **And they** drew out the staves of
the ark,
that the ends of the staves were
seen from the ark before the
oracle;
but they were not seen without.
And there it is unto this day.
10 **There** was nothing in the ark save
the two tables which Moses put
therein at Horeb,
when the LORD made a covenant
with the children of Israel,
when they came out of Egypt.
11 **And it** came to pass,
when the priests were come out of
the holy place:
(for all the priests that were present
were sanctified,
and did not then wait by course:
12 Also the Levites which were the
singers, all of them of Asaph, of
Heman, of Jeduthun, with their
sons and their brethren, {being
arrayed in white linen}, {having
cymbals and psalteries and
harps}, stood at the east end of
the altar, and with them an
hundred and twenty priests
sounding with trumpets:)
13 **It** came even to pass,
as the trumpeters and singers
were as one,
to make one sound to be heard in
praising and thanking the LORD;
and when they lifted up their voice
with the trumpets and cymbals
and instruments of musick,
and praised the LORD,
saying,
For he is good;
for his mercy endureth for ever:
that then the house was filled with
a cloud, even the house of the
LORD;
14 **So that the priests** could not
stand to minister by reason of the
cloud:
for the glory of the LORD had
filled the house of God.

6 **Then** said Solomon,
The LORD hath said
that he would dwell in the thick
darkness.
2 **But I** have built an house of
habitation for thee, and a place
for thy dwelling for ever.
3 **And the king** turned his face,
and blessed the whole congregation
of Israel:
and all the congregation of Israel
stood.
4 **And he** said,
Blessed be the LORD God of Israel,
who hath with his hands fulfilled
that which he spake with his
mouth to my father David,
saying,
5 **Since the day that I brought
forth my people out of the land
of Egypt** I chose no city among all
the tribes of Israel to build an
house in,
that my name might be there;
neither chose I any man to be a
ruler over my people Israel:
6 **But I** have chosen Jerusalem,
that my name might be there;
and have chosen David to be over
my people Israel.
7 **Now it was in the heart of David
my father** to build an house for
the name of the LORD God of
Israel.
8 **But the LORD** said to David my
father,
**Forasmuch as it was in thine
heart** to build an house for my
name,
thou didst well in that it was in
thine heart:
9 **Notwithstanding thou** shalt not
build the house;
**but thy son which shall come
forth out of thy loins,** he shall
build the house for my name.
10 **The LORD** therefore hath
performed his word that he hath
spoken:
for I am risen up in the room of
David my father,
and am set on the throne of Israel,
as the LORD promised,
and have built the house for the
name of the LORD God of Israel.
11 **And in it** have I put the ark,
wherein is the covenant of the
LORD,
that he made with the children of
Israel.
12 **And he** stood before the altar of
the LORD in the presence of all
the congregation of Israel,
and spread forth his hands:
13 **For Solomon** had made a brasen
scaffold of five cubits long, and
five cubits broad, and three cubits
high,
and had set it in the midst of the
court:
and upon it he stood,
and kneeled down upon his knees
before all the congregation of
Israel,
and spread forth his hands toward
heaven.
14 **And** said,
O LORD God of Israel, there is no
God like thee in the heaven, nor in
the earth;
which keepest covenant,
and shewest mercy unto thy
servants,
that walk before thee with all their
hearts:
15 Thou which hast kept with thy
servant David my father that
which thou hast promised him;
and spakest with thy mouth,
and hast fulfilled it with thine
hand,
as it is this day.

16 **Now therefore, O LORD God of Israel, keep** with thy servant David my father that which thou hast promised him,
saying,
There shall not fail thee a man in my sight
to sit upon the throne of Israel;
yet so that thy children take heed to their way to walk in my law,
as thou hast walked before me.

17 **Now then, O LORD God of Israel, let thy word** be verified,
which thou hast spoken unto thy servant David.

18 **But will God in very deed** dwell with men on the earth?
behold,
heaven and the heaven of heavens cannot contain thee;
how much less this house which I have built!

19 **Have** respect therefore to the prayer of thy servant, and to his supplication, O LORD my God,
to hearken unto the cry and the prayer which thy servant prayeth before thee:
20 **That thine eyes** may be open upon this house day and night, upon the place whereof thou hast said that thou wouldest put thy name there;
to hearken unto the prayer which thy servant prayeth toward this place.

21 **Hearken** therefore unto the supplications of thy servant, and of thy people Israel,
which they shall make toward this place:
hear thou from thy dwelling place, even from heaven;
and when thou hearest,
forgive.

22 **If a man** sin against his neighbour,
and an oath be laid upon him to make him swear,
and the oath come before thine altar in this house;
23 **Then hear thou** from heaven,
and do,
and judge thy servants,
by requiting the wicked,
by recompensing his way upon his own head;
and by justifying the righteous,
by giving him according to his righteousness.

24 **And if thy people Israel** be put to the worse before the enemy,
because they have sinned against thee;
and shall return and confess thy name,
and pray and make supplication before thee in this house;
25 **Then hear thou** from the heavens,
and forgive the sin of thy people Israel,
and bring them again unto the land which thou gavest to them and to their fathers.

26 **When the heaven** is shut up,
and there is no rain,
because they have sinned against thee;
yet if they pray toward this place,
and confess thy name,
and turn from their sin,
when thou dost afflict them;
27 **Then hear thou** from heaven,
and forgive the sin of thy servants, and of thy people Israel,
when thou hast taught them the good way, wherein they should walk;
and send rain upon thy land,
which thou hast given unto thy people for an inheritance.

28 **If there** be dearth in the land,
if there be pestilence,
if there be blasting, or mildew, locusts, or caterpillers;
if their enemies besiege them in the cities of their land;
whatsoever sore or whatsoever sickness there be:
29 **Then what prayer or what supplication soever** shall be made of any man, or of all thy people Israel,
when every one shall know his own sore and his own grief,
and shall spread forth his hands in this house:
30 **Then hear thou** from heaven thy dwelling place,
and forgive,
and render unto every man according unto all his ways,
whose heart thou knowest; (for thou only knowest the hearts of the children of men:)
31 **That they** may fear thee,
to walk in thy ways,
so long as they live in the land which thou gavest unto our fathers.

32 **Moreover concerning the stranger**, {which is not of thy people Israel}, {but is come from a far country for thy great name's sake, and thy mighty hand, and thy stretched out arm}; if they come and pray in this house;
33 **Then hear thou** from the heavens, even from thy dwelling place,
and do according to all that the stranger calleth to thee for;
that all people of the earth may know thy name,
and fear thee,
as doth thy people Israel,
and may know
that this house which I have built is called by thy name.

34 **If thy people** go out to war against their enemies by the way that thou shalt send them,
and they pray unto thee toward this city which thou hast chosen, and the house which I have built for thy name;
35 **Then hear thou** from the heavens their prayer and their supplication,
and maintain their cause.

36 **If they** sin against thee, (for there is no man which sinneth not,)
and thou be angry with them,
and deliver them over before their enemies,
and they carry them away captives unto a land far off or near;
37 **Yet if they** bethink themselves in the land whither they are carried captive,
and turn and pray unto thee in the land of their captivity,
saying,
We have sinned,
we have done amiss,
and have dealt wickedly;
38 **If they** return to thee with all their heart and with all their soul in the land of their captivity,
whither they have carried them captives,
and pray toward their land,
which thou gavest unto their fathers, and toward the city which thou hast chosen, and toward the house which I have built for thy name:
39 **Then hear thou** from the heavens, even from thy dwelling place, their prayer and their supplications,

and maintain their cause,
and forgive thy people which have sinned against thee.

40 **Now, my God, let, {I beseech thee}, thine eyes** be open,
and let thine ears be attent unto the prayer that is made in this place.

41 **Now therefore arise**, O LORD God, into thy resting place, thou, and the ark of thy strength:
let thy priests, O LORD God, be clothed with salvation,
and let thy saints rejoice in goodness.

42 **O LORD God, turn not away** the face of thine anointed:
remember the mercies of David thy servant.

7 **Now when Solomon** had made an end of praying,
the fire came down from heaven,
and consumed the burnt offering and the sacrifices;
and the glory of the LORD filled the house.

2 **And the priests** could not enter into the house of the LORD,
because the glory of the LORD had filled the LORD's house.

3 **And when all the children of Israel** saw how the fire came down, and the glory of the LORD upon the house,
they bowed themselves with their faces to the ground upon the pavement,
and worshipped,
and praised the LORD,
saying,
For he is good;
for his mercy endureth for ever.

4 **Then the king and all the people** offered sacrifices before the LORD.

5 **And king Solomon** offered a sacrifice of twenty and two thousand oxen, and an hundred and twenty thousand sheep:
so the king and all the people dedicated the house of God.

6 **And the priests** waited on their offices: the Levites also with instruments of musick of the LORD,
which David the king had made to praise the LORD,
because his mercy endureth for ever,
when David praised by their ministry;
and the priests sounded trumpets before them,
and all Israel stood.

7 **Moreover Solomon** hallowed the middle of the court that was before the house of the LORD:
for there he offered burnt offerings, and the fat of the peace offerings,
because the brasen altar which Solomon had made was not able to receive the burnt offerings, and the meat offerings, and the fat.

8 **Also at the same time** Solomon kept the feast seven days, and all Israel with him, a very great congregation, from the entering in of Hamath unto the river of Egypt.

9 **And in the eighth day** they made a solemn assembly:
for they kept the dedication of the altar seven days, and the feast seven days.

10 **And on the three and twentieth day of the seventh month** he sent the people away into their tents, glad and merry in heart for the goodness that the LORD had shewed unto David, and to Solomon, and to Israel his people.

11 **Thus Solomon** finished the house of the LORD, and the king's house:
and all that came into Solomon's heart to make in the house of the LORD, and in his own house, he prosperously effected.

12 **And the LORD** appeared to Solomon by night,
and said unto him,
I have heard thy prayer,
and have chosen this place to myself for an house of sacrifice.

13 **If I** shut up heaven
that there be no rain,
or if I command the locusts to devour the land,
or if I send pestilence among my people;

14 **If my people**, {which are called by my name}, shall humble themselves,
and pray,
and seek my face,
and turn from their wicked ways;
then will I hear from heaven,
and will forgive their sin,
and will heal their land.

15 **Now mine eyes** shall be open, and mine ears attent unto the prayer that is made in this place.

16 **For now** have I chosen and sanctified this house,
that my name may be there for ever:
and mine eyes and mine heart shall be there perpetually.

17 **And as for thee,** if thou wilt walk before me,
as David thy father walked,
and do according to all that I have commanded thee,
and shalt observe my statutes and my judgments;

18 **Then** will I stablish the throne of thy kingdom,
according as I have covenanted with David thy father,
saying,
There shall not fail thee a man to be ruler in Israel.

19 **But if ye** turn away,
and forsake my statutes and my commandments,
which I have set before you,
and shall go and serve other gods,
and worship them;

20 **Then** will I pluck them up by the roots out of my land which I have given them;
and this house, {which I have sanctified for my name}, will I cast out of my sight,
and will make it to be a proverb and a byword among all nations.

21 **And this house**, {which is high}, shall be an astonishment to every one that passeth by it;
so that he shall say,
Why hath the LORD done thus unto this land, and unto this house?

22 **And it** shall be answered,
Because they forsook the LORD God of their fathers,
which brought them forth out of the land of Egypt,
and laid hold on other gods,
and worshipped them,
and served them:
therefore hath he brought all this evil upon them.

8 **And it** came to pass at the end of twenty years,
wherein Solomon had built the house of the LORD, and his own house,

2 **That the cities which Huram had restored to Solomon,** Solomon built them,
and caused the children of Israel to dwell there.

3 **And Solomon** went to Hamathzobah,
and prevailed against it.

4 **And he** built Tadmor in the wilderness, and all the store cities,
which he built in Hamath.

5 **Also he** built Bethhoron the upper, and Bethhoron the nether, fenced cities, with walls, gates, and bars;
6 And Baalath, and all the store cities that Solomon had, and all the chariot cities, and the cities of the horsemen, and all that Solomon desired to build in Jerusalem, and in Lebanon, and throughout all the land of his dominion.

7 **As for all the people that were left of the Hittites, and the Amorites, and the Perizzites, and the Hivites, and the Jebusites,** {which were not of Israel},
8 But of their children, {who were left after them in the land}, {whom the children of Israel consumed not}, them did Solomon make to pay tribute until this day.

9 **But of the children of Israel** did Solomon make no servants for his work;
but they were men of war, and chief of his captains, and captains of his chariots and horsemen.

10 **And these** were the chief of king Solomon's officers, even two hundred and fifty,
that bare rule over the people.

11 **And Solomon** brought up the daughter of Pharaoh out of the city of David unto the house that he had built for her:
for he said,
My wife shall not dwell in the house of David king of Israel,
because the places are holy,
whereunto the ark of the LORD hath come.

12 **Then Solomon** offered burnt offerings unto the LORD on the altar of the LORD,
which he had built before the porch,

13 Even after a certain rate every day,
offering according to the commandment of Moses, on the sabbaths, and on the new moons, and on the solemn feasts, three times in the year, even in the feast of unleavened bread, and in the feast of weeks, and in the feast of tabernacles.

14 **And he** appointed, according to the order of David his father, the courses of the priests to their service, and the Levites to their charges,
to praise and minister before the priests,
as the duty of every day required: the porters also by their courses at every gate:
for so had David the man of God commanded.

15 **And they** departed not from the commandment of the king unto the priests and Levites concerning any matter, or concerning the treasures.

16 **Now all the work of Solomon** was prepared unto the day of the foundation of the house of the LORD,
and until it was finished.

So the house of the LORD was perfected.

17 **Then** went Solomon to Eziongeber, and to Eloth, at the sea side in the land of Edom.

18 **And Huram** sent him by the hands of his servants ships, and servants that had knowledge of the sea;
and they went with the servants of Solomon to Ophir,
and took thence four hundred and fifty talents of gold,
and brought them to king Solomon.

9 **And when the queen of Sheba** heard of the fame of Solomon,
she came to prove Solomon with hard questions at Jerusalem, with a very great company, and camels that bare spices, and gold in abundance, and precious stones:
and when she was come to Solomon,
she communed with him of all that was in her heart.

2 **And Solomon** told her all her questions:
and there was nothing hid from Solomon which he told her not.

3 **And when the queen of Sheba** had seen the wisdom of Solomon, and the house that he had built,
4 And the meat of his table, and the sitting of his servants, and the attendance of his ministers, and their apparel; his cupbearers also, and their apparel; and his ascent by which he went up into the house of the LORD;
there was no more spirit in her.

5 **And she** said to the king,
It was a true report which I heard in mine own land of thine acts, and of thy wisdom:
6 **Howbeit I** believed not their words,
until I came,
and mine eyes had seen it:
and, {behold}, the one half of the greatness of thy wisdom was not told me:
for thou exceedest the fame that I heard.

7 **Happy** are thy men,
and happy are these thy servants,
which stand continually before thee,
and hear thy wisdom.

8 **Blessed** be the LORD thy God,
which delighted in thee to set thee on his throne, to be king for the LORD thy God:
because thy God loved Israel,
to establish them for ever,
therefore made he thee king over them,
to do judgment and justice.

9 **And she** gave the king an hundred and twenty talents of gold, and of spices great abundance, and precious stones:
neither was there any such spice as the queen of Sheba gave king Solomon.

10 **And the servants also of Huram, and the servants of Solomon,** {which brought gold from Ophir}, brought algum trees and precious stones.

11 **And the king** made of the algum trees terraces to the house of the LORD, and to the king's palace, and harps and psalteries for singers:
and there were none such seen before in the land of Judah.

12 **And king Solomon** gave to the queen of Sheba all her desire,
whatsoever she asked, beside that which she had brought unto the king.
So she turned,
and went away to her own land, she and her servants.

13 **Now the weight of gold that came to Solomon in one year** was six hundred and threescore and six talents of gold;
14 Beside that which chapmen and merchants brought.
And all the kings of Arabia and governors of the country brought gold and silver to Solomon.

15 **And king Solomon** made two hundred targets of beaten gold:
six hundred shekels of beaten gold went to one target.

16 **And three hundred shields** made he of beaten gold:
three hundred shekels of gold went to one shield.
And the king put them in the house of the forest of Lebanon.

17 **Moreover the king** made a great throne of ivory,
and overlaid it with pure gold.

18 **And there** were six steps to the throne, with a footstool of gold,
which were fastened to the throne, and stays on each side of the sitting place, and two lions standing by the stays:

19 **And twelve lions** stood there on the one side and on the other upon the six steps.
There was not the like made in any kingdom.

20 **And all the drinking vessels of king Solomon** were of gold,
and all the vessels of the house of the forest of Lebanon were of pure gold:
none were of silver;
it was not any thing accounted of in the days of Solomon.

21 **For the king's ships** went to Tarshish with the servants of Huram:
every three years once came the ships of Tarshish bringing gold, and silver, ivory, and apes, and peacocks.

22 **And king Solomon** passed all the kings of the earth in riches and wisdom.

23 **And all the kings of the earth** sought the presence of Solomon,
to hear his wisdom,
that God had put in his heart.

24 **And they** brought every man his present, vessels of silver, and vessels of gold, and raiment, harness, and spices, horses, and mules, a rate year by year.

25 **And Solomon** had four thousand stalls for horses and chariots, and twelve thousand horsemen;
whom he bestowed in the chariot cities, and with the king at Jerusalem.

26 **And he** reigned over all the kings from the river even unto the land of the Philistines, and to the border of Egypt.

27 **And the king** made silver in Jerusalem as stones,
and cedar trees made he as the sycomore trees that are in the low plains in abundance.

28 **And they** brought unto Solomon horses out of Egypt, and out of all lands.

29 **Now the rest of the acts of Solomon, first and last,** are they not written in the book of Nathan the prophet, and in the prophecy of Ahijah the Shilonite, and in the visions of Iddo the seer against Jeroboam the son of Nebat?

30 **And Solomon** reigned in Jerusalem over all Israel forty years.

31 **And Solomon** slept with his fathers,
and he was buried in the city of David his father:
and Rehoboam his son reigned in his stead.

10 **And Rehoboam** went to Shechem:
for to Shechem were all Israel come to make him king.

2 **And it** came to pass,
when Jeroboam the son of Nebat, {who was in Egypt}, {whither he fled from the presence of Solomon the king}, heard it,
that Jeroboam returned out of Egypt.

3 **And they** sent and called him.
So Jeroboam and all Israel came and spake to Rehoboam,
saying,
4 **Thy father** made our yoke grievous:
now therefore ease thou somewhat the grievous servitude of thy father, and his heavy yoke that he put upon us,
and we will serve thee.

5 **And he** said unto them,
Come again unto me after three days.
And the people departed.

6 **And king Rehoboam** took counsel with the old men that had stood before Solomon his father
while he yet lived,
saying,
What counsel give ye me to return answer to this people?

7 **And they** spake unto him,
saying,
If thou be kind to this people,
and please them,
and speak good words to them,
they will be thy servants for ever.

8 **But he** forsook the counsel which the old men gave him,
and took counsel with the young men that were brought up with him, that stood before him.

9 **And he** said unto them,
What advice give ye that we may return answer to this people,
which have spoken to me,
saying,
Ease somewhat the yoke that thy father did put upon us?

10 **And the young men that were brought up with him** spake unto him,
saying,
Thus shalt thou answer the people that spake unto thee,
saying,
Thy father made our yoke heavy,
but make thou it somewhat lighter for us;
thus shalt thou say unto them,
My little finger shall be thicker than my father's loins.

11 **For whereas my father** put a heavy yoke upon you,
I will put more to your yoke:
my father chastised you with whips,
but I will chastise you with scorpions.

[12] **So Jeroboam and all the people** came to Rehoboam on the third day,
as the king bade,
saying,
Come again to me on the third day.
[13] **And the king** answered them roughly;
and king Rehoboam forsook the counsel of the old men,
[14] **And** answered them after the advice of the young men,
saying,
My father made your yoke heavy,
but I will add thereto:
my father chastised you with whips,
but I will chastise you with scorpions.
[15] **So the king** hearkened not unto the people:
for the cause was of God,
that the LORD might perform his word,
which he spake by the hand of Ahijah the Shilonite to Jeroboam the son of Nebat.
[16] **And when all Israel** saw
that the king would not hearken unto them,
the people answered the king,
saying,
What portion have we in David?
and we have none inheritance in the son of Jesse: every man to your tents, O Israel:
and now, David, see to thine own house.
So all Israel went to their tents.
[17] **But as for the children of Israel that dwelt in the cities of Judah,** Rehoboam reigned over them.
[18] **Then king Rehoboam** sent Hadoram that was over the tribute;
and the children of Israel stoned him with stones,
that he died.
But king Rehoboam made speed to get him up to his chariot,
to flee to Jerusalem.
[19] **And Israel** rebelled against the house of David unto this day.

11 **And when Rehoboam** was come to Jerusalem,
he gathered of the house of Judah and Benjamin an hundred and fourscore thousand chosen men,
which were warriors,
to fight against Israel,
that he might bring the kingdom again to Rehoboam.
[2] **But the word of the LORD** came to Shemaiah the man of God,
saying,
[3] **Speak** unto Rehoboam the son of Solomon, king of Judah, and to all Israel in Judah and Benjamin,
saying,
[4] **Thus** saith the LORD,
Ye shall not go up,
nor fight against your brethren:
return every man to his house:
for this thing is done of me.
And they obeyed the words of the LORD,
and returned from going against Jeroboam.
[5] **And Rehoboam** dwelt in Jerusalem,
and built cities for defence in Judah.
[6] **He** built even Bethlehem, and Etam, and Tekoa,
[7] And Bethzur, and Shoco, and Adullam,
[8] And Gath, and Mareshah, and Ziph,
[9] And Adoraim, and Lachish, and Azekah,
[10] And Zorah, and Aijalon, and Hebron,
which are in Judah and in Benjamin fenced cities.
[11] **And he** fortified the strong holds,
and put captains in them, and store of victual, and of oil and wine.
[12] **And in every several city** he put shields and spears,
and made them exceeding strong,
having Judah and Benjamin on his side.
[13] **And the priests and the Levites that were in all Israel** resorted to him out of all their coasts.
[14] **For the Levites** left their suburbs and their possession,
and came to Judah and Jerusalem:
for Jeroboam and his sons had cast them off from executing the priest's office unto the LORD:
[15] **And he** ordained him priests for the high places, and for the devils, and for the calves which he had made.
[16] **And after them out of all the tribes of Israel such as set their hearts to seek the LORD God of Israel** came to Jerusalem,
to sacrifice unto the LORD God of their fathers.
[17] **So they** strengthened the kingdom of Judah,
and made Rehoboam the son of Solomon strong, three years:
for three years they walked in the way of David and Solomon.
[18] **And Rehoboam** took him Mahalath the daughter of Jerimoth the son of David to wife, and Abihail the daughter of Eliab the son of Jesse;
[19] **Which** bare him children; Jeush, and Shamariah, and Zaham.
[20] **And after her** he took Maachah the daughter of Absalom;
which bare him Abijah, and Attai, and Ziza, and Shelomith.
[21] **And Rehoboam** loved Maachah the daughter of Absalom above all his wives and his concubines:
(for he took eighteen wives, and threescore concubines;
and begat twenty and eight sons, and threescore daughters.)
[22] **And Rehoboam** made Abijah the son of Maachah the chief, to be ruler among his brethren:
for he thought
to make him king.
[23] **And he** dealt wisely,
and dispersed of all his children throughout all the countries of Judah and Benjamin, unto every fenced city:
and he gave them victual in abundance.
And he desired many wives.

12 **And it** came to pass, **when Rehoboam** had established the kingdom,
and had strengthened himself,
he forsook the law of the LORD, and all Israel with him.
[2] **And it** came to pass,
that in the fifth year of king Rehoboam Shishak king of Egypt came up against Jerusalem,
because they had transgressed against the LORD,
[3] With twelve hundred chariots, and threescore thousand horsemen:
and the people were without number that came with him out of Egypt; the Lubims, the Sukkiims, and the Ethiopians.
[4] **And he** took the fenced cities which pertained to Judah,

and came to Jerusalem.

5 **Then** came Shemaiah the prophet to Rehoboam, and to the princes of Judah,
that were gathered together to Jerusalem because of Shishak,
and said unto them,
Thus saith the LORD,
Ye have forsaken me,
and therefore have I also left you in the hand of Shishak.

6 **Whereupon the princes of Israel and the king** humbled themselves;
and they said,
The LORD is righteous.

7 **And when the LORD** saw that they humbled themselves,
the word of the LORD came to Shemaiah,
saying,
They have humbled themselves;
therefore I will not destroy them,
but I will grant them some deliverance;
and my wrath shall not be poured out upon Jerusalem by the hand of Shishak.

8 **Nevertheless they** shall be his servants;
that they may know my service, and the service of the kingdoms of the countries.

9 **So Shishak king of Egypt** came up against Jerusalem,
and took away the treasures of the house of the LORD, and the treasures of the king's house;
he took all:
he carried away also the shields of gold which Solomon had made.

10 **Instead of which king Rehoboam** made shields of brass,
and committed them to the hands of the chief of the guard,
that kept the entrance of the king's house.

11 **And when the king** entered into the house of the LORD,
the guard came and fetched them,
and brought them again into the guard chamber.

12 **And when he** humbled himself,
the wrath of the LORD turned from him,
that he would not destroy him altogether:
and also in Judah things went well.

13 **So king Rehoboam** strengthened himself in Jerusalem,
and reigned:
for Rehoboam was one and forty years old
when he began to reign,
and he reigned seventeen years in Jerusalem, the city which the LORD had chosen out of all the tribes of Israel,
to put his name there.

And his mother's name was Naamah an Ammonitess.

14 **And he** did evil,
because he prepared not his heart to seek the LORD.

15 **Now the acts of Rehoboam, first and last,** are they not written in the book of Shemaiah the prophet, and of Iddo the seer concerning genealogies?

And there were wars between Rehoboam and Jeroboam continually.

16 **And Rehoboam** slept with his fathers,
and was buried in the city of David:
and Abijah his son reigned in his stead.

13

Now in the eighteenth year of king Jeroboam began Abijah to reign over Judah.

2 **He** reigned three years in Jerusalem.

His mother's name also was Michaiah the daughter of Uriel of Gibeah.

And there was war between Abijah and Jeroboam.

3 **And Abijah** set the battle in array with an army of valiant men of war, even four hundred thousand chosen men:
Jeroboam also set the battle in array against him with eight hundred thousand chosen men,
being mighty men of valour.

4 **And Abijah** stood up upon mount Zemaraim,
which is in mount Ephraim,
and said,
Hear me, thou Jeroboam, and all Israel;

5 **Ought ye not** to know
that the LORD God of Israel gave the kingdom over Israel to David for ever, even to him and to his sons by a covenant of salt?

6 **Yet Jeroboam the son of Nebat, the servant of Solomon the son of David,** is risen up,
and hath rebelled against his lord.

7 **And there** are gathered unto him vain men, the children of Belial,
and have strengthened themselves against Rehoboam the son of Solomon,
when Rehoboam was young and tenderhearted,
and could not withstand them.

8 **And now ye** think to withstand the kingdom of the LORD in the hand of the sons of David;
and ye be a great multitude,
and there are with your golden calves,
which Jeroboam made you for gods.

9 **Have ye not** cast out the priests of the LORD, the sons of Aaron, and the Levites,
and have made you priests after the manner of the nations of other lands?
so that whosoever cometh to consecrate himself with a young bullock and seven rams,
the same may be a priest of them that are no gods.

10 **But as for us,** the LORD is our God,
and we have not forsaken him;
and the priests, {which minister unto the LORD}, are the sons of Aaron,
and the Levites wait upon their business:

11 **And they** burn unto the LORD every morning and every evening burnt sacrifices and sweet incense:
the shewbread also set they in order upon the pure table; and the candlestick of gold with the lamps thereof,
to burn every evening:
for we keep the charge of the LORD our God;
but ye have forsaken him.

12 **And, {behold}, God himself** is with us for our captain, and his priests with sounding trumpets to cry alarm against you.

O children of Israel, fight ye not against the LORD God of your fathers;
for ye shall not prosper.

13 **But Jeroboam** caused an ambushment to come about behind them:
so they were before Judah,

and the ambushment was behind them.
14 **And when Judah** looked back,
behold,
the battle was before and behind:
and they cried unto the LORD,
and the priests sounded with the trumpets.
15 **Then the men of Judah** gave a shout:
and as the men of Judah shouted,
it came to pass,
that God smote Jeroboam and all Israel before Abijah and Judah.
16 **And the children of Israel** fled before Judah:
and God delivered them into their hand.
17 **And Abijah and his people** slew them with a great slaughter:
so there fell down slain of Israel five hundred thousand chosen men.
18 **Thus the children of Israel** were brought under at that time,
and the children of Judah prevailed,
because they relied upon the LORD God of their fathers.
19 **And Abijah** pursued after Jeroboam,
and took cities from him, Bethel with the towns thereof, and Jeshanah with the towns thereof, and Ephraim with the towns thereof.
20 **Neither** did Jeroboam recover strength again in the days of Abijah:
and the LORD struck him,
and he died.
21 **But Abijah** waxed mighty,
and married fourteen wives,
and begat twenty and two sons, and sixteen daughters.
22 **And the rest of the acts of Abijah, and his ways, and his sayings,** are written in the story of the prophet Iddo.

14 **So Abijah** slept with his fathers,
and they buried him in the city of David:
and Asa his son reigned in his stead.
In his days the land was quiet ten years.
2 **And Asa** did that which was good and right in the eyes of the LORD his God:
3 **For he** took away the altars of the strange gods, and the high places,
and brake down the images,
and cut down the groves:
4 **And** commanded Judah to seek the LORD God of their fathers,
and to do the law and the commandment.
5 **Also he** took away out of all the cities of Judah the high places and the images:
and the kingdom was quiet before him.
6 **And he** built fenced cities in Judah:
for the land had rest,
and he had no war in those years;
because the LORD had given him rest.
7 **Therefore he** said unto Judah,
Let us build these cities,
and make about them walls, and towers, gates, and bars,
while the land is yet before us;
because we have sought the LORD our God,
we have sought him,
and he hath given us rest on every side.
So they built and prospered.
8 **And Asa** had an army of men that bare targets and spears, out of Judah three hundred thousand; and out of Benjamin, {that bare shields and drew bows}, two hundred and fourscore thousand:
all these were mighty men of valour.
9 **And there** came out against them Zerah the Ethiopian with an host of a thousand thousand, and three hundred chariots;
and came unto Mareshah.
10 **Then Asa** went out against him,
and they set the battle in array in the valley of Zephathah at Mareshah.
11 **And Asa** cried unto the LORD his God,
and said,
LORD, it is nothing with thee to help, whether with many, or with them that have no power:
help us, O LORD our God;
for we rest on thee,
and in thy name we go against this multitude.
O LORD, thou art our God;
let no man prevail against thee.
12 **So the LORD** smote the Ethiopians before Asa, and before Judah;
and the Ethiopians fled.
13 **And Asa and the people that were with him** pursued them unto Gerar:
and the Ethiopians were overthrown,
that they could not recover themselves;
for they were destroyed before the LORD, and before his host;
and they carried away very much spoil.
14 **And they** smote all the cities round about Gerar;
for the fear of the LORD came upon them:
and they spoiled all the cities;
for there was exceeding much spoil in them.
15 **They** smote also the tents of cattle,
and carried away sheep and camels in abundance,
and returned to Jerusalem.

15 **And the Spirit of God** came upon Azariah the son of Oded:
2 **And he** went out to meet Asa,
and said unto him,
Hear ye me, Asa, and all Judah and Benjamin;
The LORD is with you,
while ye be with him;
and if ye seek him,
he will be found of you;
but if ye forsake him,
he will forsake you.
3 **Now for a long season** Israel hath been without the true God, and without a teaching priest, and without law.
4 **But when they in their trouble** did turn unto the LORD God of Israel,
and sought him,
he was found of them.
5 **And in those times** there was no peace to him that went out, nor to him that came in,
but great vexations were upon all the inhabitants of the countries.
6 **And nation** was destroyed of nation, and city of city:
for God did vex them with all adversity.
7 **Be ye** strong therefore,

and let not your hands be weak:
for your work shall be rewarded.

8 **And when Asa** heard these words, and the prophecy of Oded the prophet,
he took courage,
and put away the abominable idols out of all the land of Judah and Benjamin, and out of the cities which he had taken from mount Ephraim,
and renewed the altar of the LORD,
that was before the porch of the LORD.

9 **And he** gathered all Judah and Benjamin, and the strangers with them out of Ephraim and Manasseh, and out of Simeon:
for they fell to him out of Israel in abundance,
when they saw that the LORD his God was with him.

10 **So they** gathered themselves together at Jerusalem in the third month, in the fifteenth year of the reign of Asa.

11 **And they** offered unto the LORD the same time, of the spoil which they had brought, seven hundred oxen and seven thousand sheep.

12 **And they** entered into a covenant to seek the LORD God of their fathers with all their heart and with all their soul;

13 **That whosoever would not seek the LORD God of Israel** should be put to death, whether small or great, whether man or woman.

14 **And they** sware unto the LORD with a loud voice, and with shouting, and with trumpets, and with cornets.

15 **And all Judah** rejoiced at the oath:
for they had sworn with all their heart,
and sought him with their whole desire;
and he was found of them:
and the LORD gave them rest round about.

16 **And also concerning Maachah the mother of Asa the king,** he removed her from being queen,
because she had made an idol in a grove:
and Asa cut down her idol,
and stamped it,
and burnt it at the brook Kidron.

17 **But the high places** were not taken away out of Israel:
nevertheless the heart of Asa was perfect all his days.

18 **And he** brought into the house of God the things that his father had dedicated, and that he himself had dedicated, silver, and gold, and vessels.

19 **And there** was no more war unto the five and thirtieth year of the reign of Asa.

16

In the six and thirtieth year of the reign of Asa Baasha king of Israel came up against Judah,
and built Ramah,
to the intent that he might let none go out or come in to Asa king of Judah.

2 **Then Asa** brought out silver and gold out of the treasures of the house of the LORD and of the king's house,
and sent to Benhadad king of Syria,
that dwelt at Damascus,
saying,

3 **There** is a league between me and thee,
as there was between my father and thy father:
behold,
I have sent thee silver and gold;
go,
break thy league with Baasha king of Israel,
that he may depart from me.

4 **And Benhadad** hearkened unto king Asa,
and sent the captains of his armies against the cities of Israel;
and they smote Ijon, and Dan, and Abelmaim, and all the store cities of Naphtali.

5 **And it** came to pass,
when Baasha heard it,
that he left off building of Ramah,
and let his work cease.

6 **Then Asa the king** took all Judah;
and they carried away the stones of Ramah, and the timber thereof,
wherewith Baasha was building;
and he built therewith Geba and Mizpah.

7 **And at that time** Hanani the seer came to Asa king of Judah,
and said unto him,
Because thou hast relied on the king of Syria,
and not relied on the LORD thy God,
therefore is the host of the king of Syria escaped out of thine hand.

8 **Were not the Ethiopians and the Lubims** a huge host, with very many chariots and horsemen?
yet, {because thou didst rely on the LORD}, he delivered them into thine hand.

9 **For the eyes of the LORD** run to and fro throughout the whole earth,
to shew himself strong in the behalf of them whose heart is perfect toward him.
Herein thou hast done foolishly:
therefore from henceforth thou shalt have wars.

10 **Then Asa** was wroth with the seer,
and put him in a prison house;
for he was in a rage with him because of this thing.
And Asa oppressed some of the people the same time.

11 **And, {behold}, the acts of Asa, first and last**, {lo}, they are written in the book of the kings of Judah and Israel.

12 **And Asa in the thirty and ninth year of his reign** was diseased in his feet,
until his disease was exceeding great:
yet in his disease he sought not to the LORD, but to the physicians.

13 **And Asa** slept with his fathers,
and died in the one and fortieth year of his reign.

14 **And they** buried him in his own sepulchres,
which he had made for himself in the city of David,
and laid him in the bed which was filled with sweet odours and divers kinds of spices prepared by the apothecaries' art:
and they made a very great burning for him.

17

And Jehoshaphat his son reigned in his stead,
and strengthened himself against Israel.

2 **And he** placed forces in all the fenced cities of Judah,
and set garrisons in the land of Judah, and in the cities of Ephraim,
which Asa his father had taken.

3 **And the LORD** was with Jehoshaphat,
because he walked in the first ways of his father David,
and sought not unto Baalim;
4 **But** sought to the LORD God of his father,
and walked in his commandments, and not after the doings of Israel.
5 **Therefore the LORD** stablished the kingdom in his hand;
and all Judah brought to Jehoshaphat presents;
and he had riches and honour in abundance.
6 **And his heart** was lifted up in the ways of the LORD:
moreover he took away the high places and groves out of Judah.
7 **Also in the third year of his reign** he sent to his princes, even to Benhail, and to Obadiah, and to Zechariah, and to Nethaneel, and to Michaiah,
to teach in the cities of Judah.
8 **And with them** he sent Levites, even Shemaiah, and Nethaniah, and Zebadiah, and Asahel, and Shemiramoth, and Jehonathan, and Adonijah, and Tobijah, and Tobadonijah, Levites; and with them Elishama and Jehoram, priests.
9 **And they** taught in Judah,
and had the book of the law of the LORD with them,
and went about throughout all the cities of Judah,
and taught the people.
10 **And the fear of the LORD** fell upon all the kingdoms of the lands that were round about Judah,
so that they made no war against Jehoshaphat.
11 **Also some of the Philistines** brought Jehoshaphat presents, and tribute silver;
and the Arabians brought him flocks, seven thousand and seven hundred rams, and seven thousand and seven hundred he goats.
12 **And Jehoshaphat** waxed great exceedingly;
and he built in Judah castles, and cities of store.
13 **And he** had much business in the cities of Judah:
and the men of war, mighty men of valour, were in Jerusalem.
14 **And these** are the numbers of them according to the house of their fathers: Of Judah, the captains of thousands; Adnah the chief, and with him mighty men of valour three hundred thousand.
15 **And next to him** was Jehohanan the captain, and with him two hundred and fourscore thousand.
16 **And next him** was Amasiah the son of Zichri,
who willingly offered himself unto the LORD; and with him two hundred thousand mighty men of valour.
17 **And of Benjamin;** Eliada a mighty man of valour, and with him armed men with bow and shield two hundred thousand.
18 **And next him** was Jehozabad, and with him an hundred and fourscore thousand ready prepared for the war.
19 **These** waited on the king, beside those whom the king put in the fenced cities throughout all Judah.

18

Now Jehoshaphat had riches and honour in abundance,
and joined affinity with Ahab.
2 **And after certain years** he went down to Ahab to Samaria.
And Ahab killed sheep and oxen for him in abundance, and for the people that he had with him,
and persuaded him to go up with him to Ramothgilead.
3 **And Ahab king of Israel** said unto Jehoshaphat king of Judah,
Wilt thou go with me to Ramothgilead?
And he answered him,
I am
as thou art, and my people as thy people;
and we will be with thee in the war.
4 **And Jehoshaphat** said unto the king of Israel,
Enquire, {I pray thee}, at the word of the LORD to day.
5 **Therefore the king of Israel** gathered together of prophets four hundred men,
and said unto them,
Shall we go to Ramothgilead to battle,
or shall I forbear?
And they said,
Go up;
for God will deliver it into the king's hand.
6 **But Jehoshaphat** said,
Is there not here a prophet of the LORD besides,
that we might enquire of him?
7 **And the king of Israel** said unto Jehoshaphat,
There is yet one man,
by whom we may enquire of the LORD:
but I hate him;
for he never prophesied good unto me, but always evil:
the same is Micaiah the son of Imla.
And Jehoshaphat said,
Let not the king say so.
8 **And the king of Israel** called for one of his officers,
and said,
Fetch quickly Micaiah the son of Imla.
9 **And the king of Israel and Jehoshaphat king of Judah** sat either of them on his throne,
clothed in their robes,
and they sat in a void place at the entering in of the gate of Samaria;
and all the prophets prophesied before them.
10 **And Zedekiah the son of Chenaanah** had made him horns of iron,
and said,
Thus saith the LORD,
With these thou shalt push Syria
until they be consumed.
11 **And all the prophets** prophesied so,
saying,
Go up to Ramothgilead,
and prosper:
for the LORD shall deliver it into the hand of the king.
12 **And the messenger that went to call Micaiah** spake to him,
saying,
Behold, the words of the prophets declare good to the king with one assent;
let thy word therefore, {I pray thee}, be like one of their's,
and speak thou good.
13 **And Micaiah** said,

As the LORD liveth,
even what my God saith,
that will I speak.

14 **And when he** was come to the king,
the king said unto him,
Micaiah, shall we go to Ramothgilead to battle,
or shall I forbear?

And he said,
Go ye up,
and prosper,
and they shall be delivered into your hand.

15 **And the king** said to him,
How many times shall I adjure thee
that thou say nothing but the truth to me in the name of the LORD?

16 **Then he** said,
I did see all Israel scattered upon the mountains, as sheep that have no shepherd:
and the LORD said,
These have no master;
let them return therefore every man to his house in peace.

17 **And the king of Israel** said to Jehoshaphat,
Did I not tell thee
that he would not prophesy good unto me, but evil?

18 **Again he** said,
Therefore hear the word of the LORD;
I saw the LORD sitting upon his throne,
and all the host of heaven standing on his right hand and on his left.

19 **And the LORD** said,
Who shall entice Ahab king of Israel,
that he may go up and fall at Ramothgilead?

And one spake saying after this manner,
and another saying after that manner.

20 **Then there** came out a spirit,
and stood before the LORD,
and said,
I will entice him.

And the LORD said unto him,
Wherewith?

21 **And he** said,
I will go out,
and be a lying spirit in the mouth of all his prophets.

And the LORD said,
Thou shalt entice him,
and thou shalt also prevail:
go out,
and do even so.

22 **Now therefore, {behold}, the LORD** hath put a lying spirit in the mouth of these thy prophets,
and the LORD hath spoken evil against thee.

23 **Then Zedekiah the son of Chenaanah** came near,
and smote Micaiah upon the cheek,
and said,
Which way went the Spirit of the LORD from me to speak unto thee?

24 **And Micaiah** said,
Behold, thou shalt see on that day
when thou shalt go into an inner chamber to hide thyself.

25 **Then the king of Israel** said,
Take ye Micaiah,
and carry him back to Amon the governor of the city, and to Joash the king's son;

26 **And say,**
Thus saith the king,
Put this fellow in the prison,
and feed him with bread of affliction and with water of affliction,
until I return in peace.

27 **And Micaiah** said,
If thou certainly return in peace,
then hath not the LORD spoken by me.

And he said,
Hearken, all ye people.

28 **So the king of Israel and Jehoshaphat the king of Judah** went up to Ramothgilead.

29 **And the king of Israel** said unto Jehoshaphat,
I will disguise myself,
and I will go to the battle;
but put thou on thy robes.

So the king of Israel disguised himself;
and they went to the battle.

30 **Now the king of Syria** had commanded the captains of the chariots that were with him,
saying,
Fight ye not with small or great,
save only with the king of Israel.

31 **And it** came to pass,
when the captains of the chariots saw Jehoshaphat,
that they said,
It is the king of Israel.

Therefore they compassed about him to fight:
but Jehoshaphat cried out,
and the LORD helped him;
and God moved them to depart from him.

32 **For it** came to pass,
that, {when the captains of the chariots perceived that it was not the king of Israel}, they turned back again from pursuing him.

33 **And a certain man** drew a bow at a venture,
and smote the king of Israel between the joints of the harness:
therefore he said to his chariot man,
Turn thine hand,
that thou mayest carry me out of the host;
for I am wounded.

34 **And the battle** increased that day:
howbeit the king of Israel stayed himself up in his chariot against the Syrians until the even:
and about the time of the sun going down he died.

19 **And Jehoshaphat the king of Judah** returned to his house in peace to Jerusalem.

2 **And Jehu the son of Hanani the seer** went out to meet him,
and said to king Jehoshaphat,
Shouldest thou help the ungodly,
and love them that hate the LORD?
therefore is wrath upon thee from before the LORD.

3 **Nevertheless there** are good things found in thee,
in that thou hast taken away the groves out of the land,
and hast prepared thine heart to seek God.

4 **And Jehoshaphat** dwelt at Jerusalem:
and he went out again through the people from Beersheba to mount Ephraim,
and brought them back unto the LORD God of their fathers.

5 **And he** set judges in the land throughout all the fenced cities of Judah, city by city,

6 **And** said to the judges,
Take heed
what ye do:

for ye judge not for man, but for the LORD,
who is with you in the judgment.
7 **Wherefore now let the fear of the LORD** be upon you;
take heed
and do it:
for there is no iniquity with the LORD our God, nor respect of persons, nor taking of gifts.
8 **Moreover in Jerusalem** did Jehoshaphat set of the Levites, and of the priests, and of the chief of the fathers of Israel, for the judgment of the LORD, and for controversies,
when they returned to Jerusalem.
9 **And he** charged them,
saying,
Thus shall ye do in the fear of the LORD, faithfully, and with a perfect heart.
10 **And what cause soever shall come to you of your brethren that dwell in your cities, between blood and blood, between law and commandment, statutes and judgments,** ye shall even warn them
that they trespass not against the LORD,
and so wrath come upon you, and upon your brethren:
this do,
and ye shall not trespass.
11 **And, {behold}, Amariah the chief priest** is over you in all matters of the LORD; and Zebadiah the son of Ishmael, the ruler of the house of Judah, for all the king's matters:
also the Levites shall be officers before you.
Deal courageously,
and the LORD shall be with the good.

20

It came to pass after this also,
that the children of Moab, and the children of Ammon, and with them other beside the Ammonites, came against Jehoshaphat to battle.
2 **Then there** came some that told Jehoshaphat,
saying,
There cometh a great multitude against thee from beyond the sea on this side Syria;
and, {behold}, they be in Hazazontamar,
which is Engedi.
3 **And Jehoshaphat** feared,
and set himself to seek the LORD,
and proclaimed a fast throughout all Judah.
4 **And Judah** gathered themselves together,
to ask help of the LORD:
even out of all the cities of Judah they came to seek the LORD.
5 **And Jehoshaphat** stood in the congregation of Judah and Jerusalem, in the house of the LORD, before the new court,
6 **And** said,
O LORD God of our fathers, art not thou God in heaven?
and rulest not thou over all the kingdoms of the heathen?
and in thine hand is there not power and might,
so that none is able to withstand thee?
7 **Art not thou** our God,
who didst drive out the inhabitants of this land before thy people Israel,
and gavest it to the seed of Abraham thy friend for ever?
8 **And they** dwelt therein,
and have built thee a sanctuary therein for thy name,
saying,
9 **If, {when evil cometh upon us, as the sword, judgment, or pestilence, or famine},** we stand before this house, and in thy presence,
(for thy name is in this house,)
and cry unto thee in our affliction,
then thou wilt hear and help.
10 **And now, behold, the children of Ammon and Moab and mount Seir**, {whom thou wouldest not let Israel invade}, {when they came out of the land of Egypt}, {but they turned from them}, {and destroyed them not};
11 {Behold}, {I say}, how they reward us,
to come to cast us out of thy possession,
which thou hast given us to inherit.
12 **O our God, wilt thou not** judge them?
for we have no might against this great company that cometh against us;
neither know we
what to do:
but our eyes are upon thee.
13 **And all Judah** stood before the LORD, with their little ones, their wives, and their children.
14 **Then upon Jahaziel the son of Zechariah, the son of Benaiah, the son of Jeiel, the son of Mattaniah, a Levite of the sons of Asaph,** came the Spirit of the LORD in the midst of the congregation;
15 **And he** said,
Hearken ye, all Judah, and ye inhabitants of Jerusalem, and thou king Jehoshaphat,
Thus saith the LORD unto you,
Be not afraid
nor dismayed by reason of this great multitude;
for the battle is not yours, but God's.
16 **To morrow** go ye down against them:
behold,
they come up by the cliff of Ziz;
and ye shall find them at the end of the brook, before the wilderness of Jeruel.
17 **Ye** shall not need to fight in this battle:
set yourselves,
stand ye still,
and see the salvation of the LORD with you, O Judah and Jerusalem:
fear not,
nor be dismayed;
to morrow go out against them:
for the LORD will be with you.
18 **And Jehoshaphat** bowed his head with his face to the ground:
and all Judah and the inhabitants of Jerusalem fell before the LORD,
worshipping the LORD.
19 **And the Levites, of the children of the Kohathites, and of the children of the Korhites,** stood up to praise the LORD God of Israel with a loud voice on high.
20 **And they** rose early in the morning,
and went forth into the wilderness of Tekoa:
and as they went forth,
Jehoshaphat stood and said,

Hear me, O Judah, and ye inhabitants of Jerusalem;
Believe in the LORD your God,
so shall ye be established;
believe his prophets,
so shall ye prosper.
21 **And when he** had consulted with the people,
he appointed singers unto the LORD,
and that should praise the beauty of holiness,
as they went out before the army,
and to say,
Praise the LORD;
for his mercy endureth for ever.
22 **And when they** began to sing and to praise,
the LORD set ambushments against the children of Ammon, Moab, and mount Seir,
which were come against Judah;
and they were smitten.
23 **For the children of Ammon and Moab** stood up against the inhabitants of mount Seir,
utterly to slay and destroy them:
and when they had made an end of the inhabitants of Seir,
every one helped to destroy another.
24 **And when Judah** came toward the watch tower in the wilderness,
they looked unto the multitude,
and, {behold}, they were dead bodies fallen to the earth,
and none escaped.
25 **And when Jehoshaphat and his people** came to take away the spoil of them,
they found among them in abundance both riches with the dead bodies, and precious jewels,
which they stripped off for themselves,
more than they could carry away:
and they were three days in gathering of the spoil,
it was so much.
26 **And on the fourth day** they assembled themselves in the valley of Berachah;
for there they blessed the LORD:
therefore the name of the same place was called, The valley of Berachah, unto this day.
27 **Then they** returned, every man of Judah and Jerusalem, and Jehoshaphat in the forefront of them,
to go again to Jerusalem with joy;
for the LORD had made them to rejoice over their enemies.
28 **And they** came to Jerusalem with psalteries and harps and trumpets unto the house of the LORD.
29 **And the fear of God** was on all the kingdoms of those countries,
when they had heard that the LORD fought against the enemies of Israel.
30 **So the realm of Jehoshaphat** was quiet:
for his God gave him rest round about.
31 **And Jehoshaphat** reigned over Judah:
he was thirty and five years old
when he began to reign,
and he reigned twenty and five years in Jerusalem.
And his mother's name was Azubah the daughter of Shilhi.
32 **And he** walked in the way of Asa his father,
and departed not from it,
doing that which was right in the sight of the LORD.
33 **Howbeit the high places** were not taken away:
for as yet the people had not prepared their hearts unto the God of their fathers.
34 **Now the rest of the acts of Jehoshaphat, first and last,** {behold}, they are written in the book of Jehu the son of Hanani,
who is mentioned in the book of the kings of Israel.
35 **And after this** did Jehoshaphat king of Judah join himself with Ahaziah king of Israel,
who did very wickedly:
36 **And he** joined himself with him to make ships to go to Tarshish:
and they made the ships in Eziongaber.
37 **Then Eliezer the son of Dodavah of Mareshah** prophesied against Jehoshaphat,
saying,
Because thou hast joined thyself with Ahaziah,
the LORD hath broken thy works.
And the ships were broken,
that they were not able to go to Tarshish.

21

Now Jehoshaphat slept with his fathers,
and was buried with his fathers in the city of David.
And Jehoram his son reigned in his stead.
2 **And he** had brethren the sons of Jehoshaphat, Azariah, and Jehiel, and Zechariah, and Azariah, and Michael, and Shephatiah:
all these were the sons of Jehoshaphat king of Israel.
3 **And their father** gave them great gifts of silver, and of gold, and of precious things, with fenced cities in Judah:
but the kingdom gave he to Jehoram;
because he was the firstborn.
4 **Now when Jehoram** was risen up to the kingdom of his father,
he strengthened himself,
and slew all his brethren with the sword, and divers also of the princes of Israel.
5 **Jehoram** was thirty and two years old
when he began to reign,
and he reigned eight years in Jerusalem.
6 **And he** walked in the way of the kings of Israel,
like as did the house of Ahab:
for he had the daughter of Ahab to wife:
and he wrought that which was evil in the eyes of the LORD.
7 **Howbeit the LORD** would not destroy the house of David,
because of the covenant that he had made with David,
and as he promised to give a light to him and to his sons for ever.
8 **In his days** the Edomites revolted from under the dominion of Judah,
and made themselves a king.
9 **Then Jehoram** went forth with his princes, and all his chariots with him:
and he rose up by night,
and smote the Edomites which compassed him in, and the captains of the chariots.
10 **So the Edomites** revolted from under the hand of Judah unto this day.

The same time also did Libnah revolt from under his hand;
because he had forsaken the LORD God of his fathers.
11 **Moreover he** made high places in the mountains of Judah
and caused the inhabitants of Jerusalem to commit fornication,
and compelled Judah thereto.
12 **And there** came a writing to him from Elijah the prophet,
saying,
Thus saith the LORD God of David thy father,
Because thou hast not walked in the ways of Jehoshaphat thy father, nor in the ways of Asa king of Judah,
13 **But** hast walked in the way of the kings of Israel,
and hast made Judah and the inhabitants of Jerusalem to go a whoring, like to the whoredoms of the house of Ahab,
and also hast slain thy brethren of thy father's house,
which were better than thyself:
14 **Behold,**
with a great plague will the LORD smite thy people, and thy children, and thy wives, and all thy goods:
15 **And thou** shalt have great sickness by disease of thy bowels,
until thy bowels fall out by reason of the sickness day by day.
16 **Moreover the LORD** stirred up against Jehoram the spirit of the Philistines, and of the Arabians,
that were near the Ethiopians:
17 **And they** came up into Judah,
and brake into it,
and carried away all the substance that was found in the king's house, and his sons also, and his wives;
so that there was never a son left him, save Jehoahaz, the youngest of his sons.
18 **And after all this** the LORD smote him in his bowels with an incurable disease.
19 **And it** came to pass,
that in process of time, after the end of two years, his bowels fell out by reason of his sickness:
so he died of sore diseases.
And his people made no burning for him, like the burning of his fathers.
20 **Thirty and two years old** was he
when he began to reign,
and he reigned in Jerusalem eight years,
and departed without being desired.
Howbeit they buried him in the city of David, but not in the sepulchres of the kings.

22

And the inhabitants of Jerusalem made Ahaziah his youngest son king in his stead:
for the band of men that came with the Arabians to the camp had slain all the eldest.
So Ahaziah the son of Jehoram king of Judah reigned.
2 **Forty and two years old** was Ahaziah
when he began to reign,
and he reigned one year in Jerusalem.
His mother's name also was Athaliah the daughter of Omri.
3 **He** also walked in the ways of the house of Ahab:
for his mother was his counsellor to do wickedly.
4 **Wherefore he** did evil in the sight of the LORD like the house of Ahab:
for they were his counsellors after the death of his father to his destruction.
5 **He** walked also after their counsel,
and went with Jehoram the son of Ahab king of Israel to war against Hazael king of Syria at Ramothgilead:
and the Syrians smote Joram.
6 **And he** returned to be healed in Jezreel because of the wounds which were given him at Ramah,
when he fought with Hazael king of Syria.
And Azariah the son of Jehoram king of Judah went down to see Jehoram the son of Ahab at Jezreel,
because he was sick.
7 **And the destruction of Ahaziah** was of God
by coming to Joram:
for when he was come,
he went out with Jehoram against Jehu the son of Nimshi,
whom the LORD had anointed to cut off the house of Ahab.
8 **And it** came to pass,
that, {when Jehu was executing judgment upon the house of Ahab}, {and found the princes of Judah, and the sons of the brethren of Ahaziah}, {that ministered to Ahaziah}, he slew them.
9 **And he** sought Ahaziah:
and they caught him, (for he was hid in Samaria,)
and brought him to Jehu:
and when they had slain him,
they buried him:
Because, {said they}, he is the son of Jehoshaphat,
who sought the LORD with all his heart.
So the house of Ahaziah had no power to keep still the kingdom.
10 **But when Athaliah the mother of Ahaziah** saw that her son was dead,
she arose and destroyed all the seed royal of the house of Judah.
11 **But Jehoshabeath, the daughter of the king,** took Joash the son of Ahaziah,
and stole him from among the king's sons that were slain,
and put him and his nurse in a bedchamber.
So Jehoshabeath, the daughter of king Jehoram, the wife of Jehoiada the priest, (for she was the sister of Ahaziah,) hid him from Athaliah,
so that she slew him not.
12 **And he** was with them hid in the house of God six years:
and Athaliah reigned over the land.

23

And in the seventh year Jehoiada strengthened himself,
and took the captains of hundreds, Azariah the son of Jeroham, and Ishmael the son of Jehohanan, and Azariah the son of Obed, and Maaseiah the son of Adaiah, and Elishaphat the son of Zichri, into covenant with him.
2 **And they** went about in Judah,
and gathered the Levites out of all the cities of Judah, and the chief of the fathers of Israel,
and they came to Jerusalem.
3 **And all the congregation** made a covenant with the king in the house of God.
And he said unto them,

Behold,
the king's son shall reign,
as the LORD hath said of the sons of David.

4 **This** is the thing that ye shall do;
A third part of you entering on the sabbath, of the priests and of the Levites, shall be porters of the doors;
5 **And a third part** shall be at the king's house; and a third part at the gate of the foundation:
and all the people shall be in the courts of the house of the LORD.

6 **But let none** come into the house of the LORD, save the priests, and they that minister of the Levites;
they shall go in,
for they are holy:
but all the people shall keep the watch of the LORD.

7 **And the Levites** shall compass the king round about, every man with his weapons in his hand;
and whosoever else cometh into the house,
he shall be put to death:
but be ye with the king
when he cometh in,
and when he goeth out.

8 **So the Levites and all Judah** did according to all things that Jehoiada the priest had commanded,
and took every man his men that were to come in on the sabbath, with them that were to go out on the sabbath:
for Jehoiada the priest dismissed not the courses.

9 **Moreover Jehoiada the priest** delivered to the captains of hundreds spears, and bucklers, and shields, **that** had been king David's,
which were in the house of God.

10 **And he** set all the people,
every man having his weapon in his hand, from the right side of the temple to the left side of the temple, along by the altar and the temple, by the king round about.

11 **Then they** brought out the king's son,
and put upon him the crown,
and gave him the testimony,
and made him king.
And Jehoiada and his sons anointed him,
and said,
God save the king.

12 **Now when Athaliah** heard the noise of the people running and praising the king,
she came to the people into the house of the LORD:
13 **And she** looked,
and, {behold}, the king stood at his pillar at the entering in, and the princes and the trumpets by the king:
and all the people of the land rejoiced,
and sounded with trumpets, also the singers with instruments of musick,
and such as taught to sing praise.
Then Athaliah rent her clothes,
and said,
Treason, Treason.

14 **Then Jehoiada the priest** brought out the captains of hundreds that were set over the host,
and said unto them,
Have her forth of the ranges:
and whoso followeth her, let him be slain with the sword.
For the priest said,
Slay her not in the house of the LORD.

15 **So they** laid hands on her;
and when she was come to the entering of the horse gate by the king's house,
they slew her there.

16 **And Jehoiada** made a covenant between him, and between all the people, and between the king,
that they should be the LORD's people.

17 **Then all the people** went to the house of Baal,
and brake it down,
and brake his altars and his images in pieces,
and slew Mattan the priest of Baal before the altars.

18 **Also Jehoiada** appointed the offices of the house of the LORD by the hand of the priests the Levites,
whom David had distributed in the house of the LORD,
to offer the burnt offerings of the LORD,
as it is written in the law of Moses, with rejoicing and with singing,
as it was ordained by David.

19 **And he** set the porters at the gates of the house of the LORD,
that none which was unclean in any thing should enter in.

20 **And he** took the captains of hundreds, and the nobles, and the governors of the people, and all the people of the land,
and brought down the king from the house of the LORD:
and they came through the high gate into the king's house,
and set the king upon the throne of the kingdom.

21 **And all the people of the land** rejoiced:
and the city was quiet,
after that they had slain Athaliah with the sword.

24

Joash was seven years old **when he** began to reign,
and he reigned forty years in Jerusalem.
His mother's name also was Zibiah of Beersheba.

2 **And Joash** did that which was right in the sight of the LORD all the days of Jehoiada the priest.

3 **And Jehoiada** took for him two wives;
and he begat sons and daughters.

4 **And it** came to pass after this,
that Joash was minded to repair the house of the LORD.

5 **And he** gathered together the priests and the Levites,
and said to them,
Go out unto the cities of Judah,
and gather of all Israel money to repair the house of your God from year to year,
and see that ye hasten the matter.
Howbeit the Levites hastened it not.

6 **And the king** called for Jehoiada the chief,
and said unto him,
Why hast thou not required of the Levites to bring in out of Judah and out of Jerusalem the collection, according to the commandment of Moses the servant of the LORD, and of the congregation of Israel, for the tabernacle of witness?

7 **For the sons of Athaliah, that wicked woman,** had broken up the house of God;

and also all the dedicated things of the house of the LORD did they bestow upon Baalim.

8 **And at the king's commandment** they made a chest,
and set it without at the gate of the house of the LORD.

9 **And they** made a proclamation through Judah and Jerusalem,
to bring in to the LORD the collection that Moses the servant of God laid upon Israel in the wilderness.

10 **And all the princes and all the people** rejoiced,
and brought in,
and cast into the chest,
until they had made an end.

11 **Now it** came to pass,
that at what time the chest was brought unto the king's office by the hand of the Levites,
and when they saw that there was much money,
the king's scribe and the high priest's officer came and emptied the chest,
and took it,
and carried it to his place again.

Thus they did day by day,
and gathered money in abundance.

12 **And the king and Jehoiada** gave it to such as did the work of the service of the house of the LORD,
and hired masons and carpenters to repair the house of the LORD,
and also such as wrought iron and brass to mend the house of the LORD.

13 **So the workmen** wrought,
and the work was perfected by them,
and they set the house of God in his state,
and strengthened it.

14 **And when they** had finished it,
they brought the rest of the money before the king and Jehoiada,
whereof were made vessels for the house of the LORD,
even vessels to minister,
and to offer withal, and spoons, and vessels of gold and silver.

And they offered burnt offerings in the house of the LORD continually all the days of Jehoiada.

15 **But Jehoiada** waxed old,
and was full of days
when he died;
an hundred and thirty years old was he
when he died.

16 **And they** buried him in the city of David among the kings,
because he had done good in Israel, both toward God, and toward his house.

17 **Now after the death of Jehoiada** came the princes of Judah,
and made obeisance to the king.

Then the king hearkened unto them.

18 **And they** left the house of the LORD God of their fathers,
and served groves and idols:
and wrath came upon Judah and Jerusalem for this their trespass.

19 **Yet he** sent prophets to them,
to bring them again unto the LORD;
and they testified against them:
but they would not give ear.

20 **And the Spirit of God** came upon Zechariah the son of Jehoiada the priest,
which stood above the people,
and said unto them,
Thus saith God,
Why transgress ye the commandments of the LORD,
that ye cannot prosper?
because ye have forsaken the LORD,
he hath also forsaken you.

21 **And they** conspired against him,
and stoned him with stones at the commandment of the king in the court of the house of the LORD.

22 **Thus Joash the king** remembered not the kindness which Jehoiada his father had done to him,
but slew his son.

And when he died,
he said,
The LORD look upon it,
and require it.

23 **And it** came to pass at the end of the year,
that the host of Syria came up against him:
and they came to Judah and Jerusalem,
and destroyed all the princes of the people from among the people,
and sent all the spoil of them unto the king of Damascus.

24 **For the army of the Syrians** came with a small company of men,
and the LORD delivered a very great host into their hand,
because they had forsaken the LORD God of their fathers.

So they executed judgment against Joash.

25 **And when they** were departed from him,
(for they left him in great diseases,)
his own servants conspired against him for the blood of the sons of Jehoiada the priest,
and slew him on his bed,
and he died:
and they buried him in the city of David,
but they buried him not in the sepulchres of the kings.

26 **And these** are they that conspired against him; Zabad the son of Shimeath an Ammonitess, and Jehozabad the son of Shimrith a Moabitess.

27 **Now concerning his sons, and the greatness of the burdens laid upon him, and the repairing of the house of God**, {behold}, they are written in the story of the book of the kings.

And Amaziah his son reigned in his stead.

25 **Amaziah** was twenty and five years old
when he began to reign,
and he reigned twenty and nine years in Jerusalem.

And his mother's name was Jehoaddan of Jerusalem.

2 **And he** did that which was right in the sight of the LORD, but not with a perfect heart.

3 **Now it** came to pass,
when the kingdom was established to him,
that he slew his servants that had killed the king his father.

4 **But he** slew not their children,
but did as it is written in the law in the book of Moses,
where the LORD commanded, saying,
The fathers shall not die for the children,
neither shall the children die for the fathers,

but every man shall die for his own sin.

5 **Moreover Amaziah** gathered Judah together,
and made them captains over thousands, and captains over hundreds, according to the houses of their fathers, throughout all Judah and Benjamin:
and he numbered them from twenty years old and above,
and found them three hundred thousand choice men,
able to go forth to war,
that could handle spear and shield.

6 **He** hired also an hundred thousand mighty men of valour out of Israel for an hundred talents of silver.

7 **But there** came a man of God to him,
saying,
O king, let not the army of Israel go with thee;
for the LORD is not with Israel, to wit, with all the children of Ephraim.

8 **But if thou** wilt go,
do it;
be strong for the battle:
God shall make thee fall before the enemy:
for God hath power to help,
and to cast down.

9 **And Amaziah** said to the man of God,
But what shall we do for the hundred talents which I have given to the army of Israel?
And the man of God answered,
The LORD is able to give thee much more than this.

10 **Then Amaziah** separated them, to wit, the army that was come to him out of Ephraim,
to go home again:
wherefore their anger was greatly kindled against Judah,
and they returned home in great anger.

11 **And Amaziah** strengthened himself,
and led forth his people,
and went to the valley of salt,
and smote of the children of Seir ten thousand.

12 **And other ten thousand left alive** did the children of Judah carry away captive,
and brought them unto the top of the rock,
and cast them down from the top of the rock,
that they all were broken in pieces.

13 **But the soldiers of the army which Amaziah sent back**, {that they} should not go with him to battle}, fell upon the cities of Judah, from Samaria even unto Bethhoron,
and smote three thousand of them,
and took much spoil.

14 **Now it** came to pass,
after that Amaziah was come from the slaughter of the Edomites,
that he brought the gods of the children of Seir,
and set them up to be his gods,
and bowed down himself before them,
and burned incense unto them.

15 **Wherefore the anger of the LORD** was kindled against Amaziah,
and he sent unto him a prophet,
which said unto him,
Why hast thou sought after the gods of the people,
which could not deliver their own people out of thine hand?

16 **And it** came to pass,
as he talked with him,
that the king said unto him,
Art thou made of the king's counsel?
forbear;
why shouldest thou be smitten?
Then the prophet forbare,
and said,
I know
that God hath determined to destroy thee,
because thou hast done this,
and hast not hearkened unto my counsel.

17 **Then Amaziah king of Judah** took advice,
and sent to Joash, the son of Jehoahaz, the son of Jehu, king of Israel,
saying,
Come,
let us see one another in the face.

18 **And Joash king of Israel** sent to Amaziah king of Judah,
saying,
The thistle that was in Lebanon sent to the cedar that was in Lebanon,
saying,
Give thy daughter to my son to wife:
and there passed by a wild beast that was in Lebanon,
and trode down the thistle.

19 **Thou** sayest,
Lo,
thou hast smitten the Edomites;
and thine heart lifteth thee up to boast:
abide now at home;
why shouldest thou meddle to thine hurt,
that thou shouldest fall, even thou, and Judah with thee?

20 **But Amaziah** would not hear;
for it came of God,
that he might deliver them into the hand of their enemies,
because they sought after the gods of Edom.

21 **So Joash the king of Israel** went up;
and they saw one another in the face, both he and Amaziah king of Judah, at Bethshemesh,
which belongeth to Judah.

22 **And Judah** was put to the worse before Israel,
and they fled every man to his tent.

23 **And Joash the king of Israel** took Amaziah king of Judah, the son of Joash, the son of Jehoahaz, at Bethshemesh,
and brought him to Jerusalem,
and brake down the wall of Jerusalem from the gate of Ephraim to the corner gate, four hundred cubits.

24 **And he** took all the gold and the silver, and all the vessels that were found in the house of God with Obededom, and the treasures of the king's house, the hostages also,
and returned to Samaria.

25 **And Amaziah the son of Joash king of Judah** lived after the death of Joash son of Jehoahaz king of Israel fifteen years.

26 **Now the rest of the acts of Amaziah, first and last,** {behold}, are they not written in the book of the kings of Judah and Israel?

27 **Now after the time that Amaziah did turn away from following the LORD** they made a

conspiracy against him in Jerusalem;
and he fled to Lachish:
but they sent to Lachish after him,
and slew him there.
28 **And they** brought him upon horses,
and buried him with his fathers in the city of Judah.

26 **Then all the people of Judah** took Uzziah,
who was sixteen years old,
and made him king in the room of his father Amaziah.
2 **He** built Eloth,
and restored it to Judah,
after that the king slept with his fathers.
3 **Sixteen years old** was Uzziah
when he began to reign,
and he reigned fifty and two years in Jerusalem.
His mother's name also was Jecoliah of Jerusalem.
4 **And he** did that which was right in the sight of the LORD, according to all that his father Amaziah did.
5 **And he** sought God in the days of Zechariah,
who had understanding in the visions of God:
and as long as he sought the LORD,
God made him to prosper.
6 **And he** went forth and warred against the Philistines,
and brake down the wall of Gath, and the wall of Jabneh, and the wall of Ashdod,
and built cities about Ashdod, and among the Philistines.
7 **And God** helped him against the Philistines, and against the Arabians that dwelt in Gurbaal, and the Mehunims.
8 **And the Ammonites** gave gifts to Uzziah:
and his name spread abroad even to the entering in of Egypt;
for he strengthened himself exceedingly.
9 **Moreover Uzziah** built towers in Jerusalem at the corner gate, and at the valley gate, and at the turning of the wall,
and fortified them.
10 **Also he** built towers in the desert,
and digged many wells:
for he had much cattle, both in the low country, and in the plains: husbandmen also, and vine dressers in the mountains, and in Carmel:
for he loved husbandry.
11 **Moreover Uzziah** had an host of fighting men,
that went out to war by bands, according to the number of their account by the hand of Jeiel the scribe and Maaseiah the ruler, under the hand of Hananiah, one of the king's captains.
12 **The whole number of the chief of the fathers of the mighty men of valour** were two thousand and six hundred.
13 **And under their hand** was an army, three hundred thousand and seven thousand and five hundred,
that made war with mighty power,
to help the king against the enemy.
14 **And Uzziah** prepared for them throughout all the host shields, and spears, and helmets, and habergeons, and bows, and slings to cast stones.
15 **And he** made in Jerusalem engines,
invented by cunning men,
to be on the towers and upon the bulwarks,
to shoot arrows and great stones withal.
And his name spread far abroad;
for he was marvellously helped,
till he was strong.
16 **But when he** was strong,
his heart was lifted up to his destruction:
for he transgressed against the LORD his God,
and went into the temple of the LORD to burn incense upon the altar of incense.
17 **And Azariah the priest** went in after him, and with him fourscore priests of the LORD,
that were valiant men:
18 **And they** withstood Uzziah the king,
and said unto him,
It appertaineth not unto thee, Uzziah, to burn incense unto the LORD, but to the priests the sons of Aaron,
that are consecrated to burn incense:
go out of the sanctuary;
for thou hast trespassed;
neither shall it be for thine honour from the LORD God.
19 **Then Uzziah** was wroth,
and had a censer in his hand to burn incense:
and while he was wroth with the priests,
the leprosy even rose up in his forehead before the priests in the house of the LORD, from beside the incense altar.
20 **And Azariah the chief priest, and all the priests,** looked upon him,
and, {behold}, he was leprous in his forehead,
and they thrust him out from thence;
yea, himself hasted also to go out,
because the LORD had smitten him.
21 **And Uzziah the king** was a leper unto the day of his death,
and dwelt in a several house,
being a leper;
for he was cut off from the house of the LORD:
and Jotham his son was over the king's house,
judging the people of the land.
22 **Now the rest of the acts of Uzziah, first and last,** did Isaiah the prophet, the son of Amoz, write.
23 **So Uzziah** slept with his fathers,
and they buried him with his fathers in the field of the burial which belonged to the kings;
for they said,
He is a leper:
and Jotham his son reigned in his stead.

27 **Jotham** was twenty and five years old
when he began to reign,
and he reigned sixteen years in Jerusalem.
His mother's name also was Jerushah, the daughter of Zadok.
2 **And he** did that which was right in the sight of the LORD, according to all that his father Uzziah did:
howbeit he entered not into the temple of the LORD.
And the people did yet corruptly.
3 **He** built the high gate of the house of the LORD,
and on the wall of Ophel he built much.

4 **Moreover he** built cities in the mountains of Judah,
and in the forests he built castles and towers.
5 **He** fought also with the king of the Ammonites,
and prevailed against them.
And the children of Ammon gave him the same year an hundred talents of silver, and ten thousand measures of wheat, and ten thousand of barley.
So much did the children of Ammon pay unto him, both the second year, and the third.
6 **So Jotham** became mighty,
because he prepared his ways before the LORD his God.
7 **Now the rest of the acts of Jotham, and all his wars, and his ways,** {lo}, they are written in the book of the kings of Israel and Judah.
8 **He** was five and twenty years old
when he began to reign,
and reigned sixteen years in Jerusalem.
9 **And Jotham** slept with his fathers,
and they buried him in the city of David:
and Ahaz his son reigned in his stead.

28 **Ahaz** was twenty years old
when he began to reign,
and he reigned sixteen years in Jerusalem:
but he did not that which was right in the sight of the LORD, like David his father:
2 **For he** walked in the ways of the kings of Israel,
and made also molten images for Baalim.
3 **Moreover he** burnt incense in the valley of the son of Hinnom,
and burnt his children in the fire, after the abominations of the heathen whom the LORD had cast out before the children of Israel.
4 **He** sacrificed also and burnt incense in the high places, and on the hills, and under every green tree.
5 **Wherefore the LORD his God** delivered him into the hand of the king of Syria;
and they smote him,
and carried away a great multitude of them captives,
and brought them to Damascus.
And he was also delivered into the hand of the king of Israel,
who smote him with a great slaughter.
6 **For Pekah the son of Remaliah** slew in Judah an hundred and twenty thousand in one day,
which were all valiant men;
because they had forsaken the LORD God of their fathers.
7 **And Zichri, a mighty man of Ephraim,** slew Maaseiah the king's son, and Azrikam the governor of the house, and Elkanah that was next to the king.
8 **And the children of Israel** carried away captive of their brethren two hundred thousand, women, sons, and daughters,
and took also away much spoil from them,
and brought the spoil to Samaria.
9 **But a prophet of the LORD** was there,
whose name was Oded:
and he went out before the host that came to Samaria,
and said unto them,
Behold,
because the LORD God of your fathers was wroth with Judah,
he hath delivered them into your hand,
and ye have slain them in a rage that reacheth up unto heaven.
10 **And now ye** purpose to keep under the children of Judah and Jerusalem for bondmen and bondwomen unto you:
but are there not with you, even with you, sins against the LORD your God?
11 **Now hear** me therefore,
and deliver the captives again,
which ye have taken captive of your brethren:
for the fierce wrath of the LORD is upon you.
12 **Then certain of the heads of the children of Ephraim, Azariah the son of Johanan, Berechiah the son of Meshillemoth, and Jehizkiah the son of Shallum, and Amasa the son of Hadlai,** stood up against them that came from the war,
13 **And** said unto them,
Ye shall not bring in the captives hither:
for whereas we have offended against the LORD already,
ye intend to add more to our sins and to our trespass:
for our trespass is great,
and there is fierce wrath against Israel.
14 **So the armed men** left the captives and the spoil before the princes and all the congregation.
15 **And the men which were expressed by name** rose up,
and took the captives,
and with the spoil clothed all that were naked among them,
and arrayed them,
and shod them,
and gave them to eat and to drink,
and anointed them,
and carried all the feeble of them upon asses,
and brought them to Jericho, the city of palm trees, to their brethren:
then they returned to Samaria.
16 **At that time** did king Ahaz send unto the kings of Assyria to help him.
17 **For again the Edomites** had come and smitten Judah,
and carried away captives.
18 **The Philistines** also had invaded the cities of the low country, and of the south of Judah,
and had taken Bethshemesh, and Ajalon, and Gederoth, and Shocho with the villages thereof, and Timnah with the villages thereof, Gimzo also and the villages thereof:
and they dwelt there.
19 **For the LORD** brought Judah low because of Ahaz king of Israel;
for he made Judah naked,
and transgressed sore against the LORD.
20 **And Tilgathpilneser king of Assyria** came unto him,
and distressed him,
but strengthened him not.
21 **For Ahaz** took away a portion out of the house of the LORD, and out of the house of the king, and of the princes,
and gave it unto the king of Assyria:
but he helped him not.

22 **And in the time of his distress** did he trespass yet more against the LORD:
this is that king Ahaz.
23 **For he** sacrificed unto the gods of Damascus,
which smote him:
and he said,
Because the gods of the kings of Syria help them,
therefore will I sacrifice to them,
that they may help me.
But they were the ruin of him, and of all Israel.
24 **And Ahaz** gathered together the vessels of the house of God,
and cut in pieces the vessels of the house of God,
and shut up the doors of the house of the LORD,
and he made him altars in every corner of Jerusalem.
25 **And in every several city of Judah** he made high places to burn incense unto other gods,
and provoked to anger the LORD God of his fathers.
26 **Now the rest of his acts and of all his ways, first and last,** {behold}, they are written in the book of the kings of Judah and Israel.
27 **And Ahaz** slept with his fathers,
and they buried him in the city, even in Jerusalem:
but they brought him not into the sepulchres of the kings of Israel:
and Hezekiah his son reigned in his stead.

29 **Hezekiah** began to reign **when he** was five and twenty years old,
and he reigned nine and twenty years in Jerusalem.
And his mother's name was Abijah, the daughter of Zechariah.
2 **And he** did that which was right in the sight of the LORD, according to all that David his father had done.
3 **He in the first year of his reign, in the first month,** opened the doors of the house of the LORD,
and repaired them.
4 **And he** brought in the priests and the Levites,
and gathered them together into the east street,
5 **And** said unto them,
Hear me, ye Levites,
sanctify now yourselves,
and sanctify the house of the LORD God of your fathers,
and carry forth the filthiness out of the holy place.
6 **For our fathers** have trespassed,
and done that which was evil in the eyes of the LORD our God,
and have forsaken him,
and have turned away their faces from the habitation of the LORD,
and turned their backs.
7 **Also they** have shut up the doors of the porch,
and put out the lamps,
and have not burned incense
nor offered burnt offerings in the holy place unto the God of Israel.
8 **Wherefore the wrath of the LORD** was upon Judah and Jerusalem,
and he hath delivered them to trouble, to astonishment, and to hissing,
as ye see with your eyes.
9 **For, {lo}, our fathers** have fallen by the sword,
and our sons and our daughters and our wives are in captivity for this.
10 **Now it is in mine heart** to make a covenant with the LORD God of Israel,
that his fierce wrath may turn away from us.
11 **My sons, be not** now negligent:
for the LORD hath chosen you to stand before him,
to serve him,
and that ye should minister unto him,
and burn incense.
12 **Then the Levites** arose, Mahath the son of Amasai, and Joel the son of Azariah, of the sons of the Kohathites: and of the sons of Merari, Kish the son of Abdi, and Azariah the son of Jehalelel: and of the Gershonites; Joah the son of Zimmah, and Eden the son of Joah:
13 And of the sons of Elizaphan; Shimri, and Jeiel: and of the sons of Asaph; Zechariah, and Mattaniah:
14 And of the sons of Heman; Jehiel, and Shimei: and of the sons of Jeduthun; Shemaiah, and Uzziel.
15 **And they** gathered their brethren,
and sanctified themselves,
and came, according to the commandment of the king, by the words of the LORD,
to cleanse the house of the LORD.
16 **And the priests** went into the inner part of the house of the LORD,
to cleanse it,
and brought out all the uncleanness that they found in the temple of the LORD into the court of the house of the LORD.
And the Levites took it,
to carry it out abroad into the brook Kidron.
17 **Now they** began on the first day of the first month to sanctify,
and on the eighth day of the month came they to the porch of the LORD:
so they sanctified the house of the LORD in eight days;
and in the sixteenth day of the first month they made an end.
18 **Then they** went in to Hezekiah the king,
and said,
We have cleansed all the house of the LORD, and the altar of burnt offering, with all the vessels thereof, and the shewbread table, with all the vessels thereof.
19 **Moreover all the vessels**, {which king Ahaz in his reign did cast away in his transgression}, have we prepared and sanctified,
and, {behold}, they are before the altar of the LORD.
20 **Then Hezekiah the king** rose early,
and gathered the rulers of the city,
and went up to the house of the LORD.
21 **And they** brought seven bullocks, and seven rams, and seven lambs, and seven he goats, for a sin offering for the kingdom, and for the sanctuary, and for Judah.
And he commanded the priests the sons of Aaron to offer them on the altar of the LORD.
22 **So they** killed the bullocks,
and the priests received the blood,
and sprinkled it on the altar:
likewise, {when they had killed the rams}, they sprinkled the blood upon the altar:
they killed also the lambs,

and they sprinkled the blood upon the altar.
23 **And they** brought forth the he goats for the sin offering before the king and the congregation;
and they laid their hands upon them:
24 **And the priests** killed them,
and they made reconciliation with their blood upon the altar,
to make an atonement for all Israel:
for the king commanded
that the burnt offering and the sin offering should be made for all Israel.
25 **And he** set the Levites in the house of the LORD with cymbals, with psalteries, and with harps, according to the commandment of David, and of Gad the king's seer, and Nathan the prophet:
for so was the commandment of the LORD by his prophets.
26 **And the Levites** stood with the instruments of David, and the priests with the trumpets.
27 **And Hezekiah** commanded to offer the burnt offering upon the altar.
And when the burnt offering began,
the song of the LORD began also with the trumpets, and with the instruments ordained by David king of Israel.
28 **And all the congregation** worshipped,
and the singers sang,
and the trumpeters sounded:
and all this continued
until the burnt offering was finished.
29 **And when they** had made an end of offering,
the king and all that were present with him bowed themselves,
and worshipped.
30 **Moreover Hezekiah the king and the princes** commanded the Levites to sing praise unto the LORD with the words of David, and of Asaph the seer.
And they sang praises with gladness,
and they bowed their heads
and worshipped.
31 **Then Hezekiah** answered and said,
Now ye have consecrated yourselves unto the LORD,
come near and bring sacrifices and thank offerings into the house of the LORD.
And the congregation brought in sacrifices and thank offerings;
and as many as were of a free heart burnt offerings.
32 **And the number of the burnt offerings**, {which the congregation brought}, was threescore and ten bullocks, an hundred rams, and two hundred lambs:
all these were for a burnt offering to the LORD.
33 **And the consecrated things** were six hundred oxen and three thousand sheep.
34 **But the priests** were too few,
so that they could not flay all the burnt offerings:
wherefore their brethren the Levites did help them,
till the work was ended,
and until the other priests had sanctified themselves:
for the Levites were more upright in heart to sanctify themselves than the priests.
35 **And also the burnt offerings** were in abundance, with the fat of the peace offerings, and the drink offerings for every burnt offering.
So the service of the house of the LORD was set in order.
36 **And Hezekiah** rejoiced, and all the people,
that God had prepared the people:
for the thing was done suddenly.

30

And Hezekiah sent to all Israel and Judah,
and wrote letters also to Ephraim and Manasseh,
that they should come to the house of the LORD at Jerusalem,
to keep the passover unto the LORD God of Israel.
2 **For the king** had taken counsel, and his princes, and all the congregation in Jerusalem,
to keep the passover in the second month.
3 **For they** could not keep it at that time,
because the priests had not sanctified themselves sufficiently,
neither had the people gathered themselves together to Jerusalem.
4 **And the thing** pleased the king and all the congregation.
5 **So they** established a decree to make proclamation throughout all Israel, from Beersheba even to Dan,
that they should come to keep the passover unto the LORD God of Israel at Jerusalem:
for they had not done it of a long time in such sort as it was written.
6 **So the posts** went with the letters from the king and his princes throughout all Israel and Judah, and according to the commandment of the king,
saying,
Ye children of Israel, turn again unto the LORD God of Abraham, Isaac, and Israel,
and he will return to the remnant of you,
that are escaped out of the hand of the kings of Assyria.
7 **And be not ye** like your fathers, and like your brethren,
which trespassed against the LORD God of their fathers,
who therefore gave them up to desolation,
as ye see.
8 **Now be ye not** stiffnecked,
as your fathers were,
but yield yourselves unto the LORD,
and enter into his sanctuary,
which he hath sanctified for ever:
and serve the LORD your God,
that the fierceness of his wrath may turn away from you.
9 **For if ye** turn again unto the LORD,
your brethren and your children shall find compassion before them that lead them captive,
so that they shall come again into this land:
for the LORD your God is gracious and merciful,
and will not turn away his face from you,
if ye return unto him.
10 **So the posts** passed from city to city through the country of Ephraim and Manasseh even unto Zebulun:
but they laughed them to scorn,

and mocked them.

11 **Nevertheless divers of Asher and Manasseh and of Zebulun** humbled themselves,
and came to Jerusalem.

12 **Also in Judah** the hand of God was to give them one heart to do the commandment of the king and of the princes, by the word of the LORD.

13 **And there** assembled at Jerusalem much people
to keep the feast of unleavened bread in the second month, a very great congregation.

14 **And they** arose and took away the altars that were in Jerusalem,
and all the altars for incense took they away,
and cast them into the brook Kidron.

15 **Then they** killed the passover on the fourteenth day of the second month:
and the priests and the Levites were ashamed,
and sanctified themselves,
and brought in the burnt offerings into the house of the LORD.

16 **And they** stood in their place after their manner, according to the law of Moses the man of God:
the priests sprinkled the blood,
which they received of the hand of the Levites.

17 **For there** were many in the congregation that were not sanctified:
therefore the Levites had the charge of the killing of the passovers for every one that was not clean,
to sanctify them unto the LORD.

18 **For a multitude of the people, even many of Ephraim, and Manasseh, Issachar, and Zebulun,** had not cleansed themselves,
yet did they eat the passover
otherwise than it was written.

But Hezekiah prayed for them, saying,
The good LORD pardon every one
19 **That** prepareth his heart to seek God, the LORD God of his fathers,
though he be not cleansed according to the purification of the sanctuary.

20 **And the LORD** hearkened to Hezekiah,
and healed the people.

21 **And the children of Israel that were present at Jerusalem** kept the feast of unleavened bread seven days with great gladness:
and the Levites and the priests praised the LORD day by day,
singing with loud instruments unto the LORD.

22 **And Hezekiah** spake comfortably unto all the Levites that taught the good knowledge of the LORD:
and they did eat throughout the feast seven days,
offering peace offerings,
and making confession to the LORD God of their fathers.

23 **And the whole assembly** took counsel to keep other seven days:
and they kept other seven days with gladness.

24 **For Hezekiah king of Judah** did give to the congregation a thousand bullocks and seven thousand sheep;
and the princes gave to the congregation a thousand bullocks and ten thousand sheep:
and a great number of priests sanctified themselves.

25 **And all the congregation of Judah, with the priests and the Levites, and all the congregation that came out of Israel, and the strangers that came out of the land of Israel, and that dwelt in Judah,** rejoiced.

26 **So there** was great joy in Jerusalem:
for since the time of Solomon the son of David king of Israel there was not the like in Jerusalem.

27 **Then the priests the Levites** arose and blessed the people:
and their voice was heard,
and their prayer came up to his holy dwelling place, even unto heaven.

31

Now when all this was finished,
all Israel that were present went out to the cities of Judah,
and brake the images in pieces,
and cut down the groves,
and threw down the high places and the altars out of all Judah and Benjamin, in Ephraim also and Manasseh,
until they had utterly destroyed them all.
Then all the children of Israel returned, every man to his possession, into their own cities.

2 **And Hezekiah** appointed the courses of the priests and the Levites after their courses, every man according to his service, the priests and Levites for burnt offerings and for peace offerings,
to minister,
and to give thanks,
and to praise in the gates of the tents of the LORD.

3 **He** appointed also the king's portion of his substance for the burnt offerings, to wit, for the morning and evening burnt offerings, and the burnt offerings for the sabbaths, and for the new moons, and for the set feasts,
as it is written in the law of the LORD.

4 **Moreover he** commanded the people that dwelt in Jerusalem to give the portion of the priests and the Levites,
that they might be encouraged in the law of the LORD.

5 **And as soon as the commandment** came abroad,
the children of Israel brought in abundance the firstfruits of corn, wine, and oil, and honey, and of all the increase of the field;
and the tithe of all things brought they in abundantly.

6 **And concerning the children of Israel and Judah,** {that dwelt in the cities of Judah}, they also brought in the tithe of oxen and sheep, and the tithe of holy things which were consecrated unto the LORD their God,
and laid them by heaps.

7 **In the third month** they began to lay the foundation of the heaps,
and finished them in the seventh month.

8 **And when Hezekiah and the princes** came and saw the heaps,
they blessed the LORD, and his people Israel.

9 **Then Hezekiah** questioned with the priests and the Levites concerning the heaps.

10 **And Azariah the chief priest of the house of Zadok** answered him,
and said,
Since the people began to bring the offerings into the house of the LORD,
we have had enough to eat,
and have left plenty:
for the LORD hath blessed his people;
and that which is left is this great store.

11 **Then Hezekiah** commanded to prepare chambers in the house of the LORD;
and they prepared them,
12 **And** brought in the offerings and the tithes and the dedicated things faithfully:
over which Cononiah the Levite was ruler,
and Shimei his brother was the next.

13 **And Jehiel, and Azaziah, and Nahath, and Asahel, and Jerimoth, and Jozabad, and Eliel, and Ismachiah, and Mahath, and Benaiah,** were overseers under the hand of Cononiah and Shimei his brother, at the commandment of Hezekiah the king, and Azariah the ruler of the house of God.

14 **And Kore the son of Imnah the Levite, the porter toward the east,** was over the freewill offerings of God,
to distribute the oblations of the LORD, and the most holy things.

15 **And next him** were Eden, and Miniamin, and Jeshua, and Shemaiah, Amariah, and Shecaniah, in the cities of the priests, in their set office,
to give to their brethren by courses, as well to the great as to the small:

16 **Beside their genealogy of males, from three years old and upward, even unto every one that entereth into the house of the LORD,** his daily portion for their service in their charges according to their courses;
17 Both to the genealogy of the priests by the house of their fathers, and the Levites from twenty years old and upward, in their charges by their courses;
18 And to the genealogy of all their little ones, their wives, and their sons, and their daughters, through all the congregation:
for in their set office they sanctified themselves in holiness:
19 **Also of the sons of Aaron the priests,** {which were in the fields of the suburbs of their cities, in every several city, the men that were expressed by name}, to give portions to all the males among the priests, and to all that were reckoned by genealogies among the Levites.

20 **And thus** did Hezekiah throughout all Judah,
and wrought that which was good and right and truth before the LORD his God.

21 **And in every work that he began in the service of the house of God, and in the law, and in the commandments,** {to seek his God}, he did it with all his heart,
and prospered.

32 ∞ **After these things, and the establishment thereof,** Sennacherib king of Assyria came,
and entered into Judah,
and encamped against the fenced cities,
and thought to win them for himself.

2 **And when Hezekiah** saw that Sennacherib was come,
and that he was purposed to fight against Jerusalem,
3 **He** took counsel with his princes and his mighty men
to stop the waters of the fountains which were without the city:
and they did help him.

4 **So there** was gathered much people together,
who stopped all the fountains, and the brook that ran through the midst of the land,
saying,
Why should the kings of Assyria come,
and find much water?

5 **Also he** strengthened himself,
and built up all the wall that was broken,
and raised it up to the towers, and another wall without,
and repaired Millo in the city of David,
and made darts and shields in abundance.

6 **And he** set captains of war over the people,
and gathered them together to him in the street of the gate of the city,
and spake comfortably to them,
saying,
7 **Be** strong and courageous,
be not afraid
nor dismayed for the king of Assyria, nor for all the multitude that is with him:
for there be more with us than with him:
8 **With him** is an arm of flesh;
but with us is the LORD our God to help us,
and to fight our battles.

And the people rested themselves upon the words of Hezekiah king of Judah.

9 **After this** did Sennacherib king of Assyria send his servants to Jerusalem, (but he himself laid siege against Lachish, and all his power with him,) unto Hezekiah king of Judah, and unto all Judah that were at Jerusalem,
saying,
10 **Thus** saith Sennacherib king of Assyria,
Whereon do ye trust,
that ye abide in the siege in Jerusalem?

11 **Doth not Hezekiah** persuade you to give over yourselves to die by famine and by thirst,
saying,
The LORD our God shall deliver us out of the hand of the king of Assyria?

12 **Hath not the same Hezekiah** taken away his high places and his altars,
and commanded Judah and Jerusalem,
saying,
Ye shall worship before one altar,
and burn incense upon it?

13 **Know ye not**
what I and my fathers have done unto all the people of other lands?
were the gods of the nations of those lands any ways able to deliver their lands out of mine hand?

14 **Who** was there among all the gods of those nations that my fathers utterly destroyed,

that could deliver his people out of mine hand,
that your God should be able to deliver you out of mine hand?
15 **Now therefore let not Hezekiah** deceive you,
nor persuade you on this manner,
neither yet believe him:
for no god of any nation or kingdom was able to deliver his people out of mine hand, and out of the hand of my fathers:
how much less shall your God deliver you out of mine hand?
16 **And his servants** spake yet more against the LORD God, and against his servant Hezekiah.
17 **He** wrote also letters to rail on the LORD God of Israel,
and to speak against him,
saying,
As the gods of the nations of other lands have not delivered their people out of mine hand,
so shall not the God of Hezekiah deliver his people out of mine hand.
18 **Then they** cried with a loud voice in the Jews' speech unto the people of Jerusalem that were on the wall,
to affright them,
and to trouble them;
that they might take the city.
19 **And they** spake against the God of Jerusalem, as against the gods of the people of the earth,
which were the work of the hands of man.
20 **And for this cause** Hezekiah the king, and the prophet Isaiah the son of Amoz, prayed and cried to heaven.
21 **And the LORD** sent an angel,
which cut off all the mighty men of valour, and the leaders and captains in the camp of the king of Assyria.
So he returned with shame of face to his own land.
And when he was come into the house of his god,
they that came forth of his own bowels slew him there with the sword.
22 **Thus the LORD** saved Hezekiah and the inhabitants of Jerusalem from the hand of Sennacherib the king of Assyria, and from the hand of all other,
and guided them on every side.
23 **And many** brought gifts unto the LORD to Jerusalem, and presents to Hezekiah king of Judah:
so that he was magnified in the sight of all nations from thenceforth.
24 **In those days** Hezekiah was sick to the death,
and prayed unto the LORD:
and he spake unto him,
and he gave him a sign.
25 **But Hezekiah** rendered not again according to the benefit done unto him;
for his heart was lifted up:
therefore there was wrath upon him, and upon Judah and Jerusalem.
26 **Notwithstanding Hezekiah** humbled himself for the pride of his heart, both he and the inhabitants of Jerusalem,
so that the wrath of the LORD came not upon them in the days of Hezekiah.
27 **And Hezekiah** had exceeding much riches and honour:
and he made himself treasuries for silver, and for gold, and for precious stones, and for spices, and for shields, and for all manner of pleasant jewels;
28 Storehouses also for the increase of corn, and wine, and oil; and stalls for all manner of beasts, and cotes for flocks.
29 **Moreover he** provided him cities, and possessions of flocks and herds in abundance:
for God had given him substance very much.
30 **This same Hezekiah** also stopped the upper watercourse of Gihon,
and brought it straight down to the west side of the city of David.
And Hezekiah prospered in all his works.
31 **Howbeit in the business of the ambassadors of the princes of Babylon**, {who sent unto him to enquire of the wonder that was done in the land}, God left him,
to try him,
that he might know all that was in his heart.
32 **Now the rest of the acts of Hezekiah, and his goodness**, {behold}, they are written in the vision of Isaiah the prophet, the son of Amoz, and in the book of the kings of Judah and Israel.
33 **And Hezekiah** slept with his fathers,
and they buried him in the chiefest of the sepulchres of the sons of David:
and all Judah and the inhabitants of Jerusalem did him honour at his death.
And Manasseh his son reigned in his stead.

33

Manasseh was twelve years old
when he began to reign,
and he reigned fifty and five years in Jerusalem:
2 **But** did that which was evil in the sight of the LORD, like unto the abominations of the heathen,
whom the LORD had cast out before the children of Israel.
3 **For he** built again the high places which Hezekiah his father had broken down,
and he reared up altars for Baalim,
and made groves,
and worshipped all the host of heaven,
and served them.
4 **Also he** built altars in the house of the LORD,
whereof the LORD had said,
In Jerusalem shall my name be for ever.
5 **And he** built altars for all the host of heaven in the two courts of the house of the LORD.
6 **And he** caused his children to pass through the fire in the valley of the son of Hinnom:
also he observed times,
and used enchantments,
and used witchcraft,
and dealt with a familiar spirit, and with wizards:
he wrought much evil in the sight of the LORD,
to provoke him to anger.
7 **And he** set a carved image, the idol which he had made, in the house of God,
of which God had said to David and to Solomon his son,

In this house, and in Jerusalem, {which I have chosen before all the tribes of Israel}, will I put my name for ever:
8 **Neither** will I any more remove the foot of Israel from out of the land which I have appointed for your fathers;
so that they will take heed to do all that I have commanded them, according to the whole law and the statutes and the ordinances by the hand of Moses.

9 **So Manasseh** made Judah and the inhabitants of Jerusalem to err,
and to do worse than the heathen,
whom the LORD had destroyed before the children of Israel.

10 **And the LORD** spake to Manasseh, and to his people:
but they would not hearken.

11 **Wherefore the LORD** brought upon them the captains of the host of the king of Assyria,
which took Manasseh among the thorns,
and bound him with fetters,
and carried him to Babylon.

12 **And when he** was in affliction,
he besought the LORD his God,
and humbled himself greatly before the God of his fathers,
13 **And** prayed unto him:
and he was intreated of him,
and heard his supplication,
and brought him again to Jerusalem into his kingdom.

Then Manasseh knew
that the LORD he was God.

14 **Now after this** he built a wall without the city of David, on the west side of Gihon, in the valley, even to the entering in at the fish gate,
and compassed about Ophel,
and raised it up a very great height,
and put captains of war in all the fenced cities of Judah.

15 **And he** took away the strange gods, and the idol out of the house of the LORD, and all the altars that he had built in the mount of the house of the LORD, and in Jerusalem,
and cast them out of the city.

16 **And he** repaired the altar of the LORD,
and sacrificed thereon peace offerings and thank offerings,
and commanded Judah to serve the LORD God of Israel.

17 **Nevertheless the people** did sacrifice still in the high places, yet unto the LORD their God only.

18 **Now the rest of the acts of Manasseh, and his prayer unto his God, and the words of the seers that spake to him in the name of the LORD God of Israel,** {behold}, they are written in the book of the kings of Israel.

19 **His prayer also, {and how God was intreated of him, and all his sins, and his trespass, and the places wherein he built high places}, {and set up groves and graven images}, {before he was humbled}:** {behold}, they are written among the sayings of the seers.

20 **So Manasseh** slept with his fathers,
and they buried him in his own house:
and Amon his son reigned in his stead.

21 **Amon** was two and twenty years old
when he began to reign,
and reigned two years in Jerusalem.

22 **But he** did that which was evil in the sight of the LORD,
as did Manasseh his father:
for Amon sacrificed unto all the carved images which Manasseh his father had made,
and served them;
23 **And** humbled not himself before the LORD,
as Manasseh his father had humbled himself;
but Amon trespassed more and more.

24 **And his servants** conspired against him,
and slew him in his own house.

25 **But the people of the land** slew all them that had conspired against king Amon;
and the people of the land made Josiah his son king in his stead.

34

Josiah was eight years old
when he began to reign,
and he reigned in Jerusalem one and thirty years.

2 **And he** did that which was right in the sight of the LORD,
and walked in the ways of David his father,
and declined neither to the right hand, nor to the left.

3 **For in the eighth year of his reign**, {while he was yet young}, he began to seek after the God of David his father:
and in the twelfth year he began to purge Judah and Jerusalem from the high places, and the groves, and the carved images, and the molten images.

4 **And they** brake down the altars of Baalim in his presence;
and the images, {that were on high above them}, he cut down;
and the groves, and the carved images, and the molten images, he brake in pieces,
and made dust of them,
and strowed it upon the graves of them that had sacrificed unto them.

5 **And he** burnt the bones of the priests upon their altars,
and cleansed Judah and Jerusalem.

6 **And so** did he in the cities of Manasseh, and Ephraim, and Simeon, even unto Naphtali, with their mattocks round about.

7 **And when he** had broken down the altars and the groves,
and had beaten the graven images into powder,
and cut down all the idols throughout all the land of Israel,
he returned to Jerusalem.

8 **Now in the eighteenth year of his reign**, {when he had purged the land, and the house}, he sent Shaphan the son of Azaliah, and Maaseiah the governor of the city, and Joah the son of Joahaz the recorder, to repair the house of the LORD his God.

9 **And when they** came to Hilkiah the high priest,
they delivered the money that was brought into the house of God,
which the Levites that kept the doors had gathered of the hand of Manasseh and Ephraim, and of all the remnant of Israel, and of all Judah and Benjamin;
and they returned to Jerusalem.

10 **And they** put it in the hand of the workmen that had the oversight of the house of the LORD,

and they gave it to the workmen that wrought in the house of the LORD,
to repair and amend the house:
11 **Even to the artificers and builders** gave they it,
to buy hewn stone, and timber for couplings,
and to floor the houses which the kings of Judah had destroyed.
12 **And the men** did the work faithfully:
and the overseers of them were Jahath and Obadiah, the Levites, of the sons of Merari; and Zechariah and Meshullam, of the sons of the Kohathites, {to set it forward}; and other of the Levites, all that could skill of instruments of musick.
13 **Also they** were over the bearers of burdens,
and were overseers of all that wrought the work in any manner of service:
and of the Levites there were scribes, and officers, and porters.
14 **And when they** brought out the money that was brought into the house of the LORD,
Hilkiah the priest found a book of the law of the LORD given by Moses.
15 **And Hilkiah** answered and said to Shaphan the scribe,
I have found the book of the law in the house of the LORD.
And Hilkiah delivered the book to Shaphan.
16 **And Shaphan** carried the book to the king,
and brought the king word back again,
saying,
All that was committed to thy servants, they do it.
17 **And they** have gathered together the money that was found in the house of the LORD,
and have delivered it into the hand of the overseers, and to the hand of the workmen.
18 **Then Shaphan the scribe** told the king,
saying,
Hilkiah the priest hath given me a book.
And Shaphan read it before the king.
19 **And it** came to pass,
when the king had heard the words of the law,
that he rent his clothes.
20 **And the king** commanded Hilkiah, and Ahikam the son of Shaphan, and Abdon the son of Micah, and Shaphan the scribe, and Asaiah a servant of the king's,
saying,
21 **Go,**
enquire of the LORD for me, and for them that are left in Israel and in Judah, concerning the words of the book that is found:
for great is the wrath of the LORD that is poured out upon us,
because our fathers have not kept the word of the LORD,
to do after all that is written in this book.
22 **And Hilkiah, and they that the king had appointed,** went to Huldah the prophetess, the wife of Shallum the son of Tikvath, the son of Hasrah, keeper of the wardrobe;
(now she dwelt in Jerusalem in the college:)
and they spake to her to that effect.
23 **And she** answered them,
Thus saith the LORD God of Israel,
Tell ye the man that sent you to me,
24 **Thus** saith the LORD,
Behold,
I will bring evil upon this place, and upon the inhabitants thereof, even all the curses that are written in the book which they have read before the king of Judah:
25 **Because they** have forsaken me,
and have burned incense unto other gods,
that they might provoke me to anger with all the works of their hands;
therefore my wrath shall be poured out upon this place,
and shall not be quenched.
26 **And as for the king of Judah,** {who sent you to enquire of the LORD}, so shall ye say unto him,
Thus saith the LORD God of Israel concerning the words which thou hast heard;
27 **Because thine heart** was tender,
and thou didst humble thyself before God,
when thou heardest his words against this place, and against the inhabitants thereof,
and humbledst thyself before me,
and didst rend thy clothes,
and weep before me;
I have even heard thee also,
saith the LORD.
28 **Behold,**
I will gather thee to thy fathers,
and thou shalt be gathered to thy grave in peace,
neither shall thine eyes see all the evil that I will bring upon this place, and upon the inhabitants of the same.
So they brought the king word again.
29 **Then the king** sent and gathered together all the elders of Judah and Jerusalem.
30 **And the king** went up into the house of the LORD, and all the men of Judah, and the inhabitants of Jerusalem, and the priests, and the Levites, and all the people, great and small:
and he read in their ears all the words of the book of the covenant that was found in the house of the LORD.
31 **And the king** stood in his place,
and made a covenant before the LORD,
to walk after the LORD,
and to keep his commandments, and his testimonies, and his statutes, with all his heart, and with all his soul,
to perform the words of the covenant which are written in this book.
32 **And he** caused all that were present in Jerusalem and Benjamin to stand to it.
And the inhabitants of Jerusalem did according to the covenant of God, the God of their fathers.
33 **And Josiah** took away all the abominations out of all the countries that pertained to the children of Israel,
and made all that were present in Israel to serve,
even to serve the LORD their God.
And all his days they departed not from following the LORD, the God of their fathers.

35

Moreover Josiah kept a passover unto the LORD in Jerusalem:
and they killed the passover on the fourteenth day of the first month.

2 **And he** set the priests in their charges,
and encouraged them to the service of the house of the LORD,

3 **And** said unto the Levites that taught all Israel,
which were holy unto the LORD,
Put the holy ark in the house which Solomon the son of David king of Israel did build;
it shall not be a burden upon your shoulders:
serve now the LORD your God, and his people Israel,

4 **And prepare** yourselves by the houses of your fathers, after your courses, according to the writing of David king of Israel, and according to the writing of Solomon his son.

5 **And stand** in the holy place according to the divisions of the families of the fathers of your brethren the people, and after the division of the families of the Levites.

6 **So kill** the passover,
and sanctify yourselves,
and prepare your brethren,
that they may do according to the word of the LORD by the hand of Moses.

7 **And Josiah** gave to the people, of the flock, lambs and kids, all for the passover offerings, for all that were present, to the number of thirty thousand, and three thousand bullocks:
these were of the king's substance.

8 **And his princes** gave willingly unto the people, to the priests, and to the Levites:
Hilkiah and Zechariah and Jehiel, rulers of the house of God, gave unto the priests for the passover offerings two thousand and six hundred small cattle and three hundred oxen.

9 **Conaniah also, and Shemaiah and Nethaneel, his brethren, and Hashabiah and Jeiel and Jozabad, chief of the Levites,** gave unto the Levites for passover offerings five thousand small cattle, and five hundred oxen.

10 **So the service** was prepared,
and the priests stood in their place, and the Levites in their courses, according to the king's commandment.

11 **And they** killed the passover,
and the priests sprinkled the blood from their hands,
and the Levites flayed them.

12 **And they** removed the burnt offerings,
that they might give according to the divisions of the families of the people,
to offer unto the LORD,
as it is written in the book of Moses.

And so did they with the oxen.

13 **And they** roasted the passover with fire according to the ordinance:
but the other holy offerings sod they in pots, and in caldrons, and in pans,
and divided them speedily among all the people.

14 **And afterward they** made ready for themselves, and for the priests:
because the priests the sons of Aaron were busied in offering of burnt offerings and the fat until night;
therefore the Levites prepared for themselves, and for the priests the sons of Aaron.

15 **And the singers the sons of Asaph** were in their place, according to the commandment of David, and Asaph, and Heman, and Jeduthun the king's seer;
and the porters waited at every gate;
they might not depart from their service;
for their brethren the Levites prepared for them.

16 **So all the service of the LORD** was prepared the same day,
to keep the passover,
and to offer burnt offerings upon the altar of the LORD, according to the commandment of king Josiah.

17 **And the children of Israel that were present** kept the passover at that time, and the feast of unleavened bread seven days.

18 **And there** was no passover like to that kept in Israel from the days of Samuel the prophet;
neither did all the kings of Israel keep such a passover as Josiah kept, and the priests, and the Levites, and all Judah and Israel that were present, and the inhabitants of Jerusalem.

19 **In the eighteenth year of the reign of Josiah** was this passover kept.

20 **After all this,** {when Josiah had prepared the temple}, Necho king of Egypt came up to fight against Charchemish by Euphrates:
and Josiah went out against him.

21 **But he** sent ambassadors to him,
saying,
What have I to do with thee, thou king of Judah?
I come not against thee this day, but against the house wherewith I have war:
for God commanded me to make haste:
forbear thee from meddling with God,
who is with me,
that he destroy thee not.

22 **Nevertheless Josiah** would not turn his face from him,
but disguised himself,
that he might fight with him,
and hearkened not unto the words of Necho from the mouth of God,
and came to fight in the valley of Megiddo.

23 **And the archers** shot at king Josiah;
and the king said to his servants,
Have me away;
for I am sore wounded.

24 **His servants** therefore took him out of that chariot,
and put him in the second chariot that he had;
and they brought him to Jerusalem,
and he died,
and was buried in one of the sepulchres of his fathers.

And all Judah and Jerusalem mourned for Josiah.

25 **And Jeremiah** lamented for Josiah:
and all the singing men and the singing women spake of Josiah in their lamentations to this day,
and made them an ordinance in Israel:
and, {behold}, they are written in the lamentations.

26 **Now the rest of the acts of Josiah, and his goodness, according to that which was written in the law of the LORD,**
27 **And his deeds, first and last,** {behold}, they are written in the book of the kings of Israel and Judah.

36 **Then the people of the land** took Jehoahaz the son of Josiah,
and made him king in his father's stead in Jerusalem.

2 **Jehoahaz** was twenty and three years old
when he began to reign,
and he reigned three months in Jerusalem.

3 **And the king of Egypt** put him down at Jerusalem,
and condemned the land in an hundred talents of silver and a talent of gold.

4 **And the king of Egypt** made Eliakim his brother king over Judah and Jerusalem,
and turned his name to Jehoiakim.
And Necho took Jehoahaz his brother,
and carried him to Egypt.

5 **Jehoiakim** was twenty and five years old
when he began to reign,
and he reigned eleven years in Jerusalem:
and he did that which was evil in the sight of the LORD his God.

6 **Against him** came up Nebuchadnezzar king of Babylon,
and bound him in fetters,
to carry him to Babylon.

7 **Nebuchadnezzar** also carried of the vessels of the house of the LORD to Babylon,
and put them in his temple at Babylon.

8 **Now the rest of the acts of Jehoiakim, and his abominations which he did, and that which was found in him,** {behold}, they are written in the book of the kings of Israel and Judah:
and Jehoiachin his son reigned in his stead.

9 **Jehoiachin** was eight years old
when he began to reign,
and he reigned three months and ten days in Jerusalem:
and he did that which was evil in the sight of the LORD.

10 **And when the year** was expired,
king Nebuchadnezzar sent,
and brought him to Babylon, with the goodly vessels of the house of the LORD,
and made Zedekiah his brother king over Judah and Jerusalem.

11 **Zedekiah** was one and twenty years old
when he began to reign,
and reigned eleven years in Jerusalem.

12 **And he** did that which was evil in the sight of the LORD his God,
and humbled not himself before Jeremiah the prophet speaking from the mouth of the LORD.

13 **And he** also rebelled against king Nebuchadnezzar,
who had made him swear by God:
but he stiffened his neck,
and hardened his heart from turning unto the LORD God of Israel.

14 **Moreover all the chief of the priests, and the people,** transgressed very much after all the abominations of the heathen;
and polluted the house of the LORD which he had hallowed in Jerusalem.

15 **And the LORD God of their fathers** sent to them by his messengers,
rising up betimes,
and sending;
because he had compassion on his people, and on his dwelling place:

16 **But they** mocked the messengers of God,
and despised his words,
and misused his prophets,
until the wrath of the LORD arose against his people,
till there was no remedy.

17 **Therefore he** brought upon them the king of the Chaldees,
who slew their young men with the sword in the house of their sanctuary,
and had no compassion upon young man or maiden, old man, or him that stooped for age:
he gave them all into his hand.

18 **And all the vessels of the house of God, great and small, and the treasures of the house of the LORD, and the treasures of the king, and of his princes;** all these he brought to Babylon.

19 **And they** burnt the house of God,
and brake down the wall of Jerusalem,
and burnt all the palaces thereof with fire,
and destroyed all the goodly vessels thereof.

20 **And them that had escaped from the sword** carried he away to Babylon;
where they were servants to him and his sons until the reign of the kingdom of Persia:

21 To fulfil the word of the LORD by the mouth of Jeremiah,
until the land had enjoyed her sabbaths:
for as long as she lay desolate
she kept sabbath,
to fulfil threescore and ten years.

22 **Now in the first year of Cyrus king of Persia,** {that the word of the LORD spoken by the mouth of Jeremiah might be accomplished}, the LORD stirred up the spirit of Cyrus king of Persia,
that he made a proclamation throughout all his kingdom,
and put it also in writing,
saying,

23 **Thus** saith Cyrus king of Persia,
All the kingdoms of the earth hath the LORD God of heaven given me;
and he hath charged me to build him an house in Jerusalem,
which is in Judah.
Who is there among you of all his people?
The LORD his God be with him,
and let him go up.

Ezra

Ezra, a direct descendant of Aaron, the brother of Moses, chronicles several key events in the Israelites' history following their return from Babylonian exile. The book opens with a momentous decree from King Cyrus of Persia, allowing the Israelites to rebuild the temple in Jerusalem. This decree, a significant turning point for the Israelites, brings a renewed sense of faith and optimism to the people.

The initial wave of exiles, led by Zerubbabel, makes their way back to Jerusalem. Despite encountering resistance from the locals, they successfully complete the temple project and hold a dedication ceremony. Roughly eighty years later, Ezra takes charge of a second group of exiles with a mission to restore religious observance among the people by reintroducing the Torah. As the bedrock of their faith, the Torah not only instructs them to follow the law but also guides them to live in accordance with God's commandments. Through his teachings, Ezra steers the Israelites towards reestablishing their covenantal relationship with God.

The book reaches its zenith when Ezra implements various reforms to bolster the people's obedience to God's law. These reforms, which include the expulsion of foreign wives, the public reading of the Torah, and the enforcement of the Sabbath, mark a significant turning point in Israel's history. They symbolize the end of the Babylonian exile and herald the dawn of a new era of revival.

1 **Now in the first year of Cyrus king of Persia,** {that the word of the LORD by the mouth of Jeremiah might be fulfilled}, the LORD stirred up the spirit of Cyrus king of Persia,
that he made a proclamation throughout all his kingdom,
and put it also in writing,
saying,
2 **Thus** saith Cyrus king of Persia,
The LORD God of heaven hath given me all the kingdoms of the earth;
and he hath charged me to build him an house at Jerusalem,
which is in Judah.

3 **Who** is there among you of all his people?
his God be with him,
and let him go up to Jerusalem,
which is in Judah,
and build the house of the LORD God of Israel,
(he is the God,)
which is in Jerusalem.

4 **And whosoever** remaineth in any place where he sojourneth,
let the men of his place help him with silver, and with gold, and with goods, and with beasts, beside the freewill offering for the house of God that is in Jerusalem.

5 **Then** rose up the chief of the fathers of Judah and Benjamin, and the priests, and the Levites, with all them whose spirit God had raised, to go up to build the house of the LORD which is in Jerusalem.

6 **And all they that were about them** strengthened their hands with vessels of silver, with gold, with goods, and with beasts, and with precious things, beside all that was willingly offered.

7 **Also Cyrus the king** brought forth the vessels of the house of the LORD,
which Nebuchadnezzar had brought forth out of Jerusalem,
and had put them in the house of his gods;
8 **Even those** did Cyrus king of Persia bring forth by the hand of Mithredath the treasurer,
and numbered them unto Sheshbazzar, the prince of Judah.

9 **And this** is the number of them: thirty chargers of gold, a thousand chargers of silver, nine and twenty knives,
10 Thirty basons of gold, silver basons of a second sort four hundred and ten, and other vessels a thousand.

11 **All the vessels of gold and of silver** were five thousand and four hundred.

All these did Sheshbazzar bring up with them of the captivity that were brought up from Babylon unto Jerusalem.

2 **Now these** are the children of the province that went up out of the captivity, of those which had been carried away,
whom Nebuchadnezzar the king of Babylon had carried away unto Babylon,
and came again unto Jerusalem and Judah, every one unto his city;
2 **Which** came with Zerubbabel: Jeshua, Nehemiah, Seraiah, Reelaiah, Mordecai, Bilshan, Mizpar, Bigvai, Rehum, Baanah.

The number of the men of the people of Israel:
3 **The children of Parosh,** two thousand an hundred seventy and two.

4 **The children of Shephatiah,** three hundred seventy and two.

5 **The children of Arah,** seven hundred seventy and five.

6 **The children of Pahathmoab,** of the children of Jeshua and Joab, two thousand eight hundred and twelve.

7 **The children of Elam,** a thousand two hundred fifty and four.

8 **The children of Zattu,** nine hundred forty and five.

9 **The children of Zaccai,** seven hundred and threescore.

10 **The children of Bani,** six hundred forty and two.

11 **The children of Bebai,** six hundred twenty and three.

12 **The children of Azgad,** a thousand two hundred twenty and two.

13 **The children of Adonikam,** six hundred sixty and six.

14 **The children of Bigvai,** two thousand fifty and six.

15 **The children of Adin,** four hundred fifty and four.

16 **The children of Ater of Hezekiah,** ninety and eight.

17 **The children of Bezai,** three hundred twenty and three.

18 **The children of Jorah,** an hundred and twelve.

19 **The children of Hashum,** two hundred twenty and three.

20 **The children of Gibbar,** ninety and five.

21 **The children of Bethlehem,** an hundred twenty and three.

22 **The men of Netophah,** fifty and six.

23 **The men of Anathoth,** an hundred twenty and eight.

24 **The children of Azmaveth,** forty and two.

25 **The children of Kirjatharim, Chephirah, and Beeroth,** seven hundred and forty and three.

26 **The children of Ramah and Gaba,** six hundred twenty and one.

27 **The men of Michmas,** an hundred twenty and two.

28 **The men of Bethel and Ai,** two hundred twenty and three.

29 **The children of Nebo,** fifty and two.

30 **The children of Magbish,** an hundred fifty and six.

31 **The children of the other Elam,** a thousand two hundred fifty and four.

32 **The children of Harim,** three hundred and twenty.

33 **The children of Lod, Hadid, and Ono,** seven hundred twenty and five.

34 **The children of Jericho,** three hundred forty and five.

35 **The children of Senaah,** three thousand and six hundred and thirty.

36 **The priests:** the children of Jedaiah, of the house of Jeshua, nine hundred seventy and three.

37 **The children of Immer,** a thousand fifty and two.

38 **The children of Pashur,** a thousand two hundred forty and seven.

39 **The children of Harim,** a thousand and seventeen.

40 **The Levites:** the children of Jeshua and Kadmiel, of the children of Hodaviah, seventy and four.

41 **The singers:** the children of Asaph, an hundred twenty and eight.

42 **The children of the porters:** the children of Shallum, the children of Ater, the children of Talmon, the children of Akkub, the children of Hatita, the children of Shobai, in all an hundred thirty and nine.

43 **The Nethinims:** the children of Ziha, the children of Hasupha, the children of Tabbaoth,

44 The children of Keros, the children of Siaha, the children of Padon,

45 The children of Lebanah, the children of Hagabah, the children of Akkub,

46 The children of Hagab, the children of Shalmai, the children of Hanan,

47 The children of Giddel, the children of Gahar, the children of Reaiah,

48 The children of Rezin, the children of Nekoda, the children of Gazzam,

49 The children of Uzza, the children of Paseah, the children of Besai,

50 The children of Asnah, the children of Mehunim, the children of Nephusim,

51 The children of Bakbuk, the children of Hakupha, the children of Harhur,

52 The children of Bazluth, the children of Mehida, the children of Harsha,

53 The children of Barkos, the children of Sisera, the children of Thamah,

54 The children of Neziah, the children of Hatipha.

55 **The children of Solomon's servants:** the children of Sotai, the children of Sophereth, the children of Peruda,

56 The children of Jaalah, the children of Darkon, the children of Giddel,

57 The children of Shephatiah, the children of Hattil, the children of Pochereth of Zebaim, the children of Ami.

58 **All the Nethinims, and the children of Solomon's servants,** were three hundred ninety and two.

59 **And these** were they which went up from Telmelah, Telharsa, Cherub, Addan, and Immer:
but they could not shew their father's house, and their seed,
whether they were of Israel:
60 The children of Delaiah, the children of Tobiah, the children of Nekoda, six hundred fifty and two.

61 **And of the children of the priests:** the children of Habaiah, the children of Koz, the children of Barzillai;
which took a wife of the daughters of Barzillai the Gileadite,
and was called after their name:
62 **These** sought their register among those that were reckoned by genealogy,
but they were not found:
therefore were they, as polluted, put from the priesthood.

63 **And the Tirshatha** said unto them,
that they should not eat of the most holy things,
till there stood up a priest with Urim and with Thummim.

64 **The whole congregation together** was forty and two thousand three hundred and threescore,
65 Beside their servants and their maids,
of whom there were seven thousand three hundred thirty and seven:
and there were among them two hundred singing men and singing women.

66 **Their horses** were seven hundred thirty and six;
their mules, two hundred forty and five;
67 **Their camels,** four hundred thirty and five;
their asses, six thousand seven hundred and twenty.

68 **And some of the chief of the fathers,** {when they came to the house of the LORD which is at

Jerusalem}, offered freely for the house of God
to set it up in his place:
69 **They** gave after their ability unto the treasure of the work threescore and one thousand drams of gold, and five thousand pound of silver, and one hundred priests' garments.
70 **So the priests, and the Levites, and some of the people, and the singers, and the porters, and the Nethinims,** dwelt in their cities, and all Israel in their cities.

3 **And when the seventh month** was come,
and the children of Israel were in the cities,
the people gathered themselves together as one man to Jerusalem.
2 **Then** stood up Jeshua the son of Jozadak, and his brethren the priests, and Zerubbabel the son of Shealtiel, and his brethren,
and builded the altar of the God of Israel,
to offer burnt offerings thereon,
as it is written in the law of Moses the man of God.
3 **And they** set the altar upon his bases;
for fear was upon them because of the people of those countries:
and they offered burnt offerings thereon unto the LORD, even burnt offerings morning and evening.
4 **They** kept also the feast of tabernacles,
as it is written,
and offered the daily burnt offerings by number, according to the custom,
as the duty of every day required;
5 **And afterward** offered the continual burnt offering, both of the new moons, and of all the set feasts of the LORD that were consecrated, and of every one that willingly offered a freewill offering unto the LORD.
6 **From the first day of the seventh month** began they to offer burnt offerings unto the LORD.
But the foundation of the temple of the LORD was not yet laid.
7 **They** gave money also unto the masons, and to the carpenters; and meat, and drink, and oil, unto them of Zidon, and to them of Tyre,
to bring cedar trees from Lebanon to the sea of Joppa, according to the grant that they had of Cyrus king of Persia.
8 **Now in the second year of their coming unto the house of God at Jerusalem, in the second month,** began Zerubbabel the son of Shealtiel, and Jeshua the son of Jozadak, and the remnant of their brethren the priests and the Levites, and all they that were come out of the captivity unto Jerusalem;
and appointed the Levites, from twenty years old and upward, to set forward the work of the house of the LORD.
9 **Then** stood Jeshua with his sons and his brethren, Kadmiel and his sons, the sons of Judah, together, to set forward the workmen in the house of God: the sons of Henadad, with their sons and their brethren the Levites.
10 **And when the builders** laid the foundation of the temple of the LORD,
they set the priests in their apparel with trumpets, and the Levites the sons of Asaph with cymbals,
to praise the LORD, after the ordinance of David king of Israel.
11 **And they** sang together by course in praising and giving thanks unto the LORD;
because he is good,
for his mercy endureth for ever toward Israel.
And all the people shouted with a great shout,
when they praised the LORD,
because the foundation of the house of the LORD was laid.
12 **But many of the priests and Levites and chief of the fathers,** {who were ancient men}, {that had seen the first house}, {when the foundation of this house was laid before their eyes}, wept with a loud voice;
and many shouted aloud for joy:
13 **So that the people** could not discern the noise of the shout of joy from the noise of the weeping of the people:
for the people shouted with a loud shout,
and the noise was heard afar off.

4 **Now when the adversaries of Judah and Benjamin** heard that the children of the captivity builded the temple unto the LORD God of Israel;
2 **Then they** came to Zerubbabel, and to the chief of the fathers,
and said unto them,
Let us build with you:
for we seek your God,
as ye do;
and we do sacrifice unto him since the days of Esarhaddon king of Assur,
which brought us up hither.
3 **But Zerubbabel, and Jeshua, and the rest of the chief of the fathers of Israel,** said unto them,
Ye have nothing to do with us to build an house unto our God;
but we ourselves together will build unto the LORD God of Israel,
as king Cyrus the king of Persia hath commanded us.
4 **Then the people of the land** weakened the hands of the people of Judah,
and troubled them in building,
5 **And** hired counsellors against them,
to frustrate their purpose, all the days of Cyrus king of Persia, even until the reign of Darius king of Persia.
6 **And in the reign of Ahasuerus, in the beginning of his reign,** wrote they unto him an accusation against the inhabitants of Judah and Jerusalem.
7 **And in the days of Artaxerxes** wrote Bishlam, Mithredath, Tabeel, and the rest of their companions, unto Artaxerxes king of Persia;
and the writing of the letter was written in the Syrian tongue,
and interpreted in the Syrian tongue.
8 **Rehum the chancellor and Shimshai the scribe** wrote a letter against Jerusalem to Artaxerxes the king in this sort:
9 **Then** wrote Rehum the chancellor, and Shimshai the scribe, and the rest of their companions; the Dinaites, the Apharsathchites, the

Tarpelites, the Apharsites, the
Archevites, the Babylonians, the
Susanchites, the Dehavites, and
the Elamites,
10 And the rest of the nations whom
the great and noble Asnapper
brought over, and set in the cities
of Samaria, and the rest that are
on this side the river, and at such
a time.
11 **This** is the copy of the letter that
they sent unto him, even unto
Artaxerxes the king; Thy servants
the men on this side the river, and
at such a time.
12 **Be it** known unto the king,
**that the Jews which came up
from thee to us** are come unto
Jerusalem,
building the rebellious and the bad
city,
and have set up the walls thereof,
and joined the foundations.
13 **Be it** known now unto the king,
**that, {if this city be builded}, {and
the walls set up again},** then will
they not pay toll, tribute, and
custom,
and so thou shalt endamage the
revenue of the kings.
14 **Now because we** have
maintenance from the king's
palace,
and it was not meet for us to see
the king's dishonour,
therefore have we sent and
certified the king;
15 **That search** may be made in the
book of the records of thy fathers:
so shalt thou find in the book of the
records,
and know that this city is a
rebellious city,
and hurtful unto kings and
provinces,
and that they have moved sedition
within the same of old time:
for which cause was this city
destroyed.
16 **We** certify the king
**that, {if this city be builded
again}, {and the walls thereof
set up},** by this means thou shalt
have no portion on this side the
river.
17 **Then** sent the king an answer
unto Rehum the chancellor, and
to Shimshai the scribe, and to the
rest of their companions that
dwell in Samaria, and unto the
rest beyond the river,
Peace, and at such a time.
18 **The letter which ye sent unto us**
hath been plainly read before me.
19 **And I** commanded,
and search hath been made,
and it is found that this city of old
time hath made insurrection
against kings, and that rebellion
and sedition have been made
therein.
20 **There** have been mighty kings
also over Jerusalem,
which have ruled over all countries
beyond the river;
and toll, tribute, and custom, was
paid unto them.
21 **Give ye** now commandment to
cause these men to cease,
and that this city be not builded,
until another commandment
shall be given from me.
22 **Take heed** now that ye fail not to
do this:
why should damage grow to the
hurt of the kings?
23 **Now when the copy of king
Artaxerxes' letter** was read
before Rehum, and Shimshai the
scribe, and their companions,
they went up in haste to Jerusalem
unto the Jews,
and made them to cease by force
and power.
24 **Then** ceased the work of the
house of God which is at
Jerusalem.
So it ceased unto the second year of
the reign of Darius king of Persia.

5 **Then the prophets, Haggai
the prophet, and Zechariah
the son of Iddo,** prophesied unto
the Jews that were in Judah and
Jerusalem in the name of the God
of Israel, even unto them.
2 **Then** rose up Zerubbabel the son
of Shealtiel, and Jeshua the son of
Jozadak,
and began to build the house of
God which is at Jerusalem:
and with them were the prophets
of God helping them.
3 **At the same time** came to them
Tatnai, governor on this side the
river, and Shetharboznai and
their companions,
and said thus unto them,
Who hath commanded you to build
this house, and to make up this
wall?
4 **Then** said we unto them after this
manner,
What are the names of the men
that make this building?
5 **But the eye of their God** was
upon the elders of the Jews,
that they could not cause them to
cease,
till the matter came to Darius:
and then they returned answer by
letter concerning this matter.
6 The copy of the letter that Tatnai,
governor on this side the river,
and Shetharboznai and his
companions the Apharsachites,
which were on this side the river,
sent unto Darius the king:
7 **They** sent a letter unto him,
wherein was written thus;
Unto Darius the king, all peace.
8 **Be it** known unto the king,
that we went into the province of
Judea, to the house of the great
God,
which is builded with great stones,
and timber is laid in the walls,
and this work goeth fast on,
and prospereth in their hands.
9 **Then** asked we those elders,
and said unto them thus,
Who commanded you to build this
house, and to make up these
walls?
10 **We** asked their names also,
to certify thee,
that we might write the names of
the men that were the chief of
them.
11 **And thus they** returned us
answer,
saying,
We are the servants of the God of
heaven and earth,
and build the house that was
builded these many years ago,
which a great king of Israel
builded and set up.
12 **But after that our fathers** had
provoked the God of heaven unto
wrath,
he gave them into the hand of
Nebuchadnezzar the king of
Babylon, the Chaldean,
who destroyed this house,
and carried the people away into
Babylon.

13 **But in the first year of Cyrus the**
king of Babylon the same king
Cyrus made a decree to build this
house of God.

14 **And the vessels also of gold and**
silver of the house of God,
{which Nebuchadnezzar took out
of the temple that was in
Jerusalem}, {and brought them
into the temple of Babylon}, those
did Cyrus the king take out of the
temple of Babylon,
and they were delivered unto one,
whose name was Sheshbazzar,
whom he had made governor;
15 **And** said unto him,
Take these vessels,
go,
carry them into the temple that is
in Jerusalem,
and let the house of God be
builded in his place.

16 **Then** came the same Sheshbazzar,
and laid the foundation of the
house of God which is in
Jerusalem:
and since that time even until
now hath it been in building,
and yet it is not finished.

17 **Now therefore, if it** seem good to
the king,
let there be search made in the
king's treasure house,
which is there at Babylon,
whether it be so,
that a decree was made of Cyrus
the king to build this house of
God at Jerusalem,
and let the king send his pleasure
to us concerning this matter.

6

Then Darius the king made a
decree,
and search was made in the house
of the rolls,
where the treasures were laid up
in Babylon.

2 **And there** was found at
Achmetha, in the palace that is in
the province of the Medes, a roll,
and therein was a record thus
written:
3 **In the first year of Cyrus the king**
the same Cyrus the king made a
decree concerning the house of
God at Jerusalem,
Let the house be builded, the place
where they offered sacrifices,
and let the foundations thereof be
strongly laid; the height thereof
threescore cubits, and the breadth
thereof threescore cubits;
4 With three rows of great stones,
and a row of new timber:
and let the expenses be given out
of the king's house:
5 **And also let the golden and silver**
vessels of the house of God,
{which Nebuchadnezzar took
forth out of the temple which is at
Jerusalem}, {and brought unto
Babylon}, be restored,
and brought again unto the temple
which is at Jerusalem, every one
to his place,
and place them in the house of God.

6 **Now therefore, Tatnai, governor**
beyond the river,
Shetharboznai, and your
companions the Apharsachites,
which are beyond the river, be
ye far from thence:
7 **Let the work of this house of God**
alone;
let the governor of the Jews and
the elders of the Jews build this
house of God in his place.

8 **Moreover I** make a decree what ye
shall do to the elders of these Jews
for the building of this house of
God:
that of the king's goods, even of
the tribute beyond the river,
forthwith expenses be given unto
these men,
that they be not hindered.

9 **And that which they have need**
of, both young bullocks, and
rams, and lambs, for the burnt
offerings of the God of heaven,
wheat, salt, wine, and oil,
according to the appointment
of the priests which are at
Jerusalem, let it be given them
day by day without fail:
10 **That they** may offer sacrifices of
sweet savours unto the God of
heaven,
and pray for the life of the king, and
of his sons.

11 **Also I** have made a decree,
that whosoever shall alter this
word,
let timber be pulled down from his
house,
and being set up,
let him be hanged thereon;
and let his house be made a
dunghill for this.
12 **And the God that hath caused**
his name to dwell there destroy
all kings and people,
that shall put to their hand to alter
and to destroy this house of God
which is at Jerusalem.
I Darius have made a decree;
let it be done with speed.

13 **Then Tatnai, governor on this**
side the river, Shetharboznai,
and their companions,
according to that which Darius
the king had sent, so they did
speedily.

14 **And the elders of the Jews**
builded,
and they prospered through the
prophesying of Haggai the
prophet and Zechariah the son of
Iddo.
And they builded,
and finished it, according to the
commandment of the God of
Israel, and according to the
commandment of Cyrus, and
Darius, and Artaxerxes king of
Persia.

15 **And this house** was finished on
the third day of the month Adar,
which was in the sixth year of the
reign of Darius the king.

16 **And the children of Israel, the**
priests, and the Levites, and the
rest of the children of the
captivity, kept the dedication of
this house of God with joy.

17 **And** offered at the dedication of
this house of God an hundred
bullocks, two hundred rams, four
hundred lambs; and for a sin
offering for all Israel, twelve he
goats, according to the number of
the tribes of Israel.

18 **And they** set the priests in their
divisions, and the Levites in their
courses, for the service of God,
which is at Jerusalem;
as it is written in the book of Moses.

19 **And the children of the captivity**
kept the passover upon the
fourteenth day of the first month.

20 **For the priests and the Levites**
were purified together,
all of them were pure,
and killed the passover for all the
children of the captivity, and for
their brethren the priests, and for
themselves.

21 **And the children of Israel, {which were come again out of captivity}, and all such as had separated themselves unto them from the filthiness of the heathen of the land, {to seek the LORD God of Israel},** did eat,
22 **And** kept the feast of unleavened bread seven days with joy:
for the LORD had made them joyful,
and turned the heart of the king of Assyria unto them,
to strengthen their hands in the work of the house of God, the God of Israel.

7 **Now after these things, in the reign of Artaxerxes king of Persia, Ezra the son of Seraiah, the son of Azariah, the son of Hilkiah,**
2 **The son of Shallum, the son of Zadok, the son of Ahitub,**
3 **The son of Amariah, the son of Azariah, the son of Meraioth,**
4 **The son of Zerahiah, the son of Uzzi, the son of Bukki,**
5 **The son of Abishua, the son of Phinehas, the son of Eleazar, the son of Aaron the chief priest:**
6 This Ezra went up from Babylon;
and he was a ready scribe in the law of Moses,
which the LORD God of Israel had given:
and the king granted him all his request, according to the hand of the LORD his God upon him.
7 **And there** went up some of the children of Israel, and of the priests, and the Levites, and the singers, and the porters, and the Nethinims, unto Jerusalem, in the seventh year of Artaxerxes the king.
8 **And he** came to Jerusalem in the fifth month,
which was in the seventh year of the king.
9 **For upon the first day of the first month** began he to go up from Babylon,
and on the first day of the fifth month came he to Jerusalem, according to the good hand of his God upon him.
10 **For Ezra** had prepared his heart
to seek the law of the LORD,
and to do it,
and to teach in Israel statutes and judgments.
11 **Now this** is the copy of the letter that the king Artaxerxes gave unto Ezra the priest, the scribe, even a scribe of the words of the commandments of the LORD, and of his statutes to Israel.
12 **Artaxerxes, king of kings,** unto Ezra the priest, a scribe of the law of the God of heaven, perfect peace, and at such a time.
13 I make a decree, **that all they of the people of Israel, and of his priests and Levites, in my realm**, {which are minded of their own freewill to go up to Jerusalem}, go with thee.
14 **Forasmuch as thou** art sent of the king, and of his seven counsellors,
to enquire concerning Judah and Jerusalem, according to the law of thy God which is in thine hand;
15 **And** to carry the silver and gold, {which the king and his counsellors have freely offered unto the God of Israel}, {whose habitation is in Jerusalem},
16 And all the silver and gold that thou canst find in all the province of Babylon, with the freewill offering of the people, and of the priests,
offering willingly for the house of their God which is in Jerusalem:
17 **That thou** mayest buy speedily with this money bullocks, rams, lambs, with their meat offerings and their drink offerings,
and offer them upon the altar of the house of your God which is in Jerusalem.
18 **And whatsoever** shall seem good to thee, and to thy brethren, to do with the rest of the silver and the gold,
that do after the will of your God.
19 **The vessels also that are given thee for the service of the house of thy God,** those deliver thou before the God of Jerusalem.
20 **And whatsoever more** shall be needful for the house of thy God,
which thou shalt have occasion to bestow,
bestow it out of the king's treasure house.
21 **And I, even I Artaxerxes the king,** do make a decree to all the treasurers which are beyond the river, **that whatsoever** Ezra the priest, the scribe of the law of the God of heaven, shall require of you,
it be done speedily,
22 Unto an hundred talents of silver, and to an hundred measures of wheat, and to an hundred baths of wine, and to an hundred baths of oil, and salt without prescribing how much.
23 **Whatsoever** is commanded by the God of heaven,
let it be diligently done for the house of the God of heaven:
for why should there be wrath against the realm of the king and his sons?
24 **Also we** certify you,
that touching any of the priests and Levites, singers, porters, Nethinims, or ministers of this house of God, it shall not be lawful to impose toll, tribute, or custom, upon them.
25 **And thou, Ezra**, after the wisdom of thy God, {that is in thine hand}, set magistrates and judges,
which may judge all the people that are beyond the river, all such as know the laws of thy God;
and teach ye them that know them not.
26 **And whosoever** will not do the law of thy God, and the law of the king,
let judgment be executed speedily upon him,
whether it be unto death, or to banishment, or to confiscation of goods, or to imprisonment.
27 **Blessed** be the LORD God of our fathers,
which hath put such a thing as this in the king's heart,
to beautify the house of the LORD which is in Jerusalem:
28 **And** hath extended mercy unto me before the king, and his counsellors, and before all the king's mighty princes.
And I was strengthened
as the hand of the LORD my God was upon me,
and I gathered together out of Israel chief men to go up with me.

8  **These** are now the chief of their fathers,

and this is the genealogy of them that went up with me from Babylon, in the reign of Artaxerxes the king.
2 Of the sons of Phinehas; Gershom: of the sons of Ithamar; Daniel: of the sons of David; Hattush.
3 Of the sons of Shechaniah, of the sons of Pharosh; Zechariah:
and with him were reckoned by genealogy of the males an hundred and fifty.
4 Of the sons of Pahathmoab; Elihoenai the son of Zerahiah, and with him two hundred males.
5 Of the sons of Shechaniah; the son of Jahaziel, and with him three hundred males.
6 Of the sons also of Adin; Ebed the son of Jonathan, and with him fifty males.
7 And of the sons of Elam; Jeshaiah the son of Athaliah, and with him seventy males.
8 And of the sons of Shephatiah; Zebadiah the son of Michael, and with him fourscore males.
9 Of the sons of Joab; Obadiah the son of Jehiel, and with him two hundred and eighteen males.
10 And of the sons of Shelomith; the son of Josiphiah, and with him an hundred and threescore males.
11 And of the sons of Bebai; Zechariah the son of Bebai, and with him twenty and eight males.
12 And of the sons of Azgad; Johanan the son of Hakkatan, and with him an hundred and ten males.
13 And of the last sons of Adonikam,
whose names are these, Eliphelet, Jeiel, and Shemaiah, and with them threescore males.
14 Of the sons also of Bigvai; Uthai, and Zabbud, and with them seventy males.
15 **And I** gathered them together to the river that runneth to Ahava;
and there abode we in tents three days:
and I viewed the people, and the priests,
and found there none of the sons of Levi.
16 **Then** sent I for Eliezer, for Ariel, for Shemaiah, and for Elnathan, and for Jarib, and for Elnathan, and for Nathan, and for Zechariah, and for Meshullam, chief men; also for Joiarib, and for Elnathan, men of understanding.
17 **And I** sent them with commandment unto Iddo the chief at the place Casiphia,
and I told them
what they should say unto Iddo, and to his brethren the Nethinims, at the place Casiphia,
that they should bring unto us ministers for the house of our God.
18 **And by the good hand of our God upon us** they brought us a man of understanding, of the sons of Mahli, the son of Levi, the son of Israel; and Sherebiah, with his sons and his brethren, eighteen;
19 And Hashabiah, and with him Jeshaiah of the sons of Merari, his brethren and their sons, twenty;
20 Also of the Nethinims, {whom David and the princes had appointed for the service of the Levites}, two hundred and twenty Nethinims:
all of them were expressed by name.
21 **Then I** proclaimed a fast there, at the river of Ahava,
that we might afflict ourselves before our God,
to seek of him a right way for us, and for our little ones, and for all our substance.
22 **For I** was ashamed to require of the king a band of soldiers and horsemen
to help us against the enemy in the way:
because we had spoken unto the king,
saying,
The hand of our God is upon all them for good that seek him;
but his power and his wrath is against all them that forsake him.
23 **So we** fasted and besought our God for this:
and he was intreated of us.
24 **Then I** separated twelve of the chief of the priests, Sherebiah, Hashabiah, and ten of their brethren with them,
25 **And** weighed unto them the silver, and the gold, and the vessels, even the offering of the house of our God,
which the king, and his counsellors, and his lords, and all Israel there present, had offered:
26 **I** even weighed unto their hand six hundred and fifty talents of silver, and silver vessels an hundred talents, and of gold an hundred talents;
27 Also twenty basons of gold, of a thousand drams; and two vessels of fine copper, precious as gold.
28 **And I** said unto them,
Ye are holy unto the LORD;
the vessels are holy also;
and the silver and the gold are a freewill offering unto the LORD God of your fathers.
29 **Watch ye,**
and keep them,
until ye weigh them before the chief of the priests and the Levites, and chief of the fathers of Israel, at Jerusalem, in the chambers of the house of the LORD.
30 **So** took the priests and the Levites the weight of the silver, and the gold, and the vessels,
to bring them to Jerusalem unto the house of our God.
31 **Then we** departed from the river of Ahava on the twelfth day of the first month,
to go unto Jerusalem:
and the hand of our God was upon us,
and he delivered us from the hand of the enemy, and of such as lay in wait by the way.
32 **And we** came to Jerusalem,
and abode there three days.
33 **Now on the fourth day** was the silver and the gold and the vessels weighed in the house of our God by the hand of Meremoth the son of Uriah the priest;
and with him was Eleazar the son of Phinehas;
and with them was Jozabad the son of Jeshua, and Noadiah the son of Binnui, Levites;
34 By number and by weight of every one:
and all the weight was written at that time.
35 **Also the children of those that had been carried away**, {which were come out of the captivity}, offered burnt offerings unto the

God of Israel, twelve bullocks for all Israel, ninety and six rams, seventy and seven lambs, twelve he goats for a sin offering:
all this was a burnt offering unto the LORD.

36 **And they** delivered the king's commissions unto the king's lieutenants, and to the governors on this side the river:
and they furthered the people, and the house of God.

9 **Now when these things** were done, **the princes** came to me, saying,
The people of Israel, and the priests, and the Levites, have not separated themselves from the people of the lands,
doing according to their abominations, even of the Canaanites, the Hittites, the Perizzites, the Jebusites, the Ammonites, the Moabites, the Egyptians, and the Amorites.

2 **For they** have taken of their daughters for themselves, and for their sons:
so that the holy seed have mingled themselves with the people of those lands:
yea, the hand of the princes and rulers hath been chief in this trespass.

3 **And when** I heard this thing,
I rent my garment and my mantle,
and plucked off the hair of my head and of my beard,
and sat down astonied.

4 **Then** were assembled unto me every one that trembled at the words of the God of Israel, because of the transgression of those that had been carried away;
and I sat astonied until the evening sacrifice.

5 **And at the evening sacrifice** I arose up from my heaviness;
and having rent my garment and my mantle,
I fell upon my knees,
and spread out my hands unto the LORD my God,

6 **And** said,
O my God, I am ashamed and blush to lift up my face to thee, my God:
for our iniquities are increased over our head,
and our trespass is grown up unto the heavens.

7 **Since the days of our fathers** have we been in a great trespass unto this day;
and for our iniquities have we, our kings, and our priests, been delivered into the hand of the kings of the lands, to the sword, to captivity, and to a spoil, and to confusion of face,
as it is this day.

8 **And now for a little space** grace hath been shewed from the LORD our God,
to leave us a remnant to escape,
and to give us a nail in his holy place,
that our God may lighten our eyes,
and give us a little reviving in our bondage.

9 **For we** were bondmen;
yet our God hath not forsaken us in our bondage,
but hath extended mercy unto us in the sight of the kings of Persia,
to give us a reviving,
to set up the house of our God,
and to repair the desolations thereof,
and to give us a wall in Judah and in Jerusalem.

10 **And now, O our God, what** shall we say after this?
for we have forsaken thy commandments,

11 **Which thou** hast commanded by thy servants the prophets,
saying,
The land, {unto which ye go to possess it}, is an unclean land with the filthiness of the people of the lands, with their abominations,
which have filled it from one end to another with their uncleanness.

12 **Now therefore give not** your daughters unto their sons,
neither take their daughters unto your sons,
nor seek their peace or their wealth for ever:
that ye may be strong,
and eat the good of the land,
and leave it for an inheritance to your children for ever.

13 **And after all that** is come upon us for our evil deeds, and for our great trespass,
seeing that thou our God hast punished us less than our iniquities deserve,
and hast given us such deliverance as this;

14 **Should we** again break thy commandments,
and join in affinity with the people of these abominations?
wouldest not thou be angry with us
till thou hadst consumed us,
so that there should be no remnant nor escaping?

15 **O LORD God of Israel, thou** art righteous:
for we remain yet escaped,
as it is this day:
behold,
we are before thee in our trespasses:
for we cannot stand before thee because of this.

10 **Now when Ezra** had prayed,
and when he had confessed,
weeping and casting himself down before the house of God,
there assembled unto him out of Israel a very great congregation of men and women and children:
for the people wept very sore.

2 **And Shechaniah the son of Jehiel, one of the sons of Elam,** answered and said unto Ezra,
We have trespassed against our God,
and have taken strange wives of the people of the land:
yet now there is hope in Israel concerning this thing.

3 **Now therefore let us** make a covenant with our God to put away all the wives, and such as are born of them, according to the counsel of my lord, and of those that tremble at the commandment of our God;
and let it be done according to the law.

4 **Arise;**
for this matter belongeth unto thee:
we also will be with thee:
be of good courage,
and do it.

5 **Then** arose Ezra,
and made the chief priests, the Levites, and all Israel, to swear
that they should do according to this word.
And they sware.

[6] **Then Ezra** rose up from before the house of God,
and went into the chamber of Johanan the son of Eliashib:
and when he came thither,
he did eat no bread,
nor drink water:
for he mourned because of the transgression of them that had been carried away.

[7] **And they** made proclamation throughout Judah and Jerusalem unto all the children of the captivity,
that they should gather themselves together unto Jerusalem;
[8] **And that whosoever** would not come within three days, according to the counsel of the princes and the elders,
all his substance should be forfeited,
and himself separated from the congregation of those that had been carried away.

[9] **Then all the men of Judah and Benjamin** gathered themselves together unto Jerusalem within three days.
It was the ninth month, on the twentieth day of the month;
and all the people sat in the street of the house of God,
trembling because of this matter, and for the great rain.

[10] **And Ezra the priest** stood up,
and said unto them,
Ye have transgressed,
and have taken strange wives,
to increase the trespass of Israel.

[11] **Now therefore make** confession unto the LORD God of your fathers,
and do his pleasure:
and separate yourselves from the people of the land, and from the strange wives.

[12] **Then all the congregation** answered and said with a loud voice,
As thou hast said,
so must we do.

[13] **But the people** are many,
and it is a time of much rain,
and we are not able to stand without,
neither is this a work of one day or two:
for we are many that have transgressed in this thing.

[14] **Let now our rulers of all the congregation** stand,
and let all them which have taken strange wives in our cities come at appointed times, and with them the elders of every city, and the judges thereof,
until the fierce wrath of our God for this matter be turned from us.

[15] **Only Jonathan the son of Asahel and Jahaziah the son of Tikvah** were employed about this matter:
and Meshullam and Shabbethai the Levite helped them.

[16] **And the children of the captivity** did so.

And Ezra the priest, with certain chief of the fathers, after the house of their fathers, and all of them by their names, were separated,
and sat down in the first day of the tenth month
to examine the matter.

[17] **And they** made an end with all the men that had taken strange wives by the first day of the first month.

[18] **And among the sons of the priests** there were found that had taken strange wives: namely, of the sons of Jeshua the son of Jozadak, and his brethren; Maaseiah, and Eliezer, and Jarib, and Gedaliah.

[19] **And they** gave their hands that they would put away their wives;
and being guilty,
they offered a ram of the flock for their trespass.

[20] And of the sons of Immer; Hanani, and Zebadiah.

[21] And of the sons of Harim; Maaseiah, and Elijah, and Shemaiah, and Jehiel, and Uzziah.

[22] And of the sons of Pashur; Elioenai, Maaseiah, Ishmael, Nethaneel, Jozabad, and Elasah.

[23] Also of the Levites; Jozabad, and Shimei, and Kelaiah, (the same is Kelita,) Pethahiah, Judah, and Eliezer.

[24] Of the singers also; Eliashib: and of the porters; Shallum, and Telem, and Uri.

[25] Moreover of Israel: of the sons of Parosh; Ramiah, and Jeziah, and Malchiah, and Miamin, and Eleazar, and Malchijah, and Benaiah.

[26] And of the sons of Elam; Mattaniah, Zechariah, and Jehiel, and Abdi, and Jeremoth, and Eliah.

[27] And of the sons of Zattu; Elioenai, Eliashib, Mattaniah, and Jeremoth, and Zabad, and Aziza.

[28] Of the sons also of Bebai; Jehohanan, Hananiah, Zabbai, and Athlai.

[29] And of the sons of Bani; Meshullam, Malluch, and Adaiah, Jashub, and Sheal, and Ramoth.

[30] And of the sons of Pahathmoab; Adna, and Chelal, Benaiah, Maaseiah, Mattaniah, Bezaleel, and Binnui, and Manasseh.

[31] And of the sons of Harim; Eliezer, Ishijah, Malchiah, Shemaiah, Shimeon,
[32] Benjamin, Malluch, and Shemariah.

[33] Of the sons of Hashum; Mattenai, Mattathah, Zabad, Eliphelet, Jeremai, Manasseh, and Shimei.

[34] Of the sons of Bani; Maadai, Amram, and Uel,
[35] Benaiah, Bedeiah, Chelluh,
[36] Vaniah, Meremoth, Eliashib,
[37] Mattaniah, Mattenai, and Jaasau,
[38] And Bani, and Binnui, Shimei,
[39] And Shelemiah, and Nathan, and Adaiah,
[40] Machnadebai, Shashai, Sharai,
[41] Azareel, and Shelemiah, Shemariah,
[42] Shallum, Amariah, and Joseph.

[43] Of the sons of Nebo; Jeiel, Mattithiah, Zabad, Zebina, Jadau, and Joel, Benaiah.

[44] **All these** had taken strange wives:
and some of them had wives by whom they had children.

Nehemiah

The Book of Nehemiah recounts the story of rebuilding Jerusalem's walls after the Babylonian Exile, as told by a political leader named Nehemiah. Written in two parts, the text first chronicles his journey to Jerusalem and his efforts to rebuild the city walls, gates, and towers. In contrast, the second part focuses on the social and religious reforms that he implements.

The narrative opens with Nehemiah, the king's cupbearer, living in the Persian capital of Susa and learning about the dire state of Jerusalem and its people. This news deeply moves him, and he seeks permission from the Persian king to return to Jerusalem and rebuild its defenses. The king grants his request. After he arrives in Jerusalem, Nehemiah faces opposition from local enemies who try to thwart his reconstruction efforts. However, he rallies the citizens of Jerusalem and completes the project in just 52 days. Nehemiah then turns his attention to the city's social and religious problems. He takes several steps to address these issues, including canceling debts, redistributing land, and ensuring the appropriate observance of the Sabbath.

The book concludes with a dedication ceremony for Jerusalem's rebuilt walls. At the celebration, Nehemiah offers a prayer of thanksgiving and praise to God for His guidance and protection. United in their commitment and shared purpose, the people of Jerusalem pledge to follow God's laws and live in peace and harmony with one another. The Book of Nehemiah provides a unique perspective into the Jewish people's social, political, and religious lives at this historical moment. It offers a testament to the power of faith, determination, and community spirit in overcoming adversity. The result is a valuable lesson for the Israelites on leadership, perseverance, and commitment to a greater cause.

1 The words of Nehemiah the son of Hachaliah.
And it came to pass in the month Chisleu, in the twentieth year,
as I was in Shushan the palace,
2 **That Hanani**, one of my brethren, came, he and certain men of Judah;
and I asked them concerning the Jews that had escaped, {which were left of the captivity}, and concerning Jerusalem.
3 **And they** said unto me,
The remnant that are left of the captivity there in the province are in great affliction and reproach:
the wall of Jerusalem also is broken down,
and the gates thereof are burned with fire.
4 **And it** came to pass,
when I heard these words,
that I sat down and wept,
and mourned certain days,
and fasted,
and prayed before the God of heaven,
5 **And** said,
I beseech thee, O LORD God of heaven, the great and terrible God,
that keepeth covenant and mercy for them that love him and observe his commandments:
6 **Let thine ear** now be attentive,
and thine eyes open,
that thou mayest hear the prayer of thy servant,
which I pray before thee now, day and night, for the children of Israel thy servants,
and confess the sins of the children of Israel,
which we have sinned against thee:
both I and my father's house have sinned.
7 **We** have dealt very corruptly against thee,
and have not kept the commandments, nor the statutes, nor the judgments,
which thou commandedst thy servant Moses.
8 **Remember**, {I beseech thee}, the word that thou commandedst thy servant Moses,
saying,
If ye transgress,
I will scatter you abroad among the nations:
9 **But if ye** turn unto me,
and keep my commandments,
and do them;
though there were of you cast out unto the uttermost part of the heaven,
yet will I gather them from thence,
and will bring them unto the place that I have chosen
to set my name there.
10 **Now these** are thy servants and thy people,
whom thou hast redeemed by thy great power, and by thy strong hand.
11 **O Lord, I** beseech thee,
let now thine ear be attentive to the prayer of thy servant, and to the prayer of thy servants,
who desire to fear thy name:
and prosper, {I pray thee}, thy servant this day,
and grant him mercy in the sight of this man.
For I was the king's cupbearer.

2 **And it** came to pass in the month Nisan, in the twentieth year of Artaxerxes the king,
that wine was before him:
and I took up the wine,
and gave it unto the king.
Now I had not been beforetime sad in his presence.
2 **Wherefore the king** said unto me,
Why is thy countenance sad,
seeing thou art not sick?

this is nothing else but sorrow of heart.
Then I was very sore afraid,
3 **And** said unto the king,
Let the king live for ever:
why should not my countenance be sad,
when the city, the place of my fathers' sepulchres, lieth waste,
and the gates thereof are consumed with fire?

4 **Then the king** said unto me,
For what dost thou make request?

So I prayed to the God of heaven.

5 **And I** said unto the king,
If it please the king,
and if thy servant have found favour in thy sight,
that thou wouldest send me unto Judah, unto the city of my fathers' sepulchres,
that I may build it.

6 **And the king** said unto me,
(the queen also sitting by him,)
For how long shall thy journey be?
and when wilt thou return?

So it pleased the king to send me;
and I set him a time.

7 **Moreover I** said unto the king,
If it please the king,
let letters be given me to the governors beyond the river, {that they may convey me over} {till I come into Judah};
8 And a letter unto Asaph the keeper of the king's forest, {that he may give me timber} {to make beams for the gates of the palace which appertained to the house, and for the wall of the city, and for the house that I shall enter into}.

And the king granted me, according to the good hand of my God upon me.

9 **Then I** came to the governors beyond the river,
and gave them the king's letters.

Now the king had sent captains of the army and horsemen with me.

10 **When Sanballat the Horonite, and Tobiah the servant, the Ammonite,** heard of it,
it grieved them exceedingly that there was come a man to seek the welfare of the children of Israel.

11 **So I** came to Jerusalem,
and was there three days.

12 **And I** arose in the night, I and some few men with me;
neither told I any man
what my God had put in my heart to do at Jerusalem:
neither was there any beast with me, save the beast that I rode upon.

13 **And I** went out by night by the gate of the valley, even before the dragon well, and to the dung port,
and viewed the walls of Jerusalem,
which were broken down,
and the gates thereof were consumed with fire.

14 **Then I** went on to the gate of the fountain, and to the king's pool:
but there was no place for the beast that was under me to pass.

15 **Then** went I up in the night by the brook,
and viewed the wall,
and turned back,
and entered by the gate of the valley,
and so returned.

16 **And the rulers** knew not
whither I went,
or what I did;
neither had I as yet told it to the Jews, nor to the priests, nor to the nobles, nor to the rulers, nor to the rest that did the work.

17 **Then** said I unto them,
Ye see the distress that we are in,
how Jerusalem lieth waste,
and the gates thereof are burned with fire:
come,
and let us build up the wall of Jerusalem,
that we be no more a reproach.

18 **Then I** told them of the hand of my God which was good upon me; as also the king's words that he had spoken unto me.

And they said,
Let us rise up and build.

So they strengthened their hands for this good work.

19 **But when Sanballat the Horonite, and Tobiah the servant, the Ammonite, and Geshem the Arabian,** heard it,
they laughed us to scorn,
and despised us,
and said,
What is this thing that ye do?
will ye rebel against the king?

20 **Then** answered I them,
and said unto them,
The God of heaven, he will prosper us;
therefore we his servants will arise and build:
but ye have no portion, nor right, nor memorial, in Jerusalem.

3 **Then Eliashib the high priest** rose up with his brethren the priests,
and they builded the sheep gate;
they sanctified it,
and set up the doors of it;
even unto the tower of Meah they sanctified it, unto the tower of Hananeel.

2 **And next unto him** builded the men of Jericho.

And next to them builded Zaccur the son of Imri.

3 **But the fish gate** did the sons of Hassenaah build,
who also laid the beams thereof,
and set up the doors thereof, the locks thereof, and the bars thereof.

4 **And next unto them** repaired Meremoth the son of Urijah, the son of Koz.

And next unto them repaired Meshullam the son of Berechiah, the son of Meshezabeel.

And next unto them repaired Zadok the son of Baana.

5 **And next unto them** the Tekoites repaired;
but their nobles put not their necks to the work of their Lord.

6 **Moreover the old gate** repaired Jehoiada the son of Paseah, and Meshullam the son of Besodeiah;
they laid the beams thereof,
and set up the doors thereof, and the locks thereof, and the bars thereof.

7 **And next unto them** repaired Melatiah the Gibeonite, and Jadon the Meronothite, the men of Gibeon, and of Mizpah, unto the throne of the governor on this side the river.

8 **Next unto him** repaired Uzziel the son of Harhaiah, of the goldsmiths.

Next unto him also repaired Hananiah the son of one of the apothecaries,
and they fortified Jerusalem unto the broad wall.

9 **And next unto them** repaired Rephaiah the son of Hur, the ruler of the half part of Jerusalem.

10 **And next unto them** repaired Jedaiah the son of Harumaph, even over against his house.

And next unto him repaired Hattush the son of Hashabniah.

11 **Malchijah the son of Harim, and Hashub the son of Pahathmoab,** repaired the other piece, and the tower of the furnaces.

12 **And next unto him** repaired Shallum the son of Halohesh, the ruler of the half part of Jerusalem, he and his daughters.

13 **The valley gate** repaired Hanun, and the inhabitants of Zanoah;
they built it,
and set up the doors thereof, the locks thereof, and the bars thereof, and a thousand cubits on the wall unto the dung gate.

14 **But the dung gate** repaired Malchiah the son of Rechab, the ruler of part of Bethhaccerem;
he built it,
and set up the doors thereof, the locks thereof, and the bars thereof.

15 **But the gate of the fountain** repaired Shallun the son of Colhozeh, the ruler of part of Mizpah;
he built it,
and covered it,
and set up the doors thereof, the locks thereof, and the bars thereof, and the wall of the pool of Siloah by the king's garden, and unto the stairs that go down from the city of David.

16 **After him** repaired Nehemiah the son of Azbuk, the ruler of the half part of Bethzur, unto the place over against the sepulchres of David, and to the pool that was made, and unto the house of the mighty.

17 **After him** repaired the Levites, Rehum the son of Bani.

Next unto him repaired Hashabiah, the ruler of the half part of Keilah, in his part.

18 **After him** repaired their brethren, Bavai the son of Henadad, the ruler of the half part of Keilah.

19 **And next to him** repaired Ezer the son of Jeshua, the ruler of Mizpah, another piece over against the going up to the armoury at the turning of the wall.

20 **After him** Baruch the son of Zabbai earnestly repaired the other piece, from the turning of the wall unto the door of the house of Eliashib the high priest.

21 **After him** repaired Meremoth the son of Urijah the son of Koz another piece, from the door of the house of Eliashib even to the end of the house of Eliashib.

22 **And after him** repaired the priests, the men of the plain.

23 **After him** repaired Benjamin and Hashub over against their house.

After him repaired Azariah the son of Maaseiah the son of Ananiah by his house.

24 **After him** repaired Binnui the son of Henadad another piece, from the house of Azariah unto the turning of the wall, even unto the corner.

25 **Palal the son of Uzai,** over against the turning of the wall, and the tower which lieth out from the king's high house,
that was by the court of the prison.

After him Pedaiah the son of Parosh.

26 **Moreover the Nethinims** dwelt in Ophel, unto the place over against the water gate toward the east, and the tower that lieth out.

27 **After them** the Tekoites repaired another piece, over against the great tower that lieth out, even unto the wall of Ophel.

28 **From above the horse gate** repaired the priests, every one over against his house.

29 **After them** repaired Zadok the son of Immer over against his house.

After him repaired also Shemaiah the son of Shechaniah, the keeper of the east gate.

30 **After him** repaired Hananiah the son of Shelemiah, and Hanun the sixth son of Zalaph, another piece.

After him repaired Meshullam the son of Berechiah over against his chamber.

31 **After him** repaired Malchiah the goldsmith's son unto the place of the Nethinims, and of the merchants, over against the gate Miphkad, and to the going up of the corner.

32 **And between the going up of the corner unto the sheep gate** repaired the goldsmiths and the merchants.

4 **But it** came to pass,
that when Sanballat heard that we builded the wall,
he was wroth,
and took great indignation,
and mocked the Jews.

2 **And he** spake before his brethren and the army of Samaria,
and said,
What do these feeble Jews?
will they fortify themselves?
will they sacrifice?
will they make an end in a day?
will they revive the stones out of the heaps of the rubbish which are burned?

3 **Now Tobiah the Ammonite** was by him,
and he said,
Even that which they build, {if a fox go up}, he shall even break down their stone wall.

4 **Hear**, O our God;
for we are despised:
and turn their reproach upon their own head,
and give them for a prey in the land of captivity:

5 **And cover not** their iniquity,
and let not their sin be blotted out from before thee:
for they have provoked thee to anger before the builders.

6 **So** built we the wall;
and all the wall was joined together unto the half thereof:
for the people had a mind to work.

7 **But it** came to pass,
that when Sanballat, and Tobiah, and the Arabians, and the Ammonites, and the Ashdodites, heard that the walls of Jerusalem were made up, and that the breaches began to be stopped,
then they were very wroth,

8 **And** conspired all of them together
to come and to fight against Jerusalem,
and to hinder it.

9 **Nevertheless we** made our prayer unto our God,

and set a watch against them day and night, because of them.
10 **And Judah** said,
The strength of the bearers of burdens is decayed,
and there is much rubbish;
so that we are not able to build the wall.
11 **And our adversaries** said,
They shall not know,
neither see,
till we come in the midst among them,
and slay them,
and cause the work to cease.
12 **And it** came to pass,
that when the Jews which dwelt by them came,
they said unto us ten times,
From all places whence ye shall return unto us they will be upon you.
13 **Therefore** set I in the lower places behind the wall, and on the higher places,
I even set the people after their families with their swords, their spears, and their bows.
14 **And I** looked,
and rose up,
and said unto the nobles, and to the rulers, and to the rest of the people,
Be not ye afraid of them:
remember the Lord,
which is great and terrible,
and fight for your brethren, your sons, and your daughters, your wives, and your houses.
15 **And it** came to pass,
when our enemies heard that it was known unto us, and God had brought their counsel to nought,
that we returned all of us to the wall, every one unto his work.
16 **And it** came to pass from that time forth,
that the half of my servants wrought in the work,
and the other half of them held both the spears, the shields, and the bows, and the habergeons;
and the rulers were behind all the house of Judah.
17 **They which builded on the wall, and they that bare burdens, with those that laded,** every one with one of his hands wrought in the work,
and with the other hand held a weapon.
18 **For the builders**, every one had his sword girded by his side,
and so builded.
And he that sounded the trumpet was by me.
19 **And I** said unto the nobles, and to the rulers, and to the rest of the people,
The work is great and large,
and we are separated upon the wall, one far from another.
20 **In what place** therefore ye hear the sound of the trumpet,
resort ye thither unto us:
our God shall fight for us.
21 **So we** laboured in the work:
and half of them held the spears from the rising of the morning till the stars appeared.
22 **Likewise at the same time** said I unto the people,
Let every one with his servant lodge within Jerusalem,
that in the night they may be a guard to us,
and labour on the day.
23 **So neither I, nor my brethren, nor my servants, nor the men of the guard which followed me,** none of us put off our clothes,
saving that every one put them off for washing.

5 **And there** was a great cry of the people and of their wives against their brethren the Jews.
2 **For there** were that said,
We, our sons, and our daughters, are many:
therefore we take up corn for them,
that we may eat,
and live.
3 **Some also there** were that said,
We have mortgaged our lands, vineyards, and houses,
that we might buy corn, because of the dearth.
4 **There** were also that said,
We have borrowed money for the king's tribute, and that upon our lands and vineyards.
5 **Yet now our flesh** is as the flesh of our brethren, our children as their children:
and, {lo}, we bring into bondage our sons and our daughters to be servants,
and some of our daughters are brought unto bondage already:
neither is it in our power to redeem them;
for other men have our lands and vineyards.
6 **And I** was very angry
when I heard their cry and these words.
7 **Then I** consulted with myself,
and I rebuked the nobles, and the rulers,
and said unto them,
Ye exact usury, every one of his brother.
And I set a great assembly against them.
8 **And I** said unto them,
We after our ability have redeemed our brethren the Jews,
which were sold unto the heathen;
and will ye even sell your brethren?
or shall they be sold unto us?
Then held they their peace,
and found nothing to answer.
9 **Also I** said,
It is not good that ye do:
ought ye not to walk in the fear of our God because of the reproach of the heathen our enemies?
10 **I likewise, and my brethren, and my servants,** might exact of them money and corn:
I pray you,
let us leave off this usury.
11 **Restore,** {I pray you}, to them, even this day, their lands, their vineyards, their oliveyards, and their houses, also the hundredth part of the money, and of the corn, the wine, and the oil,
that ye exact of them.
12 **Then** said they,
We will restore them,
and will require nothing of them;
so will we do as thou sayest.
Then I called the priests,
and took an oath of them,
that they should do according to this promise.
13 **Also I** shook my lap,
and said,
So God shake out every man from his house, and from his labour,
that performeth not this promise,
even thus be he shaken out,
and emptied.
And all the congregation said, Amen,

and praised the LORD.
And the people did according to this promise.
14 **Moreover from the time that I was appointed to be their governor in the land of Judah, from the twentieth year even unto the two and thirtieth year of Artaxerxes the king, that is, twelve years,** I and my brethren have not eaten the bread of the governor.
15 **But the former governors that had been before me** were chargeable unto the people,
and had taken of them bread and wine, beside forty shekels of silver;
yea, even their servants bare rule over the people:
but so did not I, because of the fear of God.
16 **Yea, also I** continued in the work of this wall,
neither bought we any land:
and all my servants were gathered thither unto the work.
17 **Moreover there** were at my table an hundred and fifty of the Jews and rulers, beside those that came unto us from among the heathen that are about us.
18 **Now that which was prepared for me daily** was one ox and six choice sheep;
also fowls were prepared for me, and once in ten days store of all sorts of wine:
yet for all this required not I the bread of the governor,
because the bondage was heavy upon this people.
19 **Think** upon me, my God, for good, according to all that I have done for this people.

6 **Now it** came to pass **when Sanballat, and Tobiah, and Geshem the Arabian, and the rest of our enemies,** heard that I had builded the wall, and that there was no breach left therein;
(though at that time I had not set up the doors upon the gates;)
2 **That Sanballat and Geshem** sent unto me,
saying,
Come,
let us meet together in some one of the villages in the plain of Ono.
But they thought to do me mischief.
3 **And I** sent messengers unto them,
saying,
I am doing a great work,
so that I cannot come down:
why should the work cease,
whilst I leave it,
and come down to you?
4 **Yet they** sent unto me four times after this sort;
and I answered them after the same manner.
5 **Then** sent Sanballat his servant unto me in like manner the fifth time with an open letter in his hand;
6 **Wherein** was written,
It is reported among the heathen, {and Gashmu saith it}, that thou and the Jews think to rebel:
for which cause thou buildest the wall,
that thou mayest be their king, according to these words.
7 **And thou** hast also appointed prophets to preach of thee at Jerusalem,
saying,
There is a king in Judah:
and now shall it be reported to the king according to these words.
Come now therefore,
and let us take counsel together.
8 **Then I** sent unto him,
saying,
There are no such things done as thou sayest,
but thou feignest them out of thine own heart.
9 **For they all** made us afraid,
saying,
Their hands shall be weakened from the work,
that it be not done.
Now therefore, O God, strengthen my hands.
10 **Afterward I** came unto the house of Shemaiah the son of Delaiah the son of Mehetabeel,
who was shut up;
and he said,
Let us meet together in the house of God, within the temple,
and let us shut the doors of the temple:
for they will come to slay thee;
yea, in the night will they come to slay thee.
11 **And I** said,
Should such a man as I flee?
and who is there,
that, {being as I am}, would go into the temple
to save his life?
I will not go in.
12 **And, {lo}, I** perceived
that God had not sent him;
but that he pronounced this prophecy against me:
for Tobiah and Sanballat had hired him.
13 **Therefore** was he hired,
that I should be afraid,
and do so,
and sin,
and that they might have matter for an evil report,
that they might reproach me.
14 **My God, think thou** upon Tobiah and Sanballat according to these their works, and on the prophetess Noadiah, and the rest of the prophets,
that would have put me in fear.
15 **So the wall** was finished in the twenty and fifth day of the month Elul, in fifty and two days.
16 **And it** came to pass,
that when all our enemies heard thereof,
and all the heathen that were about us saw these things,
they were much cast down in their own eyes:
for they perceived
that this work was wrought of our God.
17 **Moreover in those days** the nobles of Judah sent many letters unto Tobiah,
and the letters of Tobiah came unto them.
18 **For there** were many in Judah sworn unto him,
because he was the son in law of Shechaniah the son of Arah;
and his son Johanan had taken the daughter of Meshullam the son of Berechiah.
19 **Also they** reported his good deeds before me,
and uttered my words to him.
And Tobiah sent letters
to put me in fear.

7 **Now it** came to pass,
when the wall was built,
and I had set up the doors,
and the porters and the singers
and the Levites were appointed,

2 **That I** gave my brother Hanani,
and Hananiah the ruler of the
palace, charge over Jerusalem:
for he was a faithful man,
and feared God above many.

3 **And I** said unto them,
Let not the gates of Jerusalem be
opened until the sun be hot;
and while they stand by,
let them shut the doors,
and bar them:
and appoint watches of the
inhabitants of Jerusalem, every
one in his watch, and every one to
be over against his house.

4 **Now the city** was large and great:
but the people were few therein,
and the houses were not builded.

5 **And my God** put into mine heart
to gather together the nobles, and
the rulers, and the people,
that they might be reckoned by
genealogy.
And I found a register of the
genealogy of them which came up
at the first,
and found written therein,

6 **These** are the children of the
province, {that went up out of the
captivity}, of those that had been
carried away,
whom Nebuchadnezzar the king of
Babylon had carried away,
and came again to Jerusalem and to
Judah, every one unto his city;

7 **Who** came with Zerubbabel,
Jeshua, Nehemiah, Azariah,
Raamiah, Nahamani, Mordecai,
Bilshan, Mispereth, Bigvai,
Nehum, Baanah.
**The number, {I say}, of the men of
the people of Israel** was this;

8 **The children of Parosh,** two
thousand an hundred seventy and
two.

9 **The children of Shephatiah,**
three hundred seventy and two.

10 **The children of Arah,** six
hundred fifty and two.

11 **The children of Pahathmoab, of
the children of Jeshua and Joab,**
two thousand and eight hundred
and eighteen.

12 **The children of Elam,** a
thousand two hundred fifty and
four.

13 **The children of Zattu,** eight
hundred forty and five.

14 **The children of Zaccai,** seven
hundred and threescore.

15 **The children of Binnui,** six
hundred forty and eight.

16 **The children of Bebai,** six
hundred twenty and eight.

17 **The children of Azgad,** two
thousand three hundred twenty
and two.

18 **The children of Adonikam,** six
hundred threescore and seven.

19 **The children of Bigvai,** two
thousand threescore and seven.

20 **The children of Adin,** six
hundred fifty and five.

21 **The children of Ater of
Hezekiah,** ninety and eight.

22 **The children of Hashum,** three
hundred twenty and eight.

23 **The children of Bezai,** three
hundred twenty and four.

24 **The children of Hariph,** an
hundred and twelve.

25 **The children of Gibeon,** ninety
and five.

26 **The men of Bethlehem and
Netophah,** an hundred fourscore
and eight.

27 **The men of Anathoth,** an
hundred twenty and eight.

28 **The men of Bethazmaveth,** forty
and two.

29 **The men of Kirjathjearim,
Chephirah, and Beeroth,** seven
hundred forty and three.

30 **The men of Ramah and Gaba,**
six hundred twenty and one.

31 **The men of Michmas,** an
hundred and twenty and two.

32 **The men of Bethel and Ai,** an
hundred twenty and three.

33 **The men of the other Nebo,** fifty
and two.

34 **The children of the other Elam,**
a thousand two hundred fifty and
four.

35 **The children of Harim,** three
hundred and twenty.

36 **The children of Jericho,** three
hundred forty and five.

37 **The children of Lod, Hadid, and
Ono,** seven hundred twenty and
one.

38 **The children of Senaah,** three
thousand nine hundred and
thirty.

39 **The priests:** the children of
Jedaiah, of the house of Jeshua,
nine hundred seventy and three.

40 **The children of Immer,** a
thousand fifty and two.

41 **The children of Pashur,** a
thousand two hundred forty and
seven.

42 **The children of Harim,** a
thousand and seventeen.

43 **The Levites:** the children of
Jeshua, of Kadmiel, and of the
children of Hodevah, seventy and
four.

44 **The singers:** the children of
Asaph, an hundred forty and
eight.

45 **The porters:** the children of
Shallum, the children of Ater, the
children of Talmon, the children
of Akkub, the children of Hatita,
the children of Shobai, an
hundred thirty and eight.

46 **The Nethinims:** the children of
Ziha, the children of Hashupha,
the children of Tabbaoth,

47 The children of Keros, the children
of Sia, the children of Padon,

48 The children of Lebana, the
children of Hagaba, the children
of Shalmai,

49 The children of Hanan, the
children of Giddel, the children of
Gahar,

50 The children of Reaiah, the
children of Rezin, the children of
Nekoda,

51 The children of Gazzam, the
children of Uzza, the children of
Phaseah,

52 The children of Besai, the children
of Meunim, the children of
Nephishesim,

53 The children of Bakbuk, the
children of Hakupha, the children
of Harhur,

54 The children of Bazlith, the
children of Mehida, the children
of Harsha,

55 The children of Barkos, the
children of Sisera, the children of
Tamah,

56 The children of Neziah, the
children of Hatipha.

57 **The children of Solomon's servants:** the children of Sotai, the children of Sophereth, the children of Perida,
58 The children of Jaala, the children of Darkon, the children of Giddel,
59 The children of Shephatiah, the children of Hattil, the children of Pochereth of Zebaim, the children of Amon.

60 **All the Nethinims, and the children of Solomon's servants,** were three hundred ninety and two.

61 **And these** were they which went up also from Telmelah, Telharesha, Cherub, Addon, and Immer:
but they could not shew their father's house, nor their seed,
whether they were of Israel.

62 **The children of Delaiah, the children of Tobiah, the children of Nekoda,** six hundred forty and two.

63 **And of the priests:** the children of Habaiah, the children of Koz, the children of Barzillai,
which took one of the daughters of Barzillai the Gileadite to wife,
and was called after their name.

64 **These** sought their register among those that were reckoned by genealogy,
but it was not found:
therefore were they, as polluted, put from the priesthood.

65 **And the Tirshatha** said unto them,
that they should not eat of the most holy things,
till there stood up a priest with Urim and Thummim.

66 **The whole congregation together** was forty and two thousand three hundred and threescore,
67 Beside their manservants and their maidservants,
of whom there were seven thousand three hundred thirty and seven:
and they had two hundred forty and five singing men and singing women.

68 **Their horses,** seven hundred thirty and six:
their mules, two hundred forty and five:
69 **Their camels,** four hundred thirty and five:
six thousand seven hundred and twenty asses.

70 **And some of the chief of the fathers** gave unto the work.
The Tirshatha gave to the treasure a thousand drams of gold, fifty basons, five hundred and thirty priests' garments.

71 **And some of the chief of the fathers** gave to the treasure of the work twenty thousand drams of gold, and two thousand and two hundred pound of silver.

72 **And that which the rest of the people gave** was twenty thousand drams of gold, and two thousand pound of silver, and threescore and seven priests' garments.

73 **So the priests, and the Levites, and the porters, and the singers, and some of the people, and the Nethinims, and all Israel,** dwelt in their cities;
and when the seventh month came,
the children of Israel were in their cities.

8 **And all the people** gathered themselves together as one man into the street that was before the water gate;
and they spake unto Ezra the scribe to bring the book of the law of Moses,
which the LORD had commanded to Israel.

2 **And Ezra the priest** brought the law before the congregation both of men and women, and all that could hear with understanding, upon the first day of the seventh month.

3 **And he** read therein before the street that was before the water gate from the morning until midday, before the men and the women, and those that could understand;
and the ears of all the people were attentive unto the book of the law.

4 **And Ezra the scribe** stood upon a pulpit of wood,
which they had made for the purpose;
and beside him stood Mattithiah, and Shema, and Anaiah, and Urijah, and Hilkiah, and Maaseiah, on his right hand;
and on his left hand, Pedaiah, and Mishael, and Malchiah, and Hashum, and Hashbadana, Zechariah, and Meshullam.

5 **And Ezra** opened the book in the sight of all the people;
(for he was above all the people;)
and when he opened it,
all the people stood up:
6 **And Ezra** blessed the LORD, the great God.

And all the people answered, {Amen, Amen}, with lifting up their hands:
and they bowed their heads,
and worshipped the LORD with their faces to the ground.

7 **Also Jeshua, and Bani, and Sherebiah, Jamin, Akkub, Shabbethai, Hodijah, Maaseiah, Kelita, Azariah, Jozabad, Hanan, Pelaiah, and the Levites,** caused the people to understand the law:
and the people stood in their place.

8 **So they** read in the book in the law of God distinctly,
and gave the sense,
and caused them to understand the reading.

9 **And Nehemiah, {which is the Tirshatha}, and Ezra the priest the scribe, and the Levites that taught the people,** said unto all the people,
This day is holy unto the LORD your God;
mourn not,
nor weep.

For all the people wept,
when they heard the words of the law.

10 **Then he** said unto them,
Go your way,
eat the fat,
and drink the sweet,
and send portions unto them for whom nothing is prepared:
for this day is holy unto our Lord:
neither be ye sorry;
for the joy of the LORD is your strength.

11 **So the Levites** stilled all the people,
saying,
Hold your peace,

for the day is holy;
neither be ye grieved.
12 **And all the people** went their way to eat,
and to drink,
and to send portions,
and to make great mirth,
because they had understood the words that were declared unto them.
13 **And on the second day** were gathered together the chief of the fathers of all the people, the priests, and the Levites, unto Ezra the scribe,
even to understand the words of the law.
14 **And they** found written in the law which the LORD had commanded by Moses,
that the children of Israel should dwell in booths in the feast of the seventh month:
15 **And that they** should publish and proclaim in all their cities, and in Jerusalem,
saying,
Go forth unto the mount,
and fetch olive branches, and pine branches, and myrtle branches, and palm branches, and branches of thick trees,
to make booths,
as it is written.
16 **So the people** went forth,
and brought them,
and made themselves booths, every one upon the roof of his house, and in their courts, and in the courts of the house of God, and in the street of the water gate, and in the street of the gate of Ephraim.
17 **And all the congregation of them that were come again out of the captivity** made booths,
and sat under the booths:
for since the days of Jeshua the son of Nun unto that day had not the children of Israel done so.
And there was very great gladness.
18 **Also day by day, from the first day unto the last day,** he read in the book of the law of God.
And they kept the feast seven days;
and on the eighth day was a solemn assembly, according unto the manner.

9 **Now in the twenty and fourth day of this month** the children of Israel were assembled with fasting, and with sackclothes, and earth upon them.
2 **And the seed of Israel** separated themselves from all strangers,
and stood and confessed their sins, and the iniquities of their fathers.
3 **And they** stood up in their place,
and read in the book of the law of the LORD their God one fourth part of the day;
and another fourth part they confessed,
and worshipped the LORD their God.
4 **Then** stood up upon the stairs, of the Levites, Jeshua, and Bani, Kadmiel, Shebaniah, Bunni, Sherebiah, Bani, and Chenani,
and cried with a loud voice unto the LORD their God.
5 **Then the Levites, Jeshua, and Kadmiel, Bani, Hashabniah, Sherebiah, Hodijah, Shebaniah, and Pethahiah,** said,
Stand up and bless the LORD your God for ever and ever:
and blessed be thy glorious name,
which is exalted above all blessing and praise.
6 **Thou, even thou,** art LORD alone;
thou hast made heaven, the heaven of heavens, with all their host, the earth, and all things that are therein, the seas, and all that is therein,
and thou preservest them all;
and the host of heaven worshippeth thee.
7 **Thou** art the LORD the God,
who didst choose Abram,
and broughtest him forth out of Ur of the Chaldees,
and gavest him the name of Abraham;
8 **And** foundest his heart faithful before thee,
and madest a covenant with him to give the land of the Canaanites, the Hittites, the Amorites, and the Perizzites, and the Jebusites, and the Girgashites,
to give it, {I say}, to his seed,
and hast performed thy words;
for thou art righteous:
9 **And** didst see the affliction of our fathers in Egypt,
and heardest their cry by the Red sea;
10 **And** shewedst signs and wonders upon Pharaoh, and on all his servants, and on all the people of his land:
for thou knewest
that they dealt proudly against them.
So didst thou get thee a name,
as it is this day.
11 **And thou** didst divide the sea before them,
so that they went through the midst of the sea on the dry land;
and their persecutors thou threwest into the deeps, as a stone into the mighty waters.
12 **Moreover thou** leddest them in the day by a cloudy pillar; and in the night by a pillar of fire,
to give them light in the way wherein they should go.
13 **Thou** camest down also upon mount Sinai,
and spakest with them from heaven,
and gavest them right judgments, and true laws, good statutes and commandments:
14 **And** madest known unto them thy holy sabbath,
and commandedst them precepts, statutes, and laws, by the hand of Moses thy servant:
15 **And** gavest them bread from heaven for their hunger,
and broughtest forth water for them out of the rock for their thirst,
and promisedst them
that they should go in
to possess the land which thou hadst sworn to give them.
16 **But they and our fathers** dealt proudly,
and hardened their necks,
and hearkened not to thy commandments,
17 **And** refused to obey,
neither were mindful of thy wonders
that thou didst among them;
but hardened their necks,
and in their rebellion appointed a captain
to return to their bondage:
but thou art a God ready to pardon, gracious and merciful, slow to anger, and of great kindness,
and forsookest them not.

18 **Yea, when they** had made them a molten calf,
and said,
This is thy God that brought thee up out of Egypt,
and had wrought great provocations;

19 **Yet thou in thy manifold mercies** forsookest them not in the wilderness:
the pillar of the cloud departed not from them by day, {to lead them in the way}; neither the pillar of fire by night, {to shew them light, and the way wherein they should go}.

20 **Thou** gavest also thy good spirit
to instruct them,
and withheldest not thy manna from their mouth,
and gavest them water for their thirst.

21 **Yea, forty years** didst thou sustain them in the wilderness,
so that they lacked nothing;
their clothes waxed not old,
and their feet swelled not.

22 **Moreover thou** gavest them kingdoms and nations,
and didst divide them into corners:
so they possessed the land of Sihon, and the land of the king of Heshbon, and the land of Og king of Bashan.

23 **Their children** also multipliedst thou as the stars of heaven,
and broughtest them into the land,
concerning which thou hadst promised to their fathers,
that they should go in
to possess it.

24 **So the children** went in and possessed the land,
and thou subduedst before them the inhabitants of the land, the Canaanites,
and gavest them into their hands, with their kings, and the people of the land,
that they might do with them as they would.

25 **And they** took strong cities, and a fat land,
and possessed houses full of all goods, wells digged, vineyards, and oliveyards, and fruit trees in abundance:
so they did eat,
and were filled,
and became fat,
and delighted themselves in thy great goodness.

26 **Nevertheless they** were disobedient,
and rebelled against thee,
and cast thy law behind their backs,
and slew thy prophets
which testified against them
to turn them to thee,
and they wrought great provocations.

27 **Therefore thou** deliveredst them into the hand of their enemies,
who vexed them:
and in the time of their trouble, {when they cried unto thee}, thou heardest them from heaven;
and according to thy manifold mercies thou gavest them saviours,
who saved them out of the hand of their enemies.

28 **But after they** had rest,
they did evil again before thee:
therefore leftest thou them in the land of their enemies,
so that they had the dominion over them:
yet when they returned,
and cried unto thee,
thou heardest them from heaven;
and many times didst thou deliver them according to thy mercies;

29 **And** testifiedst against them,
that thou mightest bring them again unto thy law:
yet they dealt proudly,
and hearkened not unto thy commandments,
but sinned against thy judgments,
(which if a man do,
he shall live in them;)
and withdrew the shoulder,
and hardened their neck,
and would not hear.

30 **Yet many years** didst thou forbear them,
and testifiedst against them by thy spirit in thy prophets:
yet would they not give ear:
therefore gavest thou them into the hand of the people of the lands.

31 **Nevertheless for thy great mercies' sake** thou didst not utterly consume them,
nor forsake them;
for thou art a gracious and merciful God.

32 **Now therefore, our God, the great, the mighty, and the terrible God, {who keepest covenant and mercy}, let not all the trouble** seem little before thee,
that hath come upon us, on our kings, on our princes, and on our priests, and on our prophets, and on our fathers, and on all thy people, since the time of the kings of Assyria unto this day.

33 **Howbeit thou** art just in all that is brought upon us;
for thou hast done right,
but we have done wickedly:

34 **Neither** have our kings, our princes, our priests, nor our fathers, kept thy law,
nor hearkened unto thy commandments and thy testimonies,
wherewith thou didst testify against them.

35 **For they** have not served thee in their kingdom, and in thy great goodness that thou gavest them, and in the large and fat land which thou gavest before them,
neither turned they from their wicked works.

36 **Behold,**
we are servants this day, and for the land that thou gavest unto our fathers
to eat the fruit thereof and the good thereof,
behold,
we are servants in it:

37 **And it** yieldeth much increase unto the kings whom thou hast set over us because of our sins:
also they have dominion over our bodies, and over our cattle, at their pleasure,
and we are in great distress.

38 **And because of all this** we make a sure covenant,
and write it;
and our princes, Levites, and priests, seal unto it.

10 **Now those that sealed** were, Nehemiah, the Tirshatha, the son of Hachaliah, and Zidkijah,
2 Seraiah, Azariah, Jeremiah,
3 Pashur, Amariah, Malchijah,
4 Hattush, Shebaniah, Malluch,
5 Harim, Meremoth, Obadiah,
6 Daniel, Ginnethon, Baruch,
7 Meshullam, Abijah, Mijamin,
8 Maaziah, Bilgai, Shemaiah:

these were the priests.

9 **And the Levites:** both Jeshua the son of Azaniah, Binnui of the sons of Henadad, Kadmiel;
10 And their brethren, Shebaniah, Hodijah, Kelita, Pelaiah, Hanan,
11 Micha, Rehob, Hashabiah,
12 Zaccur, Sherebiah, Shebaniah,
13 Hodijah, Bani, Beninu.

14 **The chief of the people;** Parosh, Pahathmoab, Elam, Zatthu, Bani,
15 Bunni, Azgad, Bebai,
16 Adonijah, Bigvai, Adin,
17 Ater, Hizkijah, Azzur,
18 Hodijah, Hashum, Bezai,
19 Hariph, Anathoth, Nebai,
20 Magpiash, Meshullam, Hezir,
21 Meshezabeel, Zadok, Jaddua,
22 Pelatiah, Hanan, Anaiah,
23 Hoshea, Hananiah, Hashub,
24 Hallohesh, Pileha, Shobek,
25 Rehum, Hashabnah, Maaseiah,
26 And Ahijah, Hanan, Anan,
27 Malluch, Harim, Baanah.

28 **And the rest of the people, the priests, the Levites, the porters, the singers, the Nethinims, and all they that had separated themselves from the people of the lands unto the law of God, their wives, their sons, and their daughters, {every one having knowledge}, {and having understanding};**
29 They clave to their brethren, their nobles,
and entered into a curse, and into an oath,
to walk in God's law,
which was given by Moses the servant of God,
and to observe and do all the commandments of the LORD our Lord, and his judgments and his statutes;
30 **And that we** would not give our daughters unto the people of the land,
not take their daughters for our sons:
31 **And if the people of the land** bring ware or any victuals on the sabbath day to sell,
that we would not buy it of them on the sabbath, or on the holy day:
and that we would leave the seventh year, and the exaction of every debt.

32 **Also we** made ordinances for us,
to charge ourselves yearly with the third part of a shekel for the service of the house of our God;
33 For the shewbread, and for the continual meat offering, and for the continual burnt offering, of the sabbaths, of the new moons, for the set feasts, and for the holy things, and for the sin offerings
to make an atonement for Israel, and for all the work of the house of our God.

34 **And we** cast the lots among the priests, the Levites, and the people, for the wood offering,
to bring it into the house of our God, after the houses of our fathers, at times appointed year by year,
to burn upon the altar of the LORD our God,
as it is written in the law:
35 **And** to bring the firstfruits of our ground, and the firstfruits of all fruit of all trees, year by year, unto the house of the LORD:
36 Also the firstborn of our sons, and of our cattle, {as it is written in the law}, and the firstlings of our herds and of our flocks,
to bring to the house of our God, unto the priests that minister in the house of our God:
37 **And that we** should bring the firstfruits of our dough, and our offerings, and the fruit of all manner of trees, of wine and of oil, unto the priests, to the chambers of the house of our God; and the tithes of our ground unto the Levites,
that the same Levites might have the tithes in all the cities of our tillage.

38 **And the priest the son of Aaron** shall be with the Levites,
when the Levites take tithes:
and the Levites shall bring up the tithe of the tithes unto the house of our God, to the chambers, into the treasure house.

39 **For the children of Israel and the children of Levi** shall bring the offering of the corn, of the new wine, and the oil, unto the chambers,
where are the vessels of the sanctuary, and the priests that minister, and the porters, and the singers:
and we will not forsake the house of our God.

11

And the rulers of the people dwelt at Jerusalem:
the rest of the people also cast lots, to bring one of ten to dwell in Jerusalem the holy city,
and nine parts to dwell in other cities.

2 **And the people** blessed all the men,
that willingly offered themselves to dwell at Jerusalem.

3 **Now these** are the chief of the province that dwelt in Jerusalem:
but in the cities of Judah dwelt every one in his possession in their cities, to wit, Israel, the priests, and the Levites, and the Nethinims, and the children of Solomon's servants.

4 **And at Jerusalem** dwelt certain of the children of Judah, and of the children of Benjamin.
Of the children of Judah; Athaiah the son of Uzziah, the son of Zechariah, the son of Amariah, the son of Shephatiah, the son of Mahalaleel, of the children of Perez;
5 And Maaseiah the son of Baruch, the son of Colhozeh, the son of Hazaiah, the son of Adaiah, the son of Joiarib, the son of Zechariah, the son of Shiloni.

6 **All the sons of Perez that dwelt at Jerusalem** were four hundred threescore and eight valiant men.

7 **And these** are the sons of Benjamin; Sallu the son of Meshullam, the son of Joed, the son of Pedaiah, the son of Kolaiah, the son of Maaseiah, the son of Ithiel, the son of Jesaiah.

8 **And after him** Gabbai, Sallai, nine hundred twenty and eight.

9 **And Joel the son of Zichri** was their overseer:
and Judah the son of Senuah was second over the city.

10 **Of the priests:** Jedaiah the son of Joiarib, Jachin.

11 **Seraiah the son of Hilkiah, the son of Meshullam, the son of Zadok, the son of Meraioth, the son of Ahitub,** was the ruler of the house of God.

12 **And their brethren that did the work of the house** were eight

hundred twenty and two: and
Adaiah the son of Jeroham, the
son of Pelaliah, the son of Amzi,
the son of Zechariah, the son of
Pashur, the son of Malchiah.
13 **And his brethren, chief of the fathers,** two hundred forty and two:
and Amashai the son of Azareel, the son of Ahasai, the son of Meshillemoth, the son of Immer,
14 **And their brethren, mighty men of valour,** an hundred twenty and eight:
and their overseer was Zabdiel, the son of one of the great men.
15 **Also of the Levites:** Shemaiah the son of Hashub, the son of Azrikam, the son of Hashabiah, the son of Bunni;
16 **And Shabbethai and Jozabad, of the chief of the Levites,** had the oversight of the outward business of the house of God.
17 **And Mattaniah the son of Micha, the son of Zabdi, the son of Asaph,** was the principal to begin the thanksgiving in prayer: and Bakbukiah the second among his brethren, and Abda the son of Shammua, the son of Galal, the son of Jeduthun.
18 **All the Levites in the holy city** were two hundred fourscore and four.
19 **Moreover the porters, Akkub, Talmon, and their brethren that kept the gates,** were an hundred seventy and two.
20 **And the residue of Israel, of the priests, and the Levites,** were in all the cities of Judah, every one in his inheritance.
21 **But the Nethinims** dwelt in Ophel:
and Ziha and Gispa were over the Nethinims.
22 **The overseer also of the Levites at Jerusalem** was Uzzi the son of Bani, the son of Hashabiah, the son of Mattaniah, the son of Micha.
Of the sons of Asaph, the singers were over the business of the house of God.
23 **For it was the king's commandment concerning them,** that a certain portion should be for the singers, due for every day.
24 **And Pethahiah the son of Meshezabeel, of the children of Zerah the son of Judah,** was at the king's hand in all matters concerning the people.
25 **And for the villages, with their fields,** some of the children of Judah dwelt at Kirjatharba, and in the villages thereof, and at Dibon, and in the villages thereof, and at Jekabzeel, and in the villages thereof,
26 And at Jeshua, and at Moladah, and at Bethphelet,
27 And at Hazarshual, and at Beersheba, and in the villages thereof,
28 And at Ziklag, and at Mekonah, and in the villages thereof,
29 And at Enrimmon, and at Zareah, and at Jarmuth,
30 Zanoah, Adullam, and in their villages, at Lachish, and the fields thereof, at Azekah, and in the villages thereof.
And they dwelt from Beersheba unto the valley of Hinnom.
31 **The children also of Benjamin from Geba** dwelt at Michmash, and Aija, and Bethel, and in their villages,
32 And at Anathoth, Nob, Ananiah,
33 Hazor, Ramah, Gittaim,
34 Hadid, Zeboim, Neballat,
35 Lod, and Ono, the valley of craftsmen.
36 **And of the Levites** were divisions in Judah, and in Benjamin.

12 ✕ **Now these** are the priests and the Levites that went up with Zerubbabel the son of Shealtiel, and Jeshua: Seraiah, Jeremiah, Ezra,
2 Amariah, Malluch, Hattush,
3 Shechaniah, Rehum, Meremoth,
4 Iddo, Ginnetho, Abijah,
5 Miamin, Maadiah, Bilgah,
6 Shemaiah, and Joiarib, Jedaiah,
7 Sallu, Amok, Hilkiah, Jedaiah.
These were the chief of the priests and of their brethren in the days of Jeshua.
8 **Moreover the Levites:** Jeshua, Binnui, Kadmiel, Sherebiah, Judah, and Mattaniah,
which was over the thanksgiving, he and his brethren.
9 **Also Bakbukiah and Unni, their brethren,** were over against them in the watches.
10 **And Jeshua** begat Joiakim,
Joiakim also begat Eliashib,
and Eliashib begat Joiada,
11 **And Joiada** begat Jonathan,
and Jonathan begat Jaddua.
12 **And in the days of Joiakim** were priests, the chief of the fathers:
of Seraiah, Meraiah;
of Jeremiah, Hananiah;
13 **Of Ezra,** Meshullam;
of Amariah, Jehohanan;
14 **Of Melicu,** Jonathan;
of Shebaniah, Joseph;
15 **Of Harim,** Adna;
of Meraioth, Helkai;
16 **Of Iddo,** Zechariah;
of Ginnethon, Meshullam;
17 **Of Abijah,** Zichri;
of Miniamin, of Moadiah, Piltai:
18 **Of Bilgah,** Shammua;
of Shemaiah, Jehonathan;
19 **And of Joiarib,** Mattenai;
of Jedaiah, Uzzi;
20 **Of Sallai,** Kallai;
of Amok, Eber;
21 **Of Hilkiah,** Hashabiah;
of Jedaiah, Nethaneel.
22 **The Levites in the days of Eliashib, Joiada, and Johanan, and Jaddua,** were recorded chief of the fathers: also the priests, to the reign of Darius the Persian.
23 **The sons of Levi, the chief of the fathers,** were written in the book of the chronicles, even until the days of Johanan the son of Eliashib.
24 **And the chief of the Levites:** Hashabiah, Sherebiah, and Jeshua the son of Kadmiel, with their brethren over against them,
to praise
and to give thanks, according to the commandment of David the man of God, ward over against ward.
25 **Mattaniah, and Bakbukiah, Obadiah, Meshullam, Talmon, Akkub,** were porters keeping the ward at the thresholds of the gates.
26 **These** were in the days of Joiakim the son of Jeshua, the son of Jozadak, and in the days of Nehemiah the governor, and of Ezra the priest, the scribe.

27 **And at the dedication of the wall of Jerusalem** they sought the Levites out of all their places,
to bring them to Jerusalem,
to keep the dedication with gladness, both with thanksgivings, and with singing, with cymbals, psalteries, and with harps.

28 **And the sons of the singers** gathered themselves together, both out of the plain country round about Jerusalem, and from the villages of Netophathi;
29 Also from the house of Gilgal, and out of the fields of Geba and Azmaveth:
for the singers had builded them villages round about Jerusalem.

30 **And the priests and the Levites** purified themselves,
and purified the people, and the gates, and the wall.

31 **Then I** brought up the princes of Judah upon the wall,
and appointed two great companies of them that gave thanks,
whereof one went on the right hand upon the wall toward the dung gate:
32 **And after them** went Hoshaiah, and half of the princes of Judah,
33 And Azariah, Ezra, and Meshullam,
34 Judah, and Benjamin, and Shemaiah, and Jeremiah,
35 And certain of the priests' sons with trumpets; namely, Zechariah the son of Jonathan, the son of Shemaiah, the son of Mattaniah, the son of Michaiah, the son of Zaccur, the son of Asaph:
36 And his brethren, Shemaiah, and Azarael, Milalai, Gilalai, Maai, Nethaneel, and Judah, Hanani, with the musical instruments of David the man of God, and Ezra the scribe before them.

37 **And at the fountain gate**, {which was over against them}, they went up by the stairs of the city of David, at the going up of the wall, above the house of David, even unto the water gate eastward.

38 **And the other company of them that gave thanks** went over against them, and I after them, and the half of the people upon the wall, from beyond the tower of the furnaces even unto the broad wall;
39 And from above the gate of Ephraim, and above the old gate, and above the fish gate, and the tower of Hananeel, and the tower of Meah, even unto the sheep gate:
and they stood still in the prison gate.

40 **So** stood the two companies of them that gave thanks in the house of God, and I, and the half of the rulers with me:
41 And the priests; Eliakim, Maaseiah, Miniamin, Michaiah, Elioenai, Zechariah, and Hananiah, with trumpets;
42 And Maaseiah, and Shemaiah, and Eleazar, and Uzzi, and Jehohanan, and Malchijah, and Elam, and Ezer.
And the singers sang loud, with Jezrahiah their overseer.

43 **Also that day** they offered great sacrifices,
and rejoiced:
for God had made them rejoice with great joy:
the wives also and the children rejoiced:
so that the joy of Jerusalem was heard even afar off.

44 **And at that time** were some appointed over the chambers for the treasures, for the offerings, for the firstfruits, and for the tithes,
to gather into them out of the fields of the cities the portions of the law for the priests and Levites:
for Judah rejoiced for the priests and for the Levites that waited.

45 **And both the singers and the porters** kept the ward of their God, and the ward of the purification, according to the commandment of David, and of Solomon his son.

46 **For in the days of David and Asaph of old** there were chief of the singers, and songs of praise and thanksgiving unto God.

47 **And all Israel in the days of Zerubbabel, and in the days of Nehemiah,** gave the portions of the singers and the porters, every day his portion:
and they sanctified holy things unto the Levites;
and the Levites sanctified them unto the children of Aaron.

13 **On that day** they read in the book of Moses in the audience of the people;
and therein was found written,
that the Ammonite and the Moabite should not come into the congregation of God for ever;
2 **Because they** met not the children of Israel with bread and with water,
but hired Balaam against them,
that he should curse them:
howbeit our God turned the curse into a blessing.

3 **Now it** came to pass,
when they had heard the law,
that they separated from Israel all the mixed multitude.

4 **And before this,** Eliashib the priest, {having the oversight of the chamber of the house of our God}, was allied unto Tobiah:
5 **And he** had prepared for him a great chamber,
where aforetime they laid the meat offerings, the frankincense, and the vessels, and the tithes of the corn, the new wine, and the oil,
which was commanded to be given to the Levites, and the singers, and the porters; and the offerings of the priests.

6 **But in all this time** was not I at Jerusalem:
for in the two and thirtieth year of Artaxerxes king of Babylon came I unto the king,
and after certain days obtained I leave of the king:
7 **And I** came to Jerusalem,
and understood of the evil that Eliashib did for Tobiah,
in preparing him a chamber in the courts of the house of God.

8 **And it** grieved me sore:
therefore I cast forth all the household stuff to Tobiah out of the chamber.

9 **Then I** commanded,
and they cleansed the chambers:
and thither brought I again the vessels of the house of God, with the meat offering and the frankincense.

10 **And I** perceived
that the portions of the Levites had not been given them:

for the Levites and the singers,
{that did the work}, were fled
every one to his field.
11 **Then** contended I with the rulers,
and said,
Why is the house of God forsaken?
And I gathered them together,
and set them in their place.
12 **Then** brought all Judah the tithe
of the corn and the new wine and
the oil unto the treasuries.
13 **And I** made treasurers over the
treasuries, Shelemiah the priest,
and Zadok the scribe, and of the
Levites, Pedaiah:
and next to them was Hanan the
son of Zaccur, the son of
Mattaniah:
for they were counted faithful,
and their office was to distribute
unto their brethren.
14 **Remember** me, O my God,
concerning this,
and wipe not out my good deeds
that I have done for the house of
my God, and for the offices
thereof.
15 **In those days** saw I in Judah some
treading wine presses on the
sabbath, and bringing in sheaves,
and lading asses; as also wine,
grapes, and figs, and all manner of
burdens,
which they brought into Jerusalem
on the sabbath day:
and I testified against them in the
day wherein they sold victuals.
16 **There** dwelt men of Tyre also
therein,
which brought fish, and all manner
of ware,
and sold on the sabbath unto the
children of Judah, and in
Jerusalem.
17 **Then I** contended with the nobles
of Judah,
and said unto them,
What evil thing is this that ye do,
and profane the sabbath day?
18 **Did not your fathers** thus,
and did not our God bring all this
evil upon us, and upon this city?
yet ye bring more wrath upon Israel
by profaning the sabbath.
19 **And it** came to pass,
that when the gates of Jerusalem
began to be dark before the
sabbath,
I commanded
that the gates should be shut,
and charged
that they should not be opened till
after the sabbath:
and some of my servants set I at
the gates,
that there should no burden be
brought in on the sabbath day.
20 **So the merchants and sellers of
all kind of ware** lodged without
Jerusalem once or twice.
21 **Then I** testified against them,
and said unto them,
Why lodge ye about the wall?
If ye do so again,
I will lay hands on you.
From that time forth came they no
more on the sabbath.
22 **And I** commanded the Levites
that they should cleanse
themselves,
and that they should come and
keep the gates,
to sanctify the sabbath day.
Remember me, O my God,
concerning this also,
and spare me according to the
greatness of thy mercy.
23 **In those days** also saw I Jews that
had married wives of Ashdod, of
Ammon, and of Moab:
24 **And their children** spake half in
the speech of Ashdod,
and could not speak in the Jews'
language, but according to the
language of each people.
25 **And I** contended with them,
and cursed them,
and smote certain of them,
and plucked off their hair,
and made them swear by God,
saying,
Ye shall not give your daughters
unto their sons,
nor take their daughters unto your
sons, or for yourselves.
26 **Did not Solomon king of Israel**
sin by these things?
yet among many nations was
there no king like him,
who was beloved of his God,
and God made him king over all
Israel:
nevertheless even him did
outlandish women cause to sin.
27 **Shall we** then hearken unto you
to do all this great evil,
to transgress against our God
in marrying strange wives?
28 **And one of the sons of Joiada,
the son of Eliashib the high
priest,** was son in law to
Sanballat the Horonite:
therefore I chased him from me.
29 **Remember** them, O my God,
because they have defiled the
priesthood, and the covenant of
the priesthood, and of the Levites.
30 **Thus** cleansed I them from all
strangers,
and appointed the wards of the
priests and the Levites, every one
in his business;
31 And for the wood offering, at
times appointed, and for the
firstfruits.
Remember me, O my God, for
good.

Esther

The Book of Esther (author unknown) shares a fascinating tale of bravery, intrigue, and redemption. As a young girl, Esther is orphaned and taken in by her cousin, Mordecai, who raises her as his own daughter. Mordecai teaches Esther the importance of following God's laws and living a righteous life. One day, the king of Persia holds a beauty contest to find a new queen to replace his current wife, who had disobeyed him. Esther is chosen as one of the contestants, and she soon catches the eye of the king, who is captivated by her beauty and grace. Esther is crowned Queen, and Mordecai remains close to her, serving as her advisor.

Meanwhile, a man named Haman has risen to a position of great power in the king's court. A proud and arrogant man, he demands that everyone bow down to him. Mordecai, however, refuses to do so, as he only bows to God. A furious Haman then hatches a plot to destroy not only Mordecai but many others as well. He convinces the king to order the extermination of all Jews living in the kingdom on a particular day. When Mordecai hears about this decree, he sends word to Esther, urging her to intercede on behalf of her people. Esther hesitates, fearing for her own life because to approach the king uninvited is forbidden and punishable by death. But Mordecai reminds her that she has been placed in the position of Queen for such a time. Esther fasts and prays for three days, approaches the king, who spares her life, and then invites him and Haman to a private banquet. There she reveals her Jewish heritage, as well as Haman's plot, and asks for the king's mercy.

The king, outraged at the plan to harm the Queen and her people, orders the execution of Haman, who is then hanged on the gallows he had prepared for Mordecai. But the Jewish people are still not out of danger: according to Persian law, nobody can nullify the king's original decree. So Queen Esther intervenes once again, asking the king to protect her people. In response, the king issues a new ruling, allowing the Jewish people to defend themselves against their enemies. This act of mercy leads to confrontations between the Jewish community and their adversaries, in which the former emerges victorious. This event is celebrated even today as the annual Feast of Purim. The story about Esther demonstrates divine providence as God intercedes on behalf of his chosen people, not because of their own efforts, but because He placed Esther in the position of Queen for such a time.

1 **Now it** came to pass in the days of Ahasuerus,
(this is Ahasuerus
which reigned, from India even unto Ethiopia, over an hundred and seven and twenty provinces:)
2 **That in those days**, {when the king Ahasuerus sat on the throne of his kingdom}, {which was in Shushan the palace},
3 In the third year of his reign, he made a feast unto all his princes and his servants;
the power of Persia and Media, the nobles and princes of the provinces, being before him:
4 **When he** shewed the riches of his glorious kingdom and the honour of his excellent majesty many days, even an hundred and fourscore days.
5 **And when these days** were expired,
the king made a feast unto all the people that were present in Shushan the palace, both unto great and small, seven days, in the court of the garden of the king's palace;
6 **Where** were white, green, and blue, hangings,
fastened with cords of fine linen and purple to silver rings and pillars of marble:
the beds were of gold and silver, upon a pavement of red, and blue, and white, and black, marble.
7 **And they** gave them drink in vessels of gold, (the vessels being diverse one from another,) and royal wine in abundance, according to the state of the king.
8 **And the drinking** was according to the law;
none did compel:
for so the king had appointed to all the officers of his house,
that they should do according to every man's pleasure.
9 **Also Vashti the queen** made a feast for the women in the royal house which belonged to king Ahasuerus.
10 **On the seventh day**, {when the heart of the king was merry with wine}, he commanded Mehuman, Biztha, Harbona, Bigtha, and Abagtha, Zethar, and Carcas, the seven chamberlains that served in the presence of Ahasuerus the king,
11 To bring Vashti the queen before the king with the crown royal,
to shew the people and the princes her beauty:
for she was fair to look on.
12 **But the queen Vashti** refused to come at the king's commandment by his chamberlains:
therefore was the king very wroth,
and his anger burned in him.
13 **Then the king** said to the wise men,
which knew the times,
(for so was the king's manner toward all that knew law and judgment:
14 And the next unto him was Carshena, Shethar, Admatha, Tarshish, Meres, Marsena, and

Memucan, the seven princes of
Persia and Media,
which saw the king's face,
and which sat the first in the
kingdom;)
15 **What** shall we do unto the queen
Vashti according to law,
because she hath not performed
the commandment of the king
Ahasuerus by the chamberlains?
16 **And Memucan** answered before
the king and the princes,
Vashti the queen hath not done
wrong to the king only, but also to
all the princes, and to all the
people that are in all the
provinces of the king Ahasuerus.
17 **For this deed of the queen** shall
come abroad unto all women,
so that they shall despise their
husbands in their eyes,
when it shall be reported,
The king Ahasuerus commanded
Vashti the queen to be brought in
before him,
but she came not.
18 **Likewise** shall the ladies of Persia
and Media say this day unto all
the king's princes,
which have heard of the deed of the
queen.
Thus shall there arise too much
contempt and wrath.
19 **If it** please the king,
let there go a royal commandment
from him,
and let it be written among the
laws of the Persians and the
Medes,
that it be not altered,
That Vashti come no more before
king Ahasuerus;
and let the king give her royal
estate unto another that is better
than she.
20 **And when the king's decree
which he shall make** shall be
published throughout all his
empire,
(for it is great,)
all the wives shall give to their
husbands honour, both to great
and small.
21 **And the saying** pleased the king
and the princes;
and the king did according to the
word of Memucan:
22 **For he** sent letters into all the
king's provinces, into every
province according to the writing
thereof, and to every people after
their language,
that every man should bear rule in
his own house,
and that it should be published
according to the language of every
people.

2 **After these things**, {when the
wrath of king Ahasuerus was
appeased}, he remembered
Vashti,
and what she had done,
and what was decreed against her.
2 **Then** said the king's servants that
ministered unto him,
Let there be fair young virgins
sought for the king:
3 **And let the king** appoint officers
in all the provinces of his
kingdom,
that they may gather together all
the fair young virgins unto
Shushan the palace, to the house
of the women, unto the custody of
Hege the king's chamberlain,
keeper of the women;
**and let their things for
purification** be given them:
4 **And let the maiden which
pleaseth the king** be queen
instead of Vashti.
And the thing pleased the king;
and he did so.
5 **Now in Shushan the palace** there
was a certain Jew,
whose name was Mordecai, the son
of Jair, the son of Shimei, the son
of Kish, a Benjamite;
6 **Who** had been carried away from
Jerusalem with the captivity
which had been carried away
with Jeconiah king of Judah,
**whom Nebuchadnezzar the king
of Babylon** had carried away.
7 **And he** brought up Hadassah, that
is, Esther, his uncle's daughter:
for she had neither father nor
mother,
and the maid was fair and
beautiful;
whom Mordecai, {when her father
and mother were dead}, took for
his own daughter.
8 **So it** came to pass,
**when the king's commandment
and his decree** was heard,
and when many maidens were
gathered together unto Shushan
the palace, to the custody of
Hegai,
that Esther was brought also unto
the king's house, to the custody of
Hegai, keeper of the women.
9 **And the maiden** pleased him,
and she obtained kindness of him;
and he speedily gave her her things
for purification, with such things
as belonged to her, and seven
maidens,
which were meet to be given her,
out of the king's house:
and he preferred her and her maids
unto the best place of the house of
the women.
10 **Esther** had not shewed her
people nor her kindred:
for Mordecai had charged her
that she should not shew it.
11 **And Mordecai** walked every day
before the court of the women's
house,
to know
how Esther did,
and what should become of her.
12 **Now when every maid's turn**
was come to go in to king
Ahasuerus,
after that she had been twelve
months, according to the manner
of the women,
(for so were the days of their
purifications accomplished, to
wit, six months with oil of myrrh,
and six months with sweet
odours, and with other things for
the purifying of the women;)
13 **Then thus** came every maiden
unto the king;
whatsoever she desired was given
her to go with her out of the
house of the women unto the
king's house.
14 **In the evening** she went,
and on the morrow she returned
into the second house of the
women, to the custody of
Shaashgaz, the king's
chamberlain,
which kept the concubines:
she came in unto the king no more,
except the king delighted in her,
and that she were called by name.
15 **Now when the turn of Esther,
the daughter of Abihail the
uncle of Mordecai**, {who had
taken her for his daughter}, was
come to go in unto the king,
she required nothing

but what Hegai the king's chamberlain, the keeper of the women, appointed.
And Esther obtained favour in the sight of all them that looked upon her.

16 **So Esther** was taken unto king Ahasuerus into his house royal in the tenth month,
which is the month Tebeth, in the seventh year of his reign.

17 **And the king** loved Esther above all the women,
and she obtained grace and favour in his sight more than all the virgins;
so that he set the royal crown upon her head,
and made her queen instead of Vashti.

18 **Then the king** made a great feast unto all his princes and his servants, even Esther's feast;
and he made a release to the provinces,
and gave gifts, according to the state of the king.

19 **And when the virgins** were gathered together the second time,
then Mordecai sat in the king's gate.

20 **Esther** had not yet shewed her kindred nor her people;
as Mordecai had charged her:
for Esther did the commandment of Mordecai,
like as when she was brought up with him.

21 **In those days**, {while Mordecai sat in the king's gate}, two of the king's chamberlains, Bigthan and Teresh, of those which kept the door, were wroth,
and sought to lay hands on the king Ahasuerus.

22 **And the thing** was known to Mordecai,
who told it unto Esther the queen;
and Esther certified the king thereof in Mordecai's name.

23 **And when inquisition** was made of the matter,
it was found out;
therefore they were both hanged on a tree:
and it was written in the book of the chronicles before the king.

3

After these things did king Ahasuerus promote Haman the son of Hammedatha the Agagite,
and advanced him,
and set his seat above all the princes that were with him.

2 **And all the king's servants**, {that were in the king's gate}, bowed,
and reverenced Haman:
for the king had so commanded concerning him.
But Mordecai bowed not,
nor did him reverence.

3 **Then the king's servants**, {which were in the king's gate}, said unto Mordecai,
Why transgressest thou the king's commandment?

4 **Now it** came to pass,
when they spake daily unto him,
and he hearkened not unto them,
that they told Haman,
to see whether Mordecai's matters would stand:
for he had told them
that he was a Jew.

5 **And when Haman** saw that Mordecai bowed not,
nor did him reverence,
then was Haman full of wrath.

6 **And he** thought scorn to lay hands on Mordecai alone;
for they had shewed him the people of Mordecai:
wherefore Haman sought to destroy all the Jews that were throughout the whole kingdom of Ahasuerus, even the people of Mordecai.

7 **In the first month, that is, the month Nisan, in the twelfth year of king Ahasuerus,** they cast Pur, that is, the lot, before Haman from day to day, and from month to month, to the twelfth month, that is, the month Adar.

8 **And Haman** said unto king Ahasuerus,
There is a certain people scattered abroad and dispersed among the people in all the provinces of thy kingdom;
and their laws are diverse from all people;
neither keep they the king's laws:
therefore it is not for the king's profit to suffer them.

9 **If it** please the king,
let it be written that they may be destroyed:
and I will pay ten thousand talents of silver to the hands of those that have the charge of the business,
to bring it into the king's treasuries.

10 **And the king** took his ring from his hand,
and gave it unto Haman the son of Hammedatha the Agagite, the Jews' enemy.

11 **And the king** said unto Haman,
The silver is given to thee, the people also,
to do with them as it seemeth good to thee.

12 **Then** were the king's scribes called on the thirteenth day of the first month,
and there was written according to all that Haman had commanded unto the king's lieutenants, and to the governors that were over every province, and to the rulers of every people of every province according to the writing thereof, and to every people after their language;
in the name of king Ahasuerus was it written,
and sealed with the king's ring.

13 **And the letters** were sent by posts into all the king's provinces,
to destroy,
to kill,
and to cause to perish, all Jews, both young and old, little children and women, in one day, even upon the thirteenth day of the twelfth month,
which is the month Adar,
and to take the spoil of them for a prey.

14 **The copy of the writing for a commandment to be given in every province** was published unto all people,
that they should be ready against that day.

15 **The posts** went out,
being hastened by the king's commandment,
and the decree was given in Shushan the palace.
And the king and Haman sat down to drink;
but the city Shushan was perplexed.

4 **When Mordecai** perceived all that was done,
Mordecai rent his clothes,
and put on sackcloth with ashes,
and went out into the midst of the city,
and cried with a loud and a bitter cry;
2 **And** came even before the king's gate:
for none might enter into the king's gate clothed with sackcloth.
3 **And in every province**, {whithersoever the king's commandment and his decree came}, there was great mourning among the Jews, and fasting, and weeping, and wailing;
and many lay in sackcloth and ashes.
4 **So Esther's maids and her chamberlains** came and told it her.
Then was the queen exceedingly grieved;
and she sent raiment to clothe Mordecai,
and to take away his sackcloth from him:
but he received it not.
5 **Then** called Esther for Hatach, one of the king's chamberlains,
whom he had appointed to attend upon her,
and gave him a commandment to Mordecai,
to know
what it was,
and why it was.
6 **So Hatach** went forth to Mordecai unto the street of the city,
which was before the king's gate.
7 **And Mordecai** told him of all that had happened unto him, and of the sum of the money that Haman had promised to pay to the king's treasuries for the Jews,
to destroy them.
8 **Also he** gave him the copy of the writing of the decree that was given at Shushan to destroy them,
to shew it unto Esther,
and to declare it unto her,
and to charge her
that she should go in unto the king,
to make supplication unto him,
and to make request before him for her people.
9 **And Hatach** came and told Esther the words of Mordecai.
10 **Again Esther** spake unto Hatach,
and gave him commandment unto Mordecai;
11 **All the king's servants, and the people of the king's provinces,** do know,
that whosoever, whether man or women, shall come unto the king into the inner court,
who is not called,
there is one law of his
to put him to death,
except such to whom the king shall hold out the golden sceptre,
that he may live:
but I have not been called to come in unto the king these thirty days.
12 **And they** told to Mordecai Esther's words.
13 **Then Mordecai** commanded to answer Esther,
Think not with thyself
that thou shalt escape in the king's house, more than all the Jews.
14 **For if thou** altogether holdest thy peace at this time,
then shall there enlargement and deliverance arise to the Jews from another place;
but thou and thy father's house shall be destroyed:
and who knoweth
whether thou art come to the kingdom for such a time as this?
15 **Then Esther** bade them return Mordecai this answer,
16 **Go,**
gather together all the Jews that are present in Shushan,
and fast ye for me,
and neither eat
nor drink three days, night or day:
I also and my maidens will fast likewise;
and so will I go in unto the king,
which is not according to the law:
and if I perish,
I perish.
17 **So Mordecai** went his way,
and did according to all that Esther had commanded him.

5 **Now it** came to pass on the third day,
that Esther put on her royal apparel,
and stood in the inner court of the king's house, over against the king's house:
and the king sat upon his royal throne in the royal house, over against the gate of the house.
2 **And it** was so,
when the king saw Esther the queen standing in the court,
that she obtained favour in his sight:
and the king held out to Esther the golden sceptre that was in his hand.
So Esther drew near,
and touched the top of the sceptre.
3 **Then** said the king unto her,
What wilt thou, queen Esther?
and what is thy request?
it shall be even given thee to the half of the kingdom.
4 **And Esther** answered,
If it seem good unto the king,
let the king and Haman come this day unto the banquet that I have prepared for him.
5 **Then the king** said,
Cause Haman to make haste,
that he may do as Esther hath said.
So the king and Haman came to the banquet that Esther had prepared.
6 **And the king** said unto Esther at the banquet of wine,
What is thy petition?
and it shall be granted thee:
and what is thy request?
even to the half of the kingdom it shall be performed.
7 **Then** answered Esther,
and said,
My petition and my request is;
8 **If I** have found favour in the sight of the king,
and if it please the king to grant my petition,
and to perform my request,
let the king and Haman come to the banquet that I shall prepare for them,
and I will do to morrow as the king hath said.
9 **Then** went Haman forth that day joyful and with a glad heart:
but when Haman saw Mordecai in the king's gate,
that he stood not up,
nor moved for him,
he was full of indignation against Mordecai.
10 **Nevertheless Haman** refrained himself:
and when he came home,

he sent and called for his friends, and Zeresh his wife.
11 **And Haman** told them of the glory of his riches, and the multitude of his children, and all the things wherein the king had promoted him,
and how he had advanced him above the princes and servants of the king.
12 **Haman** said moreover,
Yea, Esther the queen did let no man come in with the king unto the banquet that she had prepared but myself;
and to morrow am I invited unto her also with the king.
13 **Yet all this** availeth me nothing,
so long as I see Mordecai the Jew sitting at the king's gate.
14 **Then** said Zeresh his wife and all his friends unto him,
Let a gallows be made of fifty cubits high,
and to morrow speak thou unto the king
that Mordecai may be hanged thereon:
then go thou in merrily with the king unto the banquet.
And the thing pleased Haman;
and he caused the gallows to be made.

6

On that night could not the king sleep,
and he commanded to bring the book of records of the chronicles;
and they were read before the king.
2 **And it was found written,** that Mordecai had told of Bigthana and Teresh, two of the king's chamberlains, the keepers of the door,
who sought to lay hand on the king Ahasuerus.
3 **And the king** said,
What honour and dignity hath been done to Mordecai for this?
Then said the king's servants that ministered unto him,
There is nothing done for him.
4 **And the king** said,
Who is in the court?
Now Haman was come into the outward court of the king's house,
to speak unto the king
to hang Mordecai on the gallows that he had prepared for him.
5 **And the king's servants** said unto him,
Behold,
Haman standeth in the court.
And the king said,
Let him come in.
6 **So Haman** came in.
And the king said unto him,
What shall be done unto the man whom the king delighteth to honour?
Now Haman thought in his heart,
To whom would the king delight to do honour more than to myself?
7 **And Haman** answered the king,
For the man whom the king delighteth to honour,
8 **Let the royal apparel** be brought which the king useth to wear, and the horse that the king rideth upon, and the crown royal which is set upon his head:
9 **And let this apparel and horse** be delivered to the hand of one of the king's most noble princes,
that they may array the man withal whom the king delighteth to honour,
and bring him on horseback through the street of the city,
and proclaim before him,
Thus shall it be done to the man whom the king delighteth to honour.
10 **Then the king** said to Haman,
Make haste,
and take the apparel and the horse,
as thou hast said,
and do even so to Mordecai the Jew,
that sitteth at the king's gate:
let nothing fail of all that thou hast spoken.
11 **Then** took Haman the apparel and the horse,
and arrayed Mordecai,
and brought him on horseback through the street of the city,
and proclaimed before him,
Thus shall it be done unto the man whom the king delighteth to honour.
12 **And Mordecai** came again to the king's gate.
But Haman hasted to his house mourning,
and having his head covered.
13 **And Haman** told Zeresh his wife and all his friends every thing that had befallen him.
Then said his wise men and Zeresh his wife unto him,
If Mordecai be of the seed of the Jews,
before whom thou hast begun to fall,
thou shalt not prevail against him,
but shalt surely fall before him.
14 **And while they** were yet talking with him,
came the king's chamberlains,
and hasted to bring Haman unto the banquet that Esther had prepared.

7

So the king and Haman came to banquet with Esther the queen.
2 **And the king** said again unto Esther on the second day at the banquet of wine,
What is thy petition, queen Esther?
and it shall be granted thee:
and what is thy request?
and it shall be performed, even to the half of the kingdom.
3 **Then Esther the queen** answered and said,
If I have found favour in thy sight, O king,
and if it please the king,
let my life be given me at my petition, and my people at my request:
4 **For we** are sold, I and my people,
to be destroyed,
to be slain,
and to perish.
But if we had been sold for bondmen and bondwomen,
I had held my tongue,
although the enemy could not countervail the king's damage.
5 **Then the king Ahasuerus** answered and said unto Esther the queen,
Who is he,
and where is he,
that durst presume in his heart to do so?
6 **And Esther** said,
The adversary and enemy is this wicked Haman.
Then Haman was afraid before the king and the queen.
7 **And the king arising from the banquet of wine in his wrath** went into the palace garden:
and Haman stood up

to make request for his life to Esther the queen;
for he saw that there was evil determined against him by the king.

[8] **Then the king** returned out of the palace garden into the place of the banquet of wine;
and Haman was fallen upon the bed whereon Esther was.

Then said the king,
Will he force the queen also before me in the house?

As the word went out of king's mouth,
they covered Haman's face.

[9] **And Harbonah, one of the chamberlains,** said before the king,
Behold also,
the gallows fifty cubits high, {which Haman had made for Mordecai}, {who spoken good for the king}, standeth in the house of Haman.

Then the king said,
Hang him thereon.

[10] **So they** hanged Haman on the gallows that he had prepared for Mordecai.

Then was the king's wrath pacified.

8 **On that day** did the king Ahasuerus give the house of Haman the Jews' enemy unto Esther the queen.

And Mordecai came before the king;
for Esther had told
what he was unto her.

[2] **And the king** took off his ring,
which he had taken from Haman,
and gave it unto Mordecai.

And Esther set Mordecai over the house of Haman.

[3] **And Esther** spake yet again before the king,
and fell down at his feet,
and besought him with tears
to put away the mischief of Haman the Agagite, and his device that he had devised against the Jews.

[4] **Then the king** held out the golden sceptre toward Esther.

So Esther arose,
and stood before the king,
[5] **And** said,
If it please the king,
and if I have favour in his sight,
and the thing seem right before the king,
and I be pleasing in his eyes,
let it be written to reverse the letters devised by Haman the son of Hammedatha the Agagite,
which he wrote
to destroy the Jews which are in all the king's provinces:

[6] **For how** can I endure to see the evil that shall come unto my people?
or how can I endure to see the destruction of my kindred?

[7] **Then the king Ahasuerus** said unto Esther the queen and to Mordecai the Jew,
Behold,
I have given Esther the house of Haman,
and him they have hanged upon the gallows,
because he laid his hand upon the Jews.

[8] **Write ye** also for the Jews, as it liketh you, in the king's name,
and seal it with the king's ring:
for the writing which is written in the king's name, and sealed with the king's ring, may no man reverse.

[9] **Then** were the king's scribes called at that time in the third month, that is, the month Sivan, on the three and twentieth day thereof;
and it was written according to all that Mordecai commanded unto the Jews, and to the lieutenants, and the deputies and rulers of the provinces which are from India unto Ethiopia, an hundred twenty and seven provinces, unto every province according to the writing thereof, and unto every people after their language, and to the Jews according to their writing, and according to their language.

[10] **And he** wrote in the king Ahasuerus' name,
and sealed it with the king's ring,
and sent letters by posts on horseback, and riders on mules, camels, and young dromedaries:

[11] **Wherein** the king granted the Jews which were in every city to gather themselves together,
and to stand for their life,
to destroy, {to slay} {and to cause to perish}, all the power of the people and province that would assault them, both little ones and women,
and to take the spoil of them for a prey,

[12] Upon one day in all the provinces of king Ahasuerus, namely, upon the thirteenth day of the twelfth month,
which is the month Adar.

[13] **The copy of the writing for a commandment to be given in every province** was published unto all people,
and that the Jews should be ready against that day
to avenge themselves on their enemies.

[14] **So the posts that rode upon mules and camels** went out,
being hastened and pressed on by the king's commandment.

And the decree was given at Shushan the palace.

[15] **And Mordecai** went out from the presence of the king in royal apparel of blue and white, and with a great crown of gold, and with a garment of fine linen and purple:
and the city of Shushan rejoiced
and was glad.

[16] **The Jews** had light, and gladness, and joy, and honour.

[17] **And in every province, and in every city**, {whithersoever the king's commandment and his decree came}, the Jews had joy and gladness, a feast and a good day.

And many of the people of the land became Jews;
for the fear of the Jews fell upon them.

9 **Now in the twelfth month, that is, the month Adar, on the thirteenth day of the same, {when the king's commandment and his decree drew near to be put in execution}, in the day that the enemies of the Jews hoped to have power over them**, ({though it was turned to the contrary}, {that the Jews had rule over them that hated them};)

[2] The Jews gathered themselves together in their cities throughout all the provinces of the king Ahasuerus,

to lay hand on such as sought their hurt:
and no man could withstand them;
for the fear of them fell upon all people.

3 **And all the rulers of the provinces, and the lieutenants, and the deputies, and officers of the king,** helped the Jews;
because the fear of Mordecai fell upon them.

4 **For Mordecai** was great in the king's house,
and his fame went out throughout all the provinces:
for this man Mordecai waxed greater and greater.

5 **Thus the Jews** smote all their enemies with the stroke of the sword, and slaughter, and destruction,
and did what they would unto those that hated them.

6 **And in Shushan the palace** the Jews slew and destroyed five hundred men.

7 **And Parshandatha, and Dalphon, and Aspatha,**
8 **And Poratha, and Adalia, and Aridatha,**
9 **And Parmashta, and Arisai, and Aridai, and Vajezatha,**
10 **The ten sons of Haman the son of Hammedatha, the enemy of the Jews,** slew they;
but on the spoil laid they not their hand.

11 **On that day** the number of those that were slain in Shushan the palace was brought before the king.

12 **And the king** said unto Esther the queen,
The Jews have slain and destroyed five hundred men in Shushan the palace, and the ten sons of Haman;
what have they done in the rest of the king's provinces?
now what is thy petition?
and it shall be granted thee:
or what is thy request further?
and it shall be done.

13 **Then** said Esther,
If it please the king,
let it be granted to the Jews which are in Shushan to do to morrow also according unto this day's decree,
and let Haman's ten sons be hanged upon the gallows.
14 **And the king** commanded it
so to be done:
and the decree was given at Shushan;
and they hanged Haman's ten sons.

15 **For the Jews that were in Shushan** gathered themselves together on the fourteenth day also of the month Adar,
and slew three hundred men at Shushan;
but on the prey they laid not their hand.

16 **But the other Jews that were in the king's provinces** gathered themselves together,
and stood for their lives,
and had rest from their enemies,
and slew of their foes seventy and five thousand,
but they laid not their hands on the prey,
17 **On the thirteenth day of the month Adar; and on the fourteenth day of the same** rested they,
and made it a day of feasting and gladness.

18 **But the Jews that were at Shushan** assembled together on the thirteenth day thereof,
and on the fourteenth thereof; and on the fifteenth day of the same they rested,
and made it a day of feasting and gladness.

19 **Therefore the Jews of the villages,** {that dwelt in the unwalled towns}, made the fourteenth day of the month Adar a day of gladness and feasting, and a good day, and of sending portions one to another.

20 **And Mordecai** wrote these things,
and sent letters unto all the Jews that were in all the provinces of the king Ahasuerus, both nigh and far,
21 To stablish this among them,
that they should keep the fourteenth day of the month Adar, and the fifteenth day of the same, yearly,
22 As the days wherein the Jews rested from their enemies, and the month which was turned unto them from sorrow to joy, and from mourning into a good day:
that they should make them days of feasting and joy, and of sending portions one to another, and gifts to the poor.

23 **And the Jews** undertook to do as they had begun, and as Mordecai had written unto them;
24 **Because Haman the son of Hammedatha, the Agagite, the enemy of all the Jews,** had devised against the Jews to destroy them,
and had cast Pur, that is, the lot, to consume them,
and to destroy them;
25 **But when Esther** came before the king,
he commanded by letters
that his wicked device, {which he devised against the Jews}, should return upon his own head,
and that he and his sons should be hanged on the gallows.

26 **Wherefore they** called these days Purim after the name of Pur.

Therefore for all the words of this letter, and of that which they had seen concerning this matter, and which had come unto them,
27 The Jews ordained, {and took upon them, and upon their seed, and upon all such as joined themselves unto them}, {so as it should not fail},
that they would keep these two days according to their writing, and according to their appointed time every year;
28 **And that these days** should be remembered and kept throughout every generation, every family, every province, and every city;
and that these days of Purim should not fail from among the Jews,
nor the memorial of them perish from their seed.

29 **Then Esther the queen, the daughter of Abihail, and Mordecai the Jew,** wrote with all authority,
to confirm this second letter of Purim.

30 **And he** sent the letters unto all the Jews, to the hundred twenty and seven provinces of the

kingdom of Ahasuerus, with
words of peace and truth,
31 To confirm these days of Purim in
their times appointed,
**according as Mordecai the Jew
and Esther the queen** had
enjoined them,
and as they had decreed for
themselves and for their seed, the
matters of the fastings and their
cry.
32 **And the decree of Esther**
confirmed these matters of Purim;
and it was written in the book.

10

And the king Ahasuerus
laid a tribute upon the
land, and upon the isles of the
sea.
2 **And all the acts of his power and
of his might, and the
declaration of the greatness of
Mordecai**, {whereunto the king
advanced him}, are they not
written in the book of the
chronicles of the kings of Media
and Persia?
3 **For Mordecai the Jew** was next
unto king Ahasuerus, and great
among the Jews, and accepted of
the multitude of his brethren,
seeking the wealth of his people,
and speaking peace to all his seed.

Job

The Book of Job (author unknown) details the life of a righteous man, Job, who undergoes a severe test of faith by God and Satan. Initially, Job is portrayed as a blameless and upright man, deeply reverent of God and avoiding evil. He is bestowed with a large family, abundant wealth, and robust health. However, Satan challenges God's assertion of Job's faithfulness, insinuating that Job's devotion is solely due to his blessings. In response, God permits Satan to test Job, leading to the loss of his wealth, health, and family.

Despite the immense suffering, Job remains unwavering in his faith and refrains from cursing God. He bemoans his fate but continues to trust in God's justice. Three of Job's friends, Eliphaz, Bildad, and Zophar, arrive to console him and offer their counsel. They argue that his suffering must be a consequence of sin, and they urge him to repent. Job defends his innocence and questions why God would permit such suffering to befall a righteous man. A young man named Elihu joins the discussion and rebukes Job's friends for their unhelpful advice, asserting that they are increasing the severity of his pain and making the situation worse. Despite Job's persistent longing for an explanation, God finally speaks to him from a whirlwind, not by directly answering his questions but by challenging his comprehension of the world and reminding him of his place in the grand scheme of events.

In a moment of profound humility, Job repents, acknowledging that he cannot fathom God's ways and must rely on God's justice, even when it appears unjust to him. Following this repentance, God restores Job's wealth, health, and family, and He bestows upon him even more than before. God also admonishes Job's friends for their misguided counsel and lack of comprehension. While the Book of Job delves into the human experience of suffering, the essence of God's justice, and the boundaries of human understanding about both, it also serves as a reminder that even in the face of immense adversity, one's faith and character can endure and remain resolute. Moreover, it imparts a crucial lesson about approaching the suffering of others with empathy and compassion rather than judgment and blame, fostering a deeper connection to the story and its lessons.

1 **There** was a man in the land of Uz,
whose name was Job;
and that man was perfect and upright, and one that feared God, and eschewed evil.
2 **And there** were born unto him seven sons and three daughters.
3 **His substance** also was seven thousand sheep, and three thousand camels, and five hundred yoke of oxen, and five hundred she asses, and a very great household;
so that this man was the greatest of all the men of the east.
4 **And his sons** went and feasted in their houses, every one his day;
and sent and called for their three sisters
to eat and to drink with them.
5 **And it** was so,
when the days of their feasting were gone about,
that Job sent and sanctified them,
and rose up early in the morning,
and offered burnt offerings according to the number of them all:
for Job said,
It may be that my sons have sinned,
and cursed God in their hearts.
Thus did Job continually.
6 **Now there** was a day
when the sons of God came to present themselves before the LORD,
and Satan came also among them.
7 **And the LORD** said unto Satan,
Whence comest thou?
Then Satan answered the LORD,
and said,
From going to and fro in the earth,
and from walking up and down in it.
8 **And the LORD** said unto Satan,
Hast thou considered my servant Job,
that there is none like him in the earth, a perfect and an upright man, one that feareth God, and escheweth evil?
9 **Then Satan** answered the LORD,
and said,
Doth Job fear God for nought?
10 **Hast not thou** made an hedge about him, and about his house, and about all that he hath on every side?
thou hast blessed the work of his hands,
and his substance is increased in the land.
11 **But put forth** thine hand now,
and touch all that he hath,
and he will curse thee to thy face.
12 **And the LORD** said unto Satan,
Behold,
all that he hath is in thy power;
only upon himself put not forth thine hand.
So Satan went forth from the presence of the LORD.
13 **And there** was a day
when his sons and his daughters were eating and drinking wine in their eldest brother's house:
14 **And there** came a messenger unto Job,
and said,
The oxen were plowing,
and the asses feeding beside them:

15 **And the Sabeans** fell upon them,
and took them away;
yea, they have slain the servants with the edge of the sword;
and I only am escaped alone to tell thee.

16 **While he** was yet speaking,
there came also another,
and said,
The fire of God is fallen from heaven,
and hath burned up the sheep, and the servants,
and consumed them;
and I only am escaped alone to tell thee.

17 **While he** was yet speaking,
there came also another,
and said,
The Chaldeans made out three bands,
and fell upon the camels,
and have carried them away,
yea, and slain the servants with the edge of the sword;
and I only am escaped alone to tell thee.

18 **While he** was yet speaking,
there came also another,
and said,
Thy sons and thy daughters were eating and drinking wine in their eldest brother's house:

19 **And, {behold}, there** came a great wind from the wilderness,
and smote the four corners of the house,
and it fell upon the young men,
and they are dead;
and I only am escaped alone to tell thee.

20 **Then Job** arose,
and rent his mantle,
and shaved his head,
and fell down upon the ground,
and worshipped,

21 **And** said,
Naked came I out of my mother's womb,
and naked shall I return thither:
the LORD gave,
and the LORD hath taken away;
blessed be the name of the LORD.

22 **In all this** Job sinned not,
nor charged God foolishly.

2 **Again there** was a day **when the sons of God** came to present themselves before the LORD,
and Satan came also among them to present himself before the LORD.

2 **And the LORD** said unto Satan,
From whence comest thou?
And Satan answered the LORD,
and said,
From going to and fro in the earth,
and from walking up and down in it.

3 **And the LORD** said unto Satan,
Hast thou considered my servant Job,
that there is none like him in the earth, a perfect and an upright man, one that feareth God, and escheweth evil?
and still he holdeth fast his integrity,
although thou movedst me against him,
to destroy him without cause.

4 **And Satan** answered the LORD,
and said,
Skin for skin, yea, all that a man hath will he give for his life.

5 **But put forth** thine hand now,
and touch his bone and his flesh,
and he will curse thee to thy face.

6 **And the LORD** said unto Satan,
Behold,
he is in thine hand;
but save his life.

7 **So** went Satan forth from the presence of the LORD,
and smote Job with sore boils from the sole of his foot unto his crown.

8 **And he** took him a potsherd to scrape himself withal;
and he sat down among the ashes.

9 **Then** said his wife unto him,
Dost thou still retain thine integrity?
curse God,
and die.

10 **But he** said unto her,
Thou speakest as one of the foolish women speaketh.
What?
shall we receive good at the hand of God,
and shall we not receive evil?
In all this did not Job sin with his lips.

11 **Now when Job's three friends** heard of all this evil that was come upon him,
they came every one from his own place; Eliphaz the Temanite, and Bildad the Shuhite, and Zophar the Naamathite:
for they had made an appointment together
to come to mourn with him
and to comfort him.

12 **And when they** lifted up their eyes afar off,
and knew him not,
they lifted up their voice,
and wept;
and they rent every one his mantle,
and sprinkled dust upon their heads toward heaven.

13 **So they** sat down with him upon the ground seven days and seven nights,
and none spake a word unto him:
for they saw that his grief was very great.

3 **After this** opened Job his mouth,
and cursed his day.

2 **And Job** spake,
and said,

3 **Let the day** perish wherein I was born, and the night in which it was said,
There is a man child conceived.

4 **Let that day** be darkness;
let not God regard it from above,
neither let the light shine upon it.

5 **Let darkness and the shadow of death** stain it;
let a cloud dwell upon it;
let the blackness of the day terrify it.

6 **As for that night,** let darkness seize upon it;
let it not be joined unto the days of the year,
let it not come into the number of the months.

7 **Lo,**
let that night be solitary,
let no joyful voice come therein.

8 **Let them** curse it that curse the day,
who are ready to raise up their mourning.

9 **Let the stars of the twilight thereof** be dark;
let it look for light,
but have none;
neither let it see the dawning of the day:

10 **Because it** shut not up the doors of my mother's womb,
nor hid sorrow from mine eyes.
11 **Why** died I not from the womb?
why did I not give up the ghost
when I came out of the belly?
12 **Why** did the knees prevent me?
or why the breasts that I should suck?
13 **For now** should I have lain still and been quiet,
I should have slept:
then had I been at rest,
14 With kings and counsellors of the earth, {which build desolate places for themselves};
15 Or with princes that had gold, {who filled their houses with silver}:
16 **Or as an hidden untimely birth** I had not been; as infants which never saw light.
17 **There** the wicked cease from troubling;
and there the weary be at rest.
18 **There** the prisoners rest together;
they hear not the voice of the oppressor.
19 **The small and great** are there;
and the servant is free from his master.
20 **Wherefore** is light given to him that is in misery, and life unto the bitter in soul;
21 **Which** long for death,
but it cometh not;
and dig for it more than for hid treasures;
22 **Which** rejoice exceedingly,
and are glad,
when they can find the grave?
23 **Why** is light given to a man whose way is hid, and whom God hath hedged in?
24 **For my sighing** cometh before I eat,
and my roarings are poured out like the waters.
25 **For the thing which I greatly feared** is come upon me,
and that which I was afraid of is come unto me.
26 **I** was not in safety,
neither had I rest,
neither was I quiet;
yet trouble came.

4 **Then Eliphaz the Temanite** answered and said,
2 **If we** assay to commune with thee,
wilt thou be grieved?
but who can withhold himself from speaking?
3 **Behold,**
thou hast instructed many,
and thou hast strengthened the weak hands.
4 **Thy words** have upholden him that was falling,
and thou hast strengthened the feeble knees.
5 **But now** it is come upon thee,
and thou faintest;
it toucheth thee,
and thou art troubled.
6 **Is not this** thy fear, thy confidence, thy hope, and the uprightness of thy ways?
7 **Remember,**
I pray thee,
who ever perished,
being innocent?
or where were the righteous cut off?
8 **Even as I** have seen,
they that plow iniquity, and sow wickedness, reap the same.
9 **By the blast of God** they perish,
and by the breath of his nostrils are they consumed.
10 **The roaring of the lion, and the voice of the fierce lion, and the teeth of the young lions,** are broken.
11 **The old lion** perisheth for lack of prey,
and the stout lion's whelps are scattered abroad.
12 **Now a thing** was secretly brought to me,
and mine ear received a little thereof.
13 **In thoughts from the visions of the night**, {when deep sleep falleth on men},
14 Fear came upon me, and trembling,
which made all my bones to shake.
15 **Then a spirit** passed before my face;
the hair of my flesh stood up:
16 **It** stood still,
but I could not discern the form thereof:
an image was before mine eyes,
there was silence,
and I heard a voice,
saying,
17 **Shall mortal man** be more just than God?
shall a man be more pure than his maker?
18 **Behold,**
he put no trust in his servants;
and his angels he charged with folly:
19 **How much less** in them that dwell in houses of clay,
whose foundation is in the dust,
which are crushed before the moth?
20 **They** are destroyed from morning to evening:
they perish for ever without any regarding it.
21 **Doth not their excellency which is in them** go away?
they die, even without wisdom.

5 **Call** now,
if there be any that will answer thee;
and to which of the saints wilt thou turn?
2 **For wrath** killeth the foolish man,
and envy slayeth the silly one.
3 **I** have seen the foolish taking root:
but suddenly I cursed his habitation.
4 **His children** are far from safety,
and they are crushed in the gate,
neither is there any to deliver them.
5 **Whose harvest** the hungry eateth up,
and taketh it even out of the thorns,
and the robber swalloweth up their substance.
6 **Although affliction** cometh not forth of the dust,
neither doth trouble spring out of the ground;
7 **Yet man** is born unto trouble,
as the sparks fly upward.
8 **I** would seek unto God,
and unto God would I commit my cause:
9 **Which** doeth great things and unsearchable; marvellous things without number:
10 **Who** giveth rain upon the earth,
and sendeth waters upon the fields:
11 To set up on high those that be low;
that those which mourn may be exalted to safety.
12 **He** disappointeth the devices of the crafty,
so that their hands cannot perform their enterprise.

[13] **He** taketh the wise in their own craftiness:
and the counsel of the froward is carried headlong.
[14] **They** meet with darkness in the day time,
and grope in the noonday as in the night.
[15] **But he** saveth the poor from the sword, from their mouth, and from the hand of the mighty.
[16] **So the poor** hath hope,
and iniquity stoppeth her mouth.
[17] **Behold,**
happy is the man whom God correcteth:
therefore despise not thou the chastening of the Almighty:
[18] **For he** maketh sore,
and bindeth up:
he woundeth,
and his hands make whole.
[19] **He** shall deliver thee in six troubles:
yea, in seven there shall no evil touch thee.
[20] **In famine** he shall redeem thee from death: and in war from the power of the sword.
[21] **Thou** shalt be hid from the scourge of the tongue:
neither shalt thou be afraid of destruction
when it cometh.
[22] **At destruction and famine** thou shalt laugh:
neither shalt thou be afraid of the beasts of the earth.
[23] **For thou** shalt be in league with the stones of the field:
and the beasts of the field shall be at peace with thee.
[24] **And thou** shalt know
that thy tabernacle shall be in peace;
and thou shalt visit thy habitation,
and shalt not sin.
[25] **Thou** shalt know also
that thy seed shall be great, and thine offspring as the grass of the earth.
[26] **Thou** shalt come to thy grave in a full age, like as a shock of corn cometh in in his season.
[27] **Lo** this,
we have searched it,
so it is;
hear it,
and know thou it for thy good.

6

But Job answered and said,
[2] **Oh that my grief** were throughly weighed,
and my calamity laid in the balances together!
[3] **For now it** would be heavier than the sand of the sea:
therefore my words are swallowed up.
[4] **For the arrows of the Almighty** are within me,
the poison whereof drinketh up my spirit:
the terrors of God do set themselves in array against me.
[5] **Doth the wild ass** bray
when he hath grass?
or loweth the ox over his fodder?
[6] **Can that which is unsavoury** be eaten without salt?
or is there any taste in the white of an egg?
[7] **The things that my soul refused to touch** are as my sorrowful meat.
[8] **Oh that I** might have my request;
and that God would grant me the thing that I long for!
[9] **Even that it would please God** to destroy me;
that he would let loose his hand,
and cut me off!
[10] **Then** should I yet have comfort;
yea, I would harden myself in sorrow:
let him not spare;
for I have not concealed the words of the Holy One.
[11] **What** is my strength,
that I should hope?
and what is mine end,
that I should prolong my life?
[12] **Is my strength** the strength of stones?
or is my flesh of brass?
[13] **Is not my help** in me?
and is wisdom driven quite from me?
[14] **To him that is afflicted** pity should be shewed from his friend;
but he forsaketh the fear of the Almighty.
[15] **My brethren** have dealt deceitfully as a brook,
and as the stream of brooks they pass away;
[16] **Which** are blackish by reason of the ice,
and wherein the snow is hid:
[17] **What time they** wax warm,
they vanish:
when it is hot,
they are consumed out of their place.
[18] **The paths of their way** are turned aside;
they go to nothing,
and perish.
[19] **The troops of Tema** looked,
the companies of Sheba waited for them.
[20] **They** were confounded
because they had hoped;
they came thither,
and were ashamed.
[21] **For now ye** are nothing;
ye see my casting down,
and are afraid.
[22] **Did I** say,
Bring unto me?
or, Give a reward for me of your substance?
[23] **Or, Deliver** me from the enemy's hand?
or, Redeem me from the hand of the mighty?
[24] **Teach** me,
and I will hold my tongue:
and cause me to understand
wherein I have erred.
[25] **How forcible** are right words!
but what doth your arguing reprove?
[26] **Do ye** imagine to reprove words, and the speeches of one that is desperate,
which are as wind?
[27] **Yea, ye** overwhelm the fatherless,
and ye dig a pit for your friend.
[28] **Now therefore be** content,
look upon me;
for it is evident unto you if I lie.
[29] **Return,**
I pray you,
let it not be iniquity;
yea, return again,
my righteousness is in it.
[30] **Is there iniquity** in my tongue?
cannot my taste discern perverse things?

7

Is there not an appointed time to man upon earth?
are not his days also like the days of an hireling?
[2] **As a servant** earnestly desireth the shadow,

and as an hireling looketh for the reward of his work:
3 **So** am I made to possess months of vanity,
and wearisome nights are appointed to me.
4 **When I** lie down,
I say,
When shall I arise,
and the night be gone?
and I am full of tossings to and fro unto the dawning of the day.
5 **My flesh** is clothed with worms and clods of dust;
my skin is broken,
and become loathsome.
6 **My days** are swifter than a weaver's shuttle,
and are spent without hope.
7 **O remember**
that my life is wind:
mine eye shall no more see good.
8 **The eye of him that hath seen me** shall see me no more:
thine eyes are upon me,
and I am not.
9 **As the cloud** is consumed and vanisheth away:
so he that goeth down to the grave shall come up no more.
10 **He** shall return no more to his house,
neither shall his place know him any more.
11 **Therefore I** will not refrain my mouth;
I will speak in the anguish of my spirit;
I will complain in the bitterness of my soul.
12 **Am I** a sea, or a whale,
that thou settest a watch over me?
13 **When I** say,
My bed shall comfort me,
my couch shall ease my complaints;
14 **Then thou** scarest me with dreams,
and terrifiest me through visions:
15 **So that my soul** chooseth strangling, and death rather than my life.
16 **I** loathe it;
I would not live alway:
let me alone;
for my days are vanity.
17 **What** is man,
that thou shouldest magnify him?
and that thou shouldest set thine heart upon him?
18 **And that thou** shouldest visit him every morning,
and try him every moment?
19 **How long** wilt thou not depart from me,
nor let me alone
till I swallow down my spittle?
20 **I** have sinned;
what shall I do unto thee, O thou preserver of men?
why hast thou set me as a mark against thee,
so that I am a burden to myself?
21 **And why** dost thou not pardon my transgression,
and take away my iniquity?
for now shall I sleep in the dust;
and thou shalt seek me in the morning,
but I shall not be.

8 ∞ **Then** answered Bildad the Shuhite,
and said,
2 **How long** wilt thou speak these things?
and how long shall the words of thy mouth be like a strong wind?
3 **Doth God** pervert judgment?
or doth the Almighty pervert justice?
4 **If thy children** have sinned against him,
and he have cast them away for their transgression;
5 **If thou** wouldest seek unto God betimes,
and make thy supplication to the Almighty;
6 **If thou** wert pure and upright;
surely now he would awake for thee,
and make the habitation of thy righteousness prosperous.
7 **Though thy beginning** was small,
yet thy latter end should greatly increase.
8 **For enquire**, {I pray thee}, of the former age,
and prepare thyself to the search of their fathers:
9 (For we are but of yesterday,
and know nothing,
because our days upon earth are a shadow:)
10 **Shall not they** teach thee,
and tell thee,
and utter words out of their heart?
11 **Can the rush** grow up without mire?
can the flag grow without water?
12 **Whilst it** is yet in his greenness,
and not cut down,
it withereth before any other herb.
13 **So** are the paths of all that forget God;
and the hypocrite's hope shall perish:
14 **Whose hope** shall be cut off,
and whose trust shall be a spider's web.
15 **He** shall lean upon his house,
but it shall not stand:
he shall hold it fast,
but it shall not endure.
16 **He** is green before the sun,
and his branch shooteth forth in his garden.
17 **His roots** are wrapped about the heap,
and seeth the place of stones.
18 **If he** destroy him from his place,
then it shall deny him,
saying,
I have not seen thee.
19 **Behold,**
this is the joy of his way,
and out of the earth shall others grow.
20 **Behold,**
God will not cast away a perfect man,
neither will he help the evil doers:
21 **Till he** fill thy mouth with laughing, and thy lips with rejoicing.
22 **They that hate thee** shall be clothed with shame;
and the dwelling place of the wicked shall come to nought.

9 **Then Job** answered and said,
2 **I** know it is so of a truth:
but how should man be just with God?
3 **If he** will contend with him,
he cannot answer him one of a thousand.
4 **He** is wise in heart, and mighty in strength:
who hath hardened himself against him,
and hath prospered?
5 **Which** removeth the mountains,
and they know not:
which overturneth them in his anger.

[6] **Which** shaketh the earth out of her place,
and the pillars thereof tremble.

[7] **Which** commandeth the sun,
and it riseth not;
and sealeth up the stars.

[8] **Which alone** spreadeth out the heavens,
and treadeth upon the waves of the sea.

[9] **Which** maketh Arcturus, Orion, and Pleiades, and the chambers of the south.

[10] **Which** doeth great things past finding out; yea, and wonders without number.

[11] **Lo,**
he goeth by me,
and I see him not:
he passeth on also,
but I perceive him not.

[12] **Behold,**
he taketh away,
who can hinder him?
who will say unto him,
What doest thou?

[13] **If God** will not withdraw his anger,
the proud helpers do stoop under him.

[14] **How much less** shall I answer him,
and choose out my words
to reason with him?

[15] **Whom, though I** were righteous,
yet would I not answer,
but I would make supplication to my judge.

[16] **If I** had called,
and he had answered me;
yet would I not believe
that he had hearkened unto my voice.

[17] **For he** breaketh me with a tempest,
and multiplieth my wounds without cause.

[18] **He** will not suffer me to take my breath,
but filleth me with bitterness.

[19] **If I** speak of strength,
lo,
he is strong:
and if of judgment, who shall set me a time to plead?

[20] **If I** justify myself,
mine own mouth shall condemn me:
if I say,
I am perfect,
it shall also prove me perverse.

[21] **Though I** were perfect,
yet would I not know my soul:
I would despise my life.

[22] **This** is one thing,
therefore I said it,
He destroyeth the perfect and the wicked.

[23] **If the scourge** slay suddenly,
he will laugh at the trial of the innocent.

[24] **The earth** is given into the hand of the wicked:
he covereth the faces of the judges thereof;
if not,
where, and who is he?

[25] **Now my days** are swifter than a post:
they flee away,
they see no good.

[26] **They** are passed away as the swift ships: as the eagle that hasteth to the prey.

[27] **If I** say,
I will forget my complaint,
I will leave off my heaviness,
and comfort myself:

[28] **I** am afraid of all my sorrows,
I know
that thou wilt not hold me innocent.

[29] **If I** be wicked,
why then labour I in vain?

[30] **If I** wash myself with snow water,
and make my hands never so clean;

[31] **Yet** shalt thou plunge me in the ditch,
and mine own clothes shall abhor me.

[32] **For he** is not a man,
as I am,
that I should answer him,
and we should come together in judgment.

[33] **Neither** is there any daysman betwixt us,
that might lay his hand upon us both.

[34] **Let him** take his rod away from me,
and let not his fear terrify me:

[35] **Then** would I speak,
and not fear him;
but it is not so with me.

10

My soul is weary of my life;
I will leave my complaint upon myself;
I will speak in the bitterness of my soul.

[2] **I** will say unto God,
Do not condemn me;
shew me
wherefore thou contendest with me.

[3] **Is it good unto thee** that thou shouldest oppress,
that thou shouldest despise the work of thine hands,
and shine upon the counsel of the wicked?

[4] **Hast thou** eyes of flesh?
or seest thou as man seeth?

[5] **Are thy days** as the days of man?
are thy years as man's days,

[6] **That thou** enquirest after mine iniquity,
and searchest after my sin?

[7] **Thou** knowest
that I am not wicked;
and there is none that can deliver out of thine hand.

[8] **Thine hands** have made me and fashioned me together round about;
yet thou dost destroy me.

[9] **Remember,**
I beseech thee,
that thou hast made me as the clay;
and wilt thou bring me into dust again?

[10] **Hast thou** not poured me out as milk,
and curdled me like cheese?

[11] **Thou** hast clothed me with skin and flesh,
and hast fenced me with bones and sinews.

[12] **Thou** hast granted me life and favour,
and thy visitation hath preserved my spirit.

[13] **And these things** hast thou hid in thine heart:
I know
that this is with thee.

[14] **If I** sin,
then thou markest me,
and thou wilt not acquit me from mine iniquity.

[15] **If I** be wicked,
woe unto me;
and if I be righteous,

yet will I not lift up my head.
I am full of confusion;
therefore see thou mine affliction;
16 **For it** increaseth.
Thou huntest me as a fierce lion:
and again thou shewest thyself marvellous upon me.
17 **Thou** renewest thy witnesses against me,
and increasest thine indignation upon me;
changes and war are against me.
18 **Wherefore** then hast thou brought me forth out of the womb?
Oh that I had given up the ghost,
and no eye had seen me!
19 **I** should have been as though I had not been;
I should have been carried from the womb to the grave.
20 **Are not my days** few?
cease then,
and let me alone,
that I may take comfort a little,
21 **Before I** go whence I shall not return, even to the land of darkness and the shadow of death;
22 A land of darkness, as darkness itself; and of the shadow of death, without any order,
and where the light is as darkness.

11

Then answered Zophar the Naamathite,
and said,
2 **Should not the multitude of words** be answered?
and should a man full of talk be justified?
3 **Should thy lies** make men hold their peace?
and when thou mockest,
shall no man make thee ashamed?
4 **For thou** hast said,
My doctrine is pure,
and I am clean in thine eyes.
5 **But oh that God** would speak,
and open his lips against thee;
6 **And that he** would shew thee the secrets of wisdom,
that they are double to that which is!
Know therefore
that God exacteth of thee less than thine iniquity deserveth.
7 **Canst thou** by searching find out God?
canst thou find out the Almighty unto perfection?
8 **It** is as high as heaven;
what canst thou do?
deeper than hell;
what canst thou know?
9 **The measure thereof** is longer than the earth, and broader than the sea.
10 **If he** cut off,
and shut up,
or gather together,
then who can hinder him?
11 **For he** knoweth vain men:
he seeth wickedness also;
will he not then consider it?
12 **For vain men** would be wise,
though man be born like a wild ass's colt.
13 **If thou** prepare thine heart,
and stretch out thine hands toward him;
14 **If iniquity** be in thine hand,
put it far away,
and let not wickedness dwell in thy tabernacles.
15 **For then** shalt thou lift up thy face without spot;
yea, thou shalt be stedfast,
and shalt not fear:
16 **Because thou** shalt forget thy misery,
and remember it as waters that pass away:
17 **And thine age** shall be clearer than the noonday:
thou shalt shine forth,
thou shalt be as the morning.
18 **And thou** shalt be secure,
because there is hope;
yea, thou shalt dig about thee,
and thou shalt take thy rest in safety.
19 **Also thou** shalt lie down,
and none shall make thee afraid;
yea, many shall make suit unto thee.
20 **But the eyes of the wicked** shall fail,
and they shall not escape,
and their hope shall be as the giving up of the ghost.

12

And Job answered and said,
2 **No doubt but ye** are the people,
and wisdom shall die with you.
3 **But I** have understanding as well as you;
I am not inferior to you:
yea, who knoweth not such things as these?
4 **I** am as one mocked of his neighbour,
who calleth upon God,
and he answereth him:
the just upright man is laughed to scorn.
5 **He that is ready to slip with his feet** is as a lamp despised in the thought of him that is at ease.
6 **The tabernacles of robbers** prosper,
and they that provoke God are secure;
into whose hand God bringeth abundantly.
7 **But ask** now the beasts, {and they shall teach thee}; and the fowls of the air, {and they shall tell thee}:
8 **Or speak** to the earth,
and it shall teach thee:
and the fishes of the sea shall declare unto thee.
9 **Who** knoweth not in all these
that the hand of the LORD hath wrought this?
10 **In whose hand** is the soul of every living thing, and the breath of all mankind.
11 **Doth not the ear** try words?
and the mouth taste his meat?
12 **With the ancient** is wisdom;
and in length of days understanding.
13 **With him** is wisdom and strength,
he hath counsel and understanding.
14 **Behold,**
he breaketh down,
and it cannot be built again:
he shutteth up a man,
and there can be no opening.
15 **Behold,**
he withholdeth the waters,
and they dry up:
also he sendeth them out,
and they overturn the earth.
16 **With him** is strength and wisdom:
the deceived and the deceiver are his.
17 **He** leadeth counsellors away spoiled,
and maketh the judges fools.
18 **He** looseth the bond of kings,
and girdeth their loins with a girdle.
19 **He** leadeth princes away spoiled,

and overthroweth the mighty.
20 **He** removeth away the speech of the trusty,
and taketh away the understanding of the aged.
21 **He** poureth contempt upon princes,
and weakeneth the strength of the mighty.
22 **He** discovereth deep things out of darkness,
and bringeth out to light the shadow of death.
23 **He** increaseth the nations,
and destroyeth them:
he enlargeth the nations,
and straiteneth them again.
24 **He** taketh away the heart of the chief of the people of the earth,
and causeth them to wander in a wilderness where there is no way.
25 **They** grope in the dark without light,
and he maketh them to stagger like a drunken man.

13

Lo,
mine eye hath seen all this,
mine ear hath heard and understood it.
2 **What** ye know,
the same do I know also:
I am not inferior unto you.
3 **Surely I** would speak to the Almighty,
and I desire to reason with God.
4 **But ye** are forgers of lies,
ye are all physicians of no value.
5 **O that ye** would altogether hold your peace!
and it should be your wisdom.
6 **Hear** now my reasoning,
and hearken to the pleadings of my lips.
7 **Will ye** speak wickedly for God?
and talk deceitfully for him?
8 **Will ye** accept his person?
will ye contend for God?
9 **Is it good** that he should search you out?
or as one man mocketh another,
do ye so mock him?
10 **He** will surely reprove you,
if ye do secretly accept persons.
11 **Shall not his excellency** make you afraid?
and his dread fall upon you?
12 **Your remembrances** are like unto ashes,
your bodies to bodies of clay.
13 **Hold** your peace,
let me alone,
that I may speak,
and let come on me what will.
14 **Wherefore** do I take my flesh in my teeth,
and put my life in mine hand?
15 **Though he** slay me,
yet will I trust in him:
but I will maintain mine own ways before him.
16 **He** also shall be my salvation:
for an hypocrite shall not come before him.
17 **Hear** diligently my speech, and my declaration with your ears.
18 **Behold** now,
I have ordered my cause;
I know
that I shall be justified.
19 **Who** is he that will plead with me?
for now, {if I hold my tongue}, I shall give up the ghost.
20 **Only** do not two things unto me:
then will I not hide myself from thee.
21 **Withdraw** thine hand far from me:
and let not thy dread make me afraid.
22 **Then call thou,**
and I will answer:
or let me speak,
and answer thou me.
23 **How many** are mine iniquities and sins?
make me to know my transgression and my sin.
24 **Wherefore** hidest thou thy face,
and holdest me for thine enemy?
25 **Wilt thou** break a leaf driven to and fro?
and wilt thou pursue the dry stubble?
26 **For thou** writest bitter things against me,
and makest me to possess the iniquities of my youth.
27 **Thou** puttest my feet also in the stocks,
and lookest narrowly unto all my paths;
thou settest a print upon the heels of my feet.
28 **And he, as a rotten thing,** consumeth, as a garment that is moth eaten.

14

Man that is born of a woman is of few days and full of trouble.
2 **He** cometh forth like a flower,
and is cut down:
he fleeth also as a shadow,
and continueth not.
3 **And doth thou** open thine eyes upon such an one,
and bringest me into judgment with thee?
4 **Who** can bring a clean thing out of an unclean?
not one.
5 **Seeing his days** are determined,
the number of his months are with thee,
thou hast appointed his bounds
that he cannot pass;
6 **Turn** from him,
that he may rest,
till he shall accomplish, as an hireling, his day.
7 **For there** is hope of a tree,
if it be cut down,
that it will sprout again,
and that the tender branch thereof will not cease.
8 **Though the root thereof** wax old in the earth,
and the stock thereof die in the ground;
9 **Yet through the scent of water** it will bud,
and bring forth boughs like a plant.
10 **But man** dieth,
and wasteth away:
yea, man giveth up the ghost,
and where is he?
11 **As the waters** fail from the sea,
and the flood decayeth and drieth up:
12 **So man** lieth down,
and riseth not:
till the heavens be no more,
they shall not awake,
nor be raised out of their sleep.
13 **O that thou** wouldest hide me in the grave,
that thou wouldest keep me secret,
until thy wrath be past,
that thou wouldest appoint me a set time,
and remember me!
14 **If a man** die,
shall he live again?

all the days of my appointed time will I wait,
till my change come.
15 **Thou** shalt call,
and I will answer thee:
thou wilt have a desire to the work of thine hands.
16 **For now thou** numberest my steps:
dost thou not watch over my sin?
17 **My transgression** is sealed up in a bag,
and thou sewest up mine iniquity.
18 **And surely the mountains falling** cometh to nought,
and the rock is removed out of his place.
19 **The waters** wear the stones:
thou washest away the things which grow out of the dust of the earth;
and thou destroyest the hope of man.
20 **Thou** prevailest for ever against him,
and he passeth:
thou changest his countenance,
and sendest him away.
21 **His sons** come to honour,
and he knoweth it not;
and they are brought low,
but he perceiveth it not of them.
22 **But his flesh upon him** shall have pain,
and his soul within him shall mourn.

15 **Then** answered Eliphaz the Temanite,
and said,
2 **Should a wise man** utter vain knowledge,
and fill his belly with the east wind?
3 **Should he** reason with unprofitable talk?
or with speeches wherewith he can do no good?
4 **Yea, thou** castest off fear,
and restrainest prayer before God.
5 **For thy mouth** uttereth thine iniquity,
and thou choosest the tongue of the crafty.
6 **Thine own mouth** condemneth thee, and not I:
yea, thine own lips testify against thee.
7 **Art thou** the first man that was born?
or wast thou made before the hills?
8 **Hast thou** heard the secret of God?
and dost thou restrain wisdom to thyself?
9 **What** knowest thou,
that we know not?
what understandest thou,
which is not in us?
10 **With us** are both the grayheaded and very aged men, much elder than thy father.
11 **Are the consolations of God** small with thee?
is there any secret thing with thee?
12 **Why** doth thine heart carry thee away?
and what do thy eyes wink at,
13 **That thou** turnest thy spirit against God,
and lettest such words go out of thy mouth?
14 **What** is man, {that he should be clean}? and he which is born of a woman, {that he should be righteous}?
15 **Behold,**
he putteth no trust in his saints;
yea, the heavens are not clean in his sight.
16 **How much more abominable and filthy** is man,
which drinketh iniquity like water?
17 **I** will shew thee,
hear me;
and that which I have seen I will declare;
18 **Which wise men** have told from their fathers,
and have not hid it:
19 **Unto whom alone** the earth was given,
and no stranger passed among them.
20 **The wicked man** travaileth with pain all his days,
and the number of years is hidden to the oppressor.
21 **A dreadful sound** is in his ears:
in prosperity the destroyer shall come upon him.
22 **He** believeth not
that he shall return out of darkness,
and he is waited for of the sword.
23 **He** wandereth abroad for bread,
saying,
Where is it?
he knoweth
that the day of darkness is ready at his hand.
24 **Trouble and anguish** shall make him afraid;
they shall prevail against him, as a king ready to the battle.
25 **For he** stretcheth out his hand against God,
and strengtheneth himself against the Almighty.
26 **He** runneth upon him, even on his neck, upon the thick bosses of his bucklers:
27 **Because he** covereth his face with his fatness,
and maketh collops of fat on his flanks.
28 **And he** dwelleth in desolate cities, and in houses which no man inhabiteth,
which are ready to become heaps.
29 **He** shall not be rich,
neither shall his substance continue,
neither shall he prolong the perfection thereof upon the earth.
30 **He** shall not depart out of darkness;
the flame shall dry up his branches,
and by the breath of his mouth shall he go away.
31 **Let not him that is deceived** trust in vanity:
for vanity shall be his recompence.
32 **It** shall be accomplished before his time,
and his branch shall not be green.
33 **He** shall shake off his unripe grape as the vine,
and shall cast off his flower as the olive.
34 **For the congregation of hypocrites** shall be desolate,
and fire shall consume the tabernacles of bribery.
35 **They** conceive mischief,
and bring forth vanity,
and their belly prepareth deceit.

16 **Then Job** answered and said,
2 **I** have heard many such things:
miserable comforters are ye all.
3 **Shall vain words** have an end?
or what emboldeneth thee
that thou answerest?
4 **I** also could speak as ye do:
if your soul were in my soul's stead,
I could heap up words against you,
and shake mine head at you.

5 **But I** would strengthen you with my mouth,
and the moving of my lips should asswage your grief.

6 **Though I** speak,
my grief is not asswaged:
and though I forbear,
what am I eased?

7 **But now he** hath made me weary:
thou hast made desolate all my company.

8 **And thou** hast filled me with wrinkles,
which is a witness against me:
and my leanness rising up in me beareth witness to my face.

9 **He** teareth me in his wrath,
who hateth me:
he gnasheth upon me with his teeth;
mine enemy sharpeneth his eyes upon me.

10 **They** have gaped upon me with their mouth;
they have smitten me upon the cheek reproachfully;
they have gathered themselves together against me.

11 **God** hath delivered me to the ungodly,
and turned me over into the hands of the wicked.

12 **I** was at ease,
but he hath broken me asunder:
he hath also taken me by my neck,
and shaken me to pieces,
and set me up for his mark.

13 **His archers** compass me round about,
he cleaveth my reins asunder,
and doth not spare;
he poureth out my gall upon the ground.

14 **He** breaketh me with breach upon breach,
he runneth upon me like a giant.

15 **I** have sewed sackcloth upon my skin,
and defiled my horn in the dust.

16 **My face** is foul with weeping,
and on my eyelids is the shadow of death;

17 Not for any injustice in mine hands:
also my prayer is pure.

18 **O earth, cover not thou** my blood,
and let my cry have no place.

19 **Also now, {behold}, my witness** is in heaven,
and my record is on high.

20 **My friends** scorn me:
but mine eye poureth out tears unto God.

21 **O that one** might plead for a man with God,
as a man pleadeth for his neighbour!

22 **When a few years** are come,
then I shall go the way whence I shall not return.

17

My breath is corrupt,
my days are extinct,
the graves are ready for me.

2 **Are there not** mockers with me?
and doth not mine eye continue in their provocation?

3 **Lay down** now,
put me in a surety with thee;
who is he that will strike hands with me?

4 **For thou** hast hid their heart from understanding:
therefore shalt thou not exalt them.

5 **He that speaketh flattery to his friends,** even the eyes of his children shall fail.

6 **He** hath made me also a byword of the people;
and aforetime I was as a tabret.

7 **Mine eye** also is dim by reason of sorrow,
and all my members are as a shadow.

8 **Upright men** shall be astonied at this,
and the innocent shall stir up himself against the hypocrite.

9 **The righteous** also shall hold on his way,
and he that hath clean hands shall be stronger and stronger.

10 **But as for you all,** do ye return,
and come now:
for I cannot find one wise man among you.

11 **My days** are past,
my purposes are broken off, even the thoughts of my heart.

12 **They** change the night into day:
the light is short because of darkness.

13 **If I** wait,
the grave is mine house:
I have made my bed in the darkness.

14 **I** have said to corruption, {Thou art my father}: to the worm, {Thou art my mother, and my sister}.

15 **And where** is now my hope?
as for my hope, who shall see it?

16 **They** shall go down to the bars of the pit,
when our rest together is in the dust.

18

Then answered Bildad the Shuhite,
and said,

2 **How long** will it be ere ye make an end of words?
mark, and afterwards we will speak.

3 **Wherefore** are we counted as beasts,
and reputed vile in your sight?

4 **He** teareth himself in his anger:
shall the earth be forsaken for thee?
and shall the rock be removed out of his place?

5 **Yea, the light of the wicked** shall be put out,
and the spark of his fire shall not shine.

6 **The light** shall be dark in his tabernacle,
and his candle shall be put out with him.

7 **The steps of his strength** shall be straitened,
and his own counsel shall cast him down.

8 **For he** is cast into a net by his own feet,
and he walketh upon a snare.

9 **The gin** shall take him by the heel,
and the robber shall prevail against him.

10 **The snare** is laid for him in the ground, and a trap for him in the way.

11 **Terrors** shall make him afraid on every side,
and shall drive him to his feet.

12 **His strength** shall be hungerbitten,
and destruction shall be ready at his side.

13 **It** shall devour the strength of his skin:
even the firstborn of death shall devour his strength.

14 **His confidence** shall be rooted
out of his tabernacle,
and it shall bring him to the king of
terrors.
15 **It** shall dwell in his tabernacle,
because it is none of his:
brimstone shall be scattered upon
his habitation.
16 **His roots** shall be dried up
beneath,
and above shall his branch be cut
off.
17 **His remembrance** shall perish
from the earth,
and he shall have no name in the
street.
18 **He** shall be driven from light into
darkness,
and chased out of the world.
19 **He** shall neither have son nor
nephew among his people,
nor any remaining in his dwellings.
20 **They that come after him** shall
be astonied at his day,
as they that went before were
affrighted.
21 **Surely such** are the dwellings of
the wicked,
and this is the place of him that
knoweth not God.

19

Then Job answered and
said,
2 **How long** will ye vex my soul,
and break me in pieces with words?
3 **These ten times** have ye
reproached me:
ye are not ashamed that ye make
yourselves strange to me.
4 **And be it indeed that I** have erred,
mine error remaineth with myself.
5 **If indeed ye** will magnify
yourselves against me,
and plead against me my reproach:
6 **Know** now
that God hath overthrown me,
and hath compassed me with his
net.
7 **Behold,**
I cry out of wrong,
but I am not heard:
I cry aloud,
but there is no judgment.
8 **He** hath fenced up my way that I
cannot pass,
and he hath set darkness in my
paths.
9 **He** hath stripped me of my glory,
and taken the crown from my head.
10 **He** hath destroyed me on every
side,
and I am gone:
and mine hope hath he removed
like a tree.
11 **He** hath also kindled his wrath
against me,
and he counteth me unto him as
one of his enemies.
12 **His troops** come together,
and raise up their way against me,
and encamp round about my
tabernacle.
13 **He** hath put my brethren far from
me,
and mine acquaintance are verily
estranged from me.
14 **My kinsfolk** have failed,
and my familiar friends have
forgotten me.
15 **They that dwell in mine house,**
and my maids, count me for a
stranger:
I am an alien in their sight.
16 **I** called my servant,
and he gave me no answer;
I intreated him with my mouth.
17 **My breath** is strange to my wife,
though I intreated for the
children's sake of mine own body.
18 **Yea, young children** despised me;
I arose,
and they spake against me.
19 **All my inward friends** abhorred
me:
and they whom I loved are turned
against me.
20 **My bone** cleaveth to my skin and
to my flesh,
and I am escaped with the skin of
my teeth.
21 **Have** pity upon me,
have pity upon me, O ye my friends;
for the hand of God hath touched
me.
22 **Why** do ye persecute me as God,
and are not satisfied with my flesh?
23 **Oh that my words** were now
written!
oh that they were printed in a
book!
24 **That they** were graven with an
iron pen and lead in the rock for
ever!
25 **For I** know
that my redeemer liveth,
and that he shall stand at the latter
day upon the earth:
26 **And though after my skin**
worms destroy this body,
yet in my flesh shall I see God:
27 **Whom** I shall see for myself,
and mine eyes shall behold, and
not another;
though my reins be consumed
within me.
28 **But ye** should say,
Why persecute we him,
seeing the root of the matter is
found in me?
29 **Be ye** afraid of the sword:
for wrath bringeth the
punishments of the sword,
that ye may know
there is a judgment.

20

Then answered Zophar
the Naamathite,
and said,
2 **Therefore** do my thoughts cause
me to answer,
and for this I make haste.
3 **I** have heard the check of my
reproach,
and the spirit of my
understanding causeth me to
answer.
4 **Knowest thou not** this of old,
since man was placed upon earth,
5 **That the triumphing of the**
wicked is short,
and the joy of the hypocrite but
for a moment?
6 **Though his excellency** mount up
to the heavens,
and his head reach unto the clouds;
7 **Yet he** shall perish for ever like his
own dung:
they which have seen him shall
say,
Where is he?
8 **He** shall fly away as a dream,
and shall not be found:
yea, he shall be chased away as a
vision of the night.
9 **The eye also which saw him** shall
see him no more;
neither shall his place any more
behold him.
10 **His children** shall seek to please
the poor,
and his hands shall restore their
goods.
11 **His bones** are full of the sin of his
youth,
which shall lie down with him in
the dust.

[12] **Though wickedness** be sweet in his mouth,
though he hide it under his tongue;
[13] **Though he** spare it,
and forsake it not;
but keep it still within his mouth:
[14] **Yet his meat in his bowels** is turned,
it is the gall of asps within him.
[15] **He** hath swallowed down riches,
and he shall vomit them up again:
God shall cast them out of his belly.
[16] **He** shall suck the poison of asps:
the viper's tongue shall slay him.
[17] **He** shall not see the rivers, the floods, the brooks of honey and butter.
[18] **That which he laboured for** shall he restore,
and shall not swallow it down:
according to his substance shall the restitution be,
and he shall not rejoice therein.
[19] **Because he** hath oppressed and hath forsaken the poor;
because he hath violently taken away an house which he builded not;
[20] **Surely he** shall not feel quietness in his belly,
he shall not save of that which he desired.
[21] **There** shall none of his meat be left;
therefore shall no man look for his goods.
[22] **In the fulness of his sufficiency** he shall be in straits:
every hand of the wicked shall come upon him.
[23] **When he** is about to fill his belly,
God shall cast the fury of his wrath upon him,
and shall rain it upon him
while he is eating.
[24] **He** shall flee from the iron weapon,
and the bow of steel shall strike him through.
[25] **It** is drawn,
and cometh out of the body;
yea, the glittering sword cometh out of his gall:
terrors are upon him.
[26] **All darkness** shall be hid in his secret places:
a fire not blown shall consume him;
it shall go ill with him that is left in his tabernacle.
[27] **The heaven** shall reveal his iniquity;
and the earth shall rise up against him.
[28] **The increase of his house** shall depart,
and his goods shall flow away in the day of his wrath.
[29] **This** is the portion of a wicked man from God, and the heritage appointed unto him by God.

21

But Job answered and said,
[2] **Hear** diligently my speech,
and let this be your consolations.
[3] **Suffer** me
that I may speak;
and after that I have spoken,
mock on.
[4] **As for me,** is my complaint to man?
and if it were so,
why should not my spirit be troubled?
[5] **Mark** me,
and be astonished,
and lay your hand upon your mouth.
[6] **Even when I** remember
I am afraid,
and trembling taketh hold on my flesh.
[7] **Wherefore** do the wicked live,
become old,
yea, are mighty in power?
[8] **Their seed** is established in their sight with them, and their offspring before their eyes.
[9] **Their houses** are safe from fear,
neither is the rod of God upon them.
[10] **Their bull** gendereth,
and faileth not;
their cow calveth,
and casteth not her calf.
[11] **They** send forth their little ones like a flock,
and their children dance.
[12] **They** take the timbrel and harp,
and rejoice at the sound of the organ.
[13] **They** spend their days in wealth,
and in a moment go down to the grave.
[14] **Therefore they** say unto God,
Depart from us;
for we desire not the knowledge of thy ways.
[15] **What** is the Almighty,
that we should serve him?
and what profit should we have,
if we pray unto him?
[16] **Lo,**
their good is not in their hand:
the counsel of the wicked is far from me.
[17] **How oft** is the candle of the wicked put out!
and how oft cometh their destruction upon them!
God distributeth sorrows in his anger.
[18] **They** are as stubble before the wind, and as chaff that the storm carrieth away.
[19] **God** layeth up his iniquity for his children:
he rewardeth him,
and he shall know it.
[20] **His eyes** shall see his destruction,
and he shall drink of the wrath of the Almighty.
[21] **For what pleasure** hath he in his house after him,
when the number of his months is cut off in the midst?
[22] **Shall any** teach God knowledge?
seeing he judgeth those that are high.
[23] **One** dieth in his full strength,
being wholly at ease and quiet.
[24] **His breasts** are full of milk,
and his bones are moistened with marrow.
[25] **And another** dieth in the bitterness of his soul,
and never eateth with pleasure.
[26] **They** shall lie down alike in the dust,
and the worms shall cover them.
[27] **Behold,**
I know your thoughts, and the devices which ye wrongfully imagine against me.
[28] **For ye** say,
Where is the house of the prince?
and where are the dwelling places of the wicked?
[29] **Have ye not** asked them that go by the way?
and do ye not know their tokens,
[30] **That the wicked** is reserved to the day of destruction?

they shall be brought forth to the day of wrath.
31 **Who** shall declare his way to his face?
and who shall repay him what he hath done?
32 **Yet** shall he be brought to the grave,
and shall remain in the tomb.
33 **The clods of the valley** shall be sweet unto him,
and every man shall draw after him,
as there are innumerable before him.
34 **How** then comfort ye me in vain,
seeing in your answers there remaineth falsehood?

22

Then Eliphaz the Temanite answered and said,
2 **Can a man** be profitable unto God,
as he that is wise may be profitable unto himself?
3 **Is it any pleasure to the Almighty,** that thou art righteous?
or is it gain to him, that thou makest thy ways perfect?
4 **Will he** reprove thee for fear of thee?
will he enter with thee into judgment?
5 **Is not thy wickedness** great?
and thine iniquities infinite?
6 **For thou** hast taken a pledge from thy brother for nought,
and stripped the naked of their clothing.
7 **Thou** hast not given water to the weary to drink,
and thou hast withholden bread from the hungry.
8 **But as for the mighty man,** he had the earth;
and the honourable man dwelt in it.
9 **Thou** hast sent widows away empty,
and the arms of the fatherless have been broken.
10 **Therefore snares** are round about thee,
and sudden fear troubleth thee;
11 Or darkness,
that thou canst not see;
and abundance of waters cover thee.
12 **Is not God** in the height of heaven?
and behold the height of the stars,
how high they are!
13 **And thou** sayest,
How doth God know?
can he judge through the dark cloud?
14 **Thick clouds** are a covering to him,
that he seeth not;
and he walketh in the circuit of heaven.
15 **Hast thou** marked the old way which wicked men have trodden?
16 **Which** were cut down out of time,
whose foundation was overflown with a flood:
17 **Which** said unto God,
Depart from us:
and what can the Almighty do for them?
18 **Yet he** filled their houses with good things:
but the counsel of the wicked is far from me.
19 **The righteous** see it,
and are glad:
and the innocent laugh them to scorn.
20 **Whereas our substance** is not cut down,
but the remnant of them the fire consumeth.
21 **Acquaint** now thyself with him,
and be at peace:
thereby good shall come unto thee.
22 **Receive**, {I pray thee}, the law from his mouth,
and lay up his words in thine heart.
23 **If thou** return to the Almighty,
thou shalt be built up,
thou shalt put away iniquity far from thy tabernacles.
24 **Then** shalt thou lay up gold as dust, and the gold of Ophir as the stones of the brooks.
25 **Yea, the Almighty** shall be thy defence,
and thou shalt have plenty of silver.
26 **For then** shalt thou have thy delight in the Almighty,
and shalt lift up thy face unto God.
27 **Thou** shalt make thy prayer unto him,
and he shall hear thee,
and thou shalt pay thy vows.
28 **Thou** shalt also decree a thing,
and it shall be established unto thee:
and the light shall shine upon thy ways.
29 **When men** are cast down,
then thou shalt say,
There is lifting up;
and he shall save the humble person.
30 **He** shall deliver the island of the innocent:
and it is delivered by the pureness of thine hands.

23

Then Job answered and said,
2 **Even to day** is my complaint bitter:
my stroke is heavier than my groaning.
3 **Oh that I** knew
where I might find him!
that I might come even to his seat!
4 **I** would order my cause before him,
and fill my mouth with arguments.
5 **I** would know the words which he would answer me,
and understand
what he would say unto me.
6 **Will he** plead against me with his great power?
No; but he would put strength in me.
7 **There the righteous** might dispute with him;
so should I be delivered for ever from my judge.
8 **Behold, I** go forward, {but he is not there}; and backward, {but I cannot perceive him}:
9 On the left hand,
where he doth work,
but I cannot behold him:
he hideth himself on the right hand,
that I cannot see him:
10 **But he** knoweth the way that I take:
when he hath tried me,
I shall come forth as gold.
11 **My foot** hath held his steps,
his way have I kept,
and not declined.
12 **Neither** have I gone back from the commandment of his lips;
I have esteemed the words of his mouth more than my necessary food.
13 **But he** is in one mind,

and who can turn him?
and what his soul desireth,
even that he doeth.
14 **For he** performeth the thing that is appointed for me:
and many such things are with him.
15 **Therefore** am I troubled at his presence:
when I consider,
I am afraid of him.
16 **For God** maketh my heart soft,
and the Almighty troubleth me:
17 **Because I** was not cut off before the darkness,
neither hath he covered the darkness from my face.

24 ✡ **Why**, {seeing times are not hidden from the Almighty}, do they that know him not see his days?
2 **Some** remove the landmarks;
they violently take away flocks,
and feed thereof.
3 **They** drive away the ass of the fatherless,
they take the widow's ox for a pledge.
4 **They** turn the needy out of the way:
the poor of the earth hide themselves together.
5 **Behold,**
as wild asses in the desert, go they forth to their work;
rising betimes for a prey:
the wilderness yieldeth food for them and for their children.
6 **They** reap every one his corn in the field:
and they gather the vintage of the wicked.
7 **They** cause the naked to lodge without clothing,
that they have no covering in the cold.
8 **They** are wet with the showers of the mountains,
and embrace the rock for want of a shelter.
9 **They** pluck the fatherless from the breast,
and take a pledge of the poor.
10 **They** cause him to go naked without clothing,
and they take away the sheaf from the hungry;
11 **Which** make oil within their walls,
and tread their winepresses,
and suffer thirst.
12 **Men** groan from out of the city,
and the soul of the wounded crieth out:
yet God layeth not folly to them.
13 **They** are of those that rebel against the light;
they know not the ways thereof,
nor abide in the paths thereof.
14 **The murderer rising with the light** killeth the poor and needy,
and in the night is as a thief.
15 **The eye also of the adulterer** waiteth for the twilight,
saying,
No eye shall see me:
and disguiseth his face.
16 **In the dark** they dig through houses,
which they had marked for themselves in the daytime:
they know not the light.
17 **For the morning** is to them even as the shadow of death:
if one know them,
they are in the terrors of the shadow of death.
18 **He** is swift as the waters;
their portion is cursed in the earth:
he beholdeth not the way of the vineyards.
19 **Drought and heat** consume the snow waters:
so doth the grave those which have sinned.
20 **The womb** shall forget him;
the worm shall feed sweetly on him;
he shall be no more remembered;
and wickedness shall be broken as a tree.
21 **He** evil entreateth the barren that beareth not:
and doeth not good to the widow.
22 **He** draweth also the mighty with his power:
he riseth up,
and no man is sure of life.
23 **Though it be given him** to be in safety,
whereon he resteth;
yet his eyes are upon their ways.
24 **They** are exalted for a little while,
but are gone and brought low;
they are taken out of the way as all other,
and cut off as the tops of the ears of corn.
25 **And if it** be not so now,
who will make me a liar,
and make my speech nothing worth?

25 **Then** answered Bildad the Shuhite,
and said,
2 **Dominion and fear** are with him,
he maketh peace in his high places.
3 **Is there** any number of his armies?
and upon whom doth not his light arise?
4 **How** then can man be justified with God?
or how can he be clean that is born of a woman?
5 **Behold** even to the moon,
and it shineth not;
yea, the stars are not pure in his sight.
6 How much less man, {that is a worm}? and the son of man, {which is a worm}?

26 **But Job** answered and said,
2 **How** hast thou helped him that is without power?
how savest thou the arm that hath no strength?
3 **How** hast thou counselled him that hath no wisdom?
and how hast thou plentifully declared the thing as it is?
4 **To whom** hast thou uttered words?
and whose spirit came from thee?
5 **Dead things** are formed from under the waters, and the inhabitants thereof.
6 **Hell** is naked before him,
and destruction hath no covering.
7 **He** stretcheth out the north over the empty place,
and hangeth the earth upon nothing.
8 **He** bindeth up the waters in his thick clouds;
and the cloud is not rent under them.
9 **He** holdeth back the face of his throne,
and spreadeth his cloud upon it.
10 **He** hath compassed the waters with bounds,
until the day and night come to an end.

11 **The pillars of heaven** tremble
and are astonished at his reproof.
12 **He** divideth the sea with his power,
and by his understanding he smiteth through the proud.
13 **By his spirit** he hath garnished the heavens;
his hand hath formed the crooked serpent.
14 **Lo,**
these are parts of his ways:
but how little a portion is heard of him?
but the thunder of his power who can understand?

27

Moreover Job continued his parable,
and said,
2 **As God** liveth, {who hath taken away my judgment}; and the Almighty, {who hath vexed my soul};
3 **All the while my breath** is in me,
and the spirit of God is in my nostrils;
4 **My lips** shall not speak wickedness,
nor my tongue utter deceit.
5 **God** forbid
that I should justify you:
till I die
I will not remove mine integrity from me.
6 **My righteousness** I hold fast,
and will not let it go:
my heart shall not reproach me so long as I live.
7 **Let mine enemy** be as the wicked,
and he that riseth up against me as the unrighteous.
8 **For what** is the hope of the hypocrite,
though he hath gained,
when God taketh away his soul?
9 **Will God** hear his cry
when trouble cometh upon him?
10 **Will he** delight himself in the Almighty?
will he always call upon God?
11 **I** will teach you by the hand of God:
that which is with the Almighty will I not conceal.
12 **Behold,**
all ye yourselves have seen it;
why then are ye thus altogether vain?
13 **This** is the portion of a wicked man with God, and the heritage of oppressors,
which they shall receive of the Almighty.
14 **If his children** be multiplied,
it is for the sword:
and his offspring shall not be satisfied with bread.
15 **Those that remain of him** shall be buried in death:
and his widows shall not weep.
16 **Though he** heap up silver as the dust,
and prepare raiment as the clay;
17 **He** may prepare it,
but the just shall put it on,
and the innocent shall divide the silver.
18 **He** buildeth his house as a moth, and as a booth that the keeper maketh.
19 **The rich man** shall lie down,
but he shall not be gathered:
he openeth his eyes,
and he is not.
20 **Terrors** take hold on him as waters,
a tempest stealeth him away in the night.
21 **The east wind** carrieth him away,
and he departeth:
and as a storm hurleth him out of his place.
22 **For God** shall cast upon him,
and not spare:
he would fain flee out of his hand.
23 **Men** shall clap their hands at him,
and shall hiss him out of his place.

28

Surely there is a vein for the silver, and a place for gold where they fine it.
2 **Iron** is taken out of the earth,
and brass is molten out of the stone.
3 **He** setteth an end to darkness,
and searcheth out all perfection: the stones of darkness, and the shadow of death.
4 **The flood** breaketh out from the inhabitant;
even the waters forgotten of the foot:
they are dried up,
they are gone away from men.
5 **As for the earth,** out of it cometh bread:
and under it is turned up as it were fire.
6 **The stones of it** are the place of sapphires:
and it hath dust of gold.
7 **There** is a path which no fowl knoweth, and which the vulture's eye hath not seen:
8 **The lion's whelps** have not trodden it,
nor the fierce lion passed by it.
9 **He** putteth forth his hand upon the rock;
he overturneth the mountains by the roots.
10 **He** cutteth out rivers among the rocks;
and his eye seeth every precious thing.
11 **He** bindeth the floods from overflowing;
and the thing that is hid bringeth he forth to light.
12 **But where** shall wisdom be found?
and where is the place of understanding?
13 **Man** knoweth not the price thereof;
neither is it found in the land of the living.
14 **The depth** saith,
It is not in me:
and the sea saith,
It is not with me.
15 **It** cannot be gotten for gold,
neither shall silver be weighed for the price thereof.
16 **It** cannot be valued with the gold of Ophir, with the precious onyx, or the sapphire.
17 **The gold and the crystal** cannot equal it:
and the exchange of it shall not be for jewels of fine gold.
18 **No mention** shall be made of coral, or of pearls:
for the price of wisdom is above rubies.
19 **The topaz of Ethiopia** shall not equal it,
neither shall it be valued with pure gold.
20 **Whence** then cometh wisdom?
and where is the place of understanding?
21 **Seeing it** is hid from the eyes of all living,

and kept close from the fowls of the air.

22 **Destruction and death** say,
We have heard the fame thereof with our ears.

23 **God** understandeth the way thereof,
and he knoweth the place thereof.

24 **For he** looketh to the ends of the earth,
and seeth under the whole heaven;
25 To make the weight for the winds;
and he weigheth the waters by measure.

26 **When he** made a decree for the rain, and a way for the lightning of the thunder:
27 **Then** did he see it,
and declare it;
he prepared it,
yea, and searched it out.

28 **And unto man** he said,
Behold, the fear of the Lord,
that is wisdom;
and to depart from evil is understanding.

29

Moreover Job continued his parable,
and said,
2 **Oh that I** were as in months past,
as in the days when God preserved me;
3 **When his candle** shined upon my head,
and when by his light I walked through darkness;
4 **As I** was in the days of my youth,
when the secret of God was upon my tabernacle;
5 **When the Almighty** was yet with me,
when my children were about me;
6 **When I** washed my steps with butter,
and the rock poured me out rivers of oil;
7 **When I** went out to the gate through the city,
when I prepared my seat in the street!

8 **The young men** saw me,
and hid themselves:
and the aged arose,
and stood up.

9 **The princes** refrained talking,
and laid their hand on their mouth.

10 **The nobles** held their peace,
and their tongue cleaved to the roof of their mouth.

11 **When the ear** heard me,
then it blessed me;
and when the eye saw me,
it gave witness to me:
12 **Because I** delivered the poor that cried, and the fatherless, and him that had none to help him.

13 **The blessing of him that was ready to perish** came upon me:
and I caused the widow's heart to sing for joy.

14 **I** put on righteousness,
and it clothed me:
my judgment was as a robe and a diadem.

15 **I** was eyes to the blind,
and feet was I to the lame.

16 **I** was a father to the poor:
and the cause which I knew not I searched out.

17 **And I** brake the jaws of the wicked,
and plucked the spoil out of his teeth.

18 **Then I** said,
I shall die in my nest,
and I shall multiply my days as the sand.

19 **My root** was spread out by the waters,
and the dew lay all night upon my branch.

20 **My glory** was fresh in me,
and my bow was renewed in my hand.

21 **Unto me** men gave ear,
and waited,
and kept silence at my counsel.

22 **After my words** they spake not again;
and my speech dropped upon them.

23 **And they** waited for me as for the rain;
and they opened their mouth wide as for the latter rain.

24 **If I** laughed on them,
they believed it not;
and the light of my countenance they cast not down.

25 **I** chose out their way,
and sat chief,
and dwelt as a king in the army, as one that comforteth the mourners.

30

But now they that are younger than I have me in derision,
whose fathers I would have disdained to have set with the dogs of my flock.

2 **Yea, whereto** might the strength of their hands profit me,
in whom old age was perished?

3 **For want and famine** they were solitary;
fleeing into the wilderness in former time desolate and waste.

4 **Who** cut up mallows by the bushes, and juniper roots for their meat.

5 **They** were driven forth from among men,
(they cried after them as after a thief;)
6 To dwell in the cliffs of the valleys, in caves of the earth, and in the rocks.

7 **Among the bushes** they brayed;
under the nettles they were gathered together.

8 **They** were children of fools, yea, children of base men:
they were viler than the earth.

9 **And now** am I their song,
yea, I am their byword.

10 **They** abhor me,
they flee far from me,
and spare not to spit in my face.

11 **Because he** hath loosed my cord,
and afflicted me,
they have also let loose the bridle before me.

12 **Upon my right hand** rise the youth;
they push away my feet,
and they raise up against me the ways of their destruction.

13 **They** mar my path,
they set forward my calamity,
they have no helper.

14 **They** came upon me as a wide breaking in of waters:
in the desolation they rolled themselves upon me.

15 **Terrors** are turned upon me:
they pursue my soul as the wind:
and my welfare passeth away as a cloud.

16 **And now my soul** is poured out upon me;
the days of affliction have taken hold upon me.

17 **My bones** are pierced in me in the night season:
and my sinews take no rest.

18 **By the great force of my disease** is my garment changed:
it bindeth me about as the collar of my coat.
19 **He** hath cast me into the mire, and I am become like dust and ashes.
20 **I** cry unto thee,
and thou dost not hear me:
I stand up,
and thou regardest me not.
21 **Thou** art become cruel to me:
with thy strong hand thou opposest thyself against me.
22 **Thou** liftest me up to the wind;
thou causest me to ride upon it,
and dissolvest my substance.
23 **For I** know
that thou wilt bring me to death, and to the house appointed for all living.
24 **Howbeit he** will not stretch out his hand to the grave,
though they cry in his destruction.
25 **Did not I** weep for him that was in trouble?
was not my soul grieved for the poor?
26 **When I** looked for good,
then evil came unto me:
and when I waited for light,
there came darkness.
27 **My bowels** boiled,
and rested not:
the days of affliction prevented me.
28 **I** went mourning without the sun:
I stood up,
and I cried in the congregation.
29 **I** am a brother to dragons, and a companion to owls.
30 **My skin** is black upon me,
and my bones are burned with heat.
31 **My harp** also is turned to mourning, and my organ into the voice of them that weep.

31

I made a covenant with mine eyes;
why then should I think upon a maid?
2 **For what portion of God** is there from above?
and what inheritance of the Almighty from on high?
3 **Is not destruction** to the wicked?
and a strange punishment to the workers of iniquity?
4 **Doth not he** see my ways,
and count all my steps?
5 **If I** have walked with vanity,
or if my foot hath hasted to deceit;
6 **Let me** be weighed in an even balance
that God may know mine integrity.
7 **If my step** hath turned out of the way,
and mine heart walked after mine eyes,
and if any blot hath cleaved to mine hands;
8 **Then let me** sow,
and let another eat;
yea, let my offspring be rooted out.
9 **If mine heart** have been deceived by a woman,
or if I have laid wait at my neighbour's door;
10 **Then let my wife** grind unto another,
and let others bow down upon her.
11 **For this** is an heinous crime;
yea, it is an iniquity to be punished by the judges.
12 **For it** is a fire that consumeth to destruction,
and would root out all mine increase.
13 **If I** did despise the cause of my manservant or of my maidservant,
when they contended with me;
14 **What** then shall I do
when God riseth up?
and when he visiteth,
what shall I answer him?
15 **Did not he that made me in the womb** make him?
and did not one fashion us in the womb?
16 **If I** have withheld the poor from their desire,
or have caused the eyes of the widow to fail;
17 **Or** have eaten my morsel myself alone,
and the fatherless hath not eaten thereof;
18 (For from my youth he was brought up with me, as with a father,
and I have guided her from my mother's womb;)
19 **If I** have seen any perish for want of clothing, or any poor without covering;
20 **If his loins** have not blessed me,
and if he were not warmed with the fleece of my sheep;
21 **If I** have lifted up my hand against the fatherless,
when I saw my help in the gate:
22 **Then let mine arm** fall from my shoulder blade,
and mine arm be broken from the bone.
23 **For destruction from God** was a terror to me,
and by reason of his highness I could not endure.
24 **If I** have made gold my hope,
or have said to the fine gold,
Thou art my confidence;
25 **If I** rejoice
because my wealth was great,
and because mine hand had gotten much;
26 **If I** beheld the sun when it shined, or the moon walking in brightness;
27 **And my heart** hath been secretly enticed,
or my mouth hath kissed my hand:
28 **This** also were an iniquity to be punished by the judge:
for I should have denied the God that is above.
29 **If I** rejoice at the destruction of him that hated me,
or lifted up myself
when evil found him:
30 **Neither** have I suffered my mouth to sin
by wishing a curse to his soul.
31 **If the men of my tabernacle** said not,
Oh that we had of his flesh!
we cannot be satisfied.
32 **The stranger** did not lodge in the street:
but I opened my doors to the traveller.
33 **If I** covered my transgressions as Adam,
by hiding mine iniquity in my bosom:
34 **Did I** fear a great multitude,
or did the contempt of families terrify me,
that I kept silence,
and went not out of the door?
35 **Oh that one** would hear me!
behold,
my desire is,
that the Almighty would answer me,
and that mine adversary had written a book.

36 **Surely I** would take it upon my shoulder,
and bind it as a crown to me.
37 **I** would declare unto him the number of my steps;
as a prince would I go near unto him.
38 **If my land** cry against me,
or that the furrows likewise thereof complain;
39 **If I** have eaten the fruits thereof without money,
or have caused the owners thereof to lose their life:
40 **Let thistles** grow instead of wheat, and cockle instead of barley.
The words of Job are ended.

32

So these three men ceased to answer Job,
because he was righteous in his own eyes.
2 **Then** was kindled the wrath of Elihu the son of Barachel the Buzite, of the kindred of Ram:
against Job was his wrath kindled,
because he justified himself rather than God.
3 **Also against his three friends** was his wrath kindled,
because they had found no answer,
and yet had condemned Job.
4 **Now Elihu** had waited till Job had spoken,
because they were elder than he.
5 **When Elihu** saw that there was no answer in the mouth of these three men,
then his wrath was kindled.
6 **And Elihu the son of Barachel the Buzite** answered and said,
I am young,
and ye are very old;
wherefore I was afraid,
and durst not shew you mine opinion.
7 **I** said,
Days should speak,
and multitude of years should teach wisdom.
8 **But there** is a spirit in man:
and the inspiration of the Almighty giveth them understanding.
9 **Great men** are not always wise:
neither do the aged understand judgment.
10 **Therefore I** said,
Hearken to me;
I also will shew mine opinion.
11 **Behold,**
I waited for your words;
I gave ear to your reasons,
whilst ye searched out what to say.
12 **Yea, I** attended unto you,
and, {behold}, there was none of you that convinced Job, or that answered his words:
13 **Lest ye** should say,
We have found out wisdom:
God thrusteth him down, not man.
14 **Now he** hath not directed his words against me:
neither will I answer him with your speeches.
15 **They** were amazed,
they answered no more:
they left off speaking.
16 **When I** had waited,
(for they spake not,
but stood still,
and answered no more;)
17 **I** said,
I will answer also my part,
I also will shew mine opinion.
18 **For I** am full of matter,
the spirit within me constraineth me.
19 **Behold,**
my belly is as wine which hath no vent;
it is ready to burst like new bottles.
20 **I** will speak,
that I may be refreshed:
I will open my lips and answer.
21 **Let me not**, {I pray you}, accept any man's person,
neither let me give flattering titles unto man.
22 **For I** know not
to give flattering titles;
in so doing my maker would soon take me away.

33

Wherefore, Job, {I pray thee}, hear my speeches,
and hearken to all my words.
2 **Behold,**
now I have opened my mouth,
my tongue hath spoken in my mouth.
3 **My words** shall be of the uprightness of my heart:
and my lips shall utter knowledge clearly.
4 **The spirit of God** hath made me,
and the breath of the Almighty hath given me life.
5 **If thou** canst answer me,
set thy words in order before me,
stand up.
6 **Behold,**
I am according to thy wish in God's stead:
I also am formed out of the clay.
7 **Behold,**
my terror shall not make thee afraid,
neither shall my hand be heavy upon thee.
8 **Surely thou** hast spoken in mine hearing,
and I have heard the voice of thy words,
saying,
9 **I** am clean without transgression,
I am innocent;
neither is there iniquity in me.
10 **Behold,**
he findeth occasions against me,
he counteth me for his enemy,
11 **He** putteth my feet in the stocks,
he marketh all my paths.
12 **Behold,**
in this thou art not just:
I will answer thee,
that God is greater than man.
13 **Why** dost thou strive against him?
for he giveth not account of any of his matters.
14 **For God** speaketh once, yea twice,
yet man perceiveth it not.
15 **In a dream, in a vision of the night**, {when deep sleep falleth upon men, in slumberings upon the bed};
16 Then he openeth the ears of men,
and sealeth their instruction,
17 **That he** may withdraw man from his purpose,
and hide pride from man.
18 **He** keepeth back his soul from the pit,
and his life from perishing by the sword.
19 **He** is chastened also with pain upon his bed, and the multitude of his bones with strong pain:
20 **So that his life** abhorreth bread,
and his soul dainty meat.
21 **His flesh** is consumed away,
that it cannot be seen;
and his bones that were not seen stick out.

22 **Yea, his soul** draweth near unto the grave, and his life to the destroyers.
23 **If there** be a messenger with him, an interpreter, one among a thousand,
to shew unto man his uprightness:
24 **Then he** is gracious unto him,
and saith,
Deliver him from going down to the pit:
I have found a ransom.
25 **His flesh** shall be fresher than a child's:
he shall return to the days of his youth:
26 **He** shall pray unto God,
and he will be favourable unto him:
and he shall see his face with joy:
for he will render unto man his righteousness.
27 **He** looketh upon men,
and if any say,
I have sinned,
and perverted that which was right,
and it profited me not;
28 **He** will deliver his soul from going into the pit,
and his life shall see the light.
29 **Lo,**
all these things worketh God oftentimes with man,
30 To bring back his soul from the pit,
to be enlightened with the light of the living.
31 **Mark well,** O Job,
hearken unto me:
hold thy peace,
and I will speak.
32 **If thou** hast anything to say,
answer me:
speak,
for I desire to justify thee.
33 **If not, hearken** unto me:
hold thy peace,
and I shall teach thee wisdom.

34

Furthermore Elihu answered and said,
2 **Hear** my words, O ye wise men;
and give ear unto me, ye that have knowledge.
3 **For the ear** trieth words,
as the mouth tasteth meat.
4 **Let us** choose to us judgment:
let us know among ourselves
what is good.
5 **For Job** hath said,
I am righteous:
and God hath taken away my judgment.
6 **Should I** lie against my right?
my wound is incurable without transgression.
7 **What man** is like Job,
who drinketh up scorning like water?
8 **Which** goeth in company with the workers of iniquity,
and walketh with wicked men.
9 **For he** hath said,
It profiteth a man nothing
that he should delight himself with God.
10 **Therefore hearken** unto me ye men of understanding:
far be it from God, {that he should do wickedness}; and from the Almighty, {that he should commit iniquity}.
11 **For the work of a man** shall he render unto him,
and cause every man to find according to his ways.
12 **Yea, surely God** will not do wickedly,
neither will the Almighty pervert judgment.
13 **Who** hath given him a charge over the earth?
or who hath disposed the whole world?
14 **If he** set his heart upon man,
if he gather unto himself his spirit and his breath;
15 **All flesh** shall perish together,
and man shall turn again unto dust.
16 **If now thou** hast understanding,
hear this:
hearken to the voice of my words.
17 **Shall even he that hateth right** govern?
and wilt thou condemn him that is most just?
18 **Is it fit** to say to a king,
Thou art wicked?
and to princes,
Ye are ungodly?
19 How much less to him that accepteth not the persons of princes, nor regardeth the rich more than the poor?
for they all are the work of his hands.
20 **In a moment** shall they die,
and the people shall be troubled at midnight,
and pass away:
and the mighty shall be taken away without hand.
21 **For his eyes** are upon the ways of man,
and he seeth all his goings.
22 **There** is no darkness, nor shadow of death,
where the workers of iniquity may hide themselves.
23 **For he** will not lay upon man more than right;
that he should enter into judgment with God.
24 **He** shall break in pieces mighty men without number,
and set others in their stead.
25 **Therefore he** knoweth their works,
and he overturneth them in the night,
so that they are destroyed.
26 **He** striketh them as wicked men in the open sight of others;
27 **Because they** turned back from him,
and would not consider any of his ways:
28 **So that they** cause the cry of the poor to come unto him,
and he heareth the cry of the afflicted.
29 **When he** giveth quietness,
who then can make trouble?
and when he hideth his face,
who then can behold him?
whether it be done against a nation, or against a man only:
30 **That the hypocrite** reign not,
lest the people be ensnared.
31 **Surely it is meet** to be said unto God,
I have borne chastisement,
I will not offend any more:
32 **That which I see not** teach thou me:
if I have done iniquity,
I will do no more.
33 **Should it** be according to thy mind?
he will recompense it,
whether thou refuse,
or whether thou choose; and not I:
therefore speak
what thou knowest.
34 **Let men of understanding** tell me,
and let a wise man hearken unto me.

[35] **Job** hath spoken without
knowledge,
and his words were without
wisdom.
[36] **My desire** is that Job may be tried
unto the end because of his
answers for wicked men.
[37] **For he** addeth rebellion unto his
sin,
he clappeth his hands among us,
and multiplieth his words against
God.

35 ∞ **Elihu** spake moreover,
and said,
[2] **Thinkest thou** this to be right,
that thou saidst,
My righteousness is more than
God's?
[3] **For thou** saidst,
What advantage will it be unto
thee?
and, What profit shall I have,
if I be cleansed from my sin?
[4] **I** will answer thee, and thy
companions with thee.
[5] **Look** unto the heavens,
and see;
and behold the clouds which are
higher than thou.
[6] **If thou** sinnest,
what doest thou against him?
or if thy transgressions be
multiplied,
what doest thou unto him?
[7] **If thou** be righteous,
what givest thou him?
or what receiveth he of thine hand?
[8] **Thy wickedness** may hurt a man
as thou art;
and thy righteousness may profit
the son of man.
[9] **By reason of the multitude of
oppressions** they make the
oppressed to cry:
they cry out by reason of the arm of
the mighty.
[10] **But none** saith,
Where is God my maker,
who giveth songs in the night;
[11] **Who** teacheth us more than the
beasts of the earth,
and maketh us wiser than the fowls
of heaven?
[12] **There** they cry,
but none giveth answer, because of
the pride of evil men.
[13] **Surely God** will not hear vanity,
neither will the Almighty regard it.
[14] **Although thou** sayest
thou shalt not see him,
yet judgment is before him;
therefore trust thou in him.
[15] **But now, {because it is not so},**
he hath visited in his anger;
yet he knoweth it not in great
extremity:
[16] **Therefore** doth Job open his
mouth in vain;
he multiplieth words without
knowledge.

36 **Elihu** also proceeded,
and said,
[2] **Suffer** me a little,
and I will shew thee
that I have yet to speak on God's
behalf.
[3] **I** will fetch my knowledge from
afar,
and will ascribe righteousness to
my Maker.
[4] **For truly my words** shall not be
false:
he that is perfect in knowledge is
with thee.
[5] **Behold,**
God is mighty,
and despiseth not any:
he is mighty in strength and
wisdom.
[6] **He** preserveth not the life of the
wicked:
but giveth right to the poor.
[7] **He** withdraweth not his eyes from
the righteous:
but with kings are they on the
throne;
yea, he doth establish them for
ever,
and they are exalted.
[8] **And if they** be bound in fetters,
and be holden in cords of affliction;
[9] **Then he** sheweth them their work,
and their transgressions that they
have exceeded.
[10] **He** openeth also their ear to
discipline,
and commandeth
that they return from iniquity.
[11] **If they** obey and serve him,
they shall spend their days in
prosperity, and their years in
pleasures.
[12] **But if they** obey not,
they shall perish by the sword,
and they shall die without
knowledge.
[13] **But the hypocrites in heart** heap
up wrath:
they cry not
when he bindeth them.
[14] **They** die in youth,
and their life is among the unclean.
[15] **He** delivereth the poor in his
affliction,
and openeth their ears in
oppression.
[16] **Even so** would he have removed
thee out of the strait into a broad
place,
where there is no straitness;
**and that which should be set on
thy table** should be full of
fatness.
[17] **But thou** hast fulfilled the
judgment of the wicked:
judgment and justice take hold on
thee.
[18] **Because there** is wrath,
beware
lest he take thee away with his
stroke:
then a great ransom cannot deliver
thee.
[19] **Will he** esteem thy riches?
no, not gold, nor all the forces of
strength.
[20] **Desire not** the night,
when people are cut off in their
place.
[21] **Take heed,**
regard not iniquity:
for this hast thou chosen rather
than affliction.
[22] **Behold,**
God exalteth by his power:
who teacheth like him?
[23] **Who** hath enjoined him his way?
or who can say,
Thou hast wrought iniquity?
[24] **Remember**
that thou magnify his work,
which men behold.
[25] **Every man** may see it;
man may behold it afar off.
[26] **Behold,**
God is great,
and we know him not,
neither can the number of his years
be searched out.
[27] **For he** maketh small the drops of
water:
they pour down rain according to
the vapour thereof:
[28] **Which the clouds** do drop and
distil upon man abundantly.

29 **Also can any** understand the spreadings of the clouds, or the noise of his tabernacle?

30 **Behold,**
he spreadeth his light upon it,
and covereth the bottom of the sea.

31 **For by them** judgeth he the people;
he giveth meat in abundance.

32 **With clouds** he covereth the light;
and commandeth it
not to shine by the cloud that cometh betwixt.

33 **The noise thereof** sheweth concerning it, the cattle also concerning the vapour.

37 **At this** also my heart trembleth,
and is moved out of his place.

2 **Hear** attentively the noise of his voice, and the sound that goeth out of his mouth.

3 **He** directeth it under the whole heaven, and his lightning unto the ends of the earth.

4 **After it** a voice roareth:
he thundereth with the voice of his excellency;
and he will not stay them
when his voice is heard.

5 **God** thundereth marvellously with his voice;
great things doeth he,
which we cannot comprehend.

6 **For he** saith to the snow,
Be thou on the earth; likewise to the small rain, and to the great rain of his strength.

7 **He** sealeth up the hand of every man;
that all men may know his work.

8 **Then the beasts** go into dens,
and remain in their places.

9 **Out of the south** cometh the whirlwind: and cold out of the north.

10 **By the breath of God** frost is given:
and the breadth of the waters is straitened.

11 **Also by watering** he wearieth the thick cloud:
he scattereth his bright cloud:

12 **And it** is turned round about by his counsels:
that they may do whatsoever he commandeth them upon the face of the world in the earth.

13 **He** causeth it to come, whether for correction, or for his land, or for mercy.

14 **Hearken** unto this, O Job:
stand still,
and consider the wondrous works of God.

15 **Dost thou** know when God disposed them,
and caused the light of his cloud to shine?

16 **Dost thou** know the balancings of the clouds, the wondrous works of him which is perfect in knowledge?

17 **How thy garments** are warm,
when he quieteth the earth by the south wind?

18 **Hast thou with him** spread out the sky,
which is strong, and as a molten looking glass?

19 **Teach** us
what we shall say unto him;
for we cannot order our speech by reason of darkness.

20 **Shall it** be told him
that I speak?
if a man speak,
surely he shall be swallowed up.

21 **And now men** see not the bright light which is in the clouds:
but the wind passeth,
and cleanseth them.

22 **Fair weather** cometh out of the north:
with God is terrible majesty.

23 **Touching the Almighty,** we cannot find him out:
he is excellent in power, and in judgment, and in plenty of justice:
he will not afflict.

24 **Men** do therefore fear him:
he respecteth not any that are wise of heart.

38 **Then the LORD** answered Job out of the whirlwind,
and said,

2 **Who** is this that darkeneth counsel by words without knowledge?

3 **Gird up** now thy loins like a man;
for I will demand of thee,
and answer thou me.

4 **Where** wast thou
when I laid the foundations of the earth?
declare,
if thou hast understanding.

5 **Who** hath laid the measures thereof,
if thou knowest?
or who hath stretched the line upon it?

6 **Whereupon** are the foundations thereof fastened?
or who laid the corner stone thereof;

7 **When the morning stars** sang together,
and all the sons of God shouted for joy?

8 **Or who** shut up the sea with doors,
when it brake forth,
as if it had issued out of the womb?

9 **When I** made the cloud the garment thereof, and thick darkness a swaddlingband for it,

10 **And** brake up for it my decreed place,
and set bars and doors,

11 **And** said,
Hitherto shalt thou come, but no further:
and here shall thy proud waves be stayed?

12 **Hast thou** commanded the morning since thy days;
and caused the dayspring to know his place;

13 **That it** might take hold of the ends of the earth,
that the wicked might be shaken out of it?

14 **It** is turned as clay to the seal;
and they stand as a garment.

15 **And from the wicked** their light is withholden,
and the high arm shall be broken.

16 **Hast thou** entered into the springs of the sea?
or hast thou walked in the search of the depth?

17 **Have the gates of death** been opened unto thee?
or hast thou seen the doors of the shadow of death?

18 **Hast thou** perceived the breadth of the earth?
declare
if thou knowest it all.

19 **Where** is the way where light dwelleth?

and as for darkness, where is the place thereof,
20 **That thou** shouldest take it to the bound thereof,
and that thou shouldest know the paths to the house thereof?
21 **Knowest thou** it,
because thou wast then born?
or because the number of thy days is great?
22 **Hast thou** entered into the treasures of the snow?
or hast thou seen the treasures of the hail,
23 **Which I** have reserved against the time of trouble, against the day of battle and war?
24 **By what way** is the light parted,
which scattereth the east wind upon the earth?
25 **Who** hath divided a watercourse for the overflowing of waters, or a way for the lightning of thunder;
26 To cause it to rain on the earth, {where no man is}; on the wilderness, {wherein there is no man};
27 To satisfy the desolate and waste ground;
and to cause the bud of the tender herb to spring forth?
28 **Hath the rain** a father?
or who hath begotten the drops of dew?
29 **Out of whose womb** came the ice?
and the hoary frost of heaven, who hath gendered it?
30 **The waters** are hid as with a stone,
and the face of the deep is frozen.
31 **Canst thou** bind the sweet influences of Pleiades,
or loose the bands of Orion?
32 **Canst thou** bring forth Mazzaroth in his season?
or canst thou guide Arcturus with his sons?
33 **Knowest thou** the ordinances of heaven?
canst thou set the dominion thereof in the earth?
34 **Canst thou** lift up thy voice to the clouds,
that abundance of waters may cover thee?
35 **Canst thou** send lightnings,
that they may go and say unto thee,
Here we are?
36 **Who** hath put wisdom in the inward parts?
or who hath given understanding to the heart?
37 **Who** can number the clouds in wisdom?
or who can stay the bottles of heaven,
38 **When the dust** groweth into hardness,
and the clods cleave fast together?
39 **Wilt thou** hunt the prey for the lion?
or fill the appetite of the young lions,
40 **When they** couch in their dens,
and abide in the covert
to lie in wait?
41 **Who** provideth for the raven his food?
when his young ones cry unto God,
they wander for lack of meat.

39 **Knowest thou** the time when the wild goats of the rock bring forth?
or canst thou mark when the hinds do calve?
2 **Canst thou** number the months that they fulfil?
or knowest thou the time when they bring forth?
3 **They** bow themselves,
they bring forth their young ones,
they cast out their sorrows.
4 **Their young ones** are in good liking,
they grow up with corn;
they go forth,
and return not unto them.
5 **Who** hath sent out the wild ass free?
or who hath loosed the bands of the wild ass?
6 **Whose house** I have made the wilderness, and the barren land his dwellings.
7 **He** scorneth the multitude of the city,
neither regardeth he the crying of the driver.
8 **The range of the mountains** is his pasture,
and he searcheth after every green thing.
9 **Will the unicorn** be willing to serve thee,
or abide by thy crib?
10 **Canst thou** bind the unicorn with his band in the furrow?
or will he harrow the valleys after thee?
11 **Wilt thou** trust him,
because his strength is great?
or wilt thou leave thy labour to him?
12 **Wilt thou** believe him,
that he will bring home thy seed,
and gather it into thy barn?
13 **Gavest thou** the goodly wings unto the peacocks?
or wings and feathers unto the ostrich?
14 **Which** leaveth her eggs in the earth,
and warmeth them in dust,
15 **And** forgetteth
that the foot may crush them,
or that the wild beast may break them.
16 **She** is hardened against her young ones,
as though they were not her's:
her labour is in vain without fear;
17 **Because God** hath deprived her of wisdom,
neither hath he imparted to her understanding.
18 **What time she** lifteth up herself on high,
she scorneth the horse and his rider.
19 **Hast thou** given the horse strength?
hast thou clothed his neck with thunder?
20 **Canst thou** make him afraid as a grasshopper?
the glory of his nostrils is terrible.
21 **He** paweth in the valley,
and rejoiceth in his strength:
he goeth on to meet the armed men.
22 **He** mocketh at fear,
and is not affrighted;
neither turneth he back from the sword.
23 **The quiver** rattleth against him,
the glittering spear and the shield.
24 **He** swalloweth the ground with fierceness and rage:
neither believeth he
that it is the sound of the trumpet.
25 **He** saith among the trumpets,
Ha, ha;

and he smelleth the battle afar off, the thunder of the captains, and the shouting.
26 **Doth the hawk** fly by thy wisdom,
and stretch her wings toward the south?
27 **Doth the eagle** mount up at thy command,
and make her nest on high?
28 **She** dwelleth and abideth on the rock, upon the crag of the rock, and the strong place.
29 **From thence** she seeketh the prey,
and her eyes behold afar off.
30 **Her young ones** also suck up blood:
and where the slain are,
there is she.

40 **Moreover the LORD** answered Job,
and said,
2 **Shall he that contendeth with the Almighty** instruct him?
he that reproveth God, let him answer it.
3 **Then Job** answered the LORD,
and said,
4 **Behold,**
I am vile;
what shall I answer thee?
I will lay mine hand upon my mouth.
5 **Once** have I spoken;
but I will not answer:
yea, twice; but I will proceed no further.
6 **Then** answered the LORD unto Job out of the whirlwind,
and said,
7 **Gird up** thy loins now like a man:
I will demand of thee,
and declare thou unto me.
8 **Wilt thou** also disannul my judgment?
wilt thou condemn me,
that thou mayest be righteous?
9 **Hast thou** an arm like God?
or canst thou thunder with a voice like him?
10 **Deck** thyself now with majesty and excellency;
and array thyself with glory and beauty.
11 **Cast abroad** the rage of thy wrath:
and behold every one that is proud,
and abase him.
12 **Look** on every one that is proud,
and bring him low;
and tread down the wicked in their place.
13 **Hide** them in the dust together;
and bind their faces in secret.
14 **Then** will I also confess unto thee
that thine own right hand can save thee.
15 **Behold** now behemoth,
which I made with thee;
he eateth grass as an ox.
16 **Lo** now,
his strength is in his loins,
and his force is in the navel of his belly.
17 **He** moveth his tail like a cedar:
the sinews of his stones are wrapped together.
18 **His bones** are as strong pieces of brass;
his bones are like bars of iron.
19 **He** is the chief of the ways of God:
he that made him can make his sword to approach unto him.
20 **Surely the mountains** bring him forth food,
where all the beasts of the field play.
21 **He** lieth under the shady trees, in the covert of the reed, and fens.
22 **The shady trees** cover him with their shadow;
the willows of the brook compass him about.
23 **Behold,**
he drinketh up a river,
and hasteth not:
he trusteth
that he can draw up Jordan into his mouth.
24 **He** taketh it with his eyes:
his nose pierceth through snares.

41 **Canst thou** draw out leviathan with an hook?
or his tongue with a cord which thou lettest down?
2 **Canst thou** put an hook into his nose?
or bore his jaw through with a thorn?
3 **Will he** make many supplications unto thee?
will he speak soft words unto thee?
4 **Will he** make a covenant with thee?
wilt thou take him for a servant for ever?
5 **Wilt thou** play with him as with a bird?
or wilt thou bind him for thy maidens?
6 **Shall the companions** make a banquet of him?
shall they part him among the merchants?
7 **Canst thou** fill his skin with barbed irons?
or his head with fish spears?
8 **Lay** thine hand upon him,
remember the battle,
do no more.
9 **Behold,**
the hope of him is in vain:
shall not one be cast down even at the sight of him?
10 **None** is so fierce that dare stir him up:
who then is able to stand before me?
11 **Who** hath prevented me,
that I should repay him?
whatsoever is under the whole heaven is mine.
12 **I** will not conceal his parts, nor his power, nor his comely proportion.
13 **Who** can discover the face of his garment?
or who can come to him with his double bridle?
14 **Who** can open the doors of his face?
his teeth are terrible round about.
15 **His scales** are his pride,
shut up together as with a close seal.
16 **One** is so near to another,
that no air can come between them.
17 **They** are joined one to another,
they stick together,
that they cannot be sundered.
18 **By his neesings** a light doth shine,
and his eyes are like the eyelids of the morning.
19 **Out of his mouth** go burning lamps,
and sparks of fire leap out.
20 **Out of his nostrils** goeth smoke, as out of a seething pot or caldron.
21 **His breath** kindleth coals,
and a flame goeth out of his mouth.
22 **In his neck** remaineth strength,

and sorrow is turned into joy
before him.
23 **The flakes of his flesh** are joined
together:
they are firm in themselves;
they cannot be moved.
24 **His heart** is as firm as a stone;
yea, as hard as a piece of the
nether millstone.
25 **When he** raiseth up himself,
the mighty are afraid:
by reason of breakings they purify
themselves.
26 **The sword of him that layeth at
him** cannot hold: the spear, the
dart, nor the habergeon.
27 **He** esteemeth iron as straw, and
brass as rotten wood.
28 **The arrow** cannot make him flee:
slingstones are turned with him
into stubble.
29 **Darts** are counted as stubble:
he laugheth at the shaking of a
spear.
30 **Sharp stones** are under him:
he spreadeth sharp pointed things
upon the mire.
31 **He** maketh the deep to boil like a
pot:
he maketh the sea like a pot of
ointment.
32 **He** maketh a path to shine after
him;
one would think the deep to be
hoary.
33 **Upon earth** there is not his like,
who is made without fear.
34 **He** beholdeth all high things:
he is a king over all the children of
pride.

42

Then Job answered the
LORD,
and said,
2 **I** know
that thou canst do every thing,
and that no thought can be
withholden from thee.
3 **Who** is he that hideth counsel
without knowledge?
therefore have I uttered
that I understood not; things too
wonderful for me,
which I knew not.
4 **Hear,**
I beseech thee,
and I will speak:
I will demand of thee,
and declare thou unto me.
5 **I** have heard of thee by the hearing
of the ear:
but now mine eye seeth thee.
6 **Wherefore I** abhor myself,
and repent in dust and ashes.
7 **And it** was so,
that after the LORD had spoken
these words unto Job,
the LORD said to Eliphaz the
Temanite,
My wrath is kindled against thee,
and against thy two friends:
for ye have not spoken of me the
thing that is right,
as my servant Job hath.
8 **Therefore take** unto you now
seven bullocks and seven rams,
and go to my servant Job,
and offer up for yourselves a burnt
offering;
and my servant Job shall pray for
you:
for him will I accept:
lest I deal with you after your folly,
in that ye have not spoken of me
the thing which is right, like my
servant Job.
9 **So Eliphaz the Temanite and
Bildad the Shuhite and Zophar
the Naamathite** went,
and did according as the LORD
commanded them:
the LORD also accepted Job.
10 **And the LORD** turned the
captivity of Job,
when he prayed for his friends:
also the LORD gave Job twice as
much as he had before.
11 **Then** came there unto him all his
brethren, and all his sisters, and
all they that had been of his
acquaintance before,
and did eat bread with him in his
house:
and they bemoaned him,
and comforted him over all the evil
that the LORD had brought upon
him:
every man also gave him a piece of
money, and every one an earring
of gold.
12 **So the LORD** blessed the latter
end of Job more than his
beginning:
for he had fourteen thousand
sheep, and six thousand camels,
and a thousand yoke of oxen, and
a thousand she asses.
13 **He** had also seven sons and three
daughters.
14 **And he** called the name of the
first, Jemima; and the name of the
second, Kezia; and the name of
the third, Kerenhappuch.
15 **And in all the land** were no
women found so fair as the
daughters of Job:
and their father gave them
inheritance among their brethren.
16 **After this** lived Job an hundred
and forty years,
and saw his sons, and his sons'
sons, even four generations.
17 **So Job** died,
being old and full of days.

Psalms

The Book of Psalms, a rich tapestry of prayers, hymns, poems, and songs, is a testament to the diverse human experiences and how people express their relationship with God. Penned by a variety of authors, including King David, each psalm carries a unique message and purpose, yet they all converge on several common themes.

Many Psalms, written by authors who have experienced the full spectrum of human emotions, praise and worship God, express gratitude for His blessings and acknowledge His greatness. Other Psalms, born out of personal sorrow, sadness, and pain, offer a window into the human experience and the struggles of life. These Psalms of lament, filled with prayers and petitions for help and guidance, can resonate deeply with the personal journeys of their readers. Several Psalms explore the topics of divine justice, punishment, and retribution, often calling for God's intervention in the face of injustice and oppression. Various other Psalms offer wisdom and guidance for living a righteous life, providing moral instruction and encouragement for those seeking to follow God's will. Finally, more than a few Psalms contain prophetic messages, offering glimpses into the future and the coming of the Messiah.

The Book of Psalms, a timeless repository of inspired literature, resonates with readers across generations. It offers a profound understanding of the human soul and its relationship with God, providing solace and comfort in times of distress and guiding the path of faith and devotion. Its wisdom and encouragement remain as relevant today as they were when first penned, a testament to its enduring power.

1 **Blessed** is the man that walketh not in the counsel of the ungodly,
nor standeth in the way of sinners,
nor sitteth in the seat of the scornful.

2 **But his delight** is in the law of the LORD;
and in his law doth he meditate day and night.

3 **And he** shall be like a tree planted by the rivers of water,
that bringeth forth his fruit in his season;
his leaf also shall not wither;
and whatsoever he doeth shall prosper.

4 **The ungodly** are not so:
but are like the chaff which the wind driveth away.

5 **Therefore the ungodly** shall not stand in the judgment, nor sinners in the congregation of the righteous.

6 **For the LORD** knoweth the way of the righteous:
but the way of the ungodly shall perish.

2 **Why** do the heathen rage,
and the people imagine a vain thing?

2 **The kings of the earth** set themselves,
and the rulers take counsel together, against the LORD, and against his anointed,
saying,

3 **Let us** break their bands asunder,
and cast away their cords from us.

4 **He that sitteth in the heavens** shall laugh:
the Lord shall have them in derision.

5 **Then** shall he speak unto them in his wrath,
and vex them in his sore displeasure.

6 **Yet** have I set my king upon my holy hill of Zion.

7 **I** will declare the decree:
the LORD hath said unto me,
Thou art my Son;
this day have I begotten thee.

8 **Ask** of me,
and I shall give thee the heathen for thine inheritance, and the uttermost parts of the earth for thy possession.

9 **Thou** shalt break them with a rod of iron;
thou shalt dash them in pieces like a potter's vessel.

10 **Be** wise now therefore,
O ye kings: be instructed, ye judges of the earth.

11 **Serve** the LORD with fear,
and rejoice with trembling.

12 **Kiss** the Son,
lest he be angry,
and ye perish from the way,
when his wrath is kindled but a little.
Blessed are all they that put their trust in him.

3 *A Psalm of David, when he fled from Absalom his son.*

LORD, how are they increased that trouble me!
many are they that rise up against me.

2 **Many** there be which say of my soul,
There is no help for him in God.
Selah.

3 **But thou,** O LORD, art a shield for me; my glory, and the lifter up of mine head.

4 **I** cried unto the LORD with my voice,
and he heard me out of his holy hill.
Selah.

5 **I** laid me down and slept;
I awaked;
for the LORD sustained me.

6 **I** will not be afraid of ten thousands of people,
that have set themselves against me round about.

7 **Arise,** O LORD;
save me, O my God:

for thou hast smitten all mine enemies upon the cheek bone;
thou hast broken the teeth of the ungodly.
8 **Salvation** belongeth unto the LORD:
thy blessing is upon thy people.
Selah.

4

To the chief Musician on Negonith, A Psalm of David.

Hear me when I call, O God of my righteousness:
thou hast enlarged me when I was in distress;
have mercy upon me,
and hear my prayer.
2 **O ye sons of men, how long** will ye turn my glory into shame?
how long will ye love vanity,
and seek after leasing?
Selah.
3 **But know**
that the LORD hath set apart him that is godly for himself:
the LORD will hear when I call unto him.
4 **Stand** in awe,
and sin not:
commune with your own heart upon your bed,
and be still.
Selah.
5 **Offer** the sacrifices of righteousness,
and put your trust in the LORD.
6 **There** be many that say,
Who will shew us any good?
LORD, lift thou up the light of thy countenance upon us.
7 **Thou** hast put gladness in my heart, more than in the time that their corn and their wine increased.
8 **I** will both lay me down in peace,
and sleep:
for thou, LORD, only makest me dwell in safety.

5

To the chief Musician upon Nehiloth, A Psalm of David.

Give ear to my words, O LORD,
consider my meditation.
2 **Hearken** unto the voice of my cry, my King, and my God:
for unto thee will I pray.
3 **My voice** shalt thou hear in the morning, O LORD;
in the morning will I direct my prayer unto thee,
and will look up.
4 **For thou** art not a God that hath pleasure in wickedness:
neither shall evil dwell with thee.
5 **The foolish** shall not stand in thy sight:
thou hatest all workers of iniquity.
6 **Thou** shalt destroy them that speak leasing:
the LORD will abhor the bloody and deceitful man.
7 **But as for me,** I will come into thy house in the multitude of thy mercy:
and in thy fear will I worship toward thy holy temple.
8 **Lead** me, O LORD, in thy righteousness because of mine enemies;
make thy way straight before my face.
9 **For there** is no faithfulness in their mouth;
their inward part is very wickedness;
their throat is an open sepulchre;
they flatter with their tongue.
10 **Destroy thou** them, O God;
let them fall by their own counsels;
cast them out in the multitude of their transgressions;
for they have rebelled against thee.
11 **But let all those that put their trust in thee** rejoice:
let them ever shout for joy,
because thou defendest them:
let them also that love thy name be joyful in thee.
12 **For thou,** LORD, wilt bless the righteous;
with favour wilt thou compass him as with a shield.

6

To the chief Musician on Neginoth upon Sheminith, A Psalm of David.

O LORD, rebuke me not in thine anger,
neither chasten me in thy hot displeasure.
2 **Have** mercy upon me, O LORD;
for I am weak:
O LORD, heal me;
for my bones are vexed.
3 **My soul** is also sore vexed:
but thou, O LORD, how long?
4 **Return,** O LORD,
deliver my soul:
oh save me for thy mercies' sake.
5 **For in death** there is no remembrance of thee:
in the grave who shall give thee thanks?
6 **I** am weary with my groaning;
all the night make I my bed to swim;
I water my couch with my tears.
7 **Mine eye** is consumed because of grief;
it waxeth old because of all mine enemies.
8 **Depart** from me, all ye workers of iniquity;
for the LORD hath heard the voice of my weeping.
9 **The LORD** hath heard my supplication;
the LORD will receive my prayer.
10 **Let all mine enemies** be ashamed and sore vexed:
let them return and be ashamed suddenly.

7

Shiggaion of David, which he sang unto the LORD, concerning the words of Cush the Benjamite.

O LORD my God, in thee do I put my trust:
save me from all them that persecute me,
and deliver me:
2 **Lest he** tear my soul like a lion,
rending it in pieces,
while there is none to deliver.
3 **O LORD my God, If I** have done this;
if there be iniquity in my hands;
4 **If I** have rewarded evil unto him that was at peace with me;
(yea, I have delivered him that without cause is mine enemy:)
5 **Let the enemy** persecute my soul,
and take it;
yea, let him tread down my life upon the earth,
and lay mine honour in the dust.
Selah.
6 **Arise,** O LORD, in thine anger,
lift up thyself because of the rage of mine enemies:
and awake for me to the judgment that thou hast commanded.
7 **So** shall the congregation of the people compass thee about:
for their sakes therefore return thou on high.

[8] **The LORD** shall judge the people:
judge me, O LORD, according to my righteousness, and according to mine integrity that is in me.

[9] **Oh let the wickedness of the wicked** come to an end;
but establish the just:
for the righteous God trieth the hearts and reins.

[10] **My defence** is of God,
which saveth the upright in heart.

[11] **God** judgeth the righteous,
and God is angry with the wicked every day.

[12] **If he** turn not,
he will whet his sword;
he hath bent his bow,
and made it ready.

[13] **He** hath also prepared for him the instruments of death;
he ordaineth his arrows against the persecutors.

[14] **Behold,**
he travaileth with iniquity,
and hath conceived mischief,
and brought forth falsehood.

[15] **He** made a pit,
and digged it,
and is fallen into the ditch which he made.

[16] **His mischief** shall return upon his own head,
and his violent dealing shall come down upon his own pate.

[17] **I** will praise the LORD according to his righteousness:
and will sing praise to the name of the LORD most high.

8

To the chief Musician upon Gittith, A Psalm of David.

O LORD, our Lord, how excellent is thy name in all the earth!
who hast set thy glory above the heavens.

[2] **Out of the mouth of babes and sucklings** hast thou ordained strength because of thine enemies,
that thou mightest still the enemy and the avenger.

[3] **When I** consider thy heavens, the work of thy fingers, the moon and the stars,
which thou hast ordained;

[4] **What** is man, {that thou art mindful of him}? and the son of man, {that thou visitest him}?

[5] **For thou** hast made him a little lower than the angels,
and hast crowned him with glory and honour.

[6] **Thou** madest him to have dominion over the works of thy hands;
thou hast put all things under his feet:

[7] All sheep and oxen, yea, and the beasts of the field;

[8] The fowl of the air, and the fish of the sea, and whatsoever passeth through the paths of the seas.

[9] **O LORD our Lord, how excellent** is thy name in all the earth!

9

To the chief Musician upon Muthlabben, A Psalm of David.

I will praise thee, O LORD, with my whole heart;
I will shew forth all thy marvellous works.

[2] **I** will be glad and rejoice in thee:
I will sing praise to thy name, O thou most High.

[3] **When mine enemies** are turned back,
they shall fall and perish at thy presence.

[4] **For thou** hast maintained my right and my cause;
thou satest in the throne judging right.

[5] **Thou** hast rebuked the heathen,
thou hast destroyed the wicked,
thou hast put out their name for ever and ever.

[6] **O thou enemy, destructions** are come to a perpetual end:
and thou hast destroyed cities;
their memorial is perished with them.

[7] **But the LORD** shall endure for ever:
he hath prepared his throne for judgment.

[8] **And he** shall judge the world in righteousness,
he shall minister judgment to the people in uprightness.

[9] **The LORD** also will be a refuge for the oppressed, a refuge in times of trouble.

[10] **And they that know thy name** will put their trust in thee:
for thou, LORD, hast not forsaken them that seek thee.

[11] **Sing** praises to the LORD,
which dwelleth in Zion:
declare among the people his doings.

[12] **When he** maketh inquisition for blood,
he remembereth them:
he forgetteth not the cry of the humble.

[13] **Have** mercy upon me, O LORD;
consider my trouble which I suffer of them that hate me, thou that liftest me up from the gates of death:

[14] **That I** may shew forth all thy praise in the gates of the daughter of Zion:
I will rejoice in thy salvation.

[15] **The heathen** are sunk down in the pit that they made:
in the net which they hid is their own foot taken.

[16] **The LORD** is known by the judgment which he executeth:
the wicked is snared in the work of his own hands. Higgaion.
Selah.

[17] **The wicked** shall be turned into hell, and all the nations that forget God.

[18] **For the needy** shall not always be forgotten:
the expectation of the poor shall not perish for ever.

[19] **Arise,** O LORD;
let not man prevail:
let the heathen be judged in thy sight.

[20] **Put** them in fear, O LORD:
that the nations may know themselves to be but men.
Selah.

10

Why standest thou afar off, O LORD?
why hidest thou thyself in times of trouble?

[2] **The wicked in his pride** doth persecute the poor:
let them be taken in the devices that they have imagined.

[3] **For the wicked** boasteth of his heart's desire,
and blesseth the covetous,
whom the LORD abhorreth.

[4] **The wicked**, through the pride of his countenance, will not seek after God:
God is not in all his thoughts.

[5] **His ways** are always grievous;

thy judgments are far above out of his sight:
as for all his enemies, he puffeth at them.
6 **He** hath said in his heart,
I shall not be moved:
for I shall never be in adversity.
7 **His mouth** is full of cursing and deceit and fraud:
under his tongue is mischief and vanity.
8 **He** sitteth in the lurking places of the villages:
in the secret places doth he murder the innocent:
his eyes are privily set against the poor.
9 **He** lieth in wait secretly as a lion in his den:
he lieth in wait
to catch the poor:
he doth catch the poor,
when he draweth him into his net.
10 **He** croucheth,
and humbleth himself,
that the poor may fall by his strong ones.
11 **He** hath said in his heart,
God hath forgotten:
he hideth his face;
he will never see it.
12 **Arise,** O LORD;
O God, lift up thine hand:
forget not the humble.
13 **Wherefore** doth the wicked contemn God?
he hath said in his heart,
Thou wilt not require it.
14 **Thou** hast seen it;
for thou beholdest mischief and spite,
to requite it with thy hand:
the poor committeth himself unto thee;
thou art the helper of the fatherless.
15 **Break thou** the arm of the wicked and the evil man:
seek out his wickedness
till thou find none.
16 **The LORD** is King for ever and ever:
the heathen are perished out of his land.
17 **LORD, thou** hast heard the desire of the humble:
thou wilt prepare their heart,
thou wilt cause thine ear to hear:
18 To judge the fatherless and the oppressed,
that the man of the earth may no more oppress.

11

To the chief Musician, A Psalm of David.

In the LORD put I my trust:
how say ye to my soul,
Flee as a bird to your mountain?
2 **For, {lo}, the wicked** bend their bow,
they make ready their arrow upon the string,
that they may privily shoot at the upright in heart.
3 **If the foundations** be destroyed,
what can the righteous do?
4 **The LORD** is in his holy temple,
the LORD's throne is in heaven:
his eyes behold,
his eyelids try, the children of men.
5 **The LORD** trieth the righteous:
but the wicked and him that loveth violence his soul hateth.
6 **Upon the wicked** he shall rain snares, fire and brimstone, and an horrible tempest:
this shall be the portion of their cup.
7 **For the righteous LORD** loveth righteousness;
his countenance doth behold the upright.

12

To the chief Musician upon Sheminith, A Psalm of David.

Help, LORD;
for the godly man ceaseth;
for the faithful fail from among the children of men.
2 **They** speak vanity every one with his neighbour:
with flattering lips and with a double heart do they speak.
3 **The LORD** shall cut off all flattering lips, and the tongue that speaketh proud things:
4 **Who** have said,
With our tongue will we prevail;
our lips are our own:
who is lord over us?
5 **For the oppression of the poor, for the sighing of the needy,** now will I arise,
saith the LORD;
I will set him in safety from him that puffeth at him.
6 **The words of the LORD** are pure words: as silver tried in a furnace of earth,
purified seven times.
7 **Thou** shalt keep them, O LORD,
thou shalt preserve them from this generation for ever.
8 **The wicked** walk on every side,
when the vilest men are exalted.

13

To the chief Musician, A Psalm of David.

How long wilt thou forget me, O LORD? for ever?
how long wilt thou hide thy face from me?
2 **How long** shall I take counsel in my soul,
having sorrow in my heart daily?
how long shall mine enemy be exalted over me?
3 **Consider and hear** me, O LORD my God:
lighten mine eyes,
lest I sleep the sleep of death;
4 **Lest mine enemy** say,
I have prevailed against him;
and those that trouble me rejoice
when I am moved.
5 **But I** have trusted in thy mercy;
my heart shall rejoice in thy salvation.
6 **I** will sing unto the LORD,
because he hath dealt bountifully with me.

14

To the chief Musician, A Psalm of David.

The fool hath said in his heart,
There is no God.
They are corrupt,
they have done abominable works,
there is none that doeth good.
2 **The LORD** looked down from heaven upon the children of men,
to see if there were any that did understand,
and seek God.
3 **They** are all gone aside,
they are all together become filthy:
there is none that doeth good, no, not one.
4 **Have all the workers of iniquity** no knowledge?
who eat up my people as they eat bread,
and call not upon the LORD.
5 **There** were they in great fear:
for God is in the generation of the righteous.
6 **Ye** have shamed the counsel of the poor,
because the LORD is his refuge.

7 **Oh that the salvation of Israel** were come out of Zion!
when the LORD bringeth back the captivity of his people,
Jacob shall rejoice,
and Israel shall be glad.

15

A Psalm of David.

LORD, who shall abide in thy tabernacle?
who shall dwell in thy holy hill?
2 He that walketh uprightly, and worketh righteousness, and speaketh the truth in his heart.
3 **He** that backbiteth not with his tongue,
nor doeth evil to his neighbour,
nor taketh up a reproach against his neighbour.
4 **In whose eyes** a vile person is contemned;
but he honoureth them that fear the LORD.
He that sweareth to his own hurt,
and changeth not.
5 **He** that putteth not out his money to usury,
nor taketh reward against the innocent.
He that doeth these things shall never be moved.

16

Michtam of David.

Preserve me, O God:
for in thee do I put my trust.
2 **O my soul, thou** hast said unto the LORD,
Thou art my Lord:
my goodness extendeth not to thee;
3 But to the saints that are in the earth, and to the excellent,
in whom is all my delight.
4 **Their sorrows** shall be multiplied that hasten after another god:
their drink offerings of blood will I not offer,
nor take up their names into my lips.
5 **The LORD** is the portion of mine inheritance and of my cup:
thou maintainest my lot.
6 **The lines** are fallen unto me in pleasant places;
yea, I have a goodly heritage.
7 **I** will bless the LORD,
who hath given me counsel:
my reins also instruct me in the night seasons.
8 **I** have set the LORD always before me:
because he is at my right hand,
I shall not be moved.
9 **Therefore my heart** is glad,
and my glory rejoiceth:
my flesh also shall rest in hope.
10 **For thou** wilt not leave my soul in hell;
neither wilt thou suffer thine Holy One to see corruption.
11 **Thou** wilt shew me the path of life:
in thy presence is fulness of joy;
at thy right hand there are pleasures for evermore.

17

A Prayer of David.

Hear the right, O LORD,
attend unto my cry,
give ear unto my prayer,
that goeth not out of feigned lips.
2 **Let my sentence** come forth from thy presence;
let thine eyes behold the things that are equal.
3 **Thou** hast proved mine heart;
thou hast visited me in the night;
thou hast tried me,
and shalt find nothing;
I am purposed
that my mouth shall not transgress.
4 **Concerning the works of men, by the word of thy lips** I have kept me from the paths of the destroyer.
5 **Hold up** my goings in thy paths,
that my footsteps slip not.
6 **I** have called upon thee,
for thou wilt hear me, O God:
incline thine ear unto me,
and hear my speech.
7 **Shew** thy marvellous lovingkindness, O thou that savest by thy right hand them which put their trust in thee from those that rise up against them.
8 **Keep** me as the apple of the eye,
hide me under the shadow of thy wings,
9 From the wicked that oppress me, from my deadly enemies,
who compass me about.
10 **They** are inclosed in their own fat:
with their mouth they speak proudly.
11 **They** have now compassed us in our steps:
they have set their eyes bowing down to the earth;
12 Like as a lion that is greedy of his prey, and as it were a young lion lurking in secret places.
13 **Arise,** O LORD,
disappoint him,
cast him down:
deliver my soul from the wicked,
which is thy sword:
14 From men which are thy hand, O LORD, from men of the world,
which have their portion in this life,
and whose belly thou fillest with thy hid treasure:
they are full of children,
and leave the rest of their substance to their babes.
15 **As for me,** I will behold thy face in righteousness:
I shall be satisfied,
when I awake, with thy likeness.

18

To the chief Musician, A Psalm of David, the servant of the LORD, who spake unto the LORD the words of this song in the day that the LORD delivered him from the hand of all his enemies, and from the hand of Saul: And he said,

I will love thee, O LORD, my strength.
2 **The LORD** is my rock, and my fortress, and my deliverer; my God, my strength,
in whom I will trust; my buckler, and the horn of my salvation, and my high tower.
3 **I** will call upon the LORD,
who is worthy to be praised:
so shall I be saved from mine enemies.
4 **The sorrows of death** compassed me,
and the floods of ungodly men made me afraid.
5 **The sorrows of hell** compassed me about:
the snares of death prevented me.
6 **In my distress** I called upon the LORD,
and cried unto my God:
he heard my voice out of his temple,
and my cry came before him, even into his ears.
7 **Then the earth** shook and trembled;
the foundations also of the hills moved and were shaken,

because he was wroth.

8 **There** went up a smoke out of his nostrils,
and fire out of his mouth devoured:
coals were kindled by it.

9 **He** bowed the heavens also,
and came down:
and darkness was under his feet.

10 **And he** rode upon a cherub,
and did fly:
yea, he did fly upon the wings of the wind.

11 **He** made darkness his secret place;
his pavilion round about him were dark waters and thick clouds of the skies.

12 **At the brightness that was before him** his thick clouds passed, hail stones and coals of fire.

13 **The LORD** also thundered in the heavens,
and the Highest gave his voice; hail stones and coals of fire.

14 **Yea, he** sent out his arrows,
and scattered them;
and he shot out lightnings,
and discomfited them.

15 **Then the channels of waters** were seen,
and the foundations of the world were discovered at thy rebuke, O LORD, at the blast of the breath of thy nostrils.

16 **He** sent from above,
he took me,
he drew me out of many waters.

17 **He** delivered me from my strong enemy, and from them which hated me:
for they were too strong for me.

18 **They** prevented me in the day of my calamity:
but the LORD was my stay.

19 **He** brought me forth also into a large place;
he delivered me,
because he delighted in me.

20 **The LORD** rewarded me according to my righteousness;
according to the cleanness of my hands hath he recompensed me.

21 **For I** have kept the ways of the LORD,
and have not wickedly departed from my God.

22 **For all his judgments** were before me,
and I did not put away his statutes from me.

23 **I** was also upright before him,
and I kept myself from mine iniquity.

24 **Therefore** hath the LORD recompensed me according to my righteousness, according to the cleanness of my hands in his eyesight.

25 **With the merciful** thou wilt shew thyself merciful;
with an upright man thou wilt shew thyself upright;

26 **With the pure** thou wilt shew thyself pure;
and with the froward thou wilt shew thyself froward.

27 **For thou** wilt save the afflicted people;
but wilt bring down high looks.

28 **For thou** wilt light my candle:
the LORD my God will enlighten my darkness.

29 **For by thee** I have run through a troop;
and by my God have I leaped over a wall.

30 **As for God,** his way is perfect:
the word of the LORD is tried:
he is a buckler to all those that trust in him.

31 **For who** is God save the LORD?
or who is a rock save our God?

32 **It** is God that girdeth me with strength,
and maketh my way perfect.

33 **He** maketh my feet like hinds' feet,
and setteth me upon my high places.

34 **He** teacheth my hands to war,
so that a bow of steel is broken by mine arms.

35 **Thou** hast also given me the shield of thy salvation:
and thy right hand hath holden me up,
and thy gentleness hath made me great.

36 **Thou** hast enlarged my steps under me,
that my feet did not slip.

37 **I** have pursued mine enemies,
and overtaken them:
neither did I turn again
till they were consumed.

38 **I** have wounded them
that they were not able to rise:
they are fallen under my feet.

39 **For thou** hast girded me with strength unto the battle:
thou hast subdued under me those that rose up against me.

40 **Thou** hast also given me the necks of mine enemies;
that I might destroy them that hate me.

41 **They** cried, {but there was none to save them}: even unto the LORD, {but he answered them not}.

42 **Then** did I beat them small as the dust before the wind:
I did cast them out as the dirt in the streets.

43 **Thou** hast delivered me from the strivings of the people;
and thou hast made me the head of the heathen:
a people whom I have not known shall serve me.

44 **As soon as they** hear of me,
they shall obey me:
the strangers shall submit themselves unto me.

45 **The strangers** shall fade away,
and be afraid out of their close places.

46 **The LORD** liveth;
and blessed be my rock;
and let the God of my salvation be exalted.

47 **It** is God that avengeth me, and subdueth the people under me.

48 **He** delivereth me from mine enemies:
yea, thou liftest me up above those that rise up against me:
thou hast delivered me from the violent man.

49 **Therefore** will I give thanks unto thee, O LORD, among the heathen,
and sing praises unto thy name.

50 **Great deliverance** giveth he to his king;
and sheweth mercy to his anointed, to David, and to his seed for evermore.

19

To the chief Musician, A Psalm of David.

The heavens declare the glory of God;
and the firmament sheweth his handywork.

2 **Day unto day** uttereth speech,
and night unto night sheweth knowledge.

3 **There** is no speech nor language,
where their voice is not heard.

4 **Their line** is gone out through all the earth, and their words to the end of the world.
In them hath he set a tabernacle for the sun,

5 **Which** is as a bridegroom coming out of his chamber,
and rejoiceth as a strong man to run a race.

6 **His going forth** is from the end of the heaven, and his circuit unto the ends of it:
and there is nothing hid from the heat thereof.

7 **The law of the LORD** is perfect,
converting the soul:
the testimony of the LORD is sure,
making wise the simple.

8 **The statutes of the LORD** are right,
rejoicing the heart:
the commandment of the LORD is pure,
enlightening the eyes.

9 **The fear of the LORD** is clean,
enduring for ever:
the judgments of the LORD are true and righteous altogether.

10 **More to be desired** are they than gold, yea, than much fine gold: sweeter also than honey and the honeycomb.

11 **Moreover by them** is thy servant warned:
and in keeping of them there is great reward.

12 **Who** can understand his errors?
cleanse thou me from secret faults.

13 **Keep back** thy servant also from presumptuous sins;
let them not have dominion over me:
then shall I be upright,
and I shall be innocent from the great transgression.

14 **Let the words of my mouth, and the meditation of my heart,** be acceptable in thy sight, O LORD, my strength, and my redeemer.

20

To the chief Musician, A Psalm of David.

The LORD hear thee in the day of trouble;
the name of the God of Jacob defend thee;

2 **Send** thee help from the sanctuary,
and strengthen thee out of Zion;

3 **Remember** all thy offerings,
and accept thy burnt sacrifice;
Selah.

4 **Grant** thee according to thine own heart,
and fulfil all thy counsel.

5 **We** will rejoice in thy salvation,
and in the name of our God we will set up our banners:
the LORD fulfil all thy petitions.

6 **Now** know I
that the LORD saveth his anointed;
he will hear him from his holy heaven with the saving strength of his right hand.

7 **Some** trust in chariots, and some in horses:
but we will remember the name of the LORD our God.

8 **They** are brought down and fallen:
but we are risen,
and stand upright.

9 **Save,** LORD:
let the king hear us when we call.

21

To the chief Musician, A Psalm of David.

The king shall joy in thy strength, O LORD;
and in thy salvation how greatly shall he rejoice!

2 **Thou** hast given him his heart's desire,
and hast not withholden the request of his lips.
Selah.

3 **For thou** preventest him with the blessings of goodness:
thou settest a crown of pure gold on his head.

4 **He** asked life of thee,
and thou gavest it him, even length of days for ever and ever.

5 **His glory** is great in thy salvation:
honour and majesty hast thou laid upon him.

6 **For thou** hast made him most blessed for ever:
thou hast made him exceeding glad with thy countenance.

7 **For the king** trusteth in the LORD,
and through the mercy of the most High he shall not be moved.

8 **Thine hand** shall find out all thine enemies:
thy right hand shall find out those that hate thee.

9 **Thou** shalt make them as a fiery oven in the time of thine anger:
the LORD shall swallow them up in his wrath,
and the fire shall devour them.

10 **Their fruit** shalt thou destroy from the earth, and their seed from among the children of men.

11 **For they** intended evil against thee:
they imagined a mischievous device,
which they are not able to perform.

12 **Therefore** shalt thou make them turn their back,
when thou shalt make ready thine arrows upon thy strings against the face of them.

13 **Be thou** exalted, LORD, in thine own strength:
so will we sing and praise thy power.

22

To the chief Musician upon Aijeleth Shahar, A Psalm of David.

My God, my God, why hast thou forsaken me?
why art thou so far from helping me, and from the words of my roaring?

2 **O my God, I** cry in the day time, {but thou hearest not}; and in the night season, {and am not silent}.

3 **But thou** art holy, O thou that inhabitest the praises of Israel.

4 **Our fathers** trusted in thee:
they trusted,
and thou didst deliver them.

5 **They** cried unto thee,
and were delivered:
they trusted in thee,
and were not confounded.

6 **But I** am a worm, and no man; a reproach of men,
and despised of the people.

7 **All they that see me** laugh me to scorn:
they shoot out the lip,
they shake the head,
saying,

8 **He** trusted on the LORD that he would deliver him:
let him deliver him,
seeing he delighted in him.

9 **But thou** art he that took me out of the womb:

thou didst make me hope
when I was upon my mother's breasts.
10 **I** was cast upon thee from the womb:
thou art my God from my mother's belly.
11 **Be not** far from me;
for trouble is near;
for there is none to help.
12 **Many bulls** have compassed me:
strong bulls of Bashan have beset me round.
13 **They** gaped upon me with their mouths, as a ravening and a roaring lion.
14 **I** am poured out like water,
and all my bones are out of joint:
my heart is like wax;
it is melted in the midst of my bowels.
15 **My strength** is dried up like a potsherd;
and my tongue cleaveth to my jaws;
and thou hast brought me into the dust of death.
16 **For dogs** have compassed me:
the assembly of the wicked have inclosed me:
they pierced my hands and my feet.
17 **I** may tell all my bones:
they look and stare upon me.
18 **They** part my garments among them,
and cast lots upon my vesture.
19 **But be not thou** far from me, O LORD: O my strength,
haste thee to help me.
20 **Deliver** my soul from the sword; my darling from the power of the dog.
21 **Save** me from the lion's mouth:
for thou hast heard me from the horns of the unicorns.
22 **I** will declare thy name unto my brethren:
in the midst of the congregation will I praise thee.
23 **Ye that fear the LORD, praise** him;
all ye the seed of Jacob, glorify him;
and fear him, all ye the seed of Israel.
24 **For he** hath not despised
nor abhorred the affliction of the afflicted;
neither hath he hid his face from him;
but when he cried unto him,
he heard.
25 **My praise** shall be of thee in the great congregation:
I will pay my vows before them that fear him.
26 **The meek** shall eat and be satisfied:
they shall praise the LORD that seek him:
your heart shall live for ever.
27 **All the ends of the world** shall remember and turn unto the LORD:
and all the kindreds of the nations shall worship before thee.
28 **For the kingdom** is the LORD's:
and he is the governor among the nations.
29 **All they that be fat upon earth** shall eat and worship:
all they that go down to the dust shall bow before him:
and none can keep alive his own soul.
30 **A seed** shall serve him;
it shall be accounted to the Lord for a generation.
31 **They** shall come,
and shall declare his righteousness unto a people that shall be born,
that he hath done this.

23

A Psalm of David.

The LORD is my shepherd;
I shall not want.
2 **He** maketh me to lie down in green pastures:
he leadeth me beside the still waters.
3 **He** restoreth my soul:
he leadeth me in the paths of righteousness for his name's sake.
4 **Yea, though I** walk through the valley of the shadow of death,
I will fear no evil:
for thou art with me;
thy rod and thy staff they comfort me.
5 **Thou** preparest a table before me in the presence of mine enemies:
thou anointest my head with oil;
my cup runneth over.
6 **Surely goodness and mercy** shall follow me all the days of my life:
and I will dwell in the house of the LORD for ever.

24

A Psalm of David.

The earth is the LORD's, and the fulness thereof; the world, and they that dwell therein.
2 **For he** hath founded it upon the seas,
and established it upon the floods.
3 **Who** shall ascend into the hill of the LORD?
or who shall stand in his holy place?
4 He that hath clean hands, and a pure heart; who hath not lifted up his soul unto vanity, nor sworn deceitfully.
5 **He** shall receive the blessing from the LORD, and righteousness from the God of his salvation.
6 **This** is the generation of them that seek him, that seek thy face, O Jacob.
Selah.
7 **Lift up** your heads, O ye gates;
and be ye lift up, ye everlasting doors;
and the King of glory shall come in.
8 **Who** is this King of glory?
The LORD strong and mighty, the LORD mighty in battle.
9 **Lift up** your heads, O ye gates;
even lift them up, ye everlasting doors;
and the King of glory shall come in.
10 **Who** is this King of glory?
The LORD of hosts, he is the King of glory.
Selah.

25

A Psalm of David.

Unto thee, O LORD, do I lift up my soul.
2 **O my God, I** trust in thee:
let me not be ashamed,
let not mine enemies triumph over me.
3 **Yea, let none that wait on thee** be ashamed:
let them be ashamed which transgress without cause.
4 **Shew** me thy ways, O LORD;
teach me thy paths.
5 **Lead** me in thy truth,

and teach me:
for thou art the God of my salvation;
on thee do I wait all the day.
6 **Remember,** O LORD, thy tender mercies and thy lovingkindnesses;
for they have been ever of old.
7 **Remember not** the sins of my youth, nor my transgressions:
according to thy mercy remember thou me for thy goodness' sake, O LORD.
8 **Good and upright** is the LORD:
therefore will he teach sinners in the way.
9 **The meek** will he guide in judgment:
and the meek will he teach his way.
10 **All the paths of the LORD** are mercy and truth unto such as keep his covenant and his testimonies.
11 **For thy name's sake,** O LORD, pardon mine iniquity;
for it is great.
12 **What man** is he that feareth the LORD?
him shall he teach in the way that he shall choose.
13 **His soul** shall dwell at ease;
and his seed shall inherit the earth.
14 **The secret of the LORD** is with them that fear him;
and he will shew them his covenant.
15 **Mine eyes** are ever toward the LORD;
for he shall pluck my feet out of the net.
16 **Turn** thee unto me,
and have mercy upon me;
for I am desolate and afflicted.
17 **The troubles of my heart** are enlarged:
O bring thou me out of my distresses.
18 **Look** upon mine affliction and my pain;
and forgive all my sins.
19 **Consider** mine enemies;
for they are many;
and they hate me with cruel hatred.
20 **O keep** my soul,
and deliver me:
let me not be ashamed;
for I put my trust in thee.
21 **Let integrity and uprightness** preserve me;
for I wait on thee.
22 **Redeem** Israel, O God, out of all his troubles.

26

A Psalm of David.

Judge me, O LORD;
for I have walked in mine integrity:
I have trusted also in the LORD;
therefore I shall not slide.
2 **Examine** me, O LORD,
and prove me;
try my reins and my heart.
3 **For thy lovingkindness** is before mine eyes:
and I have walked in thy truth.
4 **I** have not sat with vain persons,
neither will I go in with dissemblers.
5 **I** have hated the congregation of evil doers;
and will not sit with the wicked.
6 **I** will wash mine hands in innocency:
so will I compass thine altar, O LORD:
7 **That I** may publish with the voice of thanksgiving,
and tell of all thy wondrous works.
8 **LORD, I** have loved the habitation of thy house, and the place where thine honour dwelleth.
9 **Gather not** my soul with sinners, nor my life with bloody men:
10 **In whose hands** is mischief,
and their right hand is full of bribes.
11 **But as for me,** I will walk in mine integrity:
redeem me,
and be merciful unto me.
12 **My foot** standeth in an even place:
in the congregations will I bless the LORD.

27

A Psalm of David.

The LORD is my light and my salvation;
whom shall I fear?
the LORD is the strength of my life;
of whom shall I be afraid?
2 **When the wicked, even mine enemies and my foes,** came upon me to eat up my flesh,
they stumbled and fell.
3 **Though an host** should encamp against me,
my heart shall not fear:
though war should rise against me,
in this will I be confident.
4 **One thing** have I desired of the LORD,
that will I seek after;
that I may dwell in the house of the LORD all the days of my life,
to behold the beauty of the LORD,
and to enquire in his temple.
5 **For in the time of trouble** he shall hide me in his pavilion:
in the secret of his tabernacle shall he hide me;
he shall set me up upon a rock.
6 **And now** shall mine head be lifted up above mine enemies round about me:
therefore will I offer in his tabernacle sacrifices of joy;
I will sing,
yea, I will sing praises unto the LORD.
7 **Hear,** O LORD,
when I cry with my voice:
have mercy also upon me,
and answer me.
8 **When thou** saidst,
Seek ye my face;
my heart said unto thee,
Thy face, LORD, will I seek.
9 **Hide not** thy face far from me;
put not thy servant away in anger:
thou hast been my help;
leave me not, neither forsake me, O God of my salvation.
10 **When my father and my mother** forsake me,
then the LORD will take me up.
11 **Teach** me thy way, O LORD,
and lead me in a plain path, because of mine enemies.
12 **Deliver me not** over unto the will of mine enemies:
for false witnesses are risen up against me, and such as breathe out cruelty.
13 **I** had fainted,
unless I had believed
to see the goodness of the LORD in the land of the living.
14 **Wait** on the LORD:
be of good courage,
and he shall strengthen thine heart:
wait, {I say}, on the LORD.

28

A Psalm of David.

Unto thee will I cry, O LORD my rock;

be not silent to me: lest,
if thou be silent to me,
I become like them that go down into the pit.

2 **Hear** the voice of my supplications,
when I cry unto thee,
when I lift up my hands toward thy holy oracle.

3 **Draw** me not away with the wicked, and with the workers of iniquity,
which speak peace to their neighbours,
but mischief is in their hearts.

4 **Give** them according to their deeds, and according to the wickedness of their endeavours:
give them after the work of their hands;
render to them their desert.

5 **Because they** regard not the works of the LORD, nor the operation of his hands,
he shall destroy them,
and not build them up.

6 **Blessed** be the LORD,
because he hath heard the voice of my supplications.

7 **The LORD** is my strength and my shield;
my heart trusted in him,
and I am helped:
therefore my heart greatly rejoiceth;
and with my song will I praise him.

8 **The LORD** is their strength,
and he is the saving strength of his anointed.

9 **Save** thy people,
and bless thine inheritance:
feed them also,
and lift them up for ever.

29

A Psalm of David.

Give unto the LORD, O ye mighty,
give unto the LORD glory and strength.

2 **Give** unto the LORD the glory due unto his name;
worship the LORD in the beauty of holiness.

3 **The voice of the LORD** is upon the waters:
the God of glory thundereth:
the LORD is upon many waters.

4 **The voice of the LORD** is powerful;
the voice of the LORD is full of majesty.

5 **The voice of the LORD** breaketh the cedars;
yea, the LORD breaketh the cedars of Lebanon.

6 **He** maketh them also to skip like a calf; Lebanon and Sirion like a young unicorn.

7 **The voice of the LORD** divideth the flames of fire.

8 **The voice of the LORD** shaketh the wilderness;
the LORD shaketh the wilderness of Kadesh.

9 **The voice of the LORD** maketh the hinds to calve,
and discovereth the forests:
and in his temple doth every one speak of his glory.

10 **The LORD** sitteth upon the flood;
yea, the LORD sitteth King for ever.

11 **The LORD** will give strength unto his people;
the LORD will bless his people with peace.

30

A Psalm and Song at the dedication of the house of David.

I will extol thee, O LORD;
for thou hast lifted me up,
and hast not made my foes to rejoice over me.

2 **O LORD my God, I** cried unto thee,
and thou hast healed me.

3 **O LORD, thou** hast brought up my soul from the grave:
thou hast kept me alive,
that I should not go down to the pit.

4 **Sing** unto the LORD, O ye saints of his,
and give thanks at the remembrance of his holiness.

5 **For his anger** endureth but a moment;
in his favour is life:
weeping may endure for a night,
but joy cometh in the morning.

6 **And in my prosperity** I said,
I shall never be moved.

7 **LORD, by thy favour** thou hast made my mountain to stand strong:
thou didst hide thy face,
and I was troubled.

8 **I** cried to thee, O LORD;
and unto the LORD I made supplication.

9 **What profit** is there in my blood,
when I go down to the pit?
Shall the dust praise thee?
shall it declare thy truth?

10 **Hear,** O LORD,
and have mercy upon me:
LORD, be thou my helper.

11 **Thou** hast turned for me my mourning into dancing:
thou hast put off my sackcloth,
and girded me with gladness;

12 **To the end that my glory** may sing praise to thee,
and not be silent.
O LORD my God, I will give thanks unto thee for ever.

31

To the chief Musician, A Psalm of David.

In thee, O LORD, do I put my trust;
let me never be ashamed:
deliver me in thy righteousness.

2 **Bow down** thine ear to me;
deliver me speedily:
be thou my strong rock,
for an house of defence to save me.

3 **For thou** art my rock and my fortress;
therefore for thy name's sake lead me,
and guide me.

4 **Pull me out** of the net that they have laid privily for me:
for thou art my strength.

5 **Into thine hand** I commit my spirit:
thou hast redeemed me, O LORD God of truth.

6 **I** have hated them that regard lying vanities:
but I trust in the LORD.

7 **I** will be glad and rejoice in thy mercy:
for thou hast considered my trouble;
thou hast known my soul in adversities;

8 **And** hast not shut me up into the hand of the enemy:
thou hast set my feet in a large room.

9 **Have** mercy upon me, O LORD,
for I am in trouble: mine eye is consumed with grief, yea, my soul and my belly.

10 **For my life** is spent with grief, and my years with sighing:

my strength faileth because of mine iniquity,
and my bones are consumed.
11 **I** was a reproach among all mine enemies, but especially among my neighbours, and a fear to mine acquaintance:
they that did see me without fled from me.
12 **I** am forgotten as a dead man out of mind:
I am like a broken vessel.
13 **For I** have heard the slander of many:
fear was on every side:
while they took counsel together against me,
they devised to take away my life.
14 **But I** trusted in thee, O LORD:
I said,
Thou art my God.
15 **My times** are in thy hand:
deliver me from the hand of mine enemies, and from them that persecute me.
16 **Make** thy face to shine upon thy servant:
save me for thy mercies' sake.
17 **Let me** not be ashamed, O LORD;
for I have called upon thee:
let the wicked be ashamed,
and let them be silent in the grave.
18 **Let the lying lips** be put to silence;
which speak grievous things proudly and contemptuously against the righteous.
19 **Oh how great** is thy goodness,
which thou hast laid up for them that fear thee;
which thou hast wrought for them that trust in thee before the sons of men!
20 **Thou** shalt hide them in the secret of thy presence from the pride of man:
thou shalt keep them secretly in a pavilion from the strife of tongues.
21 **Blessed** be the LORD:
for he hath shewed me his marvellous kindness in a strong city.
22 **For I** said in my haste,
I am cut off from before thine eyes:
nevertheless thou heardest the voice of my supplications
when I cried unto thee.
23 **O love** the LORD, all ye his saints:
for the LORD preserveth the faithful,
and plentifully rewardeth the proud doer.
24 **Be** of good courage,
and he shall strengthen your heart, all ye that hope in the LORD.

32

A Psalm of David, Maschil.

Blessed is he whose transgression is forgiven,
whose sin is covered.
2 **Blessed** is the man unto whom the LORD imputeth not iniquity,
and in whose spirit there is no guile.
3 **When I** kept silence,
my bones waxed old through my roaring all the day long.
4 **For day and night** thy hand was heavy upon me:
my moisture is turned into the drought of summer.
Selah.
5 **I** acknowledge my sin unto thee,
and mine iniquity have I not hid.
I said,
I will confess my transgressions unto the LORD;
and thou forgavest the iniquity of my sin.
Selah.
6 **For this** shall every one that is godly pray unto thee in a time when thou mayest be found:
surely in the floods of great waters they shall not come nigh unto him.
7 **Thou** art my hiding place;
thou shalt preserve me from trouble;
thou shalt compass me about with songs of deliverance.
Selah.
8 **I** will instruct thee and teach thee in the way which thou shalt go:
I will guide thee with mine eye.
9 **Be ye not** as the horse, or as the mule,
which have no understanding:
whose mouth must be held in with bit and bridle,
lest they come near unto thee.
10 **Many sorrows** shall be to the wicked:
but he that trusteth in the LORD, mercy shall compass him about.
11 **Be** glad in the LORD,
and rejoice, ye righteous:
and shout for joy, all ye that are upright in heart.

33

Rejoice in the LORD, O ye righteous:
for praise is comely for the upright.
2 **Praise** the LORD with harp:
sing unto him with the psaltery and an instrument of ten strings.
3 **Sing** unto him a new song;
play skilfully with a loud noise.
4 **For the word of the LORD** is right;
and all his works are done in truth.
5 **He** loveth righteousness and judgment:
the earth is full of the goodness of the LORD.
6 **By the word of the LORD** were the heavens made; and all the host of them by the breath of his mouth.
7 **He** gathereth the waters of the sea together as an heap:
he layeth up the depth in storehouses.
8 **Let all the earth** fear the LORD:
let all the inhabitants of the world stand in awe of him.
9 **For he** spake,
and it was done;
he commanded,
and it stood fast.
10 **The LORD** bringeth the counsel of the heathen to nought:
he maketh the devices of the people of none effect.
11 **The counsel of the LORD** standeth for ever, the thoughts of his heart to all generations.
12 **Blessed** is the nation whose God is the LORD; and the people whom he hath chosen for his own inheritance.
13 **The LORD** looketh from heaven;
he beholdeth all the sons of men.
14 **From the place of his habitation** he looketh upon all the inhabitants of the earth.
15 **He** fashioneth their hearts alike;
he considereth all their works.
16 **There** is no king saved by the multitude of an host:
a mighty man is not delivered by much strength.
17 **An horse** is a vain thing for safety:
neither shall he deliver any by his great strength.

[18] **Behold,**
the eye of the LORD is upon them that fear him, upon them that hope in his mercy;
[19] To deliver their soul from death,
and to keep them alive in famine.
[20] **Our soul** waiteth for the LORD:
he is our help and our shield.
[21] **For our heart** shall rejoice in him,
because we have trusted in his holy name.
[22] **Let thy mercy,** O LORD, be upon us,
according as we hope in thee.

34

A Psalm of David, when he changed his behaviour before Abimelech; who drove him away, and he departed.

I will bless the LORD at all times:
his praise shall continually be in my mouth.
[2] **My soul** shall make her boast in the LORD:
the humble shall hear thereof,
and be glad.
[3] **O magnify** the LORD with me,
and let us exalt his name together.
[4] **I** sought the LORD,
and he heard me,
and delivered me from all my fears.
[5] **They** looked unto him,
and were lightened:
and their faces were not ashamed.
[6] **This poor man** cried,
and the LORD heard him,
and saved him out of all his troubles.
[7] **The angel of the LORD** encampeth round about them that fear him,
and delivereth them.
[8] **O taste and see** that the LORD is good:
blessed is the man that trusteth in him.
[9] **O fear** the LORD, ye his saints:
for there is no want to them that fear him.
[10] **The young lions** do lack,
and suffer hunger:
but they that seek the LORD shall not want any good thing.
[11] **Come,** ye children,
hearken unto me:
I will teach you the fear of the LORD.
[12] **What man** is he that desireth life,
and loveth many days,
that he may see good?
[13] **Keep** thy tongue from evil, and thy lips from speaking guile.
[14] **Depart** from evil,
and do good;
seek peace,
and pursue it.
[15] **The eyes of the LORD** are upon the righteous,
and his ears are open unto their cry.
[16] **The face of the LORD** is against them that do evil,
to cut off the remembrance of them from the earth.
[17] **The righteous** cry,
and the LORD heareth,
and delivereth them out of all their troubles.
[18] **The LORD** is nigh unto them that are of a broken heart;
and saveth such as be of a contrite spirit.
[19] **Many** are the afflictions of the righteous:
but the LORD delivereth him out of them all.
[20] **He** keepeth all his bones:
not one of them is broken.
[21] **Evil** shall slay the wicked:
and they that hate the righteous shall be desolate.
[22] **The LORD** redeemeth the soul of his servants:
and none of them that trust in him shall be desolate.

35

A Psalm of David.

Plead my cause, O LORD, with them that strive with me:
fight against them that fight against me.
[2] **Take hold** of shield and buckler,
and stand up for mine help.
[3] **Draw out** also the spear,
and stop the way against them that persecute me:
say unto my soul,
I am thy salvation.
[4] **Let them** be confounded and put to shame that seek after my soul:
let them be turned back and brought to confusion that devise my hurt.
[5] **Let them** be as chaff before the wind:
and let the angel of the LORD chase them.
[6] **Let their way** be dark and slippery:
and let the angel of the LORD persecute them.
[7] **For without cause** have they hid for me their net in a pit,
which without cause they have digged for my soul.
[8] **Let destruction** come upon him at unawares;
and let his net that he hath hid catch himself:
into that very destruction let him fall.
[9] **And my soul** shall be joyful in the LORD:
it shall rejoice in his salvation.
[10] **All my bones** shall say,
LORD, who is like unto thee,
which deliverest the poor from him that is too strong for him, yea, the poor and the needy from him that spoileth him?
[11] **False witnesses** did rise up;
they laid to my charge things that I knew not.
[12] **They** rewarded me evil for good to the spoiling of my soul.
[13] **But as for me,** {when they were sick}, my clothing was sackcloth:
I humbled my soul with fasting;
and my prayer returned into mine own bosom.
[14] **I** behaved myself
as though he had been my friend or brother:
I bowed down heavily, as one that mourneth for his mother.
[15] **But in mine adversity** they rejoiced,
and gathered themselves together:
yea, the abjects gathered themselves together against me,
and I knew it not;
they did tear me,
and ceased not:
[16] **With hypocritical mockers in feasts,** they gnashed upon me with their teeth.
[17] **Lord, how long** wilt thou look on?
rescue my soul from their destructions, my darling from the lions.
[18] **I** will give thee thanks in the great congregation:
I will praise thee among much people.

19 **Let not them that are mine enemies** wrongfully rejoice over me:
neither let them wink with the eye that hate me without a cause.
20 **For they** speak not peace:
but they devise deceitful matters against them that are quiet in the land.
21 **Yea, they** opened their mouth wide against me,
and said,
Aha, aha,
our eye hath seen it.
22 **This** thou hast seen, O LORD:
keep not silence:
O Lord, be not far from me.
23 **Stir up** thyself,
and awake to my judgment, even unto my cause, my God and my Lord.
24 **Judge** me, O LORD my God, according to thy righteousness;
and let them not rejoice over me.
25 **Let them** not say in their hearts,
Ah, so would we have it:
let them not say,
We have swallowed him up.
26 **Let them** be ashamed and brought to confusion together that rejoice at mine hurt:
let them be clothed with shame and dishonour that magnify themselves against me.
27 **Let them** shout for joy,
and be glad,
that favour my righteous cause:
yea, let them say continually,
Let the LORD be magnified,
which hath pleasure in the prosperity of his servant.
28 **And my tongue** shall speak of thy righteousness and of thy praise all the day long.

36

To the chief Musician, A Psalm of David the servant of the LORD.

The transgression of the wicked saith within my heart,
that there is no fear of God before his eyes.
2 **For he** flattereth himself in his own eyes,
until his iniquity be found to be hateful.
3 **The words of his mouth** are iniquity and deceit:
he hath left off to be wise,
and to do good.
4 **He** deviseth mischief upon his bed;
he setteth himself in a way that is not good;
he abhorreth not evil.
5 **Thy mercy,** O LORD, is in the heavens;
and thy faithfulness reacheth unto the clouds.
6 **Thy righteousness** is like the great mountains;
thy judgments are a great deep:
O LORD, thou preservest man and beast.
7 **How excellent** is thy lovingkindness, O God!
therefore the children of men put their trust under the shadow of thy wings.
8 **They** shall be abundantly satisfied with the fatness of thy house;
and thou shalt make them drink of the river of thy pleasures.
9 **For with thee** is the fountain of life:
in thy light shall we see light.
10 **O continue** thy lovingkindness unto them that know thee; and thy righteousness to the upright in heart.
11 **Let not the foot of pride** come against me,
and let not the hand of the wicked remove me.
12 **There** are the workers of iniquity fallen:
they are cast down,
and shall not be able to rise.

37

A Psalm of David.

Fret not thyself because of evildoers,
neither be thou envious against the workers of iniquity.
2 **For they** shall soon be cut down like the grass,
and wither as the green herb.
3 **Trust** in the LORD,
and do good;
so shalt thou dwell in the land,
and verily thou shalt be fed.
4 **Delight** thyself also in the LORD:
and he shall give thee the desires of thine heart.
5 **Commit** thy way unto the LORD;
trust also in him;
and he shall bring it to pass.
6 **And he** shall bring forth thy righteousness as the light, and thy judgment as the noonday.
7 **Rest** in the LORD,
and wait patiently for him:
fret not thyself because of him who prospereth in his way, because of the man who bringeth wicked devices to pass.
8 **Cease** from anger,
and forsake wrath:
fret not thyself in any wise to do evil.
9 **For evildoers** shall be cut off:
but those that wait upon the LORD, they shall inherit the earth.
10 **For yet a little while,** and the wicked shall not be:
yea, thou shalt diligently consider his place,
and it shall not be.
11 **But the meek** shall inherit the earth;
and shall delight themselves in the abundance of peace.
12 **The wicked** plotteth against the just,
and gnasheth upon him with his teeth.
13 **The Lord** shall laugh at him:
for he seeth that his day is coming.
14 **The wicked** have drawn out the sword,
and have bent their bow,
to cast down the poor and needy,
and to slay such as be of upright conversation.
15 **Their sword** shall enter into their own heart,
and their bows shall be broken.
16 **A little that a righteous man hath** is better than the riches of many wicked.
17 **For the arms of the wicked** shall be broken:
but the LORD upholdeth the righteous.
18 **The LORD** knoweth the days of the upright:
and their inheritance shall be for ever.
19 **They** shall not be ashamed in the evil time:
and in the days of famine they shall be satisfied.
20 **But the wicked** shall perish,
and the enemies of the LORD shall be as the fat of lambs:
they shall consume;

into smoke shall they consume away.
[21] **The wicked** borroweth,
and payeth not again:
but the righteous sheweth mercy,
and giveth.
[22] **For such as be blessed of him** shall inherit the earth;
and they that be cursed of him shall be cut off.
[23] **The steps of a good man** are ordered by the LORD:
and he delighteth in his way.
[24] **Though he** fall,
he shall not be utterly cast down:
for the LORD upholdeth him with his hand.
[25] **I** have been young,
and now am old;
yet have I not seen the righteous forsaken, nor his seed begging bread.
[26] **He** is ever merciful,
and lendeth;
and his seed is blessed.
[27] **Depart** from evil,
and do good;
and dwell for evermore.
[28] **For the LORD** loveth judgment,
and forsaketh not his saints;
they are preserved for ever:
but the seed of the wicked shall be cut off.
[29] **The righteous** shall inherit the land,
and dwell therein for ever.
[30] **The mouth of the righteous** speaketh wisdom,
and his tongue talketh of judgment.
[31] **The law of his God** is in his heart;
none of his steps shall slide.
[32] **The wicked** watcheth the righteous,
and seeketh to slay him.
[33] **The LORD** will not leave him in his hand,
nor condemn him
when he is judged.
[34] **Wait** on the LORD,
and keep his way,
and he shall exalt thee to inherit the land:
when the wicked are cut off,
thou shalt see it.
[35] **I** have seen the wicked in great power,
and spreading himself like a green bay tree.
[36] **Yet he** passed away,
and, {lo}, he was not:
yea, I sought him,
but he could not be found.
[37] **Mark** the perfect man,
and behold the upright:
for the end of that man is peace.
[38] **But the transgressors** shall be destroyed together:
the end of the wicked shall be cut off.
[39] **But the salvation of the righteous** is of the LORD:
he is their strength in the time of trouble.
[40] **And the LORD** shall help them,
and deliver them:
he shall deliver them from the wicked,
and save them,
because they trust in him.

38

A Psalm of David, to bring to remembrance.

O LORD, rebuke me not in thy wrath:
neither chasten me in thy hot displeasure.
[2] **For thine arrows** stick fast in me,
and thy hand presseth me sore.
[3] **There** is no soundness in my flesh because of thine anger;
neither is there any rest in my bones because of my sin.
[4] **For mine iniquities** are gone over mine head:
as an heavy burden they are too heavy for me.
[5] **My wounds** stink and are corrupt because of my foolishness.
[6] **I** am troubled;
I am bowed down greatly;
I go mourning all the day long.
[7] **For my loins** are filled with a loathsome disease:
and there is no soundness in my flesh.
[8] **I** am feeble and sore broken:
I have roared by reason of the disquietness of my heart.
[9] **Lord, all my desire** is before thee;
and my groaning is not hid from thee.
[10] **My heart** panteth,
my strength faileth me:
as for the light of mine eyes, it also is gone from me.
[11] **My lovers and my friends** stand aloof from my sore;
and my kinsmen stand afar off.
[12] **They also that seek after my life** lay snares for me:
and they that seek my hurt speak mischievous things,
and imagine deceits all the day long.
[13] **But I, as a deaf man,** heard not;
and I was as a dumb man that openeth not his mouth.
[14] **Thus I** was as a man that heareth not, and in whose mouth are no reproofs.
[15] **For in thee,** O LORD, do I hope:
thou wilt hear, O Lord my God.
[16] **For I** said,
Hear me,
lest otherwise they should rejoice over me:
when my foot slippeth,
they magnify themselves against me.
[17] **For I** am ready to halt,
and my sorrow is continually before me.
[18] **For I** will declare mine iniquity;
I will be sorry for my sin.
[19] **But mine enemies** are lively,
and they are strong:
and they that hate me wrongfully are multiplied.
[20] **They also that render evil for good** are mine adversaries;
because I follow the thing that good is.
[21] **Forsake me not,** O LORD:
O my God, be not far from me.
[22] **Make haste** to help me, O Lord my salvation.

39

To the chief Musician, even to Jeduthun, A Psalm of David.

I said,
I will take heed to my ways,
that I sin not with my tongue:
I will keep my mouth with a bridle,
while the wicked is before me.
[2] **I** was dumb with silence,
I held my peace, even from good;
and my sorrow was stirred.
[3] **My heart** was hot within me,
while I was musing the fire burned:
then spake I with my tongue,
[4] **LORD, make** me to know mine end, and the measure of my days,
what it is:

that I may know
how frail I am.

5 **Behold,**
thou hast made my days as an handbreadth;
and mine age is as nothing before thee:
verily every man at his best state is altogether vanity.
Selah.

6 **Surely every man** walketh in a vain shew:
surely they are disquieted in vain:
he heapeth up riches,
and knoweth not
who shall gather them.

7 **And now, Lord, what** wait I for?
my hope is in thee.

8 **Deliver** me from all my transgressions:
make me not the reproach of the foolish.

9 **I** was dumb,
I opened not my mouth;
because thou didst it.

10 **Remove** thy stroke away from me:
I am consumed by the blow of thine hand.

11 **When thou with rebukes** dost correct man for iniquity,
thou makest his beauty to consume away like a moth:
surely every man is vanity.
Selah.

12 **Hear** my prayer, O LORD,
and give ear unto my cry;
hold not thy peace at my tears:
for I am a stranger with thee, and a sojourner,
as all my fathers were.

13 **O spare** me,
that I may recover strength,
before I go hence,
and be no more.

40

To the chief Musician, A Psalm of David.

I waited patiently for the LORD;
and he inclined unto me,
and heard my cry.

2 **He** brought me up also out of an horrible pit, out of the miry clay,
and set my feet upon a rock,
and established my goings.

3 **And he** hath put a new song in my mouth, even praise unto our God:
many shall see it,
and fear,
and shall trust in the LORD.

4 **Blessed** is that man that maketh the LORD his trust, and respecteth not the proud, nor such as turn aside to lies.

5 **Many,** O LORD my God, are thy wonderful works which thou hast done, and thy thoughts which are to us-ward:
they cannot be reckoned up in order unto thee:
if I would declare and speak of them,
they are more than can be numbered.

6 **Sacrifice and offering** thou didst not desire;
mine ears hast thou opened:
urnt offering and sin offering hast thou not required.

7 **Then** said I,
Lo,
I come:
in the volume of the book it is written of me,

8 **I** delight to do thy will, O my God:
yea, thy law is within my heart.

9 **I** have preached righteousness in the great congregation:
lo,
I have not refrained my lips, O LORD, thou knowest.

10 **I** have not hid thy righteousness within my heart;
I have declared thy faithfulness and thy salvation:
I have not concealed thy lovingkindness and thy truth from the great congregation.

11 **Withhold not thou** thy tender mercies from me, O LORD:
let thy lovingkindness and thy truth continually preserve me.

12 **For innumerable evils** have compassed me about:
mine iniquities have taken hold upon me,
so that I am not able to look up;
they are more than the hairs of mine head:
therefore my heart faileth me.

13 **Be** pleased, O LORD, to deliver me:
O LORD, make haste to help me.

14 **Let them** be ashamed and confounded together that seek after my soul to destroy it;
let them be driven backward and put to shame that wish me evil.

15 **Let them** be desolate for a reward of their shame that say unto me,
Aha, aha.

16 **Let all those that seek thee** rejoice and be glad in thee:
let such as love thy salvation say continually,
The LORD be magnified.

17 **But I** am poor and needy;
yet the Lord thinketh upon me:
thou art my help and my deliverer;
make no tarrying, O my God.

41

To the chief Musician, A *Psalm of David.*

Blessed is he that considereth the poor:
the LORD will deliver him in time of trouble.

2 **The LORD** will preserve him,
and keep him alive;
and he shall be blessed upon the earth:
and thou wilt not deliver him unto the will of his enemies.

3 **The LORD** will strengthen him upon the bed of languishing:
thou wilt make all his bed in his sickness.

4 **I** said,
LORD, be merciful unto me:
heal my soul;
for I have sinned against thee.

5 **Mine enemies** speak evil of me,
When shall he die,
and his name perish?

6 **And if he** come to see me,
he speaketh vanity:
his heart gathereth iniquity to itself;
when he goeth abroad,
he telleth it.

7 **All that hate me** whisper together against me:
against me do they devise my hurt.

8 **An evil disease,** {say they}, cleaveth fast unto him:
and now that he lieth
he shall rise up no more.

9 **Yea, mine own familiar friend,** {in whom I trusted}, {which did eat of my bread}, hath lifted up his heel against me.

10 **But thou,** O LORD, be merciful unto me,
and raise me up,
that I may requite them.

11 **By this** I know
that thou favourest me,

because mine enemy doth not triumph over me.

12 **And as for me,** thou upholdest me in mine integrity,
and settest me before thy face for ever.

13 **Blessed** be the LORD God of Israel from everlasting, and to everlasting.
Amen, and Amen.

42

To the chief Musician, Maschil, for the sons of Korah.

As the hart panteth after the water brooks,
so panteth my soul after thee, O God.

2 **My soul** thirsteth for God, for the living God:
when shall I come and appear before God?

3 **My tears** have been my meat day and night,
while they continually say unto me,
Where is thy God?

4 **When I** remember these things,
I pour out my soul in me:
for I had gone with the multitude,
I went with them to the house of God, with the voice of joy and praise, with a multitude that kept holyday.

5 **Why** art thou cast down, O my soul?
and why art thou disquieted in me?
hope thou in God:
for I shall yet praise him for the help of his countenance.

6 **O my God, my soul** is cast down within me:
therefore will I remember thee from the land of Jordan, and of the Hermonites, from the hill Mizar.

7 **Deep** calleth unto deep at the noise of thy waterspouts:
all thy waves and thy billows are gone over me.

8 **Yet the LORD** will command his lovingkindness in the day time,
and in the night his song shall be with me, and my prayer unto the God of my life.

9 **I** will say unto God my rock,
Why hast thou forgotten me?
why go I mourning because of the oppression of the enemy?

10 **As with a sword in my bones,** mine enemies reproach me;
while they say daily unto me,
Where is thy God?

11 **Why** art thou cast down, O my soul?
and why art thou disquieted within me?
hope thou in God:
for I shall yet praise him,
who is the health of my countenance, and my God.

43

Judge me, O God,
and plead my cause against an ungodly nation:
O deliver me from the deceitful and unjust man.

2 **For thou** art the God of my strength:
why dost thou cast me off?
why go I mourning because of the oppression of the enemy?

3 **O send out** thy light and thy truth:
let them lead me;
let them bring me unto thy holy hill, and to thy tabernacles.

4 **Then** will I go unto the altar of God, unto God my exceeding joy:
yea, upon the harp will I praise thee, O God my God.

5 **Why** art thou cast down, O my soul?
and why art thou disquieted within me?
hope in God:
for I shall yet praise him,
who is the health of my countenance, and my God.

44

To the chief Musician for the sons of Korah, Maschil.

We have heard with our ears, O God,
our fathers have told us,
what work thou didst in their days, in the times of old.

2 **How thou** didst drive out the heathen with thy hand,
and plantedst them;
how thou didst afflict the people,
and cast them out.

3 **For they** got not the land in possession by their own sword,
neither did their own arm save them:
but thy right hand, and thine arm, and the light of thy countenance,
because thou hadst a favour unto them.

4 **Thou** art my King, O God:
command deliverances for Jacob.

5 **Through thee** will we push down our enemies:
through thy name will we tread them under that rise up against us.

6 **For I** will not trust in my bow,
neither shall my sword save me.

7 **But thou** hast saved us from our enemies,
and hast put them to shame that hated us.

8 **In God** we boast all the day long,
and praise thy name for ever.
Selah.

9 **But thou** hast cast off,
and put us to shame;
and goest not forth with our armies.

10 **Thou** makest us to turn back from the enemy:
and they which hate us spoil for themselves.

11 **Thou** hast given us like sheep appointed for meat;
and hast scattered us among the heathen.

12 **Thou** sellest thy people for nought,
and dost not increase thy wealth by their price.

13 **Thou** makest us a reproach to our neighbours, a scorn and a derision to them that are round about us.

14 **Thou** makest us a byword among the heathen, a shaking of the head among the people.

15 **My confusion** is continually before me,
and the shame of my face hath covered me,

16 For the voice of him that reproacheth and blasphemeth; by reason of the enemy and avenger.

17 **All this** is come upon us;
yet have we not forgotten thee,
neither have we dealt falsely in thy covenant.

18 **Our heart** is not turned back,
neither have our steps declined from thy way;

19 **Though thou** hast sore broken us in the place of dragons,
and covered us with the shadow of death.

20 **If we** have forgotten the name of our God, **or** stretched out our hands to a strange god;
21 **Shall not God** search this out?
for he knoweth the secrets of the heart.
22 **Yea, for thy sake** are we killed all the day long;
we are counted as sheep for the slaughter.
23 **Awake,**
why sleepest thou, O Lord?
arise,
cast us not off for ever.
24 **Wherefore** hidest thou thy face,
and forgettest our affliction and our oppression?
25 **For our soul** is bowed down to the dust:
our belly cleaveth unto the earth.
26 **Arise** for our help,
and redeem us for thy mercies' sake.

45

To the chief Musician upon Shoshannim, for the sons of Korah, Maschil, A Song of loves.

My heart is inditing a good matter:
I speak of the things which I have made touching the king:
my tongue is the pen of a ready writer.
2 **Thou** art fairer than the children of men:
grace is poured into thy lips:
therefore God hath blessed thee for ever.
3 **Gird** thy sword upon thy thigh, O most mighty, with thy glory and thy majesty.
4 **And in thy majesty** ride prosperously because of truth and meekness and righteousness;
and thy right hand shall teach thee terrible things.
5 **Thine arrows** are sharp in the heart of the king's enemies;
whereby the people fall under thee.
6 **Thy throne,** O God, is for ever and ever:
the sceptre of thy kingdom is a right sceptre.
7 **Thou** lovest righteousness,
and hatest wickedness:
therefore God, thy God, hath anointed thee with the oil of gladness above thy fellows.
8 **All thy garments** smell of myrrh, and aloes, and cassia, out of the ivory palaces,
whereby they have made thee glad.
9 **Kings' daughters** were among thy honourable women:
upon thy right hand did stand the queen in gold of Ophir.
10 **Hearken,** O daughter,
and consider,
and incline thine ear;
forget also thine own people, and thy father's house;
11 **So** shall the king greatly desire thy beauty:
for he is thy Lord;
and worship thou him.
12 **And the daughter of Tyre** shall be there with a gift;
even the rich among the people shall intreat thy favour.
13 **The king's daughter** is all glorious within:
her clothing is of wrought gold.
14 **She** shall be brought unto the king in raiment of needlework:
the virgins her companions that follow her shall be brought unto thee.
15 **With gladness and rejoicing** shall they be brought:
they shall enter into the king's palace.
16 **Instead of thy fathers** shall be thy children,
whom thou mayest make princes in all the earth.
17 **I** will make thy name to be remembered in all generations:
therefore shall the people praise thee for ever and ever.

46

∞ *To the chief Musician for the sons of Korah, A Song upon Alamoth.*

God is our refuge and strength, a very present help in trouble.
2 **Therefore** will not we fear,
though the earth be removed,
and though the mountains be carried into the midst of the sea;
3 **Though the waters thereof** roar and be troubled,
though the mountains shake with the swelling thereof.
Selah.
4 **There** is a river,
he streams whereof shall make glad the city of God, the holy place of the tabernacles of the most High.
5 **God** is in the midst of her;
she shall not be moved:
God shall help her, and that right early.
6 **The heathen** raged,
the kingdoms were moved:
he uttered his voice,
the earth melted.
7 **The LORD of hosts** is with us;
the God of Jacob is our refuge.
Selah.
8 **Come,**
behold the works of the LORD,
what desolations he hath made in the earth.
9 **He** maketh wars to cease unto the end of the earth;
he breaketh the bow,
and cutteth the spear in sunder;
he burneth the chariot in the fire.
10 **Be** still,
and know
that I am God:
I will be exalted among the heathen,
I will be exalted in the earth.
11 **The LORD of hosts** is with us;
the God of Jacob is our refuge.
Selah.

47

To the chief Musician, A Psalm for the sons of Korah.

O clap your hands, all ye people;
shout unto God with the voice of triumph.
2 **For the LORD most high** is terrible;
he is a great King over all the earth.
3 **He** shall subdue the people under us, and the nations under our feet.
4 **He** shall choose our inheritance for us, the excellency of Jacob whom he loved.
Selah.
5 **God** is gone up with a shout, the LORD with the sound of a trumpet.
6 **Sing** praises to God,
sing praises:
sing praises unto our King,
sing praises.
7 **For God** is the King of all the earth:
sing ye praises with understanding.
8 **God** reigneth over the heathen:

God sitteth upon the throne of his holiness.
9 **The princes of the people** are gathered together, even the people of the God of Abraham:
for the shields of the earth belong unto God:
he is greatly exalted.

48 *A Song and Psalm for the sons of Korah.*

Great is the LORD,
and greatly to be praised in the city of our God, in the mountain of his holiness.
2 **Beautiful for situation, the joy of the whole earth,** is mount Zion, on the sides of the north, the city of the great King.
3 **God** is known in her palaces for a refuge.
4 **For, {lo}, the kings** were assembled,
they passed by together.
5 **They** saw it,
and so they marvelled;
they were troubled,
and hasted away.
6 **Fear** took hold upon them there, and pain, as of a woman in travail.
7 **Thou** breakest the ships of Tarshish with an east wind.
8 **As we** have heard,
so have we seen in the city of the LORD of hosts, in the city of our God:
God will establish it for ever.
Selah.
9 **We** have thought of thy lovingkindness, O God, in the midst of thy temple.
10 **According to thy name,** O God, so is thy praise unto the ends of the earth:
thy right hand is full of righteousness.
11 **Let mount Zion** rejoice,
let the daughters of Judah be glad, because of thy judgments.
12 **Walk about** Zion,
and go round about her:
tell the towers thereof.
13 **Mark ye** well her bulwarks,
consider her palaces;
that ye may tell it to the generation following.
14 **For this God** is our God for ever and ever:
he will be our guide even unto death.

49 *To the chief Musician, A Psalm for the sons of Korah.*

Hear this, all ye people;
give ear, all ye inhabitants of the world:
2 Both low and high, rich and poor, together.
3 **My mouth** shall speak of wisdom;
and the meditation of my heart shall be of understanding.
4 **I** will incline mine ear to a parable:
I will open my dark saying upon the harp.
5 **Wherefore** should I fear in the days of evil,
when the iniquity of my heels shall compass me about?
6 **They that trust in their wealth, and boast themselves in the multitude of their riches;**
7 None of them can by any means redeem his brother,
nor give to God a ransom for him:
8 (For the redemption of their soul is precious,
and it ceaseth for ever:)
9 **That he** should still live for ever,
and not see corruption.
10 **For he** seeth that wise men die,
likewise the fool and the brutish person perish,
and leave their wealth to others.
11 **Their inward thought** is,
that their houses shall continue for ever, and their dwelling places to all generations;
they call their lands after their own names.
12 **Nevertheless man being in honour** abideth not:
he is like the beasts that perish.
13 **This their way** is their folly:
yet their posterity approve their sayings.
Selah.
14 **Like sheep** they are laid in the grave;
death shall feed on them;
and the upright shall have dominion over them in the morning;
and their beauty shall consume in the grave from their dwelling.
15 **But God** will redeem my soul from the power of the grave:
for he shall receive me.
Selah.
16 **Be not thou** afraid
when one is made rich,
when the glory of his house is increased;
17 **For when he** dieth
he shall carry nothing away:
his glory shall not descend after him.
18 **Though while he** lived
he blessed his soul:
and men will praise thee,
when thou doest well to thyself.
19 **He** shall go to the generation of his fathers;
they shall never see light.
20 **Man that is in honour, and understandeth not,** is like the beasts that perish.

50 *A Psalm of Asaph.*

The mighty God, even the LORD, hath spoken,
and called the earth from the rising of the sun unto the going down thereof.
2 **Out of Zion,** the perfection of beauty, God hath shined.
3 **Our God** shall come,
and shall not keep silence:
a fire shall devour before him,
and it shall be very tempestuous round about him.
4 **He** shall call to the heavens from above, and to the earth,
that he may judge his people.
5 **Gather** my saints together unto me; those that have made a covenant with me by sacrifice.
6 **And the heavens** shall declare his righteousness:
for God is judge himself.
Selah.
7 **Hear,** O my people,
and I will speak;
O Israel, and I will testify against thee:
I am God, even thy God.
8 **I** will not reprove thee for thy sacrifices or thy burnt offerings,
to have been continually before me.
9 **I** will take no bullock out of thy house, nor he goats out of thy folds.
10 **For every beast of the forest** is mine, and the cattle upon a thousand hills.
11 **I** know all the fowls of the mountains:

and the wild beasts of the field are
mine.
12 **If I** were hungry,
I would not tell thee:
for the world is mine, and the
fulness thereof.
13 **Will I** eat the flesh of bulls,
or drink the blood of goats?
14 **Offer** unto God thanksgiving;
and pay thy vows unto the most
High:
15 **And call upon** me in the day of
trouble:
I will deliver thee,
and thou shalt glorify me.
16 **But unto the wicked** God saith,
What hast thou to do to declare my
statutes,
or that thou shouldest take my
covenant in thy mouth?
17 **Seeing thou** hatest instruction,
and casteth my words behind thee.
18 **When thou** sawest a thief,
then thou consentedst with him,
and hast been partaker with
adulterers.
19 **Thou** givest thy mouth to evil,
and thy tongue frameth deceit.
20 **Thou** sittest and speakest against
thy brother;
thou slanderest thine own mother's
son.
21 **These things** hast thou done,
and I kept silence;
thou thoughtest
that I was altogether such an one as
thyself:
but I will reprove thee,
and set them in order before thine
eyes.
22 **Now consider** this, ye that forget
God,
lest I tear you in pieces,
and there be none to deliver.
23 **Whoso offereth praise** glorifieth
me:
**and to him that ordereth his
conversation aright** will I shew
the salvation of God.

51

To the chief Musician, A Psalm of David, when Nathan the prophet came unto him, after he had gone in to Bathsheba.

Have mercy upon me, O God,
according to thy lovingkindness:
**according unto the multitude of
thy tender mercies** blot out my
transgressions.
2 **Wash** me throughly from mine
iniquity,
and cleanse me from my sin.
3 **For I** acknowledge my
transgressions:
and my sin is ever before me.
4 **Against thee, thee only,** have I
sinned,
and done this evil in thy sight:
that thou mightest be justified
when thou speakest,
and be clear when thou judgest.
5 **Behold,**
I was shapen in iniquity;
and in sin did my mother conceive
me.
6 **Behold,**
thou desirest truth in the inward
parts:
and in the hidden part thou shalt
make me to know wisdom.
7 **Purge** me with hyssop,
and I shall be clean:
wash me,
and I shall be whiter than snow.
8 **Make** me to hear joy and gladness;
**that the bones which thou hast
broken** may rejoice.
9 **Hide** thy face from my sins,
and blot out all mine iniquities.
10 **Create** in me a clean heart, O God;
and renew a right spirit within me.
11 **Cast me not away** from thy
presence;
and take not thy holy spirit from
me.
12 **Restore** unto me the joy of thy
salvation;
and uphold me with thy free spirit.
13 **Then** will I teach transgressors
thy ways;
and sinners shall be converted unto
thee.
14 **Deliver** me from bloodguiltiness,
O God, thou God of my salvation:
and my tongue shall sing aloud of
thy righteousness.
15 **O Lord, open thou** my lips;
and my mouth shall shew forth thy
praise.
16 **For thou** desirest not sacrifice;
else would I give it:
thou delightest not in burnt
offering.
17 **The sacrifices of God** are a
broken spirit:
a broken and a contrite heart, O
God, thou wilt not despise.
18 **Do** good in thy good pleasure
unto Zion:
build thou the walls of Jerusalem.
19 **Then** shalt thou be pleased with
the sacrifices of righteousness,
with burnt offering and whole
burnt offering:
then shall they offer bullocks upon
thine altar.

52

To the chief Musician, Maschil, A Psalm of David, when Doeg the Edomite came and told Saul, and said unto him, David is come to the house of Ahimelech.

Why boastest thou thyself in
mischief, O mighty man?
the goodness of God endureth
continually.
2 **The tongue** deviseth mischiefs;
like a sharp razor,
working deceitfully.
3 **Thou** lovest evil more than good;
and lying rather than to speak
righteousness.
Selah.
4 **Thou** lovest all devouring words,
O thou deceitful tongue.
5 **God** shall likewise destroy thee for
ever,
he shall take thee away,
and pluck thee out of thy dwelling
place,
and root thee out of the land of the
living.
Selah.
6 **The righteous** also shall see,
and fear,
and shall laugh at him:
7 **Lo,**
this is the man that made not God
his strength;
but trusted in the abundance of his
riches,
and strengthened himself in his
wickedness.
8 **But I** am like a green olive tree in
the house of God:
I trust in the mercy of God for ever
and ever.
9 **I** will praise thee for ever,
because thou hast done it:
and I will wait on thy name;
for it is good before thy saints.

53

To the chief Musician upon Mahalath, Maschil, A Psalm of David.

The fool hath said in his heart,
There is no God.

Corrupt are they,
and have done abominable iniquity:
there is none that doeth good.

2 **God** looked down from heaven upon the children of men,
to see if there were any that did understand, that did seek God.

3 **Every one of them** is gone back:
they are altogether become filthy;
there is none that doeth good, no, not one.

4 **Have the workers of iniquity** no knowledge?
who eat up my people
as they eat bread:
they have not called upon God.

5 **There** were they in great fear,
where no fear was:
for God hath scattered the bones of him that encampeth against thee:
thou hast put them to shame,
because God hath despised them.

6 **Oh that the salvation of Israel** were come out of Zion!
When God bringeth back the captivity of his people,
Jacob shall rejoice,
and Israel shall be glad.

54

To the chief Musician on Neginoth, Maschil, A Psalm of David, when the Ziphims came and said to Saul, Doth not David hide himself with us?

Save me, O God, by thy name,
and judge me by thy strength.

2 **Hear** my prayer, O God;
give ear to the words of my mouth.

3 **For strangers** are risen up against me,
and oppressors seek after my soul:
they have not set God before them.
Selah.

4 **Behold,**
God is mine helper:
the Lord is with them that uphold my soul.

5 **He** shall reward evil unto mine enemies:
cut them off in thy truth.

6 **I** will freely sacrifice unto thee:
I will praise thy name, O LORD;
for it is good.

7 **For he** hath delivered me out of all trouble:
and mine eye hath seen his desire upon mine enemies.

55

To the chief Musician on Neginoth, Maschil, A Psalm of David.

Give ear to my prayer, O God;
and hide not thyself from my supplication.

2 **Attend** unto me,
and hear me:
I mourn in my complaint,
and make a noise;

3 Because of the voice of the enemy, because of the oppression of the wicked:
for they cast iniquity upon me,
and in wrath they hate me.

4 **My heart** is sore pained within me:
and the terrors of death are fallen upon me.

5 **Fearfulness and trembling** are come upon me,
and horror hath overwhelmed me.

6 **And I** said,
Oh that I had wings like a dove!
for then would I fly away,
and be at rest.

7 **Lo,**
then would I wander far off,
and remain in the wilderness.
Selah.

8 **I** would hasten my escape from the windy storm and tempest

9 **Destroy,** O Lord,
and divide their tongues:
for I have seen violence and strife in the city.

10 **Day and night** they go about it upon the walls thereof:
mischief also and sorrow are in the midst of it.

11 **Wickedness** is in the midst thereof:
deceit and guile depart not from her streets.

12 **For it** was not an enemy that reproached me;
then I could have borne it:
neither was it he that hated me that did magnify himself against me;
then I would have hid myself from him:

13 **But it** was thou, a man mine equal, my guide, and mine acquaintance.

14 **We** took sweet counsel together,
and walked unto the house of God in company.

15 **Let death** seize upon them,
and let them go down quick into hell:
for wickedness is in their dwellings, and among them.

16 **As for me,** I will call upon God;
and the LORD shall save me.

17 **Evening, and morning, and at noon,** will I pray,
and cry aloud:
and he shall hear my voice.

18 **He** hath delivered my soul in peace from the battle that was against me:
for there were many with me.

19 **God** shall hear,
and afflict them, even he that abideth of old.
Selah.
Because they have no changes,
therefore they fear not God.

20 **He** hath put forth his hands against such as be at peace with him:
he hath broken his covenant.

21 **The words of his mouth** were smoother than butter,
but war was in his heart:
his words were softer than oil,
yet were they drawn swords.

22 **Cast** thy burden upon the LORD,
and he shall sustain thee:
he shall never suffer the righteous to be moved.

23 **But thou,** O God, shalt bring them down into the pit of destruction:
bloody and deceitful men shall not live out half their days;
but I will trust in thee.

56

To the chief Musician upon Jonathelemrechokim, Michtam of David, when the Philistines took him in Gath.

Be merciful unto me, O God:
for man would swallow me up;
he fighting daily oppresseth me.

2 **Mine enemies** would daily swallow me up:
for they be many that fight against me, O thou most High.

3 **What time** I am afraid,
I will trust in thee.

4 **In God** I will praise his word,
in God I have put my trust;
I will not fear what flesh can do unto me.

5 **Every day** they wrest my words:

all their thoughts are against me
for evil.
6 **They** gather themselves together,
they hide themselves,
they mark my steps,
when they wait for my soul.
7 **Shall they** escape by iniquity?
in thine anger cast down the
people, O God.
8 **Thou** tellest my wanderings:
put thou my tears into thy bottle:
are they not in thy book?
9 **When I** cry unto thee,
then shall mine enemies turn back:
this I know;
for God is for me.
10 **In God** will I praise his word:
in the LORD will I praise his word.
11 **In God** have I put my trust:
I will not be afraid what man can do
unto me.
12 **Thy vows** are upon me, O God:
I will render praises unto thee.
13 **For thou** hast delivered my soul
from death:
wilt not thou deliver my feet from
falling,
that I may walk before God in the
light of the living?

57

To the chief Musician, Altaschith, Michtam of David, when he fled from Saul in the cave.

Be merciful unto me, O God,
be merciful unto me:
for my soul trusteth in thee:
yea, in the shadow of thy wings
will I make my refuge,
until these calamities be overpast.
2 **I** will cry unto God most high; unto
God that performeth all things for
me.
3 **He** shall send from heaven,
and save me from the reproach of
him that would swallow me up.
Selah.
God shall send forth his mercy and
his truth.
4 **My soul** is among lions:
and I lie even among them that are
set on fire, even the sons of men,
whose teeth are spears and arrows,
and their tongue a sharp sword.
5 **Be thou** exalted, O God, above the
heavens;
let thy glory be above all the earth.
6 **They** have prepared a net for my
steps;
my soul is bowed down:
they have digged a pit before me,
into the midst whereof they are
fallen themselves.
Selah.
7 **My heart** is fixed, O God,
my heart is fixed:
I will sing and give praise.
8 **Awake up,** my glory;
awake, psaltery and harp:
I myself will awake early.
9 **I** will praise thee, O Lord, among
the people:
I will sing unto thee among the
nations.
10 **For thy mercy** is great unto the
heavens, and thy truth unto the
clouds.
11 **Be thou** exalted, O God, above the
heavens:
let thy glory be above all the earth.

58

∞ *To the chief Musician, Altaschith, Michtam of David.*

Do ye indeed speak righteousness,
O congregation?
do ye judge uprightly, O ye sons of
men?
2 **Yea, in heart** ye work wickedness;
ye weigh the violence of your hands
in the earth.
3 **The wicked** are estranged from
the womb:
they go astray
as soon as they be born,
speaking lies.
4 **Their poison** is like the poison of a
serpent:
they are like the deaf adder that
stoppeth her ear;
5 **Which** will not hearken to the
voice of charmers,
charming never so wisely.
6 **Break** their teeth, O God, in their
mouth:
break out the great teeth of the
young lions, O LORD.
7 **Let them** melt away as waters
which run continually:
when he bendeth his bow to shoot
his arrows,
let them be as cut in pieces.
8 **As a snail which melteth,** let
every one of them pass away: like
the untimely birth of a woman,
that they may not see the sun.
9 **Before your pots** can feel the
thorns,
he shall take them away as with a
whirlwind, both living, and in his
wrath.
10 **The righteous** shall rejoice when
he seeth the vengeance:
he shall wash his feet in the blood
of the wicked.
11 **So that a man** shall say,
Verily there is a reward for the
righteous:
verily he is a God that judgeth in
the earth.

59

To the chief Musician, Altaschith, Michtam of David; when Saul sent, and they watched the house to kill him.

Deliver me from mine enemies, O
my God:
defend me from them that rise up
against me.
2 **Deliver** me from the workers of
iniquity,
and save me from bloody men.
3 **For, {lo}, they** lie in wait for my
soul:
the mighty are gathered against
me; not for my transgression, nor
for my sin, O LORD.
4 **They** run and prepare themselves
without my fault:
awake to help me,
and behold.
5 **Thou** therefore, O LORD God of
hosts, the God of Israel,
awake to visit all the heathen:
be not merciful to any wicked
transgressors.
Selah.
6 **They** return at evening:
they make a noise like a dog,
and go round about the city.
7 **Behold,**
they belch out with their mouth:
swords are in their lips:
for who, {say they}, doth hear?
8 **But thou,** O LORD, shalt laugh at
them;
thou shalt have all the heathen in
derision.
9 **Because of his strength** will I wait
upon thee:
for God is my defence.
10 **The God of my mercy** shall
prevent me:
God shall let me see my desire upon
mine enemies.
11 **Slay them not,**
lest my people forget:

scatter them by thy power;
and bring them down, O Lord our shield.
12 **For the sin of their mouth and the words of their lips** let them even be taken in their pride: and for cursing and lying which they speak.
13 **Consume** them in wrath,
consume them,
that they may not be:
and let them know
that God ruleth in Jacob unto the ends of the earth.
Selah.
14 **And at evening** let them return;
and let them make a noise like a dog,
and go round about the city.
15 **Let them** wander up and down for meat,
and grudge
if they be not satisfied.
16 **But I** will sing of thy power;
yea, I will sing aloud of thy mercy in the morning:
for thou hast been my defence and refuge in the day of my trouble.
17 **Unto thee,** O my strength, will I sing:
for God is my defence, and the God of my mercy.

60

To the chief Musician upon Shushaneduth, Michtam of David, to teach; when he strove with Aramnaharaim and with Aramzobah, when Joab returned, and smote of Edom in the valley of salt twelve thousand.

O God, thou hast cast us off,
thou hast scattered us,
thou hast been displeased;
O turn thyself to us again.
2 **Thou** hast made the earth to tremble;
thou hast broken it:
heal the breaches thereof;
for it shaketh.
3 **Thou** hast shewed thy people hard things:
thou hast made us to drink the wine of astonishment.
4 **Thou** hast given a banner to them that fear thee,
that it may be displayed because of the truth.
Selah.
5 **That thy beloved** may be delivered;
save with thy right hand,
and hear me.
6 **God** hath spoken in his holiness;
I will rejoice,
I will divide Shechem,
and mete out the valley of Succoth.
7 **Gilead** is mine,
and Manasseh is mine;
Ephraim also is the strength of mine head;
Judah is my lawgiver;
8 **Moab** is my washpot;
over Edom will I cast out my shoe:
Philistia, triumph thou because of me.
9 **Who** will bring me into the strong city?
who will lead me into Edom?
10 **Wilt not thou,** O God, which hadst cast us off?
and thou, O God, which didst not go out with our armies?
11 **Give** us help from trouble:
for vain is the help of man.
12 **Through God** we shall do valiantly:
for he it is that shall tread down our enemies.

61

To the chief Musician upon Neginah, A Psalm of David.

Hear my cry, O God;
attend unto my prayer.
2 **From the end of the earth** will I cry unto thee,
when my heart is overwhelmed:
lead me to the rock that is higher than I.
3 **For thou** hast been a shelter for me, and a strong tower from the enemy.
4 **I** will abide in thy tabernacle for ever:
I will trust in the covert of thy wings.
Selah.
5 **For thou,** O God, hast heard my vows:
thou hast given me the heritage of those that fear thy name.
6 **Thou** wilt prolong the king's life:
and his years as many generations.
7 **He** shall abide before God for ever:
O prepare mercy and truth,
which may preserve him.
8 **So** will I sing praise unto thy name for ever,
that I may daily perform my vows.

62

To the chief Musician, to Jeduthun, A Psalm of David.

Truly my soul waiteth upon God:
from him cometh my salvation.
2 **He only** is my rock and my salvation;
he is my defence;
I shall not be greatly moved.
3 **How long** will ye imagine mischief against a man?
ye shall be slain all of you:
as a bowing wall shall ye be, and as a tottering fence.
4 **They only** consult to cast him down from his excellency:
they delight in lies:
they bless with their mouth,
but they curse inwardly.
Selah.
5 **My soul, wait thou** only upon God;
for my expectation is from him.
6 **He only** is my rock and my salvation:
he is my defence;
I shall not be moved.
7 **In God** is my salvation and my glory:
the rock of my strength, and my refuge, is in God.
8 **Trust** in him at all times;
ye people, pour out your heart before him:
God is a refuge for us.
Selah.
9 **Surely men of low degree** are vanity,
and men of high degree are a lie:
to be laid in the balance,
they are altogether lighter than vanity.
10 **Trust not** in oppression,
and become not vain in robbery:
if riches increase,
set not your heart upon them.
11 **God** hath spoken once;
twice have I heard this;
that power belongeth unto God.
12 **Also unto thee,** O Lord, belongeth mercy:
for thou renderest to every man according to his work.

63

A Psalm of David, when he was in the wilderness of Judah.

O God, thou art my God;
early will I seek thee:
my soul thirsteth for thee,
my flesh longeth for thee in a dry and thirsty land,
where no water is;
2 To see thy power and thy glory,
so as I have seen thee in the sanctuary.
3 **Because thy lovingkindness** is better than life,
my lips shall praise thee.
4 **Thus** will I bless thee
while I live:
I will lift up my hands in thy name.
5 **My soul** shall be satisfied as with marrow and fatness;
and my mouth shall praise thee with joyful lips:
6 **When I** remember thee upon my bed,
and meditate on thee in the night watches.
7 **Because thou** hast been my help,
therefore in the shadow of thy wings will I rejoice.
8 **My soul** followeth hard after thee:
thy right hand upholdeth me.
9 **But those that seek my soul**, {to destroy it}, shall go into the lower parts of the earth.
10 **They** shall fall by the sword:
they shall be a portion for foxes.
11 **But the king** shall rejoice in God;
every one that sweareth by him shall glory:
but the mouth of them that speak lies shall be stopped.

64

To the chief Musician, A Psalm of David.

Hear my voice, O God, in my prayer:
preserve my life from fear of the enemy.
2 **Hide** me from the secret counsel of the wicked; from the insurrection of the workers of iniquity:
3 **Who** whet their tongue like a sword,
and bend their bows
to shoot their arrows, even bitter words:
4 **That they** may shoot in secret at the perfect:
suddenly do they shoot at him,
and fear not.
5 **They** encourage themselves in an evil matter:
they commune of laying snares privily;
they say,
Who shall see them?
6 **They** search out iniquities;
they accomplish a diligent search:
both the inward thought of every one of them, and the heart, is deep.
7 **But God** shall shoot at them with an arrow;
suddenly shall they be wounded.
8 **So they** shall make their own tongue to fall upon themselves:
all that see them shall flee away.
9 **And all men** shall fear,
and shall declare the work of God;
for they shall wisely consider of his doing.
10 **The righteous** shall be glad in the LORD,
and shall trust in him;
and all the upright in heart shall glory.

65

To the chief Musician, A Psalm and Song of David.

Praise waiteth for thee, O God, in Sion:
and unto thee shall the vow be performed.
2 **O thou that hearest prayer,** unto thee shall all flesh come.
3 **Iniquities** prevail against me:
as for our transgressions, thou shalt purge them away.
4 **Blessed** is the man whom thou choosest, and causest to approach unto thee,
that he may dwell in thy courts:
we shall be satisfied with the goodness of thy house, even of thy holy temple.
5 **By terrible things in righteousness** wilt thou answer us, O God of our salvation;
who art the confidence of all the ends of the earth, and of them that are afar off upon the sea:
6 **Which by his strength** setteth fast the mountains;
being girded with power:
7 **Which** stilleth the noise of the seas, the noise of their waves, and the tumult of the people.
8 **They also that dwell in the uttermost parts** are afraid at thy tokens:
thou makest the outgoings of the morning and evening to rejoice.
9 **Thou** visitest the earth,
and waterest it:
thou greatly enrichest it with the river of God,
which is full of water:
thou preparest them corn,
when thou hast so provided for it.
10 **Thou** waterest the ridges thereof abundantly:
thou settlest the furrows thereof:
thou makest it soft with showers:
thou blessest the springing thereof.
11 **Thou** crownest the year with thy goodness;
and thy paths drop fatness.
12 **They** drop upon the pastures of the wilderness:
and the little hills rejoice on every side.
13 **The pastures** are clothed with flocks;
the valleys also are covered over with corn;
they shout for joy,
they also sing.

66

To the chief Musician, A Song or Psalm.

Make a joyful noise unto God, all ye lands:
2 **Sing forth** the honour of his name:
make his praise glorious.
3 **Say** unto God,
How terrible art thou in thy works!
through the greatness of thy power shall thine enemies submit themselves unto thee.
4 **All the earth** shall worship thee,
and shall sing unto thee;
they shall sing to thy name.
Selah.
5 **Come and see** the works of God:
he is terrible in his doing toward the children of men.
6 **He** turned the sea into dry land:
they went through the flood on foot:
there did we rejoice in him.
7 **He** ruleth by his power for ever;
his eyes behold the nations:
let not the rebellious exalt themselves.
Selah.
8 **O bless** our God, ye people,
and make the voice of his praise to be heard:
9 **Which** holdeth our soul in life,

and suffereth not our feet to be moved.
10 **For thou,** O God, hast proved us:
thou hast tried us,
as silver is tried.
11 **Thou** broughtest us into the net;
thou laidst affliction upon our loins.
12 **Thou** hast caused men to ride over our heads;
we went through fire and through water:
but thou broughtest us out into a wealthy place.
13 **I** will go into thy house with burnt offerings:
I will pay thee my vows,
14 **Which my lips** have uttered,
and my mouth hath spoken,
when I was in trouble.
15 **I** will offer unto thee burnt sacrifices of fatlings, with the incense of rams;
I will offer bullocks with goats.
Selah.
16 **Come and hear,** all ye that fear God,
and I will declare
what he hath done for my soul.
17 **I** cried unto him with my mouth,
and he was extolled with my tongue.
18 **If I** regard iniquity in my heart,
the Lord will not hear me:
19 **But verily God** hath heard me;
he hath attended to the voice of my prayer.
20 **Blessed** be God,
which hath not turned away my prayer, nor his mercy from me.

67

To the chief Musician on Neginoth, A Psalm or Song.

God be merciful unto us,
and bless us;
and cause his face to shine upon us;
Selah.
2 **That thy way** may be known upon earth, thy saving health among all nations.
3 **Let the people** praise thee, O God;
let all the people praise thee.
4 **O let the nations** be glad and sing for joy:
for thou shalt judge the people righteously,
and govern the nations upon earth.
Selah.
5 **Let the people** praise thee, O God;
let all the people praise thee.
6 **Then** shall the earth yield her increase;
and God, even our own God, shall bless us.
7 **God** shall bless us;
and all the ends of the earth shall fear him.

68

To the chief Musician, A Psalm or Song of David.

Let God arise,
let his enemies be scattered:
let them also that hate him flee before him.
2 **As smoke** is driven away,
so drive them away:
as wax melteth before the fire,
so let the wicked perish at the presence of God.
3 **But let the righteous** be glad;
let them rejoice before God:
yea, let them exceedingly rejoice.
4 **Sing** unto God,
sing praises to his name:
extol him that rideth upon the heavens by his name Jah,
and rejoice before him.
5 **A father of the fatherless, and a judge of the widows,** is God in his holy habitation.
6 **God** setteth the solitary in families:
he bringeth out those which are bound with chains:
but the rebellious dwell in a dry land.
7 **O God, when thou** wentest forth before thy people,
when thou didst march through the wilderness;
Selah:
8 **The earth** shook,
the heavens also dropped at the presence of God:
even Sinai itself was moved at the presence of God, the God of Israel.
9 **Thou,** O God, didst send a plentiful rain,
whereby thou didst confirm thine inheritance,
when it was weary.
10 **Thy congregation** hath dwelt therein:
thou, O God, hast prepared of thy goodness for the poor.
11 **The Lord** gave the word:
great was the company of those that published it.
12 **Kings of armies** did flee apace:
and she that tarried at home divided the spoil.
13 **Though ye** have lien among the pots,
yet shall ye be as the wings of a dove covered with silver, and her feathers with yellow gold.
14 **When the Almighty** scattered kings in it,
it was white as snow in Salmon.
15 **The hill of God** is as the hill of Bashan; an high hill as the hill of Bashan.
16 **Why** leap ye, ye high hills?
this is the hill which God desireth to dwell in;
yea, the LORD will dwell in it for ever.
17 **The chariots of God** are twenty thousand, even thousands of angels:
the Lord is among them, as in Sinai, in the holy place.
18 **Thou** hast ascended on high,
thou hast led captivity captive:
thou hast received gifts for men; yea, for the rebellious also,
that the LORD God might dwell among them.
19 **Blessed** be the Lord,
who daily loadeth us with benefits, even the God of our salvation.
Selah.
20 **He that is our God** is the God of salvation;
and unto GOD the Lord belong the issues from death.
21 **But God** shall wound the head of his enemies, and the hairy scalp of such an one as goeth on still in his trespasses.
22 **The Lord** said,
I will bring again from Bashan,
I will bring my people again from the depths of the sea:
23 **That thy foot** may be dipped in the blood of thine enemies, and the tongue of thy dogs in the same.
24 **They** have seen thy goings, O God; even the goings of my God, my King, in the sanctuary.
25 **The singers** went before,
the players on instruments followed after;
among them were the damsels playing with timbrels.

26 **Bless ye** God in the congregations, even the Lord, from the fountain of Israel.
27 **There** is little Benjamin with their ruler, the princes of Judah and their council, the princes of Zebulun, and the princes of Naphtali.
28 **Thy God** hath commanded thy strength:
strengthen, O God, that which thou hast wrought for us.
29 **Because of thy temple at Jerusalem** shall kings bring presents unto thee.
30 **Rebuke** the company of spearmen, the multitude of the bulls, with the calves of the people,
till every one submit himself with pieces of silver:
scatter thou the people that delight in war.
31 **Princes** shall come out of Egypt;
Ethiopia shall soon stretch out her hands unto God.
32 **Sing** unto God, ye kingdoms of the earth;
O sing praises unto the Lord;
Selah:
33 To him that rideth upon the heavens of heavens,
which were of old;
lo,
he doth send out his voice, and that a mighty voice.
34 **Ascribe ye** strength unto God:
his excellency is over Israel,
and his strength is in the clouds.
35 **O God, thou** art terrible out of thy holy places:
the God of Israel is he that giveth strength and power unto his people.
Blessed be God.

69 *To the chief Musician upon Shoshannim, A Psalm of David.*

Save me, O God;
for the waters are come in unto my soul.
2 **I** sink in deep mire,
where there is no standing:
I am come into deep waters,
where the floods overflow me.
3 **I** am weary of my crying:
my throat is dried:
mine eyes fail
while I wait for my God.
4 **They that hate me without a cause** are more than the hairs of mine head:
they that would destroy me, {being mine enemies wrongfully}, are mighty:
then I restored that which I took not away.
5 **O God, thou** knowest my foolishness;
and my sins are not hid from thee.
6 **Let not them that wait on thee,** O Lord GOD of hosts, be ashamed for my sake:
let not those that seek thee be confounded for my sake, O God of Israel.
7 **Because for thy sake** I have borne reproach;
shame hath covered my face.
8 **I** am become a stranger unto my brethren, and an alien unto my mother's children.
9 **For the zeal of thine house** hath eaten me up;
and the reproaches of them that reproached thee are fallen upon me.
10 **When I** wept,
and chastened my soul with fasting,
that was to my reproach.
11 **I** made sackcloth also my garment;
and I became a proverb to them.
12 **They that sit in the gate** speak against me;
and I was the song of the drunkards.
13 **But as for me,** my prayer is unto thee, O LORD, in an acceptable time:
O God, in the multitude of thy mercy hear me, in the truth of thy salvation.
14 **Deliver** me out of the mire,
and let me not sink:
let me be delivered from them that hate me, and out of the deep waters.
15 **Let not the waterflood** overflow me,
neither let the deep swallow me up,
and let not the pit shut her mouth upon me.
16 **Hear** me, O LORD;
for thy lovingkindness is good:
turn unto me according to the multitude of thy tender mercies.
17 **And hide not** thy face from thy servant;
for I am in trouble:
hear me speedily.
18 **Draw nigh** unto my soul,
and redeem it:
deliver me because of mine enemies.
19 **Thou** hast known my reproach, and my shame, and my dishonour:
mine adversaries are all before thee.
20 **Reproach** hath broken my heart;
and I am full of heaviness:
and I looked for some to take pity, {but there was none}; and for comforters, {but I found none}.
21 **They** gave me also gall for my meat;
and in my thirst they gave me vinegar to drink.
22 **Let their table** become a snare before them:
and that which should have been for their welfare, let it become a trap.
23 **Let their eyes** be darkened,
that they see not;
and make their loins continually to shake.
24 **Pour out** thine indignation upon them,
and let thy wrathful anger take hold of them.
25 **Let their habitation** be desolate;
and let none dwell in their tents.
26 **For they** persecute him whom thou hast smitten;
and they talk to the grief of those whom thou hast wounded.
27 **Add** iniquity unto their iniquity:
and let them not come into thy righteousness.
28 **Let them** be blotted out of the book of the living,
and not be written with the righteous.
29 **But I** am poor and sorrowful:
let thy salvation, O God, set me up on high.
30 **I** will praise the name of God with a song,
and will magnify him with thanksgiving.

[31] **This** also shall please the LORD better than an ox or bullock that hath horns and hoofs.
[32] **The humble** shall see this,
and be glad:
and your heart shall live that seek God.
[33] **For the LORD** heareth the poor,
and despiseth not his prisoners.
[34] **Let the heaven and earth** praise him, the seas, and every thing that moveth therein.
[35] **For God** will save Zion,
and will build the cities of Judah:
that they may dwell there,
and have it in possession.
[36] **The seed also of his servants** shall inherit it:
and they that love his name shall dwell therein.

70

To the chief Musician, A Psalm of David, to bring to remembrance.

Make haste, O God, to deliver me;
make haste to help me, O LORD.
[2] **Let them** be ashamed and confounded that seek after my soul:
let them be turned backward,
and put to confusion,
that desire my hurt.
[3] **Let them** be turned back for a reward of their shame that say,
Aha, aha.
[4] **Let all those that seek thee** rejoice and be glad in thee:
and let such as love thy salvation say continually,
Let God be magnified.
[5] **But I** am poor and needy:
make haste unto me, O God:
thou art my help and my deliverer;
O LORD, make no tarrying.

71

In thee, O LORD, do I put my trust:
let me never be put to confusion.
[2] **Deliver** me in thy righteousness,
and cause me to escape:
incline thine ear unto me,
and save me.
[3] **Be thou** my strong habitation,
whereunto I may continually resort:
thou hast given commandment to save me;
for thou art my rock and my fortress.
[4] **Deliver** me, O my God, out of the hand of the wicked, out of the hand of the unrighteous and cruel man.
[5] **For thou** art my hope, O Lord GOD:
thou art my trust from my youth.
[6] **By thee** have I been holden up from the womb:
thou art he that took me out of my mother's bowels:
my praise shall be continually of thee.
[7] **I** am as a wonder unto many;
but thou art my strong refuge.
[8] **Let my mouth** be filled with thy praise and with thy honour all the day.
[9] **Cast me not off** in the time of old age;
forsake me not
when my strength faileth.
[10] **For mine enemies** speak against me;
and they that lay wait for my soul take counsel together,
[11] Saying,
God hath forsaken him:
persecute and take him;
for there is none to deliver him.
[12] **O God, be not** far from me:
O my God, make haste for my help.
[13] **Let them** be confounded and consumed that are adversaries to my soul;
let them be covered with reproach and dishonour that seek my hurt.
[14] **But I** will hope continually,
and will yet praise thee more and more.
[15] **My mouth** shall shew forth thy righteousness and thy salvation all the day;
for I know not the numbers thereof.
[16] **I** will go in the strength of the Lord GOD:
I will make mention of thy righteousness, even of thine only.
[17] **O God, thou** hast taught me from my youth:
and hitherto have I declared thy wondrous works.
[18] **Now also {when I am old and greyheaded}**, O God, forsake me not;
until I have shewed thy strength unto this generation, and thy power to every one that is to come.
[19] **Thy righteousness** also, O God, is very high,
who hast done great things:
O God, who is like unto thee!
[20] **Thou**, {which hast shewed me great and sore troubles}, shalt quicken me again,
and shalt bring me up again from the depths of the earth.
[21] **Thou** shalt increase my greatness,
and comfort me on every side.
[22] **I** will also praise thee with the psaltery, even thy truth, O my God:
unto thee will I sing with the harp, O thou Holy One of Israel.
[23] **My lips** shall greatly rejoice
when I sing unto thee;
and my soul, which thou hast redeemed.
[24] **My tongue** also shall talk of thy righteousness all the day long:
for they are confounded,
for they are brought unto shame,
that seek my hurt.

72

A Psalm for Solomon.

Give the king thy judgments, O God, and thy righteousness unto the king's son.
[2] **He** shall judge thy people with righteousness, and thy poor with judgment.
[3] **The mountains** shall bring peace to the people, and the little hills, by righteousness.
[4] **He** shall judge the poor of the people,
he shall save the children of the needy,
and shall break in pieces the oppressor.
[5] **They** shall fear thee
as long as the sun and moon endure, throughout all generations.
[6] **He** shall come down like rain upon the mown grass: as showers that water the earth.
[7] **In his days** shall the righteous flourish; and abundance of peace
so long as the moon endureth.
[8] **He** shall have dominion also from sea to sea, and from the river unto the ends of the earth.
[9] **They that dwell in the wilderness** shall bow before him;
and his enemies shall lick the dust.

10 **The kings of Tarshish and of the isles** shall bring presents:
the kings of Sheba and Seba shall offer gifts.
11 **Yea, all kings** shall fall down before him:
all nations shall serve him.
12 **For he** shall deliver the needy
when he crieth; the poor also, and him that hath no helper.
13 **He** shall spare the poor and needy,
and shall save the souls of the needy.
14 **He** shall redeem their soul from deceit and violence:
and precious shall their blood be in his sight.
15 **And he** shall live,
and to him shall be given of the gold of Sheba:
prayer also shall be made for him continually;
and daily shall he be praised.
16 **There** shall be an handful of corn in the earth upon the top of the mountains;
the fruit thereof shall shake like Lebanon:
and they of the city shall flourish like grass of the earth.
17 **His name** shall endure for ever:
his name shall be continued as long as the sun:
and men shall be blessed in him:
all nations shall call him blessed.
18 **Blessed** be the LORD God, the God of Israel,
who only doeth wondrous things.
19 **And blessed** be his glorious name for ever:
and let the whole earth be filled with his glory;
Amen, and Amen.
20 **The prayers of David the son of Jesse** are ended.

73

A Psalm of Asaph.

Truly God is good to Israel,
even to such as are of a clean heart.
2 **But as for me,** my feet were almost gone;
my steps had well nigh slipped.
3 **For I** was envious at the foolish,
when I saw the prosperity of the wicked.
4 **For there** are no bands in their death:
but their strength is firm.
5 **They** are not in trouble as other men;
neither are they plagued like other men.
6 **Therefore pride** compasseth them about as a chain;
violence covereth them as a garment.
7 **Their eyes** stand out with fatness:
they have more than heart could wish.
8 **They** are corrupt,
and speak wickedly concerning oppression:
they speak loftily.
9 **They** set their mouth against the heavens,
and their tongue walketh through the earth.
10 **Therefore his people** return hither:
and waters of a full cup are wrung out to them.
11 **And they** say,
How doth God know?
and is there knowledge in the most High?
12 **Behold,**
these are the ungodly,
who prosper in the world;
they increase in riches.
13 **Verily I** have cleansed my heart in vain,
and washed my hands in innocency.
14 **For all the day long** have I been plagued,
and chastened every morning.
15 **If I** say,
I will speak thus;
behold,
I should offend against the generation of thy children.
16 **When I** thought to know this,
it was too painful for me;
17 **Until I** went into the sanctuary of God;
then understood I their end.
18 **Surely thou** didst set them in slippery places:
thou castedst them down into destruction.
19 **How** are they brought into desolation, as in a moment!
they are utterly consumed with terrors.
20 **As a dream when one awaketh;**
so, O Lord, {when thou awakest},
thou shalt despise their image.
21 **Thus my heart** was grieved,
and I was pricked in my reins.
22 **So foolish** was I, and ignorant:
I was as a beast before thee.
23 **Nevertheless I** am continually with thee:
thou hast holden me by my right hand.
24 **Thou** shalt guide me with thy counsel,
and afterward receive me to glory.
25 **Whom** have I in heaven but thee?
and there is none upon earth that I desire beside thee.
26 **My flesh and my heart** faileth:
but God is the strength of my heart, and my portion for ever.
27 **For, {lo}, they** that are far from thee shall perish:
thou hast destroyed all them that go a whoring from thee.
28 **But it is good for me** to draw near to God:
I have put my trust in the Lord GOD,
that I may declare all thy works.

74

Maschil of Asaph.

O God, why hast thou cast us off for ever?
why doth thine anger smoke against the sheep of thy pasture?
2 **Remember** thy congregation,
which thou hast purchased of old;
the rod of thine inheritance,
which thou hast redeemed;
this mount Zion, wherein thou hast dwelt.
3 **Lift up** thy feet unto the perpetual desolations; even all that the enemy hath done wickedly in the sanctuary.
4 **Thine enemies** roar in the midst of thy congregations;
they set up their ensigns for signs.
5 **A man** was famous according as he had lifted up axes upon the thick trees.
6 **But now they** break down the carved work thereof at once with axes and hammers.
7 **They** have cast fire into thy sanctuary,
they have defiled by casting down the dwelling place of thy name to the ground.
8 **They** said in their hearts,
Let us destroy them together:

they have burned up all the synagogues of God in the land.

9 **We** see not our signs:
there is no more any prophet:
neither is there among us any that knoweth how long.

10 **O God, how long** shall the adversary reproach?
shall the enemy blaspheme thy name for ever?

11 **Why** withdrawest thou thy hand, even thy right hand?
pluck it out of thy bosom.

12 **For God** is my King of old,
working salvation in the midst of the earth.

13 **Thou** didst divide the sea by thy strength:
thou brakest the heads of the dragons in the waters.

14 **Thou** brakest the heads of leviathan in pieces,
and gavest him to be meat to the people inhabiting the wilderness.

15 **Thou** didst cleave the fountain and the flood:
thou driedst up mighty rivers.

16 **The day** is thine,
the night also is thine:
thou hast prepared the light and the sun.

17 **Thou** hast set all the borders of the earth:
thou hast made summer and winter.

18 **Remember** this,
that the enemy hath reproached, O LORD,
and that the foolish people have blasphemed thy name.

19 **O deliver not** the soul of thy turtledove unto the multitude of the wicked:
forget not the congregation of thy poor for ever.

20 **Have** respect unto the covenant:
for the dark places of the earth are full of the habitations of cruelty.

21 **O let not the oppressed** return ashamed:
let the poor and needy praise thy name.

22 **Arise,** O God,
plead thine own cause:
remember
how the foolish man reproacheth thee daily.

23 **Forget not** the voice of thine enemies:
the tumult of those that rise up against thee increaseth continually.

75

To the chief Musician, Altaschith, A Psalm or Song of Asaph.

Unto thee, O God, do we give thanks,
unto thee do we give thanks:
for that thy name is near
thy wondrous works declare.

2 **When I** shall receive the congregation
I will judge uprightly.

3 **The earth and all the inhabitants thereof** are dissolved:
I bear up the pillars of it.
Selah.

4 **I** said unto the fools, {Deal not foolishly}: and to the wicked, {Lift not up the horn}:

5 **Lift not up** your horn on high:
speak not with a stiff neck.

6 **For promotion** cometh neither from the east, nor from the west, nor from the south.

7 **But God** is the judge:
he putteth down one,
and setteth up another.

8 **For in the hand of the LORD** there is a cup,
and the wine is red;
it is full of mixture;
and he poureth out of the same:
but the dregs thereof, all the wicked of the earth shall wring them out,
and drink them.

9 **But I** will declare for ever;
I will sing praises to the God of Jacob.

10 **All the horns of the wicked** also will I cut off;
but the horns of the righteous shall be exalted.

76

To the chief Musician on Neginoth, A Psalm or Song of Asaph.

In Judah is God known:
his name is great in Israel.

2 **In Salem** also is his tabernacle, and his dwelling place in Zion.

3 **There** brake he the arrows of the bow, the shield, and the sword, and the battle.
Selah.

4 **Thou** art more glorious and excellent than the mountains of prey.

5 **The stouthearted** are spoiled,
they have slept their sleep:
and none of the men of might have found their hands.

6 **At thy rebuke,** O God of Jacob, both the chariot and horse are cast into a dead sleep.

7 **Thou, even thou,** art to be feared:
and who may stand in thy sight
when once thou art angry?

8 **Thou** didst cause judgment to be heard from heaven;
the earth feared,
and was still,

9 **When God** arose to judgment,
to save all the meek of the earth.
Selah.

10 **Surely the wrath of man** shall praise thee:
the remainder of wrath shalt thou restrain.

11 **Vow,**
and pay unto the LORD your God:
let all that be round about him bring presents unto him that ought to be feared.

12 **He** shall cut off the spirit of princes:
he is terrible to the kings of the earth.

77

To the chief Musician, to Jeduthun, A Psalm of Asaph.

I cried unto God with my voice, even unto God with my voice;
and he gave ear unto me.

2 **In the day of my trouble** I sought the Lord:
my sore ran in the night,
and ceased not:
my soul refused to be comforted.

3 **I** remembered God,
and was troubled:
I complained,
and my spirit was overwhelmed.
Selah.

4 **Thou** holdest mine eyes waking:
I am so troubled that I cannot speak.

5 **I** have considered the days of old, the years of ancient times.

6 **I** call to remembrance my song in the night:
I commune with mine own heart:
and my spirit made diligent search.

7 **Will the Lord** cast off for ever?
and will he be favourable no more?

8 **Is his mercy** clean gone for ever?
doth his promise fail for evermore?

9 **Hath God** forgotten to be gracious?
hath he in anger shut up his tender mercies?
Selah.

10 **And I** said,
This is my infirmity:
but I will remember the years of the right hand of the most High.

11 **I** will remember the works of the LORD:
surely I will remember thy wonders of old.

12 **I** will meditate also of all thy work,
and talk of thy doings.

13 **Thy way,** O God, is in the sanctuary:
who is so great a God as our God?

14 **Thou** art the God that doest wonders:
thou hast declared thy strength among the people.

15 **Thou** hast with thine arm redeemed thy people, the sons of Jacob and Joseph.
Selah.

16 **The waters** saw thee, O God,
the waters saw thee;
they were afraid:
the depths also were troubled.

17 **The clouds** poured out water:
the skies sent out a sound:
thine arrows also went abroad.

18 **The voice of thy thunder** was in the heaven:
the lightnings lightened the world:
the earth trembled and shook.

19 **Thy way** is in the sea, and thy path in the great waters,
and thy footsteps are not known.

20 **Thou** leddest thy people like a flock by the hand of Moses and Aaron.

78

Maschil of Asaph.

Give ear, O my people, to my law:
incline your ears to the words of my mouth.

2 **I** will open my mouth in a parable:
I will utter dark sayings of old:

3 **Which we** have heard and known,
and our fathers have told us.

4 **We** will not hide them from their children,
shewing to the generation to come the praises of the LORD, and his strength, and his wonderful works that he hath done.

5 **For he** established a testimony in Jacob,
and appointed a law in Israel,
which he commanded our fathers,
that they should make them known to their children:

6 **That the generation to come** might know them, even the children which should be born;
who should arise and declare them to their children:

7 **That they** might set their hope in God,
and not forget the works of God,
but keep his commandments:

8 **And** might not be as their fathers, a stubborn and rebellious generation; a generation that set not their heart aright, and whose spirit was not stedfast with God.

9 **The children of Ephraim**, {being armed}, {and carrying bows}, turned back in the day of battle.

10 **They** kept not the covenant of God,
and refused
to walk in his law;

11 **And** forgat his works, and his wonders that he had shewed them.

12 **Marvellous things** did he in the sight of their fathers, in the land of Egypt, in the field of Zoan.

13 **He** divided the sea,
and caused them to pass through;
and he made the waters to stand as an heap.

14 **In the daytime** also he led them with a cloud, and all the night with a light of fire.

15 **He** clave the rocks in the wilderness,
and gave them drink as out of the great depths.

16 **He** brought streams also out of the rock,
and caused waters to run down like rivers.

17 **And they** sinned yet more against him
by provoking the most High in the wilderness.

18 **And they** tempted God in their heart
by asking meat for their lust.

19 **Yea, they** spake against God;
they said,
Can God furnish a table in the wilderness?

20 **Behold,**
he smote the rock,
that the waters gushed out,
and the streams overflowed;
can he give bread also?
can he provide flesh for his people?

21 **Therefore the LORD** heard this,
and was wroth:
so a fire was kindled against Jacob,
and anger also came up against Israel;

22 **Because they** believed not in God,
and trusted not in his salvation:

23 **Though he** had commanded the clouds from above,
and opened the doors of heaven,

24 **And** had rained down manna upon them to eat,
and had given them of the corn of heaven.

25 **Man** did eat angels' food:
he sent them meat to the full.

26 **He** caused an east wind to blow in the heaven:
and by his power he brought in the south wind.

27 **He** rained flesh also upon them as dust, and feathered fowls like as the sand of the sea:

28 **And he** let it fall in the midst of their camp, round about their habitations.

29 **So they** did eat,
and were well filled:
for he gave them their own desire;

30 **They** were not estranged from their lust.
But while their meat was yet in their mouths,

31 **The wrath of God** came upon them,
and slew the fattest of them,
and smote down the chosen men of Israel.

32 **For all this** they sinned still,
and believed not for his wondrous works.

33 **Therefore their days** did he consume in vanity, and their years in trouble.

34 **When he** slew them,
then they sought him:

and they returned and enquired early after God.
35 **And they** remembered
that God was their rock, and the high God their redeemer.
36 **Nevertheless they** did flatter him with their mouth,
and they lied unto him with their tongues.
37 **For their heart** was not right with him,
neither were they stedfast in his covenant.
38 **But he**, {being full of compassion}, forgave their iniquity,
and destroyed them not:
yea, many a time turned he his anger away,
and did not stir up all his wrath.
39 **For he** remembered
that they were but flesh; a wind that passeth away, and cometh not again.
40 **How oft** did they provoke him in the wilderness,
and grieve him in the desert!
41 **Yea, they** turned back and tempted God,
and limited the Holy One of Israel.
42 **They** remembered not his hand, nor the day when he delivered them from the enemy.
43 **How he** had wrought his signs in Egypt, and his wonders in the field of Zoan.
44 **And** had turned their rivers into blood; and their floods,
that they could not drink.
45 **He** sent divers sorts of flies among them, {which devoured them}; and frogs, {which destroyed them}.
46 **He** gave also their increase unto the caterpiller, and their labour unto the locust.
47 **He** destroyed their vines with hail, and their sycomore trees with frost.
48 **He** gave up their cattle also to the hail, and their flocks to hot thunderbolts.
49 **He** cast upon them the fierceness of his anger, wrath, and indignation, and trouble,
by sending evil angels among them.
50 **He** made a way to his anger;
he spared not their soul from death,
but gave their life over to the pestilence;
51 **And** smote all the firstborn in Egypt; the chief of their strength in the tabernacles of Ham:
52 **But** made his own people to go forth like sheep,
and guided them in the wilderness like a flock.
53 **And he** led them on safely,
so that they feared not:
but the sea overwhelmed their enemies.
54 **And he** brought them to the border of his sanctuary, even to this mountain,
which his right hand had purchased.
55 **He** cast out the heathen also before them,
and divided them an inheritance by line,
and made the tribes of Israel to dwell in their tents.
56 **Yet they** tempted and provoked the most high God,
and kept not his testimonies:
57 **But** turned back,
and dealt unfaithfully like their fathers:
they were turned aside like a deceitful bow.
58 **For they** provoked him to anger with their high places,
and moved him to jealousy with their graven images.
59 **When God** heard this,
he was wroth,
and greatly abhorred Israel:
60 **So that he** forsook the tabernacle of Shiloh, the tent which he placed among men;
61 **And** delivered his strength into captivity, and his glory into the enemy's hand.
62 **He** gave his people over also unto the sword;
and was wroth with his inheritance.
63 **The fire** consumed their young men;
and their maidens were not given to marriage.
64 **Their priests** fell by the sword;
and their widows made no lamentation.
65 **Then the Lord** awaked as one out of sleep, and like a mighty man that shouteth by reason of wine.
66 **And he** smote his enemies in the hinder parts:
he put them to a perpetual reproach.
67 **Moreover he** refused the tabernacle of Joseph,
and chose not the tribe of Ephraim:
68 **But** chose the tribe of Judah, the mount Zion which he loved.
69 **And he** built his sanctuary like high palaces, like the earth which he hath established for ever.
70 **He** chose David also his servant,
and took him from the sheepfolds:
71 **From following the ewes great with young** he brought him to feed Jacob his people, and Israel his inheritance.
72 **So he** fed them according to the integrity of his heart;
and guided them by the skilfulness of his hands.

79

A Psalm of Asaph.

O god, the heathen are come into thine inheritance;
thy holy temple have they defiled;
they have laid Jerusalem on heaps.
2 **The dead bodies of thy servants** have they given to be meat unto the fowls of the heaven, the flesh of thy saints unto the beasts of the earth.
3 **Their blood** have they shed like water round about Jerusalem;
and there was none to bury them.
4 **We** are become a reproach to our neighbours, a scorn and derision to them that are round about us.
5 **How long,** LORD?
wilt thou be angry for ever?
shall thy jealousy burn like fire?
6 **Pour out** thy wrath upon the heathen that have not known thee, and upon the kingdoms that have not called upon thy name.
7 **For they** have devoured Jacob,
and laid waste his dwelling place.
8 **O remember not** against us former iniquities:
let thy tender mercies speedily prevent us:
for we are brought very low.
9 **Help** us, O God of our salvation, for the glory of thy name:
and deliver us,
and purge away our sins, for thy name's sake.

10 **Wherefore** should the heathen say,
Where is their God?
let him be known among the heathen in our sight by the revenging of the blood of thy servants which is shed.

11 **Let the sighing of the prisoner** come before thee;
according to the greatness of thy power preserve thou those that are appointed to die;

12 **And render** unto our neighbours sevenfold into their bosom their reproach,
wherewith they have reproached thee, O Lord.

13 **So we thy people and sheep of thy pasture** will give thee thanks for ever:
we will shew forth thy praise to all generations.

80

To the chief Musician upon Shoshannimeduth, A Psalm of Asaph.

Give ear, O Shepherd of Israel, thou that leadest Joseph like a flock;
thou that dwellest between the cherubims, shine forth.

2 **Before Ephraim and Benjamin and Manasseh** stir up thy strength,
and come and save us.

3 **Turn** us again, O God,
and cause thy face to shine;
and we shall be saved.

4 **O LORD God of hosts, how long** wilt thou be angry against the prayer of thy people?

5 **Thou** feedest them with the bread of tears;
and givest them tears to drink in great measure.

6 **Thou** makest us a strife unto our neighbours:
and our enemies laugh among themselves.

7 **Turn** us again, O God of hosts,
and cause thy face to shine;
and we shall be saved.

8 **Thou** hast brought a vine out of Egypt:
thou hast cast out the heathen,
and planted it.

9 **Thou** preparedst room before it,
and didst cause it to take deep root,
and it filled the land.

10 **The hills** were covered with the shadow of it,
and the boughs thereof were like the goodly cedars.

11 **She** sent out her boughs unto the sea, and her branches unto the river.

12 **Why** hast thou then broken down her hedges,
so that all they which pass by the way do pluck her?

13 **The boar out of the wood** doth waste it,
and the wild beast of the field doth devour it.

14 **Return**, {we beseech thee}, O God of hosts:
look down from heaven,
and behold,
and visit this vine;

15 And the vineyard which thy right hand hath planted, and the branch that thou madest strong for thyself.

16 **It** is burned with fire,
it is cut down:
they perish at the rebuke of thy countenance.

17 **Let thy hand** be upon the man of thy right hand, upon the son of man whom thou madest strong for thyself.

18 **So** will not we go back from thee:
quicken us,
and we will call upon thy name.

19 **Turn** us again, O LORD God of hosts,
cause thy face to shine;
and we shall be saved.

81

To the chief Musician upon Gittith, A Psalm of Asaph.

Sing aloud unto God our strength:
make a joyful noise unto the God of Jacob.

2 **Take** a psalm,
and bring hither the timbrel, the pleasant harp with the psaltery.

3 **Blow up** the trumpet in the new moon, in the time appointed, on our solemn feast day.

4 **For this** was a statute for Israel, and a law of the God of Jacob.

5 **This** he ordained in Joseph for a testimony,
when he went out through the land of Egypt:
where I heard a language that I understood not.

6 **I** removed his shoulder from the burden:
his hands were delivered from the pots.

7 **Thou** calledst in trouble,
and I delivered thee;
I answered thee in the secret place of thunder:
I proved thee at the waters of Meribah.
Selah.

8 **Hear,** O my people,
and I will testify unto thee:
O Israel, if thou wilt hearken unto me;

9 **There** shall no strange god be in thee;
neither shalt thou worship any strange god.

10 **I** am the LORD thy God,
which brought thee out of the land of Egypt:
open thy mouth wide,
and I will fill it.

11 **But my people** would not hearken to my voice;
and Israel would none of me.

12 **So I** gave them up unto their own hearts' lust:
and they walked in their own counsels.

13 **Oh that my people** had hearkened unto me,
and Israel had walked in my ways!

14 **I** should soon have subdued their enemies,
and turned my hand against their adversaries.

15 **The haters of the LORD** should have submitted themselves unto him:
but their time should have endured for ever.

16 **He** should have fed them also with the finest of the wheat:
and with honey out of the rock should I have satisfied thee.

82

A Psalm of Asaph.

God standeth in the congregation of the mighty;
he judgeth among the gods.

2 **How long** will ye judge unjustly,
and accept the persons of the wicked?
Selah.

3 **Defend** the poor and fatherless:
do justice to the afflicted and needy.

4 **Deliver** the poor and needy:

rid them out of the hand of the wicked.

5 **They** know not,
neither will they understand;
they walk on in darkness:
all the foundations of the earth are out of course.

6 **I** have said,
Ye are gods;
and all of you are children of the most High.

7 **But ye** shall die like men,
and fall like one of the princes.

8 **Arise,** O God,
judge the earth:
for thou shalt inherit all nations.

83

A Song or Psalm of Asaph.

Keep not thou silence, O God:
hold not thy peace,
and be not still, O God.

2 **For, {lo}, thine enemies** make a tumult:
and they that hate thee have lifted up the head.

3 **They** have taken crafty counsel against thy people,
and consulted against thy hidden ones.

4 **They** have said,
Come,
and let us cut them off from being a nation;
that the name of Israel may be no more in remembrance.

5 **For they** have consulted together with one consent:
they are confederate against thee:
6 **The tabernacles of Edom, and the Ishmaelites; of Moab, and the Hagarenes;**
7 **Gebal, and Ammon, and Amalek; the Philistines with the inhabitants of Tyre;**
8 **Assur** also is joined with them:
they have holpen the children of Lot.
Selah.

9 **Do** unto them as unto the Midianites; as to Sisera, as to Jabin, at the brook of Kison:
10 **Which** perished at Endor:
they became as dung for the earth.

11 **Make** their nobles like Oreb, and like Zeeb: yea, all their princes as Zebah, and as Zalmunna:
12 **Who** said,
Let us take to ourselves the houses of God in possession.

13 **O my God, make** them like a wheel; as the stubble before the wind.

14 **As the fire** burneth a wood,
and as the flame setteth the mountains on fire;
15 **So persecute** them with thy tempest,
and make them afraid with thy storm.

16 **Fill** their faces with shame;
that they may seek thy name, O LORD.

17 **Let them** be confounded and troubled for ever;
yea, let them be put to shame,
and perish:
18 **That men** may know
that thou, {whose name alone is Jehovah}, art the most high over all the earth.

84

To the chief Musician upon Gittith, A Psalm for the sons of Korah.

How amiable are thy tabernacles, O LORD of hosts!

2 **My soul** longeth,
yea, even fainteth for the courts of the LORD:
my heart and my flesh crieth out for the living God.

3 **Yea, the sparrow** hath found an house, and the swallow a nest for herself,
where she may lay her young, even thine altars, O LORD of hosts, my King, and my God.

4 **Blessed** are they that dwell in thy house:
they will be still praising thee.
Selah.

5 **Blessed** is the man whose strength is in thee;
in whose heart are the ways of them.

6 **Who passing through the valley of Baca** make it a well;
the rain also filleth the pools.

7 **They** go from strength to strength,
every one of them in Zion appeareth before God.

8 **O LORD God of hosts,** hear my prayer:
give ear, O God of Jacob.
Selah.

9 **Behold,** O God our shield,
and look upon the face of thine anointed.

10 **For a day in thy courts** is better than a thousand.
I had rather be a doorkeeper in the house of my God,
than to dwell in the tents of wickedness.

11 **For the LORD God** is a sun and shield:
the LORD will give grace and glory:
no good thing will he withhold from them that walk uprightly.

12 **O LORD of hosts, blessed** is the man that trusteth in thee.

85

To the chief Musician, A Psalm for the sons of Korah.

LORD, thou hast been favourable unto thy land:
thou hast brought back the captivity of Jacob.

2 **Thou** hast forgiven the iniquity of thy people,
thou hast covered all their sin.
Selah.

3 **Thou** hast taken away all thy wrath:
thou hast turned thyself from the fierceness of thine anger.

4 **Turn** us, O God of our salvation,
and cause thine anger toward us to cease.

5 **Wilt thou** be angry with us for ever?
wilt thou draw out thine anger to all generations?

6 **Wilt thou** not revive us again:
that thy people may rejoice in thee?

7 **Shew** us thy mercy, O LORD,
and grant us thy salvation.

8 **I** will hear what God the LORD will speak:
for he will speak peace unto his people, and to his saints:
but let them not turn again to folly.

9 **Surely his salvation** is nigh them that fear him;
that glory may dwell in our land.

10 **Mercy and truth** are met together;
righteousness and peace have kissed each other.

11 **Truth** shall spring out of the earth;
and righteousness shall look down from heaven.

12 **Yea, the LORD** shall give that which is good;
and our land shall yield her increase.

13 **Righteousness** shall go before him;
and shall set us in the way of his steps.

86

A Prayer of David.

Bow down thine ear, O LORD,
hear me:
for I am poor and needy.

2 **Preserve** my soul;
for I am holy:
O thou my God, save thy servant that trusteth in thee.

3 **Be** merciful unto me, O Lord:
for I cry unto thee daily.

4 **Rejoice** the soul of thy servant:
for unto thee, O Lord, do I lift up my soul.

5 **For thou,** Lord, art good,
and ready to forgive; and plenteous in mercy unto all them that call upon thee.

6 **Give ear,** O LORD, unto my prayer;
and attend to the voice of my supplications.

7 **In the day of my trouble** I will call upon thee:
for thou wilt answer me.

8 **Among the gods** there is none like unto thee, O Lord;
neither are there any works like unto thy works.

9 **All nations whom thou hast made** shall come and worship before thee, O Lord;
and shall glorify thy name.

10 **For thou** art great,
and doest wondrous things:
thou art God alone.

11 **Teach** me thy way, O LORD;
I will walk in thy truth:
unite my heart to fear thy name.

12 **I** will praise thee, O Lord my God, with all my heart:
and I will glorify thy name for evermore.

13 **For great** is thy mercy toward me:
and thou hast delivered my soul from the lowest hell.

14 **O God, the proud** are risen against me,
and the assemblies of violent men have sought after my soul;
and have not set thee before them.

15 **But thou,** O Lord, art a God full of compassion, and gracious, long suffering, and plenteous in mercy and truth.

16 **O turn** unto me,
and have mercy upon me;
give thy strength unto thy servant,
and save the son of thine handmaid.

17 **Shew** me a token for good;
that they which hate me may see it,
and be ashamed:
because thou, LORD, hast holpen me,
and comforted me.

87

A Psalm or Song for the sons of Korah.

His foundation is in the holy mountains.

2 **The LORD** loveth the gates of Zion more than all the dwellings of Jacob.

3 **Glorious things** are spoken of thee, O city of God.
Selah.

4 **I** will make mention of Rahab and Babylon to them that know me:
behold Philistia, and Tyre, with Ethiopia;
this man was born there.

5 **And of Zion** it shall be said,
This and that man was born in her:
and the highest himself shall establish her.

6 **The LORD** shall count,
when he writeth up the people,
that this man was born there.
Selah.

7 **As well the singers as the players on instruments** shall be there:
all my springs are in thee.

88

A Song or Psalm for the sons of Korah, to the chief Musician upon Mahalath Leannoth, Maschil of Heman the Ezrahite.

O LORD God of my salvation, I have cried day and night before thee:

2 **Let my prayer** come before thee:
incline thine ear unto my cry;

3 **For my soul** is full of troubles:
and my life draweth nigh unto the grave.

4 **I** am counted with them that go down into the pit:
I am as a man that hath no strength:

5 Free among the dead, like the slain that lie in the grave,
whom thou rememberest no more:
and they are cut off from thy hand.

6 **Thou** hast laid me in the lowest pit, in darkness, in the deeps.

7 **Thy wrath** lieth hard upon me,
and thou hast afflicted me with all thy waves.
Selah.

8 **Thou** hast put away mine acquaintance far from me;
thou hast made me an abomination unto them:
I am shut up,
and I cannot come forth.

9 **Mine eye** mourneth by reason of affliction:
LORD, I have called daily upon thee,
I have stretched out my hands unto thee.

10 **Wilt thou** shew wonders to the dead?
shall the dead arise and praise thee?
Selah.

11 **Shall thy lovingkindness** be declared in the grave? or thy faithfulness in destruction?

12 **Shall thy wonders** be known in the dark? and thy righteousness in the land of forgetfulness?

13 **But unto thee** have I cried, O LORD;
and in the morning shall my prayer prevent thee.

14 **LORD, why** castest thou off my soul?
why hidest thou thy face from me?

15 **I** am afflicted and ready to die from my youth up:
while I suffer thy terrors
am distracted.

16 **Thy fierce wrath** goeth over me;
thy terrors have cut me off.

17 **They** came round about me daily like water;
they compassed me about together.

18 **Lover and friend** hast thou put far from me, and mine acquaintance into darkness.

89

Maschil of Ethan the Ezrahite.

I will sing of the mercies of the LORD for ever:
with my mouth will I make known thy faithfulness to all generations.

[2] **For I** have said,
Mercy shall be built up for ever:
thy faithfulness shalt thou establish in the very heavens.

[3] **I** have made a covenant with my chosen,
I have sworn unto David my servant,
[4] **Thy seed** will I establish for ever,
and build up thy throne to all generations.

Selah.

[5] **And the heavens** shall praise thy wonders, O LORD: thy faithfulness also in the congregation of the saints.

[6] **For who in the heaven** can be compared unto the LORD?
who among the sons of the mighty can be likened unto the LORD?

[7] **God** is greatly to be feared in the assembly of the saints,
and to be had in reverence of all them that are about him.

[8] **O LORD God of hosts, who** is a strong LORD like unto thee? or to thy faithfulness round about thee?

[9] **Thou** rulest the raging of the sea:
when the waves thereof arise,
thou stillest them.

[10] **Thou** hast broken Rahab in pieces, as one that is slain;
thou hast scattered thine enemies with thy strong arm.

[11] **The heavens** are thine,
the earth also is thine:
as for the world and the fulness thereof, thou hast founded them.

[12] **The north and the south** thou hast created them:
Tabor and Hermon shall rejoice in thy name.

[13] **Thou** hast a mighty arm:
strong is thy hand,
and high is thy right hand.

[14] **Justice and judgment** are the habitation of thy throne:
mercy and truth shall go before thy face.

[15] **Blessed** is the people that know the joyful sound:
they shall walk, O LORD, in the light of thy countenance.

[16] **In thy name** shall they rejoice all the day:
and in thy righteousness shall they be exalted.

[17] **For thou** art the glory of their strength:
and in thy favour our horn shall be exalted.

[18] **For the LORD** is our defence;
and the Holy One of Israel is our king.

[19] **Then thou** spakest in vision to thy holy one,
and saidst,
I have laid help upon one that is mighty;
I have exalted one chosen out of the people.

[20] **I** have found David my servant;
with my holy oil have I anointed him:

[21] **With whom** my hand shall be established:
mine arm also shall strengthen him.

[22] **The enemy** shall not exact upon him;
nor the son of wickedness afflict him.

[23] **And I** will beat down his foes before his face,
and plague them that hate him.

[24] **But my faithfulness and my mercy** shall be with him:
and in my name shall his horn be exalted.

[25] **I** will set his hand also in the sea, and his right hand in the rivers.

[26] **He** shall cry unto me,
Thou art my father, my God, and the rock of my salvation.

[27] **Also I** will make him my firstborn, higher than the kings of the earth.

[28] **My mercy** will I keep for him for evermore,
and my covenant shall stand fast with him.

[29] **His seed** also will I make to endure for ever, and his throne as the days of heaven.

[30] **If his children** forsake my law,
and walk not in my judgments;
[31] **If they** break my statutes,
and keep not my commandments;
[32] **Then** will I visit their transgression with the rod, and their iniquity with stripes.

[33] **Nevertheless my lovingkindness** will I not utterly take from him,
nor suffer my faithfulness to fail.

[34] **My covenant** will I not break,
nor alter the thing that is gone out of my lips.

[35] **Once** have I sworn by my holiness
that I will not lie unto David.

[36] **His seed** shall endure for ever, and his throne as the sun before me.

[37] **It** shall be established for ever as the moon, and as a faithful witness in heaven.

Selah.

[38] **But thou** hast cast off and abhorred,
thou hast been wroth with thine anointed.

[39] **Thou** hast made void the covenant of thy servant:
thou hast profaned his crown
by casting it to the ground.

[40] **Thou** hast broken down all his hedges;
thou hast brought his strong holds to ruin.

[41] **All that pass by the way** spoil him:
he is a reproach to his neighbours.

[42] **Thou** hast set up the right hand of his adversaries;
thou hast made all his enemies to rejoice.

[43] **Thou** hast also turned the edge of his sword,
and hast not made him to stand in the battle.

[44] **Thou** hast made his glory to cease,
and cast his throne down to the ground.

[45] **The days of his youth** hast thou shortened:
thou hast covered him with shame.

Selah.

[46] **How long,** LORD?
wilt thou hide thyself for ever?
shall thy wrath burn like fire?

[47] **Remember**
how short my time is:
wherefore hast thou made all men in vain?

[48] **What man** is he that liveth,
and shall not see death?
shall he deliver his soul from the hand of the grave?

Selah.

[49] **Lord, where** are thy former lovingkindnesses,
which thou swarest unto David in thy truth?

[50] **Remember,** Lord, the reproach of thy servants;

how I do bear in my bosom the
reproach of all the mighty people;
51 **Wherewith** thine enemies have
reproached, O LORD;
wherewith they have reproached
the footsteps of thine anointed.
52 **Blessed** be the LORD for
evermore.
Amen, and Amen.

90

A Prayer of Moses the man of God.

Lord, thou hast been our dwelling
place in all generations.
2 **Before the mountains** were
brought forth,
or ever thou hadst formed the
earth and the world,
**even from everlasting to
everlasting,** thou art God.
3 **Thou** turnest man to destruction;
and sayest,
Return, ye children of men.
4 **For a thousand years in thy sight**
are but as yesterday
when it is past, and as a watch in
the night.
5 **Thou** carriest them away as with a
flood;
they are as a sleep:
in the morning they are like grass
which groweth up.
6 **In the morning** it flourisheth,
and groweth up;
in the evening it is cut down,
and withereth.
7 **For we** are consumed by thine
anger,
and by thy wrath are we troubled.
8 **Thou** hast set our iniquities before
thee, our secret sins in the light of
thy countenance.
9 **For all our days** are passed away
in thy wrath:
we spend our years as a tale that is
told.
10 **The days of our years** are
threescore years and ten;
and if by reason of strength they
be fourscore years,
yet is their strength labour and
sorrow;
for it is soon cut off,
and we fly away.
11 **Who** knoweth the power of thine
anger?
even according to thy fear, so is
thy wrath.
12 **So teach** us to number our days,
that we may apply our hearts unto
wisdom.
13 **Return,** O LORD, how long?
and let it repent thee concerning
thy servants.
14 **O satisfy** us early with thy mercy;
that we may rejoice and be glad all
our days.
15 **Make** us glad according to the
days wherein thou hast afflicted
us, and the years wherein we have
seen evil.
16 **Let thy work** appear unto thy
servants, and thy glory unto their
children.
17 **And let the beauty of the LORD
our God** be upon us:
and establish thou the work of our
hands upon us;
yea, the work of our hands
establish thou it.

91

**He that dwelleth in the
secret place of the most
High** shall abide under the
shadow of the Almighty.
2 **I** will say of the LORD,
He is my refuge and my fortress: my
God;
in him will I trust.
3 **Surely he** shall deliver thee from
the snare of the fowler, and from
the noisome pestilence.
4 **He** shall cover thee with his
feathers,
and under his wings shalt thou
trust:
his truth shall be thy shield and
buckler.
5 **Thou** shalt not be afraid for the
terror by night; nor for the arrow
that flieth by day;
6 Nor for the pestilence that walketh
in darkness; nor for the
destruction that wasteth at
noonday.
7 **A thousand** shall fall at thy side,
and ten thousand at thy right
hand;
but it shall not come nigh thee.
8 **Only with thine eyes** shalt thou
behold and see the reward of the
wicked.
9 **Because thou** hast made the
LORD,
which is my refuge, even the most
High, thy habitation;
10 **There** shall no evil befall thee,
neither shall any plague come nigh
thy dwelling.
11 **For he** shall give his angels charge
over thee,
to keep thee in all thy ways.
12 **They** shall bear thee up in their
hands,
lest thou dash thy foot against a
stone.
13 **Thou** shalt tread upon the lion
and adder:
the young lion and the dragon
shalt thou trample under feet.
14 **Because he** hath set his love upon
me,
therefore will I deliver him:
I will set him on high,
because he hath known my name.
15 **He** shall call upon me,
and I will answer him:
I will be with him in trouble;
I will deliver him,
and honour him.
16 **With long life** will I satisfy him,
and shew him my salvation.

92

A Psalm or Song for the sabbath day.

It is a good thing to give thanks
unto the LORD,
and to sing praises unto thy name,
O Most High:
2 To shew forth thy lovingkindness
in the morning, and thy
faithfulness every night,
3 Upon an instrument of ten strings,
and upon the psaltery; upon the
harp with a solemn sound.
4 **For thou,** LORD, hast made me
glad through thy work:
I will triumph in the works of thy
hands.
5 **O LORD, how great** are thy works!
and thy thoughts are very deep.
6 **A brutish man** knoweth not;
neither doth a fool understand this.
7 **When the wicked** spring as the
grass,
**and when all the workers of
iniquity** do flourish;
it is that they shall be destroyed for
ever:
8 **But thou,** LORD, art most high for
evermore.
9 **For, {lo}, thine enemies,** O LORD,
for, {lo}, thine enemies shall
perish;
all the workers of iniquity shall be
scattered.

10 **But my horn** shalt thou exalt like the horn of an unicorn:
I shall be anointed with fresh oil.
11 **Mine eye** also shall see my desire on mine enemies,
and mine ears shall hear my desire of the wicked that rise up against me.
12 **The righteous** shall flourish like the palm tree:
he shall grow like a cedar in Lebanon.
13 **Those that be planted in the house of the LORD** shall flourish in the courts of our God.
14 **They** shall still bring forth fruit in old age;
they shall be fat and flourishing;
15 To shew that the LORD is upright:
he is my rock,
and there is no unrighteousness in him.

93 **The LORD** reigneth,
he is clothed with majesty;
the LORD is clothed with strength,
wherewith he hath girded himself:
the world also is stablished,
that it cannot be moved.
2 **Thy throne** is established of old:
thou art from everlasting.
3 **The floods** have lifted up, O LORD,
the floods have lifted up their voice;
the floods lift up their waves.
4 **The LORD on high** is mightier than the noise of many waters, yea, than the mighty waves of the sea.
5 **Thy testimonies** are very sure:
holiness becometh thine house, O LORD, for ever.

94 **O LORD God, to whom** vengeance belongeth;
O God, to whom vengeance belongeth,
shew thyself.
2 **Lift up** thyself,
thou judge of the earth:
render a reward to the proud.
3 **LORD, how long** shall the wicked,
how long shall the wicked triumph?
4 **How long** shall they utter and speak hard things?
and all the workers of iniquity boast themselves?
5 **They** break in pieces thy people, O LORD,
and afflict thine heritage.
6 **They** slay the widow and the stranger,
and murder the fatherless.
7 **Yet they** say,
The LORD shall not see,
neither shall the God of Jacob regard it.
8 **Understand,** ye brutish among the people:
and ye fools, when will ye be wise?
9 **He that planted the ear,** shall he not hear?
he that formed the eye, shall he not see?
10 **He that chastiseth the heathen,** shall not he correct?
he that teacheth man knowledge, shall not he know?
11 **The LORD** knoweth the thoughts of man,
that they are vanity.
12 **Blessed** is the man whom thou chastenest, O LORD, and teachest him out of thy law;
13 **That thou** mayest give him rest from the days of adversity,
until the pit be digged for the wicked.
14 **For the LORD** will not cast off his people,
neither will he forsake his inheritance.
15 **But judgment** shall return unto righteousness:
and all the upright in heart shall follow it.
16 **Who** will rise up for me against the evildoers?
or who will stand up for me against the workers of iniquity?
17 **Unless the LORD** had been my help,
my soul had almost dwelt in silence.
18 **When I** said, My foot slippeth;
thy mercy, O LORD, held me up.
19 **In the multitude of my thoughts within me** thy comforts delight my soul.
20 **Shall the throne of iniquity** have fellowship with thee,
which frameth mischief by a law?
21 **They** gather themselves together against the soul of the righteous,
and condemn the innocent blood.
22 **But the LORD** is my defence;
and my God is the rock of my refuge.
23 **And he** shall bring upon them their own iniquity,
and shall cut them off in their own wickedness;
yea, the LORD our God shall cut them off.

95 **O come,**
let us sing unto the LORD:
let us make a joyful noise to the rock of our salvation.
2 **Let us** come before his presence with thanksgiving,
and make a joyful noise unto him with psalms.
3 **For the LORD** is a great God, and a great King above all gods.
4 **In his hand** are the deep places of the earth:
the strength of the hills is his also.
5 **The sea** is his,
and he made it:
and his hands formed the dry land.
6 **O come,**
let us worship and bow down:
let us kneel before the LORD our maker.
7 **For he** is our God;
and we are the people of his pasture, and the sheep of his hand.
To day if ye will hear his voice,
8 **Harden not** your heart, as in the provocation, and as in the day of temptation in the wilderness:
9 **When your fathers** tempted me,
proved me,
and saw my work.
10 **Forty years long** was I grieved with this generation,
and said,
It is a people that do err in their heart,
and they have not known my ways:
11 **Unto whom** I swear in my wrath
that they should not enter into my rest.

96 ∞ **O sing** unto the LORD a new song:
sing unto the LORD, all the earth.
2 **Sing** unto the LORD,
bless his name;
shew forth his salvation from day to day.
3 **Declare** his glory among the heathen, his wonders among all people.
4 **For the LORD** is great,
and greatly to be praised:

he is to be feared above all gods.
[5] **For all the gods of the nations** are idols:
but the LORD made the heavens.
[6] **Honour and majesty** are before him:
strength and beauty are in his sanctuary.
[7] **Give** unto the LORD, O ye kindreds of the people,
give unto the LORD glory and strength.
[8] **Give** unto the LORD the glory due unto his name:
bring an offering,
and come into his courts.
[9] **O worship** the LORD in the beauty of holiness:
fear before him, all the earth.
[10] **Say** among the heathen
that the LORD reigneth:
the world also shall be established
that it shall not be moved:
he shall judge the people righteously.
[11] **Let the heavens** rejoice,
and let the earth be glad;
let the sea roar, and the fulness thereof.
[12] **Let the field** be joyful, and all that is therein:
then shall all the trees of the wood rejoice
[13] Before the LORD:
for he cometh,
for he cometh
to judge the earth:
he shall judge the world with righteousness, and the people with his truth.

97

The LORD reigneth;
let the earth rejoice;
let the multitude of isles be glad thereof.
[2] **Clouds and darkness** are round about him:
righteousness and judgment are the habitation of his throne.
[3] **A fire** goeth before him,
and burneth up his enemies round about.
[4] **His lightnings** enlightened the world:
the earth saw,
and trembled.
[5] **The hills** melted like wax at the presence of the LORD, at the presence of the Lord of the whole earth.
[6] **The heavens** declare his righteousness,
and all the people see his glory.
[7] **Confounded** be all they that serve graven images, that boast themselves of idols:
worship him, all ye gods.
[8] **Zion** heard,
and was glad;
and the daughters of Judah rejoiced because of thy judgments, O LORD.
[9] **For thou**, LORD, art high above all the earth:
thou art exalted far above all gods.
[10] **Ye that love the LORD, hate** evil:
he preserveth the souls of his saints;
he delivereth them out of the hand of the wicked.
[11] **Light** is sown for the righteous, and gladness for the upright in heart.
[12] **Rejoice** in the LORD, ye righteous;
and give thanks at the remembrance of his holiness.

98

A Psalm.

O sing unto the LORD a new song;
for he hath done marvellous things:
his right hand, and his holy arm, hath gotten him the victory.
[2] **The LORD** hath made known his salvation:
his righteousness hath he openly shewed in the sight of the heathen.
[3] **He** hath remembered his mercy and his truth toward the house of Israel:
all the ends of the earth have seen the salvation of our God.
[4] **Make** a joyful noise unto the LORD, all the earth:
make a loud noise,
and rejoice,
and sing praise.
[5] **Sing** unto the LORD with the harp; with the harp, and the voice of a psalm.
[6] **With trumpets and sound of cornet** make a joyful noise before the LORD, the King.
[7] **Let the sea** roar, and the fulness thereof; the world, and they that dwell therein.
[8] **Let the floods** clap their hands:
let the hills be joyful together
[9] Before the LORD;
for he cometh
to judge the earth:
with righteousness shall he judge the world, and the people with equity.

99

The LORD reigneth;
let the people tremble:
he sitteth between the cherubims;
let the earth be moved.
[2] **The LORD** is great in Zion;
and he is high above all the people.
[3] **Let them** praise thy great and terrible name;
for it is holy.
[4] **The king's strength** also loveth judgment;
thou dost establish equity,
thou executest judgment and righteousness in Jacob.
[5] **Exalt ye** the LORD our God,
and worship at his footstool;
for he is holy.
[6] **Moses and Aaron among his priests, and Samuel among them that call upon his name;** they called upon the LORD,
and he answered them.
[7] **He** spake unto them in the cloudy pillar:
they kept his testimonies, and the ordinance that he gave them.
[8] **Thou** answeredst them, O LORD our God:
thou wast a God that forgavest them,
though thou tookest vengeance of their inventions.
[9] **Exalt** the LORD our God,
and worship at his holy hill;
for the LORD our God is holy.

100

A Psalm of praise.

Make a joyful noise unto the LORD, all ye lands.
[2] **Serve** the LORD with gladness:
come before his presence with singing.
[3] **Know ye**
that the LORD he is God:
it is he that hath made us, and not we ourselves;
we are his people, and the sheep of his pasture.
[4] **Enter** into his gates with thanksgiving, and into his courts with praise:
be thankful unto him,
and bless his name.

[5] **For the LORD** is good;
his mercy is everlasting;
and his truth endureth to all generations.

101

A Psalm of David.

I will sing of mercy and judgment:
unto thee, O LORD, will I sing.
[2] **I** will behave myself wisely in a perfect way.
O when wilt thou come unto me?
I will walk within my house with a perfect heart.
[3] **I** will set no wicked thing before mine eyes:
I hate the work of them that turn aside;
it shall not cleave to me.
[4] **A froward heart** shall depart from me:
I will not know a wicked person.
[5] **Whoso privily** slandereth his neighbour,
him will I cut off:
him that hath an high look and a proud heart will not I suffer.
[6] **Mine eyes** shall be upon the faithful of the land,
that they may dwell with me:
he that walketh in a perfect way, he shall serve me.
[7] **He that worketh deceit** shall not dwell within my house:
he that telleth lies shall not tarry in my sight.
[8] **I** will early destroy all the wicked of the land;
that I may cut off all wicked doers from the city of the LORD.

102

A Prayer of the afflicted, when he is overwhelmed, and poureth out his complaint before the LORD.

Hear my prayer, O LORD,
and let my cry come unto thee.
[2] **Hide not** thy face from me in the day when I am in trouble;
incline thine ear unto me:
in the day when I call
answer me speedily.
[3] **For my days** are consumed like smoke,
and my bones are burned as an hearth.
[4] **My heart** is smitten,
and withered like grass;
so that I forget to eat my bread.
[5] **By reason of the voice of my groaning** my bones cleave to my skin.
[6] **I** am like a pelican of the wilderness:
I am like an owl of the desert.
[7] **I** watch,
and am as a sparrow alone upon the house top.
[8] **Mine enemies** reproach me all the day;
and they that are mad against me are sworn against me.
[9] **For I** have eaten ashes like bread,
and mingled my drink with weeping.
[10] Because of thine indignation and thy wrath:
for thou hast lifted me up,
and cast me down.
[11] **My days** are like a shadow that declineth;
and I am withered like grass.
[12] **But thou,** O LORD, shall endure for ever; and thy remembrance unto all generations.
[13] **Thou** shalt arise,
and have mercy upon Zion:
for the time to favour her, yea, the set time, is come.
[14] **For thy servants** take pleasure in her stones,
and favour the dust thereof.
[15] **So the heathen** shall fear the name of the LORD, and all the kings of the earth thy glory.
[16] **When the LORD** shall build up Zion,
he shall appear in his glory.
[17] **He** will regard the prayer of the destitute,
and not despise their prayer.
[18] **This** shall be written for the generation to come:
and the people which shall be created shall praise the LORD.
[19] **For he** hath looked down from the height of his sanctuary;
from heaven did the LORD behold the earth;
[20] To hear the groaning of the prisoner;
to loose those that are appointed to death;
[21] To declare the name of the LORD in Zion, and his praise in Jerusalem;
[22] **When the people** are gathered together, and the kingdoms, to serve the LORD.
[23] **He** weakened my strength in the way;
he shortened my days.
[24] **I** said,
O my God, take me not away in the midst of my days:
thy years are throughout all generations.
[25] **Of old** hast thou laid the foundation of the earth:
and the heavens are the work of thy hands.
[26] **They** shall perish,
but thou shalt endure:
yea, all of them shall wax old like a garment;
as a vesture shalt thou change them,
and they shall be changed:
[27] **But thou** art the same,
and thy years shall have no end.
[28] **The children of thy servants** shall continue,
and their seed shall be established before thee.

103

A Psalm of David.

Bless the LORD, O my soul: and all that is within me,
bless his holy name.
[2] **Bless** the LORD, O my soul,
and forget not all his benefits:
[3] **Who** forgiveth all thine iniquities;
who healeth all thy diseases;
[4] **Who** redeemeth thy life from destruction;
who crowneth thee with lovingkindness and tender mercies;
[5] **Who** satisfieth thy mouth with good things;
so that thy youth is renewed like the eagle's.
[6] **The LORD** executeth righteousness and judgment for all that are oppressed.
[7] **He** made known his ways unto Moses, his acts unto the children of Israel.
[8] **The LORD** is merciful and gracious, slow to anger, and plenteous in mercy.
[9] **He** will not always chide:
neither will he keep his anger for ever.
[10] **He** hath not dealt with us after our sins;

nor rewarded us according to our iniquities.

11 **For as the heaven** is high above the earth,
so great is his mercy toward them that fear him.

12 **As far as the east** is from the west,
so far hath he removed our transgressions from us.

13 **Like as a father** pitieth his children,
so the LORD pitieth them that fear him.

14 **For he** knoweth our frame;
he remembereth
that we are dust.

15 **As for man,** his days are as grass: as a flower of the field,
so he flourisheth.

16 **For the wind** passeth over it,
and it is gone;
and the place thereof shall know it no more.

17 **But the mercy of the LORD** is from everlasting to everlasting upon them that fear him, and his righteousness unto children's children;

18 To such as keep his covenant, and to those that remember his commandments to do them.

19 **The LORD** hath prepared his throne in the heavens;
and his kingdom ruleth over all.

20 **Bless** the LORD, ye his angels,
that excel in strength,
that do his commandments,
hearkening unto the voice of his word.

21 **Bless ye** the LORD, all ye his hosts; ye ministers of his,
that do his pleasure.

22 **Bless** the LORD, all his works in all places of his dominion:
bless the LORD, O my soul.

104

Bless the LORD, O my soul.
O LORD my God, thou art very great;
thou art clothed with honour and majesty.

2 **Who** coverest thyself with light as with a garment:
who stretchest out the heavens like a curtain:

3 **Who** layeth the beams of his chambers in the waters:
who maketh the clouds his chariot:
who walketh upon the wings of the wind:

4 **Who** maketh his angels spirits; his ministers a flaming fire:

5 **Who** laid the foundations of the earth,
that it should not be removed for ever.

6 **Thou** coveredst it with the deep as with a garment:
the waters stood above the mountains.

7 **At thy rebuke** they fled;
at the voice of thy thunder they hasted away.

8 **They** go up by the mountains;
they go down by the valleys unto the place which thou hast founded for them.

9 **Thou** hast set a bound that they may not pass over;
that they turn not again to cover the earth.

10 **He** sendeth the springs into the valleys,
which run among the hills.

11 **They** give drink to every beast of the field:
the wild asses quench their thirst.

12 **By them** shall the fowls of the heaven have their habitation,
which sing among the branches.

13 **He** watereth the hills from his chambers:
the earth is satisfied with the fruit of thy works.

14 **He** causeth the grass to grow for the cattle, and herb for the service of man:
that he may bring forth food out of the earth;

15 And wine that maketh glad the heart of man, and oil to make his face to shine, and bread which strengtheneth man's heart.

16 **The trees of the LORD** are full of sap; the cedars of Lebanon,
which he hath planted;

17 **Where the birds** make their nests:
as for the stork, the fir trees are her house.

18 **The high hills** are a refuge for the wild goats; and the rocks for the conies.

19 **He** appointed the moon for seasons:
the sun knoweth his going down.

20 **Thou** makest darkness,
and it is night:
wherein all the beasts of the forest do creep forth.

21 **The young lions** roar after their prey,
and seek their meat from God.

22 **The sun** ariseth,
they gather themselves together,
and lay them down in their dens.

23 **Man** goeth forth unto his work and to his labour until the evening.

24 **O LORD, how manifold** are thy works!
in wisdom hast thou made them all:
the earth is full of thy riches.

25 **So** is this great and wide sea,
wherein are things creeping innumerable, both small and great beasts.

26 **There** go the ships:
there is that leviathan,
whom thou hast made to play therein.

27 **These** wait all upon thee;
that thou mayest give them their meat in due season.

28 **That thou** givest them
they gather:
thou openest thine hand,
they are filled with good.

29 **Thou** hidest thy face,
they are troubled:
thou takest away their breath,
they die,
and return to their dust.

30 **Thou** sendest forth thy spirit,
they are created:
and thou renewest the face of the earth.

31 **The glory of the LORD** shall endure for ever:
the LORD shall rejoice in his works.

32 **He** looketh on the earth,
and it trembleth:
he toucheth the hills,
and they smoke.

33 **I** will sing unto the LORD
as long as I live:
I will sing praise to my God
while I have my being.

34 **My meditation of him** shall be sweet:
I will be glad in the LORD.

35 **Let the sinners** be consumed out of the earth,

and let the wicked be no more.
Bless thou the LORD, O my soul.
Praise ye the LORD.

105

O give thanks unto the LORD;
call upon his name:
make known his deeds among the people.
2 **Sing** unto him,
sing psalms unto him:
talk ye of all his wondrous works.
3 **Glory ye** in his holy name:
let the heart of them rejoice that seek the LORD.
4 **Seek** the LORD, and his strength:
seek his face evermore.
5 **Remember** his marvellous works that he hath done; his wonders, and the judgments of his mouth;
6 O ye seed of Abraham his servant, ye children of Jacob his chosen.
7 **He** is the LORD our God:
his judgments are in all the earth.
8 **He** hath remembered his covenant for ever, the word which he commanded to a thousand generations.
9 **Which covenant** he made with Abraham, and his oath unto Isaac;
10 **And** confirmed the same unto Jacob for a law, and to Israel for an everlasting covenant:
11 Saying,
Unto thee will I give the land of Canaan, the lot of your inheritance:
12 **When they** were but a few men in number; yea, very few, and strangers in it.
13 **When they** went from one nation to another, from one kingdom to another people;
14 **He** suffered no man to do them wrong:
yea, he reproved kings for their sakes;
15 Saying,
Touch not mine anointed,
and do my prophets no harm.
16 **Moreover he** called for a famine upon the land:
he brake the whole staff of bread.
17 **He** sent a man before them, even Joseph,
who was sold for a servant:
18 **Whose feet** they hurt with fetters:
he was laid in iron:
19 **Until the time that his word came:** the word of the LORD tried him.
20 **The king** sent and loosed him; even the ruler of the people,
and let him go free.
21 **He** made him lord of his house, and ruler of all his substance:
22 To bind his princes at his pleasure;
and teach his senators wisdom.
23 **Israel** also came into Egypt;
and Jacob sojourned in the land of Ham.
24 **And he** increased his people greatly;
and made them stronger than their enemies.
25 **He** turned their heart to hate his people,
to deal subtilly with his servants.
26 **He** sent Moses his servant; and Aaron whom he had chosen.
27 **They** shewed his signs among them, and wonders in the land of Ham.
28 **He** sent darkness,
and made it dark;
and they rebelled not against his word.
29 **He** turned their waters into blood,
and slew their fish.
30 **Their land** brought forth frogs in abundance, in the chambers of their kings.
31 **He** spake,
and there came divers sorts of flies, and lice in all their coasts.
32 **He** gave them hail for rain, and flaming fire in their land.
33 **He** smote their vines also and their fig trees;
and brake the trees of their coasts.
34 **He** spake,
and the locusts came, and caterpillers, and that without number,
35 **And** did eat up all the herbs in their land,
and devoured the fruit of their ground.
36 **He** smote also all the firstborn in their land, the chief of all their strength.
37 **He** brought them forth also with silver and gold:
and there was not one feeble person among their tribes.
38 **Egypt** was glad
when they departed:
for the fear of them fell upon them.
39 **He** spread a cloud for a covering;
and fire to give light in the night.
40 **The people** asked,
and he brought quails,
and satisfied them with the bread of heaven.
41 **He** opened the rock,
and the waters gushed out;
they ran in the dry places like a river.
42 **For he** remembered his holy promise, and Abraham his servant.
43 **And he** brought forth his people with joy, and his chosen with gladness:
44 **And** gave them the lands of the heathen:
and they inherited the labour of the people;
45 **That they** might observe his statutes,
and keep his laws.
Praise ye the LORD.

106

Praise ye the LORD.
O give thanks unto the LORD;
for he is good:
for his mercy endureth for ever.
2 **Who** can utter the mighty acts of the LORD?
who can shew forth all his praise?
3 **Blessed** are they that keep judgment, and he that doeth righteousness at all times.
4 **Remember** me, O LORD, with the favour that thou bearest unto thy people:
O visit me with thy salvation;
5 **That I** may see the good of thy chosen,
that I may rejoice in the gladness of thy nation,
that I may glory with thine inheritance.
6 **We** have sinned with our fathers,
we have committed iniquity,
we have done wickedly.
7 **Our fathers** understood not thy wonders in Egypt;
they remembered not the multitude of thy mercies;
but provoked him at the sea, even at the Red sea.

8 **Nevertheless he** saved them for his name's sake,
that he might make his mighty power to be known.

9 **He** rebuked the Red sea also,
and it was dried up:
so he led them through the depths, as through the wilderness.

10 **And he** saved them from the hand of him that hated them,
and redeemed them from the hand of the enemy.

11 **And the waters** covered their enemies:
there was not one of them left.

12 **Then** believed they his words;
they sang his praise.

13 **They** soon forgat his works;
they waited not for his counsel:
14 **But** lusted exceedingly in the wilderness,
and tempted God in the desert.

15 **And he** gave them their request;
but sent leanness into their soul.

16 **They** envied Moses also in the camp, and Aaron the saint of the LORD.

17 **The earth** opened and swallowed up Dathan
and covered the company of Abiram.

18 **And a fire** was kindled in their company;
the flame burned up the wicked.

19 **They** made a calf in Horeb,
and worshipped the molten image.

20 **Thus they** changed their glory into the similitude of an ox that eateth grass.

21 **They** forgat God their saviour,
which had done great things in Egypt;
22 Wondrous works in the land of Ham, and terrible things by the Red sea.

23 **Therefore he** said
that he would destroy them,
had not Moses his chosen stood before him in the breach,
to turn away his wrath,
lest he should destroy them.

24 **Yea, they** despised the pleasant land,
they believed not his word:
25 **But** murmured in their tents,
and hearkened not unto the voice of the LORD.

26 **Therefore he** lifted up his hand against them,
to overthrow them in the wilderness:
27 To overthrow their seed also among the nations,
and to scatter them in the lands.

28 **They** joined themselves also unto Baalpeor,
and ate the sacrifices of the dead.

29 **Thus they** provoked him to anger with their inventions:
and the plague brake in upon them.

30 **Then** stood up Phinehas,
and executed judgment:
and so the plague was stayed.

31 **And that** was counted unto him for righteousness unto all generations for evermore.

32 **They** angered him also at the waters of strife,
so that it went ill with Moses for their sakes:

33 **Because they** provoked his spirit,
so that he spake unadvisedly with his lips.

34 **They** did not destroy the nations,
concerning whom the LORD commanded them:
35 **But** were mingled among the heathen,
and learned their works.

36 And they served their idols:
which were a snare unto them.

37 **Yea, they** sacrificed their sons and their daughters unto devils,
38 **And** shed innocent blood, even the blood of their sons and of their daughters,
whom they sacrificed unto the idols of Canaan:
and the land was polluted with blood.

39 **Thus** were they defiled with their own works,
and went a whoring with their own inventions.

40 **Therefore** was the wrath of the LORD kindled against his people,
insomuch that he abhorred his own inheritance.

41 **And he** gave them into the hand of the heathen;
and they that hated them ruled over them.

42 **Their enemies** also oppressed them,
and they were brought into subjection under their hand.

43 **Many times** did he deliver them;
but they provoked him with their counsel,
and were brought low for their iniquity.

44 **Nevertheless he** regarded their affliction,
when he heard their cry:
45 **And he** remembered for them his covenant,
and repented according to the multitude of his mercies.

46 **He** made them also to be pitied of all those that carried them captives.

47 **Save** us, O LORD our God,
and gather us from among the heathen,
to give thanks unto thy holy name,
and to triumph in thy praise.

48 **Blessed** be the LORD God of Israel from everlasting to everlasting:
and let all the people say, Amen.
Praise ye the LORD.

107

O give thanks unto the LORD,
for he is good:
for his mercy endureth for ever.

2 **Let the redeemed of the LORD** say so,
whom he hath redeemed from the hand of the enemy;
3 **And** gathered them out of the lands, from the east, and from the west, from the north, and from the south.

4 **They** wandered in the wilderness in a solitary way;
they found no city to dwell in.

5 **Hungry and thirsty,** their soul fainted in them.

6 **Then they** cried unto the LORD in their trouble,
and he delivered them out of their distresses.

7 **And he** led them forth by the right way,
that they might go to a city of habitation.

8 **Oh that men** would praise the LORD for his goodness, and for his wonderful works to the children of men!

9 **For he** satisfieth the longing soul,

and filleth the hungry soul with goodness.

10 **Such** as sit in darkness and in the shadow of death,
being bound in affliction and iron;

11 **Because they** rebelled against the words of God,
and contemned the counsel of the most High:

12 **Therefore he** brought down their heart with labour;
they fell down,
and there was none to help.

13 **Then they** cried unto the LORD in their trouble,
and he saved them out of their distresses.

14 **He** brought them out of darkness and the shadow of death,
and brake their bands in sunder.

15 **Oh that men** would praise the LORD for his goodness, and for his wonderful works to the children of men!

16 **For he** hath broken the gates of brass,
and cut the bars of iron in sunder.

17 **Fools because of their transgression, and because of their iniquities,** are afflicted.

18 **Their soul** abhorreth all manner of meat;
and they draw near unto the gates of death.

19 **Then they** cry unto the LORD in their trouble,
and he saveth them out of their distresses.

20 **He** sent his word,
and healed them,
and delivered them from their destructions.

21 **Oh that men** would praise the LORD for his goodness, and for his wonderful works to the children of men!

22 **And let them** sacrifice the sacrifices of thanksgiving,
and declare his works with rejoicing.

23 **They that go down to the sea in ships, that do business in great waters;**

24 These see the works of the LORD, and his wonders in the deep.

25 **For he** commandeth,
and raiseth the stormy wind,
which lifteth up the waves thereof.

26 **They** mount up to the heaven,
they go down again to the depths:
their soul is melted because of trouble.

27 **They** reel to and fro,
and stagger like a drunken man,
and are at their wit's end.

28 **Then they** cry unto the LORD in their trouble,
and he bringeth them out of their distresses.

29 **He** maketh the storm a calm,
so that the waves thereof are still.

30 **Then** are they glad
because they be quiet;
so he bringeth them unto their desired haven.

31 **Oh that men** would praise the LORD for his goodness, and for his wonderful works to the children of men!

32 **Let them** exalt him also in the congregation of the people,
and praise him in the assembly of the elders.

33 **He** turneth rivers into a wilderness, and the watersprings into dry ground;

34 A fruitful land into barrenness, for the wickedness of them that dwell therein.

35 **He** turneth the wilderness into a standing water, and dry ground into watersprings.

36 **And there** he maketh the hungry to dwell,
that they may prepare a city for habitation;

37 **And** sow the fields,
and plant vineyards,
which may yield fruits of increase.

38 **He** blesseth them also,
so that they are multiplied greatly;
and suffereth not their cattle to decrease.

39 **Again, they** are minished and brought low through oppression, affliction, and sorrow.

40 **He** poureth contempt upon princes,
and causeth them to wander in the wilderness,
where there is no way.

41 **Yet** setteth he the poor on high from affliction,
and maketh him families like a flock.

42 **The righteous** shall see it,
and rejoice:
and all iniquity shall stop her mouth.

43 **Whoso** is wise,
and will observe these things,
even they shall understand the lovingkindness of the LORD.

108

A Song or Psalm of David.

O God, my heart is fixed;
I will sing and give praise, even with my glory.

2 **Awake,** psaltery and harp:
I myself will awake early.

3 **I** will praise thee, O LORD, among the people:
and I will sing praises unto thee among the nations.

4 **For thy mercy** is great above the heavens:
and thy truth reacheth unto the clouds.

5 **Be thou** exalted, O God, above the heavens: and thy glory above all the earth;

6 **That thy beloved** may be delivered:
save with thy right hand,
and answer me.

7 **God** hath spoken in his holiness;
I will rejoice,
I will divide Shechem,
and mete out the valley of Succoth.

8 **Gilead** is mine;
Manasseh is mine;
Ephraim also is the strength of mine head;
Judah is my lawgiver;

9 **Moab** is my washpot;
over Edom will I cast out my shoe;
over Philistia will I triumph.

10 **Who** will bring me into the strong city?
who will lead me into Edom?

11 **Wilt not thou,** O God, who hast cast us off?
and wilt not thou, O God, go forth with our hosts?

12 **Give** us help from trouble:
for vain is the help of man.

13 **Through God** we shall do valiantly:
for he it is that shall tread down our enemies.

109

To the chief Musician, A Psalm of David.

Hold not thy peace, O God of my praise;

[2] **For the mouth of the wicked and the mouth of the deceitful** are opened against me:
they have spoken against me with a lying tongue.

[3] **They** compassed me about also with words of hatred;
and fought against me without a cause.

[4] **For my love** they are my adversaries:
but I give myself unto prayer.

[5] **And they** have rewarded me evil for good, and hatred for my love.

[6] **Set thou** a wicked man over him:
and let Satan stand at his right hand.

[7] **When he** shall be judged,
let him be condemned:
and let his prayer become sin.

[8] **Let his days** be few;
and let another take his office.

[9] **Let his children** be fatherless, and his wife a widow.

[10] **Let his children** be continually vagabonds,
and beg:
let them seek their bread also out of their desolate places.

[11] **Let the extortioner** catch all that he hath;
and let the strangers spoil his labour.

[12] **Let there** be none to extend mercy unto him:
neither let there be any to favour his fatherless children.

[13] **Let his posterity** be cut off;
and in the generation following let their name be blotted out.

[14] **Let the iniquity of his fathers** be remembered with the LORD;
and let not the sin of his mother be blotted out.

[15] **Let them** be before the LORD continually,
that he may cut off the memory of them from the earth.

[16] **Because that he** remembered not to shew mercy,
but persecuted the poor and needy man,
that he might even slay the broken in heart.

[17] **As he** loved cursing,
so let it come unto him:
as he delighted not in blessing,
so let it be far from him.

[18] **As he** clothed himself with cursing like as with his garment,
so let it come into his bowels like water, and like oil into his bones.

[19] **Let it** be unto him as the garment which covereth him, and for a girdle wherewith he is girded continually.

[20] **Let this** be the reward of mine adversaries from the LORD, and of them that speak evil against my soul.

[21] **But do thou** for me, O GOD the Lord, for thy name's sake:
because thy mercy is good,
deliver thou me.

[22] **For I** am poor and needy,
and my heart is wounded within me.

[23] **I** am gone like the shadow
when it declineth:
I am tossed up and down as the locust.

[24] **My knees** are weak through fasting;
and my flesh faileth of fatness.

[25] **I** became also a reproach unto them:
when they looked upon me
they shaked their heads.

[26] **Help** me, O LORD my God:
O save me according to thy mercy:

[27] **That they** may know
that this is thy hand;
that thou, LORD, hast done it.

[28] **Let them** curse,
but bless thou:
when they arise,
let them be ashamed;
but let thy servant rejoice.

[29] **Let mine adversaries** be clothed with shame,
and let them cover themselves with their own confusion, as with a mantle.

[30] **I** will greatly praise the LORD with my mouth;
yea, I will praise him among the multitude.

[31] **For he** shall stand at the right hand of the poor,
to save him from those that condemn his soul.

110

A Psalm of David.

The LORD said unto my Lord,
Sit thou at my right hand,
until I make thine enemies thy footstool.

[2] **The LORD** shall send the rod of thy strength out of Zion:
rule thou in the midst of thine enemies.

[3] **Thy people** shall be willing in the day of thy power, in the beauties of holiness from the womb of the morning:
thou hast the dew of thy youth.

[4] **The LORD** hath sworn,
and will not repent,
Thou art a priest for ever after the order of Melchizedek.

[5] **The Lord at thy right hand** shall strike through kings in the day of his wrath.

[6] **He** shall judge among the heathen,
he shall fill the places with the dead bodies;
he shall wound the heads over many countries.

[7] **He** shall drink of the brook in the way:
therefore shall he lift up the head.

111

Praise ye the LORD.
I will praise the LORD with my whole heart, in the assembly of the upright, and in the congregation.

[2] **The works of the LORD** are great,
sought out of all them that have pleasure therein.

[3] **His work** is honourable and glorious:
and his righteousness endureth for ever.

[4] **He** hath made his wonderful works to be remembered:
the LORD is gracious and full of compassion.

[5] **He** hath given meat unto them that fear him:
he will ever be mindful of his covenant.

[6] **He** hath shewed his people the power of his works,
that he may give them the heritage of the heathen.

[7] **The works of his hands** are verity and judgment;
all his commandments are sure.

[8] **They** stand fast for ever and ever,
and are done in truth and uprightness.

[9] **He** sent redemption unto his people:

he hath commanded his covenant for ever:
holy and reverend is his name.
10 **The fear of the LORD** is the beginning of wisdom:
a good understanding have all they that do his commandments:
his praise endureth for ever.

112 **Praise ye** the LORD.
Blessed is the man that feareth the LORD, that delighteth greatly in his commandments.
2 **His seed** shall be mighty upon earth:
the generation of the upright shall be blessed.
3 **Wealth and riches** shall be in his house:
and his righteousness endureth for ever.
4 **Unto the upright** there ariseth light in the darkness:
he is gracious, and full of compassion, and righteous.
5 **A good man** sheweth favour,
and lendeth:
he will guide his affairs with discretion.
6 **Surely he** shall not be moved for ever:
the righteous shall be in everlasting remembrance.
7 **He** shall not be afraid of evil tidings:
his heart is fixed,
trusting in the LORD.
8 **His heart** is established,
he shall not be afraid,
until he see his desire upon his enemies.
9 **He** hath dispersed,
he hath given to the poor;
his righteousness endureth for ever;
his horn shall be exalted with honour.
10 **The wicked** shall see it,
and be grieved;
he shall gnash with his teeth,
and melt away:
the desire of the wicked shall perish.

113 **Praise ye** the LORD.
Praise, O ye servants of the LORD,
praise the name of the LORD.
2 **Blessed** be the name of the LORD from this time forth and for evermore.
3 **From the rising of the sun unto the going down of the same** the LORD's name is to be praised.
4 **The LORD** is high above all nations, and his glory above the heavens.
5 **Who** is like unto the LORD our God,
who dwelleth on high,
6 **Who** humbleth himself to behold the things that are in heaven, and in the earth!
7 **He** raiseth up the poor out of the dust,
and lifteth the needy out of the dunghill;
8 **That he** may set him with princes, even with the princes of his people.
9 **He** maketh the barren woman to keep house,
and to be a joyful mother of children.
Praise ye the LORD.

114 **When Israel** went out of Egypt, the house of Jacob from a people of strange language;
2 **Judah** was his sanctuary, and Israel his dominion.

3 **The sea** saw it,
and fled:
Jordan was driven back.

4 **The mountains** skipped like rams, and the little hills like lambs.

5 **What** ailed thee, O thou sea, {that thou fleddest}? thou Jordan, {that thou wast driven back}?
6 Ye mountains, {that ye skipped like rams}; and ye little hills, like lambs?

7 **Tremble,** thou earth, at the presence of the Lord, at the presence of the God of Jacob;
8 **Which** turned the rock into a standing water, the flint into a fountain of waters.

115 **Not unto us, O LORD, not unto us, but unto thy name** give glory, for thy mercy, and for thy truth's sake.
2 **Wherefore** should the heathen say,
Where is now their God?
3 **But our God** is in the heavens:
he hath done whatsoever he hath pleased.
4 **Their idols** are silver and gold, the work of men's hands.
5 **They** have mouths,
but they speak not:
eyes have they,
but they see not:
6 **They** have ears,
but they hear not:
noses have they,
but they smell not:
7 **They** have hands,
but they handle not:
feet have they,
but they walk not:
neither speak they through their throat.
8 **They that make them** are like unto them;
so is every one that trusteth in them.
9 **O Israel, trust thou** in the LORD:
he is their help and their shield.
10 **O house of Aaron, trust** in the LORD:
he is their help and their shield.
11 **Ye that fear the LORD, trust** in the LORD:
he is their help and their shield.
12 **The LORD** hath been mindful of us:
he will bless us;
he will bless the house of Israel;
he will bless the house of Aaron.
13 **He** will bless them that fear the LORD, both small and great.
14 **The LORD** shall increase you more and more, you and your children.
15 **Ye** are blessed of the LORD which made heaven and earth.
16 **The heaven, even the heavens,** are the LORD's:
but the earth hath he given to the children of men.
17 **The dead** praise not the LORD, neither any that go down into silence.
18 **But we** will bless the LORD from this time forth and for evermore.
Praise the LORD.

116 **I** love the LORD,
because he hath heard my voice and my supplications.
2 **Because he** hath inclined his ear unto me,
therefore will I call upon him

as long as I live.
3 **The sorrows of death** compassed me,
and the pains of hell gat hold upon me:
I found trouble and sorrow.
4 **Then** called I upon the name of the LORD;
O LORD, I beseech thee,
deliver my soul.
5 **Gracious** is the LORD, and righteous;
yea, our God is merciful.
6 **The LORD** preserveth the simple:
I was brought low,
and he helped me.
7 **Return** unto thy rest, O my soul;
for the LORD hath dealt bountifully with thee.
8 **For thou** hast delivered my soul from death, mine eyes from tears, and my feet from falling.
9 I will walk before the LORD in the land of the living.
10 I believed,
therefore have I spoken:
I was greatly afflicted:
11 I said in my haste,
All men are liars.
12 **What** shall I render unto the LORD for all his benefits toward me?
13 I will take the cup of salvation,
and call upon the name of the LORD.
14 I will pay my vows unto the LORD now in the presence of all his people.
15 **Precious in the sight of the LORD** is the death of his saints.
16 **O LORD, truly I** am thy servant;
I am thy servant, and the son of thine handmaid:
thou hast loosed my bonds.
17 I will offer to thee the sacrifice of thanksgiving,
and will call upon the name of the LORD.
18 I will pay my vows unto the LORD now in the presence of all his people.
19 In the courts of the LORD's house, in the midst of thee, O Jerusalem.
Praise ye the LORD.

117

O praise the LORD, all ye nations:
praise him, all ye people.
2 **For his merciful kindness** is great toward us:
and the truth of the LORD endureth for ever.
Praise ye the LORD.

118

O give thanks unto the LORD;
for he is good:
because his mercy endureth for ever.
2 **Let Israel** now say,
that his mercy endureth for ever.
3 **Let the house of Aaron** now say,
that his mercy endureth for ever.
4 **Let them** now that fear the LORD say,
that his mercy endureth for ever.
5 I called upon the LORD in distress:
the LORD answered me,
and set me in a large place.
6 **The LORD** is on my side;
I will not fear:
what can man do unto me?
7 **The LORD** taketh my part with them that help me:
therefore shall I see my desire upon them that hate me.
8 **It is better** to trust in the LORD than to put confidence in man.
9 **It is better** to trust in the LORD than to put confidence in princes.
10 **All nations** compassed me about:
but in the name of the LORD will I destroy them.
11 **They** compassed me about;
yea, they compassed me about:
but in the name of the LORD I will destroy them.
12 **They** compassed me about like bees:
they are quenched as the fire of thorns:
for in the name of the LORD I will destroy them.
13 **Thou** hast thrust sore at me
that I might fall:
but the LORD helped me.
14 **The LORD** is my strength and song,
and is become my salvation.
15 **The voice of rejoicing and salvation** is in the tabernacles of the righteous:
the right hand of the LORD doeth valiantly.
16 **The right hand of the LORD** is exalted:
the right hand of the LORD doeth valiantly.
17 I shall not die,
but live,
and declare the works of the LORD.
18 **The LORD** hath chastened me sore:
but he hath not given me over unto death.
19 **Open** to me the gates of righteousness:
I will go into them,
and I will praise the LORD:
20 **This** gate of the LORD,
into which the righteous shall enter.
21 I will praise thee:
for thou hast heard me,
and art become my salvation.
22 **The stone which the builders refused** is become the head stone of the corner.
23 **This** is the LORD's doing;
it is marvellous in our eyes.
24 **This** is the day which the LORD hath made;
we will rejoice
and be glad in it.
25 **Save** now,
I beseech thee, O LORD:
O LORD, I beseech thee,
send now prosperity.
26 **Blessed** be he that cometh in the name of the LORD:
we have blessed you out of the house of the LORD.
27 **God** is the LORD,
which hath shewed us light:
bind the sacrifice with cords, even unto the horns of the altar.
28 **Thou** art my God,
and I will praise thee:
thou art my God,
I will exalt thee.
29 **O give** thanks unto the LORD;
for he is good:
for his mercy endureth for ever.

119

ℵ ALEPH.

Blessed are the undefiled in the way,
who walk in the law of the LORD.
2 **Blessed** are they that keep his testimonies, and that seek him with the whole heart.
3 **They** also do no iniquity:
they walk in his ways.
4 **Thou** hast commanded us
to keep thy precepts diligently.

5 **O that my ways** were directed to keep thy statutes!

6 **Then** shall I not be ashamed,
when I have respect unto all thy commandments.

7 **I** will praise thee with uprightness of heart,
when I shall have learned thy righteous judgments.

8 **I** will keep thy statutes:
O forsake me not utterly.

BETH

9 **Wherewithal** shall a young man cleanse his way?
by taking heed thereto according to thy word.

10 **With my whole heart** have I sought thee:
O let me not wander from thy commandments.

11 **Thy word** have I hid in mine heart,
that I might not sin against thee.

12 **Blessed** art thou, O LORD:
teach me thy statutes.

13 **With my lips** have I declared all the judgments of thy mouth.

14 **I** have rejoiced in the way of thy testimonies, as much as in all riches.

15 **I** will meditate in thy precepts,
and have respect unto thy ways.

16 **I** will delight myself in thy statutes:
I will not forget thy word.

GIMEL

17 **Deal** bountifully with thy servant,
that I may live,
and keep thy word.

18 **Open thou** mine eyes,
that I may behold wondrous things out of thy law.

19 **I** am a stranger in the earth:
hide not thy commandments from me.

20 **My soul** breaketh for the longing that it hath unto thy judgments at all times.

21 **Thou** hast rebuked the proud that are cursed,
which do err from thy commandments.

22 **Remove** from me reproach and contempt;
for I have kept thy testimonies.

23 **Princes** also did sit and speak against me:
but thy servant did meditate in thy statutes.

24 **Thy testimonies** also are my delight and my counselors.

DALETH

25 **My soul** cleaveth unto the dust:
quicken thou me according to thy word.

26 **I** have declared my ways,
and thou heardest me:
teach me thy statutes.

27 **Make** me to understand the way of thy precepts:
so shall I talk of thy wondrous works.

28 **My soul** melteth for heaviness:
strengthen thou me according unto thy word.

29 **Remove** from me the way of lying:
and grant me thy law graciously.

30 **I** have chosen the way of truth:
thy judgments have I laid before me.

31 **I** have stuck unto thy testimonies:
O LORD, put me not to shame.

32 **I** will run the way of thy commandments,
when thou shalt enlarge my heart.

HE

33 **Teach** me, O LORD, the way of thy statutes;
and I shall keep it unto the end.

34 **Give** me understanding,
and I shall keep thy law;
yea, I shall observe it with my whole heart.

35 **Make** me to go in the path of thy commandments;
for therein do I delight.

36 **Incline** my heart unto thy testimonies, and not to covetousness.

37 **Turn away** mine eyes from beholding vanity;
and quicken thou me in thy way.

38 **Stablish** thy word unto thy servant,
who is devoted to thy fear.

39 **Turn away** my reproach which I fear:
for thy judgments are good.

40 **Behold,**
I have longed after thy precepts:
quicken me in thy righteousness.

VAU

41 **Let thy mercies** come also unto me, O LORD, even thy salvation, according to thy word.

42 **So** shall I have wherewith to answer him that reproacheth me:
for I trust in thy word.

43 **And take not** the word of truth utterly out of my mouth;
for I have hoped in thy judgments.

44 **So** shall I keep thy law continually for ever and ever.

45 **And I** will walk at liberty:
for I seek thy precepts.

46 **I** will speak of thy testimonies also before kings,
and will not be ashamed.

47 **And I** will delight myself in thy commandments,
which I have loved.

48 **My hands** also will I lift up unto thy commandments,
which I have loved;
and I will meditate in thy statutes.

ZAIN

49 **Remember** the word unto thy servant,
upon which thou hast caused me to hope.

50 **This** is my comfort in my affliction:
for thy word hath quickened me.

51 **The proud** have had me greatly in derision:
yet have I not declined from thy law.

52 **I** remembered thy judgments of old, O LORD;
and have comforted myself.

53 **Horror** hath taken hold upon me because of the wicked that forsake thy law.

54 **Thy statutes** have been my songs in the house of my pilgrimage.

55 **I** have remembered thy name, O LORD, in the night,
and have kept thy law.

56 **This** I had,
because I kept thy precepts.

CHETH

57 **Thou** art my portion, O LORD:
I have said
that I would keep thy words.

58 **I** intreated thy favour with my whole heart:
be merciful unto me according to thy word.

59 **I** thought on my ways,

and turned my feet unto thy testimonies.

60 **I** made haste,
and delayed not to keep thy commandments.

61 **The bands of the wicked** have robbed me:
but I have not forgotten thy law.

62 **At midnight** I will rise to give thanks unto thee because of thy righteous judgments.

63 **I** am a companion of all them that fear thee, and of them that keep thy precepts.

64 **The earth,** O LORD, is full of thy mercy:
teach me thy statutes.

TETH

65 **Thou** hast dealt well with thy servant, O LORD, according unto thy word.

66 **Teach** me good judgment and knowledge:
for I have believed thy commandments.

67 **Before I** was afflicted
I went astray:
but now have I kept thy word.

68 **Thou** art good,
and doest good;
teach me thy statutes.

69 **The proud** have forged a lie against me:
but I will keep thy precepts with my whole heart.

70 **Their heart** is as fat as grease;
but I delight in thy law.

71 **It is good for me** that I have been afflicted;
that I might learn thy statutes.

72 **The law of thy mouth** is better unto me than thousands of gold and silver.

JOD

73 **Thy hands** have made me and fashioned me:
give me understanding,
that I may learn thy commandments.

74 **They that fear thee** will be glad
when they see me;
because I have hoped in thy word.

75 **I** know, O LORD
that thy judgments are right,
and that thou in faithfulness hast afflicted me.

76 **Let, {I pray thee}, thy merciful kindness** be for my comfort, according to thy word unto thy servant.

77 **Let thy tender mercies** come unto me,
that I may live:
for thy law is my delight.

78 **Let the proud** be ashamed;
for they dealt perversely with me without a cause:
but I will meditate in thy precepts.

79 **Let those that fear thee** turn unto me, and those that have known thy testimonies.

80 **Let my heart** be sound in thy statutes;
that I be not ashamed.

CAPH

81 **My soul** fainteth for thy salvation:
but I hope in thy word.

82 **Mine eyes** fail for thy word,
saying,
When wilt thou comfort me?

83 **For I** am become like a bottle in the smoke;
yet do I not forget thy statutes.

84 **How many** are the days of thy servant?
when wilt thou execute judgment on them that persecute me?

85 **The proud** have digged pits for me,
which are not after thy law.

86 **All thy commandments** are faithful:
they persecute me wrongfully;
help thou me.

87 **They** had almost consumed me upon earth;
but I forsook not thy precepts.

88 **Quicken** me after thy lovingkindness;
so shall I keep the testimony of thy mouth.

LAMED

▶ 89 **For ever,** O LORD, thy word is settled in heaven.

90 **Thy faithfulness** is unto all generations:
thou hast established the earth,
and it abideth.

91 **They** continue this day according to thine ordinances:
for all are thy servants.

92 **Unless thy law** had been my delights,
I should then have perished in mine affliction.

93 **I** will never forget thy precepts:
for with them thou hast quickened me.

94 **I** am thine,
save me:
for I have sought thy precepts.

95 **The wicked** have waited for me to destroy me:
but I will consider thy testimonies.

96 **I** have seen an end of all perfection:
but thy commandment is exceeding broad.

MEM

97 **O how** love I thy law!
it is my meditation all the day.

98 **Thou through thy commandments** hast made me wiser than mine enemies:
for they are ever with me.

99 **I** have more understanding than all my teachers:
for thy testimonies are my meditation.

100 **I** understand more than the ancients,
because I keep thy precepts.

101 **I** have refrained my feet from every evil way,
that I might keep thy word.

102 **I** have not departed from thy judgments:
for thou hast taught me.

103 **How sweet** are thy words unto my taste! yea, sweeter than honey to my mouth!

104 **Through thy precepts** I get understanding:
therefore I hate every false way.

NUN

105 **Thy word** is a lamp unto my feet, and a light unto my path.

106 **I** have sworn,
and I will perform it,
that I will keep thy righteous judgments.

107 **I** am afflicted very much:
quicken me, O LORD, according unto thy word.

108 **Accept,** {I beseech thee}, the freewill offerings of my mouth, O LORD,
and teach me thy judgments.

109 **My soul** is continually in my hand:
yet do I not forget thy law.

110 **The wicked** have laid a snare for me:

yet I erred not from thy precepts.

111 **Thy testimonies** have I taken as an heritage for ever:
for they are the rejoicing of my heart.

112 **I** have inclined mine heart
to perform thy statutes alway, even unto the end.

SAMECH

113 **I** hate vain thoughts:
but thy law do I love.

114 **Thou** art my hiding place and my shield:
I hope in thy word.

115 **Depart** from me, ye evildoers:
for I will keep the commandments of my God.

116 **Uphold** me according unto thy word,
that I may live:
and let me not be ashamed of my hope.

117 **Hold thou me up,**
and I shall be safe:
and I will have respect unto thy statutes continually.

118 **Thou** hast trodden down all them that err from thy statutes:
for their deceit is falsehood.

119 **Thou** puttest away all the wicked of the earth like dross:
therefore I love thy testimonies.

120 **My flesh** trembleth for fear of thee;
and I am afraid of thy judgments.

AIN

121 **I** have done judgment and justice:
leave me not to mine oppressors.

122 **Be** surety for thy servant for good:
let not the proud oppress me.

123 **Mine eyes** fail for thy salvation, and for the word of thy righteousness.

124 **Deal** with thy servant according unto thy mercy,
and teach me thy statutes.

125 **I** am thy servant;
give me understanding,
that I may know thy testimonies.

126 **It is time for thee,** LORD, to work:
for they have made void thy law.

127 **Therefore I** love thy commandments above gold; yea, above fine gold.

128 **Therefore I** esteem all thy precepts concerning all things to be right;
and I hate every false way.

PE

129 **Thy testimonies** are wonderful:
therefore doth my soul keep them.

130 **The entrance of thy words** giveth light;
it giveth understanding unto the simple.

131 **I** opened my mouth,
and panted:
for I longed for thy commandments.

132 **Look thou** upon me,
and be merciful unto me,
as thou usest to do unto those that love thy name.

133 **Order** my steps in thy word:
and let not any iniquity have dominion over me.

134 **Deliver** me from the oppression of man:
so will I keep thy precepts.

135 **Make** thy face to shine upon thy servant;
and teach me thy statutes.

136 **Rivers of waters** run down mine eyes,
because they keep not thy law.

TZADDI

137 **Righteous** art thou, O LORD,
and upright are thy judgments.

138 **Thy testimonies that thou hast commanded** are righteous and very faithful.

139 **My zeal** hath consumed me,
because mine enemies have forgotten thy words.

140 **Thy word** is very pure:
therefore thy servant loveth it.

141 **I** am small and despised:
yet do not I forget thy precepts.

142 **Thy righteousness** is an everlasting righteousness,
and thy law is the truth.

143 **Trouble and anguish** have taken hold on me:
yet thy commandments are my delights.

144 **The righteousness of thy testimonies** is everlasting:
give me understanding,
and I shall live.

KOPH

145 **I** cried with my whole heart;
hear me, O LORD:
I will keep thy statutes.

146 **I** cried unto thee;
save me,
and I shall keep thy testimonies.

147 **I** prevented the dawning of the morning,
and cried:
I hoped in thy word.

148 **Mine eyes** prevent the night watches,
that I might meditate in thy word.

149 **Hear** my voice according unto thy lovingkindness:
O LORD, quicken me according to thy judgment.

150 **They** draw nigh that follow after mischief:
they are far from thy law.

151 **Thou** art near, O LORD;
and all thy commandments are truth.

152 **Concerning thy testimonies,** I have known of old
that thou hast founded them for ever.

RESH

153 **Consider** mine affliction,
and deliver me:
for I do not forget thy law.

154 **Plead** my cause,
and deliver me:
quicken me according to thy word.

155 **Salvation** is far from the wicked:
for they seek not thy statutes.

156 **Great** are thy tender mercies, O LORD:
quicken me according to thy judgments.

157 **Many** are my persecutors and mine enemies;
yet do I not decline from thy testimonies.

158 **I** beheld the transgressors,
and was grieved;
because they kept not thy word.

159 **Consider**
how I love thy precepts:
quicken me, O LORD, according to thy lovingkindness.

160 **Thy word** is true from the beginning:
and every one of thy righteous judgments endureth for ever.

SCHIN

161 **Princes** have persecuted me without a cause:

but my heart standeth in awe of thy word.

162 I rejoice at thy word, as one that findeth great spoil.

163 I hate and abhor lying:
but thy law do I love.

164 **Seven times a day** do I praise thee because of thy righteous judgments.

165 **Great peace** have they which love thy law:
and nothing shall offend them.

166 **LORD, I** have hoped for thy salvation,
and done thy commandments.

167 **My soul** hath kept thy testimonies;
and I love them exceedingly.

168 **I** have kept thy precepts and thy testimonies:
for all my ways are before thee.

TAU

169 **Let my cry** come near before thee, O LORD:
give me understanding according to thy word.

170 **Let my supplication** come before thee:
deliver me according to thy word.

171 **My lips** shall utter praise,
when thou hast taught me thy statutes.

172 **My tongue** shall speak of thy word:
for all thy commandments are righteousness.

173 **Let thine hand** help me;
for I have chosen thy precepts.

174 **I** have longed for thy salvation, O LORD;
and thy law is my delight.

175 **Let my soul** live,
and it shall praise thee;
and let thy judgments help me.

176 **I** have gone astray like a lost sheep;
seek thy servant;
for I do not forget thy commandments.

120

A Song of degrees.

In my distress I cried unto the LORD,
and he heard me.

2 **Deliver** my soul, O LORD, from lying lips, and from a deceitful tongue.

3 **What** shall be given unto thee?
or what shall be done unto thee, thou false tongue?

4 Sharp arrows of the mighty, with coals of juniper.

5 **Woe** is me,
that I sojourn in Mesech,
that I dwell in the tents of Kedar!

6 **My soul** hath long dwelt with him that hateth peace.

7 **I** am for peace:
but when I speak,
they are for war.

121

A Song of degrees.

I will lift up mine eyes unto the hills,
from whence cometh my help.

2 **My help** cometh from the LORD,
which made heaven and earth.

3 **He** will not suffer thy foot to be moved:
he that keepeth thee will not slumber.

4 **Behold,**
he that keepeth Israel shall neither slumber
nor sleep.

5 **The LORD** is thy keeper:
the LORD is thy shade upon thy right hand.

6 **The sun** shall not smite thee by day, nor the moon by night.

7 **The LORD** shall preserve thee from all evil:
he shall preserve thy soul.

8 **The LORD** shall preserve thy going out and thy coming in from this time forth, and even for evermore.

122

A Song of degrees of David.

I was glad
when they said unto me,
Let us go into the house of the LORD.

2 **Our feet** shall stand within thy gates, O Jerusalem.

3 **Jerusalem** is builded as a city that is compact together:

4 **Whither the tribes** go up, the tribes of the LORD, unto the testimony of Israel,
to give thanks unto the name of the LORD.

5 **For there** are set thrones of judgment, the thrones of the house of David.

6 **Pray** for the peace of Jerusalem:
they shall prosper that love thee.

7 **Peace** be within thy walls, and prosperity within thy palaces.

8 **For my brethren and companions' sakes,** I will now say,
Peace be within thee.

9 **Because of the house of the LORD our God** I will seek thy good.

123

A Song of degrees.

Unto thee lift I up mine eyes, O thou that dwellest in the heavens.

2 **Behold,**
as the eyes of servants look unto the hand of their masters, and as the eyes of a maiden unto the hand of her mistress;
so our eyes wait upon the LORD our God,
until that he have mercy upon us.

3 **Have** mercy upon us, O LORD,
have mercy upon us:
for we are exceedingly filled with contempt.

4 **Our soul** is exceedingly filled with the scorning of those that are at ease, and with the contempt of the proud.

124

A Song of degrees of David.

If it had not been the LORD who was on our side,
now may Israel say;

2 **If it** had not been the LORD who was on our side,
when men rose up against us:

3 **Then they** had swallowed us up quick,
when their wrath was kindled against us:

4 **Then the waters** had overwhelmed us,
the stream had gone over our soul:

5 **Then the proud waters** had gone over our soul.

6 **Blessed** be the LORD,
who hath not given us as a prey to their teeth.

7 **Our soul** is escaped as a bird out of the snare of the fowlers:
the snare is broken,
and we are escaped.

8 **Our help** is in the name of the LORD,
who made heaven and earth.

125

A Song of degrees.

They that trust in the LORD shall be as mount Zion,
which cannot be removed,
but abideth for ever.
2 **As the mountains** are round about Jerusalem,
so the LORD is round about his people from henceforth even for ever.
3 **For the rod of the wicked** shall not rest upon the lot of the righteous;
lest the righteous put forth their hands unto iniquity.
4 **Do** good, O LORD, unto those that be good, and to them that are upright in their hearts.
5 **As for such as turn aside unto their crooked ways,** the LORD shall lead them forth with the workers of iniquity:
but peace shall be upon Israel.

126

A Song of degrees.

When the LORD turned again the captivity of Zion,
we were like them that dream.
2 **Then** was our mouth filled with laughter, and our tongue with singing:
then said they among the heathen,
The LORD hath done great things for them.
3 **The LORD** hath done great things for us;
whereof we are glad.
4 **Turn** again our captivity, O LORD, as the streams in the south.
5 **They that sow in tears** shall reap in joy.
6 **He that goeth forth and weepeth**, {bearing precious seed}, shall doubtless come again with rejoicing,
bringing his sheaves with him.

127

A Song of degrees for Solomon.

Except the LORD build the house,
they labour in vain that build it:
except the LORD keep the city,
the watchman waketh but in vain.
2 **It is vain for you** to rise up early,
to sit up late,
to eat the bread of sorrows:
for so he giveth his beloved sleep.
3 **Lo,**
children are an heritage of the LORD:
and the fruit of the womb is his reward.
4 **As arrows** are in the hand of a mighty man;
so are children of the youth.
5 **Happy** is the man that hath his quiver full of them:
they shall not be ashamed,
but they shall speak with the enemies in the gate.

128

A Song of degrees.

Blessed is every one that feareth the LORD; that walketh in his ways.
2 **For thou** shalt eat the labour of thine hands:
happy shalt thou be,
and it shall be well with thee.
3 **Thy wife** shall be as a fruitful vine by the sides of thine house: thy children like olive plants round about thy table.
4 **Behold,**
that thus shall the man be blessed that feareth the LORD.
5 **The LORD** shall bless thee out of Zion:
and thou shalt see the good of Jerusalem all the days of thy life.
6 **Yea, thou** shalt see thy children's children, and peace upon Israel.

129

A Song of degrees.

Many a time have they afflicted me from my youth,
may Israel now say:
2 **Many a time** have they afflicted me from my youth:
yet they have not prevailed against me.
3 **The plowers** plowed upon my back:
they made long their furrows.
4 **The LORD** is righteous:
he hath cut asunder the cords of the wicked.
5 **Let them all** be confounded and turned back that hate Zion.
6 **Let them** be as the grass upon the housetops,
which withereth
afore it groweth up:
7 **Wherewith** the mower filleth not his hand; nor he that bindeth sheaves his bosom.
8 **Neither** do they which go by say,
The blessing of the LORD be upon you:
we bless you in the name of the LORD.

130

A Song of degrees.

Out of the depths have I cried unto thee, O LORD.
2 **Lord, hear** my voice:
let thine ears be attentive to the voice of my supplications.
3 **If thou,** LORD, shouldest mark iniquities,
O Lord, who shall stand?
4 **But there** is forgiveness with thee,
that thou mayest be feared.
5 **I** wait for the LORD,
my soul doth wait,
and in his word do I hope.
6 **My soul** waiteth for the Lord more than they that watch for the morning: {I say}, more than they that watch for the morning.
7 **Let Israel** hope in the LORD:
for with the LORD there is mercy,
and with him is plenteous redemption.
8 **And he** shall redeem Israel from all his iniquities.

131

A Song of degrees of David.

LORD, my heart is not haughty, nor mine eyes lofty:
neither do I exercise myself in great matters, or in things too high for me.
2 **Surely I** have behaved and quieted myself, as a child that is weaned of his mother:
my soul is even as a weaned child.
3 **Let Israel** hope in the LORD from henceforth and for ever.

132

A Song of degrees.

LORD, remember David, and all his afflictions:
2 **How** he sware unto the LORD,
and vowed unto the mighty God of Jacob;
3 **Surely I** will not come into the tabernacle of my house,
nor go up into my bed;
4 **I** will not give sleep to mine eyes, or slumber to mine eyelids,
5 **Until I** find out a place for the LORD, an habitation for the mighty God of Jacob.
6 **Lo,**
we heard of it at Ephratah:

we found it in the fields of the wood.
7 **We** will go into his tabernacles:
we will worship at his footstool.
8 **Arise,** O LORD, into thy rest; thou, and the ark of thy strength.
9 **Let thy priests** be clothed with righteousness;
and let thy saints shout for joy.
10 **For thy servant David's sake** turn not away the face of thine anointed.
11 **The LORD** hath sworn in truth unto David;
he will not turn from it;
Of the fruit of thy body will I set upon thy throne.
12 **If thy children** will keep my covenant and my testimony that I shall teach them,
their children shall also sit upon thy throne for evermore.
13 **For the LORD** hath chosen Zion;
he hath desired it for his habitation.
14 **This** is my rest for ever:
here will I dwell;
for I have desired it.
15 **I** will abundantly bless her provision:
I will satisfy her poor with bread.
16 **I** will also clothe her priests with salvation:
and her saints shall shout aloud for joy.
17 **There** will I make the horn of David to bud:
I have ordained a lamp for mine anointed.
18 **His enemies** will I clothe with shame:
but upon himself shall his crown flourish.

133

A Song of degrees of David.

Behold,
how good and how pleasant it is for brethren to dwell together in unity!
2 **It** is like the precious ointment upon the head,
that ran down upon the beard, even Aaron's beard:
that went down to the skirts of his garments;
3 As the dew of Hermon, and as the dew that descended upon the mountains of Zion:
for there the LORD commanded the blessing, even life for evermore.

134

A Song of degrees.

Behold,
bless ye the LORD, all ye servants of the LORD,
which by night stand in the house of the LORD.
2 **Lift up** your hands in the sanctuary,
and bless the LORD.
3 **The LORD that made heaven and earth** bless thee out of Zion.

135

Praise ye the LORD.
Praise ye the name of the LORD;
praise him, O ye servants of the LORD.
2 Ye that stand in the house of the LORD, in the courts of the house of our God.
3 **Praise** the LORD;
for the LORD is good:
sing praises unto his name;
for it is pleasant.
4 **For the LORD** hath chosen Jacob unto himself, and Israel for his peculiar treasure.
5 **For I** know
that the LORD is great,
and that our Lord is above all gods.
6 **Whatsoever the LORD** pleased,
that did he in heaven, and in earth, in the seas, and all deep places.
7 **He** causeth the vapours to ascend from the ends of the earth;
he maketh lightnings for the rain;
he bringeth the wind out of his treasuries.
8 **Who** smote the firstborn of Egypt, both of man and beast.
9 **Who** sent tokens and wonders into the midst of thee, O Egypt, upon Pharaoh, and upon all his servants.
10 **Who** smote great nations,
and slew mighty kings;
11 Sihon king of the Amorites, and Og king of Bashan, and all the kingdoms of Canaan:
12 **And** gave their land for an heritage, an heritage unto Israel his people.
13 **Thy name,** O LORD, endureth for ever; and thy memorial, O LORD, throughout all generations.
14 **For the LORD** will judge his people,
and he will repent himself concerning his servants.
15 **The idols of the heathen** are silver and gold, the work of men's hands.
16 **They** have mouths,
but they speak not;
eyes have they,
but they see not;
17 **They** have ears,
but they hear not;
neither is there any breath in their mouths.
18 **They that make them** are like unto them:
so is every one that trusteth in them.
19 **Bless** the LORD, O house of Israel:
bless the LORD, O house of Aaron:
20 **Bless** the LORD, O house of Levi:
ye that fear the LORD, bless the LORD.
21 **Blessed** be the LORD out of Zion,
which dwelleth at Jerusalem.
Praise ye the LORD.

136

O give thanks unto the LORD;
for he is good:
for his mercy endureth for ever.
2 **O give** thanks unto the God of gods:
for his mercy endureth for ever.
3 **O give** thanks to the Lord of lords:
for his mercy endureth for ever.
4 To him who alone doeth great wonders:
for his mercy endureth for ever.
5 To him that by wisdom made the heavens:
for his mercy endureth for ever.
6 To him that stretched out the earth above the waters:
for his mercy endureth for ever.
7 To him that made great lights:
for his mercy endureth for ever:
8 **The sun** to rule by day:
for his mercy endureth for ever:
9 The moon and stars to rule by night:
for his mercy endureth for ever.
10 To him that smote Egypt in their firstborn:
for his mercy endureth for ever:
11 **And** brought out Israel from among them:
for his mercy endureth for ever:

12 With a strong hand, and with a stretched out arm:
for his mercy endureth for ever.
13 To him which divided the Red sea into parts:
for his mercy endureth for ever:
14 **And** made Israel to pass through the midst of it:
for his mercy endureth for ever:
15 **But** overthrew Pharaoh and his host in the Red sea:
for his mercy endureth for ever.
16 To him which led his people through the wilderness:
for his mercy endureth for ever.
17 To him which smote great kings:
for his mercy endureth for ever:
18 **And** slew famous kings:
for his mercy endureth for ever:
19 Sihon king of the Amorites:
for his mercy endureth for ever:
20 And Og the king of Bashan:
for his mercy endureth for ever:
21 **And** gave their land for an heritage:
for his mercy endureth for ever:
22 Even an heritage unto Israel his servant:
for his mercy endureth for ever.
23 **Who** remembered us in our low estate:
for his mercy endureth for ever:
24 **And** hath redeemed us from our enemies:
for his mercy endureth for ever.
25 **Who** giveth food to all flesh:
for his mercy endureth for ever.
26 **O give** thanks unto the God of heaven:
for his mercy endureth for ever.

137

By the rivers of Babylon, there we sat down,
yea, we wept,
when we remembered Zion.
2 **We** hanged our harps upon the willows in the midst thereof.
3 **For there** they that carried us away captive required of us a song;
and they that wasted us required of us mirth,
saying,
Sing us one of the songs of Zion.
4 **How** shall we sing the LORD's song in a strange land?
5 **If I** forget thee, O Jerusalem,
let my right hand forget her cunning.
6 **If I** do not remember thee,
let my tongue cleave to the roof of my mouth;
if I prefer not Jerusalem above my chief joy.
7 **Remember,** O LORD, the children of Edom in the day of Jerusalem;
who said,
Rase it,
rase it, even to the foundation thereof.
8 **O daughter of Babylon, who** art to be destroyed;
happy shall he be,
that rewardeth thee
as thou hast served us.
9 **Happy** shall he be,
that taketh and dasheth thy little ones against the stones.

138

A Psalm of David.

I will praise thee with my whole heart:
before the gods will I sing praise unto thee.
2 **I** will worship toward thy holy temple,
and praise thy name for thy lovingkindness and for thy truth:
for thou hast magnified thy word above all thy name.
3 **In the day when I cried** thou answeredst me,
and strengthenedst me with strength in my soul.
4 **All the kings of the earth** shall praise thee, O LORD,
when they hear the words of thy mouth.
5 **Yea, they** shall sing in the ways of the LORD:
for great is the glory of the LORD.
6 **Though the LORD** be high,
yet hath he respect unto the lowly:
but the proud he knoweth afar off.
7 **Though I** walk in the midst of trouble,
thou wilt revive me:
thou shalt stretch forth thine hand against the wrath of mine enemies,
and thy right hand shall save me.
8 **The LORD** will perfect that which concerneth me:
thy mercy, O LORD, endureth for ever:
forsake not the works of thine own hands.

139

To the chief Musician, A Psalm of David.

O LORD, thou hast searched me,
and known me.
2 **Thou** knowest my downsitting and mine uprising,
thou understandest my thought afar off.
3 **Thou** compassest my path and my lying down,
and art acquainted with all my ways.
4 **For there** is not a word in my tongue,
but, {lo}, O LORD, thou knowest it altogether.
5 **Thou** hast beset me behind and before,
and laid thine hand upon me.
6 **Such knowledge** is too wonderful for me;
it is high,
I cannot attain unto it.
7 **Whither** shall I go from thy spirit?
or whither shall I flee from thy presence?
8 **If I** ascend up into heaven,
thou art there:
if I make my bed in hell,
behold,
thou art there.
9 **If I** take the wings of the morning,
and dwell in the uttermost parts of the sea;
10 **Even there** shall thy hand lead me,
and thy right hand shall hold me.
11 **If I** say, **Surely the darkness** shall cover me;
even the night shall be light about me.
12 **Yea, the darkness** hideth not from thee;
but the night shineth as the day:
the darkness and the light are both alike to thee.
13 **For thou** hast possessed my reins:
thou hast covered me in my mother's womb.
14 **I** will praise thee;
for I am fearfully and wonderfully made:
marvellous are thy works;
and that my soul knoweth right well.
15 **My substance** was not hid from thee,
when I was made in secret,

and curiously wrought in the lowest parts of the earth.

16 **Thine eyes** did see my substance,
yet being unperfect;
and in thy book all my members were written,
which in continuance were fashioned,
when as yet there was none of them.

17 **How precious** also are thy thoughts unto me, O God!
how great is the sum of them!

18 **If I** should count them,
they are more in number than the sand:
when I awake,
I am still with thee.

19 **Surely thou** wilt slay the wicked, O God:
depart from me therefore, ye bloody men.

20 **For they** speak against thee wickedly,
and thine enemies take thy name in vain.

21 **Do not I** hate them, O LORD, that hate thee?
and am not I grieved with those that rise up against thee?

22 **I** hate them with perfect hatred:
I count them mine enemies.

23 **Search** me, O God,
and know my heart:
try me,
and know my thoughts:

24 **And see** if there be any wicked way in me,
and lead me in the way everlasting.

140

To the chief Musician, A Psalm of David.

Deliver me, O LORD, from the evil man:
preserve me from the violent man;

2 **Which** imagine mischiefs in their heart;
continually are they gathered together for war.

3 **They** have sharpened their tongues like a serpent;
adders' poison is under their lips.
Selah.

4 **Keep** me, O LORD, from the hands of the wicked;
preserve me from the violent man;
who have purposed to overthrow my goings.

5 **The proud** have hid a snare for me, and cords;
they have spread a net by the wayside;
they have set gins for me.
Selah.

6 **I** said unto the LORD,
Thou art my God:
hear the voice of my supplications, O LORD.

7 **O GOD the Lord, the strength of my salvation, thou** hast covered my head in the day of battle.

8 **Grant not,** O LORD, the desires of the wicked:
further not his wicked device;
lest they exalt themselves.
Selah.

9 **As for the head of those that compass me about,** let the mischief of their own lips cover them.

10 **Let burning coals** fall upon them:
let them be cast into the fire; into deep pits,
that they rise not up again.

11 **Let not an evil speaker** be established in the earth:
evil shall hunt the violent man
to overthrow him.

12 **I** know that the LORD will maintain the cause of the afflicted, and the right of the poor.

13 **Surely the righteous** shall give thanks unto thy name:
the upright shall dwell in thy presence.

141

A Psalm of David.

LORD, I cry unto thee:
make haste unto me;
give ear unto my voice,
when I cry unto thee.

2 **Let my prayer** be set forth before thee as incense; and the lifting up of my hands as the evening sacrifice.

3 **Set** a watch, O LORD, before my mouth;
keep the door of my lips.

4 **Incline not** my heart to any evil thing,
to practise wicked works with men that work iniquity:
and let me not eat of their dainties.

5 **Let the righteous** smite me;
it shall be a kindness:
and let him reprove me;
it shall be an excellent oil,
which shall not break my head:
for yet my prayer also shall be in their calamities.

6 **When their judges** are overthrown in stony places,
they shall hear my words;
for they are sweet.

7 **Our bones** are scattered at the grave's mouth,
as when one cutteth and cleaveth wood upon the earth.

8 **But mine eyes** are unto thee, O GOD the Lord:
in thee is my trust;
leave not my soul destitute.

9 **Keep** me from the snares which they have laid for me, and the gins of the workers of iniquity.

10 **Let the wicked** fall into their own nets,
whilst that I withal escape.

142

Maschil of David; A Prayer when he was in the cave.

I cried unto the LORD with my voice;
with my voice unto the LORD did I make my supplication.

2 **I** poured out my complaint before him;
I shewed before him my trouble.

3 **When my spirit** was overwhelmed within me,
then thou knewest my path.
In the way wherein I walked have they privily laid a snare for me.

4 **I** looked on my right hand,
and beheld,
but there was no man that would know me:
refuge failed me;
no man cared for my soul.

5 **I** cried unto thee, O LORD:
I said,
Thou art my refuge and my portion in the land of the living.

6 **Attend** unto my cry;
for I am brought very low:
deliver me from my persecutors;
for they are stronger than I.

7 **Bring** my soul out of prison,
that I may praise thy name:
the righteous shall compass me about;
for thou shalt deal bountifully with me.

143

A Psalm of David.

Hear my prayer, O LORD,
give ear to my supplications:
in thy faithfulness answer me, and in thy righteousness.
2 **And enter not** into judgment with thy servant:
for in thy sight shall no man living be justified.
3 **For the enemy** hath persecuted my soul;
he hath smitten my life down to the ground;
he hath made me to dwell in darkness, as those that have been long dead.
4 **Therefore** is my spirit overwhelmed within me;
my heart within me is desolate.
5 **I** remember the days of old;
I meditate on all thy works;
I muse on the work of thy hands.
6 **I** stretch forth my hands unto thee:
my soul thirsteth after thee, as a thirsty land.
Selah.
7 **Hear** me speedily, O LORD:
my spirit faileth:
hide not thy face from me,
lest I be like unto them that go down into the pit.
8 **Cause me** to hear thy lovingkindness in the morning;
for in thee do I trust:
cause me to know the way wherein I should walk;
for I lift up my soul unto thee.
9 **Deliver** me, O LORD, from mine enemies:
I flee unto thee to hide me.
10 **Teach** me to do thy will;
for thou art my God:
thy spirit is good;
lead me into the land of uprightness.
11 **Quicken** me, O LORD, for thy name's sake:
for thy righteousness' sake bring my soul out of trouble.
12 **And of thy mercy** cut off mine enemies,
and destroy all them that afflict my soul:
for I am thy servant.

144

A Psalmof David.

Blessed be the LORD my strength
which teacheth my hands to war, and my fingers to fight:
2 My goodness, and my fortress; my high tower, and my deliverer; my shield, and he in whom I trust;
who subdueth my people under me.
3 **LORD, what** is man, {that thou takest knowledge of him}! or the son of man, {that thou makest account of him}!
4 **Man** is like to vanity:
his days are as a shadow that passeth away.
5 **Bow** thy heavens, O LORD,
and come down:
touch the mountains,
and they shall smoke.
6 **Cast forth** lightning,
and scatter them:
shoot out thine arrows,
and destroy them.
7 **Send** thine hand from above;
rid me,
and deliver me out of great waters, from the hand of strange children;
8 **Whose mouth** speaketh vanity,
and their right hand is a right hand of falsehood.
9 **I** will sing a new song unto thee, O God:
upon a psaltery and an instrument of ten strings will I sing praises unto thee.
10 **It is he** that giveth salvation unto kings:
who delivereth David his servant from the hurtful sword.
11 **Rid** me,
and deliver me from the hand of strange children,
whose mouth speaketh vanity,
and their right hand is a right hand of falsehood:
12 **That our sons** may be as plants grown up in their youth;
that our daughters may be as corner stones,
polished after the similitude of a palace:
13 **That our garners** may be full,
affording all manner of store:
that our sheep may bring forth thousands and ten thousands in our streets:
14 **That our oxen** may be strong to labour;
that there be no breaking in,
nor going out;
that there be no complaining in our streets.
15 **Happy** is that people,
that is in such a case:
yea, happy is that people,
whose God is the LORD.

145

David's Psalm of praise.

I will extol thee, my God, O king;
and I will bless thy name for ever and ever.
2 **Every day** will I bless thee;
and I will praise thy name for ever and ever.
3 **Great** is the LORD,
and greatly to be praised;
and his greatness is unsearchable.
4 **One generation** shall praise thy works to another,
and shall declare thy mighty acts.
5 **I** will speak of the glorious honour of thy majesty, and of thy wondrous works.
6 **And men** shall speak of the might of thy terrible acts:
and I will declare thy greatness.
7 **They** shall abundantly utter the memory of thy great goodness,
and shall sing of thy righteousness.
8 **The LORD** is gracious, and full of compassion; slow to anger, and of great mercy.
9 **The LORD** is good to all:
and his tender mercies are over all his works.
10 **All thy works** shall praise thee, O LORD;
and thy saints shall bless thee.
11 **They** shall speak of the glory of thy kingdom,
and talk of thy power;
12 To make known to the sons of men his mighty acts, and the glorious majesty of his kingdom.
13 **Thy kingdom** is an everlasting kingdom,
and thy dominion endureth throughout all generations.
14 **The LORD** upholdeth all that fall,
and raiseth up all those that be bowed down.
15 **The eyes of all** wait upon thee;
and thou givest them their meat in due season.
16 **Thou** openest thine hand,
and satisfiest the desire of every living thing.

17 **The LORD** is righteous in all his ways, and holy in all his works.
18 **The LORD** is nigh unto all them that call upon him, to all that call upon him in truth.
19 **He** will fulfil the desire of them that fear him:
he also will hear their cry,
and will save them.
20 **The LORD** preserveth all them that love him:
but all the wicked will he destroy.
21 **My mouth** shall speak the praise of the LORD:
and let all flesh bless his holy name for ever and ever.

146

Praise ye the LORD. **Praise** the LORD, O my soul.
2 **While** I live
will I praise the LORD:
I will sing praises unto my God
while I have any being.
3 **Put not** your trust in princes, nor in the son of man,
in whom there is no help.
4 **His breath** goeth forth,
he returneth to his earth;
in that very day his thoughts perish.
5 **Happy** is he that hath the God of Jacob for his help,
whose hope is in the LORD his God:
6 **Which** made heaven, and earth, the sea, and all that therein is:
which keepeth truth for ever:
7 **Which** executeth judgment for the oppressed:
which giveth food to the hungry.
The LORD looseth the prisoners:
8 **The LORD** openeth the eyes of the blind:
the LORD raiseth them that are bowed down:
the LORD loveth the righteous:
9 **The LORD** preserveth the strangers;
he relieveth the fatherless and widow:
but the way of the wicked he turneth upside down.
10 **The LORD** shall reign for ever, even thy God, O Zion, unto all generations.
Praise ye the LORD.

147

Praise ye the LORD: **for it is good** to sing praises unto our God;
for it is pleasant;
and praise is comely.
2 **The LORD** doth build up Jerusalem:
he gathereth together the outcasts of Israel.
3 **He** healeth the broken in heart,
and bindeth up their wounds.
4 **He** telleth the number of the stars;
he calleth them all by their names.
5 **Great** is our Lord, and of great power:
his understanding is infinite.
6 **The LORD** lifteth up the meek:
he casteth the wicked down to the ground.
7 **Sing** unto the LORD with thanksgiving;
sing praise upon the harp unto our God:
8 **Who** covereth the heaven with clouds,
who prepareth rain for the earth,
who maketh grass to grow upon the mountains.
9 **He** giveth to the beast his food, and to the young ravens which cry.
10 **He** delighteth not in the strength of the horse:
he taketh not pleasure in the legs of a man.
11 **The LORD** taketh pleasure in them that fear him, in those that hope in his mercy.
12 **Praise** the LORD, O Jerusalem;
praise thy God, O Zion.
13 **For he** hath strengthened the bars of thy gates;
he hath blessed thy children within thee.
14 **He** maketh peace in thy borders,
and filleth thee with the finest of the wheat.
15 **He** sendeth forth his commandment upon earth:
his word runneth very swiftly.
16 **He** giveth snow like wool:
he scattereth the hoarfrost like ashes.
17 **He** casteth forth his ice like morsels:
who can stand before his cold?
18 **He** sendeth out his word,
and melteth them:
he causeth his wind to blow,
and the waters flow.
19 **He** sheweth his word unto Jacob, his statutes and his judgments unto Israel.
20 **He** hath not dealt so with any nation:
and as for his judgments, they have not known them.
Praise ye the LORD.

148

Praise ye the LORD. **Praise ye** the LORD from the heavens:
praise him in the heights.
2 **Praise ye** him, all his angels:
praise ye him, all his hosts.
3 **Praise ye** him, sun and moon:
praise him, all ye stars of light.
4 **Praise** him, ye heavens of heavens, and ye waters that be above the heavens.
5 **Let them** praise the name of the LORD:
for he commanded,
and they were created.
6 **He** hath also stablished them for ever and ever:
he hath made a decree which shall not pass.
7 **Praise** the LORD from the earth, ye dragons, and all deeps:
8 Fire, and hail; snow, and vapours; stormy wind fulfilling his word:
9 Mountains, and all hills; fruitful trees, and all cedars:
10 Beasts, and all cattle; creeping things, and flying fowl:
11 Kings of the earth, and all people; princes, and all judges of the earth:
12 Both young men, and maidens; old men, and children:
13 **Let them** praise the name of the LORD:
for his name alone is excellent;
his glory is above the earth and heaven.
14 **He** also exalteth the horn of his people, the praise of all his saints; even of the children of Israel, a people near unto him.
Praise ye the LORD.

149

Praise ye the LORD. **Sing** unto the LORD a new song, and his praise in the congregation of saints.
2 **Let Israel** rejoice in him that made him:

let the children of Zion be joyful in
their King.
3 **Let them** praise his name in the
dance:
let them sing praises unto him with
the timbrel and harp.
4 **For the LORD** taketh pleasure in
his people:
he will beautify the meek with
salvation.
5 **Let the saints** be joyful in glory:
let them sing aloud upon their
beds.
6 **Let the high praises of God** be in
their mouth, and a two-edged
sword in their hand;
7 To execute vengeance upon the
heathen, and punishments upon
the people;
8 To bind their kings with chains,
and their nobles with fetters of
iron;
9 To execute upon them the
judgment written:
this honour have all his saints.
Praise ye the LORD.

150

Praise ye the LORD.
Praise God in his
sanctuary:
praise him in the firmament of his
power.
2 **Praise** him for his mighty acts:
praise him according to his
excellent greatness.
3 **Praise** him with the sound of the
trumpet:
praise him with the psaltery and
harp.
4 **Praise** him with the timbrel and
dance:
praise him with stringed
instruments and organs.
5 **Praise** him upon the loud cymbals:
praise him upon the high sounding
cymbals.
6 **Let every thing that hath breath**
praise the LORD.
Praise ye the LORD.

Proverbs

The Book of Proverbs, authored primarily by King Solomon, is a collection of wise sayings and teachings that offer guidance on how to behave righteously and make wise decisions. Solomon believed that by following these teachings, people could avoid the pitfalls of sin and foolishness. The book offers practical advice, moral guidance, and timeless truths on navigating life's most demanding situations. These challenges include dealing with difficult people, making sound financial decisions, and avoiding the temptations of sin.

In addition to warning against the dangers of sin and folly, which lead to destruction and ruin, it also encourages people to work hard and be diligent in their pursuits, both of which can lead to success and prosperity. Finally, the book teaches that humility is not just a virtue but a key that unlocks solid relationships with others.

Ultimately, Proverbs underscores the need to obey God's commands and pursue righteousness. These two principles, it asserts, are the keys to true happiness and fulfillment. As the preeminent source of wisdom and guidance for leading a righteous life in obedience to God, the Book of Proverbs remains not just relevant but impactful today, reassuring readers that its wisdom remains as timeless and relevant as it was thousands of years ago.

1 **The proverbs of Solomon the son of David, king of Israel;**
2 To know wisdom and instruction;
to perceive the words of understanding;
3 To receive the instruction of wisdom, justice, and judgment, and equity;
4 To give subtilty to the simple, to the young man knowledge and discretion.
5 **A wise man** will hear,
and will increase learning;
and a man of understanding shall attain unto wise counsels:
6 To understand a proverb, and the interpretation; the words of the wise, and their dark sayings.
7 **The fear of the LORD** is the beginning of knowledge:
but fools despise wisdom and instruction.
8 **My son, hear** the instruction of thy father,
and forsake not the law of thy mother:
9 **For they** shall be an ornament of grace unto thy head, and chains about thy neck.
10 **My son, if sinners** entice thee,
consent thou not.
11 **If they** say,
Come with us,
let us lay wait for blood,
let us lurk privily for the innocent without cause:
12 **Let us** swallow them up alive as the grave; and whole, as those that go down into the pit:
13 **We** shall find all precious substance,
we shall fill our houses with spoil:
14 **Cast in** thy lot among us;
let us all have one purse:
15 **My son, walk not thou** in the way with them;
refrain thy foot from their path:
16 **For their feet** run to evil,
and make haste to shed blood.
17 **Surely in vain** the net is spread in the sight of any bird.
18 **And they** lay wait for their own blood;
they lurk privily for their own lives.
19 **So** are the ways of every one that is greedy of gain;
which taketh away the life of the owners thereof.
20 **Wisdom** crieth without;
she uttereth her voice in the streets:
21 **She** crieth in the chief place of concourse, in the openings of the gates:
in the city she uttereth her words, saying,
22 **How long**, ye simple ones, will ye love simplicity?
and the scorners delight in their scorning,
and fools hate knowledge?
23 **Turn you** at my reproof:
behold,
I will pour out my spirit unto you,
I will make known my words unto you.
24 **Because I** have called,
and ye refused;
I have stretched out my hand,
and no man regarded;
25 **But ye** have set at nought all my counsel,
and would none of my reproof:
26 **I** also will laugh at your calamity;
I will mock
when your fear cometh;
27 **When your fear** cometh as desolation,
and your destruction cometh as a whirlwind;
when distress and anguish cometh upon you.
28 **Then** shall they call upon me,
but I will not answer;
they shall seek me early,
but they shall not find me:
29 **For that they** hated knowledge,
and did not choose the fear of the LORD:
30 **They** would none of my counsel:
they despised all my reproof.
31 **Therefore** shall they eat of the fruit of their own way,
and be filled with their own devices.
32 **For the turning away of the simple** shall slay them,
and the prosperity of fools shall destroy them.
33 **But whoso hearkeneth unto me** shall dwell safely,
and shall be quiet from fear of evil.

2

My son, if thou wilt receive my words,
and hide my commandments with thee;
2 **So that thou** incline thine ear unto wisdom,
and apply thine heart to understanding;
3 **Yea, if thou** criest after knowledge,
and liftest up thy voice for understanding;
4 **If thou** seekest her as silver,
and searchest for her as for hid treasures;
5 **Then** shalt thou understand the fear of the LORD,
and find the knowledge of God.
6 **For the LORD** giveth wisdom:
out of his mouth cometh knowledge and understanding.
7 **He** layeth up sound wisdom for the righteous:
he is a buckler to them that walk uprightly.
8 **He** keepeth the paths of judgment,
and preserveth the way of his saints.
9 **Then** shalt thou understand righteousness, and judgment, and equity; yea, every good path.
10 **When wisdom** entereth into thine heart,
and knowledge is pleasant unto thy soul;
11 **Discretion** shall preserve thee,
understanding shall keep thee:
12 To deliver thee from the way of the evil man, from the man that speaketh froward things;
13 **Who** leave the paths of uprightness,
to walk in the ways of darkness;
14 **Who** rejoice to do evil,
and delight in the frowardness of the wicked;
15 **Whose ways** are crooked,
and they froward in their paths:
16 To deliver thee from the strange woman, even from the stranger which flattereth with her words;
17 **Which** forsaketh the guide of her youth,
and forgetteth the covenant of her God.
18 **For her house** inclineth unto death,
and her paths unto the dead.
19 **None that go unto her** return again,
neither take they hold of the paths of life.
20 **That thou** mayest walk in the way of good men,
and keep the paths of the righteous.
21 **For the upright** shall dwell in the land,
and the perfect shall remain in it.
22 **But the wicked** shall be cut off from the earth,
and the transgressors shall be rooted out of it.

3

My son, forget not my law;
but let thine heart keep my commandments:
2 **For length of days, and long life, and peace,** shall they add to thee.
3 **Let not mercy and truth** forsake thee:
bind them about thy neck;
write them upon the table of thine heart:
4 **So** shalt thou find favour and good understanding in the sight of God and man.
5 **Trust** in the LORD with all thine heart;
and lean not unto thine own understanding.
6 **In all thy ways** acknowledge him,
and he shall direct thy paths.
7 **Be not** wise in thine own eyes:
fear the LORD,
and depart from evil.
8 **It** shall be health to thy navel, and marrow to thy bones.
9 **Honour** the LORD with thy substance, and with the firstfruits of all thine increase:
10 **So** shall thy barns be filled with plenty,
and thy presses shall burst out with new wine.
11 **My son, despise not** the chastening of the LORD;
neither be weary of his correction:
12 **For whom** the LORD loveth
he correcteth;
even as a father the son in whom he delighteth.
13 **Happy** is the man that findeth wisdom, and the man that getteth understanding.
14 **For the merchandise of it** is better than the merchandise of silver,
and the gain thereof than fine gold.
15 **She** is more precious than rubies:
and all the things thou canst desire are not to be compared unto her.
16 **Length of days** is in her right hand;
and in her left hand riches and honour.
17 **Her ways** are ways of pleasantness,
and all her paths are peace.
18 **She** is a tree of life to them that lay hold upon her:
and happy is every one that retaineth her.
19 **The LORD by wisdom** hath founded the earth;
by understanding hath he established the heavens.
20 **By his knowledge** the depths are broken up,
and the clouds drop down the dew.
21 **My son, let not them** depart from thine eyes:
keep sound wisdom and discretion:
22 **So** shall they be life unto thy soul, and grace to thy neck.
23 **Then** shalt thou walk in thy way safely,
and thy foot shall not stumble.
24 **When thou** liest down,
thou shalt not be afraid:
yea, thou shalt lie down,
and thy sleep shall be sweet.
25 **Be not** afraid of sudden fear,
neither of the desolation of the wicked,
when it cometh.
26 **For the LORD** shall be thy confidence,
and shall keep thy foot from being taken.
27 **Withhold not** good from them to whom it is due,
when it is in the power of thine hand to do it.
28 **Say not** unto thy neighbour,
Go,
and come again,
and to morrow I will give;
when thou hast it by thee.
29 **Devise not** evil against thy neighbour,
seeing he dwelleth securely by thee.
30 **Strive not** with a man without cause,
if he have done thee no harm.

31 **Envy thou not** the oppressor,
and choose none of his ways.
32 **For the froward** is abomination to the LORD:
but his secret is with the righteous.
33 **The curse of the LORD** is in the house of the wicked:
but he blesseth the habitation of the just.
34 **Surely he** scorneth the scorners:
but he giveth grace unto the lowly.
35 **The wise** shall inherit glory:
but shame shall be the promotion of fools.

4 **Hear,** ye children, the instruction of a father,
and attend
to know understanding.
2 **For I** give you good doctrine,
forsake ye not my law.
3 **For I** was my father's son, tender and only beloved in the sight of my mother.
4 **He** taught me also,
and said unto me,
Let thine heart retain my words:
keep my commandments,
and live.
5 **Get** wisdom,
get understanding:
forget it not;
neither decline from the words of my mouth.
6 **Forsake her not,**
and she shall preserve thee:
love her,
and she shall keep thee.
7 **Wisdom** is the principal thing;
therefore get wisdom:
and with all thy getting get understanding.
8 **Exalt** her,
and she shall promote thee:
she shall bring thee to honour,
when thou dost embrace her.
9 **She** shall give to thine head an ornament of grace:
a crown of glory shall she deliver to thee.
10 **Hear,** O my son,
and receive my sayings;
and the years of thy life shall be many.
11 **I** have taught thee in the way of wisdom;
I have led thee in right paths.
12 **When thou** goest,
thy steps shall not be straitened;
and when thou runnest,
thou shalt not stumble.
13 **Take fast hold** of instruction;
let her not go:
keep her;
for she is thy life.
14 **Enter not** into the path of the wicked,
and go not in the way of evil men.
15 **Avoid** it,
pass not by it,
turn from it,
and pass away.
16 **For they** sleep not,
except they have done mischief;
and their sleep is taken away,
unless they cause some to fall.
17 **For they** eat the bread of wickedness,
and drink the wine of violence.
18 **But the path of the just** is as the shining light,
that shineth more and more unto the perfect day.
19 **The way of the wicked** is as darkness:
they know not
at what they stumble.
20 **My son, attend** to my words;
incline thine ear unto my sayings.
21 **Let them not** depart from thine eyes;
keep them in the midst of thine heart.
22 **For they** are life unto those that find them, and health to all their flesh.
23 **Keep** thy heart with all diligence;
for out of it are the issues of life.
24 **Put away** from thee a froward mouth,
and perverse lips put far from thee.
25 **Let thine eyes** look right on,
and let thine eyelids look straight before thee.
26 **Ponder** the path of thy feet,
and let all thy ways be established.
27 **Turn not** to the right hand nor to the left:
remove thy foot from evil.

5 **My son, attend** unto my wisdom,
and bow thine ear to my understanding:
2 **That thou** mayest regard discretion,
and that thy lips may keep knowledge.
3 **For the lips of a strange woman** drop as an honeycomb,
and her mouth is smoother than oil:
4 **But her end** is bitter as wormwood, sharp as a two-edged sword.
5 **Her feet** go down to death;
her steps take hold on hell.
6 **Lest thou** shouldest ponder the path of life,
her ways are moveable,
that thou canst not know them.
7 **Hear** me now therefore, O ye children,
and depart not from the words of my mouth.
8 **Remove** thy way far from her,
and come not nigh the door of her house:
9 **Lest thou** give thine honour unto others, and thy years unto the cruel:
10 **Lest strangers** be filled with thy wealth;
and thy labours be in the house of a stranger;
11 **And thou** mourn at the last,
when thy flesh and thy body are consumed,
12 **And** say,
How have I hated instruction,
and my heart despised reproof;
13 **And** have not obeyed the voice of my teachers,
nor inclined mine ear to them that instructed me!
14 **I** was almost in all evil in the midst of the congregation and assembly.
15 **Drink** waters out of thine own cistern,
and running waters out of thine own well.
16 **Let thy fountains** be dispersed abroad,
and rivers of waters in the streets.
17 **Let them** be only thine own, and not strangers' with thee.
18 **Let thy fountain** be blessed:
and rejoice with the wife of thy youth.
19 **Let her** be as the loving hind and pleasant roe;
let her breasts satisfy thee at all times;
and be thou ravished always with her love.

20 **And why** wilt thou, my son, be ravished with a strange woman,
and embrace the bosom of a stranger?

21 **For the ways of man** are before the eyes of the LORD,
and he pondereth all his goings.

22 **His own iniquities** shall take the wicked himself,
and he shall be holden with the cords of his sins.

23 **He** shall die without instruction;
and in the greatness of his folly he shall go astray.

6 **My son, if thou** be surety for thy friend,
if thou hast stricken thy hand with a stranger,

2 **Thou** art snared with the words of thy mouth,
thou art taken with the words of thy mouth.

3 **Do** this now, my son,
and deliver thyself,
when thou art come into the hand of thy friend;
go,
humble thyself,
and make sure thy friend.

4 **Give not** sleep to thine eyes, nor slumber to thine eyelids.

5 **Deliver** thyself as a roe from the hand of the hunter, and as a bird from the hand of the fowler.

6 **Go** to the ant, thou sluggard;
consider her ways,
and be wise:
7 **Which** {having no guide, overseer, or ruler},
8 Provideth her meat in the summer,
and gathereth her food in the harvest.

9 **How long** wilt thou sleep, O sluggard?
when wilt thou arise out of thy sleep?

10 **Yet a little sleep, a little slumber, a little folding of the hands to sleep:**
11 So shall thy poverty come as one that travelleth,
and thy want as an armed man.

12 **A naughty person, a wicked man,** walketh with a froward mouth.

13 **He** winketh with his eyes,
he speaketh with his feet,
he teacheth with his fingers;
14 **Frowardness** is in his heart,
he deviseth mischief continually;
he soweth discord.

15 **Therefore** shall his calamity come suddenly;
suddenly shall he be broken without remedy.

16 **These six things** doth the LORD hate:
yea, seven are an abomination unto him:
17 A proud look, a lying tongue, and hands that shed innocent blood,
18 An heart that deviseth wicked imaginations, feet that be swift in running to mischief,
19 A false witness that speaketh lies, and he that soweth discord among brethren.

20 **My son, keep** thy father's commandment,
and forsake not the law of thy mother:
21 **Bind** them continually upon thine heart,
and tie them about thy neck.

22 **When thou** goest,
it shall lead thee;
when thou sleepest,
it shall keep thee;
and when thou awakest,
it shall talk with thee.

23 **For the commandment** is a lamp;
and the law is light;
and reproofs of instruction are the way of life:
24 To keep thee from the evil woman, from the flattery of the tongue of a strange woman.

25 **Lust not** after her beauty in thine heart;
neither let her take thee with her eyelids.

26 **For by means of a whorish woman** a man is brought to a piece of bread:
and the adultress will hunt for the precious life.

27 **Can a man** take fire in his bosom,
and his clothes not be burned?

28 **Can one** go upon hot coals,
and his feet not be burned?

29 **So** he that goeth in to his neighbour's wife;
whosoever toucheth her shall not be innocent.

30 **Men** do not despise a thief,
if he steal
to satisfy his soul
when he is hungry;
31 **But if he** be found,
he shall restore sevenfold;
he shall give all the substance of his house.

32 **But whoso committeth adultery with a woman** lacketh understanding:
he that doeth it destroyeth his own soul.

33 **A wound and dishonour** shall he get;
and his reproach shall not be wiped away.

34 **For jealousy** is the rage of a man:
therefore he will not spare in the day of vengeance.

35 **He** will not regard any ransom;
neither will he rest content,
though thou givest many gifts.

7 **My son, keep** my words,
and lay up my commandments with thee.

2 **Keep** my commandments, {and live}; and my law as the apple of thine eye.

3 **Bind** them upon thy fingers,
write them upon the table of thine heart.

4 **Say** unto wisdom,
Thou art my sister;
and call understanding thy kinswoman:
5 **That they** may keep thee from the strange woman, from the stranger which flattereth with her words.

6 **For at the window of my house** I looked through my casement,
7 **And** beheld among the simple ones,
I discerned among the youths, a young man void of understanding,
8 Passing through the street near her corner;
and he went the way to her house,
9 In the twilight, in the evening, in the black and dark night:
10 **And, {behold}, there** met him a woman with the attire of an harlot, and subtil of heart.

11 (**She** is loud and stubborn;
her feet abide not in her house:
12 **Now** is she without,
now in the streets,
and lieth in wait at every corner.)

13 **So** she caught him,
and kissed him,

and with an impudent face said unto him,
14 I have peace offerings with me;
this day have I payed my vows.
15 **Therefore** came I forth
to meet thee,
diligently to seek thy face,
and I have found thee.
16 I have decked my bed with coverings of tapestry, with carved works, with fine linen of Egypt.
17 I have perfumed my bed with myrrh, aloes, and cinnamon.
18 **Come,**
let us take our fill of love until the morning:
let us solace ourselves with loves.
19 **For the goodman** is not at home,
he is gone a long journey:
20 **He** hath taken a bag of money with him,
and will come home at the day appointed.
21 **With her much fair speech** she caused him to yield,
with the flattering of her lips she forced him.
22 **He** goeth after her straightway,
as an ox goeth to the slaughter,
or as a fool to the correction of the stocks;
23 **Till a dart** strike through his liver;
as a bird hasteth to the snare,
and knoweth not
that it is for his life.
24 **Hearken** unto me now therefore, O ye children,
and attend to the words of my mouth.
25 **Let not thine heart** decline to her ways,
go not astray in her paths.
26 **For she** hath cast down many wounded:
yea, many strong men have been slain by her.
27 **Her house** is the way to hell,
going down to the chambers of death.

8 **Doth not wisdom** cry?
and understanding put forth her voice?
2 **She** standeth in the top of high places, by the way in the places of the paths.
3 **She** crieth at the gates, at the entry of the city, at the coming in at the doors.
4 **Unto you**, O men, I call;
and my voice is to the sons of man.
5 **O ye simple, understand** wisdom:
and, ye fools, be ye of an understanding heart.
6 **Hear;**
for I will speak of excellent things;
and the opening of my lips shall be right things.
7 **For my mouth** shall speak truth;
and wickedness is an abomination to my lips.
8 **All the words of my mouth** are in righteousness;
there is nothing froward or perverse in them.
9 **They** are all plain to him that understandeth, and right to them that find knowledge.
10 **Receive** my instruction, and not silver; and knowledge rather than choice gold.
11 **For wisdom** is better than rubies;
and all the things that may be desired are not to be compared to it.
12 **I wisdom** dwell with prudence,
and find out knowledge of witty inventions.
13 **The fear of the LORD** is to hate evil:
pride, and arrogancy, and the evil way, and the froward mouth, do I hate.
14 **Counsel** is mine, and sound wisdom:
I am understanding;
I have strength.
15 **By me** kings reign,
and princes decree justice.
16 **By me** princes rule, and nobles, even all the judges of the earth.
17 I love them that love me;
and those that seek me early shall find me.
18 **Riches and honour** are with me;
yea, durable riches and righteousness.
19 **My fruit** is better than gold, yea, than fine gold;
and my revenue than choice silver.
20 I lead in the way of righteousness, in the midst of the paths of judgment:
21 **That I** may cause those that love me to inherit substance;
and I will fill their treasures.
22 **The LORD** possessed me in the beginning of his way, before his works of old.
23 I was set up from everlasting, from the beginning,
or ever the earth was.
24 **When there** were no depths,
I was brought forth;
when there were no fountains abounding with water.
25 **Before the mountains** were settled,
before the hills was I brought forth:
26 **While as yet he** had not made the earth, nor the fields, nor the highest part of the dust of the world.
27 **When he** prepared the heavens,
I was there:
when he set a compass upon the face of the depth:
28 **When he** established the clouds above:
when he strengthened the fountains of the deep:
29 **When he** gave to the sea his decree,
that the waters should not pass his commandment:
when he appointed the foundations of the earth:
30 **Then I** was by him, as one brought up with him:
and I was daily his delight,
rejoicing always before him;
31 Rejoicing in the habitable part of his earth;
and my delights were with the sons of men.
32 **Now therefore hearken** unto me, O ye children:
for blessed are they that keep my ways.
33 **Hear** instruction,
and be wise,
and refuse it not.
34 **Blessed** is the man that heareth me,
watching daily at my gates,
waiting at the posts of my doors.
35 **For whoso findeth me** findeth life,
and shall obtain favour of the LORD.
36 **But he that sinneth against me** wrongeth his own soul:
all they that hate me love death.

9

Wisdom hath builded her house,
she hath hewn out her seven pillars:
2 **She** hath killed her beasts;
she hath mingled her wine;
she hath also furnished her table.
3 **She** hath sent forth her maidens:
she crieth upon the highest places of the city,
4 **Whoso** is simple,
let him turn in hither:
as for him that wanteth understanding, she saith to him,
5 **Come,**
eat of my bread,
and drink of the wine which I have mingled.
6 **Forsake** the foolish,
and live;
and go in the way of understanding.
7 **He that reproveth a scorner** getteth to himself shame:
and he that rebuketh a wicked man getteth himself a blot.
8 **Reprove not** a scorner,
lest he hate thee:
rebuke a wise man,
and he will love thee.
9 **Give** instruction to a wise man,
and he will be yet wiser:
teach a just man,
and he will increase in learning.
10 **The fear of the LORD** is the beginning of wisdom:
and the knowledge of the holy is understanding.
11 **For by me** thy days shall be multiplied,
and the years of thy life shall be increased.
12 **If thou** be wise,
thou shalt be wise for thyself:
but if thou scornest,
thou alone shalt bear it.
13 **A foolish woman** is clamorous:
she is simple,
and knoweth nothing.
14 **For she** sitteth at the door of her house, on a seat in the high places of the city,
15 To call passengers who go right on their ways:
16 **Whoso** is simple,
let him turn in hither:
and as for him that wanteth understanding, she saith to him,
17 **Stolen waters** are sweet,
and bread eaten in secret is pleasant.
18 **But he** knoweth not
that the dead are there;
and that her guests are in the depths of hell.

10

The proverbs of Solomon.
A wise son maketh a glad father:
but a foolish son is the heaviness of his mother.
2 **Treasures of wickedness** profit nothing:
but righteousness delivereth from death.
3 **The LORD** will not suffer the soul of the righteous to famish:
but he casteth away the substance of the wicked.
4 **He** becometh poor
that dealeth with a slack hand:
but the hand of the diligent maketh rich.
5 **He that gathereth in summer** is a wise son:
but he that sleepeth in harvest is a son that causeth shame.
6 **Blessings** are upon the head of the just:
but violence covereth the mouth of the wicked.
7 **The memory of the just** is blessed:
but the name of the wicked shall rot.
8 **The wise in heart** will receive commandments:
but a prating fool shall fall.
9 **He that walketh uprightly** walketh surely:
but he that perverteth his ways shall be known.
10 **He that winketh with the eye** causeth sorrow:
but a prating fool shall fall.
11 **The mouth of a righteous man** is a well of life:
but violence covereth the mouth of the wicked.
12 **Hatred** stirreth up strifes:
but love covereth all sins.
13 **In the lips of him that hath understanding** wisdom is found:
but a rod is for the back of him that is void of understanding.
14 **Wise men** lay up knowledge:
but the mouth of the foolish is near destruction.
15 **The rich man's wealth** is his strong city:
the destruction of the poor is their poverty.
16 **The labour of the righteous** tendeth to life:
the fruit of the wicked to sin.
17 **He** is in the way of life
that keepeth instruction:
but he that refuseth reproof erreth.
18 **He that hideth hatred with lying lips, and he that uttereth a slander,** is a fool.
19 **In the multitude of words** there wanteth not sin:
but he that refraineth his lips is wise.
20 **The tongue of the just** is as choice silver:
the heart of the wicked is little worth.
21 **The lips of the righteous** feed many:
but fools die for want of wisdom.
22 **The blessing of the LORD,** it maketh rich,
and he addeth no sorrow with it.
23 **It is as sport to a fool** to do mischief:
but a man of understanding hath wisdom.
24 **The fear of the wicked,** it shall come upon him:
but the desire of the righteous shall be granted.
25 **As the whirlwind** passeth,
so is the wicked no more:
but the righteous is an everlasting foundation.
26 **As vinegar to the teeth, and as smoke to the eyes,** so is the sluggard to them that send him.
27 **The fear of the LORD** prolongeth days:
but the years of the wicked shall be shortened.
28 **The hope of the righteous** shall be gladness:
but the expectation of the wicked shall perish.
29 **The way of the LORD** is strength to the upright:
but destruction shall be to the workers of iniquity.
30 **The righteous** shall never be removed:

but the wicked shall not inhabit
the earth.
31 **The mouth of the just** bringeth
forth wisdom:
but the froward tongue shall be
cut out.
32 **The lips of the righteous** know
what is acceptable:
but the mouth of the wicked
speaketh frowardness.

11 **A false balance** is
abomination to the LORD:
but a just weight is his delight.
2 **When pride** cometh,
then cometh shame:
but with the lowly is wisdom.
3 **The integrity of the upright** shall
guide them:
**but the perverseness of
transgressors** shall destroy them.
4 **Riches** profit not in the day of
wrath:
but righteousness delivereth from
death.
5 **The righteousness of the perfect**
shall direct his way:
but the wicked shall fall by his
own wickedness.
6 **The righteousness of the upright**
shall deliver them:
but transgressors shall be taken in
their own naughtiness.
7 **When a wicked man** dieth,
his expectation shall perish:
and the hope of unjust men
perisheth.
8 **The righteous** is delivered out of
trouble,
and the wicked cometh in his
stead.
9 **An hypocrite with his mouth**
destroyeth his neighbour:
but through knowledge shall the
just be delivered.
10 **When it** goeth well with the
righteous,
the city rejoiceth:
and when the wicked perish,
there is shouting.
11 **By the blessing of the upright**
the city is exalted:
but it is overthrown by the mouth
of the wicked.
12 **He that is void of wisdom**
despiseth his neighbour:
but a man of understanding
holdeth his peace.
13 **A talebearer** revealeth secrets:
but he that is of a faithful spirit
concealeth the matter.
14 **Where no counsel** is,
the people fall:
**but in the multitude of
counsellors** there is safety.
15 **He that is surety for a stranger**
shall smart for it:
and he that hateth suretiship is
sure.
16 **A gracious woman** retaineth
honour:
and strong men retain riches.
17 **The merciful man** doeth good to
his own soul:
but he that is cruel troubleth his
own flesh.
18 **The wicked** worketh a deceitful
work:
**but to him that soweth
righteousness** shall be a sure
reward.
19 **As righteousness** tendeth to life:
so he that pursueth evil pursueth
it to his own death.
20 **They that are of a froward heart**
are abomination to the LORD:
**but such as are upright in their
way** are his delight.
21 **Though hand** join in hand,
the wicked shall not be
unpunished:
but the seed of the righteous shall
be delivered.
22 **As a jewel of gold in a swine's
snout,** so is a fair woman which is
without discretion.
23 **The desire of the righteous** is
only good:
but the expectation of the wicked
is wrath.
24 **There** is that scattereth,
and yet increaseth;
and there is that withholdeth more
than is meet,
but it tendeth to poverty.
25 **The liberal soul** shall be made
fat:
and he that watereth shall be
watered also himself.
26 **He that withholdeth corn,** the
people shall curse him:
but blessing shall be upon the head
of him that selleth it.
27 **He that diligently seeketh good**
procureth favour:
but he that seeketh mischief, it
shall come unto him.
28 **He that trusteth in his riches**
shall fall;
but the righteous shall flourish as
a branch.
29 **He that troubleth his own
house** shall inherit the wind:
and the fool shall be servant to the
wise of heart.
30 **The fruit of the righteous** is a
tree of life;
and he that winneth souls is wise.
31 **Behold,**
the righteous shall be
recompensed in the earth: much
more the wicked and the sinner.

12 **Whoso loveth instruction**
loveth knowledge:
but he that hateth reproof is
brutish.
2 **A good man** obtaineth favour of
the LORD:
but a man of wicked devices will
he condemn.
3 **A man** shall not be established by
wickedness:
but the root of the righteous shall
not be moved.
4 **A virtuous woman** is a crown to
her husband:
but she that maketh ashamed is
as rottenness in his bones.
5 **The thoughts of the righteous**
are right:
but the counsels of the wicked are
deceit.
6 **The words of the wicked** are to
lie in wait for blood:
but the mouth of the upright shall
deliver them.
7 **The wicked** are overthrown,
and are not:
but the house of the righteous
shall stand.
8 **A man** shall be commended
according to his wisdom:
but he that is of a perverse heart
shall be despised.
9 **He that is despised, and hath a
servant,** is better than he that
honoureth himself, and lacketh
bread.
10 **A righteous man** regardeth the
life of his beast:
**but the tender mercies of the
wicked** are cruel.
11 **He that tilleth his land** shall be
satisfied with bread:

but he that followeth vain persons is void of understanding.

12 **The wicked** desireth the net of evil men:
but the root of the righteous yieldeth fruit.

13 **The wicked** is snared by the transgression of his lips:
but the just shall come out of trouble.

14 **A man** shall be satisfied with good by the fruit of his mouth:
and the recompence of a man's hands shall be rendered unto him.

15 **The way of a fool** is right in his own eyes:
but he that hearkeneth unto counsel is wise.

16 **A fool's wrath** is presently known:
but a prudent man covereth shame.

17 **He that speaketh truth** sheweth forth righteousness:
but a false witness deceit.

18 **There** is that speaketh like the piercings of a sword:
but the tongue of the wise is health.

19 **The lip of truth** shall be established for ever:
but a lying tongue is but for a moment.

20 **Deceit** is in the heart of them that imagine evil:
but to the counsellors of peace is joy.

21 **There** shall no evil happen to the just:
but the wicked shall be filled with mischief.

22 **Lying lips** are abomination to the LORD:
but they that deal truly are his delight.

23 **A prudent man** concealeth knowledge:
but the heart of fools proclaimeth foolishness.

24 **The hand of the diligent** shall bear rule:
but the slothful shall be under tribute.

25 **Heaviness in the heart of man** maketh it stoop:
but a good word maketh it glad.

26 **The righteous** is more excellent than his neighbour:
but the way of the wicked seduceth them.

27 **The slothful man** roasteth not that which he took in hunting:
but the substance of a diligent man is precious.

28 **In the way of righteousness** is life:
and in the pathway thereof there is no death.

13

A wise son heareth his father's instruction:
but a scorner heareth not rebuke.

2 **A man** shall eat good by the fruit of his mouth:
but the soul of the transgressors shall eat violence.

3 **He that keepeth his mouth** keepeth his life:
but he that openeth wide his lips shall have destruction.

4 **The soul of the sluggard** desireth, **and** hath nothing:
but the soul of the diligent shall be made fat.

5 **A righteous man** hateth lying:
but a wicked man is loathsome,
and cometh to shame.

6 **Righteousness** keepeth him that is upright in the way:
but wickedness overthroweth the sinner.

7 **There** is that maketh himself rich,
yet hath nothing:
there is that maketh himself poor,
yet hath great riches.

8 **The ransom of a man's life** are his riches:
but the poor heareth not rebuke.

9 **The light of the righteous** rejoiceth:
but the lamp of the wicked shall be put out.

10 **Only by pride** cometh contention:
but with the well advised is wisdom.

11 **Wealth gotten by vanity** shall be diminished:
but he that gathereth by labour shall increase.

12 **Hope deferred** maketh the heart sick:
but when the desire cometh,
it is a tree of life.

13 **Whoso despiseth the word** shall be destroyed:
but he that feareth the commandment shall be rewarded.

14 **The law of the wise** is a fountain of life,
to depart from the snares of death.

15 **Good understanding** giveth favour:
but the way of transgressors is hard.

16 **Every prudent man** dealeth with knowledge:
but a fool layeth open his folly.

17 **A wicked messenger** falleth into mischief:
but a faithful ambassador is health.

18 **Poverty and shame** shall be to him that refuseth instruction:
but he that regardeth reproof shall be honoured.

19 **The desire accomplished** is sweet to the soul:
but it is abomination to fools to depart from evil.

20 **He that walketh with wise men** shall be wise:
but a companion of fools shall be destroyed.

21 **Evil** pursueth sinners:
but to the righteous good shall be repayed.

22 **A good man** leaveth an inheritance to his children's children:
and the wealth of the sinner is laid up for the just.

23 **Much food** is in the tillage of the poor:
but there is that is destroyed for want of judgment.

24 **He that spareth his rod** hateth his son:
but he that loveth him chasteneth him betimes.

25 **The righteous** eateth to the satisfying of his soul:
but the belly of the wicked shall want.

14

Every wise woman buildeth her house:
but the foolish plucketh it down with her hands.

2 **He that walketh in his uprightness** feareth the LORD:

but he that is perverse in his ways despiseth him.

3 **In the mouth of the foolish** is a rod of pride:
but the lips of the wise shall preserve them.

4 **Where no oxen** are,
the crib is clean:
but much increase is by the strength of the ox.

5 **A faithful witness** will not lie:
but a false witness will utter lies.

6 **A scorner** seeketh wisdom,
and findeth it not:
but knowledge is easy unto him that understandeth.

7 **Go** from the presence of a foolish man,
when thou perceivest not in him the lips of knowledge.

8 **The wisdom of the prudent** is to understand his way:
but the folly of fools is deceit.

9 **Fools** make a mock at sin:
but among the righteous there is favour.

10 **The heart** knoweth his own bitterness;
and a stranger doth not intermeddle with his joy.

11 **The house of the wicked** shall be overthrown:
but the tabernacle of the upright shall flourish.

12 **There** is a way which seemeth right unto a man,
but the end thereof are the ways of death.

13 **Even in laughter** the heart is sorrowful;
and the end of that mirth is heaviness.

14 **The backslider in heart** shall be filled with his own ways:
and a good man shall be satisfied from himself.

15 **The simple** believeth every word:
but the prudent man looketh well to his going.

16 **A wise man** feareth,
and departeth from evil:
but the fool rageth,
and is confident.

17 **He that is soon angry** dealeth foolishly:
and a man of wicked devices is hated.

18 **The simple** inherit folly:
but the prudent are crowned with knowledge.

19 **The evil** bow before the good;
and the wicked at the gates of the righteous.

20 **The poor** is hated even of his own neighbour:
but the rich hath many friends.

21 **He that despiseth his neighbour** sinneth:
but he that hath mercy on the poor, happy is he.

22 **Do they not** err
that devise evil?
but mercy and truth shall be to them that devise good.

23 **In all labour** there is profit:
but the talk of the lips tendeth only to penury.

24 **The crown of the wise** is their riches:
but the foolishness of fools is folly.

25 **A true witness** delivereth souls:
but a deceitful witness speaketh lies.

26 **In the fear of the LORD** is strong confidence:
and his children shall have a place of refuge.

27 **The fear of the LORD** is a fountain of life,
to depart from the snares of death.

28 **In the multitude of people** is the king's honour:
but in the want of people is the destruction of the prince.

29 **He that is slow to wrath** is of great understanding:
but he that is hasty of spirit exalteth folly.

30 **A sound heart** is the life of the flesh:
but envy the rottenness of the bones.

31 **He that oppresseth the poor** reproacheth his Maker:
but he that honoureth him hath mercy on the poor.

32 **The wicked** is driven away in his wickedness:
but the righteous hath hope in his death.

33 **Wisdom** resteth in the heart of him that hath understanding:
but that which is in the midst of fools is made known.

34 **Righteousness** exalteth a nation:
but sin is a reproach to any people.

35 **The king's favour** is toward a wise servant:
but his wrath is against him that causeth shame.

15

A soft answer turneth away wrath:
but grievous words stir up anger.

2 **The tongue of the wise** useth knowledge aright:
but the mouth of fools poureth out foolishness.

3 **The eyes of the LORD** are in every place,
beholding the evil and the good.

4 **A wholesome tongue** is a tree of life:
but perverseness therein is a breach in the spirit.

5 **A fool** despiseth his father's instruction:
but he that regardeth reproof is prudent.

6 **In the house of the righteous** is much treasure:
but in the revenues of the wicked is trouble.

7 **The lips of the wise** disperse knowledge:
but the heart of the foolish doeth not so.

8 **The sacrifice of the wicked** is an abomination to the LORD:
but the prayer of the upright is his delight.

9 **The way of the wicked** is an abomination unto the LORD:
but he loveth him that followeth after righteousness.

10 **Correction** is grievous unto him that forsaketh the way:
and he that hateth reproof shall die.

11 **Hell and destruction** are before the LORD:
how much more then the hearts of the children of men?

12 **A scorner** loveth not one that reproveth him:
neither will he go unto the wise.

13 **A merry heart** maketh a cheerful countenance:
but by sorrow of the heart the spirit is broken.

14 **The heart of him that hath understanding** seeketh knowledge:
but the mouth of fools feedeth on foolishness.

15 **All the days of the afflicted** are evil:
but he that is of a merry heart hath a continual feast.

16 **Better** is little with the fear of the LORD than great treasure and trouble therewith.

17 **Better** is a dinner of herbs where love is, than a stalled ox and hatred therewith.

18 **A wrathful man** stirreth up strife:
but he that is slow to anger appeaseth strife.

19 **The way of the slothful man** is as an hedge of thorns:
but the way of the righteous is made plain.

20 **A wise son** maketh a glad father:
but a foolish man despiseth his mother.

21 **Folly** is joy to him that is destitute of wisdom:
but a man of understanding walketh uprightly.

22 **Without counsel** purposes are disappointed:
but in the multitude of counsellors they are established.

23 **A man** hath joy by the answer of his mouth:
and a word spoken in due season, how good is it!

24 **The way of life** is above to the wise,
that he may depart from hell beneath.

25 **The LORD** will destroy the house of the proud:
but he will establish the border of the widow.

26 **The thoughts of the wicked** are an abomination to the LORD:
but the words of the pure are pleasant words.

27 **He that is greedy of gain** troubleth his own house;
but he that hateth gifts shall live.

28 **The heart of the righteous** studieth to answer:
but the mouth of the wicked poureth out evil things.

29 **The LORD** is far from the wicked:
but he heareth the prayer of the righteous.

30 **The light of the eyes** rejoiceth the heart:
and a good report maketh the bones fat.

31 **The ear that heareth the reproof of life** abideth among the wise.

32 **He that refuseth instruction** despiseth his own soul:
but he that heareth reproof getteth understanding.

33 **The fear of the LORD** is the instruction of wisdom;
and before honour is humility.

16 ∞ **The preparations of the heart in man, and the answer of the tongue,** is from the LORD.

2 **All the ways of a man** are clean in his own eyes;
but the LORD weigheth the spirits.

3 **Commit** thy works unto the LORD,
and thy thoughts shall be established.

4 **The LORD** hath made all things for himself: yea, even the wicked for the day of evil.

5 **Every one that is proud in heart** is an abomination to the LORD:
though hand join in hand,
he shall not be unpunished.

6 **By mercy and truth** iniquity is purged:
and by the fear of the LORD men depart from evil.

7 **When a man's ways** please the LORD,
he maketh even his enemies to be at peace with him.

8 **Better** is a little with righteousness than great revenues without right.

9 **A man's heart** deviseth his way:
but the LORD directeth his steps.

10 **A divine sentence** is in the lips of the king:
his mouth transgresseth not in judgment.

11 **A just weight and balance** are the LORD's:
all the weights of the bag are his work.

12 **It is an abomination to kings** to commit wickedness:
for the throne is established by righteousness.

13 **Righteous lips** are the delight of kings;
and they love him that speaketh right.

14 **The wrath of a king** is as messengers of death:
but a wise man will pacify it.

15 **In the light of the king's countenance** is life;
and his favour is as a cloud of the latter rain.

16 **How much better is it** to get wisdom than gold!
and to get understanding rather to be chosen than silver!

17 **The highway of the upright** is to depart from evil:
he that keepeth his way preserveth his soul.

18 **Pride** goeth before destruction,
and an haughty spirit before a fall.

19 **Better it is** to be of an humble spirit with the lowly,
than to divide the spoil with the proud.

20 **He that handleth a matter wisely** shall find good:
and whoso trusteth in the LORD,
happy is he.

21 **The wise in heart** shall be called prudent:
and the sweetness of the lips increaseth learning.

22 **Understanding** is a wellspring of life unto him that hath it:
but the instruction of fools is folly.

23 **The heart of the wise** teacheth his mouth,
and addeth learning to his lips.

24 **Pleasant words** are as an honeycomb, sweet to the soul, and health to the bones.

25 **There** is a way that seemeth right unto a man,
but the end thereof are the ways of death.

26 **He that laboureth** laboureth for himself;
for his mouth craveth it of him.

27 **An ungodly man** diggeth up evil:
and in his lips there is as a burning fire.

28 **A froward man** soweth strife:
and a whisperer separateth chief friends.

29 **A violent man** enticeth his neighbour,
and leadeth him into the way that is not good.

30 **He** shutteth his eyes
to devise froward things:
moving his lips
he bringeth evil to pass.

31 **The hoary head** is a crown of glory,

if it be found in the way of righteousness.

32 **He that is slow to anger** is better than the mighty;
and he that ruleth his spirit than he that taketh a city.

33 **The lot** is cast into the lap;
but the whole disposing thereof is of the LORD.

17 **Better** is a dry morsel, and quietness therewith, than an house full of sacrifices with strife.

2 **A wise servant** shall have rule over a son that causeth shame,
and shall have part of the inheritance among the brethren.

3 **The fining pot** is for silver,
and the furnace for gold:
but the LORD trieth the hearts.

4 **A wicked doer** giveth heed to false lips;
and a liar giveth ear to a naughty tongue.

5 **Whoso mocketh the poor** reproacheth his Maker:
and he that is glad at calamities shall not be unpunished.

6 **Children's children** are the crown of old men;
and the glory of children are their fathers.

7 **Excellent speech** becometh not a fool:
much less do lying lips a prince.

8 **A gift** is as a precious stone in the eyes of him that hath it:
whithersoever it turneth,
it prospereth.

9 **He that covereth a transgression** seeketh love;
but he that repeateth a matter separateth very friends.

10 **A reproof** entereth more into a wise man than an hundred stripes into a fool.

11 **An evil man** seeketh only rebellion:
therefore a cruel messenger shall be sent against him.

12 **Let a bear robbed of her whelps** meet a man, rather than a fool in his folly.

13 **Whoso** rewardeth evil for good,
evil shall not depart from his house.

14 **The beginning of strife** is as when one letteth out water:
therefore leave off contention,
before it be meddled with.

15 **He that justifieth the wicked, and he that condemneth the just,** even they both are abomination to the LORD.

16 **Wherefore** is there a price in the hand of a fool to get wisdom,
seeing he hath no heart to it?

17 **A friend** loveth at all times,
and a brother is born for adversity.

18 **A man void of understanding** striketh hands,
and becometh surety in the presence of his friend.

19 **He** loveth transgression
that loveth strife:
and he that exalteth his gate seeketh destruction.

20 **He that hath a froward heart** findeth no good:
and he that hath a perverse tongue falleth into mischief.

21 **He that begetteth a fool** doeth it to his sorrow:
and the father of a fool hath no joy.

22 **A merry heart** doeth good like a medicine:
but a broken spirit drieth the bones.

23 **A wicked man** taketh a gift out of the bosom
to pervert the ways of judgment.

24 **Wisdom** is before him that hath understanding;
but the eyes of a fool are in the ends of the earth.

25 **A foolish son** is a grief to his father, and bitterness to her that bare him.

26 **Also to punish the just** is not good,
nor to strike princes for equity.

27 **He that hath knowledge** spareth his words:
and a man of understanding is of an excellent spirit.

28 **Even a fool, {when he holdeth his peace},** is counted wise:
and he that shutteth his lips is esteemed a man of understanding.

18 **Through desire** a man, {having separated himself}, seeketh and intermeddleth with all wisdom.

2 **A fool** hath no delight in understanding,
but that his heart may discover itself.

3 **When the wicked** cometh,
then cometh also contempt,
and with ignominy reproach.

4 **The words of a man's mouth** are as deep waters,
and the wellspring of wisdom as a flowing brook.

5 **It is not good** to accept the person of the wicked,
to overthrow the righteous in judgment.

6 **A fool's lips** enter into contention,
and his mouth calleth for strokes.

7 **A fool's mouth** is his destruction,
and his lips are the snare of his soul.

8 **The words of a talebearer** are as wounds,
and they go down into the innermost parts of the belly.

9 **He also that is slothful in his work** is brother to him that is a great waster.

10 **The name of the LORD** is a strong tower:
the righteous runneth into it,
and is safe.

11 **The rich man's wealth** is his strong city, and as an high wall in his own conceit.

12 **Before destruction** the heart of man is haughty,
and before honour is humility.

13 **He that answereth a matter before he heareth it,** it is folly and shame unto him.

14 **The spirit of a man** will sustain his infirmity;
but a wounded spirit who can bear?

15 **The heart of the prudent** getteth knowledge;
and the ear of the wise seeketh knowledge.

16 **A man's gift** maketh room for him,
and bringeth him before great men.

17 **He that is first in his own cause** seemeth just;
but his neighbour cometh and searcheth him.

18 **The lot** causeth contentions to cease,
and parteth between the mighty.

19 **A brother offended** is harder to be won than a strong city:

and their contentions are like the
bars of a castle.
20 **A man's belly** shall be satisfied
with the fruit of his mouth;
and with the increase of his lips
shall he be filled.
21 **Death and life** are in the power of
the tongue:
and they that love it shall eat the
fruit thereof.
22 **Whoso findeth a wife** findeth a
good thing,
and obtaineth favour of the LORD.
23 **The poor** useth intreaties;
but the rich answereth roughly.
24 **A man that hath friends** must
shew himself friendly:
and there is a friend that sticketh
closer than a brother.

19 **Better** is the poor that
walketh in his integrity,
than he that is perverse in his lips,
and is a fool.
2 **Also, that the soul** be without
knowledge,
it is not good;
and he that hasteth with his feet
sinneth.
3 **The foolishness of man**
perverteth his way:
and his heart fretteth against the
LORD.
4 **Wealth** maketh many friends;
but the poor is separated from his
neighbour.
5 **A false witness** shall not be
unpunished,
and he that speaketh lies shall not
escape.
6 **Many** will intreat the favour of the
prince:
and every man is a friend to him
that giveth gifts.
7 **All the brethren of the poor** do
hate him:
how much more do his friends go
far from him?
he pursueth them with words,
yet they are wanting to him.
8 **He that getteth wisdom** loveth
his own soul:
he that keepeth understanding
shall find good.
9 **A false witness** shall not be
unpunished,
and he that speaketh lies shall
perish.
10 **Delight** is not seemly for a fool;
much less for a servant to have
rule over princes.
11 **The discretion of a man** deferreth
his anger;
and it is his glory to pass over a
transgression.
12 **The king's wrath** is as the roaring
of a lion;
but his favour is as dew upon the
grass.
13 **A foolish son** is the calamity of
his father:
and the contentions of a wife are a
continual dropping.
14 **House and riches** are the
inheritance of fathers:
and a prudent wife is from the
LORD.
15 **Slothfulness** casteth into a deep
sleep;
and an idle soul shall suffer
hunger.
16 **He that keepeth the
commandment** keepeth his own
soul;
but he that despiseth his ways
shall die.
17 **He that hath pity upon the poor**
lendeth unto the LORD;
and that which he hath given will
he pay him again.
18 **Chasten** thy son
while there is hope,
and let not thy soul spare for his
crying.
19 **A man of great wrath** shall suffer
punishment:
for if thou deliver him,
yet thou must do it again.
20 **Hear** counsel,
and receive instruction,
that thou mayest be wise in thy
latter end.
21 **There** are many devices in a man's
heart;
**nevertheless the counsel of the
LORD,** that shall stand.
22 **The desire of a man** is his
kindness:
and a poor man is better than a
liar.
23 **The fear of the LORD** tendeth to
life:
and he that hath it shall abide
satisfied;
he shall not be visited with evil.
24 **A slothful man** hideth his hand
in his bosom,
and will not so much as bring it to
his mouth again.
25 **Smite** a scorner,
and the simple will beware:
and reprove one that hath
understanding,
and he will understand knowledge.
26 **He that wasteth his father, and
chaseth away his mother,** is a
son that causeth shame, and
bringeth reproach.
27 **Cease,** my son, to hear the
instruction that causeth to err
from the words of knowledge.
28 **An ungodly witness** scorneth
judgment:
and the mouth of the wicked
devoureth iniquity.
29 **Judgments** are prepared for
scorners,
and stripes for the back of fools.

20 **Wine** is a mocker,
strong drink is raging:
**and whosoever is deceived
thereby** is not wise.
2 **The fear of a king** is as the roaring
of a lion:
whoso provoketh him to anger
sinneth against his own soul.
3 **It is an honour** for a man to cease
from strife:
but every fool will be meddling.
4 **The sluggard** will not plow by
reason of the cold;
therefore shall he beg in harvest,
and have nothing.
5 **Counsel in the heart of man** is
like deep water;
but a man of understanding will
draw it out.
6 **Most men** will proclaim every one
his own goodness:
but a faithful man who can find?
7 **The just man** walketh in his
integrity:
his children are blessed after him.
8 **A king that sitteth in the throne
of judgment** scattereth away all
evil with his eyes.
9 **Who** can say,
I have made my heart clean,
I am pure from my sin?
10 **Divers weights, and divers
measures,** both of them are alike
abomination to the LORD.
11 **Even a child** is known by his
doings,
whether his work be pure,

and whether it be right.
12 **The hearing ear, and the seeing eye,** the LORD hath made even both of them.
13 **Love not** sleep,
lest thou come to poverty;
open thine eyes,
and thou shalt be satisfied with bread.
14 **It** is naught,
it is naught,
saith the buyer:
but when he is gone his way,
then he boasteth.
15 **There** is gold, and a multitude of rubies:
but the lips of knowledge are a precious jewel.
16 **Take** his garment that is surety for a stranger:
and take a pledge of him for a strange woman.
17 **Bread of deceit** is sweet to a man;
but afterwards his mouth shall be filled with gravel.
18 **Every purpose** is established by counsel:
and with good advice make war.
19 **He that goeth about as a talebearer** revealeth secrets:
therefore meddle not with him that flattereth with his lips.
20 **Whoso** curseth his father or his mother,
his lamp shall be put out in obscure darkness.
21 **An inheritance** may be gotten hastily at the beginning;
but the end thereof shall not be blessed.
22 **Say not thou,**
I will recompense evil;
but wait on the LORD,
and he shall save thee.
23 **Divers weights** are an abomination unto the LORD;
and a false balance is not good.
24 **Man's goings** are of the LORD;
how can a man then understand his own way?
25 **It is a snare** to the man who devoureth that which is holy,
and after vows to make enquiry.
26 **A wise king** scattereth the wicked,
and bringeth the wheel over them.
27 **The spirit of man** is the candle of the LORD,
searching all the inward parts of the belly.
28 **Mercy and truth** preserve the king:
and his throne is upholden by mercy.
29 **The glory of young men** is their strength:
and the beauty of old men is the grey head.
30 **The blueness of a wound** cleanseth away evil:
so do stripes the inward parts of the belly.

21 **The king's heart** is in the hand of the LORD, as the rivers of water:
he turneth it
whithersoever he will.
2 **Every way of a man** is right in his own eyes:
but the LORD pondereth the hearts.
3 **To do justice and judgment** is more acceptable to the LORD than sacrifice.
4 **An high look, and a proud heart, and the plowing of the wicked,** is sin.
5 **The thoughts of the diligent** tend only to plenteousness;
but of every one that is hasty only to want.
6 **The getting of treasures by a lying tongue** is a vanity tossed to and fro of them that seek death.
7 **The robbery of the wicked** shall destroy them;
because they refuse to do judgment.
8 **The way of man** is froward and strange:
but as for the pure, his work is right.
9 **It is better** to dwell in a corner of the housetop, than with a brawling woman in a wide house.
10 **The soul of the wicked** desireth evil:
his neighbour findeth no favour in his eyes.
11 **When the scorner** is punished,
the simple is made wise:
and when the wise is instructed,
he receiveth knowledge.
12 **The righteous man** wisely considereth the house of the wicked:
but God overthroweth the wicked for their wickedness.
13 **Whoso** stoppeth his ears at the cry of the poor,
he also shall cry himself,
but shall not be heard.
14 **A gift in secret** pacifieth anger:
and a reward in the bosom strong wrath.
15 **It is joy to the just** to do judgment:
but destruction shall be to the workers of iniquity.
16 **The man that wandereth out of the way of understanding** shall remain in the congregation of the dead.
17 **He that loveth pleasure** shall be a poor man:
he that loveth wine and oil shall not be rich.
18 **The wicked** shall be a ransom for the righteous,
and the transgressor for the upright.
19 **It is better** to dwell in the wilderness, than with a contentious and an angry woman.
20 **There** is treasure to be desired and oil in the dwelling of the wise;
but a foolish man spendeth it up.
21 **He that followeth after righteousness and mercy** findeth life, righteousness, and honour.
22 **A wise man** scaleth the city of the mighty,
and casteth down the strength of the confidence thereof.
23 **Whoso keepeth his mouth and his tongue** keepeth his soul from troubles.
24 **Proud and haughty scorner** is his name,
who dealeth in proud wrath.
25 **The desire of the slothful** killeth him;
for his hands refuse to labour.
26 **He** coveteth greedily all the day long:
but the righteous giveth
and spareth not.
27 **The sacrifice of the wicked** is abomination:
how much more, when he bringeth it with a wicked mind?
28 **A false witness** shall perish:

but the man that heareth
speaketh constantly.
29 **A wicked man** hardeneth his face:
but as for the upright, he directeth his way.
30 **There** is no wisdom nor understanding nor counsel against the LORD.
31 **The horse** is prepared against the day of battle:
but safety is of the LORD.

22

A good name is rather to be chosen than great riches,
and loving favour rather than silver and gold.
2 **The rich and poor** meet together:
the LORD is the maker of them all.
3 **A prudent man** foreseeth the evil,
and hideth himself:
but the simple pass on,
and are punished.
4 **By humility and the fear of the LORD** are riches, and honour, and life.
5 **Thorns and snares** are in the way of the froward:
he that doth keep his soul shall be far from them.
6 **Train up** a child in the way he should go:
and when he is old,
he will not depart from it.
7 **The rich** ruleth over the poor,
and the borrower is servant to the lender.
8 **He that soweth iniquity** shall reap vanity:
and the rod of his anger shall fail.
9 **He that hath a bountiful eye** shall be blessed;
for he giveth of his bread to the poor.
10 **Cast out** the scorner,
and contention shall go out;
yea, strife and reproach shall cease.
11 **He that loveth pureness of heart, for the grace of his lips** the king shall be his friend.
12 **The eyes of the LORD** preserve knowledge,
and he overthroweth the words of the transgressor.
13 **The slothful man** saith,
There is a lion without,
I shall be slain in the streets.
14 **The mouth of strange women** is a deep pit:
he that is abhorred of the LORD shall fall therein.
15 **Foolishness** is bound in the heart of a child;
but the rod of correction shall drive it far from him.
16 **He that oppresseth the poor to increase his riches, and he that giveth to the rich,** shall surely come to want.
17 **Bow down** thine ear,
and hear the words of the wise,
and apply thine heart unto my knowledge.
18 **For it is a pleasant thing** if thou keep them within thee;
they shall withal be fitted in thy lips.
19 **That thy trust** may be in the LORD,
I have made known to thee this day, even to thee.
20 **Have not I** written to thee excellent things in counsels and knowledge,
21 **That I** might make thee know the certainty of the words of truth;
that thou mightest answer the words of truth to them that send unto thee?
22 **Rob not** the poor,
because he is poor:
neither oppress the afflicted in the gate:
23 **For the LORD** will plead their cause,
and spoil the soul of those that spoiled them.
24 **Make** no friendship with an angry man;
and with a furious man thou shalt not go:
25 **Lest thou** learn his ways,
and get a snare to thy soul.
26 **Be not thou** one of them that strike hands, or of them that are sureties for debts.
27 **If thou** hast nothing to pay,
why should he take away thy bed from under thee?
28 **Remove not** the ancient landmark,
which thy fathers have set.
29 **Seest thou** a man diligent in his business?
he shall stand before kings;
he shall not stand before mean men.

23

When thou sittest to eat with a ruler,
consider diligently
what is before thee:
2 **And put** a knife to thy throat,
if thou be a man given to appetite.
3 **Be not** desirous of his dainties:
for they are deceitful meat.
4 **Labour not** to be rich:
cease from thine own wisdom.
5 **Wilt thou** set thine eyes upon that which is not?
for riches certainly make themselves wings;
they fly away as an eagle toward heaven.
6 **Eat thou not** the bread of him that hath an evil eye,
neither desire thou his dainty meats:
7 **For as he** thinketh in his heart,
so is he:
Eat and drink,
saith he to thee;
but his heart is not with thee.
8 **The morsel which thou hast eaten** shalt thou vomit up,
and lose thy sweet words.
9 **Speak not** in the ears of a fool:
for he will despise the wisdom of thy words.
10 **Remove not** the old landmark;
and enter not into the fields of the fatherless:
11 **For their redeemer** is mighty;
he shall plead their cause with thee.
12 **Apply** thine heart unto instruction, and thine ears to the words of knowledge.
13 **Withhold not** correction from the child:
for if thou beatest him with the rod,
he shall not die.
14 **Thou** shalt beat him with the rod,
and shalt deliver his soul from hell.
15 **My son, if thine heart** be wise,
my heart shall rejoice, even mine.
16 **Yea, my reins** shall rejoice,
when thy lips speak right things.
17 **Let not thine heart** envy sinners:
but be thou in the fear of the LORD all the day long.
18 **For surely there** is an end;
and thine expectation shall not be cut off.

19 **Hear thou,** my son,
and be wise,
and guide thine heart in the way.
20 **Be not** among winebibbers;
among riotous eaters of flesh:
21 **For the drunkard and the glutton** shall come to poverty:
and drowsiness shall clothe a man with rags.
22 **Hearken** unto thy father that begat thee,
and despise not thy mother
when she is old.
23 **Buy** the truth,
and sell it not;
also wisdom, and instruction, and understanding.
24 **The father of the righteous** shall greatly rejoice:
and he that begetteth a wise child shall have joy of him.
25 **Thy father and thy mother** shall be glad,
and she that bare thee shall rejoice.
26 **My son, give** me thine heart,
and let thine eyes observe my ways.
27 **For a whore** is a deep ditch;
and a strange woman is a narrow pit.
28 **She** also lieth in wait as for a prey,
and increaseth the transgressors among men.
29 **Who** hath woe?
who hath sorrow?
who hath contentions?
who hath babbling?
who hath wounds without cause?
who hath redness of eyes?
30 **They** that tarry long at the wine;
they that go to seek mixed wine.
31 **Look not thou** upon the wine when it is red, when it giveth his colour in the cup, when it moveth itself aright.
32 **At the last** it biteth like a serpent,
and stingeth like an adder.
33 **Thine eyes** shall behold strange women,
and thine heart shall utter perverse things.
34 **Yea, thou** shalt be as he that lieth down in the midst of the sea, or as he that lieth upon the top of a mast.
35 **They** have stricken me,
shalt thou say,
and I was not sick;
they have beaten me,
and I felt it not:
when shall I awake?
I will seek it yet again.

24 ∞ **Be not thou** envious against evil men,
neither desire to be with them.
2 **For their heart** studieth destruction,
and their lips talk of mischief.
3 **Through wisdom** is an house builded;
and by understanding it is established:
4 **And by knowledge** shall the chambers be filled with all precious and pleasant riches.
5 **A wise man** is strong;
yea, a man of knowledge increaseth strength.
6 **For by wise counsel** thou shalt make thy war:
and in multitude of counsellors there is safety.
7 **Wisdom** is too high for a fool:
he openeth not his mouth in the gate.
8 **He that deviseth to do evil** shall be called a mischievous person.
9 **The thought of foolishness** is sin:
and the scorner is an abomination to men.
10 **If thou** faint in the day of adversity,
thy strength is small.
11 **If thou** forbear to deliver them that are drawn unto death, and those that are ready to be slain;
12 **If thou** sayest,
Behold,
we knew it not;
doth not he that pondereth the heart consider it?
and he that keepeth thy soul, doth not he know it?
and shall not he render to every man according to his works?
13 **My son, eat thou** honey, {because it is good}; and the honeycomb, {which is sweet to thy taste}:
14 **So** shall the knowledge of wisdom be unto thy soul:
when thou hast found it,
then there shall be a reward,
and thy expectation shall not be cut off.
15 **Lay not wait,** O wicked man, against the dwelling of the righteous;
spoil not his resting place:
16 **For a just man** falleth seven times,
and riseth up again:
but the wicked shall fall into mischief.
17 **Rejoice not** when thine enemy falleth,
and let not thine heart be glad when he stumbleth:
18 **Lest the LORD** see it,
and it displease him,
and he turn away his wrath from him.
19 **Fret not thyself** because of evil men,
neither be thou envious at the wicked:
20 **For there** shall be no reward to the evil man;
the candle of the wicked shall be put out.
21 **My son, fear thou** the LORD and the king:
and meddle not with them that are given to change:
22 **For their calamity** shall rise suddenly;
and who knoweth the ruin of them both?
23 **These things** also belong to the wise.
It is not good to have respect of persons in judgment.
24 **He that saith unto the wicked, {Thou are righteous};** him shall the people curse,
nations shall abhor him:
25 **But to them that rebuke him** shall be delight,
and a good blessing shall come upon them.
26 **Every man** shall kiss his lips that giveth a right answer.
27 **Prepare** thy work without,
and make it fit for thyself in the field;
and afterwards build thine house.
28 **Be not** a witness against thy neighbour without cause;
and deceive not with thy lips.
29 **Say not,**
I will do so to him
as he hath done to me:
I will render to the man according to his work.

30 **I** went by the field of the slothful, and by the vineyard of the man void of understanding;
31 **And, {lo}, it** was all grown over with thorns,
and nettles had covered the face thereof,
and the stone wall thereof was broken down.
32 **Then I** saw,
and considered it well:
I looked upon it,
and received instruction.
33 **Yet a little sleep, a little slumber, a little folding of the hands to sleep:**
34 So shall thy poverty come as one that travelleth; and thy want as an armed man.

25

These are also proverbs of Solomon,
which the men of Hezekiah king of Judah copied out.
2 **It is the glory of God** to conceal a thing:
but the honour of kings is to search out a matter.
3 **The heaven for height, and the earth for depth, and the heart of kings** is unsearchable.
4 **Take away** the dross from the silver,
and there shall come forth a vessel for the finer.
5 **Take away** the wicked from before the king,
and his throne shall be established in righteousness.
6 **Put not forth** thyself in the presence of the king,
and stand not in the place of great men:
7 **For better it is** that it be said unto thee,
Come up hither;
than that thou shouldest be put lower in the presence of the prince whom thine eyes have seen.
8 **Go not forth** hastily to strive,
lest thou know not
what to do in the end thereof,
when thy neighbour hath put thee to shame.
9 **Debate** thy cause with thy neighbour himself;
and discover not a secret to another:
10 **Lest he that heareth it** put thee to shame,
and thine infamy turn not away.
11 **A word fitly spoken** is like apples of gold in pictures of silver.
12 **As an earring of gold, and an ornament of fine gold,** so is a wise reprover upon an obedient ear.
13 **As the cold of snow in the time of harvest,** so is a faithful messenger to them that send him:
for he refresheth the soul of his masters.
14 **Whoso boasteth himself of a false gift** is like clouds and wind without rain.
15 **By long forbearing** is a prince persuaded,
and a soft tongue breaketh the bone.
16 **Hast thou** found honey?
eat so much as is sufficient for thee,
lest thou be filled therewith,
and vomit it.
17 **Withdraw** thy foot from thy neighbour's house;
lest he be weary of thee,
and so hate thee.
18 **A man that beareth false witness against his neighbour** is a maul, and a sword, and a sharp arrow.
19 **Confidence in an unfaithful man in time of trouble** is like a broken tooth, and a foot out of joint.
20 **As he that taketh away a garment in cold weather, and as vinegar upon nitre,** so is he that singeth songs to an heavy heart.
21 **If thine enemy** be hungry,
give him bread to eat;
and if he be thirsty,
give him water to drink:
22 **For thou** shalt heap coals of fire upon his head,
and the LORD shall reward thee.
23 **The north wind** driveth away rain:
so doth an angry countenance a backbiting tongue.
24 **It is better** to dwell in the corner of the housetop, than with a brawling woman and in a wide house.
25 **As cold waters to a thirsty soul,** so is good news from a far country.
26 **A righteous man falling down before the wicked** is as a troubled fountain, and a corrupt spring.
27 **It is not good** to eat much honey:
so for men to search their own glory is not glory.
28 **He that hath no rule over his own spirit** is like a city that is broken down, and without walls.

26

As snow in summer, and as rain in harvest, so honour is not seemly for a fool.
2 **As the bird** by wandering,
as the swallow by flying,
so the curse causeless shall not come.
3 **A whip** for the horse,
a bridle for the ass,
and a rod for the fool's back.
4 **Answer not** a fool according to his folly,
lest thou also be like unto him.
5 **Answer** a fool according to his folly,
lest he be wise in his own conceit.
6 **He that sendeth a message by the hand of a fool** cutteth off the feet,
and drinketh damage.
7 **The legs of the lame** are not equal:
so is a parable in the mouth of fools.
8 **As he that bindeth a stone in a sling,** so is he that giveth honour to a fool.
9 **As a thorn** goeth up into the hand of a drunkard,
so is a parable in the mouths of fools.
10 **The great God that formed all things** both rewardeth the fool,
and rewardeth transgressors.
11 **As a dog** returneth to his vomit,
so a fool returneth to his folly.
12 **Seest thou** a man wise in his own conceit?
there is more hope of a fool than of him.
13 **The slothful man** saith,
There is a lion in the way;
a lion is in the streets.
14 **As the door** turneth upon his hinges,
so doth the slothful upon his bed.
15 **The slothful** hideth his hand in his bosom;

it grieveth him to bring it again to his mouth.

16 **The sluggard** is wiser in his own conceit than seven men that can render a reason.

17 **He that passeth by, and meddleth with strife belonging not to him,** is like one that taketh a dog by the ears.

18 **As a mad man who casteth firebrands, arrows, and death,**
19 So is the man that deceiveth his neighbour,
and saith,
Am not I in sport?

20 **Where no wood** is,
there the fire goeth out:
so where there is no talebearer,
the strife ceaseth.

21 **As coals** are to burning coals,
and wood to fire;
so is a contentious man to kindle strife.

22 **The words of a talebearer** are as wounds,
and they go down into the innermost parts of the belly.

23 **Burning lips and a wicked heart** are like a potsherd covered with silver dross.

24 **He that hateth** dissembleth with his lips,
and layeth up deceit within him;
25 **When he** speaketh fair,
believe him not:
for there are seven abominations in his heart.

26 **Whose hatred** is covered by deceit,
his wickedness shall be shewed before the whole congregation.

27 **Whoso diggeth a pit** shall fall therein:
and he that rolleth a stone, it will return upon him.

28 **A lying tongue** hateth those that are afflicted by it;
and a flattering mouth worketh ruin.

27

Boast not thyself of to morrow;
for thou knowest not
what a day may bring forth.

2 **Let another man** praise thee, and not thine own mouth;
a stranger, and not thine own lips.

3 **A stone** is heavy,
and the sand weighty;
but a fool's wrath is heavier than them both.

4 **Wrath** is cruel,
and anger is outrageous;
but who is able to stand before envy?

5 **Open rebuke** is better than secret love.

6 **Faithful** are the wounds of a friend;
but the kisses of an enemy are deceitful.

7 **The full soul** loatheth an honeycomb;
but to the hungry soul every bitter thing is sweet.

8 **As a bird that wandereth from her nest,** so is a man that wandereth from his place.

9 **Ointment and perfume** rejoice the heart:
so doth the sweetness of a man's friend by hearty counsel.

10 **Thine own friend, and thy father's friend,** forsake not;
neither go into thy brother's house in the day of thy calamity:
for better is a neighbour that is near than a brother far off.

11 **My son, be** wise,
and make my heart glad,
that I may answer him that reproacheth me.

12 **A prudent man** foreseeth the evil,
and hideth himself;
but the simple pass on,
and are punished.

13 **Take** his garment that is surety for a stranger,
and take a pledge of him for a strange woman.

14 **He that blesseth his friend with a loud voice,** {rising early in the morning}, it shall be counted a curse to him.

15 **A continual dropping in a very rainy day and a contentious woman** are alike.

16 **Whosoever hideth her** hideth the wind, and the ointment of his right hand,
which bewrayeth itself.

17 **Iron** sharpeneth iron;
so a man sharpeneth the countenance of his friend.

18 **Whoso keepeth the fig tree** shall eat the fruit thereof:
so he that waiteth on his master shall be honoured.

19 **As in water** face answereth to face,
so the heart of man to man.

20 **Hell and destruction** are never full;
so the eyes of man are never satisfied.

21 **As the fining pot for silver, and the furnace for gold;** so is a man to his praise.

22 **Though thou** shouldest bray a fool in a mortar among wheat with a pestle,
yet will not his foolishness depart from him.

23 **Be thou** diligent to know the state of thy flocks,
and look well to thy herds.

24 **For riches** are not for ever:
and doth the crown endure to every generation?

25 **The hay** appeareth,
and the tender grass sheweth itself,
and herbs of the mountains are gathered.

26 **The lambs** are for thy clothing,
and the goats are the price of the field.

27 **And thou** shalt have goats' milk enough for thy food, for the food of thy household, and for the maintenance for thy maidens.

28

The wicked flee **when no man** pursueth:
but the righteous are bold as a lion.

2 **For the transgression of a land** many are the princes thereof:
but by a man of understanding and knowledge the state thereof shall be prolonged.

3 **A poor man that oppresseth the poor** is like a sweeping rain which leaveth no food.

4 **They that forsake the law** praise the wicked:
but such as keep the law contend with them.

5 **Evil men** understand not judgment:
but they that seek the LORD understand all things.

6 **Better** is the poor that walketh in his uprightness, than he that is perverse in his ways,

though he be rich.
7 **Whoso keepeth the law** is a wise son:
but he that is a companion of riotous men shameth his father.
8 **He that by usury and unjust gain** increaseth his substance,
he shall gather it for him that will pity the poor.
9 **He that turneth away his ear from hearing the law,** even his prayer shall be abomination.
10 **Whoso** causeth the righteous to go astray in an evil way,
he shall fall himself into his own pit:
but the upright shall have good things in possession.
11 **The rich man** is wise in his own conceit;
but the poor that hath understanding searcheth him out.
12 **When righteous men** do rejoice,
there is great glory:
but when the wicked rise,
a man is hidden.
13 **He that covereth his sins** shall not prosper:
but whoso confesseth and forsaketh them shall have mercy.
14 **Happy** is the man that feareth alway:
but he that hardeneth his heart shall fall into mischief.
15 **As a roaring lion, and a ranging bear;** so is a wicked ruler over the poor people.
16 **The prince that wanteth understanding** is also a great oppressor:
but he that hateth covetousness shall prolong his days.
17 **A man that doeth violence to the blood of any person** shall flee to the pit;
let no man stay him.
18 **Whoso walketh uprightly** shall be saved:
but he that is perverse in his ways shall fall at once.
19 **He that tilleth his land** shall have plenty of bread:
but he that followeth after vain persons shall have poverty enough.
20 **A faithful man** shall abound with blessings:
but he that maketh haste to be rich shall not be innocent.
21 **To have respect of persons** is not good:
for for a piece of bread that man will transgress.
22 **He that hasteth to be rich** hath an evil eye,
and considereth not
that poverty shall come upon him.
23 **He that rebuketh a man afterwards** shall find more favour than he that flattereth with the tongue.
24 **Whoso** robbeth his father or his mother,
and saith,
It is no transgression;
the same is the companion of a destroyer.
25 **He that is of a proud heart** stirreth up strife:
but he that putteth his trust in the LORD shall be made fat.
26 **He that trusteth in his own heart** is a fool:
but whoso walketh wisely,
he shall be delivered.
27 **He that giveth unto the poor** shall not lack:
but he that hideth his eyes shall have many a curse.
28 **When the wicked** rise,
men hide themselves:
but when they perish,
the righteous increase.

29

He, that being often reproved hardeneth his neck, shall suddenly be destroyed, and that without remedy.
2 **When the righteous** are in authority,
the people rejoice:
but when the wicked beareth rule,
the people mourn.
3 **Whoso loveth wisdom** rejoiceth his father:
but he that keepeth company with harlots spendeth his substance.
4 **The king by judgment** establisheth the land:
but he that receiveth gifts overthroweth it.
5 **A man that flattereth his neighbour** spreadeth a net for his feet.
6 **In the transgression of an evil man** there is a snare:
but the righteous doth sing **and** rejoice.
7 **The righteous** considereth the cause of the poor:
but the wicked regardeth not to know it.
8 **Scornful men** bring a city into a snare:
but wise men turn away wrath.
9 **If a wise man** contendeth with a foolish man,
whether he rage
or laugh,
there is no rest.
10 **The bloodthirsty** hate the upright:
but the just seek his soul.
11 **A fool** uttereth all his mind:
but a wise man keepeth it in till afterwards.
12 **If a ruler** hearken to lies,
all his servants are wicked.
13 **The poor and the deceitful man** meet together:
the LORD lighteneth both their eyes.
14 **The king that faithfully judgeth the poor,** his throne shall be established for ever.
15 **The rod and reproof** give wisdom:
but a child left to himself bringeth his mother to shame.
16 **When the wicked** are multiplied,
transgression increaseth:
but the righteous shall see their fall.
17 **Correct** thy son,
and he shall give thee rest;
yea, he shall give delight unto thy soul.
18 **Where there** is no vision,
the people perish:
but he that keepeth the law, happy is he.
19 **A servant** will not be corrected by words:
for though he understand
he will not answer.
20 **Seest thou** a man that is hasty in his words?
there is more hope of a fool than of him.
21 **He that delicately bringeth up his servant from a child** shall

have him become his son at the length.

22 **An angry man** stirreth up strife,
and a furious man aboundeth in transgression.

23 **A man's pride** shall bring him low:
but honour shall uphold the humble in spirit.

24 **Whoso is partner with a thief** hateth his own soul:
he heareth cursing,
and bewrayeth it not.

25 **The fear of man** bringeth a snare:
but whoso putteth his trust in the LORD shall be safe.

26 **Many** seek the ruler's favour;
but every man's judgment cometh from the LORD.

27 **An unjust man** is an abomination to the just:
and he that is upright in the way is abomination to the wicked.

30

∞ The words of Agur the son of Jakeh, even the prophecy:
the man spake unto Ithiel, even unto Ithiel and Ucal,

2 **Surely I** am more brutish than any man,
and have not the understanding of a man.

3 **I** neither learned wisdom,
nor have the knowledge of the holy.

4 **Who** hath ascended up into heaven,
or descended?
who hath gathered the wind in his fists?
who hath bound the waters in a garment?
who hath established all the ends of the earth?
what is his name,
and what is his son's name,
if thou canst tell?

5 **Every word of God** is pure:
he is a shield unto them that put their trust in him.

6 **Add thou not** unto his words,
lest he reprove thee,
and thou be found a liar.

7 **Two things** have I required of thee;
deny me them not
before I die:

8 **Remove** far from me vanity and lies:
give me neither poverty nor riches;
feed me with food convenient for me:

9 **Lest I** be full,
and deny thee,
and say,
Who is the LORD?
or lest I be poor,
and steal,
and take the name of my God in vain.

10 **Accuse not** a servant unto his master,
lest he curse thee,
and thou be found guilty.

11 **There** is a generation that curseth their father,
and doth not bless their mother.

12 **There** is a generation that are pure in their own eyes,
and yet is not washed from their filthiness.

13 **There** is a generation,
O how lofty are their eyes!
and their eyelids are lifted up.

14 **There** is a generation,
whose teeth are as swords,
and their jaw teeth as knives,
to devour the poor from off the earth, and the needy from among men.

15 **The horseleach** hath two daughters,
crying,
Give,
give.
There are three things that are never satisfied,
yea, four things say not,
It is enough:

16 The grave; and the barren womb; the earth that is not filled with water; and the fire that saith not, {It is enough}.

17 **The eye that mocketh at his father, and despiseth to obey his mother,** the ravens of the valley shall pick it out,
and the young eagles shall eat it.

18 **There be three things** which are too wonderful for me,
yea, four which I know not:

19 The way of an eagle in the air; the way of a serpent upon a rock; the way of a ship in the midst of the sea; and the way of a man with a maid.

20 **Such** is the way of an adulterous woman;
she eateth,
and wipeth her mouth,
and saith,
I have done no wickedness.

21 **For three things** the earth is disquieted,
and for four which it cannot bear:

22 **For a servant** when he reigneth;
and a fool when he is filled with meat;

23 **For an odious woman** when she is married;
and an handmaid that is heir to her mistress.

24 **There be four things** which are little upon the earth,
but they are exceeding wise:

25 **The ants** are a people not strong,
yet they prepare their meat in the summer;

26 **The conies** are but a feeble folk,
yet make they their houses in the rocks;

27 **The locusts** have no king,
yet go they forth all of them by bands;

28 **The spider** taketh hold with her hands,
and is in kings' palaces.

29 **There be three things** which go well,
yea, four are comely in going:

30 A lion {which is strongest among beasts}, {and turneth not away for any};

31 A greyhound; an he goat also; and a king, {against whom there is no rising up}.

32 **If thou** hast done foolishly
in lifting up thyself,
or if thou hast thought evil,
lay thine hand upon thy mouth.

33 **Surely the churning of milk** bringeth forth butter,
and the wringing of the nose bringeth forth blood:
so the forcing of wrath bringeth forth strife.

31

The words of king Lemuel, the prophecy that his mother taught him.

2 **What,** my son?
and what, the son of my womb?
and what, the son of my vows?

3 **Give not** thy strength unto women, nor thy ways to that which destroyeth kings.

4 **It is not for kings,** O Lemuel, it is not for kings to drink wine;
nor for princes strong drink:

5 **Lest they** drink,
and forget the law,
and pervert the judgment of any of the afflicted.

6 **Give** strong drink unto him that is ready to perish, and wine unto those that be of heavy hearts.

7 **Let him** drink,
and forget his poverty,
and remember his misery no more.

8 **Open** thy mouth for the dumb in the cause of all such as are appointed to destruction.

9 **Open** thy mouth,
judge righteously,
and plead the cause of the poor and needy.

10 **Who** can find a virtuous woman?
for her price is far above rubies.

11 **The heart of her husband** doth safely trust in her,
so that he shall have no need of spoil.

12 **She will** do him good and not evil all the days of her life.

13 **She** seeketh wool, and flax,
and worketh willingly with her hands.

14 **She** is like the merchants' ships;
she bringeth her food from afar.

15 **She** riseth also
while it is yet night,
and giveth meat to her household, and a portion to her maidens.

16 **She** considereth a field,
and buyeth it:
with the fruit of her hands she planteth a vineyard.

17 **She** girdeth her loins with strength,
and strengtheneth her arms.

18 **She** perceiveth that her merchandise is good:
her candle goeth not out by night.

19 **She** layeth her hands to the spindle,
and her hands hold the distaff.

20 **She** stretcheth out her hand to the poor;
yea, she reacheth forth her hands to the needy.

21 **She** is not afraid of the snow for her household:
for all her household are clothed with scarlet.

22 **She** maketh herself coverings of tapestry;
her clothing is silk and purple.

23 **Her husband** is known in the gates,
when he sitteth among the elders of the land.

24 **She** maketh fine linen,
and selleth it;
and delivereth girdles unto the merchant.

25 **Strength and honour** are her clothing;
and she shall rejoice in time to come.

26 **She** openeth her mouth with wisdom;
and in her tongue is the law of kindness.

27 **She** looketh well to the ways of her household,
and eateth not the bread of idleness.

28 **Her children** arise up,
and call her blessed;
her husband also,
and he praiseth her.

29 **Many daughters** have done virtuously,
but thou excellest them all.

30 **Favour** is deceitful,
and beauty is vain:
but a woman that feareth the LORD, she shall be praised.

31 **Give** her of the fruit of her hands;
and let her own works praise her in the gates.

Ecclesiastes

Ecclesiastes, traditionally attributed to King Solomon, delves into the meaning of life, the nature of wisdom, and the ultimate futility of human endeavors when they are not directed toward God. In general, it reflects on the fleeting nature of life and the inevitability of death, underscoring the importance of making the most of one's time on earth.

Solomon begins by exploring the futility of attempting to find meaning or fulfillment in earthly pursuits, arguing that all human achievements are temporary and insignificant. At the same time, he encourages people to live their lives to the fullest and to enjoy the good things that life offers. While these two pieces of advice might seem conflicting, he reconciles them by encouraging readers to find balance and moderation in their activities. But he also cautions them to avoid the extremes of self-indulgence and self-restraint. Finally, the book emphasizes the importance of recognizing God's sovereignty and seeking His guidance in all aspects of life. It argues that one can only find true fulfillment and meaning through a relationship with Him.

The Book of Ecclesiastes is a testament to the universal human experience. It explores the innate drive to live with purpose and meaning. It also affirms the importance of seeking wisdom, primarily through pursuing righteousness and studying God's Word. And finally, it encourages everyone to reflect on their priorities and seek a deeper understanding of God and His plans, not only for their lives but also for humanity.

1 The words of the Preacher, the son of David, king in Jerusalem.

2 **Vanity of vanities,** saith the Preacher, vanity of vanities;
all is vanity.

3 **What profit** hath a man of all his labour which he taketh under the sun?

4 **One generation** passeth away,
and another generation cometh:
but the earth abideth for ever.

5 **The sun** also ariseth,
and the sun goeth down,
and hasteth to his place where he arose.

6 **The wind** goeth toward the south,
and turneth about unto the north;
it whirleth about continually,
and the wind returneth again according to his circuits.

7 **All the rivers** run into the sea;
yet the sea is not full;
unto the place from whence the rivers come,
thither they return again.

8 **All things** are full of labour;
man cannot utter it:
the eye is not satisfied with seeing,
nor the ear filled with hearing.

9 **The thing that hath been,** it is that which shall be;
and that which is done is that which shall be done:
and there is no new thing under the sun.

10 **Is there any thing** whereof it may be said,
See,
this is new?
it hath been already of old time,
which was before us.

11 **There** is no remembrance of former things;
neither shall there be any remembrance of things that are to come with those that shall come after.

12 **I the Preacher** was king over Israel in Jerusalem.

13 **And I** gave my heart to seek and search out by wisdom concerning all things that are done under heaven:
this sore travail hath God given to the sons of man to be exercised therewith.

14 **I** have seen all the works that are done under the sun;
and, {behold}, all is vanity and vexation of spirit.

15 **That which is crooked** cannot be made straight:
and that which is wanting cannot be numbered.

16 **I** communed with mine own heart,
saying,
Lo,
I am come to great estate,
and have gotten more wisdom than all they that have been before me in Jerusalem:
yea, my heart had great experience of wisdom and knowledge.

17 **And I** gave my heart to know wisdom,
and to know madness and folly:
I perceived that this also is vexation of spirit.

18 **For in much wisdom** is much grief:
and he that increaseth knowledge increaseth sorrow.

2 I said in mine heart,
Go to now,
I will prove thee with mirth,
therefore enjoy pleasure:
and, {behold}, this also is vanity.

2 **I** said of laughter,
It is mad: and of mirth,
What doeth it?

3 **I** sought in mine heart to give myself unto wine,
yet acquainting mine heart with wisdom;
and to lay hold on folly,
till I might see what was that good for the sons of men,
which they should do under the heaven all the days of their life.

4 **I** made me great works;
I builded me houses;
I planted me vineyards:

5 **I** made me gardens and orchards,

and I planted trees in them of all kind of fruits:
6 **I** made me pools of water,
to water therewith the wood that bringeth forth trees:
7 **I** got me servants and maidens,
and had servants born in my house;
also I had great possessions of great and small cattle above all that were in Jerusalem before me:
8 **I** gathered me also silver and gold, and the peculiar treasure of kings and of the provinces:
I gat me men singers and women singers, and the delights of the sons of men, as musical instruments, and that of all sorts.
9 **So I** was great,
and increased more than all that were before me in Jerusalem:
also my wisdom remained with me.
10 **And whatsoever** mine eyes desired
I kept not from them,
I withheld not my heart from any joy;
for my heart rejoiced in all my labour:
and this was my portion of all my labour.
11 **Then I** looked on all the works that my hands had wrought, and on the labour that I had laboured to do:
and, {behold}, all was vanity and vexation of spirit,
and there was no profit under the sun.
12 **And I** turned myself to behold wisdom, and madness, and folly:
for what can the man do that cometh after the king? even that which hath been already done.
13 **Then I** saw that wisdom excelleth folly,
as far as light excelleth darkness.
14 **The wise man's eyes** are in his head;
but the fool walketh in darkness:
and I myself perceived also that one event happeneth to them all.
15 **Then** said I in my heart,
As it happeneth to the fool,
so it happeneth even to me;
and why was I then more wise?
Then I said in my heart,
that this also is vanity.
16 **For there** is no remembrance of the wise more than of the fool for ever;
seeing that which now is in the days to come shall all be forgotten.
And how dieth the wise man?
as the fool.
17 **Therefore I** hated life;
because the work that is wrought under the sun is grievous unto me:
for all is vanity and vexation of spirit.
18 **Yea, I** hated all my labour which I had taken under the sun:
because I should leave it unto the man that shall be after me.
19 **And who** knoweth
whether he shall be a wise man or a fool?
yet shall he have rule over all my labour wherein I have laboured, and wherein I have shewed myself wise under the sun.
This is also vanity.
20 **Therefore I** went about to cause my heart to despair of all the labour which I took under the sun.
21 **For there** is a man whose labour is in wisdom, and in knowledge, and in equity;
yet to a man that hath not laboured therein shall he leave it for his portion.
This also is vanity and a great evil.
22 **For what** hath man of all his labour, and of the vexation of his heart,
wherein he hath laboured under the sun?
23 **For all his days** are sorrows, and his travail grief;
yea, his heart taketh not rest in the night.
This is also vanity.
24 **There** is nothing better for a man,
than that he should eat and drink,
and that he should make his soul enjoy good in his labour.
This also I saw,
that it was from the hand of God.
25 **For who** can eat,
or who else can hasten hereunto, more than I?
26 **For God** giveth to a man that is good in his sight wisdom, and knowledge, and joy:
but to the sinner he giveth travail,
to gather and to heap up,
that he may give to him that is good before God.
This also is vanity and vexation of spirit.

3 **To every thing** there is a season, and a time to every purpose under the heaven:
2 **A time** to be born,
and a time to die;
a time to plant,
and a time to pluck up that which is planted;
3 **A time** to kill,
and a time to heal;
a time to break down,
and a time to build up;
4 **A time** to weep,
and a time to laugh;
a time to mourn,
and a time to dance;
5 **A time** to cast away stones,
and a time to gather stones together;
a time to embrace,
and a time to refrain from embracing;
6 **A time** to get,
and a time to lose;
a time to keep,
and a time to cast away;
7 **A time** to rend,
and a time to sew;
a time to keep silence,
and a time to speak;
8 **A time** to love,
and a time to hate; a time of war, and a time of peace.
9 **What profit** hath he that worketh in that wherein he laboureth?
10 **I** have seen the travail,
which God hath given to the sons of men to be exercised in it.
11 **He** hath made every thing beautiful in his time:
also he hath set the world in their heart,
so that no man can find out the work that God maketh from the beginning to the end.
12 **I** know
that there is no good in them,
but for a man to rejoice,
and to do good in his life.
13 **And also that every man** should eat and drink,

and enjoy the good of all his labour,
it is the gift of God.

14 **I** know
that, {whatsoever God doeth}, it shall be for ever:
nothing can be put to it,
nor any thing taken from it:
and God doeth it,
that men should fear before him.

15 **That which hath been** is now;
and that which is to be hath already been;
and God requireth that which is past.

16 **And moreover I** saw under the sun the place of judgment, {that wickedness was there}; and the place of righteousness, {that iniquity was there}.

17 **I** said in mine heart,
God shall judge the righteous and the wicked:
for there is a time there for every purpose and for every work.

18 **I** said in mine heart concerning the estate of the sons of men,
that God might manifest them,
and that they might see that they themselves are beasts.

19 **For that which befalleth the sons of men** befalleth beasts;
even one thing befalleth them:
as the one dieth,
so dieth the other;
yea, they have all one breath;
so that a man hath no preeminence above a beast:
for all is vanity.

20 **All** go unto one place;
all are of the dust,
and all turn to dust again.

21 **Who** knoweth the spirit of man that goeth upward, and the spirit of the beast that goeth downward to the earth?

22 **Wherefore I** perceive that there is nothing better,
than that a man should rejoice in his own works;
for that is his portion:
for who shall bring him to see what shall be after him?

4

So I returned,
and considered all the oppressions that are done under the sun:
and behold the tears of such as were oppressed,
and they had no comforter;
and on the side of their oppressors there was power;
but they had no comforter.

2 **Wherefore I** praised the dead which are already dead more than the living which are yet alive.

3 **Yea, better** is he than both they,
which hath not yet been,
who hath not seen the evil work that is done under the sun.

4 **Again, I** considered all travail, and every right work,
that for this a man is envied of his neighbour.
This is also vanity and vexation of spirit.

5 **The fool** foldeth his hands together,
and eateth his own flesh.

6 **Better** is an handful with quietness,
than both the hands full with travail and vexation of spirit.

7 **Then I** returned,
and I saw vanity under the sun.

8 **There** is one alone,
and there is not a second;
yea, he hath neither child nor brother:
yet is there no end of all his labour;
neither is his eye satisfied with riches;
neither saith he,
For whom do I labour,
and bereave my soul of good?
This is also vanity, yea,
it is a sore travail.

9 **Two** are better than one;
because they have a good reward for their labour.

10 **For if they** fall,
the one will lift up his fellow:
but woe to him that is alone
when he falleth;
for he hath not another to help him up.

11 **Again, if two** lie together,
then they have heat:
but how can one be warm alone?

12 **And if one** prevail against him,
two shall withstand him;
and a threefold cord is not quickly broken.

13 **Better** is a poor and a wise child than an old and foolish king,
who will no more be admonished.

14 **For out of prison** he cometh to reign;
whereas also he that is born in his kingdom becometh poor.

15 **I** considered all the living which walk under the sun, with the second child that shall stand up in his stead.

16 **There** is no end of all the people, even of all that have been before them:
they also that come after shall not rejoice in him.
Surely this also is vanity and vexation of spirit.

5

Keep thy foot
when thou goest to the house of God,
and be more ready to hear,
than to give the sacrifice of fools:
or they consider not
that they do evil.

2 **Be not** rash with thy mouth,
and let not thine heart be hasty to utter any thing before God:
for God is in heaven, and thou upon earth:
therefore let thy words be few.

3 **For a dream** cometh through the multitude of business;
and a fool's voice is known by multitude of words.

4 **When thou** vowest a vow unto God,
defer not to pay it;
for he hath no pleasure in fools:
pay that which thou hast vowed.

5 **Better is it** that thou shouldest not vow,
than that thou shouldest vow and not pay.

6 **Suffer not** thy mouth to cause thy flesh to sin;
neither say thou before the angel,
that it was an error:
wherefore should God be angry at thy voice,
and destroy the work of thine hands?

7 **For in the multitude of dreams and many words** there are also divers vanities:
but fear thou God.

8 **If thou** seest the oppression of the poor, and violent perverting of judgment and justice in a province,
marvel not at the matter:
for he that is higher than the highest regardeth;
and there be higher than they.

[9] **Moreover the profit of the earth** is for all:
the king himself is served by the field.
[10] **He that loveth silver** shall not be satisfied with silver; nor he that loveth abundance with increase:
this is also vanity.
[11] **When goods** increase,
they are increased that eat them:
and what good is there to the owners thereof,
saving the beholding of them with their eyes?
[12] **The sleep of a labouring man** is sweet,
whether he eat little or much:
but the abundance of the rich will not suffer him to sleep.
[13] **There** is a sore evil which I have seen under the sun, namely, riches kept for the owners thereof to their hurt.
[14] **But those riches** perish by evil travail:
and he begetteth a son,
and there is nothing in his hand.
[15] **As he** came forth of his mother's womb,
naked shall he return to go as he came,
and shall take nothing of his labour,
which he may carry away in his hand.
[16] **And this** also is a sore evil,
that in all points as he came,
so shall he go:
and what profit hath he that hath laboured for the wind?
[17] **All his days** also he eateth in darkness,
and he hath much sorrow and wrath with his sickness.
[18] **Behold** that which I have seen:
it is good and comely for one to eat and to drink,
and to enjoy the good of all his labour that he taketh under the sun all the days of his life,
which God giveth him:
for it is his portion.
[19] **Every man also to whom God hath given riches and wealth, and hath given him power to eat thereof, and to take his portion, and to rejoice in his labour;** this is the gift of God.
[20] **For he** shall not much remember the days of his life;
because God answereth him in the joy of his heart.

6

There is an evil which I have seen under the sun,
and it is common among men:
[2] **A man to whom God hath given riches, wealth, and honour, {so that he wanteth nothing for his soul of all that he desireth}, {yet God giveth him not power to eat thereof}, {but a stranger eateth it}:** this is vanity,
and it is an evil disease.
[3] **If a man** beget an hundred children,
and live many years,
so that the days of his years be many,
and his soul be not filled with good,
and also that he have no burial;
I say,
that an untimely birth is better than he.
[4] **For he** cometh in with vanity,
and departeth in darkness,
and his name shall be covered with darkness.
[5] **Moreover he** hath not seen the sun,
nor known any thing:
this hath more rest than the other.
[6] **Yea, though he** live a thousand years twice told,
yet hath he seen no good:
do not all go to one place?
[7] **All the labour of man** is for his mouth,
and yet the appetite is not filled.
[8] **For what** hath the wise more than the fool?
what hath the poor,
that knoweth
to walk before the living?
[9] **Better** is the sight of the eyes than the wandering of the desire:
this is also vanity and vexation of spirit.
[10] **That which hath been** is named already,
and it is known that it is man:
neither may he contend with him that is mightier than he.
[11] **Seeing there** be many things that increase vanity,
what is man the better?
[12] **For who** knoweth
what is good for man in this life, all the days of his vain life which he spendeth as a shadow?
for who can tell a man
what shall be after him under the sun?

7

A good name is better than precious ointment; and the day of death than the day of one's birth.
[2] **It is better** to go to the house of mourning,
than to go to the house of feasting:
for that is the end of all men;
and the living will lay it to his heart.
[3] **Sorrow** is better than laughter:
for by the sadness of the countenance the heart is made better.
[4] **The heart of the wise** is in the house of mourning;
but the heart of fools is in the house of mirth.
[5] **It is better** to hear the rebuke of the wise,
than for a man to hear the song of fools.
[6] **For as the crackling of thorns under a pot,** so is the laughter of the fool:
this also is vanity.
[7] **Surely oppression** maketh a wise man mad;
and a gift destroyeth the heart.
[8] **Better** is the end of a thing than the beginning thereof:
and the patient in spirit is better than the proud in spirit.
[9] **Be not** hasty in thy spirit to be angry:
for anger resteth in the bosom of fools.
[10] **Say not thou,**
What is the cause that the former days were better than these?
for thou dost not enquire wisely concerning this.
[11] **Wisdom** is good with an inheritance:
and by it there is profit to them that see the sun.
[12] **For wisdom** is a defence,
and money is a defence:
but the excellency of knowledge is,
that wisdom giveth life to them that have it.
[13] **Consider** the work of God:
for who can make that straight,

which he hath made crooked?
14 **In the day of prosperity** be joyful,
but in the day of adversity consider:
God also hath set the one over against the other,
to the end that man should find nothing after him.
15 **All things** have I seen in the days of my vanity:
there is a just man that perisheth in his righteousness,
and there is a wicked man that prolongeth his life in his wickedness.
16 **Be not** righteous over much;
neither make thyself over wise:
why shouldest thou destroy thyself?
17 **Be not** over much wicked,
neither be thou foolish:
why shouldest thou die before thy time?
18 **It is good** that thou shouldest take hold of this;
yea, also from this withdraw not thine hand:
for he that feareth God shall come forth of them all.
19 **Wisdom** strengtheneth the wise more than ten mighty men which are in the city.
20 **For there** is not a just man upon earth,
that doeth good,
and sinneth not.
21 **Also take no heed** unto all words that are spoken;
lest thou hear thy servant curse thee:
22 **For oftentimes also thine own heart** knoweth
that thou thyself likewise hast cursed others.
23 **All this** have I proved by wisdom:
I said,
I will be wise;
but it was far from me.
24 **That which is far off, and exceeding deep,** who can find it out?
25 **I** applied mine heart to know,
and to search,
and to seek out wisdom, and the reason of things,
and to know the wickedness of folly, even of foolishness and madness:
26 **And I** find more bitter than death the woman,
whose heart is snares and nets, and her hands as bands:
whoso pleaseth God shall escape from her;
but the sinner shall be taken by her.
27 **Behold,**
this have I found,
saith the preacher,
counting one by one,
to find out the account:
28 **Which yet my soul** seeketh,
but I find not:
one man among a thousand have I found;
but a woman among all those have I not found.
29 **Lo,**
this only have I found,
that God hath made man upright;
but they have sought out many inventions.

8 **Who** is as the wise man?
and who knoweth the interpretation of a thing?
a man's wisdom maketh his face to shine,
and the boldness of his face shall be changed.
2 **I** counsel thee
to keep the king's commandment, and that in regard of the oath of God.
3 **Be not** hasty to go out of his sight:
stand not in an evil thing;
for he doeth whatsoever pleaseth him.
4 **Where the word of a king** is,
there is power:
and who may say unto him,
What doest thou?
5 **Whoso keepeth the commandment** shall feel no evil thing:
and a wise man's heart discerneth both time and judgment.
6 **Because to every purpose** there is time and judgment,
therefore the misery of man is great upon him.
7 **For he** knoweth not that which shall be:
for who can tell him
when it shall be?
8 **There is** no man that hath power over the spirit to retain the spirit;
neither hath he power in the day of death:
and there is no discharge in that war;
neither shall wickedness deliver those that are given to it.
9 **All this** have I seen,
and applied my heart unto every work that is done under the sun:
there is a time wherein one man ruleth over another to his own hurt.
10 **And so I** saw the wicked buried,
who had come and gone from the place of the holy,
and they were forgotten in the city where they had so done:
this is also vanity.
11 **Because sentence against an evil work** is not executed speedily,
therefore the heart of the sons of men is fully set in them to do evil.
12 **Though a sinner** do evil an hundred times,
and his days be prolonged,
yet surely I know
that it shall be well with them that fear God,
which fear before him:
13 **But it** shall not be well with the wicked,
neither shall he prolong his days,
which are as a shadow;
because he feareth not before God.
14 **There** is a vanity which is done upon the earth;
that there be just men,
unto whom it happeneth according to the work of the wicked;
again, there be wicked men,
to whom it happeneth according to the work of the righteous:
I said
that this also is vanity.
15 **Then I** commended mirth,
because a man hath no better thing under the sun,
than to eat,
and to drink,
and to be merry:
for that shall abide with him of his labour the days of his life,
which God giveth him under the sun.
16 **When I** applied mine heart to know wisdom,
and to see the business that is done upon the earth:

(for also there is that neither day nor night seeth sleep with his eyes:)
17 **Then I** beheld all the work of God,
that a man cannot find out the work that is done under the sun:
because though a man labour to seek it out,
yet he shall not find it;
yea farther; though a wise man think to know it,
yet shall he not be able to find it.

9

For all this I considered in my heart
even to declare all this,
that the righteous, and the wise, and their works, are in the hand of God:
no man knoweth either love or hatred by all that is before them.
2 **All things** come alike to all:
there is one event to the righteous, and to the wicked; to the good and to the clean, and to the unclean; to him that sacrificeth, and to him that sacrificeth not:
as is the good,
so is the sinner;
and he that sweareth, as he that feareth an oath.
3 **This** is an evil among all things that are done under the sun,
that there is one event unto all:
yea, also the heart of the sons of men is full of evil,
and madness is in their heart
while they live,
and after that they go to the dead.
4 **For to him that is joined to all the living** there is hope:
for a living dog is better than a dead lion.
5 **For the living** know
that they shall die:
but the dead know not any thing,
neither have they any more a reward;
for the memory of them is forgotten.
6 **Also their love, and their hatred, and their envy,** is now perished;
neither have they any more a portion for ever in any thing that is done under the sun.
7 **Go** thy way,
eat thy bread with joy,
and drink thy wine with a merry heart;
for God now accepteth thy works.
8 **Let thy garments** be always white;
and let thy head lack no ointment.
9 **Live** joyfully with the wife whom thou lovest all the days of the life of thy vanity,
which he hath given thee under the sun, all the days of thy vanity:
for that is thy portion in this life, and in thy labour which thou takest under the sun.
10 **Whatsoever** thy hand findeth to do,
do it with thy might;
for there is no work, nor device, nor knowledge, nor wisdom, in the grave,
whither thou goest.
11 **I** returned,
and saw under the sun,
that the race is not to the swift, nor the battle to the strong, neither yet bread to the wise, nor yet riches to men of understanding, nor yet favour to men of skill;
but time and chance happeneth to them all.
12 **For man** also knoweth not his time:
as the fishes that are taken in an evil net, and as the birds that are caught in the snare; so are the sons of men snared in an evil time,
when it falleth suddenly upon them.
13 **This wisdom** have I seen also under the sun,
and it seemed great unto me:
14 **There** was a little city, and few men within it;
and there came a great king against it,
and besieged it,
and built great bulwarks against it:
15 **Now there** was found in it a poor wise man,
and he by his wisdom delivered the city;
yet no man remembered that same poor man.
16 **Then** said I,
Wisdom is better than strength:
nevertheless the poor man's wisdom is despised,
and his words are not heard.
17 **The words of wise men** are heard in quiet more than the cry of him that ruleth among fools.
18 **Wisdom** is better than weapons of war:
but one sinner destroyeth much good.

10

Dead flies cause the ointment of the apothecary to send forth a stinking savour:
so doth a little folly him that is in reputation for wisdom and honour.
2 **A wise man's heart** is at his right hand; but a fool's heart at his left.
3 **Yea also, when he that is a fool** walketh by the way,
his wisdom faileth him,
and he saith to every one
that he is a fool.
4 **If the spirit of the ruler** rise up against thee,
leave not thy place;
for yielding pacifieth great offences.
5 **There** is an evil which I have seen under the sun, as an error which proceedeth from the ruler:
6 **Folly** is set in great dignity,
and the rich sit in low place.
7 **I** have seen servants upon horses, and princes walking as servants upon the earth.
8 **He that diggeth a pit** shall fall into it;
and whoso breaketh an hedge,
a serpent shall bite him.
9 **Whoso removeth stones** shall be hurt therewith;
and he that cleaveth wood shall be endangered thereby.
10 **If the iron** be blunt,
and he do not whet the edge,
then must he put to more strength:
but wisdom is profitable to direct.
11 **Surely the serpent** will bite without enchantment;
and a babbler is no better.
12 **The words of a wise man's mouth** are gracious;
but the lips of a fool will swallow up himself.
13 **The beginning of the words of his mouth** is foolishness:
and the end of his talk is mischievous madness.
14 **A fool** also is full of words:
a man cannot tell
what shall be;
and what shall be after him,
who can tell him?

15 **The labour of the foolish** wearieth every one of them,
because he knoweth not
how to go to the city.

16 **Woe** to thee, O land,
when thy king is a child,
and thy princes eat in the morning!

17 **Blessed** art thou, O land,
when thy king is the son of nobles,
and thy princes eat in due season, for strength, and not for drunkenness!

18 **By much slothfulness** the building decayeth;
and through idleness of the hands the house droppeth through.

19 **A feast** is made for laughter,
and wine maketh merry:
but money answereth all things.

20 **Curse not** the king, no not in thy thought;
and curse not the rich in thy bedchamber:
for a bird of the air shall carry the voice,
and that which hath wings shall tell the matter.

11 **Cast** thy bread upon the waters:
for thou shalt find it after many days.

2 **Give** a portion to seven, and also to eight;
for thou knowest not
what evil shall be upon the earth.

3 **If the clouds** be full of rain,
they empty themselves upon the earth:
and if the tree fall toward the south, or toward the north, in the place where the tree falleth,
there it shall be.

4 **He that observeth the wind** shall not sow;
and he that regardeth the clouds shall not reap.

5 **As thou** knowest not
what is the way of the spirit,
nor how the bones do grow in the womb of her that is with child:
even so thou knowest not the works of God who maketh all.

6 **In the morning** sow thy seed,
and in the evening withhold not thine hand:
for thou knowest not
whether shall prosper, either this or that,
or whether they both shall be alike good.

7 **Truly the light** is sweet,
and a pleasant thing it is for the eyes to behold the sun:

8 **But if a man** live many years,
and rejoice in them all;
yet let him remember the days of darkness;
for they shall be many.
All that cometh is vanity.

9 **Rejoice,** O young man, in thy youth;
and let thy heart cheer thee in the days of thy youth,
and walk in the ways of thine heart, and in the sight of thine eyes:
but know thou,
that for all these things God will bring thee into judgment.

10 **Therefore remove** sorrow from thy heart,
and put away evil from thy flesh:
for childhood and youth are vanity.

12 **Remember** now thy Creator in the days of thy youth,
while the evil days come not,
nor the years draw nigh,
when thou shalt say,
I have no pleasure in them;

2 **While the sun, or the light, or the moon, or the stars,** be not darkened,
nor the clouds return after the rain:

3 **In the day when the keepers of the house** shall tremble,
and the strong men shall bow themselves,
and the grinders cease
because they are few,
and those that look out of the windows be darkened,

4 **And the doors** shall be shut in the streets,
when the sound of the grinding is low,
and he shall rise up at the voice of the bird,
and all the daughters of musick shall be brought low;

5 **Also when they** shall be afraid of that which is high,
and fears shall be in the way,
and the almond tree shall flourish,
and the grasshopper shall be a burden,
and desire shall fail:
because man goeth to his long home,
and the mourners go about the streets:

6 **Or ever the silver cord** be loosed,
or the golden bowl be broken,
or the pitcher be broken at the fountain,
or the wheel broken at the cistern.

7 **Then** shall the dust return to the earth as it was:
and the spirit shall return unto God who gave it.

8 **Vanity of vanities,** saith the preacher;
all is vanity.

9 **And moreover, {because the preacher was wise},** he still taught the people knowledge;
yea, he gave good heed,
and sought out,
and set in order many proverbs.

10 **The preacher** sought to find out acceptable words:
and that which was written was upright, even words of truth.

11 **The words of the wise** are as goads, and as nails fastened by the masters of assemblies,
which are given from one shepherd.

12 **And further, by these,** my son, be admonished:
of making many books there is no end;
and much study is a weariness of the flesh.

13 **Let us** hear the conclusion of the whole matter:
Fear God,
and keep his commandments:
for this is the whole duty of man.

14 **For God** shall bring every work into judgment, with every secret thing,
whether it be good,
or whether it be evil.

Song of Solomon

The Song of Solomon, a literary masterpiece traditionally attributed to King Solomon, has left a lasting mark on literature and culture. Its influence is evident in the works of Shakespeare, Dante, Milton, Spenser, and many others. This collection of love poems and songs delves into the themes of romantic love, passion, and desire, tracing the journey from initial attraction and courtship to the deepening of love and commitment.

The book is a testament to the beauty, complexity, and intensifying emotions that love can bring. It does so by weaving rich metaphors and imagery, drawing comparisons to nature and more abstract concepts, such as the strength of love and the power of passion. Solomon portrays the two lovers as intense, passionate, and deeply committed to each other. They share their thoughts, feelings, and desires openly and honestly, inviting readers to empathize with their journey.

While the book is primarily a celebration of romantic love and sexual desire, Jewish and Christian traditions often interpret it as an allegory for the love between God and His people. Its inclusion in the Old Testament serves as a powerful reminder for readers to embrace love, passion, and devotion in all aspects of life, be it in their relationships with others or with God.

1 The song of songs,
which is Solomon's.

2 **Let him** kiss me with the kisses of his mouth:
for thy love is better than wine.

3 **Because of the savour of thy good ointments** thy name is as ointment poured forth,
therefore do the virgins love thee.

4 **Draw** me,
we will run after thee:
the king hath brought me into his chambers:
we will be glad
and rejoice in thee,
we will remember thy love more than wine:
the upright love thee.

5 **I** am black, but comely, O ye daughters of Jerusalem, as the tents of Kedar, as the curtains of Solomon.

6 **Look not** upon me,
because I am black,
because the sun hath looked upon me:
my mother's children were angry with me;
they made me the keeper of the vineyards;
but mine own vineyard have I not kept.

7 **Tell** me, O thou whom my soul loveth,
where thou feedest,
where thou makest thy flock to rest at noon:
for why should I be as one that turneth aside by the flocks of thy companions?

8 **If thou** know not, O thou fairest among women,
go thy way forth by the footsteps of the flock,
and feed thy kids beside the shepherds' tents.

9 **I** have compared thee, O my love, to a company of horses in Pharaoh's chariots.

10 **Thy cheeks** are comely with rows of jewels,
thy neck with chains of gold.

11 **We** will make thee borders of gold with studs of silver.

12 **While the king** sitteth at his table,
my spikenard sendeth forth the smell thereof.

13 **A bundle of myrrh** is my well-beloved unto me;
he shall lie all night betwixt my breasts.

14 **My beloved** is unto me as a cluster of camphire in the vineyards of Engedi.

15 **Behold,**
thou art fair, my love;
behold,
thou art fair;
thou hast doves' eyes.

16 **Behold,**
thou art fair, my beloved, yea, pleasant:
also our bed is green.

17 **The beams of our house** are cedar,
and our rafters of fir.

2 I am the rose of Sharon, and the lily of the valleys.

2 **As the lily among thorns,** so is my love among the daughters.

3 **As the apple tree among the trees of the wood,** so is my beloved among the sons.
I sat down under his shadow with great delight,
and his fruit was sweet to my taste.

4 **He** brought me to the banqueting house,
and his banner over me was love.

5 **Stay** me with flagons,
comfort me with apples:
for I am sick of love.

6 **His left hand** is under my head,
and his right hand doth embrace me.

7 **I** charge you, O ye daughters of Jerusalem, by the roes, and by the hinds of the field,
that ye stir not up,
nor awake my love,
till he please.

8 The voice of my beloved!
behold,
he cometh
leaping upon the mountains,
skipping upon the hills.

9 **My beloved** is like a roe or a young hart:
behold,
he standeth behind our wall,
he looketh forth at the windows,

shewing himself through the
lattice.

10 **My beloved** spake,
and said unto me,
Rise up, my love, my fair one,
and come away.

11 **For, {lo}, the winter** is past,
the rain is over and gone;
12 **The flowers** appear on the earth;
the time of the singing of birds is
come,
and the voice of the turtle is heard
in our land;
13 **The fig tree** putteth forth her
green figs,
**and the vines with the tender
grape** give a good smell.
Arise, my love, my fair one,
and come away.

14 **O my dove, {that art in the clefts
of the rock, in the secret places
of the stairs}, let me** see thy
countenance,
let me hear thy voice;
for sweet is thy voice,
and thy countenance is comely.

15 **Take** us the foxes, the little foxes,
that spoil the vines:
for our vines have tender grapes.

16 **My beloved** is mine,
and I am his:
he feedeth among the lilies.

17 **Until the day** break,
and the shadows flee away,
turn, my beloved,
and be thou like a roe or a young
hart upon the mountains of
Bether.

3

By night on my bed I sought
him whom my soul loveth:
I sought him,
but I found him not.

2 **I** will rise now,
and go about the city in the streets,
and in the broad ways I will seek
him whom my soul loveth:
I sought him,
but I found him not.

3 **The watchmen that go about the
city** found me:
to whom I said,
Saw ye him whom my soul loveth?

4 **It was but a little** that I passed
from them,
but I found him whom my soul
loveth:
I held him,
and would not let him go,
until I had brought him into my
mother's house, and into the
chamber of her that conceived
me.

5 **I** charge you, O ye daughters of
Jerusalem, by the roes, and by the
hinds of the field,
that ye stir not up,
nor awake my love,
till he please.

6 **Who** is this that cometh out of the
wilderness like pillars of smoke,
perfumed with myrrh and
frankincense, with all powders of
the merchant?

7 **Behold** his bed,
which is Solomon's;
threescore valiant men are about
it, of the valiant of Israel.

8 **They all** hold swords,
being expert in war:
every man hath his sword upon his
thigh because of fear in the night.

9 **King Solomon** made himself a
chariot of the wood of Lebanon.

10 **He** made the pillars thereof of
silver, the bottom thereof of gold,
the covering of it of purple,
the midst thereof being paved with
love, for the daughters of
Jerusalem.

11 **Go forth,** O ye daughters of Zion,
and behold king Solomon with the
crown wherewith his mother
crowned him in the day of his
espousals, and in the day of the
gladness of his heart.

4

Behold,
thou art fair, my love;
behold,
thou art fair;
thou hast doves' eyes within thy
locks:
thy hair is as a flock of goats,
that appear from mount Gilead.

2 **Thy teeth** are like a flock of sheep
that are even shorn,
which came up from the washing;
whereof every one bear twins,
and none is barren among them.

3 **Thy lips** are like a thread of scarlet,
and thy speech is comely:
thy temples are like a piece of a
pomegranate within thy locks.

4 **Thy neck** is like the tower of David
builded for an armoury,
whereon there hang a thousand
bucklers, all shields of mighty
men.

5 **Thy two breasts** are like two
young roes that are twins,
which feed among the lilies.

6 **Until the day** break,
and the shadows flee away,
I will get me to the mountain of
myrrh, and to the hill of
frankincense.

7 **Thou** art all fair, my love;
there is no spot in thee.

8 **Come** with me from Lebanon, my
spouse, with me from Lebanon:
look from the top of Amana, from
the top of Shenir and Hermon,
from the lions' dens, from the
mountains of the leopards.

9 **Thou** hast ravished my heart, my
sister, my spouse;
thou hast ravished my heart with
one of thine eyes, with one chain
of thy neck.

10 **How fair** is thy love, my sister, my
spouse!
how much better is thy love than
wine!
and the smell of thine ointments
than all spices!

11 **Thy lips,** O my spouse, drop as the
honeycomb:
honey and milk are under thy
tongue;
and the smell of thy garments is
like the smell of Lebanon.

12 **A garden inclosed** is my sister,
my spouse; a spring shut up, a
fountain sealed.

13 **Thy plants** are an orchard of
pomegranates, with pleasant
fruits; camphire, with spikenard,
14 Spikenard and saffron; calamus
and cinnamon, with all trees of
frankincense; myrrh and aloes,
with all the chief spices:
15 A fountain of gardens, a well of
living waters, and streams from
Lebanon.

16 **Awake,** O north wind;
and come, thou south;
blow upon my garden,
that the spices thereof may flow
out.
Let my beloved come into his
garden,
and eat his pleasant fruits.

5

I am come into my garden, my
sister, my spouse:
I have gathered my myrrh with my
spice;

I have eaten my honeycomb with my honey;
I have drunk my wine with my milk:
eat, O friends;
drink,
yea, drink abundantly, O beloved.

2 **I** sleep,
but my heart waketh:
it is the voice of my beloved that knocketh,
saying,
Open to me, my sister, my love, my dove, my undefiled:
for my head is filled with dew,
and my locks with the drops of the night.

3 **I** have put off my coat;
how shall I put it on?
I have washed my feet;
how shall I defile them?

4 **My beloved** put in his hand by the hole of the door,
and my bowels were moved for him.

5 **I** rose up to open to my beloved;
and my hands dropped with myrrh,
and my fingers with sweet smelling myrrh, upon the handles of the lock.

6 **I** opened to my beloved;
but my beloved had withdrawn himself,
and was gone:
my soul failed
when he spake:
I sought him,
but I could not find him;
I called him,
but he gave me no answer.

7 **The watchmen that went about the city** found me,
they smote me,
they wounded me;
the keepers of the walls took away my veil from me.

8 **I** charge you, O daughters of Jerusalem,
if ye find my beloved,
that ye tell him,
that I am sick of love.

9 **What** is thy beloved more than another beloved, O thou fairest among women?
what is thy beloved more than another beloved,
that thou dost so charge us?

10 **My beloved** is white and ruddy, the chiefest among ten thousand.

11 **His head** is as the most fine gold,
his locks are bushy, and black as a raven.

12 **His eyes** are as the eyes of doves by the rivers of waters,
washed with milk,
and fitly set.

13 **His cheeks** are as a bed of spices, as sweet flowers:
his lips like lilies,
dropping sweet smelling myrrh.

14 **His hands** are as gold rings set with the beryl:
his belly is as bright ivory overlaid with sapphires.

15 **His legs** are as pillars of marble,
set upon sockets of fine gold:
his countenance is as Lebanon, excellent as the cedars.

16 **His mouth** is most sweet:
yea, he is altogether lovely.
This is my beloved,
and this is my friend, O daughters of Jerusalem.

6 **Whither** is thy beloved gone, O thou fairest among women?
whither is thy beloved turned aside?
that we may seek him with thee.

2 **My beloved** is gone down into his garden, to the beds of spices,
to feed in the gardens,
and to gather lilies.

3 **I** am my beloved's,
and my beloved is mine:
he feedeth among the lilies.

4 **Thou** art beautiful, O my love, as Tirzah, comely as Jerusalem, terrible as an army with banners.

5 **Turn away** thine eyes from me,
for they have overcome me:
thy hair is as a flock of goats that appear from Gilead.

6 **Thy teeth** are as a flock of sheep which go up from the washing,
whereof every one beareth twins,
and there is not one barren among them.

7 **As a piece of a pomegranate** are thy temples within thy locks.

8 **There** are threescore queens, and fourscore concubines, and virgins without number.

9 **My dove, my undefiled** is but one;
she is the only one of her mother,
she is the choice one of her that bare her.
The daughters saw her,
and blessed her; yea, the queens and the concubines,
and they praised her.

10 **Who** is she that looketh forth as the morning, fair as the moon, clear as the sun, and terrible as an army with banners?

11 **I** went down into the garden of nuts
to see the fruits of the valley,
and to see whether the vine flourished and the pomegranates budded.

12 **Or ever I** was aware,
my soul made me like the chariots of Amminadib.

13 **Return,**
return, O Shulamite;
return,
return,
that we may look upon thee.
What will ye see in the Shulamite?
As it were the company of two armies.

7 **How beautiful** are thy feet with shoes, O prince's daughter!
the joints of thy thighs are like jewels, the work of the hands of a cunning workman.

2 **Thy navel** is like a round goblet,
which wanteth not liquor:
thy belly is like an heap of wheat set about with lilies.

3 **Thy two breasts** are like two young roes that are twins.

4 **Thy neck** is as a tower of ivory;
thine eyes like the fishpools in Heshbon, by the gate of Bathrabbim:
thy nose is as the tower of Lebanon
which looketh toward Damascus.

5 **Thine head upon thee** is like Carmel,
and the hair of thine head like purple;
the king is held in the galleries.

6 **How fair and how pleasant** art thou, O love, for delights!

7 **This thy stature** is like to a palm tree,
and thy breasts to clusters of grapes.

8 **I** said,
I will go up to the palm tree,
I will take hold of the boughs thereof:

now also thy breasts shall be as
clusters of the vine,
and the smell of thy nose like
apples;
9 **And the roof of thy mouth** like
the best wine for my beloved,
that goeth down sweetly,
causing the lips of those that are
asleep to speak.
10 **I** am my beloved's,
and his desire is toward me.
11 **Come,** my beloved,
let us go forth into the field;
let us lodge in the villages.
12 **Let us** get up early to the
vineyards;
let us see if the vine flourish,
whether the tender grape appear,
and the pomegranates bud forth:
there will I give thee my loves.
13 **The mandrakes** give a smell,
and at our gates are all manner of
pleasant fruits, new and old,
which I have laid up for thee, O my
beloved.

8 **O that thou** wert as my
brother,
that sucked the breasts of my
mother!
when I should find thee without,
I would kiss thee;
yea, I should not be despised.
2 **I** would lead thee,
and bring thee into my mother's
house,
who would instruct me:
I would cause thee to drink of
spiced wine of the juice of my
pomegranate.
3 **His left hand** should be under my
head,
and his right hand should embrace
me.
4 **I** charge you, O daughters of
Jerusalem,
that ye stir not up,
nor awake my love,
until he please.
5 **Who** is this that cometh up from
the wilderness,
leaning upon her beloved?
I raised thee up under the apple
tree:
there thy mother brought thee
forth:
there she brought thee forth that
bare thee.
6 **Set** me as a seal upon thine heart,
as a seal upon thine arm:
for love is strong as death;
jealousy is cruel as the grave:
the coals thereof are coals of fire,
which hath a most vehement
flame.
7 **Many waters** cannot quench love,
neither can the floods drown it:
if a man would give all the
substance of his house for love,
it would utterly be contemned.
8 **We** have a little sister,
and she hath no breasts:
what shall we do for our sister in
the day when she shall be spoken
for?
9 **If she** be a wall,
we will build upon her a palace of
silver:
and if she be a door,
we will inclose her with boards of
cedar.
10 **I** am a wall,
and my breasts like towers:
then was I in his eyes as one that
found favour.
11 **Solomon** had a vineyard at
Baalhamon;
he let out the vineyard unto
keepers;
every one for the fruit thereof was
to bring a thousand pieces of
silver.
12 **My vineyard**, {which is mine}, is
before me:
thou, O Solomon, must have a
thousand,
**and those that keep the fruit
thereof** two hundred.
13 **Thou that dwellest in the
gardens, the companions**
hearken to thy voice:
cause me to hear it.
14 **Make haste,** my beloved,
and be thou like to a roe or to a
young hart upon the mountains
of spices.

Isaiah

The Book of Isaiah, a collection of prophetic texts attributed to the prophet Isaiah, speaks to the Israelites during a time of moral decline and spiritual corruption. The people, who have turned away from God, are indulging in idolatry, immorality, and injustice. They also face external threats from neighboring countries and unstable political alliances. In response, Isaiah emphasizes the need for the Israelites to abandon their idolatrous practices and return to worshipping the one true God. This theme of repentance is central to the book and a recurring message throughout its chapters.

The prophetic messages in Isaiah predict some of the most significant and consequential events for the nation, such as the Babylonian exile and the eventual return of the people to their homeland. Perhaps the most important prediction involves the coming of the Messiah, Who will establish a new covenant with the people of Israel and bring salvation to them, a theme particularly prominent in the book's second part. Isaiah also warns about the dangers of disobeying God's commandments, and he outlines the severe consequences the people will face if they continue to stray from His path. These negative repercussions are not to instill fear but to underscore the importance of obedience and faith.

Overall, the Book of Isaiah provides guidance and instruction for the people of Israel in their spiritual journey while underscoring the importance of faith, repentance, and the power of belief in God. These virtues are not just suggestions but a roadmap for the people, reminding them to turn away from their sins and to trust in God and His promises, even in times of hardship and suffering. This emphasis on faith and repentance is not a burden but a source of strength and reassurance, guiding the people through difficult times.

1 The vision of Isaiah the son of Amoz,
which he saw concerning Judah and Jerusalem in the days of Uzziah, Jotham, Ahaz, and Hezekiah, kings of Judah.

2 **Hear,** O heavens,
and give ear, O earth:
for the LORD hath spoken,
I have nourished and brought up children,
and they have rebelled against me.

3 **The ox** knoweth his owner, and the ass his master's crib:
but Israel doth not know,
my people doth not consider.

4 **Ah sinful nation, a people laden with iniquity, a seed of evildoers, children that are corrupters:** they have forsaken the LORD,
they have provoked the Holy One of Israel unto anger,
they are gone away backward.

5 **Why** should ye be stricken any more?
ye will revolt more and more:
the whole head is sick,
and the whole heart faint.

6 **From the sole of the foot even unto the head** there is no soundness in it;
but wounds, and bruises, and putrifying sores: they have not been closed,
neither bound up,
neither mollified with ointment.

7 **Your country** is desolate,
your cities are burned with fire:
your land, strangers devour it in your presence,
and it is desolate, as overthrown by strangers.

8 **And the daughter of Zion** is left as a cottage in a vineyard, as a lodge in a garden of cucumbers, as a besieged city.

9 **Except the LORD of hosts** had left unto us a very small remnant,
we should have been as Sodom,
and we should have been like unto Gomorrah.

10 **Hear** the word of the LORD, ye rulers of Sodom;
give ear unto the law of our God, ye people of Gomorrah.

11 **To what purpose** is the multitude of your sacrifices unto me?
saith the LORD:
I am full of the burnt offerings of rams, and the fat of fed beasts;
and I delight not in the blood of bullocks, or of lambs, or of he goats.

12 **When ye** come to appear before me,
who hath required this at your hand,
to tread my courts?

13 **Bring** no more vain oblations;
incense is an abomination unto me;
the new moons and sabbaths, the calling of assemblies, I cannot away with;
it is iniquity, even the solemn meeting.

14 **Your new moons and your appointed feasts** my soul hateth:
they are a trouble unto me;
I am weary to bear them.

15 **And when ye** spread forth your hands,
I will hide mine eyes from you:
yea, when ye make many prayers,
I will not hear:
your hands are full of blood.

16 **Wash** you,
make you clean;
put away the evil of your doings from before mine eyes;
cease to do evil;
17 **Learn** to do well;
seek judgment,
relieve the oppressed,
judge the fatherless,
plead for the widow.

18 **Come** now,
and let us reason together,
saith the LORD:
though your sins be as scarlet,

they shall be as white as snow;
though they be red like crimson,
they shall be as wool.

19 **If ye** be willing and obedient,
ye shall eat the good of the land:
20 **But if ye** refuse and rebel,
ye shall be devoured with the sword:
for the mouth of the LORD hath spoken it.

21 **How** is the faithful city become an harlot!
it was full of judgment;
righteousness lodged in it; but now murderers.

22 **Thy silver** is become dross, thy wine mixed with water:
23 **Thy princes** are rebellious, and companions of thieves:
every one loveth gifts,
and followeth after rewards:
they judge not the fatherless,
neither doth the cause of the widow come unto them.

24 **Therefore** saith the Lord, the LORD of hosts, the mighty One of Israel,
Ah, I will ease me of mine adversaries,
and avenge me of mine enemies:
25 **And I** will turn my hand upon thee,
and purely purge away thy dross,
and take away all thy tin:
26 **And I** will restore thy judges as at the first, and thy counsellors as at the beginning:
afterward thou shalt be called,
The city of righteousness, the faithful city.

27 **Zion** shall be redeemed with judgment, and her converts with righteousness.

28 **And the destruction of the transgressors and of the sinners** shall be together,
and they that forsake the LORD shall be consumed.

29 **For they** shall be ashamed of the oaks which ye have desired,
and ye shall be confounded for the gardens that ye have chosen.

30 **For ye** shall be as an oak whose leaf fadeth, and as a garden that hath no water.

31 **And the strong** shall be as tow, and the maker of it as a spark,
and they shall both burn together,
and none shall quench them.

2 **The word that Isaiah the son of Amoz** saw concerning Judah and Jerusalem.

2 **And it** shall come to pass in the last days,
that the mountain of the LORD's house shall be established in the top of the mountains,
and shall be exalted above the hills;
and all nations shall flow unto it.
3 **And many people** shall go and say,
Come ye,
and let us go up to the mountain of the LORD, to the house of the God of Jacob;
and he will teach us of his ways,
and we will walk in his paths:
for out of Zion shall go forth the law, and the word of the LORD from Jerusalem.

4 **And he** shall judge among the nations,
and shall rebuke many people:
and they shall beat their swords into plowshares, and their spears into pruninghooks:
nation shall not lift up sword against nation,
neither shall they learn war any more.

5 **O house of Jacob, come ye,**
and let us walk in the light of the LORD.

6 **Therefore thou** hast forsaken thy people the house of Jacob,
because they be replenished from the east,
and are soothsayers like the Philistines,
and they please themselves in the children of strangers.

7 **Their land** also is full of silver and gold,
neither is there any end of their treasures;
their land is also full of horses,
neither is there any end of their chariots:
8 **Their land** also is full of idols;
they worship the work of their own hands, that which their own fingers have made:
9 **And the mean man** boweth down,
and the great man humbleth himself:
therefore forgive them not.

10 **Enter** into the rock, {and hide thee in the dust}, for fear of the LORD, and for the glory of his majesty.

11 **The lofty looks of man** shall be humbled,
and the haughtiness of men shall be bowed down,
and the LORD alone shall be exalted in that day.

12 **For the day of the LORD of hosts** shall be upon every one that is proud and lofty, and upon every one that is lifted up;
and he shall be brought low:
13 And upon all the cedars of Lebanon, {that are high and lifted up}, and upon all the oaks of Bashan,
14 And upon all the high mountains, and upon all the hills that are lifted up,
15 And upon every high tower, and upon every fenced wall,
16 And upon all the ships of Tarshish, and upon all pleasant pictures.

17 **And the loftiness of man** shall be bowed down,
and the haughtiness of men shall be made low:
and the LORD alone shall be exalted in that day.

18 **And the idols** he shall utterly abolish.

19 **And they** shall go into the holes of the rocks, and into the caves of the earth, for fear of the LORD, and for the glory of his majesty,
when he ariseth to shake terribly the earth.

20 **In that day** a man shall cast his idols of silver, and his idols of gold,
which they made each one for himself to worship, to the moles and to the bats;
21 To go into the clefts of the rocks, and into the tops of the ragged rocks, for fear of the LORD, and for the glory of his majesty,
when he ariseth to shake terribly the earth.

22 **Cease ye** from man,
whose breath is in his nostrils:
for wherein is he to be accounted of?

3 **For, {behold}, the Lord, the LORD of hosts,** doth take away from Jerusalem and from Judah the stay and the staff, the

whole stay of bread, and the whole stay of water,
2 The mighty man, and the man of war, the judge, and the prophet, and the prudent, and the ancient,
3 The captain of fifty, and the honourable man, and the counsellor, and the cunning artificer, and the eloquent orator.

4 **And I** will give children to be their princes,
and babes shall rule over them.

5 **And the people** shall be oppressed, every one by another, and every one by his neighbour:
the child shall behave himself proudly against the ancient, and the base against the honourable.

6 **When a man** shall take hold of his brother of the house of his father, saying,
Thou hast clothing,
be thou our ruler,
and let this ruin be under thy hand:
7 **In that day** shall he swear, saying,
I will not be an healer;
for in my house is neither bread nor clothing:
make me not a ruler of the people.

8 **For Jerusalem** is ruined,
and Judah is fallen:
because their tongue and their doings are against the LORD,
to provoke the eyes of his glory.

9 **The shew of their countenance** doth witness against them;
and they declare their sin as Sodom,
they hide it not.

Woe unto their soul!
for they have rewarded evil unto themselves.

10 **Say ye** to the righteous,
that it shall be well with him:
for they shall eat the fruit of their doings.

11 **Woe** unto the wicked!
it shall be ill with him:
for the reward of his hands shall be given him.

12 **As for my people,** children are their oppressors,
and women rule over them.

O my people, they which lead thee cause thee to err,
and destroy the way of thy paths.

13 **The LORD** standeth up to plead,
and standeth to judge the people.

14 **The LORD** will enter into judgment with the ancients of his people, and the princes thereof:
for ye have eaten up the vineyard;
the spoil of the poor is in your houses.

15 **What** mean ye
that ye beat my people to pieces,
and grind the faces of the poor?
saith the Lord GOD of hosts.

16 **Moreover the LORD** saith,
Because the daughters of Zion are haughty,
and walk with stretched forth necks and wanton eyes,
walking and mincing as they go,
and making a tinkling with their feet:
17 **Therefore the Lord** will smite with a scab the crown of the head of the daughters of Zion,
and the LORD will discover their secret parts.

18 **In that day** the Lord will take away the bravery of their tinkling ornaments about their feet, and their cauls, and their round tires like the moon,
19 The chains, and the bracelets, and the mufflers,
20 The bonnets, and the ornaments of the legs, and the headbands, and the tablets, and the earrings,
21 The rings, and nose jewels,
22 The changeable suits of apparel, and the mantles, and the wimples, and the crisping pins,
23 The glasses, and the fine linen, and the hoods, and the vails.

24 **And it** shall come to pass,
that instead of sweet smell there shall be stink;
and instead of a girdle a rent;
and instead of well set hair baldness;
and instead of a stomacher a girding of sackcloth;
and burning instead of beauty.

25 **Thy men** shall fall by the sword, and thy mighty in the war.

26 **And her gates** shall lament and mourn;
and she being desolate shall sit upon the ground.

4

And in that day seven women shall take hold of one man, saying,
We will eat our own bread,
and wear our own apparel:
only let us be called by thy name,
to take away our reproach.

2 **In that day** shall the branch of the LORD be beautiful and glorious,
and the fruit of the earth shall be excellent and comely for them that are escaped of Israel.

3 **And it** shall come to pass,
that he that is left in Zion, and he that remaineth in Jerusalem, shall be called holy, even every one that is written among the living in Jerusalem:
4 **When the Lord** shall have washed away the filth of the daughters of Zion,
and shall have purged the blood of Jerusalem from the midst thereof by the spirit of judgment, and by the spirit of burning.

5 **And the LORD** will create upon every dwelling place of mount Zion, and upon her assemblies, a cloud and smoke by day, and the shining of a flaming fire by night:
for upon all the glory shall be a defence.

6 **And there** shall be a tabernacle for a shadow in the day time from the heat, and for a place of refuge, and for a covert from storm and from rain.

5

Now will I sing to my wellbeloved a song of my beloved touching his vineyard.

My wellbeloved hath a vineyard in a very fruitful hill:
2 **And he** fenced it,
and gathered out the stones thereof,
and planted it with the choicest vine,
and built a tower in the midst of it,
and also made a winepress therein:
and he looked that it should bring forth grapes,
and it brought forth wild grapes.

3 **And now, O inhabitants of Jerusalem, and men of Judah, judge**, {I pray you}, betwixt me and my vineyard.

4 **What** could have been done more to my vineyard,
that I have not done in it?
wherefore, {when I looked that it should bring forth grapes}, brought it forth wild grapes?

5 **And now go to; I** will tell you

what I will do to my vineyard:
I will take away the hedge thereof,
and it shall be eaten up;
and break down the wall thereof,
and it shall be trodden down:
6 **And I** will lay it waste:
it shall not be pruned,
nor digged;
but there shall come up briers and thorns:
I will also command the clouds
that they rain no rain upon it.

7 **For the vineyard of the LORD of hosts** is the house of Israel, and the men of Judah his pleasant plant:
and he looked for judgment, {but behold oppression}; for righteousness, {but behold a cry}.

8 **Woe** unto them that join house to house,
that lay field to field,
till there be no place,
that they may be placed alone in the midst of the earth!

9 **In mine ears** said the LORD of hosts,
Of a truth many houses shall be desolate, even great and fair, without inhabitant.

10 **Yea, ten acres of vineyard** shall yield one bath,
and the seed of an homer shall yield an ephah.

11 **Woe** unto them that rise up early in the morning,
that they may follow strong drink;
that continue until night,
till wine inflame them!

12 **And the harp, and the viol, the tabret, and pipe, and wine,** are in their feasts:
but they regard not the work of the LORD,
neither consider the operation of his hands.

13 **Therefore my people** are gone into captivity,
because they have no knowledge:
and their honourable men are famished,
and their multitude dried up with thirst.

14 **Therefore hell** hath enlarged herself,
and opened her mouth without measure:
and their glory, and their multitude, and their pomp, and he that rejoiceth, shall descend into it.

15 **And the mean man** shall be brought down,
and the mighty man shall be humbled,
and the eyes of the lofty shall be humbled:
16 **But the LORD of hosts** shall be exalted in judgment,
and God that is holy shall be sanctified in righteousness.

17 **Then** shall the lambs feed after their manner,
and the waste places of the fat ones shall strangers eat.

18 **Woe** unto them that draw iniquity with cords of vanity, and sin as it were with a cart rope:
19 **That** say,
Let him make speed,
and hasten his work,
that we may see it:
and let the counsel of the Holy One of Israel draw nigh and come,
that we may know it!

20 **Woe** unto them that call evil good, and good evil;
that put darkness for light, and light for darkness;
that put bitter for sweet, and sweet for bitter!

21 **Woe** unto them that are wise in their own eyes,
and prudent in their own sight!
22 **Woe** unto them that are mighty to drink wine,
and men of strength to mingle strong drink:
23 **Which** justify the wicked for reward,
and take away the righteousness of the righteous from him!

24 **Therefore as the fire** devoureth the stubble,
and the flame consumeth the chaff,
so their root shall be as rottenness,
and their blossom shall go up as dust:
because they have cast away the law of the LORD of hosts,
and despised the word of the Holy One of Israel.

25 **Therefore** is the anger of the LORD kindled against his people,
and he hath stretched forth his hand against them,
and hath smitten them:
and the hills did tremble,
and their carcases were torn in the midst of the streets.
For all this his anger is not turned away,
but his hand is stretched out still.

26 **And he** will lift up an ensign to the nations from far,
and will hiss unto them from the end of the earth:
and, {behold}, they shall come with speed swiftly:
27 **None** shall be weary
nor stumble among them;
none shall slumber
nor sleep;
neither shall the girdle of their loins be loosed,
nor the latchet of their shoes be broken:
28 **Whose arrows** are sharp,
and all their bows bent,
their horses' hoofs shall be counted like flint,
and their wheels like a whirlwind:
29 **Their roaring** shall be like a lion,
they shall roar like young lions:
yea, they shall roar,
and lay hold of the prey,
and shall carry it away safe,
and none shall deliver it.

30 **And in that day** they shall roar against them like the roaring of the sea:
and if one look unto the land,
behold darkness and sorrow,
and the light is darkened in the heavens thereof.

6 **In the year that king Uzziah** died
I saw also the Lord
sitting upon a throne, high and lifted up,
and his train filled the temple.

2 **Above it** stood the seraphims:
each one had six wings;
with twain he covered his face,
and with twain he covered his feet,
and with twain he did fly.

3 **And one** cried unto another,
and said,
Holy, holy, holy, is the LORD of hosts:
the whole earth is full of his glory.

4 **And the posts of the door** moved at the voice of him that cried,
and the house was filled with smoke.

5 **Then** said I,
Woe is me!

for I am undone;
because I am a man of unclean lips,
and I dwell in the midst of a people of unclean lips:
for mine eyes have seen the King, the LORD of hosts.

6 **Then** flew one of the seraphims unto me,
having a live coal in his hand,
which he had taken with the tongs from off the altar:
7 **And he** laid it upon my mouth,
and said,
Lo,
this hath touched thy lips;
and thine iniquity is taken away,
and thy sin purged.

8 **Also I** heard the voice of the Lord,
saying,
Whom shall I send,
and who will go for us?

Then said I,
Here am I;
send me.

9 **And he** said,
Go,
and tell this people,
Hear ye indeed,
but understand not;
and see ye indeed,
but perceive not.

10 **Make** the heart of this people fat,
and make their ears heavy,
and shut their eyes;
lest they see with their eyes,
and hear with their ears,
and understand with their heart,
and convert,
and be healed.

11 **Then** said I,
Lord, how long?

And he answered,
Until the cities be wasted without inhabitant, and the houses without man,
and the land be utterly desolate,
12 **And the LORD** have removed men far away,
and there be a great forsaking in the midst of the land.

13 **But yet in it** shall be a tenth,
and it shall return,
and shall be eaten: as a teil tree, and as an oak,
whose substance is in them,
when they cast their leaves:
so the holy seed shall be the substance thereof.

7

And it came to pass in the days of Ahaz the son of Jotham, the son of Uzziah, king of Judah,
that Rezin the king of Syria, and Pekah the son of Remaliah, king of Israel, went up toward Jerusalem
to war against it,
but could not prevail against it.

2 **And it** was told the house of David,
saying,
Syria is confederate with Ephraim.

And his heart was moved, and the heart of his people,
as the trees of the wood are moved with the wind.

3 **Then** said the LORD unto Isaiah,
Go forth now to meet Ahaz, thou, and Shearjashub thy son, at the end of the conduit of the upper pool in the highway of the fuller's field;
4 **And say** unto him,
Take heed,
and be quiet;
fear not,
neither be fainthearted for the two tails of these smoking firebrands, for the fierce anger of Rezin with Syria, and of the son of Remaliah.

5 **Because Syria, Ephraim, and the son of Remaliah,** have taken evil counsel against thee,
saying,
6 **Let us** go up against Judah,
and vex it,
and let us make a breach therein for us,
and set a king in the midst of it, even the son of Tabeal:
7 **Thus** saith the Lord GOD,
It shall not stand,
neither shall it come to pass.

8 **For the head of Syria** is Damascus,
and the head of Damascus is Rezin;
and within threescore and five years shall Ephraim be broken,
that it be not a people.

9 **And the head of Ephraim** is Samaria,
and the head of Samaria is Remaliah's son.
If ye will not believe,
surely ye shall not be established.

10 **Moreover the LORD** spake again unto Ahaz,
saying,

11 **Ask thee** a sign of the LORD thy God;
ask it either in the depth, or in the height above.

12 **But Ahaz** said,
I will not ask,
neither will I tempt the LORD.

13 **And he** said,
Hear ye now, O house of David;
Is it a small thing for you to weary men,
but will ye weary my God also?

14 **Therefore the Lord himself** shall give you a sign;
Behold,
a virgin shall conceive,
and bear a son,
and shall call his name Immanuel.

15 **Butter and honey** shall he eat,
that he may know
to refuse the evil,
and choose the good.

16 **For before the child** shall know
to refuse the evil,
and choose the good,
the land that thou abhorrest shall be forsaken of both her kings.

17 **The LORD** shall bring upon thee, and upon thy people, and upon thy father's house, days that have not come, from the day that Ephraim departed from Judah; even the king of Assyria.

18 **And it** shall come to pass in that day,
that the LORD shall hiss for the fly that is in the uttermost part of the rivers of Egypt, and for the bee that is in the land of Assyria.

19 **And they** shall come,
and shall rest all of them in the desolate valleys, and in the holes of the rocks, and upon all thorns, and upon all bushes.

20 **In the same day** shall the Lord shave with a razor that is hired, namely, by them beyond the river, by the king of Assyria, the head, and the hair of the feet:
and it shall also consume the beard.

21 **And it** shall come to pass in that day,
that a man shall nourish a young cow, and two sheep;
22 **And it** shall come to pass,
for the abundance of milk that they shall give he shall eat butter:

for butter and honey shall every one eat that is left in the land.

23 **And it** shall come to pass in that day,
that every place shall be,
where there were a thousand vines at a thousand silverlings,
it shall even be for briers and thorns.

24 **With arrows and with bows** shall men come thither;
because all the land shall become briers and thorns.

25 **And on all hills that shall be digged with the mattock,** there shall not come thither the fear of briers and thorns:
but it shall be for the sending forth of oxen, and for the treading of lesser cattle.

8 **Moreover the LORD** said unto me,
Take thee a great roll,
and write in it with a man's pen concerning Mahershalalhashbaz.

2 **And I** took unto me faithful witnesses to record, Uriah the priest, and Zechariah the son of Jeberechiah.

3 **And I** went unto the prophetess;
and she conceived,
and bare a son.

Then said the LORD to me,
Call his name Mahershalalhashbaz.

4 **For before the child** shall have knowledge to cry,
My father, and my mother,
the riches of Damascus and the spoil of Samaria shall be taken away before the king of Assyria.

5 **The LORD** spake also unto me again,
saying,

6 **Forasmuch as this people** refuseth the waters of Shiloah that go softly,
and rejoice in Rezin and Remaliah's son;

7 **Now therefore, {behold}, the Lord** bringeth up upon them the waters of the river, strong and many, even the king of Assyria, and all his glory:
and he shall come up over all his channels,
and go over all his banks:

8 **And he** shall pass through Judah;
he shall overflow and go over,
he shall reach even to the neck;
and the stretching out of his wings shall fill the breadth of thy land, O Immanuel.

9 **Associate** yourselves, O ye people,
and ye shall be broken in pieces;
and give ear, all ye of far countries:
gird yourselves,
and ye shall be broken in pieces;
gird yourselves,
and ye shall be broken in pieces.

10 **Take counsel** together,
and it shall come to nought;
speak the word,
and it shall not stand:
for God is with us.

11 **For the LORD** spake thus to me with a strong hand,
and instructed me
that I should not walk in the way of this people,
saying,

12 **Say ye not,** A confederacy, to all them to whom this people shall say, A confederacy;
neither fear ye their fear,
nor be afraid.

13 **Sanctify** the LORD of hosts himself;
and let him be your fear,
and let him be your dread.

14 **And he** shall be for a sanctuary; but for a stone of stumbling and for a rock of offence to both the houses of Israel, for a gin and for a snare to the inhabitants of Jerusalem.

15 **And many among them** shall stumble,
and fall,
and be broken,
and be snared,
and be taken.

16 **Bind up** the testimony,
seal the law among my disciples.

17 **And I** will wait upon the LORD,
that hideth his face from the house of Jacob,
and I will look for him.

18 **Behold,**
I and the children whom the LORD hath given me are for signs and for wonders in Israel from the LORD of hosts,
which dwelleth in mount Zion.

19 **And when they** shall say unto you,
Seek unto them that have familiar spirits, and unto wizards that peep, and that mutter:
should not a people seek unto their God?
for the living to the dead?

20 To the law and to the testimony:
if they speak not according to this word,
it is because there is no light in them.

21 **And they** shall pass through it, hardly bestead and hungry:
and it shall come to pass,
that when they shall be hungry,
they shall fret themselves,
and curse their king and their God,
and look upward.

22 **And they** shall look unto the earth;
and behold trouble and darkness, dimness of anguish;
and they shall be driven to darkness.

9 **Nevertheless the dimness** shall not be such as was in her vexation,
when at the first he lightly afflicted the land of Zebulun and the land of Naphtali,
and afterward did more grievously afflict her by the way of the sea, beyond Jordan, in Galilee of the nations.

2 **The people that walked in darkness** have seen a great light:
they that dwell in the land of the shadow of death, upon them hath the light shined.

3 **Thou** hast multiplied the nation,
and not increased the joy:
they joy before thee according to the joy in harvest,
and as men rejoice
when they divide the spoil.

4 **For thou** hast broken the yoke of his burden, and the staff of his shoulder, the rod of his oppressor, as in the day of Midian.

5 **For every battle of the warrior** is with confused noise, and garments rolled in blood;
but this shall be with burning and fuel of fire.

6 **For unto us** a child is born,
unto us a son is given:
and the government shall be upon his shoulder:
and his name shall be called Wonderful, Counsellor, The mighty God, The everlasting Father, The Prince of Peace.

7 **Of the increase of his government and peace** there shall be no end, upon the throne of David, and upon his kingdom,
to order it,
and to establish it with judgment and with justice from henceforth even for ever.

The zeal of the LORD of hosts will perform this.

8 **The Lord** sent a word into Jacob,
and it hath lighted upon Israel.

9 **And all the people** shall know, even Ephraim and the inhabitant of Samaria,
that say in the pride and stoutness of heart,
10 **The bricks** are fallen down,
but we will build with hewn stones:
the sycomores are cut down,
but we will change them into cedars.

11 **Therefore the LORD** shall set up the adversaries of Rezin against him,
and join his enemies together;
12 The Syrians before, and the Philistines behind;
and they shall devour Israel with open mouth.

For all this his anger is not turned away,
but his hand is stretched out still.

13 **For the people** turneth not unto him that smiteth them,
neither do they seek the LORD of hosts.

14 **Therefore the LORD** will cut off from Israel head and tail, branch and rush, in one day.

15 **The ancient and honourable,** he is the head;
and the prophet that teacheth lies,
he is the tail.

16 **For the leaders of this people** cause them to err;
and they that are led of them are destroyed.

17 **Therefore the Lord** shall have no joy in their young men,
neither shall have mercy on their fatherless and widows:
for every one is an hypocrite and an evildoer,
and every mouth speaketh folly.

For all this his anger is not turned away,
but his hand is stretched out still.

18 **For wickedness** burneth as the fire:
it shall devour the briers and thorns,
and shall kindle in the thickets of the forest,
and they shall mount up like the lifting up of smoke.

19 **Through the wrath of the LORD of hosts** is the land darkened,
and the people shall be as the fuel of the fire:
no man shall spare his brother.

20 **And he** shall snatch on the right hand,
and be hungry;
and he shall eat on the left hand,
and they shall not be satisfied:
they shall eat every man the flesh of his own arm:
21 Manasseh, Ephraim; and Ephraim, Manasseh:
and they together shall be against Judah.

For all this his anger is not turned away,
but his hand is stretched out still.

10 **Woe** unto them that decree unrighteous decrees, and that write grievousness which they have prescribed;
2 To turn aside the needy from judgment,
and to take away the right from the poor of my people,
that widows may be their prey,
and that they may rob the fatherless!

3 **And what** will ye do in the day of visitation, and in the desolation which shall come from far?
to whom will ye flee for help?
and where will ye leave your glory?

4 **Without me** they shall bow down under the prisoners,
and they shall fall under the slain.

For all this his anger is not turned away,
but his hand is stretched out still.

5 **O Assyrian, the rod of mine anger, and the staff in their hand** is mine indignation.

6 **I** will send him against an hypocritical nation,
and against the people of my wrath will I give him a charge,
to take the spoil,
and to take the prey,
and to tread them down like the mire of the streets.

7 **Howbeit he** meaneth not so,
neither doth his heart think so;
but it is in his heart to destroy and cut off nations not a few.

8 **For he** saith,
Are not my princes altogether kings?

9 **Is not Calno** as Carchemish?
is not Hamath as Arpad?
is not Samaria as Damascus?

10 **As my hand** hath found the kingdoms of the idols,
and whose graven images did excel them of Jerusalem and of Samaria;

11 **Shall I not**, {as I have done unto Samaria and her idols}, so do to Jerusalem and her idols?

12 **Wherefore it** shall come to pass,
that when the Lord hath performed his whole work upon mount Zion and on Jerusalem,
I will punish the fruit of the stout heart of the king of Assyria, and the glory of his high looks.

13 **For he** saith,
By the strength of my hand I have done it, and by my wisdom;
for I am prudent:
and I have removed the bounds of the people,
and have robbed their treasures,
and I have put down the inhabitants like a valiant man:
14 **And my hand** hath found as a nest the riches of the people:
and as one gathereth eggs that are left, have I gathered all the earth;
and there was none that moved the wing,
or opened the mouth,
or peeped.

15 **Shall the axe** boast itself against him that heweth therewith?
or shall the saw magnify itself against him that shaketh it?
as if the rod should shake itself against them that lift it up,
or as if the staff should lift up itself,
as if it were no wood.

16 **Therefore** shall the Lord, the Lord of hosts, send among his fat ones leanness;
and under his glory he shall kindle a burning like the burning of a fire.

17 **And the light of Israel** shall be for a fire, and his Holy One for a flame:
and it shall burn and devour his thorns and his briers in one day;
18 **And** shall consume the glory of his forest, and of his fruitful field, both soul and body:
and they shall be as when a standard-bearer fainteth.

19 **And the rest of the trees of his forest** shall be few,
that a child may write them.

20 **And it** shall come to pass in that day,
that the remnant of Israel, and such as are escaped of the house of Jacob, shall no more again stay upon him that smote them;
but shall stay upon the LORD, the Holy One of Israel, in truth.

21 **The remnant** shall return, even the remnant of Jacob, unto the mighty God.

22 **For though thy people Israel** be as the sand of the sea,
yet a remnant of them shall return:
the consumption decreed shall overflow with righteousness.

23 **For the Lord GOD of hosts** shall make a consumption, {even determined}, in the midst of all the land.

24 **Therefore thus** saith the Lord GOD of hosts,
O my people that dwellest in Zion, be not afraid of the Assyrian:
he shall smite thee with a rod,
and shall lift up his staff against thee, after the manner of Egypt.

25 **For yet a very little while,** and the indignation shall cease, and mine anger in their destruction.

26 **And the LORD of hosts** shall stir up a scourge for him according to the slaughter of Midian at the rock of Oreb:
and as his rod was upon the sea,
so shall he lift it up after the manner of Egypt.

27 **And it** shall come to pass in that day,
that his burden shall be taken away from off thy shoulder, and his yoke from off thy neck,
and the yoke shall be destroyed because of the anointing.

28 **He** is come to Aiath,
he is passed to Migron;
at Michmash he hath laid up his carriages:
29 **They** are gone over the passage:
they have taken up their lodging at Geba;
Ramah is afraid;
Gibeah of Saul is fled.

30 **Lift up** thy voice, O daughter of Gallim:
cause it to be heard unto Laish, O poor Anathoth.

31 **Madmenah** is removed;
the inhabitants of Gebim gather themselves to flee.

32 **As yet** shall he remain at Nob that day:
he shall shake his hand against the mount of the daughter of Zion, the hill of Jerusalem.

33 **Behold,**
the Lord, the LORD of hosts, shall lop the bough with terror:
and the high ones of stature shall be hewn down,
and the haughty shall be humbled.
34 **And he** shall cut down the thickets of the forest with iron,
and Lebanon shall fall by a mighty one.

11

And there shall come forth a rod out of the stem of Jesse,
and a Branch shall grow out of his roots:
2 **And the spirit of the LORD** shall rest upon him, the spirit of wisdom and understanding, the spirit of counsel and might, the spirit of knowledge and of the fear of the LORD;
3 **And** shall make him of quick understanding in the fear of the LORD:
and he shall not judge after the sight of his eyes,
neither reprove after the hearing of his ears:
4 **But with righteousness** shall he judge the poor,
and reprove with equity for the meek of the earth:
and he shall smite the earth:
with the rod of his mouth, and with the breath of his lips shall he slay the wicked.
5 **And righteousness** shall be the girdle of his loins, and faithfulness the girdle of his reins.

6 **The wolf** also shall dwell with the lamb,
and the leopard shall lie down with the kid; and the calf and the young lion and the fatling together;
and a little child shall lead them.
7 **And the cow and the bear** shall feed;
their young ones shall lie down together:
and the lion shall eat straw like the ox.
8 **And the sucking child** shall play on the hole of the asp,
and the weaned child shall put his hand on the cockatrice' den.
9 **They** shall not hurt
nor destroy in all my holy mountain:
for the earth shall be full of the knowledge of the LORD,
as the waters cover the sea.

10 **And in that day** there shall be a root of Jesse,
which shall stand for an ensign of the people;
to it shall the Gentiles seek:
and his rest shall be glorious.

11 **And it** shall come to pass in that day,
that the Lord shall set his hand again the second time
to recover the remnant of his people,
which shall be left, from Assyria, and from Egypt, and from Pathros, and from Cush, and from Elam, and from Shinar, and from Hamath, and from the islands of the sea.

12 **And he** shall set up an ensign for the nations,
and shall assemble the outcasts of Israel,
and gather together the dispersed of Judah from the four corners of the earth.

13 **The envy also of Ephraim** shall depart,
and the adversaries of Judah shall be cut off:
Ephraim shall not envy Judah,
and Judah shall not vex Ephraim.

14 **But they** shall fly upon the shoulders of the Philistines toward the west;
they shall spoil them of the east together:

they shall lay their hand upon Edom and Moab;
and the children of Ammon shall obey them.
15 **And the LORD** shall utterly destroy the tongue of the Egyptian sea;
and with his mighty wind shall he shake his hand over the river,
and shall smite it in the seven streams,
and make men go over dryshod.
16 **And there** shall be an highway for the remnant of his people,
which shall be left, from Assyria;
like as it was to Israel in the day that he came up out of the land of Egypt.

12 **And in that day** thou shalt say,
O LORD, I will praise thee:
though thou wast angry with me,
thine anger is turned away,
and thou comfortedst me.
2 **Behold,**
God is my salvation;
I will trust,
and not be afraid:
for the LORD Jehovah is my strength and my song;
he also is become my salvation.
3 **Therefore with joy** shall ye draw water out of the wells of salvation.
4 **And in that day** shall ye say,
Praise the LORD,
call upon his name,
declare his doings among the people,
make mention
that his name is exalted.
5 **Sing** unto the LORD;
for he hath done excellent things:
this is known in all the earth.
6 **Cry out and shout,** thou inhabitant of Zion:
for great is the Holy One of Israel in the midst of thee.

13 ∞ The burden of Babylon, {which Isaiah the son of Amoz did see.}
2 **Lift ye up** a banner upon the high mountain,
exalt the voice unto them,
shake the hand,
that they may go into the gates of the nobles.
3 **I** have commanded my sanctified ones,
I have also called my mighty ones for mine anger, even them that rejoice in my highness.
4 The noise of a multitude in the mountains, like as of a great people;
a tumultuous noise of the kingdoms of nations gathered together:
the LORD of hosts mustereth the host of the battle.
5 **They** come from a far country, from the end of heaven, even the LORD, and the weapons of his indignation,
to destroy the whole land.
6 **Howl** ye;
for the day of the LORD is at hand;
it shall come as a destruction from the Almighty.
7 **Therefore** shall all hands be faint,
and every man's heart shall melt:
8 **And they** shall be afraid:
pangs and sorrows shall take hold of them;
they shall be in pain as a woman that travaileth:
they shall be amazed one at another;
their faces shall be as flames.
9 **Behold,**
the day of the LORD cometh, cruel both with wrath and fierce anger,
to lay the land desolate:
and he shall destroy the sinners thereof out of it.
10 **For the stars of heaven and the constellations thereof** shall not give their light:
the sun shall be darkened in his going forth,
and the moon shall not cause her light to shine.
11 **And I** will punish the world for their evil, and the wicked for their iniquity;
and I will cause the arrogancy of the proud to cease,
and will lay low the haughtiness of the terrible.
12 **I** will make a man more precious than fine gold; even a man than the golden wedge of Ophir.
13 **Therefore I** will shake the heavens,
and the earth shall remove out of her place, in the wrath of the LORD of hosts, and in the day of his fierce anger.
14 **And it** shall be as the chased roe, and as a sheep that no man taketh up:
they shall every man turn to his own people,
and flee every one into his own land.
15 **Every one that is found** shall be thrust through;
and every one that is joined unto them shall fall by the sword.
16 **Their children** also shall be dashed to pieces before their eyes;
their houses shall be spoiled,
and their wives ravished.
17 **Behold,**
I will stir up the Medes against them,
which shall not regard silver;
and as for gold, they shall not delight in it.
18 **Their bows** also shall dash the young men to pieces;
and they shall have no pity on the fruit of the womb;
their eyes shall not spare children.
19 **And Babylon, the glory of kingdoms, the beauty of the Chaldees' excellency,** shall be as when God overthrew Sodom and Gomorrah.
20 **It** shall never be inhabited,
either shall it be dwelt in from generation to generation:
neither shall the Arabian pitch tent there;
neither shall the shepherds make their fold there.
21 **But wild beasts of the desert** shall lie there;
and their houses shall be full of doleful creatures;
and owls shall dwell there, and **satyrs** shall dance there.
22 **And the wild beasts of the islands** shall cry in their desolate houses, and dragons in their pleasant palaces:
and her time is near to come,
and her days shall not be prolonged.

14 **For the LORD** will have mercy on Jacob,
and will yet choose Israel,
and set them in their own land:
and the strangers shall be joined with them,
and they shall cleave to the house of Jacob.

[2] **And the people** shall take them,
and bring them to their place:
and the house of Israel shall possess them in the land of the LORD for servants and handmaids:
and they shall take them captives,
whose captives they were;
and they shall rule over their oppressors.

[3] **And it** shall come to pass in the day that the LORD shall give thee rest from thy sorrow, and from thy fear, and from the hard bondage wherein thou wast made to serve,

[4] **That thou** shalt take up this proverb against the king of Babylon,
and say,
How hath the oppressor ceased!
the golden city ceased!

[5] **The LORD** hath broken the staff of the wicked, and the sceptre of the rulers.

[6] **He who smote the people in wrath with a continual stroke, he that ruled the nations in anger,** is persecuted,
and none hindereth.

[7] **The whole earth** is at rest,
and is quiet:
they break forth into singing.

[8] **Yea, the fir trees** rejoice at thee, and the cedars of Lebanon,
saying,
Since thou art laid down,
no feller is come up against us.

[9] **Hell from beneath** is moved for thee
to meet thee at thy coming:
it stirreth up the dead for thee, even all the chief ones of the earth;
it hath raised up from their thrones all the kings of the nations.

[10] **All they** shall speak and say unto thee,
Art thou also become weak as we?
art thou become like unto us?

[11] **Thy pomp** is brought down to the grave, and the noise of thy viols:
the worm is spread under thee,
and the worms cover thee.

[12] **How** art thou fallen from heaven, O Lucifer, son of the morning!
how art thou cut down to the ground,
which didst weaken the nations!

[13] **For thou** hast said in thine heart,
I will ascend into heaven,
I will exalt my throne above the stars of God:
I will sit also upon the mount of the congregation, in the sides of the north:

[14] **I** will ascend above the heights of the clouds;
I will be like the most High.

[15] **Yet thou** shalt be brought down to hell, to the sides of the pit.

[16] **They that see thee** shall narrowly look upon thee,
and consider thee, saying,
Is this the man that made the earth to tremble, that did shake kingdoms;

[17] That made the world as a wilderness, and destroyed the cities thereof; that opened not the house of his prisoners?

[18] **All the kings of the nations, even all of them,** lie in glory, every one in his own house.

[19] **But thou** art cast out of thy grave like an abominable branch, and as the raiment of those that are slain,
thrust through with a sword,
that go down to the stones of the pit; as a carcase trodden under feet.

[20] **Thou** shalt not be joined with them in burial,
because thou hast destroyed thy land,
and slain thy people:
the seed of evildoers shall never be renowned.

[21] **Prepare** slaughter for his children for the iniquity of their fathers;
that they do not rise,
nor possess the land,
nor fill the face of the world with cities.

[22] **For I** will rise up against them,
saith the LORD of hosts,
and cut off from Babylon the name, and remnant, and son, and nephew,
saith the LORD.

[23] **I** will also make it a possession for the bittern, and pools of water:
and I will sweep it with the besom of destruction,
saith the LORD of hosts.

[24] **The LORD of hosts** hath sworn,
saying,
Surely as I have thought,
so shall it come to pass;
and as I have purposed,
so shall it stand:

[25] **That I** will break the Assyrian in my land,
and upon my mountains tread him under foot:
then shall his yoke depart from off them,
and his burden depart from off their shoulders.

[26] **This** is the purpose that is purposed upon the whole earth:
and this is the hand that is stretched out upon all the nations.

[27] **For the LORD of hosts** hath purposed,
and who shall disannul it?
and his hand is stretched out,
and who shall turn it back?

[28] **In the year that king Ahaz died** was this burden.

[29] **Rejoice not thou,** whole Palestina,
because the rod of him that smote thee is broken:
for out of the serpent's root shall come forth a cockatrice,
and his fruit shall be a fiery flying serpent.

[30] **And the firstborn of the poor** shall feed,
and the needy shall lie down in safety:
and I will kill thy root with famine,
and he shall slay thy remnant.

[31] **Howl,** O gate;
cry, O city;
thou, whole Palestina, art dissolved:
for there shall come from the north a smoke,
and none shall be alone in his appointed times.

[32] **What** shall one then answer the messengers of the nation?
That the LORD hath founded Zion,
and the poor of his people shall trust in it.

15

The burden of Moab.
Because in the night Ar of Moab is laid waste,
and brought to silence;
because in the night Kir of Moab is laid waste,
and brought to silence;

[2] **He** is gone up to Bajith, and to Dibon, the high places,
to weep:

Moab shall howl over Nebo, and over Medeba:
on all their heads shall be baldness,
and every beard cut off.
3 **In their streets** they shall gird themselves with sackcloth:
on the tops of their houses, and in their streets, every one shall howl,
weeping abundantly.
4 **And Heshbon** shall cry, and Elealeh:
their voice shall be heard even unto Jahaz:
therefore the armed soldiers of Moab shall cry out;
his life shall be grievous unto him.
5 **My heart** shall cry out for Moab;
his fugitives shall flee unto Zoar, an heifer of three years old:
for by the mounting up of Luhith with weeping shall they go it up;
for in the way of Horonaim they shall raise up a cry of destruction.
6 **For the waters of Nimrim** shall be desolate:
for the hay is withered away,
the grass faileth,
there is no green thing.
7 **Therefore the abundance they have gotten, and that which they have laid up,** shall they carry away to the brook of the willows.
8 **For the cry** is gone round about the borders of Moab; the howling thereof unto Eglaim, and the howling thereof unto Beerelim.
9 **For the waters of Dimon** shall be full of blood:
for I will bring more upon Dimon, lions upon him that escapeth of Moab, and upon the remnant of the land.

16 **Send ye** the lamb to the ruler of the land from Sela to the wilderness, unto the mount of the daughter of Zion.
2 **For it** shall be,
that, as a wandering bird cast out of the nest, so the daughters of Moab shall be at the fords of Arnon.
3 **Take counsel,**
execute judgment;
make thy shadow as the night in the midst of the noonday;
hide the outcasts;
bewray not him that wandereth.
4 **Let mine outcasts** dwell with thee, Moab;
be thou a covert to them from the face of the spoiler:
for the extortioner is at an end,
the spoiler ceaseth,
the oppressors are consumed out of the land.
5 **And in mercy** shall the throne be established:
and he shall sit upon it in truth in the tabernacle of David,
judging,
and seeking judgment,
and hasting righteousness.
6 **We** have heard of the pride of Moab;
he is very proud: even of his haughtiness, and his pride, and his wrath:
but his lies shall not be so.
7 **Therefore** shall Moab howl for Moab,
every one shall howl:
for the foundations of Kirhareseth shall ye mourn;
surely they are stricken.
8 **For the fields of Heshbon** languish, and the vine of Sibmah:
the lords of the heathen have broken down the principal plants thereof,
they are come even unto Jazer,
they wandered through the wilderness:
her branches are stretched out,
they are gone over the sea.
9 **Therefore I** will bewail with the weeping of Jazer the vine of Sibmah:
I will water thee with my tears, O Heshbon, and Elealeh:
for the shouting for thy summer fruits and for thy harvest is fallen.
10 **And gladness** is taken away, and joy out of the plentiful field;
and in the vineyards there shall be no singing,
neither shall there be shouting:
the treaders shall tread out no wine in their presses;
I have made their vintage shouting to cease.
11 **Wherefore my bowels** shall sound like an harp for Moab, and mine inward parts for Kirharesh.
12 **And it** shall come to pass,
when it is seen that Moab is weary on the high place,
that he shall come to his sanctuary to pray;
but he shall not prevail.
13 **This** is the word that the LORD hath spoken concerning Moab since that time.
14 **But now the LORD** hath spoken, saying,
Within three years, as the years of an hireling, and the glory of Moab shall be contemned, with all that great multitude;
and the remnant shall be very small and feeble.

17 The burden of Damascus.
Behold,
Damascus is taken away from being a city,
and it shall be a ruinous heap.
2 **The cities of Aroer** are forsaken:
they shall be for flocks,
which shall lie down,
and none shall make them afraid.
3 **The fortress** also shall cease from Ephraim, and the kingdom from Damascus, and the remnant of Syria:
they shall be as the glory of the children of Israel,
saith the LORD of hosts.
4 **And in that day** it shall come to pass,
that the glory of Jacob shall be made thin,
and the fatness of his flesh shall wax lean.
5 **And it** shall be
as when the harvestman gathereth the corn,
and reapeth the ears with his arm;
and it shall be as he that gathereth ears in the valley of Rephaim.
6 **Yet gleaning grapes** shall be left in it, as the shaking of an olive tree, two or three berries in the top of the uppermost bough, four or five in the outmost fruitful branches thereof,
saith the LORD God of Israel.
7 **At that day** shall a man look to his Maker,
and his eyes shall have respect to the Holy One of Israel.
8 **And he** shall not look to the altars, the work of his hands,

neither shall respect that which his fingers have made, either the groves, or the images.

9 **In that day** shall his strong cities be as a forsaken bough, and an uppermost branch,
which they left because of the children of Israel:
and there shall be desolation.

10 **Because thou** hast forgotten the God of thy salvation,
and hast not been mindful of the rock of thy strength,
therefore shalt thou plant pleasant plants,
and shalt set it with strange slips:
11 **In the day** shalt thou make thy plant to grow,
and in the morning shalt thou make thy seed to flourish:
but the harvest shall be a heap in the day of grief and of desperate sorrow.

12 **Woe** to the multitude of many people, {which make a noise like the noise of the seas}; and to the rushing of nations, {that make a rushing like the rushing of mighty waters}!

13 **The nations** shall rush like the rushing of many waters:
but God shall rebuke them,
and they shall flee far off,
and shall be chased as the chaff of the mountains before the wind, and like a rolling thing before the whirlwind.

14 **And behold** at eveningtide trouble;
and before the morning he is not.

This is the portion of them that spoil us, and the lot of them that rob us.

18 **Woe** to the land shadowing with wings,
which is beyond the rivers of Ethiopia:
2 **That** sendeth ambassadors by the sea, even in vessels of bulrushes upon the waters,
saying,
Go, ye swift messengers, to a nation scattered and peeled, to a people terrible from their beginning hitherto; a nation meted out and trodden down,
whose land the rivers have spoiled!

3 **All ye inhabitants of the world, and dwellers on the earth, see ye,**
when he lifteth up an ensign on the mountains;
and when he bloweth a trumpet,
hear ye.

4 **For so the LORD** said unto me,
I will take my rest,
and I will consider in my dwelling place like a clear heat upon herbs, and like a cloud of dew in the heat of harvest.

5 **For afore the harvest**, {when the bud is perfect}, {and the sour grape is ripening in the flower}, he shall both cut off the sprigs with pruning hooks,
and take away and cut down the branches.

6 **They** shall be left together unto the fowls of the mountains, and to the beasts of the earth:
and the fowls shall summer upon them,
and all the beasts of the earth shall winter upon them.

7 **In that time** shall the present be brought unto the LORD of hosts of a people scattered and peeled, and from a people terrible from their beginning hitherto; a nation meted out and trodden under foot,
whose land the rivers have spoiled, to the place of the name of the LORD of hosts, the mount Zion.

19 The burden of Egypt.
Behold,
the LORD rideth upon a swift cloud,
and shall come into Egypt:
and the idols of Egypt shall be moved at his presence,
and the heart of Egypt shall melt in the midst of it.

2 **And I** will set the Egyptians against the Egyptians:
and they shall fight every one against his brother, and every one against his neighbour; city against city, and kingdom against kingdom.

3 **And the spirit of Egypt** shall fail in the midst thereof;
and I will destroy the counsel thereof:
and they shall seek to the idols, and to the charmers, and to them that have familiar spirits, and to the wizards.

4 **And the Egyptians** will I give over into the hand of a cruel lord;
and a fierce king shall rule over them,
saith the Lord, the LORD of hosts.

5 **And the waters** shall fail from the sea,
and the river shall be wasted and dried up.

6 **And they** shall turn the rivers far away;
and the brooks of defence shall be emptied and dried up:
the reeds and flags shall wither.

7 **The paper reeds by the brooks, by the mouth of the brooks, and every thing sown by the brooks,** shall wither,
be driven away,
and be no more.

8 **The fishers** also shall mourn,
and all they that cast angle into the brooks shall lament,
and they that spread nets upon the waters shall languish.

9 **Moreover they that work in fine flax, and they that weave networks,** shall be confounded.

10 **And they** shall be broken in the purposes thereof, all that make sluices and ponds for fish.

11 **Surely the princes of Zoan** are fools,
the counsel of the wise counsellors of Pharaoh is become brutish:
how say ye unto Pharaoh,
I am the son of the wise, the son of ancient kings?

12 **Where** are they?
where are thy wise men?
and let them tell thee now,
and let them know
what the LORD of hosts hath purposed upon Egypt.

13 **The princes of Zoan** are become fools,
the princes of Noph are deceived;
they have also seduced Egypt, even they that are the stay of the tribes thereof.

14 **The LORD** hath mingled a perverse spirit in the midst thereof:
and they have caused Egypt to err in every work thereof, as a drunken man staggereth in his vomit.

15 **Neither** shall there be any work for Egypt,
which the head or tail, branch or rush, may do.

16 **In that day** shall Egypt be like unto women:
and it shall be afraid and fear because of the shaking of the hand of the LORD of hosts,
which he shaketh over it.

17 **And the land of Judah** shall be a terror unto Egypt,
every one that maketh mention thereof shall be afraid in himself,
because of the counsel of the LORD of hosts,
which he hath determined against it.

18 **In that day** shall five cities in the land of Egypt speak the language of Canaan,
and swear to the LORD of hosts;
one shall be called,
The city of destruction.

19 **In that day** shall there be an altar to the LORD in the midst of the land of Egypt, and a pillar at the border thereof to the LORD.

20 **And it** shall be for a sign and for a witness unto the LORD of hosts in the land of Egypt:
for they shall cry unto the LORD because of the oppressors,
and he shall send them a saviour, and a great one,
and he shall deliver them.

21 **And the LORD** shall be known to Egypt,
and the Egyptians shall know the LORD in that day,
and shall do sacrifice and oblation;
yea, they shall vow a vow unto the LORD,
and perform it.

22 **And the LORD** shall smite Egypt:
he shall smite and heal it:
and they shall return even to the LORD,
and he shall be intreated of them,
and shall heal them.

23 **In that day** shall there be a highway out of Egypt to Assyria,
and the Assyrian shall come into Egypt, and the Egyptian into Assyria,
and the Egyptians shall serve with the Assyrians.

24 **In that day** shall Israel be the third with Egypt and with Assyria, even a blessing in the midst of the land:

25 **Whom** the LORD of hosts shall bless,
saying,
Blessed be Egypt my people, and Assyria the work of my hands, and Israel mine inheritance.

20

In the year that Tartan came unto Ashdod,
(when Sargon the king of Assyria sent him,)
and fought against Ashdod,
and took it;

2 **At the same time** spake the LORD by Isaiah the son of Amoz,
saying,
Go and loose the sackcloth from off thy loins,
and put off thy shoe from thy foot.
And he did so,
walking naked and barefoot.

3 **And the LORD** said,
Like as my servant Isaiah hath walked naked and barefoot three years for a sign and wonder upon Egypt and upon Ethiopia;

4 **So** shall the king of Assyria lead away the Egyptians prisoners, and the Ethiopians captives, young and old, naked and barefoot, even with their buttocks uncovered, to the shame of Egypt.

5 **And they** shall be afraid and ashamed of Ethiopia their expectation, and of Egypt their glory.

6 **And the inhabitant of this isle** shall say in that day,
Behold,
such is our expectation,
whither we flee for help
to be delivered from the king of Assyria:
and how shall we escape?

21

The burden of the desert of the sea.
As whirlwinds in the south pass through;
so it cometh from the desert, from a terrible land.

2 **A grievous vision** is declared unto me;
the treacherous dealer dealeth treacherously,
and the spoiler spoileth.
Go up, O Elam:
besiege, O Media;
all the sighing thereof have I made to cease.

3 **Therefore** are my loins filled with pain:
pangs have taken hold upon me, as the pangs of a woman that travaileth:
I was bowed down at the hearing of it;
I was dismayed at the seeing of it.

4 **My heart** panted,
fearfulness affrighted me:
the night of my pleasure hath he turned into fear unto me.

5 **Prepare** the table,
watch in the watchtower,
eat,
drink:
arise, ye princes,
and anoint the shield.

6 **For thus** hath the Lord said unto me,
Go,
set a watchman,
let him declare
what he seeth.

7 **And he** saw a chariot with a couple of horsemen, a chariot of asses, and a chariot of camels;
and he hearkened diligently with much heed:

8 **And he** cried,
A lion:
My lord, I stand continually upon the watchtower in the daytime,
and I am set in my ward whole nights:

9 **And, {behold}, here** cometh a chariot of men, with a couple of horsemen.
And he answered and said,
Babylon is fallen,
is fallen;
and all the graven images of her gods he hath broken unto the ground.

10 O my threshing, and the corn of my floor:
that which I have heard of the LORD of hosts, the God of Israel, have I declared unto you.

11 The burden of Dumah.
He calleth to me out of Seir,
Watchman,
what of the night?
Watchman, what of the night?

12 **The watchman** said,
The morning cometh, and also the night:

if ye will enquire,
enquire ye:
return,
come.

13 The burden upon Arabia.

In the forest in Arabia shall ye lodge, O ye travelling companies of Dedanim.

14 **The inhabitants of the land of Tema** brought water to him that was thirsty,
they prevented with their bread him that fled.

15 **For they** fled from the swords, from the drawn sword, and from the bent bow, and from the grievousness of war.

16 **For thus** hath the Lord said unto me,
Within a year, according to the years of an hireling, and all the glory of Kedar shall fail:

17 **And the residue of the number of archers, the mighty men of the children of Kedar,** shall be diminished:
for the LORD God of Israel hath spoken it.

22 The burden of the valley of vision.

What aileth thee now,
that thou art wholly gone up to the housetops?

2 **Thou that art full of stirs, a tumultuous city, joyous city: thy slain men** are not slain with the sword, nor dead in battle.

3 **All thy rulers** are fled together,
they are bound by the archers:
all that are found in thee are bound together,
which have fled from far.

4 **Therefore** said I,
Look away from me;
I will weep bitterly,
labour not to comfort me, because of the spoiling of the daughter of my people.

5 **For it** is a day of trouble, and of treading down, and of perplexity by the LORD God of hosts in the valley of vision,
breaking down the walls, and of crying to the mountains.

6 **And Elam** bare the quiver with chariots of men and horsemen,
and Kir uncovered the shield.

7 **And it** shall come to pass,
that thy choicest valleys shall be full of chariots,
and the horsemen shall set themselves in array at the gate.

8 **And he** discovered the covering of Judah,
and thou didst look in that day to the armour of the house of the forest.

9 **Ye** have seen also the breaches of the city of David,
that they are many:
and ye gathered together the waters of the lower pool.

10 **And ye** have numbered the houses of Jerusalem,
and the houses have ye broken down
to fortify the wall.

11 **Ye** made also a ditch between the two walls for the water of the old pool:
but ye have not looked unto the maker thereof,
neither had respect unto him that fashioned it long ago.

12 **And in that day** did the Lord GOD of hosts call to weeping, and to mourning, and to baldness, and to girding with sackcloth:

13 **And behold** joy and gladness,
slaying oxen,
and killing sheep,
eating flesh,
and drinking wine:
let us eat and drink;
for to morrow we shall die.

14 **And it** was revealed in mine ears by the LORD of hosts,
Surely this iniquity shall not be purged from you till ye die,
saith the Lord GOD of hosts.

15 **Thus** saith the Lord GOD of hosts,
Go,
get thee unto this treasurer, even unto Shebna,
which is over the house,
and say,

16 **What** hast thou here?
and whom hast thou here,
that thou hast hewed thee out a sepulchre here, as he that heweth him out a sepulchre on high, and that graveth an habitation for himself in a rock?

17 **Behold,**
the LORD will carry thee away with a mighty captivity,
and will surely cover thee.

18 **He** will surely violently turn and toss thee like a ball into a large country:
there shalt thou die,
and there the chariots of thy glory shall be the shame of thy lord's house.

19 **And I** will drive thee from thy station,
and from thy state shall he pull thee down.

20 **And it** shall come to pass in that day,
that I will call my servant Eliakim the son of Hilkiah:

21 **And I** will clothe him with thy robe,
and strengthen him with thy girdle,
and I will commit thy government into his hand:
and he shall be a father to the inhabitants of Jerusalem, and to the house of Judah.

22 **And the key of the house of David** will I lay upon his shoulder;
so he shall open,
and none shall shut;
and he shall shut,
and none shall open.

23 **And I** will fasten him as a nail in a sure place;
and he shall be for a glorious throne to his father's house.

24 **And they** shall hang upon him all the glory of his father's house, the offspring and the issue, all vessels of small quantity, from the vessels of cups, even to all the vessels of flagons.

25 **In that day**, {saith the LORD of hosts}, shall the nail that is fastened in the sure place be removed,
and be cut down,
and fall;
and the burden that was upon it shall be cut off:
for the LORD hath spoken it.

23 The burden of Tyre.
Howl, ye ships of Tarshish;
for it is laid waste,
so that there is no house,
no entering in:
from the land of Chittim it is revealed to them.

2 **Be still,** ye inhabitants of the isle;

thou whom the merchants of Zidon, {<u>that</u> pass over the sea}, have replenished.
3 **And by great waters** the seed of Sihor, the harvest of the river, is her revenue;
and she is a mart of nations.
4 **Be thou** ashamed, O Zidon:
for the sea hath spoken, even the strength of the sea,
saying,
I travail not,
nor bring forth children,
neither do I nourish up young men,
nor bring up virgins.
5 **As at the report concerning Egypt,** so shall they be sorely pained at the report of Tyre.
6 **Pass ye over** to Tarshish;
howl, ye inhabitants of the isle.
7 **Is this** your joyous city,
whose antiquity is of ancient days?
her own feet shall carry her afar off to sojourn.
8 **Who** hath taken this counsel against Tyre, the crowning city,
whose merchants are princes,
whose traffickers are the honourable of the earth?
9 **The LORD of hosts** hath purposed it,
to stain the pride of all glory,
and to bring into contempt all the honourable of the earth.
10 **Pass through** thy land as a river, O daughter of Tarshish:
there is no more strength.
11 **He** stretched out his hand over the sea,
he shook the kingdoms:
the LORD hath given a commandment against the merchant city,
to destroy the strong holds thereof.
12 **And he** said,
Thou shalt no more rejoice, O thou oppressed virgin, daughter of Zidon:
arise,
pass over to Chittim;
there also shalt thou have no rest.
13 **Behold** the land of the Chaldeans;
this people was not,
till the Assyrian founded it for them that dwell in the wilderness:
they set up the towers thereof,
they raised up the palaces thereof;
and he brought it to ruin.
14 **Howl,** ye ships of Tarshish:
for your strength is laid waste.
15 **And it** shall come to pass in that day,
that Tyre shall be forgotten seventy years, according to the days of one king:
after the end of seventy years shall Tyre sing as an harlot.
16 **Take** an harp,
go about the city, thou harlot that hast been forgotten;
make sweet melody,
sing many songs,
that thou mayest be remembered.
17 **And it** shall come to pass after the end of seventy years,
that the LORD will visit Tyre,
and she shall turn to her hire,
and shall commit fornication with all the kingdoms of the world upon the face of the earth.
18 **And her merchandise and her hire** shall be holiness to the LORD:
it shall not be treasured
nor laid up;
for her merchandise shall be for them that dwell before the LORD,
to eat sufficiently, and for durable clothing.

24

Behold,
the LORD maketh the earth empty,
and maketh it waste,
and turneth it upside down,
and scattereth abroad the inhabitants thereof.
2 **And it** shall be, as with the people, so with the priest; as with the servant, so with his master; as with the maid, so with her mistress; as with the buyer, so with the seller; as with the lender, so with the borrower; as with the taker of usury, so with the giver of usury to him.
3 **The land** shall be utterly emptied, and utterly spoiled:
for the LORD hath spoken this word.
4 **The earth** mourneth and fadeth away,
the world languisheth and fadeth away,
the haughty people of the earth do languish.
5 **The earth** also is defiled under the inhabitants thereof;
because they have transgressed the laws,
changed the ordinance,
broken the everlasting covenant.
6 **Therefore** hath the curse devoured the earth,
and they that dwell therein are desolate:
therefore the inhabitants of the earth are burned,
and few men left.
7 **The new wine** mourneth,
the vine languisheth,
all the merryhearted do sigh.
8 **The mirth of tabrets** ceaseth,
the noise of them that rejoice endeth,
the joy of the harp ceaseth.
9 **They** shall not drink wine with a song;
strong drink shall be bitter to them that drink it.
10 **The city of confusion** is broken down:
every house is shut up,
that no man may come in.
11 **There** is a crying for wine in the streets;
all joy is darkened,
the mirth of the land is gone.
12 **In the city** is left desolation,
and the gate is smitten with destruction.
13 **When thus** it shall be in the midst of the land among the people,
there shall be as the shaking of an olive tree, and as the gleaning grapes
when the vintage is done.
14 **They** shall lift up their voice,
they shall sing for the majesty of the LORD,
they shall cry aloud from the sea.
15 **Wherefore glorify ye** the LORD in the fires, even the name of the LORD God of Israel in the isles of the sea.
16 **From the uttermost part of the earth** have we heard songs, even glory to the righteous.
But I said,
My leanness, my leanness, woe unto me!
the treacherous dealers have dealt treacherously;
yea, the treacherous dealers have dealt very treacherously.

[17] **Fear, and the pit, and the snare,**
are upon thee, O inhabitant of the earth.
[18] **And it** shall come to pass,
that he who fleeth from the noise of the fear shall fall into the pit;
and he that cometh up out of the midst of the pit shall be taken in the snare:
for the windows from on high are open,
and the foundations of the earth do shake.
[19] **The earth** is utterly broken down,
the earth is clean dissolved,
the earth is moved exceedingly.
[20] **The earth** shall reel to and fro like a drunkard,
and shall be removed like a cottage;
and the transgression thereof shall be heavy upon it;
and it shall fall,
and not rise again.
[21] **And it** shall come to pass in that day,
that the LORD shall punish the host of the high ones that are on high, and the kings of the earth upon the earth.
[22] **And they** shall be gathered together,
as prisoners are gathered in the pit,
and shall be shut up in the prison,
and after many days shall they be visited.
[23] **Then the moon** shall be confounded,
and the sun ashamed,
when the LORD of hosts shall reign in mount Zion, and in Jerusalem, and before his ancients gloriously.

25 **O LORD, thou** art my God;
I will exalt thee,
I will praise thy name;
for thou hast done wonderful things;
thy counsels of old are faithfulness and truth.
[2] **For thou** hast made of a city an heap; of a defenced city a ruin:
a palace of strangers to be no city;
it shall never be built.
[3] **Therefore** shall the strong people glorify thee,
the city of the terrible nations shall fear thee.
[4] **For thou** hast been a strength to the poor, a strength to the needy in his distress, a refuge from the storm, a shadow from the heat,
when the blast of the terrible ones is as a storm against the wall.
[5] **Thou** shalt bring down the noise of strangers, as the heat in a dry place; even the heat with the shadow of a cloud:
the branch of the terrible ones shall be brought low.
[6] **And in this mountain** shall the LORD of hosts make unto all people a feast of fat things, a feast of wines on the lees, of fat things full of marrow, of wines on the lees well refined.
[7] **And he** will destroy in this mountain the face of the covering cast over all people, and the vail that is spread over all nations.
[8] **He** will swallow up death in victory;
and the Lord GOD will wipe away tears from off all faces;
and the rebuke of his people shall he take away from off all the earth:
for the LORD hath spoken it.
[9] **And it** shall be said in that day,
Lo,
this is our God;
we have waited for him,
and he will save us:
this is the LORD;
we have waited for him,
we will be glad
and rejoice in his salvation.
[10] **For in this mountain** shall the hand of the LORD rest,
and Moab shall be trodden down under him,
even as straw is trodden down for the dunghill.
[11] **And he** shall spread forth his hands in the midst of them, as he that swimmeth spreadeth forth his hands to swim:
and he shall bring down their pride together with the spoils of their hands.
[12] **And the fortress of the high fort of thy walls** shall he bring down,
lay low,
and bring to the ground, even to the dust.

26 **In that day** shall this song be sung in the land of Judah;
We have a strong city;
salvation will God appoint for walls and bulwarks.
[2] **Open ye** the gates,
that the righteous nation which keepeth the truth may enter in.
[3] **Thou** wilt keep him in perfect peace,
whose mind is stayed on thee:
because he trusteth in thee.
[4] **Trust ye** in the LORD for ever:
for in the LORD Jehovah is everlasting strength:
[5] **For he** bringeth down them that dwell on high;
the lofty city, he layeth it low;
he layeth it low, even to the ground;
he bringeth it even to the dust.
[6] **The foot** shall tread it down, even the feet of the poor, and the steps of the needy.
[7] **The way of the just** is uprightness:
thou, most upright, dost weigh the path of the just.
[8] **Yea, in the way of thy judgments, O LORD,** have we waited for thee;
the desire of our soul is to thy name, and to the remembrance of thee.
[9] **With my soul** have I desired thee in the night;
yea, with my spirit within me will I seek thee early:
for when thy judgments are in the earth,
the inhabitants of the world will learn righteousness.
[10] **Let favour** be shewed to the wicked,
yet will he not learn righteousness:
in the land of uprightness will he deal unjustly,
and will not behold the majesty of the LORD.
[11] **LORD, when thy hand** is lifted up,
they will not see:
but they shall see,
and be ashamed for their envy at the people;
yea, the fire of thine enemies shall devour them.
[12] **LORD, thou** wilt ordain peace for us:
for thou also hast wrought all our works in us.

13 **O LORD our God, other lords beside thee** have had dominion over us:
but by thee only will we make mention of thy name.
14 **They** are dead,
they shall not live;
they are deceased,
they shall not rise:
therefore hast thou visited and destroyed them,
and made all their memory to perish.
15 **Thou** hast increased the nation, O LORD,
thou hast increased the nation:
thou art glorified:
thou hadst removed it far unto all the ends of the earth.
16 **LORD, in trouble** have they visited thee,
they poured out a prayer
when thy chastening was upon them.
17 **Like as a woman with child,** {that draweth near the time of her delivery}, is in pain,
and crieth out in her pangs;
so have we been in thy sight, O LORD.
18 **We** have been with child,
we have been in pain,
we have as it were brought forth wind;
we have not wrought any deliverance in the earth;
neither have the inhabitants of the world fallen.
19 **Thy dead men** shall live,
together with my dead body shall they arise.
Awake and sing, ye that dwell in dust:
for thy dew is as the dew of herbs,
and the earth shall cast out the dead.
20 **Come,** my people,
enter thou into thy chambers,
and shut thy doors about thee:
hide thyself as it were for a little moment,
until the indignation be overpast.
21 **For, {behold}, the LORD** cometh out of his place
to punish the inhabitants of the earth for their iniquity:
the earth also shall disclose her blood,
and shall no more cover her slain.

27

In that day the LORD with his sore and great and strong sword shall punish leviathan the piercing serpent, even leviathan that crooked serpent;
and he shall slay the dragon that is in the sea.
2 **In that day** sing ye unto her,
A vineyard of red wine.
3 **I** the LORD do keep it;
I will water it every moment:
lest any hurt it,
I will keep it night and day.
4 **Fury** is not in me:
who would set the briers and thorns against me in battle?
I would go through them,
I would burn them together.
5 **Or let him** take hold of my strength,
that he may make peace with me;
and he shall make peace with me.
6 **He** shall cause them that come of Jacob to take root:
Israel shall blossom and bud,
and fill the face of the world with fruit.
7 **Hath he** smitten him,
as he smote those that smote him?
or is he slain according to the slaughter of them that are slain by him?
8 **In measure,** {when it shooteth forth}, thou wilt debate with it:
he stayeth his rough wind in the day of the east wind.
9 **By this** therefore shall the iniquity of Jacob be purged;
and this is all the fruit to take away his sin;
when he maketh all the stones of the altar as chalkstones that are beaten in sunder,
the groves and images shall not stand up.
10 **Yet the defenced city** shall be desolate, and the habitation forsaken,
and left like a wilderness:
there shall the calf feed,
and there shall he lie down,
and consume the branches thereof.
11 **When the boughs thereof** are withered,
they shall be broken off:
the women come,
and set them on fire:
for it is a people of no understanding:
therefore he that made them will not have mercy on them,
and he that formed them will shew them no favour.
12 **And it** shall come to pass in that day,
that the LORD shall beat off from the channel of the river unto the stream of Egypt,
and ye shall be gathered one by one, O ye children of Israel.
13 **And it** shall come to pass in that day,
that the great trumpet shall be blown,
and they shall come which were ready to perish in the land of Assyria, and the outcasts in the land of Egypt,
and shall worship the LORD in the holy mount at Jerusalem.

28

Woe to the crown of pride, to the drunkards of Ephraim,
whose glorious beauty is a fading flower,
which are on the head of the fat valleys of them that are overcome with wine!
2 **Behold,**
the Lord hath a mighty and strong one,
which as a tempest of hail and a destroying storm, as a flood of mighty waters overflowing, shall cast down to the earth with the hand.
3 **The crown of pride, the drunkards of Ephraim,** shall be trodden under feet:
4 **And the glorious beauty,** {which is on the head of the fat valley}, shall be a fading flower, and as the hasty fruit before the summer; which when he that looketh upon it seeth,
while it is yet in his hand
he eateth it up.
5 **In that day** shall the LORD of hosts be for a crown of glory, and for a diadem of beauty, unto the residue of his people,
6 And for a spirit of judgment to him that sitteth in judgment, and for strength to them that turn the battle to the gate.
7 **But they** also have erred through wine,

and through strong drink are out of the way;
the priest and the prophet have erred through strong drink,
they are swallowed up of wine,
they are out of the way through strong drink;
they err in vision,
they stumble in judgment.

8 **For all tables** are full of vomit and filthiness,
so that there is no place clean.

9 **Whom** shall he teach knowledge?
and whom shall he make to understand doctrine?
them that are weaned from the milk, and drawn from the breasts.

10 **For precept** must be upon precept, precept upon precept; line upon line, line upon line; here a little, and there a little:

11 **For with stammering lips and another tongue** will he speak to this people.

12 **To whom** he said,
This is the rest wherewith ye may cause the weary to rest;
and this is the refreshing:
yet they would not hear.

13 **But the word of the LORD** was unto them precept upon precept, precept upon precept; line upon line, line upon line; here a little, and there a little;
that they might go,
and fall backward,
and be broken,
and snared,
and taken.

14 **Wherefore hear** the word of the LORD, ye scornful men, that rule this people which is in Jerusalem.

15 **Because ye** have said,
We have made a covenant with death,
and with hell are we at agreement;
when the overflowing scourge shall pass through,
it shall not come unto us:
for we have made lies our refuge,
and under falsehood have we hid ourselves:

16 **Therefore thus** saith the Lord GOD,
Behold,
I lay in Zion for a foundation a stone, a tried stone, a precious corner stone, a sure foundation:
he that believeth shall not make haste.

17 **Judgment** also will I lay to the line, and righteousness to the plummet:
and the hail shall sweep away the refuge of lies,
and the waters shall overflow the hiding place.

18 **And your covenant with death** shall be disannulled,
and your agreement with hell shall not stand;
when the overflowing scourge shall pass through,
then ye shall be trodden down by it.

19 **From the time that it goeth forth** it shall take you:
for morning by morning shall it pass over, by day and by night:
and it shall be a vexation only to understand the report.

20 **For the bed** is shorter than that a man can stretch himself on it:
and the covering narrower than that he can wrap himself in it.

21 **For the LORD** shall rise up as in mount Perazim,
he shall be wroth as in the valley of Gibeon,
that he may do his work, his strange work;
and bring to pass his act, his strange act.

22 **Now therefore be ye not** mockers,
lest your bands be made strong:
for I have heard from the Lord GOD of hosts a consumption,
even determined upon the whole earth.

23 **Give ye ear,**
and hear my voice;
hearken,
and hear my speech.

24 **Doth the plowman** plow all day to sow?
doth he open and break the clods of his ground?

25 **When he** hath made plain the face thereof,
doth he not cast abroad the fitches,
and scatter the cummin,
and cast in the principal wheat and the appointed barley and the rie in their place?

26 **For his God** doth instruct him to discretion,
and doth teach him.

27 **For the fitches** are not threshed with a threshing instrument,
neither is a cart wheel turned about upon the cummin;
but the fitches are beaten out with a staff, and the cummin with a rod.

28 **Bread corn** is bruised;
because he will not ever be threshing it,
nor break it with the wheel of his cart,
nor bruise it with his horsemen.

29 **This** also cometh forth from the LORD of hosts,
which is wonderful in counsel, and excellent in working.

29 **Woe** to Ariel, to Ariel, the city where David dwelt!
add ye year to year;
let them kill sacrifices.

2 **Yet I** will distress Ariel,
and there shall be heaviness and sorrow:
and it shall be unto me as Ariel.

3 **And I** will camp against thee round about,
and will lay siege against thee with a mount,
and I will raise forts against thee.

4 **And thou** shalt be brought down,
and shalt speak out of the ground,
and thy speech shall be low out of the dust,
and thy voice shall be, as of one that hath a familiar spirit, out of the ground,
and thy speech shall whisper out of the dust.

5 **Moreover the multitude of thy strangers** shall be like small dust,
and the multitude of the terrible ones shall be as chaff that passeth away:
yea, it shall be at an instant suddenly.

6 **Thou** shalt be visited of the LORD of hosts with thunder, and with earthquake, and great noise, with storm and tempest, and the flame of devouring fire.

7 **And the multitude of all the nations that fight against Ariel, even all that fight against her and her munition, and that distress her,** shall be as a dream of a night vision.

8 **It** shall even be as when an hungry man dreameth, {and, {{behold}}, he eateth}; {but he awaketh}, {and his soul is empty}: or as

when a thirsty man dreameth, {and, {{behold}}, he drinketh}; {but he awaketh}, {and, {{behold}}, he is faint}, {and his soul hath appetite}:
so shall the multitude of all the nations be,
that fight against mount Zion.

9 **Stay** yourselves,
and wonder;
cry ye out,
and cry:
they are drunken, but not with wine;
they stagger, but not with strong drink.

10 **For the LORD** hath poured out upon you the spirit of deep sleep,
and hath closed your eyes:
the prophets and your rulers, the seers hath he covered.

11 **And the vision of all** is become unto you as the words of a book that is sealed,
which men deliver to one that is learned,
saying,
Read this,
I pray thee:
and he saith
I cannot;
for it is sealed:

12 **And the book** is delivered to him that is not learned,
saying,
Read this,
I pray thee:
and he saith,
I am not learned.

13 **Wherefore the Lord** said,
Forasmuch as this people draw near me with their mouth,
and with their lips do honour me,
but have removed their heart far from me,
and their fear toward me is taught by the precept of men:

14 **Therefore, {behold}, I** will proceed to do a marvellous work among this people, even a marvellous work and a wonder:
for the wisdom of their wise men shall perish,
and the understanding of their prudent men shall be hid.

15 **Woe** unto them that seek deep to hide their counsel from the LORD,
and their works are in the dark,
and they say,
Who seeth us?
and who knoweth us?

16 **Surely your turning of things upside down** shall be esteemed as the potter's clay:
for shall the work say of him that made it,
He made me not?
or shall the thing framed say of him that framed it,
He had no understanding?

17 **Is it not** yet a very little while,
and Lebanon shall be turned into a fruitful field,
and the fruitful field shall be esteemed as a forest?

18 **And in that day** shall the deaf hear the words of the book,
and the eyes of the blind shall see out of obscurity, and out of darkness.

19 **The meek** also shall increase their joy in the LORD,
and the poor among men shall rejoice in the Holy One of Israel.

20 **For the terrible one** is brought to nought,
and the scorner is consumed,
and all that watch for iniquity are cut off:

21 **That** make a man an offender for a word,
and lay a snare for him that reproveth in the gate,
and turn aside the just for a thing of nought.

22 **Therefore thus** saith the LORD,
who redeemed Abraham,
concerning the house of Jacob,
Jacob shall not now be ashamed,
neither shall his face now wax pale.

23 **But when he** seeth his children, the work of mine hands, in the midst of him,
they shall sanctify my name,
and sanctify the Holy One of Jacob,
and shall fear the God of Israel.

24 **They also that erred in spirit** shall come to understanding,
and they that murmured shall learn doctrine.

30

Woe to the rebellious children,
saith the LORD,
that take counsel, but not of me;
and that cover with a covering, but not of my spirit,
that they may add sin to sin:
2 **That** walk to go down into Egypt,
and have not asked at my mouth;
to strengthen themselves in the strength of Pharaoh,
and to trust in the shadow of Egypt!

3 **Therefore** shall the strength of Pharaoh be your shame,
and the trust in the shadow of Egypt your confusion.

4 **For his princes** were at Zoan,
and his ambassadors came to Hanes.

5 **They** were all ashamed of a people that could not profit them,
nor be an help nor profit, but a shame, and also a reproach.

6 The burden of the beasts of the south:
into the land of trouble and anguish, {from whence come the young and old lion, the viper and fiery flying serpent}, they will carry their riches upon the shoulders of young asses, and their treasures upon the bunches of camels, to a people that shall not profit them.

7 **For the Egyptians** shall help in vain, and to no purpose:
therefore have I cried concerning this,
Their strength is to sit still.

8 **Now go,**
write it before them in a table,
and note it in a book,
that it may be for the time to come for ever and ever:

9 **That this** is a rebellious people, lying children, children that will not hear the law of the LORD:

10 **Which** say to the seers, {See not}; and to the prophets, {Prophesy not unto us right things},
speak unto us smooth things,
prophesy deceits:
11 **Get you** out of the way,
turn aside out of the path,
cause the Holy One of Israel to cease from before us.

12 **Wherefore thus** saith the Holy One of Israel,
Because ye despise this word,
and trust in oppression and perverseness,
and stay thereon:
13 **Therefore this iniquity** shall be to you as a breach ready to fall,
swelling out in a high wall,
whose breaking cometh suddenly at an instant.

14 **And he** shall break it as the breaking of the potters' vessel that is broken in pieces;
he shall not spare:
so that there shall not be found in the bursting of it a sherd to take fire from the hearth, or to take water withal out of the pit.
15 **For thus** saith the Lord GOD, the Holy One of Israel;
In returning and rest shall ye be saved;
in quietness and in confidence shall be your strength:
and ye would not.
16 **But ye** said,
No;
for we will flee upon horses;
therefore shall ye flee:
and, We will ride upon the swift;
therefore shall they that pursue you be swift.
17 **One thousand** shall flee at the rebuke of one;
at the rebuke of five shall ye flee:
till ye be left as a beacon upon the top of a mountain, and as an ensign on an hill.
18 **And therefore** will the LORD wait,
that he may be gracious unto you,
and therefore will he be exalted,
that he may have mercy upon you:
for the LORD is a God of judgment:
blessed are all they that wait for him.
19 **For the people** shall dwell in Zion at Jerusalem:
thou shalt weep no more:
he will be very gracious unto thee at the voice of thy cry;
when he shall hear it,
he will answer thee.
20 **And though the Lord** give you the bread of adversity, and the water of affliction,
yet shall not thy teachers be removed into a corner any more,
but thine eyes shall see thy teachers:
21 **And thine ears** shall hear a word behind thee,
saying,
This is the way,
walk ye in it,
when ye turn to the right hand,
and when ye turn to the left.
22 **Ye** shall defile also the covering of thy graven images of silver, and the ornament of thy molten images of gold:
thou shalt cast them away as a menstruous cloth;
thou shalt say unto it,
Get thee hence.
23 **Then** shall he give the rain of thy seed,
that thou shalt sow the ground withal; and bread of the increase of the earth,
and it shall be fat and plenteous:
in that day shall thy cattle feed in large pastures.
24 **The oxen likewise and the young asses that ear the ground** shall eat clean provender,
which hath been winnowed with the shovel and with the fan.
25 **And there** shall be upon every high mountain, and upon every high hill, rivers and streams of waters in the day of the great slaughter,
when the towers fall.
26 **Moreover the light of the moon** shall be as the light of the sun,
and the light of the sun shall be sevenfold, as the light of seven days, in the day that the LORD bindeth up the breach of his people, and healeth the stroke of their wound.
27 **Behold,**
the name of the LORD cometh from far,
burning with his anger,
and the burden thereof is heavy:
his lips are full of indignation, and his tongue as a devouring fire:
28 **And his breath, as an overflowing stream,** shall reach to the midst of the neck,
to sift the nations with the sieve of vanity:
and there shall be a bridle in the jaws of the people,
causing them to err.
29 **Ye** shall have a song, as in the night when a holy solemnity is kept; and gladness of heart, {as when one goeth with a pipe} {to come into the mountain of the LORD}, to the mighty One of Israel.
30 **And the LORD** shall cause his glorious voice to be heard,
and shall shew the lighting down of his arm, with the indignation of his anger, and with the flame of a devouring fire, with scattering, and tempest, and hailstones.
31 **For through the voice of the LORD** shall the Assyrian be beaten down,
which smote with a rod.
32 **And in every place where the grounded staff shall pass,** {which the LORD shall lay upon him}, it shall be with tabrets and harps:
and in battles of shaking will he fight with it.
33 **For Tophet** is ordained of old;
yea, for the king it is prepared;
he hath made it deep and large:
the pile thereof is fire and much wood;
the breath of the LORD, like a stream of brimstone, doth kindle it.

31 **Woe** to them that go down to Egypt for help;
and stay on horses,
and trust in chariots, {because they are many}; and in horsemen, {because they are very strong};
but they look not unto the Holy One of Israel,
neither seek the LORD!
2 **Yet he** also is wise,
and will bring evil,
and will not call back his words:
but will arise against the house of the evildoers, and against the help of them that work iniquity.
3 **Now the Egyptians** are men, and not God;
and their horses flesh, and not spirit.
When the LORD shall stretch out his hand,
both he that helpeth shall fall, and he that is holpen shall fall down,
and they all shall fail together.
4 **For thus** hath the LORD spoken unto me, Like as the lion and the young lion roaring on his prey,
when a multitude of shepherds is called forth against him,
he will not be afraid of their voice,
nor abase himself for the noise of them:
so shall the LORD of hosts come down to fight for mount Zion, and for the hill thereof.
5 **As birds** flying,

so will the LORD of hosts defend Jerusalem;
defending also
he will deliver it;
and passing over
he will preserve it.

6 **Turn ye** unto him from whom the children of Israel have deeply revolted.

7 **For in that day** every man shall cast away his idols of silver, and his idols of gold,
which your own hands have made unto you for a sin.

8 **Then shall** the Assyrian fall with the sword, not of a mighty man;
and the sword, not of a mean man, shall devour him:
but he shall flee from the sword,
and his young men shall be discomfited.

9 **And he** shall pass over to his strong hold for fear,
and his princes shall be afraid of the ensign,
saith the LORD,
whose fire is in Zion, and his furnace in Jerusalem.

32

Behold,
a king shall reign in righteousness,
and princes shall rule in judgment.

2 **And a man** shall be as an hiding place from the wind, and a covert from the tempest; as rivers of water in a dry place, as the shadow of a great rock in a weary land.

3 **And the eyes of them that see** shall not be dim,
and the ears of them that hear shall hearken.

4 **The heart also of the rash** shall understand knowledge,
and the tongue of the stammerers shall be ready to speak plainly.

5 **The vile person** shall be no more called liberal,
nor the churl said to be bountiful.

6 **For the vile person** will speak villany,
and his heart will work iniquity,
to practise hypocrisy,
and to utter error against the LORD,
to make empty the soul of the hungry,
and he will cause the drink of the thirsty to fail.

7 **The instruments also of the churl** are evil:
he deviseth wicked devices
to destroy the poor with lying words,
even when the needy speaketh right.

8 **But the liberal** deviseth liberal things;
and by liberal things shall he stand.

9 **Rise up,** ye women that are at ease;
hear my voice, ye careless daughters;
give ear unto my speech.

10 **Many days and years** shall ye be troubled, ye careless women:
for the vintage shall fail,
the gathering shall not come.

11 **Tremble,** ye women that are at ease;
be troubled, ye careless ones:
strip you,
and make you bare,
and gird sackcloth upon your loins.

12 **They** shall lament for the teats, for the pleasant fields, for the fruitful vine.

13 **Upon the land of my people** shall come up thorns and briers; yea, upon all the houses of joy in the joyous city:

14 **Because the palaces** shall be forsaken;
the multitude of the city shall be left;
the forts and towers shall be for dens for ever, a joy of wild asses, a pasture of flocks;

15 **Until the spirit** be poured upon us from on high,
and the wilderness be a fruitful field,
and the fruitful field be counted for a forest.

16 **Then judgment** shall dwell in the wilderness,
and righteousness remain in the fruitful field.

17 **And the work of righteousness** shall be peace; and the effect of righteousness quietness and assurance for ever.

18 **And my people** shall dwell in a peaceable habitation, and in sure dwellings, and in quiet resting places;

19 **When it** shall hail,
coming down on the forest;
and the city shall be low in a low place.

20 **Blessed** are ye that sow beside all waters, that send forth thither the feet of the ox and the ass.

33

Woe to thee that spoilest,
and thou wast not spoiled;
and dealest treacherously,
and they dealt not treacherously with thee!
when thou shalt cease to spoil,
thou shalt be spoiled;
and when thou shalt make an end to deal treacherously,
they shall deal treacherously with thee.

2 **O LORD, be** gracious unto us;
we have waited for thee:
be thou their arm every morning, our salvation also in the time of trouble.

3 **At the noise of the tumult** the people fled;
at the lifting up of thyself the nations were scattered.

4 **And your spoil** shall be gathered like the gathering of the caterpiller:
as the running to and fro of locusts shall he run upon them.

5 **The LORD** is exalted;
for he dwelleth on high:
he hath filled Zion with judgment and righteousness.

6 **And wisdom and knowledge** shall be the stability of thy times, and strength of salvation:
the fear of the LORD is his treasure.

7 **Behold,**
their valiant ones shall cry without:
the ambassadors of peace shall weep bitterly.

8 **The highways** lie waste,
the wayfaring man ceaseth:
he hath broken the covenant,
he hath despised the cities,
he regardeth no man.

9 **The earth** mourneth and languisheth:
Lebanon is ashamed and hewn down:
Sharon is like a wilderness;
and Bashan and Carmel shake off their fruits.

10 **Now** will I rise,
saith the LORD;
now will I be exalted;

now will I lift up myself.
11 **Ye** shall conceive chaff,
ye shall bring forth stubble:
your breath, as fire, shall devour you.
12 **And the people** shall be as the burnings of lime:
as thorns cut up shall they be burned in the fire.
13 **Hear,** ye that are far off,
what I have done;
and, ye that are near, acknowledge my might.
14 **The sinners in Zion** are afraid;
fearfulness hath surprised the hypocrites.
Who among us shall dwell with the devouring fire?
who among us shall dwell with everlasting burnings?
15 He that walketh righteously, and speaketh uprightly; he that despiseth the gain of oppressions, that shaketh his hands from holding of bribes, that stoppeth his ears from hearing of blood, and shutteth his eyes from seeing evil;
16 **He** shall dwell on high:
his place of defence shall be the munitions of rocks:
bread shall be given him;
his waters shall be sure.
17 **Thine eyes** shall see the king in his beauty:
they shall behold the land that is very far off.
18 **Thine heart** shall meditate terror.
Where is the scribe?
where is the receiver?
where is he that counted the towers?
19 **Thou shalt** not see a fierce people, a people of a deeper speech than thou canst perceive; of a stammering tongue,
that thou canst not understand.
20 **Look** upon Zion, the city of our solemnities:
thine eyes shall see Jerusalem a quiet habitation, a tabernacle that shall not be taken down;
not one of the stakes thereof shall ever be removed,
neither shall any of the cords thereof be broken.
21 **But there** the glorious LORD will be unto us a place of broad rivers and streams;
wherein shall go no galley with oars,
neither shall gallant ship pass thereby.
22 **For the LORD** is our judge,
the LORD is our lawgiver,
the LORD is our king;
he will save us.
23 **Thy tacklings** are loosed;
they could not well strengthen their mast,
they could not spread the sail:
then is the prey of a great spoil divided;
the lame take the prey.
24 **And the inhabitant** shall not say,
I am sick:
the people that dwell therein shall be forgiven their iniquity.

34 **Come** near, ye nations, to hear;
and hearken, ye people:
let the earth hear, and all that is therein; the world, and all things that come forth of it.
2 **For the indignation of the LORD** is upon all nations, and his fury upon all their armies:
he hath utterly destroyed them,
he hath delivered them to the slaughter.
3 **Their slain** also shall be cast out,
and their stink shall come up out of their carcases,
and the mountains shall be melted with their blood.
4 **And all the host of heaven** shall be dissolved,
and the heavens shall be rolled together as a scroll:
and all their host shall fall down, as the leaf falleth off from the vine, and as a falling fig from the fig tree.
5 **For my sword** shall be bathed in heaven:
behold,
it shall come down upon Idumea, and upon the people of my curse, to judgment.
6 **The sword of the LORD** is filled with blood,
it is made fat with fatness, and with the blood of lambs and goats, with the fat of the kidneys of rams:
for the LORD hath a sacrifice in Bozrah, and a great slaughter in the land of Idumea.
7 **And the unicorns** shall come down with them, and the bullocks with the bulls;
and their land shall be soaked with blood,
and their dust made fat with fatness.
8 **For it** is the day of the LORD's vengeance, and the year of recompences for the controversy of Zion.
9 **And the streams thereof** shall be turned into pitch, and the dust thereof into brimstone,
and the land thereof shall become burning pitch.
10 **It** shall not be quenched night nor day;
the smoke thereof shall go up for ever:
from generation to generation it shall lie waste;
none shall pass through it for ever and ever.
11 **But the cormorant and the bittern** shall possess it;
the owl also and the raven shall dwell in it:
and he shall stretch out upon it the line of confusion, and the stones of emptiness.
12 **They** shall call the nobles thereof to the kingdom,
but none shall be there,
and all her princes shall be nothing.
13 **And thorns** shall come up in her palaces, nettles and brambles in the fortresses thereof:
and it shall be an habitation of dragons, and a court for owls.
14 **The wild beasts of the desert** shall also meet with the wild beasts of the island,
and the satyr shall cry to his fellow;
the screech owl also shall rest there,
and find for herself a place of rest.
15 **There** shall the great owl make her nest,
and lay,
and hatch,
and gather under her shadow:
there shall the vultures also be gathered, every one with her mate.
16 **Seek ye out** of the book of the LORD,
and read:
no one of these shall fail,

none shall want her mate:
for my mouth it hath commanded,
and his spirit it hath gathered them.
17 **And he** hath cast the lot for them,
and his hand hath divided it unto them by line:
they shall possess it for ever,
from generation to generation shall they dwell therein.

35 **The wilderness and the solitary place** shall be glad for them;
and the desert shall rejoice,
and blossom as the rose.
2 **It** shall blossom abundantly,
and rejoice even with joy and singing:
the glory of Lebanon shall be given unto it,
the excellency of Carmel and Sharon, they shall see the glory of the LORD, and the excellency of our God.
3 **Strengthen ye** the weak hands,
and confirm the feeble knees.
4 **Say** to them that are of a fearful heart,
Be strong,
fear not:
behold,
your God will come with vengeance, even God with a recompence;
he will come and save you.
5 **Then the eyes of the blind** shall be opened,
and the ears of the deaf shall be unstopped.
6 **Then** shall the lame man leap as an hart,
and the tongue of the dumb sing:
for in the wilderness shall waters break out, and streams in the desert.
7 **And the parched ground** shall become a pool, and the thirsty land springs of water:
in the habitation of dragons, {where each lay}, shall be grass with reeds and rushes.
8 **And an highway** shall be there, and a way,
and it shall be called The way of holiness;
the unclean shall not pass over it;
but it shall be for those:
the wayfaring men, though fools, shall not err therein.
9 **No lion** shall be there,
nor any ravenous beast shall go up thereon,
it shall not be found there;
but the redeemed shall walk there:
10 **And the ransomed of the LORD** shall return,
and come to Zion with songs and everlasting joy upon their heads:
they shall obtain joy and gladness, and sorrow and sighing shall flee away.

36 **Now it** came to pass in the fourteenth year of king Hezekiah,
that Sennacherib king of Assyria came up against all the defenced cities of Judah,
and took them.
2 **And the king of Assyria** sent Rabshakeh from Lachish to Jerusalem unto king Hezekiah with a great army.
And he stood by the conduit of the upper pool in the highway of the fuller's field.
3 **Then** came forth unto him Eliakim, Hilkiah's son,
which was over the house, and Shebna the scribe, and Joah, Asaph's son, the recorder.
4 **And Rabshakeh** said unto them,
Say ye now to Hezekiah,
Thus saith the great king, the king of Assyria,
What confidence is this wherein thou trustest?
5 **I** say,
sayest thou,
(but they are but vain words)
I have counsel and strength for war:
now on whom dost thou trust,
that thou rebellest against me?
6 **Lo,**
thou trustest in the staff of this broken reed, on Egypt;
whereon if a man lean,
it will go into his hand,
and pierce it:
so is Pharaoh king of Egypt to all that trust in him.
7 **But if thou** say to me,
We trust in the LORD our God:
is it not he,
whose high places and whose altars Hezekiah hath taken away,
and said to Judah and to Jerusalem,
Ye shall worship before this altar?
8 **Now therefore give** pledges, {I pray thee}, to my master the king of Assyria,
and I will give thee two thousand horses,
if thou be able on thy part to set riders upon them.
9 **How** then wilt thou turn away the face of one captain of the least of my master's servants,
and put thy trust on Egypt for chariots and for horsemen?
10 **And** am I now come up without the LORD against this land
to destroy it?
the LORD said unto me,
Go up against this land,
and destroy it.
11 **Then** said Eliakim and Shebna and Joah unto Rabshakeh,
Speak, {I pray thee}, unto thy servants in the Syrian language;
for we understand it:
and speak not to us in the Jews' language, in the ears of the people that are on the wall.
12 **But Rabshakeh** said,
Hath my master sent me to thy master and to thee to speak these words?
hath he not sent me to the men that sit upon the wall,
that they may eat their own dung,
and drink their own piss with you?
13 **Then Rabshakeh** stood,
and cried with a loud voice in the Jews' language,
and said,
Hear ye the words of the great king, the king of Assyria.
14 **Thus** saith the king,
Let not Hezekiah deceive you:
for he shall not be able to deliver you.
15 **Neither let Hezekiah** make you trust in the LORD,
saying,
The LORD will surely deliver us:
this city shall not be delivered into the hand of the king of Assyria.
16 **Hearken not** to Hezekiah:
for thus saith the king of Assyria,
Make an agreement with me by a present,
and come out to me:
and eat ye every one of his vine, and every one of his fig tree,
and drink ye every one the waters of his own cistern;

[17] **Until I** come and take you away to
a land like your own land, a land
of corn and wine, a land of bread
and vineyards.
[18] **Beware**
lest Hezekiah persuade you,
saying,
the LORD will deliver us.
Hath any of the gods of the
nations delivered his land out of
the hand of the king of Assyria?
[19] **Where** are the gods of Hamath
and Arphad?
where are the gods of Sepharvaim?
and have they delivered Samaria
out of my hand?
[20] **Who** are they among all the gods
of these lands,
that have delivered their land out of
my hand,
that the LORD should deliver
Jerusalem out of my hand?
[21] **But they** held their peace,
and answered him not a word:
for the king's commandment was,
saying,
Answer him not.
[22] **Then** came Eliakim, the son of
Hilkiah,
that was over the household, and
Shebna the scribe, and Joah, the
son of Asaph, the recorder, to
Hezekiah with their clothes rent,
and told him the words of
Rabshakeh.

37 **And it** came to pass,
when king Hezekiah
heard it,
that he rent his clothes,
and covered himself with sackcloth,
and went into the house of the
LORD.
[2] **And he** sent Eliakim,
who was over the household, and
Shebna the scribe, and the elders
of the priests covered with
sackcloth, unto Isaiah the prophet
the son of Amoz.
[3] **And they** said unto him,
Thus saith Hezekiah,
This day is a day of trouble, and of
rebuke, and of blasphemy:
for the children are come to the
birth,
and there is not strength to bring
forth.
[4] **It may be** the LORD thy God will
hear the words of Rabshakeh,
whom the king of Assyria his
master hath sent to reproach the
living God,
and will reprove the words which
the LORD thy God hath heard:
wherefore lift up thy prayer for the
remnant that is left.
[5] **So the servants of king Hezekiah**
came to Isaiah.
[6] **And Isaiah** said unto them,
Thus shall ye say unto your master,
Thus saith the LORD,
Be not afraid of the words that thou
hast heard,
wherewith the servants of the king
of Assyria have blasphemed me.
[7] **Behold,**
I will send a blast upon him,
and he shall hear a rumour,
and return to his own land;
and I will cause him to fall by the
sword in his own land.
[8] **So Rabshakeh** returned,
and found the king of Assyria
warring against Libnah:
for he had heard that he was
departed from Lachish.
[9] **And he** heard say concerning
Tirhakah king of Ethiopia,
He is come forth to make war with
thee.
And when he heard it,
he sent messengers to Hezekiah,
saying,
[10] **Thus** shall ye speak to Hezekiah
king of Judah,
saying,
Let not thy God, {in whom thou
trustest}, deceive thee,
saying,
Jerusalem shall not be given into
the hand of the king of Assyria.
[11] **Behold,**
thou hast heard what the kings of
Assyria have done to all lands
by destroying them utterly;
and shalt thou be delivered?
[12] **Have the gods of the nations**
delivered them which my fathers
have destroyed, as Gozan, and
Haran, and Rezeph, and the
children of Eden which were in
Telassar?
[13] **Where** is the king of Hamath, and
the king of Arphad, and the king
of the city of Sepharvaim, Hena,
and Ivah?
[14] **And Hezekiah** received the letter
from the hand of the messengers,
and read it:
and Hezekiah went up unto the
house of the LORD,
and spread it before the LORD.
[15] **And Hezekiah** prayed unto the
LORD,
saying,
[16] **O LORD of hosts, God of Israel,**
{that dwellest between the
cherubims}, thou art the God,
even thou alone, of all the
kingdoms of the earth:
thou hast made heaven and earth.
[17] **Incline** thine ear, O LORD,
and hear;
open thine eyes, O LORD,
and see:
and hear all the words of
Sennacherib,
which hath sent to reproach the
living God.
[18] **Of a truth, LORD, the kings of**
Assyria have laid waste all the
nations, and their countries,
[19] **And** have cast their gods into the
fire:
for they were no gods, but the work
of men's hands, wood and stone:
therefore they have destroyed
them.
[20] **Now therefore, O LORD our**
God, save us from his hand,
that all the kingdoms of the earth
may know
that thou art the LORD, even thou
only.
[21] **Then Isaiah the son of Amoz**
sent unto Hezekiah,
saying,
Thus saith the LORD God of Israel,
Whereas thou hast prayed to me
against Sennacherib king of
Assyria:
[22] **This** is the word which the LORD
hath spoken concerning him;
The virgin, the daughter of Zion,
hath despised thee,
and laughed thee to scorn;
the daughter of Jerusalem hath
shaken her head at thee.
[23] **Whom** hast thou reproached and
blasphemed?
and against whom hast thou
exalted thy voice,
and lifted up thine eyes on high?
even against the Holy One of
Israel.
[24] **By thy servants** hast thou
reproached the Lord,
and hast said,

By the multitude of my chariots am I come up to the height of the mountains, to the sides of Lebanon;
and I will cut down the tall cedars thereof, and the choice fir trees thereof:
and I will enter into the height of his border, and the forest of his Carmel.

25 **I** have digged,
and drunk water;
and with the sole of my feet have I dried up all the rivers of the besieged places.

26 **Hast thou** not heard long ago, {how I have done it}; and of ancient times, {that I have formed it}?
now have I brought it to pass,
that thou shouldest be to lay waste defenced cities into ruinous heaps.

27 **Therefore their inhabitants** were of small power,
they were dismayed and confounded:
they were as the grass of the field, and as the green herb, as the grass on the housetops, and as corn blasted before it be grown up.

28 **But I** know thy abode, and thy going out, and thy coming in, and thy rage against me.

29 **Because thy rage against me, and thy tumult,** is come up into mine ears,
therefore will I put my hook in thy nose, and my bridle in thy lips,
and I will turn thee back by the way by which thou camest.

30 **And this** shall be a sign unto thee,
Ye shall eat this year such as groweth of itself; and the second year that which springeth of the same:
and in the third year sow ye,
and reap,
and plant vineyards,
and eat the fruit thereof.

31 **And the remnant that is escaped of the house of Judah** shall again take root downward,
and bear fruit upward:
32 **For out of Jerusalem** shall go forth a remnant, and they that escape out of mount Zion:
the zeal of the LORD of hosts shall do this.

33 **Therefore thus** saith the LORD concerning the king of Assyria,
He shall not come into this city,
nor shoot an arrow there,
nor come before it with shields,
nor cast a bank against it.

34 **By the way that he came,** by the same shall he return,
and shall not come into this city, saith the LORD.

35 **For I** will defend this city
to save it for mine own sake, and for my servant David's sake.

36 **Then the angel of the LORD** went forth,
and smote in the camp of the Assyrians a hundred and fourscore and five thousand:
and when they arose early in the morning,
behold,
they were all dead corpses.

37 **So Sennacherib king of Assyria** departed,
and went and returned,
and dwelt at Nineveh.

38 **And it** came to pass,
as he was worshipping in the house of Nisroch his god,
that Adrammelech and Sharezer his sons smote him with the sword;
and they escaped into the land of Armenia:
and Esarhaddon his son reigned in his stead.

38

In those days was Hezekiah sick unto death.
And Isaiah the prophet the son of Amoz came unto him,
and said unto him,
Thus saith the LORD,
Set thine house in order:
for thou shalt die,
and not live.

2 **Then Hezekiah** turned his face toward the wall,
and prayed unto the LORD,
3 **And** said,
Remember now, O LORD,
I beseech thee,
how I have walked before thee in truth and with a perfect heart,
and have done that which is good in thy sight.

And Hezekiah wept sore.

4 **Then** came the word of the LORD to Isaiah,
saying,
5 **Go,**
and say to Hezekiah,
Thus saith the LORD, the God of David thy father,
I have heard thy prayer,
I have seen thy tears:
behold,
I will add unto thy days fifteen years.

6 **And I** will deliver thee and this city out of the hand of the king of Assyria:
and I will defend this city.

7 **And this** shall be a sign unto thee from the LORD,
that the LORD will do this thing that he hath spoken;
8 **Behold,**
I will bring again the shadow of the degrees,
which is gone down in the sun dial of Ahaz, ten degrees backward.

So the sun returned ten degrees,
by which degrees it was gone down.

9 The writing of Hezekiah king of Judah,
when he had been sick,
and was recovered of his sickness:
10 **I** said in the cutting off of my days,
I shall go to the gates of the grave:
I am deprived of the residue of my years.

11 **I** said,
I shall not see the LORD, even the LORD, in the land of the living:
I shall behold man no more with the inhabitants of the world.

12 **Mine age** is departed,
and is removed from me as a shepherd's tent:
I have cut off like a weaver my life:
he will cut me off with pining sickness:
from day even to night wilt thou make an end of me.

13 **I** reckoned till morning,
that, as a lion, so will he break all my bones:
from day even to night wilt thou make an end of me.

14 **Like a crane or a swallow**, so did I chatter:
I did mourn as a dove:
mine eyes fail with looking upward:
O LORD, I am oppressed;
undertake for me.

15 **What** shall I say?
he hath both spoken unto me,

and himself hath done it:
I shall go softly all my years in the bitterness of my soul.
16 **O Lord, by these things** men live,
and in all these things is the life of my spirit:
so wilt thou recover me, and make me to live.
17 **Behold,**
for peace I had great bitterness:
but thou hast in love to my soul delivered it from the pit of corruption:
for thou hast cast all my sins behind thy back.
18 **For the grave** cannot praise thee,
death can not celebrate thee:
they that go down into the pit cannot hope for thy truth.
19 **The living, the living,** he shall praise thee,
as I do this day:
the father to the children shall make known thy truth.
20 **The LORD** was ready to save me:
therefore we will sing my songs to the stringed instruments all the days of our life in the house of the LORD.
21 **For Isaiah** had said,
Let them take a lump of figs,
and lay it for a plaister upon the boil,
and he shall recover.
22 **Hezekiah** also had said,
What is the sign that I shall go up to the house of the LORD?

39 **At that time** Merodachbaladan, the son of Baladan, king of Babylon, sent letters and a present to Hezekiah:
for he had heard that he had been sick,
and was recovered.
2 **And Hezekiah** was glad of them,
and shewed them the house of his precious things, the silver, and the gold, and the spices, and the precious ointment, and all the house of his armour, and all that was found in his treasures:
there was nothing in his house, nor in all his dominion,
that Hezekiah shewed them not.
3 **Then** came Isaiah the prophet unto king Hezekiah,
and said unto him,
What said these men?
and from whence came they unto thee?
And Hezekiah said,
They are come from a far country unto me, even from Babylon.
4 **Then** said he,
What have they seen in thine house?
And Hezekiah answered,
All that is in mine house have they seen:
there is nothing among my treasures that I have not shewed them.
5 **Then** said Isaiah to Hezekiah,
Hear the word of the LORD of hosts:
6 **Behold,**
the days come,
that all that is in thine house, and that which thy fathers have laid up in store until this day, shall be carried to Babylon:
nothing shall be left,
saith the LORD.
7 **And of thy sons that shall issue from thee,** {which thou shalt beget}, shall they take away;
and they shall be eunuchs in the palace of the king of Babylon.
8 **Then** said Hezekiah to Isaiah,
Good is the word of the LORD which thou hast spoken.
He said moreover,
For there shall be peace and truth in my days.

40 **Comfort ye, comfort ye** my people,
saith your God.
2 **Speak ye** comfortably to Jerusalem,
and cry unto her,
that her warfare is accomplished,
that her iniquity is pardoned:
for she hath received of the LORD's hand double for all her sins.
3 The voice of him that crieth in the wilderness,
Prepare ye the way of the LORD,
make straight in the desert a highway for our God.
4 **Every valley** shall be exalted,
and every mountain and hill shall be made low:
and the crooked shall be made straight, and the rough places plain:
5 **And the glory of the LORD** shall be revealed,
and all flesh shall see it together:
for the mouth of the LORD hath spoken it.
6 **The voice** said,
Cry.
And he said,
What shall I cry?
All flesh is grass,
and all the goodliness thereof is as the flower of the field:
7 **The grass** withereth,
the flower fadeth:
because the spirit of the LORD bloweth upon it:
surely the people is grass.
8 **The grass** withereth,
the flower fadeth:
but the word of our God shall stand for ever.
9 **O Zion, {that bringest good tidings}, get thee up** into the high mountain;
O Jerusalem, {that bringest good tidings}, lift up thy voice with strength;
lift it up,
be not afraid;
say unto the cities of Judah,
Behold your God!
10 **Behold,**
the Lord GOD will come with strong hand,
and his arm shall rule for him:
behold,
his reward is with him, and his work before him.
11 **He** shall feed his flock like a shepherd:
he shall gather the lambs with his arm,
and carry them in his bosom,
and shall gently lead those that are with young.
12 **Who** hath measured the waters in the hollow of his hand,
and meted out heaven with the span,
and comprehended the dust of the earth in a measure,
and weighed the mountains in scales, and the hills in a balance?
13 **Who** hath directed the Spirit of the LORD,
or {being his counsellor} hath taught him?
14 **With whom** took he counsel,
and who instructed him,
and taught him in the path of judgment,
and taught him knowledge,

and shewed to him the way of understanding?
15 **Behold,**
the nations are as a drop of a bucket,
and are counted as the small dust of the balance:
behold,
he taketh up the isles as a very little thing.
16 **And Lebanon** is not sufficient to burn,
nor the beasts thereof sufficient for a burnt offering.
17 **All nations before him** are as nothing;
and they are counted to him less than nothing, and vanity.
18 **To whom** then will ye liken God?
or what likeness will ye compare unto him?
19 **The workman** melteth a graven image,
and the goldsmith spreadeth it over with gold,
and casteth silver chains.
20 **He that is so impoverished that he hath no oblation** chooseth a tree that will not rot;
he seeketh unto him a cunning workman to prepare a graven image,
that shall not be moved.
21 **Have ye** not known?
have ye not heard?
hath it not been told you from the beginning?
have ye not understood from the foundations of the earth?
22 **It** is he that sitteth upon the circle of the earth,
and the inhabitants thereof are as grasshoppers;
that stretcheth out the heavens as a curtain,
and spreadeth them out as a tent to dwell in:
23 **That** bringeth the princes to nothing;
he maketh the judges of the earth as vanity.
24 **Yea, they** shall not be planted;
yea, they shall not be sown:
yea, their stock shall not take root in the earth:
and he shall also blow upon them,
and they shall wither,
and the whirlwind shall take them away as stubble.
25 **To whom** then will ye liken me,
or shall I be equal?
saith the Holy One.
26 **Lift up** your eyes on high,
and behold who hath created these things,
that bringeth out their host by number:
he calleth them all by names by the greatness of his might,
for that he is strong in power;
not one faileth.
27 **Why** sayest thou, O Jacob,
and speakest, O Israel,
My way is hid from the LORD,
and my judgment is passed over from my God?
28 **Hast thou not** known?
hast thou not heard,
that the everlasting God, the LORD, the Creator of the ends of the earth, fainteth not,
neither is weary?
there is no searching of his understanding.
29 **He** giveth power to the faint;
and to them that have no might he increaseth strength.
30 **Even the youths** shall faint and be weary,
and the young men shall utterly fall:
31 **But they that wait upon the LORD** shall renew their strength;
they shall mount up with wings as eagles;
they shall run,
and not be weary;
and they shall walk,
and not faint.

41 **Keep** silence before me, O islands;
and let the people renew their strength:
let them come near;
then let them speak:
let us come near together to judgment.
2 **Who** raised up the righteous man from the east,
called him to his foot,
gave the nations before him,
and made him rule over kings?
he gave them as the dust to his sword, and as driven stubble to his bow.
3 **He** pursued them,
and passed safely; even by the way that he had not gone with his feet.
4 **Who** hath wrought and done it,
calling the generations from the beginning?
I the LORD, the first, and with the last;
I am he.
5 **The isles** saw it,
and feared;
the ends of the earth were afraid,
drew near,
and came.
6 **They** helped every one his neighbour;
and every one said to his brother,
Be of good courage.
7 **So the carpenter** encouraged the goldsmith,
and he that smootheth with the hammer him that smote the anvil,
saying,
It is ready for the sodering:
and he fastened it with nails,
that it should not be moved.
8 **But thou,** Israel, art my servant, Jacob whom I have chosen, the seed of Abraham my friend.
9 **Thou whom I have taken from the ends of the earth, and called thee from the chief men thereof, and said unto thee, {Thou art my servant};** I have chosen thee,
and not cast thee away.
10 **Fear thou not;**
for I am with thee:
be not dismayed;
for I am thy God:
I will strengthen thee;
yea, I will help thee; yea,
I will uphold thee with the right hand of my righteousness.
11 **Behold,**
all they that were incensed against thee shall be ashamed and confounded:
they shall be as nothing;
and they that strive with thee shall perish.
12 **Thou** shalt seek them,
and shalt not find them, even them that contended with thee:
they that war against thee shall be as nothing, and as a thing of nought.
13 **For I the LORD thy God** will hold thy right hand,
saying unto thee,
Fear not;

I will help thee.

14 **Fear not,** thou worm Jacob, and ye men of Israel;
I will help thee,
saith the LORD, and thy redeemer, the Holy One of Israel.

15 **Behold,**
I will make thee a new sharp threshing instrument having teeth:
thou shalt thresh the mountains,
and beat them small,
and shalt make the hills as chaff.

16 **Thou** shalt fan them,
and the wind shall carry them away,
and the whirlwind shall scatter them:
and thou shalt rejoice in the LORD,
and shalt glory in the Holy One of Israel.

17 **When the poor and needy** seek water,
and there is none,
and their tongue faileth for thirst,
I the LORD will hear them,
I the God of Israel will not forsake them.

18 **I** will open rivers in high places, and fountains in the midst of the valleys:
I will make the wilderness a pool of water, and the dry land springs of water.

19 **I** will plant in the wilderness the cedar, the shittah tree, and the myrtle, and the oil tree;
I will set in the desert the fir tree, and the pine, and the box tree together:

20 **That they** may see,
and know,
and consider,
and understand together,
that the hand of the LORD hath done this,
and the Holy One of Israel hath created it.

21 **Produce** your cause,
saith the LORD;
bring forth your strong reasons,
saith the King of Jacob.

22 **Let them** bring them forth,
and shew us what shall happen:
let them shew the former things,
what they be,
that we may consider them,
and know the latter end of them;
or declare us things for to come.

23 **Shew** the things that are to come hereafter,
that we may know
that ye are gods:
yea, do good,
or do evil,
that we may be dismayed,
and behold it together.

24 **Behold,**
ye are of nothing,
and your work of nought:
an abomination is he that chooseth you.

25 **I** have raised up one from the north,
and he shall come:
from the rising of the sun shall he call upon my name:
and he shall come upon princes as upon morter, and as the potter treadeth clay.

26 **Who** hath declared from the beginning,
that we may know?
and beforetime, that we may say,
He is righteous?
yea, there is none that sheweth,
yea, there is none that declareth,
yea, there is none that heareth your words.

27 **The first** shall say to Zion,
Behold,
behold them:
and I will give to Jerusalem one that bringeth good tidings.

28 **For I** beheld,
and there was no man; even among them,
and there was no counsellor,
that, {when I asked of them}, could answer a word.

29 **Behold,**
they are all vanity;
their works are nothing:
their molten images are wind and confusion.

42 ∞ **Behold** my servant, {whom I uphold}; mine elect, {in whom my soul delighteth};
I have put my spirit upon him:
he shall bring forth judgment to the Gentiles.

2 **He** shall not cry,
nor lift up,
nor cause his voice to be heard in the street.

3 **A bruised reed** shall he not break,
and the smoking flax shall he not quench:
he shall bring forth judgment unto truth.

4 **He** shall not fail
nor be discouraged,
till he have set judgment in the earth:
and the isles shall wait for his law.

5 **Thus** saith God the LORD, he that created the heavens, {and stretched them out}; he that spread forth the earth, and that which cometh out of it; he that giveth breath unto the people upon it, and spirit to them that walk therein:

6 **I** the LORD have called thee in righteousness,
and will hold thine hand,
and will keep thee,
and give thee for a covenant of the people, for a light of the Gentiles;

7 To open the blind eyes,
to bring out the prisoners from the prison, and them that sit in darkness out of the prison house.

8 **I** am the LORD:
that is my name:
and my glory will I not give to another, neither my praise to graven images.

9 **Behold,**
the former things are come to pass,
and new things do I declare:
before they spring forth I tell you of them.

10 **Sing** unto the LORD a new song, and his praise from the end of the earth, ye that go down to the sea, and all that is therein; the isles, and the inhabitants thereof.

11 **Let the wilderness and the cities thereof** lift up their voice,
the villages that Kedar doth inhabit:
let the inhabitants of the rock sing,
let them shout from the top of the mountains.

12 **Let them** give glory unto the LORD,
and declare his praise in the islands.

13 **The LORD** shall go forth as a mighty man,
he shall stir up jealousy like a man of war:
he shall cry,
yea, roar;
he shall prevail against his enemies.

14 **I** have long time holden my peace;
I have been still,
and refrained myself:
now will I cry like a travailing woman;
I will destroy and devour at once.

15 **I** will make waste mountains and hills,
and dry up all their herbs;
and I will make the rivers islands,
and I will dry up the pools.

16 **And I** will bring the blind by a way that they knew not;
I will lead them in paths that they have not known:
I will make darkness light before them, and crooked things straight.

These things will I do unto them,
and not forsake them.

17 **They** shall be turned back,
they shall be greatly ashamed,
that trust in graven images,
that say to the molten images,
Ye are our gods.

18 **Hear,** ye deaf;
and look, ye blind,
that ye may see.

19 **Who** is blind, but my servant?
or deaf, as my messenger that I sent?
who is blind as he that is perfect, and blind as the LORD's servant?

20 Seeing many things,
but thou observest not;
opening the ears,
but he heareth not.

21 **The LORD** is well pleased for his righteousness' sake;
he will magnify the law,
and make it honourable.

22 **But this** is a people robbed and spoiled;
they are all of them snared in holes,
and they are hid in prison houses:
they are for a prey, {and none delivereth}; for a spoil, {and none saith}, {Restore}.

23 **Who among you** will give ear to this?
who will hearken and hear for the time to come?

24 **Who** gave Jacob for a spoil, and Israel to the robbers?
did not the LORD, he against whom we have sinned?
for they would not walk in his ways,
neither were they obedient unto his law.

25 **Therefore he** hath poured upon him the fury of his anger, and the strength of battle:
and it hath set him on fire round about,
yet he knew not;
and it burned him,
yet he laid it not to heart.

43

But now thus saith the LORD that created thee, O Jacob, and he that formed thee, O Israel,
Fear not:
for I have redeemed thee,
I have called thee by thy name;
thou art mine.

2 **When thou** passest through the waters, {I will be with thee}; and through the rivers, {they shall not overflow thee}:
when thou walkest through the fire,
thou shalt not be burned;
neither shall the flame kindle upon thee.

3 **For I** am the LORD thy God, the Holy One of Israel, thy Saviour:
I gave Egypt for thy ransom, Ethiopia and Seba for thee.

4 **Since thou** wast precious in my sight,
thou hast been honourable,
and I have loved thee:
therefore will I give men for thee, and people for thy life.

5 **Fear not:**
for I am with thee:
I will bring thy seed from the east,
and gather thee from the west;

6 **I** will say to the north, {Give up}; and to the south, {Keep not back}:
bring my sons from far, and my daughters from the ends of the earth;

7 Even every one that is called by my name:
for I have created him for my glory,
I have formed him;
yea, I have made him.

8 **Bring forth** the blind people that have eyes, and the deaf that have ears.

9 **Let all the nations** be gathered together,
and let the people be assembled:
who among them can declare this,
and shew us former things?
let them bring forth their witnesses,
that they may be justified:
or let them hear,
and say,
It is truth.

10 **Ye** are my witnesses, {saith the LORD}, and my servant whom I have chosen:
that ye may know and believe me,
and understand
that I am he:
before me there was no God formed,
neither shall there be after me.

11 **I, even I,** am the LORD;
and beside me there is no saviour.

12 **I** have declared,
and have saved,
and I have shewed,
when there was no strange god among you:
therefore ye are my witnesses,
saith the LORD,
that I am God.

13 **Yea, before the day** was
I am he;
and there is none that can deliver out of my hand:
I will work,
and who shall let it?

14 **Thus** saith the LORD, your redeemer, the Holy One of Israel;
For your sake I have sent to Babylon,
and have brought down all their nobles, and the Chaldeans,
whose cry is in the ships.

15 **I** am the LORD, your Holy One, the creator of Israel, your King.

16 **Thus** saith the LORD,
which maketh a way in the sea, and a path in the mighty waters;

17 **Which** bringeth forth the chariot and horse, the army and the power;
they shall lie down together,
they shall not rise:
they are extinct,
they are quenched as tow.

18 **Remember ye not** the former things,
neither consider the things of old.

19 **Behold,**
I will do a new thing;
now it shall spring forth;
shall ye not know it?

I will even make a way in the wilderness, and rivers in the desert.

20 **The beast of the field** shall honour me, the dragons and the owls:
because I give waters in the wilderness, and rivers in the desert,
to give drink to my people, my chosen.

21 **This people** have I formed for myself;
they shall shew forth my praise.

22 **But thou** hast not called upon me, O Jacob;
but thou hast been weary of me, O Israel.

23 **Thou** hast not brought me the small cattle of thy burnt offerings;
neither hast thou honoured me with thy sacrifices.

I have not caused thee to serve with an offering,
nor wearied thee with incense.

24 **Thou** hast bought me no sweet cane with money,
neither hast thou filled me with the fat of thy sacrifices:
but thou hast made me to serve with thy sins,
thou hast wearied me with thine iniquities.

25 **I, even I,** am he that blotteth out thy transgressions for mine own sake,
and will not remember thy sins.

26 **Put** me in remembrance:
let us plead together:
declare thou,
that thou mayest be justified.

27 **Thy first father** hath sinned,
and thy teachers have transgressed against me.

28 **Therefore I** have profaned the princes of the sanctuary,
and have given Jacob to the curse, and Israel to reproaches.

44

Yet now hear, O Jacob my servant; and Israel,
whom I have chosen:

2 **Thus** saith the LORD
that made thee,
and formed thee from the womb,
which will help thee;
Fear not, O Jacob, my servant; and thou, Jesurun,
whom I have chosen.

3 **For I** will pour water upon him that is thirsty, and floods upon the dry ground:
I will pour my spirit upon thy seed, and my blessing upon thine offspring:

4 **And they** shall spring up as among the grass, as willows by the water courses.

5 **One** shall say,
I am the LORD's;
and another shall call himself by the name of Jacob;
and another shall subscribe with his hand unto the LORD,
and surname himself by the name of Israel.

6 **Thus** saith the LORD the King of Israel, and his redeemer the LORD of hosts;
I am the first,
and I am the last;
and beside me there is no God.

7 **And who, as I,** shall call,
and shall declare it,
and set it in order for me,
since I appointed the ancient people?
and the things that are coming, and shall come, let them shew unto them.

8 **Fear ye not,**
neither be afraid:
have not I told thee from that time,
and have declared it?
ye are even my witnesses.

Is there a God beside me?
yea, there is no God;
I know not any.

9 **They that make a graven image** are all of them vanity;
and their delectable things shall not profit;
and they are their own witnesses;
they see not,
nor know;
that they may be ashamed.

10 **Who** hath formed a god,
or molten a graven image that is profitable for nothing?

11 **Behold,**
all his fellows shall be ashamed:
and the workmen, they are of men:
let them all be gathered together,
let them stand up;
yet they shall fear,
and they shall be ashamed together.

12 **The smith with the tongs** both worketh in the coals,
and fashioneth it with hammers,
and worketh it with the strength of his arms:
yea, he is hungry,
and his strength faileth:
he drinketh no water,
and is faint.

13 **The carpenter** stretcheth out his rule;
he marketh it out with a line;
he fitteth it with planes,
and he marketh it out with the compass,
and maketh it after the figure of a man, according to the beauty of a man;
that it may remain in the house.

14 **He** heweth him down cedars,
and taketh the cypress and the oak,
which he strengtheneth for himself among the trees of the forest:
he planteth an ash,
and the rain doth nourish it.

15 **Then** shall it be for a man to burn:
for he will take thereof,
and warm himself;
yea, he kindleth it,
and baketh bread;
yea, he maketh a god,
and worshippeth it;
he maketh it a graven image,
and falleth down thereto.

16 **He** burneth part thereof in the fire;
with part thereof he eateth flesh;
he roasteth roast,
and is satisfied:
yea, he warmeth himself,
and saith,
Aha, I am warm,
I have seen the fire:

17 **And the residue thereof** he maketh a god, even his graven image:
he falleth down unto it,
and worshippeth it,
and prayeth unto it,
and saith,
Deliver me;
for thou art my god.

18 **They** have not known
nor understood:
for he hath shut their eyes, {that they cannot see}; and their hearts, {that they cannot understand}.

19 **And none** considereth in his heart,
neither is there knowledge nor understanding to say,
I have burned part of it in the fire;

yea, also I have baked bread upon the coals thereof;
I have roasted flesh,
and eaten it:
and shall I make the residue thereof an abomination?
shall I fall down to the stock of a tree?

20 **He** feedeth on ashes:
a deceived heart hath turned him aside,
that he cannot deliver his soul,
nor say,
Is there not a lie in my right hand?

21 **Remember** these, O Jacob and Israel;
for thou art my servant:
I have formed thee;
thou art my servant: O Israel,
thou shalt not be forgotten of me.

22 **I** have blotted out, as a thick cloud, thy transgressions, and, as a cloud, thy sins:
return unto me;
for I have redeemed thee.

23 **Sing,** O ye heavens;
for the LORD hath done it:
shout, ye lower parts of the earth:
break forth into singing, ye mountains, O forest, and every tree therein:
for the LORD hath redeemed Jacob,
and glorified himself in Israel.

24 **Thus** saith the LORD, thy redeemer, and he that formed thee from the womb,
I am the LORD
that maketh all things;
that stretcheth forth the heavens alone;
that spreadeth abroad the earth by myself;

25 **That** frustrateth the tokens of the liars,
and maketh diviners mad;
that turneth wise men backward,
and maketh their knowledge foolish;

26 **That** confirmeth the word of his servant,
and performeth the counsel of his messengers;
that saith to Jerusalem, {Thou shalt be inhabited}; and to the cities of Judah, {Ye shall be built}, {and I will raise up the decayed places thereof}:

27 **That** saith to the deep, {Be dry}, {and I will dry up thy rivers}:

28 **That** saith of Cyrus, {He is my shepherd}, {and shall perform all my pleasure}:
even saying to Jerusalem, {Thou shalt be built}; and to the temple, {Thy foundation shall be laid}.

45

Thus saith the LORD to his anointed, to Cyrus,
whose right hand I have holden,
to subdue nations before him;
and I will loose the loins of kings,
to open before him the two leaved gates;
and the gates shall not be shut;

2 **I** will go before thee,
and make the crooked places straight:
I will break in pieces the gates of brass,
and cut in sunder the bars of iron:

3 **And I** will give thee the treasures of darkness, and hidden riches of secret places,
that thou mayest know
that I, the LORD, {which call thee by thy name}, am the God of Israel.

4 **For Jacob my servant's sake, and Israel mine elect,** I have even called thee by thy name:
I have surnamed thee,
though thou hast not known me.

5 **I** am the LORD,
and there is none else,
there is no God beside me:
I girded thee,
though thou hast not known me:

6 **That they** may know from the rising of the sun, and from the west,
that there is none beside me.
I am the LORD,
and there is none else.

7 **I** form the light,
and create darkness:
I make peace,
and create evil:
I the LORD do all these things.

8 **Drop down,** ye heavens, from above,
and let the skies pour down righteousness:
let the earth open,
and let them bring forth salvation,
and let righteousness spring up together;
I the LORD have created it.

9 **Woe** unto him that striveth with his Maker!
Let the potsherd strive with the potsherds of the earth.
Shall the clay say to him that fashioneth it,
What makest thou?
or thy work,
He hath no hands?

10 **Woe** unto him that saith unto his father, {What begettest thou}? or to the woman, {What hast thou brought forth}?

11 **Thus** saith the LORD, the Holy One of Israel, and his Maker,
Ask me of things to come concerning my sons,
and concerning the work of my hands command ye me.

12 **I** have made the earth,
and created man upon it:
I, even my hands, have stretched out the heavens,
and all their host have I commanded.

13 **I** have raised him up in righteousness,
and I will direct all his ways:
he shall build my city,
and he shall let go my captives,
not for price nor reward, saith the LORD of hosts.

14 **Thus** saith the LORD,
The labour of Egypt, and merchandise of Ethiopia and of the Sabeans, men of stature, shall come over unto thee,
and they shall be thine:
they shall come after thee;
in chains they shall come over,
and they shall fall down unto thee,
they shall make supplication unto thee,
saying,
Surely God is in thee;
and there is none else,
there is no God.

15 **Verily thou** art a God that hidest thyself, O God of Israel, the Saviour.

16 **They** shall be ashamed,
and also confounded, all of them:
they shall go to confusion together that are makers of idols.

17 **But Israel** shall be saved in the LORD with an everlasting salvation:
ye shall not be ashamed
nor confounded world without end.

18 **For thus** saith the LORD that created the heavens;

God himself that formed the earth and made it;
he hath established it,
he created it not in vain,
he formed it to be inhabited:
I am the LORD;
and there is none else.
19 **I** have not spoken in secret, in a dark place of the earth:
I said not unto the seed of Jacob,
Seek ye me in vain:
I the LORD speak righteousness,
I declare things that are right.
20 **Assemble** yourselves and come;
draw near together, ye that are escaped of the nations:
they have no knowledge that set up the wood of their graven image,
and pray unto a god that cannot save.
21 **Tell ye,**
and bring them near; yea,
let them take counsel together:
who hath declared this from ancient time?
who hath told it from that time?
have not I the LORD?
and there is no God else beside me; a just God and a Saviour;
there is none beside me.
22 **Look** unto me,
and be ye saved, all the ends of the earth:
for I am God,
and there is none else.
23 **I** have sworn by myself,
the word is gone out of my mouth in righteousness,
and shall not return,
That unto me every knee shall bow,
every tongue shall swear.
24 **Surely, {shall one say},** in the LORD have I righteousness and strength:
even to him shall men come;
and all that are incensed against him shall be ashamed.
25 **In the LORD** shall all the seed of Israel be justified,
and shall glory.

46 **Bel** boweth down,
Nebo stoopeth,
their idols were upon the beasts, and upon the cattle:
your carriages were heavy loaden;
they are a burden to the weary beast.
2 **They** stoop,
they bow down together;
they could not deliver the burden,
but themselves are gone into captivity.
3 **Hearken** unto me, O house of Jacob, and all the remnant of the house of Israel,
which are borne by me from the belly,
which are carried from the womb:
4 **And even to your old age** I am he;
and even to hoar hairs will I carry you:
I have made,
and I will bear;
even I will carry,
and will deliver you.
5 **To whom** will ye liken me,
and make me equal,
and compare me,
that we may be like?
6 **They** lavish gold out of the bag,
and weigh silver in the balance,
and hire a goldsmith;
and he maketh it a god:
they fall down,
yea, they worship.
7 **They** bear him upon the shoulder,
they carry him,
and set him in his place,
and he standeth;
from his place shall he not remove:
yea, one shall cry unto him,
yet can he not answer,
nor save him out of his trouble.
8 **Remember** this,
and shew yourselves men:
bring it again to mind, O ye transgressors.
9 **Remember** the former things of old:
for I am God,
and there is none else;
I am God,
and there is none like me,
10 Declaring the end from the beginning, and from ancient times the things that are not yet done,
saying,
My counsel shall stand,
and I will do all my pleasure:
11 Calling a ravenous bird from the east, the man that executeth my counsel from a far country:
yea, I have spoken it,
I will also bring it to pass;
I have purposed it,
I will also do it.
12 **Hearken** unto me, ye stouthearted,
that are far from righteousness:
13 **I** bring near my righteousness;
it shall not be far off,
and my salvation shall not tarry:
and I will place salvation in Zion for Israel my glory.

47 **Come down,**
and sit in the dust, O virgin daughter of Babylon,
sit on the ground:
there is no throne, O daughter of the Chaldeans:
for thou shalt no more be called tender and delicate.
2 **Take** the millstones,
and grind meal:
uncover thy locks,
make bare the leg,
uncover the thigh,
pass over the rivers.
3 **Thy nakedness** shall be uncovered,
yea, thy shame shall be seen:
I will take vengeance,
and I will not meet thee as a man.
4 **As for our redeemer,** the LORD of hosts is his name, the Holy One of Israel.
5 **Sit thou** silent,
and get thee into darkness, O daughter of the Chaldeans:
for thou shalt no more be called,
The lady of kingdoms.
6 **I** was wroth with my people,
I have polluted mine inheritance,
and given them into thine hand:
thou didst shew them no mercy;
upon the ancient hast thou very heavily laid thy yoke.
7 **And thou** saidst,
I shall be a lady for ever:
so that thou didst not lay these things to thy heart,
neither didst remember the latter end of it.
8 **Therefore hear** now this, thou that art given to pleasures, that dwellest carelessly, that sayest in thine heart, {I am, and none else beside me};
I shall not sit as a widow,
neither shall I know the loss of children:
9 **But these two things** shall come to thee in a moment in one day, the loss of children, and widowhood:
they shall come upon thee in their perfection for the multitude of

thy sorceries, and for the great abundance of thine enchantments.

10 **For thou** hast trusted in thy wickedness:
thou hast said,
None seeth me.

Thy wisdom and thy knowledge, it hath perverted thee;
and thou hast said in thine heart,
I am, and none else beside me.

11 **Therefore** shall evil come upon thee;
thou shalt not know
from whence it riseth:
and mischief shall fall upon thee;
thou shalt not be able to put it off:
and desolation shall come upon thee suddenly,
which thou shalt not know.

12 **Stand** now with thine enchantments, and with the multitude of thy sorceries,
wherein thou hast laboured from thy youth;
if so be thou shalt be able to profit,
if so be thou mayest prevail.

13 **Thou** art wearied in the multitude of thy counsels.

Let now the astrologers, the stargazers, the monthly prognosticators, stand up,
and save thee from these things that shall come upon thee.

14 **Behold,**
they shall be as stubble;
the fire shall burn them;
they shall not deliver themselves from the power of the flame:
there shall not be a coal to warm at,
nor fire to sit before it.

15 **Thus** shall they be unto thee with whom thou hast laboured, even thy merchants, from thy youth:
they shall wander every one to his quarter;
none shall save thee.

48

Hear ye this, O house of Jacob,
which are called by the name of Israel,
and are come forth out of the waters of Judah,
which swear by the name of the LORD, and make mention of the God of Israel, but not in truth, nor in righteousness.

2 **For they** call themselves of the holy city,
and stay themselves upon the God of Israel;
The LORD of hosts is his name.

3 **I** have declared the former things from the beginning;
and they went forth out of my mouth,
and I shewed them;
I did them suddenly,
and they came to pass.

4 **Because I** knew
that thou art obstinate,
and thy neck is an iron sinew, and thy brow brass;

5 **I** have even from the beginning declared it to thee;
before it came to pass
I shewed it thee:
lest thou shouldest say,
Mine idol hath done them,
and my graven image, and my molten image, hath commanded them.

6 **Thou** hast heard,
see all this;
and will not ye declare it?

I have shewed thee new things from this time, even hidden things,
and thou didst not know them.

7 **They** are created now, and not from the beginning; even before the day when thou heardest them not;
lest thou shouldest say,
Behold,
I knew them.

8 **Yea, thou** heardest not;
yea, thou knewest not; yea, from that time that thine ear was not opened:
for I knew
that thou wouldest deal very treacherously,
and wast called a transgressor from the womb.

9 **For my name's sake** will I defer mine anger,
and for my praise will I refrain for thee,
that I cut thee not off.

10 **Behold,**
I have refined thee, but not with silver;
I have chosen thee in the furnace of affliction.

11 **For mine own sake, even for mine own sake,** will I do it:
for how should my name be polluted?
and I will not give my glory unto another.

12 **Hearken** unto me, O Jacob and Israel, my called;
I am he;
I am the first,
I also am the last.

13 **Mine hand** also hath laid the foundation of the earth,
and my right hand hath spanned the heavens:
when I call unto them,
they stand up together.

14 **All ye, assemble** yourselves,
and hear;
which among them hath declared these things?

The LORD hath loved him:
he will do his pleasure on Babylon,
and his arm shall be on the Chaldeans.

15 **I, even I,** have spoken;
yea, I have called him:
I have brought him,
and he shall make his way prosperous.

16 **Come ye** near unto me,
hear ye this;
I have not spoken in secret from the beginning;
from the time that it was, there am I:
and now the Lord GOD, and his Spirit, hath sent me.

17 **Thus** saith the LORD, thy Redeemer, the Holy One of Israel;
I am the LORD thy God
which teacheth thee to profit,
which leadeth thee by the way that thou shouldest go.

18 **O that thou** hadst hearkened to my commandments!
then had thy peace been as a river, and thy righteousness as the waves of the sea:

19 **Thy seed** also had been as the sand, and the offspring of thy bowels like the gravel thereof;
his name should not have been cut off {nor destroyed} from before me.

20 **Go ye forth** of Babylon,
flee ye from the Chaldeans,
with a voice of singing declare ye,
tell this,
utter it even to the end of the earth;
say ye,

The LORD hath redeemed his servant Jacob.
21 **And they** thirsted not
when he led them through the deserts:
he caused the waters to flow out of the rock for them:
he clave the rock also,
and the waters gushed out.
22 **There** is no peace, {saith the LORD}, unto the wicked.

49 **Listen,** O isles, unto me;
and hearken, ye people, from far;
The LORD hath called me from the womb;
from the bowels of my mother hath he made mention of my name.
2 **And he** hath made my mouth like a sharp sword;
in the shadow of his hand hath he hid me,
and made me a polished shaft;
in his quiver hath he hid me;
3 **And** said unto me,
Thou art my servant, O Israel,
in whom I will be glorified.
4 **Then I** said,
I have laboured in vain,
I have spent my strength for nought, and in vain:
yet surely my judgment is with the LORD, and my work with my God.
5 **And now,** saith the LORD that formed me from the womb to be his servant,
to bring Jacob again to him,
Though Israel be not gathered,
yet shall I be glorious in the eyes of the LORD,
and my God shall be my strength.
6 **And he** said,
It is a light thing that thou shouldest be my servant
to raise up the tribes of Jacob,
and to restore the preserved of Israel:
I will also give thee for a light to the Gentiles,
that thou mayest be my salvation unto the end of the earth.
7 **Thus** saith the LORD, the Redeemer of Israel, and his Holy One, to him whom man despiseth, to him whom the nation abhorreth, to a servant of rulers,
Kings shall see and arise,
princes also shall worship, because of the LORD that is faithful, and the Holy One of Israel,
and he shall choose thee.
8 **Thus** saith the LORD,
In an acceptable time have I heard thee,
and in a day of salvation have I helped thee:
and I will preserve thee,
and give thee for a covenant of the people,
to establish the earth,
to cause to inherit the desolate heritages;
9 **That thou** mayest say to the prisoners,
Go forth;
to them that are in darkness, Shew yourselves.
They shall feed in the ways,
and their pastures shall be in all high places.
10 **They** shall not hunger nor thirst;
neither shall the heat nor sun smite them:
for he that hath mercy on them shall lead them,
even by the springs of water shall he guide them.
11 **And I** will make all my mountains a way,
and my highways shall be exalted.
12 **Behold,**
these shall come from far: and, {lo}, these from the north and from the west; and these from the land of Sinim.
13 **Sing,** O heavens;
and be joyful, O earth;
and break forth into singing, O mountains:
for the LORD hath comforted his people,
and will have mercy upon his afflicted.
14 **But Zion** said,
The LORD hath forsaken me,
and my Lord hath forgotten me.
15 **Can a woman** forget her sucking child,
that she should not have compassion on the son of her womb?
yea, they may forget,
yet will I not forget thee.
16 **Behold,**
I have graven thee upon the palms of my hands;
thy walls are continually before me.
17 **Thy children** shall make haste;
thy destroyers and they that made thee waste shall go forth of thee.
18 **Lift up** thine eyes round about,
and behold:
all these gather themselves together,
and come to thee.
As I live,
saith the LORD
thou shalt surely clothe thee with them all, as with an ornament,
and bind them on thee,
as a bride doeth.
19 **For thy waste and thy desolate places, and the land of thy destruction,** shall even now be too narrow by reason of the inhabitants,
and they that swallowed thee up shall be far away.
20 **The children which thou shalt have,** {after thou hast lost the other}, shall say again in thine ears,
The place is too strait for me:
give place to me
that I may dwell.
21 **Then** shalt thou say in thine heart,
Who hath begotten me these,
seeing I have lost my children,
and am desolate, a captive,
and removing to and fro?
and who hath brought up these?
Behold,
I was left alone;
these, where had they been?
22 **Thus** saith the Lord GOD,
Behold,
I will lift up mine hand to the Gentiles,
and set up my standard to the people:
and they shall bring thy sons in their arms,
and thy daughters shall be carried upon their shoulders.
23 **And kings** shall be thy nursing fathers, and their queens thy nursing mothers:
they shall bow down to thee with their face toward the earth,
and lick up the dust of thy feet;
and thou shalt know
that I am the LORD:
for they shall not be ashamed that wait for me.
24 **Shall the prey** be taken from the mighty,

or the lawful captive delivered?
25 **But thus** saith the LORD,
Even the captives of the mighty shall be taken away,
and the prey of the terrible shall be delivered:
for I will contend with him that contendeth with thee,
and I will save thy children.
26 **And I** will feed them that oppress thee with their own flesh;
and they shall be drunken with their own blood, as with sweet wine:
and all flesh shall know
that I the LORD am thy Saviour and thy Redeemer, the mighty One of Jacob.

50 **Thus** saith the LORD,
Where is the bill of your mother's divorcement,
whom I have put away?
or which of my creditors is it
to whom I have sold you?
Behold,
for your iniquities have ye sold yourselves,
and for your transgressions is your mother put away.
2 **Wherefore,** {when I came}, was there no man?
when I called,
was there none to answer?
Is my hand shortened at all,
that it cannot redeem?
or have I no power to deliver?
behold,
at my rebuke I dry up the sea,
I make the rivers a wilderness:
their fish stinketh,
because there is no water,
and dieth for thirst.
3 **I** clothe the heavens with blackness,
and I make sackcloth their covering.
4 **The Lord GOD** hath given me the tongue of the learned,
that I should know
how to speak a word in season to him that is weary:
he wakeneth morning by morning,
he wakeneth mine ear to hear as the learned.
5 **The Lord GOD** hath opened mine ear,
and I was not rebellious,
neither turned away back.
6 **I** gave my back to the smiters, and my cheeks to them that plucked off the hair:
I hid not my face from shame and spitting.
7 **For the LORD God** will help me;
therefore shall I not be confounded:
therefore have I set my face like a flint,
and I know
that I shall not be ashamed.
8 **He** is near that justifieth me;
who will contend with me?
let us stand together:
who is mine adversary?
let him come near to me.
9 **Behold,**
the Lord GOD will help me;
who is he that shall condemn me?
lo,
they all shall wax old as a garment;
the moth shall eat them up.
10 **Who** is among you that feareth the LORD,
that obeyeth the voice of his servant,
that walketh in darkness,
and hath no light?
let him trust in the name of the LORD,
and stay upon his God.
11 **Behold,** all ye that kindle a fire, that compass yourselves about with sparks:
walk in the light of your fire, and in the sparks that ye have kindled.
This shall ye have of mine hand;
ye shall lie down in sorrow.

51 **Hearken** to me, ye that follow after righteousness, ye that seek the LORD:
look unto the rock whence ye are hewn, and to the hole of the pit whence ye are digged.
2 **Look** unto Abraham your father, and unto Sarah that bare you:
for I called him alone,
and blessed him,
and increased him.
3 **For the LORD** shall comfort Zion:
he will comfort all her waste places;
and he will make her wilderness like Eden, and her desert like the garden of the LORD;
joy and gladness shall be found therein, thanksgiving, and the voice of melody.
4 **Hearken** unto me, my people;
and give ear unto me, O my nation:
for a law shall proceed from me,
and I will make my judgment to rest for a light of the people.
5 **My righteousness** is near;
my salvation is gone forth,
and mine arms shall judge the people;
the isles shall wait upon me,
and on mine arm shall they trust.
6 **Lift up** your eyes to the heavens,
and look upon the earth beneath:
for the heavens shall vanish away like smoke,
and the earth shall wax old like a garment,
and they that dwell therein shall die in like manner:
but my salvation shall be for ever,
and my righteousness shall not be abolished.
7 **Hearken** unto me, ye that know righteousness, the people in whose heart is my law;
fear ye not the reproach of men,
neither be ye afraid of their revilings.
8 **For the moth** shall eat them up like a garment,
and the worm shall eat them like wool:
but my righteousness shall be for ever, and my salvation from generation to generation.
9 **Awake,**
awake,
put on strength, O arm of the LORD;
awake, as in the ancient days, in the generations of old.
Art thou not it that hath cut Rahab, and wounded the dragon?
10 **Art thou not** it which hath dried the sea, the waters of the great deep;
that hath made the depths of the sea a way
for the ransomed to pass over?
11 **Therefore the redeemed of the LORD** shall return,
and come with singing unto Zion;
and everlasting joy shall be upon their head:
they shall obtain gladness and joy;
and sorrow and mourning shall flee away.
12 **I, even I,** am he that comforteth you:
who art thou,

that thou shouldest be afraid of a man that shall die, and of the son of man which shall be made as grass;
13 **And** forgettest the LORD thy maker,
that hath stretched forth the heavens,
and laid the foundations of the earth;
and hast feared continually every day because of the fury of the oppressor,
as if he were ready to destroy?
and where is the fury of the oppressor?
14 **The captive exile** hasteneth
that he may be loosed,
and that he should not die in the pit,
nor that his bread should fail.
15 **But I** am the LORD thy God,
that divided the sea,
whose waves roared:
The LORD of hosts is his name.
16 **And I** have put my words in thy mouth,
and I have covered thee in the shadow of mine hand,
that I may plant the heavens,
and lay the foundations of the earth,
and say unto Zion,
Thou art my people.
17 **Awake,**
awake,
stand up, O Jerusalem,
which hast drunk at the hand of the LORD the cup of his fury;
thou hast drunken the dregs of the cup of trembling,
and wrung them out.
18 **There** is none to guide her among all the sons whom she hath brought forth;
neither is there any that taketh her by the hand of all the sons that she hath brought up.
19 **These two things** are come unto thee;
who shall be sorry for thee?
desolation, and destruction, and the famine, and the sword:
by whom shall I comfort thee?
20 **Thy sons** have fainted,
they lie at the head of all the streets, as a wild bull in a net:
they are full of the fury of the LORD, the rebuke of thy God.
21 **Therefore hear** now this, thou afflicted, and drunken, but not with wine:
22 **Thus** saith thy Lord the LORD, and thy God that pleadeth the cause of his people,
Behold,
I have taken out of thine hand the cup of trembling, even the dregs of the cup of my fury;
thou shalt no more drink it again:
23 **But I** will put it into the hand of them that afflict thee;
which have said to thy soul,
Bow down,
that we may go over:
and thou hast laid thy body as the ground, and as the street, to them that went over.

52

Awake, awake;
put on thy strength, O Zion;
put on thy beautiful garments, O Jerusalem, the holy city:
for henceforth there shall no more come into thee the uncircumcised and the unclean.
2 **Shake** thyself from the dust; arise,
and sit down, O Jerusalem:
loose thyself from the bands of thy neck, O captive daughter of Zion.
3 **For thus** saith the LORD,
Ye have sold yourselves for nought;
and ye shall be redeemed without money.
4 **For thus** saith the Lord GOD,
My people went down aforetime into Egypt
to sojourn there;
and the Assyrian oppressed them without cause.
5 **Now therefore, what** have I here, saith the LORD,
that my people is taken away for nought?
they that rule over them make them to howl,
saith the LORD;
and my name continually every day is blasphemed.
6 **Therefore my people** shall know my name:
therefore they shall know in that day
that I am he that doth speak:
behold,
it is I.
7 **How beautiful upon the mountains** are the feet of him that bringeth good tidings,
that publisheth peace;
that bringeth good tidings of good,
that publisheth salvation;
that saith unto Zion,
Thy God reigneth!
8 **Thy watchmen** shall lift up the voice;
with the voice together shall they sing:
for they shall see eye to eye,
when the LORD shall bring again Zion.
9 **Break forth** into joy,
sing together, ye waste places of Jerusalem:
for the LORD hath comforted his people,
he hath redeemed Jerusalem.
10 **The LORD** hath made bare his holy arm in the eyes of all the nations;
and all the ends of the earth shall see the salvation of our God.
11 **Depart ye,**
depart ye,
go ye out from thence,
touch no unclean thing;
go ye out of the midst of her;
be ye clean,
that bear the vessels of the LORD.
12 **For ye** shall not go out with haste,
nor go by flight:
for the LORD will go before you;
and the God of Israel will be your reward.
13 **Behold,**
my servant shall deal prudently,
he shall be exalted
and extolled,
and be very high.
14 **As many** were astonied at thee;
his visage was so marred more than any man, and his form more than the sons of men:
15 **So** shall he sprinkle many nations;
the kings shall shut their mouths at him:
for that which had not been told them shall they see;
and that which they had not heard shall they consider.

53

Who hath believed our report?
and to whom is the arm of the LORD revealed?
2 **For he** shall grow up before him as a tender plant, and as a root out of a dry ground:
he hath no form nor comeliness;

and when we shall see him,
there is no beauty
that we should desire him.

3 **He** is despised and rejected of men; a man of sorrows,
and acquainted with grief:
and we hid as it were our faces from him;
he was despised,
and we esteemed him not.

4 **Surely he** hath borne our griefs,
and carried our sorrows:
yet we did esteem him stricken,
smitten of God,
and afflicted.

5 **But he** was wounded for our transgressions,
he was bruised for our iniquities:
the chastisement of our peace was upon him;
and with his stripes we are healed.

6 **All we like sheep** have gone astray;
we have turned every one to his own way;
and the LORD hath laid on him the iniquity of us all.

7 **He** was oppressed,
and he was afflicted,
yet he opened not his mouth:
he is brought as a lamb to the slaughter, and as a sheep before her shearers is dumb,
so he openeth not his mouth.

8 **He** was taken from prison and from judgment:
and who shall declare his generation?
for he was cut off out of the land of the living:
for the transgression of my people was he stricken.

9 **And he** made his grave with the wicked, and with the rich in his death;
because he had done no violence,
neither was any deceit in his mouth.

10 **Yet it pleased the LORD** to bruise him;
he hath put him to grief:
when thou shalt make his soul an offering for sin,
he shall see his seed,
he shall prolong his days,
and the pleasure of the LORD shall prosper in his hand.

11 **He** shall see of the travail of his soul,
and shall be satisfied:
by his knowledge shall my righteous servant justify many;
for he shall bear their iniquities.

12 **Therefore** will I divide him a portion with the great,
and he shall divide the spoil with the strong;
because he hath poured out his soul unto death:
and he was numbered with the transgressors;
and he bare the sin of many,
and made intercession for the transgressors.

54

Sing, O barren, thou that didst not bear;
break forth into singing,
and cry aloud, thou that didst not travail with child:
for more are the children of the desolate than the children of the married wife,
saith the LORD.

2 **Enlarge** the place of thy tent,
and let them stretch forth the curtains of thine habitations:
spare not,
lengthen thy cords,
and strengthen thy stakes;

3 **For thou** shalt break forth on the right hand and on the left;
and thy seed shall inherit the Gentiles,
and make the desolate cities to be inhabited.

4 **Fear not;**
for thou shalt not be ashamed:
neither be thou confounded;
for thou shalt not be put to shame:
for thou shalt forget the shame of thy youth,
and shalt not remember the reproach of thy widowhood any more.

5 **For thy Maker** is thine husband;
the LORD of hosts is his name; and thy Redeemer the Holy One of Israel;
The God of the whole earth shall he be called.

6 **For the LORD** hath called thee as a woman forsaken and grieved in spirit, and a wife of youth,
when thou wast refused,
saith thy God.

7 **For a small moment** have I forsaken thee;
but with great mercies will I gather thee.

8 **In a little wrath** I hid my face from thee for a moment;
but with everlasting kindness will I have mercy on thee,
saith the LORD thy Redeemer.

9 **For this** is as the waters of Noah unto me:
for as I have sworn
that the waters of Noah should no more go over the earth;
so have I sworn
that I would not be wroth with thee,
nor rebuke thee.

10 **For the mountains** shall depart,
and the hills be removed;
but my kindness shall not depart from thee,
neither shall the covenant of my peace be removed,
saith the LORD that hath mercy on thee.

11 **O thou afflicted, {tossed with tempest}, {and not comforted}, behold,**
I will lay thy stones with fair colours,
and lay thy foundations with sapphires.

12 **And I** will make thy windows of agates, and thy gates of carbuncles, and all thy borders of pleasant stones.

13 **And all thy children** shall be taught of the LORD;
and great shall be the peace of thy children.

14 **In righteousness** shalt thou be established:
thou shalt be far from oppression; {for thou shalt not fear}: and from terror; {for it shall not come near thee}.

15 **Behold,**
they shall surely gather together, but not by me:
whosoever shall gather together against thee shall fall for thy sake.

16 **Behold,**
I have created the smith that bloweth the coals in the fire, and that bringeth forth an instrument for his work;
and I have created the waster to destroy.

17 **No weapon that is formed against thee** shall prosper;

and every tongue that shall rise against thee in judgment thou shalt condemn.
This is the heritage of the servants of the LORD,
and their righteousness is of me,
saith the LORD.

55 Ho,
every one that thirsteth, come ye to the waters,
and he that hath no money; come ye,
buy,
and eat;
yea,
come,
buy wine and milk without money and without price.

2 **Wherefore** do ye spend money for that which is not bread?
and your labour for that which satisfieth not?
hearken diligently unto me,
and eat ye that which is good,
and let your soul delight itself in fatness.

3 **Incline** your ear,
and come unto me:
hear,
and your soul shall live;
and I will make an everlasting covenant with you, even the sure mercies of David.

4 **Behold,**
I have given him for a witness to the people, a leader and commander to the people.

5 **Behold,**
thou shalt call a nation that thou knowest not,
and nations that knew not thee shall run unto thee because of the LORD thy God, and for the Holy One of Israel;
for he hath glorified thee.

6 **Seek ye** the LORD
while he may be found,
call ye upon him
while he is near:

7 **Let the wicked** forsake his way, and the unrighteous man his thoughts:
and let him return unto the LORD, {and he will have mercy upon him}; and to our God, {for he will abundantly pardon}.

8 **For my thoughts** are not your thoughts,
neither are your ways my ways,
saith the LORD.

9 **For as the heavens** are higher than the earth,
so are my ways higher than your ways, and my thoughts than your thoughts.

10 **For as the rain** cometh down, and the snow from heaven,
and returneth not thither,
but watereth the earth,
and maketh it bring forth and bud,
that it may give seed to the sower, and bread to the eater:

11 **So** shall my word be that goeth forth out of my mouth:
it shall not return unto me void,
but it shall accomplish that which I please,
and it shall prosper in the thing whereto I sent it.

12 **For ye** shall go out with joy,
and be led forth with peace:
the mountains and the hills shall break forth before you into singing,
and all the trees of the field shall clap their hands.

13 **Instead of the thorn** shall come up the fir tree,
and instead of the brier shall come up the myrtle tree:
and it shall be to the LORD for a name, for an everlasting sign that shall not be cut off.

56 **Thus** saith the LORD,
Keep ye judgment,
and do justice:
for my salvation is near to come,
and my righteousness to be revealed.

2 **Blessed** is the man that doeth this, and the son of man that layeth hold on it;
that keepeth the sabbath from polluting it,
and keepeth his hand from doing any evil.

3 **Neither let the son of the stranger,** {that hath joined himself to the LORD}, speak,
saying,
The LORD hath utterly separated me from his people:
neither let the eunuch say,
Behold,
I am a dry tree.

4 **For thus** saith the LORD unto the eunuchs that keep my sabbaths,
and choose the things that please me,
and take hold of my covenant;

5 **Even unto them** will I give in mine house and within my walls a place and a name better than of sons and of daughters:
I will give them an everlasting name,
that shall not be cut off.

6 **Also the sons of the stranger, {that join themselves to the LORD}, {to serve him}, {and to love the name of the LORD}, {to be his servants}, every one that keepeth the sabbath from polluting it, and taketh hold of my covenant;**

7 Even them will I bring to my holy mountain,
and make them joyful in my house of prayer:
their burnt offerings and their sacrifices shall be accepted upon mine altar;
for mine house shall be called an house of prayer for all people.

8 **The Lord GOD**, {which gathereth the outcasts of Israel} saith,
Yet will I gather others to him, beside those that are gathered unto him.

9 **All ye beasts of the field,** come to devour, yea, all ye beasts in the forest.

10 **His watchmen** are blind:
they are all ignorant,
they are all dumb dogs,
they cannot bark;
sleeping,
lying down,
loving to slumber.

11 **Yea, they** are greedy dogs which can never have enough,
and they are shepherds that cannot understand:
they all look to their own way, every one for his gain, from his quarter.

12 **Come ye,**
say they,
I will fetch wine,
and we will fill ourselves with strong drink;
and to morrow shall be as this day, and much more abundant.

57 **The righteous** perisheth,
and no man layeth it to heart:
and merciful men are taken away,

none considering
that the righteous is taken away from the evil to come.
2 **He** shall enter into peace:
they shall rest in their beds,
each one walking in his uprightness.
3 **But draw near** hither, ye sons of the sorceress, the seed of the adulterer and the whore.
4 **Against whom** do ye sport yourselves?
against whom make ye a wide mouth,
and draw out the tongue?
are ye not children of transgression, a seed of falsehood.
5 Enflaming yourselves with idols under every green tree,
slaying the children in the valleys under the clifts of the rocks?
6 **Among the smooth stones of the stream** is thy portion;
they, they are thy lot:
even to them hast thou poured a drink offering,
thou hast offered a meat offering.
Should I receive comfort in these?
7 **Upon a lofty and high mountain** hast thou set thy bed:
even thither wentest thou up
to offer sacrifice.
8 **Behind the doors also and the posts** hast thou set up thy remembrance:
for thou hast discovered thyself to another than me,
and art gone up;
thou hast enlarged thy bed,
and made thee a covenant with them;
thou lovedst their bed
where thou sawest it.
9 **And thou** wentest to the king with ointment,
and didst increase thy perfumes,
and didst send thy messengers far off,
and didst debase thyself even unto hell.
10 **Thou** art wearied in the greatness of thy way;
yet saidst thou not,
There is no hope:
thou hast found the life of thine hand;
therefore thou wast not grieved.
11 **And of whom** hast thou been afraid or feared,
that thou hast lied,
and hast not remembered me,
nor laid it to thy heart?
have not I held my peace even of old,
and thou fearest me not?
12 **I** will declare thy righteousness, and thy works;
for they shall not profit thee.
13 **When thou** criest,
let thy companies deliver thee;
but the wind shall carry them all away;
vanity shall take them:
but he that putteth his trust in me shall possess the land,
and shall inherit my holy mountain;
14 **And** shall say,
Cast ye up,
cast ye up,
prepare the way,
take up the stumblingblock out of the way of my people.
15 **For thus** saith the high and lofty One that inhabiteth eternity,
whose name is Holy;
I dwell in the high and holy place, with him also that is of a contrite and humble spirit,
to revive the spirit of the humble,
and to revive the heart of the contrite ones.
16 **For I** will not contend for ever,
neither will I be always wroth:
for the spirit should fail before me, and the souls which I have made.
17 **For the iniquity of his covetousness** was I wroth,
and smote him:
I hid me,
and was wroth,
and he went on frowardly in the way of his heart.
18 **I** have seen his ways,
and will heal him:
I will lead him also,
and restore comforts unto him and to his mourners.
19 **I** create the fruit of the lips;
Peace, peace to him that is far off, and to him that is near, saith the LORD;
and I will heal him.
20 **But the wicked** are like the troubled sea,
when it cannot rest,
whose waters cast up mire and dirt.
21 **There** is no peace, {saith my God}, to the wicked.

58

Cry aloud,
spare not,
lift up thy voice like a trumpet,
and shew my people their transgression, and the house of Jacob their sins.
2 **Yet they** seek me daily,
and delight to know my ways, as a nation that did righteousness,
and forsook not the ordinance of their God:
they ask of me the ordinances of justice;
they take delight in approaching to God.
3 **Wherefore have we** fasted,
say they,
and thou seest not?
wherefore have we afflicted our soul,
and thou takest no knowledge?
Behold,
in the day of your fast ye find pleasure,
and exact all your labours.
4 **Behold,**
ye fast for strife and debate,
and to smite with the fist of wickedness:
ye shall not fast
as ye do this day,
to make your voice to be heard on high.
5 **Is it** such a fast that I have chosen?
a day for a man to afflict his soul?
is it to bow down his head as a bulrush,
and to spread sackcloth and ashes under him?
wilt thou call this a fast, and an acceptable day to the LORD?
6 **Is not this** the fast that I have chosen?
to loose the bands of wickedness,
to undo the heavy burdens,
and to let the oppressed go free,
and that ye break every yoke?
7 **Is it not** to deal thy bread to the hungry,
and that thou bring the poor that are cast out to thy house?
when thou seest the naked,
that thou cover him;
and that thou hide not thyself from thine own flesh?
8 **Then** shall thy light break forth as the morning,
and thine health shall spring forth speedily:

and thy righteousness shall go
before thee;
the glory of the LORD shall be thy
reward.
9 **Then** shalt thou call,
and the LORD shall answer;
thou shalt cry,
and he shall say,
Here I am.
If thou take away from the midst of
thee the yoke, the putting forth of
the finger,
and speaking vanity;
10 **And if thou** draw out thy soul to
the hungry,
and satisfy the afflicted soul;
then shall thy light rise in
obscurity,
and thy darkness be as the noon
day:
11 **And the LORD** shall guide thee
continually,
and satisfy thy soul in drought,
and make fat thy bones:
and thou shalt be like a watered
garden, and like a spring of water,
whose waters fail not.
12 **And they that shall be of thee**
shall build the old waste places:
thou shalt raise up the foundations
of many generations;
and thou shalt be called,
The repairer of the breach,
The restorer of paths to dwell in.
13 **If thou** turn away thy foot from
the sabbath,
from doing thy pleasure on my holy
day;
and call the sabbath a delight, the
holy of the LORD, honourable;
and shalt honour him,
not doing thine own ways,
nor finding thine own pleasure,
nor speaking thine own words:
14 **Then** shalt thou delight thyself in
the LORD;
and I will cause thee to ride upon
the high places of the earth,
and feed thee with the heritage of
Jacob thy father:
for the mouth of the LORD hath
spoken it.

59

Behold, the LORD's
hand is not shortened,
that it cannot save;
neither his ear heavy,
that it cannot hear:
2 **But your iniquities** have
separated between you and your
God,
and your sins have hid his face
from you,
that he will not hear.
3 **For your hands** are defiled with
blood, and your fingers with
iniquity;
your lips have spoken lies,
your tongue hath muttered
perverseness.
4 **None** calleth for justice,
nor any pleadeth for truth:
they trust in vanity,
and speak lies;
they conceive mischief,
and bring forth iniquity.
5 **They** hatch cockatrice' eggs,
and weave the spider's web:
he that eateth of their eggs dieth,
and that which is crushed
breaketh out into a viper.
6 **Their webs** shall not become
garments,
neither shall they cover themselves
with their works:
their works are works of iniquity,
and the act of violence is in their
hands.
7 **Their feet** run to evil,
and they make haste to shed
innocent blood:
their thoughts are thoughts of
iniquity;
wasting and destruction are in
their paths.
8 **The way of peace** they know not;
and there is no judgment in their
goings:
they have made them crooked
paths:
whosoever goeth therein shall not
know peace.
9 **Therefore** is judgment far from us,
neither doth justice overtake us:
we wait for light, {but behold
obscurity}; for brightness, {but we
walk in darkness}.
10 **We** grope for the wall like the
blind,
and we grope as if we had no eyes:
we stumble at noon day as in the
night;
we are in desolate places as dead
men.
11 **We** roar all like bears,
and mourn sore like doves:
we look for judgment, {but there is
none}; for salvation, {but it is far
off from us}.
12 **For our transgressions** are
multiplied before thee,
and our sins testify against us:
for our transgressions are with us;
and as for our iniquities, we know
them;
13 **In** transgressing and lying against
the LORD,
and departing away from our God,
speaking oppression and revolt,
conceiving and uttering from the
heart words of falsehood.
14 **And judgment** is turned away
backward,
and justice standeth afar off:
for truth is fallen in the street,
and equity cannot enter.
15 **Yea, truth** faileth;
and he that departeth from evil
maketh himself a prey:
and the LORD saw it,
and it displeased him that there
was no judgment.
16 **And he saw** that there was no
man,
and wondered that there was no
intercessor:
therefore his arm brought
salvation unto him;
and his righteousness, it sustained
him.
17 **For he** put on righteousness as a
breastplate, and an helmet of
salvation upon his head;
and he put on the garments of
vengeance for clothing,
and was clad with zeal as a cloak.
18 **According to their deeds,**
accordingly he will repay, fury to
his adversaries, recompence to his
enemies;
to the islands he will repay
recompence.
19 **So** shall they fear the name of the
LORD from the west, and his
glory from the rising of the sun.
When the enemy shall come in like
a flood,
the Spirit of the LORD shall lift up
a standard against him.
20 **And the Redeemer** shall come to
Zion, and unto them that turn
from transgression in Jacob,
saith the LORD.
21 **As for me,** this is my covenant
with them,
saith the LORD;
**My spirit that is upon thee, and
my words which I have put in
thy mouth,** shall not depart out

of thy mouth, nor out of the mouth of thy seed, nor out of the mouth of thy seed's seed, {saith the LORD}, from henceforth and for ever.

60

Arise, shine;
for thy light is come,
and the glory of the LORD is risen upon thee.
2 **For, {behold}, the darkness** shall cover the earth, and gross darkness the people:
but the LORD shall arise upon thee,
and his glory shall be seen upon thee.
3 **And the Gentiles** shall come to thy light, and kings to the brightness of thy rising.
4 **Lift up** thine eyes round about,
and see:
all they gather themselves together, they come to thee:
thy sons shall come from far,
and thy daughters shall be nursed at thy side.
5 **Then thou** shalt see,
and flow together,
and thine heart shall fear,
and be enlarged;
because the abundance of the sea shall be converted unto thee,
the forces of the Gentiles shall come unto thee.
6 **The multitude of camels** shall cover thee, the dromedaries of Midian and Ephah;
all they from Sheba shall come:
they shall bring gold and incense;
and they shall shew forth the praises of the LORD.
7 **All the flocks of Kedar** shall be gathered together unto thee,
the rams of Nebaioth shall minister unto thee:
they shall come up with acceptance on mine altar,
and I will glorify the house of my glory.
8 **Who** are these that fly as a cloud, and as the doves to their windows?
9 **Surely the isles** shall wait for me, and the ships of Tarshish first,
to bring thy sons from far, their silver and their gold with them, unto the name of the LORD thy God, and to the Holy One of Israel,
because he hath glorified thee.
10 **And the sons of strangers** shall build up thy walls,
and their kings shall minister unto thee:
for in my wrath I smote thee,
but in my favour have I had mercy on thee.
11 **Therefore thy gates** shall be open continually;
they shall not be shut day nor night;
that men may bring unto thee the forces of the Gentiles,
and that their kings may be brought.
12 **For the nation and kingdom that will not serve thee** shall perish; yea,
those nations shall be utterly wasted.
13 **The glory of Lebanon** shall come unto thee, the fir tree, the pine tree, and the box together,
to beautify the place of my sanctuary;
and I will make the place of my feet glorious.
14 **The sons also of them that afflicted thee** shall come bending unto thee;
and all they that despised thee shall bow themselves down at the soles of thy feet;
and they shall call thee;
The city of the LORD, The Zion of the Holy One of Israel.
15 **Whereas thou** has been forsaken and hated,
so that no man went through thee,
I will make thee an eternal excellency, a joy of many generations.
16 **Thou** shalt also suck the milk of the Gentiles,
and shalt suck the breast of kings:
and thou shalt know
that I the LORD am thy Saviour and thy Redeemer, the mighty One of Jacob.
17 **For brass** I will bring gold,
and for iron I will bring silver, and for wood brass, and for stones iron:
I will also make thy officers peace, and thine exactors righteousness.
18 **Violence** shall no more be heard in thy land, wasting nor destruction within thy borders;
but thou shalt call thy walls Salvation, and thy gates Praise.
19 **The sun** shall be no more thy light by day;
neither for brightness shall the moon give light unto thee:
but the LORD shall be unto thee an everlasting light, and thy God thy glory.
20 **Thy sun** shall no more go down;
neither shall thy moon withdraw itself:
for the LORD shall be thine everlasting light,
and the days of thy mourning shall be ended.
21 **Thy people** also shall be all righteous:
they shall inherit the land for ever, the branch of my planting, the work of my hands,
that I may be glorified.
22 **A little one** shall become a thousand, and a small one a strong nation:
I the LORD will hasten it in his time.

61

The Spirit of the Lord GOD is upon me;
because the LORD hath anointed me to preach good tidings unto the meek;
he hath sent me to bind up the brokenhearted,
to proclaim liberty to the captives, and the opening of the prison to them that are bound;
2 To proclaim the acceptable year of the LORD, and the day of vengeance of our God;
to comfort all that mourn;
3 To appoint unto them that mourn in Zion,
to give unto them beauty for ashes, the oil of joy for mourning, the garment of praise for the spirit of heaviness;
that they might be called trees of righteousness, the planting of the LORD,
that he might be glorified.
4 **And they** shall build the old wastes,
they shall raise up the former desolations,
and they shall repair the waste cities, the desolations of many generations.
5 **And strangers** shall stand and feed your flocks,

and the sons of the alien shall be your lowmen and your vinedressers.
6 **But ye** shall be named the Priests of the LORD:
men shall call you the Ministers of our God:
ye shall eat the riches of the Gentiles,
and in their glory shall ye boast yourselves.
7 **For your shame** ye shall have double;
and for confusion they shall rejoice in their portion:
therefore in their land they shall possess the double:
everlasting joy shall be unto them.
8 **For I the LORD** love judgment,
I hate robbery for burnt offering;
and I will direct their work in truth,
and I will make an everlasting covenant with them.
9 **And their seed** shall be known among the Gentiles, and their offspring among the people:
all that see them shall acknowledge them,
that they are the seed which the LORD hath blessed.
10 **I** will greatly rejoice in the LORD,
my soul shall be joyful in my God;
for he hath clothed me with the garments of salvation,
he hath covered me with the robe of righteousness, as a bridegroom decketh himself with ornaments, and as a bride adorneth herself with her jewels.
11 **For as the earth** bringeth forth her bud,
and as the garden causeth the things that are sown in it to spring forth;
so the Lord GOD will cause righteousness and praise to spring forth before all the nations.

62 **For Zion's sake** will I not hold my peace,
and for Jerusalem's sake I will not rest,
until the righteousness thereof go forth as brightness, and the salvation thereof as a lamp that burneth.
2 **And the Gentiles** shall see thy righteousness, and all kings thy glory:
and thou shalt be called by a new name,
which the mouth of the LORD shall name.
3 **Thou** shalt also be a crown of glory in the hand of the LORD, and a royal diadem in the hand of thy God.
4 **Thou** shalt no more be termed Forsaken;
neither shall thy land any more be termed Desolate:
but thou shalt be called Hephzibah, and thy land Beulah:
for the LORD delighteth in thee,
and thy land shall be married.
5 **For as a young man** marrieth a virgin,
so shall thy sons marry thee:
and as the bridegroom rejoiceth over the bride,
so shall thy God rejoice over thee.
6 **I** have set watchmen upon thy walls, O Jerusalem,
which shall never hold their peace day nor night:
ye that make mention of the LORD, keep not silence,
7 **And give** him no rest,
till he establish,
and till he make Jerusalem a praise in the earth.
8 **The LORD** hath sworn by his right hand, and by the arm of his strength,
Surely I will no more give thy corn to be meat for thine enemies;
and the sons of the stranger shall not drink thy wine,
for the which thou hast laboured:
9 **But they that have gathered it** shall eat it,
and praise the LORD;
and they that have brought it together shall drink it in the courts of my holiness.
10 **Go through,**
go through the gates;
prepare ye the way of the people;
cast up,
cast up the highway;
gather out the stones;
lift up a standard for the people.
11 **Behold,**
the LORD hath proclaimed unto the end of the world,
Say ye to the daughter of Zion,
Behold,
thy salvation cometh;
behold,
his reward is with him, and his work before him.
12 **And they** shall call them,
The holy people,
The redeemed of the LORD:
and thou shalt be called,
Sought out,
A city not forsaken.

63 **Who** is this that cometh from Edom, with dyed garments from Bozrah?
this that is glorious in his apparel,
travelling in the greatness of his strength?
I that speak in righteousness,
mighty to save.
2 **Wherefore** art thou red in thine apparel, and thy garments like him that treadeth in the winefat?
3 **I** have trodden the winepress alone;
and of the people there was none with me:
for I will tread them in mine anger,
and trample them in my fury;
and their blood shall be sprinkled upon my garments,
and I will stain all my raiment.
4 **For the day of vengeance** is in mine heart,
and the year of my redeemed is come.
5 **And I** looked,
and there was none to help;
and I wondered
that there was none to uphold:
therefore mine own arm brought salvation unto me;
and my fury, it upheld me.
6 **And I** will tread down the people in mine anger,
and make them drunk in my fury,
and I will bring down their strength to the earth.
7 **I** will mention the lovingkindnesses of the LORD, and the praises of the LORD, according to all that the LORD hath bestowed on us, and the great goodness toward the house of Israel,
which he hath bestowed on them according to his mercies, and according to the multitude of his lovingkindnesses.
8 **For he** said,
Surely they are my people, children that will not lie:
so he was their Saviour.

9 **In all their affliction** he was afflicted,
and the angel of his presence saved them:
in his love and in his pity he redeemed them;
and he bare them,
and carried them all the days of old.
10 **But they** rebelled,
and vexed his holy Spirit:
therefore he was turned to be their enemy,
and he fought against them.
11 **Then he** remembered the days of old, Moses, and his people,
saying,
Where is he that brought them up out of the sea with the shepherd of his flock?
where is he that put his holy Spirit within him?
12 **That** led them by the right hand of Moses with his glorious arm,
dividing the water before them,
to make himself an everlasting name?
13 **That** led them through the deep, as an horse in the wilderness,
that they should not stumble?
14 **As a beast** goeth down into the valley,
the Spirit of the LORD caused him to rest:
so didst thou lead thy people,
to make thyself a glorious name.
15 **Look down** from heaven,
and behold from the habitation of thy holiness and of thy glory:
where is thy zeal and thy strength, the sounding of thy bowels and of thy mercies toward me?
are they restrained?
16 **Doubtless thou** art our father,
though Abraham be ignorant of us,
and Israel acknowledge us not:
thou, O LORD, art our father, our redeemer;
thy name is from everlasting.
17 **O LORD, why** hast thou made us to err from thy ways,
and hardened our heart from thy fear?
Return for thy servants' sake, the tribes of thine inheritance.
18 **The people of thy holiness** have possessed it but a little while:
our adversaries have trodden down thy sanctuary.
19 **We** are thine:
thou never barest rule over them;
they were not called by thy name.

64 ∞ **Oh that thou** wouldest rend the heavens,
that thou wouldest come down,
that the mountains might flow down at thy presence,
2 **As when the melting fire** burneth,
the fire causeth the waters to boil,
to make thy name known to thine adversaries,
that the nations may tremble at thy presence!
3 **When thou** didst terrible things which we looked not for,
thou camest down,
the mountains flowed down at thy presence.
4 **For since the beginning of the world** men have not heard,
nor perceived by the ear,
neither hath the eye seen, O God, beside thee,
what he hath prepared for him that waiteth for him.
5 **Thou** meetest him that rejoiceth and worketh righteousness, those that remember thee in thy ways:
behold,
thou art wroth;
for we have sinned:
in those is continuance,
and we shall be saved.
6 **But we** are all as an unclean thing,
and all our righteousnesses are as filthy rags;
and we all do fade as a leaf;
and our iniquities, like the wind, have taken us away.
7 **And there** is none that calleth upon thy name,
that stirreth up himself
to take hold of thee:
for thou hast hid thy face from us,
and hast consumed us, because of our iniquities.
8 **But now, O LORD, thou** art our father;
we are the clay, and thou our potter;
and we all are the work of thy hand.
9 **Be not** wroth very sore, O LORD,
neither remember iniquity for ever:
behold,
see,
we beseech thee,
we are all thy people.
10 **Thy holy cities** are a wilderness,
Zion is a wilderness, Jerusalem a desolation.
11 **Our holy and our beautiful house,** {where our fathers praised thee}, is burned up with fire:
and all our pleasant things are laid waste.
12 **Wilt thou** refrain thyself for these things, O LORD?
wilt thou hold thy peace,
and afflict us very sore?

65 I am sought of them that asked not for me;
I am found of them that sought me not:
I said,
Behold me,
behold me, unto a nation that was not called by my name.
2 **I** have spread out my hands all the day unto a rebellious people,
which walketh in a way that was not good, after their own thoughts;
3 A people that provoketh me to anger continually to my face;
that sacrificeth in gardens,
and burneth incense upon altars of brick;
4 **Which** remain among the graves,
and lodge in the monuments,
which eat swine's flesh,
and broth of abominable things is in their vessels;
5 **Which** say,
Stand by thyself,
come not near to me;
for I am holier than thou.
These are a smoke in my nose, a fire that burneth all the day.
6 **Behold,**
it is written before me:
I will not keep silence,
but will recompense, even recompense into their bosom,
7 Your iniquities, and the iniquities of your fathers together,
saith the LORD,
which have burned incense upon the mountains,
and blasphemed me upon the hills:
therefore will I measure their former work into their bosom.
8 **Thus** saith the LORD,
As the new wine is found in the cluster,
and one saith,

Destroy it not;
for a blessing is in it:
so will I do for my servants' sakes,
that I may not destroy them all.

9 **And I** will bring forth a seed out of Jacob, and out of Judah an inheritor of my mountains:
and mine elect shall inherit it,
and my servants shall dwell there.

10 **And Sharon** shall be a fold of flocks, and the valley of Achor a place for the herds to lie down in, for my people that have sought me.

11 **But ye** are they that forsake the LORD, that forget my holy mountain, that prepare a table for that troop, and that furnish the drink offering unto that number.

12 **Therefore** will I number you to the sword,
and ye shall all bow down to the slaughter:
because when I called,
ye did not answer;
when I spake,
ye did not hear;
but did evil before mine eyes,
and did choose that wherein I delighted not.

13 **Therefore thus** saith the Lord GOD,
Behold,
my servants shall eat,
but ye shall be hungry:
behold,
my servants shall drink,
but ye shall be thirsty:
behold,
my servants shall rejoice,
but ye shall be ashamed:
14 **Behold,**
my servants shall sing for joy of heart,
but ye shall cry for sorrow of heart,
and shall howl for vexation of spirit.

15 **And ye** shall leave your name for a curse unto my chosen:
for the Lord GOD shall slay thee,
and call his servants by another name:
16 **That he who blesseth himself in the earth** shall bless himself in the God of truth;
and he that sweareth in the earth shall swear by the God of truth;
because the former troubles are forgotten,
and because they are hid from mine eyes.

17 **For, {behold}, I** create new heavens and a new earth:
and the former shall not be remembered,
nor come into mind.

18 **But** be ye glad
and rejoice for ever in that which I create:
for, {behold}, I create Jerusalem a rejoicing, and her people a joy.

19 **And I** will rejoice in Jerusalem, and joy in my people:
and the voice of weeping shall be no more heard in her, nor the voice of crying.

20 **There** shall be no more thence an infant of days, nor an old man that hath not filled his days:
for the child shall die an hundred years old;
but the sinner {being an hundred years old} shall be accursed.

21 **And they** shall build houses,
and inhabit them;
and they shall plant vineyards,
and eat the fruit of them.

22 **They** shall not build,
and another inhabit;
they shall not plant,
and another eat:
for as the days of a tree are the days of my people,
and mine elect shall long enjoy the work of their hands.

23 **They** shall not labour in vain,
nor bring forth for trouble;
for they are the seed of the blessed of the LORD, and their offspring with them.

24 **And it** shall come to pass,
that before they call,
I will answer;
and while they are yet speaking,
I will hear.

25 **The wolf and the lamb** shall feed together,
and the lion shall eat straw like the bullock:
and dust shall be the serpent's meat.
They shall not hurt {nor destroy} in all my holy mountain,
saith the LORD.

66

Thus saith the LORD,
The heaven is my throne,
and the earth is my footstool:
where is the house that ye build unto me?
and where is the place of my rest?

2 **For all those things** hath mine hand made,
and all those things have been,
saith the LORD:
but to this man will I look, even to him that is poor and of a contrite spirit,
and trembleth at my word.

3 **He that killeth an ox** is as if he slew a man;
he that sacrificeth a lamb, as if he cut off a dog's neck;
he that offereth an oblation, as if he offered swine's blood;
he that burneth incense, as if he blessed an idol.
Yea, they have chosen their own ways,
and their soul delighteth in their abominations.

4 **I** also will choose their delusions,
and will bring their fears upon them;
because when I called,
none did answer;
when I spake,
they did not hear:
but they did evil before mine eyes,
and chose that in which I delighted not.

5 **Hear** the word of the LORD, ye that tremble at his word;
Your brethren that hated you, that cast you out for my name's sake, said,
Let the LORD be glorified:
but he shall appear to your joy,
and they shall be ashamed.

6 A voice of noise from the city,
a voice from the temple,
a voice of the LORD that rendereth recompence to his enemies.

7 **Before she** travailed,
she brought forth;
before her pain came,
she was delivered of a man child.

8 **Who** hath heard such a thing?
who hath seen such things?
Shall the earth be made to bring forth in one day?
or shall a nation be born at once?
for as soon as Zion travailed,
she brought forth her children.

9 **Shall I** bring to the birth,
and not cause to bring forth?
saith the LORD:

shall I cause to bring forth,
and shut the womb?
saith thy God.
10 **Rejoice ye** with Jerusalem,
and be glad with her, all ye that love her:
rejoice for joy with her, all ye that mourn for her:
11 **That ye** may suck,
and be satisfied with the breasts of her consolations;
that ye may milk out,
and be delighted with the abundance of her glory.
12 **For thus** saith the LORD,
Behold,
I will extend peace to her like a river, and the glory of the Gentiles like a flowing stream:
then shall ye suck,
ye shall be borne upon her sides,
and be dandled upon her knees.
13 **As one whom his mother comforteth,** so will I comfort you;
and ye shall be comforted in Jerusalem.
14 **And when ye** see this,
your heart shall rejoice,
and your bones shall flourish like an herb:
and the hand of the LORD shall be known toward his servants, and his indignation toward his enemies.
15 **For, {behold}, the LORD** will come with fire, and with his chariots like a whirlwind,
to render his anger with fury, and his rebuke with flames of fire.
16 **For by fire and by his sword** will the LORD plead with all flesh:
and the slain of the LORD shall be many.
17 **They that sanctify themselves, and purify themselves in the gardens behind one tree in the midst**, {eating swine's flesh, and the abomination, and the mouse}, shall be consumed together,
saith the LORD.
18 **For I** know their works and their thoughts:
it shall come,
that I will gather all nations and tongues;
and they shall come,
and see my glory.
19 **And I** will set a sign among them,
and I will send those that escape of them unto the nations, to Tarshish, Pul, and Lud, {that draw the bow}, to Tubal, and Javan, to the isles afar off, {that have not heard my fame}, {neither have seen my glory};
and they shall declare my glory among the Gentiles.
20 **And they** shall bring all your brethren for an offering unto the LORD out of all nations upon horses, and in chariots, and in litters, and upon mules, and upon swift beasts, to my holy mountain Jerusalem,
saith the LORD,
as the children of Israel bring an offering in a clean vessel into the house of the LORD.
21 **And I** will also take of them for priests and for Levites,
saith the LORD.
22 **For as the new heavens and the new earth**, {which I will make}, shall remain before me,
saith the LORD,
so shall your seed and your name remain.
23 **And it** shall come to pass,
that from one new moon to another, and from one sabbath to another, shall all flesh come to worship before me,
saith the LORD.
24 **And they** shall go forth,
and look upon the carcases of the men that have transgressed against me:
for their worm shall not die,
neither shall their fire be quenched;
and they shall be an abhorring unto all flesh.

Jeremiah

The Book of Jeremiah is a collection of prophecies and teachings attributed to Jeremiah. It begins with Jeremiah's call to be a prophet, during which the Lord, God of Israel, gives him a message to deliver to the people of Judah. This call is on display throughout the book as Jeremiah delivers messages of judgment and hope to the people of Judah.

In terms of judgment, he warns of Jerusalem's impending destruction. He later provides an account of its fall, a grim consequence and reminder of their disobedience to God. Jeremiah also prophesies the Babylonian Captivity, during which many Judeans are forced into exile. While he describes the suffering and hardship of the exiles, he also offers hope for restoration and redemption, including an eventual return to the land of Judah. One of the book's most significant prophecies highlights God's promise to make a new covenant with his people, one that He will write on their hearts rather than on stone tablets. This New Covenant, an essential precursor to the Christian understanding of salvation through faith in Jesus Christ, will bring about a fresh era of peace and prosperity.

The Book of Jeremiah offers a rich tapestry of prophecies, teachings, and historical events. However, the overall tenet of Jeremiah's message is unmistakable: he seeks to awaken the people of Judah to the reality of their dire situation, to help them understand the importance of following God's commands . . . and the consequences of not doing so.

1 **The words of Jeremiah the son of Hilkiah,** of the priests that were in Anathoth in the land of Benjamin:
2 **To whom** the word of the LORD came in the days of Josiah the son of Amon king of Judah, in the thirteenth year of his reign.
3 **It** came also in the days of Jehoiakim the son of Josiah king of Judah, unto the end of the eleventh year of Zedekiah the son of Josiah king of Judah, unto the carrying away of Jerusalem captive in the fifth month.
4 **Then the word of the LORD** came unto me,
saying,
5 **Before I** formed thee in the belly
I knew thee;
and before thou camest forth out of the womb
I sanctified thee,
and I ordained thee a prophet unto the nations.
6 **Then** said I,
Ah, Lord GOD!
behold,
I cannot speak:
for I am a child.
7 **But the LORD** said unto me,
Say not, I am a child:
for thou shalt go to all that I shall send thee,
and whatsoever I command thee
thou shalt speak.
8 **Be not** afraid of their faces:
for I am with thee to deliver thee,
saith the LORD.
9 **Then the LORD** put forth his hand,
and touched my mouth.
And the LORD said unto me,
Behold,
I have put my words in thy mouth.
10 **See, I** have this day set thee over the nations and over the kingdoms,
to root out,
and to pull down,
and to destroy,
and to throw down,
to build,
and to plant.
11 **Moreover the word of the LORD** came unto me,
saying,
Jeremiah, what seest thou?
And I said, **I** see a rod of an almond tree.
12 **Then** said the LORD unto me,
Thou hast well seen:
for I will hasten my word to perform it.
13 **And the word of the LORD** came unto me the second time,
saying,
What seest thou?
And I said,
I see a seething pot;
and the face thereof is toward the north.
14 **Then the LORD** said unto me,
Out of the north an evil shall break forth upon all the inhabitants of the land.
15 **For, {lo}, I** will call all the families of the kingdoms of the north,
saith the LORD;
and they shall come,
and they shall set every one his throne at the entering of the gates of Jerusalem, and against all the walls thereof round about, and against all the cities of Judah.
16 **And I** will utter my judgments against them touching all their wickedness,
who have forsaken me,
and have burned incense unto other gods,
and worshipped the works of their own hands.
17 **Thou** therefore gird up thy loins,
and arise,
and speak unto them all that I command thee:
be not dismayed at their faces,
lest I confound thee before them.
18 **For, {behold}, I** have made thee this day a defenced city, and an iron pillar, and brasen walls against the whole land, against the kings of Judah, against the princes thereof, against the priests thereof, and against the people of the land.
19 **And they** shall fight against thee;
but they shall not prevail against thee;

for I am with thee,
saith the LORD,
to deliver thee.

2 **Moreover the word of the
LORD** came to me,
saying,
2 **Go and cry** in the ears of
Jerusalem,
saying,
Thus saith the LORD;
I remember thee, the kindness of
thy youth, the love of thine
espousals,
when thou wentest after me in the
wilderness, in a land that was not
sown.
3 **Israel** was holiness unto the
LORD, and the firstfruits of his
increase:
all that devour him shall offend;
evil shall come upon them,
saith the LORD.
4 **Hear ye** the word of the LORD, O
house of Jacob, and all the
families of the house of Israel:
5 **Thus** saith the LORD,
What iniquity have your fathers
found in me,
that they are gone far from me,
and have walked after vanity,
and are become vain?
6 **Neither** said they,
Where is the LORD that brought us
up out of the land of Egypt, that
led us through the wilderness,
through a land of deserts and of
pits, through a land of drought,
and of the shadow of death,
through a land that no man
passed through,
and where no man dwelt?
7 **And I** brought you into a plentiful
country,
to eat the fruit thereof and the
goodness thereof;
but when ye entered,
ye defiled my land,
and made mine heritage an
abomination.
8 **The priests** said not,
Where is the LORD?
and they that handle the law
knew me not:
the pastors also transgressed
against me,
and the prophets prophesied by
Baal,
and walked after things that do not
profit.
9 **Wherefore I** will yet plead with
you,
saith the LORD,
and with your children's children
will I plead.
10 **For pass over** the isles of Chittim,
and see;
and send unto Kedar,
and consider diligently,
and see if there be such a thing.
11 **Hath a nation** changed their gods,
which are yet no gods?
but my people have changed their
glory for that which doth not
profit.
12 **Be** astonished, O ye heavens, at
this,
and be horribly afraid,
be ye very desolate,
saith the LORD.
13 **For my people** have committed
two evils;
they have forsaken me the fountain
of living waters,
and hewed them out cisterns,
broken cisterns,
that can hold no water.
14 **Is Israel** a servant?
is he a homeborn slave?
why is he spoiled?
15 **The young lions** roared upon
him,
and yelled,
and they made his land waste:
his cities are burned without
inhabitant.
16 **Also the children of Noph and
Tahapanes** have broken the
crown of thy head.
17 **Hast thou not** procured this unto
thyself,
in that thou hast forsaken the
LORD thy God,
when he led thee by the way?
18 **And now what** hast thou to do in
the way of Egypt,
to drink the waters of Sihor?
or what hast thou to do in the way
of Assyria,
to drink the waters of the river?
19 **Thine own wickedness** shall
correct thee,
and thy backslidings shall reprove
thee:
know therefore and see
that it is an evil thing and bitter,
that thou hast forsaken the LORD
thy God,
and that my fear is not in thee,
saith the Lord GOD of hosts.
20 **For of old time** I have broken thy
yoke,
and burst thy bands;
and thou saidst,
I will not transgress;
**when upon every high hill and
under every green tree** thou
wanderest,
playing the harlot.
21 **Yet I** had planted thee a noble
vine, wholly a right seed:
how then art thou turned into the
degenerate plant of a strange vine
unto me?
22 **For though thou** wash thee with
nitre,
and take thee much soap,
yet thine iniquity is marked before
me,
saith the Lord GOD.
23 **How** canst thou say,
I am not polluted,
I have not gone after Baalim?
see thy way in the valley,
know
what thou hast done:
thou art a swift dromedary
traversing her ways;
24 A wild ass used to the wilderness,
that snuffeth up the wind at her
pleasure;
in her occasion who can turn her
away?
all they that seek her will not
weary themselves;
in her month they shall find her.
25 **Withhold** thy foot from being
unshod, and thy throat from
thirst:
but thou saidst,
There is no hope:
no; for I have loved strangers,
and after them will I go.
26 **As the thief** is ashamed
when he is found,
so is the house of Israel ashamed;
they, their kings, their princes,
and their priests, and their
prophets.
27 Saying to a stock, {Thou art my
father}; and to a stone, {Thou hast
brought me forth}:
for they have turned their back
unto me, and not their face:
but in the time of their trouble
they will say,
Arise,
and save us.

28 **But where** are thy gods that thou hast made thee?
let them arise,
if they can save thee in the time of thy trouble:
for according to the number of thy cities are thy gods, O Judah.
29 **Wherefore** will ye plead with me?
ye all have transgressed against me,
saith the LORD.
30 **In vain** have I smitten your children;
they received no correction:
your own sword hath devoured your prophets, like a destroying lion.
31 **O generation, see ye** the word of the LORD.
Have I been a wilderness unto Israel?
a land of darkness?
wherefore say my people,
We are lords;
we will come no more unto thee?
32 **Can a maid** forget her ornaments, or a bride her attire?
yet my people have forgotten me days without number.
33 **Why** trimmest thou thy way to seek love?
therefore hast thou also taught the wicked ones thy ways.
34 **Also in thy skirts** is found the blood of the souls of the poor innocents:
I have not found it by secret search, but upon all these.
35 **Yet thou** sayest,
Because I am innocent,
surely his anger shall turn from me.
Behold,
I will plead with thee,
because thou sayest,
I have not sinned.
36 **Why** gaddest thou about so much to change thy way?
thou also shalt be ashamed of Egypt,
as thou wast ashamed of Assyria.
37 **Yea, thou** shalt go forth from him, and thine hands upon thine head:
for the LORD hath rejected thy confidences,
and thou shalt not prosper in them.

3 **They** say,
If a man put away his wife,
and she go from him,
and become another man's,
shall he return unto her again?
shall not that land be greatly polluted?
but thou hast played the harlot with many lovers;
yet return again to me,
saith the LORD.
2 **Lift up** thine eyes unto the high places,
and see where thou hast not been lien with.
In the ways hast thou sat for them, as the Arabian in the wilderness;
and thou hast polluted the land with thy whoredoms and with thy wickedness.
3 **Therefore the showers** have been withholden,
and there hath been no latter rain;
and thou hadst a whore's forehead,
thou refusedst to be ashamed.
4 **Wilt thou not** from this time cry unto me,
My father, thou art the guide of my youth?
5 **Will he** reserve his anger for ever?
will he keep it to the end?
Behold,
thou hast spoken and done evil things as thou couldest.
6 **The LORD** said also unto me in the days of Josiah the king,
Hast thou seen that which backsliding Israel hath done?
she is gone up upon every high mountain and under every green tree,
and there hath played the harlot.
7 **And I** said after she had done all these things,
Turn thou unto me.
But she returned not.
And her treacherous sister Judah saw it.
8 **And I** saw,
when for all the causes whereby backsliding Israel committed adultery I had put her away,
and given her a bill of divorce;
yet her treacherous sister Judah feared not,
but went and played the harlot also.
9 **And it** came to pass through the lightness of her whoredom,
that she defiled the land,
and committed adultery with stones and with stocks.
10 **And yet for all this** her treacherous sister Judah hath not turned unto me with her whole heart, but feignedly,
saith the LORD.
11 **And the LORD** said unto me,
The backsliding Israel hath justified herself more than treacherous Judah.
12 **Go and proclaim** these words toward the north,
and say,
Return, thou backsliding Israel,
saith the LORD;
and I will not cause mine anger to fall upon you:
for I am merciful,
saith the LORD,
and I will not keep anger for ever.
13 **Only acknowledge** thine iniquity,
that thou hast transgressed against the LORD thy God,
and hast scattered thy ways to the strangers under every green tree,
and ye have not obeyed my voice,
saith the LORD.
14 **Turn,** O backsliding children,
saith the LORD;
for I am married unto you:
and I will take you one of a city, and two of a family,
and I will bring you to Zion:
15 **And I** will give you pastors according to mine heart,
which shall feed you with knowledge and understanding.
16 **And it** shall come to pass,
when ye be multiplied and increased in the land,
in those days, {saith the LORD}, they shall say no more,
The ark of the covenant of the LORD:
neither shall it come to mind:
neither shall they remember it;
neither shall they visit it;
neither shall that be done any more.
17 **At that time** they shall call Jerusalem the throne of the LORD;
and all the nations shall be gathered unto it, to the name of the LORD, to Jerusalem:
neither shall they walk any more after the imagination of their evil heart.
18 **In those days** the house of Judah shall walk with the house of Israel,
and they shall come together out of the land of the north to the land

that I have given for an inheritance unto your fathers.
19 **But I** said,
How shall I put thee among the children,
and give thee a pleasant land, a goodly heritage of the hosts of nations?
and I said,
Thou shalt call me,
My father;
and shalt not turn away from me.
20 **Surely as a wife** treacherously departeth from her husband,
so have ye dealt treacherously with me, O house of Israel,
saith the LORD.
21 **A voice** was heard upon the high places, weeping and supplications of the children of Israel:
for they have perverted their way,
and they have forgotten the LORD their God.
22 **Return,** ye backsliding children,
and I will heal your backslidings.
Behold,
we come unto thee;
for thou art the LORD our God.
23 **Truly in vain** is salvation hoped for from the hills, and from the multitude of mountains:
truly in the LORD our God is the salvation of Israel.
24 **For shame** hath devoured the labour of our fathers from our youth; their flocks and their herds, their sons and their daughters.
25 **We** lie down in our shame,
and our confusion covereth us:
for we have sinned against the LORD our God, we and our fathers, from our youth even unto this day,
and have not obeyed the voice of the LORD our God.

4 **If thou** wilt return, O Israel,
saith the LORD,
return unto me:
and if thou wilt put away thine abominations out of my sight,
then shalt thou not remove.
2 **And thou** shalt swear,
The LORD liveth, in truth, in judgment, and in righteousness;
and the nations shall bless themselves in him,
and in him shall they glory.
3 **For thus** saith the LORD to the men of Judah and Jerusalem,
Break up your fallow ground,
and sow not among thorns.
4 **Circumcise** yourselves to the LORD,
and take away the foreskins of your heart, ye men of Judah and inhabitants of Jerusalem:
lest my fury come forth like fire,
and burn that none can quench it, because of the evil of your doings.
5 **Declare ye** in Judah,
and publish in Jerusalem;
and say,
Blow ye the trumpet in the land:
cry,
gather together,
and say,
Assemble yourselves,
and let us go into the defenced cities.
6 **Set up** the standard toward Zion:
retire,
stay not:
for I will bring evil from the north, and a great destruction.
7 **The lion** is come up from his thicket,
and the destroyer of the Gentiles is on his way;
he is gone forth from his place to make thy land desolate;
and thy cities shall be laid waste, without an inhabitant.
8 **For this** gird you with sackcloth,
lament and howl:
for the fierce anger of the LORD is not turned back from us.
9 **And it** shall come to pass at that day,
saith the LORD,
that the heart of the king shall perish, and the heart of the princes;
and the priests shall be astonished,
and the prophets shall wonder.
10 **Then** said I,
Ah, Lord GOD!
surely thou hast greatly deceived this people and Jerusalem,
saying,
Ye shall have peace;
whereas the sword reacheth unto the soul.
11 **At that time** shall it be said to this people and to Jerusalem,
A dry wind of the high places in the wilderness toward the daughter of my people,
not to fan,
nor to cleanse,
12 **Even a full wind from those places** shall come unto me:
now also will I give sentence against them.
13 **Behold,**
he shall come up as clouds,
and his chariots shall be as a whirlwind:
his horses are swifter than eagles.
Woe unto us!
for we are spoiled.
14 **O Jerusalem, wash** thine heart from wickedness,
that thou mayest be saved.
How long shall thy vain thoughts lodge within thee?
15 **For a voice** declareth from Dan,
and publisheth affliction from mount Ephraim.
16 **Make ye mention** to the nations;
behold,
publish against Jerusalem,
that watchers come from a far country,
and give out their voice against the cities of Judah.
17 **As keepers of a field,** are they against her round about;
because she hath been rebellious against me,
saith the LORD.
18 **Thy way and thy doings** have procured these things unto thee;
this is thy wickedness,
because it is bitter,
because it reacheth unto thine heart.
19 My bowels, my bowels!
I am pained at my very heart;
my heart maketh a noise in me;
I cannot hold my peace,
because thou hast heard, O my soul, the sound of the trumpet, the alarm of war.
20 **Destruction upon destruction** is cried;
for the whole land is spoiled:
suddenly are my tents spoiled, and my curtains in a moment.
21 **How long** shall I see the standard,
and hear the sound of the trumpet?
22 **For my people** is foolish,
they have not known me;
they are sottish children,

and they have none understanding:
they are wise to do evil,
but to do good
they have no knowledge.
23 **I** beheld the earth, {and, {{lo}}, it was without form, and void}; and the heavens,
and they had no light.
24 **I** beheld the mountains,
and, {lo}, they trembled,
and all the hills moved lightly.
25 **I** beheld,
and, {lo}, there was no man,
and all the birds of the heavens were fled.
26 **I** beheld,
and, {lo}, the fruitful place was a wilderness,
and all the cities thereof were broken down at the presence of the LORD, and by his fierce anger.
27 **For thus** hath the LORD said,
The whole land shall be desolate;
yet will I not make a full end.
28 **For this** shall the earth mourn,
and the heavens above be black;
because I have spoken it,
I have purposed it,
and will not repent,
neither will I turn back from it.
29 **The whole city** shall flee for the noise of the horsemen and bowmen;
they shall go into thickets,
and climb up upon the rocks:
every city shall be forsaken,
and not a man dwell therein.
30 **And when thou** art spoiled,
what wilt thou do?
Though thou clothest thyself with crimson,
though thou deckest thee with ornaments of gold,
though thou rentest thy face with painting,
in vain shalt thou make thyself fair;
thy lovers will despise thee,
they will seek thy life.
31 **For I** have heard a voice as of a woman in travail, and the anguish as of her that bringeth forth her first child, the voice of the daughter of Zion,
that bewaileth herself,
that spreadeth her hands,
saying,
Woe is me now!
for my soul is wearied because of murderers.

5 **Run ye** to and fro through the streets of Jerusalem,
and see now,
and know,
and seek in the broad places thereof,
if ye can find a man,
if there be any that executeth judgment,
that seeketh the truth;
and I will pardon it.
2 **And though they** say,
The LORD liveth;
surely they swear falsely.
3 **O LORD, are not thine eyes** upon the truth?
thou hast stricken them,
but they have not grieved;
thou hast consumed them,
but they have refused to receive correction:
they have made their faces harder than a rock;
they have refused to return.
4 **Therefore I** said,
Surely these are poor;
they are foolish:
for they know not the way of the LORD, nor the judgment of their God.
5 **I** will get me unto the great men,
and will speak unto them;
for they have known the way of the LORD, and the judgment of their God:
but these have altogether broken the yoke,
and burst the bonds.
6 **Wherefore a lion out of the forest** shall slay them,
and a wolf of the evenings shall spoil them,
a leopard shall watch over their cities:
every one that goeth out thence shall be torn in pieces:
because their transgressions are many,
and their backslidings are increased.
7 **How** shall I pardon thee for this?
thy children have forsaken me,
and sworn by them that are no gods:
when I had fed them to the full,
they then committed adultery,
and assembled themselves by troops in the harlots' houses.
8 **They** were as fed horses in the morning:
every one neighed after his neighbour's wife.
9 **Shall I not** visit for these things?
saith the LORD:
and shall not my soul be avenged on such a nation as this?
10 **Go ye up** upon her walls,
and destroy;
but make not a full end:
take away her battlements;
for they are not the LORD's.
11 **For the house of Israel and the house of Judah** have dealt very treacherously against me,
saith the LORD.
12 **They** have belied the LORD,
and said,
It is not he;
neither shall evil come upon us;
neither shall we see sword nor famine:
13 **And the prophets** shall become wind,
and the word is not in them:
thus shall it be done unto them.
14 **Wherefore thus** saith the LORD God of hosts,
Because ye speak this word,
behold,
I will make my words in thy mouth fire, and this people wood,
and it shall devour them.
15 **Lo,**
I will bring a nation upon you from far, O house of Israel,
saith the LORD:
it is a mighty nation,
it is an ancient nation,
a nation whose language thou knowest not,
neither understandest
what they say.
16 **Their quiver** is as an open sepulchre,
they are all mighty men.
17 **And they** shall eat up thine harvest, and thy bread,
which thy sons and thy daughters should eat:
they shall eat up thy flocks and thine herds:
they shall eat up thy vines and thy fig trees:
they shall impoverish thy fenced cities, {wherein thou trustedst}, with the sword.
18 **Nevertheless in those days,** {saith the LORD}, I will not make a full end with you.

19 **And it** shall come to pass,
when ye shall say,
Wherefore doeth the LORD our God all these things unto us?
then shalt thou answer them,
Like as ye have forsaken me,
and served strange gods in your land,
so shall ye serve strangers in a land that is not your's.

20 **Declare** this in the house of Jacob,
and publish it in Judah,
saying,
21 **Hear** now this, O foolish people, and without understanding;
which have eyes,
and see not;
which have ears,
and hear not:
22 **Fear ye not** me?
saith the LORD:
will ye not tremble at my presence,
which have placed the sand for the bound of the sea by a perpetual decree,
that it cannot pass it:
and though the waves thereof toss themselves,
yet can they not prevail;
though they roar,
yet can they not pass over it?

23 **But this people** hath a revolting and a rebellious heart;
they are revolted and gone.

24 **Neither** say they in their heart,
Let us now fear the LORD our God,
that giveth rain, both the former and the latter, in his season:
he reserveth unto us the appointed weeks of the harvest.

25 **Your iniquities** have turned away these things,
and your sins have withholden good things from you.

26 **For among my people** are found wicked men:
they lay wait, as he that setteth snares;
they set a trap,
they catch men.

27 **As a cage** is full of birds,
so are their houses full of deceit:
therefore they are become great,
and waxen rich.

28 **They** are waxen fat,
they shine:
yea, they overpass the deeds of the wicked:
they judge not the cause, the cause of the fatherless,
yet they prosper;
and the right of the needy do they not judge.

29 **Shall I not** visit for these things?
saith the LORD:
shall not my soul be avenged on such a nation as this?

30 **A wonderful and horrible thing** is committed in the land;
31 **The prophets** prophesy falsely,
and the priests bear rule by their means;
and my people love to have it so:
and what will ye do in the end thereof?

6 **O ye children of Benjamin,**
gather yourselves to flee out of the midst of Jerusalem,
and blow the trumpet in Tekoa,
and set up a sign of fire in Bethhaccerem:
for evil appeareth out of the north, and great destruction.

2 I have likened the daughter of Zion to a comely and delicate woman.

3 **The shepherds with their flocks** shall come unto her;
they shall pitch their tents against her round about;
they shall feed every one in his place.

4 **Prepare ye** war against her;
arise,
and let us go up at noon.
Woe unto us!
for the day goeth away,
for the shadows of the evening are stretched out.

5 **Arise,**
and let us go by night,
and let us destroy her palaces.

6 **For thus** hath the LORD of hosts said,
Hew ye down trees,
and cast a mount against Jerusalem:
this is the city to be visited;
she is wholly oppression in the midst of her.

7 **As a fountain** casteth out her waters,
so she casteth out her wickedness:
violence and spoil is heard in her;
before me continually is grief and wounds.

8 **Be thou** instructed, O Jerusalem,
lest my soul depart from thee;
lest I make thee desolate, a land not inhabited.

9 **Thus** saith the LORD of hosts,
They shall throughly glean the remnant of Israel as a vine:
turn back thine hand as a grapegatherer into the baskets.

10 **To whom** shall I speak,
and give warning,
that they may hear?
behold,
their ear is uncircumcised,
and they cannot hearken:
behold,
the word of the LORD is unto them a reproach;
they have no delight in it.

11 **Therefore I** am full of the fury of the LORD;
I am weary with holding in:
I will pour it out upon the children abroad, and upon the assembly of young men together:
for even the husband with the wife shall be taken, the aged with him that is full of days.

12 **And their houses** shall be turned unto others, with their fields and wives together:
for I will stretch out my hand upon the inhabitants of the land,
saith the LORD.

13 **For from the least of them even unto the greatest of them** every one is given to covetousness;
and from the prophet even unto the priest every one dealeth falsely.

14 **They** have healed also the hurt of the daughter of my people slightly,
saying,
Peace, peace;
when there is no peace.

15 **Were they** ashamed
hen they had committed abomination?
nay, they were not at all ashamed,
neither could they blush:
therefore they shall fall among them that fall:
at the time that I visit them they shall be cast down,
saith the LORD.

16 **Thus** saith the LORD,
Stand ye in the ways,
and see,
and ask for the old paths,
where is the good way,
and walk therein,
and ye shall find rest for your souls.
But they said,

We will not walk therein.

17 **Also I** set watchmen over you,
saying,
Hearken to the sound of the trumpet.
But they said,
We will not hearken.

18 **Therefore hear,** ye nations,
and know, O congregation,
what is among them.

19 **Hear,** O earth:
behold,
I will bring evil upon this people, even the fruit of their thoughts,
because they have not hearkened unto my words, nor to my law,
but rejected it.

20 **To what purpose** cometh there to me incense from Sheba, and the sweet cane from a far country?
your burnt offerings are not acceptable,
nor your sacrifices sweet unto me.

21 **Therefore thus** saith the LORD,
Behold,
I will lay stumblingblocks before this people,
and the fathers and the sons together shall fall upon them;
the neighbour and his friend shall perish.

22 **Thus** saith the LORD,
Behold,
a people cometh from the north country,
and a great nation shall be raised from the sides of the earth.

23 **They** shall lay hold on bow and spear;
they are cruel,
and have no mercy;
their voice roareth like the sea;
and they ride upon horses,
set in array as men for war against thee, O daughter of Zion.

24 **We** have heard the fame thereof:
our hands wax feeble:
anguish hath taken hold of us, and pain, as of a woman in travail.

25 **Go not forth** into the field,
nor walk by the way;
for the sword of the enemy and fear is on every side.

26 **O daughter of my people, gird thee** with sackcloth,
and wallow thyself in ashes:
make thee mourning, as for an only son, most bitter lamentation:
for the spoiler shall suddenly come upon us.

27 I have set thee for a tower and a fortress among my people,
that thou mayest know and try their way.

28 **They** are all grievous revolters,
walking with slanders:
they are brass and iron;
they are all corrupters.

29 **The bellows** are burned,
the lead is consumed of the fire;
the founder melteth in vain:
for the wicked are not plucked away.

30 **Reprobate silver** shall men call them,
because the LORD hath rejected them.

7 The word that came to Jeremiah from the LORD,
saying,

2 **Stand** in the gate of the LORD's house,
and proclaim there this word,
and say,
Hear the word of the LORD, all ye of Judah,
that enter in at these gates
to worship the LORD.

3 **Thus** saith the LORD of hosts, the God of Israel,
Amend your ways and your doings,
and I will cause you to dwell in this place.

4 **Trust ye not** in lying words,
saying,
The temple of the LORD, The temple of the LORD, The temple of the LORD, are these.

5 **For if ye** throughly amend your ways and your doings;
if ye throughly execute judgment between a man and his neighbour;

6 **If ye** oppress not the stranger, the fatherless, and the widow,
and shed not innocent blood in this place,
neither walk after other gods to your hurt:

7 **Then** will I cause you to dwell in this place, in the land that I gave to your fathers, for ever and ever.

8 **Behold,**
ye trust in lying words,
that cannot profit.

9 **Will ye** steal, murder,
and commit adultery,
and swear falsely,
and burn incense unto Baal,
and walk after other gods
whom ye know not;

10 **And** come and stand before me in this house,
which is called by my name,
and say,
We are delivered to do all these abominations?

11 **Is this house**, {which is called by my name}, become a den of robbers in your eyes?
Behold,
even I have seen it,
saith the LORD.

12 **But go ye** now unto my place which was in Shiloh,
where I set my name at the first,
and see what I did to it for the wickedness of my people Israel.

13 **And now, {because ye have done all these works}, {saith the LORD}, {and I spake unto you}, {rising up early and speaking}, {but ye heard not}; {and I called you}, {but ye answered not};**

14 Therefore will I do unto this house,
which is called by my name,
wherein ye trust, and unto the place which I gave to you and to your fathers,
as I have done to Shiloh.

15 **And I** will cast you out of my sight,
as I have cast out all your brethren, even the whole seed of Ephraim.

16 **Therefore pray not thou** for this people,
neither lift up cry nor prayer for them,
neither make intercession to me:
for I will not hear thee.

17 **Seest thou not** what they do in the cities of Judah and in the streets of Jerusalem?

18 **The children** gather wood,
and the fathers kindle the fire,
and the women knead their dough,
to make cakes to the queen of heaven,
and to pour out drink offerings unto other gods,
that they may provoke me to anger.

19 **Do they** provoke me to anger?
saith the LORD:
do they not provoke themselves to the confusion of their own faces?

20 **Therefore thus** saith the Lord GOD;
Behold,
mine anger and my fury shall be poured out upon this place, upon man, and upon beast, and upon the trees of the field, and upon the fruit of the ground;
and it shall burn,
and shall not be quenched.
21 **Thus** saith the LORD of hosts, the God of Israel;
Put your burnt offerings unto your sacrifices,
and eat flesh.
22 **For I** spake not unto your fathers,
nor commanded them in the day that I brought them out of the land of Egypt, concerning burnt offerings or sacrifices:
23 **But this thing** commanded I them,
saying,
Obey my voice,
and I will be your God,
and ye shall be my people:
and walk ye in all the ways that I have commanded you,
that it may be well unto you.
24 **But they** hearkened not,
nor inclined their ear,
but walked in the counsels and in the imagination of their evil heart,
and went backward, and not forward.
25 **Since the day that your fathers came forth out of the land of Egypt unto this day** I have even sent unto you all my servants the prophets,
daily rising up early
and sending them:
26 **Yet they** hearkened not unto me,
nor inclined their ear,
but hardened their neck:
they did worse than their fathers.
27 **Therefore thou** shalt speak all these words unto them;
but they will not hearken to thee:
thou shalt also call unto them;
but they will not answer thee.
28 **But thou** shalt say unto them,
This is a nation that obeyeth not the voice of the LORD their God,
nor receiveth correction:
truth is perished,
and is cut off from their mouth.
29 **Cut off** thine hair, O Jerusalem,
and cast it away,
and take up a lamentation on high places;
for the LORD hath rejected and forsaken the generation of his wrath.
30 **For the children of Judah** have done evil in my sight,
saith the LORD:
they have set their abominations in the house which is called by my name,
to pollute it.
31 **And they** have built the high places of Tophet,
which is in the valley of the son of Hinnom, to burn their sons and their daughters in the fire;
which I commanded them not,
neither came it into my heart.
32 **Therefore, {behold}, the days** come,
saith the LORD,
that it shall no more be called Tophet, nor the valley of the son of Hinnom, but the valley of slaughter:
for they shall bury in Tophet,
till there be no place.
33 **And the carcases of this people** shall be meat for the fowls of the heaven, and for the beasts of the earth;
and none shall fray them away.
34 **Then** will I cause to cease from the cities of Judah, and from the streets of Jerusalem, the voice of mirth, and the voice of gladness, the voice of the bridegroom, and the voice of the bride:
for the land shall be desolate.

8

At that time, {saith the LORD}, they shall bring out the bones of the kings of Judah, and the bones of his princes, and the bones of the priests, and the bones of the prophets, and the bones of the inhabitants of Jerusalem, out of their graves:
2 **And they** shall spread them before the sun, and the moon, and all the host of heaven,
whom they have loved,
and whom they have served,
and after whom they have walked,
and whom they have sought,
and whom they have worshipped:
they shall not be gathered,
nor be buried;
they shall be for dung upon the face of the earth.
3 **And death** shall be chosen rather than life by all the residue of them that remain of this evil family,
which remain in all the places whither I have driven them,
saith the LORD of hosts.
4 **Moreover thou** shalt say unto them,
Thus saith the LORD;
Shall they fall,
and not arise?
shall he turn away,
and not return?
5 **Why** then is this people of Jerusalem slidden back by a perpetual backsliding?
they hold fast deceit,
they refuse to return.
6 **I** hearkened and heard,
but they spake not aright:
no man repented him of his wickedness,
saying,
What have I done?
every one turned to his course,
as the horse rusheth into the battle.
7 **Yea, the stork in the heaven** knoweth her appointed times;
and the turtle and the crane and the swallow observe the time of their coming;
but my people know not the judgment of the LORD.
8 **How** do ye say,
We are wise,
and the law of the LORD is with us?
Lo,
certainly in vain made he it;
the pen of the scribes is in vain.
9 **The wise men** are ashamed,
they are dismayed and taken:
lo,
they have rejected the word of the LORD;
and what wisdom is in them?
10 **Therefore** will I give their wives unto others, and their fields to them that shall inherit them:
for every one from the least even unto the greatest is given to covetousness,
from the prophet even unto the priest every one dealeth falsely.
11 **For they** have healed the hurt of the daughter of my people slightly,
saying,
Peace, peace;

when there is no peace.

12 **Were they** ashamed
when they had committed abomination?
nay, they were not at all ashamed,
neither could they blush:
therefore shall they fall among them that fall:
in the time of their visitation they shall be cast down,
saith the LORD.

13 **I** will surely consume them,
saith the LORD:
there shall be no grapes on the vine, nor figs on the fig tree,
and the leaf shall fade;
and the things that I have given them shall pass away from them.

14 **Why** do we sit still?
assemble yourselves,
and let us enter into the defenced cities,
and let us be silent there:
for the LORD our God hath put us to silence,
and given us water of gall to drink,
because we have sinned against the LORD.

15 **We** looked for peace, {but no good came}; and for a time of health, {and behold trouble}!

16 **The snorting of his horses** was heard from Dan:
the whole land trembled at the sound of the neighing of his strong ones;
for they are come,
and have devoured the land, and all that is in it; the city, and those that dwell therein.

17 **For, {behold}, I** will send serpents, cockatrices, among you,
which will not be charmed,
and they shall bite you,
saith the LORD.

18 **When I** would comfort myself against sorrow,
my heart is faint in me.

19 **Behold** the voice of the cry of the daughter of my people because of them that dwell in a far country:
Is not the LORD in Zion?
is not her king in her?

Why have they provoked me to anger with their graven images, and with strange vanities?

20 **The harvest** is past,
the summer is ended,
and we are not saved.

21 **For the hurt of the daughter of my people** am I hurt;
I am black;
astonishment hath taken hold on me.

22 **Is there** no balm in Gilead;
is there no physician there?
why then is not the health of the daughter of my people recovered?

9

Oh that my head were waters, and mine eyes a fountain of tears,
that I might weep day and night for the slain of the daughter of my people!

2 **Oh that I** had in the wilderness a lodging place of wayfaring men;
that I might leave my people,
and go from them!
for they be all adulterers, an assembly of treacherous men.

3 **And they** bend their tongues like their bow for lies:
but they are not valiant for the truth upon the earth;
for they proceed from evil to evil,
and they know not me,
saith the LORD.

4 **Take ye heed** every one of his neighbour,
and trust ye not in any brother:
for every brother will utterly supplant,
and every neighbour will walk with slanders.

5 **And they** will deceive every one his neighbour,
and will not speak the truth:
they have taught their tongue to speak lies,
and weary themselves to commit iniquity.

6 **Thine habitation** is in the midst of deceit;
through deceit they refuse to know me,
saith the LORD.

7 **Therefore thus** saith the LORD of hosts,
Behold,
I will melt them,
and try them;
for how shall I do for the daughter of my people?

8 **Their tongue** is as an arrow shot out;
it speaketh deceit:
one speaketh peaceably to his neighbour with his mouth,
but in heart he layeth his wait.

9 **Shall I not** visit them for these things?
saith the LORD:
shall not my soul be avenged on such a nation as this?

10 **For the mountains** will I take up a weeping and wailing, and for the habitations of the wilderness a lamentation,
because they are burned up,
so that none can pass through them;
neither can men hear the voice of the cattle;
both the fowl of the heavens and the beast are fled;
they are gone.

11 **And I** will make Jerusalem heaps, and a den of dragons;
and I will make the cities of Judah desolate, without an inhabitant.

12 **Who** is the wise man,
that may understand this?
and who is he to whom the mouth of the LORD hath spoken,
that he may declare it,
for what the land perisheth
and is burned up like a wilderness,
that none passeth through?

13 **And the LORD** saith,
Because they have forsaken my law which I set before them,
and have not obeyed my voice,
neither walked therein;
14 **But** have walked after the imagination of their own heart, and after Baalim,
which their fathers taught them:
15 **Therefore thus** saith the LORD of hosts, the God of Israel;
Behold,
I will feed them, even this people, with wormwood,
and give them water of gall to drink.

16 **I** will scatter them also among the heathen,
whom neither they nor their fathers have known:
and I will send a sword after them,
till I have consumed them.

17 **Thus** saith the LORD of hosts,
Consider ye,
and call for the mourning women,
that they may come;
and send for cunning women,
that they may come:
18 **And let them** make haste,
and take up a wailing for us,

that our eyes may run down with tears,
and our eyelids gush out with waters.
19 **For a voice of wailing** is heard out of Zion,
How are we spoiled!
we are greatly confounded,
because we have forsaken the land,
because our dwellings have cast us out.
20 **Yet hear** the word of the LORD, O ye women,
and let your ear receive the word of his mouth,
and teach your daughters wailing, and every one her neighbour lamentation.
21 **For death** is come up into our windows,
and is entered into our palaces,
to cut off the children from without, and the young men from the streets.
22 **Speak,**
Thus saith the LORD,
Even the carcases of men shall fall as dung upon the open field, and as the handful after the harvestman,
and none shall gather them.
23 **Thus** saith the LORD,
Let not the wise man glory in his wisdom,
neither let the mighty man glory in his might,
let not the rich man glory in his riches:
24 **But let him that glorieth** glory in this,
that he understandeth and knoweth me,
that I am the LORD which exercise lovingkindness, judgment, and righteousness, in the earth:
for in these things I delight,
saith the LORD.
25 **Behold,**
the days come,
saith the LORD,
that I will punish all them which are circumcised with the uncircumcised;
26 Egypt, and Judah, and Edom, and the children of Ammon, and Moab, and all that are in the utmost corners,
that dwell in the wilderness:
for all these nations are uncircumcised,
and all the house of Israel are uncircumcised in the heart.

10 **Hear ye** the word which the LORD speaketh unto you, O house of Israel:
2 **Thus** saith the LORD,
Learn not the way of the heathen,
and be not dismayed at the signs of heaven;
for the heathen are dismayed at them.
3 **For the customs of the people** are vain:
for one cutteth a tree out of the forest, the work of the hands of the workman, with the axe.
4 **They** deck it with silver and with gold;
they fasten it with nails and with hammers,
that it move not.
5 **They** are upright as the palm tree,
but speak not:
they must needs be borne,
because they cannot go.
Be not afraid of them;
for they cannot do evil,
neither also is it in them to do good.
6 **Forasmuch as there** is none like unto thee, O LORD;
thou art great,
and thy name is great in might.
7 **Who** would not fear thee, O King of nations?
for to thee doth it appertain:
forasmuch as among all the wise men of the nations, and in all their kingdoms, there is none like unto thee.
8 **But they** are altogether brutish and foolish:
the stock is a doctrine of vanities.
9 **Silver spread into plates** is brought from Tarshish, and gold from Uphaz, the work of the workman, and of the hands of the founder:
blue and purple is their clothing:
they are all the work of cunning men.
10 **But the LORD** is the true God,
he is the living God, and an everlasting king:
at his wrath the earth shall tremble,
and the nations shall not be able to abide his indignation.
11 **Thus** shall ye say unto them,
The gods that have not made the heavens and the earth, even they shall perish from the earth, and from under these heavens.
12 **He** hath made the earth by his power,
he hath established the world by his wisdom,
and hath stretched out the heavens by his discretion.
13 **When he** uttereth his voice,
there is a multitude of waters in the heavens,
and he causeth the vapours to ascend from the ends of the earth;
he maketh lightnings with rain,
and bringeth forth the wind out of his treasures.
14 **Every man** is brutish in his knowledge:
every founder is confounded by the graven image:
for his molten image is falsehood,
and there is no breath in them.
15 **They** are vanity, and the work of errors:
in the time of their visitation they shall perish.
16 **The portion of Jacob** is not like them:
for he is the former of all things;
and Israel is the rod of his inheritance:
The LORD of hosts is his name.
17 **Gather up** thy wares out of the land, O inhabitant of the fortress.
18 **For thus** saith the LORD,
Behold,
I will sling out the inhabitants of the land at this once,
and will distress them,
that they may find it so.
19 **Woe** is me for my hurt!
my wound is grievous;
but I said,
Truly this is a grief,
and I must bear it.
20 **My tabernacle** is spoiled,
and all my cords are broken:
my children are gone forth of me,
and they are not:
there is none to stretch forth my tent any more,
and to set up my curtains.
21 **For the pastors** are become brutish,
and have not sought the LORD:
therefore they shall not prosper,

and all their flocks shall be
scattered.
22 **Behold,**
the noise of the bruit is come, and
a great commotion out of the
north country,
to make the cities of Judah desolate,
and a den of dragons.
23 **O LORD, I** know
that the way of man is not in
himself:
it is not in man that walketh to
direct his steps.
24 **O LORD, correct** me, but with
judgment; not in thine anger,
lest thou bring me to nothing.
25 **Pour out** thy fury upon the
heathen that know thee not, and
upon the families that call not on
thy name:
for they have eaten up Jacob,
and devoured him,
and consumed him,
and have made his habitation
desolate.

11 The word that came to
Jeremiah from the LORD
saying,
2 **Hear ye** the words of this
covenant,
and speak unto the men of Judah,
and to the inhabitants of
Jerusalem;
3 **And say thou** unto them,
Thus saith the LORD God of Israel;
Cursed be the man that obeyeth
not the words of this covenant,
4 **Which I** commanded your fathers
in the day that I brought them
forth out of the land of Egypt,
from the iron furnace,
saying,
Obey my voice,
and do them, according to all which
I command you:
so shall ye be my people,
and I will be your God:
5 **That I** may perform the oath
which I have sworn unto your
fathers,
to give them a land flowing with
milk and honey,
as it is this day.
Then answered I,
and said,
So be it, O LORD.
6 **Then the LORD** said unto me,
Proclaim all these words in the
cities of Judah, and in the streets
of Jerusalem,
saying,
Hear ye the words of this covenant,
and do them.
7 **For I** earnestly protested unto your
fathers in the day that I brought
them up out of the land of Egypt,
even unto this day,
rising early
and protesting,
saying,
Obey my voice.
8 **Yet they** obeyed not,
nor inclined their ear,
but walked every one in the
imagination of their evil heart:
therefore I will bring upon them all
the words of this covenant,
which I commanded them to do:
but they did them not.
9 **And the LORD** said unto me,
A conspiracy is found among the
men of Judah, and among the
inhabitants of Jerusalem.
10 **They** are turned back to the
iniquities of their forefathers,
which refused to hear my words;
and they went after other gods to
serve them:
**the house of Israel and the house
of Judah** have broken my
covenant which I made with their
fathers.
11 **Therefore thus** saith the LORD,
Behold,
I will bring evil upon them,
which they shall not be able to
escape;
and though they shall cry unto me,
I will not hearken unto them.
12 **Then** shall the cities of Judah and
inhabitants of Jerusalem go,
and cry unto the gods unto whom
they offer incense:
but they shall not save them at all
in the time of their trouble.
13 **For according to the number of
thy cities** were thy gods, O Judah;
**and according to the number of
the streets of Jerusalem** have ye
set up altars to that shameful
thing,
even altars to burn incense unto
Baal.
14 **Therefore pray not thou** for this
people,
neither lift up a cry or prayer for
them:
for I will not hear them in the time
that they cry unto me for their
trouble.
15 **What** hath my beloved to do in
mine house,
seeing she hath wrought lewdness
with many,
and the holy flesh is passed from
thee?
when thou doest evil,
then thou rejoicest.
16 **The LORD** called thy name,
A green olive tree, fair, and of
goodly fruit:
with the noise of a great tumult
he hath kindled fire upon it,
and the branches of it are broken.
17 **For the LORD of hosts**, {that
planted thee}, hath pronounced
evil against thee, for the evil of
the house of Israel and of the
house of Judah,
which they have done against
themselves
to provoke me to anger in offering
incense unto Baal.
18 **And the LORD** hath given me
knowledge of it,
and I know it:
then thou shewedst me their
doings.
19 **But I** was like a lamb or an ox that
is brought to the slaughter;
and I knew not
that they had devised devices
against me,
saying,
Let us destroy the tree with the
fruit thereof,
and let us cut him off from the land
of the living,
that his name may be no more
remembered.
20 **But, O LORD of hosts, that
judgest righteously, that triest
the reins and the heart, let me**
see thy vengeance on them:
for unto thee have I revealed my
cause.
21 **Therefore thus** saith the LORD of
the men of Anathoth,
that seek thy life,
saying,
Prophesy not in the name of the
LORD,
that thou die not by our hand:
22 **Therefore thus** saith the LORD of
hosts,
Behold,
I will punish them:
the young men shall die by the
sword;

their sons and their daughters shall die by famine:
23 **And there** shall be no remnant of them:
for I will bring evil upon the men of Anathoth, even the year of their visitation.

12

Righteous art thou, O LORD,
when I plead with thee:
yet let me talk with thee of thy judgments:
Wherefore doth the way of the wicked prosper?
wherefore are all they happy that deal very treacherously?
2 **Thou** hast planted them,
yea, they have taken root:
they grow,
yea, they bring forth fruit:
thou art near in their mouth, and far from their reins.
3 **But thou,** O LORD, knowest me:
thou hast seen me,
and tried mine heart toward thee:
pull them out like sheep for the slaughter,
and prepare them for the day of slaughter.
4 **How long** shall the land mourn,
and the herbs of every field wither, for the wickedness of them that dwell therein?
the beasts are consumed, and the birds;
because they said,
He shall not see our last end.
5 **If thou** hast run with the footmen,
and they have wearied thee,
then how canst thou contend with horses?
and if in the land of peace, {wherein thou trustedst}, they wearied thee,
then how wilt thou do in the swelling of Jordan?
6 **For even thy brethren, and the house of thy father,** even they have dealt treacherously with thee;
yea, they have called a multitude after thee:
believe them not,
though they speak fair words unto thee.
7 **I** have forsaken mine house,
I have left mine heritage;
I have given the dearly beloved of my soul into the hand of her enemies.
8 **Mine heritage** is unto me as a lion in the forest;
it crieth out against me:
therefore have I hated it.
9 **Mine heritage** is unto me as a speckled bird,
the birds round about are against her;
come ye,
assemble all the beasts of the field,
come to devour.
10 **Many pastors** have destroyed my vineyard,
they have trodden my portion under foot,
they have made my pleasant portion a desolate wilderness.
11 **They** have made it desolate,
and being desolate
it mourneth unto me;
the whole land is made desolate,
because no man layeth it to heart.
12 **The spoilers** are come upon all high places through the wilderness:
for the sword of the LORD shall devour from the one end of the land even to the other end of the land:
no flesh shall have peace.
13 **They** have sown wheat,
but shall reap thorns:
they have put themselves to pain,
but shall not profit:
and they shall be ashamed of your revenues because of the fierce anger of the LORD.
14 **Thus** saith the LORD against all mine evil neighbours,
that touch the inheritance which I have caused my people Israel to inherit;
Behold,
I will pluck them out of their land,
and pluck out the house of Judah from among them.
15 **And it** shall come to pass,
after that I have plucked them out
I will return,
and have compassion on them,
and will bring them again, every man to his heritage, and every man to his land.
16 **And it** shall come to pass,
if they will diligently learn the ways of my people,
to swear by my name,
The LORD liveth;
as they taught my people to swear by Baal;
then shall they be built in the midst of my people.
17 **But if they** will not obey,
I will utterly pluck up
and destroy that nation,
saith the LORD.

13

Thus saith the LORD unto me,
Go and get thee a linen girdle,
and put it upon thy loins,
and put it not in water.
2 **So I** got a girdle according to the word of the LORD,
and put it on my loins.
3 **And the word of the LORD** came unto me the second time,
saying,
4 **Take** the girdle that thou hast got,
which is upon thy loins,
and arise,
go to Euphrates,
and hide it there in a hole of the rock.
5 **So I** went,
and hid it by Euphrates,
as the LORD commanded me.
6 **And it** came to pass after many days,
that the LORD said unto me,
Arise,
go to Euphrates,
and take the girdle from thence,
which I commanded thee to hide there.
7 **Then I** went to Euphrates,
and digged,
and took the girdle from the place where I had hid it:
and, {behold}, the girdle was marred,
it was profitable for nothing.
8 **Then the word of the LORD** came unto me,
saying,
9 **Thus** saith the LORD,
After this manner will I mar the pride of Judah, and the great pride of Jerusalem.
10 **This evil people**, {which refuse to hear my words}, {which walk in the imagination of their heart}, {and walk after other gods,} {to serve them}, {and to worship them}, shall even be as this girdle,
which is good for nothing.
11 **For as the girdle** cleaveth to the loins of a man,

so have I caused to cleave unto me
the whole house of Israel and the
whole house of Judah,
saith the LORD;
that they might be unto me for a
people, and for a name, and for a
praise, and for a glory:
but they would not hear.

12 **Therefore thou** shalt speak unto
them this word;
Thus saith the LORD God of Israel,
Every bottle shall be filled with
wine:
and they shall say unto thee,
Do we not certainly know
that every bottle shall be filled
with wine?

13 **Then** shalt thou say unto them,
Thus saith the LORD,
Behold,
I will fill all the inhabitants of this
land, even the kings that sit upon
David's throne, and the priests,
and the prophets, and all the
inhabitants of Jerusalem, with
drunkenness.

14 **And I** will dash them one against
another, even the fathers and the
sons together,
saith the LORD:
I will not pity,
nor spare,
nor have mercy,
but destroy them.

15 **Hear ye,**
and give ear;
be not proud:
for the LORD hath spoken.

16 **Give** glory to the LORD your God,
before he cause darkness,
and before your feet stumble upon
the dark mountains,
and, {while ye look for light}, he
turn it into the shadow of death,
and make it gross darkness.

17 **But if ye** will not hear it,
my soul shall weep in secret places
for your pride;
and mine eye shall weep sore,
and run down with tears,
because the LORD's flock is
carried away captive.

18 **Say** unto the king and to the
queen,
Humble yourselves,
sit down:
for your principalities shall come
down, even the crown of your
glory.

19 **The cities of the south** shall be
shut up,
and none shall open them:
Judah shall be carried away captive
all of it,
it shall be wholly carried away
captive.

20 **Lift up** your eyes,
and behold them that come from
the north:
where is the flock that was given
thee, thy beautiful flock?

21 **What** wilt thou say
when he shall punish thee?
for thou hast taught them to be
captains, and as chief over thee:
shall not sorrows take thee, as a
woman in travail?

22 **And if thou** say in thine heart,
Wherefore come these things upon
me?
For the greatness of thine iniquity
are thy skirts discovered,
and thy heels made bare.

23 **Can the Ethiopian** change his
skin, or the leopard his spots?
then may ye also do good,
that are accustomed to do evil.

24 **Therefore** will I scatter them as
the stubble that passeth away by
the wind of the wilderness.

25 **This** is thy lot, the portion of thy
measures from me,
saith the LORD;
because thou hast forgotten me,
and trusted in falsehood.

26 **Therefore** will I discover thy
skirts upon thy face,
that thy shame may appear.

27 **I** have seen thine adulteries, and
thy neighings, the lewdness of thy
whoredom, and thine
abominations on the hills in the
fields.

Woe unto thee, O Jerusalem!
wilt thou not be made clean?
when shall it once be?

14

The word of the LORD
that came to Jeremiah
concerning the dearth.

2 **Judah** mourneth,
and the gates thereof languish;
they are black unto the ground;
and the cry of Jerusalem is gone
up.

3 **And their nobles** have sent their
little ones to the waters:
they came to the pits,
and found no water;
they returned with their vessels
empty;
they were ashamed and
confounded,
and covered their heads.

4 **Because the ground** is chapt,
for there was no rain in the earth,
the plowmen were ashamed,
they covered their heads.

5 **Yea, the hind** also calved in the
field,
and forsook it,
because there was no grass.

6 **And the wild asses** did stand in
the high places,
they snuffed up the wind like
dragons;
their eyes did fail,
because there was no grass.

7 **O LORD, though our iniquities**
testify against us,
do thou it for thy name's sake:
for our backslidings are many;
we have sinned against thee.

8 **O the hope of Israel, the saviour**
thereof in time of trouble, why
shouldest thou be as a stranger in
the land, and as a wayfaring man
that turneth aside to tarry for a
night?

9 **Why** shouldest thou be as a man
astonied, as a mighty man that
cannot save?
yet thou, O LORD, art in the midst
of us,
and we are called by thy name;
leave us not.

10 **Thus** saith the LORD unto this
people,
Thus have they loved to wander,
they have not refrained their feet,
therefore the LORD doth not
accept them;
he will now remember their
iniquity,
and visit their sins.

11 **Then** said the LORD unto me,
Pray not for this people for their
good.

12 **When they** fast,
I will not hear their cry;
and when they offer burnt offering
and an oblation,
I will not accept them:
but I will consume them by the
sword, and by the famine, and by
the pestilence.

13 **Then** said I,

Ah, Lord GOD!
behold,
the prophets say unto them,
Ye shall not see the sword,
neither shall ye have famine;
but I will give you assured peace in this place.

14 **Then the LORD** said unto me,
The prophets prophesy lies in my name:
I sent them not,
neither have I commanded them,
neither spake unto them:
they prophesy unto you a false vision and divination, and a thing of nought, and the deceit of their heart.

15 **Therefore thus** saith the LORD concerning the prophets that prophesy in my name,
and I sent them not,
yet they say,
Sword and famine shall not be in this land;
By sword and famine shall those prophets be consumed.

16 **And the people to whom they prophesy** shall be cast out in the streets of Jerusalem because of the famine and the sword;
and they shall have none to bury them, them, their wives, nor their sons, nor their daughters:
for I will pour their wickedness upon them.

17 **Therefore thou** shalt say this word unto them;
Let mine eyes run down with tears night and day,
and let them not cease:
for the virgin daughter of my people is broken with a great breach, with a very grievous blow.

18 **If I** go forth into the field,
then behold the slain with the sword!
and if I enter into the city,
then behold them that are sick with famine!
yea, both the prophet and the priest go about into a land that they know not.

19 **Hast thou** utterly rejected Judah?
hath thy soul lothed Zion?
why hast thou smitten us,
and there is no healing for us?
we looked for peace,
and there is no good; and for the time of healing,
and behold trouble!

20 **We** acknowledge, O LORD, our wickedness, and the iniquity of our fathers:
for we have sinned against thee.

21 **Do not** abhor us, for thy name's sake,
do not disgrace the throne of thy glory:
remember,
break not thy covenant with us.

22 **Are there** any among the vanities of the Gentiles that can cause rain?
or can the heavens give showers?
art not thou he, O LORD our God?
therefore we will wait upon thee:
for thou hast made all these things.

15

Then said the LORD unto me,
Though Moses and Samuel stood before me,
yet my mind could not be toward this people:
cast them out of my sight,
and let them go forth.

2 **And it** shall come to pass,
if they say unto thee,
Whither shall we go forth?
then thou shalt tell them,
Thus saith the LORD;
Such as are for death, to death;
and such as are for the sword, to the sword;
and such as are for the famine, to the famine;
and such as are for the captivity, to the captivity.

3 **And I** will appoint over them four kinds,
saith the LORD:
the sword to slay,
and the dogs to tear, and the fowls of the heaven, and the beasts of the earth,
to devour and destroy.

4 **And I** will cause them to be removed into all kingdoms of the earth, because of Manasseh the son of Hezekiah king of Judah, for that which he did in Jerusalem.

5 **For who** shall have pity upon thee, O Jerusalem?
or who shall bemoan thee?
or who shall go aside to ask
how thou doest?

6 **Thou** hast forsaken me,
saith the LORD,
thou art gone backward:
therefore will I stretch out my hand against thee,
and destroy thee;
I am weary with repenting.

7 **And I** will fan them with a fan in the gates of the land;
I will bereave them of children,
I will destroy my people
since they return not from their ways.

8 **Their widows** are increased to me above the sand of the seas:
I have brought upon them against the mother of the young men a spoiler at noonday:
I have caused him to fall upon it suddenly, and terrors upon the city.

9 **She that hath borne seven** languisheth:
she hath given up the ghost;
her sun is gone down
while it was yet day:
she hath been ashamed and confounded:
and the residue of them will I deliver to the sword before their enemies,
saith the LORD.

10 **Woe** is me, my mother,
that thou hast borne me a man of strife and a man of contention to the whole earth!
I have neither lent on usury,
nor men have lent to me on usury;
yet every one of them doth curse me.

11 **The LORD** said,
Verily it shall be well with thy remnant;
verily I will cause the enemy to entreat thee well in the time of evil and in the time of affliction.

12 **Shall iron** break the northern iron and the steel?

13 **Thy substance and thy treasures** will I give to the spoil without price, and that for all thy sins, even in all thy borders.

14 **And I** will make thee to pass with thine enemies into a land which thou knowest not:
for a fire is kindled in mine anger,
which shall burn upon you.

15 **O LORD, thou** knowest:
remember me,
and visit me,
and revenge me of my persecutors;

take me not away in thy longsuffering:
know
that for thy sake I have suffered rebuke.
16 **Thy words** were found,
and I did eat them;
and thy word was unto me the joy and rejoicing of mine heart:
for I am called by thy name, O LORD God of hosts.
17 **I** sat not in the assembly of the mockers,
nor rejoiced;
I sat alone because of thy hand:
for thou hast filled me with indignation.
18 **Why** is my pain perpetual, and my wound incurable,
which refuseth to be healed?
wilt thou be altogether unto me as a liar, and as waters that fail?
19 **Therefore thus** saith the LORD,
If thou return,
then will I bring thee again,
and thou shalt stand before me:
and if thou take forth the precious from the vile,
thou shalt be as my mouth:
let them return unto thee;
ut return not thou unto them.
20 **And I** will make thee unto this people a fenced brasen wall:
and they shall fight against thee,
but they shall not prevail against thee:
for I am with thee to save thee and to deliver thee,
saith the LORD.
21 **And I** will deliver thee out of the hand of the wicked,
and I will redeem thee out of the hand of the terrible.

16

The word of the LORD came also unto me,
saying,
2 **Thou** shalt not take thee a wife,
neither shalt thou have sons or daughters in this place.
3 **For thus** saith the LORD concerning the sons and concerning the daughters that are born in this place, and concerning their mothers that bare them, and concerning their fathers that begat them in this land;
4 **They** shall die of grievous deaths;
they shall not be lamented;
neither shall they be buried;
but they shall be as dung upon the face of the earth:
and they shall be consumed by the sword, and by famine;
and their carcases shall be meat for the fowls of heaven, and for the beasts of the earth.
5 **For thus** saith the LORD,
Enter not into the house of mourning,
either go to lament nor bemoan them:
for I have taken away my peace from this people,
saith the LORD, even lovingkindness and mercies.
6 **Both the great and the small** shall die in this land:
they shall not be buried,
neither shall men lament for them,
nor cut themselves,
nor make themselves bald for them:
7 **Neither** shall men tear themselves for them in mourning,
to comfort them for the dead;
neither shall men give them the cup of consolation to drink for their father or for their mother.
8 **Thou** shalt not also go into the house of feasting,
to sit with them to eat and to drink.
9 **For thus** saith the LORD of hosts, the God of Israel;
Behold,
I will cause to cease out of this place in your eyes, and in your days, the voice of mirth, and the voice of gladness, the voice of the bridegroom, and the voice of the bride.
10 **And it** shall come to pass,
when thou shalt shew this people all these words,
and they shall say unto thee,
Wherefore hath the LORD pronounced all this great evil against us?
or what is our iniquity?
or what is our sin that we have committed against the LORD our God?
11 **Then** shalt thou say unto them,
Because your fathers have forsaken me,
saith the LORD,
and have walked after other gods,
and have served them,
and have worshipped them,
and have forsaken me,
and have not kept my law;
12 **And ye** have done worse than your fathers;
for, {behold}, ye walk every one after the imagination of his evil heart,
that they may not hearken unto me:
13 **Therefore** will I cast you out of this land into a land that ye know not, neither ye nor your fathers;
and there shall ye serve other gods day and night;
where I will not shew you favour.
14 **Therefore, {behold}, the days** come,
saith the LORD,
that it shall no more be said,
The LORD liveth,
that brought up the children of Israel out of the land of Egypt;
15 **But, The LORD** liveth,
that brought up the children of Israel from the land of the north, and from all the lands whither he had driven them:
and I will bring them again into their land that I gave unto their fathers.
16 **Behold,**
I will send for many fishers,
saith the LORD,
and they shall fish them;
and after will I send for many hunters,
and they shall hunt them from every mountain, and from every hill, and out of the holes of the rocks.
17 **For mine eyes** are upon all their ways:
they are not hid from my face,
neither is their iniquity hid from mine eyes.
18 **And first** I will recompense their iniquity and their sin double;
because they have defiled my land,
they have filled mine inheritance with the carcases of their detestable and abominable things.
19 **O LORD, my strength, and my fortress, and my refuge in the day of affliction, the Gentiles** shall come unto thee from the ends of the earth,
and shall say,
Surely our fathers have inherited lies, vanity, and things wherein there is no profit.

20 **Shall a man** make gods unto himself,
and they are no gods?
21 **Therefore, {<u>behold</u>}, I** will this once cause them to know,
I will cause them to know mine hand and my might;
and they shall know
that my name is The LORD.

17

The sin of Judah is written with a pen of iron, and with the point of a diamond:
it is graven upon the table of their heart, and upon the horns of your altars;
2 **Whilst their children** remember their altars and their groves by the green trees upon the high hills.
3 **O my mountain in the field, I** will give thy substance and all thy treasures to the spoil, and thy high places for sin, throughout all thy borders.
4 **And thou, even thyself,** shalt discontinue from thine heritage that I gave thee;
and I will cause thee to serve thine enemies in the land which thou knowest not:
for ye have kindled a fire in mine anger,
which shall burn for ever.
5 **Thus** saith the LORD;
Cursed be the man that trusteth in man,
and maketh flesh his arm,
and whose heart departeth from the LORD.
6 **For he** shall be like the heath in the desert,
and shall not see when good cometh;
but shall inhabit the parched places in the wilderness, in a salt land and not inhabited.
7 **Blessed** is the man that trusteth in the LORD,
and whose hope the LORD is.
8 **For he** shall be as a tree planted by the waters, and that spreadeth out her roots by the river,
and shall not see when heat cometh,
but her leaf shall be green;
and shall not be careful in the year of drought,
neither shall cease from yielding fruit.
9 **The heart** is deceitful above all things, and desperately wicked:
who can know it?
10 **I the LORD** search the heart,
I try the reins,
even to give every man according to his ways, and according to the fruit of his doings.
11 **As the partridge** sitteth on eggs,
and hatcheth them not;
so he that getteth riches, and not by right, shall leave them in the midst of his days,
and at his end shall be a fool.
12 **A glorious high throne from the beginning** is the place of our sanctuary.
13 **O LORD, the hope of Israel, all that forsake thee** shall be ashamed,
and they that depart from me shall be written in the earth,
because they have forsaken the LORD, the fountain of living waters.
14 **Heal** me, O LORD,
and I shall be healed;
save me,
and I shall be saved:
for thou art my praise.
15 **Behold,**
they say unto me,
Where is the word of the LORD?
let it come now.
16 **As for me,** I have not hastened from being a pastor to follow thee:
neither have I desired the woeful day;
thou knowest:
that which came out of my lips was right before thee.
17 **Be not** a terror unto me:
thou art my hope in the day of evil.
18 **Let them** be confounded that persecute me,
but let not me be confounded:
let them be dismayed,
but let not me be dismayed:
bring upon them the day of evil,
and destroy them with double destruction.
19 **Thus** said the LORD unto me;
Go and stand in the gate of the children of the people,
whereby the kings of Judah come in,
and by the which they go out, and in all the gates of Jerusalem;
20 **And say** unto them,
Hear ye the word of the LORD, ye kings of Judah, and all Judah, and all the inhabitants of Jerusalem,
that enter in by these gates:
21 **Thus** saith the LORD;
Take heed to yourselves,
and bear no burden on the sabbath day,
nor bring it in by the gates of Jerusalem;
22 **Neither carry forth** a burden out of your houses on the sabbath day,
neither do ye any work,
but hallow ye the sabbath day,
as I commanded your fathers.
23 **But they** obeyed not,
neither inclined their ear,
but made their neck stiff,
that they might not hear,
nor receive instruction.
24 **And it** shall come to pass,
if ye diligently hearken unto me,
saith the LORD,
to bring in no burden through the gates of this city on the sabbath day,
but hallow the sabbath day,
to do no work therein;
25 **Then** shall there enter into the gates of this city kings and princes sitting upon the throne of David, riding in chariots and on horses, they, and their princes, the men of Judah, and the inhabitants of Jerusalem:
and this city shall remain for ever.
26 **And they** shall come from the cities of Judah, and from the places about Jerusalem, and from the land of Benjamin, and from the plain, and from the mountains, and from the south,
bringing burnt offerings, and sacrifices, and meat offerings, and incense, {<u>and</u> bringing sacrifices of praise}, unto the house of the LORD.
27 **But if ye** will not hearken unto me to hallow the sabbath day,
and not to bear a burden,
even entering in at the gates of Jerusalem on the sabbath day;
then will I kindle a fire in the gates thereof,
and it shall devour the palaces of Jerusalem,
and it shall not be quenched.

18 The word which came to Jeremiah from the LORD,
saying,
2 **Arise,**
and go down to the potter's house,
and there I will cause thee to hear my words.
3 **Then I** went down to the potter's house,
and, {behold}, he wrought a work on the wheels.
4 **And the vessel that he made of clay** was marred in the hand of the potter:
so he made it again another vessel,
as seemed good to the potter to make it.
5 **Then the word of the LORD** came to me,
saying,
6 **O house of Israel, cannot I** do with you as this potter?
saith the LORD.
Behold,
as the clay is in the potter's hand,
so are ye in mine hand, O house of Israel.
7 **At what instant** I shall speak concerning a nation, and concerning a kingdom,
to pluck up,
and to pull down,
and to destroy it;
8 **If that nation,** {against whom I have pronounced}, turn from their evil,
I will repent of the evil that I thought to do unto them.
9 **And at what instant** I shall speak concerning a nation, and concerning a kingdom,
to build and to plant it;
10 **If it** do evil in my sight,
that it obey not my voice,
then I will repent of the good,
wherewith I said
I would benefit them.
11 **Now therefore go** to,
speak to the men of Judah, and to the inhabitants of Jerusalem,
saying,
Thus saith the LORD;
Behold,
I frame evil against you,
and devise a device against you:
return ye now every one from his evil way,
and make your ways and your doings good.
12 **And they** said,
There is no hope:
but we will walk after our own devices,
and we will every one do the imagination of his evil heart.
13 **Therefore thus** saith the LORD;
Ask ye now among the heathen,
who hath heard such things:
the virgin of Israel hath done a very horrible thing.
14 **Will a man** leave the snow of Lebanon which cometh from the rock of the field?
or shall the cold flowing waters that come from another place be forsaken?
15 **Because my people** hath forgotten me,
they have burned incense to vanity,
and they have caused them to stumble in their ways from the ancient paths,
to walk in paths, in a way not cast up;
16 To make their land desolate, and a perpetual hissing;
every one that passeth thereby shall be astonished,
and wag his head.
17 **I** will scatter them as with an east wind before the enemy;
I will shew them the back, and not the face, in the day of their calamity.
18 **Then** said they,
Come and let us devise devices against Jeremiah;
for the law shall not perish from the priest, nor counsel from the wise, nor the word from the prophet.
Come,
and let us smite him with the tongue,
and let us not give heed to any of his words.
19 **Give heed** to me, O LORD,
and hearken to the voice of them that contend with me.
20 **Shall evil** be recompensed for good?
for they have digged a pit for my soul.
Remember
that I stood before thee to speak good for them,
and to turn away thy wrath from them.
21 **Therefore deliver up** their children to the famine,
and pour out their blood by the force of the sword;
and let their wives be bereaved of their children,
and be widows;
and let their men be put to death;
let their young men be slain by the sword in battle.
22 **Let a cry** be heard from their houses,
when thou shalt bring a troop suddenly upon them:
for they have digged a pit to take me,
and hid snares for my feet.
23 **Yet, LORD, thou** knowest all their counsel against me to slay me:
forgive not their iniquity,
neither blot out their sin from thy sight,
but let them be overthrown before thee;
deal thus with them in the time of thine anger.

19 **Thus** saith the LORD,
Go and get a potter's earthen bottle,
and take of the ancients of the people, and of the ancients of the priests;
2 **And go forth** unto the valley of the son of Hinnom,
which is by the entry of the east gate,
and proclaim there the words that I shall tell thee,
3 **And say,**
Hear ye the word of the LORD, O kings of Judah, and inhabitants of Jerusalem;
Thus saith the LORD of hosts, the God of Israel;
Behold,
I will bring evil upon this place,
the which whosoever heareth,
his ears shall tingle.
4 **Because they** have forsaken me,
and have estranged this place,
and have burned incense in it unto other gods,
whom neither they nor their fathers have known, nor the kings of Judah,
and have filled this place with the blood of innocents;
5 **They** have built also the high places of Baal,

to burn their sons with fire for burnt offerings unto Baal,
which I commanded not,
nor spake it,
neither came it into my mind:
[6] **Therefore, {behold}, the days** come,
saith the LORD,
that this place shall no more be called Tophet, nor The valley of the son of Hinnom, but The valley of slaughter.
[7] **And I** will make void the counsel of Judah and Jerusalem in this place;
and I will cause them to fall by the sword before their enemies, and by the hands of them that seek their lives:
and their carcases will I give to be meat for the fowls of the heaven, and for the beasts of the earth.
[8] **And I** will make this city desolate, and an hissing;
every one that passeth thereby shall be astonished and hiss because of all the plagues thereof.
[9] **And I** will cause them to eat the flesh of their sons and the flesh of their daughters,
and they shall eat every one the flesh of his friend in the siege and straitness,
wherewith their enemies, and they that seek their lives, shall straiten them.
[10] **Then** shalt thou break the bottle in the sight of the men that go with thee,
[11] **And** shalt say unto them,
Thus saith the LORD of hosts;
Even so will I break this people and this city,
as one breaketh a potter's vessel,
that cannot be made whole again:
and they shall bury them in Tophet,
till there be no place to bury.
[12] **Thus** will I do unto this place,
saith the LORD, and to the inhabitants thereof,
and even make this city as Tophet:
[13] **And the houses of Jerusalem, and the houses of the kings of Judah**, shall be defiled as the place of Tophet, because of all the houses upon whose roofs they have burned incense unto all the host of heaven, and have poured out drink offerings unto other gods.
[14] **Then** came Jeremiah from Tophet,
whither the LORD had sent him to prophesy;
and he stood in the court of the LORD's house;
and said to all the people,
[15] **Thus** saith the LORD of hosts, the God of Israel;
Behold,
I will bring upon this city and upon all her towns all the evil that I have pronounced against it,
because they have hardened their necks,
that they might not hear my words.

20

Now Pashur the son of Immer the priest, {who was also chief governor in the house of the LORD}, heard that Jeremiah prophesied these things.
[2] **Then Pashur** smote Jeremiah the prophet,
and put him in the stocks that were in the high gate of Benjamin,
which was by the house of the LORD.
[3] **And it** came to pass on the morrow,
that Pashur brought forth Jeremiah out of the stocks.
Then said Jeremiah unto him,
The LORD hath not called thy name Pashur, but Magormissabib.
[4] **For thus** saith the LORD,
Behold,
I will make thee a terror to thyself, and to all thy friends:
and they shall fall by the sword of their enemies,
and thine eyes shall behold it:
and I will give all Judah into the hand of the king of Babylon,
and he shall carry them captive into Babylon,
and shall slay them with the sword.
[5] **Moreover I** will deliver all the strength of this city, and all the labours thereof, and all the precious things thereof,
and all the treasures of the kings of Judah will I give into the hand of their enemies,
which shall spoil them,
and take them,
and carry them to Babylon.
[6] **And thou, Pashur, and all that dwell in thine house** shall go into captivity:
and thou shalt come to Babylon,
and there thou shalt die,
and shalt be buried there, thou, and all thy friends,
to whom thou hast prophesied lies.
[7] **O LORD, thou** hast deceived me,
and I was deceived;
thou art stronger than I,
and hast prevailed:
I am in derision daily,
every one mocketh me.
[8] **For since I** spake,
I cried out,
I cried violence and spoil;
because the word of the LORD was made a reproach unto me, and a derision, daily.
[9] **Then I** said,
I will not make mention of him,
nor speak any more in his name.
But his word was in mine heart as a burning fire shut up in my bones,
and I was weary with forbearing,
and I could not stay.
[10] **For I** heard the defaming of many, fear on every side.
Report,
say they,
and we will report it.
All my familiars watched for my halting,
saying,
Peradventure he will be enticed,
and we shall prevail against him,
and we shall take our revenge on him.
[11] **But the LORD** is with me as a mighty terrible one:
therefore my persecutors shall stumble,
and they shall not prevail:
they shall be greatly ashamed;
for they shall not prosper:
their everlasting confusion shall never be forgotten.
[12] **But, O LORD of hosts, {that triest the righteous}, {and seest the reins and the heart}, let me** see thy vengeance on them:
for unto thee have I opened my cause.
[13] **Sing** unto the LORD,
praise ye the LORD:
for he hath delivered the soul of the poor from the hand of evildoers.
[14] **Cursed** be the day wherein I was born:
let not the day wherein my mother bare me be blessed.
[15] **Cursed** be the man who brought tidings to my father,

saying,
A man child is born unto thee;
making him very glad.
16 **And let that man** be as the cities which the LORD overthrew, and repented not:
and let him hear the cry in the morning, and the shouting at noontide;
17 **Because he** slew me not from the womb;
or that my mother might have been my grave,
and her womb to be always great with me.
18 **Wherefore** came I forth out of the womb to see labour and sorrow,
that my days should be consumed with shame?

21 The word which came unto Jeremiah from the LORD,
when king Zedekiah sent unto him Pashur the son of Melchiah, and Zephaniah the son of Maaseiah the priest,
saying,
2 **Enquire**, {I pray thee}, of the LORD for us;
for Nebuchadrezzar king of Babylon maketh war against us;
if so be that the LORD will deal with us according to all his wondrous works,
that he may go up from us.
3 **Then** said Jeremiah unto them,
Thus shall ye say to Zedekiah:
4 **Thus** saith the LORD God of Israel;
Behold,
I will turn back the weapons of war that are in your hands,
wherewith ye fight against the king of Babylon, and against the Chaldeans,
which besiege you without the walls,
and I will assemble them into the midst of this city.
5 **And I myself** will fight against you with an outstretched hand and with a strong arm, even in anger, and in fury, and in great wrath.
6 **And I** will smite the inhabitants of this city, both man and beast:
they shall die of a great pestilence.
7 **And afterward**, {saith the LORD}, I will deliver Zedekiah king of Judah, and his servants, and the people, and such as are left in this city from the pestilence, from the sword, and from the famine, into the hand of Nebuchadrezzar king of Babylon, and into the hand of their enemies, and into the hand of those that seek their life:
and he shall smite them with the edge of the sword;
he shall not spare them,
neither have pity,
nor have mercy.
8 **And unto this people** thou shalt say,
Thus saith the LORD;
Behold,
I set before you the way of life, and the way of death.
9 **He that abideth in this city** shall die by the sword, and by the famine, and by the pestilence:
but he that goeth out, and falleth to the Chaldeans that besiege you, he shall live,
and his life shall be unto him for a prey.
10 **For I** have set my face against this city for evil, and not for good,
saith the LORD:
it shall be given into the hand of the king of Babylon,
and he shall burn it with fire.
11 **And touching the house of the king of Judah,** say,
Hear ye the word of the LORD;
12 **O house of David, thus** saith the LORD;
Execute judgment in the morning,
and deliver him that is spoiled out of the hand of the oppressor,
lest my fury go out like fire,
and burn
that none can quench it, because of the evil of your doings.
13 **Behold, I** am against thee, O inhabitant of the valley, and rock of the plain,
saith the LORD;
which say,
Who shall come down against us?
or who shall enter into our habitations?
14 **But I** will punish you according to the fruit of your doings,
saith the LORD:
and I will kindle a fire in the forest thereof,
and it shall devour all things round about it.

22 **Thus** saith the LORD;
Go down to the house of the king of Judah,
and speak there this word,
2 **And say,**
Hear the word of the LORD, O king of Judah,
that sittest upon the throne of David, thou, and thy servants, and thy people that enter in by these gates:
3 **Thus** saith the LORD;
Execute ye judgment and righteousness,
and deliver the spoiled out of the hand of the oppressor:
and do no wrong,
do no violence to the stranger, the fatherless, nor the widow,
neither shed innocent blood in this place.
4 **For if ye** do this thing indeed,
then shall there enter in by the gates of this house kings sitting upon the throne of David,
riding in chariots and on horses, he, and his servants, and his people.
5 **But if ye** will not hear these words,
I swear by myself,
saith the LORD,
that this house shall become a desolation.
6 **For thus** saith the LORD unto the king's house of Judah;
Thou art Gilead unto me, and the head of Lebanon:
yet surely I will make thee a wilderness, and cities which are not inhabited.
7 **And I** will prepare destroyers against thee, every one with his weapons:
and they shall cut down thy choice cedars,
and cast them into the fire.
8 **And many nations** shall pass by this city,
and they shall say every man to his neighbour,
Wherefore hath the LORD done thus unto this great city?
9 **Then they** shall answer,
Because they have forsaken the covenant of the LORD their God,
and worshipped other gods,
and served them.
10 **Weep ye not** for the dead,
neither bemoan him:
but weep sore for him that goeth away:
for he shall return no more,
nor see his native country.

11 **For thus** saith the LORD touching Shallum the son of Josiah king of Judah,
which reigned instead of Josiah his father,
which went forth out of this place;
He shall not return thither any more:
12 **But he** shall die in the place whither they have led him captive,
and shall see this land no more.
13 **Woe** unto him that buildeth his house by unrighteousness, and his chambers by wrong; that useth his neighbour's service without wages, {and giveth him not for his work};
14 That saith, {I will build me a wide house and large chambers}, {and cutteth him out windows}; {and it is cieled with cedar}, {and painted with vermilion}.
15 **Shalt thou** reign,
because thou closest thyself in cedar?
did not thy father eat and drink,
and do judgment and justice,
and then it was well with him?
16 **He** judged the cause of the poor and needy;
then it was well with him:
was not this to know me?
saith the LORD.
17 **But thine eyes and thine heart** are not but for thy covetousness,
and for to shed innocent blood, and for oppression, and for violence,
to do it.
18 **Therefore thus** saith the LORD concerning Jehoiakim the son of Josiah king of Judah;
They shall not lament for him,
saying,
Ah my brother!
or, Ah sister!
they shall not lament for him,
saying,
Ah lord!
or, Ah his glory!
19 **He** shall be buried with the burial of an ass,
drawn and cast forth beyond the gates of Jerusalem.
20 **Go up** to Lebanon,
and cry;
and lift up thy voice in Bashan,
and cry from the passages:
for all thy lovers are destroyed.
21 **I** spake unto thee in thy prosperity;
but thou saidst,
I will not hear.
This hath been thy manner from thy youth,
that thou obeyedst not my voice.
22 **The wind** shall eat up all thy pastors,
and thy lovers shall go into captivity:
surely then shalt thou be ashamed and confounded for all thy wickedness.
23 **O inhabitant of Lebanon, {that makest thy nest in the cedars}, how gracious** shalt thou be
when pangs come upon thee, the pain as of a woman in travail!
24 **As I** live,
saith the LORD,
though Coniah the son of Jehoiakim king of Judah were the signet upon my right hand,
yet would I pluck thee thence;
25 **And I** will give thee into the hand of them that seek thy life, and into the hand of them whose face thou fearest, even into the hand of Nebuchadrezzar king of Babylon, and into the hand of the Chaldeans.
26 **And I** will cast thee out, and thy mother that bare thee, into another country,
where ye were not born;
and there shall ye die.
27 **But to the land whereunto they desire to return,** thither shall they not return.
28 **Is this man Coniah** a despised broken idol?
is he a vessel wherein is no pleasure?
wherefore are they cast out, he and his seed,
and are cast into a land which they know not?
29 **O earth, earth, earth, hear** the word of the LORD.
30 **Thus** saith the LORD,
Write ye this man childless, a man that shall not prosper in his days:
for no man of his seed shall prosper,
sitting upon the throne of David,
and ruling any more in Judah.

23

Woe be unto the pastors that destroy and scatter the sheep of my pasture!
saith the LORD.
2 **Therefore thus** saith the LORD God of Israel against the pastors that feed my people;
Ye have scattered my flock,
and driven them away,
and have not visited them:
behold,
I will visit upon you the evil of your doings,
saith the LORD.
3 **And I** will gather the remnant of my flock out of all countries whither I have driven them,
and will bring them again to their folds;
and they shall be fruitful and increase.
4 **And I** will set up shepherds over them which shall feed them:
and they shall fear no more,
nor be dismayed,
neither shall they be lacking,
saith the LORD.
5 **Behold,**
the days come,
saith the LORD,
that I will raise unto David a righteous Branch,
and a King shall reign and prosper,
and shall execute judgment and justice in the earth.
6 **In his days** Judah shall be saved,
and Israel shall dwell safely:
and this is his name whereby he shall be called,
The LORD Our Righteousness.
7 **Therefore, behold, the days** come,
saith the LORD,
that they shall no more say,
The LORD liveth,
which brought up the children of Israel out of the land of Egypt;
8 **But, The LORD** liveth,
which brought up and which led the seed of the house of Israel out of the north country, and from all countries whither I had driven them;
and they shall dwell in their own land.
9 **Mine heart within me** is broken because of the prophets;
all my bones shake;
I am like a drunken man, and like a man whom wine hath overcome,

because of the LORD, and because of the words of his holiness.
10 **For the land** is full of adulterers;
for because of swearing the land mourneth;
the pleasant places of the wilderness are dried up,
and their course is evil,
and their force is not right.
11 **For both prophet and priest** are profane;
yea, in my house have I found their wickedness,
saith the LORD.
12 **Wherefore their way** shall be unto them as slippery ways in the darkness:
they shall be driven on,
and fall therein:
for I will bring evil upon them, even the year of their visitation,
saith the LORD.
13 **And I** have seen folly in the prophets of Samaria;
they prophesied in Baal,
and caused my people Israel to err.
14 **I** have seen also in the prophets of Jerusalem an horrible thing:
they commit adultery,
and walk in lies:
they strengthen also the hands of evildoers,
that none doth return from his wickedness;
they are all of them unto me as Sodom, and the inhabitants thereof as Gomorrah.
15 **Therefore thus** saith the LORD of hosts concerning the prophets;
Behold,
I will feed them with wormwood,
and make them drink the water of gall:
for from the prophets of Jerusalem is profaneness gone forth into all the land.
16 **Thus** saith the LORD of hosts,
Hearken not unto the words of the prophets that prophesy unto you:
they make you vain:
they speak a vision of their own heart, and not out of the mouth of the LORD.
17 **They** say still unto them that despise me,
The LORD hath said,
Ye shall have peace;
and they say unto every one that walketh after the imagination of his own heart,
No evil shall come upon you.
18 **For who** hath stood in the counsel of the LORD,
and hath perceived and heard his word?
who hath marked his word,
and heard it?
19 **Behold,**
a whirlwind of the LORD is gone forth in fury, even a grievous whirlwind:
it shall fall grievously upon the head of the wicked.
20 **The anger of the LORD** shall not return,
until he have executed,
and till he have performed the thoughts of his heart:
in the latter days ye shall consider it perfectly.
21 **I** have not sent these prophets,
yet they ran:
I have not spoken to them,
yet they prophesied.
22 **But if they** had stood in my counsel,
and had caused my people to hear my words,
then they should have turned them from their evil way, and from the evil of their doings.
23 **Am I** a God at hand,
saith the LORD, and not a God afar off?
24 **Can any** hide himself in secret places that I shall not see him?
saith the LORD.
Do not I fill heaven and earth?
saith the LORD.
25 **I** have heard what the prophets said,
that prophesy lies in my name,
saying,
I have dreamed,
I have dreamed.
26 **How long** shall this be in the heart of the prophets that prophesy lies?
yea, they are prophets of the deceit of their own heart;
27 **Which** think to cause my people to forget my name by their dreams which they tell every man to his neighbour,
as their fathers have forgotten my name for Baal.
28 **The prophet that hath a dream,** let him tell a dream;
and he that hath my word, let him speak my word faithfully.
What is the chaff to the wheat?
saith the LORD.
29 **Is not my word** like as a fire?
{saith the LORD}; and like a hammer that breaketh the rock in pieces?
30 **Therefore, {behold}, I** am against the prophets,
saith the LORD,
that steal my words every one from his neighbour.
31 **Behold,**
I am against the prophets,
saith the LORD,
that use their tongues,
and say,
He saith.
32 **Behold,**
I am against them that prophesy false dreams,
saith the LORD,
and do tell them,
and cause my people to err by their lies, and by their lightness;
yet I sent them not,
nor commanded them:
therefore they shall not profit this people at all,
saith the LORD.
33 **And when this people, or the prophet, or a priest,** shall ask thee,
saying,
What is the burden of the LORD?
thou shalt then say unto them,
What burden?
I will even forsake you,
saith the LORD.
34 **And as for the prophet, and the priest, and the people, {that shall say, The burden of the LORD},** I will even punish that man and his house.
35 **Thus** shall ye say every one to his neighbour, and every one to his brother,
What hath the LORD answered?
and, What hath the LORD spoken?
36 **And the burden of the LORD** shall ye mention no more:
for every man's word shall be his burden;
for ye have perverted the words of the living God, of the LORD of hosts our God.
37 **Thus** shalt thou say to the prophet,

What hath the LORD answered thee?
and, What hath the LORD spoken?
38 **But since ye** say,
The burden of the LORD;
therefore thus saith the LORD;
Because ye say this word,
The burden of the LORD,
and I have sent unto you,
saying,
Ye shall not say,
The burden of the LORD;
39 **Therefore, {behold}, I, even I,** will utterly forget you,
and I will forsake you, and the city that I gave you and your fathers,
and cast you out of my presence:
40 **And I** will bring an everlasting reproach upon you, and a perpetual shame,
which shall not be forgotten.

24 **The LORD** shewed me,
and, {behold}, two baskets of figs were set before the temple of the LORD,
after that Nebuchadrezzar king of Babylon had carried away captive Jeconiah the son of Jehoiakim king of Judah, and the princes of Judah, with the carpenters and smiths, from Jerusalem,
and had brought them to Babylon.
2 **One basket** had very good figs, even like the figs that are first ripe:
and the other basket had very naughty figs,
which could not be eaten,
they were so bad.
3 **Then** said the LORD unto me,
What seest thou, Jeremiah?
And I said,
Figs;
the good figs, very good;
and the evil, very evil,
that cannot be eaten,
they are so evil.
4 **Again the word of the LORD** came unto me,
saying,
5 **Thus** saith the LORD, the God of Israel;
Like these good figs, so will I acknowledge them that are carried away captive of Judah,
whom I have sent out of this place into the land of the Chaldeans for their good.
6 **For I** will set mine eyes upon them for good,
and I will bring them again to this land:
and I will build them,
and not pull them down;
and I will plant them,
and not pluck them up.
7 **And I** will give them an heart to know me,
that I am the LORD:
and they shall be my people,
and I will be their God:
for they shall return unto me with their whole heart.
8 **And as the evil figs**, {which cannot be eaten}, they are so evil;
surely thus saith the LORD,
So will I give Zedekiah the king of Judah, and his princes, and the residue of Jerusalem,
that remain in this land, and them that dwell in the land of Egypt:
9 **And I** will deliver them to be removed into all the kingdoms of the earth for their hurt,
to be a reproach and a proverb, a taunt and a curse, in all places whither I shall drive them.
10 **And I** will send the sword, the famine, and the pestilence, among them,
till they be consumed from off the land that I gave unto them and to their fathers.

25 The word that came to Jeremiah concerning all the people of Judah in the fourth year of Jehoiakim the son of Josiah king of Judah,
that was the first year of Nebuchadrezzar king of Babylon;
2 **The which Jeremiah the prophet** spake unto all the people of Judah, and to all the inhabitants of Jerusalem,
saying,
3 **From the thirteenth year of Josiah the son of Amon king of Judah, even unto this day, that is the three and twentieth year,** the word of the LORD hath come unto me,
and I have spoken unto you,
rising early and speaking;
but ye have not hearkened.
4 **And the LORD** hath sent unto you all his servants the prophets,
rising early and sending them;
but ye have not hearkened,
nor inclined your ear to hear.
5 **They** said,
Turn ye again now every one from his evil way, and from the evil of your doings,
and dwell in the land that the LORD hath given unto you and to your fathers for ever and ever:
6 **And go not** after other gods to serve them,
and to worship them,
and provoke me not to anger with the works of your hands;
and I will do you no hurt.
7 **Yet ye** have not hearkened unto me,
saith the LORD;
that ye might provoke me to anger with the works of your hands to your own hurt.
8 **Therefore thus** saith the LORD of hosts;
Because ye have not heard my words,
9 **Behold,**
I will send and take all the families of the north, {saith the LORD}, and Nebuchadrezzar the king of Babylon, my servant,
and will bring them against this land, and against the inhabitants thereof, and against all these nations round about,
and will utterly destroy them,
and make them an astonishment, and an hissing, and perpetual desolations.
10 **Moreover I** will take from them the voice of mirth, and the voice of gladness, the voice of the bridegroom, and the voice of the bride, the sound of the millstones, and the light of the candle.
11 **And this whole land** shall be a desolation, and an astonishment;
and these nations shall serve the king of Babylon seventy years.
12 **And it** shall come to pass,
when seventy years are accomplished,
that I will punish the king of Babylon, and that nation, {saith the LORD}, for their iniquity, and the land of the Chaldeans,
and will make it perpetual desolations.
13 **And I** will bring upon that land all my words which I have pronounced against it, even all that is written in this book,
which Jeremiah hath prophesied against all the nations.

14 **For many nations and great kings** shall serve themselves of them also:
and I will recompense them according to their deeds, and according to the works of their own hands.
15 **For thus** saith the LORD God of Israel unto me;
Take the wine cup of this fury at my hand,
and cause all the nations, {to whom I send thee}, to drink it.
16 **And they** shall drink,
and be moved,
and be mad, because of the sword that I will send among them.
17 **Then** took I the cup at the LORD's hand,
and made all the nations to drink,
unto whom the LORD had sent me:
18 To wit, Jerusalem, and the cities of Judah, and the kings thereof, and the princes thereof,
to make them a desolation, an astonishment, an hissing, and a curse;
as it is this day;
19 Pharaoh king of Egypt, and his servants, and his princes, and all his people;
20 And all the mingled people, and all the kings of the land of Uz, and all the kings of the land of the Philistines, and Ashkelon, and Azzah, and Ekron, and the remnant of Ashdod,
21 Edom, and Moab, and the children of Ammon,
22 And all the kings of Tyrus, and all the kings of Zidon, and the kings of the isles which are beyond the sea,
23 Dedan, and Tema, and Buz, and all that are in the utmost corners,
24 And all the kings of Arabia, and all the kings of the mingled people that dwell in the desert,
25 And all the kings of Zimri, and all the kings of Elam, and all the kings of the Medes,
26 And all the kings of the north, far and near, one with another, and all the kingdoms of the world,
which are upon the face of the earth:
and the king of Sheshach shall drink after them.
27 **Therefore thou** shalt say unto them,
Thus saith the LORD of hosts, the God of Israel;
Drink ye,
and be drunken,
and spue,
and fall,
and rise no more, because of the sword which I will send among you.
28 **And it** shall be,
if they refuse to take the cup at thine hand to drink,
then shalt thou say unto them,
Thus saith the LORD of hosts;
Ye shall certainly drink.
29 **For, {lo}, I** begin to bring evil on the city which is called by my name,
and should ye be utterly unpunished?
Ye shall not be unpunished:
for I will call for a sword upon all the inhabitants of the earth,
saith the LORD of hosts.
30 **Therefore prophesy thou** against them all these words,
and say unto them,
The LORD shall roar from on high,
and utter his voice from his holy habitation;
he shall mightily roar upon his habitation;
he shall give a shout, as they that tread the grapes, against all the inhabitants of the earth.
31 **A noise** shall come even to the ends of the earth;
for the LORD hath a controversy with the nations,
he will plead with all flesh;
he will give them that are wicked to the sword,
saith the LORD.
32 **Thus** saith the LORD of hosts,
Behold,
evil shall go forth from nation to nation,
and a great whirlwind shall be raised up from the coasts of the earth.
33 **And the slain of the LORD** shall be at that day from one end of the earth even unto the other end of the earth:
they shall not be lamented,
neither gathered,
nor buried;
they shall be dung upon the ground.
34 **Howl,** ye shepherds,
and cry;
and wallow yourselves in the ashes, ye principal of the flock:
for the days of your slaughter and of your dispersions are accomplished;
and ye shall fall like a pleasant vessel.
35 **And the shepherds** shall have no way to flee, nor the principal of the flock to escape.
36 **A voice of the cry of the shepherds, and an howling of the principal of the flock,** shall be heard:
for the LORD hath spoiled their pasture.
37 **And the peaceable habitations** are cut down because of the fierce anger of the LORD.
38 **He** hath forsaken his covert, as the lion:
for their land is desolate because of the fierceness of the oppressor, and because of his fierce anger.

26

In the beginning of the reign of Jehoiakim the son of Josiah king of Judah came this word from the LORD,
saying,
2 **Thus** saith the LORD;
Stand in the court of the LORD's house,
and speak unto all the cities of Judah,
which come to worship in the LORD's house, all the words that I command thee to speak unto them;
diminish not a word:
3 **If so be they** will hearken,
and turn every man from his evil way,
that I may repent me of the evil,
which I purpose to do unto them because of the evil of their doings.
4 **And thou** shalt say unto them,
Thus saith the LORD;
If ye will not hearken to me,
to walk in my law,
which I have set before you,
5 To hearken to the words of my servants the prophets,
whom I sent unto you,
both rising up early,
and sending them,
but ye have not hearkened;
6 **Then** will I make this house like Shiloh,

and will make this city a curse to all the nations of the earth.

7 **So the priests and the prophets and all the people** heard Jeremiah speaking these words in the house of the LORD.

8 **Now it** came to pass,
when Jeremiah had made an end of speaking all that the LORD had commanded him to speak unto all the people,
that the priests and the prophets and all the people took him,
saying,
Thou shalt surely die.

9 **Why** hast thou prophesied in the name of the LORD,
saying,
This house shall be like Shiloh,
and this city shall be desolate without an inhabitant?

And all the people were gathered against Jeremiah in the house of the LORD.

10 **When the princes of Judah** heard these things,
then they came up from the king's house unto the house of the LORD,
and sat down in the entry of the new gate of the LORD's house.

11 **Then** spake the priests and the prophets unto the princes and to all the people,
saying,
This man is worthy to die;
for he hath prophesied against this city,
as ye have heard with your ears.

12 **Then** spake Jeremiah unto all the princes and to all the people,
saying,
The LORD sent me to prophesy against this house and against this city all the words that ye have heard.

13 **Therefore now amend** your ways and your doings,
and obey the voice of the LORD your God;
and the LORD will repent him of the evil that he hath pronounced against you.

14 **As for me**, {behold}, I am in your hand:
do with me
as seemeth good and meet unto you.

15 **But know ye** for certain,
that if ye put me to death,
ye shall surely bring innocent blood upon yourselves, and upon this city, and upon the inhabitants thereof:
for of a truth the LORD hath sent me unto you
to speak all these words in your ears.

16 **Then** said the princes and all the people unto the priests and to the prophets;
This man is not worthy to die:
for he hath spoken to us in the name of the LORD our God.

17 **Then** rose up certain of the elders of the land,
and spake to all the assembly of the people,
saying,

18 **Micah the Morasthite** prophesied in the days of Hezekiah king of Judah,
and spake to all the people of Judah,
saying,
Thus saith the LORD of hosts;
Zion shall be plowed like a field,
and Jerusalem shall become heaps, and the mountain of the house as the high places of a forest.

19 **Did Hezekiah king of Judah and all Judah** put him at all to death?
did he not fear the LORD,
and besought the LORD,
and the LORD repented him of the evil which he had pronounced against them?

Thus might we procure great evil against our souls.

20 **And there** was also a man that prophesied in the name of the LORD, Urijah the son of Shemaiah of Kirjathjearim,
who prophesied against this city and against this land according to all the words of Jeremiah.

21 **And when Jehoiakim the king, with all his mighty men, and all the princes,** heard his words,
the king sought to put him to death:
but when Urijah heard it,
he was afraid,
and fled,
and went into Egypt;

22 **And Jehoiakim the king** sent men into Egypt, namely, Elnathan the son of Achbor, and certain men with him into Egypt.

23 **And they** fetched forth Urijah out of Egypt,
and brought him unto Jehoiakim the king;
who slew him with the sword,
and cast his dead body into the graves of the common people.

24 **Nevertheless the hand of Ahikam the son of Shaphan** was with Jeremiah,
that they should not give him into the hand of the people to put him to death.

27

In the beginning of the reign of Jehoiakim the son of Josiah king of Judah came this word unto Jeremiah from the LORD,
saying,

2 **Thus** saith the LORD to me;
Make thee bonds and yokes,
and put them upon thy neck,

3 **And send** them to the king of Edom, and to the king of Moab, and to the king of the Ammonites, and to the king of Tyrus, and to the king of Zidon, by the hand of the messengers which come to Jerusalem unto Zedekiah king of Judah;

4 **And command** them to say unto their masters,
Thus saith the LORD of hosts, the God of Israel;
Thus shall ye say unto your masters;

5 **I** have made the earth, the man and the beast that are upon the ground, by my great power and by my outstretched arm,
and have given it unto whom it seemed meet unto me.

6 **And now** have I given all these lands into the hand of Nebuchadnezzar the king of Babylon, my servant;
and the beasts of the field have I given him also to serve him.

7 **And all nations** shall serve him, and his son, and his son's son,
until the very time of his land come:
and then many nations and great kings shall serve themselves of him.

8 **And it** shall come to pass,
that the nation and kingdom which will not serve the same Nebuchadnezzar the king of Babylon, and that will not put

their neck under the yoke of the king of Babylon, that nation will I punish, {saith the LORD}, with the sword, and with the famine, and with the pestilence,
until I have consumed them by his hand.

9 **Therefore hearken not ye** to your prophets, nor to your diviners, nor to your dreamers, nor to your enchanters, nor to your sorcerers,
which speak unto you,
saying,
Ye shall not serve the king of Babylon:
10 **For they** prophesy a lie unto you,
to remove you far from your land;
and that I should drive you out,
and ye should perish.

11 **But the nations that bring their neck under the yoke of the king of Babylon, and serve him,** those will I let remain still in their own land,
saith the LORD;
and they shall till it,
and dwell therein.

12 **I** spake also to Zedekiah king of Judah according to all these words,
saying,
Bring your necks under the yoke of the king of Babylon,
and serve him and his people,
and live.

13 **Why** will ye die, thou and thy people, by the sword, by the famine, and by the pestilence,
as the LORD hath spoken against the nation that will not serve the king of Babylon?

14 **Therefore hearken not** unto the words of the prophets that speak unto you,
saying,
Ye shall not serve the king of Babylon:
for they prophesy a lie unto you.

15 **For I** have not sent them,
saith the LORD,
yet they prophesy a lie in my name;
that I might drive you out,
and that ye might perish, ye, and the prophets that prophesy unto you.

16 **Also I** spake to the priests and to all this people,
saying,
Thus saith the LORD;
Hearken not to the words of your prophets that prophesy unto you,
saying,
Behold,
the vessels of the LORD's house shall now shortly be brought again from Babylon:
for they prophesy a lie unto you.
17 **Hearken not** unto them;
serve the king of Babylon,
and live:
wherefore should this city be laid waste?
18 **But if they** be prophets,
and if the word of the LORD be with them,
let them now make intercession to the LORD of hosts,
that the vessels which are left in the house of the LORD, and in the house of the king of Judah, and at Jerusalem, go not to Babylon.

19 **For thus** saith the LORD of hosts concerning the pillars, and concerning the sea, and concerning the bases, and concerning the residue of the vessels that remain in this city.

20 **Which Nebuchadnezzar king of Babylon** took not,
when he carried away captive Jeconiah the son of Jehoiakim king of Judah from Jerusalem to Babylon, and all the nobles of Judah and Jerusalem;
21 **Yea, thus** saith the LORD of hosts, the God of Israel, concerning the vessels that remain in the house of the LORD, and in the house of the king of Judah and of Jerusalem;
22 **They** shall be carried to Babylon,
and there shall they be until the day that I visit them,
saith the LORD;
then will I bring them up,
and restore them to this place.

28 **And it** came to pass the same year, in the beginning of the reign of Zedekiah king of Judah, in the fourth year, and in the fifth month,
that Hananiah the son of Azur the prophet, {which was of Gibeon}, spake unto me in the house of the LORD, in the presence of the priests and of all the people,
saying,
2 **Thus** speaketh the LORD of hosts, the God of Israel,
saying,
I have broken the yoke of the king of Babylon.

3 **Within two full years** will I bring again into this place all the vessels of the LORD's house,
that Nebuchadnezzar king of Babylon took away from this place,
and carried them to Babylon:
4 **And I** will bring again to this place Jeconiah the son of Jehoiakim king of Judah, with all the captives of Judah,
that went into Babylon,
saith the LORD:
for I will break the yoke of the king of Babylon.

5 **Then the prophet Jeremiah** said unto the prophet Hananiah in the presence of the priests, and in the presence of all the people that stood in the house of the LORD,
6 **Even the prophet Jeremiah** said,
Amen:
the LORD do so:
the LORD perform thy words which thou hast prophesied,
to bring again the vessels of the LORD's house, and all that is carried away captive, from Babylon into this place.

7 **Nevertheless hear thou** now this word that I speak in thine ears, and in the ears of all the people;
8 **The prophets that have been before me and before thee of old** prophesied both against many countries, and against great kingdoms, of war, and of evil, and of pestilence.

9 **The prophet which prophesieth of peace**, {when the word of the prophet shall come to pass}, then shall the prophet be known,
that the LORD hath truly sent him.

10 **Then Hananiah the prophet** took the yoke from off the prophet Jeremiah's neck,
and brake it.

11 **And Hananiah** spake in the presence of all the people,
saying,
Thus saith the LORD;
Even so will I break the yoke of Nebuchadnezzar king of Babylon from the neck of all nations within the space of two full years.

And the prophet Jeremiah went his way.

12 **Then the word of the LORD** came unto Jeremiah the prophet,
after that Hananiah the prophet had broken the yoke from off the neck of the prophet Jeremiah,
saying,
13 **Go and tell** Hananiah,
saying,
Thus saith the LORD;
Thou hast broken the yokes of wood;
but thou shalt make for them yokes of iron.

14 **For thus** saith the LORD of hosts, the God of Israel;
I have put a yoke of iron upon the neck of all these nations,
that they may serve Nebuchadnezzar king of Babylon;
and they shall serve him:
and I have given him the beasts of the field also.

15 **Then** said the prophet Jeremiah unto Hananiah the prophet,
Hear now, Hananiah;
The LORD hath not sent thee;
but thou makest this people to trust in a lie.

16 **Therefore thus** saith the LORD;
Behold,
I will cast thee from off the face of the earth:
this year thou shalt die,
because thou hast taught rebellion against the LORD.

17 **So Hananiah the prophet** died the same year in the seventh month.

29

Now these are the words of the letter that Jeremiah the prophet sent from Jerusalem unto the residue of the elders which were carried away captives, and to the priests, and to the prophets, and to all the people whom Nebuchadnezzar had carried away captive from Jerusalem to Babylon;
2 (After that Jeconiah the king, and the queen, and the eunuchs, the princes of Judah and Jerusalem, and the carpenters, and the smiths, were departed from Jerusalem;)
3 By the hand of Elasah the son of Shaphan, and Gemariah the son of Hilkiah, (whom Zedekiah king of Judah sent unto Babylon to Nebuchadnezzar king of Babylon)
saying,
4 **Thus** saith the LORD of hosts, the God of Israel, unto all that are carried away captives,
whom I have caused to be carried away from Jerusalem unto Babylon;
5 **Build ye** houses,
and dwell in them;
and plant gardens,
and eat the fruit of them;
6 **Take ye** wives,
and beget sons and daughters;
and take wives for your sons,
and give your daughters to husbands,
that they may bear sons and daughters;
that ye may be increased there,
and not diminished.

7 **And seek** the peace of the city whither I have caused you to be carried away captives,
and pray unto the LORD for it:
for in the peace thereof shall ye have peace.

8 **For thus** saith the LORD of hosts, the God of Israel;
Let not your prophets and your diviners, {that be in the midst of you}, deceive you,
neither hearken to your dreams which ye cause to be dreamed.

9 **For they** prophesy falsely unto you in my name:
I have not sent them,
saith the LORD.

10 **For thus** saith the LORD,
That after seventy years be accomplished at Babylon
I will visit you,
and perform my good word toward you,
in causing you to return to this place.

11 **For I** know the thoughts
that I think toward you,
saith the LORD, thoughts of peace, and not of evil,
to give you an expected end.

12 **Then** shall ye call upon me,
and ye shall go and pray unto me,
and I will hearken unto you.

13 **And ye** shall seek me,
and find me,
when ye shall search for me with all your heart.

14 **And I** will be found of you,
saith the LORD:
and I will turn away your captivity,
and I will gather you from all the nations, and from all the places whither I have driven you,
saith the LORD;
and I will bring you again into the place whence I caused you to be carried away captive.

15 **Because ye** have said,
The LORD hath raised us up prophets in Babylon;
16 **Know**
that thus saith the LORD of the king that sitteth upon the throne of David, and of all the people that dwelleth in this city, and of your brethren that are not gone forth with you into captivity;
17 **Thus** saith the LORD of hosts;
Behold,
I will send upon them the sword, the famine, and the pestilence,
and will make them like vile figs,
that cannot be eaten,
they are so evil.

18 **And I** will persecute them with the sword, with the famine, and with the pestilence,
and will deliver them to be removed to all the kingdoms of the earth,
to be a curse, and an astonishment, and an hissing, and a reproach, among all the nations whither I have driven them:
19 **Because they** have not hearkened to my words,
saith the LORD,
which I sent unto them by my servants the prophets,
rising up early and sending them;
but ye would not hear,
saith the LORD.

20 **Hear ye** therefore the word of the LORD, all ye of the captivity,
whom I have sent from Jerusalem to Babylon:
21 **Thus** saith the LORD of hosts, the God of Israel, of Ahab the son of Kolaiah, and of Zedekiah the son of Maaseiah,
which prophesy a lie unto you in my name;
Behold,
I will deliver them into the hand of Nebuchadrezzar king of Babylon;
and he shall slay them before your eyes;
22 **And of them** shall be taken up a curse by all the captivity of Judah which are in Babylon,
saying,

The LORD make thee like Zedekiah and like Ahab,
whom the king of Babylon roasted in the fire;
23 **Because they** have committed villany in Israel,
and have committed adultery with their neighbours' wives,
and have spoken lying words in my name,
which I have not commanded them;
even I know,
and am a witness,
saith the LORD.
24 **Thus** shalt thou also speak to Shemaiah the Nehelamite,
saying,
25 **Thus** speaketh the LORD of hosts, the God of Israel,
saying,
Because thou hast sent letters in thy name unto all the people that are at Jerusalem, and to Zephaniah the son of Maaseiah the priest, and to all the priests,
saying,
26 **The LORD** hath made thee priest in the stead of Jehoiada the priest,
that ye should be officers in the house of the LORD, for every man that is mad, and maketh himself a prophet,
that thou shouldest put him in prison, and in the stocks.
27 **Now therefore why** hast thou not reproved Jeremiah of Anathoth,
which maketh himself a prophet to you?
28 **For therefore he** sent unto us in Babylon,
saying,
This captivity is long:
build ye houses,
and dwell in them;
and plant gardens,
and eat the fruit of them.
29 **And Zephaniah the priest** read this letter in the ears of Jeremiah the prophet.
30 **Then** came the word of the LORD unto Jeremiah,
saying,
31 **Send** to all them of the captivity,
saying,
Thus saith the LORD concerning Shemaiah the Nehelamite;
Because that Shemaiah hath prophesied unto you,
and I sent him not,
and he caused you to trust in a lie:
32 **Therefore thus** saith the LORD;
Behold,
I will punish Shemaiah the Nehelamite, and his seed:
he shall not have a man to dwell among this people;
neither shall he behold the good that I will do for my people,
saith the LORD;
because he hath taught rebellion against the LORD.

30 ✡ The word that came to Jeremiah from the LORD,
saying,
2 **Thus** speaketh the LORD God of Israel,
saying,
Write thee all the words that I have spoken unto thee in a book.
3 **For, {lo}, the days** come,
saith the LORD,
that I will bring again the captivity of my people Israel and Judah,
saith the LORD:
and I will cause them to return to the land that I gave to their fathers,
and they shall possess it.
4 **And these** are the words that the LORD spake concerning Israel and concerning Judah.
5 **For thus** saith the LORD;
We have heard a voice of trembling, of fear, and not of peace.
6 **Ask ye** now,
and see whether a man doth travail with child?
wherefore do I see every man with his hands on his loins, as a woman in travail,
and all faces are turned into paleness?
7 Alas!
for that day is great,
so that none is like it:
it is even the time of Jacob's trouble,
but he shall be saved out of it.
8 **For it** shall come to pass in that day,
saith the LORD of hosts,
that I will break his yoke from off thy neck,
and will burst thy bonds,
and strangers shall no more serve themselves of him:
9 **But they** shall serve the LORD their God, and David their king,
whom I will raise up unto them.
10 **Therefore fear thou not,** O my servant Jacob,
saith the LORD;
neither be dismayed, O Israel:
for, {lo}, I will save thee from afar, and thy seed from the land of their captivity;
and Jacob shall return,
and shall be in rest,
and be quiet,
and none shall make him afraid.
11 **For I** am with thee,
saith the LORD,
to save thee:
though I make a full end of all nations whither I have scattered thee,
yet I will not make a full end of thee:
but I will correct thee in measure,
and will not leave thee altogether unpunished.
12 **For thus** saith the LORD,
Thy bruise is incurable,
and thy wound is grievous.
13 **There** is none to plead thy cause,
that thou mayest be bound up:
thou hast no healing medicines.
14 **All thy lovers** have forgotten thee;
they seek thee not;
for I have wounded thee with the wound of an enemy, with the chastisement of a cruel one, for the multitude of thine iniquity;
because thy sins were increased.
15 **Why** criest thou for thine affliction?
thy sorrow is incurable for the multitude of thine iniquity:
because thy sins were increased,
I have done these things unto thee.
16 **Therefore all they that devour thee** shall be devoured;
and all thine adversaries, every one of them, shall go into captivity;
and they that spoil thee shall be a spoil,
and all that prey upon thee will I give for a prey.
17 **For I** will restore health unto thee,
and I will heal thee of thy wounds,
saith the LORD;
because they called thee an Outcast,
saying,
This is Zion,
whom no man seeketh after.
18 **Thus** saith the LORD;
Behold,

I will bring again the captivity of Jacob's tents,
and have mercy on his dwellingplaces;
and the city shall be builded upon her own heap,
and the palace shall remain after the manner thereof.
19 **And out of them** shall proceed thanksgiving and the voice of them that make merry:
and I will multiply them,
and they shall not be few;
I will also glorify them,
and they shall not be small.
20 **Their children** also shall be as aforetime,
and their congregation shall be established before me,
and I will punish all that oppress them.
21 **And their nobles** shall be of themselves,
and their governor shall proceed from the midst of them;
and I will cause him to draw near,
and he shall approach unto me:
for who is this that engaged his heart to approach unto me?
saith the LORD.
22 **And ye** shall be my people,
and I will be your God.
23 **Behold,**
the whirlwind of the LORD goeth forth with fury, a continuing whirlwind:
it shall fall with pain upon the head of the wicked.
24 **The fierce anger of the LORD** shall not return,
until he hath done it,
and until he have performed the intents of his heart:
in the latter days ye shall consider it.

31 **At the same time**, {saith the LORD}, will I be the God of all the families of Israel,
and they shall be my people.
2 **Thus** saith the LORD,
The people which were left of the sword found grace in the wilderness; even Israel,
when I went to cause him to rest.
3 **The LORD** hath appeared of old unto me,
saying,
Yea, I have loved thee with an everlasting love:
therefore with lovingkindness have I drawn thee.
4 **Again I** will build thee,
and thou shalt be built, O virgin of Israel:
thou shalt again be adorned with thy tabrets,
and shalt go forth in the dances of them that make merry.
5 **Thou** shalt yet plant vines upon the mountains of Samaria:
the planters shall plant,
and shall eat them as common things.
6 **For there** shall be a day,
that the watchmen upon the mount Ephraim shall cry,
Arise ye,
and let us go up to Zion unto the LORD our God.
7 **For thus** saith the LORD;
Sing with gladness for Jacob,
and shout among the chief of the nations:
publish ye,
praise ye,
and say, O LORD,
save thy people, the remnant of Israel.
8 **Behold, I** will bring them from the north country,
and gather them from the coasts of the earth, and with them the blind and the lame, the woman with child and her that travaileth with child together:
a great company shall return thither.
9 **They** shall come with weeping,
and with supplications will I lead them:
I will cause them to walk by the rivers of waters in a straight way,
wherein they shall not stumble:
for I am a father to Israel,
and Ephraim is my firstborn.
10 **Hear** the word of the LORD, O ye nations,
and declare it in the isles afar off,
and say,
He that scattered Israel will gather him,
and keep him,
as a shepherd doth his flock.
11 **For the LORD** hath redeemed Jacob,
and ransomed him from the hand of him that was stronger than he.
12 **Therefore they** shall come and sing in the height of Zion,
and shall flow together to the goodness of the LORD, for wheat, and for wine, and for oil, and for the young of the flock and of the herd:
and their soul shall be as a watered garden;
and they shall not sorrow any more at all.
13 **Then** shall the virgin rejoice in the dance, both young men and old together:
for I will turn their mourning into joy,
and will comfort them,
and make them rejoice from their sorrow.
14 **And I** will satiate the soul of the priests with fatness,
and my people shall be satisfied with my goodness,
saith the LORD.
15 **Thus** saith the LORD;
A voice was heard in Ramah, lamentation, and bitter weeping;
Rahel weeping for her children refused to be comforted for her children,
because they were not.
16 **Thus** saith the LORD;
Refrain thy voice from weeping, and thine eyes from tears:
for thy work shall be rewarded,
saith the LORD;
and they shall come again from the land of the enemy.
17 **And there** is hope in thine end,
saith the LORD,
that thy children shall come again to their own border.
18 **I** have surely heard Ephraim bemoaning himself thus;
Thou hast chastised me,
and I was chastised, as a bullock unaccustomed to the yoke:
turn thou me,
and I shall be turned;
for thou art the LORD my God.
19 **Surely after that I** was turned,
I repented;
and after that I was instructed,
I smote upon my thigh:
I was ashamed, yea, even confounded,
because I did bear the reproach of my youth.
20 **Is Ephraim** my dear son?
is he a pleasant child?
for since I spake against him,
I do earnestly remember him still:

therefore my bowels are troubled
for him;
I will surely have mercy upon him,
saith the LORD.
21 **Set thee up** waymarks,
make thee high heaps:
set thine heart toward the
highway, even the way which
thou wentest:
turn again, O virgin of Israel,
turn again to these thy cities.
22 **How long** wilt thou go about, O
thou backsliding daughter?
for the LORD hath created a new
thing in the earth,
A woman shall compass a man.
23 **Thus** saith the LORD of hosts, the
God of Israel;
As yet they shall use this speech in
the land of Judah and in the cities
thereof,
when I shall bring again their
captivity;
The LORD bless thee, O habitation
of justice, and mountain of
holiness.
24 **And there** shall dwell in Judah
itself, and in all the cities thereof
together, husbandmen, and they
that go forth with flocks.
25 **For I** have satiated the weary soul,
and I have replenished every
sorrowful soul.
26 **Upon this** I awaked,
and beheld;
and my sleep was sweet unto me.
27 **Behold,**
the days come,
saith the LORD,
that I will sow the house of Israel
and the house of Judah with the
seed of man, and with the seed of
beast.
28 **And it** shall come to pass,
that like as I have watched over
them,
to pluck up,
and to break down,
and to throw down,
and to destroy,
and to afflict;
so will I watch over them,
to build,
and to plant,
saith the LORD.
29 **In those days** they shall say no
more,
The fathers have eaten a sour
grape,
and the children's teeth are set on
edge.
30 **But every one** shall die for his
own iniquity:
**every man that eateth the sour
grape,** his teeth shall be set on
edge.
31 **Behold,**
the days come,
saith the LORD,
that I will make a new covenant
with the house of Israel, and with
the house of Judah:
32 Not according to the covenant
that I made with their fathers in
the day that I took them by the
hand to bring them out of the
land of Egypt;
which my covenant they brake,
although I was an husband unto
them,
saith the LORD:
33 **But this** shall be the covenant
that I will make with the house of
Israel;
After those days, {saith the LORD},
I will put my law in their inward
parts,
and write it in their hearts;
and will be their God,
and they shall be my people.
34 **And they** shall teach no more
every man his neighbour, and
every man his brother,
saying,
Know the LORD:
for they shall all know me, from the
least of them unto the greatest of
them,
saith the LORD:
for I will forgive their iniquity,
and I will remember their sin no
more.
35 **Thus** saith the LORD,
which giveth the sun for a light by
day, and the ordinances of the
moon and of the stars for a light
by night,
which divideth the sea
when the waves thereof roar;
The LORD of hosts is his name:
36 **If those ordinances** depart from
before me,
saith the LORD,
then the seed of Israel also shall
cease from being a nation before
me for ever.
37 **Thus** saith the LORD;
If heaven above can be measured,
and the foundations of the earth
searched out beneath,
I will also cast off all the seed of
Israel for all that they have done,
saith the LORD.
38 **Behold,**
the days come,
saith the LORD,
that the city shall be built to the
LORD from the tower of Hananeel
unto the gate of the corner.
39 **And the measuring line** shall yet
go forth over against it upon the
hill Gareb,
and shall compass about to Goath.
40 **And the whole valley of the
dead bodies, and of the ashes,
and all the fields unto the brook
of Kidron, unto the corner of
the horse gate toward the east,**
shall be holy unto the LORD;
it shall not be plucked up,
nor thrown down any more for
ever.

32 The word that came to
Jeremiah from the LORD in
the tenth year of Zedekiah king of
Judah,
which was the eighteenth year of
Nebuchadrezzar.
2 **For then the king of Babylon's
army** besieged Jerusalem:
and Jeremiah the prophet was
shut up in the court of the prison,
which was in the king of Judah's
house.
3 **For Zedekiah king of Judah** had
shut him up,
saying,
Wherefore dost thou prophesy,
and say,
Thus saith the LORD,
Behold,
I will give this city into the hand of
the king of Babylon,
and he shall take it;
4 **And Zedekiah king of Judah** shall
not escape out of the hand of the
Chaldeans,
but shall surely be delivered into
the hand of the king of Babylon,
and shall speak with him mouth to
mouth,
and his eyes shall behold his eyes;
5 **And he** shall lead Zedekiah to
Babylon,
and there shall he be until I visit
him,
saith the LORD:

though ye fight with the Chaldeans,
ye shall not prosper.
6 **And Jeremiah** said,
The word of the LORD came unto me,
saying,
7 **Behold,**
Hanameel the son of Shallum thine uncle shall come unto thee
saying,
Buy thee my field that is in Anathoth:
for the right of redemption is thine to buy it.
8 **So Hanameel mine uncle's son** came to me in the court of the prison according to the word of the LORD,
and said unto me,
Buy my field, {I pray thee}, that is in Anathoth,
which is in the country of Benjamin:
for the right of inheritance is thine,
and the redemption is thine;
buy it for thyself.
Then I knew
that this was the word of the LORD.
9 **And I** bought the field of Hanameel my uncle's son,
that was in Anathoth,
and weighed him the money, even seventeen shekels of silver.
10 **And I** subscribed the evidence,
and sealed it,
and took witnesses,
and weighed him the money in the balances.
11 **So I** took the evidence of the purchase, both that which was sealed according to the law and custom, and that which was open:
12 **And I** gave the evidence of the purchase unto Baruch the son of Neriah, the son of Maaseiah, in the sight of Hanameel mine uncle's son, and in the presence of the witnesses that subscribed the book of the purchase, before all the Jews that sat in the court of the prison.
13 **And I** charged Baruch before them,
saying,
14 **Thus** saith the LORD of hosts, the God of Israel;
Take these evidences, this evidence of the purchase, both which is sealed, and this evidence which is open;
and put them in an earthen vessel,
that they may continue many days.
15 **For thus** saith the LORD of hosts, the God of Israel;
Houses and fields and vineyards shall be possessed again in this land.
16 **Now when I** had delivered the evidence of the purchase unto Baruch the son of Neriah,
I prayed unto the LORD,
saying,
17 Ah Lord GOD!
behold,
thou hast made the heaven and the earth by thy great power and stretched out arm,
and there is nothing too hard for thee:
18 **Thou** shewest lovingkindness unto thousands,
and recompensest the iniquity of the fathers into the bosom of their children after them:
the Great, the Mighty God, the LORD of hosts, is his name,
19 Great in counsel, and mighty in work:
for thine eyes are open upon all the ways of the sons of men:
to give every one according to his ways, and according to the fruit of his doings:
20 **Which** hast set signs and wonders in the land of Egypt, even unto this day, and in Israel, and among other men;
and hast made thee a name, as at this day;
21 **And** hast brought forth thy people Israel out of the land of Egypt with signs, and with wonders, and with a strong hand, and with a stretched out arm, and with great terror;
22 **And** hast given them this land,
which thou didst swear to their fathers to give them, a land flowing with milk and honey;
23 **And they** came in,
and possessed it;
but they obeyed not thy voice,
neither walked in thy law;
they have done nothing of all that thou commandedst them to do:
therefore thou hast caused all this evil to come upon them:
24 **Behold** the mounts,
they are come unto the city
to take it;
and the city is given into the hand of the Chaldeans,
that fight against it, because of the sword, and of the famine, and of the pestilence:
and what thou hast spoken is come to pass;
and, {behold}, thou seest it.
25 **And thou** hast said unto me,
O Lord GOD, Buy thee the field for money,
and take witnesses;
for the city is given into the hand of the Chaldeans.
26 **Then** came the word of the LORD unto Jeremiah,
saying,
27 **Behold,**
I am the LORD, the God of all flesh:
is there any thing too hard for me?
28 **Therefore thus** saith the LORD;
Behold,
I will give this city into the hand of the Chaldeans, and into the hand of Nebuchadrezzar king of Babylon,
and he shall take it:
29 **And the Chaldeans**, {that fight against this city}, shall come and set fire on this city,
and burn it with the houses,
upon whose roofs they have offered incense unto Baal,
and poured out drink offerings unto other gods,
to provoke me to anger.
30 **For the children of Israel and the children of Judah** have only done evil before me from their youth:
for the children of Israel have only provoked me to anger with the work of their hands,
saith the LORD.
31 **For this city** hath been to me as a provocation of mine anger and of my fury from the day that they built it even unto this day;
that I should remove it from before my face,
32 Because of all the evil of the children of Israel and of the children of Judah, {which they have done to provoke me to anger}, they, their kings, their princes, their priests, and their

prophets, and the men of Judah,
and the inhabitants of Jerusalem.
33 **And they** have turned unto me
the back, and not the face:
though I taught them,
rising up early and teaching them,
yet they have not hearkened to
receive instruction.
34 **But they** set their abominations
in the house,
which is called by my name,
to defile it.
35 **And they** built the high places of
Baal,
which are in the valley of the son of
Hinnom,
to cause their sons and their
daughters to pass through the fire
unto Molech;
which I commanded them not,
neither came it into my mind,
that they should do this
abomination,
to cause Judah to sin.
36 **And now therefore thus** saith
the LORD, the God of Israel,
concerning this city,
whereof ye say,
It shall be delivered into the hand of
the king of Babylon by the sword,
and by the famine, and by the
pestilence;
37 **Behold, I** will gather them out of
all countries,
whither I have driven them in mine
anger, and in my fury, and in great
wrath;
and I will bring them again unto
this place,
and I will cause them to dwell
safely:
38 **And they** shall be my people,
and I will be their God:
39 **And I** will give them one heart,
and one way,
that they may fear me for ever, for
the good of them, and of their
children after them:
40 **And I** will make an everlasting
covenant with them,
that I will not turn away from
them,
to do them good;
but I will put my fear in their
hearts,
that they shall not depart from me.
41 **Yea, I** will rejoice over them
to do them good,
and I will plant them in this land
assuredly with my whole heart
and with my whole soul.
42 **For thus** saith the LORD;
Like as I have brought all this great
evil upon this people,
so will I bring upon them all the
good that I have promised them.
43 **And fields** shall be bought in this
land,
whereof ye say,
It is desolate without man or beast;
it is given into the hand of the
Chaldeans.
44 **Men** shall buy fields for money,
and subscribe evidences,
and seal them,
and take witnesses in the land of
Benjamin, and in the places about
Jerusalem, and in the cities of
Judah, and in the cities of the
mountains, and in the cities of the
valley, and in the cities of the
south:
for I will cause their captivity to
return,
saith the LORD.

33 **Moreover the word of the**
LORD came unto Jeremiah
the second time,
while he was yet shut up in the
court of the prison,
saying,
2 **Thus** saith the LORD the maker
thereof, the LORD that formed it,
to establish it;
the LORD is his name;
3 **Call** unto me,
and I will answer thee,
and show thee great and mighty
things,
which thou knowest not.
4 **For thus** saith the LORD, the God
of Israel, concerning the houses of
this city, and concerning the
houses of the kings of Judah,
which are thrown down by the
mounts, and by the sword;
5 **They** come to fight with the
Chaldeans,
but it is to fill them with the dead
bodies of men,
whom I have slain in mine anger
and in my fury,
and for all whose wickedness I
have hid my face from this city.
6 **Behold,**
I will bring it health and cure,
and I will cure them,
and will reveal unto them the
abundance of peace and truth.
7 **And I** will cause the captivity of
Judah and the captivity of Israel
to return,
and will build them, as at the first.
8 **And I** will cleanse them from all
their iniquity,
whereby they have sinned against
me;
and I will pardon all their
iniquities,
whereby they have sinned,
and whereby they have
transgressed against me.
9 **And it** shall be to me a name of joy,
a praise and an honour before all
the nations of the earth,
which shall hear all the good that I
do unto them:
and they shall fear and tremble for
all the goodness and for all the
prosperity that I procure unto it.
10 **Thus** saith the LORD;
Again there shall be heard in this
place,
which ye say shall be desolate
without man and without beast,
even in the cities of Judah, and in
the streets of Jerusalem,
that are desolate, without man, and
without inhabitant, and without
beast,
11 The voice of joy, and the voice of
gladness, the voice of the
bridegroom, and the voice of the
bride, the voice of them that shall
say,
Praise the LORD of hosts:
for the LORD is good;
for his mercy endureth for ever:
and of them that shall bring the
sacrifice of praise into the house
of the LORD.
For I will cause to return the
captivity of the land, as at the
first,
saith the LORD.
12 **Thus** saith the LORD of hosts;
Again in this place, {which is
desolate without man and
without beast, and in all the cities
thereof}, shall be an habitation of
shepherds causing their flocks to
lie down.
13 **In the cities of the mountains, in
the cities of the vale, and in the
cities of the south, and in the
land of Benjamin, and in the
places about Jerusalem, and in**

the cities of Judah, shall the
flocks pass again under the hands
of him that telleth them,
saith the LORD.
14 **Behold,**
the days come,
saith the LORD,
that I will perform that good thing
which I have promised unto the
house of Israel and to the house of
Judah.
15 **In those days, and at that time,**
will I cause the Branch of
righteousness to grow up unto
David;
and he shall execute judgment and
righteousness in the land.
16 **In those days** shall Judah be
saved,
and Jerusalem shall dwell safely:
and this is the name wherewith she
shall be called,
The LORD our righteousness.
17 **For thus** saith the LORD;
David shall never want a man to sit
upon the throne of the house of
Israel;
18 **Neither** shall the priests the
Levites want a man before me to
offer burnt offerings,
and to kindle meat offerings,
and to do sacrifice continually.
19 **And the word of the LORD** came
unto Jeremiah,
saying,
20 **Thus** saith the LORD;
If ye can break my covenant of the
day, and my covenant of the
night,
and that there should not be day
and night in their season;
21 **Then** may also my covenant be
broken with David my servant,
that he should not have a son to
reign upon his throne; and with
the Levites the priests, my
ministers.
22 **As the host of heaven** cannot be
numbered,
neither the sand of the sea
measured:
so will I multiply the seed of David
my servant, and the Levites that
minister unto me.
23 **Moreover the word of the LORD**
came to Jeremiah,
saying,
24 **Considerest thou not**
what this people have spoken,
saying,
The two families which the LORD
hath chosen, he hath even cast
them off?
thus they have despised my people,
that they should be no more a
nation before them.
25 **Thus** saith the LORD;
If my covenant be not with day and
night,
and if I have not appointed the
ordinances of heaven and earth;
26 **Then** will I cast away the seed of
Jacob and David my servant,
so that I will not take any of his
seed to be rulers over the seed of
Abraham, Isaac, and Jacob:
for I will cause their captivity to
return,
and have mercy on them.

34 The word which came
unto Jeremiah from the
LORD,
when Nebuchadnezzar king of
Babylon, and all his army, and
all the kingdoms of the earth of
his dominion, and all the
people, fought against Jerusalem,
and against all the cities thereof,
saying,
2 **Thus** saith the LORD, the God of
Israel;
Go and speak to Zedekiah king of
Judah,
and tell him,
Thus saith the LORD;
Behold,
I will give this city into the hand of
the king of Babylon,
and he shall burn it with fire:
3 **And thou** shalt not escape out of
his hand,
but shalt surely be taken,
and delivered into his hand;
and thine eyes shall behold the
eyes of the king of Babylon,
and he shall speak with thee mouth
to mouth,
and thou shalt go to Babylon.
4 **Yet hear** the word of the LORD, O
Zedekiah king of Judah;
Thus saith the LORD of thee,
Thou shalt not die by the sword:
5 **But thou** shalt die in peace:
and with the burnings of thy
fathers, the former kings which
were before thee, so shall they
burn odours for thee;
and they will lament thee,
saying,
Ah lord!
for I have pronounced the word,
saith the LORD.
6 **Then Jeremiah the prophet** spake
all these words unto Zedekiah
king of Judah in Jerusalem,
7 **When the king of Babylon's**
army fought against Jerusalem,
and against all the cities of Judah
that were left, against Lachish,
and against Azekah:
for these defenced cities remained
of the cities of Judah.
8 **This** is the word that came unto
Jeremiah from the LORD,
after that the king Zedekiah had
made a covenant with all the
people which were at Jerusalem,
to proclaim liberty unto them;
9 **That every man** should let his
manservant, and every man his
maidservant, {being an Hebrew or
an Hebrewess}, go free;
that none should serve himself of
them, to wit, of a Jew his brother.
10 **Now when all the princes, and**
all the people, {which had
entered into the covenant}, heard
that every one should let his
manservant, and every one his
maidservant, go free, that none
should serve themselves of them
any more,
then they obeyed,
and let them go.
11 **But afterward they** turned,
and caused the servants and the
handmaids, {whom they had let
go free}, to return,
and brought them into subjection
for servants and for handmaids.
12 **Therefore the word of the LORD**
came to Jeremiah from the LORD,
saying,
13 **Thus** saith the LORD, the God of
Israel;
I made a covenant with your fathers
in the day that I brought them
forth out of the land of Egypt, out
of the house of bondmen,
saying,
14 **At the end of seven years** let ye
go every man his brother an
Hebrew,
which hath been sold unto thee;
and when he hath served thee six
years,
thou shalt let him go free from thee:
but your fathers hearkened not
unto me,
neither inclined their ear.

15 **And ye** were now turned,
and had done right in my sight,
in proclaiming liberty every man to his neighbour;
and ye had made a covenant before me in the house which is called by my name:
16 **But ye** turned and polluted my name,
and caused every man his servant, and every man his handmaid, {whom he had set at liberty at their pleasure}, to return,
and brought them into subjection, to be unto you for servants and for handmaids.
17 **Therefore thus** saith the LORD;
Ye have not hearkened unto me,
in proclaiming liberty, every one to his brother, and every man to his neighbour:
behold,
I proclaim a liberty for you, {saith the LORD}, to the sword, to the pestilence, and to the famine;
and I will make you to be removed into all the kingdoms of the earth.
18 **And I** will give the men that have transgressed my covenant, {which have not performed the words of the covenant which they had made before me}, {when they cut the calf in twain}, {and passed between the parts thereof},
19 The princes of Judah, and the princes of Jerusalem, the eunuchs, and the priests, and all the people of the land,
which passed between the parts of the calf;
20 **I** will even give them into the hand of their enemies, and into the hand of them that seek their life:
and their dead bodies shall be for meat unto the fowls of the heaven, and to the beasts of the earth.
21 **And Zedekiah king of Judah and his princes** will I give into the hand of their enemies, and into the hand of them that seek their life, and into the hand of the king of Babylon's army,
which are gone up from you.
22 **Behold, I** will command, {saith the LORD}, and cause them to return to this city;
and they shall fight against it,
and take it,
and burn it with fire:
and I will make the cities of Judah a desolation without an inhabitant.

35

The word which came unto Jeremiah from the LORD in the days of Jehoiakim the son of Josiah king of Judah,
saying,
2 **Go** unto the house of the Rechabites,
and speak unto them,
and bring them into the house of the LORD, into one of the chambers,
and give them wine to drink.
3 **Then I** took Jaazaniah the son of Jeremiah, the son of Habaziniah, and his brethren, and all his sons, and the whole house of the Rechabites;
4 **And I** brought them into the house of the LORD, into the chamber of the sons of Hanan, the son of Igdaliah, a man of God,
which was by the chamber of the princes,
which was above the chamber of Maaseiah the son of Shallum, the keeper of the door:
5 **And I** set before the sons of the house of the Rechabites pots full of wine, and cups,
and I said unto them,
Drink ye wine.
6 **But they** said,
We will drink no wine:
for Jonadab the son of Rechab our father commanded us,
saying,
Ye shall drink no wine, neither ye, nor your sons for ever:
7 **Neither** shall ye build house,
nor sow seed,
nor plant vineyard,
nor have any:
but all your days ye shall dwell in tents;
that ye may live many days in the land where ye be strangers.
8 **Thus** have we obeyed the voice of Jonadab the son of Rechab our father in all that he hath charged us,
to drink no wine all our days, we, our wives, our sons, nor our daughters;
9 **Nor** to build houses for us to dwell in:
neither have we vineyard, nor field, nor seed:
10 **But we** have dwelt in tents,
and have obeyed,
and done according to all that Jonadab our father commanded us.
11 **But it** came to pass,
when Nebuchadrezzar king of Babylon came up into the land,
that we said,
Come,
and let us go to Jerusalem for fear of the army of the Chaldeans, and for fear of the army of the Syrians:
so we dwell at Jerusalem.
12 **Then** came the word of the LORD unto Jeremiah,
saying,
13 **Thus** saith the LORD of hosts, the God of Israel;
Go and tell the men of Judah and the inhabitants of Jerusalem,
Will ye not receive instruction to hearken to my words?
saith the LORD.
14 **The words of Jonadab the son of Rechab**, {that he commanded his sons not to drink wine}, are performed;
for unto this day they drink none,
but obey their father's commandment:
notwithstanding I have spoken unto you,
rising early and speaking;
but ye hearkened not unto me.
15 **I** have sent also unto you all my servants the prophets,
rising up early and sending them,
saying,
Return ye now every man from his evil way,
and amend your doings,
and go not after other gods to serve them,
and ye shall dwell in the land which I have given to you and to your fathers:
but ye have not inclined your ear,
nor hearkened unto me.
16 **Because the sons of Jonadab the son of Rechab** have performed the commandment of their father,
which he commanded them;
but this people hath not hearkened unto me:
17 **Therefore thus** saith the LORD God of hosts, the God of Israel;
Behold,
I will bring upon Judah and upon all the inhabitants of Jerusalem all

the evil that I have pronounced against them:
because I have spoken unto them,
but they have not heard;
and I have called unto them,
but they have not answered.

18 **And Jeremiah** said unto the house of the Rechabites,
Thus saith the LORD of hosts, the God of Israel;
Because ye have obeyed the commandment of Jonadab your father,
and kept all his precepts,
and done according unto all that he hath commanded you:
19 **Therefore thus** saith the LORD of hosts, the God of Israel;
Jonadab the son of Rechab shall not want a man to stand before me for ever.

36 **And it** came to pass in the fourth year of Jehoiakim the son of Josiah king of Judah,
that this word came unto Jeremiah from the LORD,
saying,
2 **Take thee** a roll of a book,
and write therein all the words that I have spoken unto thee against Israel, and against Judah, and against all the nations, from the day I spake unto thee, from the days of Josiah, even unto this day.
3 **It may be that the house of Judah** will hear all the evil which I purpose to do unto them;
that they may return every man from his evil way;
that I may forgive their iniquity and their sin.
4 **Then Jeremiah** called Baruch the son of Neriah:
and Baruch wrote from the mouth of Jeremiah all the words of the LORD, {which he had spoken unto him}, upon a roll of a book.
5 **And Jeremiah** commanded Baruch,
saying,
I am shut up;
I cannot go into the house of the LORD:
6 **Therefore go thou,**
and read in the roll, {which thou hast written from my mouth}, the words of the LORD in the ears of the people in the LORD's house upon the fasting day:
and also thou shalt read them in the ears of all Judah that come out of their cities.
7 **It may be they** will present their supplication before the LORD,
and will return every one from his evil way:
for great is the anger and the fury that the LORD hath pronounced against this people.
8 **And Baruch the son of Neriah** did according to all that Jeremiah the prophet commanded him,
reading in the book the words of the LORD in the LORD's house.
9 **And it** came to pass in the fifth year of Jehoiakim the son of Josiah king of Judah, in the ninth month,
that they proclaimed a fast before the LORD to all the people in Jerusalem, and to all the people that came from the cities of Judah unto Jerusalem.
10 **Then** read Baruch in the book the words of Jeremiah in the house of the LORD, in the chamber of Gemariah the son of Shaphan the scribe, in the higher court, at the entry of the new gate of the LORD's house, in the ears of all the people.
11 **When Michaiah the son of Gemariah, the son of Shaphan,** had heard out of the book all the words of the LORD,
12 **Then he** went down into the king's house, into the scribe's chamber:
and, {lo}, all the princes sat there, even Elishama the scribe, and Delaiah the son of Shemaiah, and Elnathan the son of Achbor, and Gemariah the son of Shaphan, and Zedekiah the son of Hananiah, and all the princes.
13 **Then Michaiah** declared unto them all the words that he had heard,
when Baruch read the book in the ears of the people.
14 **Therefore all the princes** sent Jehudi the son of Nethaniah, the son of Shelemiah, the son of Cushi, unto Baruch,
saying,
Take in thine hand the roll wherein thou hast read in the ears of the people,
and come.
So Baruch the son of Neriah took the roll in his hand,
and came unto them.
15 **And they** said unto him,
Sit down now,
and read it in our ears.
So Baruch read it in their ears.

16 **Now it** came to pass,
when they had heard all the words,
they were afraid both one and other,
and said unto Baruch,
We will surely tell the king of all these words.
17 **And they** asked Baruch,
saying,
Tell us now,
How didst thou write all these words at his mouth?
18 **Then Baruch** answered them,
He pronounced all these words unto me with his mouth,
and I wrote them with ink in the book.
19 **Then** said the princes unto Baruch,
Go,
hide thee, thou and Jeremiah; and let no man know where ye be.
20 **And they** went in to the king into the court,
but they laid up the roll in the chamber of Elishama the scribe,
and told all the words in the ears of the king.
21 **So the king** sent Jehudi to fetch the roll:
and he took it out of Elishama the scribe's chamber.
And Jehudi read it in the ears of the king, and in the ears of all the princes which stood beside the king.
22 **Now the king** sat in the winterhouse in the ninth month:
and there was a fire on the hearth burning before him.
23 **And it** came to pass,
that when Jehudi had read three or four leaves,
he cut it with the penknife,
and cast it into the fire that was on the hearth,
until all the roll was consumed in the fire that was on the hearth.
24 **Yet they** were not afraid,
nor rent their garments, neither the king, nor any of his servants that heard all these words.

25 **Nevertheless Elnathan and Delaiah and Gemariah** had made intercession to the king
that he would not burn the roll:
but he would not hear them.

26 **But the king** commanded Jerahmeel the son of Hammelech, and Seraiah the son of Azriel, and Shelemiah the son of Abdeel,
to take Baruch the scribe and Jeremiah the prophet:
but the LORD hid them.

27 **Then the word of the LORD** came to Jeremiah,
after that the king had burned the roll, and the words which Baruch wrote at the mouth of Jeremiah,
saying,
28 **Take thee** again another roll,
and write in it all the former words that were in the first roll,
which Jehoiakim the king of Judah hath burned.

29 **And thou** shalt say to Jehoiakim king of Judah,
Thus saith the LORD;
Thou hast burned this roll,
saying,
Why hast thou written therein,
saying,
The king of Babylon shall certainly come and destroy this land,
and shall cause to cease from thence man and beast?

30 **Therefore thus** saith the LORD of Jehoiakim king of Judah;
He shall have none to sit upon the throne of David:
and his dead body shall be cast out in the day to the heat, and in the night to the frost.

31 **And I** will punish him and his seed and his servants for their iniquity;
and I will bring upon them, and upon the inhabitants of Jerusalem, and upon the men of Judah, all the evil that I have pronounced against them;
but they hearkened not.

32 **Then** took Jeremiah another roll,
and gave it to Baruch the scribe, the son of Neriah;
who wrote therein from the mouth of Jeremiah all the words of the book which Jehoiakim king of Judah had burned in the fire:
and there were added besides unto them many like words.

37

And king Zedekiah the son of Josiah reigned instead of Coniah the son of Jehoiakim,
whom Nebuchadrezzar king of Babylon made king in the land of Judah.

2 **But neither he, nor his servants, nor the people of the land,** did hearken unto the words of the LORD,
which he spake by the prophet Jeremiah.

3 **And Zedekiah the king** sent Jehucal the son of Shelemiah and Zephaniah the son of Maaseiah the priest to the prophet Jeremiah,
saying,
Pray now unto the LORD our God for us.

4 **Now Jeremiah** came in and went out among the people:
for they had not put him into prison.

5 **Then Pharaoh's army** was come forth out of Egypt:
and when the Chaldeans that besieged Jerusalem heard tidings of them,
they departed from Jerusalem.

6 **Then** came the word of the LORD unto the prophet Jeremiah
saying,
7 **Thus** saith the LORD, the God of Israel;
Thus shall ye say to the king of Judah,
that sent you unto me to enquire of me;
Behold,
Pharaoh's army, {which is come forth to help you}, shall return to Egypt into their own land.

8 **And the Chaldeans** shall come again,
and fight against this city,
and take it,
and burn it with fire.

9 **Thus** saith the LORD;
Deceive not yourselves,
saying,
The Chaldeans shall surely depart from us:
for they shall not depart.

10 **For though ye** had smitten the whole army of the Chaldeans that fight against you,
and there remained but wounded men among them,
yet should they rise up every man in his tent,
and burn this city with fire.

11 **And it** came to pass,
that when the army of the Chaldeans was broken up from Jerusalem for fear of Pharaoh's army,
12 **Then Jeremiah** went forth out of Jerusalem to go into the land of Benjamin,
to separate himself thence in the midst of the people.

13 **And when he** was in the gate of Benjamin,
a captain of the ward was there,
whose name was Irijah, the son of Shelemiah, the son of Hananiah;
and he took Jeremiah the prophet,
saying,
Thou fallest away to the Chaldeans.

14 **Then** said Jeremiah,
It is false;
I fall not away to the Chaldeans.

But he hearkened not to him:
so Irijah took Jeremiah,
and brought him to the princes.

15 **Wherefore the princes** were wroth with Jeremiah,
and smote him,
and put him in prison in the house of Jonathan the scribe:
for they had made that the prison.

16 **When Jeremiah** was entered into the dungeon, and into the cabins,
and Jeremiah had remained there many days;
17 **Then Zedekiah the king** sent,
and took him out:
and the king asked him secretly in his house,
and said,
Is there any word from the LORD?

And Jeremiah said,
There is:
for, {said he}, thou shalt be delivered into the hand of the king of Babylon.

18 **Moreover Jeremiah** said unto king Zedekiah,
What have I offended against thee, or against thy servants, or against this people,
that ye have put me in prison?

19 **Where** are now your prophets which prophesied unto you,
saying,
The king of Babylon shall not come against you, nor against this land?

20 **Therefore hear** now, {I pray thee}, O my lord the king:
let my supplication, {I pray thee}, be accepted before thee;
that thou cause me not to return to the house of Jonathan the scribe,
lest I die there.

21 **Then Zedekiah the king** commanded
that they should commit Jeremiah into the court of the prison,
and that they should give him daily a piece of bread out of the bakers' street,
until all the bread in the city were spent.

Thus Jeremiah remained in the court of the prison.

38 **Then Shephatiah the son of Mattan, and Gedaliah the son of Pashur, and Jucal the son of Shelemiah, and Pashur the son of Malchiah,** heard the words that Jeremiah had spoken unto all the people,
saying,
2 **Thus** saith the LORD,
He that remaineth in this city shall die by the sword, by the famine, and by the pestilence:
but he that goeth forth to the Chaldeans shall live;
for he shall have his life for a prey,
and shall live.

3 **Thus** saith the LORD,
This city shall surely be given into the hand of the king of Babylon's army,
which shall take it.

4 **Therefore the princes** said unto the king,
We beseech thee,
let this man be put to death:
for thus he weakeneth the hands of the men of war that remain in this city, and the hands of all the people,
in speaking such words unto them:
for this man seeketh not the welfare of this people, but the hurt.

5 **Then Zedekiah the king** said,
Behold,
he is in your hand:
for the king is not he that can do any thing against you.

6 **Then** took they Jeremiah,
and cast him into the dungeon of Malchiah the son of Hammelech,
that was in the court of the prison:
and they let down Jeremiah with cords.

And in the dungeon there was no water, but mire:
so Jeremiah sunk in the mire.

7 **Now when Ebedmelech the Ethiopian, one of the eunuchs which was in the king's house,** heard that they had put Jeremiah in the dungeon;
the king then sitting in the gate of Benjamin;
8 **Ebedmelech** went forth out of the king's house,
and spake to the king
saying,
9 **My lord the king, these men** have done evil in all that they have done to Jeremiah the prophet,
whom they have cast into the dungeon;
and he is like to die for hunger in the place where he is:
for there is no more bread in the city.

10 **Then the king** commanded Ebedmelech the Ethiopian,
saying,
Take from hence thirty men with thee,
and take up Jeremiah the prophet out of the dungeon,
before he die.

11 **So Ebedmelech** took the men with him,
and went into the house of the king under the treasury,
and took thence old cast clouts and old rotten rags,
and let them down by cords into the dungeon to Jeremiah.

12 **And Ebedmelech the Ethiopian** said unto Jeremiah,
Put now these old cast clouts and rotten rags under thine armholes under the cords.

And Jeremiah did so.

13 **So they** drew up Jeremiah with cords,
and took him up out of the dungeon:
and Jeremiah remained in the court of the prison.

14 **Then Zedekiah the king** sent,
and took Jeremiah the prophet unto him into the third entry that is in the house of the LORD:
and the king said unto Jeremiah,
I will ask thee a thing;
hide nothing from me.

15 **Then Jeremiah** said unto Zedekiah,
If I declare it unto thee,
wilt thou not surely put me to death?
and if I give thee counsel,
wilt thou not hearken unto me?

16 **So Zedekiah the king** sware secretly unto Jeremiah,
saying,
As the LORD liveth,
that made us this soul,
I will not put thee to death,
neither will I give thee into the hand of these men that seek thy life.

17 **Then** said Jeremiah unto Zedekiah,
Thus saith the LORD, the God of hosts, the God of Israel;
If thou wilt assuredly go forth unto the king of Babylon's princes,
then thy soul shall live,
and this city shall not be burned with fire;
and thou shalt live, and thine house:
18 **But if thou** wilt not go forth to the king of Babylon's princes,
then shall this city be given into the hand of the Chaldeans,
and they shall burn it with fire,
and thou shalt not escape out of their hand.

19 **And Zedekiah the king** said unto Jeremiah,
I am afraid of the Jews that are fallen to the Chaldeans,
lest they deliver me into their hand,
and they mock me.

20 **But Jeremiah** said,
They shall not deliver thee.
Obey, {I beseech thee}, the voice of the LORD,
which I speak unto thee:
so it shall be well unto thee,
and thy soul shall live.

21 **But if thou** refuse to go forth,
this is the word that the LORD hath shewed me:
22 **And, {behold}, all the women that are left in the king of Judah's house** shall be brought forth to the king of Babylon's princes,
and those women shall say,
Thy friends have set thee on,
and have prevailed against thee:
thy feet are sunk in the mire,
and they are turned away back.

[23] **So they** shall bring out all thy wives and thy children to the Chaldeans:
and thou shalt not escape out of their hand,
but shalt be taken by the hand of the king of Babylon:
and thou shalt cause this city to be burned with fire.

[24] **Then** said Zedekiah unto Jeremiah,
Let no man know of these words,
and thou shalt not die.

[25] **But if the princes** hear that I have talked with thee,
and they come unto thee,
and say unto thee,
Declare unto us now
what thou hast said unto the king,
hide it not from us,
and we will not put thee to death;
also what the king said unto thee:
[26] **Then thou** shalt say unto them,
I presented my supplication before the king,
that he would not cause me to return to Jonathan's house,
to die there.

[27] **Then** came all the princes unto Jeremiah,
and asked him:
and he told them according to all these words that the king had commanded.

So they left off speaking with him;
for the matter was not perceived.

[28] **So Jeremiah** abode in the court of the prison until the day that Jerusalem was taken:
and he was there
when Jerusalem was taken.

39

In the ninth year of Zedekiah king of Judah, in the tenth month, came Nebuchadrezzar king of Babylon and all his army against Jerusalem,
and they besieged it.

[2] **And in the eleventh year of Zedekiah, in the fourth month, the ninth day of the month,** the city was broken up.

[3] **And all the princes of the king of Babylon** came in,
and sat in the middle gate, even Nergalsharezer, Samgarnebo, Sarsechim, Rabsaris, Nergalsharezer, Rabmag, with all the residue of the princes of the king of Babylon.

[4] **And it** came to pass,
that when Zedekiah the king of Judah saw them, and all the men of war,
then they fled,
and went forth out of the city by night, by the way of the king's garden, by the gate betwixt the two walls:
and he went out the way of the plain.

[5] **But the Chaldeans' army** pursued after them,
and overtook Zedekiah in the plains of Jericho:
and when they had taken him,
they brought him up to Nebuchadnezzar king of Babylon to Riblah in the land of Hamath,
where he gave judgment upon him.

[6] **Then the king of Babylon** slew the sons of Zedekiah in Riblah before his eyes:
also the king of Babylon slew all the nobles of Judah.

[7] **Moreover he** put out Zedekiah's eyes,
and bound him with chains,
to carry him to Babylon.

[8] **And the Chaldeans** burned the king's house, and the houses of the people, with fire,
and brake down the walls of Jerusalem.

[9] **Then Nebuzaradan the captain of the guard** carried away captive into Babylon the remnant of the people that remained in the city, and those that fell away, that fell to him, with the rest of the people that remained.

[10] **But Nebuzaradan the captain of the guard** left of the poor of the people, {which had nothing}, in the land of Judah,
and gave them vineyards and fields at the same time.

[11] **Now Nebuchadrezzar king of Babylon** gave charge concerning Jeremiah to Nebuzaradan the captain of the guard,
saying,
[12] **Take** him,
and look well to him,
and do him no harm;
but do unto him
even as he shall say unto thee.

[13] **So Nebuzaradan the captain of the guard** sent,
and Nebushasban, Rabsaris, and Nergalsharezer, Rabmag, and all the king of Babylon's princes;
[14] Even they sent,
and took Jeremiah out of the court of the prison,
and committed him unto Gedaliah the son of Ahikam the son of Shaphan,
that he should carry him home:
so he dwelt among the people.

[15] **Now the word of the LORD** came unto Jeremiah,
while he was shut up in the court of the prison,
saying,
[16] **Go and speak** to Ebedmelech the Ethiopian,
saying,
Thus saith the LORD of hosts, the God of Israel;
Behold,
I will bring my words upon this city for evil, and not for good;
and they shall be accomplished in that day before thee.

[17] **But I** will deliver thee in that day,
saith the LORD:
and thou shalt not be given into the hand of the men of whom thou art afraid.

[18] **For I** will surely deliver thee,
and thou shalt not fall by the sword,
but thy life shall be for a prey unto thee:
because thou hast put thy trust in me,
saith the LORD.

40

The word that came to Jeremiah from the LORD,
after that Nebuzaradan the captain of the guard had let him go from Ramah,
when he had taken him being bound in chains among all that were carried away captive of Jerusalem and Judah,
which were carried away captive unto Babylon.

[2] **And the captain of the guard** took Jeremiah,
and said unto him,
The LORD thy God hath pronounced this evil upon this place.

[3] **Now the LORD** hath brought it,
and done according as he hath said:

because ye have sinned against the LORD,
and have not obeyed his voice,
therefore this thing is come upon you.
4 **And now, {behold}, I** loose thee this day from the chains which were upon thine hand.
If it seem good unto thee to come with me into Babylon,
come;
and I will look well unto thee:
but if it seem ill unto thee to come with me into Babylon,
forbear:
behold,
all the land is before thee:
whither it seemeth good and convenient for thee to go,
thither go.
5 **Now while he** was not yet gone back,
he said,
Go back also to Gedaliah the son of Ahikam the son of Shaphan,
whom the king of Babylon hath made governor over the cities of Judah,
and dwell with him among the people:
or go
wheresoever it seemeth convenient unto thee to go.
So the captain of the guard gave him victuals and a reward,
and let him go.
6 **Then** went Jeremiah unto Gedaliah the son of Ahikam to Mizpah;
and dwelt with him among the people that were left in the land.
7 **Now when all the captains of the forces which were in the fields, even they and their men,** heard that the king of Babylon had made Gedaliah the son of Ahikam governor in the land,
and had committed unto him men, and women, and children, and of the poor of the land, of them that were not carried away captive to Babylon;
8 **Then they** came to Gedaliah to Mizpah, even Ishmael the son of Nethaniah, and Johanan and Jonathan the sons of Kareah, and Seraiah the son of Tanhumeth, and the sons of Ephai the Netophathite, and Jezaniah the son of a Maachathite, they and their men.
9 **And Gedaliah the son of Ahikam the son of Shaphan** sware unto them and to their men,
saying,
Fear not to serve the Chaldeans:
dwell in the land,
and serve the king of Babylon,
and it shall be well with you.
10 **As for me**, {behold}, I will dwell at Mizpah,
to serve the Chaldeans,
which will come unto us:
but ye, gather ye wine, and summer fruits, and oil,
and put them in your vessels,
and dwell in your cities that ye have taken.
11 **Likewise when all the Jews that were in Moab, and among the Ammonites, and in Edom, and that were in all the countries,** heard that the king of Babylon had left a remnant of Judah, and that he had set over them Gedaliah the son of Ahikam the son of Shaphan;
12 **Even all the Jews** returned out of all places whither they were driven,
and came to the land of Judah, to Gedaliah, unto Mizpah,
and gathered wine and summer fruits very much.
13 **Moreover Johanan the son of Kareah, and all the captains of the forces that were in the fields,** came to Gedaliah to Mizpah,
14 **And** said unto him,
Dost thou certainly know
that Baalis the king of the Ammonites hath sent Ishmael the son of Nethaniah to slay thee?
But Gedaliah the son of Ahikam believed them not.
15 **Then Johanan the son of Kareah** spake to Gedaliah in Mizpah
secretly saying,
Let me go,
I pray thee,
and I will slay Ishmael the son of Nethaniah,
and no man shall know it:
wherefore should he slay thee,
that all the Jews which are gathered unto thee should be scattered,
and the remnant in Judah perish?
16 **But Gedaliah the son of Ahikam** said unto Johanan the son of Kareah,
Thou shalt not do this thing:
for thou speakest falsely of Ishmael.

41

Now it came to pass in the seventh month,
that Ishmael the son of Nethaniah the son of Elishama, of the seed royal, and the princes of the king, even ten men with him, came unto Gedaliah the son of Ahikam to Mizpah;
and there they did eat bread together in Mizpah.
2 **Then** arose Ishmael the son of Nethaniah, and the ten men that were with him,
and smote Gedaliah the son of Ahikam the son of Shaphan with the sword,
and slew him,
whom the king of Babylon had made governor over the land.
3 **Ishmael** also slew all the Jews that were with him, even with Gedaliah, at Mizpah, and the Chaldeans that were found there, and the men of war.
4 **And it** came to pass the second day after he had slain Gedaliah,
and no man knew it,
5 **That there** came certain from Shechem, from Shiloh, and from Samaria, even fourscore men,
having their beards shaven,
and their clothes rent,
and having cut themselves, with offerings and incense in their hand,
to bring them to the house of the LORD.
6 **And Ishmael the son of Nethaniah** went forth from Mizpah to meet them,
weeping all along as he went:
and it came to pass,
as he met them,
he said unto them,
Come to Gedaliah the son of Ahikam.
7 **And it** was so,
when they came into the midst of the city,
that Ishmael the son of Nethaniah slew them,
and cast them into the midst of the pit, he, and the men that were with him.

8 **But ten men** were found among them that said unto Ishmael,
Slay us not:
for we have treasures in the field, of wheat, and of barley, and of oil, and of honey.

So he forbare,
and slew them not among their brethren.

9 **Now the pit wherein Ishmael had cast all the dead bodies of the men**, {whom he had slain because of Gedaliah}, was it which Asa the king had made for fear of Baasha king of Israel:
and Ishmael the son of Nethaniah filled it with them that were slain.

10 **Then Ishmael** carried away captive all the residue of the people that were in Mizpah, even the king's daughters, and all the people that remained in Mizpah,
whom Nebuzaradan the captain of the guard had committed to Gedaliah the son of Ahikam:
and Ishmael the son of Nethaniah carried them away captive,
and departed to go over to the Ammonites.

11 **But when Johanan the son of Kareah, and all the captains of the forces that were with him,** heard of all the evil that Ishmael the son of Nethaniah had done,
12 **Then they** took all the men,
and went to fight with Ishmael the son of Nethaniah,
and found him by the great waters that are in Gibeon.

13 **Now it** came to pass,
that when all the people which were with Ishmael saw Johanan the son of Kareah, and all the captains of the forces that were with him,
then they were glad.

14 **So all the people that Ishmael had carried away captive from Mizpah** cast about and returned,
and went unto Johanan the son of Kareah.

15 **But Ishmael the son of Nethaniah** escaped from Johanan with eight men,
and went to the Ammonites.

16 **Then** took Johanan the son of Kareah, and all the captains of the forces that were with him, all the remnant of the people whom he had recovered from Ishmael the son of Nethaniah, from Mizpah,
after that he had slain Gedaliah the son of Ahikam, even mighty men of war, and the women, and the children, and the eunuchs,
whom he had brought again from Gibeon:
17 **And they** departed,
and dwelt in the habitation of Chimham,
which is by Bethlehem,
to go to enter into Egypt,
18 Because of the Chaldeans:
for they were afraid of them,
because Ishmael the son of Nethaniah had slain Gedaliah the son of Ahikam,
whom the king of Babylon made governor in the land.

42

Then all the captains of the forces, and Johanan the son of Kareah, and Jezaniah the son of Hoshaiah, and all the people from the least even unto the greatest, came near,
2 **And** said unto Jeremiah the prophet,
Let, {we beseech thee}, our supplication be accepted before thee,
and pray for us unto the LORD thy God, even for all this remnant;
(for we are left but a few of many, as thine eyes do behold us:)
3 **That the LORD thy God** may shew us the way wherein we may walk, and the thing that we may do.

4 **Then Jeremiah the prophet** said unto them,
I have heard you;
behold,
I will pray unto the LORD your God according to your words;
and it shall come to pass,
that whatsoever thing the LORD shall answer you,
I will declare it unto you;
I will keep nothing back from you.

5 **Then they** said to Jeremiah,
The LORD be a true and faithful witness between us,
if we do not even according to all things for the which the LORD thy God shall send thee to us.

6 **Whether it** be good,
or whether it be evil,
we will obey the voice of the LORD our God,
to whom we send thee;
that it may be well with us,
when we obey the voice of the LORD our God.

7 **And it** came to pass after ten days,
that the word of the LORD came unto Jeremiah.

8 **Then** called he Johanan the son of Kareah, and all the captains of the forces which were with him, and all the people from the least even to the greatest,
9 **And** said unto them,
Thus saith the LORD, the God of Israel,
unto whom ye sent me to present your supplication before him;
10 **If ye** will still abide in this land,
then will I build you,
and not pull you down,
and I will plant you,
and not pluck you up:
for I repent me of the evil that I have done unto you.

11 **Be not** afraid of the king of Babylon,
of whom ye are afraid;
be not afraid of him,
saith the LORD:
for I am with you
to save you,
and to deliver you from his hand.

12 **And I** will shew mercies unto you,
that he may have mercy upon you,
and cause you to return to your own land.

13 **But if ye** say,
We will not dwell in this land,
neither obey the voice of the LORD your God,
14 Saying,
No;
but we will go into the land of Egypt,
where we shall see no war,
nor hear the sound of the trumpet,
nor have hunger of bread;
and there will we dwell:
15 **And now therefore hear** the word of the LORD, ye remnant of Judah;
Thus saith the LORD of hosts, the God of Israel;
If ye wholly set your faces to enter into Egypt,
and go to sojourn there;
16 **Then it** shall come to pass,

that the sword, {which ye feared},
shall overtake you there in the
land of Egypt,
and the famine, {whereof ye were
afraid}, shall follow close after
you there in Egypt;
and there ye shall die.
17 **So** shall it be with all the men that
set their faces to go into Egypt to
sojourn there;
they shall die by the sword, by the
famine, and by the pestilence:
and none of them shall remain or
escape from the evil that I will
bring upon them.
18 **For thus** saith the LORD of hosts,
the God of Israel;
As mine anger and my fury hath
been poured forth upon the
inhabitants of Jerusalem;
so shall my fury be poured forth
upon you,
when ye shall enter into Egypt:
and ye shall be an execration, and
an astonishment, and a curse, and
a reproach;
and ye shall see this place no more.
19 **The LORD** hath said concerning
you, O ye remnant of Judah;
Go ye not into Egypt:
know certainly
that I have admonished you this
day.
20 **For ye** dissembled in your hearts,
when ye sent me unto the LORD
your God,
saying,
Pray for us unto the LORD our God;
and according unto all that the
LORD our God shall say,
so declare unto us,
and we will do it.
21 **And now I** have this day declared
it to you;
but ye have not obeyed the voice of
the LORD your God, nor any thing
for the which he hath sent me
unto you.
22 **Now therefore know** certainly
that ye shall die by the sword, by
the famine, and by the pestilence,
in the place whither ye desire to
go and to sojourn.

43 **And it** came to pass,
that when Jeremiah had
made an end of speaking unto all
the people all the words of the
LORD their God,
for which the LORD their God had
sent him to them, even all these
words,
2 **Then** spake Azariah the son of
Hoshaiah, and Johanan the son of
Kareah, and all the proud men,
saying unto Jeremiah,
Thou speakest falsely:
the LORD our God hath not sent
thee to say,
Go not into Egypt to sojourn there:
3 **But Baruch the son of Neriah**
setteth thee on against us,
for to deliver us into the hand of the
Chaldeans,
that they might put us to death,
and carry us away captives into
Babylon.
4 **So Johanan the son of Kareah,
and all the captains of the
forces, and all the people,**
obeyed not the voice of the LORD,
to dwell in the land of Judah.
5 **But Johanan the son of Kareah,
and all the captains of the
forces,** took all the remnant of
Judah,
that were returned from all nations,
whither they had been driven,
to dwell in the land of Judah;
6 Even men, and women, and
children, and the king's
daughters, and every person that
Nebuzaradan the captain of the
guard had left with Gedaliah the
son of Ahikam the son of
Shaphan, and Jeremiah the
prophet, and Baruch the son of
Neriah.
7 **So they** came into the land of
Egypt:
for they obeyed not the voice of the
LORD:
thus came they even to Tahpanhes.
8 **Then** came the word of the LORD
unto Jeremiah in Tahpanhes,
saying,
9 **Take** great stones in thine hand,
and hide them in the clay in the
brickkiln,
which is at the entry of Pharaoh's
house in Tahpanhes, in the sight
of the men of Judah;
10 **And say** unto them,
Thus saith the LORD of hosts, the
God of Israel;
Behold,
I will send and take
Nebuchadrezzar the king of
Babylon, my servant,
and will set his throne upon these
stones that I have hid;
and he shall spread his royal
pavilion over them.
11 **And when he** cometh,
he shall smite the land of Egypt,
and deliver such as are for death to
death;
and such as are for captivity to
captivity;
and such as are for the sword to the
sword.
12 **And I** will kindle a fire in the
houses of the gods of Egypt;
and he shall burn them,
and carry them away captives:
and he shall array himself with the
land of Egypt,
as a shepherd putteth on his
garment;
and he shall go forth from thence in
peace.
13 **He** shall break also the images of
Bethshemesh,
that is in the land of Egypt;
**and the houses of the gods of the
Egyptians** shall he burn with fire.

44 The word that came to
Jeremiah concerning all
the Jews which dwell in the land
of Egypt,
which dwell at Migdol, and at
Tahpanhes, and at Noph, and in
the country of Pathros,
saying,
2 **Thus** saith the LORD of hosts, the
God of Israel;
Ye have seen all the evil that I have
brought upon Jerusalem, and
upon all the cities of Judah;
and, {behold}, this day they are a
desolation,
and no man dwelleth therein,
3 Because of their wickedness which
they have committed
to provoke me to anger,
in that they went to burn incense,
and to serve other gods,
whom they knew not, neither they,
ye, nor your fathers.
4 **Howbeit I** sent unto you all my
servants the prophets,
rising early and sending them,
saying,
Oh, do not this abominable thing
that I hate.
5 **But they** hearkened not,
nor inclined their ear to turn from
their wickedness,
to burn no incense unto other gods.
6 **Wherefore my fury and mine
anger** was poured forth,

and was kindled in the cities of Judah and in the streets of Jerusalem;
and they are wasted and desolate, as at this day.

7 **Therefore now thus** saith the LORD, the God of hosts, the God of Israel;
Wherefore commit ye this great evil against your souls,
to cut off from you man and woman, child and suckling, out of Judah,
to leave you none to remain;
8 **In that ye** provoke me unto wrath with the works of your hands,
burning incense unto other gods in the land of Egypt,
whither ye be gone to dwell,
that ye might cut yourselves off,
and that ye might be a curse and a reproach among all the nations of the earth?

9 **Have ye** forgotten the wickedness of your fathers, and the wickedness of the kings of Judah, and the wickedness of their wives, and your own wickedness, and the wickedness of your wives,
which they have committed in the land of Judah, and in the streets of Jerusalem?

10 **They** are not humbled even unto this day,
neither have they feared,
nor walked in my law, nor in my statutes,
that I set before you and before your fathers.

11 **Therefore thus** saith the LORD of hosts, the God of Israel;
Behold,
I will set my face against you for evil,
and to cut off all Judah.

12 **And I** will take the remnant of Judah,
that have set their faces to go into the land of Egypt to sojourn there,
and they shall all be consumed,
and fall in the land of Egypt;
they shall even be consumed by the sword and by the famine:
they shall die, from the least even unto the greatest, by the sword and by the famine:
and they shall be an execration, and an astonishment, and a curse, and a reproach.

13 **For I** will punish them that dwell in the land of Egypt,
as I have punished Jerusalem, by the sword, by the famine, and by the pestilence:

14 **So that none of the remnant of Judah**, {which are gone into the land of Egypt to sojourn there}, shall escape or remain,
that they should return into the land of Judah,
to the which they have a desire to return to dwell there:
for none shall return but such as shall escape.

15 **Then all the men which knew that their wives had burned incense unto other gods, and all the women that stood by, a great multitude, even all the people that dwelt in the land of Egypt, in Pathros,** answered Jeremiah,
saying,
16 **As for the word that thou hast spoken unto us in the name of the LORD,** we will not hearken unto thee.

17 **But we** will certainly do whatsoever thing goeth forth out of our own mouth,
to burn incense unto the queen of heaven,
and to pour out drink offerings unto her,
as we have done, we, and our fathers, our kings, and our princes, in the cities of Judah, and in the streets of Jerusalem:
for then had we plenty of victuals,
and were well,
and saw no evil.

18 **But since we** left off to burn incense to the queen of heaven,
and to pour out drink offerings unto her,
we have wanted all things,
and have been consumed by the sword and by the famine.

19 **And when we** burned incense to the queen of heaven,
and poured out drink offerings unto her,
did we make her cakes to worship her,
and pour out drink offerings unto her, without our men?

20 **Then Jeremiah** said unto all the people, to the men, and to the women, and to all the people which had given him that answer,
saying,
21 **The incense that ye burned in the cities of Judah, and in the streets of Jerusalem, ye, and your fathers, your kings, and your princes, and the people of the land,** did not the LORD remember them,
and came it not into his mind?

22 **So that the LORD** could no longer bear, because of the evil of your doings, and because of the abominations which ye have committed;
therefore is your land a desolation, and an astonishment, and a curse, without an inhabitant, as at this day.

23 **Because ye** have burned incense,
and because ye have sinned against the LORD,
and have not obeyed the voice of the LORD,
nor walked in his law, nor in his statutes, nor in his testimonies;
therefore this evil is happened unto you, as at this day.

24 **Moreover Jeremiah** said unto all the people, and to all the women,
Hear the word of the LORD, all Judah that are in the land of Egypt:
25 **Thus** saith the LORD of hosts, the God of Israel,
saying;
Ye and your wives have both spoken with your mouths,
and fulfilled with your hand,
saying,
We will surely perform our vows that we have vowed,
to burn incense to the queen of heaven,
and to pour out drink offerings unto her:
ye will surely accomplish your vows,
and surely perform your vows.

26 **Therefore hear ye** the word of the LORD, all Judah that dwell in the land of Egypt;
Behold,
I have sworn by my great name,
saith the LORD,
that my name shall no more be named in the mouth of any man of Judah in all the land of Egypt,
saying,
The Lord GOD liveth.

27 **Behold,**
I will watch over them for evil, and not for good:
and all the men of Judah that are in the land of Egypt shall be consumed by the sword and by the famine,
until there be an end of them.
28 **Yet a small number that escape the sword** shall return out of the land of Egypt into the land of Judah,
and all the remnant of Judah, {that are gone into the land of Egypt to sojourn there}, shall know
whose words shall stand, mine, or their's.
29 **And this** shall be a sign unto you,
saith the LORD,
that I will punish you in this place,
that ye may know
that my words shall surely stand against you for evil:
30 **Thus** saith the LORD;
Behold,
I will give Pharaohhophra king of Egypt into the hand of his enemies, and into the hand of them that seek his life;
as I gave Zedekiah king of Judah into the hand of Nebuchadrezzar king of Babylon, his enemy,
and that sought his life.

45 The word that Jeremiah the prophet spake unto Baruch the son of Neriah,
when he had written these words in a book at the mouth of Jeremiah, in the fourth year of Jehoiakim the son of Josiah king of Judah,
saying,
2 **Thus** saith the LORD, the God of Israel, unto thee, O Baruch:
3 **Thou** didst say,
Woe is me now!
for the LORD hath added grief to my sorrow;
I fainted in my sighing,
and I find no rest.
4 **Thus** shalt thou say unto him,
The LORD saith thus;
Behold,
that which I have built will I break down,
and that which I have planted I will pluck up, even this whole land.
5 **And seekest thou** great things for thyself?
seek them not:
for, {behold}, I will bring evil upon all flesh,
saith the LORD:
but thy life will I give unto thee for a prey in all places whither thou goest.

46 ∞ The word of the LORD which came to Jeremiah the prophet against the Gentiles;
2 Against Egypt, against the army of Pharaohnecho king of Egypt,
which was by the river Euphrates in Carchemish,
which Nebuchadrezzar king of Babylon smote in the fourth year of Jehoiakim the son of Josiah king of Judah.
3 **Order ye** the buckler and shield,
and draw near to battle.
4 **Harness** the horses;
and get up, ye horsemen,
and stand forth with your helmets;
furbish the spears,
and put on the brigandines.
5 **Wherefore** have I seen them dismayed and turned away back?
and their mighty ones are beaten down,
and are fled apace,
and look not back:
for fear was round about,
saith the LORD.
6 **Let not the swift** flee away,
nor the mighty man escape;
they shall stumble,
and fall toward the north by the river Euphrates.
7 **Who** is this that cometh up as a flood,
whose waters are moved as the rivers?
8 **Egypt** riseth up like a flood,
and his waters are moved like the rivers;
and he saith,
I will go up,
and will cover the earth;
I will destroy the city and the inhabitants thereof.
9 **Come up,** ye horses;
and rage, ye chariots;
and let the mighty men come forth; the Ethiopians and the Libyans, {that handle the shield}; and the Lydians, {that handle and bend the bow}.
10 **For this** is the day of the Lord GOD of hosts, a day of vengeance,
that he may avenge him of his adversaries:
and the sword shall devour,
and it shall be satiate and made drunk with their blood:
for the Lord GOD of hosts hath a sacrifice in the north country by the river Euphrates.
11 **Go up** into Gilead,
and take balm, O virgin, the daughter of Egypt:
in vain shalt thou use many medicines;
for thou shalt not be cured.
12 **The nations** have heard of thy shame,
and thy cry hath filled the land:
for the mighty man hath stumbled against the mighty,
and they are fallen both together.
13 The word that the LORD spake to Jeremiah the prophet,
how Nebuchadrezzar king of Babylon should come and smite the land of Egypt.
14 **Declare ye** in Egypt,
and publish in Migdol,
and publish in Noph and in Tahpanhes:
say ye,
Stand fast,
and prepare thee;
for the sword shall devour round about thee.
15 **Why** are thy valiant men swept away?
they stood not,
because the LORD did drive them.
16 **He** made many to fall,
yea, one fell upon another:
and they said,
Arise,
and let us go again to our own people, and to the land of our nativity, from the oppressing sword.
17 **They** did cry there,
Pharaoh king of Egypt is but a noise;
he hath passed the time appointed.
18 **As I** live,
saith the King,
whose name is the LORD of hosts,
Surely as Tabor is among the mountains, and as Carmel by the sea,
so shall he come.

19 **O thou daughter dwelling in Egypt, furnish** thyself to go into captivity:
for Noph shall be waste and desolate without an inhabitant.

20 **Egypt** is like a very fair heifer,
but destruction cometh;
it cometh out of the north.

21 **Also her hired men** are in the midst of her like fatted bullocks;
for they also are turned back,
and are fled away together:
they did not stand,
because the day of their calamity was come upon them, and the time of their visitation.

22 **The voice thereof** shall go like a serpent;
for they shall march with an army,
and come against her with axes, as hewers of wood.

23 **They shall** cut down her forest,
saith the LORD,
though it cannot be searched;
because they are more than the grasshoppers,
and are innumerable.

24 **The daughter of Egypt** shall be confounded;
she shall be delivered into the hand of the people of the north.

25 **The LORD of hosts, the God of Israel,** saith;
Behold,
I will punish the multitude of No, and Pharaoh, and Egypt, with their gods, and their kings; even Pharaoh, and all them that trust in him:

26 **And I** will deliver them into the hand of those that seek their lives, and into the hand of Nebuchadrezzar king of Babylon, and into the hand of his servants:
and afterward it shall be inhabited, as in the days of old,
saith the LORD.

27 **But fear not thou,** O my servant Jacob,
and be not dismayed, O Israel:
for, {behold}, I will save thee from afar off, and thy seed from the land of their captivity;
and Jacob shall return,
and be in rest and at ease,
and none shall make him afraid.

28 **Fear thou not,** O Jacob my servant,
saith the LORD:
for I am with thee;
for I will make a full end of all the nations whither I have driven thee:
but I will not make a full end of thee,
but correct thee in measure;
yet will I not leave thee wholly unpunished.

47 The word of the LORD that came to Jeremiah the prophet against the Philistines,
before that Pharaoh smote Gaza.

2 **Thus** saith the LORD;
Behold,
waters rise up out of the north,
and shall be an overflowing flood,
and shall overflow the land, and all that is therein; the city, and them that dwell therein:
then the men shall cry,
and all the inhabitants of the land shall howl.

3 **At the noise of the stamping of the hoofs of his strong horses, at the rushing of his chariots, and at the rumbling of his wheels,** the fathers shall not look back to their children for feebleness of hands;

4 Because of the day that cometh to spoil all the Philistines,
and to cut off from Tyrus and Zidon every helper that remaineth:
for the LORD will spoil the Philistines, the remnant of the country of Caphtor.

5 **Baldness** is come upon Gaza;
Ashkelon is cut off with the remnant of their valley:
how long wilt thou cut thyself?

6 **O thou sword of the LORD, how long** will it be ere thou be quiet?
put up thyself into thy scabbard,
rest,
and be still.

7 **How** can it be quiet,
seeing the LORD hath given it a charge against Ashkelon, and against the sea shore?
there hath he appointed it.

48 **Against Moab** thus saith the LORD of hosts, the God of Israel;
Woe unto Nebo!
for it is spoiled:
Kiriathaim is confounded and taken:
Misgab is confounded and dismayed.

2 **There** shall be no more praise of Moab:
in Heshbon they have devised evil against it;
come,
and let us cut it off from being a nation.
Also thou shalt be cut down, O Madmen;
the sword shall pursue thee.

3 **A voice of crying** shall be from Horonaim, spoiling and great destruction.

4 **Moab** is destroyed;
her little ones have caused a cry to be heard.

5 **For in the going up of Luhith** continual weeping shall go up;
for in the going down of Horonaim the enemies have heard a cry of destruction.

6 **Flee,**
save your lives,
and be like the heath in the wilderness.

7 **For because thou** hast trusted in thy works and in thy treasures,
thou shalt also be taken:
and Chemosh shall go forth into captivity with his priests and his princes together.

8 **And the spoiler** shall come upon every city,
and no city shall escape:
the valley also shall perish,
and the plain shall be destroyed,
as the LORD hath spoken.

9 **Give wings** unto Moab,
that it may flee and get away:
for the cities thereof shall be desolate,
without any to dwell therein.

10 **Cursed** be he that doeth the work of the LORD deceitfully,
and cursed be he that keepeth back his sword from blood.

11 **Moab** hath been at ease from his youth,
and he hath settled on his lees,
and hath not been emptied from vessel to vessel,
neither hath he gone into captivity:
therefore his taste remained in him,
and his scent is not changed.

12 **Therefore, {behold}, the days** come,
saith the LORD,

that I will send unto him wanderers,
that shall cause him to wander,
and shall empty his vessels,
and break their bottles.
13 **And Moab** shall be ashamed of Chemosh,
as the house of Israel was ashamed of Bethel their confidence.
14 **How** say ye,
We are mighty and strong men for the war?
15 **Moab** is spoiled,
and gone up out of her cities,
and his chosen young men are gone down to the slaughter,
saith the King,
whose name is the LORD of hosts.
16 **The calamity of Moab** is near to come,
and his affliction hasteth fast.
17 **All ye that are about him, bemoan** him;
and all ye that know his name, say,
How is the strong staff broken, and the beautiful rod!
18 **Thou daughter that dost inhabit Dibon, come down** from thy glory,
and sit in thirst;
for the spoiler of Moab shall come upon thee,
and he shall destroy thy strong holds.
19 **O inhabitant of Aroer, stand** by the way,
and espy;
ask him that fleeth, and her that escapeth,
and say,
What is done?
20 **Moab** is confounded;
for it is broken down:
howl and cry;
tell ye it in Arnon,
that Moab is spoiled,
21 **And judgment** is come upon the plain country; upon Holon, and upon Jahazah, and upon Mephaath,
22 And upon Dibon, and upon Nebo, and upon Bethdiblathaim,
23 And upon Kiriathaim, and upon Bethgamul, and upon Bethmeon,
24 And upon Kerioth, and upon Bozrah, and upon all the cities of the land of Moab, far or near.
25 **The horn of Moab** is cut off,
and his arm is broken,
saith the LORD.
26 **Make ye** him drunken:
for he magnified himself against the LORD:
Moab also shall wallow in his vomit,
and he also shall be in derision.
27 **For was not Israel** a derision unto thee?
was he found among thieves?
for since thou spakest of him,
thou skippedst for joy.
28 **O ye that dwell in Moab, leave** the cities,
and dwell in the rock,
and be like the dove that maketh her nest in the sides of the hole's mouth.
29 **We** have heard the pride of Moab, (he is exceeding proud) his loftiness, and his arrogancy, and his pride, and the haughtiness of his heart.
30 **I** know his wrath,
saith the LORD;
but it shall not be so;
his lies shall not so effect it.
31 **Therefore** will I howl for Moab,
and I will cry out for all Moab;
mine heart shall mourn for the men of Kirheres.
32 **O vine of Sibmah, I** will weep for thee with the weeping of Jazer:
thy plants are gone over the sea,
they reach even to the sea of Jazer:
the spoiler is fallen upon thy summer fruits and upon thy vintage.
33 **And joy and gladness** is taken from the plentiful field, and from the land of Moab,
and I have caused wine to fail from the winepresses:
none shall tread with shouting;
their shouting shall be no shouting.
34 **From the cry of Heshbon even unto Elealeh, and even unto Jahaz,** have they uttered their voice, from Zoar even unto Horonaim, as an heifer of three years old:
for the waters also of Nimrim shall be desolate.
35 **Moreover I** will cause to cease in Moab, {saith the LORD}, him that offereth in the high places, and him that burneth incense to his gods.
36 **Therefore mine heart** shall sound for Moab like pipes,
and mine heart shall sound like pipes for the men of Kirheres:
because the riches that he hath gotten are perished.
37 **For every head** shall be bald,
and every beard clipped:
upon all the hands shall be cuttings, and upon the loins sackcloth.
38 **There** shall be lamentation generally upon all the housetops of Moab, and in the streets thereof:
for I have broken Moab like a vessel wherein is no pleasure,
saith the LORD.
39 **They** shall howl,
saying,
How is it broken down!
how hath Moab turned the back with shame!
so shall Moab be a derision and a dismaying to all them about him.
40 **For thus** saith the LORD;
Behold,
he shall fly as an eagle,
and shall spread his wings over Moab.
41 **Kerioth** is taken,
and the strong holds are surprised,
and the mighty men's hearts in Moab at that day shall be as the heart of a woman in her pangs.
42 **And Moab** shall be destroyed from being a people,
because he hath magnified himself against the LORD.
43 **Fear, and the pit, and the snare,** shall be upon thee, O inhabitant of Moab,
saith the LORD.
44 **He that fleeth from the fear** shall fall into the pit;
and he that getteth up out of the pit shall be taken in the snare:
for I will bring upon it, even upon Moab, the year of their visitation,
saith the LORD.
45 **They that fled** stood under the shadow of Heshbon because of the force:
but a fire shall come forth out of Heshbon, and a flame from the midst of Sihon,
and shall devour the corner of Moab, and the crown of the head of the tumultuous ones.

46 **Woe** be unto thee, O Moab!
the people of Chemosh perisheth:
for thy sons are taken captives, and thy daughters captives.

47 **Yet** will I bring again the captivity of Moab in the latter days,
saith the LORD.

Thus far is the judgment of Moab.

49

Concerning the Ammonites, thus saith the LORD;
Hath Israel no sons?
hath he no heir?
why then doth their king inherit Gad,
and his people dwell in his cities?

2 **Therefore, {behold}, the days** come,
saith the LORD,
that I will cause an alarm of war to be heard in Rabbah of the Ammonites;
and it shall be a desolate heap,
and her daughters shall be burned with fire:
then shall Israel be heir unto them that were his heirs,
saith the LORD.

3 **Howl,** O Heshbon,
for Ai is spoiled:
cry, ye daughters of Rabbah,
gird you with sackcloth;
lament,
and run to and fro by the hedges;
for their king shall go into captivity, and his priests and his princes together.

4 **Wherefore** gloriest thou in the valleys, thy flowing valley, O backsliding daughter?
that trusted in her treasures,
saying,
Who shall come unto me?

5 **Behold,**
I will bring a fear upon thee, {saith the Lord GOD of hosts}, from all those that be about thee;
and ye shall be driven out every man right forth;
and none shall gather up him that wandereth.

6 **And afterward I** will bring again the captivity of the children of Ammon,
saith the LORD.

7 **Concerning Edom,** thus saith the LORD of hosts;
Is wisdom no more in Teman?
is counsel perished from the prudent?
is their wisdom vanished?

8 **Flee ye,**
turn back,
dwell deep, O inhabitants of Dedan;
for I will bring the calamity of Esau upon him, the time that I will visit him.

9 **If grapegatherers** come to thee,
would they not leave some gleaning grapes?
if thieves by night,
they will destroy till they have enough.

10 **But I** have made Esau bare,
I have uncovered his secret places,
and he shall not be able to hide himself:
his seed is spoiled, and his brethren, and his neighbours,
and he is not.

11 **Leave** thy fatherless children,
I will preserve them alive;
and let thy widows trust in me.

12 **For thus** saith the LORD;
Behold,
they whose judgment was not to drink of the cup have assuredly drunken;
and art thou he that shall altogether go unpunished?
thou shalt not go unpunished,
but thou shalt surely drink of it.

13 **For I** have sworn by myself,
saith the LORD,
that Bozrah shall become a desolation, a reproach, a waste, and a curse;
and all the cities thereof shall be perpetual wastes.

14 **I** have heard a rumour from the LORD,
and an ambassador is sent unto the heathen,
saying,
Gather ye together,
and come against her,
and rise up to the battle.

15 **For, {lo}, I** will make thee small among the heathen,
and despised among men.

16 **Thy terribleness** hath deceived thee, and the pride of thine heart, O thou that dwellest in the clefts of the rock, that holdest the height of the hill:
though thou shouldest make thy nest as high as the eagle,
I will bring thee down from thence,
saith the LORD.

17 **Also Edom** shall be a desolation:
every one that goeth by it shall be astonished,
and shall hiss at all the plagues thereof.

18 **As in the overthrow of Sodom and Gomorrah and the neighbour cities thereof,** {saith the LORD}, no man shall abide there,
neither shall a son of man dwell in it.

19 **Behold,**
he shall come up like a lion from the swelling of Jordan against the habitation of the strong:
but I will suddenly make him run away from her:
and who is a chosen man,
that I may appoint over her?
for who is like me?
and who will appoint me the time?
and who is that shepherd that will stand before me?

20 **Therefore hear** the counsel of the LORD, {that he hath taken against Edom}; and his purposes, {that he hath purposed against the inhabitants of Teman}:
Surely the least of the flock shall draw them out:
surely he shall make their habitations desolate with them.

21 **The earth** is moved at the noise of their fall,
at the cry the noise thereof was heard in the Red sea.

22 **Behold,**
he shall come up and fly as the eagle,
and spread his wings over Bozrah:
and at that day shall the heart of the mighty men of Edom be as the heart of a woman in her pangs.

23 Concerning Damascus.

Hamath is confounded, and Arpad:
for they have heard evil tidings:
they are fainthearted;
there is sorrow on the sea;
it cannot be quiet.

24 **Damascus** is waxed feeble,
and turneth herself to flee,
and fear hath seized on her:
anguish and sorrows have taken her, as a woman in travail.

25 **How** is the city of praise not left,
the city of my joy!

26 **Therefore her young men** shall fall in her streets,
and all the men of war shall be cut off in that day,
saith the LORD of hosts.

27 **And I** will kindle a fire in the wall of Damascus,
and it shall consume the palaces of Benhadad.

28 **Concerning Kedar, and concerning the kingdoms of Hazor**, {which Nebuchadrezzar king of Babylon shall smite},
thus saith the LORD;
Arise ye,
go up to Kedar,
and spoil the men of the east.

29 **Their tents and their flocks** shall they take away:
they shall take to themselves their curtains, and all their vessels, and their camels;
and they shall cry unto them,
Fear is on every side.

30 **Flee,**
get you far off,
dwell deep, O ye inhabitants of Hazor,
saith the LORD;
for Nebuchadrezzar king of Babylon hath taken counsel against you,
and hath conceived a purpose against you.

31 **Arise,**
get you up unto the wealthy nation,
that dwelleth without care,
saith the LORD,
which have neither gates nor bars,
which dwell alone.

32 **And their camels** shall be a booty, and the multitude of their cattle a spoil:
and I will scatter into all winds them that are in the utmost corners;
and I will bring their calamity from all sides thereof,
saith the LORD.

33 **And Hazor** shall be a dwelling for dragons, and a desolation for ever:
there shall no man abide there,
nor any son of man dwell in it.

34 The word of the LORD that came to Jeremiah the prophet against Elam in the beginning of the reign of Zedekiah king of Judah,
saying,

35 **Thus** saith the LORD of hosts;
Behold,
I will break the bow of Elam, the chief of their might.

36 **And upon Elam** will I bring the four winds from the four quarters of heaven,
and will scatter them toward all those winds;
and there shall be no nation whither the outcasts of Elam shall not come.

37 **For I** will cause Elam to be dismayed before their enemies, and before them that seek their life:
and I will bring evil upon them, even my fierce anger,
saith the LORD;
and I will send the sword after them,
till I have consumed them:

38 **And I** will set my throne in Elam,
and will destroy from thence the king and the princes,
saith the LORD.

39 **But it** shall come to pass in the latter days,
that I will bring again the captivity of Elam,
saith the LORD.

50 The word that the LORD spake against Babylon and against the land of the Chaldeans by Jeremiah the prophet.

2 **Declare ye** among the nations,
and publish,
and set up a standard;
publish,
and conceal not:
say,
Babylon is taken,
Bel is confounded,
Merodach is broken in pieces;
her idols are confounded,
her images are broken in pieces.

3 **For out of the north** there cometh up a nation against her,
which shall make her land desolate,
and none shall dwell therein:
they shall remove,
they shall depart, both man and beast.

4 **In those days, and in that time**, {saith the LORD}, the children of Israel shall come, they and the children of Judah together,
going and weeping:
they shall go,
and seek the LORD their God.

5 **They** shall ask the way to Zion with their faces thitherward,
saying,
Come,
and let us join ourselves to the LORD in a perpetual covenant that shall not be forgotten.

6 **My people** hath been lost sheep:
their shepherds have caused them to go astray,
they have turned them away on the mountains:
they have gone from mountain to hill,
they have forgotten their restingplace.

7 **All that found them** have devoured them:
and their adversaries said,
We offend not,
because they have sinned against the LORD, the habitation of justice, even the LORD, the hope of their fathers.

8 **Remove** out of the midst of Babylon,
and go forth out of the land of the Chaldeans,
and be as the he goats before the flocks.

9 **For, {lo}, I** will raise and cause to come up against Babylon an assembly of great nations from the north country:
and they shall set themselves in array against her;
from thence she shall be taken:
their arrows shall be as of a mighty expert man;
none shall return in vain.

10 **And Chaldea** shall be a spoil:
all that spoil her shall be satisfied,
saith the LORD.

11 **Because ye** were glad,
because ye rejoiced, O ye destroyers of mine heritage,
because ye are grown fat as the heifer at grass,
and bellow as bulls;

12 **Your mother** shall be sore confounded;
she that bare you shall be ashamed:
behold,
the hindermost of the nations shall be a wilderness, a dry land, and a desert.

13 **Because of the wrath of the LORD** it shall not be inhabited,

but it shall be wholly desolate:
every one that goeth by Babylon shall be astonished,
and hiss at all her plagues.

14 **Put** yourselves in array against Babylon round about:
all ye that bend the bow, shoot at her,
spare no arrows:
for she hath sinned against the LORD.

15 **Shout** against her round about:
she hath given her hand:
her foundations are fallen,
her walls are thrown down:
for it is the vengeance of the LORD:
take vengeance upon her;
as she hath done,
do unto her.

16 **Cut off** the sower from Babylon, and him that handleth the sickle in the time of harvest:
for fear of the oppressing sword they shall turn every one to his people,
and they shall flee every one to his own land.

17 **Israel** is a scattered sheep;
the lions have driven him away:
first the king of Assyria hath devoured him;
and last this Nebuchadrezzar king of Babylon hath broken his bones.

18 **Therefore thus** saith the LORD of hosts, the God of Israel;
Behold,
I will punish the king of Babylon and his land,
as I have punished the king of Assyria.

19 **And I** will bring Israel again to his habitation,
and he shall feed on Carmel and Bashan,
and his soul shall be satisfied upon mount Ephraim and Gilead.

20 **In those days, and in that time,** {saith the LORD}, the iniquity of Israel shall be sought for, {and there shall be none}; and the sins of Judah, {and they shall not be found}:
for I will pardon them whom I reserve.

21 **Go up against** the land of Merathaim, even against it, and against the inhabitants of Pekod:
waste and utterly destroy after them,
saith the LORD,
and do according to all that I have commanded thee.

22 **A sound of battle** is in the land, and of great destruction.

23 **How** is the hammer of the whole earth cut asunder and broken!
is Babylon become a desolation among the nations!

24 **I** have laid a snare for thee,
and thou art also taken, O Babylon,
and thou wast not aware:
thou art found,
and also caught,
because thou hast striven against the LORD.

25 **The LORD** hath opened his armoury,
and hath brought forth the weapons of his indignation:
for this is the work of the Lord GOD of hosts in the land of the Chaldeans.

26 **Come against** her from the utmost border,
open her storehouses:
cast her up as heaps,
and destroy her utterly:
let nothing of her be left.

27 **Slay** all her bullocks;
let them go down to the slaughter:
woe unto them!
for their day is come, the time of their visitation.

28 The voice of them that flee and escape out of the land of Babylon,
to declare in Zion the vengeance of the LORD our God, the vengeance of his temple.

29 **Call together** the archers against Babylon:
all ye that bend the bow, camp against it round about;
let none thereof escape:
recompense her according to her work;
according to all that she hath done, do unto her:
for she hath been proud against the LORD, against the Holy One of Israel.

30 **Therefore** shall her young men fall in the streets,
and all her men of war shall be cut off in that day,
saith the LORD.

31 **Behold,**
I am against thee, O thou most proud,
saith the Lord GOD of hosts:
for thy day is come, the time that I will visit thee.

32 **And the most proud** shall stumble and fall,
and none shall raise him up:
and I will kindle a fire in his cities,
and it shall devour all round about him.

33 **Thus** saith the LORD of hosts;
The children of Israel and the children of Judah were oppressed together:
and all that took them captives held them fast;
they refused to let them go.

34 **Their Redeemer** is strong;
the LORD of hosts is his name:
he shall throughly plead their cause,
that he may give rest to the land,
and disquiet the inhabitants of Babylon.

35 **A sword** is upon the Chaldeans, {saith the LORD}, and upon the inhabitants of Babylon, and upon her princes, and upon her wise men.

36 **A sword** is upon the liars;
and they shall dote:
a sword is upon her mighty men;
and they shall be dismayed.

37 **A sword** is upon their horses, and upon their chariots, and upon all the mingled people that are in the midst of her;
and they shall become as women:
a sword is upon her treasures;
and they shall be robbed.

38 **A drought** is upon her waters;
and they shall be dried up:
for it is the land of graven images,
and they are mad upon their idols.

39 **Therefore the wild beasts of the desert with the wild beasts of the islands** shall dwell there,
and the owls shall dwell therein:
and it shall be no more inhabited for ever;
neither shall it be dwelt in from generation to generation.

40 **As God** overthrew Sodom and Gomorrah and the neighbour cities thereof,
saith the LORD;
so shall no man abide there,
neither shall any son of man dwell therein.

41 **Behold,**

a people shall come from the north,
and a great nation,
and many kings shall be raised up
from the coasts of the earth.
42 **They** shall hold the bow and the
lance:
they are cruel,
and will not shew mercy:
their voice shall roar like the sea,
and they shall ride upon horses,
every one put in array, like a man to
the battle, against thee, O
daughter of Babylon.
43 **The king of Babylon** hath heard
the report of them,
and his hands waxed feeble:
anguish took hold of him, and
pangs as of a woman in travail.
44 **Behold,**
he shall come up like a lion from the
swelling of Jordan unto the
habitation of the strong:
but I will make them suddenly run
away from her:
and who is a chosen man,
that I may appoint over her?
for who is like me?
and who will appoint me the time?
and who is that shepherd that will
stand before me?
45 **Therefore hear ye** the counsel of
the LORD, {that he hath taken
against Babylon}; and his
purposes, {that he hath purposed
against the land of the
Chaldeans}:
Surely the least of the flock shall
draw them out:
surely he shall make their
habitation desolate with them.
46 **At the noise of the taking of
Babylon** the earth is moved,
and the cry is heard among the
nations.

51

Thus saith the LORD;
Behold,
I will raise up against Babylon, and
against them that dwell in the
midst of them that rise up against
me, a destroying wind;
2 **And** will send unto Babylon
fanners,
that shall fan her,
and shall empty her land:
for in the day of trouble they shall
be against her round about.
3 **Against him that bendeth** let the
archer bend his bow, and against
him that lifteth himself up in his
brigandine:
and spare ye not her young men;
destroy ye utterly all her host.
4 **Thus the slain** shall fall in the
land of the Chaldeans, and they
that are thrust through in her
streets.
5 **For Israel** hath not been forsaken,
nor Judah of his God, of the LORD
of hosts;
though their land was filled with
sin against the Holy One of Israel.
6 **Flee** out of the midst of Babylon,
and deliver every man his soul:
be not cut off in her iniquity;
for this is the time of the LORD's
vengeance;
he will render unto her a
recompence.
7 **Babylon** hath been a golden cup in
the LORD's hand,
that made all the earth drunken:
the nations have drunken of her
wine;
therefore the nations are mad.
8 **Babylon** is suddenly fallen and
destroyed:
howl for her;
take balm for her pain,
if so be she may be healed.
9 **We** would have healed Babylon,
but she is not healed:
forsake her,
and let us go every one into his own
country:
for her judgment reacheth unto
heaven,
and is lifted up even to the skies.
10 **The LORD** hath brought forth our
righteousness:
come,
and let us declare in Zion the work
of the LORD our God.
11 **Make bright** the arrows;
gather the shields:
the LORD hath raised up the spirit
of the kings of the Medes:
for his device is against Babylon,
to destroy it;
because it is the vengeance of the
LORD, the vengeance of his
temple.
12 **Set up** the standard upon the
walls of Babylon,
make the watch strong,
set up the watchmen,
prepare the ambushes:
for the LORD hath both devised
and done that which he spake
against the inhabitants of
Babylon.
13 **O thou that dwellest upon many
waters, abundant in treasures,
thine end** is come, and the
measure of thy covetousness.
14 **The LORD of hosts** hath sworn
by himself,
saying,
Surely I will fill thee with men, as
with caterpillers;
and they shall lift up a shout
against thee.
15 **He** hath made the earth by his
power,
he hath established the world by
his wisdom,
and hath stretched out the heaven
by his understanding.
16 **When he** uttereth his voice,
there is a multitude of waters in the
heavens;
and he causeth the vapours to
ascend from the ends of the earth:
he maketh lightnings with rain,
and bringeth forth the wind out of
his treasures.
17 **Every man** is brutish by his
knowledge;
every founder is confounded by the
graven image:
for his molten image is falsehood,
and there is no breath in them.
18 **They** are vanity, the work of
errors:
in the time of their visitation they
shall perish.
19 **The portion of Jacob** is not like
them;
for he is the former of all things:
and Israel is the rod of his
inheritance:
the LORD of hosts is his name.
20 **Thou** art my battle axe and
weapons of war:
for with thee will I break in pieces
the nations,
and with thee will I destroy
kingdoms;
21 **And with thee** will I break in
pieces the horse and his rider;
and with thee will I break in pieces
the chariot and his rider;
22 **With thee** also will I break in
pieces man and woman;
and with thee will I break in pieces
old and young;
and with thee will I break in pieces
the young man and the maid;
23 **I** will also break in pieces with
thee the shepherd and his flock;

and with thee will I break in pieces the husbandman and his yoke of oxen;
and with thee will I break in pieces captains and rulers.

24 **And I** will render unto Babylon and to all the inhabitants of Chaldea all their evil that they have done in Zion in your sight,
saith the LORD.

25 **Behold,**
I am against thee, O destroying mountain,
saith the LORD,
which destroyest all the earth:
and I will stretch out mine hand upon thee,
and roll thee down from the rocks,
and will make thee a burnt mountain.

26 **And they** shall not take of thee a stone for a corner, nor a stone for foundations;
but thou shalt be desolate for ever,
saith the LORD.

27 **Set ye up** a standard in the land,
blow the trumpet among the nations,
prepare the nations against her,
call together against her the kingdoms of Ararat, Minni, and Ashchenaz;
appoint a captain against her;
ause the horses to come up as the rough caterpillers.

28 **Prepare** against her the nations with the kings of the Medes, the captains thereof, and all the rulers thereof, and all the land of his dominion.

29 **And the land** shall tremble and sorrow:
for every purpose of the LORD shall be performed against Babylon,
to make the land of Babylon a desolation without an inhabitant.

30 **The mighty men of Babylon** have forborn to fight,
they have remained in their holds:
their might hath failed;
they became as women:
they have burned her dwellingplaces;
her bars are broken.

31 **One post** shall run to meet another, and one messenger to meet another,
to shew the king of Babylon
that his city is taken at one end,

32 **And that the passages** are stopped,
and the reeds they have burned with fire,
and the men of war are affrighted.

33 **For thus** saith the LORD of hosts, the God of Israel;
The daughter of Babylon is like a threshingfloor,
it is time to thresh her:
yet a little while, and the time of her harvest shall come.

34 **Nebuchadrezzar the king of Babylon** hath devoured me,
he hath crushed me,
he hath made me an empty vessel,
he hath swallowed me up like a dragon,
he hath filled his belly with my delicates,
he hath cast me out.

35 **The violence done to me and to my flesh** be upon Babylon,
shall the inhabitant of Zion say;
and my blood upon the inhabitants of Chaldea,
shall Jerusalem say.

36 **Therefore thus** saith the LORD;
Behold,
I will plead thy cause,
and take vengeance for thee;
and I will dry up her sea,
and make her springs dry.

37 **And Babylon** shall become heaps, a dwellingplace for dragons, an astonishment, and an hissing, without an inhabitant.

38 **They** shall roar together like lions:
they shall yell as lions' whelps.

39 **In their heat** I will make their feasts,
and I will make them drunken,
that they may rejoice,
and sleep a perpetual sleep,
and not wake,
saith the LORD.

40 **I** will bring them down like lambs to the slaughter, like rams with he goats.

41 **How** is Sheshach taken!
and how is the praise of the whole earth surprised!
how is Babylon become an astonishment among the nations!

42 **The sea** is come up upon Babylon:
she is covered with the multitude of the waves thereof.

43 **Her cities** are a desolation, a dry land, and a wilderness, a land wherein no man dwelleth,
neither doth any son of man pass thereby.

44 **And I** will punish Bel in Babylon,
and I will bring forth out of his mouth that which he hath swallowed up:
and the nations shall not flow together any more unto him:
yea, the wall of Babylon shall fall.

45 **My people, go ye out** of the midst of her,
and deliver ye every man his soul from the fierce anger of the LORD.

46 **And lest your heart** faint,
and ye fear for the rumour that shall be heard in the land;
a rumour shall both come one year,
and after that in another year shall come a rumour, and violence in the land, ruler against ruler.

47 **Therefore, {behold}, the days** come,
that I will do judgment upon the graven images of Babylon:
and her whole land shall be confounded,
and all her slain shall fall in the midst of her.

48 **Then the heaven and the earth, and all that is therein,** shall sing for Babylon:
for the spoilers shall come unto her from the north,
saith the LORD.

49 **As Babylon** hath caused the slain of Israel to fall,
so at Babylon shall fall the slain of all the earth.

50 **Ye that have escaped the sword, go away,**
stand not still:
remember the LORD afar off,
and let Jerusalem come into your mind.

51 **We** are confounded,
because we have heard reproach:
shame hath covered our faces:
for strangers are come into the sanctuaries of the LORD's house.

52 **Wherefore, {behold}, the days** come,
saith the LORD,
that I will do judgment upon her graven images:
and through all her land the wounded shall groan.

53 **Though Babylon** should mount up to heaven,
and though she should fortify the height of her strength,
yet from me shall spoilers come unto her,
saith the LORD.

54 **A sound of a cry** cometh from Babylon, and great destruction from the land of the Chaldeans:
55 **Because the LORD** hath spoiled Babylon,
and destroyed out of her the great voice;
when her waves do roar like great waters,
a noise of their voice is uttered:
56 **Because the spoiler** is come upon her, even upon Babylon,
and her mighty men are taken,
every one of their bows is broken:
for the LORD God of recompences shall surely requite.

57 **And I** will make drunk her princes, and her wise men, her captains, and her rulers, and her mighty men:
and they shall sleep a perpetual sleep,
and not wake,
saith the King,
whose name is the LORD of hosts.

58 **Thus** saith the LORD of hosts;
The broad walls of Babylon shall be utterly broken,
and her high gates shall be burned with fire;
and the people shall labour in vain, and the folk in the fire,
and they shall be weary.

59 The word which Jeremiah the prophet commanded Seraiah the son of Neriah, the son of Maaseiah,
when he went with Zedekiah the king of Judah into Babylon in the fourth year of his reign.

And this Seraiah was a quiet prince.

60 **So Jeremiah** wrote in a book all the evil that should come upon Babylon, even all these words that are written against Babylon.

61 **And Jeremiah** said to Seraiah,
When thou comest to Babylon,
and shalt see,
and shalt read all these words;
62 **Then** shalt thou say,
O LORD, thou hast spoken against this place, to cut it off,
that none shall remain in it, neither man nor beast,
but that it shall be desolate for ever.

63 **And it** shall be,
when thou hast made an end of reading this book,
that thou shalt bind a stone to it,
and cast it into the midst of Euphrates:
64 **And thou** shalt say,
Thus shall Babylon sink,
and shall not rise from the evil that I will bring upon her:
and they shall be weary.

Thus far are the words of Jeremiah.

52

Zedekiah was one and twenty years old
when he began to reign,
and he reigned eleven years in Jerusalem.

And his mother's name was Hamutal the daughter of Jeremiah of Libnah.

2 **And he** did that which was evil in the eyes of the LORD, according to all that Jehoiakim had done.

3 **For through the anger of the LORD** it came to pass in Jerusalem and Judah,
till he had cast them out from his presence,
that Zedekiah rebelled against the king of Babylon.

4 **And it** came to pass in the ninth year of his reign, in the tenth month, in the tenth day of the month,
that Nebuchadrezzar king of Babylon came, he and all his army, against Jerusalem,
and pitched against it,
and built forts against it round about.

5 **So the city** was besieged unto the eleventh year of king Zedekiah.

6 **And in the fourth month, in the ninth day of the month,** the famine was sore in the city,
so that there was no bread for the people of the land.

7 **Then the city** was broken up,
and all the men of war fled,
and went forth out of the city by night by the way of the gate between the two walls,
which was by the king's garden;
(now the Chaldeans were by the city round about:)
and they went by the way of the plain.

8 **But the army of the Chaldeans** pursued after the king,
and overtook Zedekiah in the plains of Jericho;
and all his army was scattered from him.

9 **Then they** took the king,
and carried him up unto the king of Babylon to Riblah in the land of Hamath;
where he gave judgment upon him.

10 **And the king of Babylon** slew the sons of Zedekiah before his eyes:
he slew also all the princes of Judah in Riblah.

11 **Then he** put out the eyes of Zedekiah;
and the king of Babylon bound him in chains,
and carried him to Babylon,
and put him in prison till the day of his death.

12 **Now in the fifth month, in the tenth day of the month**, {which was the nineteenth year of Nebuchadrezzar king of Babylon}, came Nebuzaradan, captain of the guard, {which served the king of Babylon}, into Jerusalem,
13 **And** burned the house of the LORD, and the king's house;
and all the houses of Jerusalem, and all the houses of the great men, burned he with fire:
14 **And all the army of the Chaldeans**, {that were with the captain of the guard}, brake down all the walls of Jerusalem round about.

15 **Then Nebuzaradan the captain of the guard** carried away captive certain of the poor of the people, and the residue of the people that remained in the city, and those that fell away, that fell to the king of Babylon, and the rest of the multitude.

16 **But Nebuzaradan the captain of the guard** left certain of the poor of the land for vinedressers and for husbandmen.

17 **Also the pillars of brass that were in the house of the LORD, and the bases, and the brasen sea that was in the house of the LORD,** the Chaldeans brake,

and carried all the brass of them to Babylon.

18 **The caldrons also, and the shovels, and the snuffers, and the bowls, and the spoons, and all the vessels of brass wherewith they ministered,** took they away.

19 **And the basons, and the firepans, and the bowls, and the caldrons, and the candlesticks, and the spoons, and the cups; that which was of gold in gold, and that which was of silver in silver,** took the captain of the guard away.

20 **The two pillars, one sea, and twelve brasen bulls that were under the bases,** {which king Solomon had made in the house of the LORD}: the brass of all these vessels was without weight.

21 **And concerning the pillars,** the height of one pillar was eighteen cubits;
and a fillet of twelve cubits did compass it;
and the thickness thereof was four fingers:
it was hollow.

22 **And a chapiter of brass** was upon it;
and the height of one chapiter was five cubits, with network and pomegranates upon the chapiters round about, all of brass.
The second pillar also and the pomegranates were like unto these.

23 **And there** were ninety and six pomegranates on a side;
and all the pomegranates upon the network were an hundred round about.

24 **And the captain of the guard** took Seraiah the chief priest, and Zephaniah the second priest, and the three keepers of the door:

25 **He** took also out of the city an eunuch, {which had the charge of the men of war}; and seven men of them that were near the king's person, {which were found in the city}; and the principal scribe of the host, {who mustered the people of the land}; and threescore men of the people of the land, {that were found in the midst of the city}.

26 **So Nebuzaradan the captain of the guard** took them,
and brought them to the king of Babylon to Riblah.

27 **And the king of Babylon** smote them,
and put them to death in Riblah in the land of Hamath.

Thus Judah was carried away captive out of his own land.

28 **This** is the people whom Nebuchadrezzar carried away captive: in the seventh year three thousand Jews and three and twenty:

29 **In the eighteenth year of Nebuchadrezzar** he carried away captive from Jerusalem eight hundred thirty and two persons:

30 **In the three and twentieth year of Nebuchadrezzar** Nebuzaradan the captain of the guard carried away captive of the Jews seven hundred forty and five persons:
all the persons were four thousand and six hundred.

31 **And it** came to pass in the seven and thirtieth year of the captivity of Jehoiachin king of Judah, in the twelfth month, in the five and twentieth day of the month,
that Evilmerodach king of Babylon in the first year of his reign lifted up the head of Jehoiachin king of Judah,
and brought him forth out of prison.

32 **And** spake kindly unto him,
and set his throne above the throne of the kings that were with him in Babylon,

33 **And** changed his prison garments:
and he did continually eat bread before him all the days of his life.

34 **And for his diet,** there was a continual diet given him of the king of Babylon, every day a portion until the day of his death, all the days of his life.

Lamentations

In Lamentations, the prophet Jeremiah pours out his grief and sorrow over the ruin of Jerusalem and the Babylonian captivity. Crafted in a poetic style, using figurative language and metaphor, the book is a collection of five chapters, each one a lament for the devastation that has befallen the city and its people. It opens with a painful description of the Babylonian invasion, a calamitous event that left an indelible mark on Jewish history. The obliteration of Jerusalem and Solomon's temple is a profound loss for the prophet, as these landmarks embody the center of Jewish worship.

Jeremiah then describes the suffering and deportation of Jerusalem's citizens to Babylon. This period of exile is not only physically painful but also spiritually devastating, as the people are cut off from their land and their God. The displacement causes the prophet to lament the disappearance of homes, families, and Jewish culture. In a third lament, Jeremiah highlights the consequences of sin and disobedience as he mourns Israel's abandonment of their covenant with God, the source of all that is happening to the nation and its people. He calls for the people to return to God and seek His mercy and forgiveness.

Amidst Jeremiah's call for repentance, the book's final chapter offers a stark contrast: a glimmer of hope. The prophet envisions a future where the people of Israel are not only returned to their land but also to God's favor. While Lamentations underscores the ongoing consequences of sin and the urgent need to repent, its closing message of hope shines through. It is a hope that is not dependent on the people's ability to improve their situation but on the unchanging nature of God. His everlasting love and mercy towards a chosen people will one day lead to forgiveness and restoration.

1 ✡ **How** doth the city sit solitary,
that was full of people!
how is she become as a widow!
she that was great among the nations, and princess among the provinces, how is she become tributary!

2 **She** weepeth sore in the night,
and her tears are on her cheeks:
among all her lovers she hath none to comfort her:
all her friends have dealt treacherously with her,
they are become her enemies.

3 **Judah** is gone into captivity because of affliction, and because of great servitude:
she dwelleth among the heathen,
she findeth no rest:
all her persecutors overtook her between the straits.

4 **The ways of Zion** do mourn,
because none come to the solemn feasts:
all her gates are desolate:
her priests sigh,
her virgins are afflicted,
and she is in bitterness.

5 **Her adversaries** are the chief,
her enemies prosper;
for the LORD hath afflicted her for the multitude of her transgressions:
her children are gone into captivity before the enemy.

6 **And from the daughter of Zion** all her beauty is departed:
her princes are become like harts that find no pasture,
and they are gone without strength before the pursuer.

7 **Jerusalem** remembered in the days of her affliction and of her miseries all her pleasant things that she had in the days of old,
when her people fell into the hand of the enemy,
and none did help her:
the adversaries saw her,
and did mock at her sabbaths.

8 **Jerusalem** hath grievously sinned;
therefore she is removed:
all that honoured her despise her,
because they have seen her nakedness:
yea, she sigheth,
and turneth backward.

9 **Her filthiness** is in her skirts;
she remembereth not her last end;
therefore she came down wonderfully:
she had no comforter.
O LORD, behold my affliction:
for the enemy hath magnified himself.

10 **The adversary** hath spread out his hand upon all her pleasant things:
for she hath seen that the heathen entered into her sanctuary,
whom thou didst command
that they should not enter into thy congregation.

11 **All her people** sigh,
they seek bread;
they have given their pleasant things for meat
to relieve the soul:
see, O LORD,
and consider;
for I am become vile.

12 **Is it** nothing to you, all ye that pass by?
behold,
and see if there be any sorrow like unto my sorrow,
which is done unto me,
wherewith the LORD hath afflicted me in the day of his fierce anger.

13 **From above** hath he sent fire into my bones,
and it prevaileth against them:
he hath spread a net for my feet,
he hath turned me back:
he hath made me desolate and faint all the day.

14 **The yoke of my transgressions** is bound by his hand:
they are wreathed,

and come up upon my neck:
he hath made my strength to fall,
the Lord hath delivered me into their hands,
from whom I am not able to rise up.

15 **The Lord** hath trodden under foot all my mighty men in the midst of me:
he hath called an assembly against me
to crush my young men:
the Lord hath trodden the virgin, the daughter of Judah, as in a winepress.

16 **For these things** I weep;
mine eye, mine eye runneth down with water,
because the comforter that should relieve my soul is far from me:
my children are desolate,
because the enemy prevailed.

17 **Zion** spreadeth forth her hands,
and there is none to comfort her:
the LORD hath commanded concerning Jacob,
that his adversaries should be round about him:
Jerusalem is as a menstruous woman among them.

18 **The LORD** is righteous;
for I have rebelled against his commandment:
hear, {I pray you}, all people,
and behold my sorrow:
my virgins and my young men are gone into captivity.

19 **I** called for my lovers,
but they deceived me:
my priests and mine elders gave up the ghost in the city,
while they sought their meat
to relieve their souls.

20 **Behold,** O LORD;
for I am in distress:
my bowels are troubled;
mine heart is turned within me;
for I have grievously rebelled:
abroad the sword bereaveth,
at home there is as death.

21 **They** have heard that I sigh:
there is none to comfort me:
all mine enemies have heard of my trouble;
they are glad that thou hast done it:
thou wilt bring the day that thou hast called,
and they shall be like unto me.

22 **Let all their wickedness** come before thee;
and do unto them,
as thou hast done unto me for all my transgressions:
for my sighs are many,
and my heart is faint.

2

How hath the Lord covered the daughter of Zion with a cloud in his anger,
and cast down from heaven unto the earth the beauty of Israel,
and remembered not his footstool in the day of his anger!

2 **The Lord** hath swallowed up all the habitations of Jacob,
and hath not pitied:
he hath thrown down in his wrath the strong holds of the daughter of Judah;
he hath brought them down to the ground:
he hath polluted the kingdom and the princes thereof.

3 **He** hath cut off in his fierce anger all the horn of Israel:
he hath drawn back his right hand from before the enemy,
and he burned against Jacob like a flaming fire,
which devoureth round about.

4 **He** hath bent his bow like an enemy:
he stood with his right hand as an adversary,
and slew all that were pleasant to the eye in the tabernacle of the daughter of Zion:
he poured out his fury like fire.

5 **The Lord** was as an enemy:
he hath swallowed up Israel,
he hath swallowed up all her palaces:
he hath destroyed his strong holds,
and hath increased in the daughter of Judah mourning and lamentation.

6 **And he** hath violently taken away his tabernacle,
as if it were of a garden:
he hath destroyed his places of the assembly:
the LORD hath caused the solemn feasts and sabbaths to be forgotten in Zion,
and hath despised in the indignation of his anger the king and the priest.

7 **The Lord** hath cast off his altar,
he hath abhorred his sanctuary,
he hath given up into the hand of the enemy the walls of her palaces;
they have made a noise in the house of the LORD, as in the day of a solemn feast.

8 **The LORD** hath purposed to destroy the wall of the daughter of Zion:
he hath stretched out a line,
he hath not withdrawn his hand from destroying:
therefore he made the rampart and the wall to lament;
they languished together.

9 **Her gates** are sunk into the ground;
he hath destroyed and broken her bars:
her king and her princes are among the Gentiles:
the law is no more;
her prophets also find no vision from the LORD.

10 **The elders of the daughter of Zion** sit upon the ground,
and keep silence:
they have cast up dust upon their heads;
they have girded themselves with sackcloth:
the virgins of Jerusalem hang down their heads to the ground.

11 **Mine eyes** do fail with tears,
my bowels are troubled,
my liver is poured upon the earth,
for the destruction of the daughter of my people;
because the children and the sucklings swoon in the streets of the city.

12 **They** say to their mothers,
Where is corn and wine?
when they swooned as the wounded in the streets of the city,
when their soul was poured out into their mothers' bosom.

13 **What thing** shall I take to witness for thee?
what thing shall I liken to thee, O daughter of Jerusalem?
what shall I equal to thee,
that I may comfort thee, O virgin daughter of Zion?
for thy breach is great like the sea:
who can heal thee?

14 **Thy prophets** have seen vain and foolish things for thee:
and they have not discovered thine iniquity,

to turn away thy captivity;
but have seen for thee false burdens and causes of banishment.

15 **All that pass by** clap their hands at thee;
they hiss and wag their head at the daughter of Jerusalem,
saying,
Is this the city that men call The perfection of beauty, The joy of the whole earth?

16 **All thine enemies** have opened their mouth against thee:
they hiss
and gnash the teeth:
they say,
We have swallowed her up:
certainly this is the day that we looked for;
we have found,
we have seen it.

17 **The LORD** hath done that which he had devised;
he hath fulfilled his word that he had commanded in the days of old:
he hath thrown down,
and hath not pitied:
and he hath caused thine enemy to rejoice over thee,
he hath set up the horn of thine adversaries.

18 **Their heart** cried unto the Lord,
O wall of the daughter of Zion, let tears run down like a river day and night:
give thyself no rest;
let not the apple of thine eye cease.

19 **Arise,**
cry out in the night:
in the beginning of the watches pour out thine heart like water before the face of the Lord:
lift up thy hands toward him for the life of thy young children,
that faint for hunger in the top of every street.

20 **Behold,** O LORD,
and consider
to whom thou hast done this.
Shall the women eat their fruit, and children of a span long?
shall the priest and the prophet be slain in the sanctuary of the Lord?

21 **The young and the old** lie on the ground in the streets:
my virgins and my young men are fallen by the sword;
thou hast slain them in the day of thine anger;
thou hast killed,
and not pitied.

22 **Thou** hast called as in a solemn day my terrors round about,
so that in the day of the LORD's anger none escaped
nor remained:
those that I have swaddled and brought up hath mine enemy consumed.

3

ALEPH I Am the man that hath seen affliction by the rod of his wrath.

2 **He** hath led me,
and brought me into darkness, but not into light.

3 **Surely against me** is he turned;
he turneth his hand against me all the day.

4 **My flesh and my skin** hath he made old;
he hath broken my bones.

5 **He** hath builded against me,
and compassed me with gall and travail.

6 **He** hath set me in dark places, as they that be dead of old.

7 **He** hath hedged me about,
that I cannot get out:
he hath made my chain heavy.

8 **Also when I** cry and shout,
he shutteth out my prayer.

9 **He** hath inclosed my ways with hewn stone,
he hath made my paths crooked.

10 **He** was unto me as a bear lying in wait, and as a lion in secret places.

11 **He** hath turned aside my ways,
and pulled me in pieces:
he hath made me desolate.

12 **He** hath bent his bow,
and set me as a mark for the arrow.

13 **He** hath caused the arrows of his quiver to enter into my reins.

14 **I** was a derision to all my people; and their song all the day.

15 **He** hath filled me with bitterness,
he hath made me drunken with wormwood.

16 **He** hath also broken my teeth with gravel stones,
he hath covered me with ashes.

17 **And thou** hast removed my soul far off from peace:
I forgat prosperity.

18 **And I** said,
My strength and my hope is perished from the LORD:

19 Remembering mine affliction and my misery, the wormwood and the gall.

20 **My soul** hath them still in remembrance,
and is humbled in me.

21 **This** I recall to my mind,
therefore have I hope.

22 **It is of the LORD's mercies** that we are not consumed,
because his compassions fail not.

23 **They** are new every morning:
great is thy faithfulness.

24 **The LORD** is my portion,
saith my soul;
therefore will I hope in him.

25 **The LORD** is good unto them that wait for him, to the soul that seeketh him.

26 **It is good** that a man should both hope and quietly wait for the salvation of the LORD.

27 **It is good for a man** that he bear the yoke in his youth.

28 **He** sitteth alone
and keepeth silence,
because he hath borne it upon him.

29 **He** putteth his mouth in the dust;
if so be there may be hope.

30 **He** giveth his cheek to him that smiteth him:
he is filled full with reproach.

31 **For the Lord** will not cast off for ever:

32 **But though he** cause grief,
yet will he have compassion according to the multitude of his mercies.

33 **For he** doth not afflict willingly
nor grieve the children of men.

34 To crush under his feet all the prisoners of the earth,

35 To turn aside the right of a man before the face of the most High,

36 To subvert a man in his cause,
the Lord approveth not.

37 **Who** is he that saith,
and it cometh to pass,
when the Lord commandeth it not

38 **Out of the mouth of the most High** proceedeth not evil and good?

39 **Wherefore** doth a living man complain, a man for the punishment of his sins?

[40] **Let us** search and try our ways,
and turn again to the LORD.
[41] **Let us** lift up our heart with our hands unto God in the heavens.
[42] **We** have transgressed
and have rebelled:
thou hast not pardoned.
[43] **Thou** hast covered with anger,
and persecuted us:
thou hast slain,
thou hast not pitied.
[44] **Thou** hast covered thyself with a cloud,
that our prayer should not pass through.
[45] **Thou** hast made us as the offscouring and refuse in the midst of the people.
[46] **All our enemies** have opened their mouths against us.
[47] **Fear and a snare** is come upon us, desolation and destruction.
[48] **Mine eye** runneth down with rivers of water for the destruction of the daughter of my people.
[49] **Mine eye** trickleth down, {and ceaseth not}, without any intermission.
[50] **Till the LORD** look down,
and behold from heaven.
[51] **Mine eye** affecteth mine heart because of all the daughters of my city.
[52] **Mine enemies** chased me sore, like a bird, without cause.
[53] **They** have cut off my life in the dungeon,
and cast a stone upon me.
[54] **Waters** flowed over mine head;
then I said,
I am cut off.
[55] **I** called upon thy name, O LORD, out of the low dungeon.
[56] **Thou** hast heard my voice:
hide not thine ear at my breathing, at my cry.
[57] **Thou** drewest near in the day that I called upon thee:
thou saidst,
Fear not.
[58] **O Lord, thou** hast pleaded the causes of my soul;
thou hast redeemed my life.
[59] **O LORD, thou** hast seen my wrong:
judge thou my cause.
[60] **Thou** hast seen all their vengeance and all their imaginations against me.
[61] **Thou** hast heard their reproach, O LORD, and all their imaginations against me;
[62] The lips of those that rose up against me, and their device against me all the day.
[63] **Behold** their sitting down, and their rising up;
I am their musick.
[64] **Render** unto them a recompence, O LORD, according to the work of their hands.
[65] **Give** them sorrow of heart,
thy curse unto them.
[66] **Persecute and destroy** them in anger from under the heavens of the LORD.

4 **How** is the gold become dim! **how** is the most fine gold changed!
the stones of the sanctuary are poured out in the top of every street.
[2] **The precious sons of Zion, comparable to fine gold,** how are they esteemed as earthen pitchers, the work of the hands of the potter!
[3] **Even the sea monsters** draw out the breast,
they give suck to their young ones:
the daughter of my people is become cruel, like the ostriches in the wilderness.
[4] **The tongue of the sucking child** cleaveth to the roof of his mouth for thirst:
the young children ask bread,
and no man breaketh it unto them.
[5] **They that did feed delicately** are desolate in the streets:
they that were brought up in scarlet embrace dunghills.
[6] **For the punishment of the iniquity of the daughter of my people** is greater than the punishment of the sin of Sodom,
that was overthrown as in a moment,
and no hands stayed on her.
[7] **Her Nazarites** were purer than snow,
they were whiter than milk,
they were more ruddy in body than rubies,
their polishing was of sapphire:
[8] **Their visage** is blacker than a coal;
they are not known in the streets:
their skin cleaveth to their bones;
it is withered,
it is become like a stick.
[9] **They that be slain with the sword** are better than they that be slain with hunger:
for these pine away,
stricken through for want of the fruits of the field.
[10] **The hands of the pitiful women** have sodden their own children:
they were their meat in the destruction of the daughter of my people.
[11] **The LORD** hath accomplished his fury;
he hath poured out his fierce anger,
and hath kindled a fire in Zion,
and it hath devoured the foundations thereof.
[12] **The kings of the earth, and all the inhabitants of the world,** would not have believed
that the adversary and the enemy should have entered into the gates of Jerusalem.
[13] **For the sins of her prophets, and the iniquities of her priests**, {that have shed the blood of the just in the midst of her},
[14] They have wandered as blind men in the streets,
they have polluted themselves with blood,
so that men could not touch their garments.
[15] **They** cried unto them,
Depart ye;
it is unclean;
depart,
depart,
touch not:
when they fled away
and wandered,
they said among the heathen,
They shall no more sojourn there.
[16] **The anger of the LORD** hath divided them;
he will no more regard them:
they respected not the persons of the priests,
they favoured not the elders.
[17] **As for us,** our eyes as yet failed for our vain help:
in our watching we have watched for a nation that could not save us.
[18] **They** hunt our steps,

that we cannot go in our streets:
our end is near,
our days are fulfilled;
for our end is come.

19 **Our persecutors** are swifter than the eagles of the heaven:
they pursued us upon the mountains,
they laid wait for us in the wilderness.

20 **The breath of our nostrils, the anointed of the LORD,** was taken in their pits,
of whom we said,
Under his shadow we shall live among the heathen.

21 **Rejoice and be glad,** O daughter of Edom,
that dwellest in the land of Uz;
the cup also shall pass through unto thee:
thou shalt be drunken,
and shalt make thyself naked.

22 **The punishment of thine iniquity** is accomplished, O daughter of Zion;
he will no more carry thee away into captivity:
he will visit thine iniquity, O daughter of Edom;
he will discover thy sins.

5

Remember, O LORD,
what is come upon us:
consider,
and behold our reproach.

2 **Our inheritance** is turned to strangers,
our houses to aliens.

3 **We** are orphans and fatherless,
our mothers are as widows.

4 **We** have drunken our water for money;
our wood is sold unto us.

5 **Our necks** are under persecution:
we labour,
and have no rest.

6 **We** have given the hand to the Egyptians, and to the Assyrians,
to be satisfied with bread.

7 **Our fathers** have sinned,
and are not;
and we have borne their iniquities.

8 **Servants** have ruled over us:
there is none that doth deliver us out of their hand.

9 **We** gat our bread with the peril of our lives because of the sword of the wilderness.

10 **Our skin** was black like an oven because of the terrible famine.

11 **They** ravished the women in Zion, and the maids in the cities of Judah.

12 **Princes** are hanged up by their hand:
the faces of elders were not honoured.

13 **They** took the young men to grind,
and the children fell under the wood.

14 **The elders** have ceased from the gate,
the young men from their musick.

15 **The joy of our heart** is ceased;
our dance is turned into mourning.

16 **The crown** is fallen from our head:
woe unto us,
that we have sinned!

17 **For this** our heart is faint;
for these things our eyes are dim.

18 **Because of the mountain of Zion**, {which is desolate}, the foxes walk upon it.

19 **Thou, O LORD,** remainest for ever;
thy throne from generation to generation.

20 **Wherefore** dost thou forget us for ever,
and forsake us so long time?

21 **Turn thou** us unto thee, O LORD,
and we shall be turned;
renew our days as of old.

22 **But thou** hast utterly rejected us;
thou art very wroth against us.

Ezekiel

The Book of Ezekiel, traditionally attributed to the prophet Ezekiel, is a collection of prophetic oracles and visions written during the Babylonian exile. These divine revelations address Israel's spiritual and moral state, the consequences of their sins and disobedience, and the promise of hope, forgiveness, and restoration. The book begins with Ezekiel's call to prophecy, in which he receives a vision of God's glory and is commissioned to speak on God's behalf.

The remainder of the book focuses primarily on the prophecies that God commands Ezekiel to deliver to the people of Israel. One such prophetic message predicts the imminent fall of Jerusalem to the Babylonians. However, amidst this bleak prediction is a glimmer of hope. Another prophecy, based on a vision, involves a valley filled with dry bones that God brings back to life. It serves as a metaphor for Israel's restoration and a reminder that God can bring new life to even the most desolate and hopeless situations. In another vision, Ezekiel describes a newly rebuilt temple in Jerusalem after the exile, symbolizing the hope and a promise of a new beginning for Israel. Ezekiel also envisions a future invasion of Israel by a powerful enemy, Gog and Magog, whom God will defeat. This prophecy often foreshadows the coming of the Messiah, Who will establish God's kingdom on earth.

While the Book of Ezekiel shares many similarities with other prophetic books of the Bible, it also stands out with its unique characteristics. Ezekiel's visions, for instance, are not just prophetic but vivid and detailed, offering a unique window into the prophet's experience. The prophet also emphasizes the personal responsibility of each individual to turn away from sin and seek God's forgiveness, a departure from other books that often focus on the nation's sins as a whole. Finally, Ezekiel's writing style, frequently poetic, is filled with metaphors and images that stand in stark contrast to the other prophetic books, which can sometimes be dry and technical. These unique aspects make the book a compelling read as the prophet's primary purpose for writing unfolds. He wants to offer guidance and hope to the people of Israel during a time of great turmoil and upheaval. He accomplishes this desire through three key themes.

The first theme reminds the Israelites that God is always ready to forgive those who turn to him with a humble heart and that the path to redemption is open to all who seek it. The second theme underscores that God is the ultimate authority in the universe and that His will and purposes are always at work, even when unseen. The third theme reminds the people of Israel that God is always with them and will never abandon them. In short, these messages of hope provide the Israelites with a much-needed reminder of God's love and faithfulness and the need for each individual to repent and seek a closer relationship with Him.

1 **Now it** came to pass in the thirtieth year, in the fourth month, in the fifth day of the month,
as I was among the captives by the river of Chebar,
that the heavens were opened,
and I saw visions of God.
2 **In the fifth day of the month,** {which was the fifth year of king Jehoiachin's captivity},
3 The word of the LORD came expressly unto Ezekiel the priest, the son of Buzi, in the land of the Chaldeans by the river Chebar;
and the hand of the LORD was there upon him.
4 **And I** looked,
and, {behold}, a whirlwind came out of the north, a great cloud, and a fire infolding itself,
and a brightness was about it, and out of the midst thereof as the colour of amber, out of the midst of the fire.
5 **Also out of the midst thereof** came the likeness of four living creatures.
And this was their appearance;
they had the likeness of a man.
6 **And every one** had four faces,
and every one had four wings.
7 **And their feet** were straight feet;
and the sole of their feet was like the sole of a calf's foot:
and they sparkled like the colour of burnished brass.
8 **And they** had the hands of a man under their wings on their four sides;
and they four had their faces and their wings.
9 **Their wings** were joined one to another;
they turned not
when they went;
they went every one straight forward.
10 **As for the likeness of their faces,** they four had the face of a man, and the face of a lion, on the right side:
and they four had the face of an ox on the left side;
they four also had the face of an eagle.
11 **Thus** were their faces:
and their wings were stretched upward;

two wings of every one were joined one to another,
and two covered their bodies.

12 **And they** went every one straight forward:
whither the spirit was to go,
they went;
and they turned not
when they went.

13 **As for the likeness of the living creatures,** their appearance was like burning coals of fire, and like the appearance of lamps:
it went up and down among the living creatures;
and the fire was bright,
and out of the fire went forth lightning.

14 **And the living creatures** ran and returned as the appearance of a flash of lightning.

15 **Now as I** beheld the living creatures,
behold one wheel upon the earth by the living creatures, with his four faces.

16 **The appearance of the wheels and their work** was like unto the colour of a beryl:
and they four had one likeness:
and their appearance and their work was as it were a wheel in the middle of a wheel.

17 **When they** went,
they went upon their four sides:
and they turned not
when they went.

18 **As for their rings,** they were so high
that they were dreadful;
and their rings were full of eyes round about them four.

19 **And when the living creatures** went,
the wheels went by them:
and when the living creatures were lifted up from the earth,
the wheels were lifted up.

20 **Whithersoever the spirit** was to go,
they went,
thither was their spirit to go;
and the wheels were lifted up over against them:
for the spirit of the living creature was in the wheels.

21 **When those** went,
these went;
and when those stood,
these stood;
and when those were lifted up from the earth,
the wheels were lifted up over against them:
for the spirit of the living creature was in the wheels.

22 **And the likeness of the firmament upon the heads of the living creature** was as the colour of the terrible crystal,
stretched forth over their heads above.

23 **And under the firmament** were their wings straight, the one toward the other:
every one had two,
which covered on this side,
and every one had two,
which covered on that side, their bodies.

24 **And when they** went,
I heard the noise of their wings, like the noise of great waters, as the voice of the Almighty, the voice of speech, as the noise of an host:
when they stood,
they let down their wings.

25 **And there** was a voice from the firmament that was over their heads,
when they stood,
and had let down their wings.

26 **And above the firmament that was over their heads** was the likeness of a throne, as the appearance of a sapphire stone:
and upon the likeness of the throne was the likeness as the appearance of a man above upon it.

27 **And I** saw as the colour of amber, as the appearance of fire round about within it, from the appearance of his loins even upward, and from the appearance of his loins even downward,
I saw as it were the appearance of fire,
and it had brightness round about.

28 **As the appearance of the bow that is in the cloud in the day of rain,** so was the appearance of the brightness round about.
This was the appearance of the likeness of the glory of the LORD.
And when I saw it,
I fell upon my face,
and I heard a voice of one that spake.

2 **And he** said unto me,
Son of man, stand upon thy feet,
and I will speak unto thee.

2 **And the spirit** entered into me
when he spake unto me,
and set me upon my feet,
that I heard him that spake unto me.

3 **And he** said unto me,
Son of man, I send thee to the children of Israel, to a rebellious nation that hath rebelled against me:
they and their fathers have transgressed against me, even unto this very day.

4 **For they** are impudent children and stiffhearted.
I do send thee unto them;
and thou shalt say unto them,
Thus saith the Lord GOD.

5 **And they**, {whether they will hear}, {or whether they will forbear}, (for they are a rebellious house,) yet shall know
that there hath been a prophet among them.

6 **And thou, son of man,** be not afraid of them,
neither be afraid of their words,
though briers and thorns be with thee,
and thou dost dwell among scorpions:
be not afraid of their words,
nor be dismayed at their looks,
though they be a rebellious house.

7 **And thou** shalt speak my words unto them,
whether they will hear,
or whether they will forbear:
for they are most rebellious.

8 **But thou,** son of man, hear what I say unto thee;
Be not thou rebellious like that rebellious house:
open thy mouth,
and eat that I give thee.

9 **And when I** looked,
behold,
an hand was sent unto me;
and, {lo}, a roll of a book was therein;

10 **And he** spread it before me;
and it was written within and without:
and there was written therein lamentations, and mourning, and woe.

3 **Moreover he** said unto me,
Son of man, eat that thou findest;
eat this roll,
and go speak unto the house of Israel.
2 **So I** opened my mouth,
and he caused me to eat that roll.
3 **And he** said unto me,
Son of man, cause thy belly to eat,
and fill thy bowels with this roll that I give thee.
Then did I eat it;
and it was in my mouth as honey for sweetness.
4 **And he** said unto me,
Son of man, go,
get thee unto the house of Israel,
and speak with my words unto them.
5 **For thou** art not sent to a people of a strange speech and of an hard language, but to the house of Israel;
6 Not to many people of a strange speech and of an hard language,
whose words thou canst not understand.
Surely, had I sent thee to them,
they would have hearkened unto thee.
7 **But the house of Israel** will not hearken unto thee;
for they will not hearken unto me:
for all the house of Israel are impudent and hardhearted.
8 **Behold,**
I have made thy face strong against their faces, and thy forehead strong against their foreheads.
9 **As an adamant harder than flint** have I made thy forehead:
fear them not,
neither be dismayed at their looks,
though they be a rebellious house.
10 **Moreover he** said unto me,
Son of man, all my words that I shall speak unto thee receive in thine heart,
and hear with thine ears.
11 **And go,**
get thee to them of the captivity, unto the children of thy people,
and speak unto them,
and tell them,
Thus saith the Lord GOD;
whether they will hear,
or whether they will forbear.
12 **Then the spirit** took me up,
and I heard behind me a voice of a great rushing,
saying,
Blessed be the glory of the LORD from his place.
13 **I** heard also the noise of the wings of the living creatures that touched one another, and the noise of the wheels over against them, and a noise of a great rushing.
14 **So the spirit** lifted me up,
and took me away,
and I went in bitterness, in the heat of my spirit;
but the hand of the LORD was strong upon me.
15 **Then I** came to them of the captivity at Telabib,
that dwelt by the river of Chebar,
and I sat where they sat,
and remained there astonished among them seven days.
16 **And it** came to pass at the end of seven days,
that the word of the LORD came unto me,
saying,
17 **Son of man, I** have made thee a watchman unto the house of Israel:
therefore hear the word at my mouth,
and give them warning from me.
18 **When I** say unto the wicked,
Thou shalt surely die;
and thou givest him not warning,
nor speakest to warn the wicked from his wicked way,
to save his life;
the same wicked man shall die in his iniquity;
but his blood will I require at thine hand.
19 **Yet if thou** warn the wicked,
and he turn not from his wickedness, nor from his wicked way,
he shall die in his iniquity;
but thou hast delivered thy soul.
20 **Again, When a righteous man** doth turn from his righteousness,
and commit iniquity,
and I lay a stumbling-block before him,
he shall die:
because thou hast not given him warning,
he shall die in his sin,
and his righteousness which he hath done shall not be remembered;
but his blood will I require at thine hand.
21 **Nevertheless if thou** warn the righteous man,
that the righteous sin not,
and he doth not sin,
he shall surely live,
because he is warned;
also thou hast delivered thy soul.
22 **And the hand of the LORD** was there upon me;
and he said unto me,
Arise,
go forth into the plain,
and I will there talk with thee.
23 **Then I** arose,
and went forth into the plain:
and, {behold}, the glory of the LORD stood there, as the glory which I saw by the river of Chebar:
and I fell on my face.
24 **Then the spirit** entered into me,
and set me upon my feet,
and spake with me,
and said unto me,
Go,
shut thyself within thine house.
25 **But thou,** O son of man,
behold,
they shall put bands upon thee,
and shall bind thee with them,
and thou shalt not go out among them:
26 **And I** will make thy tongue cleave to the roof of thy mouth,
that thou shalt be dumb,
and shalt not be to them a reprover:
for they are a rebellious house.
27 **But when I** speak with thee,
I will open thy mouth,
and thou shalt say unto them,
Thus saith the Lord GOD;
He that heareth, let him hear;
and he that forbeareth, let him forbear:
for they are a rebellious house.

4 **Thou** also, son of man, take thee a tile,
and lay it before thee,
and pourtray upon it the city, even Jerusalem:
2 **And lay** siege against it,
and build a fort against it,
and cast a mount against it;
set the camp also against it,

and set battering rams against it round about.

[3] **Moreover take thou** unto thee an iron pan,
and set it for a wall of iron between thee and the city:
and set thy face against it,
and it shall be besieged,
and thou shalt lay siege against it.
This shall be a sign to the house of Israel.

[4] **Lie thou** also upon thy left side,
and lay the iniquity of the house of Israel upon it:
according to the number of the days that thou shalt lie upon it thou shalt bear their iniquity.

[5] **For I** have laid upon thee the years of their iniquity, according to the number of the days, three hundred and ninety days:
so shalt thou bear the iniquity of the house of Israel.

[6] **And when thou** hast accomplished them,
lie again on thy right side,
and thou shalt bear the iniquity of the house of Judah forty days:
I have appointed thee each day for a year.

[7] **Therefore thou** shalt set thy face toward the siege of Jerusalem,
and thine arm shall be uncovered,
and thou shalt prophesy against it.

[8] **And, {behold}, I** will lay bands upon thee,
and thou shalt not turn thee from one side to another,
till thou hast ended the days of thy siege.

[9] **Take thou** also unto thee wheat, and barley, and beans, and lentiles, and millet, and fitches,
and put them in one vessel,
and make thee bread thereof, according to the number of the days that thou shalt lie upon thy side,
three hundred and ninety days shalt thou eat thereof.

[10] **And thy meat which thou shalt eat** shall be by weight, twenty shekels a day:
from time to time shalt thou eat it.

[11] **Thou** shalt drink also water by measure, the sixth part of an hin:
from time to time shalt thou drink.

[12] **And thou** shalt eat it as barley cakes,
and thou shalt bake it with dung that cometh out of man, in their sight.

[13] **And the LORD** said,
Even thus shall the children of Israel eat their defiled bread among the Gentiles,
whither I will drive them.

[14] **Then** said I,
Ah Lord GOD!
behold,
my soul hath not been polluted:
for from my youth up even till now have I not eaten of that which dieth of itself, or is torn in pieces;
neither came there abominable flesh into my mouth.

[15] **Then he** said unto me,
Lo,
I have given thee cow's dung for man's dung,
and thou shalt prepare thy bread therewith.

[16] **Moreover he** said unto me,
Son of man, behold,
I will break the staff of bread in Jerusalem:
and they shall eat bread by weight, and with care;
and they shall drink water by measure, and with astonishment:

[17] **That they** may want bread and water,
and be astonied one with another,
and consume away for their iniquity.

5

And thou, son of man, take thee a sharp knife,
take thee a barber's razor,
and cause it to pass upon thine head and upon thy beard:
then take thee balances to weigh,
and divide the hair.

[2] **Thou** shalt burn with fire a third part in the midst of the city,
when the days of the siege are fulfilled:
and thou shalt take a third part,
and smite about it with a knife:
and a third part thou shalt scatter in the wind;
and I will draw out a sword after them.

[3] **Thou** shalt also take thereof a few in number,
and bind them in thy skirts.

[4] **Then take** of them again,
and cast them into the midst of the fire,
and burn them in the fire;
for thereof shall a fire come forth into all the house of Israel.

[5] **Thus** saith the Lord GOD;
This is Jerusalem:
I have set it in the midst of the nations and countries that are round about her.

[6] **And she** hath changed my judgments into wickedness more than the nations, and my statutes more than the countries that are round about her:
for they have refused my judgments and my statutes,
they have not walked in them.

[7] **Therefore thus** saith the Lord GOD;
Because ye multiplied more than the nations that are round about you,
and have not walked in my statutes,
neither have kept my judgments,
neither have done according to the judgments of the nations that are round about you;

[8] **Therefore thus** saith the Lord GOD;
Behold,
I, even I, am against thee,
and will execute judgments in the midst of thee in the sight of the nations.

[9] **And I** will do in thee that which I have not done,
and whereunto I will not do any more the like, because of all thine abominations.

[10] **Therefore the fathers** shall eat the sons in the midst of thee,
and the sons shall eat their fathers;
and I will execute judgments in thee,
and the whole remnant of thee will I scatter into all the winds.

[11] **Wherefore, as I** live,
saith the Lord GOD;
Surely, because thou hast defiled my sanctuary with all thy detestable things, and with all thine abominations,
therefore will I also diminish thee;
neither shall mine eye spare,
neither will I have any pity.

[12] **A third part of thee** shall die with the pestilence,
and with famine shall they be consumed in the midst of thee:

and a third part shall fall by the sword round about thee;
and I will scatter a third part into all the winds,
and I will draw out a sword after them.

13 **Thus** shall mine anger be accomplished,
and I will cause my fury to rest upon them,
and I will be comforted:
and they shall know
that I the LORD have spoken it in my zeal,
when I have accomplished my fury in them.

14 **Moreover I** will make thee waste, and a reproach among the nations that are round about thee, in the sight of all that pass by.

15 **So it** shall be a reproach and a taunt, an instruction and an astonishment unto the nations that are round about thee,
when I shall execute judgments in thee in anger and in fury and in furious rebukes.

I the LORD have spoken it.

16 **When I** shall send upon them the evil arrows of famine,
which shall be for their destruction,
and which I will send to destroy you:
and I will increase the famine upon you,
and will break your staff of bread:
17 **So** will I send upon you famine and evil beasts,
and they shall bereave thee:
and pestilence and blood shall pass through thee;
and I will bring the sword upon thee.

I the LORD have spoken it.

6

And the word of the LORD came unto me,
saying,
2 **Son of man, set** thy face toward the mountains of Israel,
and prophesy against them,
3 **And say,**
Ye mountains of Israel, hear the word of the Lord GOD;
Thus saith the Lord GOD to the mountains, and to the hills, to the rivers, and to the valleys;
Behold,
I, even I, will bring a sword upon you,
and I will destroy your high places.

4 **And your altars** shall be desolate,
and your images shall be broken:
and I will cast down your slain men before your idols.

5 **And I** will lay the dead carcases of the children of Israel before their idols;
and I will scatter your bones round about your altars.

6 **In all your dwellingplaces** the cities shall be laid waste,
and the high places shall be desolate;
that your altars may be laid waste
and made desolate,
and your idols may be broken and cease,
and your images may be cut down,
and your works may be abolished.

7 **And the slain** shall fall in the midst of you,
and ye shall know
that I am the LORD.

8 **Yet** will I leave a remnant,
that ye may have some that shall escape the sword among the nations,
when ye shall be scattered through the countries.

9 **And they that escape of you** shall remember me among the nations whither they shall be carried captives,
because I am broken with their whorish heart, {which hath departed from me}, and with their eyes, {which go a whoring after their idols}:
and they shall lothe themselves for the evils which they have committed in all their abominations.

10 **And they** shall know
that I am the LORD,
and that I have not said in vain
that I would do this evil unto them.

11 **Thus** saith the Lord GOD;
Smite with thine hand,
and stamp with thy foot,
and say,
Alas for all the evil abominations of the house of Israel!
for they shall fall by the sword, by the famine, and by the pestilence.

12 **He that is far off** shall die of the pestilence;
and he that is near shall fall by the sword;
and he that remaineth and is besieged shall die by the famine:
thus will I accomplish my fury upon them.

13 **Then** shall ye know
that I am the LORD,
when their slain men shall be among their idols round about their altars, upon every high hill, in all the tops of the mountains, and under every green tree, and under every thick oak, the place where they did offer sweet savour to all their idols.

14 **So** will I stretch out my hand upon them,
and make the land desolate, yea, more desolate than the wilderness toward Diblath, in all their habitations:
and they shall know
that I am the LORD.

7

Moreover the word of the LORD came unto me,
saying,
2 **Also, thou son of man, thus** saith the Lord GOD unto the land of Israel;
An end, the end is come upon the four corners of the land.

3 **Now** is the end come upon thee,
and I will send mine anger upon thee,
and will judge thee according to thy ways,
and will recompense upon thee all thine abominations.

4 **And mine eye** shall not spare thee,
neither will I have pity:
but I will recompense thy ways upon thee,
and thine abominations shall be in the midst of thee:
and ye shall know
that I am the LORD.

5 **Thus** saith the Lord GOD;
An evil, an only evil, {behold}, is come.

6 **An end** is come,
the end is come:
it watcheth for thee;
behold,
it is come.

7 **The morning** is come unto thee, O thou that dwellest in the land:
the time is come,
the day of trouble is near, and not the sounding again of the mountains.

8 **Now** will I shortly pour out my fury upon thee,

and accomplish mine anger upon thee:
and I will judge thee according to thy ways,
and will recompense thee for all thine abominations.
9 **And mine eye** shall not spare,
neither will I have pity:
I will recompense thee according to thy ways and thine abominations that are in the midst of thee;
and ye shall know
that I am the LORD that smiteth.
10 **Behold** the day,
behold,
it is come:
the morning is gone forth;
the rod hath blossomed,
pride hath budded.
11 **Violence** is risen up into a rod of wickedness:
none of them shall remain, nor of their multitude, nor of any of their's:
neither shall there be wailing for them.
12 **The time** is come,
the day draweth near:
let not the buyer rejoice,
nor the seller mourn:
for wrath is upon all the multitude thereof.
13 **For the seller** shall not return to that which is sold,
although they were yet alive:
for the vision is touching the whole multitude thereof,
which shall not return;
neither shall any strengthen himself in the iniquity of his life.
14 **They** have blown the trumpet,
even to make all ready;
but none goeth to the battle:
for my wrath is upon all the multitude thereof.
15 **The sword** is without, and the pestilence and the famine within:
he that is in the field shall die with the sword;
and he that is in the city, famine and pestilence shall devour him.
16 **But they that escape of them** shall escape,
and shall be on the mountains like doves of the valleys,
all of them mourning, every one for his iniquity.
17 **All hands** shall be feeble,
and all knees shall be weak as water.
18 **They** shall also gird themselves with sackcloth,
and horror shall cover them;
and shame shall be upon all faces, and baldness upon all their heads.
19 **They** shall cast their silver in the streets,
and their gold shall be removed:
their silver and their gold shall not be able to deliver them in the day of the wrath of the LORD:
they shall not satisfy their souls,
neither fill their bowels:
because it is the stumblingblock of their iniquity.
20 **As for the beauty of his ornament,** he set it in majesty:
but they made the images of their abominations and of their detestable things therein:
therefore have I set it far from them.
21 **And I** will give it into the hands of the strangers for a prey, and to the wicked of the earth for a spoil;
and they shall pollute it.
22 **My face** will I turn also from them,
and they shall pollute my secret place:
for the robbers shall enter into it,
and defile it.
23 **Make** a chain:
for the land is full of bloody crimes,
and the city is full of violence.
24 **Wherefore I** will bring the worst of the heathen,
and they shall possess their houses:
I will also make the pomp of the strong to cease;
and their holy places shall be defiled.
25 **Destruction** cometh;
and they shall seek peace,
and there shall be none.
26 **Mischief** shall come upon mischief,
and rumour shall be upon rumour;
then shall they seek a vision of the prophet;
but the law shall perish from the priest, and counsel from the ancients.
27 **The king** shall mourn,
and the prince shall be clothed with desolation,
and the hands of the people of the land shall be troubled:
I will do unto them after their way,
and according to their deserts will I judge them;
and they shall know
that I am the LORD.

8 **And it** came to pass in the sixth year, in the sixth month, in the fifth day of the month,
as I sat in mine house,
and the elders of Judah sat before me,
that the hand of the Lord GOD fell there upon me.
2 **Then I** beheld, and {lo} a likeness as the appearance of fire: from the appearance of his loins even downward, fire; and from his loins even upward, as the appearance of brightness, as the colour of amber.
3 **And he** put forth the form of an hand,
and took me by a lock of mine head;
and the spirit lifted me up between the earth and the heaven,
and brought me in the visions of God to Jerusalem, to the door of the inner gate that looketh toward the north;
where was the seat of the image of jealousy,
which provoketh to jealousy.
4 **And, {behold}, the glory of the God of Israel** was there, according to the vision that I saw in the plain.
5 **Then** said he unto me,
Son of man, lift up thine eyes now the way toward the north.
So I lifted up mine eyes the way toward the north,
and behold northward at the gate of the altar this image of jealousy in the entry.
6 **He** said furthermore unto me,
Son of man, seest thou what they do?
even the great abominations that the house of Israel committeth here,
that I should go far off from my sanctuary?
but turn thee yet again,
and thou shalt see greater abominations.
7 **And he** brought me to the door of the court;
and when I looked,
behold a hole in the wall.
8 **Then** said he unto me,

Son of man, dig now in the wall:
and when I had digged in the wall,
behold a door.
9 **And he** said unto me,
Go in,
and behold the wicked abominations that they do here.
10 **So I** went in and saw;
and behold every form of creeping things, and abominable beasts, and all the idols of the house of Israel,
pourtrayed upon the wall round about.
11 **And there** stood before them seventy men of the ancients of the house of Israel,
and in the midst of them stood Jaazaniah the son of Shaphan, with every man his censer in his hand;
and a thick cloud of incense went up.
12 **Then** said he unto me,
Son of man, hast thou seen what the ancients of the house of Israel do in the dark, every man in the chambers of his imagery?
for they say,
the LORD seeth us not;
the LORD hath forsaken the earth.
13 **He** said also unto me,
Turn thee yet again,
and thou shalt see greater abominations that they do.
14 **Then he** brought me to the door of the gate of the LORD's house which was toward the north;
and, {behold}, there sat women weeping for Tammuz.
15 **Then** said he unto me,
Hast thou seen this, O son of man?
turn thee yet again,
and thou shalt see greater abominations than these.
16 **And he** brought me into the inner court of the LORD's house,
and, {behold}, at the door of the temple of the LORD, between the porch and the altar, were about five and twenty men, with their backs toward the temple of the LORD, and their faces toward the east;
and they worshipped the sun toward the east.
17 **Then he** said unto me,
Hast thou seen this, O son of man?
Is it a light thing to the house of Judah that they commit the abominations which they commit here?
for they have filled the land with violence,
and have returned
to provoke me to anger:
and, {lo}, they put the branch to their nose.
18 **Therefore** will I also deal in fury:
mine eye shall not spare,
neither will I have pity:
and though they cry in mine ears with a loud voice,
yet will I not hear them.

9 **He** cried also in mine ears with a loud voice,
saying,
Cause them that have charge over the city to draw near, even every man with his destroying weapon in his hand.
2 **And, {behold}, six men** came from the way of the higher gate,
which lieth toward the north, and every man a slaughter weapon in his hand;
and one man among them was clothed with linen, with a writer's inkhorn by his side:
and they went in,
and stood beside the brasen altar.
3 **And the glory of the God of Israel** was gone up from the cherub, {whereupon he was}, to the threshold of the house.
And he called to the man clothed with linen,
which had the writer's inkhorn by his side;
4 **And the LORD** said unto him,
Go through the midst of the city, through the midst of Jerusalem,
and set a mark upon the foreheads of the men that sigh and that cry for all the abominations that be done in the midst thereof.
5 **And to the others** he said in mine hearing,
Go ye after him through the city,
and smite:
let not your eye spare,
neither have ye pity:
6 **Slay** utterly old and young, both maids, and little children, and women:
but come not near any man upon whom is the mark;
and begin at my sanctuary.
Then they began at the ancient men which were before the house.
7 **And he** said unto them,
Defile the house,
and fill the courts with the slain:
go ye forth.
And they went forth,
and slew in the city.
8 **And it** came to pass,
while they were slaying them,
and I was left,
that I fell upon my face,
and cried,
and said,
Ah Lord GOD!
wilt thou destroy all the residue of Israel
in thy pouring out of thy fury upon Jerusalem?
9 **Then** said he unto me,
The iniquity of the house of Israel and Judah is exceeding great,
and the land is full of blood, and the city full of perverseness:
for they say,
The LORD hath forsaken the earth, and
the LORD seeth not.
10 **And as for me** also, mine eye shall not spare,
neither will I have pity,
but I will recompense their way upon their head.
11 **And, {behold}, the man clothed with linen,** {which had the inkhorn by his side}, reported the matter,
saying,
I have done as thou hast commanded me.

10 **Then I** looked,
and, {behold}, in the firmament that was above the head of the cherubims there appeared over them as it were a sapphire stone, as the appearance of the likeness of a throne.
2 **And he** spake unto the man clothed with linen,
and said,
Go in between the wheels, even under the cherub,
and fill thine hand with coals of fire from between the cherubims,
and scatter them over the city.
And he went in in my sight.
3 **Now the cherubims** stood on the right side of the house,
when the man went in;

and the cloud filled the inner court.

4 **Then the glory of the LORD** went up from the cherub,
and stood over the threshold of the house;
and the house was filled with the cloud,
and the court was full of the brightness of the LORD's glory.

5 **And the sound of the cherubims' wings** was heard even to the outer court, as the voice of the Almighty God
when he speaketh.

6 **And it** came to pass,
that when he had commanded the man clothed with linen,
saying,
Take fire from between the wheels, from between the cherubims;
then he went in,
and stood beside the wheels.

7 **And one cherub** stretched forth his hand from between the cherubims unto the fire that was between the cherubims,
and took thereof,
and put it into the hands of him that was clothed with linen:
who took it,
and went out.

8 **And there** appeared in the cherubims the form of a man's hand under their wings.

9 **And when I** looked,
behold the four wheels by the cherubims, one wheel by one cherub, and another wheel by another cherub:
and the appearance of the wheels was as the colour of a beryl stone.

10 **And as for their appearances,** they four had one likeness,
as if a wheel had been in the midst of a wheel.

11 **When they** went,
they went upon their four sides;
they turned not
as they went,
but to the place whither the head looked they followed it;
they turned not
as they went.

12 **And their whole body, and their backs, and their hands, and their wings, and the wheels,** were full of eyes round about, even the wheels that they four had.

13 **As for the wheels,** it was cried unto them in my hearing, O wheel.

14 **And every one** had four faces:
the first face was the face of a cherub,
and the second face was the face of a man,
and the third the face of a lion,
and the fourth the face of an eagle.

15 **And the cherubims** were lifted up.
This is the living creature that I saw by the river of Chebar.

16 **And when the cherubims** went,
the wheels went by them:
and when the cherubims lifted up their wings
to mount up from the earth,
the same wheels also turned not from beside them.

17 **When they** stood,
these stood;
and when they were lifted up,
these lifted up themselves also:
for the spirit of the living creature was in them.

18 **Then the glory of the LORD** departed from off the threshold of the house,
and stood over the cherubims.

19 **And the cherubims** lifted up their wings,
and mounted up from the earth in my sight:
when they went out,
the wheels also were beside them,
and every one stood at the door of the east gate of the LORD's house;
and the glory of the God of Israel was over them above.

20 **This** is the living creature that I saw under the God of Israel by the river of Chebar;
and I knew
that they were the cherubims.

21 **Every one** had four faces apiece, and every one four wings;
and the likeness of the hands of a man was under their wings.

22 **And the likeness of their faces** was the same faces which I saw by the river of Chebar, their appearances and themselves:
they went every one straight forward.

11 **Moreover the spirit** lifted me up,
and brought me unto the east gate of the LORD's house,
which looketh eastward:
and {behold} at the door of the gate five and twenty men;
among whom I saw Jaazaniah the son of Azur, and Pelatiah the son of Benaiah, princes of the people.

2 **Then** said he unto me,
Son of man, these are the men that devise mischief,
and give wicked counsel in this city:
3 **Which** say,
It is not near;
let us build houses:
this city is the caldron,
and we be the flesh.

4 **Therefore prophesy** against them,
prophesy, O son of man.

5 **And the Spirit of the LORD** fell upon me,
and said unto me,
Speak;
Thus saith the LORD;
Thus have ye said, O house of Israel:
for I know the things that come into your mind, every one of them.

6 **Ye** have multiplied your slain in this city,
and ye have filled the streets thereof with the slain.

7 **Therefore thus** saith the Lord GOD;
Your slain whom ye have laid in the midst of it, they are the flesh,
and this city is the caldron:
but I will bring you forth out of the midst of it.

8 **Ye** have feared the sword;
and I will bring a sword upon you,
saith the Lord GOD.

9 **And I** will bring you out of the midst thereof,
and deliver you into the hands of strangers,
and will execute judgments among you.

10 **Ye** shall fall by the sword;
I will judge you in the border of Israel;
and ye shall know
that I am the LORD.

11 **This city** shall not be your caldron,
neither shall ye be the flesh in the midst thereof;
but I will judge you in the border of Israel:
12 **And ye** shall know

that I am the LORD:
for ye have not walked in my statutes,
neither executed my judgments,
but have done after the manners of the heathen that are round about you.
13 **And it** came to pass,
when I prophesied,
that Pelatiah the son of Benaiah died.
Then fell I down upon my face,
and cried with a loud voice,
and said,
Ah Lord GOD!
wilt thou make a full end of the remnant of Israel?
14 **Again the word of the LORD** came unto me,
saying,
15 **Son of man, thy brethren, even thy brethren, the men of thy kindred, and all the house of Israel wholly,** are they unto whom the inhabitants of Jerusalem have said,
Get you far from the LORD:
unto us is this land given in possession.
16 **Therefore say,**
Thus saith the Lord GOD;
Although I have cast them far off among the heathen,
and although I have scattered them among the countries,
yet will I be to them as a little sanctuary in the countries where they shall come.
17 **Therefore say,**
Thus saith the Lord GOD;
I will even gather you from the people,
and assemble you out of the countries where ye have been scattered,
and I will give you the land of Israel.
18 **And they** shall come thither,
and they shall take away all the detestable things thereof and all the abominations thereof from thence.
19 **And I** will give them one heart,
and I will put a new spirit within you;
and I will take the stony heart out of their flesh,
and will give them an heart of flesh:
20 **That they** may walk in my statutes,
and keep mine ordinances,
and do them:
and they shall be my people,
and I will be their God.
21 **But as for them whose heart walketh after the heart of their detestable things and their abominations,** I will recompense their way upon their own heads,
saith the Lord GOD.
22 **Then** did the cherubims lift up their wings, and the wheels beside them;
and the glory of the God of Israel was over them above.
23 **And the glory of the LORD** went up from the midst of the city,
and stood upon the mountain which is on the east side of the city.
24 **Afterwards the spirit** took me up,
and brought me in a vision by the Spirit of God into Chaldea, to them of the captivity.
So the vision that I had seen went up from me.
25 **Then I** spake unto them of the captivity all the things that the LORD had shewed me.

12 **The word of the LORD** also came unto me,
saying,
2 **Son of man, thou** dwellest in the midst of a rebellious house,
which have eyes to see,
and see not;
they have ears to hear,
and hear not:
for they are a rebellious house.
3 **Therefore, thou son of man, prepare** thee stuff for removing,
and remove by day in their sight;
and thou shalt remove from thy place to another place in their sight:
it may be they will consider,
though they be a rebellious house.
4 **Then** shalt thou bring forth thy stuff by day in their sight, as stuff for removing:
and thou shalt go forth at even in their sight, as they that go forth into captivity.
5 **Dig** thou through the wall in their sight,
and carry out thereby.
6 **In their sight** shalt thou bear it upon thy shoulders,
and carry it forth in the twilight:
thou shalt cover thy face,
that thou see not the ground:
for I have set thee for a sign unto the house of Israel.
7 **And I** did so
as I was commanded:
I brought forth my stuff by day, as stuff for captivity,
and in the even I digged through the wall with mine hand;
I brought it forth in the twilight,
and I bare it upon my shoulder in their sight.
8 **And in the morning** came the word of the LORD unto me,
saying,
9 **Son of man, hath not the house of Israel, the rebellious house,** said unto thee,
What doest thou?
10 **Say thou** unto them,
Thus saith the Lord GOD;
This burden concerneth the prince in Jerusalem, and all the house of Israel that are among them.
11 **Say, I** am your sign:
like as I have done,
so shall it be done unto them:
they shall remove
and go into captivity.
12 **And the prince that is among them** shall bear upon his shoulder in the twilight,
and shall go forth:
they shall dig through the wall
to carry out thereby:
he shall cover his face,
that he see not the ground with his eyes.
13 **My net** also will I spread upon him,
and he shall be taken in my snare:
and I will bring him to Babylon to the land of the Chaldeans;
yet shall he not see it,
though he shall die there.
14 **And I** will scatter toward every wind all that are about him to help him, and all his bands;
and I will draw out the sword after them.
15 **And they** shall know
that I am the LORD,
when I shall scatter them among the nations,
and disperse them in the countries.
16 **But I** will leave a few men of them from the sword, from the famine, and from the pestilence;

that they may declare all their
abominations among the heathen
whither they come;
and they shall know
that I am the LORD.

17 **Moreover the word of the LORD**
came to me,
saying,
18 **Son of man, eat** thy bread with
quaking,
and drink thy water with trembling
and with carefulness;
19 **And say** unto the people of the
land,
Thus saith the Lord GOD of the
inhabitants of Jerusalem, and of
the land of Israel;
They shall eat their bread with
carefulness,
and drink their water with
astonishment,
that her land may be desolate from
all that is therein, because of the
violence of all them that dwell
therein.

20 **And the cities that are inhabited**
shall be laid waste,
and the land shall be desolate;
and ye shall know
that I am the LORD.

21 **And the word of the LORD** came
unto me,
saying,
22 **Son of man, what** is that proverb
that ye have in the land of Israel,
saying,
The days are prolonged,
and every vision faileth?
23 **Tell** them therefore,
Thus saith the Lord GOD;
I will make this proverb to cease,
nd they shall no more use it as a
proverb in Israel;
but say unto them,
The days are at hand, and the effect
of every vision.

24 **For there** shall be no more any
vain vision nor flattering
divination within the house of
Israel.

25 **For I** am the LORD:
I will speak,
and the word that I shall speak
shall come to pass;
it shall be no more prolonged:
for in your days, O rebellious
house, will I say the word,
and will perform it,
saith the Lord GOD.

26 **Again the word of the LORD**
came to me,
saying,
27 **Son of man, {behold}, they of
the house of Israel** say,
The vision that he seeth is for
many days to come,
and he prophesieth of the times
that are far off.

28 **Therefore say** unto them,
Thus saith the Lord GOD;
There shall none of my words be
prolonged any more,
but the word which I have spoken
shall be done,
saith the Lord GOD.

13

**And the word of the
LORD** came unto me,
saying,
2 **Son of man, prophesy** against the
prophets of Israel that prophesy,
and say thou unto them that
prophesy out of their own hearts,
Hear ye the word of the LORD;
3 **Thus** saith the Lord GOD;
Woe unto the foolish prophets,
that follow their own spirit,
and have seen nothing!

4 **O Israel, thy prophets** are like the
foxes in the deserts.

5 **Ye** have not gone up into the gaps,
neither made up the hedge for the
house of Israel
to stand in the battle in the day of
the LORD.

6 **They** have seen vanity and lying
divination,
saying,
The LORD saith:
and the LORD hath not sent them:
and they have made others to hope
that they would confirm the
word.

7 **Have ye not** seen a vain vision,
and have ye not spoken a lying
divination,
whereas ye say,
The LORD saith it;
albeit I have not spoken?

8 **Therefore thus** saith the Lord
GOD;
Because ye have spoken vanity,
and seen lies,
therefore, {behold}, I am against
you,
saith the Lord GOD.

9 **And mine hand** shall be upon the
prophets that see vanity, and that
divine lies:
they shall not be in the assembly of
my people,
neither shall they be written in the
writing of the house of Israel,
neither shall they enter into the
land of Israel;
and ye shall know
that I am the Lord GOD.

10 **Because, even because they** have
seduced my people,
saying,
Peace;
and there was no peace;
and one built up a wall,
and, {lo}, others daubed it with
untempered morter:
11 **Say** unto them which daub it with
untempered morter,
that it shall fall:
there shall be an overflowing
shower;
and ye, O great hailstones, shall
fall;
and a stormy wind shall rend it.
12 **Lo,**
when the wall is fallen,
shall it not be said unto you,
Where is the daubing wherewith ye
have daubed it?
13 **Therefore thus** saith the Lord
GOD;
I will even rend it with a stormy
wind in my fury;
and there shall be an overflowing
shower in mine anger,
and great hailstones in my fury to
consume it.

14 **So** will I break down the wall that
ye have daubed with untempered
morter,
and bring it down to the ground,
so that the foundation thereof
shall be discovered,
and it shall fall,
and ye shall be consumed in the
midst thereof:
and ye shall know
that I am the LORD.

15 **Thus** will I accomplish my wrath
upon the wall, and upon them
that have daubed it with
untempered morter,
and will say unto you,
The wall is no more, neither they
that daubed it;
16 To wit, the prophets of Israel
which prophesy concerning
Jerusalem, and which see visions
of peace for her,
and there is no peace,

saith the Lord GOD.

17 **Likewise, thou son of man, set** thy face against the daughters of thy people,
which prophesy out of their own heart;
and prophesy thou against them,
18 **And say,**
Thus saith the Lord GOD;
Woe to the women that sew pillows to all armholes,
and make kerchiefs upon the head of every stature
to hunt souls!

Will ye hunt the souls of my people,
and will ye save the souls alive that come unto you?

19 **And will ye** pollute me among my people for handfuls of barley and for pieces of bread,
to slay the souls that should not die,
and to save the souls alive that should not live,
by your lying to my people that hear your lies?

20 **Wherefore thus** saith the Lord GOD;
Behold,
I am against your pillows,
wherewith ye there hunt the souls
to make them fly,
and I will tear them from your arms,
and will let the souls go, even the souls that ye hunt
to make them fly.

21 **Your kerchiefs** also will I tear,
and deliver my people out of your hand,
and they shall be no more in your hand to be hunted;
and ye shall know
that I am the LORD.

22 **Because with lies** ye have made the heart of the righteous sad,
whom I have not made sad;
and strengthened the hands of the wicked,
that he should not return from his wicked way,
by promising him life:
23 **Therefore ye** shall see no more vanity, nor divine divinations:
for I will deliver my people out of your hand:
and ye shall know
that I am the LORD.

14

Then came certain of the elders of Israel unto me,
and sat before me.

2 **And the word of the LORD** came unto me,
saying,
3 **Son of man, these men** have set up their idols in their heart,
and put the stumblingblock of their iniquity before their face:
should I be enquired of at all by them?

4 **Therefore speak** unto them,
and say unto them,
Thus saith the Lord GOD;
Every man of the house of Israel that setteth up his idols in his heart, and putteth the stumblingblock of his iniquity before his face, and cometh to the prophet; I the LORD will answer him that cometh according to the multitude of his idols;
5 **That** I may take the house of Israel in their own heart,
because they are all estranged from me through their idols.

6 **Therefore say** unto the house of Israel,
Thus saith the Lord GOD;
Repent,
and turn yourselves from your idols;
and turn away your faces from all your abominations.

7 **For every one of the house of Israel, or of the stranger that sojourneth in Israel**, {which separateth himself from me}, {and setteth up his idols in his heart}, {and putteth the stumblingblock of his iniquity before his face}, {and cometh to a prophet to enquire of him concerning me}; I the LORD will answer him by myself:
8 **And I** will set my face against that man,
and will make him a sign and a proverb,
and I will cut him off from the midst of my people;
and ye shall know
that I am the LORD.

9 **And if the prophet** be deceived
when he hath spoken a thing,
I the LORD have deceived that prophet,
and I will stretch out my hand upon him,
and will destroy him from the midst of my people Israel.

10 **And they** shall bear the punishment of their iniquity:
the punishment of the prophet shall be even as the punishment of him that seeketh unto him;
11 **That the house of Israel** may go no more astray from me,
neither be polluted any more with all their transgressions;
but that they may be my people,
and I may be their God,
saith the Lord GOD.

12 **The word of the LORD** came again to me,
saying,
13 **Son of man, when the land** sinneth against me
by trespassing grievously,
then will I stretch out mine hand upon it,
and will break the staff of the bread thereof,
and will send famine upon it,
and will cut off man and beast from it:
14 **Though these three men, Noah, Daniel, and Job,** were in it,
they should deliver but their own souls by their righteousness,
saith the Lord GOD.

15 **If I** cause noisome beasts to pass through the land,
and they spoil it,
so that it be desolate,
that no man may pass through because of the beasts:
16 **Though these three men** were in it,
as I live,
saith the Lord GOD,
they shall deliver neither sons nor daughters;
they only shall be delivered,
but the land shall be desolate.

17 **Or if I** bring a sword upon that land,
and say,
Sword, go through the land;
so that I cut off man and beast from it:
18 **Though these three men** were in it,
as I live,
saith the Lord GOD,
they shall deliver neither sons nor daughters,
but they only shall be delivered themselves.

19 **Or if I** send a pestilence into that land,

and pour out my fury upon it in blood,
to cut off from it man and beast:
20 **Though Noah, Daniel, and Job** were in it,
as I live,
saith the Lord GOD,
they shall deliver neither son nor daughter;
they shall but deliver their own souls by their righteousness.
21 **For thus** saith the Lord GOD;
How much more when I send my four sore judgments upon Jerusalem, the sword, and the famine, and the noisome beast, and the pestilence,
to cut off from it man and beast?
22 **Yet, {behold}, therein** shall be left a remnant that shall be brought forth, both sons and daughters:
behold,
they shall come forth unto you,
and ye shall see their way and their doings:
and ye shall be comforted concerning the evil that I have brought upon Jerusalem, even concerning all that I have brought upon it.
23 **And they** shall comfort you,
when ye see their ways and their doings:
and ye shall know
that I have not done without cause all that I have done in it,
saith the Lord GOD.

15 **And the word of the LORD** came unto me,
saying,
2 **Son of man, what** is the vine tree more than any tree, or than a branch which is among the trees of the forest?
3 **Shall wood** be taken thereof to do any work?
or will men take a pin of it to hang any vessel thereon?
4 **Behold,**
it is cast into the fire for fuel;
the fire devoureth both the ends of it,
and the midst of it is burned.
Is it meet for any work?
5 **Behold, when it** was whole,
it was meet for no work:
how much less shall it be meet yet for any work,
when the fire hath devoured it,
and it is burned?
6 **Therefore thus** saith the Lord GOD;
As the vine tree among the trees of the forest, {which I have given to the fire for fuel}, so will I give the inhabitants of Jerusalem.
7 **And I** will set my face against them;
they shall go out from one fire,
and another fire shall devour them;
and ye shall know
that I am the LORD,
when I set my face against them.
8 **And I** will make the land desolate,
because they have committed a trespass,
saith the Lord GOD.

16 ∞ **Again the word of the LORD** came unto me,
saying,
2 **Son of man, cause** Jerusalem to know her abominations,
3 **And say,**
Thus saith the Lord GOD unto Jerusalem;
Thy birth and thy nativity is of the land of Canaan;
thy father was an Amorite, and thy mother an Hittite.
4 **And as for thy nativity,** in the day thou wast born
thy navel was not cut,
neither wast thou washed in water to supple thee;
thou wast not salted at all,
nor swaddled at all.
5 **None eye** pitied thee,
to do any of these unto thee,
to have compassion upon thee;
but thou wast cast out in the open field, to the lothing of thy person, in the day that thou wast born.
6 **And when I** passed by thee,
and saw thee polluted in thine own blood,
I said unto thee
when thou wast in thy blood,
Live;
yea, I said unto thee
when thou wast in thy blood,
Live.
7 **I** have caused thee to multiply as the bud of the field,
and thou hast increased
and waxen great,
and thou art come to excellent ornaments:
thy breasts are fashioned,
and thine hair is grown,
whereas thou wast naked and bare.
8 **Now when** I passed by thee,
and looked upon thee,
behold,
thy time was the time of love;
and I spread my skirt over thee,
and covered thy nakedness:
yea, I sware unto thee,
and entered into a covenant with thee,
saith the Lord GOD,
and thou becamest mine.
9 **Then** washed I thee with water;
yea, I throughly washed away thy blood from thee,
and I anointed thee with oil.
10 **I** clothed thee also with broidered work,
and shod thee with badgers' skin,
and I girded thee about with fine linen,
and I covered thee with silk.
11 **I** decked thee also with ornaments,
and I put bracelets upon thy hands, and a chain on thy neck.
12 **And I** put a jewel on thy forehead, and earrings in thine ears, and a beautiful crown upon thine head.
13 **Thus** wast thou decked with gold and silver;
and thy raiment was of fine linen, and silk, and broidered work;
thou didst eat fine flour, and honey, and oil:
and thou wast exceeding beautiful,
and thou didst prosper into a kingdom.
14 **And thy renown** went forth among the heathen for thy beauty:
for it was perfect through my comeliness,
which I had put upon thee,
saith the Lord GOD.
15 **But thou** didst trust in thine own beauty,
and playedst the harlot because of thy renown,
and pouredst out thy fornications on every one that passed by;
his it was.
16 **And of thy garments** thou didst take,
and deckedst thy high places with divers colours,

and playedst the harlot thereupon:
the like things shall not come,
neither shall it be so.
17 **Thou** hast also taken thy fair
jewels of my gold and of my silver,
which I had given thee,
and madest to thyself images of
men,
and didst commit whoredom with
them,
18 **And** tookest thy broidered
garments,
and coveredst them:
and thou hast set mine oil and
mine incense before them.
19 **My meat also which I gave thee,**
fine flour, and oil, and honey,
{wherewith I fed thee}, thou hast
even set it before them for a sweet
savour:
and thus it was,
saith the Lord GOD.
20 **Moreover thou** hast taken thy
sons and thy daughters,
whom thou hast borne unto me,
and these hast thou sacrificed unto
them to be devoured.
Is this of thy whoredoms a small
matter,
21 **That thou** hast slain my children,
and delivered them
to cause them to pass through the
fire for them?
22 **And in all thine abominations**
and thy whoredoms thou hast
not remembered the days of thy
youth,
when thou wast naked and bare,
and wast polluted in thy blood.
23 **And it** came to pass after all thy
wickedness,
(woe, woe unto thee!
saith the Lord GOD;)
24 **That thou** hast also built unto
thee an eminent place,
and hast made thee an high place in
every street.
25 **Thou** hast built thy high place at
every head of the way,
and hast made thy beauty to be
abhorred,
and hast opened thy feet to every
one that passed by,
and multiplied thy whoredoms.
26 **Thou** hast also committed
fornication with the Egyptians
thy neighbours, great of flesh;
and hast increased thy whoredoms,
to provoke me to anger.
27 **Behold,**
therefore I have stretched out my
hand over thee,
and have diminished thine ordinary
food,
and delivered thee unto the will of
them that hate thee, the
daughters of the Philistines,
which are ashamed of thy lewd
way.
28 **Thou** hast played the whore also
with the Assyrians,
because thou wast unsatiable;
yea, thou hast played the harlot
with them,
and yet couldest not be satisfied.
29 **Thou** hast moreover multiplied
thy fornication in the land of
Canaan unto Chaldea;
and yet thou wast not satisfied
therewith.
30 **How weak** is thine heart,
saith the Lord GOD,
seeing thou doest all these things,
the work of an imperious whorish
woman;
31 **In that thou** buildest thine
eminent place in the head of every
way,
and makest thine high place in
every street;
and hast not been as an harlot,
in that thou scornest hire;
32 But as a wife that committeth
adultery,
which taketh strangers instead of
her husband!
33 **They** give gifts to all whores:
but thou givest thy gifts to all thy
lovers,
and hirest them,
that they may come unto thee on
every side for thy whoredom.
34 **And the contrary** is in thee from
other women in thy whoredoms,
whereas none followeth thee to
commit whoredoms:
and in that thou givest a reward,
and no reward is given unto thee,
therefore thou art contrary.
35 **Wherefore, O harlot, hear** the
word of the LORD:
36 **Thus** saith the Lord GOD;
Because thy filthiness was poured
out,
and thy nakedness discovered
through thy whoredoms with thy
lovers, and with all the idols of
thy abominations, and by the
blood of thy children,
which thou didst give unto them;
37 **Behold,**
therefore I will gather all thy
lovers,
with whom thou hast taken
pleasure, and all them that thou
hast loved, with all them that
thou hast hated;
I will even gather them round about
against thee,
and will discover thy nakedness
unto them,
that they may see all thy
nakedness.
38 **And I** will judge thee,
as women that break wedlock
and shed blood are judged;
and I will give thee blood in fury
and jealousy.
39 **And I** will also give thee into their
hand,
and they shall throw down thine
eminent place,
and shall break down thy high
places:
they shall strip thee also of thy
clothes,
and shall take thy fair jewels,
and leave thee naked and bare.
40 **They** shall also bring up a
company against thee,
and they shall stone thee with
stones,
and thrust thee through with their
swords.
41 **And they** shall burn thine houses
with fire,
and execute judgments upon thee
in the sight of many women:
and I will cause thee to cease from
playing the harlot,
and thou also shalt give no hire any
more.
42 **So** will I make my fury toward
thee to rest,
and my jealousy shall depart from
thee,
and I will be quiet,
and will be no more angry.
43 **Because thou** hast not
remembered the days of thy
youth,
but hast fretted me in all these
things;
behold,
therefore I also will recompense
thy way upon thine head,
saith the Lord GOD:
and thou shalt not commit this
lewdness above all thine
abominations.

44 **Behold,**
every one that useth proverbs shall use this proverb against thee,
saying,
As is the mother,
so is her daughter.

45 **Thou** art thy mother's daughter,
that lotheth her husband and her children;
and thou art the sister of thy sisters,
which lothed their husbands and their children:
your mother was an Hittite, and your father an Amorite.

46 **And thine elder sister** is Samaria, she and her daughters that dwell at thy left hand:
and thy younger sister, {that dwelleth at thy right hand}, is Sodom and her daughters.

47 **Yet** hast thou not walked after their ways,
nor done after their abominations:
but, {as if that were a very little thing}, thou wast corrupted more than they in all thy ways.

48 **As I** live,
saith the Lord GOD,
Sodom thy sister hath not done, she nor her daughters,
as thou hast done, thou and thy daughters.

49 **Behold,**
this was the iniquity of thy sister Sodom,
pride, fulness of bread, and abundance of idleness was in her and in her daughters,
neither did she strengthen the hand of the poor and needy.

50 **And they** were haughty,
and committed abomination before me:
therefore I took them away
as I saw good.

51 **Neither** hath Samaria committed half of thy sins;
but thou hast multiplied thine abominations more than they,
and hast justified thy sisters in all thine abominations which thou hast done.

52 **Thou** also, {which hast judged thy sisters}, bear thine own shame for thy sins that thou hast committed more abominable than they:
they are more righteous than thou:
yea, be thou confounded also,
and bear thy shame,
in that thou hast justified thy sisters.

53 **When I** shall bring again their captivity, the captivity of Sodom and her daughters, and the captivity of Samaria and her daughters,
then will I bring again the captivity of thy captives in the midst of them:

54 **That thou** mayest bear thine own shame,
and mayest be confounded in all that thou hast done,
in that thou art a comfort unto them.

55 **When thy sisters, Sodom and her daughters,** shall return to their former estate,
and Samaria and her daughters shall return to their former estate,
then thou and thy daughters shall return to your former estate.

56 **For thy sister Sodom** was not mentioned by thy mouth in the day of thy pride,

57 **Before thy wickedness** was discovered, as at the time of thy reproach of the daughters of Syria, and all that are round about her, the daughters of the Philistines,
which despise thee round about.

58 **Thou** hast borne thy lewdness and thine abominations,
saith the LORD.

59 **For thus** saith the Lord GOD;
I will even deal with thee
as thou hast done,
which hast despised the oath in breaking the covenant.

60 **Nevertheless I** will remember my covenant with thee in the days of thy youth,
and I will establish unto thee an everlasting covenant.

61 **Then thou** shalt remember thy ways,
and be ashamed,
when thou shalt receive thy sisters, thine elder and thy younger:
and I will give them unto thee for daughters, but not by thy covenant.

62 **And I** will establish my covenant with thee;
and thou shalt know
that I am the LORD:

63 **That thou** mayest remember,
and be confounded,
and never open thy mouth any more because of thy shame,
when I am pacified toward thee for all that thou hast done,
saith the Lord GOD.

17 **And the word of the LORD** came unto me,
saying,

2 **Son of man, put forth** a riddle,
and speak a parable unto the house of Israel;

3 **And say,**
Thus saith the Lord GOD;
A great eagle with great wings, longwinged, full of feathers, {which had divers colours}, came unto Lebanon,
and took the highest branch of the cedar:

4 **He** cropped off the top of his young twigs,
and carried it into a land of traffick;
he set it in a city of merchants.

5 **He** took also of the seed of the land,
and planted it in a fruitful field;
he placed it by great waters,
and set it as a willow tree.

6 **And it** grew,
and became a spreading vine of low stature,
whose branches turned toward him,
and the roots thereof were under him:
so it became a vine,
and brought forth branches,
and shot forth sprigs.

7 **There** was also another great eagle with great wings and many feathers:
and, {behold}, this vine did bend her roots toward him,
and shot forth her branches toward him,
that he might water it by the furrows of her plantation.

8 **It** was planted in a good soil by great waters,
that it might bring forth branches,
and that it might bear fruit,
that it might be a goodly vine.

9 **Say thou,**
Thus saith the Lord GOD;
Shall it prosper?
shall he not pull up the roots thereof,
and cut off the fruit thereof,

that it wither?
it shall wither in all the leaves of her spring,
even without great power or many people to pluck it up by the roots thereof.
10 **Yea, behold,**
being planted,
shall it prosper?
shall it not utterly wither,
when the east wind toucheth it?
it shall wither in the furrows where it grew.
11 **Moreover the word of the LORD** came unto me,
saying,
12 **Say** now to the rebellious house,
Know ye not
what these things mean?
tell them,
Behold,
the king of Babylon is come to Jerusalem,
and hath taken the king thereof, and the princes thereof,
and led them with him to Babylon;
13 **And** hath taken of the king's seed,
and made a covenant with him,
and hath taken an oath of him:
he hath also taken the mighty of the land:
14 **That the kingdom** might be base,
that it might not lift itself up,
but that by keeping of his covenant it might stand.
15 **But he** rebelled against him in sending his ambassadors into Egypt,
that they might give him horses and much people.
Shall he prosper?
shall he escape that doeth such things?
or shall he break the covenant,
and be delivered?
16 **As I** live,
saith the Lord GOD,
surely in the place {where the king dwelleth} that made him king, {whose oath he despised}, {and whose covenant he brake}, even with him in the midst of Babylon he shall die.
17 **Neither** shall Pharaoh with his mighty army and great company make for him in the war,
by casting up mounts
and building forts,
to cut off many persons:
18 **Seeing he** despised the oath
by breaking the covenant,
when, {lo}, he had given his hand,
and hath done all these things,
he shall not escape.
19 **Therefore thus** saith the Lord GOD;
As I live,
surely mine oath that he hath despised, and my covenant that he hath broken, even it will I recompense upon his own head.
20 **And I** will spread my net upon him,
and he shall be taken in my snare,
and I will bring him to Babylon,
and will plead with him there for his trespass that he hath trespassed against me.
21 **And all his fugitives with all his bands** shall fall by the sword,
and they that remain shall be scattered toward all winds:
and ye shall know
that I the LORD have spoken it.
22 **Thus** saith the Lord GOD;
I will also take of the highest branch of the high cedar,
and will set it;
I will crop off from the top of his young twigs a tender one,
and will plant it upon an high mountain and eminent:
23 **In the mountain of the height of Israel** will I plant it:
and it shall bring forth boughs,
and bear fruit,
and be a goodly cedar:
and under it shall dwell all fowl of every wing;
in the shadow of the branches thereof shall they dwell.
24 **And all the trees of the field** shall know
that I the LORD have brought down the high tree,
have exalted the low tree,
have dried up the green tree,
and have made the dry tree to flourish:
I the LORD have spoken
and have done it.

18 **The word of the LORD** came unto me again,
saying,
2 **What** mean ye,
that ye use this proverb concerning the land of Israel,
saying,
The fathers have eaten sour grapes,
and the children's teeth are set on edge?
3 **As I** live,
saith the Lord GOD,
ye shall not have occasion any more to use this proverb in Israel.
4 **Behold,**
all souls are mine;
as the soul of the father, so also the soul of the son is mine:
the soul that sinneth, it shall die.
5 **But if a man** be just,
and do that which is lawful and right,
6 **And** hath not eaten upon the mountains,
neither hath lifted up his eyes to the idols of the house of Israel,
neither hath defiled his neighbour's wife,
neither hath come near to a menstruous woman,
7 **And** hath not oppressed any,
but hath restored to the debtor his pledge,
hath spoiled none by violence,
hath given his bread to the hungry,
and hath covered the naked with a garment;
8 **He** that hath not given forth upon usury,
neither hath taken any increase,
that hath withdrawn his hand from iniquity,
hath executed true judgment between man and man,
9 Hath walked in my statutes,
and hath kept my judgments,
to deal truly;
he is just,
he shall surely live,
saith the Lord GOD.
10 **If he** beget a son that is a robber, a shedder of blood,
and that doeth the like to any one of these things,
11 **And that** doeth not any of those duties,
but even hath eaten upon the mountains,
and defiled his neighbour's wife,
12 Hath oppressed the poor and needy,
hath spoiled by violence,
hath not restored the pledge,
and hath lifted up his eyes to the idols,
hath committed abomination,
13 Hath given forth upon usury,
and hath taken increase:
shall he then live?

he shall not live:
he hath done all these abominations;
he shall surely die;
his blood shall be upon him.

14 **Now, {lo}, if he** beget a son,
that seeth all his father's sins which he hath done,
and considereth,
and doeth not such like,
15 **That** hath not eaten upon the mountains,
neither hath lifted up his eyes to the idols of the house of Israel,
hath not defiled his neighbour's wife,
16 **Neither** hath oppressed any,
hath not withholden the pledge,
neither hath spoiled by violence,
but hath given his bread to the hungry,
and hath covered the naked with a garment,
17 **That** hath taken off his hand from the poor,
that hath not received usury nor increase,
hath executed my judgments,
hath walked in my statutes;
he shall not die for the iniquity of his father,
he shall surely live.

18 **As for his father**, {because he cruelly oppressed}, {spoiled his brother by violence}, {and did that which is not good among his people}, {lo}, even he shall die in his iniquity.

19 **Yet say ye,**
Why?
doth not the son bear the iniquity of the father?

When the son hath done that which is lawful and right,
and hath kept all my statutes,
and hath done them,
he shall surely live.

20 **The soul that sinneth,** it shall die.

The son shall not bear the iniquity of the father,
neither shall the father bear the iniquity of the son:
the righteousness of the righteous shall be upon him,
and the wickedness of the wicked shall be upon him.

21 **But if the wicked** will turn from all his sins that he hath committed,
and keep all my statutes,
and do that which is lawful and right,
he shall surely live,
he shall not die.

22 **All his transgressions that he hath committed,** they shall not be mentioned unto him:
in his righteousness that he hath done he shall live.

23 **Have I** any pleasure at all
that the wicked should die?
saith the Lord GOD:
and not that he should return from his ways,
and live?

24 **But when the righteous** turneth away from his righteousness,
and committeth iniquity,
and doeth according to all the abominations that the wicked man doeth,
shall he live?

All his righteousness that he hath done shall not be mentioned:
in his trespass that he hath trespassed, and in his sin that he hath sinned, in them shall he die.

25 **Yet ye** say,
The way of the Lord is not equal.

Hear now, O house of Israel;
Is not my way equal?
are not your ways unequal?

26 **When a righteous man** turneth away from his righteousness,
and committeth iniquity,
and dieth in them;
for his iniquity that he hath done shall he die.

27 **Again, when the wicked man** turneth away from his wickedness that he hath committed,
and doeth that which is lawful and right,
he shall save his soul alive.

28 **Because he** considereth,
and turneth away from all his transgressions that he hath committed,
he shall surely live,
he shall not die.

29 **Yet** saith the house of Israel,
The way of the Lord is not equal.

O house of Israel, are not my ways equal?
are not your ways unequal?

30 **Therefore I** will judge you, O house of Israel, every one according to his ways,
saith the Lord GOD.

Repent,
and turn yourselves from all your transgressions;
so iniquity shall not be your ruin.

31 **Cast away** from you all your transgressions,
whereby ye have transgressed;
and make you a new heart and a new spirit:
for why will ye die, O house of Israel?

32 **For I** have no pleasure in the death of him that dieth,
saith the Lord GOD:
wherefore turn yourselves,
and live ye.

19

Moreover take thou up a lamentation for the princes of Israel,
2 **And say,**
What is thy mother?

A lioness:
she lay down among lions,
she nourished her whelps among young lions.

3 **And she** brought up one of her whelps:
it became a young lion,
and it learned to catch the prey;
it devoured men.

4 **The nations** also heard of him;
he was taken in their pit,
and they brought him with chains unto the land of Egypt.

5 **Now when she** saw that she had waited,
and her hope was lost,
then she took another of her whelps,
and made him a young lion.

6 **And he** went up and down among the lions,
he became a young lion,
and learned to catch the prey,
and devoured men.

7 **And he** knew their desolate palaces,
and he laid waste their cities;
and the land was desolate, and the fulness thereof, by the noise of his roaring.

8 **Then the nations** set against him on every side from the provinces,
and spread their net over him:
he was taken in their pit.

[9] **And they** put him in ward in chains,
and brought him to the king of Babylon:
they brought him into holds,
that his voice should no more be heard upon the mountains of Israel.

[10] **Thy mother** is like a vine in thy blood,
planted by the waters:
she was fruitful and full of branches by reason of many waters.

[11] **And she** had strong rods for the sceptres of them that bare rule,
and her stature was exalted among the thick branches,
and she appeared in her height with the multitude of her branches.

[12] **But she** was plucked up in fury,
she was cast down to the ground,
and the east wind dried up her fruit:
her strong rods were broken and withered;
the fire consumed them.

[13] **And now she** is planted in the wilderness, in a dry and thirsty ground.

[14] **And fire** is gone out of a rod of her branches,
which hath devoured her fruit,
so that she hath no strong rod to be a sceptre to rule.
This is a lamentation,
and shall be for a lamentation.

20 **And it** came to pass in the seventh year, in the fifth month, the tenth day of the month,
that certain of the elders of Israel came to enquire of the LORD,
and sat before me.

[2] **Then** came the word of the LORD unto me,
saying,

[3] **Son of man, speak** unto the elders of Israel,
and say unto them,
Thus saith the Lord GOD;
Are ye come to enquire of me?
As I live,
saith the Lord GOD,
I will not be enquired of by you.

[4] **Wilt thou** judge them, son of man,
wilt thou judge them?
cause them to know the abominations of their fathers:

[5] **And say** unto them,
Thus saith the Lord GOD;
In the day when I chose Israel,
and lifted up mine hand unto the seed of the house of Jacob,
and made myself known unto them in the land of Egypt,
when I lifted up mine hand unto them,
saying,
I am the LORD your God;

[6] **In the day that I lifted up mine hand unto them,** {to bring them forth of the land of Egypt into a land that I had espied for them}, {flowing with milk and honey}, {which is the glory of all lands}:

[7] Then said I unto them,
Cast ye away every man the abominations of his eyes,
and defile not yourselves with the idols of Egypt:
I am the LORD your God.

[8] **But they** rebelled against me,
and would not hearken unto me:
they did not every man cast away the abominations of their eyes,
neither did they forsake the idols of Egypt:
then I said,
I will pour out my fury upon them,
to accomplish my anger against them in the midst of the land of Egypt.

[9] **But I** wrought for my name's sake,
that it should not be polluted before the heathen,
among whom they were,
in whose sight I made myself known unto them,
in bringing them forth out of the land of Egypt.

[10] **Wherefore I** caused them to go forth out of the land of Egypt,
and brought them into the wilderness.

[11] **And I** gave them my statutes,
and shewed them my judgments,
which if a man do,
he shall even live in them.

[12] **Moreover also I** gave them my sabbaths,
to be a sign between me and them,
that they might know
that I am the LORD that sanctify them.

[13] **But the house of Israel** rebelled against me in the wilderness:
they walked not in my statutes,
and they despised my judgments,
which if a man do,
he shall even live in them;
and my sabbaths they greatly polluted:
then I said,
I would pour out my fury upon them in the wilderness,
to consume them.

[14] **But I** wrought for my name's sake,
that it should not be polluted before the heathen,
in whose sight I brought them out.

[15] **Yet also I** lifted up my hand unto them in the wilderness,
that I would not bring them into the land which I had given them,
flowing with milk and honey,
which is the glory of all lands;

[16] **Because they** despised my judgments,
and walked not in my statutes,
but polluted my sabbaths:
for their heart went after their idols.

[17] **Nevertheless mine eye** spared them from destroying them,
neither did I make an end of them in the wilderness.

[18] **But I** said unto their children in the wilderness,
Walk ye not in the statutes of your fathers,
neither observe their judgments,
nor defile yourselves with their idols:

[19] **I** am the LORD your God;
walk in my statutes,
and keep my judgments,
and do them;

[20] **And hallow** my sabbaths;
and they shall be a sign between me and you,
that ye may know
that I am the LORD your God.

[21] **Notwithstanding the children** rebelled against me:
they walked not in my statutes,
neither kept my judgments to do them,
which if a man do,
he shall even live in them;
they polluted my sabbaths:
then I said,
I would pour out my fury upon them,
to accomplish my anger against them in the wilderness.

[22] **Nevertheless I** withdrew mine hand,
and wrought for my name's sake,

that it should not be polluted in the sight of the heathen,
in whose sight I brought them forth.
23 **I** lifted up mine hand unto them also in the wilderness,
that I would scatter them among the heathen,
and disperse them through the countries;
24 **Because they** had not executed my judgments,
but had despised my statutes,
and had polluted my sabbaths,
and their eyes were after their fathers' idols.
25 **Wherefore I** gave them also statutes that were not good, and judgments whereby they should not live;
26 **And I** polluted them in their own gifts,
in that they caused to pass through the fire all that openeth the womb,
that I might make them desolate,
to the end that they might know
that I am the LORD.
27 **Therefore, son of man, speak** unto the house of Israel,
and say unto them,
Thus saith the Lord GOD;
Yet in this your fathers have blasphemed me,
in that they have committed a trespass against me.
28 **For when I** had brought them into the land,
for the which I lifted up mine hand to give it to them,
then they saw every high hill, and all the thick trees,
and they offered there their sacrifices,
and there they presented the provocation of their offering:
there also they made their sweet savour,
and poured out there their drink offerings.
29 **Then I** said unto them,
What is the high place whereunto ye go?
And the name whereof is called Bamah unto this day.
30 **Wherefore say** unto the house of Israel,
Thus saith the Lord GOD;
Are ye polluted after the manner of your fathers?
and commit ye whoredom after their abominations?
31 **For when ye** offer your gifts,
when ye make your sons to pass through the fire,
ye pollute yourselves with all your idols, even unto this day:
and shall I be enquired of by you, O house of Israel?
As I live,
saith the Lord GOD,
I will not be enquired of by you.
32 **And that which cometh into your mind** shall not be at all,
that ye say,
We will be as the heathen, as the families of the countries,
to serve wood and stone.
33 **As I** live,
saith the Lord GOD,
surely with a mighty hand, and with a stretched out arm, and with fury poured out, will I rule over you:
34 **And I** will bring you out from the people,
and will gather you out of the countries wherein ye are scattered, with a mighty hand, and with a stretched out arm, and with fury poured out.
35 **And I** will bring you into the wilderness of the people,
and there will I plead with you face to face.
36 **Like as I** pleaded with your fathers in the wilderness of the land of Egypt,
so will I plead with you,
saith the Lord GOD.
37 **And I** will cause you to pass under the rod,
and I will bring you into the bond of the covenant:
38 **And I** will purge out from among you the rebels, and them that transgress against me:
I will bring them forth out of the country where they sojourn,
and they shall not enter into the land of Israel:
and ye shall know
that I am the LORD.
39 **As for you, O house of Israel,**
thus saith the Lord GOD;
Go ye,
serve ye every one his idols, and hereafter also,
if ye will not hearken unto me:
but pollute ye my holy name no more with your gifts, and with your idols.
40 **For in mine holy mountain, in the mountain of the height of Israel**, {saith the Lord GOD}, there shall all the house of Israel, all of them in the land, serve me:
there will I accept them,
and there will I require your offerings, and the firstfruits of your oblations, with all your holy things.
41 **I** will accept you with your sweet savour,
when I bring you out from the people,
and gather you out of the countries wherein ye have been scattered;
and I will be sanctified in you before the heathen.
42 **And ye** shall know
that I am the LORD,
when I shall bring you into the land of Israel, into the country for the which I lifted up mine hand to give it to your fathers.
43 **And there** shall ye remember your ways, and all your doings,
wherein ye have been defiled;
and ye shall lothe yourselves in your own sight for all your evils that ye have committed.
44 **And ye** shall know
that I am the LORD
when I have wrought with you for my name's sake, not according to your wicked ways, nor according to your corrupt doings, O ye house of Israel,
saith the Lord GOD.
45 **Moreover the word of the LORD** came unto me,
saying,
46 **Son of man, set** thy face toward the south,
and drop thy word toward the south,
and prophesy against the forest of the south field;
47 **And say** to the forest of the south,
Hear the word of the LORD;
Thus saith the Lord GOD;
Behold,
I will kindle a fire in thee,
and it shall devour every green tree in thee, and every dry tree:
the flaming flame shall not be quenched,

and all faces from the south to the north shall be burned therein.
48 **And all flesh** shall see that I the LORD have kindled it:
it shall not be quenched.
49 **Then** said I,
Ah Lord GOD!
they say of me,
Doth he not speak parables?

21

And the word of the LORD came unto me,
saying,
2 **Son of man, set** thy face toward Jerusalem,
and drop thy word toward the holy places,
and prophesy against the land of Israel,
3 **And say** to the land of Israel,
Thus saith the LORD;
Behold,
I am against thee,
and will draw forth my sword out of his sheath,
and will cut off from thee the righteous and the wicked.
4 **Seeing then that I** will cut off from thee the righteous and the wicked,
therefore shall my sword go forth out of his sheath against all flesh from the south to the north:
5 **That all flesh** may know
that I the LORD have drawn forth my sword out of his sheath:
it shall not return any more.
6 **Sigh** therefore, thou son of man, with the breaking of thy loins;
and with bitterness sigh before their eyes.
7 And it shall be,
when they say unto thee,
Wherefore sighest thou?
that thou shalt answer,
For the tidings;
because it cometh:
and every heart shall melt,
and all hands shall be feeble,
and every spirit shall faint,
and all knees shall be weak as water:
behold,
it cometh,
and shall be brought to pass,
saith the Lord GOD.
8 **Again the word of the LORD** came unto me,
saying,
9 **Son of man, prophesy,**
and say,
Thus saith the LORD;
Say,
A sword, a sword is sharpened,
and also furbished:
10 **It** is sharpened
to make a sore slaughter;
it is furbished
that it may glitter:
should we then make mirth?
it contemneth the rod of my son, as every tree.
11 **And he** hath given it to be furbished,
that it may be handled:
this sword is sharpened,
and it is furbished,
to give it into the hand of the slayer.
12 **Cry and howl,** son of man:
for it shall be upon my people,
it shall be upon all the princes of Israel:
terrors by reason of the sword shall be upon my people:
smite therefore upon thy thigh.
13 **Because it** is a trial,
and what if the sword contemn even the rod?
it shall be no more,
saith the Lord GOD.
14 **Thou** therefore, son of man, prophesy,
and smite thine hands together,
and let the sword be doubled the third time, the sword of the slain:
it is the sword of the great men that are slain,
which entereth into their privy chambers.
15 **I** have set the point of the sword against all their gates,
that their heart may faint,
and their ruins be multiplied:
ah!
it is made bright,
it is wrapped up for the slaughter.
16 **Go thee** one way or other, either on the right hand, or on the left,
whithersoever thy face is set.
17 **I** will also smite mine hands together,
and I will cause my fury to rest:
I the LORD have said it.
18 **The word of the LORD** came unto me again,
saying,
19 **Also, thou son of man, appoint** thee two ways,
that the sword of the king of Babylon may come:
both twain shall come forth out of one land:
and choose thou a place,
choose it at the head of the way to the city.
20 **Appoint** a way,
that the sword may come to Rabbath of the Ammonites, and to Judah in Jerusalem the defenced.
21 **For the king of Babylon** stood at the parting of the way, at the head of the two ways,
to use divination:
he made his arrows bright,
he consulted with images,
he looked in the liver.
22 **At his right hand** was the divination for Jerusalem,
to appoint captains,
to open the mouth in the slaughter,
to lift up the voice with shouting,
to appoint battering rams against the gates,
to cast a mount,
and to build a fort.
23 **And it** shall be unto them as a false divination in their sight, to them that have sworn oaths:
but he will call to remembrance the iniquity,
that they may be taken.
24 **Therefore thus** saith the Lord GOD;
Because ye have made your iniquity to be remembered,
in that your transgressions are discovered,
so that in all your doings your sins do appear;
because, {I say}, that ye are come to remembrance,
ye shall be taken with the hand.
25 **And thou, profane wicked prince of Israel**, {whose day is come}, {when iniquity shall have an end},
26 Thus saith the Lord GOD;
Remove the diadem,
and take off the crown:
this shall not be the same:
exalt him that is low,
and abase him that is high.
27 **I** will overturn, overturn, overturn, it:
and it shall be no more,
until he come whose right it is;
and I will give it him.
28 **And thou,** son of man, prophesy and say,

Thus saith the Lord GOD concerning the Ammonites, and concerning their reproach;
even say thou,
The sword, the sword is drawn:
for the slaughter it is furbished,
to consume because of the glittering:
29 **Whiles they** see vanity unto thee,
whiles they divine a lie unto thee,
to bring thee upon the necks of them that are slain, of the wicked,
whose day is come,
when their iniquity shall have an end.
30 **Shall I** cause it to return into his sheath?
I will judge thee in the place where thou wast created, in the land of thy nativity.
31 **And I** will pour out mine indignation upon thee,
I will blow against thee in the fire of my wrath,
and deliver thee into the hand of brutish men,
and skilful to destroy.
32 **Thou** shalt be for fuel to the fire;
thy blood shall be in the midst of the land;
thou shalt be no more remembered:
for I the LORD have spoken it.

22

Moreover the word of the LORD came unto me,
saying,
2 **Now, thou son of man, wilt thou** judge,
wilt thou judge the bloody city?
yea, thou shalt shew her all her abominations.
3 **Then say thou,**
Thus saith the Lord GOD,
The city sheddeth blood in the midst of it,
that her time may come,
and maketh idols against herself
to defile herself.
4 **Thou** art become guilty in thy blood that thou hast shed;
and hast defiled thyself in thine idols which thou hast made;
and thou hast caused thy days to draw near,
and art come even unto thy years:
therefore have I made thee a reproach unto the heathen, and a mocking to all countries.
5 **Those that be near, and those that be far from thee,** shall mock thee,
which art infamous and much vexed.
6 **Behold,**
the princes of Israel, every one were in thee to their power
to shed blood.
7 **In thee** have they set light by father and mother:
in the midst of thee have they dealt by oppression with the stranger:
in thee have they vexed the fatherless and the widow.
8 **Thou** hast despised mine holy things,
and hast profaned my sabbaths.
9 **In thee** are men that carry tales
to shed blood:
and in thee they eat upon the mountains:
in the midst of thee they commit lewdness.
10 **In thee** have they discovered their fathers' nakedness:
in thee have they humbled her that was set apart for pollution.
11 **And one** hath committed abomination with his neighbour's wife;
and another hath lewdly defiled his daughter in law;
and another in thee hath humbled his sister, his father's daughter.
12 **In thee** have they taken gifts
to shed blood;
thou hast taken usury and increase,
and thou hast greedily gained of thy neighbours by extortion,
and hast forgotten me,
saith the Lord GOD.
13 **Behold,**
therefore I have smitten mine hand at thy dishonest gain which thou hast made, and at thy blood which hath been in the midst of thee.
14 **Can thine heart** endure,
or can thine hands be strong, in the days that I shall deal with thee?
I the LORD have spoken it,
and will do it.
15 **And I** will scatter thee among the heathen,
and disperse thee in the countries,
and will consume thy filthiness out of thee.
16 **And thou** shalt take thine inheritance in thyself in the sight of the heathen,
and thou shalt know
that I am the LORD.
17 **And the word of the LORD** came unto me,
saying,
18 **Son of man, the house of Israel** is to me become dross:
all they are brass, and tin, and iron, and lead, in the midst of the furnace;
they are even the dross of silver.
19 **Therefore thus** saith the Lord GOD;
Because ye are all become dross,
behold,
therefore I will gather you into the midst of Jerusalem.
20 **As they** gather silver, and brass, and iron, and lead, and tin, into the midst of the furnace,
to blow the fire upon it,
to melt it;
so will I gather you in mine anger and in my fury,
and I will leave you there,
and melt you.
21 **Yea, I** will gather you,
and blow upon you in the fire of my wrath,
and ye shall be melted in the midst therof.
22 **As silver** is melted in the midst of the furnace,
so shall ye be melted in the midst thereof;
and ye shall know
that I the LORD have poured out my fury upon you.
23 **And the word of the LORD** came unto me,
saying,
24 **Son of man, say** unto her,
Thou art the land that is not cleansed, nor rained upon in the day of indignation.
25 **There** is a conspiracy of her prophets in the midst thereof, like a roaring lion ravening the prey;
they have devoured souls;
they have taken the treasure and precious things;
they have made her many widows in the midst thereof.
26 **Her priests** have violated my law,
and have profaned mine holy things:

they have put no difference between the holy and profane,
neither have they shewed difference between the unclean and the clean,
and have hid their eyes from my sabbaths,
and I am profaned among them.

27 **Her princes in the midst thereof** are like wolves ravening the prey,
to shed blood,
and to destroy souls,
to get dishonest gain.

28 **And her prophets** have daubed them with untempered morter,
seeing vanity,
and divining lies unto them,
saying,
Thus saith the Lord GOD,
when the LORD hath not spoken.

29 **The people of the land** have used oppression,
and exercised robbery,
and have vexed the poor and needy:
yea, they have oppressed the stranger wrongfully.

30 **And I** sought for a man among them,
that should make up the hedge,
and stand in the gap before me for the land,
that I should not destroy it:
but I found none.

31 **Therefore** have I poured out mine indignation upon them;
I have consumed them with the fire of my wrath:
their own way have I recompensed upon their heads,
saith the Lord GOD.

23

The word of the LORD came again unto me,
saying,

2 **Son of man, there** were two women, the daughters of one mother:

3 **And they** committed whoredoms in Egypt;
they committed whoredoms in their youth:
there were their breasts pressed,
and there they bruised the teats of their virginity.

4 **And the names of them** were Aholah the elder, and Aholibah her sister:
and they were mine,
and they bare sons and daughters.
Thus were their names;
Samaria is Aholah, and Jerusalem Aholibah.

5 **And Aholah** played the harlot
when she was mine;
and she doted on her lovers, on the Assyrians her neighbours,

6 **Which** were clothed with blue, captains and rulers, all of them desirable young men, horsemen riding upon horses.

7 **Thus she** committed her whoredoms with them, with all them that were the chosen men of Assyria, and with all on whom she doted:
with all their idols she defiled herself.

8 **Neither** left she her whoredoms brought from Egypt:
for in her youth they lay with her,
and they bruised the breasts of her virginity,
and poured their whoredom upon her.

9 **Wherefore I** have delivered her into the hand of her lovers, into the hand of the Assyrians,
upon whom she doted.

10 **These** discovered her nakedness:
they took her sons and her daughters,
and slew her with the sword:
and she became famous among women;
for they had executed judgment upon her.

11 **And when her sister Aholibah** saw this,
she was more corrupt in her inordinate love than she, and in her whoredoms more than her sister in her whoredoms.

12 **She** doted upon the Assyrians her neighbours, captains and rulers clothed most gorgeously, horsemen riding upon horses, all of them desirable young men.

13 **Then I** saw that she was defiled,
that they took both one way,

14 **And that she** increased her whoredoms:
for when she saw men pourtrayed upon the wall, the images of the Chaldeans pourtrayed with vermilion,

15 Girded with girdles upon their loins, exceeding in dyed attire upon their heads, all of them princes to look to, after the manner of the Babylonians of Chaldea, the land of their nativity:

16 **And as soon as she** saw them with her eyes,
she doted upon them,
and sent messengers unto them into Chaldea.

17 **And the Babylonians** came to her into the bed of love,
and they defiled her with their whoredom,
and she was polluted with them,
and her mind was alienated from them.

18 **So she** discovered her whoredoms,
and discovered her nakedness:
then my mind was alienated from her,
like as my mind was alienated from her sister.

19 **Yet she** multiplied her whoredoms,
in calling to remembrance the days of her youth,
wherein she had played the harlot in the land of Egypt.

20 **For she** doted upon their paramours,
whose flesh is as the flesh of asses,
and whose issue is like the issue of horses.

21 **Thus thou** calledst to remembrance the lewdness of thy youth,
in bruising thy teats by the Egyptians for the paps of thy youth.

22 **Therefore, O Aholibah, thus** saith the Lord GOD;
Behold,
I will raise up thy lovers against thee,
from whom thy mind is alienated,
and I will bring them against thee on every side;

23 The Babylonians, and all the Chaldeans, Pekod, and Shoa, and Koa, and all the Assyrians with them: all of them desirable young men, captains and rulers, great lords and renowned,
all of them riding upon horses.

24 **And they** shall come against thee with chariots, wagons, and wheels, and with an assembly of people, **which** shall set against thee buckler and shield and helmet round about:

and I will set judgment before them,
and they shall judge thee according to their judgments.
25 **And I** will set my jealousy against thee,
and they shall deal furiously with thee:
they shall take away thy nose and thine ears;
and thy remnant shall fall by the sword:
they shall take thy sons and thy daughters;
and thy residue shall be devoured by the fire.
26 **They** shall also strip thee out of thy clothes,
and take away thy fair jewels.
27 **Thus** will I make thy lewdness to cease from thee,
and thy whoredom brought from the land of Egypt:
so that thou shalt not lift up thine eyes unto them,
nor remember Egypt any more.
28 **For thus** saith the Lord GOD;
Behold,
I will deliver thee into the hand of them whom thou hatest, into the hand of them from whom thy mind is alienated:
29 **And they** shall deal with thee hatefully,
and shall take away all thy labour,
and shall leave thee naked and bare:
and the nakedness of thy whoredoms shall be discovered, both thy lewdness and thy whoredoms.
30 **I** will do these things unto thee,
because thou hast gone a whoring after the heathen,
and because thou art polluted with their idols.
31 **Thou** hast walked in the way of thy sister;
therefore will I give her cup into thine hand.
32 **Thus** saith the Lord GOD;
Thou shalt drink of thy sister's cup deep and large:
thou shalt be laughed to scorn
and had in derision;
it containeth much.
33 **Thou** shalt be filled with drunkenness and sorrow, with the cup of astonishment and desolation, with the cup of thy sister Samaria.
34 **Thou** shalt even drink it
and suck it out,
and thou shalt break the sherds thereof,
and pluck off thine own breasts:
for I have spoken it,
saith the Lord GOD.
35 **Therefore thus** saith the Lord GOD;
Because thou hast forgotten me,
and cast me behind thy back,
therefore bear thou also thy lewdness and thy whoredoms.
36 **The LORD** said moreover unto me;
Son of man, wilt thou judge Aholah and Aholibah?
yea, declare unto them their abominations;
37 **That they** have committed adultery,
and blood is in their hands,
and with their idols have they committed adultery,
and have also caused their sons,
whom they bare unto me,
to pass for them through the fire,
to devour them.
38 **Moreover this** they have done unto me:
they have defiled my sanctuary in the same day,
and have profaned my sabbaths.
39 **For when they** had slain their children to their idols,
then they came the same day into my sanctuary
to profane it;
and, {lo}, thus have they done in the midst of mine house.
40 **And furthermore, that ye** have sent for men to come from far,
unto whom a messenger was sent;
and, {lo}, they came:
for whom thou didst wash thyself,
paintedst thy eyes,
and deckedst thyself with ornaments,
41 **And** satest upon a stately bed, and a table prepared before it,
whereupon thou hast set mine incense and mine oil.
42 **And a voice of a multitude** being at ease was with her:
and with the men of the common sort were brought Sabeans from the wilderness,
which put bracelets upon their hands, and beautiful crowns upon their heads.
43 **Then** said I unto her that was old in adulteries,
Will they now commit whoredoms with her,
and she with them?
44 **Yet they** went in unto her,
as they go in unto a woman that playeth the harlot:
so went they in unto Aholah and unto Aholibah, the lewd women.
45 **And the righteous men,** they shall judge them after the manner of adulteresses, and after the manner of women that shed blood;
because they are adulteresses,
and blood is in their hands.
46 **For thus** saith the Lord GOD;
I will bring up a company upon them,
and will give them to be removed and spoiled.
47 **And the company** shall stone them with stones,
and dispatch them with their swords;
they shall slay their sons and their daughters,
and burn up their houses with fire.
48 **Thus** will I cause lewdness to cease out of the land,
that all women may be taught
not to do after your lewdness.
49 **And they** shall recompense your lewdness upon you,
and ye shall bear the sins of your idols:
and ye shall know
that I am the Lord GOD.

24

Again in the ninth year, in the tenth month, in the tenth day of the month, the word of the LORD came unto me, saying,
2 **Son of man, write thee** the name of the day, even of this same day:
the king of Babylon set himself against Jerusalem this same day.
3 **And utter** a parable unto the rebellious house,
and say unto them,
Thus saith the Lord GOD;
Set on a pot,
set it on,
and also pour water into it:
4 **Gather** the pieces thereof into it, even every good piece, the thigh, and the shoulder;
fill it with the choice bones.

5 **Take** the choice of the flock,
and burn also the bones under it,
and make it boil well,
and let them seethe the bones of it therein.

6 **Wherefore thus** saith the Lord GOD;
Woe to the bloody city, to the pot whose scum is therein, and whose scum is not gone out of it!
bring it out piece by piece;
let no lot fall upon it.

7 **For her blood** is in the midst of her;
she set it upon the top of a rock;
she poured it not upon the ground,
to cover it with dust;

8 **That it** might cause fury to come up
to take vengeance;
I have set her blood upon the top of a rock,
that it should not be covered.

9 **Therefore thus** saith the Lord GOD;
Woe to the bloody city!
I will even make the pile for fire great.

10 **Heap** on wood,
kindle the fire,
consume the flesh,
and spice it well,
and let the bones be burned.

11 **Then set** it empty upon the coals thereof,
that the brass of it may be hot,
and may burn,
and that the filthiness of it may be molten in it,
that the scum of it may be consumed.

12 **She** hath wearied herself with lies,
and her great scum went not forth out of her:
her scum shall be in the fire.

13 **In thy filthiness** is lewdness:
because I have purged thee,
and thou wast not purged,
thou shalt not be purged from thy filthiness any more,
till I have caused my fury to rest upon thee.

14 **I** the LORD have spoken it:
it shall come to pass,
and I will do it;
I will not go back,
neither will I spare,
neither will I repent;
according to thy ways, and according to thy doings, shall they judge thee,
saith the Lord GOD.

15 **Also the word of the LORD** came unto me,
saying,

16 **Son of man, {behold}, I** take away from thee the desire of thine eyes with a stroke:
yet neither shalt thou mourn
nor weep,
neither shall thy tears run down.

17 **Forbear** to cry,
make no mourning for the dead,
bind the tire of thine head upon thee,
and put on thy shoes upon thy feet,
and cover not thy lips,
and eat not the bread of men.

18 **So I** spake unto the people in the morning:
and at even my wife died;
and I did in the morning as I was commanded.

19 **And the people** said unto me,
Wilt thou not tell us
what these things are to us,
that thou doest so?

20 **Then I** answered them,
The word of the LORD came unto me,
saying,

21 **Speak** unto the house of Israel,
Thus saith the Lord GOD;
Behold,
I will profane my sanctuary, the excellency of your strength, the desire of your eyes, and that which your soul pitieth;
and your sons and your daughters whom ye have left shall fall by the sword.

22 **And ye** shall do as I have done:
ye shall not cover your lips,
nor eat the bread of men.

23 **And your tires** shall be upon your heads, and your shoes upon your feet:
ye shall not mourn
nor weep;
but ye shall pine away for your iniquities,
and mourn one toward another.

24 **Thus Ezekiel** is unto you a sign:
according to all that he hath done shall ye do:
and when this cometh,
ye shall know
that I am the Lord GOD.

25 **Also, thou son of man, shall it not** be in the day
when I take from them their strength, the joy of their glory, the desire of their eyes, and that whereupon they set their minds, their sons and their daughters,

26 **That he that escapeth in that day** shall come unto thee,
to cause thee to hear it with thine ears?

27 **In that day** shall thy mouth be opened to him which is escaped,
and thou shalt speak,
and be no more dumb:
and thou shalt be a sign unto them;
and they shall know
that I am the LORD.

25

The word of the LORD came again unto me,
saying,

2 **Son of man, set** thy face against the Ammonites,
and prophesy against them;

3 **And say** unto the Ammonites,
Hear the word of the Lord GOD;
Thus saith the Lord GOD;
Because thou saidst, Aha, against my sanctuary, {when it was profaned}; and against the land of Israel, {when it was desolate}; and against the house of Judah, {when they went into captivity};

4 **Behold,**
therefore I will deliver thee to the men of the east for a possession,
and they shall set their palaces in thee,
and make their dwellings in thee:
they shall eat thy fruit,
and they shall drink thy milk.

5 **And I** will make Rabbah a stable for camels, and the Ammonites a couching place for flocks:
and ye shall know
that I am the LORD.

6 **For thus** saith the Lord GOD;
Because thou hast clapped thine hands,
and stamped with the feet,
and rejoiced in heart with all thy despite against the land of Israel;

7 **Behold,**
therefore I will stretch out mine hand upon thee,
and will deliver thee for a spoil to the heathen;
and I will cut thee off from the people,

and I will cause thee to perish out of the countries:
I will destroy thee;
and thou shalt know
that I am the LORD.

8 **Thus** saith the Lord GOD;
Because that Moab and Seir do say,
Behold,
the house of Judah is like unto all the heathen;
9 **Therefore, {behold}, I** will open the side of Moab from the cities, from his cities which are on his frontiers, the glory of the country, Bethjeshimoth, Baalmeon, and Kiriathaim,
10 Unto the men of the east with the Ammonites,
and will give them in possession,
that the Ammonites may not be remembered among the nations.

11 **And I** will execute judgments upon Moab;
and they shall know
that I am the LORD.

12 **Thus** saith the Lord GOD;
Because that Edom hath dealt against the house of Judah
by taking vengeance,
and hath greatly offended,
and revenged himself upon them;
13 **Therefore thus** saith the Lord GOD;
I will also stretch out mine hand upon Edom,
and will cut off man and beast from it;
and I will make it desolate from Teman;
and they of Dedan shall fall by the sword.

14 **And I** will lay my vengeance upon Edom by the hand of my people Israel:
and they shall do in Edom according to mine anger and according to my fury;
and they shall know my vengeance,
saith the Lord GOD.

15 **Thus** saith the Lord GOD;
Because the Philistines have dealt by revenge,
and have taken vengeance with a despiteful heart,
to destroy it for the old hatred;
16 **Therefore thus** saith the Lord GOD;
Behold,
I will stretch out mine hand upon the Philistines,
and I will cut off the Cherethims,
and destroy the remnant of the sea coast.

17 **And I** will execute great vengeance upon them with furious rebukes;
and they shall know
that I am the LORD,
when I shall lay my vengeance upon them.

26

And it came to pass in the eleventh year, in the first day of the month,
that the word of the LORD came unto me,
saying,
2 **Son of man, because that Tyrus** hath said against Jerusalem, Aha,
she is broken that was the gates of the people:
she is turned unto me:
I shall be replenished,
now she is laid waste:
3 **Therefore thus** saith the Lord GOD;
Behold,
I am against thee, O Tyrus,
and will cause many nations to come up against thee,
as the sea causeth his waves to come up.

4 **And they** shall destroy the walls of Tyrus,
and break down her towers:
I will also scrape her dust from her,
and make her like the top of a rock.

5 **It** shall be a place for the spreading of nets in the midst of the sea:
for I have spoken it,
saith the Lord GOD:
and it shall become a spoil to the nations.

6 **And her daughters which are in the field** shall be slain by the sword;
and they shall know
that I am the LORD.

7 **For thus** saith the Lord GOD;
Behold,
I will bring upon Tyrus Nebuchadrezzar king of Babylon, a king of kings, from the north, with horses, and with chariots, and with horsemen, and companies, and much people.

8 **He** shall slay with the sword thy daughters in the field:
and he shall make a fort against thee,
and cast a mount against thee,
and lift up the buckler against thee.

9 **And he** shall set engines of war against thy walls,
and with his axes he shall break down thy towers.

10 **By reason of the abundance of his horses** their dust shall cover thee:
thy walls shall shake at the noise of the horsemen, and of the wheels, and of the chariots,
when he shall enter into thy gates,
as men enter into a city wherein is made a breach.

11 **With the hoofs of his horses** shall he tread down all thy streets:
he shall slay thy people by the sword,
and thy strong garrisons shall go down to the ground.

12 **And they** shall make a spoil of thy riches,
and make a prey of thy merchandise:
and they shall break down thy walls,
and destroy thy pleasant houses:
and they shall lay thy stones and thy timber and thy dust in the midst of the water.

13 **And I** will cause the noise of thy songs to cease;
and the sound of thy harps shall be no more heard.

14 **And I** will make thee like the top of a rock:
thou shalt be a place to spread nets upon;
thou shalt be built no more:
for I the LORD have spoken it,
saith the Lord GOD.

15 **Thus** saith the Lord GOD to Tyrus;
Shall not the isles shake at the sound of thy fall,
when the wounded cry,
when the slaughter is made in the midst of thee?

16 **Then all the princes of the sea** shall come down from their thrones,
and lay away their robes,
and put off their broidered garments:
they shall clothe themselves with trembling;
they shall sit upon the ground,

and shall tremble at every moment,
and be astonished at thee.

17 **And they** shall take up a lamentation for thee,
and say to thee,
How art thou destroyed,
that wast inhabited of seafaring men, the renowned city,
which wast strong in the sea, she and her inhabitants,
which cause their terror to be on all that haunt it!

18 **Now** shall the isles tremble in the day of thy fall;
yea, the isles that are in the sea shall be troubled at thy departure.

19 **For thus** saith the Lord GOD;
When I shall make thee a desolate city, like the cities that are not inhabited;
when I shall bring up the deep upon thee, and great waters shall cover thee;

20 **When I** shall bring thee down with them that descend into the pit, with the people of old time,
and shall set thee in the low parts of the earth, in places desolate of old, with them that go down to the pit,
that thou be not inhabited;
and I shall set glory in the land of the living;

21 **I** will make thee a terror,
and thou shalt be no more:
though thou be sought for,
yet shalt thou never be found again,
saith the Lord GOD.

27

The word of the LORD came again unto me, saying,

2 **Now, thou son of man, take up** a lamentation for Tyrus;

3 **And say** unto Tyrus,
O thou that art situate at the entry of the sea, {which art a merchant of the people for many isles}, Thus saith the Lord GOD;
O Tyrus, thou hast said,
I am of perfect beauty.

4 **Thy borders** are in the midst of the seas,
thy builders have perfected thy beauty.

5 **They** have made all thy ship boards of fir trees of Senir:
they have taken cedars from Lebanon
to make masts for thee.

6 **Of the oaks of Bashan** have they made thine oars;
the company of the Ashurites have made thy benches of ivory,
brought out of the isles of Chittim.

7 **Fine linen with broidered work from Egypt** was that which thou spreadest forth to be thy sail;
blue and purple from the isles of Elishah was that which covered thee.

8 **The inhabitants of Zidon and Arvad** were thy mariners:
thy wise men, O Tyrus, that were in thee, were thy pilots.

9 **The ancients of Gebal and the wise men thereof** were in thee thy calkers:
all the ships of the sea with their mariners were in thee
to occupy thy merchandise.

10 **They of Persia and of Lud and of Phut** were in thine army, thy men of war:
they hanged the shield and helmet in thee;
they set forth thy comeliness.

11 **The men of Arvad with thine army** were upon thy walls round about,
and the Gammadims were in thy towers:
they hanged their shields upon thy walls round about;
they have made thy beauty perfect.

12 **Tarshish** was thy merchant by reason of the multitude of all kind of riches;
with silver, iron, tin, and lead, they traded in thy fairs.

13 **Javan, Tubal, and Meshech,** they were thy merchants:
they traded the persons of men and vessels of brass in thy market.

14 **They of the house of Togarmah** traded in thy fairs with horses and horsemen and mules.

15 **The men of Dedan** were thy merchants;
many isles were the merchandise of thine hand:
they brought thee for a present horns of ivory and ebony.

16 **Syria** was thy merchant by reason of the multitude of the wares of thy making:
they occupied in thy fairs with emeralds, purple, and broidered work, and fine linen, and coral, and agate.

17 **Judah, and the land of Israel,** they were thy merchants:
they traded in thy market wheat of Minnith, and Pannag, and honey, and oil, and balm.

18 **Damascus** was thy merchant in the multitude of the wares of thy making, for the multitude of all riches; in the wine of Helbon, and white wool.

19 **Dan also and Javan going to and fro** occupied in thy fairs:
bright iron, cassia, and calamus, were in thy market.

20 **Dedan** was thy merchant in precious clothes for chariots.

21 **Arabia, and all the princes of Kedar,** they occupied with thee in lambs, and rams, and goats:
in these were they thy merchants.

22 **The merchants of Sheba and Raamah,** they were thy merchants:
they occupied in thy fairs with chief of all spices, and with all precious stones, and gold.

23 **Haran, and Canneh, and Eden, the merchants of Sheba, Asshur, and Chilmad,** were thy merchants.

24 **These** were thy merchants in all sorts of things, in blue clothes, and broidered work, and in chests of rich apparel, bound with cords, {and made of cedar}, among thy merchandise.

25 **The ships of Tarshish** did sing of thee in thy market:
and thou wast replenished,
and made very glorious in the midst of the seas.

26 **Thy rowers** have brought thee into great waters:
the east wind hath broken thee in the midst of the seas.

27 **Thy riches, and thy fairs, thy merchandise, thy mariners, and thy pilots, thy calkers, and the occupiers of thy merchandise, and all thy men of war, {that are in thee}, and in all thy company which is in the midst of thee,** shall fall into the midst of the seas in the day of thy ruin.

28 **The suburbs** shall shake at the sound of the cry of thy pilots.

29 **And all that handle the oar, the mariners, and all the pilots of the sea,** shall come down from their ships,
they shall stand upon the land;
30 **And** shall cause their voice to be heard against thee,
and shall cry bitterly,
and shall cast up dust upon their heads,
they shall wallow themselves in the ashes:
31 **And they** shall make themselves utterly bald for thee,
and gird them with sackcloth,
and they shall weep for thee with bitterness of heart and bitter wailing.
32 **And in their wailing** they shall take up a lamentation for thee,
and lament over thee,
saying,
What city is like Tyrus, like the destroyed in the midst of the sea?
33 **When thy wares** went forth out of the seas,
thou filledst many people;
thou didst enrich the kings of the earth with the multitude of thy riches and of thy merchandise.
34 **In the time when thou shalt be broken by the seas in the depths of the waters** thy merchandise and all thy company in the midst of thee shall fall.
35 **All the inhabitants of the isles** shall be astonished at thee,
and their kings shall be sore afraid,
they shall be troubled in their countenance.
36 **The merchants among the people** shall hiss at thee;
thou shalt be a terror,
and never shalt be any more.

28

The word of the LORD came again unto me,
saying,
2 **Son of man, say** unto the prince of Tyrus,
Thus saith the Lord GOD;
Because thine heart is lifted up,
and thou hast said,
I am a God,
I sit in the seat of God, in the midst of the seas;
yet thou art a man, and not God,
though thou set thine heart as the heart of God:
3 **Behold,**
thou art wiser than Daniel;
there is no secret that they can hide from thee:
4 **With thy wisdom and with thine understanding** thou hast gotten thee riches,
and hast gotten gold and silver into thy treasures:
5 **By thy great wisdom and by thy traffick** hast thou increased thy riches,
and thine heart is lifted up because of thy riches:
6 **Therefore thus** saith the Lord GOD;
Because thou hast set thine heart as the heart of God;
7 **Behold,**
therefore I will bring strangers upon thee, the terrible of the nations:
and they shall draw their swords against the beauty of thy wisdom,
and they shall defile thy brightness.
8 **They** shall bring thee down to the pit,
and thou shalt die the deaths of them that are slain in the midst of the seas.
9 **Wilt thou** yet say before him that slayeth thee,
I am God?
but thou shalt be a man, and no God, in the hand of him that slayeth thee.
10 **Thou** shalt die the deaths of the uncircumcised by the hand of strangers:
for I have spoken it,
saith the Lord GOD.
11 **Moreover the word of the LORD** came unto me,
saying,
12 **Son of man, take up** a lamentation upon the king of Tyrus,
and say unto him,
Thus saith the Lord GOD;
Thou sealest up the sum, full of wisdom, and perfect in beauty.
13 **Thou** hast been in Eden the garden of God;
every precious stone was thy covering, the sardius, topaz, and the diamond, the beryl, the onyx, and the jasper, the sapphire, the emerald, and the carbuncle, and gold:
the workmanship of thy tabrets and of thy pipes was prepared in thee in the day that thou wast created.
14 **Thou** art the anointed cherub that covereth;
and I have set thee so:
thou wast upon the holy mountain of God;
thou hast walked up and down in the midst of the stones of fire.
15 **Thou** wast perfect in thy ways from the day that thou wast created,
till iniquity was found in thee.
16 **By the multitude of thy merchandise** they have filled the midst of thee with violence,
and thou hast sinned:
therefore I will cast thee as profane out of the mountain of God:
and I will destroy thee, O covering cherub, from the midst of the stones of fire.
17 **Thine heart** was lifted up because of thy beauty,
thou hast corrupted thy wisdom by reason of thy brightness:
I will cast thee to the ground,
I will lay thee before kings,
that they may behold thee.
18 **Thou** hast defiled thy sanctuaries by the multitude of thine iniquities, by the iniquity of thy traffick;
therefore will I bring forth a fire from the midst of thee,
it shall devour thee,
and I will bring thee to ashes upon the earth in the sight of all them that behold thee.
19 **All they that know thee among the people** shall be astonished at thee:
thou shalt be a terror,
and never shalt thou be any more.
20 **Again the word of the LORD** came unto me,
saying,
21 **Son of man, set** thy face against Zidon,
and prophesy against it,
22 **And say,**
Thus saith the Lord GOD;
Behold,
I am against thee, O Zidon;
and I will be glorified in the midst of thee:
and they shall know
that I am the LORD,
when I shall have executed judgments in her,

and shall be sanctified in her.

23 **For I** will send into her pestilence, and blood into her streets;
and the wounded shall be judged in the midst of her by the sword upon her on every side;
and they shall know
that I am the LORD.

24 **And there** shall be no more a pricking brier unto the house of Israel, nor any grieving thorn of all that are round about them,
that despised them;
and they shall know
that I am the Lord GOD.

25 **Thus** saith the Lord GOD;
When I shall have gathered the house of Israel from the people among whom they are scattered,
and shall be sanctified in them in the sight of the heathen,
then shall they dwell in their land that I have given to my servant Jacob.

26 **And they** shall dwell safely therein,
and shall build houses,
and plant vineyards;
yea, they shall dwell with confidence,
when I have executed judgments upon all those that despise them round about them;
and they shall know
that I am the LORD their God.

29

In the tenth year, in the tenth month, in the twelfth day of the month, the word of the LORD came unto me, saying,

2 **Son of man, set** thy face against Pharaoh king of Egypt,
and prophesy against him, and against all Egypt:

3 **Speak,**
and say,
Thus saith the Lord GOD;
Behold,
I am against thee, Pharaoh king of Egypt, the great dragon that lieth in the midst of his rivers,
which hath said,
My river is mine own,
and I have made it for myself.

4 **But I** will put hooks in thy jaws,
and I will cause the fish of thy rivers to stick unto thy scales,
and I will bring thee up out of the midst of thy rivers,
and all the fish of thy rivers shall stick unto thy scales.

5 **And I** will leave thee thrown into the wilderness, thee and all the fish of thy rivers:
thou shalt fall upon the open fields;
thou shalt not be brought together,
nor gathered:
I have given thee for meat to the beasts of the field and to the fowls of the heaven.

6 **And all the inhabitants of Egypt** shall know
that I am the LORD,
because they have been a staff of reed to the house of Israel.

7 **When they** took hold of thee by thy hand,
thou didst break,
and rend all their shoulder:
and when they leaned upon thee,
thou brakest,
and madest all their loins to be at a stand.

8 **Therefore thus** saith the Lord GOD;
Behold,
I will bring a sword upon thee,
and cut off man and beast out of thee.

9 **And the land of Egypt** shall be desolate and waste;
and they shall know
that I am the LORD:
because he hath said,
The river is mine,
and I have made it.

10 **Behold,**
therefore I am against thee, and against thy rivers,
and I will make the land of Egypt utterly waste and desolate, from the tower of Syene even unto the border of Ethiopia.

11 **No foot of man** shall pass through it,
nor foot of beast shall pass through it,
neither shall it be inhabited forty years.

12 **And I** will make the land of Egypt desolate in the midst of the countries that are desolate,
and her cities among the cities that are laid waste shall be desolate forty years:
and I will scatter the Egyptians among the nations,
and will disperse them through the countries.

13 **Yet thus** saith the Lord GOD;
At the end of forty years will I gather the Egyptians from the people whither they were scattered:

14 **And I** will bring again the captivity of Egypt,
and will cause them to return into the land of Pathros, into the land of their habitation;
and they shall be there a base kingdom.

15 **It** shall be the basest of the kingdoms;
neither shall it exalt itself any more above the nations:
for I will diminish them,
that they shall no more rule over the nations.

16 **And it** shall be no more the confidence of the house of Israel,
which bringeth their iniquity to remembrance,
when they shall look after them:
but they shall know
that I am the Lord GOD.

17 **And it** came to pass in the seven and twentieth year, in the first month, in the first day of the month,
the word of the LORD came unto me,
saying,

18 **Son of man, Nebuchadrezzar king of Babylon** caused his army to serve a great service against Tyrus:
every head was made bald,
and every shoulder was peeled:
yet had he no wages, nor his army, for Tyrus, for the service that he had served against it:

19 **Therefore thus** saith the Lord GOD;
Behold,
I will give the land of Egypt unto Nebuchadrezzar king of Babylon;
and he shall take her multitude,
and take her spoil,
and take her prey;
and it shall be the wages for his army.

20 **I** have given him the land of Egypt for his labour wherewith he served against it,
because they wrought for me,
saith the Lord GOD.

21 **In that day** will I cause the horn of the house of Israel to bud forth,

and I will give thee the opening of the mouth in the midst of them;
and they shall know
that I am the LORD.

30

The word of the LORD came again unto me,
saying,
2 **Son of man, prophesy and say,**
Thus saith the Lord GOD;
Howl ye,
Woe worth the day!
3 **For the day** is near,
even the day of the LORD is near, a cloudy day;
it shall be the time of the heathen.
4 **And the sword** shall come upon Egypt,
and great pain shall be in Ethiopia,
when the slain shall fall in Egypt,
and they shall take away her multitude,
and her foundations shall be broken down.
5 **Ethiopia, and Libya, and Lydia, and all the mingled people, and Chub, and the men of the land that is in league,** shall fall with them by the sword.
6 **Thus** saith the LORD;
They also that uphold Egypt shall fall;
and the pride of her power shall come down:
from the tower of Syene shall they fall in it by the sword,
saith the Lord GOD.
7 **And they** shall be desolate in the midst of the countries that are desolate,
and her cities shall be in the midst of the cities that are wasted.
8 **And they** shall know
that I am the LORD,
when I have set a fire in Egypt,
and when all her helpers shall be destroyed.
9 **In that day** shall messengers go forth from me in ships
to make the careless Ethiopians afraid,
and great pain shall come upon them, as in the day of Egypt:
for, {lo}, it cometh.
10 **Thus** saith the Lord GOD;
I will also make the multitude of Egypt to cease by the hand of Nebuchadrezzar king of Babylon.
11 **He and his people with him, the terrible of the nations,** shall be brought to destroy the land:
and they shall draw their swords against Egypt,
and fill the land with the slain.
12 **And I** will make the rivers dry,
and sell the land into the hand of the wicked:
and I will make the land waste, and all that is therein, by the hand of strangers:
I the LORD have spoken it.
13 **Thus** saith the Lord GOD;
I will also destroy the idols,
and I will cause their images to cease out of Noph;
and there shall be no more a prince of the land of Egypt:
and I will put a fear in the land of Egypt.
14 **And I** will make Pathros desolate,
and will set fire in Zoan,
and will execute judgments in No.
15 **And I** will pour my fury upon Sin, the strength of Egypt;
and I will cut off the multitude of No.
16 **And I** will set fire in Egypt:
Sin shall have great pain,
and No shall be rent asunder,
and Noph shall have distresses daily.
17 **The young men of Aven and of Pibeseth** shall fall by the sword:
and these cities shall go into captivity.
18 **At Tehaphnehes** also the day shall be darkened,
when I shall break there the yokes of Egypt:
and the pomp of her strength shall cease in her:
as for her, a cloud shall cover her,
and her daughters shall go into captivity.
19 **Thus** will I execute judgments in Egypt:
and they shall know
that I am the LORD.
20 **And it** came to pass in the eleventh year, in the first month, in the seventh day of the month,
that the word of the LORD came unto me,
saying,
21 **Son of man, I** have broken the arm of Pharaoh king of Egypt;
and, {lo}, it shall not be bound up to be healed,
to put a roller to bind it,
to make it strong to hold the sword.
22 **Therefore thus** saith the Lord GOD;
Behold,
I am against Pharaoh king of Egypt,
and will break his arms, the strong, and that which was broken;
and I will cause the sword to fall out of his hand.
23 **And I** will scatter the Egyptians among the nations,
and will disperse them through the countries.
24 **And I** will strengthen the arms of the king of Babylon,
and put my sword in his hand:
but I will break Pharaoh's arms,
and he shall groan before him with the groanings of a deadly wounded man.
25 **But I** will strengthen the arms of the king of Babylon,
and the arms of Pharaoh shall fall down;
and they shall know
that I am the LORD,
when I shall put my sword into the hand of the king of Babylon,
and he shall stretch it out upon the land of Egypt.
26 **And I** will scatter the Egyptians among the nations,
and disperse them among the countries;
and they shall know
that I am the LORD.

31

And it came to pass in the eleventh year, in the third month, in the first day of the month,
that the word of the LORD came unto me,
saying,
2 **Son of man, speak** unto Pharaoh king of Egypt, and to his multitude;
Whom art thou like in thy greatness?
3 **Behold,**
the Assyrian was a cedar in Lebanon with fair branches, and with a shadowing shroud, and of an high stature;
and his top was among the thick boughs.
4 **The waters** made him great,
the deep set him up on high with her rivers running round about his plants,
and sent her little rivers unto all the trees of the field.

5 **Therefore his height** was exalted above all the trees of the field,
and his boughs were multiplied,
and his branches became long because of the multitude of waters,
when he shot forth.
6 **All the fowls of heaven** made their nests in his boughs,
and under his branches did all the beasts of the field bring forth their young,
and under his shadow dwelt all great nations.
7 **Thus** was he fair in his greatness, in the length of his branches:
for his root was by great waters.
8 **The cedars in the garden of God** could not hide him:
the fir trees were not like his boughs,
and the chestnut trees were not like his branches;
nor any tree in the garden of God was like unto him in his beauty.
9 **I** have made him fair by the multitude of his branches:
so that all the trees of Eden, {that were in the garden of God}, envied him.
10 **Therefore thus** saith the Lord GOD;
Because thou hast lifted up thyself in height,
and he hath shot up his top among the thick boughs,
and his heart is lifted up in his height;
11 **I** have therefore delivered him into the hand of the mighty one of the heathen;
he shall surely deal with him:
I have driven him out for his wickedness.
12 **And strangers, the terrible of the nations,** have cut him off,
and have left him:
upon the mountains and in all the valleys his branches are fallen,
and his boughs are broken by all the rivers of the land;
and all the people of the earth are gone down from his shadow,
and have left him.
13 **Upon his ruin** shall all the fowls of the heaven remain,
and all the beasts of the field shall be upon his branches:
14 **To the end that none of all the trees by the waters** exalt themselves for their height,
neither shoot up their top among the thick boughs,
neither their trees stand up in their height, all that drink water:
for they are all delivered unto death, to the nether parts of the earth, in the midst of the children of men, with them that go down to the pit.
15 **Thus** saith the Lord GOD;
In the day when he went down to the grave I caused a mourning:
I covered the deep for him,
and I restrained the floods thereof,
and the great waters were stayed:
and I caused Lebanon to mourn for him,
and all the trees of the field fainted for him.
16 **I** made the nations to shake at the sound of his fall,
when I cast him down to hell with them that descend into the pit:
and all the trees of Eden, the choice and best of Lebanon, all that drink water, shall be comforted in the nether parts of the earth.
17 **They** also went down into hell with him unto them that be slain with the sword; and they that were his arm, that dwelt under his shadow in the midst of the heathen.
18 **To whom** art thou thus like in glory and in greatness among the trees of Eden?
yet shalt thou be brought down with the trees of Eden unto the nether parts of the earth:
thou shalt lie in the midst of the uncircumcised with them that be slain by the sword.
This is Pharaoh and all his multitude,
saith the Lord GOD.

32

And it came to pass in the twelfth year, in the twelfth month, in the first day of the month,
that the word of the LORD came unto me,
saying,
2 **Son of man, take up** a lamentation for Pharaoh king of Egypt,
and say unto him,
Thou art like a young lion of the nations,
and thou art as a whale in the seas:
and thou camest forth with thy rivers,
and troubledst the waters with thy feet,
and fouledst their rivers.
3 **Thus** saith the Lord GOD;
I will therefore spread out my net over thee with a company of many people;
and they shall bring thee up in my net.
4 **Then** will I leave thee upon the land,
I will cast thee forth upon the open field,
and will cause all the fowls of the heaven to remain upon thee,
and I will fill the beasts of the whole earth with thee.
5 **And I** will lay thy flesh upon the mountains,
and fill the valleys with thy height.
6 **I** will also water with thy blood the land wherein thou swimmest, even to the mountains;
and the rivers shall be full of thee.
7 **And when I** shall put thee out,
I will cover the heaven,
and make the stars thereof dark;
I will cover the sun with a cloud,
and the moon shall not give her light.
8 **All the bright lights of heaven** will I make dark over thee,
and set darkness upon thy land,
saith the Lord GOD.
9 **I** will also vex the hearts of many people,
when I shall bring thy destruction among the nations, into the countries which thou hast not known.
10 **Yea, I** will make many people amazed at thee,
and their kings shall be horribly afraid for thee,
when I shall brandish my sword before them;
and they shall tremble at every moment, every man for his own life, in the day of thy fall.
11 **For thus** saith the Lord GOD;
The sword of the king of Babylon shall come upon thee.

12 **By the swords of the mighty** will I cause thy multitude to fall, the terrible of the nations, all of them:
and they shall spoil the pomp of Egypt,
and all the multitude thereof shall be destroyed.
13 **I** will destroy also all the beasts thereof from beside the great waters;
neither shall the foot of man trouble them any more,
nor the hoofs of beasts trouble them.
14 **Then** will I make their waters deep,
and cause their rivers to run like oil,
saith the Lord GOD.
15 **When I** shall make the land of Egypt desolate,
and the country shall be destitute of that whereof it was full,
when I shall smite all them that dwell therein,
then shall they know
that I am the LORD.
16 **This** is the lamentation wherewith they shall lament her:
the daughters of the nations shall lament her:
they shall lament for her, even for Egypt, and for all her multitude,
saith the Lord GOD.
17 **It** came to pass also in the twelfth year, in the fifteenth day of the month,
that the word of the LORD came unto me,
saying,
18 **Son of man, wail** for the multitude of Egypt,
and cast them down, even her, and the daughters of the famous nations, unto the nether parts of the earth, with them that go down into the pit.
19 **Whom** dost thou pass in beauty?
go down,
and be thou laid with the uncircumcised.
20 **They** shall fall in the midst of them that are slain by the sword:
she is delivered to the sword:
draw her and all her multitudes.
21 **The strong among the mighty** shall speak to him out of the midst of hell with them that help him:
they are gone down,
they lie uncircumcised,
slain by the sword.
22 **Asshur** is there and all her company:
his graves are about him:
all of them slain,
fallen by the sword:
23 **Whose graves** are set in the sides of the pit,
and her company is round about her grave:
all of them slain,
fallen by the sword,
which caused terror in the land of the living.
24 **There** is Elam and all her multitude round about her grave,
all of them slain,
fallen by the sword,
which are gone down uncircumcised into the nether parts of the earth,
which caused their terror in the land of the living;
yet have they borne their shame with them that go down to the pit.
25 **They** have set her a bed in the midst of the slain with all her multitude:
her graves are round about him: all of them uncircumcised,
slain by the sword:
though their terror was caused in the land of the living,
yet have they borne their shame with them that go down to the pit:
he is put in the midst of them that be slain.
26 **There** is Meshech, Tubal, and all her multitude:
her graves are round about him: all of them uncircumcised,
slain by the sword,
though they caused their terror in the land of the living.
27 **And they** shall not lie with the mighty that are fallen of the uncircumcised,
which are gone down to hell with their weapons of war:
and they have laid their swords under their heads,
but their iniquities shall be upon their bones,
though they were the terror of the mighty in the land of the living.
28 **Yea, thou** shalt be broken in the midst of the uncircumcised,
and shalt lie with them that are slain with the sword.
29 **There** is Edom, her kings, and all her princes,
which with their might are laid by them that were slain by the sword:
they shall lie with the uncircumcised, and with them that go down to the pit.
30 **There** be the princes of the north, all of them, and all the Zidonians,
which are gone down with the slain;
with their terror they are ashamed of their might;
and they lie uncircumcised with them that be slain by the sword,
and bear their shame with them that go down to the pit.
31 **Pharaoh** shall see them,
and shall be comforted over all his multitude, even Pharaoh and all his army slain by the sword,
saith the Lord GOD.
32 **For I** have caused my terror in the land of the living:
and he shall be laid in the midst of the uncircumcised with them that are slain with the sword, even Pharaoh and all his multitude,
saith the Lord GOD.

33

Again the word of the LORD came unto me,
saying,
2 **Son of man, speak** to the children of thy people,
and say unto them,
When I bring the sword upon a land,
if the people of the land take a man of their coasts,
and set him for their watchman:
3 **If when he** seeth the sword come upon the land,
he blow the trumpet,
and warn the people;
4 **Then whosoever** heareth the sound of the trumpet,
and taketh not warning;
if the sword come,
and take him away,
his blood shall be upon his own head.
5 **He** heard the sound of the trumpet,
and took not warning;
his blood shall be upon him.
But he that taketh warning shall deliver his soul.

[6] **But if the watchman** see the sword come,
and blow not the trumpet,
and the people be not warned;
if the sword come,
and take any person from among them,
he is taken away in his iniquity;
but his blood will I require at the watchman's hand.

[7] **So thou,** O son of man, I have set thee a watchman unto the house of Israel;
therefore thou shalt hear the word at my mouth,
and warn them from me.

[8] **When I** say unto the wicked,
O wicked man, thou shalt surely die;
if thou dost not speak to warn the wicked from his way,
that wicked man shall die in his iniquity;
but his blood will I require at thine hand.

[9] **Nevertheless, if thou** warn the wicked of his way
to turn from it;
if he do not turn from his way,
he shall die in his iniquity;
but thou hast delivered thy soul.

[10] **Therefore, O thou son of man, speak** unto the house of Israel;
Thus ye speak,
saying,
If our transgressions and our sins be upon us,
and we pine away in them,
how should we then live?

[11] **Say** unto them,
As I live,
saith the Lord GOD,
I have no pleasure in the death of the wicked;
but that the wicked turn from his way and live:
turn ye,
turn ye from your evil ways;
for why will ye die, O house of Israel?

[12] **Therefore, thou son of man, say** unto the children of thy people,
The righteousness of the righteous shall not deliver him in the day of his transgression:
as for the wickedness of the wicked, he shall not fall thereby in the day that he turneth from his wickedness;
neither shall the righteous be able to live for his righteousness in the day that he sinneth.

[13] **When I** shall say to the righteous,
that he shall surely live;
if he trust to his own righteousness,
and commit iniquity,
all his righteousnesses shall not be remembered;
but for his iniquity that he hath committed, he shall die for it.

[14] **Again, when I** say unto the wicked,
Thou shalt surely die;
if he turn from his sin,
and do that which is lawful and right;

[15] **If the wicked** restore the pledge,
give again that he had robbed,
walk in the statutes of life,
without committing iniquity;
he shall surely live,
he shall not die.

[16] **None of his sins that he hath committed** shall be mentioned unto him:
he hath done that which is lawful and right;
he shall surely live.

[17] **Yet the children of thy people** say,
The way of the Lord is not equal:
but as for them, their way is not equal.

[18] **When the righteous** turneth from his righteousness,
and committeth iniquity,
he shall even die thereby.

[19] **But if the wicked** turn from his wickedness,
and do that which is lawful and right,
he shall live thereby.

[20] **Yet ye** say,
The way of the Lord is not equal.
O ye house of Israel, I will judge you every one after his ways.

[21] **And it** came to pass in the twelfth year of our captivity, in the tenth month, in the fifth day of the month,
that one that had escaped out of Jerusalem came unto me,
saying,
The city is smitten.

[22] **Now the hand of the LORD** was upon me in the evening,
afore he that was escaped came;
and had opened my mouth,
until he came to me in the morning;
and my mouth was opened,
and I was no more dumb.

[23] **Then the word of the LORD** came unto me,
saying,

[24] **Son of man, they that inhabit those wastes of the land of Israel** speak,
saying,
Abraham was one,
and he inherited the land:
but we are many;
the land is given us for inheritance.

[25] **Wherefore say** unto them,
Thus saith the Lord GOD;
Ye eat with the blood,
and lift up your eyes toward your idols,
and shed blood:
and shall ye possess the land?

[26] **Ye** stand upon your sword,
ye work abomination,
and ye defile every one his neighbour's wife:
and shall ye possess the land?

[27] **Say thou** thus unto them,
Thus saith the Lord GOD;
As I live,
surely they that are in the wastes shall fall by the sword,
and him that is in the open field will I give to the beasts to be devoured,
and they that be in the forts and in the caves shall die of the pestilence.

[28] **For I** will lay the land most desolate,
and the pomp of her strength shall cease;
and the mountains of Israel shall be desolate,
that none shall pass through.

[29] **Then** shall they know
that I am the LORD,
when I have laid the land most desolate because of all their abominations which they have committed.

[30] **Also, thou son of man, the children of thy people** still are talking against thee by the walls and in the doors of the houses,
and speak one to another, every one to his brother,
saying,
Come,
I pray you,

and hear what is the word that cometh forth from the LORD.
31 **And they** come unto thee as the people cometh,
and they sit before thee as my people,
and they hear thy words,
but they will not do them:
for with their mouth they shew much love,
but their heart goeth after their covetousness.
32 **And, {lo}, thou** art unto them as a very lovely song of one that hath a pleasant voice, and can play well on an instrument:
for they hear thy words,
but they do them not.
33 **And when this** cometh to pass,
(lo,
it will come,)
then shall they know
that a prophet hath been among them.

34

And the word of the LORD came unto me,
saying,
2 **Son of man, prophesy** against the shepherds of Israel,
prophesy,
and say unto them,
Thus saith the Lord GOD unto the shepherds;
Woe be to the shepherds of Israel that do feed themselves!
should not the shepherds feed the flocks?
3 **Ye** eat the fat,
and ye clothe you with the wool,
ye kill them that are fed:
but ye feed not the flock.
4 **The diseased** have ye not strengthened,
neither have ye healed that which was sick,
neither have ye bound up that which was broken,
neither have ye brought again that which was driven away,
neither have ye sought that which was lost;
but with force and with cruelty have ye ruled them.
5 **And they** were scattered,
because there is no shepherd:
and they became meat to all the beasts of the field,
when they were scattered.
6 **My sheep** wandered through all the mountains, and upon every high hill:
yea, my flock was scattered upon all the face of the earth,
and none did search or seek after them.
7 **Therefore, ye shepherds, hear** the word of the LORD;
8 **As I** live,
saith the Lord GOD,
surely because my flock became a prey,
and my flock became meat to every beast of the field,
because there was no shepherd,
neither did my shepherds search for my flock,
but the shepherds fed themselves,
and fed not my flock;
9 **Therefore, O ye shepherds, hear** the word of the LORD;
10 **Thus** saith the Lord GOD;
Behold,
I am against the shepherds;
and I will require my flock at their hand,
and cause them to cease from feeding the flock;
neither shall the shepherds feed themselves any more;
for I will deliver my flock from their mouth,
that they may not be meat for them.
11 **For thus** saith the Lord GOD;
Behold,
I, even I, will both search my sheep,
and seek them out.
12 **As a shepherd** seeketh out his flock in the day that he is among his sheep that are scattered;
so will I seek out my sheep,
and will deliver them out of all places where they have been scattered in the cloudy and dark day.
13 **And I** will bring them out from the people,
and gather them from the countries,
and will bring them to their own land,
and feed them upon the mountains of Israel by the rivers, and in all the inhabited places of the country.
14 **I** will feed them in a good pasture,
and upon the high mountains of Israel shall their fold be:
there shall they lie in a good fold,
and in a fat pasture shall they feed upon the mountains of Israel.
15 **I** will feed my flock,
and I will cause them to lie down,
saith the Lord GOD.
16 **I** will seek that which was lost,
and bring again that which was driven away,
and will bind up that which was broken,
and will strengthen that which was sick:
but I will destroy the fat and the strong;
I will feed them with judgment.
17 **And as for you, O my flock,** thus saith the Lord GOD;
Behold,
I judge between cattle and cattle, between the rams and the he goats.
18 **Seemeth it a small thing unto you** to have eaten up the good pasture,
but ye must tread down with your feet the residue of your pastures?
and to have drunk of the deep waters,
but ye must foul the residue with your feet?
19 **And as for my flock,** they eat that which ye have trodden with your feet;
and they drink that which ye have fouled with your feet.
20 **Therefore thus** saith the Lord GOD unto them;
Behold,
I, even I, will judge between the fat cattle and between the lean cattle.
21 **Because ye** have thrust with side and with shoulder,
and pushed all the diseased with your horns,
till ye have scattered them abroad;
22 **Therefore** will I save my flock,
and they shall no more be a prey;
and I will judge between cattle and cattle.
23 **And I** will set up one shepherd over them,
and he shall feed them, even my servant David;
he shall feed them,
and he shall be their shepherd.
24 **And I** the LORD will be their God, and my servant David a prince among them;

I the LORD have spoken it.

25 **And I** will make with them a covenant of peace,
and will cause the evil beasts to cease out of the land:
and they shall dwell safely in the wilderness,
and sleep in the woods.

26 **And I** will make them and the places round about my hill a blessing;
and I will cause the shower to come down in his season;
there shall be showers of blessing.

27 **And the tree of the field** shall yield her fruit,
and the earth shall yield her increase,
and they shall be safe in their land,
and shall know
that I am the LORD,
when I have broken the bands of their yoke,
and delivered them out of the hand of those that served themselves of them.

28 **And they** shall no more be a prey to the heathen,
neither shall the beast of the land devour them;
but they shall dwell safely,
and none shall make them afraid.

29 **And I** will raise up for them a plant of renown,
and they shall be no more consumed with hunger in the land,
neither bear the shame of the heathen any more.

30 **Thus** shall they know
that I the LORD their God am with them,
and that they, even the house of Israel, are my people,
saith the Lord GOD.

31 **And ye my flock, the flock of my pasture,** are men,
and I am your God,
saith the Lord GOD.

35 **Moreover the word of the LORD** came unto me,
saying,

2 **Son of man, set** thy face against mount Seir,
and prophesy against it,

3 **And say** unto it,
Thus saith the Lord GOD;
Behold, O mount Seir,
I am against thee,
and I will stretch out mine hand against thee,
and I will make thee most desolate.

4 **I** will lay thy cities waste,
and thou shalt be desolate,
and thou shalt know
that I am the LORD.

5 **Because thou** hast had a perpetual hatred,
and hast shed the blood of the children of Israel by the force of the sword in the time of their calamity, in the time that their iniquity had an end:

6 **Therefore, {as I live}, {saith the Lord GOD},** I will prepare thee unto blood,
and blood shall pursue thee:
sith thou hast not hated blood,
even blood shall pursue thee.

7 **Thus** will I make mount Seir most desolate,
and cut off from it him that passeth out and him that returneth.

8 **And I** will fill his mountains with his slain men:
in thy hills, and in thy valleys, and in all thy rivers, shall they fall that are slain with the sword.

9 **I** will make thee perpetual desolations,
and thy cities shall not return:
and ye shall know
that I am the LORD.

10 **Because thou** hast said,
These two nations and these two countries shall be mine,
and we will possess it;
whereas the LORD was there:

11 **Therefore, {as I live}, {saith the Lord GOD},** I will even do according to thine anger, and according to thine envy which thou hast used out of thy hatred against them;
and I will make myself known among them,
when I have judged thee.

12 **And thou** shalt know
that I am the LORD,
and that I have heard all thy blasphemies which thou hast spoken against the mountains of Israel,
saying,
They are laid desolate,
they are given us to consume.

13 **Thus with your mouth** ye have boasted against me,
and have multiplied your words against me:
I have heard them.

14 **Thus** saith the Lord GOD;
When the whole earth rejoiceth,
I will make thee desolate.

15 **As thou** didst rejoice at the inheritance of the house of Israel,
because it was desolate,
so will I do unto thee:
thou shalt be desolate, O mount Seir, and all Idumea, even all of it:
and they shall know
that I am the LORD.

36 **Also, thou son of man, prophesy** unto the mountains of Israel,
and say,
Ye mountains of Israel, hear the word of the LORD:

2 **Thus** saith the Lord GOD;
Because the enemy hath said against you, Aha,
even the ancient high places are ours in possession:

3 **Therefore prophesy and say,**
Thus saith the Lord GOD;
Because they have made you desolate,
and swallowed you up on every side,
that ye might be a possession unto the residue of the heathen,
and ye are taken up in the lips of talkers,
and are an infamy of the people:

4 **Therefore, ye mountains of Israel, hear** the word of the Lord GOD;
Thus saith the Lord GOD to the mountains, and to the hills, to the rivers, and to the valleys, to the desolate wastes, and to the cities that are forsaken,
which became a prey and derision to the residue of the heathen that are round about;

5 **Therefore thus** saith the Lord GOD;
Surely in the fire of my jealousy have I spoken against the residue of the heathen, and against all Idumea,
which have appointed my land into their possession with the joy of all their heart, with despiteful minds,
to cast it out for a prey.

6 **Prophesy** therefore concerning the land of Israel,

and say unto the mountains, and to the hills, to the rivers, and to the valleys,
Thus saith the Lord GOD;
Behold,
I have spoken in my jealousy and in my fury,
because ye have borne the shame of the heathen:
7 **Therefore thus** saith the Lord GOD;
I have lifted up mine hand,
Surely the heathen that are about you, they shall bear their shame.
8 **But ye, O mountains of Israel,** ye shall shoot forth your branches,
and yield your fruit to my people of Israel;
for they are at hand to come.
9 **For, {behold}, I** am for you,
and I will turn unto you,
and ye shall be tilled and sown:
10 **And I** will multiply men upon you, all the house of Israel, even all of it:
and the cities shall be inhabited,
and the wastes shall be builded:
11 **And I** will multiply upon you man and beast;
and they shall increase
and bring fruit:
and I will settle you after your old estates,
and will do better unto you than at your beginnings:
and ye shall know
that I am the LORD.
12 **Yea, I** will cause men to walk upon you, even my people Israel;
and they shall possess thee,
and thou shalt be their inheritance,
and thou shalt no more henceforth bereave them of men.
13 **Thus** saith the Lord GOD;
Because they say unto you,
Thou land devourest up men,
and hast bereaved thy nations:
14 **Therefore thou** shalt devour men no more,
neither bereave thy nations any more,
saith the Lord GOD.
15 **Neither** will I cause men to hear in thee the shame of the heathen any more,
neither shalt thou bear the reproach of the people any more,
neither shalt thou cause thy nations to fall any more,
saith the Lord GOD.
16 **Moreover the word of the LORD** came unto me,
saying,
17 **Son of man, when the house of Israel** dwelt in their own land,
they defiled it by their own way and by their doings:
their way was before me as the uncleanness of a removed woman.
18 **Wherefore I** poured my fury upon them for the blood that they had shed upon the land, and for their idols wherewith they had polluted it:
19 **And I** scattered them among the heathen,
and they were dispersed through the countries:
according to their way and according to their doings I judged them.
20 **And when they** entered unto the heathen,
whither they went,
they profaned my holy name,
when they said to them,
These are the people of the LORD,
and are gone forth out of his land.
21 **But I** had pity for mine holy name,
which the house of Israel had profaned among the heathen,
whither they went.
22 **Therefore say** unto the house of Israel,
thus saith the Lord GOD;
I do not this for your sakes, O house of Israel, but for mine holy name's sake,
which ye have profaned among the heathen,
whither ye went.
23 **And I** will sanctify my great name,
which was profaned among the heathen,
which ye have profaned in the midst of them;
and the heathen shall know
that I am the LORD,
saith the Lord GOD,
when I shall be sanctified in you before their eyes.
24 **For I** will take you from among the heathen,
and gather you out of all countries,
and will bring you into your own land.
25 **Then** will I sprinkle clean water upon you,
and ye shall be clean:
from all your filthiness, and from all your idols, will I cleanse you.
26 **A new heart** also will I give you,
and a new spirit will I put within you:
and I will take away the stony heart out of your flesh,
and I will give you an heart of flesh.
27 **And I** will put my spirit within you,
and cause you to walk in my statutes,
and ye shall keep my judgments,
and do them.
28 **And ye** shall dwell in the land that I gave to your fathers;
and ye shall be my people,
and I will be your God.
29 **I** will also save you from all your uncleannesses:
and I will call for the corn,
and will increase it,
and lay no famine upon you.
30 **And I** will multiply the fruit of the tree, and the increase of the field,
that ye shall receive no more reproach of famine among the heathen.
31 **Then** shall ye remember your own evil ways, and your doings that were not good,
and shall lothe yourselves in your own sight for your iniquities and for your abominations.
32 **Not for your sakes** do I this,
saith the Lord GOD,
be it known unto you:
be ashamed and confounded for your own ways, O house of Israel.
33 **Thus** saith the Lord GOD;
In the day that I shall have cleansed you from all your iniquities I will also cause you to dwell in the cities,
and the wastes shall be builded.
34 **And the desolate land** shall be tilled,
whereas it lay desolate in the sight of all that passed by.
35 **And they** shall say,
This land that was desolate is become like the garden of Eden;
and the waste and desolate and ruined cities are become fenced,
and are inhabited.
36 **Then the heathen that are left round about you** shall know
that I the LORD build the ruined places,

and plant that that was desolate:
I the LORD have spoken it,
and I will do it.
37 **Thus** saith the Lord GOD;
I will yet for this be enquired of by the house of Israel,
to do it for them;
I will increase them with men like a flock.
38 **As the holy flock, as the flock of Jerusalem in her solemn feasts;** so shall the waste cities be filled with flocks of men:
and they shall know
that I am the LORD.

37

The hand of the LORD was upon me,
and carried me out in the spirit of the LORD,
and set me down in the midst of the valley which was full of bones,
2 **And** caused me to pass by them round about:
and, {behold}, there were very many in the open valley;
and, {lo}, they were very dry.
3 **And he** said unto me,
Son of man, can these bones live?
And I answered,
O Lord GOD, thou knowest.
4 **Again he** said unto me,
Prophesy upon these bones,
and say unto them,
O ye dry bones, hear the word of the LORD.
5 **Thus** saith the Lord GOD unto these bones;
Behold,
I will cause breath to enter into you,
and ye shall live:
6 **And I** will lay sinews upon you,
and will bring up flesh upon you,
and cover you with skin,
and put breath in you,
and ye shall live;
and ye shall know
that I am the LORD.
7 **So I** prophesied
as I was commanded:
and as I prophesied,
there was a noise,
and behold a shaking,
and the bones came together, bone to his bone.
8 **And when I** beheld,
lo,
the sinews and the flesh came up upon them,
and the skin covered them above:
but there was no breath in them.
9 **Then** said he unto me,
Prophesy unto the wind,
prophesy, son of man,
and say to the wind,
Thus saith the Lord GOD;
Come from the four winds, O breath,
and breathe upon these slain,
that they may live.
10 **So I** prophesied
as he commanded me,
and the breath came into them,
and they lived,
and stood up upon their feet, an exceeding great army.
11 **Then he** said unto me,
Son of man, these bones are the whole house of Israel:
behold,
they say,
Our bones are dried,
and our hope is lost:
we are cut off for our parts.
12 **Therefore prophesy and say** unto them,
Thus saith the Lord GOD;
Behold, O my people,
I will open your graves,
and cause you to come up out of your graves,
and bring you into the land of Israel.
13 **And ye** shall know
that I am the LORD,
when I have opened your graves, O my people,
and brought you up out of your graves,
14 **And** shall put my spirit in you,
and ye shall live,
and I shall place you in your own land:
then shall ye know
that I the LORD have spoken it,
and performed it,
saith the LORD.
15 **The word of the LORD** came again unto me,
saying,
16 **Moreover, thou son of man, take** thee one stick,
and write upon it,
For Judah, and for the children of Israel his companions:
then take another stick,
and write upon it,
For Joseph, the stick of Ephraim and for all the house of Israel his companions:
17 **And join** them one to another into one stick;
and they shall become one in thine hand.
18 **And when the children of thy people** shall speak unto thee,
saying,
Wilt thou not shew us what thou meanest by these?
19 **Say** unto them,
Thus saith the Lord GOD;
Behold,
I will take the stick of Joseph,
which is in the hand of Ephraim, and the tribes of Israel his fellows,
and will put them with him, even with the stick of Judah,
and make them one stick,
and they shall be one in mine hand.
20 **And the sticks whereon thou writest** shall be in thine hand before their eyes.
21 **And say** unto them,
Thus saith the Lord GOD;
Behold,
I will take the children of Israel from among the heathen,
whither they be gone,
and will gather them on every side,
and bring them into their own land:
22 **And I** will make them one nation in the land upon the mountains of Israel;
and one king shall be king to them all:
and they shall be no more two nations,
neither shall they be divided into two kingdoms any more at all.
23 **Neither** shall they defile themselves any more with their idols, nor with their detestable things, nor with any of their transgressions:
but I will save them out of all their dwellingplaces,
wherein they have sinned,
and will cleanse them:
so shall they be my people,
and I will be their God.
24 **And David my servant** shall be king over them;
and they all shall have one shepherd:
they shall also walk in my judgments,
and observe my statutes,
and do them.

25 **And they** shall dwell in the land that I have given unto Jacob my servant,
wherein your fathers have dwelt;
and they shall dwell therein, even they, and their children, and their children's children for ever:
and my servant David shall be their prince for ever.

26 **Moreover I** will make a covenant of peace with them;
it shall be an everlasting covenant with them:
and I will place them,
and multiply them,
and will set my sanctuary in the midst of them for evermore.

27 **My tabernacle** also shall be with them:
yea, I will be their God,
and they shall be my people.

28 **And the heathen** shall know
that I the LORD do sanctify Israel,
when my sanctuary shall be in the midst of them for evermore.

38

And the word of the LORD came unto me, saying,
2 **Son of man, set** thy face against Gog, the land of Magog, the chief prince of Meshech and Tubal,
and prophesy against him,
3 **And say,**
Thus saith the Lord GOD;
Behold,
I am against thee, O Gog, the chief prince of Meshech and Tubal:
4 **And I** will turn thee back,
and put hooks into thy jaws,
and I will bring thee forth, and all thine army, horses and horsemen, all of them clothed with all sorts of armour, even a great company with bucklers and shields, all of them handling swords:
5 Persia, Ethiopia, and Libya with them; all of them with shield and helmet:
6 Gomer, and all his bands; the house of Togarmah of the north quarters, and all his bands: and many people with thee.

7 **Be thou** prepared,
and prepare for thyself, thou, and all thy company that are assembled unto thee,
and be thou a guard unto them.

8 **After many days** thou shalt be visited:
in the latter years thou shalt come into the land that is brought back from the sword,
and is gathered out of many people, against the mountains of Israel,
which have been always waste:
but it is brought forth out of the nations,
and they shall dwell safely all of them.

9 **Thou** shalt ascend and come like a storm,
thou shalt be like a cloud to cover the land, thou, and all thy bands, and many people with thee.

10 **Thus** saith the Lord GOD;
It shall also come to pass,
that at the same time shall things come into thy mind,
and thou shalt think an evil thought:
11 **And thou** shalt say,
I will go up to the land of unwalled villages;
I will go to them that are at rest,
that dwell safely,
all of them dwelling without walls,
and having neither bars nor gates,
12 To take a spoil,
and to take a prey;
to turn thine hand upon the desolate places that are now inhabited, and upon the people that are gathered out of the nations, {which have gotten cattle and goods}, that dwell in the midst of the land.

13 **Sheba, and Dedan, and the merchants of Tarshish, with all the young lions thereof,** shall say unto thee,
Art thou come to take a spoil?
hast thou gathered thy company to take a prey?
to carry away silver and gold,
to take away cattle and goods,
to take a great spoil?

14 **Therefore, son of man, prophesy and say** unto Gog,
Thus saith the Lord GOD;
In that day when my people of Israel dwelleth safely,
shalt thou not know it?

15 **And thou** shalt come from thy place out of the north parts, thou, and many people with thee,
all of them riding upon horses, a great company, and a mighty army:

16 **And thou** shalt come up against my people of Israel,
as a cloud to cover the land;
it shall be in the latter days,
and I will bring thee against my land,
that the heathen may know me,
when I shall be sanctified in thee, O Gog, before their eyes.

17 **Thus** saith the Lord GOD;
Art thou he of whom I have spoken in old time by my servants the prophets of Israel,
which prophesied in those days many years
that I would bring thee against them?

18 **And it** shall come to pass at the same time
when Gog shall come against the land of Israel,
saith the Lord GOD,
that my fury shall come up in my face.

19 **For in my jealousy and in the fire of my wrath** have I spoken,
Surely in that day there shall be a great shaking in the land of Israel;
20 **So that the fishes of the sea, and the fowls of the heaven, and the beasts of the field, and all creeping things that creep upon the earth, and all the men that are upon the face of the earth,** shall shake at my presence,
and the mountains shall be thrown down,
and the steep places shall fall,
and every wall shall fall to the ground.

21 **And I** will call for a sword against him throughout all my mountains,
saith the Lord GOD:
every man's sword shall be against his brother.

22 **And I** will plead against him with pestilence and with blood;
and I will rain upon him, and upon his bands, and upon the many people that are with him, an overflowing rain, and great hailstones, fire, and brimstone.

23 **Thus** will I magnify myself,
and sanctify myself;
and I will be known in the eyes of many nations,
and they shall know
that I am the LORD.

39

Therefore, thou son of man, prophesy against Gog,
and say,
Thus saith the Lord GOD;
Behold,
I am against thee, O Gog, the chief prince of Meshech and Tubal:
2 **And I** will turn thee back,
and leave but the sixth part of thee,
and will cause thee to come up from the north parts,
and will bring thee upon the mountains of Israel:
3 **And I** will smite thy bow out of thy left hand,
and will cause thine arrows to fall out of thy right hand.

4 **Thou** shalt fall upon the mountains of Israel, thou, and all thy bands, and the people that is with thee:
I will give thee unto the ravenous birds of every sort, and to the beasts of the field to be devoured.

5 **Thou** shalt fall upon the open field:
for I have spoken it,
saith the Lord GOD.

6 **And I** will send a fire on Magog, and among them that dwell carelessly in the isles:
and they shall know
that I am the LORD.

7 **So** will I make my holy name known in the midst of my people Israel;
and I will not let them pollute my holy name any more:
and the heathen shall know
that I am the LORD, the Holy One in Israel.

8 **Behold,**
it is come,
and it is done,
saith the Lord GOD;
this is the day whereof I have spoken.

9 **And they that dwell in the cities of Israel** shall go forth,
and shall set on fire and burn the weapons, both the shields and the bucklers, the bows and the arrows, and the handstaves, and the spears,
and they shall burn them with fire seven years:
10 **So that they** shall take no wood out of the field,
neither cut down any out of the forests;
for they shall burn the weapons with fire:
and they shall spoil those that spoiled them,
and rob those that robbed them,
saith the Lord GOD.

11 **And it** shall come to pass in that day,
that I will give unto Gog a place there of graves in Israel, the valley of the passengers on the east of the sea:
and it shall stop the noses of the passengers:
and there shall they bury Gog and all his multitude:
and they shall call it The valley of Hamongog.

12 **And seven months** shall the house of Israel be burying of them,
that they may cleanse the land.

13 **Yea, all the people of the land** shall bury them;
and it shall be to them a renown the day that I shall be glorified,
saith the Lord GOD.

14 **And they** shall sever out men of continual employment,
passing through the land
to bury with the passengers those that remain upon the face of the earth,
to cleanse it:
after the end of seven months shall they search.

15 **And the passengers that pass through the land**, {when any seeth a man's bone}, then shall he set up a sign by it,
till the buriers have buried it in the valley of Hamongog.

16 **And also the name of the city** shall be Hamonah.
Thus shall they cleanse the land.

17 **And, thou son of man, thus** saith the Lord GOD;
Speak unto every feathered fowl, and to every beast of the field,
Assemble yourselves,
and come;
gather yourselves on every side to my sacrifice that I do sacrifice for you, even a great sacrifice upon the mountains of Israel,
that ye may eat flesh,
and drink blood.

18 **Ye** shall eat the flesh of the mighty,
and drink the blood of the princes of the earth, of rams, of lambs, and of goats, of bullocks, all of them fatlings of Bashan.

19 **And ye** shall eat fat {till ye be full}, and drink blood {till ye be drunken}, of my sacrifice which I have sacrificed for you.

20 **Thus ye** shall be filled at my table with horses and chariots, with mighty men, and with all men of war,
saith the Lord GOD.

21 **And I** will set my glory among the heathen,
and all the heathen shall see my judgment that I have executed, and my hand that I have laid upon them.

22 **So the house of Israel** shall know
that I am the LORD their God from that day and forward.

23 **And the heathen** shall know
that the house of Israel went into captivity for their iniquity:
because they trespassed against me,
therefore hid I my face from them,
and gave them into the hand of their enemies:
so fell they all by the sword.

24 **According to their uncleanness and according to their transgressions** have I done unto them,
and hid my face from them.

25 **Therefore thus** saith the Lord GOD;
Now will I bring again the captivity of Jacob,
and have mercy upon the whole house of Israel,
and will be jealous for my holy name;
26 **After that they** have borne their shame, and all their trespasses whereby they have trespassed against me,
when they dwelt safely in their land,
and none made them afraid.
27 **When I** have brought them again from the people,
and gathered them out of their enemies' lands,
and am sanctified in them in the sight of many nations;
28 **Then** shall they know

that I am the LORD their God,
which caused them to be led into captivity among the heathen:
but I have gathered them unto their own land,
and have left none of them any more there.

29 **Neither** will I hide my face any more from them:
for I have poured out my spirit upon the house of Israel,
saith the Lord GOD.

40

In the five and twentieth year of our captivity, in the beginning of the year, in the tenth day of the month, in the fourteenth year after that the city was smitten, in the selfsame day the hand of the LORD was upon me,
and brought me thither.

2 **In the visions of God** brought he me into the land of Israel,
and set me upon a very high mountain,
by which was as the frame of a city on the south.

3 **And he** brought me thither,
and, {behold}, there was a man,
whose appearance was like the appearance of brass, with a line of flax in his hand, and a measuring reed;
and he stood in the gate.

4 **And the man** said unto me,
Son of man, behold with thine eyes,
and hear with thine ears,
and set thine heart upon all that I shall shew thee;
for to the intent that I might shew them unto thee art thou brought hither:
declare all that thou seest to the house of Israel.

5 **And behold** a wall on the outside of the house round about, and in the man's hand a measuring reed of six cubits long by the cubit and an hand breadth:
so he measured the breadth of the building, one reed; and the height, one reed.

6 **Then** came he unto the gate which looketh toward the east,
and went up the stairs thereof,
and measured the threshold of the gate, {which was one reed broad}; and the other threshold of the gate, {which was one reed broad}.

7 **And every little chamber** was one reed long, and one reed broad;
and between the little chambers were five cubits;
and the threshold of the gate by the porch of the gate within was one reed.

8 **He** measured also the porch of the gate within, one reed.

9 **Then** measured he the porch of the gate, eight cubits; and the posts thereof, two cubits;
and the porch of the gate was inward.

10 **And the little chambers of the gate eastward** were three on this side, and three on that side;
they three were of one measure:
and the posts had one measure on this side and on that side.

11 **And he** measured the breadth of the entry of the gate, ten cubits; and the length of the gate, thirteen cubits.

12 **The space also before the little chambers** was one cubit on this side,
and the space was one cubit on that side:
and the little chambers were six cubits on this side, and six cubits on that side.

13 **He** measured then the gate from the roof of one little chamber to the roof of another:
the breadth was five and twenty cubits, door against door.

14 **He** made also posts of threescore cubits, even unto the post of the court round about the gate.

15 **And from the face of the gate of the entrance unto the face of the porch of the inner gate** were fifty cubits.

16 **And there** were narrow windows to the little chambers, and to their posts within the gate round about, and likewise to the arches:
and windows were round about inward:
and upon each post were palm trees.

17 **Then** brought he me into the outward court,
and, {lo}, there were chambers, and a pavement made for the court round about:
thirty chambers were upon the pavement.

18 **And the pavement by the side of the gates over against the length of the gates** was the lower pavement.

19 **Then he** measured the breadth from the forefront of the lower gate unto the forefront of the inner court without, an hundred cubits eastward and northward.

20 **And the gate of the outward court that looked toward the north,** he measured the length thereof, and the breadth thereof.

21 **And the little chambers thereof** were three on this side and three on that side;
and the posts thereof and the arches thereof were after the measure of the first gate:
the length thereof was fifty cubits, and the breadth five and twenty cubits.

22 **And their windows, and their arches, and their palm trees,** were after the measure of the gate that looketh toward the east;
and they went up unto it by seven steps;
and the arches thereof were before them.

23 **And the gate of the inner court** was over against the gate toward the north, and toward the east;
and he measured from gate to gate an hundred cubits.

24 **After that he** brought me toward the south,
and behold a gate toward the south:
and he measured the posts thereof and the arches thereof according to these measures.

25 **And there** were windows in it and in the arches thereof round about, like those windows:
the length was fifty cubits, and the breadth five and twenty cubits.

26 **And there** were seven steps to go up to it,
and the arches thereof were before them:
and it had palm trees, one on this side, and another on that side, upon the posts thereof.

27 **And there** was a gate in the inner court toward the south:
and he measured from gate to gate toward the south an hundred cubits.

28 **And he** brought me to the inner
court by the south gate:
and he measured the south gate
according to these measures;
29 And the little chambers thereof,
and the posts thereof, and the
arches thereof, according to these
measures:
and there were windows in it and
in the arches thereof round about:
it was fifty cubits long, and five and
twenty cubits broad.

30 **And the arches round about**
were five and twenty cubits long,
and five cubits broad.

31 **And the arches thereof** were
toward the utter court;
and palm trees were upon the
posts thereof:
and the going up to it had eight
steps.

32 **And he** brought me into the inner
court toward the east:
and he measured the gate
according to these measures.

33 **And the little chambers thereof,
and the posts thereof, and the
arches thereof,** were according to
these measures:
and there were windows therein
and in the arches thereof round
about:
it was fifty cubits long, and five and
twenty cubits broad.

34 **And the arches thereof** were
toward the outward court;
and palm trees were upon the
posts thereof, on this side, and on
that side:
and the going up to it had eight
steps.

35 **And he** brought me to the north
gate,
and measured it according to these
measures;
36 The little chambers thereof, the
posts thereof, and the arches
thereof, and the windows to it
round about:
the length was fifty cubits, and the
breadth five and twenty cubits.

37 **And the posts thereof** were
toward the utter court;
and palm trees were upon the
posts thereof, on this side, and on
that side:
and the going up to it had eight
steps.

38 **And the chambers and the
entries thereof** were by the posts
of the gates,
where they washed the burnt
offering.

39 **And in the porch of the gate**
were two tables on this side, and
two tables on that side,
to slay thereon the burnt offering
and the sin offering and the
trespass offering.

40 **And at the side without,** {as one
goeth up to the entry of the north
gate}, were two tables;
and on the other side, {which was
at the porch of the gate}, were two
tables.

41 **Four tables** were on this side, and
four tables on that side, by the
side of the gate; eight tables,
whereupon they slew their
sacrifices.

42 **And the four tables** were of hewn
stone for the burnt offering, of a
cubit and an half long, and a cubit
and an half broad, and one cubit
high:
whereupon also they laid the
instruments wherewith they slew
the burnt offering and the
sacrifice.

43 **And within** were hooks, an hand
broad, fastened round about:
and upon the tables was the flesh
of the offering.

44 **And without the inner gate** were
the chambers of the singers in the
inner court,
which was at the side of the north
gate;
and their prospect was toward the
south:
one at the side of the east gate
having the prospect toward the
north.

45 **And he** said unto me,
This chamber, {whose prospect is
toward the south}, is for the
priests, the keepers of the charge
of the house.

46 **And the chamber whose
prospect is toward the north** is
for the priests, the keepers of the
charge of the altar:
these are the sons of Zadok among
the sons of Levi,
which come near to the LORD
to minister unto him.

47 **So he** measured the court, an
hundred cubits long, and an
hundred cubits broad, foursquare;
and the altar that was before the
house.

48 **And he** brought me to the porch
of the house,
and measured each post of the
porch, five cubits on this side, and
five cubits on that side:
and the breadth of the gate was
three cubits on this side, and
three cubits on that side.

49 **The length of the porch** was
twenty cubits, and the breadth
eleven cubits,
and he brought me by the steps
whereby they went up to it:
and there were pillars by the posts,
one on this side, and another on
that side.

41

Afterward he brought me
to the temple,
and measured the posts, six cubits
broad on the one side, and six
cubits broad on the other side,
which was the breadth of the
tabernacle.

2 **And the breadth of the door** was
ten cubits;
and the sides of the door were five
cubits on the one side, and five
cubits on the other side:
and he measured the length
thereof, forty cubits: and the
breadth, twenty cubits.

3 **Then** went he inward,
and measured the post of the door,
two cubits; and the door, six
cubits; and the breadth of the
door, seven cubits.

4 **So he** measured the length thereof,
twenty cubits; and the breadth,
twenty cubits, before the temple:
and he said unto me,
This is the most holy place.

5 **After he** measured the wall of the
house, six cubits;
**and the breadth of every side
chamber,** four cubits, round
about the house on every side.

6 **And the side chambers** were
three, one over another, and
thirty in order;
and they entered into the wall
which was of the house for the
side chambers round about,
that they might have hold,
but they had not hold in the wall of
the house.

7 **And there** was an enlarging, and a winding about still upward to the side chambers:
for the winding about of the house went still upward round about the house:
therefore the breadth of the house was still upward,
and so increased from the lowest chamber to the highest by the midst.

8 **I** saw also the height of the house round about:
the foundations of the side chambers were a full reed of six great cubits.

9 **The thickness of the wall**, {which was for the side chamber without}, was five cubits:
and that which was left was the place of the side chambers that were within.

10 **And between the chambers** was the wideness of twenty cubits round about the house on every side.

11 **And the doors of the side chambers** were toward the place that was left, one door toward the north, and another door toward the south:
and the breadth of the place that was left was five cubits round about.

12 **Now the building that was before the separate place at the end toward the west** was seventy cubits broad;
and the wall of the building was five cubits thick round about, and the length thereof ninety cubits.

13 **So he** measured the house, an hundred cubits long; and the separate place, and the building, with the walls thereof, an hundred cubits long;

14 Also the breadth of the face of the house, and of the separate place toward the east, an hundred cubits.

15 **And he** measured the length of the building over against the separate place which was behind it, and the galleries thereof on the one side and on the other side, an hundred cubits, with the inner temple, and the porches of the court;

16 The door posts, and the narrow windows, and the galleries round about on their three stories, over against the door, {cieled with wood round about}, and from the ground up to the windows, {and the windows were covered};

17 To that above the door, even unto the inner house, and without, and by all the wall round about within and without, by measure.

18 **And it** was made with cherubims and palm trees,
so that a palm tree was between a cherub and a cherub;
and every cherub had two faces;

19 **So that the face of a man** was toward the palm tree on the one side, and the face of a young lion toward the palm tree on the other side:
it was made through all the house round about.

20 **From the ground unto above the door** were cherubims and palm trees made, and on the wall of the temple.

21 **The posts of the temple** were squared, and the face of the sanctuary; the appearance of the one as the appearance of the other.

22 **The altar of wood** was three cubits high, and the length thereof two cubits;
and the corners thereof, and the length thereof, and the walls thereof, were of wood:
and he said unto me,
This is the table that is before the LORD.

23 **And the temple and the sanctuary** had two doors.

24 **And the doors** had two leaves apiece, two turning leaves; two leaves for the one door, and two leaves for the other door.

25 **And there** were made on them, on the doors of the temple, cherubims and palm trees, like as were made upon the walls;
and there were thick planks upon the face of the porch without.

26 **And there** were narrow windows and palm trees on the one side and on the other side, on the sides of the porch, and upon the side chambers of the house, and thick planks.

42

Then he brought me forth into the utter court, the way toward the north:
and he brought me into the chamber that was over against the separate place,
and which was before the building toward the north.

2 **Before the length of an hundred cubits** was the north door,
and the breadth was fifty cubits.

3 **Over against the twenty cubits which were for the inner court, and over against the pavement which was for the utter court,** was gallery against gallery in three stories.

4 **And before the chambers** was a walk to ten cubits breadth inward, a way of one cubit; and their doors toward the north.

5 **Now the upper chambers** were shorter:
for the galleries were higher than these, than the lower, and than the middlemost of the building.

6 **For they** were in three stories,
but had not pillars as the pillars of the courts:
therefore the building was straitened more than the lowest and the middlemost from the ground.

7 **And the wall that was without over against the chambers, toward the utter court on the forepart of the chambers,** the length thereof was fifty cubits.

8 **For the length of the chambers that were in the utter court** was fifty cubits:
and, {lo}, before the temple were an hundred cubits.

9 **And from under these chambers** was the entry on the east side,
as one goeth into them from the utter court.

10 **The chambers** were in the thickness of the wall of the court toward the east, over against the separate place, and over against the building.

11 **And the way before them** was like the appearance of the chambers which were toward the north, as long as they, and as broad as they:
and all their goings out were both according to their fashions, and according to their doors.

12 **And according to the doors of the chambers that were toward the south** was a door in the head of the way, even the way directly before the wall toward the east,
as one entereth into them.

13 **Then** said he unto me,
The north chambers and the south chambers, {which are before the separate place}, they be holy chambers,
where the priests that approach unto the LORD shall eat the most holy things:
there shall they lay the most holy things, and the meat offering, and the sin offering, and the trespass offering;
for the place is holy.

14 **When the priests** enter therein,
then shall they not go out of the holy place into the utter court,
but there they shall lay their garments wherein they minister;
for they are holy;
and shall put on other garments,
and shall approach to those things which are for the people.

15 **Now when he** had made an end of measuring the inner house,
he brought me forth toward the gate whose prospect is toward the east,
and measured it round about.

16 **He** measured the east side with the measuring reed, five hundred reeds, with the measuring reed round about.

17 **He** measured the north side, five hundred reeds, with the measuring reed round about.

18 **He** measured the south side, five hundred reeds, with the measuring reed.

19 **He** turned about to the west side,
and measured five hundred reeds with the measuring reed.

20 **He** measured it by the four sides:
it had a wall round about, five hundred reeds long, and five hundred broad,
to make a separation between the sanctuary and the profane place.

43 **Afterward he** brought me to the gate, even the gate that looketh toward the east:

2 **And, {behold}, the glory of the God of Israel** came from the way of the east:
and his voice was like a noise of many waters:
and the earth shined with his glory.

3 **And it** was according to the appearance of the vision which I saw, even according to the vision that I saw
when I came to destroy the city:
and the visions were like the vision that I saw by the river Chebar;
and I fell upon my face.

4 **And the glory of the LORD** came into the house by the way of the gate whose prospect is toward the east.

5 **So the spirit** took me up,
and brought me into the inner court;
and, {behold}, the glory of the LORD filled the house.

6 **And I** heard him speaking unto me out of the house;
and the man stood by me.

7 **And he** said unto me,
Son of man, the place of my throne, and the place of the soles of my feet, {where I will dwell in the midst of the children of Israel for ever}, and my holy name, shall the house of Israel no more defile, neither they, nor their kings, by their whoredom, nor by the carcases of their kings in their high places.

8 **In their setting of their threshold by my thresholds, and their post by my posts, and the wall between me and them,** they have even defiled my holy name by their abominations that they have committed:
wherefore I have consumed them in mine anger.

9 **Now let them** put away their whoredom, and the carcases of their kings, far from me,
and I will dwell in the midst of them for ever.

10 **Thou son of man, shew** the house to the house of Israel,
that they may be ashamed of their iniquities:
and let them measure the pattern.

11 **And if they** be ashamed of all that they have done,
shew them the form of the house, and the fashion thereof, and the goings out thereof, and the comings in thereof, and all the forms thereof, and all the ordinances thereof, and all the forms thereof, and all the laws thereof:
and write it in their sight,
that they may keep the whole form thereof, and all the ordinances thereof,
and do them.

12 **This** is the law of the house;
Upon the top of the mountain the whole limit thereof round about shall be most holy.
Behold,
this is the law of the house.

13 **And these** are the measures of the altar after the cubits:
The cubit is a cubit and an hand breadth;
even the bottom shall be a cubit, and the breadth a cubit,
and the border thereof by the edge thereof round about shall be a span:
and this shall be the higher place of the altar.

14 **And from the bottom upon the ground even to the lower settle** shall be two cubits, and the breadth one cubit;
and from the lesser settle even to the greater settle shall be four cubits, and the breadth one cubit.

15 **So the altar** shall be four cubits;
and from the altar and upward shall be four horns.

16 **And the altar** shall be twelve cubits long, twelve broad, square in the four squares thereof.

17 **And the settle** shall be fourteen cubits long and fourteen broad in the four squares thereof;
and the border about it shall be half a cubit;
and the bottom thereof shall be a cubit about;
and his stairs shall look toward the east.

18 **And he** said unto me,
Son of man, thus saith the Lord GOD;
These are the ordinances of the altar in the day when they shall make it,
to offer burnt offerings thereon,
and to sprinkle blood thereon.

19 **And thou** shalt give to the priests the Levites that be of the seed of Zadok, {which approach unto me}, {to minister unto me}, {saith

the Lord GOD}, a young bullock
for a sin offering.
20 **And thou** shalt take of the blood thereof,
and put it on the four horns of it, and on the four corners of the settle, and upon the border round about:
thus shalt thou cleanse and purge it.
21 **Thou** shalt take the bullock also of the sin offering,
and he shall burn it in the appointed place of the house, without the sanctuary.
22 **And on the second day** thou shalt offer a kid of the goats without blemish for a sin offering;
and they shall cleanse the altar,
as they did cleanse it with the bullock.
23 **When thou** hast made an end of cleansing it,
thou shalt offer a young bullock without blemish, and a ram out of the flock without blemish.
24 **And thou** shalt offer them before the LORD,
and the priests shall cast salt upon them,
and they shall offer them up for a burnt offering unto the LORD.
25 **Seven days** shalt thou prepare every day a goat for a sin offering:
they shall also prepare a young bullock, and a ram out of the flock, without blemish.
26 **Seven days** shall they purge the altar
and purify it;
and they shall consecrate themselves.
27 **And when these days** are expired,
it shall be,
that upon the eighth day, and so forward, the priests shall make your burnt offerings upon the altar, and your peace offerings;
and I will accept you,
saith the Lord GOD.

44 **Then he** brought me back the way of the gate of the outward sanctuary which looketh toward the east;
and it was shut.
2 **Then** said the LORD unto me;
This gate shall be shut,
it shall not be opened,
and no man shall enter in by it;
because the LORD, the God of Israel, hath entered in by it,
therefore it shall be shut.
3 **It** is for the prince;
the prince, he shall sit in it to eat bread before the LORD;
he shall enter by the way of the porch of that gate,
and shall go out by the way of the same.
4 **Then** brought he me the way of the north gate before the house:
and I looked,
and, {behold}, the glory of the LORD filled the house of the LORD:
and I fell upon my face.
5 **And the LORD** said unto me,
Son of man, mark well,
and behold with thine eyes,
and hear with thine ears all that I say unto thee concerning all the ordinances of the house of the LORD, and all the laws thereof;
and mark well the entering in of the house, with every going forth of the sanctuary.
6 **And thou** shalt say to the rebellious, even to the house of Israel,
Thus saith the LORD God;
O ye house of Israel, let it suffice you of all your abominations,
7 **In that ye** have brought into my sanctuary strangers, uncircumcised in heart, and uncircumcised in flesh,
to be in my sanctuary,
to pollute it, even my house,
when ye offer my bread, the fat and the blood,
and they have broken my covenant because of all your abominations.
8 **And ye** have not kept the charge of mine holy things:
but ye have set keepers of my charge in my sanctuary for yourselves.
9 **Thus** saith the Lord GOD;
No stranger, uncircumcised in heart, nor uncircumcised in flesh, shall enter into my sanctuary, of any stranger that is among the children of Israel.
10 **And the Levites that are gone away far from me**, {when Israel went astray}, {which went astray away from me after their idols}; they shall even bear their iniquity.
11 **Yet they** shall be ministers in my sanctuary,
having charge at the gates of the house,
and ministering to the house:
they shall slay the burnt offering and the sacrifice for the people,
and they shall stand before them
to minister unto them.
12 **Because they** ministered unto them before their idols,
and caused the house of Israel to fall into iniquity;
therefore have I lifted up mine hand against them,
saith the Lord GOD,
and they shall bear their iniquity.
13 **And they** shall not come near unto me,
to do the office of a priest unto me,
nor to come near to any of my holy things, in the most holy place:
but they shall bear their shame, and their abominations which they have committed.
14 **But I** will make them keepers of the charge of the house, for all the service thereof, and for all that shall be done therein.
15 **But the priests the Levites, the sons of Zadok**, {that kept the charge of my sanctuary} {when the children of Israel went astray from me}, they shall come near to me to minister unto me,
and they shall stand before me to offer unto me the fat and the blood,
saith the Lord GOD:
16 **They** shall enter into my sanctuary,
and they shall come near to my table,
to minister unto me,
and they shall keep my charge.
17 **And it** shall come to pass,
that when they enter in at the gates of the inner court,
they shall be clothed with linen garments;
and no wool shall come upon them,
whiles they minister in the gates of the inner court, and within.
18 **They shall** have linen bonnets upon their heads,
and shall have linen breeches upon their loins;
they shall not gird themselves with any thing that causeth sweat.

19 **And when they** go forth into the utter court, even into the utter court to the people,
they shall put off their garments wherein they ministered,
and lay them in the holy chambers,
and they shall put on other garments;
and they shall not sanctify the people with their garments.
20 **Neither** shall they shave their heads,
nor suffer their locks to grow long;
they shall only poll their heads.
21 **Neither** shall any priest drink wine,
when they enter into the inner court.
22 **Neither** shall they take for their wives a widow, nor her that is put away:
but they shall take maidens of the seed of the house of Israel, or a widow that had a priest before.
23 **And they** shall teach my people the difference between the holy and profane,
and cause them to discern between the unclean and the clean.
24 **And in controversy** they shall stand in judgment;
and they shall judge it according to my judgments:
and they shall keep my laws and my statutes in all mine assemblies;
and they shall hallow my sabbaths.
25 **And they** shall come at no dead person to defile themselves:
but for father, or for mother, or for son, or for daughter, for brother, or for sister that hath had no husband, they may defile themselves.
26 **And after he** is cleansed,
they shall reckon unto him seven days.
27 **And in the day that he goeth into the sanctuary, unto the inner court,** {to minister in the sanctuary}, he shall offer his sin offering,
saith the Lord GOD.
28 **And it** shall be unto them for an inheritance:
I am their inheritance:
and ye shall give them no possession in Israel:
I am their possession.
29 **They** shall eat the meat offering, and the sin offering, and the trespass offering:
and every dedicated thing in Israel shall be theirs.
30 **And the first of all the firstfruits of all things, and every oblation of all, of every sort of your oblations,** shall be the priest's:
ye shall also give unto the priest the first of your dough,
that he may cause the blessing to rest in thine house.
31 **The priests** shall not eat of any thing that is dead of itself,
or torn,
whether it be fowl or beast.

45 **Moreover, when ye** shall divide by lot the land for inheritance,
ye shall offer an oblation unto the LORD, an holy portion of the land:
the length shall be the length of five and twenty thousand reeds,
and the breadth shall be ten thousand.
This shall be holy in all the borders thereof round about.
2 **Of this** there shall be for the sanctuary five hundred in length, with five hundred in breadth, square round about; and fifty cubits round about for the suburbs thereof.
3 **And of this measure** shalt thou measure the length of five and twenty thousand, and the breadth of ten thousand:
and in it shall be the sanctuary and the most holy place.
4 **The holy portion of the land** shall be for the priests the ministers of the sanctuary,
which shall come near to minister unto the LORD:
and it shall be a place for their houses, and an holy place for the sanctuary.
5 **And the five and twenty thousand of length, and the ten thousand of breadth** shall also the Levites, the ministers of the house, have for themselves, for a possession for twenty chambers.
6 **And ye** shall appoint the possession of the city five thousand broad, and five and twenty thousand long, over against the oblation of the holy portion:
it shall be for the whole house of Israel.
7 **And a portion** shall be for the prince on the one side and on the other side of the oblation of the holy portion, and of the possession of the city, before the oblation of the holy portion, and before the possession of the city, from the west side westward, and from the east side eastward:
and the length shall be over against one of the portions, from the west border unto the east border.
8 **In the land** shall be his possession in Israel:
and my princes shall no more oppress my people;
and the rest of the land shall they give to the house of Israel according to their tribes.
9 **Thus** saith the Lord GOD;
Let it suffice you, O princes of Israel:
remove violence and spoil,
and execute judgment and justice,
take away your exactions from my people,
saith the Lord GOD.
10 **Ye** shall have just balances, and a just ephah, and a just bath.
11 **The ephah and the bath** shall be of one measure,
that the bath may contain the tenth part of an homer, and the ephah the tenth part of an homer:
the measure thereof shall be after the homer.
12 **And the shekel** shall be twenty gerahs:
twenty shekels, five and twenty shekels, fifteen shekels, shall be your maneh.
13 **This** is the oblation that ye shall offer; the sixth part of an ephah of an homer of wheat,
and ye shall give the sixth part of an ephah of an homer of barley:
14 **Concerning the ordinance of oil, the bath of oil,** ye shall offer the tenth part of a bath out of the cor,
which is an homer of ten baths;
for ten baths are an homer:
15 And one lamb out of the flock, out of two hundred, out of the fat pastures of Israel; for a meat offering, and for a burnt offering, and for peace offerings,

to make reconciliation for them,
saith the Lord GOD.
16 **All the people of the land** shall give this oblation for the prince in Israel.
17 **And it** shall be the prince's part to give burnt offerings, and meat offerings, and drink offerings, in the feasts, and in the new moons, and in the sabbaths, in all solemnities of the house of Israel:
he shall prepare the sin offering, and the meat offering, and the burnt offering, and the peace offerings,
to make reconciliation for the house of Israel.
18 **Thus** saith the Lord GOD;
In the first month, in the first day of the month, thou shalt take a young bullock without blemish,
and cleanse the sanctuary:
19 **And the priest** shall take of the blood of the sin offering,
and put it upon the posts of the house, and upon the four corners of the settle of the altar, and upon the posts of the gate of the inner court.
20 **And so thou** shalt do the seventh day of the month for every one that erreth, and for him that is simple:
so shall ye reconcile the house.
21 **In the first month, in the fourteenth day of the month,** ye shall have the passover, a feast of seven days;
unleavened bread shall be eaten.
22 **And upon that day** shall the prince prepare for himself and for all the people of the land a bullock for a sin offering.
23 **And seven days of the feast** he shall prepare a burnt offering to the LORD, seven bullocks and seven rams without blemish daily the seven days; and a kid of the goats daily for a sin offering.
24 **And he** shall prepare a meat offering of an ephah for a bullock, and an ephah for a ram, and an hin of oil for an ephah.
25 **In the seventh month, in the fifteenth day of the month,** shall he do the like in the feast of the seven days, according to the sin offering, according to the burnt offering, and according to the meat offering, and according to the oil.

46

Thus saith the Lord GOD;
The gate of the inner court that looketh toward the east shall be shut the six working days;
but on the sabbath it shall be opened,
and in the day of the new moon it shall be opened.
2 **And the prince** shall enter by the way of the porch of that gate without,
and shall stand by the post of the gate,
and the priests shall prepare his burnt offering and his peace offerings,
and he shall worship at the threshold of the gate:
then he shall go forth;
but the gate shall not be shut until the evening.
3 **Likewise the people of the land** shall worship at the door of this gate before the LORD in the sabbaths and in the new moons.
4 **And the burnt offering that the prince shall offer unto the LORD in the sabbath day** shall be six lambs without blemish, and a ram without blemish.
5 **And the meat offering** shall be an ephah for a ram,
and the meat offering for the lambs as he shall be able to give, and an hin of oil to an ephah.
6 **And in the day of the new moon** it shall be a young bullock without blemish, and six lambs, and a ram:
they shall be without blemish.
7 **And he** shall prepare a meat offering, an ephah for a bullock, and an ephah for a ram,
and for the lambs according as his hand shall attain unto, and an hin of oil to an ephah.
8 **And when the prince** shall enter,
he shall go in by the way of the porch of that gate,
and he shall go forth by the way thereof.
9 **But when the people of the land** shall come before the LORD in the solemn feasts,
he that entereth in by the way of the north gate to worship shall go out by the way of the south gate;
and he that entereth by the way of the south gate shall go forth by the way of the north gate:
he shall not return by the way of the gate whereby he came in,
but shall go forth over against it.
10 **And the prince in the midst of them**, {when they go in}, shall go in;
and when they go forth,
shall go forth.
11 **And in the feasts and in the solemnities** the meat offering shall be an ephah to a bullock, and an ephah to a ram,
and to the lambs as he is able to give, and an hin of oil to an ephah.
12 **Now when the prince** shall prepare a voluntary burnt offering or peace offerings voluntarily unto the LORD,
one shall then open him the gate that looketh toward the east,
and he shall prepare his burnt offering and his peace offerings,
as he did on the sabbath day:
then he shall go forth;
and after his going forth one shall shut the gate.
13 **Thou** shalt daily prepare a burnt offering unto the LORD of a lamb of the first year without blemish:
thou shalt prepare it every morning.
14 **And thou** shalt prepare a meat offering for it every morning, the sixth part of an ephah, and the third part of an hin of oil,
to temper with the fine flour; a meat offering continually by a perpetual ordinance unto the LORD.
15 **Thus** shall they prepare the lamb, and the meat offering, and the oil, every morning for a continual burnt offering.
16 **Thus** saith the Lord GOD;
If the prince give a gift unto any of his sons,
the inheritance thereof shall be his sons';
it shall be their possession by inheritance.
17 **But if he** give a gift of his inheritance to one of his servants,
then it shall be his to the year of liberty;
after it shall return to the prince:

but his inheritance shall be his sons' for them.

18 **Moreover the prince** shall not take of the people's inheritance by oppression,
to thrust them out of their possession;
but he shall give his sons inheritance out of his own possession:
that my people be not scattered every man from his possession.

19 **After he** brought me through the entry, {which was at the side of the gate}, into the holy chambers of the priests,
which looked toward the north:
and, {behold}, there was a place on the two sides westward.

20 **Then** said he unto me,
This is the place where the priests shall boil the trespass offering and the sin offering, where they shall bake the meat offering;
that they bear them not out into the utter court,
to sanctify the people.

21 **Then he** brought me forth into the utter court,
and caused me to pass by the four corners of the court;
and, {behold}, in every corner of the court there was a court.

22 **In the four corners of the court** there were courts joined of forty cubits long and thirty broad:
these four corners were of one measure.

23 **And there** was a row of building round about in them, round about them four,
and it was made with boiling places under the rows round about.

24 **Then** said he unto me,
These are the places of them that boil,
where the ministers of the house shall boil the sacrifice of the people.

47

Afterward he brought me again unto the door of the house;
and, {behold}, waters issued out from under the threshold of the house eastward:
for the forefront of the house stood toward the east,
and the waters came down from under from the right side of the house, at the south side of the altar.

2 **Then** brought he me out of the way of the gate northward,
and led me about the way without unto the utter gate by the way that looketh eastward;
and, {behold}, there ran out waters on the right side.

3 **And when the man that had the line in his hand** went forth eastward,
he measured a thousand cubits,
and he brought me through the waters;
the waters were to the ankles.

4 **Again he** measured a thousand,
and brought me through the waters;
the waters were to the knees.

Again he measured a thousand,
and brought me through;
the waters were to the loins.

5 **Afterward he** measured a thousand;
and it was a river that I could not pass over:
for the waters were risen, waters to swim in, a river that could not be passed over.

6 **And he** said unto me,
Son of man, hast thou seen this?

Then he brought me,
and caused me to return to the brink of the river.

7 **Now when I** had returned,
behold,
at the bank of the river were very many trees on the one side and on the other.

8 **Then** said he unto me,
These waters issue out toward the east country,
and go down into the desert
and go into the sea:
which being brought forth into the sea, the waters shall be healed.

9 **And it** shall come to pass,
that every thing that liveth, {which moveth}, {whithersoever the rivers shall come}, shall live:
and there shall be a very great multitude of fish,
because these waters shall come thither:
for they shall be healed;
and every thing shall live whither the river cometh.

10 **And it** shall come to pass,
that the fishers shall stand upon it from Engedi even unto Eneglaim;
they shall be a place to spread forth nets;
their fish shall be according to their kinds, as the fish of the great sea, exceeding many.

11 **But the miry places thereof and the marishes thereof** shall not be healed;
they shall be given to salt.

12 **And by the river upon the bank thereof, on this side and on that side,** shall grow all trees for meat,
whose leaf shall not fade,
neither shall the fruit thereof be consumed:
it shall bring forth new fruit according to his months,
because their waters they issued out of the sanctuary:
and the fruit thereof shall be for meat, and the leaf thereof for medicine.

13 **Thus** saith the Lord GOD;
This shall be the border,
whereby ye shall inherit the land according to the twelve tribes of Israel:
Joseph shall have two portions.

14 **And ye** shall inherit it, one as well as another:
concerning the which I lifted up mine hand to give it unto your fathers:
and this land shall fall unto you for inheritance.

15 **And this** shall be the border of the land toward the north side, from the great sea, the way of Hethlon, {as men go to Zedad};

16 Hamath, Berothah, Sibraim, {which is between the border of Damascus and the border of Hamath}; Hazarhatticon, {which is by the coast of Hauran}.

17 **And the border from the sea** shall be Hazarenan, the border of Damascus, and the north northward, and the border of Hamath.

And this is the north side.

18 **And the east side ye** shall measure from Hauran, and from Damascus, and from Gilead, and from the land of Israel by Jordan, from the border unto the east sea.

And this is the east side.

19 **And the south side southward,** from Tamar even to the waters of strife in Kadesh, the river to the great sea.
And this is the south side southward.
20 **The west side** also shall be the great sea from the border,
till a man come over against Hamath.
This is the west side.
21 **So** shall ye divide this land unto you according to the tribes of Israel.
22 **And it** shall come to pass,
that ye shall divide it by lot for an inheritance unto you, and to the strangers that sojourn among you,
which shall beget children among you:
and they shall be unto you as born in the country among the children of Israel
they shall have inheritance with you among the tribes of Israel.
23 **And it** shall come to pass,
that in what tribe the stranger sojourneth, there shall ye give him his inheritance,
saith the Lord GOD.

48 **Now these** are the names of the tribes.
From the north end to the coast of the way of Hethlon, {as one goeth to Hamath, Hazarenan, the border of Damascus northward, to the coast of Hamath}; {for these are his sides east and west}; a portion for Dan.
2 **And by the border of Dan, from the east side unto the west side,** a portion for Asher.
3 **And by the border of Asher, from the east side even unto the west side,** a portion for Naphtali.
4 **And by the border of Naphtali, from the east side unto the west side,** a portion for Manasseh.
5 **And by the border of Manasseh, from the east side unto the west side,** a portion for Ephraim.
6 **And by the border of Ephraim, from the east side even unto the west side,** a portion for Reuben.
7 **And by the border of Reuben, from the east side unto the west side,** a portion for Judah.
8 **And by the border of Judah, from the east side unto the west side,** shall be the offering which ye shall offer of five and twenty thousand reeds in breadth, and in length as one of the other parts, from the east side unto the west side:
and the sanctuary shall be in the midst of it.
9 **The oblation that ye shall offer unto the LORD** shall be of five and twenty thousand in length, and of ten thousand in breadth.
10 **And for them, even for the priests,** shall be this holy oblation; toward the north five and twenty thousand in length, and toward the west ten thousand in breadth, and toward the east ten thousand in breadth, and toward the south five and twenty thousand in length:
and the sanctuary of the LORD shall be in the midst thereof.
11 **It** shall be for the priests that are sanctified of the sons of Zadok;
which have kept my charge,
which went not astray
when the children of Israel went astray,
as the Levites went astray.
12 **And this oblation of the land that is offered** shall be unto them a thing most holy by the border of the Levites.
13 **And over against the border of the priests** the Levites shall have five and twenty thousand in length, and ten thousand in breadth:
all the length shall be five and twenty thousand, and the breadth ten thousand.
14 **And they** shall not sell of it,
neither exchange,
nor alienate the firstfruits of the land:
for it is holy unto the LORD.
15 **And the five thousand**, {that are left in the breadth over against the five and twenty thousand}, shall be a profane place for the city, for dwelling, and for suburbs:
and the city shall be in the midst thereof.
16 **And these** shall be the measures thereof; the north side four thousand and five hundred, and the south side four thousand and five hundred, and on the east side four thousand and five hundred, and the west side four thousand and five hundred.
17 **And the suburbs of the city** shall be toward the north two hundred and fifty, and toward the south two hundred and fifty, and toward the east two hundred and fifty, and toward the west two hundred and fifty.
18 **And the residue in length over against the oblation of the holy portion** shall be ten thousand eastward, and ten thousand westward:
and it shall be over against the oblation of the holy portion;
and the increase thereof shall be for food unto them that serve the city.
19 **And they that serve the city** shall serve it out of all the tribes of Israel.
20 **All the oblation** shall be five and twenty thousand by five and twenty thousand:
ye shall offer the holy oblation foursquare, with the possession of the city.
21 **And the residue** shall be for the prince, on the one side and on the other of the holy oblation, and of the possession of the city, over against the five and twenty thousand of the oblation toward the east border, and westward over against the five and twenty thousand toward the west border, over against the portions for the prince:
and it shall be the holy oblation;
and the sanctuary of the house shall be in the midst thereof.
22 **Moreover from the possession of the Levites, and from the possession of the city**, {being in the midst of that which is the prince's, between the border of Judah and the border of Benjamin}, shall be for the prince.
23 **As for the rest of the tribes, from the east side unto the west side,** Benjamin shall have a portion.
24 **And by the border of Benjamin, from the east side unto the west side,** Simeon shall have a portion.

25 **And by the border of Simeon,**
from the east side unto the west
side, Issachar a portion.
26 **And by the border of Issachar,**
from the east side unto the west
side, Zebulun a portion.
27 **And by the border of Zebulun,**
from the east side unto the west
side, Gad a portion.
28 **And by the border of Gad, at the**
south side southward, the
border shall be even from Tamar
unto the waters of strife in
Kadesh, and to the river toward
the great sea.
29 **This** is the land which ye shall
divide by lot unto the tribes of
Israel for inheritance,
and these are their portions,
saith the Lord GOD.
30 **And these** are the goings out of
the city on the north side, four
thousand and five hundred
measures.
31 **And the gates of the city** shall be
after the names of the tribes of
Israel: three gates northward; one
gate of Reuben, one gate of Judah,
one gate of Levi.
32 **And at the east side four**
thousand and five hundred: and
three gates; and one gate of
Joseph, one gate of Benjamin, one
gate of Dan.
33 **And at the south side four**
thousand and five hundred
measures: and three gates; one
gate of Simeon, one gate of
Issachar, one gate of Zebulun.
34 **At the west side four thousand**
and five hundred, with their
three gates; one gate of Gad, one
gate of Asher, one gate of
Naphtali.
35 **It** was round about eighteen
thousand measures:
and the name of the city from that
day shall be,
The LORD is there.

Daniel

The Book of Daniel, traditionally ascribed to the prophet Daniel himself, presents the Bible's fifth and final historical and theological account of the Babylonian exile. Daniel and his companions are among the Israelites who are exiled by King Nebuchadnezzar. The young prophet, renowned for his wisdom and understanding, ascends to power and influence in the royal court. This elevation allows him to bear witness to God's power and interpret the dreams and visions of the Babylonian kings.

Daniel's writings are the origin of several well-known stories that vividly illustrate the power and protection of God. One of the most renowned historical accounts features Daniel and the lion's den. A devout follower of God, Daniel refuses to worship the king of Babylon and thus is cast into a den of lions. Yet one day later, he emerges unscathed, a powerful testament to God's power, protection, and reward for faithfulness. The book also recounts the tale of Shadrach, Meshach, and Abednego, each a faithful follower of God, who defy the Babylonian king's golden idol. They are cast into a fiery furnace, but God's protection ensures they emerge from the flames unharmed.

The Book of Daniel is also the source of many visions and prophecies. In one vision, Daniel sees four beasts representing the kingdoms of Babylon, Persia, Greece, and Rome, and he details the rise and fall of each one. This vision culminates in the appearance of the Son of Man, Who has dominion over all earthly powers, representing the ultimate triumph of good over evil. Daniel later interprets a mysterious message from God in a story that begins when King Belshazzar hosts a great feast, during which he and his guests drink from sacred vessels taken from the temple in Jerusalem. A hand suddenly appears, and a message is written on the wall. The king is terrified, and his advisors cannot interpret the message. Daniel, however, interprets it as a prophecy of God's judgment, warning the king that his reign is ending and that his kingdom will be divided among the Medes and Persians. Daniel later experiences another vision about a seventy-week period, during which various end-time events will occur, including the coming of the Messiah and the ultimate triumph of God's kingdom over all others. These visions offer a future of hope and encouragement for the people in exile.

The Books of Daniel and Ezekiel take place during the Babylonian exile, and both are filled with visions and prophecies, yet they serve distinct purposes. While Ezekiel sheds light on God's plan for the ultimate fate of the Israelites, Daniel offers a unique perspective on God's plan for the ultimate fate of humanity. Furthermore, the Book of Daniel provides a unique, personal perspective on the importance of trusting God while standing firm in one's faith.

1 **In the third year of the reign of Jehoiakim king of Judah** came Nebuchadnezzar king of Babylon unto Jerusalem,
and besieged it.

2 **And the Lord** gave Jehoiakim king of Judah into his hand, with part of the vessels of the house of God:
which he carried into the land of Shinar to the house of his god;
and he brought the vessels into the treasure house of his god.

3 **And the king** spake unto Ashpenaz the master of his eunuchs,
that he should bring certain of the children of Israel, and of the king's seed, and of the princes;

4 **Children in whom** was no blemish, but well favoured, and skilful in all wisdom, and cunning in knowledge, and understanding science,
and such as had ability in them to stand in the king's palace,
and whom they might teach the learning and the tongue of the Chaldeans.

5 **And the king** appointed them a daily provision of the king's meat, and of the wine which he drank:
so nourishing them three years,
that at the end thereof they might stand before the king.

6 **Now among these** were of the children of Judah, Daniel, Hananiah, Mishael, and Azariah:

7 **Unto whom** the prince of the eunuchs gave names:
for he gave unto Daniel the name of Belteshazzar; and to Hananiah, of Shadrach; and to Mishael, of Meshach; and to Azariah, of Abednego.

8 **But Daniel** purposed in his heart
that he would not defile himself with the portion of the king's meat, nor with the wine which he drank:
therefore he requested of the prince of the eunuchs
that he might not defile himself.

9 **Now God** had brought Daniel into favour and tender love with the prince of the eunuchs.

10 **And the prince of the eunuchs** said unto Daniel,
I fear my lord the king,
who hath appointed your meat and your drink:
for why should he see your faces worse liking than the children which are of your sort?
then shall ye make me endanger my head to the king.

11 **Then** said Daniel to Melzar,

whom the prince of the eunuchs had set over Daniel, Hananiah, Mishael, and Azariah,

12 **Prove** thy servants, {I beseech thee}, ten days;
and let them give us pulse to eat, and water to drink.

13 **Then let our countenances** be looked upon before thee, and the countenance of the children that eat of the portion of the king's meat:
and as thou seest,
deal with thy servants.

14 **So he** consented to them in this matter,
and proved them ten days.

15 **And at the end of ten days** their countenances appeared fairer and fatter in flesh than all the children which did eat the portion of the king's meat.

16 **Thus Melzar** took away the portion of their meat, and the wine that they should drink;
and gave them pulse.

17 **As for these four children,** God gave them knowledge and skill in all learning and wisdom:
and Daniel had understanding in all visions and dreams.

18 **Now at the end of the days that the king had said he should bring them in,** then the prince of the eunuchs brought them in before Nebuchadnezzar.

19 **And the king** communed with them;
and among them all was found none like Daniel, Hananiah, Mishael, and Azariah:
therefore stood they before the king.

20 **And in all matters of wisdom and understanding**, {that the king enquired of them}, he found them ten times better than all the magicians and astrologers that were in all his realm.

21 **And Daniel** continued even unto the first year of king Cyrus.

2 **And in the second year of the reign of Nebuchadnezzar** Nebuchadnezzar dreamed dreams,
wherewith his spirit was troubled,
and his sleep brake from him.

2 **Then the king** commanded to call the magicians, and the astrologers, and the sorcerers, and the Chaldeans,
for to shew the king his dreams.

So they came and stood before the king.

3 **And the king** said unto them,
I have dreamed a dream,
and my spirit was troubled to know the dream.

4 **Then** spake the Chaldeans to the king in Syriack,
O king, live for ever:
tell thy servants the dream,
and we will shew the interpretation.

5 **The king** answered and said to the Chaldeans,
The thing is gone from me:
if ye will not make known unto me the dream, with the interpretation thereof,
ye shall be cut in pieces,
and your houses shall be made a dunghill.

6 **But if ye** shew the dream, and the interpretation thereof,
ye shall receive of me gifts and rewards and great honour:
therefore shew me the dream, and the interpretation thereof.

7 **They** answered again and said,
Let the king tell his servants the dream,
and we will shew the interpretation of it.

8 **The king** answered and said,
I know of certainty
that ye would gain the time,
because ye see the thing is gone from me.

9 **But if ye** will not make known unto me the dream,
there is but one decree for you:
for ye have prepared lying and corrupt words to speak before me,
till the time be changed:
therefore tell me the dream,
and I shall know
that ye can shew me the interpretation thereof.

10 **The Chaldeans** answered before the king,
and said,
There is not a man upon the earth that can shew the king's matter:
therefore there is no king, lord, nor ruler, that asked such things at any magician, or astrologer, or Chaldean.

11 **And it** is a rare thing that the king requireth,
and there is none other that can shew it before the king, except the gods,
whose dwelling is not with flesh.

12 **For this cause** the king was angry and very furious,
and commanded to destroy all the wise men of Babylon.

13 **And the decree** went forth that the wise men should be slain;
and they sought Daniel and his fellows
to be slain.

14 **Then Daniel** answered with counsel and wisdom to Arioch the captain of the king's guard,
which was gone forth to slay the wise men of Babylon:

15 **He** answered and said to Arioch the king's captain,
Why is the decree so hasty from the king?

Then Arioch made the thing known to Daniel.

16 **Then Daniel** went in,
and desired of the king
that he would give him time,
and that he would shew the king the interpretation.

17 **Then Daniel** went to his house,
and made the thing known to Hananiah, Mishael, and Azariah, his companions:

18 **That they** would desire mercies of the God of heaven concerning this secret;
that Daniel and his fellows should not perish with the rest of the wise men of Babylon.

19 **Then** was the secret revealed unto Daniel in a night vision.

Then Daniel blessed the God of heaven.

20 **Daniel** answered and said,
Blessed be the name of God for ever and ever:
for wisdom and might are his:

21 **And he** changeth the times and the seasons:
he removeth kings,
and setteth up kings:
he giveth wisdom unto the wise, and knowledge to them that know understanding:

22 **He** revealeth the deep and secret things:
he knoweth
what is in the darkness,

and the light dwelleth with him.
23 **I** thank thee,
and praise thee, O thou God of my fathers,
who hast given me wisdom and might,
and hast made known unto me now
what we desired of thee:
for thou hast now made known unto us the king's matter.
24 **Therefore Daniel** went in unto Arioch,
whom the king had ordained to destroy the wise men of Babylon:
he went and said thus unto him;
Destroy not the wise men of Babylon:
bring me in before the king,
and I will shew unto the king the interpretation.
25 **Then Arioch** brought in Daniel before the king in haste,
and said thus unto him,
I have found a man of the captives of Judah,
that will make known unto the king the interpretation.
26 **The king** answered and said to Daniel,
whose name was Belteshazzar,
Art thou able to make known unto me the dream which I have seen, and the interpretation thereof?
27 **Daniel** answered in the presence of the king,
and said,
The secret which the king hath demanded cannot the wise men, the astrologers, the magicians, the soothsayers, shew unto the king;
28 **But there** is a God in heaven that revealeth secrets,
and maketh known to the king Nebuchadnezzar
what shall be in the latter days.
Thy dream, and the visions of thy head upon thy bed, are these;
29 **As for thee, O king,** thy thoughts came into thy mind upon thy bed,
what should come to pass hereafter:
and he that revealeth secrets maketh known to thee
what shall come to pass.
30 **But as for me,** this secret is not revealed to me for any wisdom that I have more than any living, but for their sakes that shall make known the interpretation to the king, and that thou mightest know the thoughts of thy heart.
31 **Thou, O king,** sawest,
and behold a great image.
This great image, whose brightness was excellent, stood before thee;
and the form thereof was terrible.
32 **This image's head** was of fine gold, his breast and his arms of silver, his belly and his thighs of brass,
33 His legs of iron, his feet part of iron and part of clay.
34 **Thou** sawest till that a stone was cut out without hands,
which smote the image upon his feet that were of iron and clay,
and brake them to pieces.
35 **Then** was the iron, the clay, the brass, the silver, and the gold, broken to pieces together,
and became like the chaff of the summer threshingfloors;
and the wind carried them away,
that no place was found for them:
and the stone that smote the image became a great mountain,
and filled the whole earth.
36 **This** is the dream;
and we will tell the interpretation thereof before the king.
37 **Thou, O king,** art a king of kings:
for the God of heaven hath given thee a kingdom, power, and strength, and glory.
38 **And wheresoever the children of men** dwell,
the beasts of the field and the fowls of the heaven hath he given into thine hand,
and hath made thee ruler over them all.
Thou art this head of gold.
39 **And after thee** shall arise another kingdom inferior to thee, and another third kingdom of brass,
which shall bear rule over all the earth.
40 **And the fourth kingdom** shall be strong as iron:
forasmuch as iron breaketh in pieces and subdueth all things:
and as iron that breaketh all these, shall it break in pieces and bruise.
41 **And whereas thou** sawest the feet and toes, part of potters' clay, and part of iron,
the kingdom shall be divided;
but there shall be in it of the strength of the iron,
forasmuch as thou sawest the iron mixed with miry clay.
42 **And as the toes of the feet** were part of iron, and part of clay,
so the kingdom shall be partly strong, and partly broken.
43 **And whereas thou** sawest iron mixed with miry clay,
they shall mingle themselves with the seed of men:
but they shall not cleave one to another,
even as iron is not mixed with clay.
44 **And in the days of these kings** shall the God of heaven set up a kingdom,
which shall never be destroyed:
and the kingdom shall not be left to other people,
but it shall break in pieces and consume all these kingdoms,
and it shall stand for ever.
45 **Forasmuch as thou** sawest that the stone was cut out of the mountain without hands, and that it brake in pieces the iron, the brass, the clay, the silver, and the gold;
the great God hath made known to the king
what shall come to pass hereafter:
and the dream is certain,
and the interpretation thereof sure.
46 **Then the king Nebuchadnezzar** fell upon his face,
and worshipped Daniel,
and commanded
that they should offer an oblation and sweet odours unto him.
47 **The king** answered unto Daniel,
and said,
Of a truth it is,
that your God is a God of gods, and a Lord of kings, and a revealer of secrets,
seeing thou couldest reveal this secret.
48 **Then the king** made Daniel a great man,
and gave him many great gifts,
and made him ruler over the whole province of Babylon, and chief of the governors over all the wise men of Babylon.
49 **Then Daniel** requested of the king,

and he set Shadrach, Meshach, and Abednego, over the affairs of the province of Babylon:
but Daniel sat in the gate of the king.

3 **Nebuchadnezzar the king** made an image of gold,
whose height was threescore cubits, and the breadth thereof six cubits:
he set it up in the plain of Dura, in the province of Babylon.

2 **Then Nebuchadnezzar the king** sent to gather together the princes, the governors, and the captains, the judges, the treasurers, the counsellors, the sheriffs, and all the rulers of the provinces,
to come to the dedication of the image which Nebuchadnezzar the king had set up.

3 **Then the princes, the governors, and captains, the judges, the treasurers, the counsellors, the sheriffs, and all the rulers of the provinces,** were gathered together unto the dedication of the image that Nebuchadnezzar the king had set up;
and they stood before the image that Nebuchadnezzar had set up.

4 **Then an herald** cried aloud,
To you it is commanded, O people, nations, and languages,

5 **That at what time** ye hear the sound of the cornet, flute, harp, sackbut, psaltery, dulcimer, and all kinds of musick,
ye fall down and worship the golden image that Nebuchadnezzar the king hath set up:

6 **And whoso falleth not down and worshippeth** shall the same hour be cast into the midst of a burning fiery furnace.

7 **Therefore at that time,** {when all the people heard the sound of the cornet, flute, harp, sackbut, psaltery, and all kinds of musick}, all the people, the nations, and the languages, fell down and worshipped the golden image that Nebuchadnezzar the king had set up.

8 **Wherefore at that time** certain Chaldeans came near,
and accused the Jews.

9 **They** spake and said to the king Nebuchadnezzar,
O king, live for ever.

10 **Thou, O king,** hast made a decree,
that every man that shall hear the sound of the cornet, flute, harp, sackbut, psaltery, and dulcimer, and all kinds of musick, shall fall down and worship the golden image:

11 **And whoso** falleth not down and worshippeth,
that he should be cast into the midst of a burning fiery furnace.

12 **There** are certain Jews whom thou hast set over the affairs of the province of Babylon, Shadrach, Meshach, and Abednego;
these men, O king, have not regarded thee:
they serve not thy gods,
nor worship the golden image which thou hast set up.

13 **Then Nebuchadnezzar in his rage and fury** commanded to bring Shadrach, Meshach, and Abednego.
Then they brought these men before the king.

14 **Nebuchadnezzar** spake and said unto them,
Is it true, O Shadrach, Meshach, and Abednego,
do not ye serve my gods,
nor worship the golden image which I have set up?

15 **Now if ye** be ready that at what time ye hear the sound of the cornet, flute, harp, sackbut, psaltery, and dulcimer, and all kinds of musick,
ye fall down and worship the image which I have made; well:
but if ye worship not,
ye shall be cast the same hour into the midst of a burning fiery furnace;
and who is that God that shall deliver you out of my hands?

16 **Shadrach, Meshach, and Abednego,** answered and said to the king,
O Nebuchadnezzar, we are not careful to answer thee in this matter.

17 **If it** be so,
our God whom we serve is able to deliver us from the burning fiery furnace,
and he will deliver us out of thine hand, O king.

18 **But if not,** be it known unto thee, O king,
that we will not serve thy gods,
nor worship the golden image which thou hast set up.

19 **Then** was Nebuchadnezzar full of fury,
and the form of his visage was changed against Shadrach, Meshach, and Abednego:
therefore he spake,
and commanded
that they should heat the furnace one seven times more than it was wont to be heated.

20 And he commanded the most mighty men that were in his army to bind Shadrach, Meshach, and Abednego, and to cast them into the burning fiery furnace.

21 **Then these men** were bound in their coats, their hosen, and their hats, and their other garments,
and were cast into the midst of the burning fiery furnace.

22 **Therefore because the king's commandment** was urgent, and the furnace exceeding hot,
the flames of the fire slew those men that took up Shadrach, Meshach, and Abednego.

23 **And these three men, Shadrach, Meshach, and Abednego,** fell down bound into the midst of the burning fiery furnace.

24 **Then Nebuchadnezzar the king** was astonished,
and rose up in haste,
and spake,
and said unto his counsellors,
Did not we cast three men bound into the midst of the fire?
They answered and said unto the king,
True, O king.

25 **He** answered and said,
Lo,
I see four men loose,
walking in the midst of the fire,
and they have no hurt;
and the form of the fourth is like the Son of God.

[26] **Then Nebuchadnezzar** came near to the mouth of the burning fiery furnace,
and spake,
and said,
Shadrach, Meshach, and Abednego, ye servants of the most high God, come forth,
and come hither.
Then Shadrach, Meshach, and Abednego, came forth of the midst of the fire.
[27] **And the princes, governors, and captains, and the king's counsellors,** {being gathered together}, saw these men,
upon whose bodies the fire had no power,
nor was an hair of their head singed,
neither were their coats changed,
nor the smell of fire had passed on them.
[28] **Then Nebuchadnezzar** spake,
and said,
Blessed be the God of Shadrach, Meshach, and Abednego,
who hath sent his angel,
and delivered his servants that trusted in him,
and have changed the king's word,
and yielded their bodies,
that they might not serve {nor worship} any god, except their own God.
[29] **Therefore I** make a decree,
That every people, nation, and language, {which speak any thing amiss against the God of Shadrach, Meshach, and Abednego}, shall be cut in pieces,
and their houses shall be made a dunghill:
because there is no other God that can deliver after this sort.
[30] **Then the king** promoted Shadrach, Meshach, and Abednego, in the province of Babylon.

4 **Nebuchadnezzar the king,** unto all people, nations, and languages, that dwell in all the earth;
Peace be multiplied unto you.
[2] **I thought it good** to shew the signs and wonders that the high God hath wrought toward me.
[3] **How great** are his signs!
and how mighty are his wonders!
his kingdom is an everlasting kingdom,
and his dominion is from generation to generation.
[4] **I Nebuchadnezzar** was at rest in mine house,
and flourishing in my palace:
[5] **I** saw a dream which made me afraid,
and the thoughts upon my bed and the visions of my head troubled me.
[6] **Therefore** made I a decree to bring in all the wise men of Babylon before me,
that they might make known unto me the interpretation of the dream.
[7] **Then** came in the magicians, the astrologers, the Chaldeans, and the soothsayers:
and I told the dream before them;
but they did not make known unto me the interpretation thereof.
[8] **But at the last** Daniel came in before me,
whose name was Belteshazzar, according to the name of my God,
and in whom is the spirit of the holy gods:
and before him I told the dream, saying,
[9] **O Belteshazzar, master of the magicians, because I** know
that the spirit of the holy gods is in thee,
and no secret troubleth thee,
tell me the visions of my dream that I have seen, and the interpretation thereof.
[10] **Thus** were the visions of mine head in my bed;
I saw,
and behold a tree in the midst of the earth,
and the height thereof was great.
[11] **The tree** grew,
and was strong,
and the height thereof reached unto heaven, and the sight thereof to the end of all the earth:
[12] **The leaves thereof** were fair, and the fruit thereof much,
and in it was meat for all:
the beasts of the field had shadow under it,
and the fowls of the heaven dwelt in the boughs thereof,
and all flesh was fed of it.
[13] **I** saw in the visions of my head upon my bed,
and, {behold}, a watcher and an holy one came down from heaven;
[14] **He** cried aloud,
and said thus,
Hew down the tree,
and cut off his branches,
shake off his leaves,
and scatter his fruit:
let the beasts get away from under it, and the fowls from his branches:
[15] **Nevertheless leave** the stump of his roots in the earth, even with a band of iron and brass, in the tender grass of the field;
and let it be wet with the dew of heaven,
and let his portion be with the beasts in the grass of the earth:
[16] **Let his heart** be changed from man's,
and let a beast's heart be given unto him;
and let seven times pass over him.
[17] **This matter** is by the decree of the watchers, and the demand by the word of the holy ones:
to the intent that the living may know
that the most High ruleth in the kingdom of men,
and giveth it to whomsoever he will,
and setteth up over it the basest of men.
[18] **This dream** I king Nebuchadnezzar have seen.
Now thou, O Belteshazzar, declare the interpretation thereof,
forasmuch as all the wise men of my kingdom are not able to make known unto me the interpretation:
but thou art able;
for the spirit of the holy gods is in thee.
[19] **Then Daniel, whose name was Belteshazzar,** was astonied for one hour,
and his thoughts troubled him.
The king spake,
and said,
Belteshazzar, let not the dream, or the interpretation thereof, trouble thee.
Belteshazzar answered and said,

My lord, the dream be to them that hate thee, and the interpretation thereof to thine enemies.

20 **The tree that thou sawest,** {which grew}, {and was strong}, {whose height reached unto the heaven, and the sight thereof to all the earth};

21 {Whose leaves were fair, and the fruit thereof much}, {and in it was meat for all}; {under which the beasts of the field dwelt}, {and upon whose branches the fowls of the heaven had their habitation}:

22 It is thou, O king, that art grown and become strong:
for thy greatness is grown,
and reacheth unto heaven, and thy dominion to the end of the earth.

23 **And whereas the king** saw a watcher and an holy one coming down from heaven,
and saying,
Hew the tree down,
and destroy it;
yet leave the stump of the roots thereof in the earth, even with a band of iron and brass, in the tender grass of the field;
and let it be wet with the dew of heaven,
and let his portion be with the beasts of the field,
till seven times pass over him;
24 **This** is the interpretation, O king,
and this is the decree of the most High,
which is come upon my lord the king:
25 **That they** shall drive thee from men,
and thy dwelling shall be with the beasts of the field,
and they shall make thee to eat grass as oxen,
and they shall wet thee with the dew of heaven,
and seven times shall pass over thee,
till thou know
that the most High ruleth in the kingdom of men,
and giveth it to whomsoever he will.

26 **And whereas they** commanded to leave the stump of the tree roots;
thy kingdom shall be sure unto thee,
after that thou shalt have known
that the heavens do rule.

27 **Wherefore, O king, let my counsel** be acceptable unto thee,
and break off thy sins by righteousness, and thine iniquities by shewing mercy to the poor;
if it may be a lengthening of thy tranquillity.

28 **All this** came upon the king Nebuchadnezzar.

29 **At the end of twelve months** he walked in the palace of the kingdom of Babylon.

30 **The king** spake,
and said,
Is not this great Babylon,
that I have built for the house of the kingdom by the might of my power, and for the honour of my majesty?

31 **While the word** was in the king's mouth,
there fell a voice from heaven, saying,
O king Nebuchadnezzar, to thee it is spoken;
The kingdom is departed from thee.

32 **And they** shall drive thee from men,
and thy dwelling shall be with the beasts of the field:
they shall make thee to eat grass as oxen,
and seven times shall pass over thee,
until thou know
that the most High ruleth in the kingdom of men,
and giveth it to whomsoever he will.

33 **The same hour** was the thing fulfilled upon Nebuchadnezzar:
and he was driven from men,
and did eat grass as oxen,
and his body was wet with the dew of heaven,
till his hairs were grown like eagles' feathers, and his nails like birds' claws.

34 **And at the end of the days** I Nebuchadnezzar lifted up mine eyes unto heaven,
and mine understanding returned unto me,
and I blessed the most High,
and I praised and honoured him that liveth for ever,
whose dominion is an everlasting dominion,
and his kingdom is from generation to generation:
35 **And all the inhabitants of the earth** are reputed as nothing:
and he doeth according to his will in the army of heaven, and among the inhabitants of the earth:
and none can stay his hand,
or say unto him,
What doest thou?

36 **At the same time** my reason returned unto me;
and for the glory of my kingdom, mine honour and brightness returned unto me;
and my counsellors and my lords sought unto me;
and I was established in my kingdom,
and excellent majesty was added unto me.

37 **Now I Nebuchadnezzar** praise and extol and honour the King of heaven,
all whose works are truth, and his ways judgment:
and those that walk in pride he is able to abase.

5 **Belshazzar the king** made a great feast to a thousand of his lords,
and drank wine before the thousand.

2 **Belshazzar,** {whiles he tasted the wine}, commanded to bring the golden and silver vessels which his father Nebuchadnezzar had taken out of the temple which was in Jerusalem;
that the king, and his princes, his wives, and his concubines, might drink therein.

3 **Then they** brought the golden vessels that were taken out of the temple of the house of God which was at Jerusalem;
and the king, and his princes, his wives, and his concubines, drank in them.

4 **They** drank wine,
and praised the gods of gold, and of silver, of brass, of iron, of wood, and of stone.

5 **In the same hour** came forth fingers of a man's hand,
and wrote over against the candlestick upon the plaister of the wall of the king's palace:
and the king saw the part of the hand that wrote.

6 **Then the king's countenance** was changed,
and his thoughts troubled him,
so that the joints of his loins were loosed,
and his knees smote one against another.

7 **The king** cried aloud to bring in the astrologers, the Chaldeans, and the soothsayers.
And the king spake,
and said to the wise men of Babylon,
Whosoever shall read this writing, {and shew me the interpretation thereof}, shall be clothed with scarlet,
and have a chain of gold about his neck,
and shall be the third ruler in the kingdom.

8 **Then** came in all the king's wise men:
but they could not read the writing,
nor make known to the king the interpretation thereof.

9 **Then** was king Belshazzar greatly troubled,
and his countenance was changed in him,
and his lords were astonied.

10 **Now the queen by reason of the words of the king and his lords** came into the banquet house:
and the queen spake and said,
O king, live for ever:
let not thy thoughts trouble thee,
nor let thy countenance be changed:
11 **There** is a man in thy kingdom,
in whom is the spirit of the holy gods;
and in the days of thy father light and understanding and wisdom, like the wisdom of the gods, was found in him;
whom the king Nebuchadnezzar thy father, the king, {I say}, thy father, made master of the magicians, astrologers, Chaldeans, and soothsayers;

12 **Forasmuch as an excellent spirit, and knowledge, and understanding, interpreting of dreams, and shewing of hard sentences, and dissolving of doubts,** were found in the same Daniel,
whom the king named Belteshazzar:
now let Daniel be called,
and he will shew the interpretation.

13 **Then** was Daniel brought in before the king.
And the king spake and said unto Daniel,
Art thou that Daniel,
which art of the children of the captivity of Judah,
whom the king my father brought out of Jewry?

14 **I** have even heard of thee,
that the spirit of the gods is in thee,
and that light and understanding and excellent wisdom is found in thee.

15 **And now the wise men, the astrologers,** have been brought in before me,
that they should read this writing,
and make known unto me the interpretation thereof:
but they could not shew the interpretation of the thing:
16 **And I** have heard of thee,
that thou canst make interpretations,
and dissolve doubts:
now if thou canst read the writing,
and make known to me the interpretation thereof,
thou shalt be clothed with scarlet,
and have a chain of gold about thy neck,
and shalt be the third ruler in the kingdom.

17 **Then Daniel** answered and said before the king,
Let thy gifts be to thyself,
and give thy rewards to another;
yet I will read the writing unto the king,
and make known to him the interpretation.

18 **O thou king, the most high God** gave Nebuchadnezzar thy father a kingdom, and majesty, and glory, and honour:

19 **And for the majesty that he gave him,** all people, nations, and languages, trembled and feared before him:
whom he would he slew;
and whom he would he kept alive;
and whom he would he set up;
and whom he would he put down.

20 **But when his heart** was lifted up,
and his mind hardened in pride,
he was deposed from his kingly throne,
and they took his glory from him:
21 **And he** was driven from the sons of men;
and his heart was made like the beasts,
and his dwelling was with the wild asses:
they fed him with grass like oxen,
and his body was wet with the dew of heaven;
till he knew
that the most high God ruled in the kingdom of men,
and that he appointeth over it whomsoever he will.

22 **And thou his son, O Belshazzar,** hast not humbled thine heart,
though thou knewest all this;
23 **But** hast lifted up thyself against the Lord of heaven;
and they have brought the vessels of his house before thee,
and thou, and thy lords, thy wives, and thy concubines, have drunk wine in them;
and thou hast praised the gods of silver, and gold, of brass, iron, wood, and stone,
which see not,
nor hear,
nor know:
and the God in whose hand thy breath is, and whose are all thy ways, hast thou not glorified:
24 **Then** was the part of the hand sent from him;
and this writing was written.

25 **And this** is the writing that was written, Mene, Mene, Tekel, Upharsin.

26 **This** is the interpretation of the thing:
Mene;
God hath numbered thy kingdom,
and finished it.

27 Tekel;
Thou art weighed in the balances,
and art found wanting.

28 Peres;
Thy kingdom is divided,
and given to the Medes and Persians.

29 **Then** commanded Belshazzar,
and they clothed Daniel with scarlet,
and put a chain of gold about his neck,

and made a proclamation concerning him,
that he should be the third ruler in the kingdom.
30 **In that night** was Belshazzar the king of the Chaldeans slain.
31 **And Darius the Median** took the kingdom,
being about threescore and two years old.

6 **It pleased Darius** to set over the kingdom an hundred and twenty princes,
which should be over the whole kingdom;
2 And over these three presidents;
of whom Daniel was first:
that the princes might give accounts unto them,
and the king should have no damage.
3 **Then this Daniel** was preferred above the presidents and princes,
because an excellent spirit was in him;
and the king thought to set him over the whole realm.
4 **Then the presidents and princes** sought to find occasion against Daniel concerning the kingdom;
but they could find none occasion nor fault;
forasmuch as he was faithful,
neither was there any error or fault found in him.
5 **Then** said these men,
We shall not find any occasion against this Daniel,
except we find it against him concerning the law of his God.
6 **Then these presidents and princes** assembled together to the king,
and said thus unto him,
King Darius, live for ever.
7 **All the presidents of the kingdom, the governors, and the princes, the counsellors, and the captains,** have consulted together
to establish a royal statute,
and to make a firm decree,
that whosoever shall ask a petition of any God or man for thirty days, save of thee, O king,
he shall be cast into the den of lions.
8 **Now, O king, establish** the decree,
and sign the writing,
that it be not changed, according to the law of the Medes and Persians,
which altereth not.
9 **Wherefore king Darius** signed the writing and the decree.
10 **Now when Daniel** knew that the writing was signed,
he went into his house;
and his windows being open in his chamber toward Jerusalem,
he kneeled upon his knees three times a day,
and prayed,
and gave thanks before his God,
as he did aforetime.
11 **Then these men** assembled,
and found Daniel praying and making supplication before his God.
12 **Then they** came near,
and spake before the king concerning the king's decree;
Hast thou not signed a decree,
that every man that shall ask a petition of any God or man within thirty days, save of thee, O king, shall be cast into the den of lions?
The king answered and said,
The thing is true, according to the law of the Medes and Persians,
which altereth not.
13 **Then** answered they and said before the king,
That Daniel, {which is of the children of the captivity of Judah}, regardeth not thee, O king, nor the decree that thou hast signed,
but maketh his petition three times a day.
14 **Then the king**, {when he heard these words}, was sore displeased with himself,
and set his heart on Daniel to deliver him:
and he laboured till the going down of the sun to deliver him.
15 **Then these men** assembled unto the king,
and said unto the king,
Know, O king,
that the law of the Medes and Persians is,
That no decree nor statute which the king establisheth may be changed.
16 **Then the king** commanded,
and they brought Daniel,
and cast him into the den of lions.
Now the king spake and said unto Daniel,
Thy God whom thou servest continually, he will deliver thee.
17 **And a stone** was brought,
and laid upon the mouth of the den;
and the king sealed it with his own signet, and with the signet of his lords;
that the purpose might not be changed concerning Daniel.
18 **Then the king** went to his palace,
and passed the night fasting:
neither were instruments of musick brought before him:
and his sleep went from him.
19 **Then the king** arose very early in the morning,
and went in haste unto the den of lions.
20 **And when he** came to the den,
he cried with a lamentable voice unto Daniel:
and the king spake and said to Daniel,
O Daniel, servant of the living God, is thy God, {whom thou servest continually}, able to deliver thee from the lions?
21 **Then** said Daniel unto the king,
O king, live for ever.
22 **My God** hath sent his angel,
and hath shut the lions' mouths,
that they have not hurt me:
forasmuch as before him innocency was found in me;
and also before thee, O king, have I done no hurt.
23 **Then** was the king exceedingly glad for him,
and commanded
that they should take Daniel up out of the den.
So Daniel was taken up out of the den,
and no manner of hurt was found upon him,
because he believed in his God.
24 **And the king** commanded,
and they brought those men which had accused Daniel,
and they cast them into the den of lions, them, their children, and their wives;
and the lions had the mastery of them,

and brake all their bones in pieces or ever they came at the bottom of the den.

25 **Then king Darius** wrote unto all people, nations, and languages,
that dwell in all the earth;
Peace be multiplied unto you.

26 I make a decree,
That in every dominion of my kingdom men tremble and fear before the God of Daniel:
for he is the living God,
and stedfast for ever,
and his kingdom that which shall not be destroyed,
and his dominion shall be even unto the end.

27 **He** delivereth and rescueth,
and he worketh signs and wonders in heaven and in earth,
who hath delivered Daniel from the power of the lions.

28 **So this Daniel** prospered in the reign of Darius, and in the reign of Cyrus the Persian.

7

In the first year of Belshazzar king of Babylon Daniel had a dream and visions of his head upon his bed:
then he wrote the dream,
and told the sum of the matters.

2 **Daniel** spake and said,
I saw in my vision by night,
and, {behold}, the four winds of the heaven strove upon the great sea.

3 **And four great beasts** came up from the sea, diverse one from another.

4 **The first** was like a lion,
and had eagle's wings:
I beheld till the wings thereof were plucked,
and it was lifted up from the earth,
and made stand upon the feet as a man,
and a man's heart was given to it.

5 **And** behold another beast, a second, like to a bear,
and it raised up itself on one side,
and it had three ribs in the mouth of it between the teeth of it:
and they said thus unto it,
Arise,
devour much flesh.

6 **After this** I beheld,
and lo another, like a leopard,
which had upon the back of it four wings of a fowl;
the beast had also four heads;
and dominion was given to it.

7 **After this** I saw in the night visions,
and behold a fourth beast, dreadful and terrible, and strong exceedingly;
and it had great iron teeth:
it devoured and brake in pieces,
and stamped the residue with the feet of it:
and it was diverse from all the beasts that were before it;
and it had ten horns.

8 **I** considered the horns,
and, {behold}, there came up among them another little horn,
before whom there were three of the first horns plucked up by the roots:
and, {behold}, in this horn were eyes like the eyes of man, and a mouth speaking great things.

9 **I** beheld till the thrones were cast down, and the Ancient of days did sit,
whose garment was white as snow, and the hair of his head like the pure wool:
his throne was like the fiery flame, and his wheels as burning fire.

10 **A fiery stream** issued and came forth from before him:
thousand thousands ministered unto him,
and ten thousand times ten thousand stood before him:
the judgment was set,
and the books were opened.

11 **I** beheld then because of the voice of the great words which the horn spake:
I beheld even till the beast was slain, and his body destroyed, and given to the burning flame.

12 **As concerning the rest of the beasts,** they had their dominion taken away:
yet their lives were prolonged for a season and time.

13 **I** saw in the night visions,
and, behold, one like the Son of man came with the clouds of heaven,
and came to the Ancient of days,
and they brought him near before him.

14 **And there** was given him dominion, and glory, and a kingdom,
that all people, nations, and languages, should serve him:
his dominion is an everlasting dominion,
which shall not pass away,
and his kingdom that which shall not be destroyed.

15 **I Daniel** was grieved in my spirit in the midst of my body,
and the visions of my head troubled me.

16 **I** came near unto one of them that stood by,
and asked him the truth of all this.
So he told me,
and made me know the interpretation of the things.

17 **These great beasts,** {which are four}, are four kings,
which shall arise out of the earth.

18 **But the saints of the most High** shall take the kingdom,
and possess the kingdom for ever, even for ever and ever.

19 **Then I** would know the truth of the fourth beast,
which was diverse from all the others, exceeding dreadful,
whose teeth were of iron, and his nails of brass;
which devoured, brake in pieces, and stamped the residue with his feet;

20 And of the ten horns that were in his head, and of the other which came up, and before whom three fell; even of that horn that had eyes, and a mouth that spake very great things,
whose look was more stout than his fellows.

21 **I** beheld,
and the same horn made war with the saints,
and prevailed against them;

22 **Until the Ancient of days** came,
and judgment was given to the saints of the most High;
and the time came that the saints possessed the kingdom.

23 **Thus he** said,
The fourth beast shall be the fourth kingdom upon earth,
which shall be diverse from all kingdoms,
and shall devour the whole earth,
and shall tread it down,
and break it in pieces.

24 **And the ten horns out of this kingdom** are ten kings that shall arise:
and another shall rise after them;
and he shall be diverse from the first,
and he shall subdue three kings.

25 **And he** shall speak great words against the most High,
and shall wear out the saints of the most High,
and think to change times and laws:
and they shall be given into his hand until a time and times and the dividing of time.

26 **But the judgment** shall sit,
and they shall take away his dominion,
to consume and to destroy it unto the end.

27 **And the kingdom and dominion, and the greatness of the kingdom under the whole heaven,** shall be given to the people of the saints of the most High,
whose kingdom is an everlasting kingdom,
and all dominions shall serve and obey him.

28 **Hitherto** is the end of the matter.
As for me Daniel, my cogitations much troubled me,
and my countenance changed in me:
but I kept the matter in my heart.

8

In the third year of the reign of king Belshazzar a vision appeared unto me, even unto me Daniel, after that which appeared unto me at the first.

2 **And I** saw in a vision;
and it came to pass,
when I saw,
that I was at Shushan in the palace,
which is in the province of Elam;
and I saw in a vision,
and I was by the river of Ulai.

3 **Then I** lifted up mine eyes,
and saw,
and, {behold}, there stood before the river a ram which had two horns:
and the two horns were high;
but one was higher than the other,
and the higher came up last.

4 **I** saw the ram pushing westward, and northward, and southward;
so that no beasts might stand before him,
neither was there any that could deliver out of his hand;
but he did according to his will,
and became great.

5 **And as I** was considering,
behold,
an he goat came from the west on the face of the whole earth,
and touched not the ground:
and the goat had a notable horn between his eyes.

6 **And he** came to the ram that had two horns,
which I had seen standing before the river,
and ran unto him in the fury of his power.

7 **And I** saw him come close unto the ram,
and he was moved with choler against him,
and smote the ram,
and brake his two horns:
and there was no power in the ram to stand before him,
but he cast him down to the ground,
and stamped upon him:
and there was none that could deliver the ram out of his hand.

8 **Therefore the he goat** waxed very great:
and when he was strong,
the great horn was broken;
and for it came up four notable ones toward the four winds of heaven.

9 **And out of one of them** came forth a little horn,
which waxed exceeding great, toward the south, and toward the east, and toward the pleasant land.

10 **And it** waxed great, even to the host of heaven;
and it cast down some of the host and of the stars to the ground,
and stamped upon them.

11 **Yea, he** magnified himself even to the prince of the host,
and by him the daily sacrifice was taken away,
and the place of the sanctuary was cast down.

12 **And an host** was given him against the daily sacrifice by reason of transgression,
and it cast down the truth to the ground;
and it practised,
and prospered.

13 **Then I** heard one saint speaking,
and another saint said unto that certain saint which spake,
How long shall be the vision concerning the daily sacrifice, and the transgression of desolation,
to give both the sanctuary and the host to be trodden under foot?

14 **And he** said unto me, Unto two thousand and three hundred days;
then shall the sanctuary be cleansed.

15 **And it** came to pass,
when I, even I Daniel, had seen the vision,
and sought for the meaning,
then, {behold}, there stood before me as the appearance of a man.

16 **And I** heard a man's voice between the banks of Ulai,
which called,
and said,
Gabriel, make this man to understand the vision.

17 **So he** came near where I stood:
and when he came,
I was afraid,
and fell upon my face:
but he said unto me,
Understand, O son of man:
for at the time of the end shall be the vision.

18 **Now as he** was speaking with me,
I was in a deep sleep on my face toward the ground:
but he touched me,
and set me upright.

19 **And he** said,
Behold,
I will make thee know
what shall be in the last end of the indignation:
for at the time appointed the end shall be.

20 **The ram which thou sawest having two horns** are the kings of Media and Persia.

21 **And the rough goat** is the king of Grecia:
and the great horn that is between his eyes is the first king.

22 **Now that** being broken,
whereas four stood up for it,

four kingdoms shall stand up out of the nation, but not in his power.

23 **And in the latter time of their kingdom**, {when the transgressors are come to the full}, a king of fierce countenance, and understanding dark sentences, shall stand up.

24 **And his power** shall be mighty, but not by his own power:
and he shall destroy wonderfully,
and shall prosper,
and practise,
and shall destroy the mighty and the holy people.

25 **And through his policy** also he shall cause craft to prosper in his hand;
and he shall magnify himself in his heart,
and by peace shall destroy many:
he shall also stand up against the Prince of princes;
but he shall be broken without hand.

26 **And the vision of the evening and the morning which was told** is true:
wherefore shut thou up the vision;
for it shall be for many days.

27 **And I** Daniel fainted,
and was sick certain days;
afterward I rose up,
and did the king's business;
and I was astonished at the vision,
but none understood it.

9 **In the first year of Darius the son of Ahasuerus, of the seed of the Medes, which was made king over the realm of the Chaldeans;**

2 In the first year of his reign I Daniel understood by books the number of the years,
whereof the word of the LORD came to Jeremiah the prophet,
that he would accomplish seventy years in the desolations of Jerusalem.

3 **And I** set my face unto the Lord God,
to seek by prayer and supplications, with fasting, and sackcloth, and ashes:

4 **And I** prayed unto the LORD my God,
and made my confession,
and said,
O Lord, the great and dreadful God, {keeping the covenant and mercy to them that love him, and to them that keep his commandments};

5 We have sinned,
and have committed iniquity,
and have done wickedly,
and have rebelled,
even by departing from thy precepts and from thy judgments:

6 **Neither** have we hearkened unto thy servants the prophets,
which spake in thy name to our kings, our princes, and our fathers, and to all the people of the land.

7 **O Lord, righteousness** belongeth unto thee, but unto us confusion of faces, as at this day; to the men of Judah, and to the inhabitants of Jerusalem, and unto all Israel, that are near, and that are far off, through all the countries whither thou hast driven them, because of their trespass that they have trespassed against thee.

8 **O Lord, to us** belongeth confusion of face, to our kings, to our princes, and to our fathers,
because we have sinned against thee.

9 **To the Lord our God** belong mercies and forgivenesses,
though we have rebelled against him;

10 **Neither** have we obeyed the voice of the LORD our God,
to walk in his laws,
which he set before us by his servants the prophets.

11 **Yea, all Israel** have transgressed thy law, even by departing,
that they might not obey thy voice;
therefore the curse is poured upon us, and the oath that is written in the law of Moses the servant of God,
because we have sinned against him.

12 **And he** hath confirmed his words,
which he spake against us, and against our judges that judged us,
by bringing upon us a great evil:
for under the whole heaven hath not been done as hath been done upon Jerusalem.

13 **As it** is written in the law of Moses,
all this evil is come upon us:
yet made we not our prayer before the LORD our God,
that we might turn from our iniquities,
and understand thy truth.

14 **Therefore** hath the LORD watched upon the evil,
and brought it upon us:
for the LORD our God is righteous in all his works which he doeth:
for we obeyed not his voice.

15 **And now, O Lord our God,** {that hast brought thy people forth out of the land of Egypt with a mighty hand}, {and hast gotten thee renown, as at this day}; we have sinned,
we have done wickedly.

16 **O Lord, according to all thy righteousness,** I beseech thee,
let thine anger and thy fury be turned away from thy city Jerusalem, thy holy mountain:
because for our sins, and for the iniquities of our fathers, Jerusalem and thy people are become a reproach to all that are about us.

17 **Now therefore, O our God, hear** the prayer of thy servant, and his supplications,
and cause thy face to shine upon thy sanctuary that is desolate, for the Lord's sake.

18 **O my God, incline** thine ear,
and hear;
open thine eyes,
and behold our desolations, and the city which is called by thy name:
for we do not present our supplications before thee for our righteousnesses, but for thy great mercies.

19 **O Lord, hear;**
O Lord, forgive;
O Lord, hearken and do;
defer not, for thine own sake, O my God:
for thy city and thy people are called by thy name.

20 **And whiles** I was speaking,
and praying,
and confessing my sin and the sin of my people Israel,
and presenting my supplication before the LORD my God for the holy mountain of my God;

21 **Yea, whiles I** was speaking in prayer,

even the man Gabriel, {whom I had seen in the vision at the beginning}, {being caused to fly swiftly}, touched me about the time of the evening oblation.
22 **And he** informed me,
and talked with me,
and said,
O Daniel, I am now come forth
to give thee skill and understanding.
23 **At the beginning of thy supplications** the commandment came forth,
and I am come
to shew thee;
for thou art greatly beloved:
therefore understand the matter,
and consider the vision.
24 **Seventy weeks** are determined upon thy people and upon thy holy city,
to finish the transgression,
and to make an end of sins,
and to make reconciliation for iniquity,
and to bring in everlasting righteousness,
and to seal up the vision and prophecy,
and to anoint the most Holy.
25 **Know therefore and understand,**
that from the going forth of the commandment to restore and to build Jerusalem unto the Messiah the Prince shall be seven weeks, and threescore and two weeks:
the street shall be built again, and the wall, even in troublous times.
26 **And after threescore and two weeks** shall Messiah be cut off, but not for himself:
and the people of the prince that shall come shall destroy the city and the sanctuary;
and the end thereof shall be with a flood,
and unto the end of the war desolations are determined.
27 **And he** shall confirm the covenant with many for one week:
and in the midst of the week he shall cause the sacrifice and the oblation to cease,
and for the overspreading of abominations he shall make it desolate, even until the consummation,
and that determined shall be poured upon the desolate.

10

In the third year of Cyrus king of Persia a thing was revealed unto Daniel,
whose name was called Belteshazzar;
and the thing was true,
but the time appointed was long:
and he understood the thing,
and had understanding of the vision.
2 **In those days** I Daniel was mourning three full weeks.
3 **I** ate no pleasant bread,
neither came flesh nor wine in my mouth,
neither did I anoint myself at all,
till three whole weeks were fulfilled.
4 **And in the four and twentieth day of the first month**, {as I was by the side of the great river}, {which is Hiddekel};
5 Then I lifted up mine eyes,
and looked,
and behold a certain man clothed in linen,
whose loins were girded with fine gold of Uphaz:
6 **His body** also was like the beryl, and his face as the appearance of lightning, and his eyes as lamps of fire, and his arms and his feet like in colour to polished brass, and the voice of his words like the voice of a multitude.
7 **And I Daniel alone** saw the vision:
for the men that were with me saw not the vision;
but a great quaking fell upon them,
so that they fled
to hide themselves.
8 **Therefore I** was left alone,
and saw this great vision,
and there remained no strength in me:
for my comeliness was turned in me into corruption,
and I retained no strength.
9 **Yet** heard I the voice of his words:
and when I heard the voice of his words,
then was I in a deep sleep on my face, and my face toward the ground.
10 **And, {behold}, an hand** touched me,
which set me upon my knees and upon the palms of my hands.
11 **And he** said unto me,
O Daniel, a man greatly beloved, understand the words that I speak unto thee,
and stand upright:
for unto thee am I now sent.
And when he had spoken this word unto me,
I stood trembling.
12 **Then** said he unto me,
Fear not, Daniel:
for from the first day that thou didst set thine heart to understand, and to chasten thyself before thy God, thy words were heard,
and I am come for thy words.
13 **But the prince of the kingdom of Persia** withstood me one and twenty days:
but, {lo}, Michael, one of the chief princes, came
to help me;
and I remained there with the kings of Persia.
14 **Now I** am come
to make thee understand
what shall befall thy people in the latter days:
for yet the vision is for many days.
15 **And when he** had spoken such words unto me,
I set my face toward the ground,
and I became dumb.
16 **And, {behold}, one like the similitude of the sons of men** touched my lips:
then I opened my mouth,
and spake,
and said unto him that stood before me,
O my lord, by the vision my sorrows are turned upon me,
and I have retained no strength.
17 **For how** can the servant of this my lord talk with this my lord?
for as for me, straightway there remained no strength in me,
neither is there breath left in me.
18 **Then there** came again and touched me one like the appearance of a man,
and he strengthened me,
19 **And** said,
O man greatly beloved, fear not:
peace be unto thee,

be strong,
yea, be strong.
And when he had spoken unto me,
I was strengthened,
and said,
Let my lord speak;
for thou hast strengthened me.
20 **Then** said he,
Knowest thou
wherefore I come unto thee?
and now will I return to fight with the prince of Persia:
and when I am gone forth,
lo,
the prince of Grecia shall come.
21 **But I** will shew thee that which is noted in the scripture of truth:
and there is none that holdeth with me in these things, but Michael your prince.

11

Also I in the first year of Darius the Mede, even I, stood to confirm and to strengthen him.

2 **And now** will I shew thee the truth.
Behold,
there shall stand up yet three kings in Persia;
and the fourth shall be far richer than they all:
and by his strength through his riches he shall stir up all against the realm of Grecia.
3 **And a mighty king** shall stand up,
that shall rule with great dominion,
and do according to his will.
4 **And when he** shall stand up,
his kingdom shall be broken,
and shall be divided toward the four winds of heaven; and not to his posterity, nor according to his dominion which he ruled:
for his kingdom shall be plucked up, even for others beside those.
5 **And the king of the south** shall be strong, and one of his princes;
and he shall be strong above him,
and have dominion;
his dominion shall be a great dominion.
6 **And in the end of years** they shall join themselves together;
for the king's daughter of the south shall come to the king of the north
to make an agreement:
but she shall not retain the power of the arm;
neither shall he stand, nor his arm:
but she shall be given up, and they that brought her, and he that begat her, and he that strengthened her in these times.
7 **But out of a branch of her roots** shall one stand up in his estate,
which shall come with an army,
and shall enter into the fortress of the king of the north,
and shall deal against them,
and shall prevail:
8 **And** shall also carry captives into Egypt their gods, with their princes, and with their precious vessels of silver and of gold;
and he shall continue more years than the king of the north.
9 **So the king of the south** shall come into his kingdom,
and shall return into his own land.
10 **But his sons** shall be stirred up,
and shall assemble a multitude of great forces:
and one shall certainly come,
and overflow,
and pass through:
then shall he return,
and be stirred up, even to his fortress.
11 **And the king of the south** shall be moved with choler,
and shall come forth and fight with him, even with the king of the north:
and he shall set forth a great multitude;
but the multitude shall be given into his hand.
12 **And when he** hath taken away the multitude,
his heart shall be lifted up;
and he shall cast down many ten thousands:
but he shall not be strengthened by it.
13 **For the king of the north** shall return,
and shall set forth a multitude greater than the former,
and shall certainly come after certain years with a great army and with much riches.
14 **And in those times** there shall many stand up against the king of the south:
also the robbers of thy people shall exalt themselves
to establish the vision;
but they shall fall.
15 **So the king of the north** shall come,
and cast up a mount,
and take the most fenced cities:
and the arms of the south shall not withstand, neither his chosen people,
neither shall there be any strength to withstand.
16 **But he that cometh against him** shall do according to his own will,
and none shall stand before him:
and he shall stand in the glorious land,
which by his hand shall be consumed.
17 **He** shall also set his face to enter with the strength of his whole kingdom, and upright ones with him;
thus shall he do:
and he shall give him the daughter of women,
corrupting her:
but she shall not stand on his side,
neither be for him.
18 **After this** shall he turn his face unto the isles,
and shall take many:
but a prince for his own behalf shall cause the reproach offered by him to cease;
without his own reproach he shall cause it to turn upon him.
19 **Then he** shall turn his face toward the fort of his own land:
but he shall stumble and fall,
and not be found.
20 **Then** shall stand up in his estate a raiser of taxes in the glory of the kingdom:
but within few days he shall be destroyed, neither in anger, nor in battle.
21 **And in his estate** shall stand up a vile person,
to whom they shall not give the honour of the kingdom:
but he shall come in peaceably,
and obtain the kingdom by flatteries.
22 **And with the arms of a flood** shall they be overflown from before him,
and shall be broken; yea, also the prince of the covenant.
23 **And after the league** made with him
he shall work deceitfully:
for he shall come up,

and shall become strong with a small people.

24 **He** shall enter peaceably even upon the fattest places of the province;
and he shall do that which his fathers have not done, nor his fathers' fathers;
he shall scatter among them the prey, and spoil, and riches:
yea, and he shall forecast his devices against the strong holds, even for a time.

25 **And he** shall stir up his power and his courage against the king of the south with a great army;
and the king of the south shall be stirred up to battle with a very great and mighty army;
but he shall not stand:
for they shall forecast devices against him.

26 **Yea, they that feed of the portion of his meat** shall destroy him,
and his army shall overflow:
and many shall fall down slain.

27 **And both of these kings' hearts** shall be to do mischief,
and they shall speak lies at one table;
but it shall not prosper:
for yet the end shall be at the time appointed.

28 **Then** shall he return into his land with great riches;
and his heart shall be against the holy covenant;
and he shall do exploits,
and return to his own land.

29 **At the time appointed** he shall return,
and come toward the south;
but it shall not be as the former, or as the latter.

30 **For the ships of Chittim** shall come against him:
therefore he shall be grieved,
and return,
and have indignation against the holy covenant:
so shall he do;
he shall even return,
and have intelligence with them that forsake the holy covenant.

31 **And arms** shall stand on his part,
and they shall pollute the sanctuary of strength,
and shall take away the daily sacrifice,
and they shall place the abomination that maketh desolate.

32 **And such as do wickedly against the covenant** shall he corrupt by flatteries:
but the people that do know their God shall be strong,
and do exploits.

33 **And they that understand among the people** shall instruct many:
yet they shall fall by the sword, and by flame, by captivity, and by spoil, many days.

34 **Now when they** shall fall,
they shall be holpen with a little help:
but many shall cleave to them with flatteries.

35 **And some of them of understanding** shall fall,
to try them,
and to purge,
and to make them white, even to the time of the end:
because it is yet for a time appointed.

36 **And the king** shall do according to his will;
and he shall exalt himself,
and magnify himself above every god,
and shall speak marvellous things against the God of gods,
and shall prosper till the indignation be accomplished:
for that that is determined shall be done.

37 **Neither** shall he regard the God of his fathers, nor the desire of women, nor regard any god:
for he shall magnify himself above all.

38 **But in his estate** shall he honour the God of forces:
and a god whom his fathers knew not shall he honour with gold, and silver, and with precious stones, and pleasant things.

39 **Thus** shall he do in the most strong holds with a strange god,
whom he shall acknowledge and increase with glory:
and he shall cause them to rule over many,
and shall divide the land for gain.

40 **And at the time of the end** shall the king of the south push at him:
and the king of the north shall come against him like a whirlwind, with chariots, and with horsemen, and with many ships;
and he shall enter into the countries,
and shall overflow and pass over.

41 **He** shall enter also into the glorious land,
and many countries shall be overthrown:
but these shall escape out of his hand, even Edom, and Moab, and the chief of the children of Ammon.

42 **He** shall stretch forth his hand also upon the countries:
and the land of Egypt shall not escape.

43 **But he** shall have power over the treasures of gold and of silver, and over all the precious things of Egypt:
and the Libyans and the Ethiopians shall be at his steps.

44 **But tidings out of the east and out of the north** shall trouble him:
therefore he shall go forth with great fury
to destroy,
and utterly to make away many.

45 **And he** shall plant the tabernacles of his palace between the seas in the glorious holy mountain;
yet he shall come to his end,
and none shall help him.

12 **And at that time** shall Michael stand up, the great prince which standeth for the children of thy people:
and there shall be a time of trouble,
such as never was
since there was a nation even to that same time:
and at that time thy people shall be delivered, every one that shall be found written in the book.

2 **And many of them that sleep in the dust of the earth** shall awake, some to everlasting life, and some to shame and everlasting contempt.

3 **And they that be wise** shall shine as the brightness of the firmament; and they that turn

many to righteousness as the stars for ever and ever.

4 **But thou, O Daniel,** shut up the words,
and seal the book, even to the time of the end:
many shall run to and fro,
and knowledge shall be increased.

5 **Then I Daniel** looked,
and, {behold}, there stood other two, the one on this side of the bank of the river, and the other on that side of the bank of the river.

6 **And one** said to the man clothed in linen,
which was upon the waters of the river,
How long shall it be to the end of these wonders?

7 **And I** heard the man clothed in linen,
which was upon the waters of the river,
when he held up his right hand and his left hand unto heaven,
and sware by him that liveth for ever
that it shall be for a time, times, and an half;
and when he shall have accomplished to scatter the power of the holy people,
all these things shall be finished.

8 **And I** heard,
but I understood not:
then said I,
O my Lord, what shall be the end of these things?

9 **And he** said,
Go thy way, Daniel:
for the words are closed up and sealed till the time of the end.

10 **Many** shall be purified,
and made white,
and tried;
but the wicked shall do wickedly:
and none of the wicked shall understand;
but the wise shall understand.

11 **And from the time that the daily sacrifice** shall be taken away,
and the abomination that maketh desolate set up,
there shall be a thousand two hundred and ninety days.

12 **Blessed** is he that waiteth, and cometh to the thousand three hundred and five and thirty days.

13 **But go thou** thy way till the end be:
for thou shalt rest,
and stand in thy lot at the end of the days.

Hosea

The Book of Hosea, written by the prophet Hosea, is a collection of oracles and prophecies that warn the people of Israel about the consequences of their sins and the need for repentance and deliverance. It takes place approximately 200 years before the Babylonian exile, during the same general period as the Books of Isaiah, Micah, and Jonah, all of which provide a rich and diverse understanding of the prophetic voices of the time.

Hosea's messages and visions include several directives designed to guide and instruct the people of Israel in their relationship with God. For example, Hosea uses the story of his marriage to an unfaithful wife, Gomer, as a metaphor for God's relationship with Israel, illustrating the depth of God's love and His desire for His people to return to Him. He also repeatedly calls the people of Israel to repent of their sins and turn back to God, warning them that failing to do so will result in dire consequences, including exile and utter destruction. Despite these warnings, Hosea also offers the hope of restoration and renewal, promising that God will bring His people back from exile and restore their fortunes.

Throughout his book, the prophet underscores the paramount importance of love and mercy in God's dealings with His people. He reminds the Israelites that God's compassion is boundless. He yearns to forgive and restore everyone who seeks Him with a repentant heart. Finally, Hosea predicts the future arrival of a messianic figure who will restore the fortunes of Israel and bring about a new era of peace and prosperity. This prophecy foreshadows the coming of Jesus Christ. Overall, the book serves as a profound reminder of God's unwavering love for His people, evoking a deep sense of gratitude and humility in those who repent and seek to follow God's path.

1 The word of the LORD that came unto Hosea, the son of Beeri, in the days of Uzziah, Jotham, Ahaz, and Hezekiah, kings of Judah, and in the days of Jeroboam the son of Joash, king of Israel.

2 The beginning of the word of the LORD by Hosea.
And the LORD said to Hosea,
Go,
take unto thee a wife of whoredoms and children of whoredoms:
for the land hath committed great whoredom,
departing from the LORD.

3 **So he** went and took Gomer the daughter of Diblaim;
which conceived,
and bare him a son.

4 **And the LORD** said unto him,
Call his name Jezreel;
for yet a little while, and I will avenge the blood of Jezreel upon the house of Jehu,
and will cause to cease the kingdom of the house of Israel.

5 **And it** shall come to pass at that day,
that I will break the bow of Israel, in the valley of Jezreel.

6 **And she** conceived again,
and bare a daughter.
And God said unto him,
Call her name Loruhamah:
for I will no more have mercy upon the house of Israel;
but I will utterly take them away.

7 **But I** will have mercy upon the house of Judah,
and will save them by the LORD their God,
and will not save them by bow, nor by sword, nor by battle, by horses, nor by horsemen.

8 **Now when she** had weaned Loruhamah,
she conceived,
and bare a son.

9 **Then** said God,
Call his name Loammi:
for ye are not my people,
and I will not be your God.

10 **Yet the number of the children of Israel** shall be as the sand of the sea,
which cannot be measured
nor numbered;
and it shall come to pass,
that in the place where it was said unto them, {Ye are not my people}, there it shall be said unto them, {Ye are the sons of the living God}.

11 **Then** shall the children of Judah and the children of Israel be gathered together,
and appoint themselves one head,
and they shall come up out of the land:
for great shall be the day of Jezreel.

2 **Say ye** unto your brethren, Ammi; and to your sisters, Ruhamah.

2 **Plead** with your mother,
plead:
for she is not my wife,
neither am I her husband:
let her therefore put away her whoredoms out of her sight, and her adulteries from between her breasts;

3 **Lest I** strip her naked,
and set her as in the day that she was born,
and make her as a wilderness,
and set her like a dry land,
and slay her with thirst.

4 **And I** will not have mercy upon her children;
for they be the children of whoredoms.

5 **For their mother** hath played the harlot:
she that conceived them hath done shamefully:
for she said,

I will go after my lovers,
that give me my bread and my water, my wool and my flax, mine oil and my drink.
6 **Therefore, {behold}, I** will hedge up thy way with thorns,
and make a wall,
that she shall not find her paths.
7 **And she** shall follow after her lovers,
but she shall not overtake them;
and she shall seek them,
but shall not find them:
then shall she say,
I will go and return to my first husband;
for then was it better with me than now.
8 **For she** did not know
that I gave her corn, and wine, and oil,
and multiplied her silver and gold,
which they prepared for Baal.
9 **Therefore** will I return,
and take away my corn in the time thereof, and my wine in the season thereof,
and will recover my wool and my flax given to cover her nakedness.
10 **And now** will I discover her lewdness in the sight of her lovers,
and none shall deliver her out of mine hand.
11 **I** will also cause all her mirth to cease, her feast days, her new moons, and her sabbaths, and all her solemn feasts.
12 **And I** will destroy her vines and her fig trees,
whereof she hath said,
These are my rewards that my lovers have given me:
and I will make them a forest,
and the beasts of the field shall eat them.
13 **And I** will visit upon her the days of Baalim,
wherein she burned incense to them,
and she decked herself with her earrings and her jewels,
and she went after her lovers,
and forgat me,
saith the LORD.
14 **Therefore, {behold}, I** will allure her,
and bring her into the wilderness,
and speak comfortably unto her.
15 **And I** will give her her vineyards from thence, and the valley of Achor for a door of hope:
and she shall sing there, as in the days of her youth, and as in the day when she came up out of the land of Egypt.
16 **And it** shall be at that day,
saith the LORD,
that thou shalt call me Ishi;
and shalt call me no more Baali.
17 **For I** will take away the names of Baalim out of her mouth,
and they shall no more be remembered by their name.
18 **And in that day** will I make a covenant for them with the beasts of the field and with the fowls of heaven, and with the creeping things of the ground:
and I will break the bow and the sword and the battle out of the earth,
and will make them to lie down safely.
19 **And I** will betroth thee unto me for ever;
yea, I will betroth thee unto me in righteousness, and in judgment, and in lovingkindness, and in mercies.
20 **I** will even betroth thee unto me in faithfulness:
and thou shalt know the LORD.
21 **And it** shall come to pass in that day,
I will hear,
saith the LORD,
I will hear the heavens,
and they shall hear the earth;
22 **And the earth** shall hear the corn, and the wine, and the oil;
and they shall hear Jezreel.
23 **And I** will sow her unto me in the earth;
and I will have mercy upon her that had not obtained mercy;
and I will say to them which were not my people,
Thou art my people;
and they shall say,
Thou art my God.

3

Then said the LORD unto me,
Go yet,
love a woman beloved of her friend, yet an adulteress, according to the love of the LORD toward the children of Israel,
who look to other gods,
and love flagons of wine.
2 **So I** bought her to me for fifteen pieces of silver, and for an homer of barley, and an half homer of barley:
3 **And I** said unto her,
Thou shalt abide for me many days;
thou shalt not play the harlot,
and thou shalt not be for another man:
so will I also be for thee.
4 **For the children of Israel** shall abide many days without a king, and without a prince, and without a sacrifice, and without an image, and without an ephod, and without teraphim:
5 **Afterward** shall the children of Israel return,
and seek the LORD their God, and David their king;
and shall fear the LORD and his goodness in the latter days.

4

Hear the word of the LORD, ye children of Israel:
for the LORD hath a controversy with the inhabitants of the land,
because there is no truth, nor mercy, nor knowledge of God in the land.
2 By swearing,
and lying,
and killing,
and stealing,
and committing adultery**,**
they break out,
and blood toucheth blood.
3 **Therefore** shall the land mourn,
and every one that dwelleth therein shall languish, with the beasts of the field, and with the fowls of heaven;
yea, the fishes of the sea also shall be taken away.
4 **Yet let no man** strive,
nor reprove another:
for thy people are as they that strive with the priest.
5 **Therefore** shalt thou fall in the day,
and the prophet also shall fall with thee in the night,
and I will destroy thy mother.
6 **My people** are destroyed for lack of knowledge:
because thou hast rejected knowledge,
I will also reject thee,
that thou shalt be no priest to me:

seeing thou hast forgotten the law
of thy God,
I will also forget thy children.
7 **As they** were increased,
so they sinned against me:
therefore will I change their glory
into shame.
8 **They** eat up the sin of my people,
and they set their heart on their
iniquity.
9 **And there** shall be, like people,
like priest:
and I will punish them for their
ways,
and reward them their doings.
10 **For they** shall eat,
and not have enough:
they shall commit whoredom,
and shall not increase:
because they have left off to take
heed to the LORD.
11 **Whoredom and wine and new
wine** take away the heart.
12 **My people** ask counsel at their
stocks,
and their staff declareth unto
them:
for the spirit of whoredoms hath
caused them to err,
and they have gone a whoring from
under their God.
13 **They** sacrifice upon the tops of
the mountains,
and burn incense upon the hills,
under oaks and poplars and elms,
because the shadow thereof is
good:
therefore your daughters shall
commit whoredom,
and your spouses shall commit
adultery.
14 I will not punish your daughters
when they commit whoredom,
nor your spouses when they
commit adultery:
for themselves are separated with
whores,
and they sacrifice with harlots:
**therefore the people that doth not
understand** shall fall.
15 **Though thou, Israel,** play the
harlot,
yet let not Judah offend;
and come not ye unto Gilgal,
neither go ye up to Bethaven,
nor swear,
The LORD liveth.
16 **For Israel** slideth back as a
backsliding heifer:
now the LORD will feed them as a
lamb in a large place.
17 **Ephraim** is joined to idols:
let him alone.
18 **Their drink** is sour:
they have committed whoredom
continually:
her rulers with shame do love,
Give ye.
19 **The wind** hath bound her up in
her wings, and they shall be
ashamed because of their
sacrifices.

5 **Hear ye** this, O priests;
and hearken, ye house of
Israel;
and give ye ear, O house of the
king;
for judgment is toward you,
because ye have been a snare on
Mizpah,
and a net spread upon Tabor.
2 **And the revolters** are profound to
make slaughter,
though I have been a rebuker of
them all.
3 I know Ephraim,
and Israel is not hid from me:
for now, O Ephraim, thou
committest whoredom,
and Israel is defiled.
4 **They** will not frame their doings to
turn unto their God:
for the spirit of whoredoms is in
the midst of them,
and they have not known the
LORD.
5 **And the pride of Israel** doth
testify to his face:
therefore shall Israel and Ephraim
fall in their iniquity:
Judah also shall fall with them.
6 **They** shall go with their flocks and
with their herds
to seek the LORD;
but they shall not find him;
he hath withdrawn himself from
them.
7 **They** have dealt treacherously
against the LORD:
for they have begotten strange
children:
now shall a month devour them
with their portions.
8 **Blow ye** the cornet in Gibeah, and
the trumpet in Ramah:
cry aloud at Bethaven, after thee, O
Benjamin.
9 **Ephraim** shall be desolate in the
day of rebuke:
among the tribes of Israel have I
made known that which shall
surely be.
10 **The princes of Judah** were like
them that remove the bound:
therefore I will pour out my wrath
upon them like water.
11 **Ephraim** is oppressed and broken
in judgment,
because he willingly walked after
the commandment.
12 **Therefore** will I be unto Ephraim
as a moth, and to the house of
Judah as rottenness.
13 **When Ephraim** saw his sickness,
and Judah saw his wound,
then went Ephraim to the Assyrian,
and sent to king Jareb:
yet could he not heal you,
nor cure you of your wound.
14 **For I** will be unto Ephraim as a
lion, and as a young lion to the
house of Judah:
I, even I, will tear and go away;
I will take away,
and none shall rescue him.
15 **I** will go and return to my place,
till they acknowledge their offence,
and seek my face:
in their affliction they will seek me
early.

6 **Come,**
and let us return unto the
LORD:
for he hath torn,
and he will heal us;
he hath smitten,
and he will bind us up.
2 **After two days** will he revive us:
in the third day he will raise us up,
and we shall live in his sight.
3 **Then** shall we know,
if we follow on to know the LORD:
his going forth is prepared as the
morning;
and he shall come unto us as the
rain, as the latter and former rain
unto the earth.
4 **O Ephraim, what** shall I do unto
thee?
O Judah, what shall I do unto thee?
for your goodness is as a morning
cloud,
and as the early dew it goeth away.
5 **Therefore** have I hewed them by
the prophets;

I have slain them by the words of my mouth:
and thy judgments are as the light that goeth forth.
6 **For I** desired mercy, and not sacrifice; and the knowledge of God more than burnt offerings.
7 **But they like men** have transgressed the covenant:
there have they dealt treacherously against me.
8 **Gilead** is a city of them that work iniquity,
and is polluted with blood.
9 **And as troops of robbers** wait for a man,
so the company of priests murder in the way by consent:
for they commit lewdness.
10 **I** have seen an horrible thing in the house of Israel:
there is the whoredom of Ephraim,
Israel is defiled.
11 **Also, O Judah, he** hath set an harvest for thee,
when I returned the captivity of my people.

7 **When I** would have healed Israel,
then the iniquity of Ephraim was discovered, and the wickedness of Samaria:
for they commit falsehood;
and the thief cometh in,
and the troop of robbers spoileth without.
2 **And they** consider not in their hearts
that I remember all their wickedness:
now their own doings have beset them about;
they are before my face.
3 **They** make the king glad with their wickedness, and the princes with their lies.
4 **They** are all adulterers, as an oven heated by the baker,
who ceaseth from raising after he hath kneaded the dough,
until it be leavened.
5 **In the day of our king** the princes have made him sick with bottles of wine;
he stretched out his hand with scorners.
6 **For they** have made ready their heart like an oven,
whiles they lie in wait:
their baker sleepeth all the night;
in the morning it burneth as a flaming fire.
7 **They** are all hot as an oven,
and have devoured their judges;
all their kings are fallen:
there is none among them that calleth unto me.
8 **Ephraim, he** hath mixed himself among the people;
Ephraim is a cake not turned.
9 **Strangers** have devoured his strength,
and he knoweth it not:
yea, gray hairs are here and there upon him,
yet he knoweth not.
10 **And the pride of Israel** testifieth to his face:
and they do not return to the LORD their God,
nor seek him for all this.
11 **Ephraim** also is like a silly dove without heart:
they call to Egypt,
they go to Assyria.
12 **When they** shall go,
I will spread my net upon them;
I will bring them down as the fowls of the heaven;
I will chastise them,
as their congregation hath heard.
13 **Woe** unto them!
for they have fled from me:
destruction unto them!
because they have transgressed against me:
though I have redeemed them,
yet they have spoken lies against me.
14 **And they** have not cried unto me with their heart,
when they howled upon their beds:
they assemble themselves for corn and wine,
and they rebel against me.
15 **Though I** have bound and strengthened their arms,
yet do they imagine mischief against me.
16 **They** return, but not to the most High:
they are like a deceitful bow:
their princes shall fall by the sword for the rage of their tongue:
this shall be their derision in the land of Egypt.

8 **Set** the trumpet to thy mouth.
He shall come as an eagle against the house of the LORD,
because they have transgressed my covenant,
and trespassed against my law.
2 **Israel** shall cry unto me,
My God, we know thee.
3 **Israel** hath cast off the thing that is good:
the enemy shall pursue him.
4 **They** have set up kings, but not by me:
they have made princes,
and I knew it not:
of their silver and their gold have they made them idols,
that they may be cut off.
5 **Thy calf, O Samaria,** hath cast thee off;
mine anger is kindled against them:
how long will it be ere they attain to innocency?
6 **For from Israel** was it also:
the workman made it;
therefore it is not God:
but the calf of Samaria shall be broken in pieces.
7 **For they** have sown the wind,
and they shall reap the whirlwind:
it hath no stalk;
the bud shall yield no meal:
if so be it yield,
the strangers shall swallow it up.
8 **Israel** is swallowed up:
now shall they be among the Gentiles as a vessel wherein is no pleasure.
9 **For they** are gone up to Assyria, a wild ass alone by himself:
Ephraim hath hired lovers.
10 **Yea, though they** have hired among the nations,
now will I gather them,
and they shall sorrow a little for the burden of the king of princes.
11 **Because Ephraim** hath made many altars to sin,
altars shall be unto him to sin.
12 **I** have written to him the great things of my law,
but they were counted as a strange thing.
13 **They** sacrifice flesh for the sacrifices of mine offerings,
and eat it;
but the LORD accepteth them not;
now will he remember their iniquity,

and visit their sins:
they shall return to Egypt.
14 **For Israel** hath forgotten his Maker,
and buildeth temples;
and Judah hath multiplied fenced cities:
but I will send a fire upon his cities,
and it shall devour the palaces thereof.

9 **Rejoice not, O Israel,** for joy, as other people:
for thou hast gone a whoring from thy God,
thou hast loved a reward upon every cornfloor.
2 **The floor and the winepress** shall not feed them,
and the new wine shall fail in her.
3 **They** shall not dwell in the LORD's land;
but Ephraim shall return to Egypt,
and they shall eat unclean things in Assyria.
4 **They** shall not offer wine offerings to the LORD,
neither shall they be pleasing unto him:
their sacrifices shall be unto them as the bread of mourners;
all that eat thereof shall be polluted:
for their bread for their soul shall not come into the house of the LORD.
5 **What** will ye do in the solemn day, and in the day of the feast of the LORD?
6 **For, {lo}, they** are gone because of destruction:
Egypt shall gather them up,
Memphis shall bury them:
the pleasant places for their silver, nettles shall possess them:
thorns shall be in their tabernacles.
7 **The days of visitation** are come,
the days of recompence are come;
Israel shall know it:
the prophet is a fool,
the spiritual man is mad, for the multitude of thine iniquity, and the great hatred.
8 **The watchman of Ephraim** was with my God:
but the prophet is a snare of a fowler in all his ways, and hatred in the house of his God.
9 **They** have deeply corrupted themselves, as in the days of Gibeah:
therefore he will remember their iniquity,
he will visit their sins.
10 **I** found Israel like grapes in the wilderness;
I saw your fathers as the firstripe in the fig tree at her first time:
but they went to Baalpeor,
and separated themselves unto that shame;
and their abominations were according as they loved.
11 **As for Ephraim,** their glory shall fly away like a bird, from the birth, and from the womb, and from the conception.
12 **Though they** bring up their children,
yet will I bereave them,
that there shall not be a man left:
yea, woe also to them when I depart from them!
13 **Ephraim,** {as I saw Tyrus}, is planted in a pleasant place:
but Ephraim shall bring forth his children to the murderer.
14 **Give** them, O LORD:
what wilt thou give?
give them a miscarrying womb and dry breasts.
15 **All their wickedness** is in Gilgal:
for there I hated them:
for the wickedness of their doings I will drive them out of mine house,
I will love them no more:
all their princes are revolters.
16 **Ephraim** is smitten,
their root is dried up,
they shall bear no fruit:
yea, though they bring forth,
yet will I slay even the beloved fruit of their womb.
17 **My God** will cast them away,
because they did not hearken unto him:
and they shall be wanderers among the nations.

10 **Israel** is an empty vine,
he bringeth forth fruit unto himself:
according to the multitude of his fruit he hath increased the altars;
according to the goodness of his land they have made goodly images.
2 **Their heart** is divided;
now shall they be found faulty:
he shall break down their altars,
he shall spoil their images.
3 **For now they** shall say,
We have no king,
because we feared not the LORD;
what then should a king do to us?
4 **They** have spoken words,
swearing falsely in making a covenant:
thus judgment springeth up as hemlock in the furrows of the field.
5 **The inhabitants of Samaria** shall fear because of the calves of Bethaven:
for the people thereof shall mourn over it, and the priests thereof that rejoiced on it, for the glory thereof,
because it is departed from it.
6 **It** shall be also carried unto Assyria for a present to king Jareb:
Ephraim shall receive shame,
and Israel shall be ashamed of his own counsel.
7 **As for Samaria,** her king is cut off as the foam upon the water.
8 **The high places also of Aven, the sin of Israel,** shall be destroyed:
the thorn and the thistle shall come up on their altars;
and they shall say to the mountains, {Cover us}; and to the hills, {Fall on us}.
9 **O Israel, thou** hast sinned from the days of Gibeah:
there they stood:
the battle in Gibeah against the children of iniquity did not overtake them.
10 **It is in my desire** that I should chastise them;
and the people shall be gathered against them,
when they shall bind themselves in their two furrows.
11 **And Ephraim** is as an heifer that is taught,
and loveth to tread out the corn;
but I passed over upon her fair neck:
I will make Ephraim to ride;
Judah shall plow,
and Jacob shall break his clods.
12 **Sow** to yourselves in righteousness,
reap in mercy;
break up your fallow ground:
for it is time to seek the LORD,

till he come and rain righteousness upon you.
13 **Ye** have plowed wickedness,
ye have reaped iniquity;
ye have eaten the fruit of lies:
because thou didst trust in thy way, in the multitude of thy mighty men.
14 **Therefore** shall a tumult arise among thy people,
and all thy fortresses shall be spoiled,
as Shalman spoiled Betharbel in the day of battle:
the mother was dashed in pieces upon her children.
15 **So** shall Bethel do unto you because of your great wickedness:
in a morning shall the king of Israel utterly be cut off.

11

When Israel was a child,
then I loved him,
and called my son out of Egypt.
2 **As they** called them,
so they went from them:
they sacrificed unto Baalim,
and burned incense to graven images.
3 **I** taught Ephraim also to go,
taking them by their arms;
but they knew not
that I healed them.
4 **I** drew them with cords of a man, with bands of love:
and I was to them as they that take off the yoke on their jaws,
and I laid meat unto them.
5 **He** shall not return into the land of Egypt,
and the Assyrian shall be his king,
because they refused to return.
6 **And the sword** shall abide on his cities,
and shall consume his branches,
and devour them, because of their own counsels.
7 **And my people** are bent to backsliding from me:
though they called them to the most High,
none at all would exalt him.
8 **How** shall I give thee up, Ephraim?
how shall I deliver thee, Israel?
how shall I make thee as Admah?
how shall I set thee as Zeboim?
mine heart is turned within me,
my repentings are kindled together.
9 **I** will not execute the fierceness of mine anger,
I will not return to destroy Ephraim:
for I am God, and not man; the Holy One in the midst of thee:
and I will not enter into the city.
10 **They** shall walk after the LORD:
he shall roar like a lion:
when he shall roar,
then the children shall tremble from the west.
11 **They** shall tremble as a bird out of Egypt, and as a dove out of the land of Assyria:
and I will place them in their houses,
saith the LORD.
12 **Ephraim** compasseth me about with lies, and the house of Israel with deceit:
but Judah yet ruleth with God,
and is faithful with the saints.

12

Ephraim feedeth on wind,
and followeth after the east wind:
he daily increaseth lies and desolation;
and they do make a covenant with the Assyrians,
and oil is carried into Egypt.
2 **The LORD** hath also a controversy with Judah,
and will punish Jacob according to his ways;
according to his doings will he recompense him.
3 **He** took his brother by the heel in the womb,
and by his strength he had power with God:
4 **Yea, he** had power over the angel,
and prevailed:
he wept,
and made supplication unto him:
he found him in Bethel,
and there he spake with us;
5 Even the LORD God of hosts;
the LORD is his memorial.
6 **Therefore turn thou** to thy God:
keep mercy and judgment
and wait on thy God continually.
7 **He** is a merchant,
the balances of deceit are in his hand:
he loveth to oppress.
8 **And Ephraim** said,
Yet I am become rich,
I have found me out substance:
in all my labours they shall find none iniquity in me that were sin.
9 **And I that am the LORD thy God from the land of Egypt** will yet make thee to dwell in tabernacles, as in the days of the solemn feast.
10 **I** have also spoken by the prophets,
and I have multiplied visions,
and used similitudes, by the ministry of the prophets.
11 **Is there** iniquity in Gilead?
surely they are vanity:
they sacrifice bullocks in Gilgal;
yea, their altars are as heaps in the furrows of the fields.
12 **And Jacob** fled into the country of Syria,
and Israel served for a wife,
and for a wife he kept sheep.
13 **And by a prophet** the LORD brought Israel out of Egypt,
and by a prophet was he preserved.
14 **Ephraim** provoked him to anger most bitterly:
therefore shall he leave his blood upon him,
and his reproach shall his Lord return unto him.

13

When Ephraim spake trembling,
he exalted himself in Israel;
but when he offended in Baal,
he died.
2 **And now they** sin more and more,
and have made them molten images of their silver, and idols according to their own understanding, all of it the work of the craftsmen:
they say of them,
Let the men that sacrifice kiss the calves.
3 **Therefore they** shall be as the morning cloud and as the early dew that passeth away, as the chaff that is driven with the whirlwind out of the floor, and as the smoke out of the chimney.
4 **Yet I** am the LORD thy God from the land of Egypt,
and thou shalt know no god but me:
for there is no saviour beside me.
5 **I** did know thee in the wilderness, in the land of great drought.
6 **According to their pasture,** so were they filled;
they were filled,

and their heart was exalted;
therefore have they forgotten me.
7 **Therefore I** will be unto them as a lion:
as a leopard by the way will I observe them:
8 **I** will meet them as a bear that is bereaved of her whelps,
and will rend the caul of their heart,
and there will I devour them like a lion:
the wild beast shall tear them.
9 **O Israel, thou** hast destroyed thyself;
but in me is thine help.
10 **I** will be thy king:
where is any other that may save thee in all thy cities?
and thy judges of whom thou saidst,
Give me a king and princes?
11 **I** gave thee a king in mine anger,
and took him away in my wrath.
12 **The iniquity of Ephraim** is bound up;
his sin is hid.
13 **The sorrows of a travailing woman** shall come upon him:
he is an unwise son;
for he should not stay long in the place of the breaking forth of children.
14 **I** will ransom them from the power of the grave;
I will redeem them from death:
O death, I will be thy plagues;
O grave, I will be thy destruction:
repentance shall be hid from mine eyes.
15 **Though he** be fruitful among his brethren,
an east wind shall come,
the wind of the LORD shall come up from the wilderness,
and his spring shall become dry,
and his fountain shall be dried up:
he shall spoil the treasure of all pleasant vessels.
16 **Samaria** shall become desolate;
for she hath rebelled against her God:
they shall fall by the sword:
their infants shall be dashed in pieces,
and their women with child shall be ripped up.

14 **O Israel, return** unto the LORD thy God;
for thou hast fallen by thine iniquity.
2 **Take** with you words,
and turn to the LORD:
say unto him,
Take away all iniquity,
and receive us graciously:
so will we render the calves of our lips.
3 **Asshur** shall not save us;
we will not ride upon horses:
neither will we say any more to the work of our hands,
Ye are our gods:
for in thee the fatherless findeth mercy.
4 **I** will heal their backsliding,
I will love them freely:
for mine anger is turned away from him.
5 **I** will be as the dew unto Israel:
he shall grow as the lily,
and cast forth his roots as Lebanon.
6 **His branches** shall spread,
and his beauty shall be as the olive tree, and his smell as Lebanon.
7 **They that dwell under his shadow** shall return;
they shall revive as the corn,
and grow as the vine:
the scent thereof shall be as the wine of Lebanon.
8 **Ephraim** shall say,
What have I to do any more with idols?
I have heard him,
and observed him:
I am like a green fir tree.
From me is thy fruit found.
9 **Who** is wise,
and he shall understand these things?
prudent,
and he shall know them?
for the ways of the LORD are right,
and the just shall walk in them:
but the transgressors shall fall therein.

Joel

The Book of Joel, penned by the prophet Joel to the people of the southern Kingdom of Judah, is renowned for its prophecies concerning the Day of the Lord and the paramount importance of repentance and returning to God. It vividly portrays a cataclysmic locust plague that ravages the land, decimating crops and livestock. Joel employs this calamity as a symbol of God's judgment, aiming to instill in the Judeans a profound sense of their dire situation. He intends to prompt them to return to God, seeking His forgiveness and mercy, thereby averting the dire consequences of judgment.

The book also showcases Joel's prophecies about the Day of the Lord as he delineates the harrowing events that will befall the nations that have forsaken God. This period of reckoning, when God judges the righteous and the wicked, will descend upon the world like a thief in the night. Those who have not adhered to His commandments will face His wrath. However, Joel also balances his admonition with the promise of hope and restoration for those who repent and return to God, offering comfort and reassurance.

In the concluding chapters, the prophet heralds the advent of the promised Savior and the certainty of eternal life for those who have faith. The Messiah will forge a new covenant with His people, and His arrival will herald an era of peace and prosperity. In essence, the Book of Joel underscores the importance of repentance and turning back to God while heralding the promise of salvation and restoration for those who embrace the Messiah. As the New Testament reveals, this promise is fulfilled in the Lord Jesus Christ.

1 **The word of the LORD** that came to Joel the son of Pethuel.

2 **Hear** this, ye old men,
and give ear, all ye inhabitants of the land.
Hath this been in your days, or even in the days of your fathers?
3 **Tell ye** your children of it,
and let your children tell their children, and their children another generation.
4 **That which the palmerworm hath left** hath the locust eaten;
and that which the locust hath left hath the cankerworm eaten;
and that which the cankerworm hath left hath the caterpiller eaten.
5 **Awake,** ye drunkards,
and weep;
and howl, all ye drinkers of wine, because of the new wine;
for it is cut off from your mouth.
6 **For a nation** is come up upon my land, strong, and without number,
whose teeth are the teeth of a lion,
and he hath the cheek teeth of a great lion.
7 **He** hath laid my vine waste,
and barked my fig tree:
he hath made it clean bare,
and cast it away;
the branches thereof are made white.
8 **Lament** like a virgin girded with sackcloth for the husband of her youth.
9 **The meat offering and the drink offering** is cut off from the house of the LORD;
the priests, the LORD's ministers, mourn.
10 **The field** is wasted,
the land mourneth;
for the corn is wasted:
the new wine is dried up,
the oil languisheth.
11 **Be ye** ashamed, O ye husbandmen;
howl, O ye vinedressers, for the wheat and for the barley;
because the harvest of the field is perished.
12 **The vine** is dried up,
and the fig tree languisheth;
the pomegranate tree, the palm tree also, and the apple tree, even all the trees of the field, are withered:
because joy is withered away from the sons of men.
13 **Gird** yourselves,
and lament, ye priests:
howl, ye ministers of the altar:
come,
lie all night in sackcloth, ye ministers of my God:
for the meat offering and the drink offering is withholden from the house of your God.
14 **Sanctify ye** a fast,
call a solemn assembly,
gather the elders and all the inhabitants of the land into the house of the LORD your God,
and cry unto the LORD,
15 Alas for the day!
for the day of the LORD is at hand,
and as a destruction from the Almighty shall it come.
16 **Is not the meat** cut off before our eyes, yea, joy and gladness from the house of our God?
17 **The seed** is rotten under their clods,
the garners are laid desolate,
the barns are broken down;
for the corn is withered.
18 **How** do the beasts groan!
the herds of cattle are perplexed,
because they have no pasture;
yea, the flocks of sheep are made desolate.
19 **O LORD, to thee** will I cry:
for the fire hath devoured the pastures of the wilderness,
and the flame hath burned all the trees of the field.
20 **The beasts of the field** cry also unto thee:
for the rivers of waters are dried up,

and the fire hath devoured the
pastures of the wilderness.

2 **Blow ye** the trumpet in Zion,
and sound an alarm in my
holy mountain:
let all the inhabitants of the land
tremble:
for the day of the LORD cometh,
for it is nigh at hand;
2 A day of darkness and of
gloominess, a day of clouds and of
thick darkness,
as the morning spread upon the
mountains: a great people and a
strong;
there hath not been ever the like,
neither shall be any more after it,
even to the years of many
generations.
3 **A fire** devoureth before them;
and behind them a flame burneth:
the land is as the garden of Eden
before them,
and behind them a desolate
wilderness;
yea, and nothing shall escape
them.
4 **The appearance of them** is as the
appearance of horses;
and as horsemen, so shall they run.
5 **Like the noise of chariots on the
tops of mountains** shall they
leap, like the noise of a flame of
fire that devoureth the stubble, as
a strong people set in battle array.
6 **Before their face** the people shall
be much pained:
all faces shall gather blackness.
7 **They** shall run like mighty men;
they shall climb the wall like men of
war;
and they shall march every one on
his ways,
and they shall not break their
ranks:
8 **Neither** shall one thrust another;
they shall walk every one in his
path:
and when they fall upon the
sword,
they shall not be wounded.
9 **They** shall run to and fro in the
city;
they shall run upon the wall,
they shall climb up upon the
houses;
they shall enter in at the windows
like a thief.
10 **The earth** shall quake before
them;
the heavens shall tremble:
the sun and the moon shall be
dark,
and the stars shall withdraw their
shining:
11 **And the LORD** shall utter his
voice before his army:
for his camp is very great:
for he is strong that executeth his
word:
for the day of the LORD is great
and very terrible;
and who can abide it?
12 **Therefore also now,** {saith the
LORD}, turn ye even to me with
all your heart, and with fasting,
and with weeping, and with
mourning:
13 **And rend** your heart, and not your
garments,
and turn unto the LORD your God:
for he is gracious and merciful,
slow to anger, and of great
kindness,
and repenteth him of the evil.
14 **Who** knoweth
if he will return and repent,
and leave a blessing behind him;
even a meat offering and a drink
offering unto the LORD your God?
15 **Blow** the trumpet in Zion,
sanctify a fast,
call a solemn assembly:
16 **Gather** the people,
sanctify the congregation,
assemble the elders,
gather the children, and those that
suck the breasts:
let the bridegroom go forth of his
chamber, and the bride out of her
closet.
17 **Let the priests, the ministers of
the LORD,** weep between the
porch and the altar,
and let them say,
Spare thy people, O LORD,
and give not thine heritage to
reproach,
that the heathen should rule over
them:
wherefore should they say among
the people,
Where is their God?
18 **Then** will the LORD be jealous for
his land,
and pity his people.
19 **Yea, the LORD** will answer and
say unto his people,
Behold,
I will send you corn, and wine, and
oil,
and ye shall be satisfied therewith:
and I will no more make you a
reproach among the heathen:
20 **But I** will remove far off from you
the northern army,
and will drive him into a land
barren and desolate, with his face
toward the east sea, and his
hinder part toward the utmost
sea,
and his stink shall come up,
and his ill savour shall come up,
because he hath done great things.
21 **Fear not,** O land;
be glad
and rejoice:
for the LORD will do great things.
22 **Be not** afraid, ye beasts of the
field:
for the pastures of the wilderness
do spring,
for the tree beareth her fruit,
the fig tree and the vine do yield
their strength.
23 **Be** glad then, ye children of Zion,
and rejoice in the LORD your God:
for he hath given you the former
rain moderately,
and he will cause to come down for
you the rain, the former rain, and
the latter rain in the first month.
24 **And the floors** shall be full of
wheat,
and the vats shall overflow with
wine and oil.
25 **And I** will restore to you the years
that the locust hath eaten, the
cankerworm, and the caterpiller,
and the palmerworm, my great
army which I sent among you.
26 **And ye** shall eat in plenty,
and be satisfied,
and praise the name of the LORD
your God,
that hath dealt wondrously with
you:
and my people shall never be
ashamed.
27 **And ye** shall know
that I am in the midst of Israel,
and that I am the LORD your God,
and none else:
and my people shall never be
ashamed.
28 **And it** shall come to pass
afterward,

that I will pour out my spirit upon all flesh;
and your sons and your daughters shall prophesy,
your old men shall dream dreams,
your young men shall see visions:
29 **And also upon the servants and upon the handmaids in those days** will I pour out my spirit.
30 **And I** will shew wonders in the heavens and in the earth, blood, and fire, and pillars of smoke.
31 **The sun** shall be turned into darkness,
and the moon into blood,
before the great and terrible day of the LORD come.
32 **And it** shall come to pass,
that whosoever shall call on the name of the LORD shall be delivered:
for in mount Zion and in Jerusalem shall be deliverance, {as the LORD hath said}, and in the remnant whom the LORD shall call.

3 **For, {behold}, in those days, and in that time,** {when I shall bring again the captivity of Judah and Jerusalem},
2 I will also gather all nations,
and will bring them down into the valley of Jehoshaphat,
and will plead with them there for my people and for my heritage Israel,
whom they have scattered among the nations,
and parted my land.
3 **And they** have cast lots for my people;
and have given a boy for an harlot,
and sold a girl for wine,
that they might drink.
4 **Yea, and what** have ye to do with me, O Tyre, and Zidon, and all the coasts of Palestine?
will ye render me a recompence?
and if ye recompense me,
swiftly and speedily will I return your recompence upon your own head;
5 **Because ye** have taken my silver and my gold,
and have carried into your temples my goodly pleasant things:
6 **The children also of Judah and the children of Jerusalem** have ye sold unto the Grecians,
that ye might remove them far from their border.
7 **Behold,**
I will raise them out of the place whither ye have sold them,
and will return your recompence upon your own head:
8 **And I** will sell your sons and your daughters into the hand of the children of Judah,
and they shall sell them to the Sabeans, to a people far off:
for the LORD hath spoken it.
9 **Proclaim ye** this among the Gentiles;
Prepare war,
wake up the mighty men,
let all the men of war draw near;
let them come up:
10 **Beat** your plowshares into swords and your pruninghooks into spears:
let the weak say,
I am strong.
11 **Assemble** yourselves,
and come, all ye heathen,
and gather yourselves together round about:
thither cause thy mighty ones to come down, O LORD.
12 **Let the heathen** be wakened,
and come up to the valley of Jehoshaphat:
for there will I sit to judge all the heathen round about.
13 **Put ye** in the sickle,
for the harvest is ripe:
come,
get you down;
for the press is full,
the fats overflow;
for their wickedness is great.
14 **Multitudes, multitudes** in the valley of decision:
for the day of the LORD is near in the valley of decision.
15 **The sun and the moon** shall be darkened,
and the stars shall withdraw their shining.
16 **The LORD** also shall roar out of Zion,
and utter his voice from Jerusalem;
and the heavens and the earth shall shake:
but the LORD will be the hope of his people, and the strength of the children of Israel.
17 **So** shall ye know
that I am the LORD your God
dwelling in Zion, my holy mountain:
then shall Jerusalem be holy,
and there shall no strangers pass through her any more.
18 **And it** shall come to pass in that day,
that the mountains shall drop down new wine,
and the hills shall flow with milk,
and all the rivers of Judah shall flow with waters,
and a fountain shall come forth out of the house of the LORD,
and shall water the valley of Shittim.
19 **Egypt** shall be a desolation,
and Edom shall be a desolate wilderness, for the violence against the children of Judah,
because they have shed innocent blood in their land.
20 **But Judah** shall dwell for ever,
and Jerusalem from generation to generation.
21 **For I** will cleanse their blood
that I have not cleansed:
for the LORD dwelleth in Zion.

Amos

The Book of Amos, written by the prophet Amos from the southern Kingdom of Judah, denounces the injustices and religious corruption of the Israelites. He calls the people to repentance, warning them of God's impending judgment. The book opens with Amos receiving a vision from God that calls him to prophesy against Israel and Judah. In his prophecies, he condemns the wealthy and powerful for mistreating the poor and vulnerable, and he denounces their hypocrisy in claiming to follow God.

Amos also predicts a series of natural disasters and military defeats that will befall the divided kingdoms if they do not repent. He then describes the Day of the Lord as a time of judgment and destruction for both nations rather than a day of deliverance and salvation. But his prophecy also promises that a time of restoration and renewal will follow God's judgment.

The book closes with a prediction that the Assyrians will overrun the northern Kingdom of Israel and its people taken into captivity if they do not repent and abandon their sinful ways. This prophecy comes true a generation later. While the Book of Amos seeks to awaken the people to the seriousness of their sin and to inspire them to seek God's forgiveness and restoration, it also reminds them about God's judgment. It is not limited to individuals but extends to entire societies. Furthermore, it assures the Israelites that their practice of injustice, religious corruption, and moral decay will inevitably lead to divine consequences.

1 The words of Amos,
who was among the herdmen of Tekoa,
which he saw concerning Israel in the days of Uzziah king of Judah, and in the days of Jeroboam the son of Joash king of Israel, two years before the earthquake.
2 **And he** said,
The LORD will roar from Zion,
and utter his voice from Jerusalem;
and the habitations of the shepherds shall mourn,
and the top of Carmel shall wither.
3 **Thus** saith the LORD;
For three transgressions of Damascus, and for four, I will not turn away the punishment thereof;
because they have threshed Gilead with threshing instruments of iron:
4 **But I** will send a fire into the house of Hazael,
which shall devour the palaces of Benhadad.
5 **I** will break also the bar of Damascus,
and cut off the inhabitant from the plain of Aven, and him that holdeth the sceptre from the house of Eden:
and the people of Syria shall go into captivity unto Kir,
saith the LORD.
6 **Thus** saith the LORD;
For three transgressions of Gaza, and for four, I will not turn away the punishment thereof;
because they carried away captive the whole captivity,
to deliver them up to Edom:
7 **But I** will send a fire on the wall of Gaza,
which shall devour the palaces thereof:
8 **And I** will cut off the inhabitant from Ashdod, and him that holdeth the sceptre from Ashkelon,
and I will turn mine hand against Ekron:
and the remnant of the Philistines shall perish,
saith the Lord GOD.
9 **Thus** saith the LORD;
For three transgressions of Tyrus, and for four, I will not turn away the punishment thereof;
because they delivered up the whole captivity to Edom,
and remembered not the brotherly covenant:
10 **But I** will send a fire on the wall of Tyrus,
which shall devour the palaces thereof.
11 **Thus** saith the LORD;
For three transgressions of Edom, and for four, I will not turn away the punishment thereof;
because he did pursue his brother with the sword,
and did cast off all pity,
and his anger did tear perpetually,
and he kept his wrath for ever:
12 **But I** will send a fire upon Teman,
which shall devour the palaces of Bozrah.
13 **Thus** saith the LORD;
For three transgressions of the children of Ammon, and for four, I will not turn away the punishment thereof;
because they have ripped up the women with child of Gilead,
that they might enlarge their border:
14 **But I** will kindle a fire in the wall of Rabbah,
and it shall devour the palaces thereof, with shouting in the day of battle, with a tempest in the day of the whirlwind:
15 **And their king** shall go into captivity, he and his princes together,
saith the LORD.

2 **Thus** saith the LORD;
For three transgressions of Moab, and for four, I will not turn away the punishment thereof;
because he burned the bones of the king of Edom into lime:
2 **But I** will send a fire upon Moab,
and it shall devour the palaces of Kirioth:
and Moab shall die with tumult, with shouting, and with the sound of the trumpet:

[3] **And I** will cut off the judge from the midst thereof,
and will slay all the princes thereof with him,
saith the LORD.

[4] **Thus** saith the LORD;
For three transgressions of Judah, and for four, I will not turn away the punishment thereof;
because they have despised the law of the LORD,
and have not kept his commandments,
and their lies caused them to err,
after the which their fathers have walked:
[5] **But I** will send a fire upon Judah,
and it shall devour the palaces of Jerusalem.

[6] **Thus** saith the LORD;
For three transgressions of Israel, and for four, I will not turn away the punishment thereof;
because they sold the righteous for silver, and the poor for a pair of shoes;
[7] **That** pant after the dust of the earth on the head of the poor,
and turn aside the way of the meek:
and a man and his father will go in unto the same maid,
to profane my holy name:
[8] **And they** lay themselves down upon clothes laid to pledge by every altar,
and they drink the wine of the condemned in the house of their god.

[9] **Yet** destroyed I the Amorite before them,
whose height was like the height of the cedars,
and he was strong as the oaks;
yet I destroyed his fruit from above, and his roots from beneath.
[10] **Also I** brought you up from the land of Egypt,
and led you forty years through the wilderness,
to possess the land of the Amorite.
[11] **And I** raised up of your sons for prophets, and of your young men for Nazarites.

Is it not even thus, O ye children of Israel?
saith the LORD.
[12] **But ye** gave the Nazarites wine to drink;
and commanded the prophets, saying,
Prophesy not.

[13] **Behold,**
I am pressed under you,
as a cart is pressed that is full of sheaves.
[14] **Therefore the flight** shall perish from the swift,
and the strong shall not strengthen his force,
neither shall the mighty deliver himself:
[15] **Neither** shall he stand that handleth the bow;
and he that is swift of foot shall not deliver himself:
neither shall he that rideth the horse deliver himself.
[16] **And he that is courageous among the mighty** shall flee away naked in that day,
saith the LORD.

3 **Hear** this word that the LORD hath spoken against you, O children of Israel, against the whole family which I brought up from the land of Egypt,
saying,
[2] **You only** have I known of all the families of the earth:
therefore I will punish you for all your iniquities.

[3] **Can two** walk together,
except they be agreed?
[4] **Will a lion** roar in the forest,
when he hath no prey?
will a young lion cry out of his den,
if he have taken nothing?
[5] **Can a bird** fall in a snare upon the earth,
where no gin is for him?
shall one take up a snare from the earth,
and have taken nothing at all?
[6] **Shall a trumpet** be blown in the city,
and the people not be afraid?
shall there be evil in a city,
and the LORD hath not done it?
[7] **Surely the Lord GOD** will do nothing,
but he revealeth his secret unto his servants the prophets.
[8] **The lion** hath roared,
who will not fear?
the Lord GOD hath spoken,
who can but prophesy?

[9] **Publish** in the palaces at Ashdod, and in the palaces in the land of Egypt,
and say,
Assemble yourselves upon the mountains of Samaria,
and behold the great tumults in the midst thereof, and the oppressed in the midst thereof.
[10] **For they** know not to do right,
saith the LORD,
who store up violence and robbery in their palaces.
[11] **Therefore thus** saith the Lord GOD;
An adversary there shall be even round about the land;
and he shall bring down thy strength from thee,
and thy palaces shall be spoiled.

[12] **Thus** saith the LORD;
As the shepherd taketh out of the mouth of the lion two legs, or a piece of an ear;
so shall the children of Israel be taken out
that dwell in Samaria in the corner of a bed, and in Damascus in a couch.

[13] **Hear ye,**
and testify in the house of Jacob,
saith the Lord GOD, the God of hosts,
[14] **That in the day that I shall visit the transgressions of Israel upon him** I will also visit the altars of Bethel:
and the horns of the altar shall be cut off,
and fall to the ground.
[15] **And I** will smite the winter house with the summer house;
and the houses of ivory shall perish,
and the great houses shall have an end,
saith the LORD.

4 **Hear** this word, ye kine of Bashan,
that are in the mountain of Samaria,
which oppress the poor,
which crush the needy,
which say to their masters,
Bring,
and let us drink.
[2] **The Lord GOD** hath sworn by his holiness,
that, {lo}, the days shall come upon you,
that he will take you away with hooks, and your posterity with fishhooks.

3 **And ye** shall go out at the breaches, every cow at that which is before her;
and ye shall cast them into the palace,
saith the LORD.

4 **Come** to Bethel,
and transgress;
at Gilgal multiply transgression;
and bring your sacrifices every morning, and your tithes after three years:
5 **And offer** a sacrifice of thanksgiving with leaven,
and proclaim and publish the free offerings:
for this liketh you, O ye children of Israel,
saith the Lord GOD.

6 **And I** also have given you cleanness of teeth in all your cities,
and want of bread in all your places:
yet have ye not returned unto me,
saith the LORD.

7 **And also I** have withholden the rain from you,
when there were yet three months to the harvest:
and I caused it to rain upon one city,
and caused it not to rain upon another city:
one piece was rained upon,
and the piece whereupon it rained not withered.

8 **So two or three cities** wandered unto one city,
to drink water;
but they were not satisfied:
yet have ye not returned unto me,
saith the LORD.

9 **I** have smitten you with blasting and mildew:
when your gardens and your vineyards and your fig trees and your olive trees increased,
the palmerworm devoured them:
yet have ye not returned unto me,
saith the LORD.

10 **I** have sent among you the pestilence after the manner of Egypt:
your young men have I slain with the sword,
and have taken away your horses;
and I have made the stink of your camps to come up unto your nostrils:
yet have ye not returned unto me,
saith the LORD.

11 **I** have overthrown some of you,
as God overthrew Sodom and Gomorrah,
and ye were as a firebrand plucked out of the burning:
yet have ye not returned unto me,
saith the LORD.

12 **Therefore thus** will I do unto thee, O Israel:
and because I will do this unto thee,
prepare to meet thy God, O Israel.

13 **For, {lo}, he that formeth the mountains, and createth the wind, and declareth unto man {what is his thought}, {that maketh the morning darkness}, {and treadeth upon the high places of the earth},** The LORD, The God of hosts, is his name.

5 **Hear ye** this word which I take up against you, even a lamentation, O house of Israel.
2 **The virgin of Israel** is fallen;
she shall no more rise:
she is forsaken upon her land;
there is none to raise her up.

3 **For thus** saith the Lord GOD;
The city that went out by a thousand shall leave an hundred,
and that which went forth by an hundred shall leave ten, to the house of Israel.

4 **For thus** saith the LORD unto the house of Israel,
Seek ye me,
and ye shall live:
5 **But seek not** Bethel,
nor enter into Gilgal,
and pass not to Beersheba:
for Gilgal shall surely go into captivity,
and Bethel shall come to nought.

6 **Seek** the LORD,
and ye shall live;
lest he break out like fire in the house of Joseph,
and devour it,
and there be none to quench it in Bethel.

7 **Ye who turn judgment to wormwood, and leave off righteousness in the earth,**
8 Seek him that maketh the seven stars and Orion,
and turneth the shadow of death into the morning,
and maketh the day dark with night:
that calleth for the waters of the sea,
and poureth them out upon the face of the earth:
The LORD is his name:
9 **That** strengtheneth the spoiled against the strong,
so that the spoiled shall come against the fortress.

10 **They** hate him that rebuketh in the gate,
and they abhor him that speaketh uprightly.

11 **Forasmuch therefore as your treading** is upon the poor,
and ye take from him burdens of wheat:
ye have built houses of hewn stone,
but ye shall not dwell in them;
ye have planted pleasant vineyards,
but ye shall not drink wine of them.

12 **For I** know your manifold transgressions and your mighty sins:
they afflict the just,
they take a bribe,
and they turn aside the poor in the gate from their right.

13 **Therefore the prudent** shall keep silence in that time;
for it is an evil time.

14 **Seek** good, and not evil,
that ye may live:
and so the LORD, the God of hosts, shall be with you,
as ye have spoken.

15 **Hate** the evil,
and love the good,
and establish judgment in the gate:
it may be that the LORD God of hosts will be gracious unto the remnant of Joseph.

16 **Therefore the LORD, the God of hosts, the Lord,** saith thus;
Wailing shall be in all streets;
and they shall say in all the highways,
Alas! alas!
and they shall call the husbandman to mourning, and such as are skilful of lamentation to wailing.

17 **And in all vineyards** shall be wailing:
for I will pass through thee,
saith the LORD.

18 **Woe** unto you that desire the day of the LORD!
to what end is it for you?

the day of the LORD is darkness, and not light.
19 **As if a man** did flee from a lion,
and a bear met him;
or went into the house,
and leaned his hand on the wall,
and a serpent bit him.
20 **Shall not the day of the LORD** be darkness, and not light?
even very dark, and no brightness in it?
21 **I** hate,
I despise your feast days,
and I will not smell in your solemn assemblies.
22 **Though ye** offer me burnt offerings and your meat offerings,
I will not accept them:
neither will I regard the peace offerings of your fat beasts.
23 **Take thou away** from me the noise of thy songs;
for I will not hear the melody of thy viols.
24 **But let judgment** run down as waters,
and righteousness as a mighty stream.
25 **Have ye** offered unto me sacrifices and offerings in the wilderness forty years, O house of Israel?
26 **But ye** have borne the tabernacle of your Moloch and Chiun your images, the star of your god,
which ye made to yourselves.
27 **Therefore** will I cause you to go into captivity beyond Damascus,
saith the LORD,
whose name is The God of hosts.

6

Woe to them that are at ease in Zion, and trust in the mountain of Samaria,
which are named chief of the nations,
to whom the house of Israel came!
2 **Pass ye** unto Calneh,
and see;
and from thence go ye to Hamath the great:
then go down to Gath of the Philistines:
be they better than these kingdoms?
or their border greater than your border?
3 **Ye** that put far away the evil day,
and cause the seat of violence to come near;
4 **That** lie upon beds of ivory,
and stretch themselves upon their couches,
and eat the lambs out of the flock,
and the calves out of the midst of the stall;
5 **That** chant to the sound of the viol,
and invent to themselves instruments of musick, like David;
6 **That** drink wine in bowls,
and anoint themselves with the chief ointments:
but they are not grieved for the affliction of Joseph.
7 **Therefore now** shall they go captive with the first that go captive,
and the banquet of them that stretched themselves shall be removed.
8 **The Lord GOD** hath sworn by himself,
saith the LORD the God of hosts,
I abhor the excellency of Jacob,
and hate his palaces:
therefore will I deliver up the city with all that is therein.
9 **And it** shall come to pass,
if there remain ten men in one house,
that they shall die.
10 **And a man's uncle** shall take him up, and he that burneth him,
to bring out the bones out of the house,
and shall say unto him that is by the sides of the house,
Is there yet any with thee?
and he shall say,
No.
Then shall he say,
Hold thy tongue:
for we may not make mention of the name of the LORD.
11 **For, {behold}, the LORD** commandeth,
and he will smite the great house with breaches, and the little house with clefts.
12 **Shall horses** run upon the rock?
will one plow there with oxen?
for ye have turned judgment into gall, and the fruit of righteousness into hemlock:
13 Ye which rejoice in a thing of nought,
which say,
Have we not taken to us horns by our own strength?
14 **But, {behold}, I** will raise up against you a nation, O house of Israel,
saith the LORD the God of hosts;
and they shall afflict you from the entering in of Hemath unto the river of the wilderness.

7

Thus hath the Lord GOD shewed unto me;
and, {behold}, he formed grasshoppers in the beginning of the shooting up of the latter growth;
and, {lo}, it was the latter growth after the king's mowings.
2 **And it** came to pass,
that when they had made an end of eating the grass of the land,
then I said,
O Lord GOD, forgive,
I beseech thee:
by whom shall Jacob arise?
for he is small.
3 **The LORD** repented for this:
It shall not be,
saith the LORD.
4 **Thus** hath the Lord GOD shewed unto me:
and, {behold}, the Lord GOD called to contend by fire,
and it devoured the great deep,
and did eat up a part.
5 **Then** said I,
O Lord GOD, cease,
I beseech thee:
by whom shall Jacob arise?
for he is small.
6 **The LORD** repented for this:
This also shall not be,
saith the Lord GOD.
7 **Thus he** shewed me:
and, {behold}, the Lord stood upon a wall made by a plumbline, with a plumbline in his hand.
8 **And the LORD** said unto me,
Amos, what seest thou?
And I said,
A plumbline.
Then said the Lord,
Behold,
I will set a plumbline in the midst of my people Israel:
I will not again pass by them any more:
9 **And the high places of Isaac** shall be desolate,
and the sanctuaries of Israel shall be laid waste;

and I will rise against the house of Jeroboam with the sword.
10 **Then Amaziah the priest of Bethel** sent to Jeroboam king of Israel,
saying,
Amos hath conspired against thee in the midst of the house of Israel:
the land is not able to bear all his words.
11 **For thus** Amos saith,
Jeroboam shall die by the sword,
and Israel shall surely be led away captive out of their own land.
12 **Also Amaziah** said unto Amos,
O thou seer, go,
flee thee away into the land of Judah,
and there eat bread,
and prophesy there:
13 **But prophesy not** again any more at Bethel:
for it is the king's chapel,
and it is the king's court.
14 **Then** answered Amos,
and said to Amaziah,
I was no prophet,
neither was I a prophet's son;
but I was an herdman, and a gatherer of sycomore fruit:
15 **And the LORD** took me
as I followed the flock,
and the LORD said unto me,
Go,
prophesy unto my people Israel.
16 **Now therefore hear thou** the word of the LORD:
Thou sayest,
Prophesy not against Israel,
and drop not thy word against the house of Isaac.
17 **Therefore thus** saith the LORD;
Thy wife shall be an harlot in the city,
and thy sons and thy daughters shall fall by the sword,
and thy land shall be divided by line;
and thou shalt die in a polluted land:
and Israel shall surely go into captivity forth of his land.

8 **Thus** hath the Lord GOD shewed unto me:
and behold a basket of summer fruit.
2 **And he** said,
Amos, what seest thou?
And I said,
A basket of summer fruit.
Then said the LORD unto me,
The end is come upon my people of Israel;
I will not again pass by them any more.
3 **And the songs of the temple** shall be howlings in that day,
saith the Lord GOD:
there shall be many dead bodies in every place;
they shall cast them forth with silence.
4 **Hear** this, O ye that swallow up the needy,
even to make the poor of the land to fail,
5 Saying,
When will the new moon be gone, {that we may sell corn?} and the sabbath, {that we may set forth wheat},
making the ephah small, and the shekel great,
and falsifying the balances by deceit?
6 **That we** may buy the poor for silver, and the needy for a pair of shoes;
yea, and sell the refuse of the wheat?
7 **The LORD** hath sworn by the excellency of Jacob,
Surely I will never forget any of their works.
8 **Shall not the land** tremble for this,
and every one mourn that dwelleth therein?
and it shall rise up wholly as a flood;
and it shall be cast out and drowned, as by the flood of Egypt.
9 **And it** shall come to pass in that day,
saith the Lord GOD,
that I will cause the sun to go down at noon,
and I will darken the earth in the clear day:
10 **And I** will turn your feasts into mourning, and all your songs into lamentation;
and I will bring up sackcloth upon all loins, and baldness upon every head;
and I will make it as the mourning of an only son, and the end thereof as a bitter day.
11 **Behold,**
the days come,
saith the Lord GOD,
that I will send a famine in the land, not a famine of bread, nor a thirst for water,
but of hearing the words of the LORD:
12 **And they** shall wander from sea to sea, and from the north even to the east,
they shall run to and fro
to seek the word of the LORD,
and shall not find it.
13 **In that day** shall the fair virgins and young men faint for thirst.
14 **They that swear by the sin of Samaria, and say, {Thy god, O Dan, liveth}; {and, The manner of Beersheba liveth};** even they shall fall,
and never rise up again.

9 **I** saw the Lord standing upon the altar:
and he said,
Smite the lintel of the door,
that the posts may shake:
and cut them in the head, all of them;
and I will slay the last of them with the sword:
he that fleeth of them shall not flee away,
and he that escapeth of them shall not be delivered.
2 **Though they** dig into hell,
thence shall mine hand take them;
though they climb up to heaven,
thence will I bring them down:
3 **And though they** hide themselves in the top of Carmel,
I will search and take them out thence;
and though they be hid from my sight in the bottom of the sea,
thence will I command the serpent,
and he shall bite them:
4 **And though they** go into captivity before their enemies,
thence will I command the sword,
and it shall slay them:
and I will set mine eyes upon them for evil, and not for good.
5 **And the Lord GOD of hosts** is he that toucheth the land,
and it shall melt,
and all that dwell therein shall mourn:
and it shall rise up wholly like a flood;

and shall be drowned, as by the flood of Egypt.

6 **It is he** that buildeth his stories in the heaven,
and hath founded his troop in the earth;
he that calleth for the waters of the sea,
and poureth them out upon the face of the earth:
The LORD is his name.

7 **Are ye not** as children of the Ethiopians unto me, O children of Israel?
saith the LORD.

Have not I brought up Israel out of the land of Egypt? and the Philistines from Caphtor, and the Syrians from Kir?

8 **Behold,**
the eyes of the Lord GOD are upon the sinful kingdom,
and I will destroy it from off the face of the earth;
saving that I will not utterly destroy the house of Jacob,
saith the LORD.

9 **For, {lo}, I** will command,
and I will sift the house of Israel among all nations,
like as corn is sifted in a sieve,
yet shall not the least grain fall upon the earth.

10 **All the sinners of my people** shall die by the sword,
which say,
The evil shall not overtake
nor prevent us.

11 **In that day** will I raise up the tabernacle of David that is fallen,
and close up the breaches thereof;
and I will raise up his ruins,
and I will build it as in the days of old:

12 **That they** may possess the remnant of Edom, and of all the heathen,
which are called by my name,
saith the LORD that doeth this.

13 **Behold,**
the days come,
saith the LORD,
that the plowman shall overtake the reaper,
and the treader of grapes him that soweth seed;
and the mountains shall drop sweet wine,
and all the hills shall melt.

14 **And I** will bring again the captivity of my people of Israel,
and they shall build the waste cities,
and inhabit them;
and they shall plant vineyards,
and drink the wine thereof;
they shall also make gardens,
and eat the fruit of them.

15 **And I** will plant them upon their land,
and they shall no more be pulled up out of their land which I have given them,
saith the LORD thy God.

Obadiah

The Book of Obadiah, traditionally attributed to the prophet Obadiah, responds to the destruction of Judah and its capital, Jerusalem. Spanning only 21 verses, it stands as the shortest book in the Old Testament. In his book, Obadiah warns of judgment against the nation of Edom, the descendants of Jacob's brother, Esau. He denounces their pride, arrogance, and failure to aid Israel during its foreign invasions. His warning serves as a cautionary tale about the severe consequences of such attitudes.

The prophet also offers hope and reassurance to the people of Judah, who are confronted with exile and uncertainty. He underscores the significance of unwavering faith in God and the necessity to trust in His ultimate plan for the salvation of His people. The book's overarching themes of divine justice, retribution, and restoration are brought to the forefront. Obadiah fervently urges the people of Judah to unite and cooperate for this reason: their collective efforts are crucial in rebuilding the nation and restoring their relationship with God.

The vision of Obadiah.
Thus saith the Lord GOD concerning Edom;
We have heard a rumour from the LORD,
and an ambassador is sent among the heathen,
Arise ye,
and let us rise up against her in battle.
2 **Behold,**
I have made thee small among the heathen:
thou art greatly despised.
3 **The pride of thine heart** hath deceived thee, thou that dwellest in the clefts of the rock,
whose habitation is high;
that saith in his heart,
Who shall bring me down to the ground?
4 **Though thou** exalt thyself as the eagle,
and though thou set thy nest among the stars,
thence will I bring thee down,
saith the LORD.
5 **If thieves** came to thee, if robbers by night,
(how art thou cut off!)
would they not have stolen
till they had enough?
if the grapegatherers came to thee,
would they not leave some grapes?
6 **How** are the things of Esau searched out!
how are his hidden things sought up!
7 **All the men of thy confederacy** have brought thee even to the border:
the men that were at peace with thee have deceived thee,
and prevailed against thee;
they that eat thy bread have laid a wound under thee:
there is none understanding in him.
8 **Shall I not** in that day, {saith the LORD}, even destroy the wise men out of Edom, and understanding out of the mount of Esau?
9 **And thy mighty men**, O Teman, shall be dismayed,
to the end that every one of the mount of Esau may be cut off by slaughter.
10 **For thy violence against thy brother Jacob** shame shall cover thee,
and thou shalt be cut off for ever.
11 **In the day that thou stoodest on the other side, in the day that the strangers carried away captive his forces, and foreigners entered into his gates, and cast lots upon Jerusalem,** even thou wast as one of them.
12 **But thou** shouldest not have looked on the day of thy brother in the day that he became a stranger;
neither shouldest thou have rejoiced over the children of Judah in the day of their destruction;
neither shouldest thou have spoken proudly in the day of distress.
13 **Thou** shouldest not have entered into the gate of my people in the day of their calamity;
yea, thou shouldest not have looked on their affliction in the day of their calamity,
nor have laid hands on their substance in the day of their calamity;
14 **Neither** shouldest thou have stood in the crossway,
to cut off those of his that did escape;
neither shouldest thou have delivered up those of his that did remain in the day of distress.
15 **For the day of the LORD** is near upon all the heathen:
as thou has done,
it shall be done unto thee:
thy reward shall return upon thine own head.
16 **For as ye** have drunk upon my holy mountain,
so shall all the heathen drink continually,
yea, they shall drink,
and they shall swallow down,
and they shall be as though they had not been.
17 **But upon mount Zion** shall be deliverance,
and there shall be holiness;
and the house of Jacob shall possess their possessions.
18 **And the house of Jacob** shall be a fire,
and the house of Joseph a flame,
and the house of Esau for stubble,
and they shall kindle in them,
and devour them;
and there shall not be any remaining of the house of Esau;
for the LORD hath spoken it.
19 **And they of the south** shall possess the mount of Esau;
and they of the plain the Philistines:

and they shall possess the fields of
Ephraim, and the fields of
Samaria:
and Benjamin shall possess Gilead.
20 **And the captivity of this host of
the children of Israel** shall
possess that of the Canaanites,
even unto Zarephath;
and the captivity of Jerusalem,
{which is in Sepharad}, shall
possess the cities of the south.
21 **And saviours** shall come up on
mount Zion
to judge the mount of Esau;
and the kingdom shall be the
LORD's.

Jonah

The Book of Jonah (author unknown but likely the prophet Jonah) appears to take place before the Babylonian exile, as it involves Jonah preaching to the people of Nineveh, who were part of the Assyrian Empire. This significant regional power preceded the rise of Babylon. Jonah is unique among all the prophetic books because of its narrative format, which is different from the collection of oracles or prophecies that characterize the other books. It serves as a reminder that God is not only the God of the Israelites but also the God of all nations and that He desires all people to turn away from their sinful ways and embrace His love.

The book opens with God commanding Jonah to go to Nineveh. While there, he would preach against its wickedness. Instead of obeying God's command, Jonah boards a ship headed in the opposite direction. A large storm ensues, and the sailors cast lots to determine the cause of the storm. The lot falls on Jonah, and he is thrown overboard by the ship's crew. He is then swallowed by a great fish that God has prepared for him. While inside the fish, Jonah prays to God, acknowledging his disobedience and asking for mercy. In response to Jonah's repentant heart, God causes the fish to vomit out the prophet, who then obeys God's original command.

After arriving in Ninevah, Jonah delivers a simple message of repentance, a message that carries the power of hope and redemption. He warns the people that their wickedness has reached God's ears and that they must turn from their evil ways or face destruction. The people of Nineveh, from the king to the lowest citizen, heed Jonah's warning and repent of their sins. As a result, God relents from His plan to destroy the city, thus showing His mercy to the people. Despite the successful outcome of his mission, Jonah's reaction is unexpected. He becomes angry and disappointed, even wishing that God would have destroyed the city. God, however, seizes this opportunity to teach Jonah a lesson about compassion, reminding him of His merciful nature and His desire for the salvation of all people.

The Book of Jonah imparts several lessons. It showcases the power of repentance, illustrating how even the most wicked people can turn from their sinful ways and find forgiveness and redemption. It also serves as a reminder of God's merciful nature and His concern for all people, regardless of their background or past sins. Finally, it underscores the importance of obedience to God's call and the need for active faith in His plan for spiritual growth.

1 **Now the word of the LORD** came unto Jonah the son of Amittai,
saying,
2 **Arise,**
go to Nineveh, that great city,
and cry against it;
for their wickedness is come up before me.

3 **But Jonah** rose up to flee unto Tarshish from the presence of the LORD,
and went down to Joppa;
and he found a ship going to Tarshish:
so he paid the fare thereof,
and went down into it,
to go with them unto Tarshish from the presence of the LORD.

4 **But the LORD** sent out a great wind into the sea,
and there was a mighty tempest in the sea,
so that the ship was like to be broken.

5 **Then the mariners** were afraid,
and cried every man unto his god,
and cast forth the wares that were in the ship into the sea,
to lighten it of them.

But Jonah was gone down into the sides of the ship;
and he lay,
and was fast asleep.

6 **So the shipmaster** came to him,
and said unto him,
What meanest thou, O sleeper?
arise,
call upon thy God,
if so be that God will think upon us,
that we perish not.

7 **And they** said every one to his fellow,
Come,
and let us cast lots,
that we may know
for whose cause this evil is upon us.

So they cast lots,
and the lot fell upon Jonah.

8 **Then** said they unto him,
Tell us,
we pray thee,
for whose cause this evil is upon us;
What is thine occupation?
and whence comest thou?
what is thy country?
and of what people art thou?

9 **And he** said unto them,
I am an Hebrew;
and I fear the LORD, the God of heaven,
which hath made the sea and the dry land.

10 **Then** were the men exceedingly afraid,
and said unto him.
Why hast thou done this?
For the men knew
that he fled from the presence of the LORD,
because he had told them.

11 **Then** said they unto him,
What shall we do unto thee,
that the sea may be calm unto us?
for the sea wrought,
and was tempestuous.

12 **And he** said unto them,
Take me up,
and cast me forth into the sea;
so shall the sea be calm unto you:
for I know
that for my sake this great tempest is upon you.

13 **Nevertheless the men** rowed hard
to bring it to the land;
but they could not:
for the sea wrought,
and was tempestuous against them.

14 **Wherefore they** cried unto the LORD,
and said,
We beseech thee, O LORD,
we beseech thee,
let us not perish for this man's life,
and lay not upon us innocent blood:
for thou, O LORD, hast done as it pleased thee.

15 **So they** took up Jonah,
and cast him forth into the sea:
and the sea ceased from her raging.

16 **Then the men** feared the LORD exceedingly,
and offered a sacrifice unto the LORD,
and made vows.

17 **Now the LORD** had prepared a great fish to swallow up Jonah.
And Jonah was in the belly of the fish three days and three nights.

2 **Then Jonah** prayed unto the LORD his God out of the fish's belly,
2 **And** said,
I cried by reason of mine affliction unto the LORD,
and he heard me;
out of the belly of hell cried I,
and thou heardest my voice.

3 **For thou** hadst cast me into the deep, in the midst of the seas;
and the floods compassed me about:
all thy billows and thy waves passed over me.

4 **Then I** said,
I am cast out of thy sight;
yet I will look again toward thy holy temple.

5 **The waters** compassed me about, even to the soul:
the depth closed me round about,
the weeds were wrapped about my head.

6 **I** went down to the bottoms of the mountains;
the earth with her bars was about me for ever:
yet hast thou brought up my life from corruption, O LORD my God.

7 **When my soul** fainted within me
I remembered the LORD:
and my prayer came in unto thee, into thine holy temple.

8 **They that observe lying vanities** forsake their own mercy.

9 **But I** will sacrifice unto thee with the voice of thanksgiving;
I will pay that that I have vowed.
Salvation is of the LORD.

10 **And the LORD** spake unto the fish,
and it vomited out Jonah upon the dry land.

3 **And the word of the LORD** came unto Jonah the second time,
saying,
2 **Arise,**
go unto Nineveh, that great city,
and preach unto it the preaching that I bid thee.

3 **So Jonah** arose,
and went unto Nineveh, according to the word of the LORD.
Now Nineveh was an exceeding great city of three days' journey.

4 **And Jonah** began to enter into the city a day's journey,
and he cried,
and said,
Yet forty days, and Nineveh shall be overthrown.

5 **So the people of Nineveh** believed God,
and proclaimed a fast,
and put on sackcloth, from the greatest of them even to the least of them.

6 **For word** came unto the king of Nineveh,
and he arose from his throne,
and he laid his robe from him,
and covered him with sackcloth,
and sat in ashes.

7 **And he** caused it to be proclaimed and published through Nineveh by the decree of the king and his nobles,
saying,
Let neither man nor beast, herd nor flock, taste any thing:
let them not feed,
nor drink water:
8 **But let man and beast** be covered with sackcloth,
and cry mightily unto God:
yea, let them turn every one from his evil way, and from the violence that is in their hands.

9 **Who** can tell
if God will turn and repent,
and turn away from his fierce anger,
that we perish not?

10 **And God** saw their works,
that they turned from their evil way;
and God repented of the evil,
that he had said
that he would do unto them;
and he did it not.

4 **But it** displeased Jonah exceedingly,
and he was very angry.

2 **And he** prayed unto the LORD,
and said,
I pray thee, O LORD,
was not this my saying,
when I was yet in my country?
Therefore I fled before unto Tarshish:
for I knew
that thou art a gracious God, and merciful, slow to anger, and of great kindness,
and repentest thee of the evil.

3 **Therefore now, O LORD, take,** {I beseech thee}, my life from me;
for it is better for me to die than to live.

4 **Then** said the LORD,
Doest thou well to be angry?

5 **So Jonah** went out of the city,
and sat on the east side of the city,
and there made him a booth,
and sat under it in the shadow,
till he might see what would become of the city.

6 **And the LORD God** prepared a gourd,
and made it to come up over Jonah,
that it might be a shadow over his head,
to deliver him from his grief.

So Jonah was exceeding glad of the gourd.
7 **But God** prepared a worm
when the morning rose the next day,
and it smote the gourd
that it withered.
8 **And it** came to pass,
when the sun did arise,
that God prepared a vehement east wind;
and the sun beat upon the head of Jonah,
that he fainted,
and wished in himself to die,
and said,
It is better for me to die than to live.
9 **And God** said to Jonah,
Doest thou well to be angry for the gourd?
And he said,
I do well to be angry, even unto death.
10 **Then** said the LORD,
Thou hast had pity on the gourd,
for the which thou hast not laboured,
neither madest it grow;
which came up in a night,
and perished in a night:
11 **And** should not I spare Nineveh, that great city,
wherein are more than sixscore thousand persons that cannot discern between their right hand and their left hand; and also much cattle?

Micah

The prophet Micah writes a message to the people of Israel and Judah approximately one hundred years before the Babylonian exile. He warns them about the consequences of disobeying God's law and calls them to repent and return to God. His prophecy also speaks about the invasion of a foreign army that will punish the people for their sins and destroy the land. Micah is also driven by a deep concern for the well-being of the people, especially the poor and vulnerable in society. He sees the existing injustices and inequalities, such as the exploitation of the poor by the rich and the mistreatment of widows and orphans, and feels compelled to speak out against them. He believes that a just and righteous society is essential for the people to flourish and glorify God.

In addition to these warnings, Micah offers a message of hope and restoration, promising that God will ultimately restore His people and bring them back to the land of Israel. He is one of the few prophets to specifically prophesy about the coming of a Messiah Who will bring salvation and peace to the world. In fact, his description of the Messiah as a ruler from Bethlehem in Micah 5:2 is one of the most famous prophecies in all of Scripture. Overall, Micah represents a divine call for the people to take responsibility and repent, warning them of the consequences of disobedience but also offering them hope and the vision of a better future through faith in God and salvation through the Messiah.

1 The word of the LORD that came to Micah the Morasthite in the days of Jotham, Ahaz, and Hezekiah, kings of Judah,
which he saw concerning Samaria and Jerusalem.

2 **Hear,** all ye people;
hearken, O earth, and all that therein is:
and let the Lord GOD be witness against you, the Lord from his holy temple.

3 **For, {behold}, the LORD** cometh forth out of his place,
and will come down,
and tread upon the high places of the earth.

4 **And the mountains** shall be molten under him,
and the valleys shall be cleft, as wax before the fire, and as the waters that are poured down a steep place.

5 **For the transgression of Jacob** is all this, and for the sins of the house of Israel.
What is the transgression of Jacob?
is it not Samaria?
and what are the high places of Judah?
are they not Jerusalem?

6 **Therefore I** will make Samaria as an heap of the field, and as plantings of a vineyard:
and I will pour down the stones thereof into the valley,
and I will discover the foundations thereof.

7 **And all the graven images thereof** shall be beaten to pieces,
and all the hires thereof shall be burned with the fire,
and all the idols thereof will I lay desolate:
for she gathered it of the hire of an harlot,
and they shall return to the hire of an harlot.

8 **Therefore I** will wail and howl,
I will go stripped and naked:
I will make a wailing like the dragons, and mourning as the owls.

9 **For her wound** is incurable;
for it is come unto Judah;
he is come unto the gate of my people, even to Jerusalem.

10 **Declare ye it not** at Gath,
weep ye not at all:
in the house of Aphrah roll thyself in the dust.

11 **Pass ye away,** thou inhabitant of Saphir,
having thy shame naked:
the inhabitant of Zaanan came not forth in the mourning of Bethezel;
he shall receive of you his standing.

12 **For the inhabitant of Maroth** waited carefully for good:
but evil came down from the LORD unto the gate of Jerusalem.

13 **O thou inhabitant of Lachish, bind** the chariot to the swift beast:
she is the beginning of the sin to the daughter of Zion:
for the transgressions of Israel were found in thee.

14 **Therefore** shalt thou give presents to Moreshethgath:
the houses of Achzib shall be a lie to the kings of Israel.

15 **Yet** will I bring an heir unto thee, O inhabitant of Mareshah:
he shall come unto Adullam the glory of Israel.

16 **Make thee** bald,
and poll thee for thy delicate children;
enlarge thy baldness as the eagle;
for they are gone into captivity from thee.

2 **Woe** to them that devise iniquity, and work evil upon their beds!
when the morning is light,
they practise it,
because it is in the power of their hand.

2 **And they** covet fields,
and take them by violence; and houses,
and take them away:
so they oppress a man and his house, even a man and his heritage.

3 **Therefore thus** saith the LORD;
Behold,
against this family do I devise an evil,
from which ye shall not remove your necks;
neither shall ye go haughtily:
for this time is evil.

4 **In that day** shall one take up a parable against you,
and lament with a doleful lamentation,
and say,
We be utterly spoiled:
he hath changed the portion of my people:
how hath he removed it from me!
turning away he hath divided our fields.

5 **Therefore thou** shalt have none that shall cast a cord by lot in the congregation of the LORD.

6 **Prophesy ye not,** say they to them that prophesy:
they shall not prophesy to them,
that they shall not take shame.

7 **O thou that art named the house of Jacob, is the spirit of the LORD** straitened?
are these his doings?
do not my words do good to him that walketh uprightly?

8 **Even of late** my people is risen up as an enemy:
ye pull off the robe with the garment from them that pass by securely as men averse from war.

9 **The women of my people** have ye cast out from their pleasant houses;
from their children have ye taken away my glory for ever.

10 **Arise ye,**
and depart;
for this is not your rest:
because it is polluted,
it shall destroy you, even with a sore destruction.

11 **If a man walking in the spirit and falsehood** do lie,
saying,
I will prophesy unto thee of wine and of strong drink;
he shall even be the prophet of this people.

12 **I** will surely assemble, O Jacob, all of thee;
I will surely gather the remnant of Israel;
I will put them together as the sheep of Bozrah, as the flock in the midst of their fold:
they shall make great noise by reason of the multitude of men.

13 **The breaker** is come up before them:
they have broken up,
and have passed through the gate,
and are gone out by it:
and their king shall pass before them,
and the LORD on the head of them.

3 **And I** said,
Hear, {I pray you}, O heads of Jacob, and ye princes of the house of Israel;
Is it not for you to know judgment?

2 **Who** hate the good,
and love the evil;
who pluck off their skin from off them, and their flesh from off their bones;

3 **Who** also eat the flesh of my people,
and flay their skin from off them;
and they break their bones,
and chop them in pieces, as for the pot, and as flesh within the caldron.

4 **Then** shall they cry unto the LORD,
but he will not hear them:
he will even hide his face from them at that time,
as they have behaved themselves ill in their doings.

5 **Thus** saith the LORD concerning the prophets
that make my people err,
that bite with their teeth,
and cry,
Peace;
and he that putteth not into their mouths, they even prepare war against him.

6 **Therefore night** shall be unto you,
that ye shall not have a vision;
and it shall be dark unto you,
that ye shall not divine;
and the sun shall go down over the prophets,
and the day shall be dark over them.

7 **Then** shall the seers be ashamed,
and the diviners confounded:
yea, they shall all cover their lips;
for there is no answer of God.

8 **But truly I** am full of power by the spirit of the LORD, and of judgment, and of might,
to declare unto Jacob his transgression, and to Israel his sin.

9 **Hear** this, {I pray you}, ye heads of the house of Jacob, and princes of the house of Israel,
that abhor judgment,
and pervert all equity.

10 **They** build up Zion with blood,
and Jerusalem with iniquity.

11 **The heads thereof** judge for reward,
and the priests thereof teach for hire,
and the prophets thereof divine for money:
yet will they lean upon the LORD,
and say,
Is not the LORD among us?
none evil can come upon us.

12 **Therefore** shall Zion for your sake be plowed as a field,
and Jerusalem shall become heaps,
and the mountain of the house as the high places of the forest.

4 **But in the last days** it shall come to pass,
that the mountain of the house of the LORD shall be established in the top of the mountains,
and it shall be exalted above the hills;
and people shall flow unto it.

2 **And many nations** shall come,
and say,
Come,
and let us go up to the mountain of the LORD, and to the house of the God of Jacob;
and he will teach us of his ways,
and we will walk in his paths:
for the law shall go forth of Zion,
and the word of the LORD from Jerusalem.

3 **And he** shall judge among many people,
and rebuke strong nations afar off;
and they shall beat their swords into plowshares, and their spears into pruninghooks:
nation shall not lift up a sword against nation,
neither shall they learn war any more.

4 **But they** shall sit every man under his vine and under his fig tree;
and none shall make them afraid:
for the mouth of the LORD of hosts hath spoken it.

5 **For all people** will walk every one in the name of his god,
and we will walk in the name of the LORD our God for ever and ever.

6 **In that day,** {saith the LORD}, will I assemble her that halteth,
and I will gather her that is driven

out, and her that I have afflicted;
7 **And I** will make her that halted a remnant, and her that was cast far off a strong nation:
and the LORD shall reign over them in mount Zion from henceforth, even for ever.
8 **And thou,** O tower of the flock, the strong hold of the daughter of Zion, unto thee shall it come, even the first dominion;
the kingdom shall come to the daughter of Jerusalem.
9 **Now why** dost thou cry out aloud?
is there no king in thee?
is thy counsellor perished?
for pangs have taken thee as a woman in travail.
10 **Be** in pain,
and labour to bring forth, O daughter of Zion, like a woman in travail:
for now shalt thou go forth out of the city,
and thou shalt dwell in the field,
and thou shalt go even to Babylon;
there shalt thou be delivered;
there the LORD shall redeem thee from the hand of thine enemies.
11 **Now also many nations** are gathered against thee,
that say,
Let her be defiled,
and let our eye look upon Zion.
12 **But they** know not the thoughts of the LORD,
neither understand they his counsel:
for he shall gather them as the sheaves into the floor.
13 **Arise and thresh,** O daughter of Zion:
for I will make thine horn iron,
and I will make thy hoofs brass:
and thou shalt beat in pieces many people:
and I will consecrate their gain unto the LORD, and their substance unto the Lord of the whole earth.

5 **Now gather** thyself in troops, O daughter of troops:
he hath laid siege against us:
they shall smite the judge of Israel with a rod upon the cheek.
2 **But thou,** Bethlehem Ephratah, though thou be little among the thousands of Judah,
yet out of thee shall he come forth unto me
that is to be ruler in Israel;
whose goings forth have been from of old, from everlasting.
3 **Therefore** will he give them up,
until the time that she which travaileth hath brought forth:
then the remnant of his brethren shall return unto the children of Israel.
4 **And he** shall stand and feed in the strength of the LORD, in the majesty of the name of the LORD his God;
and they shall abide:
for now shall he be great unto the ends of the earth.
5 **And this man** shall be the peace,
when the Assyrian shall come into our land:
and when he shall tread in our palaces,
then shall we raise against him seven shepherds, and eight principal men.
6 **And they** shall waste the land of Assyria with the sword, and the land of Nimrod in the entrances thereof:
thus shall he deliver us from the Assyrian,
when he cometh into our land,
and when he treadeth within our borders.
7 **And the remnant of Jacob** shall be in the midst of many people as a dew from the LORD, as the showers upon the grass,
that tarrieth not for man,
nor waiteth for the sons of men.
8 **And the remnant of Jacob** shall be among the Gentiles in the midst of many people as a lion among the beasts of the forest, as a young lion among the flocks of sheep:
who, {if he go through}, both treadeth down,
and teareth in pieces,
and none can deliver.
9 **Thine hand** shall be lifted up upon thine adversaries,
and all thine enemies shall be cut off.
10 **And it** shall come to pass in that day,
saith the LORD,
that I will cut off thy horses out of the midst of thee,
and I will destroy thy chariots:
11 **And I** will cut off the cities of thy land,
and throw down all thy strong holds:
12 **And I** will cut off witchcrafts out of thine hand;
and thou shalt have no more soothsayers:
13 **Thy graven images** also will I cut off,
and thy standing images out of the midst of thee;
and thou shalt no more worship the work of thine hands.
14 **And I** will pluck up thy groves out of the midst of thee:
so will I destroy thy cities.
15 **And I** will execute vengeance in anger and fury upon the heathen,
such as they have not heard.

6 **Hear ye** now what the LORD saith;
Arise,
contend thou before the mountains,
and let the hills hear thy voice.
2 **Hear ye,** O mountains, the LORD's controversy, and ye strong foundations of the earth:
for the LORD hath a controversy with his people,
and he will plead with Israel.
3 **O my people, what** have I done unto thee?
and wherein have I wearied thee?
testify against me.
4 **For I** brought thee up out of the land of Egypt,
and redeemed thee out of the house of servants;
and I sent before thee Moses, Aaron, and Miriam.
5 **O my people, remember** now
what Balak king of Moab consulted,
and what Balaam the son of Beor answered him from Shittim unto Gilgal;
that ye may know the righteousness of the LORD.
6 **Wherewith** shall I come before the LORD,
and bow myself before the high God?
shall I come before him with burnt offerings, with calves of a year old?

7 **Will the LORD** be pleased with thousands of rams, or with ten thousands of rivers of oil?
shall I give my firstborn for my transgression, the fruit of my body for the sin of my soul?

8 **He** hath shewed thee, O man,
what is good;
and what doth the LORD require of thee,
but to do justly,
and to love mercy,
and to walk humbly with thy God?

9 **The LORD's voice** crieth unto the city,
and the man of wisdom shall see thy name:
hear ye the rod,
and who hath appointed it.

10 **Are there** yet the treasures of wickedness in the house of the wicked, and the scant measure that is abominable?

11 **Shall I** count them pure with the wicked balances, and with the bag of deceitful weights?

12 **For the rich men thereof** are full of violence,
and the inhabitants thereof have spoken lies,
and their tongue is deceitful in their mouth.

13 **Therefore** also will I make thee sick
in smiting thee,
in making thee desolate because of thy sins.

14 **Thou** shalt eat,
but not be satisfied;
and thy casting down shall be in the midst of thee;
and thou shalt take hold,
but shalt not deliver;
and that which thou deliverest will I give up to the sword.

15 **Thou** shalt sow,
but thou shalt not reap;
thou shalt tread the olives, {but thou shalt not anoint thee with oil}; and sweet wine, {but shalt not drink wine}.

16 **For the statutes of Omri** are kept, and all the works of the house of Ahab,
and ye walk in their counsels;
that I should make thee a desolation, and the inhabitants thereof an hissing:
therefore ye shall bear the reproach of my people.

7

Woe is me!
for I am as when they have gathered the summer fruits, as the grapegleanings of the vintage:
there is no cluster to eat:
my soul desired the firstripe fruit.

2 **The good man** is perished out of the earth:
and there is none upright among men:
they all lie in wait for blood;
they hunt every man his brother with a net.

3 **That they** may do evil with both hands earnestly,
the prince asketh,
and the judge asketh for a reward;
and the great man, he uttereth his mischievous desire:
so they wrap it up.

4 **The best of them** is as a brier:
the most upright is sharper than a thorn hedge:
the day of thy watchmen and thy visitation cometh;
now shall be their perplexity.

5 **Trust ye not** in a friend,
put ye not confidence in a guide:
keep the doors of thy mouth from her that lieth in thy bosom.

6 **For the son** dishonoureth the father,
the daughter riseth up against her mother,
the daughter in law against her mother in law;
a man's enemies are the men of his own house.

7 **Therefore I** will look unto the LORD;
I will wait for the God of my salvation:
my God will hear me.

8 **Rejoice not** against me, O mine enemy:
when I fall,
I shall arise;
when I sit in darkness,
the LORD shall be a light unto me.

9 **I** will bear the indignation of the LORD,
because I have sinned against him,
until he plead my cause,
and execute judgment for me:
he will bring me forth to the light,
and I shall behold his righteousness.

10 **Then she that is mine enemy** shall see it,
and shame shall cover her which said unto me,
Where is the LORD thy God?
mine eyes shall behold her:
now shall she be trodden down as the mire of the streets.

11 **In the day that thy walls are to be built,** in that day shall the decree be far removed.

12 **In that day** also he shall come even to thee from Assyria, and from the fortified cities, and from the fortress even to the river, and from sea to sea, and from mountain to mountain.

13 **Notwithstanding the land** shall be desolate because of them that dwell therein, for the fruit of their doings.

14 **Feed** thy people with thy rod, the flock of thine heritage,
which dwell solitarily in the wood, in the midst of Carmel:
let them feed in Bashan and Gilead, as in the days of old.

15 **According to the days of thy coming out of the land of Egypt** will I shew unto him marvellous things.

16 **The nations** shall see
and be confounded at all their might:
they shall lay their hand upon their mouth,
their ears shall be deaf.

17 **They** shall lick the dust like a serpent,
they shall move out of their holes like worms of the earth:
they shall be afraid of the LORD our God,
and shall fear because of thee.

18 **Who** is a God like unto thee,
that pardoneth iniquity,
and passeth by the transgression of the remnant of his heritage?
he retaineth not his anger for ever,
because he delighteth in mercy.

19 **He** will turn again,
he will have compassion upon us;
he will subdue our iniquities;
and thou wilt cast all their sins into the depths of the sea.

20 **Thou** wilt perform the truth to Jacob, and the mercy to Abraham,
which thou hast sworn unto our fathers from the days of old.

Nahum

The Book of Nahum, written by the prophet Nahum approximately one hundred years after the fall of the northern Kingdom of Israel, sends a prophetic message of hope and comfort to the chosen people of God who are suffering under the oppression of the Assyrians. Its primary focus concerns the coming judgment against Nineveh, which was previously spared due to its people's repentance in response to Jonah's prophetic message. However, the people of Nineveh have since returned to their sinful ways and are facing God's wrath.

The book emphasizes God's righteous anger towards wickedness and His determination to punish those who defy Him. It serves as a reminder that God is just and will not let evil go unpunished. Nahum's prophecy against the Assyrians contains graphic descriptions of Nineveh's destruction, with vivid imagery of the city being overthrown and its people suffering greatly. It warns all nations that God's judgment will ultimately prevail over those who rebel against Him. Importantly, the book underscores God's sovereignty over all nations and events, instilling a sense of trust and faith that He is in control, even when evil appears to triumph.

Despite this harsh message of judgment, the book still portrays God as compassionate and merciful, Who desires repentance and offers salvation to those who turn from their wicked ways. The Book of Nahum ultimately provides hope and comfort to anyone suffering under the oppression of evil. By offering encouragement and reassurance to struggling souls, it serves as a graphic reminder that God is on the side of those who trust in Him, and He will bring about justice and deliverance in due time.

1 The burden of Nineveh.
The book of the vision of Nahum the Elkoshite.

2 **God** is jealous,
and the LORD revengeth;
the LORD revengeth,
and is furious;
the LORD will take vengeance on his adversaries,
and he reserveth wrath for his enemies.

3 **The LORD** is slow to anger, and great in power,
and will not at all acquit the wicked:
the LORD hath his way in the whirlwind and in the storm,
and the clouds are the dust of his feet.

4 **He** rebuketh the sea,
and maketh it dry,
and drieth up all the rivers:
Bashan languisheth,
and Carmel, and the flower of Lebanon languisheth.

5 **The mountains** quake at him,
and the hills melt,
and the earth is burned at his presence, yea, the world, and all that dwell therein.

6 **Who** can stand before his indignation?
and who can abide in the fierceness of his anger?
his fury is poured out like fire,
and the rocks are thrown down by him.

7 **The LORD** is good, a strong hold in the day of trouble;
and he knoweth them that trust in him.

8 **But with an overrunning flood** he will make an utter end of the place thereof,
and darkness shall pursue his enemies.

9 **What** do ye imagine against the LORD?
he will make an utter end:
affliction shall not rise up the second time.

10 **For while they** be folden together as thorns,
and while they are drunken as drunkards,
they shall be devoured as stubble fully dry.

11 **There** is one come out of thee,
that imagineth evil against the LORD, a wicked counsellor.

12 **Thus** saith the LORD;
Though they be quiet, and likewise many,
yet thus shall they be cut down,
when he shall pass through.
Though I have afflicted thee,
I will afflict thee no more.

13 **For now** will I break his yoke from off thee,
and will burst thy bonds in sunder.

14 **And the LORD** hath given a commandment concerning thee,
that no more of thy name be sown:
out of the house of thy gods will I cut off the graven image and the molten image:
I will make thy grave;
for thou art vile.

15 **Behold** upon the mountains the feet of him that bringeth good tidings, that publisheth peace!
O Judah, keep thy solemn feasts,
perform thy vows:
for the wicked shall no more pass through thee;
he is utterly cut off.

2 **He that dasheth in pieces** is come up before thy face:
keep the munition,
watch the way,
make thy loins strong,
fortify thy power mightily.

2 **For the LORD** hath turned away the excellency of Jacob, as the excellency of Israel:
for the emptiers have emptied them out,
and marred their vine branches.

3 **The shield of his mighty men** is made red,
the valiant men are in scarlet:

the chariots shall be with flaming torches in the day of his preparation,
and the fir trees shall be terribly shaken.
4 **The chariots** shall rage in the streets,
they shall justle one against another in the broad ways:
they shall seem like torches,
they shall run like the lightnings.
5 **He** shall recount his worthies:
they shall stumble in their walk;
they shall make haste to the wall thereof,
and the defence shall be prepared.
6 **The gates of the rivers** shall be opened,
and the palace shall be dissolved.
7 **And Huzzab** shall be led away captive,
she shall be brought up,
and her maids shall lead her as with the voice of doves,
tabering upon their breasts.
8 **But Nineveh** is of old like a pool of water:
yet they shall flee away.
Stand, stand, shall they cry;
but none shall look back.
9 **Take ye** the spoil of silver,
take the spoil of gold:
for there is none end of the store and glory out of all the pleasant furniture.
10 **She** is empty, and void, and waste:
and the heart melteth,
and the knees smite together,
and much pain is in all loins,
and the faces of them all gather blackness.
11 **Where** is the dwelling of the lions, and the feedingplace of the young lions,
where the lion, even the old lion, walked, and the lion's whelp,
and none made them afraid?
12 **The lion** did tear in pieces enough for his whelps,
and strangled for his lionesses,
and filled his holes with prey, and his dens with ravin.
13 **Behold,**
I am against thee,
saith the LORD of hosts,
and I will burn her chariots in the smoke,
and the sword shall devour thy young lions:
and I will cut off thy prey from the earth,
and the voice of thy messengers shall no more be heard.

3 **Woe** to the bloody city!
it is all full of lies and robbery;
the prey departeth not;
2 The noise of a whip, and the noise of the rattling of the wheels, and of the pransing horses, and of the jumping chariots.
3 **The horseman** lifteth up both the bright sword and the glittering spear:
and there is a multitude of slain, and a great number of carcases;
and there is none end of their corpses;
they stumble upon their corpses:
4 Because of the multitude of the whoredoms of the wellfavoured harlot, the mistress of witchcrafts,
that selleth nations through her whoredoms, and families through her witchcrafts.
5 **Behold,**
I am against thee,
saith the LORD of hosts;
and I will discover thy skirts upon thy face,
and I will shew the nations thy nakedness, and the kingdoms thy shame.
6 **And I** will cast abominable filth upon thee,
and make thee vile,
and will set thee as a gazingstock.
7 **And it** shall come to pass,
that all they that look upon thee shall flee from thee,
and say,
Nineveh is laid waste:
who will bemoan her?
whence shall I seek comforters for thee?
8 **Art thou** better than populous No,
that was situate among the rivers,
that had the waters round about it,
whose rampart was the sea,
and her wall was from the sea?
9 **Ethiopia and Egypt** were her strength,
and it was infinite;
Put and Lubim were thy helpers.
10 **Yet** was she carried away,
she went into captivity:
her young children also were dashed in pieces at the top of all the streets:
and they cast lots for her honourable men,
and all her great men were bound in chains.
11 **Thou** also shalt be drunken:
thou shalt be hid,
thou also shalt seek strength because of the enemy.
12 **All thy strong holds** shall be like fig trees with the firstripe figs:
if they be shaken,
they shall even fall into the mouth of the eater.
13 **Behold,**
thy people in the midst of thee are women:
the gates of thy land shall be set wide open unto thine enemies:
the fire shall devour thy bars.
14 **Draw** thee waters for the siege,
fortify thy strong holds:
go into clay,
and tread the morter,
make strong the brickkiln.
15 **There** shall the fire devour thee;
the sword shall cut thee off,
it shall eat thee up like the cankerworm:
make thyself many as the cankerworm,
make thyself many as the locusts.
16 **Thou** hast multiplied thy merchants above the stars of heaven:
the cankerworm spoileth,
and fleeth away.
17 **Thy crowned** are as the locusts,
and thy captains as the great grasshoppers,
which camp in the hedges in the cold day,
but when the sun ariseth
they flee away,
and their place is not known
where they are.
18 **Thy shepherds** slumber, O king of Assyria:
thy nobles shall dwell in the dust:
thy people is scattered upon the mountains,
and no man gathereth them.
19 **There** is no healing of thy bruise;
thy wound is grievous:
all that hear the bruit of thee shall clap the hands over thee:
for upon whom hath not thy wickedness passed continually?

Habakkuk

The Book of Habakkuk, penned by the prophet Habakkuk in the midst of his own turmoil, calls the people of Judah to repent and trust in God. He understands their pain and uncertainty, and his message may have been God's final warning to the Judeans before the Babylonian invasion. However, it certainly was not the only one.

The book opens with Habakkuk questioning and complaining to God about the injustices he sees around him. He asks how long God will allow the wicked to rule and oppress the righteous. God responds by revealing His plan to use the Babylonians as an instrument of judgment against the wicked people in Judah. He tells Habakkuk that the Babylonians will conquer Judah. Still, He promises that they, too, will be judged for their arrogance and violence. Of particular note is the book's second chapter, which contains a famous verse (2:4) that becomes a central tenet of the Protestant Reformation: the righteous will live by faith in God, not by their own strength or works.

Habakkuk also paints a vivid future where the righteous will triumph, and the wicked will be judged. This vision is a beacon of hope for the faithful, a promise that their suffering and persecution will not be in vain. Finally, the prophet concludes his message with a prayer, a testament to his unwavering trust in God's dominion and power, even in the face of adversity. The Book of Habakkuk is a reminder to the people of Judah that God's goodness and love will prevail, even in times of great hardship, and it serves as a call to repentance and a reminder of the importance of trusting in God's plan, even when it is difficult to understand.

1

The burden which Habakkuk the prophet did see.

2 **O LORD, how long** shall I cry,
and thou wilt not hear!
even cry out unto thee of violence,
and thou wilt not save!

3 **Why** dost thou shew me iniquity,
and cause me to behold grievance?
for spoiling and violence are before me:
and there are that raise up strife and contention.

4 **Therefore the law** is slacked,
and judgment doth never go forth:
for the wicked doth compass about the righteous;
therefore wrong judgment proceedeth.

5 **Behold ye** among the heathen,
and regard,
and wonder marvelously:
for I will work a work in your days
which ye will not believe,
though it be told you.

6 **For, {lo}, I** raise up the Chaldeans, that bitter and hasty nation,
which shall march through the breadth of the land,
to possess the dwellingplaces that are not their's.

7 **They** are terrible and dreadful:
their judgment and their dignity shall proceed of themselves.

8 **Their horses** also are swifter than the leopards,
and are more fierce than the evening wolves:
and their horsemen shall spread themselves,
and their horsemen shall come from far;
they shall fly as the eagle that hasteth to eat.

9 **They** shall come all for violence:
their faces shall sup up as the east wind,
and they shall gather the captivity as the sand.

10 **And they** shall scoff at the kings,
and the princes shall be a scorn unto them:
they shall deride every strong hold;
for they shall heap dust,
and take it.

11 **Then** shall his mind change,
and he shall pass over,
and offend,
imputing this his power unto his god.

12 **Art thou not** from everlasting, O LORD my God, mine Holy One?
we shall not die.
O LORD, thou hast ordained them for judgment;
and, O mighty God, thou hast established them for correction.

13 **Thou** art of purer eyes than to behold evil,
and canst not look on iniquity:
wherefore lookest thou upon them that deal treacherously,
and holdest thy tongue
when the wicked devoureth the man that is more righteous than he?

14 **And makest** men as the fishes of the sea, as the creeping things,
that have no ruler over them?

15 **They** take up all of them with the angle,
they catch them in their net,
and gather them in their drag:
therefore they rejoice
and are glad.

16 **Therefore they** sacrifice unto their net,
and burn incense unto their drag;
because by them their portion is fat,
and their meat plenteous.

17 **Shall they** therefore empty their net,
and not spare continually to slay the nations?

2

I will stand upon my watch,
and set me upon the tower,
and will watch to see what he will say unto me,
and what I shall answer
when I am reproved.

2 **And the LORD** answered me,
and said,

Write the vision,
and make it plain upon tables,
that he may run that readeth it.
[3] **For the vision** is yet for an appointed time,
but at the end it shall speak,
and not lie:
though it tarry,
wait for it;
because it will surely come,
it will not tarry.
[4] **Behold,**
his soul which is lifted up is not upright in him:
but the just shall live by his faith.
[5] **Yea also, because he** transgresseth by wine,
he is a proud man,
neither keepeth at home,
who enlargeth his desire as hell,
and is as death,
and cannot be satisfied,
but gathereth unto him all nations,
and heapeth unto him all people:
[6] **Shall not all these** take up a parable against him, and a taunting proverb against him,
and say,
Woe to him that increaseth that which is not his!
how long?
and to him that ladeth himself with thick clay!
[7] **Shall they not** rise up suddenly that shall bite thee,
and awake that shall vex thee,
and thou shalt be for booties unto them?
[8] **Because thou** hast spoiled many nations,
all the remnant of the people shall spoil thee; because of men's blood, and for the violence of the land, of the city, and of all that dwell therein.
[9] **Woe** to him that coveteth an evil covetousness to his house,
that he may set his nest on high,
that he may be delivered from the power of evil!
[10] **Thou** hast consulted shame to thy house
by cutting off many people,
and hast sinned against thy soul.
[11] **For the stone** shall cry out of the wall,
and the beam out of the timber shall answer it.
[12] **Woe** to him that buildeth a town with blood, and stablisheth a city by iniquity!
[13] **Behold,**
is it not of the LORD of hosts that the people shall labour in the very fire,
and the people shall weary themselves for very vanity?
[14] **For the earth** shall be filled with the knowledge of the glory of the LORD,
as the waters cover the sea.
[15] **Woe** unto him that giveth his neighbour drink, that puttest thy bottle to him, and makest him drunken also,
that thou mayest look on their nakedness!
[16] **Thou** art filled with shame for glory:
drink thou also,
and let thy foreskin be uncovered:
the cup of the LORD's right hand shall be turned unto thee,
and shameful spewing shall be on thy glory.

[17] **For the violence of Lebanon** shall cover thee, and the spoil of beasts, {which made them afraid}, because of men's blood, and for the violence of the land, of the city, and of all that dwell therein.
[18] **What** profiteth the graven image
that the maker thereof hath graven it; the molten image, and a teacher of lies,
that the maker of his work trusteth therein,
to make dumb idols?
[19] **Woe** unto him that saith to the wood, {Awake}; to the dumb stone, {Arise}, {it shall teach}!
Behold,
it is laid over with gold and silver,
and there is no breath at all in the midst of it.
[20] **But the LORD** is in his holy temple:
let all the earth keep silence before him.

3 A prayer of Habakkuk the prophet upon Shigionoth.
[2] **O LORD, I** have heard thy speech,
and was afraid:
O LORD, revive thy work in the midst of the years,
in the midst of the years make known;
in wrath remember mercy.
[3] **God** came from Teman,
and the Holy One from mount Paran.
Selah.
His glory covered the heavens,
and the earth was full of his praise.
[4] **And his brightness** was as the light;
he had horns coming out of his hand:
and there was the hiding of his power.
[5] **Before him** went the pestilence,
and burning coals went forth at his feet.
[6] **He** stood,
and measured the earth:
he beheld,
and drove asunder the nations;
and the everlasting mountains were scattered,
the perpetual hills did bow:
his ways are everlasting.
[7] **I** saw the tents of Cushan in affliction:
and the curtains of the land of Midian did tremble.
[8] **Was the LORD** displeased against the rivers?
was thine anger against the rivers?
was thy wrath against the sea,
that thou didst ride upon thine horses and thy chariots of salvation?
[9] **Thy bow** was made quite naked, according to the oaths of the tribes, even thy word.
Selah.
Thou didst cleave the earth with rivers.
[10] **The mountains** saw thee,
and they trembled:
the overflowing of the water passed by:
the deep uttered his voice,
and lifted up his hands on high.
[11] **The sun and moon** stood still in their habitation:
at the light of thine arrows they went, and at the shining of thy glittering spear.
[12] **Thou** didst march through the land in indignation,
thou didst thresh the heathen in anger.

13 **Thou** wentest forth for the salvation of thy people, even for salvation with thine anointed;
thou woundedst the head out of the house of the wicked,
by discovering the foundation unto the neck.
Selah.

14 **Thou** didst strike through with his staves the head of his villages:
they came out as a whirlwind to scatter me:
their rejoicing was as to devour the poor secretly.

15 **Thou** didst walk through the sea with thine horses, through the heap of great waters.

16 **When I** heard,
my belly trembled;
my lips quivered at the voice:
rottenness entered into my bones,
and I trembled in myself,
that I might rest in the day of trouble:
when he cometh up unto the people,
he will invade them with his troops.

17 **Although the fig tree** shall not blossom,
neither shall fruit be in the vines;
the labour of the olive shall fail,
and the fields shall yield no meat;
the flock shall be cut off from the fold,
and there shall be no herd in the stalls:

18 **Yet I** will rejoice in the LORD,
I will joy in the God of my salvation.

19 **The LORD God** is my strength,
and he will make my feet like hinds' feet,
and he will make me to walk upon mine high places.

To the chief singer on my stringed instruments.

Zephaniah

The Book of Zephaniah, penned by the prophet Zephaniah during the reign of King Josiah, delivers a stark warning to the people of Judah and the surrounding nations. It foretells of God's impending judgment, a dire consequence of their sins and idolatry. The prophet's words paint a picture of God sweeping away everything from the face of the earth, from the animal kingdom to humanity, a chilling reference to the imminent judgment on Judah and Jerusalem.

He refers to this affliction as the *Day of the Lord,* a time of darkness, distress, and destruction when God intervenes in human affairs to bring judgment to the wicked. Yet after Zephaniah speaks of this imminent destruction, his message takes a turn towards hope and restoration. He envisions a future of grace and prosperity for those who repent and turn to God. He passionately urges the people to pursue virtue, truth, and humility before the Lord, their only way to escape the coming affliction.

The Book of Zephaniah then closes with a promise that one day, God will deliver the people from their enemies, and He will rejoice over them with singing. It promises a glorious future for those who turn to God and seek His righteousness.

1 The word of the LORD which came unto Zephaniah the son of Cushi, the son of Gedaliah, the son of Amariah, the son of Hizkiah, in the days of Josiah the son of Amon, king of Judah.

2 **I** will utterly consume all things from off the land,
saith the LORD.

3 **I** will consume man and beast;
I will consume the fowls of the heaven, and the fishes of the sea, and the stumbling blocks with the wicked:
and I will cut off man from off the land,
saith the LORD.

4 **I** will also stretch out mine hand upon Judah, and upon all the inhabitants of Jerusalem;
and I will cut off the remnant of Baal from this place, and the name of the Chemarims with the priests;

5 And them that worship the host of heaven upon the housetops; and them that worship and that swear by the LORD, and that swear by Malcham;

6 And them that are turned back from the LORD; and those that have not sought the LORD, nor enquired for him.

7 **Hold thy peace** at the presence of the Lord GOD:
for the day of the LORD is at hand:
for the LORD hath prepared a sacrifice,
he hath bid his guests.

8 **And it** shall come to pass in the day of the LORD's sacrifice,
that I will punish the princes, and the king's children, and all such as are clothed with strange apparel.

9 **In the same day** also will I punish all those that leap on the threshold,
which fill their masters' houses with violence and deceit.

10 **And it** shall come to pass in that day,
saith the LORD,
that there shall be the noise of a cry from the fish gate, and an howling from the second, and a great crashing from the hills.

11 **Howl,** ye inhabitants of Maktesh,
for all the merchant people are cut down;
all they that bear silver are cut off.

12 **And it** shall come to pass at that time,
that I will search Jerusalem with candles,
and punish the men that are settled on their lees:
that say in their heart,
The LORD will not do good,
neither will he do evil.

13 **Therefore their goods** shall become a booty,
and their houses a desolation:
they shall also build houses,
but not inhabit them;
and they shall plant vineyards,
but not drink the wine thereof.

14 **The great day of the LORD** is near,
it is near,
and hasteth greatly, even the voice of the day of the LORD:
the mighty man shall cry there bitterly.

15 **That day** is a day of wrath, a day of trouble and distress, a day of wasteness and desolation, a day of darkness and gloominess, a day of clouds and thick darkness,

16 A day of the trumpet and alarm against the fenced cities, and against the high towers.

17 **And I** will bring distress upon men,
that they shall walk like blind men,
because they have sinned against the LORD:
and their blood shall be poured out as dust,
and their flesh as the dung.

18 **Neither their silver nor their gold** shall be able to deliver them in the day of the LORD's wrath;
but the whole land shall be devoured by the fire of his jealousy:
for he shall make even a speedy riddance of all them that dwell in the land.

2 **Gather** yourselves together, **yea, gather** together, O nation not desired;

2 **Before the decree** bring forth,
before the day pass as the chaff,
before the fierce anger of the LORD come upon you,
before the day of the LORD's anger come upon you.

3 **Seek ye** the LORD, all ye meek of the earth,

which have wrought his judgment;
seek righteousness,
seek meekness:
it may be ye shall be hid in the day of the LORD's anger.

4 **For Gaza** shall be forsaken,
and Ashkelon a desolation:
they shall drive out Ashdod at the noon day,
and Ekron shall be rooted up.

5 **Woe** unto the inhabitants of the sea coast, the nation of the Cherethites!
the word of the LORD is against you;
O Canaan, the land of the Philistines, I will even destroy thee,
that there shall be no inhabitant.

6 **And the sea coast** shall be dwellings and cottages for shepherds, and folds for flocks.

7 **And the coast** shall be for the remnant of the house of Judah;
they shall feed thereupon:
in the houses of Ashkelon shall they lie down in the evening:
for the LORD their God shall visit them,
and turn away their captivity.

8 **I** have heard the reproach of Moab, and the revilings of the children of Ammon,
whereby they have reproached my people,
and magnified themselves against their border.

9 **Therefore as I** live,
saith the LORD of hosts, the God of Israel,
Surely Moab shall be as Sodom,
and the children of Ammon as Gomorrah, even the breeding of nettles, and saltpits, and a perpetual desolation:
the residue of my people shall spoil them,
and the remnant of my people shall possess them.

10 **This** shall they have for their pride,
because they have reproached and magnified themselves against the people of the LORD of hosts.

11 **The LORD** will be terrible unto them:
for he will famish all the gods of the earth;
and men shall worship him, every one from his place, even all the isles of the heathen.

12 **Ye Ethiopians also, ye** shall be slain by my sword.

13 **And he** will stretch out his hand against the north,
and destroy Assyria;
and will make Nineveh a desolation, and dry like a wilderness.

14 **And flocks** shall lie down in the midst of her, all the beasts of the nations:
both the cormorant and the bittern shall lodge in the upper lintels of it;
their voice shall sing in the windows;
desolation shall be in the thresholds;
for he shall uncover the cedar work.

15 **This** is the rejoicing city
that dwelt carelessly,
that said in her heart,
I am,
and there is none beside me:
how is she become a desolation,
a place for beasts to lie down in!
every one that passeth by her shall hiss,
and wag his hand.

3

Woe to her that is filthy and polluted, to the oppressing city!

2 **She** obeyed not the voice;
she received not correction;
she trusted not in the LORD;
she drew not near to her God.

3 **Her princes within her** are roaring lions;
her judges are evening wolves;
they gnaw not the bones till the morrow.

4 **Her prophets** are light and treacherous persons:
her priests have polluted the sanctuary,
they have done violence to the law.

5 **The just LORD** is in the midst thereof;
he will not do iniquity:
every morning doth he bring his judgment to light,
he faileth not;
but the unjust knoweth no shame.

6 **I** have cut off the nations:
their towers are desolate;
I made their streets waste,
that none passeth by:
their cities are destroyed,
so that there is no man,
that there is none inhabitant.

7 **I** said,
Surely thou wilt fear me,
thou wilt receive instruction;
so their dwelling should not be cut off,
howsoever I punished them:
but they rose early,
and corrupted all their doings.

8 **Therefore wait ye** upon me, {saith the LORD}, until the day that I rise up to the prey:
for my determination is to gather the nations,
that I may assemble the kingdoms,
to pour upon them mine indignation, even all my fierce anger:
for all the earth shall be devoured with the fire of my jealousy.

9 **For then** will I turn to the people a pure language,
that they may all call upon the name of the LORD,
to serve him with one consent.

10 **From beyond the rivers of Ethiopia** my suppliants, even the daughter of my dispersed, shall bring mine offering.

11 **In that day** shalt thou not be ashamed for all thy doings,
wherein thou hast transgressed against me:
for then I will take away out of the midst of thee them that rejoice in thy pride,
and thou shalt no more be haughty because of my holy mountain.

12 **I** will also leave in the midst of thee an afflicted and poor people,
and they shall trust in the name of the LORD.

13 **The remnant of Israel** shall not do iniquity,
nor speak lies;
neither shall a deceitful tongue be found in their mouth:
for they shall feed
and lie down,
and none shall make them afraid.

14 **Sing,** O daughter of Zion;
shout, O Israel;
be glad
and rejoice with all the heart, O daughter of Jerusalem.

15 **The LORD** hath taken away thy judgments,

he hath cast out thine enemy:
the king of Israel, even the LORD, is in the midst of thee:
thou shalt not see evil any more.

16 **In that day** it shall be said to Jerusalem, {Fear thou not}: and to Zion, {Let not thine hands be slack}.

17 **The LORD thy God in the midst of thee** is mighty;
he will save,
he will rejoice over thee with joy;
he will rest in his love,
he will joy over thee with singing.

18 **I** will gather them that are sorrowful for the solemn assembly,
who are of thee,
to whom the reproach of it was a burden.

19 **Behold,**
at that time I will undo all that afflict thee:
and I will save her that halteth,
and gather her that was driven out;
and I will get them praise and fame in every land where they have been put to shame.

20 **At that time** will I bring you again, even in the time that I gather you:
for I will make you a name and a praise among all people of the earth,
when I turn back your captivity before your eyes,
saith the LORD.

Haggai

The Book of Haggai, written by the prophet Haggai, is a historical testament that hones in on the prophet's messages regarding the arduous journey of the Israelites in rebuilding the Temple after the Babylonian exile. Haggai's prophecy emerges at a time when the Israelites are grappling with the reconstruction of a Temple that lies in ruins, a task that seems insurmountable due to their prevalent complacency and apathy. He calls upon the people to prioritize this task and rekindle their memory of the nation's covenant with God.

Haggai's prophecies underscore the Temple's significance as a symbol of the people's relationship with God and as a means for restoring their national identity. He contends that the people's lack of progress is a testament to their spiritual decline and a failure to uphold their part of the covenant. The prophet's messages, woven with divine promises and warnings about the repercussions of disobedience, serve as a beacon of hope and a harbinger of fear. They reassure the Israelites that God will bestow peace upon them if they adhere to His commandments, and the prophet pledges God's blessing for those who revive the nation's sacred place of worship.

The book also speaks of Zerubbabel, the governor of Judah, whom the prophet envisions as a key figure in restoring Israel's fortunes and leading the people in their reconstruction efforts. Haggai, therefore, underscores that a righteous relationship with God is grounded in a faith that leads to a dedication to uphold His covenant. So how can they honor it? By rebuilding the Temple, a structure that symbolizes their spiritual connection to Him.

1 **In the second year of Darius the king, in the sixth month, in the first day of the month,** came the word of the LORD by Haggai the prophet unto Zerubbabel the son of Shealtiel, governor of Judah, and to Joshua the son of Josedech, the high priest,
saying,
2 **Thus** speaketh the LORD of hosts, saying,
This people say,
The time is not come,
the time that the LORD's house should be built.
3 **Then** came the word of the LORD by Haggai the prophet,
saying,
4 **Is it time for you**, O ye, to dwell in your cieled houses,
and this house lie waste?
5 **Now therefore thus** saith the LORD of hosts;
Consider your ways.
6 **Ye** have sown much,
and bring in little;
ye eat,
but ye have not enough;
ye drink,
but ye are not filled with drink;
ye clothe you,
but there is none warm;
and he that earneth wages earneth wages to put it into a bag with holes.
7 **Thus** saith the LORD of hosts;
Consider your ways.
8 **Go up** to the mountain,
and bring wood,
and build the house;
and I will take pleasure in it,
and I will be glorified,
saith the LORD.
9 **Ye** looked for much,
and, {lo} it came to little;
and when ye brought it home,
I did blow upon it.
Why?
saith the LORD of hosts.
Because of mine house that is waste,
and ye run every man unto his own house.
10 **Therefore the heaven over you** is stayed from dew,
and the earth is stayed from her fruit.
11 **And I** called for a drought upon the land, and upon the mountains, and upon the corn, and upon the new wine, and upon the oil, and upon that which the ground bringeth forth, and upon men, and upon cattle, and upon all the labour of the hands.
12 **Then Zerubbabel the son of Shealtiel, and Joshua the son of Josedech, the high priest, with all the remnant of the people,** obeyed the voice of the LORD their God, and the words of Haggai the prophet,
as the LORD their God had sent him,
and the people did fear before the LORD.
13 **Then** spake Haggai the LORD's messenger in the LORD's message unto the people,
saying,
I am with you,
saith the LORD.
14 **And the LORD** stirred up the spirit of Zerubbabel the son of Shealtiel, governor of Judah, and the spirit of Joshua the son of Josedech, the high priest, and the spirit of all the remnant of the people;
and they came and did work in the house of the LORD of hosts, their God,
15 In the four and twentieth day of the sixth month, in the second year of Darius the king.

2 **In the seventh month, in the one and twentieth day of the month,** came the word of the LORD by the prophet Haggai,
saying,

2 **Speak** now to Zerubbabel the son of Shealtiel, governor of Judah, and to Joshua the son of Josedech, the high priest, and to the residue of the people,
saying,
3 **Who** is left among you that saw this house in her first glory?
and how do ye see it now?
is it not in your eyes in comparison of it as nothing?

4 **Yet now be** strong, O Zerubbabel,
saith the LORD;
and be strong, O Joshua, son of Josedech, the high priest;
and be strong, all ye people of the land,
saith the LORD,
and work:
for I am with you,
saith the LORD of hosts:
5 **According to the word that I covenanted with you {when ye came out of Egypt},** so my spirit remaineth among you:
fear ye not.

6 **For thus** saith the LORD of hosts;
Yet once, {it is a little while}, and I will shake the heavens, and the earth, and the sea, and the dry land;
7 **And I** will shake all nations,
and the desire of all nations shall come:
and I will fill this house with glory,
saith the LORD of hosts.

8 **The silver** is mine,
and the gold is mine,
saith the LORD of hosts.

9 **The glory of this latter house** shall be greater than of the former,
saith the LORD of hosts:
and in this place will I give peace,
saith the LORD of hosts.

10 **In the four and twentieth day of the ninth month, in the second year of Darius,** came the word of the LORD by Haggai the prophet,
saying,
11 **Thus** saith the LORD of hosts;
Ask now the priests concerning the law,
saying,
12 **If one** bear holy flesh in the skirt of his garment,
and with his skirt do touch bread, or pottage, or wine, or oil, or any meat,
shall it be holy?

And the priests answered and said,
No.

13 **Then** said Haggai,
If one that is unclean by a dead body touch any of these,
shall it be unclean?

And the priests answered and said,
It shall be unclean.

14 **Then** answered Haggai,
and said,
So is this people,
and so is this nation before me,
saith the LORD;
and so is every work of their hands;
and that which they offer there is unclean.

15 **And now, {I pray you}, consider** from this day and upward,
from before a stone was laid upon a stone in the temple of the LORD:
16 **Since those days** were,
when one came to an heap of twenty measures,
there were but ten:
when one came to the pressfat
for to draw out fifty vessels out of the press,
there were but twenty.

17 I smote you with blasting and with mildew and with hail in all the labours of your hands;
yet ye turned not to me,
saith the LORD.

18 **Consider** now from this day and upward, from the four and twentieth day of the ninth month, even from the day that the foundation of the LORD's temple was laid,
consider it.

19 **Is the seed** yet in the barn?
yea, as yet the vine, and the fig tree, and the pomegranate, and the olive tree, hath not brought forth:
from this day will I bless you.

20 **And again the word of the LORD** came unto Haggai in the four and twentieth day of the month,
saying,
21 **Speak** to Zerubbabel, governor of Judah,
saying,
I will shake the heavens and the earth;
22 **And I** will overthrow the throne of kingdoms,
and I will destroy the strength of the kingdoms of the heathen;
and I will overthrow the chariots, and those that ride in them;
and the horses and their riders shall come down, every one by the sword of his brother.

23 **In that day,** {saith the LORD of hosts}, will I take thee, O Zerubbabel, my servant, the son of Shealtiel,
saith the LORD,
and will make thee as a signet:
for I have chosen thee,
saith the LORD of hosts.

Zechariah

The Book of Zechariah, traditionally attributed to the prophet Zechariah, was written shortly after the Israelites' return from exile in Babylon. Filled with prophetic visions and messages, it is not just a historical account but a guide for the people as they reconstruct their nation.

Zechariah's appeal to rebuild the Temple in Jerusalem is a call to action and a profound mission. He urges the people to unite their efforts and promote a collective spirit of optimism and determination. He also offers them several glimpses into the future. These revelations include prophecies about the Messiah's arrival, the restoration of Jerusalem, and the ultimate victory of God's people over their adversaries. Yet Zechariah underscores the need for repentance and a return to God in order for them to receive His blessings and protection. Obedience is the key to redemption and a brighter future, a path that must be followed without delay.

Overall, the Book of Zechariah weaves a compelling story about the power of perseverance in the face of adversity. It also serves as a testament that, with unwavering faith and divine guidance, the Israelites can conquer even the most daunting tasks. However, the responsibility for achievement rests with the people. The path to spiritual growth, redemption, and blessing is always open and accessible, but only to those nations who actively seek it.

1 **In the eighth month, in the second year of Darius,**
came the word of the LORD unto Zechariah, the son of Berechiah, the son of Iddo the prophet,
saying,
2 **The LORD** hath been sore displeased with your fathers.
3 **Therefore** say thou unto them,
Thus saith the LORD of hosts;
Turn ye unto me,
saith the LORD of hosts,
and I will turn unto you,
saith the LORD of hosts.
4 **Be ye not** as your fathers,
unto whom the former prophets have cried,
saying,
Thus saith the LORD of hosts;
Turn ye now from your evil ways, and from your evil doings:
but they did not hear,
nor hearken unto me,
saith the LORD.
5 **Your fathers,** where are they?
and the prophets, do they live for ever?
6 **But my words and my statutes,** {which I commanded my servants the prophets}, did they not take hold of your fathers?
and they returned and said,
Like as the LORD of hosts thought to do unto us, according to our ways, and according to our doings,
so hath he dealt with us.
7 **Upon the four and twentieth day of the eleventh month,** {which is the month Sebat}, in the second year of Darius, came the word of the LORD unto Zechariah, the son of Berechiah, the son of Iddo the prophet,
saying,
8 **I** saw by night,
and behold a man riding upon a red horse,
and he stood among the myrtle trees that were in the bottom;
and behind him were there red horses, speckled, and white.
9 **Then** said I,
O my lord, what are these?
And the angel that talked with me said unto me,
I will shew thee what these be.
10 **And the man that stood among the myrtle trees** answered and said,
These are they whom the LORD hath sent to walk to and fro through the earth.
11 **And they** answered the angel of the LORD that stood among the myrtle trees,
and said,
We have walked to and fro through the earth,
and, {behold}, all the earth sitteth still,
and is at rest.
12 **Then the angel of the LORD** answered and said,
O LORD of hosts, how long wilt thou not have mercy on Jerusalem and on the cities of Judah,
against which thou hast had indignation these threescore and ten years?
13 **And the LORD** answered the angel that talked with me with good words and comfortable words.
14 **So the angel that communed with me** said unto me,
Cry thou,
saying,
Thus saith the LORD of hosts;
I am jealous for Jerusalem and for Zion with a great jealousy.
15 **And I** am very sore displeased with the heathen that are at ease:
for I was but a little displeased,
and they helped forward the affliction.
16 **Therefore thus** saith the LORD;
I am returned to Jerusalem with mercies:
my house shall be built in it,
saith the LORD of hosts,
and a line shall be stretched forth upon Jerusalem.
17 **Cry** yet,
saying,
Thus saith the LORD of hosts;
My cities through prosperity shall yet be spread abroad;
and the LORD shall yet comfort Zion,
and shall yet choose Jerusalem.
18 **Then** lifted I up mine eyes,

and saw,
and behold four horns.
19 **And I** said unto the angel that talked with me,
What be these?
And he answered me,
These are the horns which have scattered Judah, Israel, and Jerusalem.
20 **And the LORD** shewed me four carpenters.
21 **Then** said I,
What come these to do?
And he spake,
saying,
These are the horns which have scattered Judah,
so that no man did lift up his head:
but these are come
to fray them,
to cast out the horns of the Gentiles,
which lifted up their horn over the land of Judah
to scatter it.

2 I lifted up mine eyes again,
and looked,
and behold a man with a measuring line in his hand.
2 **Then** said I,
Whither goest thou?
And he said unto me,
To measure Jerusalem,
to see what is the breadth thereof,
and what is the length thereof.
3 **And, {behold}, the angel that talked with me** went forth,
and another angel went out
to meet him,
4 **And** said unto him,
Run,
speak to this young man,
saying,
Jerusalem shall be inhabited as towns without walls for the multitude of men and cattle therein:
5 **For I**, {saith the LORD}, will be unto her a wall of fire round about,
and will be the glory in the midst of her.
6 Ho, ho,
come forth,
and flee from the land of the north,
saith the LORD:
for I have spread you abroad as the four winds of the heaven,
saith the LORD.
7 **Deliver** thyself, O Zion,
that dwellest with the daughter of Babylon.
8 **For thus** saith the LORD of hosts;
After the glory hath he sent me unto the nations which spoiled you:
for he that toucheth you toucheth the apple of his eye.
9 **For, {behold}, I** will shake mine hand upon them,
and they shall be a spoil to their servants:
and ye shall know
that the LORD of hosts hath sent me.
10 **Sing and rejoice,** O daughter of Zion:
for, {lo}, I come,
and I will dwell in the midst of thee,
saith the LORD.
11 **And many nations** shall be joined to the LORD in that day,
and shall be my people:
and I will dwell in the midst of thee,
and thou shalt know
that the LORD of hosts hath sent me unto thee.
12 **And the LORD** shall inherit Judah his portion in the holy land,
and shall choose Jerusalem again.
13 **Be** silent, O all flesh, before the LORD:
for he is raised up out of his holy habitation.

3 **And he** shewed me Joshua the high priest standing before the angel of the LORD, and Satan standing at his right hand to resist him.
2 **And the LORD** said unto Satan,
The LORD rebuke thee, O Satan;
even the LORD that hath chosen Jerusalem rebuke thee:
is not this a brand plucked out of the fire?
3 **Now Joshua** was clothed with filthy garments,
and stood before the angel.
4 **And he** answered and spake unto those that stood before him,
saying,
Take away the filthy garments from him.
And unto him he said,
Behold,
I have caused thine iniquity to pass from thee,
and I will clothe thee with change of raiment.
5 **And I** said,
Let them set a fair mitre upon his head.
So they set a fair mitre upon his head,
and clothed him with garments.
And the angel of the LORD stood by.
6 **And the angel of the LORD** protested unto Joshua,
saying,
7 **Thus** saith the LORD of hosts;
If thou wilt walk in my ways,
and if thou wilt keep my charge,
then thou shalt also judge my house,
and shalt also keep my courts,
and I will give thee places to walk among these that stand by.
8 **Hear** now, O Joshua the high priest, thou, and thy fellows that sit before thee:
for they are men wondered at:
for, {behold}, I will bring forth my servant the Branch.
9 **For behold** the stone that I have laid before Joshua;
upon one stone shall be seven eyes:
behold,
I will engrave the graving thereof,
saith the LORD of hosts,
and I will remove the iniquity of that land in one day.
10 **In that day**, {saith the LORD of hosts}, shall ye call every man his neighbour under the vine and under the fig tree.

4 **And the angel that talked with me** came again,
and waked me, as a man that is wakened out of his sleep.
2 **And** said unto me,
What seest thou?
And I said,
I have looked,
and behold a candlestick all of gold, with a bowl upon the top of it, and his seven lamps thereon, and seven pipes to the seven lamps, {which are upon the top thereof}:
3 And two olive trees by it, one upon the right side of the bowl, and the other upon the left side thereof.
4 **So I** answered and spake to the angel that talked with me,
saying,
What are these, my lord?
5 **Then the angel that talked with me** answered and said unto me,

Knowest thou not
what these be?

And I said,
No, my lord.

6 **Then he** answered and spake unto me,
saying,
This is the word of the LORD unto Zerubbabel,
saying,
Not by might, nor by power, but by my spirit, saith the LORD of hosts.

7 **Who** art thou, O great mountain?
before Zerubbabel thou shalt become a plain:
and he shall bring forth the headstone thereof with shoutings,
crying,
Grace, grace unto it.

8 **Moreover the word of the LORD** came unto me,
saying,
9 **The hands of Zerubbabel** have laid the foundation of this house;
his hands shall also finish it;
and thou shalt know
that the LORD of hosts hath sent me unto you.

10 **For who** hath despised the day of small things?
for they shall rejoice,
and shall see the plummet in the hand of Zerubbabel with those seven;
they are the eyes of the LORD,
which run to and fro through the whole earth.

11 **Then** answered I,
and said unto him,
What are these two olive trees upon the right side of the candlestick and upon the left side thereof?

12 **And I** answered again,
and said unto him,
What be these two olive branches which through the two golden pipes empty the golden oil out of themselves?

13 **And he** answered me and said,
Knowest thou not
what these be?

And I said,
No, my lord.

14 **Then** said he,
These are the two anointed ones,
that stand by the Lord of the whole earth.

5

Then I turned,
and lifted up mine eyes,
and looked,
and behold a flying roll.

2 **And he** said unto me,
What seest thou?

And I answered,
I see a flying roll;
the length thereof is twenty cubits, and the breadth thereof ten cubits.

3 **Then** said he unto me,
This is the curse that goeth forth over the face of the whole earth:
for every one that stealeth shall be cut off as on this side according to it;
and every one that sweareth shall be cut off as on that side according to it.

4 **I** will bring it forth,
saith the LORD of hosts,
and it shall enter into the house of the thief, and into the house of him that sweareth falsely by my name:
and it shall remain in the midst of his house,
and shall consume it with the timber thereof and the stones thereof.

5 **Then the angel that talked with me** went forth,
and said unto me,
Lift up now thine eyes,
and see what is this that goeth forth.

6 **And I** said,
What is it?

And he said,
This is an ephah that goeth forth.

He said moreover,
This is their resemblance through all the earth.

7 **And, {behold}, there** was lifted up a talent of lead:
and this is a woman that sitteth in the midst of the ephah.

8 **And he** said,
This is wickedness.

And he cast it into the midst of the ephah;
and he cast the weight of lead upon the mouth thereof.

9 **Then** lifted I up mine eyes,
and looked,
and, {behold}, there came out two women,
and the wind was in their wings;
for they had wings like the wings of a stork:
and they lifted up the ephah between the earth and the heaven.

10 **Then** said I to the angel that talked with me,
Whither do these bear the ephah?

11 **And he** said unto me,
To build it an house in the land of Shinar:
and it shall be established,
and set there upon her own base.

6

And I turned,
and lifted up mine eyes,
and looked,
and, {behold}, there came four chariots out from between two mountains;
and the mountains were mountains of brass.

2 **In the first chariot** were red horses; and in the second chariot black horses;
3 And in the third chariot white horses; and in the fourth chariot grisled and bay horses.

4 **Then I** answered and said unto the angel that talked with me,
What are these, my lord?

5 **And the angel** answered and said unto me,
These are the four spirits of the heavens,
which go forth from standing before the Lord of all the earth.

6 **The black horses which are therein** go forth into the north country;
and the white go forth after them;
and the grisled go forth toward the south country.

7 **And the bay** went forth,
and sought to go that they might walk to and fro through the earth:
and he said,
Get you hence,
walk to and fro through the earth.

So they walked to and fro through the earth.

8 **Then** cried he upon me,
and spake unto me,
saying,
Behold,
these that go toward the north country have quieted my spirit in the north country.

9 **And the word of the LORD** came unto me,

saying,
10 **Take** of them of the captivity, even of Heldai, of Tobijah, and of Jedaiah,
which are come from Babylon,
and come thou the same day,
and go into the house of Josiah the son of Zephaniah;
11 **Then take** silver and gold,
and make crowns,
and set them upon the head of Joshua the son of Josedech, the high priest;
12 **And speak** unto him,
saying,
Thus speaketh the LORD of hosts,
saying,
Behold the man whose name is The Branch;
and he shall grow up out of his place,
and he shall build the temple of the LORD:
13 **Even he** shall build the temple of the LORD;
and he shall bear the glory,
and shall sit and rule upon his throne;
and he shall be a priest upon his throne:
and the counsel of peace shall be between them both.
14 **And the crowns** shall be to Helem, and to Tobijah, and to Jedaiah, and to Hen the son of Zephaniah, for a memorial in the temple of the LORD.
15 **And they that are far off** shall come and build in the temple of the LORD,
and ye shall know
that the LORD of hosts hath sent me unto you.
And this shall come to pass,
if ye will diligently obey the voice of the LORD your God.

7 **And it** came to pass in the fourth year of king Darius,
that the word of the LORD came unto Zechariah in the fourth day of the ninth month, even in Chisleu;
2 **When they** had sent unto the house of God Sherezer and Regemmelech, and their men,
to pray before the LORD,
3 **And** to speak unto the priests which were in the house of the LORD of hosts, and to the prophets,
saying,
Should I weep in the fifth month, separating myself,
as I have done these so many years?
4 **Then** came the word of the LORD of hosts unto me,
saying,
5 **Speak** unto all the people of the land, and to the priests,
saying,
When ye fasted and mourned in the fifth and seventh month, even those seventy years,
did ye at all fast unto me, even to me?
6 **And when ye** did eat,
and when ye did drink,
did not ye eat for yourselves,
and drink for yourselves?
7 **Should ye not** hear the words which the LORD hath cried by the former prophets,
when Jerusalem was inhabited and in prosperity, and the cities thereof round about her,
when men inhabited the south and the plain?
8 **And the word of the LORD** came unto Zechariah,
saying,
9 **Thus** speaketh the LORD of hosts,
saying,
Execute true judgment,
and shew mercy and compassions every man to his brother:
10 **And oppress not** the widow, nor the fatherless, the stranger, nor the poor;
and let none of you imagine evil against his brother in your heart.
11 **But they** refused to hearken,
and pulled away the shoulder,
and stopped their ears,
that they should not hear.
12 **Yea, they** made their hearts as an adamant stone,
lest they should hear the law, and the words which the LORD of hosts hath sent in his spirit by the former prophets:
therefore came a great wrath from the LORD of hosts.
13 **Therefore it** is come to pass,
that as he cried,
and they would not hear;
so they cried,
and I would not hear,
saith the LORD of hosts:
14 **But I** scattered them with a whirlwind among all the nations whom they knew not.
Thus the land was desolate after them,
that no man passed through
nor returned:
for they laid the pleasant land desolate.

8 **Again the word of the LORD of hosts** came to me,
saying,
2 **Thus** saith the LORD of hosts;
I was jealous for Zion with great jealousy,
and I was jealous for her with great fury.
3 **Thus** saith the LORD;
I am returned unto Zion,
and will dwell in the midst of Jerusalem:
and Jerusalem shall be called a city of truth; and the mountain of the LORD of hosts the holy mountain.
4 **Thus** saith the LORD of hosts;
There shall yet old men and old women dwell in the streets of Jerusalem, and every man with his staff in his hand for very age.
5 **And the streets of the city** shall be full of boys and girls playing in the streets thereof.
6 **Thus** saith the LORD of hosts;
If it be marvellous in the eyes of the remnant of this people in these days,
should it also be marvellous in mine eyes?
saith the LORD of hosts.
7 **Thus** saith the LORD of hosts;
Behold,
I will save my people from the east country, and from the west country;
8 **And I** will bring them,
and they shall dwell in the midst of Jerusalem:
and they shall be my people,
and I will be their God, in truth and in righteousness.
9 **Thus** saith the LORD of hosts;
Let your hands be strong, ye that hear in these days these words by the mouth of the prophets,
which were in the day that the foundation of the house of the LORD of hosts was laid,
that the temple might be built.

10 **For before these days** there was
no hire for man, nor any hire for
beast;
neither was there any peace to him
that went out or came in because
of the affliction:
for I set all men every one against
his neighbour.
11 **But now I** will not be unto the
residue of this people as in the
former days,
saith the LORD of hosts.
12 **For the seed** shall be prosperous;
the vine shall give her fruit,
and the ground shall give her
increase,
and the heavens shall give their
dew;
and I will cause the remnant of this
people to possess all these things.
13 **And it** shall come to pass,
that as ye were a curse among the
heathen, O house of Judah, and
house of Israel;
so will I save you,
and ye shall be a blessing:
fear not,
but let your hands be strong.
14 **For thus** saith the LORD of hosts;
As I thought to punish you,
when your fathers provoked me to
wrath,
saith the LORD of hosts,
and I repented not:
15 **So** again have I thought in these
days to do well unto Jerusalem
and to the house of Judah:
fear ye not.
16 **These** are the things that ye shall
do;
Speak ye every man the truth to his
neighbour;
execute the judgment of truth and
peace in your gates:
17 **And let none of you** imagine evil
in your hearts against his
neighbour;
and love no false oath:
for all these are things that I hate,
saith the LORD.
18 **And the word of the LORD of
hosts** came unto me,
saying,
19 **Thus** saith the LORD of hosts;
**The fast of the fourth month, and
the fast of the fifth, and the fast
of the seventh, and the fast of
the tenth,** shall be to the house of
Judah joy and gladness, and
cheerful feasts;
therefore love the truth and peace.
20 **Thus** saith the LORD of hosts;
It shall yet come to pass,
that there shall come people, and
the inhabitants of many cities:
21 **And the inhabitants of one city**
shall go to another,
saying,
Let us go speedily
to pray before the LORD,
and to seek the LORD of hosts:
I will go also.
22 **Yea, many people and strong
nations** shall come
to seek the LORD of hosts in
Jerusalem,
and to pray before the LORD.
23 **Thus** saith the LORD of hosts;
In those days it shall come to pass,
that ten men shall take hold out of
all languages of the nations,
even shall take hold of the skirt of
him that is a Jew,
saying,
We will go with you:
for we have heard that God is with
you.

9 **The burden of the word of
the LORD in the land of
Hadrach, and Damascus** shall be
the rest thereof: **when the eyes of
man**, as of all the tribes of Israel,
shall be toward the LORD.
2 **And Hamath** also shall border
thereby; Tyrus, and Zidon,
though it be very wise.
3 **And Tyrus** did build herself a
strong hold,
and heaped up silver as the dust,
and fine gold as the mire of the
streets.
4 **Behold,**
the Lord will cast her out,
and he will smite her power in the
sea;
and she shall be devoured with fire.
5 **Ashkelon** shall see it,
and fear;
Gaza also shall see it,
and be very sorrowful,
and Ekron; for her expectation
shall be ashamed;
and the king shall perish from
Gaza,
and Ashkelon shall not be
inhabited.
6 **And a bastard** shall dwell in
Ashdod,
and I will cut off the pride of the
Philistines.
7 **And I** will take away his blood out
of his mouth, and his
abominations from between his
teeth:
but he that remaineth, even he,
shall be for our God,
and he shall be as a governor in
Judah, and Ekron as a Jebusite.
8 **And I** will encamp about mine
house because of the army,
because of him that passeth by,
and because of him that
returneth:
and no oppressor shall pass
through them any more:
for now have I seen with mine eyes.
9 **Rejoice** greatly, O daughter of
Zion;
shout, O daughter of Jerusalem:
behold,
thy King cometh unto thee:
he is just, {and having salvation};
lowly, {and riding upon an ass,
and upon a colt the foal of an ass}.
10 **And I** will cut off the chariot from
Ephraim, and the horse from
Jerusalem,
and the battle bow shall be cut off:
and he shall speak peace unto the
heathen:
and his dominion shall be from sea
even to sea, and from the river
even to the ends of the earth.
11 **As for thee also, by the blood of
thy covenant** I have sent forth
thy prisoners out of the pit
wherein is no water.
12 **Turn you** to the strong hold, ye
prisoners of hope:
even to day do I declare
that I will render double unto thee;
13 **When I** have bent Judah for me,
filled the bow with Ephraim,
and raised up thy sons, O Zion,
against thy sons, O Greece,
and made thee as the sword of a
mighty man.
14 **And the LORD** shall be seen over
them,
and his arrow shall go forth as the
lightning:
and the Lord GOD shall blow the
trumpet,
and shall go with whirlwinds of the
south.
15 **The LORD of hosts** shall defend
them;
and they shall devour,

and subdue with sling stones;
and they shall drink,
and make a noise as through wine;
and they shall be filled like bowls,
and as the corners of the altar.
16 **And the LORD their God** shall
save them in that day as the flock
of his people:
for they shall be as the stones of a
crown,
lifted up as an ensign upon his land.
17 **For how great** is his goodness,
and how great is his beauty!
corn shall make the young men
cheerful, and new wine the
maids.

10 **Ask ye** of the LORD rain in
the time of the latter rain;
so the LORD shall make bright
clouds,
and give them showers of rain, to
every one grass in the field.
2 **For the idols** have spoken vanity,
and the diviners have seen a lie,
and have told false dreams;
they comfort in vain:
therefore they went their way as a
flock,
they were troubled,
because there was no shepherd.
3 **Mine anger** was kindled against
the shepherds,
and I punished the goats:
for the LORD of hosts hath visited
his flock the house of Judah,
and hath made them as his goodly
horse in the battle.
4 **Out of him** came forth the corner,
out of him the nail, out of him the
battle bow, out of him every
oppressor together.
5 **And they** shall be as mighty men,
which tread down their enemies in
the mire of the streets in the
battle:
and they shall fight,
because the LORD is with them,
and the riders on horses shall be
confounded.
6 **And I** will strengthen the house of
Judah,
and I will save the house of Joseph,
and I will bring them again to place
them;
for I have mercy upon them:
and they shall be as though I had
not cast them off:
for I am the LORD their God,
and will hear them.
7 **And they of Ephraim** shall be like
a mighty man,
and their heart shall rejoice as
through wine:
yea, their children shall see it,
and be glad;
their heart shall rejoice in the
LORD.
8 **I** will hiss for them,
and gather them;
for I have redeemed them:
and they shall increase as they have
increased.
9 **And I** will sow them among the
people:
and they shall remember me in far
countries;
and they shall live with their
children,
and turn again.
10 **I** will bring them again also out of
the land of Egypt,
and gather them out of Assyria;
and I will bring them into the land
of Gilead and Lebanon;
and place shall not be found for
them.
11 **And he** shall pass through the sea
with affliction,
and shall smite the waves in the
sea,
and all the deeps of the river shall
dry up:
and the pride of Assyria shall be
brought down,
and the sceptre of Egypt shall
depart away.
12 **And I** will strengthen them in the
LORD;
and they shall walk up and down in
his name,
saith the LORD.

11 **Open** thy doors, O Lebanon,
that the fire may devour thy
cedars.
2 **Howl,** fir tree;
for the cedar is fallen;
because the mighty are spoiled:
howl, O ye oaks of Bashan;
for the forest of the vintage is
come down.
3 **There** is a voice of the howling of
the shepherds;
for their glory is spoiled: a voice of
the roaring of young lions;
for the pride of Jordan is spoiled.
4 **Thus** saith the LORD my God;
Feed the flock of the slaughter;
5 **Whose possessors** slay them,
and hold themselves not guilty:
and they that sell them say,
Blessed be the LORD;
for I am rich:
and their own shepherds pity
them not.
6 **For I** will no more pity the
inhabitants of the land,
saith the LORD:
but, {lo}, I will deliver the men
every one into his neighbour's
hand, and into the hand of his
king:
and they shall smite the land,
and out of their hand I will not
deliver them.
7 **And I** will feed the flock of
slaughter, even you, O poor of the
flock.
And I took unto me two staves;
the one I called Beauty,
and the other I called Bands;
and I fed the flock.
8 **Three shepherds** also I cut off in
one month;
and my soul lothed them,
and their soul also abhorred me.
9 **Then** said I,
I will not feed you:
that that dieth, let it die;
and that that is to be cut off, let it
be cut off;
and let the rest eat every one the
flesh of another.
10 **And I** took my staff, even Beauty,
and cut it asunder,
that I might break my covenant
which I had made with all the
people.
11 **And it** was broken in that day:
**and so the poor of the flock that
waited upon me** knew
that it was the word of the LORD.
12 **And I** said unto them,
If ye think good,
give me my price;
and if not, forbear.
So they weighed for my price thirty
pieces of silver.
13 **And the LORD** said unto me,
Cast it unto the potter: a goodly
price that I was prised at of them.
And I took the thirty pieces of silver,
and cast them to the potter in the
house of the LORD.
14 **Then I** cut asunder mine other
staff, even Bands,
that I might break the brotherhood
between Judah and Israel.

15 **And the LORD** said unto me,
Take unto thee yet the instruments of a foolish shepherd.
16 **For, {lo}, I** will raise up a shepherd in the land,
which shall not visit those that be cut off,
neither shall seek the young one,
nor heal that that is broken,
nor feed that that standeth still:
but he shall eat the flesh of the fat,
and tear their claws in pieces.
17 **Woe** to the idol shepherd that leaveth the flock!
the sword shall be upon his arm, and upon his right eye:
his arm shall be clean dried up,
and his right eye shall be utterly darkened.

12 The burden of the word of the LORD for Israel,
saith the LORD,
which stretcheth forth the heavens,
and layeth the foundation of the earth,
and formeth the spirit of man within him.
2 **Behold,**
I will make Jerusalem a cup of trembling unto all the people round about,
when they shall be in the siege both against Judah and against Jerusalem.
3 **And in that day** will I make Jerusalem a burdensome stone for all people:
all that burden themselves with it shall be cut in pieces,
though all the people of the earth be gathered together against it.
4 **In that day**, {saith the LORD}, I will smite every horse with astonishment, and his rider with madness:
and I will open mine eyes upon the house of Judah,
and will smite every horse of the people with blindness.
5 **And the governors of Judah** shall say in their heart,
The inhabitants of Jerusalem shall be my strength in the LORD of hosts their God.
6 **In that day** will I make the governors of Judah like an hearth of fire among the wood, and like a torch of fire in a sheaf;
and they shall devour all the people round about, on the right hand and on the left:
and Jerusalem shall be inhabited again in her own place, even in Jerusalem.
7 **The LORD** also shall save the tents of Judah first,
that the glory of the house of David and the glory of the inhabitants of Jerusalem do not magnify themselves against Judah.
8 **In that day** shall the LORD defend the inhabitants of Jerusalem;
and he that is feeble among them at that day shall be as David;
and the house of David shall be as God, as the angel of the LORD before them.
9 **And it** shall come to pass in that day,
that I will seek to destroy all the nations that come against Jerusalem.
10 **And I** will pour upon the house of David, and upon the inhabitants of Jerusalem, the spirit of grace and of supplications:
and they shall look upon me whom they have pierced,
and they shall mourn for him, as one mourneth for his only son,
and shall be in bitterness for him, as one that is in bitterness for his firstborn.
11 **In that day** shall there be a great mourning in Jerusalem, as the mourning of Hadadrimmon in the valley of Megiddon.
12 **And the land** shall mourn, every family apart; the family of the house of David apart, and their wives apart; the family of the house of Nathan apart, and their wives apart;
13 The family of the house of Levi apart, and their wives apart; the family of Shimei apart, and their wives apart;
14 All the families that remain, every family apart, and their wives apart.

13 **In that day** there shall be a fountain opened to the house of David and to the inhabitants of Jerusalem for sin and for uncleanness.
2 **And it** shall come to pass in that day,
saith the LORD of hosts,
that I will cut off the names of the idols out of the land,
and they shall no more be remembered:
and also I will cause the prophets and the unclean spirit to pass out of the land.
3 **And it** shall come to pass,
that when any shall yet prophesy,
then his father and his mother that begat him shall say unto him,
Thou shalt not live;
for thou speakest lies in the name of the LORD:
and his father and his mother that begat him shall thrust him through when he prophesieth.
4 **And it** shall come to pass in that day,
that the prophets shall be ashamed every one of his vision,
when he hath prophesied;
neither shall they wear a rough garment
to deceive:
5 **But he** shall say,
I am no prophet,
I am an husbandman;
for man taught me to keep cattle from my youth.
6 **And one** shall say unto him,
What are these wounds in thine hands?
Then he shall answer,
Those with which I was wounded in the house of my friends.
7 **Awake,** O sword, against my shepherd, and against the man that is my fellow,
saith the LORD of hosts:
smite the shepherd,
and the sheep shall be scattered:
and I will turn mine hand upon the little ones.
8 **And it** shall come to pass,
that in all the land, {saith the LORD}, two parts therein shall be cut off and die;
but the third shall be left therein.
9 **And I** will bring the third part through the fire,
and will refine them as silver is refined,
and will try them as gold is tried:
they shall call on my name,
and I will hear them:
I will say,
It is my people:

and they shall say,
The LORD is my God.

14

Behold,
the day of the LORD cometh,
and thy spoil shall be divided in the midst of thee.
2 **For I** will gather all nations against Jerusalem to battle;
and the city shall be taken,
and the houses rifled,
and the women ravished;
and half of the city shall go forth into captivity,
and the residue of the people shall not be cut off from the city.
3 **Then** shall the LORD go forth,
and fight against those nations,
as when he fought in the day of battle.
4 **And his feet** shall stand in that day upon the mount of Olives,
which is before Jerusalem on the east,
and the mount of Olives shall cleave in the midst thereof toward the east and toward the west,
and there shall be a very great valley;
and half of the mountain shall remove toward the north, and half of it toward the south.
5 **And ye** shall flee to the valley of the mountains;
for the valley of the mountains shall reach unto Azal:
yea, ye shall flee,
like as ye fled from before the earthquake in the days of Uzziah king of Judah:
and the LORD my God shall come, and all the saints with thee.
6 **And it** shall come to pass in that day,
that the light shall not be clear, nor dark:
7 **But it** shall be one day which shall be known to the LORD, not day, nor night:
but it shall come to pass,
that at evening time it shall be light.
8 **And it** shall be in that day,
that living waters shall go out from Jerusalem; half of them toward the former sea, and half of them toward the hinder sea:
in summer and in winter shall it be.
9 **And the LORD** shall be king over all the earth:
in that day shall there be one LORD, and his name one.
10 **All the land** shall be turned as a plain from Geba to Rimmon south of Jerusalem:
and it shall be lifted up,
and inhabited in her place, from Benjamin's gate unto the place of the first gate, unto the corner gate, and from the tower of Hananeel unto the king's winepresses.
11 **And men** shall dwell in it,
and there shall be no more utter destruction;
but Jerusalem shall be safely inhabited.
12 **And this** shall be the plague wherewith the LORD will smite all the people that have fought against Jerusalem;
Their flesh shall consume away
while they stand upon their feet,
and their eyes shall consume away in their holes,
and their tongue shall consume away in their mouth.
13 **And it** shall come to pass in that day,
that a great tumult from the LORD shall be among them;
and they shall lay hold every one on the hand of his neighbour,
and his hand shall rise up against the hand of his neighbour.
14 **And Judah** also shall fight at Jerusalem;
and the wealth of all the heathen round about shall be gathered together, gold, and silver, and apparel, in great abundance.
15 **And so** shall be the plague of the horse, of the mule, of the camel, and of the ass, and of all the beasts that shall be in these tents, as this plague.
16 **And it** shall come to pass,
that every one that is left of all the nations which came against Jerusalem shall even go up from year to year
to worship the King, the LORD of hosts,
and to keep the feast of tabernacles.
17 **And it** shall be,
that whoso will not come up of all the families of the earth unto Jerusalem
to worship the King, the LORD of hosts, even upon them shall be no rain.
18 **And if the family of Egypt** go not up,
and come not,
that have no rain;
there shall be the plague,
wherewith the LORD will smite the heathen that come not up to keep the feast of tabernacles.
19 **This** shall be the punishment of Egypt, and the punishment of all nations that come not up to keep the feast of tabernacles.
20 **In that day** shall there be upon the bells of the horses, Holiness Unto The LORD;
and the pots in the LORD's house shall be like the bowls before the altar.
21 **Yea, every pot in Jerusalem and in Judah** shall be holiness unto the LORD of hosts:
and all they that sacrifice shall come and take of them,
and seethe therein:
and in that day there shall be no more the Canaanite in the house of the LORD of hosts.

Malachi

The Book of Malachi, a significant text traditionally attributed to the prophet Malachi, was penned during the post-exilic period. It was a pivotal time of rebuilding and reestablishment for the people of Israel after they reconstructed the Temple in Jerusalem. It directly addresses the various issues the people face, with each of its six chapters containing a series of prophetic oracles, exhortations, and warnings that carry a weighty message designed to resonate deeply with the community.

Malachi begins by condemning the people's practice of marrying non-Jewish foreigners, which was common during that time. He warns that such marriages lead to the mixing of the holy and the profane and urges the people to repent and be faithful to God's commandments. The prophet then criticizes the people for offering sacrifices that are not pure or acceptable to God. He urges them to make their offerings worthy of God's acceptance and with the right spirit and intent. In light of these and other practices, Malachi emphasizes the importance of righteousness in the eyes of God by urging the people to seek justice and righteousness and to obey God's commandments faithfully.

He then closes with a prophecy about the arrival of a covenant messenger who will bring justice and righteousness to the world. This prophecy is often interpreted as a reference to John the Baptist in Christian theology. Other highlights of Malachi include God's expectations of righteousness from the priesthood, God's demand for faithful stewardship in the administration of His Law, and a prophecy about the ultimate triumph of God's chosen people over their enemies.

The Book of Malachi, therefore, is a call to repentance and a reminder of the importance of faithfulness to God's commandments. It looks forward to the coming of a divine emissary who will bring about a new era of fairness, honesty, integrity, and high moral standards. The prophet also desires the Israelites to understand that their actions have consequences and that they must be faithful to God to avoid punishment. At the same time, he strives to instill in the people of Israel a sense of hope for the future and a deep sense of purpose in their lives. With its prophetic warnings and exhortations, Malachi serves as a potent reminder that God's covenant with His chosen people is unbreakable, a truth that should inspire the people to embrace true worship and seek a more meaningful relationship with their Creator.

1 **The burden of the word of the LORD** to Israel by Malachi.

2 **I** have loved you,
saith the LORD.
Yet ye say,
Wherein hast thou loved us?
Was not Esau Jacob's brother?
saith the LORD:
yet I loved Jacob,
3 **And I** hated Esau,
and laid his mountains and his heritage waste for the dragons of the wilderness.
4 **Whereas Edom** saith,
We are impoverished,
but we will return
and build the desolate places;
thus saith the LORD of hosts,
They shall build,
but I will throw down;
and they shall call them, The border of wickedness, and, The people against whom the LORD hath indignation for ever.
5 **And your eyes** shall see,
and ye shall say,
The LORD will be magnified from the border of Israel.
6 **A son** honoureth his father, and a servant his master:
if then I be a father,
where is mine honour?
and if I be a master,
where is my fear?
saith the LORD of hosts unto you, O priests,
that despise my name.
And ye say,
Wherein have we despised thy name?
7 **Ye** offer polluted bread upon mine altar;
and ye say,
Wherein have we polluted thee?
In that ye say,
The table of the LORD is contemptible.
8 **And if ye** offer the blind for sacrifice,
is it not evil?
and if ye offer the lame and sick,
is it not evil?
offer it now unto thy governor;
will he be pleased with thee,
or accept thy person?
saith the LORD of hosts.
9 **And now, {I pray you}, beseech** God
that he will be gracious unto us:
this hath been by your means:
will he regard your persons?
saith the LORD of hosts.
10 **Who** is there even among you that would shut the doors for nought?
neither do ye kindle fire on mine altar for nought.
I have no pleasure in you,
saith the LORD of hosts,
neither will I accept an offering at your hand.
11 **For from the rising of the sun even unto the going down of the same** my name shall be great among the Gentiles;
and in every place incense shall be offered unto my name, and a pure offering:

for my name shall be great among the heathen,
saith the LORD of hosts.
12 **But ye** have profaned it,
in that ye say,
The table of the LORD is polluted;
and the fruit thereof, even his meat, is contemptible.
13 **Ye** said also,
Behold,
what a weariness is it!
and ye have snuffed at it,
saith the LORD of hosts;
and ye brought that which was torn, and the lame, and the sick;
thus ye brought an offering:
should I accept this of your hand?
saith the LORD.
14 **But cursed** be the deceiver,
which hath in his flock a male,
and voweth,
and sacrificeth unto the Lord a corrupt thing:
for I am a great King,
saith the LORD of hosts,
and my name is dreadful among the heathen.

2 **And now, O ye priests,** this commandment is for you.
2 **If ye** will not hear,
and if ye will not lay it to heart,
to give glory unto my name,
saith the LORD of hosts,
I will even send a curse upon you,
and I will curse your blessings:
yea, I have cursed them already,
because ye do not lay it to heart.
3 **Behold,**
I will corrupt your seed,
and spread dung upon your faces, even the dung of your solemn feasts;
and one shall take you away with it.
4 **And ye** shall know
that I have sent this commandment unto you,
that my covenant might be with Levi,
saith the LORD of hosts.
5 **My covenant** was with him of life and peace;
and I gave them to him for the fear
wherewith he feared me,
and was afraid before my name.
6 **The law of truth** was in his mouth,
and iniquity was not found in his lips:
he walked with me in peace and equity,
and did turn many away from iniquity.
7 **For the priest's lips** should keep knowledge,
and they should seek the law at his mouth:
for he is the messenger of the LORD of hosts.
8 **But ye** are departed out of the way;
ye have caused many to stumble at the law;
ye have corrupted the covenant of Levi,
saith the LORD of hosts.
9 **Therefore** have I also made you contemptible and base before all the people,
according as ye have not kept my ways,
but have been partial in the law.
10 **Have we not** all one father?
hath not one God created us?
why do we deal treacherously every man against his brother,
by profaning the covenant of our fathers?
11 **Judah** hath dealt treacherously,
and an abomination is committed in Israel and in Jerusalem;
for Judah hath profaned the holiness of the LORD which he loved,
and hath married the daughter of a strange god.
12 **The LORD** will cut off the man that doeth this, the master and the scholar, out of the tabernacles of Jacob, and him that offereth an offering unto the LORD of hosts.
13 **And this** have ye done again,
covering the altar of the LORD with tears, with weeping, and with crying out,
insomuch that he regardeth not the offering any more,
or receiveth it with good will at your hand.
14 **Yet ye** say,
Wherefore?
Because the LORD hath been witness between thee and the wife of thy youth,
against whom thou hast dealt treacherously:
yet is she thy companion, and the wife of thy covenant.
15 **And did not he** make one?
Yet had he the residue of the spirit.
And wherefore one?
That he might seek a godly seed.
Therefore take heed to your spirit,
and let none deal treacherously against the wife of his youth.
16 **For the LORD, the God of Israel,** saith
that he hateth putting away:
for one covereth violence with his garment,
saith the LORD of hosts:
therefore take heed to your spirit,
that ye deal not treacherously.
17 **Ye** have wearied the LORD with your words.
Yet ye say,
Wherein have we wearied him?
When ye say,
Every one that doeth evil is good in the sight of the LORD,
and he delighteth in them;
or, Where is the God of judgment?

3 **Behold,**
I will send my messenger,
and he shall prepare the way before me:
and the Lord, {whom ye seek}, shall suddenly come to his temple, even the messenger of the covenant,
whom ye delight in:
behold,
he shall come,
saith the LORD of hosts.
2 **But who** may abide the day of his coming?
and who shall stand
when he appeareth?
for he is like a refiner's fire, and like fullers' soap:
3 **And he** shall sit as a refiner and purifier of silver:
and he shall purify the sons of Levi,
and purge them as gold and silver,
that they may offer unto the LORD an offering in righteousness.
4 **Then** shall the offering of Judah and Jerusalem be pleasant unto the LORD, as in the days of old, and as in former years.
5 **And I** will come near to you to judgment;
and I will be a swift witness against the sorcerers, and against the adulterers, and against false swearers, and against those that oppress the hireling in his wages,

the widow, and the fatherless,
and that turn aside the stranger
from his right, and fear not me,
saith the LORD of hosts.

6 **For I** am the LORD,
I change not;
therefore ye sons of Jacob are not
consumed.

7 **Even from the days of your
fathers** ye are gone away from
mine ordinances,
and have not kept them.

Return unto me,
and I will return unto you,
saith the LORD of hosts.

But ye said,
Wherein shall we return?

8 **Will a man** rob God?

Yet ye have robbed me.

But ye say,
Wherein have we robbed thee?

In tithes and offerings.

9 **Ye** are cursed with a curse:
for ye have robbed me, even this
whole nation.

10 **Bring ye** all the tithes into the
storehouse,
that there may be meat in mine
house,
and prove me now herewith,
saith the LORD of hosts,
if I will not open you the windows
of heaven,
and pour you out a blessing,
that there shall not be room
enough to receive it.

11 **And I** will rebuke the devourer for
your sakes,
and he shall not destroy the fruits
of your ground;
neither shall your vine cast her
fruit before the time in the field,
saith the LORD of hosts.

12 **And all nations** shall call you
blessed:
for ye shall be a delightsome land,
saith the LORD of hosts.

13 **Your words** have been stout
against me,
saith the LORD.

Yet ye say,
What have we spoken so much
against thee?

14 **Ye** have said,
It is vain to serve God:
and what profit is it
that we have kept his ordinance,
and that we have walked
mournfully before the LORD of
hosts?

15 **And now** we call the proud
happy;
yea, they that work wickedness
are set up;
yea, they that tempt God are even
delivered.

16 **Then they that feared the LORD**
spake often one to another:
and the LORD hearkened,
and heard it,
and a book of remembrance was
written before him for them that
feared the LORD, and that
thought upon his name.

17 **And they** shall be mine,
saith the LORD of hosts,
in that day when I make up my
jewels;
and I will spare them,
as a man spareth his own son that
serveth him.

18 **Then** shall ye return,
and discern between the righteous
and the wicked, between him that
serveth God and him that serveth
him not.

4 **For, {behold}, the day**
cometh,
that shall burn as an oven;
**and all the proud, yea, and all
that do wickedly,** shall be
stubble:
and the day that cometh shall
burn them up,
saith the LORD of hosts,
that it shall leave them neither root
nor branch.

2 **But unto you that fear my name**
shall the Sun of righteousness
arise with healing in his wings;
and ye shall go forth,
and grow up as calves of the stall.

3 **And ye** shall tread down the
wicked;
for they shall be ashes under the
soles of your feet in the day that I
shall do this,
saith the LORD of hosts.

4 **Remember ye** the law of Moses
my servant,
which I commanded unto him in
Horeb for all Israel, with the
statutes and judgments.

5 **Behold,**
I will send you Elijah the prophet
before the coming of the great
and dreadful day of the LORD:

6 **And he** shall turn the heart of the
fathers to the children, and the
heart of the children to their
fathers,
lest I come and smite the earth with
a curse.

The New Testament

King James Version

Theme Rheme Edition

Matthew

The Gospel of Matthew, penned by the Apostle Matthew, is the first of four canonical gospels in the New Testament. Written as a narrative, the book connects Jesus's birth, life, death, and resurrection with His teachings and interactions among His disciples and followers. Matthew addresses the needs and concerns of a predominantly Jewish audience, helping them understand how Jesus Christ and his teachings are deeply rooted within their own religious tradition. Matthew's unique emphasis on the continuity between the Old and New Testaments shows how Jesus' teachings and ministry fulfill God's covenant with Israel. By presenting Jesus as both the Son of God and the Son of David, Matthew demonstrates how Jesus is the rightful heir to David's throne and the true king of Israel.

Many of the key events that unfold in Matthew are likely to resonate with Bible readers. The book begins with a genealogy of Jesus, tracing his lineage back to Abraham, the father of the Jewish people. It then moves on to the story of Jesus' birth, emphasizing the fulfillment of Old Testament prophecies and the importance of Joseph's role in accepting Jesus as his son. It also shares the story of the wise men from the East who came to worship the newborn king, Jesus, and how Joseph, Mary, and Jesus fled to Egypt to escape Herod's wrath. Prominent in the Gospel are details about the several miracles Jesus performed, including healing a leper, calming a storm, and raising the dead. Towards the end, Matthew details the story of Jesus' arrest, trial, and crucifixion, emphasizing the significance of His sacrificial death as the ultimate expression of God's love and the only means by which humanity can be reconciled to their Creator. And finally, the book concludes with the resurrection of Jesus, the ultimate proof of His divinity and the fulfillment of God's promises.

Matthew provides a clear and compelling presentation of Jesus as the long-awaited Messiah, prophesied in the Hebrew Scriptures. In this respect, his book is a testament to how Jesus fulfills God's covenant with Israel and how He is the nation's true king. As a result, he urges his readers to embrace Jesus' teachings and live according to His example. For today's readers, the Gospel of Matthew remains a vital resource for understanding Jesus' life, teachings, and ministry. It offers profound insights into the nature of Christian discipleship, the Jewish context of Jesus' ministry, and the significance of Jesus' passion and resurrection for believers.

1 The book of the generation of Jesus Christ,
the son of David,
the son of Abraham.
2 **Abraham** begat Isaac;
and Isaac begat Jacob;
and Jacob begat Judas and his brethren;
3 **And Judas** begat Phares and Zara of Thamar;
and Phares begat Esrom;
and Esrom begat Aram;
4 **And Aram** begat Aminadab;
and Aminadab begat Naasson;
and Naasson begat Salmon;
5 **And Salmon** begat Booz of Rachab;
and Booz begat Obed of Ruth;
and Obed begat Jesse;
6 **And Jesse** begat David the king;
and David the king begat Solomon of her that had been the wife of Urias;
7 **And Solomon** begat Roboam;
and Roboam begat Abia;
and Abia begat Asa;
8 **And Asa** begat Josaphat;
and Josaphat begat Joram;
and Joram begat Ozias;
9 **And Ozias** begat Joatham;
and Joatham begat Achaz;
and Achaz begat Ezekias;
10 **And Ezekias** begat Manasses;
and Manasses begat Amon;
and Amon begat Josias;
11 **And Josias** begat Jechonias and his brethren,
about the time they were carried away to Babylon:
12 **And after they** were brought to Babylon,
Jechonias begat Salathiel;
and Salathiel begat Zorobabel;
13 **And Zorobabel** begat Abiud;
and Abiud begat Eliakim;
and Eliakim begat Azor;
14 **And Azor** begat Sadoc;
and Sadoc begat Achim;
and Achim begat Eliud;
15 **And Eliud** begat Eleazar;
and Eleazar begat Matthan;
and Matthan begat Jacob;
16 **And Jacob** begat Joseph the husband of Mary,
of whom was born Jesus,
who is called Christ.
17 **So all the generations from Abraham to David** are fourteen generations;
and from David until the carrying away into Babylon are fourteen generations;
and from the carrying away into Babylon unto Christ are fourteen generations.
18 **Now the birth of Jesus Christ** was on this wise:
When as his mother Mary was espoused to Joseph,
before they came together,
she was found with child of the Holy Ghost.
19 **Then Joseph her husband**, {being a just man}, {and not willing to make her a public example}, was minded to put her away privily.
20 **But while he** thought on these things,
behold,

the angel of the Lord appeared unto him in a dream,
saying,
Joseph, thou son of David, fear not to take unto thee Mary thy wife:
for that which is conceived in her is of the Holy Ghost.
21 **And she** shall bring forth a son,
and thou shalt call his name Jesus:
for he shall save his people from their sins.
22 **Now all this** was done,
that it might be fulfilled which was spoken of the Lord by the prophet,
saying,
23 **Behold,**
a virgin shall be with child,
and shall bring forth a son,
and they shall call his name Emmanuel,
which {being interpreted} is, God with us.
24 **Then Joseph {being raised from sleep}** did as the angel of the Lord had bidden him,
and took unto him his wife:
25 **And** knew her not
till she had brought forth her firstborn son:
and he called his name Jesus.

2 **Now when Jesus** was born in Bethlehem of Judaea in the days of Herod the king,
behold,
there came wise men from the east to Jerusalem,
2 Saying,
Where is he that is born King of the Jews?
for we have seen his star in the east,
and are come to worship him.
3 **When Herod the king** had heard these things,
he was troubled, and all Jerusalem with him.
4 **And when he** had gathered all the chief priests and scribes of the people together,
he demanded of them
where Christ should be born.
5 **And they** said unto him,
In Bethlehem of Judaea:
for thus it is written by the prophet,
6 **And thou Bethlehem, in the land of Juda,** art not the least among the princes of Juda:
for out of thee shall come a Governor,
that shall rule my people Israel.
7 **Then Herod**, {when he had privily called the wise men}, enquired of them diligently
what time the star appeared.
8 **And he** sent them to Bethlehem,
and said,
Go and search diligently for the young child;
and when ye have found him,
bring me word again,
that I may come and worship him also.
9 **When they** had heard the king,
they departed;
and, {lo}, the star, {which they saw in the east}, went before them,
till it came and stood over where the young child was.
10 **When they** saw the star,
they rejoiced with exceeding great joy.
11 **And when they** were come into the house,
they saw the young child with Mary his mother,
and fell down,
and worshipped him:
and when they had opened their treasures,
they presented unto him gifts; gold, and frankincense and myrrh.
12 **And** being warned of God in a dream
that they should not return to Herod,
they departed into their own country another way.
13 **And when they** were departed,
behold,
the angel of the Lord appeareth to Joseph in a dream,
saying,
Arise,
and take the young child and his mother,
and flee into Egypt,
and be thou there
until I bring thee word:
for Herod will seek the young child to destroy him.
14 **When he** arose,
he took the young child and his mother by night,
and departed into Egypt:
15 **And** was there until the death of Herod:
that it might be fulfilled which was spoken of the Lord by the prophet,
saying,
Out of Egypt have I called my son.
16 **Then Herod**, {when he saw} {that he was mocked of the wise men}, was exceeding wroth,
and sent forth,
and slew all the children that were in Bethlehem, and in all the coasts thereof, from two years old and under, according to the time which he had diligently inquired of the wise men.
17 **Then** was fulfilled that which was spoken by Jeremiah the prophet,
saying,
18 **In Rama** was there a voice heard, lamentation, and weeping, and great mourning,
Rachel weeping for her children,
and would not be comforted,
because they are not.
19 **But when Herod** was dead,
behold,
an angel of the Lord appeareth in a dream to Joseph in Egypt,
20 Saying,
Arise,
and take the young child and his mother,
and go into the land of Israel:
for they are dead which sought the young child's life.
21 **And he** arose,
and took the young child and his mother,
and came into the land of Israel.
22 **But when he** heard that Archelaus did reign in Judaea in the room of his father Herod,
he was afraid to go thither:
notwithstanding, {being warned of God in a dream}, he turned aside into the parts of Galilee:
23 **And he** came and dwelt in a city called Nazareth:
that it might be fulfilled which was spoken by the prophets,
He shall be called a Nazarene.

3 **In those days** came John the Baptist,
preaching in the wilderness of Judaea,
2 **And** saying,
Repent ye:
for the kingdom of heaven is at hand.
3 **For this** is he that was spoken of by the prophet Esaias,
saying,

The voice of one crying in the wilderness,
Prepare ye the way of the Lord,
make his paths straight.

4 **And the same John** had his raiment of camel's hair, and a leathern girdle about his loins;
and his meat was locusts and wild honey.

5 **Then** went out to him Jerusalem, and all Judaea, and all the region round about Jordan,
6 **And** were baptized of him in Jordan,
confessing their sins.

7 **But when he** saw many of the Pharisees and Sadducees come to his baptism,
he said unto them,
O generation of vipers, who hath warned you to flee from the wrath to come?

8 **Bring forth** therefore fruits meet for repentance:
9 **And think not** to say within yourselves,
We have Abraham to our father:
for I say unto you,
that God is able of these stones to raise up children unto Abraham.

10 **And now also the axe** is laid unto the root of the trees:
therefore every tree which bringeth not forth good fruit is hewn down,
and cast into the fire.

11 **I** indeed baptize you with water unto repentance:
but he that cometh after me is mightier than I,
whose shoes I am not worthy to bear:
he shall baptize you with the Holy Ghost, and with fire:
12 **Whose fan** is in his hand,
and he will throughly purge his floor,
and gather his wheat into the garner;
but he will burn up the chaff with unquenchable fire.

13 **Then** cometh Jesus from Galilee to Jordan unto John,
to be baptized of him.

14 **But John** forbad him,
saying,
I have need to be baptized of thee,
and comest thou to me?

15 **And Jesus answering** said unto him,
Suffer it to be so now:
for thus it becometh us to fulfil all righteousness.

Then he suffered him.

16 **And Jesus**, {when he was baptized}, went up straightway out of the water:
and, {lo}, the heavens were opened unto him,
and he saw the Spirit of God descending like a dove, and lighting upon him:
17 **And lo** a voice from heaven,
saying,
This is my beloved Son,
in whom I am well pleased.

4 **Then** was Jesus led up of the Spirit into the wilderness
to be tempted of the devil.

2 **And when he** had fasted forty days and forty nights,
he was afterward an hungred.

3 **And when the tempter** came to him,
he said,
If thou be the Son of God,
command
that these stones be made bread.

4 **But he** answered and said,
It is written,
Man shall not live by bread alone, but by every word that proceedeth out of the mouth of God.

5 **Then the devil** taketh him up into the holy city,
and setteth him on a pinnacle of the temple,
6 **And** saith unto him,
If thou be the Son of God,
cast thyself down:
for it is written,
He shall give his angels charge concerning thee:
and in their hands they shall bear thee up,
lest at any time thou dash thy foot against a stone.

7 **Jesus** said unto him,
It is written again,
Thou shalt not tempt the Lord thy God.

8 **Again, the devil** taketh him up into an exceeding high mountain,
and sheweth him all the kingdoms of the world, and the glory of them;
9 **And** saith unto him,
All these things will I give thee,
if thou wilt fall down and worship me.

10 **Then** saith Jesus unto him,
Get thee hence, Satan:
for it is written,
Thou shalt worship the Lord thy God,
and him only shalt thou serve.

11 **Then the devil** leaveth him,
and, {behold}, angels came and ministered unto him.

12 **Now when Jesus** had heard that John was cast into prison,
he departed into Galilee;
13 **And** leaving Nazareth,
he came and dwelt in Capernaum,
which is upon the sea coast, in the borders of Zabulon and Nephthalim:
14 **That it** might be fulfilled which was spoken by Esaias the prophet,
saying,
15 The land of Zabulon, and the land of Nephthalim, by the way of the sea, beyond Jordan, Galilee of the Gentiles;
16 **The people which sat in darkness** saw great light;
and to them which sat in the region and shadow of death light is sprung up.

17 **From that time** Jesus began to preach,
and to say,
Repent:
for the kingdom of heaven is at hand.

18 **And Jesus**, {walking by the sea of Galilee}, saw two brethren, Simon called Peter, and Andrew his brother,
casting a net into the sea:
for they were fishers.

19 **And he** saith unto them,
Follow me,
and I will make you fishers of men.

20 **And they** straightway left their nets,
and followed him.

21 **And** going on from thence,
he saw other two brethren, James the son of Zebedee, and John his brother, in a ship with Zebedee their father,
mending their nets;
and he called them.

22 **And they** immediately left the ship and their father,
and followed him.

23 **And Jesus** went about all Galilee,
teaching in their synagogues,
and preaching the gospel of the
kingdom,
and healing all manner of sickness
and all manner of disease among
the people.
24 **And his fame** went throughout
all Syria:
and they brought unto him all sick
people that were taken with
divers diseases and torments, and
those which were possessed with
devils, and those which were
lunatick, and those that had the
palsy;
and he healed them.
25 **And there** followed him great
multitudes of people from Galilee,
and from Decapolis, and from
Jerusalem, and from Judaea, and
from beyond Jordan.

5 **And** seeing the multitudes,
he went up into a mountain:
and when he was set,
his disciples came unto him:
2 **And he** opened his mouth,
and taught them,
saying,
3 **Blessed** are the poor in spirit:
for theirs is the kingdom of heaven.
4 **Blessed** are they that mourn:
for they shall be comforted.
5 **Blessed** are the meek:
for they shall inherit the earth.
6 **Blessed** are they which do hunger
and thirst after righteousness:
for they shall be filled.
7 **Blessed** are the merciful:
for they shall obtain mercy.
8 **Blessed** are the pure in heart:
for they shall see God.
9 **Blessed** are the peacemakers:
for they shall be called the children
of God.
10 **Blessed** are they which are
persecuted for righteousness'
sake:
for theirs is the kingdom of heaven.
11 **Blessed** are ye,
when men shall revile you,
and persecute you,
and shall say all manner of evil
against you falsely, for my sake.
12 **Rejoice,**
and be exceeding glad:
for great is your reward in heaven:
for so persecuted they the prophets
which were before you.
13 **Ye** are the salt of the earth:
but if the salt have lost his savour,
wherewith shall it be salted?
it is thenceforth good for nothing,
but to be cast out,
and to be trodden under foot of
men.
14 **Ye** are the light of the world.
A city that is set on an hill cannot
be hid.
15 **Neither** do men light a candle,
and put it under a bushel, but on a
candlestick;
and it giveth light unto all that are
in the house.
16 **Let your light** so shine before
men,
that they may see your good works,
and glorify your Father which is in
heaven.
17 **Think not**
that I am come to destroy the law,
or the prophets:
I am not come
to destroy, but to fulfil.
18 **For verily I** say unto you,
Till heaven and earth pass,
one jot or one tittle shall in no
wise pass from the law,
till all be fulfilled.
19 **Whosoever** therefore shall break
one of these least
commandments,
and shall teach men so,
he shall be called the least in the
kingdom of heaven:
but whosoever shall do and teach
them,
the same shall be called great in the
kingdom of heaven.
20 **For I** say unto you,
That except your righteousness
shall exceed the righteousness of
the scribes and Pharisees,
ye shall in no case enter into the
kingdom of heaven.
21 **Ye** have heard that it was said of
them of old time,
Thou shalt not kill;
and whosoever shall kill shall be
in danger of the judgment:
22 **But I** say unto you,
**That whosoever is angry with his
brother without a cause** shall be
in danger of the judgment:
**and whosoever shall say to his
brother, Raca,** shall be in danger
of the council:
**but whosoever shall say, Thou
fool,** shall be in danger of hell fire.
23 **Therefore if thou** bring thy gift to
the altar,
and there rememberest
that thy brother hath ought
against thee;
24 **Leave** there thy gift before the
altar,
and go thy way;
first be reconciled to thy brother,
and then come and offer thy gift.
25 **Agree** with thine adversary
quickly,
whiles thou art in the way with
him;
lest at any time the adversary
deliver thee to the judge,
and the judge deliver thee to the
officer,
and thou be cast into prison.
26 **Verily I** say unto thee,
Thou shalt by no means come out
thence,
till thou hast paid the uttermost
farthing.
27 **Ye** have heard that it was said by
them of old time,
Thou shalt not commit adultery:
28 **But I** say unto you,
**That whosoever looketh on a
woman to lust after her** hath
committed adultery with her
already in his heart.
29 **And if thy right eye** offend thee,
pluck it out,
and cast it from thee:
for it is profitable for thee
that one of thy members should
perish,
and not that thy whole body
should be cast into hell.
30 **And if thy right hand** offend
thee,
cut it off,
and cast it from thee:
for it is profitable for thee
that one of thy members should
perish,
and not that thy whole body
should be cast into hell.
31 **It** hath been said,
Whosoever shall put away his wife,
let him give her a writing of
divorcement:
32 **But I** say unto you,
**That whosoever shall put away
his wife,** {saving for the cause of
fornication}, causeth her to
commit adultery:

and whosoever shall marry her that is divorced committeth adultery.

33 **Again, ye** have heard that it hath been said by them of old time,
Thou shalt not forswear thyself,
but shalt perform unto the Lord thine oaths:
34 **But I** say unto you,
Swear not at all; neither by heaven; {for it is God's throne}:
35 Nor by the earth; {for it is his footstool}: neither by Jerusalem; {for it is the city of the great King}.
36 **Neither** shalt thou swear by thy head,
because thou canst not make one hair white or black.
37 **But let your communication** be,
Yea, yea; Nay, nay:
for whatsoever is more than these cometh of evil.
38 **Ye** have heard that it hath been said,
An eye for an eye, and a tooth for a tooth:
39 **But I** say unto you,
That ye resist not evil:
but whosoever shall smite thee on thy right cheek,
turn to him the other also.
40 **And if any man** will sue thee at the law,
and take away thy coat,
let him have thy cloak also.
41 **And whosoever** shall compel thee to go a mile,
go with him twain.
42 **Give** to him that asketh thee,
and from him that would borrow of thee turn not thou away.
43 **Ye** have heard that it hath been said,
Thou shalt love thy neighbour,
and hate thine enemy.
44 **But I** say unto you,
Love your enemies,
bless them that curse you,
do good to them that hate you,
and pray for them which despitefully use you, and persecute you;
45 **That ye** may be the children of your Father which is in heaven:
for he maketh his sun to rise on the evil and on the good,
and sendeth rain on the just and on the unjust.
46 **For if ye** love them which love you,
what reward have ye?
do not even the publicans the same?
47 **And if ye** salute your brethren only,
what do ye more than others?
do not even the publicans so?
48 **Be ye** therefore perfect,
even as your Father which is in heaven is perfect.

6

Take heed that ye do not your alms before men,
to be seen of them:
otherwise ye have no reward of your Father which is in heaven.
2 **Therefore when thou** doest thine alms,
do not sound a trumpet before thee,
as the hypocrites do in the synagogues and in the streets,
that they may have glory of men.
Verily I say unto you,
They have their reward.
3 **But when thou** doest alms,
let not thy left hand know
what thy right hand doeth:
4 **That thine alms** may be in secret:
and thy Father which seeth in secret himself shall reward thee openly.
5 **And when thou** prayest,
thou shalt not be as the hypocrites are:
for they love to pray standing in the synagogues and in the corners of the streets,
that they may be seen of men.
Verily I say unto you,
They have their reward.
6 **But thou**, {when thou prayest}, enter into thy closet,
and when thou hast shut thy door,
pray to thy Father which is in secret;
and thy Father which seeth in secret shall reward thee openly.
7 **But when ye** pray,
use not vain repetitions,
as the heathen do:
for they think
that they shall be heard for their much speaking.
8 **Be not ye** therefore like unto them:
for your Father knoweth
what things ye have need of,
before ye ask him.
9 **After this manner** therefore pray ye:
Our Father which art in heaven, Hallowed be thy name.
10 **Thy kingdom** come,
Thy will be done in earth,
as it is in heaven.
11 **Give** us this day our daily bread.
12 **And forgive** us our debts,
as we forgive our debtors.
13 **And lead us not** into temptation,
but deliver us from evil:
For thine is the kingdom, and the power, and the glory, for ever.
Amen.
14 **For if ye** forgive men their trespasses,
your heavenly Father will also forgive you:
15 **But if ye** forgive not men their trespasses,
neither will your Father forgive your trespasses.
16 **Moreover when ye** fast,
be not, as the hypocrites, of a sad countenance:
for they disfigure their faces,
that they may appear unto men to fast.
Verily I say unto you,
They have their reward.
17 **But thou**, {when thou fastest}, anoint thine head,
and wash thy face;
18 **That thou** appear not unto men to fast, but unto thy Father which is in secret:
and thy Father, {which seeth in secret}, shall reward thee openly.
19 **Lay not up** for yourselves treasures upon earth,
where moth and rust doth corrupt,
and where thieves break through and steal:
20 **But lay up** for yourselves treasures in heaven,
where neither moth nor rust doth corrupt,
and where thieves do not break through nor steal:
21 **For where your treasure** is,
there will your heart be also.
22 **The light of the body** is the eye:
if therefore thine eye be single,
thy whole body shall be full of light.
23 **But if thine eye** be evil,
thy whole body shall be full of darkness.

If therefore the light that is in thee be darkness,
how great is that darkness!
24 **No man** can serve two masters:
for either he will hate the one,
and love the other;
or else he will hold to the one,
and despise the other.
Ye cannot serve God and mammon.
25 **Therefore I** say unto you,
Take no thought for your life, {what ye shall eat}, {or what ye shall drink}; nor yet for your body, {what ye shall put on}.
Is not the life more than meat, and the body than raiment?
26 **Behold** the fowls of the air:
for they sow not,
neither do they reap,
nor gather into barns;
yet your heavenly Father feedeth them.
Are ye not much better than they?
27 **Which of you** {by taking thought} can add one cubit unto his stature?
28 **And why** take ye thought for raiment?
Consider the lilies of the field,
how they grow;
they toil not,
neither do they spin:
29 **And yet I** say unto you,
That even Solomon in all his glory was not arrayed like one of these.
30 **Wherefore, if God** so clothe the grass of the field,
which to day is,
and to morrow is cast into the oven,
shall he not much more clothe you, O ye of little faith?
31 **Therefore take** no thought,
saying,
What shall we eat?
or, What shall we drink?
or, Wherewithal shall we be clothed?
32 (For after all these things do the Gentiles seek:)
for your heavenly Father knoweth
that ye have need of all these things.
33 **But seek ye** first the kingdom of God, and his righteousness;
and all these things shall be added unto you.
34 **Take therefore no thought** for the morrow:
for the morrow shall take thought for the things of itself.
Sufficient unto the day is the evil thereof.

7

Judge not,
that ye be not judged.
2 **For with what judgment** ye judge,
ye shall be judged:
and with what measure ye mete,
it shall be measured to you again.
3 **And why** beholdest thou the mote that is in thy brother's eye,
but considerest not the beam that is in thine own eye?
4 **Or how** wilt thou say to thy brother,
Let me pull out the mote out of thine eye;
and, {behold}, a beam is in thine own eye?
5 **Thou hypocrite, first** cast out the beam out of thine own eye;
and then shalt thou see clearly to cast out the mote out of thy brother's eye.
6 **Give not** that which is holy unto the dogs,
neither cast ye your pearls before swine,
lest they trample them under their feet,
and turn again
and rend you.
7 **Ask,**
and it shall be given you;
seek,
and ye shall find;
knock,
and it shall be opened unto you:
8 **For every one that asketh** receiveth;
and he that seeketh findeth;
and to him that knocketh it shall be opened.
9 **Or what man** is there of you,
whom if his son ask bread,
will he give him a stone?
10 **Or if he** ask a fish,
will he give him a serpent?
11 **If ye** then, {being evil}, know
how to give good gifts unto your children,
how much more shall your Father which is in heaven give good things to them that ask him?
12 **Therefore all things** whatsoever ye would
that men should do to you,
do ye even so to them:
for this is the law and the prophets.
13 **Enter ye** in at the strait gate:
for wide is the gate,
and broad is the way,
that leadeth to destruction,
and many there be which go in thereat:
14 **Because strait** is the gate,
and narrow is the way,
which leadeth unto life,
and few there be that find it.
15 **Beware** of false prophets,
which come to you in sheep's clothing,
but inwardly they are ravening wolves.
16 **Ye** shall know them by their fruits.
Do men gather grapes of thorns, or figs of thistles?
17 **Even so every good tree** bringeth forth good fruit;
but a corrupt tree bringeth forth evil fruit.
18 **A good tree** cannot bring forth evil fruit,
neither can a corrupt tree bring forth good fruit.
19 **Every tree that bringeth not forth good fruit** is hewn down,
and cast into the fire.
20 **Wherefore by their fruits** ye shall know them.
21 **Not every one that saith unto me, Lord, Lord,** shall enter into the kingdom of heaven;
but he that doeth the will of my Father which is in heaven.
22 **Many** will say to me in that day,
Lord, Lord, have we not prophesied in thy name?
and in thy name have cast out devils?
and in thy name done many wonderful works?
23 **And then** will I profess unto them,
I never knew you:
depart from me, ye that work iniquity.
24 **Therefore whosoever** heareth these sayings of mine,
and doeth them,
I will liken him unto a wise man,
which built his house upon a rock:
25 **And the rain** descended,
and the floods came,
and the winds blew,
and beat upon that house;

and it fell not:
for it was founded upon a rock.
26 **And every one that heareth these sayings of mine, and doeth them not,** shall be likened unto a foolish man,
which built his house upon the sand:
27 **And the rain** descended,
and the floods came,
and the winds blew,
and beat upon that house;
and it fell:
and great was the fall of it.
28 **And it** came to pass,
when Jesus had ended these sayings,
the people were astonished at his doctrine:
29 **For he** taught them as one having authority, and not as the scribes.

8

When he was come down from the mountain,
great multitudes followed him.
2 **And, {behold}, there** came a leper and worshipped him,
saying,
Lord, if thou wilt,
thou canst make me clean.
3 **And Jesus** put forth his hand,
and touched him,
saying,
I will;
be thou clean.
And immediately his leprosy was cleansed.
4 **And Jesus** saith unto him,
See thou tell no man;
but go thy way,
shew thyself to the priest,
and offer the gift that Moses commanded, for a testimony unto them.
5 **And when Jesus** was entered into Capernaum,
there came unto him a centurion, beseeching him,
6 **And** saying,
Lord, my servant lieth at home sick of the palsy,
grievously tormented.
7 **And Jesus** saith unto him,
I will come and heal him.
8 **The centurion** answered and said,
Lord, I am not worthy that thou shouldest come under my roof:
but speak the word only,
and my servant shall be healed.
9 **For I** am a man under authority, having soldiers under me:
and I say to this man, {Go}, {and he goeth}; and to another, {Come}, {and he cometh}; and to my servant, {Do this}, {and he doeth it}.
10 **When Jesus** heard it,
he marvelled,
and said to them that followed,
Verily I say unto you,
I have not found so great faith, no, not in Israel.
11 **And I** say unto you,
That many shall come from the east and west,
and shall sit down with Abraham, and Isaac, and Jacob, in the kingdom of heaven.
12 **But the children of the kingdom** shall be cast out into outer darkness:
there shall be weeping and gnashing of teeth.
13 **And Jesus** said unto the centurion,
Go thy way;
and as thou hast believed,
so be it done unto thee.
And his servant was healed in the selfsame hour.
14 **And when Jesus** was come into Peter's house,
he saw his wife's mother laid, and sick of a fever.
15 **And he** touched her hand,
and the fever left her:
and she arose,
and ministered unto them.
16 **When the even** was come,
they brought unto him many that were possessed with devils:
and he cast out the spirits with his word,
and healed all that were sick:
17 **That it** might be fulfilled which was spoken by Esaias the prophet,
saying,
Himself took our infirmities,
and bare our sicknesses.
18 **Now when Jesus** saw great multitudes about him,
he gave commandment to depart unto the other side.
19 **And a certain scribe** came,
and said unto him,
Master, I will follow thee
whithersoever thou goest.
20 **And Jesus** saith unto him,
The foxes have holes,
and the birds of the air have nests;
but the Son of man hath not where to lay his head.
21 **And another of his disciples** said unto him,
Lord, suffer me first to go and bury my father.
22 **But Jesus** said unto him,
Follow me;
and let the dead bury their dead.
23 **And when he** was entered into a ship,
his disciples followed him.
24 **And, {behold}, there** arose a great tempest in the sea,
insomuch that the ship was covered with the waves:
but he was asleep.
25 **And his disciples** came to him,
and awoke him,
saying,
Lord, save us:
we perish.
26 **And he** saith unto them,
Why are ye fearful, O ye of little faith?
Then he arose,
and rebuked the winds and the sea;
and there was a great calm.
27 **But the men** marvelled,
saying,
What manner of man is this,
that even the winds and the sea obey him!
28 **And when he** was come to the other side into the country of the Gergesenes,
there met him two possessed with devils,
coming out of the tombs, exceeding fierce,
so that no man might pass by that way.
29 **And, {behold}, they** cried out,
saying,
What have we to do with thee, Jesus, thou Son of God?
art thou come hither to torment us before the time?
30 **And there** was a good way off from them an herd of many swine feeding.
31 **So the devils** besought him,
saying,
If thou cast us out,
suffer us to go away into the herd of swine.
32 **And he** said unto them,
Go.

And when they were come out,
they went into the herd of swine:
and, {behold}, the whole herd of swine ran violently down a steep place into the sea,
and perished in the waters.

33 **And they that kept them** fled,
and went their ways into the city,
and told every thing,
and what was befallen to the possessed of the devils.

34 **And, {behold}, the whole city** came out **to meet Jesus:**
and when they saw him,
they besought him
that he would depart out of their coasts.

9 **And he** entered into a ship,
and passed over,
and came into his own city.

2 **And, {behold}, they** brought to him a man sick of the palsy,
lying on a bed:
and Jesus seeing their faith said unto the sick of the palsy;
Son, be of good cheer;
thy sins be forgiven thee.

3 **And, {behold}, certain of the scribes** said within themselves,
This man blasphemeth.

4 **And Jesus {knowing their thoughts}** said,
Wherefore think ye evil in your hearts?

5 **For whether** is easier,
to say,
Thy sins be forgiven thee;
or to say,
Arise,
and walk?

6 **But that ye** may know
that the Son of man hath power on earth to forgive sins,
(then saith he to the sick of the palsy,)
Arise,
take up thy bed,
and go unto thine house.

7 **And he** arose,
and departed to his house.

8 **But when the multitudes** saw it,
they marvelled,
and glorified God,
which had given such power unto men.

9 **And as Jesus** passed forth from thence,
he saw a man, named Matthew,
sitting at the receipt of custom:
and he saith unto him,
Follow me.

And he arose,
and followed him.

10 **And it** came to pass,
as Jesus sat at meat in the house,
behold,
many publicans and sinners came and sat down with him and his disciples.

11 **And when the Pharisees** saw it,
they said unto his disciples,
Why eateth your Master with publicans and sinners?

12 **But when Jesus** heard that,
he said unto them,
They that be whole need not a physician, but they that are sick.

13 **But go ye and learn** what that meaneth,
I will have mercy, and not sacrifice:
for I am not come to call the righteous, but sinners to repentance.

14 **Then** came to him the disciples of John,
saying,
Why do we and the Pharisees fast oft,
but thy disciples fast not?

15 **And Jesus** said unto them,
Can the children of the bridechamber mourn,
as long as the bridegroom is with them?
but the days will come,
when the bridegroom shall be taken from them,
and then shall they fast.

16 **No man** putteth a piece of new cloth unto an old garment,
for that which is put in to fill it up taketh from the garment,
and the rent is made worse.

17 **Neither** do men put new wine into old bottles:
else the bottles break,
and the wine runneth out,
and the bottles perish:
but they put new wine into new bottles,
and both are preserved.

18 **While he** spake these things unto them,
behold,
there came a certain ruler,
and worshipped him,
saying,
My daughter is even now dead:
but come and lay thy hand upon her,
and she shall live.

19 **And Jesus** arose,
and followed him,
and so did his disciples.

20 **And, {behold}, a woman**, {which was diseased with an issue of blood twelve years}, came behind him,
and touched the hem of his garment:

21 **For she** said within herself,
If I may but touch his garment,
I shall be whole.

22 **But Jesus** turned him about,
and when he saw her,
he said,
Daughter, be of good comfort;
thy faith hath made thee whole.

And the woman was made whole from that hour.

23 **And when Jesus** came into the ruler's house,
and saw the minstrels and the people making a noise,
24 **He** said unto them,
Give place:
for the maid is not dead,
but sleepeth.

And they laughed him to scorn.

25 **But when the people** were put forth,
he went in,
and took her by the hand,
and the maid arose.

26 **And the fame hereof** went abroad into all that land.

27 **And when Jesus** departed thence,
two blind men followed him,
crying,
and saying,
Thou son of David, have mercy on us.

28 **And when he** was come into the house,
the blind men came to him:
and Jesus saith unto them,
Believe ye
that I am able to do this?

They said unto him,
Yea, Lord.

29 **Then** touched he their eyes,
saying,
According to your faith be it unto you.

30 **And their eyes** were opened;
and Jesus straitly charged them,
saying,

See that no man know it.

31 **But they**, {when they were departed}, spread abroad his fame in all that country.

32 **As they** went out,
behold,
they brought to him a dumb man possessed with a devil.

33 **And when the devil** was cast out,
the dumb spake:
and the multitudes marvelled,
saying,
It was never so seen in Israel.

34 **But the Pharisees** said,
He casteth out devils through the prince of the devils.

35 **And Jesus** went about all the cities and villages,
teaching in their synagogues,
and preaching the gospel of the kingdom,
and healing every sickness and every disease among the people.

36 **But when he** saw the multitudes,
he was moved with compassion on them,
because they fainted,
and were scattered abroad,
as sheep having no shepherd.

37 **Then** saith he unto his disciples,
The harvest truly is plenteous,
but the labourers are few;

38 **Pray ye** therefore the Lord of the harvest,
that he will send forth labourers into his harvest.

10 **And when he** had called unto him his twelve disciples,
he gave them power against unclean spirits,
to cast them out,
and to heal all manner of sickness and all manner of disease.

2 **Now the names of the twelve apostles** are these; The first, Simon, {who is called Peter}, and Andrew his brother; James the son of Zebedee, and John his brother;

3 Philip, and Bartholomew; Thomas, and Matthew the publican; James the son of Alphaeus, and Lebbaeus, {whose surname was Thaddaeus};

4 Simon the Canaanite, and Judas Iscariot, {who also betrayed him}.

5 **These twelve** Jesus sent forth,
and commanded them,
saying,
Go not into the way of the Gentiles,
and into any city of the Samaritans enter ye not:

6 **But go** rather to the lost sheep of the house of Israel.

7 **And as ye** go,
preach,
saying,
The kingdom of heaven is at hand.

8 **Heal** the sick,
cleanse the lepers,
raise the dead,
cast out devils:
freely ye have received,
freely give.

9 **Provide** neither gold, nor silver, nor brass in your purses,

10 Nor scrip for your journey, neither two coats, neither shoes, nor yet staves:
for the workman is worthy of his meat.

11 **And into whatsoever city or town** ye shall enter,
enquire who in it is worthy;
and there abide
till ye go thence.

12 **And when ye** come into an house,
salute it.

13 **And if the house** be worthy,
let your peace come upon it:
but if it be not worthy,
let your peace return to you.

14 **And whosoever** shall not receive you,
nor hear your words,
when ye depart out of that house or city,
shake off the dust of your feet.

15 **Verily I** say unto you,
It shall be more tolerable for the land of Sodom and Gomorrha in the day of judgment, than for that city.

16 **Behold,**
I send you forth as sheep in the midst of wolves:
be ye therefore wise as serpents, and harmless as doves.

17 **But beware** of men:
for they will deliver you up to the councils,
and they will scourge you in their synagogues;

18 **And ye** shall be brought before governors and kings for my sake, for a testimony against them and the Gentiles.

19 **But when they** deliver you up,
take no thought how or what ye shall speak:
for it shall be given you in that same hour what ye shall speak.

20 **For it is not ye** that speak, but the Spirit of your Father which speaketh in you.

21 **And the brother** shall deliver up the brother to death, and the father the child:
and the children shall rise up against their parents,
and cause them to be put to death.

22 **And ye** shall be hated of all men for my name's sake:
but he that endureth to the end shall be saved.

23 **But when they** persecute you in this city,
flee ye into another:
for verily I say unto you,
Ye shall not have gone over the cities of Israel,
till the Son of man be come.

24 **The disciple** is not above his master, nor the servant above his lord.

25 **It is enough for the disciple** that he be as his master, and the servant as his lord.
If they have called the master of the house Beelzebub,
how much more shall they call them of his household?

26 **Fear them not** therefore:
for there is nothing covered,
that shall not be revealed;
and hid,
that shall not be known.

27 **What** I tell you in darkness,
that speak ye in light:
and what ye hear in the ear,
that preach ye upon the housetops.

28 **And fear not** them which kill the body, but are not able to kill the soul:
but rather fear him which is able to destroy both soul and body in hell.

29 **Are not two sparrows** sold for a farthing?
and one of them shall not fall on the ground without your Father.

30 **But the very hairs of your head** are all numbered.

31 **Fear ye not** therefore,
ye are of more value than many sparrows.

32 **Whosoever** therefore shall confess me before men,
him will I confess also before my Father which is in heaven.
33 **But whosoever** shall deny me before men,
him will I also deny before my Father which is in heaven.
34 **Think not**
that I am come to send peace on earth:
I came not to send peace, but a sword.
35 **For I** am come to set a man at variance against his father, and the daughter against her mother, and the daughter in law against her mother in law.
36 **And a man's foes** shall be they of his own household.
37 **He that loveth father or mother more than me** is not worthy of me:
and he that loveth son or daughter more than me is not worthy of me.
38 **And he that taketh not his cross, and followeth after me,** is not worthy of me.
39 **He that findeth his life** shall lose it:
and he that loseth his life for my sake shall find it.
40 **He that receiveth you** receiveth me,
and he that receiveth me receiveth him that sent me.
41 **He that receiveth a prophet in the name of a prophet** shall receive a prophet's reward;
and he that receiveth a righteous man in the name of a righteous man shall receive a righteous man's reward.
42 **And whosoever** shall give to drink unto one of these little ones a cup of cold water only in the name of a disciple,
verily I say unto you,
he shall in no wise lose his reward.

11

And it came to pass, **when Jesus** had made an end of commanding his twelve disciples,
he departed thence to teach and to preach in their cities.
2 **Now when John** had heard in the prison the works of Christ,
he sent two of his disciples,
3 **And** said unto him,
Art thou he that should come,
or do we look for another?
4 **Jesus** answered and said unto them,
Go and shew John again those things which ye do hear and see:
5 **The blind** receive their sight,
and the lame walk,
the lepers are cleansed,
and the deaf hear,
the dead are raised up,
and the poor have the gospel preached to them.
6 **And blessed** is he,
whosoever shall not be offended in me.
7 **And as they** departed,
Jesus began to say unto the multitudes concerning John,
What went ye out into the wilderness to see?
A reed shaken with the wind?
8 **But what** went ye out for to see?
A man clothed in soft raiment?
behold,
they that wear soft clothing are in kings' houses.
9 **But what** went ye out for to see?
A prophet?
yea, I say unto you, and more than a prophet.
10 **For this** is he,
of whom it is written,
Behold,
I send my messenger before thy face,
which shall prepare thy way before thee.
11 **Verily I** say unto you,
Among them that are born of women there hath not risen a greater than John the Baptist:
notwithstanding he that is least in the kingdom of heaven is greater than he.
12 **And from the days of John the Baptist until now** the kingdom of heaven suffereth violence,
and the violent take it by force.
13 **For all the prophets and the law** prophesied until John.
14 **And if ye** will receive it,
this is Elias,
which was for to come.
15 **He that hath ears to hear,** let him hear.
16 **But whereunto** shall I liken this generation?
It is like unto children sitting in the markets, and calling unto their fellows,
17 And saying,
We have piped unto you,
and ye have not danced;
we have mourned unto you,
and ye have not lamented.
18 **For John** came
neither eating
nor drinking,
and they say,
He hath a devil.
19 **The Son of man** came eating and drinking,
and they say,
Behold a man gluttonous, and a winebibber, a friend of publicans and sinners.
But wisdom is justified of her children.
20 **Then** began he to upbraid the cities wherein most of his mighty works were done
because they repented not:
21 **Woe** unto thee, Chorazin!
woe unto thee, Bethsaida!
for if the mighty works, {which were done in you}, had been done in Tyre and Sidon,
they would have repented long ago in sackcloth and ashes.
22 **But I** say unto you,
It shall be more tolerable for Tyre and Sidon at the day of judgment, than for you.
23 **And thou, Capernaum**, {which art exalted unto heaven}, shalt be brought down to hell:
for if the mighty works, {which have been done in thee}, had been done in Sodom,
it would have remained until this day.
24 **But I** say unto you,
That it shall be more tolerable for the land of Sodom in the day of judgment, than for thee.
25 **At that time** Jesus answered and said,
I thank thee, O Father, Lord of heaven and earth,
because thou hast hid these things from the wise and prudent,
and hast revealed them unto babes.
26 **Even so, Father: for so** it seemed good in thy sight.
27 **All things** are delivered unto me of my Father:

and no man knoweth the Son, but the Father;
neither knoweth any man the Father, save the Son, and he to whomsoever the Son will reveal him.
28 **Come** unto me, all ye that labour and are heavy laden,
and I will give you rest.
29 **Take** my yoke upon you,
and learn of me;
for I am meek and lowly in heart:
and ye shall find rest unto your souls.
30 **For my yoke** is easy,
and my burden is light.

12 **At that time** Jesus went on the sabbath day through the corn;
and his disciples were an hungred,
and began to pluck the ears of corn
and to eat.
2 **But when the Pharisees** saw it,
they said unto him,
Behold,
thy disciples do that which is not lawful to do upon the sabbath day.
3 **But he** said unto them,
Have ye not read what David did,
when he was an hungred, and they that were with him;
4 **How** he entered into the house of God,
and did eat the shewbread,
which was not lawful for him to eat, neither for them which were with him, but only for the priests?
5 **Or have ye not** read in the law,
how that on the sabbath days the priests in the temple profane the sabbath,
and are blameless?
6 **But I** say unto you,
That in this place is one greater than the temple.
7 **But if ye** had known
what this meaneth,
I will have mercy, and not sacrifice,
ye would not have condemned the guiltless.
8 **For the Son of man** is Lord even of the sabbath day.
9 **And when he** was departed thence,
he went into their synagogue:
10 **And, {behold}, there** was a man which had his hand withered.
And they asked him,
saying,
Is it lawful to heal on the sabbath days?
that they might accuse him.
11 **And he** said unto them,
What man shall there be among you,
that shall have one sheep,
and if it fall into a pit on the sabbath day,
will he not lay hold on it,
and lift it out?
12 **How much** then is a man better than a sheep?
Wherefore it is lawful to do well on the sabbath days.
13 **Then** saith he to the man,
Stretch forth thine hand.
And he stretched it forth;
and it was restored whole, like as the other.
14 **Then the Pharisees** went out,
and held a council against him,
how they might destroy him.
15 **But when Jesus** knew it,
he withdrew himself from thence:
and great multitudes followed him,
and he healed them all;
16 **And** charged them
that they should not make him known:
17 **That it** might be fulfilled which was spoken by Esaias the prophet, saying,
18 **Behold** my servant,
whom I have chosen; my beloved,
in whom my soul is well pleased:
I will put my spirit upon him,
and he shall shew judgment to the Gentiles.
19 **He** shall not strive,
nor cry;
neither shall any man hear his voice in the streets.
20 **A bruised reed** shall he not break,
and smoking flax shall he not quench,
till he send forth judgment unto victory.
21 **And in his name** shall the Gentiles trust.
22 **Then** was brought unto him one possessed with a devil, blind, and dumb:
and he healed him,
insomuch that the blind and dumb both spake and saw.
23 **And all the people** were amazed,
and said,
Is not this the son of David?
24 **But when the Pharisees** heard it,
they said,
This fellow doth not cast out devils, but by Beelzebub the prince of the devils.
25 **And Jesus** knew their thoughts,
and said unto them,
Every kingdom divided against itself is brought to desolation;
and every city or house divided against itself shall not stand:
26 **And if Satan** cast out Satan,
he is divided against himself;
how shall then his kingdom stand?
27 **And if I by Beelzebub** cast out devils,
by whom do your children cast them out?
therefore they shall be your judges.
28 **But if I** cast out devils by the Spirit of God,
then the kingdom of God is come unto you.
29 **Or else how** can one enter into a strong man's house,
and spoil his goods,
except he first bind the strong man?
and then he will spoil his house.
30 **He that is not with me** is against me;
and he that gathereth not with me scattereth abroad.
31 **Wherefore I** say unto you,
All manner of sin and blasphemy shall be forgiven unto men:
but the blasphemy against the Holy Ghost shall not be forgiven unto men.
32 **And whosoever** speaketh a word against the Son of man,
it shall be forgiven him:
but whosoever speaketh against the Holy Ghost,
it shall not be forgiven him, neither in this world, neither in the world to come.
33 **Either make** the tree good, and his fruit good;
or else make the tree corrupt, and his fruit corrupt:
for the tree is known by his fruit.
34 **O generation of vipers, how** can ye, {being evil}, speak good things?
for out of the abundance of the heart the mouth speaketh.

35 **A good man out of the good treasure of the heart** bringeth forth good things:
and an evil man out of the evil treasure bringeth forth evil things.

36 **But I** say unto you,
That every idle word that men shall speak, they shall give account thereof in the day of judgment.

37 **For by thy words** thou shalt be justified,
and by thy words thou shalt be condemned.

38 **Then certain of the scribes and of the Pharisees** answered,
saying,
Master, we would see a sign from thee.

39 **But he** answered and said unto them,
An evil and adulterous generation seeketh after a sign;
and there shall no sign be given to it, but the sign of the prophet Jonas:

40 **For as Jonas** was three days and three nights in the whale's belly;
so shall the Son of man be three days and three nights in the heart of the earth.

41 **The men of Nineveh** shall rise in judgment with this generation,
and shall condemn it:
because they repented at the preaching of Jonas;
and, {behold}, a greater than Jonas is here.

42 **The queen of the south** shall rise up in the judgment with this generation,
and shall condemn it:
for she came from the uttermost parts of the earth to hear the wisdom of Solomon;
and, {behold}, a greater than Solomon is here.

43 **When the unclean spirit** is gone out of a man,
he walketh through dry places,
seeking rest,
and findeth none.

44 **Then he** saith,
I will return into my house from whence I came out;
and when he is come,
he findeth it empty, swept, and garnished.

45 **Then** goeth he,
and taketh with himself seven other spirits more wicked than himself,
and they enter in and dwell there:
and the last state of that man is worse than the first.
Even so shall it be also unto this wicked generation.

46 **While he** yet talked to the people,
behold,
his mother and his brethren stood without,
desiring to speak with him.

47 **Then one** said unto him,
Behold,
thy mother and thy brethren stand without,
desiring to speak with thee.

48 **But he** answered and said unto him that told him,
Who is my mother?
and who are my brethren?

49 **And he** stretched forth his hand toward his disciples,
and said,
Behold my mother and my brethren!

50 **For whosoever** shall do the will of my Father which is in heaven,
the same is my brother, and sister, and mother.

13

The same day went Jesus out of the house,
and sat by the sea side.

2 **And great multitudes** were gathered together unto him,
so that he went into a ship,
and sat;
and the whole multitude stood on the shore.

3 **And he** spake many things unto them in parables,
saying,
Behold,
a sower went forth to sow;

4 **And when he** sowed,
some seeds fell by the way side,
and the fowls came and devoured them up:

5 **Some** fell upon stony places,
where they had not much earth:
and forthwith they sprung up,
because they had no deepness of earth:

6 **And when the sun** was up,
they were scorched;
and because they had no root,
they withered away.

7 **And some** fell among thorns;
and the thorns sprung up,
and choked them:

8 **But other** fell into good ground,
and brought forth fruit, some an hundredfold, some sixtyfold, some thirtyfold.

9 **Who** hath ears to hear,
let him hear.

10 **And the disciples** came,
and said unto him,
Why speakest thou unto them in parables?

11 **He** answered and said unto them,
Because it is given unto you to know the mysteries of the kingdom of heaven,
but to them it is not given.

12 **For whosoever** hath,
to him shall be given,
and he shall have more abundance:
but whosoever hath not,
from him shall be taken away even that he hath.

13 **Therefore** speak I to them in parables:
because they seeing see not;
and hearing they hear not,
neither do they understand.

14 **And in them** is fulfilled the prophecy of Esaias,
which saith,
By hearing ye shall hear,
and shall not understand;
and seeing ye shall see,
and shall not perceive:

15 **For this people's heart** is waxed gross,
and their ears are dull of hearing,
and their eyes they have closed;
lest at any time they should see with their eyes
and hear with their ears,
and should understand with their heart,
and should be converted,
and I should heal them.

16 **But blessed** are your eyes, {for they see}: and your ears, {for they hear}.

17 **For verily I** say unto you,
That many prophets and righteous men have desired to see those things which ye see,
and have not seen them;
and to hear those things which ye hear,
and have not heard them.

18 **Hear ye** therefore the parable of the sower.

19 **When any one** heareth the word of the kingdom,
and understandeth it not,
then cometh the wicked one,
and catcheth away that which was sown in his heart.

This is he which received seed by the way side.

20 **But he that received the seed into stony places,** the same is he that heareth the word,
and anon with joy receiveth it;
21 **Yet** hath he not root in himself,
but dureth for a while:
for when tribulation or persecution ariseth because of the word,
by and by he is offended.

22 **He also that received seed among the thorns** is he that heareth the word;
and the care of this world, and the deceitfulness of riches, choke the word,
and he becometh unfruitful.

23 **But he that received seed into the good ground** is he that heareth the word,
and understandeth it;
which also beareth fruit,
and bringeth forth, some an hundredfold, some sixty, some thirty.

24 **Another parable** put he forth unto them,
saying,
The kingdom of heaven is likened unto a man which sowed good seed in his field:
25 **But while men** slept,
his enemy came and sowed tares among the wheat,
and went his way.

26 **But when the blade** was sprung up,
and brought forth fruit,
then appeared the tares also.

27 **So the servants of the householder** came and said unto him,
Sir, didst not thou sow good seed in thy field?
from whence then hath it tares?

28 **He** said unto them,
An enemy hath done this.

The servants said unto him,
Wilt thou then that we go and gather them up?

29 **But he** said,
Nay;
lest while ye gather up the tares,
ye root up also the wheat with them.

30 **Let both** grow together until the harvest:
and in the time of harvest I will say to the reapers,
Gather ye together first the tares,
and bind them in bundles
to burn them:
but gather the wheat into my barn.

31 **Another parable** put he forth unto them,
saying,
The kingdom of heaven is like to a grain of mustard seed,
which a man took,
and sowed in his field:
32 **Which indeed** is the least of all seeds:
but when it is grown,
it is the greatest among herbs,
and becometh a tree,
so that the birds of the air come and lodge in the branches thereof.

33 **Another parable** spake he unto them;
The kingdom of heaven is like unto leaven,
which a woman took,
and hid in three measures of meal,
till the whole was leavened.

34 **All these things** spake Jesus unto the multitude in parables;
and without a parable spake he not unto them:
35 **That it** might be fulfilled which was spoken by the prophet,
saying,
I will open my mouth in parables;
I will utter things which have been kept secret from the foundation of the world.

36 **Then Jesus** sent the multitude away,
and went into the house:
and his disciples came unto him,
saying,
Declare unto us the parable of the tares of the field.

37 **He** answered and said unto them,
He that soweth the good seed is the Son of man;
38 **The field** is the world;
the good seed are the children of the kingdom;
but the tares are the children of the wicked one;
39 **The enemy that sowed them** is the devil;
the harvest is the end of the world;
and the reapers are the angels.

40 **As therefore the tares** are gathered and burned in the fire;
so shall it be in the end of this world.

41 **The Son of man** shall send forth his angels,
and they shall gather out of his kingdom all things that offend, and them which do iniquity;
42 **And** shall cast them into a furnace of fire:
there shall be wailing and gnashing of teeth.

43 **Then** shall the righteous shine forth as the sun in the kingdom of their Father.

Who hath ears to hear,
let him hear.

44 **Again, the kingdom of heaven** is like unto treasure hid in a field;
the which when a man hath found,
he hideth,
and for joy thereof goeth and selleth all that he hath,
and buyeth that field.

45 **Again, the kingdom of heaven** is like unto a merchant man,
seeking goodly pearls:
46 **Who**, {when he had found one pearl of great price}, went and sold all that he had,
and bought it.

47 **Again, the kingdom of heaven** is like unto a net,
that was cast into the sea,
and gathered of every kind:
48 **Which, {when it was full},** they drew to shore,
and sat down,
and gathered the good into vessels,
but cast the bad away.

49 **So** shall it be at the end of the world:
the angels shall come forth,
and sever the wicked from among the just,
50 **And** shall cast them into the furnace of fire:
there shall be wailing and gnashing of teeth.

51 **Jesus** saith unto them,
Have ye understood all these things?

They say unto him,

Yea, Lord.

52 **Then** said he unto them,
Therefore every scribe which is instructed unto the kingdom of heaven is like unto a man that is an householder,
which bringeth forth out of his treasure things new and old.

53 **And it** came to pass,
that when Jesus had finished these parables,
he departed thence.

54 **And when he** was come into his own country,
he taught them in their synagogue,
insomuch that they were astonished,
and said,
Whence hath this man this wisdom, and these mighty works?

55 **Is not this** the carpenter's son?
is not his mother called Mary?
and his brethren, James, and Joses, and Simon, and Judas?

56 **And his sisters,** are they not all with us?

Whence then hath this man all these things?

57 **And they** were offended in him.

But Jesus said unto them,
A prophet is not without honour, save in his own country, and in his own house.

58 **And he** did not many mighty works there because of their unbelief.

14

At that time Herod the tetrarch heard of the fame of Jesus,
2 **And** said unto his servants,
This is John the Baptist;
he is risen from the dead;
and therefore mighty works do shew forth themselves in him.

3 **For Herod** had laid hold on John,
and bound him,
and put him in prison for Herodias' sake, his brother Philip's wife.

4 **For John** said unto him,
It is not lawful for thee to have her.

5 **And when he** would have put him to death,
he feared the multitude,
because they counted him as a prophet.

6 **But when Herod's birthday** was kept,
the daughter of Herodias danced before them,
and pleased Herod.

7 **Whereupon he** promised with an oath to give her whatsoever she would ask.

8 **And she,** {being before instructed of her mother}, said,
Give me here John Baptist's head in a charger.

9 **And the king** was sorry:
nevertheless for the oath's sake, and them which sat with him at meat, he commanded it to be given her.

10 **And he** sent,
and beheaded John in the prison.

11 **And his head** was brought in a charger,
and given to the damsel:
and she brought it to her mother.

12 **And his disciples** came,
and took up the body,
and buried it,
and went and told Jesus.

13 **When Jesus** heard of it,
he departed thence by ship into a desert place apart:
and when the people had heard thereof,
they followed him on foot out of the cities.

14 **And Jesus** went forth,
and saw a great multitude,
and was moved with compassion toward them,
and he healed their sick.

15 **And when it** was evening,
his disciples came to him,
saying,
This is a desert place,
and the time is now past;
send the multitude away,
that they may go into the villages,
and buy themselves victuals.

16 **But Jesus** said unto them,
They need not depart;
give ye them to eat.

17 **And they** say unto him,
We have here but five loaves, and two fishes.

18 **He** said,
Bring them hither to me.

19 **And he** commanded the multitude to sit down on the grass,
and took the five loaves, and the two fishes,
and looking up to heaven,
he blessed,
and brake,
and gave the loaves to his disciples,
and the disciples to the multitude.

20 **And they** did all eat,
and were filled:
and they took up of the fragments that remained twelve baskets full.

21 **And they that had eaten** were about five thousand men, beside women and children.

22 **And straightway** Jesus constrained his disciples to get into a ship, and to go before him unto the other side,
while he sent the multitudes away.

23 **And when he** had sent the multitudes away,
he went up into a mountain apart to pray:
and when the evening was come,
he was there alone.

24 **But the ship** was now in the midst of the sea,
tossed with waves:
for the wind was contrary.

25 **And in the fourth watch of the night** Jesus went unto them,
walking on the sea.

26 **And when the disciples** saw him walking on the sea,
they were troubled,
saying,
It is a spirit;
and they cried out for fear.

27 **But straightway** Jesus spake unto them,
saying,
Be of good cheer;
it is I;
be not afraid.

28 **And Peter** answered him and said,
Lord, if it be thou,
bid me come unto thee on the water.

29 **And he** said,
Come.

And when Peter was come down out of the ship,
he walked on the water,
to go to Jesus.

30 **But when he** saw the wind boisterous,
he was afraid;
and beginning to sink,
he cried,
saying,
Lord, save me.

[31] **And immediately** Jesus stretched forth his hand,
and caught him,
and said unto him,
O thou of little faith, wherefore didst thou doubt?
[32] **And when they** were come into the ship,
the wind ceased.
[33] **Then they that were in the ship** came and worshipped him,
saying,
Of a truth thou art the Son of God.
[34] **And when they** were gone over,
they came into the land of Gennesaret.
[35] **And when the men of that place** had knowledge of him,
they sent out into all that country round about,
and brought unto him all that were diseased;
[36] **And** besought him
that they might only touch the hem of his garment:
and as many as touched were made perfectly whole.

15 **Then** came to Jesus scribes and Pharisees,
which were of Jerusalem,
saying,
[2] **Why** do thy disciples transgress the tradition of the elders?
for they wash not their hands
when they eat bread.
[3] **But he** answered and said unto them,
Why do ye also transgress the commandment of God by your tradition?
[4] **For God** commanded,
saying,
Honour thy father and mother:
and, He that curseth father or mother, let him die the death.
[5] **But ye** say,
Whosoever shall say to his father or his mother,
It is a gift,
by whatsoever thou mightest be profited by me;
[6] **And** honour not his father or his mother,
he shall be free.
Thus have ye made the commandment of God of none effect by your tradition.
[7] **Ye hypocrites, well** did Esaias prophesy of you,
saying,
[8] **This people** draweth nigh unto me with their mouth,
and honoureth me with their lips;
but their heart is far from me.
[9] **But in vain** they do worship me,
teaching for doctrines the commandments of men.
[10] **And he** called the multitude,
and said unto them,
Hear,
and understand:
[11] **Not that which goeth into the mouth** defileth a man;
but that which cometh out of the mouth, this defileth a man.
[12] **Then** came his disciples,
and said unto him,
Knowest thou
that the Pharisees were offended,
after they heard this saying?
[13] **But he** answered and said,
Every plant, {which my heavenly Father hath not planted}, shall be rooted up.
[14] **Let them** alone:
they be blind leaders of the blind.
And if the blind lead the blind,
both shall fall into the ditch.
[15] **Then** answered Peter and said unto him,
Declare unto us this parable.
[16] **And Jesus** said,
Are ye also yet without understanding?
[17] **Do not ye** yet understand,
that whatsoever entereth in at the mouth goeth into the belly,
and is cast out into the draught?
[18] **But those things which proceed out of the mouth** come forth from the heart;
and they defile the man.
[19] **For out of the heart** proceed evil thoughts, murders, adulteries, fornications, thefts, false witness, blasphemies:
[20] **These** are the things which defile a man:
but to eat with unwashen hands defileth not a man.
[21] **Then Jesus** went thence,
and departed into the coasts of Tyre and Sidon.
[22] **And, {behold}, a woman of Canaan** came out of the same coasts,
and cried unto him,
saying,
Have mercy on me, O Lord, thou son of David;
my daughter is grievously vexed with a devil.
[23] **But he** answered her not a word.
And his disciples came and besought him,
saying,
Send her away;
for she crieth after us.
[24] **But he** answered and said,
I am not sent but unto the lost sheep of the house of Israel.
[25] **Then** came she and worshipped him,
saying,
Lord, help me.
[26] **But he** answered and said,
It is not meet to take the children's bread,
and to cast it to dogs.
[27] **And she** said,
Truth, Lord:
yet the dogs eat of the crumbs which fall from their masters' table.
[28] **Then Jesus** answered and said unto her,
O woman, great is thy faith:
be it unto thee
even as thou wilt.
And her daughter was made whole from that very hour.
[29] **And Jesus** departed from thence,
and came nigh unto the sea of Galilee;
and went up into a mountain,
and sat down there.
[30] **And great multitudes** came unto him,
having with them those that were lame, blind, dumb, maimed, and many others,
and cast them down at Jesus' feet;
and he healed them:
[31] **Insomuch that the multitude** wondered,
when they saw the dumb to speak,
the maimed to be whole,
the lame to walk,
and the blind to see:
and they glorified the God of Israel.
[32] **Then Jesus** called his disciples unto him,
and said,
I have compassion on the multitude,
because they continue with me now three days,

and have nothing to eat:
and I will not send them away fasting,
lest they faint in the way.
33 **And his disciples** say unto him,
Whence should we have so much bread in the wilderness,
as to fill so great a multitude?
34 **And Jesus** saith unto them,
How many loaves have ye?
And they said,
Seven, and a few little fishes.
35 **And he** commanded the multitude to sit down on the ground.
36 **And he** took the seven loaves and the fishes,
and gave thanks,
and brake them,
and gave to his disciples,
and the disciples to the multitude.
37 **And they** did all eat,
and were filled:
and they took up of the broken meat that was left seven baskets full.
38 **And they that did eat** were four thousand men, beside women and children.
39 **And he** sent away the multitude,
and took ship,
and came into the coasts of Magdala.

16 **The Pharisees also with the Sadducees** came,
and {tempting} desired him
that he would shew them a sign from heaven.
2 **He** answered and said unto them,
When it is evening,
ye say,
It will be fair weather:
for the sky is red.
3 **And in the morning,** It will be foul weather to day:
for the sky is red and lowering.
O ye hypocrites, ye can discern the face of the sky;
but can ye not discern the signs of the times?
4 **A wicked and adulterous generation** seeketh after a sign;
and there shall no sign be given unto it, but the sign of the prophet Jonas.
And he left them,
and departed.
5 **And when his disciples** were come to the other side,
they had forgotten to take bread.
6 **Then Jesus** said unto them,
Take heed and beware of the leaven of the Pharisees and of the Sadducees.
7 **And they** reasoned among themselves,
saying,
It is because we have taken no bread.
8 **Which when Jesus** perceived,
he said unto them,
O ye of little faith, why reason ye among yourselves,
because ye have brought no bread?
9 **Do ye not** yet understand,
neither remember the five loaves of the five thousand,
and how many baskets ye took up?
10 **Neither** the seven loaves of the four thousand,
and how many baskets ye took up?
11 **How is it** that ye do not understand
that I spake it not to you concerning bread,
that ye should beware of the leaven of the Pharisees and of the Sadducees?
12 **Then** understood they
how that he bade them not beware of the leaven of bread, but of the doctrine of the Pharisees and of the Sadducees.
13 **When Jesus** came into the coasts of Caesarea Philippi,
he asked his disciples,
saying,
Whom do men say
that I the Son of man am?
14 **And they** said,
Some say
that thou art John the Baptist: some, Elias; and others, Jeremias, or one of the prophets.
15 **He** saith unto them,
But whom say ye that I am?
16 **And Simon Peter** answered and said,
Thou art the Christ, the Son of the living God.
17 **And Jesus** answered and said unto him,
Blessed art thou, Simon Barjona:
for flesh and blood hath not revealed it unto thee, but my Father which is in heaven.
18 **And I** say also unto thee,
That thou art Peter,
and upon this rock I will build my church;
and the gates of hell shall not prevail against it.
19 **And I** will give unto thee the keys of the kingdom of heaven:
and whatsoever thou shalt bind on earth shall be bound in heaven:
and whatsoever thou shalt loose on earth shall be loosed in heaven.
20 **Then** charged he his disciples
that they should tell no man
that he was Jesus the Christ.
21 **From that time forth** began Jesus to shew unto his disciples,
how that he must go unto Jerusalem,
and suffer many things of the elders and chief priests and scribes,
and be killed,
and be raised again the third day.
22 **Then Peter** took him,
and began to rebuke him,
saying,
Be it far from thee, Lord:
this shall not be unto thee.
23 **But he** turned,
and said unto Peter,
Get thee behind me, Satan:
thou art an offence unto me:
for thou savourest not the things that be of God, but those that be of men.
24 **Then** said Jesus unto his disciples,
If any man will come after me,
let him deny himself,
and take up his cross,
and follow me.
25 **For whosoever will save his life** shall lose it:
and whosoever will lose his life for my sake shall find it.
26 **For what** is a man profited,
if he shall gain the whole world,
and lose his own soul?
or what shall a man give in exchange for his soul?
27 **For the Son of man** shall come in the glory of his Father with his angels;
and then he shall reward every man according to his works.
28 **Verily I** say unto you,
There be some standing here,

which shall not taste of death,
till they see the Son of man coming
in his kingdom.

17 **And after six days** Jesus
taketh Peter, James, and
John his brother,
and bringeth them up into an high
mountain apart,
2 **And** was transfigured before them:
and his face did shine as the sun,
and his raiment was white as the
light.
3 **And, {behold}, there** appeared
unto them Moses and Elias
talking with him.
4 **Then** answered Peter,
and said unto Jesus,
Lord, it is good for us to be here:
if thou wilt,
let us make here three tabernacles;
one for thee, and one for Moses,
and one for Elias.
5 **While he** yet spake,
behold,
a bright cloud overshadowed
them:
and behold a voice out of the cloud,
which said,
This is my beloved Son,
in whom I am well pleased;
hear ye him.
6 **And when the disciples** heard it,
they fell on their face,
and were sore afraid.
7 **And Jesus** came and touched
them,
and said,
Arise,
and be not afraid.
8 **And when they** had lifted up their
eyes,
they saw no man, save Jesus only.
9 **And as they** came down from the
mountain,
Jesus charged them,
saying,
Tell the vision to no man,
until the Son of man be risen again
from the dead.
10 **And his disciples** asked him,
saying,
Why then say the scribes
that Elias must first come?
11 **And Jesus** answered and said unto
them,
Elias truly shall first come,
and restore all things.
12 **But I** say unto you,
That Elias is come already,
and they knew him not,
but have done unto him
whatsoever they listed.
Likewise shall also the Son of man
suffer of them.
13 **Then the disciples** understood
that he spake unto them of John the
Baptist.
14 **And when they** were come to the
multitude,
there came to him a certain man,
kneeling down to him,
and saying,
15 **Lord, have mercy** on my son:
for he is lunatick, and sore vexed:
for ofttimes he falleth into the fire,
and oft into the water.
16 **And I** brought him to thy
disciples,
and they could not cure him.
17 **Then Jesus** answered and said,
**O faithless and perverse
generation, how long** shall I be
with you?
how long shall I suffer you?
bring him hither to me.
18 **And Jesus** rebuked the devil;
and he departed out of him:
and the child was cured from that
very hour.
19 **Then** came the disciples to Jesus
apart,
and said,
Why could not we cast him out?
20 **And Jesus** said unto them,
Because of your unbelief:
for verily I say unto you,
If ye have faith as a grain of
mustard seed,
ye shall say unto this mountain,
Remove hence to yonder place;
and it shall remove;
and nothing shall be impossible
unto you.
21 **Howbeit this kind** goeth not out
but by prayer and fasting.
22 **And while they** abode in Galilee,
Jesus said unto them,
The Son of man shall be betrayed
into the hands of men:
23 **And they** shall kill him,
and the third day he shall be raised
again.
And they were exceeding sorry.
24 **And when they** were come to
Capernaum,
they that received tribute money
came to Peter,
and said,
Doth not your master pay tribute?
25 **He** saith,
Yes.
And when he was come into the
house,
Jesus prevented him,
saying,
What thinkest thou, Simon?
of whom do the kings of the earth
take custom or tribute?
of their own children, or of
strangers?
26 **Peter** saith unto him,
Of strangers.
Jesus saith unto him,
Then are the children free.
27 **Notwithstanding, {lest we
should offend them},** go thou to
the sea,
and cast an hook,
and take up the fish that first
cometh up;
and when thou hast opened his
mouth,
thou shalt find a piece of money:
that take,
and give unto them for me and
thee.

18 **At the same time** came
the disciples unto Jesus,
saying,
Who is the greatest in the kingdom
of heaven?
2 **And Jesus** called a little child unto
him,
and set him in the midst of them,
3 **And** said,
Verily I say unto you,
Except ye be converted,
and become as little children,
ye shall not enter into the kingdom
of heaven.
4 **Whosoever** therefore shall
humble himself as this little child,
the same is greatest in the kingdom
of heaven.
5 **And whoso shall receive one
such little child in my name**
receiveth me.
6 **But whoso** shall offend one of
these little ones which believe in
me,
it were better for him that a
millstone were hanged about his
neck,
and that he were drowned in the
depth of the sea.
7 **Woe** unto the world because of
offences!

for it must needs be that offences come;
but woe to that man by whom the offence cometh!
8 **Wherefore if thy hand or thy foot** offend thee,
cut them off,
and cast them from thee:
it is better for thee to enter into life halt or maimed,
rather than having two hands or two feet to be cast into everlasting fire.
9 **And if thine eye** offend thee,
pluck it out,
and cast it from thee:
it is better for thee to enter into life with one eye,
rather than having two eyes to be cast into hell fire.
10 **Take heed** that ye despise not one of these little ones;
for I say unto you,
That in heaven their angels do always behold the face of my Father which is in heaven.
11 **For the Son of man** is come to save that which was lost.
12 **How** think ye?
if a man have an hundred sheep,
and one of them be gone astray,
doth he not leave the ninety and nine,
and goeth into the mountains,
and seeketh that which is gone astray?
13 **And if so be that he** find it,
verily I say unto you,
he rejoiceth more of that sheep,
than of the ninety and nine which went not astray.
14 **Even so it is not the will of your Father which is in heaven,** that one of these little ones should perish.
15 **Moreover if thy brother** shall trespass against thee,
go and tell him his fault between thee and him alone:
if he shall hear thee,
thou hast gained thy brother.
16 **But if he** will not hear thee,
then take with thee one or two more,
that in the mouth of two or three witnesses every word may be established.
17 **And if he** shall neglect to hear them,
tell it unto the church:
but if he neglect to hear the church,
let him be unto thee as an heathen man and a publican.
18 **Verily I** say unto you,
Whatsoever ye shall bind on earth shall be bound in heaven:
and whatsoever ye shall loose on earth shall be loosed in heaven.
19 **Again I** say unto you,
That if two of you shall agree on earth as touching any thing that they shall ask,
it shall be done for them of my Father which is in heaven.
20 **For where two or three** are gathered together in my name,
there am I in the midst of them.
21 **Then** came Peter to him,
and said,
Lord, how oft shall my brother sin against me,
and I forgive him?
till seven times?
22 **Jesus** saith unto him,
I say not unto thee,
Until seven times: but, Until seventy times seven.
23 **Therefore** is the kingdom of heaven likened unto a certain king,
which would take account of his servants.
24 **And when he** had begun to reckon,
one was brought unto him,
which owed him ten thousand talents.
25 **But forasmuch as he** had not to pay,
his lord commanded him to be sold, and his wife, and children, and all that he had,
and payment to be made.
26 **The servant** therefore fell down,
and worshipped him,
saying,
Lord, have patience with me,
and I will pay thee all.
27 **Then the lord of that servant** was moved with compassion,
and loosed him,
and forgave him the debt.
28 **But the same servant** went out,
and found one of his fellowservants,
which owed him an hundred pence:
and he laid hands on him,
and took him by the throat,
saying,
Pay me that thou owest.
29 **And his fellowservant** fell down at his feet,
and besought him,
saying,
Have patience with me,
and I will pay thee all.
30 **And he** would not:
but went and cast him into prison,
till he should pay the debt.
31 **So when his fellowservants** saw what was done,
they were very sorry,
and came and told unto their lord all that was done.
32 **Then his lord**, {after that he had called him}, said unto him,
O thou wicked servant, I forgave thee all that debt,
because thou desiredst me:
33 **Shouldest not thou** also have had compassion on thy fellowservant,
even as I had pity on thee?
34 **And his lord** was wroth,
and delivered him to the tormentors,
till he should pay all that was due unto him.
35 **So likewise** shall my heavenly Father do also unto you,
if ye from your hearts forgive not every one his brother their trespasses.

19 **And it** came to pass,
that {when Jesus had finished these sayings}, he departed from Galilee,
and came into the coasts of Judaea beyond Jordan;
2 **And great multitudes** followed him;
and he healed them there.
3 **The Pharisees** also came unto him,
tempting him,
and saying unto him,
Is it lawful for a man to put away his wife for every cause?
4 **And he** answered and said unto them,
Have ye not read,
that he which made them at the beginning made them male and female,
5 **And** said,

For this cause shall a man leave father and mother,
and shall cleave to his wife:
and they twain shall be one flesh?

6 **Wherefore they** are no more twain, but one flesh.

What therefore God hath joined together,
let not man put asunder.

7 **They** say unto him,
Why did Moses then command to give a writing of divorcement, and to put her away?

8 **He** saith unto them,
Moses because of the hardness of your hearts suffered you to put away your wives:
but from the beginning it was not so.

9 **And I** say unto you,
Whosoever shall put away his wife, {except it be for **fornication}, {and shall marry another},** committeth adultery:
and whoso marrieth her which is put away doth commit adultery.

10 **His disciples** say unto him,
If the case of the man be so with his wife,
it is not good to marry.

11 **But he** said unto them,
All men cannot receive this saying, save they to whom it is given.

12 **For there** are some eunuchs,
which were so born from their mother's womb:
and there are some eunuchs,
which were made eunuchs of men:
and there be eunuchs,
which have made themselves eunuchs for the kingdom of heaven's sake.

He that is able to receive it, let him receive it.

13 **Then** were there brought unto him little children,
that he should put his hands on them,
and pray:
and the disciples rebuked them.

14 **But Jesus** said,
Suffer little children,
and forbid them not,
to come unto me:
for of such is the kingdom of heaven.

15 **And he** laid his hands on them,
and departed thence.

16 **And, {behold}, one** came and said unto him,
Good Master, what good thing shall I do,
that I may have eternal life?

17 **And he** said unto him,
Why callest thou me good?
there is none good but one, that is, God:
but if thou wilt enter into life,
keep the commandments.

18 **He** saith unto him,
Which?
Jesus said,
Thou shalt do no murder,
Thou shalt not commit adultery,
Thou shalt not steal,
Thou shalt not bear false witness,
19 **Honour** thy father and thy mother:
and, Thou shalt love thy neighbour as thyself.

20 **The young man** saith unto him,
All these things have I kept from my youth up:
what lack I yet?

21 **Jesus** said unto him,
If thou wilt be perfect,
go and sell that thou hast,
and give to the poor,
and thou shalt have treasure in heaven:
and come and follow me.

22 **But when the young man** heard that saying,
he went away sorrowful:
for he had great possessions.

23 **Then** said Jesus unto his disciples,
Verily I say unto you,
That a rich man shall hardly enter into the kingdom of heaven.

24 **And again I** say unto you,
It is easier for a camel to go through the eye of a needle,
than for a rich man to enter into the kingdom of God.

25 **When his disciples** heard it,
they were exceedingly amazed,
saying,
Who then can be saved?

26 **But Jesus** beheld them,
and said unto them,
With men this is impossible;
but with God all things are possible.

27 **Then** answered Peter and said unto him,
Behold,
we have forsaken all,
and followed thee;
what shall we have therefore?

28 **And Jesus** said unto them,
Verily I say unto you,
That ye which have followed me, {in the regeneration when the Son of man shall sit in the throne of his glory}, ye also shall sit upon twelve thrones,
judging the twelve tribes of Israel.

29 **And every one that hath forsaken houses, or brethren, or sisters, or father, or mother, or wife, or children, or lands, for my name's sake,** shall receive an hundredfold,
and shall inherit everlasting life.

30 **But many that are first** shall be last;
and the last shall be first.

20 ∞ **For the kingdom of heaven** is like unto a man that is an householder,
which went out early in the morning to hire labourers into his vineyard.

2 **And when he** had agreed with the labourers for a penny a day,
he sent them into his vineyard.

3 **And he** went out about the third hour,
and saw others standing idle in the marketplace,

4 **And** said unto them;
Go ye also into the vineyard,
and whatsoever is right
I will give you.

And they went their way.

5 **Again he** went out about the sixth and ninth hour,
and did likewise.

6 **And about the eleventh hour** he went out,
and found others standing idle,
and saith unto them,
Why stand ye here all the day idle?

7 **They** say unto him,
Because no man hath hired us.

He saith unto them,
Go ye also into the vineyard;
and whatsoever is right,
that shall ye receive.

8 **So when even** was come,
the lord of the vineyard saith unto his steward,
Call the labourers,
and give them their hire,
beginning from the last unto the first.

9 **And when they** came that were hired about the eleventh hour,
they received every man a penny.
10 **But when the first** came,
they supposed
that they should have received more;
and they likewise received every man a penny.
11 **And when they** had received it,
they murmured against the goodman of the house,
12 Saying,
These last have wrought but one hour,
and thou hast made them equal unto us,
which have borne the burden and heat of the day.
13 **But he** answered one of them,
and said,
Friend, I do thee no wrong:
didst not thou agree with me for a penny?
14 **Take** that thine is,
and go thy way:
I will give unto this last, even as unto thee.
15 **Is it not lawful** for me to do what I will with mine own?
Is thine eye evil,
because I am good?
16 **So the last** shall be first, and the first last:
for many be called, but few chosen.
17 **And Jesus going up to Jerusalem** took the twelve disciples apart in the way,
and said unto them,
18 **Behold,**
we go up to Jerusalem;
and the Son of man shall be betrayed unto the chief priests and unto the scribes,
and they shall condemn him to death,
19 **And** shall deliver him to the Gentiles to mock,
and to scourge,
and to crucify him:
and the third day he shall rise again.
20 **Then** came to him the mother of Zebedees children with her sons,
worshipping him,
and desiring a certain thing of him.
21 **And he** said unto her,
What wilt thou?
She saith unto him,
Grant
that these my two sons may sit, the one on thy right hand, and the other on the left, in thy kingdom.
22 **But Jesus** answered and said,
Ye know not
what ye ask.
Are ye able to drink of the cup that I shall drink of,
and to be baptized with the baptism that I am baptized with?
They say unto him,
We are able.
23 **And he** saith unto them,
Ye shall drink indeed of my cup,
and be baptized with the baptism that I am baptized with:
but to sit on my right hand, and on my left, is not mine to give,
but it shall be given to them for whom it is prepared of my Father.
24 **And when the ten** heard it,
they were moved with indignation against the two brethren.
25 **But Jesus** called them unto him,
and said,
Ye know
that the princes of the Gentiles exercise dominion over them,
and they that are great exercise authority upon them.
26 **But it** shall not be so among you:
but whosoever will be great among you,
let him be your minister;
27 **And whosoever** will be chief among you,
let him be your servant:
28 **Even as the Son of man** came not to be ministered unto,
but to minister,
and to give his life a ransom for many.
29 **And as they** departed from Jericho,
a great multitude followed him.
30 **And, {behold}, two blind men sitting by the way side,** {when they heard that Jesus passed by}, cried out,
saying,
Have mercy on us, O Lord, thou son of David.
31 **And the multitude** rebuked them,
because they should hold their peace:
but they cried the more,
saying,
Have mercy on us, O Lord, thou son of David.
32 **And Jesus** stood still,
and called them,
and said,
What will ye
that I shall do unto you?
33 **They** say unto him,
Lord, that our eyes may be opened.
34 **So Jesus** had compassion on them,
and touched their eyes:
and immediately their eyes received sight,
and they followed him.

21 **And when they** drew nigh unto Jerusalem,
and were come to Bethphage, unto the mount of Olives,
then sent Jesus two disciples,
2 Saying unto them,
Go into the village over against you,
and straightway ye shall find an ass tied, and a colt with her:
loose them,
and bring them unto me.
3 **And if any man** say ought unto you,
ye shall say,
The Lord hath need of them;
and straightway he will send them.
4 **All this** was done,
that it might be fulfilled which was spoken by the prophet,
saying,
5 **Tell ye** the daughter of Sion,
Behold,
thy King cometh unto thee, meek,
and sitting upon an ass, and a colt the foal of an ass.
6 **And the disciples** went,
and did as Jesus commanded them,
7 **And** brought the ass, and the colt,
and put on them their clothes,
and they set him thereon.
8 **And a very great multitude** spread their garments in the way;
others cut down branches from the trees,
and strawed them in the way.
9 **And the multitudes that went before, and that followed,** cried,
saying,
Hosanna to the son of David:
Blessed is he that cometh in the name of the Lord;
Hosanna in the highest.
10 **And when he** was come into Jerusalem,

all the city was moved,
saying,
Who is this?

11 **And the multitude** said,
This is Jesus the prophet of Nazareth of Galilee.

12 **And Jesus** went into the temple of God,
and cast out all them that sold and bought in the temple,
and overthrew the tables of the moneychangers, and the seats of them that sold doves,
13 **And** said unto them,
It is written,
My house shall be called the house of prayer;
but ye have made it a den of thieves.

14 **And the blind and the lame** came to him in the temple;
and he healed them.

15 **And when the chief priests and scribes** saw the wonderful things that he did, and the children crying in the temple, and saying, {Hosanna to the son of David};
they were sore displeased,
16 **And** said unto him,
Hearest thou what these say?

And Jesus saith unto them,
Yea;
have ye never read,
Out of the mouth of babes and sucklings thou hast perfected praise?

17 **And he** left them,
and went out of the city into Bethany;
and he lodged there.

18 **Now in the morning {as he returned into the city},** he hungered.

19 **And when he** saw a fig tree in the way,
he came to it,
and found nothing thereon, but leaves only,
and said unto it,
Let no fruit grow on thee henceforward for ever.

And presently the fig tree withered away.

20 **And when the disciples** saw it,
they marvelled,
saying,
How soon is the fig tree withered away!

21 **Jesus** answered and said unto them,
Verily I say unto you,
If ye have faith,
and doubt not,
ye shall not only do this which is done to the fig tree,
but also if ye shall say unto this mountain,
Be thou removed,
and be thou cast into the sea;
it shall be done.

22 **And all things**, {whatsoever ye shall ask in prayer}, {believing}, ye shall receive.

23 **And when he** was come into the temple,
the chief priests and the elders of the people came unto him as he was teaching,
and said,
By what authority doest thou these things?
and who gave thee this authority?

24 **And Jesus** answered and said unto them,
I also will ask you one thing,
which if ye tell me,
I in like wise will tell you
by what authority I do these things.

25 **The baptism of John,** whence was it?
from heaven, or of men?

And they reasoned with themselves,
saying,
If we shall say,
From heaven;
he will say unto us,
Why did ye not then believe him?

26 **But if we** shall say,
Of men;
we fear the people;
for all hold John as a prophet.

27 **And they** answered Jesus,
and said,
We cannot tell.

And he said unto them,
Neither tell I you
by what authority I do these things.

28 **But what** think ye?

A certain man had two sons;
and he came to the first,
and said,
Son, go work to day in my vineyard.

29 **He** answered and said,
I will not:
but afterward he repented,
and went.

30 **And he** came to the second,
and said likewise.

And he answered and said,
I go, sir:
and went not.

31 **Whether of them twain** did the will of his father?

They say unto him,
The first.

Jesus saith unto them,
Verily I say unto you,
That the publicans and the harlots go into the kingdom of God before you.

32 **For John** came unto you in the way of righteousness,
and ye believed him not:
but the publicans and the harlots believed him:
and ye, {when ye had seen it}, repented not afterward,
that ye might believe him.

33 **Hear** another parable:
There was a certain householder,
which planted a vineyard,
and hedged it round about,
and digged a winepress in it,
and built a tower,
and let it out to husbandmen,
and went into a far country:
34 **And when the time of the fruit** drew near,
he sent his servants to the husbandmen,
that they might receive the fruits of it.

35 **And the husbandmen** took his servants,
and beat one,
and killed another,
and stoned another.

36 **Again, he** sent other servants more than the first:
and they did unto them likewise.

37 **But last of all** he sent unto them his son,
saying,
They will reverence my son.

38 **But when the husbandmen** saw the son,
they said among themselves,
This is the heir;
come,
let us kill him,
and let us seize on his inheritance.

39 **And they** caught him,

and cast him out of the vineyard,
and slew him.
40 **When the lord therefore of the vineyard** cometh,
what will he do unto those husbandmen?
41 **They** say unto him,
He will miserably destroy those wicked men,
and will let out his vineyard unto other husbandmen,
which shall render him the fruits in their seasons.
42 **Jesus** saith unto them,
Did ye never read in the scriptures,
The stone which the builders rejected, the same is become the head of the corner:
this is the Lord's doing,
and it is marvellous in our eyes?
43 **Therefore** say I unto you,
The kingdom of God shall be taken from you,
and given to a nation bringing forth the fruits thereof.
44 **And whosoever shall fall on this stone** shall be broken:
but on whomsoever it shall fall,
it will grind him to powder.
45 **And when the chief priests and Pharisees** had heard his parables,
they perceived that he spake of them.
46 **But when they** sought to lay hands on him,
they feared the multitude,
because they took him for a prophet.

22 ∞ **And Jesus** answered and spake unto them again by parables,
and said,
2 **The kingdom of heaven** is like unto a certain king,
which made a marriage for his son,
3 **And** sent forth his servants to call them that were bidden to the wedding:
and they would not come.
4 **Again, he** sent forth other servants,
saying,
Tell them which are bidden,
Behold,
I have prepared my dinner:
my oxen and my fatlings are killed,
and all things are ready:
come unto the marriage.
5 **But they** made light of it,
and went their ways, one to his farm, another to his merchandise:
6 **And the remnant** took his servants,
and entreated them spitefully,
and slew them.
7 **But when the king** heard thereof,
he was wroth:
and he sent forth his armies,
and destroyed those murderers,
and burned up their city.
8 **Then** saith he to his servants,
The wedding is ready,
but they which were bidden were not worthy.
9 **Go ye** therefore into the highways,
and as many as ye shall find,
bid to the marriage.
10 **So those servants** went out into the highways,
and gathered together all as many as they found, both bad and good:
and the wedding was furnished with guests.
11 **And when the king** came in to see the guests,
he saw there a man which had not on a wedding garment:
12 **And he** saith unto him,
Friend, how camest thou in hither not having a wedding garment?
And he was speechless.
13 **Then** said the king to the servants,
Bind him hand and foot,
and take him away,
and cast him into outer darkness,
there shall be weeping and gnashing of teeth.
14 **For many** are called,
but few are chosen.
15 **Then** went the Pharisees,
and took counsel how they might entangle him in his talk.
16 **And they** sent out unto him their disciples with the Herodians,
saying,
Master, we know
that thou art true,
and teachest the way of God in truth,
neither carest thou for any man:
for thou regardest not the person of men.
17 **Tell** us therefore,
What thinkest thou?
Is it lawful to give tribute unto Caesar, or not?
18 **But Jesus** perceived their wickedness,
and said,
Why tempt ye me, ye hypocrites?
19 **Shew** me the tribute money.
And they brought unto him a penny.
20 **And he** saith unto them,
Whose is this image and superscription?
21 **They** say unto him,
Caesar's.
Then saith he unto them,
Render therefore unto Caesar the things which are Caesar's; and unto God the things that are God's.
22 **When they** had heard these words,
they marvelled,
and left him,
and went their way.
23 **The same day** came to him the Sadducees,
which say
that there is no resurrection,
and asked him,
24 Saying,
Master, Moses said,
If a man die,
having no children,
his brother shall marry his wife,
and raise up seed unto his brother.
25 **Now there** were with us seven brethren:
and the first, {when he had married a wife}, deceased,
and, {having no issue}, left his wife unto his brother:
26 Likewise the second also, and the third, unto the seventh.
27 **And last of all** the woman died also.
28 **Therefore in the resurrection** whose wife shall she be of the seven?
for they all had her.
29 **Jesus** answered and said unto them,
Ye do err,
not knowing the scriptures, nor the power of God.
30 **For in the resurrection** they neither marry,
nor are given in marriage,
but are as the angels of God in heaven.
31 **But as touching the resurrection of the dead,** have ye not read that

which was spoken unto you by God,
saying,
32 **I** am the God of Abraham, and the God of Isaac, and the God of Jacob?
God is not the God of the dead, but of the living.
33 **And when the multitude** heard this,
they were astonished at his doctrine.
34 **But when the Pharisees** had heard that he had put the Sadducees to silence,
they were gathered together.
35 **Then one of them**, {which was a lawyer}, asked him a question,
tempting him,
and saying,
36 **Master, which** is the great commandment in the law?
37 **Jesus** said unto him,
Thou shalt love the Lord thy God with all thy heart, and with all thy soul, and with all thy mind.
38 **This** is the first and great commandment.
39 **And the second** is like unto it,
Thou shalt love thy neighbour as thyself.
40 **On these two commandments** hang all the law and the prophets.
41 **While the Pharisees** were gathered together,
Jesus asked them,
42 Saying,
What think ye of Christ?
whose son is he?
They say unto him,
The son of David.
43 **He** saith unto them,
How then doth David in spirit call him Lord,
saying,
44 **The LORD** said unto my Lord,
Sit thou on my right hand,
till I make thine enemies thy footstool?
45 **If David** then call him Lord,
how is he his son?
46 **And no man** was able to answer him a word,
neither durst any man from that day forth ask him any more questions.

23 **Then** spake Jesus to the multitude, and to his disciples,
2 Saying
The scribes and the Pharisees sit in Moses' seat:
3 **All therefore whatsoever they** bid you observe,
that observe and do;
but do not ye after their works:
for they say,
and do not.
4 **For they** bind heavy burdens and grievous to be borne,
and lay them on men's shoulders;
but they themselves will not move them with one of their fingers.
5 **But all their works** they do
for to be seen of men:
they make broad their phylacteries,
and enlarge the borders of their garments,
6 **And** love the uppermost rooms at feasts, and the chief seats in the synagogues,
7 And greetings in the markets,
and to be called of men, Rabbi, Rabbi.
8 **But be not ye** called Rabbi:
for one is your Master, even Christ;
and all ye are brethren.
9 **And call** no man your father upon the earth:
for one is your Father,
which is in heaven.
10 **Neither be ye called** masters:
for one is your Master, even Christ.
11 **But he that is greatest among you** shall be your servant.
12 **And whosoever shall exalt himself** shall be abased;
and he that shall humble himself shall be exalted.
13 **But woe** unto you, scribes and Pharisees, hypocrites!
for ye shut up the kingdom of heaven against men:
for ye neither go in yourselves,
neither suffer ye them that are entering to go in.
14 **Woe** unto you, scribes and Pharisees, hypocrites!
for ye devour widows' houses,
and for a pretence make long prayer:
therefore ye shall receive the greater damnation.
15 **Woe** unto you, scribes and Pharisees, hypocrites!
for ye compass sea and land to make one proselyte,
and when he is made,
ye make him twofold more the child of hell than yourselves.
16 **Woe** unto you, ye blind guides,
which say,
Whosoever shall swear by the temple,
it is nothing;
but whosoever shall swear by the gold of the temple,
he is a debtor!
17 **Ye fools and blind: for whether** is greater, the gold, or the temple that sanctifieth the gold?
18 **And, Whosoever** shall swear by the altar,
it is nothing;
but whosoever sweareth by the gift that is upon it,
he is guilty.
19 **Ye fools and blind: for whether** is greater, the gift, or the altar that sanctifieth the gift?
20 **Whoso therefore shall swear by the altar,** sweareth by it, and by all things thereon.
21 **And whoso shall swear by the temple,** sweareth by it, and by him that dwelleth therein.
22 **And he that shall swear by heaven,** sweareth by the throne of God, and by him that sitteth thereon.
23 **Woe** unto you, scribes and Pharisees, hypocrites!
for ye pay tithe of mint and anise and cummin,
and have omitted the weightier matters of the law, judgment, mercy, and faith:
these ought ye to have done,
and not to leave the other undone.
24 Ye blind guides,
which strain at a gnat,
and swallow a camel.
25 **Woe** unto you, scribes and Pharisees, hypocrites!
for ye make clean the outside of the cup and of the platter,
but within they are full of extortion and excess.
26 **Thou blind Pharisee, cleanse** first that which is within the cup and platter,
that the outside of them may be clean also.
27 **Woe** unto you, scribes and Pharisees, hypocrites!

for ye are like unto whited sepulchres,
which indeed appear beautiful outward,
but are within full of dead men's bones, and of all uncleanness.

28 **Even so ye** also outwardly appear righteous unto men,
but within ye are full of hypocrisy and iniquity.

29 **Woe** unto you, scribes and Pharisees, hypocrites!
because ye build the tombs of the prophets,
and garnish the sepulchres of the righteous,
30 **And** say,
If we had been in the days of our fathers,
we would not have been partakers with them in the blood of the prophets.

31 **Wherefore ye** be witnesses unto yourselves,
that ye are the children of them which killed the prophets.

32 **Fill ye up** then the measure of your fathers.

33 **Ye serpents, ye generation of vipers, how** can ye escape the damnation of hell?

34 **Wherefore, {behold}, I** send unto you prophets, and wise men, and scribes:
and some of them ye shall kill
and crucify;
and some of them shall ye scourge in your synagogues,
and persecute them from city to city:
35 **That upon you** may come all the righteous blood shed upon the earth, from the blood of righteous Abel unto the blood of Zacharias son of Barachias,
whom ye slew between the temple and the altar.

36 **Verily I** say unto you,
All these things shall come upon this generation.

37 **O Jerusalem, Jerusalem, thou that killest the prophets, and stonest them which are sent unto thee, how often** would I have gathered thy children together,
even as a hen gathereth her chickens under her wings,
and ye would not!

38 **Behold,**
your house is left unto you desolate.

39 **For I** say unto you,
Ye shall not see me henceforth,
till ye shall say,
Blessed is he that cometh in the name of the Lord.

24

And Jesus went out,
and departed from the temple:
and his disciples came to him
for to shew him the buildings of the temple.

2 **And Jesus** said unto them,
See ye not all these things?
verily I say unto you,
There shall not be left here one stone upon another,
that shall not be thrown down.

3 **And as he** sat upon the mount of Olives,
the disciples came unto him privately,
saying,
Tell us,
when shall these things be?
and what shall be the sign of thy coming, and of the end of the world?

4 **And Jesus** answered and said unto them,
Take heed that no man deceive you.

5 **For many** shall come in my name,
saying,
I am Christ;
and shall deceive many.

6 **And ye** shall hear of wars and rumours of wars:
see that ye be not troubled:
for all these things must come to pass,
but the end is not yet.

7 **For nation** shall rise against nation, and kingdom against kingdom:
and there shall be famines, and pestilences, and earthquakes, in divers places.

8 **All these** are the beginning of sorrows.

9 **Then** shall they deliver you up to be afflicted,
and shall kill you:
and ye shall be hated of all nations for my name's sake.

10 **And then** shall many be offended,
and shall betray one another,
and shall hate one another.

11 **And many false prophets** shall rise,
and shall deceive many.

12 **And because iniquity** shall abound,
the love of many shall wax cold.

13 **But he that shall endure unto the end,** the same shall be saved.

14 **And this gospel of the kingdom** shall be preached in all the world for a witness unto all nations;
and then shall the end come.

15 **When ye** therefore shall see the abomination of desolation,
spoken of by Daniel the prophet,
stand in the holy place,
(whoso readeth,
let him understand:)
16 **Then let them which be in Judaea** flee into the mountains:
17 **Let him which is on the housetop** not come down to take any thing out of his house:
18 **Neither let him which is in the field** return back to take his clothes.

19 **And woe** unto them that are with child, and to them that give suck in those days!

20 **But pray ye**
that your flight be not in the winter, neither on the sabbath day:
21 **For then** shall be great tribulation,
such as was not since the beginning of the world to this time,
no, nor ever shall be.

22 **And except those days** should be shortened,
there should no flesh be saved:
but for the elect's sake those days shall be shortened.

23 **Then if any man** shall say unto you,
Lo,
here is Christ, or there;
believe it not.

24 **For there** shall arise false Christs, and false prophets,
and shall shew great signs and wonders;
insomuch that, {if it were possible}, they shall deceive the very elect.

25 **Behold,**
I have told you before.

26 **Wherefore if they** shall say unto you,

Behold,
he is in the desert;
go not forth:
behold,
he is in the secret chambers;
believe it not.
27 **For as the lightning** cometh out of the east,
and shineth even unto the west;
so shall also the coming of the Son of man be.
28 **For wheresoever the carcase** is,
there will the eagles be gathered together.
29 **Immediately after the tribulation of those days** shall the sun be darkened,
and the moon shall not give her light,
and the stars shall fall from heaven,
and the powers of the heavens shall be shaken:
30 **And then** shall appear the sign of the Son of man in heaven:
and then shall all the tribes of the earth mourn,
and they shall see the Son of man coming in the clouds of heaven with power and great glory.
31 **And he** shall send his angels with a great sound of a trumpet,
and they shall gather together his elect from the four winds, from one end of heaven to the other.
32 **Now learn** a parable of the fig tree;
When his branch is yet tender,
and putteth forth leaves,
ye know
that summer is nigh:
33 **So likewise ye**, {when ye shall see all these things}, know
that it is near, even at the doors.
34 **Verily I** say unto you,
This generation shall not pass,
till all these things be fulfilled.
35 **Heaven and earth** shall pass away,
but my words shall not pass away.
36 **But of that day and hour** knoweth no man, no, not the angels of heaven, but my Father only.
37 **But as the days of Noah** were,
so shall also the coming of the Son of man be.
38 **For as in the days that were before the flood** they were eating and drinking,
marrying and giving in marriage,
until the day that Noe entered into the ark,
39 **And** knew not
until the flood came,
and took them all away;
so shall also the coming of the Son of man be.
40 **Then** shall two be in the field;
the one shall be taken, and the other left.
41 **Two women** shall be grinding at the mill;
the one shall be taken, and the other left.
42 **Watch** therefore:
for ye know not
what hour your Lord doth come.
43 **But know** this,
that if the goodman of the house had known
in what watch the thief would come,
he would have watched,
and would not have suffered his house to be broken up.
44 **Therefore be ye** also ready:
for in such an hour as ye think not the Son of man cometh.
45 **Who** then is a faithful and wise servant,
whom his lord hath made ruler over his household,
to give them meat in due season?
46 **Blessed** is that servant,
whom his lord {when he cometh} shall find so doing.
47 **Verily I** say unto you,
That he shall make him ruler over all his goods.
48 **But and if that evil servant** shall say in his heart,
My lord delayeth his coming;
49 **And** shall begin to smite his fellowservants,
and to eat and drink with the drunken;
50 **The lord of that servant** shall come in a day when he looketh not for him, and in an hour that he is not aware of,
51 **And** shall cut him asunder,
and appoint him his portion with the hypocrites:
there shall be weeping and gnashing of teeth.

25 **Then** shall the kingdom of heaven be likened unto ten virgins,
which took their lamps,
and went forth to meet the bridegroom.
2 **And five of them** were wise,
and five were foolish.
3 **They that were foolish** took their lamps,
and took no oil with them:
4 **But the wise** took oil in their vessels with their lamps.
5 **While the bridegroom** tarried,
they all slumbered and slept.
6 **And at midnight** there was a cry made,
Behold,
the bridegroom cometh;
go ye out to meet him.
7 **Then all those virgins** arose,
and trimmed their lamps.
8 **And the foolish** said unto the wise,
Give us of your oil;
for our lamps are gone out.
9 **But the wise** answered,
saying,
Not so;
lest there be not enough for us and you:
but go ye rather to them that sell,
and buy for yourselves.
10 **And while they** went to buy,
the bridegroom came;
and they that were ready went in with him to the marriage:
and the door was shut.
11 **Afterward** came also the other virgins,
saying,
Lord, Lord, open to us.
12 **But he** answered and said,
Verily I say unto you,
I know you not.
13 **Watch** therefore,
for ye know neither the day nor the hour wherein the Son of man cometh.
14 **For the kingdom of heaven** is as a man travelling into a far country,
who called his own servants,
and delivered unto them his goods.
15 **And unto one** he gave five talents, to another two, and to another one; to every man according to his several ability;
and straightway took his journey.

16 **Then he that had received the five talents** went and traded with the same,
and made them other five talents.
17 **And likewise he that had received two,** he also gained other two.
18 **But he that had received one** went and digged in the earth,
and hid his lord's money.
19 **After a long time** the lord of those servants cometh,
and reckoneth with them.
20 **And so he that had received five talents** came and brought other five talents,
saying,
Lord, thou deliveredst unto me five talents:
behold,
I have gained beside them five talents more.
21 **His lord** said unto him,
Well done, thou good and faithful servant:
thou hast been faithful over a few things,
I will make thee ruler over many things:
enter thou into the joy of thy lord.
22 **He also that had received two talents** came and said,
Lord, thou deliveredst unto me two talents:
behold,
I have gained two other talents beside them.
23 **His lord** said unto him,
Well done, good and faithful servant;
thou hast been faithful over a few things,
I will make thee ruler over many things:
enter thou into the joy of thy lord.
24 **Then he which had received the one talent** came and said,
Lord, I knew thee
that thou art an hard man,
reaping where thou hast not sown,
and gathering where thou hast not strawed:
25 **And I** was afraid,
and went and hid thy talent in the earth:
lo,
there thou hast that is thine.
26 **His lord** answered and said unto him,
Thou wicked and slothful servant, thou knewest
that I reap where I sowed not,
and gather where I have not strawed:
27 **Thou** oughtest therefore to have put my money to the exchangers,
and then at my coming I should have received mine own with usury.
28 **Take** therefore the talent from him,
and give it unto him which hath ten talents.
29 **For unto every one that hath** shall be given,
and he shall have abundance:
but from him that hath not shall be taken away even that which he hath.
30 **And cast ye** the unprofitable servant into outer darkness:
there shall be weeping and gnashing of teeth.
31 **When the Son of man** shall come in his glory, and all the holy angels with him,
then shall he sit upon the throne of his glory:
32 **And before him** shall be gathered all nations:
and he shall separate them one from another,
as a shepherd divideth his sheep from the goats:
33 **And he** shall set the sheep on his right hand, but the goats on the left.
34 **Then** shall the King say unto them on his right hand,
Come, ye blessed of my Father,
inherit the kingdom prepared for you from the foundation of the world:
35 **For I** was an hungred,
and ye gave me meat:
I was thirsty,
and ye gave me drink:
I was a stranger,
and ye took me in:
36 Naked,
and ye clothed me:
I was sick,
and ye visited me:
I was in prison,
and ye came unto me.
37 **Then** shall the righteous answer him,
saying,
Lord, when saw we thee an hungred, {and fed thee}? or thirsty, {and gave thee drink}?
38 **When** saw we thee a stranger, {and took thee in}? or naked, {and clothed thee}?
39 **Or when** saw we thee sick, or in prison,
and came unto thee?
40 **And the King** shall answer and say unto them,
Verily I say unto you,
Inasmuch as ye have done it unto one of the least of these my brethren,
ye have done it unto me.
41 **Then** shall he say also unto them on the left hand,
Depart from me, ye cursed, into everlasting fire,
prepared for the devil and his angels:
42 **For I** was an hungred,
and ye gave me no meat:
I was thirsty,
and ye gave me no drink:
43 **I** was a stranger, {and ye took me not in}: naked, {and ye clothed me not}: sick, and in prison, {and ye visited me not}.
44 **Then** shall they also answer him,
saying,
Lord, when saw we thee an hungred, or athirst, or a stranger, or naked, or sick, or in prison,
and did not minister unto thee?
45 **Then** shall he answer them,
saying,
Verily I say unto you,
Inasmuch as ye did it not to one of the least of these,
ye did it not to me.
46 **And these** shall go away into everlasting punishment: but the righteous into life eternal.

26 **And it** came to pass, **when Jesus** had finished all these sayings,
he said unto his disciples,
2 **Ye** know
that after two days is the feast of the passover,
and the Son of man is betrayed to be crucified.
3 **Then** assembled together the chief priests, and the scribes, and the elders of the people, unto the palace of the high priest,
who was called Caiaphas,

4 **And** consulted
that they might take Jesus by subtilty,
and kill him.

5 **But they** said,
Not on the feast day,
lest there be an uproar among the people.

6 **Now when Jesus** was in Bethany, in the house of Simon the leper,
7 **There** came unto him a woman having an alabaster box of very precious ointment, and poured it on his head, as he sat at meat.

8 **But when his disciples** saw it,
they had indignation,
saying,
To what purpose is this waste?

9 **For this ointment** might have been sold for much,
and given to the poor.

10 **When Jesus** understood it,
he said unto them,
Why trouble ye the woman?
for she hath wrought a good work upon me.

11 **For ye** have the poor always with you;
but me ye have not always.

12 **For in that she** hath poured this ointment on my body,
she did it for my burial.

13 **Verily I** say unto you,
Wheresoever this gospel shall be preached in the whole world,
there shall also this, {that this woman hath done}, be told for a memorial of her.

14 **Then one of the twelve, called Judas Iscariot,** went unto the chief priests,
15 **And** said unto them,
What will ye give me,
and I will deliver him unto you?
And they covenanted with him for thirty pieces of silver.

16 **And from that time** he sought opportunity to betray him.

17 **Now the first day of the feast of unleavened bread** the disciples came to Jesus,
saying unto him,
Where wilt thou that we prepare for thee to eat the passover?

18 **And he** said,
Go into the city to such a man,
and say unto him,
The Master saith,
My time is at hand;
I will keep the passover at thy house with my disciples.

19 **And the disciples** did as Jesus had appointed them;
and they made ready the passover.

20 **Now when the even** was come,
he sat down with the twelve.

21 **And as they** did eat,
he said,
Verily I say unto you,
that one of you shall betray me.

22 **And they** were exceeding sorrowful,
and began every one of them to say unto him,
Lord, is it I?

23 **And he** answered and said,
He that dippeth his hand with me in the dish, the same shall betray me.

24 **The Son of man** goeth as it is written of him:
but woe unto that man by whom the Son of man is betrayed!
it had been good for that man
if he had not been born.

25 **Then Judas**, {which betrayed him}, answered and said,
Master, is it I?
He said unto him,
Thou hast said.

26 **And as they** were eating,
Jesus took bread,
and blessed it,
and brake it,
and gave it to the disciples,
and said,
Take,
eat;
this is my body.

27 **And he** took the cup,
and gave thanks,
and gave it to them,
saying,
Drink ye all of it;
28 **For this** is my blood of the new testament,
which is shed for many for the remission of sins.

29 **But I** say unto you,
I will not drink henceforth of this fruit of the vine,
until that day when I drink it new with you in my Father's kingdom.

30 **And when they** had sung an hymn,
they went out into the mount of Olives.

31 **Then** saith Jesus unto them,
All ye shall be offended because of me this night:
for it is written,
I will smite the shepherd,
and the sheep of the flock shall be scattered abroad.

32 **But after I** am risen again,
I will go before you into Galilee.

33 **Peter** answered and said unto him,
Though all men shall be offended because of thee,
yet will I never be offended.

34 **Jesus** said unto him,
Verily I say unto thee,
That this night, {before the cock crow}, thou shalt deny me thrice.

35 **Peter** said unto him,
Though I should die with thee,
yet will I not deny thee.
Likewise also said all the disciples.

36 **Then** cometh Jesus with them unto a place called Gethsemane,
and saith unto the disciples,
Sit ye here,
while I go and pray yonder.

37 **And he** took with him Peter and the two sons of Zebedee,
and began to be sorrowful and very heavy.

38 **Then** saith he unto them,
My soul is exceeding sorrowful, even unto death:
tarry ye here,
and watch with me.

39 **And he** went a little farther,
and fell on his face,
and prayed,
saying,
O my Father, if it be possible,
let this cup pass from me:
nevertheless not as I will,
but as thou wilt.

40 **And he** cometh unto the disciples,
and findeth them asleep,
and saith unto Peter,
What, could ye not watch with me one hour?

41 **Watch and pray,**
that ye enter not into temptation:
the spirit indeed is willing,
but the flesh is weak.

42 **He** went away again the second time,
and prayed,
saying,
O my Father, if this cup may not pass away from me,

except I drink it,
thy will be done.
43 **And he** came and found them asleep again:
for their eyes were heavy.
44 **And he** left them,
and went away again,
and prayed the third time,
saying the same words.
45 **Then** cometh he to his disciples,
and saith unto them,
Sleep on now,
and take your rest:
behold,
the hour is at hand,
and the Son of man is betrayed into the hands of sinners.
46 **Rise,**
let us be going:
behold,
he is at hand that doth betray me.
47 **And while he** yet spake,
lo,
Judas, one of the twelve, came,
and with him a great multitude with swords and staves, from the chief priests and elders of the people.
48 **Now he that betrayed him** gave them a sign,
saying,
Whomsoever I shall kiss,
that same is he:
hold him fast.
49 **And forthwith** he came to Jesus,
and said,
Hail, master;
and kissed him.
50 **And Jesus** said unto him,
Friend, wherefore art thou come?
Then came they,
and laid hands on Jesus
and took him.
51 **And, {behold}, one of them which were with Jesus** stretched out his hand,
and drew his sword,
and struck a servant of the high priest's,
and smote off his ear.
52 **Then** said Jesus unto him,
Put up again thy sword into his place:
for all they that take the sword shall perish with the sword.
53 **Thinkest thou**
that I cannot now pray to my Father,
and he shall presently give me more than twelve legions of angels?
54 **But how** then shall the scriptures be fulfilled,
that thus it must be?
55 **In that same hour** said Jesus to the multitudes,
Are ye come out as against a thief with swords and staves
for to take me?
I sat daily with you
teaching in the temple,
and ye laid no hold on me.
56 **But all this** was done,
that the scriptures of the prophets might be fulfilled.
Then all the disciples forsook him,
and fled.
57 **And they that had laid hold on Jesus** led him away to Caiaphas the high priest,
where the scribes and the elders were assembled.
58 **But Peter** followed him afar off unto the high priest's palace,
and went in,
and sat with the servants,
to see the end.
59 **Now the chief priests, and elders, and all the council,** sought false witness against Jesus,
to put him to death;
60 **But** found none:
yea, though many false witnesses came,
yet found they none.
At the last came two false witnesses,
61 **And** said,
This fellow said,
I am able to destroy the temple of God,
and to build it in three days.
62 **And the high priest** arose,
and said unto him,
Answerest thou nothing?
what is it which these witness against thee?
63 **But Jesus** held his peace,
And the high priest answered and said unto him,
I adjure thee by the living God,
that thou tell us
whether thou be the Christ, the Son of God.
64 **Jesus** saith unto him,
Thou hast said:
nevertheless I say unto you,
Hereafter shall ye see the Son of man sitting on the right hand of power, and coming in the clouds of heaven.
65 **Then the high priest** rent his clothes,
saying,
He hath spoken blasphemy;
what further need have we of witnesses?
behold,
now ye have heard his blasphemy.
66 **What** think ye?
They answered and said,
He is guilty of death.
67 **Then** did they spit in his face,
and buffeted him;
and others smote him with the palms of their hands,
68 Saying,
Prophesy unto us, thou Christ,
Who is he that smote thee?
69 **Now Peter** sat without in the palace:
and a damsel came unto him,
saying,
Thou also wast with Jesus of Galilee.
70 **But he** denied before them all,
saying,
I know not
what thou sayest.
71 **And when he** was gone out into the porch,
another maid saw him,
and said unto them that were there,
This fellow was also with Jesus of Nazareth.
72 **And again he** denied with an oath,
I do not know the man.
73 **And after a while** came unto him they that stood by,
and said to Peter,
Surely thou also art one of them;
for thy speech bewrayeth thee.
74 **Then** began he to curse and to swear,
saying,
I know not the man.
And immediately the cock crew.
75 **And Peter** remembered the word of Jesus,
which said unto him,
Before the cock crow, thou shalt deny me thrice.

And he went out,
and wept bitterly.

27 **When the morning** was come,
all the chief priests and elders of the people took counsel against Jesus
to put him to death:
2 **And when they** had bound him,
they led him away,
and delivered him to Pontius Pilate the governor.
3 **Then Judas**, {which had betrayed him}, {when he saw that he was condemned}, repented himself,
and brought again the thirty pieces of silver to the chief priests and elders,
4 Saying,
I have sinned
in that I have betrayed the innocent blood.
And they said,
What is that to us?
see thou to that.
5 **And he** cast down the pieces of silver in the temple,
and departed,
and went and hanged himself.
6 **And the chief priests** took the silver pieces,
and said,
It is not lawful for to put them into the treasury,
because it is the price of blood.
7 **And they** took counsel,
and bought with them the potter's field,
to bury strangers in.
8 **Wherefore that field** was called, The field of blood, unto this day.
9 **Then** was fulfilled that which was spoken by Jeremy the prophet,
saying,
And they took the thirty pieces of silver, the price of him that was valued,
whom they of the children of Israel did value;
10 **And** gave them for the potter's field,
as the Lord appointed me.
11 **And Jesus** stood before the governor:
and the governor asked him,
saying,
Art thou the King of the Jews?
And Jesus said unto him,
Thou sayest.
12 **And when he** was accused of the chief priests and elders,
he answered nothing.
13 **Then** said Pilate unto him,
Hearest thou not how many things they witness against thee?
14 **And he** answered him to never a word;
insomuch that the governor marvelled greatly.
15 **Now at that feast** the governor was wont to release unto the people a prisoner,
whom they would.
16 **And they** had then a notable prisoner, called Barabbas.
17 **Therefore when they** were gathered together,
Pilate said unto them,
Whom will ye
that I release unto you?
Barabbas, or Jesus which is called Christ?
18 **For he** knew
that for envy they had delivered him.
19 **When he** was set down on the judgment seat,
his wife sent unto him,
saying,
Have thou nothing to do with that just man:
for I have suffered many things this day in a dream because of him.
20 **But the chief priests and elders** persuaded the multitude
that they should ask Barabbas,
and destroy Jesus.
21 **The governor** answered and said unto them,
Whether of the twain will ye
that I release unto you?
They said,
Barabbas.
22 **Pilate** saith unto them,
What shall I do then with Jesus which is called Christ?
They all say unto him,
Let him be crucified.
23 **And the governor** said,
Why,
what evil hath he done?
But they cried out the more,
saying,
Let him be crucified.
24 **When Pilate** saw that he could prevail nothing,
but that rather a tumult was made,
he took water,
and washed his hands before the multitude,
saying,
I am innocent of the blood of this just person:
see ye to it.
25 **Then** answered all the people,
and said,
His blood be on us, and on our children.
26 **Then** released he Barabbas unto them:
and when he had scourged Jesus,
he delivered him to be crucified.
27 **Then the soldiers of the governor** took Jesus into the common hall,
and gathered unto him the whole band of soldiers.
28 **And they** stripped him,
and put on him a scarlet robe.
29 **And when they** had platted a crown of thorns,
they put it upon his head, and a reed in his right hand:
and they bowed the knee before him,
and mocked him,
saying,
Hail, King of the Jews!
30 **And they** spit upon him,
and took the reed,
and smote him on the head.
31 **And after that they** had mocked him,
they took the robe off from him,
and put his own raiment on him,
and led him away to crucify him.
32 **And as they** came out,
they found a man of Cyrene, Simon by name:
him they compelled to bear his cross.
33 **And when they** were come unto a place called Golgotha, that is to say, a place of a skull,
34 **They** gave him vinegar to drink mingled with gall:
and when he had tasted thereof,
he would not drink.
35 **And they** crucified him,
and parted his garments,
casting lots:
that it might be fulfilled which was spoken by the prophet,
They parted my garments among them,
and upon my vesture did they cast lots.

36 **And** sitting down
they watched him there;
37 **And** set up over his head his
accusation written,
This Is Jesus The King Of The Jews.
38 **Then** were there two thieves
crucified with him, one on the
right hand, and another on the
left.
39 **And they that passed by** reviled
him,
wagging their heads,
40 **And** saying,
**Thou that destroyest the temple,
and buildest it in three days,
save** thyself.
If thou be the Son of God,
come down from the cross.
41 **Likewise also the chief priests
mocking him, with the scribes
and elders,** said,
42 **He** saved others;
himself he cannot save.
If he be the King of Israel,
let him now come down from the
cross,
and we will believe him.
43 **He** trusted in God;
let him deliver him now,
if he will have him:
for he said,
I am the Son of God.
44 **The thieves** also, {which were
crucified with him}, cast the same
in his teeth.
45 **Now from the sixth hour** there
was darkness over all the land
unto the ninth hour.
46 **And about the ninth hour** Jesus
cried with a loud voice,
saying,
Eli, Eli, lama sabachthani?
that is to say,
My God, my God, why hast thou
forsaken me?
47 **Some of them that stood there,**
{when they heard that}, said,
This man calleth for Elias.
48 **And straightway** one of them
ran,
and took a spunge,
and filled it with vinegar,
and put it on a reed,
and gave him to drink.
49 **The rest** said,
Let be,
let us see whether Elias will come
to save him.
50 **Jesus**, {when he had cried again
with a loud voice}, yielded up the
ghost.
51 **And, {behold}, the veil of the
temple** was rent in twain from
the top to the bottom;
and the earth did quake,
and the rocks rent;
52 **And the graves** were opened;
**and many bodies of the saints
which slept** arose,
53 **And** came out of the graves after
his resurrection,
and went into the holy city,
and appeared unto many.
54 **Now when the centurion, and
they that were with him,**
{watching Jesus}, saw the
earthquake, and those things that
were done,
they feared greatly,
saying,
Truly this was the Son of God.
55 **And many women** were there
beholding afar off,
which followed Jesus from Galilee,
ministering unto him:
56 Among which was Mary
Magdalene, and Mary the mother
of James and Joses, and the
mother of Zebedees children.
57 **When the even** was come,
there came a rich man of
Arimathaea, named Joseph,
who also himself was Jesus'
disciple:
58 **He** went to Pilate,
and begged the body of Jesus.
Then Pilate commanded the body
to be delivered.
59 **And when Joseph** had taken the
body,
he wrapped it in a clean linen cloth,
60 **And** laid it in his own new tomb,
which he had hewn out in the rock:
and he rolled a great stone to the
door of the sepulchre,
and departed.
61 **And there** was Mary Magdalene,
and the other Mary,
sitting over against the sepulchre.
62 **Now the next day**, {that followed
the day of the preparation}, the
chief priests and Pharisees came
together unto Pilate,
63 Saying,
Sir, we remember
that that deceiver said,
while he was yet alive,
After three days I will rise again.
64 **Command** therefore
that the sepulchre be made sure
until the third day,
lest his disciples come by night,
and steal him away,
and say unto the people,
He is risen from the dead:
so the last error shall be worse
than the first.
65 **Pilate** said unto them,
Ye have a watch:
go your way,
make it as sure as ye can.
66 **So they** went,
and made the sepulchre sure,
sealing the stone,
and setting a watch.

28 **In the end of the
sabbath**, {as it began to
dawn toward the first day of the
week}, came Mary Magdalene
and the other Mary to see the
sepulchre.
2 **And, {behold}, there** was a great
earthquake:
for the angel of the Lord
descended from heaven,
and came and rolled back the stone
from the door,
and sat upon it.
3 **His countenance** was like
lightning, and his raiment white
as snow:
4 **And for fear of him** the keepers
did shake,
and became as dead men.
5 **And the angel** answered and said
unto the women,
**Fear not ye:
for I** know
that ye seek Jesus,
which was crucified.
6 **He** is not here:
for he is risen,
as he said.
**Come,
see** the place where the Lord lay.
7 **And go** quickly,
and tell his disciples
that he is risen from the dead;
and, {behold}, he goeth before you
into Galilee;
there shall ye see him:
**lo,
I** have told you.
8 **And they** departed quickly from
the sepulchre with fear and great
joy;

and did run to bring his disciples word.

9 **And as they** went to tell his disciples,
behold,
Jesus met them,
saying,
All hail.

And they came and held him by the feet,
and worshipped him.

10 **Then** said Jesus unto them,
Be not afraid:
go tell my brethren
that they go into Galilee,
and there shall they see me.

11 **Now when they** were going,
behold,
some of the watch came into the city,
and shewed unto the chief priests all the things that were done.

12 **And when they** were assembled with the elders,
and had taken counsel,
they gave large money unto the soldiers,
13 Saying,
Say ye,
His disciples came by night,
and stole him away
while we slept.

14 **And if this** come to the governor's ears,
we will persuade him,
and secure you.

15 **So they** took the money,
and did as they were taught:
and this saying is commonly reported among the Jews until this day.

16 **Then the eleven disciples** went away into Galilee, into a mountain where Jesus had appointed them.

17 **And when they** saw him,
they worshipped him:
but some doubted.

18 **And Jesus** came and spake unto them,
saying,
All power is given unto me in heaven and in earth.

19 **Go ye** therefore,
and teach all nations,
baptizing them in the name of the Father, and of the Son, and of the Holy Ghost:
20 Teaching them to observe all things whatsoever I have commanded you:
and, {lo}, I am with you always, even unto the end of the world.

Amen.

Mark

John Mark, a scribe and companion of Peter and later a close associate of Paul, penned the Gospel of Mark. Despite not being an apostle, his proximity to the apostles and his contributions to the New Testament elevated his status in early Christianity. Mark's Gospel, the second of the four canonical gospels, stands out for its simplicity and directness. It offers a distinct viewpoint on the life and teachings of Jesus Christ, tailored for both Jewish and Gentile audiences. Its central theme is the universal need for repentance and acceptance of God's forgiveness and grace.

The Gospel of Mark commences with John the Baptist baptizing Jesus in the Jordan River, followed by the Holy Spirit descending on Him, signaling the start of Jesus' public ministry. The Holy Spirit then leads Jesus into the wilderness, where Satan tempts him for forty days. After overcoming this trial, Jesus calls his first disciples, including Peter, Andrew, James, and John. These disciples, who later become His closest followers, play a pivotal role in continuing His mission and spreading the Gospel after His death and resurrection. Mark's narrative is punctuated with numerous miracles performed by Jesus, demonstrating His power and authority over both the physical and spiritual realms. He also narrates Jesus' transfiguration, a significant event that anticipates His future glory and the arrival of the kingdom of God.

Toward the end of the book, Mark describes how Jesus is betrayed, arrested, and ultimately crucified on a cross. He then concludes with his account of Jesus rising from the dead on the third day, appearing to His disciples, and commissioning them to spread the good news to all nations. It marks the beginning of the Christian Church and the promise of eternal life for those who believe in Jesus. These key events form the core message of the Gospel of Mark, that Jesus is the Son of God, Who came to earth to save sinners, and that through faith in Him, anyone can have forgiveness and eternal life.

The Gospel of Mark remains an integral part of the New Testament scriptures as it offers a concise and vivid account of Jesus' ministry, including the well-known parables of the sower, the mustard seed, and the lost sheep. It enriches readers' understanding of Who Jesus is and the historical events that led to His crucifixion and resurrection. Mark wrote his Gospel during a time when the early Christian community was experiencing persecution and thus needed encouragement and guidance. In this respect, his narrative serves as a reminder that hope and salvation are found in the redemptive power of Christ and the transformative grace He extends to all who believe in Him. This grace, which can change lives and bring about a new beginning, is a key aspect of Jesus' teachings that Mark highlights with great success.

1 The beginning of the gospel of Jesus Christ, the Son of God;
2 **As it** is written in the prophets,
Behold,
I send my messenger before thy face,
which shall prepare thy way before thee.

3 The voice of one crying in the wilderness,
Prepare ye the way of the Lord,
make his paths straight.

4 **John** did baptize in the wilderness,
and preach the baptism of repentance for the remission of sins.

5 **And there** went out unto him all the land of Judaea, and they of Jerusalem,
and were all baptized of him in the river of Jordan,
confessing their sins.

6 **And John** was clothed with camel's hair, and with a girdle of a skin about his loins;
and he did eat locusts and wild honey;
7 **And** preached,
saying,
There cometh one mightier than I after me,
the latchet of whose shoes I am not worthy to stoop down and unloose.

8 **I** indeed have baptized you with water:
but he shall baptize you with the Holy Ghost.

9 **And it** came to pass in those days,
that Jesus came from Nazareth of Galilee,
and was baptized of John in Jordan.
10 **And straightway** coming up out of the water,
he saw the heavens opened, and the Spirit like a dove descending upon him:
11 **And there** came a voice from heaven,
saying,
Thou art my beloved Son,
in whom I am well pleased.

12 **And immediately** the spirit driveth him into the wilderness.

13 **And he** was there in the wilderness forty days,
tempted of Satan;
and was with the wild beasts;
and the angels ministered unto him.

14 **Now after that John** was put in prison,
Jesus came into Galilee,
preaching the gospel of the kingdom of God,
15 **And** saying,

The time is fulfilled,
and the kingdom of God is at hand:
repent ye,
and believe the gospel.

16 **Now as he** walked by the sea of Galilee,
he saw Simon and Andrew his brother casting a net into the sea:
for they were fishers.

17 **And Jesus** said unto them,
Come ye after me,
and I will make you to become fishers of men.

18 **And straightway** they forsook their nets,
and followed him.

19 **And when he** had gone a little farther thence,
he saw James the son of Zebedee, and John his brother,
who also were in the ship mending their nets.

20 **And straightway** he called them:
and they left their father Zebedee in the ship with the hired servants,
and went after him.

21 **And they** went into Capernaum;
and straightway on the sabbath day he entered into the synagogue,
and taught.

22 **And they** were astonished at his doctrine:
for he taught them as one that had authority, and not as the scribes.

23 **And there** was in their synagogue a man with an unclean spirit;
and he cried out,
24 Saying,
Let us alone;
what have we to do with thee, thou Jesus of Nazareth?
art thou come to destroy us?
I know thee who thou art, the Holy One of God.

25 **And Jesus** rebuked him,
saying,
Hold thy peace,
and come out of him.

26 **And when the unclean spirit** had torn him,
and cried with a loud voice,
he came out of him.

27 **And they** were all amazed,
insomuch that they questioned among themselves,
saying,
What thing is this?
what new doctrine is this?
for with authority commandeth he even the unclean spirits,
and they do obey him.

28 **And immediately** his fame spread abroad throughout all the region round about Galilee.

29 **And forthwith,** {when they were come out of the synagogue}, they entered into the house of Simon and Andrew, with James and John.

30 **But Simon's wife's mother** lay sick of a fever,
and anon they tell him of her.

31 **And he** came and took her by the hand,
and lifted her up;
and immediately the fever left her,
and she ministered unto them.

32 **And at even,** {when the sun did set}, they brought unto him all that were diseased, and them that were possessed with devils.

33 **And all the city** was gathered together at the door.

34 **And he** healed many that were sick of divers diseases,
and cast out many devils;
and suffered not the devils to speak,
because they knew him.

35 **And in the morning,** {rising up a great while before day}, he went out,
and departed into a solitary place,
and there prayed.

36 **And Simon and they that were with him** followed after him.

37 **And when they** had found him,
they said unto him,
All men seek for thee.

38 **And he** said unto them,
Let us go into the next towns,
that I may preach there also:
for therefore came I forth.

39 **And he** preached in their synagogues throughout all Galilee,
and cast out devils.

40 **And there** came a leper to him,
beseeching him,
and kneeling down to him,
and saying unto him,
If thou wilt,
thou canst make me clean.

41 **And Jesus,** {moved with compassion}, put forth his hand,
and touched him,
and saith unto him,
I will;
be thou clean.

42 **And as soon as he** had spoken,
immediately the leprosy departed from him,
and he was cleansed.

43 **And he** straitly charged him,
and forthwith sent him away;
44 **And** saith unto him,
See thou say nothing to any man:
but go thy way,
shew thyself to the priest,
and offer for thy cleansing those things which Moses commanded, for a testimony unto them.

45 **But he** went out,
and began to publish it much,
and to blaze abroad the matter,
insomuch that Jesus could no more openly enter into the city,
but was without in desert places:
and they came to him from every quarter.

2 **And again he** entered into Capernaum after some days;
and it was noised that he was in the house.

2 **And straightway** many were gathered together,
insomuch that there was no room to receive them, no, not so much as about the door:
and he preached the word unto them.

3 **And they** come unto him,
bringing one sick of the palsy,
which was borne of four.

4 **And when they** could not come nigh unto him for the press,
they uncovered the roof where he was:
and when they had broken it up,
they let down the bed wherein the sick of the palsy lay.

5 **When Jesus** saw their faith,
he said unto the sick of the palsy,
Son, thy sins be forgiven thee.

6 **But there** was certain of the scribes sitting there,
and reasoning in their hearts,
7 **Why** doth this man thus speak blasphemies?
who can forgive sins but God only?

8 **And immediately** when Jesus perceived in his spirit
that they so reasoned within themselves,
he said unto them,

Why reason ye these things in your hearts?

9 **Whether** is it easier to say to the sick of the palsy,
Thy sins be forgiven thee;
or to say,
Arise,
and take up thy bed,
and walk?

10 **But that ye** may know
that the Son of man hath power on earth to forgive sins,
(he saith to the sick of the palsy,)
11 **I** say unto thee,
Arise,
and take up thy bed,
and go thy way into thine house.

12 **And immediately** he arose,
took up the bed,
and went forth before them all;
insomuch that they were all amazed,
and glorified God,
saying,
We never saw it on this fashion.

13 **And he** went forth again by the sea side;
and all the multitude resorted unto him,
and he taught them.

14 **And as he** passed by,
he saw Levi the son of Alphaeus sitting at the receipt of custom,
and said unto him,
Follow me.

And he arose and followed him.

15 **And it** came to pass,
that, {as Jesus sat at meat in his house}, many publicans and sinners sat also together with Jesus and his disciples:
for there were many,
and they followed him.

16 **And when the scribes and Pharisees** saw him eat with publicans and sinners,
they said unto his disciples,
How is it that he eateth and drinketh with publicans and sinners?

17 **When Jesus** heard it,
he saith unto them,
They that are whole have no need of the physician, but they that are sick:
I came not to call the righteous, but sinners to repentance.

18 **And the disciples of John and of the Pharisees** used to fast:
and they come and say unto him,
Why do the disciples of John and of the Pharisees fast,
but thy disciples fast not?

19 **And Jesus** said unto them,
Can the children of the bridechamber fast,
while the bridegroom is with them?
as long as they have the bridegroom with them,
they cannot fast.

20 **But the days** will come,
when the bridegroom shall be taken away from them,
and then shall they fast in those days.

21 **No man** also seweth a piece of new cloth on an old garment:
else the new piece that filled it up taketh away from the old,
and the rent is made worse.

22 **And no man** putteth new wine into old bottles:
else the new wine doth burst the bottles,
and the wine is spilled,
and the bottles will be marred:
but new wine must be put into new bottles.

23 **And it** came to pass,
that he went through the corn fields on the sabbath day;
and his disciples began, {as they went}, to pluck the ears of corn.

24 **And the Pharisees** said unto him,
Behold,
why do they on the sabbath day that which is not lawful?

25 **And he** said unto them,
Have ye never read what David did,
when he had need,
and was an hungred, he, and they that were with him?

26 **How he** went into the house of God in the days of Abiathar the high priest,
and did eat the shewbread,
which is not lawful to eat but for the priests,
and gave also to them which were with him?

27 **And he** said unto them,
The sabbath was made for man, and not man for the sabbath:
28 **Therefore the Son of man** is Lord also of the sabbath.

3

And he entered again into the synagogue;
and there was a man there which had a withered hand.

2 **And they** watched him,
whether he would heal him on the sabbath day;
that they might accuse him.

3 **And he** saith unto the man which had the withered hand,
Stand forth.

4 **And he** saith unto them,
Is it lawful to do good on the sabbath days,
or to do evil?
to save life,
or to kill?

But they held their peace.

5 **And when he** had looked round about on them with anger,
being grieved for the hardness of their hearts,
he saith unto the man,
Stretch forth thine hand.

And he stretched it out:
and his hand was restored whole as the other.

6 **And the Pharisees** went forth,
and straightway took counsel with the Herodians against him,
how they might destroy him.

7 **But Jesus** withdrew himself with his disciples to the sea:
and a great multitude from Galilee followed him, and from Judaea,
8 And from Jerusalem, and from Idumaea, and from beyond Jordan;
and they about Tyre and Sidon, a great multitude, {when they had heard what great things he did}, came unto him.

9 **And he** spake to his disciples,
that a small ship should wait on him because of the multitude,
lest they should throng him.

10 **For he** had healed many;
insomuch that they pressed upon him
for to touch him,
as many as had plagues.

11 **And unclean spirits**, {when they saw him}, fell down before him,
and cried,
saying,
Thou art the Son of God.

12 **And he** straitly charged them

that they should not make him
known.
13 **And he** goeth up into a mountain,
and calleth unto him whom he
would:
and they came unto him.
14 **And he** ordained twelve,
that they should be with him,
and that he might send them forth
to preach,
15 **And** to have power to heal
sicknesses,
and to cast out devils:
16 **And Simon** he surnamed Peter;
17 And James the son of Zebedee, and
John the brother of James;
and he surnamed them Boanerges,
which is, The sons of thunder:
18 And Andrew, and Philip, and
Bartholomew, and Matthew, and
Thomas, and James the son of
Alphaeus, and Thaddaeus, and
Simon the Canaanite,
19 And Judas Iscariot,
which also betrayed him:
and they went into an house.
20 **And the multitude** cometh
together again,
so that they could not so much as
eat bread.
21 **And when his friends** heard of it,
they went out to lay hold on him:
for they said,
He is beside himself.
22 **And the scribes which came
down from Jerusalem** said,
He hath Beelzebub,
and by the prince of the devils
casteth he out devils.
23 **And he** called them unto him,
and said unto them in parables,
How can Satan cast out Satan?
24 **And if a kingdom** be divided
against itself,
that kingdom cannot stand.
25 **And if a house** be divided against
itself,
that house cannot stand.
26 **And if Satan** rise up against
himself,
and be divided,
he cannot stand,
but hath an end.
27 **No man** can enter into a strong
man's house,
and spoil his goods,
except he will first bind the strong
man;
and then he will spoil his house.
28 **Verily I** say unto you,
All sins shall be forgiven unto the
sons of men,
and blasphemies wherewith
soever they shall blaspheme:
29 **But he that shall blaspheme
against the Holy Ghost** hath
never forgiveness,
but is in danger of eternal
damnation.
30 **Because they** said,
He hath an unclean spirit.
31 **There** came then his brethren and
his mother,
and, {standing without}, sent
unto him,
calling him.
32 **And the multitude** sat about
him,
and they said unto him,
Behold,
**thy mother and thy brethren
without** seek for thee.
33 **And he** answered them,
saying,
Who is my mother, or my brethren?
34 **And he** looked round about on
them which sat about him,
and said,
Behold my mother and my
brethren!
35 **For whosoever** shall do the will
of God,
the same is my brother, and my
sister, and mother.

4 ∞ **And he** began again to
teach by the sea side:
and there was gathered unto him a
great multitude,
so that he entered into a ship,
and sat in the sea;
and the whole multitude was by
the sea on the land.
2 **And he** taught them many things
by parables,
and said unto them in his doctrine,
3 **Hearken;**
Behold,
there went out a sower to sow:
4 **And it** came to pass,
as he sowed,
some fell by the way side,
and the fowls of the air came and
devoured it up.
5 **And some** fell on stony ground,
where it had not much earth;
and immediately it sprang up,
because it had no depth of earth:
6 **But when the sun** was up,
it was scorched;
and because it had no root,
it withered away.
7 **And some** fell among thorns,
and the thorns grew up,
and choked it,
and it yielded no fruit.
8 **And other** fell on good ground,
and did yield fruit that sprang up
and increased;
and brought forth, some thirty, and
some sixty, and some an hundred.
9 **And he** said unto them,
He that hath ears to hear, let him
hear.
10 **And when he** was alone,
**they that were about him with
the twelve** asked of him the
parable.
11 **And he** said unto them,
Unto you it is given to know the
mystery of the kingdom of God:
but unto them that are without,
all these things are done in
parables:
12 **That** seeing
they may see,
and not perceive;
and hearing
they may hear,
and not understand;
lest at any time they should be
converted,
and their sins should be forgiven
them.
13 **And he** said unto them,
Know ye not this parable?
and how then will ye know all
parables?
14 **The sower** soweth the word.
15 **And these** are they by the way
side,
where the word is sown;
but when they have heard,
Satan cometh immediately,
and taketh away the word that was
sown in their hearts.
16 **And these** are they likewise which
are sown on stony ground;
who, {when they have heard the
word}, immediately receive it
with gladness;
17 **And** have no root in themselves,
and so endure but for a time:
**afterward, {when affliction or
persecution ariseth for the
word's sake},** immediately they
are offended.

18 **And these** are they which are
sown among thorns;
such as hear the word,
19 **And the cares of this world, and
the deceitfulness of riches, and
the lusts of other things
entering in,** choke the word,
and it becometh unfruitful.
20 **And these** are they which are
sown on good ground;
such as hear the word,
and receive it,
and bring forth fruit, some
thirtyfold, some sixty, and some
an hundred.
21 **And he** said unto them,
Is a candle brought
to be put under a bushel, or under a
bed?
and not to be set on a candlestick?
22 **For there** is nothing hid,
which shall not be manifested;
neither was any thing kept secret,
but that it should come abroad.
23 **If any man** have ears to hear,
let him hear.
24 **And he** said unto them,
Take heed what ye hear:
with what measure ye mete,
it shall be measured to you:
and unto you that hear shall more
be given.
25 **For he that hath,** to him shall be
given:
and he that hath not, from him
shall be taken even that which he
hath.
26 **And he** said,
So is the kingdom of God,
as if a man should cast seed into
the ground;
27 **And** should sleep,
and rise night and day,
and the seed should spring and
grow up,
he knoweth not how.
28 **For the earth** bringeth forth fruit
of herself; first the blade, then the
ear, after that the full corn in the
ear.
29 **But when the fruit** is brought
forth,
immediately he putteth in the
sickle,
because the harvest is come.
30 **And he** said,
Whereunto shall we liken the
kingdom of God?
or with what comparison shall we
compare it?
31 **It** is like a grain of mustard seed,
which, {when it is sown in the
earth}, is less than all the seeds
that be in the earth:
32 **But when it** is sown,
it groweth up,
and becometh greater than all
herbs,
and shooteth out great branches;
so that the fowls of the air may
lodge under the shadow of it.
33 **And with many such parables**
spake he the word unto them,
as they were able to hear it.
34 **But without a parable** spake he
not unto them:
and when they were alone,
he expounded all things to his
disciples.
35 **And the same day**, {when the
even was come}, he saith unto
them,
Let us pass over unto the other side.
36 **And when they** had sent away
the multitude,
they took him
even as he was in the ship.
And there were also with him other
little ships.
37 **And there** arose a great storm of
wind,
and the waves beat into the ship,
so that it was now full.
38 **And he** was in the hinder part of
the ship, asleep on a pillow:
and they awake him,
and say unto him,
Master, carest thou not that we
perish?
39 **And he** arose,
and rebuked the wind,
and said unto the sea,
Peace,
be still.
And the wind ceased,
and there was a great calm.
40 **And he** said unto them,
Why are ye so fearful?
how is it that ye have no faith?
41 **And they** feared exceedingly,
and said one to another,
What manner of man is this,
that even the wind and the sea
obey him?

5

And they came over unto the
other side of the sea, into the
country of the Gadarenes.
2 **And when he** was come out of the
ship,
immediately there met him out of
the tombs a man with an unclean
spirit,
3 **Who** had his dwelling among the
tombs;
and no man could bind him, no,
not with chains:
4 **Because that he** had been often
bound with fetters and chains,
and the chains had been plucked
asunder by him,
and the fetters broken in pieces:
neither could any man tame him.
5 **And always, night and day,** he
was in the mountains, and in the
tombs,
crying,
and cutting himself with stones.
6 **But when he** saw Jesus afar off,
he ran and worshipped him,
7 **And** cried with a loud voice,
and said,
What have I to do with thee, Jesus,
thou Son of the most high God?
I adjure thee by God,
that thou torment me not.
8 **For he** said unto him,
Come out of the man, thou unclean
spirit.
9 **And he** asked him,
What is thy name?
And he answered,
saying,
My name is Legion:
for we are many.
10 **And he** besought him much
that he would not send them away
out of the country.
11 **Now there** was there nigh unto
the mountains a great herd of
swine feeding.
12 **And all the devils** besought him,
saying,
Send us into the swine,
that we may enter into them.
13 **And forthwith** Jesus gave them
leave.
And the unclean spirits went out,
and entered into the swine:
and the herd ran violently down a
steep place into the sea,
(they were about two thousand;)
and were choked in the sea.
14 **And they that fed the swine** fled,
and told it in the city, and in the
country.

And they went out to see what it was that was done.

15 **And they** come to Jesus,
and see him that was possessed with the devil,
and had the legion,
sitting,
and clothed,
and in his right mind:
and they were afraid.

16 **And they that saw it** told them
how it befell to him that was possessed with the devil, and also concerning the swine.

17 **And they** began to pray him to depart out of their coasts.

18 **And when he** was come into the ship,
he that had been possessed with the devil prayed him
that he might be with him.

19 **Howbeit Jesus** suffered him not,
but saith unto him,
Go home to thy friends,
and tell them
how great things the Lord hath done for thee,
and hath had compassion on thee.

20 **And he** departed,
and began to publish in Decapolis
how great things Jesus had done for him:
and all men did marvel.

21 **And when Jesus** was passed over again by ship unto the other side,
much people gathered unto him:
and he was nigh unto the sea.

22 **And, {behold}, there** cometh one of the rulers of the synagogue, Jairus by name;
and when he saw him,
he fell at his feet,
23 **And** besought him greatly,
saying,
My little daughter lieth at the point of death:
I pray thee,
come and lay thy hands on her,
that she may be healed;
and she shall live.

24 **And Jesus** went with him;
and much people followed him,
and thronged him.

25 **And a certain woman**, {which had an issue of blood twelve years},
26 {And had suffered many things of many physicians},
{and had spent all that she had},
{and was nothing bettered},
{but rather grew worse},
27 {When she had heard of Jesus},
came in the press behind,
and touched his garment.

28 **For she** said,
If I may touch but his clothes,
I shall be whole.

29 **And straightway** the fountain of her blood was dried up;
and she felt in her body that she was healed of that plague.

30 **And Jesus**, {immediately knowing in himself} {that virtue had gone out of him}, turned him about in the press,
and said,
Who touched my clothes?

31 **And his disciples** said unto him,
Thou seest the multitude thronging thee,
and sayest thou,
Who touched me?

32 **And he** looked round about to see her that had done this thing.

33 **But the woman** {fearing and trembling}, {knowing} {what was done in her}, came and fell down before him,
and told him all the truth.

34 **And he** said unto her,
Daughter, thy faith hath made thee whole;
go in peace,
and be whole of thy plague.

35 **While he** yet spake,
there came from the ruler of the synagogue's house certain which said,
Thy daughter is dead:
why troublest thou the Master any further?

36 **As soon as Jesus** heard the word that was spoken,
he saith unto the ruler of the synagogue,
Be not afraid,
only believe.

37 **And he** suffered no man to follow him, save Peter, and James, and John the brother of James.

38 **And he** cometh to the house of the ruler of the synagogue,
and seeth the tumult, and them that wept and wailed greatly.

39 **And when he** was come in,
he saith unto them,
Why make ye this ado,
and weep?
the damsel is not dead,
but sleepeth.

40 **And they** laughed him to scorn.

But when he had put them all out,
he taketh the father and the mother of the damsel, and them that were with him,
and entereth in where the damsel was lying.

41 **And he** took the damsel by the hand,
and said unto her,
Talitha cumi;
which is,
being interpreted,
Damsel, I say unto thee,
arise.

42 **And straightway** the damsel arose,
and walked;
for she was of the age of twelve years.

And they were astonished with a great astonishment.

43 **And he** charged them straitly
that no man should know it;
and commanded
that something should be given her to eat.

6

And he went out from thence,
and came into his own country;
and his disciples follow him.

2 **And when the sabbath day** was come,
he began to teach in the synagogue:
and many hearing him were astonished,
saying,
From whence hath this man these things?
and what wisdom is this which is given unto him,
that even such mighty works are wrought by his hands?

3 **Is not this** the carpenter, the son of Mary, the brother of James, and Joses, and of Juda, and Simon?
and are not his sisters here with us?

And they were offended at him.

4 **But Jesus,** said unto them,
A prophet is not without honour, but in his own country, and among his own kin, and in his own house.

5 **And he** could there do no mighty work,

save that he laid his hands upon a few sick folk,
and healed them.

6 **And he** marvelled because of their unbelief.

And he went round about the villages,
teaching.

7 **And he** called unto him the twelve,
and began to send them forth by two and two;
and gave them power over unclean spirits;
8 **And** commanded them
that they should take nothing for their journey, save a staff only; no scrip, no bread, no money in their purse:
9 **But** be shod with sandals;
and not put on two coats.

10 **And he** said unto them,
In what place soever ye enter into an house,
there abide
till ye depart from that place.

11 **And whosoever** shall not receive you,
nor hear you,
when ye depart thence,
shake off the dust under your feet for a testimony against them.

Verily I say unto you,
It shall be more tolerable for Sodom and Gomorrha in the day of judgment, than for that city.

12 **And they** went out,
and preached
that men should repent.

13 **And they** cast out many devils,
and anointed with oil many that were sick,
and healed them.

14 **And king Herod** heard of him;
(for his name was spread abroad:)
and he said,
That John the Baptist was risen from the dead,
and therefore mighty works do shew forth themselves in him.

15 **Others** said,
That it is Elias.

And others said,
That it is a prophet, or as one of the prophets.

16 **But when Herod** heard thereof,
he said,
It is John,
whom I beheaded:
he is risen from the dead.

17 **For Herod himself** had sent forth
and laid hold upon John,
and bound him in prison for Herodias' sake, his brother Philip's wife:
for he had married her.

18 **For John** had said unto Herod,
It is not lawful for thee to have thy brother's wife.

19 **Therefore Herodias** had a quarrel against him,
and would have killed him;
but she could not:
20 **For Herod** feared John,
knowing
that he was a just man and an holy,
and observed him;
and when he heard him,
he did many things,
and heard him gladly.

21 **And when a convenient day** was come,
that Herod on his birthday made a supper to his lords, high captains, and chief estates of Galilee;
22 **And when the daughter of the said Herodias** came in,
and danced,
and pleased Herod and them that sat with him,
the king said unto the damsel,
Ask of me
whatsoever thou wilt,
and I will give it thee.

23 **And he** sware unto her,
Whatsoever thou shalt ask of me,
I will give it thee, unto the half of my kingdom.

24 **And she** went forth,
and said unto her mother,
What shall I ask?

And she said,
The head of John the Baptist.

25 **And she** came in straightway with haste unto the king,
and asked,
saying,
I will
that thou give me by and by in a charger the head of John the Baptist.

26 **And the king** was exceeding sorry;
yet for his oath's sake, and for their sakes which sat with him, he would not reject her.

27 **And immediately** the king sent an executioner,
and commanded
his head to be brought:
and he went and beheaded him in the prison,
28 **And** brought his head in a charger,
and gave it to the damsel:
and the damsel gave it to her mother.

29 **And when his disciples** heard of it,
they came and took up his corpse,
and laid it in a tomb.

30 **And the apostles** gathered themselves together unto Jesus,
and told him all things,
both what they had done,
and what they had taught.

31 **And he** said unto them,
Come ye yourselves apart into a desert place,
and rest a while:
for there were many coming and going,
and they had no leisure so much as to eat.

32 **And they** departed into a desert place by ship privately.

33 **And the people** saw them departing,
and many knew him,
and ran afoot thither out of all cities,
and outwent them,
and came together unto him.

34 **And Jesus**, {when he came out},
saw much people,
and was moved with compassion toward them,
because they were as sheep not having a shepherd:
and he began to teach them many things.

35 **And when the day** was now far spent,
his disciples came unto him,
and said,
This is a desert place,
and now the time is far passed:
36 **Send** them away,
that they may go into the country round about, and into the villages,
and buy themselves bread:
for they have nothing to eat.

37 **He** answered and said unto them,
Give ye them to eat.

And they say unto him,
Shall we go and buy two hundred pennyworth of bread,
and give them to eat?

38 **He** saith unto them,
How many loaves have ye?
go and see.
And when they knew,
they say,
Five, and two fishes.

39 **And he** commanded them to make all sit down by companies upon the green grass.

40 **And they** sat down in ranks, by hundreds, and by fifties.

41 **And when he** had taken the five loaves and the two fishes,
he looked up to heaven,
and blessed,
and brake the loaves,
and gave them to his disciples to set before them;
and the two fishes divided he among them all.

42 **And they** did all eat,
and were filled.

43 **And they** took up twelve baskets full of the fragments, and of the fishes.

44 **And they that did eat of the loaves** were about five thousand men.

45 **And straightway** he constrained his disciples to get into the ship,
and to go to the other side before unto Bethsaida,
while he sent away the people.

46 **And when he** had sent them away,
he departed into a mountain to pray.

47 **And when even** was come,
the ship was in the midst of the sea, and he alone on the land.

48 **And he** saw them toiling in rowing;
for the wind was contrary unto them:
and about the fourth watch of the night he cometh unto them,
walking upon the sea,
and would have passed by them.

49 **But when they** saw him walking upon the sea,
they supposed
it had been a spirit,
and cried out:
50 **For they all** saw him,
and were troubled.

And immediately he talked with them,
and saith unto them,
Be of good cheer:
it is I;
be not afraid.

51 **And he** went up unto them into the ship;
and the wind ceased:
and they were sore amazed in themselves beyond measure,
and wondered.

52 **For they** considered not the miracle of the loaves:
for their heart was hardened.

53 **And when they** had passed over,
they came into the land of Gennesaret,
and drew to the shore.

54 **And when they** were come out of the ship,
straightway they knew him,
55 **And** ran through that whole region round about,
and began to carry about in beds those that were sick,
where they heard he was.

56 **And whithersoever he** entered, into villages, or cities, or country,
they laid the sick in the streets,
and besought him
that they might touch if it were but the border of his garment:
and as many as touched him were made whole.

7

Then came together unto him the Pharisees, and certain of the scribes,
which came from Jerusalem.

2 **And when they** saw some of his disciples eat bread with defiled, that is to say, with unwashen, hands,
they found fault.

3 **For the Pharisees, and all the Jews,** {except they wash their hands oft}, eat not,
holding the tradition of the elders.

4 **And when they** come from the market,
except they wash,
they eat not.

And many other things there be,
which they have received to hold, as the washing of cups, and pots, brasen vessels, and of tables.

5 **Then the Pharisees and scribes** asked him,
Why walk not thy disciples according to the tradition of the elders,
but eat bread with unwashen hands?

6 **He** answered and said unto them,
Well hath Esaias prophesied of you hypocrites,
as it is written,
This people honoureth me with their lips,
but their heart is far from me.

7 **Howbeit in vain** do they worship me,
teaching for doctrines the commandments of men.

8 **For** laying aside the commandment of God,
ye hold the tradition of men, as the washing of pots and cups:
and many other such like things ye do.

9 **And he** said unto them,
Full well ye reject the commandment of God,
that ye may keep your own tradition.

10 **For Moses** said,
Honour thy father and thy mother;
and, Whoso curseth father or mother,
let him die the death:
11 **But ye** say,
If a man shall say to his father or mother,
It is Corban, that is to say, a gift,
by whatsoever thou mightest be profited by me;
he shall be free.

12 **And ye** suffer him no more to do ought for his father or his mother;
13 Making the word of God of none effect through your tradition,
which ye have delivered:
and many such like things do ye.

14 **And when he** had called all the people unto him,
he said unto them,
Hearken unto me every one of you,
and understand:
15 **There** is nothing from without a man,
that entering into him can defile him:
but the things which come out of him, those are they that defile the man.

16 **If any man** have ears to hear,
let him hear.

17 **And when he** was entered into the house from the people,
his disciples asked him concerning the parable.

18 **And he** saith unto them,

Are ye so without understanding also?

Do ye not perceive,
that whatsoever thing from without entereth into the man,
it cannot defile him;
19 **Because it** entereth not into his heart, but into the belly,
and goeth out into the draught,
purging all meats?

20 **And he** said,
That which cometh out of the man, that defileth the man.

21 **For from within, out of the heart of men,** proceed evil thoughts, adulteries, fornications, murders,
22 Thefts, covetousness, wickedness, deceit, lasciviousness, an evil eye, blasphemy, pride, foolishness:
23 **All these evil things** come from within,
and defile the man.

24 **And from thence** he arose,
and went into the borders of Tyre and Sidon,
and entered into an house,
and would have no man know it:
but he could not be hid.

25 **For a certain woman**, {whose young daughter had an unclean spirit}, heard of him,
and came and fell at his feet:
26 **The woman** was a Greek, a Syrophenician by nation;
and she besought him
that he would cast forth the devil out of her daughter.

27 **But Jesus** said unto her,
Let the children first be filled:
for it is not meet to take the children's bread,
and to cast it unto the dogs.

28 **And she** answered and said unto him,
Yes, Lord: yet the dogs under the table eat of the children's crumbs.

29 **And he** said unto her,
For this saying go thy way;
the devil is gone out of thy daughter.

30 **And when she** was come to her house,
she found the devil gone out,
and her daughter laid upon the bed.

31 **And again, {departing from the coasts of Tyre and Sidon},** he came unto the sea of Galilee, through the midst of the coasts of Decapolis.

32 **And they** bring unto him one that was deaf,
and had an impediment in his speech;
and they beseech him to put his hand upon him.

33 **And he** took him aside from the multitude,
and put his fingers into his ears,
and he spit,
and touched his tongue;
34 **And** looking up to heaven,
he sighed,
and saith unto him,
Ephphatha, that is,
Be opened.

35 **And straightway** his ears were opened,
and the string of his tongue was loosed,
and he spake plain.

36 **And he** charged them
that they should tell no man:
but the more he charged them,
so much the more a great deal they published it;
37 **And** were beyond measure astonished,
saying,
He hath done all things well:
he maketh
both the deaf to hear,
and the dumb to speak.

8

In those days {the multitude being very great}, {and having nothing to eat}, Jesus called his disciples unto him,
and saith unto them,
2 **I** have compassion on the multitude,
because they have now been with me three days,
and have nothing to eat:
3 **And if I** send them away fasting to their own houses,
they will faint by the way:
for divers of them came from far.

4 **And his disciples** answered him,
From whence can a man satisfy these men with bread here in the wilderness?

5 **And he** asked them,
How many loaves have ye?

And they said,
Seven.

6 **And he** commanded the people to sit down on the ground:
and he took the seven loaves,
and gave thanks,
and brake,
and gave to his disciples to set before them;
and they did set them before the people.

7 **And they** had a few small fishes:
and he blessed,
and commanded to set them also before them.

8 **So they** did eat,
and were filled:
and they took up of the broken meat that was left seven baskets.

9 **And they that had eaten** were about four thousand:
and he sent them away.

10 **And straightway** he entered into a ship with his disciples,
and came into the parts of Dalmanutha.

11 **And the Pharisees** came forth,
and began to question with him,
seeking of him a sign from heaven,
tempting him.

12 **And he** sighed deeply in his spirit,
and saith,
Why doth this generation seek after a sign?
verily I say unto you,
There shall no sign be given unto this generation.

13 **And he** left them,
and entering into the ship again departed to the other side.

14 **Now the disciples** had forgotten to take bread,
neither had they in the ship with them more than one loaf.

15 **And he** charged them,
saying,
Take heed,
beware of the leaven of the Pharisees, and of the leaven of Herod.

16 **And they** reasoned among themselves,
saying,
It is because we have no bread.

17 **And when Jesus** knew it,
he saith unto them,
Why reason ye,
because ye have no bread?
perceive ye not yet,
neither understand?
have ye your heart yet hardened?

18 Having eyes,
see ye not?

and having ears,
hear ye not?
and do ye not remember?
19 **When I** brake the five loaves among five thousand,
how many baskets full of fragments took ye up?
They say unto him,
Twelve.
20 **And when** the seven among four thousand,
how many baskets full of fragments took ye up?
And they said,
Seven.
21 **And he** said unto them,
How is it that ye do not understand?
22 **And he** cometh to Bethsaida;
and they bring a blind man unto him,
and besought him to touch him.
23 **And he** took the blind man by the hand,
and led him out of the town;
and when he had spit on his eyes,
and put his hands upon him,
he asked him
if he saw ought.
24 **And he** looked up,
and said,
I see men as trees,
walking.
25 **After that he** put his hands again upon his eyes,
and made him look up:
and he was restored,
and saw every man clearly.
26 **And he** sent him away to his house,
saying,
Neither go into the town,
nor tell it to any in the town.
27 **And Jesus** went out, and his disciples, into the towns of Caesarea Philippi:
and by the way he asked his disciples,
saying unto them,
Whom do men say
that I am?
28 **And they** answered,
John the Baptist;
but some say, Elias; and others, One of the prophets.
29 **And he** saith unto them,
But whom say ye
that I am?
And Peter answereth and saith unto him,
Thou art the Christ.
30 **And he** charged them
that they should tell no man of him.
31 **And he** began to teach them,
that the Son of man must suffer many things,
and be rejected of the elders, and of the chief priests, and scribes,
and be killed,
and after three days rise again.
32 **And he** spake that saying openly.
And Peter took him,
and began to rebuke him.
33 **But when he** had turned about and looked on his disciples,
he rebuked Peter,
saying,
Get thee behind me, Satan:
for thou savourest not the things that be of God, but the things that be of men.
34 **And when he** had called the people unto him with his disciples also,
he said unto them,
Whosoever will come after me,
let him deny himself,
and take up his cross,
and follow me.
35 **For whosoever will save his life** shall lose it;
but whosoever shall lose his life for my sake and the gospel's,
the same shall save it.
36 **For what** shall it profit a man,
if he shall gain the whole world,
and lose his own soul?
37 **Or what** shall a man give in exchange for his soul?
38 **Whosoever** therefore shall be ashamed of me and of my words in this adulterous and sinful generation;
of him also shall the Son of man be ashamed,
when he cometh in the glory of his Father with the holy angels.

9

And he said unto them,
Verily I say unto you,
That there be some of them that stand here,
which shall not taste of death,
till they have seen the kingdom of God come with power.
2 **And after six days** Jesus taketh with him Peter, and James, and John,
and leadeth them up into an high mountain apart by themselves:
and he was transfigured before them.
3 **And his raiment** became shining, exceeding white as snow;
so as no fuller on earth can white them.
4 **And there** appeared unto them Elias with Moses:
and they were talking with Jesus.
5 **And Peter** answered and said to Jesus,
Master, it is good for us to be here:
and let us make three tabernacles; one for thee, and one for Moses, and one for Elias.
6 **For he** wist not
what to say;
for they were sore afraid.
7 **And there** was a cloud that overshadowed them:
and a voice came out of the cloud,
saying,
This is my beloved Son:
hear him.
8 **And suddenly**, {when they had looked round about}, they saw no man any more, save Jesus only with themselves.
9 **And as they** came down from the mountain,
he charged them
that they should tell no man
what things they had seen,
till the Son of man were risen from the dead.
10 **And they** kept that saying with themselves,
questioning one with another
what the rising from the dead should mean.
11 **And they** asked him,
saying,
Why say the scribes
that Elias must first come?
12 **And he** answered and told them,
Elias verily cometh first,
and restoreth all things;
and how it is written of the Son of man,
that he must suffer many things,
and be set at nought.
13 **But I** say unto you,
That Elias is indeed come,
and they have done unto him whatsoever they listed,
as it is written of him.

14 **And when he** came to his disciples,
he saw a great multitude about them, and the scribes questioning with them.

15 **And straightway** all the people, {when they beheld him}, were greatly amazed,
and {running to him} saluted him.

16 **And he** asked the scribes,
What question ye with them?

17 **And one of the multitude** answered and said,
Master, I have brought unto thee my son,
which hath a dumb spirit;

18 **And wheresoever he** taketh him,
he teareth him:
and he foameth,
and gnasheth with his teeth,
and pineth away:
and I spake to thy disciples
that they should cast him out;
and they could not.

19 **He** answereth him,
and saith,
O faithless generation, how long shall I be with you?
how long shall I suffer you?
bring him unto me.

20 **And they** brought him unto him:
and when he saw him,
straightway the spirit tare him;
and he fell on the ground,
and wallowed foaming.

21 **And he** asked his father,
How long is it ago
since this came unto him?

And he said,
Of a child.

22 **And ofttimes it** hath cast him into the fire, and into the waters,
to destroy him:
but if thou canst do any thing,
have compassion on us,
and help us.

23 **Jesus** said unto him,
If thou canst believe,
all things are possible to him that believeth.

24 **And straightway** the father of the child cried out,
and said with tears,
Lord, I believe;
help thou mine unbelief.

25 **When Jesus** saw that the people came running together,
he rebuked the foul spirit,
saying unto him,
Thou dumb and deaf spirit, I charge thee,
come out of him,
and enter no more into him.

26 **And the spirit** cried,
and rent him sore,
and came out of him:
and he was as one dead;
insomuch that many said,
He is dead.

27 **But Jesus** took him by the hand,
and lifted him up;
and he arose.

28 **And when he** was come into the house,
his disciples asked him privately,
Why could not we cast him out?

29 **And he** said unto them,
This kind can come forth by nothing, but by prayer and fasting.

30 **And they** departed thence,
and passed through Galilee;
and he would not
that any man should know it.

31 **For he** taught his disciples,
and said unto them,
The Son of man is delivered into the hands of men,
and they shall kill him;
and after that he is killed,
he shall rise the third day.

32 **But they** understood not that saying,
and were afraid to ask him.

33 **And he** came to Capernaum:
and being in the house
he asked them,
What was it that ye disputed among yourselves by the way?

34 **But they** held their peace:
for by the way they had disputed among themselves,
who should be the greatest.

35 **And he** sat down,
and called the twelve,
and saith unto them,
If any man desire to be first,
the same shall be last of all, and servant of all.

36 **And he** took a child,
and set him in the midst of them:
and when he had taken him in his arms,
he said unto them,

37 **Whosoever shall receive one of such children in my name,** receiveth me:
and whosoever shall receive me, receiveth not me, but him that sent me.

38 **And John** answered him,
saying,
Master, we saw one casting out devils in thy name,
and he followeth not us:
and we forbad him,
because he followeth not us.

39 **But Jesus** said,
Forbid him not:
for there is no man which shall do a miracle in my name,
that can lightly speak evil of me.

40 **For he that is not against us** is on our part.

41 **For whosoever** shall give you a cup of water to drink in my name,
because ye belong to Christ,
verily I say unto you,
he shall not lose his reward.

42 **And whosoever** shall offend one of these little ones that believe in me,
it is better for him that a millstone were hanged about his neck,
and he were cast into the sea.

43 **And if thy hand** offend thee,
cut it off:
it is better for thee to enter into life maimed,
than having two hands to go into hell, into the fire that never shall be quenched:

44 **Where their worm** dieth not,
and the fire is not quenched.

45 **And if thy foot** offend thee,
cut it off:
it is better for thee to enter halt into life,
than having two feet to be cast into hell, into the fire that never shall be quenched:

46 **Where their worm** dieth not,
and the fire is not quenched.

47 **And if thine eye** offend thee,
pluck it out:
it is better for thee to enter into the kingdom of God with one eye,
than having two eyes to be cast into hell fire:

48 **Where their worm** dieth not,
and the fire is not quenched.

49 **For every one** shall be salted with fire,
and every sacrifice shall be salted with salt.

50 **Salt** is good:

but if the salt have lost his saltness,
wherewith will ye season it?
Have salt in yourselves,
and have peace one with another.

10

And he arose from thence,
and cometh into the coasts of Judaea by the farther side of Jordan:
and the people resort unto him again;
and, {as he was wont}, he taught them again.
2 **And the Pharisees** came to him,
and asked him,
Is it lawful for a man to put away his wife?
tempting him.
3 **And he** answered and said unto them,
What did Moses command you?
4 **And they** said,
Moses suffered to write a bill of divorcement, and to put her away.
5 **And Jesus** answered and said unto them,
For the hardness of your heart he wrote you this precept.
6 **But from the beginning of the creation** God made them male and female.
7 **For this cause** shall a man leave his father and mother,
and cleave to his wife;
8 **And they twain** shall be one flesh:
so then they are no more twain, but one flesh.
9 **What therefore God** hath joined together,
let not man put asunder.
10 **And in the house** his disciples asked him again of the same matter.
11 **And he** saith unto them,
Whosoever shall put away his wife, and marry another, committeth adultery against her.
12 **And if a woman** shall put away her husband,
and be married to another,
she committeth adultery.
13 **And they** brought young children to him,
that he should touch them:
and his disciples rebuked those that brought them.
14 **But when Jesus** saw it,
he was much displeased,
and said unto them,
Suffer the little children to come unto me,
and forbid them not:
for of such is the kingdom of God.
15 **Verily I** say unto you,
Whosoever shall not receive the kingdom of God as a little child,
he shall not enter therein.
16 **And he** took them up in his arms,
put his hands upon them,
and blessed them.
17 **And when he** was gone forth into the way,
there came one running,
and kneeled to him,
and asked him,
Good Master, what shall I do
that I may inherit eternal life?
18 **And Jesus** said unto him,
Why callest thou me good?
there is none good but one, that is, God.
19 **Thou** knowest the commandments,
Do not commit adultery,
Do not kill,
Do not steal,
Do not bear false witness,
Defraud not,
Honour thy father and mother.
20 **And he** answered and said unto him,
Master, all these have I observed from my youth.
21 **Then Jesus** {beholding him} loved him,
and said unto him,
One thing thou lackest:
go thy way,
sell whatsoever thou hast,
and give to the poor,
and thou shalt have treasure in heaven:
and come,
take up the cross,
and follow me.
22 **And he** was sad at that saying,
and went away grieved:
for he had great possessions.
23 **And Jesus** looked round about,
and saith unto his disciples,
How hardly shall they that have riches enter into the kingdom of God!
24 **And the disciples** were astonished at his words.
But Jesus answereth again,
and saith unto them,
Children, how hard is it for them that trust in riches to enter into the kingdom of God!
25 **It is easier** for a camel to go through the eye of a needle,
than for a rich man to enter into the kingdom of God.
26 **And they** were astonished out of measure,
saying among themselves,
Who then can be saved?
27 **And Jesus** {looking upon them} saith,
With men it is impossible, but not with God:
for with God all things are possible.
28 **Then Peter** began to say unto him,
Lo,
we have left all,
and have followed thee.
29 **And Jesus** answered and said,
Verily I say unto you,
There is no man that hath left house, or brethren, or sisters, or father, or mother, or wife, or children, or lands, for my sake, and the gospel's,
30 **But he** shall receive an hundredfold now in this time, houses, and brethren, and sisters, and mothers, and children, and lands, with persecutions; and in the world to come eternal life.
31 **But many that are first** shall be last; and the last first.
32 **And they** were in the way going up to Jerusalem;
and Jesus went before them:
and they were amazed;
and as they followed,
they were afraid.
And he took again the twelve,
and began to tell them
what things should happen unto him,
33 Saying,
Behold,
we go up to Jerusalem;
and the Son of man shall be delivered unto the chief priests, and unto the scribes;
and they shall condemn him to death,
and shall deliver him to the Gentiles:
34 **And they** shall mock him,
and shall scourge him,
and shall spit upon him,
and shall kill him:

and the third day he shall rise again.

35 **And James and John, the sons of Zebedee,** come unto him,
saying,
Master, we would
that thou shouldest do for us
whatsoever we shall desire.

36 **And he** said unto them,
What would ye
that I should do for you?

37 **They** said unto him,
Grant unto us
that we may sit, one on thy right hand, and the other on thy left hand, in thy glory.

38 **But Jesus** said unto them,
Ye know not
what ye ask:
can ye drink of the cup that I drink of?
and be baptized with the baptism that I am baptized with?

39 **And they** said unto him,
We can.

And Jesus said unto them,
Ye shall indeed drink of the cup that I drink of;
and with the baptism that I am baptized withal shall ye be baptized:
40 **But to sit on my right hand and on my left hand** is not mine to give;
but it shall be given to them for whom it is prepared.

41 **And when the ten** heard it,
they began to be much displeased with James and John.

42 **But Jesus** called them to him,
and saith unto them,
Ye know
that they which are accounted to rule over the Gentiles exercise lordship over them;
and their great ones exercise authority upon them.

43 **But so** shall it not be among you:
but whosoever will be great among you, shall be your minister:

44 **And whosoever of you will be the chiefest,** shall be servant of all.

45 **For even the Son of man** came not to be ministered unto,
but to minister,
and to give his life a ransom for many.

46 **And they** came to Jericho:
and as he went out of Jericho with his disciples and a great number of people,
blind Bartimaeus, the son of Timaeus, sat by the highway side begging.

47 **And when he** heard that it was Jesus of Nazareth,
he began to cry out,
and say,
Jesus, thou son of David, have mercy on me.

48 **And many** charged him
that he should hold his peace:
but he cried the more a great deal,
Thou son of David, have mercy on me.

49 **And Jesus** stood still,
and commanded him to be called.

And they call the blind man,
saying unto him,
Be of good comfort,
rise;
he calleth thee.

50 **And he,** {casting away his garment}, rose,
and came to Jesus.

51 **And Jesus** answered and said unto him,
What wilt thou
that I should do unto thee?

The blind man said unto him,
Lord, that I might receive my sight.

52 **And Jesus** said unto him,
Go thy way;
thy faith hath made thee whole.

And immediately he received his sight,
and followed Jesus in the way.

11 **And when they** came nigh to Jerusalem, unto Bethphage and Bethany, at the mount of Olives,
he sendeth forth two of his disciples,
2 **And** saith unto them,
Go your way into the village over against you:
and as soon as ye be entered into it,
ye shall find a colt tied,
whereon never man sat;
loose him,
and bring him.

3 **And if any man** say unto you,
Why do ye this?
say ye
that the Lord hath need of him;
and straightway he will send him hither.

4 **And they** went their way,
and found the colt tied by the door without in a place where two ways met;
and they loose him.

5 **And certain of them that stood there** said unto them,
What do ye,
loosing the colt?

6 **And they** said unto them
even as Jesus had commanded:
and they let them go.

7 **And they** brought the colt to Jesus,
and cast their garments on him;
and he sat upon him.

8 **And many** spread their garments in the way:
and others cut down branches off the trees,
and strawed them in the way.

9 **And they that went before, and they that followed,** cried,
saying,
Hosanna;
Blessed is he that cometh in the name of the Lord:
10 **Blessed** be the kingdom of our father David,
that cometh in the name of the Lord: Hosanna in the highest.

11 **And Jesus** entered into Jerusalem, and into the temple:
and when he had looked round about upon all things,
and now the eventide was come,
he went out unto Bethany with the twelve.

12 **And on the morrow,** {when they were come from Bethany}, he was hungry:
13 **And** seeing a fig tree afar off having leaves,
he came,
if haply he might find any thing thereon:
and when he came to it,
he found nothing but leaves;
for the time of figs was not yet.

14 **And Jesus** answered and said unto it,
No man eat fruit of thee hereafter for ever.

And his disciples heard it.

15 **And they** come to Jerusalem:
and Jesus went into the temple,
and began to cast out them that sold and bought in the temple,

and overthrew the tables of the moneychangers, and the seats of them that sold doves;

16 **And** would not suffer that any man should carry any vessel through the temple.

17 **And he** taught,
saying unto them,
Is it not written,
My house shall be called of all nations the house of prayer?
but ye have made it a den of thieves.

18 **And the scribes and chief priests** heard it,
and sought how they might destroy him:
for they feared him,
because all the people was astonished at his doctrine.

19 **And when even** was come,
he went out of the city.

20 **And in the morning,** {as they passed by}, they saw the fig tree dried up from the roots.

21 **And Peter** {calling to remembrance} saith unto him,
Master, {behold}, the fig tree which thou cursedst is withered away.

22 **And Jesus answering** saith unto them,
Have faith in God.

23 **For verily I** say unto you,
That whosoever shall say unto this mountain,
Be thou removed,
and be thou cast into the sea;
and shall not doubt in his heart,
but shall believe
that those things which he saith shall come to pass;
he shall have whatsoever he saith.

24 **Therefore I** say unto you,
What things soever ye desire,
when ye pray,
believe
that ye receive them,
and ye shall have them.

25 **And when ye** stand praying,
forgive,
if ye have ought against any:
that your Father also which is in heaven may forgive you your trespasses.

26 **But if ye** do not forgive,
neither will your Father which is in heaven forgive your trespasses.

27 **And they** come again to Jerusalem:
and as he was walking in the temple,
there come to him the chief priests, and the scribes, and the elders,

28 **And** say unto him,
By what authority doest thou these things?
and who gave thee this authority to do these things?

29 **And Jesus** answered and said unto them,
I will also ask of you one question,
and answer me,
and I will tell you
by what authority I do these things.

30 **The baptism of John,** was it from heaven, or of men?
answer me.

31 **And they** reasoned with themselves,
saying,
If we shall say,
From heaven;
he will say,
Why then did ye not believe him?

32 **But if we** shall say,
Of men;
they feared the people:
for all men counted John,
that he was a prophet indeed.

33 **And they** answered and said unto Jesus,
We cannot tell.
And Jesus answering saith unto them,
Neither do I tell you
by what authority I do these things.

12

And he began to speak unto them by parables.
A certain man planted a vineyard,
and set an hedge about it,
and digged a place for the winefat,
and built a tower,
and let it out to husbandmen,
and went into a far country.

2 **And at the season** he sent to the husbandmen a servant,
that he might receive from the husbandmen of the fruit of the vineyard.

3 **And they** caught him,
and beat him,
and sent him away empty.

4 **And again he** sent unto them another servant;
and at him they cast stones,
and wounded him in the head,
and sent him away shamefully handled.

5 **And again he** sent another;
and him they killed, and many others;
beating some,
and killing some.

6 Having yet therefore one son, his wellbeloved,
he sent him also last unto them,
saying,
They will reverence my son.

7 **But those husbandmen** said among themselves,
This is the heir;
come,
let us kill him,
and the inheritance shall be ours.

8 **And they** took him,
and killed him,
and cast him out of the vineyard.

9 **What** shall therefore the lord of the vineyard do?
he will come and destroy the husbandmen,
and will give the vineyard unto others.

10 **And have ye not** read this scripture;
The stone which the builders rejected is become the head of the corner:

11 **This** was the Lord's doing,
and it is marvellous in our eyes?

12 **And they** sought to lay hold on him,
but feared the people:
for they knew
that he had spoken the parable against them:
and they left him,
and went their way.

13 **And they** send unto him certain of the Pharisees and of the Herodians,
to catch him in his words.

14 **And when they** were come,
they say unto him,
Master, we know
that thou art true,
and carest for no man:
for thou regardest not the person of men,
but teachest the way of God in truth:
Is it lawful to give tribute to Caesar, or not?

15 **Shall we** give,
or shall we not give?
But he, {knowing their hypocrisy}, said unto them,
Why tempt ye me?
bring me a penny,
that I may see it.
16 **And they** brought it.
And he saith unto them,
Whose is this image and superscription?
And they said unto him,
Caesar's.
17 **And Jesus answering** said unto them,
Render to Caesar the things that are Caesar's, and to God the things that are God's.
And they marvelled at him.
18 **Then** come unto him the Sadducees,
which say there is no resurrection;
and they asked him,
saying,
19 **Master, Moses** wrote unto us,
If a man's brother die,
and leave his wife behind him,
and leave no children,
that his brother should take his wife,
and raise up seed unto his brother.
20 **Now there** were seven brethren:
and the first took a wife,
and dying left no seed.
21 **And the second** took her,
and died,
neither left he any seed: and the third likewise.
22 **And the seven** had her,
and left no seed:
last of all the woman died also.
23 **In the resurrection** therefore, {when they shall rise}, whose wife shall she be of them?
for the seven had her to wife.
24 **And Jesus answering** said unto them,
Do ye not therefore err,
because ye know not the scriptures, neither the power of God?
25 **For when they** shall rise from the dead,
they neither marry,
nor are given in marriage;
but are as the angels which are in heaven.
26 **And as touching the dead**, {that they rise}: have ye not read in the book of Moses,
how in the bush God spake unto him,
saying,
I am the God of Abraham, and the God of Isaac, and the God of Jacob?
27 **He** is not the God of the dead, but the God of the living:
ye therefore do greatly err.
28 **And one of the scribes** came,
and having heard them reasoning together,
and perceiving that he had answered them well,
asked him,
Which is the first commandment of all?
29 **And Jesus** answered him,
The first of all the commandments is,
Hear, O Israel;
The Lord our God is one Lord:
30 **And thou** shalt love the Lord thy God with all thy heart, and with all thy soul, and with all thy mind, and with all thy strength:
this is the first commandment.
31 **And the second** is like, namely this,
Thou shalt love thy neighbour as thyself.
There is none other commandment greater than these.
32 **And the scribe** said unto him,
Well, Master, thou hast said the truth:
for there is one God;
and there is none other but he:
33 **And to love him with all the heart, and with all the understanding, and with all the soul, and with all the strength, and to love his neighbour as himself,** is more than all whole burnt offerings and sacrifices.
34 **And when Jesus** saw that he answered discreetly,
he said unto him,
Thou art not far from the kingdom of God.
And no man after that durst ask him any question.
35 **And Jesus** answered and said,
while he taught in the temple,
How say the scribes
that Christ is the son of David?
36 **For David himself** said by the Holy Ghost,
The LORD said to my Lord,
Sit thou on my right hand,
till I make thine enemies thy footstool.
37 **David** therefore himself calleth him Lord;
and whence is he then his son?
And the common people heard him gladly.
38 **And he** said unto them in his doctrine,
Beware of the scribes,
which love to go in long clothing,
and love salutations in the marketplaces,
39 And the chief seats in the synagogues, and the uppermost rooms at feasts:
40 **Which** devour widows' houses,
and for a pretence make long prayers:
these shall receive greater damnation.
41 **And Jesus** sat over against the treasury,
and beheld how the people cast money into the treasury:
and many that were rich cast in much.
42 **And there** came a certain poor widow,
and she threw in two mites,
which make a farthing.
43 **And he** called unto him his disciples,
and saith unto them,
Verily I say unto you,
That this poor widow hath cast more in, than all they which have cast into the treasury:
44 **For all they** did cast in of their abundance;
but she of her want did cast in all that she had, even all her living.

13

And as he went out of the temple,
one of his disciples saith unto him,
Master, see what manner of stones and what buildings are here!
2 **And Jesus answering** said unto him,
Seest thou these great buildings?
there shall not be left one stone upon another,
that shall not be thrown down.
3 **And as he** sat upon the mount of Olives over against the temple,

Peter and James and John and Andrew asked him privately,
4 **Tell** us,
when shall these things be?
and what shall be the sign
when all these things shall be fulfilled?

5 **And Jesus answering them** began to say,
Take heed lest any man deceive you:
6 **For many** shall come in my name, saying,
I am Christ;
and shall deceive many.

7 **And when ye** shall hear of wars and rumours of wars,
be ye not troubled:
for such things must needs be;
but the end shall not be yet.

8 **For nation** shall rise against nation, and kingdom against kingdom:
and there shall be earthquakes in divers places,
and there shall be famines and troubles:
these are the beginnings of sorrows.

9 **But take heed** to yourselves:
for they shall deliver you up to councils;
and in the synagogues ye shall be beaten:
and ye shall be brought before rulers and kings for my sake, for a testimony against them.

10 **And the gospel** must first be published among all nations.

11 **But when they** shall lead you,
and deliver you up,
take no thought beforehand what ye shall speak,
neither do ye premeditate:
but whatsoever shall be given you in that hour,
that speak ye:
for it is not ye that speak, but the Holy Ghost.

12 **Now the brother** shall betray the brother to death, and the father the son;
and children shall rise up against their parents,
and shall cause them to be put to death.

13 **And ye** shall be hated of all men for my name's sake:
but he that shall endure unto the end, the same shall be saved.

14 **But when ye** shall see the abomination of desolation,
spoken of by Daniel the prophet,
standing where it ought not,
(let him that readeth understand,)
then let them that be in Judaea flee to the mountains:
15 **And let him that is on the housetop** not go down into the house,
neither enter therein,
to take any thing out of his house:
16 **And let him that is in the field** not turn back again
for to take up his garment.

17 **But woe** to them that are with child, and to them that give suck in those days!

18 **And pray ye**
that your flight be not in the winter.

19 **For in those days** shall be affliction,
such as was not from the beginning of the creation which God created unto this time,
neither shall be.

20 **And except that the Lord** had shortened those days,
no flesh should be saved:
but for the elect's sake, {whom he hath chosen}, he hath shortened the days.

21 **And then if any man** shall say to you,
Lo,
here is Christ;
or, lo,
he is there;
believe him not:
22 **For false Christs and false prophets** shall rise,
and shall shew signs and wonders,
to seduce, {if it were possible}, even the elect.

23 **But take ye heed:**
behold,
I have foretold you all things.

24 **But in those days**, after that tribulation, the sun shall be darkened,
and the moon shall not give her light,
25 **And the stars of heaven** shall fall,
and the powers that are in heaven shall be shaken.

26 **And then** shall they see the Son of man coming in the clouds with great power and glory.

27 **And then** shall he send his angels,
and shall gather together his elect from the four winds, from the uttermost part of the earth to the uttermost part of heaven.

28 **Now learn** a parable of the fig tree;
When her branch is yet tender,
and putteth forth leaves,
ye know
that summer is near:
29 **So ye in like manner**, {when ye shall see these things come to pass}, know
that it is nigh, even at the doors.

30 **Verily I** say unto you,
that this generation shall not pass,
till all these things be done.

31 **Heaven and earth** shall pass away:
but my words shall not pass away.

32 **But of that day and that hour** knoweth no man, no, not the angels which are in heaven, neither the Son, but the Father.

33 **Take ye heed,**
watch and pray:
for ye know not
when the time is.

34 **For the Son of Man** is as a man taking a far journey,
who left his house,
and gave authority to his servants, and to every man his work,
and commanded the porter to watch.

35 **Watch ye** therefore:
for ye know not
when the master of the house cometh, at even, or at midnight, or at the cockcrowing, or in the morning:
36 **Lest** coming suddenly
he find you sleeping.

37 **And what** I say unto you
I say unto all,
Watch.

14

After two days was the feast of the passover, and of unleavened bread:
and the chief priests and the scribes sought how they might take him by craft,
and put him to death.

2 **But they** said,
Not on the feast day,
lest there be an uproar of the people.

3 **And** being in Bethany in the house of Simon the leper,

as he sat at meat,
there came a woman having an alabaster box of ointment of spikenard very precious;
and she brake the box,
and poured it on his head.

4 **And there** were some that had indignation within themselves,
and said,
Why was this waste of the ointment made?

5 **For it** might have been sold for more than three hundred pence,
and have been given to the poor.

And they murmured against her.

6 **And Jesus** said,
Let her alone;
why trouble ye her?
she hath wrought a good work on me.

7 **For ye** have the poor with you always,
and whensoever ye will
ye may do them good:
but me ye have not always.

8 **She** hath done what she could:
she is come aforehand to anoint my body to the burying.

9 **Verily I** say unto you,
Wheresoever this gospel shall be preached throughout the whole world,
this also that she hath done shall be spoken of for a memorial of her.

10 **And Judas Iscariot, one of the twelve,** went unto the chief priests,
to betray him unto them.

11 **And when they** heard it,
they were glad,
and promised to give him money.

And he sought how he might conveniently betray him.

12 **And the first day of unleavened bread**, {when they killed the passover}, his disciples said unto him,
Where wilt thou that we go and prepare
that thou mayest eat the passover?

13 **And he** sendeth forth two of his disciples,
and saith unto them,
Go ye into the city,
and there shall meet you a man bearing a pitcher of water:
follow him.

14 **And wheresoever he** shall go in,
say ye to the goodman of the house,
The Master saith,
Where is the guestchamber,
where I shall eat the passover with my disciples?

15 **And he** will shew you a large upper room furnished and prepared:
there make ready for us.

16 **And his disciples** went forth,
and came into the city,
and found as he had said unto them:
and they made ready the passover.

17 **And in the evening** he cometh with the twelve.

18 **And as they** sat and did eat,
Jesus said,
Verily I say unto you,
One of you which eateth with me shall betray me.

19 **And they** began to be sorrowful,
and to say unto him one by one,
Is it I?
and another said,
Is it I?

20 **And he** answered and said unto them,
It is one of the twelve,
that dippeth with me in the dish.

21 **The Son of man** indeed goeth,
as it is written of him:
but woe to that man
by whom the Son of man is betrayed!
good were it for that man
if he had never been born.

22 **And as they** did eat,
Jesus took bread,
and blessed,
and brake it,
and gave to them,
and said,
Take,
eat:
this is my body.

23 **And he** took the cup,
and when he had given thanks,
he gave it to them:
and they all drank of it.

24 **And he** said unto them,
This is my blood of the new testament,
which is shed for many.

25 **Verily I** say unto you,
I will drink no more of the fruit of the vine,
until that day that I drink it new in the kingdom of God.

26 **And when they** had sung an hymn,
they went out into the mount of Olives.

27 **And Jesus** saith unto them,
All ye shall be offended because of me this night:
for it is written,
I will smite the shepherd,
and the sheep shall be scattered.

28 **But after that I** am risen,
I will go before you into Galilee.

29 **But Peter** said unto him,
Although all shall be offended,
yet will not I.

30 **And Jesus** saith unto him,
Verily I say unto thee,
That this day, even in this night, {before the cock crow twice}, thou shalt deny me thrice.

31 **But he** spake the more vehemently,
If I should die with thee,
I will not deny thee in any wise.

Likewise also said they all.

32 **And they** came to a place which was named Gethsemane:
and he saith to his disciples,
Sit ye here,
while I shall pray.

33 **And he** taketh with him Peter and James and John,
and began to be sore amazed,
and to be very heavy;
34 **And** saith unto them,
My soul is exceeding sorrowful unto death:
tarry ye here,
and watch.

35 **And he** went forward a little,
and fell on the ground,
and prayed
that, {if it were possible}, the hour might pass from him.

36 **And he** said,
Abba, Father, all things are possible unto thee;
take away this cup from me:
nevertheless not what I will,
but what thou wilt.

37 **And he** cometh,
and findeth them sleeping,
and saith unto Peter,
Simon, sleepest thou?
couldest not thou watch one hour?

38 **Watch ye and pray,**
lest ye enter into temptation.

The spirit truly is ready,
but the flesh is weak.

39 **And again he** went away,
and prayed,
and spake the same words.

40 **And when he** returned,
he found them asleep again,
(for their eyes were heavy,)
neither wist they
what to answer him.

41 **And he** cometh the third time,
and saith unto them,
Sleep on now,
and take your rest:
it is enough,
the hour is come;
behold,
the Son of man is betrayed into the hands of sinners.

42 **Rise up,**
let us go;
lo,
he that betrayeth me is at hand.

43 **And immediately**, {while he yet spake}, cometh Judas, one of the twelve, and with him a great multitude with swords and staves, from the chief priests and the scribes and the elders.

44 **And he that betrayed him** had given them a token,
saying,
Whomsoever I shall kiss,
that same is he;
take him,
and lead him away safely.

45 **And as soon as he** was come,
he goeth straightway to him,
and saith,
Master, master;
and kissed him.

46 **And they** laid their hands on him,
and took him.

47 **And one of them that stood by** drew a sword,
and smote a servant of the high priest,
and cut off his ear.

48 **And Jesus** answered and said unto them,
Are ye come out, as against a thief, with swords and with staves to take me?

49 **I** was daily with you in the temple teaching,
and ye took me not:
but the scriptures must be fulfilled.

50 **And they all** forsook him,
and fled.

51 **And there** followed him a certain young man,
having a linen cloth cast about his naked body;
and the young men laid hold on him:

52 **And he** left the linen cloth,
and fled from them naked.

53 **And they** led Jesus away to the high priest:
and with him were assembled all the chief priests and the elders and the scribes.

54 **And Peter** followed him afar off, even into the palace of the high priest:
and he sat with the servants,
and warmed himself at the fire.

55 **And the chief priests and all the council** sought for witness against Jesus
to put him to death;
and found none.

56 **For many** bare false witness against him,
but their witness agreed not together.

57 **And there** arose certain,
and bare false witness against him,
saying,

58 **We** heard him say,
I will destroy this temple that is made with hands,
and within three days I will build another made without hands.

59 **But neither so** did their witness agree together.

60 **And the high priest** stood up in the midst,
and asked Jesus,
saying,
Answerest thou nothing?
what is it which these witness against thee?

61 **But he** held his peace,
and answered nothing.

Again the high priest asked him,
and said unto him,
Art thou the Christ, the Son of the Blessed?

62 **And Jesus** said,
I am:
and ye shall see the Son of man sitting on the right hand of power, and coming in the clouds of heaven.

63 **Then the high priest** rent his clothes,
and saith,
What need we any further witnesses?

64 **Ye** have heard the blasphemy:
what think ye?

And they all condemned him to be guilty of death.

65 **And some** began to spit on him,
and to cover his face,
and to buffet him,
and to say unto him,
Prophesy:
and the servants did strike him with the palms of their hands.

66 **And as Peter** was beneath in the palace,
there cometh one of the maids of the high priest:

67 **And when she** saw Peter warming himself,
she looked upon him,
and said,
And thou also wast with Jesus of Nazareth.

68 **But he** denied,
saying,
I know not,
neither understand I
what thou sayest.

And he went out into the porch;
and the cock crew.

69 **And a maid** saw him again,
and began to say to them that stood by,
This is one of them.

70 **And he** denied it again.

And a little after, they that stood by said again to Peter,
Surely thou art one of them:
for thou art a Galilaean,
and thy speech agreeth thereto.

71 **But he** began to curse and to swear,
saying,
I know not this man of whom ye speak.

72 **And the second time** the cock crew.

And Peter called to mind the word that Jesus said unto him,
Before the cock crow twice,
thou shalt deny me thrice.

And when he thought thereon,
he wept.

15 **And straightway in the morning** the chief priests held a consultation with the elders and scribes and the whole council,

and bound Jesus,
and carried him away,
and delivered him to Pilate.
2 **And Pilate** asked him,
Art thou the King of the Jews?
And he answering said unto them,
Thou sayest it.
3 **And the chief priests** accused him of many things:
but he answered nothing.
4 **And Pilate** asked him again,
saying,
Answerest thou nothing?
behold how many things they witness against thee.
5 **But Jesus** yet answered nothing;
so that Pilate marvelled.
6 **Now at that feast** he released unto them one prisoner,
whomsoever they desired.
7 **And there** was one named Barabbas,
which lay bound with them that had made insurrection with him,
who had committed murder in the insurrection.
8 **And the multitude crying aloud** began to desire him to do as he had ever done unto them.
9 **But Pilate** answered them,
saying,
Will ye
that I release unto you the King of the Jews?
10 **For he** knew
that the chief priests had delivered him for envy.
11 **But the chief priests** moved the people,
that he should rather release Barabbas unto them.
12 **And Pilate** answered and said again unto them,
What will ye then
that I shall do unto him whom ye call the King of the Jews?
13 **And they** cried out again,
Crucify him.
14 **Then Pilate** said unto them,
Why,
what evil hath he done?
And they cried out the more exceedingly,
Crucify him.
15 **And so Pilate**, {willing to content the people}, released Barabbas unto them,
and delivered Jesus,
when he had scourged him,
to be crucified.
16 **And the soldiers** led him away into the hall, called Praetorium;
and they call together the whole band.
17 **And they** clothed him with purple,
and platted a crown of thorns,
and put it about his head,
18 **And** began to salute him,
Hail, King of the Jews!
19 **And they** smote him on the head with a reed,
and did spit upon him,
and bowing their knees worshipped him.
20 **And when they** had mocked him,
they took off the purple from him,
and put his own clothes on him,
and led him out
to crucify him.
21 **And they** compel one Simon a Cyrenian, {who passed by}, {coming out of the country}, the father of Alexander and Rufus, to bear his cross.
22 **And they** bring him unto the place Golgotha,
which is, {being interpreted}, The place of a skull.
23 **And they** gave him to drink wine mingled with myrrh:
but he received it not.
24 **And when they** had crucified him,
they parted his garments,
casting lots upon them,
what every man should take.
25 **And it** was the third hour,
and they crucified him.
26 **And the superscription of his accusation** was written over,
The King Of The Jews.
27 **And with him** they crucify two thieves; the one on his right hand, and the other on his left.
28 **And the scripture** was fulfilled,
which saith,
And he was numbered with the transgressors.
29 **And they that passed by** railed on him,
wagging their heads,
and saying,
Ah, thou that destroyest the temple, and buildest it in three days,
30 Save thyself,
and come down from the cross.
31 **Likewise also the chief priests mocking** said among themselves with the scribes,
He saved others;
himself he cannot save.
32 **Let Christ the King of Israel** descend now from the cross,
that we may see and believe.
And they that were crucified with him reviled him.
33 **And when the sixth hour** was come,
there was darkness over the whole land until the ninth hour.
34 **And at the ninth hour** Jesus cried with a loud voice,
saying,
Eloi, Eloi, lama sabachthani?
which is,
being interpreted,
My God, my God, why hast thou forsaken me?
35 **And some of them that stood by**, {when they heard it}, said,
Behold,
he calleth Elias.
36 **And one** ran and filled a spunge full of vinegar,
and put it on a reed,
and gave him to drink,
saying,
Let alone;
let us see
whether Elias will come to take him down.
37 **And Jesus** cried with a loud voice,
and gave up the ghost.
38 **And the veil of the temple** was rent in twain from the top to the bottom.
39 **And when the centurion**, {which stood over against him}, saw that he so cried out, and gave up the ghost,
he said,
Truly this man was the Son of God.
40 **There** were also women looking on afar off:
among whom was Mary Magdalene, and Mary the mother of James the less and of Joses, and Salome;
41 (Who also, {when he was in Galilee}, followed him,
and ministered unto him;)
and many other women which came up with him unto Jerusalem.

42 **And now when the even** was come,
because it was the preparation, that is, the day before the sabbath,
43 **Joseph of Arimathaea, an honourable counsellor,** {which also waited for the kingdom of God}, came,
and went in boldly unto Pilate,
and craved the body of Jesus.
44 **And Pilate** marvelled
if he were already dead:
and calling unto him the centurion,
he asked him
whether he had been any while dead.
45 **And when he** knew it of the centurion,
he gave the body to Joseph.
46 **And he** bought fine linen,
and took him down,
and wrapped him in the linen,
and laid him in a sepulchre which was hewn out of a rock,
and rolled a stone unto the door of the sepulchre.
47 **And Mary Magdalene and Mary the mother of Joses** beheld where he was laid.

16 **And when the sabbath** was past,
Mary Magdalene, and Mary the mother of James, and Salome, had bought sweet spices,
that they might come and anoint him.
2 **And very early in the morning the first day of the week,** they came unto the sepulchre at the rising of the sun.
3 **And they** said among themselves,
Who shall roll us away the stone from the door of the sepulchre?
4 **And when they** looked,
they saw that the stone was rolled away:
for it was very great.
5 **And entering into the sepulchre,** they saw a young man sitting on the right side,
clothed in a long white garment;
and they were affrighted.
6 **And he** saith unto them,
Be not affrighted:
Ye seek Jesus of Nazareth,
which was crucified:
he is risen;
he is not here:
behold the place where they laid him.
7 **But go** your way,
tell his disciples and Peter
that he goeth before you into Galilee:
there shall ye see him,
as he said unto you.
8 **And they** went out quickly,
and fled from the sepulchre;
for they trembled and were amazed:
neither said they any thing to any man;
for they were afraid.
9 **Now when Jesus** was risen early the first day of the week,
he appeared first to Mary Magdalene,
out of whom he had cast seven devils.
10 **And she** went and told them that had been with him,
as they mourned and wept.
11 **And they,** {when they had heard that he was alive}, {and had been seen of her}, believed not.
12 **After that** he appeared in another form unto two of them,
as they walked,
and went into the country.
13 **And they** went and told it unto the residue:
neither believed they them.
14 **Afterward he** appeared unto the eleven
as they sat at meat,
and upbraided them with their unbelief and hardness of heart,
because they believed not them which had seen him after he was risen.
15 **And he** said unto them,
Go ye into all the world,
and preach the gospel to every creature.
16 **He that believeth and is baptized** shall be saved;
but he that believeth not shall be damned.
17 **And these signs** shall follow them that believe;
In my name shall they cast out devils;
they shall speak with new tongues;
18 **They** shall take up serpents;
and if they drink any deadly thing,
it shall not hurt them;
they shall lay hands on the sick,
and they shall recover.
19 **So then after the Lord** had spoken unto them,
he was received up into heaven,
and sat on the right hand of God.
20 **And they** went forth,
and preached every where,
the Lord working with them,
and confirming the word with signs following.
Amen.

Luke

Luke, a physician and a close associate of the Apostle Paul, wrote the Gospel of Luke. Like John Mark, Luke was not one of the apostles. However, he was a meticulous researcher and writer who sought to provide an accurate and comprehensive account of Jesus' life, teachings, and ministry. While his relationship with Paul lent credibility to his Gospel and helped ensure its acceptance within Christian communities, Luke witnessed firsthand the struggles and triumphs of the early Christian movement and the challenges the apostles faced in spreading the Gospel. This close association with Paul also gave Luke access to the apostle's unique perspectives on Jesus' life and teachings, which he incorporated into his Gospel.

Luke's Gospel stands out among the four gospels in several ways. His narrative places a strong emphasis on Jesus' interactions with and acceptance of marginalized groups, such as women, the poor, and the sick. He also provides more detailed accounts of specific events and parables, such as the births of both John the Baptist and Jesus. And he includes several unique parables, such as The Prodigal Son and The Good Samaritan. Furthermore, the structure and order of events in Luke's Gospel include a longer journey to Jerusalem, which allows him to present a more comprehensive picture of Jesus' ministry. Finally, Luke presents the life of Jesus not as an isolated event but within a broader historical context, offering a more comprehensive understanding of the political and social environment in which Jesus lived and ministered.

While the Gospel of Luke is unique in many ways, it also corroborates significant events found in the other Gospels. For example, his Sermon on the Plain is his own telling of the Sermon on the Mount, and he also provides details about the Last Supper and Jesus' crucifixion, resurrection, and ascension into heaven. Overall, Luke presents a narrative of Jesus Christ's life and ministry that delves deep into compassion, empathy, and a thorough understanding of the human condition. It doesn't just portray Christ as a divine figure but as a human being who experienced the full spectrum of human emotions and struggles. However, his Gospel is not just a narrative but a call to action, empowering believers to live out their faith daily, to treat others with kindness and respect, and to be a source of light and hope in a world that can often be dark and uncertain.

Moreover, the Gospel of Luke is a testament to the transformative power of storytelling. It skillfully weaves a rich tapestry of characters, events, and teachings to create a compelling narrative. It reminds readers that stories have the power to change hearts and minds, to inspire them to be better versions of themselves, and to connect them to something greater than themselves. Luke's Gospel, therefore, serves as a divine guide that inspires believers to live with compassion, humility, and service to others, thus encouraging them to reflect the love and grace of Jesus in every aspect of their lives.

1 **Forasmuch as many** have taken in hand to set forth in order a declaration of those things which are most surely believed among us,

2 **Even as they** delivered them unto us,
which from the beginning were eyewitnesses, and ministers of the word;

3 **It seemed good to me** also, {having had perfect understanding of all things from the very first}, to write unto thee
in order, most excellent Theophilus,

4 **That thou** mightest know the certainty of those things,
wherein thou hast been instructed.

5 **There** was in the days of Herod, the king of Judaea, a certain priest named Zacharias, of the course of Abia:
and his wife was of the daughters of Aaron,
and her name was Elisabeth.

6 **And they** were both righteous before God,
walking in all the commandments and ordinances of the Lord blameless.

7 **And they** had no child,
because that Elisabeth was barren,
and they both were now well stricken in years.

8 **And it** came to pass,
that while he executed the priest's office before God in the order of his course,

9 According to the custom of the priest's office,
his lot was to burn incense
when he went into the temple of the Lord.

10 **And the whole multitude of the people** were praying without at the time of incense.

11 **And there** appeared unto him an angel of the Lord standing on the right side of the altar of incense.

12 **And when Zacharias** saw him,
he was troubled,
and fear fell upon him.

13 **But the angel** said unto him,
Fear not, Zacharias:
for thy prayer is heard;
and thy wife Elisabeth shall bear thee a son,

and thou shalt call his name John.
14 **And thou** shalt have joy and gladness;
and many shall rejoice at his birth.
15 **For he** shall be great in the sight of the Lord,
and shall drink neither wine nor strong drink;
and he shall be filled with the Holy Ghost, even from his mother's womb.
16 **And many of the children of Israel** shall he turn to the Lord their God.
17 **And he** shall go before him in the spirit and power of Elias,
to turn the hearts of the fathers to the children, and the disobedient to the wisdom of the just;
to make ready a people prepared for the Lord.
18 **And Zacharias** said unto the angel,
Whereby shall I know this?
for I am an old man,
and my wife well stricken in years.
19 **And the angel answering** said unto him,
I am Gabriel,
that stand in the presence of God;
and am sent to speak unto thee,
and to shew thee these glad tidings.
20 **And, {behold}, thou** shalt be dumb,
and not able to speak,
until the day that these things shall be performed,
because thou believest not my words,
which shall be fulfilled in their season.
21 **And the people** waited for Zacharias,
and marvelled
that he tarried so long in the temple.
22 **And when he** came out,
he could not speak unto them:
and they perceived that he had seen a vision in the temple:
for he beckoned unto them,
and remained speechless.
23 **And it** came to pass,
that, {as soon as the days of his ministration were accomplished}, he departed to his own house.
24 **And after those days** his wife Elisabeth conceived,
and hid herself five months,
saying,
25 **Thus** hath the Lord dealt with me in the days wherein he looked on me,
to take away my reproach among men.
26 **And in the sixth month** the angel Gabriel was sent from God unto a city of Galilee, named Nazareth,
27 To a virgin espoused to a man whose name was Joseph, of the house of David;
and the virgin's name was Mary.
28 **And the angel** came in unto her,
and said,
Hail, thou that art highly favoured,
the Lord is with thee:
blessed art thou among women.
29 **And when she** saw him,
she was troubled at his saying,
and cast in her mind
what manner of salutation this should be.
30 **And the angel** said unto her,
Fear not, Mary:
for thou hast found favour with God.
31 **And, {behold}, thou** shalt conceive in thy womb,
and bring forth a son,
and shalt call his name Jesus.
32 **He** shall be great,
and shall be called the Son of the Highest:
and the Lord God shall give unto him the throne of his father David:
33 **And he** shall reign over the house of Jacob for ever;
and of his kingdom there shall be no end.
34 **Then** said Mary unto the angel,
How shall this be,
seeing I know not a man?
35 **And the angel** answered and said unto her,
The Holy Ghost shall come upon thee,
and the power of the Highest shall overshadow thee:
therefore also that holy thing which shall be born of thee shall be called the Son of God.
36 **And, {behold}, thy cousin Elisabeth,** she hath also conceived a son in her old age:
and this is the sixth month with her,
who was called barren.
37 **For with God** nothing shall be impossible.
38 **And Mary** said,
Behold the handmaid of the Lord;
be it unto me according to thy word.
And the angel departed from her.
39 **And Mary** arose in those days,
and went into the hill country with haste, into a city of Juda;
40 **And** entered into the house of Zacharias,
and saluted Elisabeth.
41 **And it** came to pass,
that, {when Elisabeth heard the salutation of Mary}, the babe leaped in her womb;
and Elisabeth was filled with the Holy Ghost:
42 **And she** spake out with a loud voice,
and said,
Blessed art thou among women,
and blessed is the fruit of thy womb.
43 **And whence** is this to me,
that the mother of my Lord should come to me?
44 **For, {lo}, as soon as the voice of thy salutation** sounded in mine ears,
the babe leaped in my womb for joy.
45 **And blessed** is she that believed:
for there shall be a performance of those things which were told her from the Lord.
46 **And Mary** said,
My soul doth magnify the Lord,
47 **And my spirit** hath rejoiced in God my Saviour.
48 **For he** hath regarded the low estate of his handmaiden:
for, {behold}, from henceforth all generations shall call me blessed.
49 **For he that is mighty** hath done to me great things;
and holy is his name.
50 **And his mercy** is on them that fear him from generation to generation.
51 **He** hath shewed strength with his arm;
he hath scattered the proud in the imagination of their hearts.
52 **He** hath put down the mighty from their seats,
and exalted them of low degree.
53 **He** hath filled the hungry with

good things;
and the rich he hath sent empty away.
54 **He** hath helped his servant Israel, in remembrance of his mercy;
55 **As he** spake to our fathers, to Abraham, and to his seed for ever.
56 **And Mary** abode with her about three months,
and returned to her own house.
57 **Now Elisabeth's full time** came that she should be delivered;
and she brought forth a son.
58 **And her neighbours and her cousins** heard how the Lord had shewed great mercy upon her;
and they rejoiced with her.
59 **And it** came to pass,
that on the eighth day they came to circumcise the child;
and they called him Zacharias, after the name of his father.
60 **And his mother** answered and said,
Not so;
but he shall be called John.
61 **And they** said unto her,
There is none of thy kindred that is called by this name.
62 **And they** made signs to his father,
how he would have him called.
63 **And he** asked for a writing table,
and wrote,
saying,
His name is John.
And they marvelled all.
64 **And his mouth** was opened immediately,
and his tongue loosed,
and he spake,
and praised God.
65 **And fear** came on all that dwelt round about them:
and all these sayings were noised abroad throughout all the hill country of Judaea.
66 **And all they that heard them** laid them up in their hearts,
saying,
What manner of child shall this be!
And the hand of the Lord was with him.
67 **And his father Zacharias** was filled with the Holy Ghost,
and prophesied,
saying,
68 **Blessed** be the Lord God of Israel;
for he hath visited and redeemed his people,
69 **And** hath raised up an horn of salvation for us in the house of his servant David;
70 **As he** spake by the mouth of his holy prophets,
which have been since the world began:
71 **That we** should be saved from our enemies, and from the hand of all that hate us;
72 To perform the mercy promised to our fathers,
and to remember his holy covenant;
73 The oath which he sware to our father Abraham,
74 **That he** would grant unto us,
that we being delivered out of the hand of our enemies might serve him without fear,
75 In holiness and righteousness before him, all the days of our life.
76 **And thou, child,** shalt be called the prophet of the Highest:
for thou shalt go before the face of the Lord
to prepare his ways;
77 To give knowledge of salvation unto his people by the remission of their sins,
78 Through the tender mercy of our God;
whereby the dayspring from on high hath visited us,
79 To give light to them that sit in darkness and in the shadow of death,
to guide our feet into the way of peace.
80 **And the child** grew,
and waxed strong in spirit,
and was in the deserts till the day of his shewing unto Israel.

2 **And it** came to pass in those days,
that there went out a decree from Caesar Augustus
that all the world should be taxed.
2 (**And this taxing** was first made
when Cyrenius was governor of Syria.)
3 **And all** went to be taxed, every one into his own city.
4 **And Joseph** also went up from Galilee, out of the city of Nazareth, into Judaea, unto the city of David,
which is called Bethlehem;
(because he was of the house and lineage of David:)
5 To be taxed with Mary his espoused wife,
being great with child.
6 **And so** it was,
that, {while they were there}, the days were accomplished that she should be delivered.
7 **And she** brought forth her firstborn son,
and wrapped him in swaddling clothes,
and laid him in a manger;
because there was no room for them in the inn.
8 **And there** were in the same country shepherds abiding in the field,
keeping watch over their flock by night.
9 **And, {lo}, the angel of the Lord** came upon them,
and the glory of the Lord shone round about them:
and they were sore afraid.
10 **And the angel** said unto them,
Fear not:
for, {behold}, I bring you good tidings of great joy,
which shall be to all people.
11 **For unto you** is born this day in the city of David a Saviour,
which is Christ the Lord.
12 **And this** shall be a sign unto you;
Ye shall find the babe wrapped in swaddling clothes,
lying in a manger.
13 **And suddenly** there was with the angel a multitude of the heavenly host praising God,
and saying,
14 **Glory** to God in the highest, and on earth peace, good will toward men.
15 **And it** came to pass,
as the angels were gone away from them into heaven,
the shepherds said one to another,
Let us now go even unto Bethlehem,
and see this thing which is come to pass,
which the Lord hath made known unto us.
16 **And they** came with haste,
and found Mary, and Joseph, and the babe lying in a manger.
17 **And when they** had seen it,

they made known abroad the saying which was told them concerning this child.

18 **And all they that heard it** wondered at those things which were told them by the shepherds.

19 **But Mary** kept all these things,
and pondered them in her heart.

20 **And the shepherds** returned,
glorifying and praising God for all the things that they had heard and seen,
as it was told unto them.

21 **And when eight days** were accomplished for the circumcising of the child,
his name was called Jesus,
which was so named of the angel
before he was conceived in the womb.

22 **And when the days of her purification according to the law of Moses** were accomplished,
they brought him to Jerusalem,
to present him to the Lord;

23 (As it is written in the law of the Lord,
Every male that openeth the womb shall be called holy to the Lord;)

24 **And** to offer a sacrifice according to that which is said in the law of the Lord, A pair of turtledoves, or two young pigeons.

25 **And, {behold}, there** was a man in Jerusalem,
whose name was Simeon;
and the same man was just and devout,
waiting for the consolation of Israel:
and the Holy Ghost was upon him.

26 **And it was revealed unto him by the Holy Ghost,** that he should not see death,
before he had seen the Lord's Christ.

27 **And he** came by the Spirit into the temple:
and when the parents brought in the child Jesus,
to do for him after the custom of the law,

28 **Then** took he him up in his arms,
and blessed God,
and said,

29 **Lord, now lettest thou thy servant** depart in peace, according to thy word:

30 **For mine eyes** have seen thy salvation,

31 **Which thou** hast prepared before the face of all people;

32 **A light** to lighten the Gentiles, and the glory of thy people Israel.

33 **And Joseph and his mother** marvelled at those things which were spoken of him.

34 **And Simeon** blessed them,
and said unto Mary his mother,
Behold,
this child is set for the fall and rising again of many in Israel; and for a sign which shall be spoken against;

35 (Yea, a sword shall pierce through thy own soul also,)
that the thoughts of many hearts may be revealed.

36 **And there** was one Anna, a prophetess, the daughter of Phanuel, of the tribe of Aser:
she was of a great age,
and had lived with an husband seven years from her virginity;

37 **And she** was a widow of about fourscore and four years,
which departed not from the temple,
but served God with fastings and prayers night and day.

38 **And she coming in that instant** gave thanks likewise unto the Lord,
and spake of him to all them that looked for redemption in Jerusalem.

39 **And when they** had performed all things according to the law of the Lord,
they returned into Galilee, to their own city Nazareth.

40 **And the child** grew,
and waxed strong in spirit,
filled with wisdom:
and the grace of God was upon him.

41 **Now his parents** went to Jerusalem every year at the feast of the passover.

42 **And when he** was twelve years old,
they went up to Jerusalem after the custom of the feast.

43 **And when they** had fulfilled the days,
as they returned,
the child Jesus tarried behind in Jerusalem;
and Joseph and his mother knew not of it.

44 **But they**, {supposing him to have been in the company}, went a day's journey;
and they sought him among their kinsfolk and acquaintance.

45 **And when they** found him not,
they turned back again to Jerusalem,
seeking him.

46 **And it** came to pass,
that after three days they found him in the temple,
sitting in the midst of the doctors,
both hearing them,
and asking them questions.

47 **And all that heard him** were astonished at his understanding and answers.

48 **And when they** saw him,
they were amazed:
and his mother said unto him,
Son, why hast thou thus dealt with us?
behold,
thy father and I have sought thee sorrowing.

49 **And he** said unto them,
How is it that ye sought me?
wist ye not
that I must be about my Father's business?

50 **And they** understood not the saying which he spake unto them.

51 **And he** went down with them,
and came to Nazareth,
and was subject unto them:
but his mother kept all these sayings in her heart.

52 **And Jesus** increased in wisdom and stature, and in favour with God and man.

3

Now in the fifteenth year of the reign of Tiberius Caesar, {Pontius Pilate being governor of Judaea}, {and Herod being tetrarch of Galilee}, {and his brother Philip tetrarch of Ituraea and of the region of Trachonitis}, {and Lysanias the tetrarch of Abilene},

2 {Annas and Caiaphas being the high priests}, the word of God came unto John the son of Zacharias in the wilderness.

3 **And he** came into all the country about Jordan,
preaching the baptism of repentance for the remission of sins;

[4] **As it** is written in the book of the words of Esaias the prophet,
saying,
The voice of one crying in the wilderness,
Prepare ye the way of the Lord,
make his paths straight.

[5] **Every valley** shall be filled,
and every mountain and hill shall be brought low;
and the crooked shall be made straight,
and the rough ways shall be made smooth;

[6] **And all flesh** shall see the salvation of God.

[7] **Then** said he to the multitude that came forth to be baptized of him,
O generation of vipers, who hath warned you to flee from the wrath to come?

[8] **Bring forth** therefore fruits worthy of repentance,
and begin not to say within yourselves,
We have Abraham to our father:
for I say unto you,
That God is able of these stones to raise up children unto Abraham.

[9] **And now also the axe** is laid unto the root of the trees:
every tree therefore which bringeth not forth good fruit is hewn down,
and cast into the fire.

[10] **And the people** asked him,
saying,
What shall we do then?

[11] **He** answereth and saith unto them,
He that hath two coats, let him impart to him that hath none;
and he that hath meat, let him do likewise.

[12] **Then** came also publicans to be baptized,
and said unto him,
Master, what shall we do?

[13] **And he** said unto them,
Exact no more than that which is appointed you.

[14] **And the soldiers** likewise demanded of him,
saying,
And what shall we do?

And he said unto them,
Do violence to no man,
neither accuse any falsely;
and be content with your wages.

[15] **And as the people** were in expectation,
and all men mused in their hearts of John,
whether he were the Christ, or not;
[16] **John** answered,
saying unto them all,
I indeed baptize you with water;
but one mightier than I cometh,
the latchet of whose shoes I am not worthy to unloose:
he shall baptize you with the Holy Ghost and with fire:
[17] **Whose fan** is in his hand,
and he will throughly purge his floor,
and will gather the wheat into his garner;
but the chaff he will burn with fire unquenchable.

[18] **And many other things in his exhortation** preached he unto the people.

[19] **But Herod the tetrarch**, {being reproved by him for Herodias his brother Philip's wife, and for all the evils which Herod had done},
[20] Added yet this above all,
that he shut up John in prison.

[21] **Now when all the people** were baptized,
it came to pass,
that {Jesus also being baptized}, {and praying}, the heaven was opened,
[22] **And the Holy Ghost** descended in a bodily shape like a dove upon him,
and a voice came from heaven,
which said,
Thou art my beloved Son;
in thee I am well pleased.

[23] **And Jesus himself** began to be about thirty years of age,
being (as was supposed) the son of Joseph,
which was the son of Heli,
[24] **Which** was the son of Matthat,
which was the son of Levi,
which was the son of Melchi,
which was the son of Janna,
which was the son of Joseph,
[25] **Which** was the son of Mattathias,
which was the son of Amos,
which was the son of Naum,
which was the son of Esli,
which was the son of Nagge,
[26] **Which** was the son of Maath,
which was the son of Mattathias,
which was the son of Semei,
which was the son of Joseph,
which was the son of Juda,
[27] **Which** was the son of Joanna,
which was the son of Rhesa,
which was the son of Zorobabel,
which was the son of Salathiel,
which was the son of Neri,
[28] **Which** was the son of Melchi,
which was the son of Addi,
which was the son of Cosam,
which was the son of Elmodam,
which was the son of Er,
[29] **Which** was the son of Jose,
which was the son of Eliezer,
which was the son of Jorim,
which was the son of Matthat,
which was the son of Levi,
[30] **Which** was the son of Simeon,
which was the son of Juda,
which was the son of Joseph,
which was the son of Jonan,
which was the son of Eliakim,
[31] **Which** was the son of Melea,
which was the son of Menan,
which was the son of Mattatha,
which was the son of Nathan,
which was the son of David,
[32] **Which** was the son of Jesse,
which was the son of Obed,
which was the son of Booz,
which was the son of Salmon,
which was the son of Naasson,
[33] **Which** was the son of Aminadab,
which was the son of Aram,
which was the son of Esrom,
which was the son of Phares,
which was the son of Juda,
[34] **Which** was the son of Jacob,
which was the son of Isaac,
which was the son of Abraham,
which was the son of Thara,
which was the son of Nachor,
[35] **Which** was the son of Saruch,
which was the son of Ragau,
which was the son of Phalec,
which was the son of Heber,
which was the son of Sala,
[36] **Which** was the son of Cainan,
which was the son of Arphaxad,
which was the son of Sem,
which was the son of Noe,
which was the son of Lamech,
[37] **Which** was the son of Mathusala,
which was the son of Enoch,
which was the son of Jared,
which was the son of Maleleel,
which was the son of Cainan,
[38] **Which** was the son of Enos,
which was the son of Seth,
which was the son of Adam,
which was the son of God.

4 ⟴ **And Jesus being full of the Holy Ghost** returned from Jordan,
and was led by the Spirit into the wilderness,
2 Being forty days tempted of the devil.
And in those days he did eat nothing:
and when they were ended,
he afterward hungered.
3 **And the devil** said unto him,
If thou be the Son of God,
command this stone
that it be made bread.
4 **And Jesus** answered him,
saying,
It is written,
That man shall not live by bread alone,
but by every word of God.
5 **And the devil**, {taking him up into an high mountain}, shewed unto him all the kingdoms of the world in a moment of time.
6 **And the devil** said unto him,
All this power will I give thee, and the glory of them:
for that is delivered unto me;
and to whomsoever I will
I give it.
7 **If thou** therefore wilt worship me,
all shall be thine.
8 **And Jesus** answered and said unto him,
Get thee behind me, Satan:
for it is written,
Thou shalt worship the Lord thy God,
and him only shalt thou serve.
9 **And he** brought him to Jerusalem,
and set him on a pinnacle of the temple,
and said unto him,
If thou be the Son of God,
cast thyself down from hence:
10 **For it** is written,
He shall give his angels charge over thee,
to keep thee:
11 **And in their hands** they shall bear thee up,
lest at any time thou dash thy foot against a stone.
12 **And Jesus answering** said unto him,
It is said,
Thou shalt not tempt the Lord thy God.
13 **And when the devil** had ended all the temptation,
he departed from him for a season.
14 **And Jesus** returned in the power of the Spirit into Galilee:
and there went out a fame of him through all the region round about.
15 **And he** taught in their synagogues,
being glorified of all.
16 **And he** came to Nazareth,
where he had been brought up:
and, {as his custom was}, he went into the synagogue on the sabbath day,
and stood up for to read.
17 **And there** was delivered unto him the book of the prophet Esaias.
And when he had opened the book,
he found the place where it was written,
18 **The Spirit of the Lord** is upon me,
because he hath anointed me to preach the gospel to the poor;
he hath sent me to heal the brokenhearted,
to preach deliverance to the captives, and recovering of sight to the blind,
to set at liberty them that are bruised,
19 To preach the acceptable year of the Lord.
20 **And he** closed the book,
and he gave it again to the minister,
and sat down.
And the eyes of all them that were in the synagogue were fastened on him.
21 **And he** began to say unto them,
This day is this scripture fulfilled in your ears.
22 **And all** bare him witness,
and wondered at the gracious words which proceeded out of his mouth.
And they said,
Is not this Joseph's son?
23 **And he** said unto them,
Ye will surely say unto me this proverb,
Physician, heal thyself:
whatsoever we have heard done in Capernaum,
do also here in thy country.
24 **And he** said,
Verily I say unto you,
No prophet is accepted in his own country.
25 **But I** tell you of a truth,
many widows were in Israel in the days of Elias,
when the heaven was shut up three years and six months,
when great famine was throughout all the land;
26 **But unto none of them** was Elias sent, save unto Sarepta, a city of Sidon, unto a woman that was a widow.
27 **And many lepers** were in Israel in the time of Eliseus the prophet;
and none of them was cleansed, saving Naaman the Syrian.
28 **And all they in the synagogue**, {when they heard these things}, were filled with wrath,
29 **And** rose up,
and thrust him out of the city,
and led him unto the brow of the hill whereon their city was built,
that they might cast him down headlong.
30 **But he passing through the midst of them** went his way,
31 **And** came down to Capernaum, a city of Galilee,
and taught them on the sabbath days.
32 **And they** were astonished at his doctrine:
for his word was with power.
33 **And in the synagogue** there was a man,
which had a spirit of an unclean devil,
and cried out with a loud voice,
34 Saying,
Let us alone;
what have we to do with thee, thou Jesus of Nazareth?
art thou come to destroy us?
I know thee
who thou art; the Holy One of God.
35 **And Jesus** rebuked him,
saying,
Hold thy peace,
and come out of him.
And when the devil had thrown him in the midst,
he came out of him,
and hurt him not.
36 **And they** were all amazed,
and spake among themselves,
saying,
What a word is this!

for with authority and power he
commandeth the unclean spirits,
and they come out.

37 **And the fame of him** went out
into every place of the country
round about.

38 **And he** arose out of the
synagogue,
and entered into Simon's house.

And Simon's wife's mother was
taken with a great fever;
and they besought him for her.

39 **And he** stood over her,
and rebuked the fever;
and it left her:
and immediately she arose
and ministered unto them.

40 **Now when the sun** was setting,
**all they that had any sick with
divers diseases** brought them
unto him;
and he laid his hands on every one
of them,
and healed them.

41 **And devils** also came out of many,
crying out,
and saying,
Thou art Christ the Son of God.

And he rebuking them suffered
them not to speak:
for they knew
that he was Christ.

42 **And when it** was day,
he departed and went into a desert
place:
and the people sought him,
and came unto him,
and stayed him,
that he should not depart from
them.

43 **And he** said unto them,
I must preach the kingdom of God
to other cities also:
for therefore am I sent.

44 **And he** preached in the
synagogues of Galilee.

5 **And it** came to pass,
**that, {as the people pressed
upon him to hear the word of
God}**, he stood by the lake of
Gennesaret,

2 **And** saw two ships standing by the
lake:
but the fishermen were gone out of
them,
and were washing their nets.

3 **And he** entered into one of the
ships,
which was Simon's,
and prayed him
that he would thrust out a little
from the land.

And he sat down,
and taught the people out of the
ship.

4 **Now when he** had left speaking,
he said unto Simon,
Launch out into the deep,
and let down your nets for a
draught.

5 **And Simon answering** said unto
him,
Master, we have toiled all the
night,
and have taken nothing:
nevertheless at thy word I will let
down the net.

6 **And when they** had this done,
they inclosed a great multitude of
fishes:
and their net brake.

7 **And they** beckoned unto their
partners,
which were in the other ship,
that they should come and help
them.

And they came,
and filled both the ships,
so that they began to sink.

8 **When Simon Peter** saw it,
he fell down at Jesus' knees,
saying,
Depart from me;
for I am a sinful man, O Lord.

9 **For he** was astonished, and all
that were with him, at the
draught of the fishes which they
had taken:

10 **And so** was also James, and John,
the sons of Zebedee,
which were partners with Simon.

And Jesus said unto Simon,
Fear not;
from henceforth thou shalt catch
men.

11 **And when they** had brought their
ships to land,
they forsook all,
and followed him.

12 **And it** came to pass,
when he was in a certain city,
behold a man full of leprosy:
who {seeing Jesus} fell on his face,
and besought him,
saying,
Lord, if thou wilt,
thou canst make me clean.

13 **And he** put forth his hand,
and touched him,
saying,
I will:
be thou clean.

And immediately the leprosy
departed from him.

14 **And he** charged him to tell no
man:
but go,
and shew thyself to the priest,
and offer for thy cleansing,
{according as Moses
commanded}, for a testimony
unto them.

15 **But so much the more** went
there a fame abroad of him:
and great multitudes came
together to hear,
and to be healed by him of their
infirmities.

16 **And he** withdrew himself into the
wilderness,
and prayed.

17 **And it** came to pass on a certain
day,
as he was teaching,
that there were Pharisees and
doctors of the law sitting by,
which were come out of every town
of Galilee, and Judaea, and
Jerusalem:
and the power of the Lord was
present to heal them.

18 **And, {behold}, men** brought in a
bed a man which was taken with
a palsy:
and they sought means to bring
him in,
and to lay him before him.

19 **And when they** could not find by
what way they might bring him in
because of the multitude,
they went upon the housetop,
and let him down through the tiling
with his couch into the midst
before Jesus.

20 **And when he** saw their faith,
he said unto him,
Man, thy sins are forgiven thee.

21 **And the scribes and the
Pharisees** began to reason,
saying,
Who is this which speaketh
blasphemies?

Who can forgive sins, but God
alone?

22 **But when Jesus** perceived their
thoughts,
he answering said unto them,

What reason ye in your hearts?
23 **Whether** is easier,
to say,
Thy sins be forgiven thee;
or to say,
Rise up and walk?
24 **But that ye** may know
that the Son of man hath power upon earth to forgive sins,
(he said unto the sick of the palsy,)
I say unto thee,
Arise,
and take up thy couch,
and go into thine house.
25 **And immediately** he rose up before them,
and took up that whereon he lay,
and departed to his own house,
glorifying God.
26 **And they** were all amazed,
and they glorified God,
and were filled with fear,
saying,
We have seen strange things to day.
27 **And after these things** he went forth,
and saw a publican, named Levi, sitting at the receipt of custom:
and he said unto him,
Follow me.
28 **And he** left all,
rose up,
and followed him.
29 **And Levi** made him a great feast in his own house:
and there was a great company of publicans and of others that sat down with them.
30 **But their scribes and Pharisees** murmured against his disciples,
saying,
Why do ye eat and drink with publicans and sinners?
31 **And Jesus answering** said unto them,
They that are whole need not a physician; but they that are sick.
32 **I** came not to call the righteous, but sinners to repentance.
33 **And they** said unto him,
Why do the disciples of John fast often,
and make prayers, and likewise the disciples of the Pharisees;
but thine eat and drink?
34 **And he** said unto them,
Can ye make the children of the bridechamber fast,
while the bridegroom is with them?
35 **But the days** will come,
when the bridegroom shall be taken away from them,
and then shall they fast in those days.
36 **And he** spake also a parable unto them;
No man putteth a piece of a new garment upon an old;
if otherwise, then both the new maketh a rent,
and the piece that was taken out of the new agreeth not with the old.
37 **And no man** putteth new wine into old bottles;
else the new wine will burst the bottles,
and be spilled,
and the bottles shall perish.
38 **But new wine** must be put into new bottles;
and both are preserved.
39 **No man also having drunk old wine** straightway desireth new:
for he saith,
The old is better.

6 **And it** came to pass on the second sabbath after the first,
that he went through the corn fields;
and his disciples plucked the ears of corn,
and did eat,
rubbing them in their hands.
2 **And certain of the Pharisees** said unto them,
Why do ye that which is not lawful to do on the sabbath days?
3 **And Jesus answering them** said,
Have ye not read so much as this,
what David did,
when himself was an hungred, and they which were with him;
4 **How he** went into the house of God,
and did take and eat the shewbread,
and gave also to them that were with him;
which it is not lawful to eat but for the priests alone?
5 **And he** said unto them,
That the Son of man is Lord also of the sabbath.
6 **And it** came to pass also on another sabbath,
that he entered into the synagogue and taught:
and there was a man whose right hand was withered.
7 **And the scribes and Pharisees** watched him,
whether he would heal on the sabbath day;
that they might find an accusation against him.
8 **But he** knew their thoughts,
and said to the man which had the withered hand,
Rise up,
and stand forth in the midst.
And he arose and stood forth.
9 **Then** said Jesus unto them,
I will ask you one thing;
Is it lawful on the sabbath days to do good,
or to do evil?
to save life,
or to destroy it?
10 **And** looking round about upon them all,
he said unto the man,
Stretch forth thy hand.
And he did so:
and his hand was restored whole as the other.
11 **And they** were filled with madness;
and communed one with another
what they might do to Jesus.
12 **And it** came to pass in those days,
that he went out into a mountain to pray,
and continued all night in prayer to God.
13 **And when it was day,** he called unto him his disciples:
and of them he chose twelve,
whom also he named apostles;
14 Simon, (whom he also named Peter,) and Andrew his brother, James and John, Philip and Bartholomew,
15 Matthew and Thomas, James the son of Alphaeus, and Simon called Zelotes,
16 And Judas the brother of James, and Judas Iscariot,
which also was the traitor.
17 **And he** came down with them,
and stood in the plain, and the company of his disciples, and a great multitude of people out of all Judaea and Jerusalem, and from the sea coast of Tyre and Sidon,

which came to hear him,
and to be healed of their diseases;
18 And they that were vexed with
unclean spirits:
and they were healed.
19 **And the whole multitude** sought
to touch him:
for there went virtue out of him,
and healed them all.
20 **And he** lifted up his eyes on his
disciples,
and said,
Blessed be ye poor:
for yours is the kingdom of God.
21 **Blessed** are ye that hunger now:
for ye shall be filled.
Blessed are ye that weep now:
for ye shall laugh.
22 **Blessed** are ye,
when men shall hate you,
and when they shall separate you
from their company,
and shall reproach you,
and cast out your name as evil, for
the Son of man's sake.
23 **Rejoice ye** in that day,
and leap for joy:
for, {behold}, your reward is great
in heaven:
for in the like manner did their
fathers unto the prophets.
24 **But woe** unto you that are rich!
for ye have received your
consolation.
25 **Woe** unto you that are full!
for ye shall hunger.
Woe unto you that laugh now!
for ye shall mourn and weep.
26 **Woe** unto you,
when all men shall speak well of
you!
for so did their fathers to the false
prophets.
27 **But I** say unto you which hear,
Love your enemies,
do good to them which hate you,
28 **Bless** them that curse you,
and pray for them which
despitefully use you.
29 **And unto him that smiteth thee
on the one cheek** offer also the
other;
**and him that taketh away thy
cloak** forbid not to take thy coat
also.
30 **Give** to every man that asketh of
thee;
**and of him that taketh away thy
goods** ask them not again.
31 **And as ye** would
that men should do to you,
do ye also to them likewise.
32 **For if ye** love them which love
you,
what thank have ye?
for sinners also love those that love
them.
33 **And if ye** do good to them which
do good to you,
what thank have ye?
for sinners also do even the same.
34 **And if ye** lend to them of whom
ye hope to receive,
what thank have ye?
for sinners also lend to sinners,
to receive as much again.
35 **But love ye** your enemies,
and do good,
and lend,
hoping for nothing again;
and your reward shall be great,
and ye shall be the children of the
Highest:
for he is kind unto the unthankful
and to the evil.
36 **Be ye** therefore merciful,
as your Father also is merciful.
37 **Judge not,**
and ye shall not be judged:
condemn not,
and ye shall not be condemned:
forgive,
and ye shall be forgiven:
38 **Give,**
and it shall be given unto you;
**good measure, {pressed down},
{and shaken together}, {and
running over},** shall men give
into your bosom.
**For with the same measure that
ye mete withal** it shall be
measured to you again.
39 **And he** spake a parable unto
them,
Can the blind lead the blind?
shall they not both fall into the
ditch?
40 **The disciple** is not above his
master:
but every one that is perfect shall
be as his master.
41 **And why** beholdest thou the mote
that is in thy brother's eye,
but perceivest not the beam that is
in thine own eye?
42 **Either how** canst thou say to thy
brother,
Brother, let me pull out the mote
that is in thine eye,
when thou thyself beholdest not
the beam that is in thine own eye?
Thou hypocrite, cast out first the
beam out of thine own eye,
and then shalt thou see clearly to
pull out the mote that is in thy
brother's eye.
43 **For a good tree** bringeth not forth
corrupt fruit;
neither doth a corrupt tree bring
forth good fruit.
44 **For every tree** is known by his
own fruit.
For of thorns men do not gather
figs,
nor of a bramble bush gather they
grapes.
45 **A good man out of the good
treasure of his heart** bringeth
forth that which is good;
**and an evil man out of the evil
treasure of his heart** bringeth
forth that which is evil:
for of the abundance of the heart
his mouth speaketh.
46 **And why** call ye me, Lord, Lord,
and do not the things which I say?
47 **Whosoever** cometh to me,
and heareth my sayings,
and doeth them,
I will shew you
to whom he is like:
48 **He** is like a man which built an
house,
and digged deep,
and laid the foundation on a rock:
and when the flood arose,
the stream beat vehemently upon
that house,
and could not shake it:
for it was founded upon a rock.
49 **But he that heareth, and doeth
not,** is like a man that without a
foundation built an house upon
the earth;
against which the stream did beat
vehemently,
and immediately it fell;
and the ruin of that house was
great.

7 **Now when he** had ended all
his sayings in the audience of
the people,
he entered into Capernaum.
2 **And a certain centurion's
servant,** {who was dear unto
him}, was sick,
and ready to die.

3 **And when he** heard of Jesus,
he sent unto him the elders of the Jews,
beseeching him
that he would come and heal his servant.
4 **And when they** came to Jesus,
they besought him instantly,
saying,
That he was worthy for whom he should do this:
5 **For he** loveth our nation,
and he hath built us a synagogue.
6 **Then Jesus** went with them.
And when he was now not far from the house,
the centurion sent friends to him,
saying unto him,
Lord, trouble not thyself:
for I am not worthy that thou shouldest enter under my roof:
7 **Wherefore neither** thought I myself worthy to come unto thee:
but say in a word,
and my servant shall be healed.
8 **For I** also am a man set under authority,
having under me soldiers,
and I say unto one, {Go}, {and he goeth}; and to another, {Come}, {and he cometh}; and to my servant, {Do this}, {and he doeth it}.
9 **When Jesus** heard these things,
he marvelled at him,
and turned him about,
and said unto the people that followed him,
I say unto you,
I have not found so great faith, no, not in Israel.
10 **And they that were sent**, {returning to the house}, found the servant whole that had been sick.
11 **And it** came to pass the day after,
that he went into a city called Nain;
and many of his disciples went with him, and much people.
12 **Now when he** came nigh to the gate of the city,
behold,
there was a dead man carried out, the only son of his mother,
and she was a widow:
and much people of the city was with her.
13 **And when the Lord** saw her,
he had compassion on her,
and said unto her,
Weep not.
14 **And he** came and touched the bier:
and they that bare him stood still.
And he said,
Young man, I say unto thee,
Arise.
15 **And he that was dead** sat up,
and began to speak.
And he delivered him to his mother.
16 **And there** came a fear on all:
and they glorified God,
saying,
That a great prophet is risen up among us;
and, That God hath visited his people.
17 **And this rumour of him** went forth throughout all Judaea,
and throughout all the region round about.
18 **And the disciples of John** shewed him of all these things.
19 **And John calling unto him two of his disciples** sent them to Jesus,
saying,
Art thou he that should come?
or look we for another?
20 **When the men** were come unto him,
they said,
John Baptist hath sent us unto thee,
saying,
Art thou he that should come?
or look we for another?
21 **And in that same hour** he cured many of their infirmities and plagues, and of evil spirits;
and unto many that were blind he gave sight.
22 **Then Jesus answering** said unto them,
Go your way,
and tell John
what things ye have seen and heard;
how that the blind see,
the lame walk,
the lepers are cleansed,
the deaf hear,
the dead are raised,
to the poor the gospel is preached.
23 **And blessed** is he,
whosoever shall not be offended in me.
24 **And when the messengers of John** were departed,
he began to speak unto the people concerning John,
What went ye out into the wilderness for to see?
A reed shaken with the wind?
25 **But what** went ye out for to see?
A man clothed in soft raiment?
Behold,
they which are gorgeously apparelled, and live delicately, are in kings' courts.
26 **But what** went ye out for to see?
A prophet?
Yea, {I say unto you}, and much more than a prophet.
27 **This** is he,
of whom it is written,
Behold,
I send my messenger before thy face,
which shall prepare thy way before thee.
28 **For I** say unto you,
Among those that are born of women there is not a greater prophet than John the Baptist:
but he that is least in the kingdom of God is greater than he.
29 **And all the people that heard him, and the publicans,** justified God,
being baptized with the baptism of John.
30 **But the Pharisees and lawyers** rejected the counsel of God against themselves,
being not baptized of him.
31 **And the Lord** said,
Whereunto then shall I liken the men of this generation?
and to what are they like?
32 **They** are like unto children sitting in the marketplace, and calling one to another,
and saying,
We have piped unto you,
and ye have not danced;
we have mourned to you,
and ye have not wept.
33 **For John the Baptist** came
neither eating bread
nor drinking wine;
and ye say,
He hath a devil.
34 **The Son of man** is come eating and drinking;
and ye say,

Behold a gluttonous man, and a winebibber, a friend of publicans and sinners!

35 **But wisdom** is justified of all her children.

36 **And one of the Pharisees** desired him
that he would eat with him.

And he went into the Pharisee's house,
and sat down to meat.

37 **And, {behold}, a woman in the city**, {which was a sinner}, {when she knew} {that Jesus sat at meat in the Pharisee's house}, brought an alabaster box of ointment,
38 **And** stood at his feet behind him weeping,
and began to wash his feet with tears,
and did wipe them with the hairs of her head,
and kissed his feet,
and anointed them with the ointment.

39 **Now when the Pharisee which had bidden him** saw it,
he spake within himself,
saying,
This man, {if he were a prophet}, would have known
who and what manner of woman this is that toucheth him:
for she is a sinner.

40 **And Jesus answering** said unto him,
Simon, I have somewhat to say unto thee.

And he saith,
Master, say on.

41 **There** was a certain creditor which had two debtors:
the one owed five hundred pence,
and the other fifty.

42 **And when they** had nothing to pay,
he frankly forgave them both.

Tell me therefore,
which of them will love him most?

43 **Simon** answered and said,
I suppose that he,
to whom he forgave most.

And he said unto him,
Thou hast rightly judged.

44 **And he** turned to the woman,
and said unto Simon,
Seest thou this woman?

I entered into thine house,
thou gavest me no water for my feet:
but she hath washed my feet with tears,
and wiped them with the hairs of her head.

45 **Thou** gavest me no kiss:
but this woman since the time I came in hath not ceased to kiss my feet.

46 **My head with oil** thou didst not anoint:
but this woman hath anointed my feet with ointment.

47 **Wherefore I** say unto thee,
Her sins, {which are many}, are forgiven;
for she loved much:
but to whom little is forgiven,
the same loveth little.

48 **And he** said unto her,
Thy sins are forgiven.

49 **And they that sat at meat with him** began to say within themselves,
Who is this that forgiveth sins also?

50 **And he** said to the woman,
Thy faith hath saved thee;
go in peace.

8 **And it** came to pass afterward,
that he went throughout every city and village,
preaching and shewing the glad tidings of the kingdom of God:
and the twelve were with him,
2 And certain women,
which had been healed of evil spirits and infirmities, Mary called Magdalene,
out of whom went seven devils,
3 And Joanna the wife of Chuza Herod's steward, and Susanna, and many others,
which ministered unto him of their substance.

4 **And when much people** were gathered together,
and were come to him out of every city,
he spake by a parable:
5 **A sower** went out to sow his seed:
and as he sowed,
some fell by the way side;
and it was trodden down,
and the fowls of the air devoured it.

6 **And some** fell upon a rock;
and as soon as it was sprung up,
it withered away,
because it lacked moisture.

7 **And some** fell among thorns;
and the thorns sprang up with it,
and choked it.

8 **And other** fell on good ground,
and sprang up,
and bare fruit an hundredfold.

And when he had said these things,
he cried,
He that hath ears to hear, let him hear.

9 **And his disciples** asked him,
saying,
What might this parable be?

10 **And he** said,
Unto you it is given to know the mysteries of the kingdom of God:
but to others in parables;
that seeing
they might not see,
and hearing
they might not understand.

11 **Now the parable** is this:
The seed is the word of God.

12 **Those by the way side** are they that hear;
then cometh the devil,
and taketh away the word out of their hearts,
lest they should believe and be saved.

13 **They on the rock** are they,
which, {when they hear}, receive the word with joy;
and these have no root,
which for a while believe,
and in time of temptation fall away.

14 **And that which fell among thorns** are they,
which, {when they have heard}, go forth,
and are choked with cares and riches and pleasures of this life,
and bring no fruit to perfection.

15 **But that on the good ground** are they,
which in an honest and good heart, {having heard the word}, keep it,
and bring forth fruit with patience.

16 **No man**, {when he hath lighted a candle}, covereth it with a vessel,
or putteth it under a bed;
but setteth it on a candlestick,
that they which enter in may see the light.

17 **For nothing** is secret,
that shall not be made manifest;

neither any thing hid,
that shall not be known and come abroad.
18 **Take heed** therefore how ye hear:
for whosoever hath,
to him shall be given;
and whosoever hath not,
from him shall be taken even that which he seemeth to have.
19 **Then** came to him his mother and his brethren,
and could not come at him for the press.
20 **And it** was told him by certain which said,
Thy mother and thy brethren stand without,
desiring to see thee.
21 **And he** answered and said unto them,
My mother and my brethren are these which hear the word of God,
and do it.
22 **Now it** came to pass on a certain day,
that he went into a ship with his disciples:
and he said unto them,
Let us go over unto the other side of the lake.
And they launched forth.
23 **But as they** sailed
he fell asleep:
and there came down a storm of wind on the lake;
and they were filled with water,
and were in jeopardy.
24 **And they** came to him,
and awoke him,
saying,
Master, master, we perish.
Then he arose,
and rebuked the wind and the raging of the water:
and they ceased,
and there was a calm.
25 **And he** said unto them,
Where is your faith?
And they being afraid wondered,
saying one to another,
What manner of man is this!
for he commandeth even the winds and water,
and they obey him.
26 **And they** arrived at the country of the Gadarenes,
which is over against Galilee.
27 **And when he** went forth to land,
there met him out of the city a certain man,
which had devils long time,
and ware no clothes,
neither abode in any house, but in the tombs.
28 **When he** saw Jesus,
he cried out,
and fell down before him,
and with a loud voice said,
What have I to do with thee, Jesus, thou Son of God most high?
I beseech thee,
torment me not.
29 (**For he** had commanded the unclean spirit to come out of the man.
For oftentimes it had caught him:
and he was kept bound with chains and in fetters;
and he brake the bands,
and was driven of the devil into the wilderness.)
30 **And Jesus** asked him,
saying,
What is thy name?
And he said,
Legion:
because many devils were entered into him.
31 **And they** besought him
that he would not command them to go out into the deep.
32 **And there** was there an herd of many swine feeding on the mountain:
and they besought him
that he would suffer them to enter into them.
And he suffered them.
33 **Then** went the devils out of the man,
and entered into the swine:
and the herd ran violently down a steep place into the lake,
and were choked.
34 **When they that fed them** saw what was done,
they fled,
and went and told it in the city and in the country.
35 **Then they** went out to see what was done;
and came to Jesus,
and found the man,
out of whom the devils were departed,
sitting at the feet of Jesus,
clothed,
and in his right mind:
and they were afraid.
36 **They also which saw it** told them
by what means he that was possessed of the devils was healed.
37 **Then the whole multitude of the country of the Gadarenes round about** besought him to depart from them;
for they were taken with great fear:
and he went up into the ship,
and returned back again.
38 **Now the man out of whom the devils were departed** besought him
that he might be with him:
but Jesus sent him away,
saying,
39 **Return** to thine own house,
and shew how great things God hath done unto thee.
And he went his way,
and published throughout the whole city
how great things Jesus had done unto him.
40 **And it** came to pass,
that, {when Jesus was returned}, the people gladly received him:
for they were all waiting for him.
41 **And, {behold}, there** came a man named Jairus,
and he was a ruler of the synagogue:
and he fell down at Jesus' feet,
and besought him
that he would come into his house:
42 **For he** had one only daughter, about twelve years of age,
and she lay a dying.
But as he went
the people thronged him.
43 **And a woman having an issue of blood twelve years**, {which had spent all her living upon physicians}, {neither could be healed of any},
44 Came behind him,
and touched the border of his garment:
and immediately her issue of blood stanched.
45 **And Jesus** said,
Who touched me?
When all denied,
Peter and they that were with him said,

Master, the multitude throng thee and press thee,
and sayest thou,
Who touched me?

46 **And Jesus** said,
Somebody hath touched me:
for I perceive that virtue is gone out of me.

47 **And when the woman** saw that she was not hid,
she came trembling,
and falling down before him,
she declared unto him before all the people
for what cause she had touched him,
and how she was healed immediately.

48 **And he** said unto her,
Daughter, be of good comfort:
thy faith hath made thee whole;
go in peace.

49 **While he** yet spake,
there cometh one from the ruler of the synagogue's house,
saying to him,
Thy daughter is dead;
trouble not the Master.

50 **But when Jesus** heard it,
he answered him,
saying,
Fear not:
believe only,
and she shall be made whole.

51 **And when he** came into the house,
he suffered no man to go in, save Peter, and James, and John, and the father and the mother of the maiden.

52 **And all** wept,
and bewailed her:
but he said,
Weep not;
she is not dead,
but sleepeth.

53 **And they** laughed him to scorn,
knowing
that she was dead.

54 **And he** put them all out,
and took her by the hand,
and called,
saying,
Maid, arise.

55 **And her spirit** came again,
and she arose straightway:
and he commanded to give her meat.

56 **And her parents** were astonished:
but he charged them
that they should tell no man
what was done.

9

Then he called his twelve disciples together,
and gave them power and authority over all devils,
and to cure diseases.

2 **And he** sent them to preach the kingdom of God,
and to heal the sick.

3 **And he** said unto them,
Take nothing for your journey, neither staves, nor scrip, neither bread, neither money;
neither have two coats apiece.

4 **And whatsoever house** ye enter into,
there abide,
and thence depart.

5 **And whosoever** will not receive you,
when ye go out of that city,
shake off the very dust from your feet for a testimony against them.

6 **And they** departed,
and went through the towns,
preaching the gospel,
and healing every where.

7 **Now Herod the tetrarch** heard of all that was done by him:
and he was perplexed,
because that it was said of some, that John was risen from the dead;

8 **And of some,** that Elias had appeared;
and of others, that one of the old prophets was risen again.

9 **And Herod** said,
John have I beheaded:
but who is this,
of whom I hear such things?

And he desired to see him.

10 **And the apostles,** {when they were returned}, told him all that they had done.

And he took them,
and went aside privately into a desert place belonging to the city called Bethsaida.

11 **And the people,** {when they knew it}, followed him:
and he received them,
and spake unto them of the kingdom of God,
and healed them that had need of healing.

12 **And when the day** began to wear away,
then came the twelve,
and said unto him,
Send the multitude away,
that they may go into the towns and country round about,
and lodge,
and get victuals:
for we are here in a desert place.

13 **But he** said unto them,
Give ye them to eat.

And they said,
We have no more but five loaves and two fishes;
except we should go and buy meat for all this people.

14 **For they** were about five thousand men.

And he said to his disciples,
Make them sit down by fifties in a company.

15 **And they** did so,
and made them all sit down.

16 **Then he** took the five loaves and the two fishes,
and looking up to heaven,
he blessed them,
and brake,
and gave to the disciples to set before the multitude.

17 **And they** did eat,
and were all filled:
and there was taken up of fragments that remained to them twelve baskets.

18 **And it** came to pass,
as he was alone praying,
his disciples were with him:
and he asked them,
saying,
Whom say the people
that I am?

19 **They answering** said,
John the Baptist;
but some say,
Elias;
and others say,
that one of the old prophets is risen again.

20 **He** said unto them,
But whom say ye
that I am?

Peter answering said,
The Christ of God.

21 **And he** straitly charged them,
and commanded them to tell no man that thing;

22 Saying,

The Son of man must suffer many things,
and be rejected of the elders and chief priests and scribes,
and be slain,
and be raised the third day.
23 **And he** said to them all,
If any man will come after me,
let him deny himself,
and take up his cross daily,
and follow me.
24 **For whosoever will save his life** shall lose it:
but whosoever will lose his life for my sake,
the same shall save it.
25 **For what** is a man advantaged,
if he gain the whole world,
and lose himself,
or be cast away?
26 **For whosoever** shall be ashamed of me and of my words,
of him shall the Son of man be ashamed,
when he shall come in his own glory, and in his Father's, and of the holy angels.
27 **But I** tell you of a truth,
there be some standing here,
which shall not taste of death,
till they see the kingdom of God.
28 **And it** came to pass about an eight days after these sayings,
he took Peter and John and James,
and went up into a mountain to pray.
29 **And as he** prayed,
the fashion of his countenance was altered,
and his raiment was white and glistering.
30 **And, {behold}, there** talked with him two men,
which were Moses and Elias:
31 **Who** appeared in glory,
and spake of his decease which he should accomplish at Jerusalem.
32 **But Peter and they that were with him** were heavy with sleep:
and when they were awake,
they saw his glory, and the two men that stood with him.
33 **And it** came to pass,
as they departed from him,
Peter said unto Jesus,
Master, it is good for us to be here:
and let us make three tabernacles; one for thee, and one for Moses, and one for Elias:
not knowing
what he said.
34 **While he** thus spake,
there came a cloud,
and overshadowed them:
and they feared
as they entered into the cloud.
35 **And there** came a voice out of the cloud,
saying,
This is my beloved Son:
hear him.
36 **And when the voice** was past,
Jesus was found alone.
And they kept it close,
and told no man in those days any of those things which they had seen.
37 **And it** came to pass,
that on the next day, {when they were come down from the hill},
much people met him.
38 **And, {behold}, a man of the company** cried out,
saying,
Master, I beseech thee,
look upon my son:
for he is mine only child.
39 **And, {lo}, a spirit** taketh him,
and he suddenly crieth out;
and it teareth him
that he foameth again,
and bruising him hardly departeth from him.
40 **And I** besought thy disciples to cast him out;
and they could not.
41 **And Jesus answering** said,
O faithless and perverse generation, how long shall I be with you,
and suffer you?
Bring thy son hither.
42 **And as he** was yet a coming,
the devil threw him down,
and tare him.
And Jesus rebuked the unclean spirit,
and healed the child,
and delivered him again to his father.
43 **And they** were all amazed at the mighty power of God.
But while they wondered every one at all things which Jesus did,
he said unto his disciples,
44 **Let these sayings** sink down into your ears:
for the Son of man shall be delivered into the hands of men.
45 **But they** understood not this saying,
and it was hid from them,
that they perceived it not:
and they feared to ask him of that saying.
46 **Then there** arose a reasoning among them,
which of them should be greatest.
47 **And Jesus**, {perceiving the thought of their heart}, took a child,
and set him by him,
48 **And** said unto them,
Whosoever shall receive this child in my name receiveth me:
and whosoever shall receive me receiveth him that sent me:
for he that is least among you all, the same shall be great.
49 **And John** answered and said,
Master, we saw one casting out devils in thy name;
and we forbad him,
because he followeth not with us.
50 **And Jesus** said unto him,
Forbid him not:
for he that is not against us is for us.
51 **And it** came to pass,
when the time was come that he should be received up,
he stedfastly set his face to go to Jerusalem,
52 **And** sent messengers before his face:
and they went,
and entered into a village of the Samaritans,
to make ready for him.
53 **And they** did not receive him,
because his face was as though he would go to Jerusalem.
54 **And when his disciples James and John** saw this,
they said,
Lord, wilt thou
that we command fire to come down from heaven,
and consume them,
even as Elias did?
55 **But he** turned,
and rebuked them,
and said,
Ye know not
what manner of spirit ye are of.
56 **For the Son of man** is not come to destroy men's lives,

but to save them.

And they went to another village.

57 **And it** came to pass,
that, {as they went in the way}, a certain man said unto him,
Lord, I will follow thee
whithersoever thou goest.

58 **And Jesus** said unto him,
Foxes have holes,
and birds of the air have nests;
but the Son of man hath not where to lay his head.

59 **And he** said unto another,
Follow me.

But he said,
Lord, suffer me first to go and bury my father.

60 **Jesus** said unto him,
Let the dead bury their dead:
but go thou and preach the kingdom of God.

61 **And another** also said,
Lord, I will follow thee;
but let me first go bid them farewell,
which are at home at my house.

62 **And Jesus** said unto him,
No man, {having put his hand to the plough}, {and looking back},
is fit for the kingdom of God.

10

After these things the Lord appointed other seventy also,
and sent them two and two before his face into every city and place,
whither he himself would come.

2 **Therefore** said he unto them,
The harvest truly is great,
but the labourers are few:
pray ye therefore the Lord of the harvest,
that he would send forth labourers into his harvest.

3 **Go** your ways:
behold,
I send you forth as lambs among wolves.

4 **Carry** neither purse, nor scrip, nor shoes:
and salute no man by the way.

5 **And into whatsoever house** ye enter,
first say,
Peace be to this house.

6 **And if the son of peace** be there,
your peace shall rest upon it:
if not, it shall turn to you again.

7 **And in the same house** remain,
eating and drinking such things as they give:
for the labourer is worthy of his hire.

Go not from house to house.

8 **And into whatsoever city** ye enter,
and they receive you,
eat such things as are set before you:

9 **And heal** the sick that are therein,
and say unto them,
The kingdom of God is come nigh unto you.

10 **But into whatsoever city** ye enter,
and they receive you not,
go your ways out into the streets of the same,
and say,

11 **Even the very dust of your city,** {which cleaveth on us}, we do wipe off against you:
notwithstanding be ye sure of this,
that the kingdom of God is come nigh unto you.

12 **But I** say unto you,
that it shall be more tolerable in that day for Sodom, than for that city.

13 **Woe** unto thee, Chorazin!
woe unto thee, Bethsaida!
for if the mighty works had been done in Tyre and Sidon,
which have been done in you,
they had a great while ago repented,
sitting in sackcloth and ashes.

14 **But** it shall be more tolerable for Tyre and Sidon at the judgment, than for you.

15 **And thou, Capernaum,** {which art exalted to heaven}, shalt be thrust down to hell.

16 **He that heareth you** heareth me;
and he that despiseth you despiseth me;
and he that despiseth me despiseth him that sent me.

17 **And the seventy** returned again with joy,
saying,
Lord, even the devils are subject unto us through thy name.

18 **And he** said unto them,
I beheld Satan as lightning fall from heaven.

19 **Behold,**
I give unto you power to tread on serpents and scorpions, and over all the power of the enemy:
and nothing shall by any means hurt you.

20 **Notwithstanding in this** rejoice not,
that the spirits are subject unto you;
but rather rejoice,
because your names are written in heaven.

21 **In that hour** Jesus rejoiced in spirit,
and said,
I thank thee, O Father, Lord of heaven and earth,
that thou hast hid these things from the wise and prudent,
and hast revealed them unto babes: even so, Father;
for so it seemed good in thy sight.

22 **All things** are delivered to me of my Father:
and no man knoweth
who the Son is, but the Father;
and who the Father is, but the Son, and he to whom the Son will reveal him.

23 **And he** turned him unto his disciples,
and said privately,
Blessed are the eyes which see the things that ye see:

24 **For I** tell you,
that many prophets and kings have desired to see those things which ye see,
and have not seen them;
and to hear those things which ye hear,
and have not heard them.

25 **And, {behold}, a certain lawyer** stood up,
and tempted him,
saying,
Master, what shall I do to inherit eternal life?

26 **He** said unto him,
What is written in the law?
how readest thou?

27 **And he answering** said,
Thou shalt love the Lord thy God with all thy heart, and with all thy soul, and with all thy strength, and with all thy mind; and thy neighbour as thyself.

28 **And he** said unto him,
Thou hast answered right:
this do,
and thou shalt live.

29 **But he**, {willing to justify himself}, said unto Jesus,
And who is my neighbour?

30 **And Jesus answering** said,
A certain man went down from Jerusalem to Jericho,
and fell among thieves,
which stripped him of his raiment,
and wounded him,
and departed,
leaving him half dead.

31 **And by chance** there came down a certain priest that way:
and when he saw him,
he passed by on the other side.

32 **And likewise a Levite**, {when he was at the place}, came and looked on him,
and passed by on the other side.

33 **But a certain Samaritan**, {as he journeyed}, came where he was:
and when he saw him,
he had compassion on him,
34 **And** went to him,
and bound up his wounds,
pouring in oil and wine,
and set him on his own beast,
and brought him to an inn,
and took care of him.

35 **And on the morrow** {when he departed}, he took out two pence,
and gave them to the host,
and said unto him,
Take care of him;
and whatsoever thou spendest more,
when I come again,
I will repay thee.

36 **Which now of these three**, {thinkest thou}, was neighbour unto him that fell among the thieves?

37 **And he** said,
He that shewed mercy on him.

Then said Jesus unto him,
Go,
and do thou likewise.

38 **Now it** came to pass,
as they went,
that he entered into a certain village:
and a certain woman named Martha received him into her house.

39 **And she** had a sister called Mary,
which also sat at Jesus' feet,
and heard his word.

40 **But Martha** was cumbered about much serving,
and came to him,
and said,
Lord, dost thou not care that my sister hath left me to serve alone?
bid her therefore
that she help me.

41 **And Jesus** answered and said unto her,
Martha, Martha, thou art careful and troubled about many things:
42 **But one thing** is needful:
and Mary hath chosen that good part,
which shall not be taken away from her.

11 **And it** came to pass,
that, {as he was praying in a certain place}, {when he ceased}, one of his disciples said unto him,
Lord, teach us to pray,
as John also taught his disciples.

2 **And he** said unto them,
When ye pray,
say,
Our Father which art in heaven, Hallowed be thy name.

Thy kingdom come.

Thy will be done, as in heaven, so in earth.

3 **Give** us day by day our daily bread.

4 **And forgive** us our sins;
for we also forgive every one that is indebted to us.

And lead us not into temptation;
but deliver us from evil.

5 **And he** said unto them,
Which of you shall have a friend,
and shall go unto him at midnight,
and say unto him,
Friend, lend me three loaves;
6 **For a friend of mine in his journey** is come to me,
and I have nothing to set before him?

7 **And he from within** shall answer and say,
Trouble me not:
the door is now shut,
and my children are with me in bed;
I cannot rise and give thee.

8 **I** say unto you,
Though he will not rise and give him,
because he is his friend,
yet because of his importunity he will rise and give him as many as he needeth.

9 **And I** say unto you,
Ask,
and it shall be given you;
seek,
and ye shall find;
knock,
and it shall be opened unto you.

10 **For every one that asketh** receiveth;
and he that seeketh findeth;
and to him that knocketh it shall be opened.

11 **If a son** shall ask bread of any of you that is a father,
will he give him a stone?
or if he ask a fish,
will he for a fish give him a serpent?

12 **Or if he** shall ask an egg,
will he offer him a scorpion?

13 **If ye** then, {being evil}, know
how to give good gifts unto your children:
how much more shall your heavenly Father give the Holy Spirit to them that ask him?

14 **And he** was casting out a devil,
and it was dumb.

And it came to pass,
when the devil was gone out,
the dumb spake;
and the people wondered.

15 **But some of them** said,
He casteth out devils through Beelzebub the chief of the devils.

16 **And others**, {tempting him}, sought of him a sign from heaven.

17 **But he**, {knowing their thoughts}, said unto them,
Every kingdom divided against itself is brought to desolation;
and a house divided against a house falleth.

18 **If Satan** also be divided against himself,
how shall his kingdom stand?
because ye say
that I cast out devils through Beelzebub.

19 **And if I by Beelzebub** cast out devils,
by whom do your sons cast them out?
therefore shall they be your judges.

20 **But if I with the finger of God** cast out devils,
no doubt the kingdom of God is come upon you.

21 **When a strong man armed** keepeth his palace,

his goods are in peace:
22 **But when a stronger than he** shall come upon him,
and overcome him,
he taketh from him all his armour wherein he trusted,
and divideth his spoils.
23 **He that is not with me** is against me:
and he that gathereth not with me scattereth.
24 **When the unclean spirit** is gone out of a man,
he walketh through dry places,
seeking rest;
and finding none,
he saith,
I will return unto my house whence I came out.
25 **And when he** cometh,
he findeth it swept and garnished.
26 **Then** goeth he,
and taketh to him seven other spirits more wicked than himself;
and they enter in,
and dwell there:
and the last state of that man is worse than the first.
27 **And it** came to pass,
as he spake these things,
a certain woman of the company lifted up her voice,
and said unto him,
Blessed is the womb that bare thee,
and the paps which thou hast sucked.
28 **But he** said,
Yea rather, blessed are they that hear the word of God,
and keep it.
29 **And when the people** were gathered thick together,
he began to say,
This is an evil generation:
they seek a sign;
and there shall no sign be given it, but the sign of Jonas the prophet.
30 **For as Jonas** was a sign unto the Ninevites,
so shall also the Son of man be to this generation.
31 **The queen of the south** shall rise up in the judgment with the men of this generation,
and condemn them:
for she came from the utmost parts of the earth to hear the wisdom of Solomon;
and, {behold}, a greater than Solomon is here.
32 **The men of Nineve** shall rise up in the judgment with this generation,
and shall condemn it:
for they repented at the preaching of Jonas;
and, {behold}, a greater than Jonas is here.
33 **No man**, {when he hath lighted a candle}, putteth it in a secret place, neither under a bushel, but on a candlestick,
that they which come in may see the light.
34 **The light of the body** is the eye:
therefore when thine eye is single,
thy whole body also is full of light;
but when thine eye is evil,
thy body also is full of darkness.
35 **Take heed** therefore that the light which is in thee be not darkness.
36 **If thy whole body** therefore be full of light,
having no part dark,
the whole shall be full of light,
as when the bright shining of a candle doth give thee light.
37 **And as he** spake,
a certain Pharisee besought him to dine with him:
and he went in,
and sat down to meat.
38 **And when the Pharisee** saw it,
he marvelled that he had not first washed before dinner.
39 **And the Lord** said unto him,
Now do ye Pharisees make clean the outside of the cup and the platter;
but your inward part is full of ravening and wickedness.
40 **Ye fools, did not he that made that which is without** make that which is within also?
41 **But rather give** alms of such things
as ye have;
and, {behold}, all things are clean unto you.
42 **But woe** unto you, Pharisees!
for ye tithe mint and rue and all manner of herbs,
and pass over judgment and the love of God:
these ought ye to have done,
and not to leave the other undone.
43 **Woe** unto you, Pharisees!
for ye love the uppermost seats in the synagogues, and greetings in the markets.
44 **Woe** unto you, scribes and Pharisees, hypocrites!
for ye are as graves which appear not,
and the men that walk over them are not aware of them.
45 **Then** answered one of the lawyers,
and said unto him,
Master, thus saying
thou reproachest us also.
46 **And he** said,
Woe unto you also, ye lawyers!
for ye lade men with burdens grievous to be borne,
and ye yourselves touch not the burdens with one of your fingers.
47 **Woe** unto you!
for ye build the sepulchres of the prophets,
and your fathers killed them.
48 **Truly ye** bear witness that ye allow the deeds of your fathers:
for they indeed killed them,
and ye build their sepulchres.
49 **Therefore also** said the wisdom of God,
I will send them prophets and apostles,
and some of them they shall slay and persecute:
50 **That the blood of all the prophets**, {which was shed from the foundation of the world}, may be required of this generation;
51 From the blood of Abel unto the blood of Zacharias which perished between the altar and the temple:
verily I say unto you,
It shall be required of this generation.
52 **Woe** unto you, lawyers!
for ye have taken away the key of knowledge:
ye entered not in yourselves,
and them that were entering in ye hindered.
53 **And as he** said these things unto them,
the scribes and the Pharisees began to urge him vehemently,
and to provoke him to speak of many things:
54 Laying wait for him,
and seeking to catch something out of his mouth,
that they might accuse him.

12 **In the mean time, {when there were gathered together an innumerable multitude of people}**, {insomuch that they trode one upon another}, he began to say unto his disciples first of all,
Beware ye of the leaven of the Pharisees,
which is hypocrisy.
2 **For there** is nothing covered,
that shall not be revealed;
neither hid,
that shall not be known.
3 **Therefore whatsoever ye have spoken in darkness** shall be heard in the light;
and that which ye have spoken in the ear in closets shall be proclaimed upon the housetops.
4 **And I** say unto you my friends,
Be not afraid of them that kill the body,
and after that have no more that they can do.
5 **But I** will forewarn you
whom ye shall fear:
Fear him,
which after he hath killed hath power to cast into hell;
yea, I say unto you,
Fear him.
6 **Are not five sparrows** sold for two farthings,
and not one of them is forgotten before God?
7 **But even the very hairs of your head** are all numbered.
Fear not therefore:
ye are of more value than many sparrows.
8 **Also I** say unto you,
Whosoever shall confess me before men,
him shall the Son of man also confess before the angels of God:
9 **But he that denieth me before men** shall be denied before the angels of God.
10 **And whosoever** shall speak a word against the Son of man,
it shall be forgiven him:
but unto him that blasphemeth against the Holy Ghost it shall not be forgiven.
11 **And when they** bring you unto the synagogues, and unto magistrates, and powers,
take ye no thought
how or what thing ye shall answer,
or what ye shall say:
12 **For the Holy Ghost** shall teach you in the same hour what ye ought to say.
13 **And one of the company** said unto him,
Master, speak to my brother,
that he divide the inheritance with me.
14 **And he** said unto him,
Man, who made me a judge or a divider over you?
15 **And he** said unto them,
Take heed,
and beware of covetousness:
for a man's life consisteth not in the abundance of the things which he possesseth.
16 **And he** spake a parable unto them,
saying,
The ground of a certain rich man brought forth plentifully:
17 **And he** thought within himself,
saying,
What shall I do,
because I have no room where to bestow my fruits?
18 **And he** said,
This will I do:
I will pull down my barns,
and build greater;
and there will I bestow all my fruits and my goods.
19 **And I** will say to my soul,
Soul, thou hast much goods laid up for many years;
take thine ease,
eat,
drink,
and be merry.
20 **But God** said unto him,
Thou fool, this night thy soul shall be required of thee:
then whose shall those things be,
which thou hast provided?
21 **So** is he that layeth up treasure for himself,
and is not rich toward God.
22 **And he** said unto his disciples,
Therefore I say unto you,
Take no thought for your life,
what ye shall eat; neither for the body,
what ye shall put on.
23 **The life** is more than meat,
and the body is more than raiment.
24 **Consider** the ravens:
for they neither sow nor reap;
which neither have storehouse nor barn;
and God feedeth them:
how much more are ye better than the fowls?
25 **And which of you with taking thought** can add to his stature one cubit?
26 **If ye** then be not able to do that thing which is least,
why take ye thought for the rest?
27 **Consider** the lilies
how they grow:
they toil not,
they spin not;
and yet I say unto you,
that Solomon in all his glory was not arrayed like one of these.
28 **If then God** so clothe the grass,
which is to day in the field,
and to morrow is cast into the oven;
how much more will he clothe you, O ye of little faith?
29 **And seek not ye** what ye shall eat, or what ye shall drink,
neither be ye of doubtful mind.
30 **For all these things** do the nations of the world seek after:
and your Father knoweth
that ye have need of these things.
31 **But rather seek ye** the kingdom of God;
and all these things shall be added unto you.
32 **Fear not,** little flock;
for it is your Father's good pleasure to give you the kingdom.
33 **Sell** that ye have,
and give alms;
provide yourselves bags which wax not old, a treasure in the heavens that faileth not,
where no thief approacheth,
neither moth corrupteth.
34 **For where your treasure** is,
there will your heart be also.
35 **Let your loins** be girded about,
and your lights burning;
36 **And ye yourselves** like unto men that wait for their lord,
when he will return from the wedding;
that when he cometh and knocketh,
they may open unto him immediately.

37 **Blessed** are those servants,
whom the lord {when he cometh} shall find watching:
verily I say unto you,
that he shall gird himself,
and make them to sit down to meat,
and will come forth and serve them.

38 **And if he** shall come in the second watch,
or come in the third watch,
and find them so,
blessed are those servants.

39 **And this** know,
that if the goodman of the house had known
what hour the thief would come,
he would have watched,
and not have suffered his house to be broken through.

40 **Be ye** therefore ready also:
for the Son of man cometh at an hour when ye think not.

41 **Then Peter** said unto him,
Lord, speakest thou this parable unto us, or even to all?

42 **And the Lord** said,
Who then is that faithful and wise steward,
whom his lord shall make ruler over his household,
to give them their portion of meat in due season?

43 **Blessed** is that servant,
whom his lord {when he cometh} shall find so doing.

44 **Of a truth I** say unto you,
that he will make him ruler over all that he hath.

45 **But and if that servant** say in his heart,
My lord delayeth his coming;
and shall begin to beat the menservants and maidens,
and to eat
and drink,
and to be drunken;

46 **The lord of that servant** will come in a day when he looketh not for him, and at an hour when he is not aware,
and will cut him in sunder,
and will appoint him his portion with the unbelievers.

47 **And that servant**, {which knew his lord's will}, {and prepared not himself}, {neither did according to his will}, shall be beaten with many stripes.

48 **But he that knew not, and did commit things worthy of stripes,** shall be beaten with few stripes.
For unto whomsoever much is given,
of him shall be much required:
and to whom men have committed much,
of him they will ask the more.

49 **I** am come to send fire on the earth;
and what will I,
if it be already kindled?

50 **But I** have a baptism to be baptized with;
and how am I straitened
till it be accomplished!

51 **Suppose ye**
that I am come to give peace on earth?
I tell you,
Nay; but rather division:

52 **For from henceforth** there shall be five in one house divided, three against two, and two against three.

53 **The father** shall be divided against the son, and the son against the father; the mother against the daughter, and the daughter against the mother; the mother in law against her daughter in law, and the daughter in law against her mother in law.

54 **And he** said also to the people,
When ye see a cloud rise out of the west,
straightway ye say,
There cometh a shower;
and so it is.

55 **And when ye** see the south wind blow,
ye say,
There will be heat;
and it cometh to pass.

56 **Ye hypocrites, ye** can discern the face of the sky and of the earth;
but how is it that ye do not discern this time?

57 **Yea, and why even of yourselves** judge ye not
what is right?

58 **When thou** goest with thine adversary to the magistrate,
as thou art in the way,
give diligence
that thou mayest be delivered from him;
lest he hale thee to the judge,
and the judge deliver thee to the officer,
and the officer cast thee into prison.

59 **I** tell thee,
thou shalt not depart thence,
till thou hast paid the very last mite.

13 **There** were present at that season some that told him of the Galilaeans,
whose blood Pilate had mingled with their sacrifices.

2 **And Jesus answering** said unto them,
Suppose ye
that these Galilaeans were sinners above all the Galilaeans,
because they suffered such things?

3 **I** tell you,
Nay:
but, {except ye repent}, ye shall all likewise perish.

4 **Or those eighteen,** {upon whom the tower in Siloam fell}, {and slew them}, think ye
that they were sinners above all men that dwelt in Jerusalem?

5 **I** tell you,
Nay:
but, {except ye repent}, ye shall all likewise perish.

6 **He** spake also this parable;
A certain man had a fig tree planted in his vineyard;
and he came and sought fruit thereon,
and found none.

7 **Then** said he unto the dresser of his vineyard,
Behold,
these three years I come seeking fruit on this fig tree,
and find none:
cut it down;
why cumbereth it the ground?

8 **And he answering** said unto him,
Lord, let it alone this year also,
till I shall dig about it,
and dung it:

9 **And if it** bear fruit, well:
and if not, then after that thou shalt cut it down.

10 **And he** was teaching in one of the synagogues on the sabbath.

11 **And, {behold}, there** was a woman which had a spirit of infirmity eighteen years,
and was bowed together,

and could in no wise lift up herself.

12 **And when Jesus** saw her,
he called her to him,
and said unto her,
Woman, thou art loosed from thine infirmity.

13 **And he** laid his hands on her:
and immediately she was made straight,
and glorified God.

14 **And the ruler of the synagogue** answered with indignation,
because that Jesus had healed on the sabbath day,
and said unto the people,
There are six days in which men ought to work:
in them therefore come and be healed, and not on the sabbath day.

15 **The Lord** then answered him,
and said,
Thou hypocrite, doth not each one of you on the sabbath loose his ox or his ass from the stall,
and lead him away to watering?

16 **And ought not this woman,** {being a daughter of Abraham}, {whom Satan hath bound, {{lo}}, these eighteen years}, be loosed from this bond on the sabbath day?

17 **And when he** had said these things,
all his adversaries were ashamed:
and all the people rejoiced for all the glorious things that were done by him.

18 **Then** said he,
Unto what is the kingdom of God like?
and whereunto shall I resemble it?

19 **It** is like a grain of mustard seed,
which a man took,
and cast into his garden;
and it grew,
and waxed a great tree;
and the fowls of the air lodged in the branches of it.

20 **And again he** said,
Whereunto shall I liken the kingdom of God?

21 **It** is like leaven,
which a woman took and hid in three measures of meal,
till the whole was leavened.

22 **And he** went through the cities and villages,
teaching,
and journeying toward Jerusalem.

23 **Then** said one unto him,
Lord, are there few that be saved?
And he said unto them,

24 **Strive** to enter in at the strait gate:
for many, {I say unto you}, will seek to enter in,
and shall not be able.

25 **When once the master of the house** is risen up,
and hath shut to the door,
and ye begin to stand without,
and to knock at the door,
saying,
Lord, Lord, open unto us;
and he shall answer and say unto you,
I know you not
whence ye are:

26 **Then** shall ye begin to say,
We have eaten and drunk in thy presence,
and thou hast taught in our streets.

27 **But he** shall say,
I tell you,
I know you not
whence ye are;
depart from me, all ye workers of iniquity.

28 **There** shall be weeping and gnashing of teeth,
when ye shall see Abraham, and Isaac, and Jacob, and all the prophets, in the kingdom of God,
and you yourselves thrust out.

29 **And they** shall come from the east, and from the west, and from the north, and from the south,
and shall sit down in the kingdom of God.

30 **And, {behold}, there** are last which shall be first,
and there are first which shall be last.

31 **The same day** there came certain of the Pharisees,
saying unto him,
Get thee out,
and depart hence:
for Herod will kill thee.

32 **And he** said unto them,
Go ye,
and tell that fox,
Behold,
I cast out devils,
and I do cures to day and to morrow,
and the third day I shall be perfected.

33 **Nevertheless I** must walk to day, and to morrow, and the day following:
for it cannot be that a prophet perish out of Jerusalem.

34 **O Jerusalem, Jerusalem, which** killest the prophets,
and stonest them that are sent unto thee;
how often would I have gathered thy children together,
as a hen doth gather her brood under her wings,
and ye would not!

35 **Behold,**
your house is left unto you desolate:
and verily I say unto you,
Ye shall not see me,
until the time come when ye shall say,
Blessed is he that cometh in the name of the Lord.

14 ∞ **And it** came to pass,
as he went into the house of one of the chief Pharisees to eat bread on the sabbath day,
that they watched him.

2 **And, {behold}, there** was a certain man before him which had the dropsy.

3 **And Jesus answering** spake unto the lawyers and Pharisees,
saying,
Is it lawful to heal on the sabbath day?

4 **And they** held their peace.
And he took him,
and healed him,
and let him go;

5 **And** answered them,
saying,
Which of you shall have an ass or an ox fallen into a pit,
and will not straightway pull him out on the sabbath day?

6 **And they** could not answer him again to these things.

7 **And he** put forth a parable to those which were bidden,
when he marked how they chose out the chief rooms;
saying unto them.

8 **When thou** art bidden of any man to a wedding,
sit not down in the highest room;
lest a more honourable man than thou be bidden of him;

9 **And he that bade thee and him**

come and say to thee,
Give this man place;
and thou begin with shame to take the lowest room.

10 **But when thou** art bidden,
go and sit down in the lowest room;
that when he that bade thee cometh,
he may say unto thee,
Friend, go up higher:
then shalt thou have worship in the presence of them that sit at meat with thee.

11 **For whosoever exalteth himself** shall be abased;
and he that humbleth himself shall be exalted.

12 **Then** said he also to him that bade him,
When thou makest a dinner or a supper,
call not thy friends, nor thy brethren, neither thy kinsmen, nor thy rich neighbours;
lest they also bid thee again,
and a recompence be made thee.

13 **But when thou** makest a feast,
call the poor, the maimed, the lame, the blind:

14 **And thou** shalt be blessed;
for they cannot recompense thee:
for thou shalt be recompensed at the resurrection of the just.

15 **And when one of them that sat at meat with him** heard these things,
he said unto him,
Blessed is he that shall eat bread in the kingdom of God.

16 **Then** said he unto him,
A certain man made a great supper,
and bade many:

17 **And** sent his servant at supper time to say to them that were bidden,
Come;
for all things are now ready.

18 **And they all with one consent** began to make excuse.

The first said unto him,
I have bought a piece of ground,
and I must needs go and see it:
I pray thee
have me excused.

19 **And another** said,
I have bought five yoke of oxen,
and I go to prove them:
I pray thee
have me excused.

20 **And another** said,
I have married a wife,
and therefore I cannot come.

21 **So that servant** came,
and shewed his lord these things.

Then the master of the house being angry said to his servant,
Go out quickly into the streets and lanes of the city,
and bring in hither the poor, and the maimed, and the halt, and the blind.

22 **And the servant** said,
Lord, it is done as thou hast commanded,
and yet there is room.

23 **And the lord** said unto the servant,
Go out into the highways and hedges,
and compel them to come in,
that my house may be filled.

24 **For I** say unto you,
That none of those men which were bidden shall taste of my supper.

25 **And there** went great multitudes with him:
and he turned,
and said unto them,

26 **If any man** come to me,
and hate not his father, and mother, and wife, and children, and brethren, and sisters, yea, and his own life also,
he cannot be my disciple.

27 **And whosoever doth not bear his cross**, {and come after me}, cannot be my disciple.

28 **For which of you**, {intending to build a tower}, sitteth not down first,
and counteth the cost,
whether he have sufficient to finish it?

29 **Lest haply, {after he hath laid the foundation}, {and is not able to finish it},** all that behold it begin to mock him,

30 Saying,
This man began to build,
and was not able to finish.

31 **Or what king**, {going to make war against another king}, sitteth not down first,
and consulteth
whether he be able with ten thousand to meet him that cometh against him with twenty thousand?

32 **Or else, {while the other is yet a great way off},** he sendeth an ambassage,
and desireth conditions of peace.

33 **So likewise, whosoever he be of you that forsaketh not all that he hath,** he cannot be my disciple.

34 **Salt** is good:
but if the salt have lost his savour,
wherewith shall it be seasoned?

35 **It** is neither fit for the land, nor yet for the dunghill;
but men cast it out.

He that hath ears to hear, let him hear.

15

Then drew near unto him all the publicans and sinners
for to hear him.

2 **And the Pharisees and scribes** murmured,
saying,
This man receiveth sinners,
and eateth with them.

3 **And he** spake this parable unto them,
saying,

4 **What man of you**, {having an hundred sheep}, {if he lose one of them}, doth not leave the ninety and nine in the wilderness,
and go after that which is lost,
until he find it?

5 **And when he** hath found it,
he layeth it on his shoulders,
rejoicing.

6 **And when he** cometh home,
he calleth together his friends and neighbours,
saying unto them,
Rejoice with me;
for I have found my sheep which was lost.

7 **I** say unto you,
that likewise joy shall be in heaven over one sinner that repenteth, more than over ninety and nine just persons,
which need no repentance.

8 **Either what woman having ten pieces of silver**, {if she lose one piece}, doth not light a candle,
and sweep the house,
and seek diligently
till she find it?

9 **And when she** hath found it,

she calleth her friends and her neighbours together,
saying,
Rejoice with me;
for I have found the piece which I had lost.
10 **Likewise, I** say unto you,
there is joy in the presence of the angels of God over one sinner that repenteth.
11 **And he** said,
A certain man had two sons:
12 **And the younger of them** said to his father,
Father, give me the portion of goods that falleth to me.
And he divided unto them his living.
13 **And not many days after** the younger son gathered all together,
and took his journey into a far country,
and there wasted his substance with riotous living.
14 **And when he** had spent all,
there arose a mighty famine in that land;
and he began to be in want.
15 **And he** went and joined himself to a citizen of that country;
and he sent him into his fields to feed swine.
16 **And he** would fain have filled his belly with the husks that the swine did eat:
and no man gave unto him.
17 **And when he** came to himself,
he said,
How many hired servants of my father's have bread enough and to spare,
and I perish with hunger!
18 **I** will arise and go to my father,
and will say unto him,
Father, I have sinned against heaven, and before thee,
19 **And** am no more worthy to be called thy son:
make me as one of thy hired servants.
20 **And he** arose,
and came to his father.
But when he was yet a great way off,
his father saw him,
and had compassion,
and ran,
and fell on his neck,
and kissed him.
21 **And the son** said unto him,
Father, I have sinned against heaven, and in thy sight,
and am no more worthy to be called thy son.
22 **But the father** said to his servants,
Bring forth the best robe,
and put it on him;
and put a ring on his hand, and shoes on his feet:
23 **And bring** hither the fatted calf,
and kill it;
and let us eat,
and be merry:
24 **For this my son** was dead,
and is alive again;
he was lost,
and is found.
And they began to be merry.
25 **Now his elder son** was in the field:
and as he came and drew nigh to the house,
he heard musick and dancing.
26 **And he** called one of the servants,
and asked
what these things meant.
27 **And he** said unto him,
Thy brother is come;
and thy father hath killed the fatted calf,
because he hath received him safe and sound.
28 **And he** was angry,
and would not go in:
therefore came his father out,
and intreated him.
29 **And he answering** said to his father,
Lo,
these many years do I serve thee,
neither transgressed I at any time thy commandment:
and yet thou never gavest me a kid,
that I might make merry with my friends:
30 **But as soon as this thy son** was come,
which hath devoured thy living with harlots,
thou hast killed for him the fatted calf.
31 **And he** said unto him,
Son, thou art ever with me,
and all that I have is thine.
32 **It was meet** that we should make merry,
and be glad:
for this thy brother was dead,
and is alive again;
and was lost,
and is found.

16 **And he** said also unto his disciples,
There was a certain rich man,
which had a steward;
and the same was accused unto him
that he had wasted his goods.
2 **And he** called him,
and said unto him,
How is it that I hear this of thee?
give an account of thy stewardship;
for thou mayest be no longer steward.
3 **Then the steward** said within himself,
What shall I do?
for my lord taketh away from me the stewardship:
I cannot dig;
to beg I am ashamed.
4 **I** am resolved
what to do,
that, {when I am put out of the stewardship}, they may receive me into their houses.
5 **So he** called every one of his lord's debtors unto him,
and said unto the first,
How much owest thou unto my lord?
6 **And he** said,
An hundred measures of oil.
And he said unto him,
Take thy bill,
and sit down quickly,
and write fifty.
7 **Then** said he to another,
And how much owest thou?
And he said,
An hundred measures of wheat.
And he said unto him,
Take thy bill,
and write fourscore.
8 **And the lord** commended the unjust steward,
because he had done wisely:
for the children of this world are in their generation wiser than the children of light.
9 **And I** say unto you,
Make to yourselves friends of the mammon of unrighteousness;
that, {when ye fail}, they may receive you into everlasting

habitations.

10 **He that is faithful in that which is least** is faithful also in much:
and he that is unjust in the least is unjust also in much.

11 **If therefore ye** have not been faithful in the unrighteous mammon,
who will commit to your trust the true riches?

12 **And if ye** have not been faithful in that which is another man's,
who shall give you that which is your own?

13 **No servant** can serve two masters:
for either he will hate the one,
and love the other;
or else he will hold to the one,
and despise the other.

Ye cannot serve God and mammon.

14 **And the Pharisees** also, {who were covetous}, heard all these things:
and they derided him.

15 **And he** said unto them,
Ye are they which justify yourselves before men;
but God knoweth your hearts:
for that which is highly esteemed among men is abomination in the sight of God.

16 **The law and the prophets** were until John:
since that time the kingdom of God is preached,
and every man presseth into it.

17 **And it is easier** for heaven and earth to pass, than one tittle of the law to fail.

18 **Whosoever putteth away his wife, {and marrieth another},** committeth adultery:
and whosoever marrieth her that is put away from her husband committeth adultery.

19 **There** was a certain rich man,
which was clothed in purple and fine linen,
and fared sumptuously every day:
20 **And there** was a certain beggar named Lazarus,
which was laid at his gate, full of sores,
21 **And** desiring to be fed with the crumbs which fell from the rich man's table:
moreover the dogs came and licked his sores.

22 **And it** came to pass,
that the beggar died,
and was carried by the angels into Abraham's bosom:
the rich man also died,
and was buried;
23 **And in hell** he lift up his eyes,
being in torments,
and seeth Abraham afar off, and Lazarus in his bosom.

24 **And he** cried and said,
Father Abraham, have mercy on me,
and send Lazarus,
that he may dip the tip of his finger in water,
and cool my tongue;
for I am tormented in this flame.

25 **But Abraham** said,
Son, remember
that thou in thy lifetime receivedst thy good things, and likewise Lazarus evil things:
but now he is comforted,
and thou art tormented.

26 **And beside all this,** between us and you there is a great gulf fixed:
so that they which would pass from hence to you cannot;
neither can they pass to us,
that would come from thence.

27 **Then he** said,
I pray thee therefore, father,
that thou wouldest send him to my father's house:
28 **For I** have five brethren;
that he may testify unto them,
lest they also come into this place of torment.

29 **Abraham** saith unto him,
They have Moses and the prophets;
let them hear them.

30 **And he** said,
Nay, father Abraham:
but if one went unto them from the dead,
they will repent.

31 **And he** said unto him,
If they hear not Moses and the prophets,
neither will they be persuaded,
though one rose from the dead.

17 **Then** said he unto the disciples,
It is impossible but that offences will come:
but woe unto him,
through whom they come!
2 **It were better for him** that a millstone were hanged about his neck,
and he cast into the sea,
than that he should offend one of these little ones.

3 **Take heed** to yourselves:
If thy brother trespass against thee,
rebuke him;
and if he repent,
forgive him.

4 **And if he** trespass against thee seven times in a day,
and seven times in a day turn again to thee,
saying,
I repent;
thou shalt forgive him.

5 **And the apostles** said unto the Lord,
Increase our faith.

6 **And the Lord** said,
If ye had faith as a grain of mustard seed,
ye might say unto this sycamine tree,
Be thou plucked up by the root,
and be thou planted in the sea;
and it should obey you.

7 **But which of you**, {having a servant plowing or feeding cattle}, will say unto him by and by,
when he is come from the field,
Go and sit down to meat?

8 **And** will not rather say unto him,
Make ready wherewith I may sup,
and gird thyself,
and serve me,
till I have eaten and drunken;
and afterward thou shalt eat and drink?

9 **Doth he** thank that servant
because he did the things that were commanded him?

I trow not.

10 **So likewise ye**, {when ye shall have done all those things which are commanded you}, say,
We are unprofitable servants:
we have done that which was our duty to do.

11 **And it** came to pass,
as he went to Jerusalem,
that he passed through the midst of Samaria and Galilee.

12 **And as he** entered into a certain village,
there met him ten men that were

lepers,
which stood afar off:
13 **And they** lifted up their voices,
and said,
Jesus, Master, have mercy on us.
14 **And when he** saw them,
he said unto them,
Go shew yourselves unto the priests.
And it came to pass,
that, {as they went}, they were cleansed.
15 **And one of them**, {when he saw that he was healed}, turned back,
and with a loud voice glorified God,
16 **And** fell down on his face at his feet,
giving him thanks:
and he was a Samaritan.
17 **And Jesus answering** said,
Were there not ten cleansed?
but where are the nine?
18 **There** are not found that returned to give glory to God, save this stranger.
19 **And he** said unto him,
Arise,
go thy way:
thy faith hath made thee whole.
20 **And when he** was demanded of the Pharisees,
when the kingdom of God should come,
he answered them and said,
The kingdom of God cometh not with observation:
21 **Neither** shall they say,
Lo here!
or, lo there!
for, {behold}, the kingdom of God is within you.
22 **And he** said unto the disciples,
The days will come,
when ye shall desire to see one of the days of the Son of man,
and ye shall not see it.
23 **And they** shall say to you,
See here;
or, see there:
go not after them,
nor follow them.
24 **For as the lightning**, {that lighteneth out of the one part under heaven}, shineth unto the other part under heaven;
so shall also the Son of man be in his day.
25 **But first** must he suffer many things,
and be rejected of this generation.
26 **And as it** was in the days of Noe,
so shall it be also in the days of the Son of man.
27 **They** did eat,
they drank,
they married wives,
they were given in marriage, until the day that Noah entered into the ark,
and the flood came,
and destroyed them all.
28 **Likewise also as it** was in the days of Lot;
they did eat,
they drank,
they bought,
they sold,
they planted,
they builded;
29 **But the same day that Lot went out of Sodom** it rained fire and brimstone from heaven,
and destroyed them all.
30 **Even thus** shall it be in the day when the Son of man is revealed.
31 **In that day,** he which shall be upon the housetop, and his stuff in the house, let him not come down to take it away:
and he that is in the field, let him likewise not return back.
32 **Remember** Lot's wife.
33 **Whosoever shall seek to save his life** shall lose it;
and whosoever shall lose his life shall preserve it.
34 **I** tell you,
in that night there shall be two men in one bed;
the one shall be taken,
and the other shall be left.
35 **Two women** shall be grinding together;
the one shall be taken,
and the other left.
36 **Two men** shall be in the field;
the one shall be taken,
and the other left.
37 **And they** answered and said unto him,
Where, Lord?
And he said unto them,
Wheresoever the body is,
thither will the eagles be gathered together.

18 **And he** spake a parable unto them to this end,
that men ought always to pray,
and not to faint;
2 Saying,
There was in a city a judge,
which feared not God,
neither regarded man:
3 **And there** was a widow in that city;
and she came unto him,
saying,
Avenge me of mine adversary.
4 **And he** would not for a while:
but afterward he said within himself,
Though I fear not God,
nor regard man;
5 **Yet because this widow** troubleth me,
I will avenge her,
lest by her continual coming she weary me.
6 **And the Lord** said,
Hear what the unjust judge saith.
7 **And** shall not God avenge his own elect,
which cry day and night unto him,
though he bear long with them?
8 **I** tell you
that he will avenge them speedily.
Nevertheless when the Son of man cometh,
shall he find faith on the earth?
9 **And he** spake this parable unto certain which trusted in themselves
that they were righteous,
and despised others:
10 **Two men** went up into the temple to pray; the one a Pharisee, and the other a publican.
11 **The Pharisee** stood and prayed thus with himself,
God, I thank thee,
that I am not as other men are, extortioners, unjust, adulterers, or even as this publican.
12 **I** fast twice in the week,
I give tithes of all that I possess.
13 **And the publican**, {standing afar off}, would not lift up so much as his eyes unto heaven,
but smote upon his breast,
saying,
God be merciful to me a sinner.
14 **I** tell you,
this man went down to his house

justified rather than the other:
for every one that exalteth himself shall be abased;
and he that humbleth himself shall be exalted.
15 **And they** brought unto him also infants,
that he would touch them:
but when his disciples saw it,
they rebuked them.
16 **But Jesus** called them unto him,
and said,
Suffer little children to come unto me,
and forbid them not:
for of such is the kingdom of God.
17 **Verily I** say unto you,
Whosoever shall not receive the kingdom of God as a little child shall in no wise enter therein.
18 **And a certain ruler** asked him,
saying,
Good Master, what shall I do to inherit eternal life?
19 **And Jesus** said unto him,
Why callest thou me good?
none is good, save one, that is, God.
20 **Thou** knowest the commandments,
Do not commit adultery,
Do not kill,
Do not steal,
Do not bear false witness,
Honour thy father and thy mother.
21 **And he** said,
All these have I kept from my youth up.
22 **Now when Jesus** heard these things,
he said unto him,
Yet lackest thou one thing:
sell all that thou hast,
and distribute unto the poor,
and thou shalt have treasure in heaven:
and come,
follow me.
23 **And when he** heard this,
he was very sorrowful:
for he was very rich.
24 **And when Jesus** saw that he was very sorrowful,
he said,
How hardly shall they that have riches enter into the kingdom of God!
25 **For it is easier** for a camel to go through a needle's eye, than for a rich man to enter into the kingdom of God.
26 **And they that heard it** said,
Who then can be saved?
27 **And he** said,
The things which are impossible with men are possible with God.
28 **Then Peter** said,
Lo,
we have left all,
and followed thee.
29 **And he** said unto them,
Verily I say unto you,
There is no man that hath left house, or parents, or brethren, or wife, or children, for the kingdom of God's sake,
30 **Who** shall not receive manifold more in this present time, and in the world to come life everlasting.
31 **Then he** took unto him the twelve,
and said unto them,
Behold,
we go up to Jerusalem,
and all things that are written by the prophets concerning the Son of man shall be accomplished.
32 **For he** shall be delivered unto the Gentiles,
and shall be mocked,
and spitefully entreated,
and spitted on:
33 **And they** shall scourge him,
and put him to death:
and the third day he shall rise again.
34 **And they** understood none of these things:
and this saying was hid from them,
neither knew they the things which were spoken.
35 **And it** came to pass,
that {as he was come nigh unto Jericho}, a certain blind man sat by the way side begging:
36 **And** hearing the multitude pass by,
he asked
what it meant.
37 **And they** told him,
that Jesus of Nazareth passeth by.
38 **And he** cried,
saying,
Jesus, thou son of David, have mercy on me.
39 **And they which went before** rebuked him,
that he should hold his peace:
but he cried so much the more,
Thou son of David, have mercy on me.
40 **And Jesus** stood,
and commanded him to be brought unto him:
and when he was come near,
he asked him,
41 Saying,
What wilt thou
that I shall do unto thee?
And he said,
Lord, that I may receive my sight.
42 **And Jesus** said unto him,
Receive thy sight:
thy faith hath saved thee.
43 **And immediately** he received his sight,
and followed him,
glorifying God:
and all the people, {when they saw it}, gave praise unto God.

19 **And Jesus** entered and passed through Jericho.
2 **And, {behold}, there** was a man named Zacchaeus,
which was the chief among the publicans,
and he was rich.
3 **And he** sought to see Jesus who he was;
and could not for the press,
because he was little of stature.
4 **And he** ran before,
and climbed up into a sycomore tree
to see him:
for he was to pass that way.
5 **And when Jesus** came to the place,
he looked up,
and saw him,
and said unto him,
Zacchaeus, make haste,
and come down;
for to day I must abide at thy house.
6 **And he** made haste,
and came down,
and received him joyfully.
7 **And when they** saw it,
they all murmured,
saying,
That he was gone to be guest with a man that is a sinner.
8 **And Zacchaeus** stood,
and said unto the Lord:
Behold, Lord,
the half of my goods I give to the

poor;
and if I have taken any thing from any man by false accusation,
I restore him fourfold.

9 **And Jesus** said unto him,
This day is salvation come to this house,
forsomuch as he also is a son of Abraham.

10 **For the Son of man** is come to seek and to save that which was lost.

11 **And as they** heard these things,
he added and spake a parable,
because he was nigh to Jerusalem,
and because they thought
that the kingdom of God should immediately appear.

12 **He** said therefore,
A certain nobleman went into a far country
to receive for himself a kingdom,
and to return.

13 **And he** called his ten servants,
and delivered them ten pounds,
and said unto them,
Occupy
till I come.

14 **But his citizens** hated him,
and sent a message after him,
saying,
We will not have this man to reign over us.

15 **And it** came to pass,
that {when he was returned}, {having received the kingdom}, then he commanded these servants to be called unto him,
to whom he had given the money,
that he might know
how much every man had gained by trading.

16 **Then** came the first,
saying,
Lord, thy pound hath gained ten pounds.

17 **And he** said unto him,
Well, thou good servant:
because thou hast been faithful in a very little,
have thou authority over ten cities.

18 **And the second** came,
saying,
Lord, thy pound hath gained five pounds.

19 **And he** said likewise to him,
Be thou also over five cities.

20 **And another** came,
saying,
Lord, behold,
here is thy pound,
which I have kept laid up in a napkin:

21 **For I** feared thee,
because thou art an austere man:
thou takest up that thou layedst not down,
and reapest that thou didst not sow.

22 **And he** saith unto him,
Out of thine own mouth will I judge thee, thou wicked servant.
Thou knewest
that I was an austere man,
taking up that I laid not down,
and reaping that I did not sow:
23 **Wherefore** then gavest not thou my money into the bank,
that at my coming I might have required mine own with usury?

24 **And he** said unto them that stood by,
Take from him the pound,
and give it to him that hath ten pounds.

25 (**And they** said unto him,
Lord, he hath ten pounds.)

26 **For I** say unto you,
That unto every one which hath shall be given;
and from him that hath not, even that he hath shall be taken away from him.

27 **But those mine enemies**, {which would not} {that I should reign over them}, bring hither,
and slay them before me.

28 **And when he** had thus spoken,
he went before,
ascending up to Jerusalem.

29 **And it** came to pass,
when he was come nigh to Bethphage and Bethany, at the mount called the mount of Olives,
he sent two of his disciples,
30 Saying,
Go ye into the village over against you;
in the which at your entering ye shall find a colt tied,
whereon yet never man sat:
loose him,
and bring him hither.

31 **And if any man** ask you,
Why do ye loose him?
thus shall ye say unto him,
Because the Lord hath need of him.

32 **And they that were sent** went their way,
and found
even as he had said unto them.

33 **And as they** were loosing the colt,
the owners thereof said unto them,
Why loose ye the colt?

34 **And they** said,
The Lord hath need of him.

35 **And they** brought him to Jesus:
and they cast their garments upon the colt,
and they set Jesus thereon.

36 **And as he** went,
they spread their clothes in the way.

37 **And when he** was come nigh,
even now at the descent of the mount of Olives, the whole multitude of the disciples began to rejoice and praise God with a loud voice for all the mighty works that they had seen;
38 Saying,
Blessed be the King that cometh in the name of the Lord: peace in heaven, and glory in the highest.

39 **And some of the Pharisees from among the multitude** said unto him,
Master, rebuke thy disciples.

40 **And he** answered and said unto them,
I tell you
that, {if these should hold their peace}, the stones would immediately cry out.

41 **And when he** was come near,
he beheld the city,
and wept over it,
42 Saying,
If thou hadst known, even thou, at least in this thy day, the things which belong unto thy peace!
but now they are hid from thine eyes.

43 **For the days** shall come upon thee,
that thine enemies shall cast a trench about thee,
and compass thee round,
and keep thee in on every side,
44 **And** shall lay thee even with the ground, and thy children within thee;
and they shall not leave in thee one stone upon another;
because thou knewest not the time of thy visitation.

45 **And he** went into the temple,
and began to cast out them that sold therein, and them that bought;
46 Saying unto them,
It is written,
My house is the house of prayer:
but ye have made it a den of thieves.
47 **And he** taught daily in the temple.
But the chief priests and the scribes and the chief of the people sought to destroy him,
48 **And** could not find what they might do:
for all the people were very attentive to hear him.

20

And it came to pass,
that on one of those days, {as he taught the people in the temple}, {and preached the gospel}, the chief priests and the scribes came upon him with the elders,
2 **And** spake unto him,
saying,
Tell us,
by what authority doest thou these things?
or who is he that gave thee this authority?
3 **And he** answered and said unto them,
I will also ask you one thing;
and answer me:
4 **The baptism of John,** was it from heaven, or of men?
5 **And they** reasoned with themselves,
saying,
If we shall say,
From heaven;
he will say,
Why then believed ye him not?
6 **But and if we** say,
Of men;
all the people will stone us:
for they be persuaded
that John was a prophet.
7 **And they** answered,
that they could not tell
whence it was.
8 **And Jesus** said unto them,
Neither tell I you
by what authority I do these things.
9 **Then** began he to speak to the people this parable;
A certain man planted a vineyard,
and let it forth to husbandmen,
and went into a far country for a long time.
10 **And at the season** he sent a servant to the husbandmen,
that they should give him of the fruit of the vineyard:
but the husbandmen beat him,
and sent him away empty.
11 **And again he** sent another servant:
and they beat him also,
and entreated him shamefully,
and sent him away empty.
12 **And again he** sent a third:
and they wounded him also,
and cast him out.
13 **Then** said the lord of the vineyard,
What shall I do?
I will send my beloved son:
it may be they will reverence him
when they see him.
14 **But when the husbandmen** saw him,
they reasoned among themselves,
saying,
This is the heir:
come,
let us kill him,
that the inheritance may be ours.
15 **So they** cast him out of the vineyard,
and killed him.
What therefore shall the lord of the vineyard do unto them?
16 **He** shall come and destroy these husbandmen,
and shall give the vineyard to others.
And when they heard it,
they said,
God forbid.
17 **And he** beheld them,
and said,
What is this then that is written,
The stone which the builders rejected, the same is become the head of the corner?
18 **Whosoever shall fall upon that stone** shall be broken;
but on whomsoever it shall fall,
it will grind him to powder.
19 **And the chief priests and the scribes the same hour** sought to lay hands on him;
and they feared the people:
for they perceived that he had spoken this parable against them.
20 **And they** watched him,
and sent forth spies,
which should feign themselves just men,
that they might take hold of his words,
that so they might deliver him unto the power and authority of the governor.
21 **And they** asked him,
saying,
Master, we know
that thou sayest and teachest rightly,
neither acceptest thou the person of any,
but teachest the way of God truly:
22 **Is it lawful for us** to give tribute unto Caesar, or no?
23 **But he** perceived their craftiness,
and said unto them,
Why tempt ye me?
24 **Shew** me a penny.
Whose image and superscription hath it?
They answered and said, Caesar's.
25 **And he** said unto them,
Render therefore unto Caesar the things which be Caesar's, and unto God the things which be God's.
26 **And they** could not take hold of his words before the people:
and they marvelled at his answer,
and held their peace.
27 **Then** came to him certain of the Sadducees,
which deny that there is any resurrection;
and they asked him,
28 Saying,
Master, Moses wrote unto us,
If any man's brother die,
having a wife,
and he die without children,
that his brother should take his wife,
and raise up seed unto his brother.
29 **There** were therefore seven brethren:
and the first took a wife,
and died without children.
30 **And the second** took her to wife,
and he died childless.
31 **And the third** took her; and in like manner the seven also:
and they left no children,
and died.
32 **Last of all the woman** died also.

33 **Therefore in the resurrection**
whose wife of them is she?
for seven had her to wife.

34 **And Jesus answering** said unto
them,
The children of this world marry,
and are given in marriage:
35 **But they which shall be**
accounted worthy to obtain
that world, and the
resurrection from the dead,
neither marry,
nor are given in marriage:
36 **Neither** can they die any more:
for they are equal unto the angels;
and are the children of God,
being the children of the
resurrection.

37 **Now that the dead** are raised,
even Moses shewed at the bush,
when he calleth the Lord the God of
Abraham, and the God of Isaac,
and the God of Jacob.

38 **For he** is not a God of the dead,
but of the living:
for all live unto him.

39 **Then certain of the scribes**
answering said,
Master, thou hast well said.

40 **And after that** they durst not ask
him any question at all.

41 **And he** said unto them,
How say they
that Christ is David's son?

42 **And David himself** saith in the
book of Psalms,
The LORD said unto my Lord,
Sit thou on my right hand,
43 **Till I** make thine enemies thy
footstool.

44 **David** therefore calleth him Lord,
how is he then his son?

45 **Then in the audience of all the**
people he said unto his disciples,
46 **Beware** of the scribes,
which desire to walk in long robes,
and love greetings in the markets,
and the highest seats in the
synagogues, and the chief rooms
at feasts;
47 **Which** devour widows' houses,
and for a shew make long prayers:
the same shall receive greater
damnation.

21 ∞ **And he** looked up,
and saw the rich men
casting their gifts into the
treasury.

2 **And he** saw also a certain poor
widow casting in thither two
mites.

3 **And he** said,
Of a truth I say unto you,
that this poor widow hath cast in
more than they all:
4 **For all these** have of their
abundance cast in unto the
offerings of God:
but she of her penury hath cast in
all the living that she had.

5 **And as some** spake of the temple,
how it was adorned with goodly
stones and gifts,
he said,
6 **As for these things which ye**
behold, the days will come,
in the which there shall not be left
one stone upon another,
that shall not be thrown down.

7 **And they** asked him,
saying,
Master, but when shall these
things be?
and what sign will there be
when these things shall come to
pass?

8 **And he** said,
Take heed that ye be not deceived:
for many shall come in my name,
saying,
I am Christ;
and the time draweth near:
go ye not therefore after them.

9 **But when ye** shall hear of wars
and commotions,
be not terrified:
for these things must first come to
pass;
but the end is not by and by.

10 **Then** said he unto them,
Nation shall rise against nation,
and kingdom against kingdom:
11 **And great earthquakes** shall be in
divers places, and famines, and
pestilences;
and fearful sights and great signs
shall there be from heaven.

12 **But before all these,** they shall
lay their hands on you,
and persecute you,
delivering you up to the
synagogues, and into prisons,
being brought before kings and
rulers for my name's sake.

13 **And it** shall turn to you for a
testimony.

14 **Settle** it therefore in your hearts,
not to meditate before
what ye shall answer:

15 **For I** will give you a mouth and
wisdom,
which all your adversaries shall
not be able to gainsay
nor resist.

16 **And ye** shall be betrayed both by
parents, and brethren, and
kinsfolks, and friends;
and some of you shall they cause to
be put to death.

17 **And ye** shall be hated of all men
for my name's sake.

18 **But there** shall not an hair of your
head perish.

19 **In your patience** possess ye your
souls.

20 **And when ye** shall see Jerusalem
compassed with armies,
then know
that the desolation thereof is nigh.

21 **Then let them which are in**
Judaea flee to the mountains;
and let them which are in the
midst of it depart out;
and let not them that are in the
countries enter thereinto.

22 **For these** be the days of
vengeance,
that all things which are written
may be fulfilled.

23 **But woe** unto them that are with
child, and to them that give suck,
in those days!
for there shall be great distress in
the land, and wrath upon this
people.

24 **And they** shall fall by the edge of
the sword,
and shall be led away captive into
all nations:
and Jerusalem shall be trodden
down of the Gentiles,
until the times of the Gentiles be
fulfilled.

25 **And there** shall be signs in the
sun, and in the moon, and in the
stars; and upon the earth distress
of nations, with perplexity;
the sea and the waves roaring;
26 **Men's hearts** failing them for
fear,
and for looking after those things
which are coming on the earth:
for the powers of heaven shall be
shaken.

27 **And then** shall they see the Son of
man coming in a cloud with
power and great glory.

28 **And when these things** begin to

come to pass,
then look up,
and lift up your heads;
for your redemption draweth nigh.
29 **And he** spake to them a parable;
Behold the fig tree, and all the trees;
30 **When they** now shoot forth,
ye see and know of your own selves
that summer is now nigh at hand.
31 **So likewise ye**, {when ye see these things come to pass}, know ye
that the kingdom of God is nigh at hand.
32 **Verily I** say unto you,
This generation shall not pass away,
till all be fulfilled.
33 **Heaven and earth** shall pass away:
but my words shall not pass away.
34 **And take heed** to yourselves,
lest at any time your hearts be overcharged with surfeiting, and drunkenness, and cares of this life,
and so that day come upon you unawares.
35 **For as a snare** shall it come on all them that dwell on the face of the whole earth.
36 **Watch ye** therefore,
and pray always,
that ye may be accounted worthy to escape all these things that shall come to pass, and to stand before the Son of man.
37 **And in the day time** he was teaching in the temple;
and at night he went out,
and abode in the mount that is called the mount of Olives.
38 **And all the people** came early in the morning to him in the temple,
for to hear him.

22

Now the feast of unleavened bread drew nigh,
which is called the Passover.
2 **And the chief priests and scribes** sought how they might kill him;
for they feared the people.
3 **Then** entered Satan into Judas surnamed Iscariot,
being of the number of the twelve.
4 **And he** went his way,
and communed with the chief priests and captains,
how he might betray him unto them.
5 **And they** were glad,
and covenanted to give him money.
6 **And he** promised,
and sought opportunity to betray him unto them in the absence of the multitude.
7 **Then** came the day of unleavened bread,
when the passover must be killed.
8 **And he** sent Peter and John,
saying,
Go and prepare us the passover,
that we may eat.
9 **And they** said unto him,
Where wilt thou that we prepare?
10 **And he** said unto them,
Behold,
when ye are entered into the city,
there shall a man meet you,
bearing a pitcher of water;
follow him into the house where he entereth in.
11 **And ye** shall say unto the goodman of the house,
The Master saith unto thee,
Where is the guestchamber,
where I shall eat the passover with my disciples?
12 **And he** shall shew you a large upper room furnished:
there make ready.
13 **And they** went,
and found as he had said unto them:
and they made ready the passover.
14 **And when the hour** was come,
he sat down, and the twelve apostles with him.
15 **And he** said unto them,
With desire I have desired to eat this passover with you
before I suffer:
16 **For I** say unto you,
I will not any more eat thereof,
until it be fulfilled in the kingdom of God.
17 **And he** took the cup,
and gave thanks,
and said,
Take this,
and divide it among yourselves:
18 **For I** say unto you,
I will not drink of the fruit of the vine,
until the kingdom of God shall come.
19 **And he** took bread,
and gave thanks,
and brake it,
and gave unto them,
saying,
This is my body which is given for you:
this do in remembrance of me.
20 **Likewise** also the cup after supper,
saying,
This cup is the new testament in my blood,
which is shed for you.
21 **But, {behold}, the hand of him that betrayeth me** is with me on the table.
22 **And truly the Son of man** goeth,
as it was determined:
but woe unto that man by whom he is betrayed!
23 **And they** began to enquire among themselves,
which of them it was that should do this thing.
24 **And there** was also a strife among them,
which of them should be accounted the greatest.
25 **And he** said unto them,
The kings of the Gentiles exercise lordship over them;
and they that exercise authority upon them are called benefactors.
26 **But ye** shall not be so:
but he that is greatest among you, let him be as the younger;
and he that is chief, as he that doth serve.
27 **For whether** is greater, he that sitteth at meat, or he that serveth?
is not he that sitteth at meat?
but I am among you as he that serveth.
28 **Ye** are they which have continued with me in my temptations.
29 **And I** appoint unto you a kingdom,
as my Father hath appointed unto me;
30 **That ye** may eat and drink at my table in my kingdom,
and sit on thrones
judging the twelve tribes of Israel.
31 **And the Lord** said,
Simon, Simon, behold,
Satan hath desired to have you,
that he may sift you as wheat:
32 **But I** have prayed for thee,

that thy faith fail not:
and when thou art converted,
strengthen thy brethren.
33 **And he** said unto him,
Lord, I am ready to go with thee, both into prison, and to death.
34 **And he** said,
I tell thee, Peter,
the cock shall not crow this day,
before that thou shalt thrice deny
that thou knowest me.
35 **And he** said unto them,
When I sent you without purse, and scrip, and shoes,
lacked ye any thing?
And they said,
Nothing.
36 **Then** said he unto them,
But now, he that hath a purse, let him take it, and likewise his scrip:
and he that hath no sword, let him sell his garment,
and buy one.
37 **For I** say unto you,
that this that is written must yet be accomplished in me,
And he was reckoned among the transgressors:
for the things concerning me have an end.
38 **And they** said,
Lord, {behold}, here are two swords.
And he said unto them,
It is enough.
39 **And he** came out,
and went, {as he was wont}, to the mount of Olives;
and his disciples also followed him.
40 **And when he** was at the place,
he said unto them,
Pray
that ye enter not into temptation.
41 **And he** was withdrawn from them about a stone's cast,
and kneeled down,
and prayed,
42 Saying,
Father, if thou be willing,
remove this cup from me:
nevertheless not my will, but thine, be done.
43 **And there** appeared an angel unto him from heaven,
strengthening him.
44 **And being in an agony** he prayed more earnestly:
and his sweat was as it were great drops of blood falling down to the ground.
45 **And when he** rose up from prayer,
and was come to his disciples,
he found them sleeping for sorrow,
46 **And** said unto them,
Why sleep ye?
rise and pray,
lest ye enter into temptation.
47 **And while he** yet spake,
behold a multitude,
and he that was called Judas, one of the twelve, went before them,
and drew near unto Jesus to kiss him.
48 **But Jesus** said unto him,
Judas, betrayest thou the Son of man with a kiss?
49 **When they which were about him** saw what would follow,
they said unto him,
Lord, shall we smite with the sword?
50 **And one of them** smote the servant of the high priest,
and cut off his right ear.
51 **And Jesus** answered and said,
Suffer ye thus far.
And he touched his ear,
and healed him.
52 **Then Jesus** said unto the chief priests, and captains of the temple, and the elders,
which were come to him,
Be ye come out, as against a thief, with swords and staves?
53 **When I** was daily with you in the temple,
ye stretched forth no hands against me:
but this is your hour, and the power of darkness.
54 **Then** took they him,
and led him,
and brought him into the high priest's house.
And Peter followed afar off.
55 **And when they** had kindled a fire in the midst of the hall,
and were set down together,
Peter sat down among them.
56 **But a certain maid** beheld him
as he sat by the fire,
and earnestly looked upon him,
and said,
This man was also with him.
57 **And he** denied him,
saying,
Woman, I know him not.
58 **And after a little while** another saw him,
and said,
Thou art also of them.
And Peter said,
Man, I am not.
59 **And about the space of one hour after** another confidently affirmed,
saying,
Of a truth this fellow also was with him:
for he is a Galilaean.
60 **And Peter** said,
Man, I know not
what thou sayest.
And immediately, {while he yet spake}, the cock crew.
61 **And the Lord** turned,
and looked upon Peter.
And Peter remembered the word of the Lord,
how he had said unto him,
Before the cock crow,
thou shalt deny me thrice.
62 **And Peter** went out,
and wept bitterly.
63 **And the men that held Jesus** mocked him,
and smote him.
64 **And when they** had blindfolded him,
they struck him on the face,
and asked him,
saying,
Prophesy,
who is it that smote thee?
65 **And many other things** blasphemously spake they against him.
66 **And as soon as it** was day,
the elders of the people and the chief priests and the scribes came together,
and led him into their council,
saying,
67 **Art thou** the Christ?
tell us.
And he said unto them,
If I tell you,
ye will not believe:
68 **And if I** also ask you,
ye will not answer me,
nor let me go.
69 **Hereafter** shall the Son of man sit on the right hand of the power of God.

70 **Then** said they all,
Art thou then the Son of God?
And he said unto them,
Ye say
that I am.

71 **And they** said,
What need we any further witness?
for we ourselves have heard of his
own mouth.

23

And the whole
multitude of them arose,
and led him unto Pilate.

2 **And they** began to accuse him,
saying,
We found this fellow perverting the
nation,
and forbidding to give tribute to
Caesar,
saying
that he himself is Christ a King.

3 **And Pilate** asked him,
saying,
Art thou the King of the Jews?
And he answered him and said,
Thou sayest it.

4 **Then** said Pilate to the chief
priests and to the people,
I find no fault in this man.

5 **And they** were the more fierce,
saying,
He stirreth up the people,
teaching throughout all Jewry,
beginning from Galilee to this place.

6 **When Pilate** heard of Galilee,
he asked
whether the man were a Galilaean.

7 **And as soon as he** knew
that he belonged unto Herod's
jurisdiction,
he sent him to Herod,
who himself also was at Jerusalem
at that time.

8 **And when Herod** saw Jesus,
he was exceeding glad:
for he was desirous to see him of a
long season,
because he had heard many things
of him;
and he hoped to have seen some
miracle done by him.

9 **Then he** questioned with him in
many words;
but he answered him nothing.

10 **And the chief priests and scribes**
stood and vehemently accused
him.

11 **And Herod with his men of war**
set him at nought,
and mocked him,
and arrayed him in a gorgeous robe,
and sent him again to Pilate.

12 **And the same day** Pilate and
Herod were made friends
together:
for before they were at enmity
between themselves.

13 **And Pilate**, {when he had called
together the chief priests and the
rulers and the people},

14 Said unto them,
Ye have brought this man unto me,
as one that perverteth the people:
and, {behold}, I, {having examined
him before you}, have found no
fault in this man touching those
things whereof ye accuse him:

15 **No, nor** yet Herod:
for I sent you to him;
**and, {lo}, nothing worthy of
death** is done unto him.

16 **I** will therefore chastise him,
and release him.

17 (**For of necessity** he must release
one unto them at the feast.)

18 **And they** cried out all at once,
saying,
Away with this man,
and release unto us Barabbas:

19 (Who for a certain sedition made
in the city, and for murder, was
cast into prison.)

20 **Pilate** therefore, {willing to
release Jesus}, spake again to
them.

21 **But they** cried,
saying,
Crucify him,
crucify him.

22 **And he** said unto them the third
time,
Why,
what evil hath he done?
I have found no cause of death in
him:
I will therefore chastise him,
and let him go.

23 **And they** were instant with loud
voices,
requiring
that he might be crucified.
**And the voices of them and of the
chief priests** prevailed.

24 **And Pilate** gave sentence
that it should be as they required.

25 **And he** released unto them him
that for sedition and murder was
cast into prison,
whom they had desired;
but he delivered Jesus to their will.

26 **And as they** led him away,
they laid hold upon one Simon, a
Cyrenian, coming out of the
country,
and on him they laid the cross,
that he might bear it after Jesus.

27 **And there** followed him a great
company of people, and of
women,
which also bewailed and lamented
him.

28 **But Jesus turning unto them**
said,
Daughters of Jerusalem, weep not
for me,
but weep for yourselves, and for
your children.

29 **For, {behold}, the days** are
coming,
in the which they shall say,
Blessed are the barren, and the
wombs that never bare, and the
paps which never gave suck.

30 **Then** shall they begin to say to
the mountains, {Fall on us}; and
to the hills, {Cover us}.

31 **For if they** do these things in a
green tree,
what shall be done in the dry?

32 **And there** were also two other,
malefactors, led with him
to be put to death.

33 **And when they** were come to the
place,
which is called Calvary,
there they crucified him, and the
malefactors, one on the right
hand, and the other on the left.

34 **Then** said Jesus,
Father, forgive them;
for they know not
what they do.
And they parted his raiment,
and cast lots.

35 **And the people** stood beholding.
And the rulers also with them
derided him,
saying,
He saved others;
let him save himself,
if he be Christ, the chosen of God.

36 **And the soldiers** also mocked
him,
coming to him,
and offering him vinegar,

37 **And** saying,
If thou be the king of the Jews,

save thyself.

38 **And a superscription** also was written over him in letters of Greek, and Latin, and Hebrew,
This Is The King Of The Jews.

39 **And one of the malefactors which were hanged** railed on him,
saying,
If thou be Christ,
save thyself and us.

40 **But the other answering** rebuked him,
saying,
Dost not thou fear God,
seeing thou art in the same condemnation?

41 **And we** indeed justly;
for we receive the due reward of our deeds:
but this man hath done nothing amiss.

42 **And he** said unto Jesus,
Lord, remember me
when thou comest into thy kingdom.

43 **And Jesus** said unto him,
Verily I say unto thee,
Today shalt thou be with me in paradise.

44 **And it** was about the sixth hour,
and there was a darkness over all the earth until the ninth hour.

45 **And the sun** was darkened,
and the veil of the temple was rent in the midst.

46 **And when Jesus** had cried with a loud voice,
he said,
Father, into thy hands I commend my spirit:
and having said thus,
he gave up the ghost.

47 **Now when the centurion** saw what was done,
he glorified God,
saying,
Certainly this was a righteous man.

48 **And all the people that came together to that sight,** {beholding the things which were done}, smote their breasts,
and returned.

49 **And all his acquaintance, and the women that followed him from Galilee,** stood afar off,
beholding these things.

50 **And, {behold}, there** was a man named Joseph, a counsellor;
and he was a good man, and a just:

51 (The same had not consented to the counsel and deed of them;)
he was of Arimathaea, a city of the Jews:
who also himself waited for the kingdom of God.

52 **This man** went unto Pilate,
and begged the body of Jesus.

53 **And he** took it down,
and wrapped it in linen,
and laid it in a sepulchre that was hewn in stone,
wherein never man before was laid.

54 **And that day** was the preparation,
and the sabbath drew on.

55 **And the women** also, {which came with him from Galilee}, followed after,
and beheld the sepulchre,
and how his body was laid.

56 **And they** returned,
and prepared spices and ointments;
and rested the sabbath day according to the commandment.

24 **Now upon the first day of the week**, very early in the morning, they came unto the sepulchre,
bringing the spices which they had prepared, and certain others with them.

2 **And they** found the stone rolled away from the sepulchre.

3 **And they** entered in,
and found not the body of the Lord Jesus.

4 **And it** came to pass,
as they were much perplexed thereabout,
behold,
two men stood by them in shining garments:

5 **And as they** were afraid,
and bowed down their faces to the earth,
they said unto them,
Why seek ye the living among the dead?

6 **He** is not here,
but is risen:
remember
how he spake unto you
when he was yet in Galilee,

7 Saying,
The Son of man must be delivered into the hands of sinful men,
and be crucified,
and the third day rise again.

8 **And they** remembered his words,

9 **And** returned from the sepulchre,
and told all these things unto the eleven, and to all the rest.

10 **It was Mary Magdalene and Joanna, and Mary the mother of James, and other women** that were with them,
which told these things unto the apostles.

11 **And their words** seemed to them as idle tales,
and they believed them not.

12 **Then** arose Peter,
and ran unto the sepulchre;
and stooping down,
he beheld the linen clothes laid by themselves,
and departed,
wondering in himself at that which was come to pass.

13 **And, {behold}, two of them** went that same day to a village called Emmaus,
which was from Jerusalem about threescore furlongs.

14 **And they** talked together of all these things which had happened.

15 **And it** came to pass,
that, {while they communed together and reasoned}, Jesus himself drew near,
and went with them.

16 **But their eyes** were holden that they should not know him.

17 **And he** said unto them,
What manner of communications are these that ye have one to another,
as ye walk,
and are sad?

18 **And the one of them**, {whose name was Cleopas}, answering said unto him,
Art thou only a stranger in Jerusalem,
and hast not known the things which are come to pass there in these days?

19 **And he** said unto them,
What things?
And they said unto him,
Concerning Jesus of Nazareth,
which was a prophet mighty in deed and word before God and all

the people:
20 **And how** the chief priests and our rulers delivered him to be condemned to death,
and have crucified him.

21 **But we** trusted
that it had been he which should have redeemed Israel:
and beside all this, to day is the third day
since these things were done.

22 **Yea, and certain women also of our company** made us astonished,
which were early at the sepulchre;
23 **And when they** found not his body,
they came,
saying,
that they had also seen a vision of angels,
which said
that he was alive.

24 **And certain of them which were with us** went to the sepulchre,
and found it even so
as the women had said:
but him they saw not.

25 **Then he** said unto them,
O fools, and slow of heart to believe all that the prophets have spoken:
26 **Ought not Christ** to have suffered these things,
and to enter into his glory?

27 **And beginning at Moses and all the prophets,** he expounded unto them in all the scriptures the things concerning himself.

28 **And they** drew nigh unto the village,
whither they went:
and he made as though he would have gone further.

29 **But they** constrained him,
saying,
Abide with us:
for it is toward evening,
and the day is far spent.

And he went in to tarry with them.

30 **And it** came to pass,
as he sat at meat with them,
he took bread,
and blessed it,
and brake,
and gave to them.

31 **And their eyes** were opened,
and they knew him;
and he vanished out of their sight.

32 **And they** said one to another,
Did not our heart burn within us,
while he talked with us by the way,
and while he opened to us the scriptures?

33 **And they** rose up the same hour,
and returned to Jerusalem,
and found the eleven gathered together, and them that were with them,
34 Saying,
The Lord is risen indeed,
and hath appeared to Simon.

35 **And they** told
what things were done in the way,
and how he was known of them in breaking of bread.

36 **And as they thus** spake,
Jesus himself stood in the midst of them,
and saith unto them,
Peace be unto you.

37 **But they** were terrified
and affrighted,
and supposed
that they had seen a spirit.

38 **And he** said unto them,
Why are ye troubled?
and why do thoughts arise in your hearts?

39 **Behold** my hands and my feet,
that it is I myself:
handle me,
and see;
for a spirit hath not flesh and bones,
as ye see me have.

40 **And when he** had thus spoken,
he shewed them his hands and his feet.

41 **And while they** yet believed not for joy,
and wondered,
he said unto them,
Have ye here any meat?

42 **And they** gave him a piece of a broiled fish, and of an honeycomb.

43 **And he** took it,
and did eat before them.

44 **And he** said unto them,
These are the words which I spake unto you,
while I was yet with you,
that all things must be fulfilled,
which were written in the law of Moses, and in the prophets, and in the psalms, concerning me.

45 **Then** opened he their understanding,
that they might understand the scriptures,
46 **And** said unto them,
Thus it is written,
and thus it behooved Christ to suffer,
and to rise from the dead the third day:
47 **And that repentance and remission of sins** should be preached in his name among all nations,
beginning at Jerusalem.

48 **And ye** are witnesses of these things.

49 **And, {behold}, I** send the promise of my Father upon you:
but tarry ye in the city of Jerusalem,
until ye be endued with power from on high.

50 **And he** led them out as far as to Bethany,
and he lifted up his hands,
and blessed them.

51 **And it** came to pass,
while he blessed them,
he was parted from them,
and carried up into heaven.

52 **And they** worshipped him,
and returned to Jerusalem with great joy:
53 **And** were continually in the temple,
praising and blessing God.

Amen.

John

The Gospel of John, penned by the Apostle John, stands out for its distinctive style and content. Unlike other gospels, it delves deeper into theological themes and the divine nature of Jesus as the Son of God. John's purpose in writing this gospel was to fortify the faith of believers and provide a more profound understanding of Jesus' mission and purpose on earth. His theological perspective underscores the profound significance of Jesus' life and teachings, aiming to inspire his readers to believe in Him as the Son of God and the Savior of humanity.

One of the most striking aspects of John's Gospel is its portrayal of Jesus as the Son of God, the holy Word made flesh and the Savior of the world. John's emphasis on Jesus' deity surpasses that of any other gospel. His writing is replete with symbolism and theological concepts, and he employs metaphorical language and imagery to convey these profound ideas. He also presents seven miraculous signs that Jesus performed, each meticulously designed to unveil His divine nature and strengthen the faith of believers. These miracles include turning water into wine, healing the official's son, healing the person with paralysis at Bethesda, feeding the 5000, walking on water, healing a man who was born without sight, and raising Lazarus from the dead. All serve as undeniable proof of Jesus' divinity.

Perhaps the most well-known part of John's Gospel involves his accounts of Jesus using the phrase *I am* to describe Himself and His mission. Statements such as *I am* the bread of life, *I am* the light of the world, and *I am* the resurrection and the life demonstrate Jesus' self-awareness as the Son of God and the source of eternal life. John's account of Jesus' passion, death, and resurrection, unique in detail and theological significance, emphasizes the purposeful nature of Jesus' death, presenting it as a sacrifice for the world's sins and a fulfillment of prophecy. Two other theological concepts that John shares, among many others, highlight the role of the Holy Spirit, describing His comfort, guidance, and empowerment in the lives of believers. And finally, John underscores the close relationship between Jesus and His Father, presenting Them as united in purpose and action.

Overall, the Gospel of John illuminates the transformative power of faith, demonstrating how the written Word can convey truth, inspire faith, and shape the future of the Christian faith. With its profound exploration of Jesus Christ's divine nature, it serves as a guiding light for those seeking to deepen their understanding of God and live in accordance with His will.

1 **In the beginning** was the Word,
and the Word was with God,
and the Word was God.
2 **The same** was in the beginning with God.
3 **All things** were made by him;
and without him was not any thing made that was made.
4 **In him** was life;
and the life was the light of men.
5 **And the light** shineth in darkness;
and the darkness comprehended it not.
6 **There** was a man sent from God,
whose name was John.
7 **The same** came for a witness,
to bear witness of the Light,
that all men through him might believe.
8 **He** was not that Light,
but was sent to bear witness of that Light.
9 **That** was the true Light,
which lighteth every man that cometh into the world.
10 **He** was in the world,
and the world was made by him,
and the world knew him not.
11 **He** came unto his own,
and his own received him not.
12 **But as many as** received him,
to them gave he power to become the sons of God, even to them that believe on his name:
13 **Which** were born, not of blood, nor of the will of the flesh, nor of the will of man, but of God.
14 **And the Word** was made flesh,
and dwelt among us, (and we beheld his glory, the glory as of the only begotten of the Father,) full of grace and truth.
15 **John** bare witness of him,
and cried,
saying,
This was he of whom I spake,
He that cometh after me is preferred before me:
for he was before me.
16 **And of his fulness** have all we received, and grace for grace.
17 **For the law** was given by Moses,
but grace and truth came by Jesus Christ.
18 **No man** hath seen God at any time, the only begotten Son,
which is in the bosom of the Father,
he hath declared him.
19 **And this** is the record of John,
when the Jews sent priests and Levites from Jerusalem to ask him,
Who art thou?
20 **And he** confessed,
and denied not;
but confessed,
I am not the Christ.
21 **And they** asked him,

What then?
Art thou Elias?
And he saith,
I am not.
Art thou that prophet?
And he answered,
No.
22 **Then** said they unto him,
Who art thou?
that we may give an answer to them that sent us.
What sayest thou of thyself?
23 **He** said,
I am the voice of one crying in the wilderness,
Make straight the way of the Lord,
as said the prophet Esaias.
24 **And they which were sent** were of the Pharisees.
25 **And they** asked him,
and said unto him,
Why baptizest thou then,
if thou be not that Christ, nor Elias, neither that prophet?
26 **John** answered them,
saying,
I baptize with water:
but there standeth one among you,
whom ye know not;
27 **He** it is,
who coming after me is preferred before me,
whose shoe's latchet I am not worthy to unloose.
28 **These things** were done in Bethabara beyond Jordan,
where John was baptizing.
29 **The next day** John seeth Jesus coming unto him,
and saith,
Behold the Lamb of God,
which taketh away the sin of the world.
30 **This** is he of whom I said,
After me cometh a man which is preferred before me:
for he was before me.
31 **And I** knew him not:
but that he should be made manifest to Israel,
therefore am I come baptizing with water.
32 **And John** bare record,
saying,
I saw the Spirit descending from heaven like a dove,
and it abode upon him.
33 **And I** knew him not:
but he that sent me to baptize with water, the same said unto me,
Upon whom thou shalt see the Spirit descending,
and remaining on him,
the same is he which baptizeth with the Holy Ghost.
34 **And I** saw,
and bare record that this is the Son of God.
35 **Again the next day after** John stood, and two of his disciples;
36 **And** looking upon Jesus
as he walked,
he saith,
Behold the Lamb of God!
37 **And the two disciples** heard him speak,
and they followed Jesus.
38 **Then Jesus** turned,
and saw them following,
and saith unto them,
What seek ye?
They said unto him,
Rabbi,
(which is to say, {being interpreted}, Master,)
where dwellest thou?
39 **He** saith unto them,
Come and see.
They came and saw where he dwelt,
and abode with him that day:
for it was about the tenth hour.
40 **One of the two which heard John speak, and followed him,** was Andrew, Simon Peter's brother.
41 **He first** findeth his own brother Simon,
and saith unto him,
We have found the Messias,
which is, {being interpreted}, the Christ.
42 **And he** brought him to Jesus.
And when Jesus beheld him,
he said,
Thou art Simon the son of Jona:
thou shalt be called Cephas,
which is by interpretation,
A stone.
43 **The day following** Jesus would go forth into Galilee,
and findeth Philip,
and saith unto him,
Follow me.
44 **Now Philip** was of Bethsaida, the city of Andrew and Peter.
45 **Philip** findeth Nathanael,
and saith unto him,
We have found him,
of whom Moses in the law, and the prophets, did write, Jesus of Nazareth, the son of Joseph.
46 **And Nathanael** said unto him,
Can there any good thing come out of Nazareth?
Philip saith unto him,
Come and see.
47 **Jesus** saw Nathanael coming to him,
and saith of him,
Behold an Israelite indeed,
in whom is no guile!
48 **Nathanael** saith unto him,
Whence knowest thou me?
Jesus answered and said unto him,
Before that Philip called thee,
when thou wast under the fig tree,
I saw thee.
49 **Nathanael** answered and saith unto him,
Rabbi, thou art the Son of God;
thou art the King of Israel.
50 **Jesus** answered and said unto him,
Because I said unto thee,
I saw thee under the fig tree,
believest thou?
thou shalt see greater things than these.
51 **And he** saith unto him,
Verily, verily, I say unto you,
Hereafter ye shall see heaven open, and the angels of God ascending and descending upon the Son of man.

2

And the third day there was a marriage in Cana of Galilee;
and the mother of Jesus was there:
2 **And both Jesus** was called, and his disciples, to the marriage.
3 **And when they** wanted wine,
the mother of Jesus saith unto him,
They have no wine.
4 **Jesus** saith unto her,
Woman, what have I to do with thee?
mine hour is not yet come.
5 **His mother** saith unto the servants,
Whatsoever he saith unto you,
do it.
6 **And there** were set there six waterpots of stone, after the

manner of the purifying of the Jews,
containing two or three firkins apiece.
7 **Jesus** saith unto them,
Fill the waterpots with water.
And they filled them up to the brim.
8 **And he** saith unto them,
Draw out now,
and bear unto the governor of the feast.
And they bare it.
9 **When the ruler of the feast** had tasted the water that was made wine,
and knew not
whence it was:
(but the servants which drew the water knew;)
the governor of the feast called the bridegroom,
10 **And** saith unto him,
Every man at the beginning doth set forth good wine;
and when men have well drunk, then that which is worse:
but thou hast kept the good wine until now.
11 **This beginning of miracles** did Jesus in Cana of Galilee,
and manifested forth his glory;
and his disciples believed on him.
12 **After this** he went down to Capernaum, he, and his mother, and his brethren, and his disciples:
and they continued there not many days.
13 **And the Jews' passover** was at hand,
and Jesus went up to Jerusalem.
14 **And** found in the temple those that sold oxen and sheep and doves, and the changers of money sitting:
15 **And when he** had made a scourge of small cords,
he drove them all out of the temple, and the sheep, and the oxen;
and poured out the changers' money,
and overthrew the tables;
16 **And** said unto them that sold doves,
Take these things hence;
make not my Father's house an house of merchandise.
17 **And his disciples** remembered
that it was written,
The zeal of thine house hath eaten me up.
18 **Then** answered the Jews and said unto him,
What sign shewest thou unto us,
seeing that thou doest these things?
19 **Jesus** answered and said unto them,
Destroy this temple,
and in three days I will raise it up.
20 **Then** said the Jews,
Forty and six years was this temple in building,
and wilt thou rear it up in three days?
21 **But he** spake of the temple of his body.
22 **When therefore he** was risen from the dead,
his disciples remembered
that he had said this unto them;
and they believed the scripture, and the word which Jesus had said.
23 **Now when he** was in Jerusalem at the passover, in the feast day,
many believed in his name,
when they saw the miracles which he did.
24 **But Jesus** did not commit himself unto them,
because he knew all men,
25 **And** needed not that any should testify of man:
for he knew
what was in man.

3 **There** was a man of the Pharisees, named Nicodemus, a ruler of the Jews:
2 **The same** came to Jesus by night,
and said unto him,
Rabbi, we know
that thou art a teacher come from God:
for no man can do these miracles that thou doest,
except God be with him.
3 **Jesus** answered and said unto him,
Verily, verily, I say unto thee,
Except a man be born again,
he cannot see the kingdom of God.
4 **Nicodemus** saith unto him,
How can a man be born
when he is old?
can he enter the second time into his mother's womb,
and be born?
5 **Jesus** answered,
Verily, verily, I say unto thee,
Except a man be born of water and of the Spirit,
he cannot enter into the kingdom of God.
6 **That which is born of the flesh** is flesh;
and that which is born of the Spirit is spirit.
7 **Marvel not** that I said unto thee,
Ye must be born again.
8 **The wind** bloweth where it listeth,
and thou hearest the sound thereof,
but canst not tell whence it cometh, and whither it goeth:
so is every one that is born of the Spirit.
9 **Nicodemus** answered and said unto him,
How can these things be?
10 **Jesus** answered and said unto him,
Art thou a master of Israel,
and knowest not these things?
11 **Verily, verily, I** say unto thee,
We speak
that we do know,
and testify
that we have seen;
and ye receive not our witness.
12 **If I** have told you earthly things,
and ye believe not,
how shall ye believe,
if I tell you of heavenly things?
13 **And no man** hath ascended up to heaven, but he that came down from heaven, even the Son of man which is in heaven.
14 **And as Moses** lifted up the serpent in the wilderness,
even so must the Son of man be lifted up:
15 **That whosoever believeth in him** should not perish,
but have eternal life.
16 **For God** so loved the world,
that he gave his only begotten Son,
that whosoever believeth in him should not perish,
but have everlasting life.
17 **For God** sent not his Son into the world
to condemn the world;
but that the world through him might be saved.
18 **He that believeth on him** is not condemned:

but he that believeth not is condemned already,
because he hath not believed in the name of the only begotten Son of God.

19 **And this** is the condemnation,
that light is come into the world,
and men loved darkness rather than light,
because their deeds were evil.

20 **For every one that doeth evil** hateth the light,
neither cometh to the light,
lest his deeds should be reproved.

21 **But he that doeth truth** cometh to the light,
that his deeds may be made manifest,
that they are wrought in God.

22 **After these things** came Jesus and his disciples into the land of Judaea;
and there he tarried with them,
and baptized.

23 **And John** also was baptizing in Aenon near to Salim,
because there was much water there:
and they came,
and were baptized.

24 **For John** was not yet cast into prison.

25 **Then there** arose a question between some of John's disciples and the Jews about purifying.

26 **And they** came unto John,
and said unto him,
Rabbi, he that was with thee beyond Jordan, {to whom thou barest witness}, {behold}, the same baptizeth,
and all men come to him.

27 **John** answered and said,
A man can receive nothing,
except it be given him from heaven.

28 **Ye yourselves** bear me witness,
that I said,
I am not the Christ,
but that I am sent before him.

29 **He that hath the bride** is the bridegroom:
but the friend of the bridegroom, {which standeth} {and heareth him}, rejoiceth greatly because of the bridegroom's voice:
this my joy therefore is fulfilled.

30 **He** must increase,
but I must decrease.

31 **He that cometh from above** is above all:
he that is of the earth is earthly,
and speaketh of the earth:
he that cometh from heaven is above all.

32 **And what he** hath seen and heard,
that he testifieth;
and no man receiveth his testimony.

33 **He that hath received his testimony** hath set to his seal that God is true.

34 **For he whom God hath sent** speaketh the words of God:
for God giveth not the Spirit by measure unto him.

35 **The Father** loveth the Son,
and hath given all things into his hand.

36 **He that believeth on the Son** hath everlasting life:
and he that believeth not the Son shall not see life;
but the wrath of God abideth on him.

4

When therefore the Lord knew
how the Pharisees had heard that Jesus made and baptized more disciples than John,

2 (Though Jesus himself baptized not, but his disciples,)

3 **He** left Judaea,
and departed again into Galilee.

4 **And he** must needs go through Samaria.

5 **Then** cometh he to a city of Samaria,
which is called Sychar, near to the parcel of ground that Jacob gave to his son Joseph.

6 **Now Jacob's well** was there.
Jesus therefore, {being wearied with his journey}, sat thus on the well:
and it was about the sixth hour.

7 **There** cometh a woman of Samaria to draw water:
Jesus saith unto her,
Give me to drink.

8 (**For his disciples** were gone away unto the city
to buy meat.)

9 **Then** saith the woman of Samaria unto him,
How is it that thou, {being a Jew}, askest drink of me,
which am a woman of Samaria?
for the Jews have no dealings with the Samaritans.

10 **Jesus** answered and said unto her,
If thou knewest the gift of God,
and who it is that saith to thee,
Give me to drink;
thou wouldest have asked of him,
and he would have given thee living water.

11 **The woman** saith unto him,
Sir, thou hast nothing to draw with,
and the well is deep:
from whence then hast thou that living water?

12 **Art thou** greater than our father Jacob,
which gave us the well,
and drank thereof himself, and his children, and his cattle?

13 **Jesus** answered and said unto her,
Whosoever drinketh of this water shall thirst again:

14 **But whosoever drinketh of the water that I shall give him** shall never thirst;
but the water that I shall give him shall be in him a well of water springing up into everlasting life.

15 **The woman** saith unto him,
Sir, give me this water,
that I thirst not,
neither come hither to draw.

16 **Jesus** saith unto her,
Go,
call thy husband,
and come hither.

17 **The woman** answered and said,
I have no husband.
Jesus said unto her,
Thou hast well said,
I have no husband:

18 **For thou** hast had five husbands;
and he whom thou now hast is not thy husband:
in that saidst thou truly.

19 **The woman** saith unto him,
Sir, I perceive that thou art a prophet.

20 **Our fathers** worshipped in this mountain;
and ye say,
that in Jerusalem is the place where men ought to worship.

21 **Jesus** saith unto her,
Woman, believe me,

the hour cometh,
when ye shall neither in this mountain, nor yet at Jerusalem, worship the Father.
22 **Ye** worship ye know not what:
we know
what we worship:
for salvation is of the Jews.
23 **But the hour** cometh,
and now is,
when the true worshippers shall worship the Father in spirit and in truth:
for the Father seeketh such to worship him.
24 **God** is a Spirit:
and they that worship him must worship him in spirit and in truth.
25 **The woman** saith unto him,
I know
that Messias cometh,
which is called Christ:
when he is come,
he will tell us all things.
26 **Jesus** saith unto her,
I that speak unto thee am he.
27 **And upon this** came his disciples,
and marvelled that he talked with the woman:
yet no man said,
What seekest thou?
or, Why talkest thou with her?
28 **The woman** then left her waterpot,
and went her way into the city,
and saith to the men,
29 **Come,**
see a man,
which told me all things that ever I did:
is not this the Christ?
30 **Then they** went out of the city,
and came unto him.
31 **In the mean while his disciples** prayed him,
saying,
Master, eat.
32 **But he** said unto them,
I have meat to eat
that ye know not of.
33 **Therefore** said the disciples one to another,
Hath any man brought him ought to eat?
34 **Jesus** saith unto them,
My meat is to do the will of him that sent me,
and to finish his work.
35 **Say not ye,**
There are yet four months,
and then cometh harvest?
behold,
I say unto you,
Lift up your eyes,
and look on the fields;
for they are white already to harvest.
36 **And he that reapeth** receiveth wages,
and gathereth fruit unto life eternal:
that both he that soweth and he that reapeth may rejoice together.
37 **And herein** is that saying true,
One soweth,
and another reapeth.
38 **I** sent you to reap that whereon ye bestowed no labour:
other men laboured,
and ye are entered into their labours.
39 **And many of the Samaritans of that city** believed on him for the saying of the woman,
which testified,
He told me all that ever I did.
40 **So when the Samaritans** were come unto him,
they besought him
that he would tarry with them:
and he abode there two days.
41 **And many more** believed because of his own word;
42 **And** said unto the woman,
Now we believe, not because of thy saying:
for we have heard him ourselves,
and know
that this is indeed the Christ, the Saviour of the world.
43 **Now after two days** he departed thence,
and went into Galilee.
44 **For Jesus himself** testified,
that a prophet hath no honour in his own country.
45 **Then when he** was come into Galilee,
the Galilaeans received him,
having seen all the things that he did at Jerusalem at the feast:
for they also went unto the feast.
46 **So Jesus** came again into Cana of Galilee,
where he made the water wine.
And there was a certain nobleman,
whose son was sick at Capernaum.
47 **When he** heard that Jesus was come out of Judaea into Galilee,
he went unto him,
and besought him
that he would come down,
and heal his son:
for he was at the point of death.
48 **Then** said Jesus unto him,
Except ye see signs and wonders,
ye will not believe.
49 **The nobleman** saith unto him,
Sir, come down
ere my child die.
50 **Jesus** saith unto him,
Go thy way;
thy son liveth.
And the man believed the word that Jesus had spoken unto him,
and he went his way.
51 **And as he** was now going down,
his servants met him,
and told him,
saying,
Thy son liveth.
52 **Then** enquired he of them the hour when he began to amend.
And they said unto him,
Yesterday at the seventh hour the fever left him.
53 **So the father** knew
that it was at the same hour,
in the which Jesus said unto him,
Thy son liveth:
and himself believed, and his whole house.
54 **This** is again the second miracle that Jesus did,
when he was come out of Judaea into Galilee.

5 **After this** there was a feast of the Jews;
and Jesus went up to Jerusalem.
2 **Now there** is at Jerusalem by the sheep market a pool,
which is called in the Hebrew tongue Bethesda,
having five porches.
3 **In these** lay a great multitude of impotent folk, of blind, halt, withered,
waiting for the moving of the water.
4 **For an angel** went down at a certain season into the pool,
and troubled the water:
whosoever then first after the troubling of the water stepped in was made whole of whatsoever disease he had.

5 **And a certain man** was there,
which had an infirmity thirty and eight years.
6 **When Jesus** saw him lie,
and knew
that he had been now a long time in that case,
he saith unto him,
Wilt thou be made whole?
7 **The impotent man** answered him,
Sir, I have no man,
when the water is troubled,
to put me into the pool:
but while I am coming,
another steppeth down before me.
8 **Jesus** saith unto him,
Rise,
take up thy bed,
and walk.
9 **And immediately** the man was made whole,
and took up his bed,
and walked:
and on the same day was the sabbath.
10 **The Jews** therefore said unto him that was cured,
It is the sabbath day:
it is not lawful for thee to carry thy bed.
11 **He** answered them,
He that made me whole, the same said unto me,
Take up thy bed,
and walk.
12 **Then** asked they him,
What man is that which said unto thee,
Take up thy bed,
and walk?
13 **And he that was healed** wist not
who it was:
for Jesus had conveyed himself away,
a multitude being in that place.
14 **Afterward Jesus** findeth him in the temple,
and said unto him,
Behold,
thou art made whole:
sin no more,
lest a worse thing come unto thee.
15 **The man** departed,
and told the Jews
that it was Jesus,
which had made him whole.
16 **And therefore** did the Jews persecute Jesus,
and sought to slay him,
because he had done these things on the sabbath day.
17 **But Jesus** answered them,
My Father worketh hitherto,
and I work.
18 **Therefore the Jews** sought the more to kill him,
because he not only had broken the sabbath,
but said also
that God was his Father,
making himself equal with God.
19 **Then** answered Jesus and said unto them,
Verily, verily, I say unto you,
The Son can do nothing of himself,
but what he seeth the Father do:
for what things soever he doeth,
these also doeth the Son likewise.
20 **For the Father** loveth the Son,
and sheweth him all things that himself doeth:
and he will shew him greater works than these,
that ye may marvel.
21 **For as the Father** raiseth up the dead,
and quickeneth them;
even so the Son quickeneth whom he will.
22 **For the Father** judgeth no man,
but hath committed all judgment unto the Son:
23 **That all men** should honour the Son,
even as they honour the Father.
He that honoureth not the Son honoureth not the Father which hath sent him.
24 **Verily, verily, I** say unto you,
He that heareth my word, and believeth on him that sent me, hath everlasting life,
and shall not come into condemnation;
but is passed from death unto life.
25 **Verily, verily, I** say unto you,
The hour is coming,
and now is,
when the dead shall hear the voice of the Son of God:
and they that hear shall live.
26 **For as the Father** hath life in himself;
so hath he given to the Son to have life in himself;
27 **And** hath given him authority to execute judgment also,
because he is the Son of man.
28 **Marvel not** at this:
for the hour is coming,
in the which all that are in the graves shall hear his voice,
29 **And** shall come forth; they that have done good, unto the resurrection of life; and they that have done evil, unto the resurrection of damnation.
30 **I** can of mine own self do nothing:
as I hear,
I judge:
and my judgment is just;
because I seek not mine own will, but the will of the Father which hath sent me.
31 **If I** bear witness of myself,
my witness is not true.
32 **There** is another that beareth witness of me;
and I know
that the witness which he witnesseth of me is true.
33 **Ye** sent unto John,
and he bare witness unto the truth.
34 **But I** receive not testimony from man:
but these things I say,
that ye might be saved.
35 **He** was a burning and a shining light:
and ye were willing for a season to rejoice in his light.
36 **But I** have greater witness than that of John:
for the works which the Father hath given me to finish, the same works that I do, bear witness of me,
that the Father hath sent me.
37 **And the Father himself**, {which hath sent me}, hath borne witness of me.
Ye have neither heard his voice at any time,
nor seen his shape.
38 **And ye** have not his word abiding in you:
for whom he hath sent,
him ye believe not.
39 **Search** the scriptures;
for in them ye think
ye have eternal life:
and they are they which testify of me.
40 **And ye** will not come to me,
that ye might have life.
41 **I** receive not honour from men.
42 **But I** know you,

that ye have not the love of God in you.

[43] **I** am come in my Father's name,
and ye receive me not:
if another shall come in his own name,
him ye will receive.

[44] **How** can ye believe,
which receive honour one of another,
and seek not the honour that cometh from God only?

[45] **Do not think**
that I will accuse you to the Father:
there is one that accuseth you, even Moses,
in whom ye trust.

[46] **For** had ye believed Moses,
ye would have believed me;
for he wrote of me.

[47] **But if ye** believe not his writings,
how shall ye believe my words?

6 **After these things** Jesus went over the sea of Galilee,
which is the sea of Tiberias.

[2] **And a great multitude** followed him,
because they saw his miracles which he did on them that were diseased.

[3] **And Jesus** went up into a mountain,
and there he sat with his disciples.

[4] **And the passover, a feast of the Jews,** was nigh.

[5] **When Jesus** then lifted up his eyes,
and saw a great company come unto him,
he saith unto Philip,
Whence shall we buy bread,
that these may eat?

[6] **And this** he said
to prove him:
for he himself knew
what he would do.

[7] **Philip** answered him,
Two hundred pennyworth of bread is not sufficient for them,
that every one of them may take a little.

[8] **One of his disciples, Andrew, Simon Peter's brother,** saith unto him,

[9] **There** is a lad here,
which hath five barley loaves, and two small fishes:
but what are they among so many?

[10] **And Jesus** said,
Make the men sit down.
Now there was much grass in the place.
So the men sat down, in number about five thousand.

[11] **And Jesus** took the loaves;
and when he had given thanks,
he distributed to the disciples, and the disciples to them that were set down; and likewise of the fishes as much as they would.

[12] **When they** were filled,
he said unto his disciples,
Gather up the fragments that remain,
that nothing be lost.

[13] **Therefore they** gathered them together,
and filled twelve baskets with the fragments of the five barley loaves,
which remained over and above unto them that had eaten.

[14] **Then those men**, {when they had seen the miracle that Jesus did}, said,
This is of a truth that prophet that should come into the world.

[15] **When Jesus** therefore perceived that they would come and take him by force,
to make him a king,
he departed again into a mountain himself alone.

[16] **And when even** was now come,
his disciples went down unto the sea,

[17] **And** entered into a ship,
and went over the sea toward Capernaum.
And it was now dark,
and Jesus was not come to them.

[18] **And the sea** arose by reason of a great wind that blew.

[19] **So when they** had rowed about five and twenty or thirty furlongs,
they see Jesus walking on the sea, and drawing nigh unto the ship:
and they were afraid.

[20] **But he** saith unto them,
It is I;
be not afraid.

[21] **Then they willingly** received him into the ship:
and immediately the ship was at the land whither they went.

[22] **The day following**, {when the people which stood on the other side of the sea saw that there was none other boat there, save that one whereinto his disciples were entered}, {and that Jesus went not with his disciples into the boat}, {but that his disciples were gone away alone};

[23] (Howbeit there came other boats from Tiberias nigh unto the place where they did eat bread,
after that the Lord had given thanks:)

[24] {When the people therefore saw that Jesus was not there, neither his disciples},
they also took shipping,
and came to Capernaum,
seeking for Jesus.

[25] **And when they** had found him on the other side of the sea,
they said unto him,
Rabbi, when camest thou hither?

[26] **Jesus** answered them and said,
Verily, verily, I say unto you,
Ye seek me,
not because ye saw the miracles,
but because ye did eat of the loaves,
and were filled.

[27] **Labour not** for the meat which perisheth, but for that meat which endureth unto everlasting life,
which the Son of man shall give unto you:
for him hath God the Father sealed.

[28] **Then** said they unto him,
What shall we do,
that we might work the works of God?

[29] **Jesus** answered and said unto them,
This is the work of God,
that ye believe on him whom he hath sent.

[30] **They** said therefore unto him,
What sign shewest thou then,
that we may see,
and believe thee?
what dost thou work?

[31] **Our fathers** did eat manna in the desert;
as it is written,
He gave them bread from heaven to eat.

[32] **Then Jesus** said unto them,
Verily, verily, I say unto you,
Moses gave you not that bread from heaven;

but my Father giveth you the true bread from heaven.

33 **For the bread of God** is he which cometh down from heaven, and giveth life unto the world.

34 **Then** said they unto him,
Lord, evermore give us this bread.

35 **And Jesus** said unto them,
I am the bread of life:
he that cometh to me shall never hunger;
and he that believeth on me shall never thirst.

36 **But I** said unto you,
That ye also have seen me,
and believe not.

37 **All that the Father giveth me** shall come to me;
and him that cometh to me I will in no wise cast out.

38 **For I** came down from heaven,
not to do mine own will, but the will of him that sent me.

39 **And this** is the Father's will which hath sent me,
that of all which he hath given me I should lose nothing,
but should raise it up again at the last day.

40 **And this** is the will of him that sent me,
that every one which seeth the Son, and believeth on him, may have everlasting life:
and I will raise him up at the last day.

41 **The Jews** then murmured at him,
because he said,
I am the bread which came down from heaven.

42 **And they** said,
Is not this Jesus, the son of Joseph,
whose father and mother we know?
how is it then that he saith,
I came down from heaven?

43 **Jesus** therefore answered and said unto them,
Murmur not among yourselves.

44 **No man** can come to me,
except the Father which hath sent me draw him:
and I will raise him up at the last day.

45 **It** is written in the prophets,
And they shall be all taught of God.
Every man therefore that hath heard, and hath learned of the Father, cometh unto me.

46 **Not that any man** hath seen the Father, save he which is of God,
he hath seen the Father.

47 **Verily, verily, I** say unto you,
He that believeth on me hath everlasting life.

48 **I** am that bread of life.

49 **Your fathers** did eat manna in the wilderness,
and are dead.

50 **This** is the bread which cometh down from heaven,
that a man may eat thereof,
and not die.

51 **I** am the living bread which came down from heaven:
if any man eat of this bread,
he shall live for ever:
and the bread that I will give is my flesh,
which I will give for the life of the world.

52 **The Jews** therefore strove among themselves,
saying,
How can this man give us his flesh to eat?

53 **Then Jesus** said unto them,
Verily, verily, I say unto you,
Except ye eat the flesh of the Son of man,
and drink his blood,
ye have no life in you.

54 **Whoso eateth my flesh, and drinketh my blood,** hath eternal life;
and I will raise him up at the last day.

55 **For my flesh** is meat indeed,
and my blood is drink indeed.

56 **He that eateth my flesh, and drinketh my blood,** dwelleth in me, and I in him.

57 **As the living Father** hath sent me,
and I live by the Father:
so he that eateth me, even he shall live by me.

58 **This** is that bread which came down from heaven:
not as your fathers did eat manna,
and are dead:
he that eateth of this bread shall live for ever.

59 **These things** said he in the synagogue,
as he taught in Capernaum.

60 **Many therefore of his disciples,** {when they had heard this}, said,
This is an hard saying;
who can hear it?

61 **When Jesus** knew in himself
that his disciples murmured at it,
he said unto them,
Doth this offend you?

62 **What and if ye** shall see the Son of man ascend up where he was before?

63 **It is the spirit** that quickeneth;
the flesh profiteth nothing:
the words that I speak unto you, they are spirit,
and they are life.

64 **But there** are some of you that believe not.
For Jesus knew from the beginning
who they were that believed not,
and who should betray him.

65 **And he** said,
Therefore said I unto you,
that no man can come unto me,
except it were given unto him of my Father.

66 **From that time** many of his disciples went back,
and walked no more with him.

67 **Then** said Jesus unto the twelve,
Will ye also go away?

68 **Then Simon Peter** answered him,
Lord, to whom shall we go?
thou hast the words of eternal life.

69 **And we** believe and are sure
that thou art that Christ, the Son of the living God.

70 **Jesus** answered them,
Have not I chosen you twelve,
and one of you is a devil?

71 **He** spake of Judas Iscariot the son of Simon:
for he it was that should betray him,
being one of the twelve.

7

After these things Jesus walked in Galilee:
for he would not walk in Jewry,
because the Jews sought to kill him.

2 **Now the Jew's feast of tabernacles** was at hand.

3 **His brethren** therefore said unto him,
Depart hence,
and go into Judaea,
that thy disciples also may see the works that thou doest.

4 **For there** is no man that doeth any thing in secret,
and he himself seeketh to be known openly.

If thou do these things,
shew thyself to the world.

5 **For neither** did his brethren believe in him.

6 **Then Jesus** said unto them,
My time is not yet come:
but your time is alway ready.

7 **The world** cannot hate you;
but me it hateth,
because I testify of it,
that the works thereof are evil.

8 **Go ye up** unto this feast:
I go not up yet unto this feast:
for my time is not yet full come.

9 **When he** had said these words unto them,
he abode still in Galilee.

10 **But when his brethren** were gone up,
then went he also up unto the feast, not openly, but as it were in secret.

11 **Then the Jews** sought him at the feast,
and said,
Where is he?

12 **And there** was much murmuring among the people concerning him:
for some said,
He is a good man:
others said,
Nay;
but he deceiveth the people.

13 **Howbeit no man** spake openly of him for fear of the Jews.

14 **Now about the midst of the feast** Jesus went up into the temple,
and taught.

15 **And the Jews** marvelled,
saying,
How knoweth this man letters,
having never learned?

16 **Jesus** answered them,
and said,
My doctrine is not mine, but his that sent me.

17 **If any man** will do his will,
he shall know of the doctrine,
whether it be of God,
or whether I speak of myself.

18 **He that speaketh of himself** seeketh his own glory:
but he that seeketh his glory that sent him, the same is true,
and no unrighteousness is in him.

19 **Did not Moses** give you the law,
and yet none of you keepeth the law?

Why go ye about to kill me?

20 **The people** answered and said,
Thou hast a devil:
who goeth about to kill thee?

21 **Jesus** answered and said unto them,
I have done one work,
and ye all marvel.

22 **Moses** therefore gave unto you circumcision;
(not because it is of Moses, but of the fathers;)
and ye on the sabbath day circumcise a man.

23 **If a man on the sabbath day** receive circumcision,
that the law of Moses should not be broken;
are ye angry at me,
because I have made a man every whit whole on the sabbath day?

24 **Judge not** according to the appearance,
but judge righteous judgment.

25 **Then** said some of them of Jerusalem,
Is not this he,
whom they seek to kill?

26 **But, {lo}, he** speaketh boldly,
and they say nothing unto him.

Do the rulers know indeed
that this is the very Christ?

27 **Howbeit we** know this man whence he is:
but when Christ cometh,
no man knoweth
whence he is.

28 **Then** cried Jesus in the temple
as he taught,
saying,
Ye both know me,
and ye know
whence I am:
and I am not come of myself,
but he that sent me is true,
whom ye know not.

29 **But I** know him:
for I am from him,
and he hath sent me.

30 **Then they** sought to take him:
but no man laid hands on him,
because his hour was not yet come.

31 **And many of the people** believed on him,
and said,
When Christ cometh,
will he do more miracles than these which this man hath done?

32 **The Pharisees** heard that the people murmured such things concerning him;
and the Pharisees and the chief priests sent officers to take him.

33 **Then** said Jesus unto them,
Yet a little while am I with you,
and then I go unto him that sent me.

34 **Ye** shall seek me,
and shall not find me:
and where I am,
thither ye cannot come.

35 **Then** said the Jews among themselves,
Whither will he go,
that we shall not find him?
will he go unto the dispersed among the Gentiles,
and teach the Gentiles?

36 **What manner of saying** is this that he said,
Ye shall seek me,
and shall not find me:
and where I am,
thither ye cannot come?

37 **In the last day, that great day of the feast,** Jesus stood and cried,
saying,
If any man thirst,
let him come unto me,
and drink.

38 **He that believeth on me**, {as the scripture hath said}, out of his belly shall flow rivers of living water.

39 (**But this** spake he of the Spirit,
which they that believe on him should receive:
for the Holy Ghost was not yet given;
because that Jesus was not yet glorified.)

40 **Many of the people** therefore, {when they heard this saying}, said,
Of a truth this is the Prophet.

41 **Others** said,
This is the Christ.

But some said,
Shall Christ come out of Galilee?

42 **Hath not the scripture** said,

That Christ cometh of the seed of David, and out of the town of Bethlehem,
where David was?

43 **So there** was a division among the people because of him.

44 **And some of them** would have taken him;
but no man laid hands on him.

45 **Then** came the officers to the chief priests and Pharisees;
and they said unto them,
Why have ye not brought him?

46 **The officers** answered,
Never man spake like this man.

47 **Then** answered them the Pharisees,
Are ye also deceived?

48 **Have any of the rulers or of the Pharisees** believed on him?

49 **But this people who knoweth not the law** are cursed.

50 **Nicodemus** saith unto them,
(he that came to Jesus by night, {being one of them},)
51 **Doth our law** judge any man,
before it hear him,
and know
what he doeth?

52 **They** answered and said unto him,
Art thou also of Galilee?

Search,
and look:
for out of Galilee ariseth no prophet.

53 **And every man** went unto his own house.

8 **Jesus** went unto the mount of Olives.

2 **And early in the morning** he came again into the temple,
and all the people came unto him;
and he sat down,
and taught them.

3 **And the scribes and Pharisees** brought unto him a woman taken in adultery;
and when they had set her in the midst,
4 **They** say unto him,
Master, this woman was taken in adultery, in the very act.

5 **Now Moses in the law** commanded us,
that such should be stoned:
but what sayest thou?

6 **This they** said,
tempting him,
that they might have to accuse him.

But Jesus stooped down,
and with his finger wrote on the ground,
as though he heard them not.

7 **So when they** continued asking him,
he lifted up himself,
and said unto them,
He that is without sin among you, let him first cast a stone at her.

8 **And again he** stooped down,
and wrote on the ground.

9 **And they which heard it**, {being convicted by their own conscience}, went out one by one,
beginning at the eldest, even unto the last:
and Jesus was left alone,
and the woman standing in the midst.

10 **When Jesus** had lifted up himself,
and saw none but the woman,
he said unto her,
Woman, where are those thine accusers?
hath no man condemned thee?

11 **She** said,
No man, Lord.

And Jesus said unto her,
Neither do I condemn thee:
go,
and sin no more.

12 **Then** spake Jesus again unto them,
saying,
I am the light of the world:
he that followeth me shall not walk in darkness,
but shall have the light of life.

13 **The Pharisees** therefore said unto him,
Thou bearest record of thyself;
thy record is not true.

14 **Jesus** answered and said unto them,
Though I bear record of myself,
yet my record is true:
for I know
whence I came,
and whither I go;
but ye cannot tell
whence I come,
and whither I go.

15 **Ye** judge after the flesh;
I judge no man.

16 **And yet if I** judge,
my judgment is true:
for I am not alone, but I and the Father that sent me.

17 **It is also written in your law,** that the testimony of two men is true.

18 **I** am one that bear witness of myself,
and the Father that sent me beareth witness of me.

19 **Then** said they unto him,
Where is thy Father?

Jesus answered,
Ye neither know me, nor my Father:
if ye had known me,
ye should have known my Father also.

20 **These words** spake Jesus in the treasury,
as he taught in the temple:
and no man laid hands on him;
for his hour was not yet come.

21 **Then** said Jesus again unto them,
I go my way,
and ye shall seek me,
and shall die in your sins:
whither I go,
ye cannot come.

22 **Then** said the Jews,
Will he kill himself?
because he saith,
Whither I go,
ye cannot come.

23 **And he** said unto them,
Ye are from beneath;
I am from above:
ye are of this world;
I am not of this world.

24 **I** said therefore unto you,
that ye shall die in your sins:
for if ye believe not
that I am he,
ye shall die in your sins.

25 **Then** said they unto him,
Who art thou?

And Jesus saith unto them,
Even the same that I said unto you from the beginning.

26 **I** have many things to say and to judge of you:
but he that sent me is true;
and I speak to the world those things which I have heard of him.

27 **They** understood not
that he spake to them of the Father.

28 **Then** said Jesus unto them,
When ye have lifted up the Son of man,
then shall ye know
that I am he,

and that I do nothing of myself;
but as my Father hath taught me,
I speak these things.

29 **And he that sent me** is with me:
the Father hath not left me alone;
for I do always those things that please him.

30 **As he** spake these words,
many believed on him.

31 **Then** said Jesus to those Jews which believed on him,
If ye continue in my word,
then are ye my disciples indeed;
32 **And ye** shall know the truth,
and the truth shall make you free.

33 **They** answered him,
We be Abraham's seed,
and were never in bondage to any man:
how sayest thou,
Ye shall be made free?

34 **Jesus** answered them,
Verily, verily, I say unto you,
Whosoever committeth sin is the servant of sin.

35 **And the servant** abideth not in the house for ever:
but the Son abideth ever.

36 **If the Son** therefore shall make you free,
ye shall be free indeed.

37 **I** know
that ye are Abraham's seed;
but ye seek to kill me,
because my word hath no place in you.

38 **I** speak that which I have seen with my Father:
and ye do that which ye have seen with your father.

39 **They** answered and said unto him,
Abraham is our father.

Jesus saith unto them,
If ye were Abraham's children,
ye would do the works of Abraham.

40 **But now ye** seek to kill me, a man that hath told you the truth,
which I have heard of God:
this did not Abraham.

41 **Ye** do the deeds of your father.

Then said they to him,
We be not born of fornication;
we have one Father, even God.

42 **Jesus** said unto them,
If God were your Father,
ye would love me:
for I proceeded forth and came from God;
neither came I of myself,
but he sent me.

43 **Why** do ye not understand my speech?
even because ye cannot hear my word.

44 **Ye** are of your father the devil,
and the lusts of your father ye will do.

He was a murderer from the beginning,
and abode not in the truth,
because there is no truth in him.

When he speaketh a lie,
he speaketh of his own:
for he is a liar, and the father of it.

45 **And because I** tell you the truth,
ye believe me not.

46 **Which of you** convinceth me of sin?

And if I say the truth,
why do ye not believe me?

47 **He that is of God** heareth God's words:
ye therefore hear them not,
because ye are not of God.

48 **Then** answered the Jews,
and said unto him,
Say we not well
that thou art a Samaritan,
and hast a devil?

49 **Jesus** answered,
I have not a devil;
but I honour my Father,
and ye do dishonour me.

50 **And I** seek not mine own glory:
there is one that seeketh and judgeth.

51 **Verily, verily, I** say unto you,
If a man keep my saying,
he shall never see death.

52 **Then** said the Jews unto him,
Now we know
that thou hast a devil.

Abraham is dead, and the prophets;
and thou sayest,
If a man keep my saying,
he shall never taste of death.

53 **Art thou** greater than our father Abraham,
which is dead?
and the prophets are dead:
whom makest thou thyself?

54 **Jesus** answered,
If I honour myself,
my honour is nothing:
it is my Father that honoureth me;
of whom ye say,
that he is your God:
55 **Yet ye** have not known him;
but I know him:
and if I should say,
I know him not,
I shall be a liar like unto you:
but I know him,
and keep his saying.

56 **Your father Abraham** rejoiced to see my day:
and he saw it,
and was glad.

57 **Then** said the Jews unto him,
Thou art not yet fifty years old,
and hast thou seen Abraham?

58 **Jesus** said unto them,
Verily, verily, I say unto you,
Before Abraham was,
I am.

59 **Then** took they up stones
to cast at him:
but Jesus hid himself,
and went out of the temple,
going through the midst of them,
and so passed by.

9

And as Jesus passed by,
he saw a man which was blind from his birth.

2 **And his disciples** asked him, saying,
Master, who did sin, this man, or his parents,
that he was born blind?

3 **Jesus** answered,
Neither hath this man sinned, nor his parents:
but that the works of God should be made manifest in him.

4 **I** must work the works of him that sent me,
while it is day:
the night cometh,
when no man can work.

5 **As long as I** am in the world,
I am the light of the world.

6 **When he** had thus spoken,
he spat on the ground,
and made clay of the spittle,
and he anointed the eyes of the blind man with the clay,
7 **And** said unto him,
Go,
wash in the pool of Siloam,
(which is by interpretation, Sent).

He went his way therefore,
and washed,
and came seeing.

8 **The neighbours therefore, and they which before had seen him that he was blind,** said,
Is not this he that sat and begged?
9 **Some** said,
This is he:
others said,
He is like him:
but he said,
I am he.
10 **Therefore** said they unto him,
How were thine eyes opened?
11 **He** answered and said,
A man that is called Jesus made clay,
and anointed mine eyes,
and said unto me,
Go to the pool of Siloam,
and wash:
and I went and washed,
and I received sight.
12 **Then** said they unto him,
Where is he?
He said,
I know not.
13 **They** brought to the Pharisees him that aforetime was blind.
14 **And it** was the sabbath day
when Jesus made the clay,
and opened his eyes.
15 **Then again the Pharisees** also asked him
how he had received his sight.
He said unto them,
He put clay upon mine eyes,
and I washed,
and do see.
16 **Therefore** said some of the Pharisees,
This man is not of God,
because he keepeth not the sabbath day.
Others said,
How can a man that is a sinner do such miracles?
And there was a division among them.
17 **They** say unto the blind man again,
What sayest thou of him,
that he hath opened thine eyes?
He said,
He is a prophet.
18 **But the Jews** did not believe concerning him,
that he had been blind,
and received his sight,
until they called the parents of him that had received his sight.
19 **And they** asked them,
saying,
Is this your son,
who ye say was born blind?
how then doth he now see?
20 **His parents** answered them and said,
We know
that this is our son,
and that he was born blind:
21 **But by what means** he now seeth,
we know not;
or who hath opened his eyes,
we know not:
he is of age;
ask him:
he shall speak for himself.
22 **These words** spake his parents,
because they feared the Jews:
for the Jews had agreed already,
that if any man did confess
that he was Christ,
he should be put out of the synagogue.
23 **Therefore** said his parents,
He is of age;
ask him.
24 **Then again** called they the man that was blind,
and said unto him,
Give God the praise:
we know
that this man is a sinner.
25 **He** answered and said,
Whether he be a sinner or no,
I know not:
one thing I know,
that, {whereas I was blind}, now I see.
26 **Then** said they to him again,
What did he to thee?
how opened he thine eyes?
27 **He** answered them,
I have told you already,
and ye did not hear:
wherefore would ye hear it again?
will ye also be his disciples?
28 **Then they** reviled him,
and said,
Thou art his disciple;
but we are Moses' disciples.
29 **We** know
that God spake unto Moses:
as for this fellow, we know not
from whence he is.
30 **The man** answered and said unto them,
Why herein is a marvellous thing,
that ye know not
from whence he is,
and yet he hath opened mine eyes.
31 **Now we** know
that God heareth not sinners:
but if any man be a worshipper of God,
and doeth his will,
him he heareth.
32 **Since the world** began
was it not heard that any man opened the eyes of one that was born blind.
33 **If this man** were not of God,
he could do nothing.
34 **They** answered and said unto him,
Thou wast altogether born in sins,
and dost thou teach us?
And they cast him out.
35 **Jesus** heard that they had cast him out;
and when he had found him,
he said unto him,
Dost thou believe on the Son of God?
36 **He** answered and said,
Who is he, Lord,
that I might believe on him?
37 **And Jesus** said unto him,
Thou hast both seen him,
and it is he that talketh with thee.
38 **And he** said,
Lord, I believe.
And he worshipped him.
39 **And Jesus** said,
For judgment I am come into this world,
that they which see not might see;
and that they which see might be made blind.
40 **And some of the Pharisees which were with him** heard these words,
and said unto him,
Are we blind also?
41 **Jesus** said unto them,
If ye were blind,
ye should have no sin:
but now ye say,
We see;
therefore your sin remaineth.

10

Verily, verily, I say unto you,

He that entereth not by the door into the sheepfold, but climbeth up some other way, the same is a thief and a robber.

2 **But he that entereth in by the door** is the shepherd of the sheep.

3 **To him** the porter openeth;
and the sheep hear his voice:
and he calleth his own sheep by name,
and leadeth them out.

4 **And when he** putteth forth his own sheep,
he goeth before them,
and the sheep follow him:
for they know his voice.

5 **And a stranger** will they not follow,
but will flee from him:
for they know not the voice of strangers.

6 **This parable** spake Jesus unto them:
but they understood not
what things they were which he spake unto them.

7 **Then** said Jesus unto them again,
Verily, verily, I say unto you,
I am the door of the sheep.

8 **All that ever came before me** are thieves and robbers:
but the sheep did not hear them.

9 **I** am the door:
by me if any man enter in,
he shall be saved,
and shall go in and out,
and find pasture.

10 **The thief** cometh not,
but for to steal,
and to kill,
and to destroy:
I am come
that they might have life,
and that they might have it more abundantly.

11 **I** am the good shepherd:
the good shepherd giveth his life for the sheep.

12 **But he that is an hireling, and not the shepherd,** {whose own the sheep are not}, seeth the wolf coming,
and leaveth the sheep,
and fleeth:
and the wolf catcheth them,
and scattereth the sheep.

13 **The hireling** fleeth,
because he is an hireling,
and careth not for the sheep.

14 **I** am the good shepherd,
and know my sheep,
and am known of mine.

15 **As the Father** knoweth me,
even so know I the Father:
and I lay down my life for the sheep.

16 **And other sheep** I have,
which are not of this fold:
them also I must bring,
and they shall hear my voice;
and there shall be one fold, and one shepherd.

17 **Therefore** doth my Father love me,
because I lay down my life,
that I might take it again.

18 **No man** taketh it from me,
but I lay it down of myself.
I have power to lay it down,
and I have power to take it again.
This commandment have I received of my Father.

19 **There** was a division therefore again among the Jews for these sayings.

20 **And many of them** said,
He hath a devil,
and is mad;
why hear ye him?

21 **Others** said,
These are not the words of him that hath a devil.
Can a devil open the eyes of the blind?

22 **And it** was at Jerusalem the feast of the dedication,
and it was winter.

23 **And Jesus** walked in the temple in Solomon's porch.

24 **Then** came the Jews round about him,
and said unto him,
How long dost thou make us to doubt?
If thou be the Christ,
tell us plainly.

25 **Jesus** answered them,
I told you,
and ye believed not:
the works that I do in my Father's name, they bear witness of me.

26 **But ye** believe not,
because ye are not of my sheep,
as I said unto you.

27 **My sheep** hear my voice,
and I know them,
and they follow me:

28 **And I** give unto them eternal life;
and they shall never perish,
neither shall any man pluck them out of my hand.

29 **My Father**, {which gave them me}, is greater than all;
and no man is able to pluck them out of my Father's hand.

30 **I and my Father** are one.

31 **Then the Jews** took up stones again
to stone him.

32 **Jesus** answered them,
Many good works have I shewed you from my Father;
for which of those works do ye stone me?

33 **The Jews** answered him,
saying,
For a good work we stone thee not;
but for blasphemy;
and because that thou, {being a man}, makest thyself God.

34 **Jesus** answered them,
Is it not written in your law,
I said,
Ye are gods?

35 **If he** called them gods,
unto whom the word of God came,
and the scripture cannot be broken;

36 **Say ye** of him,
whom the Father hath sanctified,
and sent into the world,
Thou blasphemest;
because I said,
I am the Son of God?

37 **If I** do not the works of my Father,
believe me not.

38 **But if I do**, {though ye believe not me}, believe the works:
that ye may know,
and believe,
that the Father is in me, and I in him.

39 **Therefore they** sought again to take him:
but he escaped out of their hand,

40 **And** went away again beyond Jordan into the place where John at first baptized;
and there he abode.

41 **And many** resorted unto him,
and said,
John did no miracle:
but all things that John spake of this man were true.

42 **And many** believed on him there.

11 **Now a certain man** was sick, named Lazarus, of Bethany, the town of Mary and her sister Martha.

2 (**It was that Mary** which anointed the Lord with ointment, and wiped his feet with her hair,
whose brother Lazarus was sick.)

3 **Therefore his sisters** sent unto him,
saying,
Lord, {behold}, he whom thou lovest is sick.

4 **When Jesus** heard that,
he said,
This sickness is not unto death, but for the glory of God,
that the Son of God might be glorified thereby.

5 **Now Jesus** loved Martha, and her sister, and Lazarus.

6 **When he** had heard therefore that he was sick,
he abode two days still in the same place where he was.

7 **Then after that** saith he to his disciples,
Let us go into Judaea again.

8 **His disciples** say unto him,
Master, the Jews of late sought to stone thee;
and goest thou thither again?

9 **Jesus** answered,
Are there not twelve hours in the day?
If any man walk in the day,
he stumbleth not,
because he seeth the light of this world.

10 **But if a man** walk in the night,
he stumbleth,
because there is no light in him.

11 **These things** said he:
and after that he saith unto them,
Our friend Lazarus sleepeth;
but I go,
that I may awake him out of sleep.

12 **Then** said his disciples,
Lord, if he sleep,
he shall do well.

13 **Howbeit Jesus** spake of his death:
but they thought
that he had spoken of taking of rest in sleep.

14 **Then** said Jesus unto them plainly,
Lazarus is dead.

15 **And I** am glad for your sakes
that I was not there,
to the intent ye may believe;
nevertheless let us go unto him.

16 **Then** said Thomas,
which is called Didymus, unto his fellowdisciples,
Let us also go,
that we may die with him.

17 **Then when Jesus** came,
he found that he had lain in the grave four days already.

18 **Now Bethany** was nigh unto Jerusalem, about fifteen furlongs off:

19 **And many of the Jews** came to Martha and Mary,
to comfort them concerning their brother.

20 **Then Martha**, {as soon as she heard that Jesus was coming}, went and met him:
but Mary sat still in the house.

21 **Then** said Martha unto Jesus,
Lord, if thou hadst been here,
my brother had not died.

22 **But I** know,
that even now, {whatsoever thou wilt ask of God}, God will give it thee.

23 **Jesus** saith unto her,
Thy brother shall rise again.

24 **Martha** saith unto him,
I know
that he shall rise again in the resurrection at the last day.

25 **Jesus** said unto her,
I am the resurrection, and the life:
he that believeth in me, {though he were dead}, yet shall he live:

26 **And whosoever liveth and believeth in me** shall never die.
Believest thou this?

27 **She** saith unto him,
Yea, Lord:
I believe
that thou art the Christ, the Son of God,
which should come into the world.

28 **And when she** had so said,
she went her way,
and called Mary her sister secretly,
saying,
The Master is come,
and calleth for thee.

29 **As soon as she** heard that,
she arose quickly,
and came unto him.

30 **Now Jesus** was not yet come into the town,
but was in that place where Martha met him.

31 **The Jews then which were with her in the house, and comforted her, {when they saw Mary}, {that she rose up hastily and went out}**, followed her,
saying,
She goeth unto the grave
to weep there.

32 **Then when Mary** was come where Jesus was,
and saw him,
she fell down at his feet,
saying unto him,
Lord, if thou hadst been here,
my brother had not died.

33 **When Jesus** therefore saw her weeping,
and the Jews also weeping which came with her,
he groaned in the spirit,
and was troubled.

34 **And** said,
Where have ye laid him?
They said unto him,
Lord, come and see.

35 **Jesus** wept.

36 **Then** said the Jews,
Behold how he loved him!

37 **And some of them** said,
Could not this man, {which opened the eyes of the blind}, have caused that even this man should not have died?

38 **Jesus therefore again groaning in himself** cometh to the grave.
It was a cave,
and a stone lay upon it.

39 **Jesus** said,
Take ye away the stone.
Martha, the sister of him that was dead, saith unto him,
Lord, by this time he stinketh:
for he hath been dead four days.

40 **Jesus** saith unto her,
Said I not unto thee,
that, {if thou wouldest believe}, thou shouldest see the glory of God?

41 **Then they** took away the stone from the place where the dead was laid.
And Jesus lifted up his eyes,
and said,
Father, I thank thee
that thou hast heard me.

42 **And I** knew

that thou hearest me always:
but because of the people which stand by I said it,
that they may believe
that thou hast sent me.

43 **And when he** thus had spoken,
he cried with a loud voice,
Lazarus, come forth.

44 **And he that was dead** came forth,
bound hand and foot with graveclothes:
and his face was bound about with a napkin.
Jesus saith unto them,
Loose him,
and let him go.

45 **Then many of the Jews which came to Mary, and had seen the things which Jesus did,** believed on him.

46 **But some of them** went their ways to the Pharisees,
and told them
what things Jesus had done.

47 **Then** gathered the chief priests and the Pharisees a council,
and said,
What do we?
for this man doeth many miracles.

48 **If we** let him thus alone,
all men will believe on him:
and the Romans shall come and take away both our place and nation.

49 **And one of them, named Caiaphas, {being the high priest that same year},** said unto them,
Ye know nothing at all,
50 **Nor** consider
that it is expedient for us, that one man should die for the people, and that the whole nation perish not.

51 **And this** spake he not of himself:
but being high priest that year,
he prophesied
that Jesus should die for that nation;
52 And not for that nation only,
but that also he should gather together in one the children of God that were scattered abroad.

53 **Then from that day forth** they took counsel together
for to put him to death.

54 **Jesus** therefore walked no more openly among the Jews;
but went thence unto a country near to the wilderness, into a city called Ephraim,
and there continued with his disciples.

55 **And the Jews' passover** was nigh at hand:
and many went out of the country up to Jerusalem before the passover,
to purify themselves.

56 **Then** sought they for Jesus,
and spake among themselves,
as they stood in the temple,
What think ye,
that he will not come to the feast?

57 **Now both the chief priests and the Pharisees** had given a commandment,
that, {if any man knew where he were}, he should shew it,
that they might take him.

12 **Then Jesus** six days before the passover came to Bethany,
where Lazarus was,
which had been dead,
whom he raised from the dead.

2 **There they** made him a supper;
and Martha served:
but Lazarus was one of them that sat at the table with him.

3 **Then** took Mary a pound of ointment of spikenard, very costly,
and anointed the feet of Jesus,
and wiped his feet with her hair:
and the house was filled with the odour of the ointment.

4 **Then** saith one of his disciples, Judas Iscariot, Simon's son,
which should betray him,
5 **Why** was not this ointment sold for three hundred pence,
and given to the poor?

6 **This he** said,
not that he cared for the poor;
but because he was a thief,
and had the bag,
and bare what was put therein.

7 **Then** said Jesus,
Let her alone:
against the day of my burying hath she kept this.

8 **For the poor** always ye have with you;
but me ye have not always.

9 **Much people of the Jews** therefore knew
that he was there:
and they came not for Jesus' sake only,
but that they might see Lazarus also,
whom he had raised from the dead.

10 **But the chief priests** consulted that they might put Lazarus also to death;

11 **Because that by reason of him** many of the Jews went away,
and believed on Jesus.

12 **On the next day** much people that were come to the feast, {when they heard that Jesus was coming to Jerusalem},
13 Took branches of palm trees,
and went forth to meet him,
and cried,
Hosanna:
Blessed is the King of Israel that cometh in the name of the Lord.

14 **And Jesus**, {when he had found a young ass}, sat thereon;
as it is written,
15 **Fear not,** daughter of Sion:
behold,
thy King cometh,
sitting on an ass's colt.

16 **These things** understood not his disciples at the first:
but when Jesus was glorified,
then remembered they
that these things were written of him,
and that they had done these things unto him.

17 **The people therefore that was with him {when he called Lazarus out of his grave}, {and raised him from the dead},** bare record.

18 **For this cause** the people also met him,
for that they heard that he had done this miracle.

19 **The Pharisees** therefore said among themselves,
Perceive ye how ye prevail nothing?
behold,
the world is gone after him.

20 **And there** were certain Greeks among them that came up to worship at the feast:
21 **The same** came therefore to Philip,
which was of Bethsaida of Galilee,
and desired him,
saying,
Sir, we would see Jesus.

22 **Philip** cometh and telleth Andrew:
and again Andrew and Philip tell Jesus.

23 **And Jesus** answered them,
saying,
The hour is come,
that the Son of man should be glorified.

24 **Verily, verily, I** say unto you,
Except a corn of wheat fall into the ground and die,
it abideth alone:
but if it die,
it bringeth forth much fruit.
25 **He that loveth his life** shall lose it;
and he that hateth his life in this world shall keep it unto life eternal.

26 **If any man** serve me,
let him follow me;
and where I am,
there shall also my servant be:
if any man serve me,
him will my Father honour.

27 **Now** is my soul troubled;
and what shall I say?

Father, save me from this hour:
but for this cause came I unto this hour.

28 **Father, glorify** thy name.

Then came there a voice from heaven,
saying,
I have both glorified it,
and will glorify it again.

29 **The people therefore, {that stood by}, {and heard it}**, said that it thundered:
others said,
An angel spake to him.

30 **Jesus** answered and said,
This voice came not because of me, but for your sakes.

31 **Now** is the judgment of this world:
now shall the prince of this world be cast out.

32 **And I**, {if I be lifted up from the earth}, will draw all men unto me.

33 **This he** said,
signifying what death he should die.

34 **The people** answered him,
We have heard out of the law
that Christ abideth for ever:
and how sayest thou,
The Son of man must be lifted up?
who is this Son of man?

35 **Then Jesus** said unto them,
Yet a little while is the light with you.
Walk
while ye have the light,
lest darkness come upon you:
for he that walketh in darkness knoweth not whither he goeth.

36 **While ye** have light,
believe in the light,
that ye may be the children of light.

These things spake Jesus,
and departed,
and did hide himself from them.

37 **But though he** had done so many miracles before them,
yet they believed not on him:
38 **That the saying of Esaias the prophet** might be fulfilled,
which he spake,
Lord, who hath believed our report?
and to whom hath the arm of the Lord been revealed?

39 **Therefore they** could not believe,
because that Esaias said again,
40 **He** hath blinded their eyes,
and hardened their heart;
that they should not see with their eyes,
nor understand with their heart,
and be converted,
and I should heal them.

41 **These things** said Esaias,
when he saw his glory,
and spake of him.

42 **Nevertheless among the chief rulers** also many believed on him;
but because of the Pharisees they did not confess him,
lest they should be put out of the synagogue:
43 **For they** loved the praise of men more than the praise of God.

44 **Jesus** cried and said,
He that believeth on me, believeth not on me, but on him that sent me.

45 **And he that seeth me** seeth him that sent me.

46 **I** am come a light into the world,
that whosoever believeth on me should not abide in darkness.

47 **And if any man** hear my words,
and believe not,
I judge him not:
for I came not to judge the world,
but to save the world.

48 **He that rejecteth me, and receiveth not my words,** hath one that judgeth him:
the word that I have spoken, the same shall judge him in the last day.

49 **For I** have not spoken of myself;
but the Father which sent me, he gave me a commandment,
what I should say,
and what I should speak.

50 **And I** know
that his commandment is life everlasting:
whatsoever I speak therefore,
even as the Father said unto me,
so I speak.

13

Now before the feast of the passover, {when Jesus knew} {that his hour was come} {that he should depart out of this world unto the Father}, {having loved his own which were in the world}, he loved them unto the end.

2 **And supper** being ended,
the devil having now put into the heart of Judas Iscariot, Simon's son, to betray him;
3 **Jesus** knowing
that the Father had given all things into his hands,
and that he was come from God,
and went to God;
4 **He** riseth from supper,
and laid aside his garments;
and took a towel,
and girded himself.

5 **After that** he poureth water into a bason,
and began to wash the disciples' feet,
and to wipe them with the towel wherewith he was girded.

6 **Then** cometh he to Simon Peter:
and Peter saith unto him,
Lord, dost thou wash my feet?
7 **Jesus** answered and said unto him,
What I do
thou knowest not now;
but thou shalt know hereafter.
8 **Peter** saith unto him,
Thou shalt never wash my feet.

Jesus answered him,
If I wash thee not,
thou hast no part with me.

9 **Simon Peter** saith unto him, Lord, not my feet only, but also my hands and my head.

10 **Jesus** saith to him,
He that is washed needeth not save to wash his feet,
but is clean every whit:
and ye are clean, but not all.

11 **For he** knew
who should betray him;
therefore said he,
Ye are not all clean.

12 **So after he** had washed their feet,
and had taken his garments,
and was set down again,
he said unto them,
Know ye
what I have done to you?

13 **Ye** call me Master and Lord:
and ye say well;
for so I am.

14 **If I then, your Lord and Master,** have washed your feet;
ye also ought to wash one another's feet.

15 **For I** have given you an example,
that ye should do as I have done to you.

16 **Verily, verily, I** say unto you,
The servant is not greater than his lord; neither he that is sent greater than he that sent him.

17 **If ye** know these things,
happy are ye
if ye do them.

18 **I** speak not of you all:
I know
whom I have chosen:
but that the scripture may be fulfilled,
He that eateth bread with me hath lifted up his heel against me.

19 **Now I** tell you before it come,
that, {when it is come to pass}, ye may believe
that I am he.

20 **Verily, verily, I** say unto you,
He that receiveth whomsoever I send receiveth me;
and he that receiveth me receiveth him that sent me.

21 **When Jesus** had thus said,
he was troubled in spirit,
and testified,
and said,
Verily, verily, I say unto you,
that one of you shall betray me.

22 **Then the disciples** looked one on another,
doubting
of whom he spake.

23 **Now there** was leaning on Jesus' bosom one of his disciples,
whom Jesus loved.

24 **Simon Peter** therefore beckoned to him,
that he should ask
who it should be of whom he spake.

25 **He then lying on Jesus' breast** saith unto him,
Lord, who is it?

26 **Jesus** answered,
He it is,
to whom I shall give a sop,
when I have dipped it.

And when he had dipped the sop,
he gave it to Judas Iscariot, the son of Simon.

27 **And after the sop** Satan entered into him.

Then said Jesus unto him,
That thou doest,
do quickly.

28 **Now no man at the table** knew
for what intent he spake this unto him.

29 **For some of them** thought,
because Judas had the bag,
that Jesus had said unto him,
Buy those things that we have need of against the feast;
or, that he should give something to the poor.

30 **He** then {having received the sop} went immediately out:
and it was night.

31 **Therefore, when he** was gone out,
Jesus said,
Now is the Son of man glorified,
and God is glorified in him.

32 **If God** be glorified in him,
God shall also glorify him in himself,
and shall straightway glorify him.

33 **Little children, yet a little while** I am with you.

Ye shall seek me:
and as I said unto the Jews,
Whither I go,
ye cannot come;
so now I say to you.

34 **A new commandment** I give unto you,
That ye love one another;
as I have loved you,
that ye also love one another.

35 **By this** shall all men know
that ye are my disciples,
if ye have love one to another.

36 **Simon Peter** said unto him,
Lord, whither goest thou?

Jesus answered him,
Whither I go,
thou canst not follow me now;
but thou shalt follow me afterwards.

37 **Peter** said unto him,
Lord, why cannot I follow thee now?

I will lay down my life for thy sake.

38 **Jesus** answered him,
Wilt thou lay down thy life for my sake?

Verily, verily, I say unto thee,
The cock shall not crow,
till thou hast denied me thrice.

14

Let not your heart be troubled:
ye believe in God,
believe also in me.

2 **In my Father's house** are many mansions:
if it were not so,
I would have told you.

I go to prepare a place for you.

3 **And if I** go and prepare a place for you,
I will come again,
and receive you unto myself;
that where I am,
there ye may be also.

4 **And whither** I go
ye know,
and the way ye know.

5 **Thomas** saith unto him,
Lord, we know not
whither thou goest;
and how can we know the way?

6 **Jesus** saith unto him,
I am the way, the truth, and the life:
no man cometh unto the Father, but by me.

7 **If ye** had known me,
ye should have known my Father also:
and from henceforth ye know him,
and have seen him.

8 **Philip** saith unto him,
Lord, show us the Father,
and it sufficeth us.

9 **Jesus** saith unto him,
Have I been so long time with you,
and yet hast thou not known me, Philip?
he that hath seen me hath seen the Father;

and how sayest thou then,
Show us the Father?
10 **Believest thou not**
that I am in the Father, and the Father in me?
the words that I speak unto you I speak not of myself:
but the Father that dwelleth in me, he doeth the works.
11 **Believe** me
that I am in the Father, and the Father in me:
or else believe me for the very works' sake.
12 **Verily, verily, I** say unto you,
He that believeth on me, the works that I do shall he do also;
and greater works than these shall he do;
because I go unto my Father.
13 **And whatsoever ye** shall ask in my name,
that will I do,
that the Father may be glorified in the Son.
14 **If ye** shall ask any thing in my name,
I will do it.
15 **If ye** love me,
keep my commandments.
16 **And I** will pray the Father,
and he shall give you another Comforter,
that he may abide with you for ever;
17 Even the Spirit of truth;
whom the world cannot receive,
because it seeth him not,
neither knoweth him:
but ye know him;
for he dwelleth with you,
and shall be in you.
18 **I** will not leave you comfortless:
I will come to you.
19 **Yet a little while,** and the world seeth me no more;
but ye see me:
because I live,
ye shall live also.
20 **At that day** ye shall know
that I am in my Father, and ye in me, and I in you.
21 **He that hath my commandments, and keepeth them,** he it is that loveth me:
and he that loveth me shall be loved of my Father,
and I will love him,
and will manifest myself to him.

22 **Judas** saith unto him, not Iscariot,
Lord, how is it that thou wilt manifest thyself unto us, and not unto the world?
23 **Jesus** answered and said unto him,
If a man love me,
he will keep my words:
and my Father will love him,
and we will come unto him,
and make our abode with him.
24 **He that loveth me not** keepeth not my sayings:
and the word which ye hear is not mine, but the Father's which sent me.
25 **These things** have I spoken unto you,
being yet present with you.
26 **But the Comforter**, {which is the Holy Ghost}, {whom the Father will send in my name}, he shall teach you all things,
and bring all things to your remembrance,
whatsoever I have said unto you.
27 **Peace** I leave with you,
my peace I give unto you:
not as the world giveth,
give I unto you.
Let not your heart be troubled,
neither let it be afraid.
28 **Ye** have heard how I said unto you,
I go away,
and come again unto you.
If ye loved me,
ye would rejoice,
because I said,
I go unto the Father:
for my Father is greater than I.
29 **And now I** have told you
before it come to pass,
that, {when it is come to pass}, ye might believe.
30 **Hereafter I** will not talk much with you:
for the prince of this world cometh,
and hath nothing in me.
31 **But that the world** may know
that I love the Father;
and as the Father gave me commandment,
even so I do.
Arise,
let us go hence.

15

I am the true vine,
and my Father is the husbandman.
2 **Every branch in me that beareth not fruit** he taketh away:
and every branch that beareth fruit, he purgeth it,
that it may bring forth more fruit.
3 **Now ye** are clean through the word which I have spoken unto you.
4 **Abide** in me, and I in you.
As the branch cannot bear fruit of itself,
except it abide in the vine;
no more can ye,
except ye abide in me.
5 **I** am the vine,
ye are the branches:
He that abideth in me, and I in him, the same bringeth forth much fruit:
for without me ye can do nothing.
6 **If a man** abide not in me,
he is cast forth as a branch,
and is withered;
and men gather them,
and cast them into the fire,
and they are burned.
7 **If ye** abide in me,
and my words abide in you,
ye shall ask
what ye will,
and it shall be done unto you.
8 **Herein** is my Father glorified,
that ye bear much fruit;
so shall ye be my disciples.
9 **As the Father** hath loved me,
so have I loved you:
continue ye in my love.
10 **If ye** keep my commandments,
ye shall abide in my love;
even as I have kept my Father's commandments,
and abide in his love.
11 **These things** have I spoken unto you,
that my joy might remain in you,
and that your joy might be full.
12 **This** is my commandment,
That ye love one another,
as I have loved you.
13 **Greater love** hath no man than this,
that a man lay down his life for his friends.
14 **Ye** are my friends,
if ye do whatsoever I command you.

15 **Henceforth** I call you not servants;
for the servant knoweth not
what his lord doeth:
but I have called you friends;
for all things that I have heard of my Father I have made known unto you.

16 **Ye** have not chosen me,
but I have chosen you,
and ordained you,
that ye should go and bring forth fruit,
and that your fruit should remain:
that whatsoever ye shall ask of the Father in my name,
he may give it you.

17 **These things** I command you,
that ye love one another.

18 **If the world** hate you,
ye know
that it hated me
before it hated you.

19 **If ye** were of the world,
the world would love his own:
but because ye are not of the world,
but I have chosen you out of the world,
therefore the world hateth you.

20 **Remember** the word that I said unto you,
The servant is not greater than his lord.

If they have persecuted me,
they will also persecute you;
if they have kept my saying,
they will keep yours also.

21 **But all these things** will they do unto you for my name's sake,
because they know not him that sent me.

22 **If I** had not come and spoken unto them,
they had not had sin:
but now they have no cloak for their sin.

23 **He that hateth me** hateth my Father also.

24 **If I** had not done among them the works which none other man did,
they had not had sin:
but now have they both seen and hated both me and my Father.

25 **But this** cometh to pass,
that the word might be fulfilled that is written in their law,
They hated me without a cause.

26 **But when the Comforter** is come,
whom I will send unto you from the Father,
even the Spirit of truth, {which proceedeth from the Father}, he shall testify of me:

27 **And ye** also shall bear witness,
because ye have been with me from the beginning.

16 ✕ **These things** have I spoken unto you,
that ye should not be offended.

2 **They** shall put you out of the synagogues:
yea, the time cometh,
that whosoever killeth you will think
that he doeth God service.

3 **And these things** will they do unto you,
because they have not known the Father, nor me.

4 **But these things** have I told you,
that when the time shall come,
ye may remember
that I told you of them.

And these things I said not unto you at the beginning,
because I was with you.

5 **But now I** go my way to him that sent me;
and none of you asketh me,
Whither goest thou?

6 **But because I** have said these things unto you,
sorrow hath filled your heart.

7 **Nevertheless I** tell you the truth;
It is expedient for you that I go away:
for if I go not away,
the Comforter will not come unto you;
but if I depart,
I will send him unto you.

8 **And when he** is come,
he will reprove the world of sin, and of righteousness, and of judgment:

9 Of sin, {because they believe not on me};

10 Of righteousness, {because I go to my Father}, {and ye see me no more};

11 Of judgment, {because the prince of this world is judged}.

12 **I** have yet many things to say unto you,
but ye cannot bear them now.

13 **Howbeit when he, the Spirit of truth,** is come,
he will guide you into all truth:
for he shall not speak of himself;
but whatsoever he shall hear,
that shall he speak:
and he will shew you things to come.

14 **He** shall glorify me:
for he shall receive of mine,
and shall shew it unto you.

15 **All things that the Father hath** are mine:
therefore said I,
that he shall take of mine,
and shall shew it unto you.

16 **A little while,** and ye shall not see me:
and again, a little while, and ye shall see me,
because I go to the Father.

17 **Then** said some of his disciples among themselves,
What is this that he saith unto us,
A little while, and ye shall not see me:
and again, a little while, and ye shall see me:
and, Because I go to the Father?

18 **They** said therefore,
What is this that he saith,
A little while?
we cannot tell
what he saith.

19 **Now Jesus** knew
that they were desirous to ask him,
and said unto them,
Do ye enquire among yourselves of that I said,
A little while, and ye shall not see me:
and again, a little while, and ye shall see me?

20 **Verily, verily, I** say unto you,
That ye shall weep and lament,
but the world shall rejoice:
and ye shall be sorrowful,
but your sorrow shall be turned into joy.

21 **A woman {when she is in travail}** hath sorrow,
because her hour is come:
but as soon as she is delivered of the child,
she remembereth no more the anguish,
for joy that a man is born into the world.

22 **And ye** now therefore have sorrow:

but I will see you again,
and your heart shall rejoice,
and your joy no man taketh from you.
23 **And in that day** ye shall ask me nothing.
Verily, verily, I say unto you,
Whatsoever ye shall ask the Father in my name,
he will give it you.
24 **Hitherto** have ye asked nothing in my name:
ask,
and ye shall receive,
that your joy may be full.
25 **These things** have I spoken unto you in proverbs:
but the time cometh,
when I shall no more speak unto you in proverbs,
but I shall shew you plainly of the Father.
26 **At that day** ye shall ask in my name:
and I say not unto you,
that I will pray the Father for you:
27 **For the Father himself** loveth you,
because ye have loved me,
and have believed
that I came out from God.
28 **I** came forth from the Father,
and am come into the world:
again, I leave the world,
and go to the Father.
29 **His disciples** said unto him,
Lo,
now speakest thou plainly,
and speakest no proverb.
30 **Now** are we sure
that thou knowest all things,
and needest not that any man should ask thee:
by this we believe
that thou camest forth from God.
31 **Jesus** answered them,
Do ye now believe?
32 **Behold,**
the hour cometh,
yea, is now come,
that ye shall be scattered, every man to his own,
and shall leave me alone:
and yet I am not alone,
because the Father is with me.
33 **These things** I have spoken unto you,
that in me ye might have peace.
In the world ye shall have tribulation:
but be of good cheer;
I have overcome the world.

17

These words spake Jesus, **and** lifted up his eyes to heaven,
and said,
Father, the hour is come;
glorify thy Son,
that thy Son also may glorify thee:
2 **As thou** hast given him power over all flesh,
that he should give eternal life to as many as thou hast given him.
3 **And this** is life eternal,
that they might know thee the only true God, and Jesus Christ,
whom thou hast sent.
4 **I** have glorified thee on the earth:
I have finished the work which thou gavest me to do.
5 **And now, O Father, glorify thou** me with thine own self with the glory which I had with thee before the world was.
6 **I** have manifested thy name unto the men which thou gavest me out of the world:
thine they were,
and thou gavest them me;
and they have kept thy word.
7 **Now they** have known
that all things whatsoever thou hast given me are of thee.
8 **For I** have given unto them the words which thou gavest me;
and they have received them,
and have known surely
that I came out from thee,
and they have believed
that thou didst send me.
9 **I** pray for them:
I pray not for the world, but for them which thou hast given me;
for they are thine.
10 **And all mine** are thine,
and thine are mine;
and I am glorified in them.
11 **And now** I am no more in the world,
but these are in the world,
and I come to thee.
Holy Father, keep through thine own name those whom thou hast given me,
that they may be one,
as we are.
12 **While I** was with them in the world,
I kept them in thy name:
those that thou gavest me I have kept,
and none of them is lost, but the son of perdition;
that the scripture might be fulfilled.
13 **And now** come I to thee;
and these things I speak in the world,
that they might have my joy fulfilled in themselves.
14 **I** have given them thy word;
and the world hath hated them,
because they are not of the world,
even as I am not of the world.
15 **I** pray not
that thou shouldest take them out of the world,
but that thou shouldest keep them from the evil.
16 **They** are not of the world,
even as I am not of the world.
17 **Sanctify** them through thy truth:
thy word is truth.
18 **As thou** hast sent me into the world,
even so have I also sent them into the world.
19 **And for their sakes** I sanctify myself,
that they also might be sanctified through the truth.
20 **Neither** pray I for these alone, but for them also which shall believe on me through their word;
21 **That they all** may be one;
as thou, Father, art in me, and I in thee,
that they also may be one in us:
that the world may believe
that thou hast sent me.
22 **And the glory which thou gavest me** I have given them;
that they may be one,
even as we are one:
23 I in them, and thou in me,
that they may be made perfect in one;
and that the world may know
that thou hast sent me,
and hast loved them,
as thou hast loved me.
24 **Father, I** will
that they also, {whom thou hast given me}, be with me where I am;

that they may behold my glory,
which thou hast given me:
for thou lovedst me before the foundation of the world.

25 **O righteous Father, the world** hath not known thee:
but I have known thee,
and these have known
that thou hast sent me.

26 **And I** have declared unto them thy name,
and will declare it:
that the love wherewith thou hast loved me may be in them, and I in them.

18 **When Jesus** had spoken these words,
he went forth with his disciples over the brook Cedron,
where was a garden,
into the which he entered, and his disciples.

2 **And Judas** also, {which betrayed him}, knew the place:
for Jesus ofttimes resorted thither with his disciples.

3 **Judas then,** {having received a band of men and officers from the chief priests and Pharisees}, cometh thither with lanterns and torches and weapons.

4 **Jesus** therefore, {knowing all things that should come upon him}, went forth,
and said unto them,
Whom seek ye?

5 **They** answered him,
Jesus of Nazareth.

Jesus saith unto them,
I am he.

And Judas also, {which betrayed him}, stood with them.

6 **As soon then as he** had said unto them,
I am he,
they went backward,
and fell to the ground.

7 **Then** asked he them again,
Whom seek ye?

And they said,
Jesus of Nazareth.

8 **Jesus** answered,
I have told you
that I am he:
if therefore ye seek me,
let these go their way:
9 **That the saying** might be fulfilled,
which he spake,
Of them which thou gavest me have I lost none.

10 **Then Simon Peter having a sword** drew it,
and smote the high priest's servant,
and cut off his right ear.

The servant's name was Malchus.

11 **Then** said Jesus unto Peter,
Put up thy sword into the sheath:
the cup which my Father hath given me, shall I not drink it?

12 **Then the band and the captain and officers of the Jews** took Jesus,
and bound him,
13 **And** led him away to Annas first;
for he was father in law to Caiaphas,
which was the high priest that same year.

14 **Now Caiaphas** was he,
which gave counsel to the Jews,
that it was expedient that one man should die for the people.

15 **And Simon Peter** followed Jesus,
and so did another disciple:
that disciple was known unto the high priest,
and went in with Jesus into the palace of the high priest.

16 **But Peter** stood at the door without.

Then went out that other disciple,
which was known unto the high priest,
and spake unto her that kept the door,
and brought in Peter.

17 **Then** saith the damsel that kept the door unto Peter,
Art not thou also one of this man's disciples?

He saith,
I am not.

18 **And the servants and officers** stood there,
who had made a fire of coals;
for it was cold:
and they warmed themselves:
and Peter stood with them,
and warmed himself.

19 **The high priest** then asked Jesus of his disciples, and of his doctrine.

20 **Jesus** answered him,
I spake openly to the world;
I ever taught in the synagogue, and in the temple,
whither the Jews always resort;
and in secret have I said nothing.

21 **Why** askest thou me?
ask them which heard me,
what I have said unto them:
behold,
they know
what I said.

22 **And when he** had thus spoken,
one of the officers which stood by struck Jesus with the palm of his hand,
saying,
Answerest thou the high priest so?

23 **Jesus** answered him,
If I have spoken evil,
bear witness of the evil:
but if well, why smitest thou me?

24 **Now Annas** had sent him bound unto Caiaphas the high priest.

25 **And Simon Peter** stood and warmed himself.

They said therefore unto him,
Art not thou also one of his disciples?

He denied it,
and said,
I am not.

26 **One of the servants of the high priest**, {being his kinsman whose ear Peter cut off}, saith,
Did not I see thee in the garden with him?

27 **Peter** then denied again:
and immediately the cock crew.

28 **Then** led they Jesus from Caiaphas unto the hall of judgment:
and it was early;
and they themselves went not into the judgment hall,
lest they should be defiled;
but that they might eat the passover.

29 **Pilate** then went out unto them,
and said,
What accusation bring ye against this man?

30 **They** answered and said unto him,
If he were not a malefactor,
we would not have delivered him up unto thee.

31 **Then** said Pilate unto them,
Take ye him,
and judge him according to your law.

The Jews therefore said unto him,
It is not lawful for us to put any man to death:

32 **That the saying of Jesus** might
be fulfilled,
which he spake,
signifying what death he should
die.
33 **Then Pilate** entered into the
judgment hall again,
and called Jesus,
and said unto him,
Art thou the King of the Jews?
34 **Jesus** answered him,
Sayest thou this thing of thyself,
or did others tell it thee of me?
35 **Pilate** answered,
Am I a Jew?
**Thine own nation and the chief
priests** have delivered thee unto
me:
what hast thou done?
36 **Jesus** answered,
My kingdom is not of this world:
if my kingdom were of this world,
then would my servants fight,
that I should not be delivered to the
Jews:
but now is my kingdom not from
hence.
37 **Pilate** therefore said unto him,
Art thou a king then?
Jesus answered,
Thou sayest
that I am a king.
To this end was I born,
and for this cause came I into the
world,
that I should bear witness unto the
truth.
Every one that is of the truth
heareth my voice.
38 **Pilate** saith unto him,
What is truth?
And when he had said this,
he went out again unto the Jews,
and saith unto them,
I find in him no fault at all.
39 **But ye** have a custom,
that I should release unto you one
at the passover:
will ye therefore
that I release unto you the King of
the Jews?
40 **Then** cried they all again,
saying,
Not this man, but Barabbas.
Now Barabbas was a robber.

19 **Then Pilate** therefore
took Jesus,
and scourged him.
2 **And the soldiers** platted a crown
of thorns,
and put it on his head,
and they put on him a purple robe,
3 **And** said,
Hail, King of the Jews!
and they smote him with their
hands.
4 **Pilate** therefore went forth again,
and saith unto them,
Behold,
I bring him forth to you,
that ye may know
that I find no fault in him.
5 **Then** came Jesus forth,
wearing the crown of thorns, and
the purple robe.
And Pilate saith unto them,
Behold the man!
6 **When the chief priests therefore
and officers** saw him,
they cried out,
saying,
Crucify him,
crucify him.
Pilate saith unto them,
Take ye him,
and crucify him:
for I find no fault in him.
7 **The Jews** answered him,
We have a law,
and by our law he ought to die,
because he made himself the Son of
God.
8 **When Pilate** therefore heard that
saying,
he was the more afraid;
9 **And** went again into the judgment
hall,
and saith unto Jesus,
Whence art thou?
But Jesus gave him no answer.
10 **Then** saith Pilate unto him,
Speakest thou not unto me?
knowest thou not
that I have power to crucify thee,
and have power to release thee?
11 **Jesus** answered,
Thou couldest have no power at all
against me,
except it were given thee from
above:
**therefore he that delivered me
unto thee** hath the greater sin.
12 **And from thenceforth** Pilate
sought to release him:
but the Jews cried out,
saying,
If thou let this man go,
thou art not Caesar's friend:
whosoever maketh himself a king
speaketh against Caesar.
13 **When Pilate** therefore heard that
saying,
he brought Jesus forth,
and sat down in the judgment seat
in a place that is called the
Pavement, but in the Hebrew,
Gabbatha.
14 **And it** was the preparation of the
passover, and about the sixth
hour:
and he saith unto the Jews,
Behold your King!
15 **But they** cried out,
Away with him,
away with him,
crucify him.
Pilate saith unto them,
Shall I crucify your King?
The chief priests answered,
We have no king but Caesar.
16 **Then** delivered he him therefore
unto them to be crucified.
And they took Jesus,
and led him away.
17 **And he bearing his cross** went
forth into a place called the place
of a skull,
which is called in the Hebrew
Golgotha:
18 **Where they** crucified him, and
two other with him, on either side
one, and Jesus in the midst.
19 **And Pilate** wrote a title,
and put it on the cross.
And the writing was Jesus Of
Nazareth The King Of The Jews.
20 **This title** then read many of the
Jews:
**for the place where Jesus was
crucified** was nigh to the city:
and it was written in Hebrew, and
Greek, and Latin.
21 **Then** said the chief priests of the
Jews to Pilate,
Write not,
The King of the Jews;
but that he said,
I am King of the Jews.
22 **Pilate** answered,
What I have written
I have written.
23 **Then the soldiers**, {when they
had crucified Jesus}, took his
garments,
and made four parts, to every
soldier a part; and also his coat:

now the coat was without seam, woven from the top throughout.

24 **They** said therefore among themselves,
Let us not rend it,
but cast lots for it,
whose it shall be:
that the scripture might be fulfilled,
which saith,
They parted my raiment among them,
and for my vesture they did cast lots.

These things therefore the soldiers did.

25 **Now there** stood by the cross of Jesus his mother, and his mother's sister, Mary the wife of Cleophas, and Mary Magdalene.

26 **When Jesus** therefore saw his mother,
and the disciple standing by,
whom he loved,
he saith unto his mother,
Woman, behold thy son!

27 **Then** saith he to the disciple,
Behold thy mother!

And from that hour that disciple took her unto his own home.

28 **After this,** Jesus {knowing} {that all things were now accomplished}, {that the scripture might be fulfilled}, saith,
I thirst.

29 **Now there** was set a vessel full of vinegar:
and they filled a spunge with vinegar,
and put it upon hyssop,
and put it to his mouth.

30 **When Jesus** therefore had received the vinegar,
he said,
It is finished:
and he bowed his head,
and gave up the ghost.

31 **The Jews** therefore, {because it was the preparation}, {that the bodies should not remain upon the cross on the sabbath day}, (for that sabbath day was an high day,) besought Pilate
that their legs might be broken,
and that they might be taken away.

32 **Then** came the soldiers,
and brake the legs of the first, and of the other which was crucified with him.

33 **But when they** came to Jesus,
and saw that he was dead already,
they brake not his legs:

34 **But one of the soldiers with a spear** pierced his side,
and forthwith came there out blood and water.

35 **And he that saw it** bare record,
and his record is true:
and he knoweth
that he saith true,
that ye might believe.

36 **For these things** were done,
that the scripture should be fulfilled,
A bone of him shall not be broken.

37 **And again another scripture** saith,
They shall look on him whom they pierced.

38 **And after this** Joseph of Arimathaea, {being a disciple of Jesus, but secretly for fear of the Jews}, besought Pilate
that he might take away the body of Jesus:
and Pilate gave him leave.

He came therefore,
and took the body of Jesus.

39 **And there** came also Nicodemus,
which at the first came to Jesus by night,
and brought a mixture of myrrh and aloes, about an hundred pound weight.

40 **Then** took they the body of Jesus,
and wound it in linen clothes with the spices,
as the manner of the Jews is to bury.

41 **Now in the place where he was crucified** there was a garden; and in the garden a new sepulchre,
wherein was never man yet laid.

42 **There** laid they Jesus therefore because of the Jews' preparation day;
for the sepulchre was nigh at hand.

20

The first day of the week cometh Mary Magdalene early, {when it was yet dark}, unto the sepulchre,
and seeth the stone taken away from the sepulchre.

2 **Then she** runneth,
and cometh to Simon Peter, and to the other disciple,
whom Jesus loved,
and saith unto them,
They have taken away the Lord out of the sepulchre,
and we know not
where they have laid him.

3 **Peter** therefore went forth, and that other disciple,
and came to the sepulchre.

4 **So they** ran both together:
and the other disciple did outrun Peter,
and came first to the sepulchre.

5 **And he stooping down, and looking in,** saw the linen clothes lying;
yet went he not in.

6 **Then** cometh Simon Peter following him,
and went into the sepulchre,
and seeth the linen clothes lie,
7 **And the napkin,** {that was about his head}, not lying with the linen clothes,
but wrapped together in a place by itself.

8 **Then** went in also that other disciple,
which came first to the sepulchre,
and he saw,
and believed.

9 **For as yet** they knew not the scripture,
that he must rise again from the dead.

10 **Then the disciples** went away again unto their own home.

11 **But Mary** stood without at the sepulchre weeping:
and as she wept,
she stooped down,
and looked into the sepulchre,
12 **And** seeth two angels in white sitting, the one at the head, and the other at the feet,
where the body of Jesus had lain.

13 **And they** say unto her,
Woman, why weepest thou?

She saith unto them,
Because they have taken away my Lord,
and I know not
where they have laid him.

14 **And when she** had thus said,
she turned herself back,
and saw Jesus standing,
and knew not
that it was Jesus.

15 **Jesus** saith unto her,
Woman, why weepest thou?
whom seekest thou?

She, {supposing him to be the gardener}, saith unto him,
Sir, if thou have borne him hence,
tell me
where thou hast laid him,
and I will take him away.

16 **Jesus** saith unto her,
Mary.

She turned herself,
and saith unto him,
Rabboni; which is to say, Master.

17 **Jesus** saith unto her,
Touch me not;
for I am not yet ascended to my Father:
but go to my brethren,
and say unto them,
I ascend unto my Father, and your Father; and to my God, and your God.

18 **Mary Magdalene** came and told the disciples
that she had seen the Lord,
and that he had spoken these things unto her.

19 **Then the same day at evening,** {being the first day of the week}, {when the doors were shut where the disciples were assembled for fear of the Jews}, came Jesus and stood in the midst,
and saith unto them,
Peace be unto you.

20 **And when he** had so said,
he shewed unto them his hands and his side.

Then were the disciples glad,
when they saw the Lord.

21 **Then** said Jesus to them again,
Peace be unto you:
as my Father hath sent me,
even so send I you.

22 **And when he** had said this,
he breathed on them,
and saith unto them,
Receive ye the Holy Ghost:
23 **Whose soever sins** ye remit,
they are remitted unto them;
and whose soever sins ye retain,
they are retained.

24 **But Thomas, one of the twelve, called Didymus,** was not with them when Jesus came.

25 **The other disciples** therefore said unto him,
We have seen the Lord.

But he said unto them,
Except I shall see in his hands the print of the nails,
and put my finger into the print of the nails,
and thrust my hand into his side,
I will not believe.

26 **And after eight days** again his disciples were within, and Thomas with them:
then came Jesus,
the doors being shut,
and stood in the midst,
and said,
Peace be unto you.

27 **Then** saith he to Thomas,
Reach hither thy finger,
and behold my hands;
and reach hither thy hand,
and thrust it into my side:
and be not faithless, but believing.

28 **And Thomas** answered and said unto him,
My Lord and my God.

29 **Jesus** saith unto him,
Thomas, because thou hast seen me,
thou hast believed:
blessed are they that have not seen,
and yet have believed.

30 **And many other signs** truly did Jesus in the presence of his disciples,
which are not written in this book:
31 **But these** are written,
that ye might believe
that Jesus is the Christ, the Son of God;
and that believing ye might have life through his name.

21

After these things Jesus shewed himself again to the disciples at the sea of Tiberias;
and on this wise shewed he himself.

2 **There** were together Simon Peter, and Thomas called Didymus, and Nathanael of Cana in Galilee, and the sons of Zebedee, and two other of his disciples.

3 **Simon Peter** saith unto them,
I go a fishing.

They say unto him,
We also go with thee.

They went forth,
and entered into a ship immediately;
and that night they caught nothing.

4 **But when the morning** was now come,
Jesus stood on the shore:
but the disciples knew not
that it was Jesus.

5 **Then Jesus** saith unto them,
Children, have ye any meat?

They answered him,
No.

6 **And he** said unto them,
Cast the net on the right side of the ship,
and ye shall find.

They cast therefore,
and now they were not able to draw it for the multitude of fishes.

7 **Therefore that disciple whom Jesus loved** saith unto Peter,
It is the Lord.

Now when Simon Peter heard that it was the Lord,
he girt his fisher's coat unto him,
(for he was naked,)
and did cast himself into the sea.

8 **And the other disciples** came in a little ship;
(for they were not far from land, but as it were two hundred cubits,)
dragging the net with fishes.

9 **As soon then as they** were come to land,
they saw a fire of coals there, and fish laid thereon, and bread.

10 **Jesus** saith unto them,
Bring of the fish which ye have now caught.

11 **Simon Peter** went up,
and drew the net to land full of great fishes, an hundred and fifty and three:
and for all there were so many,
yet was not the net broken.

12 **Jesus** saith unto them,
Come and dine.

And none of the disciples durst ask him,
Who art thou?
knowing
that it was the Lord.

13 **Jesus** then cometh,
and taketh bread,
and giveth them, and fish likewise.

14 **This** is now the third time that Jesus shewed himself to his disciples,
after that he was risen from the dead.

15 **So when they** had dined,
Jesus saith to Simon Peter,
Simon, son of Jonas, lovest thou me more than these?

He saith unto him,
Yea, Lord;
thou knowest
that I love thee.

He saith unto him,
Feed my lambs.

16 **He** saith to him again the second time,
Simon, son of Jonas, lovest thou me?

He saith unto him,
Yea, Lord;
thou knowest
that I love thee.

He saith unto him,
Feed my sheep.

17 **He** saith unto him the third time,
Simon, son of Jonas, lovest thou me?

Peter was grieved
because he said unto him the third time,
Lovest thou me?

And he said unto him,
Lord, thou knowest all things;
thou knowest
that I love thee.

Jesus saith unto him,
Feed my sheep.

18 **Verily, verily, I** say unto thee,
When thou wast young,
thou girdest thyself,
and walkedst whither thou wouldest:
but when thou shalt be old,
thou shalt stretch forth thy hands,
and another shall gird thee,
and carry thee whither thou wouldest not.

19 **This** spake he,
signifying by what death he should glorify God.

And when he had spoken this,
he saith unto him,
Follow me.

20 **Then Peter**, {turning about}, seeth the disciple whom Jesus loved following;
which also leaned on his breast at supper,
and said,
Lord, which is he that betrayeth thee?

21 **Peter seeing him** saith to Jesus,
Lord, and what shall this man do?

22 **Jesus** saith unto him,
If I will
that he tarry
till I come,
what is that to thee?
follow thou me.

23 **Then** went this saying abroad among the brethren,
that that disciple should not die:
yet Jesus said not unto him,
He shall not die;
but, If I will
that he tarry
till I come,
what is that to thee?

24 **This** is the disciple which testifieth of these things,
and wrote these things:
and we know
that his testimony is true.

25 **And there** are also many other things which Jesus did,
the which, {if they should be written every one}, I suppose
that even the world itself could not contain the books that should be written.

Amen.

Acts

The Acts of the Apostles is a continuation of the Gospel of Luke. Both are authored by Luke, a physician and trusted friend of the Apostle Paul. While Acts begins where Luke ends, the books differ in several ways. Luke details the life and ministry of Jesus. In contrast, Acts focuses on the growth and expansion of the early Christian church. Luke is written for a Gentile audience. On the other hand, Acts is written for both a Gentile and Jewish audience. Luke is structured as a narrative. In comparison, Acts is structured more like a historical account in a story-like format. Finally, Luke emphasizes the importance of faith, compassion, and justice, while Acts highlights the importance of missionary work and spreading the Gospel message.

However, the Book of Acts stands out on its own, presenting a unique and captivating history that unfolds a series of events and experiences in the early Christian church. It commences with the Ascension of Jesus into heaven, a momentous event, followed by the descent of the Holy Spirit upon the disciples at Pentecost, a pivotal moment marking the birth of the Christian church. The book then proceeds to meticulously chronicle the church's growth in Jerusalem, Judea, and Samaria, and the subsequent missionary journeys of Paul and other apostles, which lead to the spread of the Good News throughout the Roman Empire. Luke also provides intriguing details about Saul's transformation from a persecutor of Christians into Paul, a devoted follower of Jesus and a key figure in the church's growth.

From this transformation, Acts then documents Paul's three missionary journeys, during which he preaches the Gospel, establishes churches, and faces numerous challenges and persecutions. These challenges, which Paul and the early church bravely faced, include opposition from various groups, cultural and religious differences, and even imprisonment. Luke also describes the events leading up to Paul's arrest in Jerusalem, his trials before Jewish and Roman authorities, and his journey to Rome as a prisoner, where he continues to preach the Gospel. The book's final chapters conclude with Paul under house arrest in Rome, preaching the Gospel, and awaiting trial before Caesar.

Through these detailed accounts, Luke accomplishes several specific goals. He aims to demonstrate that the events in the early church are not haphazard but rather part of God's grand plan for the salvation of humanity. By documenting an accurate and reliable testimony of them, he seeks to inspire and guide believers in their faith, reminding them of the Holy Spirit's power and the importance of living a life of obedience and service to God. Perhaps his most consequential task occurs as he tackles various theological questions and challenges that arise in the early church, including the role of Gentiles in Christianity, a significant issue as the early church was predominantly Jewish. Another related challenge concerns the relationship between Jewish and Gentile believers, which was often strained due to cultural and religious differences. Overall, Acts provides rich historical context for understanding the complexities of the early Christian movement, leading to a deeper appreciation for its struggles and triumphs.

1 **The former treatise** have I made, O Theophilus,
of all that Jesus began both to do and teach,
2 Until the day in which he was taken up,
after that he through the Holy Ghost had given commandments unto the apostles whom he had chosen:
3 **To whom** also he shewed himself alive after his passion by many infallible proofs,
being seen of them forty days,
and speaking of the things pertaining to the kingdom of God:
4 **And, {being assembled together with them},** commanded them
that they should not depart from Jerusalem,
but wait for the promise of the Father,
which, {saith he}, ye have heard of me.
5 **For John** truly baptized with water;
but ye shall be baptized with the Holy Ghost not many days hence.
6 **When they** therefore were come together,
they asked of him,
saying,
Lord, wilt thou at this time restore again the kingdom to Israel?
7 **And he** said unto them,
It is not for you to know the times or the seasons,
which the Father hath put in his own power.
8 **But ye** shall receive power,
after that the Holy Ghost is come upon you:
and ye shall be witnesses unto me both in Jerusalem, and in all Judaea, and in Samaria, and unto the uttermost part of the earth.
9 **And when he** had spoken these things,

while they beheld,
he was taken up;
and a cloud received him out of their sight.
10 **And while they** looked stedfastly toward heaven
as he went up,
behold,
two men stood by them in white apparel;
11 **Which** also said,
Ye men of Galilee, why stand ye gazing up into heaven?
this same Jesus, {which is taken up from you into heaven}, shall so come in like manner
as ye have seen him go into heaven.
12 **Then** returned they unto Jerusalem from the mount called Olivet,
which is from Jerusalem a sabbath day's journey.
13 **And when they** were come in,
they went up into an upper room,
where abode both Peter, and James, and John, and Andrew, Philip, and Thomas, Bartholomew, and Matthew, James the son of Alphaeus, and Simon Zelotes, and Judas the brother of James.
14 **These all** continued with one accord in prayer and supplication, with the women, and Mary the mother of Jesus, and with his brethren.
15 **And in those days** Peter stood up in the midst of the disciples,
and said,
(the number of names together were about an hundred and twenty,)
16 **Men and brethren, this scripture** must needs have been fulfilled,
which the Holy Ghost by the mouth of David spake before concerning Judas,
which was guide to them that took Jesus.
17 **For he** was numbered with us,
and had obtained part of this ministry.
18 **Now this man** purchased a field with the reward of iniquity;
and falling headlong,
he burst asunder in the midst,
and all his bowels gushed out.
19 **And it** was known unto all the dwellers at Jerusalem;
insomuch as that field is called in their proper tongue,
Aceldama, that is to say, The field of blood.
20 **For it** is written in the book of Psalms,
Let his habitation be desolate,
and let no man dwell therein:
and his bishoprick let another take.
21 **Wherefore of these men which have companied with us all the time that the Lord Jesus went in and out among us,**
22 {Beginning from the baptism of John, unto that same day that he was taken up from us}, must one be ordained to be a witness with us of his resurrection.
23 **And they** appointed two, Joseph called Barsabas, {who was surnamed Justus}, and Matthias.
24 **And they** prayed,
and said,
Thou, Lord, {which knowest the hearts of all men}, shew whether of these two thou hast chosen,
25 **That he** may take part of this ministry and apostleship,
from which Judas by transgression fell,
that he might go to his own place.
26 **And they** gave forth their lots;
and the lot fell upon Matthias;
and he was numbered with the eleven apostles.

2 **And when the day of Pentecost** was fully come,
they were all with one accord in one place.
2 **And suddenly** there came a sound from heaven as of a rushing mighty wind,
and it filled all the house where they were sitting.
3 **And there** appeared unto them cloven tongues like as of fire,
and it sat upon each of them.
4 **And they** were all filled with the Holy Ghost,
and began to speak with other tongues,
as the Spirit gave them utterance.
5 **And there** were dwelling at Jerusalem Jews, devout men, out of every nation under heaven.
6 **Now when this** was noised abroad,
the multitude came together,
and were confounded,
because that every man heard them speak in his own language.
7 **And they** were all amazed
and marvelled,
saying one to another,
Behold,
are not all these which speak Galilaeans?
8 **And how** hear we every man in our own tongue,
wherein we were born?
9 **Parthians, and Medes, and Elamites, and the dwellers in Mesopotamia, and in Judaea, and Cappadocia, in Pontus, and Asia,**
10 **Phrygia, and Pamphylia, in Egypt, and in the parts of Libya about Cyrene, and strangers of Rome, Jews and proselytes,**
11 **Cretes and Arabians,** we do hear them speak in our tongues the wonderful works of God.
12 **And they** were all amazed,
and were in doubt,
saying one to another,
What meaneth this?
13 **Others mocking** said,
These men are full of new wine.
14 **But Peter**, {standing up with the eleven}, lifted up his voice,
and said unto them,
Ye men of Judaea, and all ye that dwell at Jerusalem, be this known unto you,
and hearken to my words:
15 **For these** are not drunken,
as ye suppose,
seeing it is but the third hour of the day.
16 **But this** is that which was spoken by the prophet Joel;
17 **And it** shall come to pass in the last days,
saith God,
I will pour out of my Spirit upon all flesh:
and your sons and your daughters shall prophesy,
and your young men shall see visions,
and your old men shall dream dreams:
18 **And on my servants and on my handmaidens** I will pour out in those days of my Spirit;
and they shall prophesy:
19 **And I** will shew wonders in heaven above,

and signs in the earth beneath; blood, and fire, and vapour of smoke:
20 **The sun** shall be turned into darkness,
and the moon into blood,
before the great and notable day of the Lord come:
21 **And it** shall come to pass,
that whosoever shall call on the name of the Lord shall be saved.

22 **Ye men of Israel, hear** these words;
Jesus of Nazareth, a man approved of God among you by miracles and wonders and signs, {which God did by him in the midst of you}, {as ye yourselves also know}:
23 Him, {being delivered by the determinate counsel and foreknowledge of God}, ye have taken,
and by wicked hands have crucified and slain:
24 **Whom God** hath raised up,
having loosed the pains of death:
because it was not possible that he should be holden of it.

25 **For David** speaketh concerning him,
I foresaw the Lord always before my face,
for he is on my right hand,
that I should not be moved:
26 **Therefore** did my heart rejoice,
and my tongue was glad;
moreover also my flesh shall rest in hope:
27 **Because thou** wilt not leave my soul in hell,
neither wilt thou suffer thine Holy One to see corruption.

28 **Thou** hast made known to me the ways of life;
thou shalt make me full of joy with thy countenance.

29 **Men and brethren, let me** freely speak unto you of the patriarch David,
that he is both dead and buried,
and his sepulchre is with us unto this day.

30 **Therefore** being a prophet,
and knowing
that God had sworn with an oath to him,
that of the fruit of his loins, according to the flesh, he would raise up Christ to sit on his throne;
31 **He seeing this before** spake of the resurrection of Christ,
that his soul was not left in hell,
neither his flesh did see corruption.

32 **This Jesus** hath God raised up,
whereof we all are witnesses.

33 **Therefore** being by the right hand of God exalted,
and having received of the Father the promise of the Holy Ghost,
he hath shed forth this,
which ye now see
and hear.

34 **For David** is not ascended into the heavens:
but he saith himself,
The LORD said unto my Lord,
Sit thou on my right hand,
35 **Until I** make thy foes thy footstool.

36 **Therefore let all the house of Israel** know assuredly,
that God hath made the same Jesus, {whom ye have crucified}, both Lord and Christ.

37 **Now when they** heard this,
they were pricked in their heart,
and said unto Peter and to the rest of the apostles,
Men and brethren, what shall we do?

38 **Then Peter** said unto them,
Repent,
and be baptized every one of you in the name of Jesus Christ for the remission of sins,
and ye shall receive the gift of the Holy Ghost.

39 **For the promise** is unto you, and to your children, and to all that are afar off,
even as many as the LORD our God shall call.

40 **And with many other words** did he testify and exhort,
saying,
Save yourselves from this untoward generation.

41 **Then they that gladly received his word** were baptized:
and the same day there were added unto them about three thousand souls.

42 **And they** continued stedfastly in the apostles' doctrine and fellowship, and in breaking of bread, and in prayers.

43 **And fear** came upon every soul:
and many wonders and signs were done by the apostles.

44 **And all that believed** were together,
and had all things common;
45 **And** sold their possessions and goods,
and parted them to all men,
as every man had need.

46 **And they**, {continuing daily with one accord in the temple}, {and breaking bread from house to house}, did eat their meat with gladness and singleness of heart,
47 Praising God,
and having favour with all the people.

And the Lord added to the church daily such as should be saved.

3

Now Peter and John went up together into the temple at the hour of prayer,
being the ninth hour.

2 **And a certain man lame from his mother's womb** was carried,
whom they laid daily at the gate of the temple which is called Beautiful,
to ask alms of them that entered into the temple;
3 **Who seeing Peter and John about to go into the temple** asked an alms.

4 **And Peter**, {fastening his eyes upon him with John}, said,
Look on us.

5 **And he** gave heed unto them,
expecting to receive something of them.

6 **Then Peter** said,
Silver and gold have I none;
but such as I have give I thee:
In the name of Jesus Christ of Nazareth rise up
and walk.

7 **And he** took him by the right hand,
and lifted him up:
and immediately his feet and ankle bones received strength.

8 **And he leaping up** stood,
and walked,
and entered with them into the temple,
walking,
and leaping,

and praising God.

9 **And all the people** saw him walking
and praising God:
10 **And they** knew
that it was he which sat for alms at the Beautiful gate of the temple:
and they were filled with wonder and amazement at that which had happened unto him.

11 **And as the lame man which was healed** held Peter and John,
all the people ran together unto them in the porch that is called Solomon's,
greatly wondering.

12 **And when Peter** saw it,
he answered unto the people,
Ye men of Israel, why marvel ye at this?
or why look ye so earnestly on us,
as though by our own power or holiness we had made this man to walk?

13 **The God of Abraham, and of Isaac, and of Jacob, the God of our fathers,** hath glorified his Son Jesus;
whom ye delivered up,
and denied him in the presence of Pilate,
when he was determined to let him go.

14 **But ye** denied the Holy One and the Just,
and desired a murderer to be granted unto you;
15 **And** killed the Prince of life,
whom God hath raised from the dead;
whereof we are witnesses.

16 **And his name through faith in his name** hath made this man strong,
whom ye see
and know:
yea, the faith which is by him hath given him this perfect soundness in the presence of you all.

17 **And now, brethren, I** wot
that through ignorance ye did it,
as did also your rulers.

18 **But those things**, {which God before had shewed by the mouth of all his prophets}, {that Christ should suffer}, he hath so fulfilled.

19 **Repent ye** therefore,
and be converted,
that your sins may be blotted out,
when the times of refreshing shall come from the presence of the Lord.

20 **And he** shall send Jesus Christ,
which before was preached unto you:
21 **Whom the heaven** must receive until the times of restitution of all things,
which God hath spoken by the mouth of all his holy prophets
since the world began.

22 **For Moses** truly said unto the fathers,
A prophet shall the Lord your God raise up unto you of your brethren, like unto me;
him shall ye hear in all things
whatsoever he shall say unto you.

23 **And it** shall come to pass,
that every soul, {which will not hear that prophet}, shall be destroyed from among the people.

24 **Yea, and all the prophets from Samuel and those that follow after**, {as many as have spoken}, have likewise foretold of these days.

25 **Ye** are the children of the prophets,
and of the covenant which God made with our fathers,
saying unto Abraham,
And in thy seed shall all the kindreds of the earth be blessed.

26 **Unto you first** God, {having raised up his Son Jesus}, sent him to bless you,
in turning away every one of you from his iniquities.

4 **And as they** spake unto the people,
the priests, and the captain of the temple, and the Sadducees, came upon them,
2 Being grieved that they taught the people, and preached through Jesus the resurrection from the dead.

3 **And they** laid hands on them,
and put them in hold unto the next day:
for it was now eventide.

4 **Howbeit many of them which heard the word** believed;
and the number of the men was about five thousand.

5 **And it** came to pass on the morrow,
that their rulers, and elders, and scribes,
6 **And Annas the high priest, and Caiaphas, and John, and Alexander, {and as many as were of the kindred of the high priest},** were gathered together at Jerusalem.

7 **And when they** had set them in the midst,
they asked,
By what power, or by what name, have ye done this?

8 **Then Peter**, {filled with the Holy Ghost}, said unto them,
Ye rulers of the people, and elders of Israel,
9 **If we this day** be examined of the good deed done to the impotent man,
by what means he is made whole;
10 **Be it known unto you all, and to all the people of Israel**, that by the name of Jesus Christ of Nazareth, {whom ye crucified}, {whom God raised from the dead}, even by him doth this man stand here before you whole.

11 **This** is the stone which was set at nought of you builders,
which is become the head of the corner.

12 **Neither** is there salvation in any other:
for there is none other name under heaven given among men,
whereby we must be saved.

13 **Now when they** saw the boldness of Peter and John,
and perceived
that they were unlearned and ignorant men,
they marvelled;
and they took knowledge of them,
that they had been with Jesus.

14 **And** beholding the man which was healed standing with them,
they could say nothing against it.

15 **But when they** had commanded them
to go aside out of the council,
they conferred among themselves,
16 Saying,
What shall we do to these men?
for that indeed a notable miracle hath been done by them is manifest to all them that dwell in Jerusalem;

and we cannot deny it.

17 **But that it** spread no further among the people,
let us straitly threaten them,
that they speak henceforth to no man in this name.

18 **And they** called them,
and commanded them
not to speak at all
nor teach in the name of Jesus.

19 **But Peter and John** answered and said unto them,
Whether it be right in the sight of God to hearken unto you more than unto God,
judge ye.

20 **For we** cannot but speak the things which we have seen and heard.

21 **So when they** had further threatened them,
they let them go,
finding nothing how they might punish them, because of the people:
for all men glorified God for that which was done.

22 **For the man** was above forty years old,
on whom this miracle of healing was shewed.

23 **And** being let go,
they went to their own company,
and reported all that the chief priests and elders had said unto them.

24 **And when they** heard that,
they lifted up their voice to God with one accord,
and said,
Lord, thou art God,
which hast made heaven, and earth, and the sea, and all that in them is:

25 **Who by the mouth of thy servant David** hast said,
Why did the heathen rage,
and the people imagine vain things?

26 **The kings of the earth** stood up,
and the rulers were gathered together against the Lord, and against his Christ.

27 **For of a truth against thy holy child Jesus**, {whom thou hast anointed}, both Herod, and Pontius Pilate, with the Gentiles, and the people of Israel, were gathered together,

28 **For** to do whatsoever thy hand and thy counsel determined before to be done.

29 **And now, Lord, behold** their threatenings:
and grant unto thy servants,
that with all boldness they may speak thy word,

30 **By** stretching forth thine hand to heal;
and that signs and wonders may be done by the name of thy holy child Jesus.

31 **And when they** had prayed,
the place was shaken
where they were assembled together;
and they were all filled with the Holy Ghost,
and they spake the word of God with boldness.

32 **And the multitude of them that believed** were of one heart and of one soul:
neither said any of them
that ought of the things which he possessed was his own;
but they had all things common.

33 **And with great power** gave the apostles witness of the resurrection of the Lord Jesus:
and great grace was upon them all.

34 **Neither** was there any among them that lacked:
for as many as were possessors of lands or houses sold them,
and brought the prices of the things that were sold,

35 **And** laid them down at the apostles' feet:
and distribution was made unto every man
according as he had need.

36 **And Joses**, {who by the apostles was surnamed Barnabas, (which is, {being interpreted}, The son of consolation,) a Levite, and of the country of Cyprus},

37 {Having land}, sold it,
and brought the money,
and laid it at the apostles' feet.

5

But a certain man named Ananias, with Sapphira his wife, sold a possession,

2 **And** kept back part of the price,
his wife also being privy to it,
and brought a certain part,
and laid it at the apostles' feet.

3 **But Peter** said,
Ananias, why hath Satan filled thine heart back part of the price of the land?

4 **Whiles it** remained,
was it not thine own?
and after it was sold,
was it not in thine own power?
why hast thou conceived this thing in thine heart?
thou hast not lied unto men,
but unto God.

5 **And Ananias hearing these words** fell down,
and gave up the ghost:
and great fear came on all them that heard these things.

6 **And the young men** arose,
wound him up,
and carried him out,
and buried him.

7 **And it was about the space of three hours after,** when his wife, {not knowing what was done}, came in.

8 **And Peter** answered unto her,
Tell me
whether ye sold the land for so much?
And she said,
Yea, for so much.

9 **Then Peter** said unto her,
How is it that ye have agreed together to tempt the Spirit of the Lord?
behold,
the feet of them which have buried thy husband are at the door,
and shall carry thee out.

10 **Then** fell she down straightway at his feet,
and yielded up the ghost:
and the young men came in,
and found her dead,
and, {carrying her forth}, buried her by her husband.

11 **And great fear** came upon all the church,
and upon as many as heard these things.

12 **And by the hands of the apostles** were many signs and wonders wrought among the people;
(and they were all with one accord in Solomon's porch.

13 **And of the rest** durst no man join himself to them:
but the people magnified them.

14 **And believers** were the more

added to the Lord, multitudes both of men and women.)
15 **Insomuch that they** brought forth the sick into the streets,
and laid them on beds and couches,
that at the least the shadow of Peter passing by might overshadow some of them.
16 **There** came also a multitude out of the cities round about unto Jerusalem,
bringing sick folks, and them which were vexed with unclean spirits:
and they were healed every one.
17 **Then the high priest** rose up, and all they that were with him,
(which is the sect of the Sadducees,)
and were filled with indignation,
18 **And** laid their hands on the apostles,
and put them in the common prison.
19 **But the angel of the Lord by night** opened the prison doors,
and brought them forth,
and said,
20 **Go,**
stand and speak in the temple to the people all the words of this life.
21 **And when they** heard that,
they entered into the temple early in the morning,
and taught.
But the high priest came, and they that were with him,
and called the council together,
and all the senate of the children of Israel,
and sent to the prison to have them brought.
22 **But when the officers** came,
and found them not in the prison,
they returned and told,
23 Saying,
The prison truly found we shut with all safety,
and the keepers standing without before the doors:
but when we had opened,
we found no man within.
24 **Now when the high priest and the captain of the temple and the chief priests** heard these things,
they doubted of them
whereunto this would grow.
25 **Then** came one and told them, saying,
Behold,
the men whom ye put in prison are standing in the temple,
and teaching the people.
26 **Then** went the captain with the officers,
and brought them without violence:
for they feared the people,
lest they should have been stoned.
27 **And when they** had brought them,
they set them before the council:
and the high priest asked them,
28 Saying,
Did not we straitly command you
that ye should not teach in this name?
and, {behold}, ye have filled Jerusalem with your doctrine,
and intend
to bring this man's blood upon us.
29 **Then Peter and the other apostles** answered and said,
We ought to obey God rather than men.
30 **The God of our fathers** raised up Jesus,
whom ye slew and hanged on a tree.
31 **Him** hath God exalted with his right hand to be a Prince and a Saviour,
for to give repentance to Israel,
and forgiveness of sins.
32 **And we** are his witnesses of these things;
and so is also the Holy Ghost,
whom God hath given to them that obey him.
33 **When they** heard that,
they were cut to the heart,
and took counsel
to slay them.
34 **Then** stood there up one in the council, a Pharisee, named Gamaliel, a doctor of the law,
had in reputation among all the people,
and commanded
to put the apostles forth a little space;
35 **And** said unto them,
Ye men of Israel, take heed to yourselves
what ye intend to do as touching these men.
36 **For before these days** rose up Theudas,
boasting himself to be somebody;
to whom a number of men, about four hundred, joined themselves:
who was slain;
and all, {as many as obeyed him}, were scattered,
and brought to nought.
37 **After this man** rose up Judas of Galilee in the days of the taxing,
and drew away much people after him:
he also perished;
and all, {even as many as obeyed him}, were dispersed.
38 **And now I** say unto you,
Refrain from these men,
and let them alone:
for if this counsel or this work be of men,
it will come to nought:
39 **But if it** be of God,
ye cannot overthrow it;
lest haply ye be found even to fight against God.
40 **And to him** they agreed:
and when they had called the apostles,
and beaten them,
they commanded
that they should not speak in the name of Jesus,
and let them go.
41 **And they** departed from the presence of the council,
rejoicing that they were counted worthy to suffer shame for his name.
42 **And daily in the temple, and in every house,** they ceased not to teach and preach Jesus Christ.

6 **And in those days**, {when the number of the disciples was multiplied}, there arose a murmuring of the Grecians against the Hebrews,
because their widows were neglected in the daily ministration.
2 **Then the twelve** called the multitude of the disciples unto them,
and said,
It is not reason that we should leave the word of God,
and serve tables.
3 **Wherefore, brethren, look ye out** among you seven men of honest report, full of the Holy Ghost and wisdom,

whom we may appoint over this business.
4 **But we** will give ourselves continually to prayer,
and to the ministry of the word.
5 **And the saying** pleased the whole multitude:
and they chose Stephen, a man full of faith and of the Holy Ghost, and Philip, and Prochorus, and Nicanor, and Timon, and Parmenas, and Nicolas a proselyte of Antioch:
6 **Whom they** set before the apostles:
and when they had prayed,
they laid their hands on them.
7 **And the word of God** increased;
and the number of the disciples multiplied in Jerusalem greatly;
and a great company of the priests were obedient to the faith.
8 **And Stephen**, full of faith and power, did great wonders and miracles among the people.
9 **Then there** arose certain of the synagogue, {which is called the synagogue of the Libertines, and Cyrenians, and Alexandrians, and of them of Cilicia and of Asia}, disputing with Stephen.
10 **And they** were not able to resist the wisdom and the spirit by which he spake.
11 **Then they** suborned men,
which said,
We have heard him speak blasphemous words against Moses,
and against God.
12 **And they** stirred up the people, and the elders, and the scribes,
and came upon him,
and caught him,
and brought him to the council,
13 **And** set up false witnesses,
which said,
This man ceaseth not to speak blasphemous words against this holy place, and the law:
14 **For we** have heard him say,
that this Jesus of Nazareth shall destroy this place,
and shall change the customs which Moses delivered us.
15 **And all that sat in the council**, {looking stedfastly on him}, saw his face as it had been the face of an angel.

7

Then said the high priest, **Are these things** so?
2 **And he** said,
Men, brethren, and fathers, hearken;
The God of glory appeared unto our father Abraham,
when he was in Mesopotamia,
before he dwelt in Charran,
3 **And** said unto him,
Get thee out of thy country,
and from thy kindred,
and come into the land which I shall shew thee.
4 **Then** came he out of the land of the Chaldaeans,
and dwelt in Charran:
and from thence, {when his father was dead}, he removed him into this land,
wherein ye now dwell.
5 **And he** gave him none inheritance in it, no, not so much as to set his foot on:
yet he promised
that he would give it to him for a possession,
and to his seed after him,
when as yet he had no child.
6 **And God** spake on this wise,
That his seed should sojourn in a strange land;
and that they should bring them into bondage,
and entreat them evil four hundred years.
7 **And the nation to whom they shall be in bondage** will I judge, said God:
and after that shall they come forth,
and serve me in this place.
8 **And he** gave him the covenant of circumcision:
and so Abraham begat Isaac,
and circumcised him the eighth day;
and Isaac begat Jacob;
and Jacob begat the twelve patriarchs.
9 **And the patriarchs**, {moved with envy}, sold Joseph into Egypt:
but God was with him,
10 **And** delivered him out of all his afflictions,
and gave him favour and wisdom in the sight of Pharaoh king of Egypt;
and he made him governor over Egypt and all his house.
11 **Now there** came a dearth over all the land of Egypt and Chanaan,
and great affliction:
and our fathers found no sustenance.
12 **But when Jacob** heard that there was corn in Egypt,
he sent out our fathers first.
13 **And at the second time** Joseph was made known to his brethren;
and Joseph's kindred was made known unto Pharaoh.
14 **Then** sent Joseph,
and called his father Jacob to him, {and all his kindred}, threescore and fifteen souls.
15 **So Jacob** went down into Egypt,
and died, he, and our fathers,
16 **And** were carried over into Sychem,
and laid in the sepulchre that Abraham bought for a sum of money of the sons of Emmor the father of Sychem.
17 **But when the time of the promise** drew nigh,
which God had sworn to Abraham,
the people grew and multiplied in Egypt,
18 **Till another king** arose,
which knew not Joseph.
19 **The same** dealt subtilly with our kindred,
and evil entreated our fathers,
so that they cast out their young children,
to the end they might not live.
20 **In which time** Moses was born,
and was exceeding fair,
and nourished up in his father's house three months:
21 **And when he** was cast out,
Pharaoh's daughter took him up,
and nourished him for her own son.
22 **And Moses** was learned in all the wisdom of the Egyptians,
and was mighty in words and in deeds.
23 **And when he** was full forty years old,
it came into his heart to visit his brethren the children of Israel.
24 **And** seeing one of them suffer wrong,
he defended him,
and avenged him that was oppressed,
and smote the Egyptian:
25 **For he** supposed

his brethren would have understood
how that God by his hand would deliver them:
but they understood not.

26 **And the next day** he shewed himself unto them
as they strove,
and would have set them at one again,
saying,
Sirs, ye are brethren;
why do ye wrong one to another?

27 **But he that did his neighbour wrong** thrust him away,
saying,
Who made thee a ruler and a judge over us?

28 **Wilt thou** kill me,
as thou diddest the Egyptian yesterday?

29 **Then** fled Moses at this saying,
and was a stranger in the land of Madian,
where he begat two sons.

30 **And when forty years** were expired,
there appeared to him in the wilderness of mount Sina an angel of the Lord in a flame of fire in a bush.

31 **When Moses** saw it,
he wondered at the sight:
and as he drew near to behold it,
the voice of the Lord came unto him,
32 Saying,
I am the God of thy fathers, the God of Abraham, and the God of Isaac, and the God of Jacob.
Then Moses trembled,
and durst not behold.

33 **Then** said the Lord to him,
Put off thy shoes from thy feet:
for the place where thou standest is holy ground.

34 **I** have seen,
I have seen the affliction of my people which is in Egypt,
and I have heard their groaning,
and am come down to deliver them.
And now come,
I will send thee into Egypt.

35 **This Moses whom they refused,** {saying}, {Who made thee a ruler and a judge?} the same did God send to be a ruler and a deliverer by the hand of the angel which appeared to him in the bush.

36 **He** brought them out,
after that he had shewed wonders and signs in the land of Egypt, and in the Red sea, and in the wilderness forty years.

37 **This** is that Moses,
which said unto the children of Israel,
A prophet shall the Lord your God raise up unto you of your brethren, like unto me;
him shall ye hear.

38 **This** is he,
that was in the church in the wilderness with the angel which spake to him in the mount Sina, and with our fathers:
who received the lively oracles to give unto us:
39 **To whom** our fathers would not obey,
but thrust him from them,
and in their hearts turned back again into Egypt,
40 Saying unto Aaron,
Make us gods to go before us:
for as for this Moses, {which brought us out of the land of Egypt}, we wot not
what is become of him.

41 **And they** made a calf in those days,
and offered sacrifice unto the idol,
and rejoiced in the works of their own hands.

42 **Then God** turned,
and gave them up to worship the host of heaven;
as it is written in the book of the prophets,
O ye house of Israel, have ye offered to me slain beasts and sacrifices by the space of forty years in the wilderness?

43 **Yea, ye** took up the tabernacle of Moloch, {and the star of your god Remphan}, figures which ye made to worship them:
and I will carry you away beyond Babylon.

44 **Our fathers** had the tabernacle of witness in the wilderness,
as he had appointed,
speaking unto Moses,
that he should make it according to the fashion that he had seen.

45 **Which also our fathers that came after** brought in with Jesus into the possession of the Gentiles,
whom God drave out before the face of our fathers, unto the days of David;
46 **Who** found favour before God,
and desired
to find a tabernacle for the God of Jacob.

47 **But Solomon** built him an house.

48 **Howbeit the most High** dwelleth not in temples made with hands;
as saith the prophet,
49 **Heaven** is my throne,
and earth is my footstool:
what house will ye build me?
saith the Lord:
or what is the place of my rest?

50 **Hath not my hand** made all these things?

51 **Ye stiffnecked and uncircumcised in heart and ears, ye** do always resist the Holy Ghost:
as your fathers did,
so do ye.

52 **Which of the prophets** have not your fathers persecuted?
and they have slain them which shewed before of the coming of the Just One;
of whom ye have been now the betrayers and murderers:
53 **Who** have received the law by the disposition of angels,
and have not kept it.

54 **When they** heard these things,
they were cut to the heart,
and they gnashed on him with their teeth.

55 **But he,** {being full of the Holy Ghost}, looked up stedfastly into heaven,
and saw the glory of God,
and Jesus standing on the right hand of God,
56 **And** said,
Behold,
I see the heavens opened,
and the Son of man standing on the right hand of God.

57 **Then they** cried out with a loud voice,
and stopped their ears,
and ran upon him with one accord,
58 **And** cast him out of the city,
and stoned him:
and the witnesses laid down their clothes at a young man's feet,
whose name was Saul.

59 **And they** stoned Stephen,
calling upon God,

and saying,
Lord Jesus, receive my spirit.
60 **And he** kneeled down,
and cried with a loud voice,
Lord, lay not this sin to their charge.
And when he had said this,
he fell asleep.

8 **And Saul** was consenting unto his death.
And at that time there was a great persecution against the church which was at Jerusalem;
and they were all scattered abroad throughout the regions of Judaea and Samaria, except the apostles.
2 **And devout men** carried Stephen to his burial,
and made great lamentation over him.
3 **As for Saul,** he made havock of the church,
entering into every house,
and {haling men and women} committed them to prison.
4 **Therefore they that were scattered abroad** went every where preaching the word.
5 **Then Philip** went down to the city of Samaria,
and preached Christ unto them.
6 **And the people with one accord** gave heed unto those things which Philip spake,
hearing and seeing the miracles which he did.
7 **For unclean spirits**, {crying with loud voice}, came out of many that were possessed with them:
and many taken with palsies, and that were lame, were healed.
8 **And there** was great joy in that city.
9 **But there** was a certain man, called Simon,
which beforetime in the same city used sorcery,
and bewitched the people of Samaria,
giving out
that himself was some great one:
10 **To whom** they all gave heed, from the least to the greatest,
saying,
This man is the great power of God.
11 **And to him** they had regard,
because that of long time he had bewitched them with sorceries.
12 **But when they** believed Philip preaching the things concerning the kingdom of God, and the name of Jesus Christ,
they were baptized, both men and women.
13 **Then Simon himself** believed also:
and when he was baptized,
he continued with Philip,
and wondered,
beholding the miracles and signs which were done.
14 **Now when the apostles which were at Jerusalem** heard that Samaria had received the word of God,
they sent unto them Peter and John:
15 **Who,** {when they were come down}, prayed for them,
that they might receive the Holy Ghost:
16 (For as yet he was fallen upon none of them:
only they were baptized in the name of the Lord Jesus.)
17 **Then** laid they their hands on them,
and they received the Holy Ghost.
18 **And when Simon** saw that through laying on of the apostles' hands the Holy Ghost was given,
he offered them money,
19 Saying,
Give me also this power,
that on whomsoever I lay hands,
he may receive the Holy Ghost.
20 **But Peter** said unto him,
Thy money perish with thee,
because thou hast thought
that the gift of God may be purchased with money.
21 **Thou** hast neither part nor lot in this matter:
for thy heart is not right in the sight of God.
22 **Repent** therefore of this thy wickedness,
and pray God,
if perhaps the thought of thine heart may be forgiven thee.
23 **For I** perceive
that thou art in the gall of bitterness,
and in the bond of iniquity.
24 **Then** answered Simon,
and said,
Pray ye to the Lord for me,
that none of these things which ye have spoken come upon me.
25 **And they,** {when they had testified and preached the word of the Lord}, returned to Jerusalem,
and preached the gospel in many villages of the Samaritans.
26 **And the angel of the Lord** spake unto Philip,
saying,
Arise,
and go toward the south unto the way that goeth down from Jerusalem unto Gaza,
which is desert.
27 **And he** arose and went:
and, {behold}, a man of Ethiopia, an eunuch of great authority under Candace queen of the Ethiopians, {who had the charge of all her treasure}, {and had come to Jerusalem} {for to worship},
28 Was returning,
and {sitting in his chariot} read Esaias the prophet.
29 **Then the Spirit** said unto Philip,
Go near,
and join thyself to this chariot.
30 **And Philip** ran thither to him,
and heard him read the prophet Esaias,
and said,
Understandest thou
what thou readest?
31 **And he** said,
How can I,
except some man should guide me?
And he desired Philip
that he would come up and sit with him.
32 **The place of the scripture which he read** was this,
He was led as a sheep to the slaughter;
and like a lamb dumb before his shearer, so opened he not his mouth:
33 **In his humiliation** his judgment was taken away:
and who shall declare his generation?
for his life is taken from the earth.
34 **And the eunuch** answered Philip,
and said,
I pray thee,
of whom speaketh the prophet this?
of himself, or of some other man?
35 **Then Philip** opened his mouth,
and began at the same scripture,

and preached unto him Jesus.
36 **And as they** went on their way,
they came unto a certain water:
and the eunuch said,
See,
here is water;
what doth hinder me to be baptized?
37 **And Philip** said,
If thou believest with all thine heart,
thou mayest.
And he answered and said,
I believe
that Jesus Christ is the Son of God.
38 **And he** commanded
the chariot to stand still:
and they went down both into the water, both Philip and the eunuch;
and he baptized him.
39 **And when they** were come up out of the water,
the Spirit of the Lord caught away Philip,
that the eunuch saw him no more:
and he went on his way rejoicing.
40 **But Philip** was found at Azotus:
and passing through
he preached in all the cities,
till he came to Caesarea.

9 **And Saul**, {yet breathing out threatenings and slaughter against the disciples of the Lord}, went unto the high priest,
2 **And** desired of him letters to Damascus to the synagogues,
that if he found any of this way,
whether they were men or women,
he might bring them bound unto Jerusalem.
3 **And as he** journeyed,
he came near Damascus:
and suddenly there shined round about him a light from heaven:
4 **And he** fell to the earth,
and heard a voice saying unto him,
Saul, Saul, why persecutest thou me?
5 **And he** said,
Who art thou, Lord?
And the Lord said,
I am Jesus whom thou persecutest:
it is hard for thee to kick against the pricks.
6 **And he trembling and astonished** said,
Lord, what wilt thou have me to do?
And the Lord said unto him,
Arise,
and go into the city,
and it shall be told thee
what thou must do.
7 **And the men which journeyed with him** stood speechless,
hearing a voice,
but seeing no man.
8 **And Saul** arose from the earth;
and when his eyes were opened,
he saw no man:
but they led him by the hand,
and brought him into Damascus.
9 **And he** was three days without sight,
and neither did eat
nor drink.
10 **And there** was a certain disciple at Damascus, named Ananias;
and to him said the Lord in a vision,
Ananias.
And he said,
Behold,
I am here, Lord.
11 **And the Lord** said unto him,
Arise,
and go into the street which is called Straight,
and enquire in the house of Judas for one called Saul, of Tarsus:
for, {behold}, he prayeth,
12 **And** hath seen in a vision a man named Anania coming in,
and putting his hand on him,
that he might receive his sight.
13 **Then Ananias** answered,
Lord, I have heard by many of this man,
how much evil he hath done to thy saints at Jerusalem:
14 **And here he** hath authority from the chief priests to bind all that call on thy name.
15 **But the Lord** said unto him,
Go thy way:
for he is a chosen vessel unto me,
to bear my name before the Gentiles, and kings, and the children of Israel:
16 **For I** will shew him
how great things he must suffer for my name's sake.
17 **And Ananias** went his way,
and entered into the house;
and putting his hands on him said,
Brother Saul, the Lord, even Jesus, {that appeared unto thee in the way as thou camest}, hath sent me,
that thou mightest receive thy sight,
and be filled with the Holy Ghost.
18 **And immediately** there fell from his eyes as it had been scales:
and he received sight forthwith,
and arose,
and was baptized.
19 **And when he** had received meat,
he was strengthened.
Then was Saul certain days with the disciples which were at Damascus.
20 **And straightway** he preached Christ in the synagogues,
that he is the Son of God.
21 **But all that heard him** were amazed,
and said;
Is not this he that destroyed them which called on this name in Jerusalem, and came hither for that intent,
that he might bring them bound unto the chief priests?
22 **But Saul** increased the more in strength,
and confounded the Jews which dwelt at Damascus,
proving that this is very Christ.
23 **And after that many days** were fulfilled,
the Jews took counsel
to kill him:
24 **But their laying await** was known of Saul.
And they watched the gates day and night
to kill him.
25 **Then the disciples** took him by night,
and let him down by the wall in a basket.
26 **And when Saul** was come to Jerusalem,
he assayed to join himself to the disciples:
but they were all afraid of him,
and believed not
that he was a disciple.
27 **But Barnabas** took him,
and brought him to the apostles,
and declared unto them
how he had seen the Lord in the way,
and that he had spoken to him,

and how he had preached boldly at
Damascus in the name of Jesus.
28 **And he** was with them
coming in and going out at
Jerusalem.
29 **And he** spake boldly in the name
of the Lord Jesus,
and disputed against the Grecians:
but they went about to slay him.
30 **Which when the brethren** knew,
they brought him down to
Caesarea,
and sent him forth to Tarsus.
31 **Then** had the churches rest
throughout all Judaea and Galilee
and Samaria,
and were edified;
**and {walking in the fear of the
Lord, and in the comfort of the
Holy Ghost},** were multiplied.
32 **And it** came to pass,
as Peter passed throughout all
quarters,
he came down also to the saints
which dwelt at Lydda.
33 **And there** he found a certain man
named Aeneas,
which had kept his bed eight years,
and was sick of the palsy.
34 **And Peter** said unto him,
Aeneas, Jesus Christ maketh thee
whole:
arise,
and make thy bed.
And he arose immediately.
35 **And all that dwelt at Lydda and
Saron** saw him,
and turned to the Lord.
36 **Now there** was at Joppa a certain
disciple named Tabitha,
which by interpretation is called
Dorcas:
this woman was full of good works
and almsdeeds which she did.
37 **And it** came to pass in those days,
that she was sick,
and died:
whom when they had washed,
they laid her in an upper chamber.
38 **And forasmuch as Lydda** was
nigh to Joppa,
and the disciples had heard that
Peter was there,
they sent unto him two men,
desiring him
that he would not delay to come to
them.
39 **Then Peter** arose and went with
them.
When he was come,
they brought him into the upper
chamber:
and all the widows stood by him
weeping,
and shewing the coats and
garments which Dorcas made,
while she was with them.
40 **But Peter** put them all forth,
and kneeled down,
and prayed;
and {turning him to the body}
said,
Tabitha, arise.
And she opened her eyes:
and when she saw Peter,
she sat up.
41 **And he** gave her his hand,
and lifted her up,
and when he had called the saints
and widows,
presented her alive.
42 **And it** was known throughout all
Joppa;
and many believed in the Lord.
43 **And it** came to pass,
that he tarried many days in Joppa
with one Simon a tanner.

10 **There** was a certain man in
Caesarea called Cornelius,
a centurion of the band called the
Italian band,
2 A devout man, and one that feared
God with all his house,
which gave much alms to the
people,
and prayed to God alway.
3 **He** saw in a vision evidently about
the ninth hour of the day
an angel of God coming in to him,
and saying unto him,
Cornelius.
4 **And when he** looked on him,
he was afraid,
and said,
What is it, Lord?
And he said unto him,
Thy prayers and thine alms are
come up for a memorial before
God.
5 **And now send** men to Joppa,
and call for one Simon,
whose surname is Peter:
6 **He** lodgeth with one Simon a
tanner,
whose house is by the sea side:
he shall tell thee
what thou oughtest to do.
7 **And when the angel which spake
unto Cornelius** was departed,
he called two of his household
servants,
and a devout soldier of them that
waited on him continually;
8 **And when he** had declared all
these things unto them,
he sent them to Joppa.
9 **On the morrow**, {as they went on
their journey}, {and drew nigh
unto the city}, Peter went up upon
the housetop
to pray about the sixth hour:
10 **And he** became very hungry,
and would have eaten:
but while they made ready,
he fell into a trance,
11 **And** saw heaven opened,
and a certain vessel descending
upon him,
as it had been a great sheet knit at
the four corners,
and let down to the earth:
12 **Wherein** were all manner of
fourfooted beasts of the earth,
and wild beasts, and creeping
things, and fowls of the air.
13 **And there** came a voice to him,
Rise, Peter;
kill,
and eat.
14 **But Peter** said,
Not so, Lord;
for I have never eaten any thing
that is common or unclean.
15 **And the voice** spake unto him
again the second time,
What God hath cleansed,
that call not thou common.
16 **This** was done thrice:
and the vessel was received up
again into heaven.
17 **Now while Peter** doubted in
himself
**what this vision which he had
seen** should mean,
behold,
**the men which were sent from
Cornelius** had made enquiry for
Simon's house,
and stood before the gate,
18 **And** called,
and asked
whether Simon, {which was
surnamed Peter}, were lodged
there.
19 **While Peter** thought on the
vision,
the Spirit said unto him,

Behold,
three men seek thee.
20 **Arise** therefore,
and get thee down,
and go with them,
doubting nothing:
for I have sent them.
21 **Then Peter** went down to the men which were sent unto him from Cornelius;
and said,
Behold,
I am he whom ye seek:
what is the cause wherefore ye are come?
22 **And they** said,
Cornelius the centurion, a just man, and one that feareth God, and of good report among all the nation of the Jews, was warned from God by an holy angel
to send for thee into his house,
and to hear words of thee.
23 **Then** called he them in,
and lodged them.
And on the morrow Peter went away with them,
and certain brethren from Joppa accompanied him.
24 **And the morrow after** they entered into Caesarea.
And Cornelius waited for them,
and he had called together his kinsmen and near friends.
25 **And as Peter** was coming in,
Cornelius met him,
and fell down at his feet,
and worshipped him.
26 **But Peter** took him up,
saying,
Stand up;
I myself also am a man.
27 **And as he** talked with him,
he went in,
and found many that were come together.
28 **And he** said unto them,
Ye know
how that it is an unlawful thing for a man that is a Jew to keep company,
or come unto one of another nation;
but God hath shewed me
that I should not call any man common or unclean.
29 **Therefore** came I unto you without gainsaying,
as soon as I was sent for:
I ask therefore
for what intent ye have sent for me?
30 **And Cornelius** said,
Four days ago I was fasting until this hour;
and at the ninth hour I prayed in my house,
and, {behold}, a man stood before me in bright clothing,
31 **And** said,
Cornelius, thy prayer is heard,
and thine alms are had in remembrance in the sight of God.
32 **Send** therefore to Joppa,
and call hither Simon,
whose surname is Peter;
he is lodged in the house of one Simon a tanner by the sea side:
who, {when he cometh}, shall speak unto thee.
33 **Immediately** therefore I sent to thee;
and thou hast well done
that thou art come.
Now therefore are we all here present before God,
to hear all things that are commanded thee of God.
34 **Then Peter** opened his mouth,
and said,
Of a truth I perceive
that God is no respecter of persons:
35 **But in every nation** he that feareth him, and worketh righteousness, is accepted with him.
36 **The word which God sent unto the children of Israel**, {preaching peace by Jesus Christ}: (he is Lord of all:)
37 That word, {I say}, ye know,
which was published throughout all Judaea, {and began from Galilee}, after the baptism which John preached;
38 **How God** anointed Jesus of Nazareth with the Holy Ghost and with power:
who went about doing good,
and healing all that were oppressed of the devil;
for God was with him.
39 **And we** are witnesses of all things which he did both in the land of the Jews, and in Jerusalem;
whom they slew
and hanged on a tree:
40 **Him** God raised up the third day,
and shewed him openly;
41 Not to all the people, but unto witnesses chosen before God, even to us,
who did eat and drink with him
after he rose from the dead.
42 **And he** commanded us
to preach unto the people,
and to testify
that it is he which was ordained of God to be the Judge of quick and dead.
43 **To him** give all the prophets witness,
that through his name whosoever believeth in him shall receive remission of sins.
44 **While Peter** yet spake these words,
the Holy Ghost fell on all them which heard the word.
45 **And they of the circumcision which believed** were astonished,
as many as came with Peter,
because that on the Gentiles also was poured out the gift of the Holy Ghost.
46 **For they** heard them speak with tongues,
and magnify God.
Then answered Peter,
47 **Can any man** forbid water,
that these should not be baptized,
which have received the Holy Ghost as well as we?
48 **And he** commanded them
to be baptized in the name of the Lord.
Then prayed they him
to tarry certain days.

11

And the apostles and brethren that were in Judaea heard that the Gentiles had also received the word of God.
2 **And when Peter** was come up to Jerusalem,
they that were of the circumcision contended with him,
3 Saying,
Thou wentest in to men uncircumcised,
and didst eat with them.
4 **But Peter** rehearsed the matter from the beginning,
and expounded it by order unto them,
saying,
5 **I** was in the city of Joppa praying:

and in a trance I saw a vision,
A certain vessel descend,
as it had been a great sheet,
let down from heaven by four corners;
and it came even to me:

6 **Upon the which** {when I had fastened mine eyes}, I considered,
and saw fourfooted beasts of the earth, and wild beasts, and creeping things, and fowls of the air.

7 **And I** heard a voice saying unto me,
Arise, Peter;
slay
and eat.

8 **But I** said,
Not so, Lord:
for nothing common or unclean hath at any time entered into my mouth.

9 **But the voice** answered me again from heaven,
What God hath cleansed,
that call not thou common.

10 **And this** was done three times:
and all were drawn up again into heaven.

11 **And, {behold}, immediately** there were three men already come unto the house where I was,
sent from Caesarea unto me.

12 **And the Spirit** bade me go with them,
nothing doubting.

Moreover these six brethren accompanied me,
and we entered into the man's house:
13 **And he** shewed us
how he had seen an angel in his house,
which stood and said unto him,
Send men to Joppa,
and call for Simon,
whose surname is Peter;
14 **Who** shall tell thee words,
whereby thou and all thy house shall be saved.

15 **And as I** began to speak,
the Holy Ghost fell on them,
as on us at the beginning.

16 **Then** remembered I the word of the Lord,
how that he said,
John indeed baptized with water;
but ye shall be baptized with the Holy Ghost.

17 **Forasmuch then as God** gave them the like gift
as he did unto us,
who believed on the Lord Jesus Christ;
what was I,
that I could withstand God?

18 **When they** heard these things,
they held their peace,
and glorified God,
saying,
Then hath God also to the Gentiles granted repentance unto life.

19 **Now they which were scattered abroad upon the persecution that arose about Stephen** travelled as far as Phenice, and Cyprus, and Antioch,
preaching the word to none but unto the Jews only.

20 **And some of them** were men of Cyprus and Cyrene,
which, {when they were come to Antioch}, spake unto the Grecians,
preaching the Lord Jesus.

21 **And the hand of the Lord** was with them:
and a great number believed,
and turned unto the Lord.

22 **Then tidings of these things** came unto the ears of the church which was in Jerusalem:
and they sent forth Barnabas,
that he should go as far as Antioch.

23 **Who**, {when he came}, {and had seen the grace of God}, was glad,
and exhorted them all,
that with purpose of heart they would cleave unto the Lord.

24 **For he** was a good man,
and full of the Holy Ghost and of faith:
and much people was added unto the Lord.

25 **Then** departed Barnabas to Tarsus,
for to seek Saul:
26 **And when he** had found him,
he brought him unto Antioch.

And it came to pass,
that a whole year they assembled themselves with the church,
and taught much people.

And the disciples were called Christians first in Antioch.

27 **And in these days** came prophets from Jerusalem unto Antioch.

28 **And there** stood up one of them named Agabus,
and signified by the Spirit
that there should be great dearth throughout all the world:
which came to pass in the days of Claudius Caesar.

29 **Then the disciples, every man according to his ability,** determined to send relief unto the brethren which dwelt in Judaea:
30 **Which** also they did,
and sent it to the elders by the hands of Barnabas and Saul.

12

Now about that time Herod the king stretched forth his hands
to vex certain of the church.

2 **And he** killed James the brother of John with the sword.

3 **And because he** saw it pleased the Jews,
he proceeded further to take Peter also.

(**Then** were the days of unleavened bread.)

4 **And when he** had apprehended him,
he put him in prison,
and delivered him to four quaternions of soldiers
to keep him;
intending after Easter to bring him forth to the people.

5 **Peter** therefore was kept in prison:
but prayer was made without ceasing of the church unto God for him.

6 **And when Herod** would have brought him forth,
the same night Peter was sleeping between two soldiers,
bound with two chains:
and the keepers before the door kept the prison.

7 **And, {behold}, the angel of the Lord** came upon him,
and a light shined in the prison:
and he smote Peter on the side,
and raised him up,
saying,
Arise up quickly.

And his chains fell off from his hands.

8 **And the angel** said unto him,
Gird thyself,
and bind on thy sandals.

And so he did.

And he saith unto him,
Cast thy garment about thee,
and follow me.

9 **And he** went out,
and followed him;
and wist not
that it was true
which was done by the angel;
but thought
he saw a vision.

10 **When they** were past the first and the second ward,
they came unto the iron gate that leadeth unto the city;
which opened to them of his own accord:
and they went out,
and passed on through one street;
and forthwith the angel departed from him.

11 **And when Peter** was come to himself,
he said,
Now I know of a surety,
that the Lord hath sent his angel,
and hath delivered me out of the hand of Herod,
and from all the expectation of the people of the Jews.

12 **And when he** had considered the thing,
he came to the house of Mary the mother of John,
whose surname was Mark;
where many were gathered together praying.

13 **And as Peter** knocked at the door of the gate,
a damsel came to hearken,
named Rhoda.

14 **And when she** knew Peter's voice,
she opened not the gate for gladness,
but ran in,
and told
how Peter stood before the gate.

15 **And they** said unto her,
Thou art mad.

But she constantly affirmed
that it was even so.

Then said they,
It is his angel.

16 **But Peter** continued knocking:
and when they had opened the door,
and saw him,
they were astonished.

17 **But he**, {beckoning unto them with the hand to hold their peace}, declared unto them
how the Lord had brought him out of the prison.

And he said,
Go shew these things unto James,
and to the brethren.

And he departed,
and went into another place.

18 **Now as soon as it** was day,
there was no small stir among the soldiers,
what was become of Peter.

19 **And when Herod** had sought for him,
and found him not,
he examined the keepers,
and commanded
that they should be put to death.

And he went down from Judaea to Caesarea,
and there abode.

20 **And Herod** was highly displeased with them of Tyre and Sidon:
but they came with one accord to him,
and, {having made Blastus the king's chamberlain their friend}, desired peace;
because their country was nourished by the king's country.

21 **And upon a set day** Herod, {arrayed in royal apparel}, sat upon his throne,
and made an oration unto them.

22 **And the people** gave a shout,
saying,
It is the voice of a god,
and not of a man.

23 **And immediately** the angel of the Lord smote him,
because he gave not God the glory:
and he was eaten of worms,
and gave up the ghost.

24 **But the word of God** grew and multiplied.

25 **And Barnabas and Saul** returned from Jerusalem,
when they had fulfilled their ministry,
and took with them John,
whose surname was Mark.

13

Now there were in the church that was at Antioch certain prophets and teachers; as Barnabas, and Simeon that was called Niger, and Lucius of Cyrene, and Manaen,
which had been brought up with Herod the tetrarch, and Saul.

2 **As they** ministered to the Lord,
and fasted,
the Holy Ghost said,
Separate me Barnabas and Saul for the work whereunto I have called them.

3 **And when they** had fasted and prayed,
and laid their hands on them,
they sent them away.

4 **So they**, {being sent forth by the Holy Ghost}, departed unto Seleucia;
and from thence they sailed to Cyprus.

5 **And when they** were at Salamis,
they preached the word of God in the synagogues of the Jews:
and they had also John to their minister.

6 **And when they** had gone through the isle unto Paphos,
they found a certain sorcerer, a false prophet, a Jew,
whose name was Barjesus:

7 **Which** was with the deputy of the country, Sergius Paulus, a prudent man;
who called for Barnabas and Saul,
and desired to hear the word of God.

8 **But Elymas the sorcerer** (for so is his name by interpretation) withstood them,
seeking to turn away the deputy from the faith.

9 **Then Saul**, (who also is called Paul,) {filled with the Holy Ghost}, set his eyes on him.

10 **And** said,
O full of all subtilty and all mischief, thou child of the devil, thou enemy of all righteousness,
wilt thou not cease to pervert the right ways of the Lord?

11 **And now, {behold}, the hand of the Lord** is upon thee,
and thou shalt be blind,
not seeing the sun for a season.

And immediately there fell on him a mist and a darkness;
and he went about seeking some to lead him by the hand.

12 **Then the deputy**, {when he saw what was done}, believed,

being astonished at the doctrine of the Lord.

13 **Now when Paul and his company** loosed from Paphos,
they came to Perga in Pamphylia:
and John departing from them returned to Jerusalem.

14 **But when they** departed from Perga,
they came to Antioch in Pisidia,
and went into the synagogue on the sabbath day,
and sat down.

15 **And after the reading of the law and the prophets** the rulers of the synagogue sent unto them,
saying,
Ye men and brethren, if ye have any word of exhortation for the people,
say on.

16 **Then Paul** stood up,
and beckoning with his hand said,
Men of Israel, and ye that fear God, give audience.

17 **The God of this people of Israel** chose our fathers,
and exalted the people
when they dwelt as strangers in the land of Egypt,
and with an high arm brought he them out of it.

18 **And about the time of forty years** suffered he their manners in the wilderness.

19 **And when he** had destroyed seven nations in the land of Chanaan,
he divided their land to them by lot.

20 **And after that** he gave unto them judges about the space of four hundred and fifty years, until Samuel the prophet.

21 **And afterward they** desired a king:
and God gave unto them Saul the son of Cis, a man of the tribe of Benjamin, by the space of forty years.

22 **And when he** had removed him,
he raised up unto them David to be their king;
to whom also he gave their testimony,
and said,
I have found David the son of Jesse, a man after mine own heart,
which shall fulfil all my will.

23 **Of this man's seed** hath God according to his promise raised unto Israel a Saviour, Jesus:

24 **When John** had first preached before his coming the baptism of repentance to all the people of Israel.

25 **And as John** fulfilled his course,
he said,
Whom think ye
that I am?
I am not he.
But, {behold}, there cometh one after me,
whose shoes of his feet I am not worthy to loose.

26 **Men and brethren, children of the stock of Abraham, and whosoever among you feareth God, to you** is the word of this salvation sent.

27 **For they that dwell at Jerusalem, and their rulers,** {because they knew him not}, {nor yet the voices of the prophets which are read every sabbath day}, they have fulfilled them
in condemning him.

28 **And though they** found no cause of death in him,
yet desired they Pilate
that he should be slain.

29 **And when they** had fulfilled all that was written of him,
they took him down from the tree,
and laid him in a sepulchre.

30 **But God** raised him from the dead:

31 **And he** was seen many days of them which came up with him from Galilee to Jerusalem,
who are his witnesses unto the people.

32 **And we** declare unto you glad tidings,
how that the promise which was made unto the fathers,

33 God hath fulfilled the same unto us their children,
in that he hath raised up Jesus again;
as it is also written in the second psalm,
Thou art my Son,
this day have I begotten thee.

34 **And as concerning that he** raised him up from the dead,
now no more to return to corruption,
he said on this wise,
I will give you the sure mercies of David.

35 **Wherefore he** saith also in another psalm,
Thou shalt not suffer thine Holy One to see corruption.

36 **For David**, {after he had served his own generation by the will of God}, fell on sleep,
and was laid unto his fathers,
and saw corruption:

37 **But he**, {whom God raised again}, saw no corruption.

38 **Be it known unto you** therefore, men and brethren, that through this man is preached unto you the forgiveness of sins:

39 **And by him** all that believe are justified from all things,
from which ye could not be justified by the law of Moses.

40 **Beware** therefore,
lest that come upon you,
which is spoken of in the prophets;

41 **Behold,** ye despisers,
and wonder,
and perish:
for I work a work in your days, a work which ye shall in no wise believe,
though a man declare it unto you.

42 **And when the Jews** were gone out of the synagogue,
the Gentiles besought
that these words might be preached to them the next sabbath.

43 **Now when the congregation** was broken up,
many of the Jews and religious proselytes followed Paul and Barnabas:
who, {speaking to them}, persuaded them to continue in the grace of God.

44 **And the next sabbath day** came almost the whole city together to hear the word of God.

45 **But when the Jews** saw the multitudes,
they were filled with envy,
and spake against those things which were spoken by Paul,
contradicting
and blaspheming.

46 **Then Paul and Barnabas** waxed bold,
and said,

It was necessary that the word of God should first have been spoken to you:
but seeing ye put it from you,
and judge yourselves unworthy of everlasting life,
lo,
we turn to the Gentiles.
47 **For so** hath the Lord commanded us,
saying,
I have set thee to be a light of the Gentiles,
that thou shouldest be for salvation unto the ends of the earth.
48 **And when the Gentiles** heard this,
they were glad,
and glorified the word of the Lord:
and as many as were ordained to eternal life believed.
49 **And the word of the Lord** was published throughout all the region.
50 **But the Jews** stirred up the devout and honourable women,
and the chief men of the city,
and raised persecution against Paul and Barnabas,
and expelled them out of their coasts.
51 **But they** shook off the dust of their feet against them,
and came unto Iconium.
52 **And the disciples** were filled with joy,
and with the Holy Ghost.

14 **And it** came to pass in Iconium,
that they went both together into the synagogue of the Jews,
and so spake,
that a great multitude both of the Jews and also of the Greeks believed.
2 **But the unbelieving Jews** stirred up the Gentiles,
and made their minds evil affected against the brethren.
3 **Long time** therefore abode they
speaking boldly in the Lord,
which gave testimony unto the word of his grace,
and granted signs and wonders to be done by their hands.
4 **But the multitude of the city** was divided:
and part held with the Jews,
and part with the apostles.
5 **And when there** was an assault made both of the Gentiles, and also of the Jews with their rulers,
to use them despitefully,
and to stone them,
6 **They** were ware of it,
and fled unto Lystra and Derbe, cities of Lycaonia, and unto the region that lieth round about:
7 **And there** they preached the gospel.
8 **And there** sat a certain man at Lystra, impotent in his feet,
being a cripple from his mother's womb,
who never had walked:
9 **The same** heard Paul speak:
who stedfastly beholding him,
and perceiving
that he had faith to be healed,
10 Said with a loud voice,
Stand upright on thy feet.
And he leaped
and walked.
11 **And when the people** saw what Paul had done,
they lifted up their voices,
saying in the speech of Lycaonia,
The gods are come down to us in the likeness of men.
12 **And they** called Barnabas, Jupiter; and Paul, Mercurius,
because he was the chief speaker.
13 **Then the priest of Jupiter,** {which was before their city}, brought oxen and garlands unto the gates,
and would have done sacrifice with the people.
14 **Which when the apostles, Barnabas and Paul,** heard of,
they rent their clothes,
and ran in among the people,
crying out,
15 **And** saying,
Sirs, why do ye these things?
We also are men of like passions with you,
and preach unto you
that ye should turn from these vanities unto the living God,
which made heaven, and earth, and the sea, and all things that are therein:
16 **Who in times past** suffered all nations to walk in their own ways.
17 **Nevertheless he** left not himself without witness,
in that he did good,
and gave us rain from heaven, and fruitful seasons,
filling our hearts with food and gladness.
18 **And with these sayings** scarce restrained they the people,
that they had not done sacrifice unto them.
19 **And there** came thither certain Jews from Antioch and Iconium,
who persuaded the people,
and having stoned Paul,
drew him out of the city,
supposing
he had been dead.
20 **Howbeit, {as the disciples stood round about him},** he rose up,
and came into the city:
and the next day he departed with Barnabas to Derbe.
21 **And when they** had preached the gospel to that city,
and had taught many,
they returned again to Lystra, and to Iconium, and Antioch,
22 Confirming the souls of the disciples,
and exhorting them
to continue in the faith,
and that we must through much tribulation enter into the kingdom of God.
23 **And when they** had ordained them elders in every church,
and had prayed with fasting,
they commended them to the Lord,
on whom they believed.
24 **And after they** had passed throughout Pisidia,
they came to Pamphylia.
25 **And when they** had preached the word in Perga,
they went down into Attalia:
26 **And thence** sailed to Antioch,
from whence they had been recommended to the grace of God for the work which they fulfilled.
27 **And when they** were come,
and had gathered the church together,
they rehearsed all that God had done with them,
and how he had opened the door of faith unto the Gentiles.
28 **And there** they abode long time with the disciples.

15 And certain men which came down from Judaea taught the brethren,
and said,
Except ye be circumcised after the manner of Moses,
ye cannot be saved.

2 **When therefore Paul and Barnabas** had no small dissension and disputation with them,
they determined
that Paul and Barnabas, and certain other of them, should go up to Jerusalem unto the apostles and elders about this question.

3 **And** being brought on their way by the church,
they passed through Phenice and Samaria,
declaring the conversion of the Gentiles:
and they caused great joy unto all the brethren.

4 **And when they** were come to Jerusalem,
they were received of the church, and of the apostles and elders,
and they declared all things that God had done with them.

5 **But there** rose up certain of the sect of the Pharisees which believed,
saying,
That it was needful to circumcise them,
and to command them
to keep the law of Moses.

6 **And the apostles and elders** came together
for to consider of this matter.

7 **And when there** had been much disputing,
Peter rose up,
and said unto them,
Men and brethren, ye know
how that a good while ago God made choice among us,
that the Gentiles by my mouth should hear the word of the gospel,
and believe.

8 **And God,** {which knoweth the hearts}, bare them witness,
giving them the Holy Ghost,
even as he did unto us;
9 **And** put no difference between us and them,
purifying their hearts by faith.

10 **Now therefore why** tempt ye God,
to put a yoke upon the neck of the disciples,
which neither our fathers nor we were able to bear?

11 **But we** believe
that through the grace of the Lord Jesus Christ we shall be saved,
even as they.

12 **Then all the multitude** kept silence,
and gave audience to Barnabas and Paul,
declaring
what miracles and wonders God had wrought among the Gentiles by them.

13 **And after they** had held their peace,
James answered,
saying,
Men and brethren, hearken unto me:
14 **Simeon** hath declared
how God at the first did visit the Gentiles,
to take out of them a people for his name.

15 **And to this** agree the words of the prophets;
as it is written,
16 **After this** I will return,
and will build again the tabernacle of David,
which is fallen down;
and I will build again the ruins thereof,
and I will set it up:
17 **That the residue of men** might seek after the Lord, and all the Gentiles,
upon whom my name is called,
saith the Lord,
who doeth all these things.

18 **Known unto God** are all his works from the beginning of the world.

19 **Wherefore my sentence** is,
that we trouble not them,
which from among the Gentiles are turned to God:
20 **But that we** write unto them,
that they abstain from pollutions of idols, and from fornication, and from things strangled, and from blood.

21 **For Moses of old time** hath in every city them that preach him, being read in the synagogues every sabbath day.

22 **Then** pleased it the apostles and elders with the whole church,
to send chosen men of their own company to Antioch with Paul and Barnabas; namely, Judas surnamed Barsabas and Silas, chief men among the brethren:
23 **And they** wrote letters by them after this manner;
The apostles and elders and brethren send greeting unto the brethren which are of the Gentiles in Antioch and Syria and Cilicia.

24 **Forasmuch as we** have heard,
that certain which went out from us have troubled you with words,
subverting your souls,
saying,
Ye must be circumcised,
and keep the law:
to whom we gave no such commandment:
25 **It seemed good unto us,** {being assembled with one accord}, to send chosen men unto you with our beloved Barnabas and Paul,
26 Men that have hazarded their lives for the name of our Lord Jesus Christ.

27 **We** have sent therefore Judas and Silas,
who shall also tell you the same things by mouth.

28 **For it seemed good to the Holy Ghost, and to us,** to lay upon you no greater burden than these necessary things;
29 **That ye** abstain from meats offered to idols, and from blood, and from things strangled, and from fornication:
from which if ye keep yourselves,
ye shall do well.

Fare ye well.

30 **So when they** were dismissed,
they came to Antioch:
and when they had gathered the multitude together,
they delivered the epistle:
31 **Which when they** had read,
they rejoiced for the consolation.

32 **And Judas and Silas,** {being prophets also themselves}, exhorted the brethren with many words,
and confirmed them.

33 **And after they** had tarried there a space,

they were let go in peace from the brethren unto the apostles.

34 **Notwithstanding it pleased Silas** to abide there still.

35 **Paul also and Barnabas** continued in Antioch, {teaching and preaching the word of the Lord}, with many others also.

36 **And some days after** Paul said unto Barnabas,
Let us go again and visit our brethren in every city
where we have preached the word of the Lord,
and see how they do.

37 **And Barnabas** determined to take with them John,
whose surname was Mark.

38 **But Paul** thought
not good to take him with them,
who departed from them from Pamphylia,
and went not with them to the work.

39 **And the contention** was so sharp between them,
that they departed asunder one from the other:
and so Barnabas took Mark,
and sailed unto Cyprus;
40 **And Paul** chose Silas,
and departed,
being recommended by the brethren unto the grace of God.

41 **And he** went through Syria and Cilicia,
confirming the churches.

16

Then came he to Derbe and Lystra:
and, {behold}, a certain disciple was there, named Timotheus, the son of a certain woman,
which was a Jewess,
and believed;
but his father was a Greek:
2 **Which** was well reported of by the brethren that were at Lystra and Iconium.

3 **Him** would Paul have to go forth with him;
and took and circumcised him because of the Jews which were in those quarters:
for they knew all
that his father was a Greek.

4 **And as they** went through the cities,
they delivered them the decrees for to keep,
that were ordained of the apostles and elders which were at Jerusalem.

5 **And so** were the churches established in the faith,
and increased in number daily.

6 **Now when they** had gone throughout Phrygia and the region of Galatia,
and were forbidden of the Holy Ghost to preach the word in Asia,
7 **After they** were come to Mysia,
they assayed to go into Bithynia:
but the Spirit suffered them not.

8 **And they passing by Mysia** came down to Troas.

9 **And a vision** appeared to Paul in the night;
There stood a man of Macedonia,
and prayed him,
saying,
Come over into Macedonia,
and help us.

10 **And after he** had seen the vision,
immediately we endeavoured to go into Macedonia,
assuredly gathering
that the Lord had called us
for to preach the gospel unto them.

11 **Therefore** loosing from Troas,
we came with a straight course to Samothracia, and the next day to Neapolis;
12 And from thence to Philippi,
which is the chief city of that part of Macedonia,
and a colony:
and we were in that city abiding certain days.

13 **And on the sabbath** we went out of the city by a river side,
where prayer was wont to be made;
and we sat down,
and spake unto the women which resorted thither.

14 **And a certain woman named Lydia**, a seller of purple, of the city of Thyatira, {which worshipped God}, heard us:
whose heart the Lord opened,
that she attended unto the things which were spoken of Paul.

15 **And when she** was baptized,
and her household,
she besought us,
saying,
If ye have judged me to be faithful to the Lord,
come into my house,
and abide there.

And she constrained us.

16 **And it** came to pass,
as we went to prayer,
a certain damsel possessed with a spirit of divination met us,
which brought her masters much gain
by soothsaying:
17 **The same** followed Paul and us,
and cried,
saying,
These men are the servants of the most high God,
which shew unto us the way of salvation.

18 **And this** did she many days.
But Paul, {being grieved}, turned and said to the spirit,
I command thee in the name of Jesus Christ
to come out of her.

And he came out the same hour.

19 **And when her masters** saw that the hope of their gains was gone,
they caught Paul and Silas,
and drew them into the marketplace unto the rulers,
20 **And** brought them to the magistrates,
saying,
These men, {being Jews}, do exceedingly trouble our city,
21 **And** teach customs,
which are not lawful for us to receive,
neither to observe,
being Romans.

22 **And the multitude** rose up together against them:
and the magistrates rent off their clothes,
and commanded
to beat them.

23 **And when they** had laid many stripes upon them,
they cast them into prison,
charging the jailor
to keep them safely:
24 **Who**, {having received such a charge}, thrust them into the inner prison,
and made their feet fast in the stocks.

25 **And at midnight** Paul and Silas prayed,
and sang praises unto God:
and the prisoners heard them.

26 **And suddenly** there was a great earthquake,

so that the foundations of the prison were shaken:
and immediately all the doors were opened,
and every one's bands were loosed.
27 **And the keeper of the prison** awaking out of his sleep,
and seeing the prison doors open,
he drew out his sword,
and would have killed himself,
supposing
that the prisoners had been fled.
28 **But Paul** cried with a loud voice,
saying,
Do thyself no harm:
for we are all here.
29 **Then he** called for a light,
and sprang in,
and came trembling,
and fell down before Paul and Silas,
30 **And** brought them out,
and said,
Sirs, what must I do to be saved?
31 **And they** said,
Believe on the Lord Jesus Christ,
and thou shalt be saved,
and thy house.
32 **And they** spake unto him the word of the Lord,
and to all that were in his house.
33 **And he** took them the same hour of the night,
and washed their stripes;
and was baptized, he and all his, straightway.
34 **And when he** had brought them into his house,
he set meat before them,
and rejoiced,
believing in God with all his house.
35 **And when it** was day,
the magistrates sent the serjeants,
saying,
Let those men go.
36 **And the keeper of the prison** told this saying to Paul,
The magistrates have sent to let you go:
now therefore depart,
and go in peace.
37 **But Paul** said unto them,
They have beaten us openly uncondemned,
being Romans,
and have cast us into prison;
and now do they thrust us out privily?
nay verily;
but let them come themselves
and fetch us out.
38 **And the serjeants** told these words unto the magistrates:
and they feared,
when they heard that they were Romans.
39 **And they** came and besought them,
and brought them out,
and desired them
to depart out of the city.
40 **And they** went out of the prison,
and entered into the house of Lydia:
and when they had seen the brethren,
they comforted them,
and departed.

17

Now when they had passed through Amphipolis and Apollonia,
they came to Thessalonica,
where was a synagogue of the Jews:
2 **And Paul**, {as his manner was}, went in unto them,
and three sabbath days reasoned with them out of the scriptures,
3 Opening and alleging,
that Christ must needs have suffered,
and risen again from the dead;
and that this Jesus, {whom I preach unto you}, is Christ.
4 **And some of them** believed,
and consorted with Paul and Silas;
and of the devout Greeks a great multitude,
and of the chief women not a few.
5 **But the Jews which believed not**, {moved with envy}, took unto them certain lewd fellows of the baser sort,
and gathered a company,
and set all the city on an uproar,
and assaulted the house of Jason,
and sought to bring them out to the people.
6 **And when they** found them not,
they drew Jason and certain brethren unto the rulers of the city,
crying,
These that have turned the world upside down are come hither also;
7 **Whom** Jason hath received:
and these all do contrary to the decrees of Caesar,
saying
that there is another king, one Jesus.
8 **And they** troubled the people and the rulers of the city,
when they heard these things.
9 **And when they** had taken security of Jason,
and of the other,
they let them go.
10 **And the brethren** immediately sent away Paul and Silas by night unto Berea:
who {coming thither} went into the synagogue of the Jews.
11 **These** were more noble than those in Thessalonica,
in that they received the word with all readiness of mind,
and searched the scriptures daily,
whether those things were so.
12 **Therefore many of them** believed;
also of honourable women which were Greeks
and of men, not a few.
13 **But when the Jews of Thessalonica** had knowledge
that the word of God was preached of Paul at Berea,
they came thither also,
and stirred up the people.
14 **And then immediately** the brethren sent away Paul to go as it were to the sea:
but Silas and Timotheus abode there still.
15 **And they that conducted Paul** brought him unto Athens:
and receiving a commandment unto Silas and Timotheus
for to come to him with all speed,
they departed.
16 **Now while Paul** waited for them at Athens,
his spirit was stirred in him,
when he saw the city wholly given to idolatry.
17 **Therefore** disputed he in the synagogue with the Jews, and with the devout persons, and in the market daily with them that met with him.
18 **Then certain philosophers of the Epicureans, and of the Stoicks,** encountered him.
And some said,
What will this babbler say?
other some,

He seemeth to be a setter forth of strange gods:
because he preached unto them Jesus,
and the resurrection.
19 **And they** took him,
and brought him unto Areopagus, saying,
May we know
what this new doctrine, {whereof thou speakest}, is?
20 **For thou** bringest certain strange things to our ears:
we would know therefore
what these things mean.
21 (**For all the Athenians and strangers which were there** spent their time in nothing else,
but either to tell,
or to hear some new thing.)
22 **Then Paul** stood in the midst of Mars' hill,
and said,
Ye men of Athens, I perceive that in all things ye are too superstitious.
23 **For as I** passed by,
and beheld your devotions,
I found an altar with this inscription,
To The Unknown God.
Whom therefore ye ignorantly worship,
him declare I unto you.
24 **God that made the world and all things therein**, {seeing that he is Lord of heaven and earth}, dwelleth not in temples made with hands;
25 **Neither** is worshipped with men's hands,
as though he needed any thing,
seeing he giveth to all life, and breath, and all things;
26 **And** hath made of one blood all nations of men
for to dwell on all the face of the earth,
and hath determined the times before appointed,
and the bounds of their habitation;
27 **That they** should seek the Lord,
if haply they might feel after him,
and find him,
though he be not far from every one of us:
28 **For in him** we live,
and move,
and have our being;
as certain also of your own poets have said,
For we are also his offspring.
29 **Forasmuch then as we** are the offspring of God,
we ought not to think
that the Godhead is like unto gold, or silver, or stone,
graven by art and man's device.
30 **And the times of this ignorance** God winked at;
but now commandeth all men every where
to repent:
31 **Because he** hath appointed a day,
in the which he will judge the world in righteousness by that man whom he hath ordained;
whereof he hath given assurance unto all men,
in that he hath raised him from the dead.
32 **And when they** heard of the resurrection of the dead,
some mocked:
and others said,
We will hear thee again of this matter.
33 **So Paul** departed from among them.
34 **Howbeit certain men** clave unto him,
and believed:
among the which was Dionysius the Areopagite, and a woman named Damaris, and others with them.

18

After these things Paul departed from Athens,
and came to Corinth;
2 **And** found a certain Jew named Aquila,
born in Pontus,
lately come from Italy, with his wife Priscilla;
(because that Claudius had commanded all Jews
to depart from Rome:)
and came unto them.
3 **And because he** was of the same craft,
he abode with them,
and wrought:
for by their occupation they were tentmakers.
4 **And he** reasoned in the synagogue every sabbath,
and persuaded the Jews and the Greeks.
5 **And when Silas and Timotheus** were come from Macedonia,
Paul was pressed in the spirit,
and testified to the Jews
that Jesus was Christ.
6 **And when they** opposed themselves,
and blasphemed,
he shook his raiment,
and said unto them,
Your blood be upon your own heads;
I am clean;
from henceforth I will go unto the Gentiles.
7 **And he** departed thence,
and entered into a certain man's house, named Justus, one that worshipped God,
whose house joined hard to the synagogue.
8 **And Crispus, the chief ruler of the synagogue,** believed on the Lord with all his house;
and many of the Corinthians hearing believed,
and were baptized.
9 **Then** spake the Lord to Paul in the night by a vision,
Be not afraid,
but speak,
and hold not thy peace:
10 **For I** am with thee,
and no man shall set on thee to hurt thee:
for I have much people in this city.
11 **And he** continued there a year and six months,
teaching the word of God among them.
12 **And when Gallio** was the deputy of Achaia,
the Jews made insurrection with one accord against Paul,
and brought him to the judgment seat,
13 Saying,
This fellow persuadeth men
to worship God contrary to the law.
14 **And when Paul** was now about to open his mouth,
Gallio said unto the Jews,
If it were a matter of wrong or wicked lewdness, O ye Jews,
reason would that I should bear with you:
15 **But if it** be a question of words and names, and of your law,
look ye to it;
for I will be no judge of such matters.

16 **And he** drave them from the judgment seat.

17 **Then all the Greeks** took Sosthenes, the chief ruler of the synagogue,
and beat him before the judgment seat.

And Gallio cared for none of those things.

18 **And Paul after this** tarried there yet a good while,
and then took his leave of the brethren,
and sailed thence into Syria,
and with him Priscilla and Aquila;
having shorn his head in Cenchrea:
for he had a vow.

19 **And he** came to Ephesus,
and left them there:
but he himself entered into the synagogue,
and reasoned with the Jews.

20 **When they** desired him
to tarry longer time with them,
he consented not;
21 **But** bade them farewell,
saying,
I must by all means keep this feast that cometh in Jerusalem:
but I will return again unto you,
if God will.

And he sailed from Ephesus.

22 **And when he** had landed at Caesarea,
and gone up,
and saluted the church,
he went down to Antioch.

23 **And after he** had spent some time there,
he departed,
and went over all the country of Galatia and Phrygia in order,
strengthening all the disciples.

24 **And a certain Jew named Apollos**, born at Alexandria, an eloquent man, and mighty in the scriptures, came to Ephesus.

25 **This man** was instructed in the way of the Lord;
and being fervent in the spirit,
he spake and taught diligently the things of the Lord,
knowing only the baptism of John.

26 **And he** began to speak boldly in the synagogue:
whom when Aquila and Priscilla had heard,
they took him unto them,
and expounded unto him the way of God more perfectly.

27 **And when he** was disposed
to pass into Achaia,
the brethren wrote,
exhorting the disciples
to receive him:
who, {when he was come}, helped them much which had believed through grace:

28 **For he** mightily convinced the Jews, and that publicly,
shewing by the scriptures
that Jesus was Christ.

19

And it came to pass,
that, {while Apollos was at Corinth}, Paul {having passed through the upper coasts} came to Ephesus:
and finding certain disciples,
2 **He** said unto them,
Have ye received the Holy Ghost
since ye believed?

And they said unto him,
We have not so much as heard whether there be any Holy Ghost.

3 **And he** said unto them,
Unto what then were ye baptized?

And they said,
Unto John's baptism.

4 **Then** said Paul,
John verily baptized with the baptism of repentance,
saying unto the people,
that they should believe on him which should come after him, that is, on Christ Jesus.

5 **When they** heard this,
they were baptized in the name of the Lord Jesus.

6 **And when Paul** had laid his hands upon them,
the Holy Ghost came on them;
and they spake with tongues,
and prophesied.

7 **And all the men** were about twelve.

8 **And he** went into the synagogue,
and spake boldly for the space of three months,
disputing and persuading the things concerning the kingdom of God.

9 **But when divers** were hardened,
and believed not,
but spake evil of that way before the multitude,
he departed from them,
and separated the disciples,
disputing daily in the school of one Tyrannus.

10 **And this** continued by the space of two years;
so that all they which dwelt in Asia heard the word of the Lord Jesus, both Jews and Greeks.

11 **And God** wrought special miracles by the hands of Paul:

12 **So that from his body** were brought unto the sick handkerchiefs or aprons,
and the diseases departed from them,
and the evil spirits went out of them.

13 **Then certain of the vagabond Jews, exorcists,** took upon them to call over them which had evil spirits the name of the Lord Jesus,
saying,
We adjure you by Jesus whom Paul preacheth.

14 **And there** were seven sons of one Sceva, a Jew, and chief of the priests,
which did so.

15 **And the evil spirit** answered and said,
Jesus I know,
and Paul I know;
but who are ye?

16 **And the man in whom the evil spirit was** leaped on them,
and overcame them,
and prevailed against them,
so that they fled out of that house naked and wounded.

17 **And this** was known to all the Jews and Greeks also dwelling at Ephesus;
and fear fell on them all,
and the name of the Lord Jesus was magnified.

18 **And many that believed** came,
and confessed,
and shewed their deeds.

19 **Many of them also which used curious arts** brought their books together,
and burned them before all men:
and they counted the price of them,
and found it fifty thousand pieces of silver.

20 **So mightily** grew the word of God
and prevailed.

21 **After these things** were ended,
Paul purposed in the spirit,

when he had passed through Macedonia and Achaia,
to go to Jerusalem,
saying,
After I have been there,
I must also see Rome.

22 **So he** sent into Macedonia two of them that ministered unto him, Timotheus and Erastus;
but he himself stayed in Asia for a season.

23 **And the same time** there arose no small stir about that way.

24 **For a certain man named Demetrius**, a silversmith, {which made silver shrines for Diana}, brought no small gain unto the craftsmen;

25 **Whom he** called together with the workmen of like occupation,
and said,
Sirs, ye know
that by this craft we have our wealth.

26 **Moreover ye** see and hear,
that not alone at Ephesus, but almost throughout all Asia, this Paul hath persuaded and turned away much people,
saying
that they be no gods,
which are made with hands:

27 **So that not only this our craft** is in danger to be set at nought;
but also that the temple of the great goddess Diana should be despised,
and her magnificence should be destroyed,
whom all Asia and the world worshippeth.

28 **And when they** heard these sayings,
they were full of wrath,
and cried out,
saying,
Great is Diana of the Ephesians.

29 **And the whole city** was filled with confusion:
and having caught Gaius and Aristarchus, men of Macedonia, Paul's companions in travel,
they rushed with one accord into the theatre.

30 **And when Paul** would have entered in unto the people,
the disciples suffered him not.

31 **And certain of the chief of Asia,** {which were his friends}, sent unto him,
desiring him
that he would not adventure himself into the theatre.

32 **Some** therefore cried one thing,
and some another:
for the assembly was confused:
and the more part knew not
wherefore they were come together.

33 **And they** drew Alexander out of the multitude,
the Jews putting him forward.
And Alexander beckoned with the hand,
and would have made his defence unto the people.

34 **But when they** knew
that he was a Jew,
all with one voice about the space of two hours cried out,
Great is Diana of the Ephesians.

35 **And when the townclerk** had appeased the people,
he said,
Ye men of Ephesus, what man is there that knoweth not
how that the city of the Ephesians is a worshipper of the great goddess Diana,
and of the image which fell down from Jupiter?

36 **Seeing then that these things** cannot be spoken against,
ye ought to be quiet,
and to do nothing rashly.

37 **For ye** have brought hither these men,
which are neither robbers of churches, nor yet blasphemers of your goddess.

38 **Wherefore if Demetrius, and the craftsmen which are with him,** have a matter against any man,
the law is open,
and there are deputies:
let them implead one another.

39 **But if ye** enquire any thing concerning other matters,
it shall be determined in a lawful assembly.

40 **For we** are in danger to be called in question for this day's uproar,
there being no cause whereby we may give an account of this concourse.

41 **And when he** had thus spoken,
he dismissed the assembly.

20

And after the uproar was ceased,
Paul called unto him the disciples,
and embraced them,
and departed for to go into Macedonia.

2 **And when he** had gone over those parts,
and had given them much exhortation,
he came into Greece,

3 **And there** abode three months.
And when the Jews laid wait for him,
as he was about to sail into Syria,
he purposed
to return through Macedonia.

4 **And there** accompanied him into Asia Sopater of Berea; and of the Thessalonians, Aristarchus and Secundus; and Gaius of Derbe, and Timotheus; and of Asia, Tychicus and Trophimus.

5 **These going before** tarried for us at Troas.

6 **And we** sailed away from Philippi after the days of unleavened bread,
and came unto them to Troas in five days;
where we abode seven days.

7 **And upon the first day of the week,** {when the disciples came together to break bread}, Paul preached unto them,
ready to depart on the morrow;
and continued his speech until midnight.

8 **And there** were many lights in the upper chamber,
where they were gathered together.

9 **And there** sat in a window a certain young man named Eutychus,
being fallen into a deep sleep:
and as Paul was long preaching,
he sunk down with sleep,
and fell down from the third loft,
and was taken up dead.

10 **And Paul** went down,
and fell on him,
and {embracing him} said,
Trouble not yourselves;
for his life is in him.

11 **When he** therefore was come up again,
and had broken bread,
and eaten,

and talked a long while, even till break of day,
so he departed.
[12] **And they** brought the young man alive,
and were not a little comforted.
[13] **And we** went before to ship,
and sailed unto Assos,
there intending
to take in Paul:
for so had he appointed,
minding himself
to go afoot.
[14] **And when he** met with us at Assos,
we took him in,
and came to Mitylene.
[15] **And we** sailed thence,
and came the next day over against Chios;
and the next day we arrived at Samos,
and tarried at Trogyllium;
and the next day we came to Miletus.
[16] **For Paul** had determined
to sail by Ephesus,
because he would not spend the time in Asia:
for he hasted, {if it were possible for him}, to be at Jerusalem the day of Pentecost.
[17] **And from Miletus** he sent to Ephesus,
and called the elders of the church.
[18] **And when they** were come to him,
he said unto them,
Ye know,
from the first day that I came into Asia, after what manner I have been with you at all seasons,
[19] Serving the Lord with all humility of mind,
and with many tears, and temptations,
which befell me by the lying in wait of the Jews:
[20] **And how** I kept back nothing that was profitable unto you,
but have shewed you,
and have taught you publicly, and from house to house,
[21] Testifying both to the Jews, and also to the Greeks, repentance toward God, and faith toward our Lord Jesus Christ.
[22] **And now, {behold}, I** go bound in the spirit unto Jerusalem,
not knowing the things that shall befall me there:
[23] **Save that the Holy Ghost** witnesseth in every city,
saying
that bonds and afflictions abide me.
[24] **But none of these things** move me,
neither count I my life dear unto myself,
so that I might finish my course with joy,
and the ministry,
which I have received of the Lord Jesus,
to testify the gospel of the grace of God.
[25] **And now, {behold}, I** know
that ye all, {among whom I have gone preaching the kingdom of God}, shall see my face no more.
[26] **Wherefore I** take you to record this day,
that I am pure from the blood of all men.
[27] **For I** have not shunned to declare unto you all the counsel of God.
[28] **Take heed** therefore unto yourselves, and to all the flock,
over the which the Holy Ghost hath made you overseers,
to feed the church of God,
which he hath purchased with his own blood.
[29] **For I** know this,
that after my departing shall grievous wolves enter in among you,
not sparing the flock.
[30] **Also of your own selves** shall men arise,
speaking perverse things,
to draw away disciples after them.
[31] **Therefore watch,**
and remember,
that by the space of three years I ceased not to warn every one night and day with tears.
[32] **And now, brethren, I** commend you to God,
and to the word of his grace,
which is able to build you up,
and to give you an inheritance among all them which are sanctified.
[33] **I** have coveted no man's silver, or gold, or apparel.
[34] **Yea, ye yourselves** know,
that these hands have ministered unto my necessities,
and to them that were with me.
[35] **I** have shewed you all things,
how that so labouring ye ought to support the weak,
and to remember the words of the Lord Jesus,
how he said,
It is more blessed to give than to receive.
[36] **And when he** had thus spoken,
he kneeled down,
and prayed with them all.
[37] **And they all** wept sore,
and fell on Paul's neck,
and kissed him,
[38] Sorrowing most of all for the words which he spake,
that they should see his face no more.
And they accompanied him unto the ship.

21 **And it** came to pass,
that after we were gotten from them,
and had launched,
we came with a straight course unto Coos,
and the day following unto Rhodes,
and from thence unto Patara:
[2] **And** finding a ship sailing over unto Phenicia,
we went aboard,
and set forth.
[3] **Now when we** had discovered Cyprus,
we left it on the left hand,
and sailed into Syria,
and landed at Tyre:
for there the ship was to unlade her burden.
[4] **And** finding disciples,
we tarried there seven days:
who said to Paul through the Spirit,
that he should not go up to Jerusalem.
[5] **And when we** had accomplished those days,
we departed
and went our way;
and they all brought us on our way, with wives and children,
till we were out of the city:
and we kneeled down on the shore,
and prayed.
[6] **And when we** had taken our leave one of another,

we took ship;
and they returned home again.

7 **And when we** had finished our course from Tyre,
we came to Ptolemais,
and saluted the brethren,
and abode with them one day.

8 **And the next day** we that were of Paul's company departed,
and came unto Caesarea:
and we entered into the house of Philip the evangelist,
which was one of the seven;
and abode with him.

9 **And the same man** had four daughters, virgins,
which did prophesy.

10 **And as we** tarried there many days,
there came down from Judaea a certain prophet, named Agabus.

11 **And when he** was come unto us,
he took Paul's girdle,
and bound his own hands and feet,
and said,
Thus saith the Holy Ghost,
So shall the Jews at Jerusalem bind the man that owneth this girdle,
and shall deliver him into the hands of the Gentiles.

12 **And when we** heard these things,
both we, and they of that place, besought him
not to go up to Jerusalem.

13 **Then Paul** answered,
What mean ye to weep
and to break mine heart?
for I am ready not to be bound only,
but also to die at Jerusalem for the name of the Lord Jesus.

14 **And when he** would not be persuaded,
we ceased,
saying,
The will of the Lord be done.

15 **And after those days** we took up our carriages,
and went up to Jerusalem.

16 **There** went with us also certain of the disciples of Caesarea,
and brought with them one Mnason of Cyprus, an old disciple,
with whom we should lodge.

17 **And when we** were come to Jerusalem,
the brethren received us gladly.

18 **And the day following** Paul went in with us unto James;
and all the elders were present.

19 **And when he** had saluted them,
he declared particularly
what things God had wrought among the Gentiles by his ministry.

20 **And when they** heard it,
they glorified the Lord,
and said unto him,
Thou seest, brother,
how many thousands of Jews there are which believe;
and they are all zealous of the law:

21 **And they** are informed of thee,
that thou teachest all the Jews which are among the Gentiles
to forsake Moses,
saying
that they ought not to circumcise their children,
neither to walk after the customs.

22 **What** is it therefore?
the multitude must needs come together:
for they will hear that thou art come.

23 **Do** therefore this that we say to thee:
We have four men which have a vow on them;

24 **Them take,**
and purify thyself with them,
and be at charges with them,
that they may shave their heads:
and all may know
that those things, {whereof they were informed concerning thee}, are nothing;
but that thou thyself also walkest orderly,
and keepest the law.

25 **As touching the Gentiles which believe,** we have written and concluded
that they observe no such thing,
save only that they keep themselves from things offered to idols, and from blood, and from strangled, and from fornication.

26 **Then Paul** took the men,
and the next day {purifying himself with them} entered into the temple,
to signify the accomplishment of the days of purification,
until that an offering should be offered for every one of them.

27 **And when the seven days** were almost ended,
the Jews which were of Asia, {when they saw him in the temple}, stirred up all the people,
and laid hands on him,

28 Crying out,
Men of Israel, help:
This is the man,
that teacheth all men every where against the people, and the law, and this place:
and further brought Greeks also into the temple,
and hath polluted this holy place.

29 (**For they** had seen before with him in the city Trophimus an Ephesian,
whom they supposed
that Paul had brought into the temple.)

30 **And all the city** was moved,
and the people ran together:
and they took Paul,
and drew him out of the temple:
and forthwith the doors were shut.

31 **And as they** went about to kill him,
tidings came unto the chief captain of the band,
that all Jerusalem was in an uproar.

32 **Who** immediately took soldiers and centurions,
and ran down unto them:
and when they saw the chief captain and the soldiers,
they left beating of Paul.

33 **Then the chief captain** came near,
and took him,
and commanded him to be bound with two chains;
and demanded
who he was,
and what he had done.

34 **And some** cried one thing, {some another}, among the multitude:
and when he could not know the certainty for the tumult,
he commanded him
to be carried into the castle.

35 **And when he** came upon the stairs,
so it was,
that he was borne of the soldiers for the violence of the people.

36 **For the multitude of the people** followed after,
crying,
Away with him.

37 **And as Paul** was to be led into the castle,
he said unto the chief captain,
May I speak unto thee?
Who said,
Canst thou speak Greek?
38 **Art not thou** that Egyptian,
which before these days madest an uproar,
and leddest out into the wilderness four thousand men that were murderers?
39 **But Paul** said,
I am a man which am a Jew of Tarsus, a city in Cilicia, a citizen of no mean city:
and, {I beseech thee}, suffer me to speak unto the people.
40 **And when he** had given him licence,
Paul stood on the stairs,
and beckoned with the hand unto the people.
And when there was made a great silence,
he spake unto them in the Hebrew tongue,
saying,

22 **Men, brethren, and fathers, hear ye** my defence which I make now unto you.
2 (And when they heard that he spake in the Hebrew tongue to them,
they kept the more silence:
and he saith,)
3 **I** am verily a man which am a Jew,
born in Tarsus, a city in Cilicia,
yet brought up in this city at the feet of Gamaliel,
and taught according to the perfect manner of the law of the fathers,
and was zealous toward God,
as ye all are this day.
4 **And I** persecuted this way unto the death,
binding and delivering into prisons both men and women.
5 **As also the high priest** doth bear me witness,
and all the estate of the elders:
from whom also I received letters unto the brethren,
and went to Damascus,
to bring them which were there bound unto Jerusalem,
for to be punished.
6 **And it** came to pass,
that, {as I made my journey}, {and was come nigh unto Damascus about noon}, suddenly there shone from heaven a great light round about me.
7 **And I** fell unto the ground,
and heard a voice saying unto me,
Saul, Saul, why persecutest thou me?
8 **And I** answered,
Who art thou, Lord?
And he said unto me,
I am Jesus of Nazareth,
whom thou persecutest.
9 **And they that were with me** saw indeed the light,
and were afraid;
but they heard not the voice of him that spake to me.
10 **And I** said,
What shall I do, Lord?
And the Lord said unto me,
Arise,
and go into Damascus;
and there it shall be told thee of all things which are appointed for thee to do.
11 **And when I** could not see for the glory of that light,
being led by the hand of them that were with me,
I came into Damascus.
12 **And one Ananias**, a devout man according to the law, {having a good report of all the Jews which dwelt there},
13 Came unto me,
and stood,
and said unto me,
Brother Saul, receive thy sight.
And the same hour I looked up upon him.
14 **And he** said,
The God of our fathers hath chosen thee,
that thou shouldest know his will,
and see that Just One,
and shouldest hear the voice of his mouth.
15 **For thou** shalt be his witness unto all men of what thou hast seen and heard.
16 **And now why** tarriest thou?
arise,
and be baptized,
and wash away thy sins,
calling on the name of the Lord.
17 **And it** came to pass,
that, {when I was come again to Jerusalem}, {even while I prayed in the temple}, I was in a trance;
18 **And** saw him saying unto me,
Make haste,
and get thee quickly out of Jerusalem:
for they will not receive thy testimony concerning me.
19 **And I** said,
Lord, they know
that I imprisoned and beat in every synagogue them that believed on thee:
20 **And when the blood of thy martyr Stephen** was shed,
I also was standing by,
and consenting unto his death,
and kept the raiment of them that slew him.
21 **And he** said unto me,
Depart:
for I will send thee far hence unto the Gentiles.
22 **And they** gave him audience unto this word,
and then lifted up their voices,
and said,
Away with such a fellow from the earth:
for it is not fit that he should live.
23 **And as they** cried out,
and cast off their clothes,
and threw dust into the air,
24 **The chief captain** commanded him
to be brought into the castle,
and bade
that he should be examined by scourging;
that he might know
wherefore they cried so against him.
25 **And as they** bound him with thongs,
Paul said unto the centurion that stood by,
Is it lawful for you to scourge a man that is a Roman, and uncondemned?
26 **When the centurion** heard that,
he went and told the chief captain,
saying,
Take heed what thou doest:
for this man is a Roman.
27 **Then the chief captain** came,
and said unto him,
Tell me,
art thou a Roman?

He said,
Yea.

28 **And the chief captain** answered,
With a great sum obtained I this freedom.
And Paul said,
But I was free born.

29 **Then straightway** they departed from him which should have examined him:
and the chief captain also was afraid,
after he knew
that he was a Roman,
and because he had bound him.

30 **On the morrow**, {because he would have known the certainty} {wherefore he was accused of the Jews}, he loosed him from his bands,
and commanded the chief priests and all their council
to appear,
and brought Paul down,
and set him before them.

23

And Paul, {earnestly beholding the council}, said,
Men and brethren, I have lived in all good conscience before God until this day.

2 **And the high priest Ananias** commanded them that stood by him
to smite him on the mouth.

3 **Then** said Paul unto him,
God shall smite thee, thou whited wall:
for sittest thou to judge me after the law,
and commandest me
to be smitten contrary to the law?

4 **And they that stood by** said,
Revilest thou God's high priest?

5 **Then** said Paul,
I wist not, brethren,
that he was the high priest:
for it is written,
Thou shalt not speak evil of the ruler of thy people.

6 **But when Paul** perceived
that the one part were Sadducees,
and the other Pharisees,
he cried out in the council,
Men and brethren, I am a Pharisee, the son of a Pharisee:
of the hope and resurrection of the dead I am called in question.

7 **And when he** had so said,
there arose a dissension between the Pharisees and the Sadducees:
and the multitude was divided.

8 **For the Sadducees** say
that there is no resurrection, neither angel, nor spirit:
but the Pharisees confess both.

9 **And there** arose a great cry:
and the scribes that were of the Pharisees' part arose,
and strove,
saying,
We find no evil in this man:
but if a spirit or an angel hath spoken to him,
let us not fight against God.

10 **And when there** arose a great dissension,
the chief captain, {fearing lest Paul should have been pulled in pieces of them}, commanded the soldiers
to go down,
and to take him by force from among them,
and to bring him into the castle.

11 **And the night following** the Lord stood by him,
and said,
Be of good cheer, Paul:
for as thou hast testified of me in Jerusalem,
so must thou bear witness also at Rome.

12 **And when it** was day,
certain of the Jews banded together,
and bound themselves under a curse,
saying
that they would neither eat
nor drink
till they had killed Paul.

13 **And they** were more than forty
which had made this conspiracy.

14 **And they** came to the chief priests and elders,
and said,
We have bound ourselves under a great curse,
that we will eat nothing
until we have slain Paul.

15 **Now therefore ye with the council** signify to the chief captain
that he bring him down unto you to morrow,
as though ye would enquire something more perfectly concerning him:
and we, {or ever he come near}, are ready to kill him.

16 **And when Paul's sister's son** heard of their lying in wait,
he went and entered into the castle,
and told Paul.

17 **Then Paul** called one of the centurions unto him,
and said,
Bring this young man unto the chief captain:
for he hath a certain thing to tell him.

18 **So he** took him,
and brought him to the chief captain,
and said,
Paul the prisoner called me unto him,
and prayed me
to bring this young man unto thee,
who hath something to say unto thee.

19 **Then the chief captain** took him by the hand,
and went with him aside privately,
and asked him,
What is that thou hast to tell me?

20 **And he** said,
The Jews have agreed
to desire thee
that thou wouldest bring down Paul to morrow into the council,
as though they would enquire somewhat of him more perfectly.

21 **But do not thou** yield unto them:
for there lie in wait for him of them more than forty men,
which have bound themselves with an oath,
that they will neither eat
nor drink
till they have killed him:
and now are they ready,
looking for a promise from thee.

22 **So the chief captain** then let the young man depart,
and charged him,
See thou tell no man
that thou hast shewed these things to me.

23 **And he** called unto him two centurions,
saying,
Make ready two hundred soldiers to go to Caesarea, {and horsemen threescore and ten}, {and spearmen two hundred}, at the third hour of the night;

24 **And provide** them beasts,

that they may set Paul on,
and bring him safe unto Felix the governor.

25 **And he** wrote a letter after this manner:

26 **Claudius Lysias unto the most excellent governor Felix** sendeth greeting.

27 **This man** was taken of the Jews,
and should have been killed of them:
then came I with an army,
and rescued him,
having understood
that he was a Roman.

28 **And when I** would have known the cause wherefore they accused him,
I brought him forth into their council:
29 **Whom I** perceived
to be accused of questions of their law,
but to have nothing laid to his charge worthy of death or of bonds.

30 **And when it was told me** how that the Jews laid wait for the man,
I sent straightway to thee,
and gave commandment to his accusers also
to say before thee
what they had against him.
Farewell.

31 **Then the soldiers**, {as it was commanded them}, took Paul,
and brought him by night to Antipatris.

32 **On the morrow** they left the horsemen to go with him,
and returned to the castle:
33 **Who, {when they came to Caesarea} {and delivered the epistle to the governor},**
presented Paul also before him.

34 **And when the governor** had read the letter,
he asked
of what province he was.
And when he understood
that he was of Cilicia;
35 **I** will hear thee,
said he,
when thine accusers are also come.
And he commanded him
to be kept in Herod's judgment hall.

24

∞ **And after five days** Ananias the high priest descended with the elders,
and with a certain orator named Tertullus,
who informed the governor against Paul.

2 **And when he** was called forth,
Tertullus began to accuse him,
saying,
Seeing that by thee we enjoy great quietness,
and that very worthy deeds are done unto this nation by thy providence,
3 **We** accept it always, and in all places, most noble Felix, with all thankfulness.

4 **Notwithstanding, {that I be not further tedious unto thee},** I pray thee
that thou wouldest hear us of thy clemency a few words.

5 **For we** have found this man a pestilent fellow, and a mover of sedition among all the Jews throughout the world, and a ringleader of the sect of the Nazarenes:
6 **Who** also hath gone about to profane the temple:
whom we took,
and would have judged according to our law.
7 **But the chief captain Lysias** came upon us,
and with great violence took him away out of our hands,
8 Commanding his accusers
to come unto thee:
by examining
of whom thyself mayest take knowledge of all these things,
whereof we accuse him.

9 **And the Jews** also assented,
saying
that these things were so.

10 **Then Paul**, {after that the governor had beckoned unto him to speak}, answered,
Forasmuch as I know
that thou hast been of many years a judge unto this nation,
I do the more cheerfully answer for myself:
11 **Because that thou** mayest understand,
that there are yet but twelve days
since I went up to Jerusalem
for to worship.

12 **And they** neither found me in the temple disputing with any man,
neither raising up the people, neither in the synagogues, nor in the city:
13 **Neither** can they prove the things whereof they now accuse me.

14 **But this** I confess unto thee,
that after the way which they call heresy, so worship I the God of my fathers,
believing all things which are written in the law and in the prophets:
15 **And** have hope toward God,
which they themselves also allow,
that there shall be a resurrection of the dead, both of the just and unjust.

16 **And herein** do I exercise myself,
to have always a conscience void to offence toward God, and toward men.

17 **Now after many years** I came to bring alms to my nation,
and offerings.

18 **Whereupon** certain Jews from Asia found me purified in the temple, neither with multitude, nor with tumult.

19 **Who** ought to have been here before thee,
and object,
if they had ought against me.

20 **Or else let these same here** say,
if they have found any evil doing in me,
while I stood before the council,
21 **Except it** be for this one voice,
that I cried standing among them,
Touching the resurrection of the dead I am called in question by you this day.

22 **And when Felix** heard these things,
having more perfect knowledge of that way,
he deferred them,
and said,
When Lysias the chief captain shall come down,
I will know the uttermost of your matter.

23 **And he** commanded a centurion
to keep Paul,
and to let him have liberty,
and that he should forbid none of his acquaintance to minister or come unto him.

24 **And after certain days**, {when
Felix came with his wife Drusilla},
{which was a Jewess}, he sent for
Paul,
and heard him concerning the faith
in Christ.
25 **And as he** reasoned of
righteousness, temperance, and
judgment to come,
Felix trembled,
and answered,
Go thy way for this time;
when I have a convenient season,
I will call for thee.
26 **He** hoped also
that money should have been given
him of Paul,
that he might loose him:
wherefore he sent for him the
oftener,
and communed with him.
27 **But after two years** Porcius
Festus came into Felix' room:
and Felix, {willing to shew the Jews
a pleasure}, left Paul bound.

25

Now when Festus was
come into the province,
after three days he ascended from
Caesarea to Jerusalem.
2 **Then the high priest and the
chief of the Jews** informed him
against Paul,
and besought him,
3 **And** desired favour against him,
that he would send for him to
Jerusalem,
laying wait in the way to kill him.
4 **But Festus** answered,
that Paul should be kept at
Caesarea,
and that he himself would depart
shortly thither.
5 **Let them** therefore,
said he,
which among you are able,
go down with me,
and accuse this man,
if there be any wickedness in him.
6 **And when he** had tarried among
them more than ten days,
he went down unto Caesarea;
**and the next day {sitting on the
judgment seat}** commanded Paul
to be brought.
7 **And when he** was come,
**the Jews which came down from
Jerusalem** stood round about,
and laid many and grievous
complaints against Paul,
which they could not prove.
8 **While he** answered for himself,
**Neither against the law of the
Jews, neither against the
temple, nor yet against Caesar,**
have I offended any thing at all.
9 **But Festus**, {willing to do the Jews
a pleasure}, answered Paul,
and said,
Wilt thou go up to Jerusalem,
and there be judged of these things
before me?
10 **Then** said Paul,
I stand at Caesar's judgment seat,
where I ought to be judged:
to the Jews have I done no wrong,
as thou very well knowest.
11 **For if I** be an offender,
or have committed any thing
worthy of death,
I refuse
not to die:
but if there be none of these things
whereof these accuse me,
no man may deliver me unto them.
I appeal unto Caesar.
12 **Then Festus**, {when he had
conferred with the council},
answered,
Hast thou appealed unto Caesar?
unto Caesar shalt thou go.
13 **And after certain days** king
Agrippa and Bernice came unto
Caesarea to salute Festus.
14 **And when they** had been there
many days,
Festus declared Paul's cause unto
the king,
saying,
There is a certain man left in bonds
by Felix:
15 **About whom**, {when I was at
Jerusalem}, the chief priests and
the elders of the Jews informed
me,
desiring
to have judgment against him.
16 **To whom** I answered,
**It is not the manner of the
Romans** to deliver any man to
die,
before that he which is accused
have the accusers face to face,
and have licence to answer for
himself concerning the crime laid
against him.
17 **Therefore, when they** were come
hither,
without any delay on the morrow
I sat on the judgment seat,
and commanded the man
to be brought forth.
18 **Against whom** {when the
accusers stood up}, they brought
none accusation of such things
as I supposed:
19 **But** had certain questions against
him of their own superstition,
and of one Jesus,
which was dead,
whom Paul affirmed to be alive.
20 **And because I** doubted of such
manner of questions,
I asked him
whether he would go to Jerusalem,
and there be judged of these
matters.
21 **But when Paul** had appealed
to be reserved unto the hearing of
Augustus,
I commanded him
to be kept
till I might send him to Caesar.
22 **Then Agrippa** said unto Festus,
I would also hear the man myself.
To morrow, {said he}, thou shalt
hear him.
23 **And on the morrow**, {when
Agrippa was come, {{and
Bernice}}, with great pomp}, {and
was entered into the place of
hearing, with the chief captains,
and principal men of the city}, at
Festus' commandment Paul was
brought forth.
24 **And Festus** said,
**King Agrippa, and all men which
are here present with us, ye** see
this man,
about whom all the multitude of
the Jews have dealt with me, both
at Jerusalem, and also here,
crying
that he ought not to live any longer.
25 **But when I** found
that he had committed nothing
worthy of death,
and that he himself hath appealed
to Augustus,
I have determined
to send him.
26 **Of whom** I have no certain thing
to write unto my lord.
Wherefore I have brought him
forth before you, and specially
before thee, O king Agrippa,

that, {after examination had}, I might have somewhat to write.
27 **For it seemeth to me unreasonable** to send a prisoner,
and not withal to signify the crimes laid against him.

26 **Then Agrippa** said unto Paul,
Thou art permitted to speak for thyself.
Then Paul stretched forth the hand,
and answered for himself:
2 **I** think myself happy, king Agrippa,
because I shall answer for myself this day before thee touching all the things whereof I am accused of the Jews:
3 **Especially because I** know
thee to be expert in all customs and questions which are among the Jews:
wherefore I beseech thee
to hear me patiently.
4 **My manner of life from my youth**, {which was at the first among mine own nation at Jerusalem}, know all the Jews;
5 **Which** knew me from the beginning,
if they would testify,
that after the most straitest sect of our religion I lived a Pharisee.
6 **And now I** stand and am judged for the hope of the promise made of God, unto our fathers:
7 **Unto which promise** our twelve tribes, {instantly serving God day and night}, hope to come.
For which hope's sake, king Agrippa, I am accused of the Jews.
8 **Why** should it be thought a thing incredible with you,
that God should raise the dead?
9 **I** verily thought with myself,
that I ought to do many things contrary to the name of Jesus of Nazareth.
10 **Which thing** I also did in Jerusalem:
and many of the saints did I shut up in prison,
having received authority from the chief priests;
and when they were put to death,
I gave my voice against them.
11 **And I** punished them oft in every synagogue,
and compelled them to blaspheme;
and being exceedingly mad against them,
I persecuted them even unto strange cities.
12 **Whereupon {as I went to Damascus with authority and commission from the chief priests},**
13 At midday, O king, I saw in the way a light from heaven, above the brightness of the sun,
shining round about me and them which journeyed with me.
14 **And when we** were all fallen to the earth,
I heard a voice speaking unto me,
and saying in the Hebrew tongue,
Saul, Saul, why persecutest thou me?
it is hard for thee to kick against the pricks.
15 **And I** said,
Who art thou, Lord?
And he said,
I am Jesus whom thou persecutest.
16 **But rise,**
and stand upon thy feet:
for I have appeared unto thee for this purpose,
to make thee a minister and a witness both of these things which thou hast seen, and of those things in the which I will appear unto thee;
17 Delivering thee from the people,
and from the Gentiles,
unto whom now I send thee,
18 To open their eyes,
and to turn them from darkness to light,
and from the power of Satan unto God,
that they may receive forgiveness of sins,
and inheritance among them which are sanctified by faith that is in me.
19 **Whereupon, O king Agrippa, I** was not disobedient unto the heavenly vision:
20 **But** shewed first unto them of Damascus, and at Jerusalem, and throughout all the coasts of Judaea, and then to the Gentiles,
that they should repent
and turn to God,
and do works meet for repentance.
21 **For these causes** the Jews caught me in the temple,
and went about to kill me.
22 Having therefore obtained help of God,
I continue unto this day,
witnessing both to small and great,
saying none other things
than those which the prophets and Moses did say should come:
23 **That Christ** should suffer,
and that he should be the first that should rise from the dead,
and should shew light unto the people, and to the Gentiles.
24 **And as he** thus spake for himself,
Festus said with a loud voice,
Paul, thou art beside thyself;
much learning doth make thee mad.
25 **But he** said,
I am not mad, most noble Festus;
but speak forth the words of truth and soberness.
26 **For the king** knoweth of these things,
before whom also I speak freely:
for I am persuaded
that none of these things are hidden from him;
for this thing was not done in a corner.
27 **King Agrippa, believest thou** the prophets?
I know
that thou believest.
28 **Then Agrippa** said unto Paul,
Almost thou persuadest me
to be a Christian.
29 **And Paul** said,
I would to God,
that not only thou, but also all that hear me this day, were both almost, and altogether such as I am, except these bonds.
30 **And when he** had thus spoken,
the king rose up,
and the governor, and Bernice, and they that sat with them:
31 **And when they** were gone aside,
they talked between themselves,
saying,
This man doeth nothing worthy of death or of bonds.
32 **Then** said Agrippa unto Festus,
This man might have been set at liberty,
if he had not appealed unto Caesar.

27 ✂ **And when it was determined** that we should sail into Italy,
they delivered Paul and certain

other prisoners unto one named Julius, a centurion of Augustus' band.
2 **And** entering into a ship of Adramyttium,
we launched,
meaning to sail by the coasts of Asia;
one Aristarchus, a Macedonian of Thessalonica, being with us.
3 **And the next day** we touched at Sidon.
And Julius courteously entreated Paul,
and gave him liberty to go unto his friends
to refresh himself.
4 **And when we** had launched from thence,
we sailed under Cyprus,
because the winds were contrary.
5 **And when we** had sailed over the sea of Cilicia and Pamphylia,
we came to Myra, a city of Lycia.
6 **And there** the centurion found a ship of Alexandria sailing into Italy;
and he put us therein.
7 **And when we** had sailed slowly many days,
and scarce were come over against Cnidus,
the wind not suffering us,
we sailed under Crete, over against Salmone;
8 **And, {hardly passing it},** came unto a place which is called The fair havens;
nigh whereunto was the city of Lasea.
9 **Now when much time** was spent,
and when sailing was now dangerous,
because the fast was now already past,
Paul admonished them,
10 **And** said unto them,
Sirs, I perceive
that this voyage will be with hurt and much damage,
not only of the lading and ship,
but also of our lives.
11 **Nevertheless the centurion** believed the master and the owner of the ship, more than those things which were spoken by Paul.
12 **And because the haven** was not commodious to winter in,
the more part advised
to depart thence also,
if by any means they might attain to Phenice,
and there to winter;
which is an haven of Crete,
and lieth toward the south west and north west.
13 **And when the south wind** blew softly,
supposing
that they had obtained their purpose,
loosing thence,
they sailed close by Crete.
14 **But not long after** there arose against it a tempestuous wind,
called Euroclydon.
15 **And when the ship** was caught,
and could not bear up into the wind,
we let her drive.
16 **And** running under a certain island which is called Clauda,
we had much work to come by the boat:
17 **Which when they** had taken up,
they used helps,
undergirding the ship;
and, {fearing lest they should fall into the quicksands}, strake sail,
and so were driven.
18 **And we** being exceedingly tossed with a tempest,
the next day they lightened the ship;
19 **And the third day** we cast out with our own hands the tackling of the ship.
20 **And when neither sun nor stars in many days** appeared,
and no small tempest lay on us,
all hope that we should be saved was then taken away.
21 **But after long abstinence** Paul stood forth in the midst of them,
and said,
Sirs, ye should have hearkened unto me,
and not have loosed from Crete,
and to have gained this harm and loss.
22 **And now I** exhort you
to be of good cheer:
for there shall be no loss of any man's life among you,
but of the ship.
23 **For there** stood by me this night the angel of God,
whose I am,
and whom I serve,
24 Saying,
Fear not, Paul;
thou must be brought before Caesar:
and, {lo}, God hath given thee all them that sail with thee.
25 **Wherefore, sirs, be** of good cheer:
for I believe God,
that it shall be
even as it was told me.
26 **Howbeit we** must be cast upon a certain island.
27 **But when the fourteenth night** was come,
as we were driven up and down in Adria,
about midnight the shipmen deemed
that they drew near to some country;
28 **And** sounded,
and found it twenty fathoms:
and when they had gone a little further,
they sounded again,
and found it fifteen fathoms.
29 **Then** fearing lest we should have fallen upon rocks,
they cast four anchors out of the stern,
and wished for the day.
30 **And as the shipmen** were about to flee out of the ship,
when they had let down the boat into the sea,
under colour as though they would have cast anchors out of the foreship,
31 **Paul** said to the centurion and to the soldiers,
Except these abide in the ship,
ye cannot be saved.
32 **Then the soldiers** cut off the ropes of the boat,
and let her fall off.
33 **And while the day** was coming on,
Paul besought them all
to take meat,
saying,
This day is the fourteenth day that ye have tarried and continued fasting, having taken nothing.
34 **Wherefore I** pray you
to take some meat:
for this is for your health:
for there shall not an hair fall from the head of any of you.

35 **And when he** had thus spoken,
he took bread,
and gave thanks to God in presence of them all:
and when he had broken it,
he began to eat.

36 **Then** were they all of good cheer,
and they also took some meat.

37 **And we** were in all in the ship two hundred threescore and sixteen souls.

38 **And when they** had eaten enough,
they lightened the ship,
and cast out the wheat into the sea.

39 **And when it** was day,
they knew not the land:
but they discovered a certain creek with a shore,
into the which they were minded,
if it were possible,
to thrust in the ship.

40 **And when they** had taken up the anchors,
they committed themselves unto the sea,
and loosed the rudder bands,
and hoised up the mainsail to the wind,
and made toward shore.

41 **And** falling into a place where two seas met,
they ran the ship aground;
and the forepart stuck fast,
and remained unmoveable,
but the hinder part was broken with the violence of the waves.

42 **And the soldiers' counsel** was to kill the prisoners,
lest any of them should swim out,
and escape.

43 **But the centurion**, {willing to save Paul}, kept them from their purpose;
and commanded
that they which could swim should cast themselves first into the sea,
and get to land:

44 **And the rest**, some on boards, and some on broken pieces of the ship.
And so it came to pass,
that they escaped all safe to land.

28

And when they were escaped,
then they knew
that the island was called Melita.

2 **And the barbarous people** shewed us no little kindness:
for they kindled a fire,
and received us every one,
because of the present rain,
and because of the cold.

3 **And when Paul** had gathered a bundle of sticks,
and laid them on the fire,
there came a viper out of the heat,
and fastened on his hand.

4 **And when the barbarians** saw the venomous beast hang on his hand,
they said among themselves,
No doubt this man is a murderer,
whom, {though he hath escaped the sea}, yet vengeance suffereth not to live.

5 **And he** shook off the beast into the fire,
and felt no harm.

6 **Howbeit they** looked
when he should have swollen,
or fallen down dead suddenly:
but after they had looked a great while,
and saw no harm come to him,
they changed their minds,
and said
that he was a god.

7 **In the same quarters** were possessions of the chief man of the island,
whose name was Publius;
who received us,
and lodged us three days courteously.

8 **And it** came to pass,
that the father of Publius lay sick of a fever and of a bloody flux:
to whom Paul entered in,
and prayed,
and laid his hands on him,
and healed him.

9 **So when this** was done,
others also, {which had diseases in the island}, came,
and were healed:

10 **Who** also honoured us with many honours;
and when we departed,
they laded us with such things as were necessary.

11 **And after three months** we departed in a ship of Alexandria,
which had wintered in the isle,
whose sign was Castor and Pollux.

12 **And** landing at Syracuse,
we tarried there three days.

13 **And from thence** we fetched a compass,
and came to Rhegium:
and after one day the south wind blew,
and we came the next day to Puteoli:

14 **Where we** found brethren,
and were desired
to tarry with them seven days:
and so we went toward Rome.

15 **And from thence**, {when the brethren heard of us}, they came to meet us as far as Appii forum, and The three taverns:
whom when Paul saw,
he thanked God,
and took courage.

16 **And when we** came to Rome,
the centurion delivered the prisoners to the captain of the guard:
but Paul was suffered to dwell by himself with a soldier that kept him.

17 **And it** came to pass,
that after three days Paul called the chief of the Jews together:
and when they were come together,
he said unto them,
Men and brethren, though I have committed nothing against the people, or customs of our fathers,
yet was I delivered prisoner from Jerusalem into the hands of the Romans.

18 **Who**, {when they had examined me}, would have let me go,
because there was no cause of death in me.

19 **But when the Jews** spake against it,
I was constrained to appeal unto Caesar;
not that I had ought to accuse my nation of.

20 **For this cause** therefore have I called for you,
to see you,
and to speak with you:
because that for the hope of Israel I am bound with this chain.

21 **And they** said unto him,
We neither received letters out of Judaea concerning thee,
neither any of the brethren that came shewed or spake any harm of thee.

22 **But we** desire

to hear of thee
what thou thinkest:
for as concerning this sect, we know
that every where it is spoken against.
23 **And when they** had appointed him a day,
there came many to him into his lodging;
to whom he expounded
and testified the kingdom of God,
persuading them concerning Jesus, both out of the law of Moses, and out of the prophets, from morning till evening.
24 **And some** believed the things which were spoken,
and some believed not.
25 **And when they** agreed not among themselves,
they departed,
after that Paul had spoken one word,
Well spake the Holy Ghost by Esaias the prophet unto our fathers,
26 Saying,
Go unto this people,
and say,
Hearing ye shall hear,
and shall not understand;
and seeing ye shall see,
and not perceive:
27 **For the heart of this people** is waxed gross,
and their ears are dull of hearing,
and their eyes have they closed;
lest they should see with their eyes,
and hear with their ears,
and understand with their heart,
and should be converted,
and I should heal them.
28 **Be it known** therefore unto you,
that the salvation of God is sent unto the Gentiles,
and that they will hear it.
29 **And when he** had said these words,
the Jews departed,
and had great reasoning among themselves.
30 **And Paul** dwelt two whole years in his own hired house,
and received all that came in unto him,
31 Preaching the kingdom of God,
and teaching those things which concern the Lord Jesus Christ, with all confidence,
no man forbidding him.

Romans

The Epistle of Paul the Apostle to the Romans, a letter penned by Paul, formerly known as Saul, a significant figure in early Christianity, was written during a crucial period in the history of the Christian community in Rome. In his letter, Paul aims to establish his authority as a leader in the Church and to share the Gospel message with the people of Rome. His ultimate goal in writing Romans is to encourage believers and strengthen their faith. He wants to equip them with a deep understanding of their faith so they can effectively live out their Christian lives and share the Gospel message with others.

Romans is filled with profound theological insights, too many to summarize in a brief introduction. However, an overview of insights would begin with Paul explaining the concept of justification by faith, how Christians are declared righteous in God's sight not because of their own merits but because of their faith in Jesus Christ. This concept of saving faith is paramount throughout the book. Paul then mentions the importance of suffering and persecution in the life of a Christian, how it can lead to spiritual growth and endurance. He discusses the nature of sin and how it separates people from God. His follow-up on this truth clarifies how the law is given to reveal one's sinfulness and need for a Savior, not as a means for salvation. Finally, he addresses the potential divisions and conflicts within the Roman Church, urging believers to accept one another and to live in harmony.

For the life of a believer, Romans provides a comprehensive theological understanding of Christianity at a deeply personal level. Its focus on faith in Christ alone is a reminder for those who become overly focused on their efforts and achievements to earn the promise of eternal life. It highlights a valuable lesson for those who struggle with guilt or shame over past sins. Perhaps most importantly, it places into perspective the role of internal and external suffering and persecution in the lives of believers, thus providing hope for those who are going through difficult times and need encouragement to persevere. And its lessons on church unity, emphasizing the love and acceptance of all members, benefit those who are part of a diverse church community and need guidance on fostering harmony and love among its members, creating a sense of belonging and unity in the Roman community.

With its profound theological depth, Romans provides a foundational understanding of the Gospel. Furthermore, it remains a vitally important text in understanding the doctrine of justification by faith alone, a revolutionary concept that became the cornerstone of the Protestant Reformation. Finally, it illuminates the power of God's grace and the universal reach of salvation through Jesus Christ. If fully embraced by the Church, these truths will bring about far-reaching changes in the world by offering hope and reassurance to all who believe and inspiring them to live a life of faith, grace, and love.

1 **Paul, a servant of Jesus Christ**,
called to be an apostle,
separated unto the gospel of God,
2 (Which he had promised afore by his prophets in the holy scriptures,)
3 Concerning his Son Jesus Christ our Lord,
which was made of the seed of David according to the flesh;
4 And declared to be the Son of God with power, according to the spirit of holiness, by the resurrection from the dead:
5 By whom we have received grace and apostleship, for obedience to the faith among all nations, for his name:
6 Among whom are ye also the called of Jesus Christ:
7 To all that be in Rome, beloved of God,
called to be saints:
Grace to you {and peace} from God our Father,
and the Lord Jesus Christ.
8 **First, I** thank my God through Jesus Christ for you all,
that your faith is spoken of throughout the whole world.
9 **For God** is my witness,
whom I serve with my spirit in the gospel of his Son,
that without ceasing I make mention of you always in my prayers;
10 Making request,
if by any means now at length I might have a prosperous journey by the will of God to come unto you.
11 **For I** long to see you,
that I may impart unto you some spiritual gift,
to the end ye may be established;
12 That is,
that I may be comforted together with you by the mutual faith both of you and me.
13 **Now I** would not have you ignorant, brethren,
that oftentimes I purposed to come unto you,
(but was let hitherto,)
that I might have some fruit among you also, even as among other Gentiles.
14 **I** am debtor both to the Greeks, and to the Barbarians; both to the wise, and to the unwise.
15 **So, as much as in me** is,

I am ready to preach the gospel to you that are at Rome also.
16 **For I** am not ashamed of the gospel of Christ:
for it is the power of God unto salvation to every one that believeth; to the Jew first, and also to the Greek.
17 **For therein** is the righteousness of God revealed from faith to faith:
as it is written,
The just shall live by faith.
18 **For the wrath of God** is revealed from heaven against all ungodliness and unrighteousness of men,
who hold the truth in unrighteousness;
19 **Because that which may be known of God** is manifest in them;
for God hath shewed it unto them.
20 **For the invisible things of him from the creation of the world** are clearly seen,
being understood by the things that are made, even his eternal power and Godhead;
so that they are without excuse:
21 **Because that, {when they knew God},** they glorified him not as God,
neither were thankful;
but became vain in their imaginations,
and their foolish heart was darkened.
22 Professing themselves to be wise,
they became fools,
23 **And** changed the glory of the uncorruptible God into an image made like to corruptible man, and to birds, and fourfooted beasts, and creeping things.
24 **Wherefore God** also gave them up to uncleanness through the lusts of their own hearts,
to dishonour their own bodies between themselves:
25 **Who** changed the truth of God into a lie,
and worshipped and served the creature more than the Creator,
who is blessed for ever.
Amen.
26 **For this cause** God gave them up unto vile affections:
for even their women did change the natural use into that which is against nature:
27 **And likewise also the men,** {leaving the natural use of the woman}, burned in their lust one toward another;
men with men working that which is unseemly,
and receiving in themselves that recompence of their error which was meet.
28 **And even as they** did not like to retain God in their knowledge,
God gave them over to a reprobate mind,
to do those things which are not convenient;
29 Being filled with all unrighteousness, fornication, wickedness, covetousness, maliciousness; full of envy, murder, debate, deceit, malignity; whisperers,
30 Backbiters, haters of God, despiteful, proud, boasters, inventors of evil things, disobedient to parents,
31 Without understanding, covenantbreakers, without natural affection, implacable, unmerciful:
32 **Who** knowing the judgment of God,
that they which commit such things are worthy of death,
not only do the same,
but have pleasure in them that do them.

2 **Therefore thou** art inexcusable, O man,
whosoever thou art that judgest:
for wherein thou judgest another,
thou condemnest thyself;
for thou that judgest doest the same things.
2 **But we** are sure
that the judgment of God is according to truth against them which commit such things.
3 **And thinkest thou** this, O man,
that judgest them which do such things,
and doest the same,
that thou shalt escape the judgment of God?
4 **Or despisest thou** the riches of his goodness and forbearance and longsuffering;
not knowing
that the goodness of God leadeth thee to repentance?
5 **But after thy hardness and impenitent heart** treasurest up unto thyself wrath against the day of wrath and revelation of the righteous judgment of God;
6 **Who** will render to every man according to his deeds:
7 **To them who by patient continuance in well doing seek for glory and honour and immortality,** eternal life:
8 **But unto them that are contentious, and do not obey the truth, but obey unrighteousness,** indignation and wrath,
9 Tribulation and anguish, upon every soul of man that doeth evil, of the Jew first, and also of the Gentile;
10 But glory, honour, and peace, to every man that worketh good, to the Jew first, and also to the Gentile:
11 **For there** is no respect of persons with God.
12 **For as many as have sinned without law** shall also perish without law:
and as many as have sinned in the law shall be judged by the law;
13 (For not the hearers of the law are just before God,
but the doers of the law shall be justified.
14 For when the Gentiles, {which have not the law}, do by nature the things contained in the law,
these, {having not the law}, are a law unto themselves:
15 Which shew the work of the law written in their hearts,
their conscience also bearing witness,
and their thoughts the mean while accusing or else excusing one another;)
16 In the day when God shall judge the secrets of men by Jesus Christ according to my gospel.
17 **Behold,**
thou art called a Jew,
and restest in the law,
and makest thy boast of God,
18 **And** knowest his will,
and approvest the things that are more excellent,
being instructed out of the law;

19 **And** art confident that thou thyself art a guide of the blind, a light of them which are in darkness,
20 An instructor of the foolish, a teacher of babes,
which hast the form of knowledge and of the truth in the law.
21 **Thou therefore which teachest another,** teachest thou not thyself?
thou that preachest a man should not steal, dost thou steal?
22 **Thou that sayest a man should not commit adultery,** dost thou commit adultery?
thou that abhorrest idols, dost thou commit sacrilege?
23 **Thou that makest thy boast of the law, through breaking the law** dishonourest thou God?
24 **For the name of God** is blasphemed among the Gentiles through you,
as it is written.
25 **For circumcision** verily profiteth,
if thou keep the law:
but if thou be a breaker of the law,
thy circumcision is made uncircumcision.
26 **Therefore if the uncircumcision** keep the righteousness of the law,
shall not his uncircumcision be counted for circumcision?
27 **And shall not uncircumcision which is by nature,** {if it fulfil the law}, judge thee,
who by the letter and circumcision dost transgress the law?
28 **For he** is not a Jew,
which is one outwardly;
neither is that circumcision,
which is outward in the flesh:
29 **But he** is a Jew,
which is one inwardly;
and circumcision is that of the heart, in the spirit, and not in the letter;
whose praise is not of men, but of God.

3 **What advantage** then hath the Jew?
or what profit is there of circumcision?
2 Much every way:
chiefly, because that unto them were committed the oracles of God.
3 **For what if some** did not believe?
shall their unbelief make the faith of God without effect?
4 **God** forbid:
yea, let God be true, but every man a liar;
as it is written,
That thou mightest be justified in thy sayings,
and mightest overcome when thou art judged.
5 **But if our unrighteousness** commend the righteousness of God,
what shall we say?
Is God unrighteous who taketh vengeance?
(**I** speak as a man)
6 **God** forbid:
for then how shall God judge the world?
7 **For if the truth of God** hath more abounded through my lie unto his glory;
why yet am I also judged as a sinner?
8 **And** not rather,
(as we be slanderously reported,
and as some affirm that we say,)
Let us do evil,
that good may come?
whose damnation is just.
9 What then?
are we better than they?
No, in no wise:
for we have before proved both Jews and Gentiles,
that they are all under sin;
10 **As it** is written,
There is none righteous, no, not one:
11 **There** is none that understandeth,
there is none that seeketh after God.
12 **They** are all gone out of the way,
they are together become unprofitable;
there is none that doeth good, no, not one.
13 **Their throat** is an open sepulchre;
with their tongues they have used deceit;
the poison of asps is under their lips:
14 **Whose mouth** is full of cursing and bitterness:
15 **Their feet** are swift to shed blood:
16 **Destruction and misery** are in their ways:
17 **And the way of peace** have they not known:
18 **There** is no fear of God before their eyes.
19 **Now we** know
that what things soever the law saith,
it saith to them who are under the law:
that every mouth may be stopped,
and all the world may become guilty before God.
20 **Therefore by the deeds of the law** there shall no flesh be justified in his sight:
for by the law is the knowledge of sin.
21 **But now the righteousness of God without the law** is manifested,
being witnessed by the law and the prophets;
22 Even the righteousness of God which is by faith of Jesus Christ unto all and upon all them that believe:
for there is no difference:
23 **For all** have sinned,
and come short of the glory of God;
24 Being justified freely by his grace through the redemption that is in Christ Jesus:
25 **Whom** God hath set forth to be a propitiation through faith in his blood,
to declare his righteousness for the remission of sins that are past, through the forbearance of God;
26 To declare, {I say}, at this time his righteousness:
that he might be just, and the justifier of him which believeth in Jesus.
27 **Where** is boasting then?
It is excluded.
By what law?
of works?
Nay: but by the law of faith.
28 **Therefore we** conclude
that a man is justified by faith without the deeds of the law.
29 **Is he** the God of the Jews only?
is he not also of the Gentiles?
Yes, of the Gentiles also:
30 **Seeing it** is one God,
which shall justify the circumcision by faith, and uncircumcision through faith.

31 **Do we** then make void the law through faith?
God forbid:
yea, we establish the law.

4

What shall we say then **that Abraham our father, as pertaining to the flesh,** hath found?
2 **For if Abraham** were justified by works,
he hath whereof to glory; but not before God.
3 **For what** saith the scripture?
Abraham believed God,
and it was counted unto him for righteousness.
4 **Now to him that worketh** is the reward not reckoned of grace, but of debt.
5 **But to him that worketh not, but believeth on him that justifieth the ungodly,** his faith is counted for righteousness.
6 **Even as David** also describeth the blessedness of the man,
unto whom God imputeth righteousness without works,
7 Saying,
Blessed are they whose iniquities are forgiven, and whose sins are covered.
8 **Blessed** is the man to whom the Lord will not impute sin.
9 **Cometh this blessedness** then upon the circumcision only, or upon the uncircumcision also?
for we say
that faith was reckoned to Abraham for righteousness.
10 **How** was it then reckoned?
when he was in circumcision, or in uncircumcision?
Not in circumcision, but in uncircumcision.
11 **And he** received the sign of circumcision, a seal of the righteousness of the faith which he had yet being uncircumcised:
that he might be the father of all them that believe,
though they be not circumcised;
that righteousness might be imputed unto them also:
12 And the father of circumcision to them who are not of the circumcision only,
but who also walk in the steps of that faith of our father Abraham,
which he had being yet uncircumcised.
13 **For the promise**, {that he should be the heir of the world}, was not to Abraham, or to his seed, through the law, but through the righteousness of faith.
14 **For if they which are of the law** be heirs,
faith is made void,
and the promise made of none effect:
15 **Because the law** worketh wrath:
for where no law is,
there is no transgression.
16 **Therefore it** is of faith,
that it might be by grace;
to the end the promise might be sure to all the seed; not to that only which is of the law, but to that also which is of the faith of Abraham;
who is the father of us all,
17 (As it is written,
I have made thee a father of many nations,)
before him whom he believed, even God,
who quickeneth the dead,
and calleth those things which be not as though they were.
18 **Who against hope** believed in hope,
that he might become the father of many nations, according to that which was spoken,
So shall thy seed be.
19 **And** being not weak in faith,
he considered not his own body now dead,
when he was about an hundred years old, neither yet the deadness of Sarah's womb:
20 **He** staggered not at the promise of God through unbelief;
but was strong in faith,
giving glory to God;
21 **And** being fully persuaded that, {what he had promised}, he was able also to perform.
22 **And therefore it** was imputed to him for righteousness.
23 **Now it** was not written for his sake alone,
that it was imputed to him;
24 But for us also,
to whom it shall be imputed,
if we believe on him that raised up Jesus our Lord from the dead;
25 **Who** was delivered for our offences,
and was raised again for our justification.

5

Therefore being justified by faith,
we have peace with God through our Lord Jesus Christ:
2 **By whom** also we have access by faith into this grace wherein we stand,
and rejoice in hope of the glory of God.
3 **And not only so,** but we glory in tribulations also:
knowing
that tribulation worketh patience;
4 And patience, experience; and experience, hope:
5 **And hope** maketh not ashamed;
because the love of God is shed abroad in our hearts by the Holy Ghost which is given unto us.
6 **For when we** were yet without strength,
in due time Christ died for the ungodly.
7 **For scarcely for a righteous man** will one die:
yet peradventure for a good man some would even dare to die.
8 **But God** commendeth his love toward us,
in that, {while we were yet sinners}, Christ died for us.
9 **Much more then, {being now justified by his blood},** we shall be saved from wrath through him.
10 **For if, {when we were enemies},** we were reconciled to God by the death of his Son,
much more, {being reconciled}, we shall be saved by his life.
11 **And not only so,** but we also joy in God through our Lord Jesus Christ,
by whom we have now received the atonement.
12 **Wherefore, as by one man** sin entered into the world, and death by sin;
and so death passed upon all men,
for that all have sinned:
13 (For until the law sin was in the world:
but sin is not imputed when there is no law.
14 Nevertheless death reigned from Adam to Moses, even over them

that had not sinned after the
similitude of Adam's
transgression,
who is the figure of him that was to
come.
15 But not as the offence, so also is
the free gift.
For if through the offence of one
many be dead,
much more the grace of God, and
the gift by grace, {which is by one
man, Jesus Christ}, hath
abounded unto many.
16 And not as it was by one that
sinned,
so is the gift:
for the judgment was by one to
condemnation,
but the free gift is of many offences
unto justification.
17 For if by one man's offence death
reigned by one;
much more they which receive
abundance of grace and of the gift
of righteousness shall reign in life
by one, Jesus Christ.)
18 **Therefore as by the offence of
one judgment** came upon all
men to condemnation;
**even so by the righteousness of
one** the free gift came upon all
men unto justification of life.
19 **For as by one man's
disobedience** many were made
sinners,
so by the obedience of one shall
many be made righteous.
20 **Moreover the law** entered,
that the offence might abound.
But where sin abounded,
grace did much more abound:
21 **That as sin** hath reigned unto
death,
even so might grace reign through
righteousness unto eternal life by
Jesus Christ our Lord.

6 **What** shall we say then?
Shall we continue in sin,
that grace may abound?
2 **God** forbid.
How shall we, {that are dead to
sin}, live any longer therein?
3 **Know ye not,**
**that so many of us as were
baptized into Jesus Christ** were
baptized into his death?
4 **Therefore we** are buried with him
by baptism into death:
that like as Christ was raised up
from the dead by the glory of the
Father,
even so we also should walk in
newness of life.
5 **For if we** have been planted
together in the likeness of his
death,
we shall be also in the likeness of
his resurrection:
6 Knowing this,
that our old man is crucified with
him,
that the body of sin might be
destroyed,
that henceforth we should not
serve sin.
7 **For he that is dead** is freed from
sin.
8 **Now if we** be dead with Christ,
we believe
that we shall also live with him:
9 Knowing
**that Christ being raised from the
dead** dieth no more;
death hath no more dominion over
him.
10 **For in that he** died,
he died unto sin once:
but in that he liveth,
he liveth unto God.
11 **Likewise reckon ye** also
yourselves to be dead indeed unto
sin, but alive unto God through
Jesus Christ our Lord.
12 **Let not sin** therefore reign in your
mortal body,
that ye should obey it in the lusts
thereof.
13 **Neither yield ye** your members as
instruments of unrighteousness
unto sin:
but yield yourselves unto God, as
those that are alive from the dead,
and your members as
instruments of righteousness
unto God.
14 **For sin** shall not have dominion
over you:
for ye are not under the law, but
under grace.
15 What then?
shall we sin,
because we are not under the law,
but under grace?
God forbid.
16 **Know ye not,**
that to whom ye yield yourselves
servants to obey,
his servants ye are to whom ye
obey; whether of sin unto death,
or of obedience unto
righteousness?
17 **But God** be thanked,
that ye were the servants of sin,
but ye have obeyed from the heart
that form of doctrine which was
delivered you.
18 Being then made free from sin,
ye became the servants of
righteousness.
19 **I** speak after the manner of men
because of the infirmity of your
flesh:
for as ye have yielded your
members servants to uncleanness
and to iniquity unto iniquity;
even so now yield your members
servants to righteousness unto
holiness.
20 **For when ye** were the servants of
sin,
ye were free from righteousness.
21 **What fruit** had ye then in those
things whereof ye are now
ashamed?
for the end of those things is
death.
22 **But now** being made free from
sin,
and become servants to God,
ye have your fruit unto holiness,
and the end everlasting life.
23 **For the wages of sin** is death;
but the gift of God is eternal life
through Jesus Christ our Lord.

7 **Know ye not, brethren,**
(for I speak to them that know
the law,)
how that the law hath dominion
over a man as long as he liveth?
2 **For the woman which hath an
husband** is bound by the law to
her husband
so long as he liveth;
but if the husband be dead,
she is loosed from the law of her
husband.
3 **So then if, {while her husband
liveth},** she be married to another
man,
she shall be called an adulteress:
but if her husband be dead,
she is free from that law;
so that she is no adulteress,
though she be married to another
man.

4 **Wherefore, my brethren, ye** also are become dead to the law by the body of Christ;
that ye should be married to another, even to him who is raised from the dead,
that we should bring forth fruit unto God.

5 **For when we** were in the flesh,
the motions of sins, {which were by the law}, did work in our members
to bring forth fruit unto death.

6 **But now we** are delivered from the law,
that being dead wherein we were held;
that we should serve in newness of spirit, and not in the oldness of the letter.

7 **What** shall we say then?

Is the law sin?

God forbid.

Nay, I had not known sin, but by the law:
for I had not known lust,
except the law had said,
Thou shalt not covet.

8 **But sin**, {taking occasion by the commandment}, wrought in me all manner of concupiscence.

For without the law sin was dead.

9 **For I** was alive without the law once:
but when the commandment came,
sin revived,
and I died.

10 **And the commandment**, {which was ordained to life}, I found to be unto death.

11 **For sin**, {taking occasion by the commandment}, deceived me,
and by it slew me.

12 **Wherefore the law** is holy, and the commandment holy, and just, and good.

13 **Was then that which is good** made death unto me?

God forbid.

But sin, {that it might appear sin}, working death in me by that which is good;
that sin by the commandment might become exceeding sinful.

14 **For we** know
that the law is spiritual:
but I am carnal, sold under sin.

15 **For that which I do** I allow not:
for what I would,
that do I not;
but what I hate,
that do I.

16 **If then I** do that which I would not,
I consent unto the law
that it is good.

17 **Now then it** is no more I that do it, but sin that dwelleth in me.

18 **For I** know
that in me (that is, in my flesh,) dwelleth no good thing:
for to will is present with me;
but how to perform that which is good
I find not.

19 **For the good that I would** I do not:
but the evil which I would not, that I do.

20 **Now if I** do that I would not,
it is no more I that do it, but sin that dwelleth in me.

21 **I** find then a law,
that, {when I would do good}, evil is present with me.

22 **For I** delight in the law of God after the inward man:

23 **But I** see another law in my members,
warring against the law of my mind,
and bringing me into captivity to the law of sin which is in my members.

24 O wretched man that I am!
who shall deliver me from the body of this death?

25 **I** thank God through Jesus Christ our Lord.

So then with the mind I myself serve the law of God; but with the flesh the law of sin.

8

There is therefore now no condemnation to them which are in Christ Jesus,
who walk not after the flesh, but after the Spirit.

2 **For the law of the Spirit of life in Christ Jesus** hath made me free from the law of sin and death.

3 **For what the law** could not do,
in that it was weak through the flesh,
God sending his own Son in the likeness of sinful flesh, and for sin, condemned sin in the flesh:

4 **That the righteousness of the law** might be fulfilled in us,
who walk not after the flesh, but after the Spirit.

5 **For they that are after the flesh** do mind the things of the flesh; but they that are after the Spirit the things of the Spirit.

6 **For to be carnally minded** is death;
but to be spiritually minded is life and peace.

7 **Because the carnal mind** is enmity against God:
for it is not subject to the law of God,
neither indeed can be.

8 **So then they that are in the flesh** cannot please God.

9 **But ye** are not in the flesh, but in the Spirit,
if so be that the Spirit of God dwell in you.

Now if any man have not the Spirit of Christ,
he is none of his.

10 **And if Christ** be in you,
the body is dead because of sin;
but the Spirit is life because of righteousness.

11 **But if the Spirit of him that raised up Jesus from the dead** dwell in you,
he that raised up Christ from the dead shall also quicken your mortal bodies by his Spirit that dwelleth in you.

12 **Therefore, brethren, we** are debtors,
not to the flesh, to live after the flesh.

13 **For if ye** live after the flesh,
ye shall die:
but if ye through the Spirit do mortify the deeds of the body,
ye shall live.

14 **For as many as are led by the Spirit of God**, they are the sons of God.

15 **For ye** have not received the spirit of bondage again to fear;
but ye have received the Spirit of adoption,
whereby we cry,
Abba, Father.

16 **The Spirit itself** beareth witness with our spirit,
that we are the children of God:
17 And if children, then heirs; heirs of God, and joint-heirs with Christ;
if so be that we suffer with him,
that we may be also glorified together.

18 **For I** reckon
that the sufferings of this present time are not worthy to be compared with the glory which shall be revealed in us.

19 **For the earnest expectation of the creature** waiteth for the manifestation of the sons of God.

20 **For the creature** was made subject to vanity, not willingly, but by reason of him who hath subjected the same in hope,
21 **Because the creature itself** also shall be delivered from the bondage of corruption into the glorious liberty of the children of God.

22 **For we** know
that the whole creation groaneth and travaileth in pain together until now.

23 And not only they, but ourselves also,
which have the firstfruits of the Spirit,
even we ourselves groan within ourselves,
waiting for the adoption, to wit, the redemption of our body.

24 **For we** are saved by hope:
but hope that is seen is not hope:
for what a man seeth,
why doth he yet hope for?

25 **But if we** hope for that we see not,
then do we with patience wait for it.

26 **Likewise the Spirit** also helpeth our infirmities:
for we know not
what we should pray for as we ought:
but the Spirit itself maketh intercession for us with groanings which cannot be uttered.

27 **And he that searcheth the hearts** knoweth
what is the mind of the Spirit,
because he maketh intercession for the saints according to the will of God.

28 **And we** know
that all things work together for good to them that love God, to them who are the called according to his purpose.

29 **For whom** he did foreknow,
he also did predestinate to be conformed to the image of his Son,
that he might be the firstborn among many brethren.

30 **Moreover whom** he did predestinate,
them he also called:
and whom he called,
them he also justified:
and whom he justified,
them he also glorified.

31 **What** shall we then say to these things?
If God be for us,
who can be against us?

32 **He that spared not his own Son, but delivered him up for us all,** how shall he not with him also freely give us all things?

33 **Who** shall lay any thing to the charge of God's elect?
It is God that justifieth.

34 **Who** is he that condemneth?
It is Christ that died, yea rather, that is risen again,
who is even at the right hand of God,
who also maketh intercession for us.

35 **Who** shall separate us from the love of Christ?
shall tribulation, or distress, or persecution, or famine, or nakedness, or peril, or sword?

36 **As it** is written,
For thy sake we are killed all the day long;
we are accounted as sheep for the slaughter.

37 **Nay, in all these things** we are more than conquerors through him that loved us.

38 **For I** am persuaded,
that neither death, nor life, nor angels, nor principalities, nor powers, nor things present, nor things to come,
39 **Nor height, nor depth, nor any other creature,** shall be able to separate us from the love of God,
which is in Christ Jesus our Lord.

9 **I** say the truth in Christ,
I lie not,
my conscience also bearing me witness in the Holy Ghost,
2 **That I** have great heaviness and continual sorrow in my heart.

3 **For I** could wish
that myself were accursed from Christ for my brethren, my kinsmen according to the flesh:
4 **Who** are Israelites;
to whom pertaineth the adoption, and the glory, and the covenants, and the giving of the law, and the service of God, and the promises;
5 **Whose** are the fathers,
and of whom as concerning the flesh Christ came,
who is over all, God blessed for ever.

Amen.

6 **Not as though the word of God** hath taken none effect.
For they are not all Israel,
which are of Israel:
7 **Neither, {because they are the seed of Abraham},** are they all children:
but, In Isaac shall thy seed be called.

8 That is,
They which are the children of the flesh, these are not the children of God:
but the children of the promise are counted for the seed.

9 **For this** is the word of promise,
At this time will I come,
and Sarah shall have a son.

10 And not only this;
but when Rebecca also had conceived by one, even by our father Isaac;
11 ({For the children being not yet born},
{neither having done any good or evil},
{that the purpose of God according to election might stand, not of works, but of him that calleth};)
12 It was said unto her,
The elder shall serve the younger.

13 **As it** is written,
Jacob have I loved,
but Esau have I hated.

14 **What** shall we say then?

Is there unrighteousness with God?

God forbid.

15 **For he** saith to Moses,
I will have mercy
on whom I will have mercy,
and I will have compassion
on whom I will have compassion.
16 **So then it** is not of him that willeth, nor of him that runneth, but of God that sheweth mercy.
17 **For the scripture** saith unto Pharaoh,
Even for this same purpose have I raised thee up,
that I might shew my power in thee,
and that my name might be declared throughout all the earth.
18 **Therefore** hath he mercy
on whom he will have mercy,
and whom he will
he hardeneth.
19 **Thou** wilt say then unto me,
Why doth he yet find fault?
For who hath resisted his will?
20 **Nay but, O man, who** art thou that repliest against God?
Shall the thing formed say to him that formed it,
Why hast thou made me thus?
21 **Hath not the potter** power over the clay,
of the same lump to make one vessel unto honour, and another unto dishonour?
22 **What if God**, {willing to shew his wrath}, {and to make his power known}, endured with much longsuffering the vessels of wrath fitted to destruction:
23 **And that he** might make known the riches of his glory on the vessels of mercy,
which he had afore prepared unto glory,
24 Even us,
whom he hath called, not of the Jews only, but also of the Gentiles?
25 **As he** saith also in Osee,
I will call them my people, {which were not my people}; and her beloved, {which was not beloved}.
26 **And it** shall come to pass,
that in the place where it was said unto them, {Ye are not my people}; there shall they be called the children of the living God.
27 **Esaias** also crieth concerning Israel,
Though the number of the children of Israel be as the sand of the sea,
a remnant shall be saved:
28 **For he** will finish the work,
and cut it short in righteousness:
because a short work will the Lord make upon the earth.
29 **And as Esaias** said before,
Except the Lord of Sabaoth had left us a seed,
we had been as Sodoma,
and been made like unto Gomorrha.
30 **What** shall we say then?
That the Gentiles, {which followed not after righteousness}, have attained to righteousness, even the righteousness which is of faith.
31 **But Israel**, {which followed after the law of righteousness}, hath not attained to the law of righteousness.
32 Wherefore?
Because they sought it not by faith, but as it were by the works of the law.
For they stumbled at that stumblingstone;
33 **As it** is written,
Behold,
I lay in Sion a stumblingstone and rock of offence:
and whosoever believeth on him shall not be ashamed.

10 **Brethren, my heart's desire and prayer to God for Israel** is,
that they might be saved.
2 **For I** bear them record
that they have a zeal of God, but not according to knowledge.
3 **For they being ignorant of God's righteousness, and going about to establish their own righteousness**, have not submitted themselves unto the righteousness of God.
4 **For Christ** is the end of the law for righteousness to every one that believeth.
5 **For Moses** describeth the righteousness which is of the law,
That the man which doeth those things shall live by them.
6 **But the righteousness which is of faith** speaketh on this wise,
Say not in thine heart,
Who shall ascend into heaven?
(that is, to bring Christ down from above:)
7 **Or, Who** shall descend into the deep?
(that is, to bring up Christ again from the dead.)
8 **But what** saith it?
The word is nigh thee, even in thy mouth, and in thy heart: that is, the word of faith,
which we preach;
9 **That if thou** shalt confess with thy mouth the Lord Jesus,
and shalt believe in thine heart
that God hath raised him from the dead,
thou shalt be saved.
10 **For with the heart** man believeth unto righteousness;
and with the mouth confession is made unto salvation.
11 **For the scripture** saith,
Whosoever believeth on him shall not be ashamed.
12 **For there** is no difference between the Jew and the Greek:
for the same Lord over all is rich unto all that call upon him.
13 **For whosoever shall call upon the name of the Lord** shall be saved.
14 **How** then shall they call on him in whom they have not believed?
and how shall they believe in him of whom they have not heard?
and how shall they hear without a preacher?
15 **And how** shall they preach,
except they be sent?
as it is written,
How beautiful are the feet of them that preach the gospel of peace, and bring glad tidings of good things!
16 **But they** have not all obeyed the gospel.
For Esaias saith,
Lord, who hath believed our report?
17 **So then faith** cometh by hearing, and hearing by the word of God.
18 **But I** say,
Have they not heard?
Yes verily,
their sound went into all the earth, and their words unto the ends of the world.

19 **But I** say,
Did not Israel know?
First Moses saith,
I will provoke you to jealousy by them that are no people,
and by a foolish nation I will anger you.
20 **But Esaias** is very bold,
and saith,
I was found of them that sought me not;
I was made manifest unto them that asked not after me.
21 **But to Israel** he saith,
All day long I have stretched forth my hands unto a disobedient and gainsaying people.

11 **I** say then,
Hath God cast away his people?
God forbid.
For I also am an Israelite, of the seed of Abraham, of the tribe of Benjamin.
2 **God** hath not cast away his people which he foreknew.
Wot ye not
what the scripture saith of Elias?
how he maketh intercession to God against Israel
saying,
3 **Lord, they** have killed thy prophets,
and digged down thine altars;
and I am left alone,
and they seek my life.
4 **But what** saith the answer of God unto him?
I have reserved to myself seven thousand men,
who have not bowed the knee to the image of Baal.
5 **Even so then at this present time** also there is a remnant according to the election of grace.
6 **And if by grace**, then is it no more of works:
otherwise grace is no more grace.
But if it be of works,
then it is no more grace:
otherwise work is no more work.
7 What then?
Israel hath not obtained that which he seeketh for;
but the election hath obtained it,
and the rest were blinded
8 ({According as it is written}, {God hath given them the spirit of slumber, eyes that they should not see, and ears that they should not hear};) unto this day.
9 **And David** saith,
Let their table be made a snare, and a trap, and a stumblingblock, and a recompence unto them:
10 **Let their eyes** be darkened,
that they may not see,
and bow down their back alway.
11 **I** say then,
Have they stumbled
that they should fall?
God forbid:
but rather through their fall salvation is come unto the Gentiles,
for to provoke them to jealousy.
12 **Now if the fall of them** be the riches of the world, and the diminishing of them the riches of the Gentiles; how much more their fulness?
13 **For I** speak to you Gentiles,
inasmuch as I am the apostle of the Gentiles,
I magnify mine office:
14 **If by any means** I may provoke to emulation them which are my flesh,
and might save some of them.
15 **For if the casting away of them** be the reconciling of the world,
what shall the receiving of them be, but life from the dead?
16 **For if the firstfruit** be holy,
the lump is also holy:
and if the root be holy,
so are the branches.
17 **And if some of the branches** be broken off,
and thou, {being a wild olive tree}, wert grafted in among them,
and with them partakest of the root and fatness of the olive tree;
18 **Boast not** against the branches.
But if thou boast,
thou bearest not the root, but the root thee.
19 **Thou** wilt say then,
The branches were broken off,
that I might be grafted in.
20 Well;
because of unbelief they were broken off,
and thou standest by faith.
Be not highminded,
but fear:
21 **For if God** spared not the natural branches,
take heed lest he also spare not thee.
22 **Behold** therefore the goodness and severity of God: on them which fell, severity; but toward thee, goodness,
if thou continue in his goodness:
otherwise thou also shalt be cut off.
23 **And they also**, {if they abide not still in unbelief}, shall be grafted in:
for God is able to graft them in again.
24 **For if thou** wert cut out of the olive tree which is wild by nature,
and wert grafted contrary to nature into a good olive tree:
how much more shall these, {which be the natural branches}, be grafted into their own olive tree?
25 **For I** would not, brethren,
that ye should be ignorant of this mystery,
lest ye should be wise in your own conceits;
that blindness in part is happened to Israel,
until the fulness of the Gentiles be come in.
26 **And so all Israel** shall be saved:
as it is written,
There shall come out of Sion the Deliverer,
and shall turn away ungodliness from Jacob:
27 **For this** is my covenant unto them,
when I shall take away their sins.
28 **As concerning the gospel**, they are enemies for your sakes:
but as touching the election, they are beloved for the father's sakes.
29 **For the gifts and calling of God** are without repentance.
30 **For as ye in times past** have not believed God,
yet have now obtained mercy through their unbelief:
31 **Even so** have these also now not believed,
that through your mercy they also may obtain mercy.
32 **For God** hath concluded them all in unbelief,
that he might have mercy upon all.

33 O the depth of the riches both of the wisdom and knowledge of God!
how unsearchable are his judgments,
and his ways past finding out!

34 **For who** hath known the mind of the Lord?
or who hath been his counsellor?

35 **Or who** hath first given to him,
and it shall be recompensed unto him again?

36 **For of him, and through him, and to him**, are all things:
to whom be glory for ever.
Amen.

12 I beseech you therefore, brethren, by the mercies of God,
that ye present your bodies a living sacrifice, holy, acceptable unto God,
which is your reasonable service.

2 **And be not** conformed to this world:
but be ye transformed by the renewing of your mind,
that ye may prove what is that good, and acceptable, and perfect, will of God.

3 **For I** say,
through the grace given unto me, to every man that is among you, not to think of himself more highly than he ought to think;
but to think soberly,
according as God hath dealt to every man the measure of faith.

4 **For as we** have many members in one body,
and all members have not the same office:

5 **So we**, {being many}, are one body in Christ, and every one members one of another.

6 Having then gifts differing according to the grace that is given to us, whether prophecy,
{let us prophesy according to the proportion of faith};

7 Or ministry, {let us wait on our ministering}: or he that teacheth, on teaching;

8 Or he that exhorteth, on exhortation: he that giveth, {let him do it with simplicity}; he that ruleth, with diligence; he that sheweth mercy, with cheerfulness.

9 **Let love** be without dissimulation.
Abhor that which is evil;
cleave to that which is good.

10 **Be** kindly affectioned one to another with brotherly love;
in honour preferring one another;

11 Not slothful in business;
fervent in spirit;
serving the Lord;

12 Rejoicing in hope;
patient in tribulation;
continuing instant in prayer;

13 Distributing to the necessity of saints;
given to hospitality.

14 **Bless** them which persecute you:
bless,
and curse not.

15 **Rejoice** with them that do rejoice,
and weep with them that weep.

16 **Be** of the same mind one toward another.
Mind not high things,
but condescend to men of low estate.
Be not wise in your own conceits.

17 **Recompense** to no man evil for evil.
Provide things honest in the sight of all men.

18 **If it be possible**, {as much as lieth in you}, live peaceably with all men.

19 **Dearly beloved, avenge not** yourselves,
but rather give place unto wrath:
for it is written,
Vengeance is mine;
I will repay,
saith the Lord.

20 **Therefore if thine enemy** hunger,
feed him;
if he thirst,
give him drink:
for in so doing thou shalt heap coals of fire on his head.

21 **Be not overcome** of evil,
but overcome evil with good.

13 **Let every soul** be subject unto the higher powers.
For there is no power but of God:
the powers that be are ordained of God.

2 **Whosoever therefore resisteth the power**, resisteth the ordinance of God:
and they that resist shall receive to themselves damnation.

3 **For rulers** are not a terror to good works, but to the evil.
Wilt thou then not be afraid of the power?
do that which is good,
and thou shalt have praise of the same:

4 **For he** is the minister of God to thee for good.
But if thou do that which is evil,
be afraid;
for he beareth not the sword in vain:
for he is the minister of God,
a revenger to execute wrath upon him that doeth evil.

5 **Wherefore ye** must needs be subject, not only for wrath, but also for conscience sake.

6 **For for this cause** pay ye tribute also:
for they are God's ministers,
attending continually upon this very thing.

7 **Render** therefore to all their dues: tribute to whom tribute is due; custom to whom custom; fear to whom fear; honour to whom honour.

8 **Owe** no man any thing,
but to love one another:
for he that loveth another hath fulfilled the law.

9 For this,
Thou shalt not commit adultery,
Thou shalt not kill,
Thou shalt not steal,
Thou shalt not bear false witness,
Thou shalt not covet;
and if there be any other commandment,
it is briefly comprehended in this saying, namely,
Thou shalt love thy neighbour as thyself.

10 **Love** worketh no ill to his neighbour:
therefore love is the fulfilling of the law.

11 **And that, {knowing the time},** that now it is high time to awake out of sleep:
for now is our salvation nearer than when we believed.

12 **The night** is far spent,
the day is at hand:

let us therefore cast off the works of darkness,
and let us put on the armour of light.
13 **Let us** walk honestly, as in the day; not in rioting and drunkenness, not in chambering and wantonness, not in strife and envying.
14 **But put ye on** the Lord Jesus Christ,
and make not provision for the flesh,
to fulfil the lusts thereof.

14 **Him that is weak in the faith** receive ye, but not to doubtful disputations.
2 **For one** believeth
that he may eat all things:
another, {who is weak}, eateth herbs.
3 **Let not him that eateth** despise him that eateth not;
and let not him which eateth not judge him that eateth:
for God hath received him.
4 **Who** art thou that judgest another man's servant?
to his own master he standeth or falleth.
Yea, he shall be holden up:
for God is able to make him stand.
5 **One man** esteemeth one day above another:
another esteemeth every day alike.
Let every man be fully persuaded in his own mind.
6 **He that regardeth the day**, regardeth it unto the Lord;
and he that regardeth not the day, to the Lord he doth not regard it.
He that eateth, eateth to the Lord,
for he giveth God thanks;
and he that eateth not, to the Lord he eateth not,
and giveth God thanks.
7 **For none of us** liveth to himself,
and no man dieth to himself.
8 **For whether we** live,
we live unto the Lord;
and whether we die,
we die unto the Lord:
whether we live therefore,
or die,
we are the Lord D's.
9 **For to this end** Christ both died,
and rose,
and revived,
that he might be Lord both of the dead and living.
10 **But why** dost thou judge thy brother?
or why dost thou set at nought thy brother?
for we shall all stand before the judgment seat of Christ.
11 **For it** is written,
As I live,
saith the Lord,
every knee shall bow to me,
and every tongue shall confess to God.
12 **So then every one of us** shall give account of himself to God.
13 **Let us not** therefore judge one another any more:
but judge this rather,
that no man put a stumblingblock or an occasion to fall in his brother's way.
14 **I** know,
and am persuaded by the Lord Jesus,
that there is nothing unclean of itself:
but to him that esteemeth any thing to be unclean, to him it is unclean.
15 **But if thy brother** be grieved with thy meat,
now walkest thou not charitably.

Destroy not him with thy meat,
for whom Christ died.
16 **Let not** then your good be evil spoken of:
17 **For the kingdom of God** is not meat and drink; but righteousness, and peace, and joy in the Holy Ghost.
18 **For he that in these things serveth Christ** is acceptable to God,
and approved of men.
19 **Let us** therefore follow after the things which make for peace, and things wherewith one may edify another.
20 **For meat** destroy not the work of God.
All things indeed are pure;
but it is evil for that man who eateth with offence.
21 **It is good** neither to eat flesh, nor to drink wine, nor any thing whereby thy brother stumbleth, or is offended, or is made weak.
22 **Hast thou** faith?
have it to thyself before God.
Happy is he that condemneth not himself in that thing which he alloweth.
23 **And he that doubteth** is damned if he eat,
because he eateth not of faith:
for whatsoever is not of faith is sin.

15 **We then that are strong** ought to bear the infirmities of the weak,
and not to please ourselves.
2 **Let every one of us** please his neighbour for his good to edification.
3 **For even Christ** pleased not himself;
but, {as it is written}, The reproaches of them that reproached thee fell on me.
4 **For whatsoever things were written aforetime** were written for our learning,
that we through patience and comfort of the scriptures might have hope.
5 **Now the God of patience and consolation** grant you to be likeminded one toward another according to Christ Jesus:
6 **That ye** may with one mind and one mouth glorify God, even the Father of our Lord Jesus Christ.
7 **Wherefore receive ye** one another,
as Christ also received us to the glory of God.
8 **Now I** say
that Jesus Christ was a minister of the circumcision for the truth of God,
to confirm the promises made unto the fathers:
9 **And that the Gentiles** might glorify God for his mercy;
as it is written,
For this cause I will confess to thee among the Gentiles,
and sing unto thy name.
10 **And again he** saith,
Rejoice, ye Gentiles, with his people.
11 **And again, Praise** the Lord, all ye Gentiles;
and laud him, all ye people.
12 **And again, Esaias** saith,
There shall be a root of Jesse,

and he that shall rise to reign over the Gentiles; in him shall the Gentiles trust.

13 **Now the God of hope** fill you with all joy and peace in believing,
that ye may abound in hope, through the power of the Holy Ghost.

14 **And I myself** also am persuaded of you, my brethren,
that ye also are full of goodness,
filled with all knowledge,
able also to admonish one another.

15 **Nevertheless, brethren, I** have written the more boldly unto you in some sort,
as putting you in mind, because of the grace that is given to me of God,

16 **That I** should be the minister of Jesus Christ to the Gentiles,
ministering the gospel of God,
that the offering up of the Gentiles might be acceptable,
being sanctified by the Holy Ghost.

17 I have therefore whereof I may glory through Jesus Christ in those things which pertain to God.

18 **For I** will not dare to speak of any of those things which Christ hath not wrought by me,
to make the Gentiles obedient, by word and deed,

19 Through mighty signs and wonders, by the power of the Spirit of God;
so that from Jerusalem, and round about unto Illyricum, I have fully preached the gospel of Christ.

20 **Yea, so** have I strived to preach the gospel,
not where Christ was named,
lest I should build upon another man's foundation:

21 **But as it** is written,
To whom he was not spoken of,
they shall see:
and they that have not heard shall understand.

22 **For which cause** also I have been much hindered from coming to you.

23 **But now** having no more place in these parts,
and having a great desire these many years to come unto you;

24 **Whensoever I** take my journey into Spain,
I will come to you:
for I trust to see you in my journey,
and to be brought on my way thitherward by you,
if first I be somewhat filled with your company.

25 **But now** I go unto Jerusalem to minister unto the saints.

26 **For it hath pleased them of Macedonia and Achaia** to make a certain contribution for the poor saints which are at Jerusalem.

27 **It** hath pleased them verily;
and their debtors they are.
For if the Gentiles have been made partakers of their spiritual things,
their duty is also to minister unto them in carnal things.

28 **When therefore I** have performed this,
and have sealed to them this fruit,
I will come by you into Spain.

29 **And I** am sure that, {when I come unto you}, I shall come in the fulness of the blessing of the gospel of Christ.

30 **Now I** beseech you, brethren, for the Lord Jesus Christ's sake, and for the love of the Spirit,
that ye strive together with me in your prayers to God for me;

31 **That I** may be delivered from them that do not believe in Judaea;
and that my service which I have for Jerusalem may be accepted of the saints;

32 **That I** may come unto you with joy by the will of God,
and may with you be refreshed.

33 **Now the God of peace** be with you all.
Amen.

16 I commend unto you Phebe our sister,
which is a servant of the church which is at Cenchrea:

2 **That ye** receive her in the Lord,
as becometh saints,
and that ye assist her in whatsoever business she hath need of you:
for she hath been a succourer of many, and of myself also.

3 **Greet** Priscilla and Aquila my helpers in Christ Jesus:

4 **Who** have for my life laid down their own necks:
unto whom not only I give thanks, but also all the churches of the Gentiles.

5 **Likewise greet** the church that is in their house.
Salute my well-beloved Epaenetus,
who is the firstfruits of Achaia unto Christ.

6 **Greet** Mary,
who bestowed much labour on us.

7 **Salute** Andronicus and Junia, my kinsmen, and my fellow-prisoners,
who are of note among the apostles,
who also were in Christ before me.

8 **Greet** Amplias my beloved in the Lord.

9 **Salute** Urbane, our helper in Christ, and Stachys my beloved.

10 **Salute** Apelles approved in Christ.
Salute them which are of Aristobulus' household.

11 **Salute** Herodion my kinsman.
Greet them that be of the household of Narcissus,
which are in the Lord.

12 **Salute** Tryphena and Tryphosa,
who labour in the Lord.
Salute the beloved Persis,
which laboured much in the Lord.

13 **Salute** Rufus chosen in the Lord, and his mother and mine.

14 **Salute** Asyncritus, Phlegon, Hermas, Patrobas, Hermes, and the brethren which are with them.

15 **Salute** Philologus, and Julia, Nereus, and his sister, and Olympas, and all the saints which are with them.

16 **Salute** one another with an holy kiss.
The churches of Christ salute you.

17 **Now I** beseech you, brethren,
mark them which cause divisions and offences contrary to the doctrine which ye have learned;
and avoid them.

18 **For they that are such** serve not our Lord Jesus Christ, but their own belly;
and by good words and fair speeches deceive the hearts of the simple.

19 **For your obedience** is come
abroad unto all men.

I am glad therefore on your behalf:
but yet I would have you wise unto
that which is good, and simple
concerning evil.

20 **And the God of peace** shall
bruise Satan under your feet
shortly.

The grace of our Lord Jesus Christ
be with you.

Amen.

21 **Timotheus my workfellow, and
Lucius, and Jason, and
Sosipater, my kinsmen**, salute
you.

22 **I Tertius, who wrote this
epistle,** salute you in the Lord.

23 **Gaius mine host, and the whole
church,** soluteth you.

**Erastus the chamberlain of the
city** saluteth you, and Quartus a
brother.

24 **The grace of our Lord Jesus
Christ** be with you all.

Amen.

25 **Now to him that is of power to
stablish you according to my
gospel, and the preaching of
Jesus Christ, according to the
revelation of the mystery,
{which was kept secret since
the world began},**

26 **{But now is made manifest},
and by the scriptures of the
prophets, according to the
commandment of the
everlasting God, {made known
to all nations for the obedience
of faith}:**

27 **To God only wise,** be glory
through Jesus Christ for ever.

Amen.

1 Corinthians

The Book of First Corinthians, a letter written by the Apostle Paul during his third missionary journey, is addressed to the Church in Corinth and its surrounding areas. It offers compassionate guidance and advice on various issues facing the early Christian community. Paul writes his letter as a direct response to reports and concerns he received about the Church regarding doctrine, morality, and church organization. However, his primary goal in writing is to promote unity and harmony within the Corinthian Church.

In his letter, Paul asserts that love is the cornerstone of Christian faith and conduct. He urges the Corinthians to prioritize unity and mutual respect and to avoid divisions and personal disputes that could fracture the Church. Despite this advice, Paul addresses one such division that the Church cannot ignore. He clarifies that the gifts of the Holy Spirit exist for the common good and that spiritual gifts must strengthen the body of Christ. Furthermore, he underscores the importance of love as the ultimate goal of these gifts.

The Apostle also presents a detailed defense of the resurrection of Jesus Christ. He argues that the Christian faith is only possible with the resurrection. Throughout the letter, Paul delivers guidance on sexual immorality, idolatry, proper conduct, and other moral issues. He calls the Corinthians to live a life that is pleasing to God and consistent with their faith. Regarding Church organization and administration, Paul offers counsel on matters such as the celebration of Communion, the role of women in the Church, and the proper use of spiritual gifts. On a more personal level, the Apostle discusses the importance of integrity and self-discipline for Christian leaders. He uses his own example to demonstrate the need for humility, hard work, and accountability in service to the Church.

First Corinthians remains an important epistle in the New Testament because of its gentle advice to Corinthian believers who need spiritual growth, both personally and as a congregation. In its message, Paul creates a timeless model for navigating the complexities of faith, fellowship, and spiritual integrity within the context of the early Christian Church. This model offers invaluable lessons for believers even today.

1 **Paul called to be an apostle of Jesus Christ through the will of God, and Sosthenes our brother,**
2 Unto the church of God which is at Corinth,
to them that are sanctified in Christ Jesus,
called to be saints,
with all that in every place call upon the name of Jesus Christ our Lord, both their's and our's:
3 **Grace** be unto you, {and peace},
from God our Father,
and from the Lord Jesus Christ.
4 **I** thank my God always on your behalf, for the grace of God which is given you by Jesus Christ;
5 **That in every thing** ye are enriched by him, in all utterance, and in all knowledge;
6 **Even as the testimony of Christ** was confirmed in you:
7 **So that ye** come behind in no gift;
waiting for the coming of our Lord Jesus Christ:
8 **Who** shall also confirm you unto the end,
that ye may be blameless in the day of our Lord Jesus Christ.
9 **God** is faithful,
by whom ye were called unto the fellowship of his Son Jesus Christ our Lord.
10 **Now I** beseech you, brethren, by the name of our Lord Jesus Christ,
that ye all speak the same thing,
and that there be no divisions among you;
but that ye be perfectly joined together in the same mind and in the same judgment.
11 **For it** hath been declared unto me of you, my brethren, by them which are of the house of Chloe,
that there are contentions among you.
12 **Now this** I say,
that every one of you saith,
I am of Paul; and I of Apollos; and I of Cephas; and I of Christ.
13 **Is Christ** divided?
was Paul crucified for you?
or were ye baptized in the name of Paul?
14 **I** thank God that I baptized none of you, but Crispus and Gaius;
15 **Lest any** should say
that I had baptized in mine own name.
16 **And I** baptized also the household of Stephanas:
besides, I know not
whether I baptized any other.
17 **For Christ** sent me not to baptize,
but to preach the gospel:
not with wisdom of words, lest the cross of Christ should be made of none effect.
18 **For the preaching of the cross** is to them that perish foolishness;
but unto us which are saved it is the power of God.
19 **For it** is written,
I will destroy the wisdom of the wise,
and will bring to nothing the understanding of the prudent.
20 **Where** is the wise?

where is the scribe?
where is the disputer of this world?
hath not God made foolish the wisdom of this world?

21 **For after that in the wisdom of God the world by wisdom** knew not God,
it pleased God by the foolishness of preaching to save them that believe.

22 **For the Jews** require a sign,
and the Greeks seek after wisdom:
23 **But we** preach Christ crucified, unto the Jews a stumblingblock, and unto the Greeks foolishness;
24 But unto them which are called, both Jews and Greeks, Christ the power of God, and the wisdom of God.

25 **Because the foolishness of God** is wiser than men;
and the weakness of God is stronger than men.

26 **For ye** see your calling, brethren,
how that not many wise men after the flesh, not many mighty, not many noble, are called:
27 **But God** hath chosen the foolish things of the world
to confound the wise;
and God hath chosen the weak things of the world
to confound the things which are mighty;
28 **And base things of the world, and things which are despised,** hath God chosen, yea, and things which are not,
to bring to nought things that are:
29 **That no flesh** should glory in his presence.

30 **But of him** are ye in Christ Jesus,
who of God is made unto us wisdom, and righteousness, and sanctification, and redemption:
31 **That, {according as it is written}, He that glorieth,** let him glory in the Lord.

2

And I, brethren, {when I came to you}, came not with excellency of speech or of wisdom,
declaring unto you the testimony of God.

2 **For I** determined not to know any thing among you, save Jesus Christ, and him crucified.

3 **And I** was with you in weakness, and in fear, and in much trembling.

4 **And my speech and my preaching** was not with enticing words of man's wisdom, but in demonstration of the Spirit and of power:
5 **That your faith** should not stand in the wisdom of men, but in the power of God.

6 **Howbeit we** speak wisdom among them that are perfect: yet not the wisdom of this world, nor of the princes of this world,
that come to nought:
7 **But we** speak the wisdom of God in a mystery, even the hidden wisdom,
which God ordained before the world unto our glory:
8 **Which none of the princes of this world** knew:
for had they known it,
they would not have crucified the Lord of glory.

9 **But as it** is written,
Eye hath not seen,
nor ear heard,
neither have entered into the heart of man, the things which God hath prepared for them that love him.

10 **But God** hath revealed them unto us by his Spirit:
for the Spirit searcheth all things, yea, the deep things of God.

11 **For what man** knoweth the things of a man, save the spirit of man which is in him?
even so the things of God knoweth no man, but the Spirit of God.

12 **Now we** have received, not the spirit of the world, but the spirit which is of God;
that we might know the things that are freely given to us of God.

13 **Which things** also we speak, not in the words which man's wisdom teacheth, but which the Holy Ghost teacheth;
comparing spiritual things with spiritual.

14 **But the natural man** receiveth not the things of the Spirit of God:
for they are foolishness unto him:
neither can he know them,
because they are spiritually discerned.

15 **But he that is spiritual** judgeth all things,
yet he himself is judged of no man.
16 **For who** hath known the mind of the Lord,
that he may instruct him?
but we have the mind of Christ.

3

And I, brethren, could not speak unto you as unto spiritual, but as unto carnal, even as unto babes in Christ.

2 **I** have fed you with milk, and not with meat:
for hitherto ye were not able to bear it,
neither yet now are ye able.

3 **For ye** are yet carnal:
for whereas there is among you envying, and strife, and divisions,
are ye not carnal,
and walk as men?

4 **For while one** saith,
I am of Paul; and another,
I am of Apollos;
are ye not carnal?

5 **Who** then is Paul,
and who is Apollos,
but ministers by whom ye believed,
even as the Lord gave to every man?

6 **I** have planted,
Apollos watered;
but God gave the increase.

7 **So then neither** is he that planteth any thing, neither he that watereth; but God that giveth the increase.

8 **Now he that planteth and he that watereth** are one:
and every man shall receive his own reward according to his own labour.

9 **For we** are labourers together with God:
ye are God's husbandry,
ye are God's building.

10 **According to the grace of God which is given unto me, as a wise masterbuilder,** I have laid the foundation,
and another buildeth thereon.

But let every man take heed how he buildeth thereupon.

11 **For other foundation** can no man lay than that is laid,
which is Jesus Christ.

12 **Now if any man** build upon this foundation gold, silver, precious stones, wood, hay, stubble;

13 **Every man's work** shall be made manifest:
for the day shall declare it,
because it shall be revealed by fire;
and the fire shall try every man's work of what sort it is.

14 **If any man's work** abide which he hath built thereupon,
he shall receive a reward.

15 **If any man's work** shall be burned,
he shall suffer loss:
but he himself shall be saved; yet so as by fire.

16 **Know ye not**
that ye are the temple of God,
and that the Spirit of God dwelleth in you?

17 **If any man** defile the temple of God,
him shall God destroy;
for the temple of God is holy,
which temple ye are.

18 **Let no man** deceive himself.

If any man among you seemeth to be wise in this world,
let him become a fool,
that he may be wise.

19 **For the wisdom of this world** is foolishness with God.

For it is written,
He taketh the wise in their own craftiness.

20 **And again, The Lord** knoweth the thoughts of the wise,
that they are vain.

21 **Therefore let no man** glory in men.

For all things are your's;
22 Whether Paul, or Apollos, or Cephas, or the world, or life, or death, or things present, or things to come;
all are your's;
23 **And ye** are Christ's;
and Christ is God's.

4

Let a man so account of us, as of the ministers of Christ, and stewards of the mysteries of God.

2 **Moreover it** is required in stewards,
that a man be found faithful.

3 **But with me** it is a very small thing
that I should be judged of you, or of man's judgment:
yea, I judge not mine own self.

4 **For I** know nothing by myself;
yet am I not hereby justified:
but he that judgeth me is the Lord.

5 **Therefore judge** nothing before the time,
until the Lord come,
who both will bring to light the hidden things of darkness,
and will make manifest the counsels of the hearts:
and then shall every man have praise of God.

6 **And these things,** brethren, I have in a figure transferred to myself and to Apollos for your sakes;
that ye might learn in us not to think of men above that which is written,
that no one of you be puffed up for one against another.

7 **For who** maketh thee to differ from another?
and what hast thou that thou didst not receive?
now if thou didst receive it,
why dost thou glory,
as if thou hadst not received it?

8 **Now ye** are full,
now ye are rich,
ye have reigned as kings without us:
and I would to God ye did reign,
that we also might reign with you.

9 **For I** think
that God hath set forth us the apostles last,
as it were appointed to death:
for we are made a spectacle unto the world, and to angels, and to men.

10 **We** are fools for Christ's sake,
but ye are wise in Christ;
we are weak,
but ye are strong;
ye are honourable,
but we are despised.

11 **Even unto this present hour** we both hunger,
and thirst,
and are naked,
and are buffeted,
and have no certain dwellingplace;
12 **And** labour,
working with our own hands:
being reviled,
we bless;
being persecuted,
we suffer it:
13 Being defamed,
we intreat:
we are made as the filth of the world,
and are the offscouring of all things unto this day.

14 **I** write not these things
to shame you,
but as my beloved sons I warn you.

15 **For though ye** have ten thousand instructers in Christ,
yet have ye not many fathers:
for in Christ Jesus I have begotten you through the gospel.

16 **Wherefore I** beseech you,
be ye followers of me.

17 **For this cause** have I sent unto you Timotheus,
who is my beloved son, and faithful in the Lord,
who shall bring you into remembrance of my ways
which be in Christ,
as I teach every where in every church.

18 **Now some** are puffed up,
as though I would not come to you.

19 **But I** will come to you shortly,
if the Lord will,
and will know, not the speech of them which are puffed up, but the power.

20 **For the kingdom of God** is not in word, but in power.

21 **What** will ye?
shall I come unto you with a rod, or in love, and in the spirit of meekness?

5

It is reported commonly that there is fornication among you, and such fornication as is not so much as named among the Gentiles,
that one should have his father's wife.

2 **And ye** are puffed up,
and have not rather mourned,
that he that hath done this deed might be taken away from among you.

3 **For I verily**, {as absent in body}, {but present in spirit|, have judged already,
as though I were present,
concerning him that hath so done this deed,
4 In the name of our Lord Jesus Christ,

when ye are gathered together, and my spirit, with the power of our Lord Jesus Christ,
5 To deliver such an one unto Satan for the destruction of the flesh,
that the spirit may be saved in the day of the Lord Jesus.
6 **Your glorying** is not good.
Know ye not
that a little leaven leaveneth the whole lump?
7 **Purge out** therefore the old leaven,
that ye may be a new lump,
as ye are unleavened.
For even Christ our passover is sacrificed for us:
8 **Therefore let us** keep the feast, not with old leaven, neither with the leaven of malice and wickedness; but with the unleavened bread of sincerity and truth.
9 **I** wrote unto you in an epistle not to company with fornicators:
10 Yet not altogether with the fornicators of this world, or with the covetous, or extortioners, or with idolaters;
for then must ye needs go out of the world.
11 **But now I** have written unto you not to keep company,
if any man that is called a brother be a fornicator, or covetous, or an idolator, or a railer, or a drunkard, or an extortioner;
with such an one no not to eat.
12 **For what** have I to do to judge them also that are without?
do not ye judge them that are within?
13 **But them that are without God** judgeth.
Therefore put away from among yourselves that wicked person.

6 **Dare any of you**, {having a matter against another}, go to law before the unjust, and not before the saints?
2 **Do ye not** know
that the saints shall judge the world?
and if the world shall be judged by you,
are ye unworthy to judge the smallest matters?
3 **Know ye not**
that we shall judge angels?
how much more things that pertain to this life?
4 **If then ye** have judgments of things pertaining to this life,
set them to judge who are least esteemed in the church.
5 **I** speak to your shame.
Is it so,
that there is not a wise man among you?
no, not one that shall be able to judge between his brethren?
6 **But brother** goeth to law with brother, and that before the unbelievers.
7 **Now therefore there** is utterly a fault among you,
because ye go to law one with another.
Why do ye not rather take wrong?
why do ye not rather suffer yourselves to be defrauded?
8 **Nay, ye** do wrong,
and defraud, and that your brethren.
9 **Know ye not**
that the unrighteous shall not inherit the kingdom of God?
Be not deceived:
neither fornicators, nor idolaters, nor adulterers, nor effeminate, nor abusers of themselves with mankind,
10 **Nor thieves, nor covetous, nor drunkards, nor revilers, nor extortioners,** shall inherit the kingdom of God.
11 **And such** were some of you:
but ye are washed,
but ye are sanctified,
but ye are justified in the name of the Lord Jesus, and by the Spirit of our God.
12 **All things** are lawful unto me,
but all things are not expedient:
all things are lawful for me,
but I will not be brought under the power of any.
13 Meats for the belly, and the belly for meats:
but God shall destroy both it and them.
Now the body is not for fornication, but for the Lord; and the Lord for the body.
14 **And God** hath both raised up the Lord,
and will also raise up us by his own power.
15 **Know ye not**
that your bodies are the members of Christ?
shall I then take the members of Christ,
and make them the members of an harlot?
God forbid.
16 What?
know ye not
that he which is joined to an harlot is one body?
for two, {saith he}, shall be one flesh.
17 **But he that is joined unto the Lord** is one spirit.
18 **Flee** fornication.
Every sin that a man doeth is without the body;
but he that committeth fornication sinneth against his own body.
19 What?
know ye not
that your body is the temple of the Holy Ghost which is in you,
which ye have of God,
and ye are not your own?
20 **For ye** are bought with a price:
therefore glorify God in your body, and in your spirit,
which are God's.

7 **Now concerning the things whereof ye** wrote unto me:
It is good for a man not to touch a woman.
2 **Nevertheless, {to avoid fornication}, let every man** have his own wife,
and let every woman have her own husband.
3 **Let the husband** render unto the wife due benevolence: and likewise also the wife unto the husband.
4 **The wife** hath not power of her own body, but the husband:
and likewise also the husband hath not power of his own body, but the wife.
5 **Defraud ye not** one the other,
except it be with consent for a time,
that ye may give yourselves to fasting and prayer;
and come together again,
that Satan tempt you not for your incontinency.

6 **But I** speak this by permission, and not of commandment.

7 **For I** would
that all men were even as I myself.

But every man hath his proper gift of God, one after this manner, and another after that.

8 **I** say therefore to the unmarried and widows,
it is good for them
if they abide even as I.

9 **But if they** cannot contain,
let them marry:
for it is better to marry than to burn.

10 **And unto the married** I command, yet not I, but the Lord,
Let not the wife depart from her husband:
11 **But and if she** depart,
let her remain unmarried
or be reconciled to her husband:
and let not the husband put away his wife.

12 **But to the rest** speak I, not the Lord:
If any brother hath a wife that believeth not,
and she be pleased to dwell with him,
let him not put her away.

13 **And the woman which hath an husband that believeth not,** {and if he be pleased to dwell with her}, let her not leave him.

14 **For the unbelieving husband** is sanctified by the wife,
and the unbelieving wife is sanctified by the husband:
else were your children unclean;
but now are they holy.

15 **But if the unbelieving** depart,
let him depart.

A brother or a sister is not under bondage in such cases:
but God hath called us to peace.

16 **For what** knowest thou, O wife,
whether thou shalt save thy husband?
or how knowest thou, O man,
whether thou shalt save thy wife?

17 **But as God** hath distributed to every man,
as the Lord hath called every one,
so let him walk.

And so ordain I in all churches.

18 **Is any man** called being circumcised?
let him not become uncircumcised.
Is any called in uncircumcision?
let him not be circumcised.

19 **Circumcision** is nothing,
and uncircumcision is nothing, but the keeping of the commandments of God.

20 **Let every man** abide in the same calling wherein he was called.

21 **Art thou** called being a servant?
care not for it:
but if thou mayest be made free,
use it rather.

22 **For he that is called in the Lord,** {being a servant|, is the Lord's freeman:
likewise also he that is called, {being free}, is Christ's servant.

23 **Ye** are bought with a price;
be not ye the servants of men.

24 **Brethren, let every man,** {**wherein he is called**}, therein abide with God.

25 **Now concerning virgins** I have no commandment of the Lord:
yet I give my judgment, as one that hath obtained mercy of the Lord to be faithful.

26 **I** suppose therefore
that this is good for the present distress,
I say,
that it is good for a man so to be.

27 **Art thou** bound unto a wife?
seek not to be loosed.

Art thou loosed from a wife?
seek not a wife.

28 **But and if thou** marry,
thou hast not sinned;
and if a virgin marry,
she hath not sinned.

Nevertheless such shall have trouble in the flesh:
but I spare you.

29 **But this I** say, brethren,
the time is short:
it remaineth,
that both they that have wives be as though they had none;
30 And they that weep, {as though they wept not}; and they that rejoice, {as though they rejoiced not}; and they that buy, {as though they possessed not};
31 And they that use this world, {as not abusing it}:
for the fashion of this world passeth away.

32 **But I** would have you without carefulness.
He that is unmarried careth for the things that belong to the Lord,
how he may please the Lord:
33 **But he that is married** careth for the things that are of the world,
how he may please his wife.

34 **There** is difference also between a wife and a virgin.

The unmarried woman careth for the things of the Lord,
that she may be holy both in body and in spirit:
but she that is married careth for the things of the world,
how she may please her husband.

35 **And this** I speak for your own profit;
not that I may cast a snare upon you, but for that which is comely,
and that ye may attend upon the Lord without distraction.

36 **But if any man** think
that he behaveth himself uncomely toward his virgin,
if she pass the flower of her age,
and need so require,
let him do what he will,
he sinneth not:
let them marry.

37 **Nevertheless he that standeth stedfast in his heart,** {having no necessity}, {but hath power over his own will}, {and hath so decreed in his heart} {that he will keep his virgin}, doeth well.

38 **So then he that giveth her in marriage** doeth well;
but he that giveth her not in marriage doeth better.

39 **The wife** is bound by the law
as long as her husband liveth;
but if her husband be dead,
she is at liberty to be married to whom she will; only in the Lord.

40 **But she** is happier
if she so abide, after my judgment:
and I think also
that I have the Spirit of God.

8

Now as touching things offered unto idols,
we know
that we all have knowledge.

Knowledge puffeth up,
but charity edifieth.

2 **And if any man** think
that he knoweth any thing,
he knoweth nothing
yet as he ought to know.

3 **But if any man** love God,

the same is known of him.

4 **As concerning therefore the eating of those things that are offered in sacrifice unto idols,** we know
that an idol is nothing in the world,
and that there is none other God but one.

5 **For though there** be that are called gods, whether in heaven or in earth,
(as there be gods many, and lords many,)
6 **But to us** there is but one God, the Father,
of whom are all things, and we in him; and one Lord Jesus Christ,
by whom are all things, and we by him.

7 **Howbeit there** is not in every man that knowledge:
for some with conscience of the idol unto this hour eat it as a thing offered unto an idol;
and their conscience being weak is defiled.

8 **But meat** commendeth us not to God:
for neither, {if we eat}, are we the better;
neither, {if we eat not}, are we the worse.

9 **But take heed** lest by any means this liberty of yours become a stumblingblock to them that are weak.

10 **For if any man** see thee which hast knowledge sit at meat in the idol's temple,
shall not the conscience of him which is weak be emboldened to eat those things which are offered to idols;
11 **And through thy knowledge** shall the weak brother perish,
for whom Christ died?

12 **But when ye** sin so against the brethren,
and wound their weak conscience,
ye sin against Christ.

13 **Wherefore, if meat** make my brother to offend,
I will eat no flesh
while the world standeth,
lest I make my brother to offend.

9

Am I not an apostle?
am I not free?
have I not seen Jesus Christ our Lord?
are not ye my work in the Lord?

2 **If I** be not an apostle unto others,
yet doubtless I am to you:
for the seal of mine apostleship are ye in the Lord.

3 **Mine answer to them that do examine me** is this,
4 **Have we not** power to eat and to drink?

5 **Have we not** power to lead about a sister, a wife, as well as other apostles, and as the brethren of the Lord, and Cephas?

6 Or I only and Barnabas,
have not we power to forbear working?

7 **Who** goeth a warfare any time at his own charges?
who planteth a vineyard,
and eateth not of the fruit thereof?
or who feedeth a flock,
and eateth not of the milk of the flock?

8 **Say I** these things as a man?
or saith not the law the same also?
9 **For it** is written in the law of Moses,
thou shalt not muzzle the mouth of the ox that treadeth out the corn.

Doth God take care for oxen?
10 **Or saith he** it altogether for our sakes?

For our sakes, no doubt, this is written:
that he that ploweth should plow in hope;
and that he that thresheth in hope should be partaker of his hope.

11 **If we** have sown unto you spiritual things,
is it a great thing if we shall reap your carnal things?

12 **If others** be partakers of this power over you,
are not we rather?

Nevertheless we have not used this power;
but suffer all things,
lest we should hinder the gospel of Christ.

13 **Do ye** not know
that they which minister about holy things live of the things of the temple?
and they which wait at the altar are partakers with the altar?

14 **Even so** hath the Lord ordained that they which preach the gospel should live of the gospel.

15 **But I** have used none of these things:
neither have I written these things,
that it should be so done unto me:
for it were better for me to die,
than that any man should make my glorying void.

16 **For though I** preach the gospel,
I have nothing to glory of:
for necessity is laid upon me;
yea, woe is unto me,
if I preach not the gospel!

17 **For if I** do this thing willingly,
I have a reward:
but if against my will, a dispensation of the gospel is committed unto me.

18 **What** is my reward then?

Verily that, {when I preach the gospel}, I may make the gospel of Christ without charge,
that I abuse not my power in the gospel.

19 **For though I** be free from all men,
yet have I made myself servant unto all,
that I might gain the more.

20 **And unto the Jews** I became as a Jew, {that I might gain the Jews}; to them that are under the law, as under the law, {that I might gain them that are under the law};
21 To them that are without law, as without law, (being not without law to God, but under the law to Christ,) {that I might gain them that are without law}.

22 **To the weak** became I as weak,
that I might gain the weak:
I am made all things to all men,
that I might by all means save some.

23 **And this** I do for the gospel's sake,
that I might be partaker thereof with you.

24 **Know ye not**
that they which run in a race run all,
but one receiveth the prize?

So run,
that ye may obtain.

25 **And every man that striveth for the mastery** is temperate in all things.

Now they do it

to obtain a corruptible crown; but we an incorruptible.

26 **I** therefore so run, not as uncertainly;
so fight I, not as one that beateth the air:

27 **But I** keep under my body,
and bring it into subjection:
lest that by any means, {when I have preached to others}, I myself should be a castaway.

10 **Moreover, brethren, I** would not
that ye should be ignorant,
how that all our fathers were under the cloud,
and all passed through the sea;
2 **And** were all baptized unto Moses in the cloud and in the sea;
3 **And** did all eat the same spiritual meat;
4 **And** did all drink the same spiritual drink:
for they drank of that spiritual Rock that followed them:
and that Rock was Christ.

5 **But with many of them** God was not well pleased:
for they were overthrown in the wilderness.

6 **Now these things** were our examples,
to the intent we should not lust after evil things,
as they also lusted.

7 **Neither be ye** idolaters,
as were some of them;
as it is written,
The people sat down
to eat and drink,
and rose up
to play.

8 **Neither let us** commit fornication,
as some of them committed,
and fell in one day three and twenty thousand.

9 **Neither let us** tempt Christ,
as some of them also tempted,
and were destroyed of serpents.

10 **Neither murmur ye,**
as some of them also murmured,
and were destroyed of the destroyer.

11 **Now all these things** happened unto them for examples:
and they are written for our admonition,
upon whom the ends of the world are come.

12 **Wherefore let him that thinketh he standeth** take heed lest he fall.

13 **There hath no temptation** taken you but such as is common to man:
but God is faithful,
who will not suffer you to be tempted above that ye are able;
but will with the temptation also make a way to escape,
that ye may be able to bear it.

14 **Wherefore, my dearly beloved, flee** from idolatry.

15 **I** speak as to wise men;
judge ye
what I say.

16 **The cup of blessing which we bless,** is it not the communion of the blood of Christ?
The bread which we break, is it not the communion of the body of Christ?

17 **For we being many** are one bread, and one body:
for we are all partakers of that one bread.

18 **Behold** Israel after the flesh:
are not they which eat of the sacrifices partakers of the altar?

19 **What** say I then?
that the idol is any thing,
or that which is offered in sacrifice to idols is any thing?

20 **But I** say,
that the things which the Gentiles sacrifice, they sacrifice to devils, and not to God:
and I would not
that ye should have fellowship with devils.

21 **Ye** cannot drink the cup of the Lord, and the cup of devils:
ye cannot be partakers of the Lord's table, and of the table of devils.

22 **Do we** provoke the Lord to jealousy?
are we stronger than he?

23 **All things** are lawful for me,
but all things are not expedient:
all things are lawful for me,
but all things edify not.

24 **Let no man** seek his own, but every man another's wealth.

25 **Whatsoever** is sold in the shambles,
that eat,
asking no question for conscience sake:

26 **For the earth** is the Lord's, and the fulness thereof.

27 **If any of them that believe not** bid you to a feast,
and ye be disposed to go;
whatsoever is set before you,
eat,
asking no question for conscience sake.

28 **But if any man** say unto you,
this is offered in sacrifice unto idols,
eat not for his sake that shewed it, and for conscience sake:
for the earth is the Lord's, and the fulness thereof:
29 **Conscience,** I say, not thine own, but of the other:
for why is my liberty judged of another man's conscience?

30 **For if I by grace** be a partaker,
why am I evil spoken of for that for which I give thanks?

31 **Whether therefore ye** eat,
or drink,
or whatsoever ye do,
do all to the glory of God.

32 **Give** none offence, neither to the Jews, nor to the Gentiles, nor to the church of God:
33 **Even as I** please all men in all things,
not seeking mine own profit, but the profit of many,
that they may be saved.

11 **Be ye** followers of me,
even as I also am of Christ.

2 **Now I** praise you, brethren,
that ye remember me in all things,
and keep the ordinances,
as I delivered them to you.

3 **But I** would have you know,
that the head of every man is Christ;
and the head of the woman is the man;
and the head of Christ is God.

4 **Every man praying or prophesying, {having his head covered},** dishonoureth his head.

5 **But every woman that prayeth or prophesieth with her head uncovered** dishonoureth her head:
for that is even all one as if she were shaven.

6 **For if the woman** be not covered,
let her also be shorn:
but if it be a shame for a woman to be shorn or shaven,

let her be covered.

7 **For a man** indeed ought not to cover his head,
forasmuch as he is the image and glory of God:
but the woman is the glory of the man.

8 **For the man** is not of the woman: but the woman of the man.

9 **Neither** was the man created for the woman; but the woman for the man.

10 **For this cause** ought the woman to have power on her head because of the angels.

11 **Nevertheless neither** is the man without the woman, neither the woman without the man, in the Lord.

12 **For as the woman** is of the man,
even so is the man also by the woman; but all things of God.

13 **Judge** in yourselves:
is it comely that a woman pray unto God uncovered?

14 **Doth not even nature itself** teach you,
that, {if a man have long hair}, it is a shame unto him?

15 **But if a woman** have long hair,
it is a glory to her:
for her hair is given her for a covering.

16 **But if any man** seem to be contentious,
we have no such custom, neither the churches of God.

17 **Now in this that I declare unto you** I praise you not,
that ye come together not for the better, but for the worse.

18 **For first of all**, {when ye come together in the church}, I hear that there be divisions among you;
and I partly believe it.

19 **For there** must be also heresies among you,
that they which are approved may be made manifest among you.

20 **When ye** come together therefore into one place,
this is not to eat the Lord's supper.

21 **For in eating** every one taketh before other his own supper:
and one is hungry,
and another is drunken.

22 What?
have ye not houses to eat and to drink in?
or despise ye the church of God,
and shame them that have not?
what shall I say to you?
shall I praise you in this?
I praise you not.

23 **For I** have received of the Lord that which also I delivered unto you,
that the Lord Jesus the same night in which he was betrayed took bread:

24 **And when he** had given thanks,
he brake it,
and said,
Take,
eat:
this is my body,
which is broken for you:
this do in remembrance of me.

25 **After the same manner** also he took the cup,
when he had supped,
saying,
this cup is the new testament in my blood:
this do ye, {as oft as ye drink it}, in remembrance of me.

26 **For as often as ye** eat this bread,
and drink this cup,
ye do shew the Lord's death till he come.

27 **Wherefore whosoever shall eat this bread, and drink this cup of the Lord, unworthily,** shall be guilty of the body and blood of the Lord.

28 **But let a man** examine himself,
and so let him eat of that bread,
and drink of that cup.

29 **For he that eateth and drinketh unworthily,** eateth and drinketh damnation to himself,
not discerning the Lord's body.

30 **For this cause** many are weak and sickly among you,
and many sleep.

31 **For if we** would judge ourselves,
we should not be judged.

32 **But when we** are judged,
we are chastened of the Lord,
that we should not be condemned with the world.

33 **Wherefore, my brethren, when ye** come together to eat,
tarry one for another.

34 **And if any man** hunger,
let him eat at home;
that ye come not together unto condemnation.
And the rest will I set in order when I come.

12

Now concerning spiritual gifts, brethren, I would not have you ignorant.

2 **Ye** know
that ye were Gentiles,
carried away unto these dumb idols,
even as ye were led.

3 **Wherefore I** give you to understand,
that no man speaking by the Spirit of God calleth Jesus accursed:
and that no man can say
that Jesus is the Lord, but by the Holy Ghost.

4 **Now there** are diversities of gifts, but the same Spirit.

5 **And there** are differences of administrations, but the same Lord.

6 **And there** are diversities of operations,
but it is the same God which worketh all in all.

7 **But the manifestation of the Spirit** is given to every man
to profit withal.

8 **For to one** is given by the Spirit the word of wisdom; to another the word of knowledge by the same Spirit;

9 To another faith by the same Spirit; to another the gifts of healing by the same Spirit;

10 To another the working of miracles; to another prophecy; to another discerning of spirits; to another divers kinds of tongues; to another the interpretation of tongues:

11 **But all these** worketh that one and the selfsame Spirit,
dividing to every man severally as he will.

12 **For as the body** is one,
and hath many members,
and all the members of that one body, {being many}, are one body:
so also is Christ.

13 **For by one Spirit** are we all baptized into one body,
whether we be Jews or Gentiles,
whether we be bond or free;

and have been all made to drink into one Spirit.

14 **For the body** is not one member, but many.

15 **If the foot** shall say,
Because I am not the hand,
I am not of the body;
is it therefore not of the body?

16 **And if the ear** shall say,
Because I am not the eye,
I am not of the body;
is it therefore not of the body?

17 **If the whole body** were an eye,
where were the hearing?
If the whole were hearing,
where were the smelling?

18 **But now** hath God set the members every one of them in the body,
as it hath pleased him.

19 **And if they** were all one member,
where were the body?

20 **But now** are they many members, yet but one body.

21 **And the eye** cannot say unto the hand, {I have no need of thee}: nor again the head to the feet, {I have no need of you}.

22 **Nay, much more those members of the body, {which seem to be more feeble},** are necessary:

23 **And those members of the body, {which we think to be less honourable},** upon these we bestow more abundant honour;
and our uncomely parts have more abundant comeliness.

24 **For our comely parts** have no need:
but God hath tempered the body together,
having given more abundant honour to that part which lacked.

25 **That there** should be no schism in the body;
but that the members should have the same care one for another.

26 **And whether one member** suffer,
all the members suffer with it;
or one member be honoured,
all the members rejoice with it.

27 **Now ye** are the body of Christ, and members in particular.

28 **And God** hath set some in the church, first apostles, secondarily prophets, thirdly teachers, after that miracles, then gifts of healings, helps, governments, diversities of tongues.

29 **Are all** apostles?
are all prophets?
are all teachers?
are all workers of miracles?

30 **Have all** the gifts of healing?
do all speak with tongues?
do all interpret?

31 **But covet** earnestly the best gifts:
and yet shew I unto you a more excellent way.

13 **Though I** speak with the tongues of men and of angels,
and have not charity,
I am become as sounding brass, or a tinkling cymbal.

2 **And though I** have the gift of prophecy,
and understand all mysteries, and all knowledge;
and though I have all faith,
so that I could remove mountains,
and have not charity,
I am nothing.

3 **And though I** bestow all my goods to feed the poor,
and though I give my body to be burned,
and have not charity,
it profiteth me nothing.

4 **Charity** suffereth long,
and is kind;
charity envieth not;
charity vaunteth not itself,
is not puffed up,
5 Doth not behave itself unseemly,
seeketh not her own,
is not easily provoked,
thinketh no evil;
6 Rejoiceth not in iniquity,
but rejoiceth in the truth;
7 Beareth all things,
believeth all things,
hopeth all things,
endureth all things.

8 **Charity** never faileth:
but whether there be prophecies,
they shall fail;
whether there be tongues,
they shall cease;
whether there be knowledge,
it shall vanish away.

9 **For we** know in part,
and we prophesy in part.

10 **But when that which is perfect** is come,
then that which is in part shall be done away.

11 **When I** was a child,
I spake as a child,
I understood as a child,
I thought as a child:
but when I became a man,
I put away childish things.

12 **For now we** see through a glass, darkly; but then face to face:
now I know in part;
but then shall I know
even as also I am known.

13 **And now** abideth faith, hope, charity, these three;
but the greatest of these is charity.

14 **Follow** after charity,
and desire spiritual gifts,
but rather that ye may prophesy.

2 **For he that speaketh in an unknown tongue** speaketh not unto men, but unto God:
for no man understandeth him;
howbeit in the spirit he speaketh mysteries.

3 **But he that prophesieth** speaketh unto men to edification, and exhortation, and comfort.

4 **He that speaketh in an unknown tongue** edifieth himself;
but he that prophesieth edifieth the church.

5 **I would**
that ye all spake with tongues
but rather that ye prophesied:
for greater is he that prophesieth than he that speaketh with tongues,
except he interpret,
that the church may receive edifying.

6 **Now, brethren, if I** come unto you speaking with tongues,
what shall I profit you,
except I shall speak to you either by revelation, or by knowledge, or by prophesying, or by doctrine?

7 And even things without life giving sound, whether pipe or harp,
except they give a distinction in the sounds,
how shall it be known
what is piped or harped?

8 **For if the trumpet** give an uncertain sound,
who shall prepare himself to the battle?

9 **So likewise ye,** {except ye utter by the tongue words easy to be

understood}, how shall it be known
what is spoken?
for ye shall speak into the air.

10 **There** are, it may be, so many kinds of voices in the world,
and none of them is without signification.

11 **Therefore if I** know not the meaning of the voice,
I shall be unto him that speaketh a barbarian,
and he that speaketh shall be a barbarian unto me.

12 **Even so ye,** {forasmuch as ye are zealous of spiritual gifts}, seek that ye may excel to the edifying of the church.

13 **Wherefore let him that speaketh in an unknown tongue** pray
that he may interpret.

14 **For if I** pray in an unknown tongue,
my spirit prayeth,
but my understanding is unfruitful.

15 **What** is it then?
I will pray with the spirit,
and I will pray with the understanding also:
I will sing with the spirit,
and I will sing with the understanding also.

16 **Else when thou** shalt bless with the spirit,
how shall he that occupieth the room of the unlearned say Amen at thy giving of thanks,
seeing he understandeth not
what thou sayest?

17 **For thou** verily givest thanks well,
but the other is not edified.

18 **I** thank my God,
I speak with tongues more than ye all:

19 **Yet in the church** I had rather speak five words with my understanding, {that by my voice I might teach others also}, than ten thousand words in an unknown tongue.

20 **Brethren, be not** children in understanding:
howbeit in malice be ye children,
but in understanding be men.

21 **In the law** it is written,
With men of other tongues and other lips will I speak unto this people;
and yet for all that will they not hear me,
saith the Lord.

22 **Wherefore tongues** are for a sign, not to them that believe, but to them that believe not:
but prophesying serveth not for them that believe not, but for them which believe.

23 **If therefore the whole church** be come together into one place,
and all speak with tongues,
and there come in those that are unlearned, or unbelievers,
will they not say
that ye are mad?

24 **But if all** prophesy,
and there come in one that believeth not, or one unlearned,
he is convinced of all,
he is judged of all:

25 **And thus** are the secrets of his heart made manifest;
and so falling down on his face
he will worship God,
and report
that God is in you of a truth.

26 **How** is it then, brethren?
when ye come together,
every one of you hath a psalm,
hath a doctrine,
hath a tongue,
hath a revelation,
hath an interpretation.
Let all things be done unto edifying.

27 **If any man** speak in an unknown tongue,
let it be by two, or at the most by three, and that by course;
and let one interpret.

28 **But if there** be no interpreter,
let him keep silence in the church;
and let him speak to himself, and to God.

29 **Let the prophets** speak two or three,
and let the other judge.

30 **If any thing** be revealed to another that sitteth by,
let the first hold his peace.

31 **For ye** may all prophesy one by one,
that all may learn,
and all may be comforted.

32 **And the spirits of the prophets** are subject to the prophets.

33 **For God** is not the author of confusion, but of peace, as in all churches of the saints.

34 **Let your women** keep silence in the churches:
for it is not permitted unto them to speak;
but they are commanded to be under obedience as also saith the law.

35 **And if they** will learn any thing,
let them ask their husbands at home:
for it is a shame for women to speak in the church.

36 What?
came the word of God out from you?
or came it unto you only?

37 **If any man** think himself to be a prophet, or spiritual,
let him acknowledge that the things that I write unto you are the commandments of the Lord.

38 **But if any man** be ignorant,
let him be ignorant.

39 **Wherefore, brethren, covet** to prophesy,
and forbid not to speak with tongues.

40 **Let all things** be done decently and in order.

15

Moreover, brethren, I declare unto you the gospel which I preached unto you,
which also ye have received,
and wherein ye stand;

2 **By which** also ye are saved,
if ye keep in memory
what I preached unto you,
unless ye have believed in vain.

3 **For I** delivered unto you first of all that which I also received,
how that Christ died for our sins according to the scriptures;

4 **And that he** was buried,
and that he rose again the third day according to the scriptures:

5 **And that he** was seen of Cephas, then of the twelve:

6 **After that,** he was seen of above five hundred brethren at once;
of whom the greater part remain unto this present,
but some are fallen asleep.

7 **After that,** he was seen of James; then of all the apostles.

8 **And last of all** he was seen of me also, as of one born out of due time.

9 **For I** am the least of the apostles,
that am not meet to be called an apostle,
because I persecuted the church of God.

10 **But by the grace of God** I am what I am:
and his grace which was bestowed upon me was not in vain;
but I laboured more abundantly than they all: yet not I, but the grace of God which was with me.

11 **Therefore whether it** were I or they,
so we preach,
and so ye believed.

12 **Now if Christ** be preached
that he rose from the dead,
how say some among you
that there is no resurrection of the dead?

13 **But if there** be no resurrection of the dead,
then is Christ not risen:
14 **And if Christ** be not risen,
then is our preaching vain,
and your faith is also vain.

15 **Yea, and we** are found false witnesses of God;
because we have testified of God
that he raised up Christ:
whom he raised not up,
if so be that the dead rise not.

16 **For if the dead** rise not,
then is not Christ raised:
17 **And if Christ** be not raised,
your faith is vain;
ye are yet in your sins.

18 **Then they also which are fallen asleep in Christ** are perished.

19 **If in this life only** we have hope in Christ,
we are of all men most miserable.

20 **But now** is Christ risen from the dead,
and become the firstfruits of them that slept.

21 **For since by man** came death,
by man came also the resurrection of the dead.

22 **For as in Adam** all die,
even so in Christ shall all be made alive.

23 But every man in his own order:
Christ the firstfruits;
afterward they that are Christ's at his coming.

24 **Then** cometh the end,
when he shall have delivered up the kingdom to God, even the Father;
when he shall have put down all rule and all authority and power.

25 **For he** must reign,
till he hath put all enemies under his feet.

26 **The last enemy that shall be destroyed** is death.

27 **For he** hath put all things under his feet.
But when he saith
all things are put under him,
it is manifest that he is excepted,
which did put all things under him.

28 **And when all things** shall be subdued unto him,
then shall the Son also himself be subject unto him that put all things under him,
that God may be all in all.

29 **Else what** shall they do which are baptized for the dead,
if the dead rise not at all?
why are they then baptized for the dead?

30 **And why** stand we in jeopardy every hour?

31 **I** protest by your rejoicing which I have in Christ Jesus our Lord,
I die daily.

32 **If after the manner of men** I have fought with beasts at Ephesus,
what advantageth it me,
if the dead rise not?
let us eat and drink;
for to morrow we die.

33 **Be not** deceived:
evil communications corrupt good manners.

34 **Awake** to righteousness,
and sin not;
for some have not the knowledge of God:
I speak this to your shame.

35 **But some man** will say,
How are the dead raised up?
and with what body do they come?

36 **Thou fool, that which thou sowest** is not quickened,
except it die:
37 **And that which thou sowest,** thou sowest not that body that shall be, but bare grain,
it may chance of wheat, or of some other grain:

38 **But God** giveth it a body {as it hath pleased him}, and to every seed his own body.

39 **All flesh** is not the same flesh:
but there is one kind of flesh of men, another flesh of beasts, another of fishes, and another of birds.

40 **There** are also celestial bodies, and bodies terrestrial:
but the glory of the celestial is one,
and the glory of the terrestrial is another.

41 **There** is one glory of the sun, and another glory of the moon, and another glory of the stars:
for one star differeth from another star in glory.

42 **So** also is the resurrection of the dead.
It is sown in corruption;
it is raised in incorruption:
43 **It** is sown in dishonour;
it is raised in glory:
it is sown in weakness;
it is raised in power:
44 **It** is sown a natural body;
it is raised a spiritual body.
There is a natural body,
and there is a spiritual body.

45 **And so** it is written,
The first man Adam was made a living soul;
the last Adam was made a quickening spirit.

46 **Howbeit that** was not first which is spiritual, but that which is natural; and afterward that which is spiritual.

47 **The first man** is of the earth, earthy;
the second man is the Lord from heaven.

48 **As is the earthy,** such are they also that are earthy:
and as is the heavenly, such are they also that are heavenly.

49 **And as we** have borne the image of the earthy,
we shall also bear the image of the heavenly.

50 **Now this** I say, brethren,
that flesh and blood cannot inherit the kingdom of God;
neither doth corruption inherit incorruption.

51 **Behold,**
I shew you a mystery;

We shall not all sleep,
but we shall all be changed,
52 In a moment, in the twinkling of an eye, at the last trump:
for the trumpet shall sound,
and the dead shall be raised incorruptible,
and we shall be changed.
53 **For this corruptible** must put on incorruption,
and this mortal must put on immortality.
54 **So when this corruptible** shall have put on incorruption,
and this mortal shall have put on immortality,
then shall be brought to pass the saying that is written,
Death is swallowed up in victory.
55 **O death, where** is thy sting?
O grave, where is thy victory?
56 **The sting of death** is sin;
and the strength of sin is the law.
57 **But thanks** be to God,
which giveth us the victory through our Lord Jesus Christ.
58 **Therefore, my beloved brethren, be ye** stedfast, unmoveable,
always abounding in the work of the Lord,
forasmuch as ye know
that your labour is not in vain in the Lord.

16 **Now concerning the collection for the saints,**
{as I have given order to the churches of Galatia}, even so do ye.
2 **Upon the first day of the week** let every one of you lay by him in store,
as God hath prospered him,
that there be no gatherings when I come.
3 **And when I** come,
whomsoever ye shall approve by your letters,
them will I send to bring your liberality unto Jerusalem.
4 **And if it be meet** that I go also,
they shall go with me.
5 **Now I** will come unto you,
when I shall pass through Macedonia:
for I do pass through Macedonia.
6 **And it may be** that I will abide,
yea, and winter with you,
that ye may bring me on my journey
whithersoever I go.
7 **For I** will not see you now by the way;
but I trust to tarry a while with you,
if the Lord permit.
8 **But I** will tarry at Ephesus until Pentecost.
9 **For a great door and effectual** is opened unto me,
and there are many adversaries.
10 **Now if Timotheus** come,
see that he may be with you without fear:
for he worketh the work of the Lord,
as I also do.
11 **Let no man** therefore despise him:
but conduct him forth in peace,
that he may come unto me:
for I look for him with the brethren.
12 **As touching our brother Apollos,** I greatly desired him to come unto you with the brethren:
but his will was not at all to come at this time;
but he will come
when he shall have convenient time.
13 **Watch ye,**
stand fast in the faith,
quit you like men,
be strong.
14 **Let all your things** be done with charity.
15 **I** beseech you, brethren,
(ye know the house of Stephanas,
that it is the firstfruits of Achaia,
and that they have addicted themselves to the ministry of the saints,)
16 **That ye** submit yourselves unto such, and to every one that helpeth with us, and laboureth.
17 **I** am glad of the coming of Stephanas and Fortunatus and Achaicus:
for that which was lacking on your part they have supplied.
18 **For they** have refreshed my spirit and yours:
therefore acknowledge ye them that are such.
19 **The churches of Asia** salute you.
Aquila and Priscilla salute you much in the Lord, with the church that is in their house.
20 **All the brethren** greet you.
Greet ye one another with an holy kiss.
21 The salutation of me Paul with mine own hand.
22 **If any man** love not the Lord Jesus Christ,
let him be Anathema Maranatha.
23 **The grace of our Lord Jesus Christ** be with you.
24 **My love** be with you all in Christ Jesus.
Amen.

2 Corinthians

The Book of Second Corinthians, Paul's response to a crisis in the Church at Corinth, was penned during his third missionary journey. This epistle, far from being a mere letter, is a testament to the Apostle's commitment to address the serious challenges and divisions the Corinthian community faces. It stands as a beacon of hope, a tool to strengthen the faith of the Corinthian believers, and a testament to Paul's deep concern for their spiritual well-being.

Throughout the letter, Paul conveys his qualifications as a leader whose correspondence should carry weight. He asserts his authority as an apostle and defends the legitimacy of his ministry. He explains that his suffering and hardships are a testament to his genuine commitment to spreading the Gospel. By describing his own suffering and hardships, Paul encourages the Corinthians to see their suffering as an opportunity to grow their spiritual resilience. The Apostle also asserts that suffering is a necessary part of the Christian life that can ultimately lead to deeper faith and a closer relationship with God.

As he wrote in his first letter, Paul emphasizes the importance of genuine love in the Church, and he warns against divisions and conflicts that can arise when people focus on something other than love. He then encourages the Corinthians to be united in their love for one another and to prioritize the needs of others over their own desires. This emphasis on love and unity in the Church is not just a suggestion but a reminder of the collective strength that the Corinthians possess when they stand together in love. Paul also describes genuine Christian ministry, which needs to be marked by humility, selflessness, and a genuine concern for the well-being of others. He warns against those who seek to undermine the Gospel for their own gain, and he urges the Corinthians to support and encourage those who are truly committed to spreading the message of Christ.

Second Corinthians serves as a guide to genuine Christian ministry, offering a clear understanding of what it means to be a faithful servant of Christ. The timeless truths expressed in this epistle are not just for the Corinthians. They are relevant to the Church today, serving as a guide to navigating the challenges of the modern world.

1 **Paul, an apostle of Jesus Christ by the will of God, and Timothy our brother,** unto the church of God which is at Corinth, with all the saints which are in all Achaia:
2 **Grace** be to you {and peace} from God our Father,
and from the Lord Jesus Christ.
3 **Blessed** be God, even the Father of our Lord Jesus Christ, the Father of mercies, and the God of all comfort;
4 **Who** comforteth us in all our tribulation,
that we may be able to comfort them which are in any trouble, by the comfort wherewith we ourselves are comforted of God.
5 **For as the sufferings of Christ** abound in us,
so our consolation also aboundeth by Christ.
6 **And whether we** be afflicted,
it is for your consolation and salvation,
which is effectual in the enduring of the same sufferings which we also suffer:
or whether we be comforted,
it is for your consolation and salvation.
7 **And our hope of you** is stedfast, knowing,
that as ye are partakers of the sufferings,
so shall ye be also of the consolation.
8 **For we** would not, brethren, have you ignorant of our trouble
which came to us in Asia,
that we were pressed out of measure, above strength,
insomuch that we despaired even of life:
9 **But we** had the sentence of death in ourselves,
that we should not trust in ourselves, but in God which raiseth the dead:
10 **Who** delivered us from so great a death,
and doth deliver:
in whom we trust
that he will yet deliver us;
11 **Ye** also helping together by prayer for us,
that for the gift bestowed upon us by the means of many persons
thanks may be given by many on our behalf.
12 **For our rejoicing** is this, the testimony of our conscience,
that in simplicity and godly sincerity, not with fleshly wisdom, but by the grace of God, we have had our conversation in the world, and more abundantly to you-ward.
13 **For we** write none other things unto you,
that what ye read or acknowledge;
and I trust
ye shall acknowledge even to the end;
14 **As also ye** have acknowledged us in part,
that we are your rejoicing,
even as ye also are our's in the day of the Lord Jesus.

15 **And in this confidence** I was minded to come unto you before,
that ye might have a second benefit;

16 **And** to pass by you into Macedonia,
and to come again out of Macedonia unto you,
and of you to be brought on my way toward Judaea.

17 **When I** therefore was thus minded,
did I use lightness?
or the things that I purpose, do I purpose according to the flesh,
that with me there should be yea yea, and nay nay?

18 **But as God** is true,
our word toward you was not yea and nay.

19 **For the Son of God, Jesus Christ,** {who was preached among you by us, even by me and Silvanus and Timotheus}, was not yea and nay,
but in him was yea.

20 **For all the promises of God in him** are yea, and in him Amen, unto the glory of God by us.

21 **Now he which stablisheth us with you in Christ, and hath anointed us,** is God;

22 **Who** hath also sealed us,
and given the earnest of the Spirit in our hearts.

23 **Moreover I** call God for a record upon my soul,
that to spare you
I came not as yet unto Corinth.

24 **Not for that we** have dominion over your faith,
but are helpers of your joy:
for by faith ye stand.

2

But I determined this with myself,
that I would not come again to you in heaviness.

2 **For if I** make you sorry,
who is he then that maketh me glad, but the same which is made sorry by me?

3 **And I** wrote this same unto you,
lest, {when I came}, I should have sorrow from them of whom I ought to rejoice;
having confidence in you all,
that my joy is the joy of you all.

4 **For out of much affliction and anguish of heart** I wrote unto you with many tears;
not that ye should be grieved,
but that ye might know the love which I have more abundantly unto you.

5 **But if any** have caused grief,
he hath not grieved me, but in part:
that I may not overcharge you all.

6 **Sufficient to such a man** is this punishment,
which was inflicted of many.

7 **So that contrariwise ye** ought rather to forgive him,
and comfort him,
lest perhaps such a one should be swallowed up with overmuch sorrow.

8 **Wherefore I** beseech you
that ye would confirm your love toward him.

9 **For to this end** also did I write,
that I might know the proof of you,
whether ye be obedient in all things.

10 **To whom** ye forgive any thing,
I forgive also:
for if I forgave any thing,
to whom I forgave it,
for your sakes forgave I it in the person of Christ;

11 **Lest Satan** should get an advantage of us:
for we are not ignorant of his devices.

12 **Furthermore, when I** came to Troas
to preach Christ's gospel,
and a door was opened unto me of the Lord,

13 **I** had no rest in my spirit,
because I found not Titus my brother:
but taking my leave of them,
I went from thence into Macedonia.

14 **Now thanks** be unto God,
which always causeth us to triumph in Christ,
and maketh manifest the savour of his knowledge by us in every place.

15 **For we** are unto God a sweet savour of Christ, in them that are saved, and in them that perish:

16 **To the one** we are the savour of death unto death; and to the other the savour of life unto life.
And who is sufficient for these things?

17 **For we** are not as many,
which corrupt the word of God:
but as of sincerity, but as of God, in the sight of God speak we in Christ.

3

Do we begin again to commend ourselves?
or need we, as some others, epistles of commendation to you, or letters of commendation from you?

2 **Ye** are our epistle written in our hearts,
known and read of all men:

3 **Forasmuch as ye** are manifestly declared to be the epistle of Christ ministered by us,
written not with ink, but with the Spirit of the living God; not in tables of stone, but in fleshy tables of the heart.

4 **And such trust** have we through Christ to God-ward:

5 **Not that we** are sufficient of ourselves to think any thing as of ourselves;
but our sufficiency is of God;

6 **Who** also hath made us able ministers of the new testament; not of the letter, but of the spirit:
for the letter killeth,
but the spirit giveth life.

7 **But if the ministration of death,** {written and engraven in stones}, was glorious,
so that the children of Israel could not stedfastly behold the face of Moses for the glory of his countenance;
which glory was to be done away:

8 **How** shall not the ministration of the spirit be rather glorious?

9 **For if the ministration of condemnation** be glory,
much more doth the ministration of righteousness exceed in glory.

10 **For even that which was made glorious** had no glory in this respect, by reason of the glory that excelleth.

11 **For if that which is done away** was glorious,
much more that which remaineth is glorious.

12 **Seeing then that we** have such hope,
we use great plainness of speech:

13 And not as Moses,
which put a veil over his face,

that the children of Israel could not stedfastly look to the end of that which is abolished:

14 **But their minds** were blinded:
for until this day remaineth the same vail untaken away in the reading of the old testament;
which vail is done away in Christ.

15 **But even unto this day**, {when Moses is read}, the vail is upon their heart.

16 **Nevertheless when it** shall turn to the Lord,
the vail shall be taken away.

17 **Now the Lord** is that Spirit:
and where the Spirit of the Lord is,
there is liberty.

18 **But we all**, {with open face beholding as in a glass the glory of the Lord}, are changed into the same image from glory to glory, even as by the Spirit of the Lord.

4 **Therefore seeing we** have this ministry,
as we have received mercy,
we faint not;
2 **But** have renounced the hidden things of dishonesty,
not walking in craftiness,
nor handling the word of God deceitfully;
but by manifestation of the truth commending ourselves to every man's conscience in the sight of God.

3 **But if our gospel** be hid,
it is hid to them that are lost:
4 **In whom** the god of this world hath blinded the minds of them which believe not,
lest the light of the glorious gospel of Christ, {who is the image of God}, should shine unto them.

5 **For we** preach not ourselves, but Christ Jesus the Lord; and ourselves your servants for Jesus' sake.

6 **For God**, {who commanded the light to shine out of darkness}, hath shined in our hearts,
to give the light of the knowledge of the glory of God in the face of Jesus Christ.

7 **But we** have this treasure in earthen vessels,
that the excellency of the power may be of God, and not of us.

8 **We** are troubled on every side,
yet not distressed;
we are perplexed,
but not in despair;
9 Persecuted,
but not forsaken;
cast down,
but not destroyed;
10 **Always** bearing about in the body the dying of the Lord Jesus,
that the life also of Jesus might be made manifest in our body.

11 **For we which live** are always delivered unto death for Jesus' sake,
that the life also of Jesus might be made manifest in our mortal flesh.

12 **So then death** worketh in us, but life in you.

13 **We** having the same spirit of faith,
according as it is written,
I believed,
and therefore have I spoken;
we also believe,
and therefore speak;
14 Knowing
that he which raised up the Lord Jesus shall raise up us also by Jesus,
and shall present us with you.

15 **For all things** are for your sakes,
that the abundant grace might through the thanksgiving of many redound to the glory of God.

16 **For which cause** we faint not;
but though our outward man perish,
yet the inward man is renewed day by day.

17 **For our light affliction**, {which is but for a moment}, worketh for us a far more exceeding and eternal weight of glory;
18 **While we** look not at the things which are seen, but at the things which are not seen:
for the things which are seen are temporal;
but the things which are not seen are eternal.

5 **For we** know
that if our earthly house of this tabernacle were dissolved,
we have a building of God,
an house not made with hands, eternal in the heavens.

2 **For in this** we groan,
earnestly desiring to be clothed upon with our house which is from heaven:
3 **If so be {that being clothed}** we shall not be found naked.

4 **For we that are in this tabernacle** do groan,
being burdened:
not for that we would be unclothed,
but clothed upon,
that mortality might be swallowed up of life.

5 **Now he that hath wrought us for the selfsame thing** is God,
who also hath given unto us the earnest of the Spirit.

6 **Therefore we** are always confident,
knowing
that, {whilst we are at home in the body}, we are absent from the Lord:
7 (For we walk by faith, not by sight:)
8 **We** are confident,
I say,
and willing rather to be absent from the body,
and to be present with the Lord.

9 **Wherefore we** labour,
that, {whether present or absent}, we may be accepted of him.

10 **For we** must all appear before the judgment seat of Christ;
that every one may receive the things done in his body, according to that he hath done,
whether it be good or bad.

11 Knowing therefore the terror of the Lord,
we persuade men;
but we are made manifest unto God;
and I trust also are made manifest in your consciences.

12 **For we** commend not ourselves again unto you,
but give you occasion to glory on our behalf,
that ye may have somewhat to answer them which glory in appearance, and not in heart.

13 **For whether we** be beside ourselves,
it is to God:
or whether we be sober,
it is for your cause.

14 **For the love of Christ** constraineth us;
because we thus judge,
that if one died for all,
then were all dead:
15 **And that he** died for all,
that they which live should not henceforth live unto themselves, but unto him which died for them, and rose again.

16 **Wherefore henceforth** know we no man after the flesh:
yea, though we have known Christ after the flesh,
yet now henceforth know we him no more.

17 **Therefore if any man** be in Christ,
he is a new creature:
old things are passed away;
behold,
all things are become new.

18 **And all things** are of God,
who hath reconciled us to himself by Jesus Christ,
and hath given to us the ministry of reconciliation;
19 **To wit, that God** was in Christ,
reconciling the world unto himself,
not imputing their trespasses unto them;
and hath committed unto us the word of reconciliation.

20 **Now then we** are ambassadors for Christ,
as though God did beseech you by us:
we pray you in Christ's stead,
be ye reconciled to God.

21 **For he** hath made him to be sin for us,
who knew no sin;
that we might be made the righteousness of God in him.

6 **We then**, as workers together with him, beseech you also
that ye receive not the grace of God in vain.

2 (**For he** saith,
I have heard thee in a time accepted,
and in the day of salvation have I succoured thee:
behold,
now is the accepted time;
behold,
now is the day of salvation.)

3 Giving no offence in any thing,
that the ministry be not blamed:
4 **But in all things** approving ourselves as the ministers of God, in much patience, in afflictions, in necessities, in distresses,
5 In stripes, in imprisonments, in tumults, in labours, in watchings, in fastings;
6 By pureness, by knowledge, by long suffering, by kindness, by the Holy Ghost, by love unfeigned,
7 By the word of truth, by the power of God, by the armour of righteousness on the right hand and on the left,
8 By honour and dishonour, by evil report and good report: as deceivers, and yet true;
9 **As** unknown,
and yet well known;
as dying,
and, {behold}, we live;
as chastened,
and not killed;
10 **As** sorrowful,
yet alway rejoicing; as poor,
yet making many rich;
as having nothing,
and yet possessing all things.

11 **O ye Corinthians, our mouth** is open unto you,
our heart is enlarged.

12 **Ye** are not straitened in us,
but ye are straitened in your own bowels.

13 **Now for a recompence in the same,**
(I speak as unto my children,)
be ye also enlarged.

14 **Be ye not** unequally yoked together with unbelievers:
for what fellowship hath righteousness with unrighteousness?
and what communion hath light with darkness?

15 **And what concord** hath Christ with Belial?
or what part hath he that believeth with an infidel?

16 **And what agreement** hath the temple of God with idols?
for ye are the temple of the living God;
as God hath said,
I will dwell in them,
and walk in them;
and I will be their God,
and they shall be my people.

17 **Wherefore come out** from among them,
and be ye separate,
saith the Lord,
and touch not the unclean thing;
and I will receive you.

18 **And** will be a Father unto you,
and ye shall be my sons and daughters,
saith the Lord Almighty.

7 Having therefore these promises, dearly beloved,
let us cleanse ourselves from all filthiness of the flesh and spirit,
perfecting holiness in the fear of God.

2 **Receive** us;
we have wronged no man,
we have corrupted no man,
we have defrauded no man.

3 **I** speak not this
to condemn you:
for I have said before,
that ye are in our hearts to die and live with you.

4 **Great** is my boldness of speech toward you,
great is my glorying of you:
I am filled with comfort,
I am exceeding joyful in all our tribulation.

5 **For, {when we were come into Macedonia},** our flesh had no rest,
but we were troubled on every side;
without were fightings,
within were fears.

6 **Nevertheless God,** {that comforteth those that are cast down}, comforted us by the coming of Titus;
7 And not by his coming only, but by the consolation wherewith he was comforted in you,
when he told us your earnest desire, your mourning, your fervent mind toward me;
so that I rejoiced the more.

8 **For though I** made you sorry with a letter,
I do not repent,
though I did repent:
for I perceive that the same epistle hath made you sorry,
though it were but for a season.

9 **Now I** rejoice,
not that ye were made sorry,
but that ye sorrowed to repentance:
for ye were made sorry after a godly manner,

that ye might receive damage by us in nothing.

10 **For godly sorrow** worketh repentance to salvation not to be repented of:
but the sorrow of the world worketh death.

11 **For behold** this selfsame thing,
that ye sorrowed after a godly sort,
what carefulness it wrought in you, yea, what clearing of yourselves, yea, what indignation, yea, what fear, yea, what vehement desire, yea, what zeal, yea, what revenge!
In all things ye have approved yourselves to be clear in this matter.

12 **Wherefore, though I** wrote unto you,
I did it not for his cause that had done the wrong, nor for his cause that suffered wrong,
but that our care for you in the sight of God might appear unto you.

13 **Therefore we** were comforted in your comfort:
yea, and exceedingly the more joyed we for the joy of Titus,
because his spirit was refreshed by you all.

14 **For if I** have boasted any thing to him of you,
I am not ashamed;
but as we spake all things to you in truth,
even so our boasting, {which I made before Titus}, is found a truth.

15 **And his inward affection** is more abundant toward you,
whilst he remembereth the obedience of you all,
how with fear and trembling ye received him.

16 I rejoice therefore that I have confidence in you in all things.

8 **Moreover, brethren, we** do you to wit of the grace of God bestowed on the churches of Macedonia;

2 **How that in a great trial of affliction** the abundance of their joy and their deep poverty abounded unto the riches of their liberality.

3 **For to their power,** I bear record,
yea, and beyond their power they were willing of themselves;

4 Praying us with much intreaty
that we would receive the gift,
and take upon us the fellowship of the ministering to the saints.

5 **And this** they did,
not as we hoped,
but first gave their own selves to the Lord, and unto us by the will of God.

6 **Insomuch that we** desired Titus,
that as he had begun,
so he would also finish in you the same grace also.

7 **Therefore, as ye** abound in every thing, in faith, and utterance, and knowledge, and in all diligence, and in your love to us,
see that ye abound in this grace also.

8 **I** speak not by commandment, but by occasion of the forwardness of others,
and to prove the sincerity of your love.

9 **For ye** know the grace of our Lord Jesus Christ,
that, {though he was rich}, yet for your sakes he became poor,
that ye through his poverty might be rich.

10 **And herein** I give my advice:
for this is expedient for you,
who have begun before,
not only to do,
but also to be forward a year ago.

11 **Now therefore perform** the doing of it;
that as there was a readiness to will,
so there may be a performance also out of that which ye have.

12 **For if there** be first a willing mind,
it is accepted according to that a man hath, and not according to that he hath not.

13 **For I** mean not that other men be eased, and ye burdened:

14 But by an equality,
that now at this time your abundance may be a supply for their want,
that their abundance also may be a supply for your want:
that there may be equality:

15 **As it** is written,
He that had gathered much had nothing over;
and he that had gathered little had no lack.

16 **But thanks** be to God,
which put the same earnest care into the heart of Titus for you.

17 **For indeed he** accepted the exhortation;
but being more forward,
of his own accord he went unto you.

18 **And we** have sent with him the brother,
whose praise is in the gospel throughout all the churches;

19 **And not that only,** but who was also chosen of the churches to travel with us with this grace,
which is administered by us to the glory of the same Lord, and declaration of your ready mind:

20 Avoiding this,
that no man should blame us in this abundance which is administered by us:

21 Providing for honest things, not only in the sight of the Lord, but also in the sight of men.

22 **And we** have sent with them our brother,
whom we have oftentimes proved diligent in many things, but now much more diligent, upon the great confidence which I have in you.

23 **Whether any** do enquire of Titus,
he is my partner and fellowhelper concerning you:
or our brethren be enquired of,
they are the messengers of the churches, and the glory of Christ.

24 **Wherefore** shew ye to them, and before the churches, the proof of your love, and of our boasting on your behalf.

9 **For as touching the ministering to the saints,** it is superfluous for me to write to you:

2 **For I** know the forwardness of your mind,
for which I boast of you to them of Macedonia,
that Achaia was ready a year ago;
and your zeal hath provoked very many.

3 **Yet** have I sent the brethren,
lest our boasting of you should be in vain in this behalf;
that, {as I said}, ye may be ready:

4 **Lest haply if they of Macedonia** come with me,
and find you unprepared,
we (that we say not, ye) should be ashamed in this same confident boasting.
5 **Therefore I thought it necessary** to exhort the brethren,
that they would go before unto you,
and make up beforehand your bounty,
whereof ye had notice before,
that the same might be ready, as a matter of bounty, and not as of covetousness.
6 **But this** I say,
He which soweth sparingly shall reap also sparingly;
and he which soweth bountifully shall reap also bountifully.
7 **Every man according as he purposeth in his heart,** so let him give; not grudgingly, or of necessity:
for God loveth a cheerful giver.
8 **And God** is able to make all grace abound toward you;
that ye, {always having all sufficiency in all things}, may abound to every good work:
9 (As it is written,
He hath dispersed abroad;
he hath given to the poor:
his righteousness remaineth for ever.
10 Now he that ministereth seed to the sower both minister bread for your food,
and multiply your seed sown,
and increase the fruits of your righteousness;)
11 Being enriched in every thing to all bountifulness,
which causeth through us thanksgiving to God.
12 **For the administration of this service** not only supplieth the want of the saints,
but is abundant also by many thanksgivings unto God;
13 **Whiles by the experiment of this ministration** they glorify God for your professed subjection unto the gospel of Christ, and for your liberal distribution unto them, and unto all men;
14 And by their prayer for you,
which long after you for the exceeding grace of God in you.
15 **Thanks** be unto God for his unspeakable gift.

10 **Now I Paul myself** beseech you by the meekness and gentleness of Christ,
who in presence am base among you,
but {being absent} am bold toward you:
2 **But I** beseech you,
that I may not be bold when I am present with that confidence,
wherewith I think to be bold against some,
which think of us
as if we walked according to the flesh.
3 **For though we** walk in the flesh,
we do not war after the flesh:
4 (For the weapons of our warfare are not carnal, but mighty through God to the pulling down of strong holds;)
5 Casting down imaginations, and every high thing that exalteth itself against the knowledge of God,
and bringing into captivity every thought to the obedience of Christ;
6 **And** having in a readiness to revenge all disobedience,
when your obedience is fulfilled.
7 **Do ye** look on things after the outward appearance?
if any man trust to himself
that he is Christ's,
let him of himself think this again,
that, {as he is Christ's}, even so are we Christ's.
8 **For though I** should boast somewhat more of our authority,
which the Lord hath given us for edification, and not for your destruction,
I should not be ashamed:
9 **That I** may not seem as if I would terrify you by letters.
10 **For his letters**, {say they}, are weighty and powerful;
but his bodily presence is weak, and his speech contemptible.
11 **Let such an one** think this,
that, {such as we are in word by letters when we are absent}, such will we be also in deed when we are present.
12 **For we** dare not make ourselves of the number,
or compare ourselves with some that commend themselves:
but they measuring themselves by themselves, and comparing themselves among themselves, are not wise.
13 **But we** will not boast of things without our measure, but according to the measure of the rule which God hath distributed to us,
a measure to reach even unto you.
14 **For we** stretch not ourselves beyond our measure,
as though we reached not unto you:
for we are come as far as to you also in preaching the gospel of Christ:
15 **Not** boasting of things without our measure, that is, of other men's labours;
but having hope,
when your faith is increased,
that we shall be enlarged by you according to our rule abundantly,
16 To preach the gospel in the regions beyond you,
and not to boast in another man's line of things made ready to our hand.
17 **But he that glorieth,** let him glory in the Lord.
18 **For not he that commendeth himself** is approved,
but whom the Lord commendeth.

11 Would to God **ye** could bear with me a little in my folly:
and indeed bear with me.
2 **For I** am jealous over you with godly jealousy:
for I have espoused you to one husband,
that I may present you as a chaste virgin to Christ.
3 **But I** fear, lest by any means,
as the serpent beguiled Eve through his subtilty,
so your minds should be corrupted from the simplicity that is in Christ.
4 **For if he that cometh** preacheth another Jesus,
whom we have not preached,
or if ye receive another spirit, {which ye have not received}, or another gospel, {which ye have not accepted},
ye might well bear with him.

5 **For I** suppose
I was not a whit behind the very chiefest apostles.

6 **But though I** be rude in speech, yet not in knowledge;
but we have been throughly made manifest among you in all things.

7 **Have I** committed an offence in abasing myself that ye might be exalted,
because I have preached to you the gospel of God freely?

8 **I** robbed other churches,
taking wages of them,
to do you service.

9 **And when I** was present with you,
and wanted,
I was chargeable to no man:
for that which was lacking to me the brethren which came from Macedonia supplied:
and in all things I have kept myself from being burdensome unto you,
and so will I keep myself.

10 **As the truth of Christ** is in me,
no man shall stop me of this boasting in the regions of Achaia.

11 Wherefore?
because I love you not?

God knoweth.

12 **But what** I do,
that I will do,
that I may cut off occasion from them which desire occasion;
that wherein they glory,
they may be found even as we.

13 **For such** are false apostles, deceitful workers,
transforming themselves into the apostles of Christ.

14 And no marvel;
for Satan himself is transformed into an angel of light.

15 **Therefore it** is no great thing
if his ministers also be transformed as the ministers of righteousness;
whose end shall be according to their works.

16 **I** say again,
let no man think me a fool;
if otherwise, yet as a fool receive me,
that I may boast myself a little.

17 **That which I speak,** I speak it not after the Lord, but as it were foolishly, in this confidence of boasting.

18 **Seeing that many** glory after the flesh,
I will glory also.

19 **For ye** suffer fools gladly,
seeing ye yourselves are wise.

20 **For ye** suffer,
if a man bring you into bondage,
if a man devour you,
if a man take of you,
if a man exalt himself,
if a man smite you on the face.

21 **I** speak as concerning reproach,
as though we had been weak.

Howbeit whereinsoever any is bold,
(I speak foolishly,)
I am bold also.

22 **Are they** Hebrews?
so am I.

Are they Israelites?
so am I.

Are they the seed of Abraham?
so am I.

23 **Are they** ministers of Christ?
(I speak as a fool)
I am more; in labours more abundant, in stripes above measure, in prisons more frequent, in deaths oft.

24 **Of the Jews** five times received I forty stripes save one.

25 **Thrice** was I beaten with rods,
once was I stoned,
thrice I suffered shipwreck,
a night and a day I have been in the deep;

26 In journeyings often, in perils of waters, in perils of robbers, in perils by mine own countrymen, in perils by the heathen, in perils in the city, in perils in the wilderness, in perils in the sea, in perils among false brethren;

27 In weariness and painfulness, in watchings often, in hunger and thirst, in fastings often, in cold and nakedness.

28 **Beside those things that are without,** that which cometh upon me daily, the care of all the churches.

29 **Who** is weak,
and I am not weak?
who is offended,
and I burn not?

30 **If I** must needs glory,
I will glory of the things which concern mine infirmities.

31 **The God and Father of our Lord Jesus Christ**, {which is blessed for evermore}, knoweth
that I lie not.

32 **In Damascus** the governor under Aretas the king kept the city of the damascenes with a garrison,
desirous to apprehend me:

33 **And through a window in a basket** was I let down by the wall,
and escaped his hands.

12

It is not expedient for me doubtless to glory.
I will come to visions and revelations of the Lord.

2 **I** knew a man in Christ above fourteen years ago,
(whether in the body, I cannot tell;
or whether out of the body, I cannot tell:
God knoweth;)
such an one caught up to the third heaven.

3 **And I** knew such a man,
(whether in the body, or out of the body, I cannot tell:
God knoweth;)

4 **How that he** was caught up into paradise,
and heard unspeakable words,
which it is not lawful for a man to utter.

5 **Of such an one** will I glory:
yet of myself I will not glory, but in mine infirmities.

6 **For though I** would desire to glory,
I shall not be a fool;
for I will say the truth:
but now I forbear,
lest any man should think of me above that which he seeth me to be, or that he heareth of me.

7 **And lest I** should be exalted above measure through the abundance of the revelations,
there was given to me a thorn in the flesh,
the messenger of Satan to buffet me,
lest I should be exalted above measure.

8 **For this thing** I besought the Lord thrice,
that it might depart from me.

9 **And he** said unto me,
My grace is sufficient for thee:
for my strength is made perfect in weakness.

Most gladly therefore will I rather glory in my infirmities,

that the power of Christ may rest upon me.
10 **Therefore I** take pleasure in infirmities, in reproaches, in necessities, in persecutions, in distresses for Christ's sake:
for when I am weak,
then am I strong.
11 **I** am become a fool in glorying;
ye have compelled me:
for I ought to have been commended of you:
for in nothing am I behind the very chiefest apostles,
though I be nothing.
12 **Truly the signs of an apostle** were wrought among you in all patience, in signs, and wonders, and mighty deeds.
13 **For what is it** wherein ye were inferior to other churches,
except it be that I myself was not burdensome to you?
forgive me this wrong.
14 **Behold,**
the third time I am ready to come to you;
and I will not be burdensome to you:
for I seek not yours but you:
for the children ought not to lay up for the parents, but the parents for the children.
15 **And I** will very gladly spend and be spent for you;
though the more abundantly I love you,
the less I be loved.
16 **But** be it so,
I did not burden you:
nevertheless, {being crafty}, I caught you with guile.
17 **Did I** make a gain of you by any of them whom I sent unto you?
18 **I** desired Titus,
and with him I sent a brother.
Did Titus make a gain of you?
walked we not in the same spirit?
walked we not in the same steps?
19 **Again, think ye**
that we excuse ourselves unto you?
we speak before God in Christ:
but we do all things, dearly beloved, for your edifying.
20 **For I** fear,
lest, {when I come}, I shall not find you such as I would,
and that I shall be found unto you such as ye would not:
lest there be debates, envyings, wraths, strifes, backbitings, whisperings, swellings, tumults:
21 **And lest, {when I come again},** my God will humble me among you,
and that I shall bewail many which have sinned already,
and have not repented of the uncleanness and fornication and lasciviousness which they have committed.

13 **This** is the third time I am coming to you.
In the mouth of two or three witnesses shall every word be established.
2 **I** told you before,
and foretell you,
as if I were present, the second time;
and being absent now
I write to them which heretofore have sinned, and to all other,
that, {if I come again}, I will not spare:
3 **Since ye** seek a proof of Christ speaking in me,
which to you-ward is not weak,
but is mighty in you.
4 **For though he** was crucified through weakness,
yet he liveth by the power of God.
For we also are weak in him,
but we shall live with him by the power of God toward you.
5 **Examine** yourselves,
whether ye be in the faith;
prove your own selves.
Know ye not your own selves,
how that Jesus Christ is in you,
except ye be reprobates?
6 **But I** trust
that ye shall know
that we are not reprobates.
7 **Now I** pray to God
that ye do no evil;
not that we should appear approved,
but that ye should do that which is honest,
though we be as reprobates.
8 **For we** can do nothing against the truth, but for the truth.
9 **For we** are glad,
when we are weak,
and ye are strong:
and this also we wish, even your perfection.
10 **Therefore I** write these things being absent,
lest being present
I should use sharpness, according to the power which the Lord hath given me to edification, and not to destruction.
11 **Finally, brethren, farewell.**
Be perfect,
be of good comfort,
be of one mind,
live in peace;
and the God of love and peace shall be with you.
12 **Greet** one another with an holy kiss.
13 **All the saints** salute you.
14 **The grace of the Lord Jesus Christ, and the love of God, and the communion of the Holy Ghost,** be with you all.
Amen.

Galatians

The Apostle Paul writes the Book of Galatians to address certain issues that have arisen among the early Christian communities in the region of Galatia. Specifically, he wants to refute the teachings of some Jewish-Christian missionaries who insist that Gentile converts to Christianity must first become Jewish by adhering to Jewish law, including circumcision, before they can become full members of the Christian community. Paul's goal in writing Galatians is to emphasize that salvation comes through faith in Jesus Christ alone, not through human effort or adherence to the law. He seeks to establish that the Gospel he preaches is genuine and not a distorted version. He also hopes to reinforce church unity by emphasizing that all believers, Jewish and Gentile, are equal in Christ and share a common salvation.

The claims of this epistle are crucial for understanding Christianity and thus deserve further explanation. Paul teaches that Christians have been set free by the grace of God through faith in Christ, and he emphasizes this point by contrasting the works of the flesh with the fruit of the Spirit. He then encourages believers to live according to the Spirit and not to indulge in sinful behavior. The Apostle again reminds the Galatians of the importance of preaching the true Gospel and not being swayed by false teachings. He explains that the law was given as a tutor to lead people to Christ, but now that Christ has come, believers are no longer under the law. His letter assures the Galatians that those who believe in Christ will receive the indwelling and guidance of the Holy Spirit, Who will empower them in their Christian walk.

Galatians clearly explains the one and only Gospel and its message of salvation through faith in Jesus Christ alone. This saving faith remains a crucial foundation for anyone seeking to understand and grow in their Christian walk. The book also underscores the unity of believers in Christ, a theme that Paul reiterates throughout his letter, regardless of their background, social status, or ethnicity. No distinction exists between Jew and Gentile in Christ; therefore, all believers are one in the Spirit. Finally, Paul's message serves as a poignant reminder of the freedom found in Christ. He urges the Galatians and all believers to reject the shackles of legalism and embrace the boundless love, forgiveness, and atonement of their Creator.

1 **Paul, an apostle,** (not of men, neither by man, but by Jesus Christ, and God the Father, {who raised him from the dead};)
2 **And all the brethren which are with me,** unto the churches of Galatia:
3 **Grace** be to you {and peace} from God the Father,
and from our Lord Jesus Christ,
4 **Who** gave himself for our sins,
that he might deliver us from this present evil world, according to the will of God and our Father:
5 **To whom** be glory for ever and ever.
Amen.
6 **I** marvel
that ye are so soon removed from him that called you into the grace of Christ unto another gospel:
7 **Which** is not another;
but there be some that trouble you,
and would pervert the gospel of Christ.
8 **But though we, or an angel from heaven,** preach any other gospel unto you than that which we have preached unto you,
let him be accursed.
9 **As we** said before,
so say I now again,
if any man preach any other gospel unto you than that ye have received,
let him be accursed.
10 **For do I** now persuade men, or God?
or do I seek to please men?
for if I yet pleased men,
I should not be the servant of Christ.
11 **But I** certify you, brethren,
that the gospel which was preached of me is not after man.
12 **For I** neither received it of man,
neither was I taught it,
but by the revelation of Jesus Christ.
13 **For ye** have heard of my conversation in time past in the Jews' religion,
how that beyond measure I persecuted the church of God,
and wasted it:
14 **And** profited in the Jews' religion above many my equals in mine own nation,
being more exceedingly zealous of the traditions of my fathers.
15 **But when it** pleased God,
who separated me from my mother's womb,
and called me by his grace,
16 To reveal his Son in me,
that I might preach him among the heathen;
immediately I conferred not with flesh and blood:
17 **Neither** went I up to Jerusalem to them which were apostles before me;
but I went into Arabia,
and returned again unto Damascus.
18 **Then after three years** I went up to Jerusalem to see Peter,
and abode with him fifteen days.

19 **But other of the apostles** saw I
none, save James the Lord's
brother.
20 **Now the things which I write
unto you,** behold,
before God, I lie not.
21 **Afterwards I** came into the
regions of Syria and Cilicia;
22 **And** was unknown by face unto
the churches of Judaea which
were in Christ:
23 **But they** had heard only,
**That he which persecuted us in
times past** now preacheth the
faith which once he destroyed.
24 **And they** glorified God in me.

2

Then fourteen years after I
went up again to Jerusalem
with Barnabas,
and took Titus with me also.
2 **And I** went up by revelation,
and communicated unto them that
gospel which I preach among the
Gentiles, but privately to them
which were of reputation,
lest by any means I should run, {or
had run}, in vain.
3 **But neither Titus**, {who was with
me}, {being a Greek}, was
compelled to be circumcised:
4 **And that because of false
brethren unawares** brought in,
who came in privily to spy out our
liberty which we have in Christ
Jesus,
that they might bring us into
bondage:
5 **To whom** we gave place by
subjection, no, not for an hour;
that the truth of the gospel might
continue with you.
6 **But of these who seemed to be
somewhat,** ({whatsoever they
were}, {it maketh no matter to
me}: {God accepteth no man's
person}:) **for they who seemed
to be somewhat in conference**
added nothing to me:
7 **But contrariwise, when they** saw
that the gospel of the
uncircumcision was committed
unto me,
as the gospel of the circumcision
was unto Peter;
8 (For he that wrought effectually in
Peter to the apostleship of the
circumcision, the same was
mighty in me toward the
Gentiles:)
9 **And when James, Cephas, and
John,** {who seemed to be pillars},
perceived the grace that was
given unto me,
they gave to me and Barnabas the
right hands of fellowship;
that we should go unto the
heathen, and they unto the
circumcision.
10 **Only they** would
that we should remember the poor;
the same which I also was forward
to do.
11 **But when Peter** was come to
Antioch,
I withstood him to the face,
because he was to be blamed.
12 **For before that certain** came
from James,
he did eat with the Gentiles:
but when they were come,
he withdrew and separated himself,
fearing them which were of the
circumcision.
13 **And the other Jews** dissembled
likewise with him;
insomuch that Barnabas also was
carried away with their
dissimulation.
14 **But when I** saw that they walked
not uprightly according to the
truth of the gospel,
I said unto Peter before them all,
If thou, {being a Jew}, livest after
the manner of Gentiles, and not
as do the Jews,
why compellest thou the Gentiles
to live as do the Jews?
15 **We who are Jews by nature, and
not sinners of the Gentiles,**
16 {Knowing} {that a man is not
justified by the works of the law,
but by the faith of Jesus Christ},
even we have believed in Jesus
Christ,
that we might be justified by the
faith of Christ, and not by the
works of the law:
for by the works of the law shall
no flesh be justified.
17 **But if, {while we seek to be
justified by Christ},** we ourselves
also are found sinners,
is therefore Christ the minister of
sin?
God forbid.
18 **For if I** build again the things
which I destroyed,
I make myself a transgressor.
19 **For I through the law** am dead to
the law,
that I might live unto God.
20 **I** am crucified with Christ:
nevertheless I live; yet not I,
but Christ liveth in me:
**and the life which I now live in
the flesh** I live by the faith of the
Son of God,
who loved me,
and gave himself for me.
21 **I** do not frustrate the grace of God:
for if righteousness come by the
law,
then Christ is dead in vain.

3

O foolish Galatians, who
hath bewitched you,
that ye should not obey the truth,
before whose eyes Jesus Christ
hath been evidently set forth,
crucified among you?
2 **This only** would I learn of you,
Received ye the Spirit by the works
of the law, or by the hearing of
faith?
3 **Are ye** so foolish?
having begun in the Spirit,
are ye now made perfect by the
flesh?
4 **Have ye** suffered so many things in
vain?
if it be yet in vain.
5 **He therefore that ministereth to
you the Spirit, and worketh
miracles among you,** doeth he it
by the works of the law, or by the
hearing of faith?
6 **Even as Abraham** believed God,
and it was accounted to him for
righteousness.
7 **Know ye** therefore
that they which are of faith, the
same are the children of Abraham.
8 **And the scripture**, {foreseeing}
{that God would justify the
heathen through faith}, preached
before the gospel unto Abraham,
saying,
In thee shall all nations be blessed.
9 **So then they which be of faith**
are blessed with faithful
Abraham.
10 **For as many as are of the works
of the law** are under the curse:
for it is written,
Cursed is every one that continueth
not in all things which are written
in the book of the law to do them.

11 **But that no man** is justified by the
law in the sight of God,
it is evident:
for, The just shall live by faith.
12 **And the law** is not of faith:
but, The man that doeth them
shall live in them.
13 **Christ** hath redeemed us from the
curse of the law,
being made a curse for us:
for it is written,
Cursed is every one that hangeth on
a tree:
14 **That the blessing of Abraham**
might come on the Gentiles
through Jesus Christ;
that we might receive the promise
of the Spirit through faith.
15 **Brethren, I** speak after the
manner of men;
Though it be but a man's covenant,
yet if it be confirmed,
no man disannulleth,
or addeth thereto.
16 **Now to Abraham and his seed**
were the promises made.
He saith not,
And to seeds, as of many; but as of
one, And to thy seed,
which is Christ.
17 **And this** I say,
that the covenant, {that was
confirmed before of God in Christ,
the law}, {which was four
hundred and thirty years after},
cannot disannul,
that it should make the promise of
none effect.
18 **For if the inheritance** be of the
law,
it is no more of promise:
but God gave it to Abraham by
promise.
19 **Wherefore** then serveth the law?
It was added because of
transgressions,
till the seed should come
to whom the promise was made;
and it was ordained by angels in the
hand of a mediator.
20 **Now a mediator** is not a
mediator of one,
but God is one.
21 **Is the law** then against the
promises of God?
God forbid:
for if there had been a law given
which could have given life,
verily righteousness should have
been by the law.
22 **But the scripture** hath concluded
all under sin,
**that the promise by faith of Jesus
Christ** might be given to them
that believe.
23 **But before faith** came,
we were kept under the law,
shut up unto the faith which should
afterwards be revealed.
24 **Wherefore the law** was our
schoolmaster
to bring us unto Christ,
that we might be justified by faith.
25 **But after that faith** is come,
we are no longer under a
schoolmaster.
26 **For ye** are all the children of God
by faith in Christ Jesus.
27 **For as many of you as have been
baptized into Christ** have put on
Christ.
28 **There** is neither Jew nor Greek,
there is neither bond nor free,
there is neither male nor female:
for ye are all one in Christ Jesus.
29 **And if ye** be Christ's,
then are ye Abraham's seed, and
heirs according to the promise.

4 **Now I say,**
That the heir, {as long as he is
a child}, differeth nothing from a
servant,
though he be lord of all;
2 **But** is under tutors and governors
until the time appointed of the
father.
3 **Even so we**, {when we were
children}, were in bondage under
the elements of the world:
4 **But when the fulness of the time**
was come,
God sent forth his Son,
made of a woman,
made under the law,
5 To redeem them that were under
the law,
that we might receive the adoption
of sons.
6 **And because ye** are sons,
God hath sent forth the Spirit of his
Son into your hearts,
crying,
Abba, Father.
7 **Wherefore thou** art no more a
servant, but a son; and if a son,
then an heir of God through
Christ.
8 **Howbeit then, {when ye knew
not God},** ye did service unto
them which by nature are no
gods.
9 **But now, {after that ye have
known God}, {or rather are
known of God},** how turn ye
again to the weak and beggarly
elements,
whereunto ye desire again to be in
bondage?
10 **Ye** observe days, and months, and
times, and years.
11 **I** am afraid of you,
lest I have bestowed upon you
labour in vain.
12 **Brethren, I** beseech you,
be
as I am;
for I am
as ye are:
ye have not injured me at all.
13 **Ye** know
**how through infirmity of the
flesh** I preached the gospel unto
you at the first.
14 **And my temptation which was
in my flesh** ye despised not,
nor rejected;
but received me as an angel of God,
even as Christ Jesus.
15 **Where** is then the blessedness ye
spake of?
for I bear you record,
that, {if it had been possible}, ye
would have plucked out your own
eyes,
and have given them to me.
16 **Am I** therefore become your
enemy,
because I tell you the truth?
17 **They** zealously affect you, but not
well;
yea, they would exclude you,
that ye might affect them.
18 **But it is good** to be zealously
affected always in a good thing,
and not only when I am present
with you.
19 **My little children**, {of whom I
travail in birth again} {until
Christ be formed in you},
20 I desire to be present with you
now,
and to change my voice;
for I stand in doubt of you.
21 **Tell** me, ye that desire to be under
the law,
do ye not hear the law?

22 **For it** is written,
that Abraham had two sons, the one by a bondmaid, the other by a freewoman.
23 **But he who was of the bondwoman** was born after the flesh;
but he of the freewoman was by promise.
24 **Which things** are an allegory:
for these are the two covenants; the one from the mount Sinai,
which gendereth to bondage,
which is Agar.
25 **For this Agar** is mount Sinai in Arabia,
and answereth to Jerusalem which now is,
and is in bondage with her children.
26 **But Jerusalem which is above** is free,
which is the mother of us all.
27 **For it** is written,
Rejoice, thou barren that bearest not;
break forth and cry, thou that travailest not:
for the desolate hath many more children than she which hath an husband.
28 **Now we, brethren,** {as Isaac was}, are the children of promise.
29 **But as then he that was born after the flesh** persecuted him that was born after the Spirit,
even so it is now.
30 **Nevertheless what** saith the scripture?
Cast out the bondwoman and her son:
for the son of the bondwoman shall not be heir with the son of the freewoman.
31 **So then, brethren, we** are not children of the bondwoman, but of the free.

5

Stand fast therefore in the liberty wherewith Christ hath made us free,
and be not entangled again with the yoke of bondage.
2 **Behold,**
I Paul say unto you,
that if ye be circumcised,
Christ shall profit you nothing.
3 **For I** testify again to every man that is circumcised,
that he is a debtor to do the whole law.
4 **Christ** is become of no effect unto you,
whosoever of you are justified by the law;
ye are fallen from grace.
5 **For we through the Spirit** wait for the hope of righteousness by faith.
6 **For in Jesus Christ** neither circumcision availeth any thing, nor uncircumcision; but faith which worketh by love.
7 **Ye** did run well;
who did hinder you
that ye should not obey the truth?
8 **This persuasion** cometh not of him that calleth you.
9 **A little leaven** leaveneth the whole lump.
10 **I** have confidence in you through the Lord,
that ye will be none otherwise minded:
but he that troubleth you shall bear his judgment,
whosoever he be.
11 **And I, brethren, if I** yet preach circumcision,
why do I yet suffer persecution?
then is the offence of the cross ceased.
12 **I** would
they were even cut off which trouble you.
13 **For, brethren, ye** have been called unto liberty;
only use not liberty for an occasion to the flesh,
but by love serve one another.
14 **For all the law** is fulfilled in one word, even in this;
Thou shalt love thy neighbour as thyself.
15 **But if ye** bite and devour one another,
take heed that ye be not consumed one of another.
16 **This** I say then,
Walk in the Spirit,
and ye shall not fulfil the lust of the flesh.
17 **For the flesh** lusteth against the Spirit,
and the Spirit against the flesh:
and these are contrary the one to the other:
so that ye cannot do the things that ye would.
18 **But if ye** be led of the Spirit,
ye are not under the law.
19 **Now the works of the flesh** are manifest,
which are these; Adultery, fornication, uncleanness, lasciviousness,
20 Idolatry, witchcraft, hatred, variance, emulations, wrath, strife, seditions, heresies,
21 Envyings, murders, drunkenness, revellings, and such like:
of the which I tell you before,
as I have also told you in time past,
that they which do such things shall not inherit the kingdom of God.
22 **But the fruit of the Spirit** is love, joy, peace, longsuffering, gentleness, goodness, faith,
23 Meekness, temperance:
against such there is no law.
24 **And they that are Christ's** have crucified the flesh with the affections and lusts.
25 **If we** live in the Spirit,
let us also walk in the Spirit.
26 **Let us not** be desirous of vain glory,
provoking one another,
envying one another.

6

Brethren, if a man be overtaken in a fault,
ye which are spiritual, restore such an one in the spirit of meekness;
considering thyself,
lest thou also be tempted.
2 **Bear ye** one another's burdens,
and so fulfil the law of Christ.
3 **For if a man** think himself to be something,
when he is nothing,
he deceiveth himself.
4 **But let every man** prove his own work,
and then shall he have rejoicing in himself alone, and not in another.
5 **For every man** shall bear his own burden.
6 **Let him that is taught in the word** communicate unto him that teacheth in all good things.
7 **Be not** deceived;
God is not mocked:
for whatsoever a man soweth,

that shall he also reap.

8 **For he that soweth to his flesh**
shall of the flesh reap corruption;
but he that soweth to the Spirit
shall of the Spirit reap life
everlasting.

9 **And let us not** be weary in well
doing:
for in due season we shall reap,
if we faint not.

10 **As we** have therefore opportunity,
let us do good unto all men,
especially unto them who are of
the household of faith.

11 **Ye** see how large a letter I have
written unto you with mine own
hand.

12 **As many as** desire to make a fair
shew in the flesh,
they constrain you to be
circumcised;
only lest they should suffer
persecution for the cross of
Christ.

13 **For neither they themselves
who are circumcised** keep the
law;
but desire to have you circumcised,
that they may glory in your flesh.

14 **But God** forbid
that I should glory, save in the cross
of our Lord Jesus Christ,
by whom the world is crucified
unto me, and I unto the world.

15 **For in Christ Jesus** neither
circumcision availeth any thing,
nor uncircumcision, but a new
creature.

16 **And as many as** walk according to
this rule,
peace be on them, and mercy, and
upon the Israel of God.

17 **From henceforth let no man**
trouble me:
for I bear in my body the marks of
the Lord Jesus.

18 **Brethren, the grace of our Lord
Jesus Christ** be with your spirit.
Amen.

Ephesians

The Apostle Paul wrote the Book of Ephesians while imprisoned in Rome. He addresses his letter to the early Christian community in Ephesus, now part of modern-day Turkey. He begins by emphasizing the importance of prayer in the life of a believer and by showing the Ephesians how deeply he cares for them. Paul prays for them, asking God to strengthen their faith and grant them spiritual wisdom and understanding. This act of prayer is not just a formality but a testament to the value and importance of the Ephesians in the eyes of God. The letter then highlights the role of faith in the salvation of believers, teaching that, by grace, believers are saved through faith and not by their works. This concept is a cornerstone of Christian theology and has significant implications for how believers understand their relationship with God.

Ephesians also unveils the mystery of the gospel, a revelation that includes Gentiles in the salvation plan. Paul clarifies that the gospel is not exclusive to the Jews but is for everyone. He then underscores the need for Christians to foster unity and harmony within the body of Christ. This central theme permeates the book as Paul emphasizes the importance of collaboration and avoiding divisions and disputes. Paul also depicts the spiritual battle Christians face against evil forces. He urges believers to don God's armor and stand firm in their faith, relying on the power of the Holy Spirit for protection. Finally, Paul provides guidance on the roles of husbands and wives within the context of marriage. He teaches that husbands should love their wives as Christ loved the church. However, wives should also submit to their husbands out of respect for their leadership.

The Book of Ephesians is not a mere collection of theological concepts but a practical guide to living a life of faith. It offers valuable insights into the nature of salvation, the importance of unity, and the power of prayer. By studying these teachings, believers can cultivate a growing faith and a deepening understanding of God's plan for their lives. It also provides practical guidance on building strong relationships, particularly within marriage and the church. This emphasis on practicality serves to equip and empower believers, demonstrating that faith is a practical tool they can apply to their daily lives. The book also reminds believers that they are engaged in a spiritual battle against evil, providing a clearer understanding of the battle's nature and how to rely on the power of God to overcome it. Finally, Paul's letter is replete with encouragement and inspiration for believers who struggle or face difficult times, guiding them to understand their identity in Christ, their unity in the body of believers, and their ultimate purpose of glorifying God through actions and devotion. It reminds Christians everywhere that they are not mere spectators in this story but active participants with a divine calling.

1 **Paul, an apostle of Jesus Christ by the will of God,** to the saints which are at Ephesus,
and to the faithful in Christ Jesus:
2 **Grace** be to you, {and peace}, from God our Father,
and from the Lord Jesus Christ.
3 **Blessed** be the God and Father of our Lord Jesus Christ,
who hath blessed us with all spiritual blessings in heavenly places in Christ:
4 **According as he** hath chosen us in him before the foundation of the world,
that we should be holy and without blame before him in love:
5 Having predestinated us unto the adoption of children by Jesus Christ to himself, according to the good pleasure of his will,
6 To the praise of the glory of his grace,
wherein he hath made us accepted in the beloved.
7 **In whom** we have redemption through his blood, the forgiveness of sins, according to the riches of his grace;
8 **Wherein** he hath abounded toward us in all wisdom and prudence;
9 Having made known unto us the mystery of his will, according to his good pleasure
which he hath purposed in himself:
10 **That in the dispensation of the fulness of times** he might gather together in one all things in Christ,
both which are in heaven,
and which are on earth; even in him:
11 **In whom** also we have obtained an inheritance,
being predestinated according to the purpose of him who worketh all things after the counsel of his own will:
12 **That we** should be to the praise of his glory,
who first trusted in Christ.
13 **In whom** ye also trusted,
after that ye heard the word of truth, the gospel of your salvation:
in whom also {after that ye believed}, ye were sealed with that holy Spirit of promise,
14 **Which** is the earnest of our inheritance until the redemption

of the purchased possession, unto the praise of his glory.
15 **Wherefore I** also, {after I heard of your faith in the Lord Jesus, and love unto all the saints},
16 Cease not to give thanks for you,
making mention of you in my prayers;
17 **That the God of our Lord Jesus Christ, the Father of glory,** may give unto you the spirit of wisdom and revelation in the knowledge of him:
18 **The eyes of your understanding** being enlightened;
that ye may know
what is the hope of his calling,
and what the riches of the glory of his inheritance in the saints,
19 **And what** is the exceeding greatness of his power to us-ward who believe, according to the working of his mighty power,
20 **Which he** wrought in Christ,
when he raised him from the dead,
and set him at his own right hand in the heavenly places,
21 Far above all principality, and power, and might, and dominion, and every name that is named, not only in this world, but also in that which is to come:
22 **And** hath put all things under his feet,
and gave him to be the head over all things to the church,
23 **Which** is his body, the fulness of him that filleth all in all.

2

And you hath he quickened, **who** were dead in trespasses and sins;
2 **Wherein** in time past ye walked according to the course of this world, according to the prince of the power of the air, the spirit that now worketh in the children of disobedience:
3 **Among whom** also we all had our conversation in times past in the lusts of our flesh,
fulfilling the desires of the flesh and of the mind;
and were by nature the children of wrath, even as others.
4 **But God,** {who is rich in mercy, for his great love wherewith he loved us},
5 {Even when we were dead in sins}, hath quickened us together with Christ,
(by grace ye are saved;)
6 **And** hath raised us up together,
and made us sit together in heavenly places in Christ Jesus:
7 **That in the ages to come** he might shew the exceeding riches of his grace in his kindness toward us through Christ Jesus.
8 **For by grace** are ye saved through faith; and that not of yourselves:
it is the gift of God:
9 Not of works,
lest any man should boast.
10 **For we** are his workmanship,
created in Christ Jesus unto good works,
which God hath before ordained
that we should walk in them.
11 **Wherefore remember,**
that ye {being in time past Gentiles in the flesh}, {who are called Uncircumcision by that which is called the Circumcision in the flesh made by hands};
12 That at that time ye were without Christ,
being aliens from the commonwealth of Israel, and strangers from the covenants of promise,
having no hope, and without God in the world:
13 **But now in Christ Jesus** ye who sometimes were far off are made nigh by the blood of Christ.
14 **For he** is our peace,
who hath made both one,
and hath broken down the middle wall of partition between us;
15 Having abolished in his flesh the enmity, even the law of commandments contained in ordinances;
for to make in himself of twain one new man,
so making peace;
16 **And that he** might reconcile both unto God in one body by the cross,
having slain the enmity thereby:
17 **And** came and preached peace to you which were afar off, and to them that were nigh.
18 **For through him** we both have access by one Spirit unto the Father.
19 **Now therefore ye** are no more strangers and foreigners,
but fellowcitizens with the saints, and of the household of God;
20 **And** are built upon the foundation of the apostles and prophets,
Jesus Christ himself being the chief corner stone;
21 **In whom** all the building fitly framed together groweth unto an holy temple in the Lord:
22 **In whom** ye also are builded together for an habitation of God through the Spirit.

3

For this cause I Paul, the prisoner of Jesus Christ for you Gentiles,
2 **If ye** have heard of the dispensation of the grace of God which is given me to you-ward:
3 **How that by revelation** he made known unto me the mystery;
(as I wrote afore in few words,
4 Whereby, {when ye read}, ye may understand my knowledge in the mystery of Christ)
5 **Which in other ages** was not made known unto the sons of men,
as it is now revealed unto his holy apostles and prophets by the Spirit;
6 **That the Gentiles** should be fellowheirs, and of the same body, and partakers of his promise in Christ by the gospel:
7 **Whereof** I was made a minister, according to the gift of the grace of God given unto me by the effectual working of his power.
8 **Unto me,** {who am less than the least of all saints}, is this grace given,
that I should preach among the Gentiles the unsearchable riches of Christ;
9 **And** to make all men see
what is the fellowship of the mystery,
which from the beginning of the world hath been hid in God,
who created all things by Jesus Christ:
10 **To the intent that now unto the principalities and powers in heavenly places** might be known by the church the manifold wisdom of God,
11 According to the eternal purpose which he purposed in Christ Jesus our Lord:
12 **In whom** we have boldness and access with confidence by the faith of him.

13 **Wherefore I** desire
that ye faint not at my tribulations for you,
which is your glory.
14 **For this cause** I bow my knees unto the Father of our Lord Jesus Christ,
15 **Of whom** the whole family in heaven and earth is named,
16 **That he** would grant you, according to the riches of his glory, to be strengthened with might by his Spirit in the inner man;
17 **That Christ** may dwell in your hearts by faith;
that ye, {being rooted and grounded in love},
18 May be able to comprehend with all saints
what is the breadth, and length, and depth, and height;
19 **And** to know the love of Christ,
which passeth knowledge,
that ye might be filled with all the fulness of God.
20 **Now unto him that is able to do exceeding abundantly above all that we ask or think, according to the power that worketh in us,**
21 Unto him be glory in the church by Christ Jesus throughout all ages, world without end.
Amen.

4 **I** therefore, the prisoner of the Lord, beseech you
that ye walk worthy of the vocation wherewith ye are called,
2 With all lowliness and meekness, with longsuffering,
forbearing one another in love;
3 Endeavouring to keep the unity of the Spirit in the bond of peace.
4 **There** is one body, and one Spirit,
even as ye are called in one hope of your calling;
5 One Lord, one faith, one baptism,
6 One God and Father of all,
who is above all, and through all, and in you all.
7 **But unto every one of us** is given grace according to the measure of the gift of Christ.
8 **Wherefore he** saith,
When he ascended up on high,
he led captivity captive,
and gave gifts unto men.
9 (**Now that he** ascended,
what is it
but that he also descended first into the lower parts of the earth?
10 **He that descended** is the same also that ascended up far above all heavens,
that he might fill all things.)
11 **And he** gave some, apostles; and some, prophets; and some, evangelists; and some, pastors and teachers;
12 For the perfecting of the saints, for the work of the ministry, for the edifying of the body of Christ:
13 **Till we all** come in the unity of the faith, and of the knowledge of the Son of God, unto a perfect man, unto the measure of the stature of the fulness of Christ:
14 **That we henceforth** be no more children,
tossed to and fro,
and carried about with every wind of doctrine, by the sleight of men, and cunning craftiness,
whereby they lie in wait to deceive;
15 **But {speaking the truth in love}**, may grow up into him in all things,
which is the head, even Christ:
16 **From whom** the whole body fitly joined together and compacted by that which every joint supplieth, according to the effectual working in the measure of every part, maketh increase of the body unto the edifying of itself in love.
17 **This** I say therefore,
and testify in the Lord,
that ye henceforth walk not as other Gentiles walk, in the vanity of their mind,
18 Having the understanding darkened,
being alienated from the life of God through the ignorance that is in them, because of the blindness of their heart:
19 **Who being past feeling** have given themselves over unto lasciviousness,
to work all uncleanness with greediness.
20 **But ye** have not so learned Christ;
21 **If so be that ye** have heard him,
and have been taught by him,
as the truth is in Jesus:
22 **That ye** put off concerning the former conversation the old man,
which is corrupt according to the deceitful lusts;
23 **And** be renewed in the spirit of your mind;
24 **And that ye** put on the new man,
which after God is created in righteousness and true holiness.
25 **Wherefore putting away** lying,
speak every man truth with his neighbour:
for we are members one of another.
26 **Be ye** angry,
and sin not:
let not the sun go down upon your wrath:
27 **Neither give place** to the devil.
28 **Let him that stole** steal no more:
but rather let him labour,
working with his hands the thing which is good,
that he may have to give to him that needeth.
29 **Let no corrupt communication** proceed out of your mouth, but that which is good to the use of edifying,
that it may minister grace unto the hearers.
30 **And grieve not** the holy Spirit of God,
whereby ye are sealed unto the day of redemption.
31 **Let all bitterness, and wrath, and anger, and clamour, and evil speaking,** be put away from you, with all malice:
32 **be ye** kind one to another, tenderhearted,
forgiving one another,
even as God for Christ's sake hath forgiven you.

5 **Be ye** therefore followers of God, as dear children;
2 **And walk** in love,
as Christ also hath loved us,
and hath given himself for us an offering and a sacrifice to God for a sweetsmelling savour.
3 **But fornication, and all uncleanness, or covetousness,** let it not be once named among you,
as becometh saints;
4 Neither filthiness, nor foolish talking, nor jesting,
which are not convenient:
but rather giving of thanks.
5 **For this** ye know,
that no whoremonger, nor unclean person, nor covetous man, {who is an idolater}, hath

any inheritance in the kingdom of Christ and of God.
6 **Let no man** deceive you with vain words:
for because of these things cometh the wrath of God upon the children of disobedience.
7 **Be not ye** therefore partakers with them.
8 **For ye** were sometimes darkness,
but now are ye light in the Lord:
walk as children of light:
9 (For the fruit of the Spirit is in all goodness and righteousness and truth;)
10 Proving what is acceptable unto the Lord.
11 **And have** no fellowship with the unfruitful works of darkness,
but rather reprove them.
12 **For it is a shame** even to speak of those things which are done of them in secret.
13 **But all things that are reproved** are made manifest by the light:
for whatsoever doth make manifest is light.
14 **Wherefore he** saith,
Awake thou that sleepest,
and arise from the dead,
and Christ shall give thee light.
15 **See** then
that ye walk circumspectly, not as fools, but as wise,
16 Redeeming the time,
because the days are evil.
17 **Wherefore be ye not** unwise,
but understanding
what the will of the Lord is.
18 **And be not** drunk with wine,
wherein is excess;
but be filled with the Spirit;
19 Speaking to yourselves in psalms and hymns and spiritual songs,
singing and making melody in your heart to the Lord;
20 Giving thanks always for all things unto God and the Father in the name of our Lord Jesus Christ;
21 Submitting yourselves one to another in the fear of God.
22 **Wives, submit** yourselves unto your own husbands, as unto the Lord.
23 **For the husband** is the head of the wife,
even as Christ is the head of the church:
and he is the saviour of the body.
24 **Therefore as the church** is subject unto Christ,
so let the wives be to their own husbands in every thing.
25 **Husbands, love** your wives,
even as Christ also loved the church,
and gave himself for it;
26 **That he** might sanctify and cleanse it with the washing of water by the word,
27 **That he** might present it to himself a glorious church,
not having spot, or wrinkle, or any such thing;
but that it should be holy and without blemish.
28 **So** ought men to love their wives as their own bodies.
He that loveth his wife loveth himself.
29 **For no man** ever yet hated his own flesh;
but nourisheth and cherisheth it, even as the Lord the church:
30 **For we** are members of his body, of his flesh, and of his bones.
31 **For this cause** shall a man leave his father and mother,
and shall be joined unto his wife,
and they two shall be one flesh.
32 **This** is a great mystery:
but I speak concerning Christ and the church.
33 **Nevertheless let every one of you** in particular so love his wife even as himself;
and the wife see that she reverence her husband.

6

Children, obey your parents in the Lord:
for this is right.
2 **Honour** thy father and mother;
which is the first commandment with promise;
3 **That it** may be well with thee,
and thou mayest live long on the earth.
4 **And, ye fathers, provoke not** your children to wrath:
but bring them up in the nurture and admonition of the Lord.
5 **Servants, be** obedient to them that are your masters according to the flesh, with fear and trembling, in singleness of your heart, as unto Christ;
6 Not with eyeservice, as menpleasers; but as the servants of Christ,
doing the will of God from the heart;
7 **With good will** doing service, as to the Lord, and not to men:
8 Knowing
that whatsoever good thing any man doeth,
the same shall he receive of the Lord,
whether he be bond or free.
9 **And, ye masters, do** the same things unto them,
forbearing threatening:
knowing
that your Master also is in heaven;
neither is there respect of persons with him.
10 **Finally, my brethren, be** strong in the Lord, and in the power of his might.
11 **Put on** the whole armour of God,
that ye may be able to stand against the wiles of the devil.
12 **For we** wrestle not against flesh and blood, but against principalities, against powers, against the rulers of the darkness of this world, against spiritual wickedness in high places.
13 **Wherefore take unto you** the whole armour of God,
that ye may be able to withstand in the evil day,
and having done all,
to stand.
14 **Stand** therefore,
having your loins girt about with truth,
and having on the breastplate of righteousness;
15 **And your feet** shod with the preparation of the gospel of peace;
16 **Above all,** taking the shield of faith,
wherewith ye shall be able to quench all the fiery darts of the wicked.
17 **And take** the helmet of salvation, and the sword of the Spirit,
which is the word of God:
18 Praying always with all prayer and supplication in the Spirit,
and watching thereunto with all perseverance and supplication for all saints;
19 **And for me,** that utterance may be given unto me,
that I may open my mouth boldly,

to make known the mystery of the
gospel,
20 **For which** I am an ambassador in
bonds:
that therein I may speak boldly,
as I ought to speak.
21 **But that ye** also may know my
affairs,
and how I do,
**Tychicus, a beloved brother and
faithful minister in the Lord,**
shall make known to you all
things:
22 **Whom** I have sent unto you for
the same purpose,
that ye might know our affairs,
and that he might comfort your
hearts.
23 **Peace** be to the brethren, and love
with faith, from God the Father
and the Lord Jesus Christ.
24 **Grace** be with all them that love
our Lord Jesus Christ in sincerity.
Amen.

Philippians

The Apostle Paul writes the Book of Philippians while imprisoned in Rome. He addresses the letter to the Christian community in Philippi, a city in ancient Macedonia whose ruins today are located in northeastern Greece. His primary purpose in writing the epistle is to express gratitude and affection for the Christian community in Philippi and to accomplish several goals. First, he wants to strengthen the Philippian church's unity and address any conflicts or divisions that might have arisen within the community. Second, he aims to encourage the Philippians to hold firm in their faith despite the challenges of persecution and hardship. Third, he wants to share his experience of imprisonment as a testament to the power of faith and the importance of endurance. He believes that his suffering is not in vain but serves as an opportunity to preach the gospel and bring glory to God. Fourth, Paul hopes to express his gratitude for the financial support the Philippian Church has provided him and to emphasize the importance of generosity and unity within the broader body of Christ.

Philippians accomplishes these goals in various ways, all of which have impacted Christian theology and practice. The Apostle emphasizes the importance of finding joy and contentment in all circumstances, even in the face of hardship and persecution. He encourages the Philippians to always rejoice in the Lord and find their strength and joy in their relationship with Christ. Paul urges the Church to attain unity and harmony within their community, reminding them that they are all part of the same body of believers. He encourages them to work together, serve one another, and put aside any possible divisions.

He also teaches that true greatness in the kingdom of God is found in humility and service to others, and he uses his own example of service to Christ and His disiciples as a model to follow. In addition, Paul emphasizes the need for prayer in the life of a believer, both for personal growth and for the well-being of others. He then encourages the Philippians to pray for him and one another and to remain steadfast in their faith through prayer. Finally, throughout the letter, Paul exalts the person and work of Jesus Christ, emphasizing His preeminence and the importance of knowing Him. He encourages the Philippians to have the mind of Christ, to live in a manner worthy of the gospel, and to hold fast to the truth of the faith.

The Book of Philippians is a powerful and encouraging letter that provides valuable insights into the nature of the Christian faith. Within its pages, the Church in Philippi and Christians everywhere will find a comforting reminder that one's true citizenship is in heaven and that believers are called to live a life of humility, love, and unity, always seeking to honor and glorify Jesus Christ. It also declares that finding joy in every circumstance and living a life worthy of the gospel will release the power of faith. Finally, it argues that even in the midst of adversity, one can find contentment and peace through a solid commitment to Jesus Christ. Therefore, it urges all believers to embrace the divine purpose that unites them all.

1 **Paul and Timotheus, the servants of Jesus Christ,** to all the saints in Christ Jesus which are at Philippi, with the bishops and deacons:

2 **Grace** be unto you, {and peace}, from God our Father,
and from the Lord Jesus Christ.

3 **I** thank my God upon every remembrance of you,
4 **Always in every prayer of mine for you all** making request with joy,
5 For your fellowship in the gospel from the first day until now;
6 Being confident of this very thing,
that he which hath begun a good work in you will perform it until the day of Jesus Christ:
7 **Even as it is meet for me** to think this of you all,
because I have you in my heart;
inasmuch as both in my bonds, and in the defence and confirmation of the gospel, ye all are partakers of my grace.

8 **For God** is my record,
how greatly I long after you all in the bowels of Jesus Christ.

9 **And this** I pray,
that your love may abound yet more and more in knowledge and in all judgment;
10 **That ye** may approve things that are excellent;
that ye may be sincere and without offence till the day of Christ.

11 Being filled with the fruits of righteousness,
which are by Jesus Christ, unto the glory and praise of God.

12 **But I** would ye should understand, brethren,
that the things which happened unto me have fallen out rather unto the furtherance of the gospel;
13 **So that my bonds in Christ** are manifest in all the palace, and in all other places;

14 **And many of the brethren in the Lord**, {waxing confident by my bonds}, are much more bold to speak the word without fear.

15 **Some** indeed preach Christ even of envy and strife; and some also of good will:

16 **The one** preach Christ of contention, not sincerely,
supposing to add affliction to my bonds:

17 But the other of love,
knowing
that I am set for the defence of the gospel.

18 What then?
notwithstanding, every way, whether in pretence, or in truth, Christ is preached;
and I therein do rejoice,
yea, and will rejoice.

19 **For I** know
that this shall turn to my salvation through your prayer, and the supply of the Spirit of Jesus Christ,

20 According to my earnest expectation and my hope,
that in nothing I shall be ashamed,
but that with all boldness, as always, so now also Christ shall be magnified in my body,
whether it be by life, or by death.

21 **For to me** to live is Christ,
and to die is gain.

22 **But if I** live in the flesh,
this is the fruit of my labour:
yet what I shall choose
I wot not.

23 **For I** am in a strait betwixt two,
having a desire to depart,
and to be with Christ;
which is far better:

24 **Nevertheless to abide in the flesh** is more needful for you.

25 **And** having this confidence,
I know
that I shall abide and continue with you all for your furtherance and joy of faith;

26 **That your rejoicing** may be more abundant in Jesus Christ for me by my coming to you again.

27 **Only let your conversation** be as it becometh the gospel of Christ:
that whether I come and see you,
or else be absent,
I may hear of your affairs,
that ye stand fast in one spirit, with one mind striving together for the faith of the gospel;

28 **And in nothing** terrified by your adversaries:
which is to them an evident token of perdition, but to you of salvation, and that of God.

29 **For unto you** it is given in the behalf of Christ,
not only to believe on him,
but also to suffer for his sake;

30 Having the same conflict
which ye saw in me,
and now hear to be in me.

2 **If there** be therefore any consolation in Christ, if any comfort of love, if any fellowship of the Spirit, if any bowels and mercies,

2 **Fulfil ye** my joy,
that ye be likeminded,
having the same love,
being of one accord, of one mind.

3 **Let nothing** be done through strife or vainglory;
but in lowliness of mind let each esteem other better than themselves.

4 **Look not** every man on his own things, but every man also on the things of others.

5 **Let this mind** be in you,
which was also in Christ Jesus:

6 **Who**, {being in the form of God}, thought it not robbery to be equal with God:

7 **But** made himself of no reputation,
and took upon him the form of a servant,
and was made in the likeness of men:

8 **And** being found in fashion as a man,
he humbled himself,
and became obedient unto death, even the death of the cross.

9 **Wherefore God** also hath highly exalted him,
and given him a name which is above every name:

10 **That at the name of Jesus** every knee should bow, of things in heaven, and things in earth, and things under the earth;

11 **And that every tongue** should confess
that Jesus Christ is Lord, to the glory of God the Father.

12 **Wherefore, my beloved, {as ye have always obeyed}, not as in my presence only, but now much more in my absence,** work out your own salvation with fear and trembling.

13 **For it is God** which worketh in you
both to will
and to do of his good pleasure.

14 **Do** all things without murmurings and disputings:

15 **That ye** may be blameless and harmless, the sons of God, without rebuke, in the midst of a crooked and perverse nation,
among whom ye shine as lights in the world;

16 Holding forth the word of life;
that I may rejoice in the day of Christ,
that I have not run in vain,
neither laboured in vain.

17 **Yea, and if I** be offered upon the sacrifice and service of your faith,
I joy,
and rejoice with you all.

18 **For the same cause** also do ye joy,
and rejoice with me.

19 **But I** trust in the Lord Jesus to send Timotheus shortly unto you,
that I also may be of good comfort,
when I know your state.

20 **For I** have no man likeminded,
who will naturally care for your state.

21 **For all** seek their own, not the things which are Jesus Christ's.

22 **But ye** know the proof of him,
that, as a son with the father, he hath served with me in the gospel.

23 **Him** therefore I hope to send presently,
so soon as I shall see how it will go with me.

24 **But I** trust in the Lord
that I also myself shall come shortly.

25 **Yet I** supposed it necessary to send to you Epaphroditus, my brother, and companion in labour, and fellowsoldier, but your messenger, and he that ministered to my wants.

26 **For he** longed after you all,
and was full of heaviness,
because that ye had heard that he had been sick.

[27] **For indeed he** was sick nigh unto death:
but God had mercy on him; and not on him only, but on me also,
lest I should have sorrow upon sorrow.

[28] **I** sent him therefore the more carefully,
that, {when ye see him again}, ye may rejoice,
and that I may be the less sorrowful.

[29] **Receive** him therefore in the Lord with all gladness;
and hold such in reputation:
[30] **Because for the work of Christ** he was nigh unto death,
not regarding his life,
to supply your lack of service toward me.

3

Finally, my brethren, rejoice in the Lord.
To write the same things to you, to me indeed is not grievous,
but for you it is safe.

[2] **Beware** of dogs,
beware of evil workers,
beware of the concision.

[3] **For we** are the circumcision,
which worship God in the spirit,
and rejoice in Christ Jesus,
and have no confidence in the flesh.

[4] **Though I** might also have confidence in the flesh.

If any other man thinketh
that he hath whereof he might trust in the flesh, I more:
[5] Circumcised the eighth day, of the stock of Israel, of the tribe of Benjamin, an Hebrew of the Hebrews; as touching the law, a Pharisee;
[6] **Concerning zeal,** persecuting the church;
touching the righteousness which is in the law, blameless.

[7] **But what things** were gain to me,
those I counted loss for Christ.

[8] **Yea doubtless, and I** count all things but loss for the excellency of the knowledge of Christ Jesus my Lord:
for whom I have suffered the loss of all things,
and do count them but dung,
that I may win Christ,
[9] **And** be found in him,
not having mine own righteousness, {which is of the law}, but that which is through the faith of Christ, the righteousness which is of God by faith:
[10] **That I** may know him, and the power of his resurrection, and the fellowship of his sufferings,
being made conformable unto his death;
[11] **If by any means** I might attain unto the resurrection of the dead.

[12] **Not as though I** had already attained,
either were already perfect:
but I follow after,
if that I may apprehend that for which also I am apprehended of Christ Jesus.

[13] **Brethren, I** count not myself to have apprehended:
but this one thing I do,
forgetting those things which are behind,
and reaching forth unto those things which are before,
[14] I press toward the mark for the prize of the high calling of God in Christ Jesus.

[15] **Let us** therefore, {as many as be perfect}, be thus minded:
and if in any thing ye be otherwise minded,
God shall reveal even this unto you.

[16] **Nevertheless, whereto we** have already attained,
let us walk by the same rule,
let us mind the same thing.

[17] **Brethren, be** followers together of me,
and mark them which walk
so as ye have us for an ensample.

[18] (**For many** walk,
of whom I have told you often,
and now tell you even weeping,
that they are the enemies of the cross of Christ:
[19] **Whose end** is destruction,
whose God is their belly,
and whose glory is in their shame,
who mind earthly things.)

[20] **For our conversation** is in heaven;
from whence also we look for the Saviour, the Lord Jesus Christ:
[21] **Who** shall change our vile body,
that it may be fashioned like unto his glorious body, according to the working whereby he is able even to subdue all things unto himself.

4

Therefore, my brethren dearly beloved and longed for, my joy and crown, so stand fast in the Lord, my dearly beloved.

[2] **I** beseech Euodias,
and beseech Syntyche,
that they be of the same mind in the Lord.

[3] **And I** intreat thee also, true yokefellow,
help those women which laboured with me in the gospel, with Clement also, and with other my fellowlabourers,
whose names are in the book of life.

[4] **Rejoice** in the Lord always:
and again I say,
Rejoice.

[5] **Let your moderation** be known unto all men.

The Lord is at hand.

[6] **Be careful** for nothing;
but in every thing by prayer and supplication with thanksgiving let your requests be made known unto God.

[7] **And the peace of God**, {which passeth all understanding}, shall keep your hearts and minds through Christ Jesus.

[8] **Finally, brethren, whatsoever things** are true,
whatsoever things are honest,
whatsoever things are just,
whatsoever things are pure,
whatsoever things are lovely,
whatsoever things are of good report;
if there be any virtue,
and if there be any praise,
think on these things.

[9] **Those things**, {which ye have both learned}, {and received}, {and heard}, {and seen in me}, do:
and the God of peace shall be with you.

[10] **But I** rejoiced in the Lord greatly,
that now at the last your care of me hath flourished again;
wherein ye were also careful,
but ye lacked opportunity.

[11] **Not that I** speak in respect of want:
for I have learned,
in whatsoever state I am,
therewith to be content.

[12] **I** know

both how to be abased,
and I know
how to abound:
every where and in all things I am instructed
both to be full
and to be hungry,
both to abound
and to suffer need.
13 **I** can do all things through Christ which strengtheneth me.
14 **Notwithstanding ye** have well done,
that ye did communicate with my affliction.
15 **Now ye Philippians** know also,
that in the beginning of the gospel, {when I departed from Macedonia}, no church communicated with me as concerning giving and receiving, but ye only.
16 **For even in Thessalonica** ye sent once and again unto my necessity.
17 **Not because I** desire a gift:
but I desire fruit that may abound to your account.
18 **But I** have all,
and abound:
I am full,
having received of Epaphroditus the things which were sent from you, an odour of a sweet smell, a sacrifice acceptable, wellpleasing to God.
19 **But my God** shall supply all your need according to his riches in glory by Christ Jesus.
20 **Now unto God and our Father** be glory for ever and ever.
Amen.
21 **Salute** every saint in Christ Jesus.
The brethren which are with me greet you.
22 **All the saints** salute you, chiefly they that are of Caesar's household.
23 **The grace of our Lord Jesus Christ** be with you all.
Amen.

Colossians

The Book of Colossians, written by the Apostle Paul while imprisoned in Rome, is addressed to the Church in Colossae, a city in the Roman province of Asia Minor or modern-day Turkey. Paul writes the letter to address specific issues and concerns within the Church about some false teachings possibly influenced by Gnosticism, a belief system that promotes secret knowledge and spiritual enlightenment. In his correspondence, he tackles this concern by clarifying the true nature of Christ and the Christian faith. He emphasizes that Christ is supreme and sufficient and that believers don't need additional knowledge or secret teachings to access God's grace and salvation.

Paul opens his letter with a powerful declaration of Christ's preeminence by presenting Him as the image of God, the Creator and sustainer of all things, and the head of the Church. He underscores the importance of Christ's supremacy in the life of believers, a fact that empowers them in their spiritual journey. The Apostle then warns against being deceived by false teachings and emphasizes that through faith in Christ, believers are forgiven of their sins and granted new life. He also instructs believers on how to live a life that is pleasing to God by putting to death sinful behaviors and adopting Christ-like virtues, such as love, compassion, and forgiveness. Furthermore, he reassures believers that prayer is a powerful tool for strengthening faith and spreading the gospel. Paul closes his letter by underscoring the importance of the Christian community, teaching that believers should support one another, live in harmony, and work together to spread the gospel.

The Book of Colossians provides a clear and persuasive argument about the supremacy and sufficiency of Christ. It helps believers understand who Christ is and why He is central to the Christian faith. With insightful teaching and wisdom, Paul reminds all Christians about their divine calling to seek the truth and live in communion with their Creator and each other.

1 **Paul, an apostle of Jesus Christ by the will of God, and Timotheus our brother,**
2 To the saints and faithful brethren in Christ which are at Colosse:
Grace be unto you, {and peace}, from God our Father and the Lord Jesus Christ.
3 **We** give thanks to God and the Father of our Lord Jesus Christ,
praying always for you,
4 **Since we** heard of your faith in Christ Jesus, and of the love which ye have to all the saints,
5 For the hope which is laid up for you in heaven,
whereof ye heard before in the word of the truth of the gospel;
6 **Which** is come unto you,
as it is in all the world;
and bringeth forth fruit,
as it doth also in you,
since the day ye heard of it,
and knew the grace of God in truth:
7 **As ye** also learned of Epaphras our dear fellowservant,
who is for you a faithful minister of Christ;
8 **Who** also declared unto us your love in the Spirit.
9 **For this cause** we also, {since the day we heard it}, do not cease to pray for you,
and to desire
that ye might be filled with the knowledge of his will in all wisdom and spiritual understanding;
10 **That ye** might walk worthy of the Lord unto all pleasing,
being fruitful in every good work,
and increasing in the knowledge of God;
11 Strengthened with all might, according to his glorious power, unto all patience and longsuffering with joyfulness;
12 Giving thanks unto the Father,
which hath made us meet to be partakers of the inheritance of the saints in light:
13 **Who** hath delivered us from the power of darkness,
and hath translated us into the kingdom of his dear Son:
14 **In whom** we have redemption through his blood, even the forgiveness of sins:
15 **Who** is the image of the invisible God, the firstborn of every creature:
16 **For by him** were all things created,
that are in heaven,
and that are in earth, visible and invisible,
whether they be thrones, or dominions, or principalities, or powers:
all things were created by him, and for him:
17 **And he** is before all things,
and by him all things consist.
18 **And he** is the head of the body, the church:
who is the beginning, the firstborn from the dead;
that in all things he might have the preeminence.
19 **For it pleased the Father** that in him should all fulness dwell;
20 **And, {having made peace through the blood of his cross}**, by him to reconcile all things unto himself; by him,
I say,
whether they be things in earth, or things in heaven.
21 **And you**, {that were sometime alienated and enemies in your mind by wicked works}, yet now hath he reconciled
22 In the body of his flesh through death,

to present you holy and
unblameable and unreproveable
in his sight:
23 **If ye** continue in the faith
grounded and settled,
and be not moved away from the
hope of the gospel,
which ye have heard,
and which was preached to every
creature which is under heaven;
whereof I Paul am made a minister;
24 **Who** now rejoice in my sufferings
for you,
and fill up that which is behind of
the afflictions of Christ in my
flesh for his body's sake,
which is the church:
25 **Whereof** I am made a minister,
according to the dispensation of
God which is given to me for you,
to fulfil the word of God;
26 Even the mystery which hath
been hid from ages and from
generations,
but now is made manifest to his
saints:
27 **To whom** God would make
known
what is the riches of the glory of
this mystery among the Gentiles;
which is Christ in you, the hope of
glory:
28 **Whom** we preach,
warning every man,
and teaching every man in all
wisdom;
that we may present every man
perfect in Christ Jesus:
29 **Whereunto** I also labour,
striving according to his working,
which worketh in me mightily.

2 **For I** would
that ye knew
what great conflict I have for you,
and for them at Laodicea, and for
as many as have not seen my face
in the flesh;
2 **That their hearts** might be
comforted,
being knit together in love, and
unto all riches of the full
assurance of understanding, to
the acknowledgement of the
mystery of God, and of the Father,
and of Christ;
3 **In whom** are hid all the treasures
of wisdom and knowledge.
4 **And this** I say,
lest any man should beguile you
with enticing words.
5 **For though I** be absent in the
flesh,
yet am I with you in the spirit,
joying and beholding your order,
and the stedfastness of your faith
in Christ.
6 **As ye** have therefore received
Christ Jesus the Lord,
so walk ye in him:
7 Rooted and built up in him,
and stablished in the faith,
as ye have been taught,
abounding therein with
thanksgiving.
8 **Beware**
lest any man spoil you through
philosophy and vain deceit, after
the tradition of men, after the
rudiments of the world, and not
after Christ.
9 **For in him** dwelleth all the fulness
of the Godhead bodily.
10 **And ye** are complete in him,
which is the head of all principality
and power:
11 **In whom** also ye are circumcised
with the circumcision made
without hands,
in putting off the body of the sins of
the flesh by the circumcision of
Christ:
12 Buried with him in baptism,
wherein also ye are risen with him
through the faith of the operation
of God,
who hath raised him from the dead.
13 **And you,** {being dead in your sins
and the uncircumcision of your
flesh}, hath he quickened
together with him,
having forgiven you all trespasses;
14 Blotting out the handwriting of
ordinances that was against us,
which was contrary to us,
and took it out of the way,
nailing it to his cross;
15 **And** having spoiled principalities
and powers,
he made a shew of them openly,
triumphing over them in it.
16 **Let no man** therefore judge you in
meat, or in drink, or in respect of
an holyday, or of the new moon,
or of the sabbath days:
17 **Which** are a shadow of things to
come;
but the body is of Christ.
18 **Let no man** beguile you of your
reward in a voluntary humility
and worshipping of angels,
intruding into those things which
he hath not seen,
vainly puffed up by his fleshly mind,
19 **And** not holding the Head,
from which all the body {by joints
and bands having nourishment
ministered}, {and knit together},
increaseth with the increase of
God.
20 **Wherefore if ye** be dead with
Christ from the rudiments of the
world,
why, {as though living in the
world}, are ye subject to
ordinances,
21 ({Touch not}; {taste not}; {handle
not};
22 {Which all are to perish with the
using};) after the commandments
and doctrines of men?
23 **Which things** have indeed a
shew of wisdom in will worship,
and humility, and neglecting of
the body: not in any honour to the
satisfying of the flesh.

3 **If ye** then be risen with Christ,
seek those things which are
above,
where Christ sitteth on the right
hand of God.
2 **Set** your affection on things above,
not on things on the earth.
3 **For ye** are dead,
and your life is hid with Christ in
God.
4 **When Christ**, {who is our life},
shall appear,
then shall ye also appear with him
in glory.
5 **Mortify** therefore your members
which are upon the earth;
fornication, uncleanness,
inordinate affection, evil
concupiscence, and covetousness,
which is idolatry:
6 **For which things' sake** the wrath
of God cometh on the children of
disobedience:
7 **In the which** ye also walked some
time,
when ye lived in them.
8 **But now** ye also put off all these;
anger, wrath, malice, blasphemy,
filthy communication out of your
mouth.
9 **Lie not** one to another,
seeing that ye have put off the old
man with his deeds;
10 **And** have put on the new man,

which is renewed in knowledge after the image of him that created him:
11 **Where there** is neither Greek nor Jew, circumcision nor uncircumcision, Barbarian, Scythian, bond nor free:
but Christ is all, and in all.

12 **Put on** therefore, as the elect of God, holy and beloved, bowels of mercies, kindness, humbleness of mind, meekness, longsuffering;
13 Forbearing one another,
and forgiving one another,
if any man have a quarrel against any:
even as Christ forgave you,
so also do ye.

14 **And above all these things** put on charity,
which is the bond of perfectness.

15 **And let the peace of God** rule in your hearts,
to the which also ye are called in one body;
and be ye thankful.

16 **Let the word of Christ** dwell in you richly in all wisdom;
teaching and admonishing one another in psalms and hymns and spiritual songs,
singing with grace in your hearts to the Lord.

17 **And whatsoever ye** do in word or deed,
do all in the name of the Lord Jesus,
giving thanks to God and the Father by him.

18 **Wives, submit** yourselves unto your own husbands,
as it is fit in the Lord.

19 **Husbands, love** your wives,
and be not bitter against them.

20 **Children, obey** your parents in all things:
for this is well pleasing unto the Lord.

21 **Fathers, provoke not** your children to anger,
lest they be discouraged.

22 **Servants, obey** in all things your masters according to the flesh;
not with eyeservice, as menpleasers; but in singleness of heart,
fearing God;
23 **And whatsoever ye** do,
do it heartily, as to the Lord, and not unto men;
24 Knowing
that of the Lord ye shall receive the reward of the inheritance:
for ye serve the Lord Christ.

25 **But he that doeth wrong** shall receive for the wrong which he hath done:
and there is no respect of persons.

4 **Masters, give** unto your servants that which is just and equal;
knowing
that ye also have a Master in heaven.

2 **Continue** in prayer,
and watch in the same with thanksgiving;
3 **Withal** praying also for us,
that God would open unto us a door of utterance,
to speak the mystery of Christ,
for which I am also in bonds:
4 **That I** may make it manifest,
as I ought to speak.

5 **Walk** in wisdom toward them that are without,
redeeming the time.

6 **Let your speech** be always with grace,
seasoned with salt,
that ye may know
how ye ought to answer every man.

7 **All my state** shall Tychicus declare unto you,
who is a beloved brother, and a faithful minister and fellowservant in the Lord:
8 **Whom** I have sent unto you for the same purpose,
that he might know your estate,
and comfort your hearts;

9 With Onesimus, a faithful and beloved brother,
who is one of you.

They shall make known unto you all things which are done here.

10 **Aristarchus my fellowprisoner** saluteth you, and Marcus, sister's son to Barnabas,
(touching whom ye received commandments:
if he come unto you,
receive him;)
11 And Jesus,
which is called Justus,
who are of the circumcision.

These only are my fellowworkers unto the kingdom of God,
which have been a comfort unto me.

12 **Epaphras,** {who is one of you, a servant of Christ}, saluteth you,
always labouring fervently for you in prayers,
that ye may stand perfect and complete in all the will of God.

13 **For I** bear him record,
that he hath a great zeal for you, and them that are in Laodicea, and them in Hierapolis.

14 **Luke, the beloved physician, and Demas,** greet you.

15 **Salute** the brethren which are in Laodicea, and Nymphas, and the church which is in his house.

16 **And when this epistle** is read among you,
cause that it be read also in the church of the Laodiceans;
and that ye likewise read the epistle from Laodicea.

17 **And say** to Archippus,
Take heed to the ministry which thou hast received in the Lord,
that thou fulfil it.

18 **The salutation** by the hand of me Paul.

Remember my bonds.

Grace be with you.

Amen.

1 Thessalonians

The Apostle Paul wrote the Book of First Thessalonians during his second missionary journey. He encourages the believers in Thessalonica to remain steadfast in their faith and provides guidance on how to live as Christians in a challenging world. Despite not being physically present, he expresses his unwavering love and concern for the Church at Thessalonica. He then addresses their questions about the timing of Jesus' return, assuring them that nobody knows the exact time and they should remain steadfast in their faith. To encourage them along this path, he reminds them to maintain their faith in the face of persecution and adversity by living in a manner that is pleasing to God. Doing so will also provide an example to others. Furthermore, he offers practical advice about how they should behave as Christians, including warnings against living in idleness and engaging in immoral behavior.

Paul addresses another pressing concern of the Thessalonians: the fate of their departed loved ones. He assures them that those who have died in Christ will not be left behind when Jesus returns. They will be raised to meet Him in the air, a promise that brings solace and hope in the face of loss. He also writes about the Holy Spirit as a source of comfort, guidance, and strength for the believers, reminding them of the divine presence always with them. Paul then encourages the Thessalonians to continually pray and give thanks to God for their faith and the blessings they have already received. Finally, he underscores the need for unity and love among believers and offers the following practical advice: treat one another with kindness, patience, and understanding. It can provide solace and strength in their current circumstances.

First Thessalonians is not just a theoretical treatise but a practical guide that directs believers everywhere to a deeper understanding of righteous living. It teaches followers of Christ to stand firm in their faith, endure persecution, and hold on to the hope of His return as they eagerly await the establishment of God's kingdom for themselves and their loved ones. However, its most significant impact lies in its practicality, which empowers believers by showing them they can live as Christians in a challenging world.

1 **Paul, and Silvanus, and Timotheus,** unto the church of the Thessalonians which is in God the Father and in the Lord Jesus Christ:
Grace be unto you, {and peace}, from God our Father,
and the Lord Jesus Christ.
2 **We** give thanks to God always for you all,
making mention of you in our prayers;
3 Remembering without ceasing your work of faith, and labour of love, and patience of hope in our Lord Jesus Christ, in the sight of God and our Father;
4 Knowing, brethren beloved, your election of God.
5 **For our gospel** came not unto you in word only, but also in power, and in the Holy Ghost, and in much assurance;
as ye know
what manner of men we were among you for your sake.
6 **And ye** became followers of us, and of the Lord,
having received the word in much affliction, with joy of the Holy Ghost.
7 **So that ye** were ensamples to all that believe in Macedonia and Achaia.
8 **For from you** sounded out the word of the Lord not only in Macedonia and Achaia, but also in every place your faith to God-ward is spread abroad;
so that we need not to speak any thing.
9 **For they themselves** shew of us
what manner of entering in we had unto you,
and how ye turned to God from idols
to serve the living and true God;
10 **And** to wait for his Son from heaven,
whom he raised from the dead, even Jesus,
which delivered us from the wrath to come.

2 **For yourselves, brethren,** know our entrance in unto you,
that it was not in vain:
2 **But even after that we** had suffered before,
and were shamefully entreated,
as ye know, at Philippi,
we were bold in our God to speak unto you the gospel of God with much contention.
3 **For our exhortation** was not of deceit, nor of uncleanness, nor in guile:
4 **But as we** were allowed of God to be put in trust with the gospel,
even so we speak;
not as pleasing men, but God,
which trieth our hearts.
5 **For neither at any time** used we flattering words, {as ye know}, nor a cloke of covetousness;
God is witness:
6 **Nor of men** sought we glory, neither of you, nor yet of others,
when we might have been burdensome, as the apostles of Christ.
7 **But we** were gentle among you,
even as a nurse cherisheth her children:

8 **So** being affectionately desirous of
you,
we were willing to have imparted
unto you, not the gospel of God
only, but also our own souls,
because ye were dear unto us.
9 **For ye** remember, brethren, our
labour and travail:
for labouring night and day,
because we would not be
chargeable unto any of you,
we preached unto you the gospel of
God.
10 **Ye** are witnesses, and God also,
**how holily and justly and
unblameably** we behaved
ourselves among you that believe:
11 **As ye** know
how we exhorted and comforted
and charged every one of you,
as a father doth his children,
12 **That ye** would walk worthy of
God,
who hath called you unto his
kingdom and glory.
13 **For this cause** also thank we God
without ceasing,
**because, {when ye received the
word of God which ye heard of
us},** ye received it not as the word
of men,
but as it is in truth, the word of
God,
which effectually worketh also in
you that believe.
14 **For ye**, brethren, became
followers of the churches of God
which in Judaea are in Christ
Jesus:
for ye also have suffered like things
of your own countrymen,
even as they have of the Jews:
15 **Who** both killed the Lord Jesus,
and their own prophets,
and have persecuted us;
and they please not God,
and are contrary to all men:
16 Forbidding us to speak to the
Gentiles
that they might be saved,
to fill up their sins alway:
for the wrath is come upon them to
the uttermost.
17 **But we**, brethren, {being taken
from you for a short time in
presence, not in heart},
endeavoured the more
abundantly to see your face with
great desire.
18 **Wherefore we** would have come
unto you, even I Paul, once and
again;
but Satan hindered us.
19 **For what** is our hope, or joy, or
crown of rejoicing?
Are not even ye in the presence of
our Lord Jesus Christ at his
coming?
20 **For ye** are our glory and joy.

3 **Wherefore when we** could no
longer forbear,
we thought it good to be left at
Athens alone;
2 **And** sent Timotheus, our brother,
and minister of God, and our
fellowlabourer in the gospel of
Christ,
to establish you,
and to comfort you concerning your
faith:
3 **That no man** should be moved by
these afflictions:
for yourselves know
that we are appointed thereunto.
4 **For verily, {when we were with
you},** we told you before
that we should suffer tribulation;
even as it came to pass,
and ye know.
5 **For this cause**, {when I could no
longer forbear}, I sent
to know your faith,
lest by some means the tempter
have tempted you,
and our labour be in vain.
6 **But now when Timotheus** came
from you unto us,
and brought us good tidings of your
faith and charity,
and that ye have good
remembrance of us always,
desiring greatly to see us,
as we also to see you:
7 **Therefore, brethren, we** were
comforted over you in all our
affliction and distress by your
faith:
8 **For now we** live,
if ye stand fast in the Lord.
9 **For what thanks** can we render to
God again for you, for all the joy
wherewith we joy for your sakes
before our God;
10 **Night and day** praying
exceedingly
that we might see your face,
and might perfect that which is
lacking in your faith?
11 **Now God himself and our
Father, and our Lord Jesus
Christ,** direct our way unto you.
12 **And the Lord** make you to
increase and abound in love one
toward another, and toward all
men,
even as we do toward you:
13 **To the end he** may stablish your
hearts unblameable in holiness
before God, even our Father, at
the coming of our Lord Jesus
Christ with all his saints.

4 **Furthermore then we**
beseech you, brethren,
and exhort you by the Lord Jesus,
that as ye have received of us how
ye ought to walk and to please
God,
so ye would abound more and
more.
2 **For ye** know
what commandments we gave you
by the Lord Jesus.
3 **For this** is the will of God, even
your sanctification,
that ye should abstain from
fornication:
4 **That every one of you** should
know
how to possess his vessel in
sanctification and honour;
5 Not in the lust of concupiscence,
even as the Gentiles which know
not God:
6 **That no man** go beyond and
defraud his brother in any matter:
because that the Lord is the
avenger of all such,
as we also have forewarned you and
testified.
7 **For God** hath not called us unto
uncleanness, but unto holiness.
8 **He therefore that despiseth,**
despiseth not man, but God,
who hath also given unto us his
holy Spirit.
9 **But as touching brotherly love** ye
need not that I write unto you:
for ye yourselves are taught of God
to love one another.
10 **And indeed ye** do it toward all the
brethren which are in all
Macedonia:
but we beseech you, brethren,
that ye increase more and more;
11 **And that ye** study to be quiet,
and to do your own business,
and to work with your own hands,

as we commanded you;
12 **That ye** may walk honestly toward them that are without,
and that ye may have lack of nothing.
13 **But I** would not have you to be ignorant, brethren, concerning them which are asleep,
that ye sorrow not, even as others which have no hope.
14 **For if we** believe
that Jesus died and rose again,
even so them also which sleep in Jesus will God bring with him.
15 **For this** we say unto you by the word of the Lord,
that we which are alive and remain unto the coming of the Lord shall not prevent them which are asleep.
16 **For the Lord himself** shall descend from heaven with a shout, with the voice of the archangel, and with the trump of God:
and the dead in Christ shall rise first:
17 **Then we which are alive and remain** shall be caught up together with them in the clouds,
to meet the Lord in the air:
and so shall we ever be with the Lord.
18 **Wherefore comfort** one another with these words.

5 **But of the times and the seasons**, brethren, ye have no need that I write unto you.
2 **For yourselves** know perfectly
that the day of the Lord so cometh as a thief in the night.
3 **For when they** shall say,
Peace and safety;
then sudden destruction cometh upon them, as travail upon a woman with child;
and they shall not escape.
4 **But ye**, brethren, are not in darkness,
that that day should overtake you as a thief.
5 **Ye** are all the children of light, and the children of the day:
we are not of the night, nor of darkness.
6 **Therefore let us** not sleep, as do others;
but let us watch and be sober.
7 **For they that sleep** sleep in the night;
and they that be drunken are drunken in the night.
8 **But let us**, {who are of the day}, be sober,
putting on the breastplate of faith and love; and for an helmet, the hope of salvation.
9 **For God** hath not appointed us to wrath,
but to obtain salvation by our Lord Jesus Christ,
10 **Who** died for us,
that, {whether we wake or sleep}, we should live together with him.
11 **Wherefore comfort** yourselves together,
and edify one another,
even as also ye do.
12 **And we** beseech you, brethren,
to know them which labour among you,
and are over you in the Lord,
and admonish you;
13 **And** to esteem them very highly in love for their work's sake.
And be at peace among yourselves.
14 **Now we** exhort you, brethren,
warn them that are unruly,
comfort the feebleminded,
support the weak,
be patient toward all men.
15 **See** that none render evil for evil unto any man;
but ever follow that which is good, both among yourselves, and to all men.
16 **Rejoice** evermore.
17 **Pray** without ceasing.
18 **In every thing** give thanks:
for this is the will of God in Christ Jesus concerning you.
19 **Quench not** the Spirit.
20 **Despise not** prophesyings.
21 **Prove** all things;
hold fast that which is good.
22 **Abstain** from all appearance of evil.
23 **And the very God of peace** sanctify you wholly;
and I pray God
your whole spirit and soul and body be preserved blameless unto the coming of our Lord Jesus Christ.
24 **Faithful** is he that calleth you,
who also will do it.
25 **Brethren, pray** for us.
26 **Greet** all the brethren with an holy kiss.
27 **I** charge you by the Lord
that this epistle be read unto all the holy brethren.
28 **The grace of our Lord Jesus Christ** be with you.
Amen.

2 Thessalonians

The Book of Second Thessalonians, authored by the Apostle Paul, is one of the earliest epistles in the New Testament. In his letter, Paul addresses the community of Thessalonica for the second time. His key reason for writing is to once again correct misunderstandings about Jesus Christ's second coming, as some members of the Thessalonian Church were confused, believing that the day of the Lord had already arrived. Paul wants to assure them that this event has yet to occur and that they should not be deceived by false teachings or misinterpretations of his earlier letters. He encourages them to remain vigilant and not be caught off guard when the day of the Lord does arrive.

Paul's letter not only addresses the issue of the second coming but also serves as a source of inspiration for the believers in Thessalonica. Despite their persecution, Paul reminds them of their pivotal role in maintaining unity and standing firm in the face of adversity. He urges them to continue their diligent work and mutual support as they await the return of Christ. Paul's guidance further underscores the Church's role as a community of believers, called to minister to one another and the world. He encourages them to persist in their efforts to share the Gospel and serve others. His letter reminds them that God will ultimately judge all people, both those who have accepted Christ and those who have rejected Him. Finally, Paul underscores the significance of prayer, urging the Thessalonians to pray for one another, for the spread of the Gospel, and for God's continued guidance and protection.

Paul's letter provides a wealth of guidance and encouragement for believers, both in the ancient Church of Thessalonica and in the modern Church today. It offers profound insights and lessons that can fortify the faith of believers and inspire them in the face of persecution. Moreover, it can help them to remain steadfast and united in their devotion to Christ, and to gain a deeper understanding of their role in the Church and the world. With its timeless wisdom, encouragement, and guidance, Second Thessalonians reminds Christians everywhere about the ultimate triumph of good over evil and provides them with the assurance that their unwavering faith will lead to eternal salvation through Jesus Christ as they eagerly await the second arrival of His glorious coming.

1 **Paul, and Silvanus, and Timotheus,** unto the church of the Thessalonians in God our Father and the Lord Jesus Christ:
2 **Grace** unto you, {and peace}, from God our Father and the Lord Jesus Christ.
3 **We** are bound to thank God always for you, brethren,
as it is meet,
because that your faith groweth exceedingly,
and the charity of every one of you all toward each other aboundeth;
4 **So that we ourselves** glory in you in the churches of God for your patience and faith in all your persecutions and tribulations that ye endure:
5 **Which** is a manifest token of the righteous judgment of God,
that ye may be counted worthy of the kingdom of God,
for which ye also suffer:
6 **Seeing it is a righteous thing with God** to recompense tribulation to them that trouble you;
7 **And to you who are troubled** rest with us,
when the Lord Jesus shall be revealed from heaven with his mighty angels,
8 **In flaming fire** taking vengeance on them that know not God, and that obey not the gospel of our Lord Jesus Christ:
9 **Who** shall be punished with everlasting destruction from the presence of the Lord, and from the glory of his power;
10 **When he** shall come to be glorified in his saints,
and to be admired in all them that believe (because our testimony among you was believed) in that day.
11 **Wherefore also we** pray always for you,
that our God would count you worthy of this calling,
and fulfil all the good pleasure of his goodness, and the work of faith with power:
12 **That the name of our Lord Jesus Christ** may be glorified in you, and ye in him, according to the grace of our God and the Lord Jesus Christ.

2 **Now we** beseech you, brethren, by the coming of our Lord Jesus Christ, and by our gathering together unto him,
2 **That ye** be not soon shaken in mind,
or be troubled, neither by spirit, nor by word, nor by letter as from us,
as that the day of Christ is at hand.
3 **Let no man** deceive you by any means:
for that day shall not come,
except there come a falling away first,
and that man of sin be revealed, the son of perdition;
4 **Who** opposeth and exalteth himself above all that is called God, or that is worshipped;
so that he as God sitteth in the temple of God,
shewing himself

that he is God.

5 **Remember ye not,**
that, {when I was yet with you}, I told you these things?

6 **And now ye** know
what withholdeth
that he might be revealed in his time.

7 **For the mystery of iniquity** doth already work:
only he who now letteth will let,
until he be taken out of the way.

8 **And then** shall that Wicked be revealed,
whom the Lord shall consume with the spirit of his mouth,
and shall destroy with the brightness of his coming:
9 Even him,
whose coming is after the working of Satan with all power and signs and lying wonders,
10 And with all deceivableness of unrighteousness in them that perish;
because they received not the love of the truth,
that they might be saved.

11 **And for this cause** God shall send them strong delusion,
that they should believe a lie:
12 **That they all** might be damned
who believed not the truth,
but had pleasure in unrighteousness.

13 **But we** are bound to give thanks alway to God for you, brethren beloved of the Lord,
because God hath from the beginning chosen you to salvation through sanctification of the Spirit and belief of the truth:
14 **Whereunto** he called you by our gospel, to the obtaining of the glory of our Lord Jesus Christ.

15 **Therefore, brethren, stand fast,**
and hold the traditions which ye have been taught, whether by word, or our epistle.

16 **Now our Lord Jesus Christ himself, and God, even our Father,** {which hath loved us}, {and hath given us everlasting consolation and good hope through grace},
17 Comfort your hearts,
and stablish you in every good word and work.

3 **Finally, brethren, pray** for us,
that the word of the Lord may have free course,
and be glorified,
even as it is with you:
2 **And that we** may be delivered from unreasonable and wicked men:
for all men have not faith.

3 **But the Lord** is faithful,
who shall stablish you,
and keep you from evil.

4 **And we** have confidence in the Lord touching you,
that ye both do and will do the things which we command you.

5 **And the Lord** direct your hearts into the love of God, and into the patient waiting for Christ.

6 **Now we** command you, brethren, in the name of our Lord Jesus Christ,
that ye withdraw yourselves from every brother that walketh disorderly, and not after the tradition which he received of us.

7 **For yourselves** know
how ye ought to follow us:
for we behaved not ourselves disorderly among you;
8 **Neither** did we eat any man's bread for nought;
but wrought with labour and travail night and day,
that we might not be chargeable to any of you:
9 **Not because we** have not power,
but to make ourselves an ensample unto you
to follow us.

10 **For even when we** were with you,
this we commanded you,
that if any would not work,
neither should he eat.

11 **For we** hear that there are some which walk among you disorderly,
working not at all,
but are busybodies.

12 **Now them that are such** we command and exhort by our Lord Jesus Christ,
that with quietness they work,
and eat their own bread.

13 **But ye**, brethren, be not weary in well doing.

14 **And if any man** obey not our word by this epistle,
note that man,
and have no company with him,
that he may be ashamed.

15 **Yet count him not** as an enemy,
but admonish him as a brother.

16 **Now the Lord of peace himself** give you peace always by all means.

The Lord be with you all.

17 The salutation of Paul with mine own hand,
which is the token in every epistle:
so I write.

18 **The grace of our Lord Jesus Christ** be with you all.

Amen.

1 Timothy

The Book of First Timothy, penned by the Apostle Paul, was written as a pastoral epistle during Paul's first imprisonment in Rome. It provides guidance and instruction to Timothy, a young pastor mentored by Paul, empowering him to lead his congregation and maintain the integrity of the Christian faith. Paul's primary goal is to ensure that the teachings of Jesus Christ are upheld and properly understood by his followers and to protect the early Christian communities from false teachings and doctrines. He hopes to accomplish several goals through his letter to Timothy, recognizing his crucial role in this mission.

First, Paul wants to ensure that Timothy understands the importance of maintaining order and discipline within the Church. He provides practical advice on selecting leaders, dealing with conflicts, and managing the congregation's affairs. Second, he is concerned about the spread of false teachings and heresies within the early Christian communities. Paul wants to equip him with the tools necessary to recognize and combat these teachings, ensuring that the true message of Jesus Christ is preserved. Third, Paul understands the challenges and difficulties of being a spiritual leader and wants to encourage Timothy to persevere in his work. He emphasizes the importance of Timothy's faith and his need to remain steadfast in the face of adversity. Fourth, Paul wants to ensure that Timothy and his congregation understand how to live by the teachings of Jesus Christ. He provides guidance on prayer, worship, and the practice of good works, emphasizing the need to live a life that reflects Christian values and beliefs.

In addition to these primary goals, Paul addresses the role of women in the Church, stating that they should dress modestly, refrain from braided hair and gold jewelry, and focus on good works. While some of these teachings on women may be seen as controversial or difficult to apply in a modern context, First Timothy offers valuable insights into the Biblical perspective on the role of women in the Church and how they can contribute to its growth and development. Another area that Paul addresses concerns the importance of prayer. He encourages Timothy to pray for others, including government officials, and to lead the Church in prayer. Paul then urges Timothy and his congregation to be active in doing good deeds and to pattern one's life after the principles taught by Jesus Christ. Finally, he outlines the nature of the Church as a body of believers united in faith and dedicated to the spread of the Gospel.

Paul's first letter to Timothy not only provides Christians with a better understanding of early Church beliefs and practices but also motivates them to produce good works as a reflection of genuine faith. Notably, his letter serves as a guide for believers about the enduring principles that underpin their faith and the standards by which they should conduct their lives.

1 **Paul, an apostle of Jesus Christ by the commandment of God our Saviour, and Lord Jesus Christ,** {which is our hope};
2 Unto Timothy, my own son in the faith:
Grace, mercy, and peace, from God our Father and Jesus Christ our Lord.

3 **As I** besought thee to abide still at Ephesus,
when I went into Macedonia,
that thou mightest charge some that they teach no other doctrine,
4 **Neither** give heed to fables and endless genealogies,
which minister questions, rather than godly edifying which is in faith:
so do.

5 **Now the end of the commandment** is charity out of a pure heart, and of a good conscience, and of faith unfeigned:
6 **From which** some {having swerved} have turned aside unto vain jangling;
7 Desiring to be teachers of the law;
understanding
neither what they say,
nor whereof they affirm.

8 **But we** know
that the law is good,
if a man use it lawfully;
9 Knowing this,
that the law is not made for a righteous man, but for the lawless and disobedient, for the ungodly and for sinners, for unholy and profane, for murderers of fathers and murderers of mothers, for manslayers,
10 For whoremongers, for them that defile themselves with mankind, for menstealers, for liars, for perjured persons,
and if there be any other thing that is contrary to sound doctrine;
11 According to the glorious gospel of the blessed God,
which was committed to my trust.

12 **And I** thank Christ Jesus our Lord,
who hath enabled me,
for that he counted me faithful,
putting me into the ministry;
13 **Who** was before a blasphemer, and a persecutor, and injurious:
but I obtained mercy,

because I did it ignorantly in unbelief.

14 **And the grace of our Lord** was exceeding abundant with faith and love which is in Christ Jesus.

15 **This** is a faithful saying, and worthy of all acceptation,
that Christ Jesus came into the world to save sinners;
of whom I am chief.

16 **Howbeit for this cause** I obtained mercy,
that in me first Jesus Christ might shew forth all longsuffering, for a pattern to them which should hereafter believe on him to life everlasting.

17 **Now unto the King eternal, immortal, invisible, the only wise God,** be honour and glory for ever and ever.

Amen.

18 **This charge** I commit unto thee, son Timothy, according to the prophecies which went before on thee,
that thou by them mightest war a good warfare;
19 Holding faith, and a good conscience;
which some {having put away concerning faith} have made shipwreck:
20 **Of whom** is Hymenaeus and Alexander;
whom I have delivered unto Satan,
that they may learn not to blaspheme.

2

I exhort therefore,
that, first of all, supplications, prayers, intercessions, and giving of thanks, be made for all men;
2 For kings, and for all that are in authority;
that we may lead a quiet and peaceable life in all godliness and honesty.

3 **For this** is good and acceptable in the sight of God our Saviour;
4 **Who** will have all men to be saved,
and to come unto the knowledge of the truth.

5 **For there** is one God, and one mediator between God and men, the man Christ Jesus;
6 **Who** gave himself a ransom for all,
to be testified in due time.

7 **Whereunto** I am ordained a preacher, and an apostle, ({I speak the truth in Christ}, {and lie not};) a teacher of the Gentiles in faith and verity.

8 **I** will therefore
that men pray every where,
lifting up holy hands, without wrath and doubting.

9 **In like manner also, that women** adorn themselves in modest apparel, with shamefacedness and sobriety; not with broided hair, or gold, or pearls, or costly array;
10 But (which becometh women professing godliness) with good works.

11 **Let the woman** learn in silence with all subjection.

12 **But I** suffer not a woman to teach,
nor to usurp authority over the man,
but to be in silence.

13 **For Adam** was first formed, then Eve.

14 **And Adam** was not deceived,
but the woman being deceived was in the transgression.

15 **Notwithstanding she** shall be saved in childbearing,
if they continue in faith and charity and holiness with sobriety.

3

This is a true saying,
if a man desire the office of a bishop,
he desireth a good work.

2 **A bishop** then must be blameless, the husband of one wife, vigilant, sober, of good behaviour, given to hospitality, apt to teach;
3 Not given to wine, no striker, not greedy of filthy lucre; but patient, not a brawler, not covetous;
4 **One** that ruleth well his own house,
having his children in subjection with all gravity;
5 (For if a man know not
how to rule his own house,
how shall he take care of the church of God?)
6 Not a novice,
lest being lifted up with pride
he fall into the condemnation of the devil.

7 **Moreover he** must have a good report of them which are without;
lest he fall into reproach and the snare of the devil.

8 **Likewise** must the deacons be grave, not doubletongued, not given to much wine, not greedy of filthy lucre;
9 Holding the mystery of the faith in a pure conscience.

10 **And let these** also first be proved;
then let them use the office of a deacon,
being found blameless.

11 **Even so** must their wives be grave, not slanderers, sober, faithful in all things.

12 **Let the deacons** be the husbands of one wife,
ruling their children and their own houses well.

13 **For they that have used the office of a deacon well** purchase to themselves a good degree, and great boldness in the faith which is in Christ Jesus.

14 **These things** write I unto thee,
hoping to come unto thee shortly:
15 **But if I** tarry long,
that thou mayest know
how thou oughtest to behave thyself in the house of God,
which is the church of the living God, the pillar and ground of the truth.

16 **And without controversy great** is the mystery of godliness:
God was manifest in the flesh,
justified in the Spirit,
seen of angels,
preached unto the Gentiles,
believed on in the world,
received up into glory.

4

Now the Spirit speaketh expressly,
that in the latter times some shall depart from the faith,
giving heed to seducing spirits, and doctrines of devils;
2 Speaking lies in hypocrisy;
having their conscience seared with a hot iron;
3 Forbidding to marry,
and commanding to abstain from meats,
which God hath created to be received with thanksgiving of them which believe and know the truth.

4 **For every creature of God** is good,
and nothing to be refused,

if it be received with thanksgiving:
5 **For it** is sanctified by the word of God and prayer.

6 **If thou** put the brethren in remembrance of these things,
thou shalt be a good minister of Jesus Christ,
nourished up in the words of faith and of good doctrine,
whereunto thou hast attained.

7 **But refuse** profane and old wives' fables,
and exercise thyself rather unto godliness.

8 **For bodily exercise** profiteth little:
but godliness is profitable unto all things,
having promise of the life that now is, and of that which is to come.

9 **This** is a faithful saying and worthy of all acceptation.

10 **For therefore we both** labour and suffer reproach,
because we trust in the living God,
who is the Saviour of all men,
specially of those that believe.

11 **These things** command and teach.

12 **Let no man** despise thy youth;
but be thou an example of the believers, in word, in conversation, in charity, in spirit, in faith, in purity.

13 **Till I** come,
give attendance to reading, to exhortation, to doctrine.

14 **Neglect not** the gift that is in thee,
which was given thee by prophecy, with the laying on of the hands of the presbytery.

15 **Meditate** upon these things;
give thyself wholly to them;
that thy profiting may appear to all.

16 **Take heed** unto thyself, and unto the doctrine;
continue in them:
for in doing this thou shalt both save thyself, and them that hear thee.

5 **Rebuke not** an elder,
but intreat him as a father;
and the younger men as brethren;
2 The elder women as mothers; the younger as sisters, with all purity.

3 **Honour** widows that are widows indeed.

4 **But if any widow** have children or nephews,
let them learn first to shew piety at home, and to requite their parents:
for that is good and acceptable before God.

5 **Now she that is a widow indeed, and desolate,** trusteth in God,
and continueth in supplications and prayers night and day.

6 **But she that liveth in pleasure** is dead
while she liveth.

7 **And these things** give in charge,
that they may be blameless.

8 **But if any** provide not for his own, and specially for those of his own house,
he hath denied the faith,
and is worse than an infidel.

9 **Let not** a widow be taken into the number under threescore years old,
having been the wife of one man,
10 Well reported of for good works;
if she have brought up children,
if she have lodged strangers,
if she have washed the saints' feet,
if she have relieved the afflicted,
if she have diligently followed every good work.

11 **But the younger widows** refuse:
for when they have begun to wax wanton against Christ,
they will marry;
12 Having damnation,
because they have cast off their first faith.

13 **And withal they** learn to be idle,
wandering about from house to house; and not only idle, but tattlers also and busybodies,
speaking things which they ought not.

14 **I** will therefore
that the younger women marry,
bear children,
guide the house,
give none occasion to the adversary to speak reproachfully.

15 **For some** are already turned aside after Satan.

16 **If any man or woman that believeth** have widows,
let them relieve them,
and let not the church be charged;
that it may relieve them that are widows indeed.

17 **Let the elders that rule well** be counted worthy of double honour, especially they who labour in the word and doctrine.

18 **For the scripture** saith,
thou shalt not muzzle the ox that treadeth out the corn.

And, The labourer is worthy of his reward.

19 **Against an elder** receive not an accusation, but before two or three witnesses.

20 **Them that sin** rebuke before all,
that others also may fear.

21 **I** charge thee before God, and the Lord Jesus Christ, and the elect angels,
that thou observe these things without preferring one before another,
doing nothing by partiality.

22 **Lay hands** suddenly on no man,
neither be partaker of other men's sins:
keep thyself pure.

23 **Drink no longer** water,
but use a little wine for thy stomach's sake and thine often infirmities.

24 **Some men's sins** are open beforehand,
going before to judgment;
and some men they follow after.
25 **Likewise also the good works of some** are manifest beforehand;
and they that are otherwise cannot be hid.

6 **Let as many servants as are under the yoke** count their own masters worthy of all honour,
that the name of God and his doctrine be not blasphemed.

2 **And they that have believing masters,** let them not despise them,
because they are brethren;
but rather do them service,
because they are faithful and beloved, partakers of the benefit.
These things teach and exhort.

3 **If any man** teach otherwise,
and consent not to wholesome words, even the words of our Lord Jesus Christ, and to the doctrine which is according to godliness;
4 **He** is proud,
knowing nothing,

but doting about questions and
strifes of words,
whereof cometh envy, strife,
railings, evil surmisings,
5 Perverse disputings of men of
corrupt minds, and destitute of
the truth,
supposing
that gain is godliness:
from such withdraw thyself.

6 **But godliness with contentment**
is great gain.

7 **For we** brought nothing into this
world,
and it is certain we can carry
nothing out.

8 **And** having food and raiment
let us be therewith content.

9 **But they that will be rich** fall into
temptation and a snare, and into
many foolish and hurtful lusts,
which drown men in destruction
and perdition.

10 **For the love of money** is the root
of all evil:
which while some coveted after,
they have erred from the faith,
and pierced themselves through
with many sorrows.

11 **But thou, O man of God,** flee
these things;
and follow after righteousness,
godliness, faith, love, patience,
meekness.

12 **Fight** the good fight of faith,
lay hold on eternal life,
whereunto thou art also called,
and hast professed a good
profession before many
witnesses.

13 **I** give thee charge in the sight of
God,
who quickeneth all things, and
before Christ Jesus,
who before Pontius Pilate
witnessed a good confession;
14 **That thou** keep this
commandment without spot,
unrebukable, until the appearing
of our Lord Jesus Christ:
15 **Which in his times** he shall shew,
who is the blessed and only
Potentate, the King of kings, and
Lord of lords;
16 **Who** only hath immortality,
dwelling in the light which no man
can approach unto;
whom no man hath seen,
nor can see:
to whom be honour and power
everlasting.

Amen.

17 **Charge** them that are rich in this
world,
that they be not highminded,
nor trust in uncertain riches, but in
the living God,
who giveth us richly all things to
enjoy;
18 **That they** do good,
that they be rich in good works,
ready to distribute,
willing to communicate;
19 Laying up in store for themselves
a good foundation against the
time to come,
that they may lay hold on eternal
life.

20 **O Timothy, keep** that which is
committed to thy trust,
avoiding profane and vain
babblings, and oppositions of
science falsely so called:
21 **Which some professing** have
erred concerning the faith.

Grace be with thee.

Amen.

2 Timothy

The Book of Second Timothy, penned by the Apostle Paul, holds a special place in the New Testament as one of its last-written books. The letter reveals Paul's deep bond and concern for the Church's future. In the face of his impending death, Paul writes with a sense of urgency and a burning desire to equip Timothy to continue spreading the Gospel.

Paul's letter is not just a collection of advice and encouragement but a deeply personal testament. The Apostle underscores the significance of faith in God and Jesus Christ, urging Timothy to remain unwavering in his beliefs and to trust in God's plan for his life. Paul also delves into the role of the Holy Spirit in a believer's life, portraying the Spirit as a source of strength and guidance. He advises believers to be receptive to the Spirit's leading. Paul's words of encouragement to Timothy to persevere in his ministry, despite opposition and persecution, would resonate with believers facing similar challenges throughout the ancient world. He reminds Timothy that suffering is a natural part of the Christian life but should not deter believers from doing God's work. Paul then underscores the importance of sound doctrine and the necessity for Christian leaders to be well-versed and knowledgeable in the teachings of the faith. He encourages Timothy to study the Scriptures and to preach the true Gospel. Lastly, Paul advises Timothy to foster godly relationships with other believers and to steer clear of those individuals who might lead him astray.

The Book of Second Timothy, a letter of encouragement and guidance, is not just for Timothy but for Christians of all ages, eras, and backgrounds. It reminds believers about their need for faith, perseverance, and sound doctrine. Above all, it stands as a powerful testimonial by a soon-to-be-martyred apostle, one that leads Christians toward a Spirit-filled life of virtue, grace, wisdom, fellowship, evangelism, and eternal salvation through Jesus Christ.

1 **Paul, an apostle of Jesus Christ by the will of God, according to the promise of life which is in Christ Jesus,**
2 To Timothy, my dearly beloved son:
Grace, mercy, and peace, from God the Father and Christ Jesus our Lord.
3 **I** thank God,
whom I serve from my forefathers with pure conscience,
that without ceasing I have remembrance of thee in my prayers night and day;
4 Greatly desiring to see thee,
being mindful of thy tears,
that I may be filled with joy;
5 **When I** call to remembrance the unfeigned faith that is in thee,
which dwelt first in thy grandmother Lois, and thy mother Eunice;
and I am persuaded that in thee also.
6 **Wherefore** I put thee in remembrance
that thou stir up the gift of God,
which is in thee by the putting on of my hands.
7 **For God** hath not given us the spirit of fear; but of power, and of love, and of a sound mind.
8 **Be not thou** therefore ashamed of the testimony of our Lord, nor of me his prisoner:
but be thou partaker of the afflictions of the gospel according to the power of God;
9 **Who** hath saved us,
and called us with an holy calling, not according to our works, but according to his own purpose and grace,
which was given us in Christ Jesus before the world began,
10 **But** is now made manifest by the appearing of our Saviour Jesus Christ,
who hath abolished death,
and hath brought life and immortality to light through the gospel:
11 **Whereunto** I am appointed a preacher, and an apostle, and a teacher of the Gentiles.
12 **For the which cause** I also suffer these things:
nevertheless I am not ashamed:
for I know
whom I have believed,
and am persuaded
that he is able to keep that which I have committed unto him against that day.
13 **Hold fast** the form of sound words,
which thou hast heard of me, in faith and love which is in Christ Jesus.
14 **That good thing which was committed unto thee** keep by the Holy Ghost which dwelleth in us.
15 **This** thou knowest,
that all they which are in Asia be turned away from me;
of whom are Phygellus and Hermogenes.
16 **The Lord** give mercy unto the house of Onesiphorus;
for he oft refreshed me,
and was not ashamed of my chain:
17 **But, {when he was in Rome},** he sought me out very diligently,
and found me.
18 **The Lord** grant unto him that he may find mercy of the Lord in that day:
and in how many things he ministered unto me at Ephesus,
thou knowest very well.

2 **Thou** therefore, my son, be strong in the grace that is in Christ Jesus.
2 **And the things that thou hast heard of me among many witnesses,** the same commit thou to faithful men,
who shall be able to teach others also.
3 **Thou** therefore endure hardness, as a good soldier of Jesus Christ.
4 **No man that warreth** entangleth himself with the affairs of this life;
that he may please him who hath chosen him to be a soldier.
5 **And if a man** also strive for masteries,
yet is he not crowned,
except he strive lawfully.
6 **The husbandman that laboureth** must be first partaker of the fruits.
7 **Consider**
what I say;
and the Lord give thee understanding in all things.
8 **Remember**
that Jesus Christ of the seed of David was raised from the dead according to my gospel:
9 **Wherein** I suffer trouble, as an evil doer, even unto bonds;
but the word of God is not bound.
10 **Therefore I** endure all things for the elect's sakes,
that they may also obtain the salvation which is in Christ Jesus with eternal glory.
11 **It** is a faithful saying:
For if we be dead with him,
we shall also live with him:
12 **If we** suffer,
we shall also reign with him:
if we deny him,
he also will deny us:
13 **If we** believe not,
yet he abideth faithful:
he cannot deny himself.
14 **Of these things** put them in remembrance,
charging them before the Lord
that they strive not about words to no profit, but to the subverting of the hearers.
15 **Study** to shew thyself approved unto God, a workman that needeth not to be ashamed,
rightly dividing the word of truth.
16 **But shun** profane and vain babblings:
for they will increase unto more ungodliness.
17 **And their word** will eat as doth a canker:
of whom is Hymenaeus and Philetus;
18 **Who** concerning the truth have erred,
saying
that the resurrection is past already;
and overthrow the faith of some.
19 **Nevertheless the foundation of God** standeth sure,
having this seal,
The Lord knoweth them that are his.
And, let every one that nameth the name of Christ depart from iniquity.
20 **But in a great house** there are not only vessels of gold and of silver, but also of wood and of earth; and some to honour, and some to dishonour.
21 **If a man** therefore purge himself from these,
he shall be a vessel unto honour,
sanctified,
and meet for the master's use,
and prepared unto every good work.
22 **Flee** also youthful lusts:
but follow righteousness, faith, charity, peace, with them that call on the Lord out of a pure heart.
23 **But foolish and unlearned questions** avoid,
knowing
that they do gender strifes.
24 **And the servant of the Lord** must not strive;
but be gentle unto all men, apt to teach, patient,
25 **In meekness** instructing those that oppose themselves;
if God peradventure will give them repentance to the acknowledging of the truth;
26 **And that they** may recover themselves out of the snare of the devil,
who are taken captive by him at his will.

3 **This** know also,
that in the last days perilous times shall come.
2 **For men** shall be lovers of their own selves, covetous, boasters, proud, blasphemers, disobedient to parents, unthankful, unholy,
3 Without natural affection, trucebreakers, false accusers, incontinent, fierce, despisers of those that are good,
4 Traitors, heady, highminded, lovers of pleasures more than lovers of God;
5 Having a form of godliness,
but denying the power thereof:
from such turn away.
6 **For of this sort** are they which creep into houses,
and lead captive silly women laden with sins,
led away with divers lusts,
7 **Ever** learning,
and never able to come to the knowledge of the truth.
8 **Now as Jannes and Jambres** withstood Moses,
so do these also resist the truth:
men of corrupt minds, reprobate concerning the faith.
9 **But they** shall proceed no further:
for their folly shall be manifest unto all men,
as their's also was.
10 **But thou** hast fully known my doctrine, manner of life, purpose, faith, longsuffering, charity, patience,
11 Persecutions, afflictions,
which came unto me at Antioch, at Iconium, at Lystra;
what persecutions I endured:
but out of them all the Lord delivered me.
12 **Yea, and all that will live godly in Christ Jesus** shall suffer persecution.
13 **But evil men and seducers** shall wax worse and worse,
deceiving,
and being deceived.
14 **But continue thou** in the things which thou hast learned and hast been assured of,
knowing
of whom thou hast learned them;
15 **And that from a child** thou hast known the holy scriptures,
which are able to make thee wise unto salvation through faith which is in Christ Jesus.
16 **All scripture** is given by inspiration of God,

and is profitable for doctrine, for reproof, for correction, for instruction in righteousness:
17 **That the man of God** may be perfect,
thoroughly furnished unto all good works.

4 I charge thee therefore before God, and the Lord Jesus Christ,
who shall judge the quick and the dead at his appearing and his kingdom;
2 **Preach** the word;
be instant in season, out of season;
reprove,
rebuke,
exhort with all long suffering and doctrine.
3 **For the time** will come when they will not endure sound doctrine;
but after their own lusts shall they heap to themselves teachers,
having itching ears;
4 **And they** shall turn away their ears from the truth,
and shall be turned unto fables.
5 **But watch thou** in all things,
endure afflictions,
do the work of an evangelist,
make full proof of thy ministry.
6 **For I** am now ready to be offered,
and the time of my departure is at hand.
7 **I** have fought a good fight,
I have finished my course,
I have kept the faith:
8 **Henceforth** there is laid up for me a crown of righteousness,
which the Lord, the righteous judge, shall give me at that day: and not to me only, but unto all them also that love his appearing.
9 **Do** thy diligence to come shortly unto me:
10 **For Demas** hath forsaken me,
having loved this present world,
and is departed unto Thessalonica; Crescens to Galatia, Titus unto Dalmatia.
11 **Only Luke** is with me.
Take Mark,
and bring him with thee:
for he is profitable to me for the ministry.
12 **And Tychicus** have I sent to Ephesus.
13 **The cloke that I left at Troas with Carpus,** {when thou comest}, bring with thee, and the books, but especially the parchments.
14 **Alexander the coppersmith** did me much evil:
the Lord reward him according to his works:
15 **Of whom** be thou ware also;
for he hath greatly withstood our words.
16 **At my first answer** no man stood with me,
but all men forsook me:
I pray God
that it may not be laid to their charge.
17 **Notwithstanding the Lord** stood with me,
and strengthened me;
that by me the preaching might be fully known,
and that all the Gentiles might hear:
and I was delivered out of the mouth of the lion.
18 **And the Lord** shall deliver me from every evil work,
and will preserve me unto his heavenly kingdom:
to whom be glory for ever and ever.
Amen.
19 **Salute** Prisca and Aquila, and the household of Onesiphorus.
20 **Erastus** abode at Corinth:
but Trophimus have I left at Miletum sick.
21 **Do** thy diligence to come before winter.
Eubulus greeteth thee, and Pudens, and Linus, and Claudia, and all the brethren.
22 **The Lord Jesus Christ** be with thy spirit.
Grace be with you.
Amen.

Titus

The Book of Titus, a letter penned by the Apostle Paul, offers invaluable guidance and instruction to Titus, a young pastor and disciple of Paul, who is ministering on the island of Crete. In this epistle, Paul underscores the importance of sound teaching, good works, and godly leadership, thereby underscoring Titus' crucial role in the mission.

Paul hopes to accomplish several goals by writing this letter. First, he wants to encourage Titus to appoint elders in every town on Crete, ensuring that the church is led by godly, qualified men who can teach and guide the flock. Paul keenly understands the need for strong leadership in early Christian communities. He wants to ensure the Cretan church is built on a solid foundation. Second, Paul seeks to address the unique challenges facing the Cretan believers. The island of Crete is known for its immorality and pagan influences. Paul knows that the Christians there need to be reminded of the importance of living a life marked by good works, moral purity, and a strong testimony. Third, Paul wants to emphasize the centrality of sound doctrine in the church's life. He urges Titus to teach the believers to adhere to the truth of the Gospel, to reject false teachings, and to focus on the things that truly matter: faith, love, and godliness. And fourth, Paul's letter to Titus serves as a reminder of the importance of evangelism and mission. He encourages Titus to preach the Gospel to the Cretans, to proclaim the message of salvation, and to demonstrate the power of Christ in their lives.

Overall, the Book of Titus stresses the importance of good works, moral purity, and a strong testimony in the life of believers. It also highlights the importance of living a life consistent with the Gospel, the role of older women in the Church teaching and mentoring younger women, and the importance of grace in the Christian life. As believers strive to live a life pleasing to God, Paul reminds them that sound doctrine and good works are intimately intertwined. He stresses how the public demonstration of Christ's love in one's actions becomes a beacon of hope in a world torn by darkness and despair. Furthermore, these manifestations of Christ's love illuminate the path to a Gospel-centered faith that transforms lives, strengthens churches, and shines as a radiant witness to the world.

1 **Paul, a servant of God, and an apostle of Jesus Christ,**
according to the faith of God's elect, and the acknowledging of the truth which is after godliness;
2 In hope of eternal life,
{which God, {{that cannot lie}}, promised before the world began};
3 {But hath in due times manifested his word through preaching},
{which is committed unto me according to the commandment of God our Saviour};
4 To Titus, mine own son after the common faith:
Grace, mercy, and peace, from God the Father and the Lord Jesus Christ our Saviour.
5 **For this cause** left I thee in Crete,
that thou shouldest set in order the things that are wanting,
and ordain elders in every city,
as I had appointed thee:
6 **If any** be blameless, the husband of one wife,
having faithful children not accused of riot or unruly.
7 **For a bishop** must be blameless, as the steward of God; not selfwilled, not soon angry, not given to wine, no striker, not given to filthy lucre;
8 But a lover of hospitality, a lover of good men, sober, just, holy, temperate;
9 Holding fast the faithful word as he hath been taught,
that he may be able by sound doctrine
both to exhort
and to convince the gainsayers.
10 **For there** are many unruly and vain talkers and deceivers, specially they of the circumcision:
11 **Whose mouths** must be stopped,
who subvert whole houses,
{teaching things which they ought not}, for filthy lucre's sake.
12 **One of themselves, even a prophet of their own,** said,
the Cretians are alway liars, evil beasts, slow bellies.
13 **This witness** is true.
Wherefore rebuke them sharply,
that they may be sound in the faith;
14 Not giving heed to Jewish fables, and commandments of men,
that turn from the truth.
15 **Unto the pure** all things are pure:
but unto them that are defiled and unbelieving is nothing pure;
but even their mind and conscience is defiled.
16 **They** profess
that they know God;
but in works they deny him,
being abominable, and disobedient, and unto every good work reprobate.

2 **But speak thou** the things which become sound doctrine:
2 **That the aged men** be sober, grave, temperate, sound in faith, in charity, in patience.
3 The aged women likewise,
that they be in behaviour as becometh holiness, not false accusers, not given to much wine, teachers of good things;
4 **That they** may teach the young women to be sober,
to love their husbands,
to love their children,

[5] To be discreet, chaste, keepers at home, good, obedient to their own husbands,
that the word of God be not blasphemed.

[6] **Young men** likewise exhort to be sober minded.

[7] **In all things** shewing thyself a pattern of good works:
in doctrine shewing uncorruptness, gravity, sincerity,
[8] Sound speech,
that cannot be condemned;
that he that is of the contrary part may be ashamed,
having no evil thing to say of you.

[9] **Exhort** servants to be obedient unto their own masters,
and to please them well in all things;
not answering again;
[10] Not purloining,
but shewing all good fidelity;
that they may adorn the doctrine of God our Saviour in all things.

[11] **For the grace of God that bringeth salvation** hath appeared to all men,
[12] Teaching us that, {denying ungodliness and worldly lusts}, we should live soberly, righteously, and godly, in this present world;
[13] Looking for that blessed hope, and the glorious appearing of the great God and our Saviour Jesus Christ;
[14] **Who** gave himself for us,
that he might redeem us from all iniquity,
and purify unto himself a peculiar people, zealous of good works.

[15] **These things speak,**
and exhort,
and rebuke with all authority.
Let no man despise thee.

3 **Put them in mind** to be subject to principalities and powers,
to obey magistrates,
to be ready to every good work,
[2] To speak evil of no man,
to be no brawlers, but gentle,
shewing all meekness unto all men.

[3] **For we ourselves** also were sometimes foolish, disobedient, deceived,
serving divers lusts and pleasures,
living in malice and envy, hateful,
and hating one another.

[4] **But after that the kindness and love of God our Saviour toward man** appeared,
[5] Not by works of righteousness which we have done,
but according to his mercy he saved us, by the washing of regeneration, and renewing of the Holy Ghost;
[6] **Which he** shed on us abundantly through Jesus Christ our Saviour;
[7] **That** being justified by his grace,
we should be made heirs according to the hope of eternal life.

[8] **This** is a faithful saying,
and these things I will
that thou affirm constantly,
that they which have believed in God might be careful to maintain good works.
These things are good and profitable unto men.

[9] **But avoid** foolish questions, and genealogies, and contentions, and strivings about the law;
for they are unprofitable and vain.

[10] **A man that is an heretick after the first and second admonition** reject;
[11] Knowing
that he that is such is subverted,
and sinneth,
being condemned of himself.

[12] **When I** shall send Artemas unto thee, or Tychicus,
be diligent to come unto me to Nicopolis:
for I have determined there to winter.

[13] **Bring** Zenas the lawyer and Apollos on their journey diligently,
that nothing be wanting unto them.

[14] **And let our's** also learn to maintain good works for necessary uses,
that they be not unfruitful.

[15] **All that are with me** salute thee.

Greet them that love us in the faith.

Grace be with you all.

Amen.

Philemon

The Book of Philemon, written by the Apostle Paul during his imprisonment in Rome, is addressed to Philemon, a Christian slave owner. It deals with forgiveness and reconciliation, as Paul urges Philemon to receive back his runaway slave, Onesimus, who found salvation and is returning home to make matters right with his master. But Paul wants Philemon to do more than receive him back. He urges his friend to demonstrate the power of Christian love and forgiveness by embracing Onesimus as a brother in Christ rather than a slave.

Paul knows that Philemon embracing Onesimus as a brother will create a powerful image where the bonds of Christian love transcend all social and economic distinctions. This bold societal and spiritual move underscores the unwavering strength of Paul's leadership in the early Church. It's a leadership that guides and reassures, where relationships are transformed, forgiveness is extended, and the power of the Gospel shines in all its glory.

Paul, a prisoner of Jesus Christ, and Timothy our brother, unto Philemon our dearly beloved, and fellowlabourer,
2 **And** to our beloved Apphia,
and Archippus our fellowsoldier,
and to the church in thy house:
3 **Grace** to you, {and peace}, from God our Father and the Lord Jesus Christ.

4 **I** thank my God,
making mention of thee always in my prayers,
5 Hearing of thy love and faith,
which thou hast toward the Lord Jesus,
and toward all saints;
6 **That the communication of thy faith** may become effectual by the acknowledging of every good thing which is in you in Christ Jesus.

7 **For we** have great joy and consolation in thy love,
because the bowels of the saints are refreshed by thee, brother.

8 **Wherefore, though I** might be much bold in Christ to enjoin thee that which is convenient,
9 **Yet for love's sake** I rather beseech thee,
being such an one as Paul the aged,
and now also a prisoner of Jesus Christ.
10 **I** beseech thee for my son Onesimus,
whom I have begotten in my bonds:
11 **Which in time past** was to thee unprofitable,
but now profitable to thee and to me:
12 **Whom I** have sent again:
thou therefore receive him, that is, mine own bowels:
13 **Whom I** would have retained with me,
that in thy stead he might have ministered unto me in the bonds of the gospel:
14 **But without thy mind** would I do nothing;
that thy benefit should not be as it were of necessity,
but willingly.

15 **For perhaps he** therefore departed for a season,
that thou shouldest receive him for ever;
16 Not now as a servant, but above a servant, a brother beloved, specially to me, but how much more unto thee, both in the flesh, and in the Lord?

17 **If thou** count me therefore a partner,
receive him as myself.
18 **If he** hath wronged thee,
or oweth thee ought,
put that on mine account;
19 **I Paul** have written it with mine own hand,
I will repay it:
albeit I do not say to thee
how thou owest unto me even thine own self besides.

20 **Yea, brother, let me** have joy of thee in the Lord:
refresh my bowels in the Lord.

21 Having confidence in thy obedience
I wrote unto thee,
knowing
that thou wilt also do more than I say.

22 **But withal prepare** me also a lodging:
for I trust
that through your prayers I shall be given unto you.

23 **There salute thee** Epaphras, my fellowprisoner in Christ Jesus;
24 Marcus, Aristarchus, Demas, Lucas, my fellowlabourers.

25 **The grace of our Lord Jesus Christ** be with your spirit.
Amen.

Hebrews

The Book of Hebrews, author unknown, is a masterpiece of Christian theology. It offers profound insights into the nature of Christ, the significance of His sacrifice, and the hope of salvation that He offers to all humanity. The author writes the epistle to address a concern weighing heavily on his heart. He is deeply troubled that many Jewish Christians are considering returning to the familiar comforts of Judaism. These Jewish believers are facing intense persecution and hardship, and some are beginning to doubt the efficacy of Christ's sacrifice. They are tempted to revert to the old covenant, with its familiar rituals and practices, to escape the difficulties and uncertainties of following Jesus. Hebrews, therefore, is meant to encourage these wavering believers to persevere in their faith and remind them of Christ's surpassing greatness.

The author accomplishes this goal by first demonstrating the superiority of Christ over the old covenant. He argues that Jesus is the ultimate High Priest, Who has offered a once-for-all sacrifice that supersedes the repeated sacrifices of the Levitical priesthood. The letter aims to reassure readers that their sufferings are not in vain. It reminds them that Jesus, too, had suffered and been tempted and that He can sympathize with their weaknesses. The author also urges his readers to hold fast to their confession and to avoid the temptation to backslide. He warns them of the dangers of falling away from the faith and encourages them to press on toward maturity in Christ. Finally, Hebrews seeks to inspire its readers to live a life of faith, hope, and love, even in adversity. It reminds them that they are witnesses who have lived and died for their faith and that they, too, can persevere through the power of Christ.

The Book of Hebrews stands as a beacon of hope and reassurance, reminding believers everywhere that Christ's sacrifice is the ultimate fulfillment of God's plan and that their understanding of His divine nature is incomplete without embracing the mystery of His humanity. In short, it creates a rich tapestry of spiritual truth, woven from the very fabric of God's redemptive plan. It provides an anchor for weary souls, enabling Christians to gain a deeper understanding of Christ's sacrifice, a clearer appreciation for the role of faith, and a powerful encouragement to live a life worthy of the Gospel.

1 ∞ **God**, {who at sundry times and in divers manners spake in time past unto the fathers by the prophets},
2 Hath in these last days spoken unto us by his Son,
whom he hath appointed heir of all things,
by whom also he made the worlds;
3 **Who** {being the brightness of his glory, and the express image of his person}, {and upholding all things by the word of his power}, {when he had by himself purged our sins}, sat down on the right hand of the Majesty on high:
4 Being made so much better than the angels,
as he hath by inheritance obtained a more excellent name than they.

5 **For unto which of the angels** said he at any time,
Thou art my Son,
this day have I begotten thee?

And again, I will be to him a Father,
and he shall be to me a Son?

6 **And again, {when he bringeth in the firstbegotten into the world},** he saith,
And let all the angels of God worship him.

7 **And of the angels** he saith,
Who maketh his angels spirits, and his ministers a flame of fire.

8 **But unto the Son** he saith,
Thy throne, O God, is for ever and ever:
a sceptre of righteousness is the sceptre of thy kingdom.

9 **Thou** hast loved righteousness,
and hated iniquity;
therefore God, even thy God, hath anointed thee with the oil of gladness above thy fellows.

10 **And, Thou, Lord, in the beginning** hast laid the foundation of the earth;
and the heavens are the works of thine hands:
11 **They** shall perish;
but thou remainest;
and they all shall wax old as doth a garment;

12 **And as a vesture** shalt thou fold them up,
and they shall be changed:
but thou art the same,
and thy years shall not fail.

13 **But to which of the angels** said he at any time,
Sit on my right hand,
until I make thine enemies thy footstool?

14 **Are they not all** ministering spirits,
sent forth
to minister for them who shall be heirs of salvation?

2 **Therefore we** ought to give the more earnest heed to the things which we have heard,
lest at any time we should let them slip.

2 **For if the word spoken by angels** was stedfast,
and every transgression and disobedience received a just recompence of reward;
3 **How** shall we escape,
if we neglect so great salvation;

which at the first began to be spoken by the Lord,
and was confirmed unto us by them that heard him;
4 **God** also bearing them witness, both with signs and wonders, and with divers miracles, and gifts of the Holy Ghost, according to his own will?

5 **For unto the angels** hath he not put in subjection the world to come,
whereof we speak.

6 **But one in a certain place** testified,
saying,
What is man, {that thou art mindful of him?} or the son of man {that thou visitest him?}

7 **Thou** madest him a little lower than the angels;
thou crownedst him with glory and honour,
and didst set him over the works of thy hands:
8 **Thou** hast put all things in subjection under his feet.

For in that he put all in subjection under him,
he left nothing that is not put under him.

But now we see not yet all things put under him.

9 **But we** see Jesus,
who was made a little lower than the angels for the suffering of death,
crowned with glory and honour;
that he by the grace of God should taste death for every man.

10 **For it** became him,
for whom are all things,
and by whom are all things,
in bringing many sons unto glory,
to make the captain of their salvation perfect through sufferings.

11 **For both he that sanctifieth and they who are sanctified** are all of one:
for which cause he is not ashamed to call them brethren,
12 Saying,
I will declare thy name unto my brethren,
in the midst of the church will I sing praise unto thee.

13 **And again, I** will put my trust in him.
And again, Behold I and the children which God hath given me.

14 **Forasmuch then as the children** are partakers of flesh and blood,
he also himself likewise took part of the same;
that through death he might destroy him that had the power of death, that is, the devil;
15 **And** deliver them who through fear of death were all their lifetime subject to bondage.

16 **For verily he** took not on him the nature of angels;
but he took on him the seed of Abraham.

17 **Wherefore in all things** it behoved him to be made like unto his brethren,
that he might be a merciful and faithful high priest in things pertaining to God,
to make reconciliation for the sins of the people.

18 **For in that he himself** hath suffered being tempted,
he is able to succour them that are tempted.

3 **Wherefore, holy brethren, partakers of the heavenly calling, consider** the Apostle and High Priest of our profession, Christ Jesus;
2 **Who** was faithful to him that appointed him,
as also Moses was faithful in all his house.

3 **For this man** was counted worthy of more glory than Moses,
inasmuch as he who hath builded the house hath more honour than the house.

4 **For every house** is builded by some man;
but he that built all things is God.

5 **And Moses** verily was faithful in all his house, as a servant, for a testimony of those things which were to be spoken after;
6 **But Christ** as a son over his own house;
whose house are we,
if we hold fast the confidence and the rejoicing of the hope firm unto the end.

7 **Wherefore**
({as the Holy Ghost saith},
{To day if ye will hear his voice},
8 {Harden not your hearts, as in the provocation, in the day of temptation in the wilderness:}
9 {When your fathers tempted me},
{proved me},
{and saw my works forty years}.
10 {Wherefore I was grieved with that generation},
{and said},
{They do alway err in their heart};
{and they have not known my ways}.
11 {So I sware in my wrath},
{They shall not enter into my rest}.)
12 **Take heed**, brethren,
lest there be in any of you an evil heart of unbelief,
in departing from the living God.

13 **But exhort** one another daily,
while it is called To day;
lest any of you be hardened through the deceitfulness of sin.

14 **For we** are made partakers of Christ,
if we hold the beginning of our confidence stedfast unto the end;
15 **While it** is said,
To day if ye will hear his voice,
harden not your hearts, as in the provocation.

16 **For some**, {when they had heard}, did provoke: howbeit not all that came out of Egypt by Moses.

17 **But with whom** was he grieved forty years?
was it not with them that had sinned,
whose carcases fell in the wilderness?

18 **And to whom** sware he
that they should not enter into his rest, but to them that believed not?

19 **So we** see that they could not enter in because of unbelief.

4 **Let us** therefore fear,
lest, {a promise being left us of entering into his rest}, any of you should seem to come short of it.

2 **For unto us** was the gospel preached, as well as unto them:
but the word preached did not profit them,
not being mixed with faith in them that heard it.

3 **For we which have believed** do enter into rest,
as he said,

As I have sworn in my wrath,
if they shall enter into my rest:
although the works were finished from the foundation of the world.

4 **For he** spake in a certain place of the seventh day on this wise,
And God did rest the seventh day from all his works.

5 **And in this place again,** If they shall enter into my rest.

6 **Seeing therefore it** remaineth that some must enter therein,
and they to whom it was first preached entered not in because of unbelief:

7 **Again, he** limiteth a certain day,
saying in David,
To day, after so long a time; {as it is said}, **To day if ye will hear his voice,**
harden not your hearts.

8 **For if Jesus** had given them rest,
then would he not afterward have spoken of another day.

9 **There** remaineth therefore a rest to the people of God.

10 **For he that is entered into his rest,** he also hath ceased from his own works,
as God did from his.

11 **Let us** labour therefore to enter into that rest,
lest any man fall after the same example of unbelief.

12 **For the word of God** is quick, and powerful, and sharper than any twoedged sword,
piercing even to the dividing asunder of soul and spirit, and of the joints and marrow,
and is a discerner of the thoughts and intents of the heart.

13 **Neither** is there any creature that is not manifest in his sight:
but all things are naked and opened unto the eyes of him with whom we have to do.

14 **Seeing then that we** have a great high priest,
that is passed into the heavens, Jesus the Son of God,
let us hold fast our profession.

15 **For we** have not an high priest which cannot be touched with the feeling of our infirmities;
but was in all points tempted like as we are, yet without sin.

16 **Let us** therefore come boldly unto the throne of grace,
that we may obtain mercy,
and find grace
to help in time of need.

5 **For every high priest taken from among men** is ordained for men in things pertaining to God,
that he may offer both gifts and sacrifices for sins:

2 **Who** can have compassion on the ignorant, and on them that are out of the way;
for that he himself also is compassed with infirmity.

3 **And by reason hereof** he ought, as for the people, so also for himself, to offer for sins.

4 **And no man** taketh this honour unto himself, but he that is called of God,
as was Aaron.

5 **So also Christ** glorified not himself
to be made an high priest;
but he that said unto him,
Thou art my Son,
to day have I begotten thee.

6 **As he** saith also in another place,
Thou art a priest for ever after the order of Melchisedec.

7 **Who in the days of his flesh,** {when he had offered up prayers and supplications with strong crying and tears unto him that was able to save him from death}, and was heard in that he feared;

8 **Though he** were a Son,
yet learned he obedience by the things which he suffered;

9 **And** being made perfect,
he became the author of eternal salvation unto all them that obey him;

10 Called of God an high priest after the order of Melchisedec.

11 **Of whom** we have many things to say,
and hard to be uttered,
seeing ye are dull of hearing.

12 **For when for the time** ye ought to be teachers,
ye have need that one teach you again which be the first principles of the oracles of God;
and are become such as have need of milk, and not of strong meat.

13 **For every one that useth milk** is unskilful in the word of righteousness:
for he is a babe.

14 **But strong meat** belongeth to them that are of full age,
even those who by reason of use have their senses exercised
to discern both good and evil.

6 **Therefore {leaving the principles of the doctrine of Christ},** let us go on unto perfection;
not laying again the foundation of repentance from dead works, and of faith toward God,

2 Of the doctrine of baptisms, and of laying on of hands, and of resurrection of the dead, and of eternal judgment.

3 **And this** will we do,
if God permit.

4 **For it is impossible** for those who were once enlightened, and have tasted of the heavenly gift, and were made partakers of the Holy Ghost,

5 And have tasted the good word of God, and the powers of the world to come,

6 If they shall fall away,
to renew them again unto repentance;
seeing they crucify to themselves the Son of God afresh,
and put him to an open shame.

7 **For the earth which drinketh in the rain that cometh oft upon it, and bringeth forth herbs meet for them by whom it is dressed,** receiveth blessing from God:

8 **But that which beareth thorns and briers** is rejected,
and is nigh unto cursing;
whose end is to be burned.

9 **But, beloved, we** are persuaded better things of you, and things that accompany salvation,
though we thus speak.

10 **For God** is not unrighteous to forget your work and labour of love,
which ye have shewed toward his name,
in that ye have ministered to the saints,
and do minister.

11 **And we** desire
that every one of you do shew the same diligence to the full assurance of hope unto the end:

12 **That ye** be not slothful, but followers of them who through faith and patience inherit the promises.
13 **For when God** made promise to Abraham,
because he could swear by no greater,
he sware by himself,
14 Saying,
Surely blessing I will bless thee,
and multiplying I will multiply thee.
15 **And so, {after he had patiently endured},** he obtained the promise.
16 **For men** verily swear by the greater:
and an oath for confirmation is to them an end of all strife.
17 **Wherein God**, {willing more abundantly to shew unto the heirs of promise the immutability of his counsel}, confirmed it by an oath:
18 **That by two immutable things,** {in which it was impossible for God to lie}, we might have a strong consolation,
who have fled for refuge
to lay hold upon the hope set before us:
19 **Which hope** we have as an anchor of the soul, both sure and stedfast,
and which entereth into that within the veil;
20 **Whither the forerunner** is for us entered, even Jesus,
made an high priest for ever after the order of Melchisedec.

7 **For this Melchisedec, king of Salem, priest of the most high God,** {who met Abraham returning from the slaughter of the kings}, {and blessed him};
2 {To whom also Abraham gave a tenth part of all}; {first being by interpretation King of righteousness, and after that also King of Salem}, {which is, King of peace};
3 {Without father, without mother, without descent, having neither beginning of days, nor end of life}; {but made like unto the Son of God}; abideth a priest continually.
4 **Now consider** how great this man was,
unto whom even the patriarch Abraham gave the tenth of the spoils.
5 **And verily they that are of the sons of Levi**, {who receive the office of the priesthood}, have a commandment to take tithes of the people according to the law, that is, of their brethren,
though they come out of the loins of Abraham:
6 **But he whose descent is not counted from them** received tithes of Abraham,
and blessed him that had the promises.
7 **And without all contradiction** the less is blessed of the better.
8 **And here men that die** receive tithes;
but there he receiveth them,
of whom it is witnessed that he liveth.
9 **And as I** may so say,
Levi also, {who receiveth tithes}, payed tithes in Abraham.
10 **For he** was yet in the loins of his father,
when Melchisedec met him.
11 **If therefore perfection** were by the Levitical priesthood,
(for under it the people received the law,)
what further need was there
that another priest should rise after the order of Melchisedec,
and not be called after the order of Aaron?
12 **For the priesthood** being changed,
there is made of necessity a change also of the law.
13 **For he of whom these things are spoken** pertaineth to another tribe,
of which no man gave attendance at the altar.
14 **For it is evident** that our Lord sprang out of Juda;
of which tribe Moses spake nothing concerning priesthood.
15 **And it** is yet far more evident:
for that after the similitude of Melchisedec there ariseth another priest,
16 **Who** is made, not after the law of a carnal commandment, but after the power of an endless life.
17 **For he** testifieth,
Thou art a priest for ever after the order of Melchisedec.
18 **For there** is verily a disannulling of the commandment going before for the weakness and unprofitableness thereof.
19 **For the law** made nothing perfect,
but the bringing in of a better hope did;
by the which we draw nigh unto God.
20 **And inasmuch as not without an oath** he was made priest:
21 (For those priests were made without an oath; but this with an oath by him that said unto him,
The Lord sware and will not repent,
Thou art a priest for ever after the order of Melchisedec:)
22 **By so much** was Jesus made a surety of a better testament.
23 **And they** truly were many priests,
because they were not suffered to continue by reason of death:
24 **But this man**, {because he continueth ever}, hath an unchangeable priesthood.
25 **Wherefore he** is able also to save them to the uttermost that come unto God by him,
seeing he ever liveth
to make intercession for them.
26 **For such an high priest** became us,
who is holy, harmless, undefiled, separate from sinners,
and made higher than the heavens;
27 **Who** needeth not daily, as those high priests, to offer up sacrifice, first for his own sins, and then for the people's:
for this he did once,
when he offered up himself.
28 **For the law** maketh men high priests which have infirmity;
but the word of the oath, {which was since the law}, maketh the Son,
who is consecrated for evermore.

8 **Now of the things which we have spoken** this is the sum:
We have such an high priest,
who is set on the right hand of the throne of the Majesty in the heavens;
2 A minister of the sanctuary, and of the true tabernacle,

which the Lord pitched, and not man.

3 **For every high priest** is ordained
to offer gifts and sacrifices:
wherefore it is of necessity that this man have somewhat also to offer.

4 **For if he** were on earth,
he should not be a priest,
seeing that there are priests that offer gifts according to the law:
5 **Who** serve unto the example and shadow of heavenly things,
as Moses was admonished of God when he was about to make the tabernacle:
for, {See}, saith he,
that thou make all things according to the pattern shewed to thee in the mount.

6 **But now** hath he obtained a more excellent ministry,
by how much also he is the mediator of a better covenant,
which was established upon better promises.

7 **For if that first covenant** had been faultless,
then should no place have been sought for the second.

8 **For finding fault with them,** he saith,
Behold,
the days come, saith the Lord,
when I will make a new covenant with the house of Israel and with the house of Judah:
9 Not according to the covenant that I made with their fathers in the day when I took them by the hand
to lead them out of the land of Egypt;
because they continued not in my covenant,
and I regarded them not,
saith the Lord.

10 **For this** is the covenant that I will make with the house of Israel after those days,
saith the Lord;
I will put my laws into their mind,
and write them in their hearts:
and I will be to them a God,
and they shall be to me a people:
11 **And they** shall not teach every man his neighbour, and every man his brother,
saying,
Know the Lord:
for all shall know me, from the least to the greatest.

12 **For I** will be merciful to their unrighteousness,
and their sins and their iniquities will I remember no more.

13 **In that he** saith,
A new covenant,
he hath made the first old.

Now that which decayeth and waxeth old is ready to vanish away.

9 **Then verily the first covenant** had also ordinances of divine service, and a worldly sanctuary.

2 **For there** was a tabernacle made;
the first, wherein was the candlestick, and the table, and the shewbread;
which is called the sanctuary.

3 **And after the second veil,** the tabernacle which is called the Holiest of all;

4 **Which** had the golden censer, and the ark of the covenant overlaid round about with gold,
wherein was the golden pot that had manna, and Aaron's rod that budded, and the tables of the covenant;
5 And over it the cherubims of glory shadowing the mercyseat;
of which we cannot now speak particularly.

6 **Now when these things** were thus ordained,
the priests went always into the first tabernacle,
accomplishing the service of God.

7 **But into the second** went the high priest alone once every year, not without blood,
which he offered for himself, and for the errors of the people:
8 **The Holy Ghost** this signifying,
that the way into the holiest of all was not yet made manifest,
while as the first tabernacle was yet standing:
9 **Which** was a figure for the time then present,
in which were offered both gifts and sacrifices,
that could not make him that did the service perfect, as pertaining to the conscience;

10 **Which** stood only in meats and drinks, and divers washings, and carnal ordinances,
imposed on them until the time of reformation.

11 **But Christ** being come an high priest of good things to come, by a greater and more perfect tabernacle,
not made with hands, that is to say, not of this building;
12 **Neither by the blood of goats and calves, but by his own blood** he entered in once into the holy place,
having obtained eternal redemption for us.

13 **For if the blood of bulls and of goats, {and the ashes of an heifer sprinkling the unclean},** sanctifieth to the purifying of the flesh:
14 **How much more shall the blood of Christ**, {who through the eternal Spirit offered himself without spot to God}, purge your conscience from dead works
to serve the living God?

15 **And for this cause** he is the mediator of the new testament,
that by means of death, for the redemption of the transgressions that were under the first testament, they which are called might receive the promise of eternal inheritance.

16 **For where a testament** is,
there must also of necessity be the death of the testator.

17 **For a testament** is of force after men are dead:
otherwise it is of no strength at all
while the testator liveth.

18 **Whereupon** neither the first testament was dedicated without blood.

19 **For when Moses** had spoken every precept to all the people according to the law,
he took the blood of calves and of goats, with water, and scarlet wool, and hyssop,
and sprinkled both the book, and all the people,
20 Saying,
This is the blood of the testament which God hath enjoined unto you.

21 **Moreover he** sprinkled with blood both the tabernacle, and all the vessels of the ministry.

22 **And almost all things** are by the law purged with blood;
and without shedding of blood is no remission.
23 **It was therefore necessary** that the patterns of things in the heavens should be purified with these; but the heavenly things themselves with better sacrifices than these.
24 **For Christ** is not entered into the holy places made with hands, {which are the figures of the true}; but into heaven itself,
now to appear in the presence of God for us:
25 **Nor yet that he** should offer himself often,
as the high priest entereth into the holy place every year with blood of others;
26 **For then** must he often have suffered since the foundation of the world:
but now once in the end of the world hath he appeared
to put away sin by the sacrifice of himself.
27 **And as it** is appointed unto men once to die, but after this the judgment:
28 **So Christ** was once offered
to bear the sins of many;
and unto them that look for him shall he appear the second time without sin unto salvation.

10 **For the law having a shadow of good things to come, and not the very image of the things,** can never with those sacrifices which they offered year by year continually make the comers thereunto perfect.
2 **For then would they not** have ceased to be offered?
because that the worshippers once purged should have had no more conscience of sins.
3 **But in those sacrifices** there is a remembrance again made of sins every year.
4 **For it is not possible** that the blood of bulls and of goats should take away sins.
5 **Wherefore when he** cometh into the world,
he saith,
Sacrifice and offering thou wouldest not,
but a body hast thou prepared me:
6 **In burnt offerings and sacrifices for sin** thou hast had no pleasure.
7 **Then** said I,
Lo,
I come (in the volume of the book it is written of me,) to do thy will, O God.
8 **Above when he** said,
Sacrifice and offering and burnt offerings and offering for sin thou wouldest not,
neither hadst pleasure therein;
which are offered by the law;
9 **Then** said he,
Lo,
I come to do thy will, O God.
He taketh away the first,
that he may establish the second.
10 **By the which will** we are sanctified through the offering of the body of Jesus Christ once for all.
11 **And every priest** standeth daily ministering and offering oftentimes the same sacrifices,
which can never take away sins:
12 **But this man**, {after he had offered one sacrifice for sins for ever}, sat down on the right hand of God;
13 **From henceforth** expecting till his enemies be made his footstool.
14 **For by one offering** he hath perfected for ever them that are sanctified.
15 **Whereof the Holy Ghost** also is a witness to us:
for after that he had said before,
16 **This** is the covenant that I will make with them after those days,
saith the Lord,
I will put my laws into their hearts,
and in their minds will I write them;
17 **And their sins and iniquities** will I remember no more.
18 **Now where remission of these** is,
there is no more offering for sin.
19 Having therefore, brethren, boldness to enter into the holiest by the blood of Jesus,
20 By a new and living way,
which he hath consecrated for us, through the veil, that is to say, his flesh;
21 **And** having an high priest over the house of God;
22 **Let us** draw near with a true heart in full assurance of faith,
having our hearts sprinkled from an evil conscience,
and our bodies washed with pure water.
23 **Let us** hold fast the profession of our faith without wavering;
(for he is faithful that promised;)
24 **And let us** consider one another
to provoke unto love and to good works:
25 Not forsaking the assembling of ourselves together,
as the manner of some is;
but exhorting one another: and so much the more,
as ye see the day approaching.
26 **For if we** sin wilfully
after that we have received the knowledge of the truth,
there remaineth no more sacrifice for sins,
27 But a certain fearful looking for of judgment and fiery indignation,
which shall devour the adversaries.
28 **He that despised Moses' law** died without mercy under two or three witnesses:
29 **Of how much sorer punishment**, {suppose ye}, shall he be thought worthy,
who hath trodden under foot the Son of God,
and hath counted the blood of the covenant,
wherewith he was sanctified, an unholy thing,
and hath done despite unto the Spirit of grace?
30 **For we** know him that hath said,
Vengeance belongeth unto me,
I will recompense,
saith the Lord.
And again, The Lord shall judge his people.
31 **It is a fearful thing** to fall into the hands of the living God.
32 **But call to remembrance** the former days,
in which, {after ye were illuminated}, ye endured a great fight of afflictions;
33 **Partly,** whilst ye were made a gazingstock both by reproaches and afflictions;
and partly, whilst ye became companions of them that were so used.

34 **For ye** had compassion of me in
my bonds,
and took joyfully the spoiling of
your goods,
knowing in yourselves
that ye have in heaven a better and
an enduring substance.
35 **Cast not away** therefore your
confidence,
which hath great recompence of
reward.
36 **For ye** have need of patience,
**that, {after ye have done the will
of God},** ye might receive the
promise.
37 **For yet a little while,** and he that
shall come will come,
and will not tarry.
38 **Now the just** shall live by faith:
but if any man draw back,
my soul shall have no pleasure in
him.
39 **But we** are not of them who draw
back unto perdition; but of them
that believe to the saving of the
soul.

11

Now faith is the
substance of things hoped
for, the evidence of things not
seen.
2 **For by it** the elders obtained a
good report.
3 **Through faith** we understand
that the worlds were framed by the
word of God,
so that things which are seen
were not made of things which do
appear.
4 **By faith** Abel offered unto God a
more excellent sacrifice than
Cain,
by which he obtained witness that
he was righteous,
God testifying of his gifts:
and by it he {being dead} yet
speaketh.
5 **By faith** Enoch was translated
that he should not see death;
and was not found,
because God had translated him:
for before his translation he had
this testimony,
that he pleased God.
6 **But without faith** it is impossible
to please him:
for he that cometh to God must
believe that he is,
and that he is a rewarder of them
that diligently seek him.
7 **By faith** Noah, {being warned of
God of things not seen as yet},
{moved with fear}, prepared an
ark to the saving of his house;
by the which he condemned the
world,
and became heir of the
righteousness which is by faith.
8 **By faith** Abraham, {when he was
called to go out into a place which
he should after receive for an
inheritance}, obeyed;
and he went out,
not knowing
whither he went.
9 **By faith** he sojourned in the land
of promise, as in a strange
country,
dwelling in tabernacles with Isaac
and Jacob, the heirs with him of
the same promise:
10 **For he** looked for a city which
hath foundations,
whose builder and maker is God.
11 **Through faith** also Sara herself
received strength to conceive
seed,
and was delivered of a child
when she was past age,
because she judged him faithful
who had promised.
12 **Therefore** sprang there even of
one, and him as good as dead, so
many as the stars of the sky in
multitude, and as the sand which
is by the sea shore innumerable.
13 **These all** died in faith,
not having received the promises,
but having seen them afar off,
and were persuaded of them,
and embraced them,
and confessed
that they were strangers and
pilgrims on the earth.
14 **For they that say such things**
declare plainly
that they seek a country.
15 **And truly, {if they had been
mindful of that country from
whence they came out},** they
might have had opportunity to
have returned.
16 **But now they** desire a better
country, that is, an heavenly:
wherefore God is not ashamed to
be called their God:
for he hath prepared for them a
city.
17 **By faith** Abraham, {when he was
tried}, offered up Isaac:
**and he that had received the
promises** offered up his only
begotten son,
18 **Of whom** it was said,
That in Isaac shall thy seed be
called:
19 Accounting
that God was able to raise him up,
even from the dead;
from whence also he received him
in a figure.
20 **By faith** Isaac blessed Jacob and
Esau concerning things to come.
21 **By faith** Jacob, {when he was a
dying}, blessed both the sons of
Joseph;
and worshipped,
leaning upon the top of his staff.
22 **By faith** Joseph, {when he died},
made mention of the departing of
the children of Israel;
and gave commandment
concerning his bones.
23 **By faith** Moses, {when he was
born}, was hid three months of
his parents,
because they saw he was a proper
child;
and they were not afraid of the
king's commandment.
24 **By faith** Moses, {when he was
come to years}, refused to be
called the son of Pharaoh's
daughter;
25 Choosing rather to suffer
affliction with the people of God,
than to enjoy the pleasures of sin
for a season;
26 Esteeming the reproach of Christ
greater riches than the treasures
in Egypt:
for he had respect unto the
recompence of the reward.
27 **By faith** he forsook Egypt,
not fearing the wrath of the king:
for he endured,
as seeing him who is invisible.
28 **Through faith** he kept the
passover, and the sprinkling of
blood,
**lest he that destroyed the
firstborn** should touch them.
29 **By faith** they passed through the
Red sea as by dry land:
which the Egyptians {assaying to
do} were drowned.
30 **By faith** the walls of Jericho fell
down,
after they were compassed about
seven days.

31 **By faith** the harlot Rahab perished not with them that believed not,
when she had received the spies with peace.

32 **And what** shall I more say?
for the time would fail me to tell of Gedeon, and of Barak, and of Samson, and of Jephthae; of David also, and Samuel, and of the prophets:
33 **Who through faith** subdued kingdoms,
wrought righteousness,
obtained promises,
stopped the mouths of lions.
34 Quenched the violence of fire,
escaped the edge of the sword,
out of weakness were made strong,
waxed valiant in fight,
turned to flight the armies of the aliens.

35 **Women** received their dead raised to life again:
and others were tortured,
not accepting deliverance;
that they might obtain a better resurrection:
36 **And others** had trial of cruel mockings and scourgings, yea, moreover of bonds and imprisonment:
37 **They** were stoned,
they were sawn asunder,
were tempted,
were slain with the sword:
they wandered about in sheepskins and goatskins;
being destitute,
afflicted,
tormented;
38 (Of whom the world was not worthy:)
they wandered in deserts, and in mountains, and in dens and caves of the earth.

39 **And these all**, {having obtained a good report through faith}, received not the promise:
40 **God** having provided some better thing for us,
that they without us should not be made perfect.

12

Wherefore seeing we also are compassed about with so great a cloud of witnesses,
let us lay aside every weight, and the sin which doth so easily beset us,
and let us run with patience the race that is set before us,
2 Looking unto Jesus the author and finisher of our faith;
who for the joy that was set before him endured the cross,
despising the shame,
and is set down at the right hand of the throne of God.

3 **For consider** him that endured such contradiction of sinners against himself,
lest ye be wearied and faint in your minds.

4 **Ye** have not yet resisted unto blood,
striving against sin.

5 **And ye** have forgotten the exhortation which speaketh unto you as unto children,
My son, despise not thou the chastening of the Lord,
nor faint when thou art rebuked of him:
6 **For whom** the Lord loveth
he chasteneth,
and scourgeth every son whom he receiveth.

7 **If ye** endure chastening,
God dealeth with you as with sons;
for what son is he whom the father chasteneth not?

8 **But if ye** be without chastisement,
whereof all are partakers,
then are ye bastards, and not sons.

9 **Furthermore we** have had fathers of our flesh which corrected us,
and we gave them reverence:
shall we not much rather be in subjection unto the Father of spirits,
and live?

10 **For they** verily for a few days chastened us after their own pleasure; but he for our profit,
that we might be partakers of his holiness.

11 **Now no chastening for the present** seemeth to be joyous, but grievous:
nevertheless afterward it yieldeth the peaceable fruit of righteousness unto them which are exercised thereby.

12 **Wherefore lift up** the hands which hang down, and the feeble knees;
13 **And make straight** paths for your feet,
lest that which is lame be turned out of the way;
but let it rather be healed.

14 **Follow** peace with all men, and holiness,
without which no man shall see the Lord:
15 Looking diligently
lest any man fail of the grace of God;
lest any root of bitterness springing up trouble you,
and thereby many be defiled;
16 **Lest there** be any fornicator, or profane person, as Esau,
who for one morsel of meat sold his birthright.

17 **For ye** know
how that afterward, {when he would have inherited the blessing}, he was rejected:
for he found no place of repentance,
though he sought it carefully with tears.

18 **For ye** are not come unto the mount that might be touched, and that burned with fire, nor unto blackness, and darkness, and tempest,
19 And the sound of a trumpet, and the voice of words;
which voice they that heard intreated
that the word should not be spoken to them any more:
20 (For they could not endure that which was commanded,
And if so much as a beast touch the mountain,
it shall be stoned,
or thrust through with a dart:
21 And so terrible was the sight,
that Moses said,
I exceedingly fear and quake:)

22 **But ye** are come unto mount Sion, and unto the city of the living God, the heavenly Jerusalem, and to an innumerable company of angels,
23 To the general assembly and church of the firstborn, {which are written in heaven}, and to God the Judge of all, and to the spirits of just men made perfect,
24 And to Jesus the mediator of the new covenant, and to the blood of sprinkling, {that speaketh better things than that of Abel}.

25 **See** that ye refuse not him that speaketh.

For if they escaped not who refused him that spake on earth,
much more shall not we escape,
if we turn away from him that speaketh from heaven:
26 **Whose voice** then shook the earth:
but now he hath promised,
saying,
Yet once more I shake not the earth only, but also heaven.
27 **And this word, Yet once more,** signifieth the removing of those things that are shaken, as of things that are made,
that those things which cannot be shaken may remain.
28 **Wherefore we** receiving a kingdom which cannot be moved,
let us have grace,
whereby we may serve God acceptably with reverence and godly fear:
29 **For our God** is a consuming fire.

13

Let brotherly love continue.
2 **Be not** forgetful to entertain strangers:
for thereby some have entertained angels unawares.
3 **Remember** them that are in bonds, {as bound with them}; and them which suffer adversity,
as being yourselves also in the body.
4 **Marriage** is honourable in all,
and the bed undefiled:
but whoremongers and adulterers God will judge.
5 **Let your conversation** be without covetousness;
and be content with such things as ye have:
for he hath said,
I will never leave thee,
nor forsake thee.
6 **So that we** may boldly say,
The Lord is my helper,
and I will not fear
what man shall do unto me.
7 **Remember** them which have the rule over you,
who have spoken unto you the word of God:
whose faith follow,
considering the end of their conversation.
8 **Jesus Christ** the same yesterday, and to day, and for ever.
9 **Be not carried about** with divers and strange doctrines.
For it is a good thing that the heart be established with grace; not with meats,
which have not profited them that have been occupied therein.
10 **We** have an altar,
whereof they have no right to eat which serve the tabernacle.
11 **For the bodies of those beasts**, {whose blood is brought into the sanctuary by the high priest for sin}, are burned without the camp.
12 **Wherefore Jesus** also, {that he might sanctify the people with his own blood}, suffered without the gate.
13 **Let us** go forth therefore unto him without the camp,
bearing his reproach.
14 **For here** have we no continuing city,
but we seek one to come.
15 **By him** therefore let us offer the sacrifice of praise to God continually, that is,
the fruit of our lips giving thanks to his name.
16 **But to do good and to communicate** forget not:
for with such sacrifices God is well pleased.
17 **Obey** them that have the rule over you,
and submit yourselves:
for they watch for your souls, as they that must give account,
that they may do it with joy, and not with grief:
for that is unprofitable for you.
18 **Pray** for us:
for we trust we have a good conscience,
in all things willing to live honestly.
19 **But I** beseech you the rather to do this,
that I may be restored to you the sooner.
20 **Now the God of peace**, {that brought again from the dead our Lord Jesus, that great shepherd of the sheep, through the blood of the everlasting covenant},
21 Make you perfect in every good work
to do his will,
working in you that which is wellpleasing in his sight, through Jesus Christ;
to whom be glory for ever and ever.
Amen.
22 **And I** beseech you, brethren,
suffer the word of exhortation:
for I have written a letter unto you in few words.
23 **Know ye**
that our brother Timothy is set at liberty;
with whom, {if he come shortly}, I will see you.
24 **Salute** all them that have the rule over you, and all the saints.
They of Italy salute you.
25 **Grace** be with you all.
Amen.

James

The Book of James, penned by James, the half-brother of Jesus, is an epistle whose wisdom and teachings remain a rich source of inspiration and guidance for believers. It reminds them of the need to live out their faith in practical ways, demonstrating their love for God and neighbors through acts of charity, compassion, and service. It also addresses the importance of controlling the tongue, avoiding the sin of partiality, and many other practical words of advice. Perhaps the most well-known of all its verses is one of the Bible's most oft-quoted phrases, "Faith without works is dead" (James 2:26), a central theme to the book.

When James writes his letter, the early Christian Church is still in its formative stages, and its members are struggling to understand the implications of their faith in a world that is often hostile to their beliefs. James is concerned about the spiritual health of these communities, which are facing various trials and temptations. His letter is a call to faithfulness, encouraging believers to persevere in their unwavering devotion to the Lord, even in the face of adversity. The book's primary aim is to inspire its readers to live out their faith in a way consistent with Jesus Christ's teachings. It emphasizes the importance of good works, not as a means of earning salvation, but as a natural outflow of a genuine faith. James also stresses the need for Christians to demonstrate their faith through acts of love, mercy, and kindness, particularly towards the poor and the marginalized. Furthermore, he is concerned about the dangers of wealth and materialism, which are beginning to creep into the Church. He warns about the corrupting influence of riches and the dangers of being seduced by worldly gain. Instead, he encourages them to seek wisdom, humility, and a deeper understanding of God's ways.

Ultimately, the Book of James offers wisdom on how to navigate the challenges of everyday life, from dealing with trials and temptations to building strong relationships and using one's words to uplift others. It also promotes a deeper understanding of the relationship between faith and action, inspiring believers to live a more Christ-like life. With its emphasis on the necessity of good works as evidence of true faith, it serves as a clarion call for Christians everywhere to move beyond empty professions and into a life of obedience, thereby demonstrating the authenticity of their salvation.

1 **James, a servant of God and of the Lord Jesus Christ,**
to the twelve tribes which are scattered abroad,
greeting.
2 **My brethren, count** it all joy
when ye fall into divers temptations;
3 Knowing this,
that the trying of your faith worketh patience.
4 **But let** patience have her perfect work,
that ye may be perfect and entire,
wanting nothing.
5 **If any of you** lack wisdom,
let him ask of God,
that giveth to all men liberally,
and upbraideth not;
and it shall be given him.
6 **But let him** ask in faith,
nothing wavering.
For he that wavereth is like a wave of the sea driven with the wind and tossed.
7 **For let not that man** think
that he shall receive any thing of the Lord.
8 **A double minded man** is unstable in all his ways.
9 **Let the brother of low degree** rejoice in that he is exalted:
10 **But the rich,** in that he is made low:
because as the flower of the grass he shall pass away.
11 **For the sun** is no sooner risen with a burning heat,
but it withereth the grass,
and the flower thereof falleth,
and the grace of the fashion of it perisheth:
so also shall the rich man fade away in his ways.
12 **Blessed** is the man that endureth temptation:
for when he is tried,
he shall receive the crown of life,
which the Lord hath promised to them that love him.
13 **Let no man** say
when he is tempted,
I am tempted of God:
for God cannot be tempted with evil,
neither tempteth he any man:
14 **But every man** is tempted,
when he is drawn away of his own lust,
and enticed.
15 **Then when lust** hath conceived,
it bringeth forth sin:
and sin, {when it is finished},
bringeth forth death.
16 **Do not err,** my beloved brethren.
17 **Every good gift and every perfect gift** is from above,
and cometh down from the Father of lights,
with whom is no variableness, neither shadow of turning.
18 **Of his own will** begat he us with the word of truth,
that we should be a kind of firstfruits of his creatures.
19 **Wherefore, my beloved brethren, let every man** be swift

to hear, slow to speak, slow to
wrath:

20 **For the wrath of man** worketh
not the righteousness of God.

21 **Wherefore lay apart** all filthiness
and superfluity of naughtiness,
and receive with meekness the
engrafted word,
which is able to save your souls.

22 **But be ye** doers of the word, and
not hearers only,
deceiving your own selves.

23 **For if any** be a hearer of the word,
and not a doer,
he is like unto a man beholding his
natural face in a glass:
24 **For he** beholdeth himself,
and goeth his way,
and straightway forgetteth
what manner of man he was.

25 **But whoso** looketh into the
perfect law of liberty,
and continueth therein,
he being not a forgetful hearer, but
a doer of the work,
this man shall be blessed in his
deed.

26 **If any man among you** seem to
be religious,
and bridleth not his tongue,
but deceiveth his own heart,
this man's religion is vain.

27 **Pure religion and undefiled
before God and the Father** is
this,
To visit the fatherless and widows
in their affliction,
and to keep himself unspotted from
the world.

2 **My brethren, have not** the
faith of our Lord Jesus Christ,
the Lord of glory, with respect of
persons.

2 **For if there** come unto your
assembly a man with a gold ring,
in goodly apparel,
and there come in also a poor man
in vile raiment;
3 **And ye** have respect to him that
weareth the gay clothing,
and say unto him,
Sit thou here in a good place;
and say to the poor,
Stand thou there,
or sit here under my footstool:
4 **Are ye not** then partial in
yourselves,
and are become judges of evil
thoughts?

5 **Hearken,** my beloved brethren,
Hath not God chosen the poor of
this world rich in faith, and heirs
of the kingdom which he hath
promised to them that love him?

6 **But ye** have despised the poor.

Do not rich men oppress you,
and draw you before the judgment
seats?

7 **Do not they** blaspheme that
worthy name by the which ye are
called?

8 **If ye** fulfil the royal law according
to the scripture,
Thou shalt love thy neighbour as
thyself,
ye do well:
9 **But if ye** have respect to persons,
ye commit sin,
and are convinced of the law as
transgressors.

10 **For whosoever** shall keep the
whole law,
and yet offend in one point,
he is guilty of all.

11 **For he that said, {Do not commit
adultery},** said also,
Do not kill.

Now if thou commit no adultery,
yet if thou kill,
thou art become a transgressor of
the law.

12 **So speak ye,** {and so do}, as they
that shall be judged by the law of
liberty.

13 **For he** shall have judgment
without mercy,
that hath shewed no mercy;
and mercy rejoiceth against
judgment.

14 **What** doth it profit, my brethren,
though a man say
he hath faith,
and have not works?
can faith save him?

15 **If a brother or sister** be naked,
and destitute of daily food,
16 **And one of you** say unto them,
Depart in peace,
be ye warmed
and filled;
notwithstanding ye give them not
those things which are needful to
the body;
what doth it profit?

17 **Even so faith,** {if it hath not
works}, is dead,
being alone.

18 **Yea, a man** may say,
Thou hast faith,
and I have works:
shew me thy faith without thy
works,
and I will shew thee my faith by my
works.

19 **Thou** believest
that there is one God;
thou doest well:
the devils also believe,
and tremble.

20 **But wilt thou** know, O vain man,
that faith without works is dead?

21 **Was not Abraham our father**
justified by works,
when he had offered Isaac his son
upon the altar?

22 **Seest thou**
how faith wrought with his works,
and by works was faith made
perfect?

23 **And the scripture** was fulfilled
which saith,
Abraham believed God,
and it was imputed unto him for
righteousness:
and he was called the Friend of
God.

24 **Ye** see then
how that by works a man is
justified, and not by faith only.

25 **Likewise also was not Rahab
the harlot** justified by works,
when she had received the
messengers,
and had sent them out another
way?

26 **For as the body without the
spirit** is dead,
so faith without works is dead
also.

3 **My brethren, be not** many
masters,
knowing
that we shall receive the greater
condemnation.

2 **For in many things** we offend all.

If any man offend not in word,
the same is a perfect man,
and able also to bridle the whole
body.

3 **Behold,**
we put bits in the horses' mouths,
that they may obey us;
and we turn about their whole
body.

4 **Behold** also the ships,
which though they be so great,

and are driven of fierce winds,
yet are they turned about with a very small helm,
whithersoever the governor listeth.

5 **Even so the tongue** is a little member,
and boasteth great things.
Behold,
how great a matter a little fire kindleth!

6 **And the tongue** is a fire, a world of iniquity:
so is the tongue among our members,
that it defileth the whole body,
and setteth on fire the course of nature;
and it is set on fire of hell.

7 **For every kind of beasts, and of birds, and of serpents, and of things in the sea,** is tamed,
and hath been tamed of mankind:
8 **But the tongue** can no man tame;
it is an unruly evil, full of deadly poison.

9 **Therewith** bless we God, even the Father;
and therewith curse we men,
which are made after the similitude of God.

10 **Out of the same mouth** proceedeth blessing and cursing.
My brethren, these things ought not so to be.

11 **Doth a fountain** send forth at the same place sweet water and bitter?

12 **Can the fig tree,** my brethren, bear olive berries?
either a vine, figs?
so can no fountain both yield salt water and fresh.

13 **Who** is a wise man {and endued with knowledge} among you?
let him shew out of a good conversation his works with meekness of wisdom.

14 **But if ye** have bitter envying and strife in your hearts,
glory not,
and lie not against the truth.

15 **This wisdom** descendeth not from above,
but is earthly, sensual, devilish.

16 **For where envying and strife** is,
there is confusion and every evil work.

17 **But the wisdom that is from above** is first pure, then peaceable, gentle, and easy to be intreated, full of mercy and good fruits, without partiality, and without hypocrisy.

18 **And the fruit of righteousness** is sown in peace of them that make peace.

4 **From whence** come wars and fightings among you?
come they not hence, even of your lusts that war in your members?

2 **Ye** lust,
and have not:
ye kill,
and desire to have,
and cannot obtain:
ye fight and war,
yet ye have not,
because ye ask not.

3 **Ye** ask,
and receive not,
because ye ask amiss,
that ye may consume it upon your lusts.

4 **Ye adulterers and adulteresses, know ye not**
that the friendship of the world is enmity with God?
whosoever therefore will be a friend of the world is the enemy of God.

5 **Do ye** think
that the scripture saith in vain,
The spirit that dwelleth in us lusteth to envy?

6 **But he** giveth more grace.
Wherefore he saith,
God resisteth the proud,
but giveth grace unto the humble.

7 **Submit** yourselves therefore to God.
Resist the devil,
and he will flee from you.

8 **Draw nigh** to God,
and he will draw nigh to you.
Cleanse your hands, ye sinners;
and purify your hearts, ye double minded.

9 **Be afflicted,**
and mourn,
and weep:
let your laughter be turned to mourning, and your joy to heaviness.

10 **Humble** yourselves in the sight of the Lord,
and he shall lift you up.

11 **Speak not evil** one of another, brethren.
He that speaketh evil of his brother, and judgeth his brother, speaketh evil of the law,
and judgeth the law:
but if thou judge the law,
thou art not a doer of the law, but a judge.

12 **There** is one lawgiver,
who is able to save and to destroy:
who art thou that judgest another?

13 **Go to** now, ye that say,
To day or to morrow we will go into such a city,
and continue there a year,
and buy and sell,
and get gain:
14 **Whereas ye** know not
what shall be on the morrow.
For what is your life?
It is even a vapour,
that appeareth for a little time,
and then vanisheth away.

15 **For that ye** ought to say,
If the Lord will,
we shall live,
and do this, or that.

16 **But now ye** rejoice in your boastings:
all such rejoicing is evil.

17 **Therefore to him that knoweth to do good, and doeth it not,** to him it is sin.

5 **Go to** now, ye rich men,
weep and howl for your miseries that shall come upon you.

2 **Your riches** are corrupted,
and your garments are motheaten.

3 **Your gold and silver** is cankered;
and the rust of them shall be a witness against you,
and shall eat your flesh as it were fire.
Ye have heaped treasure together for the last days.

4 **Behold,**
the hire of the labourers who have reaped down your fields, {which is of you kept back by fraud}, crieth:
and the cries of them which have reaped are entered into the ears of the Lord of sabaoth.

5 **Ye** have lived in pleasure on the earth,

and been wanton;
ye have nourished your hearts, as in a day of slaughter.
6 **Ye** have condemned and killed the just;
and he doth not resist you.
7 **Be** patient therefore, brethren, unto the coming of the Lord.
Behold,
the husbandman waiteth for the precious fruit of the earth,
and hath long patience for it,
until he receive the early and latter rain.
8 **Be ye** also patient;
stablish your hearts:
for the coming of the Lord draweth nigh.
9 **Grudge not** one against another, brethren,
lest ye be condemned:
behold,
the judge standeth before the door.
10 **Take,** my brethren, the prophets,
who have spoken in the name of the Lord, for an example of suffering affliction, and of patience.
11 **Behold,**
we count them happy which endure.
Ye have heard of the patience of Job,
and have seen the end of the Lord;
that the Lord is very pitiful, and of tender mercy.
12 **But above all things**, my brethren, swear not, neither by heaven, neither by the earth, neither by any other oath:
but let your yea be yea; and your nay, nay;
lest ye fall into condemnation.
13 **Is any** among you afflicted?
let him pray.
Is any merry?
let him sing psalms.
14 **Is any** sick among you?
let him call for the elders of the church;
and let them pray over him,
anointing him with oil in the name of the Lord:
15 **And the prayer of faith** shall save the sick,
and the Lord shall raise him up;
and if he have committed sins,
they shall be forgiven him.
16 **Confess** your faults one to another,
and pray one for another,
that ye may be healed.
The effectual fervent prayer of a righteous man availeth much.
17 **Elias** was a man subject to like passions as we are,
and he prayed earnestly
that it might not rain:
and it rained not on the earth by the space of three years and six months.
18 **And he** prayed again,
and the heaven gave rain,
and the earth brought forth her fruit.
19 **Brethren, if any of you** do err from the truth,
and one convert him;
20 **Let him** know,
that he which converteth the sinner from the error of his way shall save a soul from death,
and shall hide a multitude of sins.

1 Peter

During the reign of Emperor Nero, a time marked by intense persecution of Christians, the Apostle Peter, one of Jesus' twelve disciples, penned the Book of First Peter. His words are a lifeline to the early Christian communities in Asia Minor, who are grappling with persecution and suffering. Peter's message is clear: remain faithful to Christ, even in the face of adversity, and live a life of hope and holiness. He seeks to encourage and strengthen these believers, reminding them that their suffering is not in vain but a means of refining their faith and demonstrating a commitment to Christ. His letter is a beacon of hope with these goals in mind.

First, he seeks to remind these believers of their true identity in Christ, urging them to live as strangers and exiles in this world with their eyes fixed on their eternal inheritance. He wants to instill in them a sense of hope and perseverance despite the trials they are facing. Second, Peter aims to provide guidance on how to live a life of faithfulness and obedience to God, even amid persecution. He emphasizes the importance of submitting to authority, honoring Christ, and living a life of compassion, humility, and love. Finally, Peter hopes to counter the false teachings and heresies that are creeping into the early Christian communities. By reaffirming the apostolic teachings and the Gospel message, he seeks to safeguard the faith and ensure that these believers remain rooted in the truth of Christ.

In essence, Peter's letter is a call to faithfulness, hope, and perseverance. He wants to inspire these believers to remain faithful, even when it is difficult, and to trust in God's sovereignty and goodness, even in the midst of suffering. His letter is a powerful balm for those Christians going through trials and tribulations, reminding them that their hardship is not meaningless. For it is in the crucible of affliction that their faith is refined and their souls are purified, ultimately leading to an eternal inheritance that is imperishable, undefiled, and unfading.

1 **Peter, an apostle of Jesus Christ,** to the strangers scattered throughout Pontus, Galatia, Cappadocia, Asia, and Bithynia,
2 Elect according to the foreknowledge of God the Father, through sanctification of the Spirit, unto obedience and sprinkling of the blood of Jesus Christ:
Grace unto you, and peace, be multiplied.
3 **Blessed** be the God and Father of our Lord Jesus Christ,
which according to his abundant mercy hath begotten us again unto a lively hope by the resurrection of Jesus Christ from the dead,
4 To an inheritance incorruptible, and undefiled, and that fadeth not away,
reserved in heaven for you,
5 **Who** are kept by the power of God through faith unto salvation ready to be revealed in the last time.
6 **Wherein** ye greatly rejoice,
though now for a season, {if need be}, ye are in heaviness through manifold temptations:
7 **That the trial of your faith,** {being much more precious than of gold that perisheth}, {though it be tried with fire}, might be found unto praise and honour and glory at the appearing of Jesus Christ:
8 **Whom** having not seen,
ye love;
in whom, {though now ye see him not}, {yet believing}, ye rejoice with joy unspeakable and full of glory:
9 Receiving the end of your faith, even the salvation of your souls.
10 **Of which salvation** the prophets have enquired and searched diligently,
who prophesied of the grace that should come unto you:
11 Searching
what, or what manner of time the Spirit of Christ which was in them did signify,
when it testified beforehand the sufferings of Christ, and the glory that should follow.
12 **Unto whom** it was revealed,
that not unto themselves, but unto us they did minister the things,
which are now reported unto you by them that have preached the gospel unto you with the Holy Ghost sent down from heaven;
which things the angels desire to look into.
13 **Wherefore gird up** the loins of your mind,
be sober,
and hope to the end for the grace that is to be brought unto you at the revelation of Jesus Christ;
14 As obedient children,
not fashioning yourselves according to the former lusts in your ignorance:
15 **But as he which hath called you** is holy,
so be ye holy in all manner of conversation;
16 **Because it** is written,
Be ye holy;
for I am holy.
17 **And if ye** call on the Father,
who without respect of persons judgeth according to every man's work,

pass the time of your sojourning here in fear:
18 **Forasmuch as ye** know
that ye were not redeemed with corruptible things, as silver and gold, from your vain conversation received by tradition from your fathers;
19 But with the precious blood of Christ, as of a lamb without blemish and without spot:
20 **Who** verily was foreordained before the foundation of the world,
but was manifest in these last times for you,
21 **Who by him** do believe in God,
that raised him up from the dead,
and gave him glory;
that your faith and hope might be in God.

22 **Seeing ye** have purified your souls
in obeying the truth through the Spirit unto unfeigned love of the brethren,
see that ye love one another with a pure heart fervently:
23 Being born again, not of corruptible seed, but of incorruptible, by the word of God,
which liveth and abideth for ever.

24 **For all flesh** is as grass,
and all the glory of man as the flower of grass.

The grass withereth,
and the flower thereof falleth away:
25 **But the word of the Lord** endureth for ever.

And this is the word which by the gospel is preached unto you.

2 **Wherefore** laying aside all malice, and all guile, and hypocrisies, and envies, and all evil speakings,
2 As newborn babes,
desire the sincere milk of the word,
that ye may grow thereby:
3 **If so be ye** have tasted that the Lord is gracious.

4 **To whom** coming, as unto a living stone, {disallowed indeed of men}, {but chosen of God}, and precious,
5 **Ye** also, as lively stones, are built up a spiritual house, an holy priesthood,
to offer up spiritual sacrifices, acceptable to God by Jesus Christ.

6 **Wherefore also it** is contained in the scripture,
Behold,
I lay in Sion a chief corner stone, elect, precious:
and he that believeth on him shall not be confounded.

7 **Unto you therefore which believe** he is precious:
but unto them which be disobedient, the stone which the builders disallowed, the same is made the head of the corner,
8 And a stone of stumbling, and a rock of offence, even to them which stumble at the word,
being disobedient:
whereunto also they were appointed.

9 **But ye** are a chosen generation, a royal priesthood, an holy nation, a peculiar people;
that ye should shew forth the praises of him who hath called you out of darkness into his marvellous light;
10 **Which in time past** were not a people,
but are now the people of God:
which had not obtained mercy,
but now have obtained mercy.

11 **Dearly beloved, I** beseech you as strangers and pilgrims,
abstain from fleshly lusts,
which war against the soul;
12 Having your conversation honest among the Gentiles:
that, {whereas they speak against you as evildoers}, they may by your good works, {which they shall behold}, glorify God in the day of visitation.

13 **Submit** yourselves to every ordinance of man for the Lord's sake:
whether it be to the king, as supreme;
14 Or unto governors, as unto them that are sent by him for the punishment of evildoers, and for the praise of them that do well.

15 **For so** is the will of God,
that with well doing ye may put to silence the ignorance of foolish men:
16 As free,
and not using your liberty for a cloke of maliciousness, but as the servants of God.

17 **Honour** all men.
Love the brotherhood.
Fear God.
Honour the king.

18 **Servants, be** subject to your masters with all fear; not only to the good and gentle, but also to the froward.

19 **For this** is thankworthy,
if a man for conscience toward God endure grief,
suffering wrongfully.
20 **For what glory** is it,
if, {when ye be buffeted for your faults}, ye shall take it patiently?
but if, {when ye do well}, {and suffer for it}, ye take it patiently,
this is acceptable with God.

21 **For even hereunto** were ye called:
because Christ also suffered for us,
leaving us an example,
that ye should follow his steps:
22 **Who** did no sin,
neither was guile found in his mouth:
23 **Who, {when he was reviled},** reviled not again;
when he suffered,
he threatened not;
but committed himself to him that judgeth righteously:
24 **Who his own self** bare our sins in his own body on the tree,
that we, {being dead to sins}, should live unto righteousness:
by whose stripes ye were healed.

25 **For ye** were as sheep going astray;
but are now returned unto the Shepherd and Bishop of your souls.

3 **Likewise, ye wives, be** in subjection to your own husbands;
that, {if any obey not the word}, they also may without the word be won by the conversation of the wives;
2 **While they** behold your chaste conversation coupled with fear.

3 **Whose adorning** let it not be that outward adorning of plaiting the hair, and of wearing of gold, or of putting on of apparel;
4 **But let it** be the hidden man of the heart, in that which is not corruptible, even the ornament of a meek and quiet spirit,
which is in the sight of God of great price.

5 **For after this manner in the old time** the holy women also, {who trusted in God}, adorned themselves,
being in subjection unto their own husbands:
6 **Even as Sara** obeyed Abraham,
calling him lord:
whose daughters ye are,
as long as ye do well,
and are not afraid with any amazement.

7 **Likewise, ye husbands, dwell** with them according to knowledge,
giving honour unto the wife, as unto the weaker vessel,
and as being heirs together of the grace of life;
that your prayers be not hindered.

8 **Finally, be ye** all of one mind,
having compassion one of another,
love as brethren,
be pitiful,
be courteous:
9 Not rendering evil for evil, or railing for railing: but contrariwise blessing;
knowing
that ye are thereunto called,
that ye should inherit a blessing.

10 **For he that will love life, and see good days,** let him refrain his tongue from evil, and his lips
that they speak no guile:
11 **Let him** eschew evil,
and do good;
let him seek peace,
and ensue it.

12 **For the eyes of the Lord** are over the righteous,
and his ears are open unto their prayers:
but the face of the Lord is against them that do evil.

13 **And who** is he that will harm you,
if ye be followers of that which is good?

14 **But and if ye** suffer for righteousness' sake,
happy are ye:
and be not afraid of their terror,
neither be troubled;
15 **But sanctify** the Lord God in your hearts:
and be ready always to give an answer to every man that asketh you a reason of the hope that is in you with meekness and fear:
16 Having a good conscience;
that, {whereas they speak evil of you, as of evildoers}, they may be ashamed
that falsely accuse your good conversation in Christ.

17 **For it is better, {**if the will of God be so}, that ye suffer for well doing, than for evil doing.

18 **For Christ** also hath once suffered for sins, the just for the unjust,
that he might bring us to God,
being put to death in the flesh,
but quickened by the Spirit:
19 **By which** also he went and preached unto the spirits in prison;
20 **Which sometime** were disobedient,
when once the longsuffering of God waited in the days of Noah,
while the ark was a preparing,
wherein few, that is, eight souls were saved by water.

21 **The like figure whereunto even baptism** doth also now save us (not the putting away of the filth of the flesh, but the answer of a good conscience toward God,) by the resurrection of Jesus Christ:
22 **Who** is gone into heaven,
and is on the right hand of God;
angels and authorities and powers being made subject unto him.

4

Forasmuch then as Christ hath suffered for us in the flesh,
arm yourselves likewise with the same mind:
for he that hath suffered in the flesh hath ceased from sin;
2 **That he** no longer should live the rest of his time in the flesh to the lusts of men, but to the will of God.

3 **For the time past of our life** may suffice us to have wrought the will of the Gentiles,
when we walked in lasciviousness, lusts, excess of wine, revellings, banquetings, and abominable idolatries:
4 **Wherein** they think it strange
that ye run not with them to the same excess of riot,
speaking evil of you:
5 **Who** shall give account to him that is ready to judge the quick and the dead.

6 **For for this cause** was the gospel preached also to them that are dead,
that they might be judged according to men in the flesh,
but live according to God in the spirit.

7 **But the end of all things** is at hand:
be ye therefore sober,
and watch unto prayer.

8 **And above all things** have fervent charity among yourselves:
for charity shall cover the multitude of sins.

9 **Use** hospitality one to another without grudging.

10 **As every man** hath received the gift,
even so minister the same one to another, as good stewards of the manifold grace of God.

11 **If any man** speak,
let him speak as the oracles of God;
if any man minister,
let him do it as of the ability which God giveth:
that God in all things may be glorified through Jesus Christ,
to whom be praise and dominion for ever and ever.

Amen.

12 **Beloved, think it not strange** concerning the fiery trial which is to try you,
as though some strange thing happened unto you:
13 **But rejoice,**
inasmuch as ye are partakers of Christ's sufferings;
that, {when his glory shall be revealed}, ye may be glad also with exceeding joy.

14 **If ye** be reproached for the name of Christ,
happy are ye;
for the spirit of glory and of God resteth upon you:
on their part he is evil spoken of,
but on your part he is glorified.

15 **But let none of you** suffer as a murderer, or as a thief, or as an evildoer, or as a busybody in other men's matters.

16 **Yet if any man** suffer as a Christian,
let him not be ashamed;
but let him glorify God on this behalf.

17 **For the time** is come
that judgment must begin at the house of God:
and if it first begin at us,
what shall the end be of them that obey not the gospel of God?
18 **And if the righteous** scarcely be saved,
where shall the ungodly and the sinner appear?
19 **Wherefore let them that suffer according to the will of God** commit the keeping of their souls to him in well doing, as unto a faithful Creator.

5 **The elders which are among you** I exhort,
who am also an elder, and a witness of the sufferings of Christ, and also a partaker of the glory that shall be revealed:
2 **Feed** the flock of God which is among you,
taking the oversight thereof, not by constraint, but willingly; not for filthy lucre, but of a ready mind;
3 **Neither as** being lords over God's heritage,
but being examples to the flock.
4 **And when the chief Shepherd** shall appear,
ye shall receive a crown of glory that fadeth not away.
5 **Likewise, ye younger, submit** yourselves unto the elder.
Yea, all of you be subject one to another,
and be clothed with humility:
for God resisteth the proud,
and giveth grace to the humble.
6 **Humble** yourselves therefore under the mighty hand of God,
that he may exalt you in due time:
7 Casting all your care upon him;
for he careth for you.
8 **Be** sober,
be vigilant;
because your adversary the devil, as a roaring lion, walketh about,
seeking
whom he may devour:
9 **Whom** resist stedfast in the faith,
knowing
that the same afflictions are accomplished in your brethren that are in the world.
10 **But the God of all grace**, {who hath called us unto his eternal glory by Christ Jesus}, {after that ye have suffered a while}, make you perfect,
stablish, strengthen, settle you.
11 **To him** be glory and dominion for ever and ever.
Amen.
12 **By Silvanus, a faithful brother unto you**, {as I suppose}, I have written briefly,
exhorting,
and testifying
that this is the true grace of God
wherein ye stand.
13 **The church that is at Babylon**, {elected together with you}, saluteth you;
and so doth Marcus my son.
14 **Greet ye** one another with a kiss of charity.
Peace be with you all that are in Christ Jesus.
Amen.

2 Peter

The Book of Second Peter, written by Peter, a disciple of Jesus, is the second letter that the Apostle writes to believers suffering under the reign of Roman Emperor Nero. As the Apostle to the Jews, Peter is deeply troubled by the rise of false teachers and heretics who are spreading false doctrines and leading many astray. As a result, he aims to combat these false teachings by reaffirming the doctrine of the apostles and warning his readers against the dangers of heresy. He writes to remind them of the true Gospel, which he has preached to them, and to encourage them to remain faithful to the teachings of Christ.

More specifically, Peter hopes first to establish the authority of his own apostolic ministry and that of the other apostles to counter the claims of the false teachers. He does so by reminding his readers of his eyewitness account of Christ's life and ministry and by emphasizing the divine origin of the apostolic message. Peter then aims to encourage his readers to grow in their faith and to persevere in the face of persecution and false teaching. He reminds them of the importance of living a holy life and the need to be diligent in pursuing spiritual growth. Peter also uses his letter to correct the false teachings circulating in the early Christian communities. He specifically targets those who were denying the return of Christ and who were using this denial as a license to indulge in sinful behavior. Additionally, he forcefully argues that Christ will indeed return and that believers must be prepared to give an account of their lives when He does. Finally, Peter hopes to leave a lasting legacy for the Christian communities after his death. He knows that his time on earth is short, so he wants to ensure that his teachings and warnings are preserved for future generations.

As the Apostle Peter so eloquently warns in this second epistle, Christians must be ever vigilant against the false teachers and heretics who seek to corrupt the flock of God. For it is only through unwavering adherence to the truth of Scripture that believers may avoid the devil's snares and remain faithful to God's message of salvation. Second Peter also reminds believers that their understanding of God's truth is not merely a product of human intellect, but rather a gift of divine revelation, entrusted to them that they might increase in the love and likeness of the Lord Jesus Christ.

1 **Simon Peter, a servant and an apostle of Jesus Christ,** to them that have obtained like precious faith with us through the righteousness of God and our Saviour Jesus Christ:
2 **Grace and peace** be multiplied unto you through the knowledge of God, and of Jesus our Lord,
3 **According as his divine power** hath given unto us all things that pertain unto life and godliness, through the knowledge of him that hath called us to glory and virtue:
4 **Whereby** are given unto us exceeding great and precious promises:
that by these ye might be partakers of the divine nature,
having escaped the corruption that is in the world through lust.
5 **And beside this,** {giving all diligence}, add to your faith virtue;
and to virtue knowledge;
6 **And to knowledge** temperance;
and to temperance patience;
and to patience godliness;
7 **And to godliness** brotherly kindness;
and to brotherly kindness charity.
8 **For if these things** be in you,
and abound,
they make you that ye shall neither be barren nor unfruitful in the knowledge of our Lord Jesus Christ.
9 **But he that lacketh these things** is blind,
and cannot see afar off,
and hath forgotten
that he was purged from his old sins.
10 **Wherefore the rather, brethren, give** diligence to make your calling and election sure:
for if ye do these things,
ye shall never fall:
11 **For so an entrance** shall be ministered unto you abundantly into the everlasting kingdom of our Lord and Saviour Jesus Christ.
12 **Wherefore I** will not be negligent to put you always in remembrance of these things,
though ye know them,
and be established in the present truth.
13 **Yea, I think it meet,** {as long as I am in this tabernacle}, to stir you up by putting you in remembrance;
14 Knowing
that shortly I must put off this my tabernacle,
even as our Lord Jesus Christ hath shewed me.
15 **Moreover I** will endeavour that ye may be able after my decease to have these things always in remembrance.
16 **For we** have not followed cunningly devised fables,
when we made known unto you the power and coming of our Lord Jesus Christ,
but were eyewitnesses of his majesty.

17 **For he** received from God the Father honour and glory,
when there came such a voice to him from the excellent glory,
This is my beloved Son,
in whom I am well pleased.
18 **And this voice which came from heaven** we heard,
when we were with him in the holy mount.
19 **We** have also a more sure word of prophecy;
whereunto ye do well that ye take heed, as unto a light that shineth in a dark place,
until the day dawn,
and the day star arise in your hearts:
20 Knowing this first,
that no prophecy of the scripture is of any private interpretation.
21 **For the prophecy** came not in old time by the will of man:
but holy men of God spake
as they were moved by the Holy Ghost.

2 **But there** were false prophets also among the people,
even as there shall be false teachers among you,
who privily shall bring in damnable heresies,
even denying the Lord that bought them,
and bring upon themselves swift destruction.
2 **And many** shall follow their pernicious ways;
by reason of whom the way of truth shall be evil spoken of.
3 **And through covetousness** shall they with feigned words make merchandise of you:
whose judgment now of a long time lingereth not,
and their damnation slumbereth not.
4 **For if God** spared not the angels that sinned,
but cast them down to hell,
and delivered them into chains of darkness,
to be reserved unto judgment;
5 **And** spared not the old world,
but saved Noah the eighth person, a preacher of righteousness,
bringing in the flood upon the world of the ungodly;
6 **And** turning the cities of Sodom and Gomorrha into ashes
condemned them with an overthrow,
making them an ensample unto those that after should live ungodly;
7 **And** delivered just Lot,
vexed with the filthy conversation of the wicked:
8 (For that righteous man dwelling among them, {in seeing and hearing}, vexed his righteous soul from day to day with their unlawful deeds;)
9 **The Lord** knoweth
how to deliver the godly out of temptations,
and to reserve the unjust unto the day of judgment
to be punished:
10 But chiefly them that walk after the flesh in the lust of uncleanness, and despise government.
Presumptuous are they, selfwilled,
they are not afraid to speak evil of dignities.
11 **Whereas angels**, {which are greater in power and might}, bring not railing accusation against them before the Lord.
12 **But these, as natural brute beasts,** {made to be taken and destroyed}, speak evil of the things that they understand not;
and shall utterly perish in their own corruption;
13 **And** shall receive the reward of unrighteousness,
as they that count it pleasure to riot in the day time.
Spots they are and blemishes,
sporting themselves with their own deceivings
while they feast with you;
14 Having eyes full of adultery,
and that cannot cease from sin;
beguiling unstable souls:
an heart they have exercised with covetous practices; cursed children:
15 **Which** have forsaken the right way,
and are gone astray,
following the way of Balaam the son of Bosor,
who loved the wages of unrighteousness;
16 **But** was rebuked for his iniquity:
the dumb ass speaking with man's voice forbad the madness of the prophet.
17 **These** are wells without water, clouds that are carried with a tempest;
to whom the mist of darkness is reserved for ever.
18 **For when they** speak great swelling words of vanity,
they allure through the lusts of the flesh, through much wantonness, those that were clean escaped from them who live in error.
19 **While they** promise them liberty,
they themselves are the servants of corruption:
for of whom a man is overcome,
of the same is he brought in bondage.
20 **For if after they** have escaped the pollutions of the world through the knowledge of the Lord and Saviour Jesus Christ,
they are again entangled therein,
and overcome,
the latter end is worse with them than the beginning.
21 **For it had been better for them** not to have known the way of righteousness,
than, {after they have known it}, to turn from the holy commandment delivered unto them.
22 **But it** is happened unto them according to the true proverb,
The dog is turned to his own vomit again;
and the sow that was washed to her wallowing in the mire.

3 **This second epistle**, beloved, I now write unto you;
in both which I stir up your pure minds by way of remembrance:
2 **That ye** may be mindful of the words which were spoken before by the holy prophets, and of the commandment of us the apostles of the Lord and Saviour:
3 Knowing this first,
that there shall come in the last days scoffers,
walking after their own lusts,
4 **And** saying,
Where is the promise of his coming?
for since the fathers fell asleep,
all things continue as they were from the beginning of the creation.
5 **For this** they willingly are ignorant of,

that by the word of God the
heavens were of old,
and the earth standing out of the
water and in the water:
6 **Whereby** the world that then was,
{being overflowed with water},
perished:
7 **But the heavens and the earth,**
{which are now}, {by the same
word are kept in store}, reserved
unto fire against the day of
judgment and perdition of
ungodly men.
8 **But, beloved, be not** ignorant of
this one thing,
that one day is with the Lord as a
thousand years,
and a thousand years as one day.
9 **The Lord** is not slack concerning
his promise,
as some men count slackness;
but is longsuffering to us-ward,
not willing
that any should perish,
but that all should come to
repentance.
10 **But the day of the Lord** will come
as a thief in the night;
in the which the heavens shall pass
away with a great noise,
and the elements shall melt with
fervent heat,
**the earth also and the works that
are therein** shall be burned up.
11 **Seeing then that all these things**
shall be dissolved,
what manner of persons ought ye
to be in all holy conversation and
godliness,
12 Looking for and hasting unto the
coming of the day of God,
wherein the heavens {being on fire}
shall be dissolved,
and the elements shall melt with
fervent heat?
13 **Nevertheless we**, according to his
promise, look for new heavens
and a new earth,
wherein dwelleth righteousness.
14 **Wherefore, beloved, {seeing
that ye look for such things},** be
diligent
that ye may be found of him in
peace, without spot, and
blameless.
15 **And account**
that the longsuffering of our Lord
is salvation;
**even as our beloved brother Paul
also according to the wisdom
given unto him** hath written
unto you;
16 As also in all his epistles,
speaking in them of these things;
in which are some things hard to be
understood,
**which they that are unlearned
and unstable** wrest, {as they do
also the other scriptures}, unto
their own destruction.
17 **Ye** therefore, beloved, {seeing ye
know these things before},
beware
lest ye also, {being led away with
the error of the wicked}, fall from
your own stedfastness.
18 **But grow** in grace, and in the
knowledge of our Lord and
Saviour Jesus Christ.
To him be glory both now and for
ever.
Amen.

1 John

The Book of First John, penned by the Apostle John, tackles a critical issue that is plaguing the early Christian Church: the rapid proliferation of false teachings and heresies that pose a significant threat to the very essence of the Christian faith. Of particular concern to John is the rampant spread of Incipient Gnosticism, a heresy that not only denies the humanity of Jesus but also places undue emphasis on secret knowledge (gnosis) as the sole path to salvation. The Gnostics further propagate the notion that the material world is inherently evil, while the spiritual realm is the only realm of goodness. This false teaching is leading many Christians astray, sowing seeds of doubt about the true nature of Christ and the message of salvation.

John's primary aim in his writing is to provide a comforting reassurance to believers about the true nature of God and Jesus Christ. He reiterates that God is love and that Jesus Christ is the embodiment of that love. The Apostle underscores the significance of fellowship with God and one another, emphasizing that true believers manifest their faith through their love for others. Through his letter, John aims to debunk the erroneous doctrines of the Gnostics and other false teachers, reaffirming the orthodox Christian doctrine. He urges believers to stay steadfast in the true Gospel, cautioning them against the perils of false teachings. John also offers a clear understanding of the nature of God, underscoring His love and the importance of leading a life of love and obedience. Lastly, to foster a sense of community and unity among believers, he implores them to love one another as God has loved them.

At its core, the Book of First John is a personal plea from John to the flock of God, a heartfelt attempt to shield them from the devastating effects of false doctrine and to nurture their spiritual growth, ensuring that they remain firmly rooted in the truth of the Gospel. He reminds believers everywhere that the nature of God's divine love is not a mere doctrine to be comprehended but a vibrant, living reality to be experienced. If Christians are to discover the true purpose of their existence and the path to eternal life, they will find it in the intimate fellowship of the Father and the Son.

1 **That which was from the beginning, which we have heard, which we have seen with our eyes, which we have looked upon, and our hands have handled, of the Word of life;**
2 (For the life was manifested,
and we have seen it,
and bear witness,
and shew unto you that eternal life,
which was with the Father,
and was manifested unto us;)
3 **That which we have seen and heard** declare we unto you,
that ye also may have fellowship with us:
and truly our fellowship is with the Father,
and with his Son Jesus Christ.
4 **And these things** write we unto you,
that your joy may be full.
5 **This** then is the message which we have heard of him, and declare unto you,
that God is light,
and in him is no darkness at all.
6 **If we** say
that we have fellowship with him,
and walk in darkness,
we lie,
and do not the truth:
7 **But if we** walk in the light,
as he is in the light,
we have fellowship one with another,
and the blood of Jesus Christ his Son cleanseth us from all sin.
8 **If we** say
that we have no sin,
we deceive ourselves,
and the truth is not in us.
9 **If we** confess our sins,
he is faithful and just
to forgive us our sins,
and to cleanse us from all unrighteousness.
10 **If we** say
that we have not sinned,
we make him a liar,
and his word is not in us.

2 **My little children, these things** write I unto you,
that ye sin not.
And if any man sin,
we have an advocate with the Father, Jesus Christ the righteous:
2 **And he** is the propitiation for our sins: and not for ours only, but also for the sins of the whole world.
3 **And hereby** we do know
that we know him,
if we keep his commandments.
4 **He that saith, {I know him}, {and keepeth not his commandments},** is a liar,
and the truth is not in him.
5 **But whoso** keepeth his word,
in him verily is the love of God perfected:
hereby know we
that we are in him.
6 **He that saith he abideth in him** ought himself also so to walk,
even as he walked.
7 **Brethren, I** write no new commandment unto you, but an old commandment which ye had from the beginning.
The old commandment is the word which ye have heard from the beginning.
8 **Again, a new commandment** I write unto you,

which thing is true in him and in
you:
because the darkness is past,
and the true light now shineth.
9 **He that saith he is in the light,**
and hateth his brother, is in
darkness even until now.
10 **He that loveth his brother**
abideth in the light,
and there is none occasion of
stumbling in him.
11 **But he that hateth his brother** is
in darkness,
and walketh in darkness,
and knoweth not
whither he goeth,
because that darkness hath
blinded his eyes.
12 **I** write unto you, little children,
because your sins are forgiven you
for his name's sake.
13 **I** write unto you, fathers,
because ye have known him that is
from the beginning.
I write unto you, young men,
because ye have overcome the
wicked one.
I write unto you, little children,
because ye have known the Father.
14 **I** have written unto you, fathers,
because ye have known him that is
from the beginning.
I have written unto you, young
men,
because ye are strong,
and the word of God abideth in
you,
and ye have overcome the wicked
one.
15 **Love not** the world, neither the
things that are in the world.
If any man love the world,
the love of the Father is not in him.
16 **For all that is in the world, the**
lust of the flesh, and the lust of
the eyes, and the pride of life, is
not of the Father,
but is of the world.
17 **And the world** passeth away, and
the lust thereof:
but he that doeth the will of God
abideth for ever.
18 **Little children, it** is the last time:
and as ye have heard that antichrist
shall come,
even now are there many
antichrists;
whereby we know
that it is the last time.
19 **They** went out from us,
but they were not of us;
for if they had been of us,
they would no doubt have
continued with us:
but they went out,
that they might be made manifest
that they were not all of us.
20 **But ye** have an unction from the
Holy One,
and ye know all things.
21 **I** have not written unto you
because ye know not the truth,
but because ye know it,
and that no lie is of the truth.
22 **Who** is a liar
but he that denieth
that Jesus is the Christ?
He is antichrist,
that denieth the Father and the
Son.
23 **Whosoever** denieth the Son,
the same hath not the Father:
he that acknowledgeth the Son
hath the Father also.
24 **Let that** therefore abide in you,
which ye have heard from the
beginning.
If that which ye have heard from
the beginning shall remain in
you,
ye also shall continue in the Son,
and in the Father.
25 **And this** is the promise that he
hath promised us, even eternal
life.
26 **These things** have I written unto
you concerning them that seduce
you.
27 **But the anointing which ye have**
received of him abideth in you,
and ye need not that any man teach
you:
but as the same anointing
teacheth you of all things,
and is truth,
and is no lie,
and even as it hath taught you,
ye shall abide in him.
28 **And now, little children, abide**
in him;
that, {<u>when he</u> shall appear}, we
may have confidence,
and not be ashamed before him at
his coming.
29 **If ye** know
that he is righteous,
ye know
that every one that doeth
righteousness is born of him.

3 **Behold,**
what manner of love the
Father hath bestowed upon us,
that we should be called the sons of
God:
therefore the world knoweth us
not,
because it knew him not.
2 **Beloved, now** are we the sons of
God,
and it doth not yet appear what
we shall be:
but we know
that, {<u>when he</u> shall appear}, we
shall be like him;
for we shall see him as he is.
3 **And every man that hath this**
hope in him purifieth himself,
even as he is pure.
4 **Whosoever committeth sin**
transgresseth also the law:
for sin is the transgression of the
law.
5 **And ye** know
that he was manifested
to take away our sins;
and in him is no sin.
6 **Whosoever abideth in him**
sinneth not:
whosoever sinneth hath not seen
him,
neither known him.
7 **Little children, let no man**
deceive you:
he that doeth righteousness is
righteous,
even as he is righteous.
8 **He that committeth sin** is of the
devil;
for the devil sinneth from the
beginning.
For this purpose the Son of God
was manifested,
that he might destroy the works of
the devil.
9 **Whosoever is born of God** doth
not commit sin;
for his seed remaineth in him:
and he cannot sin,
because he is born of God.
10 **In this** the children of God are
manifest, and the children of the
devil:
whosoever doeth not
righteousness is not of God,
neither he that loveth not his
brother.

11 **For this** is the message that ye heard from the beginning,
that we should love one another.
12 Not as Cain,
who was of that wicked one,
and slew his brother.
And wherefore slew he him?
Because his own works were evil,
and his brother's righteous.
13 **Marvel not,** my brethren,
if the world hate you.
14 **We** know
that we have passed from death unto life,
because we love the brethren.
He that loveth not his brother abideth in death.
15 **Whosoever hateth his brother** is a murderer:
and ye know
that no murderer hath eternal life abiding in him.
16 **Hereby** perceive we the love of God,
because he laid down his life for us:
and we ought to lay down our lives for the brethren.
17 **But whoso** hath this world's good,
and seeth his brother have need,
and shutteth up his bowels of compassion from him,
how dwelleth the love of God in him?
18 **My little children, let us not** love in word, neither in tongue; but in deed and in truth.
19 **And hereby** we know
that we are of the truth,
and shall assure our hearts before him.
20 **For if our heart** condemn us,
God is greater than our heart,
and knoweth all things.
21 **Beloved, if our heart** condemn us not,
then have we confidence toward God.
22 **And whatsoever we** ask,
we receive of him,
because we keep his commandments,
and do those things that are pleasing in his sight.
23 **And this** is his commandment,
That we should believe on the name of his Son Jesus Christ,
and love one another,
as he gave us commandment.
24 **And he that keepeth his commandments** dwelleth in him, and he in him.
And hereby we know
that he abideth in us, by the Spirit which he hath given us.

4

Beloved, believe not every spirit,
but try the spirits
whether they are of God:
because many false prophets are gone out into the world.
2 **Hereby** know ye the Spirit of God:
Every spirit that confesseth that Jesus Christ is come in the flesh is of God:
3 **And every spirit that confesseth not that Jesus Christ is come in the flesh** is not of God:
and this is that spirit of antichrist,
whereof ye have heard that it should come;
and even now already is it in the world.
4 **Ye** are of God, little children,
and have overcome them:
because greater is he that is in you, than he that is in the world.
5 **They** are of the world:
therefore speak they of the world,
and the world heareth them.
6 **We** are of God:
he that knoweth God heareth us;
he that is not of God heareth not us.
Hereby know we the spirit of truth, and the spirit of error.
7 **Beloved, let us** love one another:
for love is of God;
and every one that loveth is born of God,
and knoweth God.
8 **He that loveth not** knoweth not God;
for God is love.
9 **In this** was manifested the love of God toward us,
because that God sent his only begotten Son into the world,
that we might live through him.
10 **Herein** is love,
not that we loved God,
but that he loved us,
and sent his Son to be the propitiation for our sins.
11 **Beloved, if God** so loved us,
we ought also to love one another.
12 **No man** hath seen God at any time.
If we love one another,
God dwelleth in us,
and his love is perfected in us.
13 **Hereby** know we
that we dwell in him, and he in us,
because he hath given us of his Spirit.
14 **And we** have seen
and do testify
that the Father sent the Son to be the Saviour of the world.
15 **Whosoever** shall confess
that Jesus is the Son of God,
God dwelleth in him, and he in God.
16 **And we** have known and believed the love that God hath to us.
God is love;
and he that dwelleth in love dwelleth in God, and God in him.
17 **Herein** is our love made perfect,
that we may have boldness in the day of judgment:
because as he is,
so are we in this world.
18 **There** is no fear in love;
but perfect love casteth out fear:
because fear hath torment.
He that feareth is not made perfect in love.
19 **We** love him,
because he first loved us.
20 **If a man** say,
I love God,
and hateth his brother,
he is a liar:
for he that loveth not his brother whom he hath seen, how can he love God whom he hath not seen?
21 **And this commandment** have we from him,
That he who loveth God love his brother also.

5

Whosoever believeth **that Jesus is the Christ** is born of God:
and every one that loveth him that begat loveth him also that is begotten of him.
2 **By this** we know
that we love the children of God,
when we love God,
and keep his commandments.
3 **For this** is the love of God,
that we keep his commandments:
and his commandments are not grievous.

4 **For whatsoever is born of God** overcometh the world:
and this is the victory that overcometh the world, even our faith.

5 **Who** is he that overcometh the world,
but he that believeth
that Jesus is the Son of God?

6 **This** is he that came by water and blood, even Jesus Christ; not by water only, but by water and blood.
And it is the Spirit that beareth witness,
because the Spirit is truth.

7 **For there** are three that bear record in heaven, the Father, the Word, and the Holy Ghost:
and these three are one.

8 **And there** are three that bear witness in earth, the Spirit, and the water, and the blood:
and these three agree in one.

9 **If we** receive the witness of men,
the witness of God is greater:
for this is the witness of God
which he hath testified of his Son.

10 **He that believeth on the Son of God** hath the witness in himself:
he that believeth not God hath made him a liar;
because he believeth not the record that God gave of his Son.

11 **And this** is the record,
that God hath given to us eternal life,
and this life is in his Son.

12 **He that hath the Son** hath life;
and he that hath not the Son of God hath not life.

13 **These things** have I written unto you that believe on the name of the Son of God;
that ye may know
that ye have eternal life,
and that ye may believe on the name of the Son of God.

14 **And this** is the confidence that we have in him,
that, {if we ask any thing according to his will}, he heareth us:

15 **And if we** know
that he hear us,
whatsoever we ask,
we know
that we have the petitions that we desired of him.

16 **If any man** see his brother sin a sin which is not unto death,
he shall ask,
and he shall give him life for them that sin not unto death.
There is a sin unto death:
I do not say
that he shall pray for it.

17 **All unrighteousness** is sin:
and there is a sin not unto death.

18 **We** know
that whosoever is born of God sinneth not;
but he that is begotten of God keepeth himself,
and that wicked one toucheth him not.

19 **And we** know
that we are of God,
and the whole world lieth in wickedness.

20 **And we** know
that the Son of God is come,
and hath given us an understanding,
that we may know him that is true,
and we are in him that is true, even in his Son Jesus Christ.
This is the true God, and eternal life.

21 **Little children, keep** yourselves from idols.

Amen.

2 John

In Second John, the Apostle John addresses a specific concern plaguing the early Christian community. A group of false teachers has emerged, denying the true nature of Jesus Christ. They claim that Jesus is not the Messiah, the Son of God, and that He did not come in the flesh. Being an eyewitness to the life and ministry of Jesus, John is compelled to write to the believers and warn them against these false teachers. He hopes to accomplish doing so in several ways.

First, John seeks to eliminate the influence of these deceivers. He wants to ensure that believers are not led astray by false doctrine and that they remain faithful to the Gospel's message. Second, he aims to reaffirm the fundamental truths of the Christian faith: Jesus Christ is the Son of God, Who came in the flesh, and Who lived a perfect, sinless life according to the commandments of God. Third, the Apostle hopes to promote unity and fellowship among the believers. He encourages them to love one another and to walk in the truth, emphasizing that those who do so are of the truth and have the Father and the Son. This emphasis on unity and love underscores the importance of community in the face of false teachings. Finally, John's letter is a call to discernment. He empowers believers to test the spirits, examine the teachings of these false prophets, and reject any doctrine that does not align with the truth of God's Word, highlighting their active role in discerning truth from falsehood.

John's overall purpose is to safeguard the orthodoxy of the Christian faith, to promote unity and love among believers, and to encourage discernment in the face of false teaching, all of which remain relevant today. However, a more profound concern emerges in the epistle. That is, John does not simply address a particular heresy; he also grapples with the fundamental nature of truth and error. He reminds Christians that their faith is not a matter of human opinion or speculation. Instead, it is rooted in the objective truth of God's revelation.

The elder unto the elect lady
and her children,
whom I love in the truth;
and not I only,
but also all they that have known
the truth;
2 For the truth's sake,
which dwelleth in us,
and shall be with us for ever.
3 **Grace** be with you, {mercy}, {and
peace}, from God the Father,
and from the Lord Jesus Christ, the
Son of the Father, in truth and
love.
4 **I** rejoiced greatly that I found of
thy children walking in truth,
as we have received a
commandment from the Father.
5 **And now I** beseech thee, lady,
not as though I wrote a new
commandment unto thee,
but that which we had from the
beginning,
that we love one another.
6 **And this** is love,
that we walk after his
commandments.
This is the commandment,
**That, {as ye have heard from the
beginning},** ye should walk in it.
7 **For many deceivers** are entered
into the world,
who confess not
that Jesus Christ is come in the
flesh.
This is a deceiver and an antichrist.
8 **Look** to yourselves,
that we lose not those things which
we have wrought,
but that we receive a full reward.
9 **Whosoever transgresseth, {and
abideth not in the doctrine of
Christ},** hath not God.
**He that abideth in the doctrine of
Christ,** he hath both the Father
and the Son.
10 **If there** come any unto you,
and bring not this doctrine,
receive him not into your house,
neither bid him God speed:
11 **For he that biddeth him God
speed** is partaker of his evil deeds.
12 Having many things to write unto
you,
I would not write with paper and
ink:
but I trust to come unto you,
and speak face to face,
that our joy may be full.
13 **The children of thy elect sister**
greet thee.
Amen.

3 John

The Book of Third John, authored by the Apostle John, was written when the early Christian Church was still in its formative stages. In his letter, John addresses a specific situation concerning a certain Diotrephes, a Church leader who is not receiving the Apostle's delegates and is even speaking maliciously against John and other believers. The epistle is written to Gaius, a faithful believer who, despite these challenges, plays a significant role in supporting and hosting traveling teachers and missionaries. John commends Gaius for his unwavering faithfulness and encourages him to continue walking in truth and love.

Driven by a sense of urgency, John sets out several crucial goals in writing his letter. He is determined to counter the influence of Diotrephes, who is causing division and strife in the Church. He also is resolute in his desire to encourage Gaius and other Christians to remain faithful to their high calling and continue showing hospitality to those spreading the good news about Jesus Christ. Moreover, John is deeply concerned about the integrity of the Gospel message and the behavior of those claiming to be Christ's followers. He remains adamant about emphasizing the importance of living a life of love, truth, and faithfulness.

Despite its brevity, Third John is a powerful testament to the early Christian faith. It not only urges believers to remain steadfast in their faith, but also warns against the deceitful ways of false teachers. This warning remains relevant even today, like it was during the early days of the Gospel, as the very fabric of Christianity is threatened by apostasy and divisions within the Church. By studying Third John, modern readers can gain a deeper, more profound appreciation for the roots of their faith, the sacrifices made by early Christians, and the letter's timeless and practical message, all of which make it a rich and rewarding read.

The elder unto the wellbeloved Gaius,
whom I love in the truth.
2 **Beloved, I** wish above all things
that thou mayest prosper
and be in health,
even as thy soul prospereth.
3 **For I** rejoiced greatly,
when the brethren came and testified of the truth that is in thee,
even as thou walkest in the truth.
4 **I** have no greater joy than to hear that my children walk in truth.
5 **Beloved, thou** doest faithfully
whatsoever thou doest to the brethren,
and to strangers;
6 **Which** have borne witness of thy charity before the church:
whom if thou bring forward on their journey after a godly sort,
thou shalt do well:
7 **Because that for his name's sake** they went forth,
taking nothing of the Gentiles.
8 **We** therefore ought to receive such,
that we might be fellowhelpers to the truth.
9 **I** wrote unto the church:
but Diotrephes, {who loveth to have the preeminence among them}, receiveth us not.
10 **Wherefore, if I** come,
I will remember his deeds which he doeth,
prating against us with malicious words:
and not content therewith,
neither doth he himself receive the brethren,
and forbiddeth them that would,
and casteth them out of the church.
11 **Beloved, follow not** that which is evil,
but that which is good.
He that doeth good is of God:
but he that doeth evil hath not seen God.
12 **Demetrius** hath good report of all men,
and of the truth itself:
yea, and we also bear record;
and ye know
that our record is true.
13 **I** had many things to write,
but I will not with ink and pen write unto thee:
14 **But I** trust
I shall shortly see thee,
and we shall speak face to face.
Peace be to thee.
Our friends salute thee.
Greet the friends by name.

Jude

The Book of Jude is unique in its authorship. It was written by Jude, also known as Judas, the half-brother of Jesus and brother of James. This familial connection to Jesus lends a special authority to his words. The epistle serves as a warning against doctrinal error and a call to action for believers to contend for the faith. Jude penned his letter in response to the corruption of faith by certain individuals who claim to be believers but are introducing false teachings and immoral practices. His primary aim is to alert believers about these false teachers, who are leading many astray.

In his book, Jude is sounding an alarm, alerting believers to the dangers of false teachings, which are denying the sovereignty of Christ and promoting licentiousness. He is not just warning about these dangers, but he is actively seeking to protect the flock from the spiritual deceivers who want to destroy the faith from within. Jude desires to encourage believers to stand firm in their faith, to contend for the Gospel, and to remain faithful to the Gospel. He reminds them about the importance of building themselves up in their faith by praying in the Holy Spirit and keeping themselves in the love of God. Furthermore, he desires to foster a sense of unity and solidarity among the believers by emphasizing their shared identity as children of God and their common salvation in Christ. Finally, Jude's letter is a call to action, urging believers to defend the faith proactively and promote the truth. He encourages them to be vigilant, to be on guard against false teachers, and to be zealous for the Gospel message.

As Christians grapple with the complexities of faith and reason, the Book of Jude stands as a timeless sentinel, a beacon of truth. It warns believers to contend fiercely for the faith, to stand unwavering against the relentless tides of apostasy, and to anchor their hope in the unchanging sovereignty of God. It reminds believers that the struggle to defend the truth is not just a duty but a sacred trust. Their unwavering commitment to the Gospel is not just a choice but the foundation upon which the Church stands. In this sense, the Book of Jude is not just a call to vigilance but a battle cry, urging believers to contend earnestly for their faith, lest the creeping shadows of heresy obscure the radiant light of the good news about Jesus Christ.

Jude, the servant of Jesus Christ, and brother of James, to them that are sanctified by God the Father,
and preserved in Jesus Christ,
and called:
2 **Mercy** unto you,
and peace, and love, be multiplied.

3 **Beloved, when I** gave all diligence to write unto you of the common salvation,
it was needful for me to write unto you,
and exhort you
that ye should earnestly contend for the faith which was once delivered unto the saints.

4 **For there** are certain men crept in unawares,
who were before of old ordained to this condemnation, ungodly men,
turning the grace of our God into lasciviousness,
and denying the only Lord God, and our Lord Jesus Christ.

5 **I** will therefore put you in remembrance,
though ye once knew this,
how that the Lord, {having saved the people out of the land of Egypt}, afterward destroyed them that believed not.

6 **And the angels which kept not their first estate, but left their own habitation,** he hath reserved in everlasting chains under darkness unto the judgment of the great day.

7 **Even as Sodom and Gomorrha, and the cities about them in like manner**, {giving themselves over to fornication}, {and going after strange flesh}, are set forth for an example,
suffering the vengeance of eternal fire.

8 **Likewise also these filthy dreamers** defile the flesh,
despise dominion,
and speak evil of dignities.

9 **Yet Michael the archangel**, {when contending with the devil} {he disputed about the body of Moses}, durst not bring against him a railing accusation,
but said,
The Lord rebuke thee.

10 **But these** speak evil of those things which they know not:
but what they know naturally, as brute beasts,
in those things they corrupt themselves.

11 **Woe** unto them!
for they have gone in the way of Cain,
and ran greedily after the error of Balaam for reward,
and perished in the gainsaying of Core.

12 **These** are spots in your feasts of charity,
when they feast with you,
feeding themselves without fear:
clouds they are without water, {carried about of winds}; trees whose fruit withereth, without fruit, twice dead, {plucked up by the roots};
13 Raging waves of the sea, {foaming out their own shame}; wandering stars, {to whom is reserved the blackness of darkness for ever}.

14 **And Enoch** also, the seventh from Adam, prophesied of these,
saying,
Behold,
the Lord cometh with ten thousands of his saints,
15 To execute judgment upon all,
and to convince all that are ungodly among them of all their ungodly deeds which they have ungodly committed, and of all their hard speeches which ungodly sinners have spoken against him.

16 **These** are murmurers, complainers,
walking after their own lusts;
and their mouth speaketh great swelling words,
having men's persons in admiration because of advantage.

17 **But, beloved, remember ye** the words which were spoken before of the apostles of our Lord Jesus Christ;
18 **How that they** told you
there should be mockers in the last time,
who should walk after their own ungodly lusts.

19 **These** be they who separate themselves, sensual,
having not the Spirit.

20 **But ye, beloved**, {building up yourselves on your most holy faith}, {praying in the Holy Ghost},
21 Keep yourselves in the love of God,
looking for the mercy of our Lord Jesus Christ unto eternal life.

22 **And of some** have compassion,
making a difference:
23 **And others** save with fear,
pulling them out of the fire;
hating even the garment spotted by the flesh.

24 **Now unto him that is able to keep you from falling,**
and to present you faultless before the presence of his glory with exceeding joy,
25 To the only wise God our Saviour, be glory and majesty, dominion and power, both now and ever.

Amen.

Revelation

The Book of Revelation, also known as the Apocalypse of John, was written by the Apostle John while exiled on the Island of Patmos. It is a prophetic and apocalyptic text that contains visions of the last days, also known as God's final judgment. With cryptic language and symbolism, the book has sparked endless interpretations and debates throughout the centuries. While its mysteries may remain partially veiled, Revelation offers a powerful testament to God's sovereignty and the ultimate triumph of good over evil.

John's purpose for writing his book is to comfort, encourage, and exhort the early Christian communities during a time of great persecution and suffering. In the late first century, the Roman Empire, under the reign of Emperor Nero and later Domitian, is actively persecuting Christians, forcing them to worship the emperor and renounce their faith in Christ. Many believers are facing imprisonment, torture, and even martyrdom. It is a time of great uncertainty and fear. John seeks to remind these persecuted Christians that God is still in control, that He is sovereign over all things, and that He will ultimately triumph over evil. His vision is meant to inspire hope, perseverance, and faithfulness in the face of adversity.

In writing Revelation, John reminds his readers that their suffering is not in vain, that it is part of a larger cosmic struggle between good and evil. He assures them that God knows their plight and will soon bring justice and redemption. John also encourages believers to remain faithful to Christ, even in the face of persecution. He warns them against compromise and apostasy, urging them to stand firm in their commitment to the Lord. His vision, meant to comfort the afflicted, offers a glimpse into the ultimate triumph of God. It describes a future where God will dwell among His people without sorrow, pain, or death. This vision of a new heaven and a new earth is meant to inspire hope and consolation amid suffering. Furthermore, the book is a call to spiritual vigilance, urging believers to be prepared for the return of Christ, which can come at any moment. John warns them to be faithful, to persevere, and to remain watchful, lest they be caught off guard by the Lord's sudden return.

John's revelation, a majestic apocalypse of Jesus Christ, stands as a ray of light, source of comfort, guiding star, anchor of faith, and lighthouse in a world beset by darkness. It illuminates the path to eternity and assures believers everywhere that, despite the trials and tribulations of this present age, the Lord Jesus Christ shall reign supreme in the end. It is a triumphant declaration of Christ's ultimate victory over the forces of darkness, and a solemn warning to the enemies of the Gospel, that God will win, that He already has won.

1 The Revelation of Jesus Christ,
which God gave unto him,
to shew unto his servants things which must shortly come to pass;
and he sent and signified it by his angel unto his servant John:
2 **Who** bare record of the word of God,
and of the testimony of Jesus Christ,
and of all things that he saw.

3 **Blessed** is he that readeth,
and they that hear the words of this prophecy, and keep those things which are written therein:
for the time is at hand.

4 **John** to the seven churches which are in Asia:
Grace be unto you, {and peace}, from him which is, and which was, and which is to come;
and from the seven Spirits which are before his throne;
5 **And** from Jesus Christ,
who is the faithful witness,
and the first begotten of the dead,
and the prince of the kings of the earth.

Unto him that loved us, and washed us from our sins in his own blood,
6 And hath made us kings and priests unto God and his Father;
to him be glory and dominion for ever and ever.

Amen.

7 **Behold,**
he cometh with clouds;
and every eye shall see him, and they also which pierced him:
and all kindreds of the earth shall wail because of him.

Even so, Amen.

8 **I** am Alpha and Omega, the beginning and the ending,
saith the Lord,
which is,
and which was,
and which is to come, the Almighty.

9 **I John**, {who also am your brother, and companion in tribulation, and in the kingdom and patience of Jesus Christ}, was in the isle that is called Patmos, for the word of God, and for the testimony of Jesus Christ.

10 **I** was in the Spirit on the Lord's day,
and heard behind me a great voice, as of a trumpet,
11 Saying,
I am Alpha and Omega, the first and the last:
and, What thou seest,

write in a book,
and send it unto the seven churches which are in Asia; unto Ephesus, and unto Smyrna, and unto Pergamos, and unto Thyatira, and unto Sardis, and unto Philadelphia, and unto Laodicea.

12 **And I** turned to see the voice that spake with me.

And being turned,
I saw seven golden candlesticks;
13 **And in the midst of the seven candlesticks one like unto the Son of man,** clothed with a garment down to the foot,
and girt about the paps with a golden girdle.

14 **His head and his hairs** were white like wool, as white as snow;
and his eyes were as a flame of fire;
15 **And his feet** like unto fine brass,
as if they burned in a furnace; and his voice as the sound of many waters.

16 **And he** had in his right hand seven stars:
and out of his mouth went a sharp twoedged sword:
and his countenance was as the sun shineth in his strength.

17 **And when I** saw him,
I fell at his feet as dead.

And he laid his right hand upon me,
saying unto me,
Fear not;
I am the first and the last:
18 **I** am he that liveth,
and was dead;
and, {behold}, I am alive for evermore, Amen;
and have the keys of hell and of death.

19 **Write** the things which thou hast seen, and the things which are, and the things which shall be hereafter;
20 The mystery of the seven stars which thou sawest in my right hand, and the seven golden candlesticks.

The seven stars are the angels of the seven churches:
and the seven candlesticks which thou sawest are the seven churches.

2 **Unto the angel of the church of Ephesus** write;
These things saith he that holdeth the seven stars in his right hand,
who walketh in the midst of the seven golden candlesticks;
2 **I** know thy works, and thy labour, and thy patience,
and how thou canst not bear them which are evil:
and thou hast tried them which say they are apostles, and are not,
and hast found them liars:
3 **And** hast borne,
and hast patience,
and for my name's sake hast laboured,
and hast not fainted.

4 **Nevertheless I** have somewhat against thee,
because thou hast left thy first love.

5 **Remember** therefore
from whence thou art fallen,
and repent,
and do the first works;
or else I will come unto thee quickly,
and will remove thy candlestick out of his place,
except thou repent.

6 **But this thou** hast,
that thou hatest the deeds of the Nicolaitanes,
which I also hate.

7 **He that hath an ear,** let him hear what the Spirit saith unto the churches;
To him that overcometh will I give to eat of the tree of life,
which is in the midst of the paradise of God.

8 **And unto the angel of the church in Smyrna** write;
These things saith the first and the last,
which was dead,
and is alive;
9 **I** know thy works, and tribulation, and poverty,
(but thou art rich)
and I know the blasphemy of them which say they are Jews, and are not,
but are the synagogue of Satan.

10 **Fear** none of those things which thou shalt suffer:
behold,
the devil shall cast some of you into prison,
that ye may be tried;
and ye shall have tribulation ten days:
be thou faithful unto death,
and I will give thee a crown of life.

11 **He that hath an ear,** let him hear what the Spirit saith unto the churches;
He that overcometh shall not be hurt of the second death.

12 **And to the angel of the church in Pergamos** write;
These things saith he which hath the sharp sword with two edges;
13 **I** know thy works,
and where thou dwellest,
even where Satan's seat is:
and thou holdest fast my name,
and hast not denied my faith,
even in those days wherein Antipas was my faithful martyr,
who was slain among you,
where Satan dwelleth.

14 **But I** have a few things against thee,
because thou hast there them that hold the doctrine of Balaam,
who taught Balac to cast a stumblingblock before the children of Israel, to eat things sacrificed unto idols, and to commit fornication.

15 **So** hast thou also them that hold the doctrine of the Nicolaitanes,
which thing I hate.

16 **Repent;**
or else I will come unto thee quickly,
and will fight against them with the sword of my mouth.

17 **He that hath an ear,** let him hear what the Spirit saith unto the churches;
To him that overcometh will I give to eat of the hidden manna,
and will give him a white stone, and in the stone a new name written,
which no man knoweth saving he that receiveth it.

18 **And unto the angel of the church in Thyatira** write;
These things saith the Son of God,
who hath his eyes like unto a flame of fire,
and his feet are like fine brass;
19 **I** know thy works, and charity, and service, and faith, and thy patience, and thy works;
and the last to be more than the first.

20 **Notwithstanding I** have a few things against thee,
because thou sufferest that woman Jezebel,
which calleth herself a prophetess,

to teach and to seduce my servants to commit fornication,
and to eat things sacrificed unto idols.
21 **And I** gave her space
to repent of her fornication;
and she repented not.
22 **Behold,**
I will cast her into a bed, and them that commit adultery with her into great tribulation,
except they repent of their deeds.
23 **And I** will kill her children with death;
and all the churches shall know
that I am he which searcheth the reins and hearts:
and I will give unto every one of you according to your works.
24 **But unto you** I say, and unto the rest in Thyatira,
as many as have not this doctrine,
and which have not known the depths of Satan,
as they speak;
I will put upon you none other burden.
25 **But that which ye have already** hold fast
till I come.
26 **And he that overcometh, and keepeth my works unto the end,** to him will I give power over the nations:
27 **And he** shall rule them with a rod of iron;
as the vessels of a potter shall they be broken to shivers:
even as I received of my Father.
28 **And I** will give him the morning star.
29 **He that hath an ear,** let him hear what the Spirit saith unto the churches.

3 **And unto the angel of the church in Sardis** write;
These things saith he that hath the seven Spirits of God, and the seven stars;
I know thy works,
that thou hast a name that thou livest,
and art dead.
2 **Be** watchful,
and strengthen the things which remain,
that are ready to die:
for I have not found thy works perfect before God.
3 **Remember** therefore
how thou hast received and heard,
and hold fast,
and repent.
If therefore thou shalt not watch,
I will come on thee as a thief,
and thou shalt not know
what hour I will come upon thee.
4 **Thou** hast a few names even in Sardis which have not defiled their garments;
and they shall walk with me in white:
for they are worthy.
5 **He that overcometh,** the same shall be clothed in white raiment;
and I will not blot out his name out of the book of life,
but I will confess his name before my Father, and before his angels.
6 **He that hath an ear,** let him hear what the Spirit saith unto the churches.
7 **And to the angel of the church in Philadelphia** write;
These things saith he that is holy, he that is true, he that hath the key of David, he that openeth, and no man shutteth; and shutteth, and no man openeth;
8 **I** know thy works:
behold,
I have set before thee an open door,
and no man can shut it:
for thou hast a little strength,
and hast kept my word,
and hast not denied my name.
9 **Behold,**
I will make them of the synagogue of Satan,
which say they are Jews,
and are not,
but do lie;
behold,
I will make them to come and worship before thy feet,
and to know
that I have loved thee.
10 **Because thou** hast kept the word of my patience,
I also will keep thee from the hour of temptation,
which shall come upon all the world,
to try them that dwell upon the earth.
11 **Behold,**
I come quickly:
hold that fast which thou hast,
that no man take thy crown.
12 **Him that overcometh** will I make a pillar in the temple of my God,
and he shall go no more out:
and I will write upon him the name of my God, and the name of the city of my God,
which is new Jerusalem,
which cometh down out of heaven from my God:
and I will write upon him my new name.
13 **He that hath an ear,** let him hear what the Spirit saith unto the churches.
14 **And unto the angel of the church of the Laodiceans** write;
These things saith the Amen, the faithful and true witness, the beginning of the creation of God;
15 **I** know thy works,
that thou art neither cold nor hot:
I would thou wert cold or hot.
16 **So then because thou** art lukewarm, and neither cold nor hot,
I will spue thee out of my mouth.
17 **Because thou** sayest,
I am rich,
and increased with goods,
and have need of nothing;
and knowest not
that thou art wretched, and miserable, and poor, and blind, and naked:
18 **I** counsel thee to buy of me gold tried in the fire,
that thou mayest be rich; and white raiment,
that thou mayest be clothed,
and that the shame of thy nakedness do not appear;
and anoint thine eyes with eyesalve,
that thou mayest see.
19 **As many as I** love,
I rebuke and chasten:
be zealous therefore,
and repent.
20 **Behold,**
I stand at the door,
and knock:
if any man hear my voice,
and open the door,
I will come in to him,
and will sup with him, and he with me.
21 **To him that overcometh** will I grant to sit with me in my throne,
even as I also overcame,

and am set down with my Father in his throne.

22 **He that hath an ear,** let him hear what the Spirit saith unto the churches.

4 **After this** I looked,
and, {behold}, a door was opened in heaven:
and the first voice which I heard was as it were of a trumpet talking with me;
which said,
Come up hither,
and I will shew thee things which must be hereafter.

2 **And immediately** I was in the spirit:
and, {behold}, a throne was set in heaven,
and one sat on the throne.

3 **And he that sat** was to look upon like a jasper and a sardine stone:
and there was a rainbow round about the throne, in sight like unto an emerald.

4 **And round about the throne** were four and twenty seats:
and upon the seats I saw four and twenty elders sitting,
clothed in white raiment;
and they had on their heads crowns of gold.

5 **And out of the throne** proceeded lightnings and thunderings and voices:
and there were seven lamps of fire burning before the throne,
which are the seven Spirits of God.

6 **And before the throne** there was a sea of glass like unto crystal:
and in the midst of the throne, and round about the throne, were four beasts full of eyes before and behind.

7 **And the first beast** was like a lion, and the second beast like a calf,
and the third beast had a face as a man,
and the fourth beast was like a flying eagle.

8 **And the four beasts** had each of them six wings about him;
and they were full of eyes within:
and they rest not day and night,
saying,
Holy, holy, holy, Lord God Almighty,
which was,
and is,
and is to come.

9 **And when those beasts** give glory and honour and thanks to him that sat on the throne, who liveth for ever and ever,

10 **The four and twenty elders** fall down before him that sat on the throne,
and worship him that liveth for ever and ever,
and cast their crowns before the throne,
saying,

11 **Thou** art worthy, O Lord, to receive glory and honour and power:
for thou hast created all things,
and for thy pleasure they are and were created.

5 **And I** saw in the right hand of him that sat on the throne a book written within and on the backside,
sealed with seven seals.

2 **And I** saw a strong angel proclaiming with a loud voice,
Who is worthy to open the book, and to loose the seals thereof?

3 **And no man in heaven, nor in earth, neither under the earth,** was able to open the book,
neither to look thereon.

4 **And I** wept much,
because no man was found worthy to open and to read the book,
neither to look thereon.

5 **And one of the elders** saith unto me,
Weep not:
behold,
the Lion of the tribe of Judah, the Root of David, hath prevailed
to open the book,
and to loose the seven seals thereof.

6 **And I** beheld,
and, {lo}, in the midst of the throne and of the four beasts, and in the midst of the elders, stood a Lamb as it had been slain,
having seven horns and seven eyes,
which are the seven Spirits of God sent forth into all the earth.

7 **And he** came and took the book out of the right hand of him that sat upon the throne.

8 **And when he** had taken the book,
the four beasts and four and twenty elders fell down before the Lamb,
having every one of them harps, and golden vials full of odours,
which are the prayers of saints.

9 **And they** sung a new song,
saying,
Thou art worthy to take the book, and to open the seals thereof:
for thou wast slain,
and hast redeemed us to God by thy blood out of every kindred, and tongue, and people, and nation;

10 **And** hast made us unto our God kings and priests:
and we shall reign on the earth.

11 **And I** beheld,
and I heard the voice of many angels round about the throne and the beasts and the elders:
and the number of them was ten thousand times ten thousand, and thousands of thousands;

12 Saying with a loud voice,
Worthy is the Lamb that was slain
to receive power, and riches, and wisdom, and strength, and honour, and glory, and blessing.

13 **And every creature which is in heaven, and under the earth, and such as are in the sea, and all that are in them,** heard I saying,
Blessing, and honour, and glory, and power, be unto him that sitteth upon the throne, and unto the Lamb for ever and ever.

14 **And the four beasts** said,
Amen.

And the four and twenty elders fell down and worshipped him that liveth for ever and ever.

6 **And I** saw when the Lamb opened one of the seals,
and I heard, as it were the noise of thunder, one of the four beasts saying,
Come and see.

2 **And I** saw,
and behold a white horse:
and he that sat on him had a bow;
and a crown was given unto him:
and he went forth conquering,
and to conquer.

3 **And when he** had opened the second seal,
I heard the second beast say,
Come and see.

4 **And there** went out another horse that was red:

and power was given to him that sat thereon to take peace from the earth,
and that they should kill one another:
and there was given unto him a great sword.
5 **And when he** had opened the third seal,
I heard the third beast say,
Come and see.
And I beheld,
and lo a black horse;
and he that sat on him had a pair of balances in his hand.
6 **And I** heard a voice in the midst of the four beasts say,
A measure of wheat for a penny, and three measures of barley for a penny;
and see thou hurt not the oil and the wine.
7 **And when he** had opened the fourth seal,
I heard the voice of the fourth beast say,
Come and see.
8 **And I** looked,
and behold a pale horse:
and his name that sat on him was Death,
and Hell followed with him.
And power was given unto them over the fourth part of the earth,
to kill with sword, and with hunger, and with death, and with the beasts of the earth.
9 **And when he** had opened the fifth seal,
I saw under the altar the souls of them that were slain for the word of God, and for the testimony which they held:
10 **And they** cried with a loud voice,
saying,
How long, O Lord, holy and true, dost thou not judge and avenge our blood on them that dwell on the earth?
11 **And white robes** were given unto every one of them;
and it was said unto them, that they should rest yet for a little season,
until their fellowservants also and their brethren, {that should be killed as they were}, should be fulfilled.
12 **And I** beheld when he had opened the sixth seal,
and, {lo}, there was a great earthquake;
and the sun became black as sackcloth of hair,
and the moon became as blood;
13 **And the stars of heaven** fell unto the earth,
even as a fig tree casteth her untimely figs,
when she is shaken of a mighty wind.
14 **And the heaven** departed as a scroll when it is rolled together;
and every mountain and island were moved out of their places.
15 **And the kings of the earth, and the great men, and the rich men, and the chief captains, and the mighty men, and every bondman, and every free man,** hid themselves in the dens and in the rocks of the mountains;
16 **And** said to the mountains and rocks,
Fall on us,
and hide us from the face of him that sitteth on the throne, and from the wrath of the Lamb:
17 **For the great day of his wrath** is come;
and who shall be able to stand?

7 **And after these things** I saw four angels standing on the four corners of the earth,
holding the four winds of the earth,
that the wind should not blow on the earth, nor on the sea, nor on any tree.
2 **And I** saw another angel ascending from the east,
having the seal of the living God:
and he cried with a loud voice to the four angels,
to whom it was given to hurt the earth and the sea,
3 Saying,
Hurt not the earth, neither the sea, nor the trees,
till we have sealed the servants of our God in their foreheads.
4 **And I** heard the number of them which were sealed:
and there were sealed an hundred and forty and four thousand of all the tribes of the children of Israel.
5 **Of the tribe of Juda** were sealed twelve thousand.
Of the tribe of Reuben were sealed twelve thousand.
Of the tribe of Gad were sealed twelve thousand.
6 **Of the tribe of Aser** were sealed twelve thousand.
Of the tribe of Nephthalim were sealed twelve thousand.
Of the tribe of Manasses were sealed twelve thousand.
7 **Of the tribe of Simeon** were sealed twelve thousand.
Of the tribe of Levi were sealed twelve thousand.
Of the tribe of Issachar were sealed twelve thousand.
8 **Of the tribe of Zabulon** were sealed twelve thousand.
Of the tribe of Joseph were sealed twelve thousand.
Of the tribe of Benjamin were sealed twelve thousand.
9 **After this** I beheld,
and, {lo}, a great multitude, {which no man could number}, of all nations, and kindreds, and people, and tongues, stood before the throne, and before the Lamb,
clothed with white robes, and palms in their hands;
10 **And** cried with a loud voice,
saying,
Salvation to our God which sitteth upon the throne, and unto the Lamb.
11 **And all the angels** stood round about the throne, and about the elders and the four beasts,
and fell before the throne on their faces,
and worshipped God,
12 Saying,
Amen:
Blessing, and glory, and wisdom, and thanksgiving, and honour, and power, and might, be unto our God for ever and ever.
Amen.
13 **And one of the elders** answered,
saying unto me,
What are these which are arrayed in white robes?
and whence came they?
14 **And I** said unto him,
Sir, thou knowest.
And he said to me,
These are they which came out of great tribulation,
and have washed their robes,

and made them white in the blood
of the Lamb.
15 **Therefore** are they before the
throne of God,
and serve him day and night in his
temple:
and he that sitteth on the throne
shall dwell among them.
16 **They** shall hunger no more,
neither thirst any more;
neither shall the sun light on them,
nor any heat.
17 **For the Lamb which is in the
midst of the throne** shall feed
them,
and shall lead them unto living
fountains of waters:
and God shall wipe away all tears
from their eyes.

8 **And when he** had opened the
seventh seal,
there was silence in heaven about
the space of half an hour.
2 **And I** saw the seven angels which
stood before God;
and to them were given seven
trumpets.
3 **And another angel** came and
stood at the altar,
having a golden censer;
and there was given unto him
much incense,
that he should offer it with the
prayers of all saints upon the
golden altar which was before the
throne.
4 **And the smoke of the incense,**
{which came with the prayers of
the saints}, ascended up before
God out of the angel's hand.
5 **And the angel** took the censer,
and filled it with fire of the altar,
and cast it into the earth:
and there were voices, and
thunderings, and lightnings, and
an earthquake.
6 **And the seven angels which had
the seven trumpets** prepared
themselves to sound.
7 **The first angel** sounded,
and there followed hail and fire
mingled with blood,
and they were cast upon the earth:
and the third part of trees was
burnt up,
and all green grass was burnt up.
8 **And the second angel** sounded,
**and as it were a great mountain
burning with fire** was cast into
the sea:
and the third part of the sea
became blood;
9 **And the third part of the
creatures which were in the sea,
and had life,** died;
and the third part of the ships
were destroyed.
10 **And the third angel** sounded,
and there fell a great star from
heaven,
burning as it were a lamp,
and it fell upon the third part of the
rivers, and upon the fountains of
waters;
11 **And the name of the star** is called
Wormwood:
and the third part of the waters
became wormwood;
and many men died of the waters,
because they were made bitter.
12 **And the fourth angel** sounded,
and the third part of the sun was
smitten, and the third part of the
moon, and the third part of the
stars;
so as the third part of them was
darkened,
and the day shone not for a third
part of it, and the night likewise.
13 **And I** beheld,
and heard an angel flying through
the midst of heaven,
saying with a loud voice,
Woe, woe, woe, to the inhabiters of
the earth by reason of the other
voices of the trumpet of the three
angels,
which are yet to sound!

9 **And the fifth angel**
sounded,
and I saw a star fall from heaven
unto the earth:
and to him was given the key of the
bottomless pit.
2 **And he** opened the bottomless pit;
and there arose a smoke out of the
pit, as the smoke of a great
furnace;
and the sun and the air were
darkened by reason of the smoke
of the pit.
3 **And there** came out of the smoke
locusts upon the earth:
and unto them was given power,
as the scorpions of the earth have
power.
4 **And it** was commanded them
that they should not hurt the grass
of the earth, neither any green
thing, neither any tree; but only
those men which have not the
seal of God in their foreheads.
5 **And to them** it was given
that they should not kill them,
but that they should be tormented
five months:
and their torment was as the
torment of a scorpion,
when he striketh a man.
6 **And in those days** shall men seek
death,
and shall not find it;
and shall desire to die,
and death shall flee from them.
7 **And the shapes of the locusts**
were like unto horses prepared
unto battle;
and on their heads were as it were
crowns like gold,
and their faces were as the faces of
men.
8 **And they** had hair as the hair of
women,
and their teeth were as the teeth of
lions.
9 **And they** had breastplates, as it
were breastplates of iron;
and the sound of their wings was
as the sound of chariots of many
horses running to battle.
10 **And they** had tails like unto
scorpions,
and there were stings in their tails:
and their power was to hurt men
five months.
11 **And they** had a king over them,
which is the angel of the
bottomless pit,
**whose name in the Hebrew
tongue** is Abaddon,
but in the Greek tongue hath his
name Apollyon.
12 **One woe** is past;
and, {behold}, there come two
woes more hereafter.
13 **And the sixth angel** sounded,
and I heard a voice from the four
horns of the golden altar which is
before God,
14 Saying to the sixth angel which
had the trumpet,
Loose the four angels which are
bound in the great river
Euphrates.
15 **And the four angels** were loosed,
which were prepared for an hour,
and a day, and a month, and a
year,

for to slay the third part of men.

16 **And the number of the army of the horsemen** were two hundred thousand thousand:
and I heard the number of them.

17 **And thus** I saw the horses in the vision, and them that sat on them,
having breastplates of fire, and of jacinth, and brimstone:
and the heads of the horses were as the heads of lions;
and out of their mouths issued fire and smoke and brimstone.

18 **By these three** was the third part of men killed, by the fire, and by the smoke, and by the brimstone,
which issued out of their mouths.

19 **For their power** is in their mouth, and in their tails:
for their tails were like unto serpents,
and had heads,
and with them they do hurt.

20 **And the rest of the men which were not killed by these plagues yet** repented not of the works of their hands,
that they should not worship devils, and idols of gold, and silver, and brass, and stone, and of wood:
which neither can see,
nor hear,
nor walk:

21 **Neither** repented they of their murders, nor of their sorceries, nor of their fornication, nor of their thefts.

10

And I saw another mighty angel come down from heaven,
clothed with a cloud:
and a rainbow was upon his head,
and his face was as it were the sun, and his feet as pillars of fire:

2 **And he** had in his hand a little book open:
and he set his right foot upon the sea, and his left foot on the earth,

3 **And** cried with a loud voice,
as when a lion roareth:
and when he had cried,
seven thunders uttered their voices.

4 **And when the seven thunders** had uttered their voices,
I was about to write:
and I heard a voice from heaven saying unto me,
Seal up those things which the seven thunders uttered,
and write them not.

5 **And the angel which I saw stand upon the sea and upon the earth** lifted up his hand to heaven,

6 **And** sware by him that liveth for ever and ever,
who created heaven, and the things that therein are, and the earth, and the things that therein are, and the sea, and the things which are therein,
that there should be time no longer:

7 **But in the days of the voice of the seventh angel**, {when he shall begin to sound}, the mystery of God should be finished,
as he hath declared to his servants the prophets.

8 **And the voice which I heard from heaven** spake unto me again,
and said,
Go and take the little book which is open in the hand of the angel which standeth upon the sea and upon the earth.

9 **And I** went unto the angel,
and said unto him,
Give me the little book.

And he said unto me,
Take it,
and eat it up;
and it shall make thy belly bitter,
but it shall be in thy mouth sweet as honey.

10 **And I** took the little book out of the angel's hand,
and ate it up;
and it was in my mouth sweet as honey:
and as soon as I had eaten it,
my belly was bitter.

11 **And he** said unto me,
Thou must prophesy again before many peoples, and nations, and tongues, and kings.

11

And there was given me a reed like unto a rod:
and the angel stood,
saying,
Rise,
and measure the temple of God, and the altar, and them that worship therein.

2 **But the court which is without the temple** leave out,
and measure it not;
for it is given unto the Gentiles:
and the holy city shall they tread under foot forty and two months.

3 **And I** will give power unto my two witnesses,
and they shall prophesy a thousand two hundred and threescore days,
clothed in sackcloth.

4 **These** are the two olive trees, and the two candlesticks standing before the God of the earth.

5 **And if any man** will hurt them,
fire proceedeth out of their mouth,
and devoureth their enemies:
and if any man will hurt them,
he must in this manner be killed.

6 **These** have power to shut heaven,
that it rain not in the days of their prophecy:
and have power over waters
to turn them to blood,
and to smite the earth with all plagues,
as often as they will.

7 **And when they** shall have finished their testimony,
the beast that ascendeth out of the bottomless pit shall make war against them,
and shall overcome them,
and kill them.

8 **And their dead bodies** shall lie in the street of the great city,
which spiritually is called Sodom and Egypt,
where also our Lord was crucified.

9 **And they of the people and kindreds and tongues and nations** shall see their dead bodies three days and an half,
and shall not suffer their dead bodies to be put in graves.

10 **And they that dwell upon the earth** shall rejoice over them,
and make merry,
and shall send gifts one to another;
because these two prophets tormented them that dwelt on the earth.

11 **And after three days and an half** the spirit of life from God entered into them,
and they stood upon their feet;
and great fear fell upon them which saw them.

12 **And they** heard a great voice from heaven saying unto them,
Come up hither.
And they ascended up to heaven in a cloud;
and their enemies beheld them.
13 **And the same hour** was there a great earthquake,
and the tenth part of the city fell,
and in the earthquake were slain of men seven thousand:
and the remnant were affrighted,
and gave glory to the God of heaven.
14 **The second woe** is past;
and, {behold}, the third woe cometh quickly.
15 **And the seventh angel** sounded;
and there were great voices in heaven,
saying,
The kingdoms of this world are become the kingdoms of our Lord, and of his Christ;
and he shall reign for ever and ever.
16 **And the four and twenty elders,** {which sat before God on their seats}, fell upon their faces,
and worshipped God,
17 Saying,
We give thee thanks, O Lord God Almighty,
which art,
and wast,
and art to come;
because thou hast taken to thee thy great power,
and hast reigned.
18 **And the nations** were angry,
and thy wrath is come, and the time of the dead,
that they should be judged,
and that thou shouldest give reward unto thy servants the prophets, and to the saints, and them that fear thy name, small and great;
and shouldest destroy them which destroy the earth.
19 **And the temple of God** was opened in heaven,
and there was seen in his temple the ark of his testament:
and there were lightnings, and voices, and thunderings, and an earthquake, and great hail.

12

And there appeared a great wonder in heaven; a woman clothed with the sun, and the moon under her feet, and upon her head a crown of twelve stars:
2 **And she being with child** cried, travailing in birth,
and pained to be delivered.
3 **And there** appeared another wonder in heaven;
and behold a great red dragon,
having seven heads and ten horns, and seven crowns upon his heads.
4 **And his tail** drew the third part of the stars of heaven,
and did cast them to the earth:
and the dragon stood before the woman which was ready to be delivered,
for to devour her child
as soon as it was born.
5 **And she** brought forth a man child,
who was to rule all nations with a rod of iron:
and her child was caught up unto God, and to his throne.
6 **And the woman** fled into the wilderness,
where she hath a place prepared of God,
that they should feed her there a thousand two hundred and threescore days.
7 **And there** was war in heaven:
Michael and his angels fought against the dragon;
and the dragon fought and his angels,
8 **And** prevailed not;
neither was their place found any more in heaven.
9 **And the great dragon** was cast out, that old serpent, called the Devil, and Satan,
which deceiveth the whole world:
he was cast out into the earth,
and his angels were cast out with him.
10 **And I** heard a loud voice saying in heaven,
Now is come salvation, and strength, and the kingdom of our God, and the power of his Christ:
for the accuser of our brethren is cast down,
which accused them before our God day and night.
11 **And they** overcame him by the blood of the Lamb, and by the word of their testimony;
and they loved not their lives unto the death.
12 **Therefore rejoice,** ye heavens, and ye that dwell in them.
Woe to the inhabiters of the earth and of the sea!
for the devil is come down unto you,
having great wrath,
because he knoweth
that he hath but a short time.
13 **And when the dragon** saw that he was cast unto the earth,
he persecuted the woman which brought forth the man child.
14 **And to the woman** were given two wings of a great eagle,
that she might fly into the wilderness, into her place,
where she is nourished for a time, and times, and half a time, from the face of the serpent.
15 **And the serpent** cast out of his mouth water as a flood after the woman,
that he might cause her to be carried away of the flood.
16 **And the earth** helped the woman,
and the earth opened her mouth,
and swallowed up the flood which the dragon cast out of his mouth.
17 **And the dragon** was wroth with the woman,
and went to make war with the remnant of her seed,
which keep the commandments of God,
and have the testimony of Jesus Christ.

13

And I stood upon the sand of the sea,
and saw a beast rise up out of the sea,
having seven heads and ten horns, and upon his horns ten crowns, and upon his heads the name of blasphemy.
2 **And the beast which I saw** was like unto a leopard,
and his feet were as the feet of a bear, and his mouth as the mouth of a lion:
and the dragon gave him his power, and his seat, and great authority.
3 **And I** saw one of his heads as it were wounded to death;
and his deadly wound was healed:

and all the world wondered after the beast.
4 **And they** worshipped the dragon which gave power unto the beast:
and they worshipped the beast, saying,
Who is like unto the beast?
who is able to make war with him?
5 **And there** was given unto him a mouth speaking great things and blasphemies;
and power was given unto him to continue forty and two months.
6 **And he** opened his mouth in blasphemy against God,
to blaspheme his name, and his tabernacle, and them that dwell in heaven.
7 **And it was given unto him** to make war with the saints,
and to overcome them:
and power was given him over all kindreds, and tongues, and nations.
8 **And all that dwell upon the earth** shall worship him,
whose names are not written in the book of life of the Lamb slain from the foundation of the world.
9 **If any man** have an ear,
let him hear.
10 **He that leadeth into captivity** shall go into captivity:
he that killeth with the sword must be killed with the sword.
Here is the patience and the faith of the saints.
11 **And I** beheld another beast coming up out of the earth;
and he had two horns like a lamb,
and he spake as a dragon.
12 **And he** exerciseth all the power of the first beast before him,
and causeth the earth and them which dwell therein to worship the first beast,
whose deadly wound was healed.
13 **And he** doeth great wonders,
so that he maketh fire come down from heaven on the earth in the sight of men,
14 **And** deceiveth them that dwell on the earth by the means of those miracles which he had power to do in the sight of the beast;
saying to them that dwell on the earth,
that they should make an image to the beast,
which had the wound by a sword,
and did live.
15 **And he** had power to give life unto the image of the beast,
that the image of the beast should both speak,
and cause that as many as would not worship the image of the beast should be killed.
16 **And he** causeth all, both small and great, rich and poor, free and bond, to receive a mark in their right hand, or in their foreheads:
17 **And that no man** might buy or sell, save he that had the mark, or the name of the beast, or the number of his name.
18 **Here** is wisdom.
Let him that hath understanding count the number of the beast:
for it is the number of a man;
and his number is Six hundred threescore and six.

14 **And I** looked,
and, {lo}, a Lamb stood on the mount Sion, and with him an hundred forty and four thousand,
having his Father's name written in their foreheads.
2 **And I** heard a voice from heaven, as the voice of many waters, and as the voice of a great thunder:
and I heard the voice of harpers harping with their harps:
3 **And they** sung as it were a new song before the throne, and before the four beasts, and the elders:
and no man could learn that song but the hundred and forty and four thousand,
which were redeemed from the earth.
4 **These** are they which were not defiled with women;
for they are virgins.
These are they which follow the Lamb
whithersoever he goeth.
These were redeemed from among men,
being the firstfruits unto God and to the Lamb.
5 **And in their mouth** was found no guile:
for they are without fault before the throne of God.
6 **And I** saw another angel fly in the midst of heaven,
having the everlasting gospel to preach unto them that dwell on the earth, and to every nation, and kindred, and tongue, and people,
7 Saying with a loud voice,
Fear God,
and give glory to him;
for the hour of his judgment is come:
and worship him that made heaven, and earth, and the sea, and the fountains of waters.
8 **And there** followed another angel, saying,
Babylon is fallen,
is fallen, that great city,
because she made all nations drink of the wine of the wrath of her fornication.
9 **And the third angel** followed them,
saying with a loud voice,
If any man worship the beast and his image,
and receive his mark in his forehead, or in his hand,
10 **The same** shall drink of the wine of the wrath of God,
which is poured out without mixture into the cup of his indignation;
and he shall be tormented with fire and brimstone in the presence of the holy angels, and in the presence of the Lamb:
11 **And the smoke of their torment** ascendeth up for ever and ever:
and they have no rest day nor night,
who worship the beast and his image,
and whosoever receiveth the mark of his name.
12 **Here** is the patience of the saints:
here are they that keep the commandments of God, and the faith of Jesus.
13 **And I** heard a voice from heaven saying unto me,
Write,
Blessed are the dead which die in the Lord from henceforth:
Yea, saith the Spirit,
that they may rest from their labours;
and their works do follow them.
14 **And I** looked,
and behold a white cloud,

and upon the cloud one sat like unto the Son of man,
having on his head a golden crown, and in his hand a sharp sickle.
15 **And another angel** came out of the temple,
crying with a loud voice to him that sat on the cloud,
Thrust in thy sickle,
and reap:
for the time is come for thee to reap;
for the harvest of the earth is ripe.
16 **And he that sat on the cloud** thrust in his sickle on the earth;
and the earth was reaped.
17 **And another angel** came out of the temple which is in heaven,
he also having a sharp sickle.
18 **And another angel** came out from the altar,
which had power over fire;
and cried with a loud cry to him that had the sharp sickle,
saying,
Thrust in thy sharp sickle,
and gather the clusters of the vine of the earth;
for her grapes are fully ripe.
19 **And the angel** thrust in his sickle into the earth,
and gathered the vine of the earth,
and cast it into the great winepress of the wrath of God.
20 **And the winepress** was trodden without the city,
and blood came out of the winepress, even unto the horse bridles, by the space of a thousand and six hundred furlongs.

15 **And I** saw another sign in heaven, great and marvellous,
seven angels having the seven last plagues;
for in them is filled up the wrath of God.
2 **And I** saw as it were a sea of glass mingled with fire:
and them that had gotten the victory over the beast, and over his image, and over his mark, and over the number of his name, stand on the sea of glass,
having the harps of God.
3 **And they** sing the song of Moses the servant of God, and the song of the Lamb,
saying,
Great and marvellous are thy works, Lord God Almighty;
just and true are thy ways, thou King of saints.
4 **Who** shall not fear thee, O Lord,
and glorify thy name?
for thou only art holy:
for all nations shall come and worship before thee;
for thy judgments are made manifest.
5 **And after that** I looked,
and, {behold}, the temple of the tabernacle of the testimony in heaven was opened:
6 **And the seven angels** came out of the temple,
having the seven plagues,
clothed in pure and white linen,
and having their breasts girded with golden girdles.
7 **And one of the four beasts** gave unto the seven angels seven golden vials full of the wrath of God,
who liveth for ever and ever.
8 **And the temple** was filled with smoke from the glory of God, and from his power;
and no man was able to enter into the temple,
till the seven plagues of the seven angels were fulfilled.

16 **And I** heard a great voice out of the temple saying to the seven angels,
Go your ways,
and pour out the vials of the wrath of God upon the earth.
2 **And the first** went,
and poured out his vial upon the earth;
and there fell a noisome and grievous sore upon the men which had the mark of the beast, and upon them which worshipped his image.
3 **And the second angel** poured out his vial upon the sea;
and it became as the blood of a dead man:
and every living soul died in the sea.
4 **And the third angel** poured out his vial upon the rivers and fountains of waters;
and they became blood.
5 **And I** heard the angel of the waters say,
Thou art righteous, O Lord,
which art,
and wast,
and shalt be,
because thou hast judged thus.
6 **For they** have shed the blood of saints and prophets,
and thou hast given them blood to drink;
for they are worthy.
7 **And I** heard another out of the altar say,
Even so, Lord God Almighty,
true and righteous are thy judgments.
8 **And the fourth angel** poured out his vial upon the sun;
and power was given unto him to scorch men with fire.
9 **And men** were scorched with great heat,
and blasphemed the name of God,
which hath power over these plagues:
and they repented not to give him glory.
10 **And the fifth angel** poured out his vial upon the seat of the beast;
and his kingdom was full of darkness;
and they gnawed their tongues for pain,
11 **And** blasphemed the God of heaven because of their pains and their sores,
and repented not of their deeds.
12 **And the sixth angel** poured out his vial upon the great river Euphrates;
and the water thereof was dried up,
that the way of the kings of the east might be prepared.
13 **And I** saw three unclean spirits like frogs come out of the mouth of the dragon, and out of the mouth of the beast, and out of the mouth of the false prophet.
14 **For they** are the spirits of devils,
working miracles,
which go forth unto the kings of the earth and of the whole world,
to gather them to the battle of that great day of God Almighty.
15 **Behold,**
I come as a thief.
Blessed is he that watcheth,

and keepeth his garments,
lest he walk naked,
and they see his shame.

16 **And he** gathered them together into a place called in the Hebrew tongue Armageddon.

17 **And the seventh angel** poured out his vial into the air;
and there came a great voice out of the temple of heaven, from the throne,
saying,
It is done.

18 **And there** were voices, and thunders, and lightnings;
and there was a great earthquake,
such as was not
since men were upon the earth, so mighty an earthquake, and so great.

19 **And the great city** was divided into three parts,
and the cities of the nations fell:
and great Babylon came in remembrance before God,
to give unto her the cup of the wine of the fierceness of his wrath.

20 **And every island** fled away,
and the mountains were not found.

21 **And there** fell upon men a great hail out of heaven, every stone about the weight of a talent:
and men blasphemed God because of the plague of the hail;
for the plague thereof was exceeding great.

17 **And there** came one of the seven angels which had the seven vials,
and talked with me,
saying unto me,
Come hither;
I will shew unto thee the judgment of the great whore that sitteth upon many waters:

2 **With whom** the kings of the earth have committed fornication,
and the inhabitants of the earth have been made drunk with the wine of her fornication.

3 **So he** carried me away in the spirit into the wilderness:
and I saw a woman sit upon a scarlet coloured beast, full of names of blasphemy,
having seven heads and ten horns.

4 **And the woman** was arrayed in purple and scarlet colour,
and decked with gold and precious stones and pearls,
having a golden cup in her hand full of abominations and filthiness of her fornication:

5 **And upon her forehead** was a name written,
Mystery, Babylon The Great, The Mother Of Harlots And Abominations Of The Earth.

6 **And I** saw the woman drunken with the blood of the saints, and with the blood of the martyrs of Jesus:
and when I saw her,
I wondered with great admiration.

7 **And the angel** said unto me,
Wherefore didst thou marvel?
I will tell thee the mystery of the woman, and of the beast that carrieth her,
which hath the seven heads and ten horns.

8 **The beast that thou sawest** was,
and is not;
and shall ascend out of the bottomless pit,
and go into perdition:
and they that dwell on the earth shall wonder,
whose names were not written in the book of life from the foundation of the world,
when they behold the beast that was, and is not, and yet is.

9 **And here** is the mind which hath wisdom.
The seven heads are seven mountains,
on which the woman sitteth.

10 **And there** are seven kings:
five are fallen,
and one is,
and the other is not yet come;
and when he cometh,
he must continue a short space.

11 **And the beast that was, and is not,** even he is the eighth,
and is of the seven,
and goeth into perdition.

12 **And the ten horns which thou sawest** are ten kings,
which have received no kingdom as yet;
but receive power as kings one hour with the beast.

13 **These** have one mind,
and shall give their power and strength unto the beast.

14 **These** shall make war with the Lamb,
and the Lamb shall overcome them:
for he is Lord of lords, and King of kings:
and they that are with him are called, and chosen, and faithful.

15 **And he** saith unto me,
The waters which thou sawest, {where the whore sitteth}, are peoples, and multitudes, and nations, and tongues.

16 **And the ten horns which thou sawest upon the beast,** these shall hate the whore,
and shall make her desolate and naked,
and shall eat her flesh,
and burn her with fire.

17 **For God** hath put in their hearts to fulfil his will, and to agree,
and give their kingdom unto the beast,
until the words of God shall be fulfilled.

18 **And the woman which thou sawest** is that great city,
which reigneth over the kings of the earth.

18 **And after these things** I saw another angel come down from heaven,
having great power;
and the earth was lightened with his glory.

2 **And he** cried mightily with a strong voice,
saying,
Babylon the great is fallen,
is fallen,
and is become the habitation of devils, and the hold of every foul spirit, and a cage of every unclean and hateful bird.

3 **For all nations** have drunk of the wine of the wrath of her fornication,
and the kings of the earth have committed fornication with her,
and the merchants of the earth are waxed rich through the abundance of her delicacies.

4 **And I** heard another voice from heaven,
saying,
Come out of her, my people,
that ye be not partakers of her sins,

and that ye receive not of her plagues.
5 **For her sins** have reached unto heaven,
and God hath remembered her iniquities.
6 **Reward** her
even as she rewarded you,
and double unto her double according to her works:
in the cup which she hath filled fill to her double.
7 **How much** she hath glorified herself,
and lived deliciously,
so much torment and sorrow give her:
for she saith in her heart,
I sit a queen,
and am no widow,
and shall see no sorrow.
8 **Therefore** shall her plagues come in one day, death, and mourning, and famine;
and she shall be utterly burned with fire:
for strong is the Lord God who judgeth her.
9 **And the kings of the earth**, {who have committed fornication} {and lived deliciously with her}, shall bewail her,
and lament for her,
when they shall see the smoke of her burning,
10 Standing afar off for the fear of her torment,
saying,
Alas, alas that great city Babylon, that mighty city!
for in one hour is thy judgment come.
11 **And the merchants of the earth** shall weep and mourn over her;
for no man buyeth their merchandise any more:
12 The merchandise of gold, and silver, and precious stones, and of pearls, and fine linen, and purple, and silk, and scarlet, and all thyine wood, and all manner vessels of ivory, and all manner vessels of most precious wood, and of brass, and iron, and marble,
13 And cinnamon, and odours, and ointments, and frankincense, and wine, and oil, and fine flour, and wheat, and beasts, and sheep, and horses, and chariots, and slaves, and souls of men.
14 **And the fruits that thy soul lusted after** are departed from thee,
and all things which were dainty and goodly are departed from thee,
and thou shalt find them no more at all.
15 **The merchants of these things**, {which were made rich by her}, shall stand afar off for the fear of her torment, weeping and wailing,
16 And saying,
Alas, alas that great city,
that was clothed in fine linen, and purple, and scarlet,
and decked with gold, and precious stones, and pearls!
17 **For in one hour** so great riches is come to nought.
And every shipmaster, and all the company in ships, and sailors, and as many as trade by sea, stood afar off,
18 **And** cried
when they saw the smoke of her burning,
saying,
What city is like unto this great city!
19 **And they** cast dust on their heads,
and cried,
weeping and wailing,
saying,
Alas, alas that great city,
wherein were made rich all that had ships in the sea by reason of her costliness!
for in one hour is she made desolate.
20 **Rejoice** over her, thou heaven, and ye holy apostles and prophets;
for God hath avenged you on her.
21 **And a mighty angel** took up a stone like a great millstone,
and cast it into the sea,
saying,
Thus with violence shall that great city Babylon be thrown down,
and shall be found no more at all.
22 **And the voice of harpers, and musicians, and of pipers, and trumpeters,** shall be heard no more at all in thee;
and no craftsman, {of whatsoever craft he be}, shall be found any more in thee;
and the sound of a millstone shall be heard no more at all in thee;
23 **And the light of a candle** shall shine no more at all in thee;
and the voice of the bridegroom and of the bride shall be heard no more at all in thee:
for thy merchants were the great men of the earth;
for by thy sorceries were all nations deceived.
24 **And in her** was found the blood of prophets, and of saints, and of all that were slain upon the earth.

19 **And after these things** I heard a great voice of much people in heaven,
saying,
Alleluia; Salvation, and glory, and honour, and power, unto the Lord our God:
2 **For true and righteous** are his judgments:
for he hath judged the great whore,
which did corrupt the earth with her fornication,
and hath avenged the blood of his servants at her hand.
3 **And again they** said,
Alleluia.
And her smoke rose up for ever and ever.
4 **And the four and twenty elders and the four beasts** fell down and worshipped God that sat on the throne,
saying,
Amen; Alleluia.
5 **And a voice** came out of the throne,
saying,
Praise our God, all ye his servants, and ye that fear him, both small and great.
6 **And I** heard as it were the voice of a great multitude, and as the voice of many waters, and as the voice of mighty thunderings,
saying,
Alleluia:
for the Lord God omnipotent reigneth.
7 **Let us** be glad and rejoice,
and give honour to him:
for the marriage of the Lamb is come,

and his wife hath made herself ready.

8 **And to her** was granted that she should be arrayed in fine linen, clean and white:
for the fine linen is the righteousness of saints.

9 **And he** saith unto me,
Write,
Blessed are they which are called unto the marriage supper of the Lamb.

And he saith unto me,
These are the true sayings of God.

10 **And I** fell at his feet
to worship him.

And he said unto me,
See thou do it not:
I am thy fellowservant, and of thy brethren that have the testimony of Jesus:
worship God:
for the testimony of Jesus is the spirit of prophecy.

11 **And I** saw heaven opened,
and behold a white horse;
and he that sat upon him was called Faithful and True,
and in righteousness he doth judge and make war.

12 **His eyes** were as a flame of fire,
and on his head were many crowns;
and he had a name written,
that no man knew, but he himself.

13 **And he** was clothed with a vesture dipped in blood:
and his name is called The Word of God.

14 **And the armies which were in heaven** followed him upon white horses,
clothed in fine linen, white and clean.

15 **And out of his mouth** goeth a sharp sword,
that with it he should smite the nations:
and he shall rule them with a rod of iron:
and he treadeth the winepress of the fierceness and wrath of Almighty God.

16 **And he** hath on his vesture and on his thigh a name written,
King Of Kings, And LORD Of LORDs.

17 **And I** saw an angel standing in the sun;
and he cried with a loud voice,
saying to all the fowls that fly in the midst of heaven,
Come and gather yourselves together unto the supper of the great God;

18 **That ye** may eat the flesh of kings, and the flesh of captains, and the flesh of mighty men, and the flesh of horses, and of them that sit on them, and the flesh of all men, both free and bond, both small and great.

19 **And I** saw the beast, and the kings of the earth, and their armies, gathered together
to make war against him that sat on the horse, and against his army.

20 **And the beast** was taken, and with him the false prophet that wrought miracles before him,
with which he deceived them that had received the mark of the beast, and them that worshipped his image.
These both were cast alive into a lake of fire burning with brimstone.

21 **And the remnant** were slain with the sword of him that sat upon the horse,
which sword proceeded out of his mouth:
and all the fowls were filled with their flesh.

20 **And I** saw an angel come down from heaven,
having the key of the bottomless pit and a great chain in his hand.

2 **And he** laid hold on the dragon, that old serpent,
which is the Devil, and Satan,
and bound him a thousand years,
3 **And** cast him into the bottomless pit,
and shut him up,
and set a seal upon him,
that he should deceive the nations no more,
till the thousand years should be fulfilled:
and after that he must be loosed a little season.

4 **And I** saw thrones,
and they sat upon them,
and judgment was given unto them:
and I saw the souls of them that were beheaded for the witness of Jesus, and for the word of God,
and which had not worshipped the beast, neither his image,
neither had received his mark upon their foreheads, or in their hands;
and they lived and reigned with Christ a thousand years.

5 **But the rest of the dead** lived not again
until the thousand years were finished.
This is the first resurrection.

6 **Blessed and holy** is he that hath part in the first resurrection:
on such the second death hath no power,
but they shall be priests of God and of Christ,
and shall reign with him a thousand years.

7 **And when the thousand years** are expired,
Satan shall be loosed out of his prison,
8 **And** shall go out
to deceive the nations which are in the four quarters of the earth, Gog, and Magog,
to gather them together to battle:
the number of whom is as the sand of the sea.

9 **And they** went up on the breadth of the earth,
and compassed the camp of the saints about, and the beloved city:
and fire came down from God out of heaven,
and devoured them.

10 **And the devil that deceived them** was cast into the lake of fire and brimstone,
where the beast and the false prophet are,
and shall be tormented day and night for ever and ever.

11 **And I** saw a great white throne, and him that sat on it,
from whose face the earth and the heaven fled away;
and there was found no place for them.

12 **And I** saw the dead, small and great,
stand before God;
and the books were opened:
and another book was opened,
which is the book of life:
and the dead were judged out of those things which were written in the books, according to their works.

13 **And the sea** gave up the dead which were in it;
and death and hell delivered up the dead which were in them:
and they were judged every man according to their works.
14 **And death and hell** were cast into the lake of fire.
This is the second death.
15 **And whosoever was not found written in the book of life** was cast into the lake of fire.

21 **And I** saw a new heaven and a new earth:
for the first heaven and the first earth were passed away;
and there was no more sea.
2 **And I John** saw the holy city, new Jerusalem,
coming down from God out of heaven,
prepared as a bride adorned for her husband.
3 **And I** heard a great voice out of heaven
saying,
Behold,
the tabernacle of God is with men,
and he will dwell with them,
and they shall be his people,
and God himself shall be with them,
and be their God.
4 **And God** shall wipe away all tears from their eyes;
and there shall be no more death, neither sorrow, nor crying,
neither shall there be any more pain:
for the former things are passed away.
5 **And he that sat upon the throne** said,
Behold,
I make all things new.
And he said unto me,
Write:
for these words are true and faithful.
6 **And he** said unto me,
It is done.
I am Alpha and Omega, the beginning and the end.
I will give unto him that is athirst of the fountain of the water of life freely.
7 **He that overcometh** shall inherit all things;
and I will be his God,
and he shall be my son.
8 **But the fearful, and unbelieving, and the abominable, and murderers, and whoremongers, and sorcerers, and idolaters, and all liars,** shall have their part in the lake which burneth with fire and brimstone:
which is the second death.
9 **And there** came unto me one of the seven angels which had the seven vials full of the seven last plagues,
and talked with me,
saying,
Come hither,
I will shew thee the bride, the Lamb's wife.
10 **And he** carried me away in the spirit to a great and high mountain,
and shewed me that great city, the holy Jerusalem,
descending out of heaven from God,
11 Having the glory of God:
and her light was like unto a stone most precious, even like a jasper stone, clear as crystal;
12 **And** had a wall great and high,
and had twelve gates, and at the gates twelve angels, and names written thereon,
which are the names of the twelve tribes of the children of Israel:
13 On the east three gates; on the north three gates; on the south three gates; and on the west three gates.
14 **And the wall of the city** had twelve foundations, and in them the names of the twelve apostles of the Lamb.
15 **And he that talked with me** had a golden reed
to measure the city, and the gates thereof, and the wall thereof.
16 **And the city** lieth foursquare,
and the length is as large as the breadth:
and he measured the city with the reed, twelve thousand furlongs.
The length and the breadth and the height of it are equal.
17 **And he** measured the wall thereof, an hundred and forty and four cubits, according to the measure of a man, that is, of the angel.
18 **And the building of the wall of it** was of jasper:
and the city was pure gold, like unto clear glass.
19 **And the foundations of the wall of the city** were garnished with all manner of precious stones.
The first foundation was jasper; the second, sapphire; the third, a chalcedony; the fourth, an emerald;
20 The fifth, sardonyx; the sixth, sardius; the seventh, chrysolyte; the eighth, beryl; the ninth, a topaz; the tenth, a chrysoprasus; the eleventh, a jacinth; the twelfth, an amethyst.
21 **And the twelve gates** were twelve pearls:
every several gate was of one pearl:
and the street of the city was pure gold,
as it were transparent glass.
22 **And I** saw no temple therein:
for the Lord God Almighty and the Lamb are the temple of it.
23 **And the city** had no need of the sun, neither of the moon,
to shine in it:
for the glory of God did lighten it,
and the Lamb is the light thereof.
24 **And the nations of them which are saved** shall walk in the light of it:
and the kings of the earth do bring their glory and honour into it.
25 **And the gates of it** shall not be shut at all by day:
for there shall be no night there.
26 **And they** shall bring the glory and honour of the nations into it.
27 **And there** shall in no wise enter into it any thing that defileth,
neither whatsoever worketh abomination,
or maketh a lie: but they which are written in the Lamb's book of life.

22 **And he** shewed me a pure river of water of life, clear as crystal,
proceeding out of the throne of God and of the Lamb.
2 **In the midst of the street of it, and on either side of the river,** was there the tree of life,
which bare twelve manner of fruits,
and yielded her fruit every month:
and the leaves of the tree were for the healing of the nations.

3 **And there** shall be no more curse:
but the throne of God and of the Lamb shall be in it;
and his servants shall serve him:
4 **And they** shall see his face;
and his name shall be in their foreheads.

5 **And there** shall be no night there;
and they need no candle, neither light of the sun;
for the Lord God giveth them light:
and they shall reign for ever and ever.

6 **And he** said unto me,
These sayings are faithful and true:
and the Lord God of the holy prophets sent his angel
to shew unto his servants the things which must shortly be done.

7 **Behold,**
I come quickly:
blessed is he that keepeth the sayings of the prophecy of this book.

8 **And I John** saw these things,
and heard them.

And when I had heard and seen,
I fell down to worship before the feet of the angel which shewed me these things.

9 **Then** saith he unto me,
See thou do it not:
for I am thy fellowservant, and of thy brethren the prophets, and of them which keep the sayings of this book:
worship God.

10 **And he** saith unto me,
Seal not the sayings of the prophecy of this book:
for the time is at hand.

11 **He that is unjust,** let him be unjust still:
and he which is filthy, let him be filthy still:
and he that is righteous, let him be righteous still:
and he that is holy, let him be holy still.

12 **And, {behold}, I** come quickly;
and my reward is with me,
to give every man according as his work shall be.

13 **I** am Alpha and Omega, the beginning and the end, the first and the last.

14 **Blessed** are they that do his commandments,
that they may have right to the tree of life,
and may enter in through the gates into the city.

15 **For without** are dogs, and sorcerers, and whoremongers, and murderers, and idolaters,
and whosoever loveth and maketh a lie.

16 **I Jesus** have sent mine angel to testify unto you these things in the churches.

I am the root and the offspring of David, and the bright and morning star.

17 **And the Spirit and the bride** say,
Come.

And let him that heareth say,
Come.

And let him that is athirst come.

And whosoever will,
let him take the water of life freely.

18 **For I** testify unto every man that heareth the words of the prophecy of this book,
If any man shall add unto these things,
God shall add unto him the plagues that are written in this book:
19 **And if any man** shall take away from the words of the book of this prophecy,
God shall take away his part out of the book of life, and out of the holy city, and from the things which are written in this book.

20 **He which testifieth these things** saith,
Surely I come quickly.

Amen.

Even so, come, Lord Jesus.

21 **The grace of our Lord Jesus Christ** be with you all.

Amen.

www.ingramcontent.com/pod-product-compliance
Lightning Source LLC
Chambersburg PA
CBHW052106020426
42335CB00021B/2664
9781964118055